UNIVERSITY CASEBOOK SERIES

CASES AND MATERIALS

INTERNET COMMERCE

THE EMERGING LEGAL FRAMEWORK

by

MARGARET JANE RADIN
William Benjamin Scott and Luna M. Scott Professor of Law
Director, Program in Law, Science and Technology
Stanford University

JOHN A. ROTHCHILD
Associate Professor of Law
Wayne State University

GREGORY M. SILVERMAN
Assistant Professor of Law
Seattle University

NEW YORK, NEW YORK

FOUNDATION PRESS

2002

395 Hudson Street
New York, NY 10014
Phone Toll Free 1–877–888–1330
Fax (212) 367–6799
fdpress.com

Printed in the United States of America

ISBN 1–58778–081–X

TEXT IS PRINTED ON 10% POST CONSUMER RECYCLED PAPER

This book is dedicated to

John W. Radin

Joan, Julia, and Daniel

Veronique, Cyril, and Alexander, *for their support and patience over the course of this project.*

*

PREFACE

Since the mid-1990s, and with increasing urgency beginning in the late 1990s, businesses large and small have been embracing the Internet as an essential component of their business and marketing plans. Online communications have become intertwined with everyday business activities in a variety of ways:

- A large and ever-increasing number of businesses have established a website as their public face, using it to convey information to present and prospective customers, to investors, and to suppliers and collaborators. Nearly every business of substantial size has a website, as do enormous numbers of small and medium-sized enterprises.
- Businesses communicate with their customers using e-mail—both incoming, as a substitute or supplement to telephone inquiries and postal mail, and outgoing, in the form of standardized newsletters and individualized messages.
- Many businesses use their websites as online catalogs, enabling orders to be placed online.
- Businesses that offer digital goods, such as software, information, and music, may deliver their products via the Internet.
- For some companies, the Internet *is* their business. This is true of Internet service providers, which connect users to the Internet, and hosting providers, which maintain the files comprising a website on a computer server that is connected to the Internet.
- The Internet has to some extent supplanted the older, proprietary Electronic Data Interchange system as a method for conducting business-to-business transactions electronically.

In addition, new businesses made possible by the Internet, premised on near-instantaneous communication of both textual and graphical material, near-universal access from remote locations, and other features of the technology, have quickly become established. The success of online auctions is perhaps the most familiar example.

Given the substantial and expanding role that the Internet plays in everyday commercial activities, any lawyer who advises businesses or litigates on their behalf must be conversant with the new legal issues that arise from commercial use of online communications. The goal of this book is to supply that knowledge. We reject the premise that use of the Internet transports one to a new and mysterious place called "cyberspace" in which all the old rules must be jettisoned. But neither has commercial use of the Internet left the legal landscape unmodified. The lawyer's task is to understand what courts and legislatures can adapt (and are adapting) from inherited legal regimes, and what they must forge (and are forging) anew.

Chapter 1 introduces you to the options for regulating the Internet so that it can support commercial transactions. In Chapters 2 and 3 you will learn about the central role of trademark law in enabling companies to establish an online identity, and you will study the law governing domain names, an important business asset that did not exist before the Internet. In Chapters 4 and 5, we turn to contract, the basis of exchange in the online world as in the offline world. Here you will study some significant legislative initiatives and how they treat basic contractual features such as consent, as well as the impact of the online environment on signatures and the statute of frauds.

Chapter 6 will show you the range of consumer protection issues brought to the fore in the online environment. Chapter 7 takes up the difficult issue of jurisdiction in the borderless environment; businesses do not want to be open to suit in every jurisdiction where their websites may be seen (that is, everywhere in the world), but what are reasonable limits? Chapter 8 is devoted to an issue of special concern to many consumers, protection of information privacy. Online businesses need data about their customers and must find ways to work within parameters that consumers can accept.

Property in information is central to online businesses in a number of different ways, and Chapters 9 through 12 explore how these property rights function. Chapter 9 addresses copyright law, Chapter 10 the law governing databases, Chapter 11 the role of technological protection of digital goods, and Chapter 12 the patent system's protection of methods of doing business.

In Chapter 13 you will study approaches to liability for online intrusions, including unwanted commercial e-mail ("spam"), and Chapter 14 introduces the topic of secondary liability for harmful or offending online conduct by users—a matter of particular concern to Internet service providers and hosting providers. Chapter 15 addresses forms of alternative dispute resolution that may be used in Internet commerce.

Central to any commercial transaction is payment for goods and services; accordingly, Chapter 16 provides an overview of methods of paying for purchases in Internet commerce, from credit cards and debit cards to "smart cards" and newer digital payment mechanisms. Tax revenues are what enable governments to carry out their functions, and the question of taxation is still unresolved in the online environment; Chapter 17 explores some important features of the issue.

This book is meant to be user-friendly. The material and discussions assume familiarity with the first-year legal courses, but legal expertise beyond that is not presumed. Because understanding the legal issues frequently depends on understanding the technology underlying Internet communications, we provide a glossary for help with technical terms that may be unfamiliar. Appendix A, on computer networking, and Appendix B, on the domain name system, will be helpful to those seeking further background on the technology of the Internet. Appendix C offers an overview and classification of the various Internet business models. For those who want to pursue further reading, a bibliography for each chapter's topics is provided. In addition, we hope our website, at www.ecommercecasebook.com, can bring together questions and answers, and keep everyone posted on the changing world of e-commerce. This is a new book in a new field, and we invite you to let us know your reactions to it.

MARGARET JANE RADIN
JOHN A. ROTHCHILD
GREGORY M. SILVERMAN

August 2002

*

ACKNOWLEDGMENTS

We would like to thank Foundation Press for recognizing the need for a book like this, and bringing us together to create it. We thank the Roberts Program in Law and Business for support in completing the final stages of the project. A number of law students helped with this project, and we thank all of them for their fine work: Yvonne Campbell, Carole Church, Genevieve Cox, Dirk Heumueller, Masako Kanazawa, Alisa Mall, Araceli Martinez-Olguín, Corynne McSherry, Melissa Raycraft, T. Marie Satterfield, Andrew Shen, and David B. Silva. We thank Professors Janet Ainsworth, Marilyn J. Berger, Eric Chiappinelli, Mark Chinen, Margaret Chon, Sidney DeLong, Paula Lustbader, Michael J. McIntyre, R. Anthony Reese, Alan Schenk, David M. Skover, Kellye Testy, R. Polk Wagner, Jonathan Weinberg, and Kenneth Wing for helpful comments on portions of the book. We would also like to thank reference librarians Robert Menanteaux and Kelly Kunsch of the Seattle University Law Library for their assistance, as well as Seattle University Dean Rudolph Hasl and former Dean James E. Bond for their financial support of this project. We are extremely grateful to Joan E. Hartman for first-class editing and encouragement.

Excerpts from the following materials are reprinted with the permission of the copyright owners:

American Bar Association, *The Commercial Use of Electronic Data Interchange—A Report and Model Trading Partner Agreement,* 45 Bus. Law 1645 (1990). Note from American Bar Association: This Model Agreement and Commentary is the subject of an extensive report that is available from the ABA Section of Business Law (see Order Information below). Permission to reprint the Model Agreement and Commentary by Foundation Press has been granted by the American Bar Association. The Model Agreement should not be used without consulting the report. The Model Agreement and Commentary may not be copied or disseminated for any purpose or by any party without the express written consent of the American Bar Association. © 1990 American Bar Association. All rights reserved. To order: Copies of The Commercial Use of Electronic Data Interchange: A Report and Model Trading Partner Agreement are available through ABA Publication Orders, PO Box 10892, Chicago, IL 60610-0892 (800/285-2221).

Ashbourn, Julian, *Biometrics and PKI,* homepage.ntlworld.com/avanti/home.htm.

Banushi, Nikoletta, Can e-mail seal a sales deal? *Shattuck v. Klotzbach,* Boston Globe, Mar. 16, 2002, at E1.

Bell, Tom W., *Fair Use vs. Fared Use: The Impact of Automated Rights Management on Copyright's Fair Use Doctrine,* 76 N.C. L. Rev. 557 (1998).

Benkler, Yochai, *Constitutional Bounds of Database Protection: The Role of Judicial Review in the Creation and Definition of Private Rights in Information,* 15 Berkeley Tech. L.J. 535 (2000).

Blasbalg, Gregory B., Note, *Master of Their Domain: Trademark Holders Now Have New Ways to Control Their Marks in Cyberspace,* 5 Roger Williams U.L. Rev. 563 (2000).

Braucher, Jean, *The Uniform Computer Information Transactions Act (UCITA): Objections From The Consumer Perspective,* 5 No. 6 Cyberspace Law. 2 (2000).

Burk, Dan L., *The Trouble with Trespass,* 4 J. Small & Emerging Bus. L. 27 (2000).

Burk, Dan L. & Julie E. Cohen, *Fair Use Infrastructure for Rights Management Systems,* 15 Harv. J.L. & Tech. 41 (2001).

Dreyfuss, Rochelle Cooper, *Are Business Method Patents Bad For Business?,* 16 Santa Clara Computer & High Tech. L.J. 263 (2000).

Fischer, Susanna Frederick, *Saving Rosencrantz and Guildenstern in a Virtual World? A Comparative Look at Recent Global Electronic Signature Legislation,* 7 B.U. J. Sci. & Tech. L. 229 (2001).

Fowler, Brendon, Cara Franklin & Bob Hyde, *Can You Yahoo!? The Internet's Digital Fences,* 2001 Duke L. & Tech. Rev. 12.

Friedman, David D. & Kerry L. Macintosh, *The Cash of the Twenty-First Century,* 17 Santa Clara Computer & High Tech. L.J. 273 (2001).

Goldsmith, Jack L., *Against Cyberanarchy,* 65 U. Chi. L. Rev. 1199 (1998).

Greve, Michael S., *Yes, Tax the 'Net; Don't subsidize e-commerce; instead, reform sales taxes,* Weekly Standard, May 15, 2000.

Grusd, Jared Earl, *Internet Business Methods: What Role Does and Should Patent Law Play?,* 4 Va. J.L. & Tech. 9 (1999).

Harris Interactive, *Harris Interactive Files Suit Against AOL, Microsoft, Qwest and Other ISPs Over Restraint of Trade* (2001).

Helfer, Laurence R. & Graeme B. Dinwoodie, *Designing Non-National Systems: The Case of the Uniform Domain Name Dispute Resolution Policy,* 43 Wm. & Mary L. Rev. 141 (2001).

Hillebrand, Gail K. (West Coast Regional Office, Consumers Union), *Uniform Electronic Transactions Act: Consumer Nightmare or Opportunity?* (1999), www.consumersunion.org/finance/899nclcwc.htm.

Hillebrand, Gail & Margot Saunders, *E-Sign and UETA: What Should States Do Now?,* 5 No. 10 Cyberspace Law. 2, 5 No. 11 Cyberspace Law. 8 (Parts I & II) (2001).

ICANN, *Registrar Accreditation Agreement* (2001), www.icann.org/registrars/ra-agreement-17may01.htm.

Johnson, David R. & David Post, *Law and Borders—The Rise of Law in Cyberspace,* 48 Stan. L. Rev. 1367 (1996).

Kuttner, Kenneth N. & James J. McAndrews, *Personal On-Line Payments,* Econ. Pol'y Rev., Dec. 1, 2001, at 35. Reprinted by permission of the Federal Reserve Bank of New York.

Laudon, Kenneth C., *Extensions to the Theory of Markets and Privacy: Mechanics of Pricing Information,* in U.S. Dep't of Commerce, Privacy and Self Regulation in the Information Age (1997).

Lemley, Mark A., *Beyond Preemption: The Law and Policy of Intellectual Property Licensing,* 87 Calif. L. Rev. 111 (1999). © 1999 by California Law Review and Mark A. Lemley. All rights reserved. Reprinted by permission of the Regents of the University of California.

Lemley, Mark A., *The Modern Lanham Act and the Death of Common Sense,* 108 Yale L.J. 1687 (1999). Reprinted by permission of The Yale Law Journal Company and William S. Hein Company.

Lessig, Lawrence, *Code and Other Laws of Cyberspace* (1999). Reprinted by permission of The Perseus Books Group.

Lessig, Lawrence, *The Problem with Patents,* The Industry Standard, Apr. 23, 1999.

Litman, Jessica, *Information Privacy/Information Property,* 52 Stan. L. Rev. 1283 (2000).

Mail Abuse Prevention System, *MAPS RBL Rationale* (2001).

McCarthy, J. Thomas, *McCarthy on Trademarks and Unfair Competition* (2002). © 2002 by West Group, all rights reserved.

Merrill, Charles R., *Proof of Who, What and When in Electronic Commerce Under the Digital Signature Guidelines,* 542 PLI/Pat 185 (1998). The author practices Information Technology law as a partner of McCarter & English, LLP, headquartered in Newark, New Jersey.

Middlebrook, Stephen T. & John Muller, *Thoughts on Bots: The Emerging Law of Electronic Agents,* 56 Bus. Law. 341 (2000). © 2000 by the American Bar Association. Reprinted by permission.

Multistate Tax Commission, *Computer Company's Provision of In-State Repair Services Creates Nexus,* NB 95-1 (Dec. 20, 1995).

National Conference of Commissioners on Uniform State Laws, *Uniform Computer Information Transactions Act* (2000). © 2000 by National Conference of Commissioners on Uniform State Laws.

National Conference of Commissioners on Uniform State Laws, *Uniform Electronic Transactions Act* (1999). © 1999 by National Conference of Commissioners on Uniform State Laws.

National Conference of Commissioners on Uniform State Laws, *Uniform Money Services Act* (2001). © 2001 by National Conference of Commissioners on Uniform State Laws.

National Notary Association, *A Position on Digital Signatures and Notarization,* www.nationalnotary.org/Digitalsignature.pdf. Published by the National Notary Association, 9350 De Soto Avenue, Chatsworth, California 91311-4926.

Nimmer, David, *A Riff on Fair Use in the Digital Millennium Copyright Act,* 148 U. Pa. L. Rev. 673 (2000). Reprinted by permission of David Nimmer, Visiting Professor, UCLA School of Law.

Nimmer, Raymond T., *UCITA: A Commercial Contract Code,* 17 No. 5 Computer Law. 3 (2000). © 2000 by Aspen Publishers, Inc.

Oakes, Chris, *Patently Absurd,* Wired News, Mar. 3, 2000.

Pontius, Kevin L., *Prior User Rights In Business Methods,* www.viennapat.com/newsletter/vol4iss1/prioruserrightsinbusinessmethods.htm.

Rappa, Michael, *Business Models on the Web,* digitalenterprise.org/models/models.html. © 2002 by Michael Rappa. Reprinted with permission.

Raskind, Leo J., *The State Street Bank Decision: The Bad Business of Unlimited Patent Protection for Methods of Doing Business,* 10 Fordham I. P., Media & Ent. L.J. 61 (1999).

Reese, R. Anthony, *Copyright and Internet Music Transmissions: Existing Law, Major Controversies, Possible Solutions,* 55 U. Miami L. Rev. 237 (2001).

Reidenberg, Joel R. & Françoise Gamet-Pol, *The Fundamental Role of Privacy and Confidence in the Network,* 30 Wake Forest L. Rev. 105 (1995).

Safire, William, *Stalking the Internet,* N.Y. Times, May 30, 2000, at A19. Originally published in The New York Times, May 30, 2000. © 2000 by The New York Times. All rights reserved.

Samuelson, Pamela, *Mapping the Digital Public Domain,* — Law & Contemp. Probs.— (2002).

Scott, Robert E., *The Rise and Fall of Article 2,* 62 La. L. Rev. — (2002).

Shirky, Clay, *The Case Against Micropayments,* www.openp2p.com/lpt/a//p2p/2000/12/19/micropayments.html.

Smedinghoff, Thomas J., *Certification Authority: Liability Analysis* (1998).

Sorkin, David E., *Payment Methods for Consumer-to-Consumer Online Transactions,* 35 Akron L. Rev. 1 (2001).

Sorkin, David E., *Technical and Legal Approaches to Unsolicited Electronic Mail,* 35 U.S.F. L. Rev. 325 (2001).

Stefik, Mark & Alex Silverman, *The Bit and the Pendulum: Balancing the Interests of Stakeholders in Digital Publishing,* 16 No. 1 Computer Law. 1 (1999). © 1999 by Aspen Publishers, Inc.

Thornburg, Elizabeth G., *Going Private: Technology, Due Process, and Internet Dispute Resolution,* 34 U.C. Davis L. Rev. 151 (2000). © 2000 by Elizabeth G. Thornburg. Journal issue © 2000 by the Regents of the University of California. Reprinted with permission.

TRUSTe, *Resolution Process,* truste.org/programs/pub_recourse.html.

TRUSTe, *TRUSTe Oversight,* truste.org/programs/pub_oversight.html.

TRUSTe, *TRUSTe Program Principles,* truste.org/programs/pub_principles.html.

TRUSTe, *Watchdog #1723—Microsoft Statement of Finding.*

VeriSign Service Agreement, Version Number 6.2.

*

SUMMARY OF CONTENTS

TABLE OF CONTENTS

*

TABLE OF CASES

Principal cases are in bold type. Non-principal cases are in roman type. References are to Pages.

*

CASES AND MATERIALS

INTERNET COMMERCE

THE EMERGING LEGAL FRAMEWORK

*

CHAPTER ONE

Regulatory Paradigms for Electronic Commerce

The government regulates many aspects of our lives. Regulation of commercial activity is particularly pervasive: state and federal governments set standards for product safety, require disclosure of information concerning products offered for sale, prohibit deceptive marketing practices, regulate banks and securities offerings, enforce contracts, prohibit pornography, and limit gambling.

The advent of the Internet as a medium for conducting commercial transactions raises questions about the role of governments in regulating online activity. Some have argued for a regime of radical laissez-faire with respect to online activity, excluding the government entirely from this realm of human interaction. Others view the Internet as nothing more than a new medium of communication, and argue that the government's authority and obligation to regulate a particular activity cannot depend on the means of communication that is used in connection with that activity. The borderless nature of the Internet, which makes international communications no slower or more expensive than local communications, and the difficulties involved in limiting certain types of online communication to a particular subgroup of the online audience, create additional dilemmas when the government does seek to regulate online activity.

The materials in this chapter focus on the differences between the Internet and other modes of human interaction, and address the question of the proper role of governments in regulating online activity.

I. Setting the Stage: The Legitimacy and Possibility of Government Regulation of Online Activity

Theorists of online regulation have established a lively dialogue on the propriety of government regulation of online activity. Consider the following perspectives:

A. Radical Separatism

John Perry Barlow, *A Declaration of the Independence of Cyberspace*

www.eff.org/~barlow/Declaration-final.html
(Feb. 8, 1996).

Governments of the Industrial World, you weary giants of flesh and steel, I come from Cyberspace, the new home of Mind. On behalf of the future, I ask you of the past to leave us alone. You are not welcome among us. You have no sovereignty where we gather.

We have no elected government, nor are we likely to have one, so I address you with no greater authority than that with which liberty itself always speaks. I declare the global social space we are building to be naturally independent of the tyrannies you seek to impose on us. You have no moral right to rule us nor do you possess any methods of enforcement we have true reason to fear.

Governments derive their just powers from the consent of the governed. You have neither solicited nor received ours. We did not invite you. You do not know us, nor do you know our world. Cyberspace does not lie within your borders. Do not think that you can build it, as though it were a public construction project. You cannot. It is an act of nature and it grows itself through our collective actions.

You have not engaged in our great and gathering conversation, nor did you create the wealth of our marketplaces. You do not know our culture, our ethics, or the unwritten codes that already provide our society more order than could be obtained by any of your impositions.

You claim there are problems among us that you need to solve. You use this claim as an excuse to invade our precincts. Many of these problems don't exist. Where there are real conflicts, where there are wrongs, we will identify them and address them by our means. We are forming our own Social Contract. This governance will arise according to the conditions of our world, not yours. Our world is different.

Cyberspace consists of transactions, relationships, and thought itself, arrayed like a standing wave in the web of our communications. Ours is a world that is both everywhere and nowhere, but it is not where bodies live.

We are creating a world that all may enter without privilege or prejudice accorded by race, economic power, military force, or station of birth.

We are creating a world where anyone, anywhere may express his or her beliefs, no matter how singular, without fear of being coerced into silence or conformity.

Your legal concepts of property, expression, identity, movement, and context do not apply to us. They are all based on matter, and there is no matter here.

Our identities have no bodies, so, unlike you, we cannot obtain order by physical coercion. We believe that from ethics, enlightened self-interest, and the commonweal, our governance will emerge. Our identities may be distributed across many of your jurisdictions. The only law that all our constituent cultures would generally recognize is the Golden Rule. We hope we will be able to build our particular solutions on that basis. But we cannot accept the solutions you are attempting to impose.

In the United States, you have today created a law, the Telecommunications Reform Act, which repudiates your own Constitution and insults the dreams of Jefferson, Washington, Mill, Madison, DeToqueville, and Brandeis. These dreams must now be born anew in us.

You are terrified of your own children, since they are natives in a world where you will always be immigrants. Because you fear them, you entrust your bureaucracies with the parental responsibilities you are too cowardly to confront yourselves. In our world, all the sentiments and expressions of humanity, from the debasing to the angelic, are parts of a seamless whole, the global conversation of bits. We cannot separate the air that chokes from the air upon which wings beat.

In China, Germany, France, Russia, Singapore, Italy and the United States, you are trying to ward off the virus of liberty by erecting guard posts at the frontiers of Cyberspace. These may keep out the contagion for a small time, but they will not work in a world that will soon be blanketed in bit-bearing media.

Your increasingly obsolete information industries would perpetuate themselves by proposing laws, in America and elsewhere, that claim to own speech itself throughout the world. These laws would declare ideas to be another industrial product, no more noble than pig iron. In our world, whatever the human mind may create can be reproduced and distributed infinitely at no cost. The global conveyance of thought no longer requires your factories to accomplish.

These increasingly hostile and colonial measures place us in the same position as those previous lovers of freedom and self-determination who had to reject the authorities of distant, uninformed powers. We must declare our virtual selves immune to your sovereignty, even as we continue to consent to your rule over our bodies. We will spread ourselves across the Planet so that no one can arrest our thoughts.

We will create a civilization of the Mind in Cyberspace. May it be more humane and fair than the world your governments have made before.

David R. Johnson and David Post, *Law and Borders—The Rise of Law in Cyberspace*

48 Stan. L. Rev. 1367 (1996).

Introduction

Global computer-based communications cut across territorial borders, creating a new realm of human activity and undermining the feasibility—

and legitimacy—of laws based on geographic boundaries. While these electronic communications play havoc with geographic boundaries, a new boundary, made up of the screens and passwords that separate the virtual world from the "real world" of atoms, emerges. This new boundary defines a distinct Cyberspace that needs and can create its own law and legal institutions. Territorially based law-makers and law-enforcers find this new environment deeply threatening. But established territorial authorities may yet learn to defer to the self-regulatory efforts of Cyberspace participants who care most deeply about this new digital trade in ideas, information, and services. Separated from doctrine tied to territorial jurisdictions, new rules will emerge to govern a wide range of new phenomena that have no clear parallel in the nonvirtual world. These new rules will play the role of law by defining legal personhood and property, resolving disputes, and crystallizing a collective conversation about online participants' core values.

I. Breaking Down Territorial Borders

A. *Territorial Borders in the "Real World"*

We take for granted a world in which geographical borders—lines separating physical spaces—are of primary importance in determining legal rights and responsibilities. Territorial borders, generally speaking, delineate areas within which different sets of legal rules apply. There has until now been a general correspondence between borders drawn in physical space (between nation states or other political entities) and borders in "law space." For example, if we were to superimpose a "law map" (delineating areas where different rules apply to particular behaviors) onto a political map of the world, the two maps would overlap to a significant degree, with clusters of homogeneous applicable law and legal institutions fitting within existing physical borders.

1. *The Trademark Example.*

Consider a specific example to which we will refer throughout this article: trademark law—schemes for the protection of the associations between words or images and particular commercial enterprises. Trademark law is distinctly based on geographical separations. Trademark rights typically arise within a given country, usually on the basis of a mark on physical goods or in connection with the provision of services in specific locations within that country. Different countries have different trademark laws, with important differences on matters as central as whether the same name can be used in different lines of business. In the United States, similar businesses can even use the same name, provided there is sufficient geographic separation of use to avoid confusion. In fact, there are many local stores, restaurants, and businesses with identical names that do not interfere with each other because their customers do not overlap. The physical cues provided by different lines of business allow a mark to be used by one line of business without diluting its value in others. There is no global registration scheme; protection of a particularly famous mark on a global basis requires registration in each country. A trademark owner must therefore also be constantly alert to territorially based claims of abandonment, and to dilution arising from uses of confusingly similar marks, and must master each country's different procedural and jurisdictional laws.

2. *When Geographic Boundaries for Law Make Sense.*

Physical borders are not, of course, simply arbitrary creations. Although they may be based on historical accident, geographic borders for law make sense in the real world. Their logical relationship to the development and enforcement of legal rules is based on a number of related considerations.

Power. Control over physical space, and the people and things located in that space, is a defining attribute of sovereignty and statehood. Lawmaking requires some mechanism for law enforcement, which in turn depends on the ability to exercise physical control over, and impose coercive sanctions on, law-violators. For example, the U.S. government does not impose its trademark law on a Brazilian business operating in Brazil, at least in part because imposing sanctions on the Brazilian business would require assertion of physical control over business owners. Such an assertion of control would conflict with the Brazilian government's recognized monopoly on the use of force over its citizens.

Effects. The correspondence between physical boundaries and "law space" boundaries also reflects a deeply rooted relationship between physical proximity and the effects of any particular behavior. That is, Brazilian trademark law governs the use of marks in Brazil because that use has a more direct impact on persons and assets within Brazil than anywhere else. For example, a large sign over "Jones' Restaurant" in Rio de Janeiro is unlikely to have an impact on the operation of "Jones' Restaurant" in Oslo, Norway, for we may assume that there is no substantial overlap between the customers, or competitors, of these two entities. Protection of the former's trademark does not—and probably should not—affect the protection afforded the latter's.

Legitimacy. We generally accept the notion that the persons within a geographically defined border are the ultimate source of law-making authority for activities within that border. The "consent of the governed" implies that those subject to a set of laws must have a role in their formulation. By virtue of the preceding considerations, those people subject to a sovereign's laws, and most deeply affected by those laws, are the individuals who are located in particular physical spaces. Similarly, allocation of responsibility among levels of government proceeds on the assumption that, for many legal problems, physical proximity between the responsible authority and those most directly affected by the law will improve the quality of decision making, and that it is easier to determine the will of those individuals in physical proximity to one another.

Notice. Physical boundaries are also appropriate for the delineation of "law space" in the physical world because they can give notice that the rules change when the boundaries are crossed. Proper boundaries have signposts that provide warning that we will be required, after crossing, to abide by different rules, and physical boundaries—lines on the geographical map—are generally well-equipped to serve this signpost function.

B. *The Absence of Territorial Borders in Cyberspace*

Cyberspace radically undermines the relationship between legally significant (online) phenomena and physical location. The rise of the global computer network is destroying the link between geographical location and: (1) the *power* of local governments to assert control over online behavior; (2) the *effects* of online behavior on individuals or things; (3) the *legitimacy* of a local sovereign's efforts to regulate global phenomena; and (4) the ability of physical location to give *notice* of which sets of rules apply. The Net thus radically subverts the system of rule-making based on borders between physical spaces, at least with respect to the claim that Cyberspace should naturally be governed by territorially defined rules.

Cyberspace has no territorially based boundaries, because the cost and speed of message transmission on the Net is almost entirely independent of physical location. Messages can be transmitted from one physical location to any other location without degradation, decay, or substantial delay, and without any physical cues or barriers that might otherwise keep certain geographically remote places and people separate from one another. The Net enables transactions between people who do not know, and in many cases cannot know, each other's physical location. Location remains vitally important, but only location within a *virtual* space consisting of the "addresses" of the machines between which messages and information are routed. The system is indifferent to the *physical* location of those machines, and there is no necessary connection between an Internet address and a physical jurisdiction. Although the domain name initially assigned to a given machine may be associated with an Internet Protocol address that corresponds to that machine's physical location (for example, a ".uk" domain name extension), the machine may be physically moved without affecting its domain name. Alternatively, the owner of the domain name might request that the name become associated with an entirely different machine, in a different physical location. Thus, a server with a ".uk" domain name need not be located in the United Kingdom, a server with a ".com" domain name may be anywhere, and users, generally speaking, are not even aware of the location of the server that stores the content that they read.

The power to control activity in Cyberspace has only the most tenuous connections to physical location. Nonetheless, many governments' first response to electronic communications crossing their territorial borders is to try to stop or regulate that flow of information. Rather than permitting self-regulation by participants in online transactions, many governments establish trade barriers, attempt to tax border-crossing cargo, and respond especially sympathetically to claims that information coming into the jurisdiction might prove harmful to local residents. As online information becomes more important to local citizens, these efforts increase. In particular, resistance to "transborder data flow" (TDF) reflects the concerns of sovereign nations that the development and use of TDF's will undermine their "informational sovereignty," will impinge upon the privacy of local citizens, and will upset private property interests in information. Even local governments in the United States have expressed concern about their loss of control over information and transactions flowing across their borders.

But efforts to control the flow of electronic information across physical borders—to map local regulation and physical boundaries onto Cyberspace—are likely to prove futile, at least in countries that hope to participate in global commerce. Individual electrons can easily, and without any realistic prospect of detection, "enter" any sovereign's territory. The volume of electronic communications crossing territorial boundaries is just too great in relation to the resources available to government authorities. United States Customs officials have generally given up. They assert jurisdiction only over the physical goods that cross the geographic borders they guard and claim no right to force declarations of the value of materials transmitted by modem. Banking and securities regulators seem likely to lose their battle to impose local regulations on a global financial marketplace. And state attorneys general face serious challenges in seeking to intercept the electrons that transmit the kinds of consumer fraud that, if conducted physically within the local jurisdiction, would be easier to shut down.

Faced with their inability to control the flow of electrons across physical borders, some authorities strive to inject their boundaries into the new electronic medium through filtering mechanisms and the establishment of electronic barriers. Others have been quick to assert the right to regulate all online trade insofar as it might adversely affect local citizens. The Attorney General of Minnesota, for example, has asserted the right to regulate gambling that occurs on a foreign web page that a local resident accessed and "brought into" the state. The New Jersey securities regulatory agency has similarly asserted the right to shut down any offending Web page accessible from within the state.

But such protective schemes will likely fail as well. First, the determined seeker of prohibited communications can simply reconfigure his connection so as to appear to reside in a location outside the particular locality, state, or country. Because the Net is engineered to work on the basis of "logical," not geographical, locations, any attempt to defeat the independence of messages from physical locations would be as futile as an effort to tie an atom and a bit together. And, moreover, assertions of law-making authority over Net activities on the ground that those activities constitute "entry into" the physical jurisdiction can just as easily be made by any territorially-based authority. If Minnesota law applies to gambling operations conducted on the World Wide Web because such operations foreseeably affect Minnesota residents, so, too, must the law of any physical jurisdiction from which those operations can be accessed. By asserting a right to regulate whatever its citizens may access on the Net, these local authorities are laying the predicate for an argument that Singapore or Iraq or any other sovereign can regulate the activities of U.S. companies operating in Cyberspace from a location physically within the United States. All such Web-based activity, in this view, must be subject simultaneously to the laws of all territorial sovereigns.

Nor are the effects of online activities tied to geographically proximate locations. Information available on the World Wide Web is available simultaneously to anyone with a connection to the global network. The notion that the effects of an activity taking place on that website radiate from a physical location over a geographic map in concentric circles of decreasing intensity, however sensible that may be in the nonvirtual world, is incoherent when applied to Cyberspace. A website physically located in Brazil, to continue with that example, has no more of an effect on individuals in Brazil than does a website physically located in Belgium or Belize that is accessible in Brazil. Usenet discussion groups, to take another example, consist of continuously changing collections of messages that are routed from one network to another, with no centralized location at all. They exist, in effect, everywhere, nowhere in particular, and only on the Net.

Territorial regulation of online activities serves neither the legitimacy nor the notice justifications. There is no geographically localized set of constituents with a stronger and more legitimate claim to regulate it than any other local group. The strongest claim to control comes from the participants themselves, and they could be anywhere. And in Cyberspace, physical borders no longer function as signposts informing individuals of the obligations assumed by entering into a new, legally significant, place. Individuals are unaware of the existence of those borders as they move through virtual space.

The rise of an electronic medium that disregards geographical boundaries throws the law into disarray by creating entirely new phenomena that need to become the subject of clear legal rules but that cannot be governed, satisfactorily, by any current territorially based sovereign. For example, although privacy on the Net may be a familiar concept, analogous to privacy doctrine for mail systems, telephone calls, and print publications, electronic communications create serious questions regarding the nature and adequacy of geographically based privacy protections. Communications that create vast new transactional records may pass through or even simultaneously exist in many different territorial jurisdictions. What substantive law should we apply to protect this new, vulnerable body of transactional data? May a French policeman lawfully access the records of communications traveling across the Net from the United States to Japan? Similarly, whether it is permissible for a commercial entity to publish a record of all of any given individual's postings to Usenet newsgroups, or whether it is permissible to implement an interactive Web page application that inspects a user's "bookmarks" to determine which other pages that user has visited, are questions not readily addressed by existing legal regimes—both because the phenomena are novel and because any given local territorial sovereign cannot readily control the relevant, globally dispersed, actors and actions.

Because events on the Net occur everywhere but nowhere in particular, are engaged in by online personae who are both "real" (possessing reputations, able to perform services, and deploy intellectual assets) and "intangible" (not necessarily or traceably tied to any particular person in the physical sense), and concern "things" (messages, databases, standing relationships) that are not necessarily separated from one another by any physical boundaries, no physical jurisdiction has a more compelling claim than any other to subject these events exclusively to its laws.

* * *

B. COMMUNICATION SPACE AS UNITARY

Jack L. Goldsmith, *Against Cyberanarchy*

65 U. CHI. L. REV. 1199 (1998).

* * *

"REAL-SPACE" JURISDICTIONAL CONFLICT MANAGEMENT

The skeptics [who argue that governments cannot regulate online activity] are in the grip of a nineteenth century territorialist conception of how "real space" is regulated and how "real-space" conflicts of law are resolved. This conception was repudiated in the middle of this century. The skeptics' first mistake, therefore, is to measure the feasibility and legitimacy of national regulation of cyberspace against a repudiated yardstick. This Section offers a more accurate picture of real-space jurisdictional conflict management as a prelude to analysis of the skeptics' claims.

* * *

* * * Today, the Constitution permits a state to apply its law if it has a "significant contact or significant aggregation of contacts, creating state interests, such that choice of its law is neither arbitrary nor fundamentally unfair." In practice, this standard is notoriously easy to satisfy. It prohibits the application of local law only when the forum state has no interest in the case because the substance of the lawsuit has no relationship to the state. Customary international law limits on a nation's regulation of extraterritorial events are less clear because there are few international decisions on point, and because state practice does not reveal a settled custom. Nonetheless, it seems clear that customary international law, like the United States Constitution, permits a nation to apply its law to extraterritorial behavior with substantial local effects. In addition, both the Constitution and international law permit a nation or state to regulate the extraterritorial conduct of a citizen or domiciliary. In short, in modern times a transaction can legitimately be regulated by the jurisdiction where the transaction occurs, the jurisdictions where significant effects of the transaction are felt, and the jurisdictions where the parties burdened by the regulation are from.

This expansion of the permissible bases for the application of local law has revolutionized conflict of laws in the second half of this century. Any number of choice-of-law regimes are now consistent with constitutional and international law. The earlier belief in a unique governing law for all transnational activities has given way to the view that more than one jurisdiction can legitimately apply its law to the same transnational activity. The uniformity promised by the traditional approach has thus been replaced by the reality of overlapping jurisdictional authority. This means that the application of one jurisdiction's law often comes at the expense of the nonapplication of the conflicting laws of other interested jurisdictions. Because choice-of-law rules often differ from jurisdiction to jurisdiction, and because a forum applies its own choice-of-law rules, the choice of forum is now often critical to the selection of governing law. In this milieu, *ex ante* notice of a specific governing law is no longer a realistic goal in many transnational situations. Not surprisingly, the Constitution and international law impose very weak notice requirements on the application of local law to extraterritorial activity.

This modern world of jurisdictional conflict poses obvious difficulties for participants in transnational transactions. * * * [C]onflicts of law can arise when parties to a transnational transaction do not specify the governing default law, or when the transaction implicates a mandatory law that conflicts with the otherwise-applicable law. Absent a governing international law, transnational activity in these contexts will usually be governed by the law of a single jurisdiction. And absent international choice-of-law rules, the forum's choice-of-law rules will determine the governing law. In regulatory contexts, the forum will invariably apply local law. But regardless of which substantive law the forum applies, the application of that law will frequently create spillover effects on activities in other countries and on the ability of other interested nations to apply their own law. In our increasingly integrated world, these spillover effects are likely to extend to many countries.

Consider, for example, the Supreme Court's decision in *Hartford Fire Insurance Co. v. California*.[50] The Court held that the concerted refusal by London reinsurers to sell certain types of reinsurance to insurers in the United States violated the Sherman Act. The reinsurers' acts in England were legal under English law. But the Court determined that the reinsurers were nonetheless subject to U.S. regulation because their actions "produced substantial effect(s)" in the United States. U.S. law thus regulated the activities of English companies in England at the expense of the nonapplication of English law. Similarly, had an English court applied English law to adjudge the reinsurers' acts to be legal, it would have produced spillover effects on consumers in the United States, and would have come at the expense of the nonapplication of U.S. law. No matter which law governed the reinsurers' acts, the application of that law would have produced spillover effects on the English reinsurers' activities in other jurisdictions,

50. 509 U.S. 764 (1993).

and on the activities of persons in other jurisdictions adversely affected by the reinsurers' acts.

A similar phenomenon occurs in many domestic and international conflicts contexts. For example, the European Commission recently imposed strict conditions on a merger (already approved by the Federal Trade Commission) between two American companies with no manufacturing facilities in Europe. Minnesota applied its pro-plaintiff stacking rules for automobile insurance coverage to an accident in Wisconsin among Wisconsin residents. A United States federal grand jury ordered the local branch of a foreign bank, a nonparty, to disclose bank records in the Bahamas in possible violation of Bahamian law. California applied its workmen's compensation law to benefit an employee of a California corporation who suffered a tort while working in Alaska—even though Alaska purported to make its worker's compensation scheme exclusive, and even though the employment contract specified that Alaska law governed. New York applied its tort law to a car accident in Canada. California taxed a British corporation based on the California portion of its world profits.

In these situations and countless others, one jurisdiction regulates extraterritorial conduct in a way that invariably affects individual behavior and regulatory efforts in other jurisdictions. These spillover effects constitute the central problem of modern conflict of laws. The problem is pervasive. It is also inevitable, because the price of eliminating these spillovers—abolishing national or subnational lawmaking entities, or eliminating transnational activity—is prohibitively high. Most of the dizzying array of modern choice-of-law methodologies are devoted to minimizing these spillovers while at the same time preserving the sovereign prerogative to regulate effects within national borders. International harmonization efforts seek to achieve similar aims, often at the expense of national prerogatives.

There is widespread debate about which approach, or combination of approaches, is preferable. Resolution of this debate is less important for present purposes than two uncontested assumptions that underlie it. The first assumption is that in the absence of consensual international solutions, prevailing concepts of territorial sovereignty permit a nation to regulate the local effects of extraterritorial conduct even if this regulation produces spillover effects in other jurisdictions. The second assumption is that such spillover effects are a commonplace consequence of the unilateral application of any particular law to transnational activity in our increasingly interconnected world. It is against this background that the skeptics' descriptive and normative claims must be assessed.

* * *

III. Is Cyberspace Regulation Feasible?

This Section argues that the skeptics' claims about the infeasibility of national regulation of cyberspace rest on an underappreciation of the realities of modern conflict of laws, and of the legal and technological tools available to resolve multijurisdictional cyberspace conflicts. From the perspective of jurisdiction and choice of law, regulation of cyberspace transactions is no less feasible than regulation of other transnational transactions.

* * *

[As explained above, private legal ordering] has the potential to resolve many, but not all, of the challenges posed by multijurisdictional cyberspace activity. Cyberspace activities for which *ex ante* consent to a governing legal regime is either infeasible or unenforceable are not amenable to private ordering. Such activities remain subject to the skeptics' concerns about multiple or extraterritorial national regulation. * * * The skeptics' concerns are further attenuated, however, by limitations on every nation's ability to enforce its laws. A nation can purport to regulate activity that takes place anywhere. The Island of Tobago can *enact* a law that purports to bind the rights of the whole world. But the effective scope of this law depends on Tobago's ability to *enforce* it. And in general a nation can only enforce its laws against: (i) persons with a presence or assets in the nation's territory; (ii) persons over whom the nation can obtain personal jurisdiction and enforce a default judgment against abroad; or (iii) persons whom the nation can successfully extradite.

A defendant's physical presence or assets within the territory remains the primary basis for a nation or state to enforce its laws. The large majority of persons who transact in cyberspace have no presence or assets in the jurisdictions that wish to regulate their information flows in cyberspace. Such regulations are thus likely to apply primarily to Internet service providers and Internet users with a physical presence in the regulating jurisdiction. Cyberspace users in other territorial jurisdictions will indirectly feel the effect of the regulations to the extent that they are dependent on service or content providers with a presence in the regulating jurisdiction. But for almost all users, there will be no threat of extraterritorial legal liability because of a lack of presence in the regulating jurisdictions.

A nation or state can also enforce its laws over an entity with no local presence or assets if it can obtain personal jurisdiction over the entity and enforce a local default judgment against that entity abroad. The domestic interstate context presents a much greater threat in this regard than does the international context. This is because the Full Faith and Credit Clause requires a state to enforce the default judgment of a sister state that had personal jurisdiction over the defendant. This threat is attenuated, however, by constitutional limits on a state's assertion of personal jurisdiction. The Due Process Clauses prohibit a state from asserting personal jurisdiction over an entity with no local presence unless the entity has purposefully directed its activities to the forum state and the assertion of jurisdiction is reasonable.

Application of this standard to cyberspace activities presents special difficulties. Under standard assumptions about cyberspace architecture, persons can upload or transmit information knowing that it could reach any and all jurisdictions, but not knowing which particular jurisdiction it might reach. Can every state where these transmissions appear assert specific personal jurisdiction over the agent of the information under the purposeful availment and reasonableness tests? * * * [T]here is relatively little reason at present, and even less reason in the near future, to believe that the mere introduction of information into cyberspace will *by itself* suffice for personal jurisdiction over the agent of the transmission in every state where the information appears. Most courts have required something more than mere placement of information on a web page in one state as a basis for personal jurisdiction in another state where the web page is accessed. For a variety of reasons, these decisions have limited specific personal jurisdiction to cases in which there are independent indicia that the out-of-state defendant knowingly and purposefully directed the effects of out-of-state conduct to a particular state where the acts were deemed illegal.

* * *

[Concerns] about the extraterritorial enforcement of local default judgments * * * are less pronounced in the international context. In contrast to the domestic interstate context, customary international law imposes few enforceable controls on a country's assertion of personal jurisdiction, and there are few treaties on the subject. However, also in contrast to domestic law, there is no full faith and credit obligation to enforce foreign judgments in the international sphere. If one country exercises personal jurisdiction on an exorbitant basis, the resulting judgment is unlikely to be enforced in another country. In addition, local public policy exceptions to the enforcement of foreign judgments are relatively commonplace in the international sphere, especially when the foreign judgment flies in the face of the enforcing state's regulatory regime. For these reasons, there is little concern that a foreign default judgment will be enforceable against cyberspace users who live outside the regulating jurisdiction.

The final way that a nation can enforce its regulations against persons outside its jurisdiction is by seeking extradition. * * * International extradition is governed largely by treaty. A pervasive feature of modern extradition treaties is the principle of double criminality. This principle requires that the charged offense be criminal in both the requesting and the requested jurisdictions. This principle, and its animating rationale, make it unlikely that there will be international cooperation in the enforcement of exorbitant unilateral criminal regulations of cyberspace events.

This review of transnational enforcement jurisdiction makes clear that the skeptics exaggerate the threat of multiple regulation of cyberspace information flows. This threat must be measured by a regulation's enforceable scope, not by its putative scope. And the enforceable scope is relatively narrow. It extends only to individual users or system operators with presence or assets in the enforcement jurisdiction, or (in the U.S.) to entities that take extra steps to target cyberspace information flows to states where such information flows are illegal. Such regulatory exposure is a significant concern for cyberspace participants. But it is precisely how regulatory exposure operates in "real space." And it is far less significant than the skeptics' hyperbolic claim that *all* users of the Web will be simultaneously subject to *all* national regulations.

* * *

John Rothchild, *Protecting the Digital Consumer: The Limits of Cyberspace Utopianism*

74 IND. L.J. 893 (1999).

The cyberspace utopians [who deny that governments have authority over online activity] reach their anti-regulatory conclusions through arguments that are flawed in several respects. First, they mischaracterize the salient aspects of online communications. Second, they exaggerate the difficulties that the special characteristics of online communications pose for extension of the existing regulatory regime to online commercial transactions, ignoring the fact that many of those characteristics apply also to other communications media. Third, they make no effort to adapt the existing regulatory regime to the requirements of the new medium. Fourth, they make unsupportable assumptions about the ability of users of online communications to control deceptive marketing practices.

1. The Special Characteristics of Online Communications Do Not Undermine the Legitimacy of Territorially Based Jurisdiction

The key flaw in the normative component of the utopians' argument is that the harmful effects of deceptive marketing practices accomplished through use of the Internet are felt not solely in the realm of cyberspace, but also and unavoidably by a flesh-and-blood resident of a real-world geographic area subject to the territorial jurisdiction of a sovereign. If a sovereign has the right and responsibility to protect its citizens from fraudulent solicitations delivered by postal mail, telephone, radio, television, or print media, it has an equal right and responsibility to protect them from fraud delivered via the Internet. * * *

The person responsible for online deceptive marketing practices is likewise a resident of a geographic territory subject to the jurisdiction of a territorial sovereign. Physical presence within the territorial jurisdiction of a sovereign has since ancient times stood as the paradigm basis for assertion of jurisdiction in personam. No reason appears why a wrongdoer should be able to nullify this basis of jurisdiction merely by choosing to communicate through the online medium, rather than through other means of communication at a distance.

a. Online Communications, Though Universally Accessible, Have Locally Differentiated Impact

The contention that "[t]he effects of cyberspace transactions are felt *everywhere*, simultaneously and equally in all corners of the global network,"[268] is factually incorrect. It is true that certain types of online communications, such as websites and newsgroup postings, are simulta-

268. *See* [David G. Post, *Governing Cyberspace,* 43 WAYNE L. REV. 155,] 162 [1996].

neously and equally *accessible* from any geographic location with the necessary online access. However, the *effects* resulting from that access may vary greatly from place to place. Most pertinently to the present context, a solicitation to enter into a fraudulent transaction has a very different effect in a jurisdiction where a resident actually enters into the proposed transaction than in other jurisdictions where residents read the solicitation but do not act upon it. In both jurisdictions there is some resulting pollution of the commercial dialogue, by virtue of the misinformation that is conveyed to consumers, but only in the former jurisdiction does any consumer suffer direct financial injury. Therefore, it is hardly "indeterminate" to speak of online conduct that " 'has or is intended to have substantial effect within [a State's] territory' "—one standard formulation of the principle governing whether a state has jurisdiction to prescribe rules applicable to a person located outside its territorial scope. We may conclude that the mere maintenance of a website, without more, does not satisfy this criterion. But there is no logical or doctrinal difficulty with a finding that one who enters into a commercial transaction with a person, knowing that person's geographic location, both has and intends to have substantial effects within that jurisdiction.

b. Cost and Speed Advantages of Online Communications Create Only Practical Issues

The fact that "the cost and speed of message transmission on the Net is almost entirely independent of physical location"[271] creates practical problems for law enforcement authorities, but does not radically undermine the territorial basis of jurisdiction. The cost of first-class postage within the United States is typically the same regardless of the geographic separation of the sender and recipient, and it may take only a few days longer for a letter to cross the country than it does to cross a state or a city. The cost of overnight mail delivery within the United States, and the length of time required for delivery, are the same or nearly the same no matter where the sender and recipient are located. The cost of an interstate telephone call within the United States varies little with the distance between the two speakers. Yet we do not consider that the use of direct mail or telemarketing as a medium for conveying commercial communications radically undermines the geographic basis for jurisdiction within the United States; we do not declare "telespace" or "mailspace" to be a "place" unconnected with any territorial jurisdiction. Instead, the legal systems of the various jurisdictions within the United States have developed a more-or-less elaborate jurisprudence for determining under what circumstances a seller located in one state may be brought within the jurisdiction of a court located in another state.

The novelty of online communications, as discussed above, is that the cost and speed of communications remain invariant even when crossing national boundaries. This factor opens the door to a great expansion of international commercial transactions that were previously infeasible, due

271. David R. Johnson & David Post, [*Law and Borders—The Rise of Law in Cyberspace*, 48 Stan. L. Rev. 1367,] 1370 [(1996)].

to the high costs and time delays associated with international mail and telephone service. But the logical and doctrinal bases of territorially based jurisdiction remain unchanged. The challenge is rather to devise jurisdictional rules applicable in the online context that take account of the factors that have traditionally been considered relevant to resolving questions of jurisdiction—such as the effects of the defendant's conduct in the forum jurisdiction, the defendant's state of mind, the burden on the defendant of being forced to defend herself in a foreign forum, the interests of the forum, and the interests of the plaintiff in obtaining a remedy—with the goal of striking an appropriate balance among the competing interests.

c. Virtual Addressing Does Not Undermine Territorial Sovereignty

The fact that "there is no necessary connection between an Internet address and a physical jurisdiction" likewise gives rise to practical difficulties, but does not call into question the territorial basis for jurisdiction. This fact may make it difficult for injured parties and enforcement authorities to identify the perpetrator of prohibited conduct, but is without any deeper significance. It is equally true that there is no necessary connection between a toll-free telephone number—the only "address" that a purchaser may ever have for a vendor that operates via telemarketing—and the physical location of the vendor communicating through that telephone number. Mail forwarding services likewise divorce a seller's address from his physical location. Yet assertion of jurisdiction by territorially based sovereigns is not thought on that account to be illegitimate.

d. Physical Location of Online Interlocutors Is Not Unknowable

The assertion that the Internet allows transactions between people "who do not and *cannot* know the physical location of the other party" is not quite correct. The statement refers to the fact, as discussed above, that an online address—whether an e-mail address, the URL of a website, or a pseudonym used in a chat session—does not itself reveal the physical location of the person who communicates using that address. In many of the most common types of interactions that occur online, it is true that neither party knows the physical location of the other. For example, the owner of a website may not know the location of those who access the site; those who access a website may not know the location of the owner of the site; those who read newsgroup postings may not know the location of the message posters; and recipients of unsolicited commercial e-mail messages may not know the location of the sender. However, it is not true that online communicators *cannot* know the location of their interlocutors. Most obviously, there is nothing to prevent a website, e-mail message, or newsgroup posting from stating the physical address of the person communicating through it.

In the more particular case of online commerce, the vendor most typically *can and does* know the location of his customers. This is because most of the online commerce that takes place at present involves shipping a physical good (flowers, computers, books, compact disks, etc.) to a geographic address. In many cases, even sellers of digital goods that are transmitted via the network likewise *can and do* know the location of their customers. This is so when there is an ongoing commercial relationship between the two parties which involves sending invoices or other physical items to the customer's geographic location. There are, it is true, commercial transactions involving digital goods in which the nature of the transaction does not *require* either party to know the location of the other—for example, the transmission of information via the network on a one-time basis, with payment by credit card or digital cash. However, even in those cases there are steps that a seller can take—some more reliable, but more cumbersome, than others—to ascertain the physical location of the buyer. For example, the seller may require the buyer to provide a telephone number or fax number, which indicates the buyer's physical location; may perform a pre-sale verification of location through postal mail; or may access motor vehicle or voter registration records. In the future, digital certificates indicating the holder's address may become available.

It is of course an everyday occurrence to communicate by telephone or postal mail without being aware of the location of one's interlocutor. A toll-free telephone number gives no indication of the location of the holder of the number. An incoming telephone call does not disclose its geographic origin, unless the recipient subscribes to a caller ID service *and* the caller elects not to have his number blocked. Commercial correspondents frequently make use of a post office box address, or a private mailbox service, that does not reveal their geographic position. This ordinarily raises no issues: when I call the toll-free number of a catalog company to order a product, it is of no concern to me where the order-taker is located; it is of no more concern to me where my e-mailed order to the same company is received or read.

The ability of wrongdoers to conceal their location when using these traditional means of communication is viewed by law enforcement officials as an impediment to law enforcement that must be handled with due regard for privacy interests; it has never been considered a factor that divests territorially based sovereigns of their authority to enforce the law. Likewise, the fact that it is possible to communicate via the Internet without revealing one's physical location does not undermine the geographic basis of jurisdiction over online transactions.

* * *

2. The Argument from Futility Refutes Only One, Particularly Poor, Enforcement Approach

Attempting to police borders within cyberspace is said to be futile because of the large number of border crossing points. "Physical roads and ports linking sovereign territories are few in number, and geographic boundaries can be fenced and policed. In contrast, the number of starting points for an electronic 'trip' out of a given country is staggering, consisting of every telephone capable of connecting outside the territory." Furthermore, the volume of online communications is so great that "a customs house on an electronic border would cause a massive traffic jam." The same is true, however, of communications by telephone and postal mail. Since both voice and data are transmitted along the same copper and fiber optic pathways, it is as infeasible to bottle up telephone conversations as it is to contain online communications. The routes by which postal mail moves from sender to recipient are likewise "staggering" in number. The volume of postal mail is so great that each item can be subjected to no more than a perfunctory customs clearance procedure, and the idea of screening all telephone calls for content is so ridiculous that it has probably never been seriously proposed.

The basic flaw in the argument from futility is that it assumes the wrong enforcement paradigm—namely, preventing prohibited communications from reaching residents of a particular territorial jurisdiction. Although governments have attempted to apply this paradigm—notably Germany, in its efforts to prevent its citizens from gaining access to pornography and hate speech, and Singapore, which requires local Internet service providers to filter out "prohibited material"—this is not the only approach available to a territorial sovereign that wishes to protect its citizens from deceptive commercial communications. The better approach is the one that is currently applied to communications at a distance. No restrictions are placed on a seller's ability to communicate with potential buyers. However, if a seller proposes or procures a commercial transaction through deceptive marketing methods, in violation of the law of the jurisdiction where a buyer is located, the seller may be subject to enforcement action by the government of that jurisdiction.

3. The Problem of Overlapping Jurisdiction Can Be Addressed Through Approaches Less Drastic Than Abdication

The problem of overlapping jurisdiction is a real one, which arises from the facts that: (1) given present technology, the maker of an online communication cannot limit the locations in which the communication may be received; and (2) laws applying to online conduct vary from one jurisdiction to another. The appropriate solution to the problem, however, is not to bar all exercises of jurisdiction by government (whether acting in a legislative, adjudicative, or enforcement role), but rather to constrain such exercises of jurisdiction in a way that balances the various interests at stake. In the case of business-to-consumer commercial transactions, the approach proposed below is to allow online sellers to "opt out" of assertions of jurisdiction by particular states by limiting the extent of their contacts with residents of those states.

4. Deceptive Marketing Practices Are Not Likely To Be Adequately Controlled by Market Forces Alone

The cyberspace utopians argue that market forces are sufficient to prevent and redress consumer injury from deceptive marketing practices, and that government intervention is therefore unnecessary. This view fails to take account of the fact that the problem of fraud—whether perpetrated online or via some other means of communication—is highly resistant to control by market forces. It also oversimplifies by failing to recognize the interaction between regulation by market forces and government regulation.

It is easy to see why online deceptive marketing practices are unlikely to be controlled by market forces alone. The main lines of defense that the market erects—consumer sovereignty, industry self-regulation, and contract—are overmatched by online swindlers. By conveying misinformation to consumers, swindlers intend to interfere with the workings of consumer sovereignty, and they often succeed. While the market has evolved several mechanisms for improving the flow of information to online consumers—certification systems have been put into practice; ratings systems allow consumers to filter out certain categories of websites; non-governmental organizations provide consumers with information about online scams—these are simply online versions of mechanisms that pre-existed the Internet. Although they can certainly help in alleviating the problem of fraud in online commercial transactions, they are not likely to be significantly more effective than their offline analogues.

Vendors have also put into effect various types of online self-regulation: trade associations have promulgated industry codes of conduct, which may be implemented through a "hallmark" program; operators of online malls offer redress to consumers who are victimized by certain types of fraud at their sites, and screen the businesses that they allow to set up shop; one large Internet service provider "has decided not to provide website hosting or Internet access services to entities engaged in Internet-based gambling or other wagered activities which are determined to be illegal"; the online industry is engaged in a coordinated effort to develop software tools enabling parents to filter the online material to which their children are exposed. Yet these initiatives too are likely to fall short of what is required to control online deceptive marketing practices, for the simple reason that self-regulation "only binds the 'good guys.' Companies that do not have a reputation at stake have no ethical or business incentive to abide by self-regulatory principles...." Legitimate marketers recognize that a reputation for honesty is a prerequisite to long-term business success. The market provides them with a strong incentive to keep their customers happy. But perpetrators of fraud have no such interest. They do not need or expect to profit from repeat business or referrals from satisfied customers, and do not expect to remain long in the market. They have no incentive to follow voluntary codes of conduct. Once a fraudulent operation becomes known in the marketplace as such, its perpetrator simply pulls up stakes and moves on to the next scam.

In addition, one important type of self-regulation that is applied by traditional communications outlets—media screening—is of doubtful effectiveness in the online context. In the case of the traditional print and broadcast media, the number of media outlets that enable a vendor to get a marketing message to a regional, national, or multinational audience is relatively limited, and the owners of these outlets are relatively well-established business concerns. But with the online media, the number of outlets available to give an advertiser access to a global audience is virtually unlimited—any Internet hosting service, located anywhere in the world, will serve equally well—and not all of these providers will perceive an interest in enforcing standards of advertising conduct that are protective of consumer interests.

Contract-based solutions to the problem of online deceptive marketing practices are also inadequate. Most consumer-vendor disputes do not involve enough money to justify bringing a breach-of-contract action, and class actions will only rarely be available. This effect will become more pronounced as a larger number of online transactions take on an international character. Even where money losses are high, the online medium makes it easy for swindlers to disguise their identity and location, rendering contract actions useless.

* * *

The cyberspace utopians' penchant for viewing cyberspace as a "place" that is separate from the sphere of ordinary discourse leads them to frame the question, wrongly, as: "Should the government regulate cyberspace?" Cyberspace is not a place, but rather an obfuscatory reference to a means by which people may communicate with each other. The right question is therefore, "What is the appropriate role of government in regulating commercial transactions that are carried out through the use of online communication technologies?"

* * *

NOTE: REGULATION BY TECHNOLOGICAL CONSTRUCTION

The preceding texts have emphasized the borderless nature of online communications as a factor tending to make it difficult to regulate online activity. The network's facilitation of anonymous communications, and the difficulty of authenticating the actions of online communicators, introduce additional challenges for regulators. Are these immutable features of the network, or are they contingent and subject to revision?

Professor Lawrence Lessig argues that the Internet has no inherent nature, but rather becomes what we make of it. "We can build, or architect, or code cyberspace to protect values that we believe are fundamental, or we can build, or architect, or code cyberspace to allow those values to disappear. * * * Code is never found; it is only ever made, and only ever made by us." LAWRENCE LESSIG, CODE AND OTHER LAWS OF CYBERSPACE 6 (1999). The Internet was originally conceived as a tool for communication among academic researchers. To fulfill that mission, uninhibited communication was important but regulability was not. The network was therefore designed with features that promoted communicational freedom, at the expense of regulability. But, according to Lessig, "the invisible hand of cyberspace is building an architecture that is quite the opposite of what it was at cyberspace's birth. The invisible hand, through commerce, is constructing an architecture that perfects control—an architecture that makes possible highly efficient regulation." *Id.* at 6. Lessig predicts that if this trend is left unchecked, "much of the 'liberty' present at cyberspace's founding will vanish in its future. Values that we now consider fundamental will not necessarily remain. Freedoms that were foundational will slowly disappear." *Id.*

The network as originally constituted made it difficult for businesses to identify, recognize, and associate characteristics with online interlocutors. Certain features of the offline world make it feasible to gather information of this sort. Natural features, such as the uniqueness of fingerprints, and constructed features, such as the requirement that cars carry license plates, help to identify and keep track of people. The basic design of the network lacks those features or their online equivalents. "This minimalism in design is intentional. It reflects both a political decision about disabling control and a technological decision about the optimal network design. The designers were not interested in advancing social control; they were concerned with network efficiency." *Id.* at 33.

The beginnings of an effort to create trackable identities on the network may be seen in the spread of passwords and cookie files. An online service can use passwords to discriminate between those who are entitled to access and those who are not. Cookies allow website visitors to be assigned a persistent identity, with which the visitor's attributes may be associated. But for e-commerce really to succeed, argues Lessig, "the Net will need a far more general architecture of trust—an architecture that makes possible secure and private transactions." *Id.* at 40. The elements of this architecture include "(1) authentication, to ensure the identity of the person you are dealing with; (2) authorization, to ensure that the person is sanctioned for a particular function; (3) privacy, to ensure that others cannot see what exchanges there are; (4) integrity, to ensure that the transmission is not altered en route; and (5) nonrepudiation, to ensure that the sender of a message cannot deny that he sent it." *Id.* These features may be implemented through digital certificates, supported by encryption and a public key infrastructure. (For a discussion of digital certificates, see Chapter 5, *infra.*) Lessig believes that commercial imperatives are likely to foster the spread of such an architecture, with or without government intervention, through the establishment of incentives that make Internet users *want* to use digital certificates. The government, if it chose, could add impetus to this process—not by directly regulating individuals, but by creating incentives for individuals and regulating intermediaries. *Id.* at 50. For example, the government could require websites to deny access to visitors who lack the proper credentials, could impose a tax on e-commerce but exempt buyers who hold a certificate showing their state of residence, or could provide online services for free to those presenting a certificate. *Id.* at 50–51.

Lessig argues that the development of an infrastructure that meets the needs of e-commerce will have the side effect of making it easier for governments to regulate the Internet: "an ID-enabled world facilitates regulation." *Id.* at 54. He offers the example of online gambling. At present, it is difficult for any one state to prevent its citizens from gambling online. If the state takes legal action against a gambling operation located in the state, the operation can easily relocate to another jurisdiction without impinging on the ability of residents of the state to access its services—an incident of the fact that addressing on the Internet is logical rather than geographical. Lessig asks us to imagine a world where each Internet user possessed a digital certificate that contained pertinent information about him, including the country and state of his residence. That would enable gambling websites to discriminate among prospective customers, denying access to those whose certificate indicated they were from a state or country that prohibited gambling by its citizens. The legal system of each country where a server hosting an online gambling site was located would require hosting services within its jurisdiction to give effect to the gambling laws of other jurisdictions, so that wherever a gambling site was hosted, it would be required by local law to honor the laws of other jurisdictions.

NOTES & QUESTIONS

1. *Grounds for objection.* The above excerpts discuss four grounds on which objection to government regulation of online activity might be based: *legitimacy* ("Governments derive their just powers from the consent of the governed. You have neither solicited nor received ours."); *efficacy* ("Lawmaking requires some mechanism for law enforcement, which in turn depends on the ability to exercise physical control over, and impose coercive sanctions on, law-violators."); *jurisdictional cacophony* ("By asserting a right to regulate whatever its citizens may access on the Net, these local authorities are laying the predicate for an argument that Singapore or Iraq or any other sovereign can regulate the activities of U.S. companies operating in Cyberspace from a location physically within the United States."); and *superfluity* ("You claim there are problems among us that you need to solve. You use this claim as an excuse to invade our precincts. Many of these problems don't exist. Where there are real conflicts, where there are wrongs, we will identify them and address them by our means."). How do the responses address these objections? Are the responses persuasive? Is there a defensible distinction between one's capacity as a citizen of a territorially defined sovereign, and one's capacity as (to use the utopian formulation) a citizen of cyberspace?

2. *Regulability.* Do you agree with Professor Lessig that e-commerce is likely to push the Internet in the direction of regulability? What forms might that take, beyond the widespread use of digital certificates? Do you agree that the process is likely to lead to all countries agreeing to require their residents to obey all foreign laws?

3. *Exit.* One version of the efficacy argument posits that an Internet user who is dissatisfied with the set of rules to which he is subject may, at negligible cost, relocate to a more congenial jurisdiction. On the network, the argument runs, physical proximity is irrelevant: a user can make full use of the Internet without regard to his physical location or the identity of the provider through which he gains access to the network.

So, for example, if the United States enacts a law banning online gambling, the owner of a gambling website can move the site to servers located in Antigua or some other jurisdiction where such operations are permissible, without making a change in the site's URL. A German proprietor of a site featuring Nazi hate speech, which is illegal under German law, can move the site to servers in the United States where it is protected by the First Amendment, and can continue to operate the site from her location in Germany. Data havens may be expected to arise—jurisdictions that place few or no restrictions on the flow of bits in and out of servers located within their borders. The ultimate expression of this tendency is illustrated by Sealand, a country consisting of an abandoned antiaircraft platform located off the cost of England, whose sole economic activity consists of hosting web servers with unequivocal guarantees of non-interference. *See* John Markoff, *Rebel Outpost on the Fringes of Cyberspace*, N.Y. TIMES, Jun. 4, 2000, at A14.

The network's facilitation of decentralized siting of business assets may also tend to increase the attractiveness of tax havens. An online business can locate its servers in a traditional tax haven, such as Bermuda or Antigua, while its owners and managers remain in their home (high-tax) countries, operating the business remotely via the network. This approach may not work well for U.S. citizens, since the United States taxes its citizens on their worldwide income. But there is as yet little precedent in the area.

If exit is truly costless, one result might be market-style competition among the promulgators of "rule sets," which will gain and lose subjects as network users vote with their feet. *See* David G. Post, *Anarchy, State, and the Internet: An Essay on Law–Making in Cyberspace*, 1995 J. ONLINE L. art. 3. What are the limitations on an Internet user's ability to "exit" a rule set that displeases him? Are the costs of exit really negligible? For an argument that they are not, see Neil Weinstock Netanel, *Cyberspace Self–Governance: A Skeptical View from Liberal Democratic Theory*, 88 CALIF. L. REV. 395, 426–27 (2000).

4. *An objection from legislative incompetence.* Consider the following additional objection:

> Even if jurisdictional issues are solved, the infrastructure of cyberspace is evolving too rapidly for governments to regulate efficiently. The unique technical and transnational nature of cyberspace justifies self-government. * * * Overall, the legislatures, regulatory agencies, and courts do not appear percipient in anticipating the economic and social impact of new technology. This lack of foresight suggests that these institutions should not unnecessarily exercise their existing authority and not seek new authority to regulate cyberspace until either the technology and its implications have become predictable or the institutions and customs of cyberspace have an opportunity to develop in response to the needs of Cyberian constituent communities and commerce.

Llewellyn Joseph Gibbons, *No Regulation, Government Regulation, or Self–Regulation: Social Enforcement or Social Contracting for Governance in Cyberspace*, 6 CORNELL J.L. & PUB. POL'Y 475, 509–10 (1997). Do you agree that online communications constitute a uniquely unpredictable subject matter for regulation? How else might legislatures deal with governance issues arising from technological change?

5. *Self–ordering reconsidered.* Some opponents of government regulation of online conduct argue that self-ordering through contract and norms represents an advance over rules imposed by "outsiders." *See* Part II(B) & (C), *infra*. Consider, however, the argument that self-ordering by participants in online transactions would result in a poorer implementation of the ideals of liberal democracy than our existing representative democracy, because (1) pure majoritarianism lacks a mechanism for protecting minorities from overreaching by majorities; (2) the aggregation of individual preferences as elicited through a plebiscite does not truly represent the popular will, which arises only through the political process; (3) the inherent limitations on human knowledge, capacities, and time that make it impossible for citizens to express meaningful views on a range of complex public policy issues are equally applicable to "cybercitizens"; (4) the relative transience of online communities makes it unlikely that effective norms governing behavior will develop; and (5) rules emerging from online contracts will be those imposed unilaterally by vendors in pursuance of their own interests. *See* Neil Weinstock Netanel, *Cyberspace Self–Governance: A Skeptical View from Liberal Democratic Theory*, 88 CALIF. L. REV. 395 (2000).

II. A PLURALIST APPROACH TO REGULATION OF ONLINE CONDUCT

In the world at large, a variety of constraints combine to regulate human behavior to an extent that makes society possible. No single constraint is alone adequate, and different types of constraints are appropriate in different situations. Parents, teachers, and religious authorities inculcate values that govern us internally. Individuals enter into contracts, and usually adhere to them; if a dispute arises, they may call upon an arbitrator or judge to determine their obligations, and may rely upon the coercive power of the state to enforce their rights. Governments promulgate rules of conduct that are likewise enforced through coercive sanctions. Neighbors generally settle their disputes peacefully without external intervention. The avenues for having an effect on others are limited by physics, geography, and technology.

The same variety of constraints must govern activity that takes place using online means of communication: a unitary approach, relying on a single method of constraining behavior, is unlikely to succeed. The task is rather to construct a toolbox of regulatory approaches that are applicable to online activity, and to select the proper tool for each job.

How shall we determine what type of constraint is likely to work best in a given situation? Professor Trotter Hardy suggests that, in view of the protean nature of online communications, "we ought to be reluctant to impose behavior control that is inflexible and uniform beyond the needs of the situation. As a general matter, the most flexible rules are those that are issued at the 'lowest' possible level: bottom up rules like those embodied in contracts or the rule of 'live and let live' can be changed more easily by their makers than statutes or judicial precedents." I. Trotter Hardy, *The Proper Legal Regime for "Cyberspace,"* 55 U. Pitt. L. Rev. 993, 1025 (1994).

Consider the following regulatory devices. In what online situations would you expect their use to be particularly appropriate? Particularly inappropriate? What combination of government actions and market forces might encourage the implementation of each mechanism?

A. Transnational Cyberspace Law

Several commentators have suggested that online activity should be regulated by a transnational law of cyberspace, analogous to the law merchant, applying to itinerant merchants, that flourished in the middle ages, or the law of admiralty. Such a law would arise from the customs and usages that have developed spontaneously through online interactions. It would be invoked and applied by existing, territorially based courts, and enforcement authorities in other nations would recognize the validity of judgments based on this law. *See, e.g.*, I. Trotter Hardy, *The Proper Legal Regime for "Cyberspace,"* 55 U. Pitt. L. Rev. 993, 1019–21 (1994).

Is a transnational law of cyberspace possible? Would it be desirable?

B. Contractual Ordering

Contracts are a common mechanism for constraining behavior, in the online world as much as anywhere else. Some have suggested a much broader role for contracts in online transactions, displacing regulation by law in certain subject matters. The Uniform Computer Information Transactions Act, for example, discussed in Chapter 4, *infra*, would allow content owners to control use of their material contractually in a manner tending to supplant the law of copyright. Others have suggested that a system of contracts between Internet users and the Internet service providers through which they gain online access, supplemented by contracts among ISPs, could control the conduct of online participants. *See* Robert L. Dunne, *Deterring Unauthorized Access to Computers: Controlling Behavior in Cyberspace Through a Contract Law Paradigm*, 35 Jurimetrics J. 1 (1994). Consistent with such an approach, contracts are integral to the functioning of the Uniform Domain Name Dispute Resolution Policy ("UDRP"), promulgated by the Internet Corporation for Assigned Names and Numbers, ("ICANN"). ICANN contractually obligates domain name registrars to agree to implement the UDRP. Domain name registrars contractually obligate domain name registrants to abide by the UDRP. *See* Part II(F), *infra*. The UDRP is examined in Chapter 3, *infra*.

Any entity that is an indispensable participant in online transactions can potentially act as a regulator of conduct through contractual restrictions. ISPs commonly state, in their Terms of Service, rules to which a subscriber must agree as a condition to using the ISP's services. Some of these terms can take the place of legal regulation. For example, most ISPs prohibit their subscribers from sending unsolicited commercial e-mail. Credit card issuers exert control over the conduct of online merchants who want to be able to use the issuer's card to accept payment from purchasers. Online auction sites place limitations on the types of goods that may be sold using their services.

Regulation by private transactional intermediaries, like other forms of self-regulation, frequently arises in response to a perceived threat of government regulation. Yahoo!'s decision to ban Nazi memorabilia from its online auctions, for example, likely was influenced by a French court's effort to curtail that activity through application of French law. *See* Part III(A), *infra*.

In what areas is regulation by private transactional intermediaries most likely to be effective? How should we expect private regulatory regimes to differ from those resulting from political processes?

Consider the following in regard to the use of contracts as a governance device:

> Many Internet observers are adopting the view that networks of contracts among participants can substitute for external regulation. * * * How can we determine whether such a contractual ordering is possible or desirable? Note that the examples above—the agreements with the [online service providers] and the content creators—are at best contracts of adhesion. A conventional approach to adhesion contracts validates them only if the terms are reasonable and/or are foreseeable by the adhering party. In the context of mass-market uniform adhesion contracts, a conventional economic analysis would validate those contracts in which the package of terms won out in a free market, indicating that the terms were preferred by consumers, and would invalidate those that were arrived at by collusion or market power. Under this economic analysis, adhesion contracts cannot be deemed valid without investigating their market context.
>
> One easy observation is that sysops [i.e., system operators, which control access to online services] and content creators may find a way tacitly to standardize on onerous "take-it-or-leave-it" terms, under threat of exclusion in the sysop case, or denial of access to digital information in the content creation case. The optimistic view is that the adhesive character is of no moment because exit is easy; thousands of flowers will bloom (and only those that users choose to pollinate will continue to exist). But a more pessimistic view is that sysops will find a way to coordinate on onerous take-it-or-leave-it terms, under the threat of exclusion.

Such coordination on uniform take-it-or-leave-it terms amounts to imposition of a rigid entitlement structure.

Externalities are another problem with these sorts of contracts. It is possible, for example, as Professor Niva Elkin–Koren and others note, that there are more and broader-ranging externalities with information than with physical goods. Indeed, this commodified mode of thought—looking solely at the economic impact on third parties—does not fully capture what is at stake here, such as the formation of self and its characteristics and preferences in the context of groups. Contracts which concern privacy, for example, touch on a range of issues beyond the economic transaction, including personal identity and freedom. Who will decide to what extent firms may gather and use information about customers? Will it be sufficient to validate these practices that the consumer "clicks" on a box in an on-line form contract?

A third important point about contractual ordering is the distinction between contracts between immediate parties and those that "run with" the object. Contracts that run with the object change the entitlement structure—not just between the immediate parties but for all parties in a chain of distribution. When contracts that "run with" the object are also mass uniform contracts of adhesion, then we do have a change in the overall social entitlement structure. In the realm of information content, we are seeing "running" contracts both that attempt to expand background intellectual property rights (e.g., by forbidding reverse engineering) and to cut them back (e.g., the copyleft General Public License). Given that schemes of "running" adhesion contracts, like adhesion contracts generally, cannot be ipso facto valid, how will we determine which of them will be enforceable (whoever is doing the enforcing)?

The analogy of "residential private government," drawn from the context of social ordering through land ownership, is instructive. Systems of private covenants, in subdivisions or condominiums, have been praised as a method of choice-based community creation. But they have also been criticized, primarily for three reasons: (1) they are imposed on would-be residents on a take-it-or-leave-it basis; (2) they have tended to standardize on exclusionary sets of rules that reinforce patterns of social power detrimental to poor and minority persons (and anyone heterodox in lifestyle); and (3) their "private" character means there is little or no constitutional check on the power of developers to set their own rules as the market (i.e., the tastes of those with money) dictates. Judge-made doctrines such as the requirement that running covenants "touch and concern land" have served to weed out some systems of "running" contractual arrangements, arguably those that are most vulnerable to these kinds of criticisms. It is true that

> Internet users can more easily exit the rules created by one sysop or content provider than condominium or subdivision dwellers can exit the rules created by the developer. The possibility of exit will not be of much use, however, if all of the desirable sites or content have similar rules.

Margaret Jane Radin & R. Polk Wagner, *The Myth Of Private Ordering: Rediscovering Legal Realism in Cyberspace*, 73 CHI.-KENT L. REV. 1295, 1310–13 (1998).

NOTES & QUESTIONS

Appropriateness of contractual ordering. Is the use of contracts as a governance device more problematic in connection with online transactions than in any other application? Consider the argument that contracts are *less* problematic in the online context, because the online medium reduces transaction costs and enables true bargaining over contract terms.

C. NORMS

Certain social groups, such as the cattle ranchers in California that Professor Robert C. Ellickson studied in *Order Without Law* (1991), settle disputes by reference to internally generated norms of behavior, which do not necessarily correspond with, and may even be contrary to, legal rules. Some commentators believe that participants in online transactions should settle their differences in the same way, by reference to "netiquette." Consider, however, the following objections to this approach: (1) Norms typically develop in small, close-knit, homogeneous communities whose membership remains static over time. The community of Internet participants, by contrast, is large, individualistic, heterogeneous, and dynamic. (2) There is no reason to expect that norms developed within the online community will adequately control negative externalities affecting offline interests. (3) Enforcement of online norms is problematic: the defects of vigilantism are well-known, courts may have difficulty discerning applicable norms, and code-based enforcement may not reflect the will of the governed. *See* Mark A. Lemley, *The Law and Economics of Internet Norms*, 73 CHI.-KENT L. REV. 1257 (1998).

D. COORDINATED PRIVATE ACTIONS: THE REALTIME BLACKHOLE LIST

A high-tech incarnation of the old-fashioned blacklist exists in the form of the Mail Abuse Prevention System Realtime Blackhole List, known for short as the MAPS RBL. The MAPS RBL consists of a list of ISPs that MAPS, a California non-profit limited liability company headed by Internet pioneer and anti-spam activist Paul Vixie, believes aid and abet senders of unsolicited commercial e-mail. Many ISPs choose voluntarily to subscribe to the list, which they use automatically to reject mail sent from a domain hosted by any of the ISPs on the list. The goal is to provide blacklisted ISPs with a powerful incentive to get themselves off the list, which they can accomplish by conforming to MAPS's rules. In most cases, ISPs are placed on the list because they operate "open relays"—mail servers configured so that third parties can commandeer them to send unsolicited commercial e-mail in bulk, thereby evading their own ISP's Terms of Service prohibiting the practice.

Here is MAPS's justification for its approach to combating spam:

Introduction

The MAPS℠ (Mail Abuse Prevention System) RBL℠ (Realtime Blackhole List) is a list of networks which are known to be friendly, or at least neutral, to spammers who use these networks either to originate or relay spam. As we discover such networks, we deny them access to the part of the Internet that we are paying for. Because our research into the attitudes and policies of network owners is hard to duplicate, many dozens of other network owners have asked for and are now receiving a real time mirror of our MAPS RBL℠.

Theft of Service

Irrespective of the laws of whatever land a spammer, or a spam victim, is in, we consider spam to be **theft of service**. Internet users do not pay their access fees for the purpose of being annoyed. None of us bought our computers or modems for the use of so-called *advertisers*. Since the original ARPAnet the written rules of the Internet community (see the Netiquette RFCs and their precursors from Usenet) have required that we each refrain from intentionally annoying other Internet citizens.

* * *

Rights to Passage

No Internet user has any fundamental **right** to send you e-mail or any other kind of traffic. All information exchange on the Internet is consensual, and unless you **opt into** some advertising feed, the automatic presumption on the part of all Internet users is that **you would be annoyed** by e-mail which promotes a unilateral cause (such as making money for the sender). By creating and maintaining the MAPS RBL℠ we are exercising our right to refuse traffic from anyone we choose. We choose not to accept any traffic at all from networks who are friendly in any way to spammers. **This is our right** as it would be **within anyone's rights** to make the same choice (or a different one, so long as only their own resources were affected by their choice).

* * *

Censorship and Free Speech

The right to **free speech**, in places which recognize it, means the right to print leaflets, stand on street corners, and offer to give them to passers by. Just as there can be no **right** to shout *fire!* in a crowded movie theatre, there is and can be no right to use someone else's printing press and delivery trucks to send your message to people who have not asked to see it. We are all, in the MAPS℠ project and in every anti-spam coalition, extreme advocates of **free speech**. However, we believe that speech is more free if the recipients hear what **they choose** to hear rather than what spammers want them to hear.

An electronic mailbox which is jammed to overflowing with spam **may not even have room** for desirable, consensual communications, but even if there are no resource constraints on a mailbox, the ability of the average Internet citizen to sift through mountains of spam, **after paying to receive it** is limited. How free is speech between two consenting parties if thousands of third parties are deliberately shouting messages at the first two?

As for censorship, we have heard the accusation many times but have failed to understand it each time. We don't care what two consenting people say in the privacy of their own channel. We don't care if people want to send each other traffic we consider boring (such as pornography or football scores). What we are trying to prevent is our paying, in money and resources and our own time, to receive and process, or relay, traffic which is **non-consensual** in nature. We do not accept unsolicited mass e-mail, **regardless of its subject matter**.

* * *

Legality of Blackholing

As dual citizens of the Internet and of the United States of America, we worry every day about the Sherman Antitrust Act. Are our actions interpretable as *conspiracy in restraint of trade*? So far, *no*. We've been threatened with legal action on about a dozen occasions, and our legal advisors have said *it will depend on the judge you get*. Thus far no one who has threatened us has done more than initial discovery motions, so, for now, **we wait**. (*No cases are pending that we know of.*)

You can bet that the community will be hearing from us if we ever need a legal defense fund. Given that the number of spam victims numbers in the tens of millions, we suspect that the spammers **don't want to sue us** because of the popularity of our cause.

* * *

Responsibility for Spamming

We lost count a while ago of the number of times someone whose network we'd blackholed complained: *we're not spammers, our* ***customers*** *are spammers* and then advised *please take your complaint up with them*. Now, to be fair and balanced about all of this, there are indeed times in life when one is expected to be one's brother's keeper, and other times when one's brother will be expected to take all the heat by themselves. But for a network owner to try to escape responsibility for spam is a bit like an arms merchant trying to escape responsibility for dead civilians: **if you knew in advance** what the customer was planning to do with your technology, then **you are culpable**. If, once told, you do nothing to stop them, then **you are culpable**.

But as satisfying as these morality games are to all who take part in them, it makes no difference to us whether you are culpable or not. The fact is, we don't like to get spammed, and if your network is **friendly or neutral** to spammers, then we can't allow your network to touch our networks at all.

* * *

Mail Abuse Prevention System, *MAPS RBL Rationale*, mail-abuse.org/rbl/rationale.html (last revised Jul. 19, 2000).

Harris Interactive, a large Internet-based market research firm, was placed on the MAPS list. As a result, a number of ISPs that subscribe to the MAPS list blocked e-mail from Harris, which severely interfered with its ability to conduct business operations. Harris responded by filing a lawsuit against several ISPs, including America Online, Hotmail, and Qwest, as well as MAPS itself, alleging several causes of action including antitrust violations, tortious interference, commercial disparagement, and defamation. Harris explained its objections to the MAPS system:

The Government Must Provide the Rules for the Internet

Self-appointed Private Groups are Prone to Subjectivity and Selective Enforcement

A Statement by Dr. Gordon S. Black, Chairman and CEO of Harris Interactive Inc.

The current Harris Interactive situation is a perfect example of why the government, and not self-appointed private groups, must create the rules which govern Internet communications. Essentially, Mail Abuse Prevention System, LLC (MAPS), and other like groups, are permitted, without any due process of law or even a fair process, to restrict companies' rights to conduct legitimate business over the Internet. These restrictions are based on complaints that may be economically motivated by our competitors. In our case, MAPS decided to apply a standard to us that it does not apply consistently to the ISP's from which we believe, they derive their income. * * *

The decision by AOL to block our emails is a particularly egregious example of market abuse by an Internet giant. AOL owns the research firm, Digital Marketing Systems (DMS), which is a direct and very active competitor of Harris Interactive. By blocking our emails, AOL can dramatically disadvantage Harris

> Interactive as a competitor, and that is precisely what has happened. We have filed an anti-trust action against AOL, and we intend to file supporting documents with the Justice Department and the Federal Trade Commission.
>
> MAPS and the ISP's have created a process that permits them effectively both to deprive us of the use of our property without any due process, to interfere with our legitimate business activities, and to allow our direct competitors to damage us without any recourse. The damage to us will be significant, and we intend to pursue redress to the highest courts if need be.
>
> The broader issue is that Congress must act to set the standards for Internet access, much the same as they have for telephone, cable, and other forms of interstate communication. Harris Interactive does not approve of spamming and we do not engage in it. However, the proper standards cannot be established through self-regulation because the current process is unfair, undemocratic, and allows anti-competitive practices to emerge. A few self-appointed zealots cannot be the dictators of standards that affect hundreds of millions of people and billions of dollars of commerce. For this reason, Harris Interactive will pursue legislative action in Congress and regulatory actions by the Federal Trade and Federal Communication Commissions in addition to the actions already taken. Finally, we intend to seek support from the many other legitimate businesses that will be injured by MAPS and similar organizations if MAPS is allowed to continue to apply unilateral, arbitrary, and capricious standards within the industry.

Harris Interactive, *Harris Interactive Files Suit Against AOL, Microsoft, Qwest and Other ISPs Over Restraint of Trade* (Jul. 31, 2000), www.harrisinteractive.com/news/allnewsbydate.asp?NewsID=127.

Consider also the following objections to the MAPS RBL: (1) MAPS applies a contestable definition of what constitutes spam: it treats commercial e-mail as unsolicited unless the sender has implemented a double opt-in procedure, while others believe that a single opt-in is sufficient; (2) placement of an ISP on the RBL results in blocking mail from all subscribers of the ISP, most of whom are not spammers; (3) the RBL lends itself to abuse, empowering MAPS to block an ISP for reasons having nothing to do with spamming. *See* Sabra–Anne Kelin, Note, *State Regulation of Unsolicited Commercial E–Mail*, 16 BERKELEY TECH. L.J. 435 (2001). For further consideration of unsolicited commercial e-mail, see Chapter 13, *infra*.

NOTES & QUESTIONS

Evaluation of control by concerted private action. Is MAPS providing a service to the community by drawing attention to ISPs that are contributing to the problem of bulk unsolicited commercial e-mail that is clogging the network, thereby enabling other ISPs to implement their voluntary decisions to avoid doing business with those who engage in such harmful practices? Is MAPS operating an illegal secondary boycott that unfairly penalizes subscribers of the blacklisted ISPs, and tortiously interferes with the ISPs' contractual relations? Has MAPS unjustifiably arrogated to itself the right to create rules establishing acceptable conduct by ISPs? Has it done any more than propose a set of rules that has come to be accepted by a substantial portion of the market? *See Media3 Technologies, LLC v. Mail Abuse Prevention System, LLC*, 2001 WL 92389 (D.Mass. Jan. 2, 2001) (denying preliminary injunction to web-hosting company that MAPS branded "spam-friendly" and placed on the RBL, finding that plaintiff had not established likelihood of success on defamation, tortious interference with business relations, or unfair trade practices claims).

E. CODE

Professor Lawrence Lessig, in *Code and Other Laws of Cyberspace* (1999), discussed in Part I, *supra,* has drawn attention to the role of what he terms "code" or "architecture" in regulating behavior. He identifies four types of constraints on behavior: laws, norms, the market, and code. The first three of these need little explanation. Laws are rules of conduct that are enforced through the coercive power of the state. Norms are rules that arise more or less spontaneously within a certain community, and are enforced primarily through a personal sense of ethics and peer pressure. The market constrains through the mechanisms of price and availability: you can buy only what the market offers to sell, and your economic resources limit what things you can acquire.

"Code," or "architecture," is a constraint that derives from the nature of the world. The impossibility of traveling faster than light constrains our ability to visit other galaxies. A lock constrains a prospective burglar's ability to break and enter. Mountain ranges constrain our ability to travel. Closer to the present context, technological facts exert a regulatory force. Liquid crystal displays enable mobile computing, which was infeasible with cathode ray tube displays. The existence of telephone caller ID limits our ability to communicate anonymously. Code can also consist of what computer programmers mean by the term: software instructions that control the operation of computing hardware. The availability of strong encryption constrains the ability of others to intercept our communications. The feature set of a software application regulates our ability to make use of it in a manner not intended by the developer.

Some types of code-based regulation are immutable—we can't overcome the constraint of the light-speed limit. But the code that is of greatest interest to regulation of online conduct is, like the Internet itself, socially constructed. That is, the code that regulates online behavior is whatever we decide to make it. Decisions about what code will be are made through several mechanisms. A commercial venture or an independent standard-setting body can propose a protocol, which becomes generally adopted either because it works better than the alternatives or because network effects create powerful incentives to adopt it. A software product may gain widespread acceptance in the market and drive out alternatives.

Of greatest interest to Lessig, a government may regulate "indirectly," by decreeing that code should be constructed to accomplish a desired regulatory effect. He offers some examples: (1) the Communications Assistance for Law Enforcement Act of 1994 requires that the digitally switched telephone network be designed to make it easy for the government to intercept telephone calls using wiretaps; (2) the Audio Home Recording Act of 1992 requires digital audio tape recorders to be equipped with a chip that limits a user's ability to make high-quality copies of copies; (3) the Digital Millennium Copyright Act of 1998 makes it a crime to create and sell software that defeats copyright management protection devices. *See* CODE, *supra*, at 44–49.

NOTES & QUESTIONS

Private indirect control. Should we be concerned that regulation by code, as an indirect form of regulation, is less visible than direct regulation, and therefore less subject to control by political constraints? Should we be more or less concerned about non-governmental creators of code, who are presumptively motivated by the desire for profit rather than by public interest considerations?

F. AN EXPERIMENT IN HYBRID GOVERNANCE: ICANN

Resources made available on the Internet are useful only to the extent they can be identified, located, and retrieved. To this end, each resource has some sort of identifier associated with it: a resource is summoned by invoking its identifier. Domain names are at the core of the system that allows identifiers to be associated with Internet resources. All website addresses, and all e-mail addresses, are built upon domain names. To access a page on the website maintained by the New York Times, I use an identifier that has the form "www.nytimes.com/page_id." To send an e-mail message to an employee of the New York Times, I use an identifier of the form "name@nytimes.com." In both cases, the domain name is "nytimes.com."

Intense controversies have arisen with respect to domain names. These controversies are explored in Chapter 3, *infra.* Trademark owners have complained about the assignment to others of domain names incorporating their trademark. Non-commercial users, and small businesses, have decried efforts by trademark holders to maintain absolute control over domain names that resemble their trademarks. Some have argued for broad expansion of the number of top-level domains—the two-or three-letter suffix, like .com, .org, or .edu, that is used to organize domain names—to make more domain name combinations available. Others have argued for a go-slow approach to expansion of the domain name space.

Governance of the mechanisms by which domain names are managed, known as the domain name system ("DNS"), has passed through several hands during the brief history of the Internet. In the 1970's and 1980's, before the Internet gained any commercial significance, the predecessor of the DNS was controlled by several academic and non-profit institutions, under contracts with agencies of the U.S. government. In 1993, the National Science Foundation ("NSF") contracted with Network Solutions, Inc. ("NSI"), a private for-profit corporation, to manage the DNS. The contract gave NSI the exclusive right to register domain names in the .com, .org, and .net global top-level domains ("gTLDs"). Beginning in 1995, NSF allowed NSI to charge registrants for its domain registration services.

Most of the policymaking relating to the DNS remained under the control of the U.S. government—including the all-important decision on whether to add new gTLDs—but NSI of necessity began to take on certain governance functions. Perhaps the most important of these was its creation of a frequently amended policy for handling trademark disputes involving domain name registrations. The need for such a policy became clear as lawsuits alleging cybersquatting began to proliferate, and NSI was sometimes named as a defendant in actions for trademark infringement. *See, e.g., Lockheed Martin Corp. v. Network Solutions, Inc.*, 194 F.3d 980 (9th Cir.1999).

Under NSI's policy, a third party could initiate a challenge to a domain name registrant's right to that name by submitting evidence that the registration of the domain name violated the third party's rights. The challenger could meet this requirement with evidence that the domain name was identical to a trademark it owned that was registered either federally or under foreign law. Upon receipt of such evidence, NSI would offer the registrant an opportunity to show that it too owned a trademark on the domain name. If the registrant could not produce such a registration, NSI would put the domain name on "hold," preventing the registrant from using it, pending resolution of the dispute.

NSI's domain name dispute policy engendered great dissatisfaction among domain name registrants, in part due to the phenomenon of "reverse domain name hijacking"—abuse of the policy by trademark owners that asserted spurious claims of infringement with the goal of preventing registrants from using domain names that they coveted.

In 1997, responding to pressure from commercial interests and foreign governments, the Clinton administration began consultations aimed at privatizing governance of the DNS. In June 1998, the U.S. Department of Commerce ("DOC") issued a policy statement, known as the DNS White Paper, that called for the creation of "a new, not-for-profit corporation formed by private sector Internet stakeholders to administer policy for the Internet name and address system." The White Paper set out several characteristics that the new corporation would have to possess before DOC would devolve DNS governance functions upon it. Among other things, the corporation would have to be incorporated and headquartered in the United States; be governed by a board of directors, with international membership, designed to represent various specified constituencies; operate "on the basis of a sound and transparent decision-making process, which protects against capture by a self-interested faction"; and rely on the advice of internal councils dedicated to specific subject areas. The White Paper also specified several policies that it "anticipated" the new corporation would implement, including requiring information identifying domain name registrants to be publicly available (for the benefit of trademark holders that might wish to challenge a registration), and setting up and requiring registrants to abide by a dispute resolution system that would resolve claims of "cyberpiracy or cybersquatting." DOC pledged to enter into an agreement with the new corporation under which it would take over certain responsibilities for management of the DNS then under the control of government contractors. *See* Management of Internet Names and Addresses, 63 Fed. Reg. 31,741 (Jun. 10, 1998), www.ntia.doc.gov/ntiahome/domainname/6_5_98dns.htm.

In October 1998, Jon Postel, an Internet pioneer who had been involved in administration of the DNS and its predecessors since the 1970's, formed a corporation—the Internet Corporation for Assigned Names and Numbers ("ICANN")—that was designed to qualify as the new corporation described in the White Paper. The DOC requested certain changes to ICANN's articles of incorporation and bylaws, to which ICANN acceded. The transfer of DNS responsibilities to ICANN was accomplished through a complex set of memoranda of understanding and contracts among DOC, ICANN, and NSI that were entered in 1998 and 1999. Those agreements gave ICANN a significant breadth of policy-making authority, but kept it on a short leash, as the agreements carried an expiration date, and DOC retained authority over perhaps the most contentious DNS-related issue, creation of new global top-level domains.

ICANN's first substantial exercise of policy-making authority was its creation of the Uniform Domain Name Dispute Resolution Policy ("UDRP"), replacing NSI's widely criticized dispute policy. The UDRP grew out of a study and recommendation from the World Intellectual Property Organization, an agency of the United Nations that represents the interests of intellectual property rights holders, upon the proposal of the United States. The UDRP is discussed in more detail in Chapter 3, *infra*. In another action of enormous consequence to Internet users, trademark holders, and others, ICANN devised and implemented a procedure for selecting new gTLDs to supplement the original eight. ICANN's first use of this procedure, in 2000, yielded seven new gTLDs: .aero, .biz, .coop, .info, .museum, .name, and .pro.

ICANN has been the target of intense criticism during its brief existence. Critics have charged: (1) ICANN's processes are not sufficiently transparent. Many of its meetings are not open to the public. When public input is solicited, insufficient notice is provided to allow meaningful participation. ICANN's supporters respond that ICANN is essentially a technical body, not a policy-making body, and therefore public participation is unnecessary. (2) ICANN's structure is not representative of the international Internet community. Nine of the 18 members of the Board of Directors are selected by ICANN's three "Supporting Organizations," each of which represents a narrow slice of the Internet community. Of the nine "At-Large" Directors, four are holdovers from the group of nine that were put in place on an interim basis by ICANN's creators at the time it was formed. The other five At–Large Directors were elected in 2000 by Internet users worldwide who registered as Members of ICANN. Although nominally democratic, the At–Large election suffered from low voter turnout: for example, in the election for the Director representing North and South America, a total of 3,449 votes were cast, and the winner, Karl Auerbach, garnered a plurality of 1,074 votes. (3) ICANN's process for selecting seven new gTLD's in 2000 was excessively slow, arbitrary, and skewed in favor of the interests of trademark owners. The non-refundable $50,000 application fee precluded applications from all but the best-funded candidates. (4) ICANN is not an independent, international entity, but remains under the control of the U.S. Department of Commerce.

For an argument that that DOC's delegation of authority to ICANN is illegal, in violation of the Administrative Procedures Act, see A. Michael Froomkin, *Wrong Turn in Cyberspace: Using ICANN to Route Around the APA and the Constitution*, 50 DUKE L.J. 17 (2000). For a discussion of ICANN's legitimacy in broader terms, see Jonathan Weinberg, *ICANN and the Problem of Legitimacy*, 50 DUKE L.J. 187 (2000).

What is the source of ICANN's authority over the DNS? This is a difficult question. The best short answer may be that it is a combination of (1) DOC's recognition of ICANN, as reflected in certain agreements among DOC, ICANN, and NSI; (2) the U.S. government's control over most of the servers that house the authoritative root of the DNS; and (3) the network effects of adhering to a single authoritative root. (For background on the technical operation of the DNS and the role of authoritative root servers, see Appendix D.) But ICANN's authority has not gone unchallenged. Several companies have tried to set up alternative domain name roots, not sanctioned or under the control of ICANN. Internet users that take their domain name resolution services from an alternative root can reach addresses under all of the ICANN-sanctioned domains, including gTLDs like .com and country code TLDs like .us, as well as those under domains not sanctioned by ICANN, like .xxx and .kids. For contrasting views on the desirability of alternative roots, see New.net, *A Proposal to Introduce Market–Based Principles into Domain Name Governance* (2001), www.new.net/NewnetPaper.pdf; ICANN, *Keeping the Internet a Reliable Global Public Resource: Response to New.net "Policy Paper,"* www.icann.org/icp/icp–3–background/response-to-new.net–09jul01.htm (2001).

NOTES & QUESTIONS

1. *Who should manage the infrastructure of the Internet?* What entity should have control of the domain name system? Should the United States, in view of its central role in creating the Internet, be accorded some preeminent role in its management, or should the Internet be treated as a truly transnational resource? Does the fact that ICANN is incorporated in the United States give the United States an unfair advantage in controlling the DNS? What types of institutional structures are available for management of transnational resources? Can useful parallels be drawn from the systems that have evolved for managing international waters? space? Antarctica? global warming?

2. *Other possibilities.* Consider a proposal for governance of the DNS that a group of existing Internet- and telecommunications-related international organizations floated in 1997, according to which "Stewardship of the gTLD space [would be] assigned to the gTLD DNS Policy Oversight Committee (POC) comprising members named by the Internet Society (ISOC), Internet Assigned Numbers Authority (IANA), Internet Architecture Board (IAB), International Telecommunications Union (ITU), International Trademark Association (INTA), World Intellectual Property Organization (WIPO), and [the Council of Registrars, a Switzerland-based association of domain name registrars]." International Ad Hoc Committee, *Final Report of the International Ad Hoc Committee: Recommendations for Administration and Management of gTLDs* (1997), www.iahc.org/txt/draft-iahc-recommend–00.txt. Would it be preferable instead for the governing body to be established under an international treaty?

III. Regulatory Reach in a Borderless World: The Problem of Controlling Activity Based Outside the Jurisdiction

A. Extraterritorial Assertions of Regulatory Authority

The Internet gives increased salience to the issue of the extraterritorial reach of domestic law—that is, the ability of a sovereign to apply its laws to activity originating from outside its territorial jurisdiction. The distance-erasing characteristics of online communications give rise to several scenarios in which conduct originating in one country may have substantial effects in another. Consider, for example: (1) A website that offers to sell goods that are legal in the country where the website is hosted, but illegal in other countries. The goods might be offered either for physical delivery, such as unapproved pharmaceuticals or Nazi memorabilia, or electronically, such as obscenity or online gambling. (2) A website that posts speech that is legal in the host country but illegal in others. Sexually explicit material, defamation, information on making bombs, or hate speech might have the status of protected speech in some countries but not in others. (3) A website that posts material that is illegal both in the country where it originates and in the country where it is received.

The controversy over Nazi memorabilia offered for sale via Yahoo!'s online auction site illustrates some of the issues. Yahoo!, like a number of other websites, provides a forum in which individuals may auction goods to a worldwide online audience. Yahoo! never possesses or takes title to the goods being sold, but earns a commission each time a sale is completed under its auspices. Two French anti-racism groups filed a lawsuit against Yahoo! in a French court, alleging violation of a French law that makes it illegal to traffic in Nazi memorabilia. The suit was based on items that were offered for sale via Yahoo!'s original, English-language site, aimed primarily at the U.S. market, and hosted at yahoo.com. Yahoo! also maintained a French-language auction site, at yahoo.fr, which did not allow the sale of items that, like Nazi memorabilia, were illegal under French law.

Yahoo! argued that it was technically infeasible to prevent citizens of France from accessing the auction site or particular items offered for sale, while still offering the items to citizens of other countries (such as the United States) where the sales were perfectly legal. It also objected that the French court had no jurisdiction over it, since its services were directed at persons located in the United States, its servers were located in the United States, and an order requiring Yahoo! to prevent access to Nazi items would violate the First Amendment and therefore be unenforceable in U.S. courts.

In May 2000, the French court ordered Yahoo! to "take all necessary measures to prevent and render impossible any access via Yahoo.com to the Nazi artifact auction service and to any other site or service that may be construed as constituting a justification of Nazism or a denial of Nazi crimes." But it stayed the effect of the order, and appointed an international panel of experts to report on the feasibility of preventing persons located in France from accessing auctions of Nazi items.

The panel of experts reported back to the court that while it was technically infeasible to identify with 100% accuracy the geographic location of website visitors, it might be possible to identify 70–80% of the French visitors. This could be done on the basis of the IP address of the visitor's computer. The experts explained that blocks of IP addresses are allocated to access providers on a systematic basis, so that it is often possible to associate a given IP address with a particular access provider. Based on their research, the experts concluded that nearly 70% of the IP addresses used by access providers located in France could be identified as such. The other 30% includes users who get access through America Online, which uses IP addresses all of which appear to be assigned to an access provider in Virginia; users who get access through corporate intranets; and those who make use of anonymous access points. It is also possible, but less likely due to the cost of international telephone calls, that a resident of France could gain access through a provider located in another country, or that a person located outside of France could gain access through a provider located in France. Thus, the experts concluded, it is technologically feasible for Yahoo! to block access by 70% of French Internet users through IP address identification.

The court also observed that, contrary to Yahoo!'s protestations of technical infeasibility, Yahoo! had already implemented a system for determining the geographic location of site visitors, as demonstrated by the fact that a visitor accessing yahoo.com from a computer located in France was greeted with banner advertisements in the French language.

Based on the experts' report, in November 2000 the court directed Yahoo! to comply with its May 2000 order within three months, or be subject to a daily fine of about $13,000. *See Association "Union des*

Etudiants Juifs de France" v. Yahoo! Inc. (Trib. gr. inst. Nov. 20, 2000), www.legalis.net/cgi-iddn/french/affiche-jnet.cgi?droite=decisions/responsabilite/ord_tgi-paris_201100.htm, unofficial translation at www.gigalaw.com/library/france-yahoo-2000-11-20-lapres.html, *upholding id.* (Trib. gr. inst. May 22, 2000), www.legalis.net/cgi-iddn/french/affiche-jnet.cgi?droite=decisions/responsabilite/ord_tgi-paris_220500.htm.

Does this case presage irreconcilable clashes between cultures, as the Internet draws aside the curtain of separation imposed by geographical distance? Consider the following:

> The Yahoo! case illustrates the growing difficulty of reconciling the growth of the Internet with international laws. Recently, Yahoo!'s German subsidiary was also investigated for offering sales of Hitler's "Mein Kampf", and Germany's Central Council of Jews is currently threatening to sue an estimated 800 ISPs that allow German citizens to access neo-Nazi websites. The Wi[e]senthal Center, which tracks hate crimes, recorded that the number of websites promoting "hate" doubled to 3,000 in 1999 alone, many of them European extremist groups going online as their countries become more wired to the Internet. The laws enacted by individual countries are fundamentally tied to the history of each nation, a fact acknowledged by Hans–Gertz Lange, a spokesman for Germany's Federal criminal agency the Verfassungsschutz. Just as America's reverence for the First Amendment stems from its long history, Germany's "laws against incitement to racial hatred are tied up with [theirs]."
>
> This clash of cultures led Mark Weitzman, director of the Wi[e]senthal Center, to remark, "I don't think one society should be able to impose its values on another." Yet does such decoupling mean that one country should not affect the values of another via the Internet, or via laws applied in response to the Internet? Neither? Both? Should companies operating internationally be subject to all laws, or to none? Unless a uniform treaty is created, the answer appears as much tied to jurisdiction as to technology.

Brendon Fowler, Cara Franklin and Bob Hyde, *Can You Yahoo!? The Internet's Digital Fences*, 2001 DUKE L. & TECH. REV. 12.

NOTES & QUESTIONS

1. *Approaches to controlling offensive foreign content.* Consider some other approaches that national governments might take to prevent offensive foreign content from reaching its citizens via the Internet: (1) establishing a national filtering system; (2) requiring domestic ISPs to implement filtering; (3) making it illegal for its residents to receive the content; (4) establishing uniform global restrictions that all countries will enforce against content providers located within their jurisdiction. What are the pros and cons of each approach, from the standpoints of efficacy and enforceability?

What avenues does the French court have for enforcing its judgment? Could the court have achieved the result it desired, while avoiding the legal and practical difficulties with extraterritorial application of French law, by ordering French access providers to filter the offending content of yahoo.com?

In *Yahoo!, Inc. v. La Ligue Contre Le Racisme et L'Antisemitisme*, 169 F.Supp.2d 1181 (N.D.Cal.2001), *appeal pending*, Yahoo! sought a declaratory judgment that the French court's order was unenforceable in United States courts, and an injunction against the French plaintiffs directing them not to seek enforcement. Yahoo! argued that the French court order was not enforceable in the United States because, among other things, enforcement would be contrary to the public policy of protecting free speech, as expressed in the First Amendment. The court, on summary judgment, agreed with Yahoo! The court characterized the issue presented as "whether it is consistent with the Constitution and laws of the United States for another nation to regulate speech by a United States resident within the United States on the basis that such speech can be accessed by Internet users in that nation." It found that enforcement of the French order would violate the First Amendment, since it amounts to viewpoint-based regulation, and is so vague that enforcement would chill protected speech. It then held that "the principle of comity is outweighed by the Court's obligation to uphold the First Amendment," and declared that the order was unenforceable.

In January 2001, Yahoo! announced that it was banning from its auctions items that might incite racism, including items associated with Naziism and the Ku Klux Klan. Its Auction Guidelines were modified to prohibit:

> Any item that promotes, glorifies, or is directly associated with groups or individuals known principally for hateful or violent positions or acts, such as Nazis or the Ku Klux Klan. Official government-issue stamps and coins are not prohibited under this policy. Expressive media, such as books and films, may be subject to more permissive standards as determined by Yahoo! in its sole discretion.

Yahoo!, *Yahoo!Auctions Guidelines*, user.auctions.yahoo.com/html/guidelines.html viewed Jul. 26, 2002). Those guidelines also ban a range of other items, including "[a]ny item that is harmful to minors, obscene, or otherwise objectionable," guns and other weapons, cigarettes, illegal drugs, drug paraphernalia, prescription drugs and medical devices, items that infringe trademark or copyright, counterfeit items, body parts, explosives, fake or non-fake government-issued IDs, gambling items, used underwear, and "[a]ny other item that violates any applicable federal, state or local law or regulation or which Yahoo! determines, in it sole discretion, is inappropriate for sale through the services provided by Yahoo!". *Id.*

Yahoo! said that the new policy was not in response to the French court order, but rather due to complaints from users and from anti-racism organizations. The ban on Nazi items does not fully comply with the

French court's order, since it does not cover books, movies, music, or government-issued coins and stamps, and does not extend to Yahoo!'s non-commercial communication forums.

2. *Extraterritorial reach of U.S. constitutional principles.* Do you agree with the U.S. court's formulation of the issue in the Yahoo! case as one of unconstitutional viewpoint discrimination? Does this case validate the extraterritorial application of the First Amendment to speech occurring in France? Suppose a French court held a U.S. citizen liable for defamation, based on speech she uttered while physically located in France, under standards inconsistent with the First Amendment. Could a U.S. court enforce that order? *See Matusevitch v. Telnikoff*, 877 F.Supp. 1 (D.D.C. 1995), *aff'd*, 159 F.3d 636 (D.C.Cir.1998) (Table). If not, is the court's decision here supportable on the same grounds?

B. COUNTRY-OF-ORIGIN VS. COUNTRY-OF-DESTINATION REGULATION

One of the more intractable issues relating to regulation of online activity is whether a cross-border transaction should be governed by the substantive rules of the *country of origin*, where the seller or content provider is located, or those of the *country of destination*, where the purchaser or viewer of the content is located. The debate pits representatives of business interests and proponents of free speech against advocates of consumer protection and cultural protectionism.

The former camp argues that, since websites are globally accessible, a rule of country-of-destination regulation would mean that businesses would have to conform their behavior with the sometimes-inconsistent rules of some 200 countries around the world. Keeping up with all these rules, let alone complying with them, would put an enormous burden on businesses, particularly small businesses, making global e-commerce economically infeasible. In addition, application of foreign content restrictions would mean that a content provider could not use the Web to distribute certain content that is allowable in his home country.

In the view of the latter camp, a country-of-origin approach would strip consumers of the legal protections offered by their home jurisdictions, leaving them at the mercy of unscrupulous traders, and would give an unfair advantage to foreign sellers, which would not be bound by consumer protection rules applying to domestic sellers. Such an approach would also disregard local mores, making it impossible for a country to protect its citizens from content that it deems harmful.

Consider some proposed solutions to this dilemma:

(1) *Targeting*. A country may apply its rules to an online participant located outside its borders only if that participant has "targeted" its activity at residents of the regulating country. Defining what constitutes

targeting would raise difficulties: for example, if you put up a website in Spanish, have you targeted all countries where Spanish is the national language? Countries with a substantial Spanish-speaking population? What if you put up a website in Finnish? This difficulty might be addressed through an international agreement on targeting. *See* Progressive Policy Institute, *A Third Way Framework for Global E–Commerce* 11–12 (2001), www.ndol.org/documents/global_ecommerce.pdf.

(2) *Two-tier approach.* A general country-of-origin regime might be subject to derogation by a country-of-destination rule applicable to particular classes of plaintiffs. For example, the European Union's Brussels Regulation, discussed in Chapter 7, *infra*, generally enforces forum-selection clauses, but makes forum-selection clauses in most consumer contracts unenforceable. *See* Council Regulation (EC) No. 44/2001 of 22 December 2000 on jurisdiction and the recognition and enforcement of judgments in civil and commercial matters, art. 17, 2001 O.J. (L 12) 1. Likewise, the Regulation generally requires lawsuits to be brought in the country where the defendant is located, but allows consumers to bring actions in their own country of domicile. *Id.*, art. 16.

Similarly, the Rome Convention generally effectuates the parties' choice of law, but in the case of qualifying consumer contracts a contractual choice of law does not deprive the consumer of the protection of the rules of law of his home country that cannot be derogated from by contract. If there is no contractual choice of law, the applicable law is generally that of the country with which the contract is most closely connected, but with consumer contracts the law of the consumer's country governs. *See* Convention on the Law Applicable to Contractual Obligations, Jun. 19, 1980, art. 5, 1980 O.J. (L 266) 1.

Analogous issues arise in the context of taxation—the prerequisite to government regulation, and to government operations of any sort. When online commercial transactions involve more than one taxing authority (e.g., two states of the United States, or two countries), questions can arise as to which authority has the right to tax the transaction. Within the United States, the Dormant Commerce Clause plays an important role in allocating taxing authority; internationally, this is the realm of treaty. Taxation of electronic commerce is considered in Chapter 17, *infra*.

C. Commerce Clause Limitations on State Power to Regulate Online Activities

Statement of Minnesota Attorney General on Internet Jurisdiction

(1995).

WARNING TO ALL INTERNET USERS AND PROVIDERS

THIS MEMORANDUM SETS FORTH THE ENFORCEMENT POSITION OF THE MINNESOTA ATTORNEY GENERAL'S OFFICE

WITH RESPECT TO CERTAIN ILLEGAL ACTIVITIES ON THE INTERNET.

PERSONS OUTSIDE OF MINNESOTA WHO TRANSMIT INFORMATION VIA THE INTERNET KNOWING THAT INFORMATION WILL BE DISSEMINATED IN MINNESOTA ARE SUBJECT TO JURISDICTION IN MINNESOTA COURTS FOR VIOLATIONS OF STATE CRIMINAL AND CIVIL LAWS.

American Libraries Association v. Pataki

969 F.Supp. 160 (1997).

■ PRESKA, DISTRICT JUDGE.

The Internet may well be the premier technological innovation of the present age. Judges and legislators faced with adapting existing legal standards to the novel environment of cyberspace struggle with terms and concepts that the average American five-year-old tosses about with breezy familiarity. Not surprisingly, much of the legal analysis of Internet-related issues has focused on seeking a familiar analogy for the unfamiliar. Commentators reporting on the recent oral argument before the Supreme Court of the United States, which is considering a First Amendment challenge to the Communications Decency Act, noted that the Justices seemed bent on finding the appropriate analogy which would tie the Internet to some existing line of First Amendment jurisprudence: is the Internet more like a television? a radio? a newspaper? a 900–line? a village green? * * * This case, too, depends on the appropriate analogy. I find, as described more fully below, that the Internet is analogous to a highway or railroad. This determination means that the phrase "information superhighway" is more than a mere buzzword; it has legal significance, because the similarity between the Internet and more traditional instruments of interstate commerce leads to analysis under the Commerce Clause.

BACKGROUND

The plaintiffs in the present case filed this action challenging New York Penal Law § 235.21(3) (the "Act" or the "New York Act"), seeking declaratory and injunctive relief. Plaintiffs contend that the Act is unconstitutional both because it unduly burdens free speech in violation of the First Amendment and because it unduly burdens interstate commerce in violation of the Commerce Clause. Plaintiffs moved for a preliminary injunction enjoining enforcement of the Act; defendants opposed the motion. * * * For the reasons that follow, the motion for a preliminary injunction is granted.

I. Parties to the Action

Plaintiffs in the present action represent a spectrum of individuals and organizations who use the Internet to communicate, disseminate, display, and access a broad range of communications. All of the plaintiffs communicate online both within and outside the State of New York, and each plaintiff's communications are accessible from within and outside New York. * * *

II. The Challenged Statute

The Act in question amended N.Y. Penal Law § 235.21 by adding a new subdivision. The amendment makes it a crime for an individual:

> Knowing the character and content of the communication which, in whole or in part, depicts actual or simulated nudity, sexual conduct or sado-masochistic abuse, and which is harmful to minors, [to] intentionally use[] any computer communication system allowing the input, output, examination or transfer, of computer data or computer programs from one computer to another, to initiate or engage in such communication with a person who is a minor.

Violation of the Act is a Class E felony, punishable by one to four years of incarceration. The Act applies to both commercial and non-commercial disseminations of material.

* * *

The statute provides six defenses to liability. First, § 235.15(1) provides the following affirmative defense to prosecution under § 235.21(3):

> In any prosecution for obscenity, or disseminating indecent material to minors in the second degree in violation of subdivision three of § 235.21 of this article, it is an affirmative defense that the persons to whom the allegedly obscene or indecent material was disseminated, or the audience to an allegedly obscene performance, consisted of persons or institutions having scientific, educational, governmental or other similar justification for possessing, disseminating or viewing the same.

The statute further provides four regular defenses to prosecution:

> (a) The defendant made a reasonable effort to ascertain the true age of the minor and was unable to do so as a result of the actions taken by the minor; or
>
> (b) The defendant has taken, in good faith, reasonable, effective and appropriate actions under the circumstances to restrict or prevent access by minors to materials specified in such subdivision, which may involve any appropriate measures to restrict minors from access to such communications, including any method which is feasible under available technology; or
>
> (c) The defendant has restricted access to such materials by requiring use of a verified credit card, debit account, adult access code or adult personal identification number; or
>
> (d) The defendant has in good faith established a mechanism such that the labelling, segregation or other mechanism enables such material to be automatically blocked or screened by software or other capabilities reasonably available to responsible adults

> wishing to effect such blocking or screening and the defendant has not otherwise solicited minors not subject to such screening or blocking capabilities to access that material or circumvent any such screening or blocking.

N.Y. Penal Law § 235.23(3). And, finally, § 235.24 provides that no individual shall be held liable:

> Solely for providing access or connection to or from a facility, system, or network not under that person's control, including transmission, downloading, intermediate storage, access software, or other related capabilities that are incidental to providing such access or connection that do not include the creation of the content of the communication.

N.Y. Penal Law § 235.24. Exceptions to this defense for conspirators or co-owners and an additional employer liability defense are set forth in § 235.24(1)(a)–(b) and (2).

III. The Internet

The Internet is a decentralized, global communications medium linking people, institutions, corporations, and governments all across the world. * * * [The court describes the various modes of communication via the Internet, including e-mail, mailing lists, USENET newsgroups, chat rooms, and the Web.]

* * *

Regardless of the aspect of the Internet they are using, Internet users have no way to determine the characteristics of their audience that are salient under the New York Act—age and geographic location. In fact, in online communications through newsgroups, mailing lists, chat rooms, and the Web, the user has no way to determine with certainty that any particular person has accessed the user's speech. * * * As the poet said, "I shot an arrow into the air; it fell to the earth I know not where."

This highly simplified description of the Internet is not intended to minimize its marvels. While no one should lose sight of the inventiveness that has made this complex of resources available to just about anyone, the innovativeness of the technology does not preclude the application of traditional legal principles—provided that those principles are adaptable to cyberspace. In the present case, as discussed more fully below, the Internet fits easily within the parameters of interests traditionally protected by the Commerce Clause. The New York Act represents an unconstitutional intrusion into interstate commerce; plaintiffs are therefore entitled to the preliminary injunction that they seek.

DISCUSSION

* * *

II. Federalism and the Internet: The Commerce Clause

The borderless world of the Internet raises profound questions concerning the relationship among the several states and the relationship of the federal government to each state, questions that go to the heart of "our federalism." * * * The Act at issue in the present case is only one of many efforts by state legislators to control the chaotic environment of the Internet. For example, the Georgia legislature has enacted a recent law prohibiting Internet users from "falsely identifying" themselves online. Ga. Stat. [16–9–93.1].[1] Similar legislation is pending in California. * * * Texas and Florida have concluded that law firm web pages (apparently including those of out of state firms) are subject to the rules of professional conduct applicable to attorney advertising. See Texas Bar Advertising Comm., Interpretive Comment on Attorney Internet Advertising (1996); see also *Texans Against Censorship v. State Bar of Texas,* 888 F. Supp. 1328, 1369–70 (E.D.Tex.1995) (discussing applicability of Texas lawyers advertising regulation to the Internet), *aff'd,* 100 F.3d 953 (5th Cir.1996); Ethics Update, Fla. Bar News, January 1, 1996. Further, states have adopted widely varying approaches in the application of general laws to communications taking place over the Internet. Minnesota has aggressively pursued out-of-state advertisers and service providers who reach Minnesotans via the Internet; Illinois has also been assertive in using existing laws to reach out-of-state actors whose connection to Illinois occurs only by virtue of an Internet communication. See Mark Eckenwiler, States Get Entangled in the Web, Legal Times, Jan. 22, 1996, at S35, S37. Florida has taken the opposite route, declining to venture into online law enforcement until various legal issues (including, perhaps, the one discussed in the present opinion) have been determined. Id. at S37.

The unique nature of the Internet highlights the likelihood that a single actor might be subject to haphazard, uncoordinated, and even outright inconsistent regulation by states that the actor never intended to reach and possibly was unaware were being accessed. Typically, states' jurisdictional limits are related to geography; geography, however, is a virtually meaningless construct on the Internet. The menace of inconsistent state regulation invites analysis under the Commerce Clause of the Constitution, because that clause represented the framers' reaction to overreaching by the individual states that might jeopardize the growth of the nation—and in particular, the national infrastructure of communications and trade—as a whole. See *Quill Corp. v. North Dakota,* 504 U.S. 298 (1992) ("Under the Articles of Confederation, state taxes and duties hindered and suppressed interstate commerce; the Framers intended the Commerce Clause as a cure for these structural ills."); see also The Federalist Nos. 7, 11 (A. Hamilton).

The Commerce Clause is more than an affirmative grant of power to Congress. * * * In what commentators have come to term its negative or

1. [In *ACLU v. Miller,* 977 F.Supp. 1228 (N.D.Ga.1997), the District Court enjoined enforcement of this statute, finding that plaintiffs were likely to prevail on their claim that the statute violates the First Amendment.—Eds.]

"dormant" aspect, the Commerce Clause restricts the individual states interference with the flow of interstate commerce in two ways. The Clause prohibits discrimination aimed directly at interstate commerce, *see, e.g., Philadelphia v. New Jersey,* 437 U.S. 617 (1978), and bars state regulations that, although facially nondiscriminatory, unduly burden interstate commerce, *see, e.g., Kassel v. Consolidated Freightways Corp. of Del.,* 450 U.S. 662 (1981). Moreover, courts have long held that state regulation of those aspects of commerce that by their unique nature demand cohesive national treatment is offensive to the Commerce Clause. *See, e.g., Wabash, St. L. & P. Ry. Co. v. Illinois,* 118 U.S. 557 (1887) (holding railroad rates exempt from state regulation).

Thus, as will be discussed in more detail below, the New York Act is concerned with interstate commerce and contravenes the Commerce Clause for three reasons. First, the Act represents an unconstitutional projection of New York law into conduct that occurs wholly outside New York. Second, the Act is invalid because although protecting children from indecent material is a legitimate and indisputably worthy subject of state legislation, the burdens on interstate commerce resulting from the Act clearly exceed any local benefit derived from it. Finally, the Internet is one of those areas of commerce that must be marked off as a national preserve to protect users from inconsistent legislation that, taken to its most extreme, could paralyze development of the Internet altogether. Thus, the Commerce Clause ordains that only Congress can legislate in this area, subject, of course, to whatever limitations other provisions of the Constitution (such as the First Amendment) may require.

A. The Act Concerns Interstate Commerce

At oral argument, the defendants advanced the theory that the Act is aimed solely at intrastate conduct. This argument is unsupportable in light of the text of the statute itself, its legislative history, and the reality of Internet communications. * * *

* * *

The conclusion that the Act must apply to interstate as well as intrastate communications receives perhaps its strongest support from the nature of the Internet itself. The Internet is wholly insensitive to geographic distinctions. In almost every case, users of the Internet neither know nor care about the physical location of the Internet resources they access. Internet protocols were designed to ignore rather than document geographic location; while computers on the network do have "addresses," they are logical addresses on the network rather than geographic addresses in real space. The majority of Internet addresses contain no geographic clues and, even where an Internet address provides such a clue, it may be misleading. For example, in his article, Federalism in Cyberspace, 28 Conn. L. Rev. 1095, 1112 (1996), Professor Dan Burk described how he uses Seton Hall University's computer system to access the Internet, providing anyone who communicates with him (and is aware of Seton Hall's locale) a hint that he is in New Jersey. However, Professor Burk also has a guest account at a university in California which he continues to use even when he is in New Jersey; any clue derived from the California university's name within the Internet address would therefore be deceptive. In a similar vein, Ms. Kovacs testified that as she was using her computer to give an in-court demonstration of various Internet applications, she received an e-mail from a colleague who believed she was sending the message to Cincinnati, Ohio (where Ms. Kovacs is normally located); in fact, Ms. Kovacs was in New York and received the message here. (4/4/97 Tr., p. 61).

Moreover, no aspect of the Internet can feasibly be closed off to users from another state. An internet user who posts a Web page cannot prevent New Yorkers or Oklahomans or Iowans from accessing that page and will not even know from what state visitors to that site hail. Nor can a participant in a chat room prevent other participants from a particular state from joining the conversation. Someone who uses a mail exploder is similarly unaware of the precise contours of the mailing list that will ultimately determine the recipients of his or her message, because users can add or remove their names from a mailing list automatically. Thus, a person could choose a list believed not to include any New Yorkers, but an after-added New Yorker would still receive the message.

E-mail, because it is a one-to-one messaging system, stands on a slightly different footing than the other aspects of the Internet. Even in the context of e-mail, however, a message from one New Yorker to another New Yorker may well pass through a number of states en route. The Internet is, as described above, a redundant series of linked computers. Thus, a message from an Internet user sitting at a computer in New York may travel via one or more other states before reaching a recipient who is also sitting at a terminal in New York.

The system is further complicated by two Internet practices: packet switching and caching. "Packet switching" protocols subdivide individual messages into smaller packets that are then sent independently to the destination, where they are automatically reassembled by the receiving computer. If computers along the route become overloaded, packets may be rerouted to computers with greater capacity. A single message may—but does not always—travel several different pathways before reaching the receiving computer. "Caching" is the Internet practice of storing partial or complete duplicates of materials from frequently accessed sites to avoid repeatedly requesting copies from the original server. The recipient has no means of distinguishing between the cached materials and the original. Thus, the user may be accessing materials at the original site, or he may be accessing copies of those materials cached on a different machine located anywhere in the world.

The New York Act, therefore, cannot effectively be limited to purely intrastate communications over the Internet because no such communications exist. No user could reliably restrict her communications only to New York recipients. Moreover, no user could avoid liability under the New York Act simply by directing his or her communications elsewhere, given that there is no feasible way to preclude New Yorkers from accessing a website, receiving a mail exploder message or a newsgroup posting, or participating in a chat room. Similarly, a user has no way to ensure that an e-mail does not pass through New York even if the ultimate recipient is not located there, or that a message never leaves New York even if both sender and recipient are located there.

* * *

The Act is therefore necessarily concerned with interstate communications. * * * The next question that requires an answer as a threshold matter is whether the types of communication involved constitute "commerce" within the meaning of the Clause.

The definition of commerce in the Supreme Court's decisions has been notably broad. * * * In the present case, the parties have stipulated that:

> The Internet is not exclusively, or even primarily, a means of commercial communication. Many commercial entities maintain websites to inform potential consumers about their goods and services, or to solicit purchases, but many other websites exist solely for the dissemination of non-commercial information. The other forms of Internet communication—e-mail, bulletin boards, newsgroups, and chat rooms—frequently have non-commercial goals. * * *

(Joint Stipulation of Facts, ¶ 79). This stipulation, however inartfully worded, cannot insulate the statute at issue from Commerce Clause scrutiny. The non-profit nature of certain entities that use the Internet or of certain transactions that take place over the Internet does not take the Internet outside the Commerce Clause. * * * The Supreme Court has expressly held that the dormant commerce clause is applicable to activities undertaken without a profit motive. * * *

Commercial use of the Internet, moreover, is a growing phenomenon. * * * In addition, many of those users who are communicating for private, noncommercial purposes are nonetheless participants in interstate commerce by virtue of their Internet consumption. Many users obtain access to the Internet by means of an on-line service provider, such as America Online, which charges a fee for its services. "Internet service providers," including plaintiffs Panix, Echo, and NYC NET, also offer Internet access for a monthly or hourly fee. Patrons of storefront "computer coffee shops," such as New York's own CyberCafe, similarly pay for their access to the Internet, in addition to partaking of food and beverages sold by the cafe. Dial-in bulletin board systems often charge a fee for access. *See Katzenbach v. McClung,* 379 U.S. 294, 300–301 (1964) (holding that an entity that purchases goods used in the provision of its services from interstate sources is an actor in interstate commerce even in connection with the provision of services within a single state).

The courts have long recognized that railroads, trucks, and highways are themselves "instruments of commerce," because they serve as conduits for the transport of products and services. *See Kassel v. Consolidated Freightways Corp.,* 450 U.S. 662 (1981); *Southern Pacific Co. v. Arizona,*

325 U.S. 761, 780 (1945). The Internet is more than a means of communication; it also serves as a conduit for transporting digitized goods, including software, data, music, graphics, and videos which can be downloaded from the provider's site to the Internet user's computer. For example, plaintiff BiblioBytes and members of plaintiff IDSA both sell and deliver their products over the Internet.

The inescapable conclusion is that the Internet represents an instrument of interstate commerce, albeit an innovative one; the novelty of the technology should not obscure the fact that regulation of the Internet impels traditional Commerce Clause considerations. The New York Act is therefore closely concerned with interstate commerce, and scrutiny of the Act under the Commerce Clause is entirely appropriate. As discussed in the following sections, the Act cannot survive such scrutiny, because it places an undue burden on interstate traffic, whether that traffic be in goods, services, or ideas.

B. *New York Has Overreached by Enacting a Law That Seeks To Regulate Conduct Occurring Outside its Borders*

The interdiction against direct interference with interstate commerce by state legislative overreaching is apparent in a number of the Supreme Court's decisions. In *Baldwin v. G.A.F. Seelig, Inc.,* 294 U.S. 511, 521 (1935), for example, Justice Cardozo authored an opinion enjoining enforcement of a law that prohibited a dealer from selling within New York milk purchased from the producer in Vermont at less than the minimum price fixed for milk produced in New York. Justice Cardozo sternly admonished, "New York has no power to project its legislation into Vermont by regulating the price to be paid in that state for milk," finding that "such a power, if exerted, [would] set a barrier to traffic between one state and another as effective as if customs duties, equal to the price differential, had been laid upon the thing transported." Id.

The Court has more recently confirmed that the Commerce Clause precludes a state from enacting legislation that has the practical effect of exporting that state's domestic policies. In *Edgar v. MITE,* 457 U.S. 624 (1982), the Court examined the constitutionality of an Illinois anti-takeover statute that required a tender offeror to notify the Secretary of State and the target company of its intent to make a tender offer and the terms of the offer 20 days before the offer became effective. During the twenty-day period, the offeror was barred from communicating its offer to the shareholders, but the target company was free to disseminate information to its shareholders concerning the impending offer. *Id. at 633.* The statute defined "target company" as a corporation of which Illinois shareholders own 10% of the class of securities subject to the takeover offer, or for which any two of the following conditions are met: the corporation has its principal office in Illinois, is organized under Illinois law, or has at least 10% of its stated capital and paid-in surplus within Illinois. *Id.* at 625. The Court acknowledged that states traditionally retained the power to regulate intrastate securities transactions by enacting "blue-sky laws." *Id.* at 641.

Nonetheless, the Court asserted that "the Illinois Act differs substantially from state blue-sky laws in that it directly regulates transactions which take place across state lines, even if wholly outside the State of Illinois." *Id.* In striking the law as violative of the Commerce Clause, the Court found particularly egregious the fact that the Illinois law on its face would apply to a transaction that would not affect a single Illinois shareholder if a corporation fit within the definition of a "target company." *Id.* at 642. The Court concluded "the Illinois statute is a direct restraint on interstate commerce and has a sweeping extraterritorial effect," because the statute would prevent a tender offeror from communicating its offer to shareholders both within and outside Illinois. Acceptance of the offer by any of the shareholders would result in interstate transactions; the Illinois statute effectively stifled such transactions during the waiting period and thereby disrupted prospective interstate commerce. Under the Commerce Clause, the projection of these extraterritorial "practical effect[s]," regardless of the legislators' intentions, " 'exceeded the inherent limits of the State's power.' " *Id.* at 642–43 (quoting *Shaffer v. Heitner,* 433 U.S. 186 (1977)).

In the present case, a number of witnesses testified to the chill that they felt as a result of the enactment of the New York statute; these witnesses refrained from engaging in particular types of interstate commerce. In particular, I note the testimony of Rudolf Kinsky, an artist with a virtual studio on Art on the Net's Website. Mr. Kinsky testified that he removed several images from his virtual studio because he feared prosecution under the New York Act. (4/7/97 Tr., at 231–35). As described above, no Web siteholder is able to close his site to New Yorkers. Thus, even if Mr. Kinsky were located in California and wanted to display his work to a prospective purchaser in Oregon, he could not employ his virtual studio to do so without risking prosecution under the New York law.

* * *

The "extraterritoriality" analysis of the *Edgar* opinion commanded only a plurality of the Court. Later majority holdings, however, expressly adopted the underlying principles on which Justice White relied in *Edgar. See Healy v. The Beer Institute,* 491 U.S. 324 (1989); *Brown-Forman Distillers Corp. v. New York State Liquor Authority,* 476 U.S. 573 (1986).* * *

The *Edgar/Healy* extraterritoriality analysis rests on the premise that the Commerce Clause has two aspects: it subordinates each state's authority over interstate commerce to the federal power of regulation (a vertical limitation), and it embodies a principle of comity that mandates that one state not expand its regulatory powers in a manner that encroaches upon the sovereignty of its fellow states (a horizontal limitation). * * *

The nature of the Internet makes it impossible to restrict the effects of the New York Act to conduct occurring within New York. An Internet user may not intend that a message be accessible to New Yorkers, but lacks the ability to prevent New Yorkers from visiting a particular website or viewing a particular newsgroup posting or receiving a particular mail exploder. Thus, conduct that may be legal in the state in which the user acts can subject the user to prosecution in New York and thus subordinate the user's home state's policy—perhaps favoring freedom of expression over a more protective stance—to New York's local concerns. * * * New York has deliberately imposed its legislation on the Internet and, by doing so, projected its law into other states whose citizens use the Net. * * * This encroachment upon the authority which the Constitution specifically confers upon the federal government and upon the sovereignty of New York's sister states is per se violative of the Commerce Clause.

C. *The Burdens the Act Imposes on Interstate Commerce Exceed Any Local Benefit*

Even if the Act were not a per se violation of the Commerce Clause by virtue of its extraterritorial effects, the Act would nonetheless be an invalid indirect regulation of interstate commerce, because the burdens it imposes on interstate commerce are excessive in relation to the local benefits it confers. The Supreme Court set forth the balancing test applicable to indirect regulations of interstate commerce in *Pike v. Bruce Church,* 397 U.S. 137 (1970). *Pike* requires a two-fold inquiry. The first level of examination is directed at the legitimacy of the state's interest. The next, and more difficult, determination weighs the burden on interstate commerce in light of the local benefit derived from the statute.

In the present case, I accept that the protection of children against pedophilia is a quintessentially legitimate state objective—a proposition with which I believe even the plaintiffs have expressed no quarrel. * * * Even with the fullest recognition that the protection of children from sexual exploitation is an indisputably valid state goal, however, the present statute cannot survive even the lesser scrutiny to which indirect regulations of interstate commerce are subject under the Constitution. * * *.

The local benefits likely to result from the New York Act are not overwhelming. The Act can have no effect on communications originating outside the United States. As the three-judge panel that struck the federal analog of the New York Act, the Communications Decency Act, on First Amendment grounds concluded:

> [The Act] will almost certainly fail to accomplish the Government's interest in shielding children from pornography on the Internet. Nearly half of Internet communications originate outside the United States, and some percentage of that figure represents pornography. Pornography from, say, Amsterdam, will be no less appealing to a child on the Internet than pornography from New York City, and residents of Amsterdam have little incentive to comply with the [Act].

American Civil Liberties Union v. Reno, 929 F. Supp. 824, 882 (E.D.Pa. 1996). Further, in the present case, New York's prosecution of parties from out of state who have allegedly violated the Act, but whose only contact with New York occurs via the Internet, is beset with practical difficulties, even if New York is able to exercise criminal jurisdiction over such parties. The prospect of New York bounty hunters dragging pedophiles from the other 49 states into New York is not consistent with traditional concepts of comity.

Moreover, the State has espoused an interpretation of the Act that, if accepted, would further undermine its effectiveness. According to defendant, the Act reaches only pictorial messages that are harmful to minors and has no impact on purely textual communications. Were this interpretation adopted, Mr. Barlow, whose conduct supposedly motivated the supporters of the Act, would escape prosecution because his messages were verbal. * * *

The Act is, of course, not the only law in New York's statute books designed to protect children against sexual exploitation. The State is able to protect children through vigorous enforcement of the existing laws criminalizing obscenity and child pornography. *See United States v. Thomas,* 74 F.3d 701, 704–05 (6th Cir.1995), *cert. denied,* 519 U.S. 820 (1996). Moreover, plaintiffs do not challenge the sections of the statute that criminalize the sale of obscene materials to children, over the Internet or otherwise, and prohibit adults from luring children into sexual contact by communicating with them via the Internet. See N.Y. Penal Law § 235.21(1); N.Y. Penal Law § 235.22(2). The local benefit to be derived from the challenged section of the statute is therefore confined to that narrow class of cases that does not fit within the parameters of any other law. The efficacy of the statute is further limited, as discussed above, to those cases which New York is realistically able to prosecute.

The conclusion that the New York Act has a very limited effect was bolstered by the testimony of Michael McCartney, an investigator with the New York State Attorney General's office. Mr. McCartney testified that he personally had logged over 600 hours investigating on-line criminal activity. (4/3/97 Tr., p. 12). Despite this extensive investment of time, Mr. McCartney admitted that he had investigated only two cases involving the dissemination of indecent materials to minors over the Internet that did not fall into the category of child pornography (which is, of course, subject to prosecution under other laws). (Id., p. 36). * * *

Balanced against the limited local benefits resulting from the Act is an extreme burden on interstate commerce. The New York Act casts its net worldwide; moreover, the chilling effect that it produces is bound to exceed the actual cases that are likely to be prosecuted, as Internet users will steer clear of the Act by significant margin. *See ACLU,* 929 F. Supp. at 863 (holding that individuals, uncertain of the reach of the CDA, will undoubtedly " 'steer far wider of the unlawful zone' ") (citing *Baggett v. Bullitt,* 377 U.S. 360 (1964)) * * *. At oral argument, the State asserted that only a small percentage of Internet communications are "harmful to minors" and would fall within the proscriptions of the statute; therefore, the State argued, the burden on interstate commerce is small. On the record before me, I conclude that the range of Internet communications potentially affected by the Act is far broader than the State suggests. I note that in the past, various communities within the United States have found works including I Know Why the Caged Bird Sings by Maya Angelou, Funhouse by Dean Koontz, The Adventures of Huckleberry Finn by Mark Twain, and The Color Purple by Alice Walker to be indecent. (Teicher Decl., p. 3). Even assuming, arguendo, that the Act applies only to pictures, a number of Internet users take advantage of the medium's capabilities to communicate images to one another and, again, I find that the range of images that might subject the communicator to prosecution (or reasonably cause a communicator to fear prosecution) is far broader than defendants assert. For example, many libraries, museums and academic institutions post art on the Internet that some might conclude was "harmful to minors." Famous nude works by Botticelli, Manet, Matisse, Cezanne and others can be found on the Internet. In this regard, I point out that a famous painting by Manet which shows a nude woman having lunch with two fully clothed men was the subject of considerable protest when it first was unveiled in Paris, as many observers believed that it was "scandalous." (Declaration of Judith F. Krug, sworn to in March, 1997, at p. 5). Lesser known artists who post work over the Internet may face an even greater risk of prosecution, because the mantle of respectability that has descended on Manet is not associated with their as yet obscure names. * * *

* * *

The severe burden on interstate commerce resulting from the New York statute is not justifiable in light of the attenuated local benefits arising from it. The alternative analysis of the Act as an indirect regulation on interstate commerce therefore also mandates the issuance of the preliminary injunction sought by plaintiffs.

D. The Act Unconstitutionally Subjects Interstate Use of the Internet to Inconsistent Regulations

Finally, a third mode of Commerce Clause analysis further confirms that the plaintiffs are likely to succeed on the merits of their claim that the New York Act is unconstitutional. The courts have long recognized that certain types of commerce demand consistent treatment and are therefore susceptible to regulation only on a national level. The Internet represents one of those areas; effective regulation will require national, and more likely global, cooperation. Regulation by any single state can only result in chaos, because at least some states will likely enact laws subjecting Internet users to conflicting obligations. Without the limitations imposed by the Commerce Clause, these inconsistent regulatory schemes could paralyze the development of the Internet altogether.

In numerous cases, the Supreme Court has acknowledged the need for coordination in the regulation of certain areas of commerce. As long ago as 1886, the Supreme Court stated:

> Commerce with foreign countries and among the states, strictly considered, consists in intercourse and traffic, including in these terms navigation, and the transportation and transit of persons and property, as well as the purchase, sale, and exchange of commodities. For the regulation of commerce, as thus defined, there can be only one system of rules, applicable alike to the whole

> country; and the authority which can act for the whole country can alone adopt such a system. Action upon it by separate states is not, therefore, permissible.

Wabash, St. L. & P. Ry. Co. v. Illinois, 118 U.S. 557, 574–75 (1886). The Court in Wabash struck the Illinois statute at issue, which purported to establish interstate railway rates, stating "that this species of regulation is one which must be, if established at all, of a general and national character, and cannot be safely and wisely remitted to local rules and regulations, we think is clear from what has already been said." *Id.* at 577.

* * *

In *Bibb v. Navajo Freight Lines, Inc.,* 359 U.S. 520 (1959), the Court examined an Illinois statute that required the use of contour mudguards on trucks in Illinois. The Court took note of the fact that straight or conventional mudguards were permissible in most other states and actually required in Arkansas. *Id.* 359 U.S. at 526. Recognizing the need for coordinated legislation, the Court stated that "the conflict between the Arkansas regulation and the Illinois regulation * * * suggests that this regulation of mudguards is not one of those matters 'admitting of diversity of treatment, according to the special requirements of local conditions.' " *Id.* at 528 (quoting *Sproles v. Binford,* 286 U.S. 374, 390 (1932)). The Court struck the Illinois law as imposing an undue burden on interstate commerce, in part because Illinois was insisting upon "a design out of line with the requirements of almost all the other states." Id.

The Internet, like the rail and highway traffic at issue in the cited cases, requires a cohesive national scheme of regulation so that users are reasonably able to determine their obligations. Regulation on a local level, by contrast, will leave users lost in a welter of inconsistent laws, imposed by different states with different priorities. New York is not the only state to enact a law purporting to regulate the content of communications on the Internet. Already Oklahoma and Georgia have enacted laws designed to protect minors from indecent communications over the Internet; as might be expected, the states have selected different methods to accomplish their aims. Georgia has made it a crime to communicate anonymously over the Internet, while Oklahoma, like New York, has prohibited the online transmission of material deemed harmful to minors. See Ga. Code Ann. § 16–19–93.1 (1996); Okla. Stat. tit. 21, § 1040.76 (1996).

Moreover, the regulation of communications that may be "harmful to minors" taking place over the Internet poses particular difficulties. New York has defined "harmful to minors" as including:

> that quality of any description or representation, in whatever form, of nudity, sexual conduct, sexual excitement, or sado-masochistic abuse, when it:
>
> (a) Considered as a whole, appeals to the prurient interest in sex of minors; and

(b) Is patently offensive to prevailing standards in the adult community as a whole with respect to what is suitable material for minors; and

(c) Considered as a whole, lacks serious literary, artistic, political and scientific value for minors.

N.Y. Penal Law § 235.20(6). Courts have long recognized, however, that there is no single "prevailing community standard" in the United States. Thus, even were all 50 states to enact laws that were verbatim copies of the New York Act, Internet users would still be subject to discordant responsibilities. To use an example cited by the court in *ACLU v. Reno*, the Broadway play Angels in America, which concerns homosexuality and AIDS and features graphic language, was immensely popular in New York and in fact earned two Tony awards and a Pulitzer prize. *ACLU,* 929 F. Supp. at 852–53. In Charlotte, North Carolina, however, a production of the drama caused such a public outcry that the Mecklenberg County Commission voted to withhold all public funding from arts organizations whose works "expose the public to perverted forms of sexuality." Eric Harrison, Charlotte Ban on Funding Questions Community Culture Commission—Boycotts "Perverted Sexuality", Milwaukee J. & Sentinel, April 21, 1997, at 3. The Supreme Court has always recognized that "our nation is simply too big and too diverse for this Court to reasonably expect that such standards [of what is patently offensive] could be articulated for all 50 states in a single formulation." *Miller,* 413 U.S. 15 at 30.

As discussed at length above, an Internet user cannot foreclose access to her work from certain states or send differing versions of her communication to different jurisdictions. In this sense, the Internet user is in a worse position than the truck driver or train engineer who can steer around Illinois or Arizona, or change the mudguard or train configuration at the state line; the Internet user has no ability to bypass any particular state. The user must thus comply with the regulation imposed by the state with the most stringent standard or forego Internet communication of the message that might or might not subject her to prosecution. For example, a teacher might invite discussion of Angels In America from a Usenet newsgroup dedicated to the literary interests of high school students. Quotations from the play might not subject her to prosecution in New York—but could qualify as "harmful to minors" according to the community standards prevailing in Oklahoma. The teacher cannot tailor her message on a community-specific basis and thus must take her chances or avoid the discussion altogether.

Further development of the Internet requires that users be able to predict the results of their Internet use with some degree of assurance. Haphazard and uncoordinated state regulation can only frustrate the growth of cyberspace. The need for uniformity in this unique sphere of commerce requires that New York's law be stricken as a violation of the Commerce Clause.

* * *

State of Washington v. Heckel

24 P.3d 404 (Wash.2001) (en banc).

■ OWENS, J.—The State of Washington filed suit against Oregon resident Jason Heckel, alleging that his transmissions of electronic mail (e-mail) to Washington residents violated Washington's commercial electronic mail act, chapter 19.190 RCW (the Act). On cross-motions for summary judgment, the trial court dismissed the State's suit against Heckel, concluding that the Act violated the dormant Commerce Clause of the United States Constitution. This court granted the State's request for direct review. We hold that the Act does not unduly burden interstate commerce. We reverse the trial court's dismissal of the State's suit, vacate the order on attorney fees, and remand this matter for trial.

FACTS

As early as February 1996, defendant Jason Heckel, an Oregon resident doing business as Natural Instincts, began sending unsolicited commercial e-mail (UCE), or "spam," over the Internet.[1] In 1997, Heckel developed a 46–page on-line booklet entitled "How to Profit from the Internet." The booklet described how to set up an on-line promotional business, acquire free e-mail accounts, and obtain software for sending bulk e-mail. From June 1998, Heckel marketed the booklet by sending between 100,000 and 1,000,000 UCE messages per week. To acquire the large volume of e-mail addresses, Heckel used the Extractor Pro software program, which harvests e-mail addresses from various on-line sources and enables a spammer to direct a bulk-mail message to those addresses by entering a simple command. The Extractor Pro program requires the spammer to enter a return e-mail address, a subject line, and the text of the message to be sent. The text of Heckel's UCE was a lengthy sales pitch that included testimonials from satisfied purchasers and culminated in an order form that the recipient could download and print. The order form included the Salem, Oregon, mailing address for Natural Instincts. Charging $39.95 for the booklet, Heckel made 30 to 50 sales per month.

In June 1998, the Consumer Protection Division of the Washington State Attorney General's Office received complaints from Washington recipients of Heckel's UCE messages. The complaints alleged that Heckel's messages contained misleading subject lines and false transmission paths. Responding to the June complaints, David Hill, an inspector from the Consumer Protection Division, sent Heckel a letter advising him of the existence of the Act. The Act provides that anyone sending a commercial e-mail message from a computer located in Washington or to an e-mail address held by a Washington resident may not use a third-party's domain name without permission, misrepresent or disguise in any other way the message's point of origin or transmission path, or use a misleading subject

1. "'Commercial electronic mail message' means an electronic mail message sent for the purpose of promoting real property, goods, or services for sale or lease." RCW 19.190.010(2). * * *

line.[6] RCW 19.190.030 makes a violation of the Act a per se violation of the Consumer Protection Act, chapter 19.86 RCW (CPA).

Responding to Hill's letter, Heckel telephoned Hill on or around June 25, 1998. According to Hill, he discussed with Heckel the provisions of the Act and the procedures bulk e-mailers can follow to identify e-mail addressees who are Washington residents. Nevertheless, the Attorney General's Office continued to receive consumer complaints alleging that Heckel's bulk e-mailings from Natural Instincts appeared to contain misleading subject lines, false or unusable return e-mail addresses, and false or misleading transmission paths. Between June and September 1998, the Consumer Protection Division of the Attorney General's Office documented 20 complaints from 17 recipients of Heckel's UCE messages.

On October 22, 1998, the State filed suit against Heckel, stating three causes of action. First, the State alleged that Heckel had violated RCW 19.190.020(1)(b) and, in turn, the CPA, by using false or misleading information in the subject line of his UCE messages. Heckel used one of two subject lines to introduce his solicitations: "Did I get the right e-mail address?" and "For your review—HANDS OFF!" Clerk's Papers (CP) at 6, 92, 113. In the State's view, the first subject line falsely suggested that an acquaintance of the recipient was trying to make contact, while the second subject line invited the misperception that the message contained classified information for the particular recipient's review.

As its second cause of action, the State alleged that Heckel had violated RCW 19.190.020(1)(a), and thus the CPA, by misrepresenting information defining the transmission paths of his UCE messages. Heckel routed his spam through at least a dozen different domain names without receiving permission to do so from the registered owners of those names. For example, of the 20 complaints the Attorney General's Office received concerning Heckel's spam, 9 of the messages showed "13.com" as the initial ISP to transmit his spam. CP at 44, 113. The 13.com domain name, however, was registered as early as November 1995 to another individual, from whom Heckel had not sought or received permission to use the registered name. In fact, because the owner of 13.com had not yet even activated that domain name, no messages could have been sent or received through 13.com.

6. "(1) No person may initiate the transmission, conspire with another to initiate the transmission, or assist the transmission, of a commercial electronic mail message from a computer located in Washington or to an electronic mail address that the sender knows, or has reason to know, is held by a Washington resident that:

"(a) Uses a third party's internet domain name without permission of the third party, or otherwise misrepresents or obscures any information in identifying the point of origin or the transmission path of a commercial electronic mail message; or

"(b) Contains false or misleading information in the subject line.

"(2) For purposes of this section, a person knows that the intended recipient of a commercial electronic mail message is a Washington resident if that information is available, upon request, from the registrant of the Internet domain name contained in the recipient's electronic mail address." RCW 19.190.020.

Additionally, the State alleged that Heckel had violated the CPA by failing to provide a valid return e-mail address to which bulk-mail recipients could respond. When Heckel created his spam with the Extractor Pro software, he used at least a dozen different return e-mail addresses with the domain name "juno.com" (Heckel used the Juno accounts in part because they were free). CP at 88–89. None of the Juno e-mail accounts was readily identifiable as belonging to Heckel; the user names that he registered generally consisted of a name or a name plus a number (*e.g.*, "marlin1374," "cindyt5667," "howardwesley13," "johnjacobson1374," and "sjtowns"). CP at 88–89. During August and September 1998, Heckel's Juno addresses were canceled within two days of his sending out a bulk e-mail message on the account. According to Heckel, when Juno canceled one e-mail account, he would simply open a new one and send out another bulk mailing. Because Heckel's accounts were canceled so rapidly, recipients who attempted to reply were unsuccessful. The State thus contended that Heckel's practice of cycling through e-mail addresses ensured that those addresses were useless to the recipients of his UCE messages. During the months that Heckel was sending out bulk e-mail solicitations on the Juno accounts, he maintained a personal e-mail account from which he sent no spam, but that e-mail address was not included in any of his spam messages. The State asserted that Heckel's use of such ephemeral e-mail addresses in his UCE amounted to a deceptive practice in violation of RCW 19.86.020.

The State sought a permanent injunction and, pursuant to RCW 19.86.140 and .080 of the CPA, requested civil penalties, as well as costs and a reasonable attorney fee. In early 2000, the parties cross-moved for summary judgment. On March 10, 2000, the trial court entered an order granting Heckel's motion and denying the State's cross motion. The court found that the Act violated the Commerce Clause (U.S. CONST. art. I, § 8, cl. 3) and was "unduly restrictive and burdensome." * * * Challenging the trial court's finding that the Act violated the Commerce Clause, the State sought this court's direct review. * * *

ISSUE

Does the Act, which prohibits misrepresentation in the subject line or transmission path of any commercial e-mail message sent to Washington residents or from a Washington computer, unconstitutionally burden interstate commerce?

ANALYSIS

* * *

Heckel's Challenge under the Commerce Clause. The Commerce Clause grants Congress the "power * * * [t]o regulate commerce with foreign nations, and among the several states." U.S. CONST. art. I, § 8, cl. 3. Implicit in this affirmative grant is the negative or "dormant" Commerce Clause—the principle that the states impermissibly intrude on this federal power when they enact laws that unduly burden interstate commerce. *See*

Franks & Son, Inc. v. State, 136 Wn.2d 737, 747, 966 P.2d 1232 (1998). Analysis of a state law under the dormant Commerce Clause generally follows a two-step process. We first determine whether the state law openly discriminates against interstate commerce in favor of intrastate economic interests. If the law is facially neutral, applying impartially to in-state and out-of-state businesses, the analysis moves to the second step, a balancing of the local benefits against the interstate burdens * * * [*Pike v. Bruce Church, Inc.*].

The Act is not facially discriminatory. The Act applies evenhandedly to in-state and out-of-state spammers: "*No person*" may transmit the proscribed commercial e-mail messages "from a computer located in Washington or to an electronic mail address that the sender knows, or has reason to know, is held by a Washington resident." *RCW 19.190.020(1)* (emphasis added). Thus, just as the statute applied to Heckel, an Oregon resident, it is enforceable against a Washington business engaging in the same practices.

Because we conclude that the Act's local benefits surpass any alleged burden on interstate commerce, the statute likewise survives the *Pike* balancing test. The Act protects the interests of three groups—ISPs, actual owners of forged domain names, and e-mail users. The problems that spam causes have been discussed in prior cases and legislative hearings. A federal district court described the harms a mass e-mailer caused ISP CompuServe:

> In the present case, any value CompuServe realizes from its computer equipment is wholly derived from the extent to which that equipment can serve its subscriber base.... [H]andling the enormous volume of mass mailings that CompuServe receives places a tremendous burden on its equipment. Defendants' more recent practice of evading CompuServe's filters by disguising the origin of their messages commandeers even more computer resources because CompuServe's computers are forced to store undeliverable e-mail messages and labor in vain to return the messages to an address that does not exist. To the extent that defendants' multitudinous electronic mailings demand the disk space and drain the processing power of plaintiff's computer equipment, those resources are not available to serve CompuServe subscribers. Therefore, the value of that equipment to CompuServe is diminished even though it is not physically damaged by defendants' conduct.

CompuServe Inc. v. Cyber Promotions, Inc., 962 F. Supp. 1015, 1022 (S.D.Ohio 1997) (citations omitted) (granting preliminary injunction against bulk e-mailer on theory of trespass to chattels); *see also Am. Online, Inc. v. IMS,* 24 F. Supp. 2d 548, 550 (E.D.Va.1998) ("rely[ing] on the reasoning of *CompuServe*" and finding that bulk e-mailer "injured AOL's business goodwill and diminished the value of its possessory interest in its computer network"). To handle the increased e-mail traffic attributable to deceptive spam, ISPs must invest in more computer equipment. Operational costs likewise increase as ISPs hire more customer service representatives to field spam complaints and more system administrators to detect accounts being used to send spam.

Along with ISPs, the owners of impermissibly used domain names and e-mail addresses suffer economic harm. For example, the registered owner of "localhost.com" alleged that his computer system was shut down for three days by 7,000 responses to a bulk-mail message in which the spammer had forged the e-mail address "nobody@localhost.com" into his spam's header. *Seidl v. Greentree Mortgage Co.,* 30 F. Supp. 2d 1292, 1297–98 (D.Colo.1998) * * *.

Deceptive spam harms individual Internet users as well. When a spammer distorts the point of origin or transmission path of the message, e-mail recipients cannot promptly and effectively respond to the message (and thereby opt out of future mailings); their efforts to respond take time, cause frustration, and compound the problems that ISPs face in delivering and storing the bulk messages. And the use of false or misleading subject lines further hampers an individual's ability to use computer time most efficiently. When spammers use subject lines "such as 'Hi There!,' 'Information Request,' and 'Your Business Records,'" it becomes "virtually impossible" to distinguish spam from legitimate personal or business messages. Individuals who do not have flat-rate plans for Internet access but pay instead by the minute or hour are harmed more directly, but all Internet users (along with their ISPs) bear the cost of deceptive spam.

This cost-shifting—from deceptive spammers to businesses and e-mail users—has been likened to sending junk mail with postage due or making telemarketing calls to someone's pay-per-minute cellular phone. In a case involving the analogous practice of junk faxing (sending unsolicited faxes that contain advertisements), the Ninth Circuit acknowledged "the government's substantial interest in preventing the shifting of advertising costs to consumers." *Destination Ventures, Ltd. v. F.C.C.,* 46 F.3d 54, 56 (9th Cir.1995) (holding that the Telephone Consumer Protection Act's (47 U.S.C. § 227) limitations on commercial speech did not violate the First Amendment). We thus recognize that the Act serves the "legitimate local purpose" of banning the cost-shifting inherent in the sending of deceptive spam.

Under the *Pike* balancing test, "[i]f a legitimate local purpose is found, then the question becomes one of degree." 397 U.S. at 142. In the present case, the trial court questioned whether the Act's requirement of truthfulness (in the subject lines and header information) would redress the costs associated with bulk e-mailings. As legal commentators have observed, however, "the truthfulness requirements (such as the requirement not to misrepresent the message's Internet origin) make spamming unattractive to the many fraudulent spammers, thereby reducing the volume of spam." Jack L. Goldsmith & Alan O. Sykes, *The Internet and the Dormant Commerce Clause*, 110 Yale L.J. 785, 819 (2001). Calling "simply wrong" the trial court's view "that truthful identification in the subject header would do little to relieve the annoyance of spam," the commentators assert that "[t]his identification alone would allow many people to delete the message without opening it (which takes time) and perhaps being offended by the content." *Id.* The Act's truthfulness requirements thus appear to advance the Act's aim of protecting ISPs and consumers from the problems associated with commercial bulk e-mail.

To be weighed against the Act's local benefits, the only burden the Act places on spammers is the requirement of truthfulness, a requirement that does not burden commerce at all but actually "facilitates it by eliminating fraud and deception." *Id.* Spammers must use an accurate, nonmisleading subject line, and they must not manipulate the transmission path to disguise the origin of their commercial messages. While spammers incur no costs in complying with the Act, they do incur costs for noncompliance, because they must take steps to introduce forged information into the header of their message. In finding the Act "unduly burdensome," CP at 175, the trial court apparently focused not on what spammers must do to comply with the Act but on what they must do if they choose to use deceptive subject lines or to falsify elements in the transmission path. To initiate *deceptive* spam without violating the Act, a spammer must weed out Washington residents by contacting the registrant of the domain name contained in the recipient's e-mail address. This focus on the burden of *non*compliance is contrary to the approach in the *Pike* balancing test, where the United States Supreme Court assessed the cost of compliance with a challenged statute. *Pike,* 397 U.S. at 143. Indeed, the trial court could have appropriately considered the filtering requirement a burden only if Washington's statute had banned outright the sending of UCE messages to Washington residents. We therefore conclude that Heckel has failed to prove that "the burden imposed on * * * commerce [by the Act] is *clearly excessive* in relation to the putative local benefits." *Id.* at 142 (emphasis added).

Drawing on two "unsettled and poorly understood" aspects of the dormant Commerce Clause analysis, Heckel contended that the Act (1) created inconsistency among the states and (2) regulated conduct occurring wholly outside of Washington. The inconsistent-regulations test and the extraterritoriality analysis are appropriately regarded as facets of the *Pike* balancing test. The Act survives both inquiries. At present, 17 other states have passed legislation regulating electronic solicitations. The truthfulness requirements of the Act do not conflict with any of the requirements in the other states' statutes, and it is inconceivable that any state would ever pass a law requiring spammers to use misleading subject lines or transmission paths. Some states' statutes do include additional requirements; for example, some statutes require spammers to provide contact information (for opt-out purposes) or to introduce subject lines with such labels as "ADV" or "ADV–ADLT." But because such statutes "merely create additional, but not irreconcilable, obligations," they "are not considered to be 'inconsistent' " for purposes of the dormant Commerce Clause analysis. *Instructional Sys., Inc. v. Computer Curriculum Corp.,* 35 F.3d 813, 826 (3d Cir.1994). The inquiry under the dormant Commerce Clause is not whether the states have enacted different anti-spam statutes but whether those differences create compliance costs that are "clearly excessive in relation to the putative local benefits." *Pike,* 397 U.S. at 142. We do not believe that the differences between the Act and the anti-spam laws of other states impose extraordinary costs on businesses deploying spam.

Nor does the Act violate the extraterritoriality principle in the dormant Commerce Clause analysis. Here, there is no "sweeping extraterritorial effect" that would outweigh the local benefits of the Act. *Edgar v. MITE Corp.,* 457 U.S. 624, 642 (1982). Heckel offers the hypothetical of a Washington resident who downloads and reads the deceptive spam while in Portland or Denver. He contends that the dormant Commerce Clause is offended because the Act would regulate the recipient's conduct while out of state. However, the Act does not burden interstate commerce by regulating when or where recipients may open the proscribed UCE messages. Rather, the Act addresses the conduct of spammers in targeting Washington consumers. Moreover, the hypothetical mistakenly presumes that the Act must be construed to apply to Washington residents when they are out of state, a construction that creates a jurisdictional question not at issue in this case.

In sum, we reject the trial court's conclusion that the Act violates the dormant Commerce Clause. Although the trial court found particularly persuasive *American Libraries Association v. Pataki,* 969 F. Supp. 160 (S.D.N.Y.1997), that decision—the first to apply the dormant Commerce Clause to a state law on Internet use—is distinguishable in a key respect. At issue in *American Libraries* was a New York statute that made it a crime to use a computer to distribute harmful, sexually explicit content to minors. The statute applied not just to initiation of e-mail messages but to all Internet activity, including the creation of websites. Thus, under the New York statute, a website creator in California could inadvertently violate the law simply because the site could be viewed in New York. Concerned with the statute's "chilling effect," *id.* at 179, the court observed that, if an artist "were located in California and wanted to display his work to a prospective purchaser in Oregon, he could not employ his virtual [Internet] studio to do so without risking prosecution under the New York law." 969 F. Supp. at 174. In contrast to the New York statute, which could reach all content posted on the Internet and therefore subject individuals to liability based on unintended access, the Act reaches only those deceptive UCE messages directed to a Washington resident or initiated from a computer located in Washington; in other words, the Act does not impose liability for messages that are merely routed through Washington or that are read by a Washington resident who was not the actual addressee.

* * *

NOTES & QUESTIONS

1. *Geolocation technologies.* The *Pataki* court's analysis is based in part on its premise that "[t]he nature of the Internet makes it impossible to restrict the effects of the New York Act to conduct occurring within New York * * * [since an] Internet user * * * lacks the ability to prevent New

Yorkers from visiting a particular website or viewing a particular newsgroup posting or receiving a particular mail exploder." New geolocation technologies, which enable a website operator to ascertain the geographic location of a website visitor based on the IP address of the visitor's computer, undermine that premise at least with respect to websites. Companies offering geolocation services claim accuracy rates of better than 99% in identifying the visitor's country, and 80–85% in identifying the visitor's city. It is also possible, but more expensive, for a website operator to allow website access only to those visitors who have established their location by some offline means of communication, such as by telephoning from an ascertainable area code or mailing a form of identification that establishes one's residency. *See* Jack L. Goldsmith & Alan O. Sykes, *The Internet and the Dormant Commerce Clause*, 110 Yale L.J. 785 (2001). What criteria should a court use to determine whether the availability of such technologies lowers the costs of compliance by out-of-state parties to the point where those costs do not outweigh the local benefits?

2. *Need for national regulation.* Consider the implications of the *Pataki* court's statement: "The Internet * * * requires a cohesive national scheme of regulation so that users are reasonably able to determine their obligations." Does it mean that states could not enforce (1) consumer protection statutes against deceptive marketing practices transmitted via the Internet? (2) criminal conspiracy laws against conspiracies carried out online? (3) a statute criminalizing use of the Internet to "importune, invite or induce a minor to engage in sexual intercourse"? Does it matter whether the state law is applied against a resident of the state, rather than an out-of-stater?

3. *Distinguishing* Pataki. The *Heckel* court distinguished *Pataki* on the ground that the New York indecency statute reached potentially all content posted on the Internet, while the Washington spam statute addressed only e-mail messages sent to or from a Washington computer. Does a sender of bulk e-mail have any practical means of determining whether any of the addressees are Washington residents?

4. *Proposed "Jurisdictional Certainty Over Digital Commerce Act."* In 2001 a bill was introduced in Congress that would prevent states from regulating digital commerce. The bill defined a "digital commercial transaction" as a transaction for a good or service that is delivered or provided entirely by means of the Internet. The bill recited findings that "[s]tate regulation of * * * digital commercial transactions creates significant and harmful burdens on interstate commerce [and] will seriously impede the growth of such transactions, decreasing the viability of electronic commerce as an alternative instrument or channel of commerce." It accordingly preempted state regulation: "No State or political subdivision thereof may enact or enforce any law, rule, regulation, standard, or other provision having the force or effect of law that regulates, or has the effect of regulating, digital commercial transactions." H.R. 2421, 107th Cong. (2001).

Do the problems posed by state regulation of digital commerce justify complete preemption of such regulation? Why does the bill distinguish between online transactions in *digital* goods and services and online transactions in other types of goods and services?

IV. COMPETITION POLICY AND COOPERATIVE BUSINESS MODELS

Business-to-business ("B2B") electronic exchanges are virtual marketplaces in which companies can buy and sell goods and services over the Internet. B2B exchanges promise efficiency gains through, among other things, reduced administrative costs in processing orders and correcting mistakes, reduced search and negotiation costs for both buyers and sellers, lower prices from joint purchasing, and lower manufacturing costs from a better integrated supply chain. With business-to-business commerce accounting for, by some estimates, as much as seventy percent of the regular economy, even small gains in efficiency would generate huge corporate savings. Encouraged by these potential savings, B2B exchanges are forming in every sector of the economy, including, to name just a few, the automotive, airlines, metals, chemicals, plastics, energy, construction and telecommunications industries.

B2B exchanges pose a challenge to existing regulatory paradigms, in particular to competition policy. Many of these electronic marketplaces are being formed as collaborative ventures among long-standing competitors. Thus, for example, on February 25, 2000, General Motors Corp., Ford Motor Co., and DaimlerChrysler AG announced the formation of Covisint, a B2B exchange providing services for firms in the automotive industry supply chain. The venture's core offerings include services to assist in product design, supply chain management and procurement functions performed by auto manufacturers and their direct and indirect suppliers. Since its announcement, Renault SA, and Nissan Motor Co. Ltd. have also joined the venture. Together, these five companies account for roughly one-half of worldwide automobile production. In 2001, transactions worth $51 billion were conducted via Covisint.

With such potentially huge concentrations of market power in a single venture, B2B exchanges—and Covisint, in particular—have attracted the attention of federal antitrust regulators. While recognizing that B2B exchanges "have the potential to generate significant efficiencies, winning lower prices, improved quality and greater innovation for consumers," antitrust regulators are concerned that these exchanges may also afford new opportunities for collusion and price-fixing.[2]

In this Part we first provide an overview of B2B concepts and the various kinds of electronic marketplaces that are being developed. Then we

2. FEDERAL TRADE COMMISSION, ENTERING THE 21ST CENTURY: COMPETITION POLICY IN THE WORLD OF B2B ELECTRONIC MARKETPLACES, ES–5 (2000), www.ftc.gov/os/2000/10/index.htm#26 ["FTC, ENTERING THE 21ST CENTURY"].

introduce the two forms of antitrust analysis used in the United States and explore some of the concerns about B2Bs voiced by antitrust regulators.

A. AN INTRODUCTION TO B2B ONLINE EXCHANGES

Direct and Indirect Goods

B2B electronic marketplaces are forums for the sale of both direct and indirect goods. Direct goods are components or raw materials used directly in the manufacture or assembly of a company's finished products. Indirect goods (or "operating inputs") are all other items necessary to run the business that do not become part of the manufacturer's end products. Indirect goods are purchased more frequently than direct goods, but the total dollar value of purchases of direct goods is larger. While the purchase of indirect goods (e.g., paper clips) does not typically require special training or knowledge, such training or knowledge is often essential for the procurement of direct inputs (e.g., microprocessors). Direct goods are purchased principally by firms in the manufacturing and retail sectors, while indirect goods are bought principally by firms in the service sector. Differences in transactional volume, value, purchaser profile and expertise required for procurement explain why B2B electronic marketplaces emphasizing one or the other typically will adopt different market orientations.

Market Orientation and Scope

A B2B electronic marketplace may orient itself horizontally or vertically. The electronic marketplace is oriented horizontally when it targets firms in many different industries. The "product focus" of a horizontal electronic marketplace is generally broader than a single category. It offers buyers not only a variety of goods but also a consistent purchasing interface across many product categories. The marketplace is oriented vertically when it focuses on steps in the supply chain of one product category. Vertical electronic marketplaces usually "provide product expertise and in-depth content knowledge for a [particular] industry."[3] Horizontal B2B electronic marketplaces tend to emphasize indirect goods, while vertical electronic marketplaces emphasize direct or manufacturing inputs.

As with their orientation, the *scope* of B2B electronic marketplaces also varies. A B2B exchange may be global or regional. While a global electronic marketplace serves a potentially worldwide constituency, a regional B2B exchange attempts to address regional needs, of, for example, utilities, hospitals or universities. Thus, a regional, horizontal B2B electronic marketplace would serve the needs of a wide range of regionally or locally focused entities regardless of industry.

Order and Pricing Mechanisms

B2B electronic marketplaces use four basic types of transactional mechanisms to implement the ordering and pricing of goods and services: electronic catalogs, auctions, exchanges and negotiation. Catalogs generally

3. *Id.* at 7.

involve fixed or static pricing, while the other three mechanisms implement a form of dynamic pricing. We consider each in turn.

Metacatalogs. A B2B electronic marketplace using a catalog format to present the price and facilitate the ordering of goods typically uses catalog aggregators or metacatalogs to combine the product offerings of numerous vendors in a single, standard format. Its consistent user interface permits buyers to compare the goods of different vendors with relative ease, while at the same time permitting sellers to offer price lists customized to individual buyers.

Online uniform product catalogs are particularly well-suited for offering low-priced items that are purchased in small quantities, where the transaction costs of "face-to-face" negotiation would make such negotiation impractical. Online catalogs also permit frequent revisions and updates without the associated costs of printing and distribution. As a result, websites emphasizing indirect inputs tend to dominate this category.

Auctions. Online auctions are particularly appropriate for items that are both unique and differentiated and also simple to describe and understand. There are four principal kinds of auctions. The most popular is the *forward* or *English auction.* In a forward auction, a seller offers an item for sale and multiple buyers bid competitively to purchase it. Prices move up with each bid and the highest bid wins. By contrast, a *reverse English auction* is one in which the buyer indicates the need or desire for a particular product or service and multiple sellers bid competitively to provide it. Prices move down with each bid and the lowest bid generally wins. In a reverse English auction, the buyer usually issues a "request for quotation" that includes product or service specifications and commercial terms. The sellers are often prequalified, and the buyer reserves the right to select a bid other than the lowest so long as the higher price is justified by difference in quality, location or other relevant considerations.

In addition to the forward and reverse English auctions, there are also the *Dutch* and *Japanese auctions.* A Dutch auction involves one seller and many buyers in which the auctioneer reduces the price (from a high starting point) until a bidder agrees to buy at that price. In a Japanese auction, by contrast, the auctioneer raises the price (from a low starting point) and buyers must bid at each price to stay in the auction.

Auctions may be further distinguished by considering the manner and extent of information that is shared with the bidders. Bidders may be privy to the identity of other bidders or not. Bidders may be told the amount of other bids or simply that theirs has been outdone. Finally, bidders may be told to which bidder each bid belongs even if that bidder's true identity has been masked by use of an alias. Depending upon the kind of good or service being auctioned and the nature of the market, different choices will be optimal.

Exchanges. Modeled on the Chicago Board of Trade or the NASDAQ, an online exchange is a two-sided marketplace where buyers and suppliers negotiate prices, usually with a bid and ask system, and where prices can move both up and down. They provide a potentially volatile dynamic pricing mechanism that is ideal for commodities or commodity-like products. The phrase "B2B exchange" is generally used to refer to any kind of B2B electronic marketplace and is not restricted to B2Bs using an exchange order and pricing mechanism.

Negotiation. The negotiation model includes any arrangement in which buyers and sellers directly negotiate the terms of the transaction. Vendors might post requests for proposals, and potential buyers could search these posted requests according to specific criteria and obtain a list of all the requests for proposals satisfying them. A buyer could then select and contact one of these vendors and begin the process of negotiation. While minimizing the search costs involved in identifying an appropriate vendor, this model's use of direct negotiation—a less efficient process than the others just considered—suggests that it is most appropriate for goods and services that must be customized for the buyer's use or are otherwise difficult to treat as a commodity.

Ownership and Control

Ownership. The evolving ownership models adopted by B2B electronic marketplaces fall roughly into two categories: those owned by participants in the industries that the B2B serves and those owned by nonparticipants such as technology service providers, venture capitalists and management. Those in the latter category are frequently referred to as third-party or independent electronic marketplaces, while those in the former category are called coalition or consortium B2Bs. Coalition B2Bs may be further divided into buyer-owned or seller-owned electronic marketplaces. Among coalition B2Bs, those owned by groups of buyers are more numerous. Large industrial players such as the five automakers that formed Covisint can guarantee a high liquidity and transaction volume for their sites and attract the participation of many suppliers. Nonetheless, one can find seller-owned B2Bs in industries with a high concentration of suppliers and diffused buyers. Even in coalition B2Bs, however, there is often equity participation by technology firms providing the e-commerce platform and related services. In Covisint, for example, both CommerceOne Inc. and Oracle Corporation are equity partners.

Control. While the control of corporate boards and the day-to-day operations of the website are commonly exercised by the owners, some B2B exchanges have deliberately developed management teams whose members do not have prior ties to any of the owner-participants. Still others have adopted advisory boards of participants that lack an ownership interest in the exchange. Such a board may advise the B2B on matters as varied as acceptable business practices and technology requirements. As discussed in Part IV(B), *infra*, the practice of industry competitors jointly owning and collaboratively operating B2B electronic marketplaces has been a significant cause for concern among antitrust regulators.

Revenue Sources

B2B electronic marketplaces may derive revenue from several sources, including transaction fees, membership fees, service fees, advertising and marketing fees, hosting fees and the sale of data or information. A transaction fee is a flat per-transaction charge or one based on a percentage of the transaction's value. A membership or subscription fee is simply a periodic charge for access to and participation in the B2B electronic marketplace. Service fees are charges for value-added services such as logistical support (e.g., shipping services), system integration (e.g., connecting legacy systems to B2Bs), financial services (e.g., credit assessments), and industry information (e.g., notice of new products and services, industry news, upcoming trade shows and conferences, lists of industry resources on the Web, etc.). Advertising and marketing fees are charges for banner advertising and e-mail marketing services targeted at the exchange's participants. Hosting fees, also called listing fees, are charges for providing an exchange member, usually a supplier, with a virtual storefront on the B2B's site.

When goods are purchased online, every action of the buyer can be monitored and recorded digitally. Accordingly, a B2B electronic marketplace can capture information regarding, for example, which web pages the exchange member visited, which products it compared, whether the desired item was in stock, how long a buyer is willing to wait for backordered items, supplier responses to product and price changes, which items are ultimately purchased, how they are shipped, the manner of payment, and so forth. All of this data may be aggregated into valuable industry statistics. Never before have the participants in a market had the ability to analyze it so completely, identifying problems and bottlenecks as well as opportunities. While market participants may demand that their individual transaction data be kept confidential, the sale of aggregated statistics derived from the transactions conducted on the site could provide an important source of revenue for B2B electronic marketplaces. One B2B currently serving the cut-flower industry, for example, accumulates sales price data for each variety of flower on a daily basis and sells that information to a wire service which in turn makes it available internationally. Data concerning the purchasing decisions of a particular exchange member can also be sold to that member for its internal use. The management of a restaurant chain, for example, might use such data to monitor purchasing decisions of store managers.

As electronic marketplaces mature, fees for value-added services such as procurement services that include reporting, fulfillment, payment systems, and other back-office integration will also become a significant source of B2B revenue. Revenue from transaction fees is simply too limited—in 1998, for example, the New York Stock Exchange supported a trading volume of $7.3 trillion but generated only $101 million in income. B2B exchanges offering only standardized and frequently traded goods become commodities themselves and are forced by competitive pressures to accept small transaction fees. B2B exchanges that supplement their trading platform with value-added services, by contrast, can command much higher fees. For example, in the energy and petrochemical industries, "energy" B2B Altra Energy charges 0.05% on transactions, and "chemicals" B2B ChemConnect charges rates as low as 0.1%. By contrast, multi-industry B2B VerticalNet's Asset Remarketing business goes beyond making auction markets by providing value-added services such as warehousing, assessment, and inventory reporting and is therefore able to charge 10% on every sale.

B. B2B Online Exchanges and Competition Policy

Notwithstanding the potential efficiency gains of cooperative organization of business infrastructure, such organization also may thwart competition. Agreements among competitors that generate more anticompetitive harm than procompetitive benefits are illegal under the antitrust laws of the United States. In assessing the lawfulness of different B2B arrangements, two provisions of the antitrust law are especially relevant: Section 1 of the Sherman Act and Section 7 of the Clayton Act. Section 1 of the Sherman Act outlaws "every contract, combination * * * or conspiracy, in restraint of trade," but long ago, the Supreme Court decided that the Sherman Act prohibits only those contracts or agreements that restrain trade unreasonably. Section 7 of the Clayton Act prohibits mergers and acquisitions where the effect "may be substantially to lessen competition, or to tend to create a monopoly." The formation of a new joint venture such as a B2B electronic marketplace could fall within the scope of this provision.

Per Se Illegality and Rule of Reason Analysis

To assess the lawfulness of agreements among competitors under the antitrust laws of the United States and these two provisions in particular, the Federal Trade Commission and the United States Department of Justice ("the Agencies") have adopted two different approaches. Under the first, the *per se* approach, the Agencies consider whether the agreement is "so likely to harm competition and to have no significant procompetitive benefit" that it "do[es] not warrant the time and expense required for particularized inquiry" into its effects on competition.[4] Such agreements are challenged as per se illegal. Per se illegal agreements "include agreements among competitors to fix prices or output, rig bids, or share or divide markets by allocating customers, suppliers, territories, or lines of commerce."[5] These types of agreements are conclusively presumed "to be illegal, without inquiring into their claimed business purposes, anticompetitive harms, procompetitive benefits, or overall competitive effects."[6]

Under the second approach, *the rule of reason* analysis, the Agencies conduct "a factual inquiry into an agreement's overall competitive ef-

4. Federal Trade Commission and the United States Department of Justice, Antitrust Guidelines for Collaborations Among Competitors 3 (2000), www.ftc.gov/os/2000/04/ftcdojguidelines.pdf.

5. *Id.*

6. *Id.*

fects."[7] The central question of this inquiry is whether the agreement harms the state of competition by increasing the ability or incentive to profitably raise prices above or reduce output, quality, service, or innovation below what likely would prevail in the absence of the agreement.[8] "Rule of reason analysis focuses on only those factors, and undertakes only the degree of factual inquiry, necessary to assess accurately the overall competitive effect of the relevant agreement."[9] The Agencies begin with an examination of the agreement. "[W]here the likelihood of anticompetitive harm is evident from the nature of the agreement, or anticompetitive harm has resulted from an agreement already in operation, then, absent overriding benefits that could offset the anticompetitive harm, the Agencies challenge such agreements without a detailed market analysis."[10] Where the agreement raises possible competitive concerns, but is not one that would be challenged without a detailed market analysis, the Agencies analyze the agreement in greater depth. If this market analysis "indicates anticompetitive harm, the Agencies examine whether the relevant agreement is reasonably necessary to achieve procompetitive benefits that likely would offset anticompetitive harms."[11] If it is not, then the Agencies may challenge the agreement as illegal, seeking a court order enjoining the anticompetitive practices. Where the collaboration among competitors involves two or more agreements, the Agencies will consider the competitive effects of the overall collaboration.[12]

In applying the antitrust laws to a B2B electronic marketplace, the first question that must be asked is whether the marketplace is a collaboration among competitors. According to the Antitrust Guidelines for Collaborations Among Competitors published by the FTC and Department of Justice ("the Guidelines"), a collaboration among competitors "comprises a set of one or more agreements, other than merger agreements, between or among competitors to engage in economic activity, and the economic activity resulting therefrom."[13] Under this definition, a B2B electronic marketplace is likely to be a collaboration among competitors.[14]

Like any other collaboration among competitors, the lawfulness of a B2B electronic marketplace may be evaluated under either a per se or rule of reason analysis. If a B2B is formed for the illegitimate purpose of fixing prices or allocating markets, customers or suppliers among the competitors, then it is per se illegal. If, however, a B2B is formed as a legitimate joint venture, it should be evaluated under a rule of reason analysis. The Guidelines state that if "participants in an efficiency-enhancing integration of economic activity enter into an agreement that is reasonably related to

7. *Id.*

8. *Id.* at 4.

9. *Id.* at 7–8.

10. *Id.* at 4.

11. *Id.*

12. *Id.* at 6.

13. *Id.* at 2.

14. For the purposes of this discussion, we are assuming that the B2B exchange is owned and operated by a group of industry participants that compete with each other for buyers or sellers. If the exchange is owned and operated by third parties who are not industry participants, then there are unlikely to be any antitrust issues arising from their collaboration.

the integration and reasonably necessary to achieve its procompetitive benefits, the Agencies analyze the agreement under the rule of reason."[15] A B2B electronic marketplace would seek to be viewed as an efficiency-enhancing integration of economic activity. The Guidelines define such an integration as one in which participants "combine, by contract or otherwise, significant capital, technology, or other complementary assets to achieve procompetitive benefits that the participants could not achieve separately."[16]

To avoid potential antitrust difficulties under a per se or rule of reason analysis, a B2B electronic marketplace must be structured and adopt operating procedures to avoid, *inter alia*, (1) the development of monopsony power through joint purchasing, (2) group boycotts that result from denying a firm access to the B2B, (3) opportunities for collusion that might arise from information sharing among the B2B's members, and (4) exclusivity requirements that create barriers to entry for competing B2B electronic marketplaces and other threats of monopoly power.

Monopsony Power

An attractive feature of doing business online for many small and medium-size enterprises is the opportunity to purchase goods and services in concert with other firms in order to obtain volume discounts. Joint purchasing not only provides savings for buyers, but combining many small purchases into one large one can reduce the costs of manufacturers and suppliers as well. To this extent joint purchasing is procompetitive. In some cases, however, joint purchasing can create quasi-monopsony power in the buyers, and this can lead to significant anticompetitive effects. Monopsony is literally a market in which there is a single buyer of a particular product; it is the equivalent of a monopoly from the seller's side. Uniting of all the buyers in a market within a B2B exchange can create the economic equivalent of monopsony.

It is very difficult to determine when joint purchasers become monopsonists. Accordingly, the FTC and Department of Justice have created a "safe harbor" rule. Under the Guidelines, "[a]bsent extraordinary circumstances, the Agencies do not challenge a competitor collaboration when the market shares of the collaboration and its participants collectively account for no more than twenty percent of each relevant market in which competition may be affected."[17] While creating a safe harbor, this provision does not release a B2B from its duties under the antitrust laws. Nor does it mean that a B2B like Covisint that falls outside this safety zone is necessarily in violation of the antitrust laws. As the two agencies emphasize, "many competitor collaborations falling outside the safety zone are procompetitive or competitively neutral."[18] Nonetheless, if the purchases of a group of buyers engaged in joint purchasing fall outside this safety zone, then the B2B could reduce concerns over monopsony power by limiting

15. *Id.* at 8.

16. *Id.*

17. *Id.* at 26.

18. *Id.* at 25.

either the number of buyers that may participate in this group or the percentage of their purchases that each member of this group could make through the B2B.

Exclusionary Practices

In most industries the market for electronic marketplaces is likely to be dominated by one or only a few B2Bs. If the owners of a dominant B2B exchange are also participants, one can imagine a strong temptation on their part to disadvantage their competitors by excluding them from this B2B. Similarly, we can imagine other B2Bs courting possible participants who refuse to join unless their competitors are excluded. In such cases, a B2B, responding to its participants, might deny these competitors access to the B2B or permit them access on terms that prevent them from reaping the full benefits of participation. Such terms could range from higher membership fees to only partial access to the B2B's electronic interchange standards—thereby reducing the site's functionality for these competitors. While such exclusionary practices do not necessarily involve antitrust violations, the FTC has concluded that the "demand-side scale economies associated with networks warrant a heightened degree of scrutiny in assessing denials of access to joint venture membership."[19]

Exclusionary practices involve antitrust violations only when they harm competition and not merely particular competitors. *See, e.g., Associated Press v. United States*, 326 U.S. 1, 13, 18–19 (1945). Competition is harmed if the competitors excluded are important to maintaining downstream competition and the exclusionary conduct significantly raises the competitors' costs.[20] These two conditions are met when participating in the B2B exchange is the only way competitors can obtain needed inputs at comparable prices and the denial or limitation of access would give the B2B's participants the power to raise or maintain the price of their products above what otherwise would likely prevail.[21] This entire issue can be avoided if a B2B simply adopts a policy of open and equal membership for all businesses that desire to participate in it.

Information Sharing and Collusion

A B2B electronic marketplace is an information network comprising buyers, sellers, owners, managers, employees, directors, and various service providers. Each of these participants in a B2B can potentially receive information about product prices, quantities available, delivery dates, warehouse space, and materials costs. They may also learn the details of individual transactions, such as quantity purchased, payment options, payment dates, financing terms, warranties, and the identity of the members involved in them. When information and market data of this kind are shared among participants that occupy different levels in the supply chain,

19. FEDERAL TRADE COMMISSION, ANTICIPATING THE 21ST CENTURY: COMPETITION POLICY IN THE NEW HIGH-TECH, GLOBAL MARKETPLACE 9–8 (1996).

20. FTC, ENTERING THE 21ST CENTURY, at 3–19 and 3–22.

21. *Id.* at 3–20 to 3–22.

such sharing can promote competition through a more efficient supply chain. Such information shared among competitors, however, facilitates collusion, price-fixing, price-signaling, and other forms of anticompetitive behavior. Information sharing "facilitate[s] collusion by standardizing participants' costs or by enhancing the ability to project or monitor a participant's output level through knowledge of its input purchases."[22] Moreover, access to such information by participant-owners of the B2B when it is not generally available to nonequity members gives the former an unfair competitive advantage over the latter in the marketplace.

Developing policies and procedures for B2B exchanges that strike the proper balance between the procompetitive benefits of information sharing and market transparency, on the one hand, and the risks of facilitating illegal anticompetitive behavior, on the other, is difficult. Recognizing this same difficulty in the health care industry, the FTC and Department of Justice developed a safe harbor for sharing fee-related information among health care service providers, requiring information exchanges among competing providers to satisfy three conditions: first, the collection of information must be managed by a neutral third party such as a purchaser, government agency, health care consultant, academic institution, or trade association; second, any information that is shared among or is available to the competing providers must be more than three months old; and third, any statistical data available to competing providers must aggregate the individual data of at least five providers, no individual provider's data may represent more than 25 percent on a weighted basis of that statistic, and any information disseminated must be sufficiently aggregated such that it would not allow recipients to identify the prices charged by any individual provider.

While most e-commerce platforms are sufficiently powerful to support forms of information sharing that will run afoul of the antitrust laws, a B2B's board of directors or management can restrict such uses with appropriate operating rules and policies. These policies and procedures might require compliance with conditions analogous to the three conditions that must be satisfied to enjoy the safe harbor created for health care service providers. They might also require that the identity of bidders in online auctions and exchanges be masked. They might use firewalls and other network security measures to allow access only to aggregated data and information concerning one's own transactions. A B2B exchange can also reduce the likelihood of unwanted information sharing by hiring a management team with no prior affiliation to any participants, by keeping sensitive information from directors affiliated with participant-owners, and by submitting to compliance audits by independent third parties. Moreover, buyers and sellers can insist that their trading partners sign nondisclosure and confidentiality agreements to keep their sensitive information private. Finally, stiff penalties can be adopted and enforced for violations of these policies and procedures, such as requiring participant-owners to divest their equity interest.

22. *Id.* at 3–6.

Exclusivity Agreements and the Threat of Monopoly

To attract members, some B2Bs entice potential participants with equity interests, rebates or other revenue-sharing devices in return for commitments to transact a certain volume of business on the site. Some B2Bs also place requirements on members to encourage their loyalty such as minimum volume or minimum percentage requirements, bans on investments in other B2Bs and significant up-front membership fees. Penalties such as divestment of any equity interest or being barred from doing business on the site may attach to violations of these requirements.

These types of arrangements are designed to keep a member's business on the site by creating significant switching costs for members that might decide to participate in other B2Bs. To the extent that such arrangements help a B2B achieve liquidity, they are procompetitive; but to the extent that they erect barriers to entry for potential competitors, they are anticompetitive. Exclusivity agreements cause antitrust regulators much concern since the switching costs they impose combined with the network effects and economies of scale inherent in the nature of a B2B electronic marketplace act to deprive new B2Bs of the buyers and sellers they need to succeed. With potential competitors unable to attract a critical mass of buyers and sellers, and to maintain liquidity sufficient to continue in business, the B2B enjoying the protection of these exclusivity agreements is likely to develop monopoly power in the industry that it serves. Obviously, to reduce the likelihood of antitrust difficulties, a B2B should abjure such agreements.

Even without exclusivity agreements, monopoly power may develop. A B2B is fundamentally a network of buyers and sellers, and the greater a B2B's network, the greater the gains in efficiency and value it can offer its participants. With a first mover advantage or the nonexclusive participation of a majority of large industry players, a B2B can eclipse the attractiveness of any competing B2B. As participants in these competing B2Bs switch to the B2B with the larger network, the networks offered by these competing B2Bs become even smaller and less attractive until they finally fail for lack of liquidity. At the same time, the network of the larger B2B grows still larger and even more attractive, ultimately developing monopoly power in the industry that it serves.

The growth of a B2B into a natural monopoly may be prevented in two ways. On the one hand, a growing B2B may ensure that its network is interoperable with the smaller networks of competing B2Bs. By making its own network interoperable with those of others, a growing B2B not only obviates the pernicious effects of its network on others but does so by creating a still larger and socially more valuable network: an internetwork of B2Bs. On the other hand, a growing B2B may stem the growth of its monopoly power by not accepting new members once it reaches a particular size.

NOTES & QUESTIONS

1. *Breaking the rules.* As noted above, exclusionary practices merit a heightened scrutiny by antitrust regulators. To what extent might such heightened scrutiny prevent a B2B exchange from enforcing its operating rules and regulations? For example, imagine the following apparent abuses of an online B2B exchange: (1) a member of a B2B exchange frequents the online exchange only to gather information about its competitors but never to transact business; (2) a member of a B2B exchange uses the online exchange to identify and negotiate with trading partners but then approaches these companies offline in order to close the deal without paying the required transaction fees to the exchange; or (3) a member of a B2B online exchange enters into agreements with other members of the exchange but never fulfills its obligations under the agreements. Do the antitrust laws prevent a B2B online exchange from combating these types of abuses by excluding such members from the exchange? In these kinds of situations, how would you advise the management of a B2B online exchange to proceed?

2. *How large is too large*? In our discussion of B2B exchanges and the threat of monopoly power, we noted that one way in which B2B exchanges might attempt to avoid antitrust scrutiny is to limit its membership so that it does not grow too large. How large is too large? If you were advising the owners or managers of a B2B exchange, how would you determine the size beyond which they should not grow? See Federal Trade Commission and Department of Justice, ANTITRUST GUIDELINES FOR COLLABORATIONS AMONG COMPETITORS § 4.2 (2000).

3. *Safe harbors*. In our discussion of B2B exchanges, we noted that the Federal Trade Commission and the Department of Justice have created a safe harbor provision for the health care industry which permits health care service providers to share information about fees when certain conditions are met. Exactly what function is served by safe harbors in a regulatory scheme? Do they benefit industries to which they apply or not? Do they encourage or discourage innovation and competition within an industry?

CHAPTER TWO

Protecting Commercial Identity Online: Trademarks

In the world of bricks and mortar, it is widely held that the success of a retail establishment is highly dependent on its physical location. In the virtual world of electronic commerce, by contrast, physical location is almost irrelevant. From the standpoint of access by potential customers, it matters very little whether a company's web server is located in New York, Paris, Hong Kong or some remote region of Siberia. On the Web, every store is as close as the nearest network access device—whether it be a desktop computer, a laptop, a personal digital assistant, a television with a set-top box or a Web-enabled cell phone. Only when e-commerce must rely upon the traditional commercial infrastructure of brick-and-mortar companies does location matter. If I buy a television from an e-commerce website, the cost of that television and the time required for its delivery to my home will depend in part on the distance of that company's distribution center from my house. By contrast, for transactions involving information goods such as software, music and other digital products that can be delivered as well as purchased online, the physical location of the company does not matter to the consumer, though it may matter to taxing and regulatory authorities.

If physical location is not an essential predicate to commercial success online, what is? While there is no consensus answer to this question, many observers believe that developing and protecting one's commercial identity is critical. A strong brand seamlessly integrated into the search and navigation technologies with which consumers identify and connect to e-commerce websites is as important online as physical location is offline.

Brand identities serve an efficiency-enhancing role by reducing the costs that consumers incur locating goods and services that meet their needs. A brand identity reduces consumer search costs by conveying important information to consumers, at a very low cost. Within a product category, a strong brand signifies that the item it marks originates from a particular company, has a known level of quality, and enjoys a specific array of product features and characteristics. Such information is important for making informed and rational choices in the marketplace.

Branding is even more important in the online commercial environment than it has been in the world of bricks and mortar. In the offline world, consumers might become physically familiar with a store they frequent, might come to know the employees personally, might even live in the same neighborhood with them. In the online world, branding is the main thing consumers have to go on in deciding whether to trust a company or its product. Moreover, in the offline world, if a product is unsatisfactory, a consumer may have some confidence that it can be exchanged if there is a known physical store the consumer can return to, but trying to fix transactions that have gone wrong becomes more uncertain in the online environment, because electronic presence seems much more shadowy and ephemeral. Brand X website might fail to deliver a satisfactory product, and might be here today and gone tomorrow.

For these reasons, trademark law is one of the most important areas of law for Internet commerce, and the advent of Internet commerce has seen significant developments in trademark law. Perhaps the most significant of these developments is the creation of an entirely new form of intangible asset, the Internet domain name, and the disputes that have arisen over who owns and controls this asset. Among the most significant features of the most popular domain names, giving rise to difficult governance questions, are their uniqueness and international scope—even if many companies around the world have the same corporate name, there is only one dot-com for that name. We will take up the issues surrounding domain names in Chapter 3.

Meanwhile, in this chapter we explore how established trademark law applies to online businesses and their efforts to protect their brands, in two different ways. Traditional trademark law is based on the danger of confusing consumers about the source and quality of the product they are buying. Contemporary trademark protection has, in the case of powerful, well-established, "famous" brands, provided additional protection in the form of actions for trademark dilution. Dilution does not turn on consumer confusion, so it establishes much broader exclusion rights for those brands that can make use of it.

In this chapter we also explore the limits of trademark protection; that is, the balance between the exclusion rights afforded to the brand owner and the needs of competitors or the general public to use the words or images that constitute or are similar to the trademark. For example, generic words for a product cannot be trademarks because competitors need to use the word to describe their own products. "Computer" cannot be the trademark for a computer product. In fact, if a trademark becomes so popular that it becomes a generic word for the product—"aspirin" is one example—trademark protection ceases. In addition to economic issues of the scope that must be afforded to competitors, free speech issues also arise. For example, can a company use trademark law to quash a parody site like chasemanhattansucks.com?

Introduction—Trademark Basics

A trademark is "a word, name, symbol, device, or other designation * * * that is distinctive of a person's goods or services and that is used in a manner that identifies those goods or services and distinguishes them from the goods or services of others." Restatement (Third) of Unfair Competition

§ 9 (1995). In addition to words and names, such designations may include, *inter alia*, numbers, letters, slogans, pictures, characters, sounds, graphic designs, and product and packaging features.

Trademarks are protectible under both state and federal law. While trademarks were originally a creature of the common law, and common-law trademarks still exist, Congress and state legislatures have enacted statutes providing for their registration and protection. At common law and under these statutes, the trademark owner has, subject to certain limitations, the exclusive right to use the protected mark in commerce.

> The purpose underlying any trade-mark statute is twofold. One is to protect the public so that it may be confident that, in purchasing a product bearing a particular trade-mark which it favorably knows, it will get the product which it asks for and wants to get. Secondly, where the owner of a trade-mark has spent energy, time, and money in presenting to the public the product, he is protected in his investment from its misappropriation by pirates and cheats.

Id. § 9 (Reporter's Notes, cmt. c) (quoting S. REP. NO. 79–1333, at 3 (1946)).

To qualify for protection, a word, name or other designation must (1) be distinctive, (2) be used in commerce, (3) be affixed or otherwise associated with goods and services, and (4) signify the source or origin of those goods and services with which it is associated.

As to the first criterion, distinctiveness, marks may be either inherently distinctive, or may acquire distinctiveness through their use in commerce. Courts refer to inherently distinctive marks as *arbitrary, fanciful* or *suggestive*. EXXON is a fanciful mark, while APPLE, when applied to computers, is an arbitrary mark. The use of fanciful or arbitrary marks in connection with the goods and services with which they are associated has no meaning or significance other than as a trademark. Suggestive marks, in contrast, suggest some attribute or characteristic of the goods and services with which they are associated. For example, THE MONEY STORE suggests that the company with which it is associated provides money lending services. Similarly, EVERREADY when applied to batteries suggests that the batteries will have a long life.

Other marks, while not inherently distinctive, may acquire distinctiveness through their use in commerce. Courts call these marks *descriptive*. Descriptive marks are so called because they purport to describe some attribute or characteristic of the goods and services with which they are associated. For example, TENDER VITTLES applied to cat food suggests that the product has a certain desirable consistency. A descriptive mark that acquires distinctiveness is said to have "secondary meaning," and it is only the "secondary meaning" that is protected, not the term's primary meaning in ordinary language:

> There are but a limited number of words and images suitable for use in describing a product, and sellers own neither the English language nor common depictions of goods. * * * If descriptive words and pictures could be appropriated without evidence of a secondary meaning, sellers could snatch for themselves the riches

of the language and make it more difficult for new entrants to identify their own products; consumers would be worse off.

Scandia Down Corp. v. Euroquilt, Inc., 772 F.2d 1423, 1430 (7th Cir.1985).

A word, name, symbol or other designation that is generic is not protectible as a trademark. For example, APPLE, when applied to apples, is not protectible, and neither is SHREDDED WHEAT when applied to small edible "pillows" of shredded wheat. While a generic term can never become a trademark, a protectible trademark may lose its protection if it becomes generic. This process is sometimes called "genericide." THERMOS, ASPIRIN and DRY ICE are examples of marks that lost their protection in this fashion. The potential loss of trademark protection through genericide explains why employees of 3M and Xerox always say, respectively, "clear cellophane tape" instead of "scotch tape" and "photocopies" instead of "xeroxes." Since the use of a generic term is not protected under the law of trademark, if a term is or becomes generic, anyone can use it.

Generally, the owner of a protectible mark is the person or entity that first adopts and uses that mark in commerce. For this reason, the trademark owner is sometimes called the senior user of the mark. Anyone who subsequently uses the same or a confusingly similar mark is referred to as a junior user. Senior users have priority of use, and therefore priority of right, over junior users. Since the effective date of the Trademark Revision Act of 1988, one can establish priority of use for inherently distinctive marks that one has not yet used in commerce by filing an intent-to-use application to obtain a federal trademark registration. *See* Lanham Act § 1(b), 15 U.S.C. § 1051(b). Under this application process, the registrant must actually adopt and use the mark in commerce within six months, a period which the U.S. Patent and Trademark Office ("PTO") may extend for six month periods, up to three years. *See* 15 U.S.C. § 1051(d).

The senior user of a protectible mark may significantly increase its level of protection by registering that trademark on the Principal Register of the PTO. There are two application procedures through which one can request registration of a trademark: a use-based application pursuant to 15 U.S.C. § 1051(a) (under which the applicant must specify the date it first used the mark and the date it first used the mark in commerce, and the goods in connection with which the mark is used), and an intent-to-use application pursuant to 15 U.S.C. § 1051(b) (under which the applicant must specify the goods in connection with which the applicant has a bona fide intention to use the mark). Both types of applicants must specify the class of goods and services in connection with which the mark will be used, and must provide an actual specimen of such good.

PTO Trademark Examining Attorneys review applications to determine whether they satisfy statutory requirements and whether they are subject to any of the statutory bars set forth in 15 U.S.C. § 1052(a)–(e). These provisions of the Lanham Act prohibit the registration of marks that comprise or consist of, *inter alia,* (a) immoral, deceptive or scandalous matter, (b) the flag or coat of arms or other insignia of the United States, or any state, municipality, or foreign country, (c) the name, portrait or signature of a living person without that person's consent, (d) a word, name or other designation that is confusingly similar to another mark already registered, or (e) matter that applied to the applicant's goods is merely descriptive, deceptively misdescriptive, primarily geographically descriptive (unless it is a mark indicating regional origin such as "Made in America"), primarily geographically deceptively misdescriptive, primarily a surname, or primarily functional. If the Examining Attorney determines that the application is barred under one of these provisions, he or she will then determine whether the claimed mark has acquired secondary meaning and may nevertheless be registered under exceptions to the statutory bar set forth in 15 U.S.C. § 1052(f). If the application satisfies statutory requirements for registration, it is published in the Official Gazette of the PTO.[1] Upon publication, anyone who believes that he or she would be damaged by the registration may file an opposition. If all opposition proceedings are resolved in the applicant's favor, then a certificate of registration will be issued. Adverse determinations by the Examining Attorney may be appealed to the Trademark Trial and Appeals Board and then to the Court of Appeals for the Federal Circuit.

Federal registration of a trademark on the Principal Register confers substantial benefits on the trademark owner. The trademark owner may bring actions for trademark infringement in federal court, 15 U.S.C. § 1121(a), and may recover damages, 15 U.S.C. § 1117(a)–(c). In any legal proceeding, the trademark owner's registration is "prima facie evidence of the validity of the registered mark and of the registration of the mark, of the registrant's ownership of the mark, and of the registrant's exclusive right to use the registered mark in commerce on or in connection with the goods or services specified in the registration subject to any conditions or limitations stated therein." 15 U.S.C. § 1115(a). Moreover, under the incontestability provision of the Lanham Act, after five years the registration becomes conclusive evidence of those matters. 15 U.S.C. § 1115(c). Finally, the defenses that a junior user can raise against a trademark owner with a federal registration are significantly reduced. 15 U.S.C § 1115(b).

Descriptive marks that have not yet acquired secondary meaning may not be registered on the Principal Register but may be placed on the Supplemental Register. Once they acquire secondary meaning they may then be registered on the Principal Register. While not conferring as many benefits as the Principal Register, registration on the Supplemental Register nonetheless provides some advantages. For example, it allows the trademark owner to bring an action for infringement in federal court, prevents the registration of other marks that may cause confusion, permits registration abroad based on the United States registration, gives notice of use to all those who perform trademark searches, and permits the trademark owner to use the ® symbol. *See generally* 15 U.S.C. §§ 1091–96.

1. Sometimes a claimed mark will comprise both registrable and unregistrable matter. In such cases, the applicant may be required to disclaim any federal trademark rights in the unregistrable matter before the Examining Attorney will approve the application for publication in the Official Gazette. 15 U.S.C. § 1056.

Trademarks that are deemed "famous" are also entitled, under federal law and the law of many states, to protection against dilution. The Federal Trademark Dilution Act of 1995 defines "dilution" as "the lessening of the capacity of a famous mark to identify and distinguish goods or services, regardless of the presence or absence of (1) competition between the owner of the famous mark and other parties, or (2) likelihood of confusion, mistake, or deception." 15 U.S.C. § 1127. Trademark dilution can occur even when there is no infringement—that is, there is no likelihood of confusion between the diluting mark and the trademark being diluted.

Registration of a trademark with the PTO or use in commerce in the United States confers protection against infringing use only in the United States. Because there is no international registration regime, a trademark owner that wants to protect its mark must register the mark in every country where it does business. Many countries allow registration of a mark before the owner has made any use of it. This has resulted in situations where trademark owners in one country had to buy rights to marks in other countries they wanted to enter from registrants who anticipated them.

From the foregoing discussion of trademark law, we may discern a tripartite framework in which to consider the possible commercial exploitation of trademarks and other symbols, words and names. If a term is generic, then one may freely use it. No one may claim an exclusive right to use a generic term, word or symbol. If, however, a term is distinctive—inherently or because it has acquired secondary meaning—and has been used as a trademark, then one may not use in commerce or otherwise commercially exploit that mark or any other possible mark that is confusingly similar to it. Finally, if a mark has become famous from its use as a trademark, then one may not use in commerce or otherwise commercially exploit any other mark that would dilute the famous mark even if there is no likelihood of confusion between the famous mark and the possible diluting mark. The laws barring the commercial use of infringing and diluting marks are not absolute and some uses are permitted as exceptions to these rules. These exceptions are characterized as affirmative defenses that may be raised in actions for trademark infringement and trademark dilution.

The organization of the present chapter conforms to the structure of this general framework. In Part I of this chapter, we consider traditional trademark infringement. In Part II, we focus on trademark dilution. Finally, in Part III we consider various defenses that have been raised in actions for trademark infringement and dilution online.

I. TRADITIONAL TRADEMARK INFRINGEMENT: THE REQUIREMENT OF CONSUMER CONFUSION

A. INFRINGEMENT RESULTING FROM TRADITIONAL CONFUSION

As Oliver Wendell Holmes noted in 1890, the law of trademarks was created "to prevent one man from palming off his goods as another's, from getting another's business or injuring his reputation by unfair means and, perhaps, from defrauding the public." *Chadwick v. Covell*, 23 N.E. 1068, 1069 (Mass.1890). The law of trademarks may therefore be viewed as a branch of unfair competition law. As the First Circuit has observed, the law of unfair competition comprises a "broad class of business torts of which trademark infringement is one species." *Keebler Co. v. Rovira Biscuit Corp.*, 624 F.2d 366 (1st Cir.1980).

In a typical trademark infringement lawsuit, the senior user of a mark sues a junior user of the same or similar mark, alleging that consumers are likely to confuse the senior user's goods and services with those of the junior user. *See, e.g.,* Lanham Act § 32(1), 15 U.S.C. § 1114(1). "When comparing marks to determine the likelihood of consumer confusion, 'the correct test is whether a consumer who is somewhat familiar with the plaintiff's mark would likely be confused when presented with defendant's mark alone.'" *Clinique Laboratories, Inc. v. Dep Corp.,* 945 F.Supp. 547, 552 (S.D.N.Y.1996). Usually, the alleged consumer confusion concerns the source or origin of the goods or services in question. Equally actionable, however, is consumer confusion about whether there is an affiliation, relation of sponsorship or other connection between the senior and junior users of the mark. *See, e.g.,* Lanham Act § 43(a), 15 U.S.C. § 1125(a).

The following cases highlight the fact that infringing uses of a trademark are possible online as well as off.

Playboy Enterprises, Inc. v. Universal Tel–A–Talk, Inc.

1998 WL 767440 (E.D.Pa.1998).

■ McGLYNN, DISTRICT JUDGE.

Plaintiff, Playboy Enterprises, Inc. ("PEI") filed this action on October 2, 1996, alleging trademark infringement and related causes of action under the Lanham Act, 15 U.S.C. §§ 1114–1125 and Pennsylvania's anti-dilution law, 54 Pa.C.S.A. § 1124, *et seq.* at defendant's web site "adult-sex.com/playboy." The Court entered a temporary restraining order and later a consent decree enjoining the defendants use of PEI's trademarks. Thereafter, the complaint was amended to include a counterfeiting claim under 15 U.S.C. § 1116(d). * * *

FINDINGS OF FACT

1. Plaintiff Playboy Enterprises, Inc. (PEI), is a Delaware corporation having offices at 730 Fifth Avenue, New York, New York and a principal place of business in Chicago, Illinois.

2. Defendant Universal Tel–A–Talk, Inc. is a Pennsylvania corporation having a principal place of business in Philadelphia, Pennsylvania. Defendant Stanley Huberman is the president and sole shareholder.

3. Defendant Adult Discount Toys is a business entity having a principal place of business in Philadelphia, Pennsylvania and is owned by defendant Stanley Huberman.

* * *

5. Since 1953, PEI has published *Playboy* magazine. *Playboy* magazine is read by approximately 10 million readers each month and is published worldwide in 16 international editions.

6. *Playboy* magazine is known for its display of erotic and provocative pictorials of PEI models and adult entertainment material.

7. PEI and its licensees have sold a wide variety of merchandise; such as, wearing apparel, cosmetics, sunglasses, watches and other personal accessories under the trademark PLAYBOY, in interstate commerce, including the Commonwealth of Pennsylvania.

8. PEI is the owner of a number of U.S. trademark registrations for the mark PLAYBOY * * *.

9. Over the years, PEI has sold merchandise bearing the PLAYBOY trademark. Through its licenses, products bearing the PLAYBOY trademark are sold throughout the United States and in more than 50 countries around the world. PEI and its licensees have and continue to spend considerable time and money promoting the PLAYBOY trademark. As a result of PEI's longstanding use of the PLAYBOY trademark, the PLAYBOY trademark has become well known and has developed a secondary meaning, such that the public has come to associate it with PEI.

10. In addition to the PLAYBOY trademark, PEI also utilizes a Rabbit Head Design trademark (hereafter the "RABBIT HEAD DESIGN") in connection with *Playboy* magazine and a wide variety of goods sold by PEI and/or its licensees. Since 1954, PEI has used the RABBIT HEAD DESIGN mark in connection with *Playboy* magazine. The RABBIT HEAD DESIGN mark traditionally appears in the masthead of *Playboy* magazine. PEI has also used the RABBIT HEAD DESIGN in connection with a wide variety of merchandise and services.

11. PEI also owns a number of U.S. trademark registrations for the RABBIT HEAD DESIGN mark * * *.

12. In addition to the PLAYBOY trademarks and RABBIT HEAD DESIGN, the mark "BUNNY" has been registered by PEI with the United States Patent and Trademark Office.

* * *

14. Over the years, PEI has sold merchandise bearing the RABBIT HEAD DESIGN mark. Through its licensees, products bearing the RABBIT HEAD DESIGN mark are sold throughout the United States and in more than 50 countries around the world. Products bearing the RABBIT HEAD DESIGN mark are available worldwide by mail order catalog and through PLAYBOY specialty boutiques, department stores, art galleries and museum shops. PEI and its licensees have spent considerable time and money promoting products bearing the RABBIT HEAD DESIGN mark nationwide and throughout the world. As a result of PEI's longstanding use of the RABBIT HEAD DESIGN mark, the RABBIT HEAD DESIGN mark has become famous and has developed significant goodwill and secondary meaning, such that the public has come to associate it exclusively with PEI.

15. As a result of PEI's use and promotion of the RABBIT HEAD DESIGN mark, the mark BUNNY has also become associated with PEI in connection with adult entertainment services. Indeed, the RABBIT HEAD DESIGN trademark is commonly referred to by the public as the "Playboy Bunny."

16. The Internet is an international computer "super-network" of over 15,000 computer networks which is used by 30 million or more individuals, corporations, organization and educational institutions worldwide. Users of the Internet can access each others computers, can communicate directly with each other (by means of electronic mail or "e-mail"), and can access various types of data and information. Each Internet user has an address, consisting of one or more address components, which address is otherwise commonly referred to within the Internet as a "domain" or "domain name."

17. Domain names serve as an address for sending and receiving e-mail and for posting information or providing other services. On the Internet, a domain name serves as the primary identifier of the source of information, products or services. It is common practice for companies to form Internet domain names by combining their trade name or one of their famous trademarks as a prefix and their business category as a suffix. The suffix ".com" (usually pronounced "dot com") identifies a service provider as commercial in nature.

18. The domain name is one component of the "Uniform Resource Locator" ("URL"). The URL may also include root directories and subdirectories which serve as a guide to the contents of a website.

19. In August, 1994, PEI launched www.playboy.com on the Internet on the World Wide Web. The website currently receives approximately six million "hits" a day. The trademark www.playboy.com offers access to some of PEI's copyrighted images and other contents from *Playboy* magazine and other PEI publications. www.playboy.com has also been registered with the U.S. Patent and Trademark Office.

20. PEI also operates cyber.playboy.com, a subscription and pay per visit website (the "PLAYBOY CYBER CLUB") which allows members access to individual PLAYMATE home pages, video clips from PLAYMATE home pages, video clips from PLAYBOY home video and PLAYBOY TV and contents of *Playboy* magazine.

21. Both www.playboy.com and cyber.playboy.com are used by PEI to promote subscriptions to its monthly *Playboy* magazine, to display erotic pictorials of PEI models, and to advertise and sell PEI's merchandise and other services under PEI's trademarks. PEI's websites prominently feature the PEI trademarks PLAYBOY and RABBIT HEAD DESIGN, as well as photographs, articles of interest, PEI merchandise, videos and subscription information for *Playboy* magazine. PEI's Website contains electronic versions of *Playboy* magazine in that it displays the contents of *Playboy* magazine on-line. An Internet user is able to view the contents of *Playboy* magazine by visiting www.playboy.com or the PLAYBOY CYBER CLUB.

22. Defendant Universal Tel–A–Talk, Inc. created and is maintaining several Internet World Wide Web sites which may be accessed throughout the United States, including the Commonwealth of Pennsylvania.

23. On or about October 2, 1996, PEI learned that Universal–Tel–A–Talk, Inc. was using PEI's registered trademarks PLAYBOY and BUNNY in conjunction with their website to advertise on-line a collection of photographs, which both plaintiff and defendant describe as "hard core." However, neither side has defined that term, at least on this record, except as a modifier of the term sexually explicit photographs.

24. Defendant Universal Tel–A–Talk, Inc.'s website advertises and offers a subscription service called "Playboy's Private Collection" (located at www.adult-sex.com) (hereafter "Defendant's website") for a charge of $3.95 per month, which features hard core photographs. The PLAYBOY trademark is prominently featured in defendants' website. Defendants also used the term "Bunny" on the navigational bar of the introductory page of the defendants' website. The navigational bar serves as a table of contents and appears on the bottom of the introductory screens and web pages. When a user clicks onto one of six "Bunny" segments of the navigational bar on the introductory page, the user becomes connected to another level of hard core on-line services offered by Defendants.

25. A subscriber to defendants' "Playboy's Private Collection" service is greeted by a "home page" which is the equivalent of the cover and table of contents page of a magazine in that it displays the name of the site and a menu of information that is available for review. A subscriber to defendants' Playboy subscription service, upon assessing the URL "adult-sex.com/playboy/members" is welcomed by defendants' home page which reads: "Welcome to PLAYBOYS PRIVATE COLLECTION." Defendants' website www.adult-sex.com is an on-line collection of "hard core" photographs sold under the PLAYBOY and BUNNY trademarks and portrayed as an extension of PEI's *Playboy* magazine. Defendants' unlawful use of the PLAYBOY trademark also appears at least twice on every printed web page. "Playboys Private Collection" appears on the upper left-hand corner and the URL "adult-sex.com/playboy/members/pictures" appears at the upper right-hand corner.

26. Subscribers can "click" onto a portion of the home page which reads: "Let me see the pictures in Playboys Private Collection" and obtain a lengthy list of hard core photographs on a variety of topics which may be viewed on screen, downloaded to disk or printed.

27. Defendants also provided an electronic mail address which utilizes the PLAYBOY trademark in the text of defendants' website. The home page of defendants' service invites subscribers to "Send E-mail to Playboy @adult-sex.com."

28. Defendant has also "linked" their adult-sex website to PEI's website at "Playboy.com." A "link" is a connection of one website to another.

29. Defendants are not now and never have been authorized by PEI to use the PLAYBOY trademark or the BUNNY trademark in connection with any business or service.

* * *

DISCUSSION

* * *

PEI has alleged infringement of the PLAYBOY trademark under § 32 of the Lanham Act (Count I), § 43(a) of the Lanham Act (Count II) and the common law of the Commonwealth of Pennsylvania (Count IV). The test for infringement is the same for each count, namely, whether the alleged infringement creates a likelihood of confusion. *See Scott Paper Co. v. Scott's Liquid Gold,* 589 F.2d 1225 (3d Cir.1978).

In order to succeed on the merits, a plaintiff must establish that: "(1) the marks are valid and legally protectible; (2) the marks are owned by the plaintiff; and (3) the defendants' use of the marks to identify goods or services is likely to create confusion concerning the origin of the goods and services." *Opticians Ass'n v. Independent Opticians,* 920 F.2d 187, 192 (3d Cir.1990).

The trademark PLAYBOY has attained incontestable status pursuant to 15 U.S.C. § 1065. PEI's ownership of incontestable U.S. Registrations for the PLAYBOY trademark constitutes prima facie evidence of PEI's ownership of the PLAYBOY trademark and the validity of the mark. *Optician's Ass'n v. Independent Opticians,* 920 F.2d at 194.

In determining whether a likelihood of confusion exists, the court may take into account

(1) the degree of similarity between the owner's mark and the alleged infringing mark; (2) the strength of owner's mark; (3) the price of the goods and other factors indicative of the care and attention expected of consumers when making a purchase; (4) the length of time the defendant has used the mark without evidence of actual confusion arising; (5) the intent of the defendant in adopting the mark; (6) the evidence of actual confusion; (7) whether the goods, though not competing, are marketed through the same channels of trade and advertised through [sic] the same media; (8) the extent to which the targets of the parties' sales efforts are the same; (9) the relationship of the goods in the minds of the public because of the similarity of function; (10) other facts suggesting that the consuming public might expect the prior owner to manufacture a product in the defendant's market. *Scott Paper Co. v. Scott's Liquid Gold, supra* at 1229.

Defendants' use of the words "Playboy" and "Bunny" in their website and in the identifying directories of defendants' URL's are identical to PEI's duly registered trademarks PLAYBOY and BUNNY. PEI's registered trademarks have previously been adjudicated as very strong. *See, Playboy Enterprise, Inc. v. Chuckleberry Pub., Inc.,* 687 F.2d 563 (2d Cir.1982). Suggestive marks are entitled to protection without proof of secondary meaning. *See e.g., Dominion Bankshares Corp. v. Devon Holding Co., Inc.,* 690 F.Supp. 338, 345 (E.D.Pa.1988); *American Diabetes Assn. v. National Diabetes Ass'n,* 533 F.Supp. 16, 214 U.S.P.Q. 231, 233 (E.D.Pa.1981).

Even if secondary meaning were required, PEI has established that the PLAYBOY trademark and the RABBIT HEAD DESIGN trademark for adult entertainment goods and services have become famous, and have acquired significant secondary meaning, such that the public has come to associate these trademarks with PEI.

Defendants' intentionally adopted PLAYBOY and BUNNY trademarks in an effort to capitalize on PEI's established reputation in the PLAYBOY and RABBIT HEAD DESIGN marks. This is evidenced by defendant's establishment of a "link" between their website and PEI's actual PLAYBOY website at "Playboy.com" and their appropriation of the words "playboy" and "Bunny" to advertise their own on-line service.

Evidence of actual confusion is not required. It has long been recognized that because evidence of confusion is notoriously difficult to obtain, it is not necessary to find a likelihood of confusion. *See, e.g., Coach Leatherware Co. v. Ann Taylor, Inc.,* 933 F.2d 162 (2d Cir.1991); *Lois Sportswear U.S.A., Inc. v. Levi Strauss & Co.,* 631 F.Supp. 735, 743 (S.D.N.Y.), *aff'd,* 799 F.2d 867 (2d Cir.1986); *Brockum Co. v. Blaylock,* 729 F.Supp. 438, 445 (E.D.Pa.1990) (lack of evidence of actual confusion is not a bar to injunctive relief). PEI and defendant market their services through the same channel of trade: the Internet. The consuming public is likely to believe the PEI is connected with defendants' hard core. * * *

* * *

"Trademark policies are designed to '(1) to protect consumers from being misled as to the enterprise, or enterprises, from which the goods or services emanate or with which they are associated; (2) to prevent an impairment of the value of the enterprise which owns the trademark; and (3) to achieve these ends in a manner consistent with the objectives of free competition.'" *Intel Corp. v. Terabyte International, Inc.,* 6 F.3d 614, 618 (9th Cir.1993) (quoting *Anti-Poly, Inc. v. General Mills Fun Group,* 611 F.2d 296, 300–01 (9th Cir.1979)).

* * *

Accordingly, the Court arrives at the following

CONCLUSIONS OF LAW

* * *

2. Defendants have infringed on Plaintiff's PLAYBOY trademark.

* * *

Albert v. Spencer

1998 WL 483462 (S.D.N.Y.1998).

■ JOHN S. MARTIN, JR., DISTRICT JUDGE.

Plaintiff and defendant both use the title AISLE SAY for theater reviews. Plaintiff whose reviews currently appear regularly in "Singles

Almanac," a magazine distributed to approximately 40,000 people in the greater New York area, has used the title AISLE SAY for nineteen years. Defendant has published theater reviews on an Internet web cite using the title AISLE SAY since 1995.

The Court is faced with the situation of two good faith users of the same trade name who operate in distinct markets. Plaintiff has never registered AISLE SAY. While the Court accepts plaintiff's testimony that she introduced herself to defendant in 1992 and mentioned AISLE SAY to him, the Court also credits the testimony of defendant that he has no recollection of this event and was not aware of the plaintiff's use of the name at the time he established his website. To avoid confusion, defendant has added a disclaimer to his web page stating that it is not connected to the plaintiff's column. Plaintiff did, however, introduce the testimony of two theater professionals who had been confused by the fact that two reviewers were using the name AISLE SAY.

DISCUSSION

As in all such cases, the parties have placed emphasis on the eight factors set forth by the Second Circuit in *Polaroid Corp. v. Polarad Elecs. Corp.*, 287 F.2d 492, 495 (2d Cir.), *cert. denied*, 368 U.S. 820 (1961). The factors are: (1) the strength of the plaintiff's mark; (2) the similarity between the two marks; (3) the proximity of the products in the marketplace; (4) the likelihood that the prior user will bridge the gap between the two products; (5) evidence of actual confusion; (6) defendant's bad faith; (7) the quality of the defendant's product; and (8) the sophistication of the relevant consumer group. *Id.*

A review of the *Polaroid* factors does not provide a clear guide to the proper outcome of this dispute:

1. Strength of the mark. A mark's strength is defined as its tendency to identify goods as emanating from a particular source. This is assessed according to two factors: first, the degree to which the mark is inherently distinctive; and second, the degree to which it is distinctive in the marketplace. The inherent distinctiveness of a mark is gauged according to whether it is generic, descriptive, suggestive or fanciful.

Plaintiff argues that AISLE SAY is a strong mark because it is fanciful, and defendant argues that it is weak because plaintiff's column is known to a relatively small number of persons. While the Court would consider the mark as more suggestive than fanciful, the mark is original enough that plaintiff would have the right to register it and enforce it against a bad faith user. Defendant is correct, however, that plaintiff's use of the mark is not widely known. Still, this factor favors plaintiff.

2. Similarity of the marks. There is no question that the marks are for practical purposes identical, and this factor favors plaintiff.

3. *The competitive proximity of the products.* If one considers the product simply as theater reviews, plaintiff and defendant's products are in direct competition. However, it is more appropriate to ask whether plaintiff's reviews compete with defendant's reviews for readers. The answer to that question is no, because plaintiff's reviews appear in print in a specific magazine while defendant publishes his reviews only at his website. Thus, this factor favors defendant.

4. *The likelihood that plaintiff will bridge the gap.* Plaintiff does not contend that she has any plans to distribute her reviews on the Internet. Thus, this factor favors defendant.

5. *Actual confusion.* While there was evidence showing some confusion involving two theater professionals, there was no evidence that either the magazine readers of plaintiff's reviews or the Internet visitors to the defendant's website were confused. Thus, this factor appears neutral at best.

6. *The defendant's good faith.* The Court is persuaded that defendant acted in complete good faith in adopting the name AISLE SAY for his website, and this factor strongly favors defendant.

7. *The quality of the defendant's product.* While the evidence indicates that the defendant's reviews are highly regarded, this is a subjective matter and one can understand why someone like plaintiff, who takes great pride in her work, would be concerned that someone else's reviews would be attributed to her. Thus, this factor favors plaintiff.

8. *The sophistication of the buyers.* To the extent that this factor focuses on the likelihood that the purchaser will be so familiar with the relevant market that he or she will not be confused as to the source of the review, it favors plaintiff, since a sophisticated playgoer may still be unsophisticated concerning the difference between reviews on the Internet and reviews in a magazine.

While four of the eight factors favor plaintiff and only three favor defendant, most of the factors favoring plaintiff tilt only slightly in her favor. Moreover, the eight factor test is not exclusive, and is not to be applied mechanically by totting up the number of factors weighing in each party's favor. * * *

"The essence of ... unfair competition claims, under both federal and New York law 'is that the use of the infringing term creates the likelihood of consumer confusion ... The essential inquiry is whether an appreciable number of ordinary prudent prospective [customers] are likely to be confused or misled.'" *Marshak v. Green*, 505 F. Supp. 1054, 1058 (S.D.N.Y. 1981). * * *

Here, a balancing of the relevant factors suggests that defendant should not be prohibited from using a name that he adopted in good faith, because there is no danger that an appreciable number of consumers will be misled as to the source of the review they are reading.

Given the fact that there is no real competition between plaintiff's and defendant's reviews and that defendant has added a disclaimer to his website, it is unlikely that plaintiff will suffer any real economic disadvantage or damage to her reputation if defendant is permitted to continue to use AISLE SAY to identify his website. To enjoin defendant from using the name AISLE SAY would cause him far greater harm.

CONCLUSION

For the foregoing reasons, the complaint is dismissed.

Niton Corp. v. Radiation Monitoring Devices, Inc.

27 F.Supp.2d 102 (D.Mass.1998).

■ ROBERT E. KEETON, DISTRICT JUDGE.

Two innovative enterprises of modest size are coexisting almost side-by-side without friction. They are not in direct competition. Each, however, has possibilities for success and expansion. The success of both will, some months or years away, bring them to competing with each other and with larger entities whose operations may, by then, be international or global in scope.

Enter upon this tranquil scene the Internet and its inducements to each of the two modest enterprises to obtain web sites. They do so, and soon begin to worry about each other. As they learn more, one comes into a United States district court with a complaint and prayer for preliminary injunction against the other. They accept a suggestion from the judge that the request for injunctive relief be tried along with all other claims and defenses on an expedited discovery and trial schedule.

One soon learns, by chance, that the other's web sites and means of attracting Internet users to them are deceptive and immediately harmful. Forthwith, the matter is back before the district court with a renewed request for immediate intervention.

This is a classic illustration of a new kind of litigation for which nothing in past experience comes even close to preparing trial judges and the advocates appearing before them. But the case must be decided, and quickly, unless mediation within or outside court sponsorship produces an even quicker solution.

In the matter before me, I conclude that court intervention is appropriate but not in a classic form of preliminary injunction. For the reasons summarized here, my order is more provisional and tentative in nature and is entitled Preliminary Injunction Subject to Modification.

* * *

Plaintiff Niton Corporation is in the business of manufacturing and selling x-ray fluorescence ("XRF") instruments and software designed to detect the presence or absence of lead in paint. Defendant Radiation Monitoring Devices ("RMD") is in the business of manufacturing XRF instruments that detect lead in paint. One of these products is called the LPA–1. Niton's product employs the "L–Shell" and "K-shell" methods while RMD's product employs only the "K–Shell" method. By the time this civil action is commenced, Niton and RMD are aiming to sell to the same potential entities, in many instances, one or more of their respective products. Niton contends, and RMD denies, that the two companies are the only companies in the American market for XRF instruments and software.

In its complaint, Niton alleges that RMD uses false and misleading statements in RMD's advertising, marketing and promotion of its own product in Massachusetts and interstate commerce. Niton asserts that these statements "misrepresent the true nature, characteristics, capabilities, and qualities of RMD's product" and, as a result, reflect on Niton's products. Niton further contends that these misleading statements are contained on RMD's World Wide Web page on the Internet. * * *

* * *

Furthermore, Niton maintains that RMD has made false, misleading, and deceptive statements to third parties about Niton's products. * * *

* * *

In response, RMD has filed in this civil action a counterclaim against Niton for using false and misleading statements in its advertising, marketing and promotion of Niton products.

As stated above, the two companies were involved in this litigation when Niton learned, by chance, that RMD's web sites and the means of attracting Internet users to the sites were deceptive and misleading. In an affidavit, a Niton employee in charge of maintaining Niton's Internet web site, Robert Bowley, asserts that, on November 5, 1998, he discovered that the "META" descriptions of RMD's web sites included references to Niton's home page that were unusual. The term "META description" refers to words that identify an Internet site, and the term "META" keywords refers to keywords that are listed by the web page creator when creating the web site. An Internet user then uses a web search engine that searches the "META" keywords and identifies a match or a "hit".

Upon further inspection of the "META" descriptions, Bowley found that several of the web addresses appeared to be for Niton's home page, but were actually for pages of RMD's web sites. Although no links to Niton were visible in the surface text of the RMD web sites, Bowley was able to use Netscape's "View Source" command to look at the source code for the RMD web sites.

Using this feature, Bowley discovered that the "META" descriptions of RMD's web sites were identical to those he had used when creating the Niton web site. Bowley discovered that several keywords, such as "radon", that were relevant to products Niton sold, but not to products sold or marketed by RMD, nevertheless appeared in RMD's web site source code.

After this discovery, Bowley asserts that he performed an Internet web search using the phrase "home page of Niton Corporation" and turned up several "hits". Only three of the "hits" were for pages on Niton's web site. The other five matches referred him to pages on RMD's web sites. According to Bowley, the "META" description of the five RMD pages is "The Home Page of Niton Corporation, makers of the finest lead, radon, and multi-element detectors."

In his affidavit, Bowley states that he repeated the search for "home page of Niton Corporation" using several other web search engines and came up with the same results. Finally, Bowley asserts that he performed a search for "Niton Corporation" and "home page" and came up with hits that described themselves as being the "Home Page of Niton Corporation" but gave the web address of RMD's web site.

I find a likelihood of success of plaintiff in establishing before the finder of fact, at trial, the credibility of Bowley's findings recited here.

For the foregoing reasons, the Clerk is directed to enter forthwith on a separate document a Preliminary Injunction Subject to Modification in the form attached to this Opinion.

Preliminary Injunction Subject to Modification

* * *

On the basis of all the oral and filed submissions, the court finds: (a) that plaintiff has shown a likelihood of success on the merits of its contention that RMD's Internet web sites and means of attracting users of the Internet to examine these web sites have been used by RMD in a way likely to lead users to believe that the employees of RMD are "makers of the finest radon detectors," that RMD is also known as Niton Corporation, that RMD is affiliated with Niton Corporation, that RMD makes for Niton products marketed by Niton, and that RMD web sites are Niton web sites * * *. For the reasons expressed here and orally at the hearings of November 13 and 18, 1998, it is ORDERED:

Defendant Radiation Monitoring Devices, Inc. ("RMD"), its officers, directors, agents, servants, employees, and those persons in active concert or participation with them who receive notice in fact of this Order are hereby enjoined from using RMD's Internet web sites and means of attracting users of the Internet to examine those web sites in a way that is likely to lead users to believe:

(1) that the employees of RMD are "makers of the finest radon detectors," or

(2) that RMD is also known as Niton Corporation, or

(3) that RMD is affiliated with Niton Corporation, or

(4) that RMD makes for Niton any product marketed by Niton, or

(5) that RMD web sites are Niton web sites.

* * *

This Order is subject to modification by this court upon motion of an interested party for good cause shown. RMD may, at any time, apply to this court for a modification of this Order upon a showing of good cause for determining that an alternative form of relief is more appropriate than an injunction. Such a showing of good cause may be made by RMD's showing that it has developed or proposes to develop a modification of its web sites and means of attracting users of the Internet to examine those web sites

(a) that, if practiced, would not be a violation of this order, or

(b) that would be a violation of the terms of this Order, absent modification, but for special reasons shown, an alternative form of remedy allowing RMD to proceed on specified conditions, including compensation or security to Niton against harm, is more appropriate than an injunction.

NOTE: METATAGGING AND SEARCH ENGINES

The most direct way to view a web site in your web browser is to type that site's web address (also known as its Uniform Resource Locator, or "URL") into the text box on the address bar of a web browser. The principal reason why so many businesses desire to use their trademark as a domain name is because it provides a highly intuitive, direct link to their company website. But not all websites have such obvious addresses, and we often find ourselves at a loss as we try to guess the URL that points to the website we are trying to locate.

After a few unsuccessful guesses, most people enlist the aid of Internet search engines and directories. A *search engine* or *directory* is a searchable index of resources available on the Internet. A large majority of these resources are web pages, but one can also locate postings to USENET newsgroups, documents on FTP servers, and even the content of some databases. The user interface for this searchable index is usually a simple text box on a web page with a button labeled "search." The user types one or more search terms into the text box and presses the button to initiate a search. These terms, called *keywords*, are then passed off to the software that searches the index for Internet resources that contain those terms. It is not unusual for hundreds and even thousands of matches to be discovered. The web addresses of these resources are then arranged in a descending order of relevance according to relevance criteria adopted by the particular search engine or directory and returned to the user as a list of hyperlinks on a series of web pages. Often these hyperlinks are accompanied by additional information about the website. Reviewing these results pages, the user can often identify the website or other resource that she is attempting to locate and with a click of the mouse proceed directly to it.

The central difference between a search engine and a directory is that a search engine is compiled by an autonomous software agent called a *spider*. A spider moves through the Internet by following links from one website to another, searching for and retrieving various Internet resources. The manner in which a particular spider conducts its search and the decision criteria by which it decides which resources to retrieve are both determined by the programming logic and algorithms composing that spider. Well-known search engines include Altavista, Excite, Google, Hot-

Bot, Lycos and Northern Light. A directory, by contrast, is an index that is compiled by human beings. Because directories are compiled by humans, they tend to have fewer, but higher quality, links. The most widely used directories as of this writing are Yahoo!, LookSmart, Open Directory Project (ODP), NBCi and Ask Jeeves. Recognizing that their strengths are complementary, search engines and directories have begun to partner with one another, forming so-called hybrid search engines. For example, Google now provides search results for Yahoo! and is powered in part by the Open Directory Project.

The relevance ranking that a web page receives from a search engine is determined by an algorithm built into that search engine's software. As a result, if a website operator understands how a search engine's relevancy algorithm works, the operator can design and optimize the website to receive a higher ranking on the results pages that search engine returns to its users. Many search engines employ relevancy algorithms that take account of the presence of search terms (1) in certain "tagged" locations within the HTML code that comprises the web page, (2) in the text of the web page, and (3) in the URL of the web page.

Web site designers can try to increase their relevancy score under the first criterion by including as many likely keywords as possible within the HTML tags—even when the keywords have little or nothing to do with the content of the web page. This strategy, often referred to as "metatagging," has become so ubiquitous that many search engines now discount the presence of keywords within these tags.

The IBM corporate website provides a good example of how metatags are used.

```
<meta name=''DESCRIPTION'' content=''The IBM corpo-
rate home page, entry point to information about IBM
products and services''/>
<meta name='''KEYWORDS'' content=''ibm, interna-
tional business machines, internet, e-business, ebu-
siness, personal computer, personal system, e-com-
merce, ecommerce, pc, workstation, mainframe, unix,
technical support, homepage, home page''/>
```

www.ibm.com (page source code) (viewed July 26, 2002).

To enhance the relevance ranking of a web page under the second criterion, some website operators repeat likely keywords over and over again on a web page. To prevent this repetitive text from being seen by visitors to this website, site operators set the color of this text to the color of the background. Thus, while the repeated keywords remain invisible to humans viewing the web page through a browser, they are nonetheless visible to a search engine's spider. Keywords repeated in this fashion are sometimes referred to as buried code or invisible or hidden text.

The third strategy for enhancing the relevance ranking of a website—obtaining a domain name that contains a likely keyword, or using the keyword as part of the directory structure of the website—can be seen in

Playboy v. Universal Tel–A–Talk, supra ("www.adult-sex.com/playboy"). (Domain names are considered in Chapter 3, *infra*).

Recognizing the value that website operators place on a high relevance ranking, some search engines and directories have attempted to sell higher rankings directly. For a price, some search engines will guarantee a premium relevance ranking for searches containing certain keywords. Others allow companies to bid on keywords, giving the highest relevance ranking to the highest bidder. *See, e.g.*, www.overture.com. In a related practice, some search engines and directories sell premium placements for banner ads on the results pages of searches involving certain keywords. For example, let us say a search engine user types in the keyword "washing machine." If Maytag has purchased a premium placement for its banner ad on results pages generated from a search using the keyword "washing machine," then the results pages returned to the user would prominently display Maytag's banner ad.

Metatagging raises several trademark issues, including: Is it trademark infringement or dilution to embed another's trademark in HTML tags on your web page? What about repeating another's trademark as buried code or invisible text on your web page? Is it unlawful for a search engine or directory to sell premium placements for banner ads keyed to another's trademark? How about the sale of an enhanced relevancy ranking for searches keyed to another's trademark?

B. INFRINGEMENT RESULTING FROM INITIAL INTEREST CONFUSION

Brookfield Communications, Inc. v. West Coast Entertainment Corp.

174 F.3d 1036 (9th Cir.1999).

■ O'SCANNLAIN, CIRCUIT JUDGE:

We must venture into cyberspace to determine whether federal trademark and unfair competition laws prohibit a video rental store chain from using an entertainment-industry information provider's trademark in the domain name of its web site and in its web site's metatags.

I

Brookfield Communications, Inc. ("Brookfield") appeals the district court's denial of its motion for a preliminary injunction prohibiting West Coast Entertainment Corporation ("West Coast") from using in commerce terms confusingly similar to Brookfield's trademark, "MovieBuff." Brookfield gathers and sells information about the entertainment industry. Founded in 1987 for the purpose of creating and marketing software and services for professionals in the entertainment industry, Brookfield initially offered software applications featuring information such as recent film submissions, industry credits, professional contacts, and future projects.

These offerings targeted major Hollywood film studios, independent production companies, agents, actors, directors, and producers.

Brookfield expanded into the broader consumer market with computer software featuring a searchable database containing entertainment-industry related information marketed under the "MovieBuff" mark around December 1993. Brookfield's "MovieBuff" software now targets smaller companies and individual consumers who are not interested in purchasing Brookfield's professional level alternative, The Studio System, and includes comprehensive, searchable, entertainment-industry databases and related software applications containing information such as movie credits, box office receipts, films in development, film release schedules, entertainment news, and listings of executives, agents, actors, and directors. This "MovieBuff" software comes in three versions—(1) the MovieBuff Pro Bundle, (2) the MovieBuff Pro, and (3) MovieBuff—and is sold through various retail stores, such as Borders, Virgin Megastores, Nobody Beats the Wiz, The Writer's Computer Store, Book City, and Samuel French Bookstores.

Sometime in 1996, Brookfield attempted to register the World Wide Web ("the Web") domain name "moviebuff.com" with Network Solutions, Inc. ("Network Solutions"), but was informed that the requested domain name had already been registered by West Coast. Brookfield subsequently registered "brookfieldcomm.com" in May 1996 and "moviebuffonline.com" in September 1996. Sometime in 1996 or 1997, Brookfield began using its web sites to sell its "MovieBuff" computer software and to offer an Internet-based searchable database marketed under the "MovieBuff" mark. Brookfield sells its "MovieBuff" computer software through its "brookfieldcomm.com" and "moviebuffonline.com" web sites and offers subscribers online access to the MovieBuff database itself at its "inhollywood.com" web site.

On August 19, 1997, Brookfield applied to the Patent and Trademark Office (PTO) for federal registration of "MovieBuff" as a mark to designate both goods and services. Its trademark application describes its product as "computer software providing data and information in the field of the motion picture and television industries." Its service mark application describes its service as "providing multiple-user access to an on-line network database offering data and information in the field of the motion picture and television industries." Both federal trademark registrations issued on September 29, 1998. Brookfield had previously obtained a California state trademark registration for the mark "MovieBuff" covering "computer software" in 1994.

In October 1998, Brookfield learned that West Coast—one of the nation's largest video rental store chains with over 500 stores—intended to launch a web site at "moviebuff.com" containing, *inter alia,* a searchable entertainment database similar to "MovieBuff." West Coast had registered "moviebuff.com" with Network Solutions on February 6, 1996 and claims that it chose the domain name because the term "Movie Buff" is part of its service mark, "The Movie Buff's Movie Store," on which a federal registration issued in 1991 covering "retail store services featuring video cassettes and video game cartridges" and "rental of video cassettes and video game cartridges." West Coast notes further that, since at least 1988, it has also used various phrases including the term "Movie Buff" to promote goods and services available at its video stores in Massachusetts, including "The Movie Buff's Gift Guide"; "The Movie Buff's Gift Store"; "Calling All Movie Buffs!"; "Good News Movie Buffs!"; "Movie Buffs, Show Your Stuff!"; "the Perfect Stocking Stuffer for the Movie Buff!"; "A Movie Buff's Top Ten"; "The Movie Buff Discovery Program"; "Movie Buff Picks"; "Movie Buff Series"; "Movie Buff Selection Program"; and "Movie Buff Film Series."

On November 10, Brookfield delivered to West Coast a cease-and-desist letter alleging that West Coast's planned use of the "moviebuff.com" would violate Brookfield's trademark rights; as a "courtesy" Brookfield attached a copy of a complaint that it threatened to file if West Coast did not desist.

The next day, West Coast issued a press release announcing the imminent launch of its web site full of "movie reviews, Hollywood news and gossip, provocative commentary, and coverage of the independent film scene and films in production." The press release declared that the site would feature "an extensive database, which aids consumers in making educated decisions about the rental and purchase of" movies and would also allow customers to purchase movies, accessories, and other entertainment-related merchandise on the web site.

Brookfield fired back immediately with a visit to the United States District Court for the Central District of California, and this lawsuit was born. In its first amended complaint filed on November 18, 1998, Brookfield alleged principally that West Coast's proposed offering of online services at "moviebuff.com" would constitute trademark infringement and unfair competition in violation of §§ 32 and 43(a) of the Lanham Act, 15 U.S.C. §§ 1114, 1125(a). Soon thereafter, Brookfield applied *ex parte* for a temporary restraining order ("TRO") enjoining West Coast "[f]rom using . . . in any manner . . . the mark MOVIEBUFF, or any other term or terms likely to cause confusion therewith, including *moviebuff.com,* as West Coast's domain name, . . . as the name of West Coast's website service, in buried code or metatags on their home page or web pages, or in connection with the retrieval of data or information on other goods or services."

* * *

V

* * *

B

[The court concluded that West Coast's use of the domain name *moviebuff.com* infringes the trademark of Brookfield.] Because Brookfield requested that we also preliminarily enjoin West Coast from using marks confusingly similar to "MovieBuff" in metatags and buried code, we must also decide whether West Coast can, consistently with the trademark and unfair competition laws, use "MovieBuff" or "moviebuff.com" in its HTML code.

At first glance, our resolution of the infringement issues in the domain name context would appear to dictate a similar conclusion of likelihood of confusion with respect to West Coast's use of "moviebuff.com" in its metatags. Indeed, all eight likelihood of confusion factors outlined [above]—with the possible exception of purchaser care, which we discuss below—apply here as they did in our analysis of domain names; we are, after all, dealing with the same marks, the same products and services, the same consumers, etc. Disposing of the issue so readily, however, would ignore the fact that the likelihood of confusion in the domain name context resulted largely from the associational confusion between West Coast's domain name "moviebuff.com" and Brookfield's trademark "MovieBuff." The question in the metatags context is quite different. Here, we must determine whether West Coast can use "MovieBuff" or "moviebuff.com" in the metatags of its web site at "westcoastvideo.com" or at any other domain address *other than* "moviebuff.com" (which we have determined that West Coast may not use).

Although entering "MovieBuff" into a search engine is likely to bring up a list including "westcoastvideo.com" if West Coast has included that term in its metatags, the resulting confusion is not as great as where West Coast uses the "moviebuff.com" domain name. First, when the user inputs "MovieBuff" into an Internet search engine, the list produced by the search engine is likely to include both West Coast's and Brookfield's web sites. Thus, in scanning such list, the Web user will often be able to find the particular web site he is seeking. Moreover, even if the Web user chooses the web site belonging to West Coast, he will see that the domain name of the web site he selected is "westcoastvideo.com." Since there is no confusion resulting from the domain address, and since West Coast's initial web page prominently displays its own name, it is difficult to say that a consumer is likely to be confused about whose site he has reached or to think that Brookfield somehow sponsors West Coast's web site.

Nevertheless, West Coast's use of "moviebuff.com" in metatags will still result in what is known as initial interest confusion. Web surfers looking for Brookfield's "MovieBuff" products who are taken by a search engine to "westcoastvideo.com" will find a database similar enough to "MovieBuff" such that a sizeable number of consumers who were originally looking for Brookfield's product will simply decide to utilize West Coast's offerings instead. Although there is no source confusion in the sense that consumers know they are patronizing West Coast rather than Brookfield, there is nevertheless initial interest confusion in the sense that, by using "moviebuff.com" or "MovieBuff" to divert people looking for "MovieBuff" to its web site, West Coast improperly benefits from the goodwill that Brookfield developed in its mark. Recently in *Dr. Seuss,* we explicitly recognized that the use of another's trademark in a manner calculated "to capture initial consumer attention, even though no actual sale is finally completed as a result of the confusion, may be still an infringement." *Dr.*

Seuss, 109 F.3d at 1405 (citing *Mobil Oil Corp. v. Pegasus Petroleum Corp.,* 818 F.2d 254, 257–58 (2d Cir.1987)).

The *Dr. Seuss* court, in recognizing that the diversion of consumers' initial interest is a form of confusion against which the Lanham Act protects, relied upon *Mobil Oil.* In that case, Mobil Oil Corporation ("Mobil") asserted a federal trademark infringement claim against Pegasus Petroleum, alleging that Pegasus Petroleum's use of "Pegasus" was likely to cause confusion with Mobil's trademark, a flying horse symbol in the form of the Greek mythological Pegasus. Mobil established that "potential purchasers would be misled into an initial interest in Pegasus Petroleum" because they thought that Pegasus Petroleum was associated with Mobil. *Id.* at 260. But these potential customers would generally learn that Pegasus Petroleum was unrelated to Mobil well before any actual sale was consummated. *See id.* Nevertheless, the Second Circuit held that "[s]uch initial confusion works a sufficient trademark injury." *Id.*

Mobil Oil relied upon its earlier opinion in *Grotrian, Helfferich, Schulz, Th. Steinweg Nachf. v. Steinway & Sons,* 523 F.2d 1331, 1341–42 (2d Cir.1975). Analyzing the plaintiff's claim that the defendant, through its use of the "Grotrian–Steinweg" mark, attracted people really interested in plaintiff's "Steinway" pianos, the Second Circuit explained:

> We decline to hold, however, that actual or potential confusion at the time of purchase necessarily must be demonstrated to establish trademark infringement under the circumstances of this case.
>
> The issue here is not the possibility that a purchaser would buy a Grotrian-Steinweg thinking it was actually a Steinway or that Grotrian had some connection with Steinway and Sons. The harm to Steinway, rather, is the likelihood that a consumer, hearing the "Grotrian–Steinweg" name and thinking it had some connection with "Steinway," would consider it on that basis. The "Grotrian–Steinweg" name therefore would attract potential customers based on the reputation built up by Steinway in this country for many years.

Grotrian, 523 F.2d at 1342.

Both *Dr. Seuss* and the Second Circuit hold that initial interest confusion is actionable under the Lanham Act, which holdings are bolstered by the decisions of many other courts which have similarly recognized that the federal trademark and unfair competition laws do protect against this form of consumer confusion. *See Green Prods.,* 992 F.Supp. 1070, 1076 (N.D.Iowa 1997) ("In essence, ICBP is capitalizing on the strong similarity between Green Products' trademark and ICBP's domain name to lure customers onto its web page."). [Eight other citations omitted.] *But see Astra Pharm. Prods., Inc. v. Beckman Instruments, Inc.,* 718 F.2d 1201, 1206–08 (1st Cir.1983) (suggesting that only confusion that affects "the ultimate decision of a purchaser whether to buy a particular product" is actionable); *Teletech Customer Care Mgmt. (Cal.), Inc. v. Tele–*

Tech Co., 977 F.Supp. 1407, 1410, 1414 (C.D.Cal.1997) (finding likelihood of initial interest confusion but concluding that such "brief confusion is not cognizable under the trademark laws").

Using another's trademark in one's metatags is much like posting a sign with another's trademark in front of one's store. Suppose West Coast's competitor (let's call it "Blockbuster") puts up a billboard on a highway reading—"West Coast Video: 2 miles ahead at Exit 7"—where West Coast is really located at Exit 8 but Blockbuster is located at Exit 7. Customers looking for West Coast's store will pull off at Exit 7 and drive around looking for it. Unable to locate West Coast, but seeing the Blockbuster store right by the highway entrance, they may simply rent there. Even consumers who prefer West Coast may find it not worth the trouble to continue searching for West Coast since there is a Blockbuster right there. Customers are not confused in the narrow sense: they are fully aware that they are purchasing from Blockbuster and they have no reason to believe that Blockbuster is related to, or in any way sponsored by, West Coast. Nevertheless, the fact that there is only initial consumer confusion does not alter the fact that Blockbuster would be misappropriating West Coast's acquired goodwill. *See Blockbuster Entertainment Group, Div. of Viacom, Inc. v. Laylco, Inc.,* 869 F.Supp. 505, 513 (E.D.Mich.1994) (finding trademark infringement where the defendant, a video rental store, attracted customers' initial interest by using a sign confusingly [similar] to its competitor's even though confusion would end long before the point of sale or rental); *see also Dr. Seuss,* 109 F.3d at 1405; *Mobil Oil,* 818 F.2d at 260; *Green Prods.,* 992 F.Supp. at 1076.

The few courts to consider whether the use of another's trademark in one's metatags constitutes trademark infringement have ruled in the affirmative. For example, in a case in which Playboy Enterprises, Inc. ("Playboy") sued AsiaFocus International, Inc. ("AsiaFocus") for trademark infringement resulting from AsiaFocus's use of the federally registered trademarks "Playboy" and "Playmate" in its HTML code, a district court granted judgment in Playboy's favor, reasoning that AsiaFocus intentionally misled viewers into believing that its web site was connected with, or sponsored by, Playboy. *See Playboy Enters. v. Asiafocus Int'l, Inc.,* No. CIV.A. 97–734–A, 1998 WL 724000, at *3, *6–*7 (E.D.Va. Apr.10, 1998).

In a similar case also involving Playboy, a district court in California concluded that Playboy had established a likelihood of success on the merits of its claim that defendants' repeated use of "Playboy" within "machine readable code in Defendants' Internet Web pages, so that the PLAYBOY trademark [was] accessible to individuals or Internet search engines which attempt[ed] to access Plaintiff under Plaintiff's PLAYBOY registered trademark" constituted trademark infringement. *See Playboy Enters. v. Calvin Designer Label,* 985 F.Supp. 1220, 1221 (N.D.Cal.1997). The court accordingly enjoined the defendants from using Playboy's marks in buried code or metatags. *See id.* at 1221–22.

In a metatags case with an interesting twist, a district court in Massachusetts also enjoined the use of metatags in a manner that resulted in initial interest confusion. *See Niton,* 27 F.Supp.2d at 102–05. In that case, the defendant Radiation Monitoring Devices ("RMD") did not simply use Niton Corporation's ("Niton") trademark in its metatags. Instead, RMD's web site directly copied Niton's web site's metatags and HTML code. As a result, whenever a search performed on an Internet search engine listed Niton's web site, it also listed RMD's site. Although the opinion did not speak in terms of initial consumer confusion, the court made clear that its issuance of preliminary injunctive relief was based on the fact that RMD was purposefully diverting people looking for Niton to its web site. *See id.* at 104–05.

Consistently with *Dr. Seuss,* the Second Circuit, and the cases which have addressed trademark infringement through metatags use, we conclude that the Lanham Act bars West Coast from including in its metatags any term confusingly similar with Brookfield's mark. West Coast argues that our holding conflicts with *Holiday Inns,* in which the Sixth Circuit held that there was no trademark infringement where an alleged infringer merely took advantage of a situation in which confusion was likely to exist and did not affirmatively act to create consumer confusion. *See Holiday Inns, Inc. v. 800 Reservation, Inc.* 86 F.3d 619, 622 (6th Cir.1996) (holding that the use of "1–800–405–4329"—which is equivalent to "1–800–H[zero]LIDAY"—did not infringe Holiday Inn's trademark, "1–800–HOLIDAY"). Unlike the defendant in *Holiday Inns,* however, West Coast was not a passive figure; instead, it acted affirmatively in placing Brookfield's trademark in the metatags of its web site, thereby *creating* the initial interest confusion. Accordingly, our conclusion comports with *Holiday Inns.* * * *

* * *

VI

[The court concludes that "[p]reliminary injunctive relief is appropriate here to prevent irreparable injury to Brookfield's interests in its trademark 'MovieBuff' and to promote the public interest in protecting trademarks generally as well."]

* * *

Bihari v. Gross

119 F.Supp.2d 309 (S.D.N.Y.2000).

■ SCHEINDLIN, DISTRICT JUDGE.

Plaintiffs Marianne Bihari and Bihari Interiors, Inc. (collectively "Bihari") move to preliminarily enjoin defendants Craig Gross and Yolanda Truglio (collectively "Gross") from using the names "Bihari" or "Bihari Interiors" in the domain names or metatags of any of their websites ("the Gross websites"), claiming that such use violates the Anticybersquatting Consumer Protection Act ("ACPA"), 15 U.S.C. § 1125(d)(1), and infringes on Bihari's common-law service mark in violation of § 43(a) of the Lanham Act, 15 U.S.C. § 1125(a)(1)(A). * * * Neither party has requested an evidentiary hearing. For the reasons set forth below, Bihari's motion for preliminary injunctive relief is denied.

I. Introduction

[The court presents a brief description of the Internet, domain names and metatags.]

II. Background

A. The Failed Contract

Marianne Bihari is an interior designer who has been providing interior design services in New York City, New Jersey, Connecticut, California, Florida and Italy since 1984. Since 1989, she has been continuously doing business as Bihari Interiors or Marianne Bihari d/b/a Bihari Interiors. The Bihari Interiors name is well known, particularly in the New York City high-end residential interior design market. Bihari does not engage in paid advertising to promote her services; rather, she relies on referrals from clients and other design-industry professionals.

Craig Gross is a former client of Bihari Interiors. Yolanda Truglio is Gross's girlfriend. On February 12, 1998, Gross, on behalf of 530 East 76th Street, Inc., retained Bihari Interiors to provide interior and architectural design services for his condominium apartment on East 76th Street ("the Contract"). For various reasons not relevant to this action, the relationship between Bihari and Gross soured, and the Contract was never completed.

On June 14, 1999, Gross filed suit against Marianne Bihari and Bihari Interiors in New York State Supreme Court alleging fraud and breach of contract ("the State Suit"). On August 12, 1999, Gross submitted an amended verified complaint in the State Suit. On April 3, 2000, the state court dismissed two of the fraud claims, but granted Gross a right to replead one of those claims. Gross has since filed a second amended complaint which is currently pending in New York State Supreme Court * * *.

B. The Alleged Harassment

Approximately two months after Gross first filed the complaint in the State Suit, on August 10, 1999, Bihari, Gross and Truglio engaged in settlement negotiations, which were ultimately unsuccessful. Four days later, Gross registered the domain names "bihari.com" and "bihariinteriors.com". On August 16, 1999, Bihari received an anonymous facsimile alerting her to the website. The following day, Bihari accessed the website "www.bihariinteriors.com". Disturbed by the unauthorized use of her name and her business name in the domain name, as well as the disparaging statements on the website, Bihari contacted her attorney. On August 31, 1999, Bihari's attorney sent a letter to Gross demanding that he terminate the website. *See* Amended Complaint Rather than complying with Bihari's demand, Gross delivered to Bihari's residence pens bearing the words "www.bihariinteriors.com". In addition, Bihari alleges that subsequent to the delivery of the pens, Bihari received frequent "hang-up telephone calls'' which lasted until approximately November 22, 1999. Bihari filed a criminal complaint for aggravated harassment against Gross and Truglio on October 3, 1999, but the District Attorney's office declined to prosecute.

Bihari was the subject of a criminal complaint several months later. Before the contract relationship between Gross and Bihari deteriorated, Bihari Interiors sold Gross three sofas purchased from a vendor. Bihari Interiors made the initial payments for the sofas. By the terms of the Contract, if Bihari Interiors failed to pay in full by a certain date, the vendor would be free to resell the sofas. After the payment deadline expired, Gross paid the vendor the balance due on the sofas, thereby avoiding payment of Bihari Interiors' commission. The sofas, however, were not delivered to Gross, but to Bihari, who took possession of them pending resolution of the State Suit. Bihari alleges that Gross then filed a criminal complaint against her for theft of the sofas. On December 20, 1999, Bihari was arrested, held for approximately six hours, and ''charged with criminal possession of stolen property in the fifth degree, a misdemeanor offense.'' On January 24, 2000, Bihari was informed that the District Attorney's office had declined to prosecute her case.

C. The Websites

On March 7, 2000, Bihari served Gross with the instant Complaint and motion for injunctive relief. Gross then offered to take down the ''bihariinteriors.com'' website pending a preliminary injunction hearing. He has since relinquished the domain names ''bihari.com'' and ''bihariinteriors.com'' and is taking all necessary steps to return those domain names to Network Solutions, Inc., the provider of domain name registrations.

On March 7, 2000, the day that Bihari served Gross with the Complaint, Bihari also learned of another website created by Gross, ''designscam.com'', by using an Internet search engine and searching for the words ''Bihari Interiors''. Bihari discovered that the ''designscam.com'' website contained the same content as the ''bihariinteriors.com'' website. Then, on March 11, 2000, Gross registered a fourth website, ''manhattaninteriordesign.com'', containing the identical material as ''designscam.com''.

All of the Gross websites use ''Bihari Interiors'' as metatags embedded within the websites' HTML code. The description metatags of the Gross websites state ''This site deals with the problems experienced when hiring a new [sic] York City (Manhattan) designer. It discusses Marianne Bihari [,] fraud and deceit and interior decorating.''

D. The Website Content

Each of the Gross websites is critical of Bihari and her interior design services. An Internet user accessing any of the websites first sees a large caption reading ''The Real Story Behind Marianne Bihari & Bihari Interiors.'' Directly beneath this title are three photographic reproductions of scenic New York. Beneath the photographs is a counter indicating how many visitors the website has had. As of June 26, 2000, the counter indicated that 9,774 people have visited the website since August 15, 1999. Also appearing on the first page of the websites are various hyperlinks including "Tips on Picking a Designer," "New York City Information," "Who's Who in Interior Design," "Kabalarians Philosophy," "A Humorous Look," "Tell A Friend," "Send E–Mail," "Sign or Read the Guest Book," and "Participate in the Bihari Poll."

A long block of text appears beneath these hyperlinks and it states:

> Welcome to the first website designed to protect people from the alleged ill intentions of Marianne Bihari & Bihari Interiors. Keep in mind that this site reflects only the view points and experiences of one Manhattan couple that allegedly fell prey to Marianne Bihari & Bihari Interiors. There possibly may be others that have experienced similar alleged fraud and deceit from Marianne Bihari & Bihari Interiors. Please feel free to e-mail us if you think you were victimized by Marianne Bihari & Bihari Interiors. Our goal is to protect you from experiencing the overwhelming grief and aggravation in dealing with someone that allegedly only has intentions to defraud. If you think you need advice before entering into a contract with Marianne Bihari & Bihari Interiors—Please Click Here.

Below this text a viewer finds additional hyperlinks to "The Initial Meeting," "The Contract," "The Scam," and "The Law Suit" [sic]. Viewers who connect with these links do not immediately receive the information, but are told that if they send an e-mail, they will receive a copy of the requested information.

In addition to these comments, the Gross websites contain a "guestbook" where visitors leave messages for other visitors to the websites. Some of the guestbook entries indicate that potential clients declined to retain Bihari's services because of the Gross websites. Other messages simply comment or inquire about the Gross websites' design. Many other entries disparage Bihari and Bihari Interiors. Bihari alleges that many of the guestbook entries were written by Gross and Truglio, and do not reflect true dissatisfaction with Bihari or Bihari Interiors.

The "designscam.com" and "manhattaninteriordesign.com" websites also contain a box which presents in blinking green letters the following incomplete statement quoted from Bihari's March 3, 2000 Affidavit: "I was arrested and charged with criminal possession of stolen property in the Fifth Degree." Gross neither includes the rest of the sentence—which reveals that the arrest was for a misdemeanor offense—nor informs the reader that the District Attorney's Office declined to prosecute the case.

In June 2000, Gross launched amended versions of the "designscam.com" and "manhattaninteriordesign.com" websites. The new websites are substantially identical to the former version, with two exceptions. Gross deleted the statement, "Our goal is to protect you from experiencing the overwhelming grief and aggravation in dealing with someone that allegedly only has intentions to defraud." *Second,* he added two hyperlinks—from the words "alleged fraud" and "lawsuit"—to a copy of the First Amended Complaint in the State Suit.

E. Motive and Intent

The parties dispute defendants' motive and intent in creating the websites. Bihari alleges that Gross's motive was to harass Bihari and to pressure her into settling the State Suit. Gross counters that he created the websites because he was disturbed by Bihari's "deceitful practices," and was "dedicated to assisting consumers who are in the process of choosing a designer in New York City, as well as informing others of my experiences with Bihari." While there is no direct proof that Gross's motive is to pressure Bihari to settle the State Suit, there is proof that Gross intends to harm Bihari's business. Gross's specific intent, as memorialized in his own words on his websites, is to warn potential customers of Bihari's "alleged ill intentions" and to "protect" them from experiencing "the overwhelming grief and aggravation" he has experienced in dealing with Bihari. Undeniably, Gross's intent is to cause Bihari commercial harm. * * *

IV. Discussion

* * *

A claim of trademark infringement under § 43(a) of the Lanham Act requires the plaintiff to show (1) that she has a valid mark that is entitled to protection under the Lanham Act, and (2) that use of that mark by another "is likely to cause confusion ... as to the affiliation, connection, or association of such person with another person, or as to the origin, sponsorship, or approval of [the defendant's] goods, services, or commercial activities by another person." 15 U.S.C. § 1125(a)(1)(A); *Estee Lauder Inc. v. The Gap, Inc.,* 108 F.3d 1503, 1508–09 (2d Cir.1997). As discussed more fully below, Bihari has failed to demonstrate a likelihood of success on the merits of this claim because Gross's use of the "Bihari Interiors" mark in the metatags is not likely to cause confusion and is protected as a fair use.

* * *

d. Initial Interest Confusion

Even if actual confusion is unlikely, Plaintiffs argue that there is a likelihood of "initial interest confusion." Accepting, arguendo, the concept of initial interest confusion in an Internet case,[14] Bihari has failed to prove a likelihood of initial interest confusion.

14. Although the Second Circuit has not explicitly applied this doctrine in an Internet case, the Ninth Circuit has. *See Brookfield Communications,* 174 F.3d at 1062–63 (relying on *Mobil Oil Corp. v. Pegasus Petroleum Corp.,* 818 F.2d 254, 257–58 (2d Cir. 1987)). In addition, at least two courts in the Second Circuit have analyzed a trademark case involving metatags by applying the initial interest confusion doctrine. *See New York State Society of Certified Public Accountants,* 79 F.Supp.2d at 341; *OBH, Inc. v. Spotlight Magazine, Inc.,* 86 F.Supp.2d 176, 190 (W.D.N.Y.2000); *but see BigStar Entertainment, Inc. v. Next Big Star, Inc.,* 105 F.Supp.2d 185, 207–210 (S.D.N.Y.2000) (refusing to apply initial interest confusion doctrine).

An infringement action may be based on a claim that the alleged infringement creates initial consumer interest, even if no actual sale is completed as a result of the confusion. In the cyberspace context, the concern is that potential customers of one website will be diverted and distracted to a competing website. The harm is that the potential customer believes that the competing website is associated with the website the customer was originally searching for and will not resume searching for the original website.

The Ninth Circuit recently provided a useful metaphor for explaining the harm of initial interest confusion in cyberspace:

> Using another's trademark in one's metatags is much like posting a sign with another's trademark in front of one's store. Suppose West Coast's, [the defendant], competitor (let's call it "Blockbuster") puts up a billboard on a highway reading—"West Coast Video: 2 miles ahead at Exit 7"—where West Coast is really located at Exit 8 but Blockbuster is located at Exit 7. Customers looking for West Coast's store will pull off at Exit 7 and drive around looking for it. Unable to locate West Coast, but seeing the Blockbuster store right by the highway entrance, they may simply rent there. Even consumers who prefer West Coast may find it not worth the trouble to continue searching for West Coast since there is a Blockbuster right there.

Brookfield Communications, 174 F.3d at 1064.[15]

The highway analogy pinpoints what is missing in this case. Inserting "Bihari Interiors" in the metatags is not akin to a misleading "billboard," which diverts drivers to a competing store and "misappropriat[es] [plaintiff's] acquired goodwill." *Id.* ("[T]he fact that there is only initial consumer confusion does not alter the fact that [the defendant] would be misappropriating [the plaintiff's] good will."). Far from diverting "people looking for information on Bihari Interiors," as plaintiffs allege, the Gross websites provide users with information about Bihari Interiors. Furthermore, the Gross websites cannot divert Internet users away from Bihari's website because Bihari does not have a competing website. *See BigStar Entertainment,* 105 F.Supp.2d at 209–10 (stating that initial interest confusion does not arise where parties are not in close competitive proximity).

Furthermore, users are unlikely to experience initial interest confusion when searching the Internet for information about Bihari Interiors. In support of their motion, Plaintiffs' counsel provided a typical search result when "Bihari Interiors" is entered into the search field. The search revealed twelve websites, eight of which appear to be the Gross websites. Of those eight, five bear the heading "Manhattan Interior Design Scam—

15. Use of the highway billboard metaphor is not the best analogy to a metatag on the Internet. The harm caused by a misleading billboard on the highway is difficult to correct. In contrast, on the information superhighway, resuming one's search for the correct website is relatively simple. With one click of the mouse and a few seconds delay, a viewer can return to the search engine's results and resume searching for the original website.

Bihari Interiors." Each website with that heading contains the following description underneath the title: "This site deals with the problems experienced when hiring a New York City (Manhattan) designer. It discusses Marianne Bihari[,] fraud and deceit and...." An Internet user who reads this text, and then sees the domain name of "designscam.com" or "manhattaninteriordesign.com", is unlikely to believe that these websites belong to Bihari Interiors or Bihari. * * *

The few decisions holding that use of another entity's trademark in metatags constitutes trademark infringement involved very different circumstances. *Niton Corp. v. Radiation Monitoring Devices, Inc.,* 27 F.Supp.2d 102 (D.Mass.1998), for example, provides a good example of the use of metatags to divert a competitor's customers. *First,* Radiation Monitoring Devices ("RMD") and Niton Corporation ("Niton") were direct competitors. *Second,* RMD did not simply use Niton's trademark in its metatag. Rather, RMD directly copied Niton's metatags and HTML code. As a result, an Internet search using the phrase "home page of Niton Corporation" revealed three matches for Niton's website and five for RMD's website. *See id.* at 104. RMD obviously was taking advantage of Niton's good will to divert customers to the RMD website.

Similarly, in *Playboy Enters., Inc. v. Asiafocus Int'l, Inc.,* No. Civ. A. 97–734–A, 1998 WL 724000, at *3, **6–7 (E.D.Va. Apr.10, 1998), the court enjoined use of the marks "Playboy" and "Playmate" in the domain name and metatags of defendant's website. The defendant provided adult nude photos on web pages located at "asian-playmates.com" and "playmates-asian.com". The "Playboy" and "Playmate" trademarks were embedded in the metatags such that a search for Playboy Enterprises Inc.'s ("Playboy") website would produce a list that included "asian-playmates.com". *See also Playboy Enters., Inc. v. Calvin Designer Label,* 985 F.Supp. 1220, 1221 (N.D.Cal.1997) (preliminarily enjoining defendant's website, "www.playboyxxx.com" and repeated use of the "Playboy" trademark in defendant's metatags). Defendants in these cases were clearly attempting to divert potential customers from Playboy's website to their own.

Even *Brookfield Communications,* where initial interest confusion was first applied to metatags, presents convincing proof of diversion. Brookfield sought to protect its trademark in its "MovieBuff" software, which provides entertainment-industry information. Brookfield had created a website offering an Internet-based searchable database under the "Moviebuff" mark. The defendant, West Coast, a video rental store chain, registered a site at "moviebuff.com" which also contained a searchable entertainment database. The court held that defendant's use of the "moviebuff.com" domain name constituted trademark infringement. The court also enjoined West Coast from using any term confusingly similar to "moviebuff" in the metatags based on the initial interest confusion caused by the use of Brookfield's mark, which would redound to West Coast's financial benefit.

In each of these cases, the defendant was using the plaintiff's mark to trick Internet users into visiting defendant's website, believing either that they were visiting plaintiff's website or that the defendant's website was sponsored by the plaintiff. [In contrast to those cases,] Gross's use of the "Bihari Interiors" mark in the metatags is not a bad-faith attempt to trick users into visiting his websites, but rather a means of cataloging those sites.

* * *

V. Conclusion

For the foregoing reasons, Bihari's motion for a preliminary injunction is denied in its entirety. * * *

NOTES & QUESTIONS

1. *Initial interest confusion and metatags.* In *Bihari v. Gross*, the court rejects plaintiffs' argument that the defendant's websites cause initial interest confusion and are, therefore, infringing. One reason for the court's conclusion is that the plaintiff had no website. Would the result have changed if the plaintiff did have a website? Five of the eight websites operated by the defendant appear to have included a "description" metatag which contained the statement that "This site deals with the problems experienced when hiring a New York City (Manhattan) Designer. It discusses Marianne Bihari fraud and deceit * * *." Assuming that this description was presented on the results page containing links to defendant's websites, would this strengthen or weaken plaintiffs' argument for finding initial interest confusion?

2. *More initial interest confusion.* The only circuit court to have embraced the initial interest confusion doctrine in the Internet context is the Ninth Circuit. For another case that applies this doctrine, see *Green Products Co. v. Independence Corn By-Products Co.*, 992 F.Supp. 1070 (N.D.Iowa 1997), excerpted in Chapter 3, *infra*.

II. TRADEMARK DILUTION

Trademark infringement protects a trademark owner from another using his or her mark in connection with competing goods and services. It does not, however, prohibit another from using that mark in connection with noncompeting goods and services. So long as the trademark is used in connection with goods and services that do not compete with the goods and services of the trademark owner, the trademark has not been infringed. A cause of action for *trademark dilution* may, however, be available to certain trademark owners to prevent use by others even absent infringement.

Trademark dilution was federalized by the Federal Trademark Dilution Act of 1995, 15 U.S.C. § 1125(c). (Previously, dilution had been available in some states under common law or by statute.) In its federal incarnation, dilution is defined as "the lessening of the capacity of a famous mark to identify and distinguish goods or services." 15 U.S.C. § 1127. Significantly, the use of another's trademark on noncompeting goods or services may dilute that trademark even if that use does not involve consumer confusion, mistake or deception. *Id.* Equally significant, however, is the limitation of this cause of action to *famous* trademarks. As we note below, attempts to define fame for the purposes of federal trademark dilution have occasioned a split in the circuits.

Historically, courts have recognized only two forms of trademark dilution: *blurring* and *tarnishment*. Thus, for example, Section 25 of the *Restatement (Third) of Unfair Competition* states:

> An actor is subject to liability under an antidilution statute if the actor uses [the trademark of another] in a manner that is likely to associate the other's mark with the goods, services, or business of the actor and:
>
> (a) the other's mark is highly distinctive and the association of the mark with the actor's goods, services, or business is likely to cause a reduction in that distinctiveness; or
>
> (b) the association of the other's mark with the actor's goods, services, or business, or the nature of the actor's use, is likely to disparage the other's goods, services, or business or tarnish the images associated with the other's mark.

RESTATEMENT (THIRD) OF UNFAIR COMPETITION § 25(1) (1995). The *Restatement* distinguishes between blurring and tarnishment in paragraphs (a) and (b) respectively. In dilution by blurring,

> the assumption is that the relevant public sees the junior user's use, and intuitively knows, because of the context of the junior user's use, that there is no connection between the owners of the respective marks. However, even with those who perceive distinct sources and affiliation, the ability of the senior user's mark to serve as a unique identifier of the plaintiff's goods or services is weakened because the relevant public now also associates that designation with a new and different source. Hence, the unique and distinctive link between the plaintiff's mark and its goods or services is "blurred."

4 J. THOMAS MCCARTHY, MCCARTHY ON TRADEMARKS AND UNFAIR COMPETITION § 24:70 (4th ed.2002). In dilution by tarnishment, "[t]he selling power of a trademark * * * [is] undermined by a use of the mark with goods or services such as illicit drugs or pornography that 'tarnish' the mark's image through inherently negative or unsavory associations, or with goods or services that produce a negative response when linked in the minds of prospective purchasers with the goods or services of the [senior] user, such as the use on insecticide of a trademark similar to one previously used by [the senior user] on food products." RESTATEMENT (THIRD) OF UNFAIR COMPETITION § 25(1), cmt. c (1995). While both blurring and tarnishment require that the diluted trademark become associated with the goods or services of another, blurring occurs when this association is likely to reduce the distinctive quality of that mark, whereas tarnishment is found when this association is likely to tarnish that mark's image.

Some proponents of the Federal Trademark Dilution Act heralded it as, among other things, a means of combating "cybersquatting"—the practice of registering another's trademark as a domain name with the intent of selling it for a profit, usually to the trademark owner. In the remainder of this Part, we consider domain name disputes involving claims of dilution. In reading the following materials, consider when dilution can appropriately be found absent blurring or tarnishment. (Cybersquatting is considered in more detail in Chapter 3, *infra.*)

Federal Trademark Dilution Act

15 U.S.C. §§ 1125(c) & 1127 (§§ 43(c) & 45 of the Lanham Act).

§ 1125

(c) Remedies for dilution of famous marks.

(1) The owner of a famous mark shall be entitled, subject to the principles of equity and upon such terms as the court deems reasonable, to an injunction against another person's commercial use in commerce of a mark or trade name, if such use begins after the mark has become famous and causes dilution of the distinctive quality of the mark, and to obtain such other relief as is provided in this subsection. In determining whether a mark is distinctive and famous, a court may consider factors such as, but not limited to—

(A) the degree of inherent or acquired distinctiveness of the mark;

(B) the duration and extent of use of the mark in connection with the goods or services with which the mark is used;

(C) the duration and extent of advertising and publicity of the mark;

(D) the geographical extent of the trading area in which the mark is used;

(E) the channels of trade for the goods or services with which the mark is used;

(F) the degree of recognition of the mark in the trading areas and channels of trade used by the mark's owner and the person against whom the injunction is sought;

(G) the nature and extent of use of the same or similar marks by third parties; and

(H) whether the mark was registered under the Act of March 3, 1881, or: the Act of February 20, 1905, or on the principal register.

(2) In an action brought under this subsection, the owner of the famous mark shall be entitled only to injunctive relief as set forth in § 1116 of this title unless the person against whom

the injunction is sought willfully intended to trade on the owner's reputation or to cause dilution of the famous mark. If such willful intent is proven, the owner of the famous mark shall also be entitled to the remedies set forth in §§ 1117(a) and 1118 of this title, subject to the discretion of the court and the principles of equity.

(3) The ownership by a person of a valid registration under the Act of March 3, 1881, or the Act of February 20, 1905, or on the principal register shall be a complete bar to an action against that person, with respect to that mark, that is brought by another person under the common law or a statute of a State and that seeks to prevent dilution of the distinctiveness of a mark, label, or form of advertisement.

(4) The following shall not be actionable under this section:

(A) Fair use of a famous mark by another person in comparative commercial advertising or promotion to identify the competing goods or services of the owner of the famous mark.

(B) Noncommercial use of a mark.

(C) All forms of news reporting and news commentary.

§ 1127

The term "dilution" means the lessening of the capacity of a famous mark to identify and distinguish goods or services, regardless of the presence or absence of—

(1) competition between the owner of the famous mark and other parties, or

(2) likelihood of confusion, mistake, or deception.

Toys "R" Us, Inc. v. Feinberg

26 F.Supp.2d 639 (S.D.N.Y.1998), *vacated & remanded*, 201 F.3d 432 (2d Cir.1999).

■ SCHWARTZ, DISTRICT JUDGE.

* * *

Plaintiff Geoffrey, Inc. is a wholly owned subsidiary of Toys "R" Us, Inc. Geoffrey owns the rights to the Toys "R" Us and related trademarks, licensing their use to Toys "R" Us and its various subsidiaries. Plaintiffs have been making use of the Toys "R" Us mark for over 35 years. The range of products sold in Toys "R" Us stores has grown and now includes, in addition to toys, over 11,000 different items such as clothing, lamps, telephones, stereos, calculators, computers, audio and visual tapes, pools, and sporting goods. The Toys "R" Us mark is prominently featured in national and regional advertising, and throughout Toys "R" Us stores. Since 1983, Toys "R" Us has owned and operated a chain of retail children's clothing stores under the mark Kids "R" Us. There are 698 Toys "R" Us stores in the United States, and 443 in foreign countries, with annual sales over $11 billion. As a result of over $100 million in advertising annually, and an intensive effort to maintain high quality goods and services, Toys "R" Us has become one of the most famous and widely known marks in the world.

Toys "R" Us has also worked diligently to maintain its reputation as a family oriented store with a wholesome image. Toys "R" Us has sought to project the image of a store where children are the first concern, and was one of the first stores to refuse to carry or sell toy guns—a fact widely publicized.

Plaintiff Geoffrey, Inc., in addition to the Toys "R" Us mark which it licenses to its co-plaintiff, owns a number of federal trademark registrations containing the phrase " 'R' Us." For example, Geoffrey has registered Babies "R" Us, Bikes "R" Us, Books "R" Us, Computers "R" Us, Dolls "R" Us, Games "R" Us, Mathematics "R" Us, Movies "R" Us, Parties "R" Us, Portraits "R" Us, Shoes "R" Us, and Sports "R" Us. Plaintiffs also own common law rights over various other "R" Us marks, such as Treats "R" Us, Gifts "R" Us, and 1–800–Toys–R–Us, by virtue of the exclusive use of those marks.

Finally, Geoffrey also owns various internet domain names including tru.com, toysrus.com, kidsrus.com, boysrus.com, dollsrus.com, galsrus.com, girlsrus.com, babiesrus.com, computersrus.com, guysrus.com, mathematicsrus.com, moviesrus.com, opportunitiesrus.com, partiesrus.com, poolsrus.com, portraitsrus.com, racersrus.com, supervaluesrus.com, treatsrus.com, tykesrus.com, sportsrus.com, giftsrus.com, and toysrusregistry.com. Toys "R" Us operates an internet website located at www.toysrus.com

Plaintiffs make use of various of these marks and others through ownership or licensing, resulting in the extensive use of the "R" Us family of marks, under the control and supervision of plaintiffs.

Defendant Richard Feinberg is the sole proprietor of codefendant We Are Guns, a firearms store doing business at 15 Farm Lane, Norton, Massachusetts. Feinberg runs his business predominantly in Massachusetts, but also sells products on the internet and has, "on occasion, shipped products to New York firearms dealers." Feinberg's business had been previously known as "Guns Are Us." The business's name was changed to "Guns are We" and then to "We Are Guns" in response to objections by plaintiffs. Feinberg maintains a website located at www.gunsareus.com and has registered the domain name "gunsareus.com" with InterNIC.

Plaintiffs brought this suit seeking damages and an injunction prohibiting defendants from operating the website at gunsareus.com and from reverting back to either of the trade names "Guns are Us" or "Guns Are We." * * *

The Court finds no issue of material fact as to whether defendants' use of the internet domain name gunsareus.com can serve as the basis for a dilution claim under * * * § 43(c) of the Lanham Act, 15 U.S.C. § 1125(c), * * * There are two types of dilution claims, (1) blurring, and (2) tarnishment. As a matter of law, plaintiff has failed to present a prima facie case under either theory.

The owner of a famous mark is entitled to an injunction "against another person's commercial use in commerce of a mark or trade name, if such use begins after the mark has become famous and causes dilution of the distinctive quality of the mark." *See Toys "R" Us, Inc. v. Akkaoui,* 1996 WL 772709 (N.D.Cal., Oct.29, 1996) (barring the use by defendants of the name "Adults 'R Us"), *citing* 15 U.S.C. § 1125(c)(1). Dilution does not depend on a showing of either likelihood of confusion between the marks, or competition between the owner of the mark and other parties. *See* 15 U.S.C. § 1127.

First, plaintiffs have failed to establish the existence of a triable issue of fact as to whether maintaining a website with the domain name "gunsareus.com" will blur, or lessen the capacity of plaintiffs' marks to identify and distinguish their goods or services. While it is conceivable that the proliferation of trade names ending in " 'R' Us," unassociated with plaintiffs, might cause such blurring, this case is nowhere near such a situation. This case involves a website that merely uses the letters "gunsareus" as its internet domain name. Defendants neither make use of the single letter "R" nor do they space or color the letters and words in a manner remotely related to plaintiffs. The name "gunsareus" appears in all lower case letters with no spaces in between the letters. The Court finds that the use of such an internet domain name, without naming the website itself "Guns 'R' Us" or "Guns Are Us," will not, as a matter of law, blur the distinctiveness of plaintiffs' "R" Us family of marks.

Second, the Court also finds an absence of a triable issue of fact as to whether defendants have diluted plaintiffs' mark by tarnishment. Dilution by tarnishment occurs when "a famous mark is improperly associated with an inferior or offensive product or service." *See Ringling Bros.,* 937 F.Supp. at 209 (*citing Hormel Foods Corp. v. Jim Henson Prods., Inc.,* 73 F.3d 497, 506 (2d Cir.1996)). Courts have found such negative connotations in situations where a mark was used in the context of drugs, nudity, and sex. *See e.g., Dallas Cowboys Cheerleaders, Inc. v. Pussycat Cinema, Ltd.,* 467 F.Supp. 366 (S.D.N.Y.1979) (pornography); *Coca–Cola Co. v. Gemini Rising, Inc.,* 346 F.Supp. 1183 (E.D.N.Y.1972) (cocaine); *Eastman Kodak Co. v. Rakow,* 739 F.Supp. 116, 118 (W.D.N.Y.1989) (crude comedy routine).

The Court, however, finds it unlikely that defendants' website will be associated with plaintiffs' stores and products at all. As stated earlier, the differing product areas, absence of the single letter "R" in the name, and peculiarities of an internet domain name make any association with plaintiffs' products extremely unlikely. In addition, defendant does not sell to the general public outside of Massachusetts. Its internet site is used almost exclusively to sell to firearms dealers.

In sum, the parties have demonstrated an absence of any material issues of fact, requiring judgment to be issued as a matter of law. Defendants' decision to cease using the trade names "Guns Are Us" and "Guns Are We" eliminates the need or basis for the Court to decide whether those trade names infringe on or dilute plaintiffs marks. Defendants' website, entitled Guns Are We, but with the domain name gunsareus.com, does not violate any of plaintiffs' rights under federal or state trademark and unfair competition law.

CONCLUSION

For the reasons set forth above, plaintiffs' motion for summary judgment is denied in its entirety, and summary judgment is granted in favor of defendants.

Avery Dennison Corp. v. Sumpton

189 F.3d 868 (9th Cir.1999).

■ TROTT, CIRCUIT JUDGE:

Jerry Sumpton and Freeview Listings Ltd. (together, "Appellants") appeal an injunction in favor of Avery Dennison Corp., entered after summary judgment for Avery Dennison on its claims of trademark dilution under the Federal Trademark Dilution Act of 1995, 15 U.S.C. § 1125(c) (Supp. II 1996) (amending the Lanham Trademark Act of 1946, 15 U.S.C. §§ 1051–1127 (1994)), and the California dilution statute, Cal. Bus. & Prof. Code § 14330 (West 1987). The district court published an opinion, 999 F.Supp. 1337 (C.D.Cal.1998), holding that Appellants' maintenance of domain name registrations for <avery.net> and <dennison.net> diluted two of Avery Dennison's separate trademarks, "Avery" and "Dennison." (Note that when referencing Internet addresses, domain-name combinations, e-mail addresses, and other Internet-related character strings, we use the caret symbols ("< >"), in order to avoid possible confusion.) The district court then entered an injunction ordering Appellants to transfer the domain-name registrations to Avery Dennison in exchange for $300 each.

We have jurisdiction under 28 U.S.C. § 1291 (1994). Because Avery Dennison failed to create a genuine issue of fact on required elements of the dilution cause of action, we reverse and remand with instructions to enter summary judgment for Appellants and to consider Appellants' request for attorneys' fees in light of this decision.

I. Background

We are the third panel of this court in just over a year faced with the challenging task of applying centuries-old trademark law to the newest medium of communication—the Internet. (*See Brookfield Communications, Inc. v. West Coast Enter. Corp.*, 174 F.3d 1036 (9th Cir.1999), and *Panavision Int'l, L.P. v. Toeppen,* 141 F.3d 1316 (9th Cir.1998).) Although we attempt to set out the background facts as clearly as possible, the interested reader may wish to review some of the following sources for a more complete understanding of the Internet: *Brookfield,* 174 F.3d at 1044–45;

Intermatic, Inc. v. Toeppen, 947 F.Supp. 1227, 1230–32 (N.D.Ill.1996); and Marshall Leaffer, *Domain Names, Globalization and Internet Commerce,* 6 Ind. J. Global Legal Stud. 139, 139–46 (1998).

Two communicative functions of the Internet are relevant to this appeal: the capacity to support web sites and the corollary capacity to support electronic mail ("e-mail"). A web site, which is simply an interactive presentation of data which a user accesses by dialing into the host computer, can be created by any user who reserves an Internet location—called an Internet protocol address—and does the necessary programming. Because an Internet protocol address is a string of integer numbers separated by periods, for example, <129.137.84.101>, for ease of recall and use a user relies on a "domain-name combination" to reach a given web site. The registrar of Internet domain names, Network Solutions, Inc. ("NSI"),[1] maintains a database of registrations and translates entered domain-name combinations into Internet protocol addresses. When accessing a web site, a user enters the character string <http://www.>, followed by the reserved domain-name combination. The domain-name combination must include a top-level domain ("TLD"), which can be <.com>, <.net>, <.org>, <.gov> or <.edu>, among others, although some, like <.gov> and <.edu>, are reserved for specific purposes. The combination also includes a second-level domain ("SLD"), which can be any word not already reserved in combination with the TLD. Once a domain-name combination is reserved, it cannot be used by anybody else, unless the first registrant voluntarily or otherwise relinquishes its registration.

A web site can be programmed for multiple purposes. Some merchants maintain a form of "electronic catalog" on the Internet, permitting Internet users to review products and services for sale. A web site can also be programmed for e-mail, where the provider licenses e-mail addresses in the format <alias@SLD.TLD>, with <alias> selected by the e-mail user. A person or company maintaining a web site makes money in a few different ways. A site that aids in marketing goods and services is an asset to a merchant. E-mail providers make money from licensing fees paid by e-mail users. Money is also made from advertising and links to other web sites.

II. Facts

Sumpton is the president of Freeview, an Internet e-mail provider doing business as "Mailbank." Mailbank offers "vanity" e-mail addresses to users for an initial fee of $19.95 and $4.95 per year thereafter, and has registered thousands of domain-name combinations for this purpose. Most SLDs that Mailbank has registered are common surnames, although some represent hobbies, careers, pets, sports interests, favorite music, and the like. One category of SLDs is titled "Rude" and includes lewd SLDs, and another category, titled "Business," includes some common trademark SLDs. Mailbank's TLDs consist mainly of <.net> and <.org>, but some

1. At the time of publication of this opinion, NSI is no longer the exclusive registrar of domain names. A new competitive scheme is being implemented by the Commerce Department, and one competitor, "register.com," is currently in operation. * * *

registered domain name combinations, including most in the "Business" and "Rude" categories, use the TLD <.com>. Mailbank's surname archives include the domain-name combinations <avery.net> and <dennison.net>.

Avery Dennison sells office products and industrial fasteners under the registered trademarks "Avery" and "Dennison," respectively. "Avery" has been in continuous use since the 1930s and registered since 1963, and "Dennison" has been in continuous use since the late 1800s and registered since 1908. Avery Dennison spends more than $5 million per year advertising its products, including those marketed under the separate "Avery" and "Dennison" trademarks, and the company boasts in the neighborhood of $3 billion in sales of all of its trademarks annually. No evidence indicates what percentage of these dollar figures apply to the "Avery" or "Dennison" trademarks. Avery Dennison maintains a commercial presence on the Internet, marketing its products at <avery.com> and <averydennison.com>, and maintaining registrations for several other domain-name combinations, all using the TLD <.com>.

Avery Dennison sued Appellants, alleging trademark dilution under the Federal Trademark Dilution Act and California Business and Professional Code § 14330. Avery Dennison also sued NSI, alleging contributory dilution and contributory infringement. The district court granted summary judgment to NSI on Avery Dennison's claims. The district court then concluded as a matter of law that the disputed trademarks were famous and denied summary judgment to Appellants and granted summary judgment to Avery Dennison on its dilution claims, entering an injunction requiring Appellants to transfer the registrations to Avery Dennison. 999 F.Supp. at 1342.

III. Trademark Law

Trademark protection is "the law's recognition of the psychological function of symbols." *Mishawaka Rubber & Woolen Mfg. Co. v. S.S. Kresge Co.,* 316 U.S. 203 (1942). Two goals of trademark law are reflected in the federal scheme. On the one hand, the law seeks to protect consumers who have formed particular associations with a mark. On the other hand, trademark law seeks to protect the investment in a mark made by the owner.

Until recently, federal law provided protection only against infringement of a registered trademark, or the unregistered trademark analog, unfair competition. *See* §§ 32 and 43(a) of the Lanham Trademark Act of 1946, as amended, 15 U.S.C. §§ 1114, 1125(a) (1994). These causes of action require a plaintiff to prove that the defendant is using a mark confusingly similar to a valid, protectable trademark of the plaintiff's. *Brookfield,* 174 F.3d at 1046.

Many states, however, have long recognized another cause of action designed to protect trademarks: trademark dilution. Lori Krafte–Jacobs, Comment, Judicial Interpretation of the Federal Trademark Dilution Act of 1995, 66 U. Cin. L.Rev. 659, 660–62 (1998) (discussing the evolution of the dilution doctrine). With the 1995 enactment of the Federal Trademark

Dilution Act, dilution became a federal-law concern. Unlike infringement and unfair competition laws, in a dilution case competition between the parties and a likelihood of confusion are not required to present a claim for relief. *See* 15 U.S.C. § 1127 (Supp. II 1996) (definition of "dilution"); Leslie F. Brown, *Note, Avery Dennison Corp. v. Sumpton,* 14 Berkeley Tech. L.J. 247, 249 (1999). Rather, injunctive relief is available under the Federal Trademark Dilution Act if a plaintiff can establish that (1) its mark is famous; (2) the defendant is making commercial use of the mark in commerce; (3) the defendant's use began after the plaintiff's mark became famous; and (4) the defendant's use presents a likelihood of dilution of the distinctive value of the mark. *Panavision Int'l, L.P. v. Toeppen,* 141 F.3d 1316, 1324 (9th Cir.1998) (interpreting 15 U.S.C. § 1125(c)(1)).

California's dilution cause of action is substantially similar, providing relief if the plaintiff can demonstrate a "[l]ikelihood of injury to business reputation or of dilution of the distinctive quality of a mark ..., notwithstanding the absence of competition between the parties or the absence of confusion as to the source of goods or services." Cal. Bus. & Prof. Code § 14330. We have interpreted § 14330, like the Federal Trademark Dilution Act, to protect only famous marks. *Fruit of the Loom, Inc. v. Girouard,* 994 F.2d 1359, 1362–63 (9th Cir.1993); *see* 3 J. Thomas McCarthy, *Trademarks and Unfair Competition* § 24:108 (Supp.1998).

* * *

V. Dilution Protection

We now turn to the dilution causes of action at issue in this case, brought under the Federal Trademark Dilution Act and California Business and Professional Code § 14330.

In *Panavision,* we held that both the Federal Trademark Dilution Act and § 14330 were implicated when the defendant registered domain-name combinations using famous trademarks and sought to sell the registrations to the trademark owners. 141 F.3d at 1318, 1327. Three differences made *Panavision* easier than the instant case. First, the defendant did not mount a challenge on the famousness prong of the dilution tests. *Panavision,* 141 F.3d at 1324. Second, the *Panavision* defendant did not challenge the factual assertion that he sought to profit by arbitrage with famous trademarks. *Id.* at 1324–25. Third, the diluting registrations in *Panavision* both involved the TLD <.com>. In the instant case, by contrast, Appellants contest Avery Dennison's claim of famousness, Appellants contend that the nature of their business makes the trademark status of "Avery" and "Dennison" irrelevant, and the complained-of registrations involve the TLD <. net>.

A. Famousness

The district court considered evidence submitted by Avery Dennison regarding marketing efforts and consumer association with its marks and concluded as a matter of law that "Avery" and "Dennison" were famous marks entitled to dilution protection. 999 F.Supp. at 1339. We hold that

Avery Dennison failed to create a genuine issue of fact on the famousness element of both dilution statutes.[4]

Dilution is a cause of action invented and reserved for a select class of marks—those marks with such powerful consumer associations that even non-competing uses can impinge on their value. *See generally* Frank L. Schechter, *The Rational Basis for Trademark Protection,* 40 Harv. L.Rev. 813 (1927) (proposing a cause of action for dilution); Krafte–Jacobs, *supra,* at 689–91. Dilution causes of action, much more so than infringement and unfair competition laws, tread very close to granting "rights in gross" in a trademark. *See* 3 McCarthy, *supra,* § 24:108. In the infringement and unfair competition scenario, where the less famous a trademark, the less the chance that consumers will be confused as to origin, *see AMF Inc. v. Sleekcraft Boats,* 599 F.2d 341, 349 (9th Cir.1979), a carefully-crafted balance exists between protecting a trademark and permitting non-infringing uses. In the dilution context, likelihood of confusion is irrelevant. *See* 15 U.S.C. § 1127; Cal. Bus. and Prof.Code § 14330; *Panavision,* 141 F.3d at 1326. If dilution protection were accorded to trademarks based only on a showing of inherent or acquired distinctiveness, we would upset the balance in favor of over-protecting trademarks, at the expense of potential non-infringing uses. *See Fruit of the Loom,* 994 F.2d at 1363 ("[The plaintiff] would sweep clean the many business uses of this quotidian word.").

We view the famousness prong of both dilution analyses as reinstating the balance—by carefully limiting the class of trademarks eligible for dilution protection, Congress and state legislatures granted the most potent form of trademark protection in a manner designed to minimize undue impact on other uses. *See San Francisco Arts & Athletics, Inc. v. United States Olympic Comm.,* 483 U.S. 522, 564 n. 25 (1987) (Brennan, J., dissenting) (citing 2 J. McCarthy, *Trademarks & Unfair Competition* § 24:16, at 229 (2d ed.1984)) (discussing limits on the dilution doctrine that help prevent overprotection of trademarks).

Therefore, to meet the "famousness" element of protection under the dilution statutes, " 'a mark [must] be truly prominent and renowned.' " *I.P. Lund Trading ApS v. Kohler Co.,* 163 F.3d 27, 46 (1st Cir.1998) (quoting 3 McCarthy, *supra,* § 24.91). In a 1987 report, which recommended an amendment to the Lanham Act to provide a federal dilution cause of action, the Trademark Review Commission of the United States Trademark Association emphasized the narrow reach of a dilution cause of action: "We believe that a limited category of trademarks, those which are truly famous and registered,[5] are deserving of national protection from

4. Although the famousness of "Avery" and "Dennison" is disputed, no dispute exists on the third element of dilution under *Panavision:* Appellants' use must begin after the marks became famous. Any fame that Avery Dennison's marks have acquired existed before November, 1996, when Appellants' use began.

5. The Trademark Review Commission's recommended amendment is very similar to the language of the eventually-enacted Federal Trademark Dilution Act. The main difference relevant to the famousness inquiry

dilution." Trademark Review Commission, *Report & Recommendations,* 77 Trademark Rep. 375, 455 (Sept.-Oct.1987).

The Federal Trademark Dilution Act lists eight non-exclusive considerations for the famousness inquiry, 15 U.S.C. § 1125(c)(1)(A)–(H), which are equally relevant to a famousness determination under Business and Professional Code § 14330, *see Panavision,* 141 F.3d at 1324 ("Panavision's state law dilution claim is subject to the same analysis as its federal claim.").

* * *

We note the overlap between the statutory famousness considerations and the factors relevant to establishing acquired distinctiveness, which is attained "when the purchasing public associates the [mark] with a single producer or source rather than just the product itself." *First Brands Corp. v. Fred Meyer, Inc.,* 809 F.2d 1378, 1383 (9th Cir.1987). Proof of acquired distinctiveness is a difficult empirical inquiry which a factfinder must undertake, *Taco Cabana Int'l, Inc. v. Two Pesos, Inc.,* 932 F.2d 1113, 1119–20 & n. 7 (5th Cir.1991), *aff'd,* 505 U.S. 763 (1992), considering factors including:

[1] whether actual purchasers ... associate the [mark] with [the plaintiff];

[2] the degree and manner of [the plaintiff's] advertising;

[3] the length and manner of [the plaintiff's] use of the [mark]; and

[4] whether [the plaintiff's] use of the [mark] has been exclusive.

Clamp Mfg. Co. v. Enco Mfg. Co., 870 F.2d 512, 517 (9th Cir.1989). Furthermore, registration on the principal register creates a presumption of distinctiveness—in the case of a surname trademark, acquired distinctiveness. 15 U.S.C. § 1057(b) (1994); *Americana Trading Inc. v. Russ Berrie & Co.,* 966 F.2d 1284, 1287 (9th Cir.1992) ("[R]egistration carries a presumption of secondary meaning.").

However, the Federal Trademark Dilution Act and Business and Professional Code § 14330 apply "only to those marks which are both truly distinctive *and* famous, and therefore most likely to be adversely affected by dilution." S. Rep. No. 100–515, at 42 (emphasis added). The Trademark Review Commission stated that "a higher standard must be employed to gauge the fame of a trademark eligible for this extraordinary remedy." 77 Trademark Rep. at 461. Thus, "[t]o be capable of being diluted, a mark must have a degree of distinctiveness and 'strength' beyond that needed to serve as a trademark." 3 McCarthy, *supra,* § 24:109; *see also* Krafte–Jacobs, *supra,* at 690 ("If all marks are distinctive, and a showing of distinctiveness meets the element of fame, what marks would be outside the protection of the FTDA? [T]he FTDA does not indicate that any particular degree of distinctiveness should end the inquiry." (interpreting the Federal Trademark Dilution Act)). We have previously held likewise

is that the Commission's recommendation only permitted a cause of action to the owner of a registered mark, while the owner of any protectable mark or trade name can bring a cause of action under the enacted version of the Federal Trademark Dilution Act.

under California Business and Professional Code § 14330. *Accuride Int'l, Inc. v. Accuride Corp.*, 871 F.2d 1531, 1539 (9th Cir.1989) (requiring more than mere distinctiveness).

Applying the famousness factors from the Federal Trademark Dilution Act to the facts of the case at bench, we conclude that Avery Dennison likely establishes acquired distinctiveness in the "Avery" and "Dennison" trademarks, but goes no further. Because the Federal Trademark Dilution Act requires a showing greater than distinctiveness to meet the threshold element of fame, as a matter of law Avery Dennison has failed to fulfill this burden.

1. *Distinctiveness*

We begin with the first factor in the statutory list: "inherent or acquired distinctiveness." § 1125(c)(1)(A). No dispute exists that "Avery" and "Dennison" are common surnames—according to evidence presented by Appellants, respectively the 775th and 1768th most common in the United States. A long-standing principle of trademark law is the right of a person to use his or her own name in connection with a business. *See Howe Scale Co. v. Wyckoff, Seamans & Benedict,* 198 U.S. 118, 140 (1905). This principle was incorporated into the Lanham Act, which states that a mark that is "primarily merely a surname" is not protectable unless it acquires secondary meaning. 15 U.S.C. § 1052(e)(4), (f) (1994); *Abraham Zion Corp. v. Lebow,* 761 F.2d 93, 104 (2d Cir.1985); *see L.E. Waterman Co. v. Modern Pen Co.,* 235 U.S. 88, 94 (1914) (pre-Lanham Act case stating that protection from confusion is available to the holder of a surname trademark that has acquired public recognition); *Horlick's Malted Milk Corp. v. Horluck's, Inc.,* 59 F.2d 13, 15 (9th Cir.1932) (pre-Lanham Act case limiting the defendant's right to use his surname as a trademark where the name had acquired public recognition from the efforts of a competitor). Avery Dennison cannot claim that "Avery" and "Dennison" are inherently distinctive, but must demonstrate acquired distinctiveness through secondary meaning.

The drafters of the Federal Trademark Dilution Act continued the concern for surnames when adding protection against trademark dilution to the federal scheme. On early consideration of the Act, the report from the Senate Judiciary Committee emphasized: "[T]he committee intended to give special protection to an individual's ability to use his or her own name in good faith." S. Rep. No. 100–515, at 43 (1988). The Federal Trademark Dilution Act imports, at a minimum, the threshold secondary-meaning requirement for registration of a surname trademark.

Avery Dennison maintains registrations of both "Avery" and "Dennison" on the principal register, prima facie evidence that these marks have achieved the secondary meaning required for protection from infringement and unfair competition. *See Americana Trading,* 966 F.2d at 1287. We reject Appellants' argument that the distinctiveness required for famousness under the Federal Trademark Dilution Act is inherent, not merely acquired distinctiveness. *See* 15 U.S.C. § 1125(c)(1)(A) (referring to "inherent or acquired distinctiveness"). However, because famousness requires a showing greater than mere distinctiveness, the presumptive secondary meaning associated with "Avery" and "Dennison" fails to persuade us that the famousness prong is met in this case.

2. Overlapping Channels of Trade

We next consider the fifth and sixth factors of the statutory inquiry: the channels of trade for the plaintiff's goods and the degree of recognition of the mark in the trading areas and channels of trade used by plaintiff and defendant. § 1125(c)(1)(E), (F). The drafters of the Federal Trademark Dilution Act broke from the Trademark Review Commission's recommendation that only marks "which have become famous throughout a substantial part of the United States" could qualify for protection. *Report & Recommendation,* 77 Trademark Rep. at 456. Instead, fame in a localized trading area may meet the threshold element under the Act if plaintiff's trading area includes the trading area of the defendant. S.Rep. No. 100–515, at 43; *Washington Speakers Bureau, Inc. v. Leading Auths., Inc.,* 33 F.Supp.2d 488, 503–04 (E.D.Va.1999) (*citing I.P. Lund,* 163 F.3d at 46; *Teletech Customer Care Mgt., Inc. v. Tele–Tech Co.,* 977 F.Supp. 1407, 1413 (C.D.Cal.1997)). The rule is likewise for specialized market segments: specialized fame can be adequate only if the "diluting uses are directed narrowly at the same market segment." *Washington Speakers,* 33 F.Supp.2d at 503. No evidence on the record supports Avery Dennison's position on these two prongs of the famousness inquiry.

In *Teletech,* fame in a narrow market segment was present when the plaintiff showed "that the Teletech Companies may be the largest provider of primarily inbound integrated telephone and Internet customer care nationwide." 977 F.Supp. at 1409. The defendant was "a contractor providing engineering and installation services to the telecommunications industry," and maintained the domain-name combination, <teletech.com>. *Id.* at 1409–10. The court held that the showing on the threshold element under the Federal Trademark Dilution Act was adequate to qualify for a preliminary injunction. *Id.* at 1413. In *Washington Speakers,* both the plaintiff and defendant were in the business of scheduling speaking engagements for well-known lecturers. 33 F.Supp.2d at 490, 503 and n. 31 (citing cases). In the instant case, by contrast, Appellants' sought-after customer base is Internet users who desire vanity e-mail addresses, and Avery Dennison's customer base includes purchasers of office products and industrial fasteners. No evidence demonstrates that Avery Dennison possesses any degree of recognition among Internet users or that Appellants direct their e-mail services at Avery Dennison's customer base.

3. Use of the Marks by Third Parties

The seventh factor, "the nature and extent of use of the same ... marks by third parties," § 1125(c)(1)(G), undercuts the district court's conclusion as well. All relevant evidence on the record tends to establish that both "Avery" and "Dennison" are commonly used as trademarks, both on and off of the Internet, by parties other than Avery Dennison. This evidence is relevant because, when "a mark is in widespread use, it may not be famous for the goods or services of one business." *Report & Recommendation,* 77 Trademark Rep. at 461; *see Accuride,* 871 F.2d at 1539 (affirming the district court's holding that widespread use of elements of a trademark helped to defeat a dilution claim).

The record includes copies of five trademark registrations for "Avery" and "Averys," a computer printout of a list of several businesses with "Avery" in their names who market products on the Internet, and a list of business names including "Avery," which, according to a declaration submitted by NSI, is a representative sample of over 800 such businesses. The record also contains a computer printout of a list of several businesses with "Dennison" in their names which market products on the Internet and a list of business names including "Dennison," a representative sample of over 200 such businesses. Such widespread use of "Avery" and "Dennison" makes it unlikely that either can be considered a famous mark eligible for the dilution cause of action.

4. Other Famousness Factors

Avery Dennison argues that evidence of extensive advertising and sales, international operations, and consumer awareness suffices to establish fame. We agree that the remaining four statutory factors in the famousness inquiry likely support Avery Dennison's position. Both "Avery" and "Dennison" have been used as trademarks for large fractions of a century and registered for decades. Avery Dennison expends substantial sums annually advertising each mark, with some presumable degree of success due to Avery Dennison's significant annual volume of sales. In addition, Avery Dennison markets its goods internationally. *See* 15 U.S.C. § 1125(c)(1)(B)–(D), (G). However, we disagree that Avery Dennison's showing establishes fame.

Avery Dennison submitted three market research studies regarding perceptions of the "Avery" and "Avery Dennison" brands. Discussion groups through which one study was conducted were formed "using Avery client lists," and produced the conclusion that the "Avery" name has "positive associations . . . among current customers." Surveyed persons in the other two studies were mostly "users and purchasers of office products" and "[o]ffice supply consumers." The one consumer group that did not necessarily include office supply purchasers for businesses was still required to be "somewhat" or "very" familiar with Avery products in order to be counted.

Avery Dennison's marketing reports are comparable to a survey we discussed in *Anti–Monopoly, Inc. v. General Mills Fun Group, Inc.,* 684 F.2d 1316 (9th Cir.1982), proving only the near tautology that consumers already acquainted with Avery and Avery Dennison products are familiar with Avery Dennison. *See id.* at 1323–24. The marketing reports add nothing to the discussion of whether consumers in general have any brand association with "Avery" and "Avery Dennison," and no evidence of product awareness relates specifically to the "Dennison" trademark. Although proper consumer surveys might be highly relevant to a showing of fame, we reject any reliance on the flawed reports submitted by Avery Dennison.

Finally, Avery Dennison—like any company marketing on the Internet—markets its products worldwide. *See* 15 U.S.C. § 1125(c)(1)(D). By itself, this factor carries no weight; worldwide use of a non-famous mark does not establish fame. Because famousness requires more than mere distinctiveness, and Avery Dennison's showing goes no further than establishing secondary meaning, we hold that Avery Dennison has not met its burden to create a genuine issue of fact that its marks are famous. Avery Dennison's failure to fulfill its burden on this required element of both dilution causes of action mandates summary judgment for Appellants.

5. *Likelihood of Confusion Remains Irrelevant*

We recognize that our discussion of the breadth of fame and overlapping market segments begins to sound like a likelihood of confusion analysis, and we agree with Avery Dennison that likelihood of confusion should not be considered under either the Federal Trademark Dilution Act or Business and Professional Code § 14330. However, as we discuss above, the famousness element of the dilution causes of action serves the same general purpose as the likelihood of confusion element of an infringement or unfair competition analysis—preventing the trademark scheme from granting excessively broad protection at the expense of legitimate uses. *See Fruit of the Loom,* 994 F.2d at 1363 ("Whittling away will not occur unless there is at least some subliminal connection in a buyer's mind between the two parties' uses of their marks."). The close parallels between the two analyses are therefore not surprising; nor do they cause us concern.

B. *Commercial Use*

Addressing the second element of a cause of action under the Federal Trademark Dilution Act, the district court held that Appellants' registration of <avery.net> and <dennison.net> constituted commercial use. 999 F.Supp. at 1339–40. We disagree.

Commercial use under the Federal Trademark Dilution Act requires the defendant to be using the trademark as a trademark, capitalizing on its trademark status. *See Panavision,* 141 F.3d at 1325. Courts have phrased this requirement in various ways. In a classic "cybersquatter" case, one court referenced the defendants "intention to arbitrage" the registration which included the plaintiff's trademark. *Intermatic,* 947 F.Supp. at 1239. Another court, whose decision we affirmed, noted that the defendant "traded on the value of marks as marks." *Panavision Int'l, L.P. v. Toeppen,* 945 F.Supp. 1296, 1303 (C.D.Cal.1996), *aff'd,* 141 F.3d 1316 (9th Cir.1998). In our *Panavision* decision, we considered the defendant's "attempt to sell the trademarks themselves." 141 F.3d at 1325.

All evidence in the record indicates that Appellants register common surnames in domain-name combinations and license e-mail addresses using those surnames, with the consequent intent to capitalize on the surname status of "Avery" and "Dennison." Appellants do not use trademarks qua trademarks as required by the caselaw to establish commercial use. Rather, Appellants use words that happen to be trademarks for their non-trademark value. The district court erred in holding that Appellants' use of <avery.net> and <dennison.net> constituted commercial use under the Federal Trademark Dilution Act, and this essential element of the dilution causes of action likewise mandates summary judgment for Appellants.

C. Dilution

The district court then considered the dilution requirement under both statutes, holding that Appellants' use of <avery.net> and <dennison.net> caused dilution, or a likelihood of dilution, of "Avery" and "Dennison." 999 F.Supp. at 1340–41. We hold that genuine issues of fact on this element of the causes of action should have precluded summary judgment for Avery Dennison.

Two theories of dilution are implicated in this case. First, Avery Dennison argues that Appellants' conduct is the cybersquatting dilution that we recognized in *Panavision. See* 141 F.3d at 1326–27. Second, Avery Dennison argues that Appellants' conduct in housing the <avery.net> and <dennison.net> domain names in the same database as various lewd SLDs causes tarnishment of the "Avery" and "Dennison" marks.

1. Cybersquatting

Cybersquatting dilution is the diminishment of " 'the capacity of the [plaintiff's] marks to identify and distinguish the [plaintiff's] goods and services on the Internet.' " *Panavision,* 141 F.3d at 1326 (quoting the *Panavision* district court, 945 F.Supp. at 1304). We recognized that this can occur if potential customers cannot find a web page at <trademark.com.> *Id.* at 1327; *see also Brookfield,* 174 F.3d at 1045 ("The Web surfer who assumes that 'X.com' will always correspond to the web site of company X or trademark X will, however, sometimes be misled."). Dilution occurs because " '[p]rospective users of plaintiff's services . . . may fail to continue to search for plaintiff's own home page, due to anger, frustration or the belief that plaintiff's home page does not exist.' " *Panavision,* 141 F.3d at 1327 (quoting *Jews for Jesus v. Brodsky,* 993 F.Supp. 282, 306–07 (D.N.J. 1998)).

In the instant case, Appellants registered the TLD <.net>, rather than <.com>, with the SLDs <avery> and <dennison>. As we recognized in *Panavision,* <.net> applies to networks and <.com> applies to commercial entities. 141 F.3d at 1318. Evidence on the record supports this distinction, and courts applying the dilution cause of action to domain-name registrations have universally considered <trademark.com> registrations. *See* Brown, *Note, supra,* at 251–54 (discussing cases); *id.* at 262–63 (addressing the <.com> versus <.net> distinction). Although evidence on the record also demonstrates that the <.com> and <.net> distinction is illusory, a factfinder could infer that dilution does not occur with a <trademark.net> registration. This genuine issue of fact on the question of cybersquatting dilution should have prevented summary judgment for Avery Dennison.

2. *Tarnishment*

Tarnishment occurs when a defendant's use of a mark similar to a plaintiff's presents a danger that consumers will form unfavorable associations with the mark. *See Hasbro, Inc. v. Internet Ent. Group, Ltd.,* 40 U.S.P.Q.2d 1479, 1480, 1996 WL 84853 (W.D.Wash.1996) (<candyland.com> as a domain-name combination for a sexually explicit web site diluted plaintiff's trademark, "Candyland," for a children's game); 3 McCarthy, *supra,* § 24:104. The district court did not reach Avery Dennison's claims regarding tarnishment.

Avery Dennison offers, as an alternative ground for affirming the district court, the fact that Appellants house <avery.net> and <dennison.net> at the same web site as lewd domain-name registrations. However, the evidence likewise indicates that to move from <avery.net> or <dennison.net> to a lewd SLD requires "linking" through the Mailbank home page, which might remove any association with the "Avery" and "Dennison" trademarks that the Internet user might have had. *See Fruit of the Loom,* 994 F.2d at 1363 (requiring some connection between the two parties' uses of their marks). Whether Appellants' use of the registrations presents a danger of tarnishment is an issue of fact that could not be decided on summary judgment. * * *

VII. Conclusion

We reverse the district court's summary judgment in favor of Avery Dennison and remand with instructions to enter summary judgment for Sumpton and Freeview.

REVERSED and REMANDED.

NOTES & QUESTIONS

1. *Cybersquatters or entrepreneurs?* In *Avery Dennison v. Sumpton*, the district court held that "Avery" and "Dennison" were famous marks, and that defendants had made commercial use of them. These holdings were reversed on appeal. The district court went on to address the equities of the parties' claims to the two domain names. The court expressed great skepticism concerning defendants' explanation of their business model:

> Defendants allege that they have invested approximately $1,200,000 in their business. They allege that they are providing internet services to their licensees that the licensees could not offer for themselves, i.e., the ability to allow multiple uses of the same surnames as domain names, and the ability to spread the cost of maintaining the domain name registrations among all of the users.
>
> Defendants also point out that their use of the ".net" designation does not deny plaintiff access to the internet through use of its trademarks as domain names. Plaintiff has registered names corresponding to its trademarks under the ".com" designation,

> which is the designation specified for commercial use. According to the defendants, the internet registration system contemplates that the ".net" designation will be reserved for use by Internet service providers, and that it will not be used for marketing of commercial products. Defendants argue that their own use of the ".net" designation is within the contemplation of the internet registration system.
>
> Plaintiffs contend that none of defendants' arguments is apt. They contend that the internet registration system simply does not authorize "cybersquatting." They contend that it does not authorize the registration of *any* domain names that are commonly used by others to identify themselves, not for the purpose of use by the registrant as domain names, but rather for sale or license to others.
>
> The court agrees. This is not a case involving a dispute over a domain name between persons or entities that have previously used the name to identify themselves or their products. Defendants' claimed "service" depends on their first having preempted 12,000 domain names, so that others who customarily use a name to identify themselves can use a domain name for that purpose only with the permission of the defendants. Moreover, anyone who desires to use any of those 12,000 names for any purpose, other than as an e-mail address, is entirely precluded from doing so. In light of the fact that many of the most popular on-line services provide e-mail addresses without charge, limiting domain name registrations to this purpose is almost certainly not the highest and best use. Finally, the ".net" designation has not been preserved according to the original intent, and many registrants, including trademark holders, have registered domain names with ".net" designations that are not internet providers.
>
> The court is extremely dubious that licensing domain names for use as e-mail addresses is defendants' true business. As previously noted, this limitation is voluntary. It would be extremely difficult to enforce if defendants' right to the exclusive use of these domain names was ever held to exist. Thereafter, it would appear that the laws of economics would require the defendants to sell or license each of their 12,000 names to the highest bidder for whatever use the buyer or licensee wished to make of them.

Avery Dennison v. Sumpton, 999 F.Supp. 1337, 1341–42 (C.D.Cal.1998), *rev'd*, 189 F.3d 868 (9th Cir.1999).

Do you agree that defendants' purported business model is a sham? Was the district court too facile in condemning defendants as cybersquatters? Consider the district court's explanation: "Defendants are 'cybersquatters,' as that term has come to be commonly understood. They have registered over 12,000 internet domain names not for their own use, but rather to prevent others from using those names without defendants' consent." Is cybersquatting, as thus understood, more worthy of condemnation than the action of any other entrepreneur who gains control of a resource that is in limited supply (real estate, stock in a corporation, chromium) and makes it available to others for a price?

2. *Trademark combinatorics and domain permutations.* The court in *Toys "R" Us v. Feinberg* notes that "Geoffrey also owns various internet domain names including tru.com, toysrus.com, kidsrus.com, boysrus.com, dollsrus.com, galsrus.com, girlsrus.com, babiesrus.com, computersrus.com, guysrus.com, mathematicsrus.com, moviesrus.com, opportunitiesrus.com, partiesrus.com, poolsrus.com, portraitsrus.com, racersrus.com, supervalues-rus.com, treatsrus.com, tykesrus.com, sportsrus.com, giftsrus.com, and toysrusregistry.com." Would the registration or use of these domain names by somebody other than Geoffrey constitute trademark infringement?

3. *Fame.* While it is unsurprising that "Toys 'R' Us" is viewed as a "famous" trademark, you might find it odd that the court in *Teletech Customer Care Management v. Tele–Tech,* 977 F.Supp. 1407 (C.D.Cal.1997), excerpted in Chapter 3, *infra,* found "TeleTech" to be a famous mark. If "TeleTech" is a famous mark, one might conclude that the legal threshold for fame under 15 U.S.C. § 1125(c) is very low, but the Ninth Circuit in *Avery Dennison v. Sumpton, supra,* applied a rather more rigorous standard. The Seventh Circuit wrestled with this question in *Syndicate Sales, Inc. v. Hampshire Paper Corp.,* 192 F.3d 633 (7th Cir.1999):

> At an initial glance, there appears to be a wide variation of authority on this issue. Some cases apparently hold that fame in a niche market is insufficient for a federal dilution claim, while some hold that such fame is sufficient. However, a closer look indicates that the different lines of authority are addressing two different contexts. Cases holding that niche-market fame is insufficient generally address the context in which the plaintiff and defendant are using the mark in separate markets. On the other hand, cases stating that niche-market renown is a factor indicating fame address a context like the one here, in which the plaintiff and defendant are using the mark in the same or related markets. *See Teletech Customer Care Management, Inc. v. Tele–Tech Co.,* 977 F.Supp. 1407, 1413 (C.D.Cal.1997). The validity of this distinction is supported by the Restatement and a commentator:
>
> > A mark that is highly distinctive only to a select class or group of purchasers may be protected from diluting uses directed at that particular class or group. For example, a mark may be highly distinctive among purchasers of a specific type of product. In such circumstances, protection against a dilution of the mark's distinctiveness is ordinarily appropriate only against uses specifically directed at that particular class of purchasers; uses of the mark in broader markets, although they may produce an incidental diluting effect in the protected market, are not normally actionable.

> Restatement (Third) of Unfair Competition § 25 cmt. e (1995); *see also* 4 J. Thomas McCarthy, *McCarthy on Trademarks and Unfair Competition* § 24:112, at 24–204 to 24–205 (1999).
>
> Moreover, one of the factors in § 1125(c) for determining the existence of fame indicates that fame may be constricted to a particular market. That factor is "the degree of recognition of the mark in the trading areas and channels of trade used by the marks' owner and the person against whom the injunction is sought." 15 U.S.C. § 1125(c)(1)(F). We acknowledge, of course, that the narrowness of the market in which a plaintiff's mark has fame is a factor that must be considered in the balance. * * * However, when the defendant allegedly uses a mark in the same market as the plaintiff, the narrowness of that market is less important. We therefore hold that the district court erred in concluding that the trade dress was not famous based solely on the niche-market status of the baskets.

Syndicate Sales, Inc. v. Hampshire Paper Corp., 192 F.3d at 640–41. Do you find the Seventh Circuit's explanation of the *TeleTech* holding convincing? Apparently the Second Circuit did not. In *TCPIP Holding Company, Inc. v. Haar Communications, Inc.*, 244 F.3d 88 (2d Cir.2001), the Second Circuit notes that

> the benefits of the [Federal Trademark] Dilution Act are available to owners of a "famous" mark. The Act does not tell *how* famous a mark must be. Nor does it provide any direct guidance as to how courts should answer the question. The word "famous" is susceptible to many widely different understandings. If a hypothetical Grendel's Coffee Shop in Smalltown, U.S.A. has for years been the favorite hangout of Smalltown high school students, Grendel's may well be famous among the students and graduates of Smalltown High. Or another mark for a catalogue selling rare plant specimens may be famous among 100,000 collectors scattered throughout the country. Are those then "famous" marks within the meaning of the statute? The argument might be made that if the plaintiff's mark is "famous" in any sense coming within a dictionary definition, it qualifies for the statute's protection. * * *
>
> It seems most unlikely that Congress intended to confer on marks that have enjoyed only brief fame in a small part of the country, or among a small segment of the population, the power to enjoin all other users throughout the nation in all realms of commerce. The examples of eligible "famous marks" given in the House Report—Dupont, Buick, and Kodak, *see* H.R.Rep. No. 104–374, at 3 (1995), *reprinted in* 1995 U.S.C.C.A.N. 1029, 1030—are marks that for the major part of the century have been household words throughout the United States. They are representative of the best known marks in commerce. Once again, we recognize that examples in a legislative report cannot be taken as defining the limits of a statute's coverage. Putting together the extraordinary

> power the Act confers on a "famous" mark and the improbability that Congress intended to grant such outright exclusivity to marks that are famous in only a small area or segment of the nation, with the hints to be gleaned from the House Report, we think Congress envisioned that marks would qualify as "famous" only if they carried a substantial degree of fame.

TCPIP Holding Company, Inc. v. Haar Communications, Inc., 244 F.3d at 98–99. Is it possible to reconcile the Second and Seventh Circuit discussions of congressional intent? If not, which do you find more convincing?

4. *Actual harm v. likelihood of harm.* A split in the circuits has developed over the issue whether a claim for trademark dilution under the Federal Trademark Dilution Act requires proof of actual harm or merely a showing that harm is likely. In *Ringling Bros.-Barnum & Bailey Combined Shows, Inc. v. Utah Div. of Travel Development*, 170 F.3d 449 (4th Cir.1999), the Fourth Circuit required a showing of actual harm.

By contrast, in *Nabisco, Inc. v. PF Brands, Inc.*, 191 F.3d 208 (2d Cir.1999), the court held that likelihood of future harm is sufficient to support an injunction. How would you resolve this split in the circuits?

5. *A split in the circuits over descriptive trademarks.* Does a trademark have to be inherently distinctive to qualify for protection under the Federal Trademark Dilution Act? In the cases discussed above, none of the marks was descriptive (i.e., none of them had acquired distinctiveness; all were inherently distinctive). Does this mean that descriptive marks that have acquired secondary meaning are not protected under 15 U.S.C. § 1125(c)? That is exactly the conclusion reached by the Second Circuit in *TCPIP Holding Company, Inc. v. Haar Communications, Inc.*, 244 F.3d 88 (2d Cir.2001):

> In order to qualify for the Act's protection, the mark must be famous. By definition, every mark that is famous, in the sense intended by the Act, has a high degree of acquired distinctiveness. Thus, no mark can qualify for the Act's protection without acquired distinctiveness. If that acquired distinctiveness satisfies not only the fame requirement, but also the distinctiveness requirement, then there will never be a case when a court needs to consider whether the mark has inherent distinctiveness. The statute's invitation to courts to consider the mark's degree of inherent distinctiveness would serve no function.
>
> We therefore understand Clause (A) of § 1125(c)(1) to invite two inquiries: (1) Has the plaintiff's mark achieved a sufficient degree of consumer recognition ("acquired distinctiveness") to satisfy the Act's requirement of fame? (2) Does the mark possess a sufficient degree of "inherent distinctiveness" to satisfy the Act's requirement of "distinctive quality." The latter requirement cannot be satisfied by the mere fact that the public has come to associate the mark with the source. Thus, weak, non-distinctive,

descriptive marks do not qualify for the Act's protection, even if famous.

TCPIP Holding Company, Inc. v. Haar Communications, Inc., 244 F.3d at 98. In *Times Mirror Magazines, Inc. v. Las Vegas Sports News, L.L.C.,* 212 F.3d 157 (3d Cir.2000), the Third Circuit reached the opposite conclusion: that a descriptive trademark that had acquired secondary meaning was indeed covered by the Federal Trademark Dilution Act. Rejecting the idea that 15 U.S.C. § 1125(c) involves a test for distinctiveness separate and apart from its test for fame, the Third Circuit noted that

> [t]o be a "mark" eligible in the first place for protection under [§ 1125(c)(1)], basic trademark principles dictate that a designation has to be "distinctive" either inherently or through acquisition of secondary meaning.

4 *McCarthy on Trademarks and Unfair Competition* § 24:91 (footnotes omitted).

McCarthy explains the legislative history behind § 1125(c)(1)'s "distinctive and famous" language:

> The 1987 Trademark Review Commission Report, the genesis of the language contained in the 1996 federal Act, said that the dual mention of both "distinctive and famous" in the introduction to the list of factors was inserted to emphasize the policy goal that to be protected, a mark had to be truly prominent and renowned. The double-barreled language "distinctive and famous" reflected the goal that protection should be confined to marks "which are both distinctive, as established by federal registration at a minimum, and famous, as established by separate evidence." The Commission inserted the term "distinctive" as hyperbole to emphasize the requirement that the mark be registered, for without inherent or acquired distinctiveness, the designation would not have been a mark that should have federally registered in the first place. The Trademark Review Commission Report reveals that the Commission saw distinctiveness and fame as two sides of the same evidentiary coin which requires widespread and extensive customer recognition of the plaintiff's mark. However, when in the 1995 House amendment, the requirement of federal registration was dropped from the Bill, Congress neglected to also drop the mention of "distinctive" introducing the list of factors. Thus, the word "distinctive" was left floating in the statute, unmoored to either any statutory requirement or underlying policy goal.

Id. (footnotes omitted).

Accordingly, we are not persuaded that a mark be subject to separate tests for fame and distinctiveness. * * * Having decided

> that Times Mirror has proved that its mark had gained secondary meaning and a high degree of distinctiveness in the market, there is no necessity for proving an additional test of distinctiveness.

Times Mirror Magazines, Inc. v. Las Vegas Sports News, L.L.C., 212 F.3d at 167–68. Is there a conflict here between the language of the federal statute and the statute's legislative history? Is the statutory language sufficiently unclear so that the Third Circuit's primary reliance on the legislative history is warranted? Which approach makes the most sense to you?

III. Trademark Defenses Online

A. Traditional Fair Use

Brookfield Communications, Inc. v. West Coast Entertainment Corp.

174 F.3d 1036 (9th Cir.1999).

■ O'Scannlain, Circuit Judge:

[The statement of facts and the Lanham Act claims are excerpted in Part I(B), *supra*.]

* * *

Contrary to West Coast's contentions, we are not in any way restricting West Coast's right to use terms in a manner which would constitute fair use under the Lanham Act. *See New Kids on the Block v. News America Pub., Inc.*, 971 F.2d 302, 306–09 (9th Cir.1992); *see also August Storck K.G. v. Nabisco, Inc.*, 59 F.3d 616, 617–18 (7th Cir.1995). It is well established that the Lanham Act does not prevent one from using a competitor's mark truthfully to identify the competitor's goods, *see, e.g., Smith v. Chanel, Inc.*, 402 F.2d 562, 563 (9th Cir.1968) (stating that a copyist may use the originator's mark to identify the product that it has copied), or in comparative advertisements, *see New Kids on the Block*, 971 F.2d at 306–09. This fair use doctrine applies in cyberspace as it does in the real world. *See Radio Channel Networks, Inc. v. Broadcast.Com, Inc.*, No. 98 Civ. 4799, 1999 WL 124455, at *5–*6 (S.D.N.Y. Mar.8, 1999); *Bally Total Fitness Holding Corp. v. Faber*, 29 F.Supp.2d 1161 (C.D.Cal.1998); *Playboy Enterprises, Inc. v. Terri Welles*, 7 F.Supp.2d 1098, 1103–04 (S.D.Cal.1998).

In *Welles*, the case most on point, Playboy sought to enjoin former Playmate of the Year Terri Welles ("Welles") from using "Playmate" or "Playboy" on her website featuring photographs of herself. *See* 7 F.Supp.2d at 1100. Welles's website advertised the fact that she was a former Playmate of the Year, but minimized the use of Playboy's marks; it also contained numerous disclaimers stating that her site was neither endorsed by nor affiliated with Playboy. The district court found that Welles was using "Playboy" and "Playmate" not as trademarks, but rather as descriptive terms fairly and accurately describing her web page, and that her use of "Playboy" and "Playmate" in her website's metatags was a permissible, good faith attempt to index the content of her website. It accordingly concluded that her use was permissible under the trademark laws. *See id.* at 1103–04.[2]

We agree that West Coast can legitimately use an appropriate descriptive term in its metatags. But "MovieBuff" is not such a descriptive term. Even though it differs from "Movie Buff" by only a single space, that difference is pivotal. The term "Movie Buff" is a descriptive term, which is routinely used in the English language to describe a movie devotee. "MovieBuff" is not. The term "MovieBuff" is not in the dictionary. *See Merriam–Webster's Collegiate Dictionary* 762 (10th ed.1998); *American Heritage College Dictionary* 893 (3d ed.1997); *Webster's New World College Dictionary* 889 (3d ed.1997); *Webster's Third New Int'l Dictionary* 1480 (unabridged 1993). Nor has that term been used in any published federal or state court opinion. In light of the fact that it is not a word in the English language, when the term "MovieBuff" *is* employed, it is used to refer to Brookfield's products and services, rather than to mean "motion picture enthusiast." The proper term for the "motion picture enthusiast" is "Movie Buff," which West Coast certainly *can* use. It cannot, however, omit the space.

Moreover, West Coast is not absolutely barred from using the term "MovieBuff." As we explained above, that term can be legitimately used to describe Brookfield's product. For example, its web page might well include an advertisement banner such as "Why pay for MovieBuff when you can get the same thing here for FREE?" which clearly employs "MovieBuff" to refer to Brookfield's products. West Coast, however, presently uses Brookfield's trademark not to reference Brookfield's products, but instead to describe its own product (in the case of the domain name) and to attract people to its website in the case of the metatags. That is not fair use.

* * *

Bihari v. Gross

119 F.Supp.2d 309 (S.D.N.Y.2000).

■ SCHEINDLIN, DISTRICT JUDGE.

[The statement of facts and the Lanham Act claims are excerpted in Part I(B), *supra*.]

* * *

e. The Fair Use Doctrine

Even if the Gross websites cause consumer confusion, use of the "Bihari Interiors" mark in the metatags is protected as a fair use. The

2. [The district court subsequently entered summary judgment in favor of Welles, and the court of appeals affirmed in substantial part. *See Playboy Enterprises, Inc. v. Welles*, 78 F.Supp.2d 1066 (S.D.Cal.1999), *aff'd in part, rev'd in part, & remanded*, 279 F.3d 796 (9th Cir.2002). The appellate decision is excerpted in Part III(B), *infra*.—Eds.]

Lanham Act codified a common law fair use defense in 15 U.S.C. § 1115(b)(4). The fair use doctrine applies to the Internet as readily as to the print media. *See Radio Channel Networks, Inc. v. Broadcast.Com, Inc.*, 98 Civ. 4799, 1999 WL 124455, at **5–6 (S.D.N.Y. Mar.8, 1999) (permitting defendant's fair use of the term "The Radio Channel" on its website, which transmits broadcasts over the Internet, even though plaintiff had registered the service mark "The Radio Channel").

"Fair use is established when the challenged term is a use, otherwise than as a mark, ... of a term or device which is descriptive of and used fairly and in good faith only to describe the goods or services of such party...." 15 U.S.C. § 1115(b)(4). In other words, "fair use permits others to use a protected mark to describe aspects of their own goods." *Car-Freshner Corp. v. S.C. Johnson & Son, Inc.*, 70 F.3d 267, 270 (2d Cir.1995). It is not necessary that the plaintiff's mark be classified as "descriptive" to benefit from the fair use defense. Instead, the central considerations are whether the defendant has used the mark (1) in its descriptive sense, and (2) in good faith. *See id.*

(i) Use of the Term in its Descriptive Sense

The requirement that a trademark be used in its descriptive sense is met where the mark is used in an index or catalog, or to describe the defendant's connection to the business claiming trademark protection. *See Nihon Keizai Shimbun, Inc. v. Comline Bus. Data, Inc.*, 166 F.3d 65, 73–74 (2d Cir.1999) (permitting fair use defense where defendant, a company that gathers news articles and sells "abstracts" summarizing the articles, routinely used the plaintiff's mark in the reference line of its abstracts to identify the source of the article abstracted by the defendant); Restatement (Third) of Unfair Competition § 28 cmt. a (1995) (fair use defense protects a subsequent user's use of a personal name designation "if the name is used solely to indicate truthfully the named person's connection with the goods, services, or business."). Applying this general rule to the metatag context, Professor McCarthy states: "[T]he fair use defense applies ... if another's trademark is used in a meta tag solely to describe the defendant or defendant's goods or services...." 4 J. Thomas McCarthy, *McCarthy on Trademarks and Unfair Competition* ("McCarthy"), § 25:69 at 25–137 (4th ed.1999). This position finds support in recent cases. In *Playboy Enters., Inc. v. Welles*, 7 F.Supp.2d 1098 (S.D.Cal.1998), Playboy sought to enjoin Terri Welles, a former "Playmate of the Month" and "Playmate of the Year", from utilizing the trademarked terms "Playboy" and "Playmate" in the metatags of Welles' website. The court denied the injunction, holding that use of the trademarked terms in the metatags is a fair use. * * * *See also Brookfield Communications*, 174 F.3d at 1066 (stating that West Coast can use Brookfield's trademark on its website to "legitimately ... describe Brookfield's product. For example, [West Coast can] ... include an advertisement banner such as 'Why pay for MovieBuff when you can get the same thing here for FREE?' ").

Here, Gross has included "Bihari Interiors" in the metatags of his websites because the websites provide information about Bihari Interiors and Marianne Bihari. Gross has not used the terms "Bihari Interiors" and "Bihari" in the metatags as a mark, but rather, to fairly identify the content of his websites. In short, Gross uses the "Bihari Interiors" mark in its descriptive sense only.

Moreover, use of the "Bihari Interiors" mark in the metatags of his websites is the only way Gross can get his message to the public. *See Bally Total Fitness,* 29 F.Supp.2d at 1165 ("Prohibiting [the defendant] from using Bally's name in the machine readable code would effectively isolate him from all but the most savvy of Internet users."). A broad rule prohibiting use of "Bihari Interiors" in the metatags of websites not sponsored by Bihari would effectively foreclose all discourse and comment about Bihari Interiors, including fair comment. Courts must be particularly cautious of overextending the reach of the Lanham Act and intruding on First Amendment values. *Cf. Rogers v. Grimaldi,* 875 F.2d 994, 998 (2d Cir.1989) (holding that movie titles using a celebrity's name will not be actionable under the Lanham Act unless the title has no artistic relevance to the underlying work or if the title misleads as to the source or the content of the work); 4 *McCarthy,* § 27:91 at 27–140 ("Whether through the use of statutory interpretation or concern for free speech, traditional protections for commentators and critics on business and commercial affairs must not be jettisoned. It is important to create critical breathing space for legitimate comment and criticism about products and services."). The Second Circuit's warning in a recent Internet case to proceed cautiously when dealing with the frontier of expressive speech on the Internet is particularly instructive:

> In considering whether domain names constitute expressive speech, we observe that the lightning speed development of the Internet poses challenges for the common-law adjudicative process—a process which, ideally while grounded in the past, governs the present and offers direction for the future based on understandings of current circumstances. Mindful of the often unforeseeable impact of rapid technological change, we are wary of making legal pronouncements based on highly fluid circumstances, which almost certainly will give way to tomorrow's new realities.

Name.Space, Inc. v. Network Solutions, Inc., 202 F.3d 573 (2d Cir.2000) (stating that top level domain names may, one day, constitute expressive speech).

(ii) Gross's Good Faith

To benefit from the defense of fair use, Gross must have acted in good faith. The inquiry into a defendant's good faith focuses on whether "the defendant adopted its mark with the intention of capitalizing on plaintiff's reputation and goodwill and any confusion between his and the senior user's product." *Lang v. Retirement Living Pub. Co., Inc.,* 949 F.2d 576, 583 (2d Cir.1991).

Bihari argues, in a conclusory fashion, that Gross did not adopt the "Bihari Interiors" mark in good faith. Rather, Gross intended to divert individuals searching for information about Bihari Interiors to his websites. This argument is not persuasive. Metatags serve as a cataloging system for a search engine. Gross has the right to catalog the contents of his websites. Furthermore, the fact that Gross knew of the prior use of the "Bihari Interiors" mark does not in itself prove a lack of good faith. "[P]rior knowledge of [plaintiff's] trade name does not give rise to a necessary inference of bad faith, because adoption of a trademark with actual knowledge of another's prior registration ... may be consistent with good faith." *Lang,* 949 F.2d at 583–84; Restatement (Third) of Unfair Competition § 28 cmt. d ("Knowledge of a prior trademark use of the term does not in itself prove a lack of good faith.").

In addition, the domain names of the Gross websites and the disclaimer prove that Gross is using "Bihari Interiors" in good faith. The domain names of his websites in no way confuse Internet users into believing that his site is actually that of Bihari Interiors. *See, e.g., Planned Parenthood,* 1997 WL 133313, at **8–10 (defendant's anti-abortion website violates the Lanham Act because, among other reasons, it was registered at "www.plannedparenthood.com", and the site greeted users with "Welcome to the PLANNED PARENTHOOD HOME PAGE"). Moreover, the Gross websites include a disclaimer: "Keep in mind that this site reflects only the view points and experiences of one Manhattan couple...." Although a disclaimer cannot insulate Gross from liability, it indicates good faith use of the service marks and weighs in Gross's favor. *See Consumers Union of United States, Inc. v. General Signal Corp.,* 724 F.2d 1044, 1053 (2d Cir.1983) ("Disclaimers are a favored way of alleviating consumer confusion as to source or sponsorship"). Even if the Gross websites are mean-spirited and vindictive, bad faith cannot be imputed as well to Gross's use of the "Bihari Interiors" mark in the metatags. *See Nihon Keizai Shimbun,* 166 F.3d at 74 (holding that use of plaintiff's mark is in good faith even though "other aspects of defendants' behavior may have evidenced bad faith."). * * *

NOTES & QUESTIONS

1. *Fair use and metatags.* In *Bihari v. Gross,* Gross was successful in his fair use defense, while in *Brookfield Communications v. West Coast Entertainment,* West Coast was not. Why was one successful and the other not? Do both courts understand the fair use defense in the same way? If West Coast Entertainment had had a discussion and critique of the plaintiff's MovieBuff database on its website, would the Ninth Circuit have permitted West Coast to succeed on its fair use defense? Does it matter that the word "MovieBuff" is not a descriptive term that can be found in a dictionary? For a case where a defendant that used an affiliate's trademark as a keyword in a metatag succeeded in its fair use defense, *see Trans Union LLC v. Credit Research, Inc.,* 142 F.Supp.2d 1029 (N.D.Ill.2001).

2. *Fair use and dilution.* Is the fair use defense effective against claims of trademark dilution under 15 U.S.C. § 1125(c)? *See* 15 U.S.C. § 1125(c)(4). Does this provision resolve the question? What if the mark is being used to identify the defendant's goods and services? What if the mark is being used to identify the defendant rather than the defendant's goods and services?

B. NOMINATIVE USE

Playboy Enterprises, Inc. v. Welles

279 F.3d 796 (9th Cir.2002).

■ T.G. NELSON, CIRCUIT JUDGE.

Playboy Enterprises, Inc. (PEI), appeals the district court's grant of summary judgment as to its claims of trademark infringement [and trademark dilution]* * * against Terri Welles [and] Terri Welles, Inc. * * * We have jurisdiction pursuant to 28 U.S.C. § 1291, and we affirm in part and reverse in part. * * *

I. Background

Terri Welles was on the cover of Playboy in 1981 and was chosen to be the Playboy Playmate of the Year for 1981. Her use of the title "Playboy Playmate of the Year 1981," and her use of other trademarked terms on her website are at issue in this suit. During the relevant time period, Welles' website offered information about and free photos of Welles, advertised photos for sale, advertised memberships in her photo club, and promoted her services as a spokesperson. A biographical section described Welles' selection as Playmate of the Year in 1981 and her years modeling for PEI. After the lawsuit began, Welles included discussions of the suit and criticism of PEI on her website and included a note disclaiming any association with PEI.[1]

PEI complains of four different uses of its trademarked terms on Welles' website: (1) the terms "Playboy" and "Playmate" in the metatags of the website; (2) the phrase "Playmate of the Year 1981" on the masthead of the website; (3) the phrases "Playboy Playmate of the Year 1981" and "Playmate of the Year 1981" on various banner ads, which may be transferred to other websites; and (4) the repeated use of the abbreviation "PMOY '81" as the watermark on the pages of the website.[3] PEI

1. The disclaimer reads as follows: "This site is neither endorsed, nor sponsored, nor affiliated with Playboy Enterprises, Inc. PLAYBOY® PLAYMATE OF THE YEAR® AND PLAYMATE OF THE MONTH® ARE REGISTERED trademarks of Playboy Enterprises, Inc."

3. PEI claims that "PMOY" is an unregistered trademark of PEI, standing for "Playmate of the Year."

claimed that these uses of its marks constituted trademark infringement, dilution, false designation of origin, and unfair competition. The district court granted defendants' motion for summary judgment. PEI appeals the grant of summary judgment on its infringement and dilution claims. We affirm in part and reverse in part.

* * *

III. Discussion

A. Trademark Infringement

Except for the use of PEI's protected terms in the wallpaper of Welles' website, we conclude that Welles' uses of PEI's trademarks are permissible, nominative uses. They imply no current sponsorship or endorsement by PEI. Instead, they serve to identify Welles as a past PEI "Playmate of the Year."

We articulated the test for a permissible, nominative use in *New Kids On The Block v. New America Publishing, Inc.*[8] The band, New Kids On The Block, claimed trademark infringement arising from the use of their trademarked name by several newspapers. The newspapers had conducted polls asking which member of the band New Kids On The Block was the best and most popular. The papers' use of the trademarked term did not fall within the traditional fair use doctrine. Unlike a traditional fair use scenario, the defendant newspaper was using the trademarked term to describe not its own product, but the plaintiff's. Thus, the factors used to evaluate fair use were inapplicable. The use was nonetheless permissible, we concluded, based on its nominative nature.

We adopted the following test for nominative use:

> First, the product or service in question must be one not readily identifiable without use of the trademark; second, only so much of the mark or marks may be used as is reasonably necessary to identify the product or service; and third, the user must do nothing that would, in conjunction with the mark, suggest sponsorship or endorsement by the trademark holder.

We noted in *New Kids* that a nominative use may also be a commercial one.

In cases in which the defendant raises a nominative use defense, the above three-factor test should be applied instead of the test for likelihood of

8. 971 F.2d 302 (9th Cir.1992).

confusion set forth in [*AMF Inc. v. Sleekcraft Boats*, 599 F.2d 341 (9th Cir.1979)]. The three-factor test better evaluates the likelihood of confusion in nominative use cases. When a defendant uses a trademark nominally, the trademark will be identical to the plaintiff's mark, at least in terms of the words in question. Thus, application of the *Sleekcraft* test, which focuses on the similarity of the mark used by the plaintiff and the defendant, would lead to the incorrect conclusion that virtually all nominative uses are confusing. The three-factor test—with its requirements that the defendant use marks only when no descriptive substitute exists, use no more of the mark than necessary, and do nothing to suggest sponsorship or endorsement by the mark holder—better addresses concerns regarding the likelihood of confusion in nominative use cases.

We group the uses of PEI's trademarked terms into three for the purpose of applying the test for nominative use. First, we analyze Welles' use of the terms in headlines and banner advertisements. We conclude that those uses are clearly nominative. Second, we analyze the use of the terms in the metatags for Welles' website, which we conclude are nominative as well. Finally, we analyze the terms as used in the wall-paper of the website. We conclude that this use is not nominative and remand for a determination of whether it infringes on a PEI trademark.

1. Headlines and banner advertisements.

To satisfy the first part of the test for nominative use, "the product or service in question must be one not readily identifiable without use of the trademark[.]" This situation arises "when a trademark also describes a person, a place or an attribute of a product" and there is no descriptive substitute for the trademark. In such a circumstance, allowing the trademark holder exclusive rights would allow the language to "be depleted in much the same way as if generic words were protectable." In *New Kids,* we gave the example of the trademarked term, "Chicago Bulls." We explained that "one might refer to the 'two-time world champions' or 'the professional basketball team from Chicago,' but it's far simpler (and more likely to be understood) to refer to the Chicago Bulls." Moreover, such a use of the trademark would "not imply sponsorship or endorsement of the product because the mark is used only to describe the thing, rather than to identify its source." Thus, we concluded, such uses must be excepted from trademark infringement law.

The district court properly identified Welles' situation as one which must also be excepted. No descriptive substitute exists for PEI's trademarks in this context. The court explained:

> [T]here is no other way that Ms. Welles can identify or describe herself and her services without venturing into absurd descriptive phrases. To describe herself as the "nude model selected by Mr. Hefner's magazine as its number-one prototypical woman for the year 1981" would be impractical as well as ineffectual in identifying Terri Welles to the public.

We agree. Just as the newspapers in *New Kids* could only identify the band clearly by using its trademarked name, so can Welles only identify herself clearly by using PEI's trademarked title.

The second part of the nominative use test requires that "only so much of the mark or marks may be used as is reasonably necessary to identify the product or service[.]" *New Kids* provided the following examples to explain this element: "[A] soft drink competitor would be entitled to compare its product to Coca–Cola or Coke, but would not be entitled to use Coca–Cola's distinctive lettering." Similarly, in a past case, an auto shop was allowed to use the trademarked term "Volkswagen" on a sign describing the cars it repaired, in part because the shop "did not use Volkswagen's distinctive lettering style or color scheme, nor did he display the encircled 'VW' emblem." Welles' banner advertisements and headlines satisfy this element because they use only the trademarked words, not the font or symbols associated with the trademarks.

The third element requires that the user do "nothing that would, in conjunction with the mark, suggest sponsorship or endorsement by the trademark holder." As to this element, we conclude that aside from the wallpaper, which we address separately, Welles does nothing in conjunction with her use of the marks to suggest sponsorship or endorsement by PEI. The marks are clearly used to describe the title she received from PEI in 1981, a title that helps describe who she is. It would be unreasonable to assume that the Chicago Bulls sponsored a website of Michael Jordan's simply because his name appeared with the appellation "former Chicago Bull." Similarly, in this case, it would be unreasonable to assume that PEI currently sponsors or endorses someone who describes herself as a "Playboy Playmate of the Year in 1981." The designation of the year, in our case, serves the same function as the "former" in our example. It shows that any sponsorship or endorsement occurred in the past.[25]

In addition to doing nothing in conjunction with her use of the marks to suggest sponsorship or endorsement by PEI, Welles affirmatively disavows any sponsorship or endorsement. Her site contains a clear statement disclaiming any connection to PEI. Moreover, the text of the site describes her ongoing legal battles with the company.[26]

25. We express no opinion regarding whether an individual's use of a current title would suggest sponsorship or endorsement.

26. By noting Welles' affirmative actions, we do not mean to imply that affirmative actions of this type are necessary to establish nominative use. *New Kids* sets forth no such requirement, and we do not impose one here.

For the foregoing reasons, we conclude that Welles' use of PEI's marks in her headlines and banner advertisements is a nominative use excepted from the law of trademark infringement.

2. Metatags.

Welles includes the terms "playboy" and "playmate" in her metatags. Metatags describe the contents of a website using keywords. Some search engines search metatags to identify websites relevant to a search. Thus, when an internet searcher enters "playboy" or "playmate" into a search engine that uses metatags, the results will include Welles' site.[28] Because Welles' metatags do not repeat the terms extensively, her site will not be at the top of the list of search results. Applying the three-factor test for nominative use, we conclude that the use of the trademarked terms in Welles' metatags is nominative.

As we discussed above with regard to the headlines and banner advertisements, Welles has no practical way of describing herself without using trademarked terms. In the context of metatags, we conclude that she has no practical way of identifying the content of her website without referring to PEI's trademarks.

A large portion of Welles' website discusses her association with Playboy over the years. Thus, the trademarked terms accurately describe the contents of Welles' website, in addition to describing Welles. Forcing Welles and others to use absurd turns of phrase in their metatags, such as those necessary to identify Welles, would be particularly damaging in the internet search context. Searchers would have a much more difficult time locating relevant websites if they could do so only by correctly guessing the long phrases necessary to substitute for trademarks. We can hardly expect someone searching for Welles' site to imagine the same phrase proposed by the district court to describe Welles without referring to Playboy—"the nude model selected by Mr. Hefner's organization...." Yet if someone could not remember her name, that is what they would have to do. Similarly, someone searching for critiques of Playboy on the internet would have a difficult time if internet sites could not list the object of their critique in their metatags.

There is simply no descriptive substitute for the trademarks used in Welles' metatags. Precluding their use would have the unwanted effect of hindering the free flow of information on the internet, something which is certainly not a goal of trademark law. Accordingly, the use of trademarked terms in the metatags meets the first part of the test for nominative use.

We conclude that the metatags satisfy the second and third elements of the test as well. The metatags use only so much of the marks as reasonably necessary[30] and nothing is done in conjunction with them to suggest

28. We note that search engines that use their own summaries of websites, or that search the entire text of sites, are also likely to identify Welles' site as relevant to a search for "playboy" or "playmate," given the content of the site.

30. It is hard to imagine how a metatag could use more of a mark than the words sponsorship or endorsement by the trademark holder. We note that our decision might differ if the metatags listed the trademarked term so repeatedly that Welles' site would regularly appear above PEI's in searches for one of the trademarked terms.

3. Wallpaper/watermark.

The background, or wallpaper, of Welles' site consists of the repeated abbreviation "PMOY '81," which stands for "Playmate of the Year 1981." Welles' name or likeness does not appear before or after "PMOY '81." The pattern created by the repeated abbreviation appears as the background of the various pages of the website. Accepting, for the purposes of this appeal, that the abbreviation "PMOY" is indeed entitled to protection, we conclude that the repeated, stylized use of this abbreviation fails the nominative use test.

The repeated depiction of "PMOY '81" is not necessary to describe Welles. "Playboy Playmate of the Year 1981" is quite adequate. Moreover, the term does not even appear to describe Welles—her name or likeness do not appear before or after each "PMOY '81." Because the use of the abbreviation fails the first prong of the nominative use test, we need not apply the next two prongs of the test.

Because the defense of nominative use fails here, and we have already determined that the doctrine of fair use does not apply, we remand to the district court. The court must determine whether trademark law protects the abbreviation "PMOY," as used in the wallpaper.

B. Trademark Dilution

The district court granted summary judgment to Welles as to PEI's claim of trademark dilution. We affirm on the ground that all of Welles' uses of PEI's marks, with the exception of the use in the wallpaper which we address separately, are proper, nominative uses. We hold that nominative uses, by definition, do not dilute the trademarks.

Federal law provides protection against trademark dilution:

> The owner of a famous mark shall be entitled, subject to the principles of equity and upon such terms as the court deems reasonable, to an injunction against another person's commercial use in commerce of a mark or trade name, if such use begins after the mark has become famous and causes dilution of the distinctive quality of the mark....

Dilution, which was not defined by the statute, has been described by the courts as "the gradual 'whittling away' of a trademark's value." * * *

Dilution works its harm not by causing confusion in consumers' minds regarding the source of a good or service, but by creating an association in consumers' minds between a mark and a different good or service. * * *

contained in it, but we recently learned that some search engines are now using pictures. Searching for symbols, such as the Playboy bunny, cannot be far behind. That problem does not arise in this case, however, and we need not address it.

Uses that do not create an improper association between a mark and a new product but merely identify the trademark holder's products should be excepted from the reach of the anti-dilution statute. Such uses cause no harm. The anti-dilution statute recognizes this principle and specifically excepts users of a trademark who compare their product in "commercial advertising or promotion to identify the competing goods or services of the owner of the famous mark."[40]

For the same reason uses in comparative advertising are excepted from anti-dilution law, we conclude that nominative uses are also excepted. A nominative use, by definition, refers to the trademark holder's product. It does not create an improper association in consumers' minds between a new product and the trademark holder's mark.

When Welles refers to her title, she is in effect referring to a product of PEI's. She does not dilute the title by truthfully identifying herself as its one-time recipient any more than Michael Jordan would dilute the name "Chicago Bulls" by referring to himself as a former member of that team, or the two-time winner of an Academy Award would dilute the award by referring to him or herself as a "two-time Academy Award winner." Awards are not diminished or diluted by the fact that they have been awarded in the past. Similarly, they are not diminished or diluted when past recipients truthfully identify themselves as such. It is in the nature of honors and awards to be identified with the people who receive them. Of course, the conferrer of such honors and awards is free to limit the honoree's use of the title or references to the award by contract. So long as a use is nominative, however, trademark law is unavailing.

The one exception to the above analysis in this case is Welles' use of the abbreviation "PMOY" on her wallpaper. Because we determined that this use is not nominative, it is not excepted from the anti-dilution provisions. Thus, we reverse as to this issue and remand for further proceedings. We note that if the district court determines that "PMOY" is not entitled to trademark protection, PEI's claim for dilution must fail. The trademarked term, "Playmate of the Year" is not identical or nearly identical to the term "PMOY." Therefore, use of the term "PMOY" cannot, as a matter of law, dilute the trademark "Playmate of the Year."

* * *

NOTES & QUESTIONS

1. *Traditional fair use vs. nominative use.* Is Welles's use of the trademarks belonging to Playboy Enterprises protected under the traditional fair use defense as well as the nominative use defense? In *Brookfield Communications*, the court appears to suggest that the traditional fair use test privileges Welles's use of these marks when it writes:

> The district court found that Welles was using "Playboy" and "Playmate" not as trademarks, but rather as descriptive terms fairly and accurately describing her web page, and that her use of

40. 15 U.S.C. § 1125(c)(4)(A).

"Playboy" and "Playmate" in her website's metatags was a permissible, good faith attempt to index the content of her website. It accordingly concluded that her use was permissible under the trademark laws.

Is the court in *Brookfield Communications* correct that the marks were being used to describe Welles's website? How else might one view their use?

2. *Reference, necessity and repetition.* The first prong of the nominative use test is that "the product or service in question must be one not readily identifiable without use of the trademark." The Ninth Circuit points out that "[t]he background, or wallpaper, of Welles' site consists of the repeated abbreviation 'PMOY '81,' which stands for 'Playmate of the Year 1981.' " It then concludes that the use of "PMOY '81" as wallpaper fails the first prong of the nominative use test because "[t]he repeated depiction of 'PMOY '81' is not necessary to describe Welles. 'Playboy Playmate of the Year 1981' is quite adequate." Does the court mean that the abbreviation is not necessary because one can use the unabbreviated phrase? Is the court perhaps actually objecting to the repeated use of the abbreviation rather than to the abbreviation itself?

C. GENERICITY

Playboy Enterprises, Inc. v. Netscape Communications Corp.

55 F.Supp.2d 1070 (S.D.Cal.1999).

■ STOTLER, DISTRICT JUDGE.

I. PROCEDURAL BACKGROUND

On April 15, 1999, plaintiff Playboy Enterprises, Inc. ("PEI") filed a Motion for Preliminary Injunction against defendant Netscape Communications Corp. and against defendant Excite, Inc. On May 10, 1999, defendants filed a joint opposition. PEI filed its reply on May 17, 1999. The Court heard oral argument on the motion on May 24, 1999. At the end of the hearing, the Court took the matter under advisement, and ordered the parties to lodge proposed Findings of Fact and Conclusions of Law. Plaintiff lodged its proposed Findings on June 1, 1999; defendants lodged theirs on June 8, 1999. The Court has considered all of the parties' submissions, as well as arguments presented at the hearing.

II. FACTUAL BACKGROUND

Defendants operate search engines on the Internet.[1] When a person searches for a particular topic in either search engine, the search engine

1. The Court notes that Netscape's search engine is co-branded with Excite, and programmed by Excite, but for purposes of this Motion, the Court treats them both as search engine operators.

compiles a list of sites matching or related to the user's search terms, and then posts the list of sites, known as "search results."

Defendants sell advertising space on the search result pages. Known as "banner ads," the advertisements are commonly found at the top of the screen. The ads themselves are often animated and whimsical, and designed to entice the Internet user to "click here." If the user does click on the ad, she is transported to the website of the advertiser.

As with other media, advertisers seek to maximize the efficacy of their ads by targeting consumers matching a certain demographic profile. Savvy website operators accommodate the advertisers by "keying" ads to search terms entered by users. That is, instead of posting ads in a random rotation, defendants program their servers to link a pre-selected set of banner ads to certain "key" search terms. Defendants market this context-sensitive advertising ability as a value-added service and charge a premium.

Defendants key various adult entertainment ads to a group of over 450 terms related to adult entertainment, including the terms "playboy" and "playmate." Plaintiff contends that inclusion of those terms violates plaintiff's trademarks rights in those words.

III. PARTIES' CONTENTIONS

Plaintiff has a trademark on "Playboy®" and "Playmate®." Plaintiff contends that defendants are infringing and diluting its trademarks (1) by marketing and selling the group of over 450 words, including "playboy" and "playmate," to advertisers, (2) by programming the banner ads to run in response to the search terms "playboy" and "playmate" (i.e., "keying"), and (3) by actually displaying the banner ad on the search results page. As a result, plaintiff contends, Internet users are diverted from plaintiff's official website and websites sponsored or approved by plaintiff, which generally will be listed as search results, to other adult entertainment websites. Plaintiff further argues that defendants intend to divert the users to the non-PEI sites. Plaintiff does not contend, however, that defendants infringe or dilute the marks when defendants' search engines generate a list of websites related to "playboy" or "playmate."

Defendants respond that while plaintiff may have a trademark on "Playboy®" and "Playmate®," defendants do not actually "use" the trademarks qua trademarks. Moreover, even if defendants do use the trademarks, defendants argue that a trademark does not confer an absolute property right on all uses of the protected terms, and that defendants' use of the terms is permitted. Finally, defendants dispute that they have any intent to divert users from clicking on search results (such as PEI's sites) to clicking on banner ads.

IV. DISCUSSION

A. Legal Standard for Preliminary Injunction

In order for plaintiff to obtain a preliminary injunction, it "must show either (1) a combination of probable success on the merits and a possibility of irreparable harm, or (2) the existence of serious questions on the merits and the balance of hardships weighing heavily in its favor." *PEI v. Welles*, 7

F.Supp.2d 1098, 1099 (S.D.Cal.1998), *aff'd without opinion,* 162 F.3d 1169, 1998 WL 750954 (9th Cir.1998).

B. *Law and The Internet*

"The Internet is 'a unique and wholly new medium of worldwide human communication.'" *Reno v. ACLU,* 521 U.S. 844 (1997) (citation omitted). The parties and the Court are conversant with the workings of the Internet, as well as with the constantly expanding body of law that seeks to craft a legal contour for it. The Court is mindful of the difficulty of applying well-established doctrines to what can only be described as an amorphous situs of information, anonymous messenger of communication, and seemingly endless stream of commerce. Indeed, the very vastness, and manipulability, of the Internet forms the mainspring of plaintiff's lawsuit.

C. *Trademark Use*

Integral to plaintiff's success on the merits of its case, on either the infringement or dilution theory, is a showing that defendants use plaintiff's trademarks in commerce. Plaintiff does not so show. Rather, plaintiff can only contend that the use of the words "playboy" and "playmate," as keywords or search terms, is equivalent to the use of the trademarks "Playboy®" and "Playmate®." However, it is undisputed that an Internet user cannot conduct a search using the trademark form of the words, i.e., Playboy® and Playmate®. Rather, the user enters the generic word "playboy" or "playmate." It is also undisputed that the words "playboy" and "playmate" are English words in their own right, and that there exist other trademarks on the words wholly unrelated to PEI. Thus, whether the user is looking for goods and services covered by PEI's trademarks or something altogether unrelated to PEI is anybody's guess. Plaintiff guesses that most users searching the Web for "playboy" and "playmate" are indeed looking for PEI sites, goods and services. Based on that theory, plaintiff argues that since defendants also speculate that users searching for "playboy" and "playmate" are looking for things related to Playboy® and Playmate®, defendants use the trademarks when they key competing adult entertainment goods and services to the generic "playboy" and "playmate."

Plaintiff has not shown that defendants use the terms in their trademark form, i.e., Playboy® and Playmate®, when marketing to advertisers or in the algorithm that effectuates the keying of the ads to the keywords. Thus, plaintiff's argument that defendants "use" plaintiff's trademarks falls short.

D. *Trademark Infringement* * * *

Even if use of the generic "playboy" and "playmate" were construed to use the trademark terms Playboy® and Playmate®, plaintiff still must show that the use violates trademark law. Plaintiff has asserted * * * trademark infringement * * *

1. *Infringement*

"The core element of trademark infringement is the likelihood of confusion, i.e., whether the similarity of the marks is likely to confuse customers about the source of the products.'' *Official Airline Guides, Inc. v. Goss,* 6 F.3d 1385, 1391 (9th Cir.1993). Assuming arguendo that defendants' use of ''playboy'' and ''playmate'' is use of plaintiff's marks, plaintiff must still show that confusion is likely to result from that use. Plaintiff has not so shown.

Rather, plaintiff relies on the recent case from the Court of Appeals for the Ninth Circuit, *Brookfield Communications, Inc. v. West Coast Entertainment Corp.,* 174 F.3d 1036, 1062–64 (9th Cir.1999), for the proposition that defendants cause ''initial interest confusion'' by the use of the words ''playboy'' and ''playmate.'' Initial interest confusion, as coined by the Ninth Circuit, is a brand of confusion particularly applicable to the Internet. Generally speaking, initial interest confusion may result when a user conducts a search using a trademark term and the results of the search include websites not sponsored by the holder of the trademark search term, but rather of competitors. *Id.* The Ninth Circuit reasoned that the user may be diverted to an unsponsored site, and only realize that she has been diverted upon arriving at the competitor's site. Once there, however, even though the user knows she is not in the site initially sought, she may stay. In that way, the competitor has captured the trademark holder's potential visitors or customers. *Id.*

Brookfield is distinguishable from this case, and where applicable, supportive of defendants' position.

First, the trademark at issue in *Brookfield* was not an English word in its own right. In *Brookfield,* the Court compared Brookfield's trademark ''MovieBuff'' with competitor West Coast's use of the domain name ''moviebuff.com,'' and found them to be ''essentially identical'' despite the differences in capitalization, which the Court considered ''inconsequential in light of the fact that Web addresses are not caps-sensitive . . .'' *Id.* at 1054. However, the Court held that West Coast could use the term ''Movie Buff'' (or, presumably, ''movie buff'') with the space, as such is the ''proper term for the 'motion picture enthusiast'. . . . It cannot, however, omit the space.'' *Id.* at 1065. On the other hand, ''[i]n light of the fact that it is not a word in the English language, when the term 'MovieBuff' is employed, it is used to refer to Brookfield's products and services, rather than to mean 'motion picture enthusiast.' '' *Id.* at 1065.

As English words, ''playboy'' and ''playmate'' cannot be said to suggest sponsorship or endorsement of either the websites that appear as search results (as in *Brookfield*) or the banner ads that adorn the search results page. Although the trademark terms and the English language words are undisputedly identical, which, presumably, leads plaintiff to believe that the use of the English words is akin to use of the trademarks, the holder of a trademark may not remove a word from the English language merely by acquiring trademark rights in it. *Id.*

Second, the use by defendant of plaintiff's trademark in *Brookfield* was more suspect because the parties compete in the same market—as online providers of film industry information. *See Id.,* at 1056–57 (''[n]ot only are they not non-competitors, the competitive proximity of their products is actually quite high"). The Ninth Circuit analogized the capture of unsuspecting Internet users by a competitor to highways and billboards:

> Suppose West Coast's competitor ... puts up a billboard on a highway reading—"West Coast Video: 2 miles ahead at Exit 7"—where West Coast is really located at Exit 8 but Blockbuster is located at Exit 7. Customers looking for West Coast's store will pull off at Exit 7 and drive around looking for it. Unable to locate West Coast, but seeing the Blockbuster store right by the highway entrance, they may simply rent there.

Brookfield, at 1064. Although the customer is not confused as to where she ultimately rents a video, Blockbuster has misappropriated West Coast's goodwill through causing initial consumer confusion. *Id.* The customer has been captured by the competitor in much the same way that defendant in *Brookfield* captures Internet users looking for plaintiff's website.

Here, the analogy is quite unlike that of a devious placement of a road sign bearing false information. This case presents a scenario more akin to a driver pulling off the freeway in response to a sign that reads "Fast Food Burgers" to find a well-known fast food burger restaurant, next to which stands a billboard that reads: "Better Burgers: 1 Block Further." The driver, previously enticed by the prospect of a burger from the well-known restaurant, now decides she wants to explore other burger options. Assuming that the same entity owns the land on which both the burger restaurant and the competitor's billboard stand, should that entity be liable to the burger restaurant for diverting the driver? That is the rule PEI contends the Court should adopt. * * *

CONCLUSION

Accordingly, and for the foregoing reasons, the plaintiff's motion is denied. * * *

NOTES & QUESTIONS

1. *Keywords and domain names.* Central to the court's decision in *Playboy v. Netscape Communications Corp.* is its conclusion that the Plaintiff has not shown that "defendants use plaintiff's trademarks in commerce." The court argues that the words "playboy" and "playmate" are different from the registered trademarks Playboy® and Playmate® and that plaintiffs have only shown that defendants have keyed banner ads to the former. The court notes that technical limitations on the search technologies prevent the use of registered trademarks as keywords—one cannot include the registered trademark symbol ® in a search. Do you find this argument convincing? If I had registered the domain name playboy.com, would I be liable for trademark infringement? After all, the domain name playboy.com is different from the domain name Playboy®.com. Is there any reason why domain names and keywords should be treated differently?

2. *Searching for Playboy.* The court in *Playboy v. Netscape Communications Corp.* states that "whether the user [of a search engine] is looking for goods and services covered by [Playboy Enterprises'] trademarks or something altogether unrelated is anybody's guess." Reacting to this and similar statements in the opinion, one commentator has stated:

> In the author's opinion, it is highly unlikely that a teenage boy typing the word "playboy" in a search engine does not intend to look for information about the magazine, Playmate of the Month and all of the other products of Playboy Enterprises. I think that it is highly probable that most teenage boys have never even heard of the generic dictionary meaning of "playboy" as "a wealthy, carefree man who devotes most of his time to leisure, self-amusement and hedonistic pleasures, conventionally frequenting parties and night clubs, romancing a rapid succession of attractive young women and racing speedboats or sports cars."[3] Thus, the Playboy decision did not really grapple with the substantive issues raised by the sale of banner advertising.

4 J. THOMAS MCCARTHY, MCCARTHY ON TRADEMARKS AND UNFAIR COMPETITION § 25:70.1 (4th ed.2002). Do you agree with this analysis? Do you think the result would have been different if the court had found as a fact that most people using the search term "playboy" were searching for the goods and services of Playboy Enterprises, Inc.?

3. *Banner ads keyed to trademark.* Ought we to recognize a redressable harm to a trademark owner when a search engine keys a banner ad to the owner's trademark? How would you characterize this harm? Given that the average search engine user does not know that banner ads may be keyed to likely search terms, is there any likelihood of confusion regarding origin, sponsorship, or affiliation sufficient to support a claim of trademark infringement? If the trademark is famous, given that the average user does not associate the appearance of a particular banner ad with the entry of a particular search term, is keying this banner ad to a trademark dilutive of that mark in any way? Is either the search engine or the producer of the banner ad trading on the goodwill associated with the trademark to which the banner ad is keyed?

4. *Keyed relevancy rankings.* Is any harm suffered by a trademark owner when a search engine awards a higher relevancy ranking to a website when that owner's trademark is used in a search? Does it matter whether the search engine charges a fee for this higher ranking?

D. FIRST AMENDMENT

Planned Parenthood Federation of America, Inc. v. Bucci

42 U.S.P.Q.2d (BNA) 1430 (S.D.N.Y.1997).

■ KIMBA M. WOOD, DISTRICT JUDGE.

Plaintiff Planned Parenthood Federation of America, Inc. ("Planned Parenthood") has moved to preliminarily enjoin defendant Richard Bucci

3. Random House Unabridged Dictionary of the English Language 1104 (1983 rev.).

("Bucci"), doing business as Catholic Radio, from using the domain name "plannedparenthood.com," and from identifying his web site on the Internet under the name "www.plannedparenthood.com." The Court held a hearing on February 20, 1997 and February 21, 1997, and now issues the preliminary injunction sought by Planned Parenthood.

I. Undisputed Facts

The parties do not dispute the following facts. Plaintiff Planned Parenthood, founded in 1922, is a non-profit, reproductive health care organization that has used its present name since 1942. Plaintiff registered the stylized service mark "Planned Parenthood" on the Principal Register of the United States Patent and Trademark Office on June 28, 1955, and registered the block service mark "Planned Parenthood" on the Principal Register of the United States Patent and Trademark Office on September 9, 1975. Plaintiff's 146 separately incorporated affiliates, in 48 states and the District of Columbia, are licensed to use the mark "Planned Parenthood." Plaintiff expends a considerable sum of money in promoting and advertising its services. The mark "Planned Parenthood" is strong and incontestable.

Plaintiff operates a web site at "www.ppfa.org," using the domain name "ppfa.org." Plaintiff's home page offers Internet users resources regarding sexual and reproductive health, contraception and family planning, pregnancy, sexually transmitted diseases, and abortion, as well as providing links to other relevant web sites. In addition, plaintiff's home page offers Internet users suggestions on how to get involved with plaintiff's mission and solicits contributions.

Defendant Bucci is the host of "Catholic Radio," a daily radio program broadcast on the WVOA radio station in Syracuse, New York. Bucci is an active participant in the anti-abortion movement. Bucci operates web sites at "www.catholicradio.com" and at "lambsofchrist.com." On August 28, 1996, Bucci registered the domain name "plannedparenthood.com" with Network Solutions, Inc. ("NSI"), a corporation that administers the assignment of domain names on the Internet. After registering the domain name, Bucci set up a web site and home page on the Internet at the address "www.plannedparenthood.com."

Internet users who type in the address "www.plannedparenthood.com," or who use a search engine such as Yahoo! or Lycos to find web sites containing the term "planned parenthood," can reach Bucci's web site and home page. Once a user accesses Bucci's home page, she sees on the computer screen the words "Welcome to the PLANNED PARENTHOOD HOME PAGE!" These words appear on the screen first, because the text of a home page downloads from top to bottom. Tr. 2/20/97 at 47. Once the whole home page has loaded, the user sees a scanned image of the cover of a book entitled *The Cost of Abortion,* by Lawrence Roberge ("Roberge"), under which appear several links: "Foreword," "Afterword," "About the Author," "Book Review," and "Biography."

After clicking on a link, the user accesses text related to that link. By clicking on "Foreword" or "Afterword," the Internet user simply accesses the foreword or afterword of the book *The Cost of Abortion.* That text eventually reveals that *The Cost of Abortion* is an anti-abortion book. The text entitled "About the Author" contains the curriculum vitae of author Roberge. It also notes that "Mr. Roberge is available for interview and speaking engagements," and provides his telephone number. The "Book Review" link brings the Internet user to a selection of quotations by various people endorsing *The Cost of Abortion.* Those quotations include exhortations to read the book and obtain the book. "Biography" offers more information about Roberge's background.

II. Disputed Facts

The parties dispute defendant's motive in choosing plaintiff's mark as his domain name. Plaintiff alleges that defendant used plaintiff's mark with the "specific intent to damage Planned Parenthood's reputation and to confuse unwitting users of the Internet." Pl. Rep. Mem. at 2. Discussing the difference between the domain name at issue here and defendant's other web sites, defendant's counsel states that "[t]he WWWPLANNNED-PARENTHOOD.COM [sic] website ... enables Defendant's message to reach a broader audience." Def. Mem. in Opp. at 3. Defendant's counsel made the following statement to the Court regarding defendant's use of plaintiff's mark to designate his web site:

> My belief is that it was intended to reach people who would be sympathetic to the proabortion position.... [I]t is an effort to get the ... political and social message to people we might not have been otherwise able to reach. I think it's analogous to putting an advertisement in the New York Times rather than The National Review. You are more likely to get people who are sympathetic to the proabortion position, and that's who you want to reach. I believe that is exactly what Mr. Bucci did when he selected Planned Parenthood. Tr. 2/5/97 at 23.

Defendant did not dispute that his counsel was correct in that statement. Tr. 2/21/97 at 35. Defendant's counsel also admitted that Bucci was trying to reach Internet users who thought, in accessing his web site, that they would be getting information from plaintiff. *Id.* at 23–24.

* * *

2. The First Amendment Exception

Defendant also argues that his use of the "planned parenthood" mark is protected by the First Amendment. As defendant argues, trademark infringement law does not curtail or prohibit the exercise of the First Amendment right to free speech. I note that plaintiff has not sought, in any way, to restrain defendant from speech that criticizes Planned Parenthood or its mission, or that discusses defendant's beliefs regarding reproduction, family, and religion. The sole purpose of the Court's inquiry has been to determine whether the use of the "planned parenthood" mark as defendant's domain name and home page address constitutes an infringement of plaintiff's trademark. Defendant's use of another entity's mark is entitled to First Amendment protection when his use of that mark is part of a communicative message, not when it is used to identify the source of a product. *Yankee Publishing. Inc. v. News America Publishing, Inc.,* 809 F.Supp. 267, 275 (S.D.N.Y.1992). By using the mark as a domain name and home page address and by welcoming Internet users to the home page with the message "Welcome to the Planned Parenthood Home Page!" defendant identifies the web site and home page as being the product, or forum, of plaintiff. I therefore determine that, because defendant's use of the term "planned parenthood" is not part of a communicative message, his infringement on plaintiff's mark is not protected by the First Amendment.

Defendant argues that his use of the "Planned Parenthood" name for his web site is entitled to First Amendment protection, relying primarily on the holding of *Yankee Publishing,* 809 F.Supp. at 275. In that case, Judge Leval noted that the First Amendment can protect unauthorized use of a trademark when such use is part of an expression of a communicative message: "the Second Circuit has construed the Lanham Act narrowly when the unauthorized use of the trademark is for the purpose of a communicative message, rather than identification of product origin." *Id.* Defendant argues that his use of the "Planned Parenthood" name for his web site is a communicative message.

However, *Yankee Publishing* carefully draws a distinction between communicative messages and product labels or identifications:

> When another's trademark ... is used without permission for the purpose of source identification, the trademark law generally prevails over the First Amendment. Free speech rights do not extend to labelling or advertising products in a manner that conflicts with the trademark rights of others.

Id. at 276. Defendant offers no argument in his papers as to why the Court should determine that defendant's use of "plannedparenthood.com" is a communicative message rather than a source identifier. His use of "plannedparenthood.com" as a domain name to identify his web site is on its face more analogous to source identification than to a communicative message; in essence, the name identifies the web site, which contains defendant's home page. The statement that greets Internet users who access defendant's web site, "Welcome to the Planned Parenthood Home Page," is also more analogous to an identifier than to a communication. For those reasons, defendant's use of the trademarked term "planned parenthood" is not part of a communicative message, but rather, serves to identify a product or item, defendant's web site and home page, as originating from Planned Parenthood.

Defendant's use of plaintiff's mark is not protected as a title under *Rogers v. Grimaldi,* 875 F.2d 994, 998 (2d Cir.1989). There, the Court of Appeals determined that the title of the film "Ginger and Fred" was not a misleading infringement, despite the fact that the film was not about Ginger Rogers and Fred Astaire, because of the artistic implications of a title. The Court of Appeals noted that "[f]ilmmakers and authors frequently rely on word-play, ambiguity, irony, and allusion in titling their works." *Id.* The Court of Appeals found that the use of a title such as the one at issue in *Rogers* was acceptable "unless the title has no artistic relevance to the underlying work"; even when the title has artistic relevance, it may not be used to "explicitly mislead[ ] [the consumer] as to the source or content of the work." *Id.* Here, even treating defendant's domain name and home page address as titles, rather than as source identifiers, I find that the title "plannedparenthood.com" has no artistic implications, and that the title is being used to attract some consumers by misleading them as to the web site's source or content. Given defendant's testimony indicating that he knew, and intended, that his use of the domain name "plannedparenthood.com" would cause some "pro-abortion" Internet users to access his web site, Tr. 2/21/97 at 36, he cannot demonstrate that his use of "planned parenthood" is entitled to First Amendment protection.

* * *

Bally Total Fitness Holding Corp. v. Faber

29 F.Supp.2d 1161 (C.D.Cal.1998).

■ PREGERSON, DISTRICT JUDGE.

Andrew S. Faber's motion for summary judgment came before the Court for oral argument on November 23, 1998. After reviewing and considering the materials submitted by the parties and hearing oral argument, the Court GRANTS Faber's motion for summary judgment.

BACKGROUND

Bally Total Fitness Holding Corp. ("Bally") brings this action for trademark infringement, unfair competition, and dilution against Andrew S. Faber ("Faber") in connection with Bally's federally registered trademarks and service marks in the terms "Bally," "Bally's Total Fitness," and "Bally Total Fitness," including the name and distinctive styles of these marks. Bally is suing Faber based on his use of Bally's marks in a website he designed.

Faber calls his site "Bally sucks." The website is dedicated to complaints about Bally's health club business. When the website is accessed, the viewer is presented with Bally's mark with the word "sucks" printed across it. Immediately under this, the website states "Bally Total Fitness Complaints! Un–Authorized."

Faber has several websites in addition to the "Bally sucks" site. The domain in which Faber has placed his websites is "www.compupix.com." Faber's other websites within "www.compupix.com" include the "Bally sucks" site (URL address "www.compupix.com/ballysucks"); "Images of Men," a website displaying and selling photographs of nude males (URL address "www.compupix.com/index.html"); a website containing information regarding the gay community (URL address "www.compupix.com/gay"); a website containing photographs of flowers and landscapes (URL address "www.compupix.com/fl/index.html"); and a website advertising "Drew Faber Web Site Services" (URL address "www.compupix.com/biz.htm").

On April 22, 1998, Bally applied for a temporary restraining order directing Faber to withdraw his website from the Internet. Bally represents that when its application for a TRO was initially filed, the "Bally sucks" site contained a direct link to Faber's "Images of Men" site. In his opposition to the application for a TRO, Faber indicated that this link had been removed. The Court denied Bally's application on April 30, 1998.

Bally brought a motion for summary judgment on its claims of trademark infringement, trademark dilution, and unfair competition which the Court denied on October 20, 1998. In that order, the Court ordered Faber to bring a motion for summary judgment. This motion is now before the Court.

DISCUSSION

* * *

g. *Defendant's intent in selecting the mark*

Here, Faber purposely chose to use Bally's mark to build a "web site that is 'dedicated to complaint, issues, problems, beefs, grievances, grumblings, accusations, and gripes with Bally Total Fitness health clubs.'" Faber, however, is exercising his right to publish critical commentary about Bally. He cannot do this without making reference to Bally.[4] In this regard, Professor McCarthy states:

> The main remedy of the trademark owner is not an injunction to suppress the message, but a rebuttal to the message. As Justice Brandeis long ago stated, "If there be time to expose through discussion the falsehood and fallacies, to avert the evil by the process of education, the remedy to be applied is more speech, not enforced silence."

5 McCarthy, § 31:148 at 31–216.

4. Bally concedes that Faber has some right to use Bally's name as part of his consumer commentary. However, Bally argues that Faber uses more than is necessary when making his commentary and that he has alternative means of communication. Specifically, Bally argues that Faber could use the name "Bally" or "Bally Total Fitness" in block lettering without using Bally's stylized "B" mark or distinctive script. This argument, however, would create an artificial distinction that does not exist under trademark law. Trademarks are defined broadly to include both names and stylized renditions of those names or other symbols. 15 U.S.C. §§ 1051, 1127 (1997). Furthermore, the purpose of a trademark is to identify the source of goods. *Id.* § 1127. An individual who wishes to engage in consumer commentary must have the full range of marks that the trademark owner has to identify the trademark owner as the object of the criticism. (*See infra* Part I–C.)

Applying Bally's argument would extend trademark protection to eclipse First Amendment rights. The courts, however, have rejected this approach by holding that trademark rights may be limited by First Amendment concerns. *See L.L. Bean, Inc. v. Drake Publishers, Inc.,* 811 F.2d 26 (1st Cir.), *cert. denied,* 483 U.S. 1013 (1987).

* * *

C. *Trademark Dilution*

* * *

[T]he courts have held that trademark owners may not quash unauthorized use of the mark by a person expressing a point of view. *See L.L. Bean,* 811 F.2d at 29, *citing Lucasfilm Ltd. v. High Frontier,* 622 F.Supp. 931, 933–35 (D.D.C.1985). This is so even if the opinion may come in the form of a commercial setting. *See Id.* at 33 (discussing Maine's anti-dilution statute). In *L.L. Bean,* the First Circuit held that a sexually-oriented parody of L.L. Bean's catalog in a commercial adult-oriented magazine was noncommercial use of the trademark. *See Id.* The court stated:

> If the anti-dilution statute were construed as permitting a trademark owner to enjoin the use of his mark in a noncommercial context found to be negative or offensive, then a corporation could shield itself from criticism by forbidding the use of its name in commentaries critical of its conduct. The legitimate aim of the anti-dilution statute is to prohibit the unauthorized use of another's trademark in order to market incompatible products or services. The Constitution does not, however, permit the range of the anti-dilution statute to encompass the unauthorized use of a trademark in a noncommercial setting such as an editorial or artistic context.

Id.

Here, Bally wants to protect its valuable marks and ensure that they are not tarnished or otherwise diluted. This is an understandable goal. However, for the reasons set forth above, Faber's "Bally sucks" site is not a commercial use.

Even if Faber's use of Bally's mark is a commercial use, Bally also cannot show tarnishment. Bally cites several cases such as the "Enjoy Cocaine" and "Mutant of Omaha" cases for the proposition that this site and its relationship to other sites tarnishes their mark. *See Mutual of Omaha Ins. Co. v. Novak,* 648 F.Supp. 905 (D.Neb.1986) (discussing both infringement and disparagement), *aff'd* 836 F.2d 397 (8th Cir.1987) (addressing infringement, but not disparagement); *Coca–Cola v. Gemini Rising, Inc.,* 346 F.Supp. 1183 (E.D.N.Y.1972).

There are, however, two flaws with Bally's argument. First, none of the cases that Bally cites involve consumer commentary. In *Coca–Cola,* the court enjoined the defendant's publication of a poster stating "Enjoy Cocaine" in the same script as Coca–Cola's trademark. *See Coca–Cola,* 346 F.Supp. at 1192. Likewise, in *Mutual of Omaha,* the court prohibited the use of the words "Mutual of Omaha," with a picture of an emaciated human head resembling the Mutual of Omaha's logo on a variety of products as a means of protesting the arms race. *See Mutual of Omaha,* 836 F.2d at 398. Here, however, Faber is using Bally's mark in the context of a consumer commentary to say that Bally engages in business practices which Faber finds distasteful or unsatisfactory. This is speech protected by the First Amendment. *See L.L. Bean,* 811 F.2d at 29; McCarthy, § 24:105 at 24–191. As such, Faber can use Bally's mark to identify the source of the goods or services of which he is complaining. This use is necessary to maintain broad opportunities for expression. *See Restatement (Third) of Unfair Competition* § 25(2), cmt. i (1995) (stating "extension of the antidilution statutes to protect against damaging nontrademark uses raises substantial free speech issues and duplicates other potential remedies better suited to balance the relevant interests").

* * *

Name.Space, Inc. v. Network Solutions, Inc.

202 F.3d 573 (2d Cir.2000).

■ KATZMANN, CIRCUIT JUDGE:

[Plaintiff Name.Space, Inc. set up an alternative system of domain names, including 530 new global top-level domains ("gTLDs") that were not included within the official domain name system. Some of the new domain names, such as ".forpresident," ".formayor," and ".microsoft.free.zone," had arguably expressive content, contrasting in that respect with the existing three-letter gTLDs, such as .com, .net, and .org. Name.Space asked Network Solutions, Inc. ("NSI"), then the sole domain-name registrar, to include references to the new gTLDs in the zone files of the root servers that it maintained, which would make the new gTLDs available to virtually all Internet users, but NSI refused. Name.Space filed an action against NSI, charging it with antitrust violations. NSI then sought authorization from the National Science Foundation, the federal agency that then supervised the domain name system, to comply with Name.Space's request, but NSF declined, whereupon Name.Space added NSF as a defendant. In one count of the complaint, Name.Space alleged that by refusing to incorporate the new gTLDs into the domain name system, NSF had infringed its rights under the First Amendment. In the following excerpt the court discusses the First Amendment claim.]

* * *

II. First Amendment

Name.Space challenges the district court's holding that it "has not met the burden of demonstrating that the three letter top level domain portion of an Internet domain name is expressive speech." *PGMedia,* 51 F.Supp.2d at 407 (*citing Clark v. Community for Creative Non–Violence,* 468 U.S. 288, 293 n. 5 (1984)). Although we affirm the district court's dismissal of Name.Space's First Amendment claims, we do so for different reasons. "We may, of course, affirm on any basis for which there is a record sufficient to permit conclusions of law, including grounds upon which the district court did not rely." *Cromwell Assocs. v. Oliver Cromwell Owners, Inc.,* 941 F.2d 107, 111 (2d Cir.1991) (citations omitted).

In considering whether domain names constitute expressive speech, we observe that the lightning speed development of the Internet poses challenges for the common-law adjudicative process—a process which, ideally while grounded in the past, governs the present and offers direction for the future based on understandings of current circumstances. Mindful of the often unforeseeable impact of rapid technological change, we are wary of making legal pronouncements based on highly fluid circumstances, which almost certainly will give way to tomorrow's new realities. *Cf. Columbia Broad. Sys., Inc. v. Democratic Nat'l Comm.,* 412 U.S. 94, 102 (1973) ("The problems of regulation are rendered more difficult because the broadcast industry is dynamic in terms of technological change; solutions adequate a decade ago are not necessarily so now, and those acceptable today may well be outmoded 10 years hence."). "A law that changes every day is worse than no law at all." LON L. FULLER, THE MORALITY OF LAW 37, 79–81 (rev. ed.1969).

The district court adopted an analogy between Internet alphanumeric addresses and telephone numbers, and held that domain names are akin to source identifiers rather than to communicative messages. *See PGMedia,* 51 F.Supp.2d at 407–08. We disagree. It is certainly true that while "[i]t is possible to find some kernel of expression in almost every activity a person undertakes[,] ... such a kernel is not sufficient to bring the activity within the protection of the First Amendment." *City of Dallas v. Stanglin,* 490 U.S. 19, 25 (1989). Further, the district court is not alone in suggesting that an analogy between Internet domain names and telephone number mnemonics (for example, 1–800–FLOWERS) may be appropriate. *See, e.g., Panavision Int'l, L.P. v. Toeppen,* 141 F.3d 1316, 1325 (9th Cir.1998) (comparing domain name to 1–800–HOLIDAY); *PGMedia,* 51 F.Supp.2d at 407–08 (citing cases). However, the nature of domain names is not susceptible to such a uniform, monolithic characterization. As the Supreme Court has stated in an analogous and related context, "aware as we are of the changes taking place in the law, the technology, and the industrial structure related to telecommunications, ... we believe it unwise and unnecessary definitively to pick one analogy or one specific set of words now."[12] *Denver Area Educ. Telecomms. Consortium, Inc. v. Federal Communications Comm'n,* 518 U.S. 727, 742 (1996) (Breyer, J., plurality) (citations omitted). The existing gTLDs are not protected speech, but only because the current DNS and Amendment No. 11 limit them to three-letter afterthoughts such as .com and .net, which are lacking in expressive content. The district court did not address the possibility that longer and more contentful gTLDs like ".jones_for_president" and ".smith_for_senate" may constitute protected speech, such as political speech or parody. *See, e.g., Cliffs Notes, Inc. v. Bantam Doubleday Dell Publ'g Group, Inc.,* 886 F.2d

12. Therefore, different analogies, including analogies to book and movie titles, street addresses, and telephone numbers may be appropriate in different circumstances.

490, 493 (2d Cir.1989) (noting that title of book "Spy Notes" is parody constituting protected speech); *Rogers v. Grimaldi,* 875 F.2d 994, 998 (2d Cir.1989) (holding that title of movie "Ginger and Fred" contained "expressive element" implicating First Amendment).

The Internet in general, and the DNS in particular, is marked by extraordinary plasticity. The DNS has already undergone considerable change in the Internet's brief history to date, and may undergo even more radical changes in the near future under the auspices of ICANN and DNSO. There is nothing inherent in the architecture of the Internet that prevents new gTLDs from constituting expressive speech. How broad the permissible bandwidth of expression is in this context depends on the future direction of the DNS. Therefore, "we should be shy about saying the final word today about what will be accepted as reasonable tomorrow," particularly "when we know too little to risk the finality of precision." *Denver Area,* 518 U.S. at 777–78 (Souter, J., concurring).

Further, the functionality of domain names does not automatically place them beyond the reach of the First Amendment. Although domain names do have a functional purpose, whether the mix of functionality and expression is "sufficiently imbued with the elements of communication" depends on the domain name in question, the intentions of the registrant, the contents of the website, and the technical protocols that govern the DNS. *Spence v. Washington,* 418 U.S. 405, 409–10 (1974) ("[T]he context in which a symbol is used for purposes of expression is important, for the context may give meaning to the symbol." (citation omitted)). Functionality and expression are therefore not mutually exclusive: for example, automobile license plates have a functional purpose, but that function can be served as well by vanity plates, which in a small way can also be expressive. Similarly, domain names may be employed for a variety of communicative purposes with both functional and expressive elements, ranging from the truly mundane street address or telephone number-like identification of the specific business that is operating the website, to commercial speech and even core political speech squarely implicating First Amendment concerns.

In short, while we hold that the existing gTLDs do not constitute protected speech under the First Amendment, we do not preclude the possibility that certain domain names and new gTLDs, could indeed amount to protected speech. The time may come when new gTLDs could be used for "an expressive purpose such as commentary, parody, news reporting or criticism," comprising communicative messages by the author and/or operator of the website in order to influence the public's decision to visit that website, or even to disseminate a particular point of view. *United We Stand Am., Inc. v. United We Stand Am. N. Y., Inc.,* 128 F.3d 86, 93 (2d Cir.1997) (citation omitted).

We do not view *Planned Parenthood Federation of America v. Bucci* as holding to the contrary. *See* No. 97 Civ. 0629, 1997 WL 133313, at *10–11 (S.D.N.Y. Mar. 24, 1997), *aff'd,* 152 F.3d 920 (2d Cir.1998) (unpublished table decision). In *Bucci,* a trademark infringement case, the court held that the defendant's particular use of the domain name "plannedparenthood.com" was as a "source identifier" rather than a "communicative message," while leaving open the possibility that a domain name could constitute such a message under other circumstances. *See id.* In reaching this conclusion, the *Bucci* court conducted precisely the kind of particularistic, context-sensitive analysis that is appropriate here, including analyses of the domain name itself, the way the domain name is being used, the motivations of the author of the website in question, the contents of the website, and so on. *See id.* Domain names and gTLDs *per se* are neither automatically entitled to nor excluded from the protections of the First Amendment, and the appropriate inquiry is one that fully addresses particular circumstances presented with respect to each domain name.

NOTES & QUESTIONS

1. *Communication vs. source identification. Planned Parenthood v. Bucci* sets out the rule that a defendant's "use of another entity's mark is entitled to First Amendment protection when his use of that mark is part of a communicative message, not when it is used to identify the source of a product." It held that the defendant's use of "plannedparenthood.com" was not expressive. If the defendant had instead registered "plannedparenthoodsucks.com," would the case have come out the other way?

2. *Trademark as part of a URL.* In *Bally v. Faber*, the defendant used plaintiff's trademark not as part of the domain name, which is compupix.com, but rather as a subdirectory under that domain, www.compupix.com/ballysucks. Does the trademark serve as a source identifier when used in this role? Does the court recognize any distinction between use of the trademark in the URL, and use of it in the text of the website? Recognizing that the plaintiff was entitled to identify Bally as the target of its criticism, was it entitled to do so by including its trademark in the URL?

3. *Trademarks as purchasable search terms.* In *Playboy Enterprises, Inc. v. Netscape Communications Corp.*, 55 F.Supp.2d 1070 (C.D.Cal.1999), excerpted in Part III(C), *supra.*, Playboy challenged the defendant's use of its trademarks "Playboy" and "Playmate" as purchasable keywords in connection with its search engine. The court held that this use of the trademarked terms did not infringe or dilute them. It had this to say about the First Amendment implications of upholding the claims that Playboy advanced:

> Here, PEI is seeking to leverage its trademarks "Playboy®" and "Playmate®" (which cannot be searched on the Internet) into a monopoly on the *words* "playboy" and "playmate." Indeed, by seeking a prohibition on all advertisements that appear in response to the search words "playboy" and "playmate," PEI would effectively monopolize the use of these words on the Internet. This violates the First Amendment rights of (a) Excite and Netscape; (b) *other* trademark holders of "playboy" and "playmate"; as well as (c) members of the public who conduct Internet searches. *See generally Bally Total Fitness Corp. v. Faber*, 29 F.Supp.2d 1161, 1165 (C.D.Cal.1998) ("prohibiting [defendant] from using [plaintiff's] name in the machine readable code would effectively isolate him from all but the most savvy of Internet users").

CHAPTER THREE

PROTECTING COMMERCIAL IDENTITY ONLINE: DOMAIN NAMES

In the offline world, as long as I know the physical location of a store, I can find my way to it even if I have forgotten its name. On the Web, however, a company's name or online brand often *is* the way to its website. For example, I reach the website of Amazon.com by typing "www.amazon.com" into the address bar of my web browser. The text string "www.amazon.com" is called a *uniform resource locator*, or "URL". Typically a company's URL includes the company name or a reference to a product or brand for which the company is known. A company's domain name becomes, in effect, its brand identity on the Web.[1]

If I want to locate the website of a particular company or a brand, but do not know the site's URL, I can try several expedients. I might start by guessing that the URL will be the company's name, followed by a .com, and preceded by a www. This will frequently work. If that fails, I can enter the company or brand name into a search engine such as Google, HotBot, Yahoo! or MSN Search. After completing my search, the search engine returns a list of hyperlinks. If the search engine is well designed, the URL I am seeking should be among the first group of hyperlinks that is returned.

When this system works as expected, my search costs are very low: typing in a URL is quick and easy, and using a search engine is only slightly more involved. But suppose a well-known company or brand name is registered as a domain name by a person who has no affiliation with the company or brand. In that case, my search costs may be significantly increased. Typing in "www.company_name.com" will not yield the desired website, but may instead lead to the site of a competitor; to a website offering to sell the domain name; or to a site with content completely unrelated to the company, such as one offering sexually explicit images. I may fare better typing the company name into a search engine, but depending on the search algorithm employed the link I am looking for may lie somewhere beyond the first page of returned links, and my patience may

1. A domain name consists of two parts separated by a period: a second-level domain ("SLD") and a top-level domain name ("TLD"). The SLD occurs to the left of the TLD. Thus, in the domain name "amazon.com," "amazon" is the SLD and "com" is the TLD. The name associated with the company or its products is typically used as the SLD. TLDs are not unique to a particular company but are used to organize SLDs into groups for the purpose of administering the Internet address system—called the domain name system—much as house numbers are grouped by street, city and state for the purpose of the postal address system.

run out before reaching it. The situation is complicated by the fact that in the world of bricks and mortar many different companies may share the same or similar trademarks under certain circumstances, whereas there is only one dot-com domain name for each word that might be a trademark. If I type www.apple.com into my browser, I could be looking for Apple Bank or Apple Records, but the site belongs to Apple Computer.

When somebody other than a trademark owner obtains a domain name consisting of or incorporating a trademark, several types of costs may arise: (1) increased search costs for consumers; (2) consumer confusion, as may occur if a consumer reaches the website of a competitor rather than that of the company he is seeking; (3) efficiency losses due to the diminished capacity of trademarks to identify companies and products; and (4) harm to companies identified by trademarks, who may lose potential customers.

The practice of obtaining domain names containing words identical or similar to trademarks owned by somebody else commenced soon after the Internet became a commercialized venue. Some people, recognizing the value of a domain name containing a certain word before the owner of a corresponding trademark did, obtained domain names by the dozen, the hundred, and in some cases even by the thousand. This entailed a modest investment—usually $35–50 a year per domain name—which these people hoped to recoup many-fold by selling the domain names to the owners of the corresponding trademarks. In some quarters (particularly among owners of well-established trademarks), it was assumed that domain names corresponding to a trademark ought "naturally" to belong to the trademark owner (or one of the owners, in case the word corresponded to more than one trademark, as in Apple Computer, Apple Bank, and Apple Records). Those who obtained such domain names hoping to sell them to trademark owners were branded as "cybersquatters" or "cyberpirates," and harshly criticized as unethically and illegally seeking to capitalize on goodwill in a trademark that was built up by somebody else. In fact, Congress responded to this practice by enacting a statute designed specifically to end it—the Anticybersquatting Consumer Protection Act ("ACPA"), Pub. L. No. 106–113 (1999), which is addressed in detail in Part II, *infra*. In other quarters (particularly among academics seeking to preserve a robust public domain), the practice has been viewed more benignly: simply a case of one group of entrepreneurs reacting more quickly to a market opportunity than others.

As mentioned earlier, difficulties arise when different companies have the same or similar words in their trademarks and thus feel that they have legitimate claims to the same web address. Just as every house has a unique street address, every website must be built on a unique domain name. Given the obvious advantages of having a Web address built around a company's name, it often happens that two companies with similar names desire the same domain name. The oldest feminist bookstore in the United States is the Amazon Bookstore in Minneapolis, Minnesota. Once it recognized the growing importance of the Web as a distribution channel, it wanted a website with the address "www.amazon.com." The Amazon Bookstore believed its claim to this Web address was superior to that of the Internet company of similar name. After all, the Amazon Bookstore is the older and more established business—a fact of some significance under the law of trademark. While this dispute was ultimately settled out of court, other disputes over web addresses have not ended so amicably. In fact, another judgmental term, "reverse domain name hijacking," has been applied to some second-comers who try to wrest a domain name from a company with a similar trademark that got there first.

Difficulties also arise when individuals have an interest in making noncommercial uses of names and symbols that are either identical or confusingly similar to somebody's trademark. For example, consider a person whose nickname is very similar to some company's trade name. One might expect that such an individual should be able to use his or her nickname as a domain name, provided it is not already claimed by another. As a noncommercial use, it should fall outside the strictures of trademark law. Yet many trademark owners have argued that the use of any domain name on the Internet is necessarily a commercial use and some courts have been receptive to these arguments.

In response to perceived abuses by both trademark owners and cybersquatters, a new body of law has developed to provide needed regulation and dispute resolution. In this chapter, we focus on these legal issues and developments.

I. TRADITIONAL TRADEMARK LAW AND DOMAIN NAMES

As Internet-based e-commerce began to gather steam, it wasn't long before enterprising individuals and companies recognized the value of a well-chosen domain name. Soon the domain name gold rush was on, as individuals and corporations staked their claim to control various domain names. As a group, corporate trademark owners were relatively late to the party, and often found that their trademark or brand name had already been claimed as a domain name by another. While some companies simply purchased the right to use their trademark as a domain name from the person who previously obtained it, other companies refused to negotiate, arguing that the use of their trademarks as domain names was a form of trademark infringement or dilution. Trademark owners filed lawsuits, and the courts had to come to grips with the relationship between the domain name system and the law of trademarks, balancing the interest of the public to make noncommercial use of these new and evolving digital technologies with the interests of trademark owners in preserving the commercial value of their brands. In this section, we explore how the courts have grappled with this issue and evaluate the balance that they have struck.

A. TRADEMARK INFRINGEMENT

Lockheed Martin Corp. v. Network Solutions, Inc.

985 F.Supp. 949 (C.D.Ca.1997), *aff'd*, 194 F.3d 980 (9th Cir.1999).

■ PREGERSON, DISTRICT JUDGE.

The motion by defendant Network Solutions, Inc. ("NSI") for summary judgment came before the Court on October 6, 1997. After reviewing and considering the materials submitted by the parties and hearing oral argument, the Court grants the motion in its entirety.

I. Background

The issue presented by this litigation is whether NSI violated federal trademark law by accepting registrations of Internet domain names that are identical or similar to Lockheed Martin Corporation's ("Lockheed") SKUNK WORKS service mark. Lockheed asserts that NSI directly infringed and diluted its mark by accepting the registrations. Lockheed also asserts that NSI is liable as a contributory infringer because NSI did not comply with Lockheed's demands to cancel the registrations.

As to direct infringement, the Court concludes that NSI has not used Lockheed's service mark in connection with the sale, offering for sale, distribution or advertising of goods or services, and therefore cannot be liable for infringement under 15 U.S.C. § 1114(1)(a) or for unfair competition under 15 U.S.C. § 1125(a).

As to dilution, the Court finds that NSI has not made a commercial use of domain names as trademarks, and therefore cannot satisfy the commercial use element of dilution under 15 U.S.C. § 1125(c).

As to contributory infringement, there are two potential bases for liability. First, a defendant is liable if it intentionally induced others to infringe a mark. Second, a defendant is liable if it continued to supply a product to others when the defendant knew or had reason to know that the party receiving the product used it to infringe a mark.

Lockheed has not presented evidence that NSI induced others to infringe Lockheed's service mark. Therefore, NSI is not liable under the first basis.

As to the knowledge basis, the Court concludes that NSI's limited role as a registrar of domain names coupled with the inherent uncertainty in defining the scope of intellectual property rights in a trademark militates against finding that NSI knew or had reason to know of potentially infringing uses by others. Furthermore, contributory infringement doctrine does not impose upon NSI an affirmative duty to seek out potentially infringing uses of domain names by registrants.

A. The Parties

For over 50 years, plaintiff Lockheed and its predecessors have operated "Skunk Works," an aerospace development and production facility. Lockheed owns the federally registered "SKUNK WORKS" service mark.

Defendant NSI is a publicly traded corporation with its principal place of business in Herndon, Virginia. Under a contract with the National Science Foundation, NSI is the exclusive registrar of most Internet domain names.

B. The Internet

* * *

1. The Domain Name System

Web sites, like other information resources on the Internet, are currently addressed using the Internet "domain name system." A numbering system called the "Internet Protocol" gives each individual computer or network a unique numerical address on the Internet. The "Internet Protocol number," also known as an "IP number," consists of four groups of digits separated by periods, such as "192.215.247.50." For the convenience of users, individual resources on the Internet are also given names. Specialized computers known as "domain name servers" maintain tables linking domain names to IP numbers.

Domain names are arranged so that reading from right to left, each part of the name points to a more localized area of the Internet. For example, in the domain name "cacd.uscourts.gov," "gov" is the top-level domain, reserved for all networks associated with the federal government. The "uscourts" part specifies a second-level domain, a set of the networks used by the federal courts. The "cacd" part specifies a sub-network or computer used by the United States District Court for the Central District of California.

If a user knows or can deduce the domain name associated with a web site, the user can directly access the web site by typing the domain name into a Web browser, without having to conduct a time-consuming search. Because most businesses with a presence on the Internet use the ".com" top-level domain, Internet users intuitively try to find businesses by typing in the corporate or trade name as the second-level domain name, as in "acme.com." Second-level domain names, the name just to the left of ".com," must be exclusive. Therefore, although two companies can have non-exclusive trademark rights in a name, only one company can have a second-level domain name that corresponds to its trademark. For example, Juno Lighting, a maker of lamps, sought to establish a web site with the address "juno.com," a domain name already in use by Juno Online Services, which uses the domain name as part of e-mail addresses for hundreds of thousands of e-mail customers. *See Juno Online Servs., L.P. v. Juno Lighting, Inc.*, 979 F. Supp. 684 (N.D.Ill.1997). In short, the exclusive quality of second-level domain names has set trademark owners against each other in the struggle to establish a commercial presence on the Internet, and has set businesses against domain name holders who seek to continue the traditional use of the Internet as a non-commercial medium of communication.

2. NSI's Role in the Domain Naming System

Under a contract with the National Science Foundation, NSI manages domain name registrations for the ".com," ".net," ".org," ".edu," and ".gov" top-level domains. The contract authorizes NSI to charge $100 for an initial two-year registration and $50 annually starting the third year. NSI registers approximately 100,000 Internet domain names per month.

(Graves Decl. ¶ 5.) Registration applications are made via e-mail and in more than 90% of registrations no human intervention takes place. (Graves Depo. at 54.) On average, a new registration occurs approximately once every 20 seconds. (Id. at 47–48.)

NSI performs two functions in the domain name system. First, it screens domain name applications against its registry to prevent repeated registrations of the same name. Second, it maintains a directory linking domain names with the IP numbers of domain name servers. The domain name servers, which are outside of NSI's control, connect domain names with Internet resources such as web sites and e-mail systems.

NSI does not make an independent determination of an applicant's right to use a domain name. Nor does NSI assign domain names; users may choose any available second-level domain name. In 1995, NSI responded to the problem of conflicting claims to domain names by instituting a domain name dispute policy. Under the current policy, in effect since September 9, 1996,[2] NSI requires applicants to represent and warrant that their use of a particular domain name does not interfere with the intellectual property rights of third parties. (Graves Decl. Ex. 1.) Under the policy, if a trademark holder presents NSI with a United States Patent and Trademark Office registration of a trademark identical to a currently registered domain name, NSI will require the domain name holder to prove that it has a pre-existing right to use the name. If the domain name holder fails to do so, NSI will cancel the registration. (Id.) NSI's policy has been criticized as favoring trademark owners over domain name holders, and favoring owners of federally registered marks over owners of non-registered marks, because owners of federally registered marks can invoke NSI's policy to effectively enjoin the use of identical domain name's without having to make any showing of infringement or dilution. 2 Jerome Gilson & Jeffrey M. Samuels, Trademark Protection and Practice, §§ 5.11[4][B], at 5–239, 5.11[5], at 5–243 (1997) (noting that NSI's policy is tilted in favor of trademark owners, who can deprive registrants of domain names without meeting the likelihood of confusion test for infringement or showing that the domain name dilutes the mark); Gayle Weiswasser, Domain Names, the Internet, and Trademarks: Infringement in Cyberspace, 13 Santa Clara Computer & High Tech. L. J. 137, 172–73 (1997).

If a trademark holder and domain name registrant take their dispute to court, NSI will deposit the domain name in the registry of the court. This process maintains the status quo; the domain name remains active while in the registry of the court.

C. *Factual Background*

Most of the underlying facts of this case are not in dispute. The dispute at summary judgment is over the interpretation of the law and the

2. [NSI's domain name dispute policy was superseded in 1999 by the Uniform Domain Name Dispute Resolution Policy, instituted by the Internet Corporation for Assigned Names and Numbers. *See* Part III, *infra*; *see also* Chapter 1, Part II(F), *supra*, and Chapter 15, Part II(C), *infra*.—Eds.]

application of the law to the facts. The Court finds that there is no genuine issue as to the following facts:

1. Lockheed owns the federally registered SKUNK WORKS service mark for "engineering, technical consulting, and advisory services with respect to designing, building, equipping, and testing commercial and military aircraft and related equipment."

* * *

6. On May 7, 1996, Lockheed sent NSI a letter advising NSI that Lockheed owned the SKUNK WORKS mark and requesting that NSI cease registering domain names that referred to or included the names "skunk works" or "skunkworks" or otherwise infringed Lockheed's mark. Lockheed also requested that NSI provide Lockheed with a list of registered domain names that contain the words "skunk works" or any variation thereof. Lockheed's letter did not include a certified copy of its trademark registration.

7. On June 18, 1996, Lockheed sent NSI a second letter, informing NSI that the registrant of "skunkworks.com" had agreed to stop using the domain name, and that the registrant of "skunkworks.net" was being sued in federal district court. (Quinto Decl. Ex. C.) The letter did not refer to the lawsuit by docket number or caption, nor did it include a copy of the complaint or other pleading.

* * *

9. On September 18, 1996, NSI's Internet business manager, David Graves, wrote to Lockheed's counsel in response to the May 7 and June 18 letters. NSI informed Lockheed that NSI could not provide a list of all domain names that included "skunk works" or any variation thereof, but that Lockheed could use the public "Whois" database of domain name registrations to find this information. NSI further informed Lockheed that upon receipt of a file-stamped copy of the complaint in the "skunkworks.net" case, NSI would immediately deposit the domain name in the registry of the court, maintaining the status quo until the court ordered otherwise.

[Paragraphs 2–5, 8, 10 and 11 describe specific individuals and the domain names that they registered with NSI. The domain names included skunkworks.com, skunkwrks.com, skunkwerks.com, skunkworx.com, and the-skunkworks.com.]

D. Procedural Background

Lockheed filed this action on October 22, 1996, alleging infringement, unfair competition, dilution and contributory infringement under the Lanham Act, and seeking injunctive and declaratory relief. NSI answered the complaint and counterclaimed for declaratory relief.

On March 19, 1997, this Court denied NSI's motion to dismiss for failure to join the domain name registrants as indispensable parties under

Federal Rule of Civil Procedure 19(b). *Lockheed Martin Corp. v. Network Solutions, Inc.,* 43 U.S.P.Q.2d 1056 (C.D.Cal.1997).

On September 29, 1997, this Court denied Lockheed's motion to file a first amended complaint adding a cause of action for "contributory dilution." The Court denied the motion on the bases of futility, undue delay and prejudice.

NSI's present motion seeks summary judgment on all of Lockheed's claims.

II. Discussion

This Court has subject matter jurisdiction over Lanham Act claims pursuant to 28 U.S.C. §§ 1331 and 1338(a). NSI has consented to personal jurisdiction by appearing in this action. Fed.R.Civ.P. 12(h)(1).

* * *

B. Trademark Infringement Under Lanham Act § 32, 15 U.S.C. § 1114(1)

Section 32 of the Lanham Act prohibits any person from using another's mark without permission "in connection with the sale, offering for sale, distribution or advertising of any goods or services on or in connection with which such use is likely to cause confusion, or to cause mistake, or to deceive...." 15 U.S.C. § 1114(1). To be liable under § 32, a person must use the mark on competing or related goods in a way that creates a likelihood of confusion. *AMF Inc. v. Sleekcraft Boats,* 599 F.2d 341, 348 (9th Cir.1979). Before considering the likelihood of confusion, however, the Court must determine whether NSI, by accepting registrations, has used the SKUNK WORKS mark in connection with the sale, distribution or advertising of goods or services. *See Planned Parenthood Fed'n of America, Inc. v. Bucci,* 42 U.S.P.Q.2d 1430, 1434 (S.D.N.Y.1997).

Domain names present a special problem under the Lanham Act because they are used for both a non-trademark technical purpose, to designate a set of computers on the Internet, and for trademark purposes, to identify an Internet user who offers goods or services on the Internet. *See* 2 Gilson, *supra,* §§ 5.11[3], at 5–235, 5.11[5], at 5–243–44 (distinguishing the technical use of domain names from the trademark use to identify goods or services). When a domain name is used only to indicate an address on the Internet, the domain name is not functioning as a trademark.[3] *See Walt-West Enters., Inc. v. Gannett Co., Inc.,* 695 F.2d 1050, 1059–60 (7th Cir.1982) (radio station frequency used in "utilitarian sense of calling the listener's attention to a location on the FM dial" is not protectable under trademark law). Like trade names, domain names can function as trademarks, and therefore can be used to infringe trademark rights. Domain names, like trade names, do not act as trademarks when they are used

3. [*See* § II.A of the PTO's Examination Guide No. 2-99, excerpted in Part V, *infra.*—Eds.]

merely to identify a business entity; in order to infringe they must be used to identify the source of goods or services. *Cf. In re Unclaimed Salvage & Freight Co.,* 192 U.S.P.Q. 165, 168 (T.T.A.B.1976) (affirming refusal of registration of trade name as trademark where specimen demonstrated use only to identify applicant as a business); U.S. Dept. of Commerce, Patent and Trademark Office, Trademark Manual of Examining Procedure § 1202.02, at 1202–4 (2d ed. May 1993) (directing examiners to refuse registration of material that functions only to identify a business).

NSI's acceptance of domain name registrations is connected only with the names' technical function on the Internet to designate a set of computers. By accepting registrations of domain names containing the words "skunk works," NSI is not using the SKUNK WORKS mark in connection with the sale, distribution or advertising of goods and services. NSI merely uses domain names to designate host computers on the Internet. This is the type of purely "nominative" function that is not prohibited by trademark law. *See New Kids on the Block v. New America Pub., Inc.,* 971 F.2d 302, 307 (9th Cir.1992) (noting that laws against infringement do not apply to "non-trademark use of a mark"); *Lucasfilm, Ltd. v. High Frontier,* 622 F.Supp. 931, 933 (D.D.C.1985) (holding that property rights in a trademark do not extend to the use of the trademark to express ideas unconnected with the sale or offer for sale of goods or services).

This is not to say that a domain name can never be used to infringe a trademark. However, something more than the registration of the name is required before the use of a domain name is infringing. In *Planned Parenthood Fed'n of America. Inc. v. Bucci,* for example, the defendant registered the domain name "plannedparenthood.com" and used it as the address of a web site promoting his book on abortion. 42 U.S.P.Q.2d 1430, 1432 (S.D.N.Y.1997). The defendant admitted that he used the domain name hoping that people looking for the Planned Parenthood's site would find his site. *Id.* at 1433. The defendant argued that registration without more is not a commercial use of a mark. *Id.* at 1436–37. The court, however, found that the defendant did "more than merely register a domain name; he has created a home page that uses plaintiff's mark as its address, conveying the impression to Internet users that plaintiff is the sponsor of defendant's web site." *Id.* at 1437. The infringing use in *Planned Parenthood* was not registration of the plaintiff's mark with NSI, but rather the use of the plaintiff's trademark "as a domain name to identify his web site" in a manner that confused Internet users as to the source or sponsorship of the products offered there. *Id.* at 1440; *cf. Teletech Customer Care Management (California), Inc. v. Tele–Tech Co.,* 977 F.Supp. 1407 (C.D.Cal.1997) (finding that the plaintiff was not likely to prevail on the merits of an infringement claim because the plaintiff demonstrated only that customers were likely to be confused as to location of web site, not as to source of goods or services).

The cases dealing with vanity telephone numbers are consistent with the conclusion that registration of a domain name, without more, does not constitute use of the name as a trademark. A toll-free telephone number with an easy-to-remember letter equivalent is a valuable business asset. As with domain names, courts have held that the promotion of a confusingly similar telephone number may be enjoined as trademark infringement and unfair competition. *Dial–A–Mattress Franchise Corp. v. Page,* 880 F.2d 675, 678 (2d Cir.1989); *American Airlines, Inc. v. A 1–800–A–M–E–R–I–C–A–N Corp.,* 622 F.Supp. 673 (N.D.Ill.1985). The infringing act, however, is not the mere possession and use of the telephone number. If it were, trademark holders would be able to eliminate every toll-free number whose letter equivalent happens to correspond to a trademark. In *Holiday Inns, Inc., v. 800 Reservation, Inc.,* 86 F.3d 619 (6th Cir.1996), the district court held that the defendant's use of 1–800 H[zero]LIDAY infringed the plaintiff's trademark in the telephone number 1–800–HOLIDAY. *Id.* at 620. The court of appeals reversed, holding that Holiday Inns's trademark rights in its vanity telephone number did not allow it to control use by others of confusingly similar telephone numbers. Although the defendant's toll-free number was often misdialed by customers seeking 1–800–HOLIDAY, the defendant never promoted the number in connection with the HOLIDAY trademark; but only promoted it as 1–800–405–4329. *Id.* at 623. Because the defendant had used the number only as a telephone number, and not as a trademark, the court of appeals held that the defendant had not infringed the plaintiff's trademark. *Id.* at 625–26.

Domain names and vanity telephone numbers both have dual functions. Domain names, like telephone numbers, allow one machine to connect to another machine. Domain names, like telephone numbers, are also valuable to trademark holders when they make it easier for customers to find the trademark holder. Where the holder of a vanity telephone number promotes it in a way that causes a likelihood of confusion, the holder has engaged in an infringing use. *American Airlines,* 622 F.Supp. at 682 (mere use of telephone number is not infringing, but misleading use of trademarked term in yellow pages advertisement is infringing). But, where, as with NSI, the pure machine-linking function is the only use at issue, there is no trademark use and there can be no infringement.

In the ordinary trademark infringement case, where there is no question that the defendant used the mark, the analysis proceeds directly to the issue of whether there is a likelihood of confusion. Here, however, because NSI has not used Lockheed's service mark in connection with goods or services, the Court need not apply the test for likelihood of confusion. NSI, therefore, is entitled to judgment as a matter of law on the § 32 claim.

1. Printer and Publisher Liability Under 15 U.S.C. § 1114(2)(A), (B)

Lockheed asserts that NSI has infringed its service mark as a "printer" of the mark under 15 U.S.C. § 1114(2)(A). This assertion misapprehends NSI's function as a domain name registrar. To the extent that registrants of SKUNK WORKS-type domain names infringed the mark, they did so by using it on web sites or other Internet resources in a way that created a likelihood of confusion as to source or sponsorship. NSI is not an Internet service provider. It does not provide host computers for web sites or other Internet resources. NSI's role is restricted to publishing a list of domain names, their holders, and the IP numbers of the domain name servers that perform the directory functions associated with the domain names. (Graves Decl. ¶ 10.)

NSI's role is fundamentally dissimilar from that of telephone directory publishers whose conduct has been found enjoinable under § 1114(2)(A). *See Century 21 Real Estate Corp. of Northern Illinois v. R.M. Post Inc.,* 8 U.S.P.Q.2d 1614, 1617 (N.D.Ill.1988) (denying motion to dismiss where yellow pages' publishers were alleged to have printed infringing trademark in listing of former licensee who no longer had right to use trademark). There, the telephone directory printers supplied the material that directly caused the likelihood of confusion. In the domain name context, the domain name registration itself does not infringe the trademark. Infringement occurs when the domain name is used in certain ways. For example, a domain name may infringe trademark rights when it is used in connection with a web site that advertises services in competition with those of the trademark owner. *See, e.g., Cardservice International, Inc. v. McGee,* 950 F.Supp. 737, 738 (E.D.Va.1997); *Comp Examiner Agency, Inc. v. Juris, Inc.,* 1996 WL 376600 (C.D.Cal.1996). Where domain names are used to infringe, the infringement does not result from NSI's publication of the domain name list, but from the registrant's use of the name on a web site or other Internet form of communication in connection with goods or services. NSI is not a "printer or publisher" of web sites, or any other form of Internet "publication." As discussed below in the section on contributory infringement, NSI's involvement with the use of domain names does not extend beyond registration. NSI's liability cannot be premised on an argument that it prints or publishes the list of domain names, because the list is not the instrument or forum for infringement. NSI's liability, if it exists at all, would stem from registrants' use of domain names in connection with other services not provided by NSI. This type of liability is properly analyzed under contributory liability doctrine, not as printer and publisher liability under § 1114(2)(A).

C. Unfair Competition Under Lanham Act § 43(a), 15 U.S.C. § 1125(a)

Lockheed has followed the common practice of alleging unfair competition under § 43(a) of the Lanham Act along with trademark infringement under § 32. Both causes of action depend on a demonstration of a likelihood of confusion. 1 J. Thomas McCarthy, *McCarthy on Trademarks and Unfair Competition* § 2:8 (1997). Federal unfair competition requires use of the mark in connection with goods or services. 15 U.S.C. § 1125(a)(1). As discussed above, NSI's acceptance of registrations for domain names resembling SKUNK WORKS is not a use of the mark in connection with goods or services.

A recent district court decision illustrates the application of federal unfair competition law to the domain name context. *Juno Online Servs., L.P. v. Juno Lighting, Inc.,* 979 F.Supp. 684 (N.D.Ill. Sept.29, 1997). During a dispute over the domain name "juno.com," Juno Lighting registered the domain name "juno-online.com" in the hopes of persuading Juno

Online Services to switch its e-mail service to that domain name. Juno Online sued Juno Lighting for federal unfair competition. The district court dismissed the unfair competition claim because Juno Online alleged only that Juno Lighting registered the name with NSI, and did not allege further use of the name to create a web site or to advertise its services. *Id.* at 690–92. The court held that registration of a trademark as a domain name does not constitute use of the trademark on the Internet in connection with goods or services, and therefore was not prohibited by § 43(a). *Id.* This reasoning applies more strongly to NSI, which has not registered domain names resembling SKUNK WORKS for its own use, but has merely accepted domain name registrations from others.

[The court next considered Lockheed's trademark dilution claim and concluded that "NSI's acceptance of domain name registrations is not a 'commercial use' within the meaning of the Federal Trademark Dilution Act."]

[The court also dismissed Lockheed's contributory infringement claim, finding that Lockheed lacked the requisite knowledge of the infringing activity. The Court of Appeals affirmed the ruling on contributory infringement, holding that a registrar's registration of a domain name does not constitute the supply of an infringing "product," as would be necessary for the registrar to be found a contributory infringer.]

III. Conclusion

* * *

Because summary judgment on the above claims is based on Lockheed's lack of a legal right to control the domain name registration process, there is no case or controversy between these parties. Therefore, the Court grants NSI's motion for summary judgment as to Lockheed's declaratory judgment cause of action.

If the Internet were a technically ideal system for commercial exploitation, then every trademark owner would be able to have a domain name identical to its trademark. But the parts of the Internet that perform the critical addressing functions still operate on the 1960s and 1970s technologies that were adequate when the Internet's function was to facilitate academic and military research. Commerce has entered the Internet only recently. In response, the Internet's existing addressing systems will have to evolve to accommodate conflicts among holders of intellectual property rights, and conflicts between commercial and non-commercial users of the Internet. "In the long run, the most appropriate technology to access web sites and e-mail will be directories that point to the desired Internet address. Directory technology of the necessary scale and complexity is not yet available, but when it is developed it will relieve much of the pressure on domain names." *Domain Name System, Hearings Before the Subcommittee on Basic Research of the House Science Committee,* 105th Cong., 1997 WL 14151463 (September 30, 1997) (testimony of Barbara A. Dooley, Executive Director, Commercial Internet Exchange Association). No doubt trademark owners would like to make the Internet safe for their intellectual property rights by reordering the allocation of existing domain names so that each trademark owner automatically owned the domain name corresponding to the owner's mark. Creating an exact match between Internet addresses and trademarks will require overcoming the problem of concurrent uses of the same trademark in different classes of goods and geographical areas. Various solutions to this problem are being discussed, such as a graphically-based Internet directory that would allow the presentation of trademarks in conjunction with distinguishing logos, new top-level domains for each class of goods, or a new top-level domain for trademarks only. The solution to the current difficulties faced by trademark owners on the Internet lies in this sort of technical innovation, not in attempts to assert trademark rights over legitimate non-trademark uses of this important new means of communication.

Green Products Co. v. Independence Corn By–Products Co.

992 F.Supp. 1070 (N.D.Iowa 1997).

■ MELLOY, CHIEF JUDGE.

The sole issue before the Court is whether to compel Independence Corn By–Products Co. (ICBP) to convey the domain name "greenproducts.com" to the plaintiff, Green Products Co. (Green Products), for its use during the pendency of this litigation.

Green Products claims that ICBP violated § 43(a) of the Lanham Trademark Act, 15 U.S.C. § 1125(a), as well as state laws, when ICBP registered the domain name "greenproducts.com" as one of its own domain names on the internet. Green Products moved for a preliminary injunction: (1) to enjoin ICBP from using the domain name "greenproducts.com", (2) to enjoin ICBP from using the expressions "green products" and "green pet products" as the whole or part of a trademark, trade name, or domain name, and (3) to compel ICBP to convey the ownership of the domain name "greenproducts.com" to Green Products.

In response, ICBP agreed to the first and second parts of Green Products' request, but it resisted the third part. During the pendency of the litigation, ICBP has consented (1) not to use the domain name "greenproducts.com", and (2) not to use the expressions "green products" and "green pet products" as the whole or part of any trademark, trade name, or domain name, but ICBP will continue to use those names "in ways that do not constitute trademark infringement, such as comparative advertising." In order to analyze the merits of Green Products' motion to compel ICBP to transfer ownership of the domain name "greenproducts.com" during the pendency of the litigation, the Court will begin with a brief background of relevant language and information.

Background

[The court begins with a description of the Internet and domain names.]

In the case before this Court, Green Products and ICBP are direct competitors in the corncob by-products industry. On May 30, 1997, ICBP registered two domain names, "icbp.com" and "bestcob.com", with the goal of eventually designing a website that users could find through either domain name. On June 9, 1997, ICBP registered seven other domain names—five of which are formed by using the trade names of ICBP's competitors: e.g., "greenproducts.com." On July 16, 1997, Green Products tried to register "greenproducts.com" and "freshnest.com" (a sister company's name), but was told that ICBP had already registered those two domain names. Green Products then filed a complaint and a motion for a preliminary injunction against ICBP.

Discussion

A. Preliminary Injunction Standards

To decide whether to grant the motion for a preliminary injunction, the Court must consider: (1) the probability that Green Products will succeed on the merits; (2) the threat of irreparable harm to Green Products; (3) the state of the balance between this harm and the injury that granting the injunction will inflict on other parties; and (4) the public interest. *See Dataphase Sys., Inc. v. CL Sys., Inc.*, 640 F.2d 109, 113 (8th Cir.1981) (en banc). When weighing these factors, "no single factor is itself dispositive; in each case all factors must be considered to determine on balance whether they weigh towards granting the injunction." *Calvin Klein Cosmetics Corp. v. Lenox Labs., Inc.*, 815 F.2d 500, 503 (8th Cir.1987).

* * *

B. Analysis of Dataphase Factors

1. Probability that Green Products will succeed on the merits

* * *

An essential element to a trademark infringement action is that the plaintiff must prove that a defendant's use of a particular name " 'creates a likelihood of confusion, deception, or mistake among an appreciable number of ordinary buyers as to the source or association' between the two names." *Maritz, Inc. v. Cybergold, Inc.*, 947 F.Supp. 1338, 1339 (E.D.Mo. 1996) (quoting *Duluth News–Tribune v. Mesabi Publ'g Co.*, 84 F.3d 1093, 1096 (8th Cir.1996)). Factors relevant to determine the likelihood of confusion or deception are:

(1) the strength of the trademark;

(2) the similarity between the plaintiff's and defendant's marks;

(3) the competitive proximity of the parties' products;

(4) the alleged infringer's intent to confuse the public;

(5) evidence of any actual confusion; and

(6) the degree of care reasonably expected of the plaintiff's potential customers.

Maritz, 947 F.Supp. at 1340, *citing Anheuser–Busch, Inc. v. Balducci Publications,* 28 F.3d 769, 774 (8th Cir.1994), *cert. denied,* 513 U.S. 1112 (1995). The Court will next examine each of these factors in turn, although not all of the factors are applicable in this case.

In order to determine whether the trademark is entitled to protection, the Court examines the first factor—strength of the trademark—and classifies the plaintiffs mark as either (1) arbitrary or fanciful, (2) suggestive, (3) descriptive, or (4) generic. An arbitrary or fanciful mark is the strongest type of mark and is afforded the highest level of protection. At the other end, a generic term is used by the general public to identify a category of goods, so it does not receive trademark protection. Suggestive and descriptive marks fall somewhere in between. A suggestive mark is one that requires some measure of imagination to reach a conclusion about the nature of the product. In contrast, a descriptive mark "immediately conveys the nature or function of the product and is entitled to protection only if it has become distinctive by acquiring a secondary meaning." Here, the Court finds that Green Products' trademark—the name "Green Products' "—is at least suggestive. The name "Green Products' " requires at least some imagination to connect it with corncob by-products.

The next factor requires the Court to consider the similarity between the plaintiffs and defendant's marks. ICBP concedes that its domain name "greenproducts.com" is "undisputedly similar to the mark Green Products Co." However, ICBP also argues that its use of the mark must be viewed in the context of the marketplace, and that the "domain name only has meaning as an Internet address linking to ICBP's future web site and the web site will take every precaution to ensure there is no consumer confusion."

In essence, ICBP's argument is that the Court should only compare the similarity of domain names and websites linked to those domain names—not the similarity of ICBP's domain name and Green Products' trademark—because ICBP is not "selling a product on store shelves using the mark 'greenproducts.com'."

The Court finds ICBP's argument clever, but ultimately unpersuasive. ICBP's argument is analogous to saying that ICBP has the right to hang a sign in front of its store that reads, "Green Products." When customers enter the store expecting to be able to see (and possibly, to buy) products made by Green Products, ICBP then announces, "Actually, this store isn't owned by Green Products; it's owned by ICBP. We don't sell anything made by Green Products, but as long as you're here, we'll tell you how our products are better than Green Products." In essence, ICBP is capitalizing on the strong similarity between Green Products' trademark and ICBP's domain name to lure customers onto its web page.

Turning to the third factor, the competitive proximity of the parties' products, ICBP concedes that ICBP and Green Products are both competitors in the corncob byproducts industry. Despite being direct competitors, ICBP argues that this Court should not focus on their similar corn byproducts, but on domain names and their respective websites: "the relevant 'products' for the likelihood of confusion analysis are not corncob products because ICBP does not sell any corncob products with the mark 'greenproducts.com' on a label or package design." Instead, ICBP suggests, the Court should analyze whether a website located at "greenproducts.com" is proximate to a website located at "green-products.com" or "greenproducts-co.com." ICBP believes that these domain names are not proximate, because anyone who knows Green Products' domain name can use that name to go directly to Green Products' website and "will likely never even see ICBP's web site." ICBP does, however, concede that the websites are "proximate in the sense that a person guessing at Green Product Co.'s domain name might access ICBP's website if it first tries 'greenproducts.com'...."

ICBP's argument basically boils down to the idea that the Court should view the domain names as mere addresses which—along with the websites attached to each name—are products in and of themselves. The Court disagrees. There is a close competitive proximity between the products that the two companies sell, and there is also a close competitive proximity between the domain name "greenproducts.com" and the trademark "Green Products". The domain name "greenproducts.com" identifies the internet site to those who reach it, "much like a person's name identifies a particular person, or, more relevant to trademark disputes, a company's name identifies a specific company." *Cardservice,* 950 F.Supp. 737. Because customers who do not know what a company's domain name is will often guess that the domain name is the same as the company's name, a "domain name mirroring a corporate name may be a valuable corporate asset, as it facilitates communication with a customer base." *MTV Networks,* 867 F.Supp. at 203–204 n. 2.

Alternatively, even if this Court were persuaded that it should only compare the alphanumeric domain names (and not the products that each company sells, nor the similarity between ICBP's domain name and Green Products' trademark), this Court would still find a close proximity between the domain name "greenproducts.com" and any of the alternative domain names that ICBP suggests, such as "green-products.com", "greenproducts-co.com", or "greenproducts-co.com." Under either analysis, there is a close competitive proximity, and that close competitive proximity further increases the opportunity of consumer confusion.

Fourth, this Court examines whether ICBP intended to cause consumer confusion by creating an ICBP website accessed through the domain name "greenproducts.com." ICBP maintains that it had no intent to "pass off" its products as those of Green Products, and that its only intent was to distinguish ICBP's products from those of Green Products through comparative advertising. ICBP believes that there will be no consumer confusion because internet users will immediately know that the website belongs to ICBP once the actual web page appears on the screen (after users have typed the domain name "greenproducts.com"). To support this argument, ICBP distinguishes its planned website from that in *Planned Parenthood Fed. of Am., Inc. v. Bucci,* 42 U.S.P.Q.2d 1430 (S.D.N.Y.1997), where an anti-abortion activist who registered the domain name "plannedparenthood.com" to lure pro-abortion internet users onto his website designed a web page that deceptively announced that it was "Planned Parenthood's" site—instead of clearly announcing that the Planned Parenthood Federation of America had nothing to do with it.

While it is true that the *Planned Parenthood* court discussed how the graphics and design of the web page misled users into believing that the Planned Parenthood Federation was operating an anti-abortion web page, *see* 42 U.S.P.Q.2d at 1432, ICBP overlooks the fact that the *Planned Parenthood* court also found that a disclaimer would not have cured the confusion caused by the domain name:

> Due to the nature of Internet use, defendant's appropriation of plaintiffs mark as a domain name and home page address cannot adequately be remedied by a disclaimer. Defendant's domain name and home page address are external labels that, on their face, cause confusion among Internet users and may cause Internet users who seek plaintiffs website to expend time and energy accessing defendant's website. Therefore, I determine that a disclaimer on defendant's home page would not be sufficient to dispel the confusion induced by his home page address and domain name.

Planned Parenthood, 42 U.S.P.Q.2d at 1441.

Because ICBP's website has not been designed yet, this Court will make no finding as to whether ICBP's web page is likely to cause consumer confusion between the products of ICBP and those of Green Products. However, based on the briefs, affidavits, and evidence presented at the hearing, this Court finds that the use of plaintiff's trademark as defendant's own domain name is likely to cause consumer confusion as to who owns the site. Just as customers entering a store that advertises "Green Products" as its store name would be initially confused to find, upon entering the store, that ICBP actually owned it, so will customers typing the domain name "greenproducts.com" be initially confused to find that ICBP owns the website.

The Court acknowledges that such an interpretation of "consumer confusion" is somewhat different than that typically used to find consumer confusion in trademark infringement cases. Typically, the courts examine whether a company intended to confuse consumers into thinking that its own products were made by a competitor company. *See, e.g., SquirtCo v. Seven-Up Co.,* 628 F.2d 1086, 1091 (8th Cir.1980) ("Intent on the part of the alleged infringer to pass off its goods as the product of another raises an inference of likelihood of confusion, but intent is not an element of a claim for trademark infringement.").

Here, ICBP did not intend to sell its corn by-products by passing them off as having been made by Green Products. However, ICBP did intend to pass off its domain name as though it belonged to Green Products. As a result of the confusion in thinking that Green Products' website could be found through the "greenproducts.com" domain name, ICBP could deceptively lure potential customers onto its own turf, where customers would be told how ICBP is better than Green Products. This Court finds that such a deceptive use of a competitor's trademark as a way to lure customers away from the competitor is a kind of consumer confusion.

Moreover, even if such an interpretation of "consumer confusion" is not the relevant mode of inquiry, this Court also finds that ICBP's ownership of the domain name "greenproducts.com"—even without an adjoining website—could cause consumer confusion about the corporate status of Green Products. Currently, if internet users browsing the web type the domain name "greenproducts.com", they are told that "[n]o documents match the query." After reading this message, users might randomly input other domain names, guessing that Green Products is registered under some variation of its trademark. Other users might try to find out who owns the domain name "greenproducts.com" by using various functions on the web where people can type specific domain names and find out who owns them.[4] Users who do this will learn that ICBP owns the "greenproducts.com" website, and they will also learn the address and phone number of ICBP. Potential customers who see this information may be confused into thinking that ICBP has taken over Green Products, or that Green Products has merged into ICBP. As a result, customers may decide to buy from ICBP, believing that Green Products no longer exists or that ICBP now owns it. The consumer confusion thereby caused by ICBP's ownership of the domain name "greenproducts.com" during the pendency of litigation would cause Green Products to lose customers.

The fifth factor is incidents of actual confusion. Green Products concedes that because the website is not yet operational, there have been no incidents of actual confusion, so the Court need not examine this factor further.

The last factor is the degree of care reasonably expected of Green Products' potential customers. To determine this, the Court looks at the "ordinary purchaser, buying under the normally prevalent conditions of the market and giving the attention such purchasers usually give in buying that class of goods." *General Mills, Inc. v. Kellogg Co.*, 824 F.2d 622, 627 (8th Cir.1987). * * * Based on all the evidence before it at this point in the proceedings * * * this Court finds that ordinary internet users do not undergo a highly sophisticated analysis when searching for domain names [and that] * * * an ordinary internet user trying to find Green Products' website would likely guess that Green Products' domain name was the same as its trademark, and thus type "greenproducts.com". * * *

Based on this overall balancing, this Court finds a substantial probability that Green Products will prevail on the merits.

2. *Irreparable harm to Green Products*

The Court next analyzes the degree of harm, if any, that Green Products would suffer if not granted a preliminary injunction. The Eighth

4. [Here the court is referring to a "whois" search.—Eds.]

Circuit has held that a district court can presume irreparable injury from a finding of probable success on the merits of a § 43(a) Lanham Trademark Act case. *Sports Design,* 871 F.Supp. at 1165, *citing Sanborn Mfg.,* 997 F.2d at 489. While this Court could thus presume irreparable injury based on its finding of probable success on the merits, it will also examine the specific circumstances of this case in order to decide whether allowing ICBP to retain ownership of the domain name "greenproducts.com" during the pendency of litigation would cause irreparable harm to Green Products.

Although ICBP has consented to putting the domain name "greenproducts.com" on hold until the final merits are determined, Green Products is concerned that even though ICBP would not have an actual website that could be viewed by typing the domain name "greenproducts.com", customers could use other functions on the web to discover that ICBP owns that domain name. (Hearing, Sept. 11, 1997.) As a result, potential or actual customers might mistakenly conclude that ICBP has purchased the Green Products corporation, or that Green Products has merged with ICBP. This confusion could result in Green Products losing both customers and revenue during the pendency of the litigation, and it would be impossible to calculate how much money or how many customers were lost.

For these reasons, in addition to the fact that the Court believes that Green Products is likely to succeed on the merits, the Court finds that it would cause Green Products irreparable harm if ICBP were allowed to retain ownership of the domain name "greenproducts.com" during the pendency of the litigation.

3. Balance between this harm and the injury that granting the injunction will inflict on other parties

ICBP has not finalized what its web page will look like, has not advertised that it owns a web page that can be viewed by typing the domain name "greenproducts.com", and has not listed "greenproducts.com" as one of its domain names in the Thomas Register. If ICBP is compelled to relinquish ownership of the domain name "greenproducts.com" to Green Products during the pendency of the litigation, ICBP would still be able to launch its own website via its registered domain names "icbp.com" or "bestcob.com". Furthermore, the act of transferring ownership of "greenproducts.com" would not hinder ICBP's ability to launch a website that compares its products to those of Green Products: ICBP could still design and implement a website that compares the products of ICBP to those of Green Products, and internet users could access this website through ICBP's other registered domain names.

While these factors weigh in support of compelling ICBP to transfer ownership of the domain name, there are also certain factors that weigh against the transfer. For example, if ICBP were to prevail at trial, Green Products would have to transfer the "greenproducts.com" domain name back to ICBP. This could cause some initial confusion, and possibly hostility, from customers who might have become accustomed to accessing Green Products' website through the "greenproducts.com" domain name. In addition, because Green Products would like to advertise its domain name "greenproducts.com" in the Thomas Register, and because final changes to the printed version of the Thomas Register must be made by November 1, 1997, neither Green Products nor ICBP will be able to change the 1998 edition of the printed Thomas Register if ICBP prevails at trial. As a result, ICBP worries that it "would risk incurring the anger of these customers if that domain name was suddenly switched...."

After weighing the potential harm that ICBP would experience by not being able to use its competitor's trademark as its own domain name, against the harm Green Products would experience by not being able to use its own trademark as its domain name, this Court finds that the harm to Green Products is more extensive and severe than the harm to ICBP. Although ICBP would experience some harm by transferring ownership of the domain name during the pendency of litigation, the transfer is not irreversible; if ICBP ultimately prevails on the merits, the Court will transfer ownership of the domain name back to ICBP. Additionally, even though some customers who may have become accustomed to finding Green Products' web page through the "greenproducts.com" domain name may be initially upset when they find that the domain name "greenproducts.com" has become the domain name for ICBP's web page (if ICBP prevails at trial), any harm that ICBP may experience because of Green Products' temporary ownership of the domain name could be tempered by a carefully designed web page or by hyperlinks to Green Products' web page. Moreover, given ICBP's goal of distinguishing its products from those of Green Products, the opportunity for ICBP to establish a comparative advertising website located through the "greenproducts.com" domain name could be even more advantageous to ICBP if Green Products has already attracted customers to the "greenproducts.com" domain name.

For all of the above reasons, and especially considering the fact that the transfer of ownership is not irreversible because the Court will order the domain name transferred back to ICBP if ICBP prevails in litigation, the Court finds that the harm to Green Products is more extensive and severe than the harm to ICBP.

* * *

Cardservice International, Inc. v. McGee

950 F.Supp. 737 (E.D.Va.1997), *aff'd mem.*, 129 F.3d 1258 (4th Cir.1997).

■ CLARKE, DISTRICT JUDGE.

This matter comes before this Court for the hearing of evidence in the bench trial of whether Plaintiff Cardservice International, Inc., is entitled to a permanent injunction pursuant to 15 U.S.C. § 1116 against Defendants Webster R. McGee and WRM & Associates banning the use by the Defendants of words similar to Plaintiff's trademark "Cardservice". * * *

I.

This action was brought by Cardservice International seeking injunctive relief and damages for alleged infringements of its trademark "Cardservice" by the Defendants. Cardservice International provides credit and debit card processing and processes "billions of dollars in transactions annually." Plaintiff's Exhibit 3 at 2. Cardservice International registered the trademark "Cardservice International" with the United States Patent and Trademark Office as Reg. No. 1,864,924 effective Nov. 29, 1994. Plaintiff's Exhibit 1. No claim was made to the exclusive right to the word "international."

McGee, through his sole proprietorship WRM & Associates has also provided credit and debit card services. Cardservice International claims that in 1994, McGee applied to become a representative of Cardservice International. McGee claims that he was only associated with an agent of Cardservice International, but never sought to become associated with Cardservice International itself. In March of 1995 and without the permission of Cardservice International, McGee registered the internet domain name "cardservice.com" with Network Solutions, Inc., the company responsible for regulating use of domain names on the internet. In advertisements located at the internet site "cardservice.com", McGee advertised merchant card services through a company held out to be "EMS—Card Service on the Caprock".

In May and August 1995, Cardservice International contacted McGee by letter demanding that McGee "cease and desist all Cardservice related activity." Subsequent discussions between Cardservice International and McGee focused on McGee's use of "cardservice.com". When McGee refused to surrender the domain name, Cardservice International retained counsel, who called McGee's attention to Cardservice International's trademark and again demanded that McGee cease and desist use of the term "Cardservice" and any variation of it on the internet.

McGee refused to relinquish "cardservice.com" or to cease use of "Card Service" on the internet. McGee claimed that the name of his business inserts a space between "card" and "service" and that he is therefore not in violation of the trademark laws. He further claimed that "cardservice.com" was one word because the internet does not allow spaces in domain names. When Cardservice International expanded its services onto the internet, it was forced to use the domain name "cardsvc.com".

Cardservice International then filed this action in September 1996. Cardservice International filed counts alleging violations of § 32 of the Lanham Act, 15 U.S.C. § 1114, for trademark infringement; § 43(a) of the Lanham Act, 42 U.S.C. § 1125(a), for unfair competition; and common law unfair competition, misappropriation, and unjust enrichment. McGee answered these allegations and filed counterclaims seeking declaratory relief that he was the proper owner of the domain name "cardservice.com.", that Cardservice International had interfered with Defendants' business relationships by attempting to have the domain name "cardservice.com" transferred from McGee to Cardservice International, and that Cardservice International had engaged in trademark misuse and wire fraud. * * *

On January 13, 1997, the Court also proceeded with the bench trial on the merits of Cardservice International's claim in which Cardservice International sought attorneys fees and a permanent injunction. McGee indicated his desire to end the litigation and stated that he would not contest Cardservice International's evidence.

II.

The Court ruled from the Bench that Cardservice International is entitled to a permanent injunction against McGee and WRM & Associates requiring the Defendants to cease use of any variation of the registered mark "Cardservice" and to relinquish any interest in the domain name "cardservice.com". Federal Rule of Civil Procedure 65(d) requires this Court to state the reasons for the grant of the permanent injunction.

First, the Court addresses a preliminary issue. McGee has argued that because he registered the domain name "cardservice.com" with Network Solutions, he is entitled to the domain name. McGee cites Network Solutions' policy of granting domain names on a first-come-first-served basis. Such a policy cannot trump federal law. Holders of valid trademarks under federal law are not subject to company policy, nor can the rights of those trademark holders be changed without congressional actions. If trademark laws apply to domain names, anyone who obtains a domain name under Network Solutions' "first-come-first-served" policy must do so subject to whatever liability is provided for by federal law.

* * *

* * * The Fourth Circuit has stated that in order to prevail in actions under [Sections 32 and 43 of the Lanham Act, 15 U.S.C. §§ 1114(1) and 1125(a)], "a complainant must demonstrate that it has a valid, protectable trademark and that the defendant's use of a colorable imitation of the trademark is likely to cause confusion among consumers." *Lone Star Steakhouse & Saloon v. Alpha of Virginia,* 43 F.3d 922 (4th Cir.1995).

It is undisputed that Cardservice International owns a valid, protectable trademark. Until McGee informed the Court that he would not contest Cardservice International's evidence, he primarily argued that his use of "cardservice.com" and "Card Service on the Caprock" would not cause confusion on the internet. The Court disagrees and finds that there is a likelihood of confusion between Cardservice International's registered mark and McGee's use of "cardservice.com" and "Card Service" on the internet.

The factors relevant to a determination of whether there is a likelihood of confusion are as follows:

a) the strength or distinctiveness of the mark;

b) the similarity of the two marks;

c) the similarity of the goods/services the marks identify;

d) the similarity of the facilities the two parties use in their businesses;

e) the similarity of the advertising used by the two parties;

f) the defendant's intent;

g) actual confusion.

Pizzeria Uno Corp. v. Temple, 747 F.2d 1522, 1527 (4th Cir.1984). Not all of these factors are relevant to any given set of facts, nor must all factors be in the registrant's favor for a finding of confusion. *Id.*

In this case, several of the *Pizzeria Uno* factors favor a finding that McGee's use of "cardservice.com" and "Card Service" is likely to cause confusion. It is clear that McGee's use of "cardservice.com" and "Card Service on the Caprock" are strikingly similar to Cardservice International's registered mark. Although McGee's use of the term "Card Service" does not exactly duplicate "Cardservice", minor differences between the registered mark and the unauthorized use of the mark do not preclude liability under the Lanham Act when the unauthorized use is likely to cause confusion. *See Lone Star Steakhouse, supra* (finding use of "Lone Star Grill" to be an infringement of registered mark "Lone Star Steakhouse and Saloon"). The use of the term "cardservice" in Defendants' domain name exactly duplicates the registered mark "Cardservice".

Further, both parties are using the internet as the facility to provide their services. Because of the nature of the internet and domain names in particular, this factor becomes even more important in cases of trademark infringement over the internet. Domain names present a unique circumstance when determining the likelihood of confusion caused by possible trademark violations. Traditionally, trademark disputes involved two or more parties using the same or similar mark. *Intermatic Inc. v. Toeppen,* 947 F.Supp. 1227, 1233–34 (N.D.Ill.1996) (Williams, Mag.). With regard to domain names, however, only one party can hold any particular domain name. *Id.* Who has access to that domain name is made even more important by the fact that there is nothing on the internet equivalent to a phone book or directory assistance. A customer who is unsure about a company's domain name will often guess that the domain name is also the company's name. For this reason, "a domain name mirroring a corporate name may be a valuable corporate asset, as it facilitates communication with a customer base." *MTV Networks, Inc. v. Curry,* 867 F.Supp. 202, 203–04 n. 2 (S.D.N.Y.1994). Thus, a domain name is more than a mere internet address. It also identifies the internet site to those who reach it, much like a person's name identifies a particular person, or, more relevant to trademark disputes, a company's name identifies a specific company.

Because of McGee's use of "cardservice.com", Cardservice International has no access to an internet domain name containing its registered mark, and must use a different domain name. Cardservice International's customers who wish to take advantage of its internet services but do not know its domain name are likely to assume that "cardservice.com" belongs to Cardservice International. These customers would instead reach McGee and see a home page for "Card Service". They would find that McGee's internet site offers advertisements for and provides access to the same services as Cardservice International—credit and debit card processing. Many would assume that they have reached Cardservice International or, even if they realize that is not who they have reached, take advantage of McGee's services because they do not otherwise know how to reach Cardservice International. Such confusion is not only likely, but, according to McGee, has actually occurred at least four or five times since he began using "cardservice.com". Transcript of Preliminary Injunction Hearing at 366.

Such a result is exactly what the trademark laws were designed to protect against. Cardservice International has obtained a trademark to ensure that the name "cardservice" will be associated by consumers only with Cardservice International. Regardless of the fact that McGee's business is small compared to Cardservice International's, confusion will result among consumers who are seeking Cardservice International by searching for its trademark as a domain name on the internet. The fact that Cardservice International has been awarded a trademark means that it should not be forced to compete with others who would also use the words "cardservice". The terms of the Lanham Act do not limit themselves in any way which would preclude application of federal trademark law to the internet. Unauthorized use of a domain name which includes a protected trademark to engage in commercial activity over the internet constitutes use "in commerce", 15 U.S.C. § 1114(1), of a registered mark. Such use is in direct conflict with federal trademark law. *See ActMedia, Inc. v. Active Media Int'l,* No. 96c3448, 1996 WL 466527 (N.D.Ill. July 17, 1996) (finding defendant's use of domain name "actmedia.com" precluded plaintiff from reserving the domain name incorporating its registered mark and therefore violated 15 U.S.C. § 1125); *see also Panavision Int'l v. Toeppen,* 945 F.Supp. 1296 (C.D.Cal.1996) (finding defendant's reservation of domain name "panavision.com" which incorporated registered mark of plaintiff to be in violation of the Federal Trademark Dilution Act of 1995, 15 U.S.C. § 1125(c)).

Accordingly, the Court finds that McGee's use of "cardservice.com" and "Card Service on the Caprock" constitutes trademark infringement in violation of the Lanham Act and that Cardservice International is entitled to a permanent injunction against such use pursuant to 15 U.S.C. § 1116. The Court emphasizes that its finding against McGee is based on evidence which McGee ultimately chose not to contest at trial.

* * *

NOTES & QUESTIONS

1. *Is registration "commercial use"?* In *Lockheed Martin Corp. v. Network Solutions, Inc.,* the court holds that mere registration of a domain name is not use "in connection with any goods or services" or "commercial use," and therefore cannot constitute trademark infringement or dilution. In *Green Products Co. v. Independence Corn By-Products Co.,* in contrast, the court finds commercial use even though the defendant has done no more than register a domain name that is similar to a trademark owned by Green Products. The *Green Products* court reasons that the act of registering a domain name creates a public record showing that the registrant owns that domain name. By conducting a "whois" search, members of the public will see this record and erroneously infer that the registrant has acquired that company and that the goods and services of this company now originate from and are affiliated with this registrant—thereby establishing a connection to goods and services as well as consumer confusion over their origin and affiliation. Which view do you find more convincing?

2. *Similar approach in U.K.* The courts in the United Kingdom have embraced the reasoning of the *Green Products* case and held that mere registration of a domain name can constitute trademark infringement. *See British Telecommunications plc v. One in a Million Ltd.*, [1998] 4 All E.R. 476 (C.A.):

> It is accepted that the name Marks & Spencer denotes Marks & Spencer plc and nobody else. Thus anybody seeing or hearing the name realises that what is being referred to is the business of Marks & Spencer plc. It follows that registration by the appellants of a domain name including the name Marks & Spencer makes a false representation that they are associated or connected with Marks & Spencer plc. This can be demonstrated by considering the reaction of a person who taps into his computer the domain name marksandspencer.co.uk and presses a button to execute a "whois" search. He will be told that the registrant is One In A Million Limited. A substantial number of persons will conclude that One In A Million Limited must be connected or associated with Marks & Spencer plc. That amounts to a false representation which constitutes passing off.

3. *Initial interest confusion and disclaimers.* Offline, initial interest confusion is sometimes condemned as a form of "bait and switch." In holding that a bar named "The Velvet Elvis" infringed trademarks held by the Elvis Presley estate, a court noted: "[O]nce in the door, the confusion has succeeded because some patrons may stay, despite realizing that the bar has no relationship with" the Elvis Presley estate. *Elvis Presley Enters. v. Capece*, 141 F.3d 188, 204 (5th Cir.1998). Does initial interest confusion have the same consequence and significance online as it does in the world of bricks and mortar? Would the presence of disclaimers on the website affect your answer? The court in *Green Products* quotes the court in *Planned Parenthood Fed. Of Am., Inc. v. Bucci*, 42 U.S.P.Q.2d (BNA) 1430 (S.D.N.Y.1997), for the proposition that disclaimers on a website will not cure confusion caused by that website's domain name. Therein the court argued that "Defendant's domain name and home page address * * * may cause Internet users who seek plaintiff's web site to expend time and energy accessing defendant's web site. Therefore, I determine that a disclaimer on defendant's home page would not be sufficient to dispel the confusion induced by his home page address and domain name." *Id.* at 1441. Do you agree with this analysis?

4. *Registration to block another's use.* Under the reasoning of the *Lockheed* court, could a company register a competitor's trademark as a domain name in order to prevent that competitor from using it as a domain name so long as the registrant did not actually use it on the Internet? *See Juno Online Services, L.P. v. Juno Lighting, Inc.,* 979 F.Supp. 684 (N.D.Ill.1997), discussed in Part II(C) of the *Lockheed Martin* opinion.

5. *E-mail addresses vs. websites.* When courts discuss the use of a domain name on the Internet, their examples involve a "fully qualified" domain name that points to a website. Is it possible to infringe another's trademark with a domain name if one only uses that domain name as part of an e-mail address? *See America Online, Inc. v. IMS,* 24 F.Supp.2d 548 (E.D.Va.1998).

6. *Directories.* Directories are the electronic file folders found on most personal computers. One can point to a directory on a host computer connected to the Internet by appending to the fully qualified domain name of that host a forward slash "/" followed by the name of the particular directory. Thus, when I type

www.whitehouse.gov/press releases/

into the address bar of my web browser, I am served the default web page contained in the "press release" directory that resides on the host computer designated by the URL www.whitehouse.gov. With respect to trademark infringement, this raises the question whether the use of another's trademark as a directory name can constitute infringement. If so, how would you defend such a lawsuit? What is the difference between using another's trademark as a domain name and as a directory name? Is the use of another's trademark as a directory name fair use? *See, e.g., Patmont Motor Werks, Inc. v. Gateway Marine, Inc.,* 1997 WL 811770 n. 6 (N.D.Cal.1997). (For material on trademark fair use, *see* Chapter 2, Part III(A), *supra.*)

B. TRADEMARK DILUTION

Teletech Customer Care Management, Inc. v. Tele–Tech Co.

977 F.Supp. 1407 (C.D.Cal.1997).

■ PFAELZER, DISTRICT JUDGE.

On April 21, 1997, Plaintiff's Motion for Preliminary Injunction came before the Court for hearing. * * * After considering the papers filed by the parties and the arguments presented at the hearing, the Court grants Plaintiff's Motion for Preliminary Injunction and makes the following findings of fact and conclusions of law:

Findings of Fact

I. Facts Relating to the Plaintiff's Business

1. Plaintiff TeleTech Customer Care Management (California), Inc. ("TeleTech" or "Plaintiff") is the owner of the federally registered service

mark TELETECH®, United States Service Mark Registration No. 1,996,-498. The Service Mark Registration is valid and current. Plaintiff has used the mark TELETECH® in commerce since 1982.

2. TeleTech Holdings, Inc. is the parent company of the Plaintiff, as well as several other entities whose names begin with "TeleTech": * * * All of these corporations shall be referred to collectively as the TeleTech Companies. TeleTech Holdings, Inc. is a publicly traded company, whose stock is listed on the NASDAQ stock exchange.

3. Plaintiff has shown that the TeleTech Companies may be the largest provider of primarily inbound integrated telephone and Internet customer care worldwide. The main business of the TeleTech Companies is providing "customer care" for the customers of TeleTech's clients, including receiving and responding to telephone and Internet inquiries from customers of TeleTech's clients. "Customer care" provided by the TeleTech Companies includes answering questions asked by the clients' customers before a sale, providing information on new products offered by TeleTech's clients, enrolling customers in clients' programs, arranging product shipments to customers of TeleTech's clients, providing 24–hour technical and help desk support for customers of TeleTech's clients, resolving customer complaints, and conducting satisfaction surveys. The TeleTech Companies handle service calls from customers of many types of businesses, including airlines, the United States Postal Service, telephone companies, banks, computer companies, utility companies, a package delivery service, and other types of businesses. Airline reservations, tracking of packages, bank transactions, and many other customer service calls are handled by TeleTech employees.

4. It appears that the TeleTech Companies have spent hundreds of thousands of dollars promoting their services and advertising under the TELETECH® Service Mark. In 1996 alone, the TeleTech Companies appear to have spent in excess of nine hundred thousand dollars promoting their services and advertising under the TELETECH® Service Mark. The TeleTech Companies have sold millions of dollars worth of services under the TELETECH® Service Mark. As a result of these efforts, it appears that TeleTech has built up and now owns valuable goodwill symbolized by the TELETECH® Service Mark.

II. Facts Relating to the Defendant's Business

5. Defendant Tele–Tech Company, Inc. ("Tele–Tech" or "Defendant") is a contractor providing engineering and installation services to the telecommunications industry. Defendant began using the name Tele–Tech (with a hyphen) in 1978.

6. Defendant has not registered the service mark TELE–TECH. Defendant has not been authorized or licensed by TeleTech to use the TELETECH® Service Mark (without a hyphen). Defendant is not affiliated with or sponsored by TeleTech.

III. Facts Relating to the Defendant's Use of the Domain Name "Teletech.Com"

7. Defendant Tele–Tech is using Plaintiff's federally registered service mark (TELETECH, without a hyphen) as an Internet domain name, "teletech.com".

8. Plaintiff has used the TELETECH® service mark for approximately fifteen years, and began using the TELETECH® service mark long before Defendant's first use of "teletech.com" (without the hyphenation which distinguishes Defendant's name from Plaintiff's TELETECH® service mark).

9. Only one entity may use the domain name "teletech.com." As a result, Defendant's use of the "teletech.com" domain name prevents Plaintiff TeleTech from using its registered service mark and company name as its domain name.

10. Plaintiff's inability to use the TELETECH® company name and registered service mark as its domain name is causing hardship to Plaintiff. Customers and potential customers of Plaintiff are unable to locate Plaintiff's website by typing in "teletech.com" as part of the Uniform Resource Locator (URL).

11. An Internet domain name may include a hyphen.

12. Use of a hyphen would distinguish the domain name "tele-tech.com" from the domain name "teletech.com." Domain names such as "teletech.com" are used to identify the location of servers on the Internet. Because the hyphen is an additional character in the domain name, its inclusion or omission changes the location of the server to which an inquiry is made.

13. Tele–Tech is not precluded from using its own name, "Tele–Tech," with its distinctive hyphenation, as its domain name. In fact, Tele–Tech appears to have established a second website that uses the domain name "tele-tech.com."

IV. Facts Relating to the Balance of Hardship

14. Injunctive relief will probably not have great negative impact on Defendant. Defendant is free to use, and in fact already appears to be using, the domain name "tele-tech.com" (which includes the hyphenation), in a second website that Defendant maintains. In fact, it may be easier for Defendant's customers to locate Defendant's website under the domain name "tele-tech.com," since that is the way the Defendant spells its name.

15. Defendant is "attempting to inform its customers to use 'tele-tech.com' for e-mail."

16. Defendant suggests that Plaintiff's presence on the Internet is not hindered by Defendant's use of Plaintiff's name and registered service mark as its domain name, because Internet users can locate Plaintiff's website using Internet "search engines," rather than typing in Plaintiff's name as part of the URL. That method of searching the Internet appears to

generate as many as 800 to 1000 matches, however. That number of locations is likely to deter web browsers from searching for Plaintiff's particular website.

17. TeleTech appears to have incurred a great deal of expense over a long period of time developing recognition of its TELETECH® mark, and users of the Internet who have become familiar with that mark will probably assume that TeleTech's website will be found at "teletech.com."

18. The balance of hardships tips sharply in Plaintiff's favor.

* * *

VI. Facts Relating to Dilution

23. The TELETECH® mark is most likely very well recognized within the teleservicing industry, because TeleTech appears to be a large provider of integrated telephone and Internet customer care worldwide and because of the extensive promotion and advertising that TeleTech has apparently undertaken.

24. The TELETECH® mark has been continuously used in commerce by TeleTech since 1982. The mark is registered on the Principal Register.

25. The TELETECH® mark appears to be famous.

* * *

Conclusions of Law

* * *

IV. Plaintiff is Likely to Succeed on the Merits.

* * *

B. TeleTech Has Demonstrated a Likelihood of Success on the Merits of Its Dilution Claims.

* * *

12. TeleTech has demonstrated that its mark is probably famous under this statute. The evidence submitted by the Plaintiff strongly suggests that the TeleTech Companies are the largest provider of integrated telephone and Internet customer care worldwide. The TeleTech Companies appear to have spent hundreds of thousands of dollars promoting their services and advertising under the TELETECH® Service Mark. The TeleTech Companies seem to have sold hundreds of millions of dollars worth of services under the TELETECH® Service Mark. TeleTech Holdings, Inc. is a publicly traded company which is listed on the NASDAQ stock exchange. The TELETECH® mark is probably very well recognized and famous within the teleservicing industry, because TeleTech is probably the largest provider of integrated telephone and Internet customer care Worldwide and because of the extensive promotion and advertising that TeleTech appears to have undertaken. The TELETECH® mark has been continuously used

in commerce by TeleTech since 1982. The mark is registered on the Principal Register.

13. TeleTech is entitled to an injunction, under § 43(c) of the Lanham Act, even without a showing of a likelihood of confusion. See Intermatic, 947 F.Supp. at 1234–41, and *Panavision* in which the court found that Toeppen had diluted the plaintiffs' marks by using the plaintiffs' registered trademarks as his domain names. In those cases, Toeppen obtained the domain names in order to force the plaintiffs to pay him money to assign those names to them. This case is somewhat different, in that Defendant claims that it obtained the "teletech.com" domain name, because it was unaware that a hyphen could be used as part of a domain name. However, Defendant in this case also demanded that Plaintiff pay money to the Defendant in order for Defendant to stop using the "teletech.com" domain name. In any event, for purposes of this motion, the reason why Defendant adopted the diluting domain name is not relevant. Plaintiff is the owner of the registered mark TELETECH®, that mark is probably famous, and Defendant's use of the "teletech.com" domain name most likely dilutes Plaintiff's mark.

* * *

15. Plaintiff is therefore entitled to an injunction under § 43(c) of the Lanham Act.

16. California Business and Professions Code § 14330 provides as follows:

> Likelihood of injury to business reputation or of dilution of the distinctive quality of a mark registered under this chapter, or a mark valid at common law, or a trade name valid at common law, shall be a ground for injunctive relief notwithstanding the absence of competition between the parties or the absence of confusion as to the source of goods or services.

17. Plaintiff is entitled to an injunction under this statute as well.

* * *

Panavision International, L.P. v. Toeppen

141 F.3d 1316 (9th Cir.1998).

■ DAVID R. THOMPSON, CIRCUIT JUDGE:

This case presents two novel issues. We are asked to apply existing rules of personal jurisdiction to conduct that occurred, in part, in "cyberspace." In addition, we are asked to interpret the Federal Trademark Dilution Act as it applies to the Internet.

Panavision accuses Dennis Toeppen of being a "cyber pirate" who steals valuable trademarks and establishes domain names on the Internet using these trademarks to sell the domain names to the rightful trademark owners.

The district court found that under the "effects doctrine," Toeppen was subject to personal jurisdiction in California. *Panavision International, L.P. v. Toeppen,* 938 F.Supp. 616, 620 (C.D.Cal.1996). The district court then granted summary judgment in favor of Panavision, concluding that Toeppen's conduct violated the Federal Trademark Dilution Act of 1995, 15 U.S.C. § 1125(c), and the California Anti-dilution statute, California Business & Professions Code § 14330. *Panavision International, L.P. v. Toeppen,* 945 F.Supp. 1296, 1306 (C.D.Cal.1996).

Toeppen appeals. He argues that the district court erred in exercising personal jurisdiction over him because any contact he had with California was insignificant, emanating solely from his registration of domain names on the Internet, which he did in Illinois. Toeppen further argues that the district court erred in granting summary judgment because his use of Panavision's trademarks on the Internet was not a commercial use and did not dilute those marks.

We have jurisdiction under 28 U.S.C. § 1291 and we affirm.

I.

BACKGROUND

[The court begins with a description of the Internet and domain names.]

Panavision holds registered trademarks to the names "Panavision" and "Panaflex" in connection with motion picture camera equipment. Panavision promotes its trademarks through motion picture and television credits and other media advertising.

In December 1995, Panavision attempted to register a website on the Internet with the domain name Panavision.com. It could not do that, however, because Toeppen had already established a website using Panavision's trademark as his domain name. Toeppen's web page for this site displayed photographs of the City of Pana, Illinois.

On December 20, 1995, Panavision's counsel sent a letter from California to Toeppen in Illinois informing him that Panavision held a trademark in the name Panavision and telling him to stop using that trademark and the domain name Panavision.com. Toeppen responded by mail to Panavision in California, stating he had the right to use the name Panavision.com on the Internet as his domain name. Toeppen stated:

> If your attorney has advised you otherwise, he is trying to screw you. He wants to blaze new trails in the legal frontier at your expense. Why do you want to fund your attorney's purchase of a new boat (or whatever) when you can facilitate the acquisition of "PanaVision.com" cheaply and simply instead?

Toeppen then offered to "settle the matter" if Panavision would pay him $13,000 in exchange for the domain name. Additionally, Toeppen stated that if Panavision agreed to his offer, he would not "acquire any other Internet addresses which are alleged by Panavision Corporation to be its property."

After Panavision refused Toeppen's demand, he registered Panavision's other trademark with NSI as the domain name Panaflex.com. Toeppen's web page for Panaflex.com simply displays the word "Hello."

Toeppen has registered domain names for various other companies including Delta Airlines, Neiman Marcus, Eddie Bauer, Lufthansa, and over 100 other marks. Toeppen has attempted to "sell" domain names for other trademarks such as intermatic.com to Intermatic, Inc. for $10,000 and americanstandard.com to American Standard, Inc. for $15,000.

* * *

II.

DISCUSSION

A. Personal Jurisdiction

[The court considers the issue of personal jurisdiction and concludes that the lower court properly exercised personal jurisdiction over Toeppen.]

B. Trademark Dilution Claims

The Federal Trademark Dilution Act provides:

> The owner of a famous mark shall be entitled ... to an injunction against another person's commercial use in commerce of a mark or trade name, if such use begins after the mark has become famous and causes dilution of the distinctive quality of the mark....

15 U.S.C. § 1125(c).

The California Anti-dilution statute is similar. *See* Cal. Bus. & Prof. Code § 14330. It prohibits dilution of "the distinctive quality" of a mark regardless of competition or the likelihood of confusion. The protection extends only to strong and well recognized marks. Panavision's state law dilution claim is subject to the same analysis as its federal claim.

In order to prove a violation of the Federal Trademark Dilution Act, a plaintiff must show that (1) the mark is famous; (2) the defendant is making a commercial use of the mark in commerce; (3) the defendant's use began after the mark became famous; and (4) the defendant's use of the mark dilutes the quality of the mark by diminishing the capacity of the mark to identify and distinguish goods and services. 15 U.S.C. § 1125(c).

Toeppen does not challenge the district court's determination that Panavision's trademark is famous, that his alleged use began after the mark became famous, or that the use was in commerce. Toeppen challenges the district court's determination that he made "commercial use" of the mark and that this use caused "dilution" in the quality of the mark.

1. Commercial Use

Toeppen argues that his use of Panavision's trademarks simply as his domain names cannot constitute a commercial use under the Act. Case law supports this argument. *See Panavision International, L.P. v. Toeppen,* 945 F.Supp. 1296, 1303 (C.D.Cal.1996) ("Registration of a trade[mark] as a domain name, without more, is not a commercial use of the trademark and therefore is not within the prohibitions of the Act."); *Academy of Motion Picture Arts & Sciences v. Network Solutions, Inc.,* 989 F.Supp. 1276, 1997 WL 810472 (C.D.Cal. Dec.22, 1997) (the mere registration of a domain name does not constitute a commercial use); *Lockheed Martin Corp. v. Network Solutions, Inc.,* 985 F.Supp. 949 (C.D.Cal.1997) (NSI's acceptance of a domain name for registration is not a commercial use within the meaning of the Trademark Dilution Act).

Developing this argument, Toeppen contends that a domain name is simply an address used to locate a web page. He asserts that entering a domain name on a computer allows a user to access a web page, but a domain name is not associated with information on a web page. If a user were to type Panavision.com as a domain name, the computer screen would display Toeppen's web page with aerial views of Pana, Illinois. The screen would not provide any information about "Panavision," other than a "location window" which displays the domain name. Toeppen argues that a user who types in Panavision.com, but who sees no reference to the plaintiff Panavision on Toeppen's web page, is not likely to conclude the web page is related in any way to the plaintiff, Panavision.

Toeppen's argument misstates his use of the Panavision mark. His use is not as benign as he suggests. Toeppen's "business" is to register trademarks as domain names and then sell them to the rightful trademark owners. He "act[s] as a 'spoiler,' preventing Panavision and others from doing business on the Internet under their trademarked names unless they pay his fee." *Panavision,* 938 F.Supp. at 621. This is a commercial use. *See Intermatic Inc. v. Toeppen,* 947 F.Supp. 1227, 1230 (N.D.Ill.1996) (stating that "[o]ne of Toeppen's business objectives is to profit by the resale or licensing of these domain names, presumably to the entities who conduct business under these names.").

As the district court found, Toeppen traded on the value of Panavision's marks. So long as he held the Internet registrations, he curtailed Panavision's exploitation of the value of its trademarks on the Internet, a value which Toeppen then used when he attempted to sell the Panavision.com domain name to Panavision.

In a nearly identical case involving Toeppen and Intermatic Inc., a federal district court in Illinois held that Toeppen's conduct violated the Federal Trademark Dilution Act. *Intermatic,* 947 F.Supp. at 1241. There, Intermatic sued Toeppen for registering its trademark on the Internet as Toeppen's domain name, intermatic.com. It was "conceded that one of Toeppen's intended uses for registering the Intermatic mark was to eventually sell it back to Intermatic or to some other party." *Id.* at 1239. The court found that "Toeppen's intention to arbitrage the 'intermatic.com' domain name constitute[d] a commercial use." *Id. See also Teletech Customer Care Management, Inc. v. Tele–Tech Co.,* 977 F.Supp. 1407 (C.D.Cal.

1997) (granting a preliminary injunction under the Trademark Dilution Act for use of a trademark as a domain name).

Toeppen's reliance on *Holiday Inns, Inc. v. 800 Reservation, Inc.*, 86 F.3d 619 (6th Cir.1996), 519 U.S. 1093 (1997) is misplaced. In *Holiday Inns,* the Sixth Circuit held that a company's use of the most commonly *misdialed* number for Holiday Inns' 1–800 reservation number was not trademark infringement.

Holiday Inns is distinguishable. There, the defendant did not use Holiday Inns' trademark. Rather, the defendant selected the most commonly misdialed telephone number for Holiday Inns and attempted to capitalize on consumer confusion.

A telephone number, moreover, is distinguishable from a domain name because a domain name is associated with a word or phrase. A domain name is similar to a "vanity number" that identifies its source. Using Holiday Inns as an example, when a customer dials the vanity number "1–800–Holiday," she expects to contact Holiday Inns because the number is associated with that company's trademark. A user would have the same expectation typing the domain name HolidayInns.com. The user would expect to retrieve Holiday Inns' web page.

Toeppen made a commercial use of Panavision's trademarks. It does not matter that he did not attach the marks to a product. Toeppen's commercial use was his attempt to sell the trademarks themselves.[5] Under the Federal Trademark Dilution Act and the California Anti-dilution statute, this was sufficient commercial use.

2. *Dilution*

"Dilution" is defined as "the lessening of the capacity of a famous mark to identify and distinguish goods or services, regardless of the presence or absence of (1) competition between the owner of the famous mark and other parties, or (2) likelihood of confusion, mistake or deception." 15 U.S.C. § 1127.

Trademark dilution on the Internet was a matter of Congressional concern. Senator Patrick Leahy (D–Vt.) stated:

> [I]t is my hope that this anti-dilution statute can help stem the use of deceptive Internet addresses taken by those who are choosing

5. *See Boston Pro. Hockey Assoc., Inc. v. Dallas Cap & Emblem Mfg., Inc.*, 510 F.2d 1004 (1975), which involved the sale of National Hockey League logos. The defendant was selling the logos themselves, unattached to a product (such as a hat or sweatshirt). The court stated: "The difficulty with this case stems from the fact that a reproduction of the trademark itself is being sold, unattached to any other goods or services." *Id.* at 1010. The court concluded that trademark law should protect the trademark itself. "Although our decision here may slightly tilt the trademark laws from the purpose of protecting the public to the protection of the business interests of plaintiffs, we think that the two become ... intermeshed...." *Id.* at 1011. "Whereas traditional trademark law sought primarily to protect consumers, dilution laws place more emphasis on protecting the investment of the trademark owners." *Panavision,* 945 F.Supp. at 1301.

marks that are associated with the products and reputations of others.

141 Cong. Rec. § 19312–01 (daily ed. Dec. 29, 1995) (statement of Sen. Leahy). *See also Teletech Customer Care Management, Inc. v. Tele–Tech Co., Inc.,* 977 F.Supp. 1407, 1413 (C.D.Cal.1997).

To find dilution, a court need not rely on the traditional definitions such as "blurring" and "tarnishment." Indeed, in concluding that Toeppen's use of Panavision's trademarks diluted the marks, the district court noted that Toeppen's conduct varied from the two standard dilution theories of blurring and tarnishment. *Panavision,* 945 F.Supp. at 1304. The court found that Toeppen's conduct diminished "the capacity of the Panavision marks to identify and distinguish Panavision's goods and services on the Internet." *Id. See also Intermatic,* 947 F.Supp. at 1240 (Toeppen's registration of the domain name, "lessens the capacity of Intermatic to identify and distinguish its goods and services by means of the Internet.").

This view is also supported by *Teletech.* There, TeleTech Customer Care Management Inc., ("TCCM"), sought a preliminary injunction against Tele–Tech Company for use of TCCM's registered service mark, "Tele-Tech," as an Internet domain name. *Teletech,* 977 F.Supp. at 1410. The district court issued an injunction, finding that TCCM had demonstrated a likelihood of success on the merits on its trademark dilution claim. *Id.* at 1412. The court found that TCCM had invested great resources in promoting its servicemark and Teletech's registration of the domain name teletech.com on the Internet would most likely dilute TCCM's mark. *Id.* at 1413.

Toeppen argues he is not diluting the capacity of the Panavision marks to identify goods or services. He contends that even though Panavision cannot use Panavision.com and Panaflex.com as its domain name addresses, it can still promote its goods and services on the Internet simply by using some other "address" and then creating its own web page using its trademarks.

We reject Toeppen's premise that a domain name is nothing more than an address. A significant purpose of a domain name is to identify the entity that owns the website. "A customer who is unsure about a company's domain name will often guess that the domain name is also the company's name." *Cardservice Int'l v. McGee,* 950 F.Supp. 737, 741 (E.D.Va.1997). "[A] domain name mirroring a corporate name may be a valuable corporate asset, as it facilitates communication with a customer base." *MTV Networks, Inc. v. Curry,* 867 F.Supp. 202, 203–204 n. 2 (S.D.N.Y.1994).

Using a company's name or trademark as a domain name is also the easiest way to locate that company's website. Use of a "search engine" can turn up hundreds of websites, and there is nothing equivalent to a phone book or directory assistance for the Internet. *See Cardservice,* 950 F.Supp. at 741.

Moreover, potential customers of Panavision will be discouraged if they cannot find its web page by typing in "Panavision.com," but instead are forced to wade through hundreds of websites. This dilutes the value of Panavision's trademark. We echo the words of Judge Lechner, quoting Judge Wood: "Prospective users of plaintiff's services who mistakenly access defendant's website may fail to continue to search for plaintiff's own home page, due to anger, frustration or the belief that plaintiff's home page does not exist." *Jews for Jesus v. Brodsky,* 993 F.Supp. 282, 306–07 (D.N.J.1998) (Lechner, J., quoting Wood, J. in *Planned Parenthood v. Bucci,* 1997 WL 133313 at *4); *see also Teletech,* 977 F.Supp. at 1410 (finding that use of a search engine can generate as many as 800 to 1000 matches and it is "likely to deter web browsers from searching for Plaintiff's particular web site").

Toeppen's use of Panavision.com also puts Panavision's name and reputation at his mercy. *See Intermatic,* 947 F.Supp. at 1240 ("If Toeppen were allowed to use 'intermatic.com,' Intermatic's name and reputation would be at Toeppen's mercy and could be associated with an unimaginable amount of messages on Toeppen's web page.").

We conclude that Toeppen's registration of Panavision's trademarks as his domain names on the Internet diluted those marks within the meaning of the Federal Trademark Dilution Act, 15 U.S.C. § 1125(c), and the California Anti-dilution statute, Cal.Bus. & Prof.Code § 14330.

* * *

Mark A. Lemley, *The Modern Lanham Act and the Death of Common Sense*

108 YALE L.J. 1687 (1999).

* * *

II. The Expanding Boundaries of Trademark Rights

Courts seem to be replacing the traditional rationale for trademark law with a conception of trademarks as property rights, in which trademark "owners" are given strong rights over the marks without much regard for the social costs of such rights. There appear to be three basic parts to this trend. First, we sometimes seem to be making trademark law for the extreme case, but we then apply that law to a large number of run-of-the-mill trademarks. Second, courts increasingly treat brands as things owned in their own right, rather than as advertising connected with a particular product. Finally, courts have not been sufficiently sensitive to legitimate free speech concerns in cases where trademark owners seek to restrict noncompetitive uses of the trademark.

A. *Making Law for the Extreme Case*

In a number of recent instances, trademark law has been expanded quite significantly by means of new legal rules that make sense in a limited number of cases, but that then enter widespread use where they make less sense. The tendency is perhaps a natural one. If Congress creates a new statute that protects some but not all trademark owners, every trademark owner will want his or her mark to be included in the new group and will seek to receive the added protections of the new rule. If courts are not careful to restrain the new doctrine, it will soon take on a life of its own. I call this the problem of "doctrinal creep."

1. *Dilution*

The most obvious example of doctrinal creep in trademark law is dilution. Dilution laws are directed against the possibility that the unique nature of a mark will be destroyed by companies who trade on the renown of the mark by selling unrelated goods, such as Kodak pianos or Buick aspirin. But because consumers need not be confused for dilution to occur, dilution laws represent a fundamental shift in the nature of trademark protection.

Dilution laws are largely a product of the last fifty years. Approximately half of the states now have dilution statutes. But most recent attention has been focused on the federal dilution statute, which was added in 1995. The federal statute, like most state dilution statutes, protects only "famous" marks. The statute offers a nonexclusive list of eight factors for courts to consider in determining whether a mark is "distinctive and famous." The clear intention seems to have been to restrict dilution doctrine to a relatively small class of nationally known trademarks whose fame is sufficiently great that the risk of blurring by multiple noncompeting uses is significant. But courts applying the state and federal dilution statutes have been quite willing to conclude that a local favorite, or a rather obscure company, is "famous" within the meaning of the Act. Thus, marks such as Intermatic, Gazette, Dennison, Nailtiques, TeleTech, Wedgewood (for new homes, not china), Papal Visit 1999, and Wawa have been declared famous. Worse, many courts seem willing to find dilution without even inquiring into the fame of the mark. Dilution doctrine has also been expanded to encompass not only noncompeting but also nonidentical marks, to protect famous trade dress and product configurations, to attack longstanding uses of descriptive marks to describe products, to aid trademark owners in ordinary cases against competitive marks by dispensing with the need to demonstrate consumer confusion, and even to create a cause of action against consumers (or the press) who do not use marks properly. While the federal law is still relatively new, and so prediction is difficult, we may be moving toward a world in which "famous" marks protected even in the absence of consumer confusion are the rule rather than the exception. The result, as one commentator has noted, is to grant a "trademark in gross"—one unconnected to a particular product—to a wide variety of owners. * * *

3. *Cybersquatters and Domain Names*

Courts have also stretched trademark doctrine to accommodate the extreme case involving Internet domain names and "cybersquatters." Cybersquatters like Dennis Toeppen acted early to lock up a number of Internet domain names that reflect trademarks or corporate names, for a variety of possible purposes. Courts that have considered suits by trademark owners against cybersquatters have uniformly held that obtaining someone else's trademark as a domain name is either trademark infringement or dilution. In many cases, this is clearly the right result. If I register my competitor's name on the Internet, so that potential customers who enter that name will arrive at my site instead, I am clearly creating confusion in an attempt to profit commercially. In other cases, though, courts have had to stretch the "commercial use in commerce" requirement to the vanishing point in order to "catch" cybersquatters. Thus, courts have held that owning a domain name that you do not use is "use in commerce" if you hope to sell the domain name to the trademark owner. And several courts have even held that noncommercial use of a domain name is "commercial use in commerce," reasoning that *any* use on the Internet is automatically a use in commerce. This is in striking contrast to the meaning of the term in ordinary trademark cases.

Toeppen and Bucci are not particularly sympathetic defendants, and trademark or some other law *should* provide a cause of action against those who capture a domain name that clearly ought to belong to someone else in order to extort money from trademark owners. Still, there is something troubling about the erosion of the commercial use and use in commerce requirements. We may find that extending trademark protection to cover noncommercial uses of a mark, however compelling the instant case, sets a dangerous precedent for the law. Indeed, we need not look too far. The cybersquatter precedents are already being used by trademark owners to take domain names away from arguably legitimate users, such as people who want to register their last names as Internet domains and those who build a "gripe site" to complain about a specific product or company.

4. *What's Going on Here?*

* * *

* * * I think the modern dilution * * * cases take a good idea and stretch it too far. * * * [M]ost trademarks are not sufficiently well-known that their use on unrelated products would create even an association in the minds of consumers. Rather, these legal doctrines are being used to serve other purposes, ones that trademark theory does not support.[91] The explosion in product configuration cases in the last twenty years has a lot more to do with acquiring or extending de facto patent and copyright protection through a back door than with protecting consumers from confusion. And the insistence by seemingly every trademark owner that its marks must be thought famous is motivated less by genuine concerns about blurring than by a desire to "keep up with the Cokes" and get the benefit

91. Kratzke argues that dilution doctrine is misguided because it ignores consumer injury. William P. Kratzke, Normative Economic Analysis of Trademark Law, 21 Memphis St. U. L. Rev. 199, 285 (1991). He has a point: Dilution statutes do not commonly require proof of consumer confusion or an appropriate substitute. Properly conceived, however, I think dilution law is protecting consumers against a real harm: the loss of the informational value of a famous trademark through crowding.

of the same property protection that truly famous marks now receive. One can understand why trademark owners want these things, of course, but we must look to the public interest, not private interests, to decide whether trademark owners should get them.[93]

* * *

III. Restoring Common Sense to Trademark Law

If I am right that trademark owners are obtaining property rights that trademark theory cannot justify, what should be done? For the most part, I believe the courts can handle this problem, if they are vigilant in relating the protection plaintiffs seek to the principles of trademark theory and rejecting claims that are not well-founded on trademark principles. We do not need new legal rules here; what we need is the principled and vigorous application of the old rules. Courts should ask, as [Professor Ralph] Brown does, exactly what new incentives do we need trademark law to create? How are consumers hurt by the conduct at issue? And what are the interests of society at large? Brown's answer to these questions still rings true today: "[T]he only interests in trade symbols worth protecting are those against loss of sales or loss of reputation."[142]

Courts should of course protect trademarks against uses that are likely to cause confusion, and against true cases of dilution. And they should be willing to recognize that trademarks can come in many forms, including product configuration, sounds, and colors. But they should resist the inevitable attempts by trademark owners to expand these categories without limit. In particular, they should recognize that the Lanham Act is not a general anti-copying statute—and indeed that not all copying of a competitor's product is bad.

Eradicating the property rationale for trademarks, and restoring common sense to the Lanham Act, will be hard work. The forces arrayed in favor of propertization are powerful indeed. And it is true, as Brown points out, that "the restraining influence of the courts is largely passive."[144] But the courts do have some tools available for this project. The federal dilution statute vests great discretion in the courts in deciding whether a mark is famous. To date, courts have not imposed significant limitations on parties seeking to designate their marks as famous, but they certainly could (and should) do so. * * * Taking the likelihood of confusion requirement, the fair use doctrine, and the doctrine of non-trademark use seriously will also help prevent unwarranted expansion of trademark rights in ways unforeseen by the drafters of the Lanham Act. Finally, the First Amendment

93. * * * For a delightful exposition of this critical fact, which seems to have gotten lost in the debate over trademark law, see Jessica Litman, *Breakfast with Batman: The Public Interest in the Advertising Age*, 108 Yale L.J. 1717, 1725, who notes: "There has been inexorable pressure to recognize as an axiom the principle that if something appears to have substantial value to someone, the law must and should protect it as property."

142. Ralph S. Brown, Jr., *Advertising and the Public Interest: Legal Protection of Trade Symbols*, 57 Yale L.J. 1165, 1201 (1948), *reprinted in* 108 Yale L.J. 1619, 1621 (1999). * * *

144. *Id.* at 1206.

stands (or should stand) as a bulwark against the increasingly common effort to use trademark law to suppress speech.

* * *

NOTES & QUESTIONS

1. *Toeppen as a reseller.* The Internet Corporation for Assigned Names and Numbers ("ICANN") controls the market for registrars through the process of accreditation. (For a description of ICANN and its function, *see* Chapter 1, Part II(F), *supra.*) Accredited registrars, however, are permitted to provide their services through unaccredited resellers so long as the accredited registrar is listed in the TLD registry as the registrar of record. Why shouldn't we construe Toeppen as such a reseller, albeit one with a limited stock of premium domain names? Looked at in this way, isn't Toeppen's business—like NSI's—"connected only with the names' technical function on the Internet"?

2. *Intent and demands for payment.* The court in *Teletech Customer Care Management v. Tele–Tech* concludes that "Defendant's use of the 'tele-tech.com' domain name most likely dilutes Plaintiff's mark." In what way does it dilute plaintiff's mark: by tarnishment, blurring, or otherwise?

3. *Commercial use.* In *Lockheed Martin v. Network Solutions,* Lockheed Martin brought a trademark dilution claim against NSI as well as a trademark infringement claim. In a part of the opinion not reproduced in the text, the court absolves NSI of liability for trademark dilution because NSI "does not make a commercial use of domain names by trading on their value as trademarks." *Lockheed Martin v. Network Solutions,* 985 F.Supp. at 960. Can we reconcile the holdings of the *Lockheed* and *Panavision* courts? If Toeppen's use is commercial, why isn't NSI's?

4. *Surnames.* Is the registration of surnames as second-level domain names and the subsequent licensing of those domain names as e-mail addresses to people with the same surname a commercial use within the meaning of the Federal Trademark Dilution Act? *See Avery Dennison Corporation v. Sumpton,* 189 F.3d 868 (9th Cir.1999), excerpted in Chapter 2, Part II, *supra.*

5. *Confusing trademarks with property?* The law of trademarks was developed to protect a company's good will, thereby creating an incentive for companies to invest in promoting and improving their products for the benefit of the public. It was a tort-like doctrine springing from the tort of unfair competition. Do you agree with Professor Lemley that trademark law as it is being applied to domain names has lost touch with its original purpose? Does the current development of trademark dilution doctrine online serve the public interest or is it a windfall to large corporate interests? How could laws designed to protect against unfair competitive practices be construed as conferring property rights?

6. *Sale of domain names.* Take a look at www.greatdomains.com, "a Verisign Company," where exchange of domain names is flourishing. Examples: On June 24, 2002, Passover.com was listed for $90,000, and

DowQuotes.com was listed for $60,000. Similar exchange sites include www.domainnames-forsale.net (advising that wine.com sold for $3.3 million and asseenontv.com sold for $5 million), www.a-1domainsales.com, and many others. Are these proprietors doing anything illegal? If not, should the law be changed to make what they are doing illegal?

7. *Domain name entrepreneurs in a market economy.* We live in a society that generally employs free markets to allocate efficiently the goods and services that our country produces. Entrepreneurial initiative and vision are generally rewarded with wealth and prestige. Is it then a bit odd that the domain name entrepreneurs have been vilified as "cybersquatters"? These entrepreneurs took some risks: they paid registration fees when the future development of Internet commerce was not yet assured. Why didn't our society permit a free market to develop in which each domain name would end up in the hands of the person or company who could put it to its highest and best use, trademark owner or not?

II. THE ANTICYBERSQUATTING CONSUMER PROTECTION ACT

Trademark infringement and dilution remain important as legal theories under which trademark owners assert rights to a domain name registered to someone else. For the trademark owner to prevail on an infringement theory, use in commerce and consumer confusion must be shown, and in some cases, these are hurdles the trademark owner might not be able to clear. For example, one who registers a domain name desired by a trademark owner but does not offer it for sale to the owner or otherwise use it in any way will likely escape liability, even if the domain name is identical or similar to the trademark. While a dilution claim does not require a showing of consumer confusion, such claims are only available to those trademark owners who can convince a court that their marks are "famous." As one scholar has commented:

> In the author's opinion, there is a very poor fit between the actions of a cybersquatter and the federal Anti-dilution Act. The prototypical cybersquatter does not use the reserved domain name as its mark before the public, so there is no traditional dilution by blurring or tarnishment. Thus, the courts have had to create a wholly new category of "dilution" in order to find a legal weapon to combat this new and different form of reprehensible commercial activity. But this legal tool only protects "famous" marks, requiring that the courts expand and devalue the category of "famous" marks in order to combat cybersquatting.

4 J. THOMAS MCCARTHY, MCCARTHY ON TRADEMARKS AND UNFAIR COMPETITION § 25:77 (4th ed.2002).

To address these problems the Congress enacted the Anticybersquatting Consumer Protection Act ("ACPA"), Pub. L. No. 106–113 (1999). While the Act codifies much of the pre–2000 caselaw, it also introduces a number of significant innovations. For example, it makes actionable the bad faith registration of a domain name that is identical or confusingly similar to another's trademark. It limits such liability, however, to domain name registrants, codifying a domain name registrar's freedom from liability established in the *Lockheed Martin* case. *See* 15 U.S.C. §§ 1125(d)(1) and 1114(D)(iii). The Act also creates an *in rem* action against offending domain names—an important new option for trademark owners when federal courts do not have *in personam* jurisdiction over the domain name registrant. *See* 15 U.S.C. § 1125(d)(2). Yet another innovation is a provision allowing the trademark owner to elect statutory damages in lieu of actual damages. *See* 15 U.S.C. §§ 1117(d). These damages can be as large as $100,000 per registered domain name. The Act also creates a cause of action against registrants who register the non-trademarked names of others without their consent with intent to profit by resale. *See* 15 U.S.C. § 1129.

In the remainder of this Part, we first consider the overview of the Act provided in the report of the United States Senate that accompanied the legislation. We then look at three cases involving, respectively, an *in personam* action against a domain name registrant, an *in rem* action against a domain name, and an action against a cybersquatter in which statutory damages are elected. While the Act clearly grants immunity to domain name registrars for acts of selling another's trademark as a domain name, it is significantly less clear whether the Act creates a statutory framework that adequately addresses the public's right to make noncommercial uses of words and names that are identical or confusingly similar to another's trademark. It also remains to be seen how the threshold requirement that registration be with "bad faith intent to profit" will be interpreted and applied.

Senate Report 106–140

The Anticybersquatting Consumer Protection Act.
(Aug. 5, 1999).

The practice of cybersquatting harms consumers, electronic commerce, and the goodwill equity of valuable U.S. brand names, upon which consumers increasingly rely to locate the true source of genuine goods and services on the Internet. Online consumers have a difficult time distinguishing a genuine site from a pirate site, given that often the only indications of source and authenticity of the site, or the goods and services made available thereon, are the graphical interface on the site itself and the Internet address at which it resides. As a result, consumers have come to rely heavily on familiar brand names when engaging in online commerce. But if someone is operating a website under another brand owner's trademark, such as a site called "cocacola.com" or "levis.com," consumers bear a significant risk of being deceived and defrauded, or at a minimum, confused. The costs associated with these risks are increasingly burdensome as more people begin selling pharmaceuticals, financial services, and even groceries over the Internet. Regardless of what is being sold, the result of online brand name abuse, as with other forms of trademark violations, is the erosion of consumer confidence in brand name identifiers and in electronic commerce generally.

Cybersquatters target distinctive marks for a variety of reasons. Some register well-known brand names as Internet domain names in order to extract payment from the rightful owners of the marks, who find their trademarks "locked up" and are forced to pay for the right to engage in electronic commerce under their own brand name. For example, * * * the Committee * * * heard testimony that Warner Bros. was reportedly asked to pay $350,000 for the rights to the names "warner-records. com", "warner-bros-records.com", "warner-pictures.com", "warner-bros-pictures", and "warnerpictures.com".

Others register well-known marks as domain names and warehouse those marks with the hope of selling them to the highest bidder, whether it be the trademark owner or someone else. For example, * * * the Committee * * * heard testimony regarding a similarly enterprising cybersquatter whose partial inventory of domain names—the listing of which was limited by the fact that Network Solutions will only display the first 50 records of a given registrant—includes names such as Coca–Cola, Pepsi, Burger King, KFC, McDonalds, Subway, Taco Bell, Wendy's, BMW, Chrysler, Dodge, General Motors, Honda, Hyundai, Jaguar, Mazda, Mercedes, Nissan, Porsche, Rolls–Royce, Saab, Saturn, Toyota, and Volvo, all of which are available to the highest bidder through an online offer sheet.

In addition, cybersquatters often register well-known marks to prey on consumer confusion by misusing the domain name to divert customers from the mark owner's site to the cybersquatter's own site, many of which are pornography sites that derive advertising revenue based on the number of visits, or "hits," the site receives. For example, the Committee was informed of a parent whose child mistakenly typed in the domain name for "dosney.com," expecting to access the family-oriented content of the Walt Disney home page, only to end up staring at a screen of hardcore pornography because a cybersquatter had registered that domain name in anticipation that consumers would make that exact mistake. Other instances of diverting unsuspecting consumers to pornographic websites involve malicious attempts to tarnish a trademark owner's mark or to extort money from the trademark owner, such as the case where a cybersquatter placed pornographic images of celebrities on a site under the name "pentium3.com" and announced that it would sell the domain name to the highest bidder. Others attempt to divert unsuspecting consumers to their sites in order to engage in unfair competition. For example, the business operating under the domain name "disneytransportation.com" greets online consumers at its site with a picture of Mickey Mouse and offers shuttle services in the Orlando area and reservations at Disney hotels, although the company is in no way affiliated with the Walt Disney Company and such fact is not clearly indicated on the site. Similarly, the domain name address "wwwcarpoint.com," without a period following "www", was used by a cybersquatter to offer a competing service to Microsoft's popular Carpoint car buying service.

Finally, and most importantly, cybersquatters target distinctive marks to defraud consumers, including to engage in counterfeiting activities. For example, the Committee heard testimony regarding a cybersquatter who registered the domain names "attphonecard.com" and "attcallingcard.com" and used those names to establish sites purporting to sell calling cards and soliciting personally identifying information, including credit card numbers. * * * Of even greater concern was the example of an online drug store selling pharmaceuticals under the name "propecia-sales.com" without any way for online consumers to tell whether what they are buying is a legitimate product, a placebo, or a dangerous counterfeit.

The need for legislation banning cybersquatting

Current law does not expressly prohibit the act of cybersquatting. The World Intellectual Property Organization (WIPO) has identified cybersquatting as a global problem and recognized in its report on the domain name process that, "[f]amous and well-known marks have been the special target of a variety of predatory and parasitical practices on the Internet."[10] * * *

Instances of cybersquatting continue to grow each year because there is no clear deterrent and little incentive for cybersquatters to discontinue their abusive practices. While the Federal Trademark Dilution Act has been useful in pursuing cybersquatters, cybersquatters have become increasingly sophisticated as the case law has developed and now take the necessary precautions to insulate themselves from liability. For example, many cybersquatters are now careful to no longer offer the domain name for sale in any manner that could implicate liability under existing trademark dilution case law. And, in cases of warehousing and trafficking in domain names, courts have sometimes declined to provide assistance to trademark holders, leaving them without adequate and effective judicial remedies. This uncertainty as to the trademark law's application to the Internet has produced inconsistent judicial decisions and created extensive monitoring obligations, unnecessary legal costs, and uncertainty for consumers and trademark owners alike.

In cases where a trademark owner can sue, the sheer number of domain name infringements, the costs associated with hundreds of litigation matters, and the difficulty of obtaining damages in standard trademark infringement and dilution actions are significant obstacles for legitimate trademark holders. Frequently, these obstacles lead trademark owners to simply "pay off" cybersquatters, in exchange for the domain name registration, rather than seek to enforce their rights in court. * * *

10. World Intellectual Property Organization, Management of Internet Names and Addresses: Intellectual Property Issues 8 (1999).

Under the bill, as amended, the abusive conduct that is made actionable is appropriately limited just to bad-faith registrations and uses of others' marks by persons who seek to profit unfairly from the goodwill associated therewith. * * *

The Committee intends the prohibited "use" of a domain name to describe the use of a domain name by the domain name registrant, with the bad-faith intent to profit from the goodwill of the mark of another. The concept of "use" does not extend to uses of the domain name made by those other than the domain name registrant, such as the person who includes the domain name as a hypertext link on a web page or as part of a directory of Internet addresses.

In addition, the bill, as amended, balances the property interests of trademark owners with the interests of Internet users who would make fair use of others' marks or otherwise engage in protected speech online. First, the bill sets forth a number of balancing factors that a court may wish to consider in deciding whether the requisite bad-faith intent is present in any given case. * * * [Codified at 15 U.S.C. § 1125(d)(1)(B)(i)(I)–(IX)], [e]ach of these factors reflect indicators that, in practice, commonly suggest bad-faith intent or a lack thereof in cybersquatting cases. * * *

Second, the amended bill underscores the bad-faith requirement by requiring a court to remit statutory damages in any case where a defendant believed, and the court finds that the defendant had reasonable grounds to believe, that the registration or use of the domain name was a fair or otherwise lawful use. In addition, the bill makes clear that the newly created statutory damages shall apply only with respect to bad-faith conduct occurring on or after the date of enactment of the bill.

Definition of "domain name"

The bill, as amended, provides a narrow definition of the term "domain name" in order to tailor the bill's reach narrowly to the problem sought to be addressed. Thus, the term "domain name" describes any alphanumeric designation which is registered with or assigned by any domain name registrar, domain name registry, or other domain name registration authority as part of an electronic address on the Internet. This definition essentially covers the second-level domain names assigned by domain name registration authorities (i.e., the name located immediately to the left of the ".com," ".net", ".edu," and ".org" generic top level domains), but is technology neutral enough to accommodate names other than second-level domains that are actually registered with domain name registration authorities, as may be the case should Internet domain name registrars begin to issue third or fourth level domains. The limited nature of the definition is important in that it excludes such things as screen names, file names, and other identifiers not assigned by a domain name registrar or registry, which have little to do with cybersquatting in practice.

In rem jurisdiction

As amended, the bill provides for in rem jurisdiction, which allows a mark owner to seek the forfeiture, cancellation, or transfer of an infringing domain name by filing an in rem action against the name itself, provided the domain name itself violates substantive Federal trademark law, where the mark owner has satisfied the court that it has exercised due diligence in trying to locate the owner of the domain name but is unable to do so. A significant problem faced by trademark owners in the fight against cybersquatting is the fact that many cybersquatters register domain names under aliases or otherwise provide false information in their registration applications in order to avoid identification and service of process by the mark owner. The bill, as amended, will alleviate this difficulty, while protecting the notions of fair play and substantial justice, by enabling a mark owner to seek an injunction against the infringing property in those cases where, after due diligence, a mark owner is unable to proceed against the domain name registrant because the registrant has provided false contact information and is otherwise not to be found.

Additionally, some have suggested that dissidents and others who are online incognito for legitimate reasons might give false information to protect themselves and have suggested the need to preserve a degree of anonymity on the Internet particularly for this reason. Allowing a trademark owner to proceed against the domain names themselves, provided they are, in fact, infringing or diluting under the Trademark Act, decreases the need for trademark owners to join the hunt to chase down and root out these dissidents or others seeking anonymity on the Net. The approach in the amended bill is a good compromise, which provides meaningful protection to trademark owners while balancing the interests of privacy and anonymity on the Internet.

Encouraging cooperation and fairness in the effort to combat cybersquatting

Like the underlying bill, the substitute amendment encourages domain name registrars and registries to work with trademark owners to prevent cybersquatting by providing a limited exemption from monetary damages for domain name registrars and registries that suspend, cancel, or transfer domain names pursuant to a court order or in the implementation of a reasonable policy prohibiting the registration of infringing domain names. The amended bill goes further, however, in order to protect the rights of domain name registrants against overreaching trademark owners. Under the amended bill, a trademark owner who knowingly and materially misrepresents to the domain name registrar or registry that a domain name is infringing is liable to the domain name registrant for damages, including costs and attorneys' fees, resulting from the suspension, cancellation, or transfer of the domain name. In addition, the court may award injunctive relief to the domain name registrant by ordering the reactivation of the domain name or the transfer of the domain name back to the domain name registrant. The bill, as amended, also promotes the continued ease and efficiency users of the current registration system enjoy by codifying current case law limiting the secondary liability of domain name registrars and registries for the act of registration of a domain name.[11]

Preservation of first amendment rights and trademark defenses

Finally, the substitute amendment includes an explicit savings clause making clear that the bill does not affect traditional trademark defenses, such as fair use, or a person's first amendment rights, and it ensures that any new remedies created by the bill will apply prospectively only.

In summary, the legislation is a balanced approach to protecting the legitimate interests of businesses, Internet users, e-commerce, and consumers.

* * *

Sporty's Farm L.L.C. v. Sportsman's Market, Inc.

202 F.3d 489 (2d Cir.2000).

■ CALABRESI, CIRCUIT JUDGE:

This case originally involved the application of the Federal Trademark Dilution Act ("FTDA") to the Internet. *See* Federal Trademark Dilution Act of 1995, Pub.L. No. 104–98, 109 Stat. 985 (codified at 15 U.S.C. §§ 1125, 1127 (Supp.1996)). While the case was pending on appeal, however, the Anticybersquatting Consumer Protection Act ("ACPA"), Pub.L. No. 106–113 (1999), *see* H.R.Rep. No. 106–479 (Nov. 18, 1999), was passed and signed into law. That new law applies to this case.

BACKGROUND

I

* * *

Over the last few years, the commercial side of the Internet has grown rapidly. Web pages are now used by companies to provide information about their products in a much more detailed fashion than can be done through a standard advertisement. Moreover, many consumers and businesses now order goods and services directly from company web pages. Given that Internet sales are paperless and have lower transaction costs than other types of retail sales, the commercial potential of this technology is vast.

For consumers to buy things or gather information on the Internet, they need an easy way to find particular companies or brand names. The most common method of locating an unknown domain name is simply to

11. *See Panavision Int'l v. Toeppen*, 141 F.3d 1316, 1319 (9th Cir.1998) (holding that NSI is not responsible for making "a determination about registrant's right to use a domain name."); *Lockheed Martin Corporation v. Networks Solutions, Inc.*, 985 F.Supp. 949 (C.D.Ca.1997) (holding registrar not liable); *Academy of Motion Picture Arts and Science v. Network Solutions, Inc.*, 989 F.Supp. 1276, (C.D.Ca.1997) (holding that holder of registered trademarks could not obtain a preliminary injunction against domain name registrar).

type in the company name or logo with the suffix .com. If this proves unsuccessful, then Internet users turn to a device called a search engine. A search engine will find all web pages on the Internet with a particular word or phrase. Given the current state of search engine technology, that search will often produce a list of hundreds of websites through which the user must sort in order to find what he or she is looking for. As a result, companies strongly prefer that their domain name be comprised of the company or brand trademark and the suffix .com. *See* H.R.Rep. No. 106–412, at 5 (1999).

Until recently, domain names with the .com top level domain could only be obtained from Network Solutions, Inc. ("NSI"). Now other registrars may also assign them. But all these registrars grant such names primarily on a first-come, first-served basis upon payment of a small registration fee. They do not generally inquire into whether a given domain name request matches a trademark held by someone other than the person requesting the name. *See id.*

Due to the lack of any regulatory control over domain name registration, an Internet phenomenon known as "cybersquatting" has become increasingly common in recent years. *See, e.g.,* Panavision Int'l, L.P. v. Toeppen, 141 F.3d 1316 (9th Cir.1998). Cybersquatting involves the registration as domain names of well-known trademarks by non-trademark holders who then try to sell the names back to the trademark owners. Since domain name registrars do not check to see whether a domain name request is related to existing trademarks, it has been simple and inexpensive for any person to register as domain names the marks of established companies. This prevents use of the domain name by the mark owners, who not infrequently have been willing to pay "ransom" in order to get "their names" back. *See* H.R.Rep. No. 106–412, at 5–7; S.Rep. No. 106–140, at 4–7 (1999).

II

Sportsman's is a mail order catalog company that is quite well-known among pilots and aviation enthusiasts for selling products tailored to their needs. In recent years, Sportsman's has expanded its catalog business well beyond the aviation market into that for tools and home accessories. The company annually distributes approximately 18 million catalogs nationwide, and has yearly revenues of about $50 million. Aviation sales account for about 60% of Sportsman's revenue, while non-aviation sales comprise the remaining 40%.

In the 1960s, Sportsman's began using the logo "*sporty*" to identify its catalogs and products. In 1985, Sportsman's registered the trademark *sporty's* with the United States Patent and Trademark Office. Since then, Sportsman's has complied with all statutory requirements to preserve its interest in the *sporty's* mark. *Sporty's* appears on the cover of all Sportsman's catalogs; Sportsman's international toll free number is 1–800–4*sportys;* and one of Sportsman's domestic toll free phone numbers is 1–

800–*Sportys*. Sportsman's spends about $10 million per year advertising its *sporty's* logo.

Omega is a mail order catalog company that sells mainly scientific process measurement and control instruments. In late 1994 or early 1995, the owners of Omega, Arthur and Betty Hollander, decided to enter the aviation catalog business and, for that purpose, formed a wholly-owned subsidiary called Pilot's Depot, LLC ("Pilot's Depot"). Shortly thereafter, Omega registered the domain name sportys.com with NSI. Arthur Hollander was a pilot who received Sportsman's catalogs and thus was aware of the *sporty's* trademark.

In January 1996, nine months after registering sportys.com, Omega formed another wholly-owned subsidiary called Sporty's Farm and sold it the rights to sportys.com for $16,200. Sporty's Farm grows and sells Christmas trees, and soon began advertising its Christmas trees on a sportys.com web page. When asked how the name Sporty's Farm was selected for Omega's Christmas tree subsidiary, Ralph S. Michael, the CEO of Omega and manager of Sporty's Farm, explained, as summarized by the district court, that

> in his own mind and among his family, he always thought of and referred to the Pennsylvania land where Sporty's Farm now operates as *Spotty's farm*. The origin of the name ... derived from a childhood memory he had of his uncle's farm in upstate New York. As a youngster, Michael owned a dog named Spotty. Because the dog strayed, his uncle took him to his upstate farm. Michael thereafter referred to the farm as Spotty's farm. The name Sporty's Farm was ... a subsequent derivation.

Joint Appendix ("JA") at 277 (emphasis added). There is, however, no evidence in the record that Hollander was considering starting a Christmas tree business when he registered sportys.com or that Hollander was ever acquainted with Michael's dog Spotty.

In March 1996, Sportsman's discovered that Omega had registered sportys.com as a domain name. Thereafter, and before Sportsman's could take any action, Sporty's Farm brought this declaratory action seeking the right to continue its use of sportys.com. Sportsman's counterclaimed and also sued Omega as a third-party defendant for, *inter alia,* (1) trademark infringement, (2) trademark dilution pursuant to the FTDA, and (3) unfair competition under state law. Both sides sought injunctive relief to force the other to relinquish its claims to sportys.com. While this litigation was ongoing, Sportsman's used "sportys-catalogs.com" as its primary domain name.

After a bench trial, the court rejected Sportsman's trademark infringement claim and all related claims that are based on a "likelihood of [consumer] confusion" since "the parties operate wholly unrelated businesses [and t]herefore, confusion in the marketplace is not likely to develop." *Id.* at 282–83. But on Sportsman's trademark dilution action, where a likelihood of confusion was not necessary, the district court found for Sportsman's. * * * The court also held, however, that Sportsman's could only get injunctive relief and was not entitled to "punitive damages ... profits, and attorney's fees and costs" pursuant to the FTDA since Sporty Farm and Omega's conduct did not constitute willful dilution under the FTDA. *Id.* at 292–93.

Finally, the district court ruled that, although Sporty's Farm had violated the FTDA, its conduct did not constitute a violation of CUTPA [the Connecticut Unfair Trade Practices Act]. * * *

The district court then issued an injunction forcing Sporty's Farm to relinquish all rights to sportys.com. And Sportsman's subsequently acquired the domain name. Both Sporty's Farm and Sportsman's appeal. Specifically, Sporty's Farm appeals the judgment insofar as the district court granted an injunction in favor of Sportsman's for the use of the domain name. Sportsman's, on the other hand, in addition to urging this court to affirm the district court's injunction, cross-appeals, quite correctly as a procedural matter, the district court's denial of damages under both the FTDA and CUPTA. * * *

III

As we noted above, while this appeal was pending, Congress passed the ACPA. That law was passed "to protect consumers and American businesses, to promote the growth of online commerce, and to provide clarity in the law for trademark owners by prohibiting the bad-faith and abusive registration of distinctive marks as Internet domain names with the intent to profit from the goodwill associated with such marks—a practice commonly referred to as 'cybersquatting'." S.Rep. No. 106–140, at 4. In particular, Congress viewed the legal remedies available for victims of cybersquatting before the passage of the ACPA as "expensive and uncertain." H.R.Rep. No. 106–412, at 6. * * * In short, the ACPA was passed to remedy the perceived shortcomings of applying the FTDA in cybersquatting cases such as this one.

The new act accordingly amends the Trademark Act of 1946, creating a specific federal remedy for cybersquatting. New 15 U.S.C. § 1125(d)(1)(A) reads:

A person shall be liable in a civil action by the owner of a mark, including a personal name which is protected as a mark under this section, if, without regard to the goods or services of the parties, that person—

(i) has a bad faith intent to profit from that mark, including a personal name which is protected as a mark under this section; and

(ii) registers, traffics in, or uses a domain name that—

(I) in the case of a mark that is distinctive at the time of registration of the domain name, is identical or confusingly similar to that mark;

(II) in the case of a famous mark that is famous at the time of registration of the domain name, is identical or confusingly similar to or dilutive of that mark; . . .

The Act further provides that "a court may order the forfeiture or cancellation of the domain name or the transfer of the domain name to the owner of the mark," 15 U.S.C. § 1125(d)(1)(C), if the domain name was "registered before, on, or after the date of the enactment of this Act," Pub.L. No. 106–113, § 3010. It also provides that damages can be awarded for violations of the Act, but that they are not "available with respect to the registration, trafficking, or use of a domain name that occurs before the date of the enactment of this Act." *Id.*

DISCUSSION

This case has three distinct features that are worth noting before we proceed further. First, our opinion appears to be the first interpretation of the ACPA at the appellate level. Second, we are asked to undertake the interpretation of this new statute even though the district court made its ruling based on the FTDA. Third, the case before us presents a factual situation that, as far as we can tell, is rare if not unique: A Competitor X of Company Y has registered Y's trademark as a domain name and then transferred that name to Subsidiary Z, which operates a business wholly unrelated to Y. These unusual features counsel that we decide no more than is absolutely necessary to resolve the case before us.

A. Application of the ACPA to this Case

The first issue before us is whether the ACPA governs this case. The district court based its holding on the FTDA since the ACPA had not been passed when it made its decision. Because the ACPA became law while this case was pending before us, we must decide how its passage affects this case. As a general rule, we apply the law that exists at the time of the appeal. *See, e.g.,* Hamm v. City of Rock Hill, 379 U.S. 306, 312–13 (1964) (" '[I]f subsequent to the judgment and before the decision of the appellate court, a law intervenes and positively changes the rule which governs, the law must be obeyed, or its obligation denied.' " (quoting United States v. Schooner Peggy, 5 U.S. (1 Cranch) 103, 110, 2 L.Ed. 49 (1801))).

But even if a new law controls, the question remains whether in such circumstances it is more appropriate for the appellate court to apply it directly or, instead, to remand to the district court to enable that court to consider the effect of the new law. We therefore asked for additional briefing from the parties regarding the applicability of the ACPA to the case before us. After receiving those briefs and fully considering the arguments there made, we think it is clear that the new law was adopted specifically to provide courts with a preferable alternative to stretching federal dilution law when dealing with cybersquatting cases. Indeed, the new law constitutes a particularly good fit with this case. Moreover, the findings of the district court, together with the rest of the record, enable us to apply the new law to the case before us without difficulty. Accordingly, we will do so and forego a remand.

B. "Distinctive" or "Famous"

Under the new Act, we must first determine whether *sporty's* is a distinctive or famous mark and thus entitled to the ACPA's protection. *See* 15 U.S.C. § 1125(d)(1)(A)(ii)(I), (II). The district court concluded that *sporty's* is both distinctive and famous. We agree that *sporty's* is a "distinctive" mark. As a result, and without casting any doubt on the district court's holding in this respect, we need not, and hence do not, decide whether *sporty's* is also a "famous" mark.

Distinctiveness refers to inherent qualities of a mark and is a completely different concept from fame. A mark may be distinctive before it has been used—when its fame is nonexistent. By the same token, even a famous mark may be so ordinary, or descriptive as to be notable for its lack of distinctiveness. See Nabisco, Inc. v. PF Brands, Inc., 191 F.3d 208, 215–26 (2d Cir.1999). We have no doubt that *sporty's,* as used in connection with Sportsman's catalogue of merchandise and advertising, is inherently distinctive. Furthermore, Sportsman's filed an affidavit under 15 U.S.C. § 1065 that rendered its registration of the *sporty's* mark incontestable, which entitles Sportsman's "to a presumption that its registered trademark is inherently distinctive." Equine Technologies, Inc. v. Equitechnology, Inc., 68 F.3d 542, 545 (1st Cir.1995). We therefore conclude that, for the purposes of § 1125(d)(1)(A)(ii)(I), the *sporty's* mark is distinctive.

C. "Identical and Confusingly Similar"

The next question is whether domain name sportys.com is "identical or confusingly similar to" the *sporty's* mark.[11] 15 U.S.C. § 1125(d)(1)(A)(ii)(I). * * * [A]postrophes cannot be used in domain names. * * * As a result, the secondary domain name in this case (sportys) is indistinguishable from the Sportsman's trademark (*sporty's*). *Cf.* Brookfield Communications, Inc. v. West Coast Entertainment Corp., 174 F.3d 1036, 1055 (9th Cir.1999) (observing that the differences between the mark "MovieBuff" and the domain name "moviebuff.com" are "inconsequential in light of the fact that Web addresses are not caps-sensitive and that the '.com' top-level domain signifies the site's commercial nature"). We therefore conclude that, although the domain name sportys.com is not precisely identical to the *sporty's* mark, it is certainly "confusingly similar" to the protected mark under § 1125(d)(1)(A)(ii)(I). *Cf. Wella Corp. v. Wella Graphics, Inc.,* 874 F.Supp. 54, 56 (E.D.N.Y.1994) (finding the new mark "Wello" confusingly similar to the trademark "Wella").

11. We note that "confusingly similar" is a different standard from the "likelihood of confusion" standard for trademark infringement adopted by this court in Polaroid Corp. v. Polarad Electronics Corp., 287 F.2d 492 (2d Cir.1961). See Wella Corp. v. Wella Graphics, Inc., 37 F.3d 46, 48 (2d Cir.1994).

D. *"Bad Faith Intent to Profit"*

We next turn to the issue of whether Sporty's Farm acted with a "bad faith intent to profit" from the mark *sporty's* when it registered the domain name sportys.com. 15 U.S.C. § 1125(d)(1)(A)(i). The statute lists nine factors to assist courts in determining when a defendant has acted with a bad faith intent to profit from the use of a mark. But we are not limited to considering just the listed factors when making our determination of whether the statutory criterion has been met. The factors are, instead, expressly described as indicia that "may" be considered along with other facts. *Id.* § 1125(d)(1)(B)(i).

We hold that there is more than enough evidence in the record below of "bad faith intent to profit" on the part of Sporty's Farm (as that term is defined in the statute), so that "no reasonable factfinder could return a verdict against" Sportsman's. Norville v. Staten Island Univ. Hosp., 196 F.3d 89, 95 (2d Cir.1999). First, it is clear that neither Sporty's Farm nor Omega had any intellectual property rights in sportys.com at the time Omega registered the domain name. *See id.* § 1125(d)(1)(B)(i)(I). Sporty's Farm was not formed until nine months after the domain name was registered, and it did not begin operations or obtain the domain name from Omega until after this lawsuit was filed. Second, the domain name does not consist of the legal name of the party that registered it, Omega. *See id.* § 1125(d)(1)(B)(i)(II). Moreover, although the domain name does include part of the name of Sporty's Farm, that entity did not exist at the time the domain name was registered.

The third factor, the prior use of the domain name in connection with the bona fide offering of any goods or services, also cuts against Sporty's Farm since it did not use the site until after this litigation began, undermining its claim that the offering of Christmas trees on the site was in good faith. *See id.* § 1125(d)(1)(B)(i)(III). Further weighing in favor of a conclusion that Sporty's Farm had the requisite statutory bad faith intent, as a matter of law, are the following: (1) Sporty's Farm does not claim that its use of the domain name was "noncommercial" or a "fair use of the mark," *see id.* § 1125(d)(1)(B)(i)(IV), (2) Omega sold the mark to Sporty's Farm under suspicious circumstances, *see* Sporty's Farm v. Sportsman's Market, No. 96CV0756 (D.Conn. Mar. 13, 1998), *reprinted in* Joint Appendix at A277 (describing the circumstances of the transfer of sportys.com); 15 U.S.C. § 1125(d)(1)(B)(i)(VI), and, (3) as we discussed above, the *sporty's* mark is undoubtedly distinctive, *see id.* § 1125(d)(1)(B)(i)(IX).

The most important grounds for our holding that Sporty's Farm acted with a bad faith intent, however, are the unique circumstances of this case, which do not fit neatly into the specific factors enumerated by Congress but may nevertheless be considered under the statute. We know from the record and from the district court's findings that Omega planned to enter into direct competition with Sportsman's in the pilot and aviation consumer market. As recipients of Sportsman's catalogs, Omega's owners, the Hollanders, were fully aware that *sporty's* was a very strong mark for consumers of those products. It cannot be doubted, as the court found below, that Omega registered sportys.com for the primary purpose of keeping Sportsman's from using that domain name. Several months later, and after this lawsuit was filed, Omega created another company in an unrelated business that received the name Sporty's Farm so that it could (1) use the sportys.com domain name in some commercial fashion, (2) keep the name away from Sportsman's, and (3) protect itself in the event that Sportsman's brought an infringement claim alleging that a "likelihood of confusion" had been created by Omega's version of cybersquatting. Finally, the explanation given for Sporty's Farm's desire to use the domain name, based on the existence of the dog Spotty, is more amusing than credible. Given these facts and the district court's grant of an equitable injunction under the FTDA, there is ample and overwhelming evidence that, as a matter of law, Sporty's Farm's acted with a "bad faith intent to profit" from the domain name sportys.com as those terms are used in the ACPA.[13] *See* Luciano v. Olsten Corp., 110 F.3d 210, 214 (2d Cir.1997) (stating that, as a matter of law, judgment may be granted where "the evidence in favor of the movant is so overwhelming that 'reasonable and fair minded [persons] could not arrive at a verdict against [it].' " (quoting Cruz v. Local Union No. 3, 34 F.3d 1148, 1154 (2d Cir.1994) (alteration in original))).

E. Remedy

Based on the foregoing, we hold that under § 1125(d)(1)(A), Sporty's Farm violated Sportsman's statutory rights by its use of the sportys.com domain name.[14] The question that remains is what remedy is Sportsman's entitled to. The Act permits a court to "order the forfeiture or cancellation of the domain name or the transfer of the domain name to the owner of the mark," § 1125(d)(1)(C) for any "domain name [ ] registered before, on, or after the date of the enactment of [the] Act," Pub.L. No. 106–113, § 3010. That is precisely what the district court did here, albeit under the pre-existing law, when it directed a) Omega and Sporty's Farm to release their interest in sportys.com and to transfer the name to Sportsman's, and b) permanently enjoined those entities from taking any action to prevent and/or hinder Sportsman's from obtaining the domain name. That relief remains appropriate under the ACPA. We therefore affirm the district court's grant of injunctive relief.

We must also determine, however, if Sportsman's is entitled to damages either under the ACPA or pre-existing law. Under the ACPA, damages are unavailable to Sportsman's since sportys.com was registered and used by Sporty's Farm prior to the passage of the new law. *See id.* (stating that

13. We expressly note that "bad faith intent to profit" are terms of art in the ACPA and hence should not necessarily be equated with "bad faith" in other contexts.

14. The statute provides that a party "shall be *liable* in a civil action by the owner of a mark" if it meets the statutory requirements. 15 U.S.C. § 1125(d)(1)(A) (emphasis added). Although the statute uses the term "liable," it does not follow that damages will be assessed. As we discuss below, damages can be awarded for violations of the Act but they are not "available with respect to the registration, trafficking, or use of a domain name that occurs [,as in this case,] before the date of the enactment of this Act." Pub.L. No. 106–113, § 3010.

damages can be awarded for violations of the Act but that they are not "available with respect to the registration, trafficking, or use of a domain name that occurs before the date of the enactment of this Act.").

But Sportsman's might, nonetheless, be eligible for damages under the FTDA since there is nothing in the ACPA that precludes, in cybersquatting cases, the award of damages under any pre-existing law. *See* 15 U.S.C. § 1125(d)(3) (providing that any remedies created by the new act are "in addition to any other civil action or remedy otherwise applicable"). Under the FTDA, "[t]he owner of the famous mark shall be entitled only to injunctive relief unless the person against whom the injunction is sought *willfully* intended to trade on the owner's reputation or to cause dilution of the famous mark." *Id.* § 1125(c)(2) (emphasis added). Accordingly, where willful intent to dilute is demonstrated, the owner of the famous mark is—subject to the principles of equity—entitled to recover (1) damages (2) the dilutor's profits, and (3) costs. *See id.; see also id.* § 1117(a) (specifying remedies).

We conclude, however, that damages are not available to Sportsman's under the FTDA. The district court found that Sporty's Farm did not act willfully. We review such findings of "willfulness" by a district court for clear error. *See* Bambu Sales, Inc. v. Ozak Trading Inc., 58 F.3d 849, 854 (2d Cir.1995). Thus, even assuming the *sporty's* mark to be famous, we cannot say that the district court clearly erred when it found that Sporty's Farm's actions were not willful. To be sure, that question is a very close one, for the facts make clear that, as a Sportsman's customer, Arthur Hollander (Omega's owner) was aware of the significance of the *sporty's* logo. And the idea of creating a Christmas tree business named Sporty's Farm, allegedly in honor of Spotty the dog, and of giving that business the sportys.com domain name seems to have occurred to Omega only several months after it had registered the name. Nevertheless, given the uncertain state of the law at the time that Sporty's Farm and Omega acted, we cannot say that the district court clearly erred in finding that their behavior did not amount to willful dilution. It follows that Sportsman's is not entitled to damages under the FTDA.

Sportsman's also argues that it is entitled to damages under state law. Because neither the FTDA nor the ACPA preempts state remedies such as CUTPA, damages under Connecticut law are not barred, and hence may be available to Sportsman's. *See* H.R.Rep. No. 104–374, at 4 (1995), *reprinted in* 1996 U.S.C.C.A.N. 1029, 1031; 15 U.S.C. § 1125(d)(3). [The court concludes that damages are not available.]

In sum, then, we hold that the injunction issued by the district court was proper under the new anticybersquatting law, but that damages are not available to Sportsman's under the ACPA, the FTDA, or CUTPA.

F. Retroactivity

Sporty Farm's also contends that even if its actions would today violate the FTDA or the ACPA, any injunction requiring it to relinquish use of sportys.com is impermissibly retroactive. We find Sporty's Farm's position to be meritless. * * *

CONCLUSION

The judgment of the district court is AFFIRMED in all particulars.

Alitalia–Linee Aeree Italiane, S.p.A. v. Casinoalitalia.Com

128 F.Supp.2d 340 (E.D.Va.2001).

■ ELLIS, DISTRICT JUDGE.

In this trademark dispute, the plaintiff, an Italian airline, has sued both the foreign registrant of an allegedly infringing domain name *in personam* and the domain name itself *in rem*. At issue on plaintiff's summary judgment motion is whether, consistent with the Anticybersquatting Consumer Protection Act (“ACPA” or the “Act”), a mark owner may maintain *in personam* claims against a domain name registrant concurrently with an *in rem* claim against the domain name. Also presented is the related question whether the Virginia long-arm statute constitutionally reaches the foreign registrant.

I.

Plaintiff Alitalia–Linee Aeree Italiane S.p.A. (“Alitalia”) is Italy's national airline and is in the business of providing air cargo service and passenger transportation between Italy and the United States, among other foreign countries. Alitalia is the owner of a United States Trademark Registration issued on March 21, 1995, for the mark “Alitalia.” Alitalia's founders coined the term “Alitalia,” which has been used by the airline since 1957, by combining the words “Ali,” which in Italian means “wings,” and “d'Italia,” which means “Italian”; the term “Alitalia,” therefore, literally means “Italian wings.”

Since Alitalia began operation in 1957, the airline has made continuous and widespread use of the mark “Alitalia” through extensive advertising and other means by which the carrier promotes and sells its services. In this regard, Alitalia spends approximately $60 million per year in advertising and promoting the “Alitalia” logo and mark. In addition, Alitalia maintains a website for its airline business at <www.alitalia.it> and has registered the Internet domain names <www.alitalia.com> and <www.alitalia.net>. A search of the Internet for the word “alitalia,” however, returns not only Alitalia's website, but also an Internet site using the domain name <casinoalitalia.com>, which has no affiliation or connection whatever to Alitalia.

Defendant Technologia JPR, Inc., (“JPR”) has registered the domain name <casinoalitalia.com> with registrar Network Solutions, Inc., (“NSI”). JPR is an entity established under the laws of the Dominican Republic, and JPR's NSI registration information lists JPR's place of business (including administrative, technical, and billing contacts) as located in Santo Domingo, Dominican Republic. JPR conducts its business entirely outside of the United States, and the company has no offices or other physical presence in the United States; it neither owns nor leases property in the United States and has no employees in the United States. Alitalia claims that JPR registered the domain name on or about October 13, 1999, although it appears from NSI's registration information that JPR registered the domain name with NSI in August 1998.

It is evident from a visit to <casinoalitalia.com> that the website exists for the purpose of conducting the business of online casino gambling. A visitor to the website can play one or more online casino games—e.g., blackjack, poker, keno, slots, craps, and roulette—by opening an account with <casinoalitalia.com> and purchasing casino "credits" that may be used to play individual games. Players can then win credits that can be redeemed for U.S. currency. In this regard, the website appears to be an attempt to simulate the experience of gambling at a conventional "brick and mortar" casino.

A visit to the website also reveals that the term "Alitalia" appears on the first page. Given this, Alitalia, which has not given JPR permission to use the mark "Alitalia" or any variation thereof for any purpose, claims that the domain name <casinoalitalia.com> and JPR's unauthorized use of the term "alitalia" create a false impression that Alitalia promotes the business of online gambling and/or any other enterprise pursued by defendants. Indeed, Alitalia claims that the word "casino" means "brothel," so that a literal translation of "casinoalitalia" is "alitalia's brothel." Thus, argues Alitalia, the site appears in the minds of consumers familiar with the Italian language to offer the services of a brothel associated or affiliated with Alitalia. In this regard, plaintiff contends, the website <casinoalitalia.com> irreparably harms, tarnishes, and dilutes the goodwill, reputation, and image of the Alitalia mark.

In March of this year, Alitalia brought a four-count complaint stating claims for (i) trademark infringement, under 15 U.S.C. § 1114 *et seq.*, against JPR (Count I); (ii) violation of the Lanham Act, 15 U.S.C. §§ 1125(a), (c), against JPR (Count II); (iii) common law unfair competition against JPR (Count III); and (iv) violation of the ACPA against JPR and <casinoalitalia.com> (Count IV). Alitalia has moved for summary judgment on all four counts. In doing so, Alitalia argues, remarkably, that the ACPA entitles it to proceed concurrently both *in rem* and *in personam*. Whether this is so presents a threshold question that must be resolved before proceeding to resolve the remaining questions of personal jurisdiction and summary judgment. JPR has entered a limited appearance for the purpose of challenging personal jurisdiction.[4]

4. See Caesars World, Inc. v. Caesars-Palace.Com, 112 F.Supp.2d 505, 509 (E.D.Va. 2000) (noting that "*in personam* jurisdiction cannot be based merely on an appearance in an *in rem* action"); Harrods Ltd. v. Sixty Internet Domain Names, 110 F.Supp.2d 420, 421–23 (E.D.Va.2000) (holding that "no personal jurisdiction over the owner of the res is acquired by bringing ... [an *in rem*] action" under the ACPA, and a plaintiff "cannot

II.

The ACPA creates two avenues by which claimants may seek a remedy for "cyberpiracy." The first, found in § 1 of the ACPA, is a remedy for owners of a mark *in personam* against a person who, with "a bad faith intent to profit from that mark[,] . . . registers, traffics in, or uses a domain name" that:

> (I) in the case of a mark that is distinctive at the time of registration of the domain name, is identical or confusingly similar to that mark;
>
> (II) in the case of a famous mark that is famous at the time of registration of the domain name, is identical or confusingly similar to or dilutive of that mark; or
>
> (III) is a trademark, work, or name protected by reason of § 706 of Title 18 or § 220506 of Title 36.

15 U.S.C. § 1125(d)(1)(A). A plaintiff proceeding under § 1 has available a full panoply of legal and equitable remedies. Specifically, such a plaintiff may seek compensatory damages, including disgorgement of defendant's profits, or elect to recover, "instead of actual damages and profits, an award of statutory damages in the amount of not less than $1,000 and not more than $100,000 per domain name, as the court considers just." 15 U.S.C. § 1117(a) and (d).[5] In addition, a § 1 plaintiff may seek injunctive relief, including "the forfeiture or cancellation of the domain name or the transfer of the domain name to the owner of the mark." 15 U.S.C. § 1125(d)(1)(C); *see Sporty's Farm LLC v. Sportsman's Market, Inc.,* 202 F.3d 489, 500 (2d Cir.2000).

A mark owner's second avenue of relief is appropriately found in § 2 of the ACPA, which provides that, where a domain name infringes a federally registered trademark or violates any right of the mark's owner under the Lanham Act, "[t]he owner . . . may file an *in rem* civil action against a domain name in the judicial district in which the domain name registrar, domain name registry, or other domain name authority that registered or assigned the domain name is located." 15 U.S.C. § 1125(d)(2)(A). But importantly, a mark owner may file an *in rem* cause of action only where the court finds that the owner of the mark either (i) "is not able to obtain *in personam* jurisdiction over a person who would have been a defendant in a civil action under [Section 1]" ("Option I") or (ii) "through due diligence was not able to find a person who would have been a defendant in a civil action under [Section 1]" ("Option II").[6] *Id.* § 1125(d)(2)(A)(i)–(ii).

pursue any cause of action with the potential to impose personal liability" simply by virtue of filing an ACPA *in rem* action).

5. The damages awarded may be "for any sum above the amount found as actual damages, not exceeding three times such amount." 15 U.S.C. § 1117(a).

6. For purposes of brevity, the term "suitable defendant" herein refers to Section 2's requirement that suit be brought against "a person who would have been a defendant in a civil action under [§ 1]"—i.e., a person who "registers, traffics in, or uses a domain name" in a way that violates the ACPA. 15 U.S.C. § 1125(d).

Thus, the ACPA limits a court's *in rem* jurisdiction over a domain name on a finding that Option I or II exists.[7] And further, as a precondition to using Option II, a mark owner is required to exercise due diligence in attempting to find a suitable defendant. *See id.* § 1125(d). This attempt must include (i) "a notice of the alleged violation and intent to proceed [*in rem*] to the registrant of the domain name at the postal and e-mail address provided by the registrant to the registrar," and (ii) "publish[ed] notice of the [*in rem*] action as the court may direct promptly after filing." *Id.* § 1125(d)(2)(A)(ii)(II). Only if the owner complies with these requirements *and* nonetheless fails to find a suitable defendant who may be sued *in personam* may the owner maintain an *in rem* action against the domain name. And significantly, the relief afforded in an ACPA *in rem* action is limited to "a court order for the forfeiture or cancellation of the domain name or the transfer of the domain name to the owner of a mark." *Id.* § 1125(d)(2)(D)(i).

These provisions, given their plain meaning, compel the conclusion that the ACPA provides mark owners with two mutually exclusive avenues for relief against putative infringers. A mark owner may proceed either *in personam* against an infringer or, in certain circumstances where this cannot be done, the owner may proceed *in rem* against the domain name; a mark owner may not proceed against both at the same time.[9] This follows from the fact that the ACPA's plain language limits the use of *in rem* jurisdiction to two situations, labeled here as Options I and II, where there is no *in personam* jurisdiction over the domain name registrant. Option I allows a mark owner to proceed *in rem* only where the identity and location of the registrant or user of an infringing domain name are known, but *in personam* jurisdiction cannot be obtained over this entity. Option II deals

7. The ACPA strangely provides that the owner of a mark may "file" an *in rem* action if the court makes a finding that the requirements of either Option I or Option II are met. 15 U.S.C. § 1125(d)(2)(A). This language suggests, nonsensically, that such a finding must precede the filing of the suit. It is evident, however, that a court cannot make such a finding *before* the *in rem* action is "filed," which ordinarily means the formality of filing a complaint with the Office of the Clerk and paying applicable filing fees. This is so because such a finding must occur within the confines of a controversy between real parties. * * * Thus, § 1125(d)(2)(A) must be interpreted to mean that a mark owner may *maintain* an *in rem* action against a domain name only if the court finds, after suit is filed, that the requirements of either Option I or Option II are met. *Cf.* Caesars World, 112 F.Supp.2d at 505 ("[T]o force plaintiff to prove its case before filing would stand the Act on its head.").

9. Alitalia's argument to the contrary mistakenly relies on § 4 of the ACPA, which provides that "[t]he *in rem* jurisdiction established under [§ 2] shall be in addition to any other jurisdiction that otherwise exists, whether *in rem* or *in personam.*" 15 U.S.C. § 1125(d)(4). * * * The better reading of § 4—one that harmonizes all of the ACPA's provisions and gives effect to the Act's animating purpose—is that the Section serves to facilitate § 2 Option II *in rem* relief by allowing a mark owner to maintain an *in rem* cause of action upon a showing that the owner through due diligence was not able to find a suitable defendant, but *in personam* jurisdiction over a suitable defendant might "otherwise exist" were such a defendant identified and found. Thus, for example, § 4 would prevent a previously unidentified suitable defendant from attacking collaterally an *in rem* proceeding by making a showing that *in personam* jurisdiction in fact existed, notwithstanding the mark owner's inability to find the defendant through due diligence. * * *

with those situations where the registrant or user of the offending domain name cannot be found and thus simply adds that this jurisdiction may be resorted to only where an infringer cannot be identified or found. In other words, the ACPA provides for *in rem* jurisdiction against a domain name only in those circumstances where *in personam* jurisdiction is not available.[10]

Further confirmation for the conclusion that *in personam* and *in rem* jurisdictions under the ACPA are mutually exclusive is found in the different remedies available under each jurisdictional grant. Where there exists *in personam* jurisdiction over a putative infringer, a mark owner has available a full panoply of remedies, including damages and injunctive relief. *See* 15 U.S.C. § 1117(a), (d). Yet, the remedy available in the event a mark owner must proceed *in rem* is far more limited; it is restricted to the forfeiture or cancellation of the domain name or the domain name's transfer to the mark owner. *See id.* § 1125(d)(2)(D)(i).[11] Significantly, this *in rem* remedy is included in the broader set of remedies available to a plaintiff proceeding *in personam* against a putative infringer. *See id.* § 1125(d)(1)(C). In other words, where *in personam* jurisdiction exists, there is no need to proceed *in rem,* for the broader *in personam* remedies include the limited *in rem* remedy. It follows from this difference in available remedies that the *in rem* and *in personam* jurisdictional grants are exclusive and may not be simultaneously invoked or pursued by a mark owner. Indeed, to conclude otherwise would attribute a nonsensical purpose to the ACPA—namely, to provide duplicative and superfluous jurisdictional grants and remedies.

Yet another factor pointing to the exclusivity of *in rem* and *in personam* jurisdiction under the ACPA is the statutory requirement in Option I that the mark owner, as a condition to proceeding *in rem,* must bear the burden of demonstrating the absence of *in personam* jurisdiction over a suitable defendant. Unless the ACPA's *in rem* and *in personam* jurisdictional grants are mutually exclusive, a mark owner pursuing both simultaneously would then be in the odd, if not absurd, position of proving at once the presence and absence of *in personam* jurisdiction over the putative infringer. A mark owner simply cannot simultaneously establish both (i) that *in personam* jurisdiction over a suitable defendant cannot be obtained

10. This result is consistent with the settled principle that *in rem* jurisdiction is an alternative basis for jurisdiction where *in personam* jurisdiction is not available. *See generally* 4 Charles A. Wright and Arthur R. Miller, Federal Practice and Procedure § 1070 (2d ed. 1987) * * *.

11. This limitation is consistent with the extraordinary nature of *in rem* relief, which adjudicates the rights of interested parties in the res *in absentia* and therefore may raise serious due process concerns in certain circumstances. See, e.g., Shaffer v. Heitner, 433 U.S. 186, 206–09, 97 S.Ct. 2569, 53 L.Ed.2d 683 (1977) (observing that "if a direct assertion of personal jurisdiction over the defendant would violate the Constitution, it would seem that an indirect assertion of that jurisdiction should be equally impermissible" and holding that the exercise of *in rem* jurisdiction must comply with the due process requirements elucidated in International Shoe Co. v. Washington, 326 U.S. 310, 66 S.Ct. 154, 90 L.Ed. 95 (1945)) * * *.

and (ii) that *in personam* jurisdiction over a putative infringer can be obtained.[13]

A hypothetical scenario helps illustrate the ACPA's operation in this regard. When a mark owner becomes aware of an infringing use, the owner's first step, typically, is to ascertain the infringer's identity and location by reference to information available from the infringing website or the pertinent domain name registrant. With this information in hand, the owner must then proceed to determine whether the circumstances of Option I or II exist. In this regard, if the owner determines that the putative infringer resides, does business, or is otherwise present in any judicial district in the United States,[14] then the inquiry is ended, and the owner, in these circumstances, must proceed *in personam* against the infringer and is precluded by the ACPA from proceeding *in rem* against the offending domain name. But Congress recognized that in many circumstances mark owners may obtain some identifying information concerning an infringer, but nonetheless may be unable to locate that entity or obtain jurisdiction over the infringer. Often these situations occur where the putative infringer is located in a foreign country and/or provided the domain name registrar with inaccurate or false identifying information. To accommodate these possibilities, Congress included § 2 of the ACPA, so that in these circumstances, an owner could still seek a remedy—albeit a more limited one—by proceeding *in rem* against the domain name itself. But, before allowing a mark owner to proceed in this extraordinary fashion, Congress required the owner to exercise due diligence in the search for the infringer. *See* 15 U.S.C. § 1125(d)(2)(A)(ii)(II).

Because the ACPA's *in rem* and *in personam* jurisdictional grants are mutually exclusive, Alitalia may not invoke and pursue both simultaneously. Either there is *in personam* jurisdiction over JPR, in which event the *in rem* count must be dismissed and JPR then afforded an opportunity to appear and contest Alitalia's summary judgment arguments, or there is no *in personam* jurisdiction over JPR,[17] in which event Alitalia may proceed

13. In this regard, a mark owner may not simultaneously file an *in rem* cause of action and an *in personam* claim in the hope that one claim will survive the court's jurisdictional inquiry. Rather, a mark owner must choose prior to filing whether to proceed *in rem* against the domain name or *in personam* against a putative infringer. Of course, if a mark owner's first choice falters, the alternative may then be pursued by refiling or seeking to amend the complaint.

14. The ACPA does not explicitly answer the question whether a mark owner must disprove the existence of *in personam* jurisdiction over a suitable defendant in any judicial district in the United States or only in the forum where the domain name registrar is located. Although this question need not be answered here, * * * the likely answer is that the mark owner must show the absence of *in personam* jurisdiction in any judicial district in the United States. *See, e.g., Heathmount A.E. Corp. v. Technodome.Com.*, 106 F.Supp.2d 860, 867 (E.D.Va.2000) ("There are two situations in which [Option I] comes into play: first, where the registrant of the domain name is not subject to personal jurisdiction *in any U.S. court* and, second, where a domain name registrant has transferred ownership of the domain name to another individual who is not subject to personal jurisdiction.") (emphasis added). * * *

17. In this regard, Alitalia bears the burden of disproving jurisdiction by a preponderance of the evidence. See Heathmount, 106 F.Supp.2d at 862–63 (holding that "[u]n-only *in rem* against the domain name <casinoalitalia.com> and Alitalia will be entitled to summary judgment if the record discloses no triable issue of fact. Thus, the next step in the analysis is to address whether JPR is subject to jurisdiction in Virginia pursuant to the Commonwealth's long-arm statute. *See* Va.Code § 8.01–328.1. [In the remainder of the opinion the court concludes that JPR is subject to *in personam* jurisdiction in Virginia, and therefore Alitalia cannot maintain its ACPA *in rem* cause of action against *casinoalitalia.com*.]

Electronics Boutique Holdings Corp. v. Zuccarini

56 U.S.P.Q.2d (BNA) 1705 (E.D.Pa.2000).

■ SCHILLER.

Presently before the court is plaintiff Electronics Boutique Holding Corporation's action for Internet cybersquatting against defendant John Zuccarini. A hearing on the merits consolidated with a hearing on damages was held on October 10, 2000. For the reasons set forth below, I find in favor of plaintiff Electronics Boutique Holdings Corporation.

I. Procedural background

On August 10, 2000, plaintiff Electronics Boutique Holding Corporation ("EB") filed a complaint against defendant John Zuccarini ("Mr. Zuccarini"), individually and trading as Cupcake Patrol and/or Cupcake Party, alleging violations of the Anticybersquatting Consumer Protection Act of 1999, 15 U.S.C. § 1125(d) ("ACPA"), violations of § 43(a) of the Lanham Act, 15 U.S.C. § 1125(a), dilution, common law service mark infringement and unfair competition.

Also on August 10, 2000, I granted EB's motion for a temporary restraining order, enjoining the use of domain names "www.electronicboutique.com," "www.eletronicsboutique.com," "www.electronicbotique.com," "www.ebwold.com," "www.ebworl.com." (collectively "domain misspellings") or any other domain name or mark identical to or confusingly similar to EB's registered service marks until August 20, 2000, and directing Mr. Zuccarini to deactivate the domain misspellings and present the Court with evidence of the deactivations within three days of the Court's Order. Additionally, I scheduled a hearing on EB's motion for a preliminary injunction to take place on August 15, 2000.

On August 15, 2000, upon representations by EB that its attempts to effect service upon Mr. Zuccarini at his home, which is also his workplace, were unsuccessful, I granted EB's motion for alternative service, extension of the temporary restraining order, and continuance of the hearing on EB's motion for a preliminary injunction. I authorized EB to effect service

der § 1125(d)(2), a plaintiff must 'disprove' the presence of personal jurisdiction in order to proceed in rem," and "bear[s] the burden to demonstrate some indicia of due diligence in trying to establish personal jurisdiction over an individual who has been identified as a potential defendant but is not subject to jurisdiction.").

through the United States Marshals' service. The hearing on EB's motion for preliminary injunction was continued until August 29, 2000.

Mr. Zuccarini failed to appear, through counsel or otherwise, for the August 29 hearing. On that date, I granted EB's motion for preliminary injunction based on its ACPA claims, finding that Mr. Zuccarini had actual notice of this matter and that the requirements for the issuance of a preliminary injunction had been satisfied. I scheduled a hearing on the merits of EB's ACPA claims for October 10, 2000.

Mr. Zuccarini failed to obtain counsel and refused to appear himself for the October 10, 2000, hearing.

II. Findings of Fact

At the October 10, 2000, hearing I found as follows: EB, a specialty retailer in video games and personal computer software, operates more than 600 retail stores, primarily in shopping malls, and also sells its products via the Internet. EB has registered several service marks on the principal register of the United States Patent and Trademark Office for goods and services of electric and computer products, including "EB" and "Electronics Boutique." EB has applications for several other service marks on the principal register of the United States Patent and Trademark Office for goods and services of electric and computer products, including "ebworld.com." EB has continuously used its service marks in its business since 1977. They have appeared in print, trade literature, advertising, and on the Internet.

EB's online store can be accessed via the Internet at "www.ebworld.com" and "www.electronicsboutique.com." EB registered its "EB-World" domain name on December 19, 1996 and its "Electronics Boutique" domain name on December 30, 1997. EB has invested heavily in promoting its website to online customers. EB has expended a considerable amount of resources towards making its website consumer friendly. An easy-to-use website is critical to EB's ability to generate revenue directly through Internet customers and indirectly as support for EB's "brick and mortar" stores. Over the last eight months, online purchases have yielded an average of more than 1.1 million in sales per month and EB has logged more than 2.6 million online visitors.

On May 23, 2000, Mr. Zuccarini registered the domain names "www.electronicboutique.com," and "www.electronicbotique.com." One week later, Mr. Zuccarini registered the domain names "www.ebwold.com" and "www.ebworl.com." When a potential or existing online customer, attempting to access EB's website, mistakenly types one of Mr. Zuccarini's domain misspellings, he is "mousetrapped"[8] in a barrage of advertising windows, featuring a variety of products, including credit cards, internet

8. The term "mousetrapped" was used by Judge Dalzell, United States District Judge for the Eastern District of Pennsylvania, to describe the situation an Internet user encounters upon accessing one of Mr. Zuccarini's domain names in a matter in which Mr. Zuccarini was sued by a different plaintiff for similar conduct. *See Shields v. Zuccarini,* 89 F.Supp.2d 634, 635 (E.D.Pa.2000).

answering machines, games, and music. The Internet user cannot exit the Internet without clicking on the succession of advertisements that appears. Simply clicking on the "X" in the top right-hand corner of the screen, a common way to close a web browser window, will not allow a user to exit. Mr. Zuccarini is paid between 10 and 25 cents by the advertisers for every click. Sometimes, after wading through as many as 15 windows, the Internet user could gain access to EB's website.

III. Conclusions of law

A. EB's request for a permanent injunction

* * *

[The court concludes that EB is entitled to a permanent injunction on its ACPA claim.]

* * *

B. EB's request for statutory damages

Pursuant to 15 U.S.C. § 1117(d), a plaintiff seeking recovery under the ACPA may elect to recover statutory damages in lieu of actual damages and profits. A court may award statutory damages in an amount between $1,000 and $100,000 per infringing domain name based on the court's determination of what is just. *See* 15 U.S.C. § 1117(d). EB has elected to recover statutory damages in this matter. The recovery of "statutory damages in cybersquatting cases, both [ ] deter[s] wrongful conduct and [ ] provide[s] adequate remedies for trademark owners who seek to enforce their rights in court." S.REP. No. 106–140 (1999).

I emphasize that the actual damages suffered by EB as a result of lost customers and goodwill is incalculable. In proceedings before this Court, Mr. Zuccarini admitted that he yields between $800,000 and $1,000,000 annually from the thousands of domain names that he has registered. *See Shields v. Zuccarini, No.00–494,* 2000 WL 1053884, at *1 (E.D.Pa. July 18, 2000). Advertisers pay Mr. Zuccarini between 10 and 25 cents each time an Internet user clicks on one of their ads posted on Mr. Zuccarini's websites. Many of the domain names registered by Mr. Zuccarini are misspellings of famous names and infringe on the marks of others. * * *

In addition, Mr. Zuccarini has victimized a wide variety of people and entities. This Court has permanently enjoined Mr. Zuccarini from using domain names that are "substantially similar" to the marks of another plaintiff, finding Mr. Zuccarini's "conduct utterly parasitic and in complete bad faith." *Shields v. Zuccarini*, No.00–494, 2000 WL 1056400, at *1 (E.D.Pa. June 5, 2000). Other cases alleging similar conduct have been brought against Mr. Zuccarini by Radio Shack, Office Depot, Nintendo, Hewlett–Packard, the Dave Matthews Band, *The Wall Street Journal, Encyclopedia Britannica,* the distributor of Guinness beers and Spiegel's catalog in various federal courts and arbitration fora. Demands regarding similar conduct have been made on Mr. Zuccarini by the Sports Authority, Calvin Klein, and Yahoo!. Mr. Zuccarini's conduct even interferes with the ability of the public to access health information by preying on hospitals and prescription drugs. *Shields v. Zuccarini,* No. 00–494, (E.D.Pa.) (admitting the registration of domain names containing misspellings of the Mayo Clinic and the weight loss drug Xenical).

I also note that Mr. Zuccarini's conduct is not easily deterred. *See Shields*, No. 00–494, 2000 WL 1053884, at *1 (E.D.Pa. July 18, 2000) (observing that Mr. Zuccarini failed to get the "crystalline message" of the Court in its March 22 Opinion and June 5 Order). Strikingly, Mr. Zuccarini registered the domain misspellings at issue in this matter after this Court preliminarily enjoined him from using misspellings of another individual's mark. *See Shields*, 89 F.Supp.2d at 642–43.

Furthermore, since this Court permanently enjoined Mr. Zuccarini from using other domain misspellings, assessed statutory damages in the amount of $10,000 per infringing domain name against him, and required him to bear the plaintiff's costs and attorneys' fees, Mr. Zuccarini has unexplainedly registered hundreds of domain names which are misspellings of famous people's names, famous brands, company names, television shows, and movies, victimizing, among others, the Survivor television show, Play Station and Carmageddon video game products, singers Kylie Minogue, Gwen Stefani and J.C. Chasez, *The National Enquirer,* and cartoon characters the Power Puff Girls. Mr. Zuccarini boldly thumbs his nose at the rulings of this court and the laws of our country. Therefore, I find that justice in this case requires that damages be assessed against Mr. Zuccarini in the amount of $100,000 per infringing domain name, for a total of $500,000.

C. Attorneys' fees and costs

EB has requested that it be awarded attorneys' fees and the costs of this litigation. The ACPA authorizes this Court to award "reasonable attorney fees to the prevailing party" in "exceptional cases." 15 U.S.C. § 1117(a). In determining whether a case is "exceptional" under § 1117(a), the Third Circuit has required "a finding of culpable conduct on the part of the losing party, such as bad faith fraud, or knowing infringement." *Ferrero U.S.A., Inc. v. Ozak Trading, Inc.*, 952 F.2d 44, 47 (3d Cir.1991). As described above, Mr. Zuccarini acted in complete bad faith by knowingly and intentionally trading on the goodwill and reputation of EB in an attempt to mislead the public. Therefore, I find that EB is entitled to attorney's fees.

* * *

I will award EB the full amount of its $30,653.34 request.

* * *

NOTES & QUESTIONS

1. *Typosquatting*. In *Electronics Boutique Holdings Corp. v. Zuccarini*, the defendant engaged in what has become known as typosquatting. A typosquatter identifies common spelling, typing and keyboarding errors that people make when entering a well-known URL into the address bar of a web browser. The typosquatter then registers these variations on the domain name in order to increase traffic to his or her own website or sell the variations to the owner of the domain name from which the variations were derived.

Typosquatting has an analogy in the brick-and-mortar world. In *Holiday Inns, Inc. v. 800 Reservation, Inc.,* 86 F.3d 619 (6th Cir.1996), the court had to determine whether it was a violation of Sections 32 or 43(a) of the Lanham Act, 15 U.S.C. §§ 1114 and 1125(a), for the defendant to use a telephone number that it had derived as a common dialing error from a competitor's vanity number:

> Holiday Inns, Inc., filed this Lanham Act suit against the defendants, alleging unfair competition and infringement of its trademark telephone number, 1–800–HOLIDAY, known as a "vanity number." The defendants, Call Management Systems, Inc. (a consulting firm that obtains and services 1–800 telephone numbers for businesses), 800 Reservations, Inc. (an agency that makes reservations for a number of hotel chains, including Holiday Inns), and Earthwinds Travel, Inc. (a travel agency) had secured the use and were engaged in using a telephone number that potential Holiday Inns customers frequently dial by mistake when they unintentionally substitute the number zero for the letter "O." That number, 1–800–405–4329, corresponds to the alphanumeric 1–800–H[zero]LIDAY, known in the trade as a "complementary number." It is referred to in this opinion as "the 405 number" to distinguish it from the Holiday Inns numeric, 1–800–465–4329. The district court, although noting that the defendants were violating only the "spirit" and not the "letter" of the Lanham Act, nevertheless granted Holiday Inns partial summary judgment and permanently enjoined 800 Reservations and Call Management from using the 405 number. * * * For the reasons stated below, we conclude that the defendants' use of the 405 number did not violate the Lanham Act * * *
>
> * * *
>
> The plain language of § 32 of the Lanham Act forbids only the "*use* in commerce [of] any reproduction, counterfeit, copy, or colorable imitation of a registered mark ... which ... is likely *to cause* confusion." 15 U.S.C. § 1114 (emphasis added). Additionally, § 43(a) of the Act provides a cause of action only against "[a] person who ... *uses* in commerce any word, term, name, symbol, or device ... or any false designation of origin, false or misleading description of fact, or false or misleading representation of fact...." 15 U.S.C. § 1125(a) (emphasis added). The defendants in this case never *used* Holiday Inns's trademark nor any facsimile of Holiday Inns's marks.
>
> Moreover, the defendants did not *create* any confusion; the confusion already existed among the misdialing public. * * *

Should the Sixth Circuit's reasoning apply to typosquatting, and if so did the court in *Electronics Boutique* reach the wrong outcome? Does it matter that in *Electronics Boutique* the court was applying the ACPA, rather than the trademark infringement provisions of the Lanham Act? Is the court's comment in *Sporty's Farm, L.L.C. v. Sportsman's Market, supra,* at n.26, "that 'confusingly similar' [under the ACPA] is a different standard from the 'likelihood of confusion' standard for trademark infringement" relevant to your answer?

2. *A pure heart and empty head defense?* The ACPA, 15 U.S.C. § 1125(d)(1)(B)(ii), states that "[b]ad faith intent described under subparagraph (A) shall not be found in any case in which the court determines that the person believed and had reasonable grounds to believe that the use of the domain name was a fair use or otherwise lawful." One commentator has remarked:

> This might be dubbed the "pure heart and empty head defense" because it might appear to reward the cybersquatter who intended no harm and mistakenly thought that his or her conduct was lawful. This defense has the potential to reward both ignorance of the law and unawareness of the fact that cybersquatting violates widely accepted standards of fair competition. Therefore, a court should, in the author's view, make use of this "reasonable belief" defense very sparingly and only in the most unusual cases. * * * Otherwise, every cybersquatter [will] solemnly aver that it [is] entitled to this defense because it believed that its conduct was lawful.

4 J. THOMAS MCCARTHY, MCCARTHY ON TRADEMARKS AND UNFAIR COMPETITION § 25:78 (4th ed.2002). Is there any way that a court might avoid this absolute ignorance-of-the-law defense and thus avoid the perverse incentives and consequences that concern Professor McCarthy? Does a cybersquatter have any duty to inquire? Should a person who is willfully blind or who deliberately fails to inquire, knowing what the answer is likely to be, avoid liability? *See, e.g., Louis Vuitton S.A. v. Lee,* 875 F.2d 584 (7th Cir.1989) (for purposes of civil damages under 15 U.S.C. § 1117(b), it is sufficient that a retailer "failed to inquire further because he was afraid of what the inquiry would yield"). On the other hand, does the statute invite courts to infer bad faith from the mere fact that the court feels that the particular conduct was unfair competition? Is this standard too loose to protect people who might have competing claims that are arguably legitimate, even if distasteful to the trademark owner?

3. *Partial bad faith.* Much human behavior is the result of mixed motives. While one motive for a particular action may be good and legitimate, another may be less laudable. A central element for liability under the ACPA is that the person have "a bad faith intent to profit from the mark." 15 U.S.C. § 1125(d)(1)(A)(i). How should the courts decide a case in which a person acts partly in good faith? In such a case the domain name registrant may have a good-faith legitimate claim to the domain name, but still realize that it might have value to another. Just this situation was presented in *Virtual Works, Inc. v. Volkswagen of America, Inc.*, 238 F.3d 264 (4th Cir.2001). In this case, the court noted that "Virtual Works chose *vw.net* over other domain names not just because 'vw' reflected the company's own initials, but also because it foresaw the ability to profit from the natural association of *vw.net* with the VW mark." 238 F.3d at 269–70.

4. *Limitations on liability*. The ACPA limits the liability of domain name registrars and registries. *See* 15 U.S.C. §§ 1114(2)(D)(iii) & 1125(d)(2)(D)(ii). One commentator has criticized this feature of the Act:

> These limitations on liability, while encouraging the resolution of domain name disputes out of court, effectively transfer the burden upon the domain name holder to prove non-infringement. This presents a real danger due to the reality that the trademark holder is likely to have resources that far exceed the owner of the domain name being challenged. In addition, these provisions encourage domain name registries to cancel registrations upon presentation of evidence of any trademark that is identical to, confusingly similar to, or dilutive of a registered domain name. Since the act leaves the determination of this complicated legal question to the registrars themselves and protects them from liability for incorrect decisions, there is little incentive for a registry to deny a request to cancel from a trademark holder. The domain name registrant may not have registered the trademark, but may be conducting a legitimate commercial non-infringing use or could raise a recognized fair use defense that is disapproved of by the mark owner. Under the new system, the domain name holder would likely find his domain registration cancelled.

Gregory B. Blasbalg, Note, *Master of Their Domain: Trademark Holders Now Have New Ways to Control Their Marks in Cyberspace*, 5 ROGER WILLIAMS U.L. REV. 563, 579–80 (2000). Do you agree with the author that the ACPA encourages domain name registrars and registries to be overly deferential to trademark holders?

5. Lockheed Martin v. NSI *reprise*. Soon after the passage of the ACPA, Lockheed Martin decided to take another bite at the apple and brought suit against Network Solutions under the ACPA. Lockheed argued that defendant violated the Act by "registering, maintaining, or trafficking in ten specific domain names that allegedly infringe its LOCKHEED MARTIN and SKUNK WORKS marks." *Lockheed Martin Corp. v. Network Solutions, Inc.*, 141 F.Supp.2d 648, 654 (N.D.Tex.2001). The court held that the word "registers" in 15 U.S.C. § 1125(d)(1)(A) "obviously refers to a person who presents a domain name for registration, not to the registrar." *Id.* The court also noted that liability for using a domain name within the meaning of 15 U.S.C. § 1125(d)(1)(A) is limited by § 1125(d)(1)(D) to "the domain name registrant or that registrant's authorized licensee." With respect to bad-faith intent, the court wrote that "[a]lthough the list [of factors under § 1125(d)(1)(B)(i)(I)–(IX) for determining bad-faith intent] is not exclusive, none of the conditions and conduct listed would be applicable to a person functioning solely as a registrar or registry of domain names." *Id.* On the basis of this analysis, the court granted summary judgment for NSI.

6. *Dilution by linking.* Imagine that an individual registers a domain name in violation of the ACPA. If I use that domain name to create a hyperlink to that person's website, am I also liable for using a domain name that is identical or confusingly similar to or dilutive of another's trademark under 15 U.S.C. § 1125(d)(1)(A)? What if I am aware that the domain name was unlawfully registered? What about individuals who operate a search engine or other directory service on the Internet: are they liable if they index a website under such a domain name?

7. *Minimum contacts and in rem jurisdiction.* In one of the first *in rem* actions brought under the ACPA, *Caesars World, Inc. v. Caesars-Palace.Com,* 112 F.Supp.2d 502 (E.D.Va.2000), the defendant challenged the constitutionality of 15 U.S.C. § 1125(d)(2) under the Due Process Clause of the United States Constitution. In this case, the court noted:

> The question before this court, therefore, is whether *in rem* jurisdiction over defendants who are not subject to the personal jurisdiction of this court, or any other, meets the due process standards under the Constitution.
>
> In this regard, defendant Casares.com argues that under *Shaffer v. Heitner,* 433 U.S. 186 (1977), *in rem* jurisdiction is only constitutional in those circumstances where the res provides minimum contacts sufficient for *in personam* jurisdiction. The court rejects this argument, and concludes that under *Shaffer,* there must be minimum contacts to support personal jurisdiction only in those *in rem* proceedings where the underlying cause of action is unrelated to the property which is located in the forum state. Here the property, that is, the domain name, is not only related to the cause of action but is its entire subject matter. Accordingly, it is unnecessary for minimum contacts to meet personal jurisdiction standards.
>
> To the extent that minimum contacts are required for *in rem* jurisdiction under *Shaffer,* moreover, the fact of domain name registration with Network Solutions, Inc., in Virginia supplies that. Given the limited relief afforded by the Act, namely "the forfeiture or cancellation of the domain name or the transfer of the domain name to the owner of the mark," no due process violation occurs here as to defendants personally. 15 U.S.C. § 1125(d)(2)(D). The court considers the enactment of the Anticybersquatting Consumer Protection Act a classic case of the distinction between *in rem* jurisdiction and *in personam* jurisdiction and a proper and constitutional use of *in rem* jurisdiction.

Caesars World, Inc. v. Caesars-Palace.Com, 112 F.Supp.2d at 504.

8. *General appearance.* If the owner of an offending domain name makes a general appearance to defend that domain name in an *in rem* action brought under 15 U.S.C. § 1125(d)(2), does that owner become subject to the *in personam* jurisdiction of the court? *See Caesars World, Inc. v. Caesars-Palace.Com,* 112 F.Supp.2d 505 (E.D.Va.2000) ("We have recently addressed that issue and determined that *in personam* jurisdiction cannot be based merely on an appearance in an *in rem* action.").

9. *Notice.* Often in an *in rem* action where the owner of the *res* is not known or cannot be found, notice of the action is effected by publication in newspapers for a certain period of time. Under 15 U.S.C. § 1125(d)(2)(B), notice and service of process is accomplished by

> (aa) sending a notice of the alleged violation and intent to proceed under this paragraph to the registrant of the domain name at the postal and e-mail address provided by the registrant to the registrar; and
>
> (bb) publishing notice of the action as the court may direct promptly after filing the action.

15 U.S.C. § 1125(d)(2)(A)(ii)(II)(aa) and (bb). If a plaintiff can confirm that the registrant received actual notice once the plaintiff sent a letter to the registrant's postal and e-mail address, may the court waive the requirement of publication under 15 U.S.C. § 1125(d)(2)(B) and (A)(ii)(II)(bb)? *See Banco Inverlat, S.A. v. www.inverlat.com,* 112 F.Supp.2d 521 (E.D.Va. 2000).

10. *Waiting period under the ACPA.* Before filing an *in rem* action under the ACPA, the trademark owner must proceed in a manner that will permit the court to find that the owner

> (I) is not able to obtain in personam jurisdiction over a person who would have been a defendant in a civil action under paragraph (1); or
>
> (II) through due diligence was not able to find a person who would have been a defendant in a civil action under paragraph (1).

15 U.S.C. § 1125(d)(2)(A)(ii). Section 1125(d)(2)(A)(ii)(II)(aa) requires that due diligence include "sending a notice of the alleged violation and intent to proceed under this paragraph to the registrant of the domain name at the postal and e-mail address provided by the registrant to the registrar." These provisions raise the question of how long a trademark owner must wait after sending the required notice before filing an *in rem* action in federal court. The ACPA is silent on this question. In *Lucent Technologies, Inc. v. Lucentsucks.com,* 95 F.Supp.2d 528 (E.D.Va.2000), the plaintiff waited only 8 days. The owner of the domain name moved to dismiss on the ground that the plaintiff had failed to exercise due diligence. In resolving this issue the court wrote:

> Where Congress has specified a waiting period by statute in situations analogous to the ACPA *in rem* provision, ten days is the shortest amount of time specified. Perhaps the statutory provision most analogous to the provision at issue is Rule C of the Federal Rules of Civil Procedure, which allows an *in rem* action "to enforce any maritime lien" or whenever a federal statute provides for "a

> maritime action in rem or a proceeding analogous thereto." Fed. R.Civ.P. C(1). The rule permits the claimant of property that is subject to an *in rem* action 10 days after the rem has been seized to file a claim and 20 days after that to serve an answer. Fed. R.Civ.P. C(6). In the standard *in personam* action, Rule 12 of the Federal Rules of Civil Procedure allows 20 days after service of process to file an answer. Fed.R.Civ.P. 12(a)(1)(A).
>
> Neither Rule C nor Rule 12 are directly on point. In our case, we are considering what notice is required before an *in rem* action is instituted, and how long a plaintiff must wait to file an *in rem* action after sending notice by mail and e-mail, which may or may not reach the addressee. In contrast, Rule C specifies the waiting period *after* an *in rem* action is instituted, and Rule 12 specifies a waiting period after service of process is complete, that is, after actual notice has occurred. Nevertheless, taken together, these rules strongly suggest that Congress would not consider eight days to be a sufficient waiting period after mailing notice of a potential *in rem* action to a person who may be affected by that action.

Lucent Technologies, Inc. v. Lucentsucks.com, 95 F.Supp.2d at 533–34. Based on the discussion in *Lucent Technologies*, what is a reasonable waiting period?

11. *Bad-faith intent and in rem actions under the ACPA.* The ACPA envisions two situations in which an *in rem* action would be appropriate. The first, described in 15 U.S.C. § 1125(d)(2)(A)(ii)(I), is a situation in which the trademark owner knows the identity of the offending domain name registrant but the federal courts cannot obtain *in personam* jurisdiction over her. The second, described in 15 U.S.C. § 1125(d)(2)(A)(ii)(II), is a situation in which the identity of the offending domain name registrant is unknown. In *BroadBridge Media, L.L.C. v. Hypercd.com,* 106 F.Supp.2d 505 (S.D.N.Y.2000), a case of the first kind in which the offending domain name registrant was known, but the court could not exercise *in personam* jurisdiction over that registrant, the trademark owner questioned whether proof of the registrant's bad faith intent was necessary in an *in rem* action under the ACPA. The court said that it understood plaintiff's argument that it need not show bad faith, but concluded that

> bad faith intent to profit is a necessary element. * * * Congress clearly intended to use the bad faith element of the statute as a way to narrow the breadth of the statute. "The bill is carefully and narrowly tailored, however, to extend only to cases where the plaintiff can demonstrate the defendant ... *used* the offending domain name with bad-faith intent to profit from the goodwill of a mark belonging to someone else. Thus, the bill does not extend to innocent domain name registrations by ... someone who is aware of the trademark status of the name but registers a domain name containing the mark for any reason other than with bad faith intent to profit from the goodwill associated with that mark." H.R. Conf. Rep. 106–412 (emphasis added); *see also Northern Light*

> *Technology, Inc. v. Northern Lights Club,* 97 F.Supp.2d 96 (D.Mass.2000). Reflecting this intent, Congress limited the in rem action against a domain name to those situations where the court finds the owner is unable "to obtain in personam jurisdiction over a the person *who would have been a defendant under paragraph (1).*" 15 U.S.C. § 1125(d)(2)(A)(i)(I) (emphasis added). To be brought in as a defendant under paragraph (1) requires, in addition to other elements, a bad faith intent to profit.

Query how one would demonstrate bad faith where the registrant is unknown. Commenting on this problem, one commentator has noted that sometimes

> an in rem procedure is needed precisely because the domain name holder cannot be located. The holder usually cannot be located precisely because little or nothing is known about that person. In that event, it may be very difficult for the plaintiff to have any evidence of bad faith. Even negative evidence may be unavailable, such as the lack of the domain name registrant's IP rights in the name. It is improbable that the trademark owner can find evidence of bad faith of a domain name owner who cannot be personally served because he or she gave a fictitious name, a non-existent address and inaccurate contact information. In such a case, the courts should interpret the "bad faith" requirement with considerable leniency and flexibility, or else the usefulness of the in rem procedure will be curtailed.

4 J. THOMAS MCCARTHY, MCCARTHY ON TRADEMARKS AND UNFAIR COMPETITION § 25:79 (4th ed.2002).

The statute provides for notice to the registrant by publication rather than by actual notice; does this lenient standard establishing who may be a defendant in an *in rem* action conflict with a narrow legal rule concluding that such defendants may not be liable absent specific proof of their bad faith?

12. *Personal names.* Section 2(b) of the ACPA, codified as 15 U.S.C. § 1129, provides protection against the registration of non-trademarked personal names by cybersquatters. It reads:

> (1) In general
>
> (A) Civil liability. Any person who registers a domain name that consists of the name of another living person, or a name substantially and confusingly similar thereto, without that person's consent, with the specific intent to profit from such name by selling the domain name for financial gain to that person or any third party, shall be liable in a civil action by such person.
>
> (B) Exception. A person who in good faith registers a domain name consisting of the name of another living person, or a name substantially and confusingly similar thereto, shall not be liable under this paragraph if such name is used in,

affiliated with, or related to a work of authorship protected under title 17 [the Copyright Act] including a work made for hire as defined in § 101 of title 17, and if the person registering the domain name is the copyright owner or licensee of the work, the person intends to sell the domain name in conjunction with the lawful exploitation of the work, and such registration is not prohibited by a contract between the registrant and the named person. The exception under this subparagraph shall apply only to a civil action brought under paragraph (1) and shall in no manner limit the protections afforded under the Trademark Act of 1946 (15 U.S.C. §§ 1051 et seq.) or other provision of Federal or State law.

(2) Remedies. In any civil action brought under paragraph (1), a court may award injunctive relief, including the forfeiture or cancellation of the domain name or the transfer of the domain name to the plaintiff. The court may also, in its discretion, award costs and attorneys fees to the prevailing party.

* * *

Is the protection afforded non-trademarked personal names as broad as the protection granted trademarks under 15 U.S.C. § 1125(d)? Is the intent requirement under 15 U.S.C. § 1129(1)(A) the same as the intent requirement under 15 U.S.C. § 1125(d)(1)(A)(i)? Are all names covered? In particular, would nicknames, stage names, and pen names be covered under 15 U.S.C. § 1129(1)(A)? Are the remedies available under 15 U.S.C. § 1129(C) the same as those available for violations under 15 U.S.C. § 1125(d)(1)? Can you describe a scenario that would fall within the exception described in 15 U.S.C. § 1129(1)(B)?

13. *The ACPA and metatags*. In *Bihari v. Gross,* 119 F.Supp.2d 309 (S.D.N.Y.2000), the court held that the ACPA does not apply to the use of another's trademark as a keyword in metatags. This result is consistent with Senate Rep. 106–140, which states that the ACPA is inapplicable to "such things as screen names, file names, and other identifiers not assigned by a domain name registrar or registry, which have little to do with cybersquatting in practice."

III. NONJUDICIAL DISPUTE RESOLUTION AND ICANN'S UNIFORM DOMAIN NAME DISPUTE RESOLUTION POLICY

To avoid becoming embroiled in disputes between trademark owners and domain name registrants—which often take the form of costly court proceedings—domain name registrars have adopted dispute resolution policies and procedures. The first domain name registrar to adopt a dispute resolution policy was Network Solutions, Inc. ("NSI"), until recently the sole registrar for the .com, .net and .org top-level domains.[5] Under this policy, NSI would suspend the use of any disputed domain name if the

5. NSI adopted its first dispute resolution policy in 1995. This policy was followed by a series of revisions of which the last was NSI Policy Revision 03, effective February

complaining party could prove that it had a trademark registration in any country in the world for a mark identical to the disputed domain name. Thus, a complaining party could register a mark in Tunisia, a country in which marks are granted by registration only, and render someone else's domain name inoperative. Once a domain name was put "on hold," it was no longer available for use by anyone and its status could only be altered by order of a court of competent jurisdiction stating which party was entitled to use the disputed domain name. The NSI policy satisfied no one. Domain name registrants complained that NSI improperly suspended use of a domain name before a court had an opportunity to determine whether use of that domain name infringed a trademark of the complaining party. Owners of registered trademarks complained that the NSI policy did not prevent the use of domain names that were confusingly similar, but not identical, to their trademarks. Finally, owners of unregistered, common law or state trademarks complained that the NSI policy did not recognize their trademark rights at all. General dissatisfaction with the NSI policy in large measure fueled the process that led to the creation of ICANN and the requirement that all ICANN-accredited domain name registrars adopt its Uniform Domain Name Dispute Resolution Policy ("UDRP").[6]

Like the predecessor NSI policy, the UDRP is intended to prevent ICANN as well as its approved registrars from becoming embroiled in disputes surrounding domain names. As Section 6 of the UDRP states unequivocally, a domain name registrar "will not participate in any way in any dispute between you and any party * * * regarding the registration and use of your domain name." That same section also provides that the domain name registrant "shall not name [the domain name registrar] as a party or otherwise include [it] in any such proceeding." To reduce the need for resort to the courts, the UDRP sets up a streamlined alternative dispute resolution process. Through this process, a trademark owner can challenge a domain name registrant's right to use a disputed domain name before an ICANN-approved administrative panel.

Under the rules of procedure governing UDRP proceedings,[7] the administrative panel must render a written decision concerning this challenge within approximately forty-five days of the commencement of the proceeding. Consistent with the streamlined character of the process, a panel's decision is usually based upon a single submission by each of the parties and neither party is given the opportunity for discovery. If the complaining party is successful and no other litigation is pending, then ten business days after receiving the decision, the domain name registrar will either cancel or transfer the disputed domain name registration in accordance with the panel's decision. If, however, the domain name registrant brings

25, 1998. Beginning in 1999, the successor regime under ICANN was put in place.

6. *See* Uniform Domain Name Dispute Resolution Policy (adopted Oct. 24, 1999), www.icann.org/dndr/udrp/policy.htm. For further discussion of ICANN, *see* Chapter 1, Part II(F), *supra*.

7. *See* Rules for Uniform Domain Name Dispute Resolution Policy (adopted Oct. 24, 1999), www.icann.org/udrp/udrp-rules-24oct99.htm.

an action in a court of competent jurisdiction before the end of this ten-day period, then the domain name registrar will continue the status quo until a final judgment is obtained. *See* UDRP §§ 3, 4(i) and (k), and 8.

While the UDRP has been the target of considerable criticism, it is nonetheless considered a significant advance over the NSI policy for at least four reasons. First, under the UDRP the use of disputed domain names is no longer suspended. A domain name registrant may continue to use his or her domain name while the complaining party's rights in the domain name are being determined before an ICANN-approved arbitration panel or a court of competent jurisdiction. *See* UDRP § 7. Second, the UDRP permits trademark owners to challenge the use of domain names that are confusingly similar to their trademarks. It is worth noting that while the UDRP expands the grounds upon which a trademark owner may challenge the use of a domain name, unlike the Anticybersquatting Consumer Protection Act, the UDRP does not permit a trademark owner to challenge the use of a domain name because it is dilutive of his or her famous trademark. *Compare* UDRP § 4(a)(i) *with* 15 U.S.C. § 1125(d)(1)(A)(ii)(II). Third, the UDRP applies not only to nationally registered trademarks but also to state and common law trademarks. Fourth, and most significantly, proceedings under the UDRP are limited to domain name disputes in which the disputed domain name "has been registered and is being used in bad faith." UDRP § 4(a)(iii). The UDRP is specifically targeted at cybersquatting. It does not apply if the domain name registrant has registered the disputed domain name in good faith. Examples of good faith registration would include those made in connection with a bona fide offering of goods or services, registration of a name by which the domain name registrant has been commonly known, as well as the registration of another's trademark so long as the domain name registrant is making a legitimate noncommercial or fair use of that mark. *See* UDRP § 4(c).

In the remainder of this Part, we focus on the general structure of the dispute resolution process created by the UDRP and how the UDRP has been interpreted by both administrative panelists and the federal courts. In particular, the first excerpt looks at whether the UDRP implements a dispute resolution framework that is conducive to the impartial resolution of disputes between trademark owners and domain name registrants and to the development of a consistent domain name jurisprudence. Next is a decision by an administrative panel that considers, among other things, the status of foreign trademarks rights under the UDRP. Finally, we consider one federal district court's view of the significance of an administrative panel's decision under the UDRP for related federal litigation involving the disputed domain name.

Laurence R. Helfer and Graeme B. Dinwoodie, *Designing Non-National Systems: The Case of the Uniform Domain Name Dispute Resolution Policy*

43 WM. & MARY L. REV. 141 (2001).

* * *

In practice as well as in construction, the UDRP has proven to be a remarkable development in the history of international dispute settlement.

Even had trademark owners filed only a handful of complaints with panels and even had those complaints concerned only core domain-name abuses, the system would be worthy of serious scrutiny. But precisely the opposite trend has occurred.

In the first twenty-one months of the UDRP's existence, panels operating under the auspices of ICANN-approved dispute settlement providers have been inundated with cases. As of September 2001, filed complaints numbered over 4300. UDRP panels have issued over 3500 published decisions, with more than three-quarters of these decisions ordering domain names transferred to the complaining trademark owners. Although domain name registrants have achieved a few sporadic (but important) victories during the last few months, beginning in the earliest days of the UDRP panels interpreted the Policy and Rules expansively in ways that generally favored intellectual property owners over domain name registrants. These rulings occurred notwithstanding the clear intent of the UDRP drafters to limit the panels' authority to core cases of domain-name abuse, and at a time when both ICANN and WIPO were considering their own expansion of the UDRP to new gTLDs and existing country code domain names (ccTLDs) as well as to names and identifiers not covered by the present Policy. * * *

[T]he UDRP is composed of elements found in judicial, arbitral, and ministerial decision-making systems. * * * Within any single judicial, arbitral, or ministerial decision-making system, a variety of checking mechanisms constrain the power of decision makers. As a working typology, we divide these mechanisms into three distinct categories, which we refer to as creational, external, and internal checking functions. These checking mechanisms serve several important objectives. They bolster the legitimacy of decision-making outcomes and the accountability of decision makers, they confine decision making within the bounds of a system's institutional capacity, they correct errors, and they ensure consistent outcomes in factually and legally comparable cases.

When elements from different decision-making systems are combined, however, the checking mechanisms that operate in any one system cannot automatically be imported into the new hybrid system. In the case of the UDRP, checking devices found in one or another of the adjudicatory, arbitral, and ministerial models are insufficient in themselves to constrain UDRP panel decision making; oftentimes, they are simply inappropriate. Moreover, ambiguities and contradictions as to the source and content of the UDRP's checking functions send conflicting messages to panels and create incentives for them to act in ways the UDRP's drafters did not intend. * * *

The success of arbitration—its speed, its decision making tailored more closely to parties' intent than to default principles of law, and its finality ensured by less intrusive external review by courts—is premised upon two important characteristics not present here. First, the parties in arbitration have consented to these reduced forms of external checks, and second, the decision of the arbitrator affects only the parties and has limited if any value in articulating broader norms or rules. Neither the parties (by virtue of their consent) nor society (because the arbitration affects only the disputants) can therefore object to the truncated external checking mechanisms that are found in the arbitral model.

By contrast, parties to non-national UDRP proceedings are strangers and have not, other than formally, consented to the arbitral procedures thereunder, and the process by which the UDRP was created cannot serve as a genuine proxy for their consent. And if UDRP decision making is to effect the creation of norms, as we (and the proponents of the UDRP) intend and as the publication of decisions makes inevitable, then some of the control features found in a traditional adjudicatory model must be incorporated.

This does not mean that we should simply adopt an adjudicatory template, however. Courts remain predominantly national in nature, and court proceedings remain slow and expensive. So the wholesale adoption of the adjudicatory model is not attractive as a solution to a non-national problem. Instead, only selective incorporation of some of the checking features of that model is advisable.

Adoption of adjudicatory features, of course, will slow down the decision-making process, and thus, one might wish to reinject speed. Here, the ministerial model has a role to play. Ministerial decision making has the advantage of speed but it is restricted to cases where the application of the relevant rules is routinized. Much of the non-national decision making that occurs in the UDRP is not so routine. Consequently, although we might wish to incorporate aspects of the ministerial model, we cannot rely wholly on it as an antecedent because the functions it delegates to decision makers assume a far less discretionary form of decision making than we contemplate here. It would appear then that the non-national model could benefit from some—but not all—aspects of this pre-existing model. * * *

[M]uch of the UDRP was built in part upon an arbitral model of decision making. The resolution of disputes between private parties pursuant to what are nominally contractual obligations; the use of lawyers, academics, and retired judges as decision makers; the creation of multiple, independent dispute settlement centers; and the role of the parties in choosing the panel all reflect arbitral antecedents. * * *

When viewed in the aggregate, the most important constraints on arbitral decision makers are ex ante creational checks rather than ex post external or internal checks. The parties' ultimate control over an arbitrator's power flows from their virtually unfettered right to choose the substantive and procedural rules according to which the arbitral panel will decide their dispute. For this reason, negotiating the terms of the agreement to arbitrate is perhaps the most effective means of preserving accountability, preventing errors and controlling excesses of arbitral power. * * *

Consider the implications of this balance of arbitral checking functions for the UDRP. By imposing uniform, mandatory dispute settlement rules upon all domain-name registrants, ICANN eliminated the ability of registrants to opt out of UDRP dispute settlement proceedings or to tailor the system to their needs. When an individual registers a domain name with any registrar of names in the three unrestricted generic top level domains anywhere in the world, she confronts a non-negotiable contract of adhesion. She cannot specify the subject matter of the disputes upon which the panel is empowered to rule or the procedures that it will follow, and she has (consistent with the inapt analogy to arbitral models) only limited control (via her selection of registrar, and hence the courts of mutual jurisdiction from which to seek redress) over the mechanisms by which panel excesses or errors may be challenged or reviewed.

In effect, all of the key substantive and procedural terms of the UDRP "arbitration" agreement are prenegotiated by ICANN, which merely heightens the importance of the content of the UDRP's two foundational documents and the legitimacy of the process by which they were drafted. If these foundational documents fairly balance the substantive interests of trademark owners and domain-name registrants and if they contain equivalent procedural rights for both parties, then using ICANN as a proxy for individualized negotiation of a dispute settlement agreement may well be an acceptable and efficient alternative. If, by contrast, these foundational documents are substantively or procedurally skewed, or if the process by which they were created is open to challenge on legitimacy and accountability grounds, then the arbitral "bargain" struck by ICANN is itself called into question and a decisive check on the authority of UDRP panels has been cast into doubt. * * *

These concerns over the UDRP's creational checking functions are further exacerbated by the fact that external checks are even more attenuated in the UDRP context than they are for international arbitration, both with respect to institutional controls and controls by national courts. Consider first the external checks imposed by the four dispute settlement providers and ICANN itself. Under many systems of institutional arbitration * * * arbitral centers retain the authority to enforce each panelist's obligation to be both independent and impartial, first by requiring panelists to disclose any circumstances giving rise to doubts over those two attributes, and second by entertaining challenges from the parties to a particular panelist.

The system of neutrality enforcement contemplated under the UDRP is substantially more attenuated. Although the UDRP Rules do impose a duty on all panelists to be impartial and independent, the means by which that duty is enforced differ according to dispute settlement provider and thus vary from case to case. One provider gives no specific provision for party challenges; another allows challenges only within a fixed period of time after the initial appointment of a panelist; whereas a third (and perhaps a fourth) permits challenges at any time during the proceedings if doubts about a particular panelist arise. In addition, the grounds upon which challenges will be recognized vary widely. The fact that ICANN permits dispute settlement providers to adopt different standards of review of a panelist's independence and impartiality suggests that providers may compete with one another over the substantive and procedural bases for panelist challenges. Whether such competition is likely to lead to more or less stringent panelist review is uncertain, however, and turns in part on the decision-making incentives created by the UDRP's panel selection rules, an issue we address [below].

The absence of meaningful external controls by national courts over UDRP proceedings is even more striking. As an initial matter, however, the claim that external checking functions are more limited for the UDRP than for international arbitration seems contrary to the plain terms of the Policy. After all, the drafters expressly designed the UDRP as a soft-law system that supplements but does not supplant national court adjudication of domain name disputes. If de novo review by a national court is possible, then it would seem that the UDRP's external checking functions are far stronger than the extremely limited national court checking mechanisms at work in arbitration. Several features of the UDRP significantly undermine this argument, however, particularly with respect to external checking functions affecting domain name registrants. These features suggest that the UDRP may be soft law in theory, but much harder law in practice.

Consider first the filing of a complaint by a respondent in a court of so-called "mutual jurisdiction" to challenge a UDRP panel decision ordering her domain name to be canceled or transferred (described somewhat loosely as an "appeal" in the preparatory documents). The extremely short ten-day window within which respondents must file such a proceeding is likely to exert a significant deterrent effect on national court review. Initiating litigation is often a time-consuming and complex process, particularly for individuals and businesses with limited financial resources who may be forced to find an attorney to litigate in a foreign jurisdiction. Of course, nothing precludes a respondent from filing national court proceedings after the ten-day window has expired. The registrant's incentives to do so once a domain name has been canceled or transferred will be substantially diminished, however, particularly when the removal of the domain name disrupts her established or planned business operations. From a cost-benefit perspective, it may be preferable to transfer operations to a different domain name or even to abandon a start-up enterprise altogether. Empirical evidence on this point is anecdotal, but the most comprehensive database of national court challenges to UDRP rulings lists only twenty-five cases in federal district court and one foreign case out of the more than 3500 UDRP panel decisions to date.

Second, it is unclear whether respondents who do muster the resources to appeal panel decisions in fact possess a cause of action against a trademark owner under national laws seeking retention of the domain name. * * * [T]he Anti-Cybersquatting Consumer Protection Act * * * permits domain-name registrants whose domain name has been canceled or transferred pursuant to the UDRP (or a similar policy) to file a civil action in U.S. federal court against the prevailing party in order to establish that the registration and use of the domain name was lawful under the Lanham Act. If the domain-name registrant is successful, the court may "grant injunctive relief to the domain name registrant, including the reactivation of the domain name or transfer of the domain name to the domain name registrant." To our knowledge, no other national law provides such a cause of action.

Third, respondents who frame their claims not as an appeal of the merits of a UDRP ruling but rather as a challenge to excesses of panel power are equally unlikely to prevail. In traditional international arbitral proceedings, nation-states have enacted detailed statutory regimes to allow losing parties to challenge awards, albeit on very limited grounds. But it is doubtful that hybrid UDRP decisions qualify as arbitral awards under these statutes, particularly given the de novo national court review contemplated by the Policy. Courts in the United States, at least, have indicated that they would not be bound by panel findings, which suggests a clear intent not to treat panel decisions as arbitral awards. For this reason, it is doubtful that national courts possess any grant of power to review UDRP panel abuses as such.

* * *

Uncertainty over the location of national court review and the substantive law to be applied raises a fourth doubt regarding national courts' ability to provide adequate external checks on UDRP panel abuses. Initially, one would expect that, as a result of the mutual jurisdiction provision in the UDRP, courts in jurisdictions where registrars are based might develop an expertise and interest in reviewing UDRP panel decisions. * * * But the mutual jurisdiction provision is unlikely over time to centralize such expertise. Even assuming that trademark owners will select the domicile of the registrar as the court of mutual jurisdiction rather than the domicile of the domain-name registrant, the geographic location of registrars is slowly diversifying under ICANN's competitive registration policy. * * *

Finally, the attenuation of national courts' external checking function is manifested by the automatic nature of UDRP enforcement. Unlike international arbitrations subject to the New York Convention, there is no requirement that prevailing UDRP complainants institute separate national court proceedings to enforce their awards—a crucial check on arbitral power. Instead, enforcement of UDRP awards in favor of trademark owners are automatic unless the respondent takes steps to appeal. This shift of the burden of enforcement removes any opportunity for a "second look" at the arbitral award, thereby destabilizing one of the features that makes the strong presumption favoring enforcement of arbitral awards acceptable in the first place.

For the foregoing reasons, national courts are unlikely to exercise significant de facto external checks on abuses of authority by UDRP panels, notwithstanding the de jure power that they are given under the terms of the Policy. This leaves internal checking functions as the principal method by which arbitral-type excesses are to be checked. Yet UDRP panels have only weak incentives to limit their own authority.

[P]anelists and institutions operating in international arbitration cases compete for business of both complaining and responding parties. They thus have an incentive to stay within the boundaries of the arbitral agreement and to issue awards that encourage repeat business from both parties. In the UDRP, by contrast, competition incentives are skewed in favor of complainant intellectual property owners. It is complainants, not respondents, who choose the dispute settlement provider and who pay panel fees in all single-panelist cases. In principle, respondents may convert a single-member panel to a three-person panel after receiving the complaint. In practice, the large number of cases in which respondents fail to appear and the added cost of choosing a three-person panel for those who do significantly diminish the impact of respondents' choice on the incentives of providers and decision makers.

Confirming fears expressed by some participants during the ICANN review-and-comment process, evidence suggests that dispute settlement providers are acting on the "irresistible incentive to . . . develop a reputation for deciding cases in favor of complainants." Providers now publish statistics on their win/loss records and other information about their decisions, information which serves as indirect advertising to trademark owners intent on choosing the most complainant-friendly provider. There is also anecdotal evidence that providers have adopted more overt methods to attract complainants by boasting of the tough stance their panelists have taken in UDRP disputes. These features have already created a public perception that some dispute settlement providers are more complainant friendly than others, a fact that the case statistics support (although the cause-and-effect dynamic is still unclear).

In addition, consider the identity of the individuals who serve as UDRP panelists. Most are practicing intellectual property attorneys, while a somewhat lower number are retired judges and legal academics. It is at least an open question whether decision makers from the private sector can sufficiently distance themselves from the milieu in which they practice to self-limit their own powers and develop balanced norms for the trademark-domain name interface. This is particularly true if panelists are permitted to trade on their UDRP expertise by representing trademark owners in future domain-name disputes.

Taken together, these skewed internal checking functions are likely to place significant pressure on UDRP decision makers to rule in favor of complaining trademark owners. If, however, the disputes subject to the UDRP were both unambiguous and narrow, then the Policy itself might exert an adequate constraining force to prevent panelists from acting on these pressures. As we explain below, however, the UDRP provides panelists with discretionary decision-making authority, making it unlikely that the text of the Policy will exert such a constraining effect. * * *

[T]he first three subsections of paragraph 4 of the Policy * * * set forth the elements that a complainant must prove to justify a transfer or cancellation of a domain name. Paragraphs 4(b) and 4(c) list the circumstances demonstrating, on the one hand, a respondent's "registration and use" of a domain name in bad faith, and on the other, her "rights or legitimate interests" in the domain name sufficient to defeat a complaint. If the UDRP were designed as a system of constrained judicial decision making, these enumerated circumstances would be dispositive of all claims and all defenses. Under such a system panels would admittedly still have interpretative discretion to decide in each dispute whether the facts presented fell within the parameters of the enumerated rules and to resolve ambiguities contained within the rules themselves. However, the exclusive nature of the categories would exert considerable constraining force, preventing panels from expanding the Policy very far beyond the heartland of cases circumscribed by the text.

The UDRP's drafters, however, did not limit panelists' discretion to these enumerated grounds. Instead, they labeled these exemplars as "circumstances" which existed only "in particular but without limitation" to other situations of bad faith, on the one hand, or rights and legitimate expectations, on the other. Such an obvious and open-ended invitation to lawmaking sends a clear message to panels that they can exercise independent authority in determining which sorts of unenumerated circumstances justify a ruling in favor of complainants or respondents. Without constraints on these open-ended clauses, panels are left with little to guide the exercise of their discretionary lawmaking powers. Not surprisingly, this omission has produced a schism between panels that strictly construe the UDRP and those that interpret the Policy more expansively to curb a broader range of conduct by domain-name registrants.[8] * * *

ICANN's conflicting signals to UDRP panels concerning their adjudicatory powers also affects their adoption of internal checking mechanisms. On a basic level, the requirement that all decisions be published and reasoned exerts a constraining effect on gross errors and excesses of authority. Panelists know that the decisions they author will be available to all potentially affected parties, including not only the litigants, but future litigants, other panelists, and ICANN. They thus have a significant interest in ensuring that their rulings meet at least minimal levels of competence and persuasiveness, particularly if they hope to receive future UDRP assignments.

8. [Later in a portion of their article not reproduced here, the authors document their claim that some panels have interpreted the UDRP more expansively to curb a broader range of conduct by domain-name registrants, noting the following: "Several panels have extended the UDRP to cases involving legitimate disputes over domain name ownership or to bad faith registration without corresponding bad faith use, categories of cases that the drafters expressly excluded from the Policy. More striking still is a line of cases permitting surname and geographic name owners to bring successful complaints against domain name registrants (either by ignoring the elements required to prove a claim or by very expansive interpretation of the notion of common law trademark rights). Not only did these rulings ignore the drafters' desire to limit the UDRP to trademark controversies, they also were issued at a time when WIPO was studying whether to recommend an expansion of the Policy to encompass these precise intellectual property rights."—Eds.]

Beyond this bare minimum level of competence, however, there are few structural incentives for panels to produce carefully reasoned decisions. Well-reasoned decisions require at least a modicum of deliberation, a quality that the time and cost-sensitive UDRP does not favor. Consider the following: Panels normally must issue a decision within less than forty-five days after a complaint is filed. Panelists are private adjudicators with other responsibilities outside of the UDRP competing for their time. Also, the modest compensation panelists receive for their services pales in comparison to the fees they can receive as practicing attorneys or deciding other arbitral matters. Each of these pressures are likely to limit the attention that panelists can devote to drafting reasoned opinions. * * *

The UDRP's hybrid decision-making structure poses a more fundamental challenge to developing a consistent domain name jurisprudence. The arbitral model upon which much of the UDRP was founded places limited weight on past awards as sources of authority. It also focuses more on resolving disputes between the parties than on articulating governing legal norms or creating a jurisprudence to guide future conduct by nonparties. * * * [The authors conclude that] it is questionable whether the UDRP as presently constituted can achieve jurisprudential coherence.

Madonna Ciccone, p/k/a Madonna v. Dan Parisi and "Madonna.com"

Case No. D2000–0847 (WIPO Oct. 12, 2000).

1. The Parties

The Complainant is Madonna Ciccone, an individual professionally known as Madonna.

The Respondent is "Madonna.com," the registrant for the disputed domain name, located in New York, New York, U.S.A. or Dan Parisi, the listed contact for the domain name.

2. The Domain Name(s) and Registrar(s)

The disputed domain name is *madonna.com*.

The registrar is Network Solutions, Inc., 505 Huntmar Park Drive, Herndon, Virginia 20170, U.S.A.

3. Procedural History

This action was brought in accordance with the ICANN Uniform Domain Name Dispute Resolution Policy, dated October 24, 1999 ("the Policy") and the ICANN Rules for Uniform Domain Name Dispute Resolution Policy, dated October 24, 1999 ("the Rules").

The Complaint was received by the WIPO Arbitration and Mediation Center on July 21, 2000 (e-mail) and on July 24, 2000 (hardcopy). The Response was received on August 23, 2000 (e-mail) and on August 28, 2000 (hardcopy). Both parties are represented by Counsel. There have been no further submissions on the merits.

Respondent elected to have the case decided by a three-member panel. David E. Sorkin was appointed as the Respondent's nominee. James W. Dabney was selected as the Complainant's nominee. Mark V.B. Partridge was appointed as presiding panelist.

It appears that all requirements of the Policy and the Rules have been satisfied by the parties, WIPO and the Panelists.

4. Factual Background

Complainant is the well-known entertainer Madonna. She is the owner of U.S. Trademark Registrations for the mark MADONNA for entertainment services and related goods (Reg. No. 1,473,554 and 1,463,601). She has used her name and mark MADONNA professionally for entertainment services since 1979. Complainant's music and other entertainment endeavors have often been controversial for featuring explicit sexual content. In addition, nude photographs of Madonna have appeared in Penthouse magazine, and Complainant has published a coffee-table book entitled "Sex" featuring sexually explicit photographs and text.

Respondent is in the business of developing web sites. On or about May 29, 1998, Respondent, through its business Whitehouse.com, Inc., purchased the registration for the disputed domain name from Pro Domains for $20,000. On June 4, 1998, Respondent registered MADONNA as a trademark in Tunisia. On or about June 8, 1998, Respondent began operating an "adult entertainment portal web site." The web site featured sexually explicit photographs and text, and contained a notice stating "Madonna.com is not affiliated or endorsed by the Catholic Church, Madonna College, Madonna Hospital or Madonna the singer." By March 4, 1999, it appears that Respondent removed the explicit sexual content from the web site. By May 31, 1999, it appears that the site merely contained the above notice, the disputed domain name and the statement "Coming soon Madonna Gaming and Sportsbook."

On June 9, 1999, Complainant, through her attorneys, objected to Respondent's use of the Madonna.com domain name. On June 14, 1999, Respondent through its counsel stated: "As I assume you also know, Mr. Parisi's website [sic] was effectively shut down before you sent your letter, and is now shut down altogether. He is in the process of donating his registration for the domain name."

The word "Madonna," which has the current dictionary definition as the Virgin Mary or an artistic depiction of the Virgin Mary, is used by others as a trademark, trade name and personal name. After Respondent's receipt of Complainant's objection, it appears that Respondent had communication with Madonna Rehabilitation Hospital regarding the transfer of the domain name to the Hospital. It further appears that Respondent has not identified all of its communications on this matter. Nevertheless, the transfer had not taken place at the time this proceeding was commenced.

By his own admission, Respondent has registered a large number of other domain names, including names that matched the trademarks of others. Other domain names registered by Respondent include <wall-streetjournal.com> and <edgaronline.com>. See Response, Exhibit A, ¶ 30, 35.

5. Parties' Contentions

A. Complainant

Complaint contends that the disputed domain name is identical to the registered and common law trademark MADONNA in which she owns rights. She further contends that Respondent has no legitimate interest or rights in the domain name. Finally, Complainant contends that Respondent obtained and used the disputed domain name with the intent to attract Internet users to a pornographic web site for commercial gain based on confusion with Complainant's name and mark.

B. Respondent

Respondent does not dispute that the disputed domain name is identical or confusingly similar to Complainant's trademark. Respondent, however, claims that Complainant cannot show a lack of legitimate interest in the domain name because Respondent (a) made demonstrable preparation to use the domain name for a bona fide business purpose; (b) holds a bona fide trademark in the word MADONNA; and (c) has attempted to make bona fide noncommercial use of the name by donating it to the Madonna Rehabilitation Hospital.

Respondent also contends that it has not registered and used the domain name in bad faith because (a) there is no evidence that its primary motivation was to sell the disputed domain name; (b) the domain name was not registered with an intent to prevent Complainant from using her mark as a domain name; (c) respondent is not engaged in a pattern of registering domain names to prevent others from doing so; (d) the use of a disclaimer on the web site precludes a finding that Respondent intentional[ly] seeks to attract users for commercial gain based on confusion with Complainant's mark; and (e) the use of a generic term to attract business is not bad faith as a matter of law. Finally, Respondent claims that Complainant cannot legitimately claim tarnishment because she has already associated herself with sexually explicit creative work.

6. Discussion and Findings

A. The Evidentiary Standard For Decision

Paragraph 4(a) of the Policy directs that the complainant must prove each of the following:

(i) that the domain name registered by the respondent is identical or confusingly similar to a trademark or service mark in which the complainant has rights; and,

(ii) that the respondent has no legitimate interests in respect of the domain name; and,

(iii) that the domain name has been registered and used in bad faith.

A threshold question in proceedings under the Policy is to identify the proper standard for reaching a decision on each of these issues. The limited submissions allowed under the Policy makes these proceedings somewhat akin to a summary judgment motion under the United States Federal Rules of Civil Procedure. On a summary judgment motion, the movant has the burden of showing that there are no disputes of material facts. All doubts are to be resolved in favor of the non-moving party. If there are material disputes of fact, the motion must be denied and the case will advance to a hearing before a trier of fact, either judge or jury.

Although the nature of the record is similar to that found on a summary judgment motion, our role is different than that of the Court on a summary judgment motion. Paragraph 15 of the Rules states that the "Panel shall decide a complaint on the basis of the statements and documents submitted and in accordance with the Policy . . ." Paragraph 10 of the Rules provides that the "Panel shall determine the admissibility, relevance, materiality and weight of the evidence." Paragraph 4 of the Policy makes repeated reference to the Panel's role in making findings of fact based on the evidence.

Based on the Policy and the Rules, we disagree with the view that disputes over material facts should not be decided in these proceedings. Rather, it is clear to us that our role is to make findings of fact as best we can based on the evidence presented provided the matters at issue are within the scope of the Policy. There may be circumstances due to the inherent limitations of the dispute resolution process or for other reasons where it would be appropriate for a panel to decline to decide a factual dispute. However, the mere existence of a genuine dispute of material fact should not preclude a panel from weighing the evidence before it and reaching a decision.

Since these proceedings are civil, rather than criminal, in nature, we believe the appropriate standard for fact finding is the civil standard of a preponderance of the evidence (and not the higher standard of "clear and convincing evidence" or "evidence beyond a reasonable doubt"). Under the "preponderance of the evidence" standard a fact is proved for the purpose of reaching a decision when it appears more likely than not to be true based on the evidence. We recognize that other standards may be employed in other jurisdictions. However, the standard of proof employed in the United States seems appropriate for these proceedings generally, and in particular for this proceeding which involves citizens of the United States, actions occurring in the United States and a domain name registered in the United States.

In this case, there are factual disputes over Respondent's intent in obtaining and using the disputed domain name. For the reasons just stated, these disputes do not preclude a decision. Instead, we reach a decision based on the preponderance of the evidence submitted by the parties on the basic issues under the Policy.

B. Similarity of the Disputed Domain Name and Complainant's Mark

As noted above, Respondent does not dispute that its domain name is identical or confusingly similar to a trademark in which the Complainant has rights. Accordingly, we find that Complainant has satisfied the requirements of Paragraph 4(c)(i) of the Policy.

C. Lack of Rights or Legitimate Interests In Domain Name

Complainant has presented evidence tending to show that Respondent lacks any rights or legitimate interest in the domain name. Respondent's claim of rights or legitimate interests is not persuasive.

First, Respondent contends that its use of the domain name for an adult entertainment web site involved prior use of the domain name in connection with a bona fide offering of goods or services. The record supports Respondent's claim that it used the domain name in connection with commercial services prior to notice of the dispute. However, Respondent has failed to provide a reasonable explanation for the selection of Madonna as a domain name. Although the word "Madonna" has an ordinary dictionary meaning not associated with Complainant, nothing in the record supports a conclusion that Respondent adopted and used the term "Madonna" in good faith based on its ordinary dictionary meaning. We find instead that name was selected and used by Respondent with the intent to attract for commercial gain Internet users to Respondent's web site by trading on the fame of Complainant's mark. We see no other plausible explanation for Respondent's conduct and conclude that use which intentionally trades on the fame of another can not constitute a "bona fide" offering of goods or services. To conclude otherwise would mean that a Respondent could rely on intentional infringement to demonstrate a legitimate interest, an interpretation that is obviously contrary to the intent of the Policy.

Second, Respondent contends that it has rights in the domain name because it registered MADONNA as a trademark in Tunisia prior to notice of this dispute. Certainly, it is possible for a Respondent to rely on a valid trademark registration to show prior rights under the Policy. However, it would be a mistake to conclude that mere registration of a trademark creates a legitimate interest under the Policy. If an American-based Respondent could establish "rights" vis a vis an American Complainant through the expedient of securing a trademark registration in Tunisia, then the ICANN procedure would be rendered virtually useless. To establish cognizable rights, the overall circumstances should demonstrate that the registration was obtained in good faith for the purpose of making bona fide use of the mark in the jurisdiction where the mark is registered, and not obtained merely to circumvent the application of the Policy.

Here, Respondent admits that the Tunisia registration was obtained merely to protect his interests in the domain name. Respondent is not located in Tunisia and the registration was not obtained for the purpose of making bona fide use of the mark in commerce in Tunisia. A Tunisian trademark registration is issued upon application without any substantive examination. Although recognized by certain treaties, registration in Tunisia does not prevent a finding of infringement in jurisdictions outside Tunisia. Under the circumstances, some might view Respondent's Tunisian registration itself as evidence of bad faith because it appears to be a pretense to justify an abusive domain name registration. We find at a minimum that it does not evidence a legitimate interest in the disputed name under the circumstances of this case.

Third, Respondent claims that its offer to transfer the domain name to the Madonna Hospital in Lincoln, Nebraska, is a legitimate noncommercial use under Paragraph 4(c)(iii) of the Policy. We disagree. The record is incomplete on these negotiations. Respondent has failed to disclose the specifics of its proposed arrangement with Madonna Hospital. Complainant asserts that the terms of the transfer include a condition that Madonna Hospital not transfer the domain name registration to Complainant. It also appears that the negotiations started after Complainant objected to Respondent's registration and use of the domain name. These circumstances do not demonstrate a legitimate interest or right in the domain name, and instead suggest that Respondent lacks any real interest in the domain name apart from its association with Complainant. Further, we do not believe these circumstances satisfy the provisions of Paragraph 4(c)(iii), which applies to situations where the Respondent is actually making noncommercial or fair use of the domain name. That certainly was not the situation at the time this dispute arose and is not the situation now.

Respondent cites examples of other parties besides Complainant who also have rights in the mark MADONNA, but that does not aid its cause. The fact that others could demonstrate a legitimate right or interest in the domain name does nothing to demonstrate that Respondent has such right or interest.

Based on the record before us, we find that Complainant has satisfied the requirements of Paragraph 4(a)(ii) of the Policy.

D. Bad Faith Registration and Use

Under Paragraph 4(b)(iv) of the Policy, evidence of bad faith registration and use of a domain name includes the following circumstances:

> (iv) by using the domain name, you have intentionally attempted to attract, for commercial gain, Internet users to your web site or other on-line location, by creating a likelihood of confusion with the complainant's mark as to the source, sponsorship, affiliation, or endorsement of your web site or location or of a product or service on your web site or location.

The pleadings in this case are consistent with Respondent's having adopted <madonna.com> for the specific purpose of trading off the name and reputation of the Complainant, and Respondent has offered no alternative explanation for his adoption of the name despite his otherwise detailed and complete submissions. Respondent has not explained why <madonna.com> was worth $20,000 to him or why that name was thought to be valuable as an attraction for a sexually explicit web site. Respondent notes that the complainant, identifying herself as Madonna, has appeared in Penthouse and has published a "Sex" book. The statement that "madonna" is a word in the English language, by itself, is no more of a defense than would be the similar statement made in reference to the word "coke". Respondent has not even attempted to tie in his web site to any dictionary definition of madonna. The only plausible explanation for Respondent's actions appears to be an intentional effort to trade upon the fame of Complainant's name and mark for commercial gain. That purpose is a violation of the Policy, as well as U.S. Trademark Law.

Respondent's use of a disclaimer on its web site is insufficient to avoid a finding of bad faith. First, the disclaimer may be ignored or misunderstood by Internet users. Second, a disclaimer does nothing to dispel initial interest confusion that is inevitable from Respondent's actions. Such confusion is a basis for finding a violation of Complainant's rights. *See Brookfield Communications Inc. v. West Coast Entertainment Corp.*, 174 F.3d 1036 (9th Cir.1999).

The Policy requires a showing of bad faith registration and use. Here, although Respondent was not the original registrant, the record shows he acquired the registration in bad faith. The result is the equivalent of registration and is sufficient to fall within the Policy. Indeed, Paragraph 4(b)(i) of the Policy treats acquisition as the same as registration for the purposes of supporting a finding of bad faith registration. We therefore conclude that bad faith acquisition satisfies the requirement of bad faith registration under the Policy.

Respondent's reliance on a previous ICANN decision involving the domain name <sting.com> is misplaced. *See Gordon Sumner p/k/a/ Sting v. Michael Urvan*, Case No. 2000–0596 (WIPO July 24, 2000). In the Sting decision there was evidence that the Respondent had made bona fide use of the name Sting prior to obtaining the domain name registration and there was no indication that he was seeking to trade on the good will of the well-known singer. Here, there is no similar evidence of prior use by Respondent and the evidence demonstrates a deliberate intent to trade on the good will of complainant. Where no plausible explanation has been provided for adopting a domain name that corresponds to the name of a famous entertainer, other Panels have found a violation of the Policy. *See Julia Fiona Roberts v. Russell Boyd*, Case No. D2000–0210 (WIPO May 29, 2000); *Helen Folsade Adu p/k/a Sade v. Quantum Computer Services Inc.*, Case No. D2000–0794 (WIPO September 26, 2000).

There is also evidence in the record which tends to support Complainant's claim that Respondent's registration of the domain name prevents Complainant from reflecting her mark in the corresponding .com domain name and that Respondent has engaged in a pattern of such conduct. It is admitted that Respondent registers a large number of domain names and that some happen to correspond to the names or marks of others. We find, however, that the record is inconclusive on this basis for finding bad faith and do not rely on this evidence for our conclusion.

Respondent asserts that we should reject Complainant's claims because she has been disingenuous in claiming that her reputation could be tarnished by Respondent's actions. Respondent suggests that her reputation cannot be tarnished because she has already associated herself with sexually explicit creative work. That argument misses the point. Even though Complainant has produced sexually explicit content of her own, Respondent's actions may nevertheless tarnish her reputation because they resulted in association with sexually explicit content which Complainant did not control and which may be contrary to her creative intent and standards of quality. In any event, we do not rely on tarnishment as a basis for our decision.

Because the evidence shows a deliberate attempt by Respondent to trade on Complainant's fame for commercial purposes, we find that Complainant has satisfied the requirements of Paragraph 4(a)(iii) of the Policy.

7. Decision

Under Paragraph 4(i) of the Policy, we find in favor of the Complainant. The disputed domain name is identical or confusingly similar to a trademark in which Complainant has rights; Respondent lacks rights or legitimate interests in the domain name; and the domain name has been registered and used in bad faith. Therefore, we decide that the disputed domain name <madonna.com> should be transferred to the Complainant.

Weber–Stephen Products Co. v. Armitage Hardware and Building Supply, Inc.

54 U.S.P.Q.2d (BNA) 1766 (N.D.Ill.2000).

■ ASPEN, CHIEF J.

Defendant Armitage Hardware (Armitage) owns a number of internet domain names that plaintiff Weber–Stephen Products Company (Weber) alleges intentionally and in bad faith use Weber's registered trademarks and service marks in a deceptive, confusing, and misleading manner. Weber initiated an administrative proceeding before the World Intellectual Property Organization (WIPO), pursuant to the Uniform Domain Name Dispute Resolution Policy of the Internet Corporation for Assigned Names and Numbers (ICANN Policy), requesting that the administrative panel issue a decision transferring Armitage's domain names to Weber or canceling Armitage's domain names. The following day, Weber also filed suit in this Court, alleging "cyberpiracy" as well as other claims, such as trademark infringement. Weber told this Court that it had commenced an ICANN proceeding to resolve the issue of whether Armitage was using its domain names in bad faith, which is the only issue that the ICANN administrative panel has power to decide under the Policy. Weber also said that because it expected a decision from the panel within 45 to 50 days from the filing of its ICANN complaint (the Policy provides for expedited review), it would not be seeking injunctive relief in this Court with respect to Armitage's registration of the Weber domain names unless the panel declines to cancel and/or to transfer the domain names to Weber.

We understand that the panel is scheduled to issue a decision as soon as May 5, 2000. Before us now is Armitage's motion to declare the administrative proceeding non-binding and to stay this case in favor of the administrative action, or alternatively—should we find the other proceeding to be binding—to stay it while we consider whether Armitage's participation in that proceeding can be compelled. Armitage's concern is that if the panel's arbitration decision is binding on this Court, Armitage will suffer irreparable harm because our review of the panel's decision will necessarily be circumscribed pursuant to the deference accorded arbitrators' decisions under the Federal Arbitration Act.

The ICANN is a new, quasi-governmental internet-regulating body, and its Policy (approved on October 24, 1999) provides for a "mandatory administrative proceeding" in disputes between domain name owners and trademark owners and purportedly applies to every domain name registrant who registers its domain names through an ICANN-accredited registrar. Armitage contends that it did not agree to the administrative proceeding and thus cannot be compelled to participate in it. However, Armitage will participate if we declare that the proceeding is non-binding, that we owe no deference to the proceeding, and that WIPO, ICANN, and Network Solutions, Inc. (Armitage's ICANN-accredited registrar) cannot take any action adverse to Armitage until this matter is resolved in this Court.

No federal court has yet considered the legal effect of a WIPO proceeding. However, the ICANN Policy and its accompanying rules do contemplate the possibility of parallel proceedings in federal court. First, the Policy provides that ICANN will cancel or transfer domain name registrations upon "our receipt of an order from a court ... of competent jurisdiction, requiring such action; *and/or* ... our receipt of a decision of an Administrative Panel requiring such action in any administrative proceeding ... conducted under this Policy." ICANN Policy at ¶ 3. Also, the procedural rules governing the Policy provide that if legal proceedings are initiated prior to or during an administrative proceeding with regard to a domain name dispute that is the subject of the administrative complaint, the panel has the discretion to decide whether to suspend or terminate the administrative proceeding or whether to proceed and make a decision. Uniform Domain Name Dispute Resolution Rules, at ¶ 18. And the language of the Policy suggests that the administrative panels' decisions are not intended to be binding on federal courts. For example, under the heading "Availability of Court Proceedings," the ICANN Policy provides:

> The mandatory administrative proceeding requirements set forth in Paragraph 4 shall not prevent either you or the complainant from submitting the dispute to a court of competent jurisdiction for independent resolution before such mandatory administrative proceeding is commenced or after such proceeding is concluded. If an Administrative Panel decides that your domain name registration should be canceled or transferred, we will wait ten (10)

> business days ... before implementing that decision. We will then implement the decision unless we have received from you during that ten (10) business day period official documentation (such as a copy of a complaint, file-stamped by the clerk of the court) that you have commenced a lawsuit against the complainant in a jurisdiction to which the complainant has submitted ... If we receive such documentation within the ten (10) business day period, we will not implement the Administrative Panel's decision, and we will take no further action, until we receive (i) evidence satisfactory to us of a resolution between the parties; (ii) evidence satisfactory to us that your lawsuit has been dismissed or withdrawn; or (iii) a copy of an order from such court dismissing your lawsuit or ordering that you do not have the right to continue to use your domain name.

ICANN Policy at ¶ 4(k).[3] Furthermore, Armitage's counsel sent an e-mail inquiry to <domain.disputes@wipo.int>, and the response from the WIPO Arbitration and Mediation Center said that the administrative panel's determination would be binding on the registrar of the domain name, but that "[t]his decision is not binding upon a court, and a court may give appropriate weight to the Administrative Panel's decision." Albeit a vague and rather unhelpful interpretation, Weber does not take issue with this WIPO statement.

We conclude that this Court is not bound by the outcome of the ICANN administrative proceedings. But at this time we decline to determine the precise standard by which we would review the panel's decision, and what degree of deference (if any) we would give that decision. Neither the ICANN Policy nor its governing rules dictate to courts what weight should be given to a panel's decision, and the WIPO e-mail message stating that "a court may give appropriate weight to the Administrative Panel's decision" confirms the breadth of our discretion.

Because both parties to this case have adequate avenues of recourse should they be unhappy with the administrative panel's imminent decision, we find no need to stay the pending ICANN administrative action. Instead, we hereby stay this case pending the outcome of those proceedings. It is so ordered.

NOTES & QUESTIONS

1. *Foreign trademark rights*. In *Madonna v. Parisi* the domain name registrant had registered the disputed domain name in Tunisia. Under Tunisian law, the registrant had legitimate trademark rights in the name. Section 4(a)(ii) of the UDRP states that the complainant must show that

3. The Policy continues: "All other disputes between you and any party other than us regarding your domain name registration that are not brought pursuant to the mandatory administrative proceeding provisions ... shall be resolved between you and such other party through any court, arbitration or other proceeding that may be available." ICANN Policy at ¶ 5.

the domain name registrant has "no rights or legitimate interests in respect of the domain name." The Panel dismissed the domain name registrant's trademark rights under Tunisian law as a source of such rights, stating:

> If an American-based Respondent could establish "rights" vis a vis an American Complainant through the expedient of securing a trademark registration in Tunisia, then the ICANN procedure would be rendered virtually useless. To establish cognizable rights, the overall circumstances should demonstrate that the registration was obtained in good faith for the purpose of making bona fide use of the mark in the jurisdiction where the mark is registered, and not obtained merely to circumvent the application of the Policy.

The Panel thus seems to concede that the UDRP, read literally, might compel a result in favor of the registrant. To avoid this result, the Panel concludes that any "rights" in the mark must be "cognizable," and to be "cognizable," they must have been acquired in good faith and used in the jurisdiction conferring those rights. How far does a UDRP panel's authority to interpret its own grant of authority extend? A UDRP panel is not a court and its power to arbitrate a dispute rests ultimately on the domain name registrant's consent to the arbitration clause contained in the domain name registration agreement. Once the domain name registrant had demonstrated trademark rights under Tunisian law, should the Panel have suggested the parties proceed to a court of law to adjudicate their respective rights in the disputed domain name?

2. *Licensing rights*. Section 4(a)(i) of the UDRP requires that the complainant prove that the disputed "domain name is identical or confusingly similar to a trademark or service mark in which the complainant has rights." What kind of rights must a complainant have under the UDRP? In *NBA Properties, Inc. v. Adirondack Software Corp.*, Case No. D2000–1211 (WIPO Dec. 8, 2000), the complainant was the exclusive licensee of the trademark owner. The disputed domain name was knicks.com. The trademark "Knicks" is owned by Madison Square Garden, L.P., the owner and operator of the New York Knicks basketball team. This trademark had been exclusively licensed to the complainant, the exclusive licensing and merchandising agent for the National Basketball Association and its member teams, including the New York Knicks. The domain name registrant had registered the disputed domain name without the consent of the trademark owner or the complainant. Notwithstanding the complainant's status as the exclusive licensee of the trademark, the Panel held that the "Complainant has not shown that it has rights in the KNICKS trademark relied upon." More specifically, the Panel stated:

> The record fails to make clear what *rights in the trademark* Complainant claims to have. The rights of a licensee are contract rights with respect to, not *in*, the licensed marks. So it is also in the case of a licensing and merchandising agent.
>
> There may well be circumstances in which the contract rights possessed by an exclusive licensee vest in him substantially all the

powers of an owner of the licensed property. However, such circumstances have not been shown to exist here.

The Policy [i.e., the UDRP] is believed by the Panel to envision a transfer of a disputed domain name to a complainant/trademark owner as a route to unification of control over the uses of the domain name and the trademark. However, Complainant's request for an order transferring the disputed name to Complainant in this case would place ownership of the domain name in an entity other than the trademark owner without consent from the trademark owner.

Should rights in a trademark under an exclusive licensing agreement be considered "rights in a trademark" for the purposes of the UDRP? If you were negotiating or drafting a trademark licensing agreement on behalf of the licensee, how would you attempt to ensure that your client could initiate a proceeding under the UDRP?

3. *Use in bad faith.* Earlier, we saw that the Anticybersquatting Consumer Protection Act imposed liability on a domain name registrant who "registers, traffics in, *or* uses a domain name" with bad-faith intent to profit from it. 15 U.S.C. § 1125(d)(1)(A)(ii) (emphasis added). By contrast, the ICANN UDRP permits a registrar to "cancel, transfer or otherwise make changes to domain name registrations" if the disputed "domain name has been registered *and* is being used in bad faith." UDRP § 4(a)(iii) (emphasis added). Consider a domain name registrant who registers another's trademark as a domain name in bad faith but who never uses it as part of an e-mail address or fully qualified domain name. Clearly, the trademark owner could bring an action under the ACPA. Could the owner also initiate proceedings under the UDRP? In *Telstra Corp. Ltd. v. Nuclear Marshmallows*, Case No. D2000-0003 (WIPO Feb. 18, 2000), the Panel had to decide just such a case. Turning to consider Section 4(a)(iii), the Panel observed:

It is less clear cut whether the Complainant has proved the third element in paragraph 4(a) of the Uniform Policy, namely that the domain name "has been registered and is being used in bad faith" by Respondent. The Administrative Panel notes two things about this provision. First, the provision contains the conjunction "and" rather than "or". Secondly, the provision refers to both the past tense ("has been registered") and the present tense ("is being used").

The significance of the use of the conjunction "and" is that paragraph 4(a)(iii) requires the Complainant to prove use in bad faith as well as registration in bad faith. That is to say, bad faith registration alone is an insufficient ground for obtaining a remedy under the Uniform Policy. * * * [T]he Second Staff Report on Implementation Documents for the Uniform Dispute Resolution Policy submitted to the ICANN Board at its meeting on October 24, 1999 * * * at paragraph 4.5, contains the following relevant statement and recommendation:

> Several comments (submitted by INTA and various trademark owners) advocated various expansions to the scope of the definition of abusive registration. For example:
>
> a. These comments suggested that the definition should be expanded to include cases of either registration or use in bad faith, rather than both registration and use in bad faith. These comments point out that cybersquatters often register names in bulk, but do not use them, yet without use the streamlined dispute-resolution procedure is not available. While that argument appears to have merit on initial impression, it would involve a change in the policy adopted by the Board. The WIPO report, the DNSO recommendation, and the registrars-group recommendation all required both registration and use in bad faith before the streamlined procedure would be invoked. Staff recommends that this requirement not be changed without study and recommendation by the DNSO.

From the fact that the ICANN Board accepted the approach recommended in the Second Staff Report, and thus adopted the Uniform Policy in the form originally proposed, it is clear that ICANN intended that bad faith registration alone not give rise to a remedy under the Uniform Policy. For a remedy to be available, the Complainant must prove both that the domain was registered in bad faith and that it is being used in bad faith.

This interpretation is confirmed, and clarified, by the use of both the past and present tenses in paragraph 4(a)(iii). * * * [T]he requirement in paragraph 4(a)(iii) that the domain name "has been registered and is being used in bad faith" will be satisfied only if the Complainant proves that the registration was undertaken in bad faith *and* that the circumstances of the case are such that Respondent is continuing to act in bad faith.

Has the Complainant proved that the domain name "has been registered in bad faith" by the Respondent? [The Panel finds that it has.].

Has the Complainant proved the additional requirement that the domain name "is being used in bad faith" by the Respondent? The [disputed] domain name * * * does not resolve to a website or other on-line presence. There is no evidence that a website or other on-line presence is in the process of being established which will use the domain name. There is no evidence of advertising, promotion or display to the public of the domain name. Finally, there is no evidence that the Respondent has offered to sell, rent or otherwise transfer the domain name to the Complainant, a competitor of the Complainant, or any other person. In short, there is no positive action being undertaken by the Respondent in relation to the domain name.

This fact does not, however, resolve the question. * * * [T]he relevant issue is not whether the Respondent is undertaking a positive action in bad faith in relation to the domain name, but instead whether, in all the circumstances of the case, it can be said that the Respondent is acting in bad faith. The distinction between undertaking a positive action in bad faith and acting in bad faith may seem a rather fine distinction, but it is an important one. The significance of the distinction is that the concept of a domain name "being used in bad faith" is not limited to positive action; inaction is within the concept. That is to say, it is possible, in certain circumstances, for inactivity by the Respondent to amount to the domain name being used in bad faith.

This understanding of paragraph 4(a)(iii) is supported by the actual provisions of the Uniform Policy. Paragraph 4(b) of the Uniform Policy identifies, without limitation, circumstances that "shall be evidence of the registration and use of a domain name in bad faith", for the purposes of paragraph 4(a)(iii). Only one of these circumstances (paragraph 4(b)(iv)), by necessity, involves a positive action post-registration undertaken in relation to the domain name (using the name to attract custom to a website or other on-line location). The other three circumstances contemplate either a positive action or inaction in relation to the domain name. That is to say, the circumstances identified in paragraphs 4(b)(i), (ii) and (iii) can be found in a situation involving a passive holding of the domain name registration. Of course, these three paragraphs require additional facts (an intention to sell, rent or transfer the registration, for paragraph 4(b)(i); a pattern of conduct preventing a trade mark owner's use of the registration, for paragraph 4(b)(ii); the primary purpose of disrupting the business of a competitor, for paragraph 4(b)(iii)). Nevertheless, the point is that paragraph 4(b) recognises that inaction (eg. passive holding) in relation to a domain name registration can, in certain circumstances, constitute a domain name being used in bad faith. Furthermore, it must be recalled that the circumstances identified in paragraph 4(b) are "without limitation"—that is, paragraph 4(b) expressly recognises that *other* circumstances can be evidence that a domain name was registered and is being used in bad faith.

The question that then arises is what circumstances of inaction (passive holding) other than those identified in paragraphs 4(b)(i), (ii) and (iii) can constitute a domain name being used in bad faith? This question cannot be answered in the abstract; the question can only be answered in respect of the particular facts of a specific case. That is to say, in considering whether the passive holding of a domain name, following a bad faith registration of it, satisfies the requirements of paragraph 4(a)(iii), the Administrative Panel must give close attention to all the circumstances of the Respondent's behaviour. A remedy can be obtained under the

> Uniform Policy only if those circumstances show that the Respondent's passive holding amounts to acting in bad faith

Based on the rationale of this decision, under what circumstances might passive holding not constitute bad-faith use?

4. *Country-code TLDs*. In addition to the .com, .net and .org gTLD domains, as well as the more recently activated .aero, .biz, .coop, .info, .museum, and .name domains, a number of ccTLD registries have adopted the UDRP. As a result the UDRP also applies to the .ag, .as, .bs, .cy, .gt, .na, .nu, .tt, .tv, .ve and .ws TLDs.

5. *Challenging an adverse UDRP decision in federal court*. The Anticybersquatting Consumer Protection Act expressly grants a domain name registrant the right to file a civil action if a registrar pursuant to a reasonable policy—such as the UDRP—suspends, disables or transfers his or her domain name. Section 32(2)(D)(v) of the Lanham Act, 15 U.S.C. § 1114(2)(D)(v), states:

> A domain name registrant whose domain name has been suspended, disabled, or transferred under a policy described under clause (ii)(II) may, upon notice to the mark owner, file a civil action to establish that the registration or use of the domain name by such registrant is not unlawful under this chapter. The court may grant injunctive relief to the domain name registrant, including the reactivation of the domain name or transfer of the domain name to the domain name registrant.

Does this provision create a right to appeal an adverse UDRP decision in federal court? What law does a federal court apply in such an action? Why do you think this provision was included in the Anticybersquatting Consumer Protection Act? Does it merely codify a contract remedy that was already available to a domain name registrant? Is it required by 15 U.S.C. § 1114(2)(D)(i)? Does it create a quasi-intellectual property right in domain names under federal law? One commentator has stated that this provision "creates a distinct federal claim for ownership of a domain name." 4 J. THOMAS MCCARTHY, MCCARTHY ON TRADEMARKS AND UNFAIR COMPETITION § 25:74.2 (4th ed. 2002). Do you agree?

6. *Reverse domain name hijacking and abuse of process*. Reverse domain name hijacking is defined in the UDRP Rules as "using the Policy in bad faith to attempt to deprive a registered domain-name holder of a domain name." *See* Rules for Uniform Domain Name Dispute Resolution Policy § 1 (Definitions) (Oct. 24, 1999). Pursuant to § 15(e) of the Rules:

> If after considering the submissions the Panel finds that the complaint was brought in bad faith, for example in an attempt at Reverse Domain Name Hijacking or was brought primarily to harass the domain-name holder, the Panel *shall* declare in its decision that the complaint was brought in bad faith and constitutes an abuse of the administrative proceeding.

(emphasis added). Although the panel is required to make this declaration, neither the UDRP nor the Rules provides any penalty for initiating a

UDRP proceeding in bad faith. In ICANN's Second Staff Report on Implementation Documents for the Uniform Dispute Resolution Policy, penalties were rejected as "outside ICANN's scope." Regarding reverse domain name hijacking the Report observed in § 4.10:

> The final point of substantive guidance in the Board's Santiago resolutions is that the policy should define and minimize reverse domain-name hijacking. The definition of "reverse domain name hijacking" is included in paragraph 1 of the rules. The implementation documents contain several measures to minimize that practice. First, paragraph 15(e) of the rules provides that an administrative panel finding that a complaint was brought in bad faith shall note that fact in its decision. A second measure to minimize reverse domain-name hijacking is the enhanced notice requirement for the initial complaint in paragraph 2(a) of the rules. The clarification that the complainant bears the burden of proof (paragraph 4(a) of the policy statement) and the lengthening of the time for a domain-name holder to seek court review of an adverse decision (paragraph 4(k) of the policy statement) should also minimize reverse domain-name hijacking. Some commentators representing non-commercial interests stated that more punitive measures should be provided to discourage reverse domain-name hijacking. Staff believes such punishment is outside ICANN's scope.

What does the ICANN staff mean by "outside ICANN's scope"? What is ICANN's role in a UDRP proceeding?

For domain name registrants in the United States, ICANN's failure to provide any remedy to the victims of those who use the UDRP process to reverse hijack domain names was rectified by the Anticybersquatting Consumer Protection Act. Section 32(2)(D)(iv) of the Lanham Act, 15 U.S.C. § 1114(2)(D)(iv), states:

> If a registrar, registry, or other registration authority takes an action described under clause (ii) based on a knowing and material misrepresentation by any other person that a domain name is identical to, confusingly similar to, or dilutive of a mark, the person making the knowing and material misrepresentation *shall be liable for any damages, including costs and attorney's fees*, incurred by the domain name registrant as a result of such action. The court may also grant injunctive relief to the domain name registrant, including the reactivation of the domain name or the transfer of the domain name to the domain name registrant.

(emphasis added). Does this provision create an action for malicious prosecution or abuse of process with respect to a UDRP proceeding? Would this remedy be available to domain name registrants who are not United States citizens and who live in foreign countries? Would it matter whether such a registrant registered the domain name with a U.S.-based domain name registrar?

7. *Charting the UDRP and ACPA.* A chart created by the International Trademark Association and providing an excellent comparison and brief overview of key provisions of ICANN's UDRP and the ACPA may be found at www.inta.org/news/compchart.shtml.

IV. Registering Domain Names with a Domain Name Registrar

A domain name can be the focus of two wholly separate and unrelated kinds of registration procedures: a domain name registration and a trademark registration. The former is required, the latter optional. When we speak simply of domain name registration we generally intend to refer to the process of creating a new second-level domain (SLD) under an established top-level domain (TLD) such as .com, .net or .org. In this process, a person or firm—the registrant—contacts a domain name registrar and requests the use of a particular name as a domain name in the DNS. The registrar then contacts the registry for that top-level domain and asks whether the desired name is still available. If no one has previously registered it, then the registrar may process the request and register the desired name to the registrant. In this Part, we consider domain name registrations. In the next Part, we consider the circumstances under which a domain name may be registered as a trademark.

Successfully registering a domain name with an accredited domain name registrar confers no legal rights to use that domain name on the registrant beyond those created by the registration agreement itself. When a registrar registers a domain name, it no more immunizes the registrant from the legal claims of others than a state immunizes a company when it grants its application for incorporation under a name that infringes the trademark or trade name of another. *See* 1 & 4 J. Thomas McCarthy, McCarthy on Trademarks and Unfair Competition §§ 9:8 & 25:73.3 (4th ed.2002). "[R]egistration of a mark or name with NSI does not itself confer any federal trademark rights on the registrant."

Although registration of a domain name does not confer on the registrant any special rights to use that domain name, one might still wonder whether the *fact* of registration would count as a use in commerce for the purpose of establishing priority under the federal trademark laws. The Ninth Circuit Court of Appeals in *Brookfield Communications, Inc. v. West Coast Entertainment Corp.*, 174 F.3d 1036 (9th Cir.1999), excerpted in Chapter 2, Part I(B), *supra*, answered this question in the negative. Brookfield's lawsuit against West Coast was precipitated by West Coast's use of the domain name "moviebuff.com" for its website. The case turned in part on who had first used the term "moviebuff" for Internet products and services. West Coast argued that it had priority because it had registered this domain name with Network Solutions before the filing date of Brookfield's application for a federal trademark registration. Rejecting this argument the court wrote:

> To resolve whether West Coast's use of "moviebuff.com" constitutes trademark infringement or unfair competition, we must first determine whether Brookfield has a valid, protectable trademark interest in the "MovieBuff" mark. Brookfield's registration of the mark on the Principal Register in the Patent and Trademark Office constitutes prima facie evidence of the validity of the registered mark and of Brookfield's exclusive right to use the mark on the goods and services specified in the registration. *See* 15 U.S.C. §§ 1057(b); 1115(a). Nevertheless, West Coast can rebut this presumption by showing that it used the mark in commerce first, since a fundamental tenet of trademark law is that ownership of an inherently distinctive mark such as "MovieBuff" is governed by priority of use. * * *
>
> Brookfield first used "MovieBuff" on its Internet-based products and services in August 1997, so West Coast can prevail only if it establishes first use earlier than that. In the literal sense of the word, West Coast "used" the term "moviebuff.com" when it registered that domain address in February 1996. Registration with Network Solutions, however, does not in itself constitute "use" for purposes of acquiring trademark priority. The Lanham Act grants trademark protection only to marks that are used to identify and to distinguish goods or services in commerce—which typically occurs when a mark is used in conjunction with the actual sale of goods or services. The purpose of a trademark is to help consumers identify the source, but a mark cannot serve a source-identifying function if the public has never seen the mark and thus is not meritorious of trademark protection until it is used in public in a manner that creates an association among consumers between the mark and the mark's owner.

Id. at 1046–51.

While it does not confer any rights other than those created by the registration contract itself, registration of a domain name in the commercial gTLDs .aero, .biz, .com, .coop, .info, .museum, .name, .net and .org (and some of the ccTLDs) does impose two significant requirements on all registrants. First, all registrants must agree to be bound by the ICANN Uniform Domain Name Dispute Resolution Policy (discussed in Part III, *supra*). Second, all registrants must agree to give the public access to their registration data. These requirements are imposed indirectly on registrants through ICANN's accreditation of registrars. ICANN's control of the root file not only permits it to appoint the registry of each top-level domain, but it also permits ICANN to dictate which companies may act as registrars for these domains. The process through which ICANN exercises this control is called *registrar accreditation*. All registrations in the commercial gTLDs must go through an ICANN-accredited registrar.

To become an accredited registrar, a registrar must enter into a standard Registrar Accreditation Agreement with ICANN. Through this agreement, ICANN obligates all accredited registrars to require domain name registrants to agree (1) to be bound by ICANN's Uniform Domain Name Dispute Resolution Policy and (2) to have personal and technical information collected as part of the registration process made available to the public. The impact with respect to these two issues of the Registrar Accreditation Agreement on an accredited registrar's registration agreement with a domain name registrant can be seen by comparing the following excerpts.

ICANN, Registrar Accreditation Agreement

www.icann.org
(May 17, 2001).

This REGISTRAR ACCREDITATION AGREEMENT ("Agreement") is by and between the Internet Corporation for Assigned Names and Numbers, a California non-profit, public benefit corporation, and [Registrar Name], a [Organization type and jurisdiction] ("Registrar"), and shall be deemed made on ______, at Los Angeles, California, USA.

* * *

3. REGISTRAR OBLIGATIONS.

* * *

3.3 *Public Access to Data on Registered Names.* During the Term of this Agreement:

3.3.1 At its expense, Registrar shall provide an interactive web page and a port 43 Whois service providing free public query-based access to up-to-date (i.e., updated at least daily) data concerning all active Registered Names sponsored by Registrar for each TLD in which it is accredited. The data accessible shall consist of elements that are designated from time to time according to an ICANN adopted specification or policy. Until ICANN otherwise specifies by means of an ICANN adopted specification or policy, this data shall consist of the following elements as contained in Registrar's database:

3.3.1.1 The name of the Registered Name;

3.3.1.2 The names of the primary nameserver and secondary nameserver(s) for the Registered Name;

3.3.1.3 The identity of Registrar (which may be provided through Registrar's website);

3.3.1.4 The original creation date of the registration;

3.3.1.5 The expiration date of the registration;

3.3.1.6 The name and postal address of the Registered Name Holder;

3.3.1.7 The name, postal address, e-mail address, voice telephone number, and (where available) fax number of the technical contact for the Registered Name; and

> 3.3.1.8 The name, postal address, e-mail address, voice telephone number, and (where available) fax number of the administrative contact for the Registered Name.
>
> * * *

3.3.4 Registrar shall abide by any ICANN specification or policy established as a Consensus Policy according to § 4 that requires registrars to cooperatively implement a distributed capability that provides query-based Whois search functionality across all registrars.
* * *

3.7 *Business Dealings, Including with Registered Name Holders.*

* * *

3.7.7 Registrar shall require all Registered Name Holders to enter into an electronic or paper registration agreement with Registrar including at least the following provisions:

> 3.7.7.1 The Registered Name Holder shall provide to Registrar accurate and reliable contact details and promptly correct and update them during the term of the Registered Name registration, including: the full name, postal address, e-mail address, voice telephone number, and fax number if available of the Registered Name Holder; name of authorized person for contact purposes in the case of a Registered Name Holder that is an organization, association, or corporation; and the data elements listed in Subsections 3.3.1.2, 3.3.1.7 and 3.3.1.8.
>
> 3.7.7.2 A Registered Name Holder's willful provision of inaccurate or unreliable information, its willful failure promptly to update information provided to Registrar, or its failure to respond for over fifteen calendar days to inquiries by Registrar concerning the accuracy of contact details associated with the Registered Name Holder's registration shall constitute a material breach of the Registered Name Holder-registrar contract and be a basis for cancellation of the Registered Name registration.
>
> 3.7.7.3 Any Registered Name Holder that intends to license use of a domain name to a third party is nonetheless the Registered Name Holder of record and is responsible for providing its own full contact information and for providing and updating accurate technical and administrative contact information adequate to facilitate timely resolution of any problems that arise in connection with the Registered Name. A Registered Name Holder licensing use of a Registered Name according to this provision shall accept liability for harm caused by wrongful use of the Registered Name, unless it promptly discloses the identity of the licensee to a party

providing the Registered Name Holder reasonable evidence of actionable harm.

* * *

3.7.7.9 The Registered Name Holder shall represent that, to the best of the Registered Name Holder's knowledge and belief, neither the registration of the Registered Name nor the manner in which it is directly or indirectly used infringes the legal rights of any third party.

3.7.7.10 For the adjudication of disputes concerning or arising from use of the Registered Name, the Registered Name Holder shall submit, without prejudice to other potentially applicable jurisdictions, to the jurisdiction of the courts (1) of the Registered Name Holder's domicile and (2) where Registrar is located.

3.7.7.11 The Registered Name Holder shall agree that its registration of the Registered Name shall be subject to suspension, cancellation, or transfer pursuant to any ICANN adopted specification or policy, or pursuant to any registrar or registry procedure not inconsistent with an ICANN adopted specification or policy, (1) to correct mistakes by Registrar or the Registry Operator in registering the name or (2) for the resolution of disputes concerning the Registered Name. * * *

VeriSign Service Agreement

Version Number 6.2.

* * *

ADDITIONAL TERMS APPLICABLE TO REGISTRANTS OF DOMAIN NAMES

* * *

4. VeriSign's Disclosure of Certain Information. Subject to the requirements of our privacy statement, in order for us to comply [with] the current rules and policies for the domain name system, you hereby grant to VeriSign the right to disclose to third parties through an interactive publicly accessible registration database the following mandatory information that you are required to provide when registering or reserving a domain name: (i) the domain name(s) registered by you; (ii) your name and postal address; (iii) the name(s), postal address(es), e-mail address(es), voice telephone number and where available the fax number(s) of the technical and administrative contacts for your domain name(s); (iv) the Internet protocol numbers of the primary nameserver and secondary nameserver(s) for such domain name(s); (v) the corresponding names of those nameservers; (vi) the original creation date of the registration; and (vii) the expiration date of the registration. We, as are all accredited domain name registrars, are also required to make this information available in bulk form to third parties who agree not to use it to (a) allow, enable or

otherwise support the transmission of mass unsolicited, commercial advertising or solicitations via telephone, facsimile, or e-mail (spam) or (b) enable high volume, automated, electronic processes that apply to our systems to register domain names.

5. Domain Name Dispute Policy. If you registered a domain name through us, you agree to be bound by our current domain name dispute policy that is incorporated herein and made a part of this Agreement by reference. The current version of the domain name dispute policy may be found at our website: www.netsol.com/en_US/legal/dispute-policy.jhtml.

6. Domain Name Dispute Policy Modifications. You agree that we, in our sole discretion, may modify our dispute policy. We will post any such revised policy on our website at least thirty (30) calendar days before it becomes effective. You agree that, by maintaining the reservation or registration of your domain name after modifications to the dispute policy become effective, you have agreed to these modifications. You acknowledge that if you do not agree to any such modification, you may terminate this Agreement. We will not refund any fees paid by you if you terminate your Agreement with us.

7. You agree that, if your use of our domain name registration services is challenged by a third party, you will be subject to the provisions specified in our dispute policy in effect at the time of the dispute. For any dispute with, or challenge by, a third party concerning or arising from your use of a domain name registered with us or your use of our domain name registration services, you agree to submit to subject matter jurisdiction, personal jurisdiction and venue of the United States District Court for the Eastern District of Virginia, Alexandria Division and the courts of your domicile. * * *

* * *

NOTES & QUESTIONS

1. *"Whois" lookups.* The contact and technical information that a domain name registrant is required to supply in the registration process is made publicly available through what is call a *whois look-up*. The information available includes the name, address and other contact information of the registrant, and the IP addresses of the domain's primary and secondary name servers. *Whois* is the name of the database that a registrar uses to make registration data available to the public. It is called a whois database because it answers the question "*who is* the registrant of this domain name?"

2. *Country code top level domains.* Each country designates the registry for its own ccTLD. Contact information for the registries and registrars of the various ccTLDs can be found at www.iana.org/cctld/cctld-whois.htm. Some ccTLDs may have a commercial value unrelated to the country for which it is the top-level domain. For example, any website having some connection to television might want to register its domain name in the .tv domain—the top-level domain for Tuvalu, a small island nation in the

South Pacific. Similarly, any holder of a federally registered trademark who wants to use it as a domain name but also want to "show" that it is a federally registered trademark might consider registering it as a domain name in the .tm domain—the top-level domain for Turkmenistan.

3. *Competition among registrars.* Beginning in 1999, ICANN introduced competition among registrars for the commercial gTLDs. A registrant can now choose from among a multitude of registrars on the basis of the fee they charge and other services they provide. Fees vary significantly among registrars; some provide free registration services in connection with other services that they offer, such as web hosting. Initial and renewal registration terms must be offered in one-year increments and no registrar may offer a term longer than ten years. Why is the market allowed to determine the fee and term of a domain name registration but not the dispute resolution policy to which the registrant is subject?

4. *Interpleader actions.* To avoid becoming embroiled in a dispute between a domain name registrant and trademark owner, registrars have filed interpleader actions in which they deposit the contested domain name with the court. Is this procedure always available to a registrar? Are there some circumstances in which an interpleader action is not appropriate? *See Network Solutions, Inc. v. Clue Computing, Inc.*, 946 F.Supp. 858 (D.Colo. 1996).

V. REGISTERING DOMAIN NAMES AS TRADEMARKS

In addition to registering a domain name for use in establishing a website or e-mail address, one may also register a domain name as a trademark under the Lanham Act of 1946, 15 U.S.C. §§ 1051–1127. In this section, we consider some of the issues that arise in connection with registering a domain name as a trademark.

Not all domain names can be registered as federal trademarks. To qualify for registration, a domain name must be within registrable subject matter. The next excerpt explores how the rules regarding registrable subject matter apply to domain names. We conclude this Part with a Federal Circuit decision that may require the PTO to modify its policy with respect to generic domain names.

U.S. Patent and Trademark Office, Examination Guide No. 2–99, Marks Composed, in Whole or in Part, of Domain Names

(Sept. 29, 1999).

* * *

Applications for registration of marks consisting of domain names are subject to the same requirements as all other applications for federal trademark registration. This Examination Guide identifies and discusses some of the issues that commonly arise in the examination of domain name mark applications.

II. Use as a Mark

A. Use Applications

A mark composed of a domain name is registrable as a trademark or service mark only if it functions as a source identifier. The mark as depicted on the specimens must be presented in a manner that will be perceived by potential purchasers as indicating source and not as merely an informational indication of the domain name address used to access a website. *See In re Eilberg,* 49 USPQ2d 1955 (TTAB 1998).[9]

In *Eilberg,* the Trademark Trial and Appeal Board (Board) held that a term that only serves to identify the applicant's domain name or the location on the Internet where the applicant's website appears, and does not separately identify applicant's services, does not function as a service mark. The applicant's proposed mark was WWW.EILBERG.COM, and the specimens showed that the mark was used on letterhead and business cards in the following manner:

WILLIAM H. EILBERG
ATTORNEY AT LAW
820 HOMESTEAD ROAD, P.O. BOX 7
JENKINTOWN, PENNSYLVANIA 19046
215-885-4600
FAX: 215-885-4603
EMAIL: WHE@EILBERG.COM

PATENTS, TRADEMARKS
AND COPYRIGHTS WWW.EILBERG.COM

The Board affirmed the examining attorney's refusal of registration on the ground that the matter presented for registration did not function as a mark, stating that:

> [T]he asserted mark, as displayed on applicant's letterhead, does not function as a service mark identifying and distinguishing applicant's legal services and, as presented, is not capable of doing so. As shown, the asserted mark identifies applicant's Internet domain name, by use of which one can access applicant's website. In other words, the asserted mark WWW.EILBERG.COM merely indicates the location on the Internet where applicant's website appears. It does not separately identify applicant's legal services as such. *Cf. In re The Signal Companies, Inc.*, 228 USPQ 956 (TTAB 1986).

9. ["TTAB" stands for Trademark Trial and Appeal Board. The TTAB is a unit of the PTO that resolves registration disputes, including appeals from decisions of trade-

> This is not to say that, if used appropriately, the asserted mark or portions thereof may not be trademarks or [service marks]. For example, if applicant's law firm name were, say, EILBERG.COM and were presented prominently on applicant's letterheads and business cards as the name under which applicant was rendering its legal services, then that mark may well be registrable.

Id. at 1956.

The examining attorney must review the specimens in order to determine how the proposed mark is actually used. It is the perception of the ordinary customer that determines whether the asserted mark functions as a mark, not the applicant's intent, hope or expectation that it do so. *See In re Standard Oil Co.,* 275 F.2d 945, 125 USPQ 227 (C.C.P.A. 1960).

If the proposed mark is used in a way that would be perceived as nothing more than an address at which the applicant can be contacted, registration must be refused. Examples of a domain name used only as an Internet address include a domain name used in close proximity to language referring to the domain name as an address, or a domain name displayed merely as part of the information on how to contact the applicant.

> Example: The mark is WWW.XYZ.COM for on-line ordering services in the field of clothing. Specimens of use consisting of an advertisement that states "visit us on the web at www.xyz.com" do not show service mark use of the proposed mark.
>
> Example: The mark is XYZ.COM for financial consulting services. Specimens of use consisting of a business card that refers to the service and lists a phone number, fax number, and the domain name sought to be registered do not show service mark use of the proposed mark.
>
> * * *

B. Advertising One's Own Products or Services on the Internet is not a Service

Advertising one's own products or services is not a service. *See In re Reichhold Chemicals, Inc.,* 167 USPQ 376 (TTAB 1970); TMEP[10] § 1301.01(a)(ii). Therefore, businesses that create a website for the sole purpose of advertising their own products or services cannot register a domain name used to identify that activity. In examination, the issue usually arises when the applicant describes the activity as a registrable service, e.g., "providing information about [a particular field]," but the specimens of use make it clear that the website merely advertises the applicant's own products or services. In this situation, the examining attorney must refuse registration because the mark is used to identify an

mark examiners refusing to register a mark.—Eds.]

10. ["TMEP" stands for Trademark Manual of Examining Procedure, which consists of the PTO's guidelines for trademark examiners.—Eds.]

activity that does not constitute a "service" within the meaning of the Trademark Act. Trademark Act §§ 1, 2, 3 and 45, 15 U.S.C. §§ 1051, 1052, 1053 and 1127.

* * *

D. Marks Comprised Solely of TLDs for Domain Name Registry Services

If a mark is composed solely of a TLD for "domain name registry services" (e.g., the services currently provided by Network Solutions, Inc. of registering .com domain names), registration should be refused under Trademark Act §§ 1, 2, 3 and 45, 15 U.S.C. §§ 1051, 1052, 1053 and 1127, on the ground that the TLD would not be perceived as a mark. The examining attorney should include evidence from the NEXIS® database, the Internet, or other sources to show that the proposed mark is currently used as a TLD or is under consideration as a new TLD.

If the TLD merely describes the subject or user of the domain space, registration should be refused under Trademark Act § 2(e)(1), 15 U.S.C. § 2(e)(1), on the ground that the TLD is merely descriptive of the registry services.

E. Intent-to-Use Applications

A refusal of registration on the ground that the matter presented for registration does not function as a mark relates to the manner in which the asserted mark is used. Therefore, generally, in an intent-to-use application, a mark that includes a domain name will not be refused on this ground until the applicant has submitted specimens of use with either an amendment to allege use under Trademark Act § 1(c), or a statement of use under Trademark Act § 1(d), 15 U.S.C. § 1051(c) or (d). However, the examining attorney should include an advisory note in the first Office Action that registration may be refused if the proposed mark, as used on the specimens, identifies only an Internet address. This is done strictly as a courtesy. If information regarding this possible ground for refusal is not provided to the applicant prior to the filing of the allegation of use, the Office is in no way precluded from refusing registration on this basis.

III. Surnames

If a mark is composed of a surname and a TLD, the examining attorney must refuse registration because the mark is primarily merely a surname under Trademark Act § 2(e)(4), 15 U.S.C. § 1052(e)(4). A TLD has no trademark significance. If the primary significance of a term is that of a surname, adding a TLD to the surname does not alter the primary significance of the mark as a surname. * * *

IV. Descriptiveness

If a proposed mark is composed of a merely descriptive term(s) combined with a TLD, the examining attorney should refuse registration under Trademark Act § 2(e)(1), 15 U.S.C. § 1052(e)(1), on the ground that the mark is merely descriptive. This applies to trademarks, service marks, collective marks and certification marks.

Example: The mark is SOFT.COM for facial tissues. The examining attorney must refuse registration under § 2(e)(1).

Example: The mark is NATIONAL BOOK OUTLET.COM for retail book store services. The examining attorney must refuse registration under § 2(e)(1).

The TLD will be perceived as part of an Internet address, and does not add source identifying significance to the composite mark. *Cf. In re Page*, 51 USPQ2d 1660 (TTAB 1999) (addition of a telephone prefix such as "800" or "888" to a descriptive term is insufficient, by itself, to render the mark inherently distinctive); *In re Patent & Trademark Services Inc.*, 49 USPQ2d 1537 (TTAB 1998) (PATENT & TRADEMARK SERVICES INC. is merely descriptive of legal services in the field of intellectual property; the term "Inc." merely indicates the type of entity that performs the services and has no significance as a mark); *In re The Paint Products Co.*, 8 USPQ2d 1863 (TTAB 1988) (PAINT PRODUCTS CO. is no more registrable as a trademark for goods emanating from a company that sells paint products than it would be as a service mark for retail paint store services offered by such a company); *In re E.I. Kane, Inc.*, 221 USPQ 1203 (TTAB 1984) (OFFICE MOVERS, INC. incapable of functioning as a mark for moving services; addition of the term "Inc." does not add any trademark significance to matter sought to be registered). *See also* TMEP § 1209.01(b)(12) regarding marks comprising in part "1–800," "888," or other telephone numbers.

V. Generic Refusals

If a mark is composed of a generic term(s) for applicant's goods or services and a TLD, the examining attorney must refuse registration on the ground that the mark is generic and the TLD has no trademark significance. *See* TMEP § 1209.01(b)(12) regarding marks comprised in part of "1–800" or other telephone numbers. Marks comprised of generic terms combined with TLDs are not eligible for registration on the Supplemental Register, or on the Principal Register under Trademark Act § 2(f), 15 U.S.C. § 1052(f). This applies to trademarks, service marks, collective marks and certification marks.

Example: TURKEY.COM for frozen turkeys is unregistrable on either the Principal or Supplemental Register.

Example: BANK.COM for banking services is unregistrable on either the Principal or Supplemental Register.

The examining attorney generally should not issue a refusal in an application for registration on the Principal Register on the ground that a mark is a generic name for the goods or services unless the applicant asserts that the mark has acquired distinctiveness under § 2(f) of the Trademark Act, 15 U.S.C. § 1052(f). Absent such a claim, the examining attorney should issue a refusal on the ground that the mark is merely descriptive of the goods or services under § 2(e)(1), and provide an advisory statement that the matter sought to be registered appears to be a generic name for the goods or services. TMEP § 1209.02.

VI. Marks Containing Geographical Matter

The examining attorney should examine marks containing geographic matter in the same manner that any mark containing geographic matter is examined. *See generally* TMEP §§ 1210.05 and 1210.06. Depending on the manner in which it is used on or in connection with the goods or services, a proposed domain name mark containing a geographic term may be primarily geographically descriptive under § 2(e)(2) of the Trademark Act, 15 U.S.C. § 1052(e)(2), or primarily geographically deceptively misdescriptive under § 2(e)(3) of the Trademark Act, 15 U.S.C. § 1052(e)(3), and/or merely descriptive or deceptively misdescriptive under § 2(e)(1) of the Trademark Act, 15 U.S.C. § 1052(e)(1).

Geographic matter may be merely descriptive of services provided on the Internet

When a geographic term is used as a mark for services that are provided on the Internet, sometimes the geographic term describes the subject of the service rather than the geographic origin of the service. Usually this occurs when the mark is composed of a geographic term that describes the subject matter of information services (e.g., NEW ORLEANS.COM for "providing vacation planning information about New Orleans, Louisiana by means of the global computer network"). In these cases, the examining attorney should refuse registration under Trademark Act § 2(e)(1) because the mark is merely descriptive of the services. * * *

IX. Likelihood of Confusion

In analyzing whether a domain name mark is likely to cause confusion with another pending or registered mark, the examining attorney must consider the marks as a whole, but generally should accord little weight to the TLD portion of the mark. *See* TMEP § 1207.01(b) *et seq.*

* * *

In re Dial-A-Mattress Operating Corp.

240 F.3d 1341 (Fed.Cir.2001).

■ MAYER, CHIEF JUDGE.

* * *

Background

Dial–A–Mattress sells mattresses and related bedding through retail stores and a telephone "shop-at-home" service. In 1996, it filed an intent-to-use application to register "1–888–M–A–T–R–E–S–S" as a service mark for "telephone shop-at-home retail services in the field of mattresses." * * *

After several office actions, the examiner rejected the "1–888–M–A–T–R–E–S–S" application because the mark is generic for the relevant services and therefore unregisterable. The examiner found that even if it is not generic, it is "merely descriptive" and Dial–A–Mattress presented insufficient evidence of acquired distinctiveness to permit registration of the mark under § 2(f) of the Trademark Act.

Dial–A–Mattress appealed the rejection to the Trademark Trial and Appeal Board, which affirmed. * * *

Discussion

* * *

The determination of whether a mark is generic is made according to a two-part inquiry: "First, what is the genus of the goods or services at issue? Second, is the term sought to be registered ... understood by the relevant public primarily to refer to that genus of goods or services?" *H. Marvin Ginn Corp.,* 782 F.2d at 990. Placement of a term on the fanciful-suggestive-descriptive-generic continuum is a question of fact. *In re Merrill Lynch, Pierce, Fenner & Smith, Inc.,* 828 F.2d at 1569–70. The Director of the United States Patent and Trademark Office (Director) bears the burden of proving a term generic. *In re The Am. Fertility Soc'y,* 188 F.3d 1341, 1345 (Fed.Cir.1999). Any competent source suffices to show the relevant purchasing public's understanding of a contested term, including purchaser testimony, consumer surveys, dictionary definitions, trade journals, newspapers and other publications.

Where a term is a "compound word" (such as "Screenwipe"), the Director may satisfy his burden of proving it generic by producing evidence that each of the constituent words is generic, and that "the separate words joined to form a compound have a meaning identical to the meaning common usage would ascribe to those words as a compound." *In re Gould Paper Corp.,* 834 F.2d 1017, 1018 (Fed.Cir.1987). * * * The *In re Gould* test is applicable only to "compound terms formed by the union of words" where the public understands the individual terms to be generic for a genus of goods or services, and the joining of the individual terms into one compound word lends "no additional meaning to the term." *Id.* at 1348–49.

Here, there is no dispute that the genus is telephone shop-at-home services for retail mattresses. Nor does Dial–A–Mattress contest the following evidence and legal conclusions offered by the Director: (1) the area code designation (888) in the proposed mark by itself is devoid of source-indicating significance; (2) "matress" is the legal "equivalent" of the word "mattress"; and (3) the word "mattress" standing alone is generic for retail services in the field of mattresses.

Instead, Dial–A–Mattress contends that the board erred in holding this quantum of evidence sufficient to demonstrate that the term "1–888–M–A–T–R–E–S–S" is generic. * * *

* * *

We conclude that the board applied the wrong test in holding that the Director meets his burden of proving an alphanumeric telephone number generic merely by showing that it is composed of a non-source-indicating area code and a generic term. "The commercial impression of a trademark is derived from it as a whole, not from its elements separated and considered in detail. For this reason, it should be considered in its entirety...." *Estate of P.D. Beckwith, Inc. v. Comm'r of Patents,* 252 U.S. 538, 545–46 (1920). The Director must produce evidence of the meaning the relevant purchasing public accords the proposed mnemonic mark "as a whole." *In re The Am. Fertility Soc'y,* 188 F.3d at 1348; *see also H. Marvin Ginn Corp.,* 782 F.2d at 990–91. *In re Gould* does not apply here because "1–888–M–A–T–R–E–S–S" a mnemonic formed by the union of a series of numbers and a word bears closer conceptual resemblance to a phrase than a compound word. *See In re The Am. Fertility Soc'y,* 188 F.3d at 1348–49 (explicitly limiting the holding of *In re Gould* to "compound terms formed by the union of words"). It is devoid of source-indicating significance, but "(888)" is not a word and is not itself a generic term for selling by telephone.

Analyzing the "1–888–M–A–T–R–E–S–S" mark as a whole, substantial evidence does not support the conclusion that the mark is generic. There is no record evidence that the relevant public refers to the class of shop-at-home telephone mattress retailers as "1–888–M–A–T–R–E–S–S." *See H. Marvin Ginn Corp.,* 782 F.2d at 991. "Telephone shop-at-home mattresses" or "mattresses by phone" would be more apt generic descriptions. Like the title "Fire Chief" for a magazine in the field of fire fighting, a phone number is not literally a genus or class name, but is at most descriptive of the class. *Id.* Moreover, like the term "cash management account," "1–888–M–A–T–R–E–S–S" does not "immediately and unequivocally" describe the service at issue. *See In re Merrill Lynch, Pierce, Fenner & Smith, Inc.,* 828 F.2d at 1571.

Finally, given that telephone numbers consist of only seven numbers and typically can be used by only one entity at a time, a competitor of a business that has obtained a telephone number corresponding to a "mattress" mnemonic for all practical purposes is already precluded from using and promoting the number. A rule precluding registerability merely shifts the race from the Trademark Office to the telephone company. * * *

[In the remainder of the opinion the court finds that 1–888–MATTRES is descriptive and that Dial–A–Mattress presented sufficient evidence of acquired distinctiveness to permit registration of the mark under § 2(f) of the Trademark Act.]

NOTES & QUESTIONS

1. *Web address as service mark.* As the above PTO *Examination Guide* makes clear, a website that merely advertises and sells the goods and services of the site owner would not constitute a separate service supporting a service mark registration under the Lanham Act. To qualify as an information service, a website must provide some additional value beyond the promotion and sale of the site owner's goods and services. Must the site owner charge for this additional value that the site provides before it will qualify as an information service sufficient to support a federal service mark registration? *See Capital Speakers, Inc. v. Capital Speakers Club*, 41 U.S.P.Q.2d (BNA) 1030 (T.T.A.B.1996).

2. *Generic term + .com.* Is a domain name comprising a generic term and the top-level domain name .com registrable as a trademark? In *In re Dial-A-Mattress Operating Corporation,* the court concluded that the *In re Gould* test did not apply to "1–888–M–A–T–R–E–S–S" because it was more like a phrase than a compound word. Do you think that the court would have reached the same conclusion if it had been considering a domain name? Recall that a domain name replaces a number, namely an IP address. Central to the court's reasoning was the fact that the proposed mnemonic mark was composed of a number and a word. How would you describe the composition of a domain name? Is .com an English word? Is .com a generic term for selling over the Internet? Are all websites with a domain name in the .com domain engaged in selling goods or services? Or is .com simply an "area code" for the domain name system?

In Part V of *Examination Guide No. 2–99*, excerpted above, the U.S. Patent and Trademark Office states that "[i]f a mark is composed of a generic term(s) for applicant's goods or services and a TLD, the examining attorney must refuse registration on the ground that the mark is generic and the TLD has no trademark significance." Is this policy consistent with *In re Dial-A-Mattress Operating Corporation*?

3. *A race to register.* The court in *In re Dial-A-Mattress Operating Corporation* also notes that since

> telephone numbers consist of only seven numbers and typically can be used by only one entity at a time, a competitor of a business that has obtained a telephone number corresponding to a "mattress" mnemonic for all practical purposes is already precluded from using and promoting the number. A rule precluding registerability merely shifts the race from the Trademark Office to the telephone company.

Does this same line of reasoning apply to domain names? Once one company registers a particular domain name, aren't all other companies for all practical purposes precluded from using and promoting that same domain name? Does a rule precluding registrability of a domain name formed from a generic term and a top-level domain name merely shift the race from the Trademark Office to a domain name registrar?

CHAPTER FOUR

CONTRACTING ONLINE

Go to a commercial website of your choice—for example, Microsoft's at www.microsoft.com—and scroll down the home page until you come to a small link at the bottom labeled something like "Terms of Use." Click on the link and watch what unfolds. Are these terms contractually binding on you?

Contracting is just as central to online exchange transactions as it is to those that take place offline. As contract law accommodates to the digital networked environment, there are a number of issues that are in the process of being sorted out, both by legislative authorities (on the state, national, and international levels) and by the courts. This chapter and the next address these issues under the following rubrics:

Binding commitment. How will interactions between people and computers create binding commitment? Can binding commitment arise through computer-to-computer interactions?

We must consider whether e-mail offer and acceptance should be treated the same way as offer and acceptance communicated by postal mail. We must consider whether electronic text constitutes "writing" for purposes of statutes, like the Statute of Frauds, that make an agreement enforceable only if it is in writing. But we must also consider new forms of contracts (or purported contracts): whether binding commitment is created by placing boilerplate terms on an interior website page; whether computers programmed with terms can interact with each other to create binding commitment; whether terms can be attached to a digital object by a seller or licensor and made binding on everyone in a chain of distribution. In these materials, these new possibilities are called browsewrap, machine-made, and viral contracts, respectively.

Authentication. How do we know who made a particular deal? How do we know what the terms are? In the online environment, especially since most transactions are conducted at a distance, new forms of identification of parties and guarantees of textual integrity are being developed. In particular, as we shall see (in Chapter 5, *infra*), digital signatures can serve both to identify parties and to guarantee textual integrity. But digital signatures carry their own costs and risks, and the most prevalent current technology, public key cryptography, requires a well-developed institutional infrastructure, known as public key infrastructure.

Limits on contractual ordering. In the online as in the offline world, certain subjects are off-limits to contract, as are certain kinds of terms; and the circumstances under which a purported contract was arrived at may determine whether it will be deemed enforceable. In the online world, the question of unconscionability arises in standardized contracts and/or situations of unequal bargaining power. What kinds of contracts, or terms in contracts, will be disallowed? What remedies are available?

In the online world, parties often attempt to select by contract the forum in which disputes will be adjudicated, the governing law under which disputes will be adjudicated, and the type of dispute resolution (whether arbitration or litigation) or remedies available. Although this kind of contractual ordering is prevalent in the offline world, it may be even more important in the online world, because of the distances at which transactions are conducted, and because of the difficulties otherwise attendant upon sorting out whose law governs and what court has jurisdiction. (*See* Chapter 7, *infra*.) But such contracts are not always held valid and enforceable. We will look at some circumstances in which they have been held to be overreaching.

Standardization. Uniform standardized "adhesion" contracts are prevalent on the Internet, perhaps even more so than in the offline world. It has thus become important to determine the circumstances in which standardized form contracts online will be enforceable. Standardization bears significantly on questions involving the limits of contractual ordering.

Although standardization has its dangers, standardization may be a necessary component of viable e-commerce. In the United States, contract law has been primarily state law. We must consider to what extent contract law is becoming national—and international.

I. Binding Commitment

Transacting electronically brings the basis of contract, binding commitment, into question. Various legislative initiatives have sought to clarify the issue.

A. UETA, ESIGN, and UCITA

To address the uncertainties created by the rise of electronic contracting, the National Conference of Commissioners on Uniform State Laws ("NCCUSL") has recommended for adoption in the several states two model statutes that were drafted under its auspices: the Uniform Electronic Transactions Act ("UETA"), and the Uniform Computer Information Transactions Act ("UCITA"). The first of these two model acts has been widely adopted (by 37 states as of this writing), albeit with significant variations among the enacting states. To encourage greater uniformity in this regard as well as to address the uncertainties regarding electronic contracting that exist in states that have yet to adopt UETA, Congress enacted the Electronic Signatures in Global and National Commerce Act ("ESIGN"), Pub. L. No. 106–229, 114 Stat. 464 (2000), which is in many respects similar to UETA. As explained below, the approach taken by both

UETA and ESIGN is largely nonregulatory and procedural: at bottom, both acts simply state that electronic records and electronic signatures may not be denied legal effect merely because they are in an electronic format.

In contrast, UCITA takes a comprehensive, regulatory approach to electronic contracting and the licensing of computer information, much as Article 2 of the Uniform Commercial Code ("UCC") takes a comprehensive and regulatory approach to the law of sales. Indeed, NCCUSL, the organization that recommended the Uniform Commercial Code for adoption in the 1950s, originally intended for UCITA to be a new article of the UCC. While it was being drafted, UCITA was known as "Proposed Article 2B," and the drafters intended it to be inserted into the UCC after Articles 2 (Sales) and 2A (Leasing). The proposed Article 2B proved extremely controversial. For example, many state attorneys general opposed it because they felt it undermined their states' law of consumer protection. And many intellectual property scholars felt that it misunderstood the proper role of intellectual property law. As a result, the American Law Institute ("ALI"), the organization responsible for the Restatements of Law as well as jointly responsible, with NCCUSL, for the UCC, refused to approve it for incorporation into the UCC. Rather than abandon the project of a uniform licensing law, NCCUSL decided to offer Proposed Article 2B, renamed UCITA, as a separate, free-standing model act for adoption by the states. As of this writing, only two states have enacted UCITA, while three others have enacted legislation aimed at nullifying its effect within their borders. In an attempt to address some of the more contentious and controversial provisions contained in UCITA, NCCUSL has formed a committee to review and propose amendments to it. Whether UCITA will ultimately be adopted by the several states remains to be seen.

In the materials that follow, we introduce the operative provisions of UETA, ESIGN, and UCITA relating to validation of electronic transactions. More detailed treatment of provisions dealing with authentication of parties and text appears in Chapter 5, *infra*, and more detailed treatment of provisions affecting consumers appears in Chapter 6, *infra*..

1. THE UNIFORM ELECTRONIC TRANSACTIONS ACT

Uniform Electronic Transactions Act, §§ 7, 5 & 3

National Conference of Commissioners on Uniform State Laws.
(1999).

SECTION 7. LEGAL RECOGNITION OF ELECTRONIC RECORDS, ELECTRONIC SIGNATURES, AND ELECTRONIC CONTRACTS.

(a) A record or signature may not be denied legal effect or enforceability solely because it is in electronic form.

(b) A contract may not be denied legal effect or enforceability solely because an electronic record was used in its formation.

(c) If a law requires a record to be in writing, an electronic record satisfies the law.

(d) If a law requires a signature, an electronic signature satisfies the law.

Comment

1. This section sets forth the fundamental premise of this Act: namely, that the medium in which a record, signature, or contract is created, presented or retained does not affect its legal significance. * * *

SECTION 5. USE OF ELECTRONIC RECORDS AND ELECTRONIC SIGNATURES; VARIATION BY AGREEMENT.

(a) This [Act] does not require a record or signature to be created, generated, sent, communicated, received, stored, or otherwise processed or used by electronic means or in electronic form.

(b) This [Act] applies only to transactions between parties each of which has agreed to conduct transactions by electronic means. Whether the parties agree to conduct a transaction by electronic means is determined from the context and surrounding circumstances, including the parties' conduct. * * *

SECTION 3. SCOPE.

(a) Except as otherwise provided in subsection (b), this [Act] applies to electronic records and electronic signatures relating to a transaction.

(b) This [Act] does not apply to a transaction to the extent it is governed by:

(1) a law governing the creation and execution of wills, codicils, or testamentary trusts;

(2) [The Uniform Commercial Code other than §§ 1–107 and 1–206, Article 2, and Article 2A];

(3) [the Uniform Computer Information Transactions Act]; and

(4) [other laws, if any, identified by State].

(c) This [Act] applies to an electronic record or electronic signature otherwise excluded from the application of this [Act] under subsection (b) to the extent it is governed by a law other than those specified in subsection (b).

(d) A transaction subject to this [Act] is also subject to other applicable substantive law.

Comment

1. The scope of this Act is inherently limited by the fact that it only applies to transactions related to business, commercial (including consumer) and governmental matters. * * *

* * *

5. Articles 3, 4 and 4A of the UCC impact payment systems and have specifically been removed from the coverage of this Act. * * *

* * *

7. This Act does apply, *in toto*, to transactions under unrevised Articles 2 and 2A. There is every reason to validate electronic contracting in these situations. Sale and lease transactions do not implicate broad systems beyond the parties to the underlying transaction, such as are present in check collection and electronic funds transfers. Further sales and leases generally do not have as far reaching effect on the rights of third parties beyond the contracting parties, such as exists in the secured transactions system. Finally, it is in the area of sales, licenses and leases that electronic commerce is occurring to its greatest extent today. To exclude these transactions would largely gut the purpose of this Act.

In the event that Articles 2 and 2A are revised and adopted in the future, UETA will only apply to the extent provided in those Acts.

* * *

Uniform Electronic Transactions Act, Prefatory Note

National Conference of Commissioners on Uniform State Laws.
(1999).

With the advent of electronic means of communication and information transfer, business models and methods for doing business have evolved to take advantage of the speed, efficiencies, and cost benefits of electronic technologies. These developments have occurred in the face of existing legal barriers to the legal efficacy of records and documents which exist solely in electronic media. Whether the legal requirement that information or an agreement or contract must be contained or set forth in a pen and paper writing derives from a statute of frauds affecting the enforceability of an agreement, or from a record retention statute that calls for keeping the paper record of a transaction, such legal requirements raise real barriers to the effective use of electronic media.

* * *

It is important to understand that the purpose of the UETA is to remove barriers to electronic commerce by validating and effectuating electronic records and signatures. It is NOT a general contracting statute—the substantive rules of contracts remain unaffected by UETA. Nor is it a digital signature statute. To the extent that a State has a Digital Signature Law, the UETA is designed to support and complement that statute.

A. Scope of the Act and Procedural Approach. The scope of this Act provides coverage which sets forth a clear framework for covered transactions, and also avoids unwarranted surprises for unsophisticated parties dealing in this relatively new media. The clarity and certainty of the scope of the Act have been obtained while still providing a solid legal framework that allows for the continued development of innovative technology to facilitate electronic transactions.

* * *

Finally, recognition that the paradigm for the Act involves two willing parties conducting a transaction electronically, makes it necessary to expressly provide that some form of acquiescence or intent on the part of a person to conduct transactions electronically is necessary before the Act can be invoked. Accordingly, Section 5 specifically provides that the Act only applies between parties that have agreed to conduct transactions electronically. In this context, the construction of the term agreement must be broad in order to assure that the Act applies whenever the circumstances show the parties' intention to transact electronically, regardless of whether the intent rises to the level of a formal agreement.

B. Procedural Approach. Another fundamental premise of the Act is that it be minimalist and procedural. The general efficacy of existing law in an electronic context, so long as biases and barriers to the medium are removed, validates this approach. The Act defers to existing substantive law. * * *

* * *

2. THE ELECTRONIC SIGNATURES IN GLOBAL AND NATIONAL COMMERCE ACT

Electronic Signatures in Global and National Commerce Act, § 101(a)

15 U.S.C. § 7001(a).

SEC. 101. GENERAL RULE OF VALIDITY

(a) In general.—Notwithstanding any statute, regulation, or other rule of law (other than this title and title II), with respect to any transaction in or affecting interstate or foreign commerce—

(1) a signature, contract, or other record relating to such transaction may not be denied legal effect, validity, or enforceability solely because it is in electronic form; and

(2) a contract relating to such transaction may not be denied legal effect, validity, or enforceability solely because an electronic signature or electronic record was used in its formation.

Senate Report 106–131 to Accompany S. 761

Senate Committee on Commerce, Science, and Transportation.
(July 30, 1999).

* * *

PURPOSE OF THE BILL[1]

The purpose of this legislation is to promote electronic commerce by providing a consistent national framework for electronic signatures and transactions.

BACKGROUND AND NEEDS

* * * Presently * * * one of the greatest barriers to the growth of Internet commerce is the lack of consistent, national rules governing the use of electronic signatures. More than forty States have enacted electronic authentication laws, and no two of these laws are the same. This inconsistency deters businesses and consumers from using electronic signature technologies to authorize contracts or transactions.

Fortunately, the National Conference of Commissioners of Uniform State Laws (NCCUSL) is preparing a model State law that adapts existing commercial law to govern electronic commerce. This "Uniform Electronic Transactions Act" (UETA) will create a market-based, technology-neutral legal framework for electronic commerce. It is currently estimated that UETA will be finalized in July of this year.

The impending release of UETA confronts the Congress with a situation similar to that which arose when NCCUSL first released its Uniform Commercial Code (UCC). The release of the UCC began a process that eventually created a predictable regime of commercial law that was adopted by all the States. However, the UCC was not adopted everywhere simultaneously. There was a transition period in which commercial law remained unsettled as States reviewed the UCC, debated its merits, and enacted it into law.

Inevitably, a similar transition period will occur in the case of UETA. This legislation is intended to protect and foster commerce during this transition period by providing a predictable legal regime governing electronic signatures. * * *

* * *

The legislation preempts State law that is inconsistent with UETA, and provides that the electronic records produced in the execution of a digital contract shall not be denied legal effect solely because they are electronic in nature. * * *

This Federal preemption of State law is designed to be an interim measure. It preempts State law until the State enacts uniform standards which are consistent with those contained in this legislation or the UETA. Once States enact the UETA or other legislation governing the use of

1. [The reference here is to the Millennium Digital Commerce Act. This bill was the Senate's version of what ultimately was passed as the Electronic Signatures in Global and National Commerce Act. The final version of the act was agreed to in conference committee.—Eds.]

electronic signatures which is consistent with the UETA, the Federal preemption is lifted. * * *

* * *

Electronic Signatures in Global and National Commerce Act, §§ 102 & 103

15 U.S.C. §§ 7002 & 7003.

SEC. 102. EXEMPTION TO PREEMPTION.

(a) In General.—A State statute, regulation, or other rule of law may modify, limit, or supersede the provisions of § 101 with respect to State law only if such statute, regulation, or rule of law—

(1) constitutes an enactment or adoption of the Uniform Electronic Transactions Act as approved and recommended for enactment in all the States by the National Conference of Commissioners on Uniform State Laws in 1999, except that any exception to the scope of such Act enacted by a State under § 3(b)(4) of such Act shall be preempted to the extent such exception is inconsistent with this title or title II, or would not be permitted under paragraph (2)(A)(ii) of this subsection; or

(2)(A) specifies the alternative procedures or requirements for the use or acceptance (or both) of electronic records or electronic signatures to establish the legal effect, validity, or enforceability of contracts or other records, if—

(i) such alternative procedures or requirements are consistent with this title and title II; and

(ii) such alternative procedures or requirements do not require, or accord greater legal status or effect to, the implementation or application of a specific technology or technical specification for performing the functions of creating, storing, generating, receiving, communicating, or authenticating electronic records or electronic signatures; and

(B) if enacted or adopted after the date of the enactment of this Act, makes specific reference to this Act.

SEC. 103. SPECIFIC EXCEPTIONS.

(a) Excepted Requirements.—The provisions of § 101 shall not apply to a contract or other record to the extent it is governed by—

(1) a statute, regulation, or other rule of law governing the creation and execution of wills, codicils, or testamentary trusts;

(2) a State statute, regulation, or other rule of law governing adoption, divorce, or other matters of family law; or

(3) the Uniform Commercial Code, as in effect in any State, other than §§ 1–107 and 1–206 and Articles 2 and 2A.

(b) Additional Exceptions.—The provisions of § 101 shall not apply to—

(1) court orders or notices, or official court documents (including briefs, pleadings, and other writings) required to be executed in connection with court proceedings;

(2) any notice of—

(A) the cancellation or termination of utility services (including water, heat, and power);

(B) default, acceleration, repossession, foreclosure, or eviction, or the right to cure, under a credit agreement secured by, or a rental agreement for, a primary residence of an individual;

(C) the cancellation or termination of health insurance or benefits or life insurance benefits (excluding annuities); or

(D) recall of a product, or material failure of a product, that risks endangering health or safety; or

(3) any document required to accompany any transportation or handling of hazardous materials, pesticides, or other toxic or dangerous materials.

(c) Review of Exceptions.—

(1) Evaluation required.—The Secretary of Commerce, acting through the Assistant Secretary for Communications and Information, shall review the operation of the exceptions in subsections (a) and (b) to evaluate, over a period of 3 years, whether such exceptions continue to be necessary for the protection of consumers. Within 3 years after the date of enactment of this Act, the Assistant Secretary shall submit a report to the Congress on the results of such evaluation.

(2) Determinations.—If a Federal regulatory agency, with respect to matter within its jurisdiction, determines after notice and an opportunity for public comment, and publishes a finding, that one or more such exceptions are no longer necessary for the protection of consumers and eliminating such exceptions will not increase the material risk of harm to consumers, such agency may extend the application of § 101 to the exceptions identified in such finding.

3. THE UNIFORM COMPUTER INFORMATION TRANSACTIONS ACT

Uniform Computer Information Transactions Act, §§ 107, 202 & 103

National Conference of Commissioners on Uniform State Laws.
(2000).

SECTION 107. LEGAL RECOGNITION OF ELECTRONIC RECORD AND AUTHENTICATION; USE OF ELECTRONIC AGENTS

(a) A record or authentication may not be denied legal effect or enforceability solely because it is in electronic form.

* * *

SECTION 202. FORMATION IN GENERAL

(a) A contract may be formed in any manner sufficient to show agreement, including offer and acceptance or conduct of both parties or operations of electronic agents which recognize the existence of a contract.

* * *

SECTION 103. SCOPE; EXCLUSIONS

(a) This [Act] applies to computer information transactions.

(b) Except for subject matter excluded in subsection (d) and as otherwise provided in § 104, if a computer information transaction includes subject matter other than computer information or subject matter excluded under subsection (d), the following rules apply:

(1) If a transaction includes computer information and goods, this [Act] applies to the part of the transaction involving computer information, informational rights in it, and creation or modification of it. However, if a copy of a computer program is contained in and sold or leased as part of goods, this [Act] applies to the copy and the computer program only if:

(A) the goods are a computer or computer peripheral; or

(B) giving the buyer or lessee of the goods access to or use of the program is ordinarily a material purpose of transactions in goods of the type sold or leased.

(2) Subject to subsection (d)(3)(A), if a transaction includes an agreement for creating, or for obtaining rights to create, computer information and a motion picture, this [Act] does not apply to the agreement if the dominant character of the agreement is to create or obtain rights to create a motion picture. In all other such agreements, this [Act] does not apply to the part of the agreement that involves a motion picture excluded under subsection (d)(3), but does apply to the computer information.

(3) In all other cases, this [Act] applies to the entire transaction if the computer information and informational rights, or access to them, is the primary subject matter, but otherwise applies only to the part of the transaction involving computer information, informational rights in it, and creation or modification of it.

(c) To the extent of a conflict between this [Act] and [Article 9 of the Uniform Commercial Code], [Article 9] governs.

(d) This [Act] does not apply to:

(1) a financial services transaction;

(2) an insurance services transaction;

(3) an agreement to create, perform or perform in, include information in, acquire, use, distribute, modify, reproduce, have access to, adapt, make available, transmit, license, or display:

(A) a motion picture or audio or visual programming, other than in (i) a mass-market transaction or (ii) a submission of an idea or information or release of informational rights that may result in making a motion picture or similar information product; or

(B) a sound recording, musical work, or phonorecord as defined or used in Title 17 of the United States Code as of July 1, 1999, or an enhanced sound recording, other than in the submission of an idea or information or release of informational rights that may result in the creation of such material or a similar information product.

(4) a compulsory license;

(5) a contract of employment of an individual, other than an individual hired as an independent contractor to create or modify computer information, unless the independent contractor is a free-lancer in the news reporting industry as that term is commonly understood in that industry;

(6) a contract that does not require that information be furnished as computer information or a contract in which, under the agreement, the form of the information as computer information is otherwise insignificant with respect to the primary subject matter of the part of the transaction pertaining to the information;

(7) unless otherwise agreed between the parties in a record:

(A) telecommunications products or services provided pursuant to federal or state tariffs; or

(B) telecommunications products or services provided pursuant to agreements required or permitted to be filed by the service provider with a federal or state authority regulating those services or under pricing subject to approval by a federal or state regulatory authority; or

(8) subject matter within the scope of [Article 3, 4, 4A, 5, [6,] 7, or 8 of the Uniform Commercial Code].

(e) As used in subsection (d)(3)(B), "enhanced sound recording" means a separately identifiable product or service the dominant character of which consists of recorded sounds, but which includes (i) statements or instructions whose purpose is to allow or control the perception, reproduction, or communication of those sounds or (ii) other information, as long as recorded sounds constitute the dominant character of the product or service.

(f) In this section:

(1) "Audio or visual programming" means audio or visual programming that is provided by broadcast, satellite, or cable, as defined or used in the Communications Act of 1934 and related regulations as they existed on July 1, 1999, or by similar methods of delivery.

(2) "Motion picture" means:

(A) "motion picture" as defined in Title 17 of the United States Code as of July 1, 1999; or

(B) a separately identifiable product or service the dominant character of which consists of a linear motion picture, but which includes (i) statements or instructions whose purpose is to allow or control the perception, reproduction, or communication of the motion picture or (ii) other information, as long as the motion picture constitutes the dominant character of the product or service.

Official Comment

* * *

2. **Transactions in Computer Information.** * * * The scope of this Act turns initially on the definition of "*computer information transaction*." Section 102(11). "Computer information transactions" are agreements that deal with the creation, modification, access to, license, or distribution of computer information. § 102(a)(11). "Computer information" is information in a form directly capable of being processed by, or obtained from, a computer and any copy, associated documentation, or packaging. § 102(a)(10). * * *

a. **Contracts to Create or Develop Computer Information.** This Act applies to contracts to develop, modify, or create software and other computer information, such as a computer database. § 102(a)(11). Except as excluded in subsection (d), the Act covers all software development contracts, thus resolving conflicts in prior case law.

b. **Computer Programs.** This Act applies to transactions involving distribution of, or grant of a right to use, a computer program, whether they involve a license or an unrestricted sale of a copy of a program. § 102(a)(11). The difference between a license and an unrestricted sale, however, is relevant within the Act. A license may involve either a more substantial retention of rights or a greater transfer of rights than an unrestricted sale of a copy. While most provisions of this Act apply to all transactions within its scope, some are limited solely to licenses. The coverage of each section is explicit in the section.

c. **Access and Internet Contracts.** This Act applies to access contracts. § 102(a)(1). This includes Internet and similar systems for access to or use of computer information on a remote system. It generally includes contracts under which data, text or images are provided to licensees by access to the provider's system or location on Internet.

d. **Digital Multimedia Works.** This Act applies to agreements to create or distribute multimedia works. § 102(a)(11). Multimedia works are those that, through digital technology, combine multiple forms of authorship and multiple types of information into an integrated, often interactive work. Interactivity is a characteristic of software-based products. For a discussion of what is a multimedia work, see Copyright Office Circular (Multimedia Circular).

e. **Data Processing Contracts.** This Act covers contracts for data processing or data analysis of computer information. § 102(a)(1)(11)(41).

3. **Transactions Outside the Act.** The scope of this Act is limited by the affirmative definitions of "computer information" and "computer information transaction," which exclude print and various other forms of information distribution, and by the exclusions in subsection (d). * * *

This Act does not apply to "information," but to contracts and agreements regarding computer information.

4. **Mixed Transactions.** A computer information transaction may involve computer information and other subject matter. This presents a question of whether all or any part of the transaction is governed by this Act, common law, or an article of the Uniform Commercial Code. The circumstance that a contract is governed by more than one source of contract law is common in modern commerce. * * *

* * *

The rules of subsection (b) do not apply if the agreement specifies to what extent this Act governs. § 104. If the parties elect coverage under this Act, that agreement generally governs as would an agreement that this Act should not apply at all. Agreement here, as elsewhere, can be found in the express terms of the contract as well as in the usage of trade or course of dealing between the parties, or as inferred from the commercial circumstances of the contracting.

* * *

Uniform Computer Information Transactions Act, Prefatory Note

National Conference of Commissioners on Uniform State Laws.
(2000).

* * * [UCC] Article 2 served as both a model and a point of departure for UCITA. Like Article 2, UCITA covers a variety of transactions, many of which take place solely between merchants. Article 2 governs sales of jet planes as well as toasters, not to mention the large-scale acquisition of jet and toaster parts. UCITA governs access by Fortune 500 businesses to sophisticated databases as well as distribution of software to the general public; it also covers custom software development and the acquisition of various rights in multimedia products.

Both UCITA and Article 2 are based upon the principle of freedom of contract: with limited exceptions, the terms and effect of a contract can be varied by agreement. Most provisions of both statutes are default rules, applicable only if the parties do not specify some other rule. * * *

To be sure, not every contract should be enforced. UCITA follows Article 2 in providing a standard of unconscionability for courts to employ in policing contract terms. UCITA goes beyond Article 2 in authorizing courts to strike down over-reaching language that conflicts with fundamental public policy. UCITA provides that common law doctrines such as fraud and duress remain effective. UCITA does not alter competition or antitrust law. It does not change trade secret law, intellectual property law, or substantive consumer law. It deals only with contracts.

* * *

UCITA is the first uniform contract law designed to deal specifically with the new information economy. Transactions in computer information involve different expectations, different industry practices, and different policies from transactions in goods. * * *

Licensing is one way in which computer information is tailored to the information marketplace. Courts have enforced contract terms that, among other things:

• preclude commercial use	• permit commercial use
• preclude making copies	• permit making multiple copies
• grant access	• limit access
• allow use throughout a site	• limit use to a specific computer
• preclude distribution of copies for a fee	• allow distribution of copies
• preclude modification	• allow modification
• allow distribution only in specific way	• limit use to internal operations

Such contract terms have helped to create the wondrous array of products and services that characterizes our modern economy. Whether specific terms are appropriate for a given transaction or set of parties is fundamentally a marketplace issue.

As noted, in computer information transactions, license terms often define the product. A software product may be provided in the same form in two transactions, but in one case the user is authorized to make 100,000 copies and in the other merely to use a single copy at home. The value of the transaction inheres not in the tangible medium (if, indeed, any is used), but rather in the license grant terms. UCITA does not require that computer information products and services be licensed; it covers sales as well. But UCITA provides a coherent contract law framework for analyzing a license, which has been the dominant contractual framework for commerce in computer information.

* * *

NOTES & QUESTIONS

1. *Compare and contrast.* How would you compare and contrast the different approaches taken by the UETA and ESIGN, on the one hand, and UCITA, on the other? Note the exemptions for certain consumer transactions in ESIGN. What do you think is the reason for them? (For further consideration of these statutes as they affect consumer protection see Chapter 6, Part V, *infra*.

2. *Uniform adoptions—UETA*. How many states have enacted UETA? *See* www.nccusl.org.

3. *Uniform adoptions—UCITA*. How many states have adopted UCITA? *See* www.nccusl.org. *See also* MD. CODE ANN., COM. LAW §§ 22–101 to 22–816 (2002); VA. CODE ANN. §§ 59.1–501.1 to 59.1–509.2 (2002).

4. *Statutory exemptions*. Does § 102 of ESIGN preempt state enactments of UCITA? *See* UCITA § 905.

5. *Patent licensing transactions*. Does UCITA cover patent licensing transactions—for example, licensing a patented business method? (*See* Chapter 12, *infra*.)

6. *Exclusions from UCITA*. What do you think is the reason for the exemption from UCITA of the financial, insurance, motion picture, and recording industries? *See* UCITA § 103(d)(1), (d)(2), (d)(3)(A), & (d)(3)(B).

7. *Impact on intellectual property law*. In the Prefatory Note, excerpted above, the drafters state that UCITA does not have any effect on the law of intellectual property. Intellectual property scholars have disagreed. *See, e.g., Symposium: Intellectual Property and Contract Law in the Information Age: The Impact of Article 2B of the Uniform Commercial Code on the Future of Transactions in Information and Electronic Commerce*, 13 BERKELEY TECH. L.J. 809 (1998). What (if anything) do you think would be UCITA's effect on intellectual property law if widely enacted? (Reconsider this question after you consider the rest of the materials in this chapter and in Chapters 9–12, *infra*).

8. *UCITA "bomb shelter" legislation*. Some believe UCITA is the licensing statute of the future, whose enactment is imperative, while others believe that it is an affront to our society's commitment to policies supporting consumer protection and a vibrant public domain, whose adoption by states must be defeated at all costs. *See, e.g.,* www.ucitaonline.com, www.ala.org/washoff/ucita, and www.nccusl.org/nccusl/pubndrafts.asp. Indeed, this debate has become so heated that Iowa, North Carolina, and West Virginia have enacted so-called UCITA "bomb shelter" legislation intended to prevent UCITA as adopted by another state from governing a transaction to which a state resident is a party. North Carolina's bomb shelter legislation reads as follows:

> A choice of law provision in a computer information agreement which provides that the contract is to be interpreted pursuant to the laws of a state that has enacted the Uniform Computer Information Transactions Act, as proposed by the National Conference of Commissioners on Uniform State Laws, or any substantially similar law, is voidable and the agreement shall be interpreted pursuant to the laws of this State if the party against whom enforcement of the choice of law provisions is sought is a resident of this State or has its principal place of business located in this State. For purposes of this section, a "computer information

> agreement" means an agreement that would be governed by the Uniform Computer Information Transactions Act or substantially similar law as enacted in the state specified in the choice of law provisions if that state's law were applied to the agreement. This section may not be varied by agreement of the parties. This section shall remain in force until such time as the North Carolina General Assembly enacts the Uniform Computer Information Transactions Act or any substantially similar law and that law becomes effective.

N.C. Gen. Stat. Ann. § 66–329 (2002); *see also* W.Va. Code § 55–8–15 (2002); Iowa Code § 554D.104.

9. *The future of UCC Article 2.* The disagreement between the ALI and NCCUSL over UCITA may be part of a general divisive trend between these two bodies. Professor Robert Scott writes:

> On August 13, 2001 the National Conference of Commissioners on Uniform State Laws voted 89 to 53 to reject the 2001 Amendments to Article 2 of the Uniform Commercial Code that had just been approved in May by the American Law Institute. The vote followed a last minute effort by the Article 2 drafting committee to amend the scope provisions of Article 2 in response to continuing criticism from representatives of the software and information industries. Several months later, at the request of the NCCUSL leadership, the revised Article 2 with its amended scope provision was withdrawn from the agenda of the ALI Council in order to avoid its certain defeat. While negotiations continue, this public split between the two bodies that have together shepherded the UCC project for over fifty years may well represent the end of the fourteen year effort to revise the law of sales as embodied in Article 2.
>
> This most recent action follows a concerted effort by the ALI and NCCUSL over the past several years to remove controversial proposals from the Article 2 revision process so as to ensure approval by both bodies and ultimate adoption by the states. In the process of downsizing the "revisions" to "amendments," the reporter and associate reporter of the original Article 2 drafting committee, who had worked on the project for over a decade, resigned in protest. But the effort to sanitize Article 2 was ultimately unsuccessful as industry and consumer interests squared off against one another to produce the current deadlock. Thus, even if the ALI and NCCUSL are eventually able to overcome their differences, Article 2 is likely to remain substantially unrevised. As a consequence, the statute that Karl Llewellyn called the "heart and soul" of the Uniform Commercial Code will inevitably become less relevant to the legal regulation of commercial sales transactions.

Robert E. Scott, *The Rise and Fall of Article 2*, 62 La. L. Rev. ___ (2002).

10. *European Union Directives.* The European Union has adopted three Directives concerning electronic contracting: (1) the Directive on Electronic

Commerce,[2] (2) the Electronic Signature Directive,[3] and (3) the Distance Selling Directive.[4] For more information on the Electronic Signature Directive, *see* Chapter 5, *infra.*

11. *International initiatives.* Much as NCCUSL develops model laws for adoption in the several states of the United States, the United Nations Commission on International Trade Law ("UNCITRAL") develops model laws intended to facilitate international commerce and trade. UNCITRAL has adopted two model laws concerning electronic commerce: (1) UNCITRAL Model Law on Electronic Commerce with Guide to Enactment (1996), with additional article 5 *bis* as adopted in 1998, www.uncitral.org/en-index.htm; and (2) UNCITRAL Model Law on Electronic Signatures (2001), www.uncitral.org/english/texts/electcom/ml-elecsig-e.pdf. UNCITRAL describes the Model Law on Electronic Commerce as follows:

> The Model Law, adopted in 1996, is intended to facilitate the use of modern means of communications and storage of information, such as electronic data interchange (EDI), electronic mail and telecopy, with or without the use of such support as the Internet. It is based on the establishment of a functional equivalent for paper-based concepts such as "writing", "signature" and "original". By providing standards by which the legal value of electronic messages can be assessed, the Model Law should play a significant role in enhancing the use of paperless communication. In addition to general norms, the Model Law also contains rules for electronic commerce in specific areas, such as carriage of goods.

UNCITRAL, *Electronic Commerce*, www.uncitral.org/english/texts/electcom/ecommerceindex.htm.

B. E-MAIL DEALS

1. MANIFESTATIONS OF MUTUAL ASSENT USING E-MAIL

Can e-mail seal a sales deal? *Shattuck v. Klotzbach*

Nikoletta Banushi, Globe Correspondent.
BOSTON GLOBE, Mar. 16, 2002, at E1.

Buyers beware, and sellers, too—especially if you communicate with each other by e-mail.

2. Directive 2000/31/EC of the European Parliament and the Council of 8 June 2000 on certain legal aspects of information society services, in particular electronic commerce, in the Internal Market, 2000 O.J. (L 178) 1, europa.eu.int/ISPO/ecommerce/legal/documents/2000_31ec_/2000_31ec_en.pdf.

3. Directive 1999/93/EC of the European Parliament and of the Council of 13 December 1999 on a Community framework for electronic signatures, 2000 O.J. (L 13) 12, europa.eu.int/information_society/topics/ebusiness/ecommerce/3information/law&ecommerce/legal/documents/1999_93/1999_93_en.pdf.

4. Directive 97/7/EC of the European Parliament and of the Council of 20 May 1997 on the protection of consumers in respect of distance contracts, 1997 O.J. (L 144) 19, europa.eu.int/comm/consumers/policy/developments/dist_sell/dist01_en.pdf.

A pretrial decision by a judge in a dispute over a multimillion-dollar home in Marion could end up making real estate deals outlined in e-mail as binding as those put on paper.

The case, Shattuck v. Klotzbach, is scheduled to be heard in May in Plymouth Superior Court by Judge Ernest B. Murphy.

The plaintiff, Jonathan P. Shattuck, alleges breach of contract. Last year, he thought he had a deal to buy the house at 5 Main St. in Marion for $1.825 million.

But in September, six months after he began negotiating with Shattuck, defendant David K. Klotzbach backed away from selling his house.

Using e-mail, Shattuck and Klotzbach had settled on the price; the e-mail referred to the purchase and sale agreement that would be prepared.

All the e-mails exchanged by the two parties ended with the "typewritten" names of the senders, according to the judge's decision in which he refused to throw out the case.

That's a crucial point, the judge ruled.

When Shattuck tried to enforce the contract he thought he had, Klotzbach and his lawyers argued that the e-mails were not signed documents, and that there was no binding contract. They sought to have the suit dismissed.

But on Dec. 11, Judge Murphy decided the e-mails, taken together, constituted a legally binding purchase and sale agreement that outlined all the necessary terms of the contract.

Klotzbach had also argued that even if the e-mails bound him, they did not bind the other owner of the house, his wife, Barbara W. Klotzbach, because she had not signed the e-mails.

The judge, though, wrote that "the correspondences suggest that the defendant-wife was aware of the ongoing negotiations concerning the sale of the property. Thus, a reasonable trier of fact could conclude that the defendant-husband's signature on the memorandum acted as a signature of both defendants . . ."

Kevin Clancy, one of the attorneys representing the Klotzbachs, declined to comment.

But Michael J. McGlone, who represents the plaintiff, said Klotzbach and his wife were negotiating to sell to other buyers for $1.96 million—even though they had already agreed to sell to Shattuck for $1.825 million.

And according to the judge's decision not to dismiss the case, the defendant had used e-mail to tell Shattuck this:

"Once we sign the P & S we'd like to close ASAP. You may have your attorney send the P & S and deposit check for 10% of purchase price ($182,500) to my attorney."

The e-mail concluded by saying, "I'm looking forward to closing and seeing you as the owner of '5 Main Street,' the prettiest spot in Marion village."

Said Beth Mitchell, a partner in the Boston law firm Nutter McClennen & Fish who manages its real estate department:

"I think what this case is saying is if you exchange e-mails about the terms of sale—even if you think later you're going to put it all down on paper so you're going to have a more thought-out comprehensive document—you may find you're bound, even though you haven't signed anything.

"I think it's a warning to people that other courts might view this the same way. They better take more care in what they put in their e-mails than what they did before."

Klotzbach may have entered into a binding contract without realizing it, though, said David Drinkwater, president of the Massachusetts Association of Realtors.

"In this case, the seller probably thought what was said in the e-mails wasn't legally binding, but through the court's observation, he intended to make this sale."

"This is the first time in Massachusetts that e-mail communication is sufficient to form a contract," added Philip Lapatin, legal counsel to the Greater Boston Real Estate Board.

"The court just took it one step further in terms of what a signature is."

The decision raises important issues, because people may be using e-mail to communicate at a quicker pace—and increasing the risk of legal complications.

Allowing people to make a legally binding contract with as much ease as the sending of an e-mail may not be in consumers' best interests, some say.

"One of the very unfortunate things about this is that by allowing consumers to casually enter into what might be the most legally important transaction of their life, consumers are not benefited," Lapatin said.

"Even though e-mail is in writing, most people still think of e-mail as an informal form of communicating," he said. "Now the court is saying that it is now a binding document."

"The process of buying and selling is a very personal one," Drinkwater said. "In doing so, they [buyers and sellers] should be seeking the help of someone who does this for a living."

2. ELECTRONIC CONTRACT FORMATION AND THE MAILBOX RULE

The question of how to evaluate the effective timing of acceptance in an electronic medium first arose in agreements for electronic data interchange ("EDI"). Even before the advent of the Internet and the Web, large firms had developed protocols for exchanging information electronically with their trading partners through private networks.

Restatement (Second) of Contracts, §§ 63 & 64

The American Law Institute.
(1979).

§ 63. TIME WHEN ACCEPTANCE TAKES EFFECT

Unless the offer provides otherwise,

(a) an acceptance made in a manner and by a medium invited by an offer is operative and completes the manifestation of mutual assent as soon as put out of the offeree's possession, without regard to whether it ever reaches the offeror; but

(b) an acceptance under an option contract is not operative until received by the offeror.

§ 64. ACCEPTANCE BY TELEPHONE OR TELETYPE

Acceptance given by telephone or other medium of substantially instantaneous two-way communication is governed by the principles applicable to acceptances where the parties are in the presence of each other.

The Electronic Messaging Task Force, American Bar Association, *The Commercial Use of Electronic Data Interchange—A Report and Model Trading Partner Agreement*

45 Bus. Law. 1645 (1990).

The technology of electronic messaging systems introduces into commercial business practices a variety of methods for achieving accurate and timely communication not possible (and perhaps not capable of having been envisioned) when the existing provisions of the Uniform Commercial Code were adopted. * * *

1. Receipt and Verification

* * * EDI agreements included in the Study showed little consensus concerning the time when electronically transmitted messages become effective or related issues. Most agreements did not define when effective delivery or receipt of any transmission occurred; a few agreements did contain precise language for when receipt could be constructively established. These examples brought to the attention of the Task Force the need to consider the proper classification of EDI when used as a medium of communication—a medium which did not clearly fit within existing applicable legal principles under the Code and the common law relating to contract formation.

The drafters of Article 2 of the Code specifically did not address the question of when a contract is effectively formed.[76] That process occurs under applicable principles of common law. [T]he Restatement (Second) of Contracts provide[s] an effective structure for analyzing the treatment of the role of the medium of communication in the contract formation process.

The Restatement allocates between contracting parties the risks relating to the method of communication chosen by each party, and identifies the relative priority of contradictory or simultaneous communications (particularly when the means of communication utilized, such as mailed writings, do not provide for instantaneous, direct interaction between the parties). The Restatement distinguishes between two situations. In the first, the parties are in each other's presence and are able to communicate without any substantial lapse of time. In the second, the parties are not in each other's presence and the means of communication utilized to transmit offers, acceptances, modifications, revocations, and other messages result in a delay between the dispatch and receipt of those communications. In the latter situation, the common law provides, for example, the "mailbox rule," pursuant to which the dispatch of a message is effective without regard to whether the message ever reaches the other party. An important premise upon which those rules are predicated is the notion that delayed media, such as mailed writings, do not provide either party the ability to verify in a timely fashion that receipt of a message has occurred and that the message as received is without errors. However, § 64 of the Restatement specifically acknowledges the use of technology in communication, in the form of "telephone or other medium of substantially instantaneous two-way communication," and sets forth the principle that communications using those technologies are governed by the same principles that apply when the parties are in the presence of each other.

As discussed, EDI has the capability to permit prompt, reliable verification that a message has been received, and that it has been received intact and without communication errors. This verification can occur immediately, and several EDI industry standards require such verification to be sent in a commercially prompt manner. If there are ambiguities or misunderstandings perceived by either party, the problems can be corrected by additional, immediate communication. If there is a failure in the communication, EDI permits one or both parties to know or have reason to know of the failure by virtue of the capability of the technology to provide timely verifications. Of course, a distinguishing characteristic of EDI is that the communication is transmitted and received in an essentially "written" format; to review the message, users "read' " the data, either electronically or by human review (presented either as a screen display or a printout on paper). The Task Force concluded that the "written" characteristic was not

76. The Code provides that a contract may be formed in any manner, including through the conduct of the parties, and has limited provisions dealing with acceptance of offers by shipment. See, e.g., U.C.C. §§ 2-204, 2-206. The Code is silent, however, on rules pertaining to the timing of contract formation, except to the extent it provides that a contract may be formed even though the time of its making is uncertain. Id. § 2-206. Consequently, common law principles of contract formation continue to apply. Id. § 1-103.

important to its analysis; the applicable legal principles focus on the immediacy of communication, and not the format. Accordingly, the use of EDI to communicate was determined to satisfy the criteria of § 64 of the Restatement. As a result, the [Task Force recommends the adoption of] rules that parallel those provided by common law for other types of technology which facilitate instantaneous communication. * * *

Uniform Electronic Transactions Act, § 15

National Conference of Commissioners on Uniform State Laws.
(1999).

SECTION 15. TIME AND PLACE OF SENDING AND RECEIPT.

(a) Unless otherwise agreed between the sender and the recipient, an electronic record is sent when it:

(1) is addressed properly or otherwise directed properly to an information processing system that the recipient has designated or uses for the purpose of receiving electronic records or information of the type sent and from which the recipient is able to retrieve the electronic record;

(2) is in a form capable of being processed by that system; and

(3) enters an information processing system outside the control of the sender or of a person that sent the electronic record on behalf of the sender or enters a region of the information processing system designated or used by the recipient which is under the control of the recipient.

(b) Unless otherwise agreed between a sender and the recipient, an electronic record is received when:

(1) it enters an information processing system that the recipient has designated or uses for the purpose of receiving electronic records or information of the type sent and from which the recipient is able to retrieve the electronic record; and

(2) it is in a form capable of being processed by that system.

* * *

(g) If a person is aware that an electronic record purportedly sent under subsection (a), or purportedly received under subsection (b), was not actually sent or received, the legal effect of the sending or receipt is determined by other applicable law. Except to the extent permitted by the other law, the requirements of this subsection may not be varied by agreement.

Uniform Computer Information Transactions Act, §§ 102(a)(28) & 215

National Conference of Commissioners on Uniform State Laws.
(2000).

SECTION 102. DEFINITIONS

(a) In this [Act]: * * *

(28) "Electronic message" means a record or display that is stored, generated, or transmitted by electronic means for the purpose of communication to another person or electronic agent.

* * *

Official Comment

* * *

24. "Electronic Message." A message is distinguished from a "record" by the fact that a message is intended for communication to another person or an electronic agent. Communication of a message may be by copying it into another location or making it available in a system shared by or accessible to the recipient. In effect, it is stored or generated for purposes of communicating to another.

SECTION 215. ELECTRONIC MESSAGE: WHEN EFFECTIVE; EFFECT OF ACKNOWLEDGMENT.

(a) Receipt of an electronic message is effective when received even if no individual is aware of its receipt.

(b) Receipt of an electronic acknowledgment of an electronic message establishes that the message was received but by itself does not establish that the content sent corresponds to the content received.

Official Comment

* * *

2. **Time of Receipt Rule**. Subsection (a) adopts a time of receipt rule; rejecting the mail box rule for electronic messages and resolving uncertainty about what common law rule would otherwise govern. * * * This time-of-receipt rule reflects both the relatively instantaneous nature of electronic messaging and places the risk on the sending party if receipt does not occur. * * * Whether the message formed a contract is determined by ordinary offer and acceptance rules and whether an existing contract has been modified is determined by ordinary rules on modification. Neither effect happens simply because receipt of a message is effective without more.

The message is "effective" when received, not when read or reviewed by the recipient, just as written notice is received even if not read or acknowledged. This applies traditional common law theories to electronic commerce. In electronic transactions, automated systems can send and react to messages without human intervention. A rule that demands human assent would add an inefficient and error prone element or inappropriately cede control to one party.

* * *

NOTES & QUESTIONS

1. *Electronic Data Interchange vs. e-mail.* The ABA Electronic Messaging Task recommends rejecting the mailbox rule in favor of a receipt rule for

EDI. One commentator argues that e-mail should not be treated as the equivalent of face-to-face communication, and should be subject to the mailbox rule. *See* Paul Fasciano, *Internet Electronic Mail: A Last Bastion for the Mailbox Rule,* 25 HOFSTRA L. REV. 971 (1997). Are these two positions inconsistent? Can you think of significant ways e-mail differs from EDI that might serve to reconcile them?

2. *UETA vs. UCITA.* How does Section 15 of UETA differ in its approach from Section 215 of UCITA?

3. *Instant messaging.* Instant Messaging ("IM") is a service that runs on the Internet and enables real-time communication between individual users. An IM user selects the name of a person on her contact list, types a message into the instant messaging client software, and clicks "Send." If the recipient is online and signed on to the IM service, the message is instantly displayed on the recipient's computer. Most of the major online services offer instant messaging, including America Online, Yahoo! and MSN. Based on this description of the technology, would you apply the mailbox rule or a receipt rule in order to determine when an acceptance by instant messaging is effective? How would an acceptance by instant messaging be treated under UCITA?

4. *Electronic revocation.* Imagine two parties negotiating a contract over the Internet by e-mail. At 4:30 p.m., one of the parties sends an e-mail message containing a legally effective offer, but immediately begins to reconsider. The offeree, happy to receive the offer, immediately clicks the reply button and accepts the offer. The e-mail acceptance is dispatched at 4:31:01 and is received at the offeror's e-mail server at 4:31:28. The offeror dispatches a second e-mail revoking the offer after the offeree's e-mail is sent but before it is received at the offeror's e-mail server. This e-mail revocation is sent at 4:31:25 and is received at the offeree's e-mail server at 4:31:35. Is the offeror's revocation legally effective?

C. SHRINKWRAP AND ITS ONLINE ANALOGUES

As the *Restatement of Contracts* reminds us, "the formation of a contract requires a bargain in which there is manifestation of mutual assent to the exchange and a consideration." RESTATEMENT (SECOND) OF CONTRACTS § 17 (1979). While there are exceptions to this rule, most contracts require a bargain involving an exchange of promises (a bilateral contract) or a promise for a performance (a unilateral contract).[5] Moreover, the parties to the contract must clearly manifest their assent to the exchange. As Professor Allan Farnsworth notes, "[s]ince it is difficult for a workable system of contract law to take account of assent unless there has been an overt expression of it, courts have required that assent to the formation of a contract be manifested in some way, by words or other

5. The exceptions to this rule include a contract under seal, recognizances, negotiable instruments, negotiable documents and letters of credit. See RESTATEMENT (SECOND) OF CONTRACTS § 6 (1979).

conduct, if it is to be effective." E. ALLAN FARNSWORTH, FARNSWORTH ON CONTRACTS § 3.1 (3d ed. 1999).

This requirement is often satisfied in two steps—offer and acceptance. Requiring a manifestation of mutual assent before a contract is formed raises two critical questions: (1) What kind of conduct constitutes a sufficiently overt manifestation of assent to an exchange for the purposes of forming a contract?; and (2) At what point in time is an offeree's acceptance effective and the offeror's power of revocation terminated? (In considering whether the mailbox rule should be applicable to electronic communications, we have already addressed the second of these questions.) These questions are especially challenging when applied to conduct on the Internet.

When determining what kind of online conduct constitutes a sufficiently overt manifestation of assent to an exchange to form a contract, courts have focused on contracts (or purported contracts) in which assent is problematic: shrinkwrap licenses and their online analogues, variously called clickwrap, click-through, and browsewrap licenses.

The term "shrinkwrap license" usually refers to a license agreement, governing a purchaser's use of software or digitized data, that is presented to the purchaser only *after* payment of the purchase price. The term takes its name from the clear plastic wrapping that typically surrounds and seals boxes of software that are offered for sale at retail stores. The license agreement is enclosed within the box, and the shrinkwrap prevents the purchaser from reading its terms until after she pays for the software and is entitled to break the seal.[6] There may or may not be a notice visible on the outside of the box, informing the prospective purchaser that additional terms are enclosed.

A clickwrap (or click-through) agreement is one in which the terms of the agreement are displayed on the computer screen and the computer user is requested to click an on-screen button to indicate assent to the displayed terms. A website that displays the terms and says, "Click here to indicate you agree to these terms," is somewhat analogous to a shrinkwrap license that is visible on the outside of the box. The website is programmed so that you won't get to use the site if you don't click the button; analogously, you won't get to use shrinkwrapped software if you don't break the shrinkwrap. But the two situations also differ in an important respect. The existence of the clickwrap agreement is brought unavoidably to the attention of the user: although she need not actually read the terms, the requirement that she click a button labeled "I agree" (or the equivalent) cues her to the fact

6. Starting in the early 1990s, license agreements were sometimes printed on the outside of the box, or on a separate card secured under the shrinkwrap, allowing the purchaser to view the terms before purchase. These licenses typically stated that breaking the shrinkwrap would signify the purchaser's assent to the terms. Certain terms, like "Upgrade Version" or "One–Year Toll–Free Support," continue to appear on the outside of the box. This method of presenting terms *pre*-purchase, which is sometimes also referred to as a shrinkwrap license, presents different legal issues from the type of shrinkwrap license in which the terms are presented only after payment.

that she is agreeing to *something*. When the license terms are on the outside of the box, however, it is quite possible for the user to break the seal and use the software without realizing that the vendor has proposed a set of terms.

Some websites disclose the existence of terms governing use of the site with nothing more than a link on the home page labeled "Terms of Use." The website owner intends that this notice will indicate to the user, "By continuing to use this site you agree to a set of terms, which you will only see if you choose to click on this link." Some courts and commentators refer to these terms as browsewrap agreements. When a process like this has been held to form a contract, it has usually been required that the user be able to unwind the deal after viewing the terms (i.e., by returning the product for a refund).

If the online contracts now coming before courts are problematic on the issue of sufficient assent to be bound, so too, it must be remembered, are a great many contracts in the offline world. There are quite a few contracts in the offline world in which the buyer doesn't see many of the terms until after buying the product. We purchase tickets, tour packages, and countless other items (including shrinkwrapped software) over the phone before we see the fine print. Consumer product warranties are often inside the box. In some classes of these contracts, such as the fine-print inserts that come with credit-card bills, new terms are imposed at the seller's will from time to time. In all of these contracts, it appears that the promisor must at least be given the option of declining after the fact to be bound, by unwinding his or her initial acceptance of the product (e.g., ceasing to use the credit card). It does not appear, though, that this option is anything more than theoretically possible. Airlines do not cheerfully refund the purchase price of nonrefundable airline tickets upon the purchaser's refusal to assent to the terms incorporated by reference on the ticket, once having viewed them post-purchase in the airline's business office.

1. SHRINKWRAP AGREEMENTS

ProCD, Inc. v. Zeidenberg

86 F.3d 1447 (7th Cir.1996).

■ EASTERBROOK, CIRCUIT JUDGE.

Must buyers of computer software obey the terms of shrinkwrap licenses? The district court held not, for two reasons: first, they are not contracts because the licenses are inside the box rather than printed on the outside; second, federal law forbids enforcement even if the licenses are contracts. 908 F.Supp. 640 (W.D.Wis.1996). The parties and numerous amici curiae have briefed many other issues, but these are the only two that matter—and we disagree with the district judge's conclusion on each. Shrinkwrap licenses are enforceable unless their terms are objectionable on grounds applicable to contracts in general (for example, if they violate a rule of positive law, or if they are unconscionable). Because no one argues that the terms of the license at issue here are troublesome, we remand with instructions to enter judgment for the plaintiff.

I

ProCD, the plaintiff, has compiled information from more than 3,000 telephone directories into a computer database. We may assume that this database cannot be copyrighted, although it is more complex, contains more information (nine-digit zip codes and census industrial codes), is organized differently, and therefore is more original than the single alphabetical directory at issue in *Feist Publications, Inc. v. Rural Telephone Service Co.*, 499 U.S. 340 (1991). See Paul J. Heald, The Vices of Originality, 1991 Sup.Ct. Rev. 143, 160–68. ProCD sells a version of the database, called SelectPhone (trademark), on CD–ROM discs. (CD–ROM means "compact disc—read only memory." The "shrinkwrap license" gets its name from the fact that retail software packages are covered in plastic or cellophane "shrinkwrap," and some vendors, though not ProCD, have written licenses that become effective as soon as the customer tears the wrapping from the package. Vendors prefer "end user license," but we use the more common term.) A proprietary method of compressing the data serves as effective encryption too. Customers decrypt and use the data with the aid of an application program that ProCD has written. This program, which is copyrighted, searches the database in response to users' criteria (such as "find all people named Tatum in Tennessee, plus all firms with 'Door Systems' in the corporate name"). The resulting lists (or, as ProCD prefers, "listings") can be read and manipulated by other software, such as word processing programs.

The database in SelectPhone (trademark) cost more than $10 million to compile and is expensive to keep current. It is much more valuable to some users than to others. The combination of names, addresses, and SIC codes enables manufacturers to compile lists of potential customers. Manufacturers and retailers pay high prices to specialized information intermediaries for such mailing lists; ProCD offers a potentially cheaper alternative. People with nothing to sell could use the database as a substitute for calling long distance information, or as a way to look up old friends who have moved to unknown towns, or just as an electronic substitute for the local phone book. ProCD decided to engage in price discrimination, selling its database to the general public for personal use at a low price (approximately $150 for the set of five discs) while selling information to the trade for a higher price. It has adopted some intermediate strategies too: access to the SelectPhone (trademark) database is available via the America Online service for the price America Online charges to its clients (approximately $3 per hour), but this service has been tailored to be useful only to the general public.

If ProCD had to recover all of its costs and make a profit by charging a single price—that is, if it could not charge more to commercial users than to the general public—it would have to raise the price substantially over $150. The ensuing reduction in sales would harm consumers who value the information at, say, $200. They get consumer surplus of $50 under the current arrangement but would cease to buy if the price rose substantially. If because of high elasticity of demand in the consumer segment of the market the only way to make a profit turned out to be a price attractive to commercial users alone, then all consumers would lose out—and so would the commercial clients, who would have to pay more for the listings because ProCD could not obtain any contribution toward costs from the consumer market.

To make price discrimination work, however, the seller must be able to control arbitrage. An air carrier sells tickets for less to vacationers than to business travelers, using advance purchase and Saturday-night-stay requirements to distinguish the categories. A producer of movies segments the market by time, releasing first to theaters, then to pay-per-view services, next to the videotape and laserdisc market, and finally to cable and commercial tv. Vendors of computer software have a harder task. Anyone can walk into a retail store and buy a box. Customers do not wear tags saying "commercial user" or "consumer user." Anyway, even a commercial-user-detector at the door would not work, because a consumer could buy the software and resell to a commercial user. That arbitrage would break down the price discrimination and drive up the minimum price at which ProCD would sell to anyone.

Instead of tinkering with the product and letting users sort themselves—for example, furnishing current data at a high price that would be attractive only to commercial customers, and two-year-old data at a low price—ProCD turned to the institution of contract. Every box containing its consumer product declares that the software comes with restrictions stated in an enclosed license. This license, which is encoded on the CD–ROM disks as well as printed in the manual, and which appears on a user's screen every time the software runs, limits use of the application program and listings to non-commercial purposes.

Matthew Zeidenberg bought a consumer package of SelectPhone (trademark) in 1994 from a retail outlet in Madison, Wisconsin, but decided to ignore the license. He formed Silken Mountain Web Services, Inc., to resell the information in the SelectPhone (trademark) database. The corporation makes the database available on the Internet to anyone willing to pay its price—which, needless to say, is less than ProCD charges its commercial customers. Zeidenberg has purchased two additional SelectPhone (trademark) packages, each with an updated version of the database, and made the latest information available over the World Wide Web, for a price, through his corporation. ProCD filed this suit seeking an injunction against further dissemination that exceeds the rights specified in the licenses (identical in each of the three packages Zeidenberg purchased). The district court held the licenses ineffectual because their terms do not appear on the outside of the packages. The court added that the second and third licenses stand no different from the first, even though they are identical, because they *might* have been different, and a purchaser does not agree to—and cannot be bound by—terms that were secret at the time of purchase. 908 F.Supp. at 654.

II

Following the district court, we treat the licenses as ordinary contracts accompanying the sale of products, and therefore as governed by the common law of contracts and the Uniform Commercial Code. Whether there are legal differences between "contracts' and "licenses' (which may matter under the copyright doctrine of first sale) is a subject for another day. *See Microsoft Corp. v. Harmony Computers & Electronics, Inc.,* 846 F.Supp. 208 (E.D.N.Y.1994). Zeidenberg does not argue that Silken Mountain Web Services is free of any restrictions that apply to Zeidenberg himself, because any effort to treat the two parties as distinct would put Silken Mountain behind the eight ball on ProCD's argument that copying the application program onto its hard disk violates the copyright laws. Zeidenberg does argue, and the district court held, that placing the package of software on the shelf is an "offer," which the customer "accepts" by paying the asking price and leaving the store with the goods. *Peeters v. State,* 154 Wis. 111, 142 N.W. 181 (1913). In Wisconsin, as elsewhere, a contract includes only the terms on which the parties have agreed. One cannot agree to hidden terms, the judge concluded. So far, so good—but one of the terms to which Zeidenberg agreed by purchasing the software is that the transaction was subject to a license. Zeidenberg's position therefore must be that the printed terms on the outside of a box are the parties' contract—except for printed terms that refer to or incorporate other terms. But why would Wisconsin fetter the parties' choice in this way? Vendors can put the entire terms of a contract on the outside of a box only by using microscopic type, removing other information that buyers might find more useful (such as what the software does, and on which computers it works), or both. The "Read Me" file included with most software, describing system requirements and potential incompatibilities, may be equivalent to ten pages of type; warranties and license restrictions take still more space. Notice on the outside, terms on the inside, and a right to return the software for a refund if the terms are unacceptable (a right that the license expressly extends), may be a means of doing business valuable to buyers and sellers alike. See E. Allan Farnsworth, 1 Farnsworth on Contracts § 4.26 (1990); Restatement (2d) of Contracts § 211 comment a (1981) ("Standardization of agreements serves many of the same functions as standardization of goods and services; both are essential to a system of mass production and distribution. Scarce and costly time and skill can be devoted to a class of transactions rather than the details of individual transactions."). Doubtless a state could forbid the use of standard contracts in the software business, but we do not think that Wisconsin has done so.

Transactions in which the exchange of money precedes the communication of detailed terms are common. Consider the purchase of insurance. The buyer goes to an agent, who explains the essentials (amount of coverage, number of years) and remits the premium to the home office, which sends back a policy. On the district judge's understanding, the terms of the policy are irrelevant because the insured paid before receiving them. Yet the device of payment, often with a "binder" (so that the insurance takes effect immediately even though the home office reserves the right to withdraw coverage later), in advance of the policy, serves buyers' interests by accelerating effectiveness and reducing transactions costs. Or consider the purchase of an airline ticket. The traveler calls the carrier or an agent, is quoted a price, reserves a seat, pays, and gets a ticket, in that order. The ticket contains elaborate terms, which the traveler can reject by canceling the reservation. To use the ticket is to accept the terms, even terms that in retrospect are disadvantageous. See *Carnival Cruise Lines, Inc. v. Shute,* 499 U.S. 585 (1991); see also *Vimar Seguros y Reaseguros, S.A. v. M/V Sky Reefer,* 515 U.S. 528 (1995) (bills of lading). Just so with a ticket to a concert. The back of the ticket states that the patron promises not to record the concert; to attend is to agree. A theater that detects a violation will confiscate the tape and escort the violator to the exit. One *could* arrange things so that every concertgoer signs this promise before forking over the money, but that cumbersome way of doing things not only would lengthen queues and raise prices but also would scotch the sale of tickets by phone or electronic data service.

Consumer goods work the same way. Someone who wants to buy a radio set visits a store, pays, and walks out with a box. Inside the box is a leaflet containing some terms, the most important of which usually is the warranty, read for the first time in the comfort of home. By Zeidenberg's lights, the warranty in the box is irrelevant; every consumer gets the standard warranty implied by the UCC in the event the contract is silent; yet so far as we are aware no state disregards warranties furnished with consumer products. Drugs come with a list of ingredients on the outside and an elaborate package insert on the inside. The package insert describes drug interactions, contraindications, and other vital information—but, if Zeidenberg is right, the purchaser need not read the package insert, because it is not part of the contract.

Next consider the software industry itself. Only a minority of sales take place over the counter, where there are boxes to peruse. A customer may place an order by phone in response to a line item in a catalog or a review in a magazine. Much software is ordered over the Internet by purchasers who have never seen a box. Increasingly software arrives by wire. There is no box; there is only a stream of electrons, a collection of information that includes data, an application program, instructions, many limitations ("MegaPixel 3.14159 cannot be used with BytePusher 2.718"), and the terms of sale. The user purchases a serial number, which activates the software's features. On Zeidenberg's arguments, these unboxed sales are unfettered by terms—so the seller has made a broad warranty and must pay consequential damages for any shortfalls in performance, two "promises" that if taken seriously would drive prices through the ceiling or return transactions to the horse-and-buggy age.

According to the district court, the UCC does not countenance the sequence of money now, terms later. (Wisconsin's version of the UCC does not differ from the Official Version in any material respect, so we use the regular numbering system. Wis. Stat. § 402.201 corresponds to UCC § 2–201, and other citations are easy to derive.) One of the court's reasons—that by proposing as part of the draft Article 2B a new UCC § 2–2203 that would explicitly validate standard-form user licenses, the American Law Institute and the National Conference of Commissioners on Uniform Laws have conceded the invalidity of shrinkwrap licenses under current law, see 908 F.Supp. at 655–56—depends on a faulty inference. To propose a change in a law's *text* is not necessarily to propose a change in the law's *effect*. New words may be designed to fortify the current rule with a more precise text that curtails uncertainty. To judge by the flux of law review articles discussing shrinkwrap licenses, uncertainty is much in need of reduction—although businesses seem to feel less uncertainty than do scholars, for only three cases (other than ours) touch on the subject, and none directly addresses it. See *Step-Saver Data Systems, Inc. v. Wyse Technology,* 939 F.2d 91 (3d Cir.1991); *Vault Corp. v. Quaid Software Ltd.,* 847 F.2d 255, 268–70 (5th Cir.1988); *Arizona Retail Systems, Inc. v. Software Link, Inc.,* 831 F.Supp. 759 (D.Ariz.1993). As their titles suggest, these are not consumer transactions. *Step-Saver* is a battle-of-the-forms case, in which the parties exchange incompatible forms and a court must decide which prevails. See *Northrop Corp. v. Litronic Industries,* 29 F.3d 1173 (7th Cir.1994) (Illinois law); Douglas G. Baird & Robert Weisberg, *Rules, Standards, and the Battle of the Forms: A Reassessment of* § 2–207, 68 Va. L.Rev. 1217, 1227–31 (1982). Our case has only one form; UCC § 2–207 is irrelevant. *Vault* holds that Louisiana's special shrinkwrap-license statute is preempted by federal law, a question to which we return. And *Arizona Retail Systems* did not reach the question, because the court found that the buyer knew the terms of the license before purchasing the software.

What then does the current version of the UCC have to say? We think that the place to start is § 2–204(1): "A contract for sale of goods may be made in any manner sufficient to show agreement, including conduct by both parties which recognizes the existence of such a contract." A vendor, as master of the offer, may invite acceptance by conduct, and may propose limitations on the kind of conduct that constitutes acceptance. A buyer may accept by performing the acts the vendor proposes to treat as acceptance. And that is what happened. ProCD proposed a contract that a buyer would accept by *using* the software after having an opportunity to read the license at leisure. This Zeidenberg did. He had no choice, because the software splashed the license on the screen and would not let him proceed without indicating acceptance. So although the district judge was right to say that a contract can be, and often is, formed simply by paying the price and walking out of the store, the UCC permits contracts to be formed in other ways. ProCD proposed such a different way, and without protest Zeidenberg agreed. Ours is not a case in which a consumer opens a package to find an insert saying "you owe us an extra $10,000" and the seller files suit to collect. Any buyer finding such a demand can prevent formation of the contract by returning the package, as can any consumer who concludes that the terms of the license make the software worth less than the purchase price. Nothing in the UCC requires a seller to maximize the buyer's net gains.

Section 2–606, which defines "acceptance of goods", reinforces this understanding. A buyer accepts goods under § 2–606(1)(b) when, after an opportunity to inspect, he fails to make an effective rejection under § 2–602(1). ProCD extended an opportunity to reject if a buyer should find the license terms unsatisfactory; Zeidenberg inspected the package, tried out the software, learned of the license, and did not reject the goods. We refer to § 2–606 only to show that the opportunity to return goods can be important; acceptance of an offer differs from acceptance of goods after delivery, see *Gillen v. Atalanta Systems, Inc.*, 997 F.2d 280, 284 n. 1 (7th Cir.1993); but the UCC consistently permits the parties to structure their relations so that the buyer has a chance to make a final decision after a detailed review.

Some portions of the UCC impose additional requirements on the way parties agree on terms. A disclaimer of the implied warranty of merchantability must be "conspicuous." UCC § 2–316(2), incorporating UCC § 1–201(10). Promises to make firm offers, or to negate oral modifications, must be "separately signed." UCC §§ 2–205, 2–209(2). These special provisos reinforce the impression that, so far as the UCC is concerned, other terms may be as inconspicuous as the forum-selection clause on the back of the cruise ship ticket in *Carnival Lines*. Zeidenberg has not located any Wisconsin case—for that matter, any case in any state—holding that under the UCC the ordinary terms found in shrinkwrap licenses require any special prominence, or otherwise are to be undercut rather than enforced. In the end, the terms of the license are conceptually identical to the contents of the package. Just as no court would dream of saying that SelectPhone (trademark) must contain 3,100 phone books rather than 3,000, or must have data no more than 30 days old, or must sell for $100 rather than $150—although any of these changes would be welcomed by the customer, if all other things were held constant—so, we believe, Wisconsin would not let the buyer pick and choose among terms. Terms of use are no less a part of "the product" than are the size of the database and the speed with which the software compiles listings. Competition among vendors, not judicial revision of a package's contents, is how consumers are protected in a market economy. *Digital Equipment Corp. v. Uniq Digital Technologies, Inc.*, 73 F.3d 756 (7th Cir.1996). ProCD has rivals, which may elect to compete by offering superior software, monthly updates, improved terms of use, lower price, or a better compromise among these elements. As we stressed above, adjusting terms in buyers' favor might help Matthew Zeidenberg today (he already has the software) but would lead to a response, such as a higher price, that might make consumers as a whole worse off.

* * *

Hill v. Gateway 2000, Inc.

105 F.3d 1147 (7th Cir.1997).

■ EASTERBROOK, CIRCUIT JUDGE.

A customer picks up the phone, orders a computer, and gives a credit card number. Presently a box arrives, containing the computer and a list of terms, said to govern unless the customer returns the computer within 30 days. Are these terms effective as the parties' contract, or is the contract term-free because the order-taker did not read any terms over the phone and elicit the customer's assent?

One of the terms in the box containing a Gateway 2000 system was an arbitration clause. Rich and Enza Hill, the customers, kept the computer more than 30 days before complaining about its components and performance. They filed suit in federal court arguing, among other things, that the product's shortcomings make Gateway a racketeer (mail and wire fraud are said to be the predicate offenses), leading to treble damages under RICO for the Hills and a class of all other purchasers. Gateway asked the district court to enforce the arbitration clause; the judge refused, writing that "[t]he present record is insufficient to support a finding of a valid arbitration agreement between the parties or that the plaintiffs were given adequate notice of the arbitration clause." Gateway took an immediate appeal, as is its right. 9 U.S.C. § 16(a)(1)(A).

The Hills say that the arbitration clause did not stand out: they concede noticing the statement of terms but deny reading it closely enough to discover the agreement to arbitrate, and they ask us to conclude that they therefore may go to court. Yet an agreement to arbitrate must be enforced "save upon such grounds as exist at law or in equity for the revocation of any contract." 9 U.S.C. § 2. *Doctor's Associates, Inc. v. Casarotto,* 517 U.S. 681 (1996), holds that this provision of the Federal Arbitration Act is inconsistent with any requirement that an arbitration clause be prominent. A contract need not be read to be effective; people who accept take the risk that the unread terms may in retrospect prove unwelcome. *Carr v. CIGNA Securities, Inc.,* 95 F.3d 544, 547 (7th Cir. 1996); *Chicago Pacific Corp. v. Canada Life Assurance Co.,* 850 F.2d 334 (7th Cir.1988). Terms inside Gateway's box stand or fall together. If they constitute the parties' contract because the Hills had an opportunity to return the computer after reading them, then all must be enforced.

ProCD, Inc. v. Zeidenberg, 86 F.3d 1447 (7th Cir.1996), holds that terms inside a box of software bind consumers who use the software after an opportunity to read the terms and to reject them by returning the product. Likewise, *Carnival Cruise Lines, Inc. v. Shute,* 499 U.S. 585 (1991), enforces a forum-selection clause that was included among three pages of terms attached to a cruise ship ticket. *ProCD* and *Carnival Cruise Lines* exemplify the many commercial transactions in which people pay for products with terms to follow; *ProCD* discusses others. 86 F.3d at 1451–52. The district court concluded in *ProCD* that the contract is formed when the consumer pays for the software; as a result, the court held, only terms known to the consumer at that moment are part of the contract, and provisos inside the box do not count. Although this is one way a contract could be formed, it is not the only way: "A vendor, as master of the offer, may invite acceptance by conduct, and may propose limitations on the kind of conduct that constitutes acceptance. A buyer may accept by performing the acts the vendor proposes to treat as acceptance." *Id.* at 1452. Gateway shipped computers with the same sort of accept-or-return offer ProCD made to users of its software. *ProCD* relied on the Uniform Commercial Code rather than any peculiarities of Wisconsin law; both Illinois and South Dakota, the two states whose law might govern relations between Gateway and the Hills, have adopted the UCC; neither side has pointed us to any atypical doctrines in those states that might be pertinent; *ProCD* therefore applies to this dispute.

Plaintiffs ask us to limit *ProCD* to software, but where's the sense in that? *ProCD* is about the law of contract, not the law of software. Payment preceding the revelation of full terms is common for air transportation, insurance, and many other endeavors. Practical considerations support allowing vendors to enclose the full legal terms with their products. Cashiers cannot be expected to read legal documents to customers before ringing up sales. If the staff at the other end of the phone for direct-sales operations such as Gateway's had to read the four-page statement of terms before taking the buyer's credit card number, the droning voice would anesthetize rather than enlighten many potential buyers. Others would hang up in a rage over the waste of their time. And oral recitation would not avoid customers' assertions (whether true or feigned) that the clerk did not read term X to them, or that they did not remember or understand it. Writing provides benefits for both sides of commercial transactions. Customers as a group are better off when vendors skip costly and ineffectual steps such as telephonic recitation, and use instead a simple approve-or-return device. Competent adults are bound by such documents, read or unread. For what little it is worth, we add that the box from Gateway was crammed with software. The computer came with an operating system, without which it was useful only as a boat anchor. See *Digital Equipment Corp. v. Uniq Digital Technologies, Inc.*, 73 F.3d 756, 761 (7th Cir.1996). Gateway also included many application programs. So the Hills' effort to limit *ProCD* to software would not avail them factually, even if it were sound legally—which it is not.

For their second sally, the Hills contend that ProCD should be limited to executory contracts (to licenses in particular), and therefore does not apply because both parties' performance of this contract was complete when the box arrived at their home. This is legally and factually wrong: legally because the question at hand concerns the *formation* of the contract rather than its *performance*, and factually because both contracts were incompletely performed. *ProCD* did not depend on the fact that the seller characterized the transaction as a license rather than as a contract; we treated it as a contract for the sale of goods and reserved the question whether for other purposes a "license" characterization might be preferable. 86 F.3d at 1450. All debates about characterization to one side, the transaction in *ProCD* was no more executory than the one here: Zeidenberg paid for the software and walked out of the store with a box under his arm, so if arrival of the box with the product ends the time for revelation of contractual terms, then the time ended in *ProCD* before Zeidenberg opened the box. But of course ProCD had not completed performance with delivery of the box, and neither had Gateway. One element of the transaction was the warranty, which obliges sellers to fix defects in their products. The Hills have invoked Gateway's warranty and are not satisfied with its response, so they are not well positioned to say that Gateway's obligations were fulfilled when the motor carrier unloaded the box. What is more, both ProCD and Gateway promised to help customers to use their products. Long-term service and information obligations are common in the computer business, on both hardware and software sides. Gateway offers "lifetime service" and has a round-the-clock telephone hotline to fulfill this promise. Some vendors spend more money helping customers use their products than on developing and manufacturing them. The document in Gateway's box includes promises of future performance that some consumers value highly; these promises bind Gateway just as the arbitration clause binds the Hills.

Next the Hills insist that *ProCD* is irrelevant because Zeidenberg was a "merchant" and they are not. Section 2–207(2) of the UCC, the infamous battle-of-the-forms section, states that "additional terms [following acceptance of an offer] are to be construed as proposals for addition to a contract. Between merchants such terms become part of the contract unless . . .". Plaintiffs tell us that *ProCD* came out as it did only because Zeidenberg was a "merchant" and the terms inside ProCD's box were not excluded by the "unless" clause. This argument pays scant attention to the opinion in *ProCD,* which concluded that, when there is only one form, "section 2–207 is irrelevant." 86 F.3d at 1452. The question in *ProCD* was not whether terms were added to a contract after its formation, but how and when the contract was formed—in particular, whether a vendor may propose that a contract of sale be formed, not in the store (or over the phone) with the payment of money or a general "send me the product," but after the customer has had a chance to inspect both the item and the terms. *ProCD* answers "yes," for merchants and consumers alike. Yet again, for what little it is worth we observe that the Hills misunderstand the setting of *ProCD.* A "merchant" under the UCC "means a person who deals in goods of the kind or otherwise by his occupation holds himself out as having knowledge or skill peculiar to the practices or goods involved in the transaction", § 2–104(1). Zeidenberg bought the product at a retail store, an uncommon place for merchants to acquire inventory. His corporation put ProCD's database on the Internet for anyone to browse, which led to the litigation but did not make Zeidenberg a software merchant.

At oral argument the Hills propounded still another distinction: the box containing ProCD's software displayed a notice that additional terms were within, while the box containing Gateway's computer did not. The difference is functional, not legal. Consumers browsing the aisles of a store can look at the box, and if they are unwilling to deal with the prospect of additional terms can leave the box alone, avoiding the transactions costs of returning the package after reviewing its contents. Gateway's box, by contrast, is just a shipping carton; it is not on display anywhere. Its function is to protect the product during transit, and the information on its sides is for the use of handlers

("Fragile!" "This Side Up!" ↑ ↑ ↑)

rather than would-be purchasers.

Perhaps the Hills would have had a better argument if they were first alerted to the bundling of hardware and legal-ware after opening the box and wanted to return the computer in order to avoid disagreeable terms, but were dissuaded by the expense of shipping. What the remedy would be in such a case—could it exceed the shipping charges—is an interesting question, but one that need not detain us because the Hills knew before they ordered the computer that the carton would include *some* important terms, and they did not seek to discover these in advance. Gateway's ads state that their products come with limited warranties and lifetime support. How limited was the warranty—30 days, with service contingent on shipping the computer back, or five years, with free onsite service? What sort of support was offered? Shoppers have three principal ways to discover these things. First, they can ask the vendor to send a copy before deciding whether to buy. The Magnuson–Moss Warranty Act requires firms to distribute their warranty terms on request, 15 U.S.C. § 2302(b)(1)(A); the Hills do not contend that Gateway would have refused to enclose the remaining terms too. Concealment would be bad for business, scaring some customers away and leading to excess returns from others. Second, shoppers can consult public sources (computer magazines, the websites of vendors) that may contain this information. Third, they may inspect the documents after the product's delivery. Like Zeidenberg, the Hills took the third option. By keeping the computer beyond 30 days, the Hills accepted Gateway's offer, including the arbitration clause.

The Hills' remaining arguments, including a contention that the arbitration clause is unenforceable as part of a scheme to defraud, do not require more than a citation to *Prima Paint Corp. v. Flood & Conklin Mfg. Co.*, 388 U.S. 395 (1967). Whatever may be said pro and con about the cost and efficacy of arbitration (which the Hills disparage) is for Congress and the contracting parties to consider. Claims based on RICO are no less arbitrable than those founded on the contract or the law of torts. *Shearson/American Express, Inc. v. McMahon,* 482 U.S. 220, 238–42 (1987). The decision of the district court is vacated, and this case is remanded with instructions to compel the Hills to submit their dispute to arbitration.

Klocek v. Gateway, Inc.

104 F.Supp.2d 1332 (D.Kan.2000).

■ VRATIL, DISTRICT JUDGE.

William S. Klocek brings suit against Gateway, Inc. and Hewlett–Packard, Inc. on claims arising from purchases of a Gateway computer and a Hewlett–Packard scanner. This matter comes before the Court on the *Motion to Dismiss* (Doc. #6) which Gateway filed November 22, 1999. * * *

A. Gateway's Motion to Dismiss

Plaintiff brings individual and class action claims against Gateway, alleging that it induced him and other consumers to purchase computers and special support packages by making false promises of technical support. Individually, plaintiff also claims breach of contract and breach of warranty, in that Gateway breached certain warranties that its computer would be compatible with standard peripherals and standard internet services.

Gateway asserts that plaintiff must arbitrate his claims under Gateway's Standard Terms and Conditions Agreement ("Standard Terms"). Whenever it sells a computer, Gateway includes a copy of the Standard Terms in the box which contains the computer battery power cables and instruction manuals. At the top of the first page, the Standard Terms include the following notice:

> NOTE TO THE CUSTOMER:
>
> This document contains Gateway 2000's Standard Terms and Conditions. By keeping your Gateway 2000 computer system beyond five (5) days after the date of delivery, you accept these Terms and Conditions.

The notice is in emphasized type and is located inside a printed box which sets it apart from other provisions of the document. The Standard Terms are four pages long and contain 16 numbered paragraphs. Paragraph 10 provides the following arbitration clause:

> DISPUTE RESOLUTION. Any dispute or controversy arising out of or relating to this Agreement or its interpretation shall be settled exclusively and finally by arbitration. The arbitration shall be conducted in accordance with the Rules of Conciliation and Arbitration of the International Chamber of Commerce. The arbitration shall be conducted in Chicago, Illinois, U.S.A. before a sole arbitrator. Any award rendered in any such arbitration proceeding shall be final and binding on each of the parties, and judgment may be entered thereon in a court of competent jurisdiction.[1]

Gateway urges the Court to dismiss plaintiff's claims under the Federal Arbitration Act ("FAA"), 9 U.S.C. § 1 *et seq.* The FAA ensures that

1. Gateway states that after it sold plaintiff's computer, it mailed all existing customers in the United States a copy of its quarterly magazine, which contained notice of a change in the arbitration policy set forth in the Standard Terms. The new arbitration policy afforded customers the option of arbitrating before the International Chamber of Commerce ("ICC"), the American Arbitration Association ("AAA"), or the National Arbitration Forum ("NAF") in Chicago, Illinois, or any other location agreed upon by the parties. Plaintiff denies receiving notice of the amended arbitration policy. Neither party explains why—if the arbitration agreement was an enforceable contract—Gateway was entitled to unilaterally amend it by sending a magazine to computer customers.

written arbitration agreements in maritime transactions and transactions involving interstate commerce are "valid, irrevocable, and enforceable." 9 U.S.C. § 2.[2] Federal policy favors arbitration agreements and requires that we "rigorously enforce" them. *Shearson/American Exp., Inc. v. McMahon,* 482 U.S. 220, 226 (1987) (quoting *Dean Witter Reynolds, Inc. v. Byrd,* 470 U.S. 213 (1985)); *Moses,* 460 U.S. at 24. "[A]ny doubts concerning the scope of arbitrable issues should be resolved in favor of arbitration." *Moses,* 460 U.S. at 24–25.

FAA § 3 states:

> If any suit or proceeding be brought in any of the courts of the United States upon any issue referable to arbitration under an agreement in writing for such arbitration, the court in which such suit is pending, upon being satisfied that the issue involved in such suit or proceeding is referable to arbitration under such agreement, shall on application of one of the parties stay the trial of the action until such arbitration has been had in accordance with the terms of the agreement, providing the applicant for the stay is not in default in proceeding with such arbitration.

9 U.S.C. § 3. Although the FAA does not expressly provide for dismissal, the Tenth Circuit has affirmed dismissal where the applicant did not request a stay. *See Armijo v. Prudential Ins. Co. of Am.,* 72 F.3d 793, 797 (10th Cir.1995). Here, neither Gateway nor plaintiff requests a stay. Accordingly, the Court concludes that dismissal is appropriate if plaintiff's claims are arbitrable.

Gateway bears an initial summary-judgment-like burden of establishing that it is entitled to arbitration. *See, e.g., Par-Knit Mills, Inc. v. Stockbridge Fabrics Co.,* 636 F.2d 51, 54 n. 9 (3d Cir.1980) (standard on motion to compel arbitration is same as summary judgment standard); *Doctor's Assoc., Inc. v. Distajo,* 944 F.Supp. 1010, 1014 (D.Conn.1996), *aff'd,* 107 F.3d 126 (2d Cir.1997) (same); *Dougherty v. Mieczkowski,* 661 F.Supp. 267, 270 n. 1 (D.Del.1987). Thus, Gateway must present evidence sufficient to demonstrate the existence of an enforceable agreement to arbitrate. *See, e.g., Oppenheimer & Co. v. Neidhardt,* 56 F.3d 352, 358 (2d Cir.1995). If Gateway makes such a showing, the burden shifts to plaintiff to submit evidence demonstrating a genuine issue for trial. *Id.* * * * In this case, Gateway fails to present evidence establishing the most basic facts regarding the transaction. The gaping holes in the evidentiary record preclude the Court from determining what state law controls the formation of the contract in this case and, consequently, prevent the Court from agreeing that Gateway's motion is well taken.

Before granting a stay or dismissing a case pending arbitration, the Court must determine that the parties have a written agreement to

2. The FAA does not create independent federal-question jurisdiction; rather, "there must be diversity of citizenship or some other independent basis for federal jurisdiction" before the Court may act. *Moses H. Cone Memorial Hosp. v. Mercury Const. Corp.,* 460 U.S. 1, 25 n. 32 (1983). In this case, plaintiff asserts diversity jurisdiction.

arbitrate. *See* 9 U.S.C. §§ 3 and 4; *Avedon Engineering, Inc. v. Seatex,* 126 F.3d 1279, 1283 (10th Cir.1997). When deciding whether the parties have agreed to arbitrate, the Court applies ordinary state law principles that govern the formation of contracts. *First Options of Chicago, Inc. v. Kaplan,* 514 U.S. 938, 944 (1995). The existence of an arbitration agreement "is simply a matter of contract between the parties; [arbitration] is a way to resolve those disputes—but only those disputes—that the parties have agreed to submit to arbitration." *Avedon,* 126 F.3d at 1283 (quoting *Kaplan,* 514 U.S. at 943–945. If the parties dispute making an arbitration agreement, a jury trial on the existence of an agreement is warranted if the record reveals genuine issues of material fact regarding the parties' agreement. *See Avedon,* 126 F.3d at 1283.

Before evaluating whether the parties agreed to arbitrate, the Court must determine what state law controls the formation of the contract in this case. *See id.* at 1284. In diversity actions, the Court applies the substantive law, including choice of law rules, that Kansas state courts would apply. *See Moore v. Subaru of Am.,* 891 F.2d 1445, 1448 (10th Cir.1989). Kansas courts apply the doctrine of *lex loci contractus,* which requires that the Court interpret the contract according to the law of the state in which the parties performed the last act necessary to form the contract. *See Missouri Pac. R.R. Co. v. Kansas Gas and Elec. Co.,* 862 F.2d 796, 798 n. 1 (10th Cir.1988) (citing *Simms v. Metropolitan Life Ins. Co.,* 9 Kan.App.2d 640, 642–43, 685 P.2d 321 (1984)).

The parties do not address the choice of law issue, and the record is unclear where they performed the last act necessary to complete the contract. Gateway presents affidavit testimony that it shipped a computer to plaintiff on or about August 31, 1997, but it provides no details regarding the transaction. Plaintiff's complaint alleges that plaintiff lives in Missouri and, if Gateway shipped his computer, it presumably shipped it to Missouri. In his response to Gateway's motion, however, plaintiff states that on August 27, 1997 he purchased the computer in person at the Gateway store in Overland Park, Kansas, and took it with him at that time. Depending on which factual version is correct, it appears that the parties may have performed the last act necessary to form the contract in Kansas (with plaintiff purchasing the computer in Kansas), Missouri (with Gateway shipping the computer to plaintiff in Missouri), or some unidentified other states (with Gateway agreeing to ship plaintiff's catalog order and/or Gateway actually shipping the order).[4]

The Court discerns no material difference between the applicable substantive law in Kansas and Missouri and—as to those two states—it perhaps would not need to resolve the choice of law issue at this time. *See Avedon,* 126 F.3d at 1284 (choice of law analysis unnecessary if relevant states have enacted identical controlling statutes); *see also Missouri Pacific,* 862 F.2d at 798 n. 1 (applying Kansas law where record did not indicate

4. While Gateway may have shipped the computer to plaintiff in Missouri, the record contains no evidence regarding how plaintiff communicated his order to Gateway, where Gateway received plaintiff's order or where the shipment originated.

where final act occurred and parties did not raise issue); *Phillips Petrol. Co. v. Shutts,* 472 U.S. 797, 816 (1985) ("There can be no injury in applying Kansas law if it is not in conflict with that of any other jurisdiction connected to this suit").[5]

The Uniform Commercial Code ("UCC") governs the parties' transaction under both Kansas and Missouri law. *See* K.S.A. § 84–2–102; V.A.M.S. § 400.2–102 (UCC applies to "transactions in goods."); Kansas Comment 1 (main thrust of Article 2 is limited to sales); K.S.A. § 84–2–105(1) V.A.M.S. § 400.2–105(1) (" 'Goods' means all things ... which are movable at the time of identification to the contract for sale...."). Regardless whether plaintiff purchased the computer in person or placed an order and received shipment of the computer, the parties agree that plaintiff paid for and received a computer from Gateway. This conduct clearly demonstrates a contract for the sale of a computer. *See, e.g., Step-Saver Data Sys., Inc. v. Wyse Techn.,* 939 F.2d 91, 98 (3d Cir.1991). Thus the issue is whether the contract of sale includes the Standard Terms as part of the agreement.

State courts in Kansas and Missouri apparently have not decided whether terms received with a product become part of the parties' agreement. Authority from other courts is split. *Compare Step–Saver,* 939 F.2d 91 (printed terms on computer software package not part of agreement); *Arizona Retail Sys., Inc. v. Software Link, Inc.,* 831 F.Supp. 759 (D.Ariz. 1993) (license agreement shipped with computer software not part of agreement); and *U.S. Surgical Corp. v. Orris, Inc.,* 5 F.Supp.2d 1201 (D.Kan.1998) (single use restriction on product package not binding agreement); *with Hill v. Gateway 2000, Inc.,* 105 F.3d 1147 (7th Cir.), *cert. denied,* 522 U.S. 808 (1997) (arbitration provision shipped with computer binding on buyer); *ProCD, Inc. v. Zeidenberg,* 86 F.3d 1447 (7th Cir.1996) (shrinkwrap license binding on buyer);[6] *and M.A. Mortenson Co., Inc. v. Timberline Software Corp.,* 140 Wash.2d 568, 998 P.2d 305 (2000) (following *Hill* and *ProCD* on license agreement supplied with software).[7] It

5. Paragraph 9 of the Standard Terms provides that "[t]his Agreement shall be governed by the laws of the State of South Dakota, without giving effect to the conflict of laws rules thereof." Both Kansas and Missouri recognize choice-of-law provisions, so long as the transaction at issue has a "reasonable relation" to the state whose law is selected. K.S.A. § 84–1–105(1); Mo.Rev.Stat. § 400.1–105(1). At this time, because it must first determine whether the parties ever agreed to the Standard Terms, the Court does not decide whether Kansas or Missouri (or some other unidentified state) would recognize the choice of law provision contained in the Standard Terms.

6. The term "shrinkwrap license" gets its name from retail software packages that are covered in plastic or cellophane "shrinkwrap" and contain licenses that purport to become effective as soon as the customer tears the wrapping from the package. *See ProCD,* 86 F.3d at 1449.

7. The *Mortenson* court also found support for its holding in the proposed Uniform Computer Information Transactions Act ("UCITA") (formerly known as proposed UCC Article 2B) (text located at www.law.upenn.edu/library/ulc/ucita/UCITA_99.htm), which the National Conference of Commissioners on Uniform State Laws approved and recommended for enactment by the states in July 1999. *See Mortenson,* 998 P.2d at 310 n. 6, 313 n. 10. The proposed UCITA,

appears that at least in part, the cases turn on whether the court finds that the parties formed their contract *before* or *after* the vendor communicated its terms to the purchaser. *Compare Step–Saver,* 939 F.2d at 98 (parties' conduct in shipping, receiving and paying for product demonstrates existence of contract; box top license constitutes proposal for additional terms under § 2–207 which requires express agreement by purchaser); *Arizona Retail,* 831 F.Supp. at 765 (vendor entered into contract by agreeing to ship goods, or at latest by shipping goods to buyer; license agreement constitutes proposal to modify agreement under § 2–209 which requires express assent by buyer); *and Orris,* 5 F.Supp.2d at 1206 (sales contract concluded when vendor received consumer orders; single-use language on product's label was proposed modification under § 2–209 which requires express assent by purchaser); *with ProCD,* 86 F.3d at 1452 (under § 2–204 vendor, as master of offer, may propose limitations on kind of conduct that constitutes acceptance; § 2–207 does not apply in case with only one form); *Hill,* 105 F.3d at 1148–49 (same); *and Mortenson,* 998 P.2d at 311–314 (where vendor and purchaser utilized license agreement in prior course of dealing, shrinkwrap license agreement constituted issue of contract formation under § 2–204, not contract alteration under § 2–207).

Gateway urges the Court to follow the Seventh Circuit decision in *Hill.* That case involved the shipment of a Gateway computer with terms similar to the Standard Terms in this case, except that Gateway gave the customer 30 days—instead of 5 days—to return the computer. In enforcing the arbitration clause, the Seventh Circuit relied on its decision in *ProCD,* where it enforced a software license which was contained inside a product box. *See Hill,* 105 F.3d at 1148–50. In *ProCD,* the Seventh Circuit noted that the exchange of money frequently precedes the communication of detailed terms in a commercial transaction. *See ProCD,* 86 F.3d at 1451. Citing UCC § 2–204, the court reasoned that by including the license with the software, the vendor proposed a contract that the buyer could accept by using the software after having an opportunity to read the license.[8] *ProCD,* 86 F.3d at 1452. Specifically, the court stated:

> A vendor, as master of the offer, may invite acceptance by conduct, and may propose limitations on the kind of conduct that constitutes acceptance. A buyer may accept by performing the acts the vendor proposes to treat as acceptance.

ProCD, 86 F.3d at 1452. The *Hill* court followed the *ProCD* analysis, noting that "[p]ractical considerations support allowing vendors to enclose the full legal terms with their products." *Hill,* 105 F.3d at 1149.[9]

however, would not apply to the Court's analysis in this case. The UCITA applies to computer information transactions, which are defined as agreements "to create, modify, transfer, or license computer information or informational rights in computer information." UCITA, §§ 102(11) and 103. In transactions involving the sale of computers, such as our case, the UCITA applies only to the computer programs and copies, not to the sale of the computer itself. *See* UCITA § 103(c)(2).

8. Section 2–204 provides: "A contract for sale of goods may be made in any manner sufficient to show agreement, including conduct by both parties which recognizes the existence of such contract." K.S.A. § 84–2–204; V.A.M.S. § 400.2–204.

9. Legal commentators have criticized the reasoning of the Seventh Circuit in this regard. *See, e.g.,* Jean R. Sternlight, *Gateway Widens Doorway to Imposing Unfair Binding Arbitration on Consumers,* Fla. Bar J., Nov.

The Court is not persuaded that Kansas or Missouri courts would follow the Seventh Circuit reasoning in *Hill* and *ProCD.* In each case the Seventh Circuit concluded without support that UCC § 2–207 was irrelevant because the cases involved only one written form. *See ProCD,* 86 F.3d at 1452 (citing no authority); *Hill,* 105 F.3d at 1150 (citing *ProCD*). This conclusion is not supported by the statute or by Kansas or Missouri law. Disputes under § 2–207 often arise in the context of a "battle of forms," *see, e.g., Diatom, Inc. v. Pennwalt Corp.,* 741 F.2d 1569, 1574 (10th Cir.1984), but nothing in its language precludes application in a case which involves only one form. The statute provides:

Additional terms in acceptance or confirmation.

(1) A definite and seasonable expression of acceptance or a written confirmation which is sent within a reasonable time operates as an acceptance even though it states terms additional to or different from those offered or agreed upon, unless acceptance is expressly made conditional on assent to the additional or different terms.

(2) The additional terms are to be construed as proposals for addition to the contract [if the contract is not between merchants]....

K.S.A. § 84–2–207; V.A.M.S. § 400.2–207. By its terms, § 2–207 applies to an acceptance or written confirmation. It states nothing which requires another form before the provision becomes effective. In fact, the official comment to the section specifically provides that §§ 2–207(1) and (2) apply "where an agreement has been reached orally ... and is followed by one or both of the parties sending formal memoranda embodying the terms so far agreed and adding terms not discussed." Official Comment 1 of UCC § 2–207. Kansas and Missouri courts have followed this analysis. *See Southwest Engineering Co. v. Martin Tractor Co.,* 205 Kan. 684, 695, 473 P.2d 18, 26 (1970) (stating in dicta that § 2–207 applies where open offer is accepted by

1997, at 8, 10–12 (outcome in *Gateway* is questionable on federal statutory, common law and constitutional grounds and as a matter of contract law and is unwise as a matter of policy because it unreasonably shifts to consumers search cost of ascertaining existence of arbitration clause and return cost to avoid such clause); Thomas J. McCarthy et al., *Survey: Uniform Commercial Code,* 53 Bus. Law. 1461, 1465–66 (Seventh Circuit finding that UCC § 2–207 did not apply is inconsistent with official comment); Batya Goodman, *Honey, I Shrink–Wrapped the Consumer: the Shrinkwrap Agreement as an Adhesion Contract,* 21 Cardozo L.Rev. 319, 344–352 (Seventh Circuit failed to consider principles of adhesion contracts); Jeremy Senderowicz, *Consumer Arbitration and Freedom of Contract: A Proposal to Facilitate Consumers' Informed Consent to Arbitration Clauses in Form Contracts,* 32 Colum. J.L. & Soc. Probs. 275, 296–299 (judiciary (in multiple decisions, including *Hill*) has ignored issue of consumer consent to an arbitration clause). Nonetheless, several courts have followed the Seventh Circuit decisions in *Hill* and *ProCD.* See, e.g., *M.A. Mortenson Co., Inc. v. Timberline Software Corp.,* 140 Wash.2d 568, 998 P.2d 305 (license agreement supplied with software); *Rinaldi v. Iomega Corp.,* 1999 WL 1442014, Case No. 98C–09–064–RRC (Del.Super. Sept. 3,1999) (warranty disclaimer included inside computer Zip drive packaging); *Westendorf v. Gateway 2000, Inc.,* 2000 WL 307369, Case No. 16913 (Del. Ch. March 16, 2000) (arbitration provision shipped with computer); *Brower v. Gateway 2000, Inc.,* 246 A.D.2d 246, 676 N.Y.S.2d 569 (N.Y.App.Div.1998) (same); *Levy v. Gateway 2000, Inc.,* 1997 WL 823611, 33 UCC Rep. Serv.2d 1060 (N.Y.Sup. Oct.31, 1997) (same).

expression of acceptance in writing or where oral agreement is later confirmed in writing);[10] *Central Bag Co. v. W. Scott and Co.,* 647 S.W.2d 828, 830 (Mo.App.1983) (§§ 2–207(1) and (2) govern cases where one or both parties send written confirmation after oral contract). Thus, the Court concludes that Kansas and Missouri courts would apply § 2–207 to the facts in this case. *Accord Avedon,* 126 F.3d at 1283 (parties agree that § 2–207 controls whether arbitration clause in sales confirmation is part of contract).

In addition, the Seventh Circuit provided no explanation for its conclusion that "the vendor is the master of the offer." *See ProCD,* 86 F.3d at 1452 (citing nothing in support of proposition); *Hill,* 105 F.3d at 1149 (citing *ProCD*). In typical consumer transactions, the purchaser is the offeror, and the vendor is the offeree. *See Brown Mach., Div. of John Brown, Inc. v. Hercules, Inc.,* 770 S.W.2d 416, 419 (Mo.App.1989) (as general rule orders are considered offers to purchase); *Rich Prods. Corp. v. Kemutec Inc.,* 66 F.Supp.2d 937, 956 (E.D.Wis.1999) (generally price quotation is invitation to make offer and purchase order is offer). While it is possible for the vendor to be the offeror, *see Brown Machine,* 770 S.W.2d at 419 (price quote can amount to offer if it reasonably appears from quote that assent to quote is all that is needed to ripen offer into contract), Gateway provides no factual evidence which would support such a finding in this case. The Court therefore assumes for purposes of the motion to dismiss that plaintiff offered to purchase the computer (either in person or through catalog order) and that Gateway accepted plaintiff's offer (either by completing the sales transaction in person or by agreeing to ship and/or shipping the computer to plaintiff).[11] *Accord Arizona Retail,* 831 F.Supp. at 765 (vendor entered into contract by agreeing to ship goods, or at latest, by shipping goods).

Under § 2–207, the Standard Terms constitute either an expression of acceptance or written confirmation. As an expression of acceptance, the Standard Terms would constitute a counter-offer only if Gateway expressly made its acceptance conditional on plaintiff's assent to the additional or different terms. K.S.A. § 84–2–207(1); V.A.M.S. § 400.2–207(1). "[T]he conditional nature of the acceptance must be clearly expressed in a manner sufficient to notify the offeror that the offeree is unwilling to proceed with

10. In *Southwest Engineering,* the court was concerned with the existence of an enforceable contract under the UCC statute of frauds and it determined that the parties' notes satisfied the writing requirement. It found that a subsequent letter which contained additional material terms did not become part of the agreement under § 2–207, however, because the parties did not expressly agree to the change in terms. *See Southwest Engineering,* 205 Kan. at 693–94, 473 P.2d at 25. The court further found that § 2–207 did not apply to its analysis because at the time of the letter, the parties had already memorialized the agreement in writing and there was no outstanding offer to accept or oral agreement to confirm. *See Southwest Engineering,* 205 Kan. at 695, 473 P.2d at 26.

11. UCC § 2–206(b) provides that "an order or other offer to buy goods for prompt or current shipment shall be construed as inviting acceptance either by a prompt promise to ship or by the prompt or current shipment ..." The official comment states that "[e]ither shipment or a prompt promise to ship is made a proper means of acceptance of an offer looking to current shipment." UCC § 2–206, Official Comment 2.

the transaction unless the additional or different terms are included in the contract." *Brown Machine,* 770 S.W.2d at 420.[12] Gateway provides no evidence that at the time of the sales transaction, it informed plaintiff that the transaction was conditioned on plaintiff's acceptance of the Standard Terms. Moreover, the mere fact that Gateway shipped the goods with the terms attached did not communicate to plaintiff any unwillingness to proceed without plaintiff's agreement to the Standard Terms. *See, e.g., Arizona Retail,* 831 F.Supp. at 765 (conditional acceptance analysis rarely appropriate where contract formed by performance but goods arrive with conditions attached); *Leighton Indus., Inc. v. Callier Steel Pipe & Tube, Inc.,* 1991 WL 18413, *6, Case No. 89–C–8235 (N.D.Ill. Feb. 6, 1991) (applying Missouri law) (preprinted forms insufficient to notify offeror of conditional nature of acceptance, particularly where form arrives after delivery of goods).

Because plaintiff is not a merchant, additional or different terms contained in the Standard Terms did not become part of the parties' agreement unless plaintiff expressly agreed to them. *See* K.S.A. § 84–2–207, Kansas Comment 2 (if either party is not a merchant, additional terms are proposals for addition to the contract that do not become part of the contract unless the original offeror expressly agrees).[13] Gateway argues that plaintiff demonstrated acceptance of the arbitration provision by keeping the computer more than five days after the date of delivery. Although the Standard Terms purport to work that result, Gateway has not presented evidence that plaintiff expressly agreed to those Standard Terms. Gateway states only that it enclosed the Standard Terms inside the computer box for plaintiff to read afterwards. It provides no evidence that it informed plaintiff of the five-day review-and-return period as a condition of the sales transaction, or that the parties contemplated additional terms to the agreement.[14] *See Step–Saver,* 939 F.2d at 99 (during negotiations leading to purchase, vendor never mentioned box-top license or obtained buyer's express assent thereto). The Court finds that the act of keeping the computer past five days was not sufficient to demonstrate that plaintiff expressly agreed to the Standard Terms. *Accord Brown Machine,* 770 S.W.2d at 421 (express assent cannot be presumed by silence or mere failure to object). Thus, because Gateway has not provided evidence sufficient to support a finding under Kansas or Missouri law that plaintiff

12. Courts are split on the standard for a conditional acceptance under § 2–207. *See Daitom,* 741 F.2d at 1576 (finding that Pennsylvania would most likely adopt "better" view that offeree must explicitly communicate unwillingness to proceed with transaction unless additional terms in response are accepted by offeror). * * *

13. The Court's decision would be the same if it considered the Standard Terms as a proposed modification under UCC § 2–209. *See, e.g., Orris,* 5 F.Supp.2d at 1206 (express assent analysis is same under §§ 2–207 and 2–209).

14. The Court is mindful of the practical considerations which are involved in commercial transactions, but it is not unreasonable for a vendor to clearly communicate to a buyer—at the time of sale—either the complete terms of the sale or the fact that the vendor will propose additional terms as a condition of sale, if that be the case.

agreed to the arbitration provision contained in Gateway's Standard Terms, the Court overrules Gateway's motion to dismiss.

* * *

NOTES & QUESTIONS

1. *Compare and contrast. ProCD* and *Hill* were both heard in the United States Court of Appeals for the Seventh Circuit and the decision in both cases was written by Judge Easterbrook. The *ProCD* case was decided before the *Hill* case. Does Judge Easterbrook simply apply the same rule in each case or does the latter case extend the former?

2. *"Layered contracting," "rolling contract."* These terms refer to an agreement in which terms are presented only after the buyer has received the product. *ProCD* and *Hill* validate layered contracting. What are the limits on this reasoning? That is, would Judge Easterbrook reject such a contract if there was no opportunity to see the terms after receiving the product? If there was an opportunity to see the terms, but no meaningful opportunity to return the product after seeing them? Are market conditions (whether the market is competitive or monopolized) relevant to Judge Easterbrook's analysis?

3. *Manifesting dissent by silence.* Preliminary Note 5 to Proposed Amended U.C.C. § 2–207 (dealing with "the battle of the forms") states:

> The section omits any specific treatment of terms on or in the container in which the goods are delivered. Amended Article 2 takes no position on the question whether a court should follow the reasoning in *Hill v. Gateway 2000*, 105 F.3d 1147 (7th Cir. 1997) (§ 2–207 does not apply to these cases; the "rolling contract" is not made until acceptance of the seller's terms after the goods and terms are delivered) or the contrary reasoning in *Step–Saver Data Systems, Inc. v. Wyse Technology*, 939 F.2d 91 (3d Cir.1991) (contract is made at time of oral or other bargain and "shrink wrap" terms or those in the container become part of the contract only if they comply with provisions like § 2–207).

Klocek v. Gateway, excerpted above, applies the same reasoning as *Step–Saver v. Wyse Technology.* Why do you think that the committee revising U.C.C. Article 2 declines to take a position on the debate represented by *ProCD* and *Hill*, on the one hand, and *Step–Saver* and *Klocek*, on the other?

4. *UCITA and rolling contracts.* In Part I(C)(4) and Part I(D), *infra*, you will find UCITA's innovative definition of "manifestation of assent," in which assent between persons is treated together with assent by electronic agents. As part of those provisions, UCITA provides in § 112:

> (a) A person manifests assent to a record or term if the person, acting with knowledge of, or after having an opportunity to review the record or term or a copy of it:
>
> (1) authenticates the record or term with intent to adopt or accept it; or

(2) intentionally engages in conduct or makes statements with reason to know that the other party or its electronic agent may infer from the conduct or statement that the person assents to the record or term.

* * *

(e) With respect to an opportunity to review, the following rules apply:

(1) A person has an opportunity to review a record or term only if it is made available in a manner that ought to call it to the attention of a reasonable person and permit review.

(2) An electronic agent has an opportunity to review a record or term only if it is made available in manner that would enable a reasonably configured electronic agent to react to the record or term.

(3) If a record or term is available for review only after a person becomes obligated to pay or begins its performance, the person has an opportunity to review only if it has a right to a return if it rejects the record. However, a right to a return is not required if:

(A) the record proposes a modification of contract or provides particulars of performance under § 305; or

(B) the primary performance is other than delivery or acceptance of a copy, the agreement is not a mass-market transaction, and the parties at the time of contracting had reason to know that a record or term would be presented after performance, use, or access to the information began.

Compare these provisions with the regime contemplated by Judge Easterbrook in the opinions excerpted above. In what ways are these provisions more restrictive in validating rolling contracts than the regime contemplated by Judge Easterbrook? In what ways are they less restrictive?

2. CLICKWRAP AGREEMENTS

I.Lan Systems, Inc. v. Netscout Service Level Corp.

183 F.Supp.2d 328 (D.Mass.2002).

■ YOUNG, CHIEF JUDGE.

Has this happened to you? You plunk down a pretty penny for the latest and greatest software, speed back to your computer, tear open the box, shove the CD–ROM into the computer, click on "install" and, after scrolling past a license agreement which would take at least fifteen minutes to read, find yourself staring at the following dialog box: "I agree." Do you click on the box? You probably do not agree in your heart of hearts, but you click anyway, not about to let some pesky legalese delay the moment for which you've been waiting. Is that "clickwrap" license agreement enforceable? Yes, at least in the case described below.

I. INTRODUCTION

The plaintiff, i.LAN Systems, Inc. ("i.LAN"), helps companies monitor their computer networks. The defendant, NetScout Service Level Corp., formerly known as NextPoint Networks, Inc. ("NextPoint"), sells sophisticated software that monitors networks. In 1998, i.LAN and NextPoint signed a detailed Value Added Reseller ("VAR") agreement whereby i.LAN agreed to resell NextPoint's software to customers. This dispute concerns a transaction that took place in 1999.

i.LAN claims that for $85,231.42 it purchased the unlimited right to use NextPoint's software, replete with perpetual upgrades and support, whereby it effectively could rent, rather than sell, NextPoint's software to customers. In support of its argument, i.LAN points to the purchase order associated with the transaction. NextPoint, in response, points to the 1998 VAR agreement and the clickwrap license agreement contained in the software itself to reach a different conclusion.

The parties continued their relationship for several months without confronting their conflicting interpretations of the 1999 purchase order, but eventually the disagreement erupted into litigation. i.LAN filed a complaint that alleges, among other things, breach of contract. * * *

i.LAN quickly took the offensive and brought a motion for summary judgment, Fed.R.Civ.P. 56(a). i.LAN argued that it should be awarded specific performance—in particular, perpetual upgrades of NextPoint's software and unlimited support. The Court heard oral argument on i.LAN's motion and took the matter under advisement. Soon after, NextPoint brought a cross-motion for summary judgment, Fed.R.Civ.P. 56(b), the subject of this memorandum. NextPoint argued that even if i.LAN's allegations were true, the clickwrap license agreement limits NextPoint's liability to the price paid for the software, in this case $85,231.42. The Court heard oral arguments on NextPoint's motion and soon after ruled in favor of NextPoint. This memorandum explains why.

II. DISCUSSION

Before turning to NextPoint's clickwrap license agreement, the stage must be set. First, the Court will identify the set of rules by which to judge this dispute. Next, the Court will examine what is at stake, in particular i.LAN's claim for specific performance and NextPoint's limitation-of-liability defense. Finally, the Court will address the enforceability of the clickwrap license agreement.

A. *What Law Governs?*

1. Precedence of the 1998, 1999, and Clickwrap Agreements

Three contracts might govern this dispute: the 1998 VAR agreement, the 1999 purchase order, and the clickwrap license agreement to which i.LAN necessarily agreed when it installed the software at issue. The key question for purposes of this memorandum is how the 1998 and 1999 agreements affect the clickwrap license agreement.

The clickwrap license agreement states that it does not affect existing or subsequent written agreements or purchase orders. The language might be read to mean that the clickwrap license agreement is a nullity if a purchase order already exists, but that reading is not the natural one. The natural reading is that to the extent the 1998 VAR agreement and 1999 purchase order are silent, the clickwrap license agreement fills the void.

2. Common Law vs. UCC

Two bodies of contract law might govern the clickwrap license agreement: Massachusetts common law and the Uniform Commercial Code ("UCC") as adopted by Massachusetts. Article 2 of the UCC applies to "transactions in goods," UCC § 2–102, Mass. Gen. Laws ch. 106, § 2–102, but "unless the context otherwise requires 'contract' and 'agreement' are limited to those relating to the present or future *sale* of goods," *id.* § 2–106(1) (emphasis added). Indeed, the title of Article 2 is "Sales" and the definition of "goods" assumes a sale: "goods" is defined as "all things (including specially manufactured goods) which are movable at the time of identification to the contract for sale...." *Id.* § 2–105(1). The purchase of software might seem like an ordinary contract for the sale of goods, but in fact the purchaser merely obtains a *license* to use the software; never is there a "passing of title from the seller to the buyer for a price," *id.* § 2–106(1). So is the purchase of software a transaction in goods? Despite Article 2's requirement of a *sale,* courts in Massachusetts have assumed, without deciding, that Article 2 governs software *licenses. See Novacore Techs., Inc. v. GST Communications Corp.,* 20 F.Supp.2d 169, 183 (D.Mass. 1998) (Saris, J.), *aff'd,* 229 F.3d 1133 (1st Cir.1999); [string cite deleted]. *See generally* Lorin Brennan, *Why Article 2 Cannot Apply to Software Transactions,* 38 Duq. L.Rev. 459, 545–77 (2000); Mark A. Lemley, *Intellectual Property and Shrinkwrap Licenses,* 68 S. Cal. L.Rev. 1239, 1244 n. 23 (1995).

Given the cases above, and others to the same effect, i.LAN argues that the UCC should govern the 1999 purchase order and clickwrap license agreement. NextPoint does not disagree with the idea that the UCC might apply to software purchases in general, but under NextPoint's theory of the case, the 1998 VAR agreement is most important to this dispute, and that agreement predominately concerns *services,* rather than the sale of goods. NextPoint, therefore, argues that the UCC should not govern any part of this dispute. *See, e.g., Cambridge Plating Co. v. Napco, Inc.,* 991 F.2d 21, 24 (1st Cir.1993) (considering "predominate factor, thrust, or purpose" of contract).

To the extent it matters—and given the facts of this case, it likely does not—the Court will examine the clickwrap license agreement through the lens of the UCC. Admittedly, the UCC technically does not govern software licenses, and very likely does not govern the 1998 VAR agreement, but with respect to the 1999 transaction, the UCC best fulfills the parties' reasonable expectations.

In Massachusetts and across most of the nation, software licenses exist in a legislative void. Legal scholars, among them the Uniform Commissioners on State Laws, have tried to fill that void, but their efforts have not kept pace with the world of business. Lawmakers began to draft a new Article 2B (licenses) for the UCC, which would have been the logical complement to Article 2 (sales) and Article 2A (leases), but after a few years of drafting, those lawmakers decided instead to draft an independent body of law for software licenses, which is now known as the Uniform Computer Information Transactions Act ("UCITA"). So far only Maryland and Virginia have adopted UCITA; Massachusetts has not. Accordingly, the Court will not spend its time considering UCITA. At the same time, the Court will not overlook Article 2 simply because its provisions are imperfect in today's world. Software licenses are entered into every day, and business persons reasonably expect that *some* law will govern them. For the time being, Article 2's familiar provisions—which are the inspiration for UCITA—better fulfill those expectations than would the common law. Article 2 technically does not, and certainly will not in the future, govern software licenses, but for the time being, the Court will assume it does.

B. What Is at Stake?

* * *

2. Limitation of Liability

* * *

[T]he clickwrap license agreement contains a 30–day limited warranty but otherwise disclaims all warranties and limits NextPoint's liability to the fees it received for the license.[3] The key question, then, is whether the clickwrap license agreement is enforceable.

3. The clickwrap license agreement provides:

IMPORTANT: NEXTPOINT IS WILLING TO LICENSE THE LICENSED PRODUCT TO LICENSEE ONLY ON THE CONDITION THAT LICENSEE ACCEPTS THE TERMS AND CONDITIONS CONTAINED IN THIS AGREEMENT. BY CLICKING THE "I AGREE" BUTTON, LICENSEE ACKNOWLEDGES THAT IT HAS READ ALL OF THE TERMS AND CONDITIONS OF THIS AGREEMENT, UNDERSTANDS THEM, AND AGREES TO BE BOUND BY THEM.

IF LICENSEE DOES NOT AGREE TO THESE TERMS AND CONDITIONS, IT MUST PROMPTLY CEASE USE OF THE LICENSED PRODUCT AND RETURN THE LICENSED PRODUCT AND ALL ACCOMPANYING ITEMS TO NEXTPOINT OR ITS RESELLER FOR A FULL REFUND OF THE LICENSE FEE WHICH LICENSEE PAID FOR THE LICENSED PRODUCT.

* * *

3. LIMITED WARRANTY.

Limited Warranty. NEXTPOINT warrants to Licensee that the Licensed Products will substantially conform to the specifications set forth in the documentation provided by NEXTPOINT with the Licensed Product ("Documentation") for a period of thirty (30) days from the date when NEXTPOINT provides the License Key to the Licensee.

* * *

Warranty Service. NEXTPOINT's sole obligation with respect to claims of nonconfor-

C. Are Clickwrap License Agreements Enforceable?

The clickwrap license agreement may be analyzed as either (i) forming a contract under UCC § 2–204[4] or (ii) adding terms to an existing contract under UCC § 2–207,[5] a method of contracting that often results in a "battle of the forms." The distinction is important.

mance with the above warranties during the applicable warranty period shall be, at NEXTPOINT's election either (a) to repair or by [sic] replace the nonconforming Licensed Product, or (b) to return the price paid for this license, resulting in termination of this Agreement.

4. LIMITATIONS OF LIABILITY

EXCEPT AS STATED IN SECTION 3 ABOVE, NEXTPOINT DISCLAIMS ALL WARRANTIES AND CONDITIONS, EITHER EXPRESS OR IMPLIED, STATUTORY OR OTHERWISE, WITH RESPECT TO THE LICENSED PRODUCT, INCLUDING ALL IMPLIED WARRANTIES AND CONDITIONS, STATUTORY OR OTHERWISE, OF MERCHANTABILITY, NONINFRINGEMENT AND FITNESS FOR A PARTICULAR PURPOSE, OR ARISING FROM A COURSE OF DEALING, USAGE OR TRADE PRACTICE.

NEXTPOINT'S LIABILITY FOR DAMAGES TO LICENSEE FOR ANY CAUSE WHATSOEVER, REGARDLESS OF THE FORM OF ANY CLAIM OR ACTION, SHALL BE LIMITED TO THE LICENSE FEES PAID FOR THE LICENSED PRODUCT.

NEXTPOINT SHALL NOT BE LIABLE HEREUNDER FOR ANY DAMAGES RESULTING FROM LOSS OF DATA, PROFITS OR USE OF EQUIPMENT, OR FOR ANY SPECIAL, INCIDENTAL, INDIRECT, EXEMPLARY OR CONSEQUENTIAL DAMAGES ARISING OUT OF OR IN CONNECTION WITH THE USE OR PERFORMANCE OF THE LICENSED PRODUCT, WHETHER OR NOT NEXTPOINT HAS BEEN MADE AWARE OF THE POSSIBILITY OF SUCH DAMAGES.

4. The Code provides:

§ 2–204. Formation in General.

(1) A contract for sale of goods may be made in any manner sufficient to show agreement, including conduct by both parties which recognizes the existence of such a contract.

(2) An agreement sufficient to constitute a contract for sale may be found even though the moment of its making is undetermined.

(3) Even though one or more terms are left open a contract for sale does not fail for indefiniteness if the parties have intended to make a contract and there is a reasonably certain basis for giving an appropriate remedy.

UCC § 2–204, Mass. Gen. Laws ch. 106, § 2–204.

5. The Code provides:

§ 2–207. Additional Terms in Acceptance or Confirmation.

(1) A definite and seasonable expression of acceptance or a written confirmation which is sent within a reasonable time operates as an acceptance even though it states terms additional to or different from those offered or agreed upon, unless acceptance is expressly made conditional on assent to the additional or different terms.

(2) The additional terms are to be construed as proposals for addition to the contract. Between merchants such terms become part of the contract unless:

(a) the offer expressly limits acceptance to the terms of the offer;

(b) they materially alter it; or

(c) notification of objection to them has already been given or is given within a reasonable time after notice of them is received.

(3) Conduct by both parties which recognizes the existence of a contract is sufficient to establish a contract for sale although the writings of the parties do not otherwise establish a contract. In such case the terms of the particular contract consist of those terms on which the writings of the parties agree, together with any supplementary terms incorporated under any other provisions of this Act.

If the proper analysis is pursuant to UCC § 2–204, the analysis is simple: i.LAN manifested assent to the clickwrap license agreement when it clicked on the box stating "I agree," so the agreement is enforceable. *See Specht v. Netscape Communications Corp.,* 150 F.Supp.2d 585, 591–96 (S.D.N.Y.2001).

If the proper analysis is pursuant to UCC § 2–207, the analysis is more complicated. *See generally* 1 James J. White & Robert S. Summers, Uniform Commercial Code § 1.3 (4th ed. 1995 and Supp.2001). UCC § 2–207 creates two forks in the road for the facts of this case. The first fork is whether or not the clickwrap license agreement is a counteroffer—an acceptance to i.LAN's purchase order "expressly made conditional on assent to the additional or different terms," UCC § 2–207(1), here the additional terms limiting NextPoint's potential liability. The second fork is whether i.LAN accepted the additional terms either explicitly, implicitly, or by default. Clicking on "I agree" could be seen as *explicit* acceptance. Between merchants, if a party never objects to the additional terms, and the additional terms are not "material," then the UCC deems the party to have accepted the additional terms *implicitly,* for lack of a better description. UCC § 2–207(2). The comment to UCC § 2–207 suggests that the test for "materiality" is whether the terms in question would result in unreasonable surprise or hardship to the party if incorporated without the party's express awareness. UCC § 2–207 cmt. 4. Finally, if the additional terms are not accepted either explicitly or implicitly, but the conduct of the parties shows recognition of a contract, then the gap-filler provisions of Article 2 kick in to fill the void with *default* terms. UCC § 2–207(3). * * *

With respect to the first fork, the clickwrap license agreement is best characterized as a counteroffer, as its language mirrors the language provided after the comma in UCC § 2–207(1): "NEXTPOINT IS WILLING TO LICENSE THE LICENSED PRODUCT TO LICENSEE ONLY ON THE CONDITION THAT LICENSEE ACCEPTS THE TERMS AND CONDITIONS CONTAINED IN THIS AGREEMENT." The first fork only has importance, however, if the parties disagree over the additional terms. In this case, i.LAN's purchase order was silent on the issue of liability, so NextPoint proposed additional terms which, to be extra cautious, NextPoint characterized as a counteroffer. In such a case, if the original offer is silent on the issue of the additional terms, and no objection ever is made to them, then it should not matter whether the additional terms are part of a counteroffer or a proposal. All that should matter in this case, then, is whether i.LAN accepted the additional terms. Article 2 does not limit liability by default, so if i.LAN accepted the clickwrap license agreement it must have done so either explicitly, by clicking on "I agree," or implicitly, as provided in UCC § 2–207(2).

The case to which i.LAN pins its hopes is *Step-Saver Data Systems, Inc. v. Wyse Technology,* 939 F.2d 91 (3d Cir.1991). *Step-Saver* considered

UCC § 2–207; *accord* Mass. Gen. Laws ch. 106, § 2–207 ("additional or different terms").

shrinkwrap license agreements, where the agreement is printed somewhere on or in the box of software, rather than *clickwrap* license agreements, where the agreement appears on the computer before the software is installed, but otherwise the facts of *Step-Saver* are similar to the facts before this Court: (i) a reseller telephoned a software manufacturer and asked for a shipment of software, which the manufacturer verbally agreed to provide, (ii) the reseller then sent a written purchase order specifying quantity, price, and shipping and payment information, and (iii) the manufacturer then shipped the software along with an invoice matching the purchase order. On the box containing the software, however, was a shrinkwrap license agreement which contained a provision limiting the manufacturer's liability to the price paid for the shipment. The question for the court was whether to enforce the provision of the shrinkwrap license agreement limiting the manufacturer's liability. The court held that the limitation of liability was not enforceable because it was merely a proposed agreement under UCC § 2–207 to which the reseller never agreed; the court refused to imply assent because the limitation of liability was material and UCC § 2–207(2)(b) does not allow *material* terms to be added by implication. *Id.* at 105. This holding was fully adopted in a later case against the same software manufacturer, *Arizona Retail Systems, Inc. v. The Software Link, Inc.,* 831 F.Supp. 759, 766 (D.Ariz.1993).

Step-Saver once was the leading case on shrinkwrap agreements. Today that distinction goes to a case favoring NextPoint, *ProCD, Inc. v. Zeidenberg,* 86 F.3d 1447 (7th Cir.1996). The holding of *ProCD* is best summarized as follows: "terms inside a box of software bind consumers who use the software after an opportunity to read the terms and to reject them by returning the product." *Hill v. Gateway 2000, Inc.,* 105 F.3d 1147, 1148 (7th Cir.1997). *ProCD* did not apply UCC § 2–207: "Our case has only one form; UCC § 2–207 is irrelevant." 86 F.3d at 1452. Instead, *ProCD* applied only UCC § 2–204 and concluded that the absence of a timely rejection was sufficient to show assent.

The analytical difference between *Step-Saver* and *ProCD* is whether "money now, terms later" forms a contract (i) at the time of the purchase order or (ii) when the purchaser receives the box of software, sees the license agreement, and does not return the software. *See, e.g., Klocek v. Gateway, Inc.,* 104 F.Supp.2d 1332, 1338–39 (D.Kan.2000) (noting distinction and rejecting *ProCD*); *M.A. Mortenson Co. v. Timberline Software Corp.,* 140 Wash.2d 568, 998 P.2d 305, 312–14 (2000) (en banc) (noting distinction and embracing *ProCD*). If the purchase order is the contract, UCC § 2–207 applies and material terms cannot be added to the contract without explicit assent. If the contract is not formed until after the purchaser sees the shrinkwrap license agreement, UCC § 2–204 applies and the act of keeping the software implicitly shows assent.

The Court will enforce NextPoint's clickwrap license agreement for two reasons. First and foremost, the Court agrees with those cases embracing the theory of *ProCD.* * * * The UCC "shall be liberally construed and applied to promote its underlying purposes and policies," which include "the continued expansion of commercial practices through custom, usage and agreement of the parties." UCC § 1–102, Mass. Gen. Laws ch. 106, § 1–102. "Money now, terms later" is a practical way to form contracts, especially with purchasers of software. If *ProCD* was correct to enforce a shrinkwrap license agreement, where any assent is implicit, then it must also be correct to enforce a clickwrap license agreement, where the assent is explicit. To be sure, shrinkwrap and clickwrap license agreements share the defect of any standardized contract—they are susceptible to the inclusion of terms that border on the unconscionable—but that is not the issue in this case. The only issue before the Court is whether clickwrap license agreements are an appropriate way to form contracts, and the Court holds they are. In short, i.LAN explicitly accepted the clickwrap license agreement when it clicked on the box stating "I agree."

Second, even if the Court were to agree with i.LAN that UCC § 2–207 governs, the Court would hold that i.LAN implicitly accepted the clickwrap license agreement because its additional terms were not material, UCC § 2–207(2)(b). In other words, there can be no unreasonable surprise or hardship to i.LAN from enforcing the limitation of liability. To understand this holding requires a bit of background. When NextPoint and i.LAN first formed their relationship, i.LAN signed the 1998 VAR agreement, which contains warranty disclaimers and limitations of liability nearly identical to those found in the clickwrap license agreement. Furthermore, the 1998 VAR agreement incorporates the clickwrap license agreement by reference and specifically states that NextPoint's liability to end users of the software will be limited by the clickwrap license agreement. Finally, i.LAN had installed the software on many occasions before the transaction in 1999, and each time i.LAN necessarily ran across the clickwrap license agreement. In short, NextPoint consistently included a warranty disclaimer and limitation of liability in every contract it made.

Every contract, that is, except the 1999 purchase order. That contract contains a price, a quantity, and five specific terms, but is silent with respect to warranties and potential liability. Thus, i.LAN argues that NextPoint's "contrived attempt to supersede the [1999 purchase order] with directly contradicting terms or a standardized click license, a license that was neither referenced in the [1999 purchase order] nor even mentioned during negotiations, is absurd." To the contrary, it would be absurd to allow silence to destroy the detailed private ordering created by the 1998 VAR and clickwrap license agreements. Indeed, the clickwrap license agreement specifically was intended to fill any gaps left by the 1999 purchase order. "There is a long tradition in contract law of reading contracts sensibly; contracts—certainly business contracts of the kind involved here—are not parlor games but the means of getting the world's work done." *R.I. Charities Trust v. Engelhard Corp.*, 267 F.3d 3, 7 (1st Cir.2001). The only sensible interpretation of the 1999 purchase order is that it did not affect the limitations of liability found in the parties' prior and subsequent agreements.

III. CONCLUSION

For the reasons set forth above, NextPoint's cross-motion for partial summary judgment was ALLOWED on September 28, 2001 with respect to i.LAN's claims for specific performance. Furthermore, the Court held that if i.LAN were to prevail on any of its other claims, it would be entitled to recover no more than the amount it paid for the software license at issue, to wit, $85,231.42.

UETA includes a strikingly broad provision for validating contracts formed by the interaction of electronic agents with one another as well as with human agents. The most pervasive form of interaction between an electronic agent and a human agent is the clickwrap agreement. The validity of contracts formed through such interactions is addressed in Section 14 of UETA, specifically in Section 14(2). We will reconsider Section 14(1) when we focus on machine-to-machine contracts in Part II, *infra.*

Uniform Electronic Transactions Act, § 14

National Conference of Commissioners on Uniform State Laws.
(1999).

SECTION 14. AUTOMATED TRANSACTION.

In an automated transaction, the following rules apply:

(1) A contract may be formed by the interaction of electronic agents of the parties, even if no individual was aware of or reviewed the electronic agents' actions or the resulting terms and agreements.

(2) A contract may be formed by the interaction of an electronic agent and an individual, acting on the individual's own behalf or for another person, including by an interaction in which the individual performs actions that the individual is free to refuse to perform and which the individual knows or has reason to know will cause the electronic agent to complete the transaction or performance.

(3) The terms of the contract are determined by the substantive law applicable to it.

Comment

1. This section confirms that contracts can be formed by machines functioning as electronic agents for parties to a transaction. It negates any claim that lack of human intent, at the time of contract formation, prevents contract formation. When machines are involved, the requisite intention flows from the programming and use of the machine. * * *

2. The process in paragraph (2) validates an anonymous click-through transaction. It is possible that an anonymous click-through process may simply result in no recognizable legal relationship, e.g., A goes to a person's website and acquires access without in any way identifying herself, or

otherwise indicating agreement or assent to any limitation or obligation, and the owner's site grants A access. In such a case no legal relationship has been created.

On the other hand it may be possible that A's actions indicate agreement to a particular term. For example, A goes to a website and is confronted by an initial screen which advises her that the information at this site is proprietary, that A may use the information for her own personal purposes, but that, by clicking below, A agrees that any other use without the site owner's permission is prohibited. If A clicks "agree" and downloads the information and then uses the information for other, prohibited purposes, should not A be bound by the click? It seems the answer properly should be, and would be, yes.

If the owner can show that the only way A could have obtained the information was from his website, and that the process to access the subject information required that A must have clicked the "I agree" button after having the ability to see the conditions on use, A has performed actions which A was free to refuse, which A knew would cause the site to grant her access, i.e., "complete the transaction." The terms of the resulting contract will be determined under general contract principles, but will include the limitation on A's use of the information, as a condition precedent to granting her access to the information.

* * *

NOTES & QUESTIONS

1. *Goods, services and software.* Is software a good or a service or something else altogether? When you purchase software from your local computer software store, have you entered into a sales agreement, a license, or both? Should Article 2 of the *Uniform Commercial Code*, which applies to sales of goods, govern the transaction? *See generally* Lorin Brennan, *Why Article 2 Cannot Apply to Software Transactions,* 38 DUQ. L. REV. 459, 545–77 (2000); Mark A. Lemley, *Intellectual Property and Shrinkwrap Licenses,* 68 S. CAL. L. REV. 1239, 1244 n. 23 (1995). If UCC Article 2 should not apply, then what law should?

2. *Methods of presenting terms.* With both the shrinkwrap licenses at issue in *ProCD v. Zeidenberg*, *Hill v. Gateway*, and *Klocek v. Gateway*, and the clickwrap license at issue in *I.Lan Systems v. Netscout*, the terms that the seller seeks to apply to the transaction are not presented to the buyer until after the purchase. How do these cases differ with respect to the method by which the terms are brought to the purchaser's attention? How do they differ with respect to what action by the purchaser is deemed to constitute a manifestation of assent to the terms? Should these differences be relevant in resolving the contracting issues presented?

3. *UETA's approach.* How would you characterize UETA's approach to clickwrap agreements? Would it require more or less clear evidence of assent than required in *I.Lan Systems v. Netscout*?

3. BROWSEWRAP AGREEMENTS

Pollstar v. Gigmania, Ltd.

170 F.Supp.2d 974 (E.D.Cal.2000).

■ COYLE, DISTRICT JUDGE.

On September 18, 2000 the court heard Defendant Gigmania Ltd.'s ("Gigmania") motion to dismiss the Complaint under Fed.R.Civ.P. 12(b)(6) for failure to state a claim. * * *

Upon due consideration of the written and oral arguments of the parties and the record herein, the court denies Gigmania's motion to dismiss for the reasons set forth herein.

I. Pollstar's Allegations

* * *

Pollstar alleges that it created and developed up-to-the-day time sensitive concert information that was published daily on its website—www.pollstar.com—at great time and expense to itself. By accessing the pollstar.com website, an Internet user can download and use the timely and up-to-date concert information pursuant to conditions of a license agreement. Pollstar alleges that Gigmania downloaded pollstar.com from the Internet and placed information that is copied from the pollstar.com website on its website at www.gigmania.com. * * *

Finally, Pollstar alleges a breach of contract claim. It alleges that any user of its pollstar.com website is immediately confronted with a notice that use of the website is subject to a license agreement, which is set forth on the website. Pollstar states that by clicking on the access button to retrieve any of the information contained in the website, Defendant agreed to be bound by the terms of the License Agreement. Pollstar further alleges that since March 9, 2000 and before, Defendant has downloaded concert information from Plaintiff's website and used the information for commercial purposes in breach of the contract. Finally, Plaintiff alleges that it has been harmed by Defendant's use of its information because it has lost sales of the information to commercial purchasers. * * *

* * *

Motion to Dismiss under Fed.R.Civ.P. 12(b)(6)

* * *

E. Breach of Contract Claim

Gigmania contends that the breach of contract claim fails as a matter of law because Pollstar cannot allege the required contract element of mutual consent. Viewing the website, the court agrees with the defendant that many visitors to the site may not be aware of the license agreement.

Notice of the license agreement is provided by small gray text on a gray background.

Moreover, unlike the shrinkwrap license held enforceable in *ProCD v. Zeidenberg,* 86 F.3d 1447 (7th Cir.1996), the license agreement at issue is a browse wrap license. * * * [A] browse wrap license is part of the website and the user assents to the contract when the user visits the website. No reported cases have ruled on the enforceability of a browse wrap license. However, the Seventh Circuit's opinion in *ProCD* provides some policy considerations that are helpful to the court. * * *

In the present case, Pollstar alleges that users of the concert information are bound by the license agreement. This license agreement is not set forth on the homepage but is on a different web page that is linked to the homepage. However, the visitor is alerted to the fact that "use is subject to license agreement" because of the notice in small gray print on gray background. Since the text is not underlined, a common Internet practice to show an active link, many users presumably are not aware that the license agreement is linked to the homepage. In addition, the homepage also has small blue text which when clicked on, does not link to another page. This may confuse visitors who may then think that all colored small text, regardless of color, do not link the homepage to a different web page.

While the court agrees with Gigmania that the user is not immediately confronted with the notice of the license agreement, this does not dispose of Pollstar's breach of contract claim. The court hesitates to declare the invalidity and unenforceability of the browse wrap license agreement at this time. Taking into consideration the examples provided by the Seventh Circuit—showing that people sometimes enter into a contract by using a service without first seeing the terms—the browser wrap license agreement may be arguably valid and enforceable. * * *

ACCORDINGLY, IT IS ORDERED that Defendant Gigmania's Motion to Dismiss be denied.

Specht v. Netscape Communications Corp.

150 F.Supp.2d 585 (S.D.N.Y.2001).

■ HELLERSTEIN, DISTRICT JUDGE.

Promises become binding when there is a meeting of the minds and consideration is exchanged. So it was at King's Bench in common law England; so it was under the common law in the American colonies; so it was through more than two centuries ~~of jurisprudence in this country;~~ and so it is today. Assent may be registered by a signature, a handshake, or a click of a computer mouse transmitted across the invisible ether of the Internet. Formality is not a requisite; any sign, symbol or action, or even willful inaction, as long as it is unequivocally referable to the promise, may create a contract.

The three related cases before me all involve this timeless issue of assent, but in the context of free software offered on the Internet. If an offeree downloads free software, and the offeror seeks a contractual understanding limiting its uses and applications, under what circumstances does the act of downloading create a contract? On the facts presented here, is there the requisite assent and consideration? My decision focuses on these issues.

In these putative class actions, Plaintiffs allege that usage of the software transmits to Defendants private information about the user's file transfer activity on the Internet, thereby effecting an electronic surveillance of the user's activity in violation of two federal statutes, the Electronic Communications Privacy Act, 18 U.S.C. § 2510 *et seq.*, and the Computer Fraud and Abuse Act, 18 U.S.C. § 1030. Defendants move to compel arbitration and stay the proceedings, arguing that the disputes reflected in the Complaint, like all others relating to use of the software, are subject to a binding arbitration clause in the End User License Agreement ("License Agreement"), the contract allegedly made by the offeror of the software and the party effecting the download. Thus, I am asked to decide if an offer of a license agreement, made independently of freely offered software and not expressly accepted by a user of that software, nevertheless binds the user to an arbitration clause contained in the license.

I. Factual and Procedural Background

Defendant Netscape, a provider of computer software programs that enable and facilitate the use of the Internet, offers its "SmartDownload" software free of charge on its web site to all those who visit the site and indicate, by clicking their mouse in a designated box, that they wish to obtain it. SmartDownload is a program that makes it easier for its users to download files from the Internet without losing their interim progress when they pause to engage in some other task, or if their Internet connection is severed. Four of the six named Plaintiffs—John Gibson, Mark Gruber, Sean Kelly and Sherry Weindorf—selected and clicked in the box indicating a decision to obtain the software, and proceeded to download the software on to the hard drives of their computers. The fifth named Plaintiff, Michael Fagan, allegedly downloaded the software from a "shareware" web site operated by a third party. The sixth named Plaintiff, Christopher Specht, never obtained or used SmartDownload, but merely maintained a web site from which other individuals could download files.

Visitors wishing to obtain SmartDownload from Netscape's web site arrive at a page pertaining to the download of the software. On this page, there appears a tinted box, or button, labeled "Download." By clicking on the box, a visitor initiates the download. The sole reference on this page to the License Agreement appears in text that is visible only if a visitor scrolls down through the page to the next screen. If a visitor does so, he or she sees the following invitation to review the License Agreement:

> Please review and agree to the terms of the *Netscape SmartDownload software license agreement* before downloading and using the software.

Visitors are not required affirmatively to indicate their assent to the License Agreement, or even to view the license agreement, before proceeding with a download of the software. But if a visitor chooses to click on the underlined text in the invitation, a hypertext link takes the visitor to a web page entitled "License & Support Agreements." The first paragraph on this page reads in pertinent part:

> The use of each Netscape software product is governed by a license agreement. You must read and agree to the license agreement terms BEFORE acquiring a product. Please click on the appropriate link below to review the current license agreement for the product of interest to you before acquisition. For products available for download, you must read and agree to the license agreement terms BEFORE you install the software. If you do not agree to the license terms, do not download, install or use the software.

Below the paragraph appears a list of license agreements, the first of which is "*License Agreement for Netscape Navigator and Netscape Communicator Product Family* (Netscape Navigator, Netscape Communicator and Netscape SmartDownload)." If the visitor then clicks on that text, he or she is brought to another web page, this one containing the full text of the License Agreement.

The License Agreement, which has been unchanged throughout the period that Netscape has made SmartDownload available to the public, grants the user a license to use and reproduce SmartDownload, and otherwise contains few restrictions on the use of the software. The first paragraph of the License Agreement describes, in upper case print, the purported manner in which a user accepts or rejects its terms.

> BY CLICKING THE ACCEPTANCE BUTTON OR INSTALLING OR USING NETSCAPE COMMUNICATOR, NETSCAPE NAVIGATOR, OR NETSCAPE SMARTDOWNLOAD SOFTWARE (THE "PRODUCT"), THE INDIVIDUAL OR ENTITY LICENSING THE PRODUCT ("LICENSEE") IS CONSENTING TO BE BOUND BY AND IS BECOMING A PARTY TO THIS AGREEMENT. IF LICENSEE DOES NOT AGREE TO ALL OF THE TERMS OF THIS AGREEMENT, THE BUTTON INDICATING NON-ACCEPTANCE MUST BE SELECTED, AND LICENSEE MUST NOT INSTALL OR USE THE SOFTWARE.

The License Agreement also contains a term requiring that virtually all disputes be submitted to arbitration in Santa Clara County, California.

> Unless otherwise agreed in writing, all disputes relating to this Agreement (excepting any dispute relating to intellectual property rights) shall be subject to final and binding arbitration in Santa Clara County, California, under the auspices of JAMS/EndDispute, with the losing party paying all costs of arbitration.

All users of SmartDownload must use it in connection with Netscape's Internet browser, which may be obtained either as an independent product, Netscape Navigator, or as part of a suite of software, Netscape Communicator. Navigator and Communicator are governed by a single license agreement, which is identical to the License Agreement for SmartDownload. By its terms, the Navigator/Communicator license is limited to disputes "relating to this Agreement."

II. Applicable Law

The Federal Arbitration Act expresses a policy strongly favoring the enforcement of arbitration clauses in contracts.

> A written provision in ... a contract evidencing a transaction involving commerce to settle by arbitration a controversy thereafter arising out of such contract or transaction, or the refusal to perform the whole or any part thereof ... shall be valid, irrevocable, and enforceable, save upon such grounds as exist at law or in equity for the revocation of any contract.

9 U.S.C. § 2. The interpretation of an arbitration agreement is governed by the federal substantive law of arbitration. * * * On this basis, Defendants argue that this motion properly is analyzed using the federal common law regarding the arbitrability of disputes, and that such federal common law "simply 'comprises generally accepted principles of contract law.'" *McPheeters v. McGinn, Smith & Co.,* 953 F.2d 771, 772 (2d Cir.1992) (citations omitted).

However, Defendants' approach elides the distinction between two separate analytical steps. First, I must determine whether the parties entered into a binding contract. Only if I conclude that a contract exists do I proceed to a second stage of analysis: interpretation of the arbitration clause and its applicability to the present case. The first stage of the analysis—whether a contract was formed—is a question of state law. If, under the law, a contract is formed, the interpretation of the scope of an arbitration clause in the contract is a question of federal law.

In determining which state law to apply, I look first to the choice-of-law doctrine of the forum state, New York. Under New York's choice-of-law rules, when determining which state's law to apply to a contract dispute, "the court evaluates the 'center of gravity' or 'grouping of contacts,' with the purpose of establishing which state has 'the most significant relationship to the transaction and the parties.'" * * * Although the record evidence on this point is sparse at best, * * * I conclude that California has the most significant connection to the litigation, and I apply California law to the issue of contract formation.

By its terms, Article 2 of the Uniform Commercial Code "applies to transactions in goods." *See* Cal. Com.Code § 2102. The parties' relationship essentially is that of a seller and a purchaser of goods. Although in this case the product was provided free of charge,[8] the roles are essentially the same

8. In order to form a contract, parties must exchange some consideration. "Among the limitations on the enforcement of promises, the most fundamental is the requirement of consideration." E. Allan Farnsworth, *Farnsworth on Contracts* § 2.2 (2d ed.2000). In general, "the formation of a contract requires a bargain in which there is a manifes-

as when an individual uses the Internet to purchase software from a company: here, the Plaintiff requested Defendant's product by clicking on an icon marked "Download," and Defendant then tendered the product. Therefore, in determining whether the parties entered into a contract, I look to California law as it relates to the sale of goods, including the Uniform Commercial Code in effect in California.

III. Did Plaintiffs Consent to Arbitration?

Unless the Plaintiffs agreed to the License Agreement, they cannot be bound by the arbitration clause contained therein. My inquiry, therefore, focuses on whether the Plaintiffs, through their acts or failures to act, manifested their assent to the terms of the License Agreement proposed by Defendant Netscape. More specifically, I must consider whether the web site gave Plaintiffs sufficient notice of the existence and terms of the License Agreement, and whether the act of downloading the software sufficiently manifested Plaintiffs' assent to be bound by the License Agreement. I will address separately the factually distinct circumstances of Plaintiffs Michael Fagan and Christopher Specht.

In order for a contract to become binding, both parties must assent to be bound. "[C]ourts have required that assent to the formation of a contract be manifested in some way, by words or other conduct, if it is to be effective." E. Allan Farnsworth, *Farnsworth on Contracts* § 3.1 (2d ed.2000). "To form a contract, a manifestation of mutual assent is necessary. Mutual assent may be manifested by written or spoken words, or by conduct." *Binder v. Aetna Life Ins. Co.*, 75 Cal.App.4th 832, 850, 89 Cal.Rptr.2d 540, 551 (Cal.Ct.App.1999) (citations omitted). "A contract for sale of goods may be made in any manner sufficient to show agreement, including conduct by both parties which recognizes the existence of such a contract." Cal. Com.Code § 2204.

These principles enjoy continuing vitality in the realm of software licensing. The sale of software, in stores, by mail, and over the Internet, has resulted in several specialized forms of license agreements. For example, software commonly is packaged in a container or wrapper that advises the purchaser that the use of the software is subject to the terms of a license agreement contained inside the package. The license agreement generally explains that, if the purchaser does not wish to enter into a contract, he or she must return the product for a refund, and that failure to return it within a certain period will constitute assent to the license terms. These so-called "shrink-wrap licenses" have been the subject of considerable litigation.

In *ProCD, Inc. v. Zeidenberg*, for example, the Seventh Circuit Court of Appeals considered a software license agreement "encoded on the CD–ROM

tation of mutual assent to the exchange and a consideration." *Restatement (Second) of Contracts*, § 17. The apparent failure of consideration on Plaintiff's side—put simply, Plaintiff's obtaining SmartDownload without giving anything in return—might support a finding that no contract exists. However, because I rely on other grounds to find that the parties did not enter into a contract, *see infra*, I need not decide this issue.

disks as well as printed in the manual, and which appears on a user's screen every time the software runs." 86 F.3d 1447, 1450 (7th Cir.1996). The absence of contract terms on the outside of the box containing the software was not material, since "[e]very box containing [the software] declares that the software comes with restrictions stated in an enclosed license." *Id.* The court accepted that placing all of the contract terms on the outside of the box would have been impractical, and held that the transaction, even though one "in which the exchange of money precedes the communication of detailed terms," was valid, in part because the software could not be used unless and until the offeree was shown the license and manifested his assent. *Id.* at 1451–52.

* * * The court concluded that "[s]hrinkwrap licenses are enforceable unless their terms are objectionable on grounds applicable to contracts in general (for example, if they violate a rule of positive law, or if they are unconscionable)." *Id.* at 1449.[9]

The Seventh Circuit expanded this holding in *Hill v. Gateway 2000, Inc.,* 105 F.3d 1147 (7th Cir.1997), *cert. denied*, 522 U.S. 808 (1997). * * * The court held that the manufacturer, Gateway, "may invite acceptance by conduct," and that "[b]y keeping the computer beyond 30 days, the Hills accepted Gateway's offer, including the arbitration clause." *Id.* at 1149, 1150.[10] Although not mentioned in the decision, the customer, by seeking to take advantage of the warranty provisions contained in the license agreement, thus could be fairly charged with the arbitration clause as well. It bears noting that unlike the plaintiffs in *Hill* and *Brower,* who grounded their claims on express warranties contained in the contracts, the Plaintiffs in this case base their claims on alleged privacy rights independent of the License Agreement for SmartDownload.

Not all courts to confront the issue have enforced shrink-wrap license agreements. In *Klocek v. Gateway, Inc.,* the court considered a standard shrink-wrap license agreement that was included in the box containing the computer ordered by the plaintiff. 104 F.Supp.2d 1332 (D.Kan.2000). The court held that Kansas and Missouri courts probably would not follow *Hill* or *ProCD, supra.* * * * Therefore, the court held, the plaintiff did not agree to the license terms and could not be compelled to arbitrate. *Id.* at 1341.

For most of the products it makes available over the Internet (but not SmartDownload), Netscape uses another common type of software license, one usually identified as "click-wrap" licensing. A click-wrap license presents the user with a message on his or her computer screen, requiring that the user manifest his or her assent to the terms of the license agreement by

9. In a breach-of-warranty suit involving software, the Supreme Court of Washington, *en banc,* enforced a license agreement that, like the agreement at issue in *ProCD,* was presented on the user's computer screen each time the software was used, and also was located on the outside of each diskette pouch and on the inside cover of the instruction manuals. *See M.A. Mortenson Co., Inc. v. Timberline Software Corp.,* 140 Wash.2d 568, 998 P.2d 305 (Wash.2000).

10. *See also Brower v. Gateway 2000, Inc.,* 246 A.D.2d 246, 676 N.Y.S.2d 569 (N.Y.App.Div.1998) (in suit for breach of warranty, enforcing shrink-wrap license agreement identical to that in *Hill*).

clicking on an icon. The product cannot be obtained or used unless and until the icon is clicked. For example, when a user attempts to obtain Netscape's Communicator or Navigator, a web page appears containing the full text of the Communicator/Navigator license agreement. Plainly visible on the screen is the query, "Do you accept all the terms of the preceding license agreement? If so, click on the Yes button. If you select No, Setup will close." Below this text are three button or icons: one labeled "Back" and used to return to an earlier step of the download preparation; one labeled "No," which if clicked, terminates the download; and one labeled "Yes," which if clicked, allows the download to proceed. Unless the user clicks "Yes," indicating his or her assent to the license agreement, the user cannot obtain the software. The few courts that have had occasion to consider click-wrap contracts have held them to be valid and enforceable. *See, e.g., In re RealNetworks, Inc. Privacy Litigation,* 2000 WL 631341 (N.D.Ill. May 8, 2000); *Hotmail Corp. v. Van$Money Pie, Inc.,* No. C 98–20064, 1998 WL 388389 (N.D.Cal. April 16, 1998).

A third type of software license, "browse-wrap," was considered by a California federal court in *Pollstar v. Gigmania Ltd.,* 2000 WL 33266437 (E.D.Cal. Oct.17, 2000). In *Pollstar,* the plaintiff's web page offered allegedly proprietary information. Notice of a license agreement appears on the plaintiff's web site. Clicking on the notice links the user to a separate web page containing the full text of the license agreement, which allegedly binds any user of the information on the site. However, the user is not required to click on an icon expressing assent to the license, or even view its terms, before proceeding to use the information on the site. The court referred to this arrangement as a "browse-wrap" license. The defendant allegedly copied proprietary information from the site. The plaintiff sued for breach of the license agreement, and the defendant moved to dismiss for lack of mutual assent sufficient to form a contract. The court, although denying the defendant's motion to dismiss, expressed concern about the enforceability of the browse-wrap license.[13] * * *

The SmartDownload License Agreement in the case before me differs fundamentally from both click-wrap and shrink-wrap licensing, and resembles more the browse-wrap license of *Pollstar*. Where click-wrap license agreements * * * require users to perform an affirmative action unambiguously expressing assent *before* they may use the software, that affirmative action is equivalent to an express declaration stating, "I assent to the terms

13. Judge Barbara Jones of this Court considered a similar license arrangement in *Register.com v. Verio, Inc.,* 126 F.Supp.2d 238 (S.D.N.Y.2000) (Jones, J.). The plaintiff posted license terms on its web site, alongside a statement that "[b]y submitting this query [to the plaintiff's database], you agree to abide by these terms." *Id.* at 248. The court held that, "in light of this sentence at the end of Register.com's terms of use, there can be no question that by proceeding to submit a [] query, Verio manifested its assent to be bound by Register.com's terms of use, and a contract was formed and subsequently breached." *Id.* Judge Jones was applying New York law. *Id.* at 241. Here, I am applying California law. But, whether under California or New York law, the promissee's assent to be bound is a required condition, and I find no such assent on the facts presented in this case.

and conditions of the license agreement" or something similar. For example, Netscape's Navigator will not function without a prior clicking of a box constituting assent. Netscape's SmartDownload, in contrast, allows a user to download and use the software without taking any action that plainly manifests assent to the terms of the associated license or indicates an understanding that a contract is being formed.

California courts carefully limit the circumstances under which a party may be bound to a contract. "[A]n offeree, regardless of apparent manifestation of his consent, is not bound by inconspicuous contractual provisions of which he was unaware, contained in a document whose contractual nature is not obvious.... This principle of knowing consent applies with particular force to provisions for arbitration." *Windsor Mills, Inc. v. Collins & Aikman Corp.*, 25 Cal.App.3d 987, 993, 101 Cal.Rptr. 347 (Cal.Ct.App. 1972).

Netscape argues that the mere act of downloading indicates assent. However, downloading is hardly an unambiguous indication of assent. The primary purpose of downloading is to obtain a product, not to assent to an agreement. In contrast, clicking on an icon stating "I assent" has no meaning or purpose other than to indicate such assent. Netscape's failure to require users of SmartDownload to indicate assent to its license as a precondition to downloading and using its software is fatal to its argument that a contract has been formed.

Furthermore, unlike the user of Netscape Navigator or other click-wrap or shrink-wrap licensees, the individual obtaining SmartDownload is not made aware that he is entering into a contract. SmartDownload is available from Netscape's web site free of charge. Before downloading the software, the user need not view any license agreement terms or even any reference to a license agreement, and need not do anything to manifest assent to such a license agreement other than actually taking possession of the product. From the user's vantage point, SmartDownload could be analogized to a free neighborhood newspaper, readily obtained from a sidewalk box or supermarket counter without any exchange with a seller or vender. It is there for the taking.

The only hint that a contract is being formed is one small box of text referring to the license agreement, text that appears below the screen used for downloading and that a user need not even see before obtaining the product:

> Please review and agree to the terms of the *Netscape SmartDownload software license agreement* before downloading and using the software.

Couched in the mild request, "Please review," this language reads as a mere invitation, not as a condition. The language does not indicate that a user *must* agree to the license terms before downloading and using the software. While clearer language appears in the License Agreement itself, the language of the invitation does not require the reading of those terms[14] or provide adequate notice either that a contract is being created or that the terms of the License Agreement will bind the user. * * *

IV. Plaintiff Michael Fagan

Unlike most of his fellow Plaintiffs, Michael Fagan alleges that he obtained SmartDownload from a shareware web site established and managed by a third party. Defendants dispute Fagan's allegations, insisting that the record shows that he must have obtained SmartDownload from Netscape's web site in the same manner as the other Plaintiffs discussed above. I need not resolve this factual dispute. If Fagan in fact obtained SmartDownload from the Netscape site, his claims are equally subject to my earlier analysis. If, however, Fagan's version of events is accurate, his argument against arbitration is stronger than that of the other Plaintiffs. While Netscape's download page for SmartDownload contains a single brief and ambiguous reference to the License Agreement, with a link to the text of the agreement, the ZDNet site contains not even such a reference.[15] The site visitor is invited to click on a hypertext link to "more information" about SmartDownload. The link leads to a Netscape web page, which in turn contains a link to the License Agreement. Assuming, for the sake of argument, that Fagan obtained SmartDownload from ZDNet, he was even less likely than the other Plaintiffs to be aware that he was entering into a contract or what its terms might be, and even less likely to have assented to be bound by the License Agreement and its arbitration clause. Therefore, Plaintiff Michael Fagan cannot be compelled to arbitrate his claims.[16] * * *

VI. Conclusion

For the reasons stated, I deny Defendants' motion to compel arbitration. * * *

14. Defendants argue that this case resembles the situation where a party has failed to read a contract and is nevertheless bound by that contract. This argument misses the point. The question before me is whether the parties have first bound themselves to the contract. If they have unequivocally agreed to be bound, the contract is enforceable whether or not they have read its terms.

15. Various companies and individuals maintain "shareware" websites containing libraries of free, publicly available software. The ZDNet site library included SmartDownload. The pages that a user would see in downloading SmartDownload from ZDNet, however, differ from the pages that a user would see in downloading SmartDownload directly from the Netscape web site. Notably, there is no reference to the License Agreement on the ZDNet pages, merely a hypertext link to "more information" about SmartDownload, which, if clicked, takes the user to a Netscape web page which, in turn, contains a link to the License Agreement. In other words, an individual could obtain SmartDownload from ZDNet without ever seeing a reference to the License Agreement, even if he or she viewed all of ZDNet's web pages. [Relocated footnote.—Eds.]

16. Netscape's acquiescence to the distribution of the SmartDownload software through shareware sites such as ZDNet—sites containing minimal or no reference to the License Agreement—demonstrates its indifference to obtaining users' assent to the terms of the License Agreement.

NOTES & QUESTIONS

1. *Reason to know.* In *Klocek,* a case involving a shrinkwrap agreement, as well as in *Pollstar* and *Specht*, cases involving browsewrap agreements, the courts voiced concern that the licensors had not given their purported licensees sufficient notice of the licensing terms that the licensors sought to enforce. How important is notice that a product's use is governed by a license to the enforceability of that license? Is it a sufficient condition on enforceability, a necessary condition on enforceability, or neither? In a similar case, one court reasoned:

> The motion to dismiss the second claim (breach of contract) is founded on the "terms and conditions" set forth on the home page of the Ticketmaster site. This provides that anyone going beyond the home page agrees to the terms and conditions set forth, which include that the information is for personal use only, may not be used for commercial purposes, and no deep linking to the site is permitted. In defending this claim, Ticketmaster makes reference to the "shrinkwrap license" cases, where the packing on the outside of the CD stated that opening the package constitutes adherence to the license agreement (restricting republication) contained therein. This has been held to be enforceable. That is not the same as this case because the "shrink-wrap license agreement" is open and obvious and in fact hard to miss. Many websites make you click on "agree" to the terms and conditions before going on, but Ticketmaster does not. Further, the terms and conditions are set forth so that the customer needs to scroll down the home page to find and read them. Many customers instead are likely to proceed to the event page of interest rather than reading the "small print." It cannot be said that merely putting the terms and conditions in this fashion necessarily creates a contract with any one using the website. The motion is granted with leave to amend in case there are facts showing Tickets' knowledge of them plus facts showing implied agreement to them.

Ticketmaster Corp. v. Tickets.Com, Inc., 2000 WL 525390, *3 (C.D.Cal. 2000).

2. *Terms and conditions of use.* A large proportion of commercial websites today contain a hyperlink at the bottom of their homepage labeled something like "Conditions of Use" or "Terms of Use" (or sometimes just "Terms"). Many websites also have another hyperlink labeled "Privacy Policy." These hyperlinks link to web pages containing an agreement on the terms and conditions for use of the website and the website's privacy policy, respectively. Based upon the cases excerpted above, are such terms and policies binding on the users of the website? Should an agreement setting forth the terms and conditions of use be treated differently from a posted privacy policy?

3. *E-commerce website audits.* Assume that the plaintiff in *Pollstar v. Gigmania* and the defendant in *Specht v. Netscape* each employed a lawyer to draft the license whose enforceability was at issue. Assume further that the lawyer drafted the license and sent it to the client, which then passed it along to the company's web development team to post on the website. Do these cases suggest that proper lawyering requires attention not only to the text of an agreement, but also to its presentation? (Would the license agreements in these cases have been held enforceable if they had been presented as clickwrap agreements, requiring the user to click "I Agree" before allowing access to the material on the websites?)

4. UCITA ON CONTRACT FORMATION

The primary questions presented in the shrinkwrap, clickwrap, and browsewrap cases discussed above are (1) Under what circumstances is a contract formed when some of the terms are disclosed only after the purchase?, and (2) What are the terms of contracts formed in this manner? UCITA attempts to resolve these questions.

UCITA's rules on contract formation seem to be informed by a few key premises:

First, the formation of a contract, and determination of the terms of a contract, are two separate events. A given action might bring about either one or the other of these events, or both simultaneously.

Second, contracts may be formed, and terms may become contract terms, as a result of various kinds of conduct by the parties, including a failure to act.

Third, contract formation is a process that can take place over an extended period of time. Formation and determination of terms need not occur at a single point in time. Contracts may be formed in a series of layers.

As we saw in Part I(A), *supra*, UCITA's basic rule of contract formation is stated in Section 202: A contract may be formed in any manner sufficient to show agreement. § 202(a). In particular, a contract may be formed by interaction of a person with a website or some other electronic agent. This occurs if the person takes some action that he should know the electronic agent will interpret as acceptance. § 206(b). It does not matter if some terms are left open: consistent with the principle that contract formation is a different event from determination of contract terms, the existence of open terms does not defeat contract formation. § 202(b), (c).

Section 202 also directly addresses the situation where terms are provided after the commencement of the transaction. If the parties intend that formation of a contract is to be contingent on their agreement upon some term that is not yet settled, and if the parties are later unable to agree with respect to that term, then no contract is formed. In that case, the transaction must be unwound: the purchaser gives back or destroys the information product, and the seller gives back the purchaser's money. § 202(e).

If the parties do agree on the post-purchase terms, a contract is formed. But what are its terms? Sections 208 and 209 are relevant here. Some of those terms will have been agreed to in the initial contacts between the parties, leading up to contract formation. In the case of a contract formed as contemplated by Section 202(e), where the parties agree that the contract will be formed only if they subsequently agree upon some yet-unadopted term, then agreement on that term both forms the contract and makes that term part of the contract. Even after the contract is formed, additional "layers" of terms may be added to it.

These terms become part of the contract through the parties' manifestation of assent to them. According to Section 208(1), if a party manifests assent to a record, then the terms of the record become terms of the contract. (A "record" is information stored in a document, electronic or paper. § 101(a)(55).) This can occur after beginning performance, as long as the parties expected there would be additional terms presented after that point in time; but if formation of the contract was intended to be contingent on agreement to such terms, then (as we already know from Section 202(e)) if there is no agreement, a contract is not formed. § 208(2).

What, then, constitutes manifestation of assent to a record? This is governed by Section 112, which says that there is a manifestation of assent if three requirements are satisfied. (Section 112 is set forth in Part I(D), *infra*.)

First, the assenting party must have an opportunity to review the terms to which she is assenting. § 112(a). The party is deemed to have an opportunity to review if two conditions are satisfied. First, the terms must be presented in a manner that ought to call them to the attention of a reasonable person. § 112(e)(1). Second, if the party is presented with the terms only after contract performance begins, she must be accorded a right to return the product if she does not agree with those terms. § 112(e)(3). This is the right of return that Judge Easterbrook assumed to exist in *ProCD v. Zeidenberg*, *supra*.

A special, safe-harbor rule regarding pre-transaction opportunity to review applies in the case of a transaction via a website. If the terms of a standard-form license are presented before payment or delivery, the purchaser is deemed to have an opportunity to review them as long as the terms, or a reference to them, are displayed "prominently and in close proximity" to the description of the product or to the ordering instructions. In other words, if the terms themselves, or a hyperlink to the terms, or apparently just a URL indicating where the terms can be found, is placed in plain view when the purchaser is considering the purchase, then she is deemed to have an opportunity to review them. § 211(1)(A). In addition, it is sufficient if the seller discloses the availability of the terms "in a prominent place on the site," and furnishes a copy promptly upon request. § 211(1)(B). Apparently this means all the seller has to do is state somewhere on the home page of the website that all standard-form terms are available upon request by writing to a specified postal address.

Second, the assenting party must take some action to indicate assent. § 112(a)(2). But that action might consist of inaction. According to the Official Comment: "Assent occurs if a person acts *or fails to act* having reason to know its behavior will be viewed by the other party as indicating assent." § 112, cmt. 3(b) (emphasis added). So a failure to return your computer after five days, as occurred in *Hill v. Gateway*, might constitute an indication of assent.

Third, the manifestation of assent has to be attributable to the assenting party. This is determined under general agency law.

Note what manifestation of assent does *not* require. The purchaser need not realize that the terms are available for her to review: it is enough that the terms are made available in a manner that ought to call them to the attention of a reasonable person. She need not actually read the record to which she is assenting. If she does read the terms, she need not understand them. She need not intend to assent to the terms: it is enough if she "intentionally engages in conduct or makes statements with reason to know that the other party or its electronic agent *may* infer from the conduct or statement that the person assents to the record or term." § 112(a)(2) (emphasis added). She need not take any action: in proper circumstances, inaction will suffice.

Some special rules apply in the case of transactions between a merchant and a consumer (or a consumer-like business purchaser) involving a standard-form contract—called "mass-market transactions." § 102(a)(45). (UCITA's treatment of this class of transactions is examined in more detail in Part II, *infra*. For discussion of UCITA from the standpoint of consumer protection, *see* Chapter 6, Part IV, *infra*.) First, manifestation of assent to the terms of such a form can only occur before or during the purchaser's initial use of the product. § 209(a). For example, if the product is a software program, then the terms must be presented to the consumer the first time he runs the program. Second, a term does not become part of the contract if it is "unconscionable," as UCITA defines the word. § 209(a)(1). Third, a term does not become part of the contract if it conflicts with a term on which the parties expressly agreed earlier in the transaction—probably limited to express agreements in writing, since a parol evidence rule comes into play here. § 209(a)(2). Fourth, if the consumer chooses to exercise his right of return, upon disagreeing with the post-purchase terms, the vendor must pay the consumer's reasonable costs of returning the item and of restoring his computer to its condition before installing the product. § 209(b).

D. CAPACITY TO CONTRACT, AGENCY, AND MACHINE-TO-MACHINE CONTRACTS

A common scenario of Internet commerce involves a human buyer communicating with a computer in order to purchase some goods or services. Consider, for example, a person buying a book from an online book retailer such as Amazon.com or Barnesandnoble.com. The book buyer never communicates with another human being. No human agent of the corporation manifests an intent to sell and ship the book in exchange for payment. The question naturally arises, therefore, whether a person can enter into a contract by negotiating with a computer, that is, by making an offer to or accepting an offer from an electronic agent of a human or corporate principal. What is the legal status of an online order recorded by a machine?

Until recently, the common law and commercial codes presumed that the parties actually negotiating would be individual human beings or legal entities (such as corporations and partnerships) that act through their human agents. Neither legislature nor court had contemplated the rise of electronic commerce and the possibility that a prospective purchaser (or seller) might be negotiating with a machine. Accordingly, the applicability to this situation of rules regarding legal capacity to contract was unclear. Was it possible to form a contract by communicating with a machine? And if so, was it binding or voidable?

The notions of agreement and the manifestation of assent stand at the heart of the law of contract. In this section we explore the transformation of these notions as transactions move online. We begin with UCITA's innovative approach to the idea of manifesting assent, in which interactions between humans are treated in the same provisions that treat interactions between human and machine and interactions between two machines. Compare UCITA's approach with that of UETA and ESIGN, which follow.

We then consider whether a computer software program can be viewed as the legal agent of its owner or licensee. As we shall see, whether a machine or software program can be the legal agent of a human or corporate principal is equally controversial and obscure.

Uniform Computer Information Transactions Act, §§ 112, 206 & 102(a)(27)

National Conference of Commissioners on Uniform State Laws.
(2000).

SECTION 112. MANIFESTING ASSENT; OPPORTUNITY TO REVIEW

(a) A person manifests assent to a record or term if the person, acting with knowledge of, or after having an opportunity to review the record or term or a copy of it:

(1) authenticates the record or term with intent to adopt or accept it; or

(2) intentionally engages in conduct or makes statements with reason to know that the other party or its electronic agent may infer from the conduct or statement that the person assents to the record or term.

(b) An electronic agent manifests assent to a record or term if, after having an opportunity to review it, the electronic agent:

(1) authenticates the record or term; or

(2) engages in operations that in the circumstances indicate acceptance of the record or term.

(c) If this [Act] or other law requires assent to a specific term, a manifestation of assent must relate specifically to the term.

(d) Conduct or operations manifesting assent may be proved in any manner, including a showing that a person or an electronic agent obtained or used the information or informational rights and that a procedure existed by which a person or an electronic agent must have engaged in the conduct or operations in order to do so. Proof of compliance with subsection (a)(2) is sufficient if there is conduct that assents and subsequent conduct that reaffirms assent by electronic means.

(e) With respect to an opportunity to review, the following rules apply:

(1) A person has an opportunity to review a record or term only if it is made available in a manner that ought to call it to the attention of a reasonable person and permit review.

(2) An electronic agent has an opportunity to review a record or term only if it is made available in manner that would enable a reasonably configured electronic agent to react to the record or term.

(3) If a record or term is available for review only after a person becomes obligated to pay or begins its performance, the person has an opportunity to review only if it has a right to a return if it rejects the record. However, a right to a return is not required if:

(A) the record proposes a modification of contract or provides particulars of performance under Section 305; or

(B) the primary performance is other than delivery or acceptance of a copy, the agreement is not a mass-market transaction, and the parties at the time of contracting had reason to know that a record or term would be presented after performance, use, or access to the information began.

* * *

Official Comment

* * *

2. **General Theme.** The term "manifesting assent" comes from *Restatement (Second) of Contracts* § 19. * * *

* * *

3. **Manifesting Assent.**

* * *

c. **Assent by Electronic Agents.** Assent may occur through automated systems ("electronic agents"). Either or both parties (including consumers) may use electronic agents. For electronic agents, assent cannot be based on knowledge or reason to know, since computer programs are capable of neither and the automated nature of the interaction may mean that no individual is aware of it. Subsection (b) focuses on the electronic agent's acts, not knowledge or reason to know. Assent occurs if the agent's operations were an authentication or if, in the circumstances, the operations indicate assent. In this Act, manifesting assent requires a prior opportunity to review. For an electronic agent, this opportunity occurs only if the record or term was presented in such a way that a reasonably configured electronic agent could react to it. Subsection (e)(2). The capability of an automated system to react and an assessment of the implications of its actions are the only appropriate measures of assent.

* * *

SECTION 206. OFFER AND ACCEPTANCE: ELECTRONIC AGENTS.

(a) A contract may be formed by the interaction of electronic agents. If the interaction results in the electronic agents' engaging in operations that under the circumstances indicate acceptance of an offer, a contract is formed, but a court may grant appropriate relief if the operations resulted from fraud, electronic mistake, or the like.

(b) A contract may be formed by the interaction of an electronic agent and an individual acting on the individual's own behalf or for another person. A contract is formed if the individual takes an action or makes a statement that the individual can refuse to take or say and that the individual has reason to know will:

(1) cause the electronic agent to perform, provide benefits, or allow the use or access that is the subject of the contract, or send instructions to do so; or

(2) indicate acceptance, regardless of other expressions or actions by the individual to which the individual has reason to know the electronic agent cannot react.

(c) The terms of a contract formed under subsection (b) are determined under §§ 208 or 209 but do not include a term provided by the individual if the individual had reason to know that the electronic agent could not react to the term.

Official Comment

* * *

2. **Interaction of Electronic Agents.** Interaction of electronic agents creates a contract if the parties use the agents for that purpose and the operations of the electronic agents indicate that a contract exists. Conduct, even automated, can create a contract. Whether a contract is formed focuses on the operations of the agents. The issue is whether those operations indicate that a contract is formed, such as by sending and

receiving the benefits of the contract, initiating orders, or indicating in records that a contract exists. The terms of the contract are determined under §§ 208 and 209 as applicable. However, a contract is formed only by operations taken with respect to a legally significant event. An electronic agent may accept an offer, but acceptance of a message that is not an offer (such as an advertisement) does not form a contract.

3. **Electronic Mistake and Fraud.** Under subsection (a), restrictions analogous to common law concepts of fraud and mistake are made applicable to this automated context to prevent abuse or clearly unexpected results. Of course, parties may allocate risk of mistake or fraud in an agreement.

Assent does not occur if the operations are induced by mistake, fraud or the like, such as where a party or its electronic agent manipulates the programming or response of the other electronic agent in a manner akin to fraud. Such acts vitiate the assent that would occur through normal operations of the agent. Similarly, the inference is vitiated if, because of aberrant programming or through an unexpected interaction of the two agents, operations indicating existence of a contract occur in circumstances that are not within the reasonable contemplation of the parties. Such circumstances are analogous to mutual mistake. Courts applying these concepts should refer to mistake or fraud doctrine, even though an electronic agent cannot actually be said to have been misled or mistaken.

4. **Interaction of Human and Electronic Agent.** Contracts may be formed by interaction of an individual (human being) and an electronic agent. Subsection (b) does not define all cases where this can occur or the results of all interactions, such as where the individual is not aware that he is dealing with an electronic agent. The section describes one setting with two elements: (1) an electronic agent programmed to make contracts, and (2) an individual, having the ability not to do so, engaging in conduct or making a statement with reason to know that this will cause the electronic agent to provide the benefits of the contract or otherwise indicate acceptance. If the individual is dealing with an electronic agent, it may be that not all statements or actions by the individual can be reacted to by the electronic agent. A contract is formed if the human makes statements or engages in conduct that indicate assent. Statements purporting to alter or vitiate agreement to which the electronic agent cannot react are ineffective.

> **Illustration.** Officer dials the telephone information system using the company credit card. A computerized voice states: "If you would like us to dial your number, press '1'; there will be an additional charge of $1.00. If you would like to dial yourself, press '2.' " Officer states into the phone that the company will not pay the $1.00 additional charge, but will pay .50. Having stated these conditions, Officer strikes "1." The computer dials the number. User's "counter offer" is ineffective, because Officer has reason to know that the program cannot react to the counter offer. The charge to dial the number includes the additional $1.00.

SECTION 102. DEFINITIONS

(a) In this [Act]: * * *

(27) "Electronic agent" means a computer program, or electronic or other automated means, used independently to initiate an action, or to respond to electronic messages or performances, on the person's behalf without review or action by an individual at the time of the action or response to the message or performance.

* * *

Official Comment

* * *

23. "Electronic agent." This term refers to an automated means for making or performing contracts. The agent must act independently in a manner relevant to creating or performing a contract. Mere use of a telephone or e-mail system is not use of an electronic agent. The automated system must have been selected, programmed or otherwise intentionally used for that purpose by the person that is bound by its operations. The legal relationship between the person and the electronic agent is not equivalent to common law agency since the "agent" is not a human. However, parties that use electronic agents are ordinarily bound by the results of their operations.

* * *

Uniform Electronic Transactions Act, § 14

[This section is presented in Part I(C)(2), *supra*.]

Uniform Electronic Transactions Act, §§ 2(2), 2(3), 2(5) & 2(6)

National Conference of Commissioners on Uniform State Laws.
(1999).

SECTION 2. DEFINITIONS

In this [Act]:

* * *

(2) "Automated transaction" means a transaction conducted or performed, in whole or in part, by electronic means or electronic records, in which the acts or records of one or both parties are not reviewed by an individual in the ordinary course in forming a contract, performing under an existing contract, or fulfilling an obligation required by the transaction.

(3) "Computer program" means a set of statements or instructions to be used directly or indirectly in an information processing system in order to bring about a certain result.

* * *

(5) "Electronic" means relating to technology having electrical, digital, magnetic, wireless, optical, electromagnetic, or similar capabilities.

(6) "Electronic agent" means a computer program or an electronic or other automated means used independently to initiate an action or respond to electronic records or performances in whole or in part, without review or action by an individual.

* * *

Comment

* * *

2. **"Automated Transaction."** An automated transaction is a transaction performed or conducted by electronic means in which machines are used without human intervention to form contracts and perform obligations under existing contracts. Such broad coverage is necessary because of the diversity of transactions to which this Act may apply.

As with electronic agents, this definition addresses the circumstance where electronic records may result in action or performance by a party although no human review of the electronic records is anticipated. Section 14 provides specific rules to assure that where one or both parties do not review the electronic records, the resulting agreement will be effective.

The critical element in this definition is the lack of a human actor on one or both sides of a transaction. For example, if one orders books from Bookseller.com through Bookseller's website, the transaction would be an automated transaction because Bookseller took and confirmed the order via its machine. Similarly, if Automaker and supplier do business through Electronic Data Interchange, Automaker's computer, upon receiving information within certain pre-programmed parameters, will send an electronic order to supplier's computer. If Supplier's computer confirms the order and processes the shipment because the order falls within pre-programmed parameters in Supplier's computer, this would be a fully automated transaction. If, instead, the Supplier relies on a human employee to review, accept, and process the Buyer's order, then only the Automaker's side of the transaction would be automated. In either case, the entire transaction falls within this definition.

* * *

4. **"Electronic."** The basic nature of most current technologies and the need for a recognized, single term warrants the use of "electronic" as the defined term. The definition is intended to assure that the Act will be applied broadly as new technologies develop. While not all technologies listed are technically "electronic" in nature (e.g., optical fiber technology), the term "electronic" is the most descriptive term available to describe the majority of current technologies. For example, the development of biological and chemical processes for communication and storage of data, while not specifically mentioned in the definition, are included within the technical definition because such processes operate on electromagnetic impulses.

However, whether a particular technology may be characterized as technically "electronic," i.e., operates on electromagnetic impulses, should not be determinative of whether records and signatures created, used and stored by means of a particular technology are covered by this Act. This Act is intended to apply to all records and signatures created, used and stored by any medium which permits the information to be retrieved in perceivable form.

5. **"Electronic agent."** This definition establishes that an electronic agent is a machine. As the term "electronic agent" has come to be recognized, it is limited to a tool function. * * *

An electronic agent, such as a computer program or other automated means employed by a person, is a tool of that person. As a general rule, the employer of a tool is responsible for the results obtained by the use of that tool since the tool has no independent volition of its own. However, an electronic agent, by definition, is capable within the parameters of its programming, of initiating, responding or interacting with other parties or their electronic agents once it has been activated by a party, without further attention of that party.

While this Act proceeds on the paradigm that an electronic agent is capable of performing only within the technical strictures of its preset programming, it is conceivable that, within the useful life of this Act, electronic agents may be created with the ability to act autonomously, and not just automatically. That is, through developments in artificial intelligence, a computer may be able to "learn through experience, modify the instructions in their own programs, and even devise new instructions." Allen and Widdison, "Can Computers Make Contracts"? 9 Harv. J.L. & Tech 25 (Winter, 1996). If such developments occur, courts may construe the definition of electronic agent accordingly, in order to recognize such new capabilities.

* * *

Electronic Signatures in Global and National Commerce Act, §§ 101(h) & 106(3)

15 U.S.C. §§ 7001(h) & 7006(3).

SEC. 101. GENERAL RULE OF VALIDITY

* * *

(h) Electronic agents. A contract or other record relating to a transaction in or affecting interstate or foreign commerce may not be denied legal effect, validity, or enforceability solely because its formation, creation, or delivery involved the action of one or more electronic agents so long as the action of any such electronic agent is legally attributable to the person to be bound.

* * *

SEC. 106. DEFINITIONS

* * *

(3) Electronic agent. The term "electronic agent" means a computer program or an electronic or other automated means used independently to initiate an action or respond to electronic records or performances in whole or in part without review or action by an individual at the time of the action or response.

* * *

Stephen T. Middlebrook & John Muller, *Thoughts on Bots: The Emerging Law of Electronic Agents*

56 BUS. LAW. 341 (2000).

* * *

AN INTRODUCTION TO BOTS

Bot is not a rigorously defined term. It is, as you may have guessed, a shortened form of the word robot. Bots are like robots for the Internet, constructed of software, however, rather than hardware. They roam cyberspace accomplishing whatever tasks their masters have set for them. Bot refers to a broad range of software which is frequently divided into narrower, but still imprecisely delineated categories. Consequently, one may read about web crawlers, spiders, worms, shopping bots, aggregators, and myriad other specialized bots. Computer science literature sometimes refers to bots as "autonomous agents" or "intelligent agents." In fact, one commentator has said that "[t]he term bot has become interchangeable with agent." When used in these contexts, the term "agent" is not meant to suggest that the parties involved share the legal relationship of agency but rather connotes the more general idea that the software does what one tells it to do; i.e., it's a bot. The nomenclature is further confused by several recently enacted pieces of legislation which use the term "electronic agent" again to refer to software intermediaries which may or may not legally be agents. In this Article, we will avoid using terms which incorporate the word "agent" to describe bots because they, by their very terms, confuse the fundamental issue of whether a bot should also be deemed to be an "agent" under the law. The legal characterization of a particular bot must be based upon a careful analysis of what the bot does and how it operates and should not be influenced by how software developers or Internet companies choose to label their creations.

In light of the caveats about nomenclature made above, one way to begin to understand what is meant by the term "bot" is to look at some examples. The following types of software are examples of some of the many types of software that are generally considered by the Internet community to be bots:

Web Crawlers. Software which indexes key words on a web page and then moves to each additional web page linked to from the starting page. The web crawler then indexes keywords on each of the newly found web pages and then moves on to every web page linked to from those web pages, ultimately locating and indexing millions of web pages. Bots operating in roughly this fashion are used to create the indexes upon which Internet search engines are built.

Data Mining Bots. Software similar to the bots described above, but whose purpose is not to index each web page found, but rather to gather a certain type of data from each web page. Several corporations are using bots of this type to scan the web for infringing use of copyrighted or trademarked materials. The Securities and Exchange Commission (SEC) has announced its intention to use a bot of this type to search websites, message boards, and chat rooms for evidence of stock manipulation and fraud.

Online Auction Services. Websites which enable buyers and sellers to find each other and negotiate a price for a particular piece of merchandise. While still thought of mostly as a consumer-oriented service offering beanie babies, movie memorabilia, and other collector's items, there are a growing number of auction sites designed to foster business-to-business (B2B) transactions.

Online Retailers. Websites which allow customers to browse an online catalog of products, place orders for selected merchandise, and arrange for delivery. While bookseller Amazon.com is the archetype of the online retailer, there is now a bounty of websites selling a vast array of merchandise. One can now even order groceries online.

Metasearch Engines. Because they use different bots to index the web, different search engines may provide different search results to the same query. A metasearch engine queries a number of search engines and then presents the combined output to the user.

Person–To–Person Payment Systems. Especially popular with auction enthusiasts, these bots allow individuals to transfer money between each other through various methods, usually including credit cards and electronic funds transfer.

Viruses. While the bots described above are all intended to have a benevolent purpose, there is no reason to believe that a bot, whether as a result of the negligence of poor programming or the malice of wrong doers, cannot have a destructive purpose. Software which surreptitiously spreads itself across the Internet sending out fake e-mail messages and erasing hard disks is as much a bot as its cousins which are indexing the web and enabling e-commerce.

What is it about the software described above that elevates it to the status of bot? Again, there is no definitive answer to this question. Professors Stan Franklin and Art Graesser, however, have compiled a list of attributes which they use to determine when software is behaving like an "autonomous agent."[3] We have adapted their list in order to construct the following table of properties which, when present in a piece of software, suggest that the software operates as a bot:

Property	Description
Reactive	Reacts to changes in the environment
Autonomous	Exercises control over its own actions
Goal-oriented	Seeks purposeful activity
Temporally Continuous	Is a continually running process
Communicative	Communicates with people and other bots
Learning	Changes its behavior based on past experience
Mobile	Transports itself from one machine to another

As a general matter, the bots described above tend to reflect most, if not all, of these properties.

There is no government agency or international standards organization which oversees the bot industry and consequently there are no comprehensive regulations. There are, however, social conventions adhered to by most programmers which dictate how the "well-behaved" bot should act. Of particular interest is a convention that has come to be known as the Standard for Robot Exclusion (SRE). The SRE establishes a voluntary process through which web masters may exclude bots from designated portions of their websites. Specifically, the SRE sets out how a website owner, by creating special files on his server or including certain code in his web pages, may dictate which bots may access his website and what they may view when they visit. Not all bots, however, are SRE compliant and adherence to the standard is strictly voluntary. Consequently, while there exists a "gentleman's agreement" as to how bots should operate, there are no rules which can be enforced through public or private means. In the absence of any controlling regulatory scheme, parties who believe they have been harmed by bots are attempting to use tort law to protect themselves. * * *

* * *

COMMON LAW PRINCIPLES OF AGENCY GOVERNING BOTS

While the recent enactments of E–SIGN at the federal level and various permutations of UETA at the state level create a framework in which contracts may be created electronically and parties may be bound by the contracts ratified by their electronic agents, these new laws do not tell us much about the relationship between an individual and the bot acting on his or her behalf. Questions of scope of authority, liability for failure to act,

3. Stan Franklin & Art Graesser, *Is it an Agent, or Just a Program? A Taxonomy for Autonomous Agents*, in THIRD INTERNATIONAL WORKSHOP ON AGENT THEORIES, ARCHITECTURES, AND LANGUAGES 4 (1996), available at <www.msci.memphis.edu/franklin/AgentProg.html>.

or the consequences of the bot committing a tort while acting on the behalf of another receive minimal treatment in the statutes. Given that we would turn to the law of agency in order to understand the relationship between a person and a human servant, it seems prudent to look to the same body of law to inform, although perhaps not to govern absolutely, the relationships between people and their software servants. This conclusion is especially appropriate to the legal analysis surrounding the use of software robots in electronic commerce because the law of agency is, at its heart, a tool by which society fosters economic growth and innovation.

> Although the agency relation may exist without reference to mercantile affairs, as in the case of domestic servants, its primary function in modern life is to make possible the commercial enterprises which could not exist otherwise. The common law has properly been responsive to the needs of commerce, permitting what older systems of law denied, namely a direct relation between the principal and a third person with whom the agent deals, even when the principal is undisclosed.[65]

Agency law should remain responsive to the economic needs of society and thus mold and adapt itself to the new requirements of modern electronic commerce.

A REVIEW OF AGENCY LAW PRINCIPLES

Agency, as defined in the Restatement (Second) of Agency, is the legal term for the relationship between two parties wherein one party, with the consent of the other, agrees to act on the behalf of and under the control of the other party. The one for whom the action is to be taken is called "the principal" while the person who is to act is deemed "the agent." Agency is wholly a legal concept which exists when the elements of the relationship are present and which is not dependant upon the parties' desire to enter into, or knowledge of, the agency relationship. While there must be agreement between principal and agent, there need not be a contract and consideration is not a requirement. The agent is said to hold certain powers on behalf of the principal. Power in this context is defined as the ability to produce a change in a given legal relation by performing or not performing a given act. In most instances, an agent's power is to modify the legal relations between the principal and a third party, although in certain situations, the agent's power may allow him to modify his own relationship with the principal. A related concept in agency law is that of "authority," which is the power of an agent to bind the principal by acts done in accordance with the principal's manifestations of consent. Thus, an agent who, at the direction of the principal, enters into a contract on behalf of that principal is said to be acting under authority. If the agent were to enter into a contract on behalf of a principal but without the principal's explicit consent, agency law might still find that the agent's actions bind the principal, but the source of the agent's power would derive from something other than authority. Sources of power other than authority

65. *Restatement (Second) of Agency* § 8A cmt. a (1958).

include apparent authority, estoppel, and inherent agency power.[73] Under § 26 of the Restatement, authority can be granted through written or oral instructions, and may also be created when the principal's conduct, reasonably interpreted, causes the agent to believe that the principal desires him to act on the principal's behalf.

When an agent acts consistent with his authority, "he has power to affect the legal relations of the principal to the same extent as if the principal had so acted."[75] Consequently, when a third party enters into a contract with a duly authorized agent, the third party may later enforce that contract against the principal.

AN EXAMPLE OF AGENCY LAW ANALYSIS OF A BOT—PROXY BIDDING ON eBAY

In order to explore the application of agency law to the world of bots and their functions in electronic commerce, we will look at one aspect of a common online commercial transaction involving a bot, namely, proxy bidding on the online auction service eBay.[87] Let's suppose that our bidder has found a large, turn of the century Navajo rug for sale on eBay. The current bid is $500 and, in this price range, bids must be made in increments of $10. Because the rug is finely woven with an intricate pattern and is in excellent condition with minimal moth damage, our bidder is willing to pay up to $750 to acquire it. He enters his maximum bid of $750 along with his user id and password on the bidding screens. eBay processes the bid through its proxy bidding system, which it explains as follows:

> Our bidding system operates as a proxy bid system. This means that a bidder can submit a maximum bid amount and our system will act as a proxy bidder in their absence, executing their bid for them and trying to keep the bid price as low as possible. This way a bidder doesn't have to be at the auction every minute.
>
> An easier way to think of this would be to think of the bidding system standing in for you as a bidder at a live auction. Let's say you need to be somewhere and can't be present to bid and you ask a friend to go to the auction and bid for you. You tell your friend that you are willing to pay $25 for an item you saw.
>
> The auctioneer starts the bidding at $5 and your friend bids the $5. Then another bidder bids $6 and your friend then bids $7 on your behalf. Then another bidder bids $12 and your friend bids $13 for you. This would keep going until either your friend wins the item for you at or below $25 or the bidding exceeds the $25 you were willing to pay.

73. For an explanation of how power deriving from authority differs from power deriving from apparent authority, estoppel, or inherent agency power, see id. § 7 cmt. a.

75. Id. § 12 cmt. a.

87. <www.ebay.com>.

> At eBay, the proxy bidding system is your friend. This system stands in for you and bids for you against other bidders until either you have won the item at or below the price you set or until another bidder bids higher than the amount you set.
>
> Under the proxy bidding system, eBay accepts our bidder's maximum bid of $750, but initially only bids the $510 necessary to be high bidder. Later that day, another collector of Native American art sees the rug on eBay and bids his maximum of $600 for the item. Following the rules of proxy bidding, eBay raises our bidder's offer to $610 in order to maintain his status as high bidder. The auction closes shortly thereafter and our bidder wins the auction at a final price of $610.

An analysis of the events which leads to our bidder acquiring a wonderful Navajo rug for $610, coupled with eBay's own explanation of the process, inevitably leads to the conclusion that eBay, acting through its automated proxy bidding software, is in a legal sense our bidder's agent.[89] Following eBay's own explanation of the system, it is standing in for the bidder at the auction, bidding on his behalf against other bidders until the point where either he has won the item or the price exceeds the maximum set by our bidder. The relationship between our bidder and eBay clearly falls within the dictates of the Restatement. While eBay does not charge the bidder for its services, placing all the fees upon the seller, consideration is not necessary for an agency relationship to exist. Because agency law binds the principal to the actions of his agent, should our bidder win the auction in which his bids are placed by eBay's proxy bidding system, he would be legally obligated to complete the transaction with the seller.

There is also a clear delegation of authority in compliance with § 17 of the Restatement when our bidder enters his maximum bid amount, user id, and password on the bidding screens and clicks the "place bid" button. Entering this information on the bidding screens and clicking on the appropriate buttons constitutes conduct which eBay can reasonably interpret to mean that our bidder wishes for eBay to act on his behalf. In addition, under the recently enacted E–SIGN, our bidder's actions may arguably be viewed as a signed, written authorization to eBay to bid up to $750 on the rug. Either way, it is clear that our bidder has instructed eBay to act as his agent, setting out the scope of the authority, and that eBay has consented to be his agent. In fact, eBay is acting as the agent of all of the individuals bidding on the rug. Moreover, eBay is also acting as the agent of the seller, making certain items available for sale, limiting bidding to a

89. A secondary issue is whether eBay, as the seller's agent, is an "auctioneer" as that term may be defined under state law. An auctioneer, while a type of agent, holds a special relationship with regard to both buyers and sellers and is subject to special rules and regulations. Several State Attorneys General have raised the question of whether eBay constitutes an auctioneer under state law. The issue is not currently resolved. See generally Ed Ritchie, License Fees for North Carolina Auctions?, AUCTIONWATCH.COM DAILY NEWS (Nov. 30, 1999), available at <www.auctionwatch.com/awdaily/dailynews/november99/1–113099.html>.

certain time period, enforcing a reserve minimum selling price, and otherwise acting under the direction of the seller.

If the bidder in our example had searched on eBay for pieces of Native American art to add to his collection, but found nothing that interested him and thus never made a purchase or even placed a bid, eBay would still be acting as his agent. Under the Restatement, a servant need not actually contract for the sale of an item on behalf of the principal to be deemed an agent. Within a principal's authorization of an agent to buy or sell merchandise is the authorization to "find a seller or purchaser from whom or to whom the principal may buy or sell."[94] When our potential bidder entered the terms "navajo rugs" into eBay's search form, he was, for purposes of the Restatement, instructing eBay to find sellers of Navajo rugs from whom he might purchase. By acting on this request and returning a listing of such items currently offered for sale, eBay has become the potential bidder's agent. The scope of the agency at this time is limited to finding items matching the current request, but the authority may be expanded by entering a bid via the online auction service.

* * *

Suzanne Smed, *Intelligent Software Agents and Agency Law*

14 SANTA CLARA COMPUTER & HIGH TECH. L.J. 503 (1998).

* * *

At least four theories exist for giving software agents legal status. Case law has shown courts contemplating the role of a computer in a transaction when attributing liability. Other theories compare software gaining rights and duties to the historical circumstances of women, slaves, and corporations gaining legal status.

Case examples show the courts using a different standard of responsibility when the action is done by an unattended machine as opposed to the same act done by a human. Case examples exist where the court decisions attributed liability to the owner for harms caused by unattended (or autonomous) machines. In one case, the court held a bank responsible for money allegedly lost during an automatic teller transaction.[9] The court placed a greater burden on the bank because the automated teller lacked the ability to corroborate each step (via recall, recountability, and judgment) as was done with human teller transactions. In another example, an insurance company was forced to pay a claim that occurred during a lapsed period of a customer's policy.[10] The court held that the computer constituted a competent agent capable of binding its principal in circumstances

94. Restatement (Second) of Agency § 53(a).

9. *McEvens v. Citibank*, 408 NYS 2d 870 (NY County Civ. Ct. 1978).

10. *State Farm Mutual Automobile Ins. Co. v. Bockhorst*, 453 F.2d 533 (10th Cir. 1972).

where a similar decision by a human agent might not.[11] And, one case held that a bank did not comply with the truth in lending regulations because their computer-generated explanation regarding loan terms, if done without a human to answer questions, was not clear enough for an ordinary borrower to understand.[12]

Therefore, it appears that the courts are willing to consider machines as participants in ordinary consumer transactions. By extending this previous court treatment of transactions conducted by autonomous machines, or by using the liability theories available under contract (where the actions of an agent bind the principal to third parties) or tort (where the principal may be vicariously liable for the actions of the agent), intelligent software agents can be treated as "legal agents."

Once intelligent software agents are viewed as having legal status with formation of the agency relationship, it follows that liability can be attributed to the actions of the software agents and the licensees will consequently be held responsible. Certain legal duties vest in the licensees as principals in the newly formed agency relationship. Therefore, any harms committed by the intelligent software agent that breach the licensee's legal duties will cause the licensee to be liable.

* * *

NOTES & QUESTIONS

1. *Subjective vs. objective approach.* An argument that has been advanced against the possibility of machine-made contracts is that a machine cannot express the intent of a party who is not present, and therefore unaware that offer and acceptance are in progress. *See* Tom Allen & Robin Widdison, *Can Computers Make Contracts?*, 9 HARV. J.L. & TECH. 25 (1996). Is this argument consistent with the reigning objectivist approach to contract formation, which depends not on any subjective meeting of the minds, but only on outward manifestations? *See* Jean–Francois Lerouge, *The Use of Electronic Agents Questioned Under Contractual Law: Suggested Solutions on a European and American Level*, 18 J. MARSHALL J. COMPUTER & INFO. L. 403 (1999). Does UCITA adopt an objective or subjective theory of contract in its provisions on manifestation of assent?

2. *Commander Data.* Commander Data is a character from *Star Trek: The Next Generation,* a television series about space exploration in the distant future. Data is an artificial intelligence in humanoid form—an android—who holds a commission in Star Fleet, the military arm of an interplanetary federation that appears to be the principal governing organization at that time. Data is self-aware, very smart, but—at least at the start of the series—does not experience emotions. Is Data capable of being a legal agent for a human or corporate principal? How sophisticated must an artificially intelligent machine be before it can qualify as the legal agent of another? If current bots lack this degree of sophistication, what additional characteris-

11. *Id.* at 535–536.

12. *Allen v. Beneficial Fin. Co.,* 531 F.2d 797 (7th Cir.1976).

tics must future bots possess before they would qualify? Does the ability to act as a legal agent entail the ability to be a legal principal as well? Would a qualifying bot also enjoy property rights, suffer tort liability, or have other legal rights? Do you think lawyers in the future will have to wrestle with these questions? For an interesting exploration of conferring legal personhood on artificial intelligences, *see* Lawrence B. Solum, *Legal Personhood for Artificial Intelligences*, 70 N.C. L. REV. 1231 (1992).

3. *On distinguishing electronic from legal agents.* In their analysis of proxy bidding on eBay, Middlebrook and Muller argue that eBay, rather than the proxy bidding bot, should be viewed as the legal agent of the bidder. Middlebrook and Muller focus attention on eBay the corporation rather than on the proxy bidding software, presumably because they view the proxy bidding software as a mere instrumentality. They write, "eBay, acting through its automated proxy bidding software, is in a legal sense our bidder's agent." Is this conclusion inescapable? If you were representing eBay and needed to argue that your client was not the legal agent of the bidder, how might you proceed using Middlebrook and Muller's apparent assumption that the proxy bidding software bot is a mere instrumentality?

4. *The Restatement (Third) of Agency.* Tentative Draft No. 1 of the Restatement (Third) of Agency addresses the question of computer agency directly. It states:

> [A] computer program is not capable of being a principal or an agent as defined by the common law. Future developments in information technology may result in software products that should be treated as sufficiently personified for purposes of the common law of agency. At present, however, computer programs are the instrumentalities of the persons who use them.

RESTATEMENT (THIRD) OF THE LAW OF AGENCY § 1.03, cmt. f (Tentative Draft No. 1, 2000). To which of the two excerpts in this section, Middlebrook & Muller or Smed, do the *Restatement* authors appear most sympathetic?

5. *Defining electronic agents.* How do the definitions of "electronic agent" in UETA, ESIGN, and UCITA differ? Are these differences significant, i.e., will they lead to different outcomes when applied? How are the acts of an electronic agent attributed to its human user under these three acts? Do these provisions effectively fill the gaps left by the common law of agency?

6. *More on bots.* If you are interested in learning more about intelligent software agents, consider the following articles: Aaron Sloman & Brian Logan, *Building Cognitively Rich Agents Using the SIM_Agent Toolkit*, COMM. OF THE ACM, vol. 42, No. 3 (Mar. 1, 1999); Bonnie A. Nardi, James R. Miller & David J. Wright, *Collaborative Programmable Intelligent Agents*, COMM. OF THE ACM, vol. 41, No. 3 (Mar. 1, 1998); M. Mitchell Waldrop, *Software Agents Prepare to Sift the Riches of Cyberspace*, SCIENCE, vol. 265, No. 5174 (August 12, 1994). Additional information is available at agents.www.media.mit.edu/groups/agents/research.html and www.bot-spot.com.

II. THE ROLE OF STANDARDIZATION IN ELECTRONIC CONTRACTING

In the past, some courts and commentators have been leery of standard-form contracts, which present the recipient with the choice of either acceding to the proposed terms or forgoing the product or service to which the terms are attached. Yet adhesion contracts (also known as take-it-or-leave-it contracts) have always offered certain advantages. Standardization of contract terms reduces transaction costs, and is practically inevitable with respect to low-value transactions. In addition, a standard-form contract may represent the package of terms that is most efficient or most valued by customers. In the online environment it is possible that even more contracts will be standardized, especially those which are formed through the interaction of machines. (*See* Part I(D), *supra*.) This Part presents some issues raised by standardization in Internet commerce, beginning with the rules for "mass-market" licensing proposed in UCITA.

Uniform Computer Information Transactions Act, §§ 102(a)(44), 102(a)(45), & 209

National Conference of Commissioners on Uniform State Laws.
(2000).

SECTION 102. DEFINITIONS

(a) In this [Act]: * * *

(44) "Mass-market license" means a standard form used in a mass-market transaction.

(45) "Mass-market transaction" means a transaction that is:

(A) a consumer contract; or

(B) any other transaction with an end-user licensee if:

(i) the transaction is for information or informational rights directed to the general public as a whole, including consumers, under substantially the same terms for the same information;

(ii) the licensee acquires the information or informational rights in a retail transaction under terms and in a quantity consistent with an ordinary transaction in a retail market; and

(iii) the transaction is not:

(I) a contract for redistribution or for public performance or public display of a copyrighted work;

(II) a transaction in which the information is customized or otherwise specially prepared by the licensor for the licensee, other than minor customization using a capability of the information intended for that purpose;

(III) a site license; or

(IV) an access contract.

Official Comment

* * *

39. "Mass-market license" and "mass-market transaction." The term "mass market license" is new and the definition must be applied in light of its intended and limited function. That function is to describe small dollar value, routine transactions involving information that is directed to the general public when the transaction occurs in a retail market available to and used by the general public. The term includes all consumer contracts and also some transactions between businesses if they are in a retail market. One purpose of the term is to avoid artificial distinctions among business and consumer transferees in an ordinary retail market. Mass-market transactions do not include commercial transactions between businesses using ordinary commercial methods, such as purchase orders, terms offered to businesses but not to consumers, or online and access systems focused on the business-business marketplace.

* * *

The computer information must be of a *type* aimed at the general public as a whole, including consumers. This does not include information earmarked for a business or professional audience and which is not ordinarily acquired by consumers, nor does it include information earmarked for members of an organization or persons with a separate relationship to the information provider. * * * Customization that is routine in mass markets or that is done by the licensee after acquiring the information does not take the transaction outside the concept of a mass-market transaction.

The transaction must be with an end user. An end user is a licensee that intends to use the information or informational rights in its own business or personal affairs. * * *

* * *

SECTION 209. MASS–MARKET LICENSE

(a) A party adopts the terms of a mass-market license for purposes of § 208 only if the party agrees to the license, such as by manifesting assent, before or during the party's initial performance or use of or access to the information. A term is not part of the license if:

(1) the term is unconscionable or is unenforceable under § 105(a) or (b); or

(2) subject to § 301, the term conflicts with a term to which the parties to the license have expressly agreed.

(b) If a mass-market license or a copy of the license is not available in a manner permitting an opportunity to review by the licensee before the licensee becomes obligated to pay and the licensee does not agree, such as by manifesting assent, to the license after having an opportunity to review, the licensee is entitled to a return under § 112 and, in addition, to:

(1) reimbursement of any reasonable expenses incurred in complying with the licensor's instructions for returning or destroying the computer information or, in the absence of instructions, expenses incurred for return postage or similar reasonable expense in returning the computer information; and

(2) compensation for any reasonable and foreseeable costs of restoring the licensee's information processing system to reverse changes in the system caused by the installation, if:

(A) the installation occurs because information must be installed to enable review of the license; and

(B) the installation alters the system or information in it but does not restore the system or information after removal of the installed information because the licensee rejected the license.

(c) In a mass-market transaction, if the licensor does not have an opportunity to review a record containing proposed terms from the licensee before the licensor delivers or becomes obligated to deliver the information, and if the licensor does not agree, such as by manifesting assent, to those terms after having that opportunity, the licensor is entitled to a return.

Official Comment

* * *

2. **General Rules.** The terms of mass-market contracts can be established in many ways. An oral agreement may suffice as would an agreement to terms in a record. Product descriptions may define the bargain. Parties may agree that terms may be specified later by a party. Three limiting concepts govern where assent to a record is relevant:

a. **Assent and Agreement.** A party adopts the terms of a mass market license only if it agrees to the record, by manifesting assent or otherwise. A party cannot do so unless it had an opportunity to review the record before it agrees. This means that the record must be available for review and called to the person's attention in a manner such that a reasonable person ought to have noticed it. See § 112.

Adopting terms of a record under this section is pursuant to § 208, with the limits stated in that section. If the terms of the record are proposed after a party commences performance, the terms are effective only if the party had reason to know that terms would be proposed and assents to the terms when proposed. For mass-market licenses, however, even if reason to know exists at the outset, the terms must be made available no later than the initial use of the information and the person has a statutory right to a return if it refuses the license.

b. **Unconscionability and Fundamental Public Policy.** Even if a party agrees to a mass market license, a court may invalidate unconscionable terms or terms against fundamental public policy under rules that apply to all contracts under this Act. * * *

* * *

5. **Terms after Initial Agreement.** Mass market licenses may be presented after initial general agreement from the licensee. In some distribution channels this allows a more efficient mode of contracting between end users and remote parties; this is especially important where the remote party controls copyright or similar rights in the information. * * *

a. **Timing of Assent.** Agreement to the mass-market record must occur no later than during the initial use of the information. This limits the time during which layered contracting may occur in the mass market and reflects customary practices in software and other industries. * * *

b. **Cost Free Return.** Under subsection (b), if terms are not available for review until after an initial agreement, the party being asked to assent must have a right to reject the terms return the information product. * * *.

* * *

NOTES & QUESTIONS

1. *Mass market licenses.* A taxicab company purchases a spreadsheet program from a local computer software retailer in a state that has enacted UCITA. The software is subject to a shrinkwrap license. If a dispute arises between the cab company and the software manufacturer concerning the software, will Section 209 of UCITA be applicable?

2. ProCD *revisited.* Review the statement of facts in *ProCD v. Zeidenberg*, excerpted in Part I(C)(1), *supra*. If that case had been adjudicated under UETA, how do you think it would have been decided? What if it had been adjudicated under UCITA?

3. Klocek *revisited.* Review the statement of facts in *Klocek v. Gateway*, excerpted in Part I(C)(1), *supra*. If that case had been adjudicated under UETA, how do you think it would have been decided? What if it had been adjudicated under UCITA?

4. *Compare and contrast.* With respect to the validity and enforceability of layered licensing agreements, how would you compare and contrast the approaches taken by UETA and UCITA?

Margaret Jane Radin, *Online Standardization and the Integration of Text and Machine*

70 FORDHAM L. REV. 1125 (2002).

* * *

A good technical standard might come about through market emergence. The best product might have won out in a competitive market. Or, we might need some standard for smooth functioning, and be indifferent about which one. On the other hand, an inferior product might have tipped the market and eliminated its competitors; we could be stuck with such a product because no one else can enter unless they can somehow take over the entire market immediately.

The very same reasoning applies to legal standardization. Contracts in an industry might be standard because those are the terms that consumers consistently choose; the standardized contract represents the package of terms that won out in a free market. On the other hand, standardized contracts may reflect collusion or some other market failure such as a "lemons equilibrium" brought about by inadequate consumer information.

Similarly, if a standard arrives by way of promulgation, that in itself also tells us nothing about how it should be evaluated. If a legal standard comes about through legislation, one might think—and courts have tended to think—that the legislative standard is entitled to a presumption that it is socially beneficial, because it was imposed by a collective process or a representative body that takes into account everyone's interests. But we do not have to be thoroughgoing public choice theorists to note the prevalence of industry capture; and to believe that, at least some of the time, interest groups capture the process and get the statute or rule written the way they want it.

This kind of capture happens both in technical and in legal standard-setting. In the technical case, sometimes a company is helpful in getting a standard promulgated, and then it turns out the company had a patent pending, so that everyone who wants to use the standard must license the patent. In the legal case, sometimes interest groups control the drafting process. This is arguably what happened with the anti-circumvention provisions of the Digital Millennium Copyright Act ("DMCA")—captured by the copyright industries—or the pending UCITA—captured by the software industry.

From a policy point of view, then, how a standard is arrived at does not tell us whether it is good or bad, whether it should be welcomed or deplored. In the real world, however, it matters a great deal how standards are arrived at, particularly for legal standards. It is a lot harder to overturn legislation once it is on the books than it is to find a reason to disallow "bottom-up" industry standardization. Not everything about either adhesion contracts or technical standardization, even if unwise, is going to turn out to rise to the level of violation of antitrust laws, federal intellectual property laws, federal consumer protection regulation, or the Constitution; in fact, very little about them will rise to that level. So, it is a very good strategy for industries to capture legislatures or standards-setting bodies, because once they get standards promulgated, it is hard to overturn them.

I believe that there is something deeper going on when it turns out that legal and technical standardization are so closely allied to each other. I believe that the digital revolution is bringing about a seismic shift in our conceptual landscape, which I want to explore here, though only preliminarily. I call this shift the breakdown of the distinction between text and technology, or between expression and functionality, or between words and machine. * * *

The prevalent economic view of contract has broken down the distinction between agreement, formerly thought of as a text, and the product being sold, formerly thought of as a functional object or a collection of functional features. This view of contract actually predates the online environment, but in the online environment it is becoming more powerful. I call this view "contract as product," and contrast it with the view of contract as consent or agreement.

In the "contract as product" view, the contract is part of the product, part of the collection of functional components, and not a separate text about that collection. What does this mean? For example, suppose you buy a cell phone that contains a chip that will wear out within a year, and the phone comes with a set of fine print terms including a clause that says in the event of any dispute arising out of the transaction you must litigate in California under California law. Both the chip and the clause are functionally the same from the economic point of view: if you know that they are there, they will help determine what you are willing to pay for the phone. Notice that in order for the market to function efficiently this view must suppose that at least the marginal consumer must understand what chips and clauses are being purchased. How the product will work, how long it is going to last, what kind of warranties it comes with, what limitations on remedies it comes with—all of these are exactly the same from the economic point of view. The product you are buying is not just the phone, but the phone plus the terms. The contract is not a text about a product, but part of a product.

This contract as product view is suited to adhesion contracts because in such a take-it-or-leave-it transaction there is no dickering over terms and no dickering over the components either. You can buy this product that is going to wear out in a year, over which you will be forced to litigate in California if a dispute arises, or you can walk away and buy something else more to your liking. In order for the market to function efficiently, in this view, one must suppose that other products and/or other terms are available. You don't get to say, "I wish you would remanufacture this so it will not wear out in a year," and you also don't get to say, "I wish you would rewrite the contract so that I can litigate in my home state."

In the offline world, most contracts have been like this for some time, and thus the economic view has suited transactional reality. Nevertheless, lay people have largely continued to conceive of contract as dickered consent between two people. This lay conception—contract as negotiated text—will, I think, be significantly eroded in the online environment, for two reasons. On the one hand, it is likely that standardized transactions will occupy even more of the transactional universe; and on the other hand, the nature of the transaction is more transparent because the fine print that comes with the functionality being purchased is more accessible to everyone. The contract is merging into the product; the text is merging into the functionality.

* * *

It also seems that DRMSs [digital rights management systems—*see* Chapter 11, *infra*] are doing their part to undermine the distinction between text and machine. A DRMS is a program that limits distribution and use of some piece of digitized content; it is essentially next-generation copy protection. That is, a DRMS could prevent content from being copied, or allow it to be copied once and sent to one recipient, but deleted from the original recipient's computer; or it could delete the content after a set time period; and many other permutations. DRMSs give rise to many policy problems that I am not discussing here, in particular the problem of overreaching by content owners who can use technological protection to prevent activities that are otherwise the right of the user (for example, copying of material that is not protected by copyright). At least it seems that DRMSs are also contributing to the undermining of the idea that a contract is a text, separate from and accompanying some machine or functionality. The DRMS is itself a machine or functionality, and it is not at all clear whether to think of it as a contract; to me it seems like non-contractual technological self-help.

* * *

NOTES & QUESTIONS

1. *Standardization or customization?* There are reasons to believe that more and more transactions online will be standardized. Computer-to-computer agreements will have to use standardized sets of terms that they can "agree" on, and if these terms become widely used in this context, they will be used in other contexts as well. Well-drafted sets of terms can be copied and proliferate on the Internet just like other kinds of content. Sets of terms that are validated through widespread use may make globalization of contracting more practical. At the same time, however, customization of terms is technologically feasible in the online environment in ways that it has not been offline. A website could offer you a choice of terms instead of a take-or-leave-it package of fine print. It could disclaim warranties, but offer you a warranty for an extra fee, if you click a box. It could provide for compulsory arbitration, but allow you to purchase the chance to litigate in your home state. And so on. Which scenario do you predict will come to pass? (Or do you think neither scenario will describe the actual state of affairs?) What policy problems do you see associated with these scenarios?

2. *Approaches to "consent."* Professor Randy Barnett made the following comment in the context of the UCC Article 2 revision process:

> Though the idea of consumers paying for goods before they examine all the terms of the agreement has spooked some academics, their concerns [do not result from] any real impairment of contractual consent. [I] speak here not only as a contracts professor who has written extensively on the importance of contractual consent, but as a frequent consumer of such goods as electronics and software. It is not a bother in the slightest to pay for a good in a store, or online, and then examine the terms in the comfort of my own home provided that I can return the good should I reject the terms. To the contrary, I cannot imagine anything other than

> an aesthetic objection to this practice. True, consumers who dislike a term in the agreement are put to some inconvenience when they must return a good, as they would in returning any good with which they are not completely satisfied upon inspection, though even they benefit from the lower prices and more specifically tailored terms that result from the practice. But this minor inconvenience in no way warrants a frontal attack on this form of contracting on the grounds of lack of assent. There is certainly assent, though it happens after initial payment. There need no be law against that.

Letter to Lawrence J. Bugge, Esquire, Chairman of the UCC Article 2 Drafting Committee of the National Conference of Commissioners on Uniform State Laws (Mar. 5, 2001). *See also* Randy E. Barnett, *A Consent Theory of Contract*, 86 COLUM. L. REV. 269 (1986).

Consider the following alternative view:

> It certainly seems that UCITA's definition of manifestation of assent stretches the ordinary concept of consent (contested as it was). That stretching starts with the substitution of the word "assent" for the word "consent." In my dictionary, "consent" is one of the meanings of "assent." Nevertheless, "assent" has connotations of acquiescence, of mere failure to remove oneself from a process; "consent," on the other hand, seems surrounded with more connotations of voluntary involvement of oneself in a process. * * * By substituting "assent," UCITA seems to be validating the take-it-or-leave-it nature of the terms that come with these mass-market transactions. By assimilating such terms to the category of contract, UCITA, insofar as it can be read as doing anything coherent, is drifting toward explicit endorsement of the contract-as-product model.

Margaret Jane Radin, *Humans, Computers, and Binding Commitment*, 75 IND. L.J. 1125, 1141–42 (2000).

Which view do you find more persuasive? Do you think that the basic normative underpinning of contract, the idea of a voluntary bargain between autonomous actors, is no longer viable? If so, what normative underpinning is taking its place?

III. THE LIMITS OF CONTRACTUAL ORDERING IN THE ONLINE ENVIRONMENT

A. UNCONSCIONABILITY

In re RealNetworks, Inc., Privacy Litigation

2000 WL 631341 (N.D.Ill.2000).

■ KOCORAS, J.

[This case concerns the enforceability of an arbitration provision contained in a clickwrap agreement. RealNetworks makes its RealPlayer and RealJukebox software available at its website for free download. Upon installing the software, the user must agree to a license agreement containing the following clause:

> This License Agreement shall be governed by the laws of the State of Washington, without regard to conflicts of law provisions, and you hereby consent to the exclusive jurisdiction of the state and federal courts sitting in the State of Washington. Any and all unresolved disputes arising under this License Agreement shall be submitted to arbitration in the State of Washington.

The court continues:]

Defendant cites this clause as binding authority for its assertions that arbitration is required. Intervenor, on the other hand, argues that this clause does not operate to require arbitration for several reasons. First, Intervenor contends that the License Agreement, including the arbitration requirement, does not constitute a "writing."[7] * * * Finally, Intervenor argues that the arbitration provision is unenforceable because it is unconscionable.

* * *

III. Unconscionability

Finally, Intervenor claims that the arbitration agreement is unenforceable because it is both procedurally and substantively unconscionable. Procedural unconscionability involves impropriety during the process of forming a contract, whereas substantive unconscionability pertains to those cases where a clause or term in a contract is allegedly one-sided or overly harsh. *See Public Employees Mutual Ins. Co. v. Hertz Corp.*, 59 Wash.App. 641, 645–46, 800 P.2d 831, 833 (1990).

Intervenor argues that the License Agreement is procedurally unconscionable because it failed to provide fair notice of its contents and did not provide a reasonable opportunity to understand its terms before it was enforced. Both of these assertions are incorrect. Intervenor claims that the arbitration provision does not provide fair notice because it is "buried" in the License Agreement. Although burying important terms in a "maze of fine print" may contribute to a contract being found unconscionable, the arbitration provision in the License Agreement is not buried. *But see Public Employees Mutual Ins.*, 59 Wash.App. at 648, 800 P.2d at 834 (it is not law of Washington that presence of small print in context of standard form agreement necessarily leads to a finding of unconscionability). The License Agreement sets out the arbitration provision in the same size font as the rest of the agreement. *Cf. id.* at 650, 800 P.2d at 836. Moreover, it is not buried in the middle of the entire agreement or located in a footnote or appendix, but rather comprises the attention-getting final provision of the agreement. Although RealNetworks could have titled the heading containing the arbitration clause, the choice of law provision, and the forum selection clause in a more descriptive manner than "Miscellaneous," Real-

7. [This aspect of the case is treated in Chapter 5, *infra*.—Eds.]

Networks' titling it such does not necessarily bury the provision. While RealNetworks did not set off the arbitration provision and purposely draw attention to it, neither did RealNetworks bury the provision in a sea of words. Although burying an arbitration clause could contribute to a finding of unconscionability, the Court is unaware of, and Intervenor has not pointed to, any Washington state caselaw that provides that an arbitration clause is unconscionable if the contract does not draw attention to it.

Moreover, Intervenor claims that the user is not given a reasonable opportunity to understand the arbitration provision because the License Agreement comes in a small pop-up window, which is visually difficult to read. * * * The Court finds that the size of the pop-up window, although smaller than the desktop, does not make the License Agreement visually difficult to read. The Court finds disingenuous Intervenor's assertion that the License Agreement appears "in very fine print, requiring the user to position himself just inches from the monitor in order to read it." The font size of the License Agreement is no smaller, and possibly larger, than the font size of all the words appearing on the computer's own display. If Intervenor needs to plaster his face against the screen to read the License Agreement, he must then have to do the same to read anything on his computer, in which case, doing so does not seem like an inordinate hardship or an adjustment out of the ordinary for him. In addition, the user has all day to review the License Agreement on the screen. The pop-up window containing the License Agreement does not disappear after a certain time period; so, the user can scroll through it and examine it to his heart's content.

Because the arbitration agreement is not buried in fine print and because a user is given ample opportunity to understand the arbitration provision, the Court does not find that the arbitration agreement is procedurally unconscionable.

In addition, Intervenor asserts that the arbitration provision is substantively unconscionable because it chooses a geographically distant forum, it fails to provide for classwide arbitration, and the costs of arbitration are prohibitive.

The Court rejects Intervenor's claim that choosing Washington state as the arbitration forum renders the arbitration agreement substantively unconscionable. The designation of any state as a forum is bound to be distant to some potential litigants of a corporation that has a nationwide reach. Intervenor would have the Court essentially preclude arbitration agreements from having any forum selection clause in order to prevent the designation of a distant forum to any of these litigants. This Court is not willing to do so. Arbitration provisions containing forum selection clauses have previously been upheld. *See Quist v. Empire Funding Corp.,* No. 98 C 8402, 1999 WL 982953, at *3 (N.D.Ill. Oct.22, 1999) (enforcing contract of Illinois resident that required arbitration in Texas); *Doctor's Ass'n. Inc. v. Hamilton,* 150 F.3d 157, 163 (2d Cir.1998) (upholding forum selection clause in arbitration clause designating Connecticut as forum). Moreover, some courts have even found that the forum non conveniens doctrine is inapplicable in the context of arbitrations covered under the FAA. *See Al–*

Salamah Arabian Agencies Co., Ltd. v. Reece, 673 F.Supp. 748, 751 (M.D.N.C.1987); *Spring Hope Rockwool v. Industrial Clean Air, Inc.,* 504 F.Supp. 1385, 1389 (E.D.N.C.1981). Thus, that Washington is a distant arbitration forum for some does not render the arbitration clause substantively unconscionable.

Intervenor also claims that because litigants cannot pursue classwide arbitration without an arbitration provision providing for it, *see Champ v. Siegel Trading Co.,* 55 F.3d 269, 275 (7th Cir.1995), RealNetworks is effectively preventing potential litigants from seeking classwide arbitration by not expressly providing for classwide arbitration. Further, Intervenor reasons that because consumers in cases such as this have relatively small claims, these consumers' rights to bring a case would essentially be vitiated because the costs of the litigation would be so prohibitive. This Court previously rejected this argument in its prior decision. *See Lieschke,* 2000 WL 198424, at *3. The Seventh Circuit, along with other courts in this district, have considered this issue and upheld arbitration agreements that do not provide for class action and have even upheld arbitration agreements that expressly prohibit class actions. *See Champ,* 55 F.3d at 275–77; *Zawikowski v. Beneficial Nat'l Bank,* No. 98 C 2178, 1999 WL 35304, at *2 (N.D.Ill. Jan.11, 1999); *see also Lopez v. Plaza Fin. Co.,* No. 95 C 7567, 1996 WL 210073, at *3 (N.D.Ill. Apr.25, 1996); *cf. Dean Witter Reynolds, Inc. v. Byrd,* 470 U.S. 213, 217 (1985) (the FAA requires district courts to compel arbitration "even where the result would be the possibly inefficient maintenance of separate proceedings in different forums"). Thus, the Court will not find the License Agreement substantively unconscionable because it does not provide for class arbitration.

Further, the Court rejects Intervenor's argument that allegedly prohibitive arbitration costs render the License Agreement unconscionable. The Seventh Circuit has found that the costs of arbitration do not prevent the enforcement of a valid arbitration agreement. *See Hill,* 105 F.3d at 1151 (whatever may be said pro and con about the cost and efficacy of arbitration is for Congress and the contracting parties to consider); *Dorsey v. H.C.P. Sales, Inc.,* 46 F.Supp.2d 804, 807 (N.D.Ill.1999); *see also Koveleskie,* 167 F.3d at 366 (expensive fees do not necessarily preclude arbitration). As such, the potential arbitration costs do not render the arbitration clause substantively unconscionable.

CONCLUSION

For the reasons set forth above, the Court rejects Intervenor's additional arguments in support of Plaintiffs' opposition to arbitration.

Uniform Computer Information Transactions Act, § 111

National Conference of Commissioners on Uniform State Laws.
(2000).

SECTION 111. UNCONSCIONABLE CONTRACT OR TERM

(a) If a court as a matter of law finds a contract or a term thereof to have been unconscionable at the time it was made, the court may refuse to enforce the contract, enforce the remainder of the contract without the unconscionable term, or limit the application of the unconscionable term so as to avoid an unconscionable result.

(b) If it is claimed or appears to the court that a contract or term thereof may be unconscionable, the parties must be afforded a reasonable opportunity to present evidence as to its commercial setting, purpose, and effect to aid the court in making the determination.

Official Comment

1. **Scope of the Section.** This section adopts the unconscionability doctrine of Uniform Commercial Code § 2–302 (1998 Official Text).

* * *

3. **Electronic commerce.** This Act confirms the enforceability of automated contracting involving "electronic agents," but in some cases automation may produce unexpected, potentially oppressive results due to errors in programs, problems in communication, or other unforeseen circumstances in the automation process. Common law concepts of mistake may apply, as may §§ 206 and 214. In addition, in appropriate cases, unconscionability doctrine may invalidate a term because a procedural breakdown in automated contract formation produces unexpected and oppressive results in the terms of the agreement.

* * *

NOTES & QUESTIONS

1. *Are substantial costs ever substantively unconscionable?* In *In re RealNetworks*, the court cites the Seventh Circuit for the claim that "the costs of arbitration do not prevent the enforcement of a valid arbitration agreement." *See Hill,* 105 F.3d at 1151 ("Whatever may be said pro and con about the cost and efficacy of arbitration * * * is for Congress and the contracting parties to consider."). Is it necessary to qualify this statement? Does the court mean that the costs of arbitration are never an adequate basis for declaring an arbitration clause substantively unconscionable? Can you imagine a case in which the costs of arbitration might be sufficient to render an arbitration clause unenforceable? *See Brower v. Gateway 2000, Inc.*, 676 N.Y.S.2d 569 (N.Y.App.Div.1998), discussed in Chapter 15, *infra*.

2. *Conscionable options.* If a court finds a provision in a contract to be unconscionable, how should it proceed? Should it invalidate the entire contract? This judicial response would encourage people not to overreach when they negotiate contracts. Should a court simply delete the provision? How would this affect contracts with unconscionable arbitration clauses? Should a court draft and impose on the parties a conscionable version of the provision that the court found unconscionable? *See Brower v. Gateway 2000, Inc.*, 676 N.Y.S.2d 569 (N.Y.App.Div.1998), discussed in Chapter 15, *infra*.

B. THE ENFORCEABILITY OF CHOICE OF LAW, CHOICE OF FORUM AND ARBITRATION CLAUSES IN CLICKWRAP AGREEMENTS

Brower v. Gateway 2000, Inc.

676 N.Y.S.2d 569 (N.Y.App.Div.1998).

[This case is discussed in Chapter 15, Part II(B), *infra*.]

Groff v. America Online, Inc.

1998 WL 307001 (R.I.Super.1998).

[This case is discussed in Chapter 7, Part IV, *infra*.]

America Online, Inc. v. Superior Court of Alameda County

108 Cal.Rptr.2d 699 (Cal.Ct.App.2001).

[This case is discussed in Chapter 7, Part IV, *infra*.]

CHAPTER FIVE

AUTHENTICATION AND DIGITAL SIGNATURES

Authentication is one of the central issues facing contract law in Internet commerce. When one party seeks to enforce a claimed agreement, and the other party denies any obligation, it becomes necessary to pin down the operative facts about the transaction: whether a bargain was actually entered into, and if so who are the parties and what are the terms. (For example, if one party says the price was $10,000 and the other says the price was $100, we need to be able to know who is telling the truth about the number of zeroes.) The English statute of frauds provided that contracts for the sale of land or for sale of goods over a certain value would be invalid unless in writing, signed, and sealed (bearing the imprint of a seal). The seal requirement gradually fell away, but statutes of frauds still exist, in a variety of contexts. These statutes make a great many contracts unenforceable unless in writing and signed by the party to be charged.

As we saw in Chapter 4, *supra*, legislative initiatives and courts have begun to address the problem of what counts as a *writing* in the digital era. The problem of what counts as a *signature* has also emerged. (Should the signature block in your e-mail be adequate to bind you to a contract?) Forgery is easier in the digital environment than with paper documents, since, in the offline world, there might be witnesses who can vouch for a document's genuineness. The purpose of technological digital signature schemes and other methods of electronic authentication, which we address in this chapter, is to supply a forgery-resistant identifier for electronic messages that are otherwise all-too-forgeable. Electronic authentication schemes function, among other things, to enable online contracting by granting legal significance to digital signatures in situations where physical signatures otherwise would be required.

In the United States, many jurisdictions have enacted or are considering some kind of legislation relating to electronic authentication, but so far this is a patchwork. The federal Electronic Signatures in Global and National Commerce Act ("ESIGN"), and the model state Uniform Electronic Transactions Act ("UETA"), introduced in the previous chapter, provide that electronic transactions will not be invalid merely because they are electronic, but they do not select which technology of authentication will suffice to render the bargain and its terms sufficiently certain to be enforceable. In this chapter, we will give further consideration to ESIGN and UETA. The European Commission has adopted a Directive that requires European Union member states to adopt electronic signature legislation. Although the Directive does not mandate the use of any particular technology of authentication, the presumptions it sets up strongly favor the use of public key encryption technology, which we will describe in this chapter. A number of states in the United States have enacted legislation favoring public key technology and its supporting infrastructure.

Laws calling for establishment of a public key infrastructure are technology-specific. Technology-specific laws pose two principal policy issues. First, such laws are often outdated before the enactment process is finished. Second, the favored technology enjoys something like a government-sanctioned monopoly. Many commentators argue, therefore, that technology-neutral laws—i.e., those that define what must be accomplished, without mandating any particular technology to accomplish it—are preferable. But technology-neutral laws run the risk of being vague and general, and therefore difficult to apply in practice.

I. DIGITAL SIGNATURES

A. THE FUNCTIONS OF SIGNATURES

In commercial documents, verifiable signatures serve three important functions: authentication of the signer, nonrepudiation, and data integrity. *Authentication* of the signer means that a recipient can know with a high degree of confidence that the signer is a specific identified person. *Nonrepudiation* means that the signer cannot unwind the deal by denying that she signed or sent the document. *Data integrity* means that neither the parties nor interlopers can get away with altering the text.

A pen-and-ink signature authenticates the signer on the assumption that only the signer can make his personal signature. A name typed into an e-mail program, or any other digital text, does not even weakly authenticate the signer since anyone can type out the letters forming the name.

Moreover, because each person's pen-and-ink signature is distinctive, placing it at the bottom of a document is *prima facie* evidence that the person in fact assented to the terms contained in the document. Doing so prevents the signer from repudiating the signature and, with it, the person's assent to the document signed. A name typed into a digital document, by contrast, could have been typed by anyone and, therefore, does not offer even a slight barrier to repudiation.

Finally, a pen-and-ink signature can serve to indicate the integrity of the document signed. Documents are signed at the bottom of the message body to prevent alteration of the document by inserting additional text, or deleting existing text. Since ink is absorbed by paper, this technique is effective for paper documents—the ink signature cannot be moved up or down or transferred to a totally different document. A name typed into a digital document, however, can be easily moved using a word processor. Accordingly, a name at the bottom of a digital document does not even weakly indicate that the document has not been altered.

B. DIGITAL SIGNATURE TECHNOLOGY

From the outset of electronic contracting the search for an effective digital substitute for the pen-and-ink signature has been a priority. An electronic signature with the commercially desirable attributes of a pen-and-ink signature is called a digital signature. The most prevalent form of digital signature today is created using encryption and related techniques.

Encryption, for present purposes, is the process of taking a textual message, written in a natural language such as English, and transforming it so that it becomes unreadable except to one who knows how to run the transformation in reverse. The transformation is accomplished through the use of a cryptographic "key." A key may be thought of as a set of rules to follow in transforming the original message into its encrypted form. For example, a very simple cryptographic key might be expressed as: "For each letter in the message, substitute the number representing the place of that letter in the alphabet." Applying this key to the message

"Hello"

would result in transforming it into the encrypted form

"8 5 12 12 15".

The encrypted form is unreadable to one who does not know the key, but anyone who knows the key may easily reverse the transformation and arrive at the original text.

The keys used in public key cryptography work on the same principle, but in a considerably more sophisticated way. Instead of a single key, encryption and decryption are accomplished using a *pair* of keys. Each key consists of a very long number, perhaps several hundred decimal digits in length. The number stands for the set of rules that is used to transform a message into encrypted form, or back again. Each person who wishes to make use of public key cryptography has his own pair of keys, and each pair of keys is unique.

Of each pair of keys, one is designated the *public key* and the other the *private key*. As the names suggest, the owner of a key pair makes his public key generally available to the world—such as by posting it on his Web page, or inserting it at the bottom of outgoing e-mail messages—while keeping the private key strictly to himself.

The two keys making up a key pair are related to each other mathematically so as to yield several useful properties. First, if you encrypt a message with the public key, it can *only* be decrypted using the corresponding private key. This allows you to send a message that can only be read by the intended recipient: you do so by encrypting the message using the recipient's public key. Second, if a message can be decrypted with a particular public key, it can *only* have been encrypted with the corresponding private key. Thus, if you are able to decrypt a message using a particular public key, it must have been encrypted using the corresponding private key (and, if the private key has been kept private, it must have been encrypted by the owner of that key pair). Third, if the keys are of sufficient length, it is impossible to derive the private key from the public key in any reasonable amount of time, no matter how many computers you have working on the problem. This means that if the owner of a key pair keeps the private key private, there is no way for anybody else to figure out what it is.

The other technique that is used in creating a digital signature is called a *hash function*. Like an encryption key, a hash function is a set of rules that transforms a text message into what looks like gibberish. But a hash function has a different set of properties. First, it transforms any text message, no matter how long, into output of a fixed length. The output is called a *message digest*. For example, a commonly used hash function turns any text message into a message digest consisting of a number with roughly 50 decimal digits. Second, if the text message is altered by even one letter, the hash function produces a different message digest. Third, it is not feasible to run the hash function backwards: starting from the message digest, one cannot reconstruct the original message.

We can now understand how to create a digital signature and use it to sign an electronic text message. This occurs in a series of steps.

First, the sender creates a text message, as an e-mail message, a word processing document, or in some other format.

Second, the sender runs the message through the hash function, transforming it into a message digest.

Third, the sender encrypts the message digest using her private key.

Fourth, the sender sends the original message, together with the encrypted message digest, to the recipient, via e-mail or some other means.

Fifth, the recipient runs the message she received through the hash function, transforming it into a message digest.

Sixth, the recipient uses the sender's public key to decrypt the message digest. This establishes that the message must have been encrypted using the sender's private key.

Seventh, the recipient compares the result of Step 5 with the result of Step 6. If they match, then she can be confident that the message she received is exactly the same as the message that the sender sent. If the message had been altered in transit, then it would have generated a message digest different from the one that the sender generated from the original message.

Although this may seem like an onerous and time-consuming process, when implemented properly it is all accomplished automatically and nearly instantaneously by the sender's and recipient's e-mail programs.

So far, we have achieved one of the goals that needs to be met if an electronic signature is to serve the functions of its pen-and-ink predecessor: *data integrity*. Like the indelibility of ink on paper, and the placement of a pen-and-ink signature physically at the end of a message, the application of cryptographic technologies assures that a text has not been tampered with.

What about authentication? Can the recipient of the message be certain that it was sent by the person whose name is attached to it in electronic text? Not yet. So far, nothing in the digital signature process forecloses the possibility that an impostor has publicly posted his own public key, and falsely attributed it to the sender. The message might then have been sent by the impostor, in the name of somebody else. Even if it was actually sent by the person who is identified in the message as the sender, the recipient cannot prove that the sender is lying if the sender seeks to repudiate the message. Thus, we have not yet achieved either authentication or nonrepudiation.

Those goals are achieved by introducing into the system a trusted third party, known as a *certification authority*, or "CA." The CA's role is to attest that a particular public key is associated with a particular individual. The CA ascertains the individual's identity through standard offline means, such as by checking her passport or driver's license while she is physically present, and the individual demonstrates ownership of a key pair. The CA then creates a *digital certificate*. The certificate consists of a text message reading something like: "The public key 467937698316 belongs to Samantha Smith." To prevent tampering with this message, the certificate is signed with the CA's own digital signature: the CA runs the attestation message through a hash function, and encrypts the resulting message digest with its private key.

Digital certificates are maintained in a centralized registry, where they may be accessed by anyone who wants to verify that a particular public key is associated with a particular person or entity. The system by which certificates are created, maintained, accessed, revoked, and otherwise managed is known as the *public key infrastructure*, or "PKI."

With the addition of this infrastructure, the electronic signature can establish both *data integrity* (as described above) and *authentication*. Upon receipt of the message, the recipient consults the digital certificate associated with the public key she used to decrypt the message digest. If the certificate states that the public key belongs to the sender, then the message has been authenticated as issuing from the sender.

The third function of pen-and-ink signatures, *nonrepudiation*, is a bit trickier to achieve. If the indicated sender of a message falsely denies having sent it, can the recipient of the message establish that she is lying? If the procedure described above is followed, the recipient can show that the message was sent by someone in possession of the private key associated with the public key that the CA attests is associated with the sender. But the putative sender might yet maintain (1) that the CA was in error, as she did not own the key pair, or (2) while she owned the key pair, somebody else must have discovered her private key and used it to impersonate her.

This is where technology leaves off and the law comes into play. The American Bar Association's 1996 *Digital Signature Guidelines: Legal Infrastructure for Certification Authorities and Secure Electronic Commerce* sets forth a suggested approach to legal issues arising in connection with digital signatures.

Charles R. Merrill, *Proof of Who, What and When in Electronic Commerce Under the Digital Signature Guidelines*

542 PLI/Pat 185 (1998).

Hypothetical Example

Bob, a securities broker, has printed out the following document from a file on the hard drive of his PC, which he claims to be a true copy of an e-mail message he received via the Internet.

Alice has an active securities trading account with Bob, in which she maintains a credit balance of securities and cash. Alice has often used Internet e-mail to instruct Bob as to purchases and sales of securities in her account.

To: Bob@securities-r-us.com

From: Alice@restaurant.com

Date: Feb 27, 1997 10:00

Please buy 100 shs of Netscape common stock for my account immediately, at the prevailing market price. /s/ Alice

On Thursday, Feb 27, Bob did buy 100 shares of Netscape common stock for Alice's account. On Friday, Feb 28, the market price of Netscape plummeted, producing a substantial loss on this transaction. Upon receipt of routine written confirmation of purchase of 100 shares for her account, Alice claims, alternatively:

(1) Bob, I never sent any e-mail message! or

(2) Bob, I sent an e-mail message, but it said "sell 100 shs of Netscape"! or

(3) Bob, I sent that e-mail message, but not till Feb 28, after the price fell!

The Challenge of Conducting Secure Electronic Commerce on the Internet

The example illustrates the challenge of conducting secure electronic commerce on the Internet, where, as the famous New Yorker cartoon says, "They can't tell you're a dog." Although the Internet is increasingly attractive as a commercial channel, the dark side is that the Internet is notoriously insecure in its normal configuration as an "open system," where there are no trusted gatekeepers to authenticate identity of users entering the system. Sophisticated hackers are demonstrably able to send messages "spoofing" the identity and e-mail address of others, and to intrude in private communications between others—intercepting, reading, modifying and sending messages along again, without detection. Many believe that if electronic commerce continues to accelerate its volume without substantial improvements in security, commercial losses through such attacks will also grow in volume—motivated not only by mischief but by the "Willie Sutton" syndrome ("Willie, why do you rob banks?" "Because the money's there.")

On August 1, 1996, the Information Security Committee of the American Bar Association Section of Science and Technology published the Digital Signature Guidelines, a four-year collaboration of more than 70 leading technologists and attorneys from all over the world. The Guidelines seek to define a system of public key infrastructure which combines the powerful technological capabilities of an asymmetric cryptosystem with legal principles of commercial law.

* * *

Remember Alice? A Summary of the Legal Issues

Our hypothetical example illustrates a classic case of where a robust system of non-repudiation is needed to block Alice's false denial that she sent the message produced by Bob. If in fact Alice did send that message, a plausible motive could be the intention to remain unfairly flexible at the expense of Bob, by waiting to see the future market price before confirming or denying that she sent the message. Such conduct (if unfair) is recognized and remediable under the equitable principle of "laches" in the Anglo–American legal system.

The problem, of course, and the central dilemma for electronic commerce in an open system, is that in a digital environment based on bits rather than atoms, the jury and the opposing counsel will be deprived of cues or clues which would normally be available for the resolution of disputes in a paper-based and human-contact-based world. Here are the three possible factual theories which face the dispute resolution authority (judge, jury, arbitrator, mediator or the like):

(A) Alice is lying and Bob is truthful. Alice did send the message, and Bob did not falsify it. Alice intended to buy the stock, but after the market dropped, she is repudiating the transaction in order to avoid the loss, committing laches at Bob's expense. (Or she sent "buy" and wants to substitute "sell". Or she sent the message Feb 27 and now claims she sent it Feb 28, after the price dropped.)

(B) Bob is lying and Alice is truthful. Bob has falsified the message and the printout, and Alice never sent it. Bob bought the stock for his own account or for another customer, and after the market dropped, he tried to put the loss on Alice. (Or she did send "buy" and Bob has substituted "sell". Or she did sent the message Feb 28 and Bob has caused his PC to substitute Feb 27.)

(C) Alice and Bob are Both Telling the Truth!! Alice did not send the message, but Bob did receive it on Feb 27. An unknown imposter (for mischievous or other unknown motives) has either:

- Spoofed Alice and sent the message, or

• Intercepted Alice's message and changed "buy" to "sell"

The fact finder could rationally decide (A) or (B) on the basis of the relative credibility of the testimony of Alice or Bob—a process with which the legal system is comfortable and familiar. The most troublesome possibility for a system of jurisprudence is Case (C), where the fact finder decides that both Alice and Bob are truthful, innocent and victimized, yet must then decide which innocent victim should bear the damage caused by an imposter who is usually unknown, judgment-proof, and/or beyond the court's jurisdiction.

Under the facts of the hypothetical example, the e-mail message is "naked" of any cryptographic authentication of any kind. What would happen if the e-mail were digitally signed, and the case were decided in a jurisdiction (e.g., the States of Utah or Washington) where rules similar to the Digital Signature Guidelines are in force?

Deciding the Case under the Digital Signature Guidelines

Step 1. Is there a digital signature on the message? GL 1.11 defines digital signature as the following:

> A transformation of a message using an asymmetric cryptosystem and a hash function such that a person having the initial message and the signer's public key can accurately determine (1) whether the transformation was created using the private key that corresponds to the signer's public key, and (2) whether the initial message has been altered since the transformation was made.

If there is a digital signature on the message, the Guidelines apply, and we proceed to Step 2. This is an "opt-in" system, where the use of digital signatures is entirely optional on the part of users. If the user has not digitally signed the message, the Guidelines do not apply, and existing law does.

Step 2. If a relying party has a message signed with a digital signature and also has a public key available, the crypto software allows the relying party to determine whether the digital signature was created by someone who used the private key corresponding to that public key. The effect is to link the digital signature to that public key. We still know nothing about who signed the document.

Step 3. Do we have a digital certificate issued by a trusted third party certification authority (CA)? * * * Depending upon the rigor of the identification procedures required for the particular class of certificates, the certificate binds the identity of the subscriber to the subscriber's public key, during the typical one-year operational period of the certificate.

Step 4. The next step is to verify the digital signature and message integrity under GL 1.37, which defines that process as:

In relation to a given digital signature, message and public key, to determine accurately:

> (1) that the digital signature was created during the operational period of a valid certificate by the private key corresponding to the public key listed in the certificate; and
>
> (2) the message has not been altered since its digital signature was created.

From Step 2, the software has already told the relying party that the digital signature is linked to the public key available to the relying party. From Step 3, the CA linked the public key of Alice to Alice's identity. Step 4 requires that the digital signature be created during the operational period of a valid certificate (i.e., not before its issue date and not after it has expired or it has been revoked), and if this requirement is satisfied, the digital signature has been "verified". Combining Step 2, Step 3 and Step 4, the digital signature has now been linked with Alice.

Step 5. At this point, the analysis becomes primarily legal, diverging from the yes/no binary approach favored by computer security professionals, into the fuzzy, analog world of the dispute resolution process which determines who wins and loses in a commercial dispute. Guideline 5.6 provides the following *rebuttable* presumption:

> In resolving a dispute involving a digital signature it is rebuttably presumed that . . .
>
> (2) a digital signature verified by reference to the public key listed in a valid certificate is the digital signature of the subscriber listed in that certificate,
>
> (3) the message associated with a verified digital signature has not been altered from its original form, ...

Under traditional paper-based law, it is often the case that the person relying on a signed document has the burden of proof (both the burden of going forward with evidence and persuading the fact finder with the preponderance of the evidence) that the document was signed by the person to whom it is attributed. Similarly, under Federal Reserve Regulations Reg E and Reg Z governing ATM devices and credit cards, the liability of even a negligent cardholder is generally limited to $50 regardless of how much loss is caused the cardholder's bank. Reflecting the robust security capabilities of asymmetric cryptosystem technology, the Digital Signature Guidelines intentionally reverse that presumption where a digital signature is properly verifiable. If the e-mail message in our hypothetical example was digitally signed and verified by reference to Alice's valid certificate as per the preceding four steps, then Alice is liable to Bob, unless she successfully rebuts the presumption that the e-mail message produced by Bob is signed by Alice and not modified since the time she signed it. There are two major ways Alice may rebut that presumption and avoid liability.

Step 6. The first and most obvious way Alice may rebut the presumption that she signed the message is to carry the burden of proof that the certification authority made a mistake in identifying Alice as the subscriber of the certificate which contains the public key. One factual theory available to Alice is that an imposter spoofed Alice's identity in applying for a certificate in the name of Alice, but bound to the imposter's public key. If Alice succeeds with this theory and the relying party has been damaged by reliance upon the incorrect certificate, then the relying party could seek redress against the CA for damages caused by the CA's error. Under a so-called "closed PKI model" (in contrast with the "open PKI model" which the Guidelines represent) it may be that no one other than the CA itself (or a government or other entity controlling the CA or outsourcing duties to the CA) is entitled to rely upon the CA's certificate.

Step 7. The second way Alice may rebut the presumption that she signed the message is to carry the burden of proof that, although Alice's private key was used to sign the message, the use of Alice's private key was unauthorized by Alice. To do this, Alice would need to overcome the non-repudiation security service provided by the dual-key asymmetric cryptosystem, and carry the burden of proving that she compromised or lost control of her private key, and that the private key was used by another to sign the message, without her authority.

Step 8. Under GL 4.3, Alice has the affirmative duty to safeguard her private key from compromise. If Alice was successful under Step 7 in showing that her private key was used by another to sign the message without her authority, then the inquiry will proceed to the issue of whether Alice's compromise of her private key was negligent. If Alice violated her duty to safeguard her key from compromise, then as between the two innocent parties—Bob the relying party and Alice the subscriber—Alice would bear the loss if reimbursement is not possible against the unauthorized user of Alice's private key. It is not clear under the Guidelines whether Alice would have the burden of proving Alice's due care or whether Bob would have the burden of proving Alice's negligence. Either rule would be a rational approach by a State or other jurisdiction which wished to tilt the playing field more in favor of one of the two parties. The required standard of care is likely to be affected by the extent to which the digital signature software comes to be embedded in smart cards and other hardware devices with the triple compromise protection of (a) tangible token required, (b) secret PIN required, and (c) biometric proof of physical presence.

Step 9. If Alice discovers that her private key has been compromised, she can perhaps cut off her liability to relying parties (at least as to future reliance) by revoking her certificate, so that the certificate becomes listed on a certificate revocation list which cuts off the operational period of the certificate so that no digital signatures created thereafter are verifiable. See GL 5.4, regarding reasonable reliance. An important issue is the extent to which relying parties have constructive notice of certificate revocation lists maintained online and elsewhere by CAs, whether or not the relying party has actual notice of the certificate's revocation.

Step 10. Finally, even if Alice for some reason fails to revoke her certificate in time to warn relying parties, under the particular circumstances there may be factual arguments available to her under GL 5.3, regarding unreliable digital signatures, as to why Bob should be required to confirm the transaction with Alice "out-of-band" (e.g., by picking up the telephone) before proceeding to rely.

Thomas J. Smedinghoff, Certification Authority: Liability Analysis

www.bmck.com/CA-Liability-Analysis.doc.
(1998).

1. Executive Summary

This memo surveys the liability issues raised by an entity's entry into the certification authority business. It is, however, in many respects an uncharted territory. As one commentator has noted "the duties and potential liabilities imposed upon a CA by U.S. law are unclear, as might be expected from the dearth of applicable legislation, the complete absence of case law, and the very small number of currently functioning CAs."[2] Accordingly, this memo addresses the major sources of law likely to provide a basis for certification of authority liability, and analyzes those areas of the law in analogous situations in an attempt to determine how they might be applied to the activities of a certification authority.

The focus of our efforts was on what appear to be the four primary areas of potential liability: negligent misrepresentation, breach of warranty, intellectual property infringement, and liability for the conduct of others. That is not to imply, however, that there are not several other areas of law and legal theories that might support a finding of liability against a certification authority. Other bases of liability might include antitrust, interference with contractual relationships, unfair competition, and defamation.

Engaging in the business of a certification authority involves entering a type of business to which the law has not yet had time to adapt. By issuing digital certificates that verify identity, a certification authority is, in essence, engaged in the business of an information provider. This is, in many respects, different from traditional businesses that involve the sale of goods, or traditional businesses that involve the provision of services. Moreover, while publishing industries have engaged in providing information, issuing digital certificates is significantly different because of the fact that they are intended to be relied upon by parties to a commercial transaction. It is this aspect of reliance that is critical. Both the certification authority that issues a certificate and the subscriber that acquires it do so with the intention that it will be used by third parties to verify identity and engage in business transactions. In fact, that is the very nature of a certificate.

Given the fact of this intended reliance, the critical issue for a certification authority becomes the accuracy of the certificate. Stated other-

2. A. Michael Froomkin, *The Essential Role of Trusted Third Parties in Electronic Commerce,* 75 Or. L. Rev. 49 (Spring 1996).

wise, what is the CA's liability for errors in the certificate, errors in a repository containing certificates, or errors in a certificate revocation list ("CRL") on which third parties rely to their detriment? Thus, the primary focus from a liability perspective is on the tort of negligent misrepresentation and contract actions for breach of warranty that are either express or implied regarding the accuracy of the information provided. Relatedly, it is also necessary to consider intellectual property issues that permeate the certification authority process. And finally, for an entity that intends to outsource a large part of its certification authority obligation to a certificate manufacturing authority, it is important to consider the liability for the conduct of the third persons acting on its behalf that might also cause injury.

The following is a summary of the findings set forth in the sections that follow in the Memorandum.

1.1 Tort Liability—Negligent Misrepresentation

When operating as a certification authority ("CA"), an entity will primarily be in the business of providing information, in the form of certificates, a repository, and a CRL. To the extent such information is incorrect due to the failure of the CA to exercise reasonable care, the CA will be liable for the tort of negligent misrepresentation to persons who rely on the information to their detriment.

Negligent misrepresentation creates a duty to exercise reasonable care to verify facts, but it does not make the CA a guarantor of the accuracy of the information provided. The CA is subject to liability only if the error results from its negligence.

Understanding the scope of the CA's potential liability for negligent misrepresentation requires consideration of two basic issues: (1) what is the legal duty, if any, owed by the CA; and (2) to whom is such duty or obligation owed?

The extent of the legal duty owed by one person to another is described as the standard of care. The standard of care to be exercised in any particular case depends upon the surrounding circumstances and the extent of foreseeable danger. There are five possible standards of care that may apply to an entity's activities as a certification authority: (1) a general standard of ordinary or reasonable care; (2) a professional standard of care; (3) a strict liability standard; (4) a statutorily-mandated standard; and (5) possibly, a standard measured against criteria established by the CA itself.

At present, it appears that CAs will most likely be held to a general standard of reasonable care. From a business perspective, reasonable care means that degree of care that an ordinarily prudent person engaged in the same line of business would exercise under similar circumstances. Unfortunately, in an industry as novel as that of the certification authority, there is no established standard of care. Appropriate standards of reasonable care take time to be established, and are based in part on the customs of the industry, what people have come to expect, and what courts will allow based on the goal of tort law to remedy harm to individuals. The fact that

CAs, by their nature, will be parties with specialized skills in whom laypersons place trust beyond that of the normal marketplace may eventually give rise to professional status, or otherwise subject them to a higher duty of care to do what is reasonable given their specialized skills.

Generally, it appears that a CA will not be permitted to set its own standards of care. A minimum standard of care applies with respect to any given activity. In most cases it is likely to be a reasonable care standard, measured by the extent to which a company's practices meet or exceed what seems reasonable in light of the risk involved in a given activity, although in some cases standards of conduct may be set by statute. For example, the Utah Digital Signature Act imposes various duties upon a licensed CA in connection with the issuance of certificates concerning identification of the parties to the certificate, the security of the private key, and the functioning of the public key. Generally, the CA will need to carefully consider the anticipated use of the certificates it issues, and ensure that its procedures are appropriate to protect against harm to others arising from those uses.

The second issue concerns to whom a duty or obligation is owed? A CA potentially has tort duties with respect to three groups of people: (1) subscribers (i.e., the persons to whom certificates are issued), (2) parties relying on certificates, repositories, and CRLs issued or maintained by the CA ("relying parties"), and (3) third party victims of fraud. Whether it actually owes a duty to each of these classes will vary depending on the jurisdiction, since liability often depends on the nature of the relationship between the information provider and the party whose reliance resulted in loss. In identifying the third parties to whom a CA owes a duty of care, courts generally take one of three approaches:

(1) *Foreseeability Standard*: One will be liable to any person for whom reliance on the false representations was reasonably foreseeable. This is the broadest standard of liability applicable to information providers.

(2) *Standard Based on Intent and Knowledge*: There is a more limited scope of liability, providing that liability is limited to loss suffered (a) by a member of the group of the persons for whose benefit and guidance one intends to supply information or knows that the recipient intends to supply it; or (b) through reliance upon it in a transaction that he intends the information to influence or knows that the recipient so intends, or in a substantially similar transaction. This standard is the most widely adopted.

(3) *Privity Standard*: This is the most limited standard, creating a duty owed solely to the client, or one with whom the information provider had specific contact. Some states adopt this approach as a matter of common law while others adopt statutory applications.

In addition to liability for incorrect information based on negligent misrepresentation, there also exists the possibility that the use of a CA's branded certificates (or the CA's logo) by subscribers may be construed as an endorsement of the subscriber by the CA in a manner that may lead to liability. Endorsers of products may be liable for negligent misrepresentation if the product fails to live up to the justifiable expectations of quality created by the endorsement and a consumer is harmed by relying on that endorsement. Independent testing laboratories, magazines that endorse products, and trade associations which lend their mark to products have all been held liable for negligent misrepresentation when the products failed to meet expectations. A certificate itself may be considered an endorsement by the CA of the subscriber or website that it is used to verify, which may make the CA analogous to an endorser. As a general matter, endorsers may only be held liable to the extent of their representation, and only if the plaintiff could prove that the endorser was negligent in making that representation. The CA might reduce the potential for such liability by carefully delineating the nature of the representation it is making with respect to the certificates it issues.

* * *

By using notices and disclaimers to define the scope of the product or services they provide, information providers may be able to put third parties on notice that any reliance on the information contrary to the notice or disclaimer may be unreasonable and thus may be undertaken at the relying party's own risk. While disclaimers will not necessarily overcome liability for intentional fraud, they may be effective to limit liability for negligence by controlling questions about the justifiability of a party's reliance. Because reasonable or justifiable reliance on provided information must be shown in a negligent misrepresentation case, the general effect of such a disclaimer may be to put third parties on notice that any reliance contrary to the disclaimer may be deemed unreasonable and thus preclude recovery in the event that errors occur.

Unfortunately, unlike an accountant's opinion letter, which can easily accommodate a conspicuous disclaimer, digital certificates are not nearly as flexible. A certificate may only be able to incorporate a disclaimer by reference. CAs may be able to contractually bind third parties to exculpatory clauses by requiring subscribers to incorporate such provisions in their contracts with third parties. However, it remains unclear whether CAs could rely merely on a non-contractual disclaimer to limit their potential liability to third parties for negligent misrepresentation liability.

Assuming that a non-contractual disclaimer by a CA is effective, then the issue becomes one of notice. Given the limited space on a certificate, and given that a relying party may not even see the certificate itself, providing adequate notice of the disclaimer to relying parties may prove difficult.

1.2 Contract Liability

A CA's contractual and warranty obligations depend, in part, on what law applies to its certification authority activities. Article 2 of the Uniform Commercial Code (UCC) governs transactions in goods, the common law (judge-made law) applies to transactions in services and to contracts pertaining specifically to the provision of information, and Proposed Article 2B[1] (a revision of the UCC that could be approved within the next year) applies specifically to the licensing of information.

Many of the CA's proposed activities, such as maintaining a repository and CRL and receiving, transmitting, revoking, suspending, and managing certificates, appear to be services and thus subject to the common law (court-made law). Other of the CA's proposed activities, including issuing certificates and authenticating subscribers, could be characterized as provision of either a service or a good and thus be subject, respectively, to the common law or to the Uniform Commercial Code (UCC), the latter of which governs transactions in goods. Yet, even when a commercial activity does not directly fall under the UCC, courts will often refer to it as persuasive authority. Because a CA's proposed activities largely constitute the provision of information, the common law and Proposed Article 2B could also be key to determining the CA's potential liability to subscribers, relying parties, and impersonated third parties.

UCC law governing contracts for *goods* is very results-oriented—certain default warranties and other obligations arise under a UCC-governed contract to ensure that the product conforms to ordinary standards of performance. Parties are free to agree otherwise on many points and thus can limit or exclude most warranties, limit remedies, and impose damage caps and other limitations on liability. Even when parties can bargain for different contract terms, certain UCC rules restrict the ways in which they disclaim or limit their liability. By and large, disclaimers and other liability limits must be conspicuous (a notice sort of issue), which raises special problems in an electronic context, particularly with regard to digital certificates. Other provisions of the UCC cannot be disclaimed. In particular, regardless of the terms of the contract, the UCC will impose an obligation of good faith, diligence, care, and reasonableness. The UCC also will not tolerate unconscionability—i.e., a surprise term that no one in his right senses would accept—especially when an unsophisticated consumer could be hurt.

The common law governing contracts for *services* is more process-oriented. Courts ask whether the provider of the service performed in a reasonably careful and workmanlike manner, especially in light of the particular trade or profession from which the service provider is drawn and of the abilities, skill, and knowledge claimed by that service provider. Because those who provide services often must deal with factors beyond their control, courts tend not to read into contracts express and implied warranties that amount to "insuring" or "guaranteeing" favorable results, unless the parties have expressly agreed to that higher standard (which often entails the payment of a higher price). Alarm/security companies, title searchers, inspectors, and others are not expected to produce infallible results; instead, they are expected to adhere to certain procedures depend-

1. [Proposed Article 2B of the Uniform Commercial Code was promulgated as the Uniform Computer Information Transactions Act, discussed in this chapter and in Chapter 4, *supra*.—Eds.]

ing on the circumstances. Likewise, *information providers* typically are not required to ensure 100% accuracy. This is especially true for those who publish for a mass-market, as a newspaper does. As the relationship between the parties gets closer, and the information provider has more reason to know of the relying party's particular needs and is compensated accordingly, the obligations regarding the provision of information increase.

Courts generally uphold exculpatory clauses that limit a party's liability under a contract unless they violate public policy or something in the social relationship between the parties dictates against it. * * *

* * *

Consumers may constitute a large number of the relying parties. If certain consumer statutes apply to these transactions, this could restrict a CA's ability to limit its obligations and potential liability. In all likelihood, however, a CA can effectively reduce its potential liability through careful use of contractual language and representations it makes in its [certification practice statement], advertisements, and the like.

1.3 Statutory Liability—Digital Signature Regulation

One potential source of liability for a CA may arise through statute, specifically from the application of provisions contained in digital signature legislation and administrative regulations promulgated pursuant thereto. Such regulation exists, or may soon exist, not only in the various states, but also at the federal and international levels.

To date, some form of digital or electronic signature legislation has now been enacted or is currently being considered in 47 states. The form and scope of this legislation varies widely. Of these states, nine have enacted or are currently considering comprehensive digital signature acts that embrace the concept of a certification authority and specifically address liability issues. Other less comprehensive acts expressly authorize the use of digital or electronic signatures either generally or in connection with communications with the state government, but may or may not expressly contemplate the use of certification authorities or specifically address liability issues. Still others merely authorize the use of digital or electronic signatures in connection with a specific context, such as filing tax returns or corporate documents with the state government, and do not specifically address certification authorities or their liability. It is difficult to gauge at this time the extent to which future legislation might affect the liability of certification authorities, or the extent to which it could impose regulatory burdens.

The Utah Digital Signature Act (the "Utah Act") was the first comprehensive digital signature act to be enacted and has since been used as a model by other states. The Utah Act establishes a voluntary licensing program for certification authorities. Certification authorities who voluntarily subject themselves to the Utah Act must comply with the various duties imposed upon them in connection with, among other things, the issuance and revocation of certificates and the maintenance of a repository. Failure to comply with these statutory duties could not only trigger administrative enforcement action, but also could serve as a basis for negligence liability in tort.

On the other hand, the Utah Act also helps to *limit* the amount of potential liability in some ways too, such as by capping the liability of a *licensed* certification authority under certain circumstances at the amount specified in the certificate as the recommended reliance limit. The Utah Act also expressly limits the types of damages available to third parties who incur losses in connection with their reliance on a certificate.

One example of the duties imposed by the Utah Act are those duties that arise in connection with the issuance of a certificate. Certification authorities licensed in Utah may issue a certificate to a subscriber only after various conditions have been satisfied. Those conditions include, among other things, that the certification authority has confirmed that: the prospective subscriber is the person to be listed in the certificate to be issued; the information in the certificate to be issued is accurate after due diligence; the prospective subscriber rightfully holds the private key corresponding to the public key to be listed in the certificate; the prospective subscriber holds a private key capable of creating a digital signature; and the public key to be listed in the certificate can be used to verify a digital signature affixed by the private key held by the prospective subscriber. Certification authorities licensed in Utah are also required to use only a "trustworthy system" and must disclose their certification practice statement.

Although only certification authorities licensed in Utah (or in states with similar digital signature legislation) are subject to these statutory duties, such legislation nevertheless may serve as a model for measuring the reasonableness of a certification authority's conduct in states where such statutes do not yet exist. Thus any certification authority would be well advised to take these and other statutory standards of care under consideration when establishing the procedures to which it will adhere in connection with offering certification authority services.

As of yet there has not been any federal legislation enacted specifically pertaining to certification authorities. However, federal regulation of certification authorities may not be very far away. One bill recently considered in Congress would establish a national association of certification authorities to which any person or group wishing to provide electronic authentication services in the United States would have to belong. The Bill would also create a standards review committee to establish and refine criteria to be applied to the emerging electronic authentication industry. This committee also would be charged with establishing and adopting guidelines, standards and codes of conduct applicable to certification authorities. Thus, the possibility exists that at some point in the future certification authorities could become subject to potentially extensive and burdensome federal regulation. * * *

* * *

NOTES & QUESTIONS

1. *A natural transition.* A certification authority ("CA") acts as a trusted third party that vouches for parties negotiating online, confirming the identity and other important attributes of persons who are sending and receiving electronic messages and payments over the Internet. Commercial banks fulfill a similar function in the brick-and-mortar economy, especially with respect to international transactions, confirming the identity and vouching for the good reputation of local businesses involved in commercial transactions with parties in other states or countries. Should commercial banks become the certification authorities of the new online economy?

2. *Open vs. closed systems.* The Office of the Comptroller of the Currency explains:

> CA systems may be characterized as primarily open or closed. A fully closed system has contracts defining the rights and obligations of all participants for authenticating messages or transactions. This type of system offers the CA operators less risk exposure because there is little uncertainty regarding obligations. Conversely, a fully open system would not have formal contracts defining the rights and obligations of relying parties in the system. In such a system, the firms that perform the CA activities could be exposed to an uncertain level of risk for each authenticated message or transaction. It is likely during early stages of development that most CA systems will be neither fully open nor fully closed, with contracts defining the rights and responsibilities of at least some, but not all, of the system participants.

OCC Bulletin 99–20, www.occ.treas.gov/ftp/bulletin/99–20.txt.

3. *Certifying risks.* Ultimately the CA's guarantee is only as good as its identification of the person who has purchased a certificate. What kind of identification should a CA require in order to issue a certificate? Should a CA be liable to a recipient who relies on a certificate that was in fact issued to an imposter? Should the state license CAs the way it licenses notaries?

In general, what are the risks involved in being a certification authority? Which of these risks are likely to expose a certification authority to legal action? *See* OCC Bulletin 99–20, *supra*; A. Michael Froomkin, *The Essential Role of Trusted Third Parties in Electronic Commerce,* 75 OR. L. REV. 49 (1996) (especially Part III).

4. *PKI and biometric identification.* A PKI-based digital signature is not the only technology that can be used to verify the identity of an individual online. Biometric technologies that can accomplish this function are also being developed. "Biometrics are best defined as measurable physiological and/or behavioural characteristics that can be utilised to verify the identity of an individual. They include fingerprints, retinal and iris scanning, hand geometry, voice patterns, facial recognition and other techniques. They are of interest in any area where it is important to verify the true identity of an individual. Initially, these techniques were employed primarily in specialist high security applications, however we are now seeing their use and proposed use in a much broader range of public facing situations." Julian Ashbourn, *The Biometric White Paper*, homepage.ntlworld.com/avanti/home.htm.

While PKI and biometrics may at first appear to be competing methods for verifying the identity of individuals, the two technologies are actually complementary. As Ashbourn observes:

> One of the often repeated concerns lies in the area of key management, and in particular, the likelihood of your private key being misused or perhaps stolen. For example, if the operation of your private key is protected by a PIN, then this may easily be compromised at your workstation by someone who wishes to pretend to be you and makes it his or her business to discover that PIN. Similarly, if the private key is stored on your computer's hard disk, then how easy is it for someone to hack into your computer and copy this file? If someone acquires and is able to use your private key, then your PKI environment is powerless to protect you as this person could intercept messages meant for you and easily decrypt them. Furthermore they could pretend to be you within the context of important transactions, with all the implications that this entails. Key management and key security therefore become paramount within a PKI environment.
>
> Biometrics offer the potential to considerably enhance the PKI model in the same way that they have brought significant benefits to the more conventional user authentication area. Let's take for example the ability to restrict the use of your private key for encryption and decryption. Using a PIN for this provides a certain level of perceived security, although the actual level is rather low. Using a biometric, such as a fingerprint for example, provides a substantially higher level of confidence. The likelihood of someone else using your workstation or mobile computer and successfully using your biometrically protected private key is reduced to almost infinitesimal proportions. * * *

Julian Ashbourn, *Biometrics and PKI*, homepage.ntlworld.com/avanti/home.htm.

II. THE STATUTE OF FRAUDS ONLINE

Various statutes of frauds have been adopted by legislative act or judicial decision in every state of the United States, as well as by the federal government. Most statutes of frauds provide that for certain kinds of contracts—such as those involving land transfer, those that cannot be performed within one year, or those involving more than a threshold dollar value—the agreement is unenforceable unless at least some memorandum of it is in writing and signed by the party to be charged. *See, e.g.,* U.C.C. § 2–201(1)("[A] contract for the sale of goods for the price of $500 or more is not enforceable by way of action or defense unless there is some writing sufficient to indicate that a contract for sale has been made between the parties and signed by the party against whom enforcement is sought * * *.").

Two questions arise in connection with the applicability of statutes of frauds to electronic commerce: (1) Does an electronic record satisfy the writing requirement of the statute of frauds?; and (2) Does an electronic signature satisfy the signature requirement? These two questions are the focus of the present section.

A. ELECTRONIC RECORDS AS WRITINGS

In re RealNetworks, Inc., Privacy Litigation

2000 WL 631341 (N.D.Ill.2000).

■ KOCORAS, J.

[The portion of this opinion addressing plaintiff's argument that the arbitration agreement is unconscionable is reproduced in Chapter 4, Part III, *supra*. The following excerpt addresses Intervenor's argument "that the License Agreement, including the arbitration requirement, does not constitute a 'writing.' "]

DISCUSSION

Although national policy encourages arbitration of disputes, submission to arbitration is consensual, not coercive. Thus, a court cannot force a party to arbitrate unless that party has entered into a contractual agreement to do so. In order to determine whether the parties intended to submit to arbitration, a court reviews the contract at issue. In so doing, a court employs the standard methods of contract interpretation, using state-law principles. Ambiguities, however, are resolved in favor of arbitration.

A party contesting the submission of the claim to arbitration must clearly show that the presumption of arbitrability does not apply. A claim will be deemed to be arbitrable if an arbitration clause is capable of any interpretation that a claim is covered. If parties have a contract providing for arbitration of some issues, questions concerning the scope of issues subject to arbitration should be resolved in favor of arbitration.

I. Writing Requirement

Intervenor claims that the License Agreement, including the arbitration provision, does not constitute a writing as required by the Federal Arbitration Act (the "FAA") and the Washington Arbitration Act (the "WAA") in order to be enforced. According to Intervenor, the License Agreement is an electronic agreement, and electronic agreements do not satisfy the "written" agreement provisions of the FAA and the WAA. Moreover, Intervenor asserts that even if some electronic agreements are acceptable, RealNetworks' electronic agreement is not because a user cannot print or save it. RealNetworks does not dispute that the arbitration provision must be written in order to be enforceable. Rather, RealNetworks argues that its License Agreement, including the arbitration provision, constitute a writing and that it may be printed and saved.

Both the Intervenor and RealNetworks agree that Congress intended the FAA to apply only to written contracts. Because the terms in the statute must be given their plain meaning and do not explicitly allow for an "electronic" agreement, Intervenor reasons that an electronic communication cannot satisfy the writing requirement, but only a written one can. However, this only begs the question, what is a written agreement? Although contract terms must be given their plain and ordinary meaning, the Court is unconvinced that the plain and ordinary meaning of "writing" or "written" necessarily cannot include any electronic writings.

Courts frequently look to dictionaries in order determine the plain meaning of words and particularly examine how a word was defined at the time the statute was drafted and enacted. The FAA was enacted in 1925. As now, words had several different definitions. In relevant part, at the time, Webster's Dictionary defined "writing" as:

> 1. The act or art of forming letters or characters on paper, wood, stone, or other material, for the purpose of recording the ideas which characters and words express, or of communicating them to others by visible signs. 2. Anything written or printed; anything expressed in characters or letters.

See WEBSTER'S DICTIONARY (1913). Webster's defined "written" as the participle of write, which it defined as:

> 1. To set down, as legible characters; to form the conveyance of meaning; to inscribe on any material by a suitable instrument; as, to write the characters called letters; to write figures.

See id.

A legal dictionary at the time provided that "The word 'written,' used in a statute, may include printing and any other mode of representing words and letters." *See* Pope, Benjamin, W., *Legal Definitions,* Callaghan and Co. (1920). Thus, although the definition of a writing included a traditional paper document, it did not exclude representations of language on other media. Because electronic communications can be letters or characters formed on the screen to record or communicate ideas * * * and can be legible characters that represent words and letters as well as form the conveyance of meaning, it would seem that the plain meaning of the word "written" does not exclude all electronic communications. That being said, the Court does not now find that all electronic communications may be considered "written." Rather, the Court examines the contract at issue in this action and finds that its easily printable and storable nature is sufficient to render it "written."

The Court rejects Intervenor's contention that the License Agreement is not printable and storable. Intervenor asserts that RealNetworks affirmatively inhibits users from printing or storing the License Agreement by failing to provide a conspicuous "print" or "save" button on the pop-up License Agreement window. However, Intervenor is incorrect in its assertions because the License Agreement may rather easily be printed and is automatically stored on the user's hard drive despite the absence of the "print" and "save" buttons. In fact, there exists more than one way to print the License Agreement. First, before the user has even accepted the License Agreement, the user can right click his mouse over the text of the

License Agreement, select all, and copy and paste it onto any word processing program. Since using the right click function is too specialized for Intervenor, he even has the option to simply click and drag the cursor over the text of the License Agreement in order to highlight it and then copy and paste the License Agreement onto any word processing program. Moreover, users have yet another way of printing the License Agreement. After a user accepts the License Agreement, it is automatically downloaded and saved to the user's hard drive. The user can then click on the License Agreement, listed separately as either "RealJukeBox License Agreement" or "RealPlayer License Agreement," depending on the product, and easily print out either agreement from the file pull down menu. Thus, Intervenor's assertion that the License Agreement cannot be saved, retrieved, or printed is incorrect. Moreover, once installed, the License Agreement is not hidden, as Intervenor claims, but is listed as prominent and separate icons under "Real" on the "Start" menu. Although any computer use can be intimidating, the process of printing the License Agreement is no more difficult or esoteric than many other basic computer functions, and the melodrama and over exaggeration with which Intervenor describes the alleged impossibility of printing the License Agreement is disingenuous.

Finally, Intervenor points to Congress' present day discussions about electronic communications in arguing that the FAA's and WAA's writing requirement cannot be satisfied by an electronic communication. However, the modern congressional discussions that Intervenor points to do not serve as evidence of Congress' intent when it enacted the FAA in 1925. That Congress may now, with some hindsight on the advance of electronic communication, explicitly provide for written and electronic agreements in new legislation, does not mean that Congress in 1925 excluded electronic communications from the category of written communications by not explicitly providing for it. Rather, "New words may be designed to fortify the current rule with a more precise text that curtails uncertainty." *See ProCD, Inc. v. Zeiderberg,* 86 F.3d 1447, 1452 (7th Cir.1996). Modern Congress' discussions indicate that it was, in fact, the "uncertain" legal effect of an electronic record or an electronic signature that prompted Congress to consider the "Electronic Signatures in Global and National Commerce Act," to which Intervenor cites. *See* House Report No. 106–341(I), September 27, 1999. Moreover, it seems that the License Agreement would, nevertheless, constitute a writing even for purposes of Congress' discussions today because the License Agreement may be printed and stored. *See* 145 Cong. Rec. S14881–01, at *S14884, November 19, 1999.

Thus, the License Agreement, including the arbitration provision, is a written agreement.

* * *

B. AUTHENTICATION AS SIGNATURE

Parma Tile Mosaic & Marble Co., Inc. v. Estate of Short

640 N.Y.S.2d 477 (N.Y.1996).

■ SMITH, JUDGE.

The issue presented on this appeal is whether the automatic imprinting, by a fax machine, of the sender's name at the top of each page transmitted, satisfies the requirement that a writing be subscribed under New York State's general Statute of Frauds (General Obligations Law § 5–701). We reverse the order of the Appellate Division because we conclude that a subscription requires an act to authenticate the writing as defendant's. Defendant did not so subscribe the writing in this case.

In September 1989, Sime Construction Co. (Sime), a subcontractor, sought to purchase from plaintiff a large quantity of ceramic tile for use in a construction project. When plaintiff expressed reluctance to enter into such a large contract without a guaranty, Sime suggested that plaintiff approach MRLS Construction Corporation (MRLS), the general contractor on the project, for a guaranty of payment. Plaintiff contacted MRLS and after several discussions, MRLS faxed a document to plaintiff which plaintiff asserts is a guaranty. MRLS contends that it merely transmitted an unsubscribed proposal for a guaranty by fax.

Plaintiff's copy of the document bore a heading at the top of each page which indicated the name "MRLS Construction," a telephone number, the date and time, an unidentified number and a page number. It is undisputed that sometime before sending the document at issue, MRLS had programmed its fax machine to automatically imprint this information on every transmitted page. By this method, the heading would appear only on the recipient's faxed copy, not on the originating document. The two-page fax document in issue was not preceded by a cover letter or any other identifying document.

After the facsimile transmission, plaintiff began furnishing Sime with quantities of ceramic tile. When Fred Short, the principal of Sime, died in April 1990, plaintiff sought payment for Sime's outstanding invoices from MRLS. MRLS refused to make payment on the ground that the document was not an enforceable guaranty.

Plaintiff commenced this action against MRLS and Sime (sued as the estate of Fred Short herein) to recover the outstanding balances for the ceramic tiles furnished to Sime. After issue was joined, plaintiff and MRLS moved for summary judgment, and the trial court, finding issues of fact, denied both motions. Both parties moved for reargument. After reargument, the trial court granted plaintiff's motion on the third cause of action, which alleged a guaranty of payment, severed the third cause of action from the rest of plaintiff's complaint, and directed entry of judgment against MRLS.

In granting summary judgment to plaintiff, the trial court rejected MRLS' contention that the fax document had not been subscribed as required by the Statute of Frauds. The court held that the heading automatically imprinted by the fax machine on plaintiff's copy of the document satisfied the subscription requirement because an intent to be bound had been demonstrated. MRLS appealed the judgment, and the Appellate Division affirmed the trial court. We granted leave to appeal.

"Every agreement, promise or undertaking is void, unless it or some note or memorandum thereof be in writing, and subscribed by the party to be charged therewith, or by his lawful agent if such agreement, promise or undertaking * * * [i]s a special promise to answer for the debt, default or miscarriage of another person" (General Obligations Law § 5–701[a][2]). MRLS argues that the heading imprinted on the top of each page transmitted by its fax machine serves merely as identification, and was not intended to serve as a subscription within that term's special meaning under the Statute of Frauds. MRLS contends that the fax document does not satisfy the requirement in § 5–701(a) that a writing be subscribed. Plaintiff, by contrast, argues that because MRLS intentionally programmed its fax machine to print its name on top of all faxed documents, the subscription requirement has been satisfied.

Plaintiff has failed to demonstrate that MRLS affixed its "signature" to the document sent by facsimile machine sufficient to fulfill the subscription requirement. As former Chief Judge Cardozo has observed, a signature for Statute of Frauds purposes may be "a name, written or printed, [but] is not to be reckoned as a signature unless inserted or adopted with an intent, actual or apparent, to authenticate a writing" (*Mesibov, Glinert & Levy v. Cohen Bros. Mfg. Co.*, 245 N.Y. 305, 310, 157 N.E. 148; *see also, Crabtree v. Elizabeth Arden Sales Corp.*, 305 N.Y. 48, 53–54, 110 N.E.2d 551; *La Mar Hosiery Mills v. Credit & Commodity Corp.*, 28 Misc.2d 764, 216 N.Y.S.2d 186). Plaintiff contends that we may infer satisfaction of this requirement because the fax machine had been programmed by MRLS to identify each page of the document with "MRLS Construction."

The act of identifying and sending a document to a particular destination does not, by itself, constitute a signing authenticating the contents of the document for Statute of Frauds purposes and we reject plaintiff's argument that such an inference is warranted here. It is undisputed that MRLS' fax machine, after being programmed to do so, automatically imprinted "MRLS Construction" on every page transmitted, without regard to the applicability of the Statute of Frauds to a particular document. We also reject plaintiff's contention that the intentional act of programming a fax machine, by itself, sufficiently demonstrates to the recipient the sender's apparent intention to authenticate every document subsequently faxed. The intent to authenticate the particular writing at issue must be demonstrated.[1]

The argument that the Statute of Frauds was not meant to permit parties to evade an obligation otherwise incurred begs the question of whether this writing satisfied the statutory requirement. "The purpose of Statutes of Frauds is to avoid fraud by preventing the enforcement of contracts that were never in fact made" (*Fox Co. v. Kaufman Org.*, 74 N.Y.2d 136, 140, 544 N.Y.S.2d 565, 542 N.E.2d 1082). To this end, General

1. The Statute of Frauds also requires that an intent to authenticate a particular document be demonstrated for qualified financial contracts. Effective as of September

Obligations Law § 5–701(a) contains two threshold requirements for proving the existence of a binding agreement, promise or undertaking: a writing, and a subscription of the writing by the party to be charged therewith. Since the Legislature selected these objective elements to determine, in the first instance, the existence of an enforceable agreement, promise or undertaking, the absence of a writing or a subscription cannot be remedied by arguing that obligations were nevertheless incurred.[2]

NOTES & QUESTIONS

Automatically inserted signatures. In *Parma Tile*, the court held that a document header identifying the sender that was automatically printed by a fax machine was not a signature for purposes of the statute of frauds because it did not evidence the intent of the signer to authenticate the document being faxed. Under this approach, would the sender's typing of his name at the bottom of an e-mail message qualify as a signature under the statute of frauds? What if the sender programs his e-mail client to insert his name at the bottom of every e-mail message that is sent? How is the recipient of e-mail or a court to determine whether name at the bottom of an e-mail message was typed by the sender or inserted automatically by the e-mail client?

C. STATUTORY UPDATES TO THE STATUTE OF FRAUDS

In Chapter 4, *supra*, we considered the effect of UETA, ESIGN, and UCITA on the establishment of binding commitment in Internet commerce. Reconsider these statutes focusing on whether they address the core problems of authentication, non-repudiation, and textual integrity that we identified earlier in this chapter.

Uniform Electronic Transactions Act, §§ 7, 2(7), 2(8), 2(13) & 5

National Conference of Commissioners on Uniform State Laws.
(1999).

SECTION 7. LEGAL RECOGNITION OF ELECTRONIC RECORDS, ELECTRONIC SIGNATURES, AND ELECTRONIC CONTRACTS.

(a) A record or signature may not be denied legal effect or enforceability solely because it is in electronic form.

18, 1994, the Legislature amended § 5–701 of the General Obligations Law to provide that: "the tangible written text produced by telex, telefacsimile, computer retrieval or other process by which electronic signals are transmitted by telephone or otherwise shall constitute a writing and any symbol executed or adopted by a party with the present intention to authenticate a writing shall constitute a signing" (General Obligations Law § 5–701[b][4]).

2. The issue of whether a properly subscribed writing adequately describes the terms of an agreement, promise or undertaking is a different question which is not before this Court.

(b) A contract may not be denied legal effect or enforceability solely because an electronic record was used in its formation.

(c) If a law requires a record to be in writing, an electronic record satisfies the law.

(d) If a law requires a signature, an electronic signature satisfies the law.

Comment

1. This section sets forth the fundamental premise of this Act: namely, that the medium in which a record, signature, or contract is created, presented or retained does not affect its legal significance. * * *

* * *

SECTION 2. DEFINITIONS.

In this [Act]:

(7) "Electronic record" means a record created, generated, sent, communicated, received, or stored by electronic means.

(8) "Electronic signature" means an electronic sound, symbol, or process attached to or logically associated with a record and executed or adopted by a person with the intent to sign the record.

* * *

(13) "Record" means information that is inscribed on a tangible medium or that is stored in an electronic or other medium and is retrievable in perceivable form.

Comment

* * *

6. **"Electronic record."** An electronic record is a subset of the broader defined term "record." It is any record created, used or stored in a medium other than paper (see definition of electronic). The defined term is also used in this Act as a limiting definition in those provisions in which it is used.

Information processing systems, computer equipment and programs, electronic data interchange, electronic mail, voice mail, facsimile, telex, telecopying, scanning, and similar technologies all qualify as electronic under this Act. Accordingly information stored on a computer hard drive or floppy disc, facsimiles, voice mail messages, messages on a telephone answering machine, audio and video tape recordings, among other records, all would be electronic records under this Act.

7. **"Electronic signature."** The idea of a signature is broad and not specifically defined. Whether any particular record is "signed" is a question of fact. Proof of that fact must be made under other applicable law. This Act simply assures that the signature may be accomplished through electronic means. No specific technology need be used in order to create a valid

signature. One's voice on an answering machine may suffice if the requisite intention is present. Similarly, including one's name as part of an electronic mail communication also may suffice, as may the firm name on a facsimile. It also may be shown that the requisite intent was not present and accordingly the symbol, sound or process did not amount to a signature. One may use a digital signature with the requisite intention, or one may use the private key solely as an access device with no intention to sign, or otherwise accomplish a legally binding act. In any case the critical element is the intention to execute or adopt the sound or symbol or process for the purpose of signing the related record.

The definition requires that the signer execute or adopt the sound, symbol, or process with the intent to sign the record. The act of applying a sound, symbol or process to an electronic record could have differing meanings and effects. The consequence of the act and the effect of the act as a signature are determined under other applicable law. However, the essential attribute of a signature involves applying a sound, symbol or process with an intent to do a legally significant act. It is that intention that is understood in the law as a part of the word "sign", without the need for a definition.

This Act establishes, to the greatest extent possible, the equivalency of electronic signatures and manual signatures. Therefore the term "signature" has been used to connote and convey that equivalency. The purpose is to overcome unwarranted biases against electronic methods of signing and authenticating records. The term "authentication," used in other laws, often has a narrower meaning and purpose than an electronic signature as used in this Act. However, an authentication under any of those other laws constitutes an electronic signature under this Act.

* * *

This definition includes as an electronic signature the standard webpage click through process. * * *

Another important aspect of this definition lies in the necessity that the electronic signature be linked or logically associated with the record. In the paper world, it is assumed that the symbol adopted by a party is attached to or located somewhere in the same paper that is intended to be authenticated, e.g., an allonge[2] firmly attached to a promissory note, or the classic signature at the end of a long contract. These tangible manifestations do not exist in the electronic environment, and accordingly, this definition expressly provides that the symbol must in some way be linked to, or connected with, the electronic record being signed. A digital signature using public key encryption technology would qualify as an electronic signature, as would the mere inclusion of one's name as a part of an e-mail

2. [An "allonge" is "[a] slip of paper sometimes attached to a negotiable instrument for the purpose of receiving further indorsements when the original paper is filled with indorsements." BLACK'S LAW DICTIONARY (7th ed. 1999).—Eds.]

message—so long as in each case the signer executed or adopted the symbol with the intent to sign.

* * *

10. **"Record."** This is a standard definition designed to embrace all means of communicating or storing information except human memory. It includes any method for storing or communicating information, including "writings." A record need not be indestructible or permanent, but the term does not include oral or other communications which are not stored or preserved by some means. * * *

SECTION 5. USE OF ELECTRONIC RECORDS AND ELECTRONIC SIGNATURES; VARIATION BY AGREEMENT.

(a) This [Act] does not require a record or signature to be created, generated, sent, communicated, received, stored, or otherwise processed or used by electronic means or in electronic form.

(b) This [Act] applies only to transactions between parties each of which has agreed to conduct transactions by electronic means. Whether the parties agree to conduct a transaction by electronic means is determined from the context and surrounding circumstances, including the parties' conduct.

(c) A party that agrees to conduct a transaction by electronic means may refuse to conduct other transactions by electronic means. The right granted by this subsection may not be waived by agreement.

(d) Except as otherwise provided in this [Act], the effect of any of its provisions may be varied by agreement. The presence in certain provisions of this [Act] of the words "unless otherwise agreed", or words of similar import, does not imply that the effect of other provisions may not be varied by agreement.

(e) Whether an electronic record or electronic signature has legal consequences is determined by this [Act] and other applicable law.

Comment

* * *

2. The paradigm of this Act is two willing parties doing transactions electronically. It is therefore appropriate that the Act is voluntary and preserves the greatest possible party autonomy to refuse electronic transactions. The requirement that party agreement be found from all the surrounding circumstances is a limitation on the scope of this Act.

3. If this Act is to serve to facilitate electronic transactions, it must be applicable under circumstances not rising to a full fledged contract to use electronics. While absolute certainty can be accomplished by obtaining an explicit contract before relying on electronic transactions, such an explicit contract should not be necessary before one may feel safe in conducting transactions electronically. Indeed, such a requirement would itself be an unreasonable barrier to electronic commerce, at odds with the fundamental

purpose of this Act. Accordingly, the requisite agreement, express or implied, must be determined from all available circumstances and evidence.

4. Subsection (b) provides that the Act applies to transactions in which the parties have agreed to conduct the transaction electronically. In this context it is essential that the parties' actions and words be broadly construed in determining whether the requisite agreement exists. Accordingly, the Act expressly provides that the party's agreement is to be found from all circumstances, including the parties' conduct. The critical element is the intent of a party to conduct a transaction electronically. * * *

* * *

7. Subsection (e) is an essential provision in the overall scheme of this Act. While this Act validates and effectuates electronic records and electronic signatures, the legal effect of such records and signatures is left to existing substantive law outside this Act except in very narrow circumstances. * * *

For example, beyond validation of records, signatures and contracts based on the medium used, § 7(a) and (b) should not be interpreted as establishing the legal effectiveness of any given record, signature or contract. Where a rule of law requires that the record contain minimum substantive content, the legal effect of such a record will depend on whether the record meets the substantive requirements of other applicable law. * * *

Electronic Signatures in Global and National Commerce Act, §§ 101, 106(4), 106(5) & 106(9)

15 U.S.C. §§ 7001 & 7006.

Sec. 101. GENERAL RULE OF VALIDITY

(a) In General.—Notwithstanding any statute, regulation, or other rule of law (other than this title and title II), with respect to any transaction in or affecting interstate or foreign commerce—

(1) a signature, contract, or other record relating to such transaction may not be denied legal effect, validity, or enforceability solely because it is in electronic form; and

(2) a contract relating to such transaction may not be denied legal effect, validity, or enforceability solely because an electronic signature or electronic record was used in its formation.

(b) Preservation of Rights and Obligations.—This title does not—

(1) limit, alter, or otherwise affect any requirement imposed by a statute, regulation, or rule of law relating to the rights and obligations of persons under such statute, regulation, or rule of law other than a requirement that contracts or other records be written, signed, or in nonelectronic form; or

(2) require any person to agree to use or accept electronic records or electronic signatures, other than a governmental agency with respect to a record other than a contract to which it is a party. * * *

(d) Retention of Contracts and Records.—

(1) Accuracy and Accessibility.—If a statute, regulation, or other rule of law requires that a contract or other record relating to a transaction in or affecting interstate or foreign commerce be retained, that requirement is met by retaining an electronic record of the information in the contract or other record that—

(A) accurately reflects the information set forth in the contract or other record; and

(B) remains accessible to all persons who are entitled to access by statute, regulation, or rule of law, for the period required by such statute, regulation, or rule of law, in a form that is capable of being accurately reproduced for later reference, whether by transmission, printing, or otherwise.

(2) Exception.—A requirement to retain a contract or other record in accordance with paragraph (1) does not apply to any information whose sole purpose is to enable the contract or other record to be sent, communicated, or received.

(3) Originals.—If a statute, regulation, or other rule of law requires a contract or other record relating to a transaction in or affecting interstate or foreign commerce to be provided, available, or retained in its original form, or provides consequences if the contract or other record is not provided, available, or retained in its original form, that statute, regulation, or rule of law is satisfied by an electronic record that complies with paragraph (1).

(4) Checks.—If a statute, regulation, or other rule of law requires the retention of a check, that requirement is satisfied by retention of an electronic record of the information on the front and back of the check in accordance with paragraph (1).

(e) Accuracy and Ability to Retain Contracts and Other Records.—Notwithstanding subsection (a), if a statute, regulation, or other rule of law requires that a contract or other record relating to a transaction in or affecting interstate or foreign commerce be in writing, the legal effect, validity, or enforceability of an electronic record of such contract or other record may be denied if such electronic record is not in a form that is capable of being retained and accurately reproduced for later reference by all parties or persons who are entitled to retain the contract or other record.

(f) Proximity.—Nothing in this title affects the proximity required by any statute, regulation, or other rule of law with respect to any warning, notice, disclosure, or other record required to be posted, displayed, or publicly affixed.

(g) Notarization and Acknowledgment.—If a statute, regulation, or other rule of law requires a signature or record relating to a transaction in or affecting interstate or foreign commerce to be notarized, acknowledged, verified, or made under oath, that requirement is satisfied if the electronic signature of the person authorized to perform those acts, together with all other information required to be included by other applicable statute, regulation, or rule of law, is attached to or logically associated with the signature or record.

SEC. 106. DEFINITIONS.

For purposes of this title:

(4) Electronic Record.—The term "electronic record" means a contract or other record created, generated, sent, communicated, received, or stored by electronic means.

(5) Electronic Signature.—The term "electronic signature" means an electronic sound, symbol, or process, attached to or logically associated with a contract or other record and executed or adopted by a person with the intent to sign the record.

* * *

(9) Record.—The term "record" means information that is inscribed on a tangible medium or that is stored in an electronic or other medium and is retrievable in perceivable form.

Uniform Computer Information Transactions Act, §§ 107, 108, 102(a)(6), 102(a)(55) & 201

National Conference of Commissioners on Uniform State Laws. (2000).

SECTION 107. LEGAL RECOGNITION OF ELECTRONIC RECORD AND AUTHENTICATION; USE OF ELECTRONIC AGENTS

(a) A record or authentication may not be denied legal effect or enforceability solely because it is in electronic form.

(b) This [Act] does not require that a record or authentication be generated, stored, sent, received, or otherwise processed by electronic means or in electronic form.

(c) In any transaction, a person may establish requirements regarding the type of authentication or record acceptable to it.

(d) A person that uses an electronic agent that it has selected for making an authentication, performance, or agreement, including manifestation of assent, is bound by the operations of the electronic agent, even if no individual was aware of or reviewed the agent's operations or the results of the operations.

SECTION 108. PROOF AND EFFECT OF AUTHENTICATION

(a) Authentication may be proven in any manner, including a showing that a party made use of information or access that could have been available only if it engaged in conduct or operations that authenticated the record or term.

(b) Compliance with a commercially reasonable attribution procedure agreed to or adopted by the parties or established by law for authenticating a record authenticates the record as a matter of law.

Official Comment

* * *

2. **Method of Proof.** Proof of authentication can occur in any manner. In electronic commerce, one important means of proving authentication is by showing that a process existed that required an authentication in order to proceed.

SECTION 102. DEFINITIONS

(a) In this [Act]:

* * *

(6) "Authenticate" means:

(A) to sign; or

(B) with the intent to sign a record, otherwise to execute or adopt an electronic symbol, sound, message, or process referring to, attached to, included in, or logically associated or linked with, that record.

* * *

(55) "Record" means information that is inscribed on a tangible medium or that is stored in an electronic or other medium and is retrievable in perceivable form.

* * *

Official Comment

* * *

4. "Authenticate." This term replaces "signature" and "signed." A similar change in terminology is made in Uniform Commercial Code Article 9 (1998 Official Text). In this Act, the term "sign" has the meaning used in Uniform Commercial Code § 1–201 (1998 Official Text), except that it is not limited to authenticating a *writing*. The definition is technologically neutral. The definition makes clear that qualifying electronic systems fulfill former paper-based requirements. This is consistent with the policies of the federal Electronic Signatures in Global and National Commerce Act which precludes discrimination against electronic records and signatures solely because they are electronic in character.

Any "signature" under other law is an authentication under this Act. In addition, authentication includes qualifying use of any identifier, such as a personal identification number (PIN) or a typed or otherwise signed name. It can include actions or sounds such as encryption, voice and biological identification, and other technologically enabled acts if done with proper intent. See *Parma Tile Mosaic & Marble Co. v. Short*, 663 N.E.2d 633 (N.Y.1996) (intent requirement not met). There is no requirement that the authenticated record be retained by a party unless that requirement exists under other law.

An authentication may be on, logically associated with, or linked to the record. With digital technology, the analogy between signing a record electronically and signing a paper is not precise. "Logically associated" makes it clear that the association between an authentication and a record need not be physical in nature. However, the association must support the inference that the authenticating party intends to adopt or accept the associated or referenced record. "Referring to" or "linked to" captures the traditional concept of incorporating a record or term by reference, as well as use of an electronic connection, such as an Internet hyperlink.

An "authentication" may express various intended effects. What effects are intended are determined by the context and objective indicia associated with that context.

* * *

48. "Record." A record must be in, or capable of being retrieved in, perceivable form. Electronic text recorded in a computer memory that could be printed or displayed from that memory constitutes a record. Similarly, a tape recording of an oral conversation or a video taping of actions could be a record.

* * *

SECTION 201. FORMAL REQUIREMENTS

(a) Except as otherwise provided in this section, a contract requiring payment of a contract fee of $5,000 or more is not enforceable by way of action or defense unless:

(1) the party against which enforcement is sought authenticated a record sufficient to indicate that a contract has been formed and which reasonably identifies the copy or subject matter to which the contract refers; or

(2) the agreement is a license for an agreed duration of one year or less or which may be terminated at will by the party against which the contract is asserted.

(b) A record is sufficient under subsection (a) even if it omits or incorrectly states a term, but the contract is not enforceable under that subsection beyond the number of copies or subject matter shown in the record.

(c) A contract that does not satisfy the requirements of subsection (a) is nevertheless enforceable under that subsection if:

(1) a performance was tendered or the information was made available by one party and the tender was accepted or the information accessed by the other; or

(2) the party against which enforcement is sought admits in court, by pleading or by testimony or otherwise under oath, facts sufficient to indicate a contract has been made, but the agreement is not enforceable under this paragraph beyond the number of copies or the subject matter admitted.

(d) Between merchants, if, within a reasonable time, a record in confirmation of the contract and sufficient against the sender is received and the party receiving it has reason to know its contents, the record satisfies subsection (a) against the party receiving it unless notice of objection to its contents is given in a record within a reasonable time after the confirming record is received.

(e) An agreement that the requirements of this section need not be satisfied as to future transactions is effective if evidenced in a record authenticated by the person against which enforcement is sought.

(f) A transaction within the scope of this [Act] is not subject to a statute of frauds contained in another law of this State.

Official Comment

1. **Scope of the Section**. This section requires an authenticated record for enforceability of certain agreements. The section blends Uniform Commercial Code concepts with common law approaches. Failure to comply with the requirements of this section does not make the contract void, it merely precludes a party from relying on it as a defense or to bring a cause of action. Under subsection (e), EDI trading partner and similar authenticated records satisfy this section. * * *

3. * * *

b. **Record Required.** A record, when required, must 1) indicate that a contract was formed, 2) reasonably identify the copy or subject matter involved, and 3) have been authenticated by the party against whom the contract is asserted. No other formalities are required.

This section does not require that the record be retained or that it contain all material terms of the contract or even that it be designated as a contract. All that is required is that the record afford a basis for believing that offered oral evidence rests on a real agreement. A memorandum that fulfills the conditions suffices. But the record must indicate that a contract was formed, not merely that a contract was being negotiated.

Merely because a record satisfies this section does not establish that a contract exists. Nor does it establish the terms of the contract, which must be determined under other sections of this Act. Fulfilling this section merely removes the formal barrier of this section and allows a party to assert the existence of a contract as a basis for a cause of action or a defense. For the contract to actually exist, contract formation rules must be met. For example, while a record need not describe all of the scope of a license to meet this section, there is no contract if there is a material dispute about scope. § 202. Satisfying the statute of frauds is merely a gateway to being able to have a court consider whether or not there is a contract.

* * *

6. **Other Laws.** Subsection (f) clarifies that the formalities required by this section supplant formalities required under other state laws for transactions within this Act. This rule applies only with respect to state law. Federal law may require more stringent formalities. For example, the Copyright Act requires that an exclusive copyright license be in a writing and makes non-exclusive licenses that are not in a writing subject to subsequent transfers of the copyright.

NOTES & QUESTIONS

1. *Record retention.* ESIGN and UETA grant electronic records the legal status of writings not only for the purposes of contract formation and the statute of frauds, but also for purposes of record retention statutes. *See* ESIGN § 101(d), 15 U.S.C. § 7001(d); UETA § 12 (1999).

2. *Office of Electronic Notary.* UETA and ESIGN both expressly allow for electronic notarization of records. UETA § 11; ESIGN § 101(g). UCITA implies the same result. UCITA §§ 105(d)(2) & 107. In response to these legal developments, the National Notary Association ("NNA") asks: "If electronic notarizations are authorized under the *Uniform Electronic Transactions Act* now being enacted into law in dozens of states, as well as under the new federal *Electronic Signatures in Global and National Commerce Act*, who exactly will perform these electronic notarial acts?" The NNA assumes that "[i]t will largely be Notaries specially commissioned for that purpose" and has "begun formulating parameters and qualifications for the office of Electronic Notary (EN) to be published in detail in a revised *Model Notary Act.*" The NNA continues:

> In the states, the allure of e-commerce and new technologies has begun to weaken vital statutory consumer protections against document fraud. In authorizing use of electronic signatures by Notaries, the widely enacted *Uniform Electronic Transactions Act* has spawned implementing laws that ignore the critical role of the trusted impartial witness. Indeed, some states are labeling as "notarization" electronic acts that do not even require a digital signer to appear before a Notary.
>
> The fundamental principles and process of notarization must remain the same regardless of the technology used to make a signature, because, while technology may be perfectible, the basic nature of the human beings who use it is not. Any process—paper-

based or electronic—that is called notarization must involve the personal physical appearance of a signer before a commissioned Notary Public.

In the electronic arena, the role of the Notary Public as a trusted impartial witness must not only be retained but strengthened so that execution of contracts and property conveyances will not be compromised by a technology that, despite its complexity, cannot make trustworthy guarantees about a signer's identity, willingness and awareness. The Notary office must be strengthened through well-conceived training, testing and certification programs that stress ethical as well as technical instruction.

Numerous experts share the NNA's view that emerging digital technology heightens rather than diminishes the role of the Notary Public.

In today's society, the Internet permits a risk-free anonymity that has emboldened a new generation of forgers and criminal identity thieves. Identity theft complaints grew from fewer than 40,000 nationwide in 1992 to 750,000 in 1999. "As identity becomes more digital, it becomes possible to reproduce and take on the identity of another (person) much more rapidly," said U.S. Treasury Secretary Laurence Summers. In such an environment, there is more need than ever before for reliable human gatekeepers to prevent the exploitation of technology.

National Notary Association, *A Position on Digital Signatures and Notarization*, www.nationalnotary.org/Digitalsignature.pdf. For more on the role of notaries in the 21st century, see Deborah M. Thaw, *The Notary Office and Its Impact in the 21st Century*, www.nationalnotary.org/news/notaryofficeandimpact.pdf.

3. *Standards for authentication.* Electronically typed signatures are more easily forged than pen-and-ink signatures. Do ESIGN, UETA and UCITA adopt any standards about what level of certainty of authentication of a signature must be achieved in order for it to support binding commitment? About the level of certainty of non-repudiation or textual integrity that must be achieved? Should states consider adopting such standards over and above the provisions of UETA and ESIGN? (Could they?)

III. DIGITAL AUTHENTICATION AROUND THE WORLD

Susanna Frederick Fischer, *Saving Rosencrantz and Guildenstern in a Virtual World? A Comparative Look at Recent Global Electronic Signature Legislation*

7 B.U. J. SCI. & TECH. L. 229 (2001).

* * *

III. A Comparative Look at Electronic Signatures Laws to Date

It took some time for a significant number of jurisdictions to enact electronic signature legislation. The earliest countries to adopt such legislation, namely Germany (1997), Italy (1997), Malaysia (1997), and Russia (1995), endorsed the prescriptive approach mandating specific technology, namely PKI. These countries were strongly influenced by the prescriptive approach taken by the State of Utah in its pioneering Digital Signature Act of 1995.[33]

A. *Prescriptive Legislation*

The prescriptive model is founded on the argument that PKI is the only mature technology that could provide adequate security to e-commerce transactions. Proponents of prescriptive legislation contend that legal certainty is key to stimulating widespread public trust in electronic signatures. Critics, on the other hand, argue that by giving legal recognition only to one type of technology, technological improvements may be stymied.

Besides its endorsement of PKI technology, another typical attribute of prescriptive legislation is that it sets out an elaborate legal framework defining the rights and liabilities of the parties to an electronic transaction, including trusted third party CAs [certification authorities]. Critics of the prescriptive approach argue that prescriptive legislation overly limits the liability of CAs and imposes excessive liability risk on consumers. Typical prescriptive laws, such as Malaysia's Digital Signature Act of 1997, provide that if a private key is lost or stolen due to the key holder's failure to exercise reasonable care, she will bear unlimited liability for consequential loss or damage. The policy reason for this is to insulate CAs from liability where the CA could not be expected to prevent such harm or insure against it.

B. *The Hybrid Model*

As these critics became more vociferous, some jurisdictions, starting with Singapore in 1998, began to move toward a more market-driven legislative model. Singapore's Electronic Transactions Act of 1998 was heavily based on the United Nations Commission on International Trade Law ("UNCITRAL") Model Law on Electronic Commerce ("MLEC"), adopted in 1996.[39] The UNCITRAL MLEC took a technology-neutral approach. This also influenced other countries adopting legislation around this time such as Bermuda (1999).[41] The Singaporean law is an example of the "hybrid" or "two-tier" approach. This hybrid approach was also endorsed by the European Union Parliament/Council Directive on a Community Framework for Electronic Signatures ("E.U. Signatures Di-

33. See Utah Digital Signature Act of 1995, Utah Code Ann. §§ 46–3–101 to –504 (1998 and Supp. 2000).

39. See Electronic Transactions Act, 1998 (Sing.), available at <www.lawnet.com.sg/freeaccess/ETA.htm>. * * *

41. See Electronic Transactions Act, 1999 (Berm.), available at <legal.06.free.bm>.

rective").[42] This directive came into force early in 2000, and must be implemented by Member States by July of 2001.

The hybrid approach is founded on a policy of limited technological neutrality, typically providing, as does the E.U. Signatures Directive, that an electronic signature may not be denied legal effectiveness or admissibility solely because it is electronic. However, certain favored technologies are afforded special presumptions, such as a presumption of authenticity if the electronic signature is verified by a qualified certificate meeting certain requirements. Although these so-called "advanced electronic signatures" are not expressly required to be created with a particular technology, the only existing technology that appears to meet the requirements laid down by hybrid legislation like the E.U. Signatures Directive, is PKI.

Hybrid legislation typically includes some rules on the rights and duties of parties to an electronic transaction. For example, the E.U. Signatures Directive requires Member States to ensure, at minimum, that CAs are liable in damages for harm caused to someone reasonably relying on a qualified certificate for the accuracy of the information in it, unless the CA did not act negligently. However, CAs must be permitted to limit their liability by specifying limitations on the use of a qualified certificate, or the value of a transaction in which it may be used.

Proponents of hybrid schemes contend that they are preferable to other legislative models because they are more flexible and adaptable to new technological developments, but they also ensure a level of legal certainty that is necessary to build and maintain sufficient public trust in electronic signatures. But critics of hybrid legislation argue that this approach does not permit sufficient breathing room for market forces, overprotects certain technologies at the expense of innovation, and amounts to excessive government regulation.

C. Minimalist Legislation

The criticism referred to above influenced the development of the third legislative model, the "minimalist" approach. This market-worshipping approach has proved particularly popular in common law jurisdictions. E–Sign endorses a minimalist approach, as does the Uniform Electronic Transactions Act ("UETA"). Australia and the United Kingdom have also recently enacted minimalist legislation.[52] New Zealand is currently considering pending legislation that is very similar to Australia's.[53]

Minimalist legislation is wholly technology-neutral. For example, E–Sign provides that no electronic signatures of whatever type may be denied legal effect, validity, or enforceability simply because it is in electronic

42. See European Parliament and Council Directive 1999/93, 2000 O.J. (L 13) 12, available at <www.fs.dk/uk/acts/eu/esign-uk.htm>.

52. See Electronic Transactions Act, 1999 § 10 (Austl.), available at <law.gov.au/publications/ ecommerce/interim3.html>; Electronic Communications Act, 2000, c. 7, § 7 (Eng.) available at <www.hmso.gov.uk/ acts/acts2000/ 20000007.htm>.

53. See Electronic Transactions Bill, 2000, (N.Z.), Jan. 18, 2001, available at <www.med.govt.nz/irdev/elcom/transactions/bill>.

form. No special presumptions are given to PKI, or any other particular technology. Moreover, no special rights or duties for parties to electronic signature creation or verification are set out in minimalist legislation.

Proponents of minimalist legislation argue that the market should determine what technology will succeed. Also, they contend, a minimalist approach encourages the use of more than just one type of technology. Different technologies may be preferable for different purposes. But critics contend that the minimalist approach is hopelessly vague and creates too much legal uncertainty. They fear that failure to endorse PKI may deny it sufficient support to allow it to thrive.

D. *The Explosion of Legislation in 2000*

In 2000, there was an explosion of electronic signature legislation in many parts of the world.[56] Some of this legislation is prescriptive, such as in India, Hong Kong, Estonia, and Peru. Some is minimalist, such as Australia, Gibraltar, and Japan. And some, including much of the European legislation, is hybrid, including Austria, Finland, France, Ireland, Luxembourg, Slovenia, and Sweden. The Tower of Babel is clearly still under construction.

IV. Conclusion

I close with a few observations on the Tower of Babel of global electronic signature laws. First, it is extremely important for Americans not to lose sight of the fact that the minimalist approach we adopted in E–Sign (which was designed to reconcile our own American Tower of Babel of state electronic signature laws) has not been universally embraced worldwide. As in the area of privacy laws, we now find ourselves on something of a collision course with Europe, as well as some other civil law jurisdictions. Many civil lawyers are concerned that the American minimalist approach cannot be reconciled with the civil law's approach to contract formalities, which generally includes far more stringent requirements than in common law jurisdictions.

Sadly, the global initiatives promoting greater harmonization of laws have really been a case of two little too late. UNCITRAL's Working Group on Electronic Commerce recently finalized a draft Model Law on Electronic Signatures ("MLES"), which is expected to be adopted without major change by the full Commission in June of 2001.[3] But the MLES is not expected to have much effect on existing legislation. Many business entities lost confidence in the MLES due to the persistence of its adherence to a prescriptive approach mandating PKI. Although this approach has finally been abandoned, it seems unlikely that these business interests will now endorse the MLES.

56. See generally Simone van der Hof, Digital Signature Law Survey, available at <rechten.kub.nl/simone/ds-lawsu.htm>.

3. [The UNCITRAL Model Law on Electronic Signatures was adopted on July 5, 2001. It is available online at www.uncitral.org/en-index.htm.—Eds.]

Finally, it should be emphasized that too much of the world is simply uninvolved in the Tower of Babel. To my knowledge, no African country has yet enacted electronic signature legislation. In the Middle East, only Israel has electronic signature legislation. In my view, it is crucial for global stability and social justice for the First World to bridge the digital divide and enable the Third World to participate to a greater extent in e-commerce. If this does not happen, we will risk becoming a world even more divided between the greedy haves and the resentful have-nots.

NOTES & QUESTIONS

1. *Types of digital authentication statutes.* Commentators characterize digital authentication legislation as minimalist, hybrid, or prescriptive. In the article excerpted above, Fischer describes UETA and ESIGN as minimalist. What are the pros and cons of the minimalist approach? Fischer does not discuss UCITA. Where would you place UCITA in this taxonomy?

2. *Need for uniformity?* What difficulties do you foresee for Internet commerce stemming from the existence of different approaches to digital authentication? Is the "Babel" metaphor an overreaction? Or does the heterogeneity of digital signature legislation indeed pose severe obstacles for Internet commerce?

3. *Efforts at standardization.* Beginning with Utah's Digital Signature Act in 1995, *see* UTAH CODE §§ 46–3–100 to –504, which was a full-blown PKI model, a number of states enacted digital signature legislation. One purpose for enacting UETA and ESIGN was to rectify the situation in which various states had quite different requirements for digital authentication. Do UETA and ESIGN accomplish this purpose?

CHAPTER SIX

CONSUMER PROTECTION ONLINE

When consumers spend their money to purchase goods and services, they must inevitably rely to some degree upon information that those who supply the items provide. Sellers sometimes provide information about their goods that is false or misleading, and sometimes fail to carry out their contractual undertakings, with the result that consumers do not receive what they were led to expect when they entered into the transaction. The law of consumer protection is the government's response to the fact that sellers sometimes engage in such deceptive marketing practices.

This chapter addresses the incidence of deceptive marketing practices, and the role of consumer protection, in business-to-consumer ("B2C") electronic commerce. E-commerce is a form of distance selling, bearing a family resemblance to the better-established techniques of telemarketing, catalog sales, and direct mail marketing. With each of these marketing methods, the buyer and seller never meet face to face—in contrast to sales occurring at brick-and-mortar retail establishments or at the purchaser's home or office. Distance selling methods offer consumers significant benefits, including efficiency gains from eliminating the time and expense involved in traveling to a retail establishment, a broader selection of goods, and potentially lower prices. Digital networks also offer consumers new techniques for defining their preferences and identifying the optimal providers of what they seek.

But distance selling via digital networks holds potential perils as well, presenting unscrupulous sellers with enhanced opportunities to engage in deceptive marketing practices and avoid getting caught. When consumers buy goods at a distance, they lose the ability to examine the goods before purchasing. A faraway seller will find it easier to be non-responsive to dissatisfied customers than will a seller in the customer's own community. A buyer who purchases long distance may not even know where the seller is physically located.

In recognition of these dangers, legislatures have enacted special regulatory regimes applying to distance selling, including the Telemarketing and Consumer Fraud and Abuse Prevention Act, 15 U.S.C. §§ 6101–08, implemented by the Telemarketing Sales Rule, 16 C.F.R. Part 310; the Telephone Disclosure and Dispute Resolution Act, 15 U.S.C. §§ 5701, 5711–14, 5721–24, implemented by the Trade Regulation Rule Pursuant to the Telephone Disclosure and Dispute Resolution Act of 1992, 16 C.F.R. Part 308; and, in the European Union, Directive 97/7/EC of the European Parliament and of the Council of 20 May 1997 on the protection of consumers in respect of distance contracts, 1997 O.J. (L 144) 19. *See* John

Rothchild, *Making the Market Work: Enhancing Consumer Sovereignty Through the Telemarketing Sales Rule and the Distance Selling Directive*, 21 J. Consumer Pol'y 279 (1998).

The discussion in this chapter will focus on several themes: How does e-commerce differ from other forms of distance selling? What is the proper role of the government in controlling online deceptive marketing practices? How can consumer protection be promoted through code-based solutions?

I. Background: Overview of Consumer Protection Regulation

A. Consumer Protection in a Market Economy

A market economy is characterized by the existence of a sphere of activity within which sellers and buyers are allowed considerable leeway to structure the terms of their commercial interactions. Market participants arrive through negotiation at a bargain that each views as advantageous: for example, the local department store would prefer to have one fewer washing machine and a little more money, while a householder would rather have a new washing machine and a little less money. A deal is struck. The consumer agrees to pay the store $500, and the store agrees to supply a certain model of washing machine. The money and machine change hands. The welfare of each participant in the exchange is enhanced, as the buyer receives a labor-saving device that he values more highly than the money he expended and the store (and ultimately the store's owners, its stockholders) gains a profit amounting to the difference between the price the consumer paid for the washing machine and the amount it cost the store to make the sale (including what it paid the manufacturer for the washing machine and its selling costs).

The transaction also has some ancillary effects. The store's competitors, which did not make the sale, receive an incremental incentive to offer better prices or service so as to gain future sales and profits. The consumer's decision to buy that particular washing machine causes economic resources to flow toward production of that model rather than others. The purchasing decisions of many consumers in aggregate insure that resources are used to produce the goods that they want, and not the ones that they do not want, since anyone who persists in making the latter will sooner or later go out of business.

Deceptive marketing practices interfere with this happy scenario at several junctures. First, if the goods are not as advertised, the transaction may decrease the purchaser's welfare. A purchaser might prefer a new washing machine to $500 if it performed as advertised, but might prefer to keep her money and her old washing machine if the new machine did not live up to its billing. At a minimum, mischaracterization of goods prevents consumers from maximizing their welfare within their budget constraints. Second, the transaction harms the seller's competitors, which might have won the sale and the accompanying profits if the seller had not misrepresented the washing machine's characteristics. Third, the deception skews the allocation of productive resources away from the welfare-maximizing allocation, by encouraging manufacturers to make more washing machines of the type that was sold only through misrepresentations of its characteristics.

Consumer protection thus has a dual function: it reduces the amount of harm suffered by consumers through being deceived into entering non-welfare-maximizing transactions, and it makes the market work better by promoting competition.

B. THE LEGAL FRAMEWORK FOR CONSUMER PROTECTION

The legal framework for controlling misleading advertising and fraudulent trade practices consists of several elements. At the federal level, the statute with the broadest subject-matter coverage is the Federal Trade Commission Act, 15 U.S.C. § 41 et seq., which prohibits "unfair or deceptive acts or practices in or affecting commerce." The FTC Act is enforced by the Federal Trade Commission, which has authority to issue administrative complaints and orders, and to bring injunctive actions in federal district court. The FTC has also promulgated and enforces a host of trade regulation rules, under authority conferred by the FTC Act, and other regulations under the authority of specific acts of Congress. Those rules and regulations appear at 16 C.F.R. Parts 300 et seq. The FTC also has enforcement authority under a variety of other statutes, most prominently those governing consumer credit, such as the Truth in Lending Act, 15 U.S.C. §§ 1601–1667f, the Fair Credit Billing Act, 15 U.S.C. 1666–1666j, and the Fair Credit Reporting Act, 15 U.S.C. §§ 1681–1681(u).

Other federal agencies have authority to protect consumers within a more circumscribed subject matter. The Food and Drug Administration works to insure the safety of food, drugs, and cosmetics. The Securities and Exchange Commission regulates the securities markets, and the Commodity Futures Trading Commission oversees the commodities markets. The Consumer Product Safety Commission is charged with reducing the risks associated with consumer products.

Complementing the federal regulatory framework are trade regulation and consumer protection statutes at the state level. These statutes, which are sometimes referred to as "little FTC Acts," prohibit a wide range of deceptive trade practices. In addition to general prohibitions against unfair and deceptive practices, many of these statutes include more detailed treatments of specific subject matters, such as pyramid sales, lotteries, prize promotions, failure to have sufficient goods to meet reasonably expectable demand, and creating confusion about the source or sponsorship of goods. These statutes are enforced by the state attorney general, or other state enforcement officials. Unlike the FTC Act, some of these statutes also give a private right of action to injured consumers and competitors.

Within the European Union, the regulatory framework for consumer protection consists of the national laws of each member state, as amplified by Directives that the European Commission promulgates.[1] The most significant Directives from the standpoint of consumer protection are the Directive on Misleading Advertising,[2] which establishes the basic rules against deceptive marketing practices, and the Directive on Distance Selling,[3] which applies to sales made at a distance via means such as direct mail, print advertising, catalogues, telephone, and e-mail, and features a pre-sale disclosure requirement, a seven-day right of withdrawal, a requirement that goods be shipped within thirty days, and other provisions. Of direct pertinence to e-commerce, the Directive on Electronic Commerce[4] requires that online advertising communications, including unsolicited commercial e-mail, be clearly identifiable as such, and calls upon member states to encourage the settlement of disputes through alternative dispute resolution mechanisms.

In 1999, the Organization for Economic Co-operation and Development released its Guidelines for Consumer Protection in the Context of Electronic Commerce. The Guidelines establish a set of principles that is intended to assist

> (i) Governments in reviewing, formulating and implementing consumer and law enforcement policies, practices, and regulations if necessary for effective consumer protection in the context of electronic commerce;
>
> (ii) Business associations, consumer groups and self-regulatory bodies, by providing guidance as to the core characteristics of effective consumer protection that should be considered in reviewing, formulating, and implementing self-regulatory schemes in the context of electronic commerce; and
>
> (iii) Individual businesses and consumers engaged in electronic commerce, by providing clear guidance as to the core characteristics of information disclosure and fair business practices that businesses should provide and consumers should expect in the context of electronic commerce.

1. An EC Directive is a set of legal rules on a particular subject, established through a lawmaking process on the EU community level, that EU member states are required by treaty to implement through enactment of national laws.

2. Council Directive 84/450/EEC of 10 September 1984 relating to the approximation of the laws, regulations and administrative provisions of the Member States concerning misleading advertising, 1984 O.J. (L 250) 17, *amended by* Directive 97/55/EC of European Parliament and of the Council of 6 October 1997 amending Directive 84/450/EEC concerning misleading advertising so as to include comparative advertising, 1997 O.J. (L 290) 18, europa.eu.int/eur-lex/en/consleg/pdf/1984/en_1984L0450_do_001.pdf.

3. Directive 97/7/EC of the European Parliament and of the Council of 20 May 1997 on the protection of consumers in respect of distance contracts, 1997 O.J. (L 144) 19, europa.eu.int/comm/consumers/policy/developments/dist_sell/dist01_en.pdf.

4. Directive 2000/31/EC of the European Parliament and of the Council of 8 June 2000 on certain legal aspects of information society services, in particular electronic commerce, in the Internal Market, 2000 O.J. (L 178) 1, europa.eu.int/ISPO/ecommerce/legal/documents/2000_31ec/2000_31ec_en.pdf.

Guidelines for Consumer Protection in the Context of Electronic Commerce (Dec. 9, 1999), www.oecd. org/ dsti/sti/it/consumer/ prod/ CPGuidelines_final. pdf. The Guidelines have had an impact on the legal framework for consumer protection in a number of OECD member countries. *See* First Report: Government and Private Sector Initiatives to Promote and Implement the OECD Guidelines for Consumer Protection in the Context of Electronic Commerce (Feb. 28, 2001), www.oecd.org.

II. THE EXTENT OF FRAUDULENT PRACTICES ONLINE

A. FRAUD-FACILITATING FEATURES OF THE ONLINE ENVIRONMENT

The Internet presents unscrupulous marketers with plenty of opportunity to engage in consumer fraud, and they are taking advantage of that opportunity. Several features of the online environment facilitate fraudulent conduct, and make it more difficult for law enforcement agencies to control such conduct. First, the low cost of setting up and conducting business on the Internet invites new entrepreneurial ventures in large numbers—many of which consist of no more than an individual armed with a computer, a connection to the Internet, and a desire for gain. Some percentage of these entrepreneurs will put profit before all else and use fraudulent techniques to separate consumers from their money. A proliferation of small operators, each obtaining small amounts of money from a few victims, creates severe difficulties for law enforcement agencies charged with controlling deceptive marketing practices. The small size of each operation makes it uneconomic to bring the traditional machinery of law enforcement to bear, yet the amount lost to fraud may be very large in the aggregate.

Second, it is cheaper and easier to simulate a respectable business on the Web than it is using other media. A professional-looking website can be created at a fraction of the cost required to create a storefront or office that conveys an aura of respectability. When making their purchasing decisions in a world of imperfect information, consumers must rely on clues of this sort, which economists refer to as "signaling." Their experience in the brick-and-mortar world—that a respectable-looking edifice betokens a trustworthy business—may lead them astray in the online world.

Third, the fact that the marginal cost of online communications approaches zero makes profitable deceptive marketing techniques that would be uneconomic using other media. Imagine yourself in the position of an entrepreneur who is assessing the viability of a money-making scheme that consists of using deceptive communications to entice consumers to pay money for a product that is worthless, or that she has no intention of delivering. The endeavor will be profitable only if the vendor's revenues exceed her costs. In an operation of this sort, a major component of the vendor's costs will be those associated with marketing her product—traditionally by direct mail, telemarketing, or advertising in the print or broadcast media. The high cost of marketing through these traditional media serves to limit such ventures, since only attractive propositions, and those marketed through the use of sophisticated targeting methods, will yield a high enough response rate to result in a profit. For example, a direct mail piece consisting of a flyer that proclaims

> MAKE $10,000 A MONTH WORKING FROM HOME, PART TIME. NO EXPERIENCE REQUIRED. SATISFACTION GUARANTEED. SEND $5 FOR INSTRUCTIONS.

would almost certainly be a money-loser, since the cost of sending such a letter is roughly one dollar, and the response rate will be considerably less than 20%, the breakeven point neglecting all other costs.

The advent of online marketing techniques, which offer a marginal cost to reach additional prospects approaching zero, radically alters the economics of the situation. If marketing costs are low enough, it becomes possible to make money using remarkably unattractive propositions delivered through unsophisticated marketing techniques. Bulk unsolicited commercial e-mail ("UCE," or "spam") is one such technique. CD–ROMs containing a million or more e-mail addresses can be purchased for less than $100, and the marginal cost of sending e-mail messages is typically zero. With extremely low marketing costs, it is possible to make a profit with an exceedingly low response rate. If the above solicitation letter were sent by e-mail to a million recipients, the marketing cost might be $300: $100 for the list of addresses, and $200 for bulk e-mail-sending software (and these costs could be amortized through additional mailings). This means that the vendor would break even with a response rate of .006 percent (1 million solicitations yielding 60 responses), and anything beyond that would be pure profit.

This same economic calculus has brought about a resurgence in the popularity of chain letters and other pyramid schemes. Chain letters soliciting money have circulated in this country since at least the 1930s.[5] A chain letter instructs the recipient that he will receive a great deal of money if he (1) sends a certain sum of money to each of several people whose names and addresses are listed, (2) crosses off one of the names and replaces it with his own, and (3) forwards a copy of the revised letter to several friends. These letters are illegal, because it is mathematically certain that all participants except those in the first few rungs will lose money. Chain letters are one of the most popular types of fraudulent bulk e-mail that circulate via the Internet. Because it is easy and costless to forward these letters in large numbers, they circulate in much larger number than those sent by postal mail, which require paper, envelopes, and postage.

Fourth, the distributed nature of online communications reduces the power of responsible speech intermediaries, by circumventing their func-

5. The popularity of the Send-a-Dime chain letter craze peaked in 1935. *See* N.Y. TIMES (May 28, 1935) (cited in Daniel W. VanArsdale, "Chain Letter Evolution" (1998), www.silcom.com/?barnowl/clevo/start.htm.)

tion of filtering out misleading and fraudulent marketing practices. For example, the television networks have highly evolved codes of acceptable advertising practices. Proposed advertising must be submitted in advance for review. If a network finds an ad to be in poor taste, misleading, or otherwise in violation of its code, it will not run the ad. Other media outlets, such as print publications, are discriminating to lesser and varying degrees, but still filter out some of the worst advertising. Online advertisers, by contrast, typically are subject only to the online service providers' Acceptable Use Policies, which are both lenient and rarely enforced. Note, however, that the online medium may *increase* the ability of payment intermediaries, like credit card systems, to mediate disputes, since all transactions are at a distance and there are at present no widely adopted non-intermediated digital payment systems.

Complaint intake services convey some idea of the types of fraud that are most prevalent on the Internet. The National Fraud Information Center, a project of the non-profit National Consumers League, collects complaints from consumers who have been defrauded in online commerce or telemarketing transactions and forwards the complaints to law enforcement authorities. During the first ten months of 2001, the great majority of the complaints it received—78 percent—concerned online auctions. The next most commonly reported frauds, in order, were those involving general merchandise, money transfer schemes, Internet access services, adult-oriented material, computer equipment and software, and work-at-home schemes. *See* Internet Fraud Watch, 2001 Internet Fraud Statistics, www.fraud.org. Fraudulent offerings that are conveyed by unsolicited commercial e-mail show a different profile. According to the FTC, the most common UCE-borne scams are business opportunities, bulk e-mail marketing opportunities, chain letters, work-at-home schemes, health and diet scams, effortless income, free goods, investment opportunities, cable descrambler kits, guaranteed loans or credit, credit repair, and vacation prize promotions. *See FTC Names Its Dirty Dozen: 12 Scams Most Likely to Arrive Via Bulk E-mail*, www.ftc.gov/bcp/conline/pubs/alerts/doznalrt.htm.

Another measure of the extent of fraud on the Internet is the results of a series of "Surf Days" led by the FTC. In a Surf Day, law enforcement investigators search the Web for sites that are involved in a particular type of commercial activity and appear to be fraudulent. Surf Days brought to light thousands of websites making questionable claims about medical products, pyramid schemes, business and investment opportunities, and even lice treatments.

The technology of online communications has made possible novel variations on the theme of consumer fraud. A couple of cases are illustrative. In *FTC v. Audiotex Connection, Inc.*, CV–97–0726 (DRH) (E.D.N.Y. 1997), the defendants operated several websites, including www.beavisbutthead.com, www.sexygirls.com, and www.1adult.com, featuring adult-oriented images. The websites stated that visitors could view these images for free if they first downloaded a viewer program called "david.exe." But david.exe was no mere viewer program. Once downloaded and executed, it stealthily turned off the computer's speakers, disconnected the computer from its Internet connection, and dialed out to a phone number in Moldova through which it reconnected to the Internet. Charges for this international call accrued at more than $2 per minute. And the call remained connected even after the user shut down the browser, until the user turned off the computer. Thousands of users consequently incurred long-distance charges totaling hundreds of thousands of dollars. The defendants received a portion of the charges that victims paid to the foreign phone company.

FTC v. Pereira, Civ. Act. No. 99–1367–A (E.D. Va. filed Sept. 14, 1999), features another fact pattern that was not possible before the Internet. According to the FTC, the defendants downloaded the contents of over 25 million web pages, inserted into the code of each a command that redirected the visitor to another site, and then uploaded the doctored pages to its own website. A user entering an innocuous term into a search engine would pull up links to the counterfeit pages, and be redirected to another website, operated by the defendants, containing sexually explicit, adult-oriented material. The defendants made it difficult for these involuntary visitors to leave the site, since the site's code rendered the "back" and "close" buttons of the visitor's browser inoperative, and forwarded visitors to other adult sites. The defendants apparently made money from the operation as a result of driving additional traffic to sites that paid commissions for referrals.

An incident involving spoofing of a website illustrates a type of fraud that is possible in the offline world, but much easier online. A would-be scammer, apparently located in South Ural, Russia, created a replica of the PayPal.com website. PayPal is an online payment system that facilitates payment for goods purchased via online auctions. The perpetrator sent e-mails to intended victims, falsely informing them that a sum of money had been transferred to their PayPal account, and inviting them to check their balance by logging on to PayPal.com. The e-mail contained a link to a bogus login page at PayPaI.com—the "l" in PayPal replaced by an "I." With many on-screen fonts, the capital "I" looks just like a lower-case "l." The victim's login information was sent to the perpetrator, which might have allowed him to access the victim's account and help himself to the victim's funds. Although some PayPal customers were tricked into entering their login information into the counterfeit screen, none reported losing any money.

The nature of the online medium makes spoofing much easier than in other contexts. The coding that creates a web page may be freely downloaded, and then uploaded to a different URL. Successfully duplicating a storefront or a mail-order catalog is a much more difficult and expensive operation, and therefore less likely to occur.

NOTE: PAYMENT MECHANISMS

Novel aspects of the online medium can create new vulnerabilities. Consider the ramifications of the introduction of new payment mechanisms. (These mechanisms are considered in Chapter 16, *infra.*) Consumers who are accustomed to the protections they receive when they make a purchase using a credit card may be surprised to find that those protections are absent when they use new, online payment mechanisms. If a purchaser makes a purchase using a credit card, and the seller does not carry out its end of the bargain, the purchaser may dispute the charge by initiating a chargeback. Under the Fair Credit Billing Act, 15 U.S.C. §§ 1666–1666j, this sets in motion a process in which the credit card issuer attempts to mediate the dispute between seller and buyer. If the parties are unable to reach a mutually agreeable resolution, the issuer may require the merchant to absorb the loss.

This dispute resolution scheme, which was mandated by federal law and has been extended more broadly on a voluntary basis by the major credit card companies, is not available when payments are made via other mechanisms, such as cash, check, money order, or debit card. As some consumers have learned to their surprise and dismay, chargebacks are also unavailable when payments are made using online payment mechanisms. One of the most popular alternative payment mechanisms for making online purchases is PayPal. To use PayPal, a customer funds an account with a deposit from a credit card, personal check, or transfer from another PayPal user. Once an account is funded, the holder can direct that a payment be made to an online seller. Funds are transferred immediately, which benefits both buyer and seller by eliminating the delay in shipment of goods that would result if the seller waited for the buyer's check to clear.

But if the seller fails to deliver, the buyer has a problem. Unlike a credit card issuer, PayPal has no responsibility to mediate disputes between buyers and sellers. This is clearly stated in PayPal's Terms of Service: "[PayPal] does not ensure the quality, safety, or legality of the merchandise received, nor that the seller will even ship the merchandise."

Do you think federal law should extend chargeback-like rights to new online payment mechanisms? If so, should similar protections be extended to debit cards? Checks? Should we expect that market forces will impel the purveyors of new payment mechanisms to extend chargeback-like protections voluntarily, as a way of competing for customers?

B. REGULATORY AGENCY RESPONSES

Law enforcement agencies have been active in enforcing the laws prohibiting deceptive marketing practices in the online context. Some representative cases that the FTC has brought include:

Pyramid schemes. In *FTC v. Fortuna Alliance, L.L.C.*, Civ. No. C96–799M (W.D. Wash. filed May 23, 1996), the FTC charged defendants with operating a pyramid investment scheme. Defendants marketed the scheme through a website, as well as with printed promotional materials. Investors paid between $250 and $1,750 to join, with promises that they would receive over $5,000 a month in profits. Defendants claimed that their scheme differed from other pyramid schemes because payouts were based on a mathematical formula called the Fibonacci Series. They encouraged participants to propagate the scheme by setting up their own websites. Consumer losses were estimated at $7–11 million. Defendants stashed much of this money in a bank account in Antigua, some of which they returned to the United States after the court issued civil arrest warrants that made it imprudent for them to return to the United States without the money.

Failure to deliver goods. In *FTC v. Hare,* Civ. No. 98–8194 CIV HURLEY (M.D. Fla. filed Mar. 30, 1998), the defendant offered goods for sale via an online auction. The FTC alleged that defendant received money from winning bidders, but failed to ship the goods they had ordered. After settling with the FTC, the defendant pled guilty to a charge of criminal wire fraud based on the same conduct.

Deceptive health claims. In *FTC v. Liverite Products,* Civ. Act. No. SA 01–778 AHS (ANx) (C.D. Cal. Aug. 21, 2001), the defendants agreed to settle charges that they made numerous unsubstantiated claims about the efficacy of their "Liverite" dietary supplement products to treat or prevent a wide range of liver diseases, such as cirrhosis and hepatitis. The products included Liverite, the Ultimate Liver Aid; Liverite 3 in 1 for Men; Liverite 3 in 1 for Women; and Liverite Sports. These products consisted chiefly of beef liver extract. They were sold via several websites, as well as in retail stores and by telephone.

Credit repair schemes. In "Operation New ID/Bad Idea," conducted in 1999, the FTC, together with more than a dozen federal, state, and local law enforcement agencies, brought 59 cases against defendants who claimed they could help consumers clean up their credit histories. The assistance that defendants provided consisted of advising consumers to set up a new identity by obtaining a new taxpayer identification number. This method, unfortunately, is quite illegal.

For a discussion of the FTC's online enforcement program, see FEDERAL TRADE COMMISSION, COMBATING INTERNET FRAUD AND DECEPTION (2001), www.ftc.gov/bcp/internet/cases-netsum.pdf; FEDERAL TRADE COMMISSION, PROTECTING CONSUMERS ONLINE 6 (1999), www.ftc.gov/os/1999/9912/fiveyearreport.pdf.

The Securities and Exchange Commission has also been active in enforcing the securities laws in the online context. The most common types of online securities fraud are the offering of phony or overvalued investments, and stock price manipulation.

Investment fraud. In *SEC v. Briden,* 99 CV 11009 RCL (D. Mass. filed May 11, 1999), the SEC charged that defendants conducted a fraudulent offering of "prime bank" securities over the Internet. Unfortunately for the investors, "prime bank" instruments do not exist. Defendants allegedly used Internet websites, electronic bulletin board postings, and e-mails to offer the phony securities, promising investors returns of as much as 100% per week with no risk.

Stock price manipulation. The Internet is a cheap and easy way of spreading misinformation about a stock for the purpose of manipulating its price. This is frequently employed in a "pump-and-dump" scheme: the perpetrator pumps up the stock price by spreading baseless positive information about it, and then dumps his own holdings at the inflated price. The price then drops back to its pre-manipulation level. The following is from an SEC Litigation Release describing one such scheme:

SECURITIES AND EXCHANGE COMMISSION

Litigation Release No. 17294/January 3, 2002

SECURITIES AND EXCHANGE COMMISSION v. NED C. SNEIDERMAN, United States District Court for the Northern District of California, Civil Action No. C–02–0001

SEC CHARGES INTERNET MESSAGE BOARD POSTER WITH FRAUD

The Securities and Exchange Commission today announced fraud charges against a 24–year-old man for posting a phony press release on the Internet announcing that Extreme Networks, Inc. ("Extreme Networks"), a Santa Clara technology company, was acquiring Viasource Communications, Inc. ("Viasource"), a small Florida technology company. The phony news caused Viasource's stock price and volume to spike until the companies denied that an acquisition was planned.

In its complaint, the Commission alleges that on October 8, 2001, Ned C. Sneiderman, of Louisville, Kentucky, posted a fake press release on a Yahoo! Finance message board, which announced a cash tender offer by Extreme Networks for the shares of Viasource. In the hour following the posting, Viasource stock doubled in price to $.22 per share, on volume of more than 950,000 shares, nearly seven times higher than the previous trading day. The fraud artificially inflated Viasource's market capitalization by almost $4.7 million.

The complaint also alleges that Sneiderman purchased shares of Viasource stock minutes before he posted the false press release. However, within an hour after the false posting, Extreme Networks and Viasource denied the existence of a tender offer, and trading in both stocks was halted temporarily, which prevented Sneiderman from realizing substantial profits from the fraud. Both companies issued corrective press releases and, once trading was resumed, the price of Viasource shares dropped by almost 50% from the day's high.

* * *

For additional information about SEC enforcement against online securities violations, see Securities and Exchange Commission, *Internet–Related Litigation Announcements*, www.sec.gov/divisions/enforce/internetenforce/litreleases.shtml; Joseph J. Cella III & John Reed Stark, *SEC Enforcement and the Internet: Meeting the Challenge of the Next Millennium*, 52 BUS. LAW. 815 (1997).

C. NEW LAW ENFORCEMENT TOOLS

If the technology of Internet communications facilitates fraudulent conduct, and makes possible entirely new types of fraud, it also gives law enforcement officials new tools with which to fight fraud. First, centralized searching technology makes it easier to monitor and detect online scams. It is a simple matter to search the entire Web for particular keywords indicating likely scams. Fraudulent unsolicited bulk e-mail is frequently forwarded to central repositories, allowing it to be archived and searched. Searching a newsgroup archive can turn up consumers who have been victimized by a scam, and who can provide evidence against the perpetrators. By contrast, it is not feasible to monitor the unthinkably large number of offline means of transmitting fraudulent schemes—print and broadcast media, direct mail, and telemarketing all put together.

Second, consumer protection agencies can use the Internet as a means of disseminating information that helps consumers protect themselves against online fraud. One innovative approach involves the use of "teaser" websites, which are designed to draw consumers' attention and to deliver an educational message. The home page of a teaser site proposes an offer that seems too good to be true, such as a get-rich-quick scheme, diet program, or discount vacation plan. As the user clicks through to subsequent pages, he may view even more outrageous claims or testimonials, and is invited to become a participant by sending money. The final page reveals that the site was constructed by a government agency for the purpose of demonstrating to consumers how easy it is to fall for scams, and directs the user to sources of further information about how to avoid becoming a victim. Examples of teaser sites cam be found at *McWhortle,* www.mcwhortle.com; *The Ultimate Prosperity Page,* www.wemarket4u.net/prosperity/index.html; *EZ Travels,* www.wemarket4u.net/eztrvlagent/index.html; and *NordiCaLite,* www.wemarket4u.net/nordicalite/index.html.

The Internet also presents consumers with additional avenues for protecting themselves. Searching newsgroup archives can provide information about other consumers' experiences with a vendor or a product. Sites like www.eComplaints.com and www.PlanetFeedback.com accept consumer complaints and post them for all to see. Ratings sites such as www.epinions.com collect consumer experiences and product reviews. The site at www.consumer.gov provides links to the full range of consumer information available from the government. Online bookstores offer book reviews just when they are needed. Online resources can even assist consumers in defining their own preferences. *See* Mark S. Nadel, *The Consumer Product Selection Process in an Internet Age: Obstacles to Maximum Effectiveness and Policy Options*, 14 HARV. J.L. & TECH. 187 (2000).

III. ONLINE ADVERTISING ISSUES

As a general matter, legal rules that regulate the content of advertising are equally applicable regardless of the medium through which an advertisement is communicated. But it is not always clear what those rules mean, when applied to the online context. Rules that were written before the dawn of the digital age frequently contain language that was clear enough when applied to traditional communications media, but that raises issues of interpretation when applied to online communications. Features of online technologies that have no obvious offline analog, such as metatags and sponsored search engine results, likewise require careful application of rules written at a time when such technologies were yet unimagined.

A. INFORMATION DISCLOSURES IN ADVERTISING

Advertising can mislead both through what it says, and through what it fails to say. If an advertisement makes a claim that, standing alone, is ambiguous or is otherwise likely to mislead a potential purchaser, then the advertiser may be required to disclose qualifying information to insure that consumers will not be misled.

A Federal Trade Commission staff report discusses how the laws against misleading advertising apply to online advertising. The report sets out the general rules governing the use of advertising disclosures, and then applies these principles to website advertising.

FEDERAL TRADE COMMISSION, DOT COM DISCLOSURES

(2000).

A. Background on Disclosures

Advertisers must identify all express and implied claims that the ad conveys to consumers. When identifying claims, advertisers should not focus only on individual phrases or statements, but should consider the ad as a whole, including the text, product name and depictions. If an ad makes express or implied claims that are likely to be misleading without certain qualifying information, the information must be disclosed. Advertisers must determine which claims might need qualification and what information should be provided in a disclosure. If qualifying information is necessary to prevent an ad from being misleading, advertisers must present the information clearly and conspicuously.

A disclosure only qualifies or limits a claim, to avoid a misleading impression. It cannot cure a false claim. If a disclosure provides information that contradicts a claim, the disclosure will not be sufficient to prevent the ad from being deceptive. In that situation, the claim itself must be modified.

Many Commission rules and guides spell out the information that must be disclosed in connection with certain claims. In many cases, these disclosures prevent a claim from being misleading or deceptive. Other rules and guides require disclosures to ensure that consumers receive material information about the terms of a transaction, or to further public policy goals. These disclosures also must be clear and conspicuous.

B. *The Clear and Conspicuous Requirement*

Disclosures that are required to prevent deception—or to provide consumers material information about a transaction—must be presented "clearly and conspicuously." Whether a disclosure meets this standard is measured by its performance—that is, how consumers actually perceive and understand the disclosure within the context of the entire ad. The key is the *overall net impression* of the ad—that is, whether the claims consumers take from the ad are truthful and substantiated.

In reviewing their online ads, advertisers should adopt the perspective of a reasonable consumer. They also should assume that consumers don't read an entire Web site, just as they don't read every word on a printed page. In addition, it is important for advertisers to draw attention to the disclosure. Making the disclosure available somewhere in the ad so that consumers who are looking for the information *might* find it doesn't meet the clear and conspicuous standard.

Even though consumers have control over what and how much information they view on Web sites, they may not be looking for—or expecting to find—disclosures. Advertisers are responsible for ensuring that their messages are truthful and not deceptive. Accordingly, disclosures must be communicated effectively so that consumers are likely to notice and understand them.

C. *What are Clear and Conspicuous Disclosures?*

There is no set formula for a clear and conspicuous disclosure. In all media, the best way to disclose information depends on what information must be provided and the nature of the advertisement. Some disclosures are quite short, while others are more detailed. Some ads use only text, while others use graphics, video and audio. Advertisers have the flexibility to be creative in designing their ads, so long as necessary disclosures are communicated effectively and the overall message conveyed to consumers is not misleading.

To evaluate whether a particular disclosure is clear and conspicuous, consider:

- the **placement** of the disclosure in an advertisement and its **proximity** to the claim it is qualifying,
- the **prominence** of the disclosure,
- whether items in other parts of the advertisement **distract attention** from the disclosure,
- whether the advertisement is so lengthy that the disclosure needs to be **repeated**,
- whether disclosures in audio messages are presented in an adequate **volume** and **cadence** and visual disclosures appear for a sufficient **duration**, and

- whether the language of the disclosure is **understandable** to the intended audience.

* * *

1. Proximity and Placement

A disclosure is more effective if it is placed near the claim it qualifies or other relevant information. Proximity increases the likelihood that consumers will see the disclosure and relate it to the relevant claim or product. For print ads, an advertiser might measure proximity in terms of whether the disclosure is placed adjacent to the claim, or whether it is separated from the claim by text or graphics. The same approach can be used for Internet ads. Websites, however, are interactive and have a certain depth—with multiple pages linked together and pop-up screens, for example—that may affect how proximity is evaluated.

a. Evaluating Proximity in the Context of a Web Page

Some disclosures must be made when an ad contains a certain claim (often referred to as a "triggering claim"). On a Web page, the disclosure is more likely to be effective if consumers view the claim and disclosure together on the same screen. Even if a disclosure is not tied to a particular word or phrase, it is more likely that consumers will notice it if it is placed next to the information, product, or service to which it relates.

In some circumstances, it may be difficult to ensure that a disclosure appears on the "same screen" as a claim or product information. Some disclosures are long and difficult to place next to the claims they qualify. In addition, computers and other information "appliances" have varying screen sizes that display Web sites differently. In these situations, consumers may need to scroll to view a disclosure. If scrolling is necessary, advertisers should ask whether consumers are likely to do it. If consumers don't scroll, they may miss important qualifying information and be misled.

In these circumstances, advertisers are advised to:

Use text or visual cues to encourage consumers to scroll. Text prompts can indicate that more information is available. An explicit instruction like "see below for important information on diamond weights" will alert consumers to scroll and look for the information. The text prompt should be tied to the disclosure that it refers to. General or vague statements, such as "see below for details," provide no indication about the subject matter or importance of the information that consumers will find and are not adequate cues.

The visual design of the page also could help alert consumers to the availability of more information. For example, text that clearly continues below the screen, whether spread over an entire page or in a column, would indicate that the reader needs to scroll for additional information. Advertisers should consider how the Web page is displayed by the default Web browser setting for which the ad is designed, as well as for different display options.

A scroll bar on the side of a computer screen is not a sufficiently effective visual cue. Although the scroll bar may indicate to some consumers that they have not reached the end of a page, many consumers may not look at the scroll bar. In fact, some consumers access the Internet with devices that don't display a scroll bar.

Avoid Web page formats that discourage scrolling. The design of some pages might indicate that there is no more information on the page and no need to continue scrolling. If the text ends before the bottom of the screen or readers see several inches of blank space, chances are they will stop scrolling and miss the disclosure. In addition, if there is a lot of unrelated information—either words or graphics—separating a claim and a disclosure, even a consumer who is prompted to scroll might miss the disclosure or not relate it to a distant claim they've already read.

b. Hyperlinking to a Disclosure

With hyperlinks, additional information, including disclosures, might be placed on a Web page entirely separate from the relevant claim. Disclosures that are an integral part of a claim or inseparable from it, however, should be placed on the same page and immediately next to the claim. In these situations, the claim and the disclosure should be read at the same time, without referring the consumer somewhere else to obtain the disclosure. This is particularly true for cost information or certain health and safety disclosures. For example, if the total cost of a product is advertised on one page, but there are significant additional fees that the consumer would not expect to be charged, the existence of those additional fees should be disclosed on the same page and immediately adjacent to the total cost claim. In other situations, it may not even be necessary to use a hyperlink to convey disclosures. Often, disclosures consist of a word or phrase that may be easily incorporated into the text, along with the claim. This placement increases the likelihood that consumers will see the disclosure and relate it to the relevant claim.

Under some conditions, however, a disclosure accessible by a hyperlink may be sufficiently proximate to the relevant claim. Hyperlinked disclosures may be particularly useful if the disclosure is lengthy or if it needs to be repeated (because of multiple triggers, for example). The key considerations for effective hyperlinks are:

- the labeling or description of the hyperlink,
- the consistency in the use of hyperlink styles,
- its placement and prominence on the Web page, and
- the handling of the disclosure on the click-through page.

Choosing the right label for the hyperlink. A hyperlink that leads to a disclosure should be labeled clearly and conspicuously. The hyperlink's label—the text or graphic assigned to it—affects whether consumers actually click on it and see and read the disclosure.

- **Make it obvious.** Consumers should be able to tell that they can click on a hyperlink to get more information.
- **Label the link to convey the importance, nature and relevance of the information it leads to.** The hyperlink should give consumers a *reason* to click on it. That is, the label should make clear that the link is related to a particular advertising claim or product and indicate the nature of the information to be found by clicking on it. The hyperlink label should use clear, understandable text. Although the label itself does not need to contain the complete disclosure, it may be useful to incorporate part of the disclosure to indicate the type and importance of the information the link leads to.
- **Don't be coy.** Some text links may provide no indication about why a claim is qualified or the nature of the disclosure. In most cases, simply hyperlinking a single word or phrase in the text of an ad may not be effective. Although some consumers may understand that there is additional information available, they may have different ideas about the nature of the information and its significance. The same may be true of hyperlinks that simply say "disclaimer," "more information," "details," or "terms and conditions."
- **Don't be subtle.** Asterisks or other symbols by themselves may not be effective. Typically, they provide no clues about why the claim is qualified or the nature of the disclosure. In fact, consumers may view an asterisk or another symbol as just another graphic on the page. Even if a Web site explains that a particular symbol is a hyperlink to important information, consumers might miss the explanation, depending on where they enter the site and how they navigate through it.

Using hyperlink styles consistently allows consumers to know when a link is available. Although the text or graphics used to signal a hyperlink may differ among Web sites, treating hyperlinks inconsistently within a single site can increase the chances that consumers will *not* notice—or click on—a disclosure hyperlink. For example, if hyperlinks usually are underlined in a site, chances are consumers wouldn't recognize italicized text as being a link, and could miss the disclosure.

Placing the link near relevant information and making it noticeable. The hyperlink should be proximate to the claim that triggers the disclosure so that consumers can notice it easily and relate it to the claim. Typically, this means that the hyperlink is adjacent to the triggering term or other relevant information. Consumers may miss disclosure hyperlinks that are separated from the relevant claim by text, graphics, blank space, or intervening hyperlinks. Format, color or other graphics treatment also can help to ensure that consumers notice the link. (See below for more information on prominence.)

Getting to the disclosure on the click-through page should be easy. The click-through page—that is, the page the hyperlink leads to—must contain the complete disclosure. The disclosure must be displayed prominently. Distracting visual factors, extraneous information, and many "click-away" opportunities to link elsewhere before viewing the disclosure can obscure an otherwise adequate disclaimer.

- **Get consumers to the message quickly.** The hyperlink should take consumers directly to the disclosure. They shouldn't have to search a click-through page or go to other pages for the information. In addition, the disclosure should be easy to understand.
- **Assessing the effectiveness of a hyperlink disclosure is important.** Tools are available to allow advertisers to evaluate the effectiveness of disclosures through hyperlinks. For example, advertisers can monitor click-through rates—how often consumers click on a hyperlink and view the click-through page—for accurate data on the efficacy of the hyperlink. Advertisers also can evaluate the amount of time visitors spend on a certain page, which may indicate whether consumers are reading the disclosure.
- **Don't ignore your data.** If hyperlinks are not followed, another method of conveying the required information would be necessary.

c. Using High Tech Methods For Proximity and Placement

Disclosures may be displayed on Web sites in many ways. For example, a disclosure may be placed in a frame that remains constant even as the consumer scrolls down the page or navigates through another part of the site. A disclosure also might be displayed in a window that pops-up or on interstitial pages that appear while another Web page is loading. New techniques for displaying information are being unveiled all the time. But there are special considerations for evaluating whether a technique is appropriate for providing required disclosures.

- **Don't ignore technological limitations.** A scrolling marquee—information that scrolls through a box on a Web site—may display differently depending on the type of browser a consumer uses. Similarly, some browsers or information appliances may not support or display frames properly, so a disclosure placed in one portion of the frame may not be viewable. Certain Internet tools may overcome this limitation by determining if a consumer's Web browser can view frames and if not, serving a page that is formatted differently. Without such tools, advertisers should be concerned about whether a required disclosure will appear; if it won't, they should choose different ways to communicate the disclosure.
- **Recognize and respond to characteristics of each technique.** Some consumers may miss information presented in a pop-up window or on an interstitial page if the window or page disappears and they are unable or unaware of how to access it. Others may inadvertently minimize a pop-up screen by clicking on the main

page and may not know how to make the pop-up screen reappear. There may be ways to get around these drawbacks, such as requiring the consumer to take some affirmative action to proceed past the pop-up or interstitial (for example, by clicking on a "continue" button).

- **Research can help.** Research may be useful to help advertisers determine whether a particular technique is an effective method of communicating information to consumers. For example, research may show that consumers don't actually read information in pop-up windows because they immediately close the pop-up on the page they want to view. It also may indicate whether consumers relate information in a pop-up window or on an interstitial page to a claim or product they haven't encountered yet. Advertisers should consider this information in determining effective methods of presenting required disclosures.

d. Displaying Disclosures Prior to Purchase

Disclosures must be effectively communicated to consumers before they make a purchase or incur a financial obligation. Disclosures are more likely to be effective if they are provided in the context of the ad, when the consumer is considering the purchase. Where advertising and selling are combined on a Web site, disclosures should be provided before the consumer makes the decision to buy, say, before clicking on an "order now" button or a link that says "add to shopping cart."

- **Don't focus only on the order page.** Some disclosures must be made in connection with a particular claim or product. Consumers may not relate a disclosure on the order page to information they viewed many pages earlier. It also is possible that after surfing a company's Web site, some consumers may decide to purchase the product from the company's "bricks and mortar" store. Those consumers would miss any disclosures placed only on the ordering page.

e. Evaluating Proximity With Banner Ads

Most banner ads displayed today are teasers. Because of their small size, they generally do not provide complete information about a product or service. Instead, consumers must click through to the Web site to get more information and learn the terms of an offer. In some instances, a banner may contain a claim that requires qualification.

- **Disclose required information in the banner itself or clearly and conspicuously on the Web site it links to.** In some cases, a required disclosure can be incorporated into a banner ad easily. Because of the space constraints of banner ads, other disclosures may be too detailed to be disclosed effectively in the banner. In some instances, these disclosures may be communicated effectively to consumers if they are made clearly and conspicuously on the Web site the banner links to and while consumers are deciding whether to buy a product or service. In determining whether the disclosure should be placed in the banner itself or on the Web site the banner links to, advertisers should consider how important the information is to prevent deception, how much information needs to be disclosed, the burden of disclosing it in the banner ad, how much information the consumer may absorb from the ad, and how effective the disclosure would be if it was made on the Web site.

- **Use creativity to incorporate or flag required information.** Scrolling text or rotating panels in a banner can present an abbreviated version of a required disclosure that indicates that there is additional important information and a more complete disclosure available on the click-through page. With lengthier disclosures, the banner can direct consumers to the Web site for more information. The full disclosure then must be clearly and conspicuously displayed on the Web site.
- **Provide any required disclosures in interactive banners.** Some banner ads allow consumers to interact within the banner, so that they may conduct a transaction without clicking through to a Web site. If consumers can get complete information about a product or make a purchase within an interactive banner, all required disclosures should be included in the banner.

2. Prominence

It's the advertiser's responsibility to draw attention to the required disclosures.

- **Display disclosures prominently so they are noticeable to consumers.** The size, color, and graphics of the disclosure affect its prominence.
    - **Size Matters.** Disclosures that are at least as large as the advertising copy are more likely to be effective.
    - **Color Counts.** A disclosure in a color that contrasts with the background emphasizes the text of the disclosure and makes it more noticeable. Information in a color that blends in with the background of the ad is likely to be missed.
    - **Graphics Help.** Although using graphics to display a disclosure is not required, they may make the disclosure more prominent.
- **Evaluate the size, color, and graphics of the disclosure in relation to other parts of the Web site.** The size of a disclosure should be compared to the type size of the claim and other text on the page. If a claim uses a particular color or graphic treatment, the disclosure can be formatted the same way to help ensure that consumers who view the claim are able to view the disclosure as well. In addition, the graphic treatment of the disclosure may be evaluated in relation to how graphics are used to convey other items in the ad.

- **Don't bury it.** The prominence of the disclosure also may be affected by other factors. A disclosure that is buried in a long paragraph of unrelated text would not be effective. The unrelated text detracts from the message and makes it unlikely that a consumer would notice the disclosure or recognize its importance. Even though the unrelated information may be useful, advertisers must ensure that the disclosure is communicated effectively.

3. Distracting Factors in Ads

The clear and conspicuous analysis does not focus only on the disclosure itself. It also is important to consider the entire ad. Elements like graphics, sound, text or even hyperlinks that lead to other pages or sites, may result in consumers not noticing, reading or listening to the disclosure.

- **Don't let other parts of an ad get in the way.** On television, moving visuals behind a text message make the text hard to read and may distract consumers' attention from the message. Using graphics online raises similar concerns: flashing images or animated graphics may reduce the prominence of a disclosure. Graphics on a Web page *alone* may not undermine the effectiveness of a disclosure. It is important, however, to consider all the elements in the ad, not just the text of the disclosure.

4. Repetition

It may be necessary to disclose important information more than once in an advertisement to convey a non-deceptive message. Repeating a disclosure makes it more likely that a consumer will notice and understand it. Still, the disclosure need not be repeated so often that consumers would ignore it and that it would clutter the ad.

- **Repeat disclosures on lengthy Web sites, as needed.** Consumers can access and navigate Web sites differently. Many consumers may access a site through its homepage, but others might enter in the middle, perhaps by linking to that page from a search engine or another Web site. Consumers also might not click-on every page of the site and may not choose to scroll to the bottom of each page. And many may not read every word on every page of a Web site. As a result, advertisers should question whether consumers who see only a portion of their ad are likely to miss a necessary disclosure and be misled.

- **Repeat disclosures with repeated claims, as needed.** If claims requiring some qualification are repeated throughout an ad, it may be necessary to repeat the disclosure too. In some situations, a disclosure is tied so closely to a claim that it must always accompany the claim to prevent deception. Depending on the disclosure, a clearly-labeled hyperlink could be repeated on various pages so that the full disclosure would be placed on only one page of the site.

5. Multimedia Messages

Internet ads may contain audio messages, video clips and other animated segments with claims that require qualification. As with radio and television ads, the disclosure should accompany the claim. In evaluating whether disclosures in these multimedia portions of online ads are clear and conspicuous, advertisers should evaluate all of the factors discussed in this paper and these special considerations:

- **For audio claims, use audio disclosures.** The disclosure should be in a volume and cadence sufficient for a reasonable consumer to hear and understand it. The volume of the disclosure can be evaluated in relation to the rest of the message, and in particular, the claim. Of course, consumers who do not have speakers, appropriate software, or appliances with audio capabilities will not hear the claim or the disclosure. Because some consumers may miss the audio portion of an ad, disclosures triggered by a claim or other information in an ad's text should not be placed solely in an audio clip.
- **Display visual disclosures for a sufficient duration.** Visual disclosures presented in video clips or other dynamic portions of online ads should appear for a duration sufficient for consumers to notice, read and understand them. As with brief video superscripts in television ads, fleeting disclosures on Web sites are not likely to be effective.

* * *

NOTES & QUESTIONS

1. *Self-monitoring.* Advertisers have the technological capability of monitoring the effectiveness of certain types of website disclosures that goes far beyond what is possible with other advertising media. Web servers may easily be configured to keep a record of each page that a site visitor accesses. If disclosure information is made available via a link from the page containing the advertising claims, the server logs will reveal how often a visitor clicks on the link and views the disclosure page. By contrast, there is no practical way of ascertaining whether the reader of a print advertisement views disclosure information that appears in fine print at the bottom of the ad. Should advertisers be required to analyze their server logs for this purpose? In a law enforcement action predicated on inadequate disclosure, should an analysis of server logs be admissible as evidence that the disclosure did not effectively convey information to site visitors?

2. *Display variables.* Websites may be viewed through a wide variety of Internet access devices, ranging in display size from a 31–inch television set down to a tiny screen on a mobile telephone, with widely varying screen resolutions, and with various versions of website browser software. Each combination of screen size, resolution, and browser software will display the information presented by a website differently. For example, some site visitors will see the entirety of an advertisement and the accompanying disclosure on a single screen, while other visitors will need to scroll down to see all of the page. Given this variety of display variables at the site visitor's end, and the inability of a website advertiser to control how the information it provides will be received, how feasible is it for a website advertiser to observe the niceties of the FTC's rules on advertising disclosures?

3. *Is more always better?* Online technology allows a seller advertising its products via a website to add almost limitless quantities of additional information about those products at minimal cost—unlike the case with print, broadcast, and most other advertising media. Is there such a thing as providing consumers with *too much* information?

4. *You be the judge*. Take a look at the mock advertising websites that are attached to the FTC's DOT COM DISCLOSURES report, www.ftc.gov/bcp/conline/pubs/buspubs/dotcom/index.pdf, applying the standards for deceptive advertising that the FTC sets out in the report. Do you agree with the FTC's views with respect to which of these are deceptive?

B. APPLICABILITY OF RULES WITH TERMS LIKE "WRITTEN," "WRITING," "PRINTED" OR "DIRECT MAIL"

The FTC has promulgated and enforces a variety of rules applying to advertising. Nearly all of these were drafted before commercial activity via the Internet became widespread. The drafters of these rules naturally chose their language on the expectation that they would apply to advertising disseminated through the existing communications media, mainly print (including periodicals and direct mail), broadcast (radio and television) and, more recently, telephone (telemarketing).

How do these rules apply to advertising appearing on websites, on electronic bulletin boards, and in e-mail? As the FTC explains in *Dot Com Disclosures, supra,* "Many rules and guides address claims about products or services or advertising in general and are not limited to any particular medium used to disseminate those claims or advertising. Therefore, the plain language of many rules and guides applies to claims made on the Internet." For example, the Television Picture Tube Rule, one of the simplest of all the rules that the FTC enforces, is completely medium-neutral. This rule states:

> [I]t is an unfair method of competition and an unfair and deceptive act or practice to use any figure or size designation to refer to the size of the picture shown by a television receiving set or the picture tube contained therein unless such indicated size is the actual size of the viewable picture area measured on a single plane basis. If the indicated size is other than the horizontal dimension of the actual viewable picture area such size designation shall be accompanied by a statement, in close connection and conjunction therewith, clearly and conspicuously showing the manner of measurement.

Deceptive Advertising as to Sizes of Viewable Pictures Shown by Television Receiving Sets, 16 C.F.R. § 410.1.

Other rules are limited to marketing conducted through a particular medium of communication. For example, the Telemarketing Sales Rule, which prohibits deceptive and abusive methods of "telemarketing," applies only to telephone solicitations. The scope of the rule is limited by its definition of "telemarketing" as "a * * * program * * * which is conducted to induce the purchase of goods or services by use of one or more telephones." 16 C.F.R. § 310.2(u).

Interestingly, the version of the Telemarketing Sales Rule that the FTC originally proposed in 1995 contained a much broader definition of "telemarketing," one that would have included online solicitations. "Telemarketing" was there defined as "a * * * program * * * which is conducted to induce payment for goods or services by use of one or more telephones (including the use of a facsimile machine, computer modem, or any other telephonic medium)." 60 Fed. Reg. 8,329 (Feb. 14, 1995). After receiving comments on the proposed rule from the public, the FTC published a revised proposed rule, which differed substantially from the initial version. Among many other changes, the revised proposed rule dropped the language from the definition of "telemarketing" that would have swept online solicitations within its scope. The FTC explained why it had dropped coverage of online solicitations:

> After considering many comments that objected to the Rule's coverage of on-line services, the Commission acknowledges that it does not have the necessary information available to it to support coverage of on-line services under the Rule.

60 Fed. Reg. 30,411 (June 8, 1995).

Still other rules have been amended to take account of technological change. Consider the Mail or Telephone Order Merchandise Rule, 16 C.F.R. Part 435. When originally promulgated in 1975, the Mail Order Rule, as it was then known, applied only to merchandise ordered by mail. It required sellers of goods that are ordered by mail to ship the goods within the time the seller specified, or within 30 days if no shipping date is specified. If the seller could not ship within the applicable period, the seller had to notify the customer of the delay, and either obtain the customer's consent to delayed shipment, or cancel the order and make a prompt refund.

In its 1993 rule review proceeding, the FTC recognized that times had changed:

> Since the [Rule] was promulgated in 1975, buying by telephone has grown enormously. Although the number of telephone order transactions annually is still fewer than the number of mail order sales, the average telephone order sale is larger than the average mail order sale. Of the approximately $48 billion consumers spend each year for mail and telephone order merchandise, roughly half the value of these sales consists of merchandise ordered by telephone.

58 Fed. Reg. 49,096 (Sept. 21, 1993).

The FTC attributed this development to several factors, including "[t]echnological innovations, particularly the introduction in 1960 of a bulk discounted telephone call service called Wide Area Telephone Service ('WATS'), which opened the way for high-volume outbound (originated by the merchant) low cost long-distance calling, and the introduction in 1967 of '800' inbound (originated by the consumer) WATS service." *Id.* at 49,099. The Commission also cited two additional reasons for the shift to telephone ordering: "The increased acceptance of the telephone as a means of shopping," and "The willingness of consumers to use credit cards in telephone sales." The latter, and perhaps also the former, reflects technological innovations in payment mechanisms.

In response to this technological change, the Commission decided to amend the Rule so that it applies to merchandise ordered both by mail and by telephone. It accomplished this by making the Rule applicable to "mail or telephone order sales," defining that term to mean "sales in which the buyer has ordered merchandise from the seller by mail or telephone, regardless of the method of payment or the method used to solicit the order." 16 C.F.R. § 435.2(a).

The Commission also added a definition of "telephone": "any direct or indirect use of the telephone to order merchandise, regardless of whether the telephone is activated by, or the language used is that of human beings, machines, or both." *Id.* § 435.2(b). The Commission intended by this rather curious locution to "reach orders placed by facsimile machines or computers with telephone modems." 58 Fed. Reg. 49,097 (1993). While the phrase sounds rather quaint to our modern ears, the Commission deserves credit for being significantly ahead of its time. The Commission proposed this definition of telephone in a Notice of Proposed Rulemaking published in 1989—at a time when the Internet was the preserve of academics, and commercial activity was prohibited. Online commerce was at that time very limited, and was conducted mostly over proprietary networks, such as CompuServe and Prodigy, and via dial-up electronic bulletin board systems.

The Rule's definition of telephone is showing its age. Users typically access the Internet without any use of a telephone. With a standard dialup account, data travels from computer memory, through a modem, into a wire that is plugged into a telephone jack, across telephone lines and fiber-optic cable, and through similar steps to the memory of the recipient computer. Although data travels through infrastructure that also carries telephone calls, there is no use of a telephone at either end. When Internet access is supplied by a cable carrying television signals or a wireless link, the resemblance to a telephone becomes even more tenuous.

NOTES & QUESTIONS

FTC rules and online transactions. In 1994, the FTC amended the Mail Order Rule to include within its scope products ordered with the use of a computer modem. In 1995, the FTC declined to include within the scope of the Telemarketing Sales Rule solicitations communicated with the use of a computer modem, on the ground that it "does not have the necessary information available to it to support coverage of on-line services." If the FTC had sufficient information to include online communications in 1994, how could it lack sufficient information in 1995? Are these two actions inconsistent?

C. DECEPTIVE USE OF A DOMAIN NAME

UNITED STATES OF AMERICA
FEDERAL TRADE COMMISSION
WASHINGTON, D.C. 20580

August 21, 1997

Mr. David M. Graves
Internet Business Manager
Network Solutions, Inc.
505 Huntmar Park Drive
Herndon, VA 22070

Re: Domain name <internic.com>

Dear Mr. Graves:

We recently received your request for a staff opinion on behalf of Network Solutions, Inc. ("Network Solutions") concerning the business practices of Internic Software, a firm that offers domain name registration services through its Internet website located at <www.internic.com>. Based on the facts set forth below, Federal Trade Commission ("Commission") staff believe that use of the domain name <internic.com> in combination with the provision of domain name registration services at the site located at <www.internic.com> is likely to mislead consumers.

I. FACTS

Your letter describes the following facts that are critical to our analysis. Network Solutions through the Internet Network Information Center ("InterNIC") has the sole authority, granted by the National Science Foundation, to register domain names within the top-level domains <.com>, <.org>, <.net>, <.edu>, and <.gov>. InterNIC is known to consumers as the "official" domain name registry. In fact, consumers who wish to register domain names directly through Network Solutions can do so online via Network Solutions' InterNIC site located at <www.internic.net>. The cost of registering a domain name directly through Network Solutions is $100 for two years.

Your letter states that consumers searching for Network Solutions' InterNIC site often enter <internic> or <internic.**com**> into their browser which in turn calls up the domain name registration service operated by Internic Software, Inc. ("Internic Software") of Sunbury, Australia, not the service operated by Network Solutions at <internic.**net**>. (Emphasis added.) Internic Software operates as a broker, registering domain names for consumers through Network Solutions. Internic Software charges $250 for a two-year domain name registration and has processed over 2,000 domain name registrations.

According to your letter, Network Solutions has received many complaints stating that the site operated by Internic Software misled consumers who believed that they were at the site operated by Network Solutions. Moreover, these consumers believed that they had registered their domain name directly through Network Solutions and not through a broker. You also stated that Network Solutions has not received payment from Internic Software for the majority of consumers who registered their domain names through Internic Software.

II. APPLICABLE LAW

The Commission has statutory authority to prohibit unfair or deceptive acts or practices pursuant to the Federal Trade Commission Act, ("FTC Act"), 15 U.S.C. § 41 *et seq.* Under § 5 of the FTC Act, 15 U.S.C. § 45, the Commission has determined that a representation, omission, or practice is deceptive if: (1) it is likely to mislead consumers acting reasonably under the circumstances; and (2) it is material—that is, likely to affect consumers' conduct or decisions with respect to the product at issue.

III. ANALYSIS AND CONCLUSION

In staff's opinion, advertising and providing Internet domain name registration services through the Internet site located at <www.internic.com> is likely to violate § 5 of the FTC Act's prohibition against deceptive acts or practices. The use of a domain name <internic.com> virtually identical to that of the official domain registration site, combined with the provision of nearly identical domain registration services to those offered by Network Solutions, is likely to create a false impression that the site is owned and operated by Network Solutions, whose site is located at <www.internic.com>. The "disclaimer" that "Internic Software is not affiliated with, or part of Network Solutions, Inc., or its InterNIC operation which can be found at www.internic.net" that appears on certain pages of Internic Software's site, to the extent that it is even seen by consumers during the registration process, is inadequate to cure this false impression.

Staff also believes that it is likely to be deceptive within § 5 of the FTC Act to offer to broker domain name registration services, accept payment for such services, and then fail to pay the official registry of domain names. If, as your letter alleges, Internic Software fails to provide payment to Network Solutions to secure domain name registrations, staff believes that Internic Software could face additional liability under § 5 of the FTC Act. Consumers reasonably expect that their payment will result in a full registration of their domain name.

Please be advised that the views expressed in this letter are those of the FTC staff. They are not binding upon the Commission.

Yours truly,

David Medine

NOTES & QUESTIONS

1. *Why the letter?* The letter says that Network Solutions, Inc. requested that the FTC provide it with this staff opinion letter. Why do you think NSI wanted this letter?

2. *Was the website deceptive?* The letter opines that Internic.com's disclosure—"Internic Software is not affiliated with, or part of Network Solutions, Inc., or its InterNIC operation which can be found at www.internic.net"—is inadequate to overcome the deception inherent in its use of the look-alike domain name. Do you agree? Would your answer differ depending on whether the disclosure appeared (1) in small print at the bottom of the internic.com home page, after the copyright notice; (2) in normal-sized print at the bottom of the page containing the order form, such that some viewers would have to scroll to see it; (3) at the top of the order form page, where it would be visible to all visitors who filled out the order form; (4) on a page reached by clicking on a hyperlink at the top of the order form page, with the hyperlink labeled "Legally required disclosure"; (5) on a page that must be traversed on the way to the order form page, with a button labeled "I have read and understand this disclosure" that must be clicked to proceed to the order form page?

3. *Proliferation of registrars.* At the time the FTC sent this staff opinion letter, Network Solutions held a monopoly on the registration of domain names in the .com, .org, and .net top-level domains. There are now numerous companies that offer this service. The www.internic.net site is now a gateway that provides access to all accredited registrars. Do you think the FTC would consider it deceptive for a company to engage today in the same conduct that gave rise to its 1997 staff opinion letter? What if a company set up a registration shop at www.register.net, charging much higher prices than the accredited registrar operating via www.register.com under the trade name Register.com?

4. *Postscript.* The owner of the website was Internic Technology Pty Ltd, an Australian company. The FTC referred the matter to its Australian counterpart, the Australian Competition and Consumer Commission, which brought a court action against the company. The ACCC settled the matter, obtaining the company's agreement to stop using the name "Internic" and to refund $161,000 to the 12,000 customers who paid it for domain registrations.

D. BLURRING OF ADVERTISING AND EDITORIAL CONTENT

Modern marketing science has devised promotional methods that increasingly blur the distinction between advertising and editorial content. The marketer's arsenal includes (a) "infomercials," program-length television features that have the look of a television program but are actually just lengthy advertisements; (b) "advertorials," print advertisements that are designed to look like editorials; and (c) "product placement," which involves marketers paying money to producers to have their products appear in television or movie scenes, as part of the script or background.

The online medium makes possible some new variations on this theme, through manipulation of search engine results. One of the best ways to locate information on the Internet is by using a search engine. The user enters a word or phrase, clicks on "Search," and the search engine returns a result, typically consisting of an ordered list of links to material on the Web. This list of links is usually lengthy, consisting of several or many screens of text, and those near the top of the list are more likely to be followed than those near the bottom. Operators of commercial websites may perceive an interest in having their site turn up high on the list of results of certain searches.

Some website owners seek to improve their rankings in search engine results by placing selected search terms in metatags and other invisible website text, and by purchasing keywords from search engines. (These practices are discussed more fully in Chapter 2, *supra.*) This is perfectly appropriate if the text that is used corresponds to the website owner's trademarks, or a truthful description of the types of goods the site offers. But metatags can also be used in a deceptive manner. This may occur when the marketer of a product seeks to draw visitors to its website by using metatags suggesting characteristics that the product does not in fact possess. In *FTC v. Lane Labs–USA, Inc.*, Civ. Ac. No. 00 CV 3174 (D.N.J. stipulated judgment entered Sept. 26, 2000), the FTC charged the defendants with deceptive trade practices based, in part, on terms that defendants used in metatags on a website promoting their products. Those products contained shark cartilage, and defendants promoted them as a cure for cancer. The metatags included the terms "cancer treatment," "prostate cancer," "chemotherapy," "cancer patients," "cancer survivors," and "non-toxic cancer therapy." The FTC alleged that claims that shark cartilage cured cancer were unsubstantiated, and that it was therefore deceptive to make such claims. According to the complaint: "Defendants' use of these metatag references increases the likelihood that consumers who research the topics of cancer and skin cancer and effective cancer and skin cancer treatments on the Internet will find information about Bene-Fin, SkinAnswer and other Lane Labs products." The district court entered a stipulated judgment, which prohibits the defendants from making false claims about its products and requires them to pay $1 million for consumer redress and to finance a clinical study of the efficacy of shark cartilage as a cancer cure.

Website operators can also affect their rankings in search engine results through sponsorship payments. Some search engines rank their results based on payments they receive from the website owners. The most prominent of these is www.overture.com. Overture explains how its ranking system works: "Advertisers choose their priority listing in the search results by paying for placement, with the highest paying advertiser's site appearing first in the results. Each advertiser pays Overture the amount of its bid whenever a consumer clicks on an advertiser's listing in the search results." If a website that turns up in a Overture search is one of Overture's advertisers, its listing in the search results indicates how much the advertiser will pay Overture each time a user clicks on the link, and includes a few lines of advertising copy. For example, a search on "personal injury lawyer" might return, as the highest listing, this item:

1. *Personal Injury Hotline.Com—PI Lawyers*

   Personal injury lawyers offer free consultation, online or through a toll-free number, to accident or malpractice victims.

   www.personalinjuryhotline.com (Cost to advertiser: $2.10)

Other sites are listed in descending order, based on the "Cost to advertiser." Below all of the paid listings are the websites that did not pay for better placement.

NOTES & QUESTIONS

1. *Metatag abuse.* What is the vice of using irrelevant terms in metatags, from the consumer protection perspective? Is a consumer misled when a search returns websites that are not relevant to her search terms? In a case like *Lane Labs*, suppose that the metatags falsely suggested product characteristics but the visible text on the site was completely truthful: would this be deceptive? Is the problem better conceptualized as bait-and-switch, rather than as deceptive advertising? *See* Ira S. Nathenson, *Internet Infoglut and Invisible Ink: Spamdexing Search Engines with Meta Tags*, 12 HARV. J.L. & TECH. 43, 93–98 (1998).

2. *Ranking.* Why would Web users choose a search engine that ranks results based on payments from the websites, rather than one that seeks to rank them in order of relevance to the user? Overture explains:[6]

> Here's why it makes sense. Advertisers bid in an open auction for placement in the results for search terms that are relevant to

6. [This explanatory text is from a previous version of Overture's website. The company's name was then GoTo.—Eds.]

> their sites. And they pay only for consumers who click on their listings. So they have an incentive to bid for top placement only on search terms where they are going to meet consumers who are looking for what they have to offer. Think of it like this: when you look for a plumber in the Yellow Pages, chances are that those with higher visibility have a more viable and relevant business. And they better be able to offer exactly what you're looking for or it's advertising money down the drain (no pun intended!)
>
> [Overture's] marketplace also offers three things to advertisers that no other search engine does: 1) it gives advertisers complete control over their placement in search results, 2) it enables them to target specifically consumers who are interested in what they are offering, and 3) it allows them to pay only the amount they decide for visitors clicking on their listings.
>
> In short, you find the site you're looking for, the advertiser gets only the visitors they're after, and we prove our business model. Yes indeed folks, it's one of those all too rare win-win-win situations.

What do you think of this explanation? Does it rely on the same "invisible hand" mechanism that is thought to steer resources to their highest-valued uses in a laissez-faire market economy? How might a website owner that chooses not to be an Overture advertiser evaluate the system? Is Overture's ranking system potentially misleading to users? Does it make a difference how prominently the explanation of the system appears on Overture's website?

3. *Deceptive metatags?* McNeil Consumer Healthcare Company manufactures the over-the-counter medication ibuprofen, which it markets under the brand name Motrin. McNeil operates a website promoting this brand at www.motrinib.com. The HTML code for the site's home page includes the following string of metatags: "Motrin IB, Children's Motrin, Junior Strength Motrin, Infant's Motrin, Motrin Sinus Headache, Motrin Cold and Flu, Ibuprofen, Pain, Fever, Sinus, Headache, High Fever, Sinus Headache, Body Ache, Back Ache, Muscle Ache, Pain Relief, Nasal Congestion, Fever Reducer, Sinusitis, Cold, Flu, Pseudoephedrine, StayCalm, Arthritis." Motrin's website is likely to be of interest to many users who search on one or more of these terms.

Suppose that Motrin's website included in its metatags the terms "Advil," "acetaminophen," and "cancer cure." Advil is the brand name under which ibuprofen is marketed by American Home Products Corporation, which is a competitor of McNeil. Acetaminophen is, like ibuprofen, a pain reliever and fever reducer that is sold over the counter. People who take ibuprofen and switch to acetaminophen may get better, similar, or worse results. Ibuprofen has not been shown to be effective in treating cancer. Should it be a deceptive trade practice to include any or all of these terms in the metatags at www.motrinib.com?

E. ONLINE SWEEPSTAKES

The use of sweepstakes is a common marketing technique, and one that is gaining popularity in the online environment. *See, e.g., Sweepstakes*

Online, www.sweepstakesonline.com. A sweepstakes is a contest that is conducted, usually by a business, to attract the attention of prospective customers. The company invites individuals to participate by submitting an entry, selects winners using some chance-based mechanism, and awards prizes to the winners.

A properly structured sweepstakes is legal, but care must be taken to insure that it does not amount to a lottery, which (if operated by a private party) is illegal in all fifty states. A lottery is a contest that includes the elements of consideration, prize, and chance. "Prize" and "chance" are the elements that sweepstakes and lotteries have in common: each type of contest awards some sort of prize, and selects the winners through a chance-based mechanism. What distinguishes a legal sweepstakes from an illegal lottery is therefore the element of "consideration," which refers to the requirements for a participant to enter. States laws vary considerably in what is deemed to be "consideration" for purposes of constituting an illegal lottery. In some states, there is "consideration" only if an entrant is required to part with something of value to him. In other states, the entrant need only expend enough effort to support formation of a contract. The two approaches are well canvassed in *Blackburn v. Ippolito*, 156 So.2d 550 (Fla.Dist.Ct.App.1963).

NOTES & QUESTIONS

Consideration. A web-based company runs a sweepstakes. The entry form is available online, at its website. The form requires entrants to supply their name, address, telephone number, and e-mail address. At the bottom of the form is a check-box, which looks like this:

Opt–In Box

☑ You may receive valuable information about our products and services. This box must remain checked to receive a sweepstakes entry.

The statement of rules applying to the sweepstakes states: "You must leave the 'Opt–In' box checked in order to receive an entry into the Sweepstakes." Does the fact that a contestant must have Internet access to enter the sweepstakes constitute an illegal "consideration" requirement? Is the rule that entrants must opt in to receiving marketing materials from the sweepstakes operator such a requirement? What if the rules required the entrant to take a tour of the operator's website and view its product offerings? What if an entrant must fill out a form disclosing demographic information, or her personal preferences?

IV. ONLINE CONTRACTING AND ITS PERILS: UCITA AND CONSUMER PROTECTION

As we saw in Chapter 4, *supra*, the proposed Uniform Computer Information Transactions Act, a uniform law designed to govern transactions involving software, databases, and other types of computerized information, has engendered enormous controversy among those interested in its effects on consumers. According to Professor Raymond Nimmer, the Reporter to UCITA's Drafting Committee and its primary drafter, UCITA is pro-consumer in several important respects:

> UCITA is a commercial code, not a consumer protection statute, but consumers are better off under UCITA than under current law. UCITA retains existing consumer protection law (except for limited e-commerce rules), adopts the consumer rules contained in [UCC] Article 2, and adds limited additional protections appropriate for issues associated with computer information transactions. * * *
>
> Whether one describes a particular rule as a consumer protection rule or not depends on one's image of what that term means. Many rules in UCITA and in general law benefit consumers. Consumer protection could be seen as an important element of the doctrines of unconscionability, good faith, and fundamental public policy. But these rules affect more than consumer transactions and respond to broader policies. So, too, the rule in UCITA and Article 2 that disclaimer of implied warranties in a record must be conspicuous, or the rule in UCITA that a contractual choice of forum is unenforceable if it is unreasonable and unjust, or the rule in UCITA that assent is not effective unless there was an opportunity to review terms prior to giving assent. All of these and other rules benefit consumers but are not typically denominated as "consumer protection" rules. Yet they contribute to the fact that UCITA creates a world in which consumers are better off than under current law.

Raymond T. Nimmer, *UCITA: A Commercial Contract Code*, 17 No. 5 COMPUTER LAW. 3, 14–15 (2000).

To its detractors, UCITA is anything but a boon to consumers:

> * * * Some of the persons and entities that submitted letters to NCCUSL [National Conference of Commissioners on Uniform State Laws] registering opposition to UCITA or stating serious concerns from the consumer perspective include: 24 State Attorneys General; Federal Trade Commission senior staff; Consumer Federation of America, Consumers Union, Consumer Project on Technology, and the U.S. Public Interest Research Group, with the National Consumer Law Center joining the opposition after UCITA was promulgated; 45 professors of contracts and commercial law (also stating objections from the perspective of business customers); and members of the Working Group on Consumer Protection of the American Bar Association's Business Law Section, Committee on the Law of Cyberspace, Subcommittee on Electronic Commerce.

No group that takes the consumer perspective has endorsed UCITA. The Federal Trade Commission has initiated an inquiry into whether new federal regulation is needed to undo the ill effects of UCITA. UCITA is so flawed and so complex that it is not a good starting point for drafting reasonable legislation.

* * *

Far from creating greater legal certainty, UCITA will require decades of litigation to sort out its meaning. Its primary effect is to give licensors new arguments to use in that long, wasteful process. UCITA, if it becomes effective nationally, will reduce competition and legal incentives to improve software quality. Consumers of software, online services and digital content would be much better served by certain rules straightforwardly protecting their reasonable interests and expectations. In the absence of such an approach, consumers are better off under current law, which includes the common law of contract, UCC Article 2, state and federal consumer law, and federal intellectual property law.

Jean Braucher, *The Uniform Computer Information Transactions Act (UCITA): Objections from the Consumer Perspective,* 5 No. 6 CYBERSPACE LAW. 2 (2000).

Some of the key objections that critics of UCITA have raised from the consumer perspective include the following.

A. DISPLACEMENT OF EXISTING CONSUMER PROTECTION LAWS

UCITA overrides pre-existing state consumer protection laws by substituting its own standards for what constitutes a writing, a signature, and consent or agreement, and for when a contract term will be deemed conspicuous. It states as a general rule, in § 105(c), that "Except as otherwise provided in subsection (d), if this [Act] or a term of a contract under this [Act] conflicts with a consumer protection statute [or administrative rule], the consumer protection statute [or rule] governs."

The subsection (d) derogations from this rule are as follows:

(d) If a law of this State in effect on the effective date of this [Act] applies to a transaction governed by this [Act], the following rules apply:

(1) A requirement that a term, waiver, notice, or disclaimer be in a writing is satisfied by a record.

(2) A requirement that a record, writing, or term be signed is satisfied by an authentication.

(3) A requirement that a term be conspicuous, or the like, is satisfied by a term that is conspicuous under this [Act].

(4) A requirement of consent or agreement to a term is satisfied by a manifestation of assent to the term in accordance with this [Act].

§ 105(d).

1. *Conspicuousness.* UCITA's substitution of its own definition of "conspicuous" is of particular importance, since the requirement that disclosures be made in a manner that is likely to convey the relevant information is a foundational principle of consumer protection regulation. UCITA says that a term is "conspicuous" if it is "so written, displayed, or presented that a reasonable person against which it is to operate ought to have noticed it." § 102(a)(14). A letter to NCCUSL signed by the Attorneys General of 24 states criticizes this definition. The AGs' letter explains that "two key principles" underlie state laws requiring disclosure of the material terms of consumer transactions. "First, disclosures are evaluated according to how likely they are to actually be communicated, based upon the totality of the context in which they are presented, rather than the specific characteristics of the disclosures alone. Second, such disclosures should be made in a timely manner to avoid deception." According to the AGs, "[t]he definition of conspicuous in § [102(a)(14)] fails to follow either of these principles." Letter from State Attorneys General to Gene Lebrun (July 23, 1999), www.2bguide.com/docs/799ags.html.

With respect to the first principle—that a disclosure serves its purpose only if the information is presented in such a way that it is likely actually to be communicated to its intended audience—the AGs' letter has this to say:

> By focusing solely on whether a term is noticeable, the definition ignores most of the basic principles of communication and is unlikely to result in disclosures actually being communicated. Noticeability is certainly a factor to consider in determining whether a term is likely to be communicated. However, there are several other factors, which if ignored, may lead to a disclosure that is not in fact likely to be communicated. These factors include: 1) readability, whether a term uses words in accordance with their generally recognized meaning and whether it is readily understandable; 2) proximity, whether a term clarifying or explaining another term is in such proximity to the term it clarifies or explains that it is as likely to be read as the term it clarifies or explains; 3) language, whether the term is expressed in the language spoken by those to whom it is presented; 4) prominence, whether the term is hidden or obscured by other terms or whether it readily stands out from other matter with which it is presented; and 5) intended audience, whether the term meets these criteria with respect to the audience for which it is intended. If disclosures are evaluated solely by their noticeability and not these other factors, sellers will be able to easily craft disclosures that meet the requirements of UCITA, but which are highly unlikely ever to be read or understood by their intended audience. Rather than serving as useful disclosures of material information, these terms will merely form the basis of a legal defense after a purchase has failed of its essential purpose.

With respect to the second principle—that the timing of a disclosure is of crucial importance—the AGs point out:

> [B]y allowing all affected disclosures to be made as contractual terms, the definition of conspicuous ignores the timeliness requirements of consumer protection laws. This is particularly problematic in light of the contract formation rules of UCITA which allow contract terms to be presented for the first time after a purchase has been made. Most consumer protection disclosure requirements are intended to prevent deception by providing information prior to purchase. For example, the fact that a word processing software program requires 64Mb of RAM to function would be a material fact under most states' consumer laws and would have to be disclosed prior to the purchase of the program. Under UCITA, that fact could be disclosed as a post-sale contract term.

UCITA supplements its definition of "conspicuous" with what amount to safe harbors for disclosures that meet certain criteria. Thus, a term is per-se "conspicuous" under UCITA if it meets these criteria.

> Conspicuous terms include the following:
>
> (A) with respect to a person:
>
> (i) a heading in capitals in a size equal to or greater than, or in contrasting type, font, or color to, the surrounding text;
>
> (ii) language in the body of a record or display in larger or other contrasting type, font, or color or set off from the surrounding text by symbols or other marks that draw attention to the language; and
>
> (iii) a term prominently referenced in an electronic record or display which is readily accessible or reviewable from the record or display; and
>
> (B) with respect to a person or an electronic agent, a term or reference to a term that is so placed in a record or display that the person or electronic agent cannot proceed without taking action with respect to the particular term or reference.

§ 102(a)(14)(A) and (B). Critics of these safe harbors fear that sellers (and courts) will deem disclosures of the following sort to be "conspicuous":

- A highly material term (e.g., exclusion of warranty) that is buried in the middle of a lengthy online recitation, as long as it is (1) in Arial type, with surrounding text in Times Roman; (2) in italics, with surrounding text in roman; or (3) in gray type, with surrounding text in black. *See* § 102(a)(14)(A)(ii).
- A term that is not at all distinguished from the surrounding text, as long as the text is placed in a scroll box with a button labeled "I Accept" that the reader must click in order to proceed to the next screen. *See* § 102(a)(14)(B).

- A term placed on a web page that may be accessed from the page containing the contract terms by clicking on a hyperlink, where the link is labeled in such a way—for example, "Legally required disclosures"—that a user is unlikely to click on it. *See* § 102(a)(14)(A)(iii).
- A disclosure that is prominently displayed but is phrased in terms that make it incomprehensible to the majority of members of its intended audience.
- A disclosure that is prominently displayed, and understandably phrased, but that is contradicted by other language in the document.

2. *Writing.* UCITA § 105(d)(1) provides that a state-law requirement "that a term, waiver, notice, or disclaimer be in a writing is satisfied by a record." A "record" is defined as "information that is inscribed on a tangible medium or that is stored in an electronic or other medium and is retrievable in perceivable form." § 102(a)(55). Therefore, if a state consumer protection law requires certain information to be provided to a consumer "in writing," under UCITA that requirement is satisfied if the information is provided using an electronic document. (For further discussion of the effect of electronic signature statutes on "writing" requirements, *see* Chapter 5, *supra.*)

What if the consumer protection law requires that information be provided to consumers at a particular time, or in proximity to some other statement? Does UCITA § 105(d)(1) mean that such requirements need not be observed if the information is provided by means of a "record" instead of in writing? On the face of the provision the answer is not clear. Official Comment 5 to § 105 provides additional data points:

> Subsection (d)(1) allows an electronic record to suffice for a writing in a transaction within this Act. This does not alter the form or content required by consumer law. It assumes that the form and presentation of material and disclosures in the record otherwise meets the substantive requirements of the relevant other statute. For example, if a consumer protection statute requires that the consumer be able to retain the writing; this subsection does not alter the retainability requirement. Similarly, some consumer statutes require that the consumer initial particular terms of the record. Subsection (d) does not alter that rule although electronic "initials" can suffice for handwritten initials. The record that substitutes for a writing must meet all underlying requirements.

Thus, according to the commentary, if a state consumer protection law requires information to be provided to a consumer "in close proximity" to some triggering representation, it is the underlying law, and not UCITA, that determines whether dangling the information at the end of a hyperlink satisfies the requirement.

Both ESIGN and UETA are clearer on this point. As we learned in Chapter 4, *supra*, ESIGN says that "a * * * record * * * may not be denied legal effect, validity, or enforceability *solely* because it is in electronic form." ESIGN § 101(a)(1), 15 U.S.C. § 7001(a) (emphasis added). ESIGN also explicitly preserves delivery, content, and timing requirements for consumer disclosures, and proximity requirements more generally. *See* ESIGN §§ 101(c)(2) & 105(f), 15 U.S.C. §§ 7001(c)(2) & 7005(f). Similarly, UETA states, in the text of the proposed statute rather than in commentary:

> (b) If a law other than this [Act] requires a record (i) to be posted or displayed in a certain manner, (ii) to be sent, communicated, or transmitted by a specified method, or (iii) to contain information that is formatted in a certain manner, the following rules apply:
>
> (1) The record must be posted or displayed in the manner specified in the other law.
>
> (2) Except as otherwise provided in subsection (d)(2), the record must be sent, communicated, or transmitted by the method specified in the other law.
>
> (3) The record must contain the information formatted in the manner specified in the other law.

UETA § 8(b).

3. *Preservation of existing consumer protections.* The general preservation of consumer protections that is stated in UCITA § 105(c) may be less serviceable than it appears. Section 105(c) provides: "Except as otherwise provided in subsection (d), if this [Act] or a term of a contract under this [Act] conflicts with a consumer protection statute [or administrative rule], the consumer protection statute [or rule] governs." This provision explicitly does *not* preserve consumer protection rules that conflict with § 105(d), which, as noted above, substitutes UCITA's definition of "conspicuous" for the interpretation of that term under consumer protection law. Therefore, UCITA *does* displace a state consumer protection law to the extent it adopts a traditional, contextual standard for gauging the conspicuousness of a disclosure.

In addition, note that UCITA characterizes transactions in computer information as "licenses" rather than sales of goods. *See* § 102(a)(40) (defining "license" as "a contract that authorizes access to, or use, distribution, performance, modification, or reproduction of, information or informational rights, but expressly limits the access or uses authorized or expressly grants fewer than all rights in the information, whether or not the transferee has title to a licensed copy"). Few if any state consumer protection statutes are explicitly applicable to licensing transactions: typically they apply to sales of goods or services. Will a state consumer protection statute that does not explicitly apply to licensing transactions be deemed to "conflict" with UCITA, and therefore be saved under UCITA § 105(c)?

As this book goes to press, UCITA has been enacted in only two states, while three others have enacted "bomb shelter" legislation intended to prohibit UCITA from governing transactions in their states. (*See* Chapter 4, Part I(A), *supra.*) In enacting UCITA, the Maryland legislature was careful to clarify the relationship between its enactment and existing consumer protection law. It did so by adding a provision to its Consumer Protection Act, stating: "The provisions of this title apply to the subject matter of a consumer contract as defined in § 22–102 of this article in the same manner they apply to consumer goods and consumer services." MD. CODE ANN., COM. LAW § 13–101.1. Thus, Maryland's consumer protection law accords transactions that UCITA characterizes as "licenses" parity of treatment with transactions in goods and services.

B. VALIDATION OF SHRINKWRAP LICENSES

UCITA, if enacted, will generally validate shrinkwrap licenses. As the law stands without UCITA, it is unsettled whether the terms of shrinkwrap license agreements become part of the contract between the software manufacturer and the purchaser. Several influential court decisions, applying Article 2 of the Uniform Commercial Code, held that these terms do become part of the contract once the purchaser engages in conduct that is construed as consent to those terms. *See, e.g., ProCD, Inc. v. Zeidenberg*, 86 F.3d 1447 (7th Cir.1996); *Hill v. Gateway 2000, Inc.*, 105 F.3d 1147 (7th Cir.1997). Other cases, however, interpreted such terms as a proposal by the seller to modify the contract that was formed upon purchase, and held that the license terms did not become part of the contract. *See Step–Saver Data Systems, Inc. v. Wyse Technology*, 939 F.2d 91 (3d Cir.1991); *Klocek v. Gateway, Inc.*, 104 F.Supp.2d 1332 (D.Kan.2000). (These cases are discussed in Chapter 4, *supra.*)

UCITA would resolve this issue, validating such shrinkwrap licenses with certain limitations. UCITA interprets the presence of a shrinkwrap license as an indication that the parties intend that a contract will be formed, if at all, at some time after the purchase transaction. A contract is formed, and the terms of the shrinkwrap license become terms of the contract, if the purchaser "manifests assent" to the license terms. UCITA § 112(a). A manifestation of assent may be inferred from the purchaser's conduct, or from the absence of conduct, such as failure to return the product. UCITA § 112(d).

The National Association of Attorneys General, in a letter to the Chair of the UCITA drafting committee, has objected to this approach as inconsistent with principles of consumer protection:

> Under UCITA a person "manifests assent" to a term if after having an "opportunity to review" the term, s/he engages in conduct with reason to know the other party may infer assent from that conduct. (§ 112(a)(2).) However, such an "opportunity to review" requires only that the term be available "in a manner that ought to call it to the attention of a reasonable person." (Comment 2, § 112.) Furthermore, such terms are binding even if

they are not available for review until after a person pays or becomes obligated to pay, so long as the person has a right of return. (§ 112(e)(3).) It is very unlikely that consumers will read through lengthy disclosures (particularly those made on a computer screen that requires pages of scrolling) and then, when dissatisfied with the terms, return the product. Such provisions seem likely to punish businesses that attempt to make full initial disclosure, placing them at a competitive disadvantage to less forthright businesses that obscure important terms.

These provisions also depart from an important principle of consumer protection law: that material terms must be disclosed prior to consummation of the transaction. In the states, this principle is enforced through each state's Unfair and Deceptive Practices Act. UCITA would permit the post-sale disclosure of material terms and conditions, including warranty terms, when a consumer purchases software at a retail location ("shrinkwrap") or online ("clickwrap"), or signs up for Internet service online. (§ 112(e)(3).) For example, UCITA allows licensors of software to disclose the terms of the contract after the consumer has paid for the software, taken it home, and loaded it on a computer. Only then can the consumer finally review the terms. UCITA thus weakens consumer rights and results in purchases for which consumers have had no real opportunity to bargain or to compare terms. Consumers who wish to make informed choices in the marketplace will be unable to do so.

We do not believe the need for such a drastic change in the way transactions are conducted has been demonstrated, particularly in light of the fact that sellers have for years found the means of making required disclosures prior to sale. For example, the federal Magnuson–Moss Warranty Act (15 U.S.C. 2301 et seq.) requires that the terms of warranties be available prior to sale so consumers have knowledge of the terms and can compare the warranties of different sellers. UCITA, however, would permit post-sale disclosure of warranty terms of software based on proponents' claim that it is too difficult to disclose the terms of the warranty on the box or by some other means. The Magnuson–Moss Act has addressed this problem for goods by having warranty terms available at the service counter, referring in catalogs to a location for the warranty terms, or posting the warranty terms online. It is difficult to understand why software sales could not be handled in the same way.

Letter from National Association of Attorneys General to Carlyle C. Ring (Nov. 13, 2001).

As the NAAG letter notes, these provisions allow the formation of a contract defining the rights of a software purchaser containing terms of which the purchaser is completely unaware. The state Attorneys General, in their own letter opposing UCITA, set forth the following nightmare scenario as one that is permitted under UCITA:

> Jane Consumer purchases a piece of software that promises analysis and advice concerning various investment options. When she installs the software, she learns from a message displayed during the installation process that she must subscribe to a proprietary information service to use it, rather than the competing service she already uses to obtain such information. Even though other similar software packages are available which do not impose such requirements, Jane is loathe to begin the shopping process over again in order to decide which of those packages to purchase, so she accepts the new terms. Jane subscribes to the new information service, selecting a discounted 1 year agreement rather than a full price month to month agreement, and logs onto the system for the first time. When she does, she is presented a screen which contains a hyperlink in the upper left hand corner labeled "important information." She is also presented with a flashing icon calling her attention to a hot stock tip. She decides to check out the tip before reviewing the information. After deciding the tip was not something she wants to pursue, she returns to the main screen, but the "important information" hyperlink is gone.
>
> She continues to use the service for a period of months. About 6 months later, a package arrives in the mail. It is an upgrade to her investment analysis software. Because she did not order the upgrade and there is nothing contained in the package advising her otherwise, she assumes it is a free bug fix upgrade. After a couple of weeks, she installs it and logs onto the service to try it out. When she does she sees the "important information" hyperlink. Because this hyperlink eluded her before, she decides to immediately review the information and discovers that the software upgrade was not free, but was sent to her on a negative option basis. She learns that she will be billed $49.95 for the software because she failed to return it within 7 days of receipt as required by the upgrade service provisions of her original contract.
>
> Confused because she was never aware of any such provision, she calls the software company's customer service line for an explanation. She is told that the term was conspicuously displayed behind the "important information" hyperlink when she first logged onto the service and that the company has a no refund policy. She is somewhat condescendingly told that she should read her contracts before she agrees to them. She asks where on the service a copy of the contract is available for her review, but is told that it is only available during the initial session of use. She angrily asks to cancel the service, but is told that she cannot do so until her 12 month term expires.
>
> The next month, she reviews her credit card statement and discovers not only the $49.95 charge for the software, but also that

the monthly fee for the service has increased by $5. She logs onto the service and goes to the customer service area to see if she can find any information about the fee increase. In the customer service area, she finds a lengthy letter from the president of the company explaining that its former business model was flawed and that the company had to choose between raising its prices or going out of business. The letter closes with a reminder that customers should periodically check the customer service area for notice of such fee changes, as required by the company's standard contract. She again calls customer service and asks to cancel the service because of the price increase, but is again told she cannot do so until her 12 month term expires.

Jane writes to her credit card company asking for charge-backs in the amounts of the unexpected fees, but when provided a copy of the agreement by the software company, her credit card company declines the charge-backs, saying that the charges were appropriate under the agreement. Jane angrily uninstalls the software and decides that she will return to the expensive but relatively trustworthy stockbroker that she had used before.

Letter from State Attorneys General to Gene Lebrun, *supra.*

NOTES & QUESTIONS

1. *Right of return as substitute for pre-sale disclosure.* UCITA counterbalances the validation of post-sale disclosures with a mandatory right of return. Under § 209(b), if the purchaser does not have an "opportunity to review" license terms before the sale, then she may return the software for a full refund, including reimbursement of the costs of making the return; and possibly also costs of restoring her computer to its pre-installation condition.

This scheme has been criticized on several grounds:

(1) Post-sale disclosure of terms, combined with a return right, is not the equivalent of pre-sale disclosure. Once a consumer buys and installs a software program, he has invested a good deal of time and effort, which is unrecoverable if he exercises his right to return. Therefore, a consumer may end up keeping software that he never would have purchased if the terms were disclosed in advance.

(2) Allowing terms to be disclosed after the sale is effectively validation of bait-and-switch marketing techniques. The seller induces the purchaser to buy the software by emphasizing its attractive aspects. By the time the purchaser discovers the additional, less favorable terms, she is psychologically committed to the purchase.

(3) The lack of pre-sale disclosure of material terms makes comparison shopping impractical, interfering with the operation of consumer sovereignty and the policy of state and federal laws that encourages early and full disclosure to enable consumers to make informed choices.

Do you think these criticisms are well taken?

2. *Returning bundled software.* Personal computers typically come pre-loaded with bundled software—an operating system at a minimum, and typically a variety of application programs as well. If the purchaser does not load the software, how is her assent to the license terms manifested? What if the box in which the computer is shipped contains a piece of paper stating license terms: does this count as disclosure-plus-consent under UCITA? If the purchaser chose to reject the terms, how would the amount of the refund be determined? Average retail price of the unbundled software? What the computer manufacturer paid for the software? What the computer manufacturer paid increased by the manufacturer's profit margin on the complete system? Who would be responsible for making the refund: the computer manufacture? the computer retailer? the software publisher?

A Linux enthusiast in Australia had to exercise an unusual degree of persistence in order to return and get a refund for the copy of Windows 95 that came pre-loaded on a Toshiba laptop computer he purchased from a retailer in 1998. The End User License Agreement that accompanied the computer stated: "If you do not agree to the terms of this EULA, PC Manufacturer and Microsoft are unwilling to license the SOFTWARE PRODUCT to you. In such event, you may not use or copy the SOFTWARE PRODUCT, and you should promptly contact PC Manufacturer for instructions on return of the unused products(s) for a refund." Taking the EULA at its word, the purchaser, Geoffrey Bennett, contacted Toshiba and requested a refund, stating: "I do not agree to the terms of the End–User License Agreement for the Windows 95 software, and would like to return the software for a refund. Please supply me with instructions on how to return the software." The Toshiba representative he contacted replied that this was not possible, since Toshiba was contractually obligated to pay Microsoft a licensing fee for each computer it manufactured, regardless of whether Windows was installed on it. After some back and forth, Bennett accepted Toshiba's offer to take back the whole computer and refund the purchase price. At that point, Toshiba reconsidered its position and offered Bennet AUS$110 in return for his copy of Windows, an offer that Bennett gladly accepted. The saga is related in amusing detail at *Toshiba/Microsoft Saga,* www.netcraft.com.au/geoffrey/toshiba.html.

3. *Post-sale disclosure nothing new?* Why are UCITA critics so concerned about post-sale disclosure of contract terms? Isn't this what happens whenever a consumer buys an item at a distance, as via mail order or telephone?

4. *Competition to the rescue?* Retailers selling a commodity product, such as shrinkwrapped software, typically must compete largely on the basis of service. Some software retailers offer an unlimited money-back guarantee, accepting returns of software after the purchaser has installed it and tried it out. Other retailers offer a limited return right, valid for a certain number of days after purchase, or charge a "restocking fee" to accept a return. Still other retailers make all sales final. Purchasers can therefore protect themselves from surprising terms in shrinkwrapped software by purchasing only from retailers offering a generous right of return. Does the existence in the marketplace of such retailers mean that UCITA's limitation of the purchaser's legal rights as against the manufacturer is of no practical concern? How likely is it that the nightmare scenario described above will actually come about? Legitimate vendors of software and computer information services depend heavily on their reputation. Would a vendor consider it to be in its self-interest to treat a customer as badly as Jane Consumer is treated in the above scenario?

5. *Is pre-sale disclosure feasible?* What is the alternative to a regime of shrinkwrap licenses, in which contractual terms are presented to the purchaser only after the purchase is made? How could lengthy license terms be provided to a consumer before purchase? Consider the various ways of purchasing software: in a retail store, from a catalog, by telephone, from a website.

C. ELECTRONIC SELF-HELP PROVISIONS

UCITA, if enacted, would validate and establish parameters for a software vendor's use of "electronic self-help" measures to enforce the terms of its license agreements. In case of a "material breach" of the license agreement, or under such other circumstances as the agreement may provide, the licensor may cancel the licensee's rights under that agreement. UCITA § 814. If the item to which the license pertains consists of software or information in electronic form, how does the licensor prevent the licensee from continuing to make use of the item after cancellation? Traditional judicial remedies for breach of contract are available, but the licensor may elect instead to take direct action to protect his rights, through what is called "electronic self-help."

Self-help can be implemented in several different ways. If the license involves use of software or information that resides on the licensor's computers, such as in the case of an application service provider, a mainframe-based system, or an information database that is accessed via the network, the licensor can exercise self-help simply by denying the licensee access to his computers. The licensor might have a service agreement with the licensee, allowing the licensor to access the licensee's system remotely via modem, and thereby disable the software. The software might contain a "logic bomb" that disables it on a certain date or after a certain number of uses unless the user enters some code that is furnished by the licensor. More sinisterly, the licensor might send a technician to the licensee's premises for the ostensible purpose of servicing the system, while secretly planting code that disables the software. *See* Esther C. Roditti, *Is Self-Help a Lawful Contractual Remedy?*, 21 RUTGERS COMP. & TECH. L.J. 431 (1995).

The legal status of electronic self-help in such circumstances is unclear under pre-UCITA law. UCITA validates the practice, but places significant limitations on it. First, the licensee must "separately manifest assent to a term authorizing use of electronic self-help." § 816(c). According to the Official Comments, it is not enough that the licensee manifests consent to the agreement as a whole: "Assent *to the term* requires that there be action with respect to the term itself, not merely general assent to the license." § 816, Official Comment (2)(a). Second, before exercising self-help the licensor must notify the licensee

> (1) that the licensor intends to resort to electronic self-help as a remedy on or after 15 days following receipt by the licensee of the notice;
>
> (2) the nature of the claimed breach that entitles the licensor to resort to self-help; and
>
> (3) the name, title, and address, including direct telephone number, facsimile number, or e-mail address, to which the licensee may communicate concerning the claimed breach.

§ 816(d).

Third, "electronic self-help may not be used if the licensor has reason to know that its use will result in substantial injury or harm to the public health or safety or grave harm to the public interest substantially affecting third persons not involved in the dispute." § 816(f).

Consumer advocates have criticized this provision as validating a practice whereby the vendor may unilaterally determine that the licensee is in breach, and may impose a penalty that can be enormously costly to the licensee. UCITA supporters say that the provision places limitations on exercise of self-help that are more stringent than under any prior law. Critics reply that codification of the procedure makes it more likely that vendors will use it, since under prior law they could be liable for damages if a court found a self-help action to be unreasonable.

In enacting UCITA, Maryland modified the model law to make electronic self-help unavailable in the context of mass-market licenses—the type of licenses to which consumers will typically be subject. The Maryland version also requires thirty days notice to the licensee, rather than the fifteen days specified in the model law. MD. CODE ANN., COM. LAW § 22-816(b), (f).

V. ELECTRONIC SIGNATURE STATUTES

Electronic signature statutes seek to promote electronic commerce by allowing parties to enter into contracts and conduct other transactions without the use of paper documentation. A general discussion of these statutes appears in Chapter 5, *supra*. Here we will address the impact of these laws on consumer protection.

The shift to paperless transactions may raise special issues in the consumer context. According to one consumer advocate, electronic signature laws such as UETA are founded on the premises that paper documents may be dispensed with in favor of electronic documents, handwritten signatures for electronic signatures, and postal communications for e-mail, without any detriment to those engaging in the transactions. But these premises may not hold in the case of consumer transactions:

> The first premise will be true in only some consumer situations. An electronic record may be just as good as a written record for an inexpensive transaction that is completed in a short time. On the other hand, a consumer entering into a five-year car loan or a 30–year mortgage needs the note and contract in a form which he or she can keep. Home computers are replaced every few years, and previously downloaded contracts are unlikely to be copied over to a new system. Change-of-terms notices for a service provider operating only on the Internet probably can be delivered by e-mail, but a notice that your car is being recalled for a safety problem should arrive in the mail.
>
> The first premise also assumes that e-mail arrives at least as reliably as regular mail, which is contrary to the experience of many consumers. Consumers currently may change e-mail addresses more frequently than they move. Those with e-mail addresses seem to check them either far more frequently or far less frequently than their daily check of the regular mail. In addition, an Internet e-mail provider may go out of business, leaving a consumer with no choice but to obtain a new e-mail address.
>
> As to the second premise, an electronic signature does not always fully serve the purposes of a written signature. Where there is a risk of forgery, a written signature may provide additional safeguards because it may be harder to forge than a purported electronic signature. An electronic click made at home may not serve the purpose of emphasizing the seriousness or the particular risks of a transaction as well as a written signature.
>
> The third premise of UETA is reflected in the broad deference it gives to the autonomy of contracting parties. It defers to the agreement without distinguishing between negotiated agreements and standard form contracts or contracts of adhesion. This approach could give wide latitude to drafters of standard form contracts to define and impose the conditions of electronic communication.
>
> For example, UETA adopts the principle that each party should be able to determine when it will receive information electronically, and when it wishes to insist on receiving a paper communication. This sounds good in theory, but in practice it allows one-sided contracts. UETA also allows an on-line seller to insist on sending all information to the consumer electronically. The seller, however, can require that the consumer communicate any complaints, refund requests, billing disputes or other communications to the same company only by regular mail.

Consumers Union, *Uniform Electronic Transactions Act: Consumer Nightmare or Opportunity?* (Aug. 23, 1999), www.consumersunion.org/finance/899nclcwc.htm.

Congress, in enacting the Electronic Signatures in Global and National Commerce Act ("ESIGN"), was highly cognizant of the impact the legislation would have on consumer protections. Consumer issues surfaced constantly during the congressional debates that led up to passage of ESIGN, and were the source of the most contentious disagreements over the shape of the legislation. Like other electronic signature legislation, ESIGN establishes a general rule of non-discrimination against electronic signatures, contracts, and documents. But ESIGN includes important derogations from this general principle in the case of laws and rules that require sellers to provide written notices and disclosures to consumers. The following discusses the most important of these consumer protections: a prescribed procedure for obtaining consumer consent to electronic disclosures, preservation of timing, proximity, and other similar requirements, and exclusion of certain important types of consumer notifications.

A. CONSUMER CONSENT TO ELECTRONIC DISCLOSURES

Electronic Signatures in Global and National Commerce Act, § 101

15 U.S.C. § 7001.

SEC. 101. GENERAL RULE OF VALIDITY

(a) In General.—Notwithstanding any statute, regulation, or other rule of law (other than this title and title II), with respect to any transaction in or affecting interstate or foreign commerce—

(1) a signature, contract, or other record relating to such transaction may not be denied legal effect, validity, or enforceability solely because it is in electronic form; and

(2) a contract relating to such transaction may not be denied legal effect, validity, or enforceability solely because an electronic signature or electronic record was used in its formation.

* * *

(c) Consumer Disclosures.—

(1) Consent to Electronic Records.—Notwithstanding subsection (a), if a statute, regulation, or other rule of law requires that information relating to a transaction or transactions in or affecting interstate or foreign commerce be provided or made available to a consumer in writing, the use of an electronic record to provide or make available (whichever is required) such information satisfies the requirement that such information be in writing if—

(A) the consumer has affirmatively consented to such use and has not withdrawn such consent;

(B) the consumer, prior to consenting, is provided with a clear and conspicuous statement—

(i) informing the consumer of (I) any right or option of the consumer to have the record provided or made available on paper or in nonelectronic form, and (II) the right of the consumer to withdraw the consent to have the record provided or made available in an electronic form and of any conditions, consequences (which may include termination of the parties' relationship), or fees in the event of such withdrawal;

(ii) informing the consumer of whether the consent applies (I) only to the particular transaction which gave rise to the obligation to provide the record, or (II) to identified categories of records that may be provided or made available during the course of the parties' relationship;

(iii) describing the procedures the consumer must use to withdraw consent as provided in clause (i) and to update information needed to contact the consumer electronically; and

(iv) informing the consumer (I) how, after the consent, the consumer may, upon request, obtain a paper copy of an electronic record, and (II) whether any fee will be charged for such copy;

(C) the consumer—

(i) prior to consenting, is provided with a statement of the hardware and software requirements for access to and retention of the electronic records; and

(ii) consents electronically, or confirms his or her consent electronically, in a manner that reasonably demonstrates that the consumer can access information in the electronic form that will be used to provide the information that is the subject of the consent; and

(D) after the consent of a consumer in accordance with subparagraph (A), if a change in the hardware or software requirements needed to access or retain electronic records creates a material risk that the consumer will not be able to access or retain a subsequent electronic record that was the subject of the consent, the person providing the electronic record—

(i) provides the consumer with a statement of (I) the revised hardware and software requirements for access to and retention of the electronic records, and (II) the right to withdraw consent without the imposition of any fees for such withdrawal and without the imposition of any condition or consequence that was not disclosed under subparagraph (B)(i); and

(ii) again complies with subparagraph (C).

(2) Other Rights.—

(A) Preservation of Consumer Protections.—Nothing in this title affects the content or timing of any disclosure or other record required to be provided or made available to any consumer under any statute, regulation, or other rule of law.

(B) Verification or Acknowledgment.—If a law that was enacted prior to this Act expressly requires a record to be provided or made available by a specified method that requires verification or acknowledgment of receipt, the record may be provided or made available electronically only if the method used provides verification or acknowledgment of receipt (whichever is required).

(3) Effect of Failure to Obtain Electronic Consent or Confirmation of Consent.—The legal effectiveness, validity, or enforceability of any contract executed by a consumer shall not be denied solely because of the failure to obtain electronic consent or confirmation of consent by that consumer in accordance with paragraph (1)(C)(ii).

* * *

(6) Oral Communications.—An oral communication or a recording of an oral communication shall not qualify as an electronic record for purposes of this subsection except as otherwise provided under applicable law.

* * *

(e) Accuracy and Ability to Retain Contracts and Other Records.—Notwithstanding subsection (a), if a statute, regulation, or other rule of law requires that a contract or other record relating to a transaction in or affecting interstate or foreign commerce be in writing, the legal effect, validity, or enforceability of an electronic record of such contract or other record may be denied if such electronic record is not in a form that is capable of being retained and accurately reproduced for later reference by all parties or persons who are entitled to retain the contract or other record.

(f) Proximity.—Nothing in this title affects the proximity required by any statute, regulation, or other rule of law with respect to any warning, notice, disclosure, or other record required to be posted, displayed, or publicly affixed.

* * *

NOTE: ESIGN AND UETA ON CONSUMER CONSENT TO ELECTRONIC NOTIFICATIONS

One of the fundamental principles of ESIGN's validation of electronic signatures and documents is that no party (other than a government agency) is *required* to use or accept them. ESIGN § 101(b)(2). As a general matter, ESIGN does not involve itself with the question of how parties may demonstrate their willingness to make use of electronic signatures and documents. But ESIGN derogates from this approach in the case of certain consumer disclosures. If a state or federal statute or rule requires a seller to furnish information to a consumer "in writing," ESIGN prescribes a special protocol that the seller must follow to obtain the consumer's consent to receive the information in electronic form. This procedure is designed to insure that a consumer's waiver of her right to receive the disclosure on paper is informed and intentional, and that the electronic disclosure will be a reasonable substitute for the written one. Before seeking the consumer's consent, the seller must provide the consumer with "a clear and conspicuous statement" containing several categories of information. The notice must:

(1) inform the consumer of any option to receive the disclosure in written form, and of her right to withdraw her consent, and the consequences thereof;

(2) inform the consumer whether the consent applies only to the instant transaction, or to a series of future transactions as well;

(3) describe the procedures the consumer must follow to withdraw consent, and to update her contact information;

(4) inform a consumer how to obtain a paper copy of the disclosure even after consenting, and whether any fee will be charged for the paper copy; and

(5) provide the consumer with a statement of the hardware and software needed to access and retain the electronic records.

§ 101(c)(1)(B) and (C).

Once the consumer receives all of this information, she must "affirmatively consent[]" to receiving electronic disclosures. Furthermore, "affirmative consent" is rigorously defined. The consumer must "consent[] electronically, or confirm[] his or her consent electronically, in a manner that reasonably demonstrates that the consumer can access information in the electronic form that will be used to provide the information that is the subject of the consent." ESIGN § 101(c)(1)(C)(ii). So if the seller intends to provide the disclosure information in the form of, say, a Corel WordPerfect Version 8 document, the consumer must consent through some action that demonstrates she can access such documents.

The seller's obligations do not end here. If, after obtaining the consumer's consent, the seller changes the manner in which it provides the disclosures, such that the consumer needs new computer hardware or software to access or retain the disclosures, the seller must notify the seller of the new hardware or software requirements, give the consumer a cost-free means of withdrawing her consent, and once again obtain the consumer's consent in a manner that demonstrates she can access the disclosure in its new format. ESIGN § 101(c)(1)(D).

Recall that UETA, like ESIGN, also provides that electronic records are valid only between parties who have consented to use of them. (*See* Chapter 4, *supra*.) Unlike ESIGN, however, UETA contains no heightened consent procedure applying to consumer disclosures. The general consent provision, applicable to all transactions, states: "This [Act] applies only to transactions between parties each of which has agreed to conduct transactions by electronic means. Whether the parties agree to conduct a transaction by electronic means is determined from the context and surrounding circumstances, including the parties' conduct." UETA § 5(b). The Comment to this provision elaborates:

> Subsection (b) provides that the Act applies to transactions in which the parties have agreed to conduct the transaction electronically. In this context it is essential that the parties' actions and words be broadly construed in determining whether the requisite agreement exists. Accordingly, the Act expressly provides that the party's agreement is to be found from all circumstances, including the parties' conduct. The critical element is the intent of a party to conduct a transaction electronically.

UETA § 5, cmt. 4

NOTES & QUESTIONS

1. *UETA and consent.* Is the UETA standard for assessing consent insufficiently protective in the context of consumer disclosures? Do you agree with the following assessment:

> E–Sign's requirement that consumer consent be given or confirmed electronically is of crucial importance. Paper consent to future electronic transactions creates a risk that consumers will be offered boilerplate paper agreements to receive future electronic notices that they may or may not be able to open and read. The federal requirement that consent be given or confirmed electronically eliminates this risk, at least for notices legally required to be in writing.
>
> In contrast, UETA merely requires agreement but does not specify how that agreement is to be proven. Instead, UETA states that agreement can be determined from the context and circumstances. UETA undercuts its own basic premise of agreement by permitting the agreement to conduct transactions electronically to be found from the context, including conduct.

Gail Hillebrand & Margot Saunders, *E-Sign and UETA: What Should States Do Now?*, 5 NO. 10 CYBERSPACE LAW. 2, 5 NO. 11 CYBERSPACE LAW. 8 (Parts I & II) (2001). Do you think, to the contrary, that the consent procedure in ESIGN § 101(c) is unduly burdensome on both sellers and consumers, a paternalistic interference with freedom of contract? For an evaluation of the consumer consent provisions, see FEDERAL TRADE COMMISSION & DEPARTMENT OF COMMERCE, ELECTRONIC SIGNATURES IN GLOBAL AND NATIONAL COMMERCE ACT: THE CONSUMER CONSENT PROVISION IN § 101(C)(1)(C)(II) (2001), www.ftc.gov/os/2001/06/esign7.htm.

2. *UETA over ESIGN.* Note that ESIGN contains a "reverse preemption" provision: § 101 is superseded by state law, if that state law happens to be an enactment of the 1999 version of UETA, or some equivalent alternative scheme. ESIGN § 102(a). This reverse preemption would extend to ESIGN § 101(c), the consumer-consent provision. Why would the drafters of ESIGN have crafted a detailed and highly protective consumer consent provision, only to allow it to be superseded by a far less protective provision of state law?

B. Preservation of Existing Consumer Protections

ESIGN demonstrates additional solicitude to consumer interests by preserving certain features of laws and rules designed to protect consumers from deceptive marketing practices. Three provisions in particular have this function.

1. *Content or timing requirements.* "Nothing in this title affects the content or timing of any disclosure or other record required to be provided or made available to any consumer under any statute, regulation, or other rule of law." § 101(c)(2)(A). One example of a "timing" requirement is the FTC's Cooling–Off Rule, which requires a door-to-door seller to furnish the buyer with a notice of his right to cancel the transaction "at the time the buyer signs the door-to-door sales contract"—that is, during the face-to-face meeting between buyer and seller. Rule Concerning Cooling–Off Period for Sales Made at Homes or at Certain Other Locations, 16 C.F.R. § 429.1(b). The ESIGN "content or timing" provision means that a seller cannot comply with the Rule by sending the notice to the buyer's e-mail address at some time after the transaction is completed, even if the buyer so consents.

2. *Verification or acknowledgment requirements.* "If a law that was enacted prior to this Act expressly requires a record to be provided or made available by a specified method that requires verification or acknowledgment of receipt, the record may be provided or made available electronically only if the method used provides verification or acknowledgment of receipt (whichever is required)." ESIGN § 101(c)(2)(B). This would apply in the case of a law requiring that a party provide information to a consumer through the use of certified mail, return receipt requested, which generates an acknowledgment of receipt.

3. *Proximity requirements.* "Nothing in this title affects the proximity required by any statute, regulation, or other rule of law with respect to any warning, notice, disclosure, or other record required to be posted, displayed, or publicly affixed." ESIGN § 101(f). The two most important types of proximity requirements in consumer disclosure rules are (1) a requirement that a disclosure be physically attached to or printed on an item, and (2) a requirement that a qualifying statement be in close proximity to the advertising claim to which it applies.

Some examples of "physically attached" requirements include (1) the FTC's Hobby Protection Rule, requiring an imitation political item to be "plainly and permanently marked with the calendar year in which such item was manufactured," and an imitation numismatic item to be "plainly and permanently marked 'COPY' "; *see* Rules and Regulations Under the Hobby Protection Act, 16 C.F.R. §§ 304.5, 304.6; (2) the Care Labeling Rule, requiring manufacturers and importers to "attach care labels so that they can be seen or easily found when the product is offered for sale"; if the label cannot be seen through the package, "the care information must also appear on the outside of the package or on a hang tag fastened to the product"; *see* Care Labeling of Textile Wearing Apparel and Certain Piece

Goods as Amended, 16 C.F.R. § 423.6; and (3) the Packaging and Labeling Rules, requiring a label to be "affixed to or appearing upon any consumer commodity or affixed to or appearing upon a package containing any consumer commodity"; *see* Regulations Under Section 4 of the Fair Packaging and Labeling Act, 16 C.F.R. § 500.2(e).

Examples of "close proximity" requirements appear in (1) the Textile Rules, requiring disclosure of the generic name of a textile fiber "in immediate proximity and conjunction with" use of a fiber trademark; see Rules and Regulations Under the Textile Fiber Products Identification Act, 16 C.F.R. § 303.41(b); and (2) the Appliance Labeling Rule, requiring disclosure of energy efficiency information "on each page [of a catalog] that lists" appliances subject to the Rule; Rule Concerning Disclosures Regarding Energy Consumption and Water Use of Certain Home Appliances and Other Products Required Under the Energy Policy and Conservation Act, 16 C.F.R. § 305.14(a).

ESIGN's preservation-of-proximity-requirements provision makes it clear that ESIGN does not negate regulatory requirements such as these—for example, by allowing a seller to make an advertising claim in a print advertisement, and refer the reader to a website address for disclosures that qualify the claim.

NOTES & QUESTIONS

ESIGN and the Cooling Off Rule. Under ESIGN, may a seller comply with the Cooling–Off Rule by e-mailing the required notice to the buyer's e-mail address, at the time of the transaction, using a handheld wireless Internet access device? By sitting down with the consumer at her own home computer, and showing her how to access the notice on the seller's website? What would be an example of a "content" provision that is preserved by ESIGN § 101(c)(2)(A)?

C. Exceptions for Certain Notifications

The general rule of ESIGN, validating communication of information using electronic signatures, does not apply to certain kinds of notices that are considered especially critical to the welfare of consumers. These are notices of "(A) the cancellation or termination of utility services (including water, heat, and power); (B) default, acceleration, repossession, foreclosure, or eviction, or the right to cure, under a credit agreement secured by, or a rental agreement for, a primary residence of an individual; (C) the cancellation or termination of health insurance or benefits or life insurance benefits (excluding annuities); or (D) recall of a product, or material failure of a product, that risks endangering health or safety." ESIGN § 103(b)(2). (ESIGN Section 103 is set out fully in Chapter 4, Part I(A)(2), *supra.*).

Note that UETA contains no exceptions applying to notices of these types. Therefore, UETA validates electronic versions of these notices as long as the general consent rule of UETA Section 5 is satisfied.

UETA specifically exempts transactions governed by laws relating to wills, codicils, and testamentary trusts, as well as (optionally) certain provisions of the Uniform Commercial Code and UCITA. It also contains a fill-in-the-blank provision, inviting the enacting state to exempt "other laws, if any." UETA § 3(b)(4). That is, a state that enacts UETA may specify that certain additional state laws will be unaffected by UETA's validation of electronic signatures and documents, with the result that "signed in writing" requirements in those statutes will continue to require the use of paper documents signed by hand. This has the effect of blunting UETA's impact on signature and writing requirements in existing state laws. California, the first state to enact UETA, filled in that blank with a long list of regulatory provisions, many of which are designed to protect consumers. As a result, these statutes continued to require that disclosures to consumers be made using paper documents. *See* CAL. CIV. CODE § 1633.3(c). Partly in reaction to this move by California, ESIGN's reverse preemption provision does not extend to state laws that a state exempts from its enactment of UETA, to the extent those laws are inconsistent with ESIGN. *See* ESIGN § 102(a)(1). Therefore, California's attempt to limit the scope of its version of UETA is nullified by ESIGN, to the extent it is deemed inconsistent with ESIGN.

NOTES & QUESTIONS

1. *Exemption of consumer notices*. ESIGN's exclusion of certain types of important consumer notices seems to reflect an assumption that electronic notices are less reliable than their paper counterparts. If so, what is the justification for validating the use of electronic notifications in other circumstances, which can involve large sums of money or be otherwise as significant to consumers as the exempted notices? If we believe that the consumer-consent procedure specified in ESIGN § 101(c) is adequate to prevent consumers from inadvertently waiving important rights, why wouldn't we reach the same conclusion with respect to notices of the exempted type? Suppose a utility, lender, or insurance company offered consumers a better price in exchange for waiver of their right to receive a paper notification. Why shouldn't a consumer be allowed to choose this option?

Unlike ESIGN, UETA does not exempt these kinds of consumer notices from electronic delivery. Does this aspect of UETA, or any other state law explicitly allowing notices of this type to be furnished electronically, survive ESIGN's exemption of such notices?

2. *Enforceability*. ESIGN § 101(c)(3) states: "The legal effectiveness, validity, or enforceability of any contract executed by a consumer shall not be denied solely because of the failure to obtain electronic consent or confirmation of consent by that consumer in accordance with paragraph [§ 101(c)(1)(C)(ii)]"—the provision that requires consent to be tendered in a manner that demonstrates that the consumer can access electronic records of the sort the seller intends to use for the disclosures. If a contract procured in violation of this provision is nevertheless enforceable, what incentive does a seller have to comply with the provision? Does § 101(c)(3) contain a negative pregnant, implying that a contract *may* be held unenforceable if the seller fails to comply with some provision of § 101(c) *other* than § 101(c)(1)(C)(ii)?

3. *Pre-transaction disclosures.* The consumer-consent provision of ESIGN § 101(c) applies to any law or rule that "requires that information relating to a transaction or transactions in or affecting interstate or foreign commerce be provided or made available to a consumer in writing." The term "transaction" is defined as:

> an action or set of actions relating to the conduct of business, consumer, or commercial affairs between two or more persons, including any of the following types of conduct—
>
> (A) the sale, lease, exchange, licensing, or other disposition of (i) personal property, including goods and intangibles, (ii) services, and (iii) any combination thereof; and
>
> (B) the sale, lease, exchange, or other disposition of any interest in real property, or any combination thereof.

ESIGN § 106(13). Does the consumer-consent provision apply to an advertisement, with respect to consumers who view the advertisement but who do not engage with the seller in any exchange of money for goods or services?

4. *Problem.* Devise a procedure, meeting the requirements of ESIGN § 101(c), for obtaining a consumer's consent to receive disclosures in the form of Adobe Acrobat .pdf files. This will include a statement or statements that provide the required pre-consent information; a description of how the statements will be presented to the consumer; and a method for obtaining the consumer's consent in a manner that demonstrates her ability to access the disclosure information.

CHAPTER SEVEN

JUDICIAL JURISDICTION OVER DISPUTES IN INTERNET COMMERCE

For a court to adjudicate a case it must have *subject-matter jurisdiction* over the matter in controversy and *personal jurisdiction* over the parties before it. This chapter concerns the application of these doctrines to cases that arise from online transactions, focusing primarily on personal jurisdiction, which has been most salient for courts attempting to adjudicate e-commerce disputes.

Several aspects of online communications have created difficulties for courts that are called upon to apply the rules of personal jurisdiction. First, because websites, newsgroups, and Internet mailing lists are accessible with equal ease from any location where there is Internet access, courts must navigate between the equally unpalatable options of holding that online activity subjects a defendant to jurisdiction in every state (and indeed every country), or that online activity is not a basis for jurisdiction at all. Second, it is often difficult to determine where an online activity should be deemed to take place. Since jurisdictional issues depend crucially on the location of the acts that give rise to a dispute, difficulty in locating actions causes difficulty in resolving jurisdictional issues.

As you read through these materials, keep the following questions in mind: (1) Are existing jurisdictional doctrines adequate to handle the issues presented when online contacts are urged as the basis for jurisdiction? Should the courts develop a new law of jurisdiction for "cyberspace"? (2) What factors should lead to a finding that a defendant, by operating a website that may be accessed everywhere, has purposely directed its activity at a particular state? (3) Should there be different standards for evaluating contacts depending on the cause of action involved? For example, should a website that defames be treated differently from one that deceptively describes products offered for sale by the site owner? (4) To what extent are the issues presented by online communications analogous to those presented by telephone, mail, and other means of communicating at a distance? To what extent are they different?

I. BACKGROUND: PERSONAL JURISDICTION

Personal jurisdiction, also sometimes referred to a jurisdiction *in personam*, jurisdiction over the person, or jurisdiction to adjudicate, refers to the power of a court to exercise authority over a particular defendant that a plaintiff seeks to bring before it. The rules establishing the circumstances under which a court may assert jurisdiction over a defendant in a civil case derive from several sources, including Rule 4 of the Federal Rules of Civil Procedure, the Due Process Clauses of the Fourteenth and Fifth Amendments to the U.S. Constitution, state statutes conferring authority on state courts to exercise jurisdiction over persons located outside of the state (known as "long-arm statutes"), and substantive law giving rise to federal causes of action. The issue that is most commonly presented is whether a court may assert jurisdiction over a defendant who is not located within the state in which the court sits.

When an action is brought in state court, the court's authority to assert jurisdiction over a defendant located outside the state's borders is determined by the state's long-arm statute and by the Due Process Clause of the Fourteenth Amendment. The same is true for most actions brought in federal court, whether the cause of action is created by state law (and the court's diversity jurisdiction is invoked) or by federal law (based on the court's federal question jurisdiction).[1] This is due to Rule 4(k)(1)(A) of the Federal Rules of Civil Procedure, which provides that service of process, a prerequisite for assertion of jurisdiction, may be effectuated only as provided by the law of the state in which the court is located.

Where the Fourteenth Amendment's Due Process Clause is applicable, the court may assert jurisdiction only if the defendant has certain "minimum contacts" with the state in which the court sits. *International Shoe Co. v. Washington*, 326 U.S. 310, 316 (1945). Courts distinguish between "general jurisdiction" and "specific jurisdiction." If the defendant's contacts with the forum state are sufficiently "continuous and systematic," the court may conclude that it has general jurisdiction over the defendant. In that case, the court may assert jurisdiction over the defendant on any cause of action, regardless of whether it arises from the forum contacts. *Helicopteros Nacionales de Colombia, S.A. v. Hall*, 466 U.S. 408 (1984).

For specific jurisdiction, the defendant's contacts with the forum state need not be so strong, but the cause of action must arise from the forum contacts. The test for specific jurisdiction consists of three components: (1) there must be "some act by which the defendant purposely avails itself of the privilege of conducting activities within the forum State," *Hanson v. Denckla*, 357 U.S. 235, 263 (1958); (2) the cause of action must " 'arise out of or relate to' " the defendant's contacts with the forum state, *Burger*

1. Some federal statutes that create a cause of action authorize service of process wherever the defendant may be found. E.g., 15 U.S.C. § 22; 15 U.S.C. § 53(b). In a federal question case arising from such a statute, the long-arm statute drops out of the picture, since Rule 4(k)(1)(D) provides for jurisdiction "when authorized by a statute of the United States." Under these circumstances, the only territorial limitation on service of process is that imposed by the Due Process Clause of the Fifth Amendment, which requires that the defendant have certain contacts with the United States. Furthermore, Rule 4(k)(2) allows jurisdiction in a federal question case to be based on national contacts, if the defendant is not subject to the jurisdiction of the courts of any state.

These grounds for jurisdiction are rarely applicable in cases where jurisdiction is based on online conduct, and will not be discussed further.

King Corp. v. Rudzewicz, 471 U.S. 462, 472 (1985) (quoting *Helicopteros Nacionales de Colombia, S.A. v. Hall*, 466 U.S. 408, 414 (1984)); and (3) assertion of jurisdiction must be reasonable, comporting with " 'fair play and substantial justice,' " *Burger King, supra* at 476 (quoting *International Shoe*, 326 U.S. at 320).

State long-arm statutes are of two general types. The first type sets forth the specific circumstances under which a court of that state may assert jurisdiction over defendants who are not residents of the state. The statutes with which we will be concerned typically authorize jurisdiction over defendants who (1) transact business in the state, (2) cause tortious injury within the state by some act or omission either within or outside the state, or (3) solicit business within the state. Long-arm statutes of the second type provide, or have been construed to mean, that jurisdiction is authorized to the full extent allowed by the Due Process Clause. Thus, where the court is in a state whose long-arm statute is not coextensive with the due process requirement, resolution of the jurisdictional issue requires a two-stage inquiry: first, whether assertion of jurisdiction is consistent with the state long-arm statute, and second, whether assertion of jurisdiction is consistent with the Due Process Clause. In a state where the long-arm statute goes to the limits of due process, the first stage of the inquiry drops out, and the only issue is whether assertion of jurisdiction is consistent with due process. In the materials that follow, we first explore (in Part II) the due process requirement, and then address (in Part III) state long-arm statutes that are not coextensive with due process. We then consider jurisdiction by contract (Part IV), choice of law (Part V), and related matters (Part VI).

II. THE DUE PROCESS REQUIREMENT APPLIED TO ONLINE ACTIVITIES

A. OPERATION OF WEBSITES

The central difficulty presented when a court's jurisdiction over the defendant is premised on defendant's operation of a website is that due process requires that the defendant purposely direct its actions at a particular state, while a website is accessible by residents of *all* states on an equal basis. The challenge for the courts has been to identify those features of websites that demonstrate that the site owner intentionally directed its activity at one or more particular states.

1. THE THREE–CATEGORY APPROACH TO WEBSITES: *ZIPPO*

Zippo Manufacturing Co. v. Zippo Dot Com, Inc.

952 F.Supp. 1119 (W.D.Pa.1997).

■ MCLAUGHLIN, DISTRICT JUDGE.

This is an Internet domain name dispute. At this stage of the controversy, we must decide the Constitutionally permissible reach of Pennsylvania's Long Arm Statute, 42 Pa.C.S.A. § 5322, through cyberspace. Plaintiff Zippo Manufacturing Corporation ("Manufacturing") has filed a five count complaint against Zippo Dot Com, Inc. ("Dot Com") alleging trademark dilution, infringement, and false designation under the Federal Trademark Act, 15 U.S.C. §§ 1051–1127. In addition, the Complaint alleges causes of action based on state law trademark dilution under 54 Pa.C.S.A. § 1124, and seeks equitable accounting and imposition of a constructive trust. Dot Com has moved to dismiss for lack of personal jurisdiction and improper venue pursuant to Fed.R.Civ.P. 12(b)(2) and (3) or, in the alternative, to transfer the case pursuant to 28 U.S.C. § 1406(a). For the reasons set forth below, Defendant's motion is denied.

I. BACKGROUND

The facts relevant to this motion are as follows. Manufacturing is a Pennsylvania corporation with its principal place of business in Bradford, Pennsylvania. Manufacturing makes, among other things, well known "Zippo" tobacco lighters. Dot Com is a California corporation with its principal place of business in Sunnyvale, California. Dot Com operates an Internet Web site and an Internet news service and has obtained the exclusive right to use the domain names "zippo.com", "zippo.net" and "zipponews.com" on the Internet.

Dot Com's Web site contains information about the company, advertisements and an application for its Internet news service. The news service itself consists of three levels of membership—public/free, "Original" and "Super." Each successive level offers access to a greater number of Internet newsgroups. A customer who wants to subscribe to either the "Original" or "Super" level of service, fills out an on-line application that asks for a variety of information including the person's name and address. Payment is made by credit card over the Internet or the telephone. The application is then processed and the subscriber is assigned a password which permits the subscriber to view and/or download Internet newsgroup messages that are stored on the Defendant's server in California.

Dot Com's contacts with Pennsylvania have occurred almost exclusively over the Internet. Dot Com's offices, employees and Internet servers are located in California. Dot Com maintains no offices, employees or agents in Pennsylvania. Dot Com's advertising for its service to Pennsylvania residents involves posting information about its service on its Web page, which is accessible to Pennsylvania residents via the Internet. Defendant has approximately 140,000 paying subscribers worldwide. Approximately two percent (3,000) of those subscribers are Pennsylvania residents. These subscribers have contracted to receive Dot Com's service by visiting its Web site and filling out the application. Additionally, Dot Com has entered into agreements with seven Internet access providers in Pennsylvania to permit their subscribers to access Dot Com's news service. Two of these providers are located in the Western District of Pennsylvania.

The basis of the trademark claims is Dot Com's use of the word "Zippo" in the domain names it holds, in numerous locations in its Web site and in the heading of Internet newsgroup messages that have been posted by Dot Com subscribers. When an Internet user views or downloads a newsgroup message posted by a Dot Com subscriber, the word "Zippo" appears in the "Message-Id" and "Organization" sections of the heading. The news message itself, containing text and/or pictures, follows. Manufacturing points out that some of the messages contain adult oriented, sexually explicit subject matter.

* * *

III. DISCUSSION

A. Personal Jurisdiction

1. The Traditional Framework

Our authority to exercise personal jurisdiction in this case is conferred by state law. Fed.R.Civ.P. 4(e); Mellon, 960 F.2d at 1221. The extent to which we may exercise that authority is governed by the Due Process Clause of the Fourteenth Amendment to the Federal Constitution. Kulko v. Superior Court of California, 436 U.S. 84, 91 (1978).

Pennsylvania's long arm jurisdiction statute is codified at 42 Pa.C.S.A. § 5322(a). The portion of the statute authorizing us to exercise jurisdiction here permits the exercise of jurisdiction over non-resident defendants upon:

> (2) Contracting to supply services or things in this Commonwealth.

42 Pa.C.S.A. § 5322(a). It is undisputed that Dot Com contracted to supply Internet news services to approximately 3,000 Pennsylvania residents and also entered into agreements with seven Internet access providers in Pennsylvania. Moreover, even if Dot Com's conduct did not satisfy a specific provision of the statute, we would nevertheless be authorized to exercise jurisdiction to the "fullest extent allowed under the Constitution of the United States." 42 Pa.C.S.A. § 5322(b).

* * *

2. The Internet and Jurisdiction

In Hanson v. Denckla, the Supreme Court noted that "[a]s technological progress has increased the flow of commerce between States, the need for jurisdiction has undergone a similar increase." Hanson v. Denckla, 357 U.S. 235, 250–51 (1958). Twenty seven years later, the Court observed that jurisdiction could not be avoided "merely because the defendant did not *physically* enter the forum state." Burger King, 471 U.S. at 476. The Court observed that:

> [I]t is an inescapable fact of modern commercial life that a substantial amount of commercial business is transacted solely by mail and wire communications across state lines, thus obviating the need for physical presence within a State in which business is conducted.

Id.

Enter the Internet, a global " 'super-network' of over 15,000 computer networks used by over 30 million individuals, corporations, organizations, and educational institutions worldwide." Panavision Intern., L.P. v. Toeppen, 938 F.Supp. 616 (C.D.Cal.1996) (citing American Civil Liberties Union v. Reno, 929 F.Supp. 824, 830–48 (E.D.Pa.1996)). "In recent years, businesses have begun to use the Internet to provide information and products to consumers and other businesses." Id. The Internet makes it possible to conduct business throughout the world entirely from a desktop. With this global revolution looming on the horizon, the development of the law concerning the permissible scope of personal jurisdiction based on Internet use is in its infant stages. The cases are scant. Nevertheless, our review of the available cases and materials reveals that the likelihood that personal jurisdiction can be constitutionally exercised is directly proportionate to the nature and quality of commercial activity that an entity conducts over the Internet. This sliding scale is consistent with well developed personal jurisdiction principles. At one end of the spectrum are situations where a defendant clearly does business over the Internet. If the defendant enters into contracts with residents of a foreign jurisdiction that involve the knowing and repeated transmission of computer files over the Internet, personal jurisdiction is proper. E.g. CompuServe, Inc. v. Patterson, 89 F.3d 1257 (6th Cir.1996). At the opposite end are situations where a defendant has simply posted information on an Internet Web site which is accessible to users in foreign jurisdictions. A passive Web site that does little more than make information available to those who are interested in it is not grounds for the exercise personal jurisdiction. E.g. Bensusan Restaurant Corp. v. King, 937 F.Supp. 295 (S.D.N.Y.1996). The middle ground is occupied by interactive Web sites where a user can exchange information with the host computer. In these cases, the exercise of jurisdiction is determined by examining the level of interactivity and commercial nature of the exchange of information that occurs on the Web site. E.g. Maritz, Inc. v. Cybergold, Inc., 947 F.Supp. 1328 (E.D.Mo.1996).

Traditionally, when an entity intentionally reaches beyond its boundaries to conduct business with foreign residents, the exercise of specific jurisdiction is proper. Burger King, 471 U.S. at 475. Different results should not be reached simply because business is conducted over the Internet. In CompuServe, Inc. v. Patterson, 89 F.3d 1257 (6th Cir.1996), the Sixth Circuit addressed the significance of doing business over the Internet. In that case, Patterson, a Texas resident, entered into a contract to distribute shareware through CompuServe's Internet server located in Ohio. CompuServe, 89 F.3d at 1260. From Texas, Patterson electronically uploaded thirty-two master software files to CompuServe's server in Ohio via the Internet. Id. at 1261. One of Patterson's software products was designed to help people navigate the Internet. Id. When CompuServe later began to market a product that Patterson believed to be similar to his own, he threatened to sue. Id. CompuServe brought an action in the Southern District of Ohio, seeking a declaratory judgment. Id. The District Court granted Patterson's motion to dismiss for lack of personal jurisdiction and

CompuServe appealed. Id. The Sixth Circuit reversed, reasoning that Patterson had purposefully directed his business activities toward Ohio by knowingly entering into a contract with an Ohio resident and then "deliberately and repeatedly" transmitted files to Ohio. Id. at 1264–66.

In Maritz, Inc. v. Cybergold, Inc., 947 F.Supp. 1328 (E.D.Mo.1996), the defendant had put up a Web site as a promotion for its upcoming Internet service. The service consisted of assigning users an electronic mailbox and then forwarding advertisements for products and services that matched the users' interests to those electronic mailboxes. Maritz, 947 F.Supp. at 1330. The defendant planned to charge advertisers and provide users with incentives to view the advertisements. Id. Although the service was not yet operational, users were encouraged to add their address to a mailing list to receive updates about the service. Id. The court rejected the defendant's contention that it operated a "passive Web site." Id. at 1333–34. The court reasoned that the defendant's conduct amounted to "active solicitations" and "promotional activities" designed to "develop a mailing list of Internet users" and that the defendant "indiscriminately responded to every user" who accessed the site. Id. at 1333–34.

Inset Systems, Inc. v. Instruction Set, 937 F.Supp. 161 (D.Conn.1996) represents the outer limits of the exercise of personal jurisdiction based on the Internet. In Inset Systems, a Connecticut corporation sued a Massachusetts corporation in the District of Connecticut for trademark infringement based on the use of an Internet domain name. Inset Systems, 937 F.Supp. at 162. The defendant's contacts with Connecticut consisted of posting a Web site that was accessible to approximately 10,000 Connecticut residents and maintaining a toll free number. Id. at 165. The court exercised personal jurisdiction, reasoning that advertising on the Internet constituted the purposeful doing of business in Connecticut because "unlike television and radio advertising, the advertisement is available continuously to any Internet user." Id. at 165.

Bensusan Restaurant Corp. v. King, 937 F.Supp. 295 (S.D.N.Y.1996) reached a different conclusion based on a similar Web site. In Bensusan, the operator of a New York jazz club sued the operator of a Missouri jazz club for trademark infringement. Bensusan, 937 F.Supp. at 297. The Internet Web site at issue contained general information about the defendant's club, a calendar of events and ticket information. Id. However, the site was not interactive. Id. If a user wanted to go to the club, she would have to call or visit a ticket outlet and then pick up tickets at the club on the night of the show. Id. The court refused to exercise jurisdiction based on the Web site alone, reasoning that it did not rise to the level of purposeful availment of that jurisdiction's laws. The court distinguished the case from CompuServe, supra, where the user had " 'reached out' from Texas to Ohio and 'originated and maintained' contacts with Ohio." Id. at 301.[2]

2. [On appeal, the district court's decision in *Bensusan* was affirmed on state-law grounds. The decision of the court of appeals is excerpted in Part III(B)(1), *infra*.—Eds.]

Pres–Kap, Inc. v. System One, Direct Access, Inc., 636 So.2d 1351 (Fla.App.1994), review denied, 645 So.2d 455 (Fla.1994) is not inconsistent with the above cases. In Pres–Kap, a majority of a three-judge intermediate state appeals court refused to exercise jurisdiction over a consumer of an on-line airline ticketing service. Pres–Kap involved a suit on a contract dispute in a Florida court by a Delaware corporation against its New York customer. Pres–Kap, 636 So.2d at 1351–52. The defendant had leased computer equipment which it used to access an airline ticketing computer located in Florida. Id. The contract was solicited, negotiated, executed and serviced in New York. Id. at 1352. The defendant's only contact with Florida consisted of logging onto the computer located in Florida and mailing payments for the leased equipment to Florida. Id. at 1353. Pres–Kap is distinguishable from the above cases and the case at bar because it addressed the exercise of jurisdiction over a consumer of on-line services as opposed to a seller. When a consumer logs onto a server in a foreign jurisdiction he is engaging in a fundamentally different type of contact than an entity that is using the Internet to sell or market products or services to residents of foreign jurisdictions. The Pres–Kap court specifically expressed concern over the implications of subjecting users of "on-line" services with contracts with out-of-state networks to suit in foreign jurisdictions. Id. at 1353.

3. Application to this Case

First, we note that this is not an Internet advertising case in the line of Inset Systems and Bensusan, supra. Dot Com has not just posted information on a Web site that is accessible to Pennsylvania residents who are connected to the Internet. This is not even an interactivity case in the line of Maritz, supra. Dot Com has done more than create an interactive Web site through which it exchanges information with Pennsylvania residents in hopes of using that information for commercial gain later. We are not being asked to determine whether Dot Com's Web site alone constitutes the purposeful availment of doing business in Pennsylvania. This is a "doing business over the Internet" case in the line of CompuServe, supra. We are being asked to determine whether Dot Com's conducting of electronic commerce with Pennsylvania residents constitutes the purposeful availment of doing business in Pennsylvania. We conclude that it does. Dot Com has contracted with approximately 3,000 individuals and seven Internet access providers in Pennsylvania. The intended object of these transactions has been the downloading of the electronic messages that form the basis of this suit in Pennsylvania.

We find Dot Com's efforts to characterize its conduct as falling short of purposeful availment of doing business in Pennsylvania wholly unpersuasive. At oral argument, Defendant repeatedly characterized its actions as merely "operating a Web site" or "advertising." Dot Com also cites to a number of cases from this Circuit which, it claims, stand for the proposition that merely advertising in a forum, without more, is not a sufficient minimal contact. This argument is misplaced. Dot Com has done more than advertise on the Internet in Pennsylvania. Defendant has sold passwords to approximately 3,000 subscribers in Pennsylvania and entered into seven contracts with Internet access providers to furnish its services to their customers in Pennsylvania.

Dot Com also contends that its contacts with Pennsylvania residents are "fortuitous" within the meaning of World–Wide Volkswagen, 444 U.S. 286 (1980). Defendant argues that it has not "actively" solicited business in Pennsylvania and that any business it conducts with Pennsylvania residents has resulted from contacts that were initiated by Pennsylvanians who visited the Defendant's Web site. The fact that Dot Com's services have been consumed in Pennsylvania is not "fortuitous" within the meaning of World–Wide Volkswagen. In World–Wide Volkswagen, a couple that had purchased a vehicle in New York, while they were New York residents, were injured while driving that vehicle through Oklahoma and brought suit in an Oklahoma state court. World–Wide Volkswagen, 444 U.S. at 288. The manufacturer did not sell its vehicles in Oklahoma and had not made an effort to establish business relationships in Oklahoma. Id. at 295. The Supreme Court characterized the manufacturer's ties with Oklahoma as fortuitous because they resulted entirely out the fact that the plaintiffs had driven their car into that state. Id.

Here, Dot Com argues that its contacts with Pennsylvania residents are fortuitous because Pennsylvanians happened to find its Web site or heard about its news service elsewhere and decided to subscribe. This argument misconstrues the concept of fortuitous contacts embodied in World–Wide Volkswagen. Dot Com's contacts with Pennsylvania would be fortuitous within the meaning of World–Wide Volkswagen if it had no Pennsylvania subscribers and an Ohio subscriber forwarded a copy of a file he obtained from Dot Com to a friend in Pennsylvania or an Ohio subscriber brought his computer along on a trip to Pennsylvania and used it to access Dot Com's service. That is not the situation here. Dot Com repeatedly and consciously chose to process Pennsylvania residents' applications and to assign them passwords. Dot Com knew that the result of these contracts would be the transmission of electronic messages into Pennsylvania. The transmission of these files was entirely within its control. Dot Com cannot maintain that these contracts are "fortuitous" or "coincidental" within the meaning of World–Wide Volkswagen. When a defendant makes a conscious choice to conduct business with the residents of a forum state, "it has clear notice that it is subject to suit there." World–Wide Volkswagen, 444 U.S. at 297. Dot Com was under no obligation to sell its services to Pennsylvania residents. It freely chose to do so, presumably in order to profit from those transactions. If a corporation determines that the risk of being subject to personal jurisdiction in a particular forum is too great, it can choose to sever its connection to the state. Id. If Dot Com had not wanted to be amenable to jurisdiction in Pennsylvania, the solution would have been simple—it could have chosen not to sell its services to Pennsylvania residents.

Next, Dot Com argues that its forum-related activities are not numerous or significant enough to create a "substantial connection" with Pennsylvania. Defendant points to the fact that only two percent of its subscribers are Pennsylvania residents. However, the Supreme Court has made clear that even a single contact can be sufficient. McGee, 355 U.S. at 223. The test has always focused on the "nature and quality" of the contacts with the forum and not the quantity of those contacts. International Shoe, 326 U.S. at 320. The Sixth Circuit also rejected a similar argument in CompuServe when it wrote that the contacts were "deliberate and repeated even if they yielded little revenue." CompuServe, 89 F.3d at 1265.

* * *

IV. CONCLUSION

We conclude that this Court may appropriately exercise personal jurisdiction over the Defendant and that venue is proper in this judicial district.

NOTES & QUESTIONS

1. *The Zippo categorization*. In *Zippo*, the court made an effort to synthesize existing decisions on the circumstances under which operation of a website can give rise to jurisdiction. It found that those decisions have arranged websites on a "spectrum," consisting of two polar situations separated by a broad middle ground: (1) "situations where a defendant clearly does business over the Internet," by "enter[ing] into contracts with residents of a foreign jurisdiction that involve the knowing and repeated transmission of computer files over the Internet," in which case "personal jurisdiction is proper"; (2) "situations where a defendant has simply posted [a] passive website that does little more than make information available to those who are interested in it," which "is not grounds for the exercise [of] personal jurisdiction"; and (3) "interactive Web sites where a user can exchange information with the host computer," in which case "the exercise of jurisdiction is determined by examining the level of interactivity and commercial nature of the exchange of information that occurs on the Web site." Numerous subsequent decisions have adopted this approach.

How helpful is this categorization? (a) Is the "level of interactivity" that a website presents an indication of purposeful activity directed at the forum state? What would be the result of applying such a rule to telephone calls, which are as "interactive" as any website? (b) What about the "commercial nature" of the interactivity? Should a non-profit entity that commits an online tort be less susceptible to extraterritorial jurisdiction than a commercial entity that engages in the same activities? What about someone who engages in defamation for spiteful, but not commercial, purposes?

Consider this evaluation: (a) The rule applying to "passive" websites is an application of existing law holding that advertising in a nationally circulated publication does not alone support jurisdiction in every state where the publication is distributed. (b) The rule applying to websites that produce contracts with forum residents is an application of existing law holding that contracts with forum residents, regardless of the means of communication through which they are entered, may be sufficient to support jurisdiction. (c) The rule applicable to the middle category of "interactive" websites focuses inappropriately on the level and commercial nature of the site's interactivity, which are poor proxies for whether the defendant has "purposely avail[ed] itself of the privilege of conducting activities within the forum State." *Hanson v. Denckla*, 357 U.S. 235, 263 (1958). Consider also the following criticism of the interactivity criterion:

> [T]he distinction drawn by the Zippo court between actively managed, telephone-like use of the Internet and less active but "interactive" websites is not entirely clear to this court. Further, the proper means to measure the site's "level of interactivity" as a guide to personal jurisdiction remains unexplained. Finally, this court observes that the need for a special Internet-focused test for "minimum contacts" has yet to be established.

Winfield Collection, Ltd. v. McCauley, 105 F.Supp.2d 746, 750 (E.D.Mich.2000).

2. *Bensusan*. One of the cases the court relied upon in formulating its three-category analysis is the district court opinion in *Bensusan Restaurant Corp. v. King*, 937 F.Supp. 295 (S.D.N.Y.1996), *aff'd*, 126 F.3d 25 (2d Cir.1997). (The appellate decision is excerpted in Part III(B), *infra*.) After finding that the relevant provisions of the long-arm statute were not satisfied, the district court went on, in what might be considered dictum, to inquire whether assertion of jurisdiction would be consistent with due process. It stated:

> Creating a site, like placing a product into the stream of commerce, may be felt nationwide—or even worldwide—but, without more, it is not an act purposefully directed toward the forum state. See Asahi Metal Indus. Co. v. Superior Court, 480 U.S. 102, 112 (1987) (plurality opinion). There are no allegations that King actively sought to encourage New Yorkers to access his site, or that he conducted any business—let alone a continuous and systematic part of its business—in New York. There is in fact no suggestion that King has any presence of any kind in New York other than the Web site that can be accessed worldwide. Bensusan's argument that King should have foreseen that users could access the site in New York and be confused as to the relationship of the two Blue Note clubs is insufficient to satisfy due process.

Id. at 301. Distinguishing *CompuServe, Inc. v. Patterson*, 89 F.3d 1257 (6th Cir.1996), discussed in Part II(C), *infra*, the court concluded that this case "contains no allegations that King in any way directed any contact to, or had any contact with, New York or intended to avail itself of any of New York's benefits." *Id.*

2. PASSIVE WEBSITES AND THE REQUIREMENT OF "SOMETHING MORE"

Cybersell, Inc. v. Cybersell, Inc.

130 F.3d 414 (9th Cir.1997).

■ RYMER, CIRCUIT JUDGE.

We are asked to hold that the allegedly infringing use of a service mark in a home page on the World Wide Web suffices for personal jurisdiction in the state where the holder of the mark has its principal place of business. Cybersell, Inc., an Arizona corporation that advertises for commercial services over the Internet, claims that Cybersell, Inc., a Florida corporation that offers web page construction services over the Internet, infringed its federally registered mark and should be amenable to suit in Arizona because cyberspace is without borders and a web site which advertises a product or service is necessarily intended for use on a world wide basis. The district court disagreed, and so do we. Instead, applying our normal "minimum contacts" analysis, we conclude that it would not comport with "traditional notions of fair play and substantial justice," Core–Vent Corp. v. Nobel Indus. AB, 11 F.3d 1482, 1485 (9th Cir.1993) (quoting International Shoe Co. v. Washington, 326 U.S. 310, 316 (1945)), for Arizona to exercise personal jurisdiction over an allegedly infringing Florida web site advertiser who has no contacts with Arizona other than maintaining a home page that is accessible to Arizonans, and everyone else, over the Internet. We therefore affirm.

I

Cybersell, Inc. is an Arizona corporation, which we will refer to as Cybersell AZ. It was incorporated in May 1994 to provide Internet and web advertising and marketing services, including consulting. The principals of Cybersell AZ are Laurence Canter and Martha Siegel, known among web users for first "spamming" the Internet. Mainstream print media carried the story of Canter and Siegel and their various efforts to commercialize the web.

On August 8, 1994, Cybersell AZ filed an application to register the name "Cybersell" as a service mark. The application was approved and the grant was published on October 30, 1995. Cybersell AZ operated a web site using the mark from August 1994 through February 1995. The site was then taken down for reconstruction.

Meanwhile, in the summer of 1995, Matt Certo and his father, Dr. Samuel C. Certo, both Florida residents, formed Cybersell, Inc., a Florida corporation (Cybersell FL), with its principal place of business in Orlando. Matt was a business school student at Rollins College, where his father was a professor; Matt was particularly interested in the Internet, and their company was to provide business consulting services for strategic management and marketing on the web. At the time the Certos chose the name "Cybersell" for their venture, Cybersell AZ had no home page on the web nor had the PTO granted their application for the service mark.

As part of their marketing effort, the Certos created a web page at http://www.cybsell.com/cybsell/index.htm. The home page has a logo at the top with "CyberSell" over a depiction of the planet earth, with the caption underneath "Professional Services for the World Wide Web" and a local (area code 407) phone number. It proclaims in large letters "Welcome to CyberSell!" A hypertext link allows the browser to introduce himself, and invites a company not on the web—but interested in getting on the web—to "Email us to find out how!"

Canter found the Cybersell FL web page and sent an e-mail on November 27, 1995 notifying Dr. Certo that "Cybersell" is a service mark of Cybersell AZ. Trying to disassociate themselves from Canter and Siegel, the Certos changed the name of Cybersell FL to WebHorizons, Inc. on December 27 (later it was changed again to WebSolvers, Inc.) and by January 4, 1996, they had replaced the CyberSell logo at the top of their web page with WebHorizons, Inc. The WebHorizons page still said "Welcome to CyberSell!"

Cybersell AZ filed the complaint in this action January 9, 1996 in the District of Arizona, alleging trademark infringement, unfair competition, fraud, and RICO violations. On the same day Cybersell FL filed suit for declaratory relief with regard to use of the name "Cybersell" in the United States District Court for the Middle District of Florida, but that action was transferred to the District of Arizona and consolidated with the Cybersell AZ action. Cybersell FL moved to dismiss for lack of personal jurisdiction. The district court denied Cybersell AZ's request for a preliminary injunction, then granted Cybersell FL's motion to dismiss for lack of personal jurisdiction. Cybersell AZ timely appealed.

II

The general principles that apply to the exercise of personal jurisdiction are well known. As there is no federal statute governing personal jurisdiction in this case, the law of Arizona applies. Under Rule 4.2(a) of the Arizona Rules of Civil Procedure, an Arizona court

> may exercise personal jurisdiction over parties, whether found within or outside the state, to the maximum extent permitted by the Constitution of this state and the Constitution of the United States.

The Arizona Supreme Court has stated that under Rule 4.2(a), "Arizona will exert personal jurisdiction over a nonresident litigant to the maximum extent allowed by the federal constitution." * * * Thus, Cybersell FL may be subject to personal jurisdiction in Arizona so long as doing so comports with due process.

A court may assert either specific or general jurisdiction over a defendant. * * * Cybersell AZ concedes that general jurisdiction over Cybersell FL doesn't exist in Arizona, so the only issue in this case is whether specific jurisdiction is available.

We use a three-part test to determine whether a district court may exercise specific jurisdiction over a nonresident defendant:

> (1) The nonresident defendant must do some act or consummate some transaction with the forum or perform some act by which he purposefully avails himself of the privilege of conducting activities in the forum, thereby invoking the benefits and protections[;] (2)[t]he claim must be one which arises out of or results from the

> defendant's forum-related activities[; and] (3)[e]xercise of jurisdiction must be reasonable.

Ballard v. Savage, 65 F.3d 1495, 1498 (9th Cir.1995) (citations omitted).

Cybersell AZ argues that the test is met because trademark infringement occurs when the passing off of the mark occurs, which in this case, it submits, happened when the name "Cybersell" was used on the Internet in connection with advertising. Cybersell FL, on the other hand, contends that a party should not be subject to nationwide, or perhaps worldwide, jurisdiction simply for using the Internet.

A

Since the jurisdictional facts are not in dispute, we turn to the first requirement, which is the most critical. As the Supreme Court emphasized in Hanson v. Denckla, "it is essential in each case that there be some act by which the defendant purposefully avails itself of the privilege of conducting activities within the forum State, thus invoking the benefits and protections of its laws." 357 U.S. 235, 253 (1958). We recently explained in Ballard that

> the "purposeful availment" requirement is satisfied if the defendant has taken deliberate action within the forum state or if he has created continuing obligations to forum residents. "It is not required that a defendant be physically present within, or have physical contacts with, the forum, provided that his efforts 'are purposefully directed' toward forum residents."

Ballard, 65 F.3d at 1498 (citations omitted).

We have not yet considered when personal jurisdiction may be exercised in the context of cyberspace, but the Second and Sixth Circuits have had occasion to decide whether personal jurisdiction was properly exercised over defendants involved in transmissions over the Internet, see CompuServe, Inc. v. Patterson, 89 F.3d 1257 (6th Cir.1996); Bensusan Restaurant Corp. v. King, 937 F.Supp. 295 (S.D.N.Y.1996), aff'd, 126 F.3d 25 (2d Cir.1997), as have a number of district courts.

* * *

"Interactive" web sites present somewhat different issues. Unlike passive sites such as the defendant's in Bensusan, users can exchange information with the host computer when the site is interactive. Courts that have addressed interactive sites have looked to the "level of interactivity and commercial nature of the exchange of information that occurs on the Web site" to determine if sufficient contacts exist to warrant the exercise of jurisdiction. See, e.g., Zippo Mfg. Co. v. Zippo Dot Com, Inc., 952 F.Supp. 1119, 1124 (W.D.Pa.1997) (finding purposeful availment based on Dot Com's interactive web site and contracts with 3000 individuals and seven Internet access providers in Pennsylvania allowing them to download the electronic messages that form the basis of the suit); Maritz, Inc. v. Cybergold, Inc., 947 F.Supp. 1328, 1332–33 (E.D.Mo.) (browsers were encouraged to add their address to a mailing list that basically subscribed the user to the service), reconsideration denied, 947 F.Supp. 1338 (1996).

Cybersell AZ points to several district court decisions which it contends have held that the mere advertisement or solicitation for sale of goods and services on the Internet gives rise to specific jurisdiction in the plaintiff's forum. However, so far as we are aware, no court has ever held that an Internet advertisement alone is sufficient to subject the advertiser to jurisdiction in the plaintiff's home state. See, e.g., Smith v. Hobby Lobby Stores, 968 F.Supp. 1356 (W.D.Ark.1997) (no jurisdiction over Hong Kong defendant who advertised in trade journal posted on the Internet without sale of goods or services in Arkansas). Rather, in each, there has been "something more" to indicate that the defendant purposefully (albeit electronically) directed his activity in a substantial way to the forum state.

Inset Systems, Inc. v. Instruction Set, Inc., 937 F.Supp. 161 (D.Conn. 1996), is the case most favorable to Cybersell AZ's position. Inset developed and marketed computer software throughout the world; Instruction Set, Inc. (ISI) provided computer technology and support. Inset owned the federal trademark "INSET"; but ISI obtained "INSET.COM" as its Internet domain address for advertising its goods and services. ISI also used the telephone number "1–800–US–INSET." Inset learned of ISI's domain address when it tried to get the same address, and filed suit for trademark infringement in Connecticut. The court reasoned that ISI had purposefully availed itself of doing business in Connecticut because it directed its advertising activities via the Internet and its toll-free number toward the state of Connecticut (and all states); Internet sites and toll-free numbers are designed to communicate with people and their businesses in every state; an Internet advertisement could reach as many as 10,000 Internet users within Connecticut alone; and once posted on the Internet, an advertisement is continuously available to any Internet user.

Cybersell AZ further points to the court's statement in EDIAS Software International, L.L.C. v. BASIS International Ltd., 947 F.Supp. 413 (D.Ariz.1996), that a defendant "should not be permitted to take advantage of modern technology through an Internet Web page and forum and simultaneously escape traditional notions of jurisdiction." Id. at 420. In that case, EDIAS (an Arizona company) alleged that BASIS (a New Mexico company) sent advertising and defamatory statements over the Internet through e-mail, its web page, and forums. However, the court did not rest its minimum contacts analysis on use of the Internet alone; in addition to the Internet, BASIS had a contract with EDIAS, it made sales to EDIAS and other Arizona customers, and its employees had visited Arizona during the course of the business relationship with EDIAS.

Some courts have also given weight to the number of "hits" received by a web page from residents in the forum state, and to other evidence that Internet activity was directed at, or bore fruit in, the forum state. See, e.g., Heroes, Inc. v. Heroes Found., 958 F.Supp. 1 (D.D.C.1996) (web page that solicited contributions and provided toll-free telephone number along with the defendant's use on the web page of the allegedly infringing trademark and logo, along with other contacts, provided sustained contact with the District), amended by No. Civ.A. 96–1260(TAF) (1997); Pres–Kap, Inc. v. System One, Direct Access, Inc., 636 So.2d 1351 (Fla.Dist.Ct.App.1994) (declining jurisdiction where defendant consumer subscribed to plaintiff's travel reservation system but was solicited and serviced instate by the supplier's local representative).

In sum, the common thread, well stated by the district court in Zippo, is that "the likelihood that personal jurisdiction can be constitutionally exercised is directly proportionate to the nature and quality of commercial activity that an entity conducts over the Internet." Zippo, 952 F.Supp. at 1124.

B

Here, Cybersell FL has conducted no commercial activity over the Internet in Arizona. All that it did was post an essentially passive home page on the web, using the name "CyberSell," which Cybersell AZ was in the process of registering as a federal service mark. While there is no question that anyone, anywhere could access that home page and thereby learn about the services offered, we cannot see how from that fact alone it can be inferred that Cybersell FL deliberately directed its merchandising efforts toward Arizona residents.

Cybersell FL did nothing to encourage people in Arizona to access its site, and there is no evidence that any part of its business (let alone a continuous part of its business) was sought or achieved in Arizona. To the contrary, it appears to be an operation where business was primarily generated by the personal contacts of one of its founders. While those contacts are not entirely local, they aren't in Arizona either. No Arizonan except for Cybersell AZ "hit" Cybersell FL's web site. There is no evidence that any Arizona resident signed up for Cybersell FL's web construction services. It entered into no contracts in Arizona, made no sales in Arizona, received no telephone calls from Arizona, earned no income from Arizona, and sent no messages over the Internet to Arizona. The only message it received over the Internet from Arizona was from Cybersell AZ. Cybersell FL did not have an "800" number, let alone a toll-free number that also used the "Cybersell" name. The interactivity of its web page is limited to receiving the browser's name and address and an indication of interest—signing up for the service is not an option, nor did anyone from Arizona do so. No money changed hands on the Internet from (or through) Arizona. In short, Cybersell FL has done no act and has consummated no transaction, nor has it performed any act by which it purposefully availed itself of the privilege of conducting activities, in Arizona, thereby invoking the benefits and protections of Arizona law.

We therefore hold that Cybersell FL's contacts are insufficient to establish "purposeful availment." Cybersell AZ has thus failed to satisfy the first prong of our three-part test for specific jurisdiction. We decline to go further solely on the footing that Cybersell AZ has alleged trademark infringement over the Internet by Cybersell FL's use of the registered name "Cybersell" on an essentially passive web page advertisement. Otherwise, every complaint arising out of alleged trademark infringement on the Internet would automatically result in personal jurisdiction wherever the plaintiff's principal place of business is located. That would not comport with traditional notions of what qualifies as purposeful activity invoking the benefits and protections of the forum state. See Peterson v. Kennedy, 771 F.2d 1244, 1262 (9th Cir.1985) (series of phone calls and letters to California physician regarding plaintiff's injuries insufficient to satisfy first prong of test).

* * *

IV

We conclude that the essentially passive nature of Cybersell FL's activity in posting a home page on the World Wide Web that allegedly used the service mark of Cybersell AZ does not qualify as purposeful activity invoking the benefits and protections of Arizona. As it engaged in no commercial activity and had no other contacts via the Internet or otherwise in Arizona, Cybersell FL lacks sufficient minimum contacts with Arizona for personal jurisdiction to be asserted over it there. Accordingly, its motion to dismiss for lack of personal jurisdiction was properly granted.

NOTES & QUESTIONS

1. *"Something more."* The *Cybersell* court, endorsing the three-category approach set forth in *Zippo*, held that mere operation of a website is insufficient to support personal jurisdiction: "something more" is required "to indicate that the defendant purposefully (albeit electronically) directed his activity in a substantial way to the forum state." It found no such "something more" in the case at hand, but identified several prior cases in which it found that "something more" was present: the placement of defendant's toll-free number on the website, receiving "hits" from Internet users in the forum state, soliciting contributions, and using the plaintiff's trademark on the website. To what extent does the presence of these features help to establish purposeful availment of a particular state? In *Cybersell* itself, the defendant's website was set up to "receiv[e] the browser's [i.e., an Internet user's] name and address and an indication of interest." Is this any less evidence of targeting of residents of a particular state than the other factors noted above?

2. *Passive websites.* In cases involving websites that are nothing more than online advertisements, most courts have had little difficulty concluding that the website could not support jurisdiction. *See, e.g., Soma Medical Int'l v. Standard Chartered Bank*, 196 F.3d 1292 (10th Cir.1999); *Mid City Bowling Lanes & Sports Palace, Inc. v. Ivercrest, Inc.*, 35 F.Supp.2d 507 (E.D.La.1999); *Fernandez v. McDaniel Controls, Inc.*, 999 F.Supp. 1365 (D.Haw.1998); *Blackburn v. Walker Oriental Rug Galleries, Inc.*, 999 F.Supp. 636 (E.D.Pa.1998); *Green v. William Mason & Co.*, 996 F.Supp. 394 (D.N.J.1998); *SF Hotel Co., L.P v. Energy Investments, Inc.*, 985 F.Supp.

1032 (D.Kan.1997); *Smith v. Hobby Lobby Stores, Inc.*, 968 F.Supp. 1356 (W.D.Ark.1997).

But: (a) *In Maritz, Inc. v. Cybergold, Inc.*, 947 F.Supp. 1328 (E.D.Mo. 1996), the court found the due process requirement satisfied based on the fact that defendant's website was accessed 131 times by residents of the forum state, and that it was intended to reach all Internet users. The court reasoned that setting up a website is a stronger basis for jurisdiction than maintaining a telephone number or a mailing address, since (i) "[a] company's establishment of a telephone number, such as an 800 number, is not as efficient, quick, or easy way to reach the global audience that the internet has the capability of reaching," and (ii) if a forum resident sends a letter to defendant, "[defendant] would have the option as to whether to mail information to the [forum] resident, [whereas defendant] automatically and indiscriminately responds to each and every internet user who accesses its web site." What could indicate an intent that a website *not* reach all Internet users? Of what significance should be the fact that a website was viewed by residents of the forum state? Are the noted differences between websites on the one hand, and telephone and mail on the other, persuasive in the jurisdictional context?

(b) In *Hasbro Inc. v. Clue Computing Inc.*, 994 F.Supp. 34 (D.Mass. 1997), jurisdiction was based on the facts that defendant stated on its website that it had done work for Digital Equipment Corp., which it knew was a company located in the forum state; that the website contained a link allowing a visitor to send an e-mail message to the site owner; and that defendant failed to take any measures to avoid contacts in the forum state. How might the owner of a website prevent it from being accessed by residents of a particular state? Why should the inclusion of a mailto link on a website demonstrate purposeful availment of any state? Would the inclusion of a mailing address lead to the same conclusion, particularly a P.O. box address that did no more than state where mail might be directed without indicating the addressee's location?

(c) In *Inset Systems, Inc. v. Instruction Set, Inc.*, 937 F.Supp. 161 (D.Conn.1996), the court found it had jurisdiction over the defendant based merely on defendant's operation of a website that displayed its toll-free telephone number, and the fact that a substantial number of forum residents had access to the Internet. What if the defendant's toll-free number was not posted on the website, but was available to anyone who dialed the toll-free directory assistance number?

Can these decisions be reconciled with *Cybersell*'s "something more" requirement?

Other cases have rejected the view that the inclusion on a website of a link enabling visitors to send e-mail to the site owner, or inclusion of the site owner's toll-free telephone number, is enough to lift the site out of the "passive" category. *See Osteotech, Inc. v. GenSci Regeneration Sciences, Inc.*, 6 F.Supp.2d 349 (D.N.J.1998) (placement of defendant's phone number or e-mail address on its website is not relevant to the jurisdictional analysis, since inclusion of this information "has no more of an impact on any particular forum than a web site without such information"); *Edberg v. Neogen Corp.*, 17 F.Supp.2d 104 (D.Conn.1998) (no jurisdiction, where site included both a toll-free number and a link for sending e-mail to the defendant); *Grutkowski v. Steamboat Lake Guides & Outfitters, Inc.*, 1998 WL 962042 (E.D.Pa.1998) (inclusion of an e-mail link and local telephone number does not make site interactive); *Conseco, Inc. v. Hickerson*, 698 N.E.2d 816 (Ind.App.1998) (no jurisdiction, where site included e-mail link); *Transcraft Corp. v. Doonan Trailer Corp.*, 45 U.S.P.Q.2d (BNA) 1097 (N.D.Ill.1997) (no jurisdiction, where site includes a toll-free number and invites inquiries by e-mail).

3. *Deliberate direction.* What should count as a "something more" that is sufficient to support jurisdiction over the owner of a website? A more specific gloss on this requirement is that the defendant must "deliberately direct" its website advertising at the residents of the forum state. *Fernandez v. McDaniel Controls, Inc.*, 999 F.Supp. 1365, 1368 (D.Haw.1998). Consider whether the following constitute "deliberate[] direct[ion]" of advertising at a particular state: (a) What if the website contains a list of shipping costs to each of the 50 states? Does this constitute purposeful availment of each state? (b) What if the site notes that a particular product that it offers may be of special interest to residents of Illinois, or to New Englanders, or to Westerners? (c) What if the site contains a map showing driving instructions from each of the states neighboring its brick- and-mortar location? What if it includes a link to a mapping site that will generate driving directions to its location from anywhere in the country? *Cf. Millennium Enterprises, Inc. v. Millennium Music, LP*, 33 F. Supp. 2d 907 (D.Or.1999) (inclusion of local map of defendant's location does not demonstrate intent to target residents of forum state 3,000 miles away); *Vitullo v. Velocity Powerboats, Inc.*, 1998 WL 246152 (N.D.Ill.1998) (exhortation on defendant boat manufacturer's website to attend upcoming boat show in Chicago constitutes "express targeting" of Illinois).

4. *Gloss on* Zippo. In *Blumenthal v. Drudge*, 992 F.Supp. 44, 56 (D.D.C. 1998), the court characterized the *Zippo* line of cases as holding that for a website to support jurisdiction (a) "it must * * * allow [users] to interact directly with the web site on some level," and (b) "there must also be some other non-Internet related contacts between the defendant and the forum state." Does statement (a) overlook the possibility of jurisdiction based on the "effects" of a non-interactive website? See discussion of the effects test in Part II(B), *infra*. Does statement (b) ignore the possibility that a contract formed and fulfilled entirely online might be enough to support jurisdiction? See discussion of online contracts, in Part II(C), *infra*.

3. THE INTERACTIVITY CRITERION

The middle category in *Zippo*'s taxonomy of website jurisdictional contacts is occupied by those sites deemed to be interactive. With the exception of a few early cases, the courts have not been willing to find that interactivity of a website alone constitutes "purposeful availment" of the forum state. Cases in which interactive features of a website were found insufficient to support jurisdiction include: *3D Systems, Inc. v. Aarotech Laboratories, Inc.*, 160 F.3d 1373 (Fed.Cir.1998) (defendant operated a website describing its subsidiary's products, and received e-mail inquiries via that site, but merely forwarded them to its subsidiary for response); *American Information Corp. v. American Infometrics, Inc.*, 139 F.Supp.2d 696 (D.Md.2001) (prospective employees could submit their resumes via the website); *Ecotecture, Inc. v. Wenz*, 2000 WL 760961 (D.Me.2000) (website allowed visitors to subscribe to an online journal); *People Solutions, Inc. v. People Solutions, Inc.*, 2000 WL 1030619 (N.D.Tex.2000) (website "contains interactive pages that allow customers to test Defendant's products, download product demos, obtain product brochures and information, and order products online"); *JB Oxford Holdings, Inc. v. Net Trade, Inc.*, 76 F.Supp.2d 1363 (S.D.Fla.1999) (visitors could apply for a securities trading account online); *Desktop Technologies, Inc. v. Colorworks Reproduction & Design, Inc.*, 1999 WL 98572 (E.D.Pa.1999) (site allowed exchange of files via FTP and e-mail); *Agar Corp. v. Multi–Fluid, Inc.*, 45 U.S.P.Q.2d (BNA) 1444 (S.D.Tex.1997) (site included links allowing visitors to provide feedback and register).

Courts that have found an interactive website to satisfy due process requirements for jurisdiction have often relied upon some additional contacts as well. For example, in *Starmedia Network, Inc. v. Star Media Inc.*, 2001 WL 417118 (S.D.N.Y.2001), the defendant's website allowed visitors to register, download dealer applications, and obtain password-protected product and pricing information. The court said that the website was an interactive one under the *Zippo* criteria, but found that its interactivity was "limited." It held, however, that the due process requirements for jurisdiction were satisfied in view of "additional contacts" that defendant had with the forum state. In *Hsin Ten Enterprise USA, Inc. v. Clark Enterprises*, 138 F.Supp.2d 449 (S.D.N.Y.2000), the court did not ground jurisdiction on defendant's interactive website alone, but noted that defendant sent representatives to attend trade shows in the forum state, maintained independent affiliates there, and had sold its products to residents of the forum state.

NOTES & QUESTIONS

Actual vs. potential interaction. Should a website be found to support jurisdiction, based on the interactivity criterion, simply because it exhibits the *potential* for interaction with residents of the forum state, or must there be *actual* interaction with forum residents? In *Millennium Enterprises, Inc. v. Millennium Music, LP*, 33 F.Supp.2d 907 (D.Or.1999), the plaintiff, which operated music stores in Oregon under the name "Music Millennium," claimed that defendant violated its trademark in that name by operating in South Carolina under the name "Millennium Music." Defendant's website allowed visitors to purchase compact disks, join a discount club, and request franchising information, but no residents of Oregon had made any purchases via the website or engaged in any online communication with the defendant. The court rejected the view that potential interactivity is sufficient to satisfy due process: it held that there must in addition be some "deliberate action" within the forum state, consisting of either transactions with residents of the forum state or other conduct purposefully directed at them. The court stated: "Until transactions with Oregon residents are consummated through defendants' Web site, defendants cannot reasonably anticipate that they will be brought before this court * * *."

On the court's rationale, would it be enough to support jurisdiction that defendant responded to a query for information via e-mail, if defendant knew that the requester was located in Oregon, or must there be an actual commercial transaction with a forum resident? If the latter, then is the court saying that no website falling in *Zippo*'s middle category is sufficient to support jurisdiction?

4. TARGETING OF THE FORUM STATE

Some courts have glossed the due process "purposeful availment" criterion as a requirement that a website be "targeted" at the forum state. What might be evidence of such targeting? In *Quokka Sports, Inc. v. Cup Int'l Ltd.*, 99 F.Supp.2d 1105 (N.D.Cal.1999), the defendants, a company and individuals based in New Zealand, operated websites under domain names that allegedly infringed plaintiff's trademarks. The court, aggregating defendants' national contacts under Fed. R. Civ. Pro. 4(k)(2), found that "[t]he content of the * * * website reflected the defendants' intention to target the U.S. market." In reaching that result the court relied on the facts that (1) defendants "purposefully went to the United States registrar, NSI, to get a '.com' " domain name, rather than staying at home and registering a .nz domain; (2) the website featured banner advertisements from ten U.S. companies; some of the ads, when clicked, displayed a page designed for U.S. consumers; (3) defendants quoted advertising rates to prospective advertisers in U.S. dollars; (4) the website offered to sell travel packages that were priced in U.S. dollars; and (5) the website offered books for sale, in affiliation with Amazon.com, a U.S. company.

Non-targeting of a particular state may be easier to establish. In *JB Oxford Holdings, Inc. v. Net Trade, Inc.*, 76 F.Supp.2d 1363 (S.D.Fla.1999), the defendant operated an online stock brokerage. It accepted account applications only from residents of the states in which it was registered to do business, which did not include Florida, the forum state. The court found that defendant had engaged in "purposeful avoidance of the privilege of conducting business in the forum state," and held that the site did not satisfy the due process requirements for jurisdiction.

For an argument favoring a "targeting" approach to jurisdiction, see Michael A. Geist, *Is There a There There? Toward Greater Certainty for Internet Jurisdiction*, 16 BERKELEY TECH. L.J. 1345 (2001).

NOTES & QUESTIONS

1. *Evaluation of due process caselaw. Zippo* and its progeny, of which we will see more later in this chapter, take a *sui generis* approach to the question whether a defendant's operation of a website can constitute the "minimum contacts" with the forum state that due process requires, resulting in a body of doctrine applying solely to websites. Consider the alternative of treating websites as a technologically more sophisticated version of older communications media, such as nationally circulated periodicals and toll-free telephone numbers, and incrementally updating the caselaw applying to those media. Would this result in a more coherent jurisprudence of website-based jurisdiction? *See* Richard S. Zembek, Comment, *Jurisdiction and the Internet: Fundamental Fairness in the Networked World of Cyberspace*, 6 ALB. L.J. SCI. & TECH. 339 (1996). Should the answer turn on whether websites are all very much like each other and very different from other media of communication?

2. *Communication by other online means.* Should the dissemination of a statement via e-mail, an electronic bulletin board system ("BBS"), Internet mailing list, chat room, or newsgroup carry the same weight, for purposes of evaluating jurisdictional contacts, as placing the same statement on a website? Consider the variations among these modes of online communication according to the following criteria:

- *Persistence.* A website persists for as long as the site owner chooses (unless it is shut down by the access provider for violation of the Terms of Service or some other reason). A message posted on a newsgroup or BBS persists as long as the manager of the forum chooses, which may be anywhere from several hours to several years. Newsgroup postings may be archived by third-party systems indefinitely. An e-mail message persists for as long as the recipient chooses. Chat sessions are normally ephemeral, though in some cases they may be persistent (as, for example, chats via a proprietary system such as ICQ, which are archived on the users' computers until they choose to delete them).

- *Mediation.* Websites, e-mail, newsgroups, and chat sessions are unmediated: no intermediary decides whether a communication will be allowed to occur. BBSs and mailing lists may or may not be mediated.

- *Accessibility.* Websites and newsgroups are accessible by anyone with Internet access. E-mail is normally available only to the intended recipient. Chat sessions may be limited to the interlocutors one selects, or may be open to the public. BBSs are often proprietary, with membership criteria determined by the board's manager. Mailing lists may be either open or closed.

- *Geographic determinacy.* One who communicates via a website, newsgroup, BBS, or (usually) a mailing list or chat session normally does not know the geographic location of those who receive the communication. Methods of limiting access to the communication based on the location of the visitor exist, but they do not always work and in most contexts are infeasible. One may direct an e-mail to a person known to reside in a particular place, but one cannot know where the recipient will be located at the time she reads the message.

B. THE "EFFECTS" OF ONLINE ACTIVITIES

1. THE EFFECTS TEST

In *Calder v. Jones*, 465 U.S. 783 (1984), the Supreme Court held that the "minimum contacts" due process requirement may be satisfied on the basis of the "effects" that out-of-state conduct has in the forum state. In that case, the Court held that a California court could assert jurisdiction over a Florida publisher that published an article defaming the plaintiff, in view of the fact that plaintiff resided in California. The Court reasoned that the defendants had engaged in "intentional, and allegedly tortious, actions [that were] expressly aimed at California," and that "they knew that the brunt of the injury would be felt" by the plaintiff in California. *Id.* at 789–90. The Ninth Circuit summarized the effects test as follows:

> personal jurisdiction can be predicated on (1) intentional actions (2) expressly aimed at the forum state (3) causing harm, the brunt of which is suffered—and which the defendant knows is likely to be suffered—in the forum state.

Core-Vent Corp. v. Nobel Industries AB, 11 F.3d 1482, 1486 (9th Cir.1993).

Plaintiffs have frequently urged courts to find jurisdiction based on the effects test in cases where the claims are based on infringement of intellectual property rights or defamation, and the alleged violations occur through use of a website or some other online means of communication. The courts have shown varying degrees of willingness to apply the effects test in the online context.

Panavision International, L.P. v. Toeppen

141 F.3d 1316 (9th Cir.1998).

■ DAVID R. THOMPSON, CIRCUIT JUDGE:

* * * We are asked to apply existing rules of personal jurisdiction to conduct that occurred, in part, in "cyberspace." * * *

* * *

Toeppen appeals. He argues that the district court erred in exercising personal jurisdiction over him because any contact he had with California was insignificant, emanating solely from his registration of domain names on the Internet, which he did in Illinois. * * *

We have jurisdiction under 28 U.S.C. § 1291 and we affirm. The district court's exercise of jurisdiction was proper and comported with the requirements of due process. Toeppen did considerably more than simply register Panavision's trademarks as his domain names on the Internet. He registered those names as part of a scheme to obtain money from Panavision. Pursuant to that scheme, he demanded $13,000 from Panavision to release the domain names to it. His acts were aimed at Panavision in California, and caused it to suffer injury there.

* * *

I

BACKGROUND

[The facts of this case are set forth in Chapter 3, *supra*.]

* * *

II

DISCUSSION

A. *Personal Jurisdiction*

* * *

California's long-arm statute permits a court to exercise personal jurisdiction over a defendant to the extent permitted by the Due Process Clause of the Constitution. * * *

* * *

2. *Specific Jurisdiction*

We apply a three-part test to determine if a district court may exercise specific jurisdiction:

> (1) The nonresident defendant must do some act or consummate some transaction with the forum or perform some act by which he purposefully avails himself of the privilege of conducting activities in the forum, thereby invoking the benefits and protections of its laws; (2) the claim must be one which arises out of or results from the defendant's forum-related activities; and (3) exercise of jurisdiction must be reasonable.

Omeluk v. Langsten Slip & Batbyggeri A/S, 52 F.3d 267, 270 (9th Cir.1995) (quotation omitted).

The first of these requirements is purposeful availment.

a. *Purposeful Availment*

The purposeful availment requirement ensures that a nonresident defendant will not be haled into court based upon "random, fortuitous or attenuated" contacts with the forum state. Burger King Corp. v. Rudzewicz, 471 U.S. 462, 475 (1985). This requirement is satisfied if the defendant "has taken deliberate action" toward the forum state. Ballard v. Savage, 65 F.3d 1495, 1498 (9th Cir.1995). It is not required that a defendant be physically present or have physical contacts with the forum, so long as his efforts are "purposefully directed" toward forum residents. Id.

i. Application to the Internet

Applying principles of personal jurisdiction to conduct in cyberspace is relatively new. "With this global revolution looming on the horizon, the development of the law concerning the permissible scope of personal jurisdiction based on Internet use is in its infant stages. The cases are scant." Zippo Mfg. Co. v. Zippo Dot Com, Inc., 952 F.Supp. 1119, 1123 (W.D.Pa.1997). We have, however, recently addressed the personal availment aspect of personal jurisdiction in a case involving the Internet. See Cybersell, Inc. v. Cybersell, Inc., 130 F.3d 414 (9th Cir.1997).

* * * We held the Arizona court could not exercise personal jurisdiction over Cybersell FL, because it had no contacts with Arizona other than maintaining a web page accessible to anyone over the Internet. Id. at 419–420.

* * *

In the present case, the district court's decision to exercise personal jurisdiction over Toeppen rested on its determination that the purposeful availment requirement was satisfied by the "effects doctrine." That doctrine was not applicable in our Cybersell case. There, we said: "Likewise unpersuasive is Cybersell AZ's reliance on Panavision International v. Toeppen, 938 F.Supp. 616 (C.D.Cal.1996), [the district court's published opinion in this case,] where the court found the 'purposeful availment' prong satisfied by the effects felt in California, the home state of Panavision, from Toeppen's alleged out-of-state scheme to register domain names using the trademarks of California companies, including Panavision, for the purpose of extorting fees from them. Again, there is nothing analogous about Cybersell FL's conduct." Cybersell, 130 F.3d at 420 n. 6.

Our reference in Cybersell to "the effects felt in California" was a reference to the effects doctrine.

ii. The Effects Doctrine

In tort cases, jurisdiction may attach if the defendant's conduct is aimed at or has an effect in the forum state. Ziegler v. Indian River County, 64 F.3d 470, 473 (9th Cir.1995); see Calder v. Jones, 465 U.S. 783 (1984) (establishing an "effects test" for intentional action aimed at the forum state). Under Calder, personal jurisdiction can be based upon: "(1) intentional actions (2) expressly aimed at the forum state (3) causing harm, the brunt of which is suffered—and which the defendant knows is likely to be suffered—in the forum state." Core–Vent Corp. v. Nobel Industries AB, 11 F.3d 1482, 1486 (9th Cir.1993).

As the district court correctly stated, the present case is akin to a tort case. Panavision, 938 F.Supp. at 621; see also Ziegler, 64 F.3d at 473 (application of the purposeful availment prong differs depending on whether the underlying claim is a tort or contract claim). Toeppen purposefully registered Panavision's trademarks as his domain names on the Internet to force Panavision to pay him money. Panavision, 938 F.Supp. at 621. The brunt of the harm to Panavision was felt in California. Toeppen knew Panavision would likely suffer harm there because, although at all relevant times Panavision was a Delaware limited partnership, its principal place of business was in California, and the heart of the theatrical motion picture and television industry is located there. Id. at 621–622.

The harm to Panavision is similar to the harm to the Indianapolis Colts football team in Indianapolis Colts, Inc. v. Metropolitan Baltimore Football Club Ltd. Partnership, 34 F.3d 410 (7th Cir.1994). There, the Indianapolis Colts brought a trademark infringement action in the district court in Indiana against the Canadian Football League's new team, the "Baltimore CFL Colts." Id. at 411. The Seventh Circuit held that the Baltimore CFL Colts team was subject to personal jurisdiction in Indiana even though its only activity directed toward Indiana was the broadcast of its games on nationwide cable television. Id. Because the Indianapolis Colts used their trademarks in Indiana, any infringement of those marks would create an injury which would be felt mainly in Indiana, and this, coupled with the defendant's "entry" into the state by the television broadcasts, was sufficient for the exercise of personal jurisdiction. Id.

Toeppen argues he has not directed any activity toward Panavision in California, much less "entered" the state. He contends that all he did was register Panavision's trademarks on the Internet and post websites using those marks; if this activity injured Panavision, the injury occurred in cyberspace.[2]

We agree that simply registering someone else's trademark as a domain name and posting a website on the Internet is not sufficient to subject a party domiciled in one state to jurisdiction in another. Cybersell, 130 F.3d at 418. As we said in Cybersell, there must be "something more" to demonstrate that the defendant directed his activity toward the forum state. Id. Here, that has been shown. Toeppen engaged in a scheme to register Panavision's trademarks as his domain names for the purpose of extorting money from Panavision. His conduct, as he knew it likely would, had the effect of injuring Panavision in California where Panavision has its principal place of business and where the movie and television industry is centered. Under the "effects test," the purposeful availment requirement necessary for specific, personal jurisdiction is satisfied.

* * *

III

CONCLUSION

Toeppen engaged in a scheme to register Panavision's trademarks as his domain names on the Internet and then to extort money from Panavi-

2. In a subset of this argument, Toeppen contends that a large organization such as Panavision does not suffer injury in one location. See Cybersell, 130 F.3d at 420 (A corporation "does not suffer harm in a particular geographic location in the same sense that an individual does."). However, in Core–Vent, we stated that Calder v. Jones, 465 U.S. 783 (1984), does not preclude a determination that a corporation suffers the brunt of harm in its principal place of business. Core–Vent, 11 F.3d at 1487. Panavision was previously a limited partnership and is now a corporation. Under either form of business organization, however, the brunt of the harm suffered by Panavision was in the state where it maintained its principal place of business, California.

sion by trading on the value of those names. Toeppen's actions were aimed at Panavision in California and the brunt of the harm was felt in California. The district court properly exercised personal jurisdiction over Toeppen.

* * *

[The portion of the court's opinion affirming the district court's summary judgment for Panavision on its trademark dilution claim is reproduced in Chapter 3, Part I(B), *supra*.]

NOTES & QUESTIONS

1. *Relevant conduct*. The effects test is satisfied where defendant's actions are intentional, expressly aimed at the forum state, and result in harm that the defendant knows will be suffered in the forum state. Which of Toeppen's actions are relevant to application of this rule: His registration of domain names corresponding to plaintiff's trademarks? Setting up websites at those domains? Seeking a payment from the plaintiff to relinquish the domain names?

2. *"Something more."* Consider the court's statement: "We agree that simply registering someone else's trademark as a domain name and posting a website on the Internet is not sufficient to subject a party domiciled in one state to jurisdiction in another. * * * As we said in *Cybersell*, there must be 'something more' to demonstrate that the defendant directed his activity toward the forum state." What was the "something more" that the court found dispositive? Requesting payment in exchange for relinquishing the domain name? Is *Panavision* consistent with *Cybersell*?

3. *Improper motivation*. Is the defendant's motivation in registering the domain names relevant to the effects test analysis? To what extent does the decision turn on the court's view that Toeppen's conduct and motivation were reprehensible? Consider the following criticism of *Panavision*:

> Panavision appears to be one of those cases where "hard cases make bad law." * * * Except perhaps in the clearest case of a cybersquatter or where intent is undisputed, this court believes it would be a serious mistake for personal jurisdiction to turn on the issue of the defendant's intent, which itself is a major merits issue. [The district court's decision in] Panavision thus is distinguishable, and to the extent it is not distinguishable, the Court declines to follow it.

Hearst Corp. v. Goldberger, 1997 WL 97097, *19 (S.D.N.Y.1997). Is the criticism valid? What would be the rationale for factoring intent into the analysis "in the clearest case of a cybersquatter or where intent is undisputed"?

Several cases have distinguished *Panavision* on the ground that unlike Toeppen the defendant was not tainted by impure motives. *See K.C.P.L., Inc. v. Nash*, 49 U.S.P.Q.2d (BNA) 1584 (S.D.N.Y.1998) ("the facts alleged do not show [defendant] to be a 'cyber pirate' "); *No Mayo—San Francisco v. Memminger*, 1998 WL 544974 (N.D.Cal.1998) (distinguishing *Panavision*, since defendant was no "cyber pirate").

4. *The requirement of wrongful conduct. Panavision*, quoting *Core-Vent*, characterizes the effects test as requiring "intentional actions" knowingly directed at the plaintiff. Is it a further requirement that those actions be wrongful? In *Bancroft & Masters, Inc. v. Augusta National Inc.*, 223 F.3d 1082 (9th Cir.2000), the plaintiff, a California computer company named Bancroft & Masters, sought a declaratory judgment that its registration and use of masters.com did not infringe defendant's trademark "Masters." The defendant, which sponsored golfing's annual Masters Tournament, had sent a letter to the domain name registrar, Network Solutions, Inc., challenging plaintiff's registration of masters.com, and invoking NSI's dispute-resolution policy. The district court held that it did not have jurisdiction based on the effects test. After noting that *Panavision* involved a purposeful scheme to extort money, it distinguished *Panavision* on the ground that "[n]o such intentional scheme or tortious conduct is alleged in this action." The court of appeals reversed. It explained that the effects test is satisfied "when the defendant is alleged to have engaged in wrongful conduct targeted at a plaintiff whom the defendant knows to be a resident of the forum state." It continued:

> Applying these concepts to the instant case, we conclude that B & M has demonstrated purposeful availment by ANI under the *Calder* effects test. ANI acted intentionally when it sent its letter to NSI. The letter was expressly aimed at California because it individually targeted B & M, a California corporation doing business almost exclusively in California. Finally, the effects of the letter were primarily felt, as ANI knew they would be, in California.
>
> This case resembles *Panavision,* in which an Illinois resident registered as his domain name a California corporation's trademark. Though this activity was conducted outside of California, it was clear that the defendant's deliberate choice of the plaintiff's trademark, and his subsequent attempts to extort compensation for his conveyance of the domain name, targeted that individual plaintiff. *See Panavision,* 141 F.3d at 1321. Here, too, ANI was well aware that B & M currently held the masters.com website and that it was B & M that would be affected if the NSI dispute resolution procedures were triggered. This is sufficient to satisfy *Calder* and thereby demonstrate the purposeful availment necessary for an exercise of specific jurisdiction.

Did the court correctly apply the effects test in this case? What was the wrongful conduct on which jurisdiction was based? Two of the three judges on the panel concurred with this observation:

> The "effects test" has normally been restricted to tortious conduct in which the "aimer" in state Y was seeking to injure wrongfully the target in state X. I concur in the opinion only on the assumption that Augusta National, through its letter to NSI,

> engaged in tortious conduct, i.e., that they intended to effect a conversion of the masters.com domain name.
>
> I am skeptical of Bancroft & Masters's selection of masters.com as its domain name. I suspect that Augusta National's initial reaction was similar. Therefore, I do not find it implausible that Augusta National, through its letter to NSI, merely intended to protect its trademark from dilution and infringement. At this point, however, there is insufficient information with which to make such a judgment. Jurisdiction in California would be ripe for challenge if following the development of trial it should appear that Augusta National acted reasonably and in good faith to protect its trademark against an infringer.

The concurrence seems to suggest that a final determination on jurisdiction should be made once the case has gone to trial. Does this adequately protect the defendant's due process rights? How else might the defendant's motion to dismiss have been handled?

5. *Registration alone.* The *Panavision* court took the position that "simply registering someone else's trademark as a domain name and posting a website on the Internet is not sufficient to subject a party domiciled in one state to jurisdiction in another." In *Ford Motor Co. v. Great Domains, Inc.*, 141 F.Supp.2d 763, 775 n. 2 (E.D.Mich.2001), the court expressed a contrary view:

> Simply registering a domain name that incorporates a trademark can be a violation of the Lanham Act, if done with "bad faith intent to profit from that mark." 15 U.S.C. § 1125(d)(1). Thus, registering a domain name that incorporates a trademark for which only the mark owner could have a legitimate use could be sufficient under *Calder* to support the assertion of personal jurisdiction in the mark owner's place of residence.

Which court got it right? Does the 1999 passage of the Anticybersquatting Consumer Protection Act, 15 U.S.C. § 1125(d)(1), *see* Chapter 3, Part II, *supra*, affect the jurisdictional analysis? Does the approach that *Ford v. Great Domains* proposes amount to a return, under the banner of the effects test, to the extremely liberal approach to website-based jurisdiction exemplified by early cases such as *Inset Systems, Inc. v. Instruction Set, Inc.*, 937 F.Supp. 161 (D.Conn.1996), and *Maritz, Inc. v. Cybergold, Inc.*, 947 F.Supp. 1328 (E.D.Mo.1996), discussed in Part II(A)(2), *supra*?

6. *Other cases.* The effects test has been held to justify jurisdiction in other cases involving infringement of intellectual property rights. *See PurCo Fleet Services, Inc. v. Towers,* 38 F.Supp.2d 1320 (D.Utah 1999) (defendant registered domain name corresponding to plaintiff's trademark, and set up website that forwarded visitors to its own site); *3DO Co. v. Poptop Software Inc.*, 49 U.S.P.Q.2d (BNA) 1469 (N.D.Cal.1998) (defendant's website allowed visitors to download software that allegedly infringed plaintiff's copyright and misappropriated plaintiff's trade secrets); *Bunn–O–Matic Corp. v. Bunn Coffee Service, Inc.*, 46 U.S.P.Q.2d (BNA)

1375 (C.D.Ill.1998) (defendant's website included terms that allegedly infringed plaintiff's trademarks); *Digital Equipment Corp. v. AltaVista Technology, Inc.*, 960 F.Supp. 456 (D.Mass.1997) (same).

The effects test has also been found applicable in cases alleging defamation claims. *See Bochan v. La Fontaine*, 68 F.Supp.2d 692 (E.D.Va. 1999) (defendant posted allegedly defamatory statements in an Internet newsgroup, knowing that the victim of the defamation was a resident of the forum state); *EDIAS Software Int'l, L.L.C. v. BASIS Int'l Ltd.*, 947 F.Supp. 413 (D.Ariz.1996) (defendant made allegedly defamatory statements via e-mail, on a website, and in a CompuServe forum); *California Software Inc. v. Reliability Research, Inc.*, 631 F.Supp. 1356 (C.D.Cal.1986) (defendant posted an allegedly defamatory statement on a proprietary bulletin board system).

7. *Scope of the effects test.* Courts have limited the scope of the effects test when applied to online conduct in several ways.

a. First, some courts have held that the test may not be applicable where the plaintiff is a corporation. Thus, in *Cybersell, Inc. v. Cybersell, Inc.*, 130 F.3d 414 (9th Cir.1997), discussed in Part II(A)(2), *supra*, the court found the effects test inapplicable, stating: "Nor does the 'effects' test apply with the same force to [the defendant corporation] as it would to an individual, because a corporation 'does not suffer harm in a particular geographic location in the same sense that an individual does.'" *Id.* at 420 (quoting *Core-Vent Corp. v. Nobel Industries AB*, 11 F.3d 1482, 1486 (9th Cir.1993)). To the same effect is *Conseco, Inc. v. Hickerson*, 698 N.E.2d 816 (Ind.App.1998) (following *Cybersell*). But in *Panavision*, decided only four months after *Cybersell*, the Ninth Circuit stated: "Panavision was previously a limited partnership and is now a corporation. Under either form of business organization, however, the brunt of the harm suffered by Panavision was in the state where it maintained its principal place of business, California." 141 F.3d at 1322 n. 2. The plaintiff in *Cybersell* was an Arizona corporation, with its principal place of business apparently in Arizona. Is *Panavision* inconsistent with *Cybersell* on this point?

b. Second, the effects test is applicable only if the defendant intentionally directs his conduct at a party that he knows to be located in the forum state. This factor will be absent from cases involving trademark infringement if each party innocently began using a mark and only later became aware of use of the mark by the other party. In *Millennium Enterprises, Inc. v. Millennium Music*, LP, 33 F.Supp.2d 907 (D.Or.1999), plaintiff operated music stores in Oregon under the name "Music Millennium," and defendant operated music stores in South Carolina under the name "Millennium Music." The parties and their trademarks collided only when they began selling goods via the Web. The court refused to apply the effects test, since there was "no evidence that defendants targeted Oregon residents with the intent or knowledge that plaintiff could be harmed through their Web site." (Why would applicability of the effects test depend on whether defendant targeted Oregon residents? Wouldn't it be enough if defendant intentionally made use of plaintiff's trademark in order to divert Web-based sales away from plaintiff?)

c. Likewise, when the conduct allegedly giving rise to liability is negligent or inadvertent, the effects test's requirement of intentional tortious conduct is not satisfied. For example, copyright infringement is a strict-liability offense: an infringement of the copyright owner's rights is actionable even if the infringement is unintentional. As one court noted, this means that "[a]lthough the distinction between negligent and intentional infringement is irrelevant for purposes of [copyright] liability, * * * it is dispositive in the *Calder* 'effects' analysis." *CoStar Group, Inc. v. LoopNet, Inc.*, 106 F.Supp.2d 780, 787 (D.Md.2000).

d. Some district courts have limited the applicability of the effects test when the plaintiff is an individual with a national reputation. In *Barrett v. Catacombs Press*, 44 F.Supp.2d 717 (E.D.Pa.1999), plaintiff, an individual residing in Pennsylvania, sued an individual residing in Oregon, based on allegedly defamatory statements that she posted on two websites that she operated, and on listservs and newsgroups. Plaintiff, a psychiatrist, operated a website called Quackwatch, which posted extensive information concerning health frauds and quackery. According to the court, the defendant "is closely associated with individuals who are interested in advocating against the fluoridation of water sources throughout the United States." The alleged defamation related to that issue. The court credited evidence that by virtue of his efforts at exposing health fraud plaintiff was "clearly a national, if not international, figure." It declined to find jurisdiction based on the effects test, explaining:

> All these defamatory statements associate Plaintiff with his work associated with the Quackwatch Web site and none as a psychiatrist practicing in Pennsylvania. Under the "effects test" of Calder, we do not find that such defamatory statements amount to actions "expressly aimed" at Pennsylvania [citing *Calder*]. If anything, the defamatory statements concern the Plaintiff's non-Pennsylvania activities and impugn his professionalism as a nationally-recognized consumer health advocate.
>
> Yet Plaintiff, without any evidentiary support, maintains that the brunt of the harm from such defamatory statements was suffered in Pennsylvania, which is the focal point of his professional and personal life. It is certainly foreseeable that some of the harm would be felt in Pennsylvania because Plaintiff lives and works there, but such foreseeability is not sufficient for an assertion of jurisdiction. * * * While we agree that Pennsylvania residents are among the recipients or viewers of such defamatory statements, they are but a fraction of

> other worldwide Internet users who have received or viewed such statements.

Id. at 731. The court apparently assumed that the harm from defamation is suffered where it is published, rather than where the victim is located. To the same effect are *Revell v. Lidov*, 2001 WL 285253 (N.D.Tex.2001) and *Bailey v. Turbine Design, Inc.*, 86 F.Supp.2d 790 (W.D.Tenn.2000). Are these cases consistent with *Calder*?

2. AN INTERNATIONAL APPLICATION OF THE EFFECTS TEST

Special issues may arise when the defendant resides outside the United States. Consider *Yahoo! Inc. v. La Ligue Contre Le Racisme Et L'Antisemitisme*, 145 F.Supp.2d 1168 (N.D.Cal.2001). (The background of this case is described more fully in Chapter 1, *supra*.) The defendant, LICRA, had sued Yahoo! in a French court, and obtained an order requiring Yahoo! to prevent citizens of France from accessing those portions of its websites containing Nazi-related materials. Yahoo! then brought an action against LICRA in the federal district court for the district in which Yahoo!'s headquarters was located, seeking a declaratory judgment stating that the French order was not enforceable in the United States. LICRA moved to dismiss, arguing that the court did not have jurisdiction over it. The court held that it had jurisdiction under the effects test. Relying on *Bancroft & Masters, Inc. v. Augusta National, Inc.*, 223 F.3d 1082 (9th Cir.2000), the court said that the effects test was met if the defendant "engaged in wrongful conduct targeted at a plaintiff whom the defendant knows to be a resident of the forum state." The court continued:

> This Court concludes that Yahoo! has made a sufficient prima facie showing of purposeful availment under the effects test. Yahoo! alleges that Defendants knowingly have engaged in actions intentionally targeted at its Santa Clara headquarters for the express purpose of causing the consequences of such actions to be felt in California, including 1) LICRA's "cease and desist" letter to Yahoo!'s Santa Clara headquarters; 2) Defendants' request of the French Court that Yahoo! be required to perform specific physical acts in Santa Clara (*e.g.*, re-engineering of its Santa Clara-based servers); and 3) Defendants' utilization of United States Marshals to effect service of process on Yahoo! in California. Yahoo! further alleges that the conscious intent of these actions was to compel it to censor "constitutionally protected content on its U.S.-based Internet services."

While recognizing that all previous Ninth Circuit cases finding jurisdiction under the effects test had involved conduct by the defendant that was tortious, the court found that it was sufficient if the conduct was "wrongful."

> While filing a lawsuit in a foreign jurisdiction may be entirely proper under the laws of that jurisdiction, such an act nonetheless may be "wrongful" from the standpoint of a court in the United

States if its primary purpose or intended effect is to deprive a United States resident of its constitutional rights. * * * Proper application of the test thus appears to require consideration not only of the nature of the defendant's conduct (i.e., whether conduct is wrongful or tortious) but also of whether there is "express aiming" of the conduct, i.e., targeting of a forum resident. * * * The focus on evidence of "express aiming" reflects the basic rationale of the effects test in that it assures that a defendant is on notice that it may be subject to suit in the forum state with respect to its forum-related or targeted activities. * * * In the present case, Yahoo! has alleged with particularity that Defendants "purposefully targeted" its Santa Clara headquarters and thus reasonably could have expected to be haled into a California forum in order to defend the Order they obtained from the French Court.

The court then addressed the international aspects of the case:

The Court is especially mindful that "[g]reat care and reserve should be exercised when extending our notions of personal jurisdiction into the international field." * * * Accordingly, the Court looks to the Restatement (Third) of Foreign Relations Law § 101 *et al.* (1987) ("Restatement"), which articulates the limitations imposed by international law upon courts determining whether or not to exercise personal jurisdiction over a foreign defendant. Although the Restatement is not binding authority, it does provide valuable guidance. Adopting in essence a broad version of the effects test, the Restatement concludes that a court may exercise jurisdiction over a person "if at the time jurisdiction is asserted . . . the person, whether natural or judicial, had carried on outside the state an activity having a substantial, direct, and foreseeable effect within the state, but only in respect to such activity." *Restatement (Third) of Foreign Relations Law* § 421(2)(j); *see also id.,* §§ 402(c), 403(2)(a). * * *

The final requirement for specific jurisdiction is that the exercise of jurisdiction be reasonable. For the exercise of jurisdiction to be reasonable it must comport with fair play and substantial justice. * * * "The reasonableness determination requires the consideration of several specific factors [including] * * * (3) the extent of the conflict with the sovereignty of the defendant's state * * *. Generally, as just noted, a plaintiff seeking to hale a foreign defendant into court in the United States must meet a "higher jurisdictional threshold" than is required when a defendant is United States resident. *See Core–Vent Corp.,* 11 F.3d at 1484. However, since sovereignty concerns inevitably arise whenever a United States court exercises jurisdiction over a foreign national, this factor is "by no means controlling," *Ballard,* 65 F.3d at 1501; otherwise "it would always prevent suit against a foreign national in a United States court." *Gates Learjet Corp. v. Jensen,* 743 F.2d 1325, 1333 (9th Cir.1984). The instant action involves only the limited question of whether this Court should recognize and enforce a French Order which requires Yahoo! to censor its U.S.-based services to conform to French penal law. While this Court must and does accord great respect and deference to France's sovereign interest in enforcing the orders and judgments of its courts, this interest must be weighed against the United States' own sovereign interest in protecting the constitutional and statutory rights of its residents. *See, e.g., Bachchan v. India Abroad Publications Inc.*, 154 Misc.2d 228, 585 N.Y.S.2d 661, 665 (1992) (English libel judgment unenforceable because it was "antithetical to the protections afforded the press by the U.S. Constitution"); *Matusevitch v. Telnikoff*, 877 F.Supp. 1 (D.D.C.1995) (granting summary judgment in favor of plaintiff seeking declaration that English libel judgment was not enforceable in U.S. because the judgment was "contrary to U.S. libel standards"); Cal.Civ.Proc. Code § 1713.4(b)(3) (court need not recognize foreign money judgment based on cause of action repugnant to public policy of state). For purposes of its jurisdictional analysis, this Court concludes that the sovereignty factor weighs in favor of this Court's exercise of personal jurisdiction.

NOTES & QUESTIONS

Bringing an action in a foreign court. Is the court's application of the effects test to this situation justified? Does bringing an action against a U.S. company in a foreign court amount to a contact with the state in which the company is headquartered that is sufficient for purposes of the "minimum contacts" test? Is this court's distinction between conduct that is tortious and conduct that is merely "wrongful" coherent? Should bringing an action in a foreign court be considered wrongful if the resulting judgment could be contrary to U.S. law or public policy? Does the court offer a workable standard for assessing the strength of the sovereignty interests that are implicated?

C. ENTERING INTO COMMERCIAL TRANSACTIONS VIA ONLINE COMMUNICATIONS

The fact that the defendant has entered into contracts or had other commercial dealings with residents of the forum state may supply the "minimum contacts" necessary for assertion of jurisdiction to comport with the requirements of due process. This rule is the basis for the "jurisdiction exists" category of the taxonomy of websites described in *Zippo Mfg. Co. v. Zippo Dot Com, Inc.*, 952 F.Supp. 1119, 1124 (W.D.Pa.1997), discussed in Part II(A)(1), *supra*: "If the defendant enters into contracts with residents of a foreign jurisdiction that involve the knowing and repeated transmission of computer files over the Internet, personal jurisdiction is proper." The high-water mark for application of the rule came in *McGee v. International Life Insurance Co.*, 355 U.S. 220 (1957), where the Supreme Court upheld jurisdiction by a California court over an insurance company defendant with its principal place of business in Texas, on the basis of a single contract of insurance that the company had with a resident of California. The Court found that the contract had the requisite "substantial connection with" California, since "[t]he contract was delivered in California, the premiums were mailed from there and the insured was a resident of that State when he died." *Id.* at 223. Commenting on the trend, during the preceding 80 years, "toward expanding the permissible scope of state jurisdiction over foreign corporations and other nonresidents," the Court observed:

> In part this is attributable to the fundamental transformation of our national economy over the years. Today many commercial transactions touch two or more States and may involve parties separated by the full continent. With this increasing nationalization of commerce has come a great increase in the amount of business conducted by mail across state lines. At the same time modern transportation and communications have made it much less burdensome for a party sued to defend himself in a State where he engages in economic activity.

Id. at 222–23. That was in 1957. During the intervening 45 years, the advent of communication via low-cost long-distance telephone service, telecopier, and e-mail, improvements in modes of transportation, and increased nationalization and globalization of commerce have accelerated the trend that the Court noted. Still, the Court continues to reject the view that "an individual's contract with an out-of-state party *alone* can automatically establish sufficient minimum contacts in the other party's home forum." *Burger King Corp. v. Rudzewicz*, 471 U.S. 462 (1985). It has instead

> emphasized the need for a "highly realistic" approach that recognizes that a "contract" is "ordinarily but an intermediate step serving to tie up prior business negotiations with future consequences which themselves are the real object of the business transaction." * * * It is these factors—prior negotiations and contemplated future consequences, along with the terms of the contract and the parties' actual course of dealing—that must be evaluated in determining whether the defendant purposefully established minimum contacts within the forum.

Id. at 479.

CompuServe, Inc. v. Patterson

89 F.3d 1257 (6th Cir.1996).

■ BAILEY BROWN, CIRCUIT JUDGE.

In a case that requires us to consider the scope of the federal courts' jurisdictional powers in a new context, a computer network giant, CompuServe, appeals the dismissal, for lack of personal jurisdiction, of its complaint in which it sought a declaratory judgment that it had not infringed on the defendants' common law copyrights or otherwise engaged in unfair competition. The district court held that the electronic links between the defendant Patterson, who is a Texan, and Ohio, where CompuServe is headquartered, were "too tenuous to support the exercise of personal jurisdiction." The district court also denied CompuServe's motion for reconsideration. Because we believe that CompuServe made a prima facie showing that the defendant's contacts with Ohio were sufficient to support the exercise of personal jurisdiction, we REVERSE the district court's dismissal and REMAND this case for further proceedings consistent with this opinion.

I. BACKGROUND

CompuServe is a computer information service headquartered in Columbus, Ohio. It contracts with individual subscribers, such as the defendant, to provide, inter alia, access to computing and information services via the Internet, and it is the second largest such provider currently operating on the so-called "information super highway." A CompuServe subscriber may use the service to gain electronic access to more than 1700 information services.

CompuServe also operates as an electronic conduit to provide its subscribers computer software products, which may originate either from CompuServe itself or from other parties. Computer software generated and distributed in this manner is, according to CompuServe, often referred to as "shareware." Shareware makes money only through the voluntary compliance of an "end user," that is, another CompuServe subscriber who may or may not pay the creator's suggested licensing fee if she uses the software beyond a specified trial period. The "end user" pays that fee directly to CompuServe in Ohio, and CompuServe takes a 15% fee for its trouble before remitting the balance to the shareware's creator.

Defendant, Richard Patterson, is an attorney and a resident of Houston, Texas who claims never to have visited Ohio. Patterson also does business as FlashPoint Development. He subscribed to CompuServe, and he also placed items of "shareware" on the CompuServe system for others to use and purchase. When he became a shareware "provider," Patterson entered into a "Shareware Registration Agreement" ("SRA") with CompuServe. Under the SRA, CompuServe provides its subscribers with access to the software, or shareware, that Patterson creates. The SRA purports to create an independent contractor relationship between Patterson and CompuServe, whereby Patterson may place software of his creation on CompuServe's system. The SRA does not mention Patterson's software by name; in fact, it leaves the content and identification of that software to Patterson.

The SRA incorporates by reference two other documents: the CompuServe Service Agreement ("Service Agreement") and the Rules of Operation, both of which are published on the CompuServe Information Service. Both the SRA and the Service Agreement expressly provide that they are entered into in Ohio, and the Service Agreement further provides that it is to "be governed by and construed in accordance with" Ohio law. These documents appear to be standardized and entirely the product of CompuServe. It bears noting, however, that the SRA asks a new shareware "provider" like Patterson to type "AGREE" at various points in the document, "[i]n recognition of your on line agreement to all the above terms and conditions." Thus, Patterson's assent to the SRA was first manifested at his own computer in Texas, then transmitted to the CompuServe computer system in Ohio.

From 1991 through 1994, Patterson electronically transmitted 32 master software files to CompuServe. These files were stored in CompuServe's system in Ohio, and they were displayed in different services for CompuServe subscribers, who could "download" them into their own computers and, if they chose to do so, pay for them. Patterson also advertised his software on the CompuServe system, and he indicated a price term in at least one of his advertisements. CompuServe asserts that Patterson marketed his software exclusively on its system. Patterson, for his part, stated that he has sold less than $650 worth of his software to only 12 Ohio residents via CompuServe.

Patterson's software product was, apparently, a program designed to help people navigate their way around the larger Internet network. CompuServe began to market a similar product, however, with markings and names that Patterson took to be too similar to his own. Thus, in December of 1993, Patterson notified CompuServe (appropriately via an electronic mail or "E-mail" message) that the terms "WinNAV," "Windows Navigator," and "FlashPoint Windows Navigator" were common law trademarks which he and his company owned. Patterson stated that CompuServe's marketing of its product infringed these trademarks, and otherwise constituted deceptive trade practices. CompuServe changed the name of its program, but Patterson continued to complain. CompuServe asserts that, if Patterson's allegations of trademark infringement are correct, they threaten CompuServe's software sales revenue with a loss of approximately $10.8 million.

After Patterson demanded at least $100,000 to settle his potential claims, CompuServe filed this declaratory judgment action in the federal district court for the Southern District of Ohio, relying on the court's diversity subject matter jurisdiction. CompuServe sought, among other things, a declaration that it had not infringed any common law trademarks of Patterson or FlashPoint Development, and that it was not otherwise guilty of unfair or deceptive trade practices. Patterson responded pro se with a consolidated motion to dismiss on several grounds, including lack of personal jurisdiction. Patterson also submitted a supporting affidavit, in which he denied many jurisdictional facts, including his having ever visited Ohio. CompuServe then filed a memorandum in opposition to Patterson's consolidated motion, along with several supporting exhibits.

The district court, considering only these pleadings and papers, granted Patterson's motion to dismiss for lack of personal jurisdiction in a thorough and thoughtful opinion. * * *

II. ANALYSIS

* * *

B. Personal Jurisdiction.

This case presents a novel question of first impression: Did CompuServe make a prima facie showing that Patterson's contacts with Ohio, which have been almost entirely electronic in nature, are sufficient, under the Due Process Clause, to support the district court's exercise of personal jurisdiction over him?

The Supreme Court has noted, on more than one occasion, the confluence of the "increasing nationalization of commerce" and "modern transportation and communication," and the resulting relaxation of the limits that the Due Process Clause imposes on courts' jurisdiction. E.g., World–Wide Volkswagen Corp. v. Woodson, 444 U.S. 286, 293 (1980) (quoting McGee v. International Life Ins. Co., 355 U.S. 220, 223 (1957)). Simply stated, there is less perceived need today for the federal constitution to protect defendants from "inconvenient litigation," because all but the most remote forums are easily accessible for the pursuit of both business and litigation. Id. The Court has also, however, reminded us that the due process rights of a defendant should be the courts' primary concern where personal jurisdiction is at issue. Insurance Corp. v. Compagnie des Bauxites de Guinee, 456 U.S. 694, 702 n. 10 (1982).

The Internet represents perhaps the latest and greatest manifestation of these historical, globe-shrinking trends. It enables anyone with the right equipment and knowledge—that is, people like Patterson—to operate an international business cheaply, and from a desktop. That business operator, however, remains entitled to the protection of the Due Process Clause, which mandates that potential defendants be able "to structure their primary conduct with some minimum assurance as to where the conduct will and will not render them liable to suit." World–Wide Volkswagen, 444 U.S. at 297. Thus, this case presents a situation where we must reconsider the scope of our jurisdictional reach.

* * *

The Ohio long-arm statute allows an Ohio court to exercise personal jurisdiction over nonresidents of Ohio on claims arising from, inter alia, the nonresident's transacting any business in Ohio. Ohio Rev. Code Ann. § 2307.382(A) (Anderson 1995). It is settled Ohio law, moreover, that the "transacting business" clause of that statute was meant to extend to the federal constitutional limits of due process, and that as a result Ohio personal jurisdiction cases require an examination of those limits. * * *

Further, personal jurisdiction may be either general or specific in nature, depending on the nature of the contacts in a given case. * * * In the instant case, because CompuServe bases its action on Patterson's act of sending his computer software to Ohio for sale on its service, CompuServe seeks to establish such specific personal jurisdiction over Patterson. Id.

As always in this context, the crucial federal constitutional inquiry is whether, given the facts of the case, the nonresident defendant has sufficient contacts with the forum state that the district court's exercise of jurisdiction would comport with "traditional notions of fair play and substantial justice." International Shoe Co. v. Washington, 326 U.S. 310, 316 (1945) (quoting Milliken v. Meyer, 311 U.S. 457, 463 (1940)); Reynolds, 23 F.3d at 1116; Theunissen, 935 F.2d at 1459. This court has repeatedly employed three criteria to make this determination:

> First, the defendant must purposefully avail himself of the privilege of acting in the forum state or causing a consequence in the forum state. Second, the cause of action must arise from the defendant's activities there. Finally, the acts of the defendant or consequences caused by the defendant must have a substantial enough connection with the forum to make the exercise of jurisdiction over the defendant reasonable.

Reynolds, 23 F.3d at 1116 (quoting In–Flight Devices, 466 F.2d at 226); see also Southern Mach. Co. v. Mohasco Indus., 401 F.2d 374, 381 (6th Cir.1968) (adopting the above test for "determining the present outer limits of in personam jurisdiction based on a single act").

We conclude that Patterson has knowingly made an effort—and, in fact, purposefully contracted—to market a product in other states, with Ohio-based CompuServe operating, in effect, as his distribution center. Thus, it is reasonable to subject Patterson to suit in Ohio, the state which is home to the computer network service he chose to employ.

To support this conclusion, we will address each of the above three criteria seriatim, bearing in mind that (1) CompuServe need only make a prima facie case of personal jurisdiction, and (2) we cannot weigh Patterson's affidavit in the analysis, given that the district court addressed his motion to dismiss without holding an evidentiary hearing. Theunissen, 935 F.2d at 1459.

1. The "purposeful availment" requirement.

* * *

There is no question that Patterson himself took actions that created a connection with Ohio in the instant case. He subscribed to CompuServe, and then he entered into the Shareware Registration Agreement when he loaded his software onto the CompuServe system for others to use and, perhaps, purchase. Once Patterson had done those two things, he was on notice that he had made contracts, to be governed by Ohio law, with an Ohio-based company. Then, he repeatedly sent his computer software, via electronic links, to the CompuServe system in Ohio, and he advertised that software on the CompuServe system. Moreover, he initiated the events that led to the filing of this suit by making demands of CompuServe via electronic and regular mail messages.

The real question is whether these connections with Ohio are "substantial" enough that Patterson should reasonably have anticipated being haled into an Ohio court. The district court did not think so. It looked to "cases involving interstate business negotiations and relationships" and held that the relationship between CompuServe and Patterson, because it was marked by a "minimal course of dealing," was insufficient to satisfy the purposeful availment test. Compare Reynolds, 23 F.3d at 1118–21 (holding that the contacts between an England-based association and an Ohio plaintiff in a contract case were "superficial" where, although mail and telephone communications had taken place, the parties had engaged in no prior negotiations and expected no future consequences) and Health Communications, Inc. v. Mariner Corp., 860 F.2d 460, 463–65 (D.C.Cir. 1988) (finding no jurisdiction over a nonresident purchaser who had bought services from a corporation in the forum state) with Burger King Corp., 471 U.S. at 479–82 (finding significant the defendant's reaching beyond Michigan to negotiate with a Florida corporation for the purchase of a long-term franchise). The district court deemed this case closer to Reynolds and Health Communications than to Burger King Corp., and thus it found no purposeful availment on the part of Patterson.

We disagree. The contract cases upon which the district court relied are both distinguishable in important ways. Patterson, unlike the nonresident defendant in Reynolds, entered into a written contract with CompuServe which provided for the application of Ohio law, and he then purposefully perpetuated the relationship with CompuServe via repeated communications with its system in Ohio. And, unlike the nonresident defendant in Health Communications, Patterson was far more than a purchaser of services; he was a third-party provider of software who used CompuServe, which is located in Columbus, to market his wares in Ohio and elsewhere.

In fact, it is Patterson's relationship with CompuServe as a software provider and marketer that is crucial to this case. The district court's analysis misses the mark because it disregards the most salient facts of that relationship: that Patterson chose to transmit his software from Texas to CompuServe's system in Ohio, that myriad others gained access to Patterson's software via that system, and that Patterson advertised and sold his product through that system. Though all this happened with a distinct paucity of tangible, physical evidence, there can be no doubt that Patterson purposefully transacted business in Ohio. See Plus System, Inc. v. New England Network, Inc., 804 F.Supp. 111, 118–19 (D.Colo.1992) (finding personal jurisdiction over a nonresident computer network defendant because, inter alia, that defendant benefitted from the intangible computer services provided by the plaintiff's own computer network system); cf. United States v. Thomas, 74 F.3d 701, 706–07 (6th Cir.1996) (upholding a conviction under federal obscenity laws where the defendants transmitted computer-generated images across state lines, despite the defendants' argument that the images were intangible), petition for cert. filed, 64 U.S.L.W. 3839 (U.S. June 10, 1996) (No. 95–1992).

Moreover, this was a relationship intended to be ongoing in nature; it was not a "one-shot affair." Mohasco Indus., 401 F.2d at 385. Patterson sent software to CompuServe repeatedly for some three years, and the record indicates that he intended to continue marketing his software on CompuServe. As this court has often stated,

> [B]usiness is transacted in a state when obligations created by the defendant or business operations set in motion by the defendant have a realistic impact on the commerce of that state; and the defendant has purposefully availed himself of the opportunity of acting there if he should have reasonably foreseen that the transaction would have consequences in that state.

Id. at 382–83 (footnote omitted). Patterson deliberately set in motion an ongoing marketing relationship with CompuServe, and he should have reasonably foreseen that doing so would have consequences in Ohio.

Admittedly, merely entering into a contract with CompuServe would not, without more, establish that Patterson had minimum contacts with Ohio. Burger King Corp., 471 U.S. at 478. By the same token, Patterson's injection of his software product into the stream of commerce, without more, would be at best a dubious ground for jurisdiction. Compare Asahi Metal Indus. Co. v. Superior Court, 480 U.S. 102 (1987) (O'Connor, J.) (plurality op.) ("The placement of a product into the stream of commerce, without more, is not an act of the defendant purposefully directed toward the forum State.") with id. at 117 (Brennan, J., concurring in part) (rejecting the plurality's position on the stream of commerce theory). Because Patterson deliberately did both of those things, however, and because of the other factors that we discuss herein, we believe that ample contacts exist to support the assertion of jurisdiction in this case, and certainly an assertion of jurisdiction by the state where the computer network service in question is headquartered.

We find support for our conclusion in the Ohio Supreme Court case of U.S. Sprint Communications Co. Limited Partnership v. Mr. K's Foods, Inc., 68 Ohio St.3d 181, 624 N.E.2d 1048, 1052–54 (1994). In that case, the court held that a foreign corporation "transacted business" in Ohio, and thus was subject to personal jurisdiction, where it frequently made long-distance telephone calls to Ohio to sell its products, had distribution facilities in Ohio for its products, and shipped goods to Ohio for ultimate sale. Similarly, Patterson frequently contacted Ohio to sell his computer software over CompuServe's Ohio-based system. Patterson repeatedly sent his "goods" to CompuServe in Ohio for their ultimate sale. CompuServe, in effect, acted as Patterson's distributor, albeit electronically and not physically.

Further, we must reject the district court's reliance on the de minimis amount of software sales which Patterson claims he enjoyed in Ohio. As this court recently stated, "It is the '*quality*' of [the] contacts," and not their number or status, that determines whether they amount to purposeful availment. Reynolds, 23 F.3d at 1119 (emphasis added) (quoting LAK, Inc. v. Deer Creek Enters., 885 F.2d 1293, 1301 (6th Cir.1989), *cert. denied*,

494 U.S. 1056 (1990)). Patterson's contacts with CompuServe here were deliberate and repeated, even if they yielded little revenue from Ohio itself.

Moreover, we should not focus solely on the sales that Patterson made in Ohio, because that ignores the sales Patterson may have made through CompuServe to others elsewhere. Patterson sought to make those sales from Texas by way of CompuServe's system in Ohio, and the sales then involved the passage of funds through Ohio to Patterson in Texas. This case is thus analogous to the Mohasco Industries case, 401 F.2d at 383–86, where this court held that jurisdiction was proper where a nonresident defendant both (a) entered a licensing contract for the plaintiff to manufacture and sell equipment in the forum state, and (b) contemplated the ongoing marketing of that equipment in the forum state and elsewhere.

We also find instructive the Supreme Court case of McGee v. International Life Insurance Co., 355 U.S. 220 (1957), which held that due process did not prohibit California from asserting jurisdiction over a Texas insurance company based upon its issuance of a single insurance contract in California and the receipt of premium payments mailed from California. The McGee Court reasoned that (1) the company had consciously sought the contract with the California insured, and (2) "the suit was based on a contract which had substantial connection with that State." Id. at 223.

Similarly, in the instant case, Patterson consciously reached out from Texas to Ohio to subscribe to CompuServe, and to use its service to market his computer software on the Internet. He entered into a contract which expressly stated that it would be governed by and construed in light of Ohio law. Ohio has written and interpreted its long-arm statute, and particularly its "transacting business" subsection, with the intent of reaching as far as the Due Process Clause will allow, and it certainly has an interest "in providing effective means of redress for its residents." Id. As the Burger King Corp. Court noted, the purposeful direction of one's activities toward a state has always been significant in personal jurisdiction cases, particularly where individuals purposefully derive benefits from interstate activities. Burger King Corp., 471 U.S. at 472–73. Moreover, the Court continued, it could be unfair to allow individuals who purposefully engage in interstate activities for profit to escape having to account in other states for the proximate consequences of those activities. Id. (citing Kulko v. Superior Court, 436 U.S. 84, 96 (1978)).

Finally, we note this court's own finding of purposeful availment based (in part) on analogous litigation threats in American Greetings Corp. v. Cohn, 839 F.2d 1164, 1170 (6th Cir.1988). The American Greetings Corp. case involved an Ohio corporation's suit, in Ohio, against a California shareholder who had threatened to file a lawsuit to invalidate an amendment to the company's articles of incorporation. Id. at 1165. The district court dismissed the case, without conducting an evidentiary hearing, for lack of personal jurisdiction, finding that the defendant merely owned stock in an Ohio company and expressed strong reservations about a matter of shareholder interest. Id. at 1166. This court reversed, finding purposeful availment because of the defendant's letters and telephone calls to Ohio, in which he had threatened suit and had sought money to release his claim. Thus, this court stated, the defendant himself had "originated and maintained the required contacts with Ohio." Id. at 1170.

In the instant case, the record demonstrates that Patterson not only purposefully availed himself of CompuServe's Ohio-based services to market his software, but that he also "originated and maintained" contacts with Ohio when he believed that CompuServe's competing product unlawfully infringed on his own software. Patterson repeatedly sent both electronic and regular mail messages to CompuServe about his claim, and he posted a message on one of CompuServe's electronic forums, which outlined his case against CompuServe for anyone who wished to read it. Moreover, the record shows that Patterson demanded at least $100,000 to settle the matter.

Thus, we believe that the facts which CompuServe has alleged, viewed in the light most favorable to CompuServe, support a finding that Patterson purposefully availed himself of the privilege of doing business in Ohio. He knowingly reached out to CompuServe's Ohio home, and he benefitted from CompuServe's handling of his software and the fees that it generated.

* * *

Finally, because of the unique nature of this case, we deem it important to note what we do not hold. We need not and do not hold that Patterson would be subject to suit in any state where his software was purchased or used; that is not the case before us. See World–Wide Volkswagen, 444 U.S. at 296 (rejecting the idea that a seller of chattels could "appoint the chattel his agent for service of process"). We also do not have before us an attempt by another party from a third state to sue Patterson in Ohio for, say, a "computer virus" caused by his software, and thus we need not address whether personal jurisdiction could be found on those facts. Finally, we need not and do not hold that CompuServe may, as the district court posited, sue any regular subscriber to its service for nonpayment in Ohio, even if the subscriber is a native Alaskan who has never left home. Each of those cases may well arise someday, but they are not before us now.

III. CONCLUSION

Because we believe that Patterson had sufficient contacts with Ohio to support the exercise of personal jurisdiction over him, we REVERSE the district court's dismissal and REMAND this case for further proceedings consistent with this opinion.

NOTES & QUESTIONS

1. *Multiple factors*. The court did not base its decision on the existence of a contract alone, since "merely entering into a contract with CompuServe would not, without more, establish that Patterson had minimum contacts with Ohio." It found that jurisdiction was justified based on a combination of factors: Patterson (1) subscribed to CompuServe, (2) entered into the

Shareware Registration Agreement, which stated that disputes would be governed by Ohio law, (3) repeatedly sent his software to CompuServe via online means, (4) advertised and made his software available for download on CompuServe's system, (5) received revenues from sales of the software via CompuServe, less a 15% fee, (6) threatened to sue CompuServe for trademark infringement and demanded $100,000 to settle his claims, and (7) made actual sales of his software through this arrangement, to people living in Ohio and elsewhere. Which, if any, of these factors was essential to the court's decision? How much guidance does the decision offer in resolving future cases?

2. *Glosses on* CompuServe. Courts have cited *CompuServe* for a variety of propositions. E.g.,

- "If the defendant enters into contracts with residents of a foreign jurisdiction that involve the knowing and repeated transmission of computer files over the Internet, personal jurisdiction is proper." *Zippo Mfg. Co. v. Zippo Dot Com*, Inc., 952 F.Supp. 1119, 1124 (W.D.Pa.1997).
- "[C]ourts generally have exercised jurisdiction * * * where the defendant 'conducted business' over the Internet by engaging in repeated or ongoing business transactions with forum residents or by entering into a contract with the plaintiff through the Internet." *Millennium Enterprises, Inc. v. Millennium Music, LP*, 33 F. Supp. 2d 907, 916 (D.Or.1999).
- "Personal jurisdiction can be exercised over a defendant which maintains an Internet site where customers can transact business." *Decker v. Circus Circus Hotel*, 49 F.Supp.2d 743, 747–48 (D.N.J. 1999).
- "[I]nternet use and entering into contract satisfies purpose [sic] availment requirement." *Bush v. Tidewater Marine Alaska, Inc.*, 1998 WL 560048, *4 n. 3 (E.D.Tex.1998).
- "[I]nternet web site plus entering into a contract in the forum satisfied purposeful availment requirement." *Fix My PC, L.L.C. v. N.F.N. Associates*, Inc., 48 F.Supp.2d 640, 643 (N.D.Tex.1999).
- "If the defendant enters into contracts with residents of a foreign jurisdiction that involve the knowing and repeated transmission of computer files, such system is interactive and personal jurisdiction is proper." *American Homecare Federation, Inc. v. Paragon Scientific Corp.*, 27 F.Supp.2d 109, 113 (D.Conn.1998).
- The required "something more" can consist of "use of an Internet provider located in the forum State." *Vitullo v. Velocity Powerboats, Inc.*, 1998 WL 246152 (N.D.Ill.1998).
- "[In] cases in which individuals enter into contracts with defendants by way of the Internet and download, transmit, or exchange files[,] the exercise of personal jurisdiction will almost always be proper." *Mieczkowski v. Masco Corp.*, 997 F.Supp. 782, 786 (E.D.Tex.1998).

- "[I]ndividual who purposefully contracted and directly communicated via Internet with computer network service provider is subject to personal jurisdiction in the service provider's home state." *Mallinckrodt Medical, Inc. v. Sonus Pharmaceuticals, Inc.*, 989 F.Supp. 265, 273 (D.D.C.1998).

Is any of these characterizations of *CompuServe* correct?

3. *Location of CompuServe's servers.* Several of the factors that the court relied upon involve Patterson's use of CompuServe's proprietary online system, including the storage of his software on CompuServe's computers so that it could be downloaded by subscribers. Would it make any difference if CompuServe's computers were located not in Ohio, but in Indiana? In Tadjikistan? Some courts have found the location of computer servers that enable online communications relevant to the jurisdictional analysis. *See* Part II(E), *infra*.

4. *Entering into contracts as grounds for jurisdiction.* In most cases where the defendant entered into contracts with residents of the forum state, and the claims arose from those contracts, the court has held the due process requisites for personal jurisdiction to be satisfied. The courts have often relied on the existence of a contract together with other online contacts that would not alone support jurisdiction. *See Alitalia–Linee Aeree Italiane S.p.A. v. Casinoalitalia.Com*, 128 F.Supp.2d 340 (E.D.Va.2001) (five residents of forum state gambled via defendant's online casino, wagering a total of $264.80 in one year); *Superguide Corp. v. Kegan*, 987 F.Supp. 481 (W.D.N.C.1997) (jurisdiction based on assumed facts that forum residents have visited defendant's website and purchased products through it); *Gary Scott Int'l, Inc. v. Baroudi*, 981 F.Supp. 714 (D.Mass.1997) (defendant advertised products on his website and sold twelve cigar humidors to forum residents); *Hall v. LaRonde*, 56 Cal.App.4th 1342 (Cal.Ct.App.1997) (defendant made royalty payments to plaintiff on a continuing basis, pursuant to a contract).

One court held that defendant's sales to residents of the forum state were insufficient to support jurisdiction, where defendant offered the items via an online auction. In *Winfield Collection, Ltd. v. McCauley*, 105 F.Supp.2d 746 (E.D.Mich.2000), plaintiff alleged that defendant infringed his copyrights on home-craft patterns by selling crafts she made using the patterns via eBay. Defendant made two sales to forum residents. The court reasoned that "the function of an auction is to permit the highest bidder to purchase the property offered for sale, and the choice of that highest bidder is therefore beyond the control of the seller." Since defendant did not choose to sell to forum residents—forum residents instead chose to buy from defendant—the sales did not demonstrate purposeful availment of the forum state. How does offering goods for sale to the highest bidder via an auction site differ, in terms of purposeful targeting of the purchasers, from offering goods for sale at a fixed price via a website?

5. *Contract with plaintiff whose location is unknown.* Does defendant's entering into a contract with plaintiff support jurisdiction in the plaintiff's home forum even if the defendant is unaware of the plaintiff's location?

This is a frequent scenario in Internet transactions, although courts rarely address the issue. If the contract involves purchase of a digital good or service that may be delivered electronically via the network, and may be paid for by credit card or using digital cash, the seller need never learn the location of the buyer. Such digital items include subscriptions to e-zines, databases that are accessed online, provision of Internet access, online gambling, software that is downloaded, music in MP3 format, and digitized photographs. In such circumstances, can a seller be found to have purposely directed her conduct at the state where the buyer is located? Does a party enter into a contract with an unlocated party at peril of being subjected to jurisdiction wherever that party happens to reside?

For example, in *Thompson v. Handa–Lopez, Inc.*, 998 F.Supp. 738 (W.D.Tex.1998), defendant operated on online casino. Plaintiff entered into a contract with defendant that allowed him to play games on the site. When plaintiff attempted to redeem the 19,372,849 "Funbucks" that he won for $193,728.40 in cash, defendant balked. Plaintiff brought an action for breach of contract in Texas, where he lived. Defendant, a California corporation with principal place of business in California, resisted the jurisdiction of the Texas court. The court held that it had jurisdiction over defendant, based on the existence of the contract, the defendant's continuous interaction with players like plaintiff, and the defendant's advertisement of its services via its website. The court's opinion does not indicate whether the defendant was aware of the plaintiff's location.

The fact that a seller is offering a digital good or service does not necessarily mean that the seller does *not* know the location of its customers. In *American Network, Inc. v. Access America/Connect Atlanta, Inc.*, 975 F.Supp. 494 (S.D.N.Y.1997), the defendant was an Internet service provider, and jurisdiction was based on the fact that it had six subscribers in the forum state, of whose location it was aware. Similarly, in *Zippo Mfg. Co. v. Zippo Dot Com, Inc.*, 952 F.Supp. 1119 (W.D.Pa.1997), excerpted in Part II(A)(1), *supra*, the defendant knew the location of its paying subscribers, who were required to supply their name and address.

6. *Manufactured contracts.* The existence of contracts with forum state residents is such a strong ground for jurisdiction that plaintiffs will go out of their way to manufacture a contract if none exists. In *Millennium Enterprises, Inc. v. Millennium Music, LP*, 33 F.Supp.2d 907 (D.Or.1999), the defendant was a South Carolina corporation that sold music CD's at retail stores in its home state and via its website. The plaintiff was an Oregon seller of music CD's, and brought suit in its home state, arguing for jurisdiction premised on defendant's sale of a lone CD to an Oregon resident. The court's opinion relates that the purchase was made by an employee of an acquaintance of plaintiff's counsel, and therefore was presumably instigated by plaintiff's counsel. The court expressed dismay at plaintiff's counsel's "lack of candor," and disregarded the sale as a basis for jurisdiction. A similar attempt to manufacture jurisdiction by orchestrating a sale into the forum state is described in *Edberg v. Neogen Corp.*, 17 F.Supp.2d 104 (D.Conn.1998).

D. DISTRIBUTION OF PUBLICATIONS ONLINE

Under the generally applicable law of personal jurisdiction, distribution of publications in the forum state can support an assertion of jurisdiction. In *Keeton v. Hustler Magazine, Inc.*, 465 U.S. 770 (1984), the Court held that defendant's sale of 10,000 to 15,000 copies of its magazine in the forum state each month "is sufficient to support an assertion of jurisdiction in a libel action based on the contents of the magazine." *Id.* at 773–74. The Court explained: "Such regular monthly sales of thousands of magazines cannot by any stretch of the imagination be characterized as random, isolated, or fortuitous." *Id.* at 774.

What are the applicable criteria when the basis for jurisdiction is the defendant's distribution of electronic publications in the forum state? One approach is illustrated in *Scherr v. Abrahams*, 1998 WL 299678 (N.D.Ill. 1998). The plaintiff brought an action alleging various business interference torts, based on defendant's distribution of a humor and satire publication called the Annals of Improbable Research. The hard-copy version of the publication had fewer than 60 subscribers in the forum state, as well as a smaller number of newsstand sales. The court quoted *Keeton, supra*, for the proposition that jurisdiction is proper " 'whenever a substantial number of copies are regularly sold and distributed' " in the forum state. Comparing the 60 to 120 (hard) copies that defendant circulated in the forum state with the 10,000 to 15,000 circulated in *Keeton* (and the 600,000 circulated in *Calder v. Jones*, 465 U.S. 783 (1984)), the court concluded that defendant's circulation was "insubstantial" and therefore did not support jurisdiction.

The court then went on to consider the *online* circulation of the magazine as an independent basis for jurisdiction. According to the court, the defendant stated that the online version of the magazine was sent, free of charge, to about 20,000 people who had placed their e-mail addresses on a mailing list, and the mailing list was accessed via the defendant's website. Perceiving the involvement of a website, the court shifted from the *Keeton* criterion of "substantiality" of the circulation in the forum state to the *Zippo* criterion of the "level of interactivity and commercial nature of the exchange of information that occurs on the Web site." It rejected defendant's characterization of the site as "passive," since the fact that visitors to the site were able to subscribe to the mailing list meant that the site was "one in which the user can exchange information with the host computer." But it found that the level of interactivity presented by the website was "rather low: the only exchange is the listing of a person's e-mail address for an electronic copy of the" magazine; and it found that the commercial nature of the exchange of information was low, since "[n]o money is exchanged," and the only commercial content of the magazine was advertisements for the hard-copy version of the magazine and other products that defendant offered for sale. The court therefore concluded that the online circulation of the magazine did not support jurisdiction.

Naxos Resources (U.S.A.) Ltd. v. Southam Inc., 1996 WL 662451 (C.D.Cal.1996), arose in a different factual context. The plaintiff claimed that it had been defamed in an article that defendants published, and premised jurisdiction on the fact that the article was made available via an online information provider. The court found that the "article was disseminated on LEXIS, which is available in California [the forum state] * * *. Thus, defendants did knowingly disseminate the allegedly tortious material in California, and thus 'purposefully availed' themselves of the privileges of conducting activities there." The court concluded, however, that it did not have jurisdiction over the defendants, since plaintiff's claim did not "arise from" the forum-related activities. The decision seems to hold that one who provides written material to an online information provider has thereby met the "purposeful availment" element of the due process jurisdictional test.

NOTES & QUESTIONS

1. *Applying* Zippo. Is the *Zippo* analysis appropriate on the facts of *Scherr v. Abrahams*? Was jurisdiction premised on the circulation of the magazine, or on defendant's use of its website as a means of obtaining subscribers to the magazine? If defendant had advertised the availability of the online magazine through a medium other than its website, how would the jurisdictional issue be analyzed? If the website had offered additional opportunities for users to "exchange information with the host computer," so that the level of interactivity was rather high, should the jurisdictional analysis have come out differently?

2. Keeton *analysis*. How would the *Keeton* analysis apply to the situation in *Naxos Resources v. Southam*? Is it sufficient that the defendant knows that by virtue of its availability on LEXIS the article *may* have a substantial circulation in California? Would the plaintiff be required to introduce evidence of how many California residents actually accessed the publication via LEXIS? Does it make a difference that the article is made available in the forum state not directly by the defendant, but by a third-party distributor? Is providing a publication to an online service like LEXIS comparable to injecting a manufactured item into the stream of commerce? Consider the applicability of *World–Wide Volkswagen Corp. v. Woodson*, 444 U.S. 286, 297–98 (1980) ("The forum State does not exceed its powers under the Due Process Clause if it asserts personal jurisdiction over a corporation that delivers its products into the stream of commerce with the expectation that they will be purchased by consumers in the forum State."). Consider also the contending opinions in *Asahi Metal Industry Co., Ltd. v. Superior Court*, 480 U.S. 102, 112 (1987) ("The placement of a product into the stream of commerce, without more, is not an act of the defendant purposefully directed toward the forum State.") (opinion of O'Connor, J.); *id.* at 117 (agreeing with the view of "most courts and commentators" that "jurisdiction premised on the placement of a product into the stream of commerce is consistent with the Due Process Clause [without any need for] a showing of additional conduct") (opinion of Brennan, J.).

E. USE OF COMPUTER EQUIPMENT LOCATED IN THE FORUM STATE

Communication via computer networks almost inevitably involves the accessing of computer equipment that is located at some distance from the person initiating the communication. This may come about in several ways: (1) When you access a website, you cause the computer hosting the website to transmit packets of information to your own computer. (2) Information that is transmitted via the network, whether consisting of the contents of a Web page, an e-mail message, or any other data, generally is relayed through one or more intermediary computers on its way from sender to recipient. (3) Accessing information located in a remote database causes activity by the computer on which the database is stored. (4) Accessing the Internet via a dial-up connection results in activity by the service provider's computers. (5) Posting a message to, or receiving a message from, a computer bulletin board system causes activity on the part of the computer on which the BBS is hosted. (6) Communication via a proprietary online service may result in activity by the service's remotely located computers.

May a person's use of a computer network that results in activity on the part of a remote piece of computer equipment constitute contacts with the state in which that equipment is located, sufficient to satisfy the due process requirements for assertion of personal jurisdiction?

1. LOCATION OF A WEB SERVER, OR LOCATION OF SERVER'S OWNER

Several courts have considered whether a court may assert jurisdiction based on the defendant's use of a service provider located in the forum state to host its website. The cases do not always clearly distinguish between the location of the computer equipment on which the files constituting a website are stored, and the location of the company (state of incorporation? principal place of business?) that owns the equipment.

In *Jewish Defense Organization, Inc. v. Superior Court*, 85 Cal.Rptr.2d 611 (Cal.Ct.App.1999), plaintiff brought an action for defamation in a California court. Defendants' only relevant contacts with California consisted of contracting with Internet service providers, "located in California," to host a website which they maintained from their residence in New York. The court concluded "that defendants' conduct of contracting, via computer, with Internet service providers, which may be California corporations or which may maintain offices or databases in California, is insufficient to constitute 'purposeful availment.' " But in *3DO Co. v. Poptop Software Inc.*, 49 U.S.P.Q.2d (BNA) 1469, 1472 (N.D.Cal.1998), the court found it relevant that "Defendants use a San Francisco-based company as a server to operate a website that distributes allegedly infringing copies of [software]."

2. LOCATION OF COMPUTER HOLDING A DATABASE

In *Pres-Kap, Inc. v. System One, Direct Access, Inc.*, 636 So.2d 1351 (Fla.Dist.Ct.App.1994), plaintiff sued a New York corporation for breach of contract. Under the contract in question, plaintiff provided defendant with computer terminals and access to a computer database that was held on a computer located in Florida. Defendant's only connections with Florida were that it made rental payments under the contract to plaintiff's Florida billing office, and it accessed data from plaintiff's computer located in Florida. The court held that these contacts do not amount to sufficient contacts with Florida to support jurisdiction. It explained:

> Indeed, a contrary decision would, we think, have far-reaching implications for business and professional people who use "on-line" computer services for which payments are made to out-of-state companies where the database is located. Across the nation, in every state, customers of "on-line" computer information networks have contractual arrangements with out-of-state supplier companies, putting such customers in a situation similar, if not identical, to the defendant in the instant case. Lawyers, journalists, teachers, physicians, courts, universities, and business people throughout the country daily conduct various types of computer-assisted research over telephone lines linked to supplier databases located in other states.[2] Based on the trial court's decision below, users of such "on-line" services could be haled into court in the state in which supplier's billing office and database happen to be located, even if such users, as here, are solicited, engaged, and serviced entirely instate by the supplier's local representatives. Such a result, in our view, is wildly beyond the reasonable expectations of such computer-information users, and, accordingly, the result offends traditional notions of fair play and substantial justice.

NOTES & QUESTIONS

Is the court's reasoning in *Pres–Kap v. System One* equally applicable to online contacts other than accessing remote databases? In *EnvisioNet Computer Services v. Microportal.com, Inc.*, 2001 WL 179882 (D.Me.2001), the court based jurisdiction on the fact that defendant had placed its proprietary customer information on a computer system located in the forum state, for plaintiff to use in providing support services to defendant's customers. What might explain the difference between these two results?

F. COMBINING OFFLINE AND ONLINE CONTACTS

A number of cases have held that the due process standard may be satisfied by a combination of online activities and other contacts with the forum state. In some of these cases, the court suggests that it would not have been able to assert jurisdiction but for the defendant's online activities. For example, in *CompuServe, Inc. v. Patterson*, 89 F.3d 1257, 1265 (6th

2. For example, Westlaw is based in St. Paul, Minnesota, and all bills are generated and paid in St. Paul. * * * Lexis is based in Dayton, Ohio, and all bills for use of the Lexis System are generated in and paid in Dayton. * * *

Cir.1996), discussed in Part II(C), *supra*, the court noted that neither Patterson's contract with CompuServe, nor his placing software into the stream of commerce by making it available online, would by itself have been sufficient to support jurisdiction, but the two actions in combination (together with other contacts) satisfied the due process requirement. In *Vitullo v. Velocity Powerboats, Inc.*, 1998 WL 246152 (N.D.Ill.1998), the court apparently concluded that defendant's website, which solicited attendance at a boat show in the forum state, supplied the "additional conduct" required under Justice O'Connor's articulation of the stream-of-commerce basis for jurisdiction in *Asahi Metal Industry Co., Ltd. v. Superior Court*, 480 U.S. 102 (1987). In *Telephone Audio Productions, Inc. v. Smith*, 1998 WL 159932 (N.D.Tex.1998), the court held that "the website combined with Defendants [sic] other contacts with Texas satisfy the jurisdictional prerequisite," but "[did] not determine if maintenance of the website alone is sufficient." In *Rubbercraft Corp. v. Rubbercraft, Inc.*, 1997 WL 835442 (C.D.Cal.1997), the court found it had jurisdiction based on the facts that defendant advertised in a nationally circulated publication, maintained a toll-free telephone number, operated a website, and made sales into the forum state. It explained that "[a]lthough each of these factors may not alone create purposeful availment, in combination" they did. As Internet commerce becomes more widespread, will this mixed mode of jurisdictional analysis become the dominant one?

III. Application of State Long-Arm Statutes to Websites

As noted above, in Part I, some state long-arm statutes are interpreted to allow jurisdiction on any basis consistent with due process, while other statutes are more restrictive than due process requires. Statutes in the latter category may prescribe a variety of grounds for jurisdiction. The types of provisions that are most likely to be called into play when jurisdiction is based on a website are those which provide for jurisdiction on claims arising from (1) the transaction of business within the state, (2) causing tortious injury within the state, by conduct either within or outside the state, and (3) soliciting business within the state.

A. Transaction of Business Within the State

Under what circumstances does operation of a website, by someone located outside the forum state, constitute transaction of business within the forum state?

The polar cases are not difficult. Merely operating a website that is accessible in the forum state does not constitute transaction of business in the state. In *Patriot Systems, Inc. v. C–Cubed Corp.*, 21 F.Supp.2d 1318 (D.Utah 1998), the court arrived at this conclusion through application of the *Zippo* analysis. It found that defendant's website was a "passive" one, and therefore did not amount to transaction of business in the state. The reliance on *Zippo*, although out of context here since *Zippo* concerned the requirements for due process, leads to a reasonable result. In *Hearst Corp. v. Goldberger*, 1997 WL 97097 (S.D.N.Y.1997), the court held that "advertisements in national publications are not sufficient to provide personal jurisdiction" under the New York long-arm provision based on transaction of business in the state.

Conversely, making sales to residents of the forum state via defendant's website *does* constitute transaction of business in the state. In *Gary Scott Int'l, Inc. v. Baroudi*, 981 F.Supp. 714 (D.Mass.1997), the defendant offered his products for sale on his website, and sold the products to a retailer in the forum state, but it is not clear from the court's opinion whether the sales resulted from the website advertising. Should it make any difference how the sales came about? *See Digital Equipment Corp. v. AltaVista Technology, Inc.*, 960 F.Supp. 456, 465 n. 18 (D.Mass.1997) ("Ultimately, it does not matter for jurisdictional purposes whether these sales were made because a computer user clicked while accessing [defendant's] Web-site, or by calling a toll-free telephone number, or by answering mail.").

Suppose the defendant offers to sell plaintiff a domain name that consists of or contains plaintiff's trademark. Does this amount to transaction of business in the state where plaintiff resides? In *PurCo Fleet Services, Inc. v. Towers*, 38 F.Supp.2d 1320 (D.Utah 1999), an individual set up a Utah corporation, plaintiff PurCo Fleet Services, Inc., in competition with his former employer, defendant Fleet Financial Corporation. Defendant, for the avowed purpose of "injur[ing] PurCo," registered the domain name "purco.com," and set it up to redirect visitors to defendant's own website. Defendant offered "to bargain away whatever rights it has in the domain name 'purco.com' and variations thereof in exchange for part of a cash settlement from PurCo involving this and other pending litigation." The court found this case similar to *Panavision Int'l, L.P. v. Toeppen*, 141 F.3d 1316 (9th Cir.1998), discussed in Part II(B), *supra*, since, as in *Panavision,* plaintiff alleged that defendants registered purco.com "to extort money" from plaintiff. The court held that by offering to sell the domain name to plaintiff, and by responding to an inquiry from an employee of plaintiff who reached defendant through the purco.com domain, defendant used its website to transact business in Utah.

Compare *PurCo* with *K.C.P.L., Inc. v. Nash*, 49 U.S.P.Q.2d (BNA) 1584 (S.D.N.Y.1998). Plaintiff, a corporation located in New York, was the owner of a trademark on "Reaction," and defendant had registered the domain "reaction.com". Defendant had set up a website at that domain, but had not yet posted any content on it, and the URL merely pointed to a generic "Under Construction" web page. Defendant claimed to be developing a business that would be operated through a website at reaction.com. When plaintiff learned that defendant had registered reaction.com, it offered to purchase the domain name. Defendant asked $8,000 for the rights, but plaintiff rejected his offer, and sent defendant a cease-and-desist letter instead. Plaintiff later offered $1,500 for the domain, which defendant rejected. Plaintiff then filed suit alleging trademark infringement and related claims. The court held that defendant's offer to sell the domain name to plaintiff did not constitute transaction of business in New York. Its reasoning appears to be based on defendant's intent in registering the domain name. Thus, the court rejected plaintiff's characterization of defendant "as a 'cyber pirate' [and] its labeling of his conduct as 'extortion,' " viewing defendant instead as an honest businessman who was having a hard time getting his startup off the ground. The court also declined to rely on *Panavision v. Toeppen*, *supra*, since "the facts alleged do not show [defendant] to be a 'cyber pirate' " like the defendant in *Panavision*.

NOTES & QUESTIONS

1. *Special rule for "cyber pirates"?* Should the existence of jurisdiction depend on the defendant's intentions in registering a domain name and offering it for sale? Should there be a special jurisdictional rule applying to "cyber-pirates," who register domain names for the sole purpose of selling them? Compare Part II(B)(1), Note 3, *supra*. For further discussion of the practice of "cybersquatting," see Chapter 3, *supra*.

2. *Domain name registration.* Does a party transact business in a state merely by registering a domain name with a domain name registrar located in that state? In *America Online, Inc. v. Huang*, 106 F.Supp.2d 848, 855 (E.D.Va.2000), the court observed that "the act of registering a domain name over the Internet, the payment of the small, annual maintenance fee, and [the registrar's] registration, seem so modest in scope and nature that it is difficult to view it as 'transacting business' in the registrar's state of residence."

B. CAUSING TORTIOUS INJURY WITHIN THE STATE, BY CONDUCT EITHER WITHIN OR OUTSIDE THE STATE

Most long-arm statutes provide for jurisdiction over a defendant who has caused tortious injury within the state. These provisions come in two varieties: those which require conduct within the state, and those which allow jurisdiction to be based on conduct occurring outside the state. The latter usually specify some additional conduct tying the defendant more closely to the forum state.

1. TORTIOUS CONDUCT IN THE STATE

Bensusan Restaurant Corporation v. King

126 F.3d 25 (2d Cir.1997).

■ VAN GRAAFEILAND, CIRCUIT JUDGE:

Bensusan Restaurant Corporation, located in New York City, appeals from a judgment of the United States District Court for the Southern

District of New York (Stein, J.) dismissing its complaint against Richard B. King, a Missouri resident, pursuant to Fed.R.Civ.P. 12(b)(2) for lack of personal jurisdiction. We affirm.

Columbia, Missouri is a small to medium size city far distant both physically and substantively from Manhattan. It is principally a white-collar community, hosting among other institutions Stephens College, Columbia College and the University of Missouri. It would appear to be an ideal location for a small cabaret featuring live entertainment, and King, a Columbia resident, undoubtedly found this to be so. Since 1980, he has operated such a club under the name "The Blue Note" at 17 North Ninth Street in Columbia.

Plaintiff alleges in its complaint that it is "the creator of an enormously successful jazz club in New York City called 'The Blue Note,'" which name "was registered as a federal trademark for cabaret services on May 14, 1985." Around 1993, a Bensusan representative wrote to King demanding that he cease and desist from calling his club The Blue Note. King's attorney informed the writer that Bensusan had no legal right to make the demand.

Nothing further was heard from Bensusan until April 1996, when King, at the suggestion of a local web site design company, ThoughtPort Authority, Inc., permitted that company to create a web site or cyberspot on the internet for King's cabaret. This work was done in Missouri. Bensusan then brought the instant action in the Southern District of New York, alleging violations of §§ 32(1) and 43(a) of the Lanham Act, 15 U.S.C. §§ 1114(1) and 1125(a), and § 3(c) of the Federal Trademark Dilution Act of 1995, 15 U.S.C. § 1125(c), as well as common law unfair competition.

In addition to seeking trebled compensatory damages, punitive damages, costs and attorney's fees, Bensusan requests that King be enjoined from:

> using the mark "The Blue Note", or any other indicia of the Blue Note in any manner likely to cause confusion, or to cause mistake, or to deceive, or from otherwise representing to the public in any way that [King's club] is in any way sponsored, endorsed, approved, or authorized by, or affiliated or connected with, Plaintiff or its CABARET, by means of using any name, trademark, or service mark of Plaintiff or any other names whatsoever, including but not limited to removal of Defendant's web site....

The web site describes King's establishment as "Mid-Missouri's finest live entertainment venue, ... [l]ocated in beautiful Columbia, Missouri," and it contains monthly calendars of future events and the Missouri telephone number of King's box office. Initially, it contained the following text:

> The Blue Note's CyberSpot should not be confused with one of the world's finest jazz club Blue Note, located in the heart of New York's Greenwich Village. If you should ever find yourself in the big apple give them a visit.

This text was followed by a hyperlink that could be used to connect a reader's computer to a web site maintained by Bensusan. When Bensusan objected to the above-quoted language, King reworded the disclaimer and removed the hyperlink, substituting the following disclaimer that continues in use:

> The Blue Note, Columbia, Missouri should not be confused in any way, shape, or form with Blue Note Records or the jazz club, Blue Note, located in New York. The CyberSpot is created to provide information for Columbia, Missouri area individuals only, any other assumptions are purely coincidental.

The district court dismissed the complaint in a scholarly opinion that was published in 937 F.Supp. 295 (1996). Although we realize that attempting to apply established trademark law in the fast-developing world of the internet is somewhat like trying to board a moving bus, we believe that well-established doctrines of personal jurisdiction law support the result reached by the district court.

* * *

The New York law dealing with personal jurisdiction based upon tortious acts of a non-domiciliary who does not transact business in New York is contained in sub-paragraphs (a)(2) and (a)(3) of CPLR § 302, and Bensusan claims jurisdiction with some degree of inconsistency under both sub-paragraphs. Because King does not transact business in New York State, Bensusan makes no claim under § 302(a)(1). The legislative intent behind the enactment of sub-paragraphs (a)(2) and (a)(3) best can be gleaned by reviewing their disparate backgrounds. Sub-paragraph (a)(2), enacted in 1962, provides in pertinent part that a New York court may exercise personal jurisdiction over a non-domiciliary who "in person or though an agent" commits a tortious act within the state. The New York Court of Appeals has construed this provision in several cases. In Feathers v. McLucas, 15 N.Y.2d 443, 458, 261 N.Y.S.2d 8, 209 N.E.2d 68 (1965), the Court held that the language "commits a tortious act within the state," as contained in sub-paragraph (a)(2), is "plain and precise" and confers personal jurisdiction over non-residents "when they commit acts within the state." Id. at 460, 261 N.Y.S.2d 8, 209 N.E.2d 68 (internal quotation marks omitted). Feathers adopted the view that CPLR § 302(a)(2) reaches only tortious acts performed by a defendant who was physically present in New York when he performed the wrongful act. The official Practice Commentary to CPLR § 302 explains that "if a New Jersey domiciliary were to lob a bazooka shell across the Hudson River at Grant's tomb, Feathers would appear to bar the New York courts from asserting personal jurisdiction over the New Jersey domiciliary in an action by an injured New York plaintiff." C302:17. The comment goes on to conclude that:

> As construed by the Feathers decision, jurisdiction cannot be asserted over a nonresident under this provision unless the nonresident commits an act in this state. This is tantamount to a requirement that the defendant or his agent be physically present in New York.... In short, the failure to perform a duty in New York is not a tortious act in this state, under the cases, unless the defendant or his agent enters the state.

* * *

Like the district court in Bulk Oil, supra, 584 F.Supp. at 41, we recognize that the interpretation of sub-paragraph (a)(2) in the line of cases above cited has not been adopted by every district judge in the Second Circuit. However, the judges who differ are in the minority. In the absence of some indication by the New York Court of Appeals that its decisions in Feathers and Platt, as interpreted and construed in the above-cited majority of cases, no longer represent the law of New York, we believe it would be impolitic for this Court to hold otherwise. Applying these principles, we conclude that Bensusan has failed to allege that King or his agents committed a tortious act in New York as required for exercise of personal jurisdiction under CPLR § 302(a)(2). The acts giving rise to Bensusan's lawsuit—including the authorization and creation of King's web site, the use of the words "Blue Note" and the Blue Note logo on the site, and the creation of a hyperlink to Bensusan's web site—were performed by persons physically present in Missouri and not in New York. Even if Bensusan suffered injury in New York, that does not establish a tortious act in the state of New York within the meaning of § 302(a)(2). See Feathers, 15 N.Y.2d at 460, 261 N.Y.S.2d 8, 209 N.E.2d 68.

Bensusan's claims under sub-paragraph (a)(3) can be quickly disposed of. Sub-paragraph (a)(2) left a substantial gap in New York's possible exercise of jurisdiction over non-residents because it did not cover the tort of a non-resident that took place outside of New York but caused injury inside the state. Accordingly, in 1966 the New York Legislature enacted sub-paragraph (a)(3), which provides in pertinent part that New York courts may exercise jurisdiction over a non-domiciliary who commits a tortious act without the state, causing injury to person or property within the state. However, once again the Legislature limited its exercise of jurisdictional largess. Insofar as is pertinent herein it restricted the exercise of jurisdiction under sub-paragraph (a)(3) to persons who expect or should reasonably expect the tortious act to have consequences in the state and in addition derive substantial revenue from interstate commerce. To satisfy the latter requirement, Bensusan relies on the arguments that King participated in interstate commerce by hiring bands of national stature and received revenue from customers—students of the University of Missouri—who, while residing in Missouri, were domiciliaries of other states. These alleged facts were not sufficient to establish that substantial revenues were derived from interstate commerce, a requirement that "is intended to exclude non-domiciliaries whose business operations are of a local character." * * * King's "Blue Note" cafe was unquestionably a local operation.

For all the reasons above stated, we affirm the judgment of the district court.

NOTES & QUESTIONS

1. *An unusually restrictive provision.* New York's Civil Practice Law and Rules § 302(a)(2), which allows jurisdiction over one who "commits a tortious act within the state," is unusual in that it has been interpreted to require the defendant's physical presence within the state. Given that interpretation, the court of appeals had little difficulty disposing of this ground of jurisdiction, since there was no claim that the defendant committed any act while physically present in New York. To the same effect is *K.C.P.L., Inc. v. Nash*, 49 U.S.P.Q.2d (BNA) 1584 (S.D.N.Y.1998) (website does not satisfy requirement of physical presence in New York).

The district court arrived at the same result through a more circuitous route. It expansively characterized the issue as "whether the creation of a Web site, which exists either in Missouri or in cyberspace—i.e., anywhere the Internet exists—with a telephone number to order the allegedly infringing product, is an offer to sell the product in New York." *Bensusan Restaurant Corp. v. King*, 937 F.Supp. 295, 299 (S.D.N.Y.1996), *aff'd*, 126 F.3d 25 (2d Cir.1997). After noting the steps that a New York resident would have to take in order to purchase tickets to defendant's club in Missouri, the court concluded that any trademark infringement "would have occurred in Missouri, not New York." *Id.*

2. *Other long-arm statutes.* Other states' long-arm provisions allowing jurisdiction based on commission of a tort within the state have not been interpreted so restrictively as New York's, giving rise to issues concerning where a tort committed through online communication is deemed to be located.

a. In *Digital Equipment Corp. v. AltaVista Technology, Inc.*, 960 F.Supp. 456 (D.Mass.1997), the court drew an analogy between trademark infringement that occurs on a website and infringement that arrives in the state via other means of communication. After citing cases holding that misrepresentations made to forum residents via telex, telephone, and mail meet the long-arm statute's requirement of tortious conduct "in" the state, the court said: "Using the Internet under the circumstances of this case is as much knowingly 'sending' into Massachusetts the allegedly infringing and therefore tortious uses of Digital's trademark as is a telex, mail, or telephonic transmission." *Id.* at 466. Likewise, in *Maritz, Inc. v. Cybergold, Inc.*, 947 F.Supp. 1328 (E.D.Mo.1996), the infringing material on defendant's website was found to be a tortious act "in" the forum state, since it was an extraterritorial act that had an effect (namely, injury of the plaintiff) in the state. If a long-arm provision requiring a tortious act "in" the state is interpreted to be met by a defendant's operation of a website outside the state, does this render meaningless those provisions allowing jurisdiction based on tortious injury arising from an act outside the state, but only if certain other conditions are met?

b. In *Playboy Enterprises, Inc. v. AsiaFocus Int'l Inc.*, 1998 WL 724000 (E.D.Va.1998), the court held that "each act of access to the defendants' Internet sites by a Virginia computer user completed a 'tortious injury by an act ... in this Commonwealth,'" quoting the applicable provision of the Virginia long-arm statute. In the court's view, the infringement was located in the state where a computer user made use of the infringing product by means of online access. Similarly, in *E-Data Corp. v. Micropatent Corp.*, 989 F.Supp. 173 (D.Conn. 1997), the court assumed that the location of the tortious conduct (patent infringement) would be in the state where a computer user made use of the infringing product by means of online access.

By contrast, in *Maritz v. Cybergold* the court assumed that the tortious conduct (trademark infringement) was located in the state where the *plaintiff* was located (rather than the state where a computer user accessed the site), since that is where the resulting injury was felt. The court in *Digital v. AltaVista* was unclear on this point: it relied on a case involving sending into a state a communication that *injures a resident* of the state, but also charged defendant with knowledge that its allegedly infringing website was *accessible* by computer users in the state. Which view is more sensible? Are they inconsistent?

2. TORTIOUS CONDUCT OUTSIDE THE STATE, PLUS ADDITIONAL CONNECTION TO THE FORUM

Statutes allowing jurisdiction based on conduct that occurs outside the state and causes tortious injury within the state generally require some additional connection between the defendant and the state. The most common such additional requirements are (1) that the defendant "regularly does or solicits business in the state," and (2) that the defendant engages in some other "persistent course of conduct in the state."

A few early decisions held that the mere operation of a website constitutes regular solicitation of business, or a persistent course of conduct, in any state from which the site may be accessed. In *TELCO Communications v. An Apple A Day*, 977 F.Supp. 404 (E.D.Va.1997), the court held that by issuing allegedly defamatory press releases via the Internet[3] the defendant met the "regularly soliciting business" provision of the long-arm statute: "Because they conducted their advertising and soliciting over the Internet, which could be accessed by a Virginia resident 24 hours a day, the Defendants did so regularly for purposes of the long-arm statute." *Id.* at 407. The court in *Digital Equipment Corp. v. AltaVista Technology, Inc.*, 960 F.Supp. 456, 467 (D.Mass.1997), reached the same result, likewise noting that defendant's website was "generally accessible twenty-four hours a day and seven days a week to all Massachusetts residents who can access the Web."

But in *Auto Channel, Inc. v. Speedvision Network, LLC*, 995 F.Supp. 761, 765 (W.D.Ky.1997), the court held that a passive website did not satisfy the "solicitation of business" requirement: "[T]he mere fact that Internet users in Kentucky can view advertisements in web pages provided by [defendants] falls far short of demonstrating that Defendants advertise in Kentucky."

3. The court's opinion is not clear on this point, but it appears that the press releases were posted on a third party's website.

NOTES & QUESTIONS

1. *Websites soliciting business.* Are *Zippo*'s analytical categories, discussed in Part I(A)(1), *supra*, relevant to the issue whether a website amounts to solicitation of business or a persistent course of conduct directed at the forum state?

Does a defendant's operation of a website amount to solicitation of business wherever it may be accessed, regardless of whether the defendant is willing to do business with residents of that state? In *Bochan v. La Fontaine*, 68 F.Supp.2d 692 (E.D.Va.1999), discussed in Part III(D), *infra*, one defendant, who sold computers through a company named Computer Works that was located in New Mexico, was sued for an allegedly defamatory statement that he posted to a newsgroup. Jurisdiction was based on his company's website. Despite the fact that the site "specifically states that Computer Works sells computers only in New Mexico," the court found that the site constitutes regular solicitation of business in Virginia, supporting jurisdiction there. In *Hasbro Inc. v. Clue Computing Inc.*, 994 F.Supp. 34 (D.Mass.1997), the website advertising defendant's Colorado-based business was found to constitute regular solicitation of business in Massachusetts, based in part on the statement appearing on the site: "Clue will go to any customer's site! Clue's own Eric Robinson traveled to Antarctica for the 1995–1996 field season."

2. *Consequences.* Under the New York long-arm statute, jurisdiction may be based on tortious conduct outside the state if the defendant "expects or reasonably should expect the act to have consequences in the state and derives substantial revenue from interstate or international commerce." In *American Network, Inc. v. Access America/Connect Atlanta, Inc.*, 975 F.Supp. 494 (S.D.N.Y.1997), the defendant was an Internet service provider that operated a website with a domain name that allegedly infringed plaintiff's trademark. The court held that defendant's operation of a website satisfied the "reasonably should expect" requirement, since defendant "stated twice on its home page that it could help customers 'across the U.S.' [and] had signed up six New York subscribers." Would this have been a harder case if defendant had no subscribers in New York? If operating a website were deemed to be an act with reasonably foreseeable consequences in all states, how would this affect the due process analysis of jurisdiction based on website contacts?

C. REGULARLY SOLICITING BUSINESS IN THE STATE

As discussed above, solicitation of business may supply the "plus" factor required by provisions that base jurisdiction on a tortious act committed outside the state. But some long-arm statutes make the regular (or repeated) solicitation of business in the forum state an independent ground for jurisdiction.

An early application of such a provision to website contacts occurred in *Inset Systems, Inc. v. Instruction Set, Inc.*, 937 F.Supp. 161 (D.Conn.1996), a trademark infringement case in which jurisdiction was premised on defendant's operation of a website using the allegedly infringing mark. The court found that the website constituted repeated solicitation of business in Connecticut, reasoning that the defendant

> has been continuously advertising over the Internet, which includes at least 10,000 access sites in Connecticut. Further, unlike hard-copy advertisements * * *, which are often quickly disposed of and reach a limited number of potential consumers, Internet advertisements are in electronic printed form so that they can be accessed again and again by many more potential consumers.

Id. at 164. The court made no reference to whether Connecticut residents actually did access the site, or whether the site offered any interactive features. The same is true in *Black & Decker (U.S.) Inc. v. Pro–Tech Power Inc.*, 26 F.Supp.2d 834 (E.D.Va.1998), which arrived at the same conclusion.

In other cases—two of them in the same district court that decided *Inset*, though before different judges—the lack of actual access by forum residents was found to be dispositive. The court in *E-Data Corp. v. Micropatent Corp.*, 989 F.Supp. 173 (D.Conn.1997), while noting *Inset*'s finding that there were at least 10,000 Internet users in Connecticut, held that "plaintiff's mere presumption that one of these 10,000 users must have visited [defendant's] Web site and viewed these solicitations is insufficient to meet plaintiff's burden" to show that defendant engaged in repeated solicitation of business. In *MacMullen v. Villa Roma Country Club*, 1998 WL 867271 (Conn.Super.Ct.1998), the court held that defendant's website did not satisfy the "solicitation of business" requirement, since "[t]here is no factual showing that any Connecticut resident actually accessed the defendant's website." And in *American Homecare Federation, Inc. v. Paragon Scientific Corp.*, 27 F.Supp.2d 109, 114 (D.Conn.1998), the court held that a website advertisement of an essay-writing contest is not "repeated solicitation of business," where "no essays were received from Connecticut and no inquiries regarding the contest were received from this State."

NOTES & QUESTIONS

1. *Does availability = solicitation?* The *Inset* court noted the persistent availability of websites as a factor in its analysis. Should this be relevant to a determination whether the site constitutes repeated solicitation? Should a website that remains unmodified be deemed to engage in *repeated* solicitation? Is there a new solicitation each time a visitor accesses the site? If so, is there a new solicitation each time a reader opens up a magazine and reads an advertisement? Compare the "single publication rule" applicable to defamation actions, which states that "[a]ny one edition of a book or newspaper, or any one radio or television broadcast, exhibition of a motion picture or similar aggregate communication is a single publication," giving rise to a single cause of action. RESTATEMENT (SECOND) OF TORTS § 577A(3) (1965). The rule likewise applies to "any similar aggregate communication that reaches a large number of persons at the same time." *Id.* cmt. c. The purpose of the rule is to "protect[] defendants and the courts from the numerous suits that might be brought for the same words if each person reached by such a large-scale communication could serve as the foundation for a new action." *Id.* Is the rationale of this rule applicable to websites, so that making a communication available via a website would not count as *repeated* solicitation?

2. *An updated long-arm statute.* In 1999, the Virginia legislature added a provision to the state long-arm statute that is aimed at extending jurisdiction to cover certain uses of computers. The provision states: "Using a computer or computer network located in the Commonwealth shall constitute an act in the Commonwealth." This statement of what shall be deemed "an act in the Commonwealth" becomes operative when combined with other provisions of the long-arm statute, such as those granting jurisdiction over a claim arising from a person's "[t]ransacting any business in this Commonwealth," "[c]ontracting to supply services or things in this Commonwealth," or "[c]ausing tortious injury by an act or omission in this Commonwealth." VA. CODE § 8.01–328.1(A)(1)–(3). A person is deemed to "use" a computer if he "[a]ttempts to cause or causes * * * [1] a computer or computer network to perform or to stop performing computer operations; [2] the withholding or denial of the use of a computer [or] computer network * * *; or [3] another person to put false information into a computer." VA. CODE § 18.2–152.2. A "computer network" is defined as "as set of related, remotely connected devices and any communications facilities including more than one computer with the capability to transmit data among them through the communications facilities." *Id.*

Does this provision succeed in overcoming the perplexities that result when attempting to ascertain the location of events that are accomplished through online communications? If a person in State A transacts business with a person in State B by sending an e-mail message that is routed through a server located in Virginia, is this "use" of the server that gives rise to jurisdiction over the person in State A? What if the person in State A defames a person in State B by posting a message in a newsgroup that is hosted on a server located in Virginia? Some of the computers that constitute America Online are located in Virginia. Under this statute, does jurisdiction arise in Virginia every time two AOL members, located anywhere in the world, transact business using their AOL accounts?

D. LOCATION OF COMPUTER EQUIPMENT AS A FACTOR UNDER LONG-ARM STATUTES

Some courts have found that the location of the computer servers that are used in posting a message on a BBS is determinative in applying state long-arm provisions. (As discussed in Part II(E), *supra*, some courts have considered the location of computer equipment relevant to the due process analysis.) In *Krantz v. Air Line Pilots Ass'n, Int'l*, 427 S.E.2d 326 (Va. 1993), the defendant posted, on a proprietary BBS operated by a labor union, a statement that allegedly tortiously interfered with plaintiff's employment. The BBS was operated by the union "from its offices in Herndon, Virginia." Other union members accessed the BBS and read the message, resulting in harm to plaintiff. The court found that, by virtue of the fact that the BBS was "a Virginia facility," defendant's posting of the message amounted to an "act * * * in this Commonwealth" that supported jurisdiction under the state's long-arm provision. Other courts have followed *Krantz* in giving great weight to the location of the computers hosting a BBS or newsgroup. *See TELCO Communications v. An Apple A Day*, 977 F.Supp. 404 (E.D.Va.1997) (jurisdiction in Virginia based on electronic distribution of press releases through various outlets, including America Online, which is headquartered in Virginia); *Mitchell v. McGowan*, 1998 U.S. Dist. LEXIS 18587 (E.D.Va. Sept. 18, 1998) (no jurisdiction in Virginia based on posting a message on a newsgroup, since "the computer bulletin board * * * is based in Texas").

In *Bochan v. La Fontaine*, 68 F.Supp.2d 692 (E.D.Va.1999), the plaintiff, Bochan, brought an action for defamation, based on messages that defendants, the La Fontaines, posted on an Internet newsgroup, alt.conspiracy.jfk. The court found that the La Fontaines' use of their America Online account to post messages to the newsgroup met the long-arm statute's provision for jurisdiction based on "tortious injury by an act or omission in this Commonwealth," VA. CODE § 8.01–328.1(A)(3). The court explained:

> [T]he question is whether the La Fontaines committed a tort (*i.e.* libel) in Virginia by posting certain messages to an Internet newsgroup via AOL and Earthlink.net. This, as it happens, is a novel question in Virginia and there do not appear to be any decisions from other jurisdictions that are factually identical. There are, however, factually analogous cases that shed some light on how the Supreme Court of Virginia would analyze this issue. In *Krantz v. Air Line Pilots Association, Int'l,* 427 S.E.2d 326, 245 Va. 202 (1993), the defendant airline pilot posted a message from New York to ACCESS, a computer bulletin board physically located in Virginia. This message called for other pilots to pass the word that plaintiff was a "scab," apparently in an attempt to sabotage plaintiff's prospective employment at another airline. The Supreme Court of Virginia concluded that defendant's use of a bulletin board based in a Virginia facility satisfied § 8.01–328.1(A)(3). In reaching this conclusion, the court stated that "[w]ithout the use of ACCESS, a Virginia facility, [defendant] could not have obtained those recruits, and there would have been no interference with [plaintiff's] prospective contract, the third required element for a prima facie showing of this sort." *See Krantz,* 427 S.E.2d at 328.
>
> Several federal district courts have applied the principles enunciated in *Krantz* to cases alleging Internet torts. In *TELCO Communications v. An Apple A Day,* 977 F.Supp. 404 (E.D.Va. 1997), the court, in dicta, concluded that jurisdiction existed under § 8.01–328.1(A)(3) on the ground that "[b]ut for the Internet

> service providers [AOL] and users present in Virginia, the alleged tort of defamation would not have occurred in Virginia." Thus, the court concluded that those defendants fell "under the jurisdictional net cast by *Krantz*." In contrast, the court in *Mitchell v. McGowan,* Civ. No. 98–1026–A, 1998 U.S. Dist. LEXIS 18587 (E.D.Va. September 18, 1998) (unpublished disposition), concluded that the defendant "appears to escape [the 'net' cast by *Krantz*] because the computer bulletin board he accessed is based in Texas," noting that this distinction, though rather "fine," was dispositive. Thus, since *Krantz* courts have focused in large measure on the location of the Internet service provider or the server on which the bulletin board is stored and the role played by this service or hardware in facilitating the alleged tort.
>
> Under this analysis, a *prima facie* showing of a sufficient act by the La Fontaines in Virginia follows from their use of the AOL account, a Virginia-based service, to publish the allegedly defamatory statements. According to Bochan's expert, because the postings were accomplished through defendant's AOL account, they were transmitted first to AOL's USENET server hardware, located in Loudon County, Virginia.[23] There, the message was apparently both stored temporarily and transmitted to other USENET servers around the world. Thus, as to the La Fontaines, because publication is a required element of defamation, and a *prima facie* showing has been made that the use of USENET server in Virginia was integral to that publication, there is a sufficient act in Virginia to satisfy § 8.01–328.1(A)(3).

Id. at 698–99.

The court went on to hold that this approach would not justify jurisdiction over another defendant, who "did not use an AOL account after accessing the Internet, or use any Virginia-based service, but instead used only the Internet service providers Earthlink, located in California, or High Fiber, located in New Mexico." *Id.* at 700.

When a newsgroup or BBS posting does not make use of computer servers located in the forum state, there is little to distinguish such a posting from a statement on a website. In *Mallinckrodt Medical, Inc. v. Sonus Pharmaceuticals, Inc.*, 989 F.Supp. 265 (D.D.C.1998), the court found it did not have jurisdiction based on an allegedly defamatory statement that defendants posted on an America Online bulletin board, and that was accessible by some 200,000 District of Columbia residents. Relying on cases analyzing passive websites, the court found that the posting did not amount to "transacting business" in the District of Columbia. It also found that the posting did not cause "tortious injury" in the District, since

23. Defendants' expert notes that the newsgroup *alt.conspiracy.jfk* was created in Clearwater, Florida, that many newsgroups are unrelated to any specific physical or geographical area, and that the vast majority of messages posted to newgroups via AOL are not specifically targeted at any particular geographical area. These statements do not, however, clarify where and how storage and transmission of the postings on the newsgroup actually occur.

nothing about the circumstances distinguished the District from any other place in the country where the posting could be accessed.

If a defendant located outside the forum state commits a tort by sending an e-mail message to a forum resident, is the tort committed *in* the state for purposes of a long-arm grant of jurisdiction? *Compare Internet Doorway, Inc. v. Parks*, 138 F.Supp.2d 773 (S.D.Miss.2001) (sending unsolicited commercial e-mail to forum resident was a tort committed "in whole or in part in this state," since the tort was not complete upon sending but only when the message was opened by the recipient) *with Northwest Airlines, Inc. v. Friday*, 617 N.W.2d 590 (Minn.Ct.App.2000) (sending defamatory e-mail to forum resident is not an "act in" the state, since the operative act is the sending, which by analogy to postal mail occurred outside the state).

NOTES & QUESTIONS

1. *Relocation of servers*. Should the geographic location of America Online's USENET server be determinative of the jurisdictional analysis? What if AOL happened to locate its USENET server outside Virginia? What if it had several servers, some in Virginia and some elsewhere, and USENET postings were routed randomly to one server or the other? What if the postings in question were to an AOL bulletin board rather than to USENET, and the BBS server was located outside Virginia? Should it matter whether defendants had knowledge of the location of the server?

2. *Remote USENET servers*. The court in *Bochan v. La Fontaine* notes that after being stored on AOL's USENET server, the allegedly defamatory messages were "transmitted to other USENET servers around the world." Is there a rationale for holding that the involvement of AOL's server justifies jurisdiction in Virginia, without concluding that the involvement of other USENET servers that propagated the message likewise justify jurisdiction wherever they may be located?

Other courts have been troubled by the notion that the automatic functioning of a USENET server should be treated as the legal equivalent of volitional conduct. For example, one court rejected a plaintiff's argument that an Internet service provider that operates a USENET server is directly liable for copyright infringement based on material that a subscriber posts to a newsgroup. It explained: "Plaintiff's theory would create many separate acts of infringement and, carried to its natural extreme, would lead to unreasonable liability * * *. [P]laintiff's theory further implicates a Usenet server that carries * * * messages to other servers regardless of whether that server acts without any human intervention beyond the initial setting up of the system. It would also result in liability for every single Usenet server in the worldwide link of computers transmitting [messages] to every other computer. * * * There is no need to construe the [Copyright] Act to make all of these parties infringers." *Religious Technology Center v. Netcom On-Line Communication Services, Inc.*, 907 F.Supp. 1361, 1369–70 (N.D.Cal.1995). (This case is excerpted and discussed in Chapter 9, *infra*.) Should similar considerations govern in the context of personal jurisdiction?

3. *E-mail servers.* Assume that any time an AOL user sends e-mail, it is routed through the company's main servers in Virginia. On the reasoning employed in *Bochan v. La Fontaine,* would the Virginia courts have jurisdiction over any lawsuit arising from e-mail messages sent between AOL users located in, say, Tennessee and California?

4. *Location of access provider.* In *Bochan v. La Fontaine,* what if the second defendant, who resided in New Mexico, had accessed the Internet and posted allegedly defamatory USENET messages via an access provider located in Virginia? Would the court have found the long-arm provision satisfied? How would the court determine where an access provider, which may have customers and local access numbers located throughout the country, is "located" for purposes of the jurisdictional analysis? In *Mitchell v. McGowan,* 1998 U.S. Dist. LEXIS 18587 (E.D. Va. Sept. 18, 1998), the court concluded that it lacked jurisdiction over defendant based on his posting of an allegedly defamatory message "to the Internet" (apparently to a USENET newsgroup), since "the computer bulletin board he accessed is based in Texas." What might have led the court to conclude that a particular newsgroup is "based" in a particular state?

5. *Location of computer equipment vs. location of equipment owner.* In *Krantz v. Air Line Pilots Ass'n, Int'l,* 427 S.E.2d 326, 327 (Va.1993), which the *Bochan v. La Fontaine* court discussed, the defendant posted, on a proprietary BBS operated by a labor union (which was itself a defendant), a statement that allegedly tortiously interfered with plaintiff's employment. The BBS was operated by the union "from its offices in Herndon, Virginia." Other union members accessed the BBS and read the message, allegedly resulting in harm to plaintiff. The court noted that the bulletin board system was "operated by ALPA from its offices in * * * Virginia." Was the court assuming that the computer equipment in question was likewise located in Virginia, or was the relevant factor the location of the owner of the equipment?

6. *Relevance of location.* Should the location of the computer servers that are used in transmitting or storing newsgroup or BBS messages be determinative in the jurisdictional inquiry? Should this even be a relevant factor? If the location of such computer equipment is deemed relevant, shouldn't the same be true for the location of the ISP through which a user obtains access to the Internet? The location of the server on which a website is hosted? The location of a proxy server that caches frequently accessed data? How about the location of the name servers that are queried each time a user accesses a website? Is it coherent to speak of the "location" of a newsgroup?

IV. JURISDICTION BY CONTRACT: FORUM-SELECTION CLAUSES

Parties to commercial transactions often seek to establish contractually which court shall have jurisdiction to decide disputes arising from their relationship. While "[f]orum-selection clauses have historically not been favored by American courts," the modern view "is that such clauses are prima facie valid and should be enforced unless enforcement is shown by the resisting party to be 'unreasonable' under the circumstances." *M/S Bremen v. Zapata Off–Shore Co.*, 407 U.S. 1, 9–10 (1972). This rule applies, under federal law, both if the clause was the result of negotiation between two business entities, and if it is contained in a form contract that a business presents to an individual on a take-it-or-leave-it basis. In *Carnival Cruise Lines, Inc. v. Shute*, 499 U.S. 585 (1991), the Court addressed the enforceability of a forum-selection clause that was among the terms set forth on several pages appended to a cruise-ship ticket. The Court held that the clause was enforceable, despite its not being the product of negotiation, as it was not unreasonable.

Companies that offer goods and services online have an especially strong incentive to define contractually the forum for resolution of disputes, since they may be engaging in transactions with purchasers located in a multiplicity of jurisdictions, and defending lawsuits in scattered locations can be very expensive. Furthermore, since courts typically (though not always) apply the law of the forum in which they sit, suit in foreign jurisdictions subjects sellers to various substantive laws, increasing their costs of complying with applicable law.

Providers of Internet access or other online services frequently include a forum-selection clause in the Terms of Service to which subscribers must indicate their assent as part of the process of gaining access to the service. The clause is often one element of a lengthy recitation of conditions that the subscriber may view by scrolling through an on-screen box. The subscriber is typically asked to indicate assent to the Terms of Service by clicking an on-screen button that says "I Agree." The forum selection clause may also be presented in other ways, such as through a hyperlink labeled "Terms and Conditions" or "Legal Notice," or by text in greater or lesser proximity to the terms of the offer. The extent to which such presentations of terms are in general sufficient for contract formation is explored in Chapter 4, *supra*.

Most courts that have ruled on the issue have enforced online forum-selection clauses. Thus, in *Groff v. America Online, Inc.*, 1998 WL 307001 (R.I. Super. Ct.1998), the plaintiff, an individual in Rhode Island who subscribed to America Online, sued the company in Rhode Island state court, alleging violations of state consumer protection legislation. The process of becoming a member of AOL includes a step in which the applicant must assent to AOL's Terms of Service by clicking an "I Agree" button. The Terms of Service "contains a forum selection clause which expressly provides that Virginia law and Virginia courts are the appropriate law and forum for the litigation between members and AOL." Citing *M/S Bremen v. Zapata*, the court looked to whether enforcement of the clause would be "unreasonable." It did so by application of a nine-factor test, including such criteria as the place of execution of the contract, public policy of the forum state, location of the parties and witnesses, relative bargaining power of the parties, and "the conduct of the parties." The court concluded that enforcement of the clause would not be unreasonable, and so dismissed the case.

In *Kilgallen v. Network Solutions, Inc.*, 99 F.Supp.2d 125 (D.Mass. 2000), the court enforced a forum-selection clause on less supportive facts. Defendant Network Solutions, Inc., which was then the monopoly registrar of domain names in the .com top-level domain, sent plaintiff a notice via e-mail stating that he would soon receive an invoice to pay his annual registration fee. The lengthy notice included a section titled "Domain Name Registration Agreement," paragraph P of which contained a forum-selection clause. A month later, plaintiff received an invoice via e-mail, which stated: "In making payment for the invoice below, Registrant agrees to the terms and conditions of the current Domain Registration Agreement." Plaintiff paid the invoice, but through a series of clerical errors NSI misapplied the payment, and subsequently cancelled the domain name for nonpayment, whereupon another person registered it. Plaintiff sued for breach of contract, and NSI sought to enforce the forum-selection clause. The court enforced the clause, finding that plaintiff had failed to demonstrate that it was unreasonable.

But in *America Online, Inc. v. Superior Court*, 108 Cal.Rptr.2d 699 (Cal.Ct.App.2001), the court declined to enforce the contractual forum-selection clause. Plaintiff Mendoza sought to represent a class of former AOL subscribers, who alleged that AOL continued to debit their credit cards for monthly subscription fees even after they cancelled their subscriptions. The complaint alleged several causes of action, including violation of the California Consumers Legal Remedies Act ("CLRA"), CAL. CIV. CODE §§ 1750 et seq., a consumer protection statute that prohibits unfair and deceptive trade practices. AOL filed a motion to stay or dismiss, based on the forum-selection clause contained in its Terms of Service. The clause stated:

> You expressly agree that exclusive jurisdiction for any claim or dispute with AOL or relating in any way to your membership or your use of AOL resides in the courts of Virginia and you further agree and expressly consent to the exercise of personal jurisdiction in the courts of Virginia in connection with any such dispute including any claim involving AOL or its affiliates, subsidiaries, employees, contractors, officers, directors, telecommunications providers and content providers * * *.

The Terms of Service also contained a choice-of-law provision: "The laws of the Commonwealth of Virginia, excluding its conflicts-of-law rules, govern this Agreement and your membership." The trial court denied AOL's motion, and AOL petitioned for a writ of mandamus.

The appeals court affirmed. It agreed with the trial court that although "[n]ormally, the burden of proof is on the party challenging the enforcement of a contractual forum selection clause," in this case the burden should shift to AOL, in view of the CLRA's non-waiver provision, which states: "Any waiver by a consumer of the provisions of this title is contrary to public policy and shall be unenforceable and void." CAL. CIV. CODE § 1751. The court found: "Where the effect of transfer to a different forum has the potential of stripping California consumers of their legal rights deemed by the Legislature to be non-waivable, the burden must be placed on the party asserting the contractual forum selection clause to prove that the CLRA's anti-waiver provisions are not violated." 108 Cal.Rptr. 2d at 707. The court continued:

> AOL correctly posits that California favors contractual forum selection clauses so long as they are entered into freely and voluntarily, and their enforcement would not be unreasonable. * * * This favorable treatment is attributed to our law's devotion to the concept of one's free right to contract, and flows from the important practical effect such contractual rights have on commerce generally. This [court] has characterized forum selection clauses as "play[ing] an important role in both national and international commerce." * * * We * * * view such clauses as likely to become even more ubiquitous as this state and nation become acculturated to electronic commerce. See [*Carnival Cruise Lines*]. Moreover, there are strong economic arguments in support of these agreements, favoring both merchants and consumers, including reduction in the costs of goods and services and the stimulation of e-commerce.
>
> But this encomium is not boundless. Our law favors forum selection agreements only so long as they are procured freely and voluntarily, with the place chosen having some logical nexus to one of the parties or the dispute, and so long as California consumers will not find their substantial legal rights significantly impaired by their enforcement. Therefore, to be enforceable, the selected jurisdiction must be "suitable," "available," and able to "accomplish substantial justice." (*The Bremen v. Zapata Off–Shore Co.* (1972) 407 U.S. 1, 17 * * *.) The trial court determined that the circumstances of contract formation did not reflect Mendoza exercised free will, and that the effect of enforcing the forum selection clause here would violate California public policy by eviscerating important legal rights afforded to this state's consumers. Our task, then, is to review the record to determine if there was a rational basis for the court's findings and the choice it made not to enforce the forum selection clause in AOL's TOS agreement. * * * California courts will refuse to defer to the selected forum if to do so would substantially diminish the rights of California residents in a way that violates our state's public policy. * * *

Id. at 707–08. The court reviewed *Hall v. Superior Court*, 197 Cal.Rptr. 757 (Cal.Ct.App.1983), which declined to enforce a forum-selection clause naming Nevada as the forum, on the ground that to do so would conflict with the anti-waiver provision of California's Corporate Securities Law of 1968. The court continued:

> The CLRA parallels the Corporate Securities Law of 1968, at issue in *Hall*, insofar as the CRLA is a legislative embodiment of a desire to protect California consumers and furthers a strong public policy of this state. * * * Certainly, the CLRA provides remedial protections *at least* as important as those under the Corporate Securities Law of 1968. Therefore, by parity of reasoning, enforcement of AOL's forum selection clause, which is also accompanied by a choice of law provision favoring Virginia, would necessitate a waiver of the statutory remedies of the CLRA, in violation of that law's anti-waiver provision * * * and California public policy. For this reason alone, we affirm the trial court's ruling.

Id. at 710. The court went on to compare the CLRA with its Virginia counterpart, finding that "Virginia's law provides significantly less consumer protection to its citizens than California law provides for our own." *Id.* In particular, the Virginia statute does not permit class actions. The court said: "[W]e cannot accept AOL's assertion that the elimination of class actions for consumer remedies if the forum selection clause is enforced is a matter of insubstantial moment. The unavailability of class action relief in this context is sufficient in and by itself to preclude enforcement of the TOS forum selection clause." The court went on to note that

> neither punitive damages, nor enhanced remedies for disabled and senior citizens are recoverable under Virginia's law. More nuanced differences are the reduced recovery under the VCPA for "unintentional" acts, a shorter period of limitations, and Virginia's use of a Lodestar formula alone to calculate attorney fees recovery. * * * Quite apart from the remedial limitations under Virginia law relating to injunctive and class action relief, the cumulative importance of even these less significant differences is substantial. Enforcement of a forum selection clause, which would impair these aggregate rights, would itself violate important California public policy. For this additional reason the trial court was correct in denying AOL's motion to stay or to dismiss.[17]

Id. at 712.

NOTES & QUESTIONS

1. *Place of execution.* One of the reasonableness factors that the court applied in *Groff v. America Online* was the place where the contract was executed. The court admitted to some perplexity on this point. "It is not clear," the court observed, "in this electronic age, where the last place the contract was executed [sic]. Was it when plaintiff clicked the 'I agree' button * * * in Rhode Island or where the message was received, at

17. Because we affirm on other grounds, we need not decide whether the trial court correctly concluded that the TOS was an unconscionable, adhesion contract * * * or Mendoza's alternative contention that the forum selection clause is unenforceable because it was induced by fraud.

defendant's mainframe in Virginia?" The court concluded: "The place where the transaction has been or are [sic] to be performed appears to take place where defendant's mainframe is located." Does the location of the execution of the contract seem like a meaningful issue in this context? Should the location of AOL's mainframe computer be determinative?

2. *Actual knowledge required?* Should it matter whether the plaintiff actually read the forum selection clause before clicking "I Agree"? The plaintiff in *Groff v. America Online* claimed in his affidavit: "I never saw, read, negotiated for or knowingly agreed to be bound by the choice of law. . . ." The court was unmoved, reciting the "general rule that a party who signs an instrument manifests his assent to it and cannot later complain that he did not read the instrument or that he did not understand its contents." Is clicking on an "I Agree" button displayed on a computer monitor the equivalent of signing a document, for purposes of indicating that the signing party recognizes the significance of his act? Should the prominence of the forum-selection clause in the sign-up process be a significant factor? The sign-up process that the plaintiff in *Groff* underwent involved numerous screens full of text, taking up 94 pages in hard-copy format. Note that in *Carnival Cruise Lines v. Shute, supra*, the existence of additional contractual terms was signaled to plaintiff by a notice on the face of the ticket that read: " 'SUBJECT TO CONDITIONS OF CONTRACT ON LAST PAGES **IMPORTANT!** PLEASE READ CONTRACT—ON LAST PAGES 1, 2, 3.' " 499 U.S. at 587.

3. *Non-waivable provisions.* The holding in *AOL v. Superior Court* turned on the California legislature's decision to make consumer rights under the CLRA non-waivable. Why would a legislature choose to interfere with consumers' freedom of contract in this way? How might AOL (or any other online seller) respond to such legislation? Contracts in consumer transactions are typically non-negotiable. Proponents of such contracts argue that the low value of the transaction cannot justify the costs of negotiation. Are there reasons to think that this factor is of less significance online? Do you think that AOL is charging subscribers a competitive market price that takes into account AOL's cost savings from expected enforcement of the forum-selection clause? Is AOL unfairly stuck with charging California subscribers the same price as subscribers in states that are willing to enforce its forum-selection clause?

4. *Contract of adhesion.* In *Spera v. America Online, Inc.*, Index No. 06716/97 (N.Y. Sup. Ct. Jan. 27, 1998), the court enforced a forum-selection clause against a defendant who claimed that AOL had engaged in misleading business practices. Applying New York law, the court rejected plaintiff's arguments that the forum-selection clause was "a contract of adhesion" and that enforcing the clause would be against public policy.

NOTE: FORUM–SELECTION CLAUSES UNDER EUROPEAN UNION LAW

The European approach to personal jurisdiction in cross-border disputes is rather different from the U.S. approach. The rules determining which country's courts have jurisdiction over a defendant are set out in a regulation issued by the Council of the European Union, known as the Brussels Regulation. Council Regulation (EC) No 44/2001 of 22 December 2000 on jurisdiction and the recognition and enforcement of judgments in civil and commercial matters, 2001 O.J. (L 12) 1. The Regulation, which became effective on March 1, 2002, is an update of a 1968 treaty among European countries, known as the Brussels Convention. Convention on jurisdiction and the enforcement of judgments in civil and commercial Matters, 1990 O.J. (C 189) 2 (consolidated).

The Regulation establishes the general rule that "[p]ersons domiciled in a Member State shall, whatever their nationality, be sued in the courts of that Member State." Art. 2. But there are a number of derogations from that general rule, allowing a person to be sued in the courts of a country other than the one where he is domiciled. For example, if the action relates to a contract, suit may be brought "in the courts for the place of performance of the obligation in question." Art. 5(1)(a). If the action relates to tort, suit may be brought "in the courts for the place where the harmful event occurred or may occur." Art. 5(3).

There are also special rules for certain consumer contracts, in keeping with the broad distinction between consumer law and commercial law that is followed in European countries. A consumer contract is one that is "concluded by a person, the consumer, for a purpose which can be regarded as being outside his trade or profession." Art. 15(1). Certain types of consumer contracts are *per se* covered by the special rules: these are contracts for the sale of goods on installment credit, and contracts for a loan made to finance the sale of goods. Art. 15(1)(a), (b). Other types of contracts are covered if

> the contract has been concluded with a person who pursues commercial or professional activities in the Member State of the consumer's domicile or, by any means, directs such activities to that Member State or to several States including that Member State, and the contract falls within the scope of such activities.

Art. 15(1)(c).

Two important special rules apply in actions relating to a covered consumer contract. First, the consumer may sue the seller either in the seller's country *or* "in the courts for the place where the consumer is domiciled." Art. 16(1). (But the seller still may sue the consumer only in the consumer's country.) Second, contractual forum-selection clauses are usually unenforceable. A forum-selection agreement is enforceable only if it is "entered into after the dispute has arisen," if it gives the *consumer* a choice of additional courts in which to bring the action, or if it confers jurisdiction on the courts of a country in which both the seller and consumer were "domiciled or habitually resident" at the time the contract was concluded. Art. 17. In other words, a forum-selection clause that deprives a consumer of the right to file suit in the courts of his own country is enforceable *only* if it is entered after the dispute has arisen. This prevents the use of take-it-or-leave-it contracts that deprive consumers of the home-court advantage—a technique that is quite commonly employed by sellers in the United States.

The general definition of consumer contracts in Art. 15(1)(c) was quite controversial. The corresponding provision of the Brussels Convention defined a consumer contract as one as to which "in the State of the consumer's domicile the conclusion of the contract was preceded by a specific invitation addressed to him or by advertising," and "the consumer took in that State the steps necessary for the conclusion of the contract." Brussels Convention, Art. 13(3). One impetus for revision of the Convention was the uncertain application of Art. 13 to consumer contracts concluded online. As the European Commission explained in its proposal for the Regulation:

> The criteria given in Article 13(3) of the Brussels Convention have been reframed to take account of developments in marketing techniques. * * * The concept of activities pursued in or directed towards a Member State is designed to make clear that [Art. 15(1)(c) of the Regulation] applies to consumer contracts concluded via an interactive website accessible in the State of the consumer's domicile. The fact that a consumer simply had knowledge of a service or possibility of buying goods via a passive website accessible in his country of domicile will not trigger the protective jurisdiction. * * * The removal of the condition in [Art. 13(3)(b) of the Convention] that the consumer must have taken necessary steps for the conclusion of the contract in his home State shall also be seen in the context of contracts concluded via an interactive website. For such contracts the place where the consumer takes these steps may be difficult or impossible to determine, and they may in any event be irrelevant to creating a link between the contract and the consumer's State. The philosophy of new Article 15 is that the cocontractor creates the necessary link when directing his activities towards the consumer's state.

Proposal for a Council Regulation (EC) on jurisdiction and the recognition and enforcement of judgments in civil and commercial matters, COM(99)348 final at 16 (Jul. 14, 1999).

NOTES & QUESTIONS

What is a consumer contract? Given the special treatment afforded consumer contracts in the European Union, it becomes important to be able to identify which transactions involve consumer contracts. Does the revised wording of the Regulation make it clear under what circumstances a seller's maintenance of a website will subject the seller to the consumer-contract exception, allowing the consumer to sue the seller in the consumer's home country? When is a website "direct[ed] to" a particular country? If it is accessible in that country? If it is written in the national language of the country? If prices are quoted in the currency of that country? Is it clear that this formulation brings more contracts within the consumer-contract exception than the Convention did?

V. CHOICE OF LAW

The transborder nature of online communications can create difficulties in determining which jurisdiction's law governs a particular dispute. Sometimes the parties to the dispute will have agreed contractually on the governing law. Often these contracts will be enforceable, especially in commercial agreements, though sometimes a court will prefer its own jurisdiction's policies over those of a foreign jurisdiction. In the absence of such an agreement, the court must apply the jurisdiction's choice-of-law rules.

John Rothchild, *Protecting the Digital Consumer: The Limits of Cyberspace Utopianism*

74 IND. L.J. 893 (1999).

* * *

A court with jurisdiction to adjudicate a particular controversy will not necessarily apply the law of the state in which it is located. If the parties are located in the forum jurisdiction, and all of the operative facts occurred there, a court will apply the *lex fori*. However, where the controversy has "a significant relationship to more than one state," the court must resort to choice-of-law principles in order to determine which jurisdiction's laws it will apply to resolve the controversy.

Choice-of-law issues are notoriously difficult to resolve even in relatively simple contexts. The complexities of transnational commercial activities conducted via the Internet may give rise to particularly thorny choice-of-law questions. Due to the nature of online communications, an online transaction may routinely involve several jurisdictions. For example, a person in State *A* may make a communication through a Web site hosted on a computer located in State *B*, that is received by a person in State *C* who obtains access to the Internet through a server located in State *D* (which is owned and operated by a company headquartered in State *E*), and that results in a transaction involving the shipment of physical goods or downloading of digital goods from a source located in State *F*.

Among states of the United States, the two most popular approaches to resolving choice-of-law issues are *lex loci delicti* and "most significant relationship." Under the rule of *lex loci delicti*, the applicable law is the law of the place "where the last event necessary to make an actor liable for an alleged tort takes place." * * * The "most significant relationship" approach involves a balancing test that is dependent on a number of factors. One standard exposition of the test that applies where the cause of action is based on fraud or misrepresentation takes cognizance of six factors: (1) the place where the plaintiff acted in reliance upon the defendant's representations, (2) the place where the plaintiff received the representations, (3) the place where the defendant made the representations, (4) the residence and nationality of the parties, (5) the place where a tangible thing which is the subject of the transaction was situated, and (6) the place where the plaintiff was to render performance under the fraudulently induced contract.[102]

Where the cause of action arises from contract, and the parties have not effectively selected the governing substantive law, the relevant criteria in a choice-of-law analysis are (1) the place of contracting, (2) the place of negotiation of the contract, (3) the place of performance, (4) the location of the subject matter of the contract, and (5) the location of the parties.

The special characteristics of online communications create difficulties in the application of these criteria. For example, does a person "make" or "receive" an online communication (a) where the maker of the communication is located at the time he transmits it, (b) where the computer through which the maker of the communication connects to the network is located, (c) where the computer through which the recipient of the communication connects to the network is located, (d) where the computer from which the purchaser downloads his e-mail is located, or (e) where the recipient of the communication is located at the time he receives it? When performance consists of the delivery of a digital good, does performance occur at the sending end or the receiving end? Is the result different if the seller transmits the good by making it available for download from the seller's Web site? What is the situs of contracting or negotiation of a contract that is arrived at through online communications?

The novel issues raised by choice-of-law analysis of online transactions will thus center around what is deemed to be the *location* of various persons and events. As is the case with jurisdiction, the location of online events and the persons who bring them about can be difficult to assess.

* * *

Jack L. Goldsmith, *Against Cyberanarchy*

65 U. CHI. L. REV. 1199 (1998).

* * *

[T]ransnational transactions in cyberspace, like transnational transactions mediated by telephone and mail, will continue to give rise to disputes that present challenging choice-of-law issues. For example: "Whose substantive legal rules apply to a defamatory message that is written by someone in Mexico, read by someone in Israel by means of an Internet server located in the United States, injuring the reputation of a Norwegian?" Similarly,

> which of the many plausibly applicable bodies of copyright law do we consult to determine whether a hyperlink on a World Wide

102. [RESTATEMENT (SECOND) OF CONFLICT OF LAWS § 148(2).]

> Web page located on a server in France and constructed by a Filipino citizen, which points to a server in Brazil that contains materials protected by German and French (but not Brazilian) copyright law, which is downloaded to a server in the United States and reposted to a Usenet newsgroup, constitutes a remediable infringement of copyright?[146]

It would be silly to try to formulate a general theory of how such issues should be resolved. One lesson of this century's many failures in top-down choice-of-law theorizing is that choice-of-law rules are most effective when they are grounded in and sensitive to the concrete details of particular legal contexts. This does not mean that standards are better than rules in this context. It simply means that in designing choice-of-law rules or standards, it is better to begin at the micro rather than macro level, and to examine recurrent fact patterns and implicated interests in discrete legal contexts rather than devise a general context-transcendent theory of conflicts.

With these caveats in mind, I want to explain in very general terms why the residual choice-of-law problems implicated by cyberspace are not significantly different from those that are non-cyberspace conflicts. Cyberspace presents two related choice-of-law problems. The first is the problem of complexity. This is the problem of how to choose a single governing law for cyberspace activity that has multijurisdictional contacts. The second problem concerns situs. This is the problem of how to choose a governing law when the locus of activity cannot easily be pinpointed in geographical space. Both problems raise similar concerns. The choice of any dispositive geographical contact or any particular law in these cases will often seem arbitrary because several jurisdictions have a legitimate claim to apply their law. Whatever law is chosen, seemingly genuine regulatory interests of the nations whose laws are not applied may be impaired.

The problems of complexity and situs are genuine. They are not, however, unique to cyberspace. Identical problems arise all the time in real space. In fact, they inhere in every true conflict of laws. Consider the problem of complexity. The hypotheticals concerning copyright infringements and multistate libels in cyberspace are no more complex than the same issues in real space. They also are no more complex or challenging than similar issues presented by increasingly prevalent real-space events such as airplane crashes, mass torts, multistate insurance coverage, or multinational commercial transactions, all of which form the bread and butter of modern conflict of laws. Indeed, they are no more complex than a simple products liability suit arising from a two-car accident among residents of the same state, which can implicate the laws of several states, including the place of the accident, the states where the car and tire manufacturers are headquartered, the states where the car and tires were manufactured, and the state where the car was purchased.

146. [David Post & David R. Johnson, *Borders, Spillover, and Complexity* (unpublished manuscript 1977).]

Resolution of choice-of-law problems in these contexts is challenging. But the skeptics overstate the challenge. Not every geographical contact is of equal significance. For example, in the copyright hypothetical above, the laws of the source country and the end-use countries have a much greater claim to governing the copyright action than the laws of the country of the person who built the server and the country of the server whose hyperlink pointed to the server that contained the infringing material. The limits on enforcement jurisdiction may further minimize the scope of the conflict. In addition, even in extraordinarily complex cases where numerous laws potentially apply, these laws will often involve similar legal standards, thus limiting the actual choice of law to two or perhaps three options. Finally, these complex transactions need not be governed by a single law. Applying different laws to different aspects of a complex transaction is a perfectly legitimate choice-of-law technique.

The application of a single law to complex multijurisdictional conflicts will sometimes seem arbitrary and will invariably produce spillover effects. But as explained above, the arbitrariness of the chosen law, and the spillovers produced by application of this law, inhere in all conflict situations in which two or more nations, on the basis of territorial or domiciliary contacts, have a legitimate claim to apply their law. When in particular contexts the arbitrariness and spillovers become too severe, a uniform international solution remains possible. Short of such harmonization, the choice-of-law issues implicated by cyberspace transactions are no more complex than the issues raised by functionally identical multijurisdictional transactions that occur in real space all the time.

Like the problem of complexity, the situs problem is a pervasive and familiar feature of real-space jurisdictional conflicts. A classic difficulty is the situs of intangibles like a debt or a bank deposit. More generally, the situs problem arises whenever legally significant activity touches on two or more states. For example, when adultery committed in one state alienates the affections of a spouse in another, the situs of the tort is not self-evident. It depends on what contact the forum's choice-of-law rule deems dispositive. Similar locus difficulties arise when the tort takes place over many states, such as when poison is administered in one state, takes effect in another, and kills in a third. The situs problem even arises when a bodily injury occurs in one state based on negligence committed in another, for there is no logical reason why the place of injury should be viewed as the place of the tort any more than should the place of negligence. In all of these situations, the importance of any particular geographical contact is never self-evident; it is a legal rather than a factual consideration that is built into the forum's choice-of-law rules. As the geographical contacts of a transaction proliferate, the choice of any one contact as dispositive runs the risk of appearing arbitrary. But again, this problem pervades real-space conflicts of law and is not unique to cyberspace conflicts.

So the complexity and situs problems inhere to some degree in all transnational conflicts, and are exacerbated in real space and cyberspace alike as jurisdictional contacts proliferate. No choice-of-law rule will prove wholly satisfactory in these situations. However, several factors diminish the skeptics' concerns about the infeasibility of applying traditional choice-of-law tools to cyberspace. For example, the skeptics are wrong to the extent that they believe that cyberspace transactions must be resolved on the basis of geographical choice-of-law criteria that are sometimes difficult to apply to cyberspace, such as where events occur or where people are located at the time of the transaction. But these are not the only choice-of-law criteria, and certainly not the best in contexts where the geographical locus of events is so unclear. Domicile (and its cognates, such as citizenship, principal place of business, habitual residence, and so on) are also valid choice-of-law criteria that have particular relevance to problems, like those in cyberspace, that involve the regulation of intangibles or of multinational transactions. The skeptics are further mistaken to the extent that their arguments assume that all choice-of-law problems must be resolved by multilateral choice-of-law methodologies. A multilateral methodology asks which of several possible laws governs a transaction, and selects one of these laws on the basis of specified criteria. Multilateral methods accentuate the situs and complexity problems. But the regulatory issues that are most relevant to the cyberspace governance debate almost always involve unilateral choice-of-law methods that alleviate these problems. A unilateral method considers only whether the dispute at issue has close enough connections to the forum to justify the application of local law. If so, local law applies; if not, the case is dismissed and the potential applicability of foreign law is not considered. For example, a jurisdiction typically does not apply foreign criminal law. If a Tennessee court has personal jurisdiction over someone from across the Virginia border who shot and killed an in-stater, the court does not consider whether Tennessee or Virginia law applies. It considers only whether Tennessee law applies. If so, the case proceeds; if not, it is dismissed.

Unilateral choice-of-law methods make the complexity and situs problems less significant. They do not require a determination of which of a number of possible laws apply. Nor do they require a court to identify where certain events occurred. What matters is simply whether the activity has local effects that are significant enough to implicate local law. By failing to recognize that courts can and will use unilateral rather than multilateral choice-of-law methods to resolve cyberspace conflicts, the skeptics again exaggerate the challenge of cyberspace regulation.

* * *

VI. RELATED MATTERS

A. SUBJECT-MATTER JURISDICTION

A court has subject-matter jurisdiction over a case if the substance of a case brings it within the court's adjudicatory authority. The involvement of online communications in the activities giving rise to a lawsuit rarely creates new issues with respect to subject matter jurisdiction. The subject-matter jurisdiction of federal district courts is established by statute (subject to certain constitutional limitations, such as the justiciability requirements). Most generally, the district courts have jurisdiction over cases in which the parties are citizens of different states, or citizens of a state and a foreign country, and cases that arise under federal law. *See* 28 U.S.C. § 1332 (diversity jurisdiction); 28 U.S.C. § 1331 (federal question jurisdiction). Questions of citizenship, and of whether a cause of action arises under federal law, are rarely affected by whether the communication relating to the cause of action takes place online or offline. The subject-matter jurisdiction of state courts is likewise generally unaffected by the involvement of online communications.

One situation in which online communications may raise novel issues is where subject-matter jurisdiction depends upon the existence of interstate commerce. The most general constitutional basis for exercise of federal legislative authority is the Commerce Clause, which authorizes Congress "To regulate Commerce with foreign Nations, and among the several States, and with the Indian Tribes." U.S.CONST. art. I, § 8, cl. 3. Many federal statutes apply by their terms only to interstate activities—e.g., 15 U.S.C. § 1125(a) & (c) (trademark infringement and dilution require use of a mark "in commerce"); 15 U.S.C. § 1263 (prohibiting "[t]he introduction or delivery for introduction into interstate commerce of any misbranded hazardous substance or banned hazardous substance"); 16 U.S.C. § 824 (regulating "the transmission of electric energy in interstate commerce"). Federal statutes that do not contain an explicit commerce limitation, but draw their authority from the Commerce Clause, likewise may be applied consistently with the Constitution only if the case arises from interstate commerce.

Several federal statutes regulate certain types of *communications* that occur in interstate commerce. For example, the Wire Fraud statute makes it illegal to "transmit[] * * * by means of wire * * * communication in interstate or foreign commerce" any communication for the purpose of executing any scheme to obtain money by fraud. 18 U.S.C. § 1343. Similarly, the federal threats statute makes it illegal to "transmit[] in interstate or foreign commerce any communication containing any threat to kidnap any person or any threat to injure the person of another." 18 U.S.C. § 875(c). Normally these statutes are applicable in situations where a person in one state engages in a communication with a person in another state, thereby satisfying the "interstate commerce" requirement. But what if the two people who are communicating are located in a single state, and they communicate via an online medium that routes the communication through another state? Is the communication in "interstate commerce"?

The court gave an affirmative answer to this question in *United States v. Kammersell*, 7 F.Supp.2d 1196 (D.Utah 1998), which involved a defendant who was charged with making a threat in violation of 18 U.S.C. § 875(c). Defendant had sent a threatening communication from his location in Utah to the target, also located in Utah. The communication, an America Online "insta-message," was routed through AOL's server in

Virginia. The court found that this communication was in interstate commerce, on a plain reading of the statute. " 'Transmits * * * in interstate commerce' is not ambiguous. * * * Its plain meaning encompasses the conduct in this case. * * * The fact that the recipient of the threat was located in the same state is of no consequence." 7 F.Supp.2d at 1199–1200, 1202.

In concluding that the location of the two communicators is irrelevant, the court relied on (a) *United States v. Whiffen*, 121 F.3d 18 (1st Cir.1997), finding that a call from a New Hampshire location to another New Hampshire phone number, which was automatically transferred so that the caller was speaking with a person located in Florida, was in interstate commerce; (b) *United States v. Alkhabaz*, 104 F.3d 1492 (6th Cir.1997), which found it indisputable that e-mail transmissions between a person located in Ontario and a person located in Michigan are in interstate or foreign commerce; and (c) *United States v. Kelner*, 534 F.2d 1020 (2d Cir.1976), which found the interstate commerce requirement satisfied by a threat transmitted via a television broadcast that was received outside the state where the broadcaster was located, though the target of the threat was located in the same state as the broadcaster.

NOTES & QUESTIONS

1. *Communication in interstate commerce.* Do you agree with the court in *U.S. v. Kammersell* that the term "interstate commerce" unambiguously includes a communication between two people located in the same state, if it is routed through another state? Do the three cases the court relies on support this conclusion? Could the term be fairly read as encompassing only communications between people located in different states? If America Online happened to have a server located in Utah, through which the message was routed, the court would presumably have concluded that the communication was not in interstate commerce. Is it sensible for subject-matter jurisdiction to turn on such a fortuity?

2. *Other scenarios.* How would the *Kammersell* court's reasoning apply in a situation where a person accesses a website whose owner is located in the same state, but the server hosting the website is located in another state? What if the web server and both communicators are located in a single state, but some of the packets constituting the communication are routed through a server located in another state? What if a person sends a threat via Federal Express to a recipient located in the same state, but the airplane carrying the letter touches down in Memphis, where Federal Express has its hub? *See* Katherine C. Sheehan, *Predicting the Future: Personal Jurisdiction for the Twenty-First Century*, 66 U. CIN. L. REV. 385, 419 (1998) (noting that at one time "most Federal Express packages, regardless of origin or destination, were routed through Memphis, Tennessee").

B. GENERAL JURISDICTION

May operation of a website constitute sufficient contacts with a state to support general jurisdiction? As discussed in Part I, *supra*, a defendant's contacts with a state will support general jurisdiction over his activities—that is, jurisdiction over any claims brought against the defendant, regardless of whether they arise from the forum contacts—if they are "continuous and systematic." This criterion presents a much higher hurdle than that which the plaintiff must clear to establish specific jurisdiction.

No court has held that a website alone may give rise to general jurisdiction, but at least one court has ruled that in circumstances where other types of forum contacts are inadequate, the presence of a website may supply the additional contacts needed to support a finding that the court has general jurisdiction over the defendant. In *Haelan Products Inc. v. Beso Biological*, 43 U.S.P.Q.2d (BNA) 1672 (E.D.La.1997), the defendant's contacts with the forum state consisted of placing advertisements in nationally circulated trade magazines, maintaining a toll-free telephone number, and operating a website. The court held: "Although [defendant's] advertisements in trade magazines alone would not be sufficient to establish minimum contacts, * * * [and] [a]lthough [defendant's] Internet site would be insufficient, * * * [the] Internet site and toll-free number, in addition to advertisements in four national trade publications, constitute a 'purposeful availment' of" the forum state, supporting general jurisdiction.

In *Mieczkowski v. Masco Corp.*, 997 F.Supp. 782 (E.D.Tex.1998), the defendant furniture seller's contacts with the forum state included selling $5.7 million of products to forum residents over a six-year period, sending direct mailings to forum residents twice a year, purchasing 0.2 percent of its furniture from a company located in the forum state, and maintaining a website. The court analyzed the significance of the website through application of the *Zippo* three-category approach: it classified the site as an interactive one, and looked to the *Zippo* factors of the "level of interactivity and commercial nature of the exchange of information." The court added: "It should be noted that the majority of courts that have addressed this issue have done so in the context of specific jurisdiction analysis. However, the Court sees no reason why the analysis should not be applied equally to cases involving a general jurisdiction analysis." *Id.* at 786 n.3. The court held that it "need not decide today whether standing alone the Web site maintained by the defendant is sufficient to satisfy a finding of general jurisdiction [, nor] must it look only to the traditional business contacts that the defendant has with * * * Texas. Rather, it is the combination of the two that leads the Court to the conclusion that the defendant maintains substantial, continuous and systematic contacts with Texas sufficient to subject it to personal jurisdiction." *Id.* at 788.

NOTES & QUESTIONS

1. Zippo *applied to general jurisdiction analysis.* Do you agree with the court in *Mieczkowski v. Masco* that the *Zippo* analysis is the appropriate tool for ascertaining whether a website supports general jurisdiction? What is the logic behind using the same criterion, namely that proposed in *Zippo*, both to determine whether a website meets the requirements for specific jurisdiction and to determine whether it meets the more stringent requirements for general jurisdiction? In the absence of the other forum contacts, under what circumstances would the "interactivity" analysis lead to a conclusion that the website contacts were sufficiently "continuous and systematic" to support general jurisdiction? The court in *Mink v. AAAA Development LLC*, 190 F.3d 333 (5th Cir.1999), likewise applied the *Zippo* analysis to evaluate whether a website supported general jurisdiction, without noting that the analysis was designed for determining whether the standards for specific jurisdiction were met.

2. *No general jurisdiction based on website alone.* Numerous cases have held that online contacts alone do not support general jurisdiction. Courts have declined to find general jurisdiction based on a passive website, *Mid City Bowling Lanes & Sports Palace, Inc. v. Ivercrest, Inc.*, 35 F.Supp.2d 507 (E.D.La.1999); an interactive website, *ESAB Group, Inc. v. Centricut*, LLC, 34 F.Supp.2d 323 (D.S.C.1999); a website that allows visitors to make hotel reservations online, *Rodriguez v. Circus Circus Casinos, Inc.*, 2001 WL 21244 (S.D.N.Y.2001); hosting a website on a server located in the forum state, *Jewish Defense Organization, Inc. v. Superior Court*, 85 Cal.Rptr.2d 611 (Cal.Ct.App.1999); online publication of an allegedly defamatory article, *Naxos Resources (U.S.A.) Ltd. v. Southam Inc.*, 1996 WL 662451 (C.D.Cal.1996); and posting messages on a proprietary bulletin board system, *California Software Inc. v. Reliability Research, Inc.*, 631 F.Supp. 1356 (C.D.Cal.1986). Another court has held that defendant's entering into 46 transactions with residents of the forum state, through its website and toll-free telephone number, did not give rise to general jurisdiction. *Robbins v. Yutopian Enterprises, Inc.*, 202 F.Supp.2d 426 (D. Md.2002).

CHAPTER EIGHT

PRIVACY ONLINE

In this chapter we explore the law and policy of protection of information privacy in a networked world. One widely cited work on information privacy defines it as "the claim of individuals, groups, or institutions to determine for themselves when, how, and to what extent information about them is communicated to others." ALAN F. WESTIN, PRIVACY AND FREEDOM 7 (1967). The commercialization of the Internet, which is awash with personal information of all types and which allows this information to be collected, manipulated, and transmitted cheaply and easily, predictably has raised a multitude of novel information privacy issues.

Some of the key issues we will address in this chapter are: Will the market take care of online privacy, or is legislation needed? Do the economic benefits of a less-restrictive online privacy policy justify the resulting privacy intrusions? Should privacy in the online world be treated differently from privacy in the offline world?

I. BACKGROUND: PRIVACY PROTECTION IN THE ONLINE COMMERCIAL ENVIRONMENT

A. LEGAL PROTECTION OF INFORMATION PRIVACY IN THE UNITED STATES

Perhaps the most salient characteristic of legal protection of information privacy in the United States is its ad hoc nature. Some types of information transfers are heavily regulated, while other types, seemingly no less significant to individual privacy interests, are unregulated and left to the mercies of the marketplace. There is no grand scheme that rationalizes the patchwork of legal protections applying to personal information, but only a series of historical accidents and political outcomes that explain them.

For example, the Video Privacy Protection Act of 1988, 18 U.S.C. § 2710, limits disclosure of records of videotape rentals.[1] Information about an individual's book purchases, however, is unregulated.

1. This statute was enacted in response to outrage over the disclosure of the video rental records of Judge Robert Bork during the Senate's consideration of his nomination to be a Justice of the Supreme Court. The disclosure of Judge Bork's video viewing habits revealed nothing racier than James Bond movies.

The General Education Provisions Act was amended in 2002 by adding a provision requiring school boards to provide parents with annual notifications of "[a]ctivities involving the collection, disclosure, or use of personal information collected from students for the purpose of marketing or for selling that information." 20 U.S.C. § 1232h(c)(2)(C)(i). Parents must be offered an opportunity "to opt the student out of participation" in such activities. 20 U.S.C. § 1232h(c)(2)(A)(ii). The requirement, which applies to both online and offline collections of information, was inspired in part by unhappiness about arrangements under which technology companies would provide schools with free computers or Internet access in exchange for the right to monitor students' activities online.

Regulations issued by the Department of Health and Human Services pursuant to statutory authority contained in Section 264(c)(1) of the Health Insurance Portability and Accountability Act of 1996, *reprinted at* 42 U.S.C. § 1320d–2 note, limit disclosure of individually identifiable health information by health care providers, health plans, and health care clearinghouses, without the consent of the individual, except in defined circumstances. 45 C.F.R. pts. 160 & 164.

Several federal laws protect the privacy of financial information. These include the Fair Credit Reporting Act of 1970, 15 U.S.C. §§ 1681–81u, which regulates the disclosure of information from a consumer's credit report; the Fair Debt Collection Practices Act of 1977, 15 U.S.C. §§ 1692–92o, which prevents debt collectors from disclosing information about a consumer's debt to third parties; the Right to Financial Privacy Act of 1978, 12 U.S.C. §§ 3401–22, which regulates the federal government's access to financial information held by a financial institution; and the Gramm–Leach–Bliley Act of 1999, 15 U.S.C. §§ 6801–10, which requires financial institutions to provide consumers with notice and an opportunity to opt out before disclosing certain types of personal financial information to nonaffiliated third parties.

Other laws protect the privacy of information transmitted via telecommunications systems. The Electronic Communications Privacy Act of 1986, 18 U.S.C. §§ 2510–22, 2701–11, prohibits unauthorized interception of electronic communications, including e-mail, and unauthorized access of stored electronic communications. The Telecommunications Act of 1996 includes a provision that protects transactional information concerning telephone calls, including amount of usage and the destination of calls. 47 U.S.C. § 222. The Cable Communications Policy Act of 1984 requires cable operators to disclose to their customers what types of personally identifiable information ("PII") they collect, and how they use and disclose such information; limits the permissible purposes for collection of PII from subscribers; limits disclosures of subscribers' PII; gives subscribers the right to access and correct PII concerning them that a cable operator holds; and requires cable operators to destroy PII that is no longer needed for its original purpose. 47 U.S.C. § 551.

The Family Education Rights and Privacy Act of 1974 regulates handling of student records by educational institutions that receive public funds. The statute limits disclosure of student records absent parental consent, and gives parents a right to access their children's records and correct inaccuracies. 20 U.S.C. § 1232g.

Other constitutional and statutory provisions affect the *government's* handling of personal information. The Fourth Amendment to the Constitution limits the government's ability to search for and seize information in which a person holds a reasonable expectation of privacy. The Privacy Act places some (not very stringent) limitations on the government's use and disclosure of personal information that it holds, and gives individuals a right to access information pertaining to them and to challenge inaccuracies. 5 U.S.C. § 552a. The Driver's Privacy Protection Act of 1974 places limitations (also not very stringent) on disclosure of personal information by a state department of motor vehicles. 18 U.S.C. § 2721.[2]

The only federal statute that specifically addresses the collection of information online is the Children's Online Privacy Protection Act, 15 U.S.C. §§ 6501–05, which regulates collection of personal information from children, as well as disclosure and use of such information. COPPA is discussed in Part V, *infra*.

To the extent that online transfers of personal information are within the scope of laws designed for the offline world, they are likewise subject to this ad hoc set of legal and marketplace controls. As we shall see, many types of online collection of information have no easy offline analog, and in the absence of new legal rules are regulated only by the marketplace.

B. What's New About the Online Environment?

Is there anything about online communications that gives rise to fundamentally new issues relating to informational privacy? Digitization of transactional information, and the use of automatic data processing, were occurring long before the Internet became widely available as a medium for commercial transactions. For decades, digitized data on consumer buying habits and credit usage have been collected in databases and used to target marketing and to make decisions on extension of credit. As long ago as 1967, Professor Alan Westin noted that "general information gathering and the dossier have been radically accelerated by the advent of the electronic digital computer, with its capacity to store more records and manipulate them more effectively and rapidly than was ever possible before." ALAN F. WESTIN, PRIVACY AND FREEDOM 160 (1967). Moreover, vast quantities of transactional information in digitized, personally identifiable form are collected in offline transactions, through widespread use of credit and debit cards and pay-per-call, in sales conducted at a distance through catalogs and telemarketing, and by means of merchant affinity cards.

Yet use of the Internet for business-to-consumer transactions has introduced some novelties that may have an important bearing on informa-

2. This statute was enacted partly in response to the murder of actress Rebecca Schaeffer, whose killer reportedly obtained her address from records made publicly available for a two-dollar fee by the California Department of Motor Vehicles.

tion privacy issues. First, widespread use of computers and open-standard networks has made the process of collecting, storing, correlating, transferring, accessing, and otherwise manipulating data much faster and cheaper. The low cost of collecting personal information means that more of it is collected. The low cost of manipulating data means that more value can be mined from it, which raises the incentives both to collect and to disclose it. The information gathered in this way may be used to create personal profiles, allowing customized advertising messages to be targeted at particular individuals.

Second, the online medium allows pre-transactional data to be captured. When you are browsing at a website, it is a simple matter for the site owner to capture your clickstream information. This includes the identity of every page you have viewed, and any text you enter into web pages, such as search strings. For example, if you research a particular medical problem, the subject of your research can be recorded. If you read an online magazine, the publisher can know which articles you read, and how long you spent on each. If you browse at an online bookstore, the store can get an idea of your reading interests. If you browse at a travel site, the site owner learns something about the travel destinations that interest you. The nature of the online medium makes it economically feasible to store and manipulate such data. By contrast, in offline shopping it is infeasible and uneconomic for merchants to follow you around as you shop, take notes on what items you look at, and record this information in digital form.[3]

Third, anonymous payment mechanisms are not widely available online. In offline shopping you can pay with cash if you want to leave no record of a purchase. When you make a purchase online, your use of a payment mechanism—usually a credit card—generates data that connect you to the purchase.

Fourth, most items that you purchase online must be shipped to you, requiring you to disclose your home address to the merchant. This is also true of other distance selling techniques such as catalog sales, direct mail, and telemarketing, but not of purchasing in brick-and-mortar stores.

Fifth, in online transactions the seller is able to capture data surreptitiously. Through the use of cookies, web bugs, and other technologies of surveillance, discussed in Part III, *infra*, a website can gather personally identifiable information about an Internet user who thinks he is browsing anonymously. By contrast, in a telephone conversation the seller gathers only the information that the consumer chooses to provide—with the possible exception of her telephone number, which can be surreptitiously collected using caller ID. When shopping in person, it is possible for the seller to collect information through spying techniques, but this is unlikely to be feasible or cost effective.

3. This may be changing. Some retailers are placing surveillance cameras and microphones in their stores to gather information on customers' shopping habits. *See* Stephanie Simon, *Shopping with Big Brother*, L.A. TIMES, May 1, 2002, at A1.

Sixth, the Internet makes it easier to gather personal information from children without a parent's authorization. In offline shopping settings a child is more likely to be accompanied by an adult, or at least to be recognized as a child.

FEDERAL TRADE COMMISSION, PRIVACY ONLINE: FAIR INFORMATION PRACTICES IN THE ELECTRONIC MARKETPLACE

(2000).
www.ftc.gov/reports/privacy2000/privacy2000text.pdf.

[In this report, the Federal Trade Commission recommends "that Congress enact legislation that, in conjunction with continuing self-regulatory programs, will ensure adequate protection of consumer privacy online."]

STATEMENT OF COMMISSIONER THOMAS B. LEARY, CONCURRING IN PART AND DISSENTING IN PART

* * *

Recognition of the privacy concerns specific to e-commerce should not obscure the fact that in significant respects online privacy concerns are identical to those raised by offline commerce. The same technology that facilitates the efficient compilation and dissemination of personal information by online companies also allows offline companies to amass, analyze and transfer vast amounts of consumers' personal information. Offline companies collect and compile information about consumers' purchases from grocery stores, pharmacies, retailers, and mail order companies, in particular.

It is also not possible to distinguish offline and online privacy concerns on the basis of the nature of the information collected. With the exception of online profiling, it is the same information. The Report's recommendation would require Amazon.com to comply with the fair information practice principles but not the local bookstore which can compile and disseminate the same information about the reading habits of its customers. The consumer polls, upon which the Report places such significant reliance, demonstrate that consumer concerns about the disclosure of personal information are not dependent on how the data has been collected.

Moreover, it is impractical to maintain such a distinction. Businesses are likely to have a strong incentive to consolidate personal information collected, regardless of the mode of collection, in order to provide potential customers with the most personalized message possible. Already, companies are seeking to merge data collected offline with data collected online. In light of this reality, the majority's recommendation would result in perverse and arbitrary enforcement. Enforcement actions would depend on the source of and method used to collect a particular piece of consumer data rather than on whether there was a clear-cut violation of a company's announced privacy policy or mandated standards.

Finally, the Report's focus only on online privacy issues could ultimately have a detrimental impact on the growth of online commerce, directly contrary to the Report's objectives. It is clear from the Advisory Committee's Report on Access and Security and from limited portions of the Commission's own Report that implementation of the fair information practices will be complex and may create significant compliance costs. Online companies will be placed at a competitive disadvantage relative to their offline counterparts that are not forced to provide consumers with the substantive rights of notice, choice, access and security. Traditional brick and mortar companies that have an online presence or are considering entry into the electronic marketplace will be forced to assess how the cost of regulation will affect their participation in that sector.

A better approach would be to establish a level playing field for online and offline competitors and to address consumers' privacy concerns through clear and conspicuous privacy disclosures. Any privacy concerns that are unique to a particular medium or that involve particular categories of information (however collected) can continue to be addressed through separate legislation.

* * *

Joel R. Reidenberg & Françoise Gamet–Pol, *The Fundamental Role of Privacy and Confidence in the Network*

30 WAKE FOREST L. REV. 105 (1995).

* * *

In the 1960s and early 1970s, computing and telecommunications were generally controlled by the federal government and large corporations. The emergence of personal computers and networking in the mid–1980s, however, contributed to a shift in power to the commercial sector. Smaller private-sector organizations gained access to sophisticated information-processing capabilities through inexpensive equipment. Individuals and small, private organizations obtained access to vast information resources through services such as Prodigy, Compuserve, and America Online. In essence, the Internet and private networks gave globalized access to information to both individuals and small organizations. Globalized access to information and real-time interactivity multiply the options available to users of information, both individuals and businesses. Interactive communications produce numerous transaction records, thereby multiplying choices regarding the use of information as well.

At the beginning of the 1990s, information processing was decentralizing even within large corporations as networks replaced mainframe computers. Today, in the mid–1990s, the decentralization of information processing has made omnipresent surveillance possible by organizations and even individuals. This decentralization enables any network participant to centralize data, for although bits of information are scattered throughout the network, they are accessible from any place on the network. This, however, is not the extent of decentralization's effects. Sophisticated information providers and intelligent networks already enable combinations of audiovisual images and sounds with other interactive services. Further, decentralization of information processing in the United States dramatically broadened the role of private-sector data processing and shifted power from the federal government to private-sector organizations. These private organizations now have exclusive control over the decisions regarding the collection and use of personal information.

* * *

NOTES & QUESTIONS

1. *Separating online and offline privacy.* Are the privacy issues presented by the online medium sufficiently different from offline privacy issues to merit independent legislative treatment? Is it feasible to disentangle the two realms and apply different rules to each? Would application of different rules to the two realms result in harmful distortion of business or consumer economic incentives?

2. *Argument for piecemeal approach.* The concept of privacy is very broad. The interest of individuals in keeping others from knowing of their reading habits may differ from their interest in keeping their medical conditions confidential, and these may differ from their interest in keeping their sexual conduct secret, and all of these may differ from their interest in keeping quiet their past brushes with the law. Even if the U.S. piecemeal approach to privacy protection has come about without serious thought to privacy as a whole, might it nevertheless turn out to be the best approach to the issue?

C. TENSIONS WITHIN THE IDEA OF PRIVACY

Like nearly all other interests that the law recognizes, the interest in privacy is not absolute. Privacy serves a number of valuable functions. Most generally, the ability to control what other people can know about you provides a sphere of free action that is a basic human necessity. The right to keep your identity information secret can help to protect you from stalkers, abusive ex-spouses, and others whose company you wish to avoid, and makes identity theft less likely.[4] Anonymity enables people to blow the whistle on wrongdoing without fear of retribution.[5]

4. Identity theft refers to the wrongful use of a person's identifying information to obtain goods and services fraudulently. An identity thief who learns the victim's name, date of birth, and Social Security number might open a credit card account in the victim's name, go on a spending spree, and then ignore the bills. Since the card is in the victim's name, the card issuer will believe the charges to have been incurred by the victim, and will seek to hold the victim accountable. Although in theory the victim should not suffer due to the actions of the identity thief, in practice it can take months or years, and enormous efforts, before the victim clears her name and regains her credit standing. The Federal Trade Commission maintains a website about identity theft at www.consumer.gov/idtheft.

5. For an extended discussion of the functions of individual privacy, under the rubrics of "personal autonomy, emotional re-

But there are also competing societal interests that may be harmed by the protection of privacy. One way to address these competing interests is to ask "how do we balance the need to use information (by government, commerce, and individuals) with the natural desire of individuals to decide what information about themselves will be exposed to others?" INFORMATION INFRASTRUCTURE TASK FORCE, INFORMATION POLICY COMMITTEE, OPTIONS FOR PROMOTING PRIVACY ON THE NATIONAL INFORMATION INFRASTRUCTURE 7 (1997). These competing interests may be organized under the headings of *accountability*, *free circulation of ideas*, and *efficiency*.

Accountability. Privacy, when it takes the form of anonymity, enables speakers to avoid being held accountable for the consequences of their speech. Although the First Amendment broadly protects the right to free expression, limits the government's authority to impose sanctions on a person based on his speech, and even guarantees anonymity in certain circumstances,[6] there are recognized exceptions. For example, the First Amendment does not prevent the government from imposing liability based on defamation, unauthorized disclosure of trade secrets, false advertising, threats of violence, blackmail, obscenity, advocacy of imminent lawless action, and other speech acts. Anonymity interferes with the law's ability to protect the interests represented by these derogations from an absolute right of freedom of expression. Laws, norms, and self-regulatory practices that protect privacy must take these same competing interests into account.

Privacy as invisibility—a person's ability to control who may learn her whereabouts or how she may be contacted—may also interfere with legitimate societal interests. Invisibility makes it harder for single mothers to track down deadbeat dads, for litigants to locate witnesses, and for law enforcement authorities to collar criminal suspects.

Free circulation of ideas. The First Amendment's Free Speech Clause serves several interests, among them encouraging the free flow of information within what is frequently referred to as the "marketplace of ideas." The Supreme Court has held that this interest is weighty enough to overcome substantial opposing interests, in view of our "profound national commitment to the principle that debate on public issues should be uninhibited, robust, and wide-open, and that it may well include vehement, caustic, and sometimes unpleasantly sharp attacks on government and public officials."[7] Protection of privacy, when it takes the form of limiting disclosure of information that is considered personal, interferes with this goal. Thus, publication of personal information that touches on matters of public concern, and that is true and was legally obtained, is almost always

lease, self-evaluation, and limited and protected communication," see ALAN F. WESTIN, PRIVACY AND FREEDOM 32–39 (1967). For another philosophical perspective on the functions of individual privacy, see ANITA L. ALLEN, UNEASY ACCESS: PRIVACY FOR WOMEN IN A FREE SOCIETY (1988).

6. *See McIntyre v. Ohio Elections Commission*, 514 U.S. 334 (1995).

7. *New York Times Co. v. Sullivan*, 376 U.S. 254, 270 (1964).

protected.[8] But, when the First Amendment right to free association—the right to nondisclosure of the identity of those with whom one chooses to associate—is opposed to society's interest in the free flow of information, free association may sometimes prevail. Thus, compelled disclosure of membership lists has been held to violate the First Amendment.[9] In addition, in the context of reproductive rights the Supreme Court has recognized a constitutionally protected privacy interest "in avoiding disclosure of personal matters."[10]

Limiting disclosure of personal information can interfere with the ability of researchers and investigative journalists to do their work. Protected private information may be newsworthy itself, or may lead to other newsworthy information.[11]

Efficiency. Privacy is also sometimes opposed to the societal interest in facilitating efficient commercial transactions. Data collected from commercial transactions involving individual consumers are used to create profiles of prospective customers that enable marketers to target promotional solicitations to consumers who are more likely to find them of interest. This results in a higher return rate, and therefore reduces the cost of marketing. Giving individuals a right to prevent the use of their transactional data for these purposes interferes with the creation of lists that permit such targeting. In addition to making marketing more expensive, it may also be contrary to the individual's own interests in minimizing the quantity of junk mail and telemarketing that she receives, since a lower return rate might mean that more solicitations must be sent out. Limiting businesses' use of transactional information can make it harder for new entrants to compete:

> Because trade in consumer information serves an important economic function, regulatory obstacles to collecting this information can have hidden economic costs. * * * The mandatory opt-in rule would favor larger and older companies at the expense of newer, smaller ones. Established companies could afford more costly lists more easily than could small companies. And established companies would also have less need for lists, since they would have been in business long enough to collect information on their own. *The brunt of an opt-in law would thus be borne by small, new businesses or nonprofits struggling to establish a customer base.* * * * Under mandatory opt-in, firms that could afford

8. *See Florida Star v. B.J.F.*, 491 U.S. 524 (1989) (First Amendment trumps state law forbidding publication of the name of a victim of a sexual offense); *Landmark Communications, Inc. v. Virginia*, 435 U.S. 829 (1978) (First Amendment overcomes law prohibiting publication of names of judges who are under investigation for misconduct).

9. *See N.A.A.C.P. v. Alabama*, 357 U.S. 449 (1958) (preventing compelled production of NAACP's membership list).

10. *Whalen v. Roe*, 429 U.S. 589, 599 (1977).

11. For a criticism from a First Amendment perspective of proposals to protect information privacy through legal restrictions on the disclosure of information, see Eugene Volokh, *Freedom of Speech and Information Privacy: The Troubling Implications of a Right to Stop People from Speaking About You*, 52 STAN. L. REV. 1049 (2000).

> to send direct mail would no longer be able to target it effectively. That would lead to fewer, more expensive options for those who shop at home—the elderly, the disabled, rural residents, and anyone without a car—because their mobility is restricted. In a world without readily available, cheap marketing lists, it is doubtful that another company like Lands' End would ever be born. Mandatory opt-in could preclude, not only the development of new businesses, but the development of whole new business models and product lines designed to serve groups of customers that could never before be identified. Had mandatory opt-in rules been in place a hundred years ago, for example, consumer credit reporting might never have developed.

Solveig Singleton, *Privacy as Censorship: A Skeptical View of Proposals to Regulate Privacy in the Private Sector*, Cato Policy Analysis No. 295 (Jan. 22, 1998), www.cato.org/pubs/pas/pa–295es.html.

Privacy of medical records can interfere with the provision of emergency medical services. If consent is required before medical personnel may access the records of a person in need of emergency treatment, and the person is in a condition that makes it impossible for her to grant that consent, provision of medical services may be delayed or based on incomplete information.

The ability to conceal information that reflects badly on yourself, in the name of privacy, can interfere with the ability of others to make rational decisions concerning you; as for example if the fact of your criminal record is unavailable to a potential employer, business associate, or spouse, or if your poor credit history is unavailable to a prospective lender.

NOTES & QUESTIONS

1. *Balancing competing values*. Evaluate the following argument: Expressing the problem of privacy protection as one of "balancing" competing values is a formulation that leads to no stable solution. We are better off thinking of it as an optimization problem, which we can approach either from a utilitarian or a moral rights perspective. From a utilitarian perspective, we should extend the right of privacy as far as it will yield benefits exceeding its costs. From a moral rights perspective, we should sometimes protect privacy for its own sake, regardless of the costs entailed.

2. *A communitarian perspective*. Professor Amitai Etzioni urges a "communitarian" approach that explicitly recognizes the claims of societal interests that conflict with privacy interests. He argues that there is no basis for privileging privacy above all other societal interests: where individual interests conflict with communal interests, in some circumstances the individual interests must yield. He proposes a methodology for ascertaining whether a particular invasion of privacy, in the service of some societal goal, is justified:

> First, a well-balanced, communitarian society will take steps to limit privacy only if it faces a *well-documented and macroscopic threat* to the common good, not a merely hypothetical danger. * * * [For example, w]hen many thousands of lives are lost and many millions more are at risk, as with HIV, we face a clear and major threat. The effects of abusing marijuana are real but of a much lower magnitude, and hence do not justify the same kind of response. * * * The second criterion is to look at how carefully a society acts to counter a tangible and macroscopic danger without *first resorting to measures that might restrict privacy.* * * * Third, to the extent that privacy-curbing measures must be introduced, a communitarian society makes them as *minimally intrusive* as possible. * * * Lastly, measures that *treat undesirable side effects* of needed privacy-diminishing measures are to be preferred over those that ignore these effects.

AMITAI ETZIONI, THE LIMITS OF PRIVACY 12–13 (1999).

Do you agree that there is no aspect of informational privacy that we should regard as absolute, indefeasible regardless of the countervailing interests?

II. FAIR INFORMATION PRACTICE PRINCIPLES

One widely followed approach to information privacy issues is to implement privacy protections that correspond to a set of principles defining fair information practices. Statements of these principles have had an important impact on policy discussions concerning information privacy on the Internet.

FEDERAL TRADE COMMISSION, PRIVACY ONLINE: A REPORT TO CONGRESS

(1998).
www.ftc.gov/reports/privacy3.

* * *

III. Fair Information Practice Principles

A. Fair Information Practice Principles Generally

Over the past quarter century, government agencies in the United States, Canada, and Europe have studied the manner in which entities collect and use personal information—their "information practices"—and the safeguards required to assure those practices are fair and provide adequate privacy protection.[27] The result has been a series of reports,

27. Fair information practice principles were first articulated in a comprehensive manner in the United States Department of Health, Education and Welfare's seminal

guidelines, and model codes that represent widely-accepted principles concerning fair information practices.

Common to all of these documents [hereinafter referred to as "fair information practice codes"] are five core principles of privacy protection: (1) Notice/Awareness; (2) Choice/Consent; (3) Access/Participation; (4) Integrity/Security; and (5) Enforcement/Redress.

1. Notice/Awareness

The most fundamental principle is notice. Consumers should be given notice of an entity's information practices before any personal information is collected from them. Without notice, a consumer cannot make an informed decision as to whether and to what extent to disclose personal information. Moreover, three of the other principles discussed below—choice/consent, access/participation, and enforcement/redress—are only meaningful when a consumer has notice of an entity's policies, and his or her rights with respect thereto.

While the scope and content of notice will depend on the entity's substantive information practices, notice of some or all of the following have been recognized as essential to ensuring that consumers are properly informed before divulging personal information:

- identification of the entity collecting the data;
- identification of the uses to which the data will be put;
- identification of any potential recipients of the data;
- the nature of the data collected and the means by which it is collected if not obvious (passively, by means of electronic monitoring, or actively, by asking the consumer to provide the information);
- whether the provision of the requested data is voluntary or required, and the consequences of a refusal to provide the requested information; and
- the steps taken by the data collector to ensure the confidentiality, integrity and quality of the data.

1973 report entitled *Records, Computers and the Rights of Citizens* (1973) [hereinafter "HEW Report"]. In the twenty-five years that have elapsed since the HEW Report, a canon of fair information practice principles has been developed by a variety of governmental and inter-governmental agencies. In addition to the HEW Report, the major reports setting forth the core fair information practice principles are: The Privacy Protection Study Commission, *Personal Privacy in an Information Society* (1977) [hereinafter *"Privacy Protection Study"*]; Organization for Economic Cooperation and Development, *OECD Guidelines on the Protection of Privacy and Transborder Flows of Personal Data* (1980) [hereinafter *"OECD Guidelines"*]; Information Infrastructure Task Force, Information Policy Committee, Privacy Working Group, *Privacy and the National Information Infrastructure: Principles for Providing and Using Personal Information* (1995) [hereinafter *"IITF Report"*]; U.S. Dept. of Commerce, *Privacy and the NII: Safeguarding Telecommunications–Related Personal Information* (1995) [hereinafter *"Commerce Report"*]; *The European Union Directive on the Protection of Personal Data* (1995) [hereinafter *"EU Directive"*]; and the Canadian Standards Association, *Model Code for the Protection of Personal Information: A National Standard of Canada* (1996) [hereinafter *"CSA Model Code"*]. * * *

Some information practice codes state that the notice should also identify any available consumer rights, including: any choice respecting the use of the data; whether the consumer has been given a right of access to the data; the ability of the consumer to contest inaccuracies; the availability of redress for violations of the practice code; and how such rights can be exercised.

In the Internet context, notice can be accomplished easily by the posting of an information practice disclosure describing an entity's information practices on a company's site on the Web. To be effective, such a disclosure should be clear and conspicuous, posted in a prominent location, and readily accessible from both the site's home page and any Web page where information is collected from the consumer. It should also be unavoidable and understandable so that it gives consumers meaningful and effective notice of what will happen to the personal information they are asked to divulge.

2. Choice/Consent

The second widely-accepted core principle of fair information practice is consumer choice or consent. At its simplest, choice means giving consumers options as to how any personal information collected from them may be used. Specifically, choice relates to secondary uses of information—*i.e.,* uses beyond those necessary to complete the contemplated transaction. Such secondary uses can be internal, such as placing the consumer on the collecting company's mailing list in order to market additional products or promotions, or external, such as the transfer of information to third parties.

Traditionally, two types of choice/consent regimes have been considered: opt-in or opt-out. Opt-in regimes require affirmative steps by the consumer to allow the collection and/or use of information; opt-out regimes require affirmative steps to prevent the collection and/or use of such information. The distinction lies in the default rule when no affirmative steps are taken by the consumer. Choice can also involve more than a binary yes/no option. Entities can, and do, allow consumers to tailor the nature of the information they reveal and the uses to which it will be put. Thus, for example, consumers can be provided separate choices as to whether they wish to be on a company's general internal mailing list or a marketing list sold to third parties. In order to be effective, any choice regime should provide a simple and easily-accessible way for consumers to exercise their choice.

In the online environment, choice easily can be exercised by simply clicking a box on the computer screen that indicates a user's decision with respect to the use and/or dissemination of the information being collected. The online environment also presents new possibilities to move beyond the opt-in/opt-out paradigm. For example, consumers could be required to specify their preferences regarding information use before entering a Web site, thus effectively eliminating any need for default rules.

3. Access/Participation

Access is the third core principle. It refers to an individual's ability both to access data about him or herself—*i.e.,* to view the data in an entity's files—and to contest that data's accuracy and completeness. Both are essential to ensuring that data are accurate and complete. To be meaningful, access must encompass timely and inexpensive access to data, a simple means for contesting inaccurate or incomplete data, a mechanism by which the data collector can verify the information, and the means by which corrections and/or consumer objections can be added to the data file and sent to all data recipients.

4. Integrity/Security

The fourth widely accepted principle is that data be accurate and secure. To assure data integrity, collectors must take reasonable steps, such as using only reputable sources of data and cross-referencing data against multiple sources, providing consumer access to data, and destroying untimely data or converting it to anonymous form.

Security involves both managerial and technical measures to protect against loss and the unauthorized access, destruction, use, or disclosure of the data. Managerial measures include internal organizational measures that limit access to data and ensure that those individuals with access do not utilize the data for unauthorized purposes. Technical security measures to prevent unauthorized access include encryption in the transmission and storage of data; limits on access through use of passwords; and the storage of data on secure servers or computers that are inaccessible by modem.

5. Enforcement/Redress

It is generally agreed that the core principles of privacy protection can only be effective if there is a mechanism in place to enforce them. Absent an enforcement and redress mechanism, a fair information practice code is merely suggestive rather than prescriptive, and does not ensure compliance with core fair information practice principles. Among the alternative enforcement approaches are industry self-regulation; legislation that would create private remedies for consumers; and/or regulatory schemes enforceable through civil and criminal sanctions.

a. Self–Regulation

To be effective, self-regulatory regimes should include both mechanisms to ensure compliance (enforcement) and appropriate means of recourse by injured parties (redress). Mechanisms to ensure compliance include making acceptance of and compliance with a code of fair information practices a condition of membership in an industry association; external audits to verify compliance; and certification of entities that have adopted and comply with the code at issue. A self-regulatory regime with many of these principles has recently been adopted by the individual reference services industry.

Appropriate means of individual redress include, at a minimum, institutional mechanisms to ensure that consumers have a simple and effective way to have their concerns addressed. Thus, a self-regulatory system should provide a means to investigate complaints from individual consumers and ensure that consumers are aware of how to access such a system.

If the self-regulatory code has been breached, consumers should have a remedy for the violation. Such a remedy can include both the righting of the wrong (*e.g.*, correction of any misinformation, cessation of unfair practices) and compensation for any harm suffered by the consumer. Monetary sanctions would serve both to compensate the victim of unfair practices and as an incentive for industry compliance. Industry codes can provide for alternative dispute resolution mechanisms to provide appropriate compensation.

b. Private Remedies

A statutory scheme could create private rights of action for consumers harmed by an entity's unfair information practices. Several of the major information practice codes, including the seminal 1973 HEW Report, call for implementing legislation. The creation of private remedies would help create strong incentives for entities to adopt and implement fair information practices and ensure compensation for individuals harmed by misuse of their personal information. Important questions would need to be addressed in such legislation, *e.g.*, the definition of unfair information practices; the availability of compensatory, liquidated and/or punitive damages; and the elements of any such cause of action.

c. Government Enforcement

Finally, government enforcement of fair information practices, by means of civil or criminal penalties, is a third means of enforcement. Fair information practice codes have called for some government enforcement, leaving open the question of the scope and extent of such powers. Whether enforcement is civil or criminal likely will depend on the nature of the data at issue and the violation committed.

* * *

NOTES & QUESTIONS

1. *A widely recognized formulation.* This formulation of the fair information practice principles underpins several industry self-regulatory efforts aimed at online privacy. See, for example, the principles implemented by the TRUSTe privacy seal program, discussed in Part IV(B), *infra*, the guidelines adopted by the Online Privacy Alliance, discussed in Part IV(A), *infra*, and the content of website privacy notices created by the Direct Marketing Association's privacy policy generator, discussed in Part IV(A), Note 2, *infra*.

2. *Substantive content of notice.* Should the "Notice" principle extend to the *content* of a website's privacy practices, or only to whether those practices are disclosed in a clear and conspicuous manner? Consider the following hypothetical privacy notice:

> We collect and retain all of the personally identifiable information we can extract from your online activities, including all of your clickstream activity. Using a cookie, we associate this information with your online identity. We also make every effort to link this information to your real-world identity, and are usually successful. We will use the information we have gathered to target-market you to whatever extent we find profitable. We will also avail ourselves of every opportunity to sell, rent, share, or trade your personal information with any other commercial entity if by doing so we can turn a buck.

Is this privacy statement objectionable from the standpoint of the fair information practice principles?

3. *Comprehensibility of notice.* Website privacy notices tend to be long, rambling, full of legalese, diluted with extraneous material, and generally incomprehensible to most people. One analysis of the privacy policies posted at some of the most heavily trafficked sites on the Web found that they were all written at a college reading level or higher, while most people in the United States read at a tenth-grade level or below. One of these policies was eight pages long, containing 3,405 words and 167 sentences. *See* Will Rodger, *Privacy Isn't Public Knowledge* (Jun. 7, 2000), www.usatoday.com/life/cyber/tech/cth818.htm. How easily comprehensible must a privacy notice be for it to be considered adequate notice? Is the subject of online privacy so complex that it is impossible for a website to disclose its practices in a brief and understandable manner?

4. *Regulation of notices?* Various provisions of consumer protection law require sellers to give notices to consumers, and regulate the content and presentation of those notices. Should privacy notices be similarly regulated? Compare Chapter 6, *supra*.

5. *Choice: Opt-in vs. opt-out.* The question whether the exercise of choice should be through an opt-in or an opt-out mechanism has provoked heated debate. Since few Internet users exercise any choice they are offered, the default option is the one that is "selected" in the vast majority of cases. Marketers therefore strongly prefer opt-out. Privacy advocates are critical of opt-out, on the ground that it does not represent the exercise of informed consent on the part of the user. Consider the following viewpoint:

> [Opt-out] puts the burden of protecting privacy on the consumer. Most people have neither the time, know-how, or gumption to examine closely the uses to which their data will be put; they are unlikely to take the initiative to direct dozens of Web sites to not shadow and share.
>
> "Opt out" is the marketer's public relations trick to provide the pretense of choice. * * * The only genuine online privacy protection is *informed, written consent*. That is when the burden of getting permission to pass around personal data falls where it belongs, on the seller, who must explain the deal and persuade or offer inducements to the buyer to choose to give permission.

William Safire, *Stalking the Internet*, N.Y. TIMES, May 30, 2000, at A19.

Marketers vigorously oppose that point of view. In a case brought by a company protesting FCC privacy regulations, the Tenth Circuit held that an FCC regulation requiring opt-in consent to the use and disclosure of customer information by telecommunications carriers is an unconstitutional regulation of speech, in violation of the First Amendment. *See U.S. West, Inc. v. Federal Communications Commission*, 182 F.3d 1224 (10th Cir. 1999). The regulation in question was an interpretation of certain elements of a consumer privacy provision enacted as part of the Telecommunication Act of 1996. The privacy provision established that a telecommunications carrier could use its customers' personal information for certain marketing purposes only "with the approval of the customer." Under the challenged regulation, this approval had to be obtained through an opt-in method. The carriers preferred to obtain the required approval through an opt-out approach, under which a customer's approval would be inferred from her failure to express disapproval. Since the speech in question consisted of marketing messages, the court analyzed the regulation under the standards that apply to commercial speech. The court held that the government had failed adequately to establish that the carriers' use of customers' personal information for marketing purposes results in any real harm to the customers' privacy interests. The court also held that the FCC had failed to establish that the opt-in requirement was "narrowly tailored" to achieve its objective, given the availability of the less-restrictive opt-out approach: "[T]he FCC record does not adequately show that an opt-out strategy would not sufficiently protect customer privacy. The respondents merely speculate that there are a substantial number of individuals who feel strongly about their privacy, yet would not bother to opt-out if given notice and the opportunity to do so. Such speculation hardly reflects the careful calculation of costs and benefits that our commercial speech jurisprudence requires." *Id.* at 1239.

6. *Access.* The question of appropriate access has been a thorny issue for U.S. policy-makers. A blue-ribbon advisory committee assembled by the FTC was able to do little more than agree to disagree on such issues as what access consists of, what information should be subject to access, how to implement access when information is shared among various third parties, and who should bear the cost of access. *See* FINAL REPORT OF THE FEDERAL TRADE COMMISSION ADVISORY COMMITTEE ON ONLINE ACCESS AND SECURITY (2000), www.ftc.gov/acoas/index.htm. The European Commission's Data Protection Directive includes an access right that is in some respects equivocal, but does give the data subject a right to "communication to him in an intelligible form of the data undergoing processing and of any available information as to their source," and also "as appropriate the rectification, erasure or blocking of data the processing of which does not comply with the provisions of this Directive, in particular because of the incomplete or inaccurate nature of the data." Directive 95/46/EC of the European Parliament and of the Council of 24 October 1995 on the protection of individuals with regard to the processing of personal data and on the free movement of such data, art. 12, 1995 O.J. (L 281) 31, at 42, discussed in Part IV(D), *infra*.

7. *The EU Data Protection Directive and supplemental fair information practice principles.* European Union member states are required to institute privacy protection for data subjects under the European Commission's Data Protection Directive, *supra*. The Data Protection Directive goes beyond the FTC's formulation of the fair information practice principles in four significant respects.

First, the Directive places a substantive limitation on the quantity of personal data that is collected, requiring that it be "not excessive in relation to the purposes for which [the data] are collected and/or further processed." Art. 6(1)(c). Second, personal data must be "kept in a form which permits identification of data subjects for no longer than is necessary for the purposes for which the data were collected or for which they are further processed." Art. 6(1)(e). Third, the processing of certain sensitive types of data is off limits: with certain exceptions, it is impermissible to process "personal data revealing racial or ethnic origin, political opinions, religious or philosophical beliefs, trade-union membership, and * * * data concerning health or sex life." Art. 8(1). Fourth, the onward transfer of personal data is subject to the limitation that in the hands of the transferee the data must retain "an adequate level of protection." Art. 25(1).

These provisions might be formulated as four additional fair information practice principles: "Minimal Collection," "Minimal Retention," "Sensitivity," and "Onward Transfer Protection." If you were devising a list of the cardinal privacy protection principles, would you include any or all of these additional principles?

III. Online Technologies of Surveillance and Their Implications for Data Privacy

A. Undisclosed Collection of Information from Internet Users

When accessing the Internet from your personal computer it is natural to assume that, unless you choose to identify yourself, your activities are anonymous. That is an illusion. Network technology has spawned mechanisms that allow a website operator to learn the identity and track the online activities of website visitors, and enable senders of e-mail to receive notification when the recipient opens the message. Cookies brand an Internet user's computer with a unique identifying number that facilitates tracking, and web bugs allow web pages and e-mail messages to "call home" and report the information they have gathered. This surveillance is carried out in a manner that is invisible to most Internet users, and that may be difficult to prevent. Privacy advocates view this surveillance as one of the most serious and intrusive threats to the privacy interests of Internet users.

1. TECHNOLOGIES OF SURVEILLANCE

a. *Cookies*

When you use your computer to access a website, your computer transmits certain information to the website, including the URL of the web page you are seeking to access (which tells the website what data you want it to send to you), the IP address of your computer (which tells the website where to send the data so that you can receive it), the URL of the web page you are viewing at the time you access the site, and certain configuration information about your computer. This information is usually not sufficient to allow the website operator to recognize you, the next time you access the site, as someone who has previously visited the site.[12] Nor does it generally allow the website operator to ascertain your real-world identity.

Cookies were designed to overcome this identity gap. A cookie is a unique identification code that a website causes to be placed on a computer as it accesses the site.[13] The next time you visit the website, it reads the cookie it left behind on your computer, and is able to recognize you—or at least the computer you are using—as one who has previously visited the site. Cookies can also contain additional information, such as a password or user preferences, that can be read by the server that placed it on your computer.

This rather simple capability has profound implications for the privacy of website visitors. Each time you access a website, you transmit clickstream information to the site, consisting at a minimum of the URL of each page you visit at the site. Once a site has assigned your computer a unique identification code, it can collect all of the clickstream data created by visits using your computer and associate those data with your identification code. Thus, a website can create a dossier of information that is associated with your computer, and can use this information to personalize its interaction with you. For example, if you visit a sporting goods site on several occasions, and view a number of web pages showing tennis racquets, the next time you visit the site it can serve you a personalized home page that features special offers on tennis racquets. Although the site does not know your real-world identity—your name, address, age, gender, or anything

12. With the dial-up connections that most people use to access the Internet from their home computers, the IP address is usually "dynamic": it may change each time the computer dials in and makes a new connection to the Internet. Since this identifier is not persistent, it does not allow a website operator to identify a visitor. Some types of broadband connections, such as digital subscriber line and cable, may use "static" IP addresses: the address of the computer is always the same, giving the computer a persistent identity. The same is true of most connections to the Internet through a local area network.

13. Cookies come in different flavors. "Session" cookies are maintained in your computer's memory while your computer is connected to the Internet, and disappear as soon as you close your browser. "Persistent" cookies are written to a file on the hard drive of your computer—usually either into a file named "cookies.txt," or into a file directory named "cookies." It is only persistent cookies that allow a website to recognize your computer in subsequent visits to the site.

else—it does recognize you as somebody who has manifested an interest in tennis racquets.

Now suppose that in one visit to the website you provide some personal information about yourself. The unique identifier contained in the cookie the site has installed on your hard drive allows the website to associate this information with all the other data it has recorded in your dossier. If, for example, you give the website your e-mail address to subscribe to a free newsletter or to enter a contest, the site will "know"—possess data revealing—that all the clickstream data it has previously collected from you belongs to a person with a particular e-mail address. It can then use the information in its dossier to send you e-mail messages containing promotional material tailored to your interests. Or the website might want to know more. Before it sends you the free newsletter, or enters you in a contest to win a vacation for two to the Bahamas, it may ask for your age, gender, and income range. Then it has more to go on: it can tailor its promotional messages taking into account this demographic information as well. The website owner may also be able to make some money by renting your e-mail address and demographic information to another company, so that it too can send you targeted direct marketing material.

Finally you break down and decide to buy yourself that tennis racquet you have been coveting each time you visit the site. You order it via the website, necessarily providing your name, address, and telephone number so that the seller can have the racquet delivered to you. Now the website knows exactly who you are, and all the information in its dossier becomes associated with your real-world identity. The website operator can now use all of the information it has collected about you to tailor special offers it conveys to you by direct mail and telemarketing, as well as via e-mail. Your dossier becomes a more valuable commodity, which can be rented to a broader range of other sellers. Your activities in visiting that website, past and future, are no longer anonymous.

b. Globally Unique Hardware Identifiers

As described above, installing cookies is a way of branding a computer with a persistent, globally unique identifier that allows the computer to be identified from across the network. A cookie is software—it is a data file that is written to a computer's hard drive. Another type of persistent globally unique identifier ("GUID") is one that is embedded in the computer's hardware. Like a cookie, hardware GUID's can be read remotely from across the network.

One common type of hardware GUID is the identifier that is inscribed on Ethernet cards. An Ethernet card is a device installed in a personal computer that allows it to interconnect with other computers through a local area network ("LAN"). The protocol that is used for routing communications within a LAN requires each of the computers belonging to the LAN to have a unique address. This address is derived from the unique serial number of each computer's Ethernet card.

Within the context of a LAN, the existence of a unique identifier on the Ethernet card raises no privacy concerns, since nobody who uses a computer on the LAN expects that his communications across the LAN will be anonymous. But in early 1999, a privacy advocate named Richard M. Smith announced his discovery of a peculiar feature of the online registration program for Microsoft's Windows 98. If the computer whose copy of Windows 98 was being registered contained an Ethernet card, the registration program would extract the card's unique identification number, place it on the computer's hard drive as a cookie, and transmit the number to Microsoft. When a user of the computer created a document using certain Microsoft application programs, including Word 98 and Excel 98, this GUID would be inserted into the document in a manner that made it invisible to the average user but easily available to those in the know. This gave Microsoft the ability to identify the author of any such document, by looking up the document's GUID in the GUID database created by the Windows 98 registration process. It would also give anybody with access to a computer the ability to identify documents as having originated with that computer, and would make it possible to prove that two particular documents originated from the same computer.

Microsoft received a good deal of criticism after this practice was revealed, and it sought to make amends by announcing it would stop collecting GUIDs in the registration process, delete the GUID database it had assembled from Windows 98 registrations, and make available a program to delete the GUID from an individual computer's Windows registry. It also pledged to remove from its Office 2000 suite of applications the ability to insert GUIDs in documents. *See* Letter from Yusuf Mehdi (Mar. 8, 1999), www.microsoft.com/PressPass/features/1999/03–08custletter2.asp.

c. *Web Bugs*

The HTML code constituting a web page with a graphic image contains an instruction that tells your browser to fetch the image from a particular location on the server hosting the website, or on any other server connected to the Internet, and to place it on the web page it is displaying to you. The HTML protocol allow your browser to append a string of text to the fetch request it sends to the server, and the server is able to read this text. A web bug is an instruction that pretends to be fetching an image to display on your web page, but in fact has the sole purpose of transmitting information from *your* computer to the server computer.[14] The image it fetches generally consists of a single pixel that is the same color as the pixel of the web page over which it is placed, and that therefore has no visible effect on the site visitor's computer. Web bugs are sometimes euphemistically referred to as "clear GIFs," "1 x 1 GIFs," or "web beacons."

A web bug can transmit a variety of information to the server it is pointed at, including the visiting computer's IP address, the URL of the

14. An instruction that is placed in the code of a web page for the bona fide purpose of fetching a graphic image may have a dual character, functioning also as a web bug.

page on which the bug is placed, the time the page containing the bug was displayed, and the identification code contained in any cookie that was placed by that server. What makes a web bug so much more powerful than a cookie alone its ability to transmit information *to a server other than the one that holds the web page the visitor is viewing*. Suppose, for example, that the sporting goods website you are visiting displays a banner advertisement from an online bookseller. In order to display the ad, the code making up the web page of the sporting goods site you are viewing contains an instruction telling your browser to fetch the image constituting the banner ad from a server maintained by the bookseller. The instruction causes your browser to transmit to the bookseller's server the URL of the page you are visiting—the one featuring the tennis racquet of your dreams. The bookseller's server is then able to place on the web page you are about to view a banner ad that it thinks will interest you, say one featuring a book on the history of racquet sports. The bookseller's server is also able to place a cookie on your computer, so that it can begin to assemble a dossier on you. Note that this transmission of information to the bookseller occurs even though you have not clicked on its banner ad or taken any other action expressing an interest in the bookseller.

Now imagine that some company managed to place web bugs on thousands of websites, including the most popular sites on the web. This company would be in a position to assemble quite a detailed profile of your online activities. Every time you viewed a page at any one of those websites, that fact would be transmitted to the company and added to your dossier. If you ever divulged your real-world identity at any of those websites, the company would be able to associate your identity with all of the data it had assembled about you. If the company were able to link this dossier with other collections of information about your offline activities, quite a lot of information about you would be available in one easily sortable, searchable, transmissible digital package, and various commercial entities might find such a package highly valuable.

As discussed below, this is the method that network advertising servers use to gather information that may be used in targeting online advertising.

d. E-mail and Document Bugs

E-mail messages that display graphics and styled text are constructed out of the same HTML code that constitutes web pages, and are equally capable of harboring web bugs. Such a bug might consist of an instruction to fetch an invisible graphic from the e-mail-sender's server, and while doing so to transmit information back to the server. For example, when you open the message the web bug can "call home" and report the time and date you opened it. The sender thereby learns that you do in fact read your e-mail, and through sending a series of messages may discern the time of day you typically check your e-mail. A job applicant could use this technique to determine whether companies to which he e-mailed his resume opened it.

A more advanced type of bug, which works only in e-mail readers with JavaScript enabled, can transmit back to the original sender any comments you add to the e-mail when you forward it to somebody else. This technique, which is known as "email wiretapping," would allow the original sender to eavesdrop on an entire e-mail conversation between two people who converse by using the "Reply" button to send messages back and forth.

An e-mail bug can be used in conjunction with a network advertising server's cookies to link personally identified information to a previously anonymous online profile. Suppose that DoubleClick, which is one of the leading network ad servers, has installed a cookie on your hard drive, and has collected clickstream information from you that is associated with your cookie's identification code, but does not know your real-world identity. Now you register to receive a free e-mail newsletter from another company that uses DoubleClick as its ad server. When you open the newsletter in your mail reader, a bug in the newsletter set by DoubleClick checks your hard drive to see whether it holds a DoubleClick cookie. If it does, then DoubleClick is able to link your cookie identification code—and all of the clickstream information it has associated with that code—to your e-mail address. If in registering to receive the newsletter you supplied your real name, address, or other personal details, DoubleClick now has data revealing exactly who you are and can associate its entire dossier with your real-world identity.

Bugs can also be inserted into documents produced by word processing, spreadsheet, presentation, and other software applications. These documents can include code that fetches a graphical image from a remote server, via the Internet. If the instruction is coded to retrieve an invisible 1 x 1 pixel dummy graphic, it can be used just like any other web bug. This sort of instruction will routinely transfer to the server the host name and IP address of the computer holding the document, and has the ability to set and read cookies. The bug would report back to the document's creator each time it is accessed on a computer with a live Internet connection. The document creator could therefore be alerted whenever the document was forwarded to and opened by somebody else. If it was a confidential document, and the bug reported that it had been opened on a computer with a different host name, the creator would know it had been leaked and might be able to determine from the host name the organization that received it. If the document was copyrighted, the creator could determine whether it has been distributed in violation of the copyright.

e. Application–Based Spyware

Some software developers have included code within their applications that causes the user's computer to transmit information back to the developer via the Internet. One use of this technology is to deliver advertising content to the user that is tailored to the information that the spyware gathers. It could also be used to scan the user's hard drive to see what other software he has installed, adding this information to a profile of the user that will be used for marketing purposes. Several developers have been discovered using this technology without informing the user or seeking his consent. In one widely publicized incident, security experts discovered that RealJukebox, free downloadable software that organizes and plays music files, was transmitting to RealNetworks, the maker of the software, information on users' listening habits, including the number of songs stored on the user's hard drive, the file formats in which they are stored, and the user's preferred music genre. Unless the user changed the software's default settings, it also transmitted the title of each CD inserted into the user's CD–ROM drive. All of this information was combined with a GUID assigned to each user, allowing dossiers to be compiled. This collection of information occurred without notice to users, either in the RealNetworks website privacy policy or in the RealJukebox license agreement. *See* Sara Robinson, *CD Software Is Said to Monitor Users' Listening Habits*, N.Y. TIMES ON THE WEB, Nov. 1, 1999. In response to the outcry over this revelation, RealNetworks modified its software to prevent this sort of information collection, rewrote its privacy policy, created an outside board to advise it on privacy issues, and joined the Online Privacy Alliance. In February 2002, a privacy investigator released a report stating that the Windows Media Player for Windows XP, an application that plays DVD movies on a computer, engaged in a similar undisclosed collection of information. *See* Richard M. Smith, *Serious Privacy Problems in Windows Media Player for Windows XP*, computerbytesman.com/privacy/wmp8dvd.htm.

Another method of implementing application-based information gathering is through subscription services that make use of network communications. One version of this has arisen in connection with digital video recorders ("DVRs"). Like the familiar videocassette recorder, the central function of a digital video recorder is to record television programs. Instead of recording on videotape, a DVR converts the program into digital format, and records it on a hard drive. DVRs have several capabilities that VCRs lack, typically including the ability to "pause" a live broadcast and continue viewing it uninterrupted in real time. In addition, the DVRs currently on the market communicate with computer servers maintained by the manufacturer in order to download information, such as the current television schedule. The DVR then makes the schedule information available to the user through an easy-to-use interface, allowing the user to select programs for recording.

The DVR manufactured by TiVo, Inc. automatically makes a telephone call to TiVo's servers once a day, and downloads the current television schedule. According to a four-month investigation by the Privacy Foundation, the information transfer runs both ways: during that daily phone call, the TiVo unit also uploads to TiVo's servers information about the user's viewing habits. The information transferred includes a serial number that identifies the user, a code indicating each program the user watches, the time during which it was watched, and a record of each button the user presses on the TiVo remote control. TiVo states that it does not at present associate the viewing information with the user's identification number, but according to the Privacy Foundation there is nothing preventing it from doing so; in its 2002 annual report to the Securities and Exchange Commission, TiVo said it expects future revenues to come from, among other sources, "targeted commercials and other forms of television advertising enabled by the TiVo Service." *See* Privacy Foundation, *TiVo's Data Collection and Privacy Practices* (Mar. 26, 2001), www.privacyfoundation.org.

NOTES & QUESTIONS

1. *GUID's.* Is the proliferation of software- and hardware-based GUID's something to be feared and fought? Is it an inevitable and largely beneficent consequence of the growing importance of network communications in all facets of life and the consequent necessity to privilege security and easy identification over privacy and anonymity?

2. *Opt-in for cookies?* In 2001, the European Commission considered adding to a Directive a provision requiring a website to ask a site visitor's permission before placing a cookie on the visitor's hard drive. How would such a provision affect the conduct of online advertising and marketing? Would consumers be better or worse off with such a provision? In answering these questions, consider the fact that the major browsers can be configured to notify the user of all cookies being sent, and give the user an opportunity to refuse to receive them. To what extent do you think users are availing themselves of this opportunity?

3. *Bugging documents.* Bugs can be inserted into documents produced by various word processing and other document-creating applications, and thus can be used to track copying. Should companies selling products on the Internet consider using bugs to keep others from copying their online catalogs and descriptive materials? If you were advising a client whether to adopt such a technology, what pros and cons would you lay out for consideration?

4. *Adequacy of privacy disclosure.* TiVo, Inc. maintains a website, at www.tivo.com, that serves as an advertisement for its TiVo DVR device. At the bottom of the website's home page is a hyperlink labeled "Privacy Policies." Clicking on this link pulls up a page with several more links, including one labeled "Digital Video Recorder with TiVo Service Privacy Policy." Clicking on that link pulls up a page that summarizes TiVo's privacy policy applying to the DVR, and links to another page on which commences the full privacy policy, which may be read in its entirety only by clicking on several additional links in succession. TiVo DVR users are not required to access TiVo's website for any purpose; to use the TiVo DVR they need not even have Internet access. Do you view this as an adequate means of disclosing the privacy implications of using the TiVo DVR? What if the manual that came with the TiVo advised purchasers that a complete privacy disclosure is available at www.tivo.com? What if it said that a complete privacy disclosure is available by writing to a specified postal address?

The website version of the privacy policy applying to the TiVo DVR ends by stating:

> This Privacy Policy supplements and is incorporated into the TiVo Service Agreement. This Privacy Policy constitutes the entire agreement, and replaces and supersedes all prior agreements, between you and TiVo concerning the subject matter discussed in this Privacy Policy. Use of your DVR with TiVo service will signify your acceptance of this Privacy Policy.

Is this statement binding on users of the TiVo DVR?

B. ONLINE PROFILING

Commercial websites frequently feature banner advertisements, which are rectangular panels appearing on website pages that contain promotional material and are usually hyperlinked to the website of the company placing the ad. As with print and broadcast media, these advertisements may be placed through a contractual arrangement between the website owner and the advertiser, according to which the advertiser pays the website owner to insert its ad into the code making up the website.

Advertisements can also be placed on websites through a third-party intermediary known as a network advertising server. The ad server contracts with advertisers who want their banner ads placed on websites, and contracts with website owners for the right to place ads on their sites. When a user pulls up a web page on a site that belongs to an ad server's network, the ad server determines what banner advertisement to display on the page based on the information that the server has obtained about the user (more accurately, about whoever uses that computer to browse the Web). The collection of information generated when Internet users browse the Web, and association of that information with a particular web-browsing computer or individual, is known as online profiling.

FEDERAL TRADE COMMISSION, ONLINE PROFILING: A REPORT TO CONGRESS

(2000).
www.ftc.gov/reports/privacy2000/privacy2000text.pdf.

* * *

II. WHAT IS ONLINE PROFILING?

A. Overview

Over the past few years, online advertising has grown exponentially in tandem with the World Wide Web. Online advertising revenues in the U.S. grew from $301 million in 1996 to $4.62 billion in 1999, and were projected to reach $11.5 billion by 2003. A large portion of that online advertising is in the form of "banner ads" displayed on Web pages—small graphic advertisements that appear in boxes above or to the side of the primary site content. Currently, tens of billions of banner ads are delivered to consumers each month as they surf the World Wide Web. Often, these ads are not selected and delivered by the Web site visited by a consumer, but by a network advertising company that manages and provides advertising for numerous unrelated Web sites. DoubleClick, Engage, and 24/7 Media, three of the largest Internet advertising networks, all estimate that over half of all online consumers have seen an ad that they delivered.

In general, these network advertising companies do not merely supply banner ads; they also gather data about the consumers who view their ads. This is accomplished primarily by the use of "cookies" and "Web bugs" which track the individual's actions on the Web. Among the types of information that can be collected by network advertisers are: information on the Web sites and pages within those sites visited by consumers; the time and duration of the visits; query terms entered into search engines; purchases; "click-through" responses to advertisements; and the Web page a consumer came from before landing on the site monitored by the particular ad network (the referring page). All of this information is gathered even if the consumer never clicks on a single ad.

The information gathered by network advertisers is often, but not always, anonymous, *i.e.*, the profiles are frequently linked to the identification number of the advertising network's cookie on the consumer's computer rather than the name of a specific person. This data is generally referred to as non-personally identifiable information ("non-PII"). In some circumstances, however, the profiles derived from tracking consumers' activities on the Web are linked or merged with personally identifiable information ("PII"). This generally occurs in one of two ways when consumers identify themselves to a Web site on which the network advertiser places banner ads.[15] First, the Web site to whom personal information is provided may, in turn, provide that information to the network advertiser. Second, depending upon how the personal information is retrieved and processed by the Web site, the personally identifying information may be incorporated into a URL string that is automatically transmitted to the network advertiser through its cookie.

Once collected, consumer data can be analyzed and combined with demographic and "psychographic"[18] data from third-party sources, data on the consumer's offline purchases, or information collected directly from

15. A previously anonymous profile can also be linked to personally identifiable information in other ways. For example, a network advertising company could operate its own Web site at which consumers are asked to provide personal information. When consumers do so, their personal information could be linked to the identification number of the cookie placed on their computer by that company, thereby making all of the data collected through that cookie personally identifiable.

18. Psychographic data links objective demographic characteristics like age and gender with more abstract characteristics related to ideas, opinions and interests. Data mining specialists analyze demographic, media, survey, purchasing and psychographic data to determine the exact groups that are most likely to buy specific products and services. * * * Psychographic profiling is also referred to in the industry as "behavioral profiling."

consumers through surveys and registration forms. This enhanced data allows the advertising networks to make a variety of inferences about each consumer's interests and preferences. The result is a detailed profile that attempts to predict the individual consumer's tastes, needs, and purchasing habits and enables the advertising companies' computers to make split-second decisions about how to deliver ads directly targeted to the consumer's specific interests.

The profiles created by the advertising networks can be extremely detailed. A cookie placed by a network advertising company can track a consumer on any Web site served by that company, thereby allowing data collection across disparate and unrelated sites on the Web. Also, because the cookies used by ad networks are generally persistent, their tracking occurs over an extended period of time, resuming each time the individual logs on to the Internet. When this "clickstream" information is combined with third-party data, these profiles can include hundreds of distinct data fields.

Although network advertisers and their profiling activities are nearly ubiquitous, they are most often invisible to consumers. All that consumers see are the Web sites they visit; banner ads appear as a seamless, integral part of the Web page on which they appear and cookies are placed without any notice to consumers. Unless the Web sites visited by consumers provide notice of the ad network's presence and data collection, consumers may be totally unaware that their activities online are being monitored.

B. An Illustration of How Network Profiling Works

Online consumer Joe Smith goes to a Web site that sells sporting goods. He clicks on the page for golf bags. While there, he sees a banner ad, which he ignores as it does not interest him. The ad was placed by USAad Network. He then goes to a travel site and enters a search on "Hawaii." USAad Network also serves ads on this site, and Joe sees an ad for rental cars there. Joe then visits an online bookstore and browses through books about the world' s best golf courses. USAad Network serves ads there, as well. A week later, Joe visits his favorite online news site, and notices an ad for golf vacation packages in Hawaii. Delighted, he clicks on the ad, which was served by the USAad Network. Later, Joe begins to wonder whether it was a coincidence that this particular ad appeared and, if not, how it happened.

At Joe's first stop on the Web, the sporting goods site, his browser will automatically send certain information to the site that the site needs in order to communicate with Joe's computer: his browser type and operating system; the language(s) accepted by the browser; and the computer's Internet address. The server hosting the sporting goods site answers by transmitting the HTTP header and HTML source code for the site's home page, which allows Joe's computer to display the page.

Embedded in the HTML code that Joe's browser receives from the sporting goods site is an invisible link to the USAad Network site which delivers ads in the banner space on the sporting goods Web site. Joe's browser is automatically triggered to send an HTTP request to USAad which reveals the following information: his browser type and operating system; the language(s) accepted by the browser; the address of the referring Web page (in this case, the home page of the sporting goods site); and the identification number and information stored in any USAad cookies already on Joe's computer. Based on this information, USAad will place an ad in the pre-set banner space on the sporting goods site's home page. The ad will appear as an integral part of the page. If an USAad cookie is not already present on Joe's computer, USAad will place a cookie with a unique identifier on Joe's hard drive. Unless he has set his browser to notify him before accepting cookies, Joe has no way to know that a cookie is being placed on his computer. When Joe clicks on the page for golf bags, the URL address of that page, which discloses its content, is also transmitted to USAad by its cookie.

When Joe leaves the sporting goods site and goes to the travel site, also serviced by USAad, a similar process occurs. The HTML source code for the travel site will contain an invisible link to USAad that requests delivery of an ad as part of the travel site's page. Because the request reveals that the referring site is travel related, USAad sends an advertisement for rental cars. USAad will also know the identification number of its cookie on Joe's machine. As Joe moves around the travel site, USAad checks his cookie and modifies the profile associated with it, adding elements based on Joe's activities. When Joe enters a search for "Hawaii," his search term is transmitted to USAad through the URL used by the travel site to locate the information Joe wants and the search term is associated with the other data collected by the cookie on Joe's machine. USAad will also record what advertisements it has shown Joe and whether he has clicked on them.

This process is repeated when Joe goes to the online bookstore. Because USAad serves banner ads on this site as well, it will recognize Joe by his cookie identification number. USAad can track what books Joe looks at, even though he does not buy anything. The fact that Joe browsed for books about golf courses around the world is added to his profile.

Based on Joe's activities, USAad infers that Joe is a golfer, that he is interested in traveling to Hawaii someday, and that he might be interested in a golf vacation. Thus, a week later, when Joe goes to his favorite online news site, also served by USAad, the cookie on his computer is recognized and he is presented with an ad for golf vacation packages in Hawaii. The ad grabs his attention and appeals to his interests, so he clicks on it.

* * *

DoubleClick, Inc., a leading network advertising server, raised the hackles of privacy advocates when it announced, in June 1999, that it was merging with Abacus Direct Corp., a direct marketing research firm that held in its databases information about catalog purchases of around 90 million U.S. households. Thereafter, in a revision to its website privacy notice, DoubleClick announced, in language indecipherable to the great majority of Internet users, that it intended to link information acquired from websites within its network with data in the Abacus databases. This would allow it to associate previously anonymous clickstream data with the real-world identities of Internet users, and to combine information about consumers' offline purchases with data about their online activities.

In March 2000, facing a barrage of criticism from privacy advocates and a round of bad publicity, DoubleClick reversed course and announced that it would not go forward with the planned information merger "until there is agreement between government and industry on privacy standards." *Statement From Kevin O'Connor, CEO of Doubleclick* (Mar. 2, 2000), www.doubleclick.net.

NOTES & QUESTIONS

1. *Benefits of network advertising.* Network advertising servers describe the benefits of the services they provide as follows:

> Effective Internet advertising is fundamental to the accessibility and dynamism of this revolutionary medium. Advertising underwrites the rich variety of online content choices available to consumers at no cost or at a far lower cost than would otherwise be possible. By delivering customized advertising, network advertisers offer substantial benefits for consumers and the advertiser. In addition, many small and emerging Web companies depend on network advertisers to compete against more well-established companies and their Web sites. Effective Internet advertising thus helps to maintain the low barriers to entry that have played a crucial role in the robust competition and innovation that have fueled this medium.

Network Advertising Initiative: Self–Regulatory Principles for Online Preference Marketing by Network Advertisers at 2, reprinted as Appendix: NAI Principles in Federal Trade Commission, Online Profiling: A Report to Congress (Part 2 Recommendations) (2000), www.ftc.gov/os/2000/07/onlineprofiling.pdf.

How would you balance the privacy interests of Internet users against the asserted benefits of information collection by network advertisers? Are Internet users entitled to meaningful notice about the practices of network advertising servers, and true, opt-in choice about whether to allow their clickstream data to be collected for purposes of online profiling? Would you favor a rule requiring opt-in consent to online profiling if the result would be a reduction in the quantity of freely available (advertiser-supported) information on the Internet?

2. *Opting out of online profiling.* The major network advertising servers allow individual Internet users to opt out of their tracking systems. *See, e.g.,* DoubleClick, *Opt-Out,* www.doubleclick.net/us/corporate/privacy/opt-out.asp?asp_object_1= & ; Engage, *Opt Out Anytime,* www.engage.com/privacy/optout_privacy.cfm. How likely is it that users will avail themselves of this option? To do so, a user must be aware that this sort of tracking is conducted, locate the website for each of the ad server companies, and follow each company's procedure for opting out. The whole procedure must be repeated if the user switches to another computer, or if she deletes her cookies file. Would it be preferable from the standpoint of fair information practices if the website that is harboring the web bug—the one that the user is actually visiting—provided the disclosure?

In its Privacy Policy, Yahoo! discloses that it allows network advertisers to collect information about visitors to its website. It advises visitors: "If you want to prevent a third-party ad server from sending and reading cookies on your computer, currently you must visit each ad network's website individually and opt out (if they offer this capability)." Yahoo!, *Network Advertisers and Third–Party Ad Servers*, privacy.yahoo.com/privacy/us/adservers/details.html. It continues with a list of links to a number of network advertisers' websites—14 of them at this writing.

3. *Network advertisers' self-regulatory plan.* In response to the FTC's study of the privacy implications of online profiling, the network advertising industry developed and proposed a self-regulatory program designed to implement the fair information practice principles. This rather complex plan can be viewed at *Network Advertising Initiative* www.networkadvertising.org. Do you think this approach offers Internet users substantial privacy benefits? For a critical appraisal of the Network Advertising Initiative, see Electronic Privacy Information Center, *Network Advertising Initiative: Principles Not Privacy* (Jul. 2000), www.epic.org/privacy/internet/NAI_analysis.html.

4. *Surreptitious collection of video rental information.* Advertising servers are capable of collecting an Internet user's clickstream information. Suppose a website that rents videotapes uses an ad server. When a visitor selects a video to rent, that information is collected by the ad server. In so doing, has the ad server violated the Video Privacy Protection Act, 18 U.S.C. § 2710, which, with certain exceptions, makes it illegal knowingly to disclose personally identifiable information about an individual's rental or purchase of videos? Has the video rental website violated the Act? Does it matter whether the video rental information is maintained in a personally identifiable manner?

5. *Application of anti-surveillance laws to ad servers.* Network advertising servers create profiles of Internet users by tapping into the clickstream information that users exchange with the websites they visit. For this to happen, the websites with which the advertising server has contractual arrangements must modify the code that constitutes their web pages by inserting statements that direct clickstream information to the ad server. In collecting this information, does the ad server violate (i) the Electronic Communication Privacy Act, 18 U.S.C. § 2511, which makes it unlawful to "intentionally intercept[] * * * any * * * electronic communication"? (ii) another provision of ECPA, 18 U.S.C. § 2701, which prescribes penalties for anyone who "(1) intentionally accesses without authorization a facility through which an electronic communication service is provided; or (2) intentionally exceeds an authorization to access that facility; and thereby obtains, alters, or prevents authorized access to a wire or electronic communication while it is in electronic storage in such system."? (iii) the Computer Fraud and Abuse Act, 18 U.S.C. § 1030(a)(2)(C), which makes it unlawful to "intentionally access[] a computer without authorization * * * and thereby obtain[] * * * information"? *See In re DoubleClick Inc. Privacy Litigation*, 154 F.Supp.2d 497 (S.D.N.Y.2001) (dismissing claims based on these provisions). Does the website that hosts the code that allows DoubleClick to collect clickstream information violate these provisions? *See In re Intuit Privacy Litigation*, 138 F.Supp.2d 1272 (C.D.Cal.2001) (dismissing claims under §§ 2511 and 1030, but permitting plaintiffs to pursue claims under § 2701).

6. *Application of consumer protection laws.* The Attorney General of Michigan took enforcement action against several websites that harbored web bugs set by DoubleClick and other network advertising servers, explaining:

> Surreptitious tracking of consumers' browsing behavior is not legal under Michigan law. The Michigan Consumer Protection Act generally applies to a wide range of transactions and practices affecting consumers. While there are over 30 different unfair practices that are prohibited under the Act, the central theme is that businesses are required to deal fairly and honestly with consumers. This includes a duty on the part of businesses to disclose important aspects of a transaction that are not reasonably obvious to consumers. * * *
>
> In the context of online privacy, the fact that consumers' browsing behavior is being monitored by unfamiliar third parties for unknown reasons [is] a material fact to consumers. Furthermore, this fact is not something that a consumer could reasonably be expected to know. For this reason, web sites that interact with Michigan consumers are required to disclose tracking of consumers' online activity.
>
> The Attorney General's office has issued Notices of Intended Action to a number of companies that operate commercial websites warning these companies that lawsuits may follow unless the websites take steps to tell consumers that they are being tracked by third parties.

Michigan Attorney General, *Privacy on the Internet*, www.ag.state.mi.us/inet_info/ii_page09.htm.

7. *Profiling not limited to ad servers.* The same surveillance techniques that network advertising servers use to target marketing can be used for other purposes as well. For example, a trade association could use a combination of web bugs and cookies to track people who visit its members' websites, and could share that information with its members.

Amazon.com has implemented a mechanism by which Internet users can make a donation to a website they visit by clicking on a "Click to Give" icon that appears on the site's home page. The graphic file that constitutes the icon is fetched from Amazon's server; the instruction that causes the fetching therefore functions like a web bug. In fact, the instruction checks for an Amazon cookie on the visitor's hard drive, and if it finds one, looks up the name that Amazon has associated with that cookie, and customizes the "Click to Give" icon with a greeting that includes the visitor's name! But Amazon explains that it has configured its servers so that it does not retain any personal information that is collected during this procedure. *See* Amazon.com, *About the Amazon Honor System*, s1.amazon.com/exec/varzea/subst/fx/help/how-we-know.html.

C. ONLINE PRIVACY POLICIES: USES AND ABUSES

1. FAILURE TO HONOR PRIVACY POLICY

Many websites post privacy policies intended to reassure visitors about use of their data. But these policies are not always honored. Existing laws that forbid deceptive marketing practices can be applied when a website makes representations in its privacy policy concerning its handling of site visitors' personal information, and then fails to honor its promises.

One such law is the Federal Trade Commission Act, which forbids "unfair or deceptive acts or practices in or affecting commerce." 15 U.S.C. § 45(a)(1). In *GeoCities*, FTC Docket No. C–3850 (Feb. 5, 1999), the FTC charged GeoCities with failing to observe its privacy promise. GeoCities offered free website hosting services, with sites organized thematically into "virtual communities." GeoCities—which was subsequently acquired by Yahoo!, and continued operating under the name Yahoo!GeoCities—provided its members (which it dubbed "homesteaders") with space on its web server, accessed through a URL of the form "www.geocities.com/member_name/. . .". When the FTC complaint was filed, GeoCities had over 1.8 million homesteaders, including 50,000 under the age of 13. To become a member, a user had to provide GeoCities with certain types of personal information, including first and last name, zip code, e-mail address, gender, and date of birth. In its privacy notice, GeoCities stated: "We will not share this information with anyone without your permission."

The complaint alleged that, contrary to this privacy statement, GeoCities "sold, rented, or otherwise marketed or disclosed this [personal identifying] information, including information collected from children, to third parties who have used this information for purposes other than those for which members have given permission. For example, third parties have targeted unrequested e-mail advertising offers to individual members based on their chosen GeoCities neighborhoods." The complaint also alleged that GeoCities represented that *it* collected certain personal identifying information from children, when in fact this information was collected by undisclosed third parties operating through GeoCities' website. The complaint alleged that these were deceptive misrepresentations, in violation of the

FTC Act. GeoCities consented to entry of an order that prohibited future misrepresentations, required it to post a website privacy policy containing specified categories of information, and required it to obtain "express parental consent" before collecting personal identifying information from children.

2. BANKRUPTCY

Suppose the owner of a website that has operated under a policy of never disclosing its customers' personal data files for bankruptcy. Does the company's customer list, with its associated transactional data, become an asset of the bankruptcy estate, subject to sale for the benefit of the company's creditors?

The issue arose in the case of Toysmart.com, an online toy retailer. Toysmart's privacy policy stated: "Personal information voluntarily submitted by visitors to our site, such as name, address, billing information and shopping preferences, is never shared with a third party." The policy also stated: "When you register with toysmart.com, you can rest assured that your information will never be shared with a third party." Toysmart was a licensee of TRUSTe, and its website displayed the TRUSTe trustmark. The company announced that it was going out of business, and offered to sell its assets, including its customer lists, to the highest bidder. Toysmart's creditors subsequently filed a petition against it for involuntary bankruptcy.

The FTC filed a lawsuit against Toysmart to prevent the sale of the customer information, alleging that to do so in the face of its privacy promise would be a deceptive practice in violation of the FTC Act. The FTC reached a settlement with Toysmart, under which the customer information could only be sold as part of a package including the entire website, and only to a purchaser that agreed to abide by the terms of Toysmart's privacy notice. But the Attorneys General of 38 states, and TRUSTe as well, objected to the settlement as being insufficiently protective of consumers, reasoning that when a company says it will "never" disclose personal information, it should be held to its word. The controversy was ultimately resolved when Walt Disney Co., the majority owner of Toysmart, agreed to pay $50,000 for the customer information and immediately to destroy that information.

NOTES & QUESTIONS

1. *Privacy as contractual obligation.* Does an undertaking in a website privacy policy give rise to an enforceable contract? If Yahoo!GeoCities discloses a member's personal information in contravention of its privacy policy, can the member sue Yahoo!GeoCities for breach of contract?

2. *What constitutes disclosure?* It is not always easy to determine whether a particular event constitutes disclosure of information to another party. Suppose Company A operates a website that provides free information about medical problems, with a privacy policy that states: "We will never sell, share, rent, trade, or otherwise disclose your personal information to anyone, ever." Is there a violation of the privacy policy if (1) Company A is sold, as a going concern, to Company B, which is also a provider of free medical information? (2) Company A is sold, as a going concern, to Company C, which is a pharmaceutical marketing company? (3) Company A acquires Company D, a pharmaceutical marketing company, as a subsidiary, and transfers the information to Company's D's marketing department? (4) Company A expands its business by beginning to sell pharmaceuticals, and uses its customer data for marketing? (5) Company A's stockholders sell a majority of the company's stock to new stockholders? (6) Company A goes out of business, and sells its database of personal information together with the rights to its trademark?

3. *Online vs. offline.* Toysmart got into trouble because its website operated under a highly protective privacy policy. If Toysmart had been a brick-and-mortar toy store that went bankrupt, it would most likely not have stated any privacy policy, and there would be not have been any objection to sale of its customer information. Does it make sense for the two situations to be treated differently? Did the FTC and the states overreact to the proposed sale of Toysmart's customer information?

4. *The lesson of Toysmart.* In view of Toysmart's difficulties, how would you advise a commercial website to structure its privacy policy? How likely is it that prospective customers would refuse to patronize a website because its privacy policy allowed customer information to be transferred without limitation in case of merger, acquisition, restructuring, or bankruptcy? Will prospective creditors be less willing to lend to an e-commerce business if its privacy policy makes customer information unavailable as an asset to satisfy debts?

3. MODIFICATION OF A WEBSITE PRIVACY POLICY

In the aftermath of the Toysmart controversy, Amazon.com implemented a change in its privacy policy. In September 2000 it sent e-mail messages to its 23 million customers announcing the change. The e-mails (with some non-substantive variations) read:

> Dear Customer,
>
> We're sorry for this intrusion. We know that you've asked not to receive certain types of e-mail from Amazon.com. From that request, it's clear that privacy issues are important to you. As we've recently updated our privacy policy, we did think it very important to contact you by e-mail to inform you of these changes.
>
> To read the revised Privacy Notice, visit:
>
> www.amazon.com/privacy-notice
>
> And again—please accept our apologies for sending you this e-mail. Thanks for shopping with us.
>
> Sincerely,

> Amazon.com

The privacy notice had previously stated:

> Amazon.com does not sell, trade or rent your personal information to others. We may choose to do so in the future with trustworthy third parties, but you can tell us not to by sending a blank e-mail message to *never@amazon.com*.

The revised policy says:

> **Business Transfers:** As we continue to develop our business, we might sell or buy stores or assets. In such transactions, customer information generally is one of the transferred business assets. Also, in the unlikely event that Amazon.com, Inc., or substantially all of its assets are acquired, customer information will of course be one of the transferred assets.

The revised policy also eliminates the option to direct Amazon not to disclose personal information to third parties.

As a result of this modification, the Electronic Privacy Information Center, a privacy advocacy group, severed its relationship with Amazon, through which Amazon was a favored distributor of EPIC's publications. In a letter to its subscribers, EPIC explained: "Recently Amazon announced that it could no longer guarantee that it would not disclose customer information to third parties. Because of this decision, and in the absence of legal or technical means to assure privacy for Amazon customers, we have decided that we can no longer continue our relationship with Amazon." Electronic Privacy Information Center, *Letter from Marc Rotenberg* (Sept. 13, 2000), www.epic.org/privacy/internet/amazon/letter.html.

Yahoo! generated controversy when, in early 2002, it notified tens of millions of its registered users that it was both modifying its privacy policy and opting its users into receiving marketing messages. The modified policy gave notice that Yahoo! may convey marketing messages not only by e-mail, but also by telephone and postal mail. Yahoo! also added 13 new categories of marketing messages that it would begin sending to users, with a selection button next to each that indicated the user wished to receive those messages. To opt out, a user would have to click on "No" 13 times.

NOTES & QUESTIONS

1. *Sufficiency of notice of change to a privacy policy.* Note that Amazon's e-mail message announcing the modified privacy policy provided a link to the (revised) policy, but gave no indication what changes were made. How useful is such an announcement to the average Internet user? Should a website that changes its privacy policy have an obligation to explain to its existing customers exactly what those changes are? Is it sufficient for a website privacy policy to state: "We may change our privacy policy at any time. Be sure to read it carefully each time you revisit the site."?

2. *No choice.* Amazon.com's revised privacy policy does not offer users any choice about whether their personal information will be disclosed. Is this aspect of the policy consistent with the FTC's articulation of the fair information practice principles? Would Amazon.com's policy qualify for a TRUSTe seal of approval? (*See* Part IV(B), *infra.*)

3. *Retroactive application of a modified privacy policy.* If a website changes its privacy policy, which policy applies to information collected before the change is announced? Consider the following statement, which appears at the end of Amazon.com's revised privacy policy:

> Our business changes constantly. This Notice and the Conditions of Use will change also, and *use of information that we gather now is subject to the Privacy Notice in effect at the time of use.* We may e-mail periodic reminders of our notices and conditions, unless you have instructed us not to, but you should check our Web site frequently to see recent changes.

(Emphasis added.) What is the meaning of the phrase in italics? Is there anything wrong with this? As part of a settlement of a class-action lawsuit against it alleging privacy violations, DoubleClick, Inc. agreed, for a period of two years, that "[a]n Internet user's online data * * * collected by DoubleClick under one version of DoubleClick's privacy policy will not be used in a manner materially inconsistent with that privacy policy, unless DoubleClick has that Internet user's permission to do otherwise." *In re DoubleClick Privacy Litigation*, Case No. 00–CIV–0641 (NRB) (S.D.N.Y. settlement approved May 21, 2002).

D. PIERCING THE VEIL OF ONLINE ANONYMITY

Many Internet users engage in online speech under a pseudonym, on the assumption that the speech cannot be associated with their real-world identity. This assumption has frequently turned out to be unwarranted. If a user furnishes her true identity when acquiring online access from an Internet service provider, when registering a domain name, or when registering at a website that offers a bulletin board or other forum for public communication, then the institution holding that identity information frequently has the capability of associating an online pseudonym, such as an e-mail address, user name, or screen name with the speaker's real-world identity.

In a number of cases, companies have brought defamation actions against individuals who have posted anonymous comments online that are critical of the company. After initiating the lawsuit, the company issues a subpoena to an ISP, online portal, or other entity that knows the online speaker's real-world identity, seeking disclosure of that identifying information. If the entity complies with the subpoena, the company learns the identity of its critic, and can proceed with the lawsuit, or pursue various other avenues of retaliation. Revelation of the critic's identity can have severe consequences if she happens to be an employee of the company, or involved in some business relationship with it. In some of these cases, the company has dropped the defamation lawsuit after learning the identity of its critic. Privacy advocates have branded this a misuse of the judicial system, claiming that the lawsuits were frivolous and were filed for the sole purpose of unmasking the critic.

In many of these cases, the subpoena recipient complies with the subpoena by divulging the speaker's identity, without giving the speaker prior notice or an opportunity to contest the subpoena. In a few cases, however, the propriety of such discovery has been challenged.

Columbia Insurance Co. v. seescandy.com

185 F.R.D. 573 (N.D.Cal.1999).

■ Jensen, District Judge.

On February 22, 1999, plaintiff Columbia Insurance Company filed a motion for a temporary restraining order and an order to show cause why a preliminary injunction should not issue. On March 4, 1999, plaintiff withdrew the motion with respect to defendants the Web Service Provider, Sidney Trayham, and Peter Jackson. The Court hereby denies the motion without prejudice to refiling and orders plaintiff to submit a brief with the Court within 14 days addressing the issue of whether the Court should authorize discovery to establish defendant's identity sufficiently such that he may be served in compliance with the Federal Rules of Civil Procedure.

I. BACKGROUND

A. *Factual-Background and Procedural History*

On February 22, 1999, plaintiff Columbia Insurance Company ("Columbia") filed this action seeking injunctive relief, damages, and an accounting of profits. Columbia is the assignee of various trademarks related to the operation of See's Candy Shops, Inc. ("See's"). See's is the predecessor in interest to the trademarks at issue in this case and holds a license from Columbia to use the marks.

The domain names "seescandy.com" and "seecandys.com" have been registered with Network Solutions, Inc. ("NSI") by someone other than plaintiff.

* * *

As of September 24, 1998, the seescandy domain name was registered to seescandy.com. The address was given only as "CA, 90706," which is for Bellflower, California. The administrative and billing contacts were listed as Salu Kalu, who could be contacted by e-mail at hostmaster@fluctuate.com. The telephone number given, 408–555–1212, is the local number for information in the San Jose area. The fluctuate.com domain, as of February 21, 1999 is registered to a Ravi Kumar of Artesia, California.

On December 22, 1998, the record was changed to show the owner as R, L of Artesia, California; however, the zip code given, 90706 is for Cerritos, California. The phone number was again given as the number for information, but the area code had been changed from 408 to 714. The contact e-mail address had been changed to RL@fluctuate.com. In addition, the domain was now shown as being hosted by websp.com.

On February 13, 1999, the record was modified again to list the address as P.O. Box 1300, Artesia, California, with the zip code changed from 90706 to 90702, which is an actual zip code for Artesia, California. The telephone number was also changed to (562) 807–0297.

As of January 22, 1999, the domain name seecandys.com was registered to Sees Candys and had the contact listed as Robby Kumar. The address was given as Tustin, California 92782; the e-mail address as dns@fluctuate.com; and the telephone number as (310) 860–0229.

On February 25, 1999, both the seescandy.com and seescandys.com domains were changed from the web host of websp.com to simplenet.net. Simplenet.net is a San Diego, California company.

Plaintiff has sued defendants for (1) infringement of federally registered service and trademarks, in particular "SEE'S," "SEE'S CANDIES," and "FAMOUS OLD TIME"; (2) federal unfair competition; (3) federal trademark dilution; (4) California State dilution under California Business and Professions Code § 14330; (5) unfair and deceptive trade practices under California Business and Professions Code § 17200; (6) California common law trade name, trademark, and service mark infringement and unfair competition; and (7) unjust enrichment.

Plaintiff seeks as relief a temporary, preliminary, and thereafter permanent injunction enjoining defendants from using any of See's marks, for goods or services or as metatags, directory names, other computer addresses, metatags, invisible data, or otherwise engaging in acts or conduct that would cause confusion to the source, sponsorship or affiliation of See's Candies with defendants.

* * *

II. DISCUSSION

The Court will not grant a temporary restraining order against defendants at this time because such a ruling would be futile. Plaintiff has not been able to collect the information necessary to serve the complaint on defendants. As a result any temporary restraining order issued could only be in effect for a limited time and would be unlikely to have any effect on defendant whom plaintiff has not yet located. Once the order expired plaintiff would be unable to obtain a preliminary injunction because such relief cannot be imposed *ex parte.*

Service of process can pose a special dilemma for plaintiffs in cases like this in which the tortious activity occurred entirely on-line. The dilemma arises because the defendant may have used a fictitious name and address in the commission of the tortious acts. Traditionally, the default requirement in federal court is that the plaintiff must be able to identify the defendant sufficiently that a summons can be served on the defendant. *See* Fed.R.Civ.P. 4. This requires that the plaintiff be able to ascertain the defendant's name and address.

As a general rule, discovery proceedings take place only after the defendant has been served; however, in rare cases, courts have made exceptions, permitting limited discovery to ensue after filing of the complaint to permit the plaintiff to learn the identifying facts necessary to permit service on the defendant. *See e.g.,* Gillespie v. Civiletti, 629 F.2d 637, 642 (9th Cir.1980) (finding the district court abused its discretion in dismissing the case with respect to the John Doe defendants without requiring the named defendants to answer interrogatories seeking the names and addresses of the supervisors in charge of the relevant facilities during the relevant time period); Estate of Rosenberg by Rosenberg v. Crandell, 56 F.3d 35, 37 (8th Cir.1995) (permitting a suit naming fictitious parties as defendants to go forward because the allegations in the complaint were "specific enough to permit the identity of the party to be ascertained after reasonable discovery"); Maclin v. Paulson, 627 F.2d 83, 87 (7th Cir.1980) (approving of fictitious name pleadings until such time as the identity of the plaintiffs "can be learned through discovery or through the aid of the trial court"). In the even rarer case, a district court has sua sponte issued an order directing revelation of facts necessary to determine the true name of a John Doe defendant. *See* Bivens v. Six Unknown Named Agents of Fed. Bureau of Narcotics, 403 U.S. 388, 390 n. 2 (1971) (noting that the trial court had ordered the United States attorney to identify "those federal agents who it is indicated by the records of the United States Attorney participated in the ... arrest of the [petitioner]") (quoting the district court's order).

In the Ninth Circuit such exceptions to the general rule have been generally disfavored. *See* Gillespie, 629 F.2d at 642. However, a district court does have jurisdiction to determine the facts relevant to whether or not it has in personam jurisdiction in a given case. *See* Wells Fargo & Co. v. Wells Fargo Express Co., 556 F.2d 406, 430 n. 24 (9th Cir.1977). A district court's decision to grant discovery to determine jurisdictional facts is a matter of discretion. *See* id.

With the rise of the Internet has come the ability to commit certain tortious acts, such as defamation, copyright infringement, and trademark infringement, entirely on-line. The tortfeasor can act pseudonymously or anonymously and may give fictitious or incomplete identifying information. Parties who have been injured by these acts are likely to find themselves chasing the tortfeasor from Internet Service Provider (ISP) to ISP, with little or no hope of actually discovering the identity of the tortfeasor.

In such cases the traditional reluctance for permitting filings against John Doe defendants or fictitious names and the traditional enforcement of strict compliance with service requirements should be tempered by the need to provide injured parties with an forum in which they may seek redress for grievances. However, this need must be balanced against the legitimate and valuable right to participate in online forums anonymously or pseudonymously. People are permitted to interact pseudonymously and anonymously with each other so long as those acts are not in violation of the law. This ability to speak one's mind without the burden of the other party knowing all the facts about one's identity can foster open communication and robust debate. Furthermore, it permits persons to obtain information relevant to a sensitive or intimate condition without fear of embarrassment. People who have committed no wrong should be able to participate online without fear that someone who wishes to harass or embarrass them can file a frivolous lawsuit and thereby gain the power of the court's order to discover their identity.

Thus some limiting princip[les] should apply to the determination of whether discovery to uncover the identity of a defendant is warranted. The following safeguards will ensure that this unusual procedure will only be employed in cases where the plaintiff has in good faith exhausted traditional avenues for identifying a civil defendant pre-service, and will prevent use of this method to harass or intimidate.

First, the plaintiff should identify the missing party with sufficient specificity such that the Court can determine that defendant is a real person or entity who could be sued in federal court. *See e.g.,* Wells Fargo, 556 F.2d at 430 n. 24 (stating that plaintiffs bear the burden of establishing jurisdictional facts). This requirement is necessary to ensure that federal requirements of jurisdiction and justiciability can be satisfied. *See* Plant v. Does, 19 F.Supp.2d 1316 (S.D.Fla.1998) (refusing to issue a temporary restraining order against unnamed and unserved bootleggers who had not yet committed an offense on the theory that plaintiffs have failed to establish that the Court had jurisdiction over defendants, to provide defendants with due process, and to demonstrate that an actual controversy existed).

Plaintiff's papers establish that the listed defendants who remain in the case after March 4, 1999 appear to be aliases for a person known as Ravi or Robby Kumar of Artesia, California ("the Kumar defendants"). Most of the addresses listed by aliases associated with the Kumar defendants show a California domicile, which indicates that the Court likely has jurisdiction over defendants. Plaintiffs are suing the following aliases, all of which are alleged to be owners or operators of the domain names seescandy.com and seescandys.com: Seescandy.com, Sees Candys, hostmaster dns, fluctuate, foolio, x2, ticker talk, RL, and Salu Kalu. Salu Kalu was listed as the contact for seescandy.com in September of 1998. RL is a person who was listed as the contact person for seescandy.com as of January 16, 1999. Hostmaster DNS is the name of the contact person listed for seescandy.com as of February 8, 1999. It is important to note that Hostmaster DNS is a common generic term used to describe the system operator in charge of running a domain name server. It is thus highly problematic as an identifier of a defendant. However, Hostmaster's e-mail address is dns@foolio.com, which ties this alias to the Kumar defendants. Fluctuate is the second level domain of fluctuate.com, which is listed in the WHOIS as registered to tickertalk, for whom the contact is Robby Kumar. Fluctuate.com is the domain that provides all the mailboxes for the e-mail addresses listed as contacts for the seescandy.com and seescandys.com domains. X2 is the listed registrant of the domain name x2.org, for whom the contact is listed as Ticker Talk with the E-mail address of dns@foolio.com. Foolio is the listed registrant for foolio.com, for whom the contact is Salu Kalu, and which is the domain hosting the E-mail address of the contact, Ticker Talk, for the x2.org domain. Most convincing of all, See's has been in contact by e-mail with a person who goes by the name "Ravi." In his e-mail message, Ravi has indicated a desire to sell the subject domain names to See's and has provided See's with evidence that consumers have been actually confused by these websites, for which Ravi claims to hold registration rights. The Court finds that there appears to be only one person behind all these registrations, a Ravi or Robby Kumar, who may also be known as Salu Kalu. The Court finds that plaintiff has made a satisfactory showing that there is an actual person behind these acts who would be amenable to suit in federal court.

Second, the party should identify all previous steps taken to locate the elusive defendant. This element is aimed at ensuring that plaintiffs make a good faith effort to comply with the requirements of service of process and specifically identifying defendants. *See* Plant, 19 F.Supp.2d at 1320 (noting that plaintiffs had failed to explain why they were unable to identify the defendants). Plaintiff's counsel has certified that the following efforts were made to contact defendants: (1) calls were made to the two non-directory information services telephone numbers. One was a non-working number and nobody answered the other one. Simultaneous with the filing of the motion for a temporary restraining order and preliminary injunction plaintiff served its complaint, brief, and all accompanying papers to the official addresses provided to NSI, only one of which was a complete mailing address. Plaintiff also served these documents, sans exhibits, by electronic mail to the e-mail addresses associated with the domains registered by Ravi Kumar, Robby Kumar, RL, Salu Kalu, and Hostmaster DNS. Although such service is not sufficient to comply with the Federal Rules of Civil Procedure, the Court finds that such acts do show that plaintiff has made a good faith effort to specifically identify defendant and to serve notice on defendant.

Third, plaintiff should establish to the Court's satisfaction that plaintiff's suit against defendant could withstand a motion to dismiss. *See* Gillespie, 629 F.2d at 642. A conclusory pleading will never be sufficient to satisfy this element. Pre-service discovery is akin to the process used during criminal investigations to obtain warrants. The requirement that the government show probable cause is, in part, a protection against the misuse of *ex parte* procedures to invade the privacy of one who has done no wrong. A similar requirement is necessary here to prevent abuse of this extraordinary application of the discovery process and to ensure that plaintiff has standing to pursue an action against defendant. *See e.g.,* Plant, 19 F.Supp.2d at 1321 n. 2 (commenting that standing was likely absent because defendants were alleging only future acts of infringement, not past acts or patterns of infringement). Thus, plaintiff must make some showing that an act giving rise to civil liability actually occurred and that the discovery is aimed at revealing specific identifying features of the person or entity who committed that act.

Plaintiff has demonstrated that their trademark infringement claim could survive a motion to dismiss and therefore have satisfied this element. The test for infringement of a federally registered trademark (Count I) and for false designation of origin (Count II) under the Lanham Act is whether the alleged infringing act creates a likelihood of confusion. * * * [P]laintiff can show actual confusion, courtesy of the 31 e-mails provided by defendant. "Evidence of actual confusion is strong proof of the fact of likelihood of confusion." 3 J. Thomas McCarthy, McCarthy on Trademarks and Unfair Competition, § 23:13 at 23–35. Defendant Ravi has informed plaintiff by e-mail that people have requested catalogs and have tried to order candy from the websites located at seescandy.com and seescandys.com.

Defendants' desire to sell the two domains back to See's Candy combined with the use of See's trademark logos, complete down to style and figuration, is a sign that defendants intended to trade on the goodwill associated with the See's marks. The Court also can infer intentional copying and bad faith simply from the similarity of the marks. See Fleishmann Distilling Corp. v. Environmental Research & Tech., Inc., 222 U.S.P.Q. 585, 588–89 (C.D.Cal.1983). Plaintiffs showing is sufficient to demonstrate that the Kumar defendants have committed an unlawful act for which a federal cause of action can subsist.

Lastly, the plaintiff should file a request for discovery with the Court, along with a statement of reasons justifying the specific discovery requested as well as identification of a limited number of persons or entities on whom discovery process might be served and for which there is a reasonable likelihood that the discovery process will lead to identifying information about defendant that would make service of process possible. *See* Gillespie, 629 F.2d at 642 (stating that discovery should not be permitted if it is not likely to uncover the identity of the defendant). As ordered below, plaintiff has 14 days to make a filing with the Court with respect to the process the Court should consider ordering.

II. CONCLUSION AND ORDER

Plaintiff shall have 14 days from the date of this order to submit a brief with the Court setting forth specifically the forms of discovery process, the justification for such process, and the persons or entities on whom they are to be served that plaintiff expects will achieve the end of providing the missing identifying information necessary for service of process. If plaintiff does not yet have sufficient information to satisfy the Court that such process should be ordered, plaintiff may so indicate and later reapply for such discovery once the facts necessary to make the required showing have been uncovered.

NOTES & QUESTIONS

1. *Balancing interests.* In *Columbia Insurance v. seescandy.com*, was there any danger that allowing discovery of the defendant's identity would chill the online speech of defendant or others similarly situated? Is the standard that the court articulates one that appropriately balances the interests of tort victims in obtaining redress and the interests of anonymous online speakers in remaining anonymous?

2. *Another standard.* In *Dendrite Int'l, Inc. v. Doe*, 775 A.2d 756 (N.J.Super.Ct.App.Div.2001), the court affirmed the motion judge's ruling that plaintiff, Dendrite, had failed to establish its entitlement to pre-service discovery aimed at ascertaining the identity of defendant John Doe No. 3, an anonymous poster of allegedly defamatory messages on a Yahoo! message board. The motion judge had adopted and applied the four-factor test set forth in *Columbia Insurance v. seescandy.com*, concluding that Dendrite did not establish that its defamation claim could survive a motion to dismiss, since Dendrite did not adduce sufficient proof of actual harm to it resulting from the alleged defamation. The appellate court, citing *seescandy.com* with approval, set forth the following four-factor test as "guidelines to trial courts when faced with an application by a plaintiff for expedited discovery seeking an order compelling an ISP to honor a subpoena and disclose the identity of anonymous Internet posters who are sued for allegedly violating the rights of individuals, corporations or businesses":

> We hold that when such an application is made, the trial court should first require the plaintiff to undertake efforts to notify the anonymous posters that they are the subject of a subpoena or application for an order of disclosure, and withhold action to afford the fictitiously-named defendants a reasonable opportunity to file and serve opposition to the application. These notification efforts should include posting a message of notification of the identity discovery request to the anonymous user on the ISP's pertinent message board.
>
> [Second,] [t]he court shall also require the plaintiff to identify and set forth the exact statements purportedly made by each anonymous poster that plaintiff alleges constitutes actionable speech.
>
> [Third,] [t]he complaint and all information provided to the court should be carefully reviewed to determine whether plaintiff has set forth a prima facie cause of action against the fictitiously-named anonymous defendants. In addition to establishing that its action can withstand a motion to dismiss for failure to state a claim upon which relief can be granted pursuant to *R.* 4:6–2(f),[15] the plaintiff must produce sufficient evidence supporting each

15. [The reference (which should be to subsection (e), not subsection (f)) is to the provision of the New Jersey Rules of Court setting forth available defenses, including "failure to state a claim upon which relief can be granted." N.J. Rules of Ct. 4:6–2(e).—Eds.]

> element of its cause of action, on a prima facie basis, prior to a court ordering the disclosure of the identity of the unnamed defendant.
>
> Finally, assuming the court concludes that the plaintiff has presented a prima facie cause of action, the court must balance the defendant's First Amendment right of anonymous free speech against the strength of the prima facie case presented and the necessity for the disclosure of the anonymous defendant's identity to allow the plaintiff to properly proceed.

Id. at 760–71. How do these four factors differ from the factors set forth in *seescandy.com*? Are the differences significant?

Dendrite argued on appeal that the motion judge had misapplied the third factor, improperly requiring Dendrite to submit *proof* that the alleged defamation resulted in actual harm, rather than merely requiring Dendrite to state a claim. The appellate court agreed that "Dendrite meets the bare minimum requirements for a defamation cause of action, and would survive a motion to dismiss under the traditional application of *R.* 4:6–2(e)." *Id.* at 770. Nevertheless, the court approved the motion judge's disposition of the issue, explaining:

> Our review of *seescandy.com* discloses that a strict application of our rules surrounding motions to dismiss is not the appropriate litmus test to apply in evaluating the disclosure issue. We conclude that the District Court [in *seescandy.com*] envisioned this four-part test to act as a flexible, non-technical, fact-sensitive mechanism for courts to use as a means of ensuring that plaintiffs do not use discovery procedures to ascertain the identities of unknown defendants in order to harass, intimidate or silence critics in the public forum opportunities presented by the Internet.

Id. at 771. Is it appropriate to require a plaintiff to adduce such proof at a stage in the litigation when it does not even know the defendant's identity?

Consider also the fourth criterion the court articulated, namely that the trial judge "balance the defendant's First Amendment right of anonymous free speech against the strength of the prima facie case presented and the necessity for the disclosure," and determine whether disclosure of the defendant's identity is warranted. Does this statement furnish adequate guidance to the trial judge?

3. *Yet another standard.* In *Melvin v. Doe,* 49 Pa. D. & C. 4th 449 (Pa.Com.Pl.2000), the plaintiff was a state judge who brought a defamation action against a person who had anonymously posted a message on an America Online bulletin board that accused her of official misconduct. Plaintiff made a discovery request, seeking the defendant's identity. Defendant objected to the discovery request on the ground that anonymous political speech is protected by the First Amendment. While recognizing that the First Amendment prevents states from barring anonymous political speech entirely, and that allowing litigants to unmask anonymous speakers has a tendency to chill speech that is at the core of First

Amendment protections, the court rejected the argument that the First Amendment places an absolute bar on discovering the identity of an anonymous online speaker. Instead, the court held that discovery would be allowed unless defendant showed that plaintiff could not make out a prima facie case, and stayed discovery to give defendant a chance to do so. The court explained that plaintiff could defeat defendant's effort to make such a showing "(1) if the plaintiff establishes that the publication appeared on the Internet and that the statements within the publication, if false, support a defamation recovery, and (2) if the plaintiff testifies that the statements are untrue and that she has experienced emotional distress as the result of the statements." 49 Pa.D.&C. 4th at 462–63. The court held that plaintiff had met this threshold, and that discovery into defendant's identity would be allowed. To limit the exposure of defendant's identity in case defendant should ultimately prevail, however, the court issued a protective order preventing disclosure of defendant's identity other than to the parties and their counsel.

When the issue is whether to allow discovery of the identity of an anonymous online speaker, is the burden of proof more appropriately placed on the plaintiff or defendant? Should a higher standard apply in cases where the speech in question is core First Amendment speech, such as speech relating to the conduct of government officials?

4. *John Doe fights back.* In *Doe a/k/a Aquacool_2000 v. Yahoo! Inc.*, Case No. CV 00–04993 WMB (RZx) (C.D. Cal. filed May 11, 2000), the plaintiff was an individual who had posted comments on a Yahoo! message board that were critical of his former employer, a company named AnswerThink Consulting Group, Inc. The comments were posted pseudonymously, attributed to "Aquacool_2000." AnswerThink filed a defamation action against Aquacool_2000 and several other unnamed defendants, and served a subpoena on Yahoo! seeking the disclosure of their identities. Yahoo! complied with the subpoena, disclosing Aquacool_2000's real-world identity, without notifying him or seeking his consent. Upon learning Aquacool_2000's identity, AnswerThink fired him and took other punitive action against him.

Aquacool_2000 then filed this action against Yahoo!, alleging that the disclosure of his identity violated his free speech rights under the U.S. and California Constitutions, and that it constituted unfair competition and false advertising under California law. He also alleged that Yahoo! was in breach of contract, and had committed negligent misrepresentation, by failing to abide by its website privacy policy. The policy stated: "We will notify you at the time of data collection or transfer if your data will be shared with a third party and you will always have the option of not permitting the transfer." It also stated that Yahoo! would disclose a member's personal information "when we believe in good faith that the law requires it."

How would you interpret the quoted provisions of Yahoo!'s Privacy Policy? Do you think Yahoo! violated the policy when it revealed Aquacool_2000's identity in response to the subpoena? Is this policy an enforceable contract? Yahoo! later modified its Privacy Policy so that it states: "We respond to subpoenas, court orders or legal process," and does not promise any notification that it is doing so.

5. *Anonymous plaintiffs?* In *America Online, Inc. v. Anonymous Publicly Traded Company*, 542 S.E.2d 377 (Va.2001), plaintiff, identified only as "Anonymous Publicly Traded Company," brought a defamation action against defendants who had anonymously posted disparaging comments concerning plaintiff. Plaintiff sought to protect its own anonymity in the litigation, arguing that disclosure of its identity would cause irreparable harm. Plaintiff caused a subpoena to be issued to America Online requiring it to identify the John Doe defendants. AOL resisted the subpoena, "arguing that APTC should not be permitted to proceed until it revealed its identity." The trial court ruled that the plaintiff could proceed anonymously, but the Virginia Supreme Court disagreed. The court began by observing that "courts must balance the need for anonymity against the general presumption that parties' identities are public information and the risk of unfairness to the opposing party." It held that the plaintiff had not made the required showing. "In the case before us, the sole reason APTC has offered in support of its request to proceed anonymously is fear of economic harm. While reasonable concern over potential economic harm is not excluded from factors to consider, APTC has not borne its burden to show special circumstances justifying anonymity." The court was not impressed by the plaintiff's assertion that " 'the filing of this lawsuit under the proper and correct legal name for the Plaintiff, where Plaintiff at this time is unable to identify the Defendants, will trigger publicity about this lawsuit, which Plaintiff believes will damage the value of the corporation.' " *Id.* at 380–85.

IV. MODELS FOR PROTECTING ONLINE PRIVACY

Nearly everybody agrees that Internet users have legitimate privacy interests. There is much less agreement about the proper approach to protecting those interests, in view of the competing interests with which privacy protection can interfere. Several different models of online privacy protection have been implemented or proposed. Most observers agree that none of these approaches is by itself sufficient, and advocate some combination. To understand their strengths and weaknesses, it will be useful to consider the approaches individually.

A. MODEL I: INDUSTRY SELF-REGULATION VIA CODES OF CONDUCT

The champions of self-regulation have been more vocal on the subject of privacy than on any other subject relating to online communications. Large segments of the business community, as well as some agencies of government, have forcefully argued that government regulation of online privacy should be the approach of last resort, and that all interested parties will be better off if regulators leave protection of privacy to the market. The Clinton Administration's 1997 policy paper on electronic commerce endorsed a combination of self-regulation and technological tools as the preferred means to implement privacy protections online. *See* WILLIAM J. CLINTON & ALBERT GORE, JR., A FRAMEWORK FOR GLOBAL ELECTRONIC COMMERCE (1997), www.ecommerce.gov/framewrk.htm.

Following a pattern exhibited in many other industries, the online industry's efforts at self-regulation to protect online privacy were driven by the perceived threat of government regulation. An early wake-up call, not widely heeded, was congressional reaction to the problem of children's access to sexually explicit material online. Congress attempted to stamp out this problem with the 1996 Communications Decency Act. The U.S. Supreme Court invalidated provisions of the Act that restricted the posting of "indecent" or "patently offensive" material, finding them unconstitutional in violation of the First Amendment. *See Reno v. American Civil Liberties Union*, 521 U.S. 844 (1997).

The Federal Trade Commission's explorations of the issue of online privacy in a series of workshops and reports, and a string of well-publicized privacy scares, hit closer to home, giving impetus to both industry self-regulation and calls for government regulation. In June 1996, the FTC held a public workshop to learn about online privacy. Sensing that the government might be gearing up to regulate in this arena, two trade associations, the Interactive Services Association and the Direct Marketing Association, announced at the workshop their release of self-regulatory guidelines on protecting privacy online, marketing to children, and use of unsolicited commercial e-mail and newsgroup postings. In July 1996, TRUSTe launched its privacy seal program. *See* Part IV(B), *infra*.

In September 1996, privacy advocates drew attention to a service called P–Trak that LexisNexis offered. When originally introduced, P–Trak allowed subscribers to enter an individual's name and address, and to retrieve personal information including the individual's Social Security number. In response to expressions of outrage that publicity about P–Trak raised, LexisNexis modified the service so that it did not return Social Security numbers, but still allowed a subscriber to enter a Social Security number and retrieve the holder's name, address, two prior addresses, telephone number, and birth month and year. This did not answer the objections, since the information P–Trak provided could still be used in aid of stalking, identity theft, and other unsavory practices. Publicity surrounding this service prompted members of Congress to request that the FTC conduct a study of the issue. The FTC's announcement that it would conduct the requested study spurred several companies in the business of furnishing personal information about individuals, known as "look-up services," to form an association, called the Individual Reference Services Group ("IRSG") for the purpose of developing a self-regulatory scheme that would respond to the perceived abuses that gave rise to the study. Among other things, the IRSG principles placed limitations on the disclosure of non-public personal information by look-up services, depending on the sensitivity of the information requested and the identity of the requester; required the services to protect against misuse of non-public information; and granted individuals access to non-public information concerning them. *See IRSG Industry Principles*, www.irsg.org/html/industry_principles_principles.htm. In a 1997 report, the FTC praised IRSG's effort as "more comprehensive and far-reaching than any other voluntary, industry-wide program in the information sector," but noted certain shortcomings in the principles and exhorted the industry to do more. *See* FEDERAL TRADE COMMISSION, INDIVIDUAL REFERENCE SERVICES: A REPORT TO CONGRESS (1997), www.ftc.gov/bcp/privacy/wkshp97/irsdoc1.htm.

The IRSG dissolved itself in late 2001, explaining that there was no further need for the self-regulatory program given Congress's enactment of the Gramm–Leach–Bliley Act of 1999, 15 U.S.C. §§ 6801–10. The Act and its implementing regulations govern the disclosure by a financial institution of a consumer's personal financial information, and the redisclosure and reuse of such information. Compliance with the regulations implementing the Act was required starting July 1, 2001.

In March 1998, the FTC conducted a survey of 1,402 commercial websites to assess the extent to which they collected personal identifying information from users, and to determine whether sites that collected personally identifiable information ("PII") gave users notice of their information-handling policies. In June 1998, the FTC issued a report detailing the results of the survey, as well as its assessment of self-regulatory guidelines that online industry had produced. It found that more than 85% of commercial websites collected PII, but only 14% of them provided any notice of their information practices. It also found that 89% of sites directed to children collected PII from children, but very few of those made any effort to obtain parental consent. Based on the results of its survey, the FTC recommended that Congress enact legislation regulating online collection and use of information from children, but deferred any recommendation on a regulatory response to collection of PII from adults. *See* FEDERAL TRADE COMMISSION, PRIVACY ONLINE: A REPORT TO CONGRESS (1998), www.ftc.gov/reports/privacy3/index.htm.

Congress responded by enacting the Children's Online Privacy Protection Act, 15 U.S.C. §§ 6501–05, discussed in Part V, *infra*. In congressional testimony discussing the report in July 1998, the FTC opined that "unless industry can demonstrate that it has developed and implemented broad-based and effective self-regulatory programs by the end of this year, additional governmental authority in this area would be appropriate and necessary." Prepared Statement of the Federal Trade Commission on "Consumer Privacy on the World Wide Web," Before the Subcommittee on Telecommunications, Trade and Consumer Protection of the House Committee on Commerce, United States House of Representatives (Jul. 21, 1998), www.ftc.gov/os/1998/9807/privac98.htm.

The online industry responded with the formation of an industry group, called the Online Privacy Alliance, with a membership including some of the biggest and best-known companies with online business activities. In June 1998, just three weeks after publication of the FTC's report, the OPA released a set of guidelines for online privacy designed to demonstrate that the industry was able to police itself, and that government regulation was not required. OPA's 50 members pledged to abide by these guidelines, which require companies engaged in online activities to adopt and implement a privacy policy that addresses the fair information practices principles of notice, choice, data security, and data quality and access. Online Privacy Alliance, *Guidelines for Online Privacy Policies* (Jun. 22, 1998), www.privacyalliance.org/resources/ppguidelines.shtml. The Guidelines were to be enforced through a third-party seal program. Online Privacy Alliance, *Effective Enforcement Of Self Regulation* (Jul. 21, 1998), www.privacyalliance.org/resources/enforcement.shtml.

In a July 1999 report to Congress on the status of self-regulation, the FTC praised the industry for the progress it had made in the prior year, and expressed the view that legislative action was not warranted, but concluded that the industry needed to do much more to protect the privacy of Internet users. The report cited two website surveys conducted in 1999 finding that a majority of websites posted at least some sort of privacy disclosure, but few (10% in one study, 22% in the other) of them addressed all four of the substantive fair information practice principles (notice, choice, access, and security). FEDERAL TRADE COMMISSION, SELF-REGULATION AND PRIVACY ONLINE: A REPORT TO CONGRESS (1999), www.ftc.gov/os/1999/9907/privacy99.pdf.

Evaluations of the efficacy of self-regulation then began to turn less favorable. A February 2000 report on the privacy practices of the most popular consumer-oriented health care websites found that "on a number of sites personally identified information is collected through the use of cookies and banner advertisements by third parties without the host sites disclosing this practice. There are also instances where personally identified data is transferred to third parties in direct violation of stated privacy policies." CALIFORNIA HEALTHCARE FOUNDATION, PRIVACY: REPORT ON THE PRIVACY POLICIES AND PRACTICES OF HEALTH WEB SITES 4 (2000), www.chcf.org/topics/view.cfm?itemID=12497. In a March 2000 cover article, *Business Week* magazine strongly endorsed federal legislation to protect online privacy. It labeled the existing state of self-regulation a "sham": Privacy policies "are usually buried at the bottom of the page, and seem to be drafted by life-forms on a distant planet"; when websites offer privacy options, they are too hard to find; few sites offer users access to the information that has been collected about them; and there is little enforcement of privacy rules. *See It's Time for Rules in Wonderland*, BUS. WK., Mar. 20, 2000, at 82.

Then in May 2000, the FTC released a report finding that self-regulation had failed, and recommending that Congress enact online privacy legislation. The report described the results of yet another survey of website privacy practices and policies. As in the 1999 studies, the FTC found that a majority of the sites (88% of a random sample and 100% of the 100 most popular sites) displayed at least one privacy disclosure. However, only a minority (20% of the former and 42% of the latter) implemented, even in part, all four of the fair information practice principles. The FTC also found that privacy seal programs had not achieved widespread adoption: 8% of the random sites, and 45% of the most popular sites, displayed a privacy seal. Based on these findings, the FTC concluded: "Because self-regulatory initiatives to date fall far short of the broad-based implementation of effective self-regulatory programs, the Commission has concluded that such efforts alone cannot ensure that the online marketplace as a whole will emulate the standards adopted by industry leaders. While there will continue to be a major role for industry self-regulation in the future, the Commission recommends that Congress enact legislation that, in conjunction with continuing self-regulatory programs, will ensure adequate protection of consumer privacy online." FEDERAL TRADE COMMISSION, PRIVACY ONLINE: FAIR INFORMATION PRACTICES IN THE ELECTRONIC MARKETPLACE ii-iii (2000), www.ftc.gov/reports/privacy2000/privacy2000.pdf.

Following issuance of this report, a number of bills addressing online privacy issues in a variety of ways were introduced in Congress, but none proceeded to enactment. In the meantime, President Bush replaced the Chairman of the FTC with an appointee favoring a market-based approach to privacy protection. In October 2001, the FTC Chairman announced that the agency no longer supported federal legislation to protect online privacy, having concluded there was a need "to develop better information about how such legislation would work and the costs and benefits it would generate." Timothy J. Muris, *Protecting Consumers' Privacy: 2002 and Beyond* (Oct. 4, 2001), www.ftc.gov/speeches/muris/privisp1002.htm.

NOTES & QUESTIONS

1. *Online privacy trends*. In March 2002, the Progress and Freedom Foundation[16] reported on a study of online privacy practices that it had commissioned Ernst & Young to perform. The study used the same methodology that the Federal Trade Commission had used in the study on which it reported to Congress in May 2000, discussed *supra*. The goal of the study was to generate data that could be compared to the FTC's results, in order to gauge how online privacy practices had changed in the intervening 21 months. The study found: (1) fewer websites were collecting personally identifying information; (2) fewer websites were using third-party cookies (typically those placed by network advertisers) to track online behavior; (3) more websites were allowing users choice over whether their information would be shared with third parties; (4) a larger percentage of sites offering choice about sharing information with third parties used opt-in choice, and a smaller percentage used opt-out. *See* WILLIAM F. ADKINSON, JR., JEFFREY A. EISENACH & THOMAS M. LENARD, PRIVACY ONLINE: A REPORT ON THE INFORMATION PRACTICES AND POLICIES OF COMMERCIAL WEBSITES (2002). Assuming the validity of these findings, to what might they be attributable? Are operators of

16. The Progress & Freedom Foundation describes itself as "a market-oriented think tank that promotes innovative policy solutions for the digital age." *See* www.pff.org.

commercial websites responding to consumer demand? Are they responding to the threat of government regulation? Could an evolution in e-commerce business models account for the trend?

At the end of 2001, DoubleClick, Inc. announced that it was dropping its targeted marketing service, through which it aimed banner advertisements at Internet users based on profiles it had assembled on them, charging advertisers a premium for this service. What might account for DoubleClick's decision to drop this service?

2. *Privacy policy generators*. In an effort at self-regulation, several organizations created privacy-policy generators: web-based tools that allow a website operator to create an individualized website privacy policy based on a template or component parts. Take a look at the privacy-policy generators located at Direct Marketing Association, *How to Construct Your Privacy Policy*, www.the-dma.org/library/privacy/creating.shtml; and Organisation for Economic Co-operation and Development, *What Is the OECD Privacy Statement Generator?*, cs3–hq.oecd.org/scripts/pwv3/pwhome.htm. Try using one of these tools to create a privacy statement. Do you think that your statement, if posted on a website at the other end of a link on the website's homepage labeled "Privacy," is something that website visitors would find useful? How could you modify it to make it more useful?

3. *Enforcement of voluntary codes*. What mechanisms does a trade association have available to enforce compliance with a code of conduct? How effective are those mechanisms likely to be?

B. MODEL II: THIRD-PARTY CERTIFICATION VIA PRIVACY SEALS

It is difficult or impossible for consumers to make an unaided rational assessment of the quality and characteristics of many goods that are offered in the marketplace. Which of the hundreds of cordless telephones offered for sale has the best sound? Which will last the longest? Which refrigerator is the most energy efficient? Which produce contains the least pesticide residues? If a consumer were to attempt to get answers to these questions through her own research, she would give up long before reaching her goal, finding that it would cost more effort than the item is worth.

The same holds for the experience of visiting a website, which may be considered to be a "product" for present purposes. One of the characteristics of this product is the website's privacy policy. Internet users may wish to "shop" for websites to visit based on a number of criteria, including what the site will do with the visitor's personal information. But how is a potential visitor to assess this characteristic? The privacy policies that websites post are frequently extremely long, complex, and difficult to understand, and most people will consider it not worth their time to decipher the verbiage. Even if someone did take the trouble to get her lawyer's opinion on a website's privacy policy, there is no simple way to determine whether the site actually adheres to its policy.

The market for goods has produced several mechanisms designed to remedy this type of information shortfall. Third-party evaluators, such as

Consumer Reports, perform tests on competing products and report their results. Other third-party evaluators, such as Underwriters Laboratories, certify that a product meets certain minimum quality standards and license the use of their trademarked seal in connection with the product to so indicate. A well-known brand may serve the same purpose: to protect the brand, a manufacturer or reseller may spend whatever it takes to make sure that purchasers are satisfied. Or a manufacturer may offer a warranty on its products, or a money-back guarantee, to assure potential purchasers that even if the product is in some way defective they will be protected.

Responding to the need to furnish website visitors with information about the privacy characteristics of websites, the market has so far relied most heavily on third-party seal systems. The best-known privacy seals are those issued by TRUSTe, a nonprofit entity that was founded by the Electronic Frontier Foundation and the CommerceNet Consortium, and the Council of Better Business Bureaus, which operates the familiar network of BBB's. TRUSTe's seal, which it refers to as a "trustmark," looks like this:

A TRUSTe licensee is also required to display another mark:

This mark is hyperlinked to TRUSTe's site, www.truste.org, so that when clicked it returns a notice indicating that the site displaying it is indeed a licensee—or an indication that the trustmark is a counterfeit.

To qualify for a TRUSTe seal, a website must comply with a set of requirements that TRUSTe has promulgated. As TRUSTe explains:

> We will approve a privacy statement written by you, and will check to see that it contains the following collection and use practices. At a minimum, your privacy statement needs to disclose:
>
> - What personal information is being gathered by your site
> - Who is collecting the information
> - How the information will be used
> - With whom the information will be shared
> - The choices available to users regarding collection, use, and distribution of their information: You must offer users an opportunity to opt-out of internal secondary uses as well as third-party distribution for secondary uses.
> - The security procedures in place to protect users' collected information from loss, misuse, or alteration: If your site collects, uses, or distributes personally identifiable informa-

tion such as credit card or social security numbers, accepted transmission protocols (e.g. encryption) must be in place.

- How users can update or correct inaccuracies in their pertinent information: Appropriate measures shall be taken to ensure that personal information collected online is accurate, complete, and timely, and that easy-to-use mechanisms are in place for users to verify that inaccuracies have been corrected.

TRUSTe, *TRUSTe Program Principles*, truste.org/programs/pub_principles.html.

TRUSTe oversees the trustmark program in several ways:

> We monitor our licensees for compliance with their posted privacy practices and TRUSTe program requirements through a variety of measures. Our oversight process includes initial and periodic Web site reviews, "seeding," and online community monitoring.
>
> *Initial and Periodic Reviews*
>
> After you have completed a formal application to become a TRUSTe licensee (see How to Join), a TRUSTe representative will initially review your site for adherence to our program principles, privacy statement requirements, and trustmark usage. A TRUSTe representative will then periodically review your site to ensure compliance with posted privacy practices and program requirements, and to check for changes to your privacy statement.
>
> *Seeding*
>
> TRUSTe regularly "seeds" Web sites, which is the process of tracking unique identifiers in the site's database. We submit unique user information ourselves and monitor results to ensure that your site is practicing information collection and use practices that are consistent with its stated policies.
>
> *Online Community Monitoring*
>
> A cornerstone of the TRUSTe program is the ability of the community at-large to report violations of posted privacy policies, misuse of the TRUSTe trustmark, or specific privacy concerns pertaining to a licensee. In fact, TRUSTe has established a convenient online Watchdog reporting form for users to report suspected violations of trustmark misuse.

TRUSTe, *TRUSTe Oversight*, truste.org/programs/pub_oversight.html. TRUSTe also has a mechanism for resolving consumer complaints about a licensee's adherence to its privacy policy, and for disciplining licensees that do not comply with TRUSTe's requirements:

> To resolve privacy concerns or complaints raised by consumers or by TRUSTe during our program oversight process, Web site licensees agree to cooperate with all our reviews and inquiries. We work with licensees, as well as with consumers, to resolve privacy-related issues quickly and fairly.

> As a licensee in the TRUSTe program, a Web site agrees to provide consumers with simple, effective means to submit their privacy concerns directly to the Web site. At a minimum, all privacy statements contain TRUSTe contact information so that consumers may direct their questions or concerns to us. We request users to contact Web sites directly before filing a report with us.
>
> If the Web site has not acknowledged the receipt of the consumer's complaint, or if a satisfactory response is not provided, we step in as the liaison between the consumer and Web site to resolve the issue. This process entails:
>
> - Notifying the licensee of the consumer's complaint and working with the site for a speedy, satisfactory resolution.
> - Notifying the consumer of the resolution or other relevant findings.
> - Pursuing the issue further if we are unable to reach a mutual resolution with the licensee.
>
> In the unlikely event that TRUSTe has reason to believe a licensee has violated its posted privacy practices or other TRUSTe program requirements, we will conduct an escalating investigation. This process may include an on-site compliance review by one of TRUSTe's official auditors, PricewaterhouseCoopers LLP or KPMG Peat Marwick LLP. If the on-site review finds that a licensee is non-compliant, TRUSTe will advise and guide the licensee on the steps to remedy the problem.
>
> If no action is taken by the licensee—depending on the severity of the breach—our investigation may also result in revocation of the TRUSTe trustmark, termination from the program, or in extreme cases, referral to the appropriate government agency.

TRUSTe, *Resolution Process*, truste.org/programs/pub_recourse.html.

The Better Business Bureau's privacy seal program has similar elements. *See* BBBOnLine, *BBBOnLine Privacy Seal*, www.bbbonline.com/privacy.

One limitation of TRUSTe's seal program was illustrated by its response to a complaint against the privacy practices of Microsoft, a TRUSTe licensee and one of its Premier Corporate Sponsors. As discussed in Part III(A), *supra*, in 1999 it was discovered that the globally unique identifier contained within a computer's Ethernet card was being transmitted to Microsoft during the Windows 98 registration process, and was being electronically stamped onto documents created with Microsoft Office 98 application programs. A privacy advocate, Jason Catlett, lodged a complaint against Microsoft with TRUSTe. Here is TRUSTe's response to the complaint:

Watchdog #1723—Microsoft Statement of Finding

* * *

Investigation Results

On March 12, 1999, Jason Catlett, President of Junkbusters e-mailed Susan Scott asking that TRUSTe initiate an investigation of a perceived breach of the TRUSTe License Agreement by Microsoft. As with any Watchdog complaint, TRUSTe enacted its escalation process to investigate the complaint. After a thorough review of Microsoft's alleged violation of its privacy policy, TRUSTe has determined that Microsoft has not violated its TRUSTe license.

* * *

Nature of Privacy Breach

One privacy breach was revealed in TRUSTe's investigation: a "bug" existed that transferred the [hardware identifier] to Microsoft's server, even if the consumer opted out of such transfer. This breach of privacy has since been corrected and did not at any time involve the Microsoft.com Web site. Microsoft has acknowledged this breach publicly.

Privacy Statement

The privacy statement governing Microsoft.com is posted at the site and accessible from the home page and the Profile Center. This privacy policy carries the TRUSTe trustmark. In this case, TRUSTe's certification process covers data that is collected specifically by Microsoft.com, a TRUSTe licensed site. Upon reviewing past Microsoft.com privacy statements, TRUSTe determined that Microsoft.com had indeed disclosed that registration information would be collected and that the [hardware identifier] would also be collected. In addition, the privacy statement explained the uses of this information in conformance with TRUSTe's "use" principle.

Conclusion

TRUSTe has determined that Microsoft.com was in compliance with all TRUSTe principles. Had TRUSTe determined that Microsoft.com had violated its stated practices, TRUSTe would have conducted an audit to ascertain that sufficient remedies had been put in place.

While the complaint itself does not pertain to the Web site, TRUSTe believes that is important to note that the transfer of Hardware IDs to the Microsoft secure server without customer consent did, in TRUSTe's opinion, compromise consumer trust and privacy.

* * *

TRUSTe, *Watchdog #1723—Microsoft Statement of Finding*, www.truste.org/news/padvisories/users_w1723.html.

NOTES & QUESTIONS

1. *Microsoft.com privacy statement.* TRUSTe's decision concludes that microsoft.com has not violated the conditions of its licensing agreement, since the site accurately disclosed what information would be collected in the registration process, and how it would be used. Is there any reason to expect that a computer user registering his copy of Windows 98 would have any occasion to view the privacy notice at microsoft.com? Take a look at the privacy statement at www.microsoft.com/info/privacy.htm. Does this clearly convey to the average Internet user the information she needs to make an informed decision whether to register a Microsoft product, or whether to register as a visitor to the microsoft.com website?

2. *Message conveyed to site visitors*. Internet users who have not taken the trouble to study the details of TRUSTe's privacy seal program are likely to assume that the presence of a TRUSTe trustmark on a website indicates that the site's information practices are in some way protective of privacy interests. Is this assumption warranted? If a site visitor views the trustmark as a proxy for a protective privacy policy, she may dispense with reading the policy statement itself. How does this impact the goal of transmitting to site visitors the information they need to make an informed decision whether to trust their personal information to a website?

C. Model III: Empowerment of Individuals Through Technological Tools

Another market-based approach to protecting online privacy is to make available to Internet users technological tools that they can use to protect themselves.

U.S. Senate Judiciary Committee, Know the Rules, Use the Tools—Privacy in the Digital Age: A Resource for Internet Users

(2000).

* * *

In the dynamic arena of Internet technology, a wide variety of exciting technological solutions exist to safeguard personally identifiable information and new ones are continually being developed. This Report's discussion of the available technologies is not intended to be a comprehensive one, but rather is intended to give consumers a sampling of the tools currently available to consumers that help empower them to safeguard their privacy to the extent they wish. * * *

* * *

1. Ways of Handling Cookies.

"[C]ookies" are electronic tags that are placed on the hard drive of a user's computer by websites he or she visits. * * * Currently available to users are a number of options to: (1) alert them as to when a cookie is placed on their hard drive, (2) block the placement of a cookie altogether, or (3) remove cookies from the user's hard drive. A few of these options are described below:

a. Internet Browser Settings.

New technology permits Internet users to see when a cookie is about to be planted on their system and make an informed choice about whether to accept it or reject it. With current versions of leading browsers such as Netscape Navigator and Internet Explorer, a user can select to have an alert box flash on the screen to inform them whenever a server is trying to place a cookie on their system. Some sites, however, send cookies for every object the user clicks on the page, requiring the user to reject cookies dozens of times for a single web page.

b. Manual Deletion Of Cookies Using Browser Files.

Internet users can locate and delete cookies that already have been placed on their computer by websites. In Netscape Navigator, the cookies are stored in a single file called "cookies.txt." This file generally is in the directory the user previously designated for Netscape to use for storing user profiles. To delete all cookies, find the "cookies.txt" file, highlight it, and delete it. To delete a specific cookie, open the file "cookies.txt" with an editor or word processor, and delete the line corresponding to the cookie you wish to delete.

For Internet Explorer, find the directory called "Cookies." To delete all cookies, delete all the files in the directory. To delete a specific cookie, find the file in the directory corresponding to the cookie and delete that file.

c. Cookie–Cutters.

Various technology-based tools exist for coping with unwanted cookies. * * *

i. Netscape Cookie Manager.

Developed by America Online, Netscape Cookie Manager, a feature of the new Netscape browser, allows users to view, block, and delete cookies based on their individual privacy preferences. For example, Cookie Manager permits a user to determine who may and who may not set cookies on his or her computer, edit and delete any of the cookies placed, and review a list and description of all of the cookies placed on the user's computer.

Other privacy technology developed by America Online includes AOL Parental Controls and AOL Instant Messenger. AOL Parental Controls permits parents to determine who their children may or may not communicate with when they use AOL by initiating specific privacy settings. AOL Instant Messenger allows a user to control his or her own privacy by limiting who is permitted to know when the user is online and who is permitted to make contact with the user.

ii. Privacy Companion.

Developed by Idcide, Inc., Privacy Companion is a browser software application that is intended to enable users to detect and block third party cookies, while allowing them to benefit from personalized services from the websites that they are visiting. Privacy Companion automatically detects and blocks cookies from third party advertisers and profiling companies which can be used to track a user's browsing behavior as he or she moves from website to website. It also provides statistics on sites which may have tracked a user's browsing behavior.

iii. NSClean Privacy Software.

NSClean Privacy Software provides products that permit the end-user to turn off the cookie warnings, accept cookies while online, and then remove them from their hard drive. "Owing to the need for legitimate cookies to be kept for the convenience of users for legitimate sites," the new NSClean products permit users control over cookies, enabling them to select which cookies they find useful and desire to keep and remove all other cookies automatically at their option.

iv. AdSubtract.

AdSubtract offers filtering to eliminate unwanted advertisements, animated images, cookies, pop-up windows, background music, and the like. By eliminating unwanted pages, AdSubtract speeds up web page download time. The downloadable software provides the user with statistics showing items filtered.

* * *

viii. WebWasher for Windows and Macintosh.

WebWasher filters the HTML data stream to automatically block ads, animation, java script and cookies. The program comes configured to automatically block "bad" cookies that leak personal information while automatically accepting "good" cookies required for efficient online shopping and quick page views. From its "traffic cop" position in the data stream, WebWasher filters both incoming cookies from website servers and outgoing cookies from the user's browser. WebWasher can be installed on an individual computer or run as a proxy-server for an entire office network.

2. Identity Scrubbers.

Various user information is instantly available to websites when users visit them. Identity scrubbers are tools developed to allow users of the Internet to remain anonymous while surfing the Internet. While a number of companies offer different options for consumer, the following is a sampling of identity scrubbing tools that are available.

a. PrivadaControl.

Privada is a digital privacy service created for Network service providers. PrivadaControl, operated on a user's personal computer, permits the user to browse the Internet anonymously and to send and receive e-mails anonymously. While using PrivadaControl during Internet use, a user's webpage requests are encrypted and sent to the Privada Network. The Privada Network then retrieves the webpage and returns it to the user. Additionally, PrivadaControl allows users to manage the placement of cookies, which are assigned to the user's individual profile on the Privada Network rather than on the user's computer. As a result, the user may take advantage of the benefits of customized browsing without privacy concerns. Users may disable PrivadaControl's privacy protections in order to share personal information with those websites they choose. PrivadaControl also allows a user to send and receive e-mail anonymously by permitting the user to create a separate identity and to establish an anonymous e-mail account with that identity on the Privada Network. A user may then send and receive e-mail from this account without disclosing his or her personal identity. E-mail messages sent by the user to the Privada Network are encrypted, and the user may choose to have the Privada Network assign his or her sent messages a random delay of 30 minutes to four hours.

b. Incogno SafeZone.

Developed by Incogno Corporation, Incogno SafeZone is a patent-pending technology that enables Internet merchants to offer anonymous checkout services to privacy-sensitive buyers. Using Incogno SafeZone, customers buy directly from the merchant's site and receive product shipments without revealing their names, addresses, e-mail addresses, or credit card information to the merchant. Additionally, because the merchant does not receive, store, or transmit the customer's credit card information in unencrypted form, the risk of credit card fraud is reduced. In using Incogno SafeZone, a merchant can request that customers disclose their personal information, but any such disclosure is fully voluntary. Incogno SafeZone currently is in the market trial stage.

* * *

d. Anonymizer.com.

Recognizing that each time an Internet user enters a website, he or she could provide certain personal information, including viewing habits, geographical location, addresses, e-mail and credit card numbers, Anonymizer.com enables users to visit sites while concealing their identity. Anonymizer protects consumer privacy by acting as an intermediary between the user and a particular website. * * *

e. Crowds.

Developed by AT & T Research, Crowds allows users to blend into a virtual crowd on the Internet by hiding an individual's actions within the actions of many users. Users are placed into a large and geographically diverse group, or "crowd," which collectively issues requests on behalf of its members. The end server is unable to identify the initiator of the request because the initiator is indistinguishable from any of the other "crowd" members.

3. Privacy Preference Technology.

Privacy preference technology allows the user to select his or her own privacy preferences, to modify those preferences, and to compare how particular websites' privacy policies match his or her own preferences.

a. AT&T Research.

AT&T Research, in conjunction with Microsoft Corporation, is developing browser software technology to be used with Microsoft's Internet Explorer. When installed by the user, this technology will add a privacy button to the top of his or her browser window. By clicking on this button, a user will be able to set his or her privacy preferences, check how well a website's privacy policy matches the user's preferences, and view a site's actual privacy policy. AT&T's technology currently is in the development stages.

* * *

NOTE: PLATFORM FOR PRIVACY PREFERENCES

The Platform for Privacy Preferences ("P3P") is another technological approach to empowering Internet users to retain control of their personal information. P3P, which was developed by the World Wide Web Consortium, is a protocol that allows a website to describe its privacy policy in a standardized format. When an Internet user accesses a P3P-compliant website, the server automatically communicates the website's privacy policy to the user's browser. The browser is configured with the user's privacy preferences. For example, if you are unwilling to have your personal information shared with any third party, you can indicate that preference in your browser settings. When you access a website, your browser compares the site's policies with your own preferences. If the site meets your privacy requirements, the browser accesses the website. If not, the browser may alert you of the mismatch, and allow you to decide whether to bypass the site.[17]

There are several important tasks relating to online privacy that P3P does not undertake. As the W3C explains: "P3P does not set minimum standards for privacy, nor can it monitor whether sites adhere to their own stated procedures. Addressing all of the complicated, fundamental issues surrounding privacy on the Web will require the appropriate combination of technology, a legal framework and self-regulatory practices." World Wide Web Consortium, *P3P 1.0: A New Standard in Online Privacy,* www.w3.org/P3P/brochure.html.

Critics of P3P note that website operators will have little incentive to take the trouble to implement P3P. Given the complexity of configuring a browser with one's privacy preferences, most users will leave their browsers in their default configurations, which will likely not be highly protec-

17. P3P does not define how a browser responds in case of a mismatch: it is only a language that allows the website to communicate with a browser. It is up to the browser developer to determine how the browser will communicate to the user the result of its comparison of the website privacy policy with the user's preferences.

tive of privacy, since that would result in denying access to a large number of popular websites. Even users who want strong privacy protection will probably leave their browsers configured to a low level of protection, since otherwise there will be few sites they can visit. As a result, P3P will not create any meaningful incentives for websites to implement fair information practices. Internet users will get only the illusion, but not the reality, of sovereignty in the marketplace for privacy. Furthermore, no mechanism currently exists for enforcement of privacy promises embedded in P3P code. For a critique of P3P, see Electronic Privacy Information Center, *Pretty Poor Privacy: An Assessment of P3P and Internet Privacy* (2000), www.epic.org/reports/prettypoorprivacy.html. For a review of the development of P3P, highlighting the role of privacy advocates in its development, see Lorrie Faith Cranor, *The Role of Privacy Advocates and Data Protection Authorities in the Design and Deployment of the Platform for Privacy Preferences*, doi.acm.org/10.1145/543482.543506.

NOTES & QUESTIONS

1. *Costs of self-empowerment.* The use of privacy control technologies entails significant costs for Internet users. A user must invest a substantial amount of time and effort to research the various tools, select the one she thinks will best suit her purposes, install it, and learn how to use it. There are likely to be significant segments of the online population that lack the skills necessary to make use of these tools: an August 2000 study found that 56 percent of web users did not know what a cookie is. *See* Pew Internet & American Life Project, *Trust and Privacy Online: Why Americans Want to Rewrite the Rules* (2000), www.pewinternet.org/reports/toc.asp?Report=19. Adding a new piece of software to one's computer always carries the risk that it will be buggy or incompatible with other software on the system, costing more time and effort. Some of these tools significantly degrade a user's experience in accessing the Web, by slowing down communications or by adding additional procedures that must be followed when accessing a new website. Some of them are free, but others carry a purchase price or subscription fee. How much burden is it appropriate for Internet users to shoulder to protect themselves from invasions of their privacy?

2. *Does individual empowerment obviate regulation?* Should the availability of tools like these lead legislators and regulators to the conclusion that government intervention to protect privacy online is unnecessary? How would you distinguish this argument from the following one? "Door locks, window bars, burglar alarms, and private guard services are widely available. Heavy-handed government intervention in the form of criminalization of burglary is therefore unnecessary. We should instead devote more resources to educating householders to make use of these tools and protect themselves."

3. *Will tools emerge without law?* Professor Lawrence Lessig argues that technology enabling automated negotiations over privacy between a website and a prospective site visitor, like P3P, will not emerge unless the law mandates it, since "[t]he power of commerce is not behind any such change." LAWRENCE LESSIG, CODE AND OTHER LAWS OF CYBERSPACE 163 (1999). Do you agree? Are the imperatives of commerce necessarily opposed to implementation of fair information practices?

D. MODEL IV: PLENARY REGULATION—THE EC DIRECTIVE

The European approach to information privacy is very different from the U.S. approach. Beginning in the 1970s, many European countries enacted "data protection" laws that were broad in scope and were backed up by data protection commissions and commissioners. These laws varied widely in their substantive provisions as well as in the associated enforcement schemes. In order to promote a more uniform legal treatment of personal data, and as part of its ongoing effort to remove barriers to trade among countries within the European Union, in 1995 (effective 1998) the European Commission promulgated a Directive addressing data protection. *See* Directive 95/46/EC of the European Parliament and of the Council of 24 October 1995 on the protection of individuals with regard to the processing of personal data and on the free movement of such data, 1995 O.J. (L 281) 31.

Consistent with the European model of regulation, the Directive is broad in scope and detailed in its prescriptions. As you read the following material, consider whether such an approach would be suited to the U.S. context.

1. PROVISIONS OF THE DIRECTIVE

The Directive places limitations on the "processing" of "personal data." "Personal data" means "any information relating to an identified or identifiable natural person"; that person is referred to as the "data subject." Art. 2(a). "Processing" of personal data is broadly defined as any operation that is performed on personal data, including "collection, recording, organization, storage, adaptation or alteration, retrieval, consultation, use, disclosure by transmission, dissemination or otherwise making available, alignment or combination, blocking, erasure or destruction." Art. 2(b). There are exceptions for certain important functions that governments perform, as well as for processing "by a natural person in the course of a purely personal or household activity." Art. 3(2).

The Directive applies to processing of personal data "wholly or partly by automatic means," and to non-automatic processing "of personal data which form part of a filing system." Art. 3(1). A "filing system" is "any structured set of personal data which are accessible according to specific criteria." Art. 2(c). Thus, any manipulation of personal data through the use of computers is covered by the Directive. Manipulation of non-computerized personal data is covered if the records are maintained in an organized format that makes it possible to retrieve records with particular characteristics. This would seem to include most business records: sending a copy of a document stored in one's file drawer that contains personal information would likely be covered.

The Directive places several types of limitations on the processing of personal data by a "data controller," which is defined as any person with a role in determining "the purposes and means of the processing of personal data." Art. 2(d). First, there are limitations on what data may be collected and how it must be maintained. Personal data may only be collected for specified purposes, and may not be processed "in a way incompatible with those purposes." The quantity of data collected must not be "excessive" in relation to those purposes. Data must be accurate and kept up to date. And data may be retained in a form that makes them identifiable to a person only for as long as necessary to accomplish the purposes for collection. Art. 6(1)(b)–(e).

Second, there is a general consent requirement: processing of personal data is allowed only if "the data subject has unambiguously given his consent." Art. 7(a). The requisite consent is strictly defined: it must be a "freely given specific and informed indication of his wishes by which the data subject signifies his agreement to personal data relating to him being processed." Art. 2(h). This consent requirement is, however, subject to a number of exceptions, including where processing is necessary (1) to the performance of a contract to which the data subject is a party, (2) for compliance with a legal obligation, (3) to protect the data subject's vital interests, (4) to further the public interest, or (5) to the achievement of the data controller's legitimate interests that are not outweighed by the data subject's fundamental rights and freedoms. Art. 7(b)–(f). The data subject also has a specifically enumerated right to object to the use of data concerning him for the purposes of direct marketing. Art. 14(b).

Third, there is a general prohibition against the processing of certain types of sensitive personal information, namely that "revealing racial or ethnic origin, political opinions, religious or philosophical beliefs, [and] trade-union membership." The prohibition also extends to *any* data, whether personal or not, "concerning health or sex life." Art. 8(1). The exceptions from this prohibition include (1) where the data subject has given explicit consent, (2) where processing is necessary to satisfy the requirements of employment laws, (3) where processing is necessary to protect vital interests, and the data subject is incapable of giving consent, (4) certain uses by non-profit entities, (5) where the data are made public by the data subject or must be revealed in connection with legal claims, and (6) use in connection with provision of medical services. Art. 8(2)–(3). The Directive also creates a limited right "not to be subject to a decision which produces legal effects concerning him or significantly affects him and which is based solely on automated processing of data intended to evaluate certain personal aspects relating to him, such as his performance at work, creditworthiness, reliability, conduct, etc." Art. 15(1).

Fourth, the data controller must furnish certain information to the data subject. Information that is required to be disclosed includes the identity of the data controller, the purposes for processing the data, and whatever additional information is required "to guarantee fair processing in respect of the data subject." Arts. 10 & 11.

Fifth, data subjects have the right to obtain from the data controller, "at reasonable intervals and without excessive delay or expense," (1) confirmation whether data concerning the subject are being processed, and if so information regarding the purposes of the processing, the categories of information processed, and the identity of the recipients of the information, (2) the data that are being processed and their source, and (3) "the logic involved in any automatic processing" of data that results in the making of decisions that significantly affect the data subject. Art. 12(a). The data subject may also demand that the controller correct inaccurate data, and if practicable advise third parties to which the data were disclosed of the correction. Art. 12(b) & (c).

Sixth, data controllers must assure the confidentiality and security of the data they process. Arts. 16 & 17.

Seventh, a data controller must notify the national supervisory authority, which the Directive requires each EU member state to set up, before commencing any automatic processing of data. Art. 18. The notification must include the name and address of the controller, the purposes of the processing, the categories of data subjects and categories of data relating to them that are involved in the processing, the categories of recipients to which the data may be disclosed, whether any data will be transferred to non-EU countries, and a description of security measures. The supervisory authority must then examine any operations involved in the proposed processing that are among those the member state has determined are "likely to present specific risks to the rights and freedoms of data subjects." Art. 20(1). The supervisory authority must also maintain a publicly accessible register of the data processing operations of which it is notified. Art. 21.

Eighth, the Directive places limitations on a controller's transfer of personal data to a country outside the European Union. Transfers of personal data to a "third country" are allowed only if "the third country in question ensures an adequate level of protection" to the data. Art. 25(1). The determination of adequacy is contextual, depending on "all the circumstances surrounding a data transfer operation," such as "the nature of the data, the purpose and duration of the proposed processing operation or operations, the country of origin and country of final destination, the rules of law, both general and sectoral, in force in the third country in question and the professional rules and security measures which are complied with in that country." Art. 25(2). Data may be transferred to a third country even absent "adequate" protection if (1) the data subject consents "unambiguously," (2) the transfer is necessary for the performance of a contract between the data subject and the controller, (3) the transfer is necessary for the performance of a contract between the controller and a third party that is for the benefit of the data subject, (4) the transfer is needed on public interest grounds or in connection with a legal claim, (5) the transfer is needed to protect the "vital interests" of the data subject, or (6) the data are publicly available. Art. 26(1). A lack of adequate protection in the third country may also be overcome if the controller puts in place "adequate safeguards" for the protection of privacy, such as through contractual arrangements with the data recipient. Art. 26(2).

The Directive's effects are profound and wide-ranging. Most commercial transactions involving individual purchasers generate transactional information that includes personal data. Businesses have a strong incentive to retain these data in a personally identifiable form, since that endows them with substantial value: the information may be used to solicit additional purchases, and may be sold or rented to other businesses for their own marketing purposes. Practically any operation that is performed on such data will fall within the scope of the Directive. Personal data are also generated in educational settings, in the provision of medical services, through charitable activities, and in other non-commercial undertakings. Most of these data are stored in a digital format and are processed by computers: this processing by "automatic means" brings it within the scope of the Directive. Even data maintained in the form of paper documents are likely to be subject to the Directive as belonging to a "filing system."

Of greatest relevance to the United States is the Article 25 limitation on transfers of personal data to "third countries," of which the United States is one. Enormous quantities of personal data are routinely transferred from European Union countries to the United States (and other "third countries"), and are therefore potentially affected by the Directive. For example:

- The Directive could apply to e-mail messages that are sent from within the EU to some country outside the EU. If a message contains personal information that relates only to the sender, then the sender's act of sending it would certainly constitute unambiguous consent in satisfaction of Art. 26(1)(a). But if the message relates to someone other than the sender, there will not necessarily be consent or satisfaction of any of the other Art. 26 exemptions. The same logic applies to paper documents that are sent via postal mail or facsimile transmission, as long as the documents form part of a "filing system."
- The Directive applies to websites that collect personal information, which is true of nearly all commercially oriented websites. If the site is operated from within the EU, there is no question of the Directive's applicability. If the site is operated from outside the EU, the question becomes trickier. It is unclear whether an EU member state can assert jurisdiction over a website that is operated by a company located in the United States, and that resides on a server located in the United States, on the ground that the site is collecting data from individuals located within that member state.
- The use of online surveillance devices, such as cookies and web bugs, would seem to fall within the Directive's scope. Placing a cookie on the hard drive of a site visitor's computer may allow a website to

identify the visitor, and to accumulate personal data about the visitor's browsing habits. If the website uses a third-party advertising server, such as DoubleClick, a visit to the site may result in the transfer of personal data to the ad server. Using web bugs, a site operator or e-mail sender can collect personal data about when the recipient accesses a web page or e-mail message. If the visitor that is located in an EU country, and the website operator, ad server, or e-mail sender is in some other country, Article 25 limitations apply.

- Corporations that operate in more than one country routinely make intra-company transfers of personal information that are also cross-border transfers. This would be true of personal data that reside on a corporate intranet, and that are accessible by employees in different countries. The company may maintain transactional information in a distributed fashion on computers located both within and outside the EU, and may need to combine the data on its "third country" computers. With client-server system architectures, a server located within the EU may routinely transfer personal data to clients outside the EU, and vice versa. Information about a company's employees is especially likely to fall within the scope of the Directive, and to undergo transfers that will be transborder if the company's operations are multi-national. The same will be true for many other corporate-wide functions, such as auditing and accounting, use of consultants, and handling of customer service.

If the European Commission determines that a particular country does not provide "adequate" protection to personal data, various effects might ensue. A company that has operations both within the EU and in the inadequately protective third country might have an incentive to move certain data processing operations from the third country to an EU country. For example, it might move its human resources office to Europe, or engage European accountants and auditors, to avoid the need to transfer personal information involved in those functions to the third country. The company might respond by de-centralizing its operations, erecting a "fire-wall" between its European operations and its activities in the third country. If the European operations are a small part of its business, the company might sell off those operations; if the third-country operations are small, it might jettison that part of its business instead. A company headquartered in the third country might find it infeasible to hire employees located in European Union countries.

On the other hand, the effects of the Directive on businesses located in countries with inadequate protections might be moderated by the exemptions provided by Art. 26. In particular, the provision allowing transborder transfers on consent of the data subject might, if expansively interpreted, overcome the most serious of the limitations imposed by Art. 25.

For more detailed treatment of the Directive, and especially of the Art. 25 limitation on transmission of personal data outside the EU, see PETER P. SWIRE & ROBERT E. LITAN, NONE OF YOUR BUSINESS: WORLD DATA FLOWS, ELECTRONIC COMMERCE, AND THE EUROPEAN PRIVACY DIRECTIVE (1998).

2. THE U.S.-EU SAFE HARBOR PRINCIPLES

The European Commission's adoption of the Directive sparked a flurry of negotiations between the United States (led by the Department of Commerce) and the EC, aimed at averting the possibility that trans-Atlantic flows of personal data would be halted by a finding that the United States does not provide adequate protections satisfying Article 25. The result of these negotiations was the EU's approval of a set of "safe harbor" principles to which U.S. companies could subscribe and thereby be deemed to ensure an adequate level of protection.

Safe Harbor Privacy Principles

(2000).
www.export.gov/safeharbor

The European Union's comprehensive privacy legislation, the Directive on Data Protection (the Directive), became effective on October 25, 1998. It requires that transfers of personal data take place only to non-EU countries that provide an "adequate" level of privacy protection. While the United States and the European Union share the goal of enhancing privacy protection for their citizens, the United States takes a different approach to privacy from that taken by the European Union. The United States uses a sectoral approach that relies on a mix of legislation, regulation, and self regulation. Given those differences, many U.S. organizations have expressed uncertainty about the impact of the EU-required "adequacy standard" on personal data transfers from the European Union to the United States.

To diminish this uncertainty and provide a more predictable framework for such data transfers, the Department of Commerce is issuing this document and Frequently Asked Questions ("the Principles") under its statutory authority to foster, promote, and develop international commerce.

* * *

Decisions by organizations to qualify for the safe harbor are entirely voluntary. * * *

* * *

"Personal data" and "personal information" are data about an identified or identifiable individual that are within the scope of the Directive, received by a U.S. organization from the European Union, and recorded in any form.

NOTICE: An organization must inform individuals about the purposes for which it collects and uses information about them, how to contact the organization with any inquiries or complaints, the types of third parties to which it discloses the information, and the choices and means the organization offers individuals for limiting its use and disclosure. This notice must be provided in clear and conspicuous language when individuals are first asked to provide personal information to the organization or as soon thereafter as is practicable, but in any event before the organization uses such information for a purpose other than that for which it was originally collected or processed by the transferring organization or discloses it for the first time to a third party.[1]

CHOICE: An organization must offer individuals the opportunity to choose (opt out) whether their personal information is (a) to be disclosed to a third party or (b) to be used for a purpose that is incompatible with the purpose(s) for which it was originally collected or subsequently authorized by the individual. Individuals must be provided with clear and conspicuous, readily available, and affordable mechanisms to exercise choice.

For sensitive information (i.e. personal information specifying medical or health conditions, racial or ethnic origin, political opinions, religious or philosophical beliefs, trade union membership or information specifying the sex life of the individual), they must be given affirmative or explicit (opt in) choice if the information is to be disclosed to a third party or used for a purpose other than those for which it was originally collected or subsequently authorized by the individual through the exercise of opt in choice. In any case, an organization should treat as sensitive any information received from a third party where the third party treats and identifies it as sensitive.

ONWARD TRANSFER: To disclose information to a third party, organizations must apply the Notice and Choice Principles. Where an organization wishes to transfer information to a third party that is acting as an agent, as described in the [footnote], it may do so if it first either ascertains that the third party subscribes to the Principles or is subject to the Directive or another adequacy finding or enters into a written agreement with such third party requiring that the third party provide at least the same level of privacy protection as is required by the relevant Principles. If the organization complies with these requirements, it shall not be held responsible (unless the organization agrees otherwise) when a third party to which it transfers such information processes it in a way contrary to any restrictions or representations, unless the organization knew or should have known the third party would process it in such a contrary way and the organization has not taken reasonable steps to prevent or stop such processing.

SECURITY: Organizations creating, maintaining, using or disseminating personal information must take reasonable precautions to protect it from loss, misuse and unauthorized access, disclosure, alteration and destruction.

DATA INTEGRITY: Consistent with the Principles, personal information must be relevant for the purposes for which it is to be used. An organization may not process personal information in a way that is incompatible with the purposes for which it has been collected or subsequently authorized by the individual. To the extent necessary for those purposes,

1. It is not necessary to provide notice or choice when disclosure is made to a third party that is acting as an agent to perform task(s) on behalf of and under the instructions of the organization. The Onward Transfer Principle, on the other hand, does apply to such disclosures.

E. MODEL V: COMMODIFICATION OF PRIVACY?

Kenneth C. Laudon, *Extensions to the Theory of Markets and Privacy: Mechanics of Pricing Information*

U.S. DEP'T OF COMMERCE, PRIVACY AND SELF-REGULATION IN THE INFORMATION AGE (1997).

* * *

The theory of markets and privacy begins with the understanding that the current crisis in the privacy of personal information is a result of market failure and not "technological progress" alone. The market failure has occurred because of a poor social choice in the allocation of property rights. Under current law, the ownership right to personal information is given to the collector of that information, and not to the individual to whom the information refers. Individuals have no property rights in their own personal information. As a result, they cannot participate in the flourishing market for personal information, i.e., they receive no compensation for the uses of their personal information. As a further consequence, the price of personal information is so low that information-intense industries become inefficient in its use. The price is low because the price of personal information does not reflect the true social costs of coping with personal information. The market is dominated by privacy-invading institutions. And as a further result, there is a disturbing growth in privacy invasion, an excessive and abusive disregard for the interests of many in keeping elements of their life private, or at least under their control.

* * *

An earlier paper attempted to lay the legal and economic foundation for a true marketplace for personal information. In this marketplace, individuals would retain the ownership in their personal information and have the right, but not the obligation, to sell this information either to institutional users directly, or more likely, to information intermediaries who would aggregate the information into useful tranches (e.g. blocks of one thousand individuals with known demographic characteristics) and sell these information baskets on a National Information Exchange.

Individual ownership of personal information can be anchored within British and American common law. The common law tort of appropriation protects the right of celebrities to own their images, likenesses, voices, and other elements of their persona. To appropriate personal images of celebrities for commercial purposes without consent or payment is recognized by the courts as an appropriation. Likewise, it is conceivable that courts and juries could be convinced to protect the personal "data images" of ordinary citizens. These data images have somewhat less resolution than a photographic image, but they are increasingly and profoundly descriptive and predictive of human behavior. As computers extend their powers, these data images will approach photographic resolutions.

The economic foundation for individual ownership of personal information can be found in the theory of markets (and related theories of governance) and the theory of externalities. Markets are likely the most efficient mechanisms for allocating scarce resources. Governments should intervene in markets only if markets fail. Markets do fail under conditions of monopoly, asymmetries in power and information, and in the case of public goods, e.g., clean air. Governments should either seek to restore markets or regulate the activity. In the case of personal information, the market has failed because of asymmetries in power and information brought about by poor social choice in the allocation of property rights to information. The price of personal information is far too low, and therefore its abuse in the form of privacy invasion is far too cost beneficial to those institutions that dominate the market. The function of government here should be to restore the power of one class of participants in the market, namely individuals, by vesting ownership of personal information in the individual. A second function of government is to ensure the orderly functioning of a personal information marketplace.

The failure of the marketplace results in significant negative externalities for individuals. These externalities are experienced as excessive indirect and direct costs involved in "coping" with information. Coping costs include tangible costs like excessively large mail handling facilities (public and private), and loss of attention, as well as intangible costs like loss of serenity, privacy, and solitude. These negative externalities must be balanced against the positive externalities of nearly unlimited exploitation of personal information which results in enormous amounts of marketing information being delivered to consumers (whether they want it or not). However, it can no longer be argued that these positive externalities fully compensate individuals or society for the negative costs of unlimited exploitation of personal information.

* * *

Jessica Litman, *Information Privacy/Information Property*

52 STAN. L. REV. 1283 (2000).

* * *

Imagine the commercial world wide web in a world that treats personal data as alienable personal property. If personal data are alienable, then by ordering that free computer, downloading that free MP3 recording of a hit song, downloading and installing that software, you will surely have consummated the transfer. We could make a rule that the terms of such a transfer must be disclosed as part of the inevitable click-through license, and just as surely, they would be, and everyone would click "I accept" without even reading them. Indeed, arguably, for any website for which access requires clicking an "I accept" box, the fact that you, for instance, read the *New York Times* on the Web at a considerable savings over the newsstand rate will support the claim of transfer.

It's no better out here in meatspace. Imagine that a person, and let's for the sake of convenience and brevity call her "I," has initial ownership of information about herself, that is, me. I sign up for a check cashing card at the supermarket, or a shopper's club discount card, and, in return for the convenience of paying by check or a steady stream of small discounts on products I may or may not buy, I waive, forfeit, or assign any ownership rights I might have in whatever information resides in an ongoing record of my purchases.

The store, meanwhile, has its own proprietary interest in the compiled purchasing records of each and all of its customers, and will rely on that interest to sell facts about me to whomever. Whomever, of course, has a property interest in those facts because it paid for them, and will be able to combine them with facts about other people and more facts about me from other sources. Whomever may use that collection of data to make up a list of people who are ripe for Discover Card® solicitations, or who might be interested in a mail order catalog for folks suffering from depression, or who, based on recent medical and pharmaceutical purchases, might be eager to purchase some no-questions-asked life insurance.

What makes the whole situation worse is that privacy is one of those things that many people don't believe they really need until they find themselves with something to keep secret. If easy assignment is the rule, they may no longer have the power to preserve their secrecy; even if they could, the exceptional nature of their asserting a privacy claim will tip off those from whom this is a secret that there is an interesting secret there. So, if someone who is deemed to have waived any property rights in the information supplied to businesses in return for product discounts should suddenly find himself diagnosed with hemorrhoids, or herpes, or HIV, he may have no practical way to recapture his secrecy.

Now, imagine the world we have made. We each owned our own personal data initially, but we've assigned them for value to some business, which has sold them to some other business, which combines them with other data to generate a profile of each of us, and sells or rents that profile out. Nor is it unrealistic to imagine those businesses asserting their property interest in their collections of data: There is a lot of that going around. In October, the *New York Times* reported that the NIH Recombinant DNA Advisory Committee had been stymied in its efforts to require more complete disclosure of the safety problems encountered in gene therapy by pharmaceutical companies' insistence that that information is proprietary.

The market in personal data is the problem. Market solutions based on a property rights model won't cure it; they'll only legitimize it.

* * *

Margaret Jane Radin, *Incomplete Commodification in the Computerized World*

THE COMMODIFICATION OF INFORMATION (Neil Netanel & Niva Elkin–Koren eds., 2002).

* * *

It makes a big difference whether privacy is thought of as a human right, attaching to persons by virtue of their personhood, or as a property right, something that can be owned and controlled by persons. The difference has to do with the rhetorical significance of alienability. Human rights are presumptively market-inalienable, whereas property rights are presumptively market-alienable.

Consider the situation if some particular type of privacy, for example data regarding a person's information buying habits, is conceived of and treated as a human right. Then to gain access to and use the private data, in ways other than sanctioned by society, violates a human right. We could think of such violation as a tort, if we have in mind torts against personal integrity rather than against business interests. If a defendant wanted to argue that the data subject had waived or transferred the right, probably by means of a contract, such an argument would face an uphill battle. As a human right, at least presumptively the right would be non-waivable and non-transferable. Human rights are rooted in a noncommodified understanding of personhood and the attributes and context necessary to constitute and maintain personhood. Because the rhetoric of human rights tends to assume inalienability, whoever wants to argue for alienability has a substantial burden. It is not the case, of course, that such rights are never in practice held to have been waived. Rather, because the rhetoric leans toward inalienability, such holdings at least require some argumentative footwork. Of course, too, if such footwork comes to be routinely performed, then the concept of inalienable human rights will be undermined.

The situation is reversed if data privacy is conceived of and treated as a property right of the data subject. In that case, to gain access to and use the private data, in ways other than those sanctioned by society, is a violation of a property right. We could think of this violation as a tort, if we have in mind torts against property or business interests—like theft of trade secrets—rather than against personal integrity. In this case, a defendant who wanted to argue that the subject's privacy rights had been transferred or waived would have a much easier time. In the PPFK [private-property-plus-free-contract] system, transferability (alienability) of property rights is presumed. The market system depends both upon private property and free contract; neither can function without the other to support a market. They are tightly connected rhetorically as well as in the actual world of exchange. Some thinkers believe that alienability is inherent in the concept of private property. At minimum, once something is conceived of as private property, arguing for market-inalienability is an uphill battle.

The difference in the presumptive starting points of these two rhetorical perspectives may say a lot about the difference between the EU and the U.S. when it comes to privacy. The data marketers in the U.S. argue that data they have collected (by the sweat of their corporate brows) belongs to them, not to the subjects. Thus, some consumer advocates in the U.S.

believe that legislation declaring that the property right belongs to the data subject will provide protection for privacy. According to the EU view, which treats privacy more like a noncommodified human right and less like a commodified property right, this would be inadequate to protect data subjects.

Indeed, defeating the property claims of the data marketers and vesting the property right in the data subject instead would be a Pyrrhic victory. In either case the issue of waiver and transferability—market alienability—is paramount. It appears that online commerce will be governed more and more by contracts between providers and users, and less by a priori (default) entitlement structures. * * * [W]aivers or transfers can turn out to be ubiquitous, in which case it will not much matter where the rights started out.

* * *

As the debate proceeds about how to conceive of and protect digital data, at least we should realize that we have had these arguments before, in the offline world, about such things as whether consumers can waive product liability, or whether form leases can have tenants waive implied warranty of habitability and live in a cheaper but unsafe and unhealthy dwelling. On the one side, PPFK rhetoric argues that users have the right to waive or transfer whatever rights they have, for a consideration; on the other side, human rights rhetoric argues that users cannot waive rights that are important to personal integrity and self-constitution, at least unless we are very sure that they are doing so in possession of full understanding of the consequences. Debate will be advanced if we work on what sort of an incomplete commodification is appropriate for various aspects of privacy; that is, which aspects of the individual's interests in various kinds of data privacy are more appropriately conceived of as human (personal) rights and which are more appropriately conceived of as property (economic) rights.

* * *

NOTES & QUESTIONS

Privacy as property in the courts. Some courts have held that individuals generally have no enforceable property right in their personal information. *See, e.g., U.S. News & World Report, Inc. v. Avrahami*, 1996 WL 1065557 (Va. Cir. Ct.1996), *reh'g denied*, *Avrahami v. U.S. News & World Report, Inc.*, No. 961837 (Va. 1996) (holding that an individual has no property right in his name, so commercial exchange of names on a mailing list does not violate state statute or common law).

V. CHILDREN'S PRIVACY: CHILDREN'S ONLINE PRIVACY PROTECTION ACT

A. ANTECEDENTS

Since the earliest policy discussions of online privacy, marketing to children has been recognized as presenting special privacy issues. The FTC first publicly broached the issue of children's privacy online in a 1996 public workshop, attended by a variety of industry and consumer representatives. While a wide range of views was presented, the FTC noted: "A consensus seemed to emerge among Workshop participants that: (1) children are a special audience; (2) information collection from children raises special concerns; (3) there is a need for some degree of notice to parents of Web sites' information practices; and (4) parents need to have some level of control over the collection of their children's information." FEDERAL TRADE COMMISSION, STAFF REPORT: PUBLIC WORKSHOP ON CONSUMER PRIVACY ON THE GLOBAL INFORMATION INFRASTRUCTURE (1996), pt. IV, www.ftc.gov/reports/privacy/privacy1.htm. There was no consensus, however, on whether government intervention was required to protect children's privacy online, or whether the market could be entrusted with that assignment. At one extreme, the Direct Marketing Association and Interactive Services Association proposed a set of guidelines that would put virtually no crimp in marketers' collection of personal information from children. At the other, the Center for Media Education and the Consumer Federation of America asked the FTC to adopt guidelines that would require parental consent before collecting personal information from children under 16, preceded by full and effective disclosure of the collector's information practices. *See id.* app. C.

The first self-regulatory effort to address children's online privacy came in 1997, when the Council of Better Business Bureaus' Children's Advertising Review Unit ("CARU") amended its *Self Regulatory Guidelines for Children's Advertising* by adding a section addressing online marketing.[18] This section, *Guidelines for Interactive Electronic Media (e.g. Internet and Online Services),* called upon online sellers to provide notice of the intended uses of the personally identifiable information they collect from children, and to make "reasonable efforts" to obtain parental consent to the collection of that information. The term "reasonable efforts" was defined as requiring different procedures "depending on the type and sensitivity of the information collected."

At about the same time, staff of the FTC addressed whether a particular website's collection of information from children was deceptive, in violation of the FTC Act. In May 1996 the Center for Media Education, a nonprofit organization concerned with children's media issues, petitioned the FTC to investigate a website called "KidsCom," at www.kidscom.com. The site, which was directed at children aged 4 to 15, induced children to provide personally identifiable information and product preference information with the promise that by doing so they would earn "KidsKash points" that could be redeemed for prizes at the "Loot Locker." The site did not disclose that "[i]nformation collected from some of these surveys was

18. The Council of Better Business Bureaus, an industry group that operates the well-known system of BBB's, created CARU in 1974 "to promote responsible children's advertising and to respond to public concerns." *Better Business Bureau Advertising Review Programs,* www.caru.bbb.org/caruguid.asp. For an assessment of the effectiveness of CARU's Guidelines, see Angela J. Campbell, *Self-Regulation and the Media,* 51 FED. COMM. L.J. 711, 735–44 (1999).

provided to private companies on an aggregate, anonymous basis." The FTC staff held that this practice likely was deceptive and unfair, in violation of the FTC Act:

> When KidsCom collected information at the KidsKash Questions area, it represented that the information collection would enable the children to earn premiums, but did not also disclose the marketing uses of this information. It is a deceptive practice to represent that a Web site is collecting personally identifiable information from a child for a particular purpose (e.g., to earn points to redeem a premium), when the information will also be used for another purpose which parents would find material, in the absence of a clear and prominent disclosure to that effect. * * *
>
> We [also] believe that it would likely be an unfair practice in violation of Section 5 [of the FTC Act] to collect personally identifiable information, such as name, e-mail address, home address or phone number, from children and sell or otherwise disclose such identifiable information to third parties without providing parents with adequate notice, as described above, and an opportunity to control the collection and use of the information.

FTC Staff, *Staff Opinion Letter re Kids.com* (Jul. 15, 1997), www.ftc.gov/os/1997/9707/cenmed.htm. Despite its finding of a likely violation, the FTC staff declined to bring an enforcement action, noting that the practices in question had been corrected, and that KidsCom had not released any personally identifiable information for commercial marketing purposes.

In a June 1998 report to Congress, the FTC recommended that Congress enact legislation to deal with children's online privacy issues. The report detailed the results of a survey of website privacy policies that FTC staff had conducted. Among the sites surveyed were 212 sites directed to children. Although 89% of these sites collected personal information from children, only 23% instructed children to ask their parents for permission before submitting personal information, and only 1% required prior parental consent. The report concluded: "The results reveal a very low level of compliance with the basic parental control principles contained in the [KidsCom] staff opinion letter and the CARU guidelines more than seven months after these documents were released." FEDERAL TRADE COMMISSION, PRIVACY ONLINE: A REPORT TO CONGRESS 38 (1998), www.ftc.gov/reports/privacy3/index.htm. In light of the failure of the market to provide appropriate protections to children's online privacy, and finding that its existing authority under the FTC Act was likely not broad enough to allow it to require such protections, the FTC recommended that Congress enact legislation requiring notice and parental consent before collecting personal identifying information from children online.

B. COPPA AND THE FTC'S IMPLEMENTING RULE

Congress responded by enacting the Children's Online Privacy Protection Act, 15 U.S.C. §§ 6501–05, which prescribes standards for the collection of personal information from children online and directs the Federal Trade Commission to promulgate a regulation implementing those standards. The FTC's Children's Online Privacy Protection Rule, 16 C.F.R. Part 312, imposes requirements on operators of websites that are "directed to children" under the age of 13, and on operators of websites who have "actual knowledge" that they are collecting "personal information" from children. 16 C.F.R. § 312.3. Only those websites that are "operated for commercial purposes" are covered. 16 C.F.R. § 312.2. "Personal information" is defined as "individually identifiable information about an individual collected online," including name, physical address, e-mail address, telephone number, social security number, and a persistent identifier (such as one contained in a cookie file or in hardware) that is associated with individually identifiable information. It also includes any information, such as age, personal interests, or transactional records, that is associated with a personal identifier. 16 C.F.R. § 312.2.

The Rule imposes several obligations on covered website operators. First, the operator must include on the home page of the website, and on any other page where personal information is collected from children, a link to a notice setting out the operator's information practices. The notice must disclose (1) identity and contact information for all operators that collect personal information from children through the site, (2) the types of personal information collected, (3) how the operator may use that information, (4) whether information is disclosed to third parties, (5) the fact that the operator may collect no more information from children than necessary for the stated purpose of the collection, and (6) a parent's right to access and delete a child's personal information. 16 C.F.R. § 312.4(b).

Second, the website operator is required to make reasonable efforts to obtain "verifiable parental consent" before collecting information from children. 16 C.F.R. § 312.5(a). The reasonableness of a method for obtaining consent will depend on the available technology. The Rule offers several examples of what might constitute acceptable methods of obtaining consent: a parent's signature on a consent form returned by postal mail or facsimile, a parent's use of a credit card, a telephone call from a parent to "trained personnel," a digital certificate, or an e-mail containing a password. Until April 21, 2005, consent for uses of information other than disclosure may also be obtained by less secure means, such as through an e-mail followed up with a confirmation. 16 C.F.R. § 312.5(b)(2). In seeking a parent's consent, the site operator must provide the parent with notice of the site's information practices. 16 C.F.R. § 312.4(c).

Third, the operator is required to give the parent of a child from whom personal information has been collected an opportunity to review that information, to direct the operator to delete it, and to withdraw consent to any future collection of information. 16 C.F.R. § 312.6.

Fourth, the operator may not condition a child's participation in any online activity on the child's disclosure of more personal information than is needed for purposes of her participation in the activity. 16 C.F.R. § 312.7.

Fifth, the operator must maintain reasonable procedures to protect the confidentiality, security, and integrity of personal information it has collected from children. 16 C.F.R. § 312.8.

The Rule also provides for a safe harbor in the form of compliance with approved self-regulatory guidelines. The guidelines must implement requirements that are "substantially similar" to those contained in the Rule, and that offer "the same or greater protections for children." There must also be a mechanism for assessment of compliance with the guidelines, and effective incentives for compliance. 16 C.F.R. § 312.10(b). The FTC has approved several safe-harbor programs, including ones operated by the Council of Better Business Bureaus' Children's Advertising Review Unit, and TRUSTe.

The FTC enforces the Rule through its existing enforcement mechanisms, which enable it to seek injunctions and civil penalties against website operators that do not comply with the Rule.

NOTES & QUESTIONS

1. *"Directed to children."* How hard is it for a website operator to ascertain whether its site is "directed to children"? The Rule states that in making this determination the FTC "will consider [the site's] subject matter, visual or audio content, age of models, language or other characteristics of the website or online service, as well as whether advertising promoting or appearing on the website or online service is directed to children. The Commission will also consider competent and reliable empirical evidence regarding audience composition; evidence regarding the intended audience; and whether a site uses animated characters and/or child-oriented activities and incentives." 16 C.F.R. § 312.2. How should the FTC classify a website that appeals to a range of visitors, say from 10 to 16? Should it depend on the percentage of visitors who state they are under 13?

2. *"Actual notice."* If a site is not "directed to children," the operator must obtain parental consent with respect to a particular visitor only if it has "actual knowledge" that the visitor is under the age of 13. Can the operator avoid acquiring such knowledge by adopting a "don't ask, don't tell" policy? Note that for marketing purposes site operators may want to know the age of each visitor.

3. *Screening for children.* The simplest mechanism by which a website can screen for visitors who are under 13 is to ask them their age. Would you expect there to be many in the under–13 crowd who are savvy enough and interested enough to lie about their age? Does this make age-screening by self-identification useless? Can you think of any better mechanism for ascertaining whether a visitor is under 13?

4. *"Verifiable parental consent."* Are the mechanisms for obtaining parental consent that the FTC endorses unduly burdensome on website operators? On parents? Websites that have implemented parental consent mechanism to comply with COPPA have found it to be an expensive proposition.

Some sites have calculated that it will cost them $100,000 to $500,000 to comply. One prominent child-oriented site, www.zeeks.com, spent $150,000 to comply, and, to add insult to injury, suffered a 20% decline in traffic as a result. Compliance may also require disabling certain features of a site, such as interactive capabilities that result in third-party disclosure of personal information. Other sites, such as www.eCrush.com and Yahoo!GeoCities, have found it impracticable to comply, and have opted instead to limit their services to users who (say they) are 13 or over. Parents may also not be too happy about being asked to disclose their credit card number before their child may get access to a website, viewing this as an invasion of their own privacy.

CHAPTER NINE

Controlling Digital Goods: Copyright

Businesses involved in e-commerce may confront copyright issues in several different contexts. First, almost all businesses, whether online or offline, and whether selling hard goods or information goods, will market their products using literature, catalog copy, images, and other materials that they wish to prevent others from copying. Second, some businesses, both online and offline, have information goods (software, movies, music, books, or other "content") as their stock in trade; these businesses want to prevent competitors and "pirates" from appropriating their products. Third, some businesses, native to the online environment, depend upon transmitting, aggregating, or repackaging digitized content, some of which is subject to copyrights owned by others. New copyright issues arise in all three of these contexts, due to the digitized format in which information goods and other materials are maintained on the network.

One of the great strengths of the Internet as a platform for commerce is the ease and efficiency with which information can be distributed in the global marketplace. If a company wishes to announce a new product to the world, it need only post the announcement on the company's website, or on electronic mailing lists or bulletin boards whose membership might have an interest in the product. In addition, the company can e-mail an announcement to those who have expressed an interest in learning of such a product, or discuss it in chat rooms and live online fora dedicated to a topic to which the product is relevant. The Internet may also be used to distribute customer service information quickly and inexpensively.

But the very ease and efficiency with which the Internet permits information to be copied and distributed is regarded by some as a great danger. To content producers—movie studios, book publishers, software producers, artists, composers, music publishers, and record companies—the Internet poses a threat that some perceive as of the greatest magnitude. Once an information product is reduced to a digital file, such as a movie on a DVD or a song on a CD, perfect copies of it can be distributed world-wide in unlimited numbers at virtually no cost—perfect because one of the characteristics of digital information products is that every copy perfectly duplicates the original. Accordingly, if a company loses control of its information assets on the Internet, the market value of those assets may drop to near zero—the marginal cost of copying and distributing them.

In part for this reason, traditional content companies have been slow to embrace the Internet as anything other than a marketing channel. While the Internet could also provide these companies with a low-cost, 24/7 distribution channel for delivering their digital goods and services, many content companies consider the risk to their principal assets simply too great.

In an analog world, the risk to a company's information assets was not nearly so great. It has been possible for decades, for example, to make copies of printed materials through xerography, and copies of recorded music on audio cassettes. But those technologies posed only a limited threat to content industries due to economic and technological constraints. It is usually cheaper to purchase an authorized copy of a book than to buy a pirated version reproduced through xerography, and the quality of the original is higher.[1] Copying via audiocassette usually costs less than buying an authorized version, but the quality degrades quickly with successive generations of copying further removed from the original. With the emergence of digital technologies, the economics and quality factors began to incline more favorably toward unauthorized copying and distribution. Floppy disks containing software or data, and CDs containing music, can be copied cheaply and easily, and with no loss in quality, even after multiple generations of copies. The need physically to distribute the media bearing the content, however, acts as a constraint on unauthorized distribution: special efforts must be made to conceal the factories needed to engage in large-scale piracy, and large shipments of physical media are susceptible to discovery and confiscation. Large-scale copying and distribution via the Internet largely eliminates these constraints.

Content companies have been reluctant to make their material available online for another reason as well: the law governing rights in information goods, the law of copyright, is less well settled online than offline. In many ways, the law of copyright applies online just as one would expect. Images and text posted on a web page are governed by copyright in the same way that images and text in a mail-order catalog are. Similarly, digital music files online generally receive the same protection as music recorded on an audio CD. What causes uncertainty online is not these established applications of copyright law, but rather the novel uses of digital goods in a purely digital environment.

For example, the use of any kind of digital information on a computer, and any transmission of information from one computer to another, involves temporary storage of that information. Is the unauthorized storage of such information a violation of the copyright owner's exclusive right to make copies? Is transmitting a digital file a violation of the copyright owner's exclusive distribution right? Does the appearance of an image in a web browser implicate the copyright owner's public display right? If the transmission of a file over the Internet requires its conversion from one file format to another, is that a violation of the copyright owner's exclusive

1. For certain types of printed works, however, such as sheet music, a photocopy may be significantly cheaper than an authorized version.

right to prepare derivative works? Also unresolved are issues concerning how the copyright laws apply to the many new and emerging business models that use, manipulate, repurpose, and repackage digital goods in ways unanticipated by the drafters of the copyright laws.

In the last few years, Congress has enacted significant amendments to federal copyright law aimed at addressing some of the unique issues raised by the Internet. Courts have also done their part, extending traditional copyright doctrine into the digital domain. Nonetheless, much uncertainty remains.

In light of these legal uncertainties and the greater threat of unauthorized copying online, some companies have embraced self-help technologies in an effort to reduce the business risks involved in making digitized content available on the Internet. Chief among these self-help measures has been the use of encryption-based software programs—sometimes called digital rights management systems or simply "trusted systems"—that control access to and copying of information goods. In recognition of the importance of these systems to the development of Internet commerce, two recent international treaties require signatory states to enact legislation making it unlawful to circumvent such systems. We address trusted systems and the laws supporting their use in Chapter 11.

In this chapter, we look at the evolving role of copyright law online. In Part I, we present an overview of the law of copyright that highlights some of the uncertainties that arise when applying it online. In Part II, we consider how the doctrines of direct, contributory, and vicarious copyright infringement apply to such online actors as website visitors, bulletin board operators, website owners, and Internet service providers. Part III reviews the defenses of fair use, the first-sale doctrine, and copyright misuse, and the right to make copies of musical sound recordings for noncommercial purposes. Part IV considers the complex statutory framework governing the streaming and downloading of music online. Finally, in Part V we consider the safe harbors that Title II of the Digital Millennium Copyright Act created for the benefit of online service providers.

I. A Brief Overview of the Law of Copyright

Copyright is a set of statutory rights that writers, artists, composers, musicians, and other authors acquire in connection with their original creations. These rights constitute a legal monopoly, allowing authors (or the transferees of their rights) to prevent others for a limited time from making certain uses of the protected works, and to condition the use of those works on whatever terms they see fit.

Federal copyright law derives from Article 1, Section 8, Clause 8 of the United States Constitution, which confers on the federal government the power "[t]o promote the Progress of Science and useful Arts, by securing for limited Times to Authors * * * the exclusive Right to their * * *

Writings * * *." Exercising this power, Congress enacted the first copyright law in 1790, and has amended it many times since.

The goal of copyright is to encourage the creation and distribution of original works of authorship, by enabling authors to exploit the economic value of their creations. Works of authorship have the special property that, once disclosed to the public, they may be reproduced by others in such a way that little of their value translates into income to the author. For example, if it were cost-free to make a perfect copy of a book, and if the law did not proscribe such copying, then it is likely the publisher would be able to sell only one copy of each book at cover price, making it economically infeasible to publish. If authors are unable to convert the fruits of their labor into income, they will cease to create, or at least create less. Because society as a whole benefits from the creation of literary, artistic, musical, and other works of authorship, the law grants authors the right to prevent others from making use of their works without paying for that privilege.

The Copyright Act of 1976 accomplishes this by granting authors a set of "exclusive rights" with respect to the works they create. These are the rights (1) to reproduce the work, (2) to prepare derivative works based on the work, (3) to distribute copies of the work to the public, (4) to perform the work publicly, (5) to display the work publicly, and (6) in the case of sound recordings, to perform the copyrighted work publicly by means of a digital audio transmission. 17 U.S.C. § 106. A person who exercises any of these rights without the permission of the copyright holder is said to "infringe" the copyright, and is liable for damages and subject to injunctive relief. The *reproduction right* may be infringed by, for example, making an unauthorized copy of a text, a musical composition, a recording of a musical performance, or a software program. The copyright holder's *right to prepare derivative works* is infringed by one who creates a new work based on the original, such as by producing a motion picture that is based on a book. The *distribution right* reserves to the copyright holder the exclusive right to transfer copies of the work to the public, by sale, rental, lease, or lending. The *public performance right* may be infringed by showing a movie, playing a sound recording, or performing a dance at a location that is open to the public, or where members of the public are gathered. Similarly, the *public display right* is infringed by showing a picture or other protected work publicly.

The works of authorship that copyright protects span the range of human imagination, including literary works, computer programs, musical compositions, dramatic works, pantomimes and choreographic works, drawings, paintings, photographs, motion pictures and other audiovisual works (including computer games), sound recordings, and architectural works. 17 U.S.C. § 102(a). Works are entitled to protection only if they are original: the author must have created the work independently rather than copying it from another, and the work must involve some minimal quantum of creativity. Only the author's *expression* is protectible; the ideas, concepts, principles, and facts communicated by that expression are not within the protection of copyright. 17 U.S.C. § 102(b).

Copyright protection exists from the moment a work of authorship is fixed in some tangible medium of expression, such as by writing a text or musical composition on paper, recording a performance on audiotape or videotape, or making a drawing or painting. The observance of formalities, such as placing a © symbol on each copy of the work or timely registering it with the Copyright Office, is not a prerequisite to copyright protection, but may yield significant advantages to the copyright holder in an infringement action. Under current law, protection generally lasts until 70 years after the death of the author. In the case of "works made for hire," which are works produced by an employee within the scope of his employment as well as certain works produced by independent contractors, copyright lasts for 95 years from publication, but no more than 120 years from creation.

Copyright seeks to maintain an appropriate balance between the interests of authors in benefiting from the economic value of their works, and the interests of the public, and of subsequent authors, in having access to the works that copyright is designed to encourage. To this end, the Copyright Act imposes certain limitations on copyright holders' exercise of their exclusive rights. The most important of these limitations is known as "fair use," which allows free use of copyrighted works in circumstances where the user derives significant benefit and the copyright owner suffers only minor harm. 17 U.S.C. § 107. The copyright laws also contain a variety of narrow exemptions for libraries, nonprofit and educational users, limited uses on business premises, non-commercial copying of musical recordings, and other circumstances. *See, e.g.*, 17 U.S.C. §§ 108, 110, & 1008. In addition, the Copyright Act grants compulsory licenses for certain uses, giving anyone the right to make use of a copyrighted work upon payment of a royalty rate determined by law. *See, e.g.*, 17 U.S.C. §§ 114 & 115.

Because the socially optimal balance between authorial rights and public access changes over time as new forms of expression emerge and new uses for copyrighted works develop, the law of copyright has been regularly amended to accommodate new and emerging technologies and forms of commerce. Historically, for example, the development and commercialization of photography, telegraphy, radio, motion pictures, broadcast and cable television, xerography, audio and video recording equipment, and the computer have all led to amendments of federal copyright law.

NOTES & QUESTIONS

1. *Fixation on the Web.* Today, many web pages are created "on the fly" using technologies such as Active Server Pages ("ASP"). These technologies are used when the information that must be displayed on a web page changes frequently, such as an e-commerce site's available inventory, sports scores, stock quotations, or the identity of the viewer. Typically, once the page is requested, an ASP application will assemble that web page by first acquiring the needed information from a database or cookie and then inserting it into appropriate HTML code. The web server will then send the newly created page to the web browser that requested it. The web page created by the ASP application may only exist momentarily in the random access memory of the server before it is sent to the requesting browser. In such a case, is the web page copyrightable subject matter? Does it meet the fixation requirement? Upon what additional facts might your answer depend?

2. *RAM copies*. Utilization of a computer inevitably involves loading software code into the machine's random access memory ("RAM"). A very significant issue in copyright law is whether this temporary storage of (generally copyrighted) code constitutes "fixation" of the code in RAM. A work (such as computer code) is "fixed" for this purpose if its embodiment in a material object (such as RAM) "is sufficiently permanent or stable to permit it to be perceived, reproduced, or otherwise communicated for a period of more than transitory duration." 17 U.S.C. § 101. If code temporarily stored in RAM is considered to be "fixed," the RAM would constitute a "copy" of the work, and making the RAM copy without authorization of the copyright owner would constitute prima facie infringement. This would mean that a wide variety of ordinary uses of computers, including particularly engaging in online communications, could involve infringement of copyrights.

This issue was addressed in *MAI Systems Corp. v. Peak Computer*, 991 F.2d 511 (9th Cir.1993), in which the copyright owner of operating system software sued a computer repair company for infringement, based on the repair company's turning on a computer running the operating system for the purpose of servicing the machine. The Ninth Circuit upheld the district court's conclusion that "the loading of copyrighted computer software * * * into the memory of a central processing unit ('CPU') causes a copy to be made," which in the absence of permission from the copyright owner constitutes infringement. *Id*. at 518.

Congress responded to the decision in *MAI v. Peak* by enacting Title III of the Digital Millennium Copyright Act, known as the Computer Maintenance Competition Assurance Act, which amends 17 U.S.C. § 117 to provide that "an independent service provider may turn on a client's computer machine in order to service its hardware components" without infringing the copyright of software that is loaded during this process. H.R. CONF. REP. NO. 105-796, at 86 (1998). This amendment, however, did not settle the more general issue of whether the temporary storage of computer code in RAM is the making of a "copy" for purposes of the Copyright Act.

The view that under current law temporary storage of a work in RAM is a "copy" for purposes of the Copyright Act has been criticized by many scholars. *See, e.g.*, Jessica Litman, *The Exclusive Right to Read*, 13 CARDOZO ARTS & ENT. L.J. 29, 41–43 (1994); Mark A. Lemley, *Dealing with Overlapping Copyrights on the Internet*, 22 U. DAYTON L. REV. 547, 550–52 (1997). Other scholars, however, argue that temporary storage in RAM does amount to the making of a "copy." *See, e.g.*, Jane C. Ginsburg, *Putting Cars on the "Information Superhighway": Authors, Exploiters, and Copyright in Cyberspace*, 95 COLUM. L. REV. 1466, 1476 (1995). The Register of

Copyrights has expressed the same view. *See* U.S. COPYRIGHT OFFICE, DMCA SECTION 104 REPORT (2001), www.copyright.gov/reports/studies/dmca/dmca_study.html.

Professor Joseph Liu explains the significance of this issue for the balance of power between copyright owners and users in the online environment:

> Driving the sharp criticism of the result in *MAI* is a broader concern that the result drastically and unthinkingly shifts the existing balance of rights in copyrighted works from users to copyright owners in the digital environment. Because computer software is copied into RAM as a necessary incident to the use of that software, the decision in *MAI* effectively gives copyright owners the right to control any and all uses of the software, unless such uses are subject to some statutory privilege. In addition, nothing in the reasoning of the opinion prevents it from being extended from computer software to any and all works stored in digital form, such as images, text documents, sound recordings, and motion pictures. Indeed, several federal courts have extended the rule in MAI to just such digital works. * * * Taken to its logical conclusion, MAI would give copyright owners broad control, at least in theory, over nearly all computer-aided uses of copyrighted works encoded in digital form.

Joseph P. Liu, *Owning Digital Copies: Copyright Law and the Incidents of Copy Ownership*, 42 WM. & MARY L. REV. 1245, 1262-1263 (2001).

3. *Framing and derivative works.* A frame is a region within the window of a web browser that can display a single web page. By employing multiple frames within a single browser window, one can display multiple web pages simultaneously. Moreover, one can design these web pages so that they appear to be a single page. Multiple frames are sometimes used to create a persistent user interface for a website. For example, it is common to see a website with navigational elements such as buttons and dropdown menus on the left side of the browser window, a narrow unchanging header for the website running across the top, and the changing content of the site displayed in the remaining part of the browser window. The navigational bar, the header, and the content displayed in the remainder of the browser window are actually separate web pages, each one displayed in a separate frame.

From the perspective of copyright law, it is unclear how one should characterize the display of multiple web pages in a single browser window. Under 17 U.S.C. § 101, a "derivative work" is "a work based upon one or more preexisting works." If one incorporates web pages created by another, is the result a derivative work? If so, then unauthorized framing of web pages created by another may infringe the copyright owner's exclusive right "to prepare derivative works based upon the copyrighted work." 17 U.S.C. § 106(2). This was the legal theory of the plaintiff in *Futuredontics, Inc. v. Applied Anagramics, Inc.*, 45 U.S.P.Q.2d (BNA) 2005 (C.D.Cal.1998), *aff'd*, 152 F.3d 925 (9th Cir.1998). The defendant, Applied Anagramics, Inc.

("AAI"), had framed a web page from the plaintiff's website. The defendant caused plaintiff's web page to appear in the window of a web browser with web pages that contained the defendant's logo, information about the defendant's business, and hypertext links to other web pages created by the defendant. In denying defendant's motion to dismiss, the court said:

> The parties sharply dispute what function AAI's framed link serves. Defendant contends that AAI's window or frame provides a "lens" which enables Internet users to view the information that Plaintiff itself placed on the Internet. Plaintiff's complaint, however, alleges that defendant reproduces its copyrighted web page by combining AAI material and Plaintiff's web site. * * *
>
> * * *
>
> The parties discuss the applicability of *Mirage Editions, Inc. v. Albuquerque A.R.T. Co.*, 856 F.2d 1341, 1343 (9th Cir.1988). In *Mirage*, the Ninth Circuit held that transferring and affixing art images with glue to ceramic tiles constituted "the creation of a derivative work in violation of the copyright laws." Id. at 1343–44. As this Court noted in its Order denying Plaintiff's request for a preliminary injunction, *Mirage* is distinguishable from the present case. In this case, AAI has not affixed an image to a ceramic tile, rather AAI appears to have placed an electronic frame or border around Plaintiff's web page.
>
> Defendants primarily rely on *Lewis Galoob Toys, Inc. v. Nintendo of America, Inc.*, 964 F.2d 965, 968 (9th Cir.1992). In that case, the Ninth Circuit held that a Game Genie which merely enhances audiovisual displays which originate in Nintendo game cartridges does not constitute a derivative work because, in part, it does "not incorporate a portion of a copyrighted work in some concrete or permanent form." * * * *Galoob* does not foreclose Plaintiff from establishing that AAI's web page incorporates Futuredontic's web page in some "concrete or permanent form" or that AAI's framed link duplicates or recasts Plaintiff's web page. Id.
>
> For these reasons, the Court finds that the cases cited by the parties do not conclusively determine whether Defendants' frame page constitutes a derivative work.

Futuredontics, Inc. v. Applied Anagramics, Inc., 45 U.S.P.Q.2d at 2010. How would you decide this case? As the plaintiff, how might you argue that AAI's web page incorporates Futuredontic's web page in some "concrete or permanent form"? As the defendant, how might you argue that AAI's framed link does not duplicate or recast plaintiff's web page?

4. *Filtering and derivative works*. Before allowing a web page to be displayed in a browser, filtering software may be used to screen the page and determine whether it contains a particular type of content. Web filtering technologies may employ a variety of approaches to ascertain the content of a web page. Such filtering software might screen a web page for particular keywords, attempt to interpret the images contained on the page, or identify the HTML tags used to format the page. Once targeted content is identified, the filtering software can either prevent the browser from displaying the web page, block the entire site, or excise the targeted content and permit the remainder of the page to be displayed. If the offending content is excised, how would you characterize the resulting web page for the purpose of copyright? Who, if anyone, owns the copyright in the cleansed web page? Does creation of the cleansed web page infringe any of the exclusive rights held by the copyright owner of the original web page?

5. *Criminal copyright infringement and the Internet.* An example of how the Internet brought about amendment of the copyright laws involves criminal copyright infringement under 17 U.S.C. § 506(a). In *United States v. LaMacchia*, 871 F.Supp. 535 (D.Mass.1994), David LaMacchia, a twenty-one-year-old student at the Massachusetts Institute of Technology,

> used MIT's computer network to gain entree to the Internet. Using pseudonyms and an encrypted address, LaMacchia set up an electronic bulletin board which he named Cynosure. He encouraged his correspondents to upload popular software applications (Excel 5.0 and WordPerfect 6.0) and computer games (Sim City 2000). These he transferred to a second encrypted address (Cynosure II) where they could be downloaded by other users with access to the Cynosure password. Although LaMacchia was at pains to impress the need for circumspection on the part of his subscribers, the worldwide traffic generated by the offer of free software attracted the notice of university and federal authorities.
>
> On April 7, 1994, a federal grand jury returned a one count indictment charging LaMacchia with conspiring with "persons unknown" to violate 18 U.S.C. § 1343, the wire fraud statute. According to the indictment, LaMacchia devised a scheme to defraud that had as its object the facilitation "on an international scale" of the "illegal copying and distribution of copyrighted software" without payment of licensing fees and royalties to software manufacturers and vendors. The indictment alleges that LaMacchia's scheme caused losses of more than one million dollars to software copyright holders. The indictment does not allege that LaMacchia sought or derived any personal benefit from the scheme to defraud.

Id. at 536–37. The government argued that LaMacchia's conduct fell within the purview of the wire fraud statute because he had used the Internet to copy and distribute software in violation of 17 U.S.C. § 506(a). Section 506(a) "requir[ed] prosecutors to prove that the defendant infringed a copyright 'willfully and for purpose of commercial advantage or private financial gain.'" *Id.* at 540. Since LaMacchia acted neither for commercial advantage nor financial gain, the elements of the crime were not present, and the court granted LaMacchia's motion to dismiss.

Congress reacted to the *LaMacchia* decision by enacting the No Electronic Theft ("NET") Act, Pub. L. No. 105–147, 111 Stat. 2678 (1997). The NET Act amended the definition of "financial gain" under 17 U.S.C. § 101 to include "receipt, or expectation of receipt, of anything of value, including the receipt of other copyrighted works." It also amended the elements for criminal copyright infringement under § 506(a). As amended, § 506(a) now reads as follows:

> **(a) Criminal Infringement.**—Any person who infringes a copyright willfully either—
>
> (1) for purposes of commercial advantage or private financial gain, or
>
> (2) by the reproduction or distribution, including by electronic means, during any 180–day period, of 1 or more copies or phonorecords of 1 or more copyrighted works, which have a total retail value of more than $1,000,
>
> shall be punished as provided under section 2319 of title 18, United States Code. For purposes of this subsection, evidence of reproduction or distribution of a copyrighted work, by itself, shall not be sufficient to establish willful infringement.

17 U.S.C. § 506(a).

6. *The display right on the Web.* When a person views a page of a website using her browser, it seems clear that a "display" has occurred. From the standpoint of copyright law, who should be deemed responsible for the display: the viewer, for pointing her browser at a particular web address? the website operator, for making material available for display? both? *See Playboy Enterprises, Inc. v. Frena*, 839 F.Supp. 1552 (M.D.Fla.1993), excerpted in Part II(A), *infra*; *Kelly v. Arriba Soft Corp.*, 280 F.3d 934 (9th Cir. 2002), excerpted in Part II(A), *infra*; and *Intellectual Reserve, Inc. v. Utah Lighthouse Ministry, Inc.*, 75 F.Supp.2d 1290 (D.Utah 1999), excerpted in Part II(B), *infra*. *See also* R. Anthony Reese, *The Public Display Right: the Copyright Act's Neglected Solution to the Controversy over RAM "Copies,"* 2001 U. ILL. L. REV. 83.

NOTE: DIGITALLY REPURPOSED WORKS

Digital works have the significant advantage that they can be easily manipulated and reused for a variety of purposes at very low cost. For example, a traditional print publication can easily reformat the content of its print edition for display on the Web. The variety of online versions of traditional print publications is indeed a testimony to the ease and low expense with which such repurposing can be accomplished. Moreover, as broadband connections to the Internet become more pervasive, we can expect to see traditional over-the-air broadcasters also repurposing their audio and video content online. The pervasive reuse and repurposing of content on the Web raises the question whether licensees of the right to use articles and other kinds of content in traditional print publications and over-the-air broadcasts also enjoy the right to use the same content on the Web if the licensing agreement between the publisher and the author is silent on this issue. *See Random House, Inc. v. Rosetta Books LLC*, 150 F.Supp.2d 613 (S.D.N.Y.2001), *denial of prelim. inj. aff'd*, 283 F.3d 490 (2d Cir.2002).

In *New York Times Co. v. Tasini*, 533 U.S. 483 (2001), the Supreme Court addressed a closely related question, namely whether a newspaper could reuse articles from its print edition in an electronic database. The litigation was commenced by six freelance authors, and concerned articles that they had contributed to three print periodicals (two newspapers and one magazine). "Under agreements with the periodicals' publishers, but without the freelancers' consent, two computer database companies placed copies of the freelancers' articles—along with all other articles from the periodicals in which the freelancers' work appeared—into three databases." *Id.* at 487. (For a discussion of the law applicable to databases and compilations online, see Chapter 10, *infra.*)

The two database companies were LEXIS/NEXIS and University Microfilms International ("UMI"). LEXIS/NEXIS placed the articles in its online text-based database known as NEXIS. "Each article appear[ed] as a separate, isolated 'story'—without any visible link to the other stories originally published in the same newspaper or magazine edition." The NEXIS version did "not contain pictures or advertisements," nor did it "reproduce the original print publication's formatting features such as headline size, page placement (*e.g.*, above or below the fold for newspapers), or location of continuation pages." UMI placed the articles in its own text-only database, called the New York Times OnDisc ("NYTO"). UMI also placed the articles in an image-based database called General Periodicals OnDisc ("GPO"). This database shows "each article exactly as it appeared on printed pages, complete with photographs, captions, advertisements, and other surrounding materials." *Id.* at 490–91.

The plaintiffs alleged that inclusion of their articles in the databases infringed their copyrights. The publishers defended by invoking Section 201(c) of the Copyright Act, which provides:

> Copyright in each separate contribution to a collective work is distinct from copyright in the collective work as a whole, and vests initially in the author of the contribution. In the absence of an express transfer of the copyright or of any rights under it, the owner of copyright in the collective work is presumed to have acquired only the privilege of reproducing and distributing the contribution as part of that particular collective work, any revision of that collective work, and any later collective work in the same series.

17 U.S.C. § 201(c). "Specifically, the publishers maintained that, as copyright owners of collective works, *i.e.*, the original print publications, they had merely exercised 'the privilege' § 201(c) accords them to 'reproduc[e] and distribut[e]' the author's discretely copyrighted contribution." 533 U.S. at 508–09.

Applying this provision, the Court noted that

> the three Databases present articles to users clear of the context provided either by the original periodical editions or by any revision of those editions. The Databases first prompt users to search the universe of their contents: thousands or millions of files containing individual articles from thousands of collective works (*i.e.,* editions), either in one series (the Times, in NYTO) or in scores of series (the sundry titles in NEXIS and GPO). When the user conducts a search, each article appears as a separate item within the search result. In NEXIS and NYTO, an article appears to a user without the graphics, formatting, or other articles with which the article was initially published. In GPO, the article appears with the other materials published on the same page or pages, but without any material published on other pages of the original periodical. In either circumstance, we cannot see how the Database perceptibly reproduces and distributes the article "as part of" either the original edition or a "revision" of that edition.

Id. at 499–500. The Court further elaborated its position by likening the databases to an imaginary library:

> For the purpose at hand—determining whether the Authors' copyrights have been infringed—an analogy to an imaginary library may be instructive. Rather than maintaining intact editions of periodicals, the library would contain separate copies of each article. Perhaps these copies would exactly reproduce the periodical pages from which the articles derive (if the model is GPO); perhaps the copies would contain only typescript characters, but still indicate the original periodical's name and date, as well as the article's headline and page number (if the model is NEXIS or NYTO). The library would store the folders containing the articles in a file room, indexed based on diverse criteria, and containing articles from vast numbers of editions. In response to patron requests, an inhumanly speedy librarian would search the room and provide copies of the articles matching patron-specified criteria.
>
> Viewing this strange library, one could not, consistent with ordinary English usage, characterize the articles "as part of" a "revision" of the editions in which the articles first appeared. In substance, however, the Databases differ from the file room only to the extent they aggregate articles in electronic packages (the LEXIS/NEXIS central discs or UMI CD–ROMs), while the file room stores articles in spatially separate files. The crucial fact is that the Databases, like the hypothetical library, store and retrieve articles separately within a vast domain of diverse texts. Such a storage and retrieval system effectively overrides the Authors' exclusive right to control the individual reproduction and distribution of each Article, 17 U.S.C. §§ 106(1), (3).

> The Publishers claim the protection of § 201(c) because users can manipulate the Databases to generate search results consisting entirely of articles from a particular periodical edition. By this logic, § 201(c) would cover the hypothetical library if, in response to a request, that library's expert staff assembled all of the articles from a particular periodical edition. However, the fact that a third party can manipulate a database to produce a noninfringing document does not mean the database is not infringing. Under § 201(c), the question is not whether a user can generate a revision of a collective work from a database, but whether the database itself perceptibly presents the author's contribution as part of a revision of the collective work. That result is not accomplished by these Databases.

Id. at 502–04. This analogy, however, was not persuasive to all members of the Court. In his dissenting opinion, Justice Stevens, joined by Justice Breyer, adopted a different analogy:

> A proper analysis of this case benefits from an incremental approach. Accordingly, I begin by discussing an issue the majority largely ignores: whether a collection of articles from a single edition of the New York Times (*i.e.*, the batch of files the Print Publishers periodically send to the Electronic Databases) constitutes a "revision" of an individual edition of the paper. In other words, does a single article within such a collection exist as "part of" a "revision"? Like the majority, I believe that the crucial inquiry is whether the article appears within the "context" of the original collective work. But this question simply raises the further issue of precisely how much "context" is enough.
>
> The record indicates that what is sent from the New York Times to the Electronic Databases (with the exception of General Periodicals on Disc (GPO)) is simply a collection of ASCII text files representing the editorial content of the New York Times for a particular day.[7] * * *
>
> I see no compelling reason why a collection of files corresponding to a single edition of the New York Times, standing alone, cannot constitute a "revision" of that day's New York Times. * * * Once one accepts the premise that a disk containing all the files from the October 31, 2000, New York Times can constitute a "revision," there is no reason to treat any differently the same set of files, stored in a folder on the hard disk of a computer at the New York Times. * * * If my hypothetical October 31, 2000, floppy disk can be a revision, I do not see why the inclusion of other editions and other periodicals is any more significant than

7. ASCII (American Standard Code for Information Interchange) is a standard means for storing textual data. It assigns a unique binary code for each letter of the alphabet, as well as for numbers, punctuation, and other characters. It cannot be used to convey graphical information. * * *

> the placement of a single edition of the New York Times in a large public library or in a book store.

Id. at 511–12, 517. Justice Stevens then reminded the majority that " 'the primary purpose of copyright is not to reward the author, but is rather to secure "the general benefits derived by the public from the labors of authors." ' " *Id.* at 519 (quoting MELVILLE B. NIMMER & DAVID NIMMER, NIMMER ON COPYRIGHT § 1.03[A]) (quoting *Fox Film Corp. v. Doyal*, 286 U.S. 123, 127 (1932)). He thought that the authors' victory "unnecessarily subverts this fundamental goal of copyright law in favor of a narrow focus on 'authorial rights.' " He said that while "the desire to protect such rights is certainly a laudable sentiment, copyright law demands that 'private motivation must ultimately serve the cause of promoting *broad public availability* of literature, music, and the other arts.' *Twentieth Century Music Corp. v. Aiken*, 422 U.S. 151, 156 (1975)." *Id.* at 520.

The *Tasini* majority and dissenting opinions suggest several questions.

1. *Authorial rights vs. public access.* To advance their arguments, both the majority and the dissent present thought experiments. The majority appeals to a hypothetical library containing a collection of individual articles, while the dissent appeals to a floppy disk containing the digitized articles from a single edition of a periodical. Which is more analogous to the case before the Court? Do you agree with the dissent that the floppy disk is a revision? If so, should storage of more than one revision on a single floppy disk or other medium cause these files to lose their status as revisions? How would you respond to the dissent's rhetorical query whether paper editions of a newspaper lose their status as editions when piled together in a library?

2. Tasini *on the Web.* How does the holding in *Tasini* apply to the *New York Times* website, which reproduces material from the *Times*'s print publications? Would your answer change if the *Times* formatted each article on its website as a separate HTML page?

II. COPYRIGHT INFRINGEMENT ONLINE

Many acts of online copyright infringement are initiated by individual Internet users—a person posting a copyrighted text on an electronic bulletin board system ("BBS"), for example. Copyright owners would find it impractical to identify and sue such individual infringers in large numbers. In many cases the defendant would be judgment-proof; investigative and legal fees would be considerable; and success on the merits would be unlikely to deter others from engaging in the same kind of behavior, given the unlikelihood that any particular individual would be targeted in a subsequent enforcement action. Therefore, rather than pursue individual infringers, copyright owners have usually preferred to sue BBS operators and other online service providers who act as conduits for such infringing activities. These entities generally have deeper pockets than the individual infringers, and forcing them either to shut down or to police the infringing activities of their users can bring about a significant reduction of infringement online.

A person who without authorization exercises one of a copyright holder's exclusive rights, or authorizes another to do so, is liable as a direct infringer. A person may also be held liable for the infringing actions of others, under the doctrines of contributory and vicarious liability. In this Part, we consider how courts have applied these doctrines to Internet users, BBS operators, search engines, and Internet service providers.

A. DIRECT INFRINGEMENT

A claim for direct copyright infringement arises when a person infringes one of the exclusive rights that 17 U.S.C. § 106 grants to the copyright owner. A person directly infringes a copyright by reproducing, adapting, distributing, publicly performing, or publicly displaying the copyrighted work of another, without authorization. To succeed in an action for direct copyright infringement, the plaintiff must prove (1) that she owns a valid copyright in the work, and (2) that the defendant copied or authorized the copying of protected elements of the work. The courts frequently refer to each of these infringing actions as "copying," even though distribution, performance, and display need not involve copying.

Playboy Enterprises, Inc. v. Frena

839 F.Supp. 1552 (M.D.Fla.1993).

■ SCHLESINGER, DISTRICT JUDGE.

* * * Plaintiff requests that the Court grant partial summary judgment that Defendant Frena infringed Plaintiff's copyrights and specifically that the 170 image files in question * * * infringed Plaintiff's copyrights in 50 of Plaintiff's copyrighted magazines. * * *

Defendant George Frena operates a subscription computer bulletin board service, Techs Warehouse BBS ("BBS"), that distributed unauthorized copies of Plaintiff Playboy Enterprises, Inc.'s ("PEI") copyrighted photographs. BBS is accessible via telephone modem to customers. For a fee, or to those who purchase certain products from Defendant Frena, anyone with an appropriately equipped computer can log onto BBS. Once logged on subscribers may browse through different BBS directories to look at the pictures and customers may also download the high quality computerized copies of the photographs and then store the copied image from Frena's computer onto their home computer. Many of the images found on BBS include adult subject matter. One hundred and seventy of the images that were available on BBS were copies of photographs taken from PEI's copyrighted materials.

Defendant Frena admits that these materials were displayed on his BBS, that he never obtained authorization or consent from PEI, and that each of the accused computer graphic files on BBS is substantially similar to copyrighted PEI photographs. Defendant Frena also admits that each of the files in question has been downloaded by one of his customers.

Subscribers can upload material onto the bulletin board so that any other subscriber, by accessing their computer, can see that material. Defendant Frena states in his Affidavit filed August 4, 1993, that he never uploaded any of PEI's photographs onto BBS and that subscribers to BBS uploaded the photographs. Defendant Frena states that as soon as he was served with a summons and made aware of this matter, he removed the photographs from BBS and has since that time monitored BBS to prevent additional photographs of PEI from being uploaded.

* * *

I. COPYRIGHT INFRINGEMENT

The Copyright Act of 1976 gives copyright owners control over most, if not all, activities of conceivable commercial value. The statute provides that

> the owner of a copyright ... has the exclusive rights to do and to authorize any of the following: (1) to reproduce the copyrighted work in copies ...; (2) to prepare derivative works based upon the copyrighted work; (3) to distribute copies ... of the copyrighted work to the public ... and (5) in the case of ... pictorial ... works ... to display the copyrighted work publicly.

17 U.S.C. § 106. Engaging in or authorizing any of these categories without the copyright owner's permission violates the exclusive rights of the copyright owner and constitutes infringement of the copyright. *See* 17 U.S.C. § 501(a).

To establish copyright infringement, PEI must show ownership of the copyright and "copying" by Defendant Frena, see *Feist Publications, Inc. v. Rural Tel. Serv. Co.,* 499 U.S. 340 (1991); *Southern Bell Tel. & Tel. v. Assoc. Telephone Directory Publishers,* 756 F.2d 801, 810 (11th Cir.1985).

There is no dispute that PEI owns the copyrights on the photographs in question. PEI owns copyright registrations for each of the 50 issues of Playboy publications that contain the photographs on BBS. The copyright registration certificate constitutes prima facie evidence in favor of Plaintiff. Once the plaintiff has established his prima facie ownership, the burden then shifts to the defendant to counter this evidence. Defendant Frena, however, failed to rebut the appropriate inference of validity.

Next, PEI must demonstrate copying by Defendant Frena. Since direct evidence of copying is rarely available in a copyright infringement action, copying may be inferentially proven by showing that Defendant Frena had access to the allegedly infringed work, that the allegedly infringing work is substantially similar to the copyrighted work, and that one of the rights statutorily guaranteed to copyright owners is implicated by Frena's actions. *See Ford Motor Co. v. Summit Motor Products, Inc.,* 930 F.2d 277, 291 (3d Cir.1991), *cert. denied,* 502 U.S. 939.

Access to the copyrighted work is not at issue. Access is essentially undeniable because every month PEI sells over 3.4 million copies of Playboy magazine throughout the United States.

Substantial similarity is also a non-issue in this case. Defendant Frena has admitted that every one of the accused images is substantially similar to the PEI copyrighted photograph from which the accused image was produced. Moreover, not only are the accused works substantially similar to the copyrighted work, but the infringing photographs are essentially exact copies. In many cases, the only difference is that PEI's written text appearing on the same page of the photograph has been removed from the infringing copy.

The next step is to determine whether Defendant Frena violated one of the rights statutorily guaranteed to copyright owners under 17 U.S.C. § 106. *See* 17 U.S.C. § 501(a).

Public distribution of a copyrighted work is a right reserved to the copyright owner, and usurpation of that right constitutes infringement. *See Cable/Home Communication Corp. v. Network Productions, Inc.*, 902 F.2d 829, 843 (11th Cir.1990). PEI's right under 17 U.S.C. § 106(3) to distribute copies to the public has been implicated by Defendant Frena. Section 106(3) grants the copyright owner "the exclusive right to sell, give away, rent or lend any material embodiment of his work." 2 MELVILLE B. NIMMER, Nimmer on Copyright § 8.11[A], at 8–124.1 (1993). There is no dispute that Defendant Frena supplied a product containing unauthorized copies of a copyrighted work. It does not matter that Defendant Frena claims he did not make the copies itself.

Furthermore, the "display" rights of PEI have been infringed upon by Defendant Frena. *See* 17 U.S.C. § 106(5). The concept of display is broad. *See* 17 U.S.C. § 101. It covers "the projection of an image on a screen or other surface by any method, the transmission of an image by electronic or other means, and the showing of an image on a cathode ray tube, or similar viewing apparatus connected with any sort of information storage and retrieval system." H.R.Rep. No. 1476, 94th Cong., 2d Sess. 64 (Sept. 3, 1976), reprinted in 1976 U.S.Code Cong. & Admin.News 5659, 5677. The display right precludes unauthorized transmission of the display from one place to another, for example, by a computer system. *See* H.R.Rep. No. 1476, 94th Cong., 2d Sess. 80 (Sept. 3, 1976), reprinted in 1976 U.S.Code Cong. & Admin.News 5659, 5694.

"Display" covers any showing of a "copy" of the work, "either directly or by means of a film, slide, television image or any other device or process." 17 U.S.C. § 101. However, in order for there to be copyright infringement, the display must be public. A "public display" is a display "at a place open to the public or ... where a substantial number of persons outside of a normal circle of family and its social acquaintenances is gathered." 2 MELVILLE B. NIMMER, Nimmer on Copyright § 8.14[C], at 8–169 (1993). A place is "open to the public" in this sense even if access is limited to paying customers.

Defendant's display of PEI's copyrighted photographs to subscribers was a public display. Though limited to subscribers, the audience consisted of "a substantial number of persons outside of a normal circle of family and its social acquaintenances." 2 MELVILLE B. NIMMER, Nimmer on Copyright § 8.14[C], at 8–169 (1993). *See also Thomas v. Pansy Ellen Products,* 672 F.Supp. 237, 240 (W.D.North Carolina 1987) (display at a trade show was public even though limited to members); *Ackee Music, Inc. v. Williams,* 650 F.Supp. 653 (D.Kan.1986) (performance of copyrighted songs at defendant's private club constituted a public performance). * * *

There is irrefutable evidence of direct copyright infringement in this case. It does not matter that Defendant Frena may have been unaware of the copyright infringement. Intent to infringe is not needed to find copyright infringement. Intent or knowledge is not an element of infringement, and thus even an innocent infringer is liable for infringement; rather, innocence is significant to a trial court when it fixes statutory damages, which is a remedy equitable in nature. * * *

Accordingly, * * * Plaintiff's First Motion for Partial Summary Judgment (Copyright Infringement) as to Defendant Frena (Doc. No. S–1) is GRANTED.

Religious Technology Center v. Netcom On–Line Communication Services, Inc.

907 F.Supp. 1361 (N.D.Cal.1995).

■ WHYTE, DISTRICT JUDGE.

This case concerns an issue of first impression regarding intellectual property rights in cyberspace. Specifically, this order addresses whether the operator of a computer bulletin board service ("BBS"), and the large Internet access provider that allows that BBS to reach the Internet, should be liable for copyright infringement committed by a subscriber of the BBS.

Plaintiffs Religious Technology Center ("RTC") and Bridge Publications, Inc. ("BPI") hold copyrights in the unpublished and published works of L. Ron Hubbard, the late founder of the Church of Scientology ("the Church"). Defendant Dennis Erlich ("Erlich") is a former minister of Scientology turned vocal critic of the Church, whose pulpit is now the Usenet newsgroup alt.religion.scientology ("a.r.s."), an on-line forum for discussion and criticism of Scientology. Plaintiffs maintain that Erlich infringed their copyrights when he posted portions of their works on a.r.s. Erlich gained his access to the Internet through defendant Thomas Klemesrud's ("Klemesrud's") BBS "support.com." Klemesrud is the operator of the BBS, which is run out of his home and has approximately 500 paying users. Klemesrud's BBS is not directly linked to the Internet, but gains its connection through the facilities of defendant Netcom On–Line Communications, Inc. ("Netcom"), one of the largest providers of Internet access in the United States.

After failing to convince Erlich to stop his postings, plaintiffs contacted defendants Klemesrud and Netcom. Klemesrud responded to plaintiffs' demands that Erlich be kept off his system by asking plaintiffs to prove that they owned the copyrights to the works posted by Erlich. However, plaintiffs refused Klemesrud's request as unreasonable. Netcom similarly refused plaintiffs' request that Erlich not be allowed to gain access to the Internet through its system. Netcom contended that it would be impossible to prescreen Erlich's postings and that to kick Erlich off the Internet meant kicking off the hundreds of users of Klemesrud's BBS. Consequently, plaintiffs named Klemesrud and Netcom in their suit against Erlich, although only on the copyright infringement claims.

* * * For the reasons set forth below, the court grants in part and denies in part Netcom's motion for summary judgment * * *

I. NETCOM'S MOTION FOR SUMMARY JUDGMENT OF NONINFRINGEMENT

* * *

B. Copyright Infringement

* * * The court has already determined that plaintiffs have established that they own the copyrights to all of the * * * works, except item 4 of Exhibit A. The court also found plaintiffs likely to succeed on their claim that defendant Erlich copied the * * * works and was not entitled to a fair use defense. Plaintiffs argue that, although Netcom was not itself the source of any of the infringing materials on its system, it nonetheless should be liable for infringement, either directly, contributorily, or vicariously. Netcom disputes these theories of infringement and further argues that it is entitled to its own fair use defense.

1. Direct Infringement

Infringement consists of the unauthorized exercise of one of the exclusive rights of the copyright holder delineated in section 106. 17 U.S.C. § 501. Direct infringement does not require intent or any particular state of mind,[10] although willfulness is relevant to the award of statutory damages. 17 U.S.C. § 504(c).

* * *

10. The strict liability for copyright infringement is in contrast to another area of liability affecting online service providers: defamation. Recent decisions have held that where a BBS exercised little control over the content of the material on its service, it was more like a "distributor" than a "republisher" and was thus only liable for defamation on its system where it knew or should have known of the defamatory statements. *Cubby, Inc. v. CompuServe, Inc.,* 776 F.Supp. 135 (S.D.N.Y.1991). By contrast, a New York state court judge found that Prodigy was a publisher because it held itself out to be controlling the content of its services and because it used software to automatically prescreen messages that were offensive or in bad taste. *Stratton Oakmont, Inc. v. Prodigy Services Co.,* 1995 WL 323710, THE RECORDER, June 1, 1995, at 7 (excerpting May 24, 1995 Order Granting Partial Summary Judgment to Plaintiffs). [For more on a service provider's liability for defamation, see Chapter 14, *infra.*—Eds.]

a. Undisputed Facts

The parties do not dispute the basic processes that occur when Erlich posts his allegedly infringing messages to a.r.s. Erlich connects to Klemesrud's BBS using a telephone and a modem. Erlich then transmits his messages to Klemesrud's computer, where they are automatically briefly stored. According to a prearranged pattern established by Netcom's software, Erlich's initial act of posting a message to the Usenet results in the automatic copying of Erlich's message from Klemesrud's computer onto Netcom's computer and onto other computers on the Usenet. In order to ease transmission and for the convenience of Usenet users, Usenet servers maintain postings from newsgroups for a short period of time—eleven days for Netcom's system and three days for Klemesrud's system. Once on Netcom's computers, messages are available to Netcom's customers and Usenet neighbors, who may then download the messages to their own computers. Netcom's local server makes available its postings to a group of Usenet servers, which do the same for other servers until all Usenet sites worldwide have obtained access to the postings, which takes a matter of hours.

Unlike some other large on-line service providers, such as CompuServe, America Online, and Prodigy, Netcom does not create or control the content of the information available to its subscribers. It also does not monitor messages as they are posted. It has, however, suspended the accounts of subscribers who violated its terms and conditions, such as where they had commercial software in their posted files. Netcom admits that, although not currently configured to do this, it may be possible to reprogram its system to screen postings containing particular words or coming from particular individuals. Netcom, however, took no action after it was told by plaintiffs that Erlich had posted messages through Netcom's system that violated plaintiffs' copyrights, instead claiming that it could not shut out Erlich without shutting out all of the users of Klemesrud's BBS.

b. Creation of Fixed Copies

The Ninth Circuit addressed the question of what constitutes infringement in the context of storage of digital information in a computer's random access memory ("RAM"). *MAI Systems Corp. v. Peak Computer, Inc.*, 991 F.2d 511, 518 (9th Cir.1993). In *MAI*, the Ninth Circuit upheld a finding of copyright infringement where a repair person, who was not authorized to use the computer owner's licensed operating system software, turned on the computer, thus loading the operating system into RAM for long enough to check an "error log." *Id.* at 518–19. Copyright protection subsists in original works of authorship "*fixed* in any tangible medium of expression, now known or later developed, from which they can be perceived, reproduced, or otherwise communicated, either directly or with the aid of a machine or device." 17 U.S.C. § 102 (emphasis added). A work is "fixed" when its "embodiment in a copy . . . is sufficiently permanent or stable to permit it to be perceived, reproduced, or otherwise communicated for a period of more than transitory duration." *Id.* § 101. *MAI* established that the loading of data from a storage device into RAM constitutes copying because that data stays in RAM long enough for it to be perceived. *MAI Systems,* 991 F.2d at 518.

In the present case, there is no question after *MAI* that "copies" were created, as Erlich's act of sending a message to a.r.s. caused reproductions of portions of plaintiffs' works on both Klemesrud's and Netcom's storage devices. Even though the messages remained on their systems for at most eleven days, they were sufficiently "fixed" to constitute recognizable copies under the Copyright Act. *See* Information Infrastructure Task Force, *Intellectual Property and the National Information Infrastructure: The Report of the Working Group on Intellectual Property Rights* 66 (1995) ("IITF Report").

c. Is Netcom Directly Liable for Making the Copies?

Accepting that copies were made, Netcom argues that Erlich, and not Netcom, is directly liable for the copying. *MAI* did not address the question raised in this case: whether possessors of computers are liable for incidental copies automatically made on their computers using their software as part of a process initiated by a third party. Netcom correctly distinguishes *MAI* on the ground that Netcom did not take any affirmative action that directly resulted in copying plaintiffs' works other than by installing and maintaining a system whereby software automatically forwards messages received from subscribers onto the Usenet, and temporarily stores copies on its system. Netcom's actions, to the extent that they created a copy of plaintiffs' works, were necessary to having a working system for transmitting Usenet postings to and from the Internet. Unlike the defendants in *MAI,* neither Netcom nor Klemesrud initiated the copying. The defendants in *MAI* turned on their customers' computers thereby creating temporary copies of the operating system, whereas Netcom's and Klemesrud's systems can operate without any human intervention. Thus, unlike *MAI,* the mere fact that Netcom's system incidentally makes temporary copies of plaintiffs' works does not mean Netcom has caused the copying. The court believes that Netcom's act of designing or implementing a system that automatically and uniformly creates temporary copies of all data sent through it is not unlike that of the owner of a copying machine who lets the public make copies with it.[12] Although some of the people using the machine may directly infringe copyrights, courts analyze the machine owner's liability

12. Netcom compares itself to a common carrier that merely acts as a passive conduit for information. In a sense, a Usenet server that forwards all messages acts like a common carrier, passively retransmitting every message that gets sent through it. Netcom would seem no more liable than the phone company for carrying an infringing facsimile transmission or storing an infringing audio recording on its voice mail. * * * In any event, common carriers are granted statutory exemptions for liability that might otherwise exist. Here, Netcom does not fall under this statutory exemption, and thus faces the usual strict liability scheme that exists for copyright. Whether a new exemption should be carved out for online service providers is to be resolved by Congress, not the courts. [Congress enacted a limited exemption for online service providers as part of the Digital Millennium Copyright Act of 1998. *See* Part V, *infra.*—Eds.]

under the rubric of contributory infringement, not direct infringement. * * * Plaintiffs' theory would create many separate acts of infringement and, carried to its natural extreme, would lead to unreasonable liability. It is not difficult to conclude that Erlich infringes by copying a protected work onto his computer and by posting a message to a newsgroup. However, plaintiffs' theory further implicates a Usenet server that carries Erlich's message to other servers regardless of whether that server acts without any human intervention beyond the initial setting up of the system. It would also result in liability for every single Usenet server in the worldwide link of computers transmitting Erlich's message to every other computer. These parties, who are liable under plaintiffs' theory, do no more than operate or implement a system that is essential if Usenet messages are to be widely distributed. There is no need to construe the Act to make all of these parties infringers. Although copyright is a strict liability statute, there should still be some element of volition or causation which is lacking where a defendant's system is merely used to create a copy by a third party.

Plaintiffs point out that the infringing copies resided for eleven days on Netcom's computer and were sent out from it onto the "Information Superhighway." However, under plaintiffs' theory, any storage of a copy that occurs in the process of sending a message to the Usenet is an infringement. While it is possible that less "damage" would have been done if Netcom had heeded plaintiffs' warnings and acted to prevent Erlich's message from being forwarded,[13] this is not relevant to its *direct* liability for copying. The same argument is true of Klemesrud and any Usenet server. Whether a defendant makes a direct copy that constitutes infringement cannot depend on whether it received a warning to delete the message. *See D.C. Comics, Inc. v. Mini Gift,* 912 F.2d 29, 35 (2d Cir.1990). This distinction may be relevant to contributory infringement, however, where knowledge is an element.

* * *

d. Playboy Case

Playboy Enterprises, Inc. v. Frena involved a suit against the operator of a small BBS whose system contained files of erotic pictures. 839 F.Supp. 1552, 1554 (M.D.Fla.1993). A subscriber of the defendant's BBS had uploaded files containing digitized pictures copied from the plaintiff's copyrighted magazine, which files remained on the BBS for other subscribers to download. *Id.* The court did not conclude, as plaintiffs suggest in this case, that the BBS is itself liable for the unauthorized *reproduction of plaintiffs' work*; instead, the court concluded that the BBS operator was liable for violating the plaintiff's right to publicly *distribute and display copies of its work. Id.* at 1556–57.

13. The court notes, however, that stopping the distribution of information once it is on the Internet is not easy. The decentralized network was designed so that if one link in the chain be closed off, the information will be dynamically rerouted through another link. This was meant to allow the system to be used for communication after a catastrophic event that shuts down part of it.

In support of their argument that Netcom is directly liable for copying plaintiffs' works, plaintiffs cite to the court's conclusion that "[t]here is no dispute that [the BBS operator] supplied a product containing unauthorized copies of a copyrighted work. It does not matter that [the BBS operator] claims he did not make the copies [him]self." *Id.* at 1556. It is clear from the context of this discussion that the *Playboy* court was looking only at the exclusive right to distribute copies to the public, where liability exists regardless of whether the defendant makes copies. Here, however, plaintiffs do not argue that Netcom is liable for its public distribution of copies. Instead, they claim that Netcom is liable because its computers in fact made copies. Therefore, the above-quoted language has no bearing on the issue of direct liability for unauthorized reproductions. Notwithstanding *Playboy*'s holding that a BBS operator may be directly liable for *distributing or displaying* to the public copies of protected works, this court holds that the storage on a defendant's system of infringing copies and retransmission to other servers is not a direct infringement by the BBS operator of the exclusive right to *reproduce* the work where such copies are uploaded by an infringing user. *Playboy* does not hold otherwise.

* * *

f. Public Distribution and Display?

Plaintiffs allege that Netcom is directly liable for making *copies* of their works. They also allege that Netcom violated their exclusive rights to publicly display copies of their works. There are no allegations that Netcom violated plaintiffs' exclusive right to publicly distribute their works. However, in their discussion of direct infringement, plaintiffs insist that Netcom is liable for "maintain[ing] copies of [Erlich's] messages on its server for eleven days for access by its subscribers and 'USENET neighbors' " and they compare this case to the *Playboy* case, which discussed the right of public distribution. Plaintiffs also argued this theory of infringement at oral argument. Because this could be an attempt to argue that Netcom has infringed plaintiffs' rights of public distribution and display, the court will address these arguments.

Playboy concluded that the defendant infringed the plaintiff's exclusive rights to publicly distribute and display copies of its works. 839 F.Supp. at 1556–57. The court is not entirely convinced that the mere possession of a digital copy on a BBS that is accessible to some members of the public constitutes direct infringement by the BBS operator. Such a holding suffers from the same problem of causation as the reproduction argument. Only the subscriber should be liable for causing the distribution of plaintiffs' work, as the contributing actions of the BBS provider are automatic and indiscriminate. Erlich could have posted his messages through countless access providers and the outcome would be the same: anyone with access to Usenet newsgroups would be able to read his messages. There is no logical reason to draw a line around Netcom and Klemesrud and say that they are uniquely responsible for distributing Erlich's messages. Netcom is not even the first link in the chain of distribution—Erlich had no direct relationship with Netcom but dealt solely with Klemesrud's BBS, which used Netcom to gain its Internet access. Every Usenet server has a role in the distribution, so plaintiffs' argument would create unreasonable liability. Where the BBS merely stores and passes along all messages sent by its subscribers and others, the BBS should not be seen as causing these works to be publicly distributed or displayed.

Even accepting the *Playboy* court's holding, the case is factually distinguishable. Unlike the BBS in that case, Netcom does not maintain an archive of files for its users. Thus, it cannot be said to be "suppl[ying] a product." In contrast to some of its larger competitors, Netcom does not create or control the content of the information available to its subscribers; it merely provides *access* to the Internet, whose content is controlled by no single entity. Although the Internet consists of many different computers networked together, some of which may contain infringing files, it does not make sense to hold the operator of each computer liable as an infringer merely because his or her computer is linked to a computer with an infringing file. It would be especially inappropriate to hold liable a service that acts more like a conduit, in other words, one that does not itself keep an archive of files for more than a short duration. Finding such a service liable would involve an unreasonably broad construction of public distribution and display rights. No purpose would be served by holding liable those who have no ability to control the information to which their subscribers have access, even though they might be in some sense helping to achieve the Internet's automatic "public distribution" and the users' "public" display of files.

g. Conclusion

The court is not persuaded by plaintiffs' argument that Netcom is directly liable for the copies that are made and stored on its computer. Where the infringing subscriber is clearly directly liable for the same act, it does not make sense to adopt a rule that could lead to the liability of countless parties whose role in the infringement is nothing more than setting up and operating a system that is necessary for the functioning of the Internet. Such a result is unnecessary as there is already a party directly liable for causing the copies to be made. Plaintiffs occasionally claim that they only seek to hold liable a party that refuses to delete infringing files after they have been warned. However, such liability cannot be based on a theory of direct infringement, where knowledge is irrelevant. The court does not find workable a theory of infringement that would hold the entire Internet liable for activities that cannot reasonably be deterred. Billions of bits of data flow through the Internet and are necessarily stored on servers throughout the network and it is thus practically impossible to screen out infringing bits from noninfringing bits. Because the court cannot see any meaningful distinction (without regard to knowledge) between what Netcom did and what every other Usenet server does, the court finds that Netcom cannot be held liable for direct infringement. *Cf.* IITF Report at 69 (noting uncertainty regarding whether BBS operator should be directly liable for reproduction or distribution of files uploaded by a subscriber).

* * *

Kelly v. Arriba Soft Corp.

280 F.3d 934 (9th Cir.2002).

■ NELSON, CIRCUIT JUDGE.

This case involves the application of copyright law to the vast world of the internet and internet search engines. The plaintiff, Leslie Kelly, is a professional photographer who has copyrighted many of his images of the American West. Some of these images are located on Kelly's web site or other web sites with which Kelly has a license agreement. The defendant, Arriba Soft Corp.,[1] operates an internet search engine that displays its results in the form of small pictures rather than the more usual form of text. Arriba obtained its database of pictures by copying images from other web sites.[2] By clicking on one of these small pictures, called "thumbnails," the user can then view a large version of that same picture within the context of the Arriba web page.

When Kelly discovered that his photographs were part of Arriba's search engine database, he brought a claim against Arriba for copyright infringement. The district court found that Kelly had established a prima facie case of copyright infringement based on Arriba's unauthorized reproduction and display of Kelly's works, but that this reproduction and display constituted a non-infringing "fair use" under Section 107 of the Copyright Act. Kelly appeals that decision, and we affirm in part and reverse in part. The creation and use of the thumbnails in the search engine is a fair use, but the display of the larger image is a violation of Kelly's exclusive right to publicly display his works. We remand with instructions to determine damages and the need for an injunction.

I.

The search engine at issue in this case is unconventional in that it displays the results of a user's query as "thumbnail" images. When a user wants to search the internet for information on a certain topic, he or she types a search term into a search engine, which then produces a list of web sites that have information relating to the search term. Normally, the list of results is in text format. The Arriba search engine, however, produces its list of results as small pictures.

To provide this functionality, Arriba developed a computer program that "crawls" the web looking for images to index. This crawler downloads full-sized copies of the images onto Arriba's server. The program then uses these copies to generate smaller, lower-resolution thumbnails of the images. Once the thumbnails are created, the program deletes the full-sized originals from the server. Although a user could copy these thumbnails to his computer or disk, he cannot increase the resolution of the thumbnail; any enlargement would result in a loss of clarity of the image.

1. Arriba Soft has changed its name since the start of this litigation. It is now known as "Ditto.com."

2. [For a discussion of the law applicable to databases and compilations online, see Chapter 10, *infra*.—Eds.]

The second component of the Arriba program occurs when the user double-clicks on the thumbnail. From January 1999 to June 1999, clicking on the thumbnail produced the "Images Attributes" page. This page contained the original full-sized image imported directly from the originating web site, along with text describing the size of the image, a link to the originating web site, the Arriba banner, and Arriba advertising. The process of importing an image from another web site is called inline linking. The image imported from another web site is displayed as though it is part of the current web page, surrounded by the current web page's text and advertising. As a result, although the image in Arriba's Image Attributes page was directly from the originating web site, and not copied onto Arriba's site, the user typically would not realize that the image actually resided on another web site.

From July 1999 until sometime after August 2000, the results page contained thumbnails accompanied by two links: "Source" and "Details." The "Details" link produced a screen similar to the Images Attributes page but with a thumbnail rather than the full-sized image. Alternatively, by clicking on the "Source" link or the thumbnail from the results page, the site produced two new windows on top of the Arriba page. The window in the forefront contained the full-sized image, imported directly from the originating web site. Underneath that was another window displaying the originating web page. This technique is known as framing. The image from a second web site is viewed within a frame that is pulled into the primary site's web page.

In January 1999, Arriba's crawler visited web sites that contained Kelly's photographs. The crawler copied thirty-five of Kelly's images to the Arriba database. Kelly had never given permission to Arriba to copy his images and objected when he found out that Arriba was using them. Arriba deleted the thumbnails of images that came from Kelly's own web sites and placed those sites on a list of sites that it would not crawl in the future. Several months later, Arriba received Kelly's complaint of copyright infringement, which identified other images of his that came from third-party web sites. Arriba subsequently deleted those thumbnails and placed those third-party sites on a list of sites that it would not crawl in the future.

The district court granted summary judgment in favor of Arriba. Although the court found that Kelly had established a prima facie case of infringement based on Arriba's reproduction and display of Kelly's photographs, the court ruled that such actions by Arriba constituted fair use. * * *

II.

* * *

This case involves two distinct actions by Arriba that warrant analysis. The first action consists of the reproduction of Kelly's images to create the thumbnails and the use of those thumbnails in Arriba's search engine. [The court held that the reproductions were prima facie infringing but came within the doctrine of fair use. This portion of the opinion is excerpted in Part III(A), *infra*.]

* * *

B.

The second part of our analysis concerns Arriba's inline linking to and framing of Kelly's full-sized images. This use of Kelly's images does not entail copying them but, rather, importing them directly from Kelly's web site. Therefore, it cannot be copyright infringement based on the reproduction of copyrighted works * * *. Instead, this use of Kelly's images infringes upon Kelly's exclusive right to "display the copyrighted work publicly."[36]

1. Public display right.

In order for Kelly to prevail, Arriba must have displayed Kelly's work without his permission and made that display available to the public. The Copyright Act defines "display" as showing a copy of a work. This would seem to preclude Kelly from arguing that showing his original images was an infringement. However, the Act defines a copy as a material object in which a work is fixed, including the material object in which the work is first fixed. The legislative history of the Act makes clear that "[s]ince 'copies' are defined as including the material object 'in which the work is first fixed,' the right of public display applies to original works of art as well as to reproductions of them."[39] By inline linking and framing Kelly's images, Arriba is showing Kelly's original works without his permission.

The legislative history goes on to state that " 'display' would include the projection of an image on a screen or other surface by any method, the transmission of an image by electronic or other means, and the showing of an image on a cathode ray tube, or similar viewing apparatus connected with any sort of information storage and retrieval system."[40] This language indicates that showing Kelly's images on a computer screen would constitute a display.

The Act's definition of the term "publicly" encompasses a transmission of a display of a work to the public "by means of any device or process, whether the members of the public capable of receiving the performance or display receive it in the same place or in separate places and at the same time or at different times."[41] A display is public even if there is no proof that any of the potential recipients was operating his receiving apparatus at the time of the transmission.[42] By making Kelly's images available on its web site, Arriba is allowing public access to those images. The ability to view those images is unrestricted to anyone with a computer and internet access.

36. 17 U.S.C. § 106(5).

39. H.R.Rep. No. 94–1476, at 64 (1976), *reprinted in* 1976 U.S.C.C.A.N. 5659, 5677.

40. *Id.*

41. 17 U.S.C. § 101.

42. H.R.Rep. No. 94–1476, at 64–65 (1976), *reprinted in* 1976 U.S.C.C.A.N. 5659, 5678.

The legislative history emphasizes the broad nature of the display right, stating that "[e]ach and every method by which the images or sounds comprising a performance or display are picked up and conveyed is a 'transmission,' and if the transmission reaches the public in [any] form, the case comes within the scope of [the public performance and display rights] of section 106."[43] Looking strictly at the language of the Act and its legislative history, it appears that when Arriba imports Kelly's images into its own web page, Arriba is infringing upon Kelly's public display right. The limited case law in this area supports this conclusion.

No cases have addressed the issue of whether inline linking or framing violates a copyright owner's public display rights. However, in *Playboy Enterprises, Inc. v. Webbworld, Inc.*,[44] the court found that the owner of an internet site infringed a magazine publisher's copyrights by displaying copyrighted images on its web site. The defendant, Webbworld, downloaded material from certain newsgroups, discarded the text and retained the images, and made those images available to its internet subscribers.[46] Playboy owned copyrights to many of the images Webbworld retained and displayed. The court found that Webbworld violated Playboy's exclusive right to display its copyrighted works, noting that allowing subscribers to view copyrighted works on their computer monitors while online was a display. The court also discounted the fact that no image existed until the subscriber downloaded it. The image existed in digital form, which made it available for decoding as an image file by the subscriber, who could view the images merely by visiting the Webbworld site.

Although Arriba does not download Kelly's images to its own server but, rather, imports them directly from other web sites, the situation is analogous to *Webbworld*. By allowing the public to view Kelly's copyrighted works while visiting Arriba's web site, Arriba created a public display of Kelly's works. Arriba argues that Kelly offered no proof that anyone ever saw his images and, therefore, there can be no display. We dispose of this argument, as did the court in *Webbworld*, because Arriba made the images available to any viewer that merely visited Arriba's site. Allowing this capability is enough to establish an infringement; the fact that no one saw the images goes to the issue of damages, not liability.

In a similar case, *Playboy Enterprises, Inc. v. Russ Hardenburgh, Inc.*,[49] the court held that the owner of an electronic bulletin board system infringed Playboy's copyrights by displaying copyrighted images on its system. The bulletin board is a central system that stores information, giving home computer users the opportunity to submit information to the system (upload) or retrieve information from the system (download). In this

43. *Id.* at 64, *reprinted in* 1976 U.S.C.C.A.N. at 5678.

44. 991 F.Supp. 543 (N.D.Texas 1997).

46. Interestingly, the images were retained as both full-sized images and thumbnails. A subscriber could view several thumbnails on one page and then view a full-sized image by clicking on the thumbnail. However, both the thumbnail and full-sized image were copied onto Webbworld's server so no inline linking or framing was used.

49. 982 F.Supp. 503 (N.D.Ohio 1997).

case, the defendant encouraged its subscribers to upload adult photographs, screened all submitted images, and moved some of the images into files from which general subscribers could download them. Because these actions resulted in subscribers being able to download copyrighted images, it violated Playboy's right of public display. Again, the court noted that adopting a policy that allowed the defendants to place images in files available to subscribers entailed a display. This conclusion indicates that it was irrelevant whether anyone actually saw the images.

Both of these cases highlighted the fact that the defendants took an active role in creating the display of the copyrighted images. The reason for this emphasis is that several other cases held that operators of bulletin board systems and internet access providers were not liable for copyright infringement.[54] These cases distinguished direct infringement from contributory infringement and held that where the defendants did not take any affirmative action that resulted in copying copyrighted works, but only maintained a system that acted as a passive conduit for third parties' copies, they were not liable for direct infringement.

The courts in *Webbworld* and *Hardenburgh* specifically noted that the defendants did more than act as mere providers of access or passive conduits. In *Webbworld,* the web site sold images after actively trolling the internet for them and deciding which images to provide to subscribers. The court stated that "Webbworld exercised total dominion over the content of its site and the product it offered its clientele."[56] Likewise, in *Hardenburgh,* the court found that by encouraging subscribers to upload images and then screening those images and selecting ones to make available for downloading, the defendants were more than passive conduits.[57]

Like the defendants in *Webbworld* and *Hardenburgh,* Arriba is directly liable for infringement. Arriba actively participated in displaying Kelly's images by trolling the web, finding Kelly's images, and then having its program inline link and frame those images within its own web site. Without this program, users would not have been able to view Kelly's images within the context of Arriba's site. Arriba acted as more than a passive conduit of the images by establishing a direct link to the copyright-

54. *See e.g. Religious Tech. Ctr. v. Netcom On–Line Communication Servs., Inc.,* 907 F.Supp. 1361, 1372–73 (N.D.Cal.1995) (holding that operator of a computer bulletin board system that forwarded messages from subscribers to other subscribers was not liable for displaying copyrighted works because it took no role in controlling the content of the information but only acted as passive conduit of the information); *Marobie–FL, Inc. v. Nat'l. Ass'n of Fire and Equip. Distribs.,* 983 F.Supp. 1167, 1176–79 (N.D.Ill.1997) (holding that company that provided a host computer for web page and access link to internet users was not directly liable for copyright infringement when administrator of web page posted copyrighted works on the page, because it only provided the means to display the works but did not engage in the activity itself); *Costar Group Inc. v. Loopnet, Inc.,* 164 F.Supp.2d 688, 695–96 (D.Md.2001) (holding that operator of a web site that hosted real estate listings and photos was not directly liable for copyright infringement because it did not actively participate in copying or displaying the images).

56. *Webbworld,* 991 F.Supp. at 552.

57. *Hardenburgh,* 982 F.Supp. at 513.

ed images. Therefore, Arriba is liable for publicly displaying Kelly's copyrighted images without his permission.

* * *

NOTES & QUESTIONS

1. *Downloading vs. photocopying.* In *Playboy v. Frena*, how does Frena's act of making the material available for download differ from the act of a library in keeping original magazines on its shelves and allowing members of the public to make copies using an on-premises photocopy machine?

2. *Unreasonable and unnecessary liability?* The *Netcom* court, in holding that Netcom is not directly liable for copying, distributing, or publicly displaying materials by virtue of maintaining them on its server, reasons that the alternative "would lead to unreasonable liability." What are the relative costs and benefits of imposing liability on Netcom? Who would be the least cost avoider of the harm resulting from infringement? Was the court's imposition of liability in *Frena* unreasonable? The *Netcom* court also states that imposing liability on Netcom is "unnecessary as there is already a party directly liable for causing the copies to be made." Is this the usual rule in tort actions?

3. *Who engages in the display and distribution?* In *Playboy v. Frena*, did the court address the question of who engaged in the public display and distribution of Playboy's pictures? Is there an argument that it was not Frena, but rather the BBS subscribers, who engaged in these actions?

In *Kelly v. Arriba Soft*, is it clear that the display of Kelly's images is attributable to Arriba Soft? As the court indicates, the files constituting the full-sized images never resided on or even passed through Arriba Soft's computer servers. Arriba Soft's website contained only links pointing to the URLs of the images where they resided on Kelly's site. When a user clicked on such a link, the user's browser sent a request to Kelly's computer, which Kelly's server interpreted as: "Please send me the image file that you are storing at the address www.goldrush1849.com/images/coloma.jpg." Kelly's server was configured so that it automatically granted such requests, by transmitting the requested image to the user, whose browser then displayed it graphically. (It is easy to configure a server otherwise. For example, many servers are configured so that certain pages are served *only* to requesters who are linking from a page within the site.) Thus the user's browser and Kelly's server communicated directly with each other; Arriba Soft was not an intermediary.

This is the same sequence of events that occurs whenever a user clicks on a link, and is served a page, image, or other resource from the linked-to site. If Arriba Soft is responsible for the display that occurs when a user clicks a link on its site that points to an image file on another site, it would seem to follow that every other website owner is equally responsible for displaying material residing on other sites simply by virtue of pointing a link at that material. If the material is copyrighted, and the copyright owner does not authorize the display, then the owner of the website containing the link would seem to be engaging in an infringing display every time a user clicks on the link. Can this be a proper application of the Copyright Act? The previous paragraph above contains a URL pointing to an image on Kelly's website; does this constitute an infringing display by the author or publisher of this book? Would it make any difference if this were an electronic book, so that the URL were a working hyperlink? Compare *Ticketmaster Corp. v. Tickets.Com,* 54 U.S.P.Q.2d (BNA) 1344 (C.D.Cal.2000) ("[H]yperlinking does not itself involve a violation of the Copyright Act * * * since no copying is involved. The customer is automatically transferred to the particular genuine web page of the original author."), *superseded and withdrawn,* 2000 Copyright L. Dec. (CCH) ¶ 28,-146 (C.D.Cal.2000).

4. *Liability under the* Netcom *standard.* In *Playboy Enterprises, Inc. v. Russ Hardenburgh, Inc.,* 982 F.Supp. 503 (N.D.Ohio 1997), the court adopted the *Netcom* approach to direct infringement but, contrary to *Netcom,* found the defendants liable under that standard. Plaintiff, Playboy Enterprises, Inc., sued a computer bulletin board system and its owner, alleging they engaged in copyright infringement by making PEI's copyrighted images available for download from the BBS. Subscribers uploaded files to the BBS, which offered them an incentive to do so: "Subscribers were given a 'credit' for each megabyte of electronic data that they uploaded onto the system. For each credit, the subscriber was entitled to download 1.5 extra megabytes of electronic information, in addition to the megabytes available under the normal terms of subscription." Once uploaded, the files were reviewed by a BBS employee, to make sure they were "not pornographic, and not blatantly protected by copyright." *Id.* at 506. Once approved, they were made available for download by other subscribers. The court expressed agreement with the principle, which it attributed to *Netcom,* "that a finding of direct copyright infringement requires some element of direct action or participation." It found the requisite "direct action or participation" in the factors that (1) defendants encouraged subscribers to upload material to the BBS, and (2) defendants employed a screening procedure before making uploaded files available for download. These two factors "transform Defendants from passive providers of a space in which infringing activities happened to occur to active participants in the process of copyright infringement." *Id.* at 512–13.

Do the two factors that the court relies upon warrant treating defendants differently from "passive providers" of a forum for infringement? Does the court's reliance on the second (screening) factor provide BBS operators with a perverse incentive to avoid screening uploads for possible copyright infringement?

B. CONTRIBUTORY INFRINGEMENT

Absent clear evidence of direct participation in acts of infringement, courts have been reluctant to hold BBS operators and Internet service providers directly liable based on the actions of their subscribers. Copyright owners have therefore argued that such entities should be held liable as contributory or vicarious infringers, based on their providing Internet access or some other service to the primary infringer. In this section and the next, we look at how courts have applied these two doctrines to the online environment.

A person is liable as a contributory infringer if the person, with knowledge of the infringing acts, induces or materially contributes to the infringing activity of another. For example, in *Eleckra Records Co. v. Gem Elec. Distributors, Inc.,* 360 F.Supp. 821 (E.D.N.Y.1973), an electronics store selling blank audio tapes was found liable for contributory infringement. The offending conduct was promoting the sale of its blank tapes by allowing tape purchasers to use its dubbing equipment to duplicate prerecorded audio tapes containing copyrighted music onto the blank tapes. The customers were the direct infringers, and the store was a contributory infringer.

Religious Technology Center v. Netcom On–Line Communication Services, Inc.

907 F.Supp. 1361 (N.D.Cal.1995).

■ WHYTE, DISTRICT JUDGE.

[The facts of this case are set forth in Part II(A), *supra.*]

* * *

2. Contributory Infringement

Netcom is not free from liability just because it did not directly infringe plaintiffs' works; it may still be liable as a contributory infringer. Although there is no statutory rule of liability for infringement committed by others,

> [t]he absence of such express language in the copyright statute does not preclude the imposition of liability for copyright infringement on certain parties who have not themselves engaged in the infringing activity. For vicarious liability is imposed in virtually all areas of the law, and the concept of contributory infringement is merely a species of the broader problem of identifying the circumstances in which it is just to hold one individual accountable for the actions of another.

Sony Corp. v. Universal City Studios, Inc., 464 U.S. 417, 435 (1984) (footnote omitted). Liability for participation in the infringement will be established where the defendant, "with knowledge of the infringing activity, induces, causes or materially contributes to the infringing conduct of another." *Gershwin Publishing Corp. v. Columbia Artists Management, Inc.,* 443 F.2d 1159, 1162 (2d Cir.1971).

a. Knowledge of Infringing Activity

Plaintiffs insist that Netcom knew that Erlich was infringing their copyrights at least after receiving notice from plaintiffs' counsel indicating that Erlich had posted copies of their works onto a.r.s.[3] through Netcom's system. Despite this knowledge, Netcom continued to allow Erlich to post messages to a.r.s. and left the allegedly infringing messages on its system so that Netcom's subscribers and other Usenet servers could access them. Netcom argues that it did not possess the necessary type of knowledge because (1) it did not know of Erlich's planned infringing activities when it agreed to lease its facilities to Klemesrud, (2) it did not know that Erlich would infringe prior to any of his postings, (3) it is unable to screen out infringing postings before they are made, and (4) its knowledge of the infringing nature of Erlich's postings was too equivocal given the difficulty in assessing whether the registrations were valid and whether Erlich's use was fair. The court will address these arguments in turn.

Netcom cites cases holding that there is no contributory infringement by the lessors of premises that are later used for infringement unless the lessor had knowledge of the intended use at the time of the signing of the lease. *See, e.g. Deutsch v. Arnold,* 98 F.2d 686, 688 (2d Cir.1938). The contribution to the infringement by the defendant in *Deutsch* was merely to lease use of the premises to the infringer. Here, Netcom not only leases space but also serves as an access provider, which includes the storage and transmission of information necessary to facilitate Erlich's postings to a.r.s. Unlike a landlord, Netcom retains some control over the use of its system. Thus, the relevant time frame for knowledge is not when Netcom entered into an agreement with Klemesrud. It should be when Netcom provided its services to allow Erlich to infringe plaintiffs' copyrights. *Cf. Screen Gems–Columbia Music, Inc. v. Mark–Fi Records, Inc.,* 256 F.Supp. 399, 403 (S.D.N.Y.1966) (analyzing knowledge at time that defendant rendered its particular service). It is undisputed that Netcom did not know that Erlich was infringing before it received notice from plaintiffs. Netcom points out that the alleged instances of infringement occurring on Netcom's system all happened prior to December 29, 1994, the date on which Netcom first received notice of plaintiffs' infringement claim against Erlich. Thus, there is no question of fact as to whether Netcom knew or should have known of Erlich's infringing activities that occurred more than 11 days before receipt of the December 28, 1994 letter.

However, the evidence reveals a question of fact as to whether Netcom knew or should have known that Erlich had infringed plaintiffs' copyrights following receipt of plaintiffs' letter. Because Netcom was arguably participating in Erlich's public distribution of plaintiffs' works, there is a genuine issue as to whether Netcom knew of any infringement by Erlich before it was too late to do anything about it. If plaintiffs can prove the knowledge element, Netcom will be liable for contributory infringement since its failure to simply cancel Erlich's infringing message and thereby stop an infringing copy from being distributed worldwide constitutes substantial participation in Erlich's public distribution of the message.

3. [Recall that "a.r.s" stands for the Usenet newsgroup alt.religion.scientology.—Eds.]

Netcom argues that its knowledge after receiving notice of Erlich's alleged infringing activities was too equivocal given the difficulty in assessing whether registrations are valid and whether use is fair. Although a mere unsupported allegation of infringement by a copyright owner may not automatically put a defendant on notice of infringing activity, Netcom's position that liability must be unequivocal is unsupportable. While perhaps the typical infringing activities of BBSs will involve copying software, where BBS operators are better equipped to judge infringement, the fact that this involves written works should not distinguish it. Where works contain copyright notices within them, as here, it is difficult to argue that a defendant did not know that the works were copyrighted. To require proof of valid registrations would be impractical and would perhaps take too long to verify, making it impossible for a copyright holder to protect his or her works in some cases, as works are automatically deleted less than two weeks after they are posted. The court is more persuaded by the argument that it is beyond the ability of a BBS operator to quickly and fairly determine when a use is not infringement where there is at least a colorable claim of fair use. Where a BBS operator cannot reasonably verify a claim of infringement, either because of a possible fair use defense, the lack of copyright notices on the copies, or the copyright holder's failure to provide the necessary documentation to show that there is a likely infringement, the operator's lack of knowledge will be found reasonable and there will be no liability for contributory infringement for allowing the continued distribution of the works on its system.

Since Netcom was given notice of an infringement claim before Erlich had completed his infringing activity, there may be a question of fact as to whether Netcom knew or should have known that such activities were infringing. Given the context of a dispute between a former minister and a church he is criticizing, Netcom may be able to show that its lack of knowledge that Erlich was infringing was reasonable. However, Netcom admits that it did not even look at the postings once given notice and that had it looked at the copyright notice and statements regarding authorship, it would have triggered an investigation into whether there was infringement. These facts are sufficient to raise a question as to Netcom's knowledge once it received a letter from plaintiffs on December 29, 1994.

b. Substantial Participation

Where a defendant has knowledge of the primary infringer's infringing activities, it will be liable if it "induces, causes or materially contributes to the infringing conduct of" the primary infringer. *Gershwin Publishing,* 443 F.2d at 1162. Such participation must be substantial. *Apple Computer, Inc. v. Microsoft Corp.,* 821 F.Supp. 616, 625 (N.D.Cal.1993), *aff'd,* 35 F.3d 1435 (9th Cir.1994).

Providing a service that allows for the automatic distribution of all Usenet postings, infringing and noninfringing, goes well beyond renting a premises to an infringer. * * * It is more akin to the radio stations that were found liable for rebroadcasting an infringing broadcast. *See, e.g.,*

Select Theatres Corp. v. Ronzoni Macoroni Co., 59 U.S.P.Q. 288, 291 (S.D.N.Y.1943). Netcom allows Erlich's infringing messages to remain on its system and be further distributed to other Usenet servers worldwide. It does not completely relinquish control over how its system is used, unlike a landlord. Thus, it is fair, assuming Netcom is able to take simple measures to prevent further damage to plaintiffs' copyrighted works, to hold Netcom liable for contributory infringement where Netcom has knowledge of Erlich's infringing postings yet continues to aid in the accomplishment of Erlich's purpose of publicly distributing the postings. Accordingly, plaintiffs do raise a genuine issue of material fact as to their theory of contributory infringement as to the postings made after Netcom was on notice of plaintiffs' infringement claim. * * *

[For similar reasons, the court also finds that the plaintiffs have raised a genuine issue of material fact as to their theory of contributory infringement against the BBS operator, Klemesrud.]

* * *

Intellectual Reserve, Inc. v. Utah Lighthouse Ministry, Inc.

75 F.Supp.2d 1290 (D.Utah 1999).

■ CAMPBELL, DISTRICT JUDGE.

This matter is before the court on plaintiff's motion for preliminary injunction. Plaintiff claims that unless a preliminary injunction issues, defendants will directly infringe and contribute to the infringement of its copyright in the *Church Handbook of Instructions* ("Handbook"). Defendants do not oppose a preliminary injunction, but argue that the scope of the injunction should be restricted to only prohibit direct infringement of plaintiff's copyright.[4]

Having fully considered the arguments of counsel, the submissions of the parties and applicable legal authorities, the court grants plaintiff's motion for a preliminary injunction. However, the scope of the preliminary injunction is limited.

Discussion

* * *

I. Likelihood of Plaintiff Prevailing on the Merits

First, the court considers whether there is a substantial likelihood that plaintiff will eventually prevail on the merits. Plaintiff alleges that the defendants infringed its copyright directly by posting substantial portions of its copyrighted material on defendants' website, and also contributed to infringement of its copyright by inducing, causing or materially contributing to the infringing conduct of another. To determine the proper scope of

4. [Plaintiff is the owner of copyrights in the Handbook and other materials used by the Church of Jesus Christ of Latter-day Saints (the Mormon Church). Defendant is an organization that is critical of the Mormon Church.—Eds.]

the preliminary injunction, the court considers the likelihood that plaintiff will prevail on either or both of its claims.

* * *

B. Contributory Infringement

According to plaintiff, after the defendants were ordered to remove the Handbook from their website, the defendants began infringing plaintiff's copyright by inducing, causing, or materially contributing to the infringing conduct of others. It is undisputed that defendants placed a notice on their website that the Handbook was online, and gave three website addresses of websites containing the material defendants were ordered to remove from their website. Defendants also posted e-mails on their website that encouraged browsing those websites, printing copies of the Handbook and sending the Handbook to others.

* * *

Liability for contributory infringement is imposed when "one who, with knowledge of the infringing activity, induces, causes or materially contributes to the infringing conduct of another." *Gershwin Publ'g Corp. v. Columbia Artists Mgt., Inc.,* 443 F.2d 1159, 1162 (2d Cir.1971). Thus, to prevail on its claim of contributory infringement, plaintiff must first be able to establish that the conduct defendants allegedly aided or encouraged could amount to infringement. *See Subafilms, Ltd. v. MGM–Pathe Comms. Co.,* 24 F.3d 1088, 1092 (9th Cir.1994). Defendants argue that they have not contributed to copyright infringement by those who posted the Handbook on websites nor by those who browsed the websites on their computers.

1. Can the Defendants Be Liable Under a Theory of Contributory Infringement for the Actions of Those Who Posted the Handbook on the Three Websites?

a. Did those who posted the Handbook on the websites infringe plaintiff's copyright?

During a hearing on the motion to vacate the temporary restraining order, defendants accepted plaintiff's proffer that the three websites contain the material which plaintiff alleges is copyrighted. Therefore, plaintiff at trial is likely to establish that those who have posted the material on the three websites are directly infringing plaintiff's copyright.

b. Did the defendants induce, cause or materially contribute to the infringement?

The evidence now before the court indicates that there is no direct relationship between the defendants and the people who operate the three websites. The defendants did not provide the website operators with the plaintiff's copyrighted material, nor are the defendants receiving any kind of compensation from them. The only connection between the defendants and those who operate the three websites appears to be the information defendants have posted on their website concerning the infringing sites.

Based on this scant evidence, the court concludes that plaintiff has not shown that defendants contributed to the infringing action of those who operate the infringing websites.

2. Can the Defendants Be Liable Under a Theory of Contributory Infringement for the Actions of Those Who Browse the Three Infringing Websites?

Defendants make two arguments in support of their position that the activities of those who browse the three websites do not make them liable under a theory of contributory infringement. First, defendants contend that those who browse the infringing websites are not themselves infringing plaintiff's copyright; and second, even if those who browse the websites are infringers, defendants have not materially contributed to the infringing conduct.

a. Do those who browse the websites infringe plaintiff's copyright?

The first question, then, is whether those who browse any of the three infringing websites are infringing plaintiff's copyright. Central to this inquiry is whether the persons browsing are merely viewing the Handbook (which is not a copyright infringement), or whether they are making a copy of the Handbook (which is a copyright infringement). *See* 17 U.S.C. § 106.

"Copy" is defined in the Copyright Act as: "material objects ... in which a work is fixed by any method now known or later developed, and from which the work can be perceived, reproduced, or otherwise communicated, either directly or with the aid of a machine or device." 17 U.S.C. § 101. "A work is 'fixed' ... when its ... [sic] sufficiently permanent or stable to permit it to be perceived, reproduced, or otherwise communicated for a period of more than transitory duration." *Id.*

When a person browses a website, and by so doing displays the Handbook, a copy of the Handbook is made in the computer's random access memory (RAM), to permit viewing of the material. And in making a copy, even a temporary one, the person who browsed infringes the copyright.[5] *See MAI Systems Corp. v. Peak Computer, Inc.*, 991 F.2d 511, 518 (9th Cir.1993) (holding that when material is transferred to a computer's RAM, copying has occurred; in the absence of ownership of the copyright or express permission by license, such an act constitutes copyright infringement); *Marobie–FL., Inc. v. National Ass'n of Fire and Equip. Distrib.*, 983 F.Supp. 1167, 1179 (N.D.Ill.1997) (noting that liability for copyright infringement is with the persons who cause the display or distribution of the infringing material onto their computer); *see also* Nimmer on Copyright § 8.08(A)(1) (stating that the infringing act of copying may occur from "loading the copyrighted material ... into the computer's random access memory (RAM)"). Additionally, a person making a printout or re-posting a

5. Although this seems harsh, the Copyright Act has provided a safeguard for innocent infringers. Where the infringer "was not aware and had no reason to believe that his or her acts constituted an infringement of copyright, the court in its discretion may reduce the award of statutory damages...." 17 U.S.C. § 504(c)(2).

copy of the Handbook on another website would infringe plaintiff's copyright.

b. Did the defendants induce, cause or materially contribute to the infringement?

The court now considers whether the defendants' actions contributed to the infringement of plaintiff's copyright by those who browse the three websites.

The following evidence establishes that defendants have actively encouraged the infringement of plaintiff's copyright[6] After being ordered to remove the Handbook from their website, defendants posted on their website: "Church Handbook of Instructions is back online!" and listed the three website addresses. Defendants also posted e-mail suggesting that the lawsuit against defendants would be affected by people logging onto one of the websites and downloading the complete handbook. One of the e-mails posted by the defendants mentioned sending a copy of the copyrighted material to the media. In response to an e-mail stating that the sender had unsuccessfully tried to browse a website that contained the Handbook, defendants gave further instruction on how to browse the material. At least one of the three websites encourages the copying and posting of copies of the allegedly infringing material on other websites. *See* Ex. 4 [to Plaintiff's Reply Brief] ("Please mirror these files.... It will be a LOT quicker for you to download the compressed version ... Needless to say, we need a LOT of mirror sites, as absolutely soon as possible.").

Based on the above, the court finds that the first element necessary for injunctive relief is satisfied.

[In the remainder of the opinion, the court finds the other elements necessary for injunctive relief also satisfied and issues a preliminary injunction.]

* * *

A & M Records, Inc. v. Napster, Inc.

239 F.3d 1004 (9th Cir.2001).

■ BEEZER, CIRCUIT JUDGE:

Plaintiffs are engaged in the commercial recording, distribution and sale of copyrighted musical compositions and sound recordings. The complaint alleges that Napster, Inc. ("Napster") is a contributory and vicarious copyright infringer. On July 26, 2000, the district court granted plaintiffs'

6. Plaintiff at this point has been unable to specifically identify persons who have infringed its copyright because they were induced or assisted by defendants' conduct, however, there is a substantial likelihood that plaintiff will be able to do so after conducting discovery. There is evidence that at least one of the websites has seen a great increase in "hits" recently. Also, plaintiff does not have to establish that the defendants' actions are the sole cause of another's infringement; rather plaintiff may prevail by establishing that defendants' conduct induces or materially contributes to the infringing conduct of another.

motion for a preliminary injunction. The injunction was slightly modified by written opinion on August 10, 2000. *A & M Records, Inc. v. Napster, Inc.*, 114 F.Supp.2d 896 (N.D.Cal.2000). The district court preliminarily enjoined Napster "from engaging in, or facilitating others in copying, downloading, uploading, transmitting, or distributing plaintiffs' copyrighted musical compositions and sound recordings, protected by either federal or state law, without express permission of the rights owner." *Id.* at 927. Federal Rule of Civil Procedure 65(c) requires successful plaintiffs to post a bond for damages incurred by the enjoined party in the event that the injunction was wrongfully issued. The district court set bond in this case at $5 million.

We entered a temporary stay of the preliminary injunction pending resolution of this appeal. We have jurisdiction pursuant to 28 U.S.C. § 1292(a)(1). We affirm in part, reverse in part and remand.

I

We have examined the papers submitted in support of and in response to the injunction application and it appears that Napster has designed and operates a system which permits the transmission and retention of sound recordings employing digital technology.

In 1987, the Moving Picture Experts Group set a standard file format for the storage of audio recordings in a digital format called MPEG–3, abbreviated as "MP3." Digital MP3 files are created through a process colloquially called "ripping." Ripping software allows a computer owner to copy an audio compact disk ("audio CD") directly onto a computer's hard drive by compressing the audio information on the CD into the MP3 format. The MP3's compressed format allows for rapid transmission of digital audio files from one computer to another by electronic mail or any other file transfer protocol.

Napster facilitates the transmission of MP3 files between and among its users. Through a process commonly called "peer-to-peer" file sharing, Napster allows its users to: (1) make MP3 music files stored on individual computer hard drives available for copying by other Napster users; (2) search for MP3 music files stored on other users' computers; and (3) transfer exact copies of the contents of other users' MP3 files from one computer to another via the Internet. These functions are made possible by Napster's MusicShare software, available free of charge from Napster's Internet site, and Napster's network servers and server-side software. Napster provides technical support for the indexing and searching of MP3 files, as well as for its other functions, including a "chat room," where users can meet to discuss music, and a directory where participating artists can provide information about their music.

A. Accessing the System

In order to copy MP3 files through the Napster system, a user must first access Napster's Internet site and download the MusicShare software to his individual computer. *See* www.Napster.com. Once the software is installed, the user can access the Napster system. A first-time user is required to register with the Napster system by creating a "user name" and password.

B. Listing Available Files

If a registered user wants to list available files stored in his computer's hard drive on Napster for others to access, he must first create a "user library" directory on his computer's hard drive. The user then saves his MP3 files in the library directory, using self-designated file names. He next must log into the Napster system using his user name and password. His MusicShare software then searches his user library and verifies that the available files are properly formatted. If in the correct MP3 format, the names of the MP3 files will be uploaded from the user's computer to the Napster servers. The content of the MP3 files remains stored in the user's computer.

Once uploaded to the Napster servers, the user's MP3 file names are stored in a server-side "library" under the user's name and become part of a "collective directory" of files available for transfer during the time the user is logged onto the Napster system. The collective directory is fluid; it tracks users who are connected in real time, displaying only file names that are immediately accessible.

C. Searching For Available Files

Napster allows a user to locate other users' MP3 files in two ways: through Napster's search function and through its "hotlist" function.

Software located on the Napster servers maintains a "search index" of Napster's collective directory. To search the files available from Napster users currently connected to the network servers, the individual user accesses a form in the MusicShare software stored in his computer and enters either the name of a song or an artist as the object of the search. The form is then transmitted to a Napster server and automatically compared to the MP3 file names listed in the server's search index. Napster's server compiles a list of all MP3 file names pulled from the search index which include the same search terms entered on the search form and transmits the list to the searching user. The Napster server does not search the contents of any MP3 file; rather, the search is limited to "a text search of the file names indexed in a particular cluster. Those file names may contain typographical errors or otherwise inaccurate descriptions of the content of the files since they are designated by other users." *Napster,* 114 F.Supp.2d at 906.

To use the "hotlist" function, the Napster user creates a list of other users' names from whom he has obtained MP3 files in the past. When logged onto Napster's servers, the system alerts the user if any user on his list (a "hotlisted user") is also logged onto the system. If so, the user can access an index of all MP3 file names in a particular hotlisted user's library and request a file in the library by selecting the file name. The contents of the hotlisted user's MP3 file are not stored on the Napster system.

D. *Transferring Copies of an MP3 file*

To transfer a copy of the contents of a requested MP3 file, the Napster server software obtains the Internet address of the requesting user and the Internet address of the "host user" (the user with the available files). *See generally Brookfield Communications, Inc. v. West Coast Entm't Corp.,* 174 F.3d 1036, 1044 (9th Cir.1999) (describing, in detail, the structure of the Internet). The Napster servers then communicate the host user's Internet address to the requesting user. The requesting user's computer uses this information to establish a connection with the host user and downloads a copy of the contents of the MP3 file from one computer to the other over the Internet, "peer-to-peer." A downloaded MP3 file can be played directly from the user's hard drive using Napster's MusicShare program or other software. The file may also be transferred back onto an audio CD if the user has access to equipment designed for that purpose. In both cases, the quality of the original sound recording is slightly diminished by transfer to the MP3 format.

This architecture is described in some detail to promote an understanding of transmission mechanics as opposed to the content of the transmissions. The content is the subject of our copyright infringement analysis. * * *

III

Plaintiffs claim Napster users are engaged in the wholesale reproduction and distribution of copyrighted works, all constituting direct infringement.[2] The district court agreed. We note that the district court's conclusion that plaintiffs have presented a prima facie case of direct infringement by Napster users is not presently appealed by Napster. We only need briefly address the threshold requirements.

A. *Infringement*

Plaintiffs must satisfy two requirements to present a prima facie case of direct infringement: (1) they must show ownership of the allegedly infringed material and (2) they must demonstrate that the alleged infringers violate at least one exclusive right granted to copyright holders under 17 U.S.C. § 106. *See* 17 U.S.C. § 501(a) (infringement occurs when alleged infringer engages in activity listed in § 106); *see also Baxter v. MCA, Inc.,* 812 F.2d 421, 423 (9th Cir.1987); *see, e.g., S.O.S., Inc. v. Payday, Inc.,* 886 F.2d 1081, 1085 n. 3 (9th Cir.1989) ("The word 'copying' is shorthand for the infringing of any of the copyright owner's five exclusive rights...."). Plaintiffs have sufficiently demonstrated ownership. The record supports the district court's determination that "as much as eighty-seven percent of

2. Secondary liability for copyright infringement does not exist in the absence of direct infringement by a third party. *Religious Tech. Ctr. v. Netcom On-Line Communication Servs., Inc.,* 907 F.Supp. 1361, 1371 (N.D.Cal.1995) ("[T]here can be no contributory infringement by a defendant without direct infringement by another."). It follows that Napster does not facilitate infringement of the copyright laws in the absence of direct infringement by its users.

the files available on Napster may be copyrighted and more than seventy percent may be owned or administered by plaintiffs." *Napster,* 114 F.Supp.2d at 911.

The district court further determined that plaintiffs' exclusive rights under § 106 were violated: "here the evidence establishes that a majority of Napster users use the service to download and upload copyrighted music.... And by doing that, it constitutes—the uses constitute direct infringement of plaintiffs' musical compositions, recordings." *A & M Records, Inc. v. Napster, Inc.,* 2000 WL 1009483, at *1 (N.D.Cal. July 26, 2000) (transcript of proceedings). The district court also noted that "it is pretty much acknowledged ... by Napster that this is infringement." *Id.* We agree that plaintiffs have shown that Napster users infringe at least two of the copyright holders' exclusive rights: the rights of reproduction, § 106(1); and distribution, § 106(3). Napster users who upload file names to the search index for others to copy violate plaintiffs' distribution rights. Napster users who download files containing copyrighted music violate plaintiffs' reproduction rights.

* * *

IV

We first address plaintiffs' claim that Napster is liable for contributory copyright infringement. Traditionally, "one who, with knowledge of the infringing activity, induces, causes or materially contributes to the infringing conduct of another, may be held liable as a 'contributory' infringer." *Gershwin Publ'g Corp. v. Columbia Artists Mgmt., Inc.,* 443 F.2d 1159, 1162 (2d Cir.1971); *see also Fonovisa, Inc. v. Cherry Auction, Inc.,* 76 F.3d 259, 264 (9th Cir.1996). Put differently, liability exists if the defendant engages in "personal conduct that encourages or assists the infringement." *Matthew Bender & Co. v. West Publ'g Co.,* 158 F.3d 693, 706 (2d Cir.1998).

The district court determined that plaintiffs in all likelihood would establish Napster's liability as a contributory infringer. The district court did not err; Napster, by its conduct, knowingly encourages and assists the infringement of plaintiffs' copyrights.

A. Knowledge

Contributory liability requires that the secondary infringer "know or have reason to know" of direct infringement. *Cable/Home Communication Corp. v. Network Prods., Inc.,* 902 F.2d 829, 845 and 846 n. 29 (11th Cir.1990); *Religious Tech. Ctr. v. Netcom On–Line Communication Servs., Inc.,* 907 F.Supp. 1361, 1373–74 (N.D.Cal.1995) (framing issue as "whether Netcom knew or should have known of" the infringing activities). The district court found that Napster had both actual and constructive knowledge that its users exchanged copyrighted music. The district court also concluded that the law does not require knowledge of "specific acts of infringement" and rejected Napster's contention that because the company cannot distinguish infringing from noninfringing files, it does not "know" of the direct infringement. 114 F.Supp.2d at 917.

It is apparent from the record that Napster has knowledge, both actual and constructive,[5] of direct infringement. Napster claims that it is nevertheless protected from contributory liability by the teaching of *Sony Corp. v. Universal City Studios, Inc.,* 464 U.S. 417 (1984). We disagree. We observe that Napster's actual, specific knowledge of direct infringement renders *Sony*'s holding of limited assistance to Napster. We are compelled to make a clear distinction between the architecture of the Napster system and Napster's conduct in relation to the operational capacity of the system.

The *Sony* Court refused to hold the manufacturer and retailers of video tape recorders liable for contributory infringement despite evidence that such machines could be and were used to infringe plaintiffs' copyrighted television shows. *Sony* stated that if liability "is to be imposed on petitioners in this case, it must rest on the fact that *they have sold equipment with constructive knowledge of the fact that their customers may use that equipment to make unauthorized copies* of copyrighted material." *Id.* at 439 (emphasis added). The *Sony* Court declined to impute the requisite level of knowledge where the defendants made and sold equipment capable of both infringing and "substantial noninfringing uses." *Id.* at 442 (adopting a modified "staple article of commerce" doctrine from patent law). *See also Universal City Studios, Inc. v. Sony Corp.,* 480 F.Supp. 429, 459 (C.D.Cal. 1979) ("This court agrees with defendants that their knowledge was insufficient to make them contributory infringers."), *rev'd,* 659 F.2d 963 (9th Cir.1981), *rev'd,* 464 U.S. 417 (1984); Alfred C. Yen, *Internet Service Provider Liability for Subscriber Copyright Infringement, Enterprise Liability, and the First Amendment,* 88 Geo. L.J. 1833, 1874 and 1893 n.210 (2000) (suggesting that, after *Sony,* most Internet service providers lack "the requisite level of knowledge" for the imposition of contributory liability).

We are bound to follow *Sony,* and will not impute the requisite level of knowledge to Napster merely because peer-to-peer file sharing technology may be used to infringe plaintiffs' copyrights. *See* 464 U.S. at 436 (rejecting argument that merely supplying the " 'means' to accomplish an infringing activity" leads to imposition of liability). We depart from the reasoning of the district court that Napster failed to demonstrate that its system is capable of commercially significant noninfringing uses. *See Napster,* 114 F.Supp.2d at 916, 917–18. The district court improperly confined the use analysis to current uses, ignoring the system's capabilities. *See generally Sony,* 464 U.S. at 442–43 (framing inquiry as whether the video tape recorder is "*capable* of commercially significant noninfringing uses") (em-

5. The district court found actual knowledge because: (1) a document authored by Napster co-founder Sean Parker mentioned "the need to remain ignorant of users' real names and IP addresses 'since they are exchanging pirated music' "; and (2) the Recording Industry Association of America ("RIAA") informed Napster of more than 12,000 infringing files, some of which are still available. 114 F.Supp.2d at 918. The district court found constructive knowledge because: (a) Napster executives have recording industry experience; (b) they have enforced intellectual property rights in other instances; (c) Napster executives have downloaded copyrighted songs from the system; and (d) they have promoted the site with "screen shots listing infringing files." *Id.* at 919.

phasis added). Consequently, the district court placed undue weight on the proportion of current infringing use as compared to current and future noninfringing use. *See generally Vault Corp. v. Quaid Software Ltd.,* 847 F.2d 255, 264–67 (5th Cir.1988) (single noninfringing use implicated *Sony*). Nonetheless, whether we might arrive at a different result is not the issue here. *See Sports Form, Inc. v. United Press Int'l, Inc.,* 686 F.2d 750, 752 (9th Cir.1982). The instant appeal occurs at an early point in the proceedings and "the fully developed factual record may be materially different from that initially before the district court...." *Id.* at 753. Regardless of the number of Napster's infringing versus noninfringing uses, the evidentiary record here supported the district court's finding that plaintiffs would likely prevail in establishing that Napster knew or had reason to know of its users' infringement of plaintiffs' copyrights.

This analysis is similar to that of *Religious Technology Center v. Netcom On–Line Communication Services, Inc.,* which suggests that in an online context, evidence of actual knowledge of specific acts of infringement is required to hold a computer system operator liable for contributory copyright infringement. 907 F.Supp. at 1371. *Netcom* considered the potential contributory copyright liability of a computer bulletin board operator whose system supported the posting of infringing material. *Id.* at 1374. The court, in denying Netcom's motion for summary judgment of noninfringement and plaintiff's motion for judgment on the pleadings, found that a disputed issue of fact existed as to whether the operator had sufficient knowledge of infringing activity. *Id.* at 1374–75.

The court determined that for the operator to have sufficient knowledge, the copyright holder must "provide the necessary documentation to show there is likely infringement." 907 F.Supp. at 1374; *cf. Cubby, Inc. v. CompuServe, Inc.,* 776 F.Supp. 135, 141 (S.D.N.Y.1991) (recognizing that online service provider does not and cannot examine every hyperlink for potentially defamatory material). If such documentation was provided, the court reasoned that Netcom would be liable for contributory infringement because its failure to remove the material "and thereby stop an infringing copy from being distributed worldwide constitutes substantial participation" in distribution of copyrighted material. *Id.*

We agree that if a computer system operator learns of specific infringing material available on his system and fails to purge such material from the system, the operator knows of and contributes to direct infringement. *See Netcom,* 907 F.Supp. at 1374. Conversely, absent any specific information which identifies infringing activity, a computer system operator cannot be liable for contributory infringement merely because the structure of the system allows for the exchange of copyrighted material. *See Sony,* 464 U.S. at 436, 442–43. To enjoin simply because a computer network allows for infringing use would, in our opinion, violate *Sony* and potentially restrict activity unrelated to infringing use.

We nevertheless conclude that sufficient knowledge exists to impose contributory liability when linked to demonstrated infringing use of the Napster system. *See Napster,* 114 F.Supp.2d at 919 ("*Religious Technology*

Center would not mandate a determination that Napster, Inc. lacks the knowledge requisite to contributory infringement."). The record supports the district court's finding that Napster has *actual* knowledge that *specific* infringing material is available using its system, that it could block access to the system by suppliers of the infringing material, and that it failed to remove the material. *See Napster,* 114 F.Supp.2d at 918, 920–21.[6]

B. Material Contribution

Under the facts as found by the district court, Napster materially contributes to the infringing activity. Relying on *Fonovisa,* the district court concluded that "[w]ithout the support services defendant provides, Napster users could not find and download the music they want with the ease of which defendant boasts." *Napster,* 114 F.Supp.2d at 919–20 ("Napster is an integrated service designed to enable users to locate and download MP3 music files."). We agree that Napster provides "the site and facilities" for direct infringement. *See Fonovisa,* 76 F.3d at 264; *cf. Netcom,* 907 F.Supp. at 1372 ("Netcom will be liable for contributory infringement since its failure to cancel [a user's] infringing message and thereby stop an infringing copy from being distributed worldwide constitutes substantial participation."). The district court correctly applied the reasoning in *Fonovisa,* and properly found that Napster materially contributes to direct infringement.

We affirm the district court's conclusion that plaintiffs have demonstrated a likelihood of success on the merits of the contributory copyright infringement claim. * * *

* * *

NOTES & QUESTIONS

1. *Knowledge of infringement.* In *RTC v. Netcom,* the court holds that Netcom may be contributorily liable for the infringement, based on application of traditional copyright principles, if it had knowledge of the infringing activity and substantially contributed to the infringement. What will constitute the requisite knowledge? The court offers several bits of guidance on this point. First, it says that "[w]here works contain copyright notices within them, as here, it is difficult to argue that a defendant did not know that the works were copyrighted." Does presence of a copyright notice necessarily imply that the posting is infringing? The court continues: "Where a BBS operator cannot reasonably verify a claim of infringement, either because of a possible fair use defense [or] the lack of copyright notices on the copies, the operator's lack of knowledge will be found

6. As stated by the district court:

> Plaintiff[s] ... demonstrate that defendant had actual notice of direct infringement because the RIAA informed it of more than 12,000 infringing files. Although Napster, Inc. purportedly terminated the users offering these files, the songs are still available using the Napster service, as are the copyrighted works which the record company plaintiffs identified in Schedules A and B of their complaint.

114 F.Supp.2d at 918.

reasonable and there will be no liability for contributory infringement for allowing the continued distribution of the works on its system." Isn't there always "a possible fair use defense"?

2. *Infringement via linking and browsing.* Based on the reasoning in *Intellectual Reserve v. Utah Lighthouse Ministry*, does a search engine "materially contribute" to infringement, for purposes of contributory infringement analysis, when it presents a user with a link to a website containing infringing material? If so, what must the search engine's operator do to avoid liability if it receives notice of the website's infringement? Also under the reasoning of this case, does an individual engage in direct infringement when she comes across infringing material while browsing a website? If so, what must she do to avoid liability?

3. Napster *and the* Sony *criterion.* In *A & M Records v. Napster*, what is the role of *Sony's* approach to contributory liability? Under the standard set forth in *Sony*: "[T]he sale of copying equipment, like the sale of other articles of commerce, does not constitute contributory infringement if the product is widely used for legitimate, unobjectionable purposes. Indeed, it need merely be capable of substantial noninfringing uses." *Sony Corp. v. Universal City Studios, Inc.*, 464 U.S. 417, 442 (1984). Is there a distinction, for present purposes, between Napster's role with respect to its file-sharing technology, and a VCR manufacturer's role with respect to its tape-copying technology?

4. *Liability for age-verification services.* Numerous websites that offer adult-oriented materials make use of online age-verification services. When a prospective customer clicks to indicate he wishes to subscribe to such a website, he is transferred to the site of the associated age-verification service, which accepts the customer's credit card information, bills the card in its own name for a membership fee, and pays a portion of the fees to the website, keeping the rest for itself. Suppose that an adult-oriented website offers copyrighted materials without the authorization of the copyright owner. Is its age-verification service contributorily or vicariously liable for the website's infringement? *See Perfect 10, Inc. v. Cybernet Ventures, Inc.*, ___ F.Supp.2d ___, 2002 WL 731721 (C.D.Cal.2002).

5. *Filtering and contributory infringement.* If a person purchases and installs Web-filtering software to excise banner ads from the web pages that are viewed, would the filtered web pages be infringing derivative works? If so, would the software manufacturer be liable for contributory copyright infringement?

C. VICARIOUS LIABILITY FOR COPYRIGHT INFRINGEMENT

In the preceding section we saw that a person who does not directly violate one of the exclusive rights of a copyright owner may nonetheless be held liable as a contributory infringer. Another form of indirect liability, vicarious liability, may be found when a person who has the right and ability to control the activities of the primary infringer receives a direct financial benefit from the infringement.

Religious Technology Center v. Netcom On–Line Communication Services, Inc.

907 F.Supp. 1361 (N.D.Cal.1995).

■ WHYTE, DISTRICT JUDGE.

[The facts of this case are set forth in Part II(A), *supra.*]

* * *

3. Vicarious Liability

Even if plaintiffs cannot prove that Netcom is contributorily liable for its participation in the infringing activity, it may still seek to prove vicarious infringement based on Netcom's relationship to Erlich. A defendant is liable for vicarious liability for the actions of a primary infringer where the defendant (1) has the right and ability to control the infringer's acts and (2) receives a direct financial benefit from the infringement. *See Shapiro, Bernstein & Co. v. H.L. Green Co.,* 316 F.2d 304, 306 (2d Cir.1963). Unlike contributory infringement, knowledge is not an element of vicarious liability. 3 NIMMER ON COPYRIGHT § 12.04[A][1], at 12–70.

a. Right and Ability To Control

The first element of vicarious liability will be met if plaintiffs can show that Netcom has the right and ability to supervise the conduct of its subscribers. Netcom argues that it does not have the right to control its users' postings before they occur. Plaintiffs dispute this and argue that Netcom's terms and conditions, to which its subscribers[22] must agree, specify that Netcom reserves the right to take remedial action against subscribers. *See, e.g., Francis Depo.* at 124–126. Plaintiffs argue that under "netiquette," the informal rules and customs that have developed on the Internet, violation of copyrights by a user is unacceptable and the access provider has a duty [to] take measures to prevent this; where the immediate service provider fails, the next service provider up the transmission stream must act. Further evidence of Netcom's right to restrict infringing activity is its prohibition of copyright infringement and its requirement that its subscribers indemnify it for any damage to third parties. Plaintiffs have thus raised a question of fact as to Netcom's right to control Erlich's use of its services.

Netcom argues that it could not possibly screen messages before they are posted given the speed and volume of the data that goes through its system. Netcom further argues that it has never exercised control over the content of its users' postings. Plaintiffs' expert opines otherwise, stating that with an easy software modification Netcom could identify postings

22. In this case, Netcom is even further removed from Erlich's activities. Erlich was in a contractual relationship only with Klemesrud. Netcom thus dealt directly only with Klemesrud. However, it is not crucial that Erlich does not obtain access directly through Netcom. The issue is Netcom's right and ability to control the use of its system, which it can do indirectly by controlling Klemesrud's use.

that contain particular words or come from particular individuals.[31] Plaintiffs further dispute Netcom's claim that it could not limit Erlich's access to Usenet without kicking off all 500 subscribers of Klemesrud's BBS. As evidence that Netcom has in fact exercised its ability to police its users' conduct, plaintiffs cite evidence that Netcom has acted to suspend subscribers' accounts on over one thousand occasions. *See* Ex. J (listing suspensions of subscribers by Netcom for commercial advertising, posting obscene materials, and off-topic postings). Further evidence shows that Netcom can delete specific postings. Whether such sanctions occurred before or after the abusive conduct is not material to whether Netcom can exercise control. The court thus finds that plaintiffs have raised a genuine issue of fact as to whether Netcom has the right and ability to exercise control over the activities of its subscribers, and of Erlich in particular.

b. Direct Financial Benefit

Plaintiffs must further prove that Netcom receives a direct financial benefit from the infringing activities of its users. For example, a landlord who has the right and ability to supervise the tenant's activities is vicariously liable for the infringements of the tenant where the rental amount is proportional to the proceeds of the tenant's sales. *Shapiro, Bernstein,* 316 F.2d at 306. However, where a defendant rents space or services on a fixed rental fee that does not depend on the nature of the activity of the lessee, courts usually find no vicarious liability because there is no direct financial benefit from the infringement. *See, e.g., Roy Export Co. v. Trustees of Columbia University,* 344 F.Supp. 1350, 1353 (S.D.N.Y.1972) (finding no vicarious liability of university because no financial benefit from allowing screening of bootlegged films); *Fonovisa,* 847 F.Supp. at 1496 (finding swap meet operators did not financially benefit from fixed fee);[5]; *see also* Kelly Tickle, Comment, *The Vicarious Liability of Electronic Bulletin Board Operators for the Copyright Infringement Occurring on Their Bulletin Boards,* 80 IOWA L.REV. 391, 415 (1995) (arguing that BBS operators "lease cyberspace" and should thus be treated like landlords, who are not liable for infringement that occurs on their premises).

* * *

* * * Plaintiffs cannot provide any evidence of a direct financial benefit received by Netcom from Erlich's infringing postings. Unlike *Shapiro, Bernstein,* and like *Fonovisa,* Netcom receives a fixed fee. There is no evidence that infringement by Erlich, or any other user of Netcom's services, in any way enhances the value of Netcom's services to subscribers

31. However, plaintiffs submit no evidence indicating Netcom, or anyone, could design software that could determine whether a posting is infringing.

5. [The district court opinion in *Fonovisa* was reversed on appeal. The Ninth Circuit held, contrary to the district court, that the operator of a swap meet *does* receive a direct financial benefit from the participation of vendors selling bootleg music recordings, by virtue of the admission fees, concession stand sales, and parking fees they receive from the additional customers attracted by the counterfeit recordings. *Fonovisa, Inc. v. Cherry Auction, Inc.*, 76 F.3d 259 (9th Cir.1996).—Eds.]

or attracts new subscribers. Plaintiffs argue, however, that Netcom somehow derives a benefit from its purported "policy of refusing to take enforcement actions against its subscribers and others who transmit infringing messages over its computer networks." Plaintiffs point to Netcom's advertisements that, compared to competitors like CompuServe and America Online, Netcom provides easy, regulation-free Internet access. Plaintiffs assert that Netcom's policy attracts copyright infringers to its system, resulting in a direct financial benefit. The court is not convinced that such an argument, if true, would constitute a direct financial benefit to Netcom from *Erlich's* infringing activities. *See Fonovisa,* 847 F.Supp. at 1496 (finding no direct financial benefit despite argument that lessees included many vendors selling counterfeit goods and that clientele sought "bargain basement prices"). Further, plaintiffs' argument is not supported by probative evidence. The only "evidence" plaintiffs cite for their supposition is the declaration of their counsel, Elliot Abelson, who states that

> [o]n April 7, 1995, in a conversation regarding Netcom's position related to this case, Randolf Rice, attorney for Netcom, informed me that Netcom's executives are happy about the publicity it is receiving in the press as a result of this case. Mr. Rice also told me that Netcom was concerned that it would lose business if it took action against Erlich or Klemesrud in connection with Erlich's infringements.

Abelson Decl. ¶ 2. Netcom objects to this declaration as hearsay and as inadmissible evidence of statements made in compromise negotiations. Fed.R.Ev. 801, 408. Whether or not this declaration is admissible, it does not support plaintiffs' argument that Netcom either has a policy of not enforcing violations of copyright laws by its subscribers or, assuming such a policy exists, that Netcom's policy directly financially benefits Netcom, such as by attracting new subscribers. Because plaintiffs have failed to raise a question of fact on this vital element, their claim of vicarious liability fails.
* * *

[For similar reasons, the court also finds that the plaintiffs have failed to raise a genuine issue of material fact on their claim of vicarious infringement against the BBS operator, Klemesrud.]

* * *

A & M Records, Inc. v. Napster, Inc.

239 F.3d 1004 (9th Cir.2001).

■ BEEZER, CIRCUIT JUDGE:

[For the facts of the case and the court's finding of direct infringement by the users of the Napster service, see Part II(B), *supra*.]

V

We turn to the question whether Napster engages in vicarious copyright infringement. Vicarious copyright liability is an "outgrowth" of respondeat superior. *Fonovisa,* 76 F.3d at 262. In the context of copyright law, vicarious liability extends beyond an employer/employee relationship to cases in which a defendant "has the right and ability to supervise the infringing activity and also has a direct financial interest in such activities." *Id.* (quoting *Gershwin,* 443 F.2d at 1162); *see also Polygram Int'l Publ'g, Inc. v. Nevada/TIG, Inc.,* 855 F.Supp. 1314, 1325–26 (D.Mass.1994) (describing vicarious liability as a form of risk allocation).

Before moving into this discussion, we note that *Sony*'s "staple article of commerce" analysis has no application to Napster's potential liability for vicarious copyright infringement. *See Sony,* 464 U.S. at 434–435; *see generally* 3 Melville B. Nimmer & David Nimmer, *Nimmer On Copyright* §§ 12.04[A][2] and [A][2][b] (2000) (confining *Sony* to contributory infringement analysis: "Contributory infringement itself is of two types—personal conduct that forms part of or furthers the infringement and contribution of machinery or goods that provide the means to infringe"). The issues of Sony's liability under the "doctrines of 'direct infringement' and 'vicarious liability' " were not before the Supreme Court, although the Court recognized that the "lines between direct infringement, contributory infringement, and vicarious liability are not clearly drawn." *Id.* at 435 n. 17. Consequently, when the *Sony* Court used the term "vicarious liability," it did so broadly and outside of a technical analysis of the doctrine of vicarious copyright infringement. *Id.* at 435 ("[V]icarious liability is imposed in virtually all areas of the law, and the concept of contributory infringement is merely a species of the broader problem of identifying the circumstances in which it is just to hold one individual accountable for the actions of another."); *see also Black's Law Dictionary* 927 (7th ed. 1999) (defining "vicarious liability" in a manner similar to the definition used in *Sony*).

A. *Financial Benefit*

The district court determined that plaintiffs had demonstrated they would likely succeed in establishing that Napster has a direct financial interest in the infringing activity. *Napster,* 114 F.Supp.2d at 921–22. We agree. Financial benefit exists where the availability of infringing material "acts as a 'draw' for customers." *Fonovisa,* 76 F.3d at 263–64 (stating that financial benefit may be shown "where infringing performances enhance the attractiveness of a venue"). Ample evidence supports the district court's finding that Napster's future revenue is directly dependent upon "increases in userbase." More users register with the Napster system as the "quality and quantity of available music increases." 114 F.Supp.2d at 902. We conclude that the district court did not err in determining that Napster financially benefits from the availability of protected works on its system.

B. *Supervision*

The district court determined that Napster has the right and ability to supervise its users' conduct. *Napster,* 114 F.Supp.2d at 920–21 (finding that Napster's representations to the court regarding "its improved methods of blocking users about whom rights holders complain ... is tantamount to an admission that defendant can, and sometimes does, police its service"). We agree in part.

The ability to block infringers' access to a particular environment for any reason whatsoever is evidence of the right and ability to supervise. *See Fonovisa,* 76 F.3d at 262 ("Cherry Auction had the right to terminate vendors for any reason whatsoever and through that right had the ability to control the activities of vendors on the premises."); *cf. Netcom,* 907 F.Supp. at 1375–76 (indicating that plaintiff raised a genuine issue of fact regarding ability to supervise by presenting evidence that an electronic bulletin board service can suspend subscriber's accounts). Here, plaintiffs have demonstrated that Napster retains the right to control access to its system. Napster has an express reservation of rights policy, stating on its website that it expressly reserves the "right to refuse service and terminate accounts in [its] discretion, including, but not limited to, if Napster believes that user conduct violates applicable law ... or for any reason in Napster's sole discretion, with or without cause."

To escape imposition of vicarious liability, the reserved right to police must be exercised to its fullest extent. Turning a blind eye to detectable acts of infringement for the sake of profit gives rise to liability. *See, e.g., Fonovisa,* 76 F.3d at 261 ("There is no dispute for the purposes of this appeal that Cherry Auction and its operators were aware that vendors in their swap meets were selling counterfeit recordings."); *see also Gershwin,* 443 F.2d at 1161–62 (citing *Shapiro, Bernstein & Co. v. H.L. Green Co.,* 316 F.2d 304 (2d Cir.1963), for the proposition that "failure to police the conduct of the primary infringer" leads to imposition of vicarious liability for copyright infringement).

The district court correctly determined that Napster had the right and ability to police its system and failed to exercise that right to prevent the exchange of copyrighted material. The district court, however, failed to recognize that the boundaries of the premises that Napster "controls and patrols" are limited. *See, e.g., Fonovisa,* 76 F.3d at 262–63 (in addition to having the right to exclude vendors, defendant "controlled and patrolled" the premises); *see also Polygram,* 855 F.Supp. at 1328–29 (in addition to having the contractual right to remove exhibitors, trade show operator reserved the right to police during the show and had its "employees walk the aisles to ensure 'rules compliance' "). Put differently, Napster's reserved "right and ability" to police is cabined by the system's current architecture. As shown by the record, the Napster system does not "read" the content of indexed files, other than to check that they are in the proper MP3 format.

Napster, however, has the ability to locate infringing material listed on its search indices, and the right to terminate users' access to the system. The file name indices, therefore, are within the "premises" that Napster has the ability to police. We recognize that the files are user-named and may not match copyrighted material exactly (for example, the artist or song could be spelled wrong). For Napster to function effectively, however, file names must reasonably or roughly correspond to the material contained in the files, otherwise no user could ever locate any desired music. As a practical matter, Napster, its users and the record company plaintiffs have equal access to infringing material by employing Napster's "search function."

Our review of the record requires us to accept the district court's conclusion that plaintiffs have demonstrated a likelihood of success on the merits of the vicarious copyright infringement claim. Napster's failure to police the system's "premises," combined with a showing that Napster financially benefits from the continuing availability of infringing files on its system, leads to the imposition of vicarious liability. * * *

* * *

NOTES & QUESTIONS

1. *Vicarious liability of corporate officers and employees.* In *Playboy Enterprises, Inc. v. Webbworld, Inc.*, 991 F.Supp. 543 (N.D.Tex.1997), *aff'd mem.*, 168 F.3d 486 (5th Cir.1999), the court held that defendant Webbworld, Inc. directly infringed the copyrights of plaintiff Playboy Enterprises, Inc. by posting Playboy's pictures on its website. The court then addressed the liability of the three individuals who acted as the corporation's principals, one of whom was the corporation's president and sole shareholder. In doing so, it applied the test for vicarious copyright liability: "To show vicarious liability, a plaintiff must prove that a defendant (1) has a direct financial interest in the infringing activity, and (2) has the right and ability to supervise the activity which causes the infringement." *Id.* at 553. The court concluded that all three of the individuals had a direct financial interest in the infringement, as they split the profits from the website's operations. It found that two of the three additionally had the requisite ability to supervise, and therefore held them, but not the third individual, liable as vicarious infringers. Did the court apply the correct test for liability of the individuals? Should it instead, or additionally, have determined whether they were liable as *direct* infringers, either because they themselves performed the actions constituting infringement, or through "piercing the corporate veil"?

2. *Vicarious liability of venture capitalists?* Venture capital firms collect money from investors and invest the money in start-up firms they think are likely to succeed. Of course, the venture capitalists (VCs) only make money if their start-ups succeed and their investors make money, rendering them willing to invest in other ventures sponsored by the VC firm. Thus, in order to keep control of a start-up's business model and operations during the crucial launch period, VCs often condition funding of a start-up on placement of a member of their firm as interim CEO of the company. For example, at the time the record companies launched their lawsuit against Napster for copyright infringement, its CEO was a member of a VC firm. If Napster is contributorily liable for its users' infringements, is the VC firm vicariously liable?

III. DEFENSES TO COPYRIGHT INFRINGEMENT

In this Part, we consider the use of four defenses to copyright infringement online: the doctrine of fair use, the first-sale doctrine,[6] the defense of copyright misuse, and the right, established by the Audio Home Recording Act, to make copies of musical sound recordings for noncommercial purposes. These defenses play an important role in marking out the shifting line of demarcation between the uses of works that are under the control of the copyright owner, and the uses that are open to competitors and the public.

A. FAIR USE ONLINE

As noted above, the law of copyright strives to accommodate two competing goals: offering sufficient incentives to motivate the creation of original works of authorship, while allowing the public access to and use of these works. One method the Copyright Act employs to maintain this balance is by granting the public the right to fair use of copyrighted materials.

Fair use is an affirmative defense that a defendant in a lawsuit for copyright infringement may raise. Fair use includes uses for such purposes as "criticism, comment, news reporting, teaching (including multiple copies for classroom use), scholarship, or research." 17 U.S.C. § 107. If a use is fair, then it "is not an infringement of copyright." *Id.* To determine whether a particular use is fair, courts evaluate it using four factors set forth in section 107.

UMG Recordings, Inc. v. MP3.com, Inc.

92 F.Supp.2d 349 (S.D.N.Y.2000).

■ RAKOFF, DISTRICT JUDGE.

The complex marvels of cyberspatial communication may create difficult legal issues; but not in this case. Defendant's infringement of plaintiffs' copyrights is clear. Accordingly, on April 28, 2000, the Court granted defendant's motion for partial summary judgment holding defendant liable for copyright infringement. This opinion will state the reasons why.

The pertinent facts, either undisputed or, where disputed, taken most favorably to defendant, are as follows:

6. In the European Union member states, and in some other countries, the doctrine that limits the extent of control by both copyright and patent holders after their products leave their hands goes by the name of "exhaustion." Thus the U.S. first-sale doctrine in copyright law is subsumed under the general concept of exhaustion in many other jurisdictions.

The technology known as "MP3" permits rapid and efficient conversion of compact disc recordings ("CDs") to computer files easily accessed over the Internet. *See generally Recording Industry Ass'n of America v. Diamond Multimedia Systems Inc.,* 180 F.3d 1072, 1073–74 (9th Cir.1999). Utilizing this technology, defendant MP3.com, on or around January 12, 2000, launched its "My.MP3.com" service, which is advertised as permitting subscribers to store, customize and listen to the recordings contained on their CDs from any place where they have an Internet connection. To make good on this offer, defendant purchased tens of thousands of popular CDs in which plaintiffs held the copyrights, and, without authorization, copied their recordings onto its computer servers so as to be able to replay the recordings for its subscribers.

Specifically, in order to first access such a recording, a subscriber to MP3.com must either "prove" that he already owns the CD version of the recording by inserting his copy of the commercial CD into his computer CD–Rom drive for a few seconds (the "Beam-it Service") or must purchase the CD from one of defendant's cooperating online retailers (the "instant Listening Service"). Thereafter, however, the subscriber can access via the Internet from a computer anywhere in the world the copy of plaintiffs' recording made by defendant. Thus, although defendant seeks to portray its service as the "functional equivalent" of storing its subscribers' CDs, in actuality defendant is re-playing for the subscribers converted versions of the recordings it copied, without authorization, from plaintiffs' copyrighted CDs. On its face, this makes out a presumptive case of infringement under the Copyright Act of 1976 ("Copyright Act"), 17 U.S.C. § 101 *et seq. See, e.g., Castle Rock Entertainment, Inc. v. Carol Publishing Group, Inc.,* 150 F.3d 132, 137 (2d Cir.1998); *Hasbro Bradley, Inc. v. Sparkle Toys, Inc.,* 780 F.2d 189, 192 (2d Cir.1985).[1]

Defendant argues, however, that such copying is protected by the affirmative defense of "fair use." *See* 17 U.S.C. § 107. In analyzing such a defense, the Copyright Act specifies four factors that must be considered: "(1) the purpose and character of the use, including whether such use is of a commercial nature or is for nonprofit educational purposes; (2) the nature of the copyrighted work; (3) the amount and substantiality of the portion used in relation to the copyrighted work as a whole; and (4) the effect of the use upon the potential market for or value of the copyrighted work." *Id.* Other relevant factors may also be considered, since fair use is an "equitable rule of reason" to be applied in light of the overall purposes

1. Defendant's only challenge to plaintiffs' *prima facie* case of infringement is the suggestion, buried in a footnote in its opposition papers, that its music computer files are not in fact "reproductions" of plaintiffs' copyrighted works within the meaning of the Copyright Act. *See, e.g.,* 17 U.S.C. § 114(b). Specifically, defendant claims that the simulated sounds on MP3–based music files are not physically identical to the sounds on the original CD recordings. Defendant concedes, however, that the human ear cannot detect a difference between the two. *Id.* Moreover, defendant admits that a goal of its copying is to create a music file that is sonically as identical to the original CD as possible. In such circumstances, some slight, humanly undetectable difference between the original and the copy does not qualify for exclusion from the coverage of the Act.

of the Copyright Act. *Sony Corporation of America v. Universal City Studios, Inc.,* 464 U.S. 417, 448, 454 (1984); *see Harper & Row, Publishers, Inc. v. Nation Enterprises,* 471 U.S. 539, 549 (1985).

Regarding the first factor—"the purpose and character of the use"—defendant does not dispute that its purpose is commercial, for while subscribers to My.MP3.com are not currently charged a fee, defendant seeks to attract a sufficiently large subscription base to draw advertising and otherwise make a profit. Consideration of the first factor, however, also involves inquiring into whether the new use essentially repeats the old or whether, instead, it "transforms" it by infusing it with new meaning, new understandings, or the like. *See, e.g., Campbell v. Acuff-Rose Music, Inc.,* 510 U.S. 569, 579 (1994); *Castle Rock,* 150 F.3d at 142; *See also* Pierre N. Leval, "Toward a Fair Use Standard," 103 *Harv.L.Rev.* 1105, 111 (1990). Here, although defendant recites that My.MP3.com provides a transformative "space shift" by which subscribers can enjoy the sound recordings contained on their CDs without lugging around the physical discs themselves, this is simply another way of saying that the unauthorized copies are being retransmitted in another medium—an insufficient basis for any legitimate claim of transformation, *See, e.g., Infinity Broadcast Corp. v. Kirkwood,* 150 F.3d 104, 108 (2d Cir.1998) (rejecting the fair use defense by operator of a service that retransmitted copyrighted radio broadcasts over telephone lines); *Los Angeles News Serv. v. Reuters Television Int'l Ltd.,* 149 F.3d 987 (9th Cir.1998) (rejecting the fair use defense where television news agencies copied copyrighted news footage and retransmitted it to news organizations), *cert. denied,* 525 U.S. 1141 (1999); *see also American Geophysical Union v. Texaco Inc.,* 60 F.3d 913, 923 (2d Cir.), *cert. dismissed,* 516 U.S. 1005 (1995).

Here, defendant adds no "new aesthetics, new insights and understandings" to the original music recordings it copies, *see Castle Rock,* 150 F.3d at 142 (internal quotation marks omitted), but simply repackages those recordings to facilitate their transmission through another medium. While such services may be innovative, they are not transformative.[2]

Regarding the second factor—"the nature of the copyrighted work"—the creative recordings here being copied are "close[ ] to the core of intended copyright protection," *Campbell,* 510 U.S. at 586, and, conversely, far removed from the more factual or descriptive work more amenable to "fair use," *see Nihon Keizai Shimbun, Inc. v. Comline Business Data, Inc.,* 166 F.3d 65, 72–73 (2d Cir.1999); *see also Castle Rock,* 150 F.3d at 143–44.

Regarding the third factor—"the amount and substantiality of the portion [of the copyrighted work] used [by the copier] in relation to the

2. Defendant's reliance on the Ninth Circuit's "reverse engineering" cases, *see Sony Computer Entertainment, Inc. v. Connectix Corp.,* 203 F.3d 596 (9th Cir.2000); *Sega Enterprises Ltd. v. Accolade, Inc.,* 977 F.2d 1510, 1527 (9th Cir.1992), is misplaced, because, among other relevant distinctions, those cases involved the copying of software in order to develop a new product, whereas here defendant copied CDs onto its servers not to create any new form of expression but rather to retransmit the same expression in a different medium.

copyrighted work as a whole''—it is undisputed that defendant copies, and replays, the entirety of the copyrighted works here in issue, thus again negating any claim of fair use.

Regarding the fourth factor—''the effect of the use upon the potential market for or value of the copyrighted work''—defendant's activities on their face invade plaintiffs' statutory right to license their copyrighted sound recordings to others for reproduction. *See* 17 U.S.C. § 106. Defendant, however, argues that, so far as the derivative market here involved is concerned, plaintiffs have not shown that such licensing is ''traditional, reasonable, or likely to be developed.'' *American Geophysical,* 60 F.3d at 930 and n. 17. Moreover, defendant argues, its activities can only enhance plaintiffs' sales, since subscribers cannot gain access to particular recordings made available by MP3.com unless they have already ''purchased'' (actually or purportedly), or agreed to purchase, their own CD copies of those recordings.

Such arguments—though dressed in the garb of an expert's ''opinion'' (that, on inspection, consists almost entirely of speculative and conclusory statements)—are unpersuasive. Any allegedly positive impact of defendant's activities on plaintiffs' prior market in no way frees defendant to usurp a further market that directly derives from reproduction of the plaintiffs' copyrighted works. *See Infinity Broadcast,* 150 F.3d at 111. This would be so even if the copyrightholder had not yet entered the new market in issue, for a copyrighterholder's ''exclusive'' rights, derived from the Constitution and the Copyright Act, include the right, within broad limits, to curb the development of such a derivative market by refusing to license a copyrighted work or by doing so only on terms the copyright owner finds acceptable. *See Castle Rock,* 150 F.3d at 145–46; *Salinger v. Random House, Inc.,* 811 F.2d 90, 99 (2d Cir.), *cert. denied,* 484 U.S. 890 (1987). Here, moreover, plaintiffs have adduced substantial evidence that they have in fact taken steps to enter that market by entering into various licensing agreements.

Finally, regarding defendant's purported reliance on other factors, *see Campbell,* 510 U.S. at 577, this essentially reduces to the claim that My.MP3.com provides a useful service to consumers that, in its absence, will be served by ''pirates.'' Copyright, however, is not designed to afford consumer protection or convenience but, rather, to protect the copyrightholders' property interests. Moreover, as a practical matter, plaintiffs have indicated no objection in principle to licensing their recordings to companies like MP3.com; they simply want to make sure they get the remuneration the law reserves for them as holders of copyrights on creative works. Stripped to its essence, defendant's ''consumer protection'' argument amounts to nothing more than a bald claim that defendant should be able to misappropriate plaintiffs' property simply because there is a consumer demand for it. This hardly appeals to the conscience of equity.

In sum, on any view, defendant's ''fair use'' defense is indefensible and must be denied as a matter of law. * * *

Accordingly, the Court, for the foregoing reasons, has determined that plaintiffs are entitled to partial summary judgment holding defendant to have infringed plaintiffs' copyrights.

* * *

A & M Records, Inc. v. Napster, Inc.

239 F.3d 1004 (9th Cir.2001).

■ Beezer, Circuit Judge:

[For the facts of the case and the court's finding of direct infringement by the users of the Napster service, see Part II(B), *supra*.]

* * *

B. Fair Use

Napster contends that its users do not directly infringe plaintiffs' copyrights because the users are engaged in fair use of the material. *See* 17 U.S.C. § 107 ("[T]he fair use of a copyrighted work ... is not an infringement of copyright."). Napster identifies three specific alleged fair uses: sampling, where users make temporary copies of a work before purchasing; space-shifting, where users access a sound recording through the Napster system that they already own in audio CD format; and permissive distribution of recordings by both new and established artists.

The district court considered factors listed in 17 U.S.C. § 107, which guide a court's fair use determination. These factors are: (1) the purpose and character of the use; (2) the nature of the copyrighted work; (3) the "amount and substantiality of the portion used" in relation to the work as a whole; and (4) the effect of the use upon the potential market for the work or the value of the work. *See* 17 U.S.C. § 107. The district court first conducted a general analysis of Napster system uses under § 107, and then applied its reasoning to the alleged fair uses identified by Napster. The district court concluded that Napster users are not fair users. We agree. * * *

1. Purpose and Character of the Use

This factor focuses on whether the new work merely replaces the object of the original creation or instead adds a further purpose or different character. In other words, this factor asks "whether and to what extent the new work is 'transformative.'" *See Campbell v. Acuff–Rose Music, Inc.*, 510 U.S. 569, 579 (1994).

The district court first concluded that downloading MP3 files does not transform the copyrighted work. *Napster*, 114 F.Supp.2d at 912. This conclusion is supportable. Courts have been reluctant to find fair use when an original work is merely retransmitted in a different medium. *See, e.g., Infinity Broadcast Corp. v. Kirkwood*, 150 F.3d 104, 108 (2d Cir.1998) (concluding that retransmission of radio broadcast over telephone lines is not transformative); *UMG Recordings, Inc. v. MP3.Com, Inc.*, 92 F.Supp.2d

349, 351 (S.D.N.Y.) (finding that reproduction of audio CD into MP3 format does not "transform" the work), *certification denied,* 2000 WL 710056 (S.D.N.Y. June 1, 2000) ("Defendant's copyright infringement was clear, and the mere fact that it was clothed in the exotic webbing of the Internet does not disguise its illegality.").

This "purpose and character" element also requires the district court to determine whether the allegedly infringing use is commercial or noncommercial. *See Campbell,* 510 U.S. at 584–85. A commercial use weighs against a finding of fair use but is not conclusive on the issue. *Id.* The district court determined that Napster users engage in commercial use of the copyrighted materials largely because (1) "a host user sending a file cannot be said to engage in a personal use when distributing that file to an anonymous requester" and (2) "Napster users get for free something they would ordinarily have to buy." *Napster,* 114 F.Supp.2d at 912. The district court's findings are not clearly erroneous.

Direct economic benefit is not required to demonstrate a commercial use. Rather, repeated and exploitative copying of copyrighted works, even if the copies are not offered for sale, may constitute a commercial use. *See Worldwide Church of God v. Philadelphia Church of God,* 227 F.3d 1110, 1118 (9th Cir.2000) (stating that church that copied religious text for its members "unquestionably profit[ed]" from the unauthorized "distribution and use of [the text] without having to account to the copyright holder"); *American Geophysical Union v. Texaco, Inc.,* 60 F.3d 913, 922 (2d Cir.1994) (finding that researchers at for-profit laboratory gained indirect economic advantage by photocopying copyrighted scholarly articles). In the record before us, commercial use is demonstrated by a showing that repeated and exploitative unauthorized copies of copyrighted works were made to save the expense of purchasing authorized copies. *See Worldwide Church,* 227 F.3d at 1117–18; *Sega Enters. Ltd. v. MAPHIA,* 857 F.Supp. 679, 687 (N.D.Cal.1994) (finding commercial use when individuals downloaded copies of video games "to avoid having to buy video game cartridges"); *see also American Geophysical,* 60 F.3d at 922. Plaintiffs made such a showing before the district court.[4]

We also note that the definition of a financially motivated transaction for the purposes of criminal copyright actions includes trading infringing copies of a work for other items, "including the receipt of other copyrighted works." *See* No Electronic Theft Act ("NET Act"), *Pub.L. No. 105–147,* 18 U.S.C. § 101 (defining "Financial Gain").

2. *The Nature of the Use*

Works that are creative in nature are "closer to the core of intended copyright protection" than are more fact-based works. *See Campbell,* 510 U.S. at 586. The district court determined that plaintiffs' "copyrighted

4. Napster counters that even if certain users engage in commercial use by downloading instead of purchasing the music, space-shifting and sampling are nevertheless *non-commercial* in nature. We address this contention in our discussion of these specific uses, *infra.*

musical compositions and sound recordings are creative in nature ... which cuts against a finding of fair use under the second factor." *Napster,* 114 F.Supp.2d at 913. We find no error in the district court's conclusion.

3. *The Portion Used*

"While 'wholesale copying does not preclude fair use per se,' copying an entire work 'militates against a finding of fair use.'" *Worldwide Church,* 227 F.3d at 1118 (quoting *Hustler Magazine, Inc. v. Moral Majority, Inc.,* 796 F.2d 1148, 1155 (9th Cir.1986)). The district court determined that Napster users engage in "wholesale copying" of copyrighted work because file transfer necessarily "involves copying the entirety of the copyrighted work." *Napster,* 114 F.Supp.2d at 913. We agree. We note, however, that under certain circumstances, a court will conclude that a use is fair even when the protected work is copied in its entirety. *See, e.g., Sony Corp. v. Universal City Studios, Inc.,* 464 U.S. 417, 449–50 (1984) (acknowledging that fair use of time-shifting necessarily involved making a full copy of a protected work).

4. *Effect of Use on Market*

"Fair use, when properly applied, is limited to copying by others which does not materially impair the marketability of the work which is copied." *Harper & Row Publishers, Inc. v. Nation Enters.,* 471 U.S. 539, 566–67 (1985). "[T]he importance of this [fourth] factor will vary, not only with the amount of harm, but also with the relative strength of the showing on the other factors." *Campbell,* 510 U.S. at 591 n. 21. The proof required to demonstrate present or future market harm varies with the purpose and character of the use:

> A challenge to a noncommercial use of a copyrighted work requires proof either that the particular use is harmful, or that if it should become widespread, it would adversely affect the potential market for the copyrighted work.... *If the intended use is for commercial gain, that likelihood [of market harm] may be presumed. But if it is for a noncommercial purpose, the likelihood must be demonstrated.*

Sony, 464 U.S. at 451 (emphases added).

Addressing this factor, the district court concluded that Napster harms the market in "at least" two ways: it reduces audio CD sales among college students and it "raises barriers to plaintiffs' entry into the market for the digital downloading of music." *Napster,* 114 F.Supp.2d at 913. The district court relied on evidence plaintiffs submitted to show that Napster use harms the market for their copyrighted musical compositions and sound recordings. In a separate memorandum and order regarding the parties' objections to the expert reports, the district court examined each report, finding some more appropriate and probative than others. *A & M Records, Inc. v. Napster, Inc.,* 2000 WL 1170106 (N.D.Cal. August 10, 2000). Notably, plaintiffs' expert, Dr. E. Deborah Jay, conducted a survey (the "Jay Report") using a random sample of college and university students to track their reasons for using Napster and the impact Napster had on their music purchases. *Id.* at *2. The court recognized that the Jay Report focused on just one segment of the Napster user population and found "evidence of lost sales attributable to college use to be probative of irreparable harm for purposes of the preliminary injunction motion." *Id.* at *3.

Plaintiffs also offered a study conducted by Michael Fine, Chief Executive Officer of Soundscan, (the "Fine Report") to determine the effect of online sharing of MP3 files in order to show irreparable harm. Fine found that online file sharing had resulted in a loss of "album" sales within college markets. After reviewing defendant's objections to the Fine Report and expressing some concerns regarding the methodology and findings, the district court refused to exclude the Fine Report insofar as plaintiffs offered it to show irreparable harm. *Id.* at *6.

Plaintiffs' expert Dr. David J. Teece studied several issues ("Teece Report"), including whether plaintiffs had suffered or were likely to suffer harm in their existing and planned businesses due to Napster use. *Id.* Napster objected that the report had not undergone peer review. The district court noted that such reports generally are not subject to such scrutiny and overruled defendant's objections. *Id.*

As for defendant's experts, plaintiffs objected to the report of Dr. Peter S. Fader, in which the expert concluded that Napster is *beneficial* to the music industry because MP3 music file-sharing stimulates more audio CD sales than it displaces. *Id.* at *7. The district court found problems in Dr. Fader's minimal role in overseeing the administration of the survey and the lack of objective data in his report. The court decided the generality of the report rendered it "of dubious reliability and value." The court did not exclude the report, however, but chose "not to rely on Fader's findings in determining the issues of fair use and irreparable harm." *Id.* at *8.

The district court cited both the Jay and Fine Reports in support of its finding that Napster use harms the market for plaintiffs' copyrighted musical compositions and sound recordings by reducing CD sales among college students. The district court cited the Teece Report to show the harm Napster use caused in raising barriers to plaintiffs' entry into the market for digital downloading of music. *Napster,* 114 F.Supp.2d at 910. The district court's careful consideration of defendant's objections to these reports and decision to rely on the reports for specific issues demonstrates a proper exercise of discretion in addition to a correct application of the fair use doctrine. Defendant has failed to show any basis for disturbing the district court's findings.

We, therefore, conclude that the district court made sound findings related to Napster's deleterious effect on the present and future digital download market. Moreover, lack of harm to an established market cannot deprive the copyright holder of the right to develop alternative markets for the works. *See L.A. Times v. Free Republic,* 54 U.S.P.Q.2d 1453, 1469–71 (C.D.Cal.2000) (stating that online market for plaintiff newspapers' articles was harmed because plaintiffs demonstrated that "[defendants] are attempting to exploit the market for viewing their articles online"); *see also UMG Recordings,* 92 F.Supp.2d at 352 ("Any allegedly positive impact of defendant's activities on plaintiffs' prior market in no way frees defendant to usurp a further market that directly derives from reproduction of the plaintiffs' copyrighted works."). Here, similar to *L.A. Times* and *UMG Recordings,* the record supports the district court's finding that the "record company plaintiffs have already expended considerable funds and effort to commence Internet sales and licensing for digital downloads." 114 F.Supp.2d at 915. Having digital downloads available for free on the Napster system necessarily harms the copyright holders' attempts to charge for the same downloads.

Judge Patel did not abuse her discretion in reaching the above fair use conclusions, nor were the findings of fact with respect to fair use considerations clearly erroneous. We next address Napster's identified uses of sampling and space-shifting.

5. *Identified Uses*

Napster maintains that its identified uses of sampling and space-shifting were wrongly excluded as fair uses by the district court.

a. Sampling

Napster contends that its users download MP3 files to "sample" the music in order to decide whether to purchase the recording. Napster argues that the district court: (1) erred in concluding that sampling is a commercial use because it conflated a noncommercial use with a personal use; (2) erred in determining that sampling adversely affects the market for plaintiffs' copyrighted music, a requirement if the use is noncommercial; and (3) erroneously concluded that sampling is not a fair use because it determined that samplers may also engage in other infringing activity.

The district court determined that sampling remains a commercial use even if some users eventually purchase the music. We find no error in the district court's determination. Plaintiffs have established that they are likely to succeed in proving that even authorized temporary downloading of individual songs for sampling purposes is commercial in nature. *See Napster,* 114 F.Supp.2d at 913. The record supports a finding that free promotional downloads are highly regulated by the record company plaintiffs and that the companies collect royalties for song samples available on retail Internet sites. *Id.* Evidence relied on by the district court demonstrates that the free downloads provided by the record companies consist of thirty-to-sixty second samples or are full songs programmed to "time out," that is, exist only for a short time on the downloader's computer. *Id.* at 913–14. In comparison, Napster users download a full, free and permanent copy of the recording. *Id.* at 914–15. The determination by the district court as to the commercial purpose and character of sampling is not clearly erroneous.

The district court further found that both the market for audio CDs and market for online distribution are adversely affected by Napster's service. As stated in our discussion of the district court's general fair use analysis: the court did not abuse its discretion when it found that, overall,

Napster has an adverse impact on the audio CD and digital download markets. Contrary to Napster's assertion that the district court failed to specifically address the market impact of sampling, the district court determined that "[e]ven if the type of sampling supposedly done on Napster were a non-commercial use, plaintiffs have demonstrated a substantial likelihood that it would adversely affect the potential market for their copyrighted works if it became widespread." *Napster,* 114 F.Supp.2d at 914. The record supports the district court's preliminary determinations that: (1) the more music that sampling users download, the less likely they are to eventually purchase the recordings on audio CD; and (2) even if the audio CD market is not harmed, Napster has adverse effects on the developing digital download market.

Napster further argues that the district court erred in rejecting its evidence that the users' downloading of "samples" increases or tends to increase audio CD sales. The district court, however, correctly noted that "any potential enhancement of plaintiffs' sales ... would not tip the fair use analysis conclusively in favor of defendant." *Id.* at 914. We agree that increased sales of copyrighted material attributable to unauthorized use should not deprive the copyright holder of the right to license the material. *See Campbell,* 510 U.S. at 591 n. 21 ("Even favorable evidence, without more, is no guarantee of fairness. Judge Leval gives the example of the film producer's appropriation of a composer's previously unknown song that turns the song into a commercial success; the boon to the song does not make the film's simple copying fair."); *see also L.A. Times,* 54 U.S.P.Q.2d at 1471–72. Nor does positive impact in one market, here the audio CD market, deprive the copyright holder of the right to develop identified alternative markets, here the digital download market. *See id.* at 1469–71.

We find no error in the district court's factual findings or abuse of discretion in the court's conclusion that plaintiffs will likely prevail in establishing that sampling does not constitute a fair use.

b. Space–Shifting

Napster also maintains that space-shifting is a fair use. Space-shifting occurs when a Napster user downloads MP3 music files in order to listen to music he already owns on audio CD. *See id.* at 915–16. Napster asserts that we have already held that space-shifting of musical compositions and sound recordings is a fair use. *See Recording Indus. Ass'n of Am. v. Diamond Multimedia Sys., Inc.,* 180 F.3d 1072, 1079 (9th Cir.1999) ("Rio [a portable MP3 player] merely makes copies in order to render portable, or 'space-shift,' those files that already reside on a user's hard drive.... Such copying is a paradigmatic noncommercial personal use."). *See also generally Sony,* 464 U.S. at 423 (holding that "time-shifting," where a video tape recorder owner records a television show for later viewing, is a fair use).

We conclude that the district court did not err when it refused to apply the "shifting" analyses of *Sony* and *Diamond.* Both *Diamond* and *Sony* are inapposite because the methods of shifting in these cases did not also simultaneously involve distribution of the copyrighted material to the general public; the time or space-shifting of copyrighted material exposed the material only to the original user. In *Diamond,* for example, the copyrighted music was transferred from the user's computer hard drive to the user's portable MP3 player. So too *Sony,* where "the majority of VCR purchasers ... did not distribute taped television broadcasts, but merely enjoyed them at home." *Napster,* 114 F.Supp.2d at 913. Conversely, it is obvious that once a user lists a copy of music he already owns on the Napster system in order to access the music from another location, the song becomes "available to millions of other individuals," not just the original CD owner. *See UMG Recordings,* 92 F.Supp.2d at 351–52 (finding space-shifting of MP3 files not a fair use even when previous ownership is demonstrated before a download is allowed); *cf. Religious Tech. Ctr. v. Lerma,* 1996 WL 633131, at *6 (E.D.Va. Oct.4, 1996) (suggesting that storing copyrighted material on computer disk for later review is not a fair use).

c. *Other Uses*

Permissive reproduction by either independent or established artists is the final fair use claim made by Napster. The district court noted that plaintiffs did not seek to enjoin this and any other noninfringing use of the Napster system, including: chat rooms, message boards and Napster's New Artist Program. *Napster,* 114 F.Supp.2d at 917. Plaintiffs do not challenge these uses on appeal.

We find no error in the district court's determination that plaintiffs will likely succeed in establishing that Napster users do not have a fair use defense. * * *

* * *

Kelly v. Arriba Soft Corporation

280 F.3d 934 (9th Cir.2002).

■ Nelson, Circuit Judge.

[The facts of this case are set forth in Part II(A), *supra.*]

* * *

II.

* * *

A.

An owner of a copyright has the exclusive right to reproduce, distribute, and publicly display copies of the work. To establish a claim of copyright infringement by reproduction, the plaintiff must show ownership of the copyright and copying by the defendant. As to the thumbnails, there is no dispute that Kelly owned the copyright to the images and that Arriba copied those images. Therefore, Kelly established a prima facie case of copyright infringement.

A claim of copyright infringement is subject to certain statutory exceptions, including the fair use exception. This exception "permits courts to avoid rigid application of the copyright statute when, on occasion, it would stifle the very creativity which that law is designed to foster."[9] The statute sets out four factors to consider in determining whether the use in a particular case is a fair use. We must balance these factors, in light of the objectives of copyright law, rather than view them as definitive or determinative tests. We now turn to the four fair use factors.

1. Purpose and character of the use.

The Supreme Court has rejected the proposition that a commercial use of the copyrighted material ends the inquiry under this factor.[12] Instead,

> [t]he central purpose of this investigation is to see ... whether the new work merely supersede[s] the objects of the original creation, or instead adds something new, with a further purpose or different character, altering the first with new expression, meaning, or message; it asks, in other words, whether and to what extent the new work is transformative.[13]

The more transformative the new work, the less important the other factors, including commercialism, become.

There is no dispute that Arriba operates its web site for commercial purposes and that Kelly's images were part of Arriba's search engine database. As the district court found, while such use of Kelly's images was commercial, it was more incidental and less exploitative in nature than more traditional types of commercial use. Arriba was neither using Kelly's images to directly promote its web site nor trying to profit by selling Kelly's images. Instead, Kelly's images were among thousands of images in Arriba's search engine database. Because the use of Kelly's images was not highly exploitative, the commercial nature of the use only slightly weighs against a finding of fair use.

The second part of the inquiry as to this factor involves the transformative nature of the use. We must determine if Arriba's use of the images merely superseded the object of the originals or instead added a further purpose or different character. We find that Arriba's use of Kelly's images for its thumbnails was transformative.

Despite the fact that Arriba made exact replications of Kelly's images, the thumbnails were much smaller, lower-resolution images that served an entirely different function than Kelly's original images. Kelly's images are artistic works used for illustrative purposes. His images are used to portray scenes from the American West in an esthetic manner. Arriba's use of Kelly's images in the thumbnails is unrelated to any esthetic purpose. Arriba's search engine functions as a tool to help index and improve access

9. *Dr. Seuss Enters., L.P. v. Penguin Books USA, Inc.*, 109 F.3d 1394, 1399 (9th Cir.1997) (internal quotation marks and citation omitted).

12. *Campbell v. Acuff–Rose Music, Inc.*, 510 U.S. 569, 579 (1994).

13. *Id.* (internal quotation marks and citation omitted) (alteration in original).

to images on the internet and their related web sites. In fact, users are unlikely to enlarge the thumbnails and use them for artistic purposes because the thumbnails are of much lower resolution than the originals; any enlargement results in a significant loss of clarity of the image, making them inappropriate as display material.

Kelly asserts that because Arriba reproduced his exact images and added nothing to them, Arriba's use cannot be transformative. It is true that courts have been reluctant to find fair use when an original work is merely retransmitted in a different medium.[17] Those cases are inapposite, however, because the resulting use of the copyrighted work in those cases was the same as the original use. For instance, reproducing music CD's into computer MP3 format does not change the fact that both formats are used for entertainment purposes. Likewise, reproducing news footage into a different format does not change the ultimate purpose of informing the public about current affairs. * * *

This case involves more than merely a retransmission of Kelly's images in a different medium. Arriba's use of the images serves a different function than Kelly's use—improving access to information on the internet versus artistic expression. Furthermore, it would be unlikely that anyone would use Arriba's thumbnails for illustrative or esthetic purposes because enlarging them sacrifices their clarity. Because Arriba's use is not superseding Kelly's use but, rather, has created a different purpose for the images, Arriba's use is transformative.

* * *

[I]n *Nunez v. Caribbean International News Corp.,*[22] the First Circuit found that copying a photograph that was intended to be used in a modeling portfolio and using it instead in a news article was a transformative use. By putting a copy of the photograph in the newspaper, the work was transformed into news, creating a new meaning or purpose for the work. The use of Kelly's images in Arriba's search engine is more analogous to the situation in *Nunez* because Arriba has created a new purpose for the images and is not simply superseding Kelly's purpose.

The Copyright Act was intended to promote creativity, thereby benefiting the artist and the public alike. To preserve the potential future use of artistic works for purposes of teaching, research, criticism, and news reporting, Congress made the fair use exception. Arriba's use of Kelly's images promotes the goals of the Copyright Act and the fair use exception. The thumbnails do not stifle artistic creativity because they are not used for illustrative or artistic purposes and therefore do not supplant the need for the originals. In addition, they benefit the public by enhancing information gathering techniques on the internet.

17. *See Infinity Broad. Corp. v. Kirkwood,* 150 F.3d 104, 108 (2d Cir.1998) (concluding that retransmission of radio broadcast over telephone lines is not transformative); *UMG Recordings, Inc. v. MP3.Com, Inc.,* 92 F.Supp.2d 349, 351 (S.D.N.Y.2000) (finding that reproduction of audio CD into computer MP3 format does not transform the work) * * *.

22. 235 F.3d 18 (1st Cir.2000).

In *Sony Computer Entertainment America, Inc. v. Bleem,*[25] we held that when Bleem copied "screen shots" from Sony computer games and used them in its own advertising, it was a fair use.[26] In finding that the first factor weighed in favor of Bleem, we noted that "comparative advertising redounds greatly to the purchasing public's benefit with very little corresponding loss to the integrity of Sony's copyrighted material."[27] Similarly, this first factor weighs in favor of Arriba due to the public benefit of the search engine and the minimal loss of integrity to Kelly's images.

2. Nature of the copyrighted work.

"Works that are creative in nature are closer to the core of intended copyright protection than are more fact-based works."[28] Photographs used for illustrative purposes, such as Kelly's, are generally creative in nature. The fact that a work is published or unpublished also is a critical element of its nature.[29] Published works are more likely to qualify as fair use because the first appearance of the artist's expression has already occurred. Kelly's images appeared on the internet before Arriba used them in its search image. When considering both of these elements, we find that this factor only slightly weighs in favor of Kelly.

3. Amount and substantiality of portion used.

"While wholesale copying does not preclude fair use per se, copying an entire work militates against a finding of fair use."[31] However, the extent of permissible copying varies with the purpose and character of the use.[32] If the secondary user only copies as much as is necessary for his or her intended use, then this factor will not weigh against him or her.

This factor will neither weigh for nor against either party because, although Arriba did copy each of Kelly's images as a whole, it was reasonable to do so in light of Arriba's use of the images. It was necessary for Arriba to copy the entire image to allow users to recognize the image and decide whether to pursue more information about the image or the originating web site. If Arriba only copied part of the image, it would be more difficult to identify it, thereby reducing the usefulness of the visual search engine.

4. Effect of the use upon the potential market for or value of the copyrighted work.

This last factor requires courts to consider "not only the extent of market harm caused by the particular actions of the alleged infringer, but

25. 214 F.3d 1022 (9th Cir.2000).

26. *Id.* at 1029.

27. *Id.* at 1027.

28. *A & M Records,* 239 F.3d at 1016 (citing *Campbell,* 510 U.S. at 586) (internal quotation marks omitted).

29. *Harper & Row, Publishers, Inc. v. Nation Enters.,* 471 U.S. 539, 564 (1985) (noting that the scope of fair use is narrower with respect to unpublished works because the author's right to control the first public appearance of his work weighs against the use of his work before its release).

31. *Worldwide Church of God,* 227 F.3d at 1118 (internal quotation marks and citation omitted).

32. *Campbell,* 510 U.S. at 586–87.

also 'whether unrestricted and widespread conduct of the sort engaged in by the defendant ... would result in a substantially adverse impact on the potential market for the original.' "[33] A transformative work is less likely to have an adverse impact on the market of the original than a work that merely supersedes the copyrighted work.

Kelly's images are related to several potential markets. One purpose of the photographs is to attract internet users to his web site, where he sells advertising space as well as books and travel packages. In addition, Kelly could sell or license his photographs to other web sites or to a stock photo database, which then could offer the images to its customers.

Arriba's use of Kelly's images in its thumbnails does not harm the market for Kelly's images or the value of his images. By showing the thumbnails on its results page when users entered terms related to Kelly's images, the search engine would guide users to Kelly's web site rather than away from it. Even if users were more interested in the image itself rather than the information on the web page, they would still have to go to Kelly's site to see the full-sized image. The thumbnails would not be a substitute for the full-sized images because when the thumbnails are enlarged, they lose their clarity. If a user wanted to view or download a quality image, he or she would have to visit Kelly's web site.[35] This would hold true whether the thumbnails are solely in Arriba's database or are more widespread and found in other search engine databases.

Arriba's use of Kelly's images also would not harm Kelly's ability to sell or license his full-sized images. Arriba does not sell or license its thumbnails to other parties. Anyone who downloaded the thumbnails would not be successful selling the full-sized images because of the low-resolution of the thumbnails. There would be no way to view, create, or sell a clear, full-sized image without going to Kelly's web sites. Therefore, Arriba's creation and use of the thumbnails does not harm the market for or value of Kelly's images. This factor weighs in favor of Arriba.

Having considered the four fair use factors and found that two weigh in favor of Arriba, one is neutral, and one weighs slightly in favor of Kelly, we conclude that Arriba's use of Kelly's images as thumbnails in its search engine is a fair use.

B.

* * *

33. *Id.* at 590 (quoting 3 M. Nimmer & D. Nimmer, *Nimmer on Copyright* § 13.05[A][4], at 13–102.61 (1993)) (ellipses in original).

35. We do not suggest that the inferior display quality of a reproduction is in any way dispositive, or will always assist an alleged infringer in demonstrating fair use. In this case, however, it is extremely unlikely that users would download thumbnails for display purposes, as the quality full-size versions are easily accessible from Kelly's web sites.

In addition, we note that in the unique context of photographic images, the quality of the reproduction may matter more than in other fields of creative endeavor. The appearance of photographic images accounts for virtually their entire esthetic value.

2. *Fair use of full-sized images.*

The last issue we must address is whether Arriba's display of Kelly's full-sized images was a fair use. Although Arriba did not address the use of the full-sized images in its fair use argument, the district court considered such use in its analysis, and we will consider Arriba's fair use defense here.

Once again, to decide whom the first factor, the purpose and character of the use, favors, we must determine whether Arriba's use of Kelly's images was transformative. Unlike the use of the images for the thumbnails, displaying Kelly's full-sized images does not enhance Arriba's search engine. The images do not act as a means to access other information on the internet but, rather, are likely the end product themselves. Although users of the search engine could link from the full-sized image to Kelly's web site, any user who is solely searching for images would not need to do so. Because the full-sized images on Arriba's site act primarily as illustrations or artistic expression and the search engine would function the same without them, they do not have a purpose different from Kelly's use of them.

Not only is the purpose the same, but Arriba did not add new expression to the images to make them transformative. Placing the images in a "frame" or locating them near text that specifies the size and originating web site is not enough to create new expression or meaning for the images. In sum, Arriba's full-sized images superseded the object of Kelly's images. Because Arriba has not changed the purpose or character of the use of the images, the first factor favors Kelly.

The analysis of the second factor, the nature of the copyrighted work, is the same as in the previous fair use discussion because Kelly's images are still the copyrighted images at issue. Therefore, as before, this factor slightly weighs in favor of Kelly.

The third fair use factor turns on the amount of the work displayed and the reasonableness of this amount in light of the purpose for the display. Arriba displayed the full images, which cuts against a finding of fair use. And while it was necessary to provide whole images to suit Arriba's purpose of giving users access to the full-sized images without having to go to another site, such a purpose is not legitimate, as we noted above. Therefore, it was not reasonable to copy the full-sized display. The third factor favors Kelly.

The fourth factor often depends upon how transformative the new use is compared to the original use. A work that is very transformative will often be in a different market from the original work and therefore is less likely to cause harm to the original work's market. Works that are not transformative, however, have the same purpose as the original work and will often have a negative effect on the original work's market.

As discussed in the previous fair use analysis, Kelly's markets for his images include using them to attract advertisers and buyers to his web site, and selling or licensing the images to other web sites or stock photo databases. By giving users access to Kelly's full-sized images on its own web site, Arriba harms all of Kelly's markets. Users will no longer have to go to Kelly's web site to see the full-sized images, thereby deterring people from visiting his web site. In addition, users would be able to download the full-sized images from Arriba's site and then sell or license those images themselves, reducing Kelly's opportunity to sell or license his own images. If the display of Kelly's images became widespread across other web sites, it would reduce the number of visitors to Kelly's web site even further and increase the chance of others exploiting his images. These actions would result in substantial adverse effects to the potential markets for Kelly's original works. For this reason, the fourth factor weighs heavily in favor of Kelly.

In conclusion, all of the fair use factors weigh in favor of Kelly. Therefore, the doctrine of fair use does not sanction Arriba's display of Kelly's images through the inline linking or framing processes that puts Kelly's original images within the context of Arriba's web site.

* * *

NOTES & QUESTIONS

1. *Private property vs. public access.* In *UMG Recordings, Inc. v. MP3.Com*, the court states that "[c]opyright * * * is not designed to afford consumer protection or convenience but, rather, to protect the copyright-holders' property interests." Dismissing Defendant's attempt to invoke the fair use defense, the court continues that "[s]tripped to its essence, defendant's 'consumer protection' argument amounts to nothing more than a bald claim that defendant should be able to misappropriate plaintiffs' property simply because there is a consumer demand for it." Should the public's desire for access be a relevant consideration in determining the scope of the monopoly conferred on the copyright owner, that is, in determining the applicability of the fair use defense? Compare Justice Stevens's statement in *New York Times v. Tasini*, 533 U.S. 483, 519 (2001): " 'the primary purpose of copyright is not to reward the author, but is rather to secure "the general benefits derived by the public from the labors of authors." ' " (quoting MELVILLE B. NIMMER & DAVID NIMMER, NIMMER ON COPYRIGHT § 1.03[A]) (quoting *Fox Film Corp. v. Doyal*, 286 U.S. 123, 127 (1932)).

2. *Fair use and digital video recorders.* ReplayTV is an updated, digital version of the familiar videocassette recorder. Like a VCR, ReplayTV connects to a television set, records broadcasts as they are received, and allows the recorded broadcast to be replayed at a later time. Rather than storing the broadcast on videotape, ReplayTV makes use of a hard drive, to which it saves a digitized version of the broadcast. Replay TV has two especially noteworthy features. First, a program that is saved on a ReplayTV can be sent by e-mail to up to 15 recipients who may play the program on their own ReplayTV, but the recipients may not retransmit the program to additional recipients. Second, when in playback mode ReplayTV can be set automatically to skip commercials. When it works properly (which it does more than 90 percent of the time), the commercials simply disappear: there is no pause or fast-forwarding through them. The broadcast, cable, and satellite television industries have expressed fears that these features threaten to undermine their business models. In *Sony Corp. of America v. Universal City Studios*, 464 U.S. 417 (1984), the Supreme Court held that recording a broadcast using a traditional VCR for home viewing (often referred to as "time-shifting") is a fair use under the Copyright Act. Should the same rationale lead the courts to hold that recording broadcasts with devices like Replay TV is also fair use? *See Paramount Pictures Corp. v. ReplayTV, Inc.*, CV 01–9358 FMC (Ex) (C.D. Cal. filed Oct. 31, 2001).

B. THE FIRST-SALE DOCTRINE

Video Pipeline, Inc. v. Buena Vista Home Entertainment, Inc.

192 F.Supp.2d 321 (D.N.J.2002).

■ SIMANDLE, DISTRICT JUDGE.

* * *

In the multi-billion dollar home video industry, an increasing amount of sales takes place over the Internet. This case examines the copyright issues that arise when an entity uses the copyrighted motion pictures to make short trailers, which are then made available for money to the entity's clients, which are video retailers, for the viewing by retail customers on the retailers' Internet websites, for the purpose of promoting sales of the copyrighted videos. In this case, the copyright owners seek a preliminary injunction against the entity which creates and sells the unauthorized trailers for their copyrighted home videos.

This matter comes before the Court upon motion by defendant Buena Vista Home Entertainment, Inc. (formerly known as Buena Vista Home Video), and counterclaim-plaintiff Miramax Film Corp. (hereinafter collectively "BVHE" or "defendants") for a preliminary injunction upon their amended counterclaim against plaintiff/counterclaim-defendant Video Pipeline, Inc. Plaintiff Video Pipeline originally brought suit against defendant Buena Vista Home Entertainment, Inc., for a declaratory judgment that plaintiff's use of trailers provided by BVHE in creating its own video clips to be commercially used by Internet video retailers does not constitute copyright infringement under the Copyright Act.

* * *

* * *For the reasons now discussed, the Court will grant defendant BVHE's motion for a preliminary injunction, pursuant to the following findings of fact and conclusions of law entered under Rules 52(a) and 65(d), Fed.R.Civ.P.

BACKGROUND

In this preliminary injunction motion, Buena Vista Home Entertainment, Inc. ("BVHE") seeks to enjoin Video Pipeline from streaming video previews it created out of motion pictures upon which BVHE owns the copyright. BVHE is a wholly-owned, indirect subsidiary of The Walt Disney Company, in the business of manufacturing, distributing, and selling home video versions of copyrighted motion pictures and other entertainment content. Since 1987, BVHE has been the exclusive licensee of Walt Disney Pictures and Television for the distribution of its products in the home video market. In addition, BVHE is the exclusive distributor for Miramax, also a wholly-owned, indirect subsidiary of The Walt Disney Company, in the home video market. Video Pipeline is a company founded in 1985 that compiles and organizes promotional previews from entertainment companies into promotional videos which retailers display in their stores to promote retail sales and rentals. Since 1985, Video Pipeline had provided promotional videos to retailers for in-store use, at times editing the material sent by the movie studios, either because it contained sales and marketing information not intended for customer viewing or because Video Pipeline's retailer clients complained about certain inappropriate previews supplied by studios.

BVHE and Video Pipeline entered into a Master Clip Agreement dated November 7, 1988, by which BVHE granted Video Pipeline permission to use certain videotape promotional previews ("trailers") in compilations to be exhibited in video stores to promote home video sales and rentals. Beginning in 1995, home video retailers began using the Internet as a means of marketing home video products. In 1997, Video Pipeline began making the promotional previews available to home video retailers' Internet websites by means of an Internet service comprised of "VideoPipeline.net" to promote sales and rentals of the home video products. VideoPipeline.net is not a website, but is the network through which retailers' customers can access and stream the previews. These previews can be viewed but cannot be downloaded by Internet users.

In general, retail customers can view the previews while on the retailers' websites by clicking on the "preview" buttons for a particular motion picture, which links them immediately to VideoPipeline.net, which then "streams" the video to the customer. (Hearing Tr. at 102.) "Video Pipeline.com" is Video Pipeline's corporate website that provides information about Video Pipeline's online promotional services for retailers, and no previews are actually shown via that site itself. "VideoDetective.com" is another website that uses VideoPipeline.net to allow Internet users to access previews and to link to retail websites by means of a "Shop Now" button. Video Pipeline has approximately 25 agreements with certain retailers, including Yahoo!Shopping, Netflix, TLA, and IMDB/Amazon to provide these services. In providing these services to Internet-based retailers, Video Pipeline charges the retailers "per Mega Byte actually shown to consumers." Thus, Video Pipeline receives its income for this service from the retailers it serves, based upon the units of time that a retailer's customer is viewing the Video Pipeline previews.

On September 13, 2000, BVHE advised Video Pipeline that it did not have permission to use the studio-supplied trailers on the Internet, nor were they cleared for online use, and requested that the previews of BVHE's motion pictures be removed from the website immediately. On October 24, 2000, Video Pipeline filed suit in this Court against BVHE, seeking a declaratory judgment that its use of promotional materials provided by BVHE to Video Pipeline did not violate any of BVHE's rights under federal copyright law or any other law. BVHE subsequently terminated the Master Clip License Agreement and demanded return of all trailers previously provided to Video Pipeline. On December 21, 2000, Video Pipeline returned to BVHE 80 promotional previews subject to the Master Clip License Agreement.

Video Pipeline removed the previews subject to the agreement from the Internet at BVHE's request, but continued to make its own previews (hereinafter "clip previews") from copies of videos of BVHE's copyrighted motion pictures owned by its retailer clients, with the exception of one clip preview of the Belgian movie "Everybody Famous," which was made from material provided directly by BVHE. Each clip preview created by Video Pipeline is approximately 120 seconds in length and consist of an opening display of the Disney or Miramax trademark, the title of the motion picture being distributed by BVHE, then two or more scenes from the motion picture, followed by another display of the title. In addition, Video Pipeline's clip previews have no voice over, no editing, no use of additional music, and no use or narration or other types of marketing techniques often found in studio-produced trailers. At issue are 62 clip previews, including those for movies such as *Fantasia, Beauty and the Beast,* and *Pretty Woman,* for purposes of this preliminary injunction. It is estimated that Internet users have streamed Video Pipeline's clip previews over 30,000 times between November 3, 2000, and April 3, 2001.

BVHE alleges that Video Pipeline's creation, distribution, and provision of online streaming of clip previews to video retailers in this fashion violates § 106 of the Copyright Act. Video Pipeline alleges that its clip previews do not infringe the copyrights on the underlying motion pictures, and that they are in any event protected by the "first sale" doctrine under § 109(a) of the Copyright Act * * *

DISCUSSION

* * * Here, it is uncontested that Disney, BVHE's licensor, owns the copyright of the full-length motion pictures on which Video Pipeline's clip previews are based, as well as the trademarks of the logos of Disney, Buena Vista, Hollywood Pictures, and Touchstone, shown at the beginning of the clip previews. To BVHE is thus conferred the exclusive rights reserved as copyright owner under § 106 of the Copyright Act.

1. Exclusive Rights Under § 106 of the Copyright Act

BVHE argues that Video Pipeline's reproduction of the video clips provided by BVHE infringes all five of the exclusive rights that are reserved to it as owner of the copyright at issue under § 106. * * *

Video Pipeline's creation of video clips is most likely a derivative work under § 106(2). *See, e.g., Lamb v. Starks,* 949 F.Supp. 753, 756 (N.D.Cal. 1996) (holding that defendant infringed copyright by copying trailer consisting of parts of scenes from plaintiff's movie). * * *

The Court finds that Video Pipeline's clip previews also constitute a public performance under § 106(4). * * *

In addition, the Court finds that Video Pipeline's service of providing clip previews online constitutes a "public display" that violates the copyright owner's exclusive right "to display the copyrighted work publicly." 17 U.S.C. § 106(5). * * *

The Court finds that because Video Pipeline's actions violate the exclusive rights of the copyright owner BVHE, plaintiff has infringed on BVHE's copyright. *See* 17 U.S.C. § 501. The next point of discussion concerns Video Pipeline's contention that, notwithstanding its violations of § 106, it is nevertheless protected by the First Sale Doctrine. * * *

2. *First Sale Doctrine*

Video Pipeline argues that its actions of creating its own clip previews from those provided by BVHE and subsequently allowing customers of its retailer clients to view them online is protected by the First Sale Doctrine. The first sale doctrine, codified at 17 U.S.C. § 109(a), prevents the copyright owner from controlling future transfers of a particular copy of a copyrighted work after he has transferred its "material ownership" to another. *Columbia Pictures v. Aveco, Inc.,* 800 F.2d 59, 63–64 (3d Cir.1986) (citing *Columbia Pictures Indus. v. Redd Horne,* 749 F.2d 154, 159 (3d Cir.1984)). Section 109(a) provides

> Notwithstanding the provisions of section 106(3), the owner of a particular copy or phonorecord lawfully made under this title, or any person authorized by such owner, is entitled, without the authority of the copyright owner, to sell or otherwise dispose of the possession of that copy or phonorecord.

17 U.S.C. § 109(a). "Section 109(a) is an extension of the principle that ownership of the material object is distinct from ownership of the copyright in this material." *Redd Horne,* 749 F.2d at 159 (citing 17 U.S.C. § 202). Under the first sale doctrine, the copyright owner cannot control the future transfer of a particular copy once its material ownership has been transferred. *See Redd Horne,* 749 F.2d at 159 (citations omitted).

Video Pipeline relies on *Quality King Distribs. v. L'anza Research Int'l,* 523 U.S. 135, 118 (1998), for the proposition that from the retailer's right to resell its lawfully purchased copyrighted products must come the retailer's right to advertise and promote sales of the products without the copyright holder's consent. The Supreme Court in *Quality King* involved a California manufacturer that sold its copyrighted hair care products to a Malta distributor, which subsequently sold them to an importer, which imported the products back into the United States to be sold at lower prices than the California manufacturer. The Supreme Court held that the importer was entitled to the first sale defense in the copyright infringement action, stating that "[t]he whole point of the first sale doctrine is that once the copyright owner places the copyrighted item in the stream of commerce by selling it, he has exhausted his exclusive statutory right to control its distribution." *Quality King,* 523 U.S. at 152.

Video Pipeline's reliance on *Quality King* is misplaced because it is not a retailer who has lawfully purchased copies of BVHE's product and therefore entitled to the protection afforded by the first sale doctrine. Rather, its clients, not Video Pipeline, are video retailers who may promote the sales or rentals of the products it has lawfully purchased from BVHE. Video Pipeline, in creating clip previews and providing an online service to its customer retailers, contends that the focus of this first sale analysis should more properly be placed on the actions of the retailers, arguing that the defenses afforded to its retailer customers should be transferred to it.

The Court agrees with BVHE that the actual nature of the relationship between Video Pipeline and its retailer customers is one of licensor and licensee, not one of agency. *See* Horovitz Aff. at Ex. 7. According to the agreement, the retailer customers are allowed access to previews provided by Video Pipeline either for "in-store use and/or internet point-of-sale promotional use." *See id.* Video Pipeline provides no support for the argument that one in a license agreement is entitled to the protection of the first sale doctrine defense that may be afforded to the other party.

* * *

Plaintiff's assertion that it should be entitled, as its retailer customers are, to the privilege of advertising video products, is addressed more appropriately within the confines of subsection (c) of § 109. Section 109(c), formerly subsection (b), provides:

> Notwithstanding the provisions of section 106(5), the owner of a particular copy lawfully made under this title, or any person authorized by such owner, is entitled, without the authority of the copyright owner, to display that copy publicly, either directly or by the projection of no more than one image at a time, to viewers present at the place where the copy is located.

17 U.S.C. § 109(c). Congress stated that this subsection "deals with the scope of the copyright owner's exclusive right to control the public display of a particular 'copy' of a work." H.R.Rep. No. 94–1476, 94th Cong., 2d Sess. 79 (1976). Congress further explained the boundaries of the right granted to owners of a particular copy under § 106(5):

> [S]ection [109(c)] takes account of the potentialities of the new communications media, notably television, cable and optical transmission devices, and information storage and retrieval devices, for replacing printed copies with visual images. First of all, the public display of an image of a copyrighted work would not be exempted from copyright control if the copy from which the image was derived were outside the presence of the viewers. In other words, *the display of a visual image of a copyrighted work would be an*

> *infringement if the image were transmitted* by any method (by closed or open circuit television, for example, or *by a computer system*) from one place to members of the public located elsewhere.

Id. Although Congress was discussing the possibility of copyright infringement as it relates to a copy owner, its discussion of copyright infringement occurring as a result of computerized transmission is instructive here nonetheless. Under this provision, Congress intended for copyright infringement to occur when images of a copy of copyrighted work are displayed to members of the public located other than where the copy is located. By providing for this provision, Congress intended "to preserve the traditional privilege of the owner of a copy to display it directly, but to place reasonable restrictions on the ability to display it indirectly in such a way that the copyright owner's market for reproduction and distribution of copies would be affected." *Id.*

In this case, the transmittal of images of BVHE's copyrighted motion pictures to customers of retailer licensees of Video Pipeline, presents a markedly similar scenario envisioned by Congress, and therefore constitutes copyright infringement notwithstanding the retailer's right to display under § 106(5). Congress could have said that the transmission of copyrighted images to customers at a distant point of sale by electronic means is within the zone of use permitted by § 109(c), but it has not done so. Thus, Video Pipeline's argument that it is entitled to the same scope of protection as its customer retailers further fails here due to the probable unavailability of the first sale doctrine defense to retailers who have the right to advertise their copies of copyrighted work, but are displaying images of their copyrighted materials at a distance over the Internet. Accordingly, Video Pipeline is not entitled to the protection of the first sale doctrine as provided in § 109 of the Copyright Act. * * *

* * *

NOTES & QUESTIONS

1. *"Copies" and the first-sale right.* 17 U.S.C. § 109(a) provides that "the owner of a particular copy * * * is entitled * * * to sell or otherwise dispose of the possession of that copy." A purchaser of a CD–ROM containing software does not thereby gain ownership of the copyright in the software, but only the right to use it in ways that do not conflict with the rights of the copyright owner. Does the purchaser gain ownership of the CD–ROM disk itself? If so, does the first-sale doctrine apply, allowing the purchaser to dispose of the CD–ROM as she chooses? *See* MELVILLE B. NIMMER & DAVID NIMMER, NIMMER ON COPYRIGHT § 8.12[B][1].

What if she purchases the software by downloading it from a website onto her computer's hard drive? Does the first-sale doctrine allow her to e-mail the software to somebody else, if she deletes it from her own computer's hard drive? Does it allow her to sell the computer without first deleting the software? Suppose she downloads the software directly to a floppy diskette. Does the first-sale doctrine allow her to give the diskette to somebody else?

Can a copyright owner use contract to extend his control over redistribution of material objects containing copyrighted works?

2. *Exceptions from the first-sale right for record and software rental.* In the early 1980s, record rental stores began to proliferate. These stores would rent you an LP record for a dollar or two, allowing you to keep it for a few days. As was clear to all, nearly everyone who patronized these establishments was making a copy of the record on audio cassette tape, and adding the tape to their collection. At the instance of music copyright holders, Congress enacted the Record Rental Amendment of 1984, Pub. L. No. 98–450, 98 Stat. 1727 (1984), which amended the Copyright Act's codification of the first-sale right, 17 U.S.C. § 109. The amendment limits the first-sale right, so that it no longer permits the rental, lease, or lending of phonorecords (that is, records, tapes, and other physical objects containing sound recordings) for commercial purposes. In 1990, Congress similarly limited the applicability of the first-sale right to computer programs, by enacting a parallel amendment of Section 109. *See* Computer Software Rental Amendments Act of 1990, Pub. L. No. 101–650, 104 Stat. 5089, 5134 (1990).

These two congressional actions exemplify a clash between an owner's right to dispose of his chattels as he sees fit, which is recognized in the common law's strong distaste for restraints on alienation, and a copyright holder's statutory right to control distribution of his works. The boundary between these two rights is fluid, and shifts with technological and societal developments. Can you think of any aspects of online technology, or the societal changes it has spawned, that call for a rethinking of where this boundary should be drawn?

3. *First-sale right and digital works.* Owners of copyrighted digital works, such as software, music files, and electronic books, increasingly seek to limit distribution of those works by incorporating access-control technology into the file constituting a work. For example, movies on DVD incorporate code that allows the DVD to be played on players designed for one region of the world, but not on players designed for other regions: a DVD that a friend in Europe gives to you may not be playable on the DVD player you have at your home in the United States. Electronic books and music files may contain code that allows them to be read or played only on the computer to which they are downloaded. You can transfer such a file to a friend, but it will not be usable on her computer. Does the use of such access-control technology effectively vitiate the first-sale right? Should Congress vindicate the first-sale right by making such technology illegal, or by making use of it cause for forfeiting the copyright on a work to which it is applied? Consider how this would affect the willingness of copyright owners to make their works available in digital form. Should Congress at least regulate such technology by mandating that access-control technologies allow transfer of one copy to a second user if it is deleted from the first user's computer? Would an affirmation of the applicability of the first-sale right to digital works inevitably interfere with the central goals of the copyright laws, namely to encourage authors to create and disseminate original works? If consumers find access-control technology objectionable, is it likely to disappear from the marketplace?

Congress's actual response to the rise of access-control technology is discussed in Chapter 11, *infra*. Under 17 U.S.C. § 1201, added by the 1998 Digital Millennium Copyright Act, one who circumvents (or provides a product that may be used to circumvent) such technology is subject to civil liability and criminal penalties.

C. COPYRIGHT MISUSE

In re Napster

191 F.Supp.2d 1087 (N.D.Cal.2002).

■ PATEL, DISTRICT JUDGE.

The recording industry plaintiffs move for summary judgment against defendant Napster, Inc. ("Napster") for willful contributory and vicarious copyright infringement. In response, Napster requests that pursuant to *Federal Rule of Civil Procedure 56(f)* the court stay any decision on the merits to allow for additional discovery. Napster's 56(f) motion asks the court to determine whether additional discovery is necessary to decide if some of largest players in the music recording industry actually own the rights to the musical works for which they allege copyright infringement by Napster. The court is also asked to permit discovery to determine whether plaintiffs have misused their copyrights by attempting to control the market for the digital distribution of music. Having considered the arguments presented, and for the reasons set forth below, the court rules as follows.

BACKGROUND

This action is one of several copyright infringement actions against Napster, an Internet service that facilitates the downloading of MP3 music files. *See In re Napster,* MDL 00–1369 MHP. Because this court and the Ninth Circuit have discussed the Napster service at length in prior orders, and because the parties are familiar with the Napster system, the court will limit this background section to information relevant to the current motions.

A. Procedural History

On December 6, 1999, A & M Records and seventeen other record companies filed a complaint for contributory and vicarious copyright infringement against Napster. These eighteen parties can be collectively grouped into five major recording companies: BMG, Sony, EMI, Universal, and Warner. *See A & M Records, Inc. v. Napster, Inc.,* 114 F.Supp.2d 896, 908 (N.D.Cal.2000). Plaintiffs' complaint alleges that Napster knew of and failed to prevent its users' unauthorized reproduction and distribution of plaintiffs' copyrighted sound recordings. Plaintiffs claim ownership to a diverse catalog of artists including many of the industry's top-grossing artists from the last five decades.

This court granted plaintiffs' request for a preliminary injunction in July 2000 and prohibited Napster from "engaging in or facilitating others in copying, downloading, uploading, transmitting, or distributing plaintiffs' copyrighted works." 114 F.Supp.2d at 927. Two days later, the Court of Appeals stayed the injunction. *See A & M Records, Inc. v. Napster, Inc.*, 2000 WL 1055915, *1 (9th Cir. July 28, 2000). In February 2001, the Ninth Circuit largely affirmed this court's findings of fact and grant of injunctive relief. *See A & M Records, Inc. v. Napster, Inc.*, 239 F.3d 1004 (9th Cir.2001). A modified preliminary injunction was entered on March 5, 2001. *See A & M Records, Inc. v. Napster, Inc.*, 2001 WL 227083 (N.D.Cal. March 5, 2001). The court continued, with the aid of a technical expert, to monitor Napster's compliance with the preliminary injunction through August 2001.

* * *

Plaintiffs filed their motion for summary judgment on liability and willfulness on July 27, 2001. On September 10, 2001, Napster filed its opposition to plaintiffs' motion for summary judgment and a corresponding Rule 56(f) motion asking to stay summary judgment to allow for further discovery. * * *

* * *

B. *Plaintiffs' Entry into the Digital Distribution Market*

* * * In mid–2001, plaintiffs announced the formation of two joint ventures, MusicNet and pressplay. The aim of these joint ventures is to provide platforms for the digital distribution of music. MusicNet is a joint venture between three of the five record company plaintiffs—EMI, BMG, and Warner. MusicNet is also owned in part by RealNetworks (and possibly another entity). Pressplay is a venture between the other two plaintiffs—Sony and Universal.

In June 2001, Napster signed a licensing agreement with MusicNet, allowing Napster access to all of the copyrighted works licensed to MusicNet. Prior to signing the MusicNet agreement, Napster was unable to obtain individual licenses from any of the recording company plaintiffs. The MusicNet agreement explicitly limits Napster's ability to obtain individual licenses from any of the five plaintiffs, including the non-MusicNet plaintiffs—Sony and Universal—until March 2002. The agreement also allows MusicNet to terminate the agreement within ninety days, even after March 2002, if Napster licenses content from any of the five recording companies other than through MusicNet. Additionally, the agreement mandates a separate pricing structure for *any* content that Napster licenses from anyone other than MusicNet. Napster has only provided the court with the MusicNet agreement and the court has no other information as to how MusicNet operates or exactly what content it will offer and to whom. Similarly, because Napster has not signed a licensing agreement with pressplay, the court has before it only information culled from the public record which reveals little about pressplay's intended operations. * * *

DISCUSSION

* * *

II. Copyright Misuse

Napster argues that the court should deny summary judgment or stay the matter to allow for further discovery because plaintiffs are engaged in copyright misuse. Copyright misuse as a defense to an infringement action finds its origins in the equitable defense of unclean hands and is similar to the patent law defense of the same name. *See Morton Salt Co. v. G.S. Suppiger,* 314 U.S. 488 (1942). This court and the Ninth Circuit dismissed Napster's misuse defense at the preliminary injunction stage, noting that copyright misuse is rarely a defense to injunctive relief and that there was not enough evidence at that stage to support a finding of misuse. *See A & M Records,* 239 F.3d at 1026–27; 114 F.Supp.2d at 923. Since those rulings, the factual and procedural landscape has changed significantly. The motion now before the court is for summary judgment, not preliminary injunctive relief. Additionally, the prior inapplicability of copyright misuse rested on the fact that none of the plaintiffs had granted licenses to Napster, let alone impermissibly restrictive ones. *See A & M Records,* 114 F.Supp.2d at 924. The evidence now shows that plaintiffs have licensed their catalogs of works for digital distribution in what could be an overreaching manner. The evidence also suggests that plaintiffs' entry into the digital distribution market may run afoul of antitrust laws.

A. The Development of the Copyright Misuse Defense

The legitimacy of copyright misuse as a valid defense to an infringement action was in question for some time. *See Lasercomb Am., Inc. v. Reynolds,* 911 F.2d 970, 976 (4th Cir.1990) (describing the history of the misuse doctrine). For years, courts shied away from applying the doctrine, either refusing to recognize the defense, or finding it inapplicable on the facts. *Id.* Recently, courts have displayed a greater willingness to find copyright misuse, employing two different, though interrelated approaches. The first approach requires a finding that plaintiff engaged in antitrust violations before the court will apply the doctrine of copyright misuse. *See, e.g., Saturday Evening Post v. Rumbleseat Press, Inc.,* 816 F.2d 1191, 1200 (7th Cir.1987). The second approach, adopted by the Ninth Circuit, focuses on public policy and has been applied to a greater range of conduct than the antitrust approach. *See Practice Mgmt. Info. Corp. v. American Med. Assoc.,* 121 F.3d 516 (9th Cir.1997). *See generally* Brett Frischmann & Dan Moylan, *The Evolving Common Law Doctrine of Copyright Misuse: A Unified Theory and Its Application to Software,* 15 Berkeley Tech.L.J. 865, 880–902 (Fall 2000) (comparing antitrust and public policy-based misuse). Under the "public policy" approach, copyright misuse exists when plaintiff expands the statutory copyright monopoly in order to gain control over areas outside the scope of the monopoly. *See Practice Mgmt.,* 121 F.3d at

520; *Lasercomb,* 911 F.2d at 977–79 (copyright misuse "forbids the use of the copyright to secure an exclusive right or limited monopoly not granted by the Copyright Office"). The test is whether plaintiff's use of his or her copyright violates the public policy embodied in the grant of a copyright, not whether the use is anti-competitive. *See Practice Mgmt.,* 121 F.3d at 521. However, as a practical matter, this test is often difficult to apply and inevitably requires courts to rely on antitrust principles or language to some degree. *See Lasercomb,* 911 F.2d at 977 (noting courts' "understandable" but misplaced reliance on antitrust principles).

The scope of the defense of copyright misuse has not been significantly tested in the Ninth Circuit. In fact, the court has been unable to find a single reported case that discusses beyond a mere citation the Ninth Circuit's adoption of the copyright misuse defense in *Practice Management. See, e.g., Sony Pictures Entm't, Inc. v. Fireworks Entm't Group, Inc.,* 156 F.Supp.2d 1148, 1156 (C.D.Cal.2001); *Pollstar v. Gigmania Ltd.,* 170 F.Supp.2d 974, 982 (E.D.Cal.2000). Nor did this court or the Ninth Circuit devote any discussion to *Practice Management* in previous rulings. *A & M Records,* 239 F.3d at 1026–7; 114 F.Supp.2d at 924. As a result, the doctrine of copyright misuse remains largely undeveloped, with little case law to aid this court in its inquiry.[11]

* * *

B. Napster's Allegations of Misuse

Napster alleges two bases for misuse. First, Napster contends that the licensing clauses in Napster's agreement with plaintiffs' joint venture, MusicNet, are unduly restrictive. In the alternative, Napster argues that even if that particular agreement is not unduly restrictive, plaintiffs' practices as they enter the market for the digital distribution of music are so anti-competitive as to give rise to a misuse defense.

1. The MusicNet Agreement

Napster contends that licensing requirements of plaintiffs' online venture, MusicNet, are unduly restrictive. MusicNet is a joint venture between three of the five record company plaintiffs (EMI, BMG, and Warner) to distribute digital music. This joint venture anticipates obtaining licenses from the other two major labels (Sony and Universal) to distribute their catalogs of copyrighted music. While Napster was unable to secure licenses from any of the individual plaintiffs, Napster reached an agreement with MusicNet that allows Napster to distribute the music from the catalogs of the three participating MusicNet plaintiffs and any other label that licenses its catalog to MusicNet.

11. In comparison, there is a substantial body of case law on patent misuse. *See, e.g., Morton Salt Co. v. G.S. Suppiger,* 314 U.S. 488 (1942). Patent misuse bases its analysis on antitrust principles and consequently is doctrinally analogous to antitrust-based copyright misuse. It is less helpful when employing the "public policy" analysis adopted by the Ninth Circuit.

Section 19.1 of the MusicNet agreement prevents Napster from entering into any licensing agreement with any individual plaintiffs until March 1, 2002. The text of the agreement calls this space of time the "Initial Exclusivity Period." *Id.* The agreement also provides that even after March 2002 if Napster enters into any individual license with any of the major labels—i.e. the plaintiffs—including the MusicNet plaintiffs, MusicNet may terminate the agreement with ninety-day notice. Additionally, section 6.3(a) lays out a pricing structure under which Napster will be charged higher fees if it fails to use MusicNet as its exclusive licensor for content.[13]

It is unclear from the text of the agreement if the exclusivity provision operates to impermissibly extend plaintiffs' control beyond the scope of their copyright monopoly. In other misuse cases, the offending provision was exclusive and the "adverse effects of the licensing agreement [were] apparent." *Practice Mgmt.,* 121 F.3d at 521 (provision prevented defendant from using any competitor's coding system); *Lasercomb,* 911 F.2d at 978 (defendant prohibited from producing any die-making software); *Alcatel,* 166 F.3d at 793–4 (software licensing provision effectively gave plaintiff control over uncopyrighted microprocessor cards). In contrast, the MusicNet provision is non-exclusive. Napster may obtain licenses from any of the record label plaintiffs, but may only do it through its agreement with MusicNet. Despite this theoretical non-exclusivity, the provision effectively grants MusicNet control over which content Napster licenses. Napster's use of other music catalogs is predicated on MusicNet's securing an individual license to those catalogs. For example, under the MusicNet agreement, Napster no longer has the ability to obtain an individual license from Sony (a non-MusicNet plaintiff). Instead, Napster must rely on MusicNet to obtain a license to Sony's catalog. And, if MusicNet chooses not to obtain such a license, Napster is effectively prevented from using Sony's catalog. The result is an expansion of the powers of the three MusicNet plaintiffs' copyrights to cover the catalogs of the two non-MusicNet plaintiffs.

The MusicNet plaintiffs argue that this restriction is unimportant because they fully expect to obtain licenses from the other two major recording companies.[14] That the restriction only applies until MusicNet contains licenses from Sony and Universal (non-MusicNet plaintiffs) or until March 2002 is irrelevant. *See Practice Mgmt.,* 121 F.3d 516, 521 ("The controlling fact is that HCFA is prohibited from using any other coding system by virtue of the binding commitment ... to use the AMA's copyrighted material exclusively."). The critical issue is that the agreement binds Napster to obtain licenses from MusicNet and not its competitors. Napster was caught in a position where its only options were to sign the agreement to gain access to the catalogs of the major record companies and

13. There are also allegations by Napster that the pricing structure of the MusicNet agreement prevents Napster from obtaining licenses from parties other than the five major record companies.

14. Plaintiffs find themselves in a catch–22 because if MusicNet does not obtain these licenses, the licensing provision may be unduly restrictive, and if MusicNet does obtain licenses from the non-MusicNet plaintiffs, such cross-licensing implicates potential antitrust concerns.

thereby incur these restrictions in all their murkiness or to refuse to sign the agreement and have virtually no access to most commercially available music.

Though the agreement is troubling on its face, too many questions remain unanswered for the court to effectively rule on the issue. It is unclear to what extent it is appropriate to impute the actions of MusicNet to plaintiffs as MusicNet is a joint venture and technically remains a separate entity from plaintiffs. However, plaintiffs cannot hide behind the shell of a joint venture to protect themselves from misuse claims. The court views with great suspicion plaintiffs' claims of ignorance as to MusicNet's activities. Surely the three parties to MusicNet discussed their joint venture before embarking on it. MusicNet did not suddenly appear full blown from the head of a fictitious entity. The evidence suggests that plaintiffs formed a joint venture to distribute digital music and simultaneously refused to enter into individual licenses with competitors, effectively requiring competitors to use MusicNet as their source for digital licensing. If this proves to be the case, the propriety of treating MusicNet as a separate entity is in question. *Cf. Copperweld Corp. v. Independence Tube Corp.,* 467 U.S. 752, 768–69 (1984).

A few of plaintiff's arguments can be disposed of summarily. First, plaintiffs argue that Napster, as a party to the MusicNet agreement, cannot now challenge an agreement that it negotiated and subsequently signed. *Practice Management* explicitly holds that it is irrelevant who includes an exclusivity provision in an agreement. 121 F.3d at 521 (even if the exclusivity provision was included at HCFA's urging, it still prohibited HCFA from using competing coding systems). That Napster is both the party alleging misuse and a party to the offending agreement does not affect the court's analysis. *See Lasercomb,* 121 F.3d at 979 ("[T]he defense of misuse is available even if the defendants have not been injured by the misuse"; "The fact that appellants were not parties to one of Lasercomb's standard license agreements is inapposite to their copyright misuse defense."); *Morton Salt,* 314 U.S. at 494 ("It is the adverse effect upon the public interest of a successful infringement suit in conjunction with the patentee's course of conduct which disqualifies him to maintain the suit, regardless of whether the particular defendant has suffered from the misuse of the patent.")[16]

Second, plaintiffs contend that because MusicNet is not yet in operation, there is no ongoing misuse. This argument fails. The issue is not whether MusicNet is yet in operation, but whether the exclusivity provision in the agreement is active. Because Napster is already bound by the

16. Plaintiffs' argument would have merit if there was any evidence that Napster introduced and negotiated for the exclusivity provision. In that scenario, it would be unseemly to allow Napster to use the same provision as protection against infringement actions. Such a rule would create perverse incentives to artificially manufacture overreaching clauses as liability shields under the misuse doctrine. However, the evidence thus far shows that the relevant provisions were inserted at MusicNet's urging and not as an end-run around copyright laws by Napster.

agreement, the restriction on Napster's ability to negotiate for licenses with individual plaintiffs is *currently* restricted.

Third, plaintiffs contend that even if they are engaged in misuse, be it through restrictive licensing or antitrust violations, they should still be able to recover for infringement that occurred prior to the MusicNet agreement. Plaintiffs misunderstand the misuse doctrine. Misuse limits enforcement of rights, not remedies. *See Practice Mgmt.,* 121 F.3d at 520 n. 9 ("Copyright misuse does not invalidate a copyright, but precludes its enforcement during the period of misuse."). If plaintiffs are engaged in misuse, they cannot bring suit based on their rights until the misuse ends. *See Lasercomb,* 911 F.2d at 979 n. 22 ("Lasercomb is free to bring a suit for infringement once it has purged itself of the misuse."); *Morton Salt,* 314 U.S. at 492 ("Equity may rightly withhold its assistance ... by declining to entertain a suit for infringement, and should do so at least until it is made to appear that the improper practice has been abandoned and that the consequences of the misuse ... have been dissipated."). The doctrine does not prevent plaintiffs from ultimately recovering for acts of infringement that occur during the period of misuse. The issue focuses on when plaintiffs can bring or pursue an action for infringement, not for which acts of infringement they can recover.

2. *Antitrust Violations As Copyright Misuse*

Napster does not confine its argument to the particular provision of the MusicNet licensing agreement. Napster also argues that plaintiffs' entry into the digital distribution market is rife with actual anti-competitive effects and potential antitrust concerns.

Antitrust violations can give rise to copyright misuse if those violations offend the public policy behind the copyright grant. *See Lasercomb,* 911 F.2d at 977 ("[A]ntitrust law is the statutory embodiment of that public policy"). However, generalized antitrust violations will not suffice. Napster must establish a "nexus between ... alleged anti-competitive actions and [plaintiffs'] power over copyrighted material." *Orth–O–Vision, Inc. v. Home Box Office,* 474 F.Supp. 672, 686 (S.D.N.Y.1979).

Napster's arguments are based primarily on the declaration of Roger Noll, a Stanford professor who specializes in antitrust economics and the recording industry. Based on Dr. Noll's review of the MusicNet agreement and facts in the public record, Napster alleges that there are a host of anti-competitive behaviors by the plaintiffs that violate antitrust laws. Dr. Noll concludes that plaintiffs' joint ventures, MusicNet and pressplay, have anti-competitive features and facilitate collusive activity between plaintiffs. Dr. Noll further asserts that plaintiffs engage in vertical foreclosure of the digital distribution market through retail price squeezes, raising costs through licensing provisions, refusals to deal, and exclusive dealing. Dr. Noll also discusses myriad other behaviors that Napster alleges provide a sufficient nexus to the copyright monopoly to invoke the doctrine of copyright misuse.

* * *

Napster has raised serious questions with respect to possible copyright misuse, based on both the MusicNet agreement and plaintiffs' possible antitrust violations in their entry into digital music delivery. Nor does the court believe Napster's motion to be merely a fishing expedition to avoid summary judgment. The same conduct by plaintiffs that Napster alleges gives rise to copyright misuse is currently under investigation by the Department of Justice. For the time being, however, neither side has sufficiently developed the factual and legal bases for their arguments. The evidence presently before the court suggests that Napster needs further discovery in order to sufficiently oppose plaintiffs' motion for summary judgment. As such, the court grants Napster's Rule 56(f) motion with respect to its misuse defense. Once such discovery is completed, both sides will have an opportunity to rebrief the issue of misuse, incorporating any new discovery and focusing on legal issues that were not adequately briefed earlier.

* * *

NOTES & QUESTIONS

Intellectual property and competition policy. Like the first-sale doctrine, the doctrine of copyright misuse can be considered a device to mark the boundary between, on the one hand, the scope of the monopoly granted to an intellectual property owner as incentive for future creators, and, on the other hand, the scope of open competition necessary for a free market. What principles do you think courts and legislators should use in drawing these boundaries? Do the boundaries shift as technology changes?

D. THE AUDIO HOME RECORDING ACT OF 1992

A & M Records, Inc. v. Napster, Inc.

239 F.3d 1004 (9th Cir.2001).

■ BEEZER, CIRCUIT JUDGE:

[For the facts of the case and the court's finding of direct infringement by the users of the Napster service, see Part II(B), *supra*.]

VI

* * * Napster asserts that its users engage in actions protected by § 1008 of the Audio Home Recording Act of 1992, 17 U.S.C. § 1008. * * *

A. Audio Home Recording Act

The statute states in part:

> *No action may be brought under this title alleging infringement of copyright* based on the manufacture, importation, or distribution of a digital audio recording device, a digital audio recording medium, an analog recording device, or an analog recording medium, or *based on the noncommercial use by a consumer*

> *of such a device or medium* for making digital musical recordings or analog musical recordings.

17 U.S.C. § 1008 (emphases added). Napster contends that MP3 file exchange is the type of "noncommercial use" protected from infringement actions by the statute. Napster asserts it cannot be secondarily liable for users' nonactionable exchange of copyrighted musical recordings.

The district court rejected Napster's argument, stating that the Audio Home Recording Act is "irrelevant" to the action because: (1) plaintiffs did not bring claims under the Audio Home Recording Act; and (2) the Audio Home Recording Act does not cover the downloading of MP3 files. *Napster,* 114 F.Supp.2d at 916 n. 19.

We agree with the district court that the Audio Home Recording Act does not cover the downloading of MP3 files to computer hard drives. First, "[u]nder the plain meaning of the Act's definition of digital audio recording devices, computers (and their hard drives) are not digital audio recording devices because their 'primary purpose' is not to make digital audio copied recordings." *Recording Indus. Ass'n of Am. v. Diamond Multimedia Sys., Inc.,* 180 F.3d 1072, 1078 (9th Cir.1999). Second, notwithstanding Napster's claim that computers are "digital audio recording devices," computers do not make "digital music recordings" as defined by the Audio Home Recording Act. *Id.* at 1077 (citing S. Rep. 102–294) ("There are simply no grounds in either the plain language of the definition or in the legislative history for interpreting the term 'digital musical recording' to include songs fixed on computer hard drives."). * * *

* * *

NOTES & QUESTIONS

1. *The Audio Home Recording Act.* The Audio Home Recording Act of 1992 ("AHRA"), Pub. L. No. 102–563, 106 Stat. 4248 (1992), was enacted in response to the release into the consumer marketplace of digital audio tape ("DAT") recorders. A DAT recorder may be used by consumers to make copies of audio recordings in digital format. Like music recorded on a CD, music recorded on DAT can be copied repeatedly, through multiple generations, with no loss of fidelity to the original. Holders of copyrights in musical works and recordings feared that availability of DAT recorders would lead to widespread copying of recorded music, cutting into sales of tapes and CDs. Manufacturers of DAT recorders entered into negotiations involving record companies, music publishers, musicians, and other participants in the music industry, arriving at a settlement that Congress ratified by enacting the AHRA.

The central feature of the AHRA is a simple quid pro quo. First, the music industry receives a technological solution to the problem of unauthorized copying of music recordings. All DAT recorders and similar devices, which in the statute are called "digital audio recording devices" ("DARDs"), must be outfitted with a Serial Copy Management System. 17 U.S.C. § 1002(a). This technology allows an original recording to be copied any number of times, but prevents the copying of a copy. Second, the music industry receives a stream of royalty payments deriving from sales of DARDs and the media (e.g., digital audio tapes) upon which these devices record. Manufacturers and importers of these devices pay a royalty of two percent of the sales price, and manufacturers and importers of recording media pay three percent of the sales price, into a fund that is distributed to music copyright holders and to recording artists. 17 U.S.C. § 1003–06.

In return, the manufacturers of the recording devices are free to market them, without the threat of being sued as contributory infringers. This is accomplished by Section 1008 of the AHRA, addressed in the above excerpt from *A & M Records v. Napster*.

2. *MP3 player not a DARD.* In rejecting Napster's argument based on the AHRA, the court relies on its earlier decision in *Recording Industry Ass'n of America v. Diamond Multimedia Systems, Inc.*, 180 F.3d 1072 (9th Cir.1999). That case addressed the question whether the Diamond Rio, a portable MP3 player, is a "digital audio recording device" ("DARD") under the AHRA; if so, the Rio would have to incorporate a Serial Copyright Management System, and its manufacturer would have to pay royalties. The court held that the Rio is not a DARD. It reached this result through analysis of the AHRA's rather complex set of nested definitions. According to these definitions, a device is a DARD only if it is capable of reproducing a "digital music recording." A "digital music recording" is defined as a material object in which sounds are fixed, but (as the court held) excludes computer hard drives. Since the Rio is capable of recording MP3's only from a hard drive, it cannot reproduce a "digital music recording," and therefore is not a DARD.

As a consumer, should you be happy or unhappy with the decision in *RIAA v. Diamond Multimedia*?

3. *Insulation for burning?* If a computer user downloads an MP3 file from the Internet, and burns it directly onto a CD–R disk using her computer's CD–RW drive, is she insulated from infringement liability under the AHRA, 17 U.S.C. § 1008? Consult the definitions of "digital audio recording device" and "digital audio recording medium" in 17 U.S.C. § 1001.

IV. WEBCASTING, MUSIC DOWNLOADS AND STATUTORY LICENSES

In the preceding Part, we saw that several defenses may serve to limit the exclusive rights conferred on the owner of a copyright under 17 U.S.C. § 106. Another device that limits the scope of these exclusive rights is the statutory, or "compulsory," license. To promote a particular socially beneficial use of a copyrighted work by persons other than the owner of the copyright, Congress may grant a license to use such a work to anyone whose use satisfies the conditions set forth in the statute creating the license and who pays the prescribed royalty.

By creating a compulsory licensing scheme for particular socially beneficial uses of copyrighted works, Congress obviates the need for licensees to negotiate directly with copyright owners. Statutory licenses, like the privilege of fair use, thereby reduce transaction costs that might otherwise prevent such socially beneficial uses. As a tool for implementing public policy, a compulsory license has certain advantages over the fair use defense. First, a compulsory license allows Congress precisely to target the particular kinds of uses that it desires to promote. The statute granting the license can include detailed conditions that must be satisfied before a person may enjoy the benefit of this license. Second, by creating a compulsory license Congress can require the licensee to pay a royalty to the copyright owner, balancing the interests of the public and copyright owners.

Finally, a compulsory license provides the user of another's work with greater certainty that the use is noninfringing. While broad in scope, the doctrine of fair use is uncertain in application: the four factors a court must weigh when determining whether a particular defendant is entitled to this defense are very general and require a nuanced analysis of the alleged infringing activity. As a result, until the matter is fully litigated, a person cannot be certain whether use of another's work is noninfringing. Such uncertainty may chill socially beneficial uses of copyrighted works.

Compulsory licenses are a derogation from the sweeping "exclusive rights" that the Copyright Act grants to copyright owners, and apply only to a few specific categories of activity. Of particular relevance for present purposes are the two statutory licenses contained in Sections 114 and 115 of the Copyright Act, which apply to webcasting (the digital transmission of sound recordings over the Internet by means of streaming audio technologies) and digital music deliveries. *See* The Digital Performance Right in Sound Recording Act of 1995, Pub. L. No. 104–39, 109 Stat. 336 (1995), and Title IV of the Digital Millennium Copyright Act, Pub. L. No. 105–304, 112 Stat. 2860, 2887 (1998). These compulsory licenses are the focus of the next excerpt.

R. Anthony Reese, *Copyright and Internet Music Transmissions: Existing Law, Major Controversies, Possible Solutions*

55 U. MIAMI L. REV. 237 (2001).

* * *

I. Copyright Law Relevant to Internet Music Transmissions

A. Musical Works and Sound Recordings: Two Separate Copyrights

Every musical recording involves two separate copyrightable works: a "musical work" and a "sound recording." A musical work is the sequence of notes, and often words, that a songwriter or composer creates. For example, when Cole Porter sat down at a piano and wrote the lyrics and music to the song "Ev'ry Time We Say Goodbye," he created a musical work protectible by copyright law. That work can be recorded in many ways, including in printed sheet music that a musician can use to play or sing the song. A sound recording, in contrast, is a fixation of sounds, including a fixation of a performance of someone playing and singing a musical work. For instance, when Ella Fitzgerald and her accompanists went into a studio in the 1950s and performed Cole Porter's song "Ev'ry Time We Say Goodbye," the recording of that performance resulted in a sound recording. When Annie Lennox recorded the same song in the 1990s, her recorded performance was another sound recording of Porter's musical work. Transmitting recorded musical performances over the Internet involves transmitting both the sound recording and the musical work embodied in the recording.[10] U.S. copyright law grants different rights and limitations to musical works and sound recordings, increasing the complexity of the copyright implications of such transmissions, particularly when the copyright rights in those works are owned or administered by different parties.

B. *The Copyright Owners' Relevant Rights: Reproduction and Public Performance*

1. *The Reproduction Right*

Copyright law grants copyright owners the right to control certain uses of their works, including the exclusive rights to reproduce and to publicly perform copyrighted works. These are the rights most relevant to Internet music transmissions. The right to reproduce a copyrighted work is the oldest right of the copyright owner and applies to both musical works and sound recordings. Copyright owners of musical works and sound recordings have the exclusive right to reproduce their works in "phonorecords," which are "material objects in which sounds ... are fixed ... and from which the sounds can be perceived, reproduced, or otherwise communicated, either directly or with the aid of a machine or device."[13] A phonorecord can be a vinyl LP, a cassette tape, a compact disc, or a hard drive or floppy diskette containing an MP3 file. These are all tangible objects in which sounds are fixed and from which, given the proper hardware (and, in some cases, software), those sounds can be made audible. The reproduction right generally encompasses making any phonorecord of a copyrighted work.

Any single phonorecord of music is a phonorecord of both the sound recording fixed in the phonorecord and any musical work performed in that sound recording. For example, a compact disc of Ella Fitzgerald's album The Cole Porter Songbook constitutes a phonorecord of Cole Porter's musical work "Ev'ry Time We Say Goodbye" and a phonorecord of Ella

10. Transmitting live musical performances would generally involve only the copyright in the musical work, since a live, unfixed performance is not protected by copyright, which extends only to fixed works. Unauthorized transmission of a live performance, however, may violate 17 U.S.C. § 1101(a)(2) (1998).

13. Id. § 101 ("phonorecords"). Musical work copyright owners also have the exclusive right to reproduce their works in copies, such as sheet music. See id. ("copies").

Fitzgerald's sound recording of that musical work. Someone who makes a tape of that compact disc therefore produces a new phonorecord, the tape, of both the musical work and the sound recording. The same is true of someone who "rips" an MP3 version of the song from a compact disc, or who downloads such a version from a Web site and stores the MP3 file on a hard drive or other storage medium.

2. Limitations on the Reproduction Right in Musical Works: The Compulsory Mechanical License and Digital Phonorecord Deliveries

The "compulsory mechanical license" limits the copyright owner's exclusive right to make phonorecords of most musical works.[15] Once the owner allows someone to make and sell phonorecords of a musical work, anyone else can make his or her own phonorecords of that work. This requires compliance with certain procedural requirements and paying a fee established by the Copyright Office.[16] This license essentially allows the making of so-called "cover" recordings, where a performer records a song that another performer previously recorded. As long as the compulsory license requirements are complied with, one can go into a recording studio and record, for example, a performance of the song "Yesterday" as it was written by John Lennon and Paul McCartney and sell compact discs of the recording without the permission of the copyright owner of that musical work. In fact, most performers who make cover recordings do not actually get a compulsory license from the Copyright Office. Instead, they usually obtain a license from the Harry Fox Agency, which acts as licensing agent for the U.S. copyright owners (usually music publishing companies) of most musical works.

The compulsory mechanical license grants reproduction and distribution rights only for musical works, not sound recordings. The license would not allow one to record and sell compact discs of the Beatles' original recording of "Yesterday" (instead of recording and selling compact discs of one's own performance of the song). Every compact disc made would be a phonorecord of both the Lennon and McCartney musical work "Yesterday" and of the Beatles' sound recording of "Yesterday." The compulsory license confers only a reproduction privilege in the musical work. In order to make the compact discs, one would need permission from the copyright owner of the Beatles' sound recording, who would be free to refuse permission or to charge any price for that permission.[19] The compulsory mechanical license

15. 17 U.S.C. § 115 (1998). The compulsory license extends to "nondramatic" musical works. Id.

16. The current rate is usually 7.55 cents for each phonorecord. For the full schedule of rates, see 37 C.F.R. §§ 255.2, 255.3 (1999). For an album containing several copyrighted musical works, the royalty would be payable for each phonorecord of each work.

19. Indeed, the compulsory mechanical license for the musical work is not available for making phonorecords of another party's sound recording unless the licensee has authorization for reproduction from the owner of the rights in the sound recording. 17 U.S.C. § 115(a)(1) (1998).

therefore primarily assists recording artists and record companies who want to make and sell their own recordings of songs by other songwriters.

In 1995, Congress amended the compulsory mechanical license to allow reproducing and distributing musical works by means of "digital phonorecord delivery" (hereinafter "DPD"). A DPD is a digital transmission of a sound recording that results in a "specifically identifiable reproduction by or for any transmission recipient of a phonorecord."[20] For example, if one connects to a Web site such as MP3.com or Emusic.com and downloads an MP3 file of the song "Yesterday," the Web site digitally transmits a sound recording of a performance of "Yesterday." At the end of the transmission that MP3 file is stored on that individual's hard drive—a phonorecord. Thus, the Web site has made a digital phonorecord delivery. If the site has obtained a compulsory mechanical license for the composition "Yesterday" and pays the specified royalty rate, then its transmission will not infringe the composition's copyright. The royalty rate, currently identical to the rate for making and selling a physical compact disc or cassette, is set every two years by a two-step process that encourages voluntary, industry-wide negotiations to establish rates to be adopted by the Copyright Office. If negotiations fail, any interested party can petition the Copyright Office to hold an arbitration proceeding to set the fees. The compulsory license only confers the right to make DPDs of the musical work, not any particular sound recording. If a little-known band tries to drum up interest in its music by allowing people to download its cover version of "Yesterday" from its Web site, the band itself will likely own the copyright in the sound recording of its performance. Therefore, the band will have the right to digitally deliver phonorecords of the sound recording, in addition to the right to digitally deliver phonorecords of the Lennon and McCartney musical work given by the compulsory mechanical license. If a Web site allows users to download the Beatles' recording of "Yesterday," then the Web site will need the permission of the owner of the copyright in that sound recording.

3. *The Public Performance Right: Musical Works*

The second exclusive right relevant to Internet music transmissions is the right to publicly perform a copyrighted work. The Copyright Act defines "performing" a work very broadly. One performs Cole Porter's song, "Ev'ry Time We Say Goodbye," if one sings the lyrics to the song, plays the song on a piano, plays a compact disc of the song on a stereo, or plays an MP3 file of the song on a personal computer or a portable playback device. Although all of those activities 'perform' the musical work, they infringe the copyright only if done "publicly." A performance can be public in two ways. First, one "publicly" performs a work by performing it in a public or semi-public place, such as by singing "Ev'ry Time We Say Goodbye" in a nightclub. Second, and more important for music on the Internet, transmitting a performance is a public performance if the transmission is "to the public, by means of any device or process, whether the members of the

20. Id. § 115(d).

public capable of receiving the performance ... receive it in the same place or in separate places and at the same time or at different times."[23] A radio station that broadcasts a performance of "Ev'ry Time We Say Goodbye" publicly performs the musical work by transmitting a performance to the public. Similarly, a Web site that transmits the recording to users in streaming audio publicly performs the musical work by transmitting a performance to the public. This is true even if each listener is located alone in her own home and only one listener hears the song at any given time. Even if the Web site limits its transmissions to subscribing users who pay a monthly fee, its transmissions will be "to the public."

No general compulsory license exists for the public performance right in musical works; to publicly perform such a work requires the permission of the copyright owner. Because public performances of musical works are fleeting and occur in widely dispersed locations, enforcement of the public performance right has challenged copyright owners. In response, copyright owners created collective rights societies to administer and enforce the public performance right. The principal societies in the United States are the American Society of Composers, Authors and Publishers ("ASCAP"), Broadcast Music, Inc. ("BMI"), and SESAC, Inc. (formerly the Society of European State Authors and Composers). The societies are made up of copyright owners (usually songwriters and music publishers) who grant the society the nonexclusive right to license public performances of their musical works. The societies, in turn, grant blanket licenses to entities that engage in public performances, such as radio and television stations, nightclubs and concert halls, restaurants and retail establishments. In return for a license fee (generally calculated as a percentage of the licensee's revenue), the licensee obtains the right to perform publicly any work in the society's repertoire, and the ASCAP, BMI, and SESAC repertoires collectively include virtually all copyrighted American music.

4. *Sound Recordings: The Digital Transmission Performance Right*

Congress granted the exclusive public performance right to copyright owners of musical works, but not to copyright owners of sound recordings.[26] As a result, a nightclub or radio station that plays a compact disc of Annie Lennox singing "Ev'ry Time We Say Goodbye" publicly performs both Cole Porter's musical work and Annie Lennox's sound recording but needs permission only from the copyright owner of Porter's music and lyrics and not from the copyright owner of Lennox's sound recording.

In 1995, Congress granted sound recording copyright owners a limited public performance right: the right to perform their sound recordings publicly "by means of a digital audio transmission."[27] A Web site that

23. *Id.* § 101 ("publicly"). The Copyright Act defines "transmit" quite broadly: "To 'transmit' a performance ... is to communicate it by any device or process whereby ... sounds are received beyond the place from which they are sent." Id.

26. 17 U.S.C. § 106(4) (1995).

27. 17 U.S.C. § 106(6) (1995). Essentially, a digital audio transmission is a transmission in any non-analog format that embodies a sound recording. 17 U.S.C. § 114(j)(5) (1994 & Supp. IV 1998).

streams a recording of Annie Lennox singing "Ev'ry Time We Say Goodbye" to listeners over the Internet publicly performs the sound recording by means of a digital audio transmission. That activity would be covered by the digital transmission performance right.

Congress also enacted significant limitations on the digital transmission performance right. The scope of the copyright owner's right varies with the type of digital transmission. There are four basic types. The first is a transmission made by an "interactive service" that either transmits a particular sound recording requested by the recipient or transmits a program specially created for the recipient. Several kinds of transmissions are interactive. The archetypal interactive service is the much-prophesied "celestial jukebox," an on-demand service that allows a recipient (who pays a monthly subscription fee or a per-use charge) to connect to a repository of sound recordings and select a particular recording that is immediately transmitted to the recipient's speakers. MusicBank.com has entered into agreements with all of the major record labels to provide, by subscription, on-demand streaming access to all of the recordings in the labels' catalogs. MusicBank will be offering an interactive service, because the subscriber will receive, on request, the transmission of a particular sound recording that she selected. Transmissions by an interactive service are subject to the sound recording copyright owner's digital transmission performance right, so the transmitter needs the permission of the copyright owner prior to making transmissions of the subject recording. The sound recording copyright owner is entitled to charge any price for such permission or to deny permission entirely.[30]

Noninteractive service transmissions basically fall into three categories. First, there are nonsubscription broadcast transmissions.[31] Such transmissions are entirely exempt from a copyright owner's digital transmission performance right, so obtaining permission from the sound recording copyright owner is not necessary.[32] Permission for the public performance of any musical work would be required, though.[33] Many radio stations, in addition to broadcasting over the radio airwaves, now have Web sites where they simultaneously transmit identical programming in streaming audio format. For example, public radio station KUT in Austin, Texas, has a Web site (www.kut.org) that allows users to hear in real time the programming that KUT is broadcasting over the airwaves to central Texas. * * * In response to a petition by the Recording Industry Association of America ("RIAA"), the trade association for the major recording labels, the Copyright Office recently amended its regulations to provide that an Internet

30. In fact, 17 U.S.C. §§ 114(d)(3) and 114(h) (1994 & Supp. IV 1998) impose some limits on the ability of sound recording copyright owners to grant exclusive licenses to interactive services and require, in certain circumstances, that owners who license the digital transmission right to affiliates make licenses available to similar services on no-less-favorable terms.

31. These are "transmission[s] made by a terrestrial broadcast station licensed as such" by the FCC. 17 U.S.C. § 114(j)(3).

32. Id. § 114(d)(1)(A). Certain other types of transmissions are also exempt. Id. §§ 114(d)(1)(B), (C).

33. Id. § 114(d)(4)(B)(i).

simulcast by a licensed AM or FM broadcaster is not within the "nonsubscription broadcast transmission" exemption from the digital transmission performance right.[35] * * *

Second, certain noninteractive transmissions other than broadcast transmissions, although not exempt from the digital transmission performance right, are eligible for a compulsory license of the digital transmission performance right.[37] For example, a hypothetical Web site, WebJazz, that runs a jazz "Web radio station" and streams jazz music to those who visit the site, just as a radio station would broadcast jazz music over the airwaves, would be eligible for such a license.[38] The transmissions are not interactive because WebJazz's programmers, not the site's listeners, select which songs are played. A noninteractive transmitter like WebJazz must adhere to a long list of detailed conditions to qualify for the compulsory license.[39] Those conditions seek to limit the license to those transmissions thought least likely to substitute for the sale of records. Therefore, the conditions attempt to prevent listeners from getting advance notice of which songs are to be transmitted so that they could record them or listen to them "on demand." Some conditions concern the programming that is transmitted. For example, WebJazz cannot transmit, during any three-hour period, more than three different tracks from any one compact disc or more than four different tracks by the same recording artist.[41] Other conditions govern the technology and interfaces used for the transmission.[42] If Web-

35. *See* Public Performance of Sound Recordings: Definition of a Service, 65 Fed. Reg. 77,292 (Dec. 11, 2000). The regulation makes clear that the compulsory license for Web transmissions of sound recordings, discussed in the next paragraph, is available to over-the-air broadcasters for their Internet simulcasts if they meet the statute's detailed conditions for the license.

37. 17 U.S.C. § 114(d)(2).

38. Both subscription and nonsubscription transmissions are eligible for the license, so the site might support itself either by limiting access to subscribers or by transmitting advertising to its listeners. See id. §§ 114(j)(9), (14). If the transmission is nonsubscription, it must, in order to qualify for the statutory license, be part of a service whose "primary purpose" is to provide audio or entertainment programming to the public and not to sell or promote particular products or services. Id. § 114(j)(6).

39. The conditions are set forth in id. §§ 114(d)(2)(A), (C).

41. 17 U.S.C. §§ 114(d)(2)(C)(i) and 114(j)(13). Other programming-related conditions include a ban on advance publication of program schedules or specific titles to be played, § 114(d)(2)(C)(ii), minimum time limits for the program of which a transmission of a sound recording is a part, § 114(d)(2)(C)(iii), a requirement to transmit recordings from lawfully made phonorecords and not from bootleg recordings, § 114(d)(2)(C)(vii), and a bar on transmitting visual images along with the audio transmission in a way likely to confuse recipients as to the endorsement or affiliation of the recording artist or copyright owner, § 114(d)(2)(C)(iv).

42. For example, the transmitter must identify, in text displayed to the recipient during the performance, the title of the recording, the title of the record from which it comes, and the name of the recording artist. 17 U.S.C. § 114(d)(2)(C)(ix). Other conditions of this type include not causing the receiving equipment to change channel, § 114(d)(2)(A)(ii), transmitting any identifying information encoded in the sound recording by the copyright owner, § 114(d)(2)(A)(iii), accommodating and not interfering with technical measures used by copyright owners to identify or protect their works, § 114(d)(2)(C)(viii), not taking any affirmative steps to cause the making of a phonorecord by the recipient of the transmission and setting the transmission equipment

Jazz meets all the conditions, then it can obtain a compulsory license to transmit any sound recording by complying with Copyright Office procedures and paying the license fee. As with the compulsory mechanical license for DPDs, the license fee is to be determined every two years by voluntary negotiations among the parties to establish an industry-wide consensus on rates that would then be adopted by the Copyright Office. Failing that, rates would be set by an arbitration proceeding in the Copyright Office.[43] Rates have not yet been set for the generally available compulsory license for eligible noninteractive transmissions.[7] The compulsory license, like the broadcast exemption, applies only to the digital transmission performance right in sound recordings and not to the public performance right in musical works. A transmitter that qualifies for the compulsory license will therefore still need to obtain musical work performance licenses, usually from ASCAP, BMI, and SESAC.

Third, noninteractive transmissions that are not broadcast transmissions and that do not meet the conditions for the compulsory license are fully subject to the digital transmission performance right. Persons making such transmissions must generally obtain the permission of the copyright owner. If WebJazz wanted to program "all Ella Fitzgerald, all the time," it would not be able to comply with the limit of four tracks by one artist in three hours. Thus, it would not qualify for the compulsory license. WebJazz would therefore need permission for its digital transmission of each sound recording from the copyright owners. * * *

II. Application of Copyright Law to Streaming and Download Transmissions

A. *Streaming Transmissions*

The provisions of U.S. copyright law outlined in Part I govern the two major types of music transmissions available over the Internet today: streaming and downloading musical files. A digital music file can be streamed to a user. Over the World Wide Web, for example, a user might connect to the Web site of the Red Hot Organization and find a streaming audio file of Annie Lennox's recording of "Ev'ry Time We Say Goodbye" from the album Red, Hot + Blue. The user might then request that the Web site transmit that file. As the site transmits the information in the file, the user's computer makes the recording audible through the computer's speakers. During the transmission, the user's computer temporarily stores or "buffers" segments of the recording before making them audible, in order to allow (usually) uninterrupted playback of the recording even if network congestion slows the transmission. As the recording is played, however, the part of the file that is played is removed from the buffer and replaced with subsequent portions of the recording. At the end of the

to limit such recording if possible, § 114(d)(2)(C)(vi), and cooperating to prevent the scanning of transmissions in order to select a particular recording to be transmitted, § 114(d)(2)(C)(v).

43. 17 U.S.C. § 114(f)(2).

7. [The Librarian of Congress established these rates in June 2002. *See* Note 5, following this excerpt.—Eds.]

transmission, the user has heard the entire recording. Generally, no copy of the recording remains stored on the computer. If the user wishes to hear the streamed recording again, she must again connect to the Red Hot Web site and request that it transmit the file again.

Such streaming transmissions may fit a wide variety of Internet music business models. A user might hear streaming transmissions from the Web site of a particular musician or record label that wishes to promote particular recordings, from a Web "radio station" that transmits a variety of music in the same way that over-the-air radio stations do, or from a "music locker" service that stores particular songs selected (and possibly purchased) by the user to provide the user access to those songs from any Internet-connected computer.

A streaming transmission over the Internet clearly constitutes a digital transmission performance of the sound recording transmitted and of any musical work embodied in that sound recording. Such a transmission will infringe the public performance rights unless the person making it has permission or is otherwise excused. For example, WebJazz may want to transmit Annie Lennox's recording of "Ev'ry Time We Say Goodbye" in streaming audio as part of its Webcast. With respect to Annie Lennox's sound recording, WebJazz will either be exempt from the digital transmission right entirely (if it makes a nonsubscription broadcast transmission), be entitled to transmit the stream under the a compulsory license (if the transmission is noninteractive and meets all the license conditions), or be required to obtain permission from the copyright owner (if the stream is available to listeners on demand). The transmitter will need to obtain permission to perform Cole Porter's musical work publicly. ASCAP, BMI, and SESAC each provide blanket licenses for such transmissions of the works in their respective repertoires.[46]

The major copyright question with respect to streaming audio transmissions is whether every such transmission constitutes not only a public performance of the works transmitted but also a reproduction of those works. The reproduction and performance rights are independent of one another. The statutory language and legislative history contemplate that a single transmission could involve the exercise of both reproduction and public performance rights. Such a transmission occurs where the recipient can both hear the song received and store a copy of it.

The more significant aspect of the question is whether every streaming audio transmission reproduces both the musical work and the sound recording transmitted, even if the recipient does not retain any copy of the music at the end of the transmission, as is the case with an ordinary streaming transmission. This possibility arises largely because of the temporary storage in random-access memory (hereinafter "RAM") that occurs in essentially every computer. As a streaming audio transmission is re-

46. See www.ascap.com/weblicense/webintro.html (last visited Feb. 10, 2001), www.bmi.com/iama/webcaster/automated/index.asp (last visited Feb. 10, 2001), www.sesac.com/licensing/internet_newmedia.htm (last visited Feb. 10, 2001).

ceived, the digits that represent the sounds to be played back by the recipient's streaming audio software will temporarily be stored in the RAM of the recipient's computer, until they are processed by the software, played back, and replaced in RAM by subsequently transmitted digits.[49] In cases not involving streaming transmissions, at least two federal appellate courts have held that storing a copyrightable work in RAM constitutes reproduction of the work in violation of the copyright owner's exclusive reproduction right.[50] Many have criticized these decisions as inconsistent with the statutory language and the legislative history of the Copyright Act. Some lower courts and government officials have, however, adopted this view, suggesting that courts may rule that temporary RAM storage that occurs automatically in the course of every streaming audio transmission constitutes a reproduction of the copyrighted works transmitted.

The legislative history of the compulsory DPD license indicates that at least some RAM storage as part of a streaming transmission will constitute the reproduction of a phonorecord. For purposes of license rates, the statute distinguishes between ordinary DPDs and "incidental" DPDs.[55] The legislative history provides the following example to explain the distinction:

> [I]f a transmission system was designed to allow transmission recipients to hear sound recordings substantially at the time of transmission, but the sound recording was transmitted in a high-speed burst of data and stored in a computer memory for prompt playback (such storage being technically the making of a phonorecord), and the transmission recipient could not retain the phonorecord for playback on subsequent occasions (or for any other purpose), delivering the phonorecord to the transmission recipient would be incidental to the transmission.[56]

Thus, at least streaming transmissions where the entire transmitted sound recording is stored at one time in the RAM of the recipient's computer for playback would appear to involve the making of a DPD. It is not clear, however, whether the temporary RAM storage of small portions of a sound recording involved in the buffering typically done by streaming software today would constitute a DPD. * * *

B. Download Transmissions

The other major type of Internet music transmission, aside from streaming audio, is the downloading of a file of recorded music. Over the World Wide Web, for example, a user might connect to the Red Hot

49. Reproduction may also occur because the streaming software may temporarily store (or cache) the received data on the hard drive of the recipient's computer, where it may remain until it is written over by other data. There is little doubt that such storage technically constitutes the reproduction of the stored work in a phonorecord.

50. *Stenograph L.L.C. v. Bossard Assocs.*, 144 F.3d 96 (D.C.Cir.1998); *MAI Systems Corp. v. Peak Computer, Inc.*, 991 F.2d 511 (9th Cir.1993).

55. 17 U.S.C. § 115(c)(3)(C), (D).

56. S. Rep. No. 104–128 at 39.

Organization's Web site and find an MP3 file of Annie Lennox's recording of "Ev'ry Time We Say Goodbye." The user can direct the Web site to transmit the music file to her, and the user's computer will store the received file, typically on the computer's hard drive. At the end of the transmission, the user has her own copy of the file on her computer hard drive, and she can listen to the recording embodied in that file whenever she wants, without any need to be connected to the Web site that originally transmitted it. With appropriate equipment, the user can copy the file onto a compact disc or onto the storage device of a portable, Walkman-like player that will allow her to listen to the recording away from her computer.

Download transmissions may be provided by various types of Internet entities. A user might download a music file from the Web site of a recording artist or record label which provides downloads for promotional purposes. The user might also download a file from a Web site specializing in downloadable music by many artists, such as Emusic.com (which has over 100,000 tracks available for download for ninety-nine cents each), MP3.com (where music files from thousands of artists can be downloaded, many for free), or DownloadsDirect (which features both free and pay downloadable files). Or, instead of downloading from a Web site, the user might download a music file directly from the hard drive of another user's computer using file-sharing software such as Napster or Gnutella.

A user who downloads an MP3 file of Annie Lennox's recording of "Ev'ry Time We Say Goodbye" reproduces in a phonorecord—the new file on the user's hard drive—both Lennox's sound recording and Cole Porter's musical work. To make that phonorecord without infringing those copyrights will generally require permission from both copyright owners. Permission to reproduce Annie Lennox's sound recording can only be obtained from the owner of the copyright in that sound recording—usually the record label that originally issued the recording. Once the sound recording copyright owner has authorized the reproduction, permission to make a phonorecord of Cole Porter's musical work by means of a digital phonorecord delivery can be obtained in the form of the compulsory mechanical license or a mechanical license from the Harry Fox Agency. Some question may exist as to who exactly is committing the act of reproduction.[72] Under any view, however, the party transmitting the file probably faces liability for copyright infringement, either direct or contributory, if the transmission is not authorized.[73] As a result, no matter who is seen, as a technical

72. One possibility would be to view the downloading end user as the party who is making the new phonorecord. The user, after all, has instructed her computer to connect to the computer where the digital musical file is stored, to request that the file be transmitted to her computer, and to store the transmitted file as it is received. Another possibility would be to view the party that transmits the file to the end user as making the reproduction: the transmission of the data from the transmitter's computer to the receiving computer's hard drive results in the new copy of the file. A third possibility would be to view both the transmitter and the downloading user as acting jointly to reproduce the file; therefore, they would be jointly liable for any infringement involved.

73. If the transmitter is considered to be the party making the new phonorecord,

matter, to be making the new phonorecord on the download recipient's hard drive, the entity transmitting the file likely will need reproduction licenses.

The major copyright question regarding download transmissions is the flip side of the question about streaming transmissions as reproductions: do download transmissions constitute not only a reproduction of the transmitted music but also a public performance by digital transmission, such that the transmitter will need permission from the owners of the public performance rights as well? Again, the statutory language contemplates that a transmission resulting in a DPD—a download—might also be a public performance of the works delivered[74] and makes clear that the compulsory DPD license does not grant the licensee any public performance rights.[75] The statutory framework, however, does not answer the question of whether any particular download transmission is a public performance.

It is easy to conceive of a download transmission that clearly would be a public performance of the works transmitted. For example, a Web site could transmit a music file to a user so that the user's computer, as it receives the transmitted information, both stores that information on the user's hard drive and makes the transmitted recording audible through the computer's speakers. Such a transmission would be both a reproduction of the sound recording and the musical work embodied in the file (by means of a digital phonorecord delivery) and a public performance of those works (by means of a digital audio transmission to the public). Thus, the transmitter would need permission to reproduce and to publicly perform both works.

Currently, however, typical download transmissions do not allow the end user to hear the song as the digital musical file is being received. Instead, the recipient's computer stores the received file, and the recipient can then, at her leisure, choose to play back the file in order to hear the recording.[76] Although widely perceived as extremely generous to copyright owners in its interpretation of copyright law in the Internet context, the Clinton Administration's White Paper addressing intellectual property rights and computer networks nevertheless took the position that such a transmission, "without the capability of simultaneous 'rendering' of the work, 'rather clearly' did not constitute a public performance." ASCAP and BMI have asserted, however, that every transmission of a musical work to the public, whether or not the transmission allows the user to hear the work in the course of the transmission, is a public performance for which

then the transmitter will be directly liable. If the end user is considered to be the party making the reproduction, then the transmitter will likely face liability for contributory infringement. * * *

74. 17 U.S.C. § 115(d) (Supp. IV 1998).

75. *Id.* § 115(c)(3)(K)(i) (Supp. IV 1998).

76. When the user plays back the recording, she will be performing the sound recording and the musical work it embodies, but unless she plays the song in a public or semi-public place, her performance will not infringe because it is a not a public performance.

permission of the copyright owner is needed—generally in the form of an ASCAP or BMI blanket license.

Neither the language of the Copyright Act, nor its legislative history, appears to resolve this question conclusively, and policy arguments exist on both sides of the matter. But answering the question of whether a download transmission constitutes a public performance may not, at the moment, be of particular urgency because the answer may make little practical difference in the business operations of most transmitters.

For performances of musical works, the practical impact turns on whether Web sites that provide download transmissions also provide streaming transmissions. For example, many download sites offer users the chance to listen to a song—or an excerpt of a song—before deciding whether to download it. Some of these sites might not hold performance licenses in the belief that the fair use doctrine excuses their public performances. Their reliance on the fair use doctrine, though, is probably misplaced because the streaming of any large-scale selection—even of thirty-second excerpts from songs—would not likely qualify as fair use. To comply with copyright law, sites that offer such streaming transmissions are likely to need a performance license. If most download sites also engage in some streaming transmissions, those sites—regardless of any download transmissions—will be publicly performing musical works and will already need licenses from the relevant performing rights societies.

Performance licenses are readily available to operators of these sites because the repertoires of ASCAP, BMI, and SESAC cover the vast majority of copyrighted music, these societies grant blanket licenses that allow the performance of any work in their respective repertoire for the same fee, and at least ASCAP and BMI must, under the antitrust consent decrees that govern their operations, grant licenses to any user willing to pay a reasonable license fee.[80] Thus, applying the performance right to downloads does not raise issues regarding the availability of a performance license but rather raises issues regarding the cost of such a license.

Because ASCAP, BMI, and SESAC grant blanket performance licenses that cover both streaming and download transmissions of all compositions in their repertories, a Web site that already needs performance licenses for its streaming transmissions will not incur any significant additional transaction costs in securing performance licenses for its download transmissions. The cost of the licenses also should not depend on whether a license is needed only for streaming transmissions or for both streaming and download transmissions. Whatever total price the licensor and the licensee are willing to agree to for the performance license can be spread over either the licensee's total transmissions (streams and downloads) or over a subset of those transmissions (streams only). For example, if all transmissions

80. *See United States v. Broad. Music, Inc.*, 1996–1 Trade Cas. (CCH) ¶ 71,378, at 76,891 (S.D.N.Y. Nov. 18, 1994); *United States v. The Am. Soc'y of Composers, Authors & Publishers,* 1950–51 Trade Cas. (CCH) P62,595, at 63, 754 (S.D.N.Y. Mar. 14, 1950). The amount of the reasonable license fee is subject to determination by the District Court, Southern District of New York. Id.

were to be considered performances and if the parties agreed on a rate of one cent per transmission, then a site that makes a thousand transmissions (both streaming and download) would incur a license fee of ten dollars. If, however, only streaming transmissions are required to be licensed, and if only one half of the licensee's transmissions are streams, then a price of two cents per transmission yields the same total price of ten dollars for one thousand total transmissions.

Thus, with respect to musical works, whether considering downloads to be performances has any practical impact on transmitters depends on whether sites that provide downloads also engage in streaming transmissions and therefore already require performance licenses. If they do engage in streaming, the impact would seem to be minimal; if they do not, then the impact is potentially greater. Currently, the larger download sites, such as EMusic.com, MP3.com, DownloadsDirect.com, Launch.com, CDNow.com, and Virgin Jamcast, do engage in both streaming and download transmissions. At the other end of the spectrum, individual Web users who use software such as Napster or Gnutella to make musical files on their hard drives available to other people may be engaged only in downloading and not streaming, so that they would not need a performance license unless their download transmissions constitute public performances. But those users' download transmissions are not licensed even under the reproduction right, which clearly applies to download transmissions, so at least at the moment considering such download transmissions to be performances seems unlikely to have any practical impact on those activities. In between the major music sites and the individual Napster user are a wide range of possible music Web sites, some of which may offer only download and not streaming transmissions. Sites that do not stream any music would not need performance licenses unless downloads are considered public performances; thus, requiring a performance license for download transmissions could impose additional costs on these sites that they otherwise would not face.[85]

Of course, the public performance question affects sound recording copyrights as well. If a download transmission is a public performance of

85. Requiring performance licenses would not have a significant impact on all music Web sites, however. For example, if those who run such sites make available their own recordings of their own compositions, then no third-party licenses will be required whatsoever. The same holds true if a third-party site makes such works available at the request of a performer because the performer will herself be able to license the reproduction and performance rights in both the sound recording and the musical work. Transmitting recordings of other people's musical works, on the other hand, will require a mechanical DPD license at a typical cost of 7.55 cents per work per transmission, and if the site transmits recordings of those works by performers other than the site owner, then a reproduction license for the sound recording (at whatever price the copyright owner charges) will also be necessary. A Web site that can afford to pay for the necessary reproduction licenses may be able to pay the cost of a performance license. Requiring a performance license for download transmissions therefore may not necessarily make download transmissions by such sites so costly that they will not be made, but instead may raise the cost of the transmission to the end user, change the allocation of revenue from the transmission between the transmitter and the copyright owner, or both.

the musical work, then it is also a digital transmission performance of the sound recording. Here again, under current conditions, characterizing a download to be a performance seems unlikely to have a significant economic impact on download Web sites. Because the download results in a reproduction of the sound recording that is transmitted, the transmitter will already need a reproduction license for the transmission. The compulsory DPD license covers only musical works, so the transmitter will have to obtain permission to transmit the sound recording directly from the copyright owner of that work. Where reproduction and digital transmission performance rights in sound recordings are owned by the same entity, as is currently the case for most sound recordings, the copyright owner—with whom the download transmitter will already have to negotiate—will be able to grant the transmitter permission to make the download under both the reproduction and performance rights. No additional transaction costs will be incurred in locating the relevant copyright owner and negotiating permission to perform. Moreover, permission is likely to be equally available (or equally unavailable) whether a download is just a reproduction or is both a reproduction and a performance because no compulsory reproduction license is available for sound recordings. And in the absence of divided ownership and any compulsory license, the price the download transmitter would pay for a reproduction and performance license for a download transmission should not be any greater than the price for a reproduction license alone for the same transmission. If the parties can agree on a price for the license, it will make little difference to either party whether that entire price is designated as the cost for a reproduction license or whether a portion is designated as the cost for a reproduction license and the remainder is designated as the cost for a performance license. It appears that ownership of the reproduction and digital transmission performance rights is not currently divided. Therefore, a transmitter generally will be able to obtain both rights from a single party.

In summary, unless a significant number of download-only sites would need performance licenses which they could not afford, the question of whether a download transmission is a public performance perhaps can await resolution until it becomes clear that answering the question will make a difference. * * *

* * *

NOTES & QUESTIONS

1. *Scope of the Section 114 statutory license.* Section 114 creates a compulsory license allowing "[t]he performance of a sound recording publicly" through certain types of digital transmissions. 17 U.S.C. § 114(d)(2). This provision also places limitations on the scope of this license:

> Nothing in this section annuls or limits in any way—
>
> (i) the exclusive right to publicly perform a musical work, including by means of a digital audio transmission, under section 106(4);

(ii) the exclusive rights in a sound recording or the musical work embodied therein under sections 106(1), 106(2) and 106(3); * * *

17 U.S.C. § 114(d)(4)(B)(i) and (ii).

Review the exclusive rights of a copyright owner set forth in 17 U.S.C. § 106(1)–(6), and bear in mind that a sound recording (the Annie Lennox recording, in Professor Reese's example) and a musical work (the Cole Porter composition) are two different copyrighted works, which receive different types of protection under Section 106. To which type of work does the Section 114 compulsory license apply? To which of the copyright holder's exclusive rights does it apply? To which rights does it not apply?

2. *Streaming as distribution and adaptation.* When a webcaster streams a sound recording over the Internet, it is clearly engaging in "public performance" of both the sound recording and the underlying musical work, thereby implicating the copyright owners' exclusive rights under 17 U.S.C. § 106(4) and (6). Professor Reese addresses the question whether a streaming transmission constitutes a "reproduction" of the two works, which would implicate the copyright owners' rights under Section 106(1), and concludes that the answer is in some circumstances unclear. Does a streaming transmission also constitute a "distribution" of the works, implicating the copyright owners' rights under Section 106(3)? Does the conversion of the sound recording into a format compatible with the recipient's software (for example, RealPlayer) constitute the preparation of a "derivative work" based on the underlying musical composition and sound recording, implicating the copyright owners' rights under Section 106(2)?

3. *Other licenses needed.* In view of your answers to the questions in the above two Notes, consider which exclusive rights, of which copyright owners, are implicated in the streaming of a sound recording over the Internet. Beyond the statutory license extended by Section 114(d)(2), what other licenses must the webcaster obtain for the transmission not to be infringing?

4. *Interactive services.* The use of the Internet to deliver music makes it technologically possible for webcasters to offer personalized programming for individual listeners. Each listener can create a channel that provides music and other programming customized in real-time to that listener's present mood and unique tastes. As a result, personalized webcasts and interactive Internet music delivery generally have caused traditional broadcasters and record companies much anxiety, fearing diversion of their customers. Reacting to the concerns of these industries, Congress limited the exemption under Section 114(d)(1) and the statutory license under Section 114(d)(2) to noninteractive services. Thus, interactive services are fully subject to the digital performance right in sound recordings. Section 114(j)(7) defines an interactive service as

> one that enables a member of the public to receive a transmission of a program specially created for the recipient, or on request, a transmission of a particular sound recording, whether or not as part of a program, which is selected by or on behalf of the

> recipient. The ability of individuals to request that particular sound recordings be performed for reception by the public at large, or in the case of a subscription service, by all subscribers of the service, does not make a service interactive, if the programming on each channel of the service does not substantially consist of sound recordings that are performed within 1 hour of the request or at a time designated by either the transmitting entity or the individual making such request. If an entity offers both interactive and noninteractive services (either concurrently or at different times), the noninteractive component shall not be treated as part of an interactive service.

17 U.S.C. § 114(j)(7). A music service that falls within the scope of this definition must negotiate licenses for the music it offers, company-by-company and recording-by-recording. To be successful and at the same time avoid these additional costs, Internet music services need to qualify for the statutory license under Section 114(d)(2) while offering value-added services and features that distinguish their music service from traditional broadcasters.

Consider one Internet music service that appears to be pushing the limits of the Section 114(d)(2) statutory license. The service allows a listener to create a "station" or "channel" with a playlist of up to twenty-five of the listener's favorite recording artists. The station then plays music by these artists and others who have a similar musical style. Listeners can use a radio timeline to select music from particular time periods, a tempo tuner to select "faster" or "slower" music depending on the listener's mood, as well as a feature to skip to the next song. In your opinion, should such a service be considered a noninteractive service that falls within the scope of the Section 114(d)(2) statutory license, or is it an interactive service?

5. *Licensing terms and royalty rates.* Under 17 U.S.C. § 114(f), the Librarian of Congress is charged with establishing the rates and terms for statutory licenses for certain nonexempt transmissions of digital audio music. In June 2002, the Librarian established royalty rates under which a webcaster must pay $0.0007 each time it streams a song to a recipient (i.e., seven cents each time it streams 100 songs). *See* Determination of Reasonable Rates and Terms for the Digital Performance of Sound Recordings and Ephemeral Recordings, 67 Fed. Reg. 45,239 (Jul. 8, 2002). Webcasters say they cannot afford to pay these rates, and will be driven out of business. The recording industry contends that the rates have been set so low they are effectively being forced to subsidize online broadcasters. *See* Jon Healey, *Net Radio, Labels At Odds Over Royalties*, L.A. TIMES, June 24, 2002, at Part 3, p.1. Should the royalty rate be set at a level that makes webcasting viable under current business models?

Should the terms and conditions set by the Librarian of Congress be reviewable by a court and, if so, what standard of review should the reviewing court employ? *See Bonneville International Corp. v. Peters,* 153 F.Supp.2d 763 (E.D.Pa.2001); *Recording Industry Association of America v. Librarian of Congress,* 176 F.3d 528 (D.C.Cir.1999).

V. A SAFE HARBOR FOR ONLINE SERVICE PROVIDERS

As we have seen, the Copyright Act confers several exclusive rights on copyright owners with the aim of encouraging authors to create original works, but limits those rights to ensure that the works created are reasonably available to the public. We have so far discussed several types of limitations: fair use, the first-sale doctrine, copyright misuse, the right to make copies of musical sound recordings for noncommercial purposes, and compulsory licenses. Another limitation on the exclusive rights of copyright owners is found in 17 U.S.C. § 512, which was added by Title II of the Digital Millennium Copyright Act, Pub. L. No. 105–304, 112 Stat. 2860, 2877 (1998).

Section 512 limits online service providers' liability for direct, contributory, and vicarious copyright infringement.

> As to direct infringement, liability is ruled out for passive, automatic acts engaged in through a technological process initiated by another. Thus, the bill essentially codifies the result in the leading and most thoughtful judicial decision to date: *Religious Technology Center v. Netcom On-Line Communication Services, Inc.,* 907 F.Supp. 1361 (N.D.Cal.1995). In doing so, it overrules those aspects of *Playboy Enterprises, Inc. v. Frena,* 839 F.Supp. 1552 (M.D.Fla.1993), insofar as that case suggests that such acts by service providers could constitute direct infringement, and provides certainty that *Netcom* and its progeny, so far only a few district court cases, will be the law of the land.
>
> As to secondary liability, the bill changes existing law in two primary respects: (1) no monetary relief can be assessed for the passive, automatic acts identified in *Religious Technology Center v. Netcom On-Line Communication Services, Inc.;* and (2) the current criteria for finding contributory infringement or vicarious liability are made clearer and somewhat more difficult to satisfy.

H.R. REP. NO. 105–551, pt. 1, at 11 (1998) (discussing an earlier version of the provision ultimately adopted). If a service provider is within the Section 512 safe harbor, it is not subject to monetary liability based on copyright infringement by users of its system, and is subject only to limited injunctive remedies.

U.S. COPYRIGHT OFFICE, SUMMARY OF THE DIGITAL MILLENNIUM COPYRIGHT ACT OF 1998

1998.
www.loc.gov/copyright/legislation/dmca.pdf.

TITLE II: ONLINE COPYRIGHT INFRINGEMENT LIABILITY LIMITATION

Title II of the DMCA adds a new section 512 to the Copyright Act to create four new limitations on liability for copyright infringement by online service providers. The limitations are based on the following four categories of conduct by a service provider:

1. Transitory communications;

2. System caching;

3. Storage of information on systems or networks at direction of users; and

4. Information location tools.

New section 512 also includes special rules concerning the application of these limitations to nonprofit educational institutions. Each limitation entails a complete bar on monetary damages, and restricts the availability of injunctive relief in various respects. (§ 512(j)). Each limitation relates to a separate and distinct function, and a determination of whether a service provider qualifies for one of the limitations does not bear upon a determination of whether the provider qualifies for any of the other three. (§ 512(n)).

The failure of a service provider to qualify for any of the limitations in § 512 does not necessarily make it liable for copyright infringement. The copyright owner must still demonstrate that the provider has infringed, and the provider may still avail itself of any of the defenses, such as fair use, that are available to copyright defendants generally. (§ 512(*l*)).

* * *

Eligibility for Limitations Generally

A party seeking the benefit of the limitations on liability in Title II must qualify as a "service provider." For purposes of the first limitation, relating to transitory communications, "service provider" is defined in § 512(k)(1)(A) as "an entity offering the transmission, routing, or providing of connections for digital online communications, between or among points specified by a user, of material of the user's choosing, without modification to the content of the material as sent or received." For purposes of the other three limitations, "service provider" is more broadly defined in § 512(k)(1)(B) as "a provider of online services or network access, or the operator of facilities therefor."

In addition, to be eligible for any of the limitations, a service provider must meet two overall conditions: (1) it must adopt and reasonably implement a policy of terminating in appropriate circumstances the accounts of subscribers who are repeat infringers; and (2) it must accommodate and not interfere with "standard technical measures." (§ 512(i)). "Standard technical measures" are defined as measures that copyright owners use to identify or protect copyrighted works, that have been developed pursuant to a broad consensus of copyright owners and service providers in an open, fair and voluntary multi-industry process, are available to anyone on reasonable nondiscriminatory terms, and do not impose substantial costs or burdens on service providers.

Limitation for Transitory Communications

In general terms, section 512(a) limits the liability of service providers in circumstances where the provider merely acts as a data conduit, transmitting digital information from one point on a network to another at someone else's request. This limitation covers acts of transmission, routing, or providing connections for the information, as well as the intermediate and transient copies that are made automatically in the operation of a network.

In order to qualify for this limitation, the service provider's activities must meet the following conditions:

- The transmission must be initiated by a person other than the provider.
- The transmission, routing, provision of connections, or copying must be carried out by an automatic technical process without selection of material by the service provider.
- The service provider must not determine the recipients of the material.
- Any intermediate copies must not ordinarily be accessible to anyone other than anticipated recipients, and must not be retained for longer than reasonably necessary.
- The material must be transmitted with no modification to its content.

Limitation for System Caching

Section 512(b) limits the liability of service providers for the practice of retaining copies, for a limited time, of material that has been made available online by a person other than the provider, and then transmitted to a subscriber at his or her direction. The service provider retains the material so that subsequent requests for the same material can be fulfilled by transmitting the retained copy, rather than retrieving the material from the original source on the network.

The benefit of this practice is that it reduces the service provider's bandwidth requirements and reduces the waiting time on subsequent requests for the same information. On the other hand, it can result in the delivery of outdated information to subscribers and can deprive website operators of accurate "hit" information—information about the number of requests for particular material on a website—from which advertising revenue is frequently calculated. For this reason, the person making the material available online may establish rules about updating it, and may utilize technological means to track the number of "hits."

The limitation applies to acts of intermediate and temporary storage, when carried out through an automatic technical process for the purpose of making the material available to subscribers who subsequently request it. It is subject to the following conditions:

- The content of the retained material must not be modified.

- The provider must comply with rules about "refreshing" material—replacing retained copies of material with material from the original location—when specified in accordance with a generally accepted industry standard data communication protocol.
- The provider must not interfere with technology that returns "hit" information to the person who posted the material, where such technology meets certain requirements.
- The provider must limit users' access to the material in accordance with conditions on access (e.g., password protection) imposed by the person who posted the material.
- Any material that was posted without the copyright owner's authorization must be removed or blocked promptly once the service provider has been notified that it has been removed, blocked, or ordered to be removed or blocked, at the originating site.

Limitation for Information Residing on Systems or Networks at the Direction of Users

Section 512(c) limits the liability of service providers for infringing material on websites (or other information repositories) hosted on their systems. It applies to storage at the direction of a user. In order to be eligible for the limitation, the following conditions must be met:

- The provider must not have the requisite level of knowledge of the infringing activity, as described below.
- If the provider has the right and ability to control the infringing activity, it must not receive a financial benefit directly attributable to the infringing activity.
- Upon receiving proper notification of claimed infringement, the provider must expeditiously take down or block access to the material.

In addition, a service provider must have filed with the Copyright Office a designation of an agent to receive notifications of claimed infringement. The Office provides a suggested form for the purpose of designating an agent (www.loc.gov/copyright/onlinesp/) and maintains a list of agents on the Copyright Office website (www.loc.gov/copyright/onlinesp/list/).

Under the knowledge standard, a service provider is eligible for the limitation on liability only if it does not have actual knowledge of the infringement, is not aware of facts or circumstances from which infringing activity is apparent, or upon gaining such knowledge or awareness, responds expeditiously to take the material down or block access to it.

The statute also establishes procedures for proper notification, and rules as to its effect. (§ 512(c)(3)). Under the notice and takedown procedure, a copyright owner submits a notification under penalty of perjury, including a list of specified elements, to the service provider's designated agent. Failure to comply substantially with the statutory requirements means that the notification will not be considered in determining the requisite level of knowledge by the service provider. If, upon receiving a proper notification, the service provider promptly removes or blocks access to the material identified in the notification, the provider is exempt from monetary liability. In addition, the provider is protected from any liability to any person for claims based on its having taken down the material. (§ 512(g)(1)).

In order to protect against the possibility of erroneous or fraudulent notifications, certain safeguards are built into section 512. Subsection (g)(1) gives the subscriber the opportunity to respond to the notice and takedown by filing a counter notification. In order to qualify for the protection against liability for taking down material, the service provider must promptly notify the subscriber that it has removed or disabled access to the material. If the subscriber serves a counter notification complying with statutory requirements, including a statement under penalty of perjury that the material was removed or disabled through mistake or misidentification, then unless the copyright owner files an action seeking a court order against the subscriber, the service provider must put the material back up within 10–14 business days after receiving the counter notification.

Penalties are provided for knowing material misrepresentations in either a notice or a counter notice. Any person who knowingly materially misrepresents that material is infringing, or that it was removed or blocked through mistake or misidentification, is liable for any resulting damages (including costs and attorneys' fees) incurred by the alleged infringer, the copyright owner or its licensee, or the service provider. (§ 512(f)).

Limitation for Information Location Tools

Section 512(d) relates to hyperlinks, online directories, search engines and the like. It limits liability for the acts of referring or linking users to a site that contains infringing material by using such information location tools, if the following conditions are met:

- The provider must not have the requisite level of knowledge that the material is infringing. The knowledge standard is the same as under the limitation for information residing on systems or networks.
- If the provider has the right and ability to control the infringing activity, the provider must not receive a financial benefit directly attributable to the activity.
- Upon receiving a notification of claimed infringement, the provider must expeditiously take down or block access to the material.

These are essentially the same conditions that apply under the previous limitation, with some differences in the notification requirements. The provisions establishing safeguards against the possibility of erroneous or fraudulent notifications, as discussed above, as well as those protecting the provider against claims based on having taken down the material apply to this limitation. (§§ 512(f)–(g)).

Special Rules Regarding Liability of Nonprofit Educational Institutions

Section 512(e) determines when the actions or knowledge of a faculty member or graduate student employee who is performing a teaching or research function may affect the eligibility of a nonprofit educational institution for one of the four limitations on liability. As to the limitations for transitory communications or system caching, the faculty member or student shall be considered a "person other than the provider," so as to avoid disqualifying the institution from eligibility. As to the other limitations, the knowledge or awareness of the faculty member or student will not be attributed to the institution. The following conditions must be met:

- The faculty member or graduate student's infringing activities do not involve providing online access to course materials that were required or recommended during the past three years;
- The institution has not received more than two notifications over the past three years that the faculty member or graduate student was infringing; and
- The institution provides all of its users with informational materials describing and promoting compliance with copyright law.

* * *

A & M Records, Inc. v. Napster, Inc.

54 U.S.P.Q.2d 1746 (N.D.Cal.2000).

■ PATEL, CHIEF J.

On December 6, 1999, plaintiff record companies filed suit alleging contributory and vicarious federal copyright infringement and related state law violations by defendant Napster, Inc. ("Napster"). Now before this court is defendant's motion for summary adjudication of the applicability of a safe harbor provision of the Digital Millennium Copyright Act ("DMCA"), 17 U.S.C. § 512(a), to its business activities. Defendant argues that the entire Napster system falls within the safe harbor and, hence, that plaintiffs may not obtain monetary damages or injunctive relief, except as narrowly specified by subparagraph 512(j)(1)(B). In the alternative, Napster asks the court to find subsection 512(a) applicable to its role in downloading MP3 music files, as opposed to searching for or indexing such files. Having considered the parties' arguments and for the reasons set forth below, the court enters the following memorandum and order.

BACKGROUND

Napster—a small Internet start-up based in San Mateo, California—makes its proprietary MusicShare software freely available for Internet users to download. Users who obtain Napster's software can then share MP3 music files with others logged-on to the Napster system. MP3 files, which reproduce nearly CD-quality sound in a compressed format, are available on a variety of websites either for a fee or free-of-charge. Napster allows users to exchange MP3 files stored on their own computer hard-drives directly, without payment, and boasts that it "takes the frustration out of locating servers with MP3 files." Def. Br. at 4.

Although the parties dispute the precise nature of the service Napster provides, they agree that using Napster typically involves the following basic steps: After downloading MusicShare software from the Napster website, a user can access the Napster system from her computer. The MusicShare software interacts with Napster's server-side software when the user logs on, automatically connecting her to one of some 150 servers that Napster operates. The MusicShare software reads a list of names of MP3 files that the user has elected to make available. This list is then added to a directory and index, on the Napster server, of MP3 files that users who are logged-on wish to share. If the user wants to locate a song, she enters its name or the name of the recording artist on the search page of the MusicShare program and clicks the "Find It" button. The Napster software then searches the current directory and generates a list of files responsive to the search request. To download a desired file, the user highlights it on the list and clicks the "Get Selected Song(s)" button. The user may also view a list of files that exist on another user's hard drive and select a file from that list. When the requesting user clicks on the name of a file, the Napster server communicates with the requesting user's and host user's[2] MusicShare browser software to facilitate a connection between the two users and initiate the downloading of the file without any further action on either user's part.

According to Napster, when the requesting user clicks on the name of the desired MP3 file, the Napster server routes this request to the host user's browser. The host user's browser responds that it either can or cannot supply the file. If the host user can supply the file, the Napster server communicates the host's address and routing information to the requesting user's browser, allowing the requesting user to make a connection with the host and receive the desired MP3 file. The parties disagree about whether this process involves a hypertext link that the Napster server-side software provides. However, plaintiffs admit that the Napster server gets the necessary IP address information from the host user, enabling the requesting user to connect to the host. The MP3 file is actually transmitted over the Internet, *see, e.g.*, Def. Reply Br. at 3, but the steps necessary to make that connection could not take place without the Napster server.

The Napster system has other functions besides allowing users to search for, request, and download MP3 files. For example, a requesting user can play a downloaded song using the MusicShare software. Napster also hosts a chat room.

2. Napster uses the term "host user" to refer to the user who makes the desired MP3 file available for downloading.

Napster has developed a policy that makes compliance with all copyright laws one of the "terms of use" of its service and warns users that:

> Napster will terminate the accounts of users who are repeat infringers of the copyrights, or other intellectual property rights, of others. In addition, Napster reserves the right to terminate the account of a user upon any single infringement of the rights of others in conjunction with use of the Napster service.

However, the parties disagree over when this policy was instituted and how effectively it bars infringers from using the Napster service. Napster claims that it had a copyright compliance policy as early as October 1999, but admits that it did not document or notify users of the existence of this policy until February 7, 2000.

* * *

DISCUSSION

Section 512 of the DMCA addresses the liability of online service and Internet access providers for copyright infringements occurring online. Subsection 512(a) exempts qualifying service providers from monetary liability for direct, vicarious, and contributory infringement and limits injunctive relief to the degree specified in subparagraph 512(j)(1)(B). Interpretation of subsection 512(a), or indeed any of the section 512 safe harbors, appears to be an issue of first impression.

Napster claims that its business activities fall within the safe harbor provided by subsection 512(a). This subsection limits liability "for infringement of copyright by reason of the [service] provider's transmitting, routing, or providing connections for, material through a system or network controlled or operated by or for the service provider, or by reason of the intermediate and transient storage of that material in the course of such transmitting, routing, or providing connections," if five conditions are satisfied:

(1) the transmission of the material was initiated by or at the direction of a person other than the service provider;

(2) the transmission, routing, provision of connections, or storage is carried out through an automatic technical process without selection of the material by the service provider;

(3) the service provider does not select the recipients of the material except as an automatic response to the request of another person;

(4) no copy of the material made by the service provider in the course of such intermediate or transient storage is maintained on the system or network in a manner ordinarily accessible to anyone other than the anticipated recipients, and no such copy is maintained on the system or network in a manner ordinarily accessible to such anticipated recipients for a longer period than is reasonably necessary for the transmission, routing, or provision of connections; and

(5) the material is transmitted through the system or network without modification of its content.

17 U.S.C. § 512(a).

Citing the "definitions" subsection of the statute, Napster argues that it is a "service provider" for the purposes of the 512(a) safe harbor. *See* 17 U.S.C. § 512(k)(1)(A).[4] First, it claims to offer the "transmission, routing, or providing of connections for digital online communications" by enabling the connection of users' hard-drives and the transmission of MP3 files "directly from the Host hard drive and Napster browser through the Internet to the user's Napster browser and hard drive." Def. Reply Br. at 3. Second, Napster states that users choose the online communication points and the MP3 files to be transmitted with no direction from Napster. Finally, the Napster system does not modify the content of the transferred files. Defendant contends that, because it meets the definition of "service provider,"[5] it need only satisfy the five remaining requirements of the safe harbor to prevail in its motion for summary adjudication.

Defendant then seeks to show compliance with these requirements by arguing: (1) a Napster user, and never Napster itself, initiates the transmission of MP3 files; (2) the transmission occurs through an automatic, technical process without any editorial input from Napster; (3) Napster does not choose the recipients of the MP3 files; (4) Napster does not make a copy of the material during transmission; and (5) the content of the material is not modified during transmission. Napster maintains that the 512(a) safe harbor thus protects its core function—"transmitting, routing and providing connections for sharing of the files its users choose." Def. Reply Br. at 2.

Plaintiffs disagree. They first argue that subsection 512(n) requires the court to analyze each of Napster's functions independently and that not all of these functions fall under the 512(a) safe harbor. In their view, Napster provides information location tools—such as a search engine, directory, index, and links—that are covered by the more stringent eligibility requirements of subsection 512(d), rather than subsection 512(a).

4. Subparagraph 512(k)(1)(A) provides:

As used in subsection (a), the term "service provider" means an entity offering the transmission, routing, or providing of connections for digital online communications, between or among points specified by a user, of material of the user's choosing, without modification to the content of the material sent or received.

Subparagraph 512(k)(1)(B) states:

As used in this section, other than subsection (a), the term "service provider" means a provider of online services or network access, or the operator of facilities therefor, and includes an entity described in subparagraph (A).

5. It is not entirely clear to the court that Napster qualifies under the narrower subparagraph 512(k)(1)(A). However, plaintiffs appear to concede that Napster is a "service provider" within the meaning of subparagraph 512(k)(1)(A), arguing instead that Napster does not satisfy the additional limitations that the prefatory language of subsection 512(a) imposes. The court assumes, but does not hold, that Napster is a "service provider" under subparagraph 512(k)(1)(A).

Plaintiffs also contend that Napster does not perform the function which the 512(a) safe harbor protects because the infringing material is not transmitted or routed *through* the Napster system, as required by subsection 512(a). They correctly note that the definition of "service provider" under subparagraph 512(k)(1)(A) is not identical to the prefatory language of subsection 512(a). The latter imposes the additional requirement that transmitting, routing, or providing connections must occur "through the system or network." Plaintiffs argue in the alternative that, if users' computers are part of the Napster system, copies of MP3 files are stored on the system longer than reasonably necessary for transmission, and thus subparagraph 512(a)(4) is not satisfied.

Finally, plaintiffs note that, under the general eligibility requirements established in subsection 512(i), a service provider must have adopted, reasonably implemented, and informed its users of a policy for terminating repeat infringers. Plaintiffs contend that Napster only adopted its copyright compliance policy after the onset of this litigation and even now does not discipline infringers in any meaningful way. Therefore, in plaintiffs' view, Napster fails to satisfy the DMCA's threshold eligibility requirements or show that the 512(a) safe harbor covers any of its functions.

I. Independent Analysis of Functions

Subsection 512(n) of the DMCA states:

> Subsections (a), (b), (c), and (d) describe separate and distinct functions for purposes of applying this section. Whether a service provider qualifies for the limitation on liability in any one of those subsections shall be based solely on the criteria in that subsection and shall not affect a determination of whether that service provider qualifies for the limitations on liability under any other such subsections.

Citing subsection 512(n), plaintiffs argue that the 512(a) safe harbor does not offer blanket protection to Napster's entire system. Plaintiffs consider the focus of the litigation to be Napster's function as an information location tool—eligible for protection, if at all, under the more rigorous subsection 512(d). They contend that the system does not operate as a passive conduit within the meaning of subsection 512(a). In this view, Napster's only possible safe harbor is subsection 512(d), which applies to service providers "referring or linking users to an online location containing infringing material or infringing activity, by using information location tools, including a directory, index, reference, pointer, or hypertext link...." Subsection 512(d) imposes more demanding eligibility requirements because it covers active assistance to users.

Defendant responds in two ways. First, it argues that subsection 512(a), rather than 512(d), applies because the information location tools it provides are incidental to its core function of automatically transmitting, routing, or providing connections for the MP3 files users select. In the alternative, defendant maintains that, even if the court decides to analyze the information location functions under 512(d), it should hold that the 512(a) safe harbor protects other aspects of the Napster service.

Napster undisputedly performs some information location functions. The Napster server stores a transient list of the files that each user currently logged-on to that server wants to share. This data is maintained until the user logs off, but the structure of the index itself continues to exist. If a user wants to find a particular song or recording artist, she enters a search, and Napster looks for the search terms in the index. Edward Kessler, Napster's Vice President of Engineering, admitted in his deposition that, at least in this context, Napster functions as a free information location tool. *Cf.* Declaration of Daniel Farmer ("Farmer Dec.") ¶ 16 (stating that "Napster operates exactly like a search engine or information location tool to the user"). Napster software also has a "hot list" function that allows users to search for other users' log-in names and receive notification when users with whom they might want to communicate have connected to the service. In short, the parties agree on the existence of a searchable directory and index, and Napster representatives have used the phrase "information location tool," which appears in the heading for subsection 512(d), to characterize some Napster functions.

There the agreement ends. According to Napster, the information location tools upon which plaintiffs base their argument are incidental to the system's core function of transmitting MP3 music files, and for this reason, the court should apply subsection 512(a). Napster also disputes the contention that it organizes files or provides links to other Internet sites in the same manner as a search engine like Yahoo!. Consequently, it deems subsection 512(d) inapplicable to its activities. *Cf.* H.R.Rep. No. 105–551(II), 105th Cong., 2d Sess. (1998), 1998 WL 414916, at *147 (using Yahoo! as an example of an information location tool covered by 512(d)). Napster contrasts its operations, which proceed automatically after initial stimuli from users, with search engines like Yahoo! that depend upon the "human judgment and editorial discretion" of the service provider's staff. *Id.*

Napster's final and most compelling argument regarding subsection 512(d) is that the DMCA safe harbors are not mutually exclusive. According to subsection 512(n), a service provider could enjoy the 512(a) safe harbor even if its information location tools were also protected by (or failed to satisfy) subsection 512(d). *See* 17 U.S.C. § 512(n) ("Whether a service provider qualifies for the limitation on liability in any one of those subsections ... shall not affect a determination of whether that service provider qualifies for the limitations on liability under any other such subsections.") Similarly, finding *some* aspects of the system outside the scope of subsection 512(a) would not preclude a ruling that *other* aspects *do* meet 512(a) criteria.

Because the parties dispute material issues regarding the operation of Napster's index, directory, and search engine, the court declines to hold that these functions are peripheral to the alleged infringement, or that they should not be analyzed separately under subsection 512(d).[6] Indeed, despite its contention that its search engine and indexing functions are incidental to the provision of connections and transmission of MP3 files, Napster has advertised the ease with which its users can locate "millions of songs" online without "wading through page after page of unknown artists." Declaration of Russell J. Frackman ("Frackman Dec."), Exh. 5, 4. Such statements by Napster to promote its service are tantamount to an admission that its search and indexing functions are essential to its marketability. Some of these essential functions—including but not limited to the search engine and index—should be analyzed under subsection 512(d).

However, the potential applicability of subsection 512(d) does not completely foreclose use of the 512(a) safe harbor as an affirmative defense. *See* 17 U.S.C. § 512(n). The court will now turn to Napster's eligibility for protection under subsection 512(a). It notes at the outset, though, that a ruling that subsection 512(a) applies to a given function would not mean that the DMCA affords the service provider blanket protection.

II. Subsection 512(a)

Plaintiffs' principal argument against application of the 512(a) safe harbor is that Napster does not perform the passive conduit function eligible for protection under this subsection. As defendant correctly notes, the words "conduit" or "passive conduit" appear nowhere in 512(a), but are found only in the legislative history and summaries of the DMCA. The court must look first to the plain language of the statute, "construing the provisions of the entire law, including its object and policy, to ascertain the intent of Congress." *United States v. Hockings,* 129 F.3d 1069, 1071 (9th Cir.1997) (quoting *Northwest Forest Resource Council v. Glickman,* 82 F.3d 825, 830 (9th Cir.1996)) (internal quotation marks omitted). If the statute is unclear, however, the court may rely on the legislative history. *See Hockings,* 129 F.3d at 1071. The language of subsection 512(a) makes the safe harbor applicable, as a threshold matter, to service providers "transmitting, routing or providing connections for, material *through a system or network* controlled or operated by or for the service provider...." 17 U.S.C. § 512(a) (emphasis added). According to plaintiffs, the use of the word "conduit" in the legislative history explains the meaning of "through a system."

Napster has expressly denied that the transmission of MP3 files ever passes through its servers. Indeed, Kessler declared that "files reside on the computers of Napster users, and are transmitted directly between those computers." MP3 files are transmitted "from the Host user's hard drive and Napster browser, *through the Internet* to the recipient's Napster browser and hard drive." Def. Reply Br. at 3 (emphasis added). The Internet cannot be considered "a system or network controlled or operated by or for the service provider," however. 17 U.S.C. § 512(a). To get around

6. The court need not rule on the applicability of subsection 512(d) to the functions plaintiffs characterize as information location tools because defendant does not rely on subsection 512(d) as grounds for its motion for summary adjudication.

this problem, Napster avers (and plaintiffs seem willing to concede) that "Napster's servers and Napster's MusicShare browsers on its users' computers are all part of Napster's overall system." Def. Reply Br. at 5. Defendant narrowly defines its system to include the browsers on users' computers. In contrast, plaintiffs argue that either (1) the system does not include the browsers, or (2) it includes not only the browsers, but also the users' computers themselves.

Even assuming that the system includes the browser on each user's computer, the MP3 files are not transmitted "through" the system within the meaning of subsection 512(a). Napster emphasizes the passivity of its role—stating that "[a]ll files transfer directly from the computer of one Napster user *through the Internet* to the computer of the requesting user." Def. Br. at 5 (emphasis added). It admits that the transmission bypasses the Napster server. This means that, even if each user's Napster browser is part of the system, the transmission goes *from* one part of the system *to* another, or *between* parts of the system, but not "through" the system. The court finds that subsection 512(a) does not protect the transmission of MP3 files.

The prefatory language of subsection 512(a) is disjunctive, however. The subsection applies to "infringement of copyright by reason of the provider's transmitting, routing, *or* providing connections through a system or network controlled or operated by or for the service provider." 17 U.S.C. § 512(a) (emphasis added). The court's finding that transmission does not occur "through" the system or network does not foreclose the possibility that subsection 512(a) applies to "routing" or "providing connections." Rather, each of these functions must be analyzed independently.

Napster contends that providing connections between users' addresses "constitutes the value of the system to the users and the public." Def. Br. at 15. This connection cannot be established without the provision of the host's address to the Napster browser software installed on the requesting user's computer. The central Napster server delivers the host's address. While plaintiffs contend that the infringing material is not *transmitted* through the Napster system, they provide no evidence to rebut the assertion that Napster supplies the requesting user's computer with information necessary to facilitate a connection with the host.

Nevertheless, the court finds that Napster does not provide connections "through" its system. Although the Napster server conveys address information to establish a connection between the requesting and host users, the connection itself occurs through the Internet. The legislative history of section 512 demonstrates that Congress intended the 512(a) safe harbor to apply only to activities "in which a service provider plays the role of a 'conduit' for the communications of others." H.R.Rep. No. 105–551(II), 105th Cong., 2d Sess. (1998), 1998 WL 414916, at *130. Drawing inferences in the light most favorable to the non-moving party, this court cannot say that Napster serves as a conduit for the connection itself, as opposed to the address information that makes the connection possible. Napster enables or facilitates the initiation of connections, but these connections do not pass through the system within the meaning of subsection 512(a).

Neither party has adequately briefed the meaning of "routing" in subsection 512(a), nor does the legislative history shed light on this issue. Defendant tries to make "routing" and "providing connections" appear synonymous—stating, for example, that "the central Napster server *routes* the transmission by providing the Host's address to the Napster browser that is installed on and in use by User's computer." Def. Br. at 16. However, the court doubts that Congress would have used the terms "routing" and "providing connections" disjunctively if they had the same meaning. It is clear from both parties' submissions that the route of the allegedly infringing material goes through the Internet from the host to the requesting user, not through the Napster server. *See, e.g.*, Def. Br. at 13 ("Indeed, the content of the MP3 files are routed without even passing through Napster's Servers."). The court holds that routing does not occur through the Napster system.

Because Napster does not transmit, route, or provide connections through its system, it has failed to demonstrate that it qualifies for the 512(a) safe harbor. The court thus declines to grant summary adjudication in its favor.

III. Copyright Compliance Policy

Even if the court had determined that Napster meets the criteria outlined in subsection 512(a), subsection 512(i) imposes additional requirements on eligibility for *any* DMCA safe harbor. This provision states:

> The limitations established by this section shall apply to a service provider only if the service provider—
>
> (A) has adopted and reasonably implemented, and informs subscribers and account holders of the service provider's system or network of, a policy that provides for the termination in appropriate circumstances of subscribers and account holders of the service provider's system or network who are repeat infringers; and
>
> (B) accommodates and does not interfere with standard technical measures.

17 U.S.C. § 512(i).

Plaintiffs challenge Napster's compliance with these threshold eligibility requirements on two grounds. First, they point to evidence from Kessler's deposition that Napster did not adopt a written policy of which its users had notice until on or around February 7, 2000—two months after the filing of this lawsuit. Kessler testified that, although Napster had a copyright compliance policy as early as October 1999, he is not aware that this policy was reflected in any document, or communicated to any user. Congress did not intend to require a service provider to "investigate possible infringements, monitor its service or make difficult judgments as to whether conduct is or is not infringing," but the notice requirement is designed to insure that flagrant or repeat infringers "know that there is a realistic threat of losing [their] access." H.R. Rep. 105–551(II), 1998 WL 414916, at *154.

Napster attempts to refute plaintiffs' argument by noting that subsection 512(i) does not specify when the copyright compliance policy must be in place. Although this characterization of subsection 512(i) is facially accurate, it defies the logic of making formal notification to users or subscribers a prerequisite to exemption from monetary liability. The fact that Napster developed and notified its users of a formal policy *after* the onset of this action should not moot plaintiffs' claim to monetary relief for past harms. Without further documentation, defendant's argument that it has satisfied subsection 512(i) is merely conclusory and does not support summary adjudication in its favor.

Summary adjudication is also inappropriate because Napster has not shown that it *reasonably* implemented a policy for terminating repeat infringers. *See* 17 U.S.C. § 512(i)(A) (requiring "reasonable" implementation of such a policy). If Napster is formally notified of infringing activity, it blocks the infringer's password so she cannot log on to the Napster service using that password. Napster does not block the IP addresses of infringing users, however, and the parties dispute whether it would be feasible or effective to do so.

Plaintiffs aver that Napster wilfully turns a blind eye to the identity of its users—that is, their real names and physical addresses—because their anonymity allows Napster to disclaim responsibility for copyright infringement. Hence, plaintiffs contend, "infringers may readily reapply to the Napster system to recommence their infringing downloading and uploading of MP3 music files." Pl. Br. at 24. Plaintiffs' expert, computer security researcher Daniel Farmer, declared that he conducted tests in which he easily deleted all traces of his former Napster identity, convincing Napster that "it had never seen me or my computer before." Farmer Dec. ¶ 29. Farmer also cast doubt on Napster's contention that blocking IP addresses is not a reasonable means of terminating infringers. He noted that Napster bans the IP addresses of users who runs "bots" on the service. *See id.* ¶ 27.

Hence, plaintiffs raise genuine issues of material fact about whether Napster has reasonably implemented a policy of terminating repeat infringers. They have produced evidence that Napster's copyright compliance policy is neither timely nor reasonable within the meaning of subparagraph 512(i)(A).

CONCLUSION

This court has determined above that Napster does not meet the requirements of subsection 512(a) because it does not transmit, route, or provide connections for allegedly infringing material through its system. The court also finds summary adjudication inappropriate due to the existence of genuine issues of material fact about Napster's compliance with subparagraph 512(i)(A), which a service provider must satisfy to enjoy the protection of *any* section 512 safe harbor. Defendant's motion for summary adjudication is DENIED.

Ellison v. Robertson

189 F.Supp.2d 1051 (C.D.Cal.2002).

■ COOPER, DISTRICT JUDGE.

Introduction

When an overenthusiastic fan uploads his favorite author's novels to a newsgroup on the internet, what is the liability of an internet service provider, such as AOL, for allowing the books to reside for two weeks on their USENET server? The impact of the Digital Millennium Copyright Act on this issue presents a question of first impression in the Ninth Circuit.

* * *

II. Background

A. *Factual History*

Plaintiff Harlan Ellison is the author of many works of fact and fiction, particularly science fiction. He is the owner of the valid copyrights to most if not all of those works and has registered his copyrights in accordance with all applicable laws. Some of his fictional works, however, have been copied and distributed on the internet without his permission.

Some time in late March or early April 2000, Stephen Robertson scanned a number of Ellison's fictional works in order to convert them to digital files. Thereafter, Robertson uploaded and copied the files onto the USENET newsgroup "alt.binaries.e-book." Robertson accessed the internet through his local internet services provider, Tehama County Online ("TCO"); his USENET service was provided by RemarQ Communities, Inc. ("RemarQ"). The USENET, an abbreviation of "User Network," is an international collection of organizations and individuals (known as "peers") whose computers connect to each other and exchange messages posted by USENET users. Messages are organized into "newsgroups," which are topic-based discussion forums where individuals exchange ideas and information. Users' messages may contain the users' analyses and opinions, copies of newspaper or magazine articles, and even binary files containing binary copies of musical and literary works. "Alt.binaries.e-book", the newsgroup at issue in this case, seems to have been used primarily to exchange pirated and unauthorized digital copies of text material, primarily works of fiction by famous authors, including Ellison.

Peers in USENET enter into peer agreements, whereby one peer's servers automatically transmit and receive newsgroup messages from another peer's servers. As most peers are parties to a large number of peer agreements, messages posted on one USENET peer's server are quickly transmitted around the world. The result is a huge informational exchange system whereby millions of users can exchange millions of messages every day.

AOL has been a USENET peer since 1994, and its USENET servers automatically transmit and receive newsgroup messages from at least 41 other peers. AOL estimates that its peer servers receive 4.5 terabytes of data in more than twenty-four million messages each week from AOL's peers. This data is automatically transmitted to and received by AOL's USENET servers, which are computers that are accessed by AOL's users when they reach the USENET system through AOL's newsgroup service. In late March and early April 2000, when Robertson posted the infringing copies of Ellison's works, AOL's retention policy provided for USENET messages containing binary files to remain on the company's servers for fourteen days.

After Robertson uploaded the infringing copies of Ellison's works to the alt.binaries.e-book newsgroup, they were then forwarded and copied throughout USENET onto servers all over the world, including those belonging to AOL. As a result, AOL users had access to the alt.binaries.e-book newsgroup containing the infringing copies of Ellison's works. As these infringing copies were in binary file form, they would have remained on AOL's servers for approximately fourteen days.

On or about April 13, 2000, Plaintiff learned of the infringing activity and contacted counsel. After researching the notification procedures of 17 U.S.C. § 512, the Digital Millennium Copyright Act ("DMCA"), Plaintiff's counsel sent an e-mail on April 17, 2000, to TCO's and AOL's agents for notice of copyright infringement. Plaintiff received an acknowledgment of receipt from TCO, but no response from AOL, which claims never to have received that e-mail.

On April 24, 2000, Plaintiff filed suit against AOL and other Defendants. After having been served by Plaintiff on April 26, 2000, AOL blocked its users' access to alt.binaries.e-book.

B. Procedural History

* * *

On November 26, 2001, AOL filed a Motion for summary judgment, alleging that Plaintiff had failed to set forth prima facie cases of copyright infringement, and also claiming various defenses under the DMCA. * * *

IV. Discussion

* * *

B. DMCA Limitations on Liability

AOL claims to qualify for two of the DMCA's "safe-harbor" provisions, subsection (a), Transitory digital network communications, and subsection (c), Information residing on systems or networks at direction of users. *See* 17 U.S.C. § 512(a), (c). These safe harbors do not confer absolute immunity upon ISPs, but do drastically limit their potential liability based on specific functions they perform (e.g. user-directed information storage). *See generally* 17 U.S.C. § 512. A party satisfying the requirements for one of the safe harbors cannot be liable for monetary relief, or, with the exception of the rather narrow relief available under subsection (j), for injunctive or other equitable relief for copyright infringement. *See id.*

1. Section 512(i)

In order to avail itself of any of section 512's limitation-on-liability safe harbors, AOL must also satisfy the two requirements laid out in section 512(i). Section 512(i) provides that all safe-harbor provisions established by the DMCA shall apply to a service provider only if the service provider:

> (A) has adopted and reasonably implemented, and informs subscribers and account holders of the service provider's system or network of, a policy that provides for the termination in appropriate circumstances of subscribers and account holders of the service provider's system or network who are repeat infringers; and
>
> (B) accommodates and does not interfere with standard technical measures.

17 U.S.C. § 512(i)(1).

Furthermore, in order for an ISP to comply with subsection (i) and avail itself of one of the DMCA's safe harbors, the ISP must have adopted, reasonably implemented, and notified its members of the repeat infringer termination policy at the time the allegedly infringing activity occurred. Doing so after the infringing activity has already occurred is insufficient if the ISP seeks a limitation of liability in connection with that infringing activity. As explained by the district court in *Napster,* to hold otherwise would be defeat the whole purpose of subsection (i):

> Napster attempts to refute plaintiffs' argument by noting that subsection (i) does not specify when the copyright compliance policy must be in place. Although this characterization of subsection (i) is factually accurate, it defies the logic of making formal notification to users or subscribers a prerequisite to exemption from monetary liability. The fact that Napster developed and notified its users of a formal policy *after* the onset of this action should not moot plaintiffs' claim to monetary relief for past harms.

Napster, 2000 WL 573136 at * 9 (original emphasis).

On its face, subsection (i) is only concerned with repeat-infringer termination policies, and not with copyright infringement in general. Nonetheless, Plaintiff urges that any reasonable policy whose goal is to put repeat infringers on notice that they face possible termination must necessarily include some procedures for actually identifying such individuals in the first place, such as a mechanism whereby the public can notify an ISP of copyright infringement occurring on its system. A termination policy could not be considered "reasonably implemented" if the ISP remained willfully ignorant of users on its system who infringe copyrights repeatedly. Although the text of section 512(i) could conceivably support such an interpretation, the legislative history demonstrates that Congress's intent was far more limited regarding subsection (i):

> the Committee does not intend this provision to undermine the principles of new subsection (l)[13] or the knowledge standard of new subsection (c) by suggesting that a provider *must investigate possible infringements, monitor its service, or make difficult judgments as to whether conduct is or is not infringing.* However, those who repeatedly or flagrantly abuse their access to the Internet through disrespect for the intellectual property rights of others should know that there is a realistic threat of losing that access.

H.R. Rep. 105–551(II), at p. 61 (July 22, 1998) (emphasis added); *see also* S.Rep. 105–190, at p. 51–52 (May 11, 1998) (providing *verbatim* the same explanation of subsection (i)). In the face of such clear guidance from the legislative history of the DMCA, subsection (i) cannot be interpreted to require ISPs to take affirmative steps to investigate potential infringement and set up notification procedures in an attempt to identify the responsible individuals. Accordingly, many of Plaintiff's argument regarding subsection (i) are irrelevant to determining whether AOL had reasonably implemented a policy for termination of repeat infringers.[14]

It is undisputed that AOL satisfies prong (B) based on its accommodation and non-interference with standard technical measures. And AOL presents evidence to support the conclusion that it has also met the requirements of prong (A). AOL's Terms of Service, to which every AOL member must agree before becoming a member, includes a notice that AOL members may not make unauthorized copies of content protected by copyrights, trademarks, or any other intellectual property rights. They also notify members that their AOL accounts could be terminated for making such unauthorized copies.

Plaintiff contends, however, that AOL cannot satisfy prong (A) of subsection 512(i)(1) because although the ISP has presented substantial evidence of compliance, most of that evidence comes from March 2001, nearly a year after the infringing conduct occurred. AOL's percipient witness, Elizabeth Compton, testified that AOL's procedures for notifying its users that their access could be terminated if they were to infringe others' copyrights has not changed substantively since April 2000. However, Plaintiff challenges the credibility and competency of Ms. Compton, whose grasp of the technical side of AOL's copyright infringement procedures was decidedly less than expert.

In addition, Plaintiff notes that although AOL claims to have complied with subsection (i) and adopted and reasonably implemented polices aimed at terminating repeat infringers, Compton testified that no individual has ever been terminated for being a repeat infringer. Given the millions of AOL users, Plaintiff argues, this lack of even a single termination for repeat infringement is evidence that AOL has failed to fulfill its obligation to reasonably implement its subsection(i) termination policy. Moreover,

13. In the version of the DMCA actually enacted, subsection (l)'s equivalent is now found at subsection (m).

14. These arguments are, however, relevant to determining whether AOL complied with the requirements of subsection (c).

Compton testified at her deposition that at the time of the infringement, AOL had not precisely defined how many times a user had to be guilty of infringement before that user could be classified as a "repeat infringer." Plaintiff claims this is further evidence that AOL had failed to comply with the reasonable-implementation requirement of subsection (i).

As noted above in the discussion of the legislative history of the DMCA, however, subsection (i) does not require AOL to actually terminate repeat infringers, or even to investigate infringement in order to determine if AOL users are behind it.[15] That is the province of subsection (c), which provides detailed requirements related to notification of infringement and the ISPs' responsibility to investigate and, in some instances, delete or block access to infringing material on their systems. Subsection (i) only requires AOL to put its users on notice that they face a realistic threat of having their Internet access terminated if they repeatedly violate intellectual property rights.

* * *

Accordingly, the Court holds that AOL had satisfied the requirements of 17 U.S.C. § 512(i) at the time of the alleged infringement of Ellison's copyrights.

2. *Section 512's limitations on liability (a) through (d)*

Section 512(n) explicitly provides that each of the four limitation-on-liability safe harbors found in subsections (a) through (d) "describe separate and distinct functions for purposes of applying this section." *Id.* As a result, "[w]hether a service provider qualifies for the limitation of liability in any one of the subsections shall be based solely on the criteria in that subsection, and shall not affect a determination of whether the service provider qualifies for the limitations on liability under any other such subsection." *Id.* The DMCA's legislative history provides the following instructional example:

> Section 512's limitations on liability are based on functions, and each limitation is intended to describe a separate and distinct function. Consider, for example, a service provider that provides a hyperlink to a site containing infringing material which it then caches on its system in order to facilitate access to it by its users. This service provider is engaging in at least three functions that may be subject to the limitation on liability: transitory digital

15. As such, the "realistic threat of losing [Internet] access" that Congress wishes ISPs to impress upon would-be infringers remains just that—a mere threat—unless the ISP decides to implement procedures aimed at identifying, investigating, and remedying infringement in hopes of meeting the requirements of subsection (c)'s safe harbor. Such an arrangement makes a certain amount of sense. If subsection (i) obligated ISPs to affirmatively seek out information regarding infringement and then investigate, eradicate, and punish infringement on their networks, then most if not all of the notice and take-down requirements of the subsection (c) safe harbor would be indirectly imported and applied to subsections (a) and (b) as well. This would upset the carefully balanced, "separate function—separate safe harbor—separate requirements" architecture of the DMCA.

> network communications under subsection (a), system caching under subsection (b), and information locating tools under subsection (d).

H.R. Rep. 105–551(II), at p. 65 (July 22, 1998). In this example, if the service provider met the threshold requirements of subsection (i), "then for its acts of system caching it is eligible for that limitation on liability with corresponding narrow injunctive relief. But if the same company is committing an infringement by using information locating tools to link its users to infringing material, then its fulfillment of the requirements to claim the system caching liability limitation does not affect whether it qualifies for the liability limitation for information location tools." 3 NIMMER ON COPYRIGHT § 12B.06[A], at 12B–53, 54.

Although AOL performs many Internet-service-provider-related functions, Plaintiff's claims against AOL are based solely on its storage of USENET messages on its servers and provision of access to those USENET messages to AOL users and others accessing the AOL system from outside.

AOL claims that it is eligible under both subsections (a) and (c) for a limitation on liability regarding Plaintiff's claims against it.

3. *Subsection (a)'s limitation on liability*

AOL contends that it meets all the criteria for the limitation-on-liability safe harbor found in subsection (a), which provides:

(a) Transitory digital network communications.—A service provider shall not be liable for monetary relief, or, except as provided in subsection (j), for injunctive or other equitable relief, for the infringement of copyright by reason of the provider's transmitting, routing, or providing connections for, material through a system or network controlled or operated by or for the service provider, or by reason of the intermediate and transient storage of that material in the course of transmitting, routing, or providing connections, if—

(1) the transmission of the material was initiated by or at the direction of a person other than the service provider;

(2) the transmission, routing, provision of connections, or storage is carried out through an automatic technical process without selection of the material by the service provider;

(3) the service provider does not select the recipients of the material except as an automatic response to the request of another person;

(4) no copy of the material made by the service provider in the course of such intermediate or transient storage is maintained on the system or network in a manner ordinarily accessible to anyone other than anticipated recipients, and no such copy is maintained on the system or network in a manner ordinarily accessible to such anticipated recipients for a longer period than is reasonably necessary for the transmission, routing, or provision of connections; and

(5) the material is transmitted through the system without modification of its content.

Subsection (a) does not require ISPs to remove or block access to infringing materials upon receiving notification of infringement, as is the case with subsections (c) and (d).

* * *

Plaintiff argues that AOL's USENET servers do not engage in "intermediate and transient storage" of USENET messages such as the one posted by Robertson. Instead, AOL stores USENET messages containing binary files on its servers for up to fourteen days. AOL, however, claims that the USENET message copies are "intermediate." AOL's role is as an intermediary between the original USENET user who posts a message, such as Robertson, and the recipient USENET users who later choose to view the message.

By itself, the term "intermediate and transient storage" is rather ambiguous. And it is unclear from reading the DMCA whether AOL's storage of USENET messages containing binary files on its servers for fourteen days in order to make those messages accessible to AOL users constitutes "intermediate and transient storage." Certain functions such as the provision of e-mail service or Internet connectivity clearly fall under the purview of subsection (a); other functions such as hosting a web site or chatroom fall under the scope of subsection (c). The question presented by this case is which subsection applies to the function performed by AOL when it stores USENET messages in order to provide USENET access to users. Faced with the ambiguous language in the statute itself, the Court looks to the DMCA's legislative history for guidance in interpretation. The only real guidance is provided in the House Judiciary Committee Report. *See* H.R. Rep. 105–551 (May 22, 1998).

* * *

[T]he section-by-section analysis found in the First House Report is relevant to interpreting whether AOL's storage of USENET messages in order to provide USENET access to AOL users constitutes (1) "intermediate and transient storage" of (2) copies that are not "maintained on the system or network . . . for a longer period than is reasonably necessary for the transmission, routing, or provision of connections." 17 U.S.C. § 512(a), (a)(4).

The First House Report answers both of those questions with a resounding yes:

> The exempted storage and transmissions are those carried out through an automatic technological process that is indiscriminate—i.e., the provider takes no part in the selection of the particular material transmitted—where the copies are retained no longer than necessary for the purpose of carrying out the transmission. This conduct would ordinarily include forwarding of customers' Usenet postings to other Internet sites in accordance with configuration settings that apply to all such postings . . .
>
> This exemption codifies the result of *Religious Technology Center v. Netcom On–Line Communication Services, Inc.*, 907

> F.Supp. 1361 (N.D.Cal.1995) ("Netcom"), with respect to liability of providers for direct copyright infrigement.[20] *See id.* at 1368–70. In Netcom the court held that a provider is not liable for direct infringement where it takes no "affirmative action that [directly results] in copying ... works other than by installing and maintaining a system whereby software automatically forwards messages received from subscribers ... and temporarily stores copies on its system." *By referring to temporary storage of copies, Netcom recognizes implicitly that intermediate copies may be retained without liability for only a limited period of time. The requirement in 512(a)(1) that "no copy be maintained on the system or network ... for a longer period than reasonably necessary for the transmission" is drawn from the facts of the Netcom case, and is intended to codify this implicit limitation in the Netcom holding.*

H.R. Rep. 105–551(I), at p. 24. (emphasis added).

In *Netcom,* infringing USENET postings were stored on Netcom's servers for up to *eleven days,* during which those postings were accessible to Netcom users. *See Netcom,* 907 F.Supp. at 1368. In AOL's case, messages containing binary files, such as the message posted by Robertson, were stored on AOL's servers for up to *fourteen days.* While "intermediate copies may be retained without liability for only a limited period of time," the three-day difference between AOL's USENET storage and that of Netcom is insufficient to distinguish the two cases.

Accordingly, the Court finds that AOL's storage of Robertson's posts on its USENET servers constitutes "intermediate and transient storage" that was not "maintained on the system or network ... for a longer period than is reasonably necessary for the transmission, routing, or provision of connections."

* * *

The Court hereby finds that AOL qualifies for the limitation-on-liability provided under subsection 512(a).

V. Conclusion

The Court hereby GRANTS Defendant AOL's Motion for summary judgment.

ALS Scan, Inc. v. RemarQ Communities, Inc.

239 F.3d 619 (4th Cir.2001).

■ NIEMEYER, CIRCUIT JUDGE:

We are presented with an issue of first impression—whether an Internet service provider enjoys a safe harbor from copyright infringement

20. Any argument that this codification of *Netcom*'s facts regarding intermediate storage was only meant to apply to direct infringement, and not to vicarious or contributory infringement, is forestalled by subsection (2) of the version of the bill then under consideration by the Judiciary Committee. For subsection (2) makes it clear that the same limitations on liability that apply under subsection (1) for direct infringement also apply to "contributory infringement or vicarious liability, based solely on conduct described in paragraph (1)." * * *

liability as provided by Title II of the Digital Millennium Copyright Act ("DMCA") when it is put on notice of infringement activity on its system by an imperfect notice. Because we conclude that the service provider was provided with a notice of infringing activity that *substantially* complied with the Act, it may not rely on a claim of defective notice to maintain the immunity defense provided by the safe harbor. Accordingly, we reverse the ruling of the district court that found the notice fatally defective, and affirm its remaining rulings.

I

ALS Scan, Inc., a Maryland corporation, is engaged in the business of creating and marketing "adult" photographs. It displays these pictures on the Internet to paying subscribers and also sells them through the media of CD ROMs and videotapes. ALS Scan is holder of the copyrights for all of these photographs.

RemarQ Communities, Inc., a Delaware corporation, is an online Internet service provider that provides access to its subscribing members. It has approximately 24,000 subscribers to its newsgroup base and provides access to over 30,000 newsgroups which cover thousands of subjects. These newsgroups, organized by topic, enable subscribers to participate in discussions on virtually any topic, such as fine arts, politics, religion, social issues, sports, and entertainment. For example, RemarQ provides access to a newsgroup entitled "Baltimore Orioles," in which users share observations or materials about the Orioles. It claims that users post over one million articles a day in these newsgroups, which RemarQ removes after about 8–10 days to accommodate its limited server capacity. In providing access to newsgroups, RemarQ does not monitor, regulate, or censor the content of articles posted in the newsgroup by subscribing members. It does, however, have the ability to filter information contained in the newsgroups and to screen its members from logging onto certain newsgroups, such as those containing pornographic material.

Two of the newsgroups to which RemarQ provides its subscribers access contain ALS Scan's name in the titles. These newsgroups—"alt.als" and "alt.binaries.pictures.erotica.als"—contain hundreds of postings that infringe ALS Scan's copyrights. These postings are placed in these newsgroups by RemarQ's subscribers.

Upon discovering that RemarQ databases contained material that infringed ALS Scan's copyrights, ALS Scan sent a letter, dated August 2, 1999, to RemarQ, stating:

> Both of these newsgroups ["alt.als" and "alt.binaries.pictures.erotica.als"] were created for the sole purpose of violating our Federally filed Copyrights and Tradename. These newsgroups contain virtually all Federally Copyrighted images.... Your servers provide access to these illegally posted images and enable the illegal transmission of these images across state lines.

> This is a cease and desist letter. You are hereby ordered to cease carrying these newsgroups within twenty-four (24) hours upon receipt of this correspondence....
>
> America Online, Erol's, Mindspring, and others have all complied with our cease and desist order and no longer carry these newsgroups.
>
> * * *
>
> Our ALS Scan models can be identified at www.alsscan.com/modlinf2.html[.] Our copyright information can be reviewed at www.alsscan.com/copyrite.html[.]

RemarQ responded by refusing to comply with ALS Scan's demand but advising ALS Scan that RemarQ would eliminate individual infringing items from these newsgroups if ALS Scan identified them "with sufficient specificity." ALS Scan answered that RemarQ had included over 10,000 copyrighted images belonging to ALS Scan in its newsgroups over the period of several months and that

> [t]hese newsgroups have apparently been created by individuals for the express sole purpose of illegally posting, transferring and disseminating photographs that have been copyrighted by my client through both its websites and its CD–ROMs. The newsgroups, on their face from reviewing messages posted thereon, serve no other purpose.

When correspondence between the parties progressed no further to resolution of the dispute, ALS Scan commenced this action, alleging violations of the Copyright Act and Title II of the DMCA, as well as unfair competition. In its complaint, ALS Scan alleged that RemarQ possessed actual knowledge that the newsgroups contained infringing material but had "steadfastly refused to remove or block access to the material." ALS Scan also alleged that RemarQ was put on notice by ALS Scan of the infringing material contained in its database. In addition to injunctive relief, ALS Scan demanded actual and statutory damages, as well as attorneys fees. It attached to its complaint affidavits establishing the essential elements of its claims.

In response, RemarQ filed a motion to dismiss the complaint or, in the alternative, for summary judgment, and also attached affidavits, stating that RemarQ was prepared to remove articles posted in its newsgroups if the allegedly infringing articles were specifically identified. It contended that because it is a provider of access to newsgroups, ALS Scan's failure to comply with the DMCA notice requirements provided it with a defense to ALS Scan's copyright infringement claim.

The district court ruled on RemarQ's motion, stating, "[RemarQ's] motion to dismiss or for summary judgment is treated as one to dismiss and, as such, is granted." In making this ruling, the district court held: (1) that RemarQ could not be held liable for *direct* copyright infringement merely because it provided access to a newsgroup containing infringing material; and (2) that RemarQ could not be held liable for *contributory* infringement because ALS Scan failed to comply with the notice requirements set forth in the DMCA, 17 U.S.C. § 512(c)(3)(A). This appeal followed.

* * *

III

For its principal argument, ALS Scan contends that it substantially complied with the notification requirements of the DMCA and thereby denied RemarQ the "safe harbor" from copyright infringement liability granted by that Act. *See* 17 U.S.C. § 512(c)(3)(A) (setting forth notification requirements). It asserts that because its notification was sufficient to put RemarQ on notice of its infringement activities, RemarQ lost its service-provider immunity from infringement liability. It argues that the district court's application of the DMCA was overly strict and that Congress did not intend to permit Internet providers to avoid copyright infringement liability "merely because a cease and desist notice failed to technically comply with the DMCA."

RemarQ argues in response that it did not have "knowledge of the infringing activity as a matter of law," stating that the DMCA protects it from liability because "ALS Scan failed to identify the infringing works in compliance with the Act, and RemarQ falls within the 'safe harbor' provisions of the Act." It notes that ALS Scan never provided RemarQ or the district court with the identity of the pictures forming the basis of its copyright infringement claim.

These contentions of the parties present the issue of whether ALS Scan complied with the notification requirements of the DMCA so as to deny RemarQ the safe-harbor defense to copyright infringement liability afforded by that Act.

* * * Neither party to this case suggests that RemarQ is not an Internet service provider for purposes of the Act.

The liability-limiting provision applicable here, 17 U.S.C. § 512(c), gives Internet service providers a safe harbor from liability for "infringement of copyright by reason of the storage at the direction of a user of material that resides on a system or network controlled or operated by or for the service provider" as long as the service provider can show that: (1) it has neither actual knowledge that its system contains infringing materials nor an awareness of facts or circumstances from which infringement is apparent, or it has expeditiously removed or disabled access to infringing material upon obtaining actual knowledge of infringement; (2) it receives no financial benefit directly attributable to infringing activity; *and* (3) it responded expeditiously to remove or disable access to material claimed to be infringing after receiving from the copyright holder a notification conforming with requirements of § 512(c)(3). *Id.* § 512(c)(1).[112] Thus, to

112. Section 512(c)(1) provides in full:

(c) Information residing on systems or networks at direction of users.—

qualify for this safe harbor protection, the Internet service provider must demonstrate that it has met all three of the safe harbor requirements, and a showing under the first prong—the lack of actual or constructive knowledge—is prior to and separate from the showings that must be made under the second and third prongs.

* * *

* * * [W]e conclude that ALS Scan substantially complied with the third prong, thereby denying RemarQ its safe harbor defense.

In evaluating the third prong, requiring RemarQ to remove materials following "notification," the district court concluded that ALS Scan's notice was defective in failing to comply strictly with two of the six requirements of a notification—(1) that ALS Scan's notice include "a list of [infringing] works" contained on the RemarQ site and (2) that the notice identify the infringing works in sufficient detail to enable RemarQ to locate and disable them. 17 U.S.C. § 512(c)(3)(A)(ii), (iii).[113]

In support of the district court's conclusion, RemarQ points to the fact that ALS Scan never provided it with a "representative list" of the

(1) In general.—A service provider shall not be liable for monetary relief, or, except as provided in subsection (j), for injunctive or other equitable relief, for infringement of copyright by reason of the storage at the direction of a user of material that resides on a system or network controlled or operated by or for the service provider, if the service provider—

(A)(i) does not have actual knowledge that the material or an activity using the material on the system or network is infringing;

(ii) in the absence of such actual knowledge, is not aware of facts or circumstances from which infringing activity is apparent; or

(iii) upon obtaining such knowledge or awareness, acts expeditiously to remove, or disable access to, the material;

(B) does not receive a financial benefit directly attributable to the infringing activity, in a case in which the service provider has the right and ability to control such activity; and

(C) upon notification of claimed infringement as described in paragraph (3), responds expeditiously to remove, or disable access to, the material that is claimed to be infringing or to be the subject of infringing activity.

113. Section 512(c)(3)(A)(ii), (iii) provides:

(3) Elements of notification.—

(A) To be effective under this subsection, a notification of claimed infringement must be a written communication provided to the designated agent of a service provider that includes substantially the following:

* * *

(ii) Identification of the copyrighted work claimed to have been infringed, or, if multiple copyrighted works at a single online site are covered by a single notification, a representative list of such works at that site.

(iii) Identification of the material that is claimed to be infringing or to be the subject of infringing activity and that is to be removed or access to which is to be disabled, and information reasonably sufficient to permit the service provider to locate the material.

infringing photographs, as required by § 512(c)(3)(A)(ii), nor did it identify those photographs with sufficient detail to enable RemarQ to locate and disable them, as required by § 512(c)(3)(A)(iii). RemarQ buttresses its contention with the observation that not all materials at the offending sites contained material to which ALS Scan held the copyrights. RemarQ's affidavit states in this regard:

> Some, but not all, of the pictures users have posted on these sites appear to be ALS Scan pictures. It also appears that users have posted other non-ALS Scan's erotic images on these newsgroups. The articles in these newsgroups also contain text messages, many of which discuss the adult images posted on the newsgroups.

ALS Scan responds that the two sites in question—"alt.als" and "alt.binaries.pictures.erotica.als"—were created solely for the purpose of publishing and exchanging ALS Scan's copyrighted images. It points out that the address of the newsgroup is defined by ALS Scan's name. As one of its affidavits states:

> [RemarQ's] subscribers going onto the two offending newsgroups for the purpose of violating [ALS Scan's] copyrights, are actually aware of the copyrighted status of [ALS Scan's] material because (1) each newsgroup has "als" as part of its title, and (2) each photograph belonging to [ALS Scan] has [ALS Scan's] name and/or the copyright symbol next to it.
>
> Each of these two newsgroups was created by unknown persons for the illegal purpose of trading the copyrighted pictures of [ALS Scan] to one another without the need for paying to either (1) become members of [ALS Scan's] web site(s) or (2) purchasing the CD ROMs produced by[ALS Scan].

ALS Scan presses the contention that these two sites serve no other purpose than to distribute ALS Scan's copyrighted materials and therefore, by directing RemarQ to these sites, it has directed RemarQ to a representative list of infringing materials.

The DMCA was enacted both to preserve copyright enforcement on the Internet and to provide immunity to service providers from copyright infringement liability for "passive," "automatic" actions in which a service provider's system engages through a technological process initiated by another without the knowledge of the service provider. H.R. Conf. Rep. No. 105–796, at 72 (1998), *reprinted in* 1998 U.S.C.C.A.N. 649; H.R.Rep. No. 105–551(I), at 11 (1998). This immunity, however, is not presumptive, but granted only to "innocent" service providers who can prove they do not have actual or constructive knowledge of the infringement, as defined under any of the three prongs of 17 U.S.C. § 512(c)(1). The DMCA's protection of an innocent service provider disappears at the moment the service provider loses its innocence, i.e., at the moment it becomes aware that a third party is using its system to infringe. At that point, the Act shifts responsibility to the service provider to disable the infringing matter, "preserv[ing] the strong incentives for service providers and copyright owners to cooperate to detect and deal with copyright infringements that take place in the digital networked environment." H.R. Conf. Rep. No. 105–796, at 72 (1998), *reprinted in* 1998 U.S.C.C.A.N. 649. In the spirit of achieving a balance between the responsibilities of the service provider and the copyright owner, the DMCA requires that a copyright owner put the service provider on notice in a detailed manner but allows notice by means that comport with the prescribed format only "substantially," rather than perfectly. The Act states: "To be effective under this subsection, a notification of claimed infringement must be a written communication provided to the designated agent of a service provider that includes *substantially* the following...." 17 U.S.C. § 512(c)(3)(A) (emphasis added). In addition to substantial compliance, the notification requirements are relaxed to the extent that, with respect to multiple works, not all must be identified—only a "representative" list. *See id.* § 512(c)(3)(A)(ii). And with respect to location information, the copyright holder must provide information that is "*reasonably* sufficient" to permit the service provider to "locate" this material. *Id.* § 512(c)(3)(A)(iii) (emphasis added). This subsection specifying the requirements of a notification does not seek to burden copyright holders with the responsibility of identifying every infringing work—or even most of them—when multiple copyrights are involved. Instead, the requirements are written so as to reduce the burden of holders of multiple copyrights who face extensive infringement of their works. Thus, when a letter provides notice equivalent to a list of representative works that can be easily identified by the service provider, the notice substantially complies with the notification requirements.

In this case, ALS Scan provided RemarQ with information that (1) identified two sites created for the sole purpose of publishing ALS Scan's copyrighted works, (2) asserted that virtually all the images at the two sites were its copyrighted material, and (3) referred RemarQ to two web addresses where RemarQ could find pictures of ALS Scan's models and obtain ALS Scan's copyright information. In addition, it noted that material at the site could be identified as ALS Scan's material because the material included ALS Scan's "name and/or copyright symbol next to it." We believe that with this information, ALS Scan substantially complied with the notification requirement of providing a representative list of infringing material as well as information reasonably sufficient to enable RemarQ to locate the infringing material. To the extent that ALS Scan's claims about infringing materials prove to be false, RemarQ has remedies for any injury it suffers as a result of removing or disabling noninfringing material. *See* 17 U.S.C. § 512(f), (g).

Accordingly, we reverse the district court's ruling granting summary judgment in favor of RemarQ on the basis of ALS Scan's non-compliance with the notification provisions of 17 U.S.C. § 512(c)(3)(A)(ii) and (iii). Because our ruling only removes the safe harbor defense, we remand for further proceedings on ALS Scan's copyright infringement claims and any other affirmative defenses that RemarQ may have. * * *

NOTES & QUESTIONS

1. *The reach of Section 512.* Subsections (a), (b), (c), and (d) of Section 512 each applies to a particular category of online activity. Under which subsection, if any, would each of the following Internet services and activities fall?

- running a chat room
- streaming video over the Internet
- operating a search engine
- hosting a website
- operating a website containing hypertext links
- hosting a bulletin board system
- operating as an Internet service provider

2. *Anticircumvention and Section 512.* Title I of the Digital Millennium Copyright Act, 17 U.S.C. §§ 1201–05, imposes liability for circumventing a technological measure that effectively controls access to a protected work, as well as for providing any technology that is primarily designed or produced for the purpose of circumventing such measures. Suppose a website makes available for download software constituting such prohibited technology. Is the website operator protected by Section 512? *See Universal City Studios, Inc. v. Reimerdes,* 82 F.Supp.2d 211 (S.D.N.Y.2000), excerpted in Chapter 11, Part II(A), *infra.*

3. *Pirates, Internet directories, and red flags.* Under Section 512(d), the safe harbor for a service provider's use of information location tools is unavailable if the service provider has actual or constructive knowledge of the infringing activity. During the legislative process leading to the enactment of Section 512, concern was expressed that a human-compiled Internet directory, such as Yahoo!'s directory, would not meet this requirement since each website cataloged is visited and evaluated by an employee of the online service provider. Responding to this concern, a House report on the bill noted:

> A question has been raised as to whether a service provider would be disqualified from the safe harbor based solely on evidence that it had viewed the infringing Internet site. If so, there is concern that on-line directories prepared by human editors and reviewers, who view and classify various Internet sites, would be denied eligibility to the information location tools safe harbor, in an unintended number of cases and circumstances. This is an important concern because such on-line directories play a valuable role in assisting Internet users to identify and locate the information they seek on the decentralized and dynamic networks of the Internet.
>
> Like the information storage safe harbor in Section 512(c), a service provider would qualify for this safe harbor if, among other requirements, it "does not have actual knowledge that the material or activity is infringing" or, in the absence of such actual

knowledge, it is "not aware of facts or circumstances from which infringing activity is apparent." Under this standard, a service provider would have no obligation to seek out copyright infringement, but it would not qualify for the safe harbor if it had turned a blind eye to "red flags" of obvious infringement.

For instance, the copyright owner could show that the provider was aware of facts from which infringing activity was apparent if the copyright owner could prove that the location was clearly, at the time the directory provider viewed it, a "pirate" site of the type described below, where sound recordings, software, movies, or books were available for unauthorized downloading, public performance, or public display. Absent such "red flags" or actual knowledge, a directory provider would not be similarly aware merely because it saw one or more well known photographs of a celebrity at a site devoted to that person. The provider could not be expected, during the course of its brief cataloguing visit, to determine whether the photograph was still protected by copyright or was in the public domain; if the photograph was still protected by copyright, whether the use was licensed; and if the use was not licensed, whether it was permitted under the fair use doctrine.

The intended objective of this standard is to exclude from the safe harbor sophisticated "pirate" directories—which refer Internet users to other selected Internet sites where pirate software, books, movies, and music can be downloaded or transmitted. Such pirate directories refer Internet users to sites that are obviously infringing because they typically use words such as "pirate," "bootleg," or slang terms in their URL and header information to make their illegal purpose obvious, in the first place, to the pirate directories as well as other Internet users. Because the infringing nature of such sites would be apparent from even a brief and casual viewing, safe harbor status for a provider that views such a site and then establishes a link to it would not be appropriate. Pirate directories do not follow the routine business practices of legitimate service providers preparing directories, and thus evidence that they have viewed the infringing site may be all that is available for copyright owners to rebut their claim to a safe harbor.

H.R. REP. NO. 105–551, pt. 2, at 57–58 (1998). How would you apply the "red flag" standard for actual or constructive knowledge to the *Napster* case?

CHAPTER TEN

CONTROLLING INFORMATION ASSETS: DATABASES

Databases are a core technology of Internet commerce. An online retailer could not function if its customers could not search an online database of its inventory. A business-to-business exchange could not function if it did not provide its members with access to a database comprising the suppliers and manufacturers of different categories of goods and services. Without databases, no company conducting business on the Internet could keep track of such critical information as the identity of its customers, the sales and other transactions into which it enters, the settlement of accounts, and the shipment and delivery of its goods and services.

Many online businesses depend on their control of information maintained in databases. For example, Westlaw and Lexis each charge fees to access their comprehensive databases of legal materials. Many companies offer free access to online databases of information in order to sell space on their websites to advertisers. Still other companies compile timely and extensive databases of commercially valuable information such as stock quotes or sports scores and sell or license them to others for use on their websites. Advertisers depend on databases of names and addresses and other marketing information. (Such databases can become problematic from the standpoint of consumer privacy; see Chapter 8, *supra*.)

Most commercial databases are compilations of facts. Facts, however, are not protected under the law of copyright. While the selection and arrangement of facts in a database *may* qualify for protection under copyright law—provided the selection and arrangement are sufficiently original—the factual contents of these databases remain unprotected. Thus, in many circumstances, a person may use the factual contents of another's database without infringing the owner's copyright. Database owners seeking alternative legal protection through state courts and legislatures may be disappointed in their attempts, because of federal copyright law's preemption of state laws, such as the law of misappropriation or unfair competition, that otherwise might provide protection. This state of affairs has led some to call for federal *sui generis* protection for databases along the lines of the European Union's Directive on the Legal Protection of Databases.

Before proceeding to these legal matters, however, it is necessary to have some background on why federal copyright law generally does not protect databases.

I. DATABASES AND THE LAW OF COPYRIGHT

Until the Supreme Court's decision in *Feist Publications v. Rural Telephone Service Co.*, 499 U.S. 340 (1991), there was some confusion over whether factual databases were protected under the law of copyright. Historically, many courts and scholars believed that compilations of facts were protected under the "sweat of the brow" doctrine, which holds that one can acquire a copyright in a compilation of facts by dint of the effort one expends to compile it. The intuitive appeal of this doctrine is nicely set forth by Justice Story, who noted that, although all maps of the same region feature the same selection and arrangement, another person "has no right, without any such surveys and labors, to sit down and copy the whole of the map already produced by the skill and labors of the first party, and thus to rob him of all the fruit of his industry, skill, and expenditures." *Gray v. Russell*, 10 F. Cas. 1035, 1038 (C.C.D.Mass.1839). As Justice Story summarized his point in a later case, "[a] man has a right to the copy-right of a map of a state or country, which he has surveyed or caused to be compiled from existing materials, at his own expense, or skill, or labor, or money." *Emerson v. Davies*, 8 F. Cas. 615, 619 (C.C.D.Mass.1845). If return to one's labor ("sweat of the brow") is grounds for granting an intellectual property right, the lack of creativity and originality in the cartographer's selection and arrangement appears irrelevant.

In 1879, however, the Supreme Court held that "originality" is an absolute prerequisite for copyright protection. In the *Trade-Mark Cases*, 100 U.S. 82 (1879), the Court determined that the federal trademark law was not a valid exercise of Congress's power under the Constitution's Copyright Clause,[1] since trademarks do not necessarily embody the requisite originality. The Court explained that "while the word *writings* [in the Copyright Clause] may be liberally construed, as it has been, to include original designs for engravings, prints, & c., it is only such as are *original*, and are founded in the creative powers of the mind." *Id.* at 94. In *Bleistein v. Donaldson Lithographing Co.*, 188 U.S. 239, 250 (1903), the Court made clear that the quantum of originality required for copyright protection is very low: "a very modest grade of art" will suffice.

When the Supreme Court embraced the originality doctrine, it did not at the same time expressly reject the "sweat of the brow" doctrine. For much of the last century, the lower courts found compilations of facts, such as law reports and directories, protectible either because they embodied the requisite degree of originality, or because substantial labor was expended in compiling them. *See, e.g. Hutchinson Tel. Co. v. Fronteer Directory Co. of Minnesota*, 770 F.2d 128 (8th Cir.1985) (originality); *Schroeder v. William Morrow & Co.*, 566 F.2d 3 (7th Cir.1977) ("sweat of the brow"); *Adventures*

1. "The Congress shall have Power * * * [t]o promote the Progress of Science and useful Arts, by securing for limited Times to Authors and Inventors the exclusive Right to their respective Writings and Discoveries." U.S. CONST., art. I, § 8, cl. 8.

in Good Eating, Inc. v. Best Places to Eat, Inc., 131 F.2d 809 (7th Cir.1942) ("sweat of the brow"); *Jeweler's Circular Publishing Co. v. Keystone Publishing Co.*, 281 F. 83 (2d Cir.1922) ("sweat of the brow"); *West Pub. Co. v. Edward Thompson Co.*, 169 F. 833 (C.C.E.D.N.Y. 1909) ("sweat of the brow"); *Edward Thompson Co. v. American Law Book Co.*, 122 F. 922 (2d Cir.1903) (originality).

With passage of the 1976 Copyright Act, Congress expressly imposed the originality doctrine on compilations protected under the Act: it defined a compilation as "a work formed by the collection and assembling of preexisting materials or of data that are selected, coordinated, or arranged in such a way that the resulting work as a whole constitutes an *original* work of authorship." 17 U.S.C. § 101 (emphasis added).

The significance of this change in the definition of a compilation was not immediately clear. Some courts continued to apply the "sweat of the brow" doctrine, *see, e.g., Illinois Bell Tel. Co. v. Haines & Co.,* 683 F.Supp. 1204 (N.D.Ill.1988), *aff'd,* 905 F.2d 1081 (7th Cir.1990), *vacated and remanded,* 499 U.S. 944 (1991), while others viewed the doctrine as superseded by the new statutory language of originality, *see, e.g., Financial Info., Inc. v. Moody's Investors Serv., Inc.*, 808 F.2d 204 (2d Cir.1986), and *Worth v. Selchow & Righter Co.,* 827 F.2d 569 (9th Cir.1987). Some courts found factual compilations such as telephone directories sufficiently original to meet this standard. *See Hutchinson Tel. Co. v. Fronteer Directory Co. of Minnesota,* 770 F.2d 128 (8th Cir.1985) ("white pages" directory copyrightable); *Southern Bell Tel. and Tel. Co. v. Associated Tel. Directory Publishers,* 756 F.2d 801 (11th Cir.1985) ("yellow pages" directory copyrightable).

Such was the state of the caselaw when, in the following case, the Supreme Court established the standards that a factual compilation must meet to qualify for copyright protection.

Feist Publications, Inc. v. Rural Telephone Service Co.

499 U.S. 340 (1991).

■ JUSTICE O'CONNOR delivered the opinion of the Court.

This case requires us to clarify the extent of copyright protection available to telephone directory white pages.

I

Rural Telephone Service Company, Inc., is a certified public utility that provides telephone service to several communities in northwest Kansas. It is subject to a state regulation that requires all telephone companies operating in Kansas to issue annually an updated telephone directory. Accordingly, as a condition of its monopoly franchise, Rural publishes a typical telephone directory, consisting of white pages and yellow pages. The white pages list in alphabetical order the names of Rural's subscribers, together with their towns and telephone numbers. The yellow pages list

Rural's business subscribers alphabetically by category and feature classified advertisements of various sizes. Rural distributes its directory free of charge to its subscribers, but earns revenue by selling yellow pages advertisements.

Feist Publications, Inc., is a publishing company that specializes in area-wide telephone directories. Unlike a typical directory, which covers only a particular calling area, Feist's area-wide directories cover a much larger geographical range, reducing the need to call directory assistance or consult multiple directories. The Feist directory that is the subject of this litigation covers 11 different telephone service areas in 15 counties and contains 46,878 white pages listings—compared to Rural's approximately 7,700 listings. Like Rural's directory, Feist's is distributed free of charge and includes both white pages and yellow pages. Feist and Rural compete vigorously for yellow pages advertising.

As the sole provider of telephone service in its service area, Rural obtains subscriber information quite easily. Persons desiring telephone service must apply to Rural and provide their names and addresses; Rural then assigns them a telephone number. Feist is not a telephone company, let alone one with monopoly status, and therefore lacks independent access to any subscriber information. To obtain white pages listings for its area-wide directory, Feist approached each of the 11 telephone companies operating in northwest Kansas and offered to pay for the right to use its white pages listings.

Of the 11 telephone companies, only Rural refused to license its listings to Feist. Rural's refusal created a problem for Feist, as omitting these listings would have left a gaping hole in its area-wide directory, rendering it less attractive to potential yellow pages advertisers. In a decision subsequent to that which we review here, the District Court determined that this was precisely the reason Rural refused to license its listings. The refusal was motivated by an unlawful purpose "to extend its monopoly in telephone service to a monopoly in yellow pages advertising." *Rural Telephone Service Co. v. Feist Publications, Inc.,* 737 F.Supp. 610, 622 (D.Kan.1990).

Unable to license Rural's white pages listings, Feist used them without Rural's consent. Feist began by removing several thousand listings that fell outside the geographic range of its area-wide directory, then hired personnel to investigate the 4,935 that remained. These employees verified the data reported by Rural and sought to obtain additional information. As a result, a typical Feist listing includes the individual's street address; most of Rural's listings do not. Notwithstanding these additions, however, 1,309 of the 46,878 listings in Feist's 1983 directory were identical to listings in Rural's 1982–1983 white pages. App. 54 (¶ 15–16), 57. Four of these were fictitious listings that Rural had inserted into its directory to detect copying.

Rural sued for copyright infringement in the District Court for the District of Kansas taking the position that Feist, in compiling its own directory, could not use the information contained in Rural's white pages. Rural asserted that Feist's employees were obliged to travel door-to-door or conduct a telephone survey to discover the same information for themselves. Feist responded that such efforts were economically impractical and, in any event, unnecessary because the information copied was beyond the scope of copyright protection. The District Court granted summary judgment to Rural, explaining that "[c]ourts have consistently held that telephone directories are copyrightable" and citing a string of lower court decisions. 663 F.Supp. 214, 218 (1987). In an unpublished opinion, the Court of Appeals for the Tenth Circuit affirmed "for substantially the reasons given by the district court." App. to Pet. for Cert. 4a, judgt. order reported at 916 F.2d 718 (1990). We granted certiorari, 498 U.S. 808 (1990), to determine whether the copyright in Rural's directory protects the names, towns, and telephone numbers copied by Feist.

II

A

This case concerns the interaction of two well-established propositions. The first is that facts are not copyrightable; the other, that compilations of facts generally are. Each of these propositions possesses an impeccable pedigree. That there can be no valid copyright in facts is universally understood. The most fundamental axiom of copyright law is that "[n]o author may copyright his ideas or the facts he narrates." *Harper & Row, Publishers, Inc. v. Nation Enterprises,* 471 U.S. 539, 556 (1985). Rural wisely concedes this point, noting in its brief that "[f]acts and discoveries, of course, are not themselves subject to copyright protection." Brief for Respondent 24. At the same time, however, it is beyond dispute that compilations of facts are within the subject matter of copyright. Compilations were expressly mentioned in the Copyright Act of 1909, and again in the Copyright Act of 1976.

There is an undeniable tension between these two propositions. Many compilations consist of nothing but raw data—*i.e.,* wholly factual information not accompanied by any original written expression. On what basis may one claim a copyright in such a work? Common sense tells us that 100 uncopyrightable facts do not magically change their status when gathered together in one place. Yet copyright law seems to contemplate that compilations that consist exclusively of facts are potentially within its scope.

The key to resolving the tension lies in understanding why facts are not copyrightable. The *sine qua non* of copyright is originality. To qualify for copyright protection, a work must be original to the author. * * * Original, as the term is used in copyright, means only that the work was independently created by the author (as opposed to copied from other works), and that it possesses at least some minimal degree of creativity. 1 M. Nimmer & D. Nimmer, Copyright §§ 2.01[A], [B] (1990) (hereinafter Nimmer). To be sure, the requisite level of creativity is extremely low; even a slight amount will suffice. The vast majority of works make the grade quite easily, as they possess some creative spark, "no matter how crude, humble or obvious" it might be. *Id.,* § 1.08[C][1]. Originality does not signify novelty; a work may be original even though it closely resembles other works so long as the similarity is fortuitous, not the result of copying. To illustrate, assume that two poets, each ignorant of the other, compose identical poems. Neither work is novel, yet both are original and, hence, copyrightable. * * *

Originality is a constitutional requirement. The source of Congress' power to enact copyright laws is Article I, § 8, cl. 8, of the Constitution, which authorizes Congress to "secur[e] for limited Times to Authors ... the exclusive Right to their respective Writings." In two decisions from the late 19th century—*The Trade-Mark Cases,* 100 U.S. 82 (1879); and *Burrow-Giles Lithographic Co. v. Sarony,* 111 U.S. 53 (1884)—this Court defined the crucial terms "authors" and "writings." In so doing, the Court made it unmistakably clear that these terms presuppose a degree of originality.

* * *

The originality requirement articulated in *The Trade–Mark Cases* and *Burrow–Giles* remains the touchstone of copyright protection today. * * *

It is this bedrock principle of copyright that mandates the law's seemingly disparate treatment of facts and factual compilations. "No one may claim originality as to facts." [Nimmer] § 2.11[A], p. 2–157. This is because facts do not owe their origin to an act of authorship. The distinction is one between creation and discovery: The first person to find and report a particular fact has not created the fact; he or she has merely discovered its existence. To borrow from *Burrow–Giles,* one who discovers a fact is not its "maker" or "originator." 111 U.S., at 58. "The discoverer merely finds and records." Nimmer § 2.03[E]. Census takers, for example, do not "create" the population figures that emerge from their efforts; in a sense, they copy these figures from the world around them. Denicola, Copyright in Collections of Facts: A Theory for the Protection of Nonfiction Literary Works, 81 Colum.L.Rev. 516, 525 (1981) (hereinafter Denicola). Census data therefore do not trigger copyright because these data are not "original" in the constitutional sense. Nimmer § 2.03[E]. The same is true of all facts—scientific, historical, biographical, and news of the day. "[T]hey may not be copyrighted and are part of the public domain available to every person." [*Miller v. Universal City Studios, Inc.*, 650 F.2d 1365, 1369 (CA5 1981).]

Factual compilations, on the other hand, may possess the requisite originality. The compilation author typically chooses which facts to include, in what order to place them, and how to arrange the collected data so that they may be used effectively by readers. These choices as to selection and arrangement, so long as they are made independently by the compiler and entail a minimal degree of creativity, are sufficiently original that Congress may protect such compilations through the copyright laws. Nimmer §§ 2.11[D], 3.03; Denicola 523, n.38. Thus, even a directory that contains absolutely no protectible written expression, only facts, meets the constitutional minimum for copyright protection if it features an original selection or arrangement. * * *

This protection is subject to an important limitation. The mere fact that a work is copyrighted does not mean that every element of the work may be protected. Originality remains the *sine qua non* of copyright; accordingly, copyright protection may extend only to those components of a work that are original to the author. [Patterson & Joyce, Monopolizing the Law: The Scope of Copyright Protection for Law Reports and Statutory Compilations, 36 UCLA L.Rev. 719, 800–02 (1989) (hereinafter Patterson & Joyce).] Ginsburg, Creation and Commercial Value: Copyright Protection of Works of Information, 90 Colum.L.Rev. 1865, 1868, and n. 12 (1990) (hereinafter Ginsburg). Thus, if the compilation author clothes facts with an original collocation of words, he or she may be able to claim a copyright in this written expression. Others may copy the underlying facts from the publication, but not the precise words used to present them. In *Harper & Row,* for example, we explained that President Ford could not prevent others from copying bare historical facts from his autobiography, see 471 U.S., at 556–557, but that he could prevent others from copying his "subjective descriptions and portraits of public figures." *Id.,* at 563. Where the compilation author adds no written expression but rather lets the facts speak for themselves, the expressive element is more elusive. The only conceivable expression is the manner in which the compiler has selected and arranged the facts. Thus, if the selection and arrangement are original, these elements of the work are eligible for copyright protection. See Patry, Copyright in Compilations of Facts (or Why the "White Pages" Are Not Copyrightable), 12 Com. & Law 37, 64 (Dec. 1990) (hereinafter Patry). No matter how original the format, however, the facts themselves do not become original through association. See Patterson & Joyce 776.

This inevitably means that the copyright in a factual compilation is thin. Notwithstanding a valid copyright, a subsequent compiler remains free to use the facts contained in another's publication to aid in preparing a competing work, so long as the competing work does not feature the same selection and arrangement. As one commentator explains it: "[N]o matter how much original authorship the work displays, the facts and ideas it exposes are free for the taking. . . . [T]he very same facts and ideas may be divorced from the context imposed by the author, and restated or reshuffled by second comers, even if the author was the first to discover the facts or to propose the ideas." Ginsburg 1868.

It may seem unfair that much of the fruit of the compiler's labor may be used by others without compensation. As Justice Brennan has correctly observed, however, this is not "some unforeseen byproduct of a statutory scheme." *Harper & Row,* 471 U.S., at 589 (dissenting opinion). It is, rather, "the essence of copyright," *ibid.,* and a constitutional requirement. The primary objective of copyright is not to reward the labor of authors, but "[t]o promote the Progress of Science and useful Arts." Art. I, § 8, cl. 8. * * * To this end, copyright assures authors the right to their original expression, but encourages others to build freely upon the ideas and information conveyed by a work. *Harper & Row, supra,* 471 U.S., at 556–557. This principle, known as the idea/expression or fact/expression dichotomy, applies to all works of authorship. As applied to a factual compilation, assuming the absence of original written expression, only the compiler's selection and arrangement may be protected; the raw facts may be copied at will. This result is neither unfair nor unfortunate. It is the means by which copyright advances the progress of science and art.

* * *

This, then, resolves the doctrinal tension: Copyright treats facts and factual compilations in a wholly consistent manner. Facts, whether alone or as part of a compilation, are not original and therefore may not be copyrighted. A factual compilation is eligible for copyright if it features an original selection or arrangement of facts, but the copyright is limited to the particular selection or arrangement. In no event may copyright extend to the facts themselves.

B

As we have explained, originality is a constitutionally mandated prerequisite for copyright protection. The Court's decisions announcing this rule predate the Copyright Act of 1909, but ambiguous language in the 1909 Act caused some lower courts temporarily to lose sight of this requirement.

* * *

Most courts construed the 1909 Act correctly, notwithstanding the less-than-perfect statutory language. They understood from this Court's decisions that there could be no copyright without originality. * * *

* * *

But some courts misunderstood the statute. * * *

Making matters worse, these courts developed a new theory to justify the protection of factual compilations. Known alternatively as "sweat of the brow" or "industrious collection," the underlying notion was that copyright was a reward for the hard work that went into compiling facts. The classic formulation of the doctrine appeared in *Jeweler's Circular Publishing Co.,* 281 F., at 88:

> "The right to copyright a book upon which one has expended labor in its preparation does not depend upon whether the materials which he has collected consist or not of matters which are publici juris, or whether such materials show literary skill *or originality,* either in thought or in language, or anything more than industrious collection. The man who goes through the streets of a town and puts down the names of each of the inhabitants, with their occupations and their street number, acquires material of which he is the author" (emphasis added).

The "sweat of the brow" doctrine had numerous flaws, the most glaring being that it extended copyright protection in a compilation beyond selection and arrangement—the compiler's original contributions—to the facts themselves. Under the doctrine, the only defense to infringement was independent creation. A subsequent compiler was "not entitled to take one word of information previously published," but rather had to "independently wor[k] out the matter for himself, so as to arrive at the same result from the same common sources of information." *Id.*, at 88–89 (internal quotation marks omitted). "Sweat of the brow" courts thereby eschewed the most fundamental axiom of copyright law—that no one may copyright facts or ideas. *See Miller v. Universal City Studios, Inc.*, 650 F.2d, at 1372 (criticizing "sweat of the brow" courts because "ensur[ing] that later writers obtain the facts independently ... is precisely the scope of protection given ... copyrighted matter, and the law is clear that facts are not entitled to such protection").

* * *

Without a doubt, the "sweat of the brow" doctrine flouted basic copyright principles. Throughout history, copyright law has "recognize[d] a greater need to disseminate factual works than works of fiction or fantasy." *Harper & Row,* 471 U.S., at 563. Accord, Gorman, Fact or Fancy: The Implications for Copyright, 29 J. Copyright Soc. 560, 563 (1982). But "sweat of the brow" courts took a contrary view; they handed out proprietary interests in facts and declared that authors are absolutely precluded from saving time and effort by relying upon the facts contained in prior works. In truth, "[i]t is just such wasted effort that the proscription against the copyright of ideas and facts ... [is] designed to prevent." *Rosemont Enterprises, Inc. v. Random House, Inc.*, 366 F.2d 303, 310 (C.A.2 1966). "Protection for the fruits of such research ... may in certain circumstances be available under a theory of unfair competition. But to accord copyright protection on this basis alone distorts basic copyright principles in that it creates a monopoly in public domain materials without the necessary justification of protecting and encouraging the creation of 'writings' by 'authors.'" Nimmer § 3.04, p. 3–23 (footnote omitted).

C

"Sweat of the brow" decisions did not escape the attention of the Copyright Office. When Congress decided to overhaul the copyright statute and asked the Copyright Office to study existing problems, * * * the Copyright Office promptly recommended that Congress clear up the confusion in the lower courts as to the basic standards of copyrightability. * * *

Congress took the Register's advice. In enacting the Copyright Act of 1976, Congress dropped the reference to "all the writings of an author" and replaced it with the phrase "original works of authorship." 17 U.S.C. § 102(a). In making explicit the originality requirement, Congress announced that it was merely clarifying existing law: "The two fundamental criteria of copyright protection [are] originality and fixation in tangible form.... The phrase 'original works of authorship,' which is purposely left undefined, is intended to incorporate without change *the standard of originality established by the courts under the present [1909] copyright statute.*" H.R.Rep. No. 94–1476, p. 51 (1976) (emphasis added) (hereinafter H.R.Rep.); S.Rep. No. 94–473, p. 50 (1975), U.S.Code Cong. & Admin.News 1976, pp. 5659, 5664 (emphasis added) (hereinafter S.Rep.). * * *

To ensure that the mistakes of the "sweat of the brow" courts would not be repeated, Congress took additional measures. * * *

First, to make clear that compilations were not copyrightable *per se,* Congress provided a definition of the term "compilation." Second, to make clear that the copyright in a compilation did not extend to the facts themselves, Congress enacted § 103.

The definition of "compilation" is found in § 101 of the 1976 Act. It defines a "compilation" in the copyright sense as "a work formed by the collection and assembling of preexisting materials or of data *that* are selected, coordinated, or arranged *in such a way that* the resulting work as a whole constitutes an original work of authorship" (emphasis added).

The purpose of the statutory definition is to emphasize that collections of facts are not copyrightable *per se.* It conveys this message through its tripartite structure, as emphasized above by the italics. The statute identifies three distinct elements and requires each to be met for a work to qualify as a copyrightable compilation: (1) the collection and assembly of pre-existing material, facts, or data; (2) the selection, coordination, or arrangement of those materials; and (3) the creation, by virtue of the particular selection, coordination, or arrangement, of an "original" work of authorship. * * *

* * *

The key to the statutory definition is the second requirement. It instructs courts that, in determining whether a fact-based work is an original work of authorship, they should focus on the manner in which the collected facts have been selected, coordinated, and arranged. This is a straightforward application of the originality requirement. Facts are never original, so the compilation author can claim originality, if at all, only in the way the facts are presented. To that end, the statute dictates that the principal focus should be on whether the selection, coordination, and arrangement are sufficiently original to merit protection.

Not every selection, coordination, or arrangement will pass muster. This is plain from the statute. It states that, to merit protection, the facts must be selected, coordinated, or arranged "in such a way" as to render the work as a whole original. This implies that some "ways" will trigger copyright, but that others will not. * * * Otherwise, the phrase "in such a way" is meaningless and Congress should have defined "compilation" simply as "a work formed by the collection and assembly of preexisting materials or data that are selected, coordinated, or arranged." * * *

As discussed earlier, however, the originality requirement is not particularly stringent. A compiler may settle upon a selection or arrangement that others have used; novelty is not required. Originality requires only that the author make the selection or arrangement independently (*i.e.,* without copying that selection or arrangement from another work), and that it display some minimal level of creativity. Presumably, the vast majority of compilations will pass this test, but not all will. There remains a narrow category of works in which the creative spark is utterly lacking or so trivial as to be virtually nonexistent. * * * Such works are incapable of sustaining a valid copyright. * * *

Even if a work qualifies as a copyrightable compilation, it receives only limited protection. This is the point of § 103 of the Act. Section 103 explains that "[t]he subject matter of copyright ... includes compilations," § 103(a), but that copyright protects only the author's original contributions—not the facts or information conveyed:

> "The copyright in a compilation ... extends only to the material contributed by the author of such work, as distinguished from the preexisting material employed in the work, and does not imply any exclusive right in the preexisting material." § 103(b).

As § 103 makes clear, copyright is not a tool by which a compilation author may keep others from using the facts or data he or she has collected. "The most important point here is one that is commonly misunderstood today: copyright ... has no effect one way or the other on the copyright or public domain status of the preexisting material." H.R.Rep., at 57; S.Rep., at 55, U.S.Code Cong. & Admin. News 1976, p. 5670. The 1909 Act did not require, as "sweat of the brow" courts mistakenly assumed, that each subsequent compiler must start from scratch and is precluded from relying on research undertaken by another. See, *e.g., Jeweler's Circular Publishing Co.,* 281 F., at 88–89. Rather, the facts contained in existing works may be freely copied because copyright protects only the elements that owe their origin to the compiler—the selection, coordination, and arrangement of facts.

In summary, the 1976 revisions to the Copyright Act leave no doubt that originality, not "sweat of the brow," is the touchstone of copyright protection in directories and other fact-based works. * * *

III

There is no doubt that Feist took from the white pages of Rural's directory a substantial amount of factual information. At a minimum, Feist copied the names, towns, and telephone numbers of 1,309 of Rural's subscribers. Not all copying, however, is copyright infringement. To establish infringement, two elements must be proven: (1) ownership of a valid copyright, and (2) copying of constituent elements of the work that are original. * * * The first element is not at issue here; Feist appears to concede that Rural's directory, considered as a whole, is subject to a valid copyright because it contains some foreword text, as well as original material in its yellow pages advertisements. * * *

The question is whether Rural has proved the second element. In other words, did Feist, by taking 1,309 names, towns, and telephone numbers from Rural's white pages, copy anything that was "original" to Rural? Certainly, the raw data does not satisfy the originality requirement. Rural may have been the first to discover and report the names, towns, and telephone numbers of its subscribers, but this data does not " 'ow[e] its origin' " to Rural. *Burrow–Giles,* 111 U.S., at 58. Rather, these bits of information are uncopyrightable facts; they existed before Rural reported them and would have continued to exist if Rural had never published a telephone directory. The originality requirement "rule[s] out protecting ... names, addresses, and telephone numbers of which the plaintiff by no stretch of the imagination could be called the author." Patterson & Joyce 776.

Rural essentially concedes the point by referring to the names, towns, and telephone numbers as "preexisting material." Brief for Respondent 17. Section 103(b) states explicitly that the copyright in a compilation does not extend to "the preexisting material employed in the work."

The question that remains is whether Rural selected, coordinated, or arranged these uncopyrightable facts in an original way. As mentioned, originality is not a stringent standard; it does not require that facts be presented in an innovative or surprising way. It is equally true, however, that the selection and arrangement of facts cannot be so mechanical or routine as to require no creativity whatsoever. The standard of originality is low, but it does exist. * * * As this Court has explained, the Constitution mandates some minimal degree of creativity, see *The Trade–Mark Cases,* 100 U.S., at 94; and an author who claims infringement must prove "the existence of ... intellectual production, of thought, and conception." *Burrow–Giles, supra,* 111 U.S., at 59–60.

The selection, coordination, and arrangement of Rural's white pages do not satisfy the minimum constitutional standards for copyright protection. As mentioned at the outset, Rural's white pages are entirely typical. Persons desiring telephone service in Rural's service area fill out an application and Rural issues them a telephone number. In preparing its white pages, Rural simply takes the data provided by its subscribers and lists it alphabetically by surname. The end product is a garden-variety white pages directory, devoid of even the slightest trace of creativity.

Rural's selection of listings could not be more obvious: It publishes the most basic information—name, town, and telephone number—about each person who applies to it for telephone service. This is "selection" of a sort, but it lacks the modicum of creativity necessary to transform mere selection into copyrightable expression. Rural expended sufficient effort to make the white pages directory useful, but insufficient creativity to make it original.

We note in passing that the selection featured in Rural's white pages may also fail the originality requirement for another reason. Feist points out that Rural did not truly "select" to publish the names and telephone numbers of its subscribers; rather, it was required to do so by the Kansas Corporation Commission as part of its monopoly franchise. * * * Accordingly, one could plausibly conclude that this selection was dictated by state law, not by Rural.

Nor can Rural claim originality in its coordination and arrangement of facts. The white pages do nothing more than list Rural's subscribers in alphabetical order. This arrangement may, technically speaking, owe its origin to Rural; no one disputes that Rural undertook the task of alphabetizing the names itself. But there is nothing remotely creative about arranging names alphabetically in a white pages directory. It is an age-old practice, firmly rooted in tradition and so commonplace that it has come to be expected as a matter of course. * * * It is not only unoriginal, it is practically inevitable. This time-honored tradition does not possess the minimal creative spark required by the Copyright Act and the Constitution.

We conclude that the names, towns, and telephone numbers copied by Feist were not original to Rural and therefore were not protected by the copyright in Rural's combined white and yellow pages directory. As a constitutional matter, copyright protects only those constituent elements of a work that possess more than a *de minimis* quantum of creativity. Rural's white pages, limited to basic subscriber information and arranged alphabetically, fall short of the mark. As a statutory matter, 17 U.S.C. § 101 does not afford protection from copying to a collection of facts that are selected, coordinated, and arranged in a way that utterly lacks originality. Given that some works must fail, we cannot imagine a more likely candidate. Indeed, were we to hold that Rural's white pages pass muster, it is hard to believe that any collection of facts could fail.

* * *

NOTES & QUESTIONS

1. *The protection of commercial databases after* Feist. In *Feist*, the Supreme Court held that a factual database or compilation satisfies the Copyright Act's originality requirement if "the author make[s] the selection or arrangement independently (*i.e.,* without copying that selection or arrangement from another work)" and if the selection and arrangement "display some minimal level of creativity." 499 U.S. at 358. The Court adds that "the vast majority of compilations will pass this test, but not all will." *Id.* at 359. In your opinion, will independently compiled electronic databases normally "pass the test," or will they fall into that "narrow category of works in which the creative spark is utterly lacking or so trivial as to be virtually nonexistent"? *Id.*

2. *Perverse incentives?* Imagine a website that provides access to a comprehensive database of all the hospitals in the United States. A user keys in her zip code, and the database returns a list of hospitals in her area, including each hospital's address and telephone number. How would the rule announced in *Feist* apply to such a national database of hospitals? *See Warren Pub., Inc. v. Microdos Data Corp.*, 115 F.3d 1509 (11th Cir.1997). Would it make a difference to your answer if the database of hospitals only listed those hospitals that had an acupuncture therapist on staff? *See Key Publications, Inc. v. Chinatown Today Publishing Enterprises Inc.*, 945 F.2d 509 (2d Cir.1991). What if the database listed all the hospitals in the United States but indicated for each one whether it had an acupuncture therapist on staff?

3. *Impact on consumers.* Is the "originality" requirement for copyrightability of collections of facts pro-consumer, in that it fosters competition among businesses that use or offer facts by preventing businesses from exercising monopoly control over facts? Is it anti-consumer, in that it reduces the incentives of businesses to compile databases of value to consumers?

4. *Interface vs. database.* In *Feist*, the Supreme Court focused on a telephone "white pages" directory, in a hard-copy book format. In book form, information is presented to the reader in the same arrangement in which it is stored. In the case of an electronic database, however, there is no necessary correspondence between the arrangement of data on a hard drive and the arrangement of returned data on a user's computer monitor. Furthermore, the arrangement of data on a hard drive may change each time the database is saved anew. Under the rule announced in *Feist*, how does one gauge the originality in the arrangement of data in an electronic database?

5. *"Thin" copyright.* Even if an electronic database's selection and arrangement of facts is sufficiently original to qualify for copyright protection, the protection afforded is extremely limited. As the Court notes, "the copyright in a factual compilation is thin. Notwithstanding a valid copyright, a subsequent compiler remains free to use the facts contained in another's publication to aid in preparing a competing work, so long as the competing work does not feature the same selection and arrangement." *Feist*, 499 U.S. at 349. In light of the "thin" protection afforded to factual databases, what is the appropriate standard for determining copyright infringement? Compare *Kregos v. Associated Press*, 937 F.2d 700, 709–10 (2d Cir.1991) and *Harper House, Inc. v. Thomas Nelson, Inc.*, 889 F.2d 197, 205 (9th Cir.1989) with *Bellsouth Advertising & Publishing Corp. v. Donnelley Information Publishing, Inc.*, 999 F.2d 1436, 1445 (11th Cir. 1993) (en banc).

6. *Overruling* Feist. Can Congress overrule *Feist* by amending the Copyright Act to provide for protection of factual databases?

II. PROTECTION FOR DATABASES UNDER STATE LAW AND THE PROBLEM OF FEDERAL COPYRIGHT PREEMPTION

In *Feist*, the Supreme Court suggested that protection for uncopyrightable databases " 'may in certain circumstances be available under a theory of [state-law] unfair competition.' " 499 U.S. at 374–75 (quoting MELVILLE B. NIMMER & DAVID NIMMER, NIMMER ON COPYRIGHT § 3.04 (1990)). While the owner of a database or compilation of facts who seeks to exclude others from using those facts might seek relief under state law, the circumstances under which a state law cause of action might offer a remedy are significantly limited by federal copyright preemption of state law.

There are two forms of preemption associated with copyright law: first, the general preemption under the supremacy clause of the Constitution afforded in favor of federal law; second, preemption deriving from a specific provision in the Copyright Act, Section 301. Constitutional preemption invalidates a state law that "stands as an obstacle to the accomplishment and execution of the full purposes and objectives of Congress." *Hines v. Davidowitz*, 312 U.S. 52, 67 (1941).

Section 301(a) of the Copyright Act preempts

> all legal or equitable rights that are equivalent to any of the exclusive rights within the general scope of copyright as specified by section 106 in works of authorship that are fixed in a tangible medium of expression and come within the subject matter of copyright as specified by sections 102 and 103.

17 U.S.C. § 301(a). Under this provision, a state cause of action is preempted, and thereby rendered invalid, if two conditions are met. First, the material that the state law purports to protect must be "within the subject matter of copyright." That is, it must be a literary work, musical work, compilation, or one of the other types of works that are capable of receiving copyright protection, as set forth in Sections 102 and 103 of the Copyright Act. A database, as long as it is "fixed in a tangible medium of expression," will meet this subject-matter requirement, even if (like the telephone white pages at issue in *Feist v. Rural Telephone Service Co.*) it lacks the requisite originality to be copyrightable.

Second, the rights that the state law protects must be "equivalent to" any of the exclusive rights granted by Section 106 of the Copyright Act, namely the rights of reproduction, adaptation, distribution, public performance, and public display. It is often unclear whether a state law satisfies this criterion. As explained in *Computer Associates International v. Altai, Inc.*, 982 F.2d 693, 716–17 (2d Cir.1992), Section 301

> preempts only those state law rights that "may be abridged by an act which, in and of itself, would infringe one of the exclusive rights" provided by federal copyright law. *See Harper & Row, Publishers, Inc. v. Nation Enters.*, 723 F.2d 195, 200 (2d Cir.1983), *rev'd on other grounds,* 471 U.S. 539 (1985). If an "extra element" is "required instead of or in addition to the acts of reproduction, performance, distribution or display, in order to constitute a state-created cause of action, then the right does not lie 'within the general scope of copyright,' and there is no preemption." 1 Nimmer [on Copyright] § 1.01[B], at 1–14–15; *see also Harper & Row, Publishers, Inc.*, 723 F.2d at 200 (where state law right "is predicated upon an act incorporating elements beyond mere reproduction or the like, the [federal and state] rights are not equivalent" and there is no preemption).
>
> A state law claim is not preempted if the "extra element" changes the "nature of the action so that it is *qualitatively* different from a copyright infringement claim." *Mayer v. Josiah Wedgwood & Sons, Ltd.*, 601 F.Supp. 1523, 1535 (S.D.N.Y.1985). To determine whether a claim meets this standard, we must determine "what plaintiff seeks to protect, the theories in which the matter is thought to be protected and the rights sought to be

> enforced." 1 Roger M. Milgrim, *Milgrim on Trade Secrets* § 2.06A[3], at 2–150 (1992) * * *. An action will not be saved from preemption by elements such as awareness or intent, which alter "the action's scope but not its nature...." *Mayer,* 601 F.Supp. at 1535.
>
> Following this "extra element" test, we have held that unfair competition and misappropriation claims grounded solely in the copying of a plaintiff's protected expression are preempted by section 301. * * * We also have held to be preempted a tortious interference with contract claim grounded in the impairment of a plaintiff's right under the Copyright Act to publish derivative works. * * *
>
> However, many state law rights that can arise in connection with instances of copyright infringement satisfy the extra element test, and thus are not preempted by section 301. These include unfair competition claims based upon breaches of confidential relationships, breaches of fiduciary duties and trade secrets.

Several types of state laws might offer database owners the protection against unauthorized use that the Copyright Act fails to provide. Among the likely candidates are state laws against misappropriation of intangible property, laws protecting trade secrets, and laws enforcing contractual restraints on the use of a database. Most recently, the common law action of trespass to chattels and computer fraud statutes have been applied to protect databases used in e-commerce.

Misappropriation. The state-law tort of misappropriation is a branch of unfair competition law, which seeks to promote the competitive process by imposing liability for forms of competition that undermine it. The competitive markets can be undermined in many ways. A company may engage in deceptive practices in order to deprive consumers of the information they need to make informed and rational choices in the marketplace, thereby undermining its efficient operation. A company may infringe the trademark of another business in order to create customer confusion over the origin of one's goods, thereby appropriating the other company's good will. A company may appropriate information from another company, thereby gaining an unfair competitive advantage. The tort of misappropriation is intended to combat this last type of harm.

A state law against misappropriation may survive preemption if it is drawn sufficiently narrowly. In *International News Service v. Associated Press*, 248 U.S. 215 (1918), the Supreme Court recognized a federal common law cause of action for misappropriation of "hot news." The hot news in question consisted of uncopyrighted news items, which were written and disseminated by a news-gathering organization, and were copied and disseminated by a competing news-gathering organization. No issue of preemption was presented in that case. But in *National Basketball Association v. Motorola, Inc.*, 105 F.3d 841 (2d Cir.1997), the court addressed the question whether Section 301 preempts a state-law cause of action for misappropriation of hot news. The NBA sought to prevent defendants from operating a service that delivered scores and other data about professional basketball games in progress to handheld pagers carried by subscribers. Defendants acquired the information from television and radio broadcasts of the games, transmitting it to subscribers with a time lag of two to three minutes. The court held that New York's misappropriation law, which protects property rights from "any form of commercial immorality," was preempted. It explained that a state misappropriation law that seeks to protect "hot news" survives preemption only if it satisfies the following conditions:

> (i) a plaintiff generates or gathers information at a cost; (ii) the information is time-sensitive; (iii) a defendant's use of the information constitutes free-riding on the plaintiff's efforts; (iv) the defendant is in direct competition with a product or service offered by the plaintiffs; and (v) the ability of other parties to free-ride on the efforts of the plaintiff or others would so reduce the incentive to produce the product or service that its existence or quality would be substantially threatened.

105 F.3d at 845. Misappropriation laws that meet these conditions, and therefore survive preemption, will offer a rather limited range of protection to database owners.

Trade Secrets. Trade secret laws are likely to survive preemption. These laws make unauthorized disclosure of trade secrets actionable if the information holder makes a reasonable effort to keep the information secret, and the defendant either acquires it by improper means or breaches a duty of confidentiality. These requirements constitute an "extra element" in the state cause of action, beyond those which are sufficient to constitute an infringement of a copyright owner's exclusive rights. *See Architectronics, Inc. v. Control Systems, Inc.*, 935 F.Supp. 425, 441 (S.D.N.Y.1996). Consequently, such a law does not meet Section 301's "equivalent rights" criterion, and it is not preempted. Like non-preempted misappropriation laws, trade secret laws will protect only a narrow category of databases, excluding, for example, all those to which subscribers are provided access.

Breach of Contract. Another state-law cause of action that has been used to protect interests in databases and other compilations of fact is breach of contract. Most providers of compilations of information in digital form, whether through online access or on a tangible medium such as a CD–ROM, require a prospective user to agree to various terms and conditions of use before providing access. Online, the terms and conditions may be presented to the user in a scrollable window, with the user manifesting assent by clicking an on-screen button labeled "I accept"; or they may be presented on an interior page of the website, indicated only by a link labeled "Terms" at the bottom of the home page. If the information product is supplied on CD–ROM, the terms and conditions might be presented on the user's computer screen the first time the product is run, or might be on a sheet of paper enclosed within the CD–ROM's packaging. (Whether such presentations of terms can give rise to binding contractual obligation is addressed in Chapter 4, *supra*.)

These clickwrap or shrinkwrap agreements, provided they are enforceable, could give information providers and database owners a significant level of control over their information assets. To the extent that such sets of terms are standardized and widespread within a market, the terms form a substitute for the background intellectual property rights that would prevail without them. The question arises, therefore, whether such terms are preempted by federal copyright law.

State laws enforcing contractual restraints on the use of information contained in a database can be expected generally to survive preemption. In *ProCD, Inc. v. Zeidenberg*, 86 F.3d 1447, 1454 (7th Cir.1996), the court held that a shrinkwrap license limiting the purchaser's use of telephone directory information contained on a CD–ROM was enforceable under state contract law. The court reasoned:

> Rights "equivalent to any of the exclusive rights within the general scope of copyright" are rights established *by law*—rights that restrict the options of persons who are strangers to the author. Copyright law forbids duplication, public performance, and so on, unless the person wishing to copy or perform the work gets permission; silence means a ban on copying. A copyright is a right against the world. Contracts, by contrast, generally affect only their parties; strangers may do as they please, so contracts do not create "exclusive rights."

The reasoning and result in *ProCD v. Zeidenberg* have drawn a good deal of criticism.

> A few courts and commentators have taken the position that federal preemption simply shouldn't apply to contract terms—or at least that it shouldn't apply in the same way—because contracts are different than state statutes. * * * Judge Easterbrook's decision in *ProCD v. Zeidenberg* seems to accept this view, and some courts have taken this logic so far as to conclude that contracts simply can't be preempted by copyright law.
>
> There are a number of problems with the "contracts are different" idea. First, the reference to "equivalence" seems to direct the analysis only at copyright field preemption under section 301, and thus to ignore both copyright conflicts preemption and any form of patent preemption. Even if contract and copyright are not equivalent, it simply does not follow that federal law places no limits on the enforceability of contracts. Courts that take this position should also be troubled by the significant number of cases that do apply intellectual property rules to preempt contracts.
>
> Second, the viability of the distinction between private contracts and public legislation is diminishing day by day. One of the main changes Article 2B[2] would make in current law would be to

2. [Article 2B, a proposed addition to the Uniform Commercial Code, was ultimately promulgated by the National Conference of Commissioners on Uniform State Laws as a

render enforceable contract "terms" to which the parties did not agree in the classic sense, and indeed of which one party may be entirely unaware. * * * In other words, Article 2B promises to usher in an era of "private legislation," in which parties who are in a position to write contracts can jointly impose uniform terms that no one can escape. * * *

* * *

Third, even truly "private" contracts affect third parties who haven't agreed to the contract terms.

Mark A. Lemley, *Beyond Preemption: The Law and Policy of Intellectual Property Licensing*, 87 CALIF. L. REV. 111, 147–49 (1999). See also David Nimmer, Elliot Brown & Gary N. Frischling, *The Metamorphosis of Contract into Expand*, 87 CALIF. L. REV. 17, 48 (1999) ("[W]hen a breach of contract cause of action—particularly one that does not result from the bargained-for agreement of both parties to its putative execution—is used as a subterfuge to control nothing other than the reproduction, adaptation, public distribution, etc., of works within the subject matter of copyright, then it too should be deemed preempted.").

For a discussion of the availability of state misappropriation and contract claims to protect databases, see Jane C. Ginsburg, *Copyright, Common Law, and Sui Generis Protection of Databases in the United States and Abroad*, 66 U. CIN. L. REV. 151 (1997).

Trespass to Chattels. Databases and compilations of fact, although themselves intangible, must reside on some tangible medium. In the case of online databases, the tangible medium is the computer system on which the database is stored, and which makes access to it possible. A computer system is tangible personal property. In part because of the limited protection factual databases receive under the law of copyright, database owners have attempted to combat unauthorized access to their online databases by bringing lawsuits predicated upon state law causes of action designed to protect against unwanted interferences with personal property. The theory is that if one can bar unauthorized access to the computer system on which one's database resides, one can bar access to the database.

In several cases, database owners have successfully invoked the common law action of trespass to chattels to prevent unauthorized access to their information. *See eBay, Inc. v. Bidder's Edge, Inc.*, 100 F.Supp.2d 1058 (N.D.Cal.2000) (entering preliminary injunction against operator of website that accessed online auction sites and aggregated information collected from them); *Register.com, Inc. v. Verio, Inc.*, 126 F.Supp.2d 238 (S.D.N.Y. 2000) (entering preliminary injunction against company that collected domain-registration information from database maintained by registrar). (These cases are excerpted and discussed in Chapter 13, *infra*.)

freestanding model state law, called the Uniform Computer Information Transactions Act. *See* Chapters 4 & 5, *supra*.—Eds.]

Under the *Restatement* version of the trespass to chattels cause of action, "[a] trespass to a chattel may be committed by intentionally (a) dispossessing another of the chattel, or (b) using or intermeddling with a chattel in the possession of another." RESTATEMENT (SECOND) OF TORTS § 217 (1965). Based on the "extra element" criterion, at least one court has held that trespass to chattels survives preemption under Section 301. *See eBay. v. Bidder's Edge, supra,* at 1072 ("The right to exclude others from using physical personal property is not equivalent to any rights protected by copyright and therefore constitutes an extra element that makes trespass qualitatively different from a copyright infringement claim.").

Computer Fraud. The federal Computer Fraud and Abuse Act, 18 U.S.C. § 1030, prohibits a range of conduct that is often referred to under the rubric of "hacking." Database owners, characterizing unauthorized access to their information as a form of hacking, have invoked several provisions of the Act to bar such access. The Act makes it illegal to "intentionally access[]" a computer "without authorization," if the access results in at least $5,000 of damage. 18 U.S.C. § 1030(a)(5)(A)(iii). It also provides an action against one who "knowingly and with intent to defraud, accesses a * * * computer without authorization, or exceeds authorized access, and by means of such conduct furthers the intended fraud and obtains anything of value," again if the result is damages of at least $5,000. 18 U.S.C. § 1030(a)(4). Courts have applied these provisions in cases involving unauthorized access to data. *See Register.com, Inc. v. Verio, Inc., supra*; *EF Cultural Travel BV v. Explorica, Inc.*, 274 F.3d 577 (1st Cir. 2001) (affirming entry of preliminary injunction against company that acquired price data from a competitor's website and used it to undercut the competitors prices). (These cases are excerpted and discussed in Chapter 13, *infra.*)

Since this cause of action clearly requires elements beyond those required for copyright infringement, it is likely to survive preemption when applied to protect databases.

NOTES & QUESTIONS

1. *Preemption and copyright management systems.* A copyright management system is a technological means of enforcing the terms and conditions of a license automatically, making recourse to the courts unnecessary. Would the widespread use of copyright management systems make the preemption doctrine irrelevant? (Copyright management systems are discussed in Chapter 11, *infra.*)

2. *Future of state-law causes of action.* As we will see in the next Part, database owners have sought legislation that would grant them control over use by others of the information in their databases. Given the availability of the various state-law causes of action described above, is such legislation necessary? If such legislation is enacted, will the state-law causes of action become superfluous?

III. *Sui Generis* Protection for Databases

In light of the limited protection provided to databases and compilations of fact under the law of copyright, and the federal preemption of state-law causes of action that might otherwise remedy this situation, many information providers and trade organizations with an interest in procuring greater legal protection for factual databases have advocated the passage of legislation that creates a *sui generis* right in databases: a legally protected interest in databases independent of federal copyright law as well as state common and statutory law. Two basic models have been proposed for such legislation: the intellectual property model and the unfair competition model.

Under the intellectual property model, the legislation would create a new exclusive property right in databases. Like a copyright or patent, an exclusive right in databases under the intellectual property model would be granted for a limited period of time, alienable by contract and subject to various statutory exceptions, defenses and compulsory licenses.

Under the unfair competition model, the legislation would prohibit particular methods of competition that undermine competitive markets for databases. Like the Lanham Act or the general doctrine of misappropriation, legislation under the unfair competition model would impose liability for conduct that unfairly appropriates commercial value of a database created by another.

Confronting a similar perceived need to strengthen the legal protection of databases and ensure Europe a strong competitive position in the emerging global information marketplace, the European Union embraced the intellectual property model for database protection and adopted a Directive according legal protection to databases. *See* Directive 96/9/EC of the European Parliament and of the Council of the European Union of 11 March, 1996, on the legal protection of databases, 1996 O.J. (L 77) 20. Under this Directive, all European Union member states were required to enact conforming database protection legislation by January 1, 1998. The details of this Directive are covered in a report published by the United States Copyright Office, excerpted below.

In the United States, the choice between the intellectual property model and the unfair competition model of database protection was presented as a choice between two bills proposed in Congress: the Collections of Information Antipiracy Act and the Consumer and Investor Access to Information Act of 1999. Although these two bills were not enacted, they are worth studying as paradigms of data protection legislation that is likely to be introduced in a future Congress.

The Collections of Information Antipiracy Act, H.R. 354, 106th Cong. (1999) ("H.R. 354"), embraces the intellectual property model and confers on the owner of a database an exclusive right in a "collection of information" enforceable in federal district court without regard to the amount in controversy. Its central provision is Section 1402, which states:

> (a) MAKING AVAILABLE OR EXTRACTING TO MAKE AVAILABLE—Any person who makes available to others, or extracts to make available to others, all or a substantial part of a collection of information gathered, organized, or maintained by another person through the investment of substantial monetary or other resources, so as to cause material harm to the primary market or a related market of that other person, or a successor in interest of that other person, for a product or service that incorporates that collection of information and is offered or intended to be offered in commerce by that other person, or a successor in interest of that person, shall be liable to that person or successor in interest for the remedies set forth in section 1406.
>
> (b) OTHER ACTS OF EXTRACTION—Any person who extracts all or a substantial part of a collection of information gathered, organized, or maintained by another person through the investment of substantial monetary or other resources, so as to cause material harm to the primary market of that other person, or a successor in interest of that other person, for a product or service that incorporates that collection of information and is offered or intended to be offered in commerce by that other person, or a successor in interest of that person, shall be liable to that person or successor in interest for the remedies set forth in section 1406.

H.R. 354, 106th Cong. § 1402 (1999). The terms "collection of information" and "information" are defined as follows:

> (1) COLLECTION OF INFORMATION—The term "collection of information" means information that has been collected and has been organized for the purpose of bringing discrete items of information together in one place or through one source so that persons may access them. The term does not include an individual work which, taken as a whole, is a work of narrative literary prose, but may include a collection of such works.
>
> (2) INFORMATION—The term "information" means facts, data, works of authorship, or any other intangible material capable of being collected and organized in a systematic way.

Id. § 1401. Section 1406 provides for injunctions, impoundment, monetary damages that can be trebled in the discretion of the court, reasonable attorney's fees and costs. Section 1403 carves out various exceptions to Section 1402, including reasonable uses understood in a manner analogous to fair use under the law of copyright. Nothing in the Act is intended to "restrict the rights of parties freely to enter into licenses or any other contracts with respect to making available or extracting collections of information," nor to "affect rights, limitations, or remedies concerning copyright, or any other rights or obligations relating to information, including laws with respect to patent, trademark, design rights, antitrust, trade secrets, privacy, access to public documents, and the law of contract." *Id.*

§ 1405. Government collections of information are excluded, as are computer programs and "collections of information gathered, organized, or maintained to address, route, forward, transmit, or store digital online communications, register addresses to be used in digital online communications, or provide or receive access to connections for digital online communications." *Id.* § 1401.

The Consumer and Investor Access to Information Act of 1999, H.R. 1858, 106th Cong. (1999) ("H.R. 1858"), embraces the unfair competition law model of database protection and prohibits the unauthorized sale or distribution of another's database. Its central provision is Section 102, which states:

> PROHIBITION AGAINST DISTRIBUTION OF DUPLICATES. It is unlawful for any person, by any means or instrumentality of interstate or foreign commerce or communications, to sell or distribute to the public a database that—
>
> (1) is a duplicate of another database that was collected and organized by another person; and
>
> (2) is sold or distributed in commerce in competition with that other database.

H.R. 1858, 106th Cong. § 102 (1999). The terms "database" and "duplicate" are defined in Section 101 as follows:

> (1) DATABASE.—The term "database" means a collection of discrete items of information that have been collected and organized in a single place, or in such a way as to be accessible through a single source, through the investment of substantial monetary or other resources, for the purpose of providing access to those discrete items of information by users of the database. However, a discrete section of a database that contains multiple discrete items of information may also be treated as a database.
>
> (2) DUPLICATE OF A DATABASE.—A database is "a duplicate" of any other database if the database is substantially the same as such other database, and was made by extracting information from such other database.

Id. § 101. Unlike H.R. 354, H.R. 1858 does not confer any rights on the owner of a database, nor does it provide a private right of action in federal district court. Instead, H.R. 1858 provides that the "Federal Trade Commission shall have jurisdiction, under section 5 of the Federal Trade Commission Act (15 U.S.C. 45), to prevent violations of section 102 of this title." *Id.* § 107(a). Section 107(b) of the Act also grants the FTC rulemaking authority, and subsection (c) states that "[a]ny violation of any rule prescribed under subsection (b) shall be treated as a violation of a rule respecting unfair or deceptive acts or practices under section 5 of the Federal Trade Commission Act (15 U.S.C. 45)."

Notwithstanding Section 102, the Act permits the sale and distribution of information contained in another's database for the purpose of law enforcement and intelligence activities, and for certain news reporting, scientific, educational, or research uses. *Id.* § 103. The Act also places limits on the liability of service providers, and denies relief to one who "has misused the protection afforded" by the Act. *Id.* § 106.

Like H.R. 354, nothing in H.R. 1858 is intended to "restrict the rights of parties freely to enter into licenses or any other contracts with respect to making available or extracting collections of information," nor to "affect rights, limitations, or remedies concerning copyright, or any other rights or obligations relating to information, including laws with respect to patent, trademark, design rights, antitrust, trade secrets, privacy, access to public documents, and the law of contract." *Id.* § 105. Also like H.R. 354, government databases are excluded. Unlike H.R. 354, however, H.R. 1858 does not prohibit sale or distribution to the public of individual items from a protected database. *Id.* § 104.

The two bills appear to offer a choice between two different models for legal protection of databases, but they both would change the balance between what information is property and what is in the public domain. Both approaches remove factual material from the public domain, a topic that Professor Pamela Samuelson addresses in the second excerpt below. Furthermore, database protection schemes may raise constitutional issues. In the third excerpt below, Professor Yochai Benkler considers the constitutional constraints imposed by the U.S. Constitution's Intellectual Property Clause and the First Amendment.

U.S. COPYRIGHT OFFICE, REPORT ON LEGAL PROTECTION FOR DATABASES

(1997).
www.copyright.gov/docs/db4.pdf

* * *

B. European Database Directive

1. *Background*

Pursuant to the action plan set out in its 1991 "Follow-up to the Green Paper,"[122] the European Commission proposed in 1992 to harmonize the national laws within the European Union regarding the protection of databases. The Commission proposal was adopted in a modified form as a directive to the member states on March 11, 1996.[123] The directive is required to be implemented by the member states by January 1, 1998.

A number of factors appear to have led the European Union (EU) to harmonize the law regarding database protection. The rapid expansion of

122. Doc. COM (90) 584 final, 17 Jan. 1991. The "Green Paper" referred to is the 1988 "Green Paper on Copyright and the Challenge of Technology," Doc. COM (88) 172 final, 7 June 1988.

123. Directive 96/9/EC of the European Parliament and of the Council of the European Union of 11 March 1996 on the legal protection of databases, 1996 O.J. (L 77/20) [hereinafter *Database Directive*].

the Internet raised the EU's awareness of "the exponential growth, in the Community and worldwide, in the amount of information generated and processed annually in all sectors of commerce and industry," and the important role of databases "in the development of an information market within the community."[125] The EU also expressed concern about the "very great imbalance in the level of investment in the database sector both as between the Member States and between the Community and the world's largest database-producing third countries."[126] In addition, the *Feist* decision in the U.S. Supreme Court galvanized concern regarding the adequacy of copyright protection for databases within the EU.

The directive covers compilations of data in any form, and thus includes hard copy compilations as well as electronic databases.[128] The Commission's original proposal was limited to electronic databases, but in the course of deliberations this approach was found unworkable, because it would subject the identical material to differing legal standards based solely on the medium employed. As one of the participants is reported to have stated, "making use of a scanner should not be decisive in granting legal protection." In addition, technologies such as scanning and optical character recognition render even hard-copy databases vulnerable to unauthorized copying and commercial reuse in both hard-copy and electronic form. Moreover, the TRIPs Agreement makes no such distinction.

As adopted, the directive establishes a dual system for protection of databases. One component is copyright protection for the "structure" of the database. The other is a *sui generis* ("of its own kind"—i.e., not falling within existing categories of legal protection) intellectual property right in the contents of the database.

2. *Copyright Protection*

The copyright portion of the directive, Chapter II, applies only to the structure or schema of a database, without prejudice to any existing protection under copyright for the database contents.[133] It seeks to harmonize the scope of copyright protection for databases throughout the European Union. It does so in two major respects: First, it sets a uniform standard

125. Database Directive, recitals (10), (9).

126. *Id.* recital (11).

128. Database Directive, art. 1(1), recital (14). The term "database" is defined in the directive as "a collection of independent works, data or other materials arranged in a systematic or methodical way and individually accessible by electronic or other means." Art. 1(2). Explicitly excluded from protection under the directive are "computer programs used in the making or operation of databases accessible by electronic means." Art. 1(3). Recital (17) expands on the definition:

[T]he term "database" should be understood to include literary, artistic, musical or other collections of works or collections of other material such as texts, sound, images, numbers, facts, and data; ... it should cover collections of independent works, data or other materials which are systematically or methodically arranged and can be individually accessed; ... this means that a recording or an audiovisual, cinematographic, literary or musical work as such does not fall within the scope of this Directive.

133. *Id.* art. 3(2).

of originality. Second, it establishes a uniform list of "restricted acts" (i.e., exclusive rights) and exceptions to restricted acts.

Prior to the directive, copyright protection for databases in the member states could be divided into two general groups. In the U.K., Ireland and the Netherlands, the threshold for protection was quite low. In particular, Anglo–Irish common law incorporated a "sweat of the brow" doctrine that developed from the same line of eighteenth and nineteenth century English cases that were cited in early U.S. compilation cases. In the remaining European countries, however, copyright imposed a fairly high threshold of originality to qualify for protection. This is in keeping with the "author's right" approach that prevails throughout most of Continental Europe, which defines originality as an expression of the author's individual personality.

The standard established by the directive requires the database to, "by reason of the selection or arrangement of [its] contents, constitute the author's own intellectual creation."[137] This language was incorporated verbatim from the EU's 1991 directive on the protection of computer programs.[138] It was originally adopted to override the very high standard of originality mandated by the German Supreme Court in the "Inkasso Programm" case and other decisions. At the same time, by requiring an "intellectual creation," the database directive imposes a higher standard of originality than that required under current law in the U.K., Ireland and the Netherlands. The directive thus charts a middle course on the level of originality required. Although the directive's standard of originality has not been tested in practice, the formulation appears to be quite similar to the criteria for protection under U.S. law, as set out in the definition of "compilation" in the Copyright Act and interpreted by the Supreme Court in *Feist*.

The "restricted acts" (exclusive rights of the copyright owner) under the directive are reproduction (temporary or permanent), adaptation, distribution, and communication, display or performance to the public.[141] Authorization is not required for a lawful user to engage in any restricted act "which is necessary for the purposes of access to the contents of the database and normal use of the contents."[142] Any contractual provision to the contrary is "null and void."[143]

In addition to this mandatory exemption, the directive permits member states to provide for limitations on the restricted acts in the following cases:

137. Database Directive, art. 3(1).

138. Council Directive 91/250/EEC of 14 May 1991 on the Legal Protection of Computer Programs, 1991 O.J. (L 122/42) [hereinafter *Software Directive*].

141. Database Directive, art. 5. The directive only covers economic rights under copyright; moral rights are beyond the scope of the directive. *Id.* recital (28).

142. Database Directive, art. 6(1). *Cf.* Software Directive, art. 5(1).

143. Database Directive, art. 15.

(a) in the case of reproduction for private purposes of a non-electronic database;

(b) where there is use for the sole purpose of illustration for teaching or scientific research, as long as the source is indicated and to the extent justified by the non-commercial purpose to be achieved;

(c) where there is use for the purposes of public security o[r] for the purposes of an administrative or judicial procedure;

(d) where other exceptions to copyright which are traditionally authorized under national law are involved, without prejudice to points (a), (b) and (c).[144]

Such exceptions are subject to an overall economic harm limitation, ensuring that they cannot "unreasonably prejudice[] the rightholder's legitimate interests or conflict[] with normal exploitation of the database."[145]

3. *Sui Generis Protection*

As a supplement to copyright, Chapter III of the directive establishes a *sui generis* form of protection for the contents of databases. The stated justification for this protection is that "in the absence of a harmonized system of unfair-competition legislation or of case-law, other measures are required in addition [to copyright] to prevent the unauthorized extraction and/or re-utilization of the contents of a database," the making of which "requires the investment of considerable human, technical and financial resources while such databases can be copied or accessed at a fraction of the cost needed to design them independently."[146]

Some of the EU member states originally advocated leaving the protection of the contents of databases to unfair competition law, and the initial Commission proposal described the *sui generis* right as a "right to prevent unfair extraction from a database" for commercial purposes.[147] By mid–

144. *Id.* art. 6(2). It has been suggested that article 6(2) "narrow[s] the educational and scientific communities' ability to invoke 'fair use' with respect to copyrightable databases under prior law." Jerome H. Reichman & Pamela Samuelson, *Intellectual Property Rights in Data?*, 50 VAND. L. REV. 51, 79 (1997). This view is based on an interpretation of points (a) through (c) as limitations on the scope of any exception permitted under point (d). *Id.* at 77, n.113. Others view point (d) as allowing "other exceptions to copyright which are traditionally permitted by the Member State concerned to continue." Jens–L. Gaster, *The New EU Directive Concerning the Legal Protection of Data Bases,* in FOURTH ANNUAL CONFERENCE ON INTERNATIONAL INTELLECTUAL PROPERTY LAW & POLICY, 35, 40 (Fordham Univ. School of Law, Apr. 11, 1996).

145. Database Directive, art. 6(3). This language is patterned after virtually identical language in the Berne Convention, art. 9(2) and TRIPs, art. 13 (which has been relied on by the United States to permit the doctrine of fair use under copyright law). *See also* WIPO Copyright Treaty, art. 10, and accompanying Agreed Statement (noting the understanding that similar treaty language would "permit Contracting Parties to carry forward and appropriately extend into the digital environment limitations and exceptions in their national laws which have been considered acceptable under the Berne Convention.")

146. Database Directive, recitals (6) and (7).

147. Proposal for a Council Directive on the Legal Protection of Databases, COM(92)24 final, art. 2 [hereinafter *1992 Proposal*].

1993, however, "an increasing majority of interested parties" were reportedly favoring the creation of a property right along the lines ultimately adopted. The rationale, at least in part, was the perceived difficulty in harmonizing unfair competition law throughout the European Union. In addition, the Commission has noted that "unfair competition rules only come into play once an act has taken place. They do not provide an economic right with clear scope which can be freely transferred."[149]

In some respects the *sui generis* right is similar to the "catalogue rule" existing in the Nordic countries, which provided a model for the Commission. That rule establishes a "related right" for factual compilations, in addition to copyright protection. The catalogue rule provides to the producer of a catalogue, table, or similar matter "in which a large number of information items have been compiled" a right against unauthorized reproduction.[150] Originality is not a requirement for protection, and the term of protection for such "catalogues" is fairly short: 10 years from publication or 15 years from creation, whichever expires sooner.

The essential features of the database directive's *sui generis* right are:

a. Protection for "substantial investment". The *sui generis* right is available for "the maker of a database which shows that there has been qualitatively and/or quantitatively a substantial investment in either the obtaining, verification or presentation of the contents ..."[151] "Substantial investment" is not defined in the directive. However, the recitals leading up to its provisions indicate that "such investment may consist in the deployment of financial resources and/or the expending of time, effort and energy."[152]

b. Protects against acts of extraction and re-utilization. The rights accorded under the directive are the rights to "prevent extraction and/or re-utilization of the whole or of a substantial part ... of the contents of that database."[153] "Extraction" is defined as "the permanent or temporary transfer of all or a substantial part of the contents of a database to another medium by any means or in any form."[154] "Re-utilization" is defined as "any form of making available to the public all or a substantial part of the contents of a database by the distribution of copies, by renting, by on-line or other forms of transmission."[155]

c. "Insubstantial parts" excluded from protection. The maker of a database "may not prevent a lawful user of the database from extracting and/or re-utilizing insubstantial parts of its contents ... for any purposes

149. Submission from the European Community and its Member States to the World Intellectual Property Organization on "An International Treaty on the Protection of Databases," p. 2 (July 1997).

150. Swedish Copyright Act, art. 49. *See also* Norwegian Copyright Act, art. 43; Danish Copyright Act, art. 71; Finnish Copyright Act, art. 49.

151. Database Directive, art. 7(1).

152. *Id.* recital (40).

153. *Id.* art. 7(1).

154. *Id.* art. 7(2)(a).

155. *Id.* art. 7(2)(b).

whatsoever."[156] Any contractual provision to the contrary is "null and void."[157] The directive does not attempt to define "insubstantial parts," but does state that substantiality is to be "evaluated qualitatively and/or quantitatively."[158]

d. Exceptions for certain uses. The directive permits member states to adopt exceptions from the *sui generis* right for lawful users in three specific categories: (a) extraction for private purposes of the contents of a non-electronic database; (b) "extraction for the purposes of illustration for teaching or scientific research, as long as the source is indicated and to the extent justified by the non-commercial purpose to be achieved"; and (c) "extraction and/or re-utilization for the purposes of public security or an administrative or judicial procedure."[159] These exceptions are similar to those permitted under copyright, but without the additional reference to "other exceptions to copyright which are traditionally authorized under national laws." Nevertheless, the recitals indicate that existing exemptions to any existing similar *sui generis* rights are grandfathered under the directive.[160]

The exceptions must be read in conjunction with provisions in the directive on "obligations of lawful users," prohibiting lawful users of databases that have been made available to the public from "performing acts which conflict with normal exploitation of the database or unreasonably prejudice the legitimate interests of the maker of the database," or "caus[ing] prejudice to the holder of a copyright or related right in respect of the works or subject matter contained in the database."[161]

e. Fifteen year term of protection. The term of protection for the *sui generis* right is fifteen years.[162] This was an increase from the ten-year term that was originally proposed in 1992.[163] Any qualitatively or quantitatively "substantial change," including one resulting from an accumulation of small changes, "which would result in the database being considered to be a substantial new investment," qualifies the resulting database for its own fifteen-year term of protection.[164]

f. Available to non-EU nationals only on the basis of reciprocity. The *sui generis* right is available only to database makers who are EU nationals or habitual residents.[165] For purposes of the directive, this would include business entities that have a business presence in the EU (defined as a

156. *Id.* art. 8(1).

157. *Id.* art. 15.

158. *Id.* art. 8(1).

159. *Id.* art. 9. While not stated explicitly in the text of the provision on exceptions, Recital (50) adds the gloss that the purpose of "such operations . . . must not be commercial."

160. *Id.* recital 52.

161. *Id.* arts. 8(2), 8(3) (again patterned after Berne Convention, art. 9(2) and TRIPs, art. 13). Recital (50) indicates that articles 8(2) and 8(3) function as a limitation on the exceptions in article 9.

162. *Id.* art. 10(1).

163. 1992 Proposal, art. 9(3).

164. 67 Database Directive, art. 10(3). It is unclear whether the new term of protection would apply to the entire database or only the "substantial new investment."

165. Database Directive, art. 11(1).

central administration or principal place of business in the EU, or a registered office in the EU plus a genuine, ongoing operational link with the economy of a member state).[166] The EU can conclude agreements to extend the right to databases made in third countries.[167] Although the provisions of the directive themselves are silent as to the basis for such agreements, the recitals make clear that protection will be offered only on the basis of reciprocity—i.e., where the third country offers "comparable protection" to EU databases.[168]

The original proposal for the directive also included a compulsory license, requiring database vendors who are the sole source of any given information to license that information to competitors on "fair and non-discriminatory terms."[169] This provision proved controversial. It was dropped after the European Court of Justice imposed a similar licensing requirement under existing principles of EU competition law in the "Magill case."[170] At the same time, apparently as part of an overall compromise, changes were made in the scope of the right and the exceptions, as well as the provision on rights of lawful users.

The recitals acknowledge the important role of competition policy in the database area.[172] In addition, the directive establishes a procedure for review every three years to determine, among other things, "whether the application of [the *sui generis*] right has led to abuse of a dominant position or other interference with free competition which would justify appropriate measures being taken, including the establishment of non-voluntary licensing arrangements."[173]

* * *

Pamela Samuelson, *Mapping the Digital Public Domain*

___ LAW & CONTEMP. PROBS. ___ (2002).

* * *

Several times in the past five years, the U.S. Congress has considered legislation to protect the contents of databases akin to that adopted by the European Union in 1996. The EU regime grants those who have invested substantial resources in making a database fifteen years of exclusive rights to control the extraction and reuse of all or substantial parts of the contents of that database. Database rights are renewable upon further expenditures of resources, and substantiality is to be judged in both qualitative as well as quantitative terms. The most recent EU-style database bill introduced into the U.S. Congress was the [Collections of Information Anti–Piracy Act ("CIAA"), H.R. 354].

166. *Id.* art. 11(2).

167. *Id.* art. 11(3).

168. *Id.* recital (56).

169. 1992 Proposal, art. 8(1).

170. Cases C–241/91 P and C–242/91 P, Radio Telefis Eireann v. Commission of the European Communities, E.C.J. (Apr. 6, 1995) (upholding an order by the Commission requiring television broadcasters to license self-generated programming information to competing publishers of program guides on a non-discriminatory basis).

172. Database Directive, recital (47) * * *.

173. *Id.*, art. 16 (3).

Although its sponsors characterize CIAA as a regulation of unfair competition, opponents characterize it as an intellectual property regime that is unconstitutional, bad public policy, or both. CIAA differs from the EU Directive in requiring proof of harm to actual or potential markets and in its "reasonable use" limit on the liability of scientific and educational users for extractions and uses of data in protected compilations, as well as in several outright exemptions (e.g., for news reporting, verification, and genealogical information). However, by conferring rights on compilers to control the use or extraction of all or a substantial part of a collection of information that is the product of substantial investment, CIAA would substantially contract the digital public domain—and not just as to items of information, but also as to public domain works (e.g., Shakespeare's plays) which fall within the meaning of "data" under the legislation. The main reason that CIAA has not been enacted is that organizations of scientists and a coalition of Internet-based firms (including prominently Yahoo!) recognized the serious threats that CIAA posed to the digital public domain and mobilized against this legislation. In the aftermath of the September 11 attacks on the World Trade Center and the Pentagon, Congress has other more urgent matters to consider, but like the Terminator, CIAA will almost certainly be back.

Although CIAA and the EU database law pose substantial threats to the digital public domain, more narrowly crafted legislation to protect data compilations against market failures would not. H.R. 1858 is the alternative bill to CIAA considered during the last Congressional session. It forbids duplicating another firm's database and then engaging in direct competition with it. While this bill would, of course, affect the public domain, it does so in a much narrower and more targeted way than CIAA. Assuming there was persuasive evidence that market failures were occurring or imminent in the database industry because firms were competitively duplicating existing databases, this limitation on the reuse of public domain information would be justifiable. This approach is consistent with the Supreme Court's ruling in *International News Service v. Associated Press* which held that INS had engaged in unfair competition with AP when its reporters took news from early editions of AP newspapers and published it verbatim in INS papers directly competing with AP papers. The Supreme Court's *Feist* decision may have said that "raw facts can be copied at will," but the Court qualified this statement with a reference to its *INS v. AP* decision.

* * *

Yochai Benkler, *Constitutional Bounds of Database Protection: The Role of Judicial Review in the Creation and Definition of Private Rights in Information*

15 Berkeley Tech. L.J. 535 (2000).

* * *

[A] law that assigns to some people rights to prevent others from accessing certain information, or communicating in certain ways, must comply with two constitutional constraints.

First, if the nature of the right is an exclusive right intended to create market incentives for its owners, or protect those owners' investments, by permitting them to exclude others from making valuable uses of the information, then Congress may act only within the confines of the Intellectual Property Clause. It may only give such rights in original works. It cannot create such rights as would enclose or burden access to information or knowledge already available to the public, and it cannot give exclusive rights to control ideas or facts. Furthermore, Congress may only enact rights under other clauses of Article I, Section 8, in particular the Commerce Clause, if these rights are different in kind from the rights that it is empowered, within constitutional bounds, to create under the Intellectual Property Clause. Creating a general right, good against the world, in "the news of the day," for example, is beyond the power of Congress.

Second, private rights to control the use of information, whether created within the confines of the Intellectual Property Clause or properly created outside of that framework, are regulations on speech. As such, they are subject to independent and cumulative review under the First Amendment. * * *

IV. CONSTITUTIONALITY OF THE DATABASE PROTECTION BILLS UNDER THE INTELLECTUAL PROPERTY CLAUSE

If the House of Representatives had purposefully tried to create a test case of the constitutional bounds imposed on it by the Intellectual Property Clause, its members could not have done better than to propose the two main opposing database protection bills reported to the House on September 30, 1999. House Bill 354, reported from the Committee on the Judiciary by Representative Coble, creates a property right in raw information in all but name. As reported, House Bill 354 prohibits extraction of information from a database, both for reuse and dissemination and simply for use, and gives database owners the right to track and prevent uses of information extracted from their database into downstream products—whether or not they compete with the database. * * * House Bill 1858, reported from the Committee on Commerce by Representative Bliley, on the other hand, assiduously shies away from property, and attempts to remain within the confines of unfair competition. It addresses competitors only, not users—either consumers or downstream creative users. It prohibits duplication, defined narrowly as slavish copying of the contents of the database without adding value, for sale of this data in competition with the source database. And it vests enforcement in the Federal Trade Commission. As one reviews the background and components of each proposed law, it becomes clear how House Bill 354 fails both the threshold test imposed by the Intellectual Property Clause and the backstop constraint imposed by the First Amendment, while House Bill 1858 survives at least the former, and probably the latter. * * *

* * *

* * * [T]he Intellectual Property Clause requires that intellectual property-like rights in information be enacted, if at all, only within the confines of that clause. In *Feist*, the Supreme Court stated that that clause did not permit recognition of property rights in the information contents of a collection. In regulating information markets under the general commerce power, Congress may only enact regulations that are different in kind from intellectual property rights, like trademark protection. House Bill 354 is functionally an intellectual property right in the information contents of databases, cannot be passed under the Commerce Clause, and is unconstitutional under the Supreme Court's interpretation of the Intellectual Property Clause throughout this century, and more specifically in *Feist*. House Bill 1858, on the other hand, is a law that regulates one particularly ruinous form of competition, and can therefore properly be passed under the Commerce Clause.

V. CONSTITUTIONALITY OF THE DATABASE PROTECTION BILLS UNDER THE FIRST AMENDMENT

* * *

Both database protection bills are regulations on information use and exchange. Both are thus regulations of speech, in the sense that they are subject to First Amendment scrutiny. For the most part, they are both content-neutral, and should be treated as functionally equivalent to structural media regulations—i.e., laws that regulate information production and exchange with the intent of improving information flows, but do so by regulating how people can and cannot, produce, use, and exchange information. These laws are subject to an intermediate level of scrutiny, most plainly stated in [*Turner Broad. Sys., Inc. v. FCC*, 512 U.S. 622 (1994)]. They must be shown to be aimed at an important government interest, to be capable of actually serving that goal, and not to serve that goal in a manner that is much more restrictive of speech than necessary.

House Bill 354 fails this level of intermediate scrutiny both because there is no basis to believe that the important government interest claimed by its drafters really exists, and because even if there were such basis, it regulates speech much more broadly than necessary to attain its stated goal. No serious evidence was presented to Congress or identified by the committee that the database industry in fact needs any new protection. Evidence identified in the Committee Report for House Bill 1858 specifically refutes the claim that there is a need for something like a property right in raw information in databases—whether it is called a sui generis property right or a robust unfair competition rule. The database industry, and in particular its commercial component, have grown robustly both before and after *Feist*. Short of generalized statements of the possibility of "piracy" there was no evidence to suggest that widespread consumer or competitor practices undercut the ability of commercial database producers to support their continued investment in the production, maintenance, and distribution of databases.

Moreover, despite this lack of evidence, House Bill 354 sweeps much more broadly than necessary given those justifications offered—if not supported—by the Committee Report on the bill. Its general prohibition on extraction, its broad definitions of primary and related markets, the sweep of productive uses it captures for the benefit of existing database owners at the expense of future database producers and their consumers, and the property-like protection (in terms of the economic function of the rights created) it provides for the information contained in databases simply cover too many ways in which people want to and can use information in databases. It prohibits or burdens with uncertainty too many valuable uses of information, both commercial and noncommercial, both amateur and professional, which do not complete with, and certainly do not undercut, commercial database producers. In the absence of serious evidence that the database industry is broken, it imposes this heavy burden for a highly speculative gain.

House Bill 1858 is similarly thin on evidence that there is a real need for a new right. Authors of the Committee Report on that bill do little to support that claim, other than begrudgingly admit that database providers sought some protection, and this seems to have been the minimal protection that would do to ameliorate the pressure whose primary product is House Bill 354. Even with respect to its second section, which creates something like a fifteen minute property right in real-time market information, most of the testimony that supported the bill came from online brokers who sought greater access to the information, while those who testified to a market need for such a right in fact supported the much broader rights created in House Bill 354. Nonetheless, the narrowness of the prohibitions created in House Bill 1858, on both its parts and its placing of enforcement responsibility with the Federal Trade Commission, thereby limiting the risk of anticompetitive abuses of the prohibition by database owners, suggest that the harm that would be imposed by this bill, if passed, would be relatively minimal.

NOTES & QUESTIONS

1. *Defining "database".* How the term "database" or "collection of information" is defined in any database protection legislation will greatly affect the nature and scope of the protection provided. Under the statutory definitions presented in H.R. 354 and H.R. 1858, consider whether the following works would be protected:

(a) websites

(b) the bits fixed on the hard drive of a computer

(c) movies on videotape or DVD, and videogame cartridges

(d) a West Reporter

(e) routing tables found on a Internet router

(f) a library

(g) a tax return

(h) a restaurant check

(i) an online discussion group among scientists

(j) a Powerpoint presentation

(k) a scientific paper presenting research results

(*l*) a scientific journal

(m) an issue of a law review

(n) an L.L.Bean catalog

(*o*) a distributed database such as the domain name system

(p) your brain

How would you draft a definition for the term "database" or "collection of information"? Try it and apply your definition to the examples listed above.

2. *Clicks vs. bricks.* Should the United States consider adopting database protection legislation that distinguishes between online and offline electronic databases? What about legislation that distinguishes between digital databases and nondigital ones, such as traditional paper-based library card catalogs?

3. *Vague scope.* The EU Directive requires member states to enact legislation creating a sui generis right in "a database which shows that there has been qualitatively and/or quantitatively a *substantial investment* in either the obtaining, verification or presentation of the contents." Directive 96/9/EC of the European Parliament and of the Council of the European Union of 11 March, 1996, on the legal protection of databases, 1996 O.J. (L 77) 20, art. 7(1) (emphasis added). H.R. 1858 applies to "items of information that have been collected and organized in a single place, or in such a way as to be accessible through a single source, through the *investment of substantial monetary or other resources*." H.R. 1858, 106th Cong. § 101 (1999) (emphasis added). Similarly, H.R. 1858 defines a duplication of a database as one that is "*substantially the same* as such other database," *id.* § 101 (emphasis added), and H.R. 354 applies to "[a]ny person who extracts all or a *substantial part* of a collection of information." H.R. 354, 106th Cong. § 1402 (1999) (emphasis added). The EU Database Directive prohibits the "extraction and/or re-utilization of the whole or of a substantial part * * * of the contents of [a] database," while at the same time requiring that "a lawful user of the database [not be prevented] from extracting and/or re-utilizing insubstantial parts of its contents." Directive Arts. 7(1) & 8(1).

Is vague language of this kind likely to strengthen or weaken the incentive to create large commercial databases? Is it likely to encourage or deter the theft of database contents? Is such language unavoidable or a legislative compromise?

4. *The proposed WIPO Database Treaty.* On August 30, 1996, the same day that the World Intellectual Property Organization ("WIPO") released proposal drafts for two treaties that would ultimately be adopted in substantially different form as the WIPO Copyright Treaty and the WIPO Performances and Phonograms Treaty, WIPO also released a third: the Basic Proposal for the Substantive Provisions of the Treaty on Intellectual Property in Respect of Databases. Unlike the other two proposals, this one was not adopted. Nonetheless, it has focused debate and discussion on whether and how to harmonize the international legal protection of databases.

Article 1 of this draft states that "Contracting Parties shall protect any database that represents a substantial investment in the collection, assembly, verification, organization or presentation of the contents of the database." Article 2 states that the term " 'database' means a collection of independent works, data or other materials arranged in a systematic or methodical way and capable of being individually accessed by electronic or other means." Article 3 states that "[t]he maker of a database eligible for protection under this Treaty shall have the right to authorize or prohibit the extraction or utilization of its contents." Article 4 states that "[t]he rights provided under this Treaty shall be owned by the maker of the database" and that they "shall be freely transferable." Article 5 allows that "Contracting Parties may, in their national legislation, provide exceptions to or limitations of the rights provided in this Treaty in certain special cases that do not conflict with the normal exploitation of the database and do not unreasonably prejudice the legitimate interests of the rightholder." Article 6 requires that "[e]ach Contracting Party shall protect according to the terms of this Treaty makers of databases who are nationals of a Contracting Party." Finally, Article 14 and the Annex to the Treaty require that Contracting Parties put in place some form of enforcement procedure the permits the rights in databases to be enforced against acts of infringement.

Based on the foregoing summary of its central provisions, what model of database protection does the proposed WIPO treaty embrace: the intellectual property model or the unfair competition model? Treaties often require implementing legislation. For example, the WIPO Copyright Treaty and the WIPO Performances and Phonograms Treaty were both implemented in the United States by Title I of the Digital Millennium Copyright Act. Given that the proposed WIPO treaty on database protection imposes an obligation on Contracting Parties to enact appropriate implementing legislation, could the United States have entered into this treaty? Or would the U.S. Constitution preclude it? Recall Professor Benkler's arguments, above.

CHAPTER ELEVEN

Technological Protection of Digital Goods

Created by a college freshman at Northeastern University in 1999, Napster used an innovative file-sharing technology to enable Internet users to download music at no cost via peer-to-peer file sharing. Napster made it easy for users to trade music encoded in the MP3 format, which compresses recordings into small and portable files without any noticeable sacrifice in sound quality. As Napster's popularity increased—at one point it claimed 60 million users—the recording industry filed multiple lawsuits, accusing Napster of encouraging the illegal copying and distribution of copyrighted music, in violation of the copyright laws. At the same time, recording artists, most notably the heavy metal group Metallica, began criticizing Napster for the large-scale distribution of copyrighted music. The company eventually shut down in response to federal court orders.[1]

Yet even after the courts' declarations that users who exchanged copyrighted music via Napster were violating the copyright laws, file sharing continued, hardly abated, through a variety of other file-trading services that sprang up to fill the void created by Napster's demise. The online sharing of digital versions of copyrighted movies has also become widespread: in some cases, pirated versions of movies are available for download from the Internet before they open on the big screen. The unauthorized uploading and downloading of copyrighted software remains a major irritant to software developers, notwithstanding years of aggressive anti-piracy efforts by industry representatives.

The Napster experience, and the persistent unauthorized trade in other information products despite copyright owners' sustained efforts to banish it from the network, suggests two propositions: first, that individuals, and in some cases businesses, are unlikely voluntarily to conform their behavior to what the courts have declared is the mandate of the copyright laws (at least under current market conditions); and second, that efforts by copyright owners to vindicate their rights by taking legal action against infringers are unlikely to reduce unauthorized reproduction and distribution to a level that copyright owners consider acceptable.

What then are copyright owners to do? One approach is to try to control unauthorized access to information products through the use of trusted systems.

1. For the legal history of these lawsuits, see Chapter 9, *supra*.

A trusted system, also known as a digital rights management system ("DRMS"), is a technological device—usually implemented through computer code—that controls access to or use of an accompanying information product. Such systems prevent a person from making any use of an information product beyond that which the copyright owner has authorized. A trusted system acts as a self-enforcement mechanism, cutting off access to the information product if the user does something not allowed by the license, such as attempting to send a copy to someone else. Developers of trusted systems envision that these programs will be able to structure the entire package of rights the content owner wishes to allow the user, and that they will be able to "negotiate" with the user's computer to arrive at an "agreement" about the package of rights and its price. To encourage the use of trusted systems, the Digital Millennium Copyright Act of 1998 added provisions to the Copyright Act making it unlawful both to circumvent the access controls employed by trusted systems, and to manufacture, import, or offer to the public products that are designed to circumvent controls on access and use.

The use of trusted systems has generated a good deal of controversy. Some argue that trusted systems will result in more digital products being available to more people at lower costs than ever before. Others maintain that permitting the use of trusted systems upsets the delicate balance between ownership rights and public access created by the law of copyright, shifting the balance in favor of copyright owners at the expense of the public, by allowing owners to prevent uses that the copyright law permits—for example, use of material that is not copyrightable or whose copyright has expired, or use of copyrighted material that is within fair use. Still others argue that the use of such systems permits industry to make unacceptable incursions into the domain of personal privacy, by tracking, recording, and ultimately commercializing users' personal preferences as reflected in their online use of information goods, such as music, electronic books, movies, and games.

In this chapter, we explore the use of trusted systems from several perspectives. In Part I, we look at the technology itself and the ways it can be used. In Part II, we examine the protections for trusted systems added by the Digital Millennium Copyright Act. In Part III, we look at some of the policy debates that the use of trusted systems has occasioned.

I. INTRODUCTION TO TRUSTED SYSTEMS

Mark Stefik & Alex Silverman, *The Bit and the Pendulum: Balancing the Interests of Stakeholders in Digital Publishing*

16 No. 1 COMPUTER LAW. 1 (1999).

Personal computers and computer networks have the potential to become an ideal basis for digital publishing. But the potential for digital publishing remains just that—a potential. The market for digital works remains nascent, because the medium has failed so far to balance the interests of important stakeholders. Computers and the digital medium are sometimes seen as the root of this problem. In this article we explore how computers designed as trusted systems could bring things more into balance.

By digital publishing, we mean the on-line sale and distribution of digital works. A digital work can be anything in digital form: an article, a book, a program, or any multimedia combination involving programming, music, text, and video. The advantages of the digital media include nearly instant distribution, low production costs, and the convenience of 24–hour automated shopping.

When personal computers and desktop publishing first appeared in the early 1980s, many publishers saw digital publishing as too risky. Although numerous factors influenced publishers' judgments in particular cases, the dominant and recurring factor was the fear of widespread unauthorized copying. Realistically concerned about loss of control over their intellectual assets, many publishers avoided the digital medium. From the publishers' perspective, the pendulum representing the balance of power between creators and consumers had swung too far towards consumers.

In the late 1990s, trusted systems began to appear from several vendors, including Folio, IBM, Intertrust, Xerox, and Wave Systems. Trusted systems vary in their hardware and software security arrangements, but in general, they automatically enforce terms and conditions under which digital works can be used. For example, rights can expire after a period of time. Different people can pay different fees for using a work, depending on digital licenses for membership in such groups as affiliated book clubs. Trusted systems differentiate between different uses such as making a digital copy, rendering a work on a screen, printing a work on a color printer, or extracting a portion of a work for inclusion in a new work. When asked to perform an operation not licensed by a work's specific terms and conditions, a trusted system refuses to carry it out. So dramatically do trusted systems alter the balance of power between publishers and consumers, some observers have suggested that the pendulum has now swung too far towards publishers.

* * *

Copyright and Trusted Systems

Beginning in the 1990s, it was realized that computers could become part of the solution to the copyright problem that they were said to cause. The key was the development of trusted systems technology.

There are two main ideas behind trusted systems: that the terms and conditions governing the authorized use of a digital work can be expressed in a computer-interpretable language, and that computers and software can be designed to enforce those terms and conditions. An example of a rights language is Xerox's DPRL (Digital Property Rights Language).

Digital rights cluster into several categories. Transport rights include rights to copy, transfer, or loan a work. Render rights include playing and printing. Derivative work rights govern extracting portions of a work, controlled editing of changes to it, and embedding of the portion in other works. Other rights govern the making and restoring of backup copies. With trusted systems, a publisher can assign rights to a digital work. Each right can specify fees that must be paid to exercise the right. Each right can specify access conditions that govern who can exercise the right.

Trusted systems enforce the terms and conditions. They also exchange copies of the work only with systems that can prove themselves trusted via challenge-response protocols. In exchanging digital works, trusted systems form a closed network of computers that exclude non-trusted systems and collectively support use of digital works under established rules of commerce. When digital works are sent between trusted systems, the works are encrypted. When digital works are rendered—by printing them on paper, displaying them on monitors, or playing them on speakers—the rendering process can embed machine-readable watermark data in the signal to make it easier to trace the source of any external copying of the works.

In general, the higher the security of a trusted system, the higher its cost. High-security trusted systems can detect any physical tampering, set off alarms, and erase secret key information inside. Intermediate security trusted systems have more modest physical, encryption, and programmatic defenses. Using challenge-response protocols, trusted systems have the capability to recognize other trusted systems and to determine their security levels. For any particular work, publishers can specify the security level required by a trusted system that can receive it. An expensive industry report might require an expensive and secure corporate trusted system with advanced security measures. A digital newspaper for wide distribution and subsidized by advertisements might require only modest security measures for home computers.

Trusted Systems and the Balance of Interests

There are many stakeholders in digital publishing. Beyond the government itself, U.S. copyright law focuses on two parties or categories of people: rights holders (that is, the authors and publishers who hold the copyrights) and the public. However, trusted systems delegate enforcement and control to computers. One of the effects of this delegation is that it introduces third parties to the arrangement, including distributors, trusted system vendors, financial clearing houses, and multiple governments. This complicates the balance of interests, in that it introduces more parties whose interests need to be considered.

The use of trusted systems to enforce terms and conditions provides a much finer grain of control than copyright law, and moves the legal basis of protection in the direction of contracts and licenses. The finer grain of control includes distinctions between different kinds of usage rights such as copying, loaning, printing, displaying, backup, and so on. It also includes provisions for identifying specific users, specific kinds of devices for rendering, and fees for uses. Further, trusted systems provide a finer grain of control in that it becomes possible for rights holders to monitor and negotiate over transactions in copyrighted works in situations where, in the past, such monitoring and negotiation would have been impractical, if not impossible.

Copyright Law

* * *

Without trusted systems, effective enforcement of copyright in the digital medium can be nearly impossible. Like a proverbial sieve with thousands of little holes, it is too hard and expensive to find all the little infringement leaks of isolated individuals making copies. Furthermore, living with the leaks has its own deep risks. By publishing without copyright enforcement in a community that routinely makes unauthorized copies, rights holders risk that, over time, such copying could become established as common practice or even sanctioned by courts as fair use.

In sum, the move toward digital media poses challenges for copyright law and creates uncertainty for rights holders, especially for would-be publishers in the new media. The uncertainty tends to hamper the adoption of the new media and to discourage publishers from publishing in it. The impracticalities of enforcing copyright on untrusted, networked systems, the gray areas of legal interpretation for digital works, the lack of fine-grained control in copyright law, and the risk of an emerging legal claim of fair use for digital copying all motivate would-be authors and publishers in the digital medium to find means other than copyright law for protecting their interests.

Contract Law and Digital Contracts

In a representative scenario of digital publication on a trusted system, an author begins by creating a digital work. When the work is ready, the author finds a publisher (possibly himself) to develop the work further and to sell it. The publisher develops a set of terms and conditions for use of the work. Using a rights management language like DPRL, the publisher specifies the time period over which the rights apply. He determines what rights to include, for example, whether printing is allowed, whether the work can be loaned out for free, whether there is a special discount for members of a particular book club. He may assign different fees for different rights. For example, he may decide either to disallow creation of derivative works or to encourage creation of such works as a source of further revenue. He may mandate that the reader of the digital work must have proof in the form of a proper digital certificate that he is over 18. In DPRL, each right specification statement includes a type of right, a time specification governing when the right is valid, an access specification governing any special licenses required to exercise the right, and a fee specification governing billing. Using a trusted system, these rights are associated with the digital work, either by bundling them together in an encrypted file or by assigning the work a unique digital identifier and by registering the work and its rights in an on-line database.

Why would a publisher or a consumer want to have a specific and detailed agreement about use? The alternative, based on copyright as used for most printed works, is to have a single fee to purchase a work and then general legal standards about how works can be used. In the previous section we considered motivations for publishers to use specialized terms and conditions for their digital works. Specialized rules also have potential economic advantages for consumers. In the established software market, a software license is typically purchased for a fixed fee. This means that a user who expects to make little use of a software product must pay the same fee as someone who would use it for many hours a day. In some markets, this situation is bad for both publishers and consumers because many low-usage consumers will decide not to purchase the software at all. Trusted systems offer the possibility of differential pricing and "metered use" in which the amount that someone pays to use software depends on how much they use it. One way to look at metered use is that it allows "renting" software, where the rental terms can be flexible enough to provide for decreasing costs or caps with increased volume of use.

Another example of mutual economic advantages concerns the first sale doctrine. When consumers buy a paper book, they receive and own the copy of the book. When they are done with the book, they are free to give it to a friend or to sell the book to someone else. The first sale doctrine from copyright law guarantees these rights. In the DPRL language, the analogous usage right is called a transfer right. When one trusted system transfers a digital work to a second trusted system, the copy on the first trusted system is deleted or deactivated so that it can no longer be used. Analogous to handing a book to a friend, a transfer operation preserves the number of usable copies of the work. Analogous to the first sale doctrine, the terms and conditions on a digital work could allow it to be transferred at no charge.

A free transfer right is exactly what a consumer might want if he or she were buying the digital work for a friend, or intended to share the work serially with others. On the other hand, from a publisher's perspective, a free transfer right is a threat to future sales. If each person who reads a copy of a digital work needs to buy their own copy, the publisher would sell more copies. A publisher could offer two different combinations of rights with a work. In one combination, the consumer pays the "standard" amount for a work, and can transfer the work without a fee just as with the first sale doctrine. In another combination, the consumer gets a discount for a non-transferable work or must pay a fee to transfer it. This discounted purchase might be preferred by a consumer who buys the work for his personal use and who does not anticipate giving it away. Arguably, the first sale doctrine is grounded in experience with paper-based works and the copies were treated as physical objects, independent of their creative content. Like tools or food, such physical objects could be resold at the owner's convenience. Enforcement of a law to prevent resale or giving of books would be difficult in any case, so the first sale doctrine makes sense for paper-based works. For digital works and trusted systems, these considerations are less relevant. The publisher and the consumer are free to enter into an agreement that each sees as economically advantageous.

In many ways, a set of terms and conditions in DPRL is much like a contract or license agreement for using a digital work. For convenience here, we will call such a set of terms and conditions a digital contract. However, it should be remembered that a digital contract differs from an ordinary contract in crucial ways. Notably, in an ordinary contract between people, compliance is not automatic and is the responsibility of the agreeing parties. There may be provisions for monitoring and checking compliance with the terms and conditions, but the responsibility for acting in accordance with the terms falls on the parties, and enforcement of the contract is ultimately the province of the courts. In contrast, with trusted systems, a substantial part of the enforcement of a digital contract is carried out by the trusted systems themselves. In the short term, at least, the consumer does not have an option to disregard a digital contract, for example, to make infringing copies of a digital work. A trusted system will refuse to exercise a right that is not sanctioned by the digital contract. Over the longer term, it may be possible for consumers or consumer advocacy groups to negotiate with publishers to obtain different terms and conditions in the digital contracts, but even then, the new digital contracts will be subject to automatic enforcement by trusted systems.

* * *

Courts provide checks and balances in contract law by deciding what contracts to enforce and how to interpret the terms and conditions of those contracts. With properly designed trusted systems, many of these checks and balances can be made available automatically. Consider a digital publishing scenario again. The author has finished the work and the publisher assigns terms and conditions. Just as there can be conventional (so-called "boilerplate") language used in putting together an agreement, there can be digital boilerplate in the form of templates and default conditions in setting up a digital contract. Suppose that the publisher has included some very unusual terms and conditions in the agreement. When the consumer's trusted system is in communication with the publisher's trusted system, it can first retrieve the terms and conditions of the digital contract. It shows these to the consumer. Before the consumer accepts receipt of the digital work, a program can check for and highlight unusual conditions in the digital contract. Because rights management languages like DPRL are simple and formal languages with limited complexity, simple grammar and predetermined meanings, this checking is straightforward for a computer. In particular, the contract checker can look for unusual or high fees on certain rights, unrealistic expiration dates, or any other requirement that is outside of the usual practice. (As a somewhat bizarre example, consider a digital work that the consumer can copy for free but, surprisingly and inconveniently, costs $10 to delete.) The consumer is given an opportunity to agree to the terms and accept delivery or to refuse the terms and not take delivery of the work. If the consumer agrees, his trusted system can digitally sign a form marking his agreement to the contract. This signing can be digitally notarized by a third party (a "digital notary") known to both parties.

The sequence of events in this example illustrates several checks and balances in the process. Both the publisher and the consumer can use computational aids to check the normalcy and appropriateness of the contract. More than being a labor-saving or time-saving procedure, this approach also helps to compensate for the somewhat less tangible nature of information inside computers. It gives increased confidence to both parties that the terms and conditions used by the trusted systems will be reasonable.

It is helpful to think of a digital contract as encompassing several distinct legal contracts. There is the contract for access to the copyrighted work itself. Further, there is a contract for the service of delivering digital data to the consumer, irrespective of whether that data is or can be copyrighted. For example, if the publisher provides an uncopyrightable database or telephone white pages directory to the consumer via a trusted system, the publisher can fairly charge for this service, even though the consumer could, in principle, get the uncopyrightable data elsewhere or put together the database himself. Similarly, the digital publisher could charge the consumer for a copy of the complete works of Shakespeare even though that is in the public domain, just as print publishers can charge for printed copies of Shakespeare's works. Put another way, like the print publisher, the digital publisher has made life more convenient for the consumer, and the consumer pays the publisher for this convenience. What the publisher of an uncopyrightable or public domain work cannot do is to prevent another publisher from offering consumers the same or a comparable work, as would be the case if the work were copyrighted. Finally, there is a third contract implicit in the digital contract, namely, the service agreement by which the consumer is entitled to access the network of trusted systems in the first place. This agreement may be arranged between the consumer and the publisher, or between the consumer and one or more network service providers who may or may not be affiliated with the publisher.

The idea that a digital contract includes multiple legal contracts provides a coherent rationale for why digital contracts ought to be enforceable, even as to uncopyrightable works. For example, suppose that a publisher provides a public domain work, such as the complete works of Shakespeare, to the consumer via a trusted system. However, the digital contract for this work prohibits the consumer from copying or further transferring the contents of the work, at least not in digital form. The consumer is unhappy about this. He knows that the work is not protected by copyright and, when the bill arrives from the publisher, he refuses to pay, or else sues to get his money back. In court, the consumer argues that for the publisher to charge for what is no longer protected by copyright is in violation of the policy of copyright to establish limited-term monopolies for authors. Therefore, says the consumer, the digital contract should be preempted by the Copyright Act and should be held unenforceable. (The consumer might also argue that, because the publisher accepts the consumer's money while providing in return only a public domain work that ought to be available for free, the agreement fails for lack of consideration). The publisher responds that what is being sold here isn't the work, but rather the service of delivering the work. The publisher says, in effect, "Consumer, by dealing with me, you save time and energy and money over other delivery mechanisms such as conventional bookstores. But if I, as vendor, want to continue successfully to provide this service to others, then I am entitled to collect revenue at every transaction, not just the first one. Therefore, I can legitimately prevent you by this digital contract from transferring the copy of the work I just sold you." We think that the publisher has the better argument here. The consumer can pay the publisher for the right to print out the contents of the book, and can then copy the contents, for example, by hand or by scanning with an untrusted optical scanner. Also, other publishers can produce similar books containing identical texts, and a not-for-profit library could make these texts available for free. In short, the publisher has not overstepped the bounds of copyright.

Another point of possible concern with a digital contract is the extent to which a user is realistically in a position to negotiate the terms of the contract. In court cases concerning the viability of shrinkwrap licenses, one of the legal arguments used to challenge the validity of the license is that a publisher has an advantaged position of power and leaves the user with only a "take it or leave it" proposition. In this situation, many consumers do not bother to read the shrinkwrap license. In the case of trusted systems, it may be important that a consumer agent could be called upon to highlight terms and conditions likely to be unacceptable. In principle, one of the options when such terms are found is for the trusted systems to open a channel for negotiation and possible change of the terms. It is worth noting, however, that one of the main advantages of digital publishing is the possibility of fully automated systems providing 24–hour shopping convenience. In that setting, one might not expect to negotiate the terms of purchase for a mass-market digital work any more than one would expect to negotiate the price of buying a best-seller paperback at a convenience store in the middle of the night. The consumer would simply have to either accept the terms as they stand, or postpone her purchase until such time as a human agent became available to negotiate the terms.

* * *

NOTES & QUESTIONS

1. *Implementation of trusted systems.* Digital rights management systems along the lines described in this article have been implemented in several contexts. The Serial Copy Management System, discussed in Chapter 9, *supra*, has been required for digital audio tape machines since 1992. More recently, some music CDs have been released with coding designed to prevent them from being copied using a CD–RW drive, or even being played on a computer. Motion pictures on DVD are protected by an encryption system called the Content Scramble System, which is designed to prevent unauthorized copying. As discussed in *Universal City Studios, Inc. v. Reimerdes*, excerpted in Part II, *infra*, CSS was cracked and circumvented by a 15-year-old Norwegian computer hobbyist, giving rise to several lawsuits and creating a cause célèbre for both proponents and opponents of trusted systems. Movie DVDs also contain regional coding, which prevents a DVD purchased in one region of the world from playing on a DVD player sold in a different region of the world. Electronic books are released with DRMS technology provided by several manufacturers, including Palm, Microsoft, and Adobe. What are the obstacles to the further implementation of systems such as these?

2. *Limiting users' rights*. The rights that one has with respect to a digital product (a music CD, a movie on DVD, software, data, a text) one purchases may be limited through several methods. First, the copyright laws limit the purchaser's right to copy, adapt, distribute, perform, and display works to which copyright applies. Second, one's rights may be limited by an accompanying set of terms, usually called a license agreement, that is deemed part of the contract between the parties. Third, one's rights may be limited by a digital rights management system incorporated into the product. In what ways do these three methods of limiting the purchaser's rights differ, from the standpoint of both vendor and purchaser? Consider the extent to which such terms may be negotiated; the ability of the parties to renegotiate disputed terms; the availability of legal defenses to enforcement; the costs of enforcement.

3. *A technological arms race*. Trusted systems, like any other technology, are susceptible to circumvention. A piece of computer code designed to prevent unauthorized access to an informational good may be defeated by another piece of computer code. The latter code may itself be neutralized by a counter-measure that plugs the loophole it exploited, giving rise to a circumvention that exploits some different loophole. This has led to a sort of technological arms race, in which trusted-system creators and hackers take turns outwitting one another. Who do you think is more likely to win this arms race: the lock-makers, or the lock-breakers? Do you agree with amateur cryptographer Edgar Allen Poe: "[I]t may be roundly asserted that human ingenuity cannot concoct a cipher which human ingenuity cannot resolve."?[2]

Suppose that the locks are effective enough to keep out all but a tiny proportion of the population, the hacker aristocracy, who are able to defeat any trusted system in existence. Should copyright owners feel safe? Do you agree with the following analogy, offered by Professor Lessig?: "[F]rom the fact that 'hackers could break any security system,' it no more follows that security systems are irrelevant than it follows from the fact that 'a locksmith can pick any lock' that locks are irrelevant. Locks, like security systems on computers, will be quite effective, even if there are norm-

2. Edgar Allan Poe, *A Few Words on Secret Writing*, GRAHAM'S MAGAZINE, July 1841, at 33, 33.

oblivious sorts who can break them." Lawrence Lessig, *Reading the Constitution in Cyberspace*, 45 Emory L.J. 869, 896 n.80 (1996). In the digital world, is there an argument that any system that is less than 100 percent effective is practically worthless?

II. Special Protection for Technological Management Systems: Title I of the Digital Millennium Copyright Act

Congress responded to the technological arms race described above, weighing in on the side of the trusted-system community, with Title I of the Digital Millennium Copyright Act of 1998 ("DMCA"), 17 U.S.C. §§ 1201–05. The drive for regulation of this kind developed in the mid–1990s when the World International Property Organization ("WIPO") Copyright Treaty and the WIPO Performances and Phonograms Treaty were negotiated. Article 11 of the WIPO Copyright Treaty, titled "Obligations concerning Technological Measures," requires:

> Contracting Parties shall provide adequate legal protection and effective legal remedies against the circumvention of effective technological measures that are used by authors in connection with the exercise of their rights under this Treaty or the Berne Convention and that restrict acts, in respect of their works, which are not authorized by the authors concerned or permitted by law.

WIPO Copyright Treaty, Dec. 20, 1996, art. 11, WIPO Doc. CRNR/DC/94, www.wipo.int/eng/diplconf/distrib/94dc.htm.

In addition, Article 12 of the same treaty, "Obligations concerning Rights Management Information," states:

> (1) Contracting Parties shall provide adequate and effective legal remedies against any person knowingly performing any of the following acts knowing, or with respect to civil remedies having reasonable grounds to know, that it will induce, enable, facilitate or conceal an infringement of any right covered by this Treaty or the Berne Convention:
>
> (i) to remove or alter any electronic rights management information without authority;
>
> (ii) to distribute, import for distribution, broadcast or communicate to the public, without authority, works or copies of works knowing that electronic rights management information has been removed or altered without authority.
>
> (2) As used in this Article, "rights management information" means information which identifies the work, the author of the work, the owner of any right in the work, or information about the terms and conditions of use of the work, and any numbers or codes that represent such information, when any of these

> items of information is attached to a copy of a work or appears in connection with the communication of a work to the public.

Id. art. 12. Nearly identical provisions can also be found in the WIPO Performances and Phonograms Treaty. *See* WIPO Performances and Phonograms Treaty, Dec. 20, 1996, arts. 18 & 19, WIPO Doc. CRNR/DC/95, www.wipo.org/eng/diplconf/distrib/95dc.htm. Enactment of Title I of the DMCA was intended to meet the obligations of the United States under both of these treaties.

A Senate Report on the DMCA describes Title I as follows:

> Title I implements the WIPO Copyright Treaty and the WIPO Performances and Phonograms Treaty. These treaties were concluded by the Clinton administration in December 1996. The treaties are best understood as supplements to the Berne Convention for the Protection of Literary and Artistic Works. The Berne Convention is the leading multilateral treaty on copyright and related rights, with 130 countries adhering to it. The United States ratified the Berne Convention in 1989. The two new WIPO treaties were adopted at a diplomatic conference by a consensus of over 150 countries. In general, the Copyright Treaty updates the Berne Convention for digital works and the growth of the Internet and other digital communications networks, and the Performances and Phonograms Treaty supplements the Berne Convention with comprehensive copyright protection for performances and sound recordings (called "phonograms" in international parlance).
>
> The importance of the treaties to the protection of American copyrighted works abroad cannot be overestimated. The treaties, as well as the Berne Convention, are based on the principle of national treatment; that is, that adhering countries are obliged to grant the same protection to foreign works that they grant to domestic works. Even more importantly, the Berne Convention and the treaties set minimum standards of protection. Thus, the promise of the treaties is that, in an increasing[ly] global digital marketplace, U.S. copyright owners will be able to rely upon strong, non-discriminatory copyright protection in most of the countries of the world.
>
> The copyright industries are one of America's largest and fastest growing economic assets. * * * In fact, the copyright industries contribute more to the U.S. economy and employ more workers than any single manufacturing sector, including chemicals, industrial equipment, electronics, food processing, textiles and apparel, and aircraft. More significantly for the WIPO treaties, in 1996 U.S. copyright industries achieved foreign sales and exports of $60.18 billion, for the first time leading all major industry sectors, including agriculture, automobiles and auto parts, and the aircraft industry.

> The WIPO treaties contain many important provisions. For example, the Copyright Treaty contains significant provisions such as: * * * (5) an obligation to provide "legal protection and effective legal remedies" against circumventing technological measures, e.g. encryption and password protection, that are used by copyright owners to protect their works from piracy; and (6) an obligation to provide "adequate and effective legal remedies" to preserve the integrity of "rights management information." * * *
>
> The Committee believes that in order to adhere to the WIPO treaties, legislation is necessary in two primary areas—anticircumvention of technological protection measures and protection of the integrity of rights management information, or "copyright management information" (CMI), as it is referred to in the bill. This view is shared by the Clinton administration. In drafting implementing legislation for the WIPO treaties, the Committee has sought to address those two areas, as well as avoid government regulation of the Internet and encourage technological solutions. The Committee is keenly aware that other countries will use U.S. legislation as a model.

S. Rep. No. 105–190, at 9–11 (1998).

A. Using and Trafficking in Circumvention Technologies

Title I of the DMCA added Chapter 12 to Title 17 of the U.S. Code. The first section of this chapter, Section 1201, deals with using and trafficking in circumvention technologies. Section 1201(a)(1)(A) makes it illegal to "circumvent a technological measure that effectively controls access to a work protected under" the Copyright Act. Section 1201(a)(2) provides:

> No person shall manufacture, import, offer to the public, provide, or otherwise traffic in any technology, product, service, device, component, or part thereof, that—
>
> > (A) is primarily designed or produced for the purpose of circumventing a technological measure that effectively controls access to a work protected under this title;
> >
> > (B) has only limited commercially significant purpose or use other than to circumvent a technological measure that effectively controls access to a work protected under this title; or
> >
> > (C) is marketed by that person or another acting in concert with that person with that person's knowledge for use in circumventing a technological measure that effectively controls access to a work protected under this title.

Section 1201(b)(1) further provides:

> No person shall manufacture, import, offer to the public, provide, or otherwise traffic in any technology, product, service, device, component, or part thereof, that—

> (A) is primarily designed or produced for the purpose of circumventing protection afforded by a technological measure that effectively protects a right of a copyright owner under this title in a work or a portion thereof;
>
> (B) has only limited commercially significant purpose or use other than to circumvent protection afforded by a technological measure that effectively protects a right of a copyright owner under this title in a work or a portion thereof; or
>
> (C) is marketed by that person or another acting in concert with that person with that person's knowledge for use in circumventing protection afforded by a technological measure that effectively protects a right of a copyright owner under this title in a work or a portion thereof.

Section 1201 thus addresses two types of technological protections of copyrighted works, and two types of forbidden conduct in connection with those protections. The two types of technological protections are those that prevent unauthorized *access* to a work, and those that prevent *use* of a work in a manner that infringes the copyright. The two types of forbidden conduct are the *act of circumventing* a technological protection, and the manufacturing or distribution of a device or software program that disables such a protection, generally referred to as *trafficking*. As a matter of logic, the combination of two technological protections with two types of prohibited conduct could yield four (two times two) prohibitions. In fact, however, Section 1201 only addresses three of those combinations. With respect to the first type of technological protection (preventing unauthorized access), it is illegal both to circumvent it and to traffic in technologies of circumvention. With respect to the second type of technological protection (preventing unauthorized use), it is illegal to traffic in technologies of circumvention, but there is no prohibition against the act of circumvention. The prohibitions of Section 1201 may be represented graphically:

		Type of technological protection	
		Access controls	Use controls
Type of prohibition	Prohibition on circumvention	§ 1201(a)(1)(A)	None
	Prohibition on trafficking	§ 1201(a)(2)	§ 1201(b)(1)

Why does Section 1201 contain no prohibition against the act of circumventing protection of the rights of a copyright owner? The Senate Report explains:

> The prohibition in 1201(a)(1) is necessary because prior to this Act, the conduct of circumvention was never before made unlawful. The device limitation in 1201(a)(2) enforces this new prohibi-

> tion on conduct. The copyright law has long forbidden copyright infringements, so no new prohibition [on conduct facilitated by the devices prohibited in 1201(b)] was necessary. The device limitation in 1201(b) enforces the longstanding prohibitions on infringements.

S. Rep. No. 105–190, *supra*, at 12.

Thus, according to the Senate Report a prohibition on the act of circumventing a technological measure that prevents infringement of a copyright—which would occupy the upper right-hand box in the above chart—is unnecessary, because it would be redundant with the central provision of the Copyright Act, 17 U.S.C. § 106.

In addition to setting forth the preceding anti-circumvention and anti-trafficking prohibitions, Section 1201 also creates a series of exceptions to them. There are exemptions from the anti-circumvention provisions for nonprofit libraries and educational institutions, law enforcement and intelligence agents, reverse engineering computer programs, encryption research, filtering Web content to determine if it is appropriate for minors, protection of privacy, and testing computer and network security. *See* 17 U.S.C. § 1201(d)–(j). (Some of these exemptions also apply, to a limited extent, to the anti-trafficking provisions.) Moreover, Section 1201(a)(1)(B)–(E) empowers the Librarian of Congress, upon recommendation from the Register of Copyrights, to create additional exceptions to the prohibition against circumventing access controls. Pursuant to this subsection, the Librarian has exempted (through October 28, 2003) two additional narrow categories of use: "(1) Compilations consisting of lists of websites blocked by filtering software applications; and (2) Literary works, including computer programs and databases, protected by access control mechanisms that fail to permit access because of malfunction, damage or obsoleteness." 37 C.F.R. § 201.40. It remains to be seen whether these exceptions can satisfy the concerns of advocates of broader rights for users of protected materials.

Beyond the prohibitions and exceptions created by this section, Section 1201(c)(1) & (2) emphasize that none of the foregoing "shall affect rights, remedies, limitations, or defenses to copyright infringement, including fair use," or "shall enlarge or diminish vicarious or contributory liability for copyright infringement in connection with any technology, product, service, device, component, or part thereof." Moreover, with one exception, Section 1201(c)(3) states that manufacturers of consumer electronics, telecommunications equipment, and computer products are not required to design their products so that they accommodate access and use controls. The one exception is created by Section 1201(k), which requires manufacturers, importers, and distributors of certain devices such as VCRs and camcorders to produce, import and traffic only in devices that employ the copy control technology developed and owned by Macrovision Corporation.[3] By requiring

3. The reference to Macrovision Corp. occurs not in the statute, but only in the legislative history. *See* H.R. Conf. Rep. No. 105–796, at 67–69 (1998).

the use of a specific technology, this provision contrasts sharply with the rest of the DMCA, which strives to remain technology-neutral.

To set the stage for examination of the continuing controversies surrounding the DMCA, consider the following portions of its legislative history. While reading it, think about how Congress characterizes the problem the legislation is supposed to solve, and how it conceives of the fit between this statute and pre-existing copyright law. Consider, as well, what role is played by Congress's understanding of existing and foreseeable encryption technology. What interest groups do you think were most influential in crafting this legislation?

Section–By–Section Analysis of H.R. 2281

House Committee on the Judiciary, 105th Congress.
(Comm. Print 1998).

* * *

Section 1201: Circumvention of Copyright Protection Systems.

Subsection (a) of new Section 1201 applies when a person who is not authorized to have access to a work seeks to gain access by circumventing a technological measure put in place by the copyright owner that effectively controls access to the work. * * *

[§ 1201(a)(1).] The act of circumventing a technological protection measure put in place by a copyright owner to control access to a copyrighted work is the electronic equivalent of breaking into a locked room in order to obtain a copy of a book. Subparagraph (A) establishes a general prohibition against gaining unauthorized access to a work by circumventing a technological measure put in place by the copyright owner where such measure effectively controls access to a work protected under Title 17 of the U.S. Code. * * *

* * *

* * * The technological measures—such as encryption, scrambling and electronic envelopes—that this bill protects can be deployed, not only to prevent piracy and other economically harmful unauthorized uses of copyrighted materials, but also to support new ways of disseminating copyrighted materials to users, and to safeguard the availability of legitimate uses of those materials by individuals. These technological measures may make more works more widely available, and the process of obtaining permissions easier.

For example, an access control technology under section 1201(a) would not necessarily prevent access to a work altogether, but could be designed to allow access during a limited time period, such as during a period of library borrowing. Technological measures are also essential to a distribution strategy that allows a consumer to purchase a copy of a single article from an electronic database, rather than having to pay more for a subscription to a journal containing many articles the consumer does not want. * * *

[§ 1201(a)(2)]. In order to provide meaningful protection and enforcement of the copyright owner's right to control access to his or her copyrighted work, this paragraph supplements the prohibition against the act of circumvention in [§ 1201(a)(1)] with prohibitions on creating and making available certain technologies, products and services used, developed or advertised to defeat technological protections against unauthorized access to a work. * * *

Specifically, [§ 1201(a)(2)] prohibits manufacturing, importing, offering to the public, providing, or otherwise trafficking in certain technologies, products, services, devices, components, or parts that can be used to circumvent a technological protection measure that otherwise effectively controls access to a work protected under Title 17. It is drafted carefully to target "black boxes," and to ensure that legitimate multipurpose devices can continue to be made and sold. For a technology, product, service, device, component, or part thereof to be prohibited under this subsection, one of three conditions must be met. It must:

(1) be primarily designed or produced for the purpose of circumventing;

(2) have only a limited commercially significant purpose or use other than to circumvent; or

(3) be marketed by the person who manufactures it, imports it, offers it to the public, provides it or otherwise traffics in it, or by another person acting in concert with that person, for use in circumventing a technological protection measure that effectively controls access to a work protected under Title 17.

This provision is designed to protect copyright owners, and simultaneously allow the development of technology.

This three-part test, established for determining when the manufacture, distribution or other provision of a product or service constitutes a violation, is the core of the anti-circumvention provisions of this legislation. This test (also spelled out in 1201(b)(1)), as explicated by the Judiciary Committee report, stands on its own. While this legislation is aimed primarily at "black boxes" that have virtually no legitimate uses, trafficking in any product or service that meets one or more of the three points in this test could lead to liability. It is not required to prove that the device in question was "expressly intended to facilitate circumvention." At the same time, the manufacturers of legitimate consumer products such as personal computers, VCR's, and the like have nothing to fear from this legislation because those legitimate devices do not meet the three-part test. The *Sony* test of "capab[ility] of substantial non-infringing uses," while still operative in cases claiming contributory infringement of copyright, is not part of this legislation, however. *Sony Corporation of America v. Universal City Studios, Inc.*, 464 U.S. 417 (1984). The relevant test, spelled out in the plain and unchanged language of the bill, is whether or not a product or service "has only limited commercially significant purpose or use other than to circumvent."

* * *

The Committee on the Judiciary, which possesses primary jurisdiction over this legislation, considered the argument that the lack of a definition of "technological measure" leaves manufacturers in the dark as to the range of protective technologies to which their products must respond. The Committee concluded that any such concern is unfounded. No legitimate manufacturer of consumer electronics devices or computer equipment could reasonably claim to be left in doubt about the course of action to be avoided, simply because the phrase "technological measure" is not itself defined in the bill. The only obligation imposed on manufacturers by this legislation is a purely negative one: to refrain from affirmatively designing a product or a component *primarily* for the purpose of circumventing a protective technology that effectively controls unauthorized access to or uses of a copyrighted work.

Any effort to read into this bill what is not there—a statutory definition of "technological measure"—or to define in terms of particular technologies what constitutes an "effective" measure, could inadvertently deprive legal protection to some of the copy or access control technologies that are or will be in widespread use for the protection of both digital and analog formats. Perhaps more importantly, this approach runs a substantial risk of discouraging innovation in the development of protective technologies. For instance, today the standard form of encryption of digital materials involves scrambling its contents so that they are unintelligible unless processed with a key supplied by the copyright owner or its agent. However, in a field that changes and advances as rapidly as encryption research, it would be short-sighted to write this definition into a statute as the exclusive technological means protected by this bill.

* * *

[§ 1201(b)] applies when a person has obtained authorized access to a copy or a phonorecord of a work, but the copyright owner has put in place technological measures that effectively protect his or her rights under Title 17 to control or limit the nature of the use of the copyrighted work.

[§ 1201(b)(1)]. Paralleling subsection (a)(2), above, [§ 1201(b)(1)] seeks to provide meaningful protection and enforcement of copyright owners' use of technological measures to protect their rights under Title 17 by prohibiting the act of making or selling the technological means to overcome these protections and facilitate copyright infringement. Paragraph (1) prohibits manufacturing, importing, offering to the public, providing, or otherwise trafficking in certain technologies, products, services, devices, components, or parts thereof that can be used to circumvent a technological measure that effectively protects a right of a copyright owner under Title 17 in a work or portion thereof. Again, for a technology, product, service, device, component, or part thereof to be prohibited under this subsection, one of three conditions must be met. It must:

(1) be primarily designed or produced for the purpose of circumventing;

(2) have only limited commercially significant purpose or use other than to circumvent; or

(3) be marketed by the person who manufactures it, imports it, offers it to the public, provides it, or otherwise traffics in it, or by another person acting in concert with that person, for use in circumventing a technological protection measure that effectively protects the right of a copyright owner under Title 17 in a work or a portion thereof.

Like subsection (a)(2), this provision is designed to protect copyright owners, and simultaneously allow the development of technology.

[§ 1201(b)(2)] defines certain terms used in subsection (b):

(1) "circumvent protection afforded by a technological measure" is defined as "avoiding, bypassing, removing, deactivating, or otherwise impairing a technological measure."

(2) "effectively protects a right of a copyright owner under Title 17"—a technological measure effectively protects a right of a copyright owner under Title 17 "if the measure, in the ordinary course of its operation, prevents, restricts, or otherwise limits the exercise of a right under Title 17 of a copyright owner."

* * *

[§ 1201(c)] provides that section 1201 shall not have any effect on rights, remedies, limitations, or defenses to copyright infringement, including fair use, under Title 17. Paragraph (2) provides that section 1201 shall not alter the existing doctrines of contributory or vicarious liability for copyright infringement in connection with any technology, product, service, device, component or part thereof. Together, these provisions are intended to ensure that none of the provisions in section 1201 affect the existing legal regime established in the Copyright Act and case law interpreting that statute.

* * *

[§ 1201(f)] is intended to allow legitimate software developers to continue engaging in certain activities for the purpose of achieving interoperability to the extent permitted by law prior to the enactment of this chapter. The objective is to ensure that the effect of current case law interpreting the Copyright Act is not changed by enactment of this legislation for certain acts of identification and analysis done in respect of computer programs. *See Sega Enterprises Ltd.* v. *Accolade, Inc.*, 977 F.2d 1510 (9th Cir.1992). The purpose of this subsection is to avoid hindering competition and innovation in the computer and software industry.

[§ 1201(f)(1)] permits the circumvention of access control technologies for the sole purpose of achieving software interoperability. For example, this subsection permits a software developer to circumvent an access control technology applied to a portion or portions of a program in order to

perform the necessary steps to identify and analyze the information needed to achieve interoperability. * * * [T]he goal of this section is to ensure that current law is not changed, and not to encourage or permit infringement. Thus, each of the acts undertaken must fall within the scope of fair use or otherwise avoid infringing the copyright of the author of the underlying computer program.

[§ 1201(f)(2)] recognizes that to accomplish the acts permitted under paragraph (1) a person may, in some instances, have to make and use certain tools. In most instances these will be generally available tools that programmers use in developing computer programs, such as compilers, trace analyzers and disassemblers, which do not fall within the prohibition of this section. In certain instances, it is possible that a person may have to develop special tools to achieve the permitted purpose of interoperability. Thus, this provision creates an exception to the prohibition on making circumvention tools contained in sections 1201(a)(2) and (b). These tools can be either software or hardware. Again, this provision is limited by a general ban on acting in a way that constitutes infringing activity.

* * *

[§ 1201(f)(4)] defines "interoperability" as the ability of computer programs to exchange information, and for such programs mutually to use the information which has been exchanged. The seamless exchange of information is a key element of creating an interoperable independently created program. This provision applies to computer programs as such, regardless of their medium of fixation and not to works generally, such as music or audiovisual works, which may be fixed and distributed in digital form. Accordingly, since the goal of interoperability is the touchstone of the exceptions contained in paragraphs (1)–(3), nothing in those paragraphs can be read to authorize the circumvention of any technological protection measure that controls access to any work other than a computer program, or the trafficking in products or services for that purpose.

[§ 1201(g)] is intended to facilitate the purpose of this bill, namely, to improve the ability of copyright owners to prevent the theft of their works, including by applying technological measures. * * *

* * * This subsection provides that generally available encryption testing tools meeting certain specifications will not be made illegal by this Act. If each of these tools has a legitimate and substantial commercial purpose—testing security and effectiveness—it is therefore explicitly excluded from the prohibition in section 1201.

In addition to the exemption contained in this subsection, the testing of specific encryption algorithms would not fall within the scope of 1201, since mathematical formulas as such are not protected by copyright. * * *

* * *

[An] example would be a company, in the course of developing a new cryptographic product, sponsoring a crypto-cracking contest with cash prizes. Contestants would not violate section 1201, since the research acts are specifically authorized.

Significantly, section 1201 does not make illegal cryptographic devices that have substantial legitimate purposes other than to circumvent technological protection measures as applied to a work. For example, many popular word processing and other computer programs include a security feature allowing users to password-protect documents (employing a low-grade form of encryption.) It is not uncommon for users of such products to forget or lose their passwords for such documents, making their own protected works unrecoverable. As a result, many independent programmers have created utilities designed to assist in the recovery of passwords or password-protected works. Several of these utilities are distributed over the Internet as freeware or shareware. Because these utilities have a substantial legitimate use, and because they would be used by persons to gain access to their own works, these devices do not violate section 1201.

* * *

Today, network and website management and security tools increasingly contain components that automatically test a system's security and identify common vulnerabilities. These programs are valuable tools for systems administrators and website operators, to use in the course of their regular testing of their systems' security. Again, because these devices are good products put to a good use, they do not fall within the scope of this statute.

In sum, the prohibition on "devices" as written does not encompass many forms of useful encryption products. Subsection (g) is specifically structured to go further, and allow the development and use of certain additional encryption products used for research purposes.

* * *

Conference Report, Digital Millennium Copyright Act

H.R. Conf. Rep. No. 105–796.
(1998).

* * *

Section 1201(j)—Security Testing. * * * It is not the intent of this act to prevent persons utilizing technological measures in respect of computers, computer systems or networks from testing the security value and effectiveness of the technological measures they employ, or from contracting with companies that specialize in such security testing.

Thus, in addition to the exception for good faith encryption research contained in Section 1201(g), the conferees have adopted Section 1201(j) to resolve additional issues related to the effect of the anti-circumvention provision on legitimate information security activities. First, the conferees were concerned that Section 1201(g)'s exclusive focus on encryption-related research does not encompass the entire range of legitimate information security activities. Not every technological means that is used to provide security relies on encryption technology, or does so to the exclusion of other methods. Moreover, an individual who is legitimately testing a security technology may be doing so not to advance the state of encryption research or to develop encryption products, but rather to ascertain the effectiveness of that particular security technology.

The conferees were also concerned that the anti-circumvention provision of Section 1201(a) could be construed to inhibit legitimate forms of security testing. It is not unlawful to test the effectiveness of a security measure before it is implemented to protect the work covered under title 17. Nor is it unlawful for a person who has implemented a security measure to test its effectiveness. In this respect, the scope of permissible security testing under the Act should be the same as permissible testing of a simple door lock: a prospective buyer may test the lock at the store with the store's consent, or may purchase the lock and test it at home in any manner that he or she sees fit—for example, by installing the lock on the front door and seeing if it can be picked. What that person may not do, however, is test the lock once it has been installed on someone else's door, without the consent of the person whose property is protected by the lock.

* * *

Section 1201(j)(4) permits an individual, notwithstanding the prohibition contained in Section 1201(a)(2), to develop, produce, distribute, or employ technological means for the sole purpose of performing acts of good faith security testing under Section 1201(j)(2), provided the technological means do not otherwise violate section 1201(a)(2). It is Congress' intent for this subsection to have application only with respect to good faith security testing. The intent is to ensure that parties engaged in good faith security testing have the tools available to them to complete such acts. The conferees understand that such tools may be coupled with additional tools that serve purposes wholly unrelated to the purposes of this Act. Eligibility for this exemption should not be precluded because these tools are coupled in such a way. The exemption would not be available, however, when such tools are coupled with a product or technology that violates section 1201(a)(2).

Section 1201(k)—Certain Analog Devices and Certain Technological Measures. The conferees included a provision in the final legislation to require that analog video cassette recorders must conform to the two forms of copy control technology that are in wide use in the market today—the automatic gain control copy control technology and the colorstripe copy control technology. Neither are currently required elements of any format of video recorder, and the ability of each technology to work as intended depends on the consistency of design of video recorders or on incorporation of specific response elements in video recorders. Moreover, they do not employ encryption or scrambling of the content being protected.

As a consequence, these analog copy control technologies may be rendered ineffective either by redesign of video recorders or by intervention of "black box" devices or software "hacks". The conferees believe, and specifically intend, that the general circumvention prohibition in Section 1201(b)(2) will prohibit the manufacture and sale of "black box" devices that defeat these technologies. Moreover, the conferees believe and intend that the term "technology" should be read to include the software "hacks" of this type, and that such "hacks" are equally prohibited by the general circumvention provision. Devices have been marketed that claim to "fix" television picture disruptions allegedly caused by these technologies. However, as described in more detail below, there is no justification for the existence of any intervention device to "fix" such problems allegedly caused by these technologies, including "fixes" allegedly related to stabilization or clean up of the picture quality. Such devices should be seen for what they are—circumvention devices prohibited by this legislation.

* * *

NOTES & QUESTIONS

1. *Interoperability.* Many products, to be useful, must be designed so as to work in tandem with some other product—they must be designed to be interoperable. Electrical plugs must fit into outlets; software must interoperate with the operating system on which it runs. In designing a plug to fit into an outlet, it is a simple matter to take apart—to disassemble—an outlet and thereby deduce how the plug must be designed to fit it. Doing so may result in destroying the outlet, but runs no risk of legal liability (as long as the dissassembler owns the outlet). In designing software to work with an operating system, it is necessary to know something about that system. The act of disassembling an operating system, to see how it works, inevitably involves copying copyrighted computer code, which may infringe rights of the copyright owner. In *Sega Enterprises Ltd. v. Accolade, Inc.*, 977 F.2d 1510 (9th Cir.1992), referenced in the House Committee's Section–By–Section Analysis of H.R. 2281, *supra*, the court considered whether the copyright holder can prevent others from engaging in copying of this sort. The manufacturer of a computer game system, Sega, sued a developer of computer game cassettes, Accolade, alleging that Accolade infringed its copyright by disassembling code contained in the game console, in order to learn how to make its game cassettes interoperate with the console. The court held that the copying involved in disassembling code for this purpose is within fair use, and therefore does not infringe Sega's copyright.

Do the anti-circumvention provisions of Section 1201 threaten to interfere with the ability of competitors to create software products that interoperate as they must in order to function? To what extent do the exemptions contained in Section 1201 allay concerns of this sort?

2. *Encryption research and security testing.* What explains the emphasis on encryption research and security testing in the legislative history? What is your prediction about whether the exemptions in Section 1201 will prove to offer sufficient safe harbors for these activities?

Consider the experience of Princeton University computer science professor Edward Felten. In September 2000, the Secure Digital Music Initiative ("SDMI"), an association of technology companies, issued a public challenge, inviting one and all to attempt to crack the digital watermarking technology that SDMI had selected as a standard for protecting digital music. SDMI offered a $10,000 prize for a successful challenger.

Professor Felten and his associates accepted the challenge, and cracked the protection scheme quite readily. Felten wrote a paper about his research on the SDMI watermarks, and planned to present his findings at an academic conference. The Recording Industry Association of American ("RIAA") asked Felten to omit the details of the SDMI watermark technology from his presentation, and sent him a letter stating that revealing his research results "could subject you and you research team to actions under the Digital Millennium Copyright Act."

In the face of this perceived threat, Felten withdrew from the conference. He subsequently filed an action against the RIAA, seeking a declaration that publication of his paper would be lawful. The RIAA and SDMI hastily insisted publicly that they never had any intention of suing Felten, and the court dismissed the case on procedural grounds.

Professor Felten subsequently presented his paper at another conference. The paper, titled "Reading Between the Lines: Lessons from the SDMI Challenge," is available at www.usenix.org/publications/library/proceedings/sec01/craver.pdf. Does presentation or publication of the paper violate Section 1201?

3. *Locked room analogy.* Consider the House Committee Report's declaration that circumventing a technological management system "is the electronic equivalent of breaking into a locked room in order to obtain a copy of a book." Do you agree with this analogy? Consider the differences between "locking up" information and locking up hard goods. To what extent can copyright protection be appropriately conceptualized in terms of traditional physical property? Who would you suppose are the proponents of this analogy?

4. *Section 1201's exemptions.* Copyright law is often described as mediating two conflicting societal interests: the promotion of original works of authorship and public access to those works. Consider the various exemptions to Section 1201's prohibition on circumvention, namely those contained in § 1201(d)–(j). What goals, beyond promoting access to works of authorship, are these exemptions directed at achieving? Does the inclusion of these exemptions ameliorate the extent to which the Section 1201(a)(1)(A) & (a)(2) prohibitions disallow circumvention for purposes that do not infringe copyright—such as fair use of a work, or copying of uncopyrightable facts or ideas?

RealNetworks, Inc. v. Streambox, Inc.

2000 WL 127311 (W.D.Wash.2000).

■ PECHMAN, J.

INTRODUCTION

Plaintiff RealNetworks, Inc. ("RealNetworks") filed this action on December 21, 1999. RealNetworks claims that Defendant Streambox has violated provisions of the Digital Millennium Copyright Act ("DMCA"), *17*

U.S.C. § 1201 et seq., by distributing and marketing products known as the Streambox VCR and the Ripper. * * *

* * *

The Court * * * concludes that a preliminary injunction should be entered to enjoin the manufacture, distribution, and sale of the Streambox VCR * * *.

FINDINGS OF FACT

RealNetworks

1. RealNetworks is a public company based in Seattle, Washington that develops and markets software products designed to enable owners of audio, video, and other multimedia content to send their content to users of personal computers over the Internet.

2. RealNetworks offers products that enable consumers to access audio and video content over the Internet through a process known as "streaming." When an audio or video clip is "streamed" to a consumer, no trace of the clip is left on the consumer's computer, unless the content owner has permitted the consumer to download the file.

3. Streaming is to be contrasted with "downloading," a process by which a complete copy of an audio or video clip is delivered to and stored on a consumer's computer. Once a consumer has downloaded a file, he or she can access the file at will, and can generally redistribute copies of that file to others.

4. In the digital era, the difference between streaming and downloading is of critical importance. A downloaded copy of a digital audio or video file is essentially indistinguishable from the original, and such copies can often be created at the touch of a button. A user who obtains a digital copy may supplant the market for the original by distributing copies of his or her own. To guard against the unauthorized copying and redistribution of their content, many copyright owners do not make their content available for downloading, and instead distribute the content using streaming technology in a manner that does not permit downloading.

5. A large majority of all Internet Web pages that deliver streaming music or video use the RealNetworks' format.

RealNetworks' Products

6. The RealNetworks' products at issue in this action include the "RealProducer," the "RealServer" and the "RealPlayer." These products may be used together to form a system for distributing, retrieving and playing digital audio and video content via the Internet.

7. Owners of audio or video content may choose to use a RealNetworks product to encode their digital content into RealNetworks' format. Once encoded in that format, the media files are called RealAudio or RealVideo (collectively "RealMedia") files.

8. After a content owner has encoded its content into the RealMedia format, it may decide to use a "RealServer" to send that content to consumers. A RealServer is software program that resides on a content owner's computer that holds RealMedia files and "serves" them to consumers through streaming.

9. The RealServer is not the only available means for distributing RealMedia files. RealMedia files may also be made available on an ordinary web server instead of a RealServer. An end-user can download content from an ordinary web server using nothing more than a freely available Internet browser such as Netscape's Navigator or Microsoft's Internet Explorer.

10. To download streaming content distributed by a RealServer, however, a consumer must employ a "RealPlayer." The RealPlayer is a software program that resides on an end-user's computer and must be used to access and play a streaming RealMedia file that is sent from a RealServer.

RealNetworks' Security Measures

11. RealNetworks' products can be used to enable owners of audio and video content to make their content available for consumers to listen to or view, while at the same time securing the content against unauthorized access or copying.

12. The first of these measures, called the "Secret Handshake" by RealNetworks, ensures that files hosted on a RealServer will only be sent to a RealPlayer. The Secret Handshake is an authentication sequence which only RealServers and RealPlayers know. By design, unless this authentication sequence takes place, the RealServer does not stream the content it holds.

13. By ensuring that RealMedia files hosted on a RealServer are streamed only to RealPlayers, RealNetworks can ensure that a second security measure, which RealNetworks calls the "Copy Switch," is given effect. The Copy Switch is a piece of data in all RealMedia files that contains the content owner's preference regarding whether or not the stream may be copied by end-users. RealPlayers are designed to read this Copy Switch and obey the content owner's wishes. If a content owner turns on the Copy Switch in a particular RealMedia file, when that file is streamed, an end-user can use the RealPlayer to save a copy of that RealMedia file to the user's computer. If a content owner does not turn on the Copy Switch in a RealMedia file, the RealPlayer will not allow an end-user to make a copy of that file. The file will simply "evaporate" as the user listens to or watches it stream.

14. Through the use of the Secret Handshake and the Copy Switch, owners of audio and video content can prevent the unauthorized copying of their content if they so choose.

15. Content owners who choose to use the security measures described above are likely to be seeking to prevent their works from being copied without their authorization. RealNetworks has proferred declara-

tions from copyright owners that they rely on RealNetworks security measures to protect their copyrighted works on the Internet. Many of these copyright owners further state that if users could circumvent the security measures and make unauthorized copies of the content, they likely would not put their content up on the Internet for end-users.

16. Many copyright owners make content available on their Web site as a means to attract end-users to the Web site; that is, to drive "traffic" to the Web site. The more traffic a Web site generates, the more it can charge for advertisements placed on the Web site. Without RealNetworks' security measures, a copyright owner could lose the traffic its content generates. An end-user could obtain a copy of the content after only one visit and listen to or view it repeatedly without ever returning to the Web site. That end-user could also redistribute the content to others who would then have no occasion to visit the site in the first instance.

17. Copyright owners also use Real Networks' technology so that end-users can listen to, but not record, music that is on sale, either at a Web site or in retail stores. Other copyright owners enable users to listen to content on a "pay-per-play" basis that requires a payment for each time the end-user wants to hear the content. Without the security measures afforded by RealNetworks, these methods of distribution could not succeed. End-users could make and redistribute digital copies of any content available on the Internet, undermining the market for the copyrighted original.

18. RealNetworks' success as a company is due in significant part to the fact that it has offered copyright owners a successful means of protecting against unauthorized duplication and distribution of their digital works.

* * *

Streambox VCR

23. The Streambox VCR enables end-users to access and download copies of RealMedia files that are streamed over the Internet. While the Streambox VCR also allows users to copy RealMedia files that are made freely available for downloading from ordinary web servers, the only function relevant to this case is the portions of the VCR that allow it to access and copy RealMedia files located on RealServers.

24. In order to gain access to RealMedia content located on a RealServer, the VCR mimics a RealPlayer and circumvents the authentication procedure, or Secret Handshake, that a RealServer requires before it will stream content. In other words, the Streambox VCR is able to convince the RealServer into thinking that the VCR is, in fact, a RealPlayer.

25. Having convinced a RealServer to begin streaming content, the Streambox VCR, like the RealPlayer, acts as a receiver. However, unlike the RealPlayer, the VCR ignores the Copy Switch that tells a RealPlayer whether an end-user is allowed to make a copy of (i.e., download) the RealMedia file as it is being streamed. The VCR thus allows the end-user to download RealMedia files even if the content owner has used the Copy Switch to prohibit end-users from downloading the files.

26. The only reason for the Streambox VCR to circumvent the Secret Handshake and interact with a RealServer is to allow an end-user to access and make copies of content that a copyright holder has placed on a RealServer in order to secure it against unauthorized copying. In this way, the Streambox VCR acts like a "black box" which descrambles cable or satellite broadcasts so that viewers can watch pay programming for free. Like the cable and satellite companies that scramble their video signals to control access to their programs, RealNetworks has employed technological measures to ensure that only users of the RealPlayer can access RealMedia content placed on a RealServer. RealNetworks has gone one step further than the cable and satellite companies, not only controlling access, but also allowing copyright owners to specify whether or not their works can be copied by end-users, even if access is permitted. The Streambox VCR circumvents both the access control and copy protection measures.

* * *

31. The Streambox VCR poses a threat to RealNetworks' relationships with existing and potential customers who wish to secure their content for transmission over the Internet and must decide whether to purchase and use RealNetworks' technology. If the Streambox VCR remains available, these customers may opt not to utilize RealNetworks' technology, believing that it would not protect their content against unauthorized copying.

* * *

CONCLUSIONS OF LAW

* * *

RealNetworks Has Demonstrated a Reasonable Likelihood of Success on its DMCA Claims With Respect to the Streambox VCR

* * *

Parts of the VCR Are Likely to Violate Sections 1201(a)(2) and 1201(b)

7. Under the DMCA, the Secret Handshake that must take place between a RealServer and a RealPlayer before the RealServer will begin streaming content to an end-user appears to constitute a "technological measure" that "effectively controls access" to copyrighted works. *See* 17 U.S.C. § 1201(a)(3)(B) (measure "effectively controls access" if it "requires the application of information or a process or a treatment, with the authority of the copyright holder, to gain access to the work"). To gain access to a work protected by the Secret Handshake, a user must employ a RealPlayer, which will supply the requisite information to the RealServer in a proprietary authentication sequence.

8. In conjunction with the Secret Handshake, the Copy Switch is a "technological measure" that effectively protects the right of a copyright owner to control the unauthorized copying of its work. *See* 17 U.S.C. § 1201(b)(2)(B) (measure "effectively protects" right of copyright holder if

it "prevents, restricts or otherwise limits the exercise of a right of a copyright owner"); 17 U.S.C. § 106(a) (granting copyright holder exclusive right to make copies of its work). To access a RealMedia file distributed by a RealServer, a user must use a RealPlayer. The RealPlayer reads the Copy Switch in the file. If the Copy Switch in the file is turned off, the RealPlayer will not permit the user to record a copy as the file is streamed. Thus, the Copy Switch may restrict others from exercising a copyright holder's exclusive right to copy its work.

9. Under the DMCA, a product or part thereof "circumvents" protections afforded a technological measure by "avoiding, bypassing, removing, deactivating or otherwise impairing" the operation of that technological measure. 17 U.S.C. §§ 1201(b)(2)(A), 1201(a)(2)(A). Under that definition, at least a part of the Streambox VCR circumvents the technological measures RealNetworks affords to copyright owners. Where a RealMedia file is stored on a RealServer, the VCR "bypasses" the Secret Handshake to gain access to the file. The VCR then circumvents the Copy Switch, enabling a user to make a copy of a file that the copyright owner has sought to protect.

10. Given the circumvention capabilities of the Streambox VCR, Streambox violates the DMCA if the product or a part thereof: (i) is primarily designed to serve this function; (ii) has only limited commercially significant purposes beyond the circumvention; or (iii) is marketed as a means of circumvention. 17 U.S.C. §§ 1201(a)(2)(A–C), [1201(b)(1)(A–C)]. These three tests are disjunctive. *Id.* A product that meets only one of the three independent bases for liability is still prohibited. Here, the VCR meets at least the first two.

11. The Streambox VCR meets the first test for liability under the DMCA because at least a part of the Streambox VCR is primarily, if not exclusively, designed to circumvent the access control and copy protection measures that RealNetworks affords to copyright owners. 17 U.S.C. §§ 1201(a)(2)(A), [1201(b)(1)(A)].

12. The second basis for liability is met because a portion of the VCR that circumvents the Secret Handshake so as to avoid the Copy Switch has no significant commercial purpose other than to enable users to access and record protected content. 17 U.S.C. § 1201(a)(2)(B), [1201(b)(1)(B)]. There does not appear to be any other commercial value that this capability affords.

13. Streambox's primary defense to Plaintiff's DMCA claims is that the VCR has legitimate uses. In particular, Streambox claims that the VCR allows consumers to make "fair use" copies of RealMedia files, notwithstanding the access control and copy protection measures that a copyright owner may have placed on that file.

14. The portions of the VCR that circumvent the secret handshake and copy switch permit consumers to obtain and redistribute perfect digital copies of audio and video files that copyright owners have made clear they do not want copied. For this reason, Streambox's VCR is not entitled to the

same "fair use" protections the Supreme Court afforded to video cassette recorders used for "time-shifting" in *Sony Corp. v. Universal City Studios, Inc.,* 464 U.S. 417 (1984).

15. The *Sony* decision turned in large part on a finding that substantial numbers of copyright holders who broadcast their works either had authorized or would not object to having their works time-shifted by private viewers. *See Sony,* 464 U.S. at 443, 446. Here, by contrast, copyright owners have specifically chosen to prevent the copying enabled by the Streambox VCR by putting their content on RealServers and leaving the Copy Switch off.

16. Moreover, the *Sony* decision did not involve interpretation of the DMCA. Under the DMCA, product developers do not have the right to distribute products that circumvent technological measures that prevent consumers from gaining unauthorized access to or making unauthorized copies of works protected by the Copyright Act. Instead, Congress specifically prohibited the distribution of the tools by which such circumvention could be accomplished. The portion of the Streambox VCR that circumvents the technological measures that prevent unauthorized access to and duplication of audio and video content therefore runs afoul of the DMCA.

* * *

18. Streambox also argues that the VCR does not violate the DMCA because the Copy Switch that it avoids does not "effectively protect" against the unauthorized copying of copyrighted works as required by [§ 1201(b)(2)(B)]. Streambox claims this "effective" protection is lacking because an enterprising end-user could potentially use other means to record streaming audio content as it is played by the end-user's computer speakers. This argument fails because the Copy Switch, in the ordinary course of its operation when it is on, restricts and limits the ability of people to make perfect digital copies of a copyrighted work. The Copy Switch therefore constitutes a technological measure that effectively protects a copyright owner's rights under section [1201(b)(2)(B)].

19. In addition, the argument ignores the fact that before the Copy Switch is even implicated, the Streambox VCR has already circumvented the Secret Handshake to gain access to a unauthorized RealMedia file. That alone is sufficient for liability under the DMCA. *See* 17 U.S.C. [§ 1201(a)(1)(A)].

20. Streambox's last defense to liability for the VCR rests on § 1201(c)(3) of the DMCA which it cites for the proposition that the VCR is not required to respond to the Copy Switch. Again, this argument fails to address the VCR's circumvention of the Secret Handshake, which is enough, by itself, to create liability under § 1201(a)(2).

21. Moreover, § 1201(c)(3) states that "[n]othing in this section shall require ... a response to any particular technological measure, so long as ... the product ... does not otherwise fall within the prohibitions of subsections (a)(2) or (b)(1)." 17 U.S.C. § 1201(c)(3). As the remainder of the statute and the leading copyright commentator make clear,

§ 1201(c)(3) does not provide immunity for products that circumvent technological measures in violation of §§ 1201(a)(2) or (b)(1). *See* 17 U.S.C. § 1201(c)(3) (a product need not respond to a particular measure "*so long as such ... product ... does not otherwise fall within the prohibitions of subsections (a)(2) or (b)(1)).*" (emphasis added); 1 *Nimmer on Copyright* (1999 Supp.), § 12A.05[C]. If the statute meant what Streambox suggests, any manufacturer of circumvention tools could avoid DMCA liability simply by claiming it chose not to respond to the particular protection that its tool circumvents.

22. As set forth above, the Streambox VCR falls within the prohibitions of §§ 1201(a)(2) and 1201(b)(1). Accordingly, § 1201(c)(3) affords Streambox no defense.

* * *

Universal City Studios, Inc. v. Reimerdes

111 F.Supp.2d 294 (S.D.N.Y.2000), *aff'd*, 273 F.3d 429 (2d Cir.2001).

■ Lewis A. Kaplan, District Judge.

Plaintiffs, eight major United States motion picture studios, distribute many of their copyrighted motion pictures for home use on digital versatile disks ("DVDs"), which contain copies of the motion pictures in digital form. They protect those motion pictures from copying by using an encryption system called CSS. CSS-protected motion pictures on DVDs may be viewed only on players and computer drives equipped with licensed technology that permits the devices to decrypt and play—but not to copy—the films.

Late last year, computer hackers devised a computer program called DeCSS that circumvents the CSS protection system and allows CSS-protected motion pictures to be copied and played on devices that lack the licensed decryption technology. Defendants quickly posted DeCSS on their Internet web site, thus making it readily available to much of the world. Plaintiffs promptly brought this action under the Digital Millennium Copyright Act (the "DMCA") to enjoin defendants from posting DeCSS and to prevent them from electronically "linking" their site to others that post DeCSS. Defendants responded with what they termed "electronic civil disobedience"—increasing their efforts to link their web site to a large number of others that continue to make DeCSS available.

Defendants contend that their actions do not violate the DMCA * * *.

Defendants argue first that the DMCA should not be construed to reach their conduct, principally because the DMCA, so applied, could prevent those who wish to gain access to technologically protected copyrighted works in order to make fair—that is, non-infringing—use of them from doing so. They argue that those who would make fair use of technologically protected copyrighted works need means, such as DeCSS, of circumventing access control measures not for piracy, but to make lawful use of those works.

Technological access control measures have the capacity to prevent fair uses of copyrighted works as well as foul. Hence, there is a potential tension between the use of such access control measures and fair use. Defendants are not the first to recognize that possibility. As the DMCA made its way through the legislative process, Congress was preoccupied with precisely this issue. Proponents of strong restrictions on circumvention of access control measures argued that they were essential if copyright holders were to make their works available in digital form because digital works otherwise could be pirated too easily. Opponents contended that strong anti-circumvention measures would extend the copyright monopoly inappropriately and prevent many fair uses of copyrighted material.

Congress struck a balance. The compromise it reached, depending upon future technological and commercial developments, may or may not prove ideal. But the solution it enacted is clear. The potential tension to which defendants point does not absolve them of liability under the statute. There is no serious question that defendants' posting of DeCSS violates the DMCA. * * *

I. The Genesis of the Controversy

As this case involves computers and technology with which many are unfamiliar, it is useful to begin by defining some of the vocabulary.

A. The Vocabulary of this Case

* * *

4. Portable Storage Media

Digital files may be stored on several different kinds of storage media, some of which are readily transportable. Perhaps the most familiar of these are so called floppy disks or "floppies," which now are 3 1/2 inch magnetic disks upon which digital files may be recorded. For present purposes, however, we are concerned principally with two more recent developments, CD–ROMs and digital versatile disks, or DVDs.

A CD–ROM is a five-inch wide optical disk capable of storing approximately 650 MB of data. To read the data on a CD–ROM, a computer must have a CD–ROM drive.

DVDs are five-inch wide disks capable of storing more than 4.7 GB of data. In the application relevant here, they are used to hold full-length motion pictures in digital form. They are the latest technology for private home viewing of recorded motion pictures and result in drastically improved audio and visual clarity and quality of motion pictures shown on televisions or computer screens.

5. The Technology Here at Issue

CSS, or Content Scramble System, is an access control and copy prevention system for DVDs developed by the motion picture companies, including plaintiffs. It is an encryption-based system that requires the use of appropriately configured hardware such as a DVD player or a computer

DVD drive to decrypt, unscramble and play back, but not copy, motion pictures on DVDs. The technology necessary to configure DVD players and drives to play CSS-protected DVDs has been licensed to hundreds of manufacturers in the United States and around the world.

DeCSS is a software utility, or computer program, that enables users to break the CSS copy protection system and hence to view DVDs on unlicensed players and make digital copies of DVD movies. The quality of motion pictures decrypted by DeCSS is virtually identical to that of encrypted movies on DVD.

DivX is a compression program available for download over the Internet. It compresses video files in order to minimize required storage space, often to facilitate transfer over The Internet or other networks.

B. Parties

Plaintiffs are eight major motion picture studios. Each is in the business of producing and distributing copyrighted material including motion pictures. Each distributes, either directly or through affiliates, copyrighted motion pictures on DVDs. Plaintiffs produce and distribute a large majority of the motion pictures on DVDs on the market today.

Defendant Eric Corley is viewed as a leader of the computer hacker community and goes by the name Emmanuel Goldstein, after the leader of the underground in George Orwell's classic, *1984.* He and his company, defendant 2600 Enterprises, Inc., together publish a magazine called *2600: The Hacker Quarterly,* which Corley founded in 1984, and which is something of a bible to the hacker community. The name "2600" was derived from the fact that hackers in the 1960's found that the transmission of a 2600 hertz tone over a long distance trunk connection gained access to "operator mode" and allowed the user to explore aspects of the telephone system that were not otherwise accessible. Mr. Corley chose the name because he regarded it as a "mystical thing," commemorating something that he evidently admired. Not surprisingly, *2600: The Hacker Quarterly* has included articles on such topics as how to steal an Internet domain name, access other people's e-mail, intercept cellular phone calls, and break into the computer systems at Costco stores and Federal Express. One issue contains a guide to the federal criminal justice system for readers charged with computer hacking. In addition, defendants operate a web site located at <http://www.2600.com> ("2600.com"), which is managed primarily by Mr. Corley and has been in existence since 1995.[47]

Prior to January 2000, when this action was commenced, defendants posted the source and object code for DeCSS on the 2600.com web site, from which they could be downloaded easily. At that time, 2600.com contained also a list of links to other web sites purporting to post DeCSS.

47. Interestingly, defendants' copyright both their magazine and the material on their web site to prevent others from copying their works.

C. The Development of DVD and CSS

The major motion picture studios typically distribute films in a sequence of so-called windows, each window referring to a separate channel of distribution and thus to a separate source of revenue. The first window generally is theatrical release, distribution, and exhibition. Subsequently, films are distributed to airlines and hotels, then to the home market, then to pay television, cable and, eventually, free television broadcast. The home market is important to plaintiffs, as it represents a significant source of revenue.

Motion pictures first were, and still are, distributed to the home market in the form of video cassette tapes. In the early 1990's, however, the major movie studios began to explore distribution to the home market in digital format, which offered substantially higher audio and visual quality and greater longevity than video cassette tapes. This technology, which in 1995 became what is known today as DVD, brought with it a new problem—increased risk of piracy by virtue of the fact that digital files, unlike the material on video cassettes, can be copied without degradation from generation to generation. In consequence, the movie studios became concerned as the product neared market with the threat of DVD piracy.

Discussions among the studios with the goal of organizing a unified response to the piracy threat began in earnest in late 1995 or early 1996. They eventually came to include representatives of the consumer electronics and computer industries, as well as interested members of the public, and focused on both legislative proposals and technological solutions. In 1996, Matsushita Electric Industrial Co. ("MEI") and Toshiba Corp., presented—and the studios adopted—CSS.

CSS involves encrypting, according to an encryption algorithm, the digital sound and graphics files on a DVD that together constitute a motion picture. A CSS-protected DVD can be decrypted by an appropriate decryption algorithm that employs a series of keys stored on the DVD and the DVD player. In consequence, only players and drives containing the appropriate keys are able to decrypt DVD files and thereby play movies stored on DVDs.

As the motion picture companies did not themselves develop CSS and, in any case, are not in the business of making DVD players and drives, the technology for making compliant devices, i.e., devices with CSS keys, had to be licensed to consumer electronics manufacturers.[60] In order to ensure that the decryption technology did not become generally available and that compliant devices could not be used to copy as well as merely to play CSS-protected movies, the technology is licensed subject to strict security requirements. Moreover, manufacturers may not, consistent with their licenses, make equipment that would supply digital output that could be

60. The licensing function initially was performed by MEI and Toshiba. Subsequently, MEI and Toshiba granted a royalty free license to the DVD Copy Control Association ("DVD CCA"), which now handles the licensing function. The motion picture companies themselves license CSS from the DVD CCA.

used in copying protected DVDs. Licenses to manufacture compliant devices are granted on a royalty-free basis subject only to an administrative fee. At the time of trial, licenses had been issued to numerous hardware and software manufacturers, including two companies that plan to release DVD players for computers running the Linux operating system.

With CSS in place, the studios introduced DVDs on the consumer market in early 1997. All or most of the motion pictures released on DVD were, and continue to be, encrypted with CSS technology. Over 4,000 motion pictures now have been released in DVD format in the United States, and movies are being issued on DVD at the rate of over 40 new titles per month in addition to re-releases of classic films. Currently, more than five million households in the United States own DVD players, and players are projected to be in ten percent of United States homes by the end of 2000.

DVDs have proven not only popular, but lucrative for the studios. Revenue from their sale and rental currently accounts for a substantial percentage of the movie studios' revenue from the home video market. Revenue from the home market, in turn, makes up a large percentage of the studios' total distribution revenue.

D. The Appearance of DeCSS

In late September 1999, Jon Johansen, a Norwegian subject then fifteen years of age, and two individuals he "met" under pseudonyms over the Internet, reverse engineered a licensed DVD player and discovered the CSS encryption algorithm and keys. They used this information to create DeCSS, a program capable of decrypting or "ripping" encrypted DVDs, thereby allowing playback on non-compliant computers as well as the copying of decrypted files to computer hard drives. Mr. Johansen then posted the executable code on his personal Internet web site and informed members of an Internet mailing list that he had done so. Neither Mr. Johansen nor his collaborators obtained a license from the DVD CCA.

Although Mr. Johansen testified at trial that he created DeCSS in order to make a DVD player that would operate on a computer running the Linux operating system, DeCSS is a Windows executable file; that is, it can be executed only on computers running the Windows operating system. Mr. Johansen explained the fact that he created a Windows rather than a Linux program by asserting that Linux, at the time he created DeCSS, did not support the file system used on DVDs. Hence, it was necessary, he said, to decrypt the DVD on a Windows computer in order subsequently to play the decrypted files on a Linux machine. Assuming that to be true, however, the fact remains that Mr. Johansen created DeCSS in the full knowledge that it could be used on computers running Windows rather than Linux. Moreover, he was well aware that the files, once decrypted, could be copied like any other computer files.

In January 1999, Norwegian prosecutors filed charges against Mr. Johansen stemming from the development of DeCSS. The disposition of the Norwegian case does not appear of record.

E. *The Distribution of DeCSS*

In the months following its initial appearance on Mr. Johansen's web site, DeCSS has become widely available on the Internet, where hundreds of sites now purport to offer the software for download. A few other applications said to decrypt CSS-encrypted DVDs also have appeared on the Internet.

In November 1999, defendants' web site began to offer DeCSS for download. It established also a list of links to several web sites that purportedly "mirrored" or offered DeCSS for download. * * *

F. *The Preliminary Injunction and Defendants' Response*

The movie studios, through the Internet investigations division of the Motion Picture Association of America ("MPAA"), became aware of the availability of DeCSS on the Internet in October 1999. The industry responded by sending out a number of cease and desist letters to web site operators who posted the software, some of which removed it from their sites. In January 2000, the studios filed this lawsuit against defendant Eric Corley and two others.[91]

After a hearing at which defendants presented no affidavits or evidentiary material, the Court granted plaintiffs' motion for a preliminary injunction barring defendants from posting DeCSS. At the conclusion of the hearing, plaintiffs sought also to enjoin defendants from linking to other sites that posted DeCSS, but the Court declined to entertain the application at that time in view of plaintiffs' failure to raise the issue in their motion papers.

Following the issuance of the preliminary injunction, defendants removed DeCSS from the 2600.com web site. In what they termed an act of "electronic civil disobedience," however, they continued to support links to other web sites purporting to offer DeCSS for download, a list which had grown to nearly five hundred by July 2000. Indeed, they carried a banner saying "Stop the MPAA" and, in a reference to this lawsuit, proclaimed: "We have to face the possibility that we could be forced into submission. For that reason it's especially important that as many of you as possible, all throughout the world, take a stand and mirror these files." Thus, defendants obviously hoped to frustrate plaintiffs' recourse to the judicial system by making effective relief difficult or impossible.

At least some of the links currently on defendants' mirror list lead the user to copies of DeCSS that, when downloaded and executed, successfully decrypt a motion picture on a CSS-encrypted DVD.

G. *Effects on Plaintiffs*

The effect on plaintiffs of defendants' posting of DeCSS depends upon the ease with which DeCSS decrypts plaintiffs' copyrighted motion pic-

91. The other two defendants entered into consent decrees with plaintiffs. Plaintiffs subsequently amended the complaint to add 2600 Enterprises, Inc. as a defendant.

tures, the quality of the resulting product, and the convenience with which decrypted copies may be transferred or transmitted.

As noted, DeCSS was available for download from defendants' web site and remains available from web sites on defendants' mirror list. Downloading is simple and quick—plaintiffs' expert did it in seconds. The program in fact decrypts at least some DVDs. Although the process is computationally intensive, plaintiffs' expert decrypted a store-bought copy of *Sleepless in Seattle* in 20 to 45 minutes. The copy is stored on the hard drive of the computer. The quality of the decrypted film is virtually identical to that of encrypted films on DVD. The decrypted file can be copied like any other.

The decryption of a CSS-protected DVD is only the beginning of the tale, as the decrypted file is very large—approximately 4.3 to 6 GB or more depending on the length of the film—and thus extremely cumbersome to transfer or to store on portable storage media. One solution to this problem, however, is DivX, a compression utility available on the Internet that is promoted as a means of compressing decrypted motion picture files to manageable size.

DivX is capable of compressing decrypted files constituting a feature length motion picture to approximately 650 MB at a compression ratio that involves little loss of quality. While the compressed sound and graphic files then must be synchronized, a tedious process that took plaintiffs' expert between 10 and 20 hours, the task is entirely feasible. Indeed, having compared a store-bought DVD with portions of a copy compressed and synchronized with DivX (which often are referred to as "DivX'd" motion pictures), the Court finds that the loss of quality, at least in some cases, is imperceptible or so nearly imperceptible as to be of no importance to ordinary consumers.

The fact that DeCSS-decrypted DVDs can be compressed satisfactorily to 650 MB is very important. A writeable CD–ROM can hold 650 MB. Hence, it is entirely feasible to decrypt a DVD with DeCSS, compress and synchronize it with DivX, and then make as many copies as one wishes by burning the resulting files onto writeable CD–ROMs, which are sold blank for about one dollar apiece. Indeed, even if one wished to use a lower compression ratio to improve quality, a film easily could be compressed to about 1.3 GB and burned onto two CD–ROMs. But the creation of pirated copies of copyrighted movies on writeable CD–ROMs, although significant, is not the principal focus of plaintiffs' concern, which is transmission of pirated copies over the Internet or other networks.

Network transmission of decrypted motion pictures raises somewhat more difficult issues because even 650 MB is a very large file that, depending upon the circumstances, may take a good deal of time to transmit. But there is tremendous variation in transmission times. Many home computers today have modems with a rated capacity of 56 kilobits per second. DSL lines, which increasingly are available to home and business users, offer transfer rates of 7 megabits per second. Cable modems also offer increased bandwidth. Student rooms in many universities are equipped with network connections rated at 10 megabits per second. Large institutions such as universities and major companies often have networks with backbones rated at 100 megabits per second. While effective transmission times generally are much lower than rated maximum capacities in consequence of traffic volume and other considerations, there are many environments in which very high transmission rates may be achieved. Hence, transmission times ranging from three to twenty minutes to six hours or more for a feature length film are readily achievable, depending upon the users' precise circumstances.

At trial, defendants repeated, as if it were a mantra, the refrain that plaintiffs, as they stipulated, have no direct evidence of a specific occasion on which any person decrypted a copyrighted motion picture with DeCSS and transmitted it over the Internet. But that is unpersuasive. Plaintiffs' expert expended very little effort to find someone in an IRC chat room who exchanged a compressed, decrypted copy of *The Matrix,* one of plaintiffs' copyrighted motion pictures, for a copy of *Sleepless in Seattle.* While the simultaneous electronic exchange of the two movies took approximately six hours, the computers required little operator attention during the interim. An MPAA investigator downloaded between five and ten DVD-sourced movies over the Internet after December 1999. At least one web site contains a list of 650 motion pictures, said to have been decrypted and compressed with DivX, that purportedly are available for sale, trade or free download. And although the Court does not accept the list, which is hearsay, as proof of the truth of the matters asserted therein, it does note that advertisements for decrypted versions of copyrighted movies first appeared on the Internet in substantial numbers in late 1999, following the posting of DeCSS.

The net of all this is reasonably plain. DeCSS is a free, effective and fast means of decrypting plaintiffs' DVDs and copying them to computer hard drives. DivX, which is available over the Internet for nothing, with the investment of some time and effort, permits compression of the decrypted files to sizes that readily fit on a writeable CD–ROM. Copies of such CD–ROMs can be produced very cheaply and distributed as easily as other pirated intellectual property. While not everyone with Internet access now will find it convenient to send or receive DivX'd copies of pirated motion pictures over the Internet, the availability of high speed network connections in many businesses and institutions, and their growing availability in homes, make Internet and other network traffic in pirated copies a growing threat.

These circumstances have two major implications for plaintiffs. First, the availability of DeCSS on the Internet effectively has compromised plaintiffs' system of copyright protection for DVDs, requiring them either to tolerate increased piracy or to expend resources to develop and implement a replacement system unless the availability of DeCSS is terminated. It is analogous to the publication of a bank vault combination in a national newspaper. Even if no one uses the combination to open the vault, its mere publication has the effect of defeating the bank's security system, forcing the bank to reprogram the lock. Development and implementation of a new

DVD copy protection system, however, is far more difficult and costly than reprogramming a combination lock and may carry with it the added problem of rendering the existing installed base of compliant DVD players obsolete.

Second, the application of DeCSS to copy and distribute motion pictures on DVD, both on CD–ROMs and via the Internet, threatens to reduce the studios' revenue from the sale and rental of DVDs. It threatens also to impede new, potentially lucrative initiatives for the distribution of motion pictures in digital form, such as video-on-demand via the Internet.

In consequence, plaintiffs already have been gravely injured. As the pressure for and competition to supply more and more users with faster and faster network connections grows, the injury will multiply.

II. The Digital Millennium Copyright Act

A. Background and Structure of the Statute

* * *

The DMCA contains two principal anticircumvention provisions. The first, Section 1201(a)(1), governs "[t]he act of circumventing a technological protection measure put in place by a copyright owner to control access to a copyrighted work," an act described by Congress as "the electronic equivalent of breaking into a locked room in order to obtain a copy of a book."[131] The second, Section 1201(a)(2), which is the focus of this case, "supplements the prohibition against the act of circumvention in paragraph (a)(1) with prohibitions on creating and making available certain technologies . . . developed or advertised to defeat technological protections against unauthorized access to a work."[132] As defendants are accused here only of posting and linking to other sites posting DeCSS, and not of using it themselves to bypass plaintiffs' access controls, it is principally the second of the anticircumvention provisions that is at issue in this case.

B. Posting of DeCSS

1. Violation of Anti–Trafficking Provision

Section 1201(a)(2) of the Copyright Act, part of the DMCA, provides that:

No person shall . . . offer to the public, provide or otherwise traffic in any technology . . . that—

(A) is primarily designed or produced for the purpose of circumventing a technological measure that effectively controls access to a work protected under [the Copyright Act];

(B) has only limited commercially significant purpose or use other than to circumvent a technological measure that effectively controls access to a work protected under [the Copyright Act]; or

131. H.R.REP. NO. 105–551(I), 105th Cong., 2d Sess. ("JUDICIARY COMM. REP."), at 17 (1998).

132. *Id.* at 18.

(C) is marketed by that person or another acting in concert with that person with that person's knowledge for use in circumventing a technological measure that effectively controls access to a work protected under [the Copyright Act].

17 U.S.C. § 1201(a)(2).

In this case, defendants concededly offered and provided and, absent a court order, would continue to offer and provide DeCSS to the public by making it available for download on the 2600.com web site. DeCSS, a computer program, unquestionably is "technology" within the meaning of the statute. "[C]ircumvent a technological measure" is defined to mean descrambling a scrambled work, decrypting an encrypted work, or "otherwise to avoid, bypass, remove, deactivate, or impair a technological measure, without the authority of the copyright owner," so DeCSS clearly is a means of circumventing a technological access control measure. In consequence, if CSS otherwise falls within paragraphs (A), (B) or (C) of Section 1201(a)(2), and if none of the statutory exceptions applies to their actions, defendants have violated and, unless enjoined, will continue to violate the DMCA by posting DeCSS.

a. Section 1201(a)(2)(A)

(1) CSS Effectively Controls Access to Copyrighted Works

During pretrial proceedings and at trial, defendants attacked plaintiffs' Section 1201(a)(2)(A) claim, arguing that CSS, which is based on a 40–bit encryption key, is a weak cipher that does not "effectively control" access to plaintiffs' copyrighted works. They reasoned from this premise that CSS is not protected under this branch of the statute at all. Their post-trial memorandum appears to have abandoned this argument. In any case, however, the contention is indefensible as a matter of law.

First, the statute expressly provides that "a technological measure 'effectively controls access to a work' if the measure, in the ordinary course of its operation, requires the application of information or a process or a treatment, with the authority of the copyright owner, to gain access to a work." One cannot gain access to a CSS-protected work on a DVD without application of the three keys that are required by the software. One cannot lawfully gain access to the keys except by entering into a license with the DVD CCA under authority granted by the copyright owners or by purchasing a DVD player or drive containing the keys pursuant to such a license. In consequence, under the express terms of the statute, CSS "effectively controls access" to copyrighted DVD movies. It does so, within the meaning of the statute, whether or not it is a strong means of protection.

This view is confirmed by the legislative history, which deals with precisely this point. The House Judiciary Committee section-by-section analysis of the House bill, which in this respect was enacted into law, makes clear that a technological measure "effectively controls access" to a copyrighted work if its *function* is to control access:

> The bill does define the *functions* of the technological measures that are covered—that is, what it means for a technological measure to "effectively control access to a work" ... and to "effectively protect a right of a copyright owner under this title".... The practical, common-sense approach taken by H.R.2281 is that if, in the ordinary course of its operation, a technology actually works in the defined ways to control access to a work ... then the "effectiveness" test is met, and the prohibitions of the statute are applicable. This test, which focuses on the function performed by the technology, provides a sufficient basis for clear interpretation.[140]

Further, the House Commerce Committee made clear that measures based on encryption or scrambling "effectively control" access to copyrighted works,[141] although it is well known that what may be encrypted or scrambled often may be decrypted or unscrambled. As CSS, in the ordinary course of its operation—that is, when DeCSS or some other decryption program is not employed—"actually works" to prevent access to the protected work, it "effectively controls access" within the contemplation of the statute.

Finally, the interpretation of the phrase "effectively controls access" offered by defendants at trial—viz., that the use of the word "effectively" means that the statute protects only successful or efficacious technological means of controlling access—would gut the statute if it were adopted. If a technological means of access control is circumvented, it is, in common parlance, ineffective. Yet defendants' construction, if adopted, would limit the application of the statute to access control measures that thwart circumvention, but withhold protection for those measures that can be circumvented. In other words, defendants would have the Court construe the statute to offer protection where none is needed but to withhold protection precisely where protection is essential. The Court declines to do so. Accordingly, the Court holds that CSS effectively controls access to plaintiffs' copyrighted works.

(2) DeCSS Was Designed Primarily to Circumvent CSS

As CSS effectively controls access to plaintiffs' copyrighted works, the only remaining question under Section 1201(a)(2)(A) is whether DeCSS was designed primarily to circumvent CSS. The answer is perfectly obvious. By the admission of both Jon Johansen, the programmer who principally wrote DeCSS, and defendant Corley, DeCSS was created solely for the purpose of decrypting CSS—that is all it does. Hence, absent satisfaction of a statutory exception, defendants clearly violated Section 1201(a)(2)(A) by posting DeCSS to their web site.

140. HOUSE COMM. ON JUDICIARY, SECTION-BY-SECTION ANALYSIS OF H.R.2281 AS PASSED BY THE UNITED STATES HOUSE OF REPRESENTATIVES ON AUGUST 4, 1998 ("SECTION-BY-SECTION ANALYSIS"), at 10 (Comm.Print 1998) (emphasis in original).

141. H.R.REP. NO. 105-551(II), 105th Cong., 2d Sess. ("COMMERCE COMM. REP."), at 39 (1998).

b. Section 1201(a)(2)(B)

As the only purpose or use of DeCSS is to circumvent CSS, the foregoing is sufficient to establish a *prima facie* violation of Section 1201(a)(2)(B) as well.

c. The Linux Argument

Perhaps the centerpiece of defendants' statutory position is the contention that DeCSS was not created for the purpose of pirating copyrighted motion pictures. Rather, they argue, it was written to further the development of a DVD player that would run under the Linux operating system, as there allegedly were no Linux compatible players on the market at the time. * * *

* * *

[T]he question whether the development of a Linux DVD player motivated those who wrote DeCSS is immaterial to the question whether the defendants now before the Court violated the anti-trafficking provision of the DMCA. The inescapable facts are that (1) CSS is a technological means that effectively controls access to plaintiffs' copyrighted works, (2) the one and only function of DeCSS is to circumvent CSS, and (3) defendants offered and provided DeCSS by posting it on their web site. Whether defendants did so in order to infringe, or to permit or encourage others to infringe, copyrighted works in violation of other provisions of the Copyright Act simply does not matter for purposes of Section 1201(a)(2). The offering or provision of the program is the prohibited conduct—and it is prohibited irrespective of why the program was written, except to whatever extent motive may be germane to determining whether their conduct falls within one of the statutory exceptions.

2. Statutory Exceptions

Earlier in the litigation, defendants contended that their activities came within several exceptions contained in the DMCA and the Copyright Act and constitute fair use under the Copyright Act. Their post-trial memorandum appears to confine their argument to the reverse engineering exception. In any case, all of their assertions are entirely without merit.

a. Reverse engineering

Defendants claim to fall under Section 1201(f) of the statute, which provides in substance that one may circumvent, or develop and employ technological means to circumvent, access control measures in order to achieve interoperability with another computer program provided that doing so does not infringe another's copyright and, in addition, that one may make information acquired through such efforts "available to others, if the person [in question] ... provides such information solely for the purpose of enabling interoperability of an independently created computer program with other programs, and to the extent that doing so does not constitute infringement...." They contend that DeCSS is necessary to achieve interoperability between computers running the Linux operating system and DVDs and that this exception therefore is satisfied. This contention fails.

First, Section 1201(f)(3) permits information acquired through reverse engineering to be made available to others only by the person who acquired the information. But these defendants did not do any reverse engineering. They simply took DeCSS off someone else's web site and posted it on their own.

Defendants would be in no stronger position even if they had authored DeCSS. The right to make the information available extends only to dissemination "solely for the purpose" of achieving interoperability as defined in the statute. It does not apply to public dissemination of means of circumvention, as the legislative history confirms. These defendants, however, did not post DeCSS "solely" to achieve interoperability with Linux or anything else.

Finally, it is important to recognize that even the creators of DeCSS cannot credibly maintain that the "sole" purpose of DeCSS was to create a Linux DVD player. DeCSS concededly was developed on and runs under Windows—a far more widely used operating system. The developers of DeCSS therefore knew that DeCSS could be used to decrypt and play DVD movies on Windows as well as Linux machines. They knew also that the decrypted files could be copied like any other unprotected computer file. Moreover, the Court does not credit Mr. Johansen's testimony that he created DeCSS solely for the purpose of building a Linux player. Mr. Johansen is a very talented young man and a member of a well known hacker group who viewed "cracking" CSS as an end it itself and a means of demonstrating his talent and who fully expected that the use of DeCSS would not be confined to Linux machines. Hence, the Court finds that Mr. Johansen and the others who actually did develop DeCSS did not do so solely for the purpose of making a Linux DVD player if, indeed, developing a Linux-based DVD player was among their purposes.

Accordingly, the reverse engineering exception to the DMCA has no application here.

* * *

d. Fair use

Finally, defendants rely on the doctrine of fair use. Stated in its most general terms, the doctrine, now codified in Section 107 of the Copyright Act, limits the exclusive rights of a copyright holder by permitting others to make limited use of portions of the copyrighted work, for appropriate purposes, free of liability for copyright infringement. For example, it is permissible for one other than the copyright owner to reprint or quote a suitable part of a copyrighted book or article in certain circumstances. The doctrine traditionally has facilitated literary and artistic criticism, teaching and scholarship, and other socially useful forms of expression. It has been viewed by courts as a safety valve that accommodates the exclusive rights conferred by copyright with the freedom of expression guaranteed by the First Amendment.

The use of technological means of controlling access to a copyrighted work may affect the ability to make fair uses of the work. Focusing specifically on the facts of this case, the application of CSS to encrypt a copyrighted motion picture requires the use of a compliant DVD player to view or listen to the movie. Perhaps more significantly, it prevents exact copying of either the video or the audio portion of all or any part of the film. This latter point means that certain uses that might qualify as "fair" for purposes of copyright infringement—for example, the preparation by a film studies professor of a single CD–ROM or tape containing two scenes from different movies in order to illustrate a point in a lecture on cinematography, as opposed to showing relevant parts of two different DVDs—would be difficult or impossible absent circumvention of the CSS encryption. Defendants therefore argue that the DMCA cannot properly be construed to make it difficult or impossible to make any fair use of plaintiffs' copyrighted works and that the statute therefore does not reach their activities, which are simply a means to enable users of DeCSS to make such fair uses.

Defendants have focused on a significant point. Access control measures such as CSS do involve some risk of preventing lawful as well as unlawful uses of copyrighted material. Congress, however, clearly faced up to and dealt with this question in enacting the DMCA.

The Court begins its statutory analysis, as it must, with the language of the statute. Section 107 of the Copyright Act provides in critical part that certain uses of copyrighted works that otherwise would be wrongful are "not . . . infringement[s] of copyright." Defendants, however, are not here sued for copyright infringement. They are sued for offering and providing technology designed to circumvent technological measures that control access to copyrighted works and otherwise violating Section 1201(a)(2) of the Act. If Congress had meant the fair use defense to apply to such actions, it would have said so. Indeed, as the legislative history demonstrates, the decision not to make fair use a defense to a claim under Section 1201(a) was quite deliberate.

Congress was well aware during the consideration of the DMCA of the traditional role of the fair use defense in accommodating the exclusive rights of copyright owners with the legitimate interests of noninfringing users of portions of copyrighted works. It recognized the contention, voiced by a range of constituencies concerned with the legislation, that technological controls on access to copyrighted works might erode fair use by preventing access even for uses that would be deemed "fair" if only access might be gained.[162] And it struck a balance among the competing interests.

The first element of the balance was the careful limitation of Section 1201(a)(1)'s prohibition of the act of circumvention to the act itself so as not to "apply to subsequent actions of a person once he or she has obtained

162. *See, e.g.,* COMMERCE COMM. REP. 25–26.

authorized access to a copy of a [copyrighted] work. . . ."[163] By doing so, it left "the traditional defenses to copyright infringement, including fair use, . . . fully applicable" provided "the access is authorized."[164]

Second, Congress delayed the effective date of Section 1201(a)(1)'s prohibition of the act of circumvention for two years pending further investigation about how best to reconcile Section 1201(a)(1) with fair use concerns. Following that investigation, which is being carried out in the form of a rule-making by the Register of Copyright, the prohibition will not apply to users of particular classes of copyrighted works who demonstrate that their ability to make noninfringing uses of those classes of works would be affected adversely by Section 1201(a)(1).

Third, it created a series of exceptions to aspects of Section 1201(a) for certain uses that Congress thought "fair," including reverse engineering, security testing, good faith encryption research, and certain uses by non-profit libraries, archives and educational institutions.

Defendants claim also that the possibility that DeCSS might be used for the purpose of gaining access to copyrighted works in order to make fair use of those works saves them under *Sony Corp. v. Universal City Studios, Inc.*, 464 U.S. 417 (1984). But they are mistaken. *Sony* does not apply to the activities with which defendants here are charged. Even if it did, it would not govern here. *Sony* involved a construction of the Copyright Act that has been overruled by the later enactment of the DMCA to the extent of any inconsistency between *Sony* and the new statute.

Sony was a suit for contributory infringement brought against manufacturers of video cassette recorders on the theory that the manufacturers were contributing to infringing home taping of copyrighted television broadcasts. The Supreme Court held that the manufacturers were not liable in view of the substantial numbers of copyright holders who either had authorized or did not object to such taping by viewers. But *Sony* has no application here.

When *Sony* was decided, the only question was whether the manufacturers could be held liable for infringement by those who purchased equipment from them in circumstances in which there were many noninfringing uses for their equipment. But that is not the question now before this Court. The question here is whether the possibility of noninfringing fair use by someone who gains access to a protected copyrighted work through a circumvention technology distributed by the defendants saves the defendants from liability under Section 1201. But nothing in Section 1201 so suggests. By prohibiting the provision of circumvention technology, the DMCA fundamentally altered the landscape. A given device or piece of technology might have "a substantial noninfringing use, and hence be immune from attack under *Sony*'s construction of the Copyright Act—but nonetheless still be subject to suppression under Section 1201."[169] Indeed,

163. JUDICIARY COMM.REP. 18.

164. *Id.*

169. *RealNetworks, Inc.*, 2000 WL 127311, at *8 * * *.

Congress explicitly noted that Section 1201 does not incorporate *Sony*.[170]

The policy concerns raised by defendants were considered by Congress. Having considered them, Congress crafted a statute that, so far as the applicability of the fair use defense to Section 1201(a) claims is concerned, is crystal clear. In such circumstances, courts may not undo what Congress so plainly has done by "construing" the words of a statute to accomplish a result that Congress rejected. The fact that Congress elected to leave technologically unsophisticated persons who wish to make fair use of encrypted copyrighted works without the technical means of doing so is a matter for Congress unless Congress' decision contravenes the Constitution * * *. Defendants' statutory fair use argument therefore is entirely without merit.

C. Linking to Sites Offering DeCSS

Plaintiffs seek also to enjoin defendants from "linking" their 2600.com web site to other sites that make DeCSS available to users. Their request obviously stems in no small part from what defendants themselves have termed their act of "electronic civil disobedience"—their attempt to defeat the purpose of the preliminary injunction by (a) offering the practical equivalent of making DeCSS available on their own web site by electronically linking users to other sites still offering DeCSS, and (b) encouraging other sites that had not been enjoined to offer the program. The dispositive question is whether linking to another web site containing DeCSS constitutes "offer[ing DeCSS] to the public" or "provid[ing] or otherwise traffic[king]" in it within the meaning of the DMCA.[171] Answering this question requires careful consideration of the nature and types of linking.

Most web pages are written in computer languages, chiefly HTML, which allow the programmer to prescribe the appearance of the web page on the computer screen and, in addition, to instruct the computer to perform an operation if the cursor is placed over a particular point on the screen and the mouse then clicked. Programming a particular point on a screen to transfer the user to another web page when the point, referred to as a hyperlink, is clicked is called linking. Web pages can be designed to link to other web pages on the same site or to web pages maintained by different sites.

[T]he links that defendants established on their web site are of several types. Some transfer the user to a web page on an outside site that contains a good deal of information of various types, does not itself contain a link to DeCSS, but that links, either directly or via a series of other pages, to another page on the same site that posts the software. It then is up to the user to follow the link or series of links on the linked-to web site in order to arrive at the page with the DeCSS link and commence the download of the software. Others take the user to a page on an outside web site on which

170. SECTION-BY-SECTION ANALYSIS 9 ("The *Sony* test of 'capab[ility] of substantial non-infringing uses,' while still operative in cases claiming contributory infringement of copyright, is not part of this legislation....").

171. 17 U.S.C. § 1201(a)(2).

there appears a direct link to the DeCSS software and which may or may not contain text or links other than the DeCSS link. The user has only to click on the DeCSS link to commence the download. Still others may directly transfer the user to a file on the linked-to web site such that the download of DeCSS to the user's computer automatically commences without further user intervention.

The statute makes it unlawful to offer, provide or otherwise traffic in described technology. To "traffic" in something is to engage in dealings in it, conduct that necessarily involves awareness of the nature of the subject of the trafficking. To "provide" something, in the sense used in the statute, is to make it available or furnish it. To "offer" is to present or hold it out for consideration. The phrase "or otherwise traffic in" modifies and gives meaning to the words "offer" and "provide." In consequence, the anti-trafficking provision of the DMCA is implicated where one presents, holds out or makes a circumvention technology or device available, knowing its nature, for the purpose of allowing others to acquire it.

To the extent that defendants have linked to sites that automatically commence the process of downloading DeCSS upon a user being transferred by defendants' hyperlinks, there can be no serious question. Defendants are engaged in the functional equivalent of transferring the DeCSS code to the user themselves.

Substantially the same is true of defendants' hyperlinks to web pages that display nothing more than the DeCSS code or present the user only with the choice of commencing a download of DeCSS and no other content. The only distinction is that the entity extending to the user the option of downloading the program is the transferee site rather than defendants, a distinction without a difference.

Potentially more troublesome might be links to pages that offer a good deal of content other than DeCSS but that offer a hyperlink for downloading, or transferring to a page for downloading, DeCSS. If one assumed, for the purposes of argument, that the *Los Angeles Times* web site somewhere contained the DeCSS code, it would be wrong to say that anyone who linked to the *Los Angeles Times* web site, regardless of purpose or the manner in which the link was described, thereby offered, provided or otherwise trafficked in DeCSS merely because DeCSS happened to be available on a site to which one linked. But that is not this case. Defendants urged others to post DeCSS in an effort to disseminate DeCSS and to inform defendants that they were doing so. Defendants then linked their site to those "mirror" sites, after first checking to ensure that the mirror sites in fact were posting DeCSS or something that looked like it, and proclaimed on their own site that DeCSS could be had by clicking on the hyperlinks on defendants' site. By doing so, they offered, provided or otherwise trafficked in DeCSS, and they continue to do so to this day.

* * *

[The court's discussion of defendants' First Amendment argument is omitted.]

VI. Conclusion

In the final analysis, the dispute between these parties is simply put if not necessarily simply resolved.

Plaintiffs have invested huge sums over the years in producing motion pictures in reliance upon a legal framework that, through the law of copyright, has ensured that they will have the exclusive right to copy and distribute those motion pictures for economic gain. They contend that the advent of new technology should not alter this long established structure.

Defendants, on the other hand, are adherents of a movement that believes that information should be available without charge to anyone clever enough to break into the computer systems or data storage media in which it is located. Less radically, they have raised a legitimate concern about the possible impact on traditional fair use of access control measures in the digital era.

Each side is entitled to its views. In our society, however, clashes of competing interests like this are resolved by Congress. For now, at least, Congress has resolved this clash in the DMCA and in plaintiffs' favor. * * * Accordingly, plaintiffs are entitled to appropriate injunctive and declaratory relief.

In the following decision, the Second Circuit affirmed the decision of the district court that is excerpted above.

Universal City Studios, Inc. v. Corley

273 F.3d 429 (2d Cir.2001).

■ JON O. NEWMAN, CIRCUIT JUDGE.

When the Framers of the First Amendment prohibited Congress from making any law "abridging the freedom of speech," they were not thinking about computers, computer programs, or the Internet. But neither were they thinking about radio, television, or movies. Just as the inventions at the beginning and middle of the 20th century presented new First Amendment issues, so does the cyber revolution at the end of that century. This appeal raises significant First Amendment issues concerning one aspect of computer technology—encryption to protect materials in digital form from unauthorized access. The appeal challenges the constitutionality of the Digital Millennium Copyright Act ("DMCA"), 17 U.S.C. § 1201 *et seq.* (Supp. V 1999) and the validity of an injunction entered to enforce the DMCA.

Defendant–Appellant Eric C. Corley and his company, 2600 Enterprises, Inc., (collectively "Corley," "the Defendants," or "the Appellants") appeal from the amended final judgment of the United States District Court for the Southern District of New York (Lewis A. Kaplan, District

Judge), entered August 23, 2000, enjoining them from various actions concerning a decryption program known as "DeCSS." *Universal City Studios, Inc. v. Reimerdes,* 111 F.Supp.2d 346 (S.D.N.Y.2000) ("*Universal II*"). The injunction primarily bars the Appellants from posting DeCSS on their web site and from knowingly linking their web site to any other web site on which DeCSS is posted. *Id.* at 346–47. We affirm.

* * *

Discussion

* * *

II. Constitutional Challenge Based on the Copyright Clause

In a footnote to their brief, the Appellants appear to contend that the DMCA, as construed by the District Court, exceeds the constitutional authority of Congress to grant authors copyrights for a "limited time," *U.S. Const. art. I, § 8, cl. 8,* because it "empower[s] copyright owners to effectively secure perpetual protection by mixing public domain works with copyrighted materials, then locking both up with technological protection measures." Brief for Appellants at 42 n.30. This argument is elaborated in the *amici curiae* brief filed by Prof. Julie E. Cohen on behalf of herself and 45 other intellectual property law professors. *See also* David Nimmer, *A Riff on Fair Use in the Digital Millennium Copyright Act,* 148 U. Pa. L. Rev. 673, 712 (2000). For two reasons, the argument provides no basis for disturbing the judgment of the District Court.

First, we have repeatedly ruled that arguments presented to us only in a footnote are not entitled to appellate consideration. * * * Although an *amicus* brief can be helpful in elaborating issues properly presented by the parties, it is normally not a method for injecting new issues into an appeal, at least in cases where the parties are competently represented by counsel. * * * Second, to whatever extent the argument might have merit at some future time in a case with a properly developed record, the argument is entirely premature and speculative at this time on this record. There is not even a claim, much less evidence, that any Plaintiff has sought to prevent copying of public domain works, or that the injunction prevents the Defendants from copying such works. As Judge Kaplan noted, the possibility that encryption would preclude access to public domain works "does not yet appear to be a problem, although it may emerge as one in the future." *Universal I,* 111 F.Supp.2d at 338 n. 245.

III. Constitutional Challenges Based on the First Amendment

A. Applicable Principles

* * *

[The court finds that computer code can merit First Amendment protection.]

3. The Scope of First Amendment Protection for Computer Code

Having concluded that computer code conveying information is "speech" within the meaning of the First Amendment, we next consider, to a limited extent, the scope of the protection that code enjoys. As the District Court recognized, *Universal I,* 111 F.Supp.2d at 327, the scope of protection for speech generally depends on whether the restriction is imposed because of the content of the speech. Content-based restrictions are permissible only if they serve compelling state interests and do so by the least restrictive means available. *See Sable Communications of California, Inc. v. FCC,* 492 U.S. 115, 126 (1989). A content-neutral restriction is permissible if it serves a substantial governmental interest, the interest is unrelated to the suppression of free expression, and the regulation is narrowly tailored, which "in this context requires ... that the means chosen do not 'burden substantially more speech than is necessary to further the government's legitimate interests.'" *Turner Broadcasting System, Inc. v. FCC,* 512 U.S. 622, 662 (1994) (*quoting Ward v. Rock Against Racism,* 491 U.S. 781, 799 (1989)).

"[G]overnment regulation of expressive activity is 'content neutral' if it is justified without reference to the content of regulated speech." *Hill v. Colorado,* 530 U.S. 703, 720, (2000). "The government's purpose is the controlling consideration. A regulation that serves purposes unrelated to the content of expression is deemed neutral, even if it has an incidental effect on some speakers or messages but not others." *Ward,* 491 U.S. at 791. * * *

* * *

The Appellants vigorously reject the idea that computer code can be regulated according to any different standard than that applicable to pure speech, *i.e.,* speech that lacks a nonspeech component. Although recognizing that code is a series of instructions to a computer, they argue that code is no different, for First Amendment purposes, than blueprints that instruct an engineer or recipes that instruct a cook. *See* Supplemental Brief for Appellants at 2, 3. We disagree. Unlike a blueprint or a recipe, which cannot yield any functional result without human comprehension of its content, human decision-making, and human action, computer code can instantly cause a computer to accomplish tasks and instantly render the results of those tasks available throughout the world via the Internet. The only human action required to achieve these results can be as limited and instantaneous as a single click of a mouse. These realities of what code is and what its normal functions are require a First Amendment analysis that treats code as combining nonspeech and speech elements, *i.e.,* functional and expressive elements. *See Red Lion Broadcasting Co. v. FCC,* 395 U.S. 367, 386 (1969) ("[D]ifferences in the characteristics of new media justify differences in the First Amendment standards applied to them." (footnote omitted)).

* * *

The functionality of computer code properly affects the scope of its First Amendment protection.

4. The Scope of First Amendment Protection for Decryption Code

In considering the scope of First Amendment protection for a decryption program like DeCSS, we must recognize that the essential purpose of encryption code is to prevent unauthorized access. Owners of all property rights are entitled to prohibit access to their property by unauthorized persons. Homeowners can install locks on the doors of their houses. Custodians of valuables can place them in safes. Stores can attach to products security devices that will activate alarms if the products are taken away without purchase. These and similar security devices can be circumvented. Burglars can use skeleton keys to open door locks. Thieves can obtain the combinations to safes. Product security devices can be neutralized.

Our case concerns a security device, CSS computer code, that prevents access by unauthorized persons to DVD movies. The CSS code is embedded in the DVD movie. Access to the movie cannot be obtained unless a person has a device, a licensed DVD player, equipped with computer code capable of decrypting the CSS encryption code. In its basic function, CSS is like a lock on a homeowner's door, a combination of a safe, or a security device attached to a store's products.

DeCSS is computer code that can decrypt CSS. In its basic function, it is like a skeleton key that can open a locked door, a combination that can open a safe, or a device that can neutralize the security device attached to a store's products. DeCSS enables anyone to gain access to a DVD movie without using a DVD player.

* * *

At first glance, one might think that Congress has as much authority to regulate the distribution of computer code to decrypt DVD movies as it has to regulate distribution of skeleton keys, combinations to safes, or devices to neutralize store product security devices. However, despite the evident legitimacy of protection against unauthorized access to DVD movies, just like any other property, regulation of decryption code like DeCSS is challenged in this case because DeCSS differs from a skeleton key in one important respect: it not only is capable of performing the function of unlocking the encrypted DVD movie, it also is a form of communication, albeit written in a language not understood by the general public. As a communication, the DeCSS code has a claim to being "speech," and as "speech," it has a claim to being protected by the First Amendment. But just as the realities of what any computer code can accomplish must inform the scope of its constitutional protection, so the capacity of a decryption program like DeCSS to accomplish unauthorized—indeed, unlawful—access to materials in which the Plaintiffs have intellectual property rights must inform and limit the scope of its First Amendment protection. * * *

With all of the foregoing considerations in mind, we next consider the Appellants' First Amendment challenge to the DMCA as applied in the specific prohibitions that have been imposed by the District Court's injunction.

B. *First Amendment Challenge*

The District Court's injunction applies the DMCA to the Defendants by imposing two types of prohibition, both grounded on the anti-trafficking provisions of the DMCA. The first prohibits posting DeCSS or any other technology for circumventing CSS on any Internet web site. *Universal II,* 111 F.Supp.2d at 346–47, ¶ 1(a), (b). The second prohibits knowingly linking any Internet web site to any other web site containing DeCSS. *Id.* at 347, ¶ 1(c). The validity of the posting and linking prohibitions must be considered separately.

1. Posting

The initial issue is whether the posting prohibition is content-neutral, since, as we have explained, this classification determines the applicable constitutional standard. The Appellants contend that the anti-trafficking provisions of the DMCA and their application by means of the posting prohibition of the injunction are content-based. They argue that the provisions "specifically target ... scientific expression based on the particular topic addressed by that expression—namely, techniques for circumventing CSS." Supplemental Brief for Appellants at 1. We disagree. The Appellants' argument fails to recognize that the target of the posting provisions of the injunction—DeCSS—has both a nonspeech and a speech component, and that the DMCA, as applied to the Appellants, and the posting prohibition of the injunction target only the nonspeech component. Neither the DMCA nor the posting prohibition is concerned with whatever capacity DeCSS might have for conveying information to a human being, and that capacity, as previously explained, is what arguably creates a speech component of the decryption code. The DMCA and the posting prohibition are applied to DeCSS solely because of its capacity to instruct a computer to decrypt CSS. That functional capability is not speech within the meaning of the First Amendment. The Government seeks to "justif[y]," *Hill,* 530 U.S. at 720, both the application of the DMCA and the posting prohibition to the Appellants solely on the basis of the functional capability of DeCSS to instruct a computer to decrypt CSS, *i.e.,* "without reference to the content of the regulated speech," *id.* This type of regulation is therefore content-neutral, just as would be a restriction on trafficking in skeleton keys identified because of their capacity to unlock jail cells, even though some of the keys happened to bear a slogan or other legend that qualified as a speech component.

As a content-neutral regulation with an incidental effect on a speech component, the regulation must serve a substantial governmental interest, the interest must be unrelated to the suppression of free expression, and the incidental restriction on speech must not burden substantially more speech than is necessary to further that interest. *Turner Broadcasting,* 512

U.S. at 662. The Government's interest in preventing unauthorized access to encrypted copyrighted material is unquestionably substantial, and the regulation of DeCSS by the posting prohibition plainly serves that interest. Moreover, that interest is unrelated to the suppression of free expression. The injunction regulates the posting of DeCSS, regardless of whether DeCSS code contains any information comprehensible by human beings that would qualify as speech. Whether the incidental regulation on speech burdens substantially more speech than is necessary to further the interest in preventing unauthorized access to copyrighted materials requires some elaboration.

Posting DeCSS on the Appellants' web site makes it instantly available at the click of a mouse to any person in the world with access to the Internet, and such person can then instantly transmit DeCSS to anyone else with Internet access. Although the prohibition on posting prevents the Appellants from conveying to others the speech component of DeCSS, the Appellants have not suggested, much less shown, any technique for barring them from making this instantaneous worldwide distribution of a decryption code that makes a lesser restriction on the code's speech component. It is true that the Government has alternative means of prohibiting unauthorized access to copyrighted materials. For example, it can create criminal and civil liability for those who gain unauthorized access, and thus it can be argued that the restriction on posting DeCSS is not absolutely necessary to preventing unauthorized access to copyrighted materials. But a content-neutral regulation need not employ the least restrictive means of accomplishing the governmental objective. *Id.* It need only avoid burdening "substantially more speech than is necessary to further the government's legitimate interests." *Id.* (internal quotation marks and citation omitted). The prohibition on the Defendants' posting of DeCSS satisfies that standard.[30]

2. Linking

* * *

In applying the DMCA to linking (via hyperlinks), Judge Kaplan recognized, as he had with DeCSS code, that a hyperlink has both a speech and a nonspeech component. It conveys information, the Internet address of the linked web page, and has the functional capacity to bring the content of the linked web page to the user's computer screen (or, as Judge Kaplan put it, to "take one almost instantaneously to the desired destination." *Id.*). As he had ruled with respect to DeCSS code, he ruled that application of the DMCA to the Defendants' linking to web sites containing DeCSS is content-neutral because it is justified without regard to the speech component of the hyperlink. *Id.* The linking prohibition applies whether or not

30. We have considered the opinion of a California intermediate appellate court in *DVD Copy Control Ass'n v. Bunner,* 93 Cal. App.4th 648, 113 Cal.Rptr.2d 338 (2001), declining, on First Amendment grounds, to issue a preliminary injunction under state trade secrets law prohibiting a web site operator from posting DeCSS. To the extent that *DVD Copy Control* disagrees with our First Amendment analysis, we decline to follow it.

the hyperlink contains any information, comprehensible to a human being, as to the Internet address of the web page being accessed. The linking prohibition is justified solely by the functional capability of the hyperlink.

Applying the *O'Brien/Ward/Turner Broadcasting* requirements for content-neutral regulation, Judge Kaplan then ruled that the DMCA, as applied to the Defendants' linking, served substantial governmental interests and was unrelated to the suppression of free expression. *Id.* We agree. He then carefully considered the "closer call," *id.,* as to whether a linking prohibition would satisfy the narrow tailoring requirement. In an especially carefully considered portion of his opinion, he observed that strict liability for linking to web sites containing DeCSS would risk two impairments of free expression. Web site operators would be inhibited from displaying links to various web pages for fear that a linked page might contain DeCSS, and a prohibition on linking to a web site containing DeCSS would curtail access to whatever other information was contained at the accessed site. *Id.* at 340.

To avoid applying the DMCA in a manner that would "burden substantially more speech than is necessary to further the government's legitimate interests," *Turner Broadcasting,* 512 U.S. at 662 (internal quotation marks and citation omitted), Judge Kaplan adapted the standards of *New York Times Co. v. Sullivan,* 376 U.S. 254, 283 (1964), to fashion a limited prohibition against linking to web sites containing DeCSS. He required clear and convincing evidence

> that those responsible for the link (a) know at the relevant time that the offending material is on the linked-to site, (b) know that it is circumvention technology that may not lawfully be offered, and (c) create or maintain the link for the purpose of disseminating that technology.

Universal I, 111 F.Supp.2d at 341. He then found that the evidence satisfied his three-part test by his required standard of proof. *Id.*

* * *

At oral argument, we asked the Government whether its undoubted power to punish the distribution of obscene materials would permit an injunction prohibiting a newspaper from printing addresses of bookstore locations carrying such materials. In a properly cautious response, the Government stated that the answer would depend on the circumstances of the publication. The Appellants' supplemental papers enthusiastically embraced the arguable analogy between printing bookstore addresses and displaying on a web page links to web sites at which DeCSS may be accessed. Supplemental Brief for Appellants at 14. They confidently asserted that publication of bookstore locations carrying obscene material cannot be enjoined consistent with the First Amendment, and that a prohibition against linking to web sites containing DeCSS is similarly invalid. *Id.*

Like many analogies posited to illuminate legal issues, the bookstore analogy is helpful primarily in identifying characteristics that *distinguish* it from the context of the pending dispute. If a bookstore proprietor is knowingly selling obscene materials, the evil of distributing such materials can be prevented by injunctive relief against the unlawful distribution (and similar distribution by others can be deterred by punishment of the distributor). And if others publish the location of the bookstore, preventive relief against a distributor can be effective before any significant distribution of the prohibited materials has occurred. The digital world, however, creates a very different problem. If obscene materials are posted on one web site and other sites post hyperlinks to the first site, the materials are available for instantaneous worldwide distribution before any preventive measures can be effectively taken.

This reality obliges courts considering First Amendment claims in the context of the pending case to choose between two unattractive alternatives: either tolerate some impairment of communication in order to permit Congress to prohibit decryption that may lawfully be prevented, or tolerate some decryption in order to avoid some impairment of communication. Although the parties dispute the extent of impairment of communication if the injunction is upheld and the extent of decryption if it is vacated, and differ on the availability and effectiveness of techniques for minimizing both consequences, the fundamental choice between impairing some communication and tolerating decryption cannot be entirely avoided.

In facing this choice, we are mindful that it is not for us to resolve the issues of public policy implicated by the choice we have identified. Those issues are for Congress. Our task is to determine whether the legislative solution adopted by Congress, as applied to the Appellants by the District Court's injunction, is consistent with the limitations of the First Amendment, and we are satisfied that it is.

IV. Constitutional Challenge Based on Claimed Restriction of Fair Use

Asserting that fair use "is rooted in and required by both the Copyright Clause and the First Amendment," Brief for Appellants at 42, the Appellants contend that the DMCA, as applied by the District Court, unconstitutionally "*eliminates* fair use" of copyrighted materials, *id.* at 41 (emphasis added). We reject this extravagant claim.

Preliminarily, we note that the Supreme Court has never held that fair use is constitutionally required, although some isolated statements in its opinions might arguably be enlisted for such a requirement. * * *

We need not explore the extent to which fair use might have constitutional protection, grounded on either the First Amendment or the Copyright Clause, because whatever validity a constitutional claim might have as to an application of the DMCA that impairs fair use of copyrighted materials, such matters are far beyond the scope of this lawsuit for several reasons. In the first place, the Appellants do not claim to be making fair use of any copyrighted materials, and nothing in the injunction prohibits them from making such fair use. They are barred from trafficking in a decryption code that enables unauthorized access to copyrighted materials.

Second, as the District Court properly noted, to whatever extent the anti-trafficking provisions of the DMCA might prevent others from copying portions of DVD movies in order to make fair use of them, "the evidence as to the impact of the anti-trafficking provision[s] of the DMCA on prospective fair users is scanty and fails adequately to address the issues." *Universal I,* 111 F.Supp.2d at 338 n. 246.

Third, the Appellants have provided no support for their premise that fair use of DVD movies is constitutionally required to be made by copying the original work in its original format. Their examples of the fair uses that they believe others will be prevented from making all involve copying in a digital format those portions of a DVD movie amenable to fair use, a copying that would enable the fair user to manipulate the digitally copied portions. One example is that of a school child who wishes to copy images from a DVD movie to insert into the student's documentary film. We know of no authority for the proposition that fair use, as protected by the Copyright Act, much less the Constitution, guarantees copying by the optimum method or in the identical format of the original. Although the Appellants insisted at oral argument that they should not be relegated to a "horse and buggy" technique in making fair use of DVD movies, the DMCA does not impose even an arguable limitation on the opportunity to make a variety of traditional fair uses of DVD movies, such as commenting on their content, quoting excerpts from their screenplays, and even recording portions of the video images and sounds on film or tape by pointing a camera, a camcorder, or a microphone at a monitor as it displays the DVD movie. The fact that the resulting copy will not be as perfect or as manipulable as a digital copy obtained by having direct access to the DVD movie in its digital form, provides no basis for a claim of unconstitutional limitation of fair use. A film critic making fair use of a movie by quoting selected lines of dialogue has no constitutionally valid claim that the review (in print or on television) would be technologically superior if the reviewer had not been prevented from using a movie camera in the theater, nor has an art student a valid constitutional claim to fair use of a painting by photographing it in a museum. Fair use has never been held to be a guarantee of access to copyrighted material in order to copy it by the fair user's preferred technique or in the format of the original.

Conclusion

We have considered all the other arguments of the Appellants and conclude that they provide no basis for disturbing the District Court's judgment. Accordingly, the judgment is affirmed.

NOTES & QUESTIONS

1. *Injunctive relief and the Internet.* From the perspective of content producers, the Internet is worrisome due to the ease and efficiency with which digital goods can be copied and distributed. A case in point is the DeCSS computer program that is the focus of the *Reimerdes* decision. In *Reimerdes*, by the time the court issued a preliminary injunction enjoining the defendants from distributing the DeCSS program, it was already available on many websites around the world. Although after the preliminary injunction one could no longer obtain a copy of the program from the defendants' websites, a visit to a search engine would have revealed numerous other sites from which the program could be downloaded. Enjoining distribution of certain digital goods over the Internet once such goods are already available online is arguably an exercise in futility—an argument that the defendants made, by observing that granting "an injunction would be comparable to locking the barn door after the horse is gone." *Reimerdes,* 111 F.Supp.2d at 344. The court admitted that it "has been troubled by that possibility," but concluded that "the countervailing arguments overcome that concern." *Id.*

> To begin with, any such conclusion effectively would create all the wrong incentives by allowing defendants to continue violating the DMCA simply because others, many doubtless at defendants' urging, are doing so as well. Were that the law, defendants confronted with the possibility of injunctive relief would be well advised to ensure that others engage in the same unlawful conduct in order to set up the argument that an injunction against the defendants would be futile because everyone else is doing the same thing.
>
> Second, and closely related, is the fact that this Court is sorely "troubled by the notion that any Internet user ... can destroy valuable intellectual property rights by posting them over the Internet."[273] While equity surely should not act where the controversy has become moot, it ought to look very skeptically at claims that the defendant or others already have done all the harm that might be done before the injunction issues.
>
> The key to reconciling these views is that the focus of injunctive relief is on the defendants before the Court. If a plaintiff seeks to enjoin a defendant from burning a pasture, it is no answer that there is a wild fire burning in its direction. If the defendant itself threatens the plaintiff with irreparable harm, then equity will enjoin the defendant from carrying out the threat even if other threats abound and even if part of the pasture already is burned.
>
> These defendants would harm plaintiffs every day on which they post DeCSS on their heavily trafficked web site and link to other sites that post it because someone who does not have DeCSS thereby might obtain it. They thus threaten plaintiffs with immediate and irreparable injury. They will not be allowed to continue to do so simply because others may do so as well. * * *

Id. Are you convinced by the court's conclusion that the controversy is not moot? Do you find the court's analogy to a wildfire apposite? Does the

273. *Religious Technology Center v. Netcom On-Line Communication Services, Inc.,* 923 F.Supp. 1231, 1256 (N.D.Cal.1995).

Internet, more than any other medium of communication, give rise to cases in which damages are inadequate and an injunction is ineffective? If so, how should the legal system respond?

2. *How much authority does a copyright owner have?* In a footnote in *Reimerdes*, the court notes that "[d]ecryption or avoidance of an access control measure is not 'circumvention' within the meaning of the statute unless it occurs 'without the authority of the copyright owner.' 17 U.S.C. § 1201(a)(3)(A)." Apparently, defendants' counsel had argued that the defendants' acts did not constitute circumvention within the meaning of § 1201(a)(3)(A). The court sets out defendants' view as follows:

> Defendants posit that purchasers of a DVD acquire the right "to perform all acts with it that are not exclusively granted to the copyright holder." Based on this premise, they argue that DeCSS does not circumvent CSS within the meaning of the statute because the Copyright Act does not grant the copyright holder the right to prohibit purchasers from decrypting. As the copyright holder has no statutory right to prohibit decryption, the argument goes, decryption cannot be understood as unlawful circumvention.

Reimerdes, 111 F.Supp.2d at 317 n.137. The court is blunt in its evaluation of this line of reasoning: "The argument is pure sophistry." Should the court have been so quick to dismiss defendants' argument? Does the applicability of the statute turn on the rights of a copyright owner qua copyright owner? If not, does the statute grant rights to a copyright owner which are over and above the rights granted by the Copyright Act? Consider also whether the result is consistent with Section 1201(c)(1), which provides: "Nothing in this section shall affect rights, remedies, limitations, or defenses to copyright infringement, including fair use, under this title."

3. *Is trafficking under Section 1201 a form of secondary liability?* Under the law of copyright, secondary liability for copyright infringement requires proof of direct infringement by another. Is this also the case for liability under Section 1201(b)? Similarly, does liability under Section 1201(a)(2) require proof of a violation of Section 1201(a)(1)? That is, in order to be liable for making or selling tools that will facilitate breaking into a technological protection system to obtain access to information, or disabling technological use restrictions on information, must unauthorized access or copyright infringement by means of those tools actually be shown?

4. *Criminal penalties under Section 1204.* Section 1204 prescribes criminal penalties for those who violate Section 1201 or 1202 "willfully and for purposes of commercial advantage or private financial gain." For a first offense, the penalties are a fine of up to $500,000, a prison term up to five years, or both. 17 U.S.C. § 1204(a)(1). In July 2001, a Russian computer programmer named Dmitri Sklyarov was arrested by the Federal Bureau of Investigation and charged with violating the anti-circumvention provisions, based on his creation of a program that defeated use controls built into electronic books distributed by Adobe Systems, Inc. The arrest occurred in Las Vegas at the annual Def Con convention, known as a gathering of hackers, where Sklyarov had presented a paper describing the research that led to his creation of the program. The program, as he explained in the paper, had grown out of research about security flaws in e-document security systems that he had done for his Ph.D. dissertation. After three weeks in jail, Sklyarov was released on bail. A grand jury returned a five-count indictment against both Sklyarov and his employer, a Russian software development company called ElcomSoft Co., Ltd., for violations of the anti-trafficking provision, Section 1201(b)(1). Under the indictment, Sklyarov was subject to up to 25 years in prison and a $2,250,000 fine. Sklyarov was not allowed to return to Russia until making a deal with prosecutors, under which he agreed to testify against his employer.

In *United States v. Elcom Ltd.*, 203 F.Supp.2d 1111 (N.D.Cal.2002), the district court rejected arguments that Section 1201 is unconstitutionally vague in violation of the Due Process Clause, that it is vague and overbroad in violation of the First Amendment, and that it is beyond Congress's legislative powers. As this book goes to press, the trial of ElcomSoft is in progress.

B. TAMPERING WITH COPYRIGHT MANAGEMENT INFORMATION

To fulfill the obligations of the United States under Article 12 of the WIPO Copyright Treaty and Article 19 of the WIPO Performances and Phonograms Treaty, Title I of the Digital Millennium Copyright Act added Section 1202 to Title 17 of the U.S. Code. The addition of Section 1202 actually exceeded the obligations of the United States as a signatory state to the two WIPO treaties. In identical provisions, the two WIPO treaties require that member states enact legislation providing effective legal remedies against persons who "remove or alter any electronic rights management information without authority" as well as against persons who "distribute, import for distribution, broadcast or communicate to the public, without authority, works or copies of works knowing that electronic rights management information has been removed or altered without authority." WIPO Copyright Treaty, Dec. 20, 1996, art. 12, WIPO Doc. CRNR/DC/94, www.wipo.int/eng/diplconf/distrib/94dc.htm; WIPO Performances and Phonograms Treaty, Dec. 20, 1996, art. 19, WIPO Doc. CRNR/DC/95, www.wipo.org/eng/diplconf/distrib/95dc.htm. Section 1202 not only provides effective legal remedies against such conduct, but also prohibits individuals from providing, distributing or importing for distribution, copyright management information that is false. This last prohibition is not required by any international obligation.

Section–By–Section Analysis of H.R. 2281

House Committee on the Judiciary, 105th Congress.
(Comm. Print. 1998).

* * *

Section 1202: Integrity of Copyright Management Information.

Subsection (a) establishes a general prohibition against knowingly providing, distributing or importing false copyright management information ("CMI"), as defined in subsection (c). There are two prerequisites that must be met for the conduct to be illegal: (1) the person providing, distributing or importing the false CMI must know the CMI is false, and (2) he or she must do so with the intent to induce, enable, facilitate or conceal an infringement of any right under Title 17. The prohibition in this subsection does not apply to the ordinary and customary practices of broadcasters or the inadvertent omission of credits from broadcasts of audiovisual works, since such acts do not involve the provision of false CMI with the requisite knowledge and intent.

Subsection (b) establishes a general prohibition against deliberately removing or altering CMI, and against distributing or importing for distribution altered CMI or distributing, importing for distribution or publicly performing works in which CMI has been removed. Three specific acts are prohibited if they are committed without the authority of the copyright owner or the law, and if they are done knowing, or with respect to civil remedies under section 1203, having reasonable grounds to know, that they will induce, enable, facilitate or conceal a copyright infringement: (1) intentionally removing or altering CMI; (2) distributing or importing for distribution CMI, knowing that it has been altered without the authority of the copyright owner or the law; or (3) distributing, importing for distribution, or publicly performing works, copies of works, or phonorecords, knowing that CMI has been removed or altered without the authority of the copyright owner or the law. As with subsection (a), the prohibition in this subsection does not include the ordinary and customary practices of broadcasters or the inadvertent omission of credits from broadcasts of audiovisual works, since such omissions do not involve the requisite knowledge and intent.

Subsection (c) defines CMI. To fall within the definition, there is a threshold requirement that the information be conveyed in connection with copies or phonorecords, performances or displays of the copyrighted work. The term "conveyed" is used in its broadest sense and is not meant to require any type of transfer, physical or otherwise, of the information. It merely requires that the information be accessible in conjunction with, or appear with, an embodiment of the work itself.

CMI is defined as any of the following: (1) the title of a work or other information that identifies the work; (2) the author's name or other information that identifies the author; (3) the copyright owner's name or other information that identifies the copyright owner; (4) with the exception of public performances of works by radio and television broadcast stations, a performer's name or other information that identifies a performer whose performance is fixed in a non-audiovisual work; (5) with the exception of public performances of works by radio and television broadcast stations, the name of or other identifying information about a writer, performer, or director who is credited in an audiovisual work; (6) terms and conditions for use of a work; and (7) numbers and symbols which refer to, link to, or represent the above information. As noted above, both treaties require that numbers and symbols be included within the definition of CMI. Links, such as embedded pointers and hyperlinks, to the above information are also included. The phrase "links to such information" was included in paragraph (7) because removing or altering a link to the information will have the same adverse effect as removing or altering the information itself. Finally, paragraph (c)(8) of the definition permits the Register of Copyrights to prescribe by regulation other information that, if conveyed in connection with a work, is to be protected as CMI. To protect the privacy of users of copyrighted works, however, the Register of Copyrights may not include within the definition of CMI any information concerning *users* of copyrighted works.

Section 1202 does not mandate the use of CMI, or of any particular type of CMI. It merely protects the integrity of CMI if a party chooses to use it in connection with a copyrighted work, by prohibiting its deliberate deletion or alteration. It also should be noted that the definition of "copyright management information" does not encompass, nor is it intended to encompass, tracking or usage information relating to the identity of users of works. It would be inconsistent with the purpose and construction of this bill and contrary to the protection of privacy to include tracking and usage information within the definition of CMI.

Section 1202 imposes liability for specified acts. It does not address the question of liability for persons who manufacture devices or provide services.

Subsection (d) makes clear that the prohibitions in section 1202 do not prohibit any lawfully authorized investigative, protective or intelligence activity by or at the direction of a federal, state or local law enforcement agency, or of an intelligence agency of the United States.

Subsection (e) recognizes special problems that certain broadcasting entities may have with the transmission of copyright management information. Under this subsection, radio and television broadcasters, cable systems, and persons who provide programming to such broadcasters or systems, who do not intend to induce, enable, facilitate or conceal infringement, are eligible for an exemption from liability for violation of the CMI provisions of subsection (b) in certain, limited circumstances.

* * *

Kelly v. Arriba Soft Corp.

77 F.Supp.2d 1116 (C.D.Cal.1999), *aff'd in part, rev'd in part, and remanded on other grounds*, 280 F.3d 934 (9th Cir.2002).

■ TAYLOR, DISTRICT JUDGE.

[The facts of this case are set forth in Chapter 9, Part II(A), *supra*.]

II. DISCUSSION

These cross motions for summary adjudication present two questions of first impression. * * * [The first, whether the display of copyrighted images by a search engine constitutes fair use, is treated in the excerpt from the opinion of the court of appeals in this case, reproduced in Chapter 9, *supra*.] The second is whether the display of such images without their copyright management information is a violation of the Digital Millennium Copyright Act.

* * *

B. Digital Millennium Copyright Act

* * * Section 1202 of the DMCA governs "integrity of copyright management information." Section 1202(a) prohibits falsification of copyright management information with the intent to aid copyright infringement. Section 1202(b) prohibits, unless authorized, several forms of knowing removal or alteration of copyright management information. Section 1203 creates a federal civil action for violations of these provisions.

Plaintiff argues Defendant violated § 1202(b) by displaying thumbnails of Plaintiff's images without displaying the corresponding copyright management information consisting of standard copyright notices in the surrounding text. Joint Stip. of Facts, ¶¶ 64–69. Because these notices do not appear in the images themselves, the Ditto crawler did not include them when it indexed the images. *Id.* ¶ 70. As a result, the images appeared in Defendant's index without the copyright management information, and any users retrieving Plaintiff's images while using Defendant's Web site would not see the copyright management information.

Section 1202(b)(1) does not apply to this case. Based on the language and structure of the statute, the Court holds this provision applies only to the removal of copyright management information on a plaintiff's product or original work. Moreover, even if § 1202(b)(1) applied, Plaintiff has not offered any evidence showing Defendant's actions were intentional, rather than merely an unintended side effect of the Ditto crawler's operation.

Here, where the issue is the absence of copyright management information from *copies* of Plaintiff's works, the applicable provision is § 1202(b)(3). To show a violation of that section, Plaintiff must show Defendant makes available to its users the thumbnails and full-size images, which were copies of Plaintiff's work separated from their copyright management information, even though it knows or should know this will lead to infringement of Plaintiff's copyrights. There is no dispute the Ditto crawler removed Plaintiff's images from the context of Plaintiff's Web sites where their copyright management information was located, and converted them to thumbnails in Defendant's index. There is also no dispute the Arriba Vista search engine allowed full-size images to be viewed without their copyright management information.

Defendant's users could obtain a full-sized version of a thumbnailed image by clicking on the thumbnail. A user who did this was given the name of the Web site from which Defendant obtained the image, where any associated copyright management information would be available, and an opportunity to link there. Users were also informed on Defendant's Web site that use restrictions and copyright limitations may apply to images retrieved by Defendant's search engine.[13]

Based on all of this, the Court finds Defendant did not have "reasonable grounds to know" it would cause its users to infringe Plaintiff's copyrights. Defendant warns its users about the possibility of use restrictions on the images in its index, and instructs them to check with the originating Web sites before copying and using those images, even in reduced thumbnail form.

Plaintiff's images are vulnerable to copyright infringement because they are displayed on Web sites. Plaintiff has not shown users of Defendant's site were any more likely to infringe his copyrights, any of these users did infringe, or Defendant should reasonably have expected infringement.

* * * The Court finds there was no violation of DMCA § 1202. Defendant's motion is GRANTED and Plaintiff's motion is DENIED on the DMCA claim.

NOTES & QUESTIONS

1. *Encouraging the use of CMI.* The House Report excerpted above notes that "Section 1202 does not mandate the use of CMI, or of any particular type of CMI." The Berne Convention[4] precludes formalities as a prerequisite to copyright validity, so that the United States as a signatory would not have been compliant with the treaty had it mandated the use of CMI as a prerequisite to copyright protection. Nevertheless, a signatory is not precluded from enacting protection for CMI once owners have chosen to use it. What economic or other policy reasons can you adduce for encouraging the use of CMI by punishing those who alter or remove it?

2. *Safe harbors.* As discussed in Chapter 9, *supra*, 17 U.S.C. § 512(d) offers the operator of a search engine a safe harbor from monetary liability "for infringement of copyright by reason of * * * referring or linking users to an online location containing infringing material or infringing activity." Could the defendant in *Kelly v. Arriba Soft* have successfully defended against the Section 1202 claim based on this provision?

13. Plaintiff argues Defendant's warnings are insufficient because they do not appear with the thumbnail images on the search result pages produced by the search engine. The Arriba Vista Web site only offered a warning if users clicked on a link to its "Copyright" page. This warning may arguably have been placed in the wrong place to deter some potential copyright infringers. But this does not necessarily mean Defendant "knew" or "should have known" for the purposes of a DMCA violation, especially since Plaintiff offers no evidence of any actual copyright infringement about which Defendant "should have known."

4. Berne Convention for the Protection of Literary and Artistic Works, July 24, 1971, S. Treaty Doc. No. 99–27 (1986), 828 U.N.T.S. 221.

3. *Civil remedies under Section 1203.* Section 1203 sets out the civil remedies available for violations of the anti-circumvention and CMI-protection provisions of Sections 1201 and 1202. In addition to awarding injunctive relief and damages, a court may "order the remedial modification or destruction of any device or product involved in the violation that is in the custody or control of the violator." § 1203(b)(6). This would apparently allow impoundment and destruction of the violator's computer. Is this an inappropriately draconian remedy? Compare 17 U.S.C. § 503(b) (in case of copyright infringement, court may order destruction "of all plates, molds, matrices, masters, tapes, film negatives, or other articles by means of which" infringing materials may be produced).

III. Trusted Systems and Fair Use

As we have seen in the preceding materials addressing the DMCA's prohibitions against circumventing technological protection measures and tampering with copyright management information, there is considerable debate among copyright owners, users of copyrighted materials, and commentators about the proper scope of legal protection for trusted systems. A recurring issue has to do with the traditional defense of fair use, and how (or if) it can be carried forward into the era of technological protection. Is the fair use doctrine still viable?

Tom W. Bell, *Fair Use vs. Fared Use: The Impact of Automated Rights Management on Copyright's Fair Use Doctrine*

76 N.C. L. Rev. 557 (1998).

* * *

1. Fair Use Is Not Free Use

Despite gross misconceptions to the contrary, fair use never comes for free. One way or another, consumers using conventional media must pay to browse magazines at newsstands, to photocopy and distribute newspaper stories for spontaneous classroom use, to search for quotes and type them into articles, and to otherwise avail themselves of the fair use doctrine. Although such acts do not entail paying licensing fees, they inevitably impose a variety of transaction costs—for personal transport, manipulating paper and ink, searching card catalogs, and so on—that follow from the very nature of conventional media. It makes no difference that consumers pay licensing fees in cash whereas they pay fair use's transaction costs in lost opportunities. Economically speaking, a cost is a cost.

The digital intermedia[3] allow consumers to avoid or reduce such transaction costs. Bits flow directly to homes and offices, copy easily into

3. This Article uses "digital intermedia" to refer to the Internet, circuit-switched networks, and other interactive channels over which digital information gets distribut-

RAM or magnetic storage, forward instantly to destinations worldwide, and submit easily to electronic searches. Transaction costs remain even here, of course. The burgeoning growth of the Internet and other digital intermedia indicates, however, that consuming bits very often costs less than consuming atoms. The increasing reliance of legal academics on commercial online services, CD–ROMs, and the Internet confirms this observation. Those who decry the advent of fared use thus err when they imply that it must impose a net cost on consumers. To the contrary, fared use offers a considerable likelihood of providing more and better verified, organized, and interlinked information, at less cost, than fair use does now.

2. Fixing Market Failure

Scholars have explained fair use in at least three ways: (1) as a proxy for a copyright owner's implied consent; (2) as part of a bargain between authors and the public, struck on their behalf first by courts and then by Congress; and (3) as a response to a market failure in private attempts to protect authors' expressions from undue copying. * * * The present subsection addresses the third explanation of fair use and argues that, as a response to market failure, the fair use doctrine can and should give way in the face of the effective enforcement of authors' rights through automated rights management.

Lawmakers enacted the Copyright Act to cure an alleged case of market failure: creating a work can cost authors a good deal, whereas copying a work costs free riders very little. Absent special protection from such copying, the argument goes, authors will underproduce and the public will suffer. * * *

Markets, like squeezed balloons, bulge outward where unconstrained. In its attempt to protect authors from the discouraging effects of unfettered copying, copyright law has thus created market failure elsewhere. The costs of avoiding infringement by obtaining permission to use a copyrighted work, and thus avoiding infringement claims, often exceed the benefits of the desired use. Such transaction costs threaten to prevent many socially beneficial uses of copyrighted works from taking place. The doctrine of fair use attempts to cure this particular market failure by excusing as non-infringing a limited (though poorly defined) class of uses of copyrighted works. * * * As Professor Gordon describes it, "courts and Congress have employed fair use to permit uncompensated transfers that are socially desirable but not capable of effectuation through the market."[121]

ed and through which automated rights management can function. "Digital intermedia" does not encompass such comparatively noninteractive distribution channels as CDs, CD–ROMs, and digital audio cassettes. [Relocated footnote.—Eds.]

121. [Wendy J. Gordon, Fair Use As Market Failure: A Structural and Economic Analysis of the Betamax Case and Its Predecessors, 82 Colum. L. Rev. 1600, 1601 (1982) (footnote omitted).]

Understanding fair use as a response to market failure does much to explain the vagaries of its development in the case law. * * * [T]he scope of the fair use defense rises and falls with the transaction costs of licensing access to copyrighted works.

Automated rights management radically reduces the transaction costs of licensing access to copyrighted works in digital intermedia. Indeed, as its name suggests, it makes licensing automatic. Insofar as it responds to market failure, therefore, fair use should have a much reduced scope when ARM takes effect. * * *

* * *

3. Maintaining Copyright's Quid Pro Quo

As courts and commentators often have noted, the Constitution demands a public benefit as the price for the limited statutory privileges that copyright creates. In contrast to the view that the fair use doctrine represents a second-best response to pervasive market failure, therefore, some commentators regard the doctrine as an integral part of this constitutional quid pro quo. On this view, fair use provides a public benefit—unbilled access to copyrighted works—to balance the State's grant of a limited monopoly.

Automated rights management at first appears to threaten this bargain. It seems as if ARM restricts the public's access to copyrighted works in digital intermedia without offering a benefit in return. As this subsection's consideration of the issue shows, however, friends of fair use should not assume that ARM will leave the public worse off. To the contrary, it appears likely to provide a net benefit to the public.

By reducing transaction costs throughout the market for copyrighted expressions, ARM benefits the public both directly and indirectly. Having emanated from an intentionally vague statute and developed in various, occasionally contradictory cases, the fair use doctrine necessarily blurs the boundary between valid and invalid copyright claims. High risks of "theft"—here, infringement—increase the insecurity of copyright's protection. Though the resultant uncertainty obviously harms producers and sellers of copyrighted works, it also harms consumers. Academics, artists, commentators, and others desirous of reusing copyrighted works without authorization must borrow at their peril, consult experts on fair use, or, sadly, forego such reuse altogether. ARM's clarifying power directly benefits those who would reuse copyrighted works—and through them their public audiences—by creating harbors safe from the threat of copyright litigation.

Moreover, ARM benefits the public indirectly by increasing the transactional efficiency of the market for expressive works. Like other markets, the market for expressive works does not constitute a zero sum game. And, as Coase observed of markets in general,

> [i]t is obviously desirable that rights should be assigned to those who can use them most productively and with incentives that lead

> them to do so. It is also desirable that, to discover (and maintain) such a distribution of rights, the costs of their transference should be low, through clarity in the law and by making the legal requirements for such transfers less onerous.[137]

ARM, by its systemic improvement of copyright's transactional efficiency, helps us discover and maintain a distribution of rights to expressive works that will increase net social wealth. ARM thus stands to benefit both producers and consumers.

In particular, because it increases the value of expressive works, ARM will put deflationary pressure on the price of accessing them. In general, an asset's current price internalizes the value of its future income stream. Copyrights therefore commonly lose present value because, with the passage of time and their wider distribution, they prove increasingly vulnerable to uncompensated uses. Because it reduces such risks, ARM tends to increase the value of copyrights. But although this windfall might initially accrue to copyright owners, competition among information providers would force access prices downward, toward the marginal costs of obtaining and distributing expressive works. Directly or indirectly, such price pressure would similarly affect the prices that copyright owners can demand. Gains that ARM provides to copyright owners would thus pass on to consumers in the form of reduced access fees.

Because ARM will increase the value of copyrighted works, moreover, it will encourage their greater production and improved distribution. Consumers will thus benefit from better access to information. Access providers will improve the information itself, too, increasing its quantity and making it better organized, verified, interlinked, diverse, up-to-date, and relevant. Although this cornucopia of information may at first come only for a fee, some of it eventually will fall into the public domain. To judge from current implementations of ARM, copyright owners might very well offer limited free access to their wares in an attempt to draw more extensive (and expensive) uses. Entrepreneurs will undoubtedly create other services, at present utterly and inevitably unforeseen, to attract and satisfy consumers of information.

* * *

David Nimmer, *A Riff on Fair Use in the Digital Millennium Copyright Act*

148 U. PA. L. REV. 673 (2000).

* * *

Historically, copyright owners have always had the right to retain their works confidentially. "The owner of the copyright, if he pleases, may

137. Ronald H. Coase, The Institutional Structure of Production, in Coase, Essays on Economics and Economists 3, 11 (1994).

refrain from vending or licensing and content himself with simply exercising the right to exclude others from using his property."[208] In this manner, United States law has accorded de facto recognition to the branch of moral rights called the *droit de divulgation*. Once those same owners consented to initial publication of the work, however, they have historically lost control over its subsequent flow. The first sale doctrine prevented them from barring or demanding a royalty upon subsequent disposition of published copies. The fair use doctrine prevented them from barring or demanding a royalty from such activities as miscellaneous quotations in the context of a review. In this manner, traditional copyright law accorded the public substantial leeway in browsing published works.

The digital revolution places unprecedented stress on those browsing activities. Potentially, it allows copyright owners to control the flow not merely of their unpublished manuscripts, but more importantly, of their published works as well. If copyright owners package their "published" goods in digital envelopes accessible only through passwords, then perhaps they can, indeed, levy a unilateral royalty upon such activities as resales and reviews. At issue here are both factual and legal variables. The former involves a prediction as to the future of technology; the latter demands unprecedented attention to the legal status of such browsing activities as were previously simply beyond practical redress.

Consider the factual angle. Publishers are free to take old works that have fallen into the public domain, to add a bit of original material to them, and to claim a copyright in the newly released whole. Thus, for example, they could collect all cookbooks published in the nineteenth century, write a new introduction to each, and then wrap the product in a digital envelope. The resulting product, considered as a whole, would be subject to copyright protection. Whether that product holds any promise or not, however, depends on how technology develops.

If lending libraries continue to flourish, then anyone with a burning interest in how shrimp was cooked in *fin de siècle* New Orleans could simply check out the relevant volume from her local repository. There is no reason for her to pay to access the digital product—unless she specifically wishes to read the newly composed introductions, as opposed to the underlying books.

On the other hand, if the world develops such that a trip to the library becomes as common as sending messages via the Pony Express, then a different dynamic pertains. If access to works via electronic or photo-optical means becomes the universal norm, and if the only way that the pertinent network allows users to view any instantiation of Louisiana cookbooks of the 1890s is through payment of a fee, then royalties to the publisher of the electronic cookbook would become essentially mandatory. By the same token, if in tomorrow's world only antiquarians maintain phonographs and CD players, the sole effective way to hear an old recording of music might be through the same network service. To the extent that the service

208. Fox Film Corp. v. Doyal, 286 U.S. 123, 127 (1932).

charged the same access fee for early 1920s jazz recordings as for new recordings subject to copyright protection, the effective result would be to convert public domain works into royalty-generating items.

In short, depending on how the future unfolds, concern about fair use in the digital environment could range from pointless to vital. The latter scenario requires payment to gain access even to works that nominally lie in the public domain, such as works from centuries past, even if the purpose of the access is for one that the law favors, such as to quote a few sentences for scholarly purposes. Under that scenario, the work itself is effectively placed under lock and key, and the proprietor can charge simply for the initial act of access. Thus arises what one senator calls "the specter of moving our Nation towards a 'pay-per-use' society."[225]

In turn, the legal issue arises of how to conceptualize the browsing activities of users in decades past. Why is it that reviewers could traditionally quote scattered passages from copyrighted works? Is it because they had a right to do so? Could chefs review the techniques of their predecessors as contained in published cookbooks of the past as a matter of right? If so, was the right of constitutional magnitude, safeguarding First Amendment interests of free speech and the advancement of knowledge? Or did the law simply allow those activities, as it would have been economically unproductive to pursue such small scale utilization?

These fundamental questions exert practical consequences. Under the first point of view, any danger to the public's right to browse posed by the digital environment must be negated. In other words, if users have a constitutional right to quote for fair use purposes, then Congress was under an obligation to frame [17 U.S.C.] section 1201 in a manner that preserves that right. Under the second point of view, by contrast, the marketplace can be left to develop—if browsing rights are extinguished in the process, the only lesson to derive is that the economics evidently have changed. Congress, under this viewpoint, need not embody into section 1201 any special solicitude for user rights.

* * *

Let us revert to the public domain cookbook or sound recording that has been combined with a new introduction or other material subject to copyright and brought under a technological protection measure. As of the year 2005, those works could be virtually unavailable through low-tech means yet accessible to those who have paid for the appropriate decryption algorithm or password. In such a world, let us further imagine that Alice hacks her way in, gaining access to the work to avoid paying the license fee associated with taking out an authorized password. Bob does the same but instead to determine if he likes the old jazz song enough to pay the freight for regular access to it. Carol is writing her Ph.D. dissertation on obscure diction and wants to quote archaisms and franglais from the mouths of Creole chefs, which she remembers (from browsing a copy of the book long ago at a second-hand shop) are contained in the cookbook. Finally, Ted is a

225. 144 Cong. Rec. S11887 (daily ed. Oct. 8, 1998) (statement of Sen. Ashcroft).

software virtuoso who boasts that he "can pick any lock." How does their conduct stack up?

Alice is the quintessential violator—hers is the precise conduct against which the basic provision [Section 1201(a)(1)(A)] is aimed. Accordingly, there is no question that her circumvention of a technological measure that effectively controls access to a work protected by a subsisting U.S. copyright places her in violation of the statute. Can she nevertheless take refuge in the fact that the publisher is actually charging for a work in the public domain rather than one protected by copyright? Inasmuch as the publisher has implemented a password scheme that prevents unauthorized access to its works, which themselves are subject to copyright by virtue of the new additions, that argument is unavailing. Although Alice would not run afoul of section 1201 by hacking her way into a domain containing no copyrightable elements, the domain to which she in fact gained unauthorized entry does contain copyrighted elements—notwithstanding that the particular components that she ultimately wished to enjoy lie outside copyright protection. Given that the language of the statute is absolute—"[n]o person shall circumvent a technological measure that effectively controls access to a work protected under this title"[297]—Alice is culpable for the anti-circumvention violation.

What about Bob? Many publishers release shareware, which customers can "try on for size" during a test period. Shareware publishers do not fall within the framework of the anti-circumvention basic provision and its coordinate trafficking offense; instead, they fall under the "additional violations" [Section 1201(b)(1)]. In that context, there is no counterpart basic offense to dovetail with the additional violations, so Bob's conduct would be nonactionable against a shareware publisher. In effect, Bob has elected to treat the subject music as shareware; an honorable listener, he has an unblemished track record of paying for all recordings that he actually adds to his collection.

Ultimately, however, Bob too falls on the wrong side of the tracks laid by section 1201. Although publishers are free to adopt the shareware paradigm, they are not obligated to do so. Bob cannot unilaterally pigeonhole purveyors of works into a category from which they have absented themselves—to make proprietary publishers into shareware publishers. Bob has no right to browse the access-protected works to determine if he wants to buy them. Section 1201 grants such browsing rights only to qualifying libraries and archives, not to individuals such as Bob.

Bob, like Alice, cannot take refuge in the fact that the recordings themselves reside in the public domain, for the language of the statute is such that Bob runs afoul of it. Given that the subject recordings are contained in a file that contains the copyrighted commentary of a renowned musicologist, that the file as a whole is protected by a technological measure that effectively controls access to it, and that Bob hacked his way into that file, all the elements for a section 1201 violation are present—

297. 17 U.S.C. § 1201(a)(1)(A).

again, notwithstanding that the particular components that Bob ultimately wished to enjoy lie outside copyright protection.

The examples of Alice and Bob seem to bear out the dissenters' initial criticism that "[t]he anti-circumvention language of H.R. 2281, even as amended, bootstraps the limited monopoly into a perpetual right."[304] To be sure, that bootstrapping is far from inevitable—it comes to bear only in a world in which the sole effective means of access to the subject cookbook and recording is through the encrypted methodology posited above. Hopefully, that state of affairs would never come to pass—just as one entity was able to obtain a copy of the subject works in order to upload them, so others should be able to do the same. The latter, moreover, can offer those works free of charge. Therefore, it might be that the first publisher's efforts at constructing its own *domaine public payant* will be doomed to failure. The point, however, is that the structure of section 1201, despite protestations to the contrary, does not categorically negate this baleful possibility—unless through the exception for adversely affected users, to which the discussion turns below.

Before reaching those points, however, consider Carol and Ted. Not only is Carol (the Ph.D. candidate) using a public domain work—a circumstance that, as observed in the cases of Alice and Bob, affords only cold comfort—but even such isolated quotation as she is drawing from the work, were it copyrighted, would itself find shelter under the fair use umbrella. Does section 1201 catch even her in its net? It does. For regardless of how lofty her purpose might be, she has violated the elements of the statute. Although, as noted in the discussion of Bob, section 1201 contains no prohibition on disabling technological measures once access to a work has been lawfully gained, as the Commerce Committee dissenters specifically complained, their effort at "legislating an equivalent fair use defense for the new right to control access" was rejected "for reasons not clear to us."[310]

But why does the fair use doctrine itself not come to Carol's rescue? Even though Congress did not add to section 1201 a specific fair use proviso that covers Carol, it at least left the existing provision undisturbed. Given that Carol's activities fall quintessentially within the protection of that defense, why is it inadequate to doom any cause of action against her? The answer lies in how the Copyright Act is structured. On the one hand, the Act forbids copyright infringement subject to a fair use defense. On the other hand, the WIPO Treaties Act adds a wholly separate tort of unauthorized circumvention, to which the fair use defense is inapplicable.

The upshot is that Carol, too, having circumvented a technological measure that effectively controls access to a work protected by U.S. copyright, falls afoul of section 1201. From a traditional copyright stand-

304. [Report of the House Comm. on Commerce, H.R. Rep. No. 105–551, pt. 2,] at 85 [(1998)] (Additional Views of Representatives Klug and Boucher). * * *

310. Commerce Rep. (DMCA), supra note [304], at 86 (Additional Views of Representatives Klug and Boucher).

point, the purportedly "fair" character of her utilization affords no defense to a charge that she is culpable of a new anti-circumvention violation.

At last reaching Ted (the hacker), to the extent that he advertises his abilities to or performs services for Alice, Bob, or Carol, he would thereby be aiding individuals who themselves fall afoul of section 1201. As such, he would be culpable of a trafficking violation.

* * *

Congress enacted section 1201 based on its perception that "the digital environment poses a unique threat to the rights of copyright owners."[349] Even if that threat is unique, however, it scarcely arises in a vacuum. The tension between property rights and user-access rights does not loom from the approaching digital millennium; it has been a ceaseless part of the millennium now ending.

The lengthy analysis of how section 1201 works in practice leads to the conclusion that its entire edifice of user exemptions is of doubtful puissance. The user safeguards so proudly heralded as securing balance between owner and user interests, on inspection, largely fail to achieve their stated goals. If the courts apply section 1201 as written, the only users whose interests are truly safeguarded are those few who personally possess sufficient expertise to counteract whatever technological measures are placed in their path.

This defect is not a small one. Many legislators characterized the Digital Millennium Copyright Act as "probably one of the most important bills that we have passed this Congress."[354] The fair use issue constitutes "one of the most important provisions of this legislation."[355] Accordingly, it is a source of disappointment to be forced to disagree with the conclusion that Congress "mastered the intricate details of this complex subject and has produced a balanced result."[356]

* * *

In the event that future technology and business models do indeed converge to produce such a pay-per-use world, then the structure of section 1201, notwithstanding pious protests to the contrary, cannot meaningfully serve as the tool to defeat universal pay-per-use and de facto perpetual protection. Instead, courts at that juncture would be called upon to apply section 1201 to that world of the future—whether by upholding it exactly as written, by interpolating into it additional exceptions to give substance to the user exemption that it already contains, or by making the determina-

349. Commerce Rep. (DMCA), supra note [304], at 25.

354. 144 Cong. Rec. H10618 (daily ed. Oct. 12, 1998) (remarks of Rep. Stearns); see also 144 Cong. Rec. S11889 (daily ed. Oct. 8, 1998) (remarks of Sen. Hatch) ("[T]he DMCA is one of the most important bills passed this session....").

355. 144 Cong. Rec. H7094 (daily ed. Aug. 4, 1998) (remarks of Rep. Bliley); see also 144 Cong. Rec. E2144 (daily ed. Oct. 13, 1998) (remarks of Rep. Tauzin) (asserting that the fair use exception is "the most important contribution that we made to this bill").

356. 144 Cong. Rec. H7096 (daily ed. Aug. 4, 1998) (remarks of Rep. Boucher).

tion that protection for user rights (traditionally protected in the analog world through such devices as fair use and the first sale doctrine) rises to constitutional levels.

* * *

Dan L. Burk & Julie E. Cohen, *Fair Use Infrastructure for Rights Management Systems*

15 HARV. J.L. & TECH. 41 (2001).

* * *

IV. OPTIONS FOR FAIR USE INFRASTRUCTURE

Currently, the DMCA's anti-circumvention provisions effectively sanction the use of private code to write the public law of fair use out of existence. But the legal regime governing rights management technologies need not be structured in such a fashion. Instead, law could be designed to shift technological development in a direction that balances the incentive structure of copyright protection with copyright's concern for the public domain and for the legitimate fair use privileges of the public. Here, we suggest modifications to the DMCA designed to create incentives for the preservation of fair use in digital media.

Realizing the promise of fair use in a digital rights management environment will require some technical mechanism to allow public access and reuse privileges equivalent to those deemed fair in previous media. In broad brush, there are two ways that such a system might be designed. First, the rights management system itself might be designed to detect and regulate fair use access. Second, a decisionmaker external to the rights management system might authorize would-be fair users to override rights management controls. We propose a fair use infrastructure that combines elements of both approaches.

A. Coding for Fair Use

The most direct method of accommodating fair use would be to mandate or prompt the development of rights management systems that directly allow purchasers of a work to make fair use of the content. Optimally, the "breathing space" required for fair uses would be programmed directly into the technical rule set that controls access to the work. The systems might, for example, include provisions allowing users to extract a certain number of bits, or display the work for certain periods of time, or partially perform the work a certain number of times. Depending on the characteristics of the desired use, users would be able to take these actions without having to seek additional permission or pay additional fees.

In reality, an algorithm-based approach to fair use is unlikely to accommodate even the shadow of fair use as formulated in current copyright law. We are not optimistic that system designers will be able to anticipate the range of access privileges that may be appropriate for fair uses to be made of a particular work. Neither are we optimistic that system designers will be able to anticipate the types of uses that would be considered fair by a court. Fair use is irreducibly a situation-specific determination. In some instances, a user may fairly take a work in its entirety—say, for example, where the work is entitled to only thin protection, the use is for a protected purpose such as scholarship, criticism, or software reverse engineering, and/or the use is expected to have no appreciable impact on the market for the work. Indeed, some uses, such as software reverse engineering or automatically searching text, music, or video files for particular words, themes, or images (a process essential for some types of academic research), are impossible if the user cannot gain access to the entire work. In other situations, where three or four of the factors weigh heavily against a particular use, taking much less might exceed fair use.

Building the range of possible uses and outcomes into computer code would require both a bewildering degree of complexity and an impossible level of prescience. There is currently no good algorithm that is capable of producing such an analysis. Relatedly, fair use is a dynamic, equitable doctrine designed to respond to changing conditions of use. Programmed fair use functionality, in contrast, is relatively static. At least for now, there is no feasible way to build rights management code that approximates both the individual results of judicial determinations and the overall dynamism of fair use jurisprudence.

* * *

B. Key Access for Fair Use

The second option for the design of fair use infrastructure involves the introduction of an external decisionmaker into the process for obtaining access to technologically secured works. At present, only human intelligence, reviewing the unique circumstances of a particular use, can determine whether it is likely to be fair. Thus, we might require users to apply for keys to access the encrypted work. This option would allow case-by-case determination of the need for access, building in judgment capabilities that cannot practically be emulated by technical defaults.

One such method might be to place the fair use determination in the rights holder's hands. We cannot, however, recommend a legal rule that would fundamentally shift the decisionmaking authority about whether to proceed with a use from users to owners. As we have described above, fair use frequently condones public access in situations where the collective public interest runs contrary to the rights holder's individual interest. Thus, there may be a strong incentive for the rights holder to deny access just when the public interest most demands access. * * *

In addition, a preauthorization system for fair use is vulnerable to three more general objections. The first and second, closely related, are that a preauthorization requirement would be costly and would chill spontaneous uses. Case by case determination of the fairness of the intended use would require a lengthy and complicated approval process. Even a quick and inexpensive pre-screening procedure, however, will impose some transaction costs and will deter some uses that otherwise would have been made. As noted above, considerable social benefit accrues from this sort of unplanned use. Research and teaching, in particular, are processes that contain an irreducible element of ad hoc adjustment.

The third objection is that application to a third party is likely to compromise the sort of anonymity that users presently enjoy. Anonymity is the current default for fair use access (and indeed for access generally) in traditional media—a copyright holder does not know who has made use of the work, or at what time, or in what manner. Even if the fair use results in publication or dissemination of a subsidiary work, the author need not reveal her name. * * * [W]e are particularly reluctant to recommend that this situation be inverted by requiring revelation to the rights holder of a user's identity and use for every fair use. More generally, there exists a wide range of situations—for example, those involving parodies or other negative critiques—in which the user may prefer to remain anonymous.

* * *

Our proposal hinges upon the concept of key escrow, that is, management of rights management keys by a trusted third party, rather than by the owner of a work. Keys to technologically protected works would be held by the trusted third party, who would release them to users applying for access to make fair use. The trusted third party would be a publicly funded institution that would be statutorily insulated from both direct and indirect copyright infringement liability and subject to regulatory oversight for compliance with its escrow and privacy obligations.

Although, as we have noted, any preauthorization requirement would impinge upon spontaneous uses and thereby threaten the overall flexibility and adaptability of the fair use system, the trusted third party's approval procedure could be designed to minimize this impact. In order to avoid difficult ex ante judgments about particular uses, and to approximate as nearly as possible the cost and incentive structure of traditional fair uses, the third party would not be required, and would not attempt, to make a determination about the bona fides of the access application. Rather, the third party would simply issue keys to applicants via a simple online procedure.

Solving the anonymity problem is far more difficult. The concept of key escrow has been vilified in the past, with good reason, when it constituted the core of a governmental plan that would have systematically undermined the integrity of private communications. But a different sort of privacy interest is at stake here, where the issue is public access to publicly distributed works of authorship, rather than governmental access to private communications. In this instance, the concept of third-party escrow works toward the public interest and could be made to work in favor of preserving privacy, rather than against both goals.

* * *

C. Mixed Fair Use Infrastructure

Each of the two possible mechanisms for preserving fair use in a digital rights management environment has advantages and drawbacks. Automatic fair use functionality does not require human intervention but is unlikely to afford the full spectrum of fair uses allowed by law. The use of a trusted third party intermediary to mediate access, in contrast, potentially allows the full spectrum of uses but is less responsive to anonymity and spontaneity concerns. The optimal result, we suggest, is an infrastructure that combines the two.

The first layer of our proposed fair use infrastructure would involve the design of rights management technologies that incorporate automatic fair use defaults based on customary norms of personal noncommercial use. The legal rule for facilitating this part of the proposal would operate in a fashion similar to current provisions of the Copyright Act designed to encourage copyright registration and deposit, by conditioning copyright enforcement for United States works on implementation of the automatic fair use defaults. To guard against a "race to the bottom" in fair use law, the law would clearly state that the level of copying permitted by the automatic defaults does not define the full extent of permitted fair use.

Those who desire greater fair use access, meanwhile, would turn to the trusted third party intermediary. Under the system, deposit of access keys into key escrow would be facilitated by conditioning anti-circumvention protection for both United States and non-United States works on such deposit. Users who failed to obtain access via the escrow agent would be subject to suit for circumventing technical measures. Those users, however, still might escape liability by successful invocation of a statutory or constitutional defense to circumvention liability. Rights holders that opt not to deposit keys with the escrow agent would be unable to invoke legal protection against circumvention. For such unescrowed works, a "right to hack" would effectively substitute for access via the escrowed keys. * * * [T]he DMCA's ban on the manufacture and distribution of circumvention technologies also would need to be modified to make this defense a realistic possibility. Finally, to preserve the relative anonymity of the key escrow system, the records of applicants and keys issued would need to be guarded by stringent legal protections along the lines described above.

The most likely and appropriate escrow agent would be a publicly funded institution, such as the Library of Congress. * * * [W]e think that a publicly funded institution would be the preferred choice because the public policies underlying fair use require some guarantees of public accountability and institutional longevity.

* * *

* * *The presence of other national laws regarding anti-circumvention highlights the fact that the balance between access and protection must be struck in a global milieu, where the U.S. approach to technical protection is not insular and where our suggestion may find broader application than the American DMCA. Although we have focused on the implementation of

a fair use infrastructure within U.S. copyright law, the escrow principles we have outlined here also might find application under the European Union's ("E.U.") new copyright directive, which in some respects reflects greater cognizance of the user access problem than does its American counterpart. Like the DMCA, the E.U. Copyright Directive requires member states to provide legal protection for rights management systems. Unlike its U.S. analogue, however, the E.U. Copyright Directive allows member states to enact legislation requiring that copyright holders provide users with the means to take advantage of exceptions or limitations to the exclusive rights granted under copyright law. These limitations and exceptions, which are enumerated in the directive, specifically include private reproduction, criticism and parody, and news reporting. To prevent user rights from being nullified by technical controls, moreover, the directive creates an incentive for content owners to design technical measures capable of facilitating permitted uses; member states may legislate to compel the provision of means for access only if content owners have not already provided such means voluntarily. The key escrow system that we propose here might be an appropriate means by which member states could ensure user access, or promote voluntary provision of access by copyright owners.

It is worth noting that the E.U. Copyright Directive contemplates nothing so broad, flexible, or indeterminate as the U.S. concept of fair use. Rather, in the European tradition of "fair dealing," the directive lists specific circumstances under which member states may allow a user to make unauthorized use of a copyrighted work. The exceptions and limitations enumerated in the directive are discrete and relatively narrow. Design of a rights management infrastructure that would allow users access commensurate with such exceptions may be less challenging than design of an infrastructure to accommodate U.S.-style fair use. Nonetheless, we expect that it would still be difficult to design an algorithm that could take into account whether, for example, a reproduction is "for private use and for ends that are neither directly nor indirectly commercial," as the directive requires. Thus, the key escrow option discussed here may remain an attractive method of providing user access.

* * *

NOTES & QUESTIONS

Assessing the threat. How great a threat to public access and fair use is posed by the use of technological management systems? What factors does Professor Nimmer suggest will determine how serious the threat is? Do you agree with his analysis? Recall that Section 1201 provides that the anti-circumvention provisions do not affect the law of fair use. 17 U.S.C. § 1201(c)(1). Does that mean that these fears are overblown? In considering this question, note that observers have expressed sharply differing views as to what policy best supports fair use. For some, such as Professor Bell, fair use is based primarily on economic efficiency. Under one application of the efficiency criterion, use of copyrighted works is fair where that use would be welfare-maximizing, but the transaction costs of acquiring authorization from the copyright owner through voluntary licensing are too high for the transaction to take place. For others, such as Professors Burk and Cohen, fair use is based on principles of free circulation of information, especially criticism and debate; i.e., fair use is an exception to the exclusive rights of copyright owners that should be retained even absent transaction costs. How much do fears about the future of fair use rest on a non-economic understanding of its purpose? Consider also the argument that if transaction costs are indeed the only basis for the fair use privilege, then there is nothing to fear if the doctrine fades away in the online world of greatly reduced transaction costs. *See* Margaret Jane Radin, *Incomplete Commodification in the Computerized World,* in THE COMMODIFICATION OF INFORMATION (Neil Netanel & Niva Elkin–Koren eds., 2002).

CHAPTER TWELVE

CONTROLLING ONLINE BUSINESS METHODS: PATENT

The application of patent protection to methods for transacting business, electronic and otherwise, is a relatively recent phenomenon, but one that has rapidly become widespread. Be Free, Inc. holds a patent on the ability to target Internet advertising based on user preferences. Priceline.com owns a patent on reverse auctions, a method of selling goods and services through an Internet bidding system whereby a customer commits to buying an item at a specified price if a seller can be found to supply it at that price. DoubleClick, Inc., owns a patent on Web-based banner advertising. And Amazon.com holds a patent on its "One–Click" ordering system, which allows online customers to save time by entering their credit and personal information only once.

Less than a decade ago, many legal experts would have considered patents such as these invalid, because business methods were believed to be specifically excluded from patent protection. In 1998, however, in *State Street Bank and Trust Co. v. Signature Financial Group, Inc.*, 149 F.3d 1368 (Fed.Cir.1998), the Court of Appeals for the Federal Circuit[1] declared that business methods are not categorically outside the subject matter of patent. In other words, an inventive business method, like any other invention, could receive patent protection if the United States Patent and Trademark Office ("PTO") found it to be new, non-obvious, and useful.

State Street Bank prompted a rapid increase in applications for patents on business methods, particularly those involving electronic commerce operations. *See* Julia King, *Patent Examiners Pending: Tech/Business Skills Combo Needed to Handle Onslaught*, COMPUTERWORLD, Sept. 13, 1999, www.idg.net/crd_idgsearch_84983.html. Some commentators have argued that the Patent Office was unprepared for the flood, and that, as a result, it has failed properly to evaluate patent applications and has issued patents for "inventions" that are obvious and/or non-novel. Others compare the current "flood" with the early years of biotechnology patents, when the patent standards were not yet clear and a solid prior-art database had not yet been established. The PTO and patent applicants may simply be experiencing a similar period of transition. In the meantime, entrepreneurs

1. The Federal Circuit, a division of the U.S. Court of Appeals, was created in 1982 through a merger of the U.S. Court of Customs and Patent Appeals and the U.S. Court of Claims. The Federal Circuit's jurisdiction is limited to cases involving patents, claims against the United States, and certain other specialized areas of law. Its jurisdiction over such cases is exclusive of the other Circuits.

all over the country are being urged to reexamine their business practices to determine (1) whether those practices might be patentable; and (2) whether those practices have been patented by others.

I. PATENT BASICS

What does it mean to gain patent protection for a business method? A patent is a limited right, granted by the federal government, to prevent others from making, using, selling or offering to sell an invention. In other words, it is a right to exclude competitors for the term of the patent. In the United States, the granting of patents is authorized by Article 1, Section 8, Clause 8 of the Constitution, which gives Congress the power "[t]o promote the Progress of Science and useful Arts, by securing for limited Times to * * * Inventors the exclusive Right to their * * * Discoveries." In the absence of some incentive to do otherwise, inventors will choose to keep their inventions secret so as to forestall direct competition. The primary goals of the patent system are to encourage inventors to reveal their secrets to the public, and to encourage investment in the development of new inventions, by granting the inventor a temporary monopoly over the use of her inventions.

Title 35 of the U.S. Code contains the statutory basis for the patent system. Sections 101, 102, 103 and 112 are particularly important. Section 101 defines patentable subject matter as any "new and useful process, machine, manufacture or composition of matter, or any new and useful improvement thereof." 35 U.S.C. § 101. (We will be particularly interested here in the first "new and useful" subject matter identified by Section 101—the process—which is defined as a "process, art or method [including] a new use of a known process, machine, manufacture, composition of matter, or material." 35 U.S.C. § 100(b).) In contrast to copyright law, in which the first creator is the owner of the derivative work right, so that subsequent creators must get the first owner's permission for follow-on works, in patent law, new and non-obvious improvements to existing technology are patentable by the improver. This means that the owner of the original technology must get the permission of the follow-on innovator in order to practice the state of the art, and vice versa—a situation known as "blocking patents."

Section 102 explains the meaning of "new": that which was not anticipated by printed literature or a patent anywhere in the world more than one year prior to the application and any time prior to the actual "invention" date shown by the applicant; not anticipated by public use in this country more than one year prior to the application date or any time before the invention date; and not commercialized in this country more than one year prior to the application date. 35 U.S.C. § 102(a) & (b). Section 102 requires that the patent applicant be the actual inventor or inventors; a patent applied for in the name of the wrong person or from which one or more co-inventors were excluded can be invalidated. Section 103 adds a non-obviousness requirement: an invention that would have been obvious at the time of invention to a person of ordinary skill in the art to which the patent pertains is not patentable. 35 U.S.C. § 103(a).[2]

Thus, in order to receive patent protection, any business method, including Internet commerce techniques and software processes, must satisfy the basic threshold requirements for patents generally:

1. *Patentable subject matter.* The types of inventions that may be entitled to patent protection include any process, machine, manufacture, or composition of matter, as well as any improvements on such inventions. 35 U.S.C. § 101. Laws of nature, physical phenomena, and abstract ideas (including mathematical algorithms) are not patentable, although a useful process that is otherwise within patentable subject matter does not lose that status merely because it implements one of the foregoing.

2. *Utility.* The process described must be "useful"—it must have a functional purpose and must produce a concrete and tangible result. 35 U.S.C. § 101.

3. *Novelty.* The method must be "new": it must be different from what is already known, and must add something new to the prior art. 35 U.S.C. §§ 101 & 102.

4. *Non-obviousness.* The described process must not be obvious (in light of the state of the prior art) to one of ordinary skill in the art at the time of invention. 35 U.S.C. § 103.

5. *Legally sufficient disclosure.* As quid pro quo for the privilege of monopoly, the patent must describe the invention in sufficient detail so that one who is skilled in the subject matter can construct it, must describe the best mode of making and using it, and must claim the invention in a clear and distinct manner which can give notice of what is to claimed to competitors and the public. 35 U.S.C. § 112.

A patent document consist of several parts: (1) an "abstract," which briefly summarizes the invention; (2) a list of references to the "prior art"—that is, citations to publications, other patents, and other inventions, which may be relevant to establishing whether the invention meets the requirements of novelty and non-obviousness; (3) the "specification," which describes the related art and the advantages of the invention with respect to that art, provides drawings of the invention, explains how to make and use the invention, and outlines the "best mode" of using it; and (4) a set of "claims," which is technically part of the specification, but is normally set out in a separate section of the patent document. The PTO makes a complete set of patent documents available via its website, www.uspto.gov.

The claims delineate exactly what is to be covered by the exclusion right and are the operative part of the patent. Claims usually consist of a preamble, a transitional phrase, and a body that lists the elements of the

2. Outside the United States, this requirement usually goes by the name of "inventive step."

invention and how they interact. If the application is successful, those claims set the bounds of the property right. Inventions must be "definitely" claimed, that is, the nature and function of the invention must be clear and clearly delimited. 35 U.S.C.A. § 112.

Claims are especially important in questions concerning infringement and validity, when a patent will be evaluated claim by claim. That is, patents may have more than one claim, and some of them have a great many. (Often the broadest claim will be the first one, and narrower claims will be further down the list.) To be liable for patent infringement, it is enough to infringe any one of the patent's claims.

Business method patents allow the owner to prevent others from making, using, selling, or offering to sell a specific operation or set of operations for transacting business. The United States is one of the few countries in which the patentability of business methods is clearly established. In other countries, some business methods have been found patentable, while others have not. Until recently the United States excluded business methods from patentable subject matter—but the exclusion was embedded in common law rather than the Patent Act, and, as we shall see in the *State Street Bank* case, *infra*, it was not robust. Put simply, judges distinguished, at least conceptually, a system for transacting business from a specific apparatus or process for implementing that system. The former was considered to be unpatentable because more akin to an abstract mathematical principle than to a machine or mechanical process. It is possible, too, that judges believed business methods were almost all already known (not novel); if so, the digital era changed that assumption.

II. BACKGROUND: THE (FORMER) BUSINESS METHOD EXCEPTION

Prior to the Federal Circuit's holding in *State Street Bank* (discussed *infra*), most patent attorneys would have advised their clients not to apply for a patent on a pure business practice. The so-called "business methods exception" precluded patentability of business practices for most of the twentieth century.

The business methods exception made an early appearance in *Hotel Security Checking Co. v. Lorraine Co.*, 160 F. 467 (2d Cir.1908), in which the Second Circuit invalidated a patent that described an accounting system designed to prevent fraud by waiters and cashiers in restaurants and hotels. The system tracked the orders handled by different workers, allowing owners to determine whether money was missing and trace its source: "If there has been no carelessness or dishonesty, the amounts will agree and if there has been, it is easy to discover where the fault lies." *Id.* at 468.

The court held that "there is no patentable novelty either in the physical means employed or in the method described and claimed":

> Section 4886 of the Revised Statutes [the predecessor of 35 U.S.C. § 101] provides, under certain conditions, that "any person who has invented or discovered any new and useful art, machine, manufacture or composition of matter" may obtain a patent therefor. It is manifest that the subject-matter of the claims is not a machine, manufacture or composition of matter. If within the language of the statute at all, it must be as a "new and useful art." One of the definitions given by Webster of the word "art" is as follows: "The employment of means to accomplish some desired end; the adaptation of things in the natural world to the uses of life; the application of knowledge or power to practical purposes." In the sense of the patent law, an art is not a mere abstraction. A system of transacting business disconnected from the means for carrying out the system is not, within the most liberal interpretation of the term, an art. Advice is not patentable. As this court said in Fowler v. City of New York, 121 Fed. 747, 58 C.C.A. 113: "No mere abstraction, no idea, however brilliant, can be the subject of a patent irrespective of the means designed to give it effect."
>
> It cannot be maintained that the physical means described by Hicks,—the sheet and the slips,—apart from the manner of their use, present any new and useful feature. A blank sheet of paper ruled vertically and numbered at the top cannot be the subject of a patent, and, if used in carrying out a method, it can impart no more novelty thereto, than the pen and ink which are also used. In other words, if the "art" described in the specification be old, the claims cannot be upheld because of novelty in the appliances used in carrying it out,—for the reason that there is no novelty.

Id. at 469.

The *Hotel Security* court characterized business methods as abstractions rather than contributions to the progress of the useful arts. Subsequent cases built the court's observation into apparently solid doctrine. In *Berardini v. Tocci*, 200 F. 1021 (2d Cir.1912), a method of transmitting money via a set of coded telegraph messages was found unpatentable on the ground that the method was simply an advisory system for devising code messages, akin to advice on how to improve the practice of painting or baseball. *Conover v. Coe*, 99 F.2d 377 (D.C.Cir.1938), stated the theory plainly, declaring it to be "a rule of universal application that an object is not patentable where its novelty consists wholly in a method of doing business." *Id.* at 379.

The exclusion was said to apply even where the business in question was arguably "new," though this was dictum in cases where the court also held the business method to be non-novel. In *Loew's Drive-In Theatres v. Park-In Theatres*, 174 F.2d 547 (1st Cir.1949), the Court of Appeals invalidated a patent for a system of parking cars in the lot of a drive-in movie theater so as to improve patrons' view of the screen. Noting that the arrangement of cars simply adapted an ancient system for arranging seats in a theater, and was therefore neither new nor non-obvious, the Court added that "a system for the transaction of business * * * however novel, useful, or commercially successful is not patentable apart from the means for making the system practically useful." *Id.* at 552.

The business method exception was buttressed by the development of the "mental steps" doctrine. The essence of this doctrine, which still has not been entirely rejected, is that patents embrace only physical effects, rather than the mental steps leading to the effects. *See, e.g.*, *Gottschalk v. Benson*, 409 U.S. 63 (1972); *In re Abrams*, 188 F.2d 165 (C.C.P.A. 1951); *In re Shao Wen Yuan*, 188 F.2d 377 (C.C.P.A. 1951); *but see In re Musgrave*, 431 F.2d 882 (C.C.P.A. 1970). Mental steps were viewed as too abstract to be acceptable subject matter for a patent. Processes that were primarily mental and/or that involved substantial human decisionmaking in their operation were seen as too difficult to describe with the reasonable definiteness required by patent law. Furthermore, human judgment, however well-trained, was seen as a general skill rather than a specific way of achieving a predictable and useful result, and therefore unpatentable. Finally, mental activity—including mental judgments involved in many business practices—was seen as more akin to writing than to machine-building, and therefore appropriately regulated by copyright law.

III. SOFTWARE PATENTS: THE CHANGING LEGAL LANDSCAPE

The business method exception was thus apparently firmly rooted in case law. To understand how this changed, it is helpful to look first to developments in the legal treatment of software. Many business method patent applications involve computer-implemented practices, and, as we will see, it was not coincidental that the demise of the business method exception occurred as a result of litigation over a computer-related invention.

Computer technologies presented serious difficulties for courts evaluating patents, principally because in the 1960s and 70s judges viewed software "inventions" as essentially comprising mathematical formulas—abstract ideas, which are unpatentable, rather than the application of ideas toward a useful end. Thus, for example, the Supreme Court firmly rejected as inherently unpatentable a method for converting binary coded decimal ("BCD") numbers into pure binary numerals that was not limited to any particular art, technology, apparatus, or even a particular end use.

> It is conceded that one may not patent an idea. But in practical effect that would be the result if the formula for converting BCD numerals to pure binary numerals were patented in this case. The mathematical formula involved here has no substantial practical application except in connection with a digital computer, which means that if the judgment below is affirmed, the patent would wholly pre-empt the mathematical formula and in practical effect would be a patent on the algorithm itself.

Gottschalk v. Benson, 409 U.S. 63, 71–72 (1972).

The Supreme Court softened its position considerably several years later, and laid out a kind of "physical transformation" test for software patentability. The crucial case was *Diamond v. Diehr*, 450 U.S. 175 (1981), in which the Court declared patentable an industrial process that automated a rubber molding process by using a computer to calculate repetitively the mathematical equation governing how long to leave the mold closed, and to open the mold automatically when the curing was complete. The Court distinguished this process from an abstract mathematical formula or algorithm by noting that the algorithm in question was used to accomplish *physical transformation* of matter (in this case, uncured rubber).

> [W]hen a claim containing a mathematical formula implements or applies that formula in a structure or process which, when considered as a whole, is performing a function which the patent laws were designed to protect (e.g., transforming or reducing an article to a different state or thing), then the claim satisfies the requirements of § 101.

Id. at 192. In a series of subsequent decisions, the Court of Customs and Patent Appeals developed a counterpart to the physical transformation inquiry established in *Diehr*. *In re Freeman*, 573 F.2d 1237 (C.C.P.A.1978); *In re Walter*, 618 F.2d 758 (C.C.P.A.1980); *In re Abele*, 684 F.2d 902 (C.C.P.A.1982). The test has been summarized as follows: "First, the claim is analyzed to determine whether a mathematical algorithm is directly or indirectly recited. Next, if a mathematical algorithm is found, the claim as a whole is further analyzed to determine whether the algorithm is 'applied in any manner to physical elements or process steps,' and, if it is, it 'passes muster under § 101.'" *In re Pardo*, 684 F.2d 912, 915 (C.C.P.A.1982).

Some members of the Court of Appeals for the Federal Circuit were suspicious of the test, however, and those suspicions were not alleviated by the increasingly attenuated nature of the physicality requirement. In one case, a claim based primarily on an algorithm that reorganized data to produce a picture of the condition of a patient's heart on a hospital monitor was accepted as patentable on the theory that converting electrocardiograph signals into digital signals involved a physical transformation and that the conversion process began with the independent physical activity of a patient's heart function. *Arrhythmia Research Technology Inc. v. Corazonix Corp.*, 958 F.2d 1053 (Fed.Cir.1992). Two years later, a programmed computer was found to be a machine that produced a "useful concrete and tangible result," even though the program in question clearly embodied a mathematical algorithm. *In re Alappat*, 33 F.3d 1526 (Fed.Cir.1994). After *Alappat*, it appeared that a patent applicant need only show practical application of an algorithm to pass as statutory subject matter. In other words, few inventions would be deemed too abstract, by definition, to be excluded from patentability.

Yet the limits of patentability remained unclear. In 1994, a system for calculating auction bids that used simple linear math to group and regroup bids was deemed unpatentable on the theory that bids were not "physical" and, therefore, their reorganization could not involve a physical effect or transformation. *In re Schrader*, 22 F.3d 290 (Fed.Cir.1994).

Schrader brought into sharper relief the potential impact of the computing technology cases—and the erosion of the mathematical algorithm exception—on the continuing viability of the business method exception. Though the opinion turned on the physical transformation test, *Schrader*'s majority made reference to the business method exception as well, prompting a prescient dissent from Judge Newman:

> [The business method exception is] an unwarranted encumbrance to the definition of statutory subject matter in § 101, * * * that [should] be discarded as error-prone, redundant, and obsolete. It merits retirement from the glossary of § 101. * * * All of the "doing business" cases could have been decided using the clearer concepts of Title 35. Patentability does not turn on whether the claimed method does "business" instead of something else, but on whether the method, viewed as a whole, meets the requirements of patentability as set forth in §§ 102, 103, and 112 of the Patent Act.

In re Schrader, 22 F.3d at 298 (Newman, J., dissenting).

IV. THE DEMISE OF THE BUSINESS METHOD EXCEPTION

Many observers have argued, as Judge Newman suggested in her *In re Schrader* dissent, that the business methods exception, though appropriately removing commonplace or obvious business practices from the realm of patentability, unfairly penalizes inventors who devise new methods of conducting business that would otherwise meet the requirements of patentability.

Though the business methods exception generally acted as a bar to patentability, some courts declined to invalidate patents that met the novelty and non-obviousness requirements, just because the invention was a "method" related to business procedures. In *Paine, Webber, Jackson & Curtis v. Merrill Lynch, Pierce, Fenner & Smith*, 564 F.Supp. 1358 (D.Del. 1983), the court rejected Paine Webber's argument that Merrill Lynch's patent on a computer-implemented, data-processing system was "nothing more than familiar business systems, that is, the financial management of individual brokerage accounts." Instead, the court found that the patent met the threshold requirements for statutory subject matter under Section 101.

The court's reasoning carved out a niche allowing some computerized business methods to be patented, by re-articulating the mechanics of the business methods test:

> the "technological" or "useful" arts inquiry *must* focus on whether the claimed subject matter (a method of operating a machine to translate) is statutory [i.e., within patentable subject matter], not on whether the product of the claimed subject matter (a translated

> text) is statutory, not on whether the prior art which the claimed subject matter purports to replace (translation by human mind) is statutory, and *not* on whether the claimed subject matter is presently perceived to be an improvement over the prior art, e.g., whether it "enhances" the operation of a machine.

Paine, Webber v. Merrill Lynch, 564 F.Supp. at 1369 (quoting *In re Toma,* 575 F.2d 872, 877–78 (C.C.P.A.1978)). Applying this reasoning, the court held that though Merrill Lynch's financial integration method "would be unpatentable if done by hand, * * * the focus of analysis should be on the operation of the program on the computer." 564 F.Supp. at 1369. Because the method was implemented through a machine—the computer—the court held that the patent was within statutory subject matter.

Paine, Webber v. Merrill Lynch demonstrates that long before the official demise of the business methods exception in *State Street Bank,* courts were avoiding the business methods bar by treating computer-implemented business methods like any other computer-implemented invention. *State Street Bank* eliminated the need for this indirect approach to business method patents.

State Street Bank & Trust Co. v. Signature Financial Group, Inc.

149 F.3d 1368 (Fed.Cir.1998).

■ Rich, Circuit Judge.

Signature Financial Group, Inc. (Signature) appeals from the decision of the United States District Court for the District of Massachusetts granting a motion for summary judgment in favor of State Street Bank & Trust Co. (State Street), finding U.S. Patent No. 5,193,056 (the '056 patent) invalid on the ground that the claimed subject matter is not encompassed by 35 U.S.C. § 101 (1994). See *State Street Bank & Trust Co. v. Signature Financial Group, Inc.,* 927 F.Supp. 502 (D.Mass.1996). We reverse and remand because we conclude that the patent claims are directed to statutory subject matter.

BACKGROUND

Signature is the assignee of the '056 patent which is entitled "Data Processing System for Hub and Spoke Financial Services Configuration." The '056 patent issued to Signature on 9 March 1993, naming R. Todd Boes as the inventor. The '056 patent is generally directed to a data processing system (the system) for implementing an investment structure which was developed for use in Signature's business as an administrator and accounting agent for mutual funds. In essence, the system, identified by the proprietary name Hub and Spoke®, facilitates a structure whereby mutual funds (Spokes) pool their assets in an investment portfolio (Hub) organized as a partnership. This investment configuration provides the administrator of a mutual fund with the advantageous combination of economies of scale in administering investments coupled with the tax advantages of a partnership.

State Street and Signature are both in the business of acting as custodians and accounting agents for multi-tiered partnership fund financial services. State Street negotiated with Signature for a license to use its patented data processing system described and claimed in the '056 patent. When negotiations broke down, State Street brought a declaratory judgment action asserting invalidity, unenforceability, and noninfringement in Massachusetts district court, and then filed a motion for partial summary judgment of patent invalidity for failure to claim statutory subject matter under § 101. The motion was granted and this appeal followed.

DISCUSSION

* * *

The following facts pertinent to the statutory subject matter issue are either undisputed or represent the version alleged by the nonmovant. See *Anderson v. Liberty Lobby, Inc.*, 477 U.S. 242, 255 (1986). The patented invention relates generally to a system that allows an administrator to monitor and record the financial information flow and make all calculations necessary for maintaining a partner fund financial services configuration. As previously mentioned, a partner fund financial services configuration essentially allows several mutual funds, or "Spokes," to pool their investment funds into a single portfolio, or "Hub," allowing for consolidation of, inter alia, the costs of administering the fund combined with the tax advantages of a partnership. In particular, this system provides means for a daily allocation of assets for two or more Spokes that are invested in the same Hub. The system determines the percentage share that each Spoke maintains in the Hub, while taking into consideration daily changes both in the value of the Hub's investment securities and in the concomitant amount of each Spoke's assets.

In determining daily changes, the system also allows for the allocation among the Spokes of the Hub's daily income, expenses, and net realized and unrealized gain or loss, calculating each day's total investments based on the concept of a book capital account. This enables the determination of a true asset value of each Spoke and accurate calculation of allocation ratios between or among the Spokes. The system additionally tracks all the relevant data determined on a daily basis for the Hub and each Spoke, so that aggregate year end income, expenses, and capital gain or loss can be determined for accounting and for tax purposes for the Hub and, as a result, for each publicly traded Spoke.

It is essential that these calculations are quickly and accurately performed. In large part this is required because each Spoke sells shares to the public and the price of those shares is substantially based on the Spoke's percentage interest in the portfolio. In some instances, a mutual fund administrator is required to calculate the value of the shares to the nearest penny within as little as an hour and a half after the market closes. Given the complexity of the calculations, a computer or equivalent device is a virtual necessity to perform the task.

* * *

* * * [C]laim 1, properly construed, claims a machine, namely, a data processing system for managing a financial services configuration of a portfolio established as a partnership * * *. A "machine" is proper statutory subject matter under § 101. We note that, for the purposes of a § 101 analysis, it is of little relevance whether claim 1 is directed to a "machine" or a "process," as long as it falls within at least one of the four enumerated categories of patentable subject matter, "machine" and "process" being such categories.

This does not end our analysis, however, because the court concluded that the claimed subject matter fell into one of two alternative judicially-created exceptions to statutory subject matter. The court refers to the first exception as the "mathematical algorithm" exception and the second exception as the "business method" exception. Section 101 reads:

> Whoever invents or discovers any new and useful process, machine, manufacture, or composition of matter, or any new and useful improvement thereof, may obtain a patent therefor, subject to the conditions and requirements of this title.

The plain and unambiguous meaning of § 101 is that any invention falling within one of the four stated categories of statutory subject matter may be patented, provided it meets the other requirements for patentability set forth in Title 35, i.e., those found in §§ 102, 103, and 112, ¶ 2.

The repetitive use of the expansive term "any" in § 101 shows Congress's intent not to place any restrictions on the subject matter for which a patent may be obtained beyond those specifically recited in § 101. Indeed, the Supreme Court has acknowledged that Congress intended § 101 to extend to "anything under the sun that is made by man." *Diamond v. Chakrabarty,* 447 U.S. 303, 309 (1980); *see also Diamond v. Diehr*, 450 U.S. 175, 182 (1981). Thus, it is improper to read limitations into § 101 on the subject matter that may be patented where the legislative history indicates that Congress clearly did not intend such limitations. See *Chakrabarty*, 447 U.S. at 308 ("We have also cautioned that courts 'should not read into the patent laws limitations and conditions which the legislature has not expressed.' " (citations omitted)).

The "Mathematical Algorithm" Exception

The Supreme Court has identified three categories of subject matter that are unpatentable, namely "laws of nature, natural phenomena, and abstract ideas." *Diehr*, 450 U.S. at 185. Of particular relevance to this case, the Court has held that mathematical algorithms are not patentable subject matter to the extent that they are merely abstract ideas. See *Diehr*, 450 U.S. 175, passim; *Parker v. Flook*, 437 U.S. 584 (1978); Gottschalk v. Benson, 409 U.S. 63 (1972). In Diehr, the Court explained that certain types of mathematical subject matter, standing alone, represent nothing more than abstract ideas until reduced to some type of practical application, i.e., "a useful, concrete and tangible result." *Alappat*, 33 F.3d at 1544.[4]

Unpatentable mathematical algorithms are identifiable by showing they are merely abstract ideas constituting disembodied concepts or truths that are not "useful." From a practical standpoint, this means that to be patentable an algorithm must be applied in a "useful" way. In *Alappat*, we held that data, transformed by a machine through a series of mathematical calculations to produce a smooth waveform display on a rasterizer monitor, constituted a practical application of an abstract idea (a mathematical algorithm, formula, or calculation), because it produced "a useful, concrete and tangible result"—the smooth waveform.

Similarly, in *Arrhythmia Research Technology Inc. v. Corazonix Corp.*, 958 F.2d 1053 (Fed.Cir.1992), we held that the transformation of electrocardiograph signals from a patient's heartbeat by a machine through a series of mathematical calculations constituted a practical application of an abstract idea (a mathematical algorithm, formula, or calculation), because it corresponded to a useful, concrete or tangible thing—the condition of a patient's heart.

Today, we hold that the transformation of data, representing discrete dollar amounts, by a machine through a series of mathematical calculations into a final share price, constitutes a practical application of a mathematical algorithm, formula, or calculation, because it produces "a useful, concrete and tangible result"—a final share price momentarily fixed for recording and reporting purposes and even accepted and relied upon by regulatory authorities and in subsequent trades.

The district court erred by applying the *Freeman–Walter–Abele* test to determine whether the claimed subject matter was an unpatentable abstract idea. The *Freeman–Walter–Abele* test was designed by the Court of Customs and Patent Appeals, and subsequently adopted by this court, to extract and identify unpatentable mathematical algorithms in the aftermath of *Benson* and *Flook*. See *In re Freeman*, 573 F.2d 1237 (CCPA 1978) as modified by *In re Walter*, 618 F.2d 758 (CCPA 1980). The test has been thus articulated:

> First, the claim is analyzed to determine whether a mathematical algorithm is directly or indirectly recited. Next, if a mathematical algorithm is found, the claim as a whole is further analyzed to determine whether the algorithm is "applied in any manner to physical elements or process steps," and, if it is, it "passes muster under § 101."

In re Pardo, 684 F.2d 912, 915 (CCPA 1982) (citing *In re Abele*, 684 F.2d 902 (CCPA 1982)).

4. This has come to be known as the mathematical algorithm exception. This designation has led to some confusion, especially given the *Freeman–Walter–Abele* analysis. By keeping in mind that the mathematical algorithm is unpatentable only to the extent that it represents an abstract idea, this confusion may be ameliorated.

After *Diehr* and *Chakrabarty*, the *Freeman–Walter–Abele* test has little, if any, applicability to determining the presence of statutory subject matter. As we pointed out in *Alappat*, 33 F.3d at 1543, application of the test could be misleading, because a process, machine, manufacture, or composition of matter employing a law of nature, natural phenomenon, or abstract idea is patentable subject matter even though a law of nature, natural phenomenon, or abstract idea would not, by itself, be entitled to such protection. The test determines the presence of, for example, an algorithm. Under *Benson*, this may have been a sufficient indicium of nonstatutory subject matter. However, after *Diehr* and *Alappat*, the mere fact that a claimed invention involves inputting numbers, calculating numbers, outputting numbers, and storing numbers, in and of itself, would not render it nonstatutory subject matter, unless, of course, its operation does not produce a "useful, concrete and tangible result." *Alappat*, 33 F.3d at 1544. After all, as we have repeatedly stated,

> every step-by-step process, be it electronic or chemical or mechanical, involves an algorithm in the broad sense of the term. Since § 101 expressly includes processes as a category of inventions which may be patented and § 100(b) further defines the word "process" as meaning "process, art or method, and includes a new use of a known process, machine, manufacture, composition of matter, or material," it follows that it is no ground for holding a claim is directed to nonstatutory subject matter to say it includes or is directed to an algorithm. This is why the proscription against patenting has been limited to mathematical algorithms....

In re Iwahashi, 888 F.2d 1370, 1374 (Fed.Cir.1989) (emphasis in the original).

The question of whether a claim encompasses statutory subject matter should not focus on which of the four categories of subject matter a claim is directed to—process, machine, manufacture, or composition of matter—but rather on the essential characteristics of the subject matter, in particular, its practical utility. Section 101 specifies that statutory subject matter must also satisfy the other "conditions and requirements" of Title 35, including novelty, nonobviousness, and adequacy of disclosure and notice. See *In re Warmerdam*, 33 F.3d 1354, 1359, (Fed.Cir.1994). For purpose of our analysis, as noted above, claim 1 is directed to a machine programmed with the Hub and Spoke software and admittedly produces a "useful, concrete, and tangible result." *Alappat*, 33 F.3d at 1544. This renders it statutory subject matter, even if the useful result is expressed in numbers, such as price, profit, percentage, cost, or loss.

The Business Method Exception

As an alternative ground for invalidating the '056 patent under § 101, the court relied on the judicially-created, so-called "business method" exception to statutory subject matter. We take this opportunity to lay this ill-conceived exception to rest. Since its inception, the "business method" exception has merely represented the application of some general, but no longer applicable legal principle, perhaps arising out of the "requirement for invention"—which was eliminated by § 103. Since the 1952 Patent Act, business methods have been, and should have been, subject to the same legal requirements for patentability as applied to any other process or method.

The business method exception has never been invoked by this court, or the CCPA, to deem an invention unpatentable. Application of this particular exception has always been preceded by a ruling based on some clearer concept of Title 35 or, more commonly, application of the abstract idea exception based on finding a mathematical algorithm. Illustrative is the CCPA's analysis in *In re Howard*, 394 F.2d 869 (CCPA 1968), wherein the court affirmed the Board of Appeals' rejection of the claims for lack of novelty and found it unnecessary to reach the Board's § 101 ground that a method of doing business is "inherently unpatentable." 394 F.2d at 872.

Similarly, *In re Schrader*, 22 F.3d 290 (Fed.Cir.1994), while making reference to the business method exception, turned on the fact that the claims implicitly recited an abstract idea in the form of a mathematical algorithm and there was no "transformation or conversion of subject matter representative of or constituting physical activity or objects." 22 F.3d at 294 (emphasis omitted).[13]

* * *

Even the case frequently cited as establishing the business method exception to statutory subject matter, *Hotel Security Checking Co. v. Lorraine Co.*, 160 F. 467 (2d Cir.1908), did not rely on the exception to strike the patent. In that case, the patent was found invalid for lack of novelty and "invention," not because it was improper subject matter for a patent. The court stated "the fundamental principle of the system is as old as the art of bookkeeping, i.e., charging the goods of the employer to the agent who takes them." *Id.* at 469. "If at the time of [the patent] application, there had been no system of bookkeeping of any kind in restaurants, we would be confronted with the question whether a new and useful system of cash registering and account checking is such an art as is patentable under the statute." *Id.* at 472.

This case is no exception. The district court announced the precepts of the business method exception as set forth in several treatises, but noted as its primary reason for finding the patent invalid under the business method exception as follows:

> If Signature's invention were patentable, any financial institution desirous of implementing a multi-tiered funding complex modelled (sic) on a Hub and Spoke configuration would be required to seek Signature's permission before embarking on such a project. *This is so because the '056 Patent is claimed [sic] sufficiently broadly to*

13. Any historical distinctions between a method of "doing" business and the means of carrying it out blur in the complexity of modern business systems. See *Paine, Webber, Jackson & Curtis v. Merrill Lynch*, 564 F.Supp. 1358 (D.Del.1983), (holding a computerized system of cash management was held to be statutory subject matter.)

> *foreclose virtually any computer-implemented accounting method necessary to manage this type of financial structure.*

927 F.Supp. 502, 516 (emphasis added). Whether the patent's claims are too broad to be patentable is not to be judged under § 101, but rather under §§ 102, 103 and 112. Assuming the above statement to be correct, it has nothing to do with whether what is claimed is statutory subject matter.

In view of this background, it comes as no surprise that in the most recent edition of the Manual of Patent Examining Procedures (MPEP) (1996), a paragraph of § 706.03(a) was deleted. In past editions it read:

> Though seemingly within the category of process or method, a method of doing business can be rejected as not being within the statutory classes. See *Hotel Security Checking Co. v. Lorraine Co.*, 160 F. 467 (2d Cir. 1908) and *In re Wait*, 73 F.2d 982, 22 C.C.P.A. 822 (1934).

MPEP § 706.03(a) (1994). This acknowledgment is buttressed by the U.S. Patent and Trademark 1996 Examination Guidelines for Computer Related Inventions which now read:

> Office personnel have had difficulty in properly treating claims directed to methods of doing business. Claims should not be categorized as methods of doing business. Instead such claims should be treated like any other process claims.

Examination Guidelines, 61 Fed. Reg. 7478, 7479 (1996). We agree that this is precisely the manner in which this type of claim should be treated. Whether the claims are directed to subject matter within § 101 should not turn on whether the claimed subject matter does "business" instead of something else.

CONCLUSION

The appealed decision is reversed and the case is remanded to the district court for further proceedings consistent with this opinion.

NOTES & QUESTIONS

1. *Limited to computer-related inventions?* State Street's patent application claimed a computer-related invention, and some commentators have characterized the Federal Circuit opinion as accepting only computer-related business methods as statutory (i.e., patentable) subject matter. Do you agree that the decision should be so interpreted? Or does the decision mean that any business method is potentially patentable?

2. *The mathematical algorithm exception.* The "tangibility" or "physicality" dimensions of the transformation inquiry, were largely abandoned in *State Street Bank*. The question whether a claim comprises statutory subject matter, the Federal Circuit insisted, should focus simply on the "practical utility" of the claim, or whether it produced a concrete, tangible and useful result. Numbers were concrete enough to "count" as such a result. What meaning is left for the word "tangible"?

The view that a numerical output can be concrete, tangible and useful was affirmed shortly thereafter, in *AT & T v. Excel Communications, Inc.*, 172 F.3d 1352 (Fed.Cir.1999), which concerned a patent on a process for transmitting billing information relating to long-distance telephone calls. The district court had found AT & T's patent to be invalid because, as a mathematical algorithm, it failed to satisfy the statutory subject matter requirements: "The court was of the view that the only physical step in the claims involves data-gathering for the algorithm. Though the court recognized that the claims require the use of switches and computers, it nevertheless concluded that use of such facilities to perform a non-substantive change in the data's format could not serve to convert non-patentable subject matter into patentable subject matter." *Id.* at 1355.

The Federal Circuit reversed, explaining that the statutory subject matter requirements were intended to exclude only "laws of nature, natural phenomena, and abstract ideas," and sharply narrowed the mathematical algorithm exception to "mathematical algorithms in the abstract." *Id.* at 1356. Further, the court interpreted *Diamond v. Diehr* as holding that "even though a mathematical algorithm is not patentable in isolation, a process that applies an equation to a new and useful end 'is at the very least not barred at the threshold by 101.' " *Id.* at 1357 (quoting *Diamond v. Diehr*, 450 U.S. at 188).

In sum, the court explicitly limited the previous "mathematical algorithm exception" to a simple inquiry of patentability: whether "the claimed subject matter as a whole is a disembodied mathematical concept representing nothing more than a 'law of nature' or an 'abstract idea,' or if the mathematical concept has been reduced to some practical application rendering it 'useful.' " *Id.* at 1357.

Applying this criterion, the Federal Circuit found that AT & T's invention fell within the purview of Section 101 statutory requirements, and reversed the holding of the district court:

> Excel argues that method claims containing mathematical algorithms are patentable subject matter only if there is a "physical transformation" or conversion of subject matter from one state into another. The physical transformation language appears in *Diehr*, *see* 450 U.S. at 184 ("That respondents' claims involve the transformation of an article, in this case raw, uncured synthetic rubber, into a different state or thing cannot be disputed."), and has been echoed by this court in *Schrader*, 22 F.3d at 294, ("Therefore, we do not find in the claim any kind of data transformation.").
>
> The notion of "physical transformation" can be misunderstood. In the first place, it is not an invariable requirement, but merely one example of how a mathematical algorithm may bring about a useful application. As the Supreme Court itself noted, "when [a claimed invention] is performing a function which the patent laws were designed to protect (e.g., transforming or reduc-

> ing an article to a different state or thing), then the claim satisfies the requirements of § 101."

172 F.3d at 1358–59. Indeed, as a Federal Circuit judge remarked a few months later: "We have come a long way from the days when judges frowned on patents as pernicious monopolies deserving scant regard. Today, patents are the backbone of much of the national economy, and, as this court has recently held, virtually anything is patentable." *Hughes Aircraft v. United States*, 148 F.3d 1384, 1385 (Fed.Cir.1998) (Clevenger, J., dissenting).

A. THE PRIOR-USER DEFENSE

In the wake of the *State Street Bank* decision, entrepreneurs in many fields expressed concern that they might have to pay license fees for the right to continue engaging in longstanding business practices, simply because they had not sought patent protection for those practices and somebody else had. The fact that a user of a practice had invented it independently would not be a defense in a patent infringement suit, unless the defendant were able to show that the patent must be invalidated. Entrepreneurs were concerned that an attempt to invalidate a competitor's patent on the basis of prior invention might not succeed if the patentee could prove that he was in fact first to reduce the method to practice; and where the prior user had been keeping the method secret, an attempt to invalidate the patent based upon prior public use might fail. Responding to these concerns, Congress enacted the First Inventor Defense Act of 1999, Pub. L. No. 106–113, 113 Stat. 1501A–555 (1999), which added Section 273 to Title 35. Section 273 provides:

> It shall be a defense to an action for infringement under section 271 of this title with respect to any subject matter that would otherwise infringe one or more claims for a method in the patent being asserted against a person, if such person had, acting in good faith, actually reduced the subject matter to practice at least 1 year before the effective filing date of such patent, and commercially used the subject matter before the effective filing date of such patent.

35 U.S.C. § 273(b)(1).

Although this provision grants prior user rights for "a method," the statute defines "method" as "a method of doing or conducting business." 35 U.S.C. § 273(a)(3).

A House Report on the bill noted that it would be "administratively and economically impossible to expect any inventor to apply for a patent on all business methods and processes now deemed patentable." H.R. REP. NO. 106–287, at 45 (1999). The person asserting the defense must prove its applicability by clear and convincing evidence. 35 U.S.C. § 273(b)(4). If the defense is asserted unsuccessfully, and the person asserting it is found not to have had a "reasonable basis" for asserting it, the defendant is liable for the plaintiff's attorney's fees. 35 U.S.C. § 273(b)(8).

To understand how the prior-user exception can be expected to work, and to appreciate its limitations, consider the following hypothetical and discussion:

> Take the example of Bugs Bunny and Yosemite Sam. Bugs invented a method of systematically marketing carrots (and other roots) via the Rabbitnet (a network of computer networks), and filed for a patent on his "carrot pushing" method on January 15, 1998. Sam, a bitter competitor of Bugs, markets various roots (including carrots) using the same method. When precisely Sam started doing so is clouded in some mystery. The only thing Bugs knows for sure is that whenever he asks Sam to purchase a license on the carrot pushing technology, he is treated to all manner of verbal abuse.
>
> Bugs receives his patent on January 18, 2000 and promptly sues Sam for patent infringement. Sam insists that he was pushing carrots via the Rabbitnet when Bugs was in diapers. How does Sam turn that tough talk into a viable defense?
>
> First, Sam must prove that he was *actually commercially exploiting* the patented method before Bugs filed his application in the Patent Office. Second, Sam must prove that he reduced the patented method to practice * * * at least one year before Bugs' filing date at the Patent Office. The real kicker is that Sam has to prove these things by evidence that meets the high standard of "clear and convincing." This elevated standard is an explicit requirement in the new law. Although Congress created a loophole, they didn't want it to be an easy one to wiggle through.
>
> Can Sam squeeze through this loophole? He has to put on testimony about events that happened over three years ago, and he needs to corroborate that testimony with objective evidence such as paper documents. That corroborating evidence is critical to meeting the clear and convincing standard, and it may not be available after such a long time, assuming that it ever existed in the first place.
>
> The worst case for Bugs is that Sam convinces the judge that he truly was a prior user. This is not the end of the world for Bugs' carrot business. Successfully proving oneself to be a prior user does not invalidate the patent, so Bugs still has his patent. He can still enforce it against other people besides Sam. Although Sam gets a free license to infringe at will, Sam is boxed in and cannot improve on his method in any way that would take advantage of any improvements that Bugs patented. Essentially, Sam's business is frozen in the form it was when Bugs filed his patent application. Even worse for Sam is that he cannot practice his rights at any sites other than the ones he was using on the day Bugs filed his patent application. And, Sam cannot sell his prior user rights; they have no market value in theory.

> Suddenly Sam doesn't sound like such a big winner. Sure he gets to stay in business, but the growth of his business is permanently hobbled. And slow growth is death for a Rabbitnet business.
>
> Let's take a look at the downside for Sam if the judge rules against him on his prior user rights defense: Sam has already *admitted* he is an infringer! Bugs doesn't have to prove this element, because Sam shot off his mouth. Unless Sam can scrape up some evidence for another defense (insanity?) he is doomed.
>
> In all seriousness, the practical effect of this new wrinkle in the law is that, in rare cases where an infringer has credible evidence that they can fit through the prior user loophole, it will promote early settlement of the lawsuit. This defense increases risks for both sides, and will motivate them to think twice before going to trial.

Kevin L. Pontius, *Prior User Rights In Business Methods*, www.viennapat.com/newsletter/vol4iss1/prioruserrightsinbusinessmethods.htm.

NOTES & QUESTIONS

1. *Limitation to business methods*. The prior-user defense is limited to business method patents. Is there a convincing reason not to extend the defense to other types of patents? Proponents of the defense have argued that it is particularly necessary in this field, where the PTO has had difficulty sorting out what is patentable and what is not. It is also arguably more difficult for prospective inventors and PTO examiners to search for relevant prior art, because a comprehensive body of prior art does not exist and prior uses may not even be documented. Business methods may be more frequently wholly "internal" to a business's operations than other processes it uses in manufacturing or marketing its products—or so it might be argued. Might a better solution be to go to the root of the problem—the Patent Office—and formulate more rigorous standards for determining patentability? While prior user rights might help resolve some of the unique problems presented by business method patents in the short-run, what effect might they have on the patent system in the long run?

2. *What exactly is a method of doing business*? What criteria should the courts use in determining whether a given method used in commerce is or is not a "method of doing business" for purposes of granting or withholding prior user rights?

3. *Patents vs. trade secrets*. Some prior users may have elected trade secrecy for their business methods because they did not realize, prior to *State Street Bank*, that such processes could be patented. When a developer of an innovative method chooses trade secrecy, it assumes the risk that someone else may obtain a patent on the method, just as it assumes the risk that the secret will leak out and be lost. The coexistence of patent (federal law) and trade secret (state law) rests partly on the fact that trade secrecy is fragile. By giving a defense to prior users of business methods who choose trade secrecy, even after *State Street Bank* made it clear that a patent may be available, has Congress undermined the balance between patent and trade secret law? *See* James R. Barney, *The Prior User Defense: A Reprieve for Trade Secret Owners or a Disaster for the Patent Law?*, 82 J. PAT. & TRADEMARK OFF. SOC'Y 261 (2000).

B. THE IMPACT OF *STATE STREET BANK* ON THE PATENT AND TRADEMARK OFFICE AND ON THE PATENT SYSTEM AS A WHOLE

Many commentators have argued that the blitz of patent applications on computer-related inventions starting in the 1970s caught the PTO unprepared—without examiners trained in computer science, without the resources to research thoroughly whether the claimed invention was original. Hence, these commentators believe that there are a large number of patents on computer-related inventions whose validity is questionable. Once it became well known that repetitive calculations are better performed by a computer, should an invention that consists of inserting a computer into a process where repetitive calculations are needed count as non-obvious?

Since the early 1990s, the number of patent examiners has increased dramatically, and the PTO reports that the bulk of new examiners are assigned to computer technologies and biotechnologies. Yet the PTO's 2000 Corporate Plan anticipates "continuing recruitment difficulties" due to budget shortfalls and competition from private industry for qualified examiners. Q. Todd Dickinson, Remarks at the American Bar Association's Summer IPL Conference (June 23, 2000), www.uspto.gov/web/offices/speches/speeches.html; USPTO Corporate Plan—FY 2001, Executive Summary at 19.

Much of the criticism of the *State Street Bank* decision and business method patents in general has centered on the problem of patent quality and prior art. Patent examiners look closely at relevant publications (including scholarly articles, issued patents, and other printed materials) to see whether an invention is either non-novel or obvious. The ability of patent examiners to conduct such a search may be hampered in the case of business method applications. Professor Rochelle Cooper Dreyfuss summarizes the problem.

> First, because business methods have not been patented in the past, there is very little patent-related prior art readily at hand to the examiner corps. More important, because knowledge about business methods resides mainly in the practices and policies of the firms that use them, even common methods may not be documented in the sorts of materials that examiners can efficiently consult. Unless these difficulties are taken care of—and it is hard to see how the latter can ever be dealt with effectively—invalid patents will inevitably issue.

Rochelle Cooper Dreyfuss, *Are Business Method Patents Bad For Business?*, 16 SANTA CLARA COMPUTER & HIGH TECH. L.J. 263, 269 (2000).

Other commentators concede the point, but note that similar complaints were advanced with respect to biotechnology patent applications in the early 1980s, until the PTO built up a good database of prior art and gained greater evaluative experience. *See, e.g.*, Robert Merges, *As Many as Six Impossible Patents Before Breakfast: Property Rights for Business Concepts and Patent System Reform*, 14 BERKELEY TECH. L.J. 577, 589 (1999). If business method patents are similarly in a transition period, patent quality will soon improve. Are there qualitative differences between biotechnological research and business method development that might undermine this "transition" analogy? Consider the following analysis, also from Professor Dreyfuss.

> One could dismiss the problem of invalid patents as ephemeral—if a patent covers a business method that is really important, it will be challenged and invalidated. But while the potential for successful challenge is certainly real, it is not clear that it is an adequate solution. After all, patents have in terrorem effects: no one wants to invest in a business that cannot succeed without first winning a lawsuit. Moreover, much can happen during the transition period between allowance and invalidation. For example, many industries experience shake outs. These have the beneficial effect of culling out those firms that are the least competent. But to some extent, business method patents protect businesses from competition. Thus, they can function in a way that preserves inefficiencies in the marketplace.
>
> In some fields, there is another, more enduring, problem[:] * * * lock in. Consider, for example, Amazon.com's patented one-click technology, which has been enforced against BarnesandNoble.com.[3] One click is very nice for shoppers because once they have inputted various bits of shipping and billing information, they can check out quickly on subsequent visits. Accordingly, if Amazon has the exclusive right to one-click, we can expect that many customers will patronize its site. What happens if the patent is eventually invalidated—will there then be effective competition? Probably not because once a book buyer has entered information at Amazon, there is no reason to go elsewhere, particularly now that Amazon has the capacity to further analyze the information and offer its patrons useful suggestions about future purchases. Buyers who rely on such services will not care if the patent is invalidated, and rival sites are permitted to utilize one-click: once locked in to Amazon, shoppers will not likely visit a site that is less informative and requires more work.
>
> Another way to make customers stick is with network effects. An example of a network effect is AOL's instant messenger. A user's ability to exchange e-mail in real time is useful only when

3. [The district court's preliminary injunction enforcing the patent against Barnesandnoble.com was overturned on appeal, and the parties subsequently settled. The case is discussed and excerpted in Part VI, *infra*.—Eds.]

the people the user wishes to reach are also on the same system. As a result, the value of the system as a whole depends directly on its size. I do not know whether AOL has protected its system with a patent, but if it has, then instant messenger is a good example of the problem with relying on invalidation. The reason is this: if there were such a patent, it would be extremely significant because it would force everyone interested in instant messenger to sign up with AOL. But once a large (and valuable) network is created, invalidation will not matter at all. True, rivals would appear, but because they would necessarily start small, they would not be able to deliver the same value to their customers. The bottom line is thus a terrible transition problem: patents do not need to be in force for long to exert a substantial effect on competition.

Dreyfuss, *supra*, 16 SANTA CLARA COMPUTER & HIGH TECH. L.J. at 270–272.

Several commentators have argued that even valid business method patents are unnecessary to encourage innovation.

> [T]he broad grant of patent protection for methods of doing business is something of a square peg in a sinkhole of uncertain dimensions. Nowhere in the substantial literature on innovation is there a statement that the United States economy suffers from a lack of innovation in methods of doing business. Compared with the business practices of comparable economies we seem to be innovators in distribution and in the service industries. By the casual empiricism of counting the number of graduate business schools, the United States is ahead of other developed economies. This datum, plus the substantial enrollment of foreign students in the graduate schools of business in the United States, permits the inference that business methods in this country as presently practiced, are considered innovative and attractive, despite the prior absence of patent protection.
>
> There is, moreover, substantial anecdotal evidence that competition alone serves as a sufficient spur to innovation in business methods. The rapid cluster of development in the following businesses casts doubt on the need for the added incentive of patents. Consider the growth of fast food restaurants, self-service gasoline stations, quick oil change facilities, supermarkets for food and office supplies, automatic teller devices and other banking services, electronic fund transfers, supplemental insurance for physician services, and alternatives for long-distance telephone services. To the argument that the economy of the United States would function even better with such patent protection, the model casts doubt. The case for broad patent protection, plausible as a matter of theory, has been qualified by the historical/empirical studies of industries in which there had been broad patent protection.
>
> Moreover, conceding the possibility of free-riding as well as outright piracy of business methods, the absence of patent protection would not leave a total void of legal remedies. There are a

> variety of federal and state alternative regimes of protection. Copyright, misappropriation, unfair competition, and deceptive practices statutes may serve as alternative means of protection. These regimes may serve to furnish the incentive of protection as well as a means of redress against "dirty tricks" by competitors.

Leo J. Raskind, *The State Street Bank Decision: The Bad Business of Unlimited Patent Protection for Methods of Doing Business*, 10 FORDHAM I. P., MEDIA & ENT. L.J. 61, 92–93 (1999).

Some commentators have hinted that the problems created by trying to apply business method patents to the Internet might be impossible to resolve—and that the Internet would be best served if allowed to develop freely (at least for the time being) without the competitive impediment of patent monopolies. Will the desire to encourage technological development in cyberspace be better served by allowing or not allowing patent protection? Considering the traditional reliance on patents to encourage innovation, could limiting or even eliminating patent protection on the Internet actually lead to *more* innovation? Here is one view.

> A patent is a form of regulation. It is a government-granted monopoly—an exclusive right backed by the power of the state. This monopoly is granted by a bureaucrat—a well-meaning, hard-working bureaucrat no doubt, but a bureaucrat nonetheless. This government employee decides whether an idea is novel, useful and nonobvious. If it is, the government guarantees the inventor an exclusive right to the idea for 20 years. Last year, some 150,000 such exclusive rights were granted, up one-third from the year before.
>
> No doubt we are better off with a patent system than without one. Lots of research and invention wouldn't occur without the government's protection. But just because some protection is good, more isn't necessarily better. Especially in cyberspace.
>
> There is growing skepticism among academics about whether such state-imposed monopolies help a rapidly evolving market such as the Internet. What is "novel," "nonobvious" or "useful" is hard enough to know in a relatively stable field. In a transforming market, it's nearly impossible for anyone—let alone an underpaid worker in the U.S. Department of Commerce who spends on average of eight hours evaluating the prior art in a patent and gets paid based on how many he processes—to identify what's "novel." Costly mistakes get made. On average it takes $1.2 million to challenge the validity of a patent, which means it is often cheaper simply to pay the royalties than to establish that the patent isn't deserved.
>
> "Bad patents" thus become the space debris of cyberspace. Nowhere is this clearer than in the context of business-method patents. At a recent conference in Israel, I watched as a lawyer terrified the assembled crowd of Internet startups with stories of

the increasing number of business-method patents that now haunt Internet space. Patent No. 5,715,314, for example, gives the holder a monopoly over "network-based sales systems"—we call that e-commerce. Patent No. 5,797,127 forms the basis for Priceline.com and effectively blocks any competitor. Patent No. 4,949,257 covers the purchase of software over a network.

To West Coast coders, it seems bizarre that East Coast coders—the Patent Office—consider these ideas nonobvious. But the real problem is the incentives such a system creates. Awarding patents of that type siphons off resources from technologists to lawyers—from people making real products to people applying for regulatory privilege and protection. An increasingly significant cost of Net startups involves both defensive and offensive lawyering—making sure you don't "steal" someone else's "idea" and quickly claiming as yours every "idea" you can describe in a patent application.

But this is absurd. When the world was given TCP/IP and the collection of protocols it induced, a billion ideas became obvious to anyone who took the time to think. These were not ideas that were discovered because some lone inventor spent years toiling away in his basement, but because TCP/IP was a language with which practically anything could be done. And with very little promise of protection by government, lots was done. The Internet revolution was born long before lawyers arrived on the scene.

Lawrence Lessig, *The Problem with Patents*, THE INDUSTRY STANDARD, Apr. 23, 1999, www.thestandard.com/article/display/0,1151,4296,00.html.

NOTES & QUESTIONS

1. *Software patents problematic*? Other than the courts' outmoded concerns with the metaphysics of patentable subject matter, which ended with *State Street Bank*, there are at least two reasons why software patents are a troubled area of patent law: (1) the fact that most software developments lose their value in a short time, so that the time it takes to get a patent may exhaust the invention's value; (2) the overlap in protection between patent law and copyright law.

Software became protectible under copyright law in the 1970s when the courts were refusing patent protection. Under copyright law, computer code—both source and object code—is protectible as a literary work. In addition, the structural elements of a computer program, if found to constitute "expression" rather than "ideas," can be copyrighted. It is arguable that patent and copyright were meant to be mutually exclusive, and that this situation is anomalous. Professor Radin argues that this anomaly is symptomatic of a broader breakdown of the distinction between text and machine:

> Computer programs are both text and machine. They are text when considered as code statements, they are machines when considered as devices for accomplishing a task. Copyright law reflects the text perspective (programs are considered literary works); patent law reflects the machine perspective (a programmed computer is a "new machine"). The fact that computer programs are both copyrightable and patentable is anomalous for intellectual property law. Copyright is supposed to exclude works that are functional; patent is supposed to focus on functionality and exclude texts. Computer programs are the only large area covered both by patent and copyright. This anomaly is obscured to some extent by the fact that copyright and patent regard programs differently: patent focuses on the protocol for accomplishing the task, however the programmer chooses to code it, whereas copyright focuses on the code statements, but also their structure, sequence and organization. The difference between structure, sequence and organization (copyrightable) and useful algorithm, protocol or method (patentable) is, however, conceptually difficult to maintain. This difficulty reflects the fact that computer programs can be understood either as text or machine. Those who write code sometimes genuinely feel that it is their speech and should be protected by the First Amendment. At the same time, it is clear that the primary *raison d'etre* for programs is their technological function, their ability to accomplish a task.

Margaret Jane Radin, *Online Standardization and the Integration of Text and Machine*, 70 FORDHAM L. REV. 1125, 1143–44 (2002).

Had software not been brought within the protection of copyright law, perhaps Congress would have enacted a new form of protection particularly suited to software, perhaps less onerous to apply for and of shorter duration than patents. Commentators argued at the time for such *sui generis* protection, but their arguments did not convince policy makers. *See, e.g.*, Pamela Samuelson, Randall Davis, Mitchell D. Kapor & J.H. Reichman, *A Manifesto Concerning the Legal Protection of Computer Programs*, 94 COLUM. L. REV. 2308 (1994).

2. *Availability of prior art.* Is Professor Dreyfuss correct to see little hope of effectively addressing the problem that prior art may reside in the heads of managers rather than the pages of any accessible publication? Would the proliferation of business method patents, perhaps ironically, help resolve the difficulty she identifies?

3. *Improving the system.* Commentators have advanced several proposals aimed at remedying the perceived flaws in the business method patent application examination process. Which of the following strategies would best answer the criticisms advanced above? Would some be harder to implement than others? What reforms would you suggest?

a. *Reforming the PTO.* Professor Robert Merges has proposed a series of changes in PTO examination procedures to improve patent quality. These include: (1) subcontracting patent examination and search procedures to outside firms that can conduct more comprehensive, efficient searches focusing on specific technologies and/or industries; (2) raising pay and benefits to encourage senior examiners to remain with the office and train new examiners; (3) restructuring the examiner bonus system, which may now encourage examiners to issue more patents and thereby raise their case completion rate, by introducing "error" tracking systems; and (4) revamping the reexamination system to allow more participation by interested third parties and to allow third parties to appeal adverse reexamination decisions. *See* Robert Merges, *As Many as Six Impossible Patents Before Breakfast: Property Rights for Business Concepts and Patent System Reform*, 14 BERKELEY TECH. L.J. 577 (1999). For an argument that putting more resources into the patent-examining process would be inefficient, see Mark A. Lemley, *Rational Ignorance at the Patent Office*, 95 NW. U. L. REV. 1495 (2001).

b. *An opposition procedure*. Many countries allow interested members of the public to file oppositions to a patent during a designated period of time. In 1999 Congress amended the Patent Act to implement such a procedure, called "inter partes reexamination." Optional Inter Partes Reexamination Procedure Act of 1999, Pub. L. No. 106–113, 113 Stat. 1501A–567 (1999), 35 U.S.C. §§ 311–18. Under this procedure, any person may at any time bring to the attention of the PTO prior art that may be relevant to a patent, and may request reexamination of the patent. If the PTO determines that the request raises a substantial new question concerning validity of the patent, it must open a reexamination of the patent. Both the person requesting reexamination and the patentee are entitled to participate in the reexamination. Reexamination may lead to invalidation of the patent. 35 U.S.C. §§ 311–18. Does this procedure address the concerns about patent quality? The procedure has so far been infrequently invoked. According to the PTO Director, as of October 24, 2000, no one had chosen to take advantage of the new reexamination procedures with respect to a business method patent.

c. *A bounty system*. Professor John R. Thomas argues that the patent system needs bounty hunters. One of the basic assumptions of the patent system is that the validity of patents will be checked by private parties. According to this assumption, a competitor that wishes to use a patented invention, and believes the patent to be invalid, will ignore it; if the patentee seeks to bring an infringement action, she will lose because the competitor will be able to show the invention in question is obvious or non-novel. But this basic assumption may ignore the reality that competitors may decide the costs or risks of litigation are too high. Thomas suggests, therefore, the development of a kind of private bounty system that would reward persons who can show a patent to be invalid. Because the bounty would be paid by the patent applicant, applicants would be encouraged to research potential prior art carefully prior to filing an application. *See* John R. Thomas,

Collusion and Collective Action in the Patent System: A Proposal for Patent Bounties, 2001 U. ILL. L. REV. 305.

Versions of a bounty system already exist. BountyQuest.com, launched in October 2000, promises to pay users a reward for finding prior art applicable to specific patents or technologies described on the site. Rewards generally range from $10,000 to $50,000, depending on the patent. Companies interested in finding relevant prior art (potential infringers of a patent, for example), and/or inventors who want to be sure their invention is really new and non-obvious, pay the reward, as well as a fee to the BountyQuest Corporation. Internet-commerce-related patents featured on the site have included those on Web-based banner advertising, the Amazon.com "One–Click" feature, the Priceline.com reverse auction, and the BountyQuest business concept itself.

The ground for BountyQuest.com's effort was paved by the Software Patent Institute ("SPI"), a nonprofit organization that collects information pertaining to software technologies. Funded primarily by small grants and subscription fees, SPI focuses specifically on the "prior art" problem with respect to all computer-related inventions, including computer-related business method inventions. SPI does not offer a bounty, but has similarly sought to build up a body of information that can be used by patent applicants and possible infringers to determine whether an invention has been anticipated by prior art. Drawing on contributions from thousands of knowledgeable members of the computing community, SPI has developed a Database of Software Technologies consisting of source documents that are generally not readily available online or in electronic form elsewhere. Because it seeks to fill in major gaps in the prior art used to evaluate computer-related inventions, SPI does not include patents and most current trade publications; rather it seeks to track and corral the "folklore" of the computing industry. Available source documents, some of which date to 1955, include computer manuals, older textbooks and older journal articles, conference proceedings, computer science theses, and other materials that can provide pointers to prior art relevant to a given technology. Anyone with access to the Web can submit new materials and search the database. *See* www.spi.org.

For an argument that the problems with the PTO are institutional, and will not be solved by approaches such as those discussed above, see Brian Kahin, *The Expansion of the Patent System: Politics and Political Economy*, FIRST MONDAY, vol. 6, no. 1 (Jan. 2001), firstmonday.org/issues/issue6_1/kahin/index.html.

C. PATENTS OUTSIDE THE UNITED STATES

In contrast to the expansiveness of the current U.S. approach to patentability of business methods, other countries are taking a more cautious approach. Many nations have been engaged in a drive toward international harmonization of intellectual property law, driven in part by the globalization of commerce, and some have begun to reconsider their limits on patentability in light of U.S. developments. The patent offices of the United States, Japan, and Europe have repeatedly met to discuss software and business method patentability. In June 2000, these three offices reported a "consensus" opinion consisting of two propositions: (1) "A technical aspect is necessary for a computer-implemented business method to be eligible for patenting." and (2) "To merely automate a known human transaction process using well known automation techniques is not patentable." *See* Report on Comparative Study Carried Out Under Trilateral Project B3b (June 14–16, 2000), www.european-patent-office.org/tws/front_page.pdf. An Appendix to the report, issued by the President of the European Patent Office, specifies guidelines for evaluating computer-implemented business methods, the key test being whether the invention solves an objective technical problem. *Id.*, app. 6. According to a September 2000 study, at least eight business method patents already have been issued in Japan, with many more expected as the number of applications increases. Economic Research Institute, *Impact of Business Model (Method) Patents: Implications for Corporate Management*, www.marubeni.co.jp/research/eindex/00082.html. The patentability of business methods outside the United States remains an open question, though it seems the trend toward patentability will continue.

Likewise uncertain is the enforceability of U.S. business method patents against infringers based in other countries. Patent law is territorial. The Patent Act includes as infringements importing an infringing product into the United States, or importing into the United States an unpatented product made abroad by a process patented in the United States. U.S. patent law also makes it an infringement to ship all of the components of a patented invention abroad and manufacture it there. 35 U.S.C. § 271. But in general, those acting outside the territory of the United States are not covered by the U.S. patent law, and may engage in activities which if they occurred in the United States would infringe a patent.

The United States is working with other countries to address these questions. An important international agreement governing patents, to which the United States is a signatory, is the Agreement on Trade–Related Aspects of Intellectual Property Rights ("TRIPS"), www.wto.org/english/tratop_e/trips_e/t_agm0_e.htm. Under Article 1 of TRIPS, signatory countries must treat citizens and foreigners equally under the law; that is, foreigners are free to file applications for U.S. patents on the same terms as U.S. citizens. TRIPS also requires signatory countries to implement certain legal standards for patentability and sets forth a uniform patent term as well. Countries are not required to enforce each other's laws, however, nor are they prevented from excluding some forms of subject matter from protection—apparently including business methods if not sufficiently technological.[4]

4. Article 27(1) of TRIPS provides:

[P]atents shall be available for any inventions, whether products or processes, in all fields of technology, provided that they are new, involve an inventive step and are capable of industrial application. * * * [P]atents shall be available and patent rights enjoyable without discrimi-

NOTES & QUESTIONS

Extraterritorial effects. Should a French Web-based company using a business method patented in the United States be liable for patent infringement if the company targets U.S. citizens in its advertising? What if does not target U.S. citizens but its website is nevertheless accessible in the United States? Does it matter if actual goods are shipped to the United States?

V. EXAMPLES OF E–COMMERCE BUSINESS METHOD PATENTS

The availability of business method patents following *State Street Bank* has had a profound effect on the operation and strategy of e-commerce, as inventors and businesses have flocked to the PTO seeking to patent their methods of doing business. Following are some examples of patents that have issued for Internet-commerce-related business methods. Note that the excerpts include only Claim One of each patent. Claim One is often the shortest and most general in wording—therefore, it often is the *broadest* of the claims of the patent. Because Claim One is often the broadest, it might be deemed by a court or a patent examiner to be invalid, while other narrower claims, more specifically delineating the actual embodiment of the invention developed by the patentee, might be upheld (remember, a patent is evaluated claim by claim).

A. AMAZON.COM'S ONE-CLICK PATENT

Patent Number: 5,960,411

Date of Patent: September 28, 1999

METHOD AND SYSTEM FOR PLACING A PURCHASE ORDER VIA A COMMUNICATIONS NETWORK

* * *

Abstract

A method and system for placing an order to purchase an item via the Internet. The order is placed by a purchaser at a client system and received by a server system. The server system receives purchaser information including identification of the purchaser, payment information, and shipment information from the client system. The server system then assigns a client identifier to the client system and associates the assigned client identifier with the received purchaser information. The server system sends to the client system the assigned client identifier and an HTML document identifying the item and including an order button. The client system receives and stores the assigned client identifier and receives and displays

nation as to the place of invention, the field of technology and whether products are imported or locally produced.

the HTML document. In response to the selection of the order button, the client system sends to the server system a request to purchase the identified item. The server system receives the request and combines the purchaser information associated with the client identifier of the client system to generate an order to purchase the item in accordance with the billing and shipment information whereby the purchaser effects the ordering of the product by selection of the order button.

* * *

BACKGROUND OF THE INVENTION

* * *

The World Wide Web is especially conducive to conducting electronic commerce. Many Web servers have been developed through which vendors can advertise and sell products. The products can include items (e.g., music) that are delivered electronically to the purchaser over the Internet and items (e.g., books) that are delivered through conventional distribution channels (e.g., a common carrier). A server computer system may provide an electronic version of a catalog that lists the items that are available. A user, who is a potential purchaser, may browse through the catalog using a browser and select various items that are to be purchased. When the user has completed selecting the items to be purchased, the server computer system then prompts the user for information to complete the ordering of the items. This purchaser-specific order information may include the purchaser's name, the purchaser's credit card number, and a shipping address for the order. The server computer system then typically confirms the order by sending a confirming Web page to the client computer system and schedules shipment of the items.

Since the purchaser-specific order information contains sensitive information (e.g., a credit card number), both vendors and purchasers want to ensure the security of such information. Security is a concern because information transmitted over the Internet may pass through various intermediate computer systems on its way to its final destination. The information could be intercepted by an unscrupulous person at an intermediate system. To help ensure the security of the sensitive information, various encryption techniques are used when transmitting such information between a client computer system and a server computer system. Even though such encrypted information can be intercepted, because the information is encrypted, it is generally useless to the interceptor. Nevertheless, there is always a possibility that such sensitive information may be successfully decrypted by the interceptor. Therefore, it would be desirable to minimize the sensitive information transmitted when placing an order.

The selection of the various items from the electronic catalogs is generally based on the "shopping cart" model. When the purchaser selects an item from the electronic catalog, the server computer system metaphorically adds that item to a shopping cart. When the purchaser is done selecting items, then all the items in the shopping cart are "checked out" (i.e., ordered) when the purchaser provides billing and shipment information. In some models, when a purchaser selects any one item, then that item is "checked out" by automatically prompting the user for the billing and shipment information. Although the shopping cart model is very flexible and intuitive, it has a downside in that it requires many interactions by the purchaser. For example, the purchaser selects the various items from the electronic catalog, and then indicates that the selection is complete. The purchaser is then presented with an order Web page that prompts the purchaser for the purchaser-specific order information to complete the order. That Web page may be prefilled with information that was provided by the purchaser when placing another order. The information is then validated by the server computer system, and the order is completed. Such an ordering model can be problematic for a couple of reasons. If a purchaser is ordering only one item, then the overhead of confirming the various steps of the ordering process and waiting for, viewing, and updating the purchaser-specific order information can be much more than the overhead of selecting the item itself. This overhead makes the purchase of a single item cumbersome. Also, with such an ordering model, each time an order is placed sensitive information is transmitted over the Internet. Each time the sensitive information is transmitted over the Internet, it is susceptible to being intercepted and decrypted.

* * *

[Claims]

We claim:

1. A method of placing an order for an item comprising:

under control of a client system,

displaying information identifying the item; and

in response to only a single action being performed, sending a request to order the item along with an identifier of a purchaser of the item to a server system;

under control of a single-action ordering component of the server system,

receiving the request;

retrieving additional information previously stored for the purchaser identified by the identifier in the received request; and

generating an order to purchase the requested item for the purchaser identified by the identifier in the received request using the retrieved additional information; and

fulfilling the generated order to complete purchase of the item whereby the item is ordered without using a shopping cart ordering model.

* * *

B. PRICELINE.COM'S PATENT ON REVERSE AUCTIONS

Patent Number: 5,794,207

Date of Patent: August 11, 1998

METHOD AND APPARATUS FOR A CRYPTOGRAPHICALLY ASSISTED COMMERCIAL NETWORK SYSTEM DESIGNED TO FACILITATE BUYER–DRIVEN CONDITIONAL PURCHASE OFFERS

Abstract

The present invention is a method and apparatus for effectuating bilateral buyer-driven commerce. The present invention allows prospective buyers of goods and services to communicate a binding purchase offer globally to potential sellers, for sellers conveniently to search for relevant buyer purchase offers, and for sellers potentially to bind a buyer to a contract based on the buyer's purchase offer. In a preferred embodiment, the apparatus of the present invention includes a controller which receives binding purchase offers from prospective buyers. The controller makes purchase offers available globally to potential sellers. Potential sellers then have the option to accept a purchase offer and thus bind the corresponding buyer to a contract. The method and apparatus of the present invention have applications on the Internet as well as conventional communications systems such as voice telephony.

* * *

SUMMARY OF THE INVENTION

In a preferred embodiment, the present invention provides a method and apparatus for prospective buyers of goods or services to communicate a binding purchase offer globally to potential sellers, for sellers conveniently to search for relevant buyer purchase offers, and for sellers to bind a buyer to a contract based on the buyer's purchase offer. Additionally, the present invention can effectuate performance of the agreement between the buyer and seller by guaranteeing buyer payment for the purchase. The present invention is therefore a highly effective bilateral buyer-driven commerce system which improves the ability of buyers to reach sellers capable of satisfying the buyers' purchasing needs and improves sellers' ability to identify interested buyers.

In one embodiment of this invention, communications between buyers and sellers are conducted using an electronic network and central controller. A buyer who wishes to make a purchase accesses the central controller located at a remote server. The buyer will then create a conditional purchase offer ("CPO") by specifying the subject of the goods he wishes to purchase, a description of the goods he wishes to obtain, and any other conditions the buyer requires. For example, a typical CPO could specify that the buyer wants to purchase a block of four airline tickets from Chicago's O'Hare Airport to Dallas, Tex., the tickets must be from any of the six largest U.S. carriers, the buyer is willing to change planes no more than once so long as the scheduled layover is less than two hours, and the buyer is willing to pay $180 per ticket, plus any applicable taxes.

The buyer then attaches a user identification to the CPO and transmits the CPO to the central controller. Under the present invention, the CPO may be transmitted via numerous means including a world-wide-web interface, electronic mail, voice mail, facsimile, or postal mail. Standard legal provisions and language are then integrated with the CPO to "fill in the gaps" of the buyer's purchase offer. Alternatively, the CPO may be developed while the buyer is on-line with the central controller.

Before communicating the CPO to potential sellers, the central controller authenticates the buyer's identification number against a buyer database. The central controller may require that the buyer provide a credit card number and may also ensure that the buyer has sufficient credit available to cover the purchase price specified in the CPO by contacting the credit card clearinghouse. The central controller then assigns a unique tracking number to the CPO and globally displays the CPO in a manner such that it is available to be viewed by any interested potential sellers. CPOs may be displayed by subject category to make it easier for potential sellers to identify relevant CPOs. Thus, a seller could log onto a website, for example, and see a listing of CPO subject categories. The seller could then choose a particular subject and have the ability to browse CPOs which correspond to that subject category. In one embodiment, the seller may be required to provide qualifications in order to view the CPOs of a given subject category.

If, after reviewing a particular CPO, a potential seller wishes to accept the CPO, the seller communicates his intent to the central controller. The central controller then timestamps the message from the seller and authenticates the identity of the seller and his capacity to deliver the goods sought by the buyer. The system then verifies that the particular CPO is still "active" and capable of being accepted. If a CPO is capable of being accepted only by one seller, it is "completed" when the first qualified seller accepts it. Subsequent sellers will not be able to accept a "completed" CPO. If a seller accepts an active CPO, a unique tracking number is assigned to the seller's acceptance. The acceptance is then stored in a database. The buyer and seller are now parties to a legally binding contract.

* * *

The present invention can also be practiced in off-line embodiments. Instead of using electronic mail or web-based servers, buyers and sellers may communicate with the central controller via telephone, facsimile, postal mail, or another off-line communication tool. For example, buyers may use telephones to create CPOs (with or without the assistance of live agents) and potential sellers may use a telephone to browse and bind CPOs.

* * *

What the present invention accomplishes, which no previous system has done before, is literally to hang buyer money on a "clothesline" for sellers to see. Attached to the money is a note describing what the seller has to agree to do in order to take the money down off the clothesline. There is no uncertainty or waste of time on the part of the seller. He knows that if he can meet the conditions set forth by the buyer, he can immediately close the sale and get paid for it. No hassles. No negotiations.

The invention also allows buyers to reach a large number of remotely located sellers who normally would not be able to afford to find the buyer, but who may be able to provide the buyer with the exact deal the buyer desires. For instance, this might be the case for a car buyer who could precisely define the car and option packages he wanted for a specified price. The present invention allows such a buyer to issue a binding purchase offer which is globally communicated to authorized dealers in the U.S. Any one of those dealers could then decide whether or not to accept the offer. The buyer's advantage is particularly significant when the sellers of products sought by the buyer have no inventory carrying costs, as is the case with insurance sales. Insurance buyers could use the present invention to cast a wide net to reach thousands of potential insurance sellers and potentially find a seller willing to satisfy the buyer's specified purchase conditions.

It is a goal of the present invention to provide a robust system which matches buyers' requirements with sellers capable of satisfying those requirements. The invention provides a global bilateral buyer-driven system for creating binding contracts incorporating various methods of communication, commerce and security for the buyer and the seller. The power of a central controller to field binding offers from buyers, communicate those offers globally in a format which can be efficiently accessed and analyzed by potential sellers, effectuate performance of resulting contracts, resolve disputes arising from those contracts, and maintain billing, collection, authentication, and anonymity makes the present invention an improvement over conventional systems.

[Claims]

What is claimed:

1. A method for using a computer to facilitate a transaction between a buyer and at least one of sellers, comprising:

inputting into the computer a conditional purchase offer which includes an offer price;

inputting into the computer a payment identifier specifying a credit card account, the payment identifier being associated with the conditional purchase offer;

outputting the conditional purchase offer to the plurality of sellers after receiving the payment identifier;

inputting into the computer an acceptance from a seller, the acceptance being responsive to the conditional purchase offer; and

providing a payment to the seller by using the payment identifier.

* * *

C. CYBERGOLD'S PAY–PER–VIEW ADVERTISING PATENT

Patent Number: 5,794,210

Date of Patent: August 11, 1998

ATTENTION BROKERAGE

Abstract

A system provides for the immediate payment to computer and other users for paying attention to an advertisement or other "negatively priced" information distributed over a computer network such as the Internet. Called Attention Brokerage, this is the business of brokering the buying and selling of the "attention" of users. A further invention, Orthogonal Sponsorship, allows advertisers to detach their messages from program content and explicitly target their audience. A special icon or other symbol displayed on a computer screen may represent compensation and allow users to choose whether they will view an ad or other negatively priced information and receive associated compensation. Targeting users may be provided by reference to a data base of digitally stored demographic profiles of potential users. Information can be routed to users based on demographics, and software agents can be used to actively seek out users on a digital network. Private profiles may be maintained for different users and user information may be released to advertisers and other marketers only based on user permission. Users may be compensated for allowing their information to be released. Competing advertisers may "bid" for the attention of users using automatic electronic systems, e.g., "an auction" protocol and these concepts can be generalized to provide an electronic trading house where buyers and sellers can actively find each other and negotiate transactions.

BACKGROUND AND SUMMARY OF THE INVENTION

Historically, advertising has involved a battle of wits between advertiser and consumer. In the mass media, producers of products and services vie with each other to capture the attention of potential consumers, while those same consumers (although generally endorsing the idea of advertising as a way of keeping entertainment and information costs down) strive to evade as many advertising messages as they can. Consumers press the mute button on their TV remotes and "zap" advertisements by flipping between channels, they mentally tune out or "zap" radio commercials, they flip advertising pages of a newspaper or magazine without paying any attention to them, and they subscribe to non-commercial information and entertainment media. Rare indeed is the consumer who actually enjoys being at the receiving end of mass-media advertising.

This state of affairs is not accidental. It is an inevitable result of the environment in which advertising came of age. To make contact with the relatively small percentage of people who might actually want to use a product or service, mass-media advertising has to impact everyone who uses the medium. For example, every reader of the New York Times has to see (though not necessarily read) the display ad for Macy's; every viewer of popular television programs such as "Roseanne" has to sit through (though not necessarily pay attention to) the commercial for Diet Coke.

Although the concept of a consumer's attention as a commodity with intrinsic value has only recently entered public discussion, it has long been implicit in advertising, marketing, and public relations. Since advertisers know that only a small percentage of the audience has a real interest in the product or service being sold, they have learned to rely on entertainment values—constant repetition, snappy jingles, blaring headlines, and sex—to attract the attention of the audience and thereby sell their wares.

In the traditional mass media advertising model, mass media (e.g., television networks, radio stations, newspapers and magazines) develop particular content of interest to certain classes of consumers. The mass media also develops and provides a mechanism to deliver the content to as many potential consumers as possible (e.g., over the air or by cable transmissions, by mass distribution of print media copies, etc.). The mass media may charge audience members for content delivery (e.g., magazine or newspaper subscription fees, cable television subscription fees, or "pay per view" fees), but mass media typically receives most of its revenue from advertisers.

Advertising "sponsorship" in this traditional mass media advertising model has been a mechanism by which economic value is passed indirectly from an advertiser to a consumer. Advertisers "sponsor" content by paying the mass media to deliver their advertisements with the content. Traditionally, advertisers often want their advertisements inextricably embedded within the content itself so the advertisements are more certain to reach the mass media audience. For example, some advertisers have television and radio commentators work advertising "pitches" into their commentary. Other advertisers have televised/photographed race car drivers emblazon their cars with advertising slogans. Still other advertisers have film actors or actresses use the advertiser's products as part of their role playing. Moreover, the now-standard technique of pacing commercial television programming to intersperse advertising at various points within the programming is designed to make it more difficult for viewers to not pay attention to the advertisements.

* * *

The advertising practices described above have a number of drawbacks, both for the advertiser and for society at large. The primary drawback for the advertiser is lack of efficiency. Mass media advertising is inherent both over-inclusive and under-inclusive. For example, the lingerie ads aired during Melrose Place are not delivered to many consumers who are prime candidates for purchasing the product (for example, fashion conscious women who buy a lot of lingerie but don't like Melrose Place and/or don't watch television). In addition, the advertisements are delivered to many consumers (e.g., men who watch Melrose Place) who have no interest in purchasing the products being advertised. From the advertiser's point of view, a lingerie company could advertise more efficiently if it could directly reach women who are explicitly interested in lingerie (or clothes, or fashion).

Society at large is also harmed by this lack of efficiency. As one example, television programming has, to a very large extent, become dictated by factors that will make it appeal to the largest possible audience so it can generate the largest possible advertising revenue. The result is a decrease in the overall diversity of information available and an alarming increase in the homogeneity and "lowest common denominator" appeal of mass media programming. Unlinking sponsorship from the content of the sponsored entertainment or service would benefit the consumer and would also provide broad benefits to society such as greater freedom of speech and making a larger diversity of opinions available to the public.

* * *

The Internet is the first medium that can claim to be both "mass," in the sense that it reaches millions of people all over the globe, and "specialized," in the sense that its technology is capable of targeting information directly to the individual consumer. This is such a fundamental change from all previous information technologies that it has the potential to transform the advertising transaction into an alliance between consumer and advertiser, based on mutual respect and mutual benefits.

The Internet is a system of linked computers that permits fast, low-cost, global communication, entertainment, and information exchange. The Internet may be considered the test-bed for a "Future Net" which will likely encompass the functions now provided by today's Internet, cable and broadcast television, telephone communications (including voice and picture) and other linear and interactive business, telecommunication and entertainment systems. This "Future Net" may be a single network or an amalgamation of two or more independent networks. It is likely that new forms of entertainment and business will emerge, made possible by the Future Net.

Even with the current form of the Information Superhighway (Internet, cable television, video conference, "zines" created by desktop publishing, etc.), competition for the public's time and attention will become increasingly keen. Consumers with hundreds of competing, independent, and widely distributed sources of entertainment and information to choose from will no longer be the passive prisoners of advertising messages that they were in the era of the centralized mass media. So far, however, advertising has been only a marginal—and somewhat unwelcome—presence on the Information Superhighway.

Many consumers of the Information Superhighway view the recent advent of advertising to the wide open spaces of the Internet with deep suspicion and an almost instinctive aversion. But the kind of advertising the skeptics are thinking about—and rejecting—bears little resemblance to the advertising of the future.

The present invention provides a new approach to advertising for the digital age. Advertising in accordance with the present invention is based on the new realities of communication and commerce on the Internet, on-line services, the Future Net, and other computer networks, including networks that distribute information via physical media such as CD–ROM.

The innovations provided by the present invention have the potential to turn what has historically been an uneasy and sometimes hostile stand-off between advertiser and consumer into an alliance based on mutual respect and mutual benefits. The approach provided by the present invention is based on four principles:

attention,

interest,

sponsorship, and

privacy.

Attention

A fundamental premise underlying the present invention is the idea that a consumer's attention is a valuable commodity. The present invention will allow advertisers to pay consumers directly for their time and attention. The notion of direct, immediate payment in this context is new. The rationale for direct payment, from the advertiser's point of view, is that direct payment is a cost-effective way of getting the attention of targeted customers as compared to mass-media advertising.

The present invention provides mechanisms for "attention brokerage"—the business of buying and selling (brokering) the "attention" of consumers. Attention brokerage establishes a market that allows advertisers to compete for the attention of a particular consumer or group of consumers—thereby maximizing efficiency and creating value.

"Negative pricing" is one means by which advertisers could compete for available attention in the system provided in accordance with the present invention. In its simplest form, negative pricing is a "passive" competition: advertisers make fixed offers and viewers select among them. Another innovative idea is "attention bidding," a mechanism by which advertisers actively compete by bidding for a viewer's attention. These bids might be based, in part, on estimates of the viewer's interest and likelihood to buy—estimates derived from access to the viewer's electronic profiles detailing preferences and past consuming behavior. Bids might also be based on other bids, via an "auction" protocol by empowered bidding "agents." The bidding may be explicit or automatic. Viewers may elect to have advertisers bid for their attention or the system may offer bidding without the viewers' knowledge.

Interest

As discussed above, traditional advertising was both under-inclusive and over-inclusive. In contrast, technology provided in accordance with the present invention permits the design of ads that are virtually custom-fitted to consumer preferences, thus ensuring that the ad messages will be welcomed and attentively viewed by the consumer. This ability to finely target (and customize) ads based on the interests of particular individual consumers maximizes efficiency and benefits both the advertisers and the consumers.

For example, when selecting ads for viewing, the consumer would be given the chance to express a preference for certain kinds of ad content. For example, if the consumer is shopping for a computer, he/she might ask to see an advertisement that provides straightforward technical specifications of specific models or configurations. For a movie commercial, one consumer might request a film clip while another asks for a plot summary. Some consumers might enjoy the entertainment value of celebrity-spokesperson ads, while a consumer viewing an ad for food or drink might ask for a list of ingredients or nutrients.

A related innovation, "demographic routing," is a mechanism by which an information package or its agent (or an agent for any goods or service) can be routed directly to interested and willing buyers. Conceptually, this is an addressing mechanism that can be used to route the information to more than one individual, e.g., to all users who are demographically suitable (e.g., "anyone who fits the following profile").

Sponsorship

Since all the ads on the list will be targeted to the consumer's needs, interests, and preferences, it is very likely that she would be inclined to view them even without a cash incentive. However, the system provided by the present invention will offer her one. The present invention provides a "consumer interface button"—for example, the image of a little gold coin ("CyberCoin") next to each title on a list. This use of a consumer interface button—the "CyberCoin"—though reminiscent of the prior art "gems" in video game adventures, is innovative and unique in that it transfers real value.

The "CyberCoin" transaction reflects a radical and innovative change in the meaning of sponsorship. In effect, the advertisers have elected to sponsor the consumer who selects the CyberCoin—that is, they have chosen to pay the consumer directly for her attention rather than using the same funds for mass-market ad campaigns that are far less likely to hit the mark. Thus, the present invention provides a method of separating advertising sponsorship from the editorial content of the medium in which the advertising appears. We call this ability to decouple the advertising content from other content "orthogonal sponsorship."

The technology offered by the present invention breaks (or makes inexplicit) the link between the ad and the content of the sponsored material. Advertisers will not necessarily know what content of entertainment or information they are sponsoring. Instead, advertisers will simply provide ads to the service, explicitly delineate their target audience, and offer some form of compensation for time and attention directly to those viewers willing to "view" ads.

In orthogonal sponsorship, how will advertisers know that they are getting their money's worth? What is to prevent a consumer from clicking the CyberGold button, collecting the credit, and NOT reading the ad? The system provided by the present invention can, as one example, have a built-in system of incentives and checks—a "carrot and stick" approach—to solve this problem. The "carrot" in this example is the consumer's interest in the product or service, which will make him or her unlikely to ignore the ad once it is presented. The "stick" is an element of interactivity designed into the ad that requires the consumer to provide a response or otherwise interact with the ad (thus allowing the service to assure the advertiser that the consumer did indeed watch and pay attention).

The present invention also introduces the concept of "negative pricing of information." In today's marketplace, entertainment and information (sometimes generically referred to as "intellectual property") carries a positive price, or is free. "Negatively priced information" pays the consumer for his or her attention. This is a generalization of direct payment for ad viewing, since the information or content need not be an advertisement in the conventional sense. There is a fine line between certain kinds of information and advertising, particularly when an advertising message can be as straightforward as the technical specs of a new car or computer, and an information message or entertainment can change minds and influence people. Negative pricing could work well for information of this type. For example, it could be used as a means of expressing a political viewpoint, raising the priority of an e-mail message, or getting potential employers to read a resume. Negatively-priced information would find its audience through personal profiles of potential consumers on file in the database.

Privacy

In the system provided by the present invention, the link between the ad and the appropriate viewer is provided by reference to a data base of digitally stored electronic demographic profiles of potential viewers. The viewer profiles are to be private, dynamic, and interactive. The system protects member privacy while at the same time maintaining the personal information files that permit specialized targeting of ads.

Many businesses keep profiles of customer interests and transactions. (For example, some supermarkets keep customer profiles via "savings cards" that allow the market to track each person's purchases and tailor individual promotions.) The system provided by the present invention offers several innovative features and applications for such profiles. Profiles can be private (pseudonymous). That is, they can be used and even marketed while protecting the customer's identity. For example, a merchant may be permitted scan a profile to determine his affinity for the customer, but cannot learn the customer's name or address. Contacts between advertisers and consumers can be brokered by a "profile bank" that protects the consumer's privacy.

The demographic profiles can be constructed through interest questionnaires that the consumer completes when subscribing to the service, and also through electronic tracking of his/her usage of the service (and other habits). Thus, the profiles can be dynamic, evolving with the customer's transaction history. A customer can choose to exclude any transaction (e.g., viewing of certain material or purchasing of certain products) from his profile. Profiles can also be interactive in that a customer may edit his profile at any time to add or delete interest features, and to delete any transaction records. Thus, for example, the customer can delete historical transaction entries evidencing her purchase of an "adult" film if desired. Similarly, the customer can change her profile to express interest in seeing certain types of automobile advertisements, and then, after she has selected and purchased a new car, delete those profile entries.

In addition to the viewer profiles, the system provided by the present invention also may keep the contact information of each member confidential. For example, if an advertiser wants a consumer's name and address, he has to offer to buy it, and the consumer has to agree to the price. Furthermore, the consumer can specify that no advertiser can resell his/her name without permission. An offer to buy a consumer's name and address might look like this: "Please accept $2.00 for your name and address so we can send you more info." If the consumer accepts (e.g., by clicking on the associated "CyberCoin"), her name and address (from her personal data) will be forwarded to the advertiser, and $2 will be transferred from the advertiser to the consumer's account.

Another aspect of the present invention provides a two step technique for the development of an accurate consumer profile. First, a consumer is asked to pro-actively describe him or herself. This forms a "base profile." Then the consumer's actions can be monitored in this example such that a representation of the consumer's actions are "overlaid" upon the self description. This combination of self description combined with monitored actions yields highly accurate and granular consumer profile which can be used to predict consumer interests and behaviors. The system also can generate a base profile from historical data as well as self description.

* * *

[Claims]

What is claimed is:

1. In an arrangement comprising plural computers connected to a digital computer network, said network carrying and routing digital information between said plural computers, said plural computers including at least one personal computer associated with at least one user, at least one

computer associated with at least one attention broker, at least one computer associated with at least one provider of negatively priced information, and at least one computer associated with at least one provider of positively priced information, said network being decentralized in that any pair of said personal and information provider computers may communicate without said communication passing through any of the other said personal and information provider computers, said personal computer having a display device and at least one user input device, the display device being capable of providing a visual display based at least in part on the digital information delivered to the personal computer via said network, said displayed information including at least one visual link associated with one of said information provider computers, said user being able to operate said user input device to select and activate said link in order to erect a network connection to said information provider computer, a method for permitting the provider of negatively priced information to orthogonally sponsor user purchases of positively priced information, the method comprising:

(1) supplying negatively priced information to the personal computer from at least one negatively priced information provider;

(2) providing said user with the opportunity to receive compensation in connection with said negatively priced information by connecting via the network to said attention broker computer;

(3) compensating, via said attention broker computer, the user in connection with the supplied negatively priced information;

(4) presenting the user, via said personal computer display, with a choice of at least one item of positively priced information, and allowing the user to select said item by operating the user input device;

(5) collecting at least one selection from step (4) and communicating, via the network, said selection to at least one computer associated with a positively priced information provider; and

(6) allowing the user to pay for the selected positively priced information at least in part using compensation provided in step (3).

* * *

NOTES & QUESTIONS

1. *Broad claims and obviousness.* After reading these sample patents, do you agree with numerous commentators who argue that Internet commerce patents have been wrongly granted with broadly sweeping claims that, if ever enforced, would severely injure e-commerce? What are the implications of allowing broad claims in Internet-related patents, as compared to broad claims in more traditional technologies?

One author has criticized the breadth of the Priceline.com patent claims as follows:

> * * * This patent could permit Priceline.com to exclude all other business methods in which buyers propose a price for a

product or service, and then sellers bid to supply it. The reach of this patent could extend beyond the airfare context (as it is currently being used) to all industries. Accordingly, it would seem as though the scope of the patent would render it too broad to satisfy the various scope provisions. The issuance of the Priceline.com patent suggests that the USPTO is willing to permit potential patentees to claim extremely broad matter in the Internet context.

The Priceline.com patent also represents a good example of the lenient treatment of the nonobviousness requirement as applied to Internet business methods. Although reverse Dutch Auctions have existed for centuries, the USPTO did not find that it was obvious for Priceline.com to apply the reverse Dutch Auction method to the Internet. The issuance of this patent implies that it would not be obvious for a firm to take any standard business practice and apply it to the Internet. Such a loose interpretation of the nonobviousness doctrine implies that the nonobviousness requirement is no longer being used as a significant bar on commonplace inventions. As such, this interpretation seems to pave the way for the issuance of many Internet business method patents on seemingly regular business methods.

Jared Earl Grusd, *Internet Business Methods: What Role Does and Should Patent Law Play?*, 4 VA. J.L. & TECH. 9, 28–29 (1999).

Do you agree that, pushed to its logical extreme, Claim One of the Priceline patent implies that "any standard business practice" would become patentable when applied to the Internet? If not, can you justify the PTO's determination that the Priceline method satisfies the requirement of non-obviousness?

In October 1999, Priceline.com filed suit against Expedia.com, claiming that Expedia's "Price–Matcher" service, which allowed customers to place bids on airline tickets and hotel rooms, violated Priceline's patent. After a little over a year, the two companies settled the lawsuit in a deal that requires Expedia to pay Priceline royalties for the right to continue to offer its "Price–Matcher" service.

Given the widespread condemnation of the Priceline.com patent, the questionable breadth of the claim, and the issue of possible obviousness, why would Expedia, in which Microsoft at the time held a majority stake, settle the lawsuit rather than seek to have the patent invalidated?

2. *Business method patent factory.* Walker Digital Corp., a creation of Jay Walker, the founder of Priceline.com, is a self-styled laboratory for new business models. The company's business is devising, obtaining, and marketing business method patents of all kinds. According to the company's website, as of mid–2002, 70 patents had been issued and hundreds more were pending. *See* www.walkerdigital.com. The patents range from an automated system for monitoring hospital patients and calling in an expert when needed, to controlling the prices charged by a vending machine. Is

Walker Digital's business model the wave of the future? Is it a development that proves our patent system has gone astray in declaring business methods to be propertizable?

3. *Strategic use of Internet commerce patents.* Priceline.com patented its reverse auction business method to solidify its first-mover advantage on the Internet, creating a legal monopoly of its market and blocking out competitors. Arguably, this strategy worked well—it (initially) bolstered investor confidence and enabled Priceline to maintain a strong hold on the reverse-auction market. Most importantly, competitors did not opt to challenge the patent.

As with all patents, Internet business method patents can be used *offensively*, to stop infringing uses by a company's competitors, or *defensively*, as part of settlement or licensing negotiations with a competitor. Competitors frequently enter into agreements to "live and let live" with respect to patent infringement, in order to avoid costly litigation.

The following excerpt addresses some possible defensive and offensive uses of a business's patent portfolio, and the misguided incentive structure that often results. The excerpt suggests that for large businesses, procuring patents is less about promoting progress and innovation than it is about preventing lawsuits:

> In the high-technology age, the patent has become more than a way to protect legitimate intellectual property. It's often the legal equivalent of a Cold War nuclear stockpile: Sue me over your patents and I'll sue you over mine.
>
> "Internet-involved enterprises of all types continue building their own patent portfolios, for both offensive and defensive purposes," said intellectual property attorney Alan Fisch.
>
> * * *
>
> As a weapon against competitors, a patent can be a potent offense. "If you have a patent and approach someone else, you can get an injunction [and] cause a lot of harm up front," [Gregory] Aharonian said.
>
> As a result, there's little incentive for companies not to patent everything they can.
>
> "People will throw something into the patent office just to see if they can get something issued," [patent attorney Virginia] Medlen said. "Once it's issued, under law the presumption is that it's valid. And to knock it down the challenger has to produce clear and convincing evidence that the patent is not valid, and that clear and convincing evidence is very difficult to prove."
>
> That's where the defensive counter-patent comes in.

A judge faced with two similar, but competing patents is likely to tell the opponents to settle the issue themselves, rather than try to wade through the subtle differences in court.

"[The counter-patent] is a relatively inexpensive way to present evidence of invalidity," Medlen said.

* * *

* * * One industry source said the practice is so common that some big-name companies chock full of communications technology patents have struck agreements not to sue each other. Their other competitors may not be so lucky.

Chris Oakes, *Patently Absurd*, WIRED NEWS (Mar. 3, 2000), www.wired.com/news/politics/0,1283,34695,00.html.

Would it be appropriate to discourage these sorts of settlements and cross-licensing? Though it is debatable whether the current system is truly rewarding and promoting innovation, as it is supposed to, allowing businesses to use patents as defensive bargaining chips might reduce the costs of litigation to both private parties and the courts. *See, e.g.*, Carl Shapiro, *Navigating the Patent Thicket: Cross Licenses, Patent Pools, and Standard Setting, in* INNOVATION POLICY AND THE ECONOMY, VOL. I (Adam B. Jaffe, Josh Lerner, & Scott Stern eds., 2001).

VI. PATENT LITIGATION: AMAZON.COM V. BARNESANDNOBLE.COM

Despite the prevalence of strategic behavior and cross-licensing to settle disputes, some cases do go to trial. To show infringement of an Internet business method patent, a plaintiff must demonstrate that the defendant's conduct matches up exactly to *all* of the elements of one (or more) of the plaintiff's patent claims—that is, that the claim "reads on" the conduct. In addition, a court might find infringement under the "doctrine of equivalents" even if no literal infringement has occurred. The doctrine of equivalents prevents would-be infringers from escaping liability by making trivial changes but copying the essence of the invention. Nonetheless, many business method patents seem to present a fairly easy opportunity to "design around" to avoid infringement.

Amazon.com brought an infringement action against Barnesandnoble.com, alleging that the latter's "Express Lane" checkout system infringed its "One–Click" business method patent, excerpted in Part V(A), *supra*. In the district court, Amazon sought and obtained a preliminary injunction preventing Barnes & Noble from using its "Express Lane" checkout. *See Amazon.com, Inc. v. Barnesandnoble.com, Inc.*, 73 F.Supp.2d 1228 (W.D.Wash.1999).

The district court rejected Barnesandnoble.com's argument that the Amazon.com patent was invalid as obvious and anticipated by the relevant prior art. After analyzing the prior art references, the court found that there were sufficient "differences between each of the prior art references cited by Defendants and the method and system described in the claims of the '411 patent" and that there was no evidence "regarding a teaching, suggestion, or motivation in the prior art that would lead one of ordinary skill in the art of e-commerce to combine the references," *id.* at 1235, which is the kind of evidence needed to establish invalidity on the ground of obviousness.

Further, Amazon.com presented other evidence of non-obviousness that the court found very convincing: "[D]espite their experience with prior art shopping cart models of on-line purchasing, both sides' technical experts acknowledged that they had never conceived of the invention." *Id.* at 1236–37. One expert testified that he found the Amazon.com One–Click technology to be "a huge leap from what was done in the past" and testified that "I've been working in electronic commerce for years now. And I've never thought of the idea of being able to turn a shopping cart or take the idea of clicking on an item and suddenly having the item ship—having the complete process done." *Id.* at 1237. The district court held that the One–Click patent "addressed an unsolved need that had been long-felt (at least in the relatively short period of time that e-commerce has existed), namely streamlining the on-line ordering process to reduce the high percentage of orders that are begun but never completed, i.e., abandoned shopping carts." *Id.* One final objective indicator of non-obviousness cited by the district court was the vast commercial success of the one-click ordering method, as used by both Amazon.com and Barnesandnoble.com. *Id.*

After Barnesandnoble.com lost on its claim of invalidity, there was little evidence to dispute that it had directly copied from Amazon.com. Barnesandnoble.com had consistently promoted its "Express Lane" feature as "One Click Ordering," both internally and to customers. The court found that continuing infringement by Barnesandnoble.com would irreparably harm Amazon.com. The court noted that "customers become loyal to sites with which they become familiar," and allowing Barnesandnoble.com to continue benefiting from the "easy-to-use and easy-to-learn consumer interfaces" Amazon.com had invented would be extremely detrimental to Amazon.com's commercial success. *Id.* at 1238. An important factor weighing in favor of issuing the injunction was the approaching holiday season:

> As many as 10 million new users are expected to make their first on-line purchases during the 1999 holiday season. Millions of these new customers are likely to be shopping at Amazon.com and Barnesandnoble.com for the first time. Long-term success in e-commerce depends on establishing positive relationships with these new on-line buyers now, to preserve the ability to compete effectively for future sales, which by some estimates will reach $78 billion by the year 2003.

Id. The district court granted Amazon.com's request for a preliminary injunction requiring Barnesandnoble.com to remove the "Express Lane" feature in time for holiday ordering. The injunction, as we will see shortly, was overturned on appeal.

Following the issuance of the preliminary injunction in Amazon.com's favor, Barnesandnoble.com changed its checkout to a two-click scheme. The decision, however, was widely criticized.

> An ad-hoc Internet-based opposition emerged to express outrage over Amazon's actions. The one-click concept, they argued, should be unpatentable—it's an utterly obvious use of cookies, which existed long before Amazon's patent application. Richard Stallman, president of the Free Software Foundation and a ringleader of the backlash, launched a boycott against the company, proclaiming that "foolish government policies gave Amazon the opportunity—but an opportunity is not an excuse. Amazon made the choice to obtain this patent, and the choice to use it in court for aggression. The ultimate moral responsibility for Amazon's actions lies with Amazon's executives."
>
> Stallman's boycott didn't get much attention until late February, when Amazon announced yet another business-method patent, this one for its "affiliate program," a revenue-sharing scheme in which other sites refer customers to Amazon's store via Web links. Again, protesters viewed the patent as obvious and absurdly broad. Tim O'Reilly, a prominent publisher of computer books, posted an open letter on his website denouncing Amazon, gathering 10,000 protest signatures in a few days. A cowed Jeff Bezos [Amazon's founder and CEO] responded with an open letter of his own, declining to "give up our patents unilaterally," but expressing concern about the role of patents in the new economy and calling for major patent reform.
>
> Bezos' move turned patents into front-page news. In March, the PTO bowed to the mounting pressure and announced a few quick-fix changes: among them, increased supervision for the patent examiners who oversee business-method patent applications, as well as a promise to hold an open discussion on patent reform with Internet leaders this summer.

Evan Ratliff, *Patent Upending*, WIRED, June 2000, www.wired.com/wired/archive/8.06/patents_pr.html

NOTES & QUESTIONS

1. *District court's analysis*. Do you agree with the district court's analysis of validity and irreparable harm? Do you believe that there was really a "long-felt" need in e-commerce to come up with a more efficient ordering method? If so, how would the existence of such a long-felt need give rise to an inference that Amazon.com's one-click method was non-obvious when invented? Should the commercial success of one-click ordering also be considered as evidence of non-obviousness? Courts routinely consider long-felt need and commercial success in evaluating non-obviousness. But is it possible to distinguish between the commercial success of the one-click method and Amazon.com's business method generally? Were people coming to the site because of the novel method of ordering, or because of the nature of the business?

2. *Responsibility to play nice?* Stallman seems to demand that Amazon.com pursue only patent applications that it truly believes are legitimate. But, if the patent examiner is willing to grant a patent, why would Amazon.com be ethically obligated to refuse it? Can convincing distinctions be drawn between companies that seek business method patents on any possible innovation, and *any* company that attempts to draft its application such that as much as possible is claimed, with as little possible disclosure, when applying for a patent? Where should the responsibility for assuring patent validity lie—with the applicant? the examiner? Congress? the courts?

The district court's ruling on validity was overturned on appeal. While the Federal Circuit agreed that Amazon.com had made a convincing case for infringement, it held that Barnesandnoble.com had raised a substantial question as to the validity of the "One–Click" patent, and remanded the case for further consideration.

Amazon.com, Inc. v. Barnesandnoble.com, Inc.

239 F.3d 1343 (Fed.Cir.2001).

■ CLEVENGER, CIRCUIT JUDGE.

This is a patent infringement suit brought by Amazon.com, Inc. ("Amazon") against barnesandnoble.com, inc., and barnesandnoble.com llc (together, "BN"). Amazon moved for a preliminary injunction to prohibit BN's use of a feature of its website called "Express Lane." BN resisted the preliminary injunction on several grounds, including that its Express Lane feature did not infringe the claims of Amazon's patent, and that substantial questions exist as to the validity of Amazon's patent. The United States District Court for the Western District of Washington rejected BN's contentions. Instead, the district court held that Amazon had presented a case showing a likelihood of infringement by BN, and that BN's challenges to the validity of the patent in suit lacked sufficient merit to avoid awarding extraordinary preliminary injunctive relief to Amazon. The district court granted Amazon's motion, and now BN brings its timely appeal from the order entering the preliminary injunction. We have jurisdiction to review the district court's order under 28 U.S.C. § 1292(c)(1) (1994).

After careful review of the district court's opinion, the record, and the arguments advanced by the parties, we conclude that BN has mounted a substantial challenge to the validity of the patent in suit. Because Amazon is not entitled to preliminary injunctive relief under these circumstances, we vacate the order of the district court that set the preliminary injunction in place and remand the case for further proceedings.

I

This case involves United States Patent No. 5,960,411 ("the '411 patent"), which issued on September 28, 1999, and is assigned to Amazon. On October 21, 1999, Amazon brought suit against BN alleging infringement of the patent and seeking a preliminary injunction.

Amazon's patent is directed to a method and system for "single action" ordering of items in a client/server environment such as the Internet. In the context of the '411 patent, a client/server environment describes the relationship between two computer systems in which a program executing on a client computer system makes a service request from another program executing on a server computer system, which fulfills the request. *See* col. 1, ll. 10–31; col. 3, ll. 31–33; col. 5, l. 56 to col. 6, l. 21; Fig. 2. Typically, the client computer system and the server computer system are located remotely from each other and communicate via a data communication network.

The '411 patent describes a method and system in which a consumer can complete a purchase order for an item via an electronic network using only a "single action," such as the click of a computer mouse button on the client computer system. Amazon developed the patent to cope with what it considered to be frustrations presented by what is known as the "shopping cart model" purchase system for electronic commerce purchasing events. In previous incarnations of the shopping cart model, a purchaser using a client computer system (such as a personal computer executing a web browser program) could select an item from an electronic catalog, typically by clicking on an "Add to Shopping Cart" icon, thereby placing the item in the "virtual" shopping cart. Other items from the catalog could be added to the shopping cart in the same manner. When the shopper completed the selecting process, the electronic commercial event would move to the check-out counter, so to speak. Then, information regarding the purchaser's identity, billing and shipping addresses, and credit payment method would be inserted into the transactional information base by the soon-to-be purchaser. Finally, the purchaser would "click" on a button displayed on the screen or somehow issue a command to execute the completed order, and the server computer system would verify and store the information concerning the transaction.

As is evident from the foregoing, an electronic commerce purchaser using the shopping cart model is required to perform several actions before achieving the ultimate goal of the placed order. The '411 patent sought to reduce the number of actions required from a consumer to effect a placed order. In the words of the written description of the '411 patent:

> The present invention provides a method and system for single-action ordering of items in a client/server environment. The single-action ordering system of the present invention reduces the number of purchaser interactions needed to place an order and reduces the amount of sensitive information that is transmitted between a client system and a server system.

Col. 3, ll. 31–37. How, one may ask, is the number of purchaser interactions reduced? The answer is that the number of purchaser interactions is reduced because the purchaser has previously visited the seller's website and has previously entered into the database of the seller all of the required billing and shipping information that is needed to effect a sales transaction. Thereafter, when the purchaser visits the seller's website and wishes to purchase a product from that site, the patent specifies that only a single action is necessary to place the order for the item. In the words of the written description, "once the description of an item is displayed, the purchaser need only take a single action to place the order to purchase that item." Col. 3, ll. 64–66.

II

* * * We set forth below the text of the claims pertinent to our deliberations (*i.e.*, claims 1, 2, 6, 9, and 11), with emphasis added to highlight the disputed claim terms:

[Claim 1 is set forth in Part V(A), *supra*. Claims 2, 6, 9, and 11 are drawn to narrower versions of the one-click method. The court emphasizes the term "single action" as used in each claim.]

The district court interpreted the key "single action" claim limitation, which appears in each of the pertinent claims, to mean:

> The term "single action" is not defined by the patent specification.... As a result, the term "single action" as used in the '411 patent appears to refer to one action (such as clicking a mouse button) that a user takes to purchase an item once the following information is displayed to the user: (1) a description of the item; and (2) a description of the single action the user must take to complete a purchase order for that item.

With this interpretation of the key claim limitation in hand, the district court turned to BN's accused ordering system. BN's short-cut ordering system, called "Express Lane," like the system contemplated by the patent, contains previously entered billing and shipping information for the customer. In one implementation, after a person is presented with BN's initial web page (referred to as the "menu page"), the person can [click] on an icon on the menu page to get to what is called the "product page." BN's product page displays an image and a description of the selected product, and also presents the person with a description of a single action that can be taken to complete a purchase order for the item. If the single action described is taken, for example by a mouse click, the person will have effected a purchase order using BN's Express Lane feature.

BN's Express Lane thus presents a product page that contains the description of the item to be purchased and a "description" of the single action to be taken to effect placement of the order. Because only a single action need be taken to complete the purchase order once the product page is displayed, the district court concluded that Amazon had made a showing of likelihood of success on its allegation of patent infringement.

In response to BN's contention that substantial questions exist as to the validity of the '411 patent, the district court reviewed the prior art references upon which BN's validity challenge rested. The district court concluded that none of the prior art references anticipated the claims of the '411 patent under 35 U.S.C. § 102 (1994) or rendered the claimed invention obvious under 35 U.S.C. § 103 (1994).

III

* * * As the moving party, Amazon is entitled to a preliminary injunction if it can succeed in showing: (1) a reasonable likelihood of success on the merits; (2) irreparable harm if an injunction is not granted; (3) a balance of hardships tipping in its favor; and (4) the injunction's favorable impact on the public interest. * * * Irreparable harm is presumed when a clear showing of patent validity and infringement has been made. * * *

Our case law and logic both require that a movant cannot be granted a preliminary injunction unless it establishes *both* of the first two factors, *i.e.*, likelihood of success on the merits and irreparable harm. * * *

In order to demonstrate a likelihood of success on the merits, Amazon must show that, in light of the presumptions and burdens that will inhere at trial on the merits, (1) Amazon will likely prove that BN infringes the '411 patent, and (2) Amazon's infringement claim will likely withstand BN's challenges to the validity and enforceability of the '411 patent. *Genentech, Inc. v. Novo Nordisk, A/S*, 108 F.3d 1361, 1364 (Fed.Cir.1997). If BN raises a substantial question concerning either infringement or validity, *i.e.*, asserts an infringement or invalidity defense that the patentee cannot prove "lacks substantial merit," the preliminary injunction should not issue. *Id.*

Of course, whether performed at the preliminary injunction stage or at some later stage in the course of a particular case, infringement and validity analyses must be performed on a claim-by-claim basis. * * *

Both infringement and validity are at issue in this appeal. It is well settled that an infringement analysis involves two steps: the claim scope is first determined, and then the properly construed claim is compared with the accused device to determine whether all of the claim limitations are present either literally or by a substantial equivalent.* * *

Only when a claim is properly understood can a determination be made whether the claim "reads on" an accused device or method, or whether the prior art anticipates and/or renders obvious the claimed invention. Because the claims of a patent measure the invention at issue, the claims must be interpreted and given the same meaning for purposes of both validity and infringement analyses. * * *

IV

BN contends on appeal that the district court committed legal errors that undermine the legitimacy of the preliminary injunction. In particular,

BN asserts that the district court construed key claim limitations one way for purposes of its infringement analysis, and another way when considering BN's validity challenges. BN asserts that under a consistent claim interpretation, its Express Lane feature either does not infringe the '411 patent, or that if the patent is interpreted so as to support the charge of infringement, then the claims of the patent are subject to a severe validity challenge. When the key claim limitations are properly interpreted, BN thus asserts, it will be clear that Amazon is not likely to succeed on the merits of its infringement claim, or that BN has succeeded in calling the validity of the '411 patent into serious question. In addition, BN asserts that the district court misunderstood the teaching of the prior art references, thereby committing clear error in the factual predicates it established for comprehension of the prior art references.

Amazon understandably aligns itself with the district court, asserting that no error of claim interpretation and no clear error in fact-finding has occurred that would undermine the grant of the preliminary injunction. We thus turn to the legal gist of this appeal.

V

It is clear from the district court's opinion that the meaning it ascribed to the "single action" limitation includes a temporal consideration. The "single action" to be taken to complete the purchase order, according to the district court, only occurs after other events have transpired. These preliminary events required pursuant to the district court's claim interpretation are the presentation of a description of the item to be purchased and the presentation of the single action the user must take to complete the purchase order for the item.

* * *

Our analysis begins with the plain language of the claims themselves. The term "single action" appears in the independent claims of the '411 patent in the following forms: "in response to only a single action being performed" (claims 1 and 9), "single-action ordering component" (claims 1, 6, and 9), "in response to performance of only a single action" (claim 6), "in response to only the indicated single action being performed" (claim 11), and "displaying an indication of a single action that is to be performed to order the identified item" (claim 11).

In claims 1, 6, and 11, the context of the claim makes it clear that the single action is performed after some information about the item is displayed. Claim 1 provides for "displaying information identifying the item," and then immediately recites that "in response to only a single action being performed," a request to purchase the item is sent to a server system. Claim 6 provides for "a display component for displaying information identifying the item," and then immediately recites "the single action ordering component that in response to performance of only a single action" sends a request to purchase the item to a server system. Claim 11 provides for "displaying information identifying the item and displaying an indication of the single action," and then immediately recites that "in response to only the indicated single action being performed" a request to purchase the item is sent to a server system. The context also indicates that the single action is performed, or is capable of being performed, after information about the item is displayed, without any intervening action. Nothing suggests, however, that the single action must be performed after every display or even immediately after the first display of information. Claim 9 does not explicitly provide for displaying information. It merely recites that a request to order an item is "sent in response to only a single action being performed." However, although claim 9 does not recite "displaying," the written description defines the claim 9 language of "single action being performed" to require that information has been displayed.

The ordinary meaning of "single action" as used in the various claims is straightforward, but the phrase alone does not indicate when to start counting actions. Therefore, we must look first to the written description of the '411 patent for further guidance.

The written description supports a construction that after information is "displayed," single-action ordering is an option available to the user, and the counting falls within the scope of the claim when single-action ordering is actually selected by the user. To the extent that the claims are considered ambiguous on this point, the written description defines "single action" to require as much. In the Summary of the Invention, the written description describes an embodiment that "displays information that identifies the item and displays an indication of an action ... [and] [i]n response to the indicated action being performed" orders the item. Col. 2, ll. 54–59. Similarly, in the Detailed Description of the Invention, the written description states that "[o]nce the description of an item is displayed, the purchaser need only take a single action." Col. 3, ll. 65–66. This is consistent for all of the disclosed embodiments.

Therefore, neither the written description nor the plain meaning of the claims require that single action ordering be possible after each and every display of information (or even immediately after the first display of information). The plain language of the claims and the written description require only that single action ordering be possible after some display of information. Indeed, the written description allows for and suggests the possibility that previous displays of information will have occurred before the display immediately preceding an order.

* * *

VI

A

When the correct meaning of the single action limitation is read on the accused BN system, it becomes apparent that the limitations of claim 1 are likely met by the accused system. The evidence on the record concerning the operation of BN's "Express Lane" feature is not in dispute. At the time that the '411 patent was issued, BN offered customers two purchasing options. One was called "Shopping Cart," and the other was called "Express Lane." The Shopping Cart option involved the steps of adding items to a "virtual" shopping cart and then "checking out" to complete the purchase. In contrast, the Express Lane option allowed customers who had registered for the feature to purchase items simply by "clicking" on the "Express Lane" button provided on the "detail page" or "product page" describing and identifying the book or other item to be purchased. The text beneath the Express Lane button invited users to "Buy it now with just 1 click!"

BN's allegedly infringing website thus may be characterized as having "page 1," (the "menu" page) which displays a catalog listing several items but which does not contain an "order" icon, and "page 2," (the "product" or "detail" page) which includes information on one item and also shows an order icon. Someone shopping at this website would look at the catalog on page 1 and perform a first click to go to page 2. Once at page 2, a second click on the ordering icon would cause the order request to be sent. Under the claim construction set forth herein, BN likely infringes claim 1 because on page 2, the item is there displayed (meeting step 1 of the claim) and only a single action thereafter causes the order request to be transmitted (meeting step 2). The method implemented on page 1 of the BN website does not infringe, but the method on page 2 does. This has nothing to do with the state of mind of the purchaser, but simply reflects the ordinary meaning of the words of the claim in the context of the written description and in light of the prosecution history.

* * *

E

After full review of the record before us, we conclude that under a proper claim interpretation, Amazon has made the showing that it is likely to succeed at trial on its infringement case. Given that we conclude that Amazon has demonstrated likely literal infringement of at least the four independent claims in the '411 patent, we need not consider infringement under the doctrine of equivalents. The question remaining, however, is whether the district court correctly determined that BN failed to mount a substantial challenge to the validity of the claims in the '411 patent.

VII

The district court considered, but ultimately rejected, the potentially invalidating impact of several prior art references cited by BN. Because the district court determined that BN likely infringed all of the asserted claims, it did not focus its analysis of the validity issue on any particular claim. Instead, in its validity analysis, the district court appears to have primarily directed its attention to determining whether the references cited by BN implemented the single action limitation.

* * *

In this case, we find that the district court committed clear error by misreading the factual content of the prior art references cited by BN and by failing to recognize that BN had raised a substantial question of invalidity of the asserted claims in view of these prior art references.

Validity challenges during preliminary injunction proceedings can be successful, that is, they may raise substantial questions of invalidity, on evidence that would not suffice to support a judgment of invalidity at trial. *See, e.g., Helifix Ltd. v. Blok–Lok, Ltd.*, 208 F.3d 1339, 1352 (Fed.Cir.2000) (holding that the allegedly anticipatory prior art references sufficiently raised a question of invalidity to deny a preliminary injunction, even though summary judgment of anticipation based on the same references was not supported). The test for invalidity at trial is by evidence that is clear and convincing. *WMS Gaming, Inc. v. Int'l Game Tech.*, 184 F.3d 1339, 1355 (Fed.Cir.1999). To succeed with a summary judgment motion of invalidity, for example, the movant must demonstrate a lack of genuine dispute about material facts and show that the facts not in dispute are clear and convincing in demonstrating invalidity. *Robotic Vision Sys., Inc. v. View Eng'g, Inc.*, 112 F.3d 1163, 1165 (Fed.Cir.1997). In resisting a preliminary injunction, however, one need not make out a case of actual invalidity. Vulnerability is the issue at the preliminary injunction stage, while validity is the issue at trial. The showing of a substantial question as to invalidity thus requires less proof than the clear and convincing showing necessary to establish invalidity itself. That this is so is plain from our cases.

* * *

When the heft of the asserted prior art is assessed in light of the correct legal standards, we conclude that BN has mounted a serious challenge to the validity of Amazon's patent. We hasten to add, however, that this conclusion only undermines the prerequisite for entry of a preliminary injunction. Our decision today on the validity issue in no way resolves the ultimate question of invalidity. That is a matter for resolution at trial. It remains to be learned whether there are other references that may be cited against the patent, and it surely remains to be learned whether any shortcomings in BN's initial preliminary validity challenge will be magnified or dissipated at trial. All we hold, in the meantime, is that BN cast enough doubt on the validity of the '411 patent to avoid a preliminary injunction, and that the validity issue should be resolved finally at trial.

A

One of the references cited by BN was the "CompuServe Trend System." The undisputed evidence indicates that in the mid–1990s, CompuServe offered a service called "Trend" whereby CompuServe subscribers could obtain stock charts for a surcharge of 50 cents per chart. Before the district court, BN argued that this system anticipated claim 11 of the '411 patent. The district court failed to recognize the substantial question of invalidity raised by BN in citing the CompuServe Trend reference, in that this system appears to have used "single action ordering technology" within the scope of the claims in the '411 patent.

First, the district court dismissed the significance of this system partly on the basis that "[t]he CompuServe system was not a world wide web application." This distinction is irrelevant, since none of the claims mention either the Internet or the World Wide Web (with the possible exception of dependent claim 15, which mentions HTML, a program commonly associated with both the Internet and the World Wide Web). Moreover, the '411 patent specification explicitly notes that "[o]ne skilled in the art would appreciate that the single-action ordering techniques can be used in various environments other than the Internet." Col. 6, ll. 22–24.

More importantly, one of the screen shots in the record (reproduced below) indicates that with the CompuServe Trend system, once the "item" to be purchased (*i.e.*, a stock chart) has been displayed (by typing in a valid stock symbol), only a single action (*i.e.*, a single mouse click on the button labeled "Chart ($.50)") is required to obtain immediate electronic delivery (*i.e.*, "fulfillment") of the item. Once the button labeled "Chart ($.50)" was activated by a purchaser, an electronic version of the requested stock chart would be transmitted to the purchaser and displayed on the purchaser's computer screen, and an automatic process to charge the purchaser's account 50 cents for the transaction would be initiated. In terms of the language of claims 2 and 11 in the CompuServe Trend system, the item to be ordered is "displayed" when the screen echoes back the characters of the stock symbol typed in by the purchaser before clicking on the ordering button.

* * *

* * * Amazon's counsel claimed that the CompuServe Trend system was different from the claims of the '411 patent because it required a user to "log in" at the beginning of each session, and therefore would not send the claimed "identifier" along with a request to purchase each item. However, claim 11 does not require transmission of an identifier along with a request to order an item. This requirement is found only in claims 1, 6, and 9, and their respective dependent claims.

On its face, the CompuServe Trend reference does not mention transmission of the claimed identifier along with a request to purchase each item. Nor does the evidence in the record at this stage indicate that the CompuServe Trend system transmitted such an identifier. BN has therefore not demonstrated that the CompuServe Trend reference anticipates the asserted claims of the '411 patent requiring transmission of such an identifier with the degree of precision necessary to obtain summary judgment on this point. However, as noted above, validity challenges during preliminary injunction proceedings can be successful on evidence that would not suffice to support a judgment of invalidity at trial. *See Helifix*, 208 F.3d at 1352. The record in this case is simply not yet developed to the point where a determination can be made whether the CompuServe Trend system transmits the claimed identifier along with a request to order an item, or whether this limitation is obvious in view of the prior art. * * *

* * *

In view of the above, we conclude that the district court erred in failing to recognize that the CompuServe Trend reference raises a substantial question of invalidity. Whether the CompuServe Trend reference either anticipates and/or renders obvious the claimed invention in view of the knowledge of one of ordinary skill in the relevant art is a matter for decision at trial.

B

In addition to the CompuServe Trend system, other prior art references were cited by BN, but ultimately rejected by the district court. For example, BN's expert, Dr. Lockwood, testified that he developed an on-line ordering system called "Web–Basket" in or around August 1996. The Web–Basket system appears to be an embodiment of a "shopping cart ordering component": it requires users to accumulate items into a virtual shopping basket and to check these items out when they are finished shopping. Because it is an implementation of a shopping cart model, Web Basket requires several confirmation steps for even pre-registered users to complete their purchases.

However, despite the fact that Web–Basket is an embodiment of a shopping cart model, it is undisputed that Web–Basket implemented the Internet Engineering Task Force ("IETF") draft "cookie" specification, and stored a customer identifier in a cookie for use by a web server to retrieve information from a database. In other words, when a user first visited the Web–Basket site, a cookie (*i.e.*, a file stored by the server system on the client system for subsequent use) was used to store an identifier on the user's computer. The first time that a user purchased an item on the Web–Basket site, the information entered by the user necessary to complete the purchase (*e.g.*, name, address) would be stored in a database on the server system indexed by an identifier stored in the cookie on the client system. On subsequent visits, the cookie could be used to retrieve the user identifier, which would serve as the key to retrieve the user's information from the database on the server system.

At the preliminary injunction stage, based on Dr. Lockwood's declaration and testimony during the hearing, BN argued that the Web–Basket reference—combined with the knowledge of one of ordinary skill in the art at the relevant time—renders obvious the claimed invention.

The district court concluded that the Web–Basket system was "inconsistent with the single-action requirements of the '411 patent" because "it requires a multiple-step ordering process from the time that an item to be purchased is displayed." However, as discussed earlier, the undisputed evidence demonstrates that the accused BN Express Lane feature also requires a multiple-step ordering process (*i.e.*, at least two "clicks") *from the time that an item to be purchased is first displayed on the menu page*, yet the district court concluded that BN's Express Lane feature infringed all of the asserted claims of the '411 patent. The district court's failure to recognize the inconsistency in these two conclusions was erroneous.

Moreover, the district court did not address the "cookie" aspects of the Web–Basket reference, and failed to recognize that a reasonable jury could find that the step of storing purchaser data on the server system for subsequent retrieval indexed by an identifier transmitted from the client system was anticipated and/or rendered obvious by the Web–Basket reference.

* * * [T]he district court apparently based its conclusion of nonobviousness on Dr. Lockwood's "admission" that he personally never thought of combining or modifying the prior art to come up with the claimed "single action" invention. This approach was erroneous as a matter of law. Whatever Dr. Lockwood did or did not *personally* realize at the time based on his actual knowledge is irrelevant. The relevant inquiry is what a hypothetical ordinarily skilled artisan would have gleaned from the cited references at the time that the patent application leading to the '411 patent was filed. *See Kimberly–Clark Corp. v. Johnson & Johnson*, 745 F.2d 1437, 1453 (Fed.Cir.1984) (discussing the origin and significance of the hypothetical ordinarily skilled artisan in detail).

C

BN also presented as a prior art reference an excerpt from a book written by Magdalena Yesil entitled *Creating the Virtual Store* that was copyrighted in 1996. Before the district court, BN argued that this reference anticipated every limitation of claim 11. Before this court, BN also alleges that many other claim limitations are disclosed in the reference, but that there was insufficient time to prepare testimony concerning these limitations, given the district court's accelerated briefing and hearing schedule at the preliminary injunction stage.

In general terms, the reference apparently discusses software to implement a shopping cart ordering model. However, BN focuses on the following passage from Appendix F of the book:

> Instant Buy Option
>
> Merchants also can provide shoppers with an Instant Buy button for some or all items, enabling them to skip check out review. This provides added appeal for customers who already know the single item they want to purchase during their shopping excursion.

The district court dismissed the significance of this passage, stating that "[r]ead in context, the few lines relied on by Defendants appear to describe only the elimination of the checkout review step, leaving at least two other required steps to complete a purchase." However, the district court failed to recognize that a reasonable jury could find that this passage provides a motivation to modify shopping cart ordering software to skip unnecessary steps. Thus, we find that this passage, viewed in light of the rest of the reference and the other prior art references cited by BN, raises a substantial question of validity with respect to the asserted claims of the '411 patent.

D

Another reference cited by BN, a print-out from a web page describing the "Oliver's Market" ordering system, generally describes a prior art multi-step shopping cart model. BN argued that this reference anticipates at least claim 9. The reference begins with an intriguing sentence:

A single click on its picture is all it takes to order an item.

Read in context, the quote emphasizes how easy it is to order things on-line. The district court failed to recognize that a reasonable jury could find that this sentence provides a motivation to modify a shopping cart model to implement "single-click" ordering as claimed in the '411 patent. In addition, the district court failed to recognize that other passages from this reference could be construed by a reasonable jury as anticipating and/or rendering obvious the allegedly novel "single action ordering technology" of the '411 patent. For example, the reference states that "[o]ur solution allows one-click ordering anywhere you see a product picture or a price." The reference also describes a system in which a user's identifying information (*e.g.*, username and password) and purchasing information (*e.g.*, name, phone number, payment method, delivery address) is captured and stored in a database "the very first time a user clicks on an item to order," and in which a corresponding cookie is stored on the client system. In this system, the stored information may be retrieved automatically during subsequent visits by reading the cookie. All of these passages further support BN's argument that a substantial question of validity is raised by this prior art reference, either alone or in combination with the other cited references.

E

* * *

The district court also cited certain "secondary considerations" to support its conclusion of nonobviousness. Specifically, the district court cited (1) "copying of the invention" by BN and other e-commerce retailers following Amazon's introduction of its "1–Click®" feature, and (2) "the need to solve the problem of abandoned shopping carts." First, we note that evidence of copying Amazon's "1–Click®" feature is legally irrelevant unless the "1–Click®" feature is shown to be an embodiment of the claims. To the extent Amazon can demonstrate that its "1–Click®" feature embodies any asserted claims of the '411 patent under the correct claim interpretation, evidence of copying by BN and others is not sufficient to demonstrate nonobviousness of the claimed invention, in view of the substantial question of validity raised by the prior art references cited by BN and discussed herein.

With respect to the abandoned shopping carts, this problem is not even mentioned in the '411 patent. Moreover, Amazon did not submit any evidence to show either that its commercial success was related to the "1–Click®" ordering feature, or that single-action ordering caused a reduction in the number of abandoned shopping carts. Therefore, we fail to see how this "consideration" supports Amazon's nonobviousness argument.

CONCLUSION

While it appears on the record before us that Amazon has carried its burden with respect to demonstrating the likelihood of success on infringement, it is also true that BN has raised substantial questions as to the validity of the '411 patent. For that reason, we must conclude that the necessary prerequisites for entry of a preliminary injunction are presently lacking. We therefore vacate the preliminary injunction and remand the case for further proceedings.

NOTES & QUESTIONS

1. *The value of questionable patents.* Litigating a patent all the way through the Federal Circuit to a final determination of validity can take several years, and cost several million dollars. A bit more than half of these litigated patents are upheld. Those who hold questionable, but colorable, patents therefore have quite a bit of room for maneuvering: they can license them cheaply enough so that prospective licensors will not have an incentive to litigate. It is therefore possible to make a good deal of money in licensing questionable patents. Is there reason to think this process will be even worse with Internet-commerce patents than with others?

2. *Computerization and patentability.* As the caselaw on "methods" patents has established, a commercial method that is unpatentable when performed in the traditional manner by hand may become patentable if performed by a computer. Nobody owns the method of writing checks to pay bills, but a method of electronic check writing and clearing might well be patentable. Nobody owns the method of payment by cash, but there are dozens of patents on e-cash implementations. This trend may be expected to continue, as nearly all commercial methods become computerized. Is the trend worrisome from the standpoint of competition policy? From the standpoint of individual liberty?

3. *Patentability of contracts.* Contracts are normally not thought of as patentable, though as texts they are generally copyrightable. Yet contracts perform a function. Can a standardized contract be patented? If it is in digital form? If it is embedded in delivery of a digital product? Is the method of achieving formation of a contract containing the desired terms, through the use of a shrinkwrap license, patentable?

CHAPTER THIRTEEN

HARMFUL ACTIVITIES ONLINE: LIABILITY FOR ELECTRONIC INTRUSIONS

Defining particular movements of information as wrongful creates potentially serious conflicts with the ideal of a society that is based on the free flow of information, epitomized in the First Amendment. It is also in tension with the historically, and some would say quintessentially, open nature of the Internet, as well as with the ideal of a free market where competition is open and unregulated. Yet flows of information can cause very real harms: even the First Amendment's prohibition on infringement of the freedom of speech is not absolute.

Informational torts committed at a distance are nothing new—the transmission of defamatory material via a publication that circulates at some place far from the speaker is a familiar example. The law of defamation walks the line between deterring harm and respecting freedom of expression. The law of defamation has impacted the Internet in cases seeking to hold third parties such as ISPs liable for defamatory messages of users, a topic we will explore in Chapter 14, *infra*. The Internet's technology also gives rise to new types of informational harms, such as damaging a service provider's network with a flood of unwanted messages. This chapter addresses the various approaches to new online informational harms that courts and legislatures have endorsed. Courts have applied statutes that were designed to counter computer crime, unfair competition, and trademark infringement, and have revived the all-but-forgotten common-law tort of trespass to chattels, in an effort to resolve these new controversies. State legislatures have responded with sui generis statutory treatment of unsolicited commercial e-mail.

I. INTRUSION ON PROPRIETARY NETWORKS: UNSOLICITED COMMERCIAL E-MAIL

Electronic mail combines the desirable features of several other modes of communication: it allows asynchronous communications like postal mail, but travels nearly as fast as a telephone call, and is priced like a face-to-face conversation. Nearly everyone with Internet access is capable of sending and receiving e-mail messages. For these and other reasons, e-mail has become an immensely popular method of both commercial and non-commercial person-to-person communication.

These same features have made e-mail an attractive medium of communication for commercial entities seeking to market their products to a broad audience. Marketers assemble lists of thousands or millions of e-mail addresses and, typically without first seeking permission from the holders of those addresses, direct commercial messages to them in large numbers. These messages are known as unsolicited commercial e-mail ("UCE"), unsolicited bulk e-mail, or, more popularly (and pejoratively), "spam."[1] If you have an e-mail account, it is extremely likely that you are a recipient of UCE.

The advent of UCE as a direct marketing tool has elicited a fierce response from consumers and service providers. Opponents of UCE argue that the sending of UCE unfairly imposes costs on Internet service providers, on recipients of the messages, and in some cases on third-party owners of domain names. They point out that UCE frequently contains deceptive elements, such as false subject lines and routing information, and often promotes objectionable goods and services, such as pornography and fraudulent get-rich-quick schemes. Proponents of UCE characterize it as a low-cost marketing tool that can help new market participants mount challenges to existing sellers and introduce new products to the marketplace. In their view, UCE is no more objectionable than telemarketing, and market forces should determine whether it continues to be sent.

UCE presents new challenges to courts, legislatures, and the online community. Courts have responded by exhuming and reviving the ancient common-law action of trespass to chattels, and by applying the more familiar doctrines of trademark and unfair competition. State legislatures have enacted a variety of statutes that respond to the issues created by UCE. Congress has considered numerous bills that would regulate UCE, but so far has failed to enact one. ISPs have applied technological solutions in an attempt to blunt the effects of UCE, sometimes giving rise to reprisal lawsuits.

This Part will examine the legal issues that UCE raises, and the various judicial, legislative, and technological responses.

A. THE COSTS OF UCE

The sending of UCE imposes costs primarily on three constituencies: individuals to whom the unsolicited messages are addressed, Internet service providers that process the outgoing and incoming messages, and

1. As a technical matter, unsolicited commercial e-mail could be sent out individually, rather than in bulk, and unsolicited bulk e-mail is not necessarily commercial in nature. In practice, however, most unsolicited commercial e-mail is sent in bulk, and most unsolicited bulk e-mail is commercial. Therefore, in this chapter "UCE" will generally refer to unsolicited e-mail messages that are commercial in nature and sent to numerous recipients.

third-party domain owners whose names are falsely incorporated in the return addresses of UCE messages.

Harm to individual users. UCE costs individuals users both time and money. The wasted-time cost borne by consumers in sorting through and deleting unwanted solicitations may be insignificant with respect to any particular message, but becomes substantial in aggregate considering the vast numbers of UCE messages that are sent—according to various estimates, from 9 to 60 billion each year. Large volumes of UCE messages may interfere with the ISP's handling of its mail, delaying the delivery of non-UCE mail. Time spent by employees reading and deleting the UCE they receive on their office computers is time diverted from more productive endeavors. Users who pay access fees based on the length of time they are connected to the Internet, or who must make a long-distance call to connect with their access provider, incur direct additional costs as a result of UCE, since it takes time to download each UCE message from the network. UCE also imposes costs on users indirectly, to the extent that ISPs pass UCE-related costs along to their subscribers in the form of higher access fees.

Some users also regard UCE as an unwarranted intrusion on their privacy. Many UCE messages contain material that recipients consider offensive, and that they prefer not to confront in their own homes. UCE that contains a hyperlink to a website with adult-oriented material is of particular concern to parents of young children.

In several related contexts, legislatures have recognized and offered protection to this privacy interest. A statutory provision governing the U.S. Postal Service allows individuals to opt out of receiving postal mail of a salacious nature. 39 U.S.C. § 3008. The Telephone Consumer Protection Act of 1991, 47 U.S.C. § 227, prohibits marketers from delivering prerecorded messages to residential telephones, and prohibits sending unsolicited advertisements to a fax machine. The Telemarketing and Consumer Fraud and Abuse Prevention Act, 15 U.S.C. § 6102(a), directs the Federal Trade Commission to promulgate regulations prohibiting deceptive and abusive practices involving telemarketing. *See* Telemarketing Sales Rule, 16 C.F.R. pt. 310. The courts have upheld these regulations. In *Rowan v. United States Post Office Dep't*, 397 U.S. 728, 736 (1970), upholding the postal statute (39 U.S.C. § 3008) against a First Amendment challenge, the Supreme Court recognized "the very basic right to be free from sights, sounds, and tangible matter we do not want."

Harm to Internet service providers. A consumer might receive several UCE messages per day, but ISPs must process through their systems tens to hundreds of millions of UCE messages every day. ISPs estimate that five to thirty percent of the incoming e-mail messages they process consists of UCE. Such large increments in the volume of e-mail traffic impose several types of costs upon ISPs. An increase in e-mail volume may require an ISP to upgrade the capacity of its connection to the Internet, or to increase its hard-drive storage capacity, at significant cost. The additional time that users spend online to download UCE messages may require the ISP to install additional dial-up lines. Additional staffing is required to handle subscribers' complaints about UCE, to install and maintain filtering systems aimed at preventing the delivery of unwanted UCE, and to respond to system problems that can result when a large influx of UCE messages overwhelms an ISP's storage or transmission capacity. Some of these costs are absorbed by the ISP, and the rest of them are passed on to consumers in the form of higher access fees. The degradation to the performance of an ISP's mail system resulting from large volumes of UCE can harm the ISP's reputation.

Harm to third parties. Many recipients of UCE find it offensive, and would respond to it with complaints or retaliation if it were easy to locate the sender. Because senders of UCE typically send messages in bulk to an enormous number of recipients, responses from offended recipients could overwhelm the sender or its ISP and make it impractical to use UCE as a marketing tool. One method UCE senders have developed to avoid this problem is to falsify the routing information contained in the UCE messages, to make it appear that they originated from some other source. When a recipient responds to an e-mail message with a falsified "From" address, the response goes to the domain indicated in that address, rather than to the actual sender of the UCE. The result is that innocent owners of domain names, who have nothing to do with the sending of UCE, are injured by the large volume of negative responses that are directed to their addresses, which can interfere with their ability to receive e-mail that is really intended for them; such owners may suffer reputational harm from the association with UCE.

Generalized harm to e-mail as a medium of communication. The various harms described above result in a generalized harm to e-mail as a means of communication. Compilers of lists of e-mail addresses that are used by senders of UCE typically make use of software robots to gather addresses from postings in USENET newsgroups and listservs, from websites, and from other online sources. To avoid having their addresses placed on these lists, many users go out of their way to prevent their e-mail addresses from appearing in publicly accessible locations online. They may do so by limiting the public fora in which they will communicate; by identifying postings with obfuscated versions of their e-mail addresses that can be read by humans, but not easily by robots[2]; or by setting up multiple e-mail accounts, reserving some for public postings and others for private use—all of which is socially unproductive activity. ISPs seeking to filter out UCE may misidentify a legitimate mailing to a large group of recipients as UCE, causing the messages not to reach the intended recipients. Blacklists identifying ISPs that they view as insufficiently diligent in blocking UCE may sweep too broadly, with the result that ISPs observing the blacklist refuse mail from innocent holders of domain names that are associated with the blacklisted ISP.

2. For example, if my e-mail address is peter@rabbit.com, I might write it instead as "peter at rabbit dot com"—confusing most of the robots, but few of the human readers.

B. Benefits of UCE

Though they are not often articulated, it is important to recognize that UCE has its benefits. UCE is a low-cost means of reaching large numbers of potential customers with marketing messages. The availability of UCE therefore may allow a new competitor to enter the market, when it would otherwise not have the resources needed to attract customers. The entry of such a new competitor may result in lower prices, or in the availability of a broader range of goods.

Potential detriments resulting from the regulation of UCE may also be viewed, if not as a benefit of UCE, at least as a reason for leaving it unregulated. UCE, as commercial speech, is protected by the First Amendment. *See Central Hudson Gas & Electric Corp. v. Public Service Commission*, 447 U.S. 557 (1980). A regulation of UCE that is not appropriately limited may violate the First Amendment: the "cure" of government regulation may be worse than the disease. We also may not want ISPs, pursuing their own economic interests, to decide what commercial speech will reach us and what will be filtered out. One could argue that some recipients of UCE must be responding to it favorably, or marketers would not continue sending UCE: although less expensive than other marketing methods, sending UCE is not free. Limiting UCE would deprive those recipients of whatever benefits they perceive in receiving it.

Consider also the following view:

> E-mail is no less than the expected replacement for a great deal of the physical mail currently sent through the postal service and a great many telephone calls, as well. As such, it will become our primary medium for person-to-person communication. As that primary medium, it deserves the highest levels of protection of the rights of free expression. As annoying as the problem of unwanted e-mail can be, we must act with the most extreme caution in applying legislative rules concerning who can send e-mail to whom, how the e-mail can be sent and, most of all, limitations on the content of e-mail messages.

Letter from the Electronic Frontier Foundation to the House Commerce Committee (Jul. 29, 1998), www.eff.org/Social_responsibility/Spamming_and_net_abuse/19980729_eff_hr3888.letter.

Another possible defense of UCE is that it is no worse than other forms of marketing, such as unsolicited commercial postal mail ("junk mail") and telemarketing. Telemarketing, in particular, is arguably considerably more intrusive than UCE, since it interrupts whatever we are doing and requires an immediate response. Though these forms of marketing are regulated, as noted above, they are not prohibited.

NOTES & QUESTIONS

1. *Spam vs. other kinds of "junk" communications.* Do you think that UCE is more of a problem than postal "junk mail" and telemarketing? Are consumers more willing to sift through and dispose of unsolicited commercial *postal* mail than they are to deal with unsolicited commercial *electronic* mail? Is the burden on e-mail recipients and ISPs any greater than the burden on mailbox holders and the U.S. Postal Service? Are consumers more willing to put up with telemarketing than they are with UCE? Are there justifications for regulating UCE more stringently than these other marketing methods?

2. *Spam vs. other kinds of Internet marketing.* The Internet is full of advertising, including the banner advertisements that are ubiquitous on the Web, and the practice of interposing a pop-up ad before one can access a web page. Is UCE any more problematic than these kinds of advertising?

C. CHALLENGING UCE IN COURT

The following sections consider several legal theories that have been advanced in litigation as a means of attacking the harms that UCE causes.

1. TRESPASS TO CHATTELS

CompuServe Inc. v. Cyber Promotions, Inc.

962 F.Supp. 1015 (S.D.Ohio 1997).

■ GRAHAM, DISTRICT JUDGE

MEMORANDUM OPINION AND ORDER

This case presents novel issues regarding the commercial use of the Internet, specifically the right of an online computer service to prevent a commercial enterprise from sending unsolicited electronic mail advertising to its subscribers.

Plaintiff CompuServe Incorporated ("CompuServe") is one of the major national commercial online computer services. It operates a computer communication service through a proprietary nationwide computer network. In addition to allowing access to the extensive content available within its own proprietary network, CompuServe also provides its subscribers with a link to the much larger resources of the Internet. This allows its subscribers to send and receive electronic messages, known as "e-mail," by the Internet. Defendants Cyber Promotions, Inc. and its president Sanford Wallace are in the business of sending unsolicited e-mail advertisements on behalf of themselves and their clients to hundreds of thousands of Internet users, many of whom are CompuServe subscribers. * * *

This matter is before the Court on the application of CompuServe for a preliminary injunction which would * * * prevent defendants from sending unsolicited advertisements to CompuServe subscribers.

For the reasons which follow, this Court holds that where defendants engaged in a course of conduct of transmitting a substantial volume of electronic data in the form of unsolicited e-mail to plaintiff's proprietary computer equipment, where defendants continued such practice after repeated demands to cease and desist, and where defendants deliberately evaded plaintiff's affirmative efforts to protect its computer equipment from such use, plaintiff has a viable claim for trespass to personal property and is entitled to injunctive relief to protect its property.

I.

* * *

Internet users often pay a fee for Internet access. However, there is no per-message charge to send electronic messages over the Internet and such messages usually reach their destination within minutes. Thus electronic mail provides an opportunity to reach a wide audience quickly and at almost no cost to the sender. It is not surprising therefore that some companies, like defendant Cyber Promotions, Inc., have begun using the Internet to distribute advertisements by sending the same unsolicited commercial message to hundreds of thousands of Internet users at once. Defendants refer to this as "bulk e-mail," while plaintiff refers to it as "junk e-mail." In the vernacular of the Internet, unsolicited e-mail advertising is sometimes referred to pejoratively as "spam."

CompuServe subscribers use CompuServe's domain name "CompuServe.com" together with their own unique alpha-numeric identifier to form a distinctive e-mail mailing address. That address may be used by the subscriber to exchange electronic mail with any one of tens of millions of other Internet users who have electronic mail capability. E-mail sent to CompuServe subscribers is processed and stored on CompuServe's proprietary computer equipment. Thereafter, it becomes accessible to CompuServe's subscribers, who can access CompuServe's equipment and electronically retrieve those messages.

Over the past several months, CompuServe has received many complaints from subscribers threatening to discontinue their subscription unless CompuServe prohibits electronic mass mailers from using its equipment to send unsolicited advertisements. CompuServe asserts that the volume of messages generated by such mass mailings places a significant burden on its equipment which has finite processing and storage capacity. CompuServe receives no payment from the mass mailers for processing their unsolicited advertising. However, CompuServe's subscribers pay for their access to CompuServe's services in increments of time and thus the process of accessing, reviewing and discarding unsolicited e-mail costs them money, which is one of the reasons for their complaints. CompuServe has notified defendants that they are prohibited from using its proprietary computer equipment to process and store unsolicited e-mail and has requested them to cease and desist from sending unsolicited e-mail to its subscribers. Nonetheless, defendants have sent an increasing volume of e-mail solicitations to CompuServe subscribers.

In an effort to shield its equipment from defendants' bulk e-mail, CompuServe has implemented software programs designed to screen out the messages and block their receipt. In response, defendants have modified their equipment and the messages they send in such a fashion as to circumvent CompuServe's screening software. Allegedly, defendants have been able to conceal the true origin of their messages by falsifying the point-of-origin information contained in the header of the electronic messages. Defendants have removed the "sender" information in the header of their messages and replaced it with another address. Also, defendants have developed the capability of configuring their computer servers to conceal their true domain name and appear on the Internet as another computer, further concealing the true origin of the messages. By manipulating this data, defendants have been able to continue sending messages to CompuServe's equipment in spite of CompuServe's protests and protective efforts.

Defendants assert that they possess the right to continue to send these communications to CompuServe subscribers. CompuServe contends that, in doing so, the defendants are trespassing upon its personal property.

* * *

IV.

This Court will now address the * * * aspect of plaintiff's motion in which it seeks to enjoin defendants Cyber Promotions, Inc. and its president Sanford Wallace from sending any unsolicited advertisements to any electronic mail address maintained by CompuServe.

CompuServe predicates this aspect of its motion for a preliminary injunction on the common law theory of trespass to personal property or to chattels, asserting that defendants' continued transmission of electronic messages to its computer equipment constitutes an actionable tort.

Trespass to chattels has evolved from its original common law application, concerning primarily the asportation of another's tangible property, to include the unauthorized use of personal property:

> Its chief importance now, is that there may be recovery ... for interferences with the possession of chattels which are not sufficiently important to be classed as conversion, and so to compel the defendant to pay the full value of the thing with which he has interfered. Trespass to chattels survives today, in other words, largely as a little brother of conversion.

Prosser & Keeton, Prosser and Keeton on Torts, § 14, 85–86 (1984).

The scope of an action for conversion recognized in Ohio may embrace the facts in the instant case. The Supreme Court of Ohio established the definition of conversion under Ohio law in *Baltimore & O. R. Co. v. O'Donnell*, 49 Ohio St. 489, 32 N.E. 476, 478 (1892) by stating that:

> In order to constitute a conversion, it was not necessary that there should have been an actual appropriation of the property by the defendant to its own use and benefit. It might arise from the exercise of a dominion over it in exclusion of the rights of the owner, or withholding it from his possession under a claim inconsistent with his rights. If one take the property of another, for a

> temporary purpose only, in disregard of the owner's right, it is a conversion. Either a wrongful taking, an assumption of ownership, an illegal use or misuse, or a wrongful detention of chattels will constitute a conversion.

Id. 49 Ohio St. at 497–98; *see also Miller v. Uhl*, 37 Ohio App. 276, 174 N.E. 591 (1929); *Great American Mut. Indem. Co. v. Meyer*, 18 Ohio App. 97 (1924); 18 O. Jur. 3d, Conversion § 17. While authority under Ohio law respecting an action for trespass to chattels is extremely meager, it appears to be an actionable tort. * * *

Both plaintiff and defendants cite the Restatement (Second) of Torts to support their respective positions. * * *

The Restatement § 217(b) states that a trespass to chattel may be committed by intentionally using or intermeddling with the chattel in possession of another. Restatement § 217, Comment e defines physical "intermeddling" as follows:

> ... intentionally bringing about a physical contact with the chattel. The actor may commit a trespass by an act which brings him into an intended physical contact with a chattel in the possession of another[.]

Electronic signals generated and sent by computer have been held to be sufficiently physically tangible to support a trespass cause of action. *Thrifty-Tel, Inc. v. Bezenek*, 46 Cal. App. 4th 1559, 1567 (1996); *State v. McGraw*, 480 N.E.2d 552, 554 (Ind.1985) (Indiana Supreme Court recognizing in dicta that a hacker's unauthorized access to a computer was more in the nature of trespass than criminal conversion) and *State v. Riley*, 121 Wash. 2d 22, 846 P.2d 1365 (1993) (computer hacking as the criminal offense of "computer trespass" under Washington law). It is undisputed that plaintiff has a possessory interest in its computer systems. Further, defendants' contact with plaintiff's computers is clearly intentional. Although electronic messages may travel through the Internet over various routes, the messages are affirmatively directed to their destination.

Defendants, citing Restatement (Second) of Torts § 221, which defines "dispossession", assert that not every interference with the personal property of another is actionable and that physical dispossession or substantial interference with the chattel is required. Defendants then argue that they did not, in this case, physically dispossess plaintiff of its equipment or substantially interfere with it. However, the Restatement (Second) of Torts § 218 defines the circumstances under which a trespass to chattels may be actionable:

> One who commits a trespass to a chattel is subject to liability to the possessor of the chattel if, but only if,
>
> (a) he dispossesses the other of the chattel, or
>
> (b) the chattel is impaired as to its condition, quality, or value, or
>
> (c) the possessor is deprived of the use of the chattel for a substantial time, or

(d) bodily harm is caused to the possessor, or harm is caused to some person or thing in which the possessor has a legally protected interest.

Therefore, an interference resulting in physical dispossession is just one circumstance under which a defendant can be found liable. Defendants suggest that "unless an alleged trespasser actually takes physical custody of the property or physically damages it, courts will not find the 'substantial interference' required to maintain a trespass to chattel claim." (Defendant's Memorandum at 13). To support this rather broad proposition, defendants cite only two cases which make any reference to the Restatement. In *Glidden v. Szybiak*, 95 N.H. 318, 63 A.2d 233 (1949), the court simply indicated that an action for trespass to chattels could not be maintained in the absence of some form of damage. The court held that where plaintiff did not contend that defendant's pulling on her pet dog's ears caused any injury, an action in tort could not be maintained. 63 A.2d at 235. In contrast, plaintiff in the present action has alleged that it has suffered several types if injury as a result of defendants' conduct. In *Koepnick v. Sears Roebuck & Co.*, 158 Ariz. 322, 762 P.2d 609 (1988) the court held that a two-minute search of an individual's truck did not amount to a "dispossession" of the truck as defined in Restatement § 221 or a deprivation of the use of the truck for a substantial time. It is clear from a reading of Restatement § 218 that an interference or intermeddling that does not fit the § 221 definition of "dispossession" can nonetheless result in defendants' liability for trespass. The *Koepnick* court did not discuss any of the other grounds for liability under Restatement § 218.

A plaintiff can sustain an action for trespass to chattels, as opposed to an action for conversion, without showing a substantial interference with its right to possession of that chattel. *Thrifty-Tel, Inc.*, 46 Cal. App. 4th at 1567 (quoting *Zaslow v. Kroenert,* 29 Cal. 2d 541, 176 P.2d 1 (Cal. 1946)). Harm to the personal property or diminution of its quality, condition, or value as a result of defendants' use can also be the predicate for liability. Restatement § 218(b).

> An unprivileged use or other intermeddling with a chattel which results in actual impairment of its physical condition, quality or value to the possessor makes the actor liable for the loss thus caused. In the great majority of cases, the actor's intermeddling with the chattel impairs the value of it to the possessor, as distinguished from the mere affront to his dignity as possessor, only by some impairment of the physical condition of the chattel. There may, however, be situations in which the value to the owner of a particular type of chattel may be impaired by dealing with it in a manner that does not affect its physical condition.... In such a case, the intermeddling is actionable even though the physical condition of the chattel is not impaired.

The Restatement (Second) of Torts § 218, comment h. In the present case, any value CompuServe realizes from its computer equipment is wholly derived from the extent to which that equipment can serve its subscriber base. Michael Mangino, a software developer for CompuServe who monitors its mail processing computer equipment, states by affidavit that handling the enormous volume of mass mailings that CompuServe receives places a tremendous burden on its equipment. (Mangino Supp. Dec. at ¶ 12). Defendants' more recent practice of evading CompuServe's filters by disguising the origin of their messages commandeers even more computer resources because CompuServe's computers are forced to store undeliverable e-mail messages and labor in vain to return the messages to an address that does not exist. (Mangino Supp. Dec. at ¶¶ 7–8). To the extent that defendants' multitudinous electronic mailings demand the disk space and drain the processing power of plaintiff's computer equipment, those resources are not available to serve CompuServe subscribers. Therefore, the value of that equipment to CompuServe is diminished even though it is not physically damaged by defendants' conduct.

Next, plaintiff asserts that it has suffered injury aside from the physical impact of defendants' messages on its equipment. Restatement § 218(d) also indicates that recovery may be had for a trespass that causes harm to something in which the possessor has a legally protected interest. Plaintiff asserts that defendants' messages are largely unwanted by its subscribers, who pay incrementally to access their e-mail, read it, and discard it. Also, the receipt of a bundle of unsolicited messages at once can require the subscriber to sift through, at his expense, all of the messages in order to find the ones he wanted or expected to receive. These inconveniences decrease the utility of CompuServe's e-mail service and are the foremost subject in recent complaints from CompuServe subscribers. Patrick Hole, a customer service manager for plaintiff, states by affidavit that in November 1996 CompuServe received approximately 9,970 e-mail complaints from subscribers about junk e-mail, a figure up from approximately two hundred complaints the previous year. (Hole 2d Supp. Dec. at ¶ 4). Approximately fifty such complaints per day specifically reference defendants. (Hole Supp. Dec. at ¶ 3). Defendants contend that CompuServe subscribers are provided with a simple procedure to remove themselves from the mailing list. However, the removal procedure must be performed by the e-mail recipient at his expense, and some CompuServe subscribers complain that the procedure is inadequate and ineffectual. (See, e.g., Hole Supp. Dec. at ¶ 8).

Many subscribers have terminated their accounts specifically because of the unwanted receipt of bulk e-mail messages. (Hole Supp. Dec. at ¶ 9, Hole 2d Supp. Dec. at ¶ 6). Defendants' intrusions into CompuServe's computer systems, insofar as they harm plaintiff's business reputation and goodwill with its customers, are actionable under Restatement § 218(d).

The reason that the tort of trespass to chattels requires some actual damage as a *prima facie* element, whereas damage is assumed where there is a trespass to real property, can be explained as follows:

> The interest of a possessor of a chattel in its inviolability, unlike the similar interest of a possessor of land, is not given legal protection by an action for nominal damages for harmless in-

> termeddlings with the chattel. In order that an actor who interferes with another's chattel may be liable, his conduct must affect some other and more important interest of the possessor. Therefore, one who intentionally intermeddles with another's chattel is subject to liability only if his intermeddling is harmful to the possessor's materially valuable interest in the physical condition, quality, or value of the chattel, or if the possessor is deprived of the use of the chattel for a substantial time, or some other legally protected interest of the possessor is affected as stated in Clause (c). *Sufficient legal protection of the possessor's interest in the mere inviolability of his chattel is afforded by his privilege to use reasonable force to protect his possession against even harmless interference.*

Restatement (Second) of Torts § 218, Comment e (emphasis added). Plaintiff CompuServe has attempted to exercise this privilege to protect its computer systems. However, defendants' persistent affirmative efforts to evade plaintiff's security measures have circumvented any protection those self-help measures might have provided. In this case CompuServe has alleged and supported by affidavit that it has suffered several types of injury as a result of defendants' conduct. The foregoing discussion simply underscores that the damage sustained by plaintiff is sufficient to sustain an action for trespass to chattels. However, this Court also notes that the implementation of technological means of self-help, to the extent that reasonable measures are effective, is particularly appropriate in this type of situation and should be exhausted before legal action is proper.

Under Restatement § 252, the owner of personal property can create a privilege in the would-be trespasser by granting consent to use the property. A great portion of the utility of CompuServe's e-mail service is that it allows subscribers to receive messages from individuals and entities located anywhere on the Internet. Certainly, then, there is at least a tacit invitation for anyone on the Internet to utilize plaintiff's computer equipment to send e-mail to its subscribers. *Buchanan Marine, Inc. v. McCormack Sand Co.*, 743 F.Supp. 139 (E.D.N.Y.1990) (whether there is consent to community use is a material issue of fact in an action for trespass to chattels). However, in or around October 1995, CompuServe employee Jon Schmidt specifically told Mr. Wallace that he was "prohibited from using CompuServe's equipment to send his junk e-mail messages." (Schmidt Dec. at ¶ 5). There is apparently some factual dispute as to this point, but it is clear from the record that Mr. Wallace became aware at about this time that plaintiff did not want to receive messages from Cyber Promotions and that plaintiff was taking steps to block receipt of those messages. (Transcript of December 15, 1996 Hearing at 81–86).

Defendants argue that plaintiff made the business decision to connect to the Internet and that therefore it cannot now successfully maintain an action for trespass to chattels. Their argument is analogous to the argument that because an establishment invites the public to enter its property for business purposes, it cannot later restrict or revoke access to that property, a proposition which is erroneous under Ohio law. *See, e.g., State v. Carriker*, 5 Ohio App. 2d 255, 214 N.E.2d 809 (1964) (the law in Ohio is that a business invitee's privilege to remain on the premises of another may be revoked upon the reasonable notification to leave by the owner or his agents); *Allstate Ins. Co. v. U.S. Associates Realty, Inc.*, 11 Ohio App. 3d 242, 464 N.E.2d 169 (1983) (notice of express restriction or limitation on invitation turns business invitee into trespasser). On or around October 1995, CompuServe notified defendants that it no longer consented to the use of its proprietary computer equipment. Defendants' continued use thereafter was a trespass. Restatement (Second) of Torts §§ 252 and 892A(5); *see also* Restatement (Second) of Torts § 217, Comment f ("The actor may commit a new trespass by continuing an intermeddling which he has already begun, with or without the consent of the person in possession. Such intermeddling may persist after the other's consent, originally given, has been terminated."); Restatement (Second) of Torts § 217, Comment g.

Further, CompuServe expressly limits the consent it grants to Internet users to send e-mail to its proprietary computer systems by denying unauthorized parties the use of CompuServe equipment to send unsolicited electronic mail messages. (Kolehmainen Dec. at ¶ 2). This policy statement, posted by CompuServe online, states as follows:

> CompuServe is a private online and communications services company. CompuServe does not permit its facilities to be used by unauthorized parties to process and store unsolicited e-mail. If an unauthorized party attempts to send unsolicited messages to e-mail addresses on a CompuServe service, CompuServe will take appropriate action to attempt to prevent those messages from being processed by CompuServe. Violations of CompuServe's policy prohibiting unsolicited e-mail should be reported to....

Id. at ¶¶ 2 and 3. Defendants Cyber Promotions, Inc. and its president Sanford Wallace have used plaintiff's equipment in a fashion that exceeds that consent. The use of personal property exceeding consent is a trespass. *City of Amsterdam v. Daniel Goldreyer, Ltd.*, 882 F.Supp. 1273 (E.D.N.Y. 1995); Restatement (Second) of Torts § 256. It is arguable that CompuServe's policy statement, insofar as it may serve as a limitation upon the scope of its consent to the use of its computer equipment, may be insufficiently communicated to potential third-party users when it is merely posted at some location on the network. However, in the present case the record indicates that defendants were actually notified that they were using CompuServe's equipment in an unacceptable manner. To prove that a would-be trespasser acted with the intent required to support liability in tort it is crucial that defendant be placed on notice that he is trespassing.

As a general matter, the public possesses a privilege to reasonably use the facilities of a public utility, Restatement (Second) of Torts § 259, but internet service providers have been held not to be common carriers. *Religious Technology Center v. Netcom On–Line Communication Services, Inc.*, 907 F.Supp. 1361 (N.D.Cal.1995). The definition of public utility status under Ohio law was recently articulated in *A & B Refuse Disposers,*

Inc. v. Bd. Of Ravenna Township Trustees, 64 Ohio St. 3d 385, 596 N.E.2d 423 (1992). The Ohio Supreme Court held that the determination of whether an entity is a "public utility" requires consideration of several factors relating to the "public service" and "public concern" characteristics of a public utility. 596 N.E.2d at 426. The public service characteristic contemplates an entity which devotes an essential good or service to the general public which the public in turn has a legal right to demand or receive. *Id.* at 425. CompuServe's network, Internet access and electronic mail services are simply not essential to society. There are many alternative forms of communication which are customarily used for the same purposes. Further, only a minority of society at large has the equipment to send and receive e-mail messages via the Internet, and even fewer actually do. The second characteristic of a public utility contemplates an entity which conducts its operations in such manner as to be a matter of public concern, that is, a public utility normally occupies a monopolistic or o[li]gopolistic position in the relevant marketplace. *Id.* at 425–426. Defendants estimate that plaintiff serves some five million Internet users worldwide. However, there are a number of major internet service providers that have very large subscriber bases, and with a relatively minor capital investment, anyone can acquire the computer equipment necessary to provide Internet access services on a smaller scale. Furthermore, Internet users are not a "captive audience" to any single service provider, but can transfer from one service to another until they find one that best suits their needs. Finally, the Ohio Supreme Court made clear that a party asserting public utility status is required to support that assertion with evidence going to the relevant aforementioned factors. *Id.* at 427. Defendants have not argued that CompuServe is a public utility, much less produced evidence tending to support such a conclusion. Therefore, CompuServe is not a public utility as that status is defined under Ohio law and defendants can not be said to enjoy a special privilege to use CompuServe's proprietary computer systems.

* * *

Having considered the relevant factors, this Court concludes that the preliminary injunction that plaintiff requests is appropriate.

* * *

NOTES & QUESTIONS

1. *The "value" of computer equipment.* The court found the impairment needed to support a claim of trespass to chattels in the effect of the unwanted e-mail on CompuServe's computer equipment: "To the extent that defendants' multitudinous electronic mailings demand the disk space and drain the processing power of plaintiff's computer equipment, those resources are not available to serve CompuServe subscribers. Therefore, the value of that equipment to CompuServe is diminished even though it is not physically damaged by defendants' conduct." Does making unauthorized use of another's property impair its value? Is this a reasonable application of the concept of "value," or an unwarranted stretch?

2. *The new property.* The trespass in this case was against CompuServe's computer hardware, which is unquestionably a form of property. Is an e-mail account a form of property that may support an action for trespass to chattels? That is, could an individual who receives unwanted UCE messages successfully maintain an action against the sender for trespass to chattels based on unauthorized interference with his e-mail account? Could the owner of a domain name that is falsely designated as the source of the UCE maintain such an action?

3. *Impairment, or just communication?* Why did the court view defendant's bulk e-mail as an impairment of CompuServe's system, rather than simply as communication of exactly the sort that the system was built to accommodate? Suppose defendants sent unsolicited bulk e-mail with a message that all or nearly all of the recipients were happy to receive: for example, coupons good for free admissions to movie theaters. Could CompuServe still maintain its claim of impairment? What is the legal import of the fact that at least some of the recipients of defendant's UCE must have responded favorably to it, since otherwise defendant would have no economic incentive to continue sending it?

4. *The King of Spam.* Sanford Wallace, the owner of the defendant in this case, became notorious in the late 1990's as the self-described King of Spam. His high-volume dispatches of UCE, as many as 25 million e-mails a day, resulted in Cyber Promotions' being kicked off the Internet by a succession of ISPs, and led to a $2 million judgment against the company. Wallace later got out of the UCE business, renounced his former way of life, lined up in support of federal regulation of UCE, and offered himself as a technical expert to litigants battling UCE.

5. *Creative use of common law, or Pandora's box?* As we shall see below, in Parts II and III, *infra,* the doctrine of trespass to chattels has been revived in other contexts besides transmission of UCE. It remains to be seen whether expansive us of this doctrine is consistent with policies of freedom of expression and free competition.

2. GENERAL COMPUTER PROTECTION STATUTES; TRADEMARK INFRINGEMENT AND DILUTION

America Online, Inc. v. LCGM, Inc.

46 F.Supp.2d 444 (E.D.Va.1998).

■ LEE, DISTRICT JUDGE

MEMORANDUM OPINION

This matter is before the Court on plaintiff's Motion for Summary Judgment as to each of the seven counts in the complaint. Plaintiff America Online, Inc. (AOL) complains that defendants sent large numbers of unauthorized and unsolicited bulk e-mail advertisements ("spam") to its members (AOL members). * * *

* * *

II. Findings of Fact and Conclusions of Law

AOL, an Internet service provider located in the Eastern District of Virginia, provides a proprietary, content-based online service that provides its members (AOL members) access to the Internet and the capability to receive as well as send e-mail messages. AOL registered "AOL" as a trademark and service mark in 1996 and has registered its domain name "aol.com" with the InterNIC. At the time this cause of action arose, defendant LCGM, Inc. was a Michigan corporation which operated and transacted business from Internet domains offering pornographic web sites. * * *

AOL alleges that defendants, in concert, sent unauthorized and unsolicited bulk e-mail advertisements ("spam") to AOL customers. AOL's Unsolicited Bulk E-mail Policy and its Terms of Service bar both members and nonmembers from sending bulk e-mail through AOL's computer systems. Plaintiff estimates that defendants, in concert with their "site partners," transmitted more than 92 million unsolicited and bulk e-mail messages advertising their pornographic Web sites to AOL members from approximately June 17, 1997 to January 21, 1998. Plaintiff bases this number on defendants' admissions that they sent approximately 300,000 e-mail messages a day at various intervals from their Michigan offices. See LCGM and Web Promo's Answers to Document Request 12; Sharrak and Drakos' Answers to Document Request 16. Plaintiff asserts that defendants provided AOL with computer disks containing a list of the addresses of 820,296 AOL members to whom defendants admitted to transmitting bulk e-mail.

Plaintiff alleges that defendants harvested, or collected, the e-mail addresses of AOL members in violation of AOL's Terms of Service. Defendants have admitted to maintaining AOL memberships to harvest or collect the e-mail addresses of other AOL members. See Defendants' Answer, para 63. Defendants have admitted to maintaining AOL accounts and to using the AOL Collector and E-mail Pro/Stealth Mailer extractor programs to collect the e-mail addresses of AOL members, alleging that they did so in targeted adult AOL chat rooms. See LCGM and Web Promo's Answers to Document Request 3. See Sharrak and Drakos' Answers to Document Requests 4 and 20. Defendants have admitted to using this software to evade AOL's filtering mechanisms. See Sharrak and Drakos' Answers to Document Request 16.

Plaintiff alleges that defendants forged the domain information "aol.com" in the "from" line of e-mail messages sent to AOL members. Defendants have admitted to creating the domain information "aol.com" through an e-mail sending program, and to causing the AOL domain to appear in electronic header information of its commercial e-mails. See LCGM and Web Promo's Answers to Document Request 17; Sharrak and

Drakos' Answers to Document Requests 13 and 21. LCGM and Web Promo's Answers to Interrogatory 14. Plaintiffs assert that as a result, many AOL members expressed confusion about whether AOL endorsed defendants' pornographic Web sites or their bulk e-mailing practices. Plaintiff also asserts that defendants' e-mail messages were sent through AOL's computer networks. Defendants have admitted to sending e-mail messages from their computers through defendants' network *via* e-mail software to AOL, which then relayed the messages to AOL members. See LCGM and Web Promo's Answers to Document Request 14.

Plaintiff alleges that AOL sent defendants two cease and desist letters, dated respectively December 8, 1997 and December 30, 1997, but that defendants continued their e-mailing practices to AOL members after receiving those letters. Defendants have admitted to receiving those letters, contending that any e-mails sent after such receipt were "lawful." See Defendants Answer, para 46–47.

Plaintiff alleges that defendants paid their "site partners" to transmit unsolicited bulk e-mail on their behalf and encouraged these site partners to advertise. Plaintiff further alleges that defendants conspired with CN Productions, another pornographic e-mailer, to transmit bulk e-mails to AOL members. Plaintiff alleges that many e-mails sent by defendants contained Hyper–Text Links both to defendants' web sites and CN Productions' web sites.

Plaintiff alleges that defendants' actions injured AOL by consuming capacity on AOL's computers, causing AOL to incur technical costs, impairing the functioning of AOL's e-mail system, forcing AOL to upgrade its computer networks to process authorized e-mails in a timely manner, damaging AOL's goodwill with its members, and causing AOL to lose customers and revenue. Plaintiff asserts that between the months of December 1997 and April 1998, defendants' unsolicited bulk e-mails generated more than 450,000 complaints by AOL members.

Count I: False Designation of Origin Under the Lanham Act

The undisputed facts establish that defendants violated 15 U.S.C. § 1125(a)(1) of the Lanham Act, which makes it unlawful to use in commerce:

> any false designation of origin ... which ... is likely to cause confusion, or to cause mistake, or to deceive as to the affiliation, connection, or association of such person with another person, or as to the origin, sponsorship, or approval of his or her goods, services, or commercial activities by another person.

The unauthorized sending of bulk e-mails has been held to constitute a violation of this section of the Lanham Act. *America Online, Inc. v. IMS, et al.*, 24 F.Supp.2d 548 (E.D.Va.1998); *See also Hotmail Corp. v. Van$Money Pie Inc., et al.*, 47 U.S.P.Q.2D (BNA) 1020 (granting injunction where plaintiff was likely to prevail on the merits under the Lanham Act). The elements necessary to establish a false designation violation under the

Lanham Act are as follows: (1) a defendant uses a designation; (2) in interstate commerce; (3) in connection with goods and services; (4) which designation is likely to cause confusion, mistake or deception as to origin, sponsorship, or approval of defendant's goods or services; and (5) plaintiff has been or is likely to be damaged by these acts. See *First Keystone Federal Savings Bank v. First Keystone Mortgage, Inc.*, 923 F.Supp. 693, 707 (E.D.Pa.1996).

Each of the false designation elements has been satisfied. First, defendants clearly used the "aol.com" designation, incorporating the registered trademark and service mark AOL in their e-mail headers. Second, defendants' activities involved interstate commerce because all e-mails sent to AOL members were routed from defendants' computers in Michigan through AOL's computers in Virginia. Third, the use of AOL's designation was in connection with goods and services as defendants' e-mails advertised their commercial web sites. Fourth, the use of "aol.com" in defendants' e-mails was likely to cause confusion as to the origin and sponsorship of defendants' goods and services. Any e-mail recipient could logically conclude that a message containing the initials "aol.com" in the header would originate from AOL's registered Internet domain, which incorporates the registered mark "AOL." *AOL v. IMS*, 24 F.Supp.2d 548. The recipient of such a message would be led to conclude the sender was an AOL member or AOL, the Internet Service Provider. Indeed, plaintiff alleges that this designation did cause such confusion among many AOL members, who believed that AOL sponsored and authorized defendants' bulk e-mailing practices and pornographic web sites. Finally, plaintiff asserts that these acts damaged AOL's technical capabilities and its goodwill. The defendants are precluded from opposing these claims due to their failure to comply with discovery orders. Therefore, there is no genuine issue of material fact in regards to this Count, and the Court holds the plaintiff is entitled to summary judgment on Count I.

Count II: Dilution of Interest in Service Marks Under the Lanham Act

The undisputed facts establish that defendants violated 15 U.S.C. § 1125(c)(1) of the Lanham Act, also known as the Federal Trademark Dilution Act of 1995, which provides relief to an owner of a mark whose mark or trade name is used by another person in commerce "if such use begins after the mark has become famous and causes dilution of the distinctive quality of the mark." The legislative history of the Act indicates that it was intended to address Internet domain name issues. *Intermatic Inc. v. Toeppen*, 947 F.Supp. 1227, 1238 (N.D.Ill.1996) (granting summary judgment to Intermatic, Inc. on its Lanham Act dilution claim against defendant who had registered "intermatic.com" as its domain name). United States Senator Leahy, in discussing the Act, stated that

> . . . it is my hope that this antidilution statute can help stem the use of *deceptive internet addresses* taken by those who are choosing marks that are associated with the products and reputations of others [emphasis added].

Id. (quoting 141 Cong. Rec. S19312–01 (daily ed. December 29, 1995) (statement of Senator Leahy)). Moreover, this Court has found the unauthorized sending of bulk e-mails constitutes a violation of § 1125(c)(1) of the Lanham Act. *AOL v. IMS*, 24 F.Supp.2d 548; *see also Hotmail*, 47 U.S.P.Q.2D (BNA) 1020 (court granted injunction, finding plaintiffs were likely to prevail on the merits under this section of the Act).

Plaintiff has satisfied the two elements necessary to establish a dilution claim: "(1) the ownership of a distinctive mark, and (2) a likelihood of dilution." *Hormel Foods Corp. v. Jim Henson Prods. Inc.*, 73 F.3d 497, 506 (2d Cir.1996) (applying New York's anti-dilution statute). Plaintiff's "AOL" mark qualifies as a distinctive mark. The "AOL" mark is registered on the principal register of the United States Patent and Trademark Office. Furthermore, the mark is recognized throughout the world in association with AOL's online products and services. Dilution can be established by "tarnishment." "The sine qua non of tarnishment is a finding that plaintiff's mark will suffer negative associations through defendant's use." *Id.* at 507. Plaintiff contends that the "AOL" mark is a valuable business asset to plaintiff. Plaintiff argues that the "AOL" mark is tarnished, and thus diluted, by association with defendants' bulk e-mail practices and submits thousands of member complaints about defendants' e-mails as evidence of tarnishment.

Count III: Exceeding Authorized Access in Violation of the Computer Fraud and Abuse Act

The facts before the Court establish that defendants violated 18 U.S.C. § 1030(a)(2)(C) of the Computer Fraud and Abuse Act, which prohibits individuals from "intentionally accessing a computer without authorization or exceeding authorized access, and thereby obtaining information from any protected computer if the conduct involved an interstate or foreign communication." Defendants' own admissions satisfy the Act's requirements. Defendants have admitted to maintaining an AOL membership and using that membership to harvest the e-mail addresses of AOL members. Defendants have stated that they acquired these e-mail addresses by using extractor software programs. Defendants' actions violated AOL's Terms of Service, and as such was unauthorized. Plaintiff contends that the addresses of AOL members are "information" within the meaning of the Act because they are proprietary in nature. Plaintiff asserts that as a result of defendants' actions, it suffered damages exceeding $5,000, the statutory threshold requirement.

Count IV: Impairing Computer Facilities In Violation of the Computer Fraud and Abuse Act

The undisputed facts establish that defendants violated 18 U.S.C. § 1030(a)(5)(C) [since redesignated § 1030(a)(5)(A)(iii)—Eds.] of the Computer Fraud and Abuse Act, which prohibits anyone from "intentionally accessing a protected computer without authorization, and as a result of such conduct, causes damage." Another court found that spamming was an actionable claim under this Act. *See Hotmail*, 47 U.S.P.Q.2D (BNA) 1020 (granting injunction to Hotmail because it was likely to prevail on the merits under this statute). Defendants have admitted to utilizing software to collect AOL members' addresses. These actions were unauthorized because they violated AOL's Terms of Service. Defendants' intent to access a protected computer, in this case computers within AOL's network, is clear under the circumstances. Defendants' access of AOL's computer network enabled defendants to send large numbers of unsolicited bulk e-mail messages to AOL members.

In addition to defendants' admissions, plaintiff alleges that by using the domain information "aol.com" in their e-mails, defendants and their "site partners" camouflaged their identities, and evaded plaintiff's blocking filters and its members' mail controls. Defendants have admitted to using extractor software to evade AOL's filtering mechanisms. As a result of these actions, plaintiff asserts damages to its computer network, reputation and goodwill in excess of the minimum $5,000 statutory requirement.

Count V: Violations of the Virginia Computer Crimes Act

The facts presented to the Court establish that defendants violated the Virginia Computer Crimes Act, Va. Code § 18.2–152.3(3), which provides that "any person who uses a computer or computer network without authority and with the intent to convert the property of another shall be guilty of the crime of computer fraud." Section 18.2–152.12 authorizes a private right of action for violations of the Act. Defendants have admitted to causing "aol.com" to appear in the electronic header information of e-mail messages which they sent. Sending such messages through AOL's computer network was unauthorized. Plaintiff alleges that defendants intended to obtain services by false pretenses and to convert AOL's property. Plaintiff alleges that the inclusion of false domain information in defendants' e-mails enabled defendants to escape detection by plaintiff's blocking filters and its members' mail controls. Plaintiff argues that as a result, defendants illegitimately obtained the unauthorized service of plaintiff's mail delivery system and obtained free advertising from AOL because AOL, not defendants, bore the costs of sending these messages. There are no genuine issues for trial with respect to this Count. As such, plaintiff's Motion for Summary Judgment must be granted on Count V.

Count VI: Trespass to Chattels under the Common Law of Virginia

[The court follows *CompuServe v. Cyber Promotions,* excerpted *supra,* finding that defendants have committed trespass to chattels.] * * *

* * *

NOTES & QUESTIONS

1. *Damage resulting from access.* What damage did the defendant's unauthorized access cause to AOL? Was there any damage to the computer system that the defendant accessed? Should it be sufficient that the access resulted proximately in some damage to the *owner* of the computer?

2. *Confusion and harm from forged return address.* The plaintiff alleged that defendant's use of the AOL mark as the return address of its UCE messages caused recipients to believe "that AOL sponsored and authorized defendants' bulk e-mailing practices and pornographic web sites." How plausible is this allegation? Would the fact that an ISP allows its members to send UCE harm the ISP's reputation?

In *Classified Ventures, L.L.C. v. Softcell Marketing, Inc.*, 109 F.Supp.2d 898 (N.D.Ill.2000), the plaintiff operated an automotive website using the domain name cars.com, and the defendant engaged in marketing using bulk UCE.

> On November 18, 1998, Softcell perpetrated a massive and intricately designed spam e-mail scheme whereby it sent at least a hundred thousand e-mail messages addressed to subscribers of the internet service provider America Online ("AOL"), located throughout the United States. Each e-mail bore the same return address: stione@cars.com. These messages were "spam" e-mail. All messages bore the return address stione@cars.com and contained an advertisement for Internet pornography services available at www.freeyellow.com/members5/hot-web. The messages varied only by their subject lines, which included such messages as "Hi," "Do it for free," "don'y fay [sic] for Video," "not kidding!.... Really Free," "free this time," and "Got your note." Classified Ventures did not create or maintain the e-mail address stione@cars.com. Classified Ventures did not authorize the use of its domain name cars.com in connection with the address designation *stione*. However, consumers who received Softcell's spam e-mails believed they were sent by Classified Ventures because the return address designated "cars.com" as the sender. Consumers were harmed by receiving unsolicited spam e-mail messages advertising Internet pornography. They received the unsolicited spam e-mail but had no way of knowing that the return e-mail address, stione@cars.com, was a false address. The spam e-mails sent a false message that Classified Ventures participates in spam e-mail campaigns and sells pornography services under its CARS.COM Service Marks.

Is such confusion on the part of the recipients of the UCE messages more plausible if the falsified return address contains the domain name of a website that sells a product, like cars.com, than if it contains the domain name of an ISP, like aol.com?

Third parties whose domain names are forged as the return address of UCE mailings may also suffer more tangible forms of harm. In *Parker v. C.N. Enterprises*, No. 97–06273 (Tex., Travis County Dist. Ct. Nov. 10, 1997), a bulk e-mailer used the plaintiff's domain name, flowers.com, as the return address of its UCE. According to the court: "Because many thousands of the Internet addresses were not valid addresses, thousands upon thousands of copies of junk mail were returned to [plaintiff's] computers. This massive, unwanted delivery of the Defendants' garbage to the Plaintiffs' doorstep inflicted substantial harm, including substantial service disruptions, lost access to communications, lost time, lost income and lost opportunities." The court enjoined defendant from further misuse of flowers.com, and awarded plaintiff actual damages in the amount of $13,910.

3. *State laws.* Some state computer crimes laws, like the Virginia statute invoked in *AOL v. LCGM,* have been interpreted to prohibit misuse of another's domain name in UCE. Other states have enacted more specific prohibitions. For example, the California computer crimes statute, discussed in Part I(D), *infra*, imposes criminal penalties against one who "[k]nowingly and without permission uses the Internet domain name of another individual, corporation, or entity in connection with the sending of one or more electronic mail messages, and thereby damages or causes damage to a computer, computer system, or computer network." CAL. PENAL CODE § 502(c)(9).

4. *Antitrust as a sword.* In *Cyber Promotions, Inc. v. America Online, Inc.*, 948 F.Supp. 456 (E.D.Pa.1996), Cyber Promotions, a large sender of unsolicited commercial e-mail (and the defendant in *CompuServe v. Cyber Promotions, supra*), argued "that AOL has obtained a monopoly in the market for providing direct marketing advertising material via electronic transmission to AOL's own subscribers in violation of Section 2 of the Sherman Act, 15 U.S.C. § 2." The court rejected Cyber Promotions' contention that AOL's network constituted an "essential facility" that was the only means of advertising to AOL's subscribers:

> In order to make out a claim under the essential facilities doctrine, Cyber must show "(1) control of the essential facility by a monopolist; (2) the competitor's inability practically or reasonably to duplicate the essential facility; (3) denial of the use of the facility to a competitor; and (4) the feasibility of providing the facility." *Ideal Dairy Farms*, 90 F.3d 737, 748.
>
> With regard to the first factor, there is little likelihood that Cyber will be able to demonstrate that AOL is a monopolist. [The court rejected Cyberpromo's argument that AOL possessed monopoly power in a relevant market, and that it willfully acquired or maintained that power. It continued:]
>
> Even if Cyber could prove AOL is a monopolist in the relevant market, there is little likelihood that Cyber could prove that AOL monopolizes an "essential facility".
>
> "An 'essential facility' is one which is not merely helpful but vital to the claimant's competitive viability." * * * The essential facility Cyber contends that AOL monopolizes is advertising to AOL's own subscribers via electronic mail. We believe there is little likelihood that Cyber will be able to show that the ability to advertise to AOL's subscribers is vital to Cyber's competitive ability.
>
> In the first instance, as mentioned above, AOL has not even completely excluded Cyber from the AOL system. AOL's Preferred

Mail simply gives the AOL subscriber the option to choose whether he wishes to view Cyber's e-mail advertisements. In addition, AOL currently has approximately seven million members who constitute no more than one-sixth to one-seventh of the current total e-mail population of 40 to 50 million and approximately one-half of the current total online population of 12 million. Cyber also has many other means of disseminating its advertising to Internet users in general and to AOL subscribers in particular besides electronic mail. Cyber can send its advertisements to the subscribers of the many other online services which compete with AOL, including CompuServe, the Microsoft Network and Prodigy. Cyber can send its advertisements to AOL members over the Internet through the World Wide Web which would allow access by AOL subscribers who want to receive Cyber's advertisements. Cyber, as an advertising agency, can disseminate its advertisements to AOL subscribers and others by non-Internet means including the United States mail, telemarketing, television, cable, newspapers, magazines, billboards and leaflets. And, of course, Cyber could attempt to lure AOL subscribers away from AOL by developing its own commercial online system or advertising website and charging a competitive rate. * * *

In short, Cyber has failed to show why its advertising to AOL subscribers is any more vital than its advertising to the subscribers of the many other commercial online services or its advertising to other individuals with an Internet e-mail address.

Even if Cyber could prove an essential facility, it is unlikely that it could satisfy the remaining elements of its essential facilities claim. With regard to the second factor—the competitor's inability practically or reasonably to duplicate the essential facility—Cyber has not shown any reason why it could not (other than perhaps because it would have to pay its own way) use its servers to create its own commercial online internet service or advertising website and attempt to lure away AOL subscribers.

With regard to the third element—denial of the use of the essential facility to a competit[or]—we reiterate that Cyber has not been completely prevented from sending its e-mail advertisements to AOL subscribers. Although the onus is on the AOL subscriber who wants to view Cyber's advertisements to click the "I want junk e-mail!" box on the screen, we do not believe this process is unreasonably burdensome to AOL subscribers.

Finally, Cyber is unlikely to be able to show the feasibility of AOL providing its facility to Cyber without the PreferedMail tool. It is clearly unfeasible for AOL's e-mail servers, which the parties have stipulated have a finite capacity, to be burdened with up to 1.9 million e-mail advertisements each day from a single advertiser such as Cyber. In addition, as we noted in our Memorandum Opinion of November 4, 1996, the Court has received a plethora of

> letters from disgruntled AOL subscribers who complain of not only having to sift through Cyber's e-mail advertisements in their e-mail boxes but also of having to pay for the time it takes to erase these messages. AOL simply should not have to incur the wrath of its paying customers and resulting damage to its reputation in order to carry millions of Cyber's e-mail advertisements free of charge.
>
> In sum, we find that there is little likelihood that Cyber will be able to establish the necessary elements of its claim under the "essential facilities" or "bottleneck" doctrine and that AOL has "refused to deal" with Cyber in violation of Section 2 of the Sherman Act.

948 F.Supp. 461–64.

5. *First Amendment as defense.* Also in *Cyber Promotions v. AOL*, Cyber Promotions argued that AOL's efforts to bar Cyber Promotions' e-mailings from AOL's network violated the First Amendment's free-speech guarantee. The court held that AOL was not a state actor, and that the First Amendment therefore did not apply to its activities.

6. *Calculating damages for illegal sending of unsolicited commercial e-mail.* What is the measure of damages to the operator of a computer network that is the target of bulk UCE? In *America Online, Inc. v. Prime Data Systems, Inc.*, 1998 WL 34016692 (E.D.Va.1998), AOL introduced evidence establishing "that its computer costs are at least $.00078 per message, without considering personnel or other costs associated with the computers' operation." The court granted AOL compensatory damages of $.00078 for each UCE message defendants sent to its subscribers, as well as punitive damages of three times that amount. Based on AOL's showing that defendants had sent it at least 130 million UCE messages, the court awarded $101,400 in compensatory damages and $304,200 in punitive damages.

In *America Online, Inc. v. National Health Care Discount, Inc.*, 174 F.Supp.2d 890 (N.D.Iowa 2001), AOL sought damages based on the market value of the marketing defendants accomplished by sending their UCE to AOL's subscribers. AOL argued for a market value based on the rate it charged advertisers to place banner advertisements on subscribers' e-mail in-boxes. That rate, $8.56 per thousand impressions, would have translated into damages of $.00856 per UCE message—more than ten times AOL's cost-to-process of $.00078. The court agreed that "AOL's damages should not be limited to the amount [defendant's] wrongful conduct cost AOL. Such a result would permit [defendant], and others in a similar position, to appropriate the use of AOL's equipment at cost, without compensating AOL for any profit." However, the court did not agree that the value of a UCE message was the same as that of a banner ad impression, noting: "Banner advertisements are much larger on a computer screen than incoming e-mail messages. Banners usually are in color, with eye-catching graphics. They often have moving text. They can be linked directly to an advertiser's website, taking the viewer to the site with a single click of the mouse." It arrived at a compromise damage figure of $.0025 per message. Multiplying that by the 135 million e-mails defendant sent resulted in damages of $337,500.

The California statute regulating UCE, discussed below, allows ISPs to recover liquidated damages of $50 for each e-mail message received, up to a maximum of $25,000 per day. Is this excessive? Assuming that 60 billion UCE messages are sent each year, this would mean that ISPs could be entitled to damages of $3 trillion each year.

D. Legislative Approaches

As this book went to press, twenty-two states had passed laws regulating the use of unsolicited commercial e-mail, and a number of other states had considered similar legislation. Restrictions vary from state to state, but most incorporate one or more of the following types of regulation:

- a requirement that UCE messages include removal instructions, allowing recipients to *opt out* of receiving future UCE messages from that sender;
- *labeling requirements*, requiring that each UCE message contain language in the subject line indicating it is an advertisement;
- prohibitions against the use of *falsified routing information*, false return addresses, or misleading subject lines;
- a prohibition against providing *software designed to facilitate falsification* of routing information;
- a prohibition against transmitting UCE messages in violation of an ISP's *Terms of Service*;
- a prohibition against *unauthorized use of a third-party's domain name*.

Violations of these statutes may result in civil liability or criminal penalties.

Congress has considered a number of bills aimed at regulating UCE, but none has been enacted. In 2000, the House passed H.R. 3113, the Unsolicited Commercial Electronic Mail Act of 2000, but the Senate failed to act on it. H.R. 3113 requires UCE to be labeled as such and to include opt-out instructions, prohibits false routing information, and makes a provider's Terms of Service enforceable. The bill was reintroduced into the 107th Congress as H.R. 95, and as this book went to press was pending.

Some senders of UCE, quick to spot an opportunity, have sought to capitalize on the House's approval of H.R. 3113, by including (false) statements in their UCE messages such as: "Under Bill H.R.3113 passed by the 106th US Congress this letter cannot be considered spam as long as the sender includes contact information and a method of removal."

California Business & Professions Code

§ 17538.4. Unsolicited fax or e-mail

(a) No person or entity conducting business in this state shall facsimile (fax) or cause to be faxed, or electronically mail (e-mail) or cause to be e-mailed, documents consisting of unsolicited advertising material for the lease, sale, rental, gift offer, or other disposition of any realty, goods, services, or extension of credit unless:

(1) In the case of a fax, that person or entity establishes a toll-free telephone number that a recipient of the unsolicited faxed documents may call to notify the sender not to fax the recipient any further unsolicited documents.

(2) In the case of e-mail, that person or entity establishes a toll-free telephone number or valid sender operated return e-mail address that the recipient of the unsolicited documents may call or e-mail to notify the sender not to e-mail any further unsolicited documents.

(b) All unsolicited faxed or e-mailed documents subject to this section shall include a statement informing the recipient of the toll-free telephone number that the recipient may call, or a valid return address to which the recipient may write or e-mail, as the case may be, notifying the sender not to fax or e-mail the recipient any further unsolicited documents to the fax number, or numbers, or e-mail address, or addresses, specified by the recipient.

In the case of faxed material, the statement shall be in at least nine-point type. In the case of e-mail, the statement shall be the first text in the body of the message and shall be of the same size as the majority of the text of the message.

(c) Upon notification by a recipient of his or her request not to receive any further unsolicited faxed or e-mailed documents, no person or entity conducting business in this state shall fax or cause to be faxed or e-mail or cause to be e-mailed any unsolicited documents to that recipient.

(d) In the case of e-mail, this section shall apply when the unsolicited e-mailed documents are delivered to a California resident via an electronic mail service provider's service or equipment located in this state. For these purposes "electronic mail service provider" means any business or organization qualified to do business in this state that provides individuals, corporations, or other entities the ability to send or receive electronic mail through equipment located in this state and that is an intermediary in sending or receiving electronic mail.

(e) As used in this section, "unsolicited e-mailed documents" means any e-mailed document or documents consisting of advertising material for the lease, sale, rental, gift offer, or other disposition of any realty, goods, services, or extension of credit that meet both of the following requirements:

(1) The documents are addressed to a recipient with whom the initiator does not have an existing business or personal relationship.

(2) The documents are not sent at the request of, or with the express consent of, the recipient.

(f) As used in this section, "fax" or "cause to be faxed" or "e-mail" or "cause to be e-mailed" does not include or refer to the transmission of any documents by a telecommunications utility or internet service provider to the extent that the telecommunications utility or internet service provider merely carries that transmission over its network.

(g) In the case of e-mail that consists of unsolicited advertising material for the lease, sale, rental, gift offer, or other disposition of any realty, goods, services, or extension of credit, the subject line of each and every message shall include "ADV:" as the first four characters. If these messages contain information that consists of unsolicited advertising material for the lease, sale, rental, gift offer, or other disposition of any realty, goods, services, or extension of credit, that may only be viewed, purchased, rented, leased, or held in possession by an individual 18 years of age and older, the subject line of each and every message shall include "ADV:ADLT" as the first eight characters.

(h) An employer who is the registered owner of more than one e-mail address may notify the person or entity conducting business in this state e-mailing or causing to be e-mailed, documents consisting of unsolicited advertising material for the lease, sale, rental, gift offer, or other disposition of any realty, goods, services, or extension of credit of the desire to cease e-mailing on behalf of all of the employees who may use employer-provided and employer-controlled e-mail addresses.

(i) This section, or any part of this section, shall become inoperative on and after the date that federal law is enacted that prohibits or otherwise regulates the transmission of unsolicited advertising by electronic mail (e-mail).

§ 17538.45. Unsolicited electronic mail advertisement

(a) For purposes of this section, the following words have the following meanings:

(1) "Electronic mail advertisement" means any electronic mail message, the principal purpose of which is to promote, directly or indirectly, the sale or other distribution of goods or services to the recipient.

(2) "Unsolicited electronic mail advertisement" means any electronic mail advertisement that meets both of the following requirements:

(A) It is addressed to a recipient with whom the initiator does not have an existing business or personal relationship.

(B) It is not sent at the request of or with the express consent of the recipient.

* * *

(b) No registered user of an electronic mail service provider shall use or cause to be used that electronic mail service provider's equipment located in this state in violation of that electronic mail service provider's policy prohibiting or restricting the use of its service or equipment for the initiation of unsolicited electronic mail advertisements.

(c) No individual, corporation, or other entity shall use or cause to be used, by initiating an unsolicited electronic mail advertisement, an electronic mail service provider's equipment located in this state in violation of that electronic mail service provider's policy prohibiting or restricting the use of its equipment to deliver unsolicited electronic mail advertisements to its registered users.

(d) An electronic mail service provider shall not be required to create a policy prohibiting or restricting the use of its equipment for the initiation or delivery of unsolicited electronic mail advertisements.

(e) Nothing in this section shall be construed to limit or restrict the rights of an electronic mail service provider under Section 230(c)(1) of Title 47 of the United States Code, or any decision of an electronic mail service provider to permit or to restrict access to or use of its system, or any exercise of its editorial function.

(f)

(1) In addition to any other action available under law, any electronic mail service provider whose policy on unsolicited electronic mail advertisements is violated as provided in this section may bring a civil action to recover the actual monetary loss suffered by that provider by reason of that violation, or liquidated damages of fifty dollars ($50) for each electronic mail message initiated or delivered in violation of this section, up to a maximum of twenty-five thousand dollars ($25,000) per day, whichever amount is greater.

(2) In any action brought pursuant to paragraph (1), the court may award reasonable attorney's fees to a prevailing party.

(3)

(A) In any action brought pursuant to paragraph (1), the electronic mail service provider shall be required to establish as an element of its cause of action that prior to the alleged violation, the defendant had actual notice of both of the following:

(i) The electronic mail service provider's policy on unsolicited electronic mail advertising.

(ii) The fact that the defendant's unsolicited electronic mail advertisements would use or cause to be used the electronic mail service provider's equipment located in this state.

(B) In this regard, the Legislature finds that with rapid advances in Internet technology, and electronic mail technology in particular, internet service providers are already experimenting with embedding policy statements directly into the software running on the computers used to provide electronic mail services in a manner that displays the policy statements every time an electronic mail delivery is requested. While the state of the technology does not support such a finding at present, the Legislature believes that, in a given case at some future date, a showing that notice was supplied via electronic means between the sending and receiving computers could be held to constitute actual notice to the sender for purposes of this paragraph.

* * *

CALIFORNIA PENAL CODE

§ 502. Computer crimes

* * *

(c) [A]ny person who commits any of the following acts is guilty of a public offense:

* * *

(9) Knowingly and without permission uses the Internet domain name of another individual, corporation, or entity in connection with the sending of one or more electronic mail messages, and thereby damages or causes damage to a computer, computer system, or computer network.

(d)

* * *

(5) Any person who violates paragraph (9) of subdivision (c) is punishable as follows:

(A) For a first violation that does not result in injury, an infraction punishable by a fine not [exceeding] one thousand dollars.

(B) For any violation that results in injury, or for a second or subsequent violation, by a fine not exceeding five thousand dollars ($5,000), or by imprisonment in a county jail not exceeding one year, or by both that fine and imprisonment.

NOTES & QUESTIONS

1. *Parallel treatment of UCE and faxes.* Note that Section 17538.4, requiring that UCE messages display opt-out information and that they be labeled as advertisements, applies a similar regulatory scheme to both unsolicited faxes and unsolicited e-mails. The section originally addressed only faxes. It was amended in 1998 to add coverage of UCE.

2. *Applicability of prohibition.* Would the actions of the defendant in *AOL v. LCGM*, excerpted in Part I(C)(2), *supra,* constitute a violation of Section 502(c)(9)? What about those of the defendant in *Parker v. C.N. Enterprises*, discussed in Part I(C)(2), Note 2, *supra*?

3. *Labeling and content restrictions.* The California statute, like several other state statutes, requires a specific label, such as "ADV:", on the subject line of UCE messages. The label allows consumers, and ISPs, automatically to filter out UCE messages, so that they do not appear in the in-box. Other statutes prohibit subject lines, such as "Re: your question," that mislead the recipient into assuming that the message is from someone they know. This helps consumers to identify and delete incoming UCE messages without having to read them. Are such requirements less problematic, from the standpoint of free speech and autonomy, than prohibitions, in that they allow the recipient or ISP to make the determination whether to accept UCE?

DELAWARE CODE

11 Del. Code § 931. Definitions

As used in this subpart:

* * *

(17) "Commercial electronic mail" or "commercial e-mail" means any electronic mail message that is sent to a receiving address or account for the purposes of advertising, promoting, marketing or otherwise attempting to solicit interest in any good service or enterprise.

11 Del. Code § 937. Unrequested or unauthorized electronic mail or use of network or software to cause same

A person is guilty of the computer crime of unrequested or unauthorized electronic mail:

(1) When that person, without authorization, intentionally or recklessly distributes any unsolicited bulk commercial electronic mail (commercial E-mail) to any receiving address or account under the control of any authorized user of a computer system. This section shall not apply to electronic mail that is sent between human beings, or when the individual has requested said information. This section shall not apply to the transmission of electronic mail from an organization to its members or where there is a preexisting business relationship. No Internet/interactive service provider shall be liable for merely transmitting an unsolicited, bulk commercial electronic mail message in its network. No internet/interactive service provider shall be held liable for any action voluntarily taken in good faith to block the receipt or transmission through its service of any unsolicited, bulk electronic mail which it believes is, or will be, sent in violation to disconnect or terminate the service of any person that is in violation of this article; or

(2) When a person uses a computer or computer network without authority with the intent to: Falsify or forge electronic mail transmission information in any manner in connection with the transmission of unsolicited bulk electronic mail through or into the computer network of an electronic mail service provider or its subscribers; or

(3) When a person sells, gives or otherwise distributes or possesses with the intent to sell, give or distribute software which:

a. Is primarily designed or produced for the purpose of facilitating or enabling the falsification of electronic mail transmission information or other routing information;

b. Has only limited commercially significant purpose or use other than to facilitate or enable the falsification of electronic mail transmission information or other routing information; or

c. Is marketed by that person or another acting in concert with that person's knowledge for use in facilitating or enabling the falsification of electronic mail transmission information or other routing information.

(4) For the purposes of this section, conduct occurring outside of the State shall be sufficient to constitute this offense if such conduct is within the terms of § 204 of this title, or if the receiving address or account was under the control of any authorized user of a computer system who was located in Delaware at the time he or she received the electronic mail or communication and the defendant was aware of circumstances which rendered the presence of such authorized user in Delaware a reasonable possibility.

COLORADO REVISED STATUTES

6–2.5–102. Definitions

As used in this article, unless the context otherwise requires:

* * *

(5) "Unsolicited commercial electronic mail message" means an electronic mail message sent without the recipient's expressed permission for the purpose of promoting real property, goods, or services for sale or lease.

6–2.5–103. Restrictions on certain commercial electronic mail—violations of article

(1) It shall be a violation of this article for any person that sends an unsolicited commercial electronic mail message to fail to disclose the actual point-of-origin electronic mail address of the unsolicited commercial electronic mail message.

(2) It shall be a violation of this article for any person that sends an unsolicited commercial electronic mail message to falsify electronic mail transmission information or other routing information for the unsolicited commercial electronic mail message.

(3) It shall be a violation of this article for any person that sends an unsolicited commercial electronic mail message to use a third party's internet address or domain name without the third party's consent for the purposes of transmitting electronic mail.

* * *

NOTES & QUESTIONS

1. *Privilege for human beings.* The Delaware statute generally forbids the sending of bulk UCE, but allows an exception for "electronic mail that is sent between human beings." To what sorts of UCE might this language apply? Consider the indubitably true, but not frequently noted, fact that senders of UCE are nearly invariably human beings. If such a person decides to send an e-mail message to one million human beings, and uses a mailing program to save himself the drudgery of hand-addressing each message, is this excluded as e-mail sent between human beings? What might fall into the category of e-mail that is *not* sent between human beings?

2. *Extraterritorial effects of state UCE laws.* State UCE laws apply, to varying degrees, to UCE sent by a sender who is located outside of the state. For example, the Delaware statute imposes criminal liability for sending UCE if the recipient is in Delaware "and the [sender] was aware of circumstances which rendered the presence of such authorized user in Delaware a reasonable possibility." 11 DEL. CODE § 937(4). Given the general knowledge that there exist e-mail users in Delaware, and the haphazard manner in which lists of e-mail addresses for addressing UCE are assembled, all senders of UCE are arguably in this category. The effect of this provision might be to discourage the sending of UCE from states in which that activity is perfectly legal. Is it appropriate for the law of one state to control the behavior of residents of other states? Several state laws regulating UCE and adult-oriented materials on the Internet have been challenged as violating the Constitution's Dormant Commerce Clause, which prohibits state laws that are found improperly to discriminate against interstate commerce or to have unwarranted extraterritorial effects. These challenges have generated mixed results. The Dormant Commerce Clause issues are discussed in Chapter 1, Part III(C), *supra.*

3. *Defining "unsolicited commercial e-mail."* Some statutes, like the Delaware statute excerpted above, apply only to UCE that is sent in "bulk." Some of these statutes do not define the term "bulk." But the Idaho statute defines "bulk electronic mail advertisement" as "an electronic message, containing the same or similar advertisement, which is contemporaneously transmitted to two (2) or more recipients." IDAHO STAT. § 48–603E(1)(a). In Louisiana, e-mail qualifies as "bulk" only if it "is sent in the same or substantially similar form to more than one thousand recipients." LA. REV. STAT. 14:73.1(13).

Consider the following view of the Electronic Frontier Foundation, expressed in a letter sent to members of the House Commerce Committee, addressing proposed federal legislation regulating UCE:

> The current bills define spam as "unsolicitied commercial e-mail." However, it is not the commercial nature of the messages that make them spam; it is the volume of the messages that make them invasive. Any anti-spamming law must recognize that only in bulk does e-mail approach the nuisance level of telemarketing. A law that attempts to prohibit or regulate person-to-person e-mail, even of a commercial nature, is almost certain to be found unconstitutional, especially since the abuse of e-mail is not limited to commercial advertising. As such, restricting single advertising messages is a poor solution to the problem and fails the constitutional tests set forth by the Supreme Court in Central Hudson Gas & Elec. v. Public Serv. Comm'n, 447 U.S. 557 (1980), and City of

> Cincinnati v. Discovery Network, Inc., 507 U.S. 410 (1993), which require that limits on commercial speech be narrowly tailored to serve a compelling state interest.

Letter from the Electronic Frontier Foundation to the House Commerce Committee (Jul. 29, 1998), www.eff.org/Social_responsibility/Spamming_and_net_abuse/19980729_eff_hr3888.letter.

What types of e-mail messages should these statutes regulate? An inappropriately broad definition of UCE would regulate more broadly than necessary to remedy the problem, and might run afoul of the First Amendment. All of the current state statutes limit their coverage to e-mail that is "unsolicited." Most statutes define "unsolicited" so as to exclude e-mail that is sent with the consent of the recipient, or that is sent between parties with a pre-existing business or professional relationship. Most statutes apply only to e-mail that has a commercial purpose. But the Connecticut statute makes it illegal to falsify routing information in connection with the sending of "unsolicited bulk electronic mail." CONN. GEN. STAT. § 53–451(b)(7). Is this restriction consistent with the First Amendment? Which of the statutes excerpted above is most sensitive to First Amendment values?

How would you craft a statute to balance the competing interests of ISPs, e-mail recipients, and marketers? Does all UCE impose equal costs, suggesting that a uniform regulation might be appropriate, or do the disparate costs of, for example, unsolicited adult-oriented e-mails compared to clearly labeled commercial e-mails suggest that regulation should varying depending on the type of UCE?

4. *Opting out.* Rather than banning UCE entirely, opt-out regulations give e-mail recipients the option of receiving or blocking unsolicited commercial e-mails. Some state statutes require that all UCE contain a toll-free number or valid e-mail address that the recipient can contact to request that the sender stop sending commercial messages to the recipient. Are such statutes likely to be effective in controlling the volume of unwanted commercial solicitations? Consider the time that recipients must spend replying to the initial UCE message from each sender, the large number of UCE senders, and the ease with which UCE senders may change their identity with new products and new sending addresses. Do the statutes we have looked at deal with this problem?

5. *Enforceability of ISP Terms of Service.* Several statutes impose liability for sending UCE in violation of an ISP's Terms of Service. (In the absence of such a statute are Terms of Service enforceable on a breach-of-contract theory?) Is it fair to hold a sender of UCE responsible for complying with Terms of Service that he may never have seen? Consider the following view:

> The difficult questions in such an approach lie in determining the circumstances under which policies should be enforced—in particular, determining what form of notice ought to be required before

> a provider's policies can be enforced with respect to a particular spammer.
>
> Several methods of providing constructive notice of such policies have been proposed. First, a provider may choose to post its policies on the web—preferably, where they can be easily located by someone who knows nothing more than the prospective recipient's e-mail address. Second, a provider may configure its SMTP server to transmit a brief reference to its policies during every session, before it will receive a message. A third approach would be for providers to register their policies with a central authority, such as a state or federal government agency; spammers could be required to consult a central registry of providers' policies before sending unsolicited messages. * * *
>
> If a law is enacted that enforces providers' anti-spam policies and one or more of these forms of constructive notice is deemed adequate, the practical result will be roughly equivalent to imposing a legal prohibition on spam, since nearly all destination operators already have anti-spam policies and nearly all likely will take advantage of the constructive notice provision.

David E. Sorkin, *Technical and Legal Approaches to Unsolicited Electronic Mail*, 35 U.S.F. L. REV. 325, 372–74 (2001).

6. *Constitutional challenge to UCE statute*. Washington State's commercial e-mail legislation was upheld against a constitutional challenge based upon the Dormant Commerce Clause in *State of Washington v. Heckel*, 24 P.3d 404 (Wash.2001) (en banc), excerpted in Chapter 1, Part III(C), *supra*.

E. SELF-HELP APPROACHES

In addition to the legal and legislative strategies, described above, that aim at stemming the flood of UCE, ISPs and e-mail users have implemented a variety of self-help measures. Some of these measures may be credited with modest success in curbing unsolicited commercial e-mailing, but the practice continues largely unabated.

Most ISPs have adopted Terms of Service that strictly prohibit the use of their facilities for sending UCE messages. A subscriber of such an ISP who violates those Terms of Service may have his subscription terminated. It is difficult, however, for ISPs to identify those who violate their Terms of Service and take steps to deny service to them. Nor does anything prevent the subscriber from moving to another ISP, perhaps under another name, and continuing to send UCE.

The informal code of Internet etiquette, sometimes referred to as "netiquette," likewise prohibits UCE. Some marketers are likely to be attentive to informal codes, but many more are not. Legitimate companies, which value their reputations, have hesitated to send UCE because they recognize that it is widely disliked by consumers. Most senders of UCE are unconcerned with their reputations: they hope to implement a successful money-making scheme, and then move on to the next scheme, under a new identity, once the first scheme stops working.

There have been various proposals, some originating with UCE senders themselves, to establish a universal opt-out list, which would contain the e-mail addresses of users who have stated they do not wish to receive UCE. Opponents have pointed to the risk that such a list would fall into the wrong hands, and would be used as a source of valid e-mail addresses to which UCE would be sent.

What incentive would a marketer have to honor an opt-out list? A marketer that values its reputation might think it counterproductive to send advertising messages to recipients who have stated they do not wish to receive them. The Direct Marketing Association, a trade association of sellers that use telemarketing, direct mail, and other direct-marketing techniques, maintains a UCE opt-out list, called "e-MPS," and requires its members to honor it. As the DMA explains:

> **Why would a marketer want to use e-MPS?** Marketers use, as at least one measure of success, the building of long term relationships with customers. They do not want to irritate consumers who might be receptive to hearing from them in other media or who might buy from them directly without being solicited.

Direct Marketing Association, *E-Mail Preference Service*, preference.the-dma.org/products/empssubscription.shtml. Most UCE senders do not belong to the DMA.

Some recipients of unwanted UCE respond by attempting to punish the sender, such as by sending abusive responses, reporting the sender to its ISP, unleashing a flood of messages ("mail bomb") or some other online attack designed to knock the sender offline, or publicizing the sender's name and personal details. These efforts have proven largely ineffective, and sometimes counterproductive. Because UCE senders frequently use false return addresses and falsified routing information, and do not disclose their physical locations, they are hard to find. A reply to a UCE message usually does not reach the sender: it is either directed to a non-existent address, goes to a real address where it is automatically deleted, or goes to the address of an innocent third-party which the sender forges as the return address.

A more sophisticated system that many ISPs have adopted is subscription to a blacklist of ISPs that are deemed to offer aid and comfort to UCE senders. The best-known such blacklist, the Mail Abuse Prevention System's Realtime Blackhole List ("RBL"), is discussed in Chapter 1, Part II(D), *supra*. ISPs that subscribe to the RBL implement an e-mail filtering system that automatically blocks the reception of e-mail messages from a sender hosted by an ISP that is on the blacklist. ISPs most commonly are placed on the RBL because they operate "open relays": mail servers that can be used by parties who are not subscribers of the ISP. Senders of UCE frequently use open relays to disguise the origin of their messages and prevent their own ISP from terminating them for violation of the Terms of Service.

The RBL's filtering is overbroad, as it may block e-mail from innocent senders who happen to subscribe to an ISP that is on the blacklist. Some ISPs have objected to their inclusion on the blacklist.

Media3 Technologies, LLC v. Mail Abuse Prevention System, LLC

2001 WL 92389 (D.Mass.2001).

■ MORRIS E. LASKER, DISTRICT JUDGE.

MEMORANDUM AND ORDER

Media3 Technologies, LLC ("Media3"), sues Mail Abuse Prevention System, LLC ("MAPS"), and Paul Vixie, MAPS's Chief Executive Officer, for redress of alleged unfair business practices. Media3 contends that its reputation has been injured and that it has lost current and anticipated business as the result of defamatory remarks related to Media3 placed in certain files on MAPS's website, located at mail-abuse.org/, as well as by MAPS's recommendation to other businesses, through its Realtime Blackhole List ("blackhole list"), not to allow access to websites hosted by Media3. Media3 alleges that these acts constitute defamation, intentional interference with existing advantageous business relations, intentional interference with prospective advantageous business relations, and a violation of M.G.L. ch. 93A.

Media3 moves for a preliminary injunction requiring MAPS to remove all websites hosted by Media3 from MAPS's blackhole list. The application for a preliminary injunction is denied.

I.

Media3 is an Internet "web-hosting" company based in Pembroke, Massachusetts, that offers services in creating and maintaining websites to those who wish to conduct electronic commerce. As a "web-hosting" company, Media3 is the owner of forty-two "Class C network address blocks." Each block is capable of holding approximately 254 "Internet protocol addresses" on which websites may be placed. Media3 rents Internet protocol addresses on these Class C networks to individuals and organizations who wish to create websites. Often with Media3's help, these customers then build websites which Media3 also assists in maintaining.

Before agreeing to host a website, Media3 follows the standard industry practice of requiring its customers to sign an Acceptable Use Policy for conducting business on the Internet. This policy contains provisions which are standard in the industry, including an "anti-spam" provision.

Spam is the industry term used to describe unwanted e-mail that is often sent en masse to e-mail addresses for commercial purposes. For obvious reasons, spam is unpopular with many in the Internet community.

One not so obvious, but critically important reason why spam is unpopular, is that while it is free to send it costs money to receive. Media3's Acceptable Use Policy prohibits not only the transmission of spam, but also the support of spam through the development of software which could be used to hide the origin of a person sending spam.

Although Media3's Acceptable Use Policy bars websites it hosts from supporting spam in some ways, it does not prohibit its hosted websites from providing other services which appear to be used primarily by spammers. These services include the sale of lists of hundreds of thousands and even millions of e-mail addresses and computer software programs which can "harvest" similar lists from the Internet. While the vast majority of Media3's customers do not offer such "spam support" services, a few do. See Def.'s Exhibits 1–4.

In May of 2000, the offending websites were brought to the attention of MAPS. MAPS is a non-profit internet service provider based in California which, like other internet service providers (such as America Online), provides Internet and e-mail access to its subscribers. While MAPS is organized like an ordinary ISP, its mission and role in the Internet community is distinct. MAPS's stated purpose is to combat spam. Its primary means for combating spam is its "Realtime Blackhole List." The blackhole list is a constantly updated list of the websites which, in MAPS's view, either send or support the sending of spam. When MAPS places a website on the blackhole list, it blocks transmission between the website and addresses in its system. MAPS has made its popular blackhole list available to other internet service providers, sometimes for a fee. It is a popular product and approximately 40 percent of all internet addresses, including those of several Massachusetts enterprises, use MAPS's blackhole list as a spam filter.

In May of 2000, when MAPS learned that Media3 was hosting ten websites on one of its Class C networks which allegedly "supported spam," it contacted Media3 and requested that Media3; (1) terminate its hosting agreements with the contested websites; and (2) revise its Acceptable Use Policy to expressly prohibit the provision of "spam support" services such as the harvesting of e-mail addresses described above. If Media3 did not comply, MAPS informed Media3 that it would place on the blackhole list not only the ten contested websites but also any other websites that were on the same Class C network as the contested websites. This prospect was of some concern to Media3 because, as a hosting company, one of the primary services that it provides to its customers is ensuring that their websites are freely accessible and can easily access the Internet. Inclusion on MAPS's blackhole list would threaten Media3's ability to deliver good access to the Internet. After some exchange back and forth via e-mail and telephone between MAPS, in California, and Media3, in Massachusetts, Media3 refused to comply with MAPS's requests. MAPS then listed the disputed websites and any other websites on the same Class C network on the blackhole list.

In October and November of 2000, a similar exchange between MAPS and Media3 occurred. MAPS asserted that seven websites, on five different Class C networks hosted by Media3, were providing spam support. Once again, after several communications back and forth, Media3 refused to terminate the disputed websites and MAPS then added five more Class C networks hosted by Media3 to the blackhole list. At present, six Class C networks, containing over 1,500 websites hosted by Media3, remain on MAPS's blackhole list.

* * *

III. Media3's Application for a Preliminary Injunction

* * *

Although it has made serious claims which may entitle it to ultimate relief, Media3 has failed to establish a likelihood of success on the merits or that it is suffering irreparable injury. Accordingly, Media3's motion for preliminary relief is denied. * * *

A. Merits

1. Defamation

Business defamation is committed when a false and defamatory statement is communicated which "prejudice[s] [the plaintiff] in the conduct of its business and deter[s] others from dealing with it." *A.F.M. Corp. v. Corporate Aircraft Mgmt.*, 626 F.Supp. 1533 (D.Mass.1985). In all other respects, the elements of a business defamation claim are those of ordinary defamation, that is, that the defendant published "a false and defamatory written communication of and concerning the plaintiff." *McAvoy v. Shufrin*, 401 Mass. 593, 597, 518 N.E.2d 513, 517 (1988).

"A threshold issue is whether the statement is reasonably susceptible of a defamatory meaning, and that determination is a question of law for the court." *Foley v. Lowell Sun Pub. Co.*, 404 Mass. 9, 11, 533 N.E.2d 196, 197 (1989) (citation omitted). "The test is, whether, in the circumstances, the writing discredits the plaintiff in the minds of any considerable and respectable class of the community." *Smith v. Suburban Rests., Inc.*, 374 Mass. 528, 529, 373 N.E.2d 215, 217 (1978) (citations omitted). There is no dispute among the parties that calling an Internet business a "spammer," or "spam-friendly," discredits the enterprise in the minds of a considerable segment of the Internet community.[7]

However, even if the statement is subject to a defamatory construction, truth is a complete defense. *Dulgarian v. Stone,* 420 Mass. 843, 847, 652 N.E.2d 603, 606 (1995). It is the defendant's burden to prove truth as an

7. Other courts have recognized that "spamming" is a practice condemned by many in the Internet community. *See CompuServe, Inc. v. Cyber Promotions, Inc.*, 962 F.Supp. 1015, 1018 (S.D.Ohio 1997) (describing spamming as a "much maligned practice" in the Internet community); *America Online, Inc. v. LCGM, Inc.*, 46 F.Supp.2d 444, 446, n. 1 (E.D.Va.1998) (describing spamming as a "practice widely condemned in the Internet community").

affirmative defense. *Maloof v. Post Publ'g Co.,* 306 Mass. 279, 280, 28 N.E.2d 458, 459 (1940). MAPS has labeled Media3 as a "spam-friendly" organization. PI Hearing Transcript. II 10, 16, 19. Media3 contends that the label is false. In attempting to prove the falsity of the statement, Media3 relies heavily on its "Acceptable Use Policy," which it requires all its hosted websites to sign. This "Acceptable Use Policy" contains an "anti-spam" provision.

MAPS responds that its assertion that Media3 is "spam-friendly" is true because Media3 does, in fact, host companies that provide services exclusively to spammers.

Media3 has not established a likelihood that it will prevail on the merits of its defamation claim because, on the present record, MAPS has made a strong showing that its characterization of Media3 as "spam-friendly," is true. Media3's actions may well be found to outweigh its "Acceptable Use Policy." As described above, Media3 hosts several websites which provide support services that are used either exclusively or predominantly by spammers. See Def.'s Exhibits 1–4. These services include the sale of hundreds of thousands and even millions of e-mail addresses which are sold without any indication whatsoever that they are sold with the permission of the e-mail user. As the record stands, there is a serious question whether MAPS's assertion that Media3 is "spam-friendly" is defamatory because the statement appears to be accurate.

2. Intentional Interference with Existing and Prospective Business Relations

The torts of intentional interference with existing and prospective business relations share the same elements:

(1) a business relationship or contemplated contract of economic benefit;

(2) the defendant's knowledge of such relationship;

(3) the defendant's interference with it through improper motive or means; and

(4) the plaintiff's loss of advantage directly resulting from the defendant's conduct.

American Private Line Servs., Inc. v. Eastern Microwave, Inc., 980 F.2d 33, 35 (1st Cir.1992) (*citing United Truck Leasing Corp. v. Geltman,* 406 Mass. 811, 551 N.E.2d 20 (1990)).

Media3 contends that MAPS has improperly and tortiously listed over 1500 websites that Media3 hosts on MAPS's blackhole list. MAPS has alleged that only seventeen of these websites actually support spam. Media3 argues that MAPS's inclusion of about 1500 websites that belong to non-spamming customers of Media3 in the blackhole list was improperly motivated by an intent to "coerce" Media3 into dropping the seventeen "spam-friendly" websites.

MAPS responds that Media3 has failed to demonstrate a likelihood of success on the merits of its intentional interference claims because Media3 has not shown that its conduct was undertaken with an improper motive or by improper means or that it has in fact suffered any actual loss of business advantage as a result of MAPS's actions.

The record to date fails to establish that Media3 is likely to prevail on the merits of its intentional interference claims because it has failed to provide any evidence of actual or imminent loss of present or future business advantage resulting from MAP's actions and a serious question remains as to whether MAPS's motive or means were intentional and culpable.

3. Unfair Trade Practices Under M.G.L. Ch. 93A, § 11

Media3's Chapter 93A claim is based on the same allegedly "sharp practice" which forms the basis of its intentional interference claims. Media3 alleges that MAPS is attempting to "coerce" Media3 into terminating seventeen accounts which allegedly provide "spam support" by placing 1500 untainted websites on the blackhole list.

MAPS asserts three defenses to Media3's Chapter 93A claim: First, that it has not engaged in any "sharp practices;" second, that because its activities were not commercial in nature, its actions do not fall within the scope of M.G.L. ch. 93A, § 11 (citing *Hubert v. Melrose–Wakefield Hosp. Ass'n*, 40 Mass. App. Ct. 172, 661 N.E.2d 1347 (1996)); and third, that Media3 has failed to establish that the allegedly unfair activities occurred "primarily and substantially" in Massachusetts.

Again, the present record fails to demonstrate that Media3 is likely to succeed on the merits of its Chapter 93A claim. There remain serious questions whether MAPS's behavior constitutes "sharp practices," as defined by the cases, as well as whether MAPS's actions occurred "primarily and substantially" in Massachusetts or involved "commercial activity" by MAPS.

* * *

IV.

For the reasons stated above, Media3's application for a preliminary injunction is denied.

NOTES & QUESTIONS

The limits of self-help? Consider who gets to decide which messages are spam, and the risks of allowing private parties to make this decision and implement self-help measures. Can a sender who feels aggrieved by having its messages treated as spam sue for redress? In a variation on the blacklist theme, Blue Mountain Arts, a company allowing users to send free online electronic greeting cards, sued Microsoft for alleged malicious filtering of its cards. According to Blue Mountain, a beta version of Microsoft's Internet Explorer web browser came equipped with a "junk" e-mail filter, designed to route incoming UCE away from the inbox and into a special junk-mail folder. The filter, Blue Mountain said, treated its greeting cards as UCE, and sent them to the junk-mail folder. The court granted Blue Mountain a preliminary injunction, and the parties later settled. *See Hartford House, Ltd. v. Microsoft Corp.*, Case No. CV 778550 (Cal. Super. Ct., Cnty. of Santa Clara, prelim. inj. issued Feb. 2, 1999).

II. Intruding on Proprietary Networks: Speech Directed at Employees via a Corporate Network

Intel Corp. v. Hamidi

114 Cal.Rptr.2d 244 (Cal.Ct.App.2001).

■ Morrison, Judge.

After Kourosh Kenneth Hamidi was fired by Intel Corporation, he began to air grievances about the company. Hamidi repeatedly flooded Intel's e-mail system. When its security department was unable to block or otherwise end Hamidi's mass e-mails, Intel filed this action. The trial court issued a permanent injunction stopping the campaign, on a theory of trespass to chattels.

On appeal Hamidi, supported by Amici Curiae Electronic Frontier Foundation (EFF) and American Civil Liberties Union (ACLU), urges trespass to chattels was not proven and, even if it was, the injunction violates free speech principles which require the elements of the tort be tempered in cases involving speech. We shall affirm.

FACTUAL AND PROCEDURAL BACKGROUND

Intel filed a brief complaint, alleging it maintains an internal, proprietary, e-mail system for use of its employees; the e-mail addresses are confidential; defendant Hamidi and FACE–Intel (Former and Current Employees of Intel, a defaulting party which did not appeal) obtained Intel's e-mail address list and on several occasions sent e-mail to up to 29,000 employees; on March 17, 1998, Intel sent a letter demanding Hamidi stop, but he refused. The complaint sought remedies based on theories of nuisance and trespass to chattels.

Intel moved for summary judgment and submitted a set of undisputed facts which Hamidi did not dispute. They establish: Hamidi is the FACE–Intel webmaster and spokesperson. He sent e-mails to between 8,000 and 35,000 Intel employees on six specific occasions. He ignored Intel's request to stop and took steps to evade its security measures. Intel's employees "spend significant amounts of time attempting to block and remove HAMIDI's e-mail from the INTEL computer systems," which are governed by policies which "limit use of the e-mail system to company business."

Hamidi filed a declaration in opposition to summary judgment, explaining "FACE–INTEL was formed to provide a medium for INTEL employees to air their grievances and concerns over employment conditions at INTEL. FACE–INTEL provides an extremely important forum for employees within an international corporation to communicate via a web page on the Internet and via electronic mail, on common labor issues, that, due to geographical and other limitations, would not otherwise be possible." His six mass e-mailings "did not originate on INTEL property, nor were they sent to INTEL property. The electronic mails were sent over the internet to an internet server. [¶] With each of the electronic mailings [he] informed each recipient that [he] would remove them from the mailing list upon request. [He] only received 450 requests[.]"

Intel dropped its nuisance theory and claim for damages, and the trial court granted summary judgment. It issued an injunction that "defendants, their agents, servants, assigns, employees, officers, directors, and all those acting in concert for or with defendants are hereby permanently restrained and enjoined from sending unsolicited e-mail to addresses on INTEL's computer systems." Hamidi timely appealed.

* * *

DISCUSSION

I. Intel Proved Hamidi Trespassed to its Chattels

* * *

We begin with Prosser, who explains: "The earliest cases in which the action of trespass was applied to chattels involved asportation, or carrying off, and a special form of the writ, known as trespass de bonis asportatis, was devised to deal with such situations. Later the action was extended to include cases where the goods were damaged but not taken—as where animals were killed or beaten. Later decisions extended the tort to include any direct and immediate intentional interference with a chattel in the possession of another. Thus, it is a trespass to damage goods or destroy them, to make an unpermitted use of them, or to move them from one place to another." (Prosser and Keeton, Torts (5th ed. 1984) Trespass to Chattels, § 14, p. 85, fns. omitted.)

Although there was litigation over who could bring suit and over formal pleading requirements, the shape of the tort is simple. A leading American court approved this definition: "1. To constitute a trespass, there must be a disturbance of the plaintiff's possession. 2. The disturbance may be by an actual taking, a physical seizing or taking hold of the goods, removing them from their owner, or by exercising a control or authority over them inconsistent with their owner's possession." (*Holmes v. Doane,* (1855) 69 Mass. 328, 329.) The most common application is for a physical taking, even if momentary. (*See Tubbs v. Delk,* (Mo.Ct.App.1996) 932 S.W.2d 454 [taking camera for five minutes, returning it with film intact].)

The Restatement is in accord, providing "A trespass to a chattel may be committed by intentionally . . . (b) using or intermeddling with a chattel in the possession of another." (Rest.2d Torts, § 217, p. 417.) Most cases involve concrete harm to a chattel, "actual impairment of its physical condition, quality or value to the possessor . . . as distinguished from the mere affront to [the owner's] dignity as possessor[.]" (§ 218, com. h, p. 422 [allowing some exceptions, such as use of another's toothbrush].)

The Restatement also provides "The interest of a possessor of a chattel in its inviolability, unlike the similar interest of a possessor of land, is not given legal protection by an action for nominal damages for harmless intermeddlings with the chattel. In order that an actor who interferes with another's chattel may be liable, his conduct must affect some other and more important interest of the possessor. Therefore, one who intentionally intermeddles with another's chattel is subject to liability only if his intermeddling is harmful to the possessor's materially valuable interest in the physical condition, quality, or value of the chattel, or if the possessor is deprived of the use of the chattel for a substantial time, or some other legally protected interest [is harmed.] Sufficient legal protection of the possessor's interest in the mere inviolability of his chattel is afforded by his privilege to use reasonable force to protect his possession against even harmless interference. [¶] Illustration: [¶] 2. A, a child, climbs upon the back of B's large dog and pulls its ears. No harm is done to the dog, or to any other legally protected interest of B. A is not liable to B." (§ 218, com. e, pp. 421–422; see *Glidden v. Szybiak,* (1949) 95 N.H. 318, 320 63 A.2d 233, 235.) This caveat speaks of "nominal damages." Intel does not seek damages, even nominal damages, to compensate for Hamidi's conduct; Intel wants to prevent him from repeating his conduct. In this case, the nature of the remedy sought colors the analysis.

* * *

As indicated, some confusion in the cases and treatises disappears when the nature of the remedy is considered. We accept that "The plaintiff, in order to recover more than nominal damages, must prove the value of the property taken, or that he has sustained some special damage." (1 Waterman, Trespass (1875) Remedy for Wrongful Taking of Property, § 596, p. 617; see *Lay v. Bayless* (1867) 44 Tenn. 246, 247; *Warner v. Capps* (1881) 37 Ark. 32.) Intel seeks no damages.

Hamidi's conduct was trespassory. Even assuming Intel has not demonstrated sufficient "harm" to trigger entitlement to nominal damages for past breaches of decorum by Hamidi, it showed he was disrupting its business by using its property and therefore is entitled to injunctive relief based on a theory of trespass to chattels. Hamidi acknowledges Intel's right to self help and urges Intel could take further steps to fend off his e-mails. He has shown he will try to evade Intel's security. We conceive of no public benefit from this wasteful cat-and-mouse game which justifies depriving Intel of an injunction. (Cf. *America Online, Inc. v. Nat. Health Care Discount, Inc.,* (N.D.Iowa 2000) 121 F.Supp.2d 1255, 1259–1260 [detailing ongoing technological struggle between spammers and system operators].) Even where a company cannot precisely measure the harm caused by an unwelcome intrusion, the fact the intrusion occurs supports a claim for trespass to chattels. (See *Register.com, Inc. v. Verio, Inc.* (S.D.N.Y.2000) 126 F.Supp.2d 238, 249–250 [applying New York law, based on the Restatement, "evidence of mere possessory interference is sufficient to demonstrate the quantum of harm necessary to establish a claim for trespass to chattels"].)

Some commentators espouse the view that "cyberspace," as they term it, is necessarily free and open, minimizing the harm caused to Intel's business. (*E.g., Comment, Developments—The Law of Cyberspace* (1999) 112 Harv.L.Rev. 1574, 1633, fn. 137.) And Amicus ACLU urges "Harm flowing from the content of the communication may not form the basis for an action for trespass to chattel." But Intel proved more than its displeasure with Hamidi's message, it showed it was hurt by the loss of productivity caused by the thousands of employees distracted from their work and by the time its security department spent trying to halt the distractions after Hamidi refused to respect Intel's request to stop invading its internal, proprietary e-mail system by sending unwanted e-mails to thousands of Intel's employees on the system. (See *Hotmail Corporation v. Van$ Money Pie, Inc.* (N.D.Cal.1998), 47 U.S.P.Q.2d 1020, 1025 (*Hotmail*) [trespass caused "added costs for personnel"].)

" 'Intermeddling' means intentionally bringing about a physical contact with the chattel." (Rest.2d Torts, § 217, com. e, p. 419.) "Electronic signals generated and sent by computer have been held to be sufficiently physically tangible to support a trespass cause of action. [Citations.] It is undisputed that plaintiff has a possessory interest in its computer systems. Further, defendants' contact with plaintiff's computers is clearly intentional. Although electronic messages may travel through the Internet over various routes, the messages are affirmatively directed to their destination." (*CompuServe Inc. v. Cyber Promotions, Inc.* (S.D.Ohio 1997) 962 F.Supp. 1015, 1021(*CompuServe*).) * * *

Amicus ACLU seeks to distinguish *CompuServe* on the ground the conduct "placed 'a tremendous burden' on *CompuServe's* equipment thus depriving CompuServe of the full use of its equipment." Elsewhere in its brief, ACLU states Hamidi did not send "a large number of e-mails. All in all, he sent a total of only six e-mails over a period spanning close to two years." Similarly, Amicus EFF states: "Assuming the veracity of Intel's allegations, on six occasions over a nearly two-year period, many Intel employees simply had one additional e-mail from Mr. Hamidi sitting in their in boxes when they came to work in the morning. This hardly constitutes physical disruption to Intel's computer system." Amici discount disruption to Intel's business system, inasmuch as the thousands of employees had to confront, read, and delete the messages even if only to tell Hamidi to send them no more, as several hundred did.

EFF states if such loss of productivity "is the applicable standard [of harm], then every personal e-mail that an employee reads at work could constitute a trespass." The answer is, where the employer has told the sender the entry is unwanted and the sender persists, the employer's petition for redress is proper. Strangely, EFF, purporting to laud the "freedom" of the Internet, emphasizes Intel allows its employees reasonable personal use of Intel's equipment for sending and receiving personal e-mail. Such tolerance by employers would vanish if they had no way to limit such personal usage of company equipment.

CompuServe relied in part on *Thrifty-Tel, Inc. v. Bezenek* (1996) 46 Cal.App.4th 1559 (*Thrifty-Tel*). *Thrifty-Tel* held the unauthorized use of telephone access numbers, which "overburdened the system, denying some subscribers access," (p. 1564) was sufficient to support liability *for actual monetary damages*. The case did not state or imply that such an extreme effect was required to establish the tort. *Thrifty-Tel* noted: "At early common law, trespass required a physical touching of another's chattel or entry onto another's land. The modern rule recognizes an indirect touching or entry; e.g., dust particles from a cement plant that migrate onto another's real and personal property may give rise to trespass. [Citing, *inter alia, Wilson v. Interlake Steel Co.* (1982) 32 Cal.3d 229, 185 Cal. Rptr. 280, 649 P.2d 922 (*Wilson*).] But the requirement of a tangible trespass has been relaxed almost to the point of being discarded. Thus, some courts have held that microscopic particles [citation] or smoke [citation] may give rise to trespass. And the California Supreme Court has intimated migrating intangibles (e.g., sound waves) may result in a trespass, provided they do not simply impede an owner's use or enjoyment of property, but cause damage. [Citing *Wilson*.] In our view, the electronic signals generated by the Bezenek boys' activities were sufficiently tangible to support a trespass cause of action." (46 Cal.App.4th at p. 1566, fn. 6.) We agree.

Amicus EFF suggests *Thrifty–Tel, supra,* 46 Cal.App.4th 1559 is based on the view "physical damages or physical disruption, even if temporary," "gives the 'electronic signal' a sufficiently tangible quality to support a cause of action for trespass," and Intel has not shown Hamidi's e-mails caused physical disruption. This is not so for two reasons. First, the footnote just quoted makes it plain that the electronic signal is "sufficiently tangible to support a trespass cause of action." The tangibility of the contact is not dependent on the harm caused. Second, Hamidi's e-mails caused disruption to Intel's workers, who were drawn away from their jobs to deal with the messages. If EFF is saying Hamidi can flood Intel's system to the penultimate extent before causing a computer crash, we disagree.

* * *

In *America Online, Inc. v. IMS* (E.D.Va.1998) 24 F.Supp.2d 548, IMS "sent unauthorized bulk e-mail advertisements ('spam') to AOL subscribers," even after AOL told IMS to stop. (*Id.* at p. 549.) Applying the common law of Virginia, the court granted summary judgment to AOL on its claim of trespass to chattels. The court relied in part on *CompuServe* to conclude AOL was harmed by the time spent processing the unwanted e-mail, and the burden to the computer equipment it caused. (*Id.* at p. 550; accord *America Online, Inc. v. GreatDeals.Net* (E.D.Va.1999) 49 F.Supp.2d 851, 864.) In *America Online, Inc. v. LCGM, Inc.* (E.D.Va.1998) 46 F.Supp.2d 444, another judge of the same court held (at page 452): "The transmission of electrical signals through a computer network is sufficiently 'physical' contact to constitute a trespass to property."

Quite recently, a California federal court reached a similar conclusion in *eBay Inc. v. Bidder's Edge, Inc.* (N.D.Cal.2000) 100 F.Supp.2d 1058, 1071: "Even if, as BE argues, its searches use only a small amount of eBay's computer system capacity, BE has nonetheless deprived eBay of the ability to use that portion of its personal property for its own purposes. The law recognizes no such right to use another's personal property."

Hamidi and EFF ask, if unwanted e-mail can constitute a trespass, why isn't unwanted first-class mail a trespass? " 'The short, though regular journey from mailbox to trash can . . . is an acceptable burden, at least as far as the Constitution is concerned.' " (*Bolger v. Youngs Drug Products Corp.* (1983) 463 U.S. 60, 72 [held, law against use of mail for advertising contraceptives invalid].) The issue is one of degree. As Hamidi impliedly concedes, he could not lawfully cause Intel's computers to crash, or overwhelm the system so that Intel's employees were unable to use the computer system. (*See Hotmail, supra,* 47 U.S.P.Q.2d at p. 1025 [threat to "fill[] up Hotmail's computer storage space and . . . damage Hotmail's ability to service its legitimate customers]".) Nor could a person send thousands of unwanted letters to a company, nor make thousands of unwelcome telephone calls. (*See Rowan v. United States Post Office* (1970) 397 U.S. 728, 736–737 [upholding statute allowing blocking of mail, "Everyman's mail today is made up overwhelmingly of material he did not seek from persons he does not know"; "To hold less would tend to license a form of trespass"].)

At oral argument counsel referred to [California] Business and Professions Code section 17538.4, which prohibits entities from barraging a person or company with unwanted commercial e-mails. The statute shows the Legislature recognizes the distraction and harm caused by unwanted electronic communications. Nothing in the statute suggests any intent to eliminate the application of common law remedies, such as trespass to chattels, to electronic communications, nor to limit common law remedies to cases of commercial speech.

We conclude the summary judgment moving papers demonstrated Intel's entitlement to an injunction based on a theory of trespass to chattels.

II. The Injunction Comports with the Federal Constitution

Hamidi and Amici insist the injunction runs afoul of the First Amendment. In like manner as the First Amendment trumps a state's power to make and enforce defamation torts (*e.g., New York Times v. Sullivan* (1964) 376 U.S. 254 (*Sullivan*)) they urge it governs a state's power to enjoin e-mails. This lawsuit does not implicate federal constitutional rights, for lack of state action.

Sullivan famously held "actual malice" was an element of the tort of libel—as a matter of federal constitutional law—in a case where a political figure sued a newspaper. *Sullivan* pit common law rights protecting reputation against the constitutional right of a newspaper to publish. In a trespass case, however, the speaker's rights are pitted against a property owner's rights—of at least equal constitutional force—to wisely govern his lands (or, in this case, his chattels). The equation is different. (376 U.S. 254.)

"The First Amendment protects individuals only from government, not private, infringements upon speech rights." (*George v. Pacific–CSC Work Furlough* (9th Cir.1996) 91 F.3d 1227, 1229.) When individuals seek protection for expressive rights, the "courts must first determine whether it is indeed government action—state or federal—that the litigants are challenging." (Tribe, American Constitutional Law (2d ed. 1988) The Problem of State Action, § 18–1, p. 1688 (Tribe).) The case law is muddled. (*See id.*, at p. 1690.) However, in some cases, including speech cases, a state-court decision in a suit between private litigants implicates federal concerns and "there seems little doubt that judges are government actors and that judicial remedies are state action." (Chemerinsky, *State Action* (1999) 618 PLI/Lit 183, 209 (Chemerinsky).)

* * *

We need not delve too far into the state action morass. Judicial enforcement of neutral trespass laws has been held *not* to constitute state action. * * *

Recent cases involving unwanted commercial e-mail support our view. In *Cyber Promotions v. American Online, Inc.* (E.D.Pa.1996) 948 F. Supp. 436 (*Cyber Promotions*), the court found no state action when an online company obtained an injunction to prevent another company from sending commercial e-mail to its members. The court rejected the e-mail sender's position that " 'the Court's participation with the litigant in issuing or enforcing an order which impinges on another's First Amendment rights' " amounted to state action. (*Id.* at pp. 444–445.) * * *

For lack of state action the federal constitution is not implicated herein. Intel has the right to exclude others from speaking on its property. Intel is not required to exercise its right in a "content-neutral" fashion. Content discrimination is part of a private property-owner's bundle of rights. Intel does not welcome Hamidi.

III. The Injunction Comports with the State Constitution

Hamidi contends his right to send e-mail to Intel employees is protected by the California analog to the First Amendment, which provides "Every person may freely speak, write or publish his or her sentiments on all subjects, being responsible for the abuse of this right. A law may not restrain or abridge liberty of speech or press." (Cal. Const., art. I, § 2, subd. (a).) This provision is "more definitive and inclusive than the First Amendment[.]" (*Wilson v. Superior Court* (1975) 13 Cal.3d 652, 658, 119 Cal. Rptr. 468, 532 P.2d 116.)

In a controversial 4–3 decision, over a vigorous dissent, the California Supreme Court held the free speech rights of students obtaining petition signatures trumped the right of the owner of a shopping center to exclude them. *Robins v. Pruneyard Shopping Center* (1979) 23 Cal.3d 899, 153 Cal.

Rptr. 854, 592 P.2d 341 (*Robins*), affd. sub nom. *PruneYard Shopping Center v. Robins* (1980) 447 U.S. 74. * * *

* * * [A]ctions to halt expressive activity on one's private property do not contravene the California Constitution unless the property is freely open to the public.

Private e-mail servers differ from the Internet; they are not traditional public forums. (*Cyber Promotions*, *supra*, 948 F.Supp. at p. 446.) Nor is a private company which chooses to use e-mail made a public forum.

Although Intel is a large company, it is not like a Pruneyard Shopping Center, in that it is not a place where the public gathers to engage in expressive activity such as gathering signatures to petition the government, nor is its e-mail system so used. The Intel e-mail system is private property used for business purposes. Intel's system is not transformed into a public forum merely because it permits some personal use by employees. (*See Perry Education Association v. Perry Local Educators' Assn.* (1983) 460 U.S. 37, 47 [limited access to outside organizations does not transform school mailbox system into a public forum].) Intel invites the public to use its e-mail system for and only for *business purposes*.

Hamidi insists Intel's act of connecting itself (and thus, its employees) to the Internet and giving its employees e-mail addresses makes Intel's e-mails a public forum. By the same reasoning, connecting one's realty to the general system of roads invites demonstrators to use the property as a public forum and buying a telephone is an invitation to receive thousands of unwanted calls. That is not the law. (*CompuServe*, *supra*, 962 F.Supp. at p. 1024; *Cyber Promotions*, *supra*, 948 F.Supp. at p. 442.) Intel is as much entitled to control its e-mail system as it is to guard its factories and hallways. No citizen has the general right to enter a private business and pester an employee trying to work. It may be a few unwanted e-mails would not be sufficient to trigger a court's equity powers. Indeed, such may be an inevitable, though regrettable, fact of modern life, like unwelcome junk mail and telephone solicitations. (*See Cyber Promotions, Inc. v. Apex Global Information Svcs., Inc.* (E.D.Pa.1997) 1997 WL 634384, p. *3 [bulk e-mail "annoying and intrusive"].) However, the massive size of Hamidi's campaign caused Intel much trouble, not the least of which was caused by the lost time of each employee who had to read or delete an unwanted message, either out of fear of a virus or a lack of desire to communicate with Hamidi. As we pointed out in another case, "When a camel's back is broken we need not weigh each straw in its load to see which one could have done the deed." (*Woodland Joint Unified School Dist. v. Commission on Professional Competence* (1992) 2 Cal.App.4th 1429, 1457.)

Finally, Hamidi has many available alternate ways to reach his target audience. (Cf. *Chico Feminist Women's Health Center v. Scully* (1989) 208 Cal. App. 3d 230, 243–248, 256 Cal. Rptr. 194. *Cf. also Golden Gateway*, *supra*, 26 Cal.4th at p. 1050 (dis. opn.) [concluding use of mail and off-site distribution were not feasible alternatives to door-to-door leafleting].)

We may safely assume most, if not all, Intel employees can reach Hamidi's website, either from their homes or from libraries or cafes which provide Internet access. Hamidi concedes the Internet has become widely accessible and affordable, at least in the United States. Employees who cannot get on the Internet can correspond with Hamidi about issues of mutual concern. According to Hamidi's website, <www.faceintel.com>, he has delivered many thousands of printed "e-mails" to Intel's headquarters by horse and buggy, both to communicate with its workers within the terms of the injunction, and to publicize this lawsuit. (*See* www.intelhamidi.com/seconddelivery.htm. See also Gaura, E–Mail Delivered by Horse–Mail, S.F. Chron. (Sep. 29, 1999) p. B–2 ["Mounted as an outrider and dressed in a red shirt and star-spangled kerchief, Hamidi handed 16 boxes of messages to Intel security officials"].) Hamidi may freely exchange ideas with Intel or Intel workers. This highlights a critical factual misstatement in Hamidi's brief, that he has been enjoined "from sending e-mail over the internet to Intel employees." The injunction prohibits Hamidi "from sending unsolicited e-mails to addresses on INTEL's computer systems." Hamidi is free to send mail—"e" or otherwise—to the homes of Intel employees, and is free to send them regular mail. The injunction simply requires that Hamidi air his views without using Intel's private property.

* * *

We conclude the injunction does not violate the California Constitution.

DISPOSITION

The judgment is affirmed.

I concur: Scotland, P.J.

■ Kolkey, J., dissenting

I respectfully dissent. The majority would apply the tort of trespass to chattel to the transmittal of unsolicited electronic mail that causes no harm to the private computer system that receives it by modifying the tort to dispense with any need for injury, or by deeming the mere reading of an unsolicited e-mail to constitute the requisite injury. (Maj. opn. at pp. 9–10.)

While common law doctrines do evolve to adapt to new circumstances, it is not too much to ask that trespass to chattel continue to require some injury to the chattel (or at least to the possessory interest in the chattel) in order to maintain the action. The only injury claimed here—the *time* spent reading an e-mail—goes beyond any injury associated with the chattel or within the tort's zone of protection. Although I understand Intel's desire to end what it deems harassment by a disgruntled former employee, "we must not throw to the winds the advantages of consistency and uniformity to do justice in the instance. We must keep within those interstitial limits which precedent and custom and the long and silent and almost indefinable practice of other judges through centuries of the common law have set to judge-made innovations." (Cardozo, The Nature of the Judicial Process (1921), p. 103, fn. omitted.)

The other appellate decisions that have applied trespass to chattel to computer systems have done so only where the transmittal of the unsolicited bulk e-mail burdened the computer equipment, thereby interfering with its operation and diminishing the chattel's value (*e.g., America Online, Inc. v. IMS* (E.D.Va.1998) 24 F.Supp.2d 548, 550–551; *America Online, Inc. v. LCGM, Inc.* (E.D.Va.1998) 46 F.Supp.2d 444, 449; *CompuServe, Inc. v. Cyber Promotions, Inc.* (S.D.Ohio 1997) 962 F.Supp. 1015), or where the unauthorized search of, and retrieval of information from, another party's database reduced the computer system's capacity, slowing response times and reducing system performance (*Register.com, Inc. v. Verio, Inc.* (S.D.N.Y.2000) 126 F.Supp.2d 238, 250; *eBay, Inc. v. Bidder's Edge, Inc.* (N.D.Cal.2000) 100 F.Supp.2d 1058, 1066, 1071). But no case has held that the requisite injury for trespass to chattel can consist of the mere receipt of an e-mail, the only damage from which consists of the time consumed to read it—assuming the recipient chooses to do so. To apply this tort to electronic signals that do not damage or interfere with the value or operation of the chattel would expand the tort of trespass to chattel in untold ways and to unanticipated circumstances.

A

California cases have consistently required actual injury as an element of the tort of trespass to chattel. * * *

* * *

The Restatement Second of Torts agrees on the need for actual damage for the tort to lie * * *.

For that reason, where a child climbs on the back of another's dog and pulls its ears, but no harm is done to the dog or to the legally protected interest of the owner, the child is not liable. (*Glidden v. Szybiak* (1949) 63 A.2d 233, 95 N.H. 318; Rest.2d Torts, § 218, com. e, illus. 2, p. 422.) On the other hand, the intermeddling is actionable where the trespass impairs the value of the chattel, even if its physical condition is unaffected. (Rest.2d Torts, § 218, com. h, p. 422.) For instance, "the use of a toothbrush by someone else ... leads a person of ordinary sensibilities to regard the article as utterly incapable of further use by him." (*Ibid.*)

The only possible exception to the requirement of actual injury is where there has been a loss of possession, which is viewed as a loss of something of value and thus actual damage * * *.

Accordingly, in conformity with the California cases, section 218 of the Restatement Second of Torts requires actual injury in order to state a cause of action for trespass to chattel—unless there is a loss of possession, which is deemed to constitute actual damage * * *.

B

In this case, however, Intel was not dispossessed, even temporarily, of its e-mail system by reason of receipt of e-mails; the e-mail system was not impaired as to its condition, quality, or value; and no actual harm was caused to a person or thing in which Intel had a legally protected interest.

The majority nonetheless suggests that "even assuming Intel has not demonstrated sufficient 'harm' to trigger entitlement to nominal damages ... it showed [the defendant] was disrupting its business by using its property and therefore is entitled to injunctive relief based on a theory of trespass to chattels." (Maj. opn. at p. 9.)

However, if the defendant's earlier transmittals of e-mail did not constitute harm, it is hard to understand what cognizable injury the injunction is designed to avoid. The fact the relief sought is injunctive does not excuse a showing of injury, whether actual or threatened. After all, injunctive relief requires a "showing that the defendant's wrongful act constitutes an actual or threatened injury to property or personal rights that cannot be compensated by an ordinary damage award." (5 Witkin, California Procedure (4th ed. 1997) Pleading § 782, p. 239.) The majority therefore cannot avoid the element of injury by relying on the fact that injunctive relief is sought here.

Alternatively, the majority suggests that injury resulted from defendant's e-mails, because Intel "was hurt by the loss of productivity caused by the thousands of employees distracted from their work [by the e-mails] and by the time its security department spent trying to halt the distractions after [defendant] refused to respect Intel's request to stop sending unwanted e-mails." (Maj. opn. at p. 10.)

But considering first Intel's efforts to stop the e-mails, it is circular to premise the damage element of a tort solely upon the steps taken to prevent the damage. Injury can only be established by the completed tort's consequences, not by the cost of the steps taken to avoid the injury and prevent the tort; otherwise, we can create injury for every supposed tort.

Nor can a loss of employees' productivity (by having to read an unwanted e-mail on six different occasions over a nearly two-year period) qualify as injury of the type that gives rise to a trespass to chattel. If that is injury, then every unsolicited communication that does not further the business's objectives (including telephone calls) interferes with the chattel to which the communication is directed simply because it must be read or heard, distracting the recipient. "Damage" of this nature—the distraction of reading or listening to an unsolicited communication—is not within the scope of the injury against which the trespass-to-chattel tort protects, and indeed trivializes it. After all, "the property interest protected by the old action of trespass was that of possession; and this has continued to affect the character of the action." (Prosser and Keeton on Torts, *supra,* § 14, p. 87.) Reading an e-mail transmitted to equipment designed to receive it, in and of itself, does not affect the possessory interest in the equipment.

Indeed, if a chattel's receipt of an electronic communication constitutes a trespass to that chattel, then not only are unsolicited telephone calls and faxes trespasses to chattel, but unwelcome radio waves and television signals also constitute a trespass to chattel every time the viewer inadvertently sees or hears the unwanted program.

At oral argument, Intel's counsel argued that the latter cases can be distinguished because Intel gave defendant notice of its objection before his final set of e-mails in September 1998. But such a notice could also be given to television and radio stations, telephone callers, and correspondents. Under Intel's theory, even lovers' quarrels could turn into trespass suits by reason of the receipt of unsolicited letters or calls from the jilted lover. Imagine what happens after the angry lover tells her fiance not to call again and violently hangs up the phone. Fifteen minutes later the phone rings. Her fiance wishing to make up? No, trespass to chattel.

No case goes so far as to hold that reading an unsolicited message transmitted to a computer screen constitutes an injury that forms the basis for trespass to chattel. * * *

* * *

In conclusion, the overwhelming weight of authority is that trespass to chattel requires injury to the chattel or to the possessor's legally protected interest in the chattel. Opening and reading unsolicited e-mails is not a cognizable injury to the chattel or to the owner's possessory interest in it.

C

One more issue remains to be addressed. If the transmittal of an unsolicited e-mail that causes no injury to the condition, value, or operation of the chattel (or to the possessory interest therein) does not rise to the level of trespass to chattel, should the requirement of injury be relaxed to allow an injunction against unwanted e-mail?

While the common law can be adapted to new circumstances, it is not infinitely malleable. Relaxation of the injury requirement would not merely adapt the tort, but change its nature. After all, "the property interest protected by the old action of trespass was that of possession; and this has continued to affect the character of the action." (Prosser and Keeton on Torts, *supra,* § 14, p. 87.) Dispensing with the requirement of injury to the value, operation, or condition of the chattel, or the possessory interest therein, would extend the tort's scope in a way that loses sight of its purpose.

* * *

The injury claimed here—the *time* spent reading an e-mail—goes beyond anything associated with the chattel or within the tort's zone of protection. Extension of the tort to protect against undesired communications, where neither the chattel nor the possessory interest therein is injured, transforms a tort meant to protect possessory interests into one that merely attacks speech. Regardless of whether restraining e-mails to a private company implicates First Amendment rights, such a metamorphosis of the tort is better suited for deliberate legislative action than judicial policymaking.

Indeed, the Legislature has enacted two statutes that restrict the e-mailing of unsolicited *advertising* materials (Bus. & Prof. Code, §§ 17538.4, 17538.45) and another that affords a civil remedy to those who suffer *damage or loss* from, inter alia, the unauthorized access to a computer system (Pen. Code, § 502, subd. (e)(1)). These statutory provisions and the Legislature's failure to extend these remedies to unsolicited e-mails in general suggests a deliberate decision by the Legislature not to reach the circumstances here. * * *

* * *

NOTES & QUESTIONS

1. *Establishing impairment.* What is the "chattel" on which the court finds Hamidi to have "trespassed"? Is the fact that Intel's employees spent time reading Hamidi's e-mails and trying to block them relevant to the determination whether the e-mails resulted in impairment of any chattel?

2. *E-mail vs. postal mail.* The majority agrees that its reasoning leads to the result that "every personal e-mail that an employee reads at work could constitute a trespass," which it considers proper. But it rejects the further implication that "unwanted first-class mail [is] a trespass," on the ground that "[t]he issue is one of degree." Can these two positions be reconciled?

3. *Substantiality of impairment.* Is the dissent correct in distinguishing *CompuServe Inc. v. Cyber Promotions, Inc.*, excerpted in Part I(C)(1), *supra*, *Register.com, Inc. v. Verio, Inc.*, excerpted in Part III, *infra*, and *eBay, Inc. v. Bidder's Edge, Inc.*, excerpted in Part III, *infra*, on the ground that in those cases the intrusions resulted in substantial interference with plaintiffs' computer systems, while the interference here—six e-mail messages, addressed to some or all of Intel's 29,000 employees over the course of two years—was trivial? Consider whether this case is like the example from the *Restatement (Second) of Torts*, which both the majority and dissenting opinions cite: "A, a child, climbs upon the back of B's large dog and pulls its ears. No harm is done to the dog, or to any other legally protected interest of B. A is not liable to B."

4. *Alternative means of communication.* Does Hamidi have any alternative means of communicating with Intel's employees, as the majority asserts? Are any of these as effective as e-mail to the employees' work addresses? If there are no reasonable alternative means of communication, should that affect the court's analysis? Should an employer have the right to determine whose messages its employees may receive via the corporate e-mail system: e.g., solicitations for contributions from the Democratic National Committee but not the Republican National Committee; from the National Rifle Association, but not from the American Civil Liberties Union?

5. *Communications relating to labor conditions.* Is it relevant in this case that Hamidi was an unhappy ex-employee who wished to communicate with employees about labor conditions? Consider Section 552.1(a) of the California Penal Code, which provides that the state law against trespass does not prohibit

> [a]ny lawful activity for the purpose of engaging in any organizational effort on behalf of any labor union, agent, or member thereof, or of any employee group, or any member thereof, employed or formerly employed in any place of business or manufacturing establishment described in this article, or for the purpose of carrying on the lawful activities of labor unions, or members thereof.

CAL. PENAL CODE § 552.1(a). Consider also Section 527.3 of the California Code of Civil Procedure, which deprives courts of jurisdiction to issue an injunction prohibiting any person from "[g]iving publicity to, and obtaining or communicating information regarding the existence of, or the facts involved in, any labor dispute, whether by advertising, speaking, patrolling any public street or any place where any person or persons may lawfully be, or by any other method not involving fraud, violence or breach of the peace." CAL. CIV. PROC. CODE § 527.3(b)(1).

6. Hamidi *on appeal*. As this book goes to press, the California Supreme Court has agreed to hear Hamidi's appeal from this decision. How should the Court rule?

7. *Trespass a nuisance?* Professor Dan Burk is highly critical of the courts' embrace of the trespass to chattels cause of action in cases such as the foregoing. He argues that "these courts essentially reversed several hundred years of legal evolution, collapsing the separate doctrines of trespass to land and trespass to chattels back into their single common law progenitor, the action for trespass. But to do so effectively creates a brand new cause of action, unknown to modern jurisprudence." Dan L. Burk, *The Trouble with Trespass*, 4 J. SMALL & EMERGING BUS. L. 27, 33 (2000). He proposes an alternative approach:

> An optimal regulatory standard, rather than imposing a blanket possessory exclusion, might provide for consideration of comparative harm, imposing liability where the harm from the use exceeded that attending exclusion.
>
> The need to balance social costs and benefits in this fashion suggests that the imposition of theories, such as trespass upon the digital commons, may tend to lead to detrimental over-propertization of the Internet. Incomplete entitlements, rather than strong exclusive rights, might better serve the balancing function. * * * [S]uch flexible or "muddy" entitlements may better accommodate diffuse societal values that would not be internalized by bright-line property rules. Economic theory indicates that in situations where the costs of locating, negotiating, and valuing transactions are high, unclear entitlements may tend to facilitate bargaining. Unclear rules will tend to facilitate innovative or informal bargaining arrangements, whereas bright-line rules appropriate to low transaction cost situations may simply lock the parties into their respective ownership positions, unable to reach a beneficial exchange. Alternatively, the unclear rule may shunt disputes into

> third-party review, as in litigation, where the court can tailor an ownership rule to the specific situation.
>
> These characteristics suggest that the correct property theory might be nuisance to web sites, rather than trespass. Nuisance lies only if the cost of the intrusive activity outweighs the benefit. The "muddy" nature of nuisance would allow computer owners on the Net to exclude unreasonably costly uses of their servers, while allowing access for socially beneficial uses, even if the server owner might otherwise object. Stated differently, nuisance would authorize computer owners to legally "defect" from the network when necessary to avoid wasteful negative network externalities, but require them to remain legally networked when necessary to generate beneficial positive network externalities. Of course, the server owner always would have the option of physically disconnecting from the network to avoid objectionable uses, so long as he was willing to forgo the positive benefits of the network as well. Presumably, proper application of the nuisance standard would make this drastic action unattractive on average to rational server owners, as they would be shielded from marginally detrimental uses, while enjoying marginally beneficial network advantages.

Id. at 52–53. Do you agree that "muddy" rules might lead to better results in disputes of this sort?

III. ACQUIRING DATA FROM ANOTHER'S WEBSITE

eBay, Inc. v. Bidder's Edge, Inc.

100 F.Supp.2d 1058 (N.D.Cal.2000).

■ WHYTE, DISTRICT JUDGE.

ORDER GRANTING PRELIMINARY INJUNCTION

Plaintiff eBay, Inc.'s ("eBay") motion for preliminary injunction was heard by the court on April 14, 2000. * * * For the reasons set forth below, the court preliminarily enjoins defendant Bidder's Edge, Inc. ("BE") from accessing eBay's computer systems by use of any automated querying program without eBay's written authorization.

I. BACKGROUND

eBay is an Internet-based, person-to-person trading site. (Jordan Decl. ¶ 3.) eBay offers sellers the ability to list items for sale and prospective buyers the ability to search those listings and bid on items. (Id.) The seller can set the terms and conditions of the auction. (Id.) The item is sold to the highest bidder. (Id.) The transaction is consummated directly between the buyer and seller without eBay's involvement. (Id.) A potential purchaser looking for a particular item can access the eBay site and perform a key word search for relevant auctions and bidding status. (Id.) eBay has also created category listings which identify items in over 2500 categories, such as antiques, computers, and dolls. (Id.) Users may browse these category listing pages to identify items of interest. (Id.)

Users of the eBay site must register and agree to the eBay User Agreement. (Id. ¶ 4.) Users agree to the seven page User Agreement by clicking on an "I Accept" button located at the end of the User Agreement. (Id. Ex. D.) The current version of the User Agreement prohibits the use of "any robot, spider, other automatic device, or manual process to monitor or copy our web pages or the content contained herein without our prior expressed written permission." (Id.) It is not clear that the version of the User Agreement in effect at the time BE began searching the eBay site prohibited such activity, or that BE ever agreed to comply with the User Agreement.

eBay currently has over 7 million registered users. (Jordan Decl. ¶ 4.) Over 400,000 new items are added to the site every day. (Id.) Every minute, 600 bids are placed on almost 3 million items. (Id.) Users currently perform, on average, 10 million searches per day on eBay's database. Bidding for and sales of items are continuously ongoing in millions of separate auctions. (Id.)

A software robot is a computer program which operates across the Internet to perform searching, copying and retrieving functions on the web sites of others.[2] (Maynor Decl. ¶ 3; Johnson–Laird Decl. P 15.) A software robot is capable of executing thousands of instructions per minute, far in excess of what a human can accomplish. (Maynor Decl. ¶ 3) Robots consume the processing and storage resources of a system, making that portion of the system's capacity unavailable to the system owner or other users. (Id.) Consumption of sufficient system resources will slow the processing of the overall system and can overload the system such that it will malfunction or "crash." (Id.) A severe malfunction can cause a loss of data and an interruption in services. (Id.)

The eBay site employs "robot exclusion headers." (Id. ¶ 5.) A robot exclusion header is a message, sent to computers programmed to detect and respond to such headers, that eBay does not permit unauthorized robotic activity. (Id.) Programmers who wish to comply with the Robot Exclusion Standard design their robots to read a particular data file, "robots.txt," and to comply with the control directives it contains. (Johnson–Laird Decl. ¶ 20.)

To enable computers to communicate with each other over the Internet, each is assigned a unique Internet Protocol ("IP") address. (Maynor Decl. ¶ 6.) When a computer requests information from another computer over the Internet, the requesting computer must offer its IP address to the responding computer in order to allow a response to be sent. (Id.) These IP addresses allow the identification of the source of incoming requests. (Id.)

2. Programs that recursively query other computers over the Internet in order to obtain a significant amount of information are referred to in the pleadings by various names, including software robots, robots, spiders and web crawlers.

eBay identifies robotic activity on its site by monitoring the number of incoming requests from each particular IP address. (Id. ¶ 7.) Once eBay identifies an IP address believed to be involved in robotic activity, an investigation into the identity, origin and owner of the IP address may be made in order to determine if the activity is legitimate or authorized. (Id. ¶ 8.) If an investigation reveals unauthorized robotic activity, eBay may attempt to ignore ("block") any further requests from that IP address. (Id.) Attempts to block requests from particular IP addresses are not always successful. (Id. ¶ 9; Johnson–Laird Decl. ¶ 27.)

Organizations often install "proxy server" software on their computers. (Johnson–Laird Decl. ¶ 12.) Proxy server software acts as a focal point for outgoing Internet requests. (Id.) Proxy servers conserve system resources by directing all outgoing and incoming data traffic through a centralized portal. (Id.) Typically, organizations limit the use of their proxy servers to local users. (Id.) However, some organizations, either as a public service or because of a failure to properly protect their proxy server through the use of a "firewall," allow their proxy servers to be accessed by remote users. (Id. ¶ 13.) Outgoing requests from remote users can be routed through such unprotected proxy servers and appear to originate from the proxy server. (Id.) Incoming responses are then received by the proxy server and routed to the remote user. (Id.) Information requests sent through such proxy servers cannot easily be traced back to the originating IP address and can be used to circumvent attempts to block queries from the originating IP address. (Id. ¶ 14.) Blocking queries from innocent third party proxy servers is both inefficient, because it creates an endless game of hide-and-seek, and potentially counterproductive, as it runs a substantial risk of blocking requests from legitimate, desirable users who use that proxy server. (Id. ¶ 22.)

BE is a company with 22 employees that was founded in 1997. (Carney Decl. ¶ 2.) The BE website debuted in November 1998. (Id. ¶ 3.) BE does not host auctions. (Id. ¶ 2.) BE is an auction aggregation site designed to offer on-line auction buyers the ability to search for items across numerous on-line auctions without having to search each host site individually. (Id.) As of March 2000, the BE website contained information on more that five million items being auctioned on more than one hundred auction sites. (Id. ¶ 3.) BE also provides its users with additional auction-related services and information. (Id. ¶ 2.) The information available on the BE site is contained in a database of information that BE compiles through access to various auction sites such as eBay. (Id. ¶ 4.) When a user enters a search for a particular item at BE, BE searches its database and generates a list of every item in the database responsive to the search, organized by auction closing date and time. (Id. ¶ 5.) Rather than going to each host auction site one at a time, a user who goes to BE may conduct a single search to obtain information about that item on every auction site tracked by BE. (Id. ¶ 6.) It is important to include information regarding eBay auctions on the BE site because eBay is by far the biggest consumer to consumer on-line auction site. (Id.)

* * *

In early 1998, eBay gave BE permission to include information regarding eBay-hosted auctions for Beanie Babies and Furbies in the BE database. (Id. ¶ 7.) In early 1999, BE added to the number of person-to-person auction sites it covered and started covering a broader range of items hosted by those sites, including eBay. (Id. ¶ 8.) On April 24, 1999, eBay verbally approved BE crawling the eBay website for a period of 90 days. (Id.) The parties contemplated that during this period they would reach a formal licensing agreement. (Id.) They were unable to do so.

It appears that the primary dispute was over the method BE uses to search the eBay database. eBay wanted BE to conduct a search of the eBay system only when the BE system was queried by a BE user. (Ploen Decl. Ex. 9.) This reduces the load on the eBay system and increases the accuracy of the BE data. (Id.) BE wanted to recursively crawl the eBay system to compile its own auction database. (Carney Decl. ¶ 18.) This increases the speed of BE searches and allows BE to track the auctions generally and automatically update its users when activity occurs in particular auctions, categories of auctions, or when new items are added. (Id.)

In late August or early September 1999, eBay requested by telephone that BE cease posting eBay auction listings on its site. (Id. ¶ 9; Rock Decl. ¶ 5.) BE agreed to do so. (Rock Decl. ¶ 5.) In October 1999, BE learned that other auction aggregations sites were including information regarding eBay auctions. (Carney Decl. ¶ 12.) On November 2, 1999, BE issued a press release indicating that it had resumed including eBay auction listings on its site. (Rock Decl. Ex. H.) On November 9, 1999, eBay sent BE a letter reasserting that BE's activities were unauthorized, insisting that BE cease accessing the eBay site, alleging that BE's activities constituted a civil trespass and offering to license BE's activities. (Id. Ex. I.) eBay and BE were again unable to agree on licensing terms. As a result, eBay attempted to block BE from accessing the eBay site; by the end of November, 1999, eBay had blocked a total of 169 IP addresses it believed BE was using to query eBay's system. (Maynor Decl. ¶ 12.) BE elected to continue crawling eBay's site by using proxy servers to evade eBay's IP blocks. (Mundy Depo. at 271:18–19 ("We eventually adopted the rotating proxy servers."))

Approximately 69% of the auction items contained in the BE database are from auctions hosted on eBay. (Carney Decl. ¶ 17.) BE estimates that it would lose one-third of its users if it ceased to cover the eBay auctions. (Id.)

The parties agree that BE accessed the eBay site approximate 100,000 times a day. (Felton Decl. ¶ 33.) eBay alleges that BE activity constituted up to 1.53% of the number of requests received by eBay, and up to 1.10% of the total data transferred by eBay during certain periods in October and November of 1999. (Johnson–Laird Decl. ¶ 64.) BE alleges that BE activity constituted no more than 1.11% of the requests received by eBay, and no more than 0.70% of the data transferred by eBay. (Felton Decl. ¶ 60.) eBay alleges that BE activity had fallen 27%, to 0.74% of requests and 0.61% of data, by February 20, 2000. (Johnson–Laird Decl. ¶ ¶ 70–71.) eBay alleges damages due to BE's activity totaling between $45,323 and $61,804 for a ten month period including seven months in 1999 and the first three months in 2000. (Meyer Decl. ¶ 28.) However, these calculations appear flawed in that they assume the maximal BE usage of eBay resources continued over all ten months. (Id.) Moreover, the calculations attribute a pro rata share of eBay expenditures to BE activity, rather than attempting to calculate the incremental cost to eBay due to BE activity. (Id.) eBay has not alleged any specific incremental damages due to BE activity. (See Rock Depo., 192:8–10.)

It appears that major Internet search engines, such as Yahoo!, Google, Excite and AltaVista, respect the Robot Exclusion Standard. (Johnson-Laird Decl. ¶ ¶ 81–85.)

eBay now moves for preliminary injunctive relief preventing BE from accessing the eBay computer system based on nine causes of action: trespass, false advertising, federal and state trademark dilution, computer fraud and abuse, unfair competition, misappropriation, interference with prospective economic advantage and unjust enrichment. However, eBay does not move, either independently or alternatively, for injunctive relief that is limited to restricting how BE can use data taken from the eBay site.

II. LEGAL STANDARD

To obtain preliminary injunctive relief, a movant must demonstrate "either a likelihood of success on the merits and the possibility of irreparable injury, or that serious questions going to the merits were raised and the balance of hardships tips sharply in its favor." * * * "The critical element in determining the test to be applied is the relative hardship to the parties. If the balance of harm tips decidedly toward the plaintiff, then the plaintiff need not show as robust a likelihood of success on the merits as when the balance tips less decidedly." * * *

III. ANALYSIS

A. Balance of Harm

* * *

According to eBay, the load on its servers resulting from BE's web crawlers represents between 1.11% and 1.53% of the total load on eBay's listing servers. eBay alleges both economic loss from BE's current activities and potential harm resulting from the total crawling of BE and others. In alleging economic harm, eBay's argument is that eBay has expended considerable time, effort and money to create its computer system, and that BE should have to pay for the portion of eBay's system BE uses. eBay attributes a pro rata portion of the costs of maintaining its entire system to the BE activity. However, eBay does not indicate that these expenses are incrementally incurred because of BE's activities, nor that any particular service disruption can be attributed to BE's activities. eBay provides no support for the proposition that the pro rata costs of obtaining an item represent the appropriate measure of damages for unauthorized use. In contrast, California law appears settled that the appropriate measure of damages is the actual harm inflicted by the conduct:

> Where the conduct complained of does not amount to a substantial interference with possession or the right thereto, but consists of intermeddling with or use of or damages to the personal property, the owner has a cause of action for trespass or case, and may recover only the actual damages suffered by reason of the impairment of the property or the loss of its use.

Zaslow v. Kroenert, 29 Cal. 2d 541, 551, 176 P.2d 1 (1946). Moreover, even if BE is inflicting incremental maintenance costs on eBay, potentially calculable monetary damages are not generally a proper foundation for a preliminary injunction. * * *

eBay's allegations of harm are based, in part, on the argument that BE's activities should be thought of as equivalent to sending in an army of 100,000 robots a day to check the prices in a competitor's store. This analogy, while graphic, appears inappropriate. Although an admittedly formalistic distinction, unauthorized robot intruders into a "brick and mortar" store would be committing a trespass to real property. There does not appear to be any doubt that the appropriate remedy for an ongoing trespass to business premises would be a preliminary injunction. *See e.g., State v. Carriker*, 5 Ohio App. 2d 255, 214 N.E.2d 809, 811–12 (Ohio App. 1964) (interpreting Ohio criminal trespass law to cover a business invitee who, with no intention of making a purchase, uses the business premises of another for his own gain after his invitation has been revoked); *General Petroleum Corp. v. Beilby*, 213 Cal. 601, 605, 2 P.2d 797 (1931). More importantly, for the analogy to be accurate, the robots would have to make up less than two out of every one-hundred customers in the store, the robots would not interfere with the customers' shopping experience, nor would the robots even be seen by the customers. Under such circumstances, there is a legitimate claim that the robots would not pose any threat of irreparable harm. However, eBay's right to injunctive relief is also based upon a much stronger argument.

If BE's activity is allowed to continue unchecked, it would encourage other auction aggregators to engage in similar recursive searching of the eBay system such that eBay would suffer irreparable harm from reduced system performance, system unavailability, or data losses. (See Spafford Decl. ¶ 32; Parker Decl. ¶ 19; Johnson–Laird Decl. ¶ 85.[14]) BE does not appear to seriously contest that reduced system performance, system unavailability or data loss would inflict irreparable harm on eBay consisting of lost profits and lost customer goodwill. Harm resulting from lost profits and lost customer goodwill is irreparable because it is neither easily calculable, nor easily compensable and is therefore an appropriate basis for injunctive relief. *See, e.g., People of State of California ex rel. Van De Kamp v. Tahoe Reg'l Planning Agency,* 766 F.2d 1316, 1319 (9th Cir.1985).

14. "Given that Bidder's Edge can be seen to have imposed a load of 1.53% on eBay's listing servers, simple arithmetic and economies reveal how only a few more such companies deploying rude robots [that do not respect the Robot Exclusion Standard] would be required before eBay would be brought to its knees by what would be then a debilitating load."

Where, as here, the denial of preliminary injunctive relief would encourage an increase in the complained of activity, and such an increase would present a strong likelihood of irreparable harm, the plaintiff has at least established a possibility of irreparable harm.

* * *

BE correctly observes that there is a dearth of authority supporting a preliminary injunction based on an ongoing to trespass to chattels. In contrast, it is black letter law in California that an injunction is an appropriate remedy for a continuing trespass to real property. *See Allred v. Harris*, 14 Cal. App. 4th 1386, 1390 (1993) (citing 5 B.E. Witkin, Summary of California Law, Torts § 605 (9th ed. 1988)). If eBay were a brick and mortar auction house with limited seating capacity, eBay would appear to be entitled to reserve those seats for potential bidders, to refuse entrance to individuals (or robots) with no intention of bidding on any of the items, and to seek preliminary injunctive relief against non-customer trespassers eBay was physically unable to exclude. The analytic difficulty is that a wrongdoer can commit an ongoing trespass of a computer system that is more akin to the traditional notion of a trespass to real property, than the traditional notion of a trespass to chattels, because even though it is ongoing, it will probably never amount to a conversion. The court concludes that under the circumstances present here, BE's ongoing violation of eBay's fundamental property right to exclude others from its computer system potentially causes sufficient irreparable harm to support a preliminary injunction.

BE argues that even if eBay is entitled to a presumption of irreparable harm, the presumption may be rebutted. The presumption may be rebutted by evidence that a party has engaged in a pattern of granting licenses to engage in the complained of activity such that it may be reasonable to expect that invasion of the right can be recompensed with a royalty rather than with an injunction, or by evidence that a party has unduly delayed in bringing suit, thereby negating the idea of irreparability. *See Polymer Technologies, Inc. v. Bridwell,* 103 F.3d 970, 974 (Fed.Cir.1996) (discussing presumption of irreparable harm in patent infringement context). BE alleges that eBay has both engaged in a pattern of licensing aggregators to crawl its site as well as delayed in seeking relief. For the reasons set forth below, the court finds that neither eBay's limited licensing activities nor its delay in seeking injunctive relief while it attempted to resolve the matter without judicial intervention are sufficient to rebut the possibility of irreparable harm.

If eBay's irreparable harm claim were premised solely on the potential harm caused by BE's current crawling activities, evidence that eBay had licensed others to crawl the eBay site would suggest that BE's activity would not result in irreparable harm to eBay. However, the gravamen of the alleged irreparable harm is that if eBay is allowed to continue to crawl the eBay site, it may encourage frequent and unregulated crawling to the point that eBay's system will be irreparably harmed. There is no evidence that eBay has indiscriminately licensed all comers. Rather, it appears that eBay has carefully chosen to permit crawling by a limited number of aggregation sites that agree to abide by the terms of eBay's licensing agreement. "The existence of such a [limited] license, unlike a general license offered to all comers, does not demonstrate a decision to relinquish all control over the distribution of the product in exchange for a readily computable fee." *Ty, Inc. v. GMA Accessories, Inc.*, 132 F.3d 1167, 1173 (7th Cir.1997) (discussing presumption of irreparable harm in copyright infringement context). eBay's licensing activities appear directed toward limiting the amount and nature of crawling activity on the eBay site. Such licensing does not support the inference that carte blanche crawling of the eBay site would pose no threat of irreparable harm.

eBay first learned of BE in late 1997 or early 1998 when BE sought to retain the same public relations firm used by eBay. (See Ploen Decl. Ex. 1.) This motion was filed on January 18, 2000. An unexplained delay of two years would certainly raise serious doubts as the irreparability of any alleged harm. See *Playboy Enters., Inc. v. Netscape Communications Corp.*, 55 F.Supp.2d 1070, 1090 (C.D.Cal.1999) (noting that delay of as little as 60 days to three months has been held sufficient to rebut the presumption of irreparable harm). Here, the circumstances establish that any delay resulted from eBay's good faith efforts to resolve this dispute without judicial intervention and do not rebut a finding of the possibility of irreparable harm.

* * *

BE argues that even if eBay will be irreparably harmed if a preliminary injunction is not granted, BE will suffer greater irreparable harm if an injunction is granted. According to BE, lack of access to eBay's database will result in a two-thirds decrease in the items listed on BE, and a one-eighth reduction in the value of BE, from $80 million to $70 million. (Sweeny Decl. PP 42, 43.) Although the potential harm to BE does not appear insignificant, BE does not appear to have suffered any irreparable harm during the period it voluntarily ceased crawling the eBay site. Barring BE from automatically querying eBay's site does not prevent BE from maintaining an aggregation site including information from eBay's site. Any potential economic harm is appropriately addressed through the posting of an adequate bond.

* * * Accordingly, the court concludes that eBay has demonstrated at least a possibility of suffering irreparable system harm and that BE has not established a balance of hardships weighing in its favor.

B. Likelihood of Success

As noted above, eBay moves for a preliminary injunction on all nine of its causes of action. * * * Since the court finds eBay is entitled to the relief requested based on its trespass claim, the court does not address the merits of the remaining claims or BE's arguments that many of these other state law causes of action are preempted by federal copyright law. The court first addresses the merits of the trespass claim, then BE's arguments regarding copyright preemption of the trespass claim, and finally the public interest.

1. Trespass

* * *

In order to prevail on a claim for trespass based on accessing a computer system, the plaintiff must establish: (1) defendant intentionally and without authorization interfered with plaintiff's possessory interest in the computer system; and (2) defendant's unauthorized use proximately resulted in damage to plaintiff. * * * Here, eBay has presented evidence sufficient to establish a strong likelihood of proving both prongs and ultimately prevailing on the merits of its trespass claim.

a. BE's Unauthorized Interference

eBay argues that BE's use was unauthorized and intentional. eBay is correct. BE does not dispute that it employed an automated computer program to connect with and search eBay's electronic database. BE admits that, because other auction aggregators were including eBay's auctions in their listing, it continued to "crawl" eBay's website even after eBay demanded BE terminate such activity.

BE argues that it cannot trespass eBay's website because the site is publicly accessible. BE's argument is unconvincing. eBay's servers are private property, conditional access to which eBay grants the public. eBay does not generally permit the type of automated access made by BE. In fact, eBay explicitly notifies automated visitors that their access is not permitted. "In general, California does recognize a trespass claim where the defendant exceeds the scope of the consent." *Baugh v. CBS, Inc.*, 828 F.Supp. 745, 756 (N.D.Cal.1993).

Even if BE's web crawlers were authorized to make individual queries of eBay's system, BE's web crawlers exceeded the scope of any such consent when they began acting like robots by making repeated queries. * * * Moreover, eBay repeatedly and explicitly notified BE that its use of eBay's computer system was unauthorized. The entire reason BE directed its queries through proxy servers was to evade eBay's attempts to stop this unauthorized access. The court concludes that BE's activity is sufficiently outside of the scope of the use permitted by eBay that it is unauthorized for the purposes of establishing a trespass. * * *

eBay argues that BE interfered with eBay's possessory interest in its computer system. Although eBay appears unlikely to be able to show a substantial interference at this time, such a showing is not required. Conduct that does not amount to a substantial interference with possession, but which consists of intermeddling with or use of another's personal property, is sufficient to establish a cause of action for trespass to chattel. *See Thrifty-Tel*, 46 Cal. App. 4th at 1567 (distinguishing the tort from conversion). Although the court admits some uncertainty as to the precise level of possessory interference required to constitute an intermeddling, there does not appear to be any dispute that eBay can show that BE's conduct amounts to use of eBay's computer systems. Accordingly, eBay has made a strong showing that it is likely to prevail on the merits of its assertion that BE's use of eBay's computer system was an unauthorized and intentional interference with eBay's possessory interest.

b. Damage to eBay's Computer System

A trespasser is liable when the trespass diminishes the condition, quality or value of personal property. *See CompuServe, Inc. v. Cyber Promotions,* 962 F.Supp. 1015 (S.D.Ohio 1997). The quality or value of personal property may be "diminished even though it is not physically damaged by defendant's conduct." *Id.* at 1022. * * *

eBay is likely to be able to demonstrate that BE's activities have diminished the quality or value of eBay's computer systems. BE's activities consume at least a portion of plaintiff's bandwidth and server capacity. Although there is some dispute as to the percentage of queries on eBay's site for which BE is responsible, BE admits that it sends some 80,000 to 100,000 requests to plaintiff's computer systems per day. (Ritchey Decl. Ex. 3 at 391:11–12.) Although eBay does not claim that this consumption has led to any physical damage to eBay's computer system, nor does eBay provide any evidence to support the claim that it may have lost revenues or customers based on this use, eBay's claim is that BE's use is appropriating eBay's personal property by using valuable bandwidth and capacity, and necessarily compromising eBay's ability to use that capacity for its own purposes. See *CompuServe*, 962 F.Supp. at 1022 ("any value [plaintiff] realizes from its computer equipment is wholly derived from the extent to which that equipment can serve its subscriber base.").

BE argues that its searches represent a negligible load on plaintiff's computer systems, and do not rise to the level of impairment to the condition or value of eBay's computer system required to constitute a trespass. However, it is undisputed that eBay's server and its capacity are personal property, and that BE's searches use a portion of this property. Even if, as BE argues, its searches use only a small amount of eBay's computer system capacity, BE has nonetheless deprived eBay of the ability to use that portion of its personal property for its own purposes. The law recognizes no such right to use another's personal property. Accordingly, BE's actions appear to have caused injury to eBay and appear likely to continue to cause injury to eBay. If the court were to hold otherwise, it would likely encourage other auction aggregators to crawl the eBay site, potentially to the point of denying effective access to eBay's customers. If preliminary injunctive relief were denied, and other aggregators began to crawl the eBay site, there appears to be little doubt that the load on eBay's computer system would qualify as a substantial impairment of condition or value. California law does not require eBay to wait for such a disaster before applying to this court for relief. The court concludes that eBay has made a strong showing that it is likely to prevail on the merits of its trespass claim, and that there is at least a possibility that it will suffer irreparable harm if preliminary injunctive relief is not granted. eBay is therefore entitled to preliminary injunctive relief.

* * *

IV. ORDER

Bidder's Edge, its officers, agents, servants, employees, attorneys and those in active concert or participation with them who receive actual notice of this order by personal service or otherwise, are hereby enjoined pending the trial of this matter, from using any automated query program, robot, web crawler or other similar device, without written authorization, to access eBay's computer systems or networks, for the purpose of copying any part of eBay's auction database. * * *

* * *

NOTES & QUESTIONS

1. *Notice via robot exclusion headers*. eBay's site contained "robot exclusion headers," which are instructions in a file named "robots.txt" that are designed to affect the operation of robot software that accesses the site. A robot's programmer may design it to read the instructions contained in the robots.txt file; if the robots.txt file bars access by robots, and the robot is programmed to heed the instructions in robots.txt files, then the robot will not access the site. Should a website's implementation of a robots.txt file be deemed notice to all who deploy robots that their accessing of the site is unauthorized? Should it only be notice as to robots that have been designed to read and honor the instructions in robots.txt files?

2. *Anticipatory harm*. Do you agree with the court's holding that trespass to chattels may be premised on the likelihood that harm will result if *additional* parties begin accessing eBay's site without authorization?

3. *Degree of interference*. In *Ticketmaster Corp. v. Tickets.com, Inc.*, 2000 WL 1887522 (C.D.Cal.2000), the plaintiff, the largest seller of events tickets in the United States, sought to prevent defendant, a much smaller seller of tickets, from using robots to extract information about events from plaintiff's site, and presenting that information on its own site. The court declined to hold that defendant's actions constituted trespass to chattels. It distinguished *eBay v. Bidders Edge* on the basis that there was no showing that defendant's accessing of plaintiff's site was substantial enough to interfere with plaintiff's business. The court also observed that the case did not present "the spectre of dozens or more parasites joining the fray, the cumulative total of which could affect the operation of [Ticketmaster's] business." Is *eBay v. Bidders Edge* distinguishable on this basis?

4. *Database copying*. The injunction that eBay sought and obtained prevents "copying * * * eBay's auction database." Could eBay have obtained relief under the law of copyright? under state law of unfair competition or misappropriation? Is trespass to chattels an appropriate instrument for database protection? Reconsider Chapter 10, *supra*.

Register.com, Inc. v. Verio, Inc.

126 F.Supp.2d 238 (S.D.N.Y.2000).

■ JONES, DISTRICT JUDGE.

Introduction

Plaintiff Register.com, a registrar of Internet domain names, moves for a preliminary injunction against the defendant, Verio, Inc. ("Verio"), a provider of Internet services. Register.com relies on claims under Section 43(a) of the Lanham Act, 15 U.S.C. § 1125(a); the Computer Fraud and Abuse Act of 1986, 18 U.S.C. § 1030, as amended; as well as trespass to chattels and breach of contract under the common law of the State of New York. In essence Register.com seeks an injunction barring Verio from using automated software processes to access and collect the registrant contact information contained in its WHOIS database and from using any of that information, however accessed, for mass marketing purposes.

I. Findings of Fact

The Parties

Plaintiff Register.com is one of over fifty domain name registrars for customers who wish to register a name in the .com, .net, and .org top-level domains. As a registrar it contracts with these second-level domain ("SLD") name holders and a registry, collecting registration data about the SLD holder and submitting zone file information for entry in the registry database. In addition to its domain name registration services, Register.com offers to its customers, both directly and through its more than 450 co-branded and private label partners, a variety of other related services, such as (i) website creation tools; (ii) website hosting; (iii) electronic mail; (iv) domain name hosting; (v) domain name forwarding, and (vi) real-time domain name management. * * *

In order to give its customers control over their receipt of commercial solicitations, Register.com provides them with the opportunity to "opt-in" during the domain name registration process to receiving sales and marketing communications from Register.com or its co-brand or private label partners. Customers who do not opt-in to such communications are not solicited by Register.com or its co-brands. Significantly, Register.com's co-brand and private label partners have contracted with Register.com for the right to have their services featured on the www.register.com website. (See Mornell Decl. ¶ 18).

Defendant Verio is one of the largest operators of web sites for businesses and a leading provider of comprehensive Internet services. Although not a registrar of domain names, Verio directly competes with Register.com and its partners to provide registration services and a variety of other Internet services including website hosting and development. Verio recently made a multimillion dollar investment in its computer system and facilities for its expanded force of telephone sales associates in its efforts to "provide recent domain name registration customers with the services they need, at the time they need them." (Eden Decl. ¶ 31).

The WHOIS database

To become an accredited domain name registrar for the .com, .net, and .org domains, all registrars, including Register.com are required to enter into a registrar Accreditation Agreement ("Agreement") with the Internet Corporation for Assigned Names and Numbers ("ICANN"). Under that Agreement, Register.com, as well as all other registrars, is required to provide an on-line, interactive WHOIS database. This database contains the names and contact information—postal address, telephone number, electronic mail address and in some cases facsimile number—for customers who register domain names through the registrar. The Agreement also requires Register.com to make the database freely accessible to the public via its web page and through an independent access port called port 43. These query-based channels of access to the WHOIS database allow the user to collect registrant contact information for one domain name at a time by entering the domain name into the provided search engine.

The primary purpose of the WHOIS database is to provide necessary information in the event of domain name disputes, such as those arising from cybersquatting or trademark infringement. (See Rony Decl. ¶ 18, Ex. B to McPherson Decl. at 13). The parties also agree that the WHOIS data may be used for market research.

Specifically, section II.F.5 of Register.com's Accreditation Agreement with ICANN requires that:

> In providing query-based public access to registration data as required by Sections II.F.1 and II.F.4, Registrar shall not impose terms and conditions on use of the data provided except as permitted by ICANN-adopted policy. Unless and until ICANN adopts a different policy, Registrar shall permit use of data it provides in response to queries *for any lawful purposes except to*: (a) *allow, enable, or otherwise support the transmission of mass unsolicited, commercial advertising or solicitations via e-mail (spam);* or (b) enable high volume, automated, electronic processes that apply to Registrar (or its systems).

(Ex. E to McPherson Decl.) (emphasis added).

Originally Register.com's terms and conditions for users of its WHOIS database were substantially the same. In April 2000, however, Register.com implemented the following more restrictive terms of use governing its WHOIS database:

> By submitting a WHOIS query, you agree that you will use this data *only for lawful purposes* and that, *under no circumstances will you use this data to: (1) allow, enable, or otherwise support the transmission of mass unsolicited, commercial advertising or solicitations* ***via direct mail****, electronic mail,* ***or by telephone****;* or (2) enable high volume, automated, electronic processes that apply to Register.com (or its systems). The compilation, repackaging, dissemination or other use of this data is expressly prohibited without the prior written consent of Register.com. Register.com reserves the right to modify these terms at any time. By submitting this query, you agree to abide by these terms.

(Ex. 27 to Pl.'s Sept. 8, 2000 Motion) (emphasis added).

Verio's Project Henhouse

In late 1999, to better target their marketing and sales efforts toward customers in need of web hosting services and to reach those customers more quickly, Verio developed an automated software program or "robot." With its search robot, Verio accessed the WHOIS database maintained by the accredited registrars, including Register.com, and collected the contact information of customers who had recently registered a domain name. Then, despite the marketing prohibitions in Register.com's terms of use, Verio utilized this data in a marketing initiative known as Project Henhouse and began to contact and solicit Register.com's customers, within the first several days after their registration, by e-mail, regular mail, and telephone.

Verio's Search Robots

In general, the process worked as follows: First, each day Verio downloaded, in compressed format, a list of all currently registered domain names, of all registrars, ending in .com, .net, and .org. That list or database is maintained by Network Solutions, Inc. ("NSI") and is published on 13 different "root zone" servers. The registry list is updated twice daily and provides the domain name, the sponsoring registrar, and the nameservers for all registered names. Using a computer program, Verio then compared the newly downloaded NSI registry with the NSI registry it downloaded a day earlier in order to isolate the domain names that had been registered in the last day and the names that had been removed. After downloading the list of new domain names, only then was a search robot used to query the NSI database to extract the name of the accredited registrar of each new name. That search robot then automatically made successive queries to the various registrars' WHOIS databases, via the port 43 access channels, to harvest the relevant contact information for each new domain name registered. (See Eden Depo. at 26–30; Eden Decl. PP36–38). Once retrieved, the WHOIS data was deposited into an information database maintained by Verio. The resulting database of sales leads was then provided to Verio's telemarketing staff.

* * *

IV. Register.com's Claims

* * *

B. Trespass To Chattels

Register.com argues that Verio's use of an automated software robot to search the "WHOIS" database constitutes trespass to chattels. Register.com states that it has made its computer system available on the Internet, and that "Verio has used 'software automation' to flood that computer system with traffic in order to retrieve the contact information of Register.com customers for the purpose of solicitation in knowing violation of Register.com's posted policies and terms of use." (Pl.'s Mem. of Law at 36.)

The standard for trespass to chattels in New York is based upon the standard set forth in the Restatement of Torts:

> One who uses a chattel with the consent of another is subject to liability in trespass for any harm to the chattel which is caused by or occurs in the course of any use exceeding the consent, even though such use is not a conversion.

City of Amsterdam v. Goldreyer, Ltd., 882 F.Supp. 1273 (E.D.N.Y.1995) (citing Restatement (Second) of Torts, § 256 (1965)).

* * *

* * * [I]t is clear since at least the date this lawsuit was filed that Register.com does not consent to Verio's use of a search robot, and Verio is on notice that its search robot is unwelcome. (Pl.'s V.C. P36)

Accordingly, Verio's future use of a search robot to access the database exceeds the scope of Register.com's consent, and Verio is liable for any harm to the chattel (Register.com's computer systems) caused by that unauthorized access. *See Compuserve,* 962 F.Supp. at 1024 (holding that defendants' continued use after CompuServe notified defendants that it no longer consented to the use of its proprietary computer equipment was a trespass) (citing Restatement (Second) of Torts §§ 252 and 892A(5)).

Having established that Verio's access to its WHOIS database by robot is unauthorized, Register.com must next demonstrate that Verio's unauthorized access caused harm to its chattels, namely its computer system. To that end, Robert Gardos, Register.com's Vice President for Technology, submitted a declaration estimating that Verio's searching of Register.com's WHOIS database has resulted in a diminishment of 2.3% of Register.com's system resources. (See Gardos Decl. P32.) However, during discovery, the basis for Gardos' estimations of the impact Verio's search robot had on Register.com's computer systems was thoroughly undercut. Gardos admitted in his deposition that he had taken measurements of neither the capacity of Register.com's computer systems nor the portion of that capacity which was consumed by Verio's search robots. Furthermore, when describing how he arrived at his conclusion that Verio's search robots occupied a certain percentage of Register.com's systems capacity, Mr. Gardos testified that the numbers he used were "all rough estimates." (Gardos Depo. at 76).

Although Register.com's evidence of any burden or harm to its computer system caused by the successive queries performed by search robots is imprecise, evidence of mere possessory interference is sufficient to demonstrate the quantum of harm necessary to establish a claim for trespass to chattels. "A trespasser is liable when the trespass diminishes the condition, quality, or value of personal property." *eBay, Inc. v. Bidder's Edge, Inc.,* 100 F.Supp.2d 1058, 1071 (N.D.Cal.2000) (*citing Compuserve,* 962 F.Supp. at 1022). "The quality or value of personal property may be 'diminished even though it is not physically damaged by defendant's conduct.'" Id. Though it does correctly dispute the trustworthiness and accuracy of Mr.

Gardos' calculations, Verio does not dispute that its search robot occupies some of Register.com's systems capacity.

Although Register.com was unable to directly measure the amount by which its systems capacity was reduced, the record evidence is sufficient to establish the possessory interference necessary to establish a trespass to chattels claim. As the *eBay* Court wrote:

> BE argues that its searches present a negligible load on plaintiff's computer systems, and do not rise to the level of impairment to the condition or value of eBay's computer system required to consitute a trespass. *However, it is undisputed that eBay's server and its capacity are personal property, and that BE's searches use a portion of this property. Even if, as BE argues, its searches only use a small amount of eBay's computer system capacity, BE has nonetheless deprived eBay of the ability to use that portion of its personal property for its own purposes. The law recognizes no such right to use another's personal property.* Accordingly, BE's actions appear to have caused injury to eBay and appear likely to continue to cause injury to eBay.

(100 F.Supp.2d at 1071.) (emphasis added).

Furthermore, Gardos also noted in his declaration "if the strain on Register.com's resources generated by Verio's searches becomes large enough, it could cause Register.com's computer systems to malfunction or crash" and "I believe that if Verio's searching of Register.com's WHOIS database were determined to be lawful, then every purveryor of Internet-based services would engage in similar conduct." (Gardos Decl. ¶ ¶ 33, 34). Gardos' concerns are supported by Verio's testimony that it sees no need to place a limit on the number of other companies that should be allowed to harvest data from Register.com's computers. (See Ayers Depo. at 71). Furthermore, Verio's own internal documents reveal that Verio was aware that its robotic queries could slow the response times of the registrars' databases and even overload them. (See Ex. 29 & to Pl.'s Sept. 8, 2000 Motion). Because of that possibility, Verio contemplated cloaking the origin of its queries by using a process called IP aliasing. (See id.; see also Ex. 64 to Pl.'s Sept. 8, 2000 Motion).

Accordingly, Register.com's evidence that Verio's search robots have presented and will continue to present an unwelcome interference with, and a risk of interruption to, its computer system and servers is sufficient to demonstrate a likelihood of success on the merits of its trespass to chattels claim.

There is no adequate remedy at law for an ongoing trespass and without an injunction the victim of such a trespass will be irreparably harmed. The *eBay* court specifically held that eBay was entitled to preliminary injunctive relief based on the claim that if such relief were denied, other companies would be encouraged to deploy search robots against eBay's servers and would further diminish eBay's server capacity to the point of denying effective access to eBay's customers. *See id.* at 1071–72.

The same reasoning applies here. Register.com, through Mr. Gardos, has expressed the fear that its servers will be flooded by search robots deployed by competitors in the absence of injunctive relief. Register.com has therefore demonstrated both a likelihood of success on the merits of its trespass to chattels claim and the existence of irreparable harm, and is entitled to a preliminary injunction against Verio based upon that claim.

C. Computer Fraud And Abuse Act §§ 1030(a)(2)(C) and (a)(5)(C)

The issue of the scope of Verio's authorization to access the WHOIS database is also central to the Court's analysis of Register.com's claims that Verio is violating two discrete provisions of the Computer Fraud and Abuse Act ("CFAA"), 18 U.S.C. § 1030 et seq.

Register.com claims both that the use of software robots to harvest customer information from its WHOIS database in violation of its terms of use violates 18 U.S.C. §§ 1030(a)(2)(C) and (a)(5)(C) [since redesignated § 1030(a)(5)(A)(iii)—Eds.], and that using the harvested information in violation of Register.com's policy forbidding the use of WHOIS data for marketing also violates those sections. That is, that both Verio's method of accessing the WHOIS data and Verio's end uses of the data violate the CFAA.

1. Verio's Use of Search Robots

Both §§ 1030(a)(2)(C) and (a)(5)(C) require that the plaintiff prove that the defendant's access to its computer system was unauthorized, or in the case of § 1030(a)(2)(C) that it was unauthorized or exceeded authorized access. However, although each section requires proof of some degree of unauthorized access, each addresses a different type of harm. Section 1030(a)(2)(C) requires Register.com to prove that Verio intentionally accessed its computers without authorization and thereby obtained information. Section 1030(a)(5)(C) requires Register.com to show that Verio intentionally accessed its computer without authorization and thereby caused damage.

As discussed more fully in the context of the trespass to chattels claim, because Register.com objects to Verio's use of search robots they represent an unauthorized access to the WHOIS database.

The type of harm that Register.com alleges is caused by the search robots, including diminished server capacity and potential system shutdowns, is better analyzed under § 1030(a)(5)(C), which specifically addresses damages to the computer system. Pursuant to the pertinent part of § 1030(e)(8), "the term 'damage' means any impairment to the integrity or availability of data, a program, a system, or information that (A) causes loss aggregating at least $5000 in value during any 1–year period to one or more individuals."

On this record Register.com has demonstrated that Verio's unauthorized use of search robots to harvest registrant contact information from Register.com's WHOIS database has diminished server capacity, however slightly, and could diminish response time, which could impair the availability of data to clients trying to get registrant contact information. Moreover, Register.com has raised the possibility that if Verio's robotic queries of Register.com's WHOIS database were determined to be lawful, then other vendors of Internet services would engage in similar conduct. This Court finds that it is highly probable that other Internet service vendors would also use robots to obtain this potential customer information were it to be permitted. The use of the robot allows a marketer to reach a potential client within the first several days of the domain name registration, an optimal time to solicit the customer for other services. In contrast, if instead of using a search robot the service vendor obtains registrant contact information pursuant to a bulk license, the vendor must wait to receive the information on a weekly basis. As Eric Eden, the director of operation Henhouse wrote in an e-mail to a Verio employee "consistent testing has found that the faster we approach someone after they register a domain name, the more likely we are to sell them hosting." (Ex. 40 to Pl.'s Sept. 8, 2000 Motion).

If the strain on Register.com's resources generated by robotic searches becomes large enough, it could cause Register.com's computer systems to malfunction or crash. Such a crash would satisfy § 1030(a)(5)(C)'s threshold requirement that a plaintiff demonstrate $5000 in economic damages[12] resulting from the violation, both because of costs relating to repair and lost data and also because of lost good will based on adverse customer reactions.

* * *

Because Register.com has demonstrated that Verio's access to its WHOIS database by means of an automated search robot is unauthorized and caused or could cause $5000 in damages by impairing the availability of data or the availability of its computer systems, Register.com has established both irreparable harm and a likelihood of success on the merits of its claim that Verio's use of the search robot violated § 1030(a)(5)(C) of the Computer Fraud And Abuse Act. Register.com is therefore entitled to injunctive relief based upon this claim.

2. Verio's Use of WHOIS Data For Marketing Purposes

With respect to its use of Register.com's WHOIS data for e-mail, direct mail and telephone marketing, Verio argues that such an act can only be analyzed under § 1030(a)(2)(C)'s provision assessing liability where a party

12. Register.com relies upon lost revenue from Verio's exploitation of the WHOIS data for marketing purposes to constitute the damages required under § 1030(a)(5)(C). Although lost good will or business could provide the loss figure required under § 1030(a)(5)(C), it could only do so if it resulted from the impairment or unavailability of data or systems. The good will losses cited by Register.com are not the result of the harm addressed by § 1030(a)(5)(C). How Verio uses the WHOIS data, once extracted, has no bearing on whether Verio has impaired the availability or integrity of Register.com's data or computer systems in extracting it. Accordingly, because violating an anti-marketing restriction on the end use of data harms neither the data nor the computer and therefore does not cause the type of harm that § 1030(a)(5)(C) addresses, the specific good will damages cited by Register.com cannot satisfy its burden under § 1030(a)(5)(C).

exceeds authorized access and obtains information it is not entitled to obtain. Verio argues that because it is authorized to access the WHOIS database for some purposes its access was authorized. Verio then argues that its conduct must meet the Act's specific definition of conduct that "exceeds authorized access." Pursuant to the definition contained in § 1030(e)(6) of the CFAA, "the term 'exceeds authorized access' means to access a computer with authorization and to use such access to obtain or alter information in the computer that the accessor is not entitled to obtain or alter." 18 U.S.C. § 1030(e)(6) (emphasis added). Verio then argues that this definition does not contemplate a violation of end use restrictions placed on data as "exceeding authorized access," and therefore that Verio has not violated § 1030(a)(2)(C).

Again, neither party disputes that Verio is not authorized under Register.com's terms of use to use the data for mass marketing purposes, and neither party disputes that Verio is authorized to obtain the data for some purposes. However, Verio's distinctions between authorized access and an unauthorized end use of information strike the Court as too fine. First, the means of access Verio employs, namely the automated search robot, is unauthorized. Second, even if Verio's means of access to the WHOIS database would otherwise be authorized, that access would be rendered unauthorized ab initio by virtue of the fact that prior to entry Verio knows that the data obtained will be later used for an unauthorized purpose.

Accordingly, the Court finds that Verio's access to the WHOIS database was unauthorized and that Verio violated § 1030(a)(2)(C) by using that unauthorized access to obtain data for mass marketing purposes. As discussed above, the harvesting and subsequent use of that data has caused and will cause Register.com irreparable harm. Therefore, because Register.com has demonstrated a likelihood of success on the merits of its claim that Verio's use of its WHOIS data for mass marketing purposes violates § 1030(a)(2)(C) of the Computer Fraud And Abuse Act and has demonstrated irreparable harm stemming from that violation, Register.com is entitled to injunctive relief based on that claim.

* * *

NOTES & QUESTIONS

The domain name system and the limits of private ordering. Does the holding of *Register.com v. Verio* give domain name registrars an effective monopoly in marketing additional services to domain name registrants? How does the court treat the contract between the domain name registrar and the registrant? The contract between ICANN and the registrar? Is the situation presented in this case any different from the usual situation in which a seller has privileged access to its customer list? Should registrars have a special duty of openness, deriving from their status as part of the global administration of the domain name space, which flows from ICANN's unilateral control over the domain name system?

EF Cultural Travel BV v. Explorica, Inc.

274 F.3d 577 (1st Cir.2001).

■ COFFIN, SENIOR CIRCUIT JUDGE.

Appellant Explorica, Inc. ("Explorica") and several of its employees challenge a preliminary injunction issued against them for alleged violations of the Computer Fraud and Abuse Act ("CFAA"), 18 U.S.C. § 1030. We affirm the district court's conclusion that appellees will likely succeed on the merits of their CFAA claim, but rest on a narrower basis than the court below.

I. Background

Explorica was formed in 2000 to compete in the field of global tours for high school students. Several of Explorica's employees formerly were employed by appellee EF, which has been in business for more than thirty-five years. EF and its partners and subsidiaries make up the world's largest private student travel organization.

Shortly after the individual defendants left EF in the beginning of 2000, Explorica began competing in the teenage tour market. The company's vice president (and former vice president of information strategy at EF), Philip Gormley, envisioned that Explorica could gain a substantial advantage over all other student tour companies, and especially EF, by undercutting EF's already competitive prices on student tours. Gormley considered several ways to obtain and utilize EF's prices: by manually keying in the information from EF's brochures and other printed materials; by using a scanner to record that same information; or, by manually searching for each tour offered through EF's website. Ultimately, however, Gormley engaged Zefer, Explorica's Internet consultant, to design a computer program called a "scraper" to glean all of the necessary information from EF's website. Zefer designed the program in three days.

The scraper has been likened to a "robot," a tool that is extensively used on the Internet. Robots are used to gather information for countless purposes, ranging from compiling results for search engines such as Yahoo! to filtering for inappropriate content. The widespread deployment of robots enables global Internet users to find comprehensive information quickly and almost effortlessly.

Like a robot, the scraper sought information through the Internet. Unlike other robots, however, the scraper focused solely on EF's website, using information that other robots would not have. Specifically, Zefer utilized tour codes whose significance was not readily understandable to the public. With the tour codes, the scraper accessed EF's website repeatedly and easily obtained pricing information for those specific tours. The scraper sent more than 30,000 inquiries to EF's website and recorded the pricing information into a spreadsheet.[2]

2. John Hawley, one of Zefer's senior technical associates, explained the technical progression of the scraper in an affidavit:

Zefer ran the scraper program twice, first to retrieve the 2000 tour prices and then the 2001 prices. All told, the scraper downloaded 60,000 lines of data, the equivalent of eight telephone directories of information.[3] Once Zefer "scraped" all of the prices, it sent a spreadsheet containing EF's pricing information to Explorica, which then systematically undercut EF's prices. Explorica thereafter printed its own brochures and began competing in EF's tour market.

The development and use of the scraper came to light about a year and a half later during state-court litigation regarding appellant Olsson's departure from appellee EFICE. EF then filed this action, alleging violations of the CFAA; the Copyright Act of 1976, 17 U.S.C. § 101; the Racketeer Influenced and Corrupt Organizations Act, 18 U.S.C. § 1961; and various related state laws. It sought a preliminary injunction barring Explorica and Zefer from using the scraper program and demanded the return of all materials generated through use of the scraper.

On May 30, 2001, the district court granted a preliminary injunction against Explorica based on the CFAA, which criminally and civilly prohibits certain access to computers. *See* 18 U.S.C. § 1030(a)(4). The court found that EF would likely prove that Explorica violated the CFAA when it used EF's website in a manner outside the "reasonable expectations" of both EF and its ordinary users. The court also concluded that EF could show that it suffered a loss, as required by the statute, consisting of reduced business, harm to its goodwill, and the cost of diagnostic measures it incurred to evaluate possible harm to EF's systems, although it could not show that Explorica's actions physically damaged its computers. In a supplemental opinion the district court further articulated its "reasonable expectations" standard and explained that copyright, contractual and technical restraints sufficiently notified Explorica that its use of a scraper would be unauthorized and thus would violate the CFAA.

The district court first relied on EF's use of a copyright symbol on one of the pages of its website and a link directing users with questions to

[a.] Open an Excel spreadsheet. The spreadsheet initially contains EFTours gateway and destination city codes, which are available on the EFTours web site.

[b.] Identify the first gateway and destination city codes [on the] Excel spreadsheet.

[c.] Create a [website address] request for the EFTours tour prices page based on a combination of gateway and destination city. Example: show me all the prices for a London trip leaving JFK.

[d.] View the requested web page which is retained in the random access memory of the requesting computer in the form of HTML [computer language] code. * * *

[e.] Search the HTML for the tour prices for each season, year, etc.

[f.] Store the prices into the Excel spreadsheet.

[g.] Identify the next gateway and city codes in the spreadsheet.

[h.] Repeat steps 3–7 for all gateway and destination city combinations.

3. Appellants dispute the relevance of the size of the printed data, arguing that 60,000 printed lines, while voluminous on paper, is not a large amount of data for a computer to store. This is a distinction without a difference. The fact is that appellants utilized the scraper program to download EF's pricing data. In June 2000, EF's website listed 154,293 prices for various tours.

contact the company,[6] finding that "such a clear statement should have dispelled any notion a reasonable person may have had that the 'presumption of open access' applied to information on EF's website." The court next found that the manner by which Explorica accessed EF's website likely violated a confidentiality agreement between appellant Gormley and EF, because Gormley provided to Zefer technical instructions concerning the creation of the scraper. Finally, the district court noted without elaboration that the scraper bypassed technical restrictions embedded in the website to acquire the information. The court therefore let stand its earlier decision granting the preliminary injunction. Appellants contend that the district court erred in taking too narrow a view of what is authorized under the CFAA and similarly mistook the reach of the confidentiality agreement. Appellants also argue that the district court erred in finding that appellees suffered a "loss," as defined by the CFAA, and that the preliminary injunction violates the First Amendment.

* * *

III. The Computer Fraud and Abuse Act

Although appellees alleged violations of three provisions of the CFAA, the district court found that they were likely to succeed only under § 1030(a)(4). That section provides

> [Whoever] knowingly and with intent to defraud, accesses a protected computer without authorization, or exceeds authorized access, and by means of such conduct furthers the intended fraud and obtains anything of value . . . shall be punished.

18 U.S.C. § 1030(a)(4).[8]

Appellees allege that the appellants knowingly and with intent to defraud accessed the server hosting EF's website more than 30,000 times to obtain proprietary pricing and tour information, and confidential information about appellees' technical abilities. At the heart of the parties' dispute is whether appellants' actions either were "without authorization" or "exceeded authorized access" as defined by the CFAA.[9] We conclude that because of the broad confidentiality agreement appellants' actions "exceeded authorized access," and so we do not reach the more general arguments

6. The notice stated in full:

Copyright © 2000 EF Cultural Travel BV

EF Educational Tours is a member of the EF group of companies.

Questions? Please contact us.

8. Although the CFAA is primarily a criminal statute, under § 1030(g), "any person who suffers damage or loss . . . may maintain a civil action . . . for compensatory damages and injunctive relief or other equitable relief."

9. At oral argument, appellants contended that they had no "intent to defraud" as defined by the CFAA. That argument was not raised in the briefs and thus has been waived. *See Garcia-Ayala v. Parenterals, Inc.*, 212 F.3d 638, 645 (1st Cir.2000) (failure to brief an argument constitutes waiver despite attempt to raise the argument at oral argument). Likewise, at oral argument Explorica attempted to adopt appellant Zefer's argument that the preliminary injunction violates the First Amendment. The lateness of Explorica's attempt renders it fruitless. *See id.*

made about statutory meaning, including whether use of a scraper alone renders access unauthorized.

A. "Exceeds authorized access"

Congress defined "exceeds authorized access," as accessing "a computer with authorization and [using] such access to obtain or alter information in the computer that the accesser is not entitled so to obtain or alter." 18 U.S.C. § 1030(e)(6). EF is likely to prove such excessive access based on the confidentiality agreement between Gormley and EF. Pertinently, that agreement provides:

> Employee agrees to maintain in strict confidence and not to disclose to any third party, either orally or in writing, any Confidential or Proprietary Information ... and never to at any time (i) directly or indirectly publish, disseminate or otherwise disclose, deliver or make available to anybody any Confidential or Proprietary Information or (ii) use such Confidential or Proprietary Information for Employee's own benefit or for the benefit of any other person or business entity other than EF.
>
> * * *
>
> As used in this Agreement, the term "Confidential or Proprietary Information" means (a) any trade or business secrets or confidential information of EF, whether or not reduced to writing ...; (b) any technical, business, or financial information, the use or disclosure of which might reasonably be construed to be contrary to the interests of EF....

The record contains at least two communications from Gormley to Zefer seeming to rely on information about EF to which he was privy only because of his employment there. First, in an e-mail to Zefer employee Joseph Alt exploring the use of a scraper, Gormley wrote: "might one of the team be able to write a program to automatically extract prices ...? I could work with him/her on the specification." Gormley also sent the following e-mail to Zefer employee John Hawley:

> Here is a link to the page where you can grab EF's prices. There are two important drop down menus on the right.... With the lowest one you select one of about 150 tours. * * * You then select your origin gateway from a list of about 100 domestic gateways (middle drop down menu). When you select your origin gateway a page with a couple of tables comes up. One table has 1999–2000 prices and the other has 2000–2001 prices. * * * On a high speed connection it is possible to move quickly from one price table to the next by hitting backspace and then the down arrow.

This documentary evidence points to Gormley's heavy involvement in the conception of the scraper program. Furthermore, the voluminous spreadsheet containing all of the scraped information includes the tour codes, which EF claims are proprietary information. Each page of the spreadsheet produced by Zefer includes the tour and gateway codes, the date of travel, and the price for the tour. An uninformed reader would regard the tour codes as nothing but gibberish.[11] Although the codes can be correlated to the actual tours and destination points, the codes standing alone need to be "translated" to be meaningful.

Explorica argues that none of the information Gormley provided Zefer was confidential and that the confidentiality agreement therefore is irrelevant. The case on which they rely, *Lanier Professional Services, Inc. v. Ricci,* 192 F.3d 1, 5 (1st Cir.1999), focused almost exclusively on an employee's non-compete agreement. The opinion mentioned in passing that there was no actionable misuse of confidential information because the only evidence that the employee had taken protected information was a "practically worthless" affidavit from the employee's successor. *Id.* at 5.

Here, on the other hand, there is ample evidence that Gormley provided Explorica proprietary information about the structure of the website and the tour codes. To be sure, gathering manually the various codes through repeated searching and deciphering of the URLs theoretically may be possible. Practically speaking, however, if proven, Explorica's wholesale use of EF's travel codes to facilitate gathering EF's prices from its website reeks of use—and, indeed, abuse—of proprietary information that goes beyond any authorized use of EF's website.[14]

Gormley voluntarily entered a broad confidentiality agreement prohibiting his disclosure of any information "which might reasonably be construed to be contrary to the interests of EF." Appellants would face an uphill battle trying to argue that it was not against EF's interests for appellants to use the tour codes to mine EF's pricing data. *See Anthony's Pier Four, Inc. v. HBC Assoc.,* 411 Mass. 451, 471, 583 N.E.2d 806, 820 (1991) (imposing a duty of good faith and fair dealing in all contracts under Massachusetts law). If EF's allegations are proven, it will likely prove that whatever authorization Explorica had to navigate around EF's site (even in a competitive vein), it exceeded that authorization by providing proprietary information and know-how to Zefer to create the scraper.[16] Accordingly, the

11. An example of the website address including the tour information is www.ef-tours.com/tours/PriceResult.asp?Gate=GTF & TourID=LPM. In this address, the proprietary codes are "GTF" and "LPM."

14. Among the several e-mails in the record is one from Zefer employee Joseph Alt to the Explorica "team" at Zefer:

> Below is the information needed to log into EF's site as a tour leader. Please use this to gather competitor information from both a business and experience design perspective. We may also be able to glean knowledge of their technical abilities. As with all of our information, this is extremely confidential. Please do not share it with anyone.

16. EF also claims that Explorica skirted the website's technical restraints. To learn about a specific tour, a user must navigate through several different web pages by "clicking" on various drop-down menus and choosing the desired departure location, date, tour destination, tour length, and price range. The district court found that the scraper circumvented the technical restraints by operating at a warp speed that the website was not normally intended to accommodate. We need not reach the argument that this alone was a violation of the CFAA, however, because the apparent transfer of information in violation of the Confidentiality Agreement furnishes a sufficient basis for injunctive relief.

district court's finding that Explorica likely violated the CFAA was not clearly erroneous.

B. Damage or Loss under § 1030(g)

Appellants also challenge the district court's finding that the appellees would likely prove they met the CFAA's "damage or loss" requirements. Under the CFAA, EF may maintain a private cause of action if it suffered "damage or loss." 18 U.S.C. § 1030(g). "Damage" is defined as "any impairment to the integrity or availability of data, a program, a system, or information that ... causes loss aggregating at least $5,000 in value during any 1–year period to one or more individuals...." 18 U.S.C. § 1030(e)(8). "Loss" is not defined.

The district court held that although EF could not show any "damage" it would likely be able to show "loss" under the statute. It reasoned that a general understanding of the word "loss" would fairly encompass a loss of business, goodwill, and the cost of diagnostic measures that EF took after it learned of Explorica's access to its website.[17] Appellants respond that such diagnostic measures cannot be included in the $5,000 threshold because their actions neither caused any physical damage nor placed any stress on EF's website.

Few courts have endeavored to resolve the contours of damage and loss under the CFAA. *See, e.g., Shaw v. Toshiba Am. Info. Sys.*, 91 F.Supp.2d 926 (E.D.Tex.1999) (noting the paucity of decisions construing the Act). Two district courts that have addressed the issue have found that expenses such as those borne by EF do fall under the statute. In *Shurgard Storage Centers v. Safeguard Self Storage, Inc.*, 119 F.Supp.2d 1121 (W.D.Wa.2000), the district court found that the need to assess whether a defendant's actions compromised the plaintiff's computers was compensable under the CFAA because the computer's integrity was called into question. The court based its finding on the legislative history of the 1996 amendments to the CFAA:

> The 1994 Amendment required both "damage" and "loss," but it is not always clear what constitutes "damage." For example, intruders often alter existing log-on programs so that user passwords are copied to a file which the hackers can retrieve later. After retrieving the newly created password file, the intruder restores the altered log-on file to its original condition. Arguably, in such a situation, neither the computer nor its information is damaged. Nonetheless, this conduct allows the intruder to accumu-

Likewise, we express no opinion on the district court's ruling that EF's copyright notice served as a "clear statement [that] should have dispelled any notion a reasonable person may have had the 'presumption of open access' " to EF's website.

17. It is undisputed that appellees paid $20,944.92 to assess whether their website had been compromised. Appellees also claim costs exceeding $40,000 that they will incur to "remedy and secure their website and computer." We need not consider whether these expenses constitute loss because the initial $20,944.92 greatly exceeds the threshold.

> late valid user passwords to the system, requires all system users to change their passwords, and requires the system administrator to devote resources to re-securing the system. Thus, although there is arguably no "damage," the victim does suffer "loss." If the loss to the victim meets the required monetary threshold, the conduct should be criminal, and the victim should be entitled to relief.

S. Rep. No. 104–357, at 11 (1996) (quoted in *Shurgard*, 119 F.Supp.2d at 1126). Another district court held that this legislative history makes "clear that Congress intended the term 'loss' to target remedial expenses borne by victims that could not properly be considered direct damage caused by a computer hacker." *In re DoubleClick Inc. Privacy Litig.*, 154 F.Supp.2d 497, 521 (S.D.N.Y.2001).

We agree with this construction of the CFAA. In the absence of a statutory definition for "loss," we apply the well-known rule of assigning undefined words their normal, everyday meaning. *See Inmates of Suffolk Cty. Jail v. Rouse,* 129 F.3d 649, 653–54 (1st Cir.1997). The word "loss" means "detriment, disadvantage, or deprivation from failure to keep, have or get." The Random House Dictionary of the English Language 1137 (2d ed. 1983). Appellees unquestionably suffered a detriment and a disadvantage by having to expend substantial sums to assess the extent, if any, of the physical damage to their website caused by appellants' intrusion. That the physical components were not damaged is fortunate, but it does not lessen the loss represented by consultant fees. Congress's use of the disjunctive, "damage or loss," confirms that it anticipated recovery in cases involving other than purely physical damage. *But see In re Intuit Privacy Litig.*, 138 F.Supp.2d 1272, 1281 (C.D.Ca.2001) (loss means "irreparable damage" and any other interpretation "would render the term 'damage' superfluous"); *Register.com, Inc. v. Verio, Inc.,* 126 F.Supp.2d 238, 252 n. 12 (S.D.N.Y.2000) (lost business or goodwill could not constitute loss absent the impairment or unavailability of data or systems). To parse the words in any other way would not only impair Congress's intended scope of the Act, but would also serve to reward sophisticated intruders. As we move into an increasingly electronic world, the instances of physical damage will likely be fewer while the value to the victim of what has been stolen and the victim's costs in shoring up its security features undoubtedly will loom ever-larger. If we were to restrict the statute as appellants urge, we would flout Congress's intent by effectively permitting the CFAA to languish in the twentieth century, as violators of the Act move into the twenty-first century and beyond.

We do not hold, however, that any loss is compensable. The CFAA provides recovery for "damage" only if it results in a loss of at least $5,000. We agree with the court in *In re DoubleClick Inc. Privacy Litigation*, 154 F.Supp.2d 497 (S.D.N.Y.2001), that Congress could not have intended other types of loss to support recovery unless that threshold were met. Indeed, the Senate Report explicitly states that "if the loss to the victim meets the required monetary threshold," the victim is entitled to relief under the

CFAA. S. Rep. 104–357, at 11. We therefore conclude that expenses of at least $5,000 resulting from a party's intrusion are "losses" for purposes of the "damage or loss" requirement of the CFAA.

IV. Conclusion

For the foregoing reasons, we agree with the district court that appellees will likely succeed on the merits of their CFAA claim under 18 U.S.C. § 1030(a)(4). Accordingly, the preliminary injunction was properly ordered.

Affirmed.

NOTES & QUESTIONS

1. *Burden on remand.* The Court of Appeals affirmed the District Court's grant of a preliminary injunction, finding that the plaintiff was likely to succeed on the merits of its claim under the Computer Fraud and Abuse Act. On remand, what will the plaintiff be required to prove in order to prevail? Based on the facts presented in this opinion, how likely do you think it is that plaintiff will succeed?

2. *De-authorization via Terms of Use.* The home page of EF Tours' website contains a link at the bottom of the page labeled Terms of Use. Clicking on the link calls up a page titled "Terms of Use," which contains, in the middle of a page of text, the following:

> You may not without the prior written permission of EF use any computer code, data mining software, "robot," "bot," "spider," "scraper" or other automatic device, or program, algorithm or methodology having similar processes or functionality, or any manual process, to monitor or copy any of the web pages, data or content found on this site or accessed through this site. You also may not: engage in the mass downloading of files from this site; use the computer processing power of this site for purposes other than those permitted above; flood this site with electronic traffic designed to slow or stop its operation; or establish links to or from other websites to this site.

Does the presence of this statement in the Terms of Use render any use of the site that is inconsistent with its strictures an access "without authorization" under the Computer Fraud and Abuse Act? If I place an unapproved link from my website to this site, and the site operator expends $7,000 in consultant costs attempting to render my link inoperative, am I in violation of § 1030(a)(5)(A)(iii), which provides that one who "intentionally accesses a protected computer without authorization, and as a result of such conduct, causes damage; and [by such conduct] caused * * * loss * * * aggregating at least $5,000 in value" is subject to criminal and civil liability?

3. *Competition in the balance.* Decisions like *eBay v. Bidders Edge*, *Register.com v. Verio*, and *EF v. Explorica* have the potential to interfere with the gathering of information that is necessary to operate price comparison sites and search engines, prevent online information-gathering by organizations like Consumer Reports, limit linking, impede efforts by sellers to price their offerings competitively, and hinder other activities aimed at improving the flow of information to consumers and promoting competition. Yet sellers have a legitimate interest in controlling information that is critical to their business operations. Do existing legal doctrines give adequate weight to each set of conflicting interests?

CHAPTER FOURTEEN

Liability of Internet Service Providers and Other Intermediaries for Online Harms

When a wrong is committed via online communications, there are, as usual, a perpetrator and a victim. But transmission of a communication online, and therefore commission of an online wrong, cannot occur without the participation of various other parties that enable the communication to occur. If the perpetrator and victim access the Internet via dial-up connections, those enablers may include the perpetrator's local exchange carrier; the perpetrator's Internet service provider or hosting provider; an interexchange carrier; operators of servers through which the packets of data constituting the communication travel; the victim's Internet service provider; the victim's local exchange carrier; and domain name registrars and registry custodians. This chapter addresses the rules that apply when a victim, or a prosecutor, seeks to hold such an intermediary liable for online wrongs.

Efforts to hold an intermediary responsible for online wrongs occur in several contexts. The most common scenarios include: (1) An Internet user posts a message on a bulletin board system ("BBS") that is defamatory, constitutes business disparagement, or is otherwise tortious. The target of the posting sues the operator of the BBS. (2) A user manipulates the market by posting false statements about a publicly traded company, causing the stock price to soar or dive. The company, or a group of investors in its stock, sues an Internet intermediary that made the postings available. (3) A website presents financial information about a company, supplied by a third party, that turns out to be erroneous. The company or a group of its investors sues the website operator. (4) A malicious attacker launches a "denial of service" attack, overwhelming a company's servers and forcing it to shut down, causing harm to the company's customers who sue the company. (5) A user posts material via a website or BBS that infringes a copyright owned by another. The copyright owner sues the website or BBS. (6) A person offers an item for sale via an online auction site. The offering is fraudulent, the seller fails to deliver, the product is harmful or defective, or the item is contraband. The purchaser sues the operator of the auction site.

The prospect of liability for conduct of this sort is a major concern for Internet service providers, and can have a significant impact on the conduct of Internet commerce. As we will see below, in Part I(C), the imposition of liability on ISPs for third-party defamation and other speech torts provoked a strong congressional response in the form of Section 509 of the Communications Decency Act of 1996, 47 U.S.C. § 230.[1] In addition, ISP liability for third-party copyright infringement brought about the safe harbors in Title II of the Digital Millennium Copyright Act, 17 U.S.C. § 512, which is discussed in Chapter 9, *supra*. The safe harbors applicable to copyright infringement grant service providers only a conditional immunity, imposing continuing obligations on them to limit the availability of infringing material. As we shall see in this Chapter, Section 230 offers immunity with fewer conditions.

In some cases, there is an easy analogy between an online intermediary and its offline equivalent. For example, the operator of an Internet backbone transmission facility has the same function in an online communication that an interexchange carrier has in a long-distance telephone conversation. It is therefore easy to argue that the backbone provider should be entitled to the same immunity from liability based on communications that traverse its facilities as is enjoyed by telecommunications common carriers.[2] In other cases, the governing analogy is not so clear. Is a service that hosts proprietary content, or the operator of an online bulletin board, more like a bookstore, a publisher, or an author?

I. LIABILITY OF SERVICE PROVIDERS FOR REPUTATIONAL HARM CAUSED BY AVAILABILITY OF HARMFUL CONTENT

A. LIABILITY AS "DISTRIBUTOR" OF DEFAMATORY MATERIAL

Cubby, Inc. v. CompuServe Inc.

776 F.Supp. 135 (S.D.N.Y.1991).

■ LEISURE, DISTRICT JUDGE.

This is a diversity action for libel, business disparagement, and unfair competition, based on allegedly defamatory statements made in a publication carried on a computerized database. Defendant CompuServe Inc.

1. Another provision of the Communications Decency Act imposed penalties for making indecent material available to minors. (Indecent material is protected by the First Amendment; obscene material is not.) In *Reno v. American Civil Liberties Union*, 521 U.S. 844 (1997), the Supreme Court invalidated this provision, holding that it violates the First Amendment. The invalidation did not involve Section 230, the ISP immunity provision.

2. Under common law, a common carrier that is required to transmit certain content is generally immune from defamation liability based on that content even if it knows of the defamation. RESTATEMENT (SECOND) OF TORTS § 612(2) (1965). Likewise, broadcasters are immune from defamation liability for equal-time material that federal law requires them to carry. *See Farmers Educational & Cooperative Union v. WDAY, Inc.*, 360 U.S. 525 (1959).

("CompuServe") has moved for summary judgment pursuant to Rule 56 of the Federal Rules of Civil Procedure. For the reasons stated below, CompuServe's motion is granted in its entirety.

Background

CompuServe develops and provides computer-related products and services, including CompuServe Information Service ("CIS"), an on-line general information service or "electronic library" that subscribers may access from a personal computer or terminal. Subscribers to CIS pay a membership fee and online time usage fees, in return for which they have access to the thousands of information sources available on CIS. Subscribers may also obtain access to over 150 special interest "forums," which are comprised of electronic bulletin boards, interactive online conferences, and topical databases.

One forum available is the Journalism Forum, which focuses on the journalism industry. Cameron Communications, Inc. ("CCI"), which is independent of CompuServe, has contracted to "manage, review, create, delete, edit and otherwise control the contents" of the Journalism Forum "in accordance with editorial and technical standards and conventions of style as established by CompuServe." Affidavit of Jim Cameron, sworn to on April 4, 1991 ("Cameron Aff."), Exhibit A.

One publication available as part of the Journalism Forum is Rumorville USA ("Rumorville"), a daily newsletter that provides reports about broadcast journalism and journalists. Rumorville is published by Don Fitzpatrick Associates of San Francisco ("DFA"), which is headed by defendant Don Fitzpatrick. CompuServe has no employment, contractual, or other direct relationship with either DFA or Fitzpatrick; DFA provides Rumorville to the Journalism Forum under a contract with CCI. The contract between CCI and DFA provides that DFA "accepts total responsibility for the contents" of Rumorville. Cameron Aff., Exhibit B. The contract also requires CCI to limit access to Rumorville to those CIS subscribers who have previously made membership arrangements directly with DFA.

CompuServe has no opportunity to review Rumorville's contents before DFA uploads it into CompuServe's computer banks, from which it is immediately available to approved CIS subscribers. CompuServe receives no part of any fees that DFA charges for access to Rumorville, nor does CompuServe compensate DFA for providing Rumorville to the Journalism Forum; the compensation CompuServe receives for making Rumorville available to its subscribers is the standard online time usage and membership fees charged to all CIS subscribers, regardless of the information services they use. CompuServe maintains that, before this action was filed, it had no notice of any complaints about the contents of the Rumorville publication or about DFA.

In 1990, plaintiffs Cubby, Inc. ("Cubby") and Robert Blanchard ("Blanchard") (collectively, "plaintiffs") developed Skuttlebut, a computer database designed to publish and distribute electronically news and gossip in the television news and radio industries. Plaintiffs intended to compete with Rumorville; subscribers gained access to Skuttlebut through their personal computers after completing subscription agreements with plaintiffs.

Plaintiffs claim that, on separate occasions in April 1990, Rumorville published false and defamatory statements relating to Skuttlebut and Blanchard, and that CompuServe carried these statements as part of the Journalism Forum. The allegedly defamatory remarks included a suggestion that individuals at Skuttlebut gained access to information first published by Rumorville "through some back door"; a statement that Blanchard was "bounced" from his previous employer, WABC; and a description of Skuttlebut as a "new start-up scam." Affidavit of Robert G. Blanchard, sworn to on July 11, 1991 ("Blanchard Aff."), ¶ ¶ 5–9.

Plaintiffs have asserted claims against CompuServe and Fitzpatrick under New York law for libel of Blanchard, business disparagement of Skuttlebut, and unfair competition as to Skuttlebut, based largely upon the allegedly defamatory statements contained in Rumorville. CompuServe has moved, pursuant to Fed.R.Civ.P. 56, for summary judgment on all claims against it. CompuServe does not dispute, solely for the purposes of this motion, that the statements relating to Skuttlebut and Blanchard were defamatory; rather, it argues that it acted as a distributor, and not a publisher, of the statements, and cannot be held liable for the statements because it did not know and had no reason to know of the statements. Plaintiffs oppose CompuServe's motion for summary judgment, claiming that genuine issues of material fact exist and that little in the way of discovery has been undertaken thus far.

Discussion

* * *

II. *Libel Claim*

A. *The Applicable Standard of Liability*

Plaintiffs base their libel claim on the allegedly defamatory statements contained in the Rumorville publication that CompuServe carried as part of the Journalism Forum. CompuServe argues that, based on the undisputed facts, it was a distributor of Rumorville, as opposed to a publisher of the Rumorville statements. CompuServe further contends that, as a distributor of Rumorville, it cannot be held liable on the libel claim because it neither knew nor had reason to know of the allegedly defamatory statements. Plaintiffs, on the other hand, argue that the Court should conclude that CompuServe is a publisher of the statements and hold it to a higher standard of liability.

Ordinarily, " 'one who repeats or otherwise republishes defamatory matter is subject to liability as if he had originally published it.' " Cianci v. New Times Publishing Co., 639 F.2d 54, 61 (2d Cir.1980) (Friendly, J.) (quoting Restatement (Second) of Torts § 578 (1977)). With respect to entities such as news vendors, book stores, and libraries, however, "New York courts have long held that vendors and distributors of defamatory publications are not liable if they neither know nor have reason to know of the defamation." Lerman v. Chuckleberry Publishing, Inc., 521 F.Supp. 228, 235 (S.D.N.Y.1981); accord Macaluso v. Mondadori Publishing Co., 527 F.Supp. 1017, 1019 (E.D.N.Y.1981).

The requirement that a distributor must have knowledge of the contents of a publication before liability can be imposed for distributing that publication is deeply rooted in the First Amendment, made applicable to the states through the Fourteenth Amendment. "[T]he constitutional guarantees of the freedom of speech and of the press stand in the way of imposing" strict liability on distributors for the contents of the reading materials they carry. Smith v. California, 361 U.S. 147, 152–53 (1959). In Smith, the Court struck down an ordinance that imposed liability on a bookseller for possession of an obscene book, regardless of whether the bookseller had knowledge of the book's contents. The Court reasoned that

> "Every bookseller would be placed under an obligation to make himself aware of the contents of every book in his shop. It would be altogether unreasonable to demand so near an approach to omniscience." And the bookseller's burden would become the public's burden, for by restricting him the public's access to reading matter would be restricted. If the contents of bookshops and periodical stands were restricted to material of which their proprietors had made an inspection, they might be depleted indeed.

Id. at 153 (citation and footnote omitted). Although Smith involved criminal liability, the First Amendment's guarantees are no less relevant to the instant action: "What a State may not constitutionally bring about by means of a criminal statute is likewise beyond the reach of its civil law of libel. The fear of damage awards ... may be markedly more inhibiting than the fear of prosecution under a criminal statute." New York Times Co. v. Sullivan, 376 U.S. 254, 277 (1964) (citation omitted).

CompuServe's CIS product is in essence an electronic, for-profit library that carries a vast number of publications and collects usage and membership fees from its subscribers in return for access to the publications. CompuServe and companies like it are at the forefront of the information industry revolution. High technology has markedly increased the speed with which information is gathered and processed; it is now possible for an individual with a personal computer, modem, and telephone line to have instantaneous access to thousands of news publications from across the United States and around the world. While CompuServe may decline to carry a given publication altogether, in reality, once it does decide to carry a publication, it will have little or no editorial control over that publication's contents. This is especially so when CompuServe carries the publication as part of a forum that is managed by a company unrelated to CompuServe.

With respect to the Rumorville publication, the undisputed facts are that DFA uploads the text of Rumorville into CompuServe's data banks and makes it available to approved CIS subscribers instantaneously. CompuServe has no more editorial control over such a publication than does a public library, book store, or newsstand, and it would be no more feasible for CompuServe to examine every publication it carries for potentially defamatory statements than it would be for any other distributor to do so. "First Amendment guarantees have long been recognized as protecting distributors of publications.... Obviously, the national distributor of hundreds of periodicals has no duty to monitor each issue of every periodical it distributes. Such a rule would be an impermissible burden on the First Amendment." Lerman v. Flynt Distributing Co., 745 F.2d 123, 139 (2d Cir.1984), *cert. denied,* 471 U.S. 1054 (1985); see also Daniel v. Dow Jones & Co., 137 Misc.2d 94, 102, 520 N.Y.S.2d 334, 340 (N.Y.Civ.Ct.1987) (computerized database service "is one of the modern, technologically interesting, alternative ways the public may obtain up-to-the-minute news" and "is entitled to the same protection as more established means of news distribution").

Technology is rapidly transforming the information industry. A computerized database is the functional equivalent of a more traditional news vendor, and the inconsistent application of a lower standard of liability to an electronic news distributor such as CompuServe than that which is applied to a public library, book store, or newsstand would impose an undue burden on the free flow of information. Given the relevant First Amendment considerations, the appropriate standard of liability to be applied to CompuServe is whether it knew or had reason to know of the allegedly defamatory Rumorville statements.

B. *CompuServe's Liability as a Distributor*

CompuServe contends that it is undisputed that it had neither knowledge nor reason to know of the allegedly defamatory Rumorville statements, especially given the large number of publications it carries and the speed with which DFA uploads Rumorville into its computer banks and makes the publication available to CIS subscribers. Affidavit of Eben L. Kent, sworn to on April 4, 1991 ("Kent Aff."), ¶¶ 7–9; Cameron Aff., ¶¶ 6–7. The burden is thus shifted to plaintiffs, who " 'must set forth specific facts showing that there is a genuine issue for trial.' " Anderson v. Liberty Lobby, Inc., 477 U.S. 242, 250 (1986) (quoting Fed.R.Civ.P. 56(e)). Plaintiffs have not set forth anything other than conclusory allegations as to whether CompuServe knew or had reason to know of the Rumorville statements, and have failed to meet their burden on this issue. Plaintiffs do contend that CompuServe was informed that persons affiliated with Skuttlebut might be "hacking" in order to obtain unauthorized access to Rumorville, but that claim is wholly irrelevant to the issue of whether CompuServe was put on notice that the Rumorville publication contained statements accusing the Skuttlebut principals of engaging in "hacking."

Plaintiffs have not set forth any specific facts showing that there is a genuine issue as to whether CompuServe knew or had reason to know of Rumorville's contents. Because CompuServe, as a news distributor, may not be held liable if it neither knew nor had reason to know of the allegedly defamatory Rumorville statements, summary judgment in favor of CompuServe on the libel claim is granted.

* * *

NOTES & QUESTIONS

1. *"Opportunity" to review material.* The court's decision to treat CompuServe like a distributor of the allegedly defamatory material is based in part on its finding that CompuServe had "no opportunity" to review the material before it became available to subscribers. The absence of such an opportunity is attributable to the system of content management that CompuServe chose to implement. For example, CompuServe could have implemented a system whereby a third-party content provider uploaded material to a holding area, from which it would be released to subscribers only after being vetted by CompuServe's in-house lawyers. How is CompuServe's defense different from, say, that of a hit-and-run driver who argues that his decision to wear a blindfold deprived him of the opportunity to see that he had run over a pedestrian?

Should it make a difference *why* CompuServe instituted the system it did? For example, CompuServe might have decided against a prior-review system because (1) such a system was technologically infeasible, (2) the system was feasible but prohibitively expensive, (3) the system would have cost a modest sum that CompuServe simply elected to avoid, (4) CompuServe's management was philosophically opposed to censorship, or (5) CompuServe intentionally avoided any conduct that might deprive it of common-carrier immunity.

2. *Constructive notice.* The court found there was no evidence that CompuServe "knew or had reason to know" of the defamatory statements contained in the publication, which was called "Rumorville." Should a distributor of a publication with a name suggesting that it engages in uncorroborated reporting be deemed on notice of its potentially defamatory contents? What if it were widely known that Rumorville had been sued several times, successfully, for defamation? Should newsstands be liable for the defamatory content of *The National Enquirer*, which has been adjudged a publisher of defamatory falsehoods on more than one occasion?

3. *Technological change.* Suppose that artificial intelligence technology improves to the point where it can flag potentially defamatory content to a degree of accuracy that makes it feasible for an online service to eliminate 90% of the defamatory statements that pass through its facilities at a modest cost. Would the balance of interests then tip away from the First Amendment interest in free speech, and in favor of providing recourse to victims of defamation? Can the "knew or should have known" standard adequately adjust for changes in technology?

4. *Availability of author of the defamation.* In addition to suing CompuServe, the plaintiffs sued the author of the allegedly defamatory content. Does the fact that a victim may always sue the originator of defamatory content justify providing blanket immunity to distributors of the content? Are the considerations any different with respect to online communications, as opposed to other means of communication?

B. LIABILITY AS "PUBLISHER" OF DEFAMATORY MATERIAL

Stratton Oakmont, Inc. v. Prodigy Services Co.

23 Media L. Rep. 1794 (N.Y.Sup.Ct.1995).

■ STUART L. AIN, JUSTICE.

Upon the foregoing papers, it is ordered that this motion by Plaintiffs for partial summary judgment against Defendant PRODIGY SERVICES COMPANY ("PRODIGY") is granted and this Court determines, as a matter of law, the following two disputed issues as follows:

(i) that PRODIGY was a "publisher" of statements concerning Plaintiffs on its "Money Talk" computer bulletin board for the purposes of Plaintiffs' libel claims; and,

(ii) that Charles Epstein, the Board Leader of PRODIGY's "Money Talk" computer bulletin board, acted as PRODIGY's agent for the purposes of the acts and omissions alleged in the complaint.

At issue in this case are statements about Plaintiffs made by an unidentified bulletin board user or "poster" on PRODIGY's "Money Talk" computer bulletin board on October 23rd and 25th of 1994. These statements included the following:

(a) STRATTON OAKMONT, INC. ("STRATTON"), a securities investment banking firm, and DANIEL PORUSH, STRATTON's president, committed criminal and fraudulent acts in connection with the initial public offering of stock of Solomon–Page Ltd.;

(b) the Solomon–Page offering was a "major criminal fraud" and "100% criminal fraud";

(c) PORUSH was "soon to be proven criminal"; and,

(d) STRATTON was a "cult of brokers who either lie for a living or get fired."

Plaintiffs commenced this action against PRODIGY, the owner and operator of the computer network on which the statements appeared, and the unidentified party who posted the aforementioned statements. The second amended complaint alleges ten (10) causes of action, including claims for per se libel. On this motion, "in order to materially advance the outcome of this litigation" (Zamansky affidavit, par. 4), Plaintiffs seek partial summary judgment on two issues, namely:

(1) whether PRODIGY may be considered a "publisher" of the aforementioned statements; and,

(2) whether Epstein, the Board Leader for the computer bulletin board on which the statements were posted, acted with actual and apparent authority as PRODIGY's "agent" for the purposes of the claims in this action.

By way of background, it is undisputed that PRODIGY's computer network has at least two million subscribers who communicate with each other and with the general subscriber population on PRODIGY's bulletin boards. "Money Talk" the board on which the aforementioned statements appeared, is allegedly the leading and most widely read financial computer bulletin board in the United States, where members can post statements regarding stocks, investments and other financial matters. PRODIGY contracts with bulletin Board Leaders, who, among other things, participate in board discussions and undertake promotional efforts to encourage usage and increase users. The Board Leader for "Money Talk" at the time the alleged libelous statements were posted was Charles Epstein.

PRODIGY commenced operations in 1990. Plaintiffs base their claim that PRODIGY is a publisher in large measure on PRODIGY's stated policy, starting in 1990, that it was a family oriented computer network. In various national newspaper articles written by Geoffrey Moore, PRODIGY's Director of Market Programs and Communications, PRODIGY held itself out as an online service that exercised editorial control over the content of messages posted on its computer bulletin boards, thereby expressly differentiating itself from its competition and expressly likening itself to a newspaper. (see, Exhibits I and J to Plaintiffs' moving papers.) In one article PRODIGY stated:

> "We make no apology for pursuing a value system that reflects the culture of the millions of American families we aspire to serve. Certainly no responsible newspaper does less when it chooses the type of advertising it publishes, the letters it prints, the degree of nudity and unsupported gossip its editors tolerate."

(Exhibit J.)

Plaintiffs characterize the aforementioned articles by PRODIGY as admissions (see, Dattner v. Pokoik, 81 A.D.2d 572, app. dsmd. 54 N.Y.2d 750) and argue that, together with certain documentation and deposition testimony, these articles establish Plaintiffs' prima facie case. In opposition, PRODIGY insists that its policies have changed and evolved since 1990 and that the latest article on the subject, dated February, 1993, did not reflect PRODIGY's policies in October, 1994, when the allegedly libelous statements were posted. Although the eighteen month lapse of time between the last article and the aforementioned statements is not insignificant, and the Court is wary of interpreting statements and admissions out of context, these considerations go solely to the weight of this evidence.

Plaintiffs further rely upon the following additional evidence in support of their claim that PRODIGY is a publisher:

(A) promulgation of "content guidelines" (the "Guidelines" found at Plaintiffs' Exhibit F) in which, inter alia, users are requested to refrain from posting notes that are "insulting" and are advised that "notes that harass other members or are deemed to be in bad taste or grossly repugnant to community standards, or are deemed harmful to maintaining a harmonious online community, will be removed when brought to PRODIGY's attention"; the Guidelines all expressly state that although "Prodigy is committed to open debate and discussion on the bulletin boards, . . . this doesn't mean that 'anything goes' ";

(B) use of a software screening program which automatically prescreens all bulletin board postings for offensive language;

(C) the use of Board Leaders such as Epstein whose duties include enforcement of the Guidelines, according to Jennifer Ambrozek, the Manager of Prodigy's bulletin boards and the person at PRODIGY responsible for supervising the Board Leaders (see Plaintiffs' Exhibit R, Ambrozek deposition transcript, at p. 191); and

(D) testimony by Epstein as to a tool for Board Leaders known as an "emergency delete function" pursuant to which a Board Leader could remove a note and send a previously prepared message of explanation "ranging from solicitation, bad advice, insulting, wrong topic, off topic, bad taste, etcetera." (Epstein deposition Transcript, p. 52).

A finding that PRODIGY is a publisher is the first hurdle for Plaintiffs to overcome in pursuit of their defamation claims, because one who repeats or otherwise republishes a libel is subject to liability as if he had originally published it. [Cianci v. New Times Pub. Co., 639 F.2d 54, 61; Restatement, Second Torts § 578 (1977).] In contrast, distributors such as book stores and libraries may be liable for defamatory statements of others only if they knew or had reason to know of the defamatory statement at issue. [Cubby Inc. v. CompuServe Inc., 776 F.Supp. 135, 139; see also Auvil v. CBS 60 Minutes, 800 F.Supp. 928, 932.] A distributor, or deliverer of defamatory material is considered a passive conduit and will not be found liable in the absence of fault. [Auvil, supra; see also Misut v. Mooney, 124 Misc.2d 95 (claims against printer of weekly newspaper containing allegedly libelous articles dismissed in absence of any evidence that printer knew or had reason to know of the allegedly libelous nature of the articles).] However, a newspaper, for example, is more than a passive receptacle or conduit for news, comment and advertising. [Miami Herald Publishing Co. v. Tornillo, 418 U.S. 241, 258.] The choice of material to go into a newspaper and the decisions made as to the content of the paper constitute the exercise of editorial control and judgment (Id.), and with this editorial control comes increased liability. (See Cubby, supra.) In short, the critical issue to be determined by this Court is whether the foregoing evidence establishes a prima facie case that PRODIGY exercised sufficient editorial control over its computer bulletin boards to render it a publisher with the same responsibilities as a newspaper.

Again, PRODIGY insists that its former policy of manually reviewing all messages prior to posting was changed "long before the messages complained of by Plaintiffs were posted". (Schneck affidavit, par. 4.) However, no documentation or detailed explanation of such a change, and the dissemination of news of such a change, has been submitted. In addition, PRODIGY argues that in terms of sheer volume—currently 60,000 messages a day are posted on PRODIGY bulletin boards—manual review of messages is not feasible. While PRODIGY admits that Board Leaders may remove messages that violate its Guidelines, it claims in conclusory manner that Board Leaders do not function as "editors". Furthermore, PRODIGY argues generally that this Court should not decide issues that can directly impact this developing communications medium without the benefit of a full record, although it fails to describe what further facts remain to be developed on this issue of whether it is a publisher.

As for legal authority, PRODIGY relies on the Cubby case, supra. There the defendant CompuServe was a computer network providing subscribers with computer related services or forums including an online general information service or "electronic library". One of the publications available on the Journalism Forum carried defamatory statements about the Plaintiff, an electronic newsletter. Interestingly, an independent entity named Cameron Communications, Inc. ("CCI") had "contracted to manage, review, create, delete, edit and otherwise control the contents of the Journalism Forum in accordance with editorial and technical standards and conventions of style as established by CompuServe". The Court noted that CompuServe had no opportunity to review the contents of the publication at issue before it was uploaded into CompuServe's computer banks. Consequently, the Court found that CompuServe's product was, "in essence, an electronic for-profit library" that carried a vast number of publications, and that CompuServe had "little or no editorial control" over the contents of those publications. In granting CompuServe's motion for summary judgment, the Cubby court held:

> A computerized database is the functional equivalent of a more traditional news vendor, and the inconsistent application of a lower standard of liability to an electronic news distributor such as CompuServe than that which is applied to a public library, book store, or newsstand would impose an undue burden on the free flow of information.

(776 F.Supp. 135, 140.)

The key distinction between CompuServe and PRODIGY is two fold. First, PRODIGY held itself out to the public and its members as controlling the content of its computer bulletin boards. Second, PRODIGY implemented this control through its automatic software screening program, and the Guidelines which Board Leaders are required to enforce. By actively utilizing technology and manpower to delete notes from its computer bulletin boards on the basis of offensiveness and "bad taste", for example, PRODIGY is clearly making decisions as to content (see, Miami Herald Publishing Co. v. Tornillo, supra), and such decisions constitute editorial control. (Id.) That such control is not complete and is enforced both as early as the notes arrive and as late as a complaint is made, does not minimize or eviscerate the simple fact that PRODIGY has uniquely arrogated to itself the role of determining what is proper for its members to post and read on its bulletin boards. Based on the foregoing, this Court is compelled to conclude that for the purposes of Plaintiffs' claims in this action, PRODIGY is a publisher rather than a distributor.

An interesting comparison may be found in Auvil v. CBS 60 Minutes (supra), where apple growers sued a television network and local affiliates because of an allegedly defamatory investigative report generated by the network and broadcast by the affiliates. The record established that the affiliates exercised no editorial control over the broadcast although they had the power to do so by virtue of their contract with CBS, they had the opportunity to do so by virtue of a three hour hiatus for the west coast time differential, they had the technical capability to do so, and they in fact had occasionally censored network programming in the past, albeit never in connection with "60 Minutes". The Auvil court found:

> It is argued that these features, coupled with the power to censor, triggered the duty to censor. That is a leap which the Court is not prepared to join in.
>
> * * *
>
> ... plaintiffs' construction would force the creation of full time editorial boards at local stations throughout the country which possess sufficient knowledge, legal acumen and access to experts to continually monitor incoming transmissions and exercise on-the-spot discretionary calls or face $75 million dollar lawsuits at every turn. That is not realistic.
>
> * * *
>
> More than merely unrealistic in economic terms, it is difficult to imagine a scenario more chilling on the media's right of expression and the public's right to know.

(800 F.Supp. at 931–932.) Consequently, the court dismissed all claims against the affiliates on the basis of "conduit liability", which could not be established therein absent fault, which was not shown.

In contrast, here PRODIGY has virtually created an editorial staff of Board Leaders who have the ability to continually monitor incoming transmissions and in fact do spend time censoring notes. Indeed, it could be said that PRODIGY's current system of automatic scanning, Guidelines and Board Leaders may have a chilling effect on freedom of communication in Cyberspace, and it appears that this chilling effect is exactly what PRODIGY wants, but for the legal liability that attaches to such censorship.

Let it be clear that this Court is in full agreement with Cubby and Auvil. Computer bulletin boards should generally be regarded in the same context as bookstores, libraries and network affiliates. [See Edward V. DiLello, Functional Equivalency and Its application to Freedom of Speech on Computer Bulletin Boards, 26 Colum.J.Law & Soc.Probs. 199, 210–211 (1993).] It is PRODIGY's own policies, technology and staffing decisions which have altered the scenario and mandated the finding that it is a publisher.

PRODIGY's conscious choice, to gain the benefits of editorial control, has opened it up to a greater liability than CompuServe and other computer networks that make no such choice. For the record, the fear that this Court's finding of publisher status for PRODIGY will compel all computer networks to abdicate control of their bulletin boards, incorrectly presumes that the market will refuse to compensate a network for its increased control and the resulting increased exposure. [See, Eric Schlachter, Cyberspace, The Free Market and The Free Marketplace of Ideas: Recognizing Legal Differences in Computer Bulletin Board Functions, 16 Hastings Communication and Entertainment L.J., 87, 138–139.] Presumably PRODIGY's decision to regulate the content of its bulletin boards was in part influenced by its desire to attract a market it perceived to exist consisting of users seeking a "family-oriented" computer service. This decision simply required that to the extent computer networks provide such services, they must also accept the concomitant legal consequences. In addition, the Court also notes that the issues addressed herein may ultimately be preempted by federal law if the Communications Decency Act of 1995, several versions of which are pending in Congress, is enacted. [See, Congressional Quarterly US S 652, Congressional Quarterly US HR 1004, and Congressional Quarterly US S 314.]

* * *

NOTES & QUESTIONS

1. *Standard of care dependent on care taken.* The court concludes that a computer BBS that holds itself out to the public as exercising editorial control over its content, and that actually does exercise such control, is liable for defamation under the standard applicable to publishers, rather than under the standard applicable to distributors. This implies the odd result that a sysop who chooses to exercise *more* care (by exercising editorial control over at least some of the BBS's content) is held to a higher standard of care—"negligence" rather than "knew or had reason to know"—than one who chooses to exercise *less* care. Why should the amount of care one *actually* exercises determine how much care she *must* exercise in order to avoid liability?

Under common law, publisher liability was strict. The First Amendment has been interpreted to exclude liability unless the defendant is at least negligent. *See Gertz v. Robert Welch, Inc.*, 418 U.S. 323 (1974); RESTATEMENT (SECOND) OF TORTS § 580B (1965). What is the practical difference between a negligence standard and a knew-or-should-have-known standard? Why do you think there is no corresponding constitutional rule applicable to copyright infringement, excluding liability unless the infringer is at least negligent?

2. *Relevance of actual review.* It seems likely that Prodigy did not in fact review the defamatory material in question. Why should the fact that it reviews *some* material result in the imposition of a higher standard of care with respect to material that it did *not* review?

3. *Offline implications.* The court's reasoning would seem to yield the conclusion that a bookstore or newsstand that reviews some of its offerings for defamation before making them available for sale would be held to the standard applicable to publishers with respect to all of its offerings. Conversely, the reasoning might imply that a publisher that chooses not to read the material it publishes—say, the publisher of a free newsletter that accepts only camera-ready text—should be treated as a distributor.

4. *Distinguishing* Auvil. Like Prodigy, the CBS affiliates in *Auvil v. CBS 60 Minutes* had the technical capability of exercising editorial control over CBS's challenged broadcast, and had actually exercised this control with respect to other broadcasts. Is the court successful in distinguishing *Auvil*?

5. *Postscript to the* Stratton Oakmont *case.* In October 1995, after receiving an apology from Prodigy, Stratton Oakmont agreed to drop its libel suit. Prodigy, wishing to have the court's opinion removed from the books, filed a motion to reargue the case, which Stratton Oakmont did not oppose. The judge, finding that there were no new facts justifying reargument, denied the motion. *Stratton Oakmont Inc. v. Prodigy Services Co.*, 24 Media L. Rep. 1126 (N.Y. Sup. Ct.1995). In April 1996, Stratton Oakmont agreed to pay a fine of $325,000 to the National Association of Securities Dealers in settlement of NASD charges that the brokerage firm had defrauded investors in connection with a 1991 initial public offering. NASD charged Stratton Oakmont with more than 1,000 violations of trading rules and federal securities laws, including taking orders from customers before trading was legally authorized and manipulating the prices of warrants to buy the stock. This was only the latest of Stratton's tangles with regulatory bodies. According to NASD records, Stratton Oakmont was disciplined for violating various stock trading rules in 1989, 1990, 1991, and 1992, and was also sued twice by the Securities and Exchange Commission. In February 1996, a federal court issued a permanent injunction against Stratton for violating previous SEC orders. Later that year, the NASD expelled Stratton Oakmont from the securities industry. In 1998, the NASD fined, suspended, or permanently barred from the industry 13 former partners and employees of Stratton. The former president of Stratton Oakmont, Daniel Porush—who was a target of the alleged defamation that gave rise to *Stratton Oakmont v. Prodigy*—and its former chairman, Jordan Belfort, later pled guilty to federal charges including conspiracy to commit stock fraud, money laundering, and price manipulation. It thus appears that had litigation proceeded in *Stratton Oakmont v. Prodigy,* the defendant might well have prevailed with truth as a defense.

C. LEGISLATIVE RESPONSE: SERVICE PROVIDER IMMUNITY

Eight months after issuance of the decision, Congress legislatively overruled *Stratton Oakmont* by enacting an ISP-immunity provision that states: "No provider or user of an interactive computer service shall be treated as the publisher or speaker of any information provided by another information content provider." 47 U.S.C. § 230(c)(1) (added by Communications Decency Act of 1996, § 509, Pub. L No. 104–104, 110 Stat. 137, 137–39 (1996)).

The terse and somewhat cryptic language of Section 230 left several issues for clarification by the courts. In negating liability based on a defendant's status as a "publisher or speaker," did Congress mean to exclude liability for *distributors* of defamatory material? That is, did it overrule *Cubby v. CompuServe* in addition to *Stratton Oakmont v. Prodigy*? Is a defendant's knowledge of the offensive nature of the material of any relevance? Are there circumstances in which an online service provider has such a substantial role in bringing content into existence (without actually producing the content itself) that the content is not "information provided by another information content provider" for purposes of Section 230(c)(1)?

Zeran v. America Online, Inc.

129 F.3d 327 (4th Cir.1997).

■ WILKINSON, CHIEF JUDGE.

Kenneth Zeran brought this action against America Online, Inc. ("AOL"), arguing that AOL unreasonably delayed in removing defamatory messages posted by an unidentified third party, refused to post retractions of those messages, and failed to screen for similar postings thereafter. The district court granted judgment for AOL on the grounds that the Communications Decency Act of 1996 ("CDA")—47 U.S.C. § 230—bars Zeran's claims. Zeran appeals, arguing that § 230 leaves intact liability for interactive computer service providers who possess notice of defamatory material posted through their services. He also contends that § 230 does not apply here because his claims arise from AOL's alleged negligence prior to the CDA's enactment. Section 230, however, plainly immunizes computer service providers like AOL from liability for information that originates with third parties. Furthermore, Congress clearly expressed its intent that § 230 apply to lawsuits, like Zeran's, instituted after the CDA's enactment. Accordingly, we affirm the judgment of the district court.

I.

"The Internet is an international network of interconnected computers," currently used by approximately 40 million people worldwide. Reno v. ACLU, 521 U.S. 844, 849 (1997). One of the many means by which individuals access the Internet is through an interactive computer service. These services offer not only a connection to the Internet as a whole, but also allow their subscribers to access information communicated and stored only on each computer service's individual proprietary network. Id. AOL is just such an interactive computer service. Much of the information transmitted over its network originates with the company's millions of subscribers. They may transmit information privately via electronic mail, or they may communicate publicly by posting messages on AOL bulletin boards, where the messages may be read by any AOL subscriber.

The instant case comes before us on a motion for judgment on the pleadings, see Fed.R.Civ.P. 12(c), so we accept the facts alleged in the complaint as true. Bruce v. Riddle, 631 F.2d 272, 273 (4th Cir.1980). On April 25, 1995, an unidentified person posted a message on an AOL bulletin board advertising "Naughty Oklahoma T–Shirts." The posting described the sale of shirts featuring offensive and tasteless slogans related to the April 19, 1995, bombing of the Alfred P. Murrah Federal Building in Oklahoma City. Those interested in purchasing the shirts were instructed to call "Ken" at Zeran's home phone number in Seattle, Washington. As a result of this anonymously perpetrated prank, Zeran received a high volume of calls, comprised primarily of angry and derogatory messages, but also including death threats. Zeran could not change his phone number because he relied on its availability to the public in running his business out of his home. Later that day, Zeran called AOL and informed a company representative of his predicament. The employee assured Zeran that the posting would be removed from AOL's bulletin board but explained that as a matter of policy AOL would not post a retraction. The parties dispute the date that AOL removed this original posting from its bulletin board.

On April 26, the next day, an unknown person posted another message advertising additional shirts with new tasteless slogans related to the Oklahoma City bombing. Again, interested buyers were told to call Zeran's phone number, to ask for "Ken," and to "please call back if busy" due to high demand. The angry, threatening phone calls intensified. Over the next four days, an unidentified party continued to post messages on AOL's bulletin board, advertising additional items including bumper stickers and key chains with still more offensive slogans. During this time period, Zeran called AOL repeatedly and was told by company representatives that the individual account from which the messages were posted would soon be closed. Zeran also reported his case to Seattle FBI agents. By April 30, Zeran was receiving an abusive phone call approximately every two minutes.

Meanwhile, an announcer for Oklahoma City radio station KRXO received a copy of the first AOL posting. On May 1, the announcer related the message's contents on the air, attributed them to "Ken" at Zeran's phone number, and urged the listening audience to call the number. After this radio broadcast, Zeran was inundated with death threats and other violent calls from Oklahoma City residents. Over the next few days, Zeran talked to both KRXO and AOL representatives. He also spoke to his local police, who subsequently surveilled his home to protect his safety. By May 14, after an Oklahoma City newspaper published a story exposing the shirt advertisements as a hoax and after KRXO made an on-air apology, the number of calls to Zeran's residence finally subsided to fifteen per day.

Zeran first filed suit on January 4, 1996, against radio station KRXO in the United States District Court for the Western District of Oklahoma. On April 23, 1996, he filed this separate suit against AOL in the same court.

Zeran did not bring any action against the party who posted the offensive messages.[1] After Zeran's suit against AOL was transferred to the Eastern District of Virginia pursuant to 28 U.S.C. § 1404(a), AOL answered Zeran's complaint and interposed 47 U.S.C. § 230 as an affirmative defense. AOL then moved for judgment on the pleadings pursuant to Fed.R.Civ.P. 12(c). The district court granted AOL's motion, and Zeran filed this appeal.

II.

A.

Because § 230 was successfully advanced by AOL in the district court as a defense to Zeran's claims, we shall briefly examine its operation here. Zeran seeks to hold AOL liable for defamatory speech initiated by a third party. He argued to the district court that once he notified AOL of the unidentified third party's hoax, AOL had a duty to remove the defamatory posting promptly, to notify its subscribers of the message's false nature, and to effectively screen future defamatory material. Section 230 entered this litigation as an affirmative defense pled by AOL. The company claimed that Congress immunized interactive computer service providers from claims based on information posted by a third party.

The relevant portion of § 230 states: "No provider or user of an interactive computer service shall be treated as the publisher or speaker of any information provided by another information content provider." 47 U.S.C. § 230(c)(1).[2] By its plain language, § 230 creates a federal immunity to any cause of action that would make service providers liable for information originating with a third-party user of the service. Specifically, § 230 precludes courts from entertaining claims that would place a computer service provider in a publisher's role. Thus, lawsuits seeking to hold a service provider liable for its exercise of a publisher's traditional editorial functions—such as deciding whether to publish, withdraw, postpone or alter content—are barred.

The purpose of this statutory immunity is not difficult to discern. Congress recognized the threat that tort-based lawsuits pose to freedom of speech in the new and burgeoning Internet medium. The imposition of tort liability on service providers for the communications of others represented, for Congress, simply another form of intrusive government regulation of

1. Zeran maintains that AOL made it impossible to identify the original party by failing to maintain adequate records of its users. The issue of AOL's record keeping practices, however, is not presented by this appeal.

2. Section 230 defines "interactive computer service" as "any information service, system, or access software provider that provides or enables computer access by multiple users to a computer server, including specifically a service or system that provides access to the Internet and such systems operated or services offered by libraries or educational institutions." 47 U.S.C. § 230(e)(2). The term "information content provider" is defined as "any person or entity that is responsible, in whole or in part, for the creation or development of information provided through the Internet or any other interactive computer service." Id. § 230(e)(3). The parties do not dispute that AOL falls within the CDA's "interactive computer service" definition and that the unidentified third party who posted the offensive messages here fits the definition of an "information content provider."

speech. Section 230 was enacted, in part, to maintain the robust nature of Internet communication and, accordingly, to keep government interference in the medium to a minimum. In specific statutory findings, Congress recognized the Internet and interactive computer services as offering "a forum for a true diversity of political discourse, unique opportunities for cultural development, and myriad avenues for intellectual activity." Id. § 230(a)(3). It also found that the Internet and interactive computer services "have flourished, to the benefit of all Americans, with a minimum of government regulation." Id. § 230(a)(4) (emphasis added). Congress further stated that it is "the policy of the United States . . . to preserve the vibrant and competitive free market that presently exists for the Internet and other interactive computer services, unfettered by Federal or State regulation." Id. § 230(b)(2) (emphasis added).

None of this means, of course, that the original culpable party who posts defamatory messages would escape accountability. While Congress acted to keep government regulation of the Internet to a minimum, it also found it to be the policy of the United States "to ensure vigorous enforcement of Federal criminal laws to deter and punish trafficking in obscenity, stalking, and harassment by means of computer." Id. § 230(b)(5). Congress made a policy choice, however, not to deter harmful online speech through the separate route of imposing tort liability on companies that serve as intermediaries for other parties' potentially injurious messages.

Congress' purpose in providing the § 230 immunity was thus evident. Interactive computer services have millions of users. See Reno v. ACLU, 521 U.S. at 850–51 (noting that at time of district court trial, "commercial online services had almost 12 million individual subscribers"). The amount of information communicated via interactive computer services is therefore staggering. The specter of tort liability in an area of such prolific speech would have an obvious chilling effect. It would be impossible for service providers to screen each of their millions of postings for possible problems. Faced with potential liability for each message republished by their services, interactive computer service providers might choose to severely restrict the number and type of messages posted. Congress considered the weight of the speech interests implicated and chose to immunize service providers to avoid any such restrictive effect.

Another important purpose of § 230 was to encourage service providers to self-regulate the dissemination of offensive material over their services. In this respect, § 230 responded to a New York state court decision, Stratton Oakmont, Inc. v. Prodigy Servs. Co., 1995 WL 323710 (N.Y.Sup.Ct. May 24, 1995). There, the plaintiffs sued Prodigy—an interactive computer service like AOL—for defamatory comments made by an unidentified party on one of Prodigy's bulletin boards. The court held Prodigy to the strict liability standard normally applied to original publishers of defamatory statements, rejecting Prodigy's claims that it should be held only to the lower "knowledge" standard usually reserved for distributors. The court reasoned that Prodigy acted more like an original publisher than a distributor both because it advertised its practice of controlling content on its service and because it actively screened and edited messages posted on its bulletin boards.

Congress enacted § 230 to remove the disincentives to self-regulation created by the Stratton Oakmont decision. Under that court's holding, computer service providers who regulated the dissemination of offensive material on their services risked subjecting themselves to liability, because such regulation cast the service provider in the role of a publisher. Fearing that the specter of liability would therefore deter service providers from blocking and screening offensive material, Congress enacted § 230's broad immunity "to remove disincentives for the development and utilization of blocking and filtering technologies that empower parents to restrict their children's access to objectionable or inappropriate online material." 47 U.S.C. § 230(b)(4). In line with this purpose, § 230 forbids the imposition of publisher liability on a service provider for the exercise of its editorial and self-regulatory functions.

B.

Zeran argues, however, that the § 230 immunity eliminates only publisher liability, leaving distributor liability intact. Publishers can be held liable for defamatory statements contained in their works even absent proof that they had specific knowledge of the statement's inclusion. W. Page Keeton et al., Prosser and Keeton on the Law of Torts § 113, at 810 (5th ed.1984). According to Zeran, interactive computer service providers like AOL are normally considered instead to be distributors, like traditional news vendors or book sellers. Distributors cannot be held liable for defamatory statements contained in the materials they distribute unless it is proven at a minimum that they have actual knowledge of the defamatory statements upon which liability is predicated. Id. at 811 (explaining that distributors are not liable "in the absence of proof that they knew or had reason to know of the existence of defamatory matter contained in matter published"). Zeran contends that he provided AOL with sufficient notice of the defamatory statements appearing on the company's bulletin board. This notice is significant, says Zeran, because AOL could be held liable as a distributor only if it acquired knowledge of the defamatory statements' existence.

Because of the difference between these two forms of liability, Zeran contends that the term "distributor" carries a legally distinct meaning from the term "publisher." Accordingly, he asserts that Congress' use of only the term "publisher" in § 230 indicates a purpose to immunize service providers only from publisher liability. He argues that distributors are left unprotected by § 230 and, therefore, his suit should be permitted to proceed against AOL. We disagree. Assuming arguendo that Zeran has satisfied the requirements for imposition of distributor liability, this theory of liability is merely a subset, or a species, of publisher liability, and is therefore also foreclosed by § 230.

The terms "publisher" and "distributor" derive their legal significance from the context of defamation law. Although Zeran attempts to artfully plead his claims as ones of negligence, they are indistinguishable from a garden variety defamation action. Because the publication of a statement is a necessary element in a defamation action, only one who publishes can be subject to this form of tort liability. Restatement (Second) of Torts § 558(b) (1977); Keeton et al., supra, § 113, at 802. Publication does not only describe the choice by an author to include certain information. In addition, both the negligent communication of a defamatory statement and the failure to remove such a statement when first communicated by another party—each alleged by Zeran here under a negligence label—constitute publication. Restatement (Second) of Torts § 577; see also Tacket v. General Motors Corp., 836 F.2d 1042, 1046–47 (7th Cir.1987). In fact, every repetition of a defamatory statement is considered a publication. Keeton et al., supra, § 113, at 799.

In this case, AOL is legally considered to be a publisher. "[E]very one who takes part in the publication ... is charged with publication." Id. Even distributors are considered to be publishers for purposes of defamation law:

> Those who are in the business of making their facilities available to disseminate the writings composed, the speeches made, and the information gathered by others may also be regarded as participating to such an extent in making the books, newspapers, magazines, and information available to others as to be regarded as publishers. They are intentionally making the contents available to others, sometimes without knowing all of the contents—including the defamatory content—and sometimes without any opportunity to ascertain, in advance, that any defamatory matter was to be included in the matter published.

Id. at 803. AOL falls squarely within this traditional definition of a publisher and, therefore, is clearly protected by § 230's immunity.

Zeran contends that decisions like Stratton Oakmont and Cubby, Inc. v. CompuServe Inc., 776 F.Supp. 135 (S.D.N.Y.1991), recognize a legal distinction between publishers and distributors. He misapprehends, however, the significance of that distinction for the legal issue we consider here. It is undoubtedly true that mere conduits, or distributors, are subject to a different standard of liability. As explained above, distributors must at a minimum have knowledge of the existence of a defamatory statement as a prerequisite to liability. But this distinction signifies only that different standards of liability may be applied within the larger publisher category, depending on the specific type of publisher concerned. See Keeton et al., supra, § 113, at 799–800 (explaining that every party involved is charged with publication, although degrees of legal responsibility differ). To the extent that decisions like Stratton and Cubby utilize the terms "publisher" and "distributor" separately, the decisions correctly describe two different standards of liability. Stratton and Cubby do not, however, suggest that distributors are not also a type of publisher for purposes of defamation law.

Zeran simply attaches too much importance to the presence of the distinct notice element in distributor liability. The simple fact of notice surely cannot transform one from an original publisher to a distributor in the eyes of the law. To the contrary, once a computer service provider receives notice of a potentially defamatory posting, it is thrust into the role of a traditional publisher. The computer service provider must decide whether to publish, edit, or withdraw the posting. In this respect, Zeran seeks to impose liability on AOL for assuming the role for which § 230 specifically proscribes liability—the publisher role.

Our view that Zeran's complaint treats AOL as a publisher is reinforced because AOL is cast in the same position as the party who originally posted the offensive messages. According to Zeran's logic, AOL is legally at fault because it communicated to third parties an allegedly defamatory statement. This is precisely the theory under which the original poster of the offensive messages would be found liable. If the original party is considered a publisher of the offensive messages, Zeran certainly cannot attach liability to AOL under the same theory without conceding that AOL too must be treated as a publisher of the statements.

Zeran next contends that interpreting § 230 to impose liability on service providers with knowledge of defamatory content on their services is consistent with the statutory purposes outlined in Part IIA. Zeran fails, however, to understand the practical implications of notice liability in the interactive computer service context. Liability upon notice would defeat the dual purposes advanced by § 230 of the CDA. Like the strict liability imposed by the Stratton Oakmont court, liability upon notice reinforces service providers' incentives to restrict speech and abstain from self-regulation.

If computer service providers were subject to distributor liability, they would face potential liability each time they receive notice of a potentially defamatory statement—from any party, concerning any message. Each notification would require a careful yet rapid investigation of the circumstances surrounding the posted information, a legal judgment concerning the information's defamatory character, and an on-the-spot editorial decision whether to risk liability by allowing the continued publication of that information. Although this might be feasible for the traditional print publisher, the sheer number of postings on interactive computer services would create an impossible burden in the Internet context. Cf. Auvil v. CBS 60 Minutes, 800 F.Supp. 928, 931 (E.D.Wash.1992) (recognizing that it is unrealistic for network affiliates to "monitor incoming transmissions and exercise on-the-spot discretionary calls"). Because service providers would be subject to liability only for the publication of information, and not for its removal, they would have a natural incentive simply to remove messages upon notification, whether the contents were defamatory or not. See Philadelphia Newspapers, Inc. v. Hepps, 475 U.S. 767, 777 (1986) (recognizing that fears of unjustified liability produce a chilling effect antithetical to First Amendment's protection of speech). Thus, like strict liability, liability upon notice has a chilling effect on the freedom of Internet speech.

Similarly, notice-based liability would deter service providers from regulating the dissemination of offensive material over their own services. Any efforts by a service provider to investigate and screen material posted on its service would only lead to notice of potentially defamatory material more frequently and thereby create a stronger basis for liability. Instead of subjecting themselves to further possible lawsuits, service providers would likely eschew any attempts at self-regulation.

More generally, notice-based liability for interactive computer service providers would provide third parties with a no-cost means to create the basis for future lawsuits. Whenever one was displeased with the speech of another party conducted over an interactive computer service, the offended party could simply "notify" the relevant service provider, claiming the information to be legally defamatory. In light of the vast amount of speech communicated through interactive computer services, these notices could produce an impossible burden for service providers, who would be faced with ceaseless choices of suppressing controversial speech or sustaining prohibitive liability. Because the probable effects of distributor liability on the vigor of Internet speech and on service provider self-regulation are directly contrary to § 230's statutory purposes, we will not assume that Congress intended to leave liability upon notice intact.

* * *

For the foregoing reasons, we affirm the judgment of the district court.

Blumenthal v. Drudge

992 F.Supp. 44 (D.D.C.1998).

■ PAUL L. FRIEDMAN, DISTRICT JUDGE.

This is a defamation case revolving around a statement published on the Internet by defendant Matt Drudge. On August 10, 1997, the following was available to all having access to the Internet:

> The DRUDGE REPORT has learned that top GOP operatives who feel there is a double-standard of only reporting republican shame believe they are holding an ace card: New White House recruit Sidney Blumenthal has a spousal abuse past that has been effectively covered up.
>
> The accusations are explosive.
>
> There are court records of Blumenthal's violence against his wife, one influential republican, who demanded anonymity, tells the DRUDGE REPORT.
>
> If they begin to use [Don] Sipple and his problems against us, against the Republican Party ... to show hypocrisy, Blumenthal would become fair game. Wasn't it Clinton who signed the Violence Against Women Act?
>
> [There goes the budget deal honeymoon.]
>
> One White House source, also requesting anonymity, says the Blumenthal wife-beating allegation is a pure fiction that has been created by Clinton enemies. [The First Lady] would not have

brought him in if he had this in his background, assures the well-placed staffer. This story about Blumenthal has been in circulation for years.

Last month President Clinton named Sidney Blumenthal an Assistant to the President as part of the Communications Team. He's brought in to work on communications strategy, special projects themeing—a newly created position.

Every attempt to reach Blumenthal proved unsuccessful.

Complaint, Ex. 4.

Currently before this Court are a motion for summary judgment filed by defendant America Online, Inc. ("AOL") and a motion to dismiss or transfer for lack of personal jurisdiction filed by defendant Matt Drudge. Upon consideration of the papers filed by the parties and the oral arguments of counsel, the Court concludes that AOL's motion should be granted and Drudge's motion should be denied.

I. BACKGROUND

* * * Sidney Blumenthal works in the White House as an Assistant to the President of the United States. His first day of work as Assistant to the President was Monday, August 11, 1997, the day after the publication of the alleged defamatory statement. * * *

* * * In early 1995, defendant Drudge created an electronic publication called the Drudge Report, a gossip column focusing on gossip from Hollywood and Washington, D.C. * * *

Access to defendant Drudge's world wide web site is available at no cost to anyone who has access to the Internet at the Internet address of "www.drudgereport.com." Drudge Decl. I ¶ 9. The front page of the web site contains the logo "Drudge Report." Defendant Drudge has also placed a hyperlink on his web site that, when activated, causes the most recently published edition of the Drudge Report to be displayed. Id. The web site also contains numerous hyperlinks to other on-line news publications and news articles that may be of interest to readers of the Drudge Report. Id. In addition, during the time period relevant to this case, Drudge had developed a list of regular readers or subscribers to whom he e-mailed each new edition of the Drudge Report. Drudge Decl. I ¶¶ 6–7. By March 1995, the Drudge Report had 1,000 e-mail subscribers, Drudge Decl. I ¶ 8; and plaintiffs allege that by 1997 Drudge had 85,000 subscribers to his e-mail service. Complaint ¶ 47.

* * *

In late May or early June of 1997, * * * defendant Drudge entered into a written license agreement with AOL. The agreement made the Drudge Report available to all members of AOL's service for a period of one year. In exchange, defendant Drudge received a flat monthly "royalty payment" of $3,000 from AOL. During the time relevant to this case, defendant Drudge has had no other source of income. Drudge Decl. I ¶¶ 13–14. Under the licensing agreement, Drudge is to create, edit, update and "otherwise manage" the content of the Drudge Report, and AOL may "remove content that AOL reasonably determine[s] to violate AOL's then standard terms of service." AOL Mem. at 7; see Exhibit C to Licensing Agreement ¶ I, Ex. A to Jennings Decl. Drudge transmits new editions of the Drudge Report by e-mailing them to AOL. AOL then posts the new editions on the AOL service. AOL Mem., Declaration of Matt Drudge ("Drudge Decl. II") ¶ 17; AOL Mem. at 9. Drudge also has continued to distribute each new edition of the Drudge Report via e-mail and his own web site. Drudge Decl. I ¶ 16; Hearing Tr. at 41–42.

Late at night on the evening of Sunday, August 10, 1997 (Pacific Daylight Time), defendant Drudge wrote and transmitted the edition of the Drudge Report that contained the alleged defamatory statement about the Blumenthals. Drudge transmitted the report from Los Angeles, California by e-mail to his direct subscribers and by posting both a headline and the full text of the Blumenthal story on his world wide web site. He then transmitted the text but not the headline to AOL, which in turn made it available to AOL subscribers. Drudge Decl. I ¶¶ 15, 16, 19.

After receiving a letter from plaintiffs' counsel on Monday, August 11, 1997, Complaint, Ex. 6, defendant Drudge retracted the story through a special edition of the Drudge Report posted on his web site and e-mailed to his subscribers. Drudge Decl. I ¶¶ 17–19. At approximately 2:00 a.m. on Tuesday, August 12, 1997, Drudge e-mailed the retraction to AOL which posted it on the AOL service. Drudge Decl. I ¶ 19; AOL Mem. at 12.[5] Defendant Drudge later publicly apologized to the Blumenthals. Drudge Decl. I ¶ 20; Complaint, Ex. 6 (Howard Kurtz, Blumenthals Get Apology, Plan Lawsuit: Web Site Retracts Story on Clinton Aide, Washington Post, August 11, 1997, at A 11).

II. AOL's MOTION FOR SUMMARY JUDGMENT

* * *

B. Communications Decency Act of 1996, Section 230

[I]n enacting the Communications Decency Act of 1996 [Congress] chose to "promote the continued development of the Internet and other interactive computer services and other interactive media" and "to preserve the vibrant and competitive free market" for such services, largely "unfettered by Federal or State regulation...." 47 U.S.C. § 230(b)(1) and (2). Whether wisely or not, it made the legislative judgment to effectively immunize providers of interactive computer services from civil liability in tort with respect to material disseminated by them but created by others. In recognition of the speed with which information may be disseminated and the near impossibility of regulating information content, Congress decided not to treat providers of interactive computer services like other

5. AOL later removed the August 10 edition of the Drudge Report from the electronic archive of previous editions of the Drudge Report available to AOL subscribers. AOL Mem. at 13.

information providers such as newspapers, magazines or television and radio stations, all of which may be held liable for publishing or distributing obscene or defamatory material written or prepared by others. While Congress could have made a different policy choice, it opted not to hold interactive computer services liable for their failure to edit, withhold or restrict access to offensive material disseminated through their medium.

Section 230(c) of the Communications Decency Act of 1996 provides:

> No provider or user of an interactive computer service shall be treated as the publisher or speaker of any information provided by another information content provider.

47 U.S.C. § 230(c)(1). The statute goes on to define the term "information content provider" as "any person or entity that is responsible, in whole or in part, for the creation or development of information provided through the Internet or any other interactive computer service." 47 U.S.C. § 230(e)(3). In view of this statutory language, plaintiffs' argument that the Washington Post would be liable if it had done what AOL did here—"publish Drudge's story without doing anything whatsoever to edit, verify, or even read it (despite knowing what Drudge did for a living and how he did it)," Plaintiff's Memorandum of Points and Authorities in Opposition to Defendant America Online, Inc.'s Motion for Summary Judgment ("Pls.' Mem.") at 1—has been rendered irrelevant by Congress.

Plaintiffs concede that AOL is a "provider ... of an interactive computer service" for purposes of Section 230, see Complaint ¶ 94; Pls.' Mem. at 3, and that if AOL acted exclusively as a provider of an interactive computer service it may not be held liable for making the Drudge Report available to AOL subscribers. See 47 U.S.C. § 230(c)(1). They also concede that Drudge is an "information content provider" because he wrote the alleged defamatory material about the Blumenthals contained in the Drudge Report. Pls.' Mem. at 4. While plaintiffs suggest that AOL is responsible along with Drudge because it had some role in writing or editing the material in the Drudge Report, they have provided no factual support for that assertion. Indeed, plaintiffs affirmatively state that "no person, other than Drudge himself, edited, checked, verified, or supervised the information that Drudge published in the Drudge Report." Plaintiffs' Statement of Material Facts ("Pls.' Stmt.") ¶ 1(ii). It also is apparent to the Court that there is no evidence to support the view originally taken by plaintiffs that Drudge is or was an employee or agent of AOL, and plaintiffs seem to have all but abandoned that argument.[9]

AOL acknowledges both that Section 230(c)(1) would not immunize AOL with respect to any information AOL developed or created entirely by itself and that there are situations in which there may be two or more information content providers responsible for material disseminated on the Internet—joint authors, a lyricist and a composer, for example. Defendant

9. Plaintiffs' Statement of Genuine Issues of Material Facts does not identify any evidence to support their conclusory assertion that there are genuine issues of fact as to whether Drudge was an employee or agent of AOL. See Pls.' Stmt. ¶¶ 3–4, 12. * * *

America Online, Inc.'s Reply Memorandum In Further Support of Its Motion for Summary Judgment ("AOL Reply Mem.") at 10; Hearing Tr. at 12. While Section 230 does not preclude joint liability for the joint development of content, AOL maintains that there simply is no evidence here that AOL had any role in creating or developing any of the information in the Drudge Report. The Court agrees. It is undisputed that the Blumenthal story was written by Drudge without any substantive or editorial involvement by AOL. Drudge Decl. II ¶¶ 46–47. AOL was nothing more than a provider of an interactive computer service on which the Drudge Report was carried, and Congress has said quite clearly that such a provider shall not be treated as a "publisher or speaker" and therefore may not be held liable in tort. 47 U.S.C. § 230(c)(1).

As Chief Judge Wilkinson recently wrote for the Fourth Circuit:

> By its plain language, § 230 creates a federal immunity to any cause of action that would make service providers liable for information originating with a third-party user of the service. * * *
>
> * * *

Zeran v. America Online, Inc., 129 F.3d 327, 330–31 (4th Cir.1997). The court in Zeran has provided a complete answer to plaintiffs' primary argument, an answer grounded in the statutory language and intent of Section 230.

Plaintiffs make the additional argument, however, that Section 230 of the Communications Decency Act does not provide immunity to AOL in this case because Drudge was not just an anonymous person who sent a message over the Internet through AOL. He is a person with whom AOL contracted, whom AOL paid $3,000 a month—$36,000 a year, Drudge's sole, consistent source of income—and whom AOL promoted to its subscribers and potential subscribers as a reason to subscribe to AOL. Pls.' Mem. at 2, 7. Furthermore, the license agreement between AOL and Drudge by its terms contemplates more than a passive role for AOL; in it, AOL reserves the "right to remove, or direct [Drudge] to remove, any content which, as reasonably determined by AOL . . . violates AOL's then-standard Terms of Service. . . ." Jennings Decl. ¶ 16 (quoting Exhibit C to Licensing Agreement ¶ I, Ex. A to Jennings Decl.). By the terms of the agreement, AOL also is "entitled to require reasonable changes to . . . content, to the extent such content will, in AOL's good faith judgment, adversely affect operations of the AOL network." Id.

In addition, shortly after it entered into the licensing agreement with Drudge, AOL issued a press release making clear the kind of material Drudge would provide to AOL subscribers—gossip and rumor—and urged potential subscribers to sign onto AOL in order to get the benefit of the Drudge Report. The press release was captioned: "AOL Hires Runaway Gossip Success Matt Drudge." Complaint, Ex. I. It noted that "[m]averick gossip columnist Matt Drudge has teamed up with America Online," and stated: "Giving the Drudge Report a home on America Online (keyword: Drudge) opens up the floodgates to an audience ripe for Drudge's brand of reporting.... AOL has made Matt Drudge instantly accessible to members who crave instant gossip and news breaks." Id. Why is this different, the Blumenthals suggest, from AOL advertising and promoting a new purveyor of child pornography or other offensive material? Why should AOL be permitted to tout someone as a gossip columnist or rumor monger who will make such rumors and gossip "instantly accessible" to AOL subscribers, and then claim immunity when that person, as might be anticipated, defames another?

If it were writing on a clean slate, this Court would agree with plaintiffs. AOL has certain editorial rights with respect to the content provided by Drudge and disseminated by AOL, including the right to require changes in content and to remove it; and it has affirmatively promoted Drudge as a new source of unverified instant gossip on AOL. Yet it takes no responsibility for any damage he may cause. AOL is not a passive conduit like the telephone company, a common carrier with no control and therefore no responsibility for what is said over the telephone wires. Because it has the right to exercise editorial control over those with whom it contracts and whose words it disseminates, it would seem only fair to hold AOL to the liability standards applied to a publisher or, at least, like a book store owner or library, to the liability standards applied to a distributor. But Congress has made a different policy choice by providing immunity even where the interactive service provider has an active, even aggressive role in making available content prepared by others. In some sort of tacit quid pro quo arrangement with the service provider community, Congress has conferred immunity from tort liability as an incentive to Internet service providers to self-police the Internet for obscenity and other offensive material, even where the self-policing is unsuccessful or not even attempted.

In Section 230(c)(2) of the Communications Decency Act, Congress provided:

> No provider or user of an interactive computer service shall be held liable on account of—
>
> (A) Any action voluntarily taken in good faith to restrict access to or availability of material that the provider or user considers to be obscene, lewd, lascivious, filthy, excessively violent, harassing, or otherwise objectionable, whether or not such material is constitutionally protected; or
>
> (B) any action taken to enable or make available to information content providers or others the technical means to restrict access to material described in paragraph (1).

47 U.S.C. § 230(c)(2). As the Fourth Circuit stated in Zeran: "Congress enacted § 230 to remove ... disincentives to self-regulation.... Fearing that the specter of liability would ... deter service providers from blocking and screening offensive material ... § 230 forbids the imposition of pub-

lisher liability on a service provider for the exercise of its editorial and selfregulatory functions." Zeran v. America Online, Inc., 129 F.3d at 331.[14]

Any attempt to distinguish between "publisher" liability and notice-based "distributor" liability and to argue that Section 230 was only intended to immunize the former would be unavailing. Congress made no distinction between publishers and distributors in providing immunity from liability. * * * While it appears to this Court that AOL in this case has taken advantage of all the benefits conferred by Congress in the Communications Decency Act, and then some, without accepting any of the burdens that Congress intended, the statutory language is clear: AOL is immune from suit, and the Court therefore must grant its motion for summary judgment.

* * *

NOTES & QUESTIONS

1. *The scope of Section 230: non-defamation causes of action.* Given Congress's explicit statement in the legislative history that it intended to override *Stratton Oakmont v. Prodigy*, it is clear that at least one significant congressional purpose in enacting Section 230 was to immunize ISPs against *defamation* liability based on third-party postings. But Section 230 itself does not refer to defamation: it speaks more broadly, forbidding treatment of an ISP "as the publisher or speaker of any information" provided by another. Consider too the Conference Report's explanation of the section's purpose:

> One of the specific purposes of this section is to overrule *Stratton Oakmont v. Prodigy* and any other similar decisions which have treated such providers and users as publishers or speakers of content that is not their own because they have restricted access to objectionable material. The conferees believe that such decisions create serious obstacles to the important federal policy of empowering parents to determine the content of communications their children receive through interactive computer services.

H.R. REP. NO. 104–458, at 194 (1996). Given the language of Section 230, and the Conference Report's explanation, can it plausibly be argued that Section 230 applies *only* to defamation claims?

The courts have not found Section 230 so limited. *Zeran* held that Section 230 immunized the defendant against a negligence claim, and explained: "By its plain language, § 230 creates a federal immunity to any cause of action that would make service providers liable for information originating with a third-party user of the service." In *Doe v. America Online, Inc.*, 783 So.2d 1010 (Fla.2001), discussed *infra*, the court held that Section 230 immunized AOL from negligence liability based on a subscrib-

14. 47 U.S.C. § 230(b)(4) provides:

It is the policy of the United States to remove disincentives for the development and utilization of blocking and filtering technologies that empower parents to restrict their children's access to objectionable or inappropriate online material.

er's use of its facilities to distribute child pornography. In *Ben Ezra, Weinstein, and Co. v. America Online Inc.*, 206 F.3d 980 (10th Cir.2000), the court held that Section 230 insulated AOL from liability based on erroneous stock information that it provided. Plaintiff had alleged causes of action sounding in negligence as well as defamation. Other courts have held that Section 230 extends to a breach-of-contract claim, *see Schneider v. Amazon.com, Inc.*, 31 P.3d 37 (Wash.Ct.App.2001); and to a taxpayer claim for waste of public funds, *see Kathleen R. v. City of Livermore*, 104 Cal.Rptr.2d 772 (Cal.Ct.App.2001).

Should a court find Section 230 immunity available where liability is predicated on (1) bad advice that a subscriber posts on a BBS, on which a third party relies to its detriment? (2) obscene material posted by a third party, which gives rise to civil liability? (3) false advertising, as for example in the description of an item offered for sale via an online auction? (4) negligent release of users' private financial information, such as credit card numbers? (5) publication of information constituting a trade secret? (6) negligent release of information that allows attackers to shut down a major portal site?

2. *The scope of Section 230: statutory exclusions.* The Section 230 immunity provision by its own terms does not extend to "any * * * Federal criminal statute," "any law pertaining to intellectual property," or enforcement of the Electronic Communications Privacy Act, 18 U.S.C. §§ 2510 et seq., 47 U.S.C. § 230(e). ISP liability for copyright infringement is treated in Title II of the Digital Millennium Copyright Act, 17 U.S.C. § 512, discussed in Chapter 9, Part V, *supra*. ISP liability for knowing disclosure of trade secrets would arguably come within the terms of the federal Economic Espionage Act of 1996, 18 U.S.C. § 1832, providing a criminal penalty for an organization that intentionally "replicates, transmits, delivers, sends, mails, communicates, or conveys" information constituting a trade secret. Since an ISP is potentially subject to criminal liability based on material made available through its system, how much benefit does Section 230 provide? Doesn't an ISP still have to police its system for content that might give rise to criminal liability?

3. *The scope of Section 230: service provider's knowledge of the wrongful conduct.* In *Doe v. America Online, Inc.*, 783 So.2d 1010 (Fla.2001), plaintiff sued AOL for allowing a subscriber, one Russell, to use its chat rooms for marketing videotapes and photographs consisting of child pornography in which plaintiff's minor son appears. The complaint alleged that AOL was negligent per se in allowing Russell to use its facilities for criminal distribution of obscene materials, and that it was likewise negligent on common-law principles. Plaintiff alleged that AOL had received complaints about Russell's use of its facilities for unlawful purposes, but that "AOL neither warned Russell to stop nor suspended his service." 783 So.2d at 1012. The Florida Supreme Court, in a 4–3 decision, affirmed the trial and appellate courts' grant of AOL's motion to dismiss based on Section 230. The majority opinion adopted the reasoning of *Zeran v. AOL*. The dissenters, disagreeing with *Zeran* and considering that it was not binding authority, explained their view at length:

> I understand that it may be somewhat attractive for the majority to follow an existing published opinion from a different jurisdiction; however, I conclude that, because the analysis upon which it is based is faulty and leads to a totally unacceptable interpretation, it should not be followed. Therefore, I dissent.
>
> It is clear that Congress, through the Communications Decency Act, 47 U.S.C. § 230 (the "CDA"), intended to shield an Internet Service Provider (an "ISP") from liability due solely to implementation of a good-faith monitoring program whose goal is to preclude dissemination of illicit and improper materials through the ISP's electronic medium. Contrary to the majority's view, however, the carefully crafted statute at issue, undergirded by a clear legislative history, does not reflect an intent to totally exonerate and insulate an ISP from responsibility where, as here, it is alleged that an ISP has acted as a knowing distributor of material leading to the purchase, sale, expansion and advancement of child pornography, after having been given actual notice of the particular activity, by taking absolutely no steps to curtail continued dissemination of the information by its specifically identified customer, when it had the right and power to do so. * * *
>
> I suggest that by interpreting the statute to provide this carte blanche immunity for wrongful conduct plainly not intended by Congress, the majority view ignores the common law underpinnings of the present controversy; fails to accommodate the traditional distinction between publishers and distributors consistently recognized in American jurisprudence; overlooks the historical timing of the subject legislation in the context of developing case law; excludes proper analysis of the careful wording of the subject legislation; and does not consider the obvious intent additionally underscored by Congress both in the stated policies underlying the statute, and in the statute's legislative history. These grounds, collectively—coupled with the rationale of the very case which the majority deems controlling—warrant a far different result.
>
> In *Zeran* (as quoted in the majority opinion), the Fourth Circuit began by explaining what Congress had intended when it enacted the Communications Decency Act, 47 U.S.C. § 230. The legislation was aimed at removing "disincentives for the development and utilization of blocking and filtering technologies that empower parents to restrict their children's access to objectionable or inappropriate online material." 47 U.S.C. § 230(b)(4). * * *
>
> * * * While the initial foray into *Zeran*'s analysis is thus promising, its eventual conclusion—and thus, the majority's corresponding conclusion in this case, patterned on the analyses contained in the two *Zeran* decisions—is, in my view, a startling non sequitur. * * * The fatal flaw in *Zeran*'s logic—and thus, in the

majority view—is its erroneous conclusion that, under section 577 of the Restatement of Torts (Second), distributors are merely an internal category of publishers.

* * *

In my view, my colleagues in the majority overlook and fail to consider this distinction between publishers and distributors, which is key to an understanding of what Congress, in 1996, intended to accomplish by enacting the CDA. Five years earlier, in 1991, a federal district court had held, in *Cubby,* that the defendant Internet service provider, CompuServe, was the equivalent of "an electronic, for profit library." 776 F.Supp. at 140. The *Cubby* court had held, therefore, that CompuServe was entitled to the same first amendment protection as a "distributor," subject to liability only if it knew or had reason to know of the allegedly defamatory statements. * * *

However, only shortly before enactment of the CDA, the court in *Stratton Oakmont,* faced with a similar question, reached a far different result. There, the court held that the ISP, Prodigy, would be treated as a "publisher," subject to liability regardless of its actual or imputed knowledge. * * * Thus, even though the courts in *Cubby* and *Stratton Oakmont* both recognized the distinction between publisher liability and distributor liability, in characterizing the ISP's function, they reached very different results. The ISP in *Stratton Oakmont,* merely by virtue of its "Good Samaritan" editorial policies, was held liable for matter published on its service by third parties, even though it was not alleged to have had actual knowledge of the content of the publication.

This was obviously the legal conclusion which Congress, in enacting the CDA promptly thereafter, sought to change.[15] It reflected this intent in two ways. First, the language of the statute itself could not be more explicit. It provides, in § 230(c) ("Protection for 'Good Samaritan' blocking and screening of offensive material") that "[n]o provider or user of an interactive computer service shall be treated *as the publisher or speaker* of any information *provided by another* information content provider." In *Zeran* and the majority view here, however, this statement that an ISP shall not be treated as a "publisher or speaker" of third-party information has been interpreted to mean not only that an ISP can never be subject to liability for negligence as a "publisher" of third-party information appearing on its service, but also that an ISP can never be subject to liability based upon its own patently irresponsible role as a distributor who has allegedly been given actual notice of materials published on its service by a specified

15. * * * While the legislative history reflects Congress's intent to "overrule" *Stratton Oakmont,* there is no similar mention of a desire to "overrule" *Cubby* (despite the fact that Congress was not only presumed to be aware of that decision, but was actually reminded of it during legislative debate). * * *

customer (in furtherance of criminal conduct as defined by Florida law) by soliciting the purchase and sale of explicit child pornography, yet has done absolutely nothing about it.

* * *

Such an absurd interpretation is totally unwarranted. If Congress had intended absolute immunity, why would it state only that no ISP "shall be treated as a *publisher* or *speaker of* any *information provided by another* information content provider?" * * * If blanket immunity were intended, why not state more broadly that no ISP "shall be held liable" for any information provided on its service by another information content provider? In fact, that very phrase was used in the subsection immediately following § 230(c)(1), which provides:

(2) Civil liability

No provider or user of an interactive computer service *shall be held liable* on account of—

(A) any action voluntarily taken in good faith to restrict access to or availability of material that the provider or user considers to be obscene, lewd, lascivious, filthy, excessively violent, harassing, or otherwise objectionable, whether or not such material is constitutionally protected; or

(B) any action taken to enable or make available to information content providers or others the technical means to restrict access to material described in paragraph (1).

(Emphasis supplied.)

The reason, pointedly, is that Congress never intended for such a broad immunity to apply. In cutting a wide swath of immunity from the cloth of this purposefully narrow language, the analysis contained in *Zeran* (and approved by the majority here) turns on its head the very goal of the Communications Decency Act. While Congress has recognized that the Internet presents a "forum for true diversity of political discourse, unique opportunities for cultural development, and myriad avenues for intellectual activity," 47 U.S.C. § 230(a)(3), the purpose of the CDA is not, as the *Zeran* court espoused, "to promote unfettered speech," *Zeran,* 129 F.3d at 334—most particularly where such alleged speech is an invitation to purchase child pornography. To the contrary, even where objectionable material may be constitutionally protected, the CDA, which was added to "extend the standards of decency which have protected telephone users to new telecommunications devices" and to "protect the sanctuary of the home from uninvited indecencies," 141 Cong. Rec. S1953 (daily ed. Feb. 1, 1995) (statement of Sen. Exon), sanctions an ISP's good-faith efforts to block its dissemination. Here, moreover, where the communications allegedly pertain to graphic sex acts involving eleven-year-old victims, First Amendment rights are not even implicated.

What *is* implicated is Congress's intent to shield ISPs from liability based solely on self-policing efforts to intercept the very type of material at issue here—conduct defined by society as criminal involving material which is invidiously and perniciously harmful to children. This is reflected in the second hallmark of Congress's intent in enacting the CDA—the statute's legislative history. As expressed in 47 U.S.C. § 230(b), "the stated policy of the United States" is "to remove disincentives for the development and utilization of blocking and filtering technologies that empower parents to restrict their children's access to objectionable or inappropriate online material." While the majority view recognizes that, as reflected in the legislative history of the CDA referenced in *Zeran,* "the 'disincentive' Congress specifically had in mind was liability of the sort described in *Stratton Oakmont,*" majority at 1016 (quoting *Zeran,* 958 F.Supp. at 1134), what it inexplicably fails to recognize is that this is *not* the distributor liability recognized in *Cubby.* Rather, it is the far stricter standard of publisher liability which was imposed in *Stratton Oakmont,* based solely on the ISP's implementation of laudable, self-regulating efforts to screen inappropriate material prior to its publication, which efforts the CDA—as expressed in the policies set forth as a preamble to the statute—unabashedly encourages.

Given the precise, limiting language of the statute, the stated policy underlying the CDA, and the CDA's explicit legislative history, it is inconceivable that Congress intended the CDA to shield from potential liability an ISP alleged to have taken absolutely no actions to curtail illicit activities in furtherance of conduct defined as criminal, despite actual knowledge that a source of child pornography was being advertised and delivered through contact information provided on its service by an identified customer, while profiting from its customer's continued use of the service. * * *

783 So.2d at 1018–28. What accounts for the differing perspectives of the court in *Zeran v. AOL,* and the dissent in *Doe v. AOL*? How does *Zeran* address the argument that Section 230 does not displace liability on a knew-or-should-have-known standard? Which opinion is more convincing?

4. *Criminal liability.* In 1998, the New York Attorney General charged BuffNET, an ISP located near Buffalo, New York, with criminal liability in connection with the distribution of child pornography via USENET newsgroups to which it proved access. The Attorney General explained that it took the action because BuffNET failed to cut off access to the newsgroup even after police informed it of the unlawful content. BuffNET said that the police had conveyed this information to a low-level employee, who failed to pass it along to the company's management. Though it initially denied liability, BuffNET later pled guilty to a misdemeanor, and paid a $5,000 fine. Is there a convincing policy rationale for insulating AOL from civil liability in *Doe v. AOL,* but imposing criminal liability on BuffNET? For a discussion of the two cases, see Kenneth M. Dreifach, *Emerging Issues in Liability for Internet Service Providers*, N.Y.L.J., July 12, 2001, at 5.

In February 2002, Representative Robert Goodlatte introduced a bill in Congress that would negate federal criminal liability for an ISP in the position of BuffNET. The bill provides, with some limitations, that "no interactive computer service provider, or corporate officer of such provider, shall be liable for an offense against the United States arising from such provider's transmitting, storing, distributing, or otherwise making available, in the ordinary course of its business activities as an interactive computer service provider, material provided by another person." Online Criminal Liability Standardization Act of 2002, H.R. 3716, 107th Cong., § 2(a) (2002). Would such a law be good policy?

Also in February 2002, the Pennsylvania Legislature enacted a statute providing:

> **(a) General rule.**—An Internet Service Provider shall remove or disable access to child pornography items residing on or accessible through its service in a manner accessible to persons located within this Commonwealth within five business days of when the Internet Service Provider is notified by the Attorney General pursuant to subsection (g) that child pornography items reside on or are accessible through its service.

18 PA. CONS. STAT. § 7330(a). The Attorney General may make such a notification only upon a finding by a court, which may be ex parte, that there is probable cause that the material in question violates state law prohibiting child pornography. *Id.* § 7330(e), (f), (g). Criminal penalties apply to an ISP that fails to take down the material upon such a notification. *Id.* § 7330(c). Does this statute establish an appropriately limited form of ISP liability for making available criminal content?

5. *The scope of Section 230: defendant's participation in creation of the offensive material.* Section 230 privileges an ISP's publication of "information provided by another information content provider," but liability still attaches to publication of material created and published by the ISP itself. Thus, under the scenario presented in *Blumenthal v. Drudge*, if Drudge were AOL's employee, the content of the Drudge Report would be attributable to AOL and the immunity would be unavailable. Since Drudge was not AOL's employee, but an independent contractor, the court found that AOL enjoyed Section 230 immunity. Is there a defensible rationale for distinguishing between these two situations? What if AOL had more of a say in the content that was produced—if it offered to pay Drudge to produce "something that will grab eyeballs, whether it is true or not"? Would it be fair for the ISP to lose its immunity once its degree of participation becomes significant enough? Is such a result possible given the language of Section 230? Consider the provision's definition of "information content provider": "any person or entity that is responsible, in whole or in part, for the creation or development of information provided through the Internet or any other interactive computer service." 47 U.S.C. § 230(e)(3). Does this definition answer the question?

What if AOL had actually exercised editorial authority over some of Drudge's reports, but not this one? What if it had edited this particular report, but left the complained-of portion unchanged? Would AOL then qualify as an "information content provider" under 47 U.S.C. Section 230(e)(3), and therefore not be entitled to Section 230(c)(1) immunity? If so, can this be squared with the clear intent of Section 230(c)(2) to protect "good Samaritans" from liability?

6. *The scope of Section 230: republishing material created by another.* Does Section 230 protect one who intentionally republishes a defamatory statement that was created by another person? In *Barrett v. Clark*, 29 Media L. Rep. 2473 (Cal. Super. Ct. 2001), two doctors who were prominent critics of medical quackery brought a defamation action against several advocates of alternative medicine, based on a variety of allegedly defamatory statements. One such statement was a posting in a USENET newsgroup, which characterized one of the plaintiffs as a stalker. The defendant who posted the statement, Ilena Rosenthal, raised Section 230 as a defense. It was undisputed that it was not she who composed the statement: it was written by another defendant, Tom Bolen, who posted it to a newsgroup. Rosenthal argued that since she had merely republished material provided by another, she was within the literal terms of the immunity provided by Section 230(c)(1): "No * * * user of an interactive computer service shall be treated as the publisher or speaker of any information provided by another information content provider." The court agreed:

> § 230(c)(1) provides immunity to users, as well as providers, of interactive computer services.
>
> It is undisputed that Rosenthal did not "create" or "develop"[4] the information in defendant Bolen's piece. Thus, as a user of an interactive computer service, that is, a newsgroup, Rosenthal is not the publisher or speaker of Bolen's piece. Thus, she cannot be civilly liable for posting it on the Internet. She is immune.

Id. at *9. Is this a proper application of the immunity? If not, in what other situations might the immunity be available for the "user" of an interactive computer service?

7. *The scope of Section 230: service providers covered.* The immunity conferred by Section 230 applies to any "provider or user of an interactive computer service." The term "interactive computer service" is defined as "any information service, system, or access software provider that provides or enables computer access by multiple users to a computer server, including specifically a service or system that provides access to the Internet and such systems operated or services offered by libraries or educational institutions." § 230(f)(2). This definition covers entities that are traditionally thought of as Internet service providers, including those that provide

4. [The words in quotation marks are apparently a reference to Section 230(f)(3)'s definition of "information content provider" as "any person or entity that is responsible, in whole or in part, for the creation or development of information provided through the Internet or any other interactive computer service."—Eds.]

nothing more than access to the Internet, such as EarthLink or UUNET; those that provide Internet access as well as proprietary content, such as America Online and MSN; and those that provide website hosting services. But is it broad enough also to include other types of entities that offer online services, such as (1) online portals, like Yahoo! and Lycos; (2) dial-up BBSs that do not connect to the Internet; (3) instant messaging systems; (4) operators of USENET servers; (5) search engines; and (6) operators of Internet mailing lists?

In *Schneider v. Amazon.com, Inc.*, 31 P.3d 37 (Wash.Ct.App.2001), an author sued Amazon.com for defamation and tortious interference with a business expectancy, based on a negative and allegedly defamatory book review posted by a third party. The plaintiff argued that Amazon.com was not a provider of an "interactive computer service," since it did not enable access to the Internet: to visit the site, a user must already be online through some other service provider. The court rejected plaintiff's argument, explaining:

> Amazon's web site postings appear indistinguishable from AOL's message board [in *Zeran v. America Online*] for § 230 purposes. Schneider points out that web site operators do not provide access to the Internet, but this is irrelevant. * * * Amazon's web site enables visitors to the site to comment about authors and their work, thus providing an information service that necessarily enables access by multiple users to a server.

31 P.3d at 40. *See also Stoner v. eBay Inc.*, 56 U.S.P.Q.2d (BNA) 1852 (2000) (undisputed that eBay's auction site is an "interactive computer service").

But in *Batzel v. Smith*, 2001 WL 1893843 (C.D.Cal.2001), *appeal pending*, the court accepted a similar argument by plaintiff, holding that the operator of an Internet mailing list, or listserv, is not a provider of an "interactive computer service." The plaintiff, Batzel, had hired defendant Smith, a building contractor, to do some work on her house. The two had a falling out. Smith then sent an e-mail message to a non-profit website called Museum Security Network ("MSN"), which provided news about art theft and related issues, and was operated from the Netherlands by defendant Cremers. The e-mail stated that Batzel had bragged to him that she was the granddaughter of "one of Hitler's right-hand men," and had inherited artworks that Smith believed were stolen from Jewish victims of Nazis during World War II. Cremers included the allegations in an e-mail newsletter that he published in conjunction with the website, which was sent to some 1,000 subscribers around the world. Batzel sued Smith, Cremers, and MSN for defamation. Cremers and MSN moved to dismiss, invoking Section 230 as a defense.

The court denied the motion, finding that MSN was not an "interactive computer service":

> Although several cases have held that, by virtue of [Section 230], internet service providers cannot be sued for defamation,

> none are applicable here because, unlike MSN/Cremers, the qualifying entities were true internet service providers, like America Online, that provided individuals with access to the internet. * * * MSN, in contrast, is clearly not an internet service provider, as it has no capability to provide internet access. To the contrary, it is plainly an "information content provider" within the meaning of [Section 230]. Thus, the Defendants' preemption argument is without merit.

Id. at *8. Is the court's reasoning supportable? Could Cremers be *both* a provider of an "interactive computer service" *and* an "information content provider"?

8. *Liability for online auctions.* Does Section 230 immunity protect the operator of an online auction site from liability, under consumer protection or unfair competition laws, based on items that users list for sale on the site? Or is the immunity unavailable, since liability is predicated on the site's *conduct* in offering the items, rather than on any speech? *See Stoner v. eBay Inc.*, 56 U.S.P.Q.2d (BNA) 1852, 1853 (2000) (Section 230 protects eBay, since liability would be based on eBay's "informing prospective purchasers" of the availability of items for sale).

9. *Lack of parity with treatment of offline publishers.* In *Blumenthal v. Drudge*, the court expressed frustration over what it viewed as Congress's policy decision to treat online publishers differently from traditional publishers: "In view of this statutory language [of § 230], plaintiffs' argument that the Washington Post would be liable if it had done what AOL did here—'publish Drudge's story without doing anything whatsoever to edit, verify, or even read it (despite knowing what Drudge did for a living and how he did it)' * * *—has been rendered irrelevant by Congress." Is this policy judgment defensible? Do you agree with the court's statement that "it would seem only fair to hold AOL to the liability standards applied to a publisher or, at least, like a book store owner or library, to the liability standards applied to a distributor." What are the arguments for distinguishing an online service provider from a publisher or book store owner? Is there a national policy to encourage book stores to police the contents of the books they carry, and to eliminate those with offensive content? Should such a policy apply to ISPs?

10. *Is Section 230 too blunt an instrument?* Does Section 230 paint with too broad a brush, lumping all providers of interactive computer services together regardless of the activities in which they engage and the source and format of the offensive material? Consider the following critique. It makes sense for an ISP to enjoy unqualified immunity from liability based on material created by third parties, and made available through its service, where the ISP is functioning essentially like a common carrier. The risk of liability under such circumstances imposes an unreasonable burden on ISPs, and threatens unduly to restrict free expression in online bulletin board systems and chat rooms, since ISPs are likely to react by (1) engaging in censorship, (2) increasing the price of access to cover expected liability for offensive content, or (3) restricting anonymous speech in order to increase the accountability of online speakers. But this rationale does not apply when an ISP chooses to make an online publication available through its service. In this role, the ISP occupies the same position as any offline distributor of publications: it is making a decision to carry certain publications, based on general information about the content and editorial policies of each publication. There is no good reason to apply different standards of liability for defamation or other speech-based torts depending on whether the liability is based on (1) an ISP's decision to make available the *New York Times* or the *National Enquirer*, (2) an ISP's decision to make available Rumorville or the Drudge Report, or (3) a newsstand's decision to make available hard copies of any of those publications. Congress was right to override *Stratton Oakmont v. Prodigy*, but it drew the line in the wrong place: ISPs should not enjoy absolute immunity when, as in *Cubby v. CompuServe* and *Blumenthal v. Drudge*, they choose to make available publications known to have offensive content.

11. *Is Section 230 logical?* One of the stated purposes of Section 230 is to eliminate the disincentive that *Stratton Oakmont v. Prodigy* creates for ISPs to police their systems for offensive content. In so doing, Section 230 also eliminates the incentive to police their systems created for traditional publishers by the fear of legal liability. Is the theory underlying Section 230 that even absent this fear ISPs will be motivated to keep offensive materials off their systems? What motivations remain operative on ISPs? Developing a reputation as a family-friendly service, or as one that contains reliable information? Is it desirable to have a spectrum of different services, including "G-rated" services that are guaranteed to contain nothing objectionable, "PG–13" services that contain mildly offensive material, "R-rated" ones that parents might want to keep their children away from, and "NC–17" services on which nothing is off limits? Is this an area in which self-regulation, impelled by market forces, is the best approach?

12. *Balancing competing interests.* One effect of Section 230, and common-law doctrines that immunize ISPs from liability based on third-party communications, is that deserving plaintiffs may have no remedy. This will be the case when the originator of the offending communication cannot be identified, as in *Zeran v. AOL*[5] and *Lunney v. Prodigy* (discussed *infra).* Does the law therefore go overboard in protecting free speech, while neglecting other important interests such as reputation? Would it be good policy to restore the balance by requiring ISPs to verify the identity of subscribers before allowing them online, enabling an ISP to disclose the identity of a subscriber in response to a subpoena or court order?

13. *Does the technology of online communications render the law of defamation obsolete?* One commentator points out that a person who is

5. Zeran was also rebuffed in his suit against the radio station that broadcast the AOL postings. The court held against him, on summary judgment, for failure to introduce evidence of reputational injury, as required by the Oklahoma statute defining a cause of action for slander. It likewise rejected, on evidentiary grounds, his claims based on false light invasion of privacy and intentional infliction of emotional distress. *See Zeran v. Diamond Broadcasting, Inc.*, 203 F.3d 714 (10th Cir.2000).

defamed by a posting on a bulletin board system has an automatic right of reply, which she may exercise simply by posting a reply message in the forum where the defamation appeared. Accordingly, he argues, we may dispense with the application of legal remedies, like defamation liability, that cut close to First Amendment protections by casting a chill upon system operators. Do you agree? *See* Edward A. Cavazos, *Computer Bulletin Board Systems and the Right of Reply: Redefining Defamation Liability for a New Technology*, 12 REV. LITIG. 231 (1992).

14. *Continuing vitality of the common law of defamation after Section 230.* Section 230 is an overlay that does not displace the limitations on liability resulting from the common (or statutory) law of defamation. In *Lunney v. Prodigy Services Co.*, 723 N.E.2d 539 (N.Y.1999), plaintiff sued Prodigy for defamation, based on messages on one of its bulletin boards that the poster falsely attributed to plaintiff. The court, applying New York common law, held that, under the circumstances presented, Prodigy was not a publisher of the posted material. In contrast to the breadth of the legislative approach followed in Section 230, the court declined to rule any more broadly than necessary to decide the case before it: "We see no occasion to hypothesize whether there may be other instances in which the role of an electronic bulletin board operator would qualify it as a publisher." The court also declined Prodigy's request that it decide the case on the basis of Section 230, and that it interpret the statutory provision "to render an ISP unconditionally free from notice-based liability." Once again, the court found that "[t]his case does not call for it."

15. *Parallel treatment for copyright liability?* In *Zeran*, the court rejected plaintiff's argument that Section 230 should be interpreted to countenance the imposition of liability on service providers that are on notice of the offending material, observing: "Because service providers would be subject to liability only for the publication of information, and not for its removal, they would have a natural incentive simply to remove messages upon notification, whether the contents were defamatory or not. * * * Thus, like strict liability, liability upon notice has a chilling effect on the freedom of Internet speech." Reconsider the notice and takedown provisions applicable to allegedly infringing postings with respect to copyright liability, considered in Chapter 9, Part V, *supra*. Do you think that these provisions will have a chilling effect on speech similar to the one the court in *Zeran* sought to avoid? That is, do you think service providers will have a "natural incentive simply to remove messages upon notification" of alleged copyright infringement? If so, has Congress simply balanced First Amendment concerns differently with respect to allegedly infringing speech than for allegedly defamatory speech? What is your evaluation of the appropriateness of this difference?

16. *Insurance as alternative.* Print publications can purchase insurance to protect themselves against liability for defamation and other torts based on what they publish. The insurance premium becomes an additional cost of doing business. Is there any reason why ISPs could not insure against similar types of liability? Would this be a better solution than the blanket immunity created by Section 230, which leaves some innocent victims without recourse? Is Section 230 itself regulatory or deregulatory?

D. A Comparative View

Outside the United States, service providers have received less favorable treatment with respect to liability for third-party content. This is illustrated by the criminal prosecution of a German CompuServe official for distribution of child pornography. In December 1995, prosecutors in Bavaria notified CompuServe's German subsidiary that they were investigating the distribution of child pornography via the Internet. In response, CompuServe blocked access to over 200 USENET newsgroups, which German prosecutors suspected of carrying pornographic images. The blocking affected all of CompuServe's 4.3 million subscribers throughout the world, as it did not have the technology to block access only by those in a specific geographic location. Authorities in Munich subsequently prosecuted the managing director of CompuServe's German subsidiary, Felix Somm, under an act prohibiting publications deemed harmful to children. Prosecutors sought to hold Somm responsible for CompuServe's provision of access to USENET newsgroups containing pornographic images illegal under German law, as well as access to computer games with violent content.

In the course of the prosecution, the German legislature passed an amendment to the law regulating telecommunications services that was designed to limit the liability of ISPs for third-party communications, but the court held this provision inapplicable. The court found Somm guilty as charged, and imposed a two-year suspended sentence—despite the fact that the prosecution had a change of heart during the proceedings, and joined the defense in arguing for acquittal. In their closing arguments, both the prosecution and defense argued that it was technically impossible to filter out all offensive material on the Internet, but the judge disagreed. The prosecutors, believing that the new law insulated Somm from liability, themselves appealed the conviction. The court of appeals agreed, and threw out the conviction.

A court decision in the United Kingdom likewise held an ISP liable for third-party content. In *Godfrey v. Demon Internet Ltd.*, [1999] E.M.L.R. 542 (Q.B.), an unknown person posted a scurrilous message on a USENET newsgroup, and signed plaintiff Lawrence Godfrey's name to it. Godfrey notified Demon Internet, an ISP carrying the newsgroup, that the posting was a forgery, and asked Demon to delete it, but Demon failed to do so. The facts of the case were thus quite similar to those in *Zeran v. AOL* and *Lunney v. Prodigy*, discussed *supra*, but the result was quite different. The U.K. Defamation Act contains an "innocent dissemination" defense, which is available only if the defendant took "reasonable care," and "did not know, and had no reason to believe," that he was publishing a defamatory statement. The court held that, since Demon was informed of the posting, it did not satisfy those two requirements, and was not entitled to the defense. The court discussed what it viewed as the relevant U.S. cases—*Cubby v. CompuServe*, *Stratton Oakmont v. Prodigy*, *Zeran v. AOL*, and

Lunney v. Prodigy—but found them inapplicable. Referring to Section 230, the ISP immunity provision of the Communications Decency Act, the court observed: "In my judgment the English 1996 [Defamation] Act did not adopt this approach or have this purpose."

The case subsequently settled: Demon agreed to pay Godfrey £15,000, plus legal costs which could exceed £200,000. Demon's own legal costs were nearly £500,000.

Shortly after this ruling, the Campaign Against Censorship of the Internet in Britain posted a story on its website describing a situation in which an ISP shut down a website it hosted after a firm of solicitors notified the ISP that it would be subject to a defamation suit if the website should publish a libel. The ISP required the website to provide a guarantee against any such wrongdoing, and when the website failed to do so shut down the website. The story on CACIB's site was headlined: "Web site suppressed: *Godfrey's* first victim." Godfrey complained to CACIB's ISP that this was defamatory, as the headline could be read to imply that the threat was issued by Godfrey personally, rather than by the *Godfrey* ruling. Fearing liability under the theory of this very ruling, the ISP shut down CACIB's website. CACIB relocated to servers located in the United States and restored the censored content.

This story illustrates two negative aspects of a legal regime making ISPs liable for third-party content. First, it tends to have a chilling effect on speech, as the specter of ruinous liability impels ISPs to pull the plug on controversial material. Second, it demonstrates the mobility of content in the borderless online world. Since the address of a website is logical, and not geographically based, a site need not be hosted on servers located within the geographic boundaries of the country with jurisdiction over the domain name. For example, a domain name ending with the country-code .uk, which is issued by the domain registration authority of the United Kingdom, may be hosted just as easily, from a technical standpoint, on a server located in the United States as on one located in the United Kingdom. The location of the server may, however, introduce practical difficulties: for example, it may be easier for a U.K. resident to contract with a website hosting service located in her own country than with one located overseas.

NOTES & QUESTIONS

The borderless world. Do the German and English experiences with different rules make you reconsider your evaluation of Section 230? Consider the question in context: England and other European countries have always had stricter laws against defamation than the United States, and fewer defenses. Will the Internet force countries to relinquish their legal culture when that culture supports regulation that is difficult to administer in the borderless online environment? Consider also in this regard Yahoo!'s efforts to have a judgment against it, issued by a French court, declared unenforceable in the United States, on the ground that enforcement would violate the First Amendment. *Yahoo!, Inc. v. La Ligue Contre Le Racisme et L'Antisemitisme*, 169 F.Supp.2d 1181 (N.D.Cal.2001), *appeal pending*, discussed in Chapter 1, Part III(A), *supra*. If the original action against Yahoo! had been brought in a U.S. court, could Yahoo! have successfully invoked a Section 230 defense?

NOTE: LIABILITY OF INTERNET SERVICE PROVIDERS IN THE EUROPEAN UNION

The European Commission's Directive on Electronic Commerce[6] contains several provisions limiting the liability of Internet service providers based on material provided by others. The Directive's treatment of ISP liability differs from the U.S. regime in several important respects. In the United States, as we have seen, the rules limiting the liability of a service provider vary depending on the subject matter of the material giving rise to the claim of liability. Thus, an ISP's liability for copyright infringement is limited by the Digital Millennium Copyright Act ("DMCA") immunity provision, 17 U.S.C. § 512, discussed in Chapter 9, Part V, *supra*. ISP liability based on most other types of material is limited by the Communications Decency Act ("CDA") immunity provision, 47 U.S.C. § 230, as discussed in this Chapter. Liability based on other subject matters that are excluded from the scope of Section 230, including criminal liability, non-copyright intellectual property, and liability based on the Electronic Communications Privacy Act, are not subject to any limitation other than what exists in the substantive rules creating liability.

The Directive, on the other hand, applies a unitary approach to all forms of ISP liability, regardless of the subject matter under which it arises.[7] The Directive bears a strong resemblance to the DMCA immunity provision, 17 U.S.C. § 512, and very little resemblance to the CDA provision, 47 U.S.C. § 230, in that it offers conditional rather than blanket immunity.

- When an ISP acts as a "mere conduit" of information provided by others, the ISP is not liable based on the information transmitted as long as it "(a) does not initiate the transmission; (b) does not select the receiver of the transmission; and (c) does not select or modify the information contained in the transmission." Art. 12(1). This immunity is applicable to the "automatic, intermediate and transient storage" of the information transmitted only if the storage is "for the sole purpose of carrying out the transmission in the communication network, and provided that the information is not stored for any

6. Directive 2000/31/EC of the European Parliament and of the Council of 8 June 2000 on certain legal aspects of information society services, in particular electronic commerce, in the Internal Market, 2000 O.J. (L 178) 1, europa.eu.int/ISPO/ecommerce/legal/documents/2000_31ec/2000_31ec_en.pdf.

7. This difference between the U.S. and EU approaches finds an analogy in the area of privacy protection. In the United States, legislation protecting privacy is sectoral, with no overarching scheme, while in the European Union privacy is regulated comprehensively by the Data Privacy Directive. *See* Chapter 8, *supra*.

period longer than is reasonably necessary for the transmission." Art. 12(2). Compare 17 U.S.C. § 512(a).

- An ISP is not liable based on "caching," that is, "the automatic, intermediate and temporary storage of that information, performed for the sole purpose of making more efficient the information's onward transmission to other recipients of the service upon their request," if certain conditions are met, including: "(c) the provider complies with rules regarding the updating of the information, specified in a manner widely recognised and used by industry; (d) the provider does not interfere with the lawful use of technology, widely recognised and used by industry, to obtain data on the use of the information; and (e) the provider acts expeditiously to remove or to disable access to the information it has stored upon obtaining actual knowledge of the fact that the information at the initial source of the transmission has been removed from the network, or access to it has been disabled, or that a court or an administrative authority has ordered such removal or disablement." Art. 13(1). Compare 17 U.S.C. § 512(b).
- An ISP is not liable based on hosting a website or other material, if "(a) the provider does not have actual knowledge of illegal activity or information and, as regards claims for damages, is not aware of facts or circumstances from which the illegal activity or information is apparent; or (b) the provider, upon obtaining such knowledge or awareness, acts expeditiously to remove or to disable access to the information." Art. 14(1). Compare 17 U.S.C. § 512(c), which includes detailed notification procedures not present in the Directive.
- Unlike the U.S. law, the Directive does not limit the liability of search engines and online directories. Compare 17 U.S.C. § 512(d).
- The forgoing immunity provisions do not prevent the issuance of injunctive relief, requiring that an ISP remove or cease providing access to the offending information. Art. 12(3), 13(2), 14(3). Compare 17 U.S.C. § 512(j).
- The Directive provides that EU member states "shall not impose a general obligation on providers, when providing the services covered by Articles 12, 13 and 14, to monitor the information which they transmit or store, nor a general obligation actively to seek facts or circumstances indicating illegal activity." Art. 15(1). This provision is consistent with the general approach of both 17 U.S.C. § 512 and 47 U.S.C. § 230.

What are the advantages and disadvantages of the Directive's unitary approach, as compared with the sectoral approach followed by U.S. law? For a comparison of the U.S. and EU approaches, see Kamiel J. Koelman, *Online Intermediary Liability, in* COPYRIGHT AND ELECTRONIC COMMERCE: LEGAL ASPECTS OF ELECTRONIC COPYRIGHT MANAGEMENT 7 (P. Bernt Hugenholtz ed., 2000).

II. LIABILITY OF INTERMEDIARIES FOR HARM CAUSED BY DENIAL OF SERVICE ATTACKS AND OTHER MALICIOUS INTRUSIONS

As we have seen in Part I, *supra*, the liability of Internet intermediaries for speech torts originating with third-party users has been largely eliminated by the Communications Decency Act immunity provision, 47 U.S.C. § 230. Service provider liability for third-party copyright infringement is strictly confined by the Digital Millennium Copyright Act's safe harbors, 17 U.S.C. § 512, as discussed in Chapter 9, Part V, *supra*.

The potential liability of intermediaries based on denial-of-service attacks perpetrated by third parties is murkier, as discussed in the following excerpt.

Margaret Jane Radin, *Distributed Denial of Service Attacks: Who Pays?*

6 No. 9 CYBERSPACE LAW. 2 (2001) (Part I) and 6 No. 10 CYBERSPACE LAW. 2 (2002) (Part II).

I. DDoS: A Lurking Problem for Business

* * *

The vulnerability of businesses to DDoS attacks hit the headlines with the attacks that brought down Yahoo!, eBay and others in February 2000. Recent attacks on Microsoft and the World Economic Forum at Davos generated further headlines. What does not make the headlines is how serious and pervasive the problem is. For example, more than one-third of the respondents in the 2001 Computer Crime and Security Survey experienced denial of service attacks. In spite of such evidence, the problem is under-reported. Many denial of service attacks go undetected. Even when attacks are detected, many organizations, fearing bad publicity and the consequent effect on their customers and shareholders, simply do not report such incidents. The tools available to intruders are becoming more sophisticated and readily available on the Web.

The costs of DDoS attacks can be staggering. The estimated direct losses from the attacks in February 2000 were $1.2 billion. Losses of customer goodwill, corporate reputation and overall public trust in the online economy were likely even greater. DDoS attacks also take their toll on productivity, user access, and lost business opportunities. These indirect costs are no less real because they are difficult to monetize.

* * *

What is a DDoS Attack?

In a DDoS attack, intruders commandeer unsuspecting users' computers and use these distributed "zombies" to flood a target site or service with junk messages. The junk messages overwhelm the servers of the victim and cause that site to experience a period of "denial of service" to its legitimate customers. The success of typical DDoS attacks involves the "cooperation" of a number of players, or *a chain of actors*. The chain consists of (1) computer users whose machines are commandeered by intruders; (2) portals, corporate and other Internet sites that are targets or "victims" of attacks; and (3) network intermediaries (i.e., various kinds of ISPs and hosting service providers) and backbone network service providers, who deliver the messages that constitute the attack.

User computers are vulnerable because their operating systems are not designed to screen out intruders. Victim sites are vulnerable for many reasons. Some are not aware of the extent of the problem; some are unable to deploy the personnel and technology needed to detect and stop attacks. Even for sophisticated sites, the task of determining the source of the unwanted messages can be like looking for a needle in a haystack; and it is difficult for security personnel to keep up with rapid development of newer and more sophisticated attack modes. Network intermediaries and backbone service providers are vulnerable too, in the sense that they are transmitting malicious packets that are part of an attack. Also, under certain circumstances the flood of messages may slow down the entire network, or further disrupt the server by directing traffic back to it.

* * *

II. *Potential Tort Liability for Damages Due to DDoS Attacks*

* * *

DDoS-Based Claims Through the Lens of Traditional Tort Law

A Hypothetical Scenario: Let's consider how liability might come before a court in the case of a DDoS attack with the following example. Suppose a securities brokerage such as E*Trade or Schwab suffers a DDoS attack. Its customers cannot complete any transactions for several hours. The attack messages have been relayed through a large hosting service provider such as Exodus or Digex. Suppose that the market is volatile on the day that this happens, so that many customers are trying to buy or sell quickly. As a result of the outage, a large number of customers suffer significant financial losses. (Significant losses could occur on account of a slowdown, as well, even if it weren't a complete outage.)

What legal claims might arise out of this event? First, the customers of the brokerage might sue the brokerage for damages on account of their financial losses. Second, the brokerage could sue its hosting or bandwidth provider, for damages on account of its own financial losses (lost revenue from transactions not completed, employee time in recovering lost data, loss of customer goodwill, and perhaps decreased market share or capitalization). In such suits, the plaintiff is said to be in *privity* with the defendant because the relationship between the plaintiff and the defendant is governed by a contract—the TOS [Terms of Service] between the brokerage and its users, the SLA [Service Level Agreement] between the network service provider and the broker.

Tort and Contract Interaction: Thus, there are two intertwined legal questions to pose in these kinds of suits: who would be liable in the absence of contract? And, has the contract successfully allocated the risk in a different way (that is, has the contract disclaimed liability on the part of the party who would otherwise be liable)? This paper examines both tort liability and contractual shifting of liability. Of the two questions, the latter is the more important for parties who are in privity with each other.

Third-Party Claims: Another class of legal claims arising out of my hypothetical example involves claims against a party not in privity with the plaintiff, which I will sometimes refer to as third-party claims. (The brokerage's customers are third parties vis-à-vis the contract between the brokerage and its service provider; and the service provider is a third party vis-à-vis the contract between the brokerage and its customers.)

A suit by the customers of the brokerage firm against the brokerage's Web hosting service and/or backbone service provider is a claim against a third party defendant. Attempted contractual disclaimer will usually not play a role in this scenario, because the plaintiffs are not a party to the contract in which the disclaimer appears; they did not agree to it, and it wasn't a part of their bargain. In this situation, however, traditional tort law developed defenses for the third party defendant based essentially upon the extent of exposure to liability, and whether the court found such exposure to be reasonable under the circumstances. (I will touch upon those defenses later in this section).

* * *

How Will Courts Analyze DDoS–Based Tort Claims?

Tort law is divided doctrinally into torts based upon intentional harm, harm caused by negligence, and liability without fault (strict liability). In the case of liability for DDoS attacks, at least for parties other than the intruders themselves, we are not dealing with intentional harm. The doctrine of strict liability is used primarily in the context of harm caused by defective products that are dangerous to the user, so it is more likely that courts will consider liability for DDoS attacks under the rubric of negligence rather than that of strict liability, and the analysis here will assume a negligence context. (In practice, however, the application of strict liability often involves inquiries that overlap with those involved in negligence.)

Actors in the Causal Chain Who Are in Privity (i.e., in a Provider/Customer Relationship): Assuming the absence of a successful contractual disclaimer, each party would owe its partner a duty of reasonable care; and if it failed to use due care it would be deemed negligent. Damages could follow if the negligence results in losses on account of a DDoS attack, if the losses are foreseeable and could have been prevented with exercise of due care. That is, a network intermediary could be held liable to its customer;

and its customer, such as a portal or other e-commerce site, could be held liable to its own customers.

My research has disclosed no cases to date (April 30, 2001) in which this issue has been litigated and reported in the context of a DDoS attack. Traditional principles of tort law direct courts to consider *foreseeability* of the damage, including the identity of the party likely to be injured and the type and extent of injury that can be foreseen. Those issues seem relatively straightforward in the case of a provider-customer (victim site) relationship, and in the case of a victim site-user relationship. That is, DDoS attacks and the types of damage they cause to a customer are reasonably foreseeable by a service provider, so liability could be found under traditional tort principles if the governing standard of care required the service provider to take precautions to prevent such attacks. The same is true in the case of the victim site vis-à-vis its users.

But it is important to keep in mind that these kinds of cases are frequently going to be governed by the contract between the parties. Exceptions are where the contract is improperly formed, or where the contract tries to exclude liability in a way the court finds contrary to public policy. (See Part III.)

Third-Party Liability: Potential tort liability in this situation—e.g., where the victim's own customers sue the victim's network service provider, Web hosting service, etc.—is somewhat more difficult to analyze. In the past the courts have sometimes rejected liability of third party defendants, especially where it appeared that the third party would expose itself to an unknown and potentially large amount of risk, inappropriate in light of its role.[11] On the other hand, some courts have found third parties liable, especially where the risk was foreseeable and particularized,[12] or where they could find a special relationship between the plaintiff and the defendant.[13]

* * *

Property Damage and Recent Cases Involving "Trespass to Chattels": Victim sites may well be able to convince a court that DDoS attacks cause them property damage. A number of recent cases suggest that courts are

11. See generally, Robert L. Rabin, Tort Recovery for Negligently Inflicted Economic Loss: A Reassessment, 37 Stanford Law Review 1513 (1985).

12. See, e.g., J'Aire Corp. v. Gregory, 24 Cal. 3d 799 (1979)(contractor who undertook construction work for owner of building had duty to tenants to complete construction on time to avoid resultant economic losses); Union Oil Co. v. Oppen 501 F. 2d 558 (9th Cir.1974) (fishermen making known commercial use of public waters may recover economic losses due to defendant's oil spill).

13. This doctrine usually comes into play in cases involving reliance by third parties on opinions of professionals such as auditors, attorneys, surveyors, inspectors, engineers, and notaries. The law has not been monolithic on the issue of whether such professionals can be held liable, but a common approach has been to ask whether the plaintiff has a special relationship between the negligent tortfeasor and the foreseeable plaintiffs who relied on the quality of defendants' work or services. See, e.g., Marc A. Franklin & Robert L. Rabin, *Tort Law and Alternatives: Cases and Materials* 278–279 (6th ed. 1996).

willing to consider receipt of unwanted messages to be a physical harm to a victim's system, and thus the requisite physical harm to property. These cases have found tort liability for slowing down a system or taking up bandwidth, by spam or data-gathering programs, under the doctrine of trespass to chattels.[14]

* * *

Can ISPs Claim Immunity from Liability?

Service providers may argue that because they are mere conduits of messages it is inappropriate to place any liabilities on them. This argument is not convincing, as the courts have not hesitated to place liability on service providers in other contexts.

In determining whether ISPs (broadly construed) could claim immunity to tort suits for DDoS attacks, we can consider [these] possible analogies: the immunities of "common carriers," [and] the safe harbor in the Communications Decency Act (CDA) * * *.

* * *

"Common Carrier": Traditionally, the government held "common carriers," who provided services to the public at large (e.g., railroads), to a high standard of care to their customers. Communications regulation designated telephone companies as "common carriers," but as communications law developed, such carriers were permitted to place disclaimers of liability for customers' loss due to denial of service or poor quality of service in their governing document (tariff). Although many in the communications field have fought over the definition of "common carrier," none of the providers in the DDoS attack scenario is likely to be considered a common carrier, because they do not hold out their service to everyone.[17]

Safe Harbor for Indecent or Defamatory Content: As e-commerce evolved, courts demonstrated willingness to hold an ISP liable for defamatory content present on its system. The Communications Decency Act (CDA) overrules this case law and grants a safe harbor to ISPs who in good faith try to filter out offending material. Among other things, this provision prevents ISPs from being sued in tort for defamation, for "publishing" defamatory content.

Several considerations distinguish ISP immunity in the context of defamation from any claimed immunity in the context of DDoS. First, Congress statutorily grants the immunity from liability for defamatory [and other offensive] content, and there is no such statutory immunity applicable to DDoS attacks. Second, and equally important, the defamation immunity is granted to foster provision of content. Congress has decided that the social desirability of content provision outweighs the interest of injured

14. [Cases finding liability based on trespass to chattels are discussed in Chapter 13, *supra*.—Eds.]

17. See, e.g., Religious Technology Center v. Netcom On-Line Communication Services, 907 F.Supp. 1361, 1370 n. 12 (rejecting Netcom's invocation of a "common carrier" analogy in order to shield itself from liability).

plaintiffs in compensation for defamation. Part of the reason for doing so is the preferred place of speech in our social order. Another reason is the fact that defamation is a murky subject area; an ISP could not be expected consistently to guess right about whether courts would find material defamatory, even if an ISP could undertake serious review of posted content (which is impossible in the ordinary course of business).

In contrast, DDoS attacks are not speech and there is no reason to think that DDoS attacks have a socially beneficial side that should be encouraged. Moreover, where technology exists that can differentiate normal from attack traffic on a consistent basis, DDoS attacks would not be hard to distinguish from the beneficial use of a network. In other words, there is no policy basis that would support immunity in a world where preventive technology exists.

* * *

III. *Contractual Risk–Shifting of Damage Liability for DDoS Attacks*

A key risk-management strategy for avoiding liability for DDoS attacks is contractual. Firms may attempt to use contracts either to force partners to take adequate precautions, or to force partners to take on the liability themselves by disclaiming whatever liability might otherwise accrue to them. Forcing a customer to take adequate precautions involves using contracts that make the customer promise to implement specific precautions as a condition of service. Forcing customers to take on the liability themselves involves using contracts that either explicitly allocate liability to the customer, or else just disclaim liability on the part of the service provider.

Requiring Customer Precautions

With respect to the first strategy, some network intermediaries and backbone service providers use Service Level Agreements (SLAs) that condition service delivery upon the customer's implementation of specific security precautions and submission to monitoring by the service provider for compliance. The success of such a strategy depends on the marketplace. If competitive providers do not impose such onerous terms in their SLAs, but rather implement effective preventive technologies themselves, they may gain market share against providers that do impose such terms.

Contractual Disclaimers of Liability

The second strategy, contractual disclaimers, is legally efficacious in some contexts, but not always. First, contractual disclaimers are not binding on third parties who are not parties to the contract. Second, not all contracts are valid and enforceable. Two ways a contract could be unenforceable are (1) invalid formation (the court finds that no agreement was formed) and (2) invalid content (the court finds that even if there was agreement, such an agreement is not legally allowable).

In general, courts determine whether a contract looks like a reasonable bargained-for exchange or whether, on the contrary, it looks onerous and coercive. SLAs between business entities of roughly equal bargaining power—for example, between a high-profile Web portal and a well-established Web hosting service—are more likely to be presumed the result of bargained-for exchange. TOSes [Terms of Service agreements] between parties of unequal bargaining power—for example, between a network service provider and individual consumers—are more likely to be scrutinized for over-reaching.

Public Policy and Choice of Law: Some contractual provisions may seem like obvious over-reaching or contrary to public policy even if they are between entities of equal bargaining power. There are also some conditions even willing parties cannot agree to enforce. For example, all courts would find it contrary to public policy for an entity to exculpate itself for its own criminal activities. Moreover, most courts would not allow contractual exculpation for gross negligence. Courts in different jurisdictions are divided, however, on whether it is permissible to disclaim liability for one's own negligence (if it does not amount to gross negligence or recklessness)—that is, to shift the risk of one's own negligence to one's contractual partner.

The question of disclaiming a party's own negligence is thus complicated by the question of choice of law: will the contract be governed by the law of a jurisdiction that permits such disclaimers, or will it be governed by the law of a jurisdiction that invalidates them? In order to deal with this issue, parties routinely include choice of law clauses, which contractually choose whose law will govern. At least in the U.S., these clauses are routinely considered valid, but may on occasion be invalidated by courts. Outside the U.S., a court may be unwilling to transfer a case brought against one of its own nationals to a U.S. jurisdiction whose public policy conflicts with its own.

Curtailment of Remedies: Many contracts also attempt to limit risk by excluding all but a limited remedy, such as the amount paid for the service. Again, whether this limitation is enforceable depends whether the court believes this is a bargained-for exchange or instead represents some sort of overreaching and attempt to foreclose the other party's right to legal redress.

Arbitration: Many contracts force customers to accept arbitration as the sole remedy for a dispute. The courts in the U.S. are very favorable to arbitration. These clauses are generally considered enforceable, at least in the U.S., assuming that the court finds the contract to be validly formed.[24]

Contractual Disclaimers Vis-à-Vis Consumers

Contractual disclaimers, or limitations of remedy and redress, that are imposed on consumers are not always enforceable. As an outgrowth of the shrink-wrap license contracts that developed in the software industry, a

24. But see Brower v. Gateway 2000, Inc., 676 N.Y.S.2d 569 (N.Y. Sup. Ct. App. Div. 1998)(consumer class action in which court held clause calling for arbitration before the International Chamber of Commerce, which required consumers to pay a filing fee of $4000, was unconscionable and therefore unenforceable). [This case is excerpted in Chapter 15, Part II(B), *infra*.—Eds.]

large percentage of commercial Web sites are using a TOS contract, often on an interior Web page that users are unlikely to see, much less read. Many of these TOSes disclaim warranties and limit remedies.

As an example, consider AOL's "Terms of Use," which can be seen by scrolling to the very bottom of its home page and clicking on a link called "Legal Notices." After disclaiming "all warranties with respect to materials, information, software, products, and services included in or available through its site," the Terms provide:

> UNDER NO CIRCUMSTANCES SHALL AMERICA ONLINE, ITS SUBSIDIARIES, OR ITS LICENSORS BE LIABLE FOR ANY DIRECT, INDIRECT, PUNITIVE, INCIDENTAL, SPECIAL, OR CONSEQUENTIAL DAMAGES THAT RESULT FROM THE USE OF, OR INABILITY TO USE, THIS SITE. THIS LIMITATION APPLIES WHETHER THE ALLEGED LIABILITY IS BASED ON CONTRACT, TORT, NEGLIGENCE, STRICT LIABILITY, OR ANY OTHER BASIS, EVEN IF AMERICA ONLINE HAS BEEN ADVISED OF THE POSSIBILITY OF SUCH DAMAGE. BECAUSE SOME JURISDICTIONS DO NOT ALLOW THE EXCLUSION OR LIMITATION OF INCIDENTAL OR CONSEQUENTIAL DAMAGES, AMERICA ONLINE'S LIABILITY IN SUCH JURISDICTIONS SHALL BE LIMITED TO THE EXTENT PERMITTED BY LAW.

These provisions purport to divest AOL of all liability to its users for unavailability of service due to Denial of Service attacks. Many service providers and high-profile Web sites have provisions like this. But are they enforceable?

That question is multi-faceted. First is the question of public policy. AOL itself informs anyone who reads these terms that there are some jurisdictions that do not permit this much risk-shifting, and that it is not trying to impose these terms on said users. Thus, the service provider recognizes that it cannot impose the terms across the board. This outcome is true whether or not AOL chose to inform readers about it.

A further wrinkle, however, is that another clause, a choice of law clause, says that the contract is to be governed by the laws of Virginia. An allied choice of forum clause says that all suits must be brought in Virginia. The laws of Virginia do not categorically outlaw the types of disclaimers that AOL has in its contract. Could AOL impose these disclaimers on everyone by virtue of the fact that the contract is governed everywhere by Virginia law?

No. A court in a jurisdiction that does not permit these kinds of disclaimers might well say that the choice of law clause is not enforceable against its residents. It might say that to enforce the clause would contravene that jurisdiction's public policy, and might allow the action to go forward in its own jurisdiction despite the choice of forum clause.[15]

15. [*See America Online, Inc. v. Superior Court*, 108 Cal.Rptr.2d 699 (Cal.Ct.App. 2001), discussed in Chapter 7, Part IV, *supra*.—Eds.]

To generalize, choice of law and choice of forum clauses are often enforceable, especially in the United States, but courts can always refuse to enforce them if doing so would be seriously contrary to the interests and policies of the state in which the court is located, or if the forum would be seriously inconvenient for the aggrieved party. Enforcement is more uncertain when the clash of policies is international, rather than between two U.S. jurisdictions.

The Issue of Contract Formation: Even if a jurisdiction does not find the terms contrary to public policy, a court could find something about the way this contract is purportedly entered into which would invalidate the entire contract, or at least the parts of it that seem too unfavorable to the recipient. In other words, an invalid process of contract formation could result in no contractual obligation being formed, or no contractual obligation with respect to the loss-shifting terms. In a nutshell, the question is whether the court finds there really was an agreement, a process that amounts to consent, or one that otherwise qualifies as giving rise to binding obligation.

Contracts of Adhesion: What causes a court to look askance at contract formation? Some judges tend to disfavor so-called "contracts of adhesion," otherwise known as "take-it-or-leave it" contracts. Thus, in some jurisdictions a purported contract might be invalid if it is a standard-form set of terms for which one party had no opportunity to negotiate, especially if that party is a consumer, and especially if the terms seem onerous. If the contract seems grossly one-sided, or if some of the terms are against public policy (such as exculpation for gross negligence), it is more likely to be unenforceable.

Some judges are most concerned about the apparent lack of consent that goes along with these "take-it-or-leave it" contracts. Thus, a purported contract might be more likely to be held invalid if one party did not even see the terms before purportedly being bound by them.[16] This, of course, applies to many of the TOS agreements we are seeing on the Web, including the AOL Terms, since, even though they are printed in capital letters to make them conspicuous, it is unlikely that many users of the site will click on the link that reveals the terms.

* * *

Most adhesion contracts would be held valid if litigated, at least in the U.S., because the modern market could not function otherwise; but other countries rely on consumer law that is less tolerant of them. Even in the U.S., because of the varying concerns about public policy and contract formation, the thoroughgoing contractual exculpation attempted by terms disclaiming liability will not turn out to be uniformly valid. (That is why AOL's Terms say that the disclaimers don't apply to users in jurisdictions that disallow them.) Even where the terms function as intended, the firm defending the terms must pay attorneys to file motions to dismiss in each

16. [See the cases discussed in Chapter 4, Parts I(C)(1) and II, *supra*.—Eds.]

case. Because of this expense, the strategy of using disclaimers to avoid liability—defending them legally in all U.S. jurisdictions as well as in foreign jurisdictions—may not be optimal from a business standpoint.

Contractual Disclaimers Between Business Parties

Many SLAs between Web hosting services and their customers attempt to limit liability and shift risk to the customer. Similar to the Terms imposed by AOL (see above), such contracts disclaim responsibility for performance issues resulting from third party actions, and may limit remedies to credits or refunds, disclaim warranties of merchantability and fitness, and also disclaim consequential damages of any kind. For example, one such clause in an SLA, similar to that used by AOL in its TOS, reads:

> [Except for breaches involving intellectual property], IN NO EVENT WILL EITHER PARTY BE LIABLE OR RESPONSIBLE TO THE OTHER FOR ANY TYPE OF INCIDENTAL, PUNITIVE, INDIRECT OR CONSEQUENTIAL DAMAGES, INCLUDING, BUT NOT LIMITED TO, LOST REVENUE, LOST PROFITS, REPLACEMENT GOODS, LOSS OF TECHNOLOGY, RIGHTS OR SERVICES, LOSS OF DATA, OR INTERRUPTION OR LOSS OF USE OF SERVICE OR EQUIPMENT, EVEN IF ADVISED OF THE POSSIBILITY OF SUCH DAMAGES, WHETHER ARISING UNDER THEORY OF CONTRACT, TORT (INCLUDING NEGLIGENCE), STRICT LIABILITY OR OTHERWISE.

This clause can be bolstered by another one that attests to bargained-for exchange by stating that the limitations of liability and the disclaimers of warranties and damages are an essential basis of the bargain between the parties. These provisions can in turn be bolstered by choice of law and choice of forum clauses selecting a friendly jurisdiction, and perhaps by an arbitration clause.

Such SLAs are drafted to shift risk from potential DDoS damages to the customer, the service provider's contractual partner, who is the party most likely to suffer losses from attacks. They are likely to stand up much of the time, especially vis-à-vis partners of roughly equal bargaining power. Nevertheless, it is conceivable that some other jurisdictions might not want to relinquish the action to the forum chosen. This is conceivable for some jurisdictions within the United States, and also for foreign jurisdictions, where courts might be reluctant to send their own aggrieved citizens to the U.S.

* * *

NOTES & QUESTIONS

1. *Liability for software developers?* The above excerpt does not address whether companies that sell software that permits DDoS attacks, such as operating system software, should be held liable to those injured by the attacks. Should they?

2. *Standard of care.* In another part of this paper, Professor Radin notes that the legal standard of care depends upon the state of the art of preventive technologies and practices. How well do you think courts can implement the standard of care in this area?

3. *Blaming the victim?* Non-lawyers often are surprised by the possibility of suits against commercial sites that are felled by attackers, because this seems like blaming the victim. How would you answer them?

CHAPTER FIFTEEN

Alternative Resolution of Online Disputes

When people engage in commercial interactions, disputes arise. This is no less true for online commercial interactions than it is for commerce conducted through other means of communication. There are disputes about performance of contractual obligations, infringement of intellectual property rights, invasion of privacy, and tortious conduct. How are such disputes to be resolved?

The traditional answer is: through law, as applied by judges, facilitated by lawyers who do their work in courthouses and other face-to-face fora. There is reason to doubt, however, that the traditional answer is the best one for resolving many types of disputes arising in offline interactions, and many people believe that judicial processes are even less well adapted to resolving online disputes. Alternative dispute resolution ("ADR") is an umbrella designation for a variety of techniques that aim to resolve disputes through methods other than judicial processes.

While the online medium has called into existence many familiar sorts of disputes, and a few new types, it has also created the potential for new methods of resolving disputes. These new methods, referred to as online dispute resolution ("ODR"), make use of the online medium as a tool to resolve disputes, whether they arise online or offline.

In this chapter we explore the use of various ADR techniques to resolve online disputes, and the use of ODR more generally. Some questions to keep in mind: Are there differences between online and offline disputes that make ADR more appropriate to the former? Which ADR methods are best suited to particular types of online disputes? Why have ODR efforts borne so little fruit, and what are the prospects for greater success from these techniques?

I. Introduction

A. Background on Alternative Dispute Resolution

The two most common forms of ADR are arbitration and mediation. In arbitration, the parties agree contractually to submit their dispute to a neutral decisionmaker, the arbitrator. In binding arbitration, the parties agree to be bound by the arbitrator's decision. In non-binding arbitration, the arbitrator's decision is advisory, presenting an outcome that the arbitrator considers a fair one, and a suggestion of how a court might rule if the dispute were litigated. A nonbinding arbitration reveals to the parties the strengths and weaknesses of each other's positions, and may incline them toward a negotiated settlement.

An arbitration proceeding typically resembles a simplified version of a trial. The arbitrator sits as a judge, hears testimony, considers the parties' legal arguments, and renders a decision, referred to as an award. Unlike a judge, an arbitrator is not a representative of the state, but rather a private individual who is paid for his time. A number of service providers are in the business of supplying arbitrators and providing administrative services to facilitate arbitrations. Among the most prominent of these are the American Arbitration Association, the CPR Institute, and the National Arbitration Forum. Arbitration is used extensively to resolve labor disputes, to resolve disputes between investors and stockbrokers, to resolve salary issues in professional sports, and in other industries.

Arbitration is a creature of contract. Parties to a transaction can agree to the use of arbitration to resolve any dispute that might arise in connection with the transaction by including an arbitration clause in the contract that defines their relationship. These clauses are common in standardized, boilerplate contracts governing business-to-consumer commercial transactions, and many negotiated business-to-business contracts also contain them. If the parties have not selected arbitration at the initiation of their relationship, they may do so at the time a dispute arises by entering an agreement to arbitrate.

Although courts were once hostile to arbitration, on the ground that it ousted them of jurisdiction, *see Kulukundis Shipping Co., S/A v. Amtorg Trading Corp.*, 126 F.2d 978 (2d Cir.1942), that hostility has been overcome by state and federal enactments that look favorably on arbitration.[1] The first such enactment was the New York Arbitration Act, in 1920. The Federal Arbitration Act was enacted in 1925, and nearly all the states now have modern arbitration statutes, many of them based on the Uniform Arbitration Act of 1955. These acts generally make agreements to arbitrate enforceable, and limit the authority of courts to review arbitral awards.

Thus, the Federal Arbitration Act makes agreements to arbitrate "valid, irrevocable, and enforceable, save upon such grounds as exist at law or in equity for the revocation of any contract." 9 U.S.C. § 2. This rule of enforceability preempts any state requirement to the contrary. *See Southland Corp. v. Keating*, 465 U.S. 1 (1984) (enforcing agreement to arbitrate a claim, despite state law requiring such claims to be resolved judicially). In the context of e-commerce, the European Union's Directive on Electronic Commerce likewise expresses a policy of support for ADR, stating: "Member States shall ensure that, in the event of disagreement between an

1. This modern attitude reinstates the older view that one should "prefer arbitration to the law court, for the arbitrator keeps equity in view, whereas the dicast [i.e., judge] looks only to the law, and the reason why arbitrators were appointed was that equity might prevail." ARISTOTLE, RHETORIC, Bk. 1, Ch. 13, 1374b (J.H. Freese trans., London, William Heinemann Ltd. 1926).

information society service provider and the recipient of the service, their legislation does not hamper the use of out-of-court schemes, available under national law, for dispute settlement, including appropriate electronic means." Directive 2000/31/EC of the European Parliament and of the Council of 8 June 2000 on certain legal aspects of information society services, in particular electronic commerce, in the Internal Market, art. 17(1), 2000 O.J. (L 178) 1, europa.eu.int/ISPO/ecommerce/legal/documents/2000_31ec/2000_31ec_en.pdf.

The state and federal arbitration statutes also provide for enforcement of arbitral awards. The party seeking enforcement applies to a court for confirmation of the award. Once confirmed, the award is transformed into a judgment, which may be enforced through standard judicial methods. Arbitral awards may also be enforced internationally, under the terms of the New York Convention, which (subject to certain defenses) generally requires signatory countries to enforce arbitration awards that are rendered in other signatory countries. *See* Convention on the Recognition and Enforcement of Foreign Arbitral Awards, June 10, 1958, 21 U.S.T. 2517, 330 U.N.T.S. 38. The United States and more than 140 other countries are signatories to this treaty.

In addition, Congress has announced a national policy favoring use of ADR methods to resolve cases that are filed as civil actions in federal district court. The Alternative Dispute Resolution Act of 1998, 28 U.S.C. §§ 651–58, requires district courts to authorize the use of ADR in all civil actions. ADR is defined in this statute as including "any process or procedure, other than an adjudication by a presiding judge, in which a neutral third party participates to assist in the resolution of issues in controversy, through processes such as early neutral evaluation, mediation, minitrial, and arbitration." 28 U.S.C. § 651(a). The district courts must require litigants to consider the use of an ADR process. If the parties consent, the court may refer a civil action to nonbinding arbitration. After an arbitral award is issued, each party has 30 days to request a trial de novo. Otherwise, the award is entered as a judgment, and has the same force and effect as any other judgment, except that it is not subject to review. *See* 28 U.S.C. §§ 652 & 657.

A mediator is a neutral third party who assists disputants in negotiating a settlement of their dispute. The activities of a mediator typically involve listening to the position of each party, which may be conveyed in the presence of the opposing party or confidentially to the mediator, encouraging parties to recognize the weaknesses of their position and to abandon unrealistic expectations, formulating settlement options for the parties' consideration, summarizing each party's position and argument, and translating the parties' statements of their positions into more helpful statements of their interests. Mediation sessions frequently shift between joint sessions and individual caucuses involving the mediator and one of the parties.

A less formal version of mediation is referred to as conciliation. Like mediation, conciliation involves a neutral third party who assists the parties in arriving at a resolution, but the conciliator's role may be limited to collecting information from the parties and passing communications back and forth between them.

The main advantages typically ascribed to ADR are that it is faster and less expensive than judicial processes. Courts often have a backlog of cases that may be months or even years in duration. Arbitration and mediation can usually be initiated much more quickly. Because of the flexibility that arbitrators have in structuring proceedings, and their less formal nature, arbitration proceedings can be conducted more expeditiously than trials. This is not inevitably the case, however, and complicated arbitrations can, like complicated trials, run for months. A skilled mediator and motivated parties can also reach a resolution in much less time than it takes to conduct a trial. Like non-binding arbitration, however, an unsuccessful mediation can consume time without yielding a resolution.

To the extent that arbitration and mediation are faster than judicial processes, they will also tend to be less expensive, since less counsel time will be required. Because of the lesser formality of these procedures, the parties may elect to forgo legal counsel altogether, with attendant cost savings. But ADR neutrals generally do not work for free; the parties must pay them for their time. This can be a significant additional expense that is not incurred by parties to traditional judicial proceedings.

There are several other aspects of binding arbitration that some parties may consider disadvantageous. It can be difficult to know in advance whether the arbitrator is truly neutral; for example, some arbitrators are drawn from the ranks of retired industry executives. Barring unusual circumstances there is no appeal from a binding arbitral decision, so the parties are stuck with the arbitrator's view of the facts and the law. Arbitral awards have no precedential value, which makes them less useful than judicial decisions from the standpoint of institutional parties that have an interest in reliable precedent.

B. ONLINE DISPUTE RESOLUTION; COMPUTER-ASSISTED DISPUTE RESOLUTION

Online dispute resolution ("ODR") is the use of online communication technologies in the resolution of disputes. ODR techniques enable dispute resolution to proceed without assembling the parties and facilitator at a single location. ODR techniques range from mediation in which the mediator communicates with the parties via e-mail, online chat, or bulletin board postings, to using electronic self-help over the Internet to disable software that is running on a remote computer system.

Computer-assisted dispute resolution ("CADR") uses software to help parties resolve their disputes. For example, a negotiation algorithm implemented through software can assist parties in negotiating a mutually acceptable settlement. Computer-assisted dispute resolution is generally designed to operate remotely, via the network, as a form of ODR.

It will be useful to distinguish clearly between ADR, ODR, and CADR, and to understand their applicability to disputes arising from online commerce. ADR refers to any method of dispute resolution that does not use traditional judicial methods. ADR may be implemented through the use of ODR or CADR, but need not be: an arbitration that is conducted with all parties and the arbitrator present at a particular location is ADR, but not ODR or CADR. ODR is a technique that is typically used to facilitate an ADR or CADR method, by allowing dispute resolution to take place with the parties located at a distance from each other. ODR might also serve as a component of traditional adjudication, such as by allowing testimony to be gathered or presented at a distance. CADR is a type of ADR that is particularly well suited to play a role in ODR.

It is also important to recognize that none of these techniques is limited to the resolution of disputes engendered online. ADR has probably always existed in some form or another, and certainly predates the existence of courts. ADR is widely hailed as a necessary concomitant to online commerce, but at present, with a few exceptions (notably domain name disputes), ADR is no more prevalent in resolving online transactions than in resolving disputes arising from any other type of distance contracting. ODR has been used experimentally in efforts to resolve online disputes, but its most successful application to date has been in settling ordinary disputes over insurance claims. The same is true of CADR.

C. ALTERNATIVE DISPUTE RESOLUTION AND ELECTRONIC COMMERCE

There are several reasons why ADR may be thought to be particularly important to online commerce.

First, most online transactions are between parties who are located at some geographical distance from each other. Traditional judicial approaches to resolving disputes, which require the parties to appear before a decision-maker, entail travel expenses that make such approaches economically infeasible in the case of typical low-value consumer transactions. This consideration is, of course, equally applicable to distance transactions carried out through other means of communication, such as telemarketing, catalog sales, or direct mail.

Second, online commerce offers the potential for greatly increasing the volume of international business-to-consumer ("B2C") transactions. Traditional judicial approaches are especially ill-suited to resolving cross-border disputes. In addition to prohibitive travel costs, there are great uncertainties and difficulties involved in asserting jurisdiction over a party located outside the country in which the court is located, determining the applicable law, and enforcing judgments against parties located outside the jurisdiction. The need to deal with an unfamiliar legal system in what may be an unfamiliar language adds to the costs. At present, this consideration is of little practical concern, since international B2C transactions represent a very small proportion of online commerce. Yet perhaps the unresolved questions about enforcement are part of what is keeping the proportion small.

Third, those who engage in electronic commerce may be more open to non-traditional methods of dispute resolution, since after all they are engaging in a non-traditional mode of commerce. Their use of online communications makes it likely that they will be comfortable with engaging in dispute resolution at a distance, via ODR.

Fourth, many consumers are hesitant to engage in online commerce because they are unfamiliar with the vendor and view online transactions as risky. This is especially likely with online auctions, where the seller is typically an individual with no institutional interest in protecting his reputation. The availability of ADR may help consumers overcome this hesitation.

We must be careful to distinguish among different categories of online disputes, since some will be more susceptible than others to resolution via ADR, and a particular method of ADR may work better with one category of dispute than with another. For example, if a dispute arises in the course of a commercial transaction that the parties have entered voluntarily, arbitration or some other form of ADR can be specified in the contract before any dispute arises. But if there is no prior relationship between the parties, then ADR is available only if the parties agree, after the dispute arises, to submit to dispute resolution. At this point, the party complained against will have an incentive not to agree to ADR, knowing that if traditional adjudication is the complainant's only option she is less likely to proceed. Yet a firm might prefer ADR to the risk of a class action brought by a determined consumer. ADR also has a better chance of succeeding if it is imposed by a third party, such as a payment intermediary or domain name authority. A party that has an interest in maintaining a good reputation will be more likely to submit to ADR than one who is in the business of fraud or who engages in a single transaction.

NOTES & QUESTIONS

ADR coming into its own online? Do you think that ADR is more needed, or more likely to be successful, in the context of disputes arising in online commerce than it is in the case of other distance-selling techniques, such as telemarketing, direct mail, and catalog sales? What about ODR?

II. ADR AND ODR IN ELECTRONIC COMMERCE

A. THE NULL OPTION: VOLUNTARY RESOLUTION OF DISPUTES BY THE PARTIES THEMSELVES

The vast majority of disputes that arise in commercial transactions are resolved by the parties themselves, without recourse to any formal dispute-resolution method. Most vendors are concerned about their reputation in the marketplace, and most purchasers are reasonable. Vendors frequently act on the principle that it is in their best interest to keep their customers happy, even if they have a legal right to do otherwise. Most customers are willing to accept a compromise if they feel the vendor is acting fairly.

In addition, most parties are averse to the time, expense, and uncertainties of engaging in dispute resolution procedures that involve a third party. They prefer to resolve their problems expeditiously, giving up the opportunity to do better by fighting longer.

The online medium in some ways interferes with the operation of these incentives to settle. Online communication technologies reduce the capital costs of going into business, making it possible for many small vendors to access a national and even international marketplace. New entrepreneurs and small businesses may not perceive as great an interest in maintaining a good reputation as do the established players, and may not have the financial resources to accept short-term costs in furtherance of long-term reputational interests. A business that is community-based will be well aware that a bad reputation will cause its customers to evaporate, while one with customers that are geographically widely distributed may believe it is less likely that dissatisfied customers will share their experiences with many potential future customers. A vendor that is located at some distance from the purchaser may feel itself insulated from any efforts by the purchaser to seek resolution of a dispute.

1. REPUTATIONAL INCENTIVES

On the other hand, the Internet creates some new avenues through which dissatisfied customers can make their voices heard in a way that affects a vendor's reputation. Internet newsgroups provide a forum where customers can post complaints against companies with which they have had a bad experience. Newsgroup postings are archived and searchable. A prospective customer who wishes to perform due diligence can search for the name of a company—whether the company does business online or offline—or a particular product and find out whether any complaints have been posted.[2] There are message boards that are devoted to particular companies, and attract a range of commentary. For example, Yahoo! maintains a separate message board for each publicly traded company in the United States. *See Yahoo! Message Boards*, messages.yahoo.com/index.html. There are also websites that solicit consumer complaints, and forward them to the complained-against company, giving the company a chance to respond. Here is an example of such an exchange:

2. One such search site is "Google Groups," groups.google.com.

Complaint Information

Complaint ID:	EXAGY012402
Company name:	Netmarket
Problem Type:	Service/Product never provided/delivered
Incident date:	10/28/2000
Complaint Info:	I order a cordless phone. The phone arrived to mailing address very quickly. However, the wrong model number arrived. I had to send it back. I was told I had to order the phone again. I decided to give it another chance. I waited about 8–9 days and the cordless had not arrived. I called NetMarket. They conferenced in UPS. Turns out the phone was sent to a wrong address. The phone was at the UPS depot. UPS would call me so that I could pick it up at the depot. I was willing, just to get this behind me. Next day I called, NetMarket again. The phone had been returned to NetMarket. The customer serv. rep said I would have to re-order the phone a third time. I said just give the credit and I'll buy this at the store. It was an ugly lesson in eCommerce.
Company Response:	Dear Marcos Pilozo: I have received notification from eComplaints.com regarding the problems you experienced in order a 900 MHz telephone from Netmarket. I sincerely apologize for those problems and would like to assure you that this is not the typical manner in which our customer orders are handled. In reviewing your orders it appears that human error was the culprit in both instances: our vendor inadvertantly sent the wrong model on the first order, and when our agent placed the second order for you it looks like the shipping address was entered incorrectly. I realize you now wish to purchase the phone locally, however I would like to offer to order the phone for you again through Netmarket, with a $10.00 discount for your inconvenience. If this acceptable to you please let me know and I will personally process the order to ensure its accuracy. I would ask that you specify the address you would like it shipped to so I can avoid the input error that occurred on the second order. If you do not want to order through us a third time, I certainly understand and I will place a $10.00 coupon in your awards account that you can use on a future Netmarket purchase. I really appreciate your feed-

back on your shopping experience with us and hope you will give us a chance to redeem ourselves. Thanks again, and I look forward to your reply.

Sincerely,

Wayne Harriman
Customer Relations Manager
Netmarket Group, Inc.
(203) 416–2527

eComplaints.com, www.ecomplaints.com/SearchComplaints/SearchingProcess/type_problem.php3?counter=012402 & lim=0 & id_search=587467 & type_search=keywords (spelling and other errors in original).

eBay, the largest online auctioneer, implements a system that enables users to rate their experiences with individual buyers and sellers. The ratings are tabulated to create a "Feedback Profile" for each rated buyer and seller. A prospective buyer or seller may consult an eBay user's Feedback Profile, and may decide to avoid doing business with that user if she has earned a poor rating. *See* eBay, *Feedback Forum*, pages.ebay.com/services/forum/feedback.html.

NOTES & QUESTIONS

BBB compared. The Better Business Bureau has for many years operated a system designed to encourage sellers to be responsive to their customers' complaints through operation of the reputational sanction. A purchaser who is dissatisfied with a company's handling of her issue may file a complaint with the BBB. The complaint is routed to the BBB office in the district where the company is located. The BBB forwards the complaint to the company. If the company is uncooperative, or has generated a pattern of unresolved complaints, the BBB records that experience in its file on the company. A consumer who is considering doing business with the company may check with the appropriate BBB, and find out whether the BBB has any negative record on file. Companies that value their reputations will have an incentive to keep their records with the BBB clean, by being responsive to consumer complaints.

How would you compare the BBB system with the mechanisms that the Internet offers for encouraging sellers to settle disputes voluntarily? Which mechanism do you think gives sellers the strongest incentive to keep their customers happy? How could online mechanisms be made to work more effectively?

2. ASSISTED NEGOTIATION

Some ODR systems are designed to reduce the time and expense involved in negotiation, and to assist the parties in arriving at a settlement that maximizes the parties' welfare. One such system is computerized blind bidding. This system works best in situations where the parties agree that one owes money to the other, but disagree on the amount—such as in the case of insurance claims. In one implementation of this system, the insurance company enters the maximum amount it is willing to pay in each of three rounds of bidding. The claimant likewise enters the minimum amount she will accept in each round. These amounts are not disclosed to the other party. The site's proprietary software then calculates what each party should bid in the first round, to maximize the likelihood of reaching a settlement that is within each party's parameters. If the two bids in a round differ by less than a pre-established percentage, typically 30 percent, the site declares a settlement at a figure that splits the difference. If settlement is not reached after the first round, the software runs through a second and, if necessary, a third round. The claimant pays a fee ranging from $100 to $1,000, depending on the settlement amount, and the insurance company pays a separate fee established by the site. *See* CyberSettle, www.cybersettle.com.

Other assisted negotiation systems are more sophisticated, and are able to handle multi-dimensional issues. With a system called One Accord, www.smartsettle.com/flash.html, the parties begin by working with a facilitator to create a "single negotiating form," which lists all of the elements that must be resolved to arrive at a settlement, with blanks representing the unresolved issues. The parties then individually confide to the software their true preferences. The software uses this information to assign a preference rating to any given settlement package, which enables it to facilitate the negotiation by proposing new settlement packages that are equivalent in the eyes of each party. Once the parties agree tentatively on a settlement package, it is submitted to the software for optimization. With the preference information it has gathered, the software may be able to generate a Pareto-superior revised settlement: one that makes both parties better off.

With SquareTrade, www.squaretrade.com, either buyer or seller initiates the process by filling out a Web-based form, describing the complaint. SquareTrade passes the complaint along to the other party, and the two parties have a chance to negotiate with each other in an effort to resolve the dispute. The service uses technological tools to facilitate the negotiation process, including a "wizard" that suggests alternatives based on the parties' responses to questions.

B. THIRD-PARTY VOLUNTARY APPROACHES

1. ARBITRATION

a. Enforceability of Contractual Arbitration Clauses

When making purchases of ordinary consumer goods, the average consumer concerns herself with only a few key terms: the price, the characteristics of the product or service purchased, and possibly warranty terms. But most consumer transactions are subject to an additional set of contractual terms that few consumers notice unless something goes wrong with the transaction. In electronic commerce transactions, these may take the form of clickwrap terms, which are displayed on the purchaser's monitor during the course of an online purchase, or shrinkwrap terms, which physically accompany a product when it is shipped, and which the purchaser sees for the first time (if at all) on receipt of the shipment. (Shrinkwrap and clickwrap agreements are discussed in Chapter 4, Part I(C), *supra.*)

One of the terms that frequently is included in clickwrap and shrinkwrap contracts is an arbitration clause: a contractual agreement to submit any dispute arising in connection with the transaction for resolution through binding arbitration. Are such clauses enforceable, against a party that wishes to have a dispute resolved in some other forum? As a general matter, the enforceability of an arbitration clause contained in a clickwrap or shrinkwrap agreement is evaluated under the same standards that apply to the other terms of the agreement. But, as in the following case, an arbitration clause may be held unenforceable on grounds that do not apply to other terms of such an agreement.

Brower v. Gateway 2000, Inc.

676 N.Y.S.2d 569 (N.Y.App.Div.1998).

■ MILONAS, JUSTICE PRESIDING.

Appeal from an order of the Supreme Court (Beatrice Shainswit, J.), entered October 21, 1997 in New York County, which, to the extent appealed from, granted defendants' motion to dismiss the complaint on the ground that there was a valid agreement to arbitrate between the parties.

Appellants are among the many consumers who purchased computers and software products from defendant Gateway 2000 through a direct-sales system, by mail or telephone order. As of July 3, 1995, it was Gateway's practice to include with the materials shipped to the purchaser along with the merchandise a copy of its "Standard Terms and Conditions Agreement" and any relevant warranties for the products in the shipment. The Agreement begins with a "NOTE TO CUSTOMER," which provides, in slightly larger print than the remainder of the document, in a box that spans the width of the page: "This document contains Gateway 2000's Standard Terms and Conditions. By keeping your Gateway 2000 computer system beyond thirty (30) days after the date of delivery, you accept these Terms and Conditions." The document consists of 16 paragraphs, and, as is relevant to this appeal, paragraph 10 of the agreement, entitled "DISPUTE RESOLUTION," reads as follows:

> Any dispute or controversy arising out of or relating to this Agreement or its interpretation shall be settled exclusively and finally by arbitration. The arbitration shall be conducted in accordance with the Rules of Conciliation and Arbitration of the International Chamber of Commerce. The arbitration shall be conducted in Chicago, Illinois, U.S.A. before a sole arbitrator. Any award rendered in any such arbitration proceeding shall be final and binding on each of the parties, and judgment may be entered thereon in a court of competent jurisdiction.

Plaintiffs commenced this action on behalf of themselves and others similarly situated for compensatory and punitive damages, alleging deceptive sales practices in seven causes of action, including breach of warranty, breach of contract, fraud and unfair trade practices. In particular, the allegations focused on Gateway's representations and advertising that promised "service when you need it," including around-the-clock free technical support, free software technical support and certain on-site services. According to plaintiffs, not only were they unable to avail themselves of this offer because it was virtually impossible to get through to a technician, but also Gateway continued to advertise this claim notwithstanding numerous complaints and reports about the problem.

Insofar as is relevant to appellants, who purchased their computers after July 3, 1995, Gateway moved to dismiss the complaint based on the arbitration clause in the Agreement. Appellants argued that the arbitration clause is invalid under UCC 2–207, unconscionable under UCC 2–302 and an unenforceable contract of adhesion. Specifically, they claimed that the provision was obscure; that a customer could not reasonably be expected to appreciate or investigate its meaning and effect; that the International Chamber of Commerce ("ICC") was not a forum commonly used for consumer matters; and that because ICC headquarters were in France, it was particularly difficult to locate the organization and its rules. To illustrate just how inaccessible the forum was, appellants advised the court that the ICC was not registered with the Secretary of State, that efforts to locate and contact the ICC had been unsuccessful and that apparently the only way to attempt to contact the ICC was through the United States Council for International Business, with which the ICC maintained some sort of relationship.

In support of their arguments, appellants submitted a copy of the ICC's Rules of Conciliation and Arbitration and contended that the cost of ICC arbitration was prohibitive, particularly given the amount of the typical consumer claim involved. For example, a claim of less than $50,000 required advance fees of $4,000 (more than the cost of most Gateway products), of which the $2000 registration fee was nonrefundable even if the consumer prevailed at the arbitration. Consumers would also incur travel expenses disproportionate to the damages sought, which appellants' counsel estimated would not exceed $1,000 per customer in this action, as well as bear the cost of Gateway's legal fees if the consumer did not prevail at the arbitration; in this respect, the ICC rules follow the "loser pays" rule used in England. Also, although Chicago was designated as the site of the actual arbitration, all correspondence must be sent to ICC headquarters in France.

The IAS court dismissed the complaint as to appellants based on the arbitration clause in the Agreements delivered with their computers. We agree with the court's decision and reasoning in all respects but for the issue of the unconscionability of the designation of the ICC as the arbitration body.

First, the court properly rejected appellants' argument that the arbitration clause was invalid under UCC 2–207. Appellants claim that when they placed their order they did not bargain for, much less accept, arbitration of any dispute, and therefore the arbitration clause in the agreement that accompanied the merchandise shipment was a "material alteration" of a preexisting oral agreement. Under UCC 2–207(2), such a material alteration constitutes "proposals for addition to the contract" that become part of the contract only upon appellants' express acceptance. However, as the court correctly concluded, the clause was not a "material alteration" of an oral agreement, but, rather, simply one provision of the sole contract that existed between the parties. That contract, the court explained, was formed and acceptance was manifested not when the order was placed but only with the retention of the merchandise beyond the 30 days specified in the Agreement enclosed in the shipment of merchandise. Accordingly, the contract was outside the scope of UCC 2–207.

In reaching its conclusion, the IAS court took note of the litigation in Federal courts on this very issue, and, indeed, on this very arbitration clause. In *Hill v. Gateway 2000, Inc.*, 105 F.3d 1147, *cert. denied* 522 U.S. 808, plaintiffs in a class action contested the identical Gateway contract in dispute before us, including the enforceability of the arbitration clause. As that court framed the issue, the "[t]erms inside Gateway's box stand or fall together. If they constitute the parties' contract because the Hills had an opportunity to return the computer after reading them, then all must be enforced" (id. at 1148). The court then concluded that the contract was not formed with the placement of a telephone order or with the delivery of the goods. Instead, an enforceable contract was formed only with the consumer's decision to retain the merchandise beyond the 30–day period specified in the agreement. Thus, the agreement as a whole, including the arbitration clause, was enforceable.

This conclusion was in keeping with the same court's decision in *ProCD, Inc. v. Zeidenberg*, 86 F.3d 1447 * * *.

* * *

Second, with respect to appellants' claim that the arbitration clause is unenforceable as a contract of adhesion, in that it involved no choice or negotiation on the part of the consumer but was a "take it or leave it" proposition (*see, e.g., Matter of State v. Ford Motor Company*, 74 N.Y.2d 495, 503, 549 N.Y.S.2d 368, 548 N.E.2d 906), we find that this argument, too, was properly rejected by the IAS court. Although the parties clearly do not possess equal bargaining power, this factor alone does not invalidate the contract as one of adhesion. * * *

While returning the goods to avoid the formation of the contract entails affirmative action on the part of the consumer, and even some expense, this may be seen as a trade-off for the convenience and savings for which the consumer presumably opted when he or she chose to make a purchase of such consequence by phone or mail as an alternative to on-site retail shopping. That a consumer does not read the agreement or thereafter claims he or she failed to understand or appreciate some term therein does not invalidate the contract any more than such claim would undo a contract formed under other circumstances. * * * We further note that appellants' claim of adhesion is identical to that made and rejected in *Filias v. Gateway 2000, Inc.*, an unreported case brought to our attention by both parties that interprets the same Gateway agreement (No. 97C 2523 [N.D.Ill., January 15, 1998], *transferred by* 1997 U.S. Dist. LEXIS 7115 [E.D.Mich., Apr. 8, 1997, Zatkoff, J.]).

Finally, we turn to appellants' argument that the IAS court should have declared the contract unenforceable, pursuant to UCC 2–302, on the ground that the arbitration clause is unconscionable due to the unduly burdensome procedure and cost for the individual consumer. The IAS court found that while a class-action lawsuit, such as the one herein, may be a less costly alternative to the arbitration (which is generally less costly than litigation), that does not alter the binding effect of the valid arbitration clause contained in the agreement * * *.

As a general matter, under New York law, unconscionability requires a showing that a contract is "both procedurally and substantively unconscionable when made" (*Gillman v. Chase Manhattan Bank*, 73 N.Y.2d 1, 10, 537 N.Y.S.2d 787, 534 N.E.2d 824). That is, there must be "some showing of 'an absence of meaningful choice on the part of one of the parties together with contract terms which are unreasonably favorable to the other party' [citation omitted]" (*Matter of State of New York v. Avco Financial Service*, 50 N.Y.2d 383, 389, 429 N.Y.S.2d 181, 406 N.E.2d 1075). The *Avco* court took pains to note, however, that the purpose of this doctrine is not to redress the inequality between the parties but simply to ensure that the more powerful party cannot "surprise" the other party with some overly oppressive term (*id.*, at 389, 429 N.Y.S.2d 181, 406 N.E.2d 1075).

As to the procedural element, a court will look to the contract formation process to determine if in fact one party lacked any meaningful choice in entering into the contract, taking into consideration such factors as the setting of the transaction, the experience and education of the party claiming unconscionability, whether the contract contained "fine print," whether the seller used "high-pressured tactics" and any disparity in the parties' bargaining power (*Gillman v. Chase Manhattan Bank, supra*, at 11, 537 N.Y.S.2d 787, 534 N.E.2d 824). None of these factors supports appellants' claim here. Any purchaser has 30 days within which to thoroughly examine the contents of their shipment, including the terms of the Agreement, and seek clarification of any term therein (*e.g., Matter of Ball, supra*, at 161, 665 N.Y.S.2d 444). The Agreement itself, which is entitled in large print "STANDARD TERMS AND CONDITIONS AGREEMENT," consists of only three pages and 16 paragraphs, all of which appear in the same size print. Moreover, despite appellants' claims to the contrary, the arbitration clause is in no way "hidden" or "tucked away" within a complex document of inordinate length, nor is the option of returning the merchandise, to avoid the contract, somehow a "precarious" one. We also reject appellants' insinuation that, by using the word "standard," Gateway deliberately meant to convey to the consumer that the terms were standard within the industry, when the document clearly purports to be no more than Gateway's "standard terms and conditions."

With respect to the substantive element, which entails an examination of the substance of the agreement in order to determine whether the terms unreasonably favor one party * * *, we do not find that the possible inconvenience of the chosen site (Chicago) alone rises to the level of unconscionability. We do find, however, that the excessive cost factor that is necessarily entailed in arbitrating before the ICC is unreasonable and surely serves to deter the individual consumer from invoking the process * * *. Barred from resorting to the courts by the arbitration clause in the first instance, the designation of a financially prohibitive forum effectively bars consumers from this forum as well; consumers are thus left with no forum at all in which to resolve a dispute. In this regard, we note that this particular claim is not mentioned in the *Hill* decision, which upheld the clause as part of an enforceable contract.

While it is true that, under New York law, unconscionability is generally predicated on the presence of both the procedural and substantive elements, the substantive element alone may be sufficient to render the terms of the provision at issue unenforceable * * *. Excessive fees, such as those incurred under the ICC procedure, have been grounds for finding an arbitration provision unenforceable or commercially unreasonable * * *.

In the *Filias* case previously mentioned, the Federal District Court stated that it was "inclined to agree" with the argument that selection of the ICC rendered the clause unconscionable, but concluded that the issue was moot because Gateway had agreed to arbitrate before the American Arbitration Association ("AAA") and sought court appointment of the AAA pursuant to Federal Arbitration Act 9 U.S.C. § 5. The court accordingly granted Gateway's motion to compel arbitration and appointed the AAA in lieu of the ICC. Plaintiffs in that action (who are represented by counsel for appellants before us) contend that costs associated with the AAA process are also excessive, given the amount of the individual consumer's damages, and their motion for reconsideration of the court's decision has not yet been decided. While the AAA rules and costs are not part of the record before us, the parties agree that there is a minimum, nonrefundable filing fee of $500, and appellants claim each consumer could spend in excess of $1,000 to arbitrate in this forum.

Gateway's agreement to the substitution of the AAA is not limited to the *Filias* plaintiffs. Gateway's brief includes the text of a new arbitration agreement that it claims has been extended to all customers, past, present and future (apparently through publication in a quarterly magazine sent to anyone who has ever purchased a Gateway product). The new arbitration agreement provides for the consumer's choice of the AAA or the ICC as the arbitral body and the designation of any location for the arbitration by agreement of the parties, which "shall not be unreasonably withheld." It also provides telephone numbers at which the AAA and the ICC may be reached for information regarding the "organizations and their procedures."

As noted, however, appellants complain that the AAA fees are also excessive and thus in no way have they accepted defendant's offer (*see,* UCC 2–209); because they make the same claim as to the AAA as they did with respect to the ICC, the issue of unconscionability is not rendered moot, as defendant suggests. We cannot determine on this record whether the AAA process and costs would be so "egregiously oppressive" that they, too, would be unconscionable * * *. Thus, we modify the order on appeal to the extent of finding that portion of the arbitration provision requiring arbitration before the ICC to be unconscionable and remand to Supreme Court so that the parties have the opportunity to seek appropriate substitution of an arbitrator pursuant to the Federal Arbitration Act (9 U.S.C. § 1 et seq.), which provides for such court designation of an arbitrator upon application of either party, where, for whatever reason, one is not otherwise designated (9 U.S.C. § 5).

Appellants make the final argument that the arbitration clause does not apply to the cause of action for false advertising (with respect to the promised round-the-clock service) under various sections of the General Business Law on the ground that there is no mention of arbitration in the technical service contract itself. Although they raise this claim for the first time on this appeal, we find the promise of technical support to be within the scope of arbitration as it is clearly a "dispute or controversy arising out or relating to [the] Agreement or its interpretation." Put another way, the service contract does not apply to some separate product that could be retained while the computer products—and the accompanying agreement—could be returned.

* * *

NOTES & QUESTIONS

1. *Why litigate?* Why would a disgruntled consumer choose to bring a lawsuit, with its attendant high costs and long delays, rather than allowing the dispute to be decided by an arbitrator?

2. *Tradeoffs and alternatives.* In *Brower*, the court says that the possible expense involved in returning the computer if the consumer does not like the contract terms accompanying it is acceptable "as a trade-off for the convenience and savings for which the consumer presumably opted when he or she chose to make a purchase of such consequence by phone or mail as an alternative to on-site retail shopping." Is the consumer likely to be aware of the existence of this trade-off at the time she makes the purchase? Does it matter whether she is aware of it?

3. *Procedural criterion.* The *Brower* court found that the presentation of the arbitration clause was not procedurally deficient. What standard did it apply in making this determination? Consider the fact that the arbitration clause stated that arbitration would be conducted in Chicago under the rules of the International Chamber of Commerce, but nowhere disclosed that those rules provided that the complainant must pay $4,000 in advance fees, $2,000 of which was nonrefundable even if the complainant prevailed, and that the complainant could be required to pay Gateway's attorney's fees if she lost. Do you agree with the court that Gateway's Standard Terms provided purchasers with the information they required to exercise a "meaningful choice"?

4. *Contrary view.* Other courts have held that the high costs of an arbitration proceeding do not render an arbitration clause unconscionable. *See, e.g., In re RealNetworks, Inc., Privacy Litigation*, 2000 WL 631341 (N.D.Ill. May 8, 2000), excerpted in Chapter 4, Part III, *supra.*

b. Arbitration via ODR

Arbitration has traditionally been a face-to-face, trial-like procedure. Can arbitration be conducted online? The first effort at online arbitration to receive widespread publicity was the Virtual Magistrate Project. The Project had its beginnings in 1995, when a working group conceived what it hoped would be a system for resolving disputes arising from online activities such as "messages, postings, and files allegedly involving copyright or trademark infringement, misappropriation of trade secrets, defamation, fraud, deceptive trade practices, inappropriate (obscene, lewd, or otherwise violative of system rules) materials, invasion of privacy, and other wrongful content." Arbitrations would take place via e-mail. The arbitrator, who would be selected from a pool by the Project's administrator, would normally render a decision within 72 hours. The Project organizers hoped that arbitral awards would be enforced by system operators, who would remove postings or deny online access, and that complaining parties would agree to be bound by the arbitrator's decision. *See* The Virtual Magistrate Project[SM], *Concept Paper* (Jul. 24, 1996), www.vmag.org/docs/concept.html.

Although the Virtual Magistrate Project received a lot of attention, it was not successful in attracting cases. In fact, the Virtual Magistrate decided only a single case: a 1996 complaint by an individual who wanted America Online to remove an advertisement that offered five million e-mail addresses for sale, to be used for sending bulk unsolicited commercial e-mail messages. The Virtual Magistrate ruled in favor of the complainant, determining that AOL should remove the offending item. This case did not do much to prove Virtual Magistrate's concept, as it had several odd features. First, the real party in interest, who posted the advertisement, did not participate. Second, since sending unsolicited commercial e-mail violated AOL's Terms of Service, and is generally regarded by Internet service providers as a scourge, AOL most likely would have been more than happy to remove the posting without the intervention of an arbitrator. Third, it turned out that the advertisement in question was not a bulletin board posting, but was rather an unsolicited commercial e-mail message itself, making it both impossible and unnecessary for AOL to implement the decision. *See* Alejandro E. Almaguer & Roland W. Baggott III, Note & Comment, *Shaping New Legal Frontiers: Dispute Resolution for the Internet*, 13 OHIO ST. J. ON DISP. RESOL. 711, 727–733 (1998).

Another model for conducting online arbitration is operated by iCourthouse. Parties to a dispute first agree contractually to submit their dispute to iCourthouse, and to be bound by the results. Jurors are volunteers, and are selected from a pool consisting of those who register at the site to become iCourthouse members. The jury selection procedure is unusual: "Each party may invite persons to serve as jurors on a case. There is no limit on the number of invitations that can be issued. * * * Persons invited to serve as juror on a case may forward the invitation to others." iCourthouse Rules of Procedure, Rule 6, www.i-courthouse.com/main.taf?area1_id=front&area2_id=rulesofproc. Members may also browse the pending cases and select those on which they wish to serve as jurors. Each party submits evidence and argument via an online "trial book," which is accessible to the other party and the jurors. The jurors can address questions to the parties, and the questions and answers become part of the trial book. Each juror renders a verdict, and if the verdict is in favor of the plaintiff an award of damages. The parties agree beforehand how the verdict will be interpreted: whether the plaintiff prevails with a simple majority vote, or whether a supermajority is required, and whether the award is the median of all the jurors' awards or some other measure. iCourthouse does not charge a fee for its standard online arbitration service.

NOTES & QUESTIONS

1. *Submitting to ADR*. What would motivate a respondent who is charged with some sort of tortious conduct using online communications to submit to an online arbitration system? Are cases involving tortious conduct more or less likely to come before an arbitrator than cases involving breach of contract? How would you characterize the kinds of disputes the Virtual Magistrate Project was designed to resolve?

2. *Enforcement of awards*. How effective is the enforcement mechanism contemplated in the Virtual Magistrate Project?

2. MEDIATION

Online technologies can enable mediation of disputes between parties that are geographically separated, while avoiding the time and expense involved in bringing all the parties together in the same room. Various services offer trained mediators who communicate with the disputants via e-mail, instant messaging, videoconferencing, chat, and bulletin board postings, and technology tools that allow private caucuses as well as plenary conversations. Fee structures vary, and may involve a flat fee, an hourly rate, a percentage of the settlement amount, or some combination.

The Online Ombuds Office, www.ombuds.org, a service of the Center for Information Technology and Dispute Resolution at the University of Massachusetts, operated a month-long pilot project in 1999 to apply online mediation techniques to disputes arising from transactions conducted through eBay, the online auction site. Using e-mail to communicate with the parties, the mediator brought about a successful result in 46% of the 108 completed mediations. The most common complaint, and the one that proved easiest to resolve, was for nondelivery of goods. The project leaders found the absence of face-to-face meetings to be a significant hindrance to mediation, and looked forward to the development of more flexible online communications technologies and videoconferencing to facilitate online mediation. For a discussion of the project, see Ethan Katsh, Janet Rifkin, & Alan Gaitenby, *E-Commerce, E-Disputes, and E-Dispute Resolution: In the Shadow of "Ebay Law,"* 15 OHIO ST. J. ON DISP. RESOL. 705 (2000).

NOTES & QUESTIONS

Telephone mediation. If meeting face-to-face or videoconferencing is not possible, people can still communicate at a distance with telephone conference calls. What are the advantages and disadvantages of online mediation compared with mediation conducted by telephone?

C. THIRD-PARTY STRUCTURAL APPROACHES

In the voluntary approaches to dispute resolution discussed above, the parties themselves decide how to go about resolving their dispute, either through negotiation, submitting the dispute to an arbitrator, or engaging the services of a mediator. The complained-against party (referred to here as the "respondent") generally can decline to engage in such processes, and be subject only to the reputational sanction. A structural approach to dispute resolution, by contrast, is one that the respondent cannot simply ignore, because it is implemented by a third party that has something the respondent wants, and therefore is in a position to impose conditions on the availability of that good.

1. UNIFORM DOMAIN NAME DISPUTE RESOLUTION POLICY

The Uniform Domain Name Dispute Resolution Policy ("UDRP"), promulgated by the Internet Corporation for Assigned Names and Numbers ("ICANN"), discussed in Chapter 3, Part III, *supra*, is a structural approach that is targeted at a narrow but very important range of disputes: claims that a domain name has been registered and is being used in bad faith, in violation of the complainant's trademark rights. Registrants of names in the commercial global top-level domains are subject to the policy whether they like it or not, because ICANN requires all registrars to impose it contractually as a condition of registering a domain name.

> Every domain name registrar accredited by ICANN must incorporate the UDRP into each individual domain name registration agreement. *See* UDRP, § 1. In effect, the UDRP binds registrants by virtue of their contracts with registrars, such as Network Solutions, Inc., "to submit" to "mandatory administrative proceedings" initiated by third-party "complainants." UDRP, § 4. The scope of such UDRP proceedings is limited to claims of "abusive" registrations of Internet domain names. The UDRP covers no other disputes. UDRP, § 5. Complainants in UDRP proceedings must prove that the disputed "domain name is identi-

> cal or confusingly similar to a trademark or service mark in which the complainant has rights," that the registrant has "no rights or legitimate interests in respect of the domain name," and that the domain name "has been registered and is being used in bad faith." UDRP, § 4(a). The UDRP identifies badges of "bad faith" and grounds for demonstrating a registrant's "rights and legitimate interests" in a domain name. UDRP, § 4(b)–(c).
>
> Complainants initiate UDRP proceedings directly with a dispute resolution service "provider" designated by ICANN.[3] *See* UDRP Rules, § 3. The UDRP and the UDRP Rules prescribe detailed procedures for appointing either a solo arbitrator or a three-member panel to conduct the inquiry. The UDRP is fashioned as an "online" procedure administered via the Internet.[4] Although a panel may opt in exceptional cases to hold live or telephonic hearings, it is expected to base its decision on "the statements and documents submitted" in accordance with the UDRP, the UDRP Rules, and any "rules and principles of law that it deems applicable." UDRP Rules, §§ 13, 15(a). In the absence of "exceptional circumstances," a panel is expected to issue its decision within fourteen days of its appointment. UDRP Rules, § 15(b).
>
> If the panel rules in the complainant's favor, the only available remedy is for the registrar to cancel the domain name registration or transfer it to the complainant. UDRP, § 4(i). A registrar may automatically implement a UDRP panel decision after ten days unless the aggrieved registrant notifies the registrar within this ten day period that it has "commenced a lawsuit against the complainant in a jurisdiction to which the complainant has submitted" as required by the UDRP Rules. *See* UDRP, § 4(k); UDRP Rules, § 5(e). Upon such notification, the registrar "will take no further action" until it receives "satisfactory" evidence of the resolution of the dispute, the dismissal or withdrawal of the lawsuit, or a court order that the registrant does "not have the right to continue using" the domain name. UDRP, § 4(k).

Parisi v. Netlearning, Inc., 139 F.Supp.2d 745, 747–48 (E.D.Va.2001).

The Federal Arbitration Act ("FAA") requires a court to enter judgment on an arbitral award, and sharply limits the circumstances under which an award may be vacated or modified. 9 U.S.C. §§ 9–12. In *Parisi v. Netlearning*, *supra*, the court held that the FAA does not prevent the losing

3. [As of this writing, four providers are accredited to handle domain-name disputes: the Asian Domain Name Dispute Resolution Centre, CPR Institute for Dispute Resolution, National Arbitration Forum, and World Intellectual Property Organization. *See* ICANN, *Approved Providers for Uniform Domain-Name Dispute-Resolution Policy*, www.icann .org/dndr/udrp/approved-providers.htm.—Eds.]

4. [In fact, the UDRP requires parties to submit documents both electronically and in hard copy. *See* Rules for Uniform Domain Name Dispute Resolution Policy §§ 3 & 5.—Eds.]

party in a UDRP proceeding from relitigating ownership of the domain name in federal district court under the Anticybersquatting Consumer Protection Act (discussed in Chapter 3, Part II, *supra*). The court reasoned that the UDRP itself contemplates relitigation at the losing party's option, and that the parties to a proceeding have not agreed to entry of judgment on a UDRP award. For an evaluation of the UDRP process, see Laurence R. Helfer & Graeme B. Dinwoodie, *Designing Non-National Systems: The Case of the Uniform Domain Name Dispute Resolution Policy*, 43 WM. & MARY L. REV. 141 (2001), excerpted in Chapter 3, Part III, *supra*.

2. THIRD-PARTY SEAL PROGRAMS

A seal is a distinctive mark, attached to or associated with a product, service, or vendor, that is intended to convey that the item or entity to which it pertains has certain desirable characteristics. As discussed in Chapter 8, Part IV(B), *supra*, seals are used to certify that a website adheres to specified privacy policies. They may also be used to vouch for other aspects of an online seller's performance, such as its customer satisfaction and dispute-resolution policies.

The BBBOnLine Reliability Program makes use of such a seal. The Better Business Bureau licenses its seal to sellers that agree to abide by a set of conditions, which include a system for resolving disputes with consumers. The seller must agree to participate in binding arbitration under the BBB rules of arbitration, if the consumer selects that option, or to participate in a non-binding informal dispute-resolution process. Under the latter, the parties present their positions to a neutral hearing officer, who makes a recommendation on how the dispute should be resolved. Although the recommendation is non-binding, participating sellers must "act in good faith in determining whether, and to what extent, they will comply with the decision." *See* BBBOnLine, *Dispute Resolution*, www.bbbonline.org/reliability/dr.asp. The consumer publication *Which?* (published in England) operates a similar system, called the Web Trader Scheme. Which?Online, *Which? Web Trader Scheme*, www.which.net.

Enforcement of seal programs is considerably less airtight than the UDRP enforcement scheme. If the seal program operator finds that a website licensee has failed to abide by the program requirements, it can require the website to come into compliance, or else lose the right to display the seal. If the website continues to display the seal despite losing its license to do so, the seal owner can proceed against the site with a trademark infringement action, which can be a costly and extended operation.

3. PAYMENT INTERMEDIARIES: CHARGEBACKS

Since cash cannot be transmitted across the network, nearly all sellers that offer goods online are dependent on some payment intermediary. While individual sellers, such as those who sell through online auctions, frequently are paid with a check sent in the mail, most institutional sellers that transact business online, as well as via telemarketing or otherwise at a distance, are highly dependent on credit cards. (For a discussion of methods of paying for transactions in Internet commerce, see Chapter 16, *infra.*)

Federal law gives credit card holders the right to dispute charges that appear on their bill, and prescribes a procedure that the card issuer must follow. The purchaser initiates the process by submitting a written complaint to the issuer, which must acknowledge the complaint in writing within 30 days after receiving it. The issuer then has two billing cycles, up to a maximum of 90 days, in which to conduct an investigation and resolve the dispute. The issuer normally does so by contacting the merchant that put through the charge, and asking for justification for the charge. For example, if the purchaser claims that an item she ordered was not delivered, the issuer may ask the merchant for evidence such as a signed delivery receipt obtained by United Parcel Service or FedEx. If the issuer finds that the purchaser's complaint is valid, it must remove the charge. Complaints within the scope of this dispute-resolution procedure include claims that a charge appearing on the bill was not authorized; a charge was authorized but the amount of the charge is wrong; a charge is for goods or services that the purchaser did not accept, or were not delivered as agreed; and math errors. *See* Fair Credit Billing Act, 15 U.S.C. § 1666; Regulation Z, 12 C.F.R. § 226.13.

Some credit card networks provide more protection to purchasers than required by the legal rules applying to disputed charges. The major U.S. credit card networks apply U.S. chargeback rules to international transactions, though they are not legally required to do so. One credit card company also has special policies applying to online sales. For goods that are to be delivered physically to the recipient's address, the company will charge back the purchase if the goods are not signed for as received by the cardmember or an authorized representative. For goods to be delivered electronically, it will charge back the purchase automatically upon complaint by the recipient, without even allowing the merchant to present its side of the story.

NOTES & QUESTIONS

Extent of chargebacks. Why would credit card networks extend chargeback rights beyond the requirements of law? Why would a credit card company decide to be especially pro-consumer in handling of chargebacks arising from online sales?

4. MERCHANT AGGREGATORS (ONLINE MALLS)

Some websites serve as a portal to a group of unaffiliated merchants. These portals may provide a variety of services that participating merchants find valuable, such as bringing prospective customers to the merchant sites, operating a payment mechanism, performing other order-processing chores, and providing merchants with a strong brand identification. Such a portal may have enough to offer participating merchants that it can impose conditions on them, including dispute-handling procedures.

America Online, which among many other roles acts as a portal to numerous online merchants, operates a dispute-resolution program on this model, which it calls the Certified Merchant Program. Merchants that choose to participate in the program receive certain benefits from AOL, including promotional placement and the right to display the Certified Merchant Seal. Participating merchants must agree to abide by AOL's standards of conduct, which are designed to minimize the likelihood that a dispute will arise, and to bring about a satisfactory conclusion in case there is a dispute. For example, merchants must post their customer service policies, process orders promptly, notify customers if an item is back-ordered, ship the exact product ordered, respond to customer service inquiries within one business day, and follow fair, ethical and responsible online marketing practices. AOL offers customers this guarantee: "If we are unable to satisfactorily resolve your issue with the merchant, we will refund your purchase price 100% (including shipping/handling and taxes up to a maximum of $10,000) ourselves." America Online, *Certified Merchant Program 100% Guarantee of Satisfaction*, webcenter.shop.aol.com/shopping-help/promise/guarantee.adp.

NOTES & QUESTIONS

Scope of the guarantee. How useful is AOL's guarantee? What types of disputes does it cover? What types of disputes might arise that could not be resolved by return of the purchase price?

D. UNILATERAL APPROACHES

Under the approaches discussed above, the parties to a dispute seek to resolve it either through direct communication with each other or with the involvement of a mediator or arbitrator. There are other approaches through which a dissatisfied party may, without any consultation with the other party, achieve the desired remedy through her own efforts.

1. ELECTRONIC SELF-HELP

A software or data vendor may be in a position to implement electronic self-help in case of a dispute with the purchaser. Self-help in this context involves reaching across the network to disable software residing on the purchaser's computer, or cutting off the purchaser's access to data located on the vendor's server. For a more detailed discussion of electronic self-help in the context of the Uniform Computer Information Transactions Act ("UCITA"), see Chapter 6, Part IV, *supra*.

Unlike negotiation and mediation, the vendor need not consult with the purchaser before taking this action, and unlike arbitration she needs no assistance or coercive authority from any third party. The status of electronic self-help under current law is not entirely clear, but it may well be permissible as long as the contract governing the sales transaction provides for it. UCITA explicitly authorizes self-help, but requires that the purchaser "separately manifest assent to a term [of the sales contract or license] authorizing use of electronic self-help," prescribes procedures that the vendor must follow when implementing self-help, and limits the circumstances in which it may be used. UCITA § 816.

2. DMCA NOTICE-AND-TAKEDOWN PROVISION

Title II of the Digital Millennium Copyright Act, 17 U.S.C. § 512, creates a notice-and-takedown regime that gives copyright owners a broad authority to resolve unilaterally disputes about whether materials made available online infringe their copyrights. Under this regime, the copyright owner sends a notice to an Internet service provider, stating that specified materials made available through the ISP's facilities infringe the copyright, and demanding that they be removed. If the ISP complies, it is insulated from monetary liability for infringement. If the ISP does not comply, then it may be liable for infringement. Since the ISP is unlikely to have a vested interest in keeping the challenged content available, it has a strong incentive to take down the challenged material. For a more detailed discussion of Section 512, see Chapter 9, Part V, *supra*.

NOTES & QUESTIONS

1. *Consumer-to-consumer transactions*. In certain types of online commercial transactions, including most prominently sales through online auction sites, both parties are typically individuals. This scenario is less often seen in distance transactions accomplished through other means of communication, where normally the seller is a business entity. When both parties to a transaction are individuals, they are less likely to have agreed in advance of the transaction to use an ADR mechanism for resolving any disputes. What mechanisms might be available for implementing ADR to resolve disputes in this context?

2. *Who bears the costs?* All forms of ADR entail some cost. Some procedures require the involvement of third parties who charge a fee for their services: mediators, arbitrators, and online dispute resolution services.[5] The allocation of these fees between the disputants may be determined by the terms of an arbitration clause, the rules of the arbitration provider specified in the arbitration clause, or a post-transaction agreement between the parties. For example, the Commercial Arbitration Rules of the American Arbitration Association provide: "The expenses of witnesses for either side shall be paid by the party producing such witnesses. All other expenses of

5. The parties may incur additional costs, such as their own time, counsel fees, and travel and witness costs. These costs may be substantial in comparison with the costs of the third-party facilitator. The potential cost-effectiveness of ADR, in comparison with judicial processes, comes largely from the possibility of doing without counsel, or at least reducing the cost of counsel as a result of simplified procedures. ODR also offers a chance to eliminate travel costs.

the arbitration, including required travel and other expenses of the arbitrator, AAA representatives, and any witness and the cost of any proof produced at the direct request of the arbitrator, shall be borne equally by the parties, unless they agree otherwise or unless the arbitrator in the award assesses such expenses or any part thereof against any specified party or parties." American Arbitration Association, *Commercial Dispute Resolution Procedures*, R–52, www.adr.org. The Uniform Domain Name Dispute Resolution Policy, on the other hand, specifies that the complaining party pays the arbitrator's fee, unless the respondent demands a three-arbitrator panel, in which case the parties split the fees. ICANN, *Uniform Domain Name Dispute Resolution Policy* § 4(g), www.icann.org/dndr/udrp/policy.htm.

Some ADR procedures spread their costs throughout the system, rather than charging an incremental fee to parties that invoke the procedure. For example, a credit card holder pays no incremental fee to invoke a chargeback. The costs of administering the chargeback system are borne by the card issuers, who may pass those costs on to merchants in the form of higher fees. Depending on market conditions, merchants may in turn pass the costs on to consumers, in the form of higher prices for the goods they sell.[6] The resulting cost-spreading is a form of insurance: everybody pays a little bit more for the right to access the chargeback system, regardless of whether they actually use it.

Similarly, seal programs and merchant aggregator programs place the costs on all participating merchants. This type of cost-spreading yields a net gain, on the assumption that the aggregate cost to the system is less than the aggregate benefits resulting from increased consumer confidence, which leads to a broader marketplace and easier entrance for new market participants.

What are the pros and cons of insurance-type cost-spreading systems for financing dispute resolution, and pay-per-use systems?

3. *The perils of privatization.* One commentator observes that all may not be well in ADR-land, pointing out some potential problems with privatized methods of dispute resolution:

> If left unchecked, these privatized systems and their probable technological extensions will have several consequences for the power of courts as institutions and for due process to litigants. First, they result in privatized justice. These processes take place independently, with little or no participation or sanction from government actors. Rather, private or even automated decision makers have sole power to control the rights of the parties. Second, the processes shift procedural advantage to certain powerful players. Rules can be designed to promote desired outcomes. Interim relief can be obtained without the need to prove irreparable injury or probable success on the merits and without a balanc-

6. Merchants must also absorb the costs of reversing transactions and refunding the purchase price in cases where the chargeback is sustained.

> ing of interests. Third, the mechanisms do not protect certain traditional components of due process in dispute resolution. Aspects of litigation such as affordable access to justice, notice, discovery, collective action, live hearings, confrontation of witnesses, a neutral decision maker, and a transparent process may be absent from these privatized processes. Fourth, by eliminating the courts as the arbiters of disputes, these processes decrease the power of government to shape and enforce substantive law. The "law" becomes what is specified in the contract or programmed into the software, and courts lose the ability to enforce mandatory rules and to subject contractual "law" to the needs of public policy. These privatized systems can result in granting trademark owners protection they would not be granted under trademark law, copyright owners rights to prevent or license publications that they could not control under copyright law, and sellers rights to impose terms they could not impose under commercial law. They need not include public interests, such as free speech, an intellectual commons, and consumer protection, that real world governments balance against private property rights.

Elizabeth G. Thornburg, *Going Private: Technology, Due Process, and Internet Dispute Resolution*, 34 U.C. DAVIS L. REV. 151, 154 (2000). Do these considerations call into question the widely accepted policy in favor of promoting ADR to settle disputes?

CHAPTER SIXTEEN

ELECTRONIC PAYMENT SYSTEMS

Every commercial transaction, whether conducted online or in the brick-and-mortar world, involves an exchange of value for some good or service. The presentation of this value to the seller is called a payment, which may be defined as " '(1) a delivery, (2) by the debtor, or his representative, (3) to the creditor or his representative, (4) of money or something accepted by the creditor as the equivalent thereof, (5) with the intention on the part of the debtor to pay the debt in whole or in part, and (6) accepted as payment by the creditor.' " *Sizemore v. E. T. Barwick Industries, Inc.*, 465 S.W.2d 873, 875 (Tenn.1971) (quoting *Sullivan v. Tigert*, 1 Tenn.App. 262 (1925)).

While cash and checks are popular methods of payment in physical point-of-sale transactions, neither is optimal for use in Internet commerce. Payment by these methods requires physical transfer of the medium of payment (banknotes or paper checks) by postal mail or some other conveyance, which cannot take place instantaneously. The delay entailed by this physical transfer, and possibly an additional delay if the seller is unwilling to ship the purchase until the check clears, would be intolerable for most types of consumer purchases in Internet commerce. In addition, it is risky to send currency by mail. While new mechanisms for making online payments have been developed, these mechanisms have not yet had a significant impact in the online marketplace—other than in the narrow, but important, area of online auctions. As a result, the payment methods most commonly used in online consumer transactions are the familiar credit and debit cards.

The use of electronic payment methods in consumer transactions is steadily increasing both here and abroad. The causes of this increase include the "development of interoperability standards among different card networks" as well as new network arrangements that "have enabled providers to share the initial costs of payment card infrastructures and given them a platform for developing new procedures and instruments." COMMITTEE ON PAYMENT AND SETTLEMENT SYSTEMS, RETAIL PAYMENTS IN SELECTED COUNTRIES: A COMPARATIVE STUDY § 4.3 (1999). An example of the latter is the use of the Automated Teller Machine ("ATM") network to process payments made by swiping a debit card through a point-of-sale card reader terminal.

In this chapter, we will survey the principal existing and emerging electronic payment systems that may be used to effect payment over the Internet. After presenting background information on money and payment systems, we continue with a discussion of the more familiar electronic payment methods, namely credit and debit cards. We then proceed to a discussion of emerging payment mechanisms, including person-to-person systems, escrow services, micropayments, stored-value cards, electronic checks, and billing to another account.

I. BACKGROUND: OUR CURRENT MONETARY SYSTEM AND THE DEVELOPMENT OF ELECTRONIC MONEY

David D. Friedman & Kerry L. Macintosh, *The Cash of the Twenty–First Century*

17 SANTA CLARA COMPUTER & HIGH TECH. L.J. 273 (2001).

I. Introduction

We live in a world of monopoly monies—in two senses. First, most trade takes place between people who are physically close to each other; thus, money is usually a geographic monopoly. Second, nations have found it profitable to seize control over the money presses. As a result, governments are the primary issuers of money. The end result is familiar to us all: Americans use dollars, Japanese use yen, the British use pounds and so forth.

As we move into the twenty-first century, on-line commerce and electronic money will grow in importance. These and other technological developments will undermine money monopolies and increase the likelihood that systems of competing monies—both public and private—will emerge.

* * *

II. The Functions of Money

Money serves three basic functions: medium of exchange, unit of account and store of value.

Consider first the primary function of money—as a medium of exchange—a way of avoiding the problems of barter. Suppose a contractor who builds houses wants to buy food. In a world without money, he must find someone who wants a house and has food—a lot of food, perhaps a year's worth or more—to offer in exchange. If a law professor wants a car, she must find someone who wants to learn law and has a car to give in exchange. This double coincidence problem—the problem of finding someone who has what you want, and wants what you have—makes barter a clumsy form of trade, especially in a complicated society with a wide variety of goods and services.

Money solves the double coincidence problem because it is a single good that everyone will accept in exchange for goods or services. Thus, a contractor or law professor can sell services to one person and use the money to buy food or a car from someone else.

* * *

The second function of money is as a unit of account, a way of stating and comparing prices and values. Here again, monopoly monies have had an advantage until now, since it is easier to compare the prices charged by alternative sellers if they are all expressed in the same units. For example, there is some evidence that the introduction of the Euro is reducing price variance across European markets by making comparison-shopping easier between sellers located in different countries.

* * *

Money's third and final function is as a store of value. Few people in a modern society hold very much of their wealth as currency since other financial assets pay interest and currency does not. However, in order to use money as a medium of exchange, we must hold some. Moreover, many other financial assets we hold are debts (e.g., bank accounts, or promissory notes) that can be repaid with money. If debtors repay us with devalued currency, our wealth is diminished.

* * *

IV. Electronic Money and On-line Commerce

Making payments by physically transferring objects, whether gold coins or paper currency, works reasonably well in the physical world, but it encounters serious problems in on-line commerce. There is no practical way to pass a twenty-dollar bill through a modem. Instead, we must transact using intangible claims to payment.

Credit cards allow us to do this. Unfortunately, credit cards pose certain disadvantages for sellers and buyers alike. On every transaction, sellers must pay percentage fees that erode their profit margins. Sellers also face the risk that buyers may attempt to reverse charges after receiving goods or services. Meanwhile, buyers who transmit credit card numbers on-line risk capture of information by interlopers. Even though federal law strictly caps liability for unauthorized charges, a stolen number can give a criminal the foothold he or she needs to commit identity theft. Finally, and perhaps most significantly, credit card transactions leave a paper trail that can result in a loss of privacy for sellers or buyers.

Electronic money can provide the on-line economy with an alternative payment system. A government—or a private company—can issue coins or notes in the form of electronic information. Each coin or note represents a claim against the issuer and can be redeemed in exchange for traditional money (e.g., dollars), commodities (e.g., gold) or any other agreed item of value.

Since electronic money is just information, geographical constraints become irrelevant. It is just as easy to transmit electronic cash to someone on the other side of the world as to someone next door. Moreover, once electronic money is loaded onto the computer chips embedded in "smart" cards, it can be used in real as well as virtual space.

In a world of electronic money, sellers need not fear that buyers might reverse credit card charges after goods have been shipped or services received. Providers of online services can charge for access as it occurs, using automated transaction systems. Buyers can trade free of the worry that credit card numbers may be stolen.

Moreover, unlike credit cards, which leave a paper trail, electronic money can be designed to provide traders with the anonymity they crave. Imagine an electronic currency that is encrypted so securely that the parties—seller, buyer and issuer—cannot identify each other. Such fully anonymous electronic cash surpasses the privacy obtained with paper bills since a properly designed set of encryption protocols do not allow the equivalent of serial number tracing.

Given the advantages, it seems likely that one or more electronic currencies will come into use for online transactions, and having done so, will also become available for real space transactions through payment technologies such as smart cards. But will the currencies be monopolies? And if so, within what boundaries? Will the issuers of the currencies be governments or is the time ripe for private companies to enter the money business?

V. How Will Technology Affect Money?

The answers to these questions depend on technology. To explain why, we discuss four factors: (1) the Internet and online commerce; (2) computers that can perform complex calculations; (3) electronic currency that is easy to create, manage and redeem and, (4) increased bandwidth leading to real-time audio and video. Each factor will play a role in determining the future of money.

The Internet makes on-line commerce possible and on-line commerce makes it easy to trade with people who are far away. As a result, geography and nationality are becoming less important to trade and traders.

As discussed above, our current system of monopoly monies is based on the premise that most trade takes place within geographic and national boundaries. On-line commerce attacks that premise at its core. Americans trade, not necessarily with other Americans, but with the Japanese, who, in turn, trade with the British and so forth.

Providing electronic money for the on-line environment is a challenge. What medium of exchange will be widely accepted within a global trading community? What unit of account will allow global traders to compare prices with ease and confidence?

In the absence of effective world government, it is hard to imagine who might issue a global monopoly money. The European Union encountered substantial economic and political difficulties in adopting the Euro, even though its member states had similar economies and cultures. Surely, the United Nations could not manage the same feat for the entire world. Many—perhaps most—nations would balk at granting the United Nations the power to fund activities through the (electronic) printing press and inflation.

A different solution seems likely in the short term. Nations are well aware that they earn seigniorage—that is, interest—on coins and paper bills in circulation. Thus, as trade goes electronic, nations will have ample incentive to issue their own monopoly monies in electronic form.

Once the Internet is flooded with alternative national monies, traders may find that exchanging from one to another is inefficient. Over time, they may come to prefer one currency that seems to enjoy the widest acceptance and greatest stability. Eventually, that one currency will emerge as the de facto global monopoly money. For example, dollars may come to dominate on-line commerce just as English has become the language of international trade, travel, journalism and diplomacy.

This development will threaten the seigniorage income and national prestige of other countries. Governments may respond by enacting laws to prevent citizens from using electronic money other than their own. But such restrictions will be difficult to enforce in a world of competing monies and strong encryption.

However, traders from other countries may also resist the electronic dollar. At best, they may view the electronic dollar as an offensive form of cultural imperialism; at worst, they may find themselves powerless to intervene, as the United States uses its currency to advance its own economic and political agenda

To get around such problems, traders may shift to a system of competing currencies based on the same commodity. By providing a common unit of account, such a system may obviate the need for a common medium of exchange. To illustrate, suppose multiple issuers (whether public or private) produce electronic cash using gold as the base commodity. The currency of reliable issuers will exchange at par—one Microsoft gold unit for one Netscape gold unit, for example. The currency of unreliable issuers (those unwilling or unable to redeem their own currency) will trade at a discount. Monies trading at a discount will be less convenient and valuable, and will go out of use rapidly.

Computer technology makes it easier to convert from one unit of account to another. Electronic money is easy to store and transmit, reducing the cost of exchange. These developments will lessen the need for money monopolies, whether public or private.

Thus far, we have assumed that a common medium of exchange and unit of account will tend to be the most efficient form of money for the Internet. In other words, we have assumed money monopolies will continue to exist.

However, another path is possible if computers eliminate or reduce the transaction costs of making conversions among different units of account.

Consider how a currency-transparent browser may work in the future. A Japanese seller lists the prices of the goods he sells in yen on his web page. A buyer in the United States accesses the page, seeking information about goods and prices. His browser, noting that the prices are in yen, automatically contacts the website of his bank, checks the current exchange rate and makes the calculation from yen to dollars. In other words, the seller writes his prices in yen, but the buyer reads them in dollars—thus overcoming the unit of account problem.

If our buyer decides to make the purchase, he still must convert his dollars to electronic yen—the requested medium of exchange. His bank will charge for this service. However, since it is relatively easy to store and transmit electronic information, the cost of operating an exchange service for electronic money should be much lower than the cost of running an exchange service for paper money. Presumably, the bank will react by lowering the exchange fee charged to the buyer. A drop in exchange fees may reduce the pressure to use a common medium of exchange.

In this example, both buyer and seller are using government monies. This is the most likely scenario, given that most transactions still take place in real space using paper money. If a consumer has to keep paper dollars in her pocket for everyday purchases, she may be more likely to prefer electronic dollars for on-line purchases.

However, as the years go by, more and more real space transactions will take place using smart cards and other electronic payment systems. This raises the possibility that Americans may one day hold electronic yen for use on-line—and in America.

More radically, * * * [p]rivate companies may begin to issue electronic currencies that are based on different commodity standards. Monies designed for general use will compete directly with each other for market share. Meanwhile, niche currencies will circulate within particular trades. For example, if an on-line community trades primarily in software, it may prefer currency that maintains a stable purchasing power relative to software.

In either case, private companies will obtain a competitive edge by designing their monies for anonymous use. Many traders will prefer currencies that protect against the prying eyes of both private parties and government officials.

* * *

How might governments react to such monetary proliferation? As explained above, some may ban competing monies in an effort to protect seigniorage and sovereignty. Moreover, governments are likely to react badly to anonymous monies that make it harder for them to monitor compliance with tax, immigration, employment or other laws that affect trade. Realistically, however, the very feature that makes such monies threatening—encryption—may make it impossible for governments to enforce the ban.

Technology will create conditions that tend to support monetary stability. First, ease of entry into the business of issuing electronic money will promote a healthy competition. Second, improved communication will make it easier to check the reputation of the issuer. Third, the ability to return electronic money for redemption at the speed of light will reduce the ability of issuers to engage successfully in hyperinflationary schemes. As a result of these technological developments, private monies will become more attractive to the public.

Let's return to the third function of money: a store of value. People prefer monies that are stable. As evidence of this, consider what happens in countries where the official local currency is inflated. Traders begin to use foreign money as their preferred medium of exchange. Efforts to outlaw foreign money are often ineffective and tend to create black markets. In some cases, foreign money emerges as a de facto unit of account. For example, at one time it was common for long-term rentals in Israel to be priced in dollars rather than Israeli pounds.

A common charge leveled against the idea of private monies is that they will not be stable. Private companies will enrich themselves by accepting value from customers and then inflating the money supply.

One way to reduce this risk is through competition among issuers. * * * This is how private banks established a stable monetary and banking system in Scotland during the eighteenth century.

Effective competition is more likely in a world of electronic money for two reasons. First, entry into the business is relatively easy and inexpensive. Issuers need not invest in gold or manage bulky paper bills. Second, on-line technology drastically reduces the cost of information and communication. A user on one side of the globe can check the reputation of an issuer on the other side (or have an intelligent software agent check it for him in a fraction of a second while deciding whether to accept a proffered payment).

Another way to reduce the risk of inflation is through contract. An issuer can promise to redeem its money at a minimum level of value expressed in commodities or other currencies. Here again, technology makes the contractual solution work better. If an issuer begins to inflate its electronic money, disgruntled users can return the money for redemption at the speed of light.

Increased bandwidth may lead to the rise of virtual communities with their own idiosyncratic currencies.

As bandwidth increases, and most Internet users gain access to real-time audio and video, we may witness the emergence of virtual communities defined by common interests or beliefs. Given the nature of the Internet, these virtual communities will have members from a variety of different countries. Rather than employ the official currency of any one nation, members may prefer to invent their own electronic money for circulation only within the community. Use of the idiosyncratic currency will help the community to form, express and maintain its own identity. Moreover, by encouraging members to trade with each other, the currency will build solidarity.

VI. Five Possible Futures for Money

If the foregoing arguments are correct, money faces five possible futures:

1. A world with the same monopoly monies we have now, but in electronic form. Governments will enact laws outlawing the use of alternative currencies in an effort to protect seigniorage revenues, bolster national prestige and control the economic lives of their citizens. However, these laws will be hard to enforce.

2. A world with a single electronic money for on-line commerce. This outcome could be difficult to achieve in the absence of effective world government. However, in a competition among different nations, one currency—say, the electronic dollar—may emerge as the victor. The resulting unitary system will be very efficient, but may be perceived as culturally and economically oppressive.

3. A world with a single commodity base for a system of competing electronic monies. This system combines the benefits of competition with the simplicity of a common standard. Its disadvantage is that the single standard may not be the right one—and could be hard to change.

4. A world of multiple competing currencies, some public and some private, with a variety of different bases, exchanging at changing rates. The optimal number of currencies may depend on how effective computers are at reducing or eliminating the costs of conversion and exchange. This system will promote competition not only among monies, but also among monetary standards. If for some reason one standard turns out to have advantages over another, issuers can shift accordingly.

5. A world with multiple currencies and standards, each standard being identified with a virtual community. This outcome is more likely if improved bandwidth fosters the development of strong virtual communities.

Governments anxious to preserve their powers and prerogatives may push for outcome one. Powerful nations or groups of nations, like the United States or the European Union, may push for outcome two. However, we conclude that technological developments, along with the self-interest of users and enforcement difficulties, are going to push us towards outcomes three and four, or possibly, given the appropriate social developments, outcome five.

BOARD OF GOVERNORS OF THE FEDERAL RESERVE SYSTEM, REPORT TO THE CONGRESS ON THE APPLICATION OF THE ELECTRONIC FUND TRANSFER ACT TO ELECTRONIC STORED-VALUE PRODUCTS

(1997).

* * *

Risks in Consumer Retail Payments

The various retail payment mechanisms available to consumers in the United States are subject to numerous risks that could result in harm to the consumer. * * *

1. *Loss of Instrument.* Some types of payment instruments have value in and of themselves, in that they are exchangeable for value by any bearer or holder. A consumer who loses a bearer instrument will incur a direct financial loss. The primary example of a bearer instrument is a Federal Reserve note (currency), which is legal tender under federal law. 31 U.S.C. § 5103. If a consumer loses currency, the Federal Reserve Banks will not replace it. If currency is stolen, the consumer generally has no recourse outside of pursuing a civil or criminal action against the thief.

* * *

2. *Unauthorized Use.* Consumers also face the risk of financial loss due to unauthorized use of a payment instrument, which may or may not result from the instrument's being lost or stolen. Unauthorized use is a relatively common problem for several types of payment instruments, such as checks, debit cards, and credit cards. * * *

* * *

3. *Errors.* If an error occurs in the processing of a payment, the payment may be made to the wrong party or for the wrong amount. With currency, the consumer generally has control over who receives the payment and how much is tendered. The consumer could make an error in the amount of currency tendered, but an error that is not detected by the consumer or the payee at the time of the transaction may be difficult to prove or correct later.

* * *

4. *Dishonor.* Consumers may face the risk that a particular payment instrument will be dishonored by the issuer or drawee. Payment instruments may also be returned because of the default of the issuer or drawee. These risks generally do not exist with currency, as Federal Reserve Banks do not dishonor notes other than those that are counterfeit (and counterfeits are rarely traceable to a particular consumer) and Reserve Banks present no default risk. A check or an ACH debit transaction might be returned by the payor's bank for various reasons, such as insufficient funds in the account, lack of authorization from the payor, or failure of the drawee bank. * * *

Credit and debit card transactions are usually verified by the payee before the transaction is completed (e.g., before a merchant releases goods to the consumer) using an on-line communications system, thereby protecting the payee and the consumer from the risk of dishonor later. * * *

* * *

Dishonor of an electronic stored-value product could arise if the financial condition of the issuer were called into question. In the event of an issuer default, merchants could face risks of loss similar to those with credit or debit card transactions. For consumers, an issuer default could lead to financial losses up to the amount of prepaid funds currently held on a stored-value product.[59] The magnitude of this risk depends on factors such as the investment policies of the issuer and the nature of the consumer's claim in bankruptcy, including whether the consumer holds a direct claim on a specified pool of assets or whether the product is covered by some third-party insurance system. Such considerations are similar to those of other prepaid payment instruments, such as travelers checks and money orders, as well as for payments drawn on bank deposits.

* * *

Fraud or counterfeiting could also lead to dishonor at the point of sale or thereafter. Some stored-value systems would be able to detect counterfeit balances or devices at the point of sale. A consumer who unknowingly accepted a fraudulent or counterfeit device might find that the device was rejected for transactions. Reimbursement policies in such situations would thus be of concern to consumers as well as to merchants.

5. *Inability to Use a Payment Mechanism.* For various reasons, a consumer might be unable to use a particular payment mechanism. This situation would not necessarily result in a financial loss to the consumer but might unexpectedly prevent a consumer from discharging a debt or obtaining goods or services, result in late fees or other penalties, or at the very least, cause embarrassment.

A consumer might be unable to use a payment instrument because of a defect in the instrument. For example, a credit card or debit card might have a demagnetized strip or a damaged chip, causing the card to be rejected at the merchant's card-reading machine. * * *

Merchants or other payees may refuse certain types of payment instruments for reasons other than defects in the instrument. Currency, which has the status of legal tender under federal law, must be accepted in payment of a debt unless the parties agree otherwise. Payees need not, however, accept credit or debit cards or checks and do so only voluntarily. Credit card and debit card issuers and associations usually attempt to sign up merchants to accept their cards to maximize the utility of the card for consumers.

Electronic stored-value products are not likely to be widely accepted for some time. Moreover, they are not legal tender and, as in the cases of checks and credit and debit cards, merchants are not obligated to accept them as payment. Thus consumers may face the risk that stored-value products cannot be used at the time and place they desire. With some stored-value products, consumers could also be left with unused balances that could not be readily converted to other forms of payment. For example, a stored-value card may be designed to expire after a certain date, with or without a window of time for the consumer to exchange the expired card for a new one. Consumers who are unable to use a card because of

59. Depending on when the consumer's obligations are deemed to be discharged, the consumer may also be liable to merchants for goods purchased with a stored-value card if the merchant is unable to collect from the defaulting issuer. * * *

malfunctions or card expirations may suffer financial losses if they cannot obtain reimbursement from the issuer.

Consumers typically reduce risks that they will be unable to make payments by carrying more than one form of payment with them. In doing so, they must weigh the benefits of maintaining access to additional payment options against any inconvenience and fees involved in doing so. The same is likely to be true of electronic stored-value products.

6. Privacy Concerns. Another potential risk to consumers is that information regarding the amount and location of payments they make will be collected and used for purposes unknown to or unauthorized by them. For example, information regarding a particular consumer's spending habits could be captured in a database and sold to a marketing or other kind of firm. This information might also be used to monitor the activities of individuals without their knowledge, either by law enforcement officials or by other third parties. Generally, electronic payments are more susceptible to this kind of risk than are other types of payments because of the relative ease of capturing electronic data. With the increase in use and sophistication of electronic payments, many consumers are becoming more concerned about the privacy of their payment information.

* * *

Consumers who are concerned about the privacy of transaction information can use paper currency and coins rather than stored-value products or other electronic payment methods. * * *

* * *

NOTES & QUESTIONS

1. *Private money.* Professors Friedman and Macintosh argue that Internet commerce is a promising environment for the emergence of forms of private money. What do they mean by private money? Do you agree that the online environment invites the development of private money?

2. *Many monies or one dominant money?* Professors Friedman and Macintosh argue that in the online environment, monies could proliferate. What features of the digital world might facilitate such a proliferation? On the other hand, they also mention the possibility that the various monies of the world might coalesce into one universal money. What features of the digital world might facilitate such a coalescence? Do you agree with Friedman and Macintosh that "competing public and private monies are the most likely development"?

3. *Evaluating risk online and off.* As the Federal Reserve Board of Governors' Report points out, payment systems involve a set of specific risks. The risks vary in severity depending upon the payment modality. What are the most serious risks of using cash? Paper checks? As we shall see in Part II, credit cards are the most frequently used payment mechanism in Internet commerce. What are the most serious risks of using credit cards in the world of bricks and mortar? In the online world?

II. COMMONLY USED ELECTRONIC PAYMENT SYSTEMS

A. CREDIT CARDS

The most widely used form of payment for consumer purchases in Internet commerce is the credit card. By one estimate, credit cards are used for more than 90% of all online purchases. Credit cards typically feature a revolving credit arrangement, in which the cardholder may carry a balance across monthly billing periods, and is charged interest on the outstanding balance. In 2000, credit cards accounted for 15 billion transactions (51% of all electronic payment transactions) with a total value of $1.235 trillion (17% of the total value of all electronic payments). *See* THE FEDERAL RESERVE SYSTEM, RETAIL PAYMENTS RESEARCH PROJECT: A SNAPSHOT OF THE U.S. PAYMENTS LANDSCAPE 9 (2001).

In offline transactions, a credit card purchase typically proceeds in the following steps. At the point of sale, the cardholder presents the merchant with her credit card. The merchant swipes the card through a card reader, called a point-of-sale terminal, which transmits an authorization request to the acquirer.[1] The acquirer routes the request, via the credit card network, to the issuing bank.[2] If the cardholder's credit line is sufficient for the purchase, and the card has not been reported as lost or stolen, the issuing bank authorizes the transaction by sending an authorization code to the acquirer. The point-of-sale terminal generates a paper charge slip, which the cardholder signs. The merchant sends an electronic record of the sale to the acquirer, which credits the merchant's account, and requests payment from the issuing bank. The issuing bank transfers payment to the acquirer, and includes the charge on the next statement that it sends to the cardholder for payment.

When a credit card is used to make a purchase in Internet commerce, the process is similar, but an additional intermediary, called a payment gateway, may be involved. The payment gateway sits between the merchant's website and the acquirer, automatically translating communications between the protocols used for Internet communications and those used for messaging on the credit card network. In lieu of using a payment gateway, the merchant may manually enter the transactional data into the credit card network.

1. The acquirer is a financial institution, such as a bank, that processes credit card transactions as described in the text. The acquirer may be the bank in which the merchant maintains the account it uses for credit card transactions, known as the merchant bank, or it may be a third-party entity with which the merchant bank contracts to provide these services.

2. The issuing bank is the bank that issues a credit card to the cardholder, and that sends the cardholder a monthly statement of charges for payment. Visa and MasterCard do not issue the cards carrying their logos, but rather authorize banks to issue them. American Express, on the other hand, issues its own cards.

The merchant pays a fee to the acquirer for its processing services. The fee is typically in the range of 1.75% to 3.5% of the amount of each transaction. Internet and mail-order sellers generally pay higher rates than established storefront retailers, due to the greater risks of unauthorized use that the former present.

Credit card transactions in which the purchaser is not in the physical presence of the merchant—including sales via the Internet, by telephone, and by mail order—are called "card-not-present" transactions. Credit card issuers typically have detailed protocols that merchants must follow in such transactions. Visa, for example, requires, where possible, that the merchant obtain the credit card's expiration date, and recommends that the merchant ask the purchaser for the three-digit security number printed on the back of the card. In addition, in a card-not-present transaction the merchant is fully liable for any fraudulent use of a card. In a face-to-face transaction, on the other hand, the bank that issues the credit card is liable for unauthorized use. For further details on Visa's card-not-present protocols, see Visa, *Fraud Control Basics*, www.usa.visa.com/business/merchants/fraud_basics_index.html#b.

In an effort to reduce the risk of loss from fraudulent use of credit cards online, some card issuers have introduced a security system that involves the generation of a card number that is valid only for a single online transaction. The cardholder presents the merchant with the single-use number, rather than the number of her credit card account. The process is transparent from the merchant's standpoint, as the card issuer handles the back-end tasks of generating the single-use number and associating it with the cardholder's account number. In addition, some issuers are offering cardholders a password that can be used to prevent unauthorized use of their credit card account numbers.

The legal relationships among the parties to a credit-card transaction are governed by a set of contracts, and by state and federal law. The relationship between the issuing bank and the cardholder is governed by the Truth in Lending Act ("TILA"), 15 U.S.C. §§ 1601–1667f, as implemented by Regulation Z, 12 C.F.R. pt. 226. The primary aim of federal regulation in this area is consumer protection. For example, TILA and Regulation Z prohibit the issuance of an unsolicited credit card[3] and impose various disclosure requirements on the issuing bank.[4]

3. Regulation Z states that "[r]egardless of the purpose for which a credit card is to be used, including business, commercial, or agricultural use, no credit card shall be issued to any person except: (1) In response to an oral or written request or application for the card; or (2) As a renewal of, or substitute for, an accepted credit card." 12 C.F.R. § 226.12(a); *see also* TILA § 132, 15 U.S.C. § 1642.

4. For example, when an individual applies for a credit card, the issuer must disclose the card's interest rate as an annual percentage rate, all fees which may be imposed, any minimum or fixed finance charges, any grace periods, and the method used to compute the balance on which the finance charge is imposed. 12 C.F.R. § 226.5a(b)(1)–(6).

Regulation Z also mandates certain procedures for the resolution of billing errors, which are errors reflected on or made in connection with a periodic statement of a cardholder's account. If a cardholder believes her statement contains a billing error, she may initiate the billing dispute procedure by providing written notice of the error to the issuer. The issuer must then investigate the complaint and arrive at a conclusion within two billing cycles. 12 C.F.R. § 226.13(c)(2). Until the resolution procedure is completed, the cardholder need not pay the disputed amount, and the issuer may not make an adverse report about the cardholder's credit standing based on the dispute. 12 C.F.R. § 226.13(d)(1) & (d)(2). If the issuer determines that a billing error occurred as asserted, it must correct the billing error and credit the cardholder's account with any disputed amount. 12 C.F.R. § 226.13(e).

Finally, Regulation Z limits a cardholder's liability for unauthorized uses of his credit card. If the cardholder reports loss of the card before any unauthorized charges are made, the cardholder has no liability. Otherwise, the cardholder's liability is limited to $50. 12 C.F.R. § 226.12(b)(1) & (b)(2). The major card companies have instituted policies under which holders of U.S.-issued cards have no liability for most fraudulent uses of their cards.

B. Debit Cards

A debit card is used to make an electronic fund transfer from a consumer's bank account to a merchant's account in payment for a purchase. The card that is used for debit transactions may also function as a credit card or an ATM card. In 2000, debit cards accounted for 8.3 billion transactions (28% of all electronic payment transactions) with a total value of $348 billion (4.8% of the total value of all electronic payment transactions). *See* The Federal Reserve System, Retail Payments Research Project: A Snapshot of the U.S. Payments Landscape 9 (2001).

There are two types of debit cards: "online" and "offline." A typical online debit transaction in the brick-and-mortar world proceeds as follows. A consumer swipes his debit card through an electronic fund transfer point-of-sale ("EFTPOS") terminal, and enters his personal identification number ("PIN"). The PIN is used to verify that the consumer is authorized to use the debit card. Next, the terminal transmits information about the transaction to the consumer's bank and seeks authorization for the purchase. If the consumer's bank confirms that the PIN is associated with the consumer's account and there are sufficient funds in that account to cover the purchase, then the bank will approve the purchase and debit the consumer's account for the amount of the purchase. The approval is transmitted to the EFTPOS terminal, and the purchase is completed. The electronic communications are made over the ATM network.

Offline debit transactions are processed through the credit card network, rather than the ATM network. Instead of using a PIN, the cardholder signs a charge slip. In an offline debit transaction, the funds are not transferred immediately, but only upon settlement, which may take several days.

As odd as it may sound, offline debit cards can be used for online purchases, but online debit cards generally cannot. Online cards, as noted above, require the use of a PIN. A card reader is required to verify that the correct PIN has been entered, but few consumers have a card reader attached to their computers. Offline debit cards, on the other hand, may be used for purchases in Internet commerce in the same manner as a credit card.

Most offline debit cards are issued by banks in association with Visa and MasterCard. These two card networks, which control more than 90% of the credit-card market, require merchants that accept their credit cards also to accept their debit cards. Many merchants would prefer not to accept these debit cards, because of the high fees involved. These fees are set by Visa and MasterCard at about the same levels as for credit card transactions. For a $100 purchase, that can mean the merchant will pay a fee of several dollars per transaction, as compared to $.59 or so for an online debit transaction. In 1999, a group of merchants, including Wal–Mart, Sears, and Circuit City, brought a class-action suit against Visa U.S.A. and MasterCard International, alleging that the rules requiring merchants to accept the defendants' offline debit cards violated the antitrust laws. The district court certified the action as a class action. *See In re Visa Check/Mastermoney Antitrust Litigation*, 192 F.R.D. 68 (E.D.N.Y.2000), *aff'd*, 280 F.3d 124 (2001), *cert. denied*, ___ U.S. ___, 122 S.Ct. 2382 (2002).

The legal relationship between the bank that issues the debit card (the "issuer") and the consumer is governed by the agreement between the issuer and the consumer, and by the Electronic Fund Transfer Act ("EFTA"), 15 U.S.C. §§ 1693–1693r, as implemented by Regulation E, 12 C.F.R. pt. 205. As with the Truth in Lending Act, the principal aim of the EFTA and Regulation E is consumer protection. Toward this end, the EFTA and Regulation E broadly define what will count as an "access device" for electronic fund transfers,[5] prohibit the issuance of an unsolicited access device,[6] and impose disclosure and documentation requirements on the issuing bank. 12 C.F.R. § 205.7.

Regulation E also mandates an error resolution procedure that is triggered if the consumer believes that any of several kinds of errors has occurred, including an unauthorized or incorrect electronic fund transfer, a computational or bookkeeping error made by the financial institution relating to an electronic fund transfer, and the consumer's receipt of an incorrect amount of money from an electronic terminal such as an ATM. 12

5. The EFTA applies not only to transfers initiated by debit cards but to electronic fund transfers initiated by any kind of access device. An access device is defined as "a card, code, or other means of access to a consumer's account, or any combination thereof, that may be used by the consumer to initiate electronic fund transfers." 12 C.F.R. § 205.2(a)(1). Thus, the account number on the face of the debit card qualifies as an access device since it is this number that the consumer must key in to access her account.

6. A financial institution may issue an access device to a consumer only (1) in response to an oral or written request for the device or (2) as a renewal of, or in substitution for, an accepted access device whether issued by the institution or a successor. 12 C.F.R. § 205.5(a).

C.F.R.§ 205.11(a). The error resolution procedure resembles in outline the procedure that applies to credit cards, as described above, but differs in the particulars. 12 C.F.R. § 205.11.

When a consumer uses a debit card to pay for goods or services in an "online" transaction at a point-of-sale terminal or over the Internet, the consumer's account is immediately debited. Once a consumer's bank authorizes an electronic fund transfer, it is absolutely liable to pay the merchant's bank the amount authorized. Under Regulation E, the consumer may not reverse an electronic fund transfer. If a consumer wishes to reverse the transaction and get her money back, then in most states the consumer's only recourse is to proceed against the merchant directly. In this respect, payment by electronic fund transfer is like payment by cash. Some states, however, have enacted laws that allow consumers to reverse electronic fund transfers under certain circumstances. *See, e.g.,* MICH. COMP. LAWS § 488.16.

Regulation E limits a consumer's liability for an unauthorized electronic fund transfer, which is defined as "an electronic fund transfer from a consumer's account initiated by a person other than the consumer without actual authority to initiate the transfer and from which the consumer receives no benefit." 12 C.F.R. § 205.2(m). Liability for unauthorized EFTs depends on the consumer's promptness in reporting the loss or theft of an access device. If the consumer notifies the financial institution before there is any unauthorized use, the consumer has no liability. If she notifies the financial institution within two business days after learning of the loss or theft of the access device, the consumer's liability is limited to $50. If the consumer fails to notify the financial institution within two business days after learning of the loss or theft of the access device, the consumer may be liable for up to $500. Finally, a consumer who fails to report an unauthorized electronic fund transfer that appears on a billing statement within 60 days of the financial institution's transmittal of the statement may be liable for the full amount of subsequent transfers. 12 C.F.R. § 205.6. A cardholder's potential liability for unauthorized use of a debit card is thus far greater than the corresponding liability with respect to credit cards.

Although the limits on consumer liability prescribed by Regulation E may not be increased by either state law or agreement, they may be reduced by such means. *See* 12 C.F.R. § 205.6(6); COLO. REV. STAT. §§ 11–6.5–109(2) & 11–48–106(2); MASS. GEN. LAWS ANN. Ch. 167B, § 18; IOWA CODE ANN. § 527.8.1 (all three statutes limit consumer liability for unauthorized transfers to $50 if an access device was lost or stolen; Colorado law further provides that if the unauthorized use occurs through no fault of the account holder, no liability is imposed).

NOTES & QUESTIONS

Need for new payment mechanisms. Given the widespread availability and near-universal acceptance of credit and debit cards online, is there any need for alternative payment mechanisms for Internet commerce? Consider the following:

> One might think * * * that traditional payment instruments are fulfilling consumers' need for a safe and easy way to make payments while cybershopping. But there are three additional hurdles to using these payment instruments online. The first and biggest barrier to online shopping is consumer reluctance to use credit and debit cards in cyberspace. One recent survey found, as is typical, that 43 percent of consumers fear cybershopping will result in the theft of their credit-card numbers (PR Newswire 2001). Another survey found that 29 percent of online shoppers think they are responsible for fraudulent Internet purchases made with their debit cards (*ATM & Debit News*, July 2001).
>
> The second hurdle is the costliness of using credit and debit cards for very small purchases (that is, micropayments) such as the one-time use of digital content, like an individual song, photograph, or magazine article. The fees merchants must pay on purchases made with these cards are so high that sellers of digital content and other very inexpensive goods cannot afford to accept the cards. Yet the demand for such purchases is potentially very large. About 38 percent of all Internet users report having downloaded music files at some point.
>
> The third hurdle is that many potential cybershoppers do not have access to the traditional payment instruments. One study found that lower income consumers—the consumers more likely to be constrained in their ability to make credit-card purchases—are the fastest growing group of Internet users. Teenagers are also likely to lack credit cards, debit cards, and checking accounts; yet they are thought to constitute the largest market of cybershoppers who look but do not buy.

Stacey L. Schreft, *Clicking with Dollars: How Consumers Can Pay for Purchases from E-tailers*, ECON. REV., First Quarter 2002, at 37, 47–48.

III. EMERGING ELECTRONIC PAYMENT SYSTEMS

A. BACKGROUND

Although credit cards are still the dominant form of payment for consumer purchases in Internet commerce, several new payment technologies that may be used for online purchases have been introduced and have experienced varying degrees of acceptance. In this Part we consider these emerging technologies and discuss how they operate, their acceptance in the marketplace, and the challenges that each system faces.

In contrast to the more familiar electronic payment systems, which are governed primarily by federal law, the emerging online payment services are regulated mainly by state law. The primary goals of state regulation of financial services businesses are consumer protection and the prevention of money laundering. States attempt to ensure that these services have sufficient funds and other resources to fulfill their obligations to their customers by imposing safety and soundness requirements, such as restricting how money deposited with such services may be used or invested, or requiring services to obtain a surety bond, letter of credit, or other similar security device. States also attempt to prevent these services from becoming conduits for money laundering by imposing licensing and reporting requirements. To encourage greater uniformity among these laws, in 2000 the National Conference of Commissioners for Uniform State Laws approved and recommended for enactment the Uniform Money Services Act. The prefatory note to this Act, which includes a brief description of some of the emerging electronic payment systems, is excerpted below.

Prefatory Note to the Uniform Money Services Act

National Conference of Commissioners on Uniform State Laws.
(2001).

A. Goals and Objectives

The Uniform Money Services Act ("UMSA" or "Act") is a state safety and soundness law that creates licensing provisions for various types of money-services businesses ("MSBs"). While many States have laws that deal with the sale of payment instruments, state regulation of money transmission, check cashers and currency exchangers is extremely varied. * * *

* * * [U]niformity of the reporting and record keeping requirements should enable industry to comply with multiple state requirements in a uniform and cost-effective manner. Uniform licensing, reporting and enforcement provisions for MSBs will serve as a larger deterrent to money laundering than will a host of varying state laws. * * *

* * *

D. Internet Payment Mechanisms and Stored Value

The UMSA takes the approach that certain cyberpayment mechanisms pose the same safety and soundness concerns as their brick and mortar counterparts. The UMSA incorporates certain Internet payment mechanisms into the statute's licensing framework. However, the Act does not include new or different licensing regimes for such payment mechanisms. The cyberpayment licensing requirements set forth in this Act are not complex and cumbersome. Rather, they are simple and meant to apply the existing licensing frameworks to new technologies. Existing definitions have been expanded *slightly* to take into account the fact that (1) Internet payment mechanisms are in many respects the functional equivalent of traditional money transmission, and (2) that the sale of stored value is in many respects analogous to the sale of traditional payment instruments such as money orders.

This Act expands upon our traditional concept of "money". With the advent of the Internet and new microchip technology it is possible to exchange value that is not "money" in the traditional sense. The UMSA consequently provides a new definition of "monetary value". Like money, monetary value can be transmitted. Similarly issuers need not sell a physical tangible payment instrument in order to issue value to consumers. It is possible for consumers to purchase redeemable value that may only exist in a computerized format. Hence, this Act contains a definition of stored value that is distinct from the traditional payment instrument. Listed below are examples of some of the new types of payment mechanisms that potentially fall within the scope of the Act.

1. Stored value

Stored-value products are a recent innovation in payment systems technology. Stored-value products possess certain basic characteristics. According to the Federal Reserve, stored-value products share three attributes: "(1) [a] card or other device electronically stores or provides access to a specified amount of funds selected by the holder of the device and available for making payments to others; (2) the device is the only means of routine access to the funds; and (3) the issuer does not record the funds associated with the device as an account in the name of (or credited to) the holder."[5]

Stored-value cards are also known as "smart" cards, prepaid cards, or value-added cards. These cards record a balance on a computer chip that is debited at a point-of-sale terminal when a consumer or individual makes a purchase. Typically, a consumer will pay a bank or other provider money in exchange for a card that is loaded with value. The value can evidence the provider's promise (typically to pay money), or can evidence the promise of a trustworthy third party. The consumer uses the card rather than paper currency to purchase goods and services. Merchants who accept smart cards can typically transfer the value of accumulated credits to their bank accounts. A smart card is not typically used for transactions over the Internet, although this may be changing with the advent of new credit-card products that include a stored-value component. Several new services, however, provide for remote payments to be made by electronic currency that is stored on the hard drive of a person's computer.

Several States have begun to include stored value within their existing money transmission law. Connecticut, for example, has defined stored value as a form of "electronic payment instrument."[6] This term would also include electronic traveler's checks. West Virginia defines "currency transmission" or "money transmission" to include "the transmission of funds through the issuance and sale of stored-value cards which are intended for general acceptance and use in commercial or consumer transactions."[7]

5. Electronic Funds Transfers (Regulation E), 61 Fed. Reg. 19, 696 (1996).

6. Conn. Gen. Stat. Ann. Section 36a–596 (West Supp. 2001). Connecticut defines electronic payment instrument as stored value, not the reverse.

7. W. Va. Code Section 32A–2–1(6) (West 1999).

Other States, such as Texas, have included stored-value providers by interpretation. The Texas Banking Department has explained, for example, its rationale for requiring nonbank issuers of open system stored-value cards to obtain a license under the Texas Sale of Checks Act:

> Stored-value cards issued by nonbanks for use in "open" systems (i.e., to purchase goods and services offered by vendors other than the issuer of the card) will generally be subject to regulation under the Sale of Checks Act because the nonbank issuer is holding the funds of third parties. Consumers are relying on the nonbank issuer that the card will be honored when presented by the purchaser of goods and services at diverse locations.[8]

Oregon is another State that has included a provision for the regulation of stored value. Section 2 of the Sale of Checks Act includes a definition of electronic instrument which "means a card or other tangible object . . . for the storage of information, that is prefunded and for which the value is decrement[ed] upon each use."[9] The term excludes "a card or other tangible object that is redeemable by the issuer in the issuer's goods and services."[10]

* * *

2. E-money and Internet payment mechanisms

New types of cyberpayments or Internet payment mechanisms have been referred to by regulators and commentators by a host of different names including electronic cash, digital cash, electronic currency, and Internet or on-line scrip ("E-money"). E-money refers to money or a money substitute that is transformed into information stored on a computer chip or a personal computer so that it can be transferred over information systems such as the Internet. Technology permits the transmission of electronic value over networks that link personal computers (PCs) and the storage of electronic cash on the hard drives of personal computers.

* * * One type of Internet-based E-money system has been described as a token or notational system. These computer-based systems involve a customer purchasing electronic tokens, which serve as cash substitutes for transactions over the Internet. With this type of system, "money" or "value" is purchased from an issuer (who may be a bank or a nonbank). The value is then stored in a digital form on a consumer's personal computer and the notational value is transferred over the Internet.

The "coin" is merely a notational series of numbers or other symbols that are transmitted over the Internet to a merchant. The merchant must then redeem the "coin" with an issuer that will verify that the coin has not been spent previously. The issuer of the Internet E-money is obligated to

8. See Remarks of Catherine A. Ghiglieri, Texas Department of Banking to the PULSE EFT Assoc. Member Conference (October 11, 1996) (visited June 15, 2001) located at <http://www.banking.state.tx.us/exec/speech10a.htm>.

9. Or. Rev. Stat. Section 717.200(7) (West 1999).

10. *Id.*

redeem these payments when received from the merchant. For example, Company A issues a certain type of E-money—Internet "cash" cards with unique personal identification numbers ("PINs"). These cash cards are purchased from vendors who are sales representatives. A consumer uses his PIN when transacting with a merchant on-line.

Commentators have noted that state money transmission statutes may, by implication, include or regulate Internet payment systems such as the notational systems described above. Others have suggested that in the future [they] might be a source of prudential regulation for nonbank entities engaged in this activity. * * *

* * *

In addition to token or notational systems, there are also "account-based" E-money systems. Account-based systems involve a consumer purchasing "E-money" by debiting an existing bank account or using a credit card to buy "coins". The value is then stored on the issuer's records and the consumer might access the records. The merchant who accepts the E-money ultimately redeems the account-based E-money with a bank or credit card company.

3. Internet scrip

Stored value cards, token or notational systems as well as account-based systems may all involve exchange of value that is not redeemable in money. The term "scrip" has been used to refer to value that may be exchanged over the Internet but which may not be redeemable for money. Scrip is more analogous to coupons or bonus points that can be exchanged by a consumer for goods or services but have no cash redemption value. Scrip can be used by merchants to sell access to value-added web pages on a per-access basis or a subscription basis. They can also use scrip to provide promotional incentives to users. Scrip can represent any form of currency, points in a frequent user program, access rights, etc.

At present, there are new micropayments systems being developed that allow customers to either earn reward points on line or to purchase points or "value" that is redeemable for goods and services rather than for money. One such example is Company B, which issues its own gift "money." Company B issues what are essentially online gift certificates. A customer opens an account and purchases a certain amount of Company B's reward "dollars." Then, the person can send the dollars to anyone with an e-mail address (along with a card). The recipient, upon receipt, opens an account and then can spend the gift "dollars" at any participating store that accepts the "dollars." What is not apparent from the website is whether Company B's "dollars" are redeemable in cash or merely in goods and services.

Another company, Company C, offers online points that are billed as web "currency." Company C's "points" are units that consumers may earn when visiting various websites, filling out surveys or engaging in other online activities for which merchants seek to reward consumers. The points accrue and are stored in an online "account" that a customer may access to redeem his or her "points" for various goods and services. The points are not redeemable for money, and the company states that it may discontinue the service at any point. Company C is offering an account-based payment system that issues non-redeemable points.

4. Internet funds transfer

New payment services offered by banks and nonbanks will transfer money over the Internet. One such service, offered by Company D, will transfer money over the Internet to anyone who has an e-mail address. Consumers who wish to send money via the Internet must first establish an online account with Company D. A consumer can fund his or her account with payments from a credit card, a debit from his bank account, or by sending in a money order or check. Company D holds the consumer's money until it receives a request to transfer the funds to a recipient. A transfer is effectuated by sending an e-mail to the recipient. The recipient then has several options for receiving payment ranging from establishing his or her own online account with Company D, having the funds transferred to an existing bank account, or, if the customer has no bank account, receiving a check from Company D.

5. Gold/precious metals transfer and payment

Somewhat similar to an Internet funds transfer system is a system whereby customers transfer precious metal via accounts on the Internet. For example, with Company E, rather than having an "account" with E-money denominated in U.S. dollars, a customer sets up an online account and buys gold, silver, platinum, or palladium. The customer then has "x" grams or troy ounces of the precious metal. One can only send money to or purchase items from an existing customer of Company E. The advantage, Company E claims, is the stability of precious metals relative to currency. Customers can utilize their precious metal accounts to buy goods and services, to receive payment from third parties, and to pay bills.

6. Internet bill payment services

Banks and nonbank[s] have began to offer Internet bill payment services. For a fee, electronic bill payment services pay certain bills for consumers, after receiving authorization from a consumer. The customer accesses the service via the Internet. Bill payments may subsequently be made for the consumer electronically. Typically, the service provider will use an automated clearinghouse (ACH) transfer to effectuate payment. However, if the designated payee does not accept electronic payment, the bill-payment service will print and mail a check on behalf of its customer. When a nonbank service is involved, the nonbank has no contractual relationship with the consumer's bank. Instead, the consumer's bank will transfer money to the bill-payment service company. The bill-payment service will, in turn, deposit the funds into its own bank account. The bill-payment service will then issue a payment instrument payable on its own account to the designated payee.

The Texas Department of Banking has required at least one bill-payment service to obtain a license under its Sale of Checks Act.[12] Texas made this decision based on the fact that the bill-payment service was holding the money of consumers in its own account and issuing payment instruments to merchants payable on the same account. The Texas Sale of Checks Act defines a check to include "an instrument for the transmission or payment of money, including a draft, traveler's check, or money order. The term also includes an instrument for the transmission or payment of money in which the purchaser or remitter of the instrument appoints or purports to appoint the seller as its agent for the receipt, transmission, or handling of money, regardless of who signs the instrument."[13] California has also required an Internet bill-payment service to obtain a license under its relevant statute.[14] By implication, Internet bill-payment services may already be included within various statutes regulating sale of payment instruments or money transmission statutes.

NOTES & QUESTIONS

1. *Adoptions.* Vermont was the first state to adopt the Uniform Money Services Act, effective January 1, 2002. *See* VT. STAT. ANN. tit. 8, §§ 2500–2555. The current status of state enactments of the UMSA is available at www.nccusl.org/nccusl/uniformact_factsheets/uniformacts-fs-msa.asp.

2. *Electronic money and criminal activity.* How does electronic money compare with other payment mechanisms, such as cash, with respect to the risk of counterfeiting and money laundering? Consider how these mechanisms compare in terms of traceability, ease of transportation, anonymity, ease of forgery, and the security of the systems through which they are transmitted.

Electronic payments in Internet commerce may involve the use of several electronic networks, in addition to the Internet itself. Credit card payments make use of proprietary networks operated by companies such as Visa, MasterCard, and American Express. Electronic fund transfers using online debit card accounts travel over ATM networks operated by banks. An additional network that may be involved in making electronic payments over the Internet is the Automated Clearing House ("ACH") Network. The ACH Network was originally developed as a paperless process to facilitate efficient interbank settlements. Today, consumers and businesses can also initiate electronic credit and debit transfers over this network. The following excerpt describes how the ACH Network functions.

12. TEX. FIN. CODE ANN. Section 152.001–152.508 (West Supp. 2001).

13. TEX. FIN. CODE ANN. Section 152.002(1) (West Supp. 2001).

14. State of California, Department of Financial Institutions (visited June 15, 2001) <http://www.sbd.ca.gov/>.

Comptroller of the Currency, ACH Transactions Involving the Internet

Appendix A—The ACH Network
OCC 2002–2 (2002).
www.occ.treas.gov/ftp/bulletin/2002-2.doc

The ACH Network is a nationwide, batch-oriented electronic transfer system that provides for the interbank clearing of payments among participating depository financial institutions. The ACH Network was developed in the early 1970s as a response to the massive growth of check payments.

NACHA [the National Automated Clearing House Association] was established in 1974 to coordinate the ACH Network. NACHA's primary roles are to develop and maintain the NACHA Operating Rules, to promote growth in ACH volume, and to provide educational services to its members and other ACH participants.

The process by which funds are transferred through the ACH Network operates from beginning to end through a series of legal agreements between the parties and pursuant to the NACHA Operating Rules. The rules are enforceable by the parties pursuant to the common law of contract. In addition, ACH entries are also subject to applicable federal and state law, such as the Electronic Fund Transfer Act (EFTA), implemented by Regulation E, and Article 4A of the Uniform Commercial Code, as enacted by a particular state.

For a given transaction, up to five entities may participate in the ACH Network—the originator, the originating depository financial institution (ODFI), the ACH operator, the receiving depository financial institution (RDFI), and the receiver. In addition, some of the entities may use a third-party service provider as part of the process.

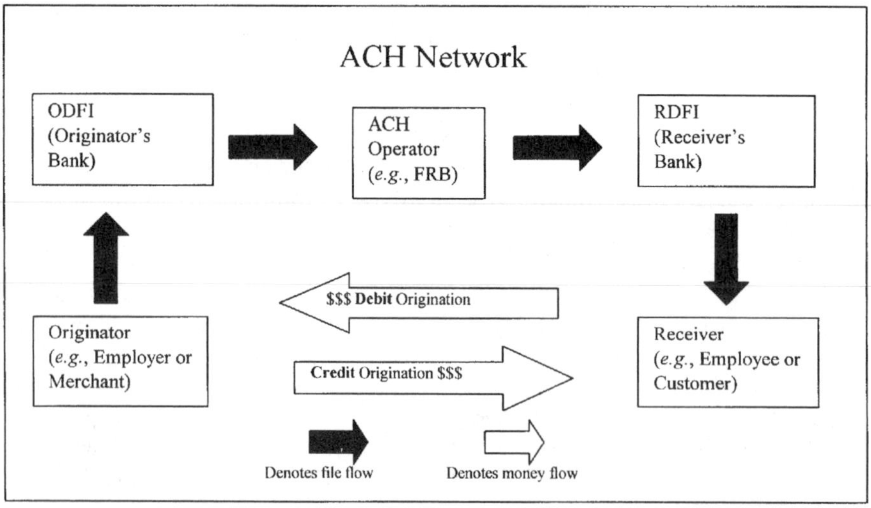

The *originator* is the party that agrees to initiate ACH entries into the payment system according to an arrangement with a receiver. The originator is usually a company directing a transfer of funds to or from a consumer's or another company's account, but may be an individual initiating funds transfers to or from the individual's own account.

The *ODFI* is the institution that receives the payment instructions from its customers, the originators, and transmits the entries to the ACH operator. An ODFI can also initiate ACH entries for itself, in which case it is both ODFI and originator.

The *ACH operator* is the central clearing facility, operated by a Federal Reserve Bank or a private organization, that receives entries from ODFIs, distributes the entries to appropriate RDFIs, and performs the settlement functions for the affected institutions.

The *RDFI* is the institution that receives entries from the ACH operator and posts them to the accounts of its depositors, the receivers.

The *receiver* is the party that has authorized an originator to initiate an ACH entry to the receiver's account with the RDFI.

Unlike the wire transfer and check systems, the ACH Network is both a credit and a debit payment system. ACH credit transactions transfer funds *from the originator to the receiver*. For example, an originator may arrange to meet its payroll obligations by causing an ODFI to transmit ACH credit entries so that employees' salaries are credited to their accounts and the originator's account is debited in the total amount of the payroll. ACH debit transactions, on the other hand, transfer funds *from the receiver to the originator*. For example, a merchant originator may permit a customer to purchase goods or services through the Internet when the customer authorizes the merchant to initiate an ACH debit to the customer's account. Although credits and debits transfer funds in different directions, the entry information and the functional processing always flows in one direction, from the originator to the receiver.

B. PERSON-TO-PERSON MONEY SERVICES

The most widely used emerging online money services are known as person-to-person ("P2P") payment services. These services enable anyone with an e-mail address to transfer funds to anyone else with an e-mail address. Depending on the service, payments may be made via credit card, personal check, debit card, or by electronic fund transfer from the payor's bank. For an annotated listing of P2P payment systems see www.payby-email.info/site/eng/index.htm.

In the following excerpt, Professor David Sorkin describes how PayPal, Billpoint, and other emerging P2P payment systems function. In reading the excerpt, consider how these payments systems differ from traditional payment systems and from one another.

David E. Sorkin, *Payment Methods for Consumer-to-Consumer Online Transactions*

35 AKRON L. REV. 1 (2001).

* * *

The payment mechanisms discussed in this section include PayPal and Billpoint, which seem to enjoy the largest popularity for online auction transactions, along with several competing systems that represent different approaches to online payments. PayPal is an independent payment service,[7] while Billpoint is owned by eBay, the largest auction site. Amazon.com and Yahoo!, eBay's primary competitors, operate their own payment services, though they generally function in a manner similar to PayPal and Billpoint. * * *

Introduced in late 1998, PayPal is the leading online payment service, with over 7 million registered users. PayPal operates in 26 countries. Its daily transaction volume is over $7 million. PayPal advertises its services as "free to consumers," although moderate and high-volume users are required to upgrade to fee-based accounts. PayPal can be used for fund transfers and purchases unrelated to auction sites, but its most common application is for online auction purchases.

A seller must be registered with PayPal in order to receive payments through the service. If the buyer is also a registered user, he or she may initiate a payment by logging into PayPal's website and entering information about the purchase, including the amount and the seller's e-mail address. The payment is deducted from the buyer's PayPal account if it contains sufficient funds; otherwise, the buyer may charge the payment to a credit card (as a purchase, with PayPal as the merchant), or authorize an ACH transfer from a checking account. If the buyer is not a registered user, the seller can still refer the buyer to PayPal's site for a one-time payment. In either case, the payment is then credited to the seller's PayPal account, after applicable fees are deducted. The seller can leave the funds in his or her PayPal account, or may direct PayPal to transfer them into a bank account. The seller never sees the buyer's credit card or bank account number, and PayPal provides the parties with little or no information about one another other than that which they choose to disclose.

Billpoint is another major online payment service, currently available for use in 37 countries. Billpoint was founded in 1998 and was acquired by eBay in 1999. As eBay's in-house online payment service, Billpoint has an inherent advantage over competing payment services, although PayPal still seems to enjoy greater popularity even on eBay.

Billpoint operates in much the same manner as PayPal, except that Billpoint does not have individual accounts where users' funds are held. Buyers therefore pay by credit card or ACH transfer, and payments (less Billpoint fees) are automatically credited to the seller's bank account immediately in the case of credit card payments, or after three business

7. [In July 2002, eBay announced it intended to purchase PayPal.—Eds.]

days for ACH transfers. Credit card charges are posted as purchases with Billpoint as the merchant of record. However, an abbreviated form of the seller's e-mail address also appears on the buyer's credit card statement. As is the case with PayPal, the seller must be a registered Billpoint user. If the buyer is not also a registered user, he or she is required to provide credit card or bank account information at the time of the payment.

ProPay takes a different approach than PayPal and Billpoint. Instead of serving as an intermediary to the transaction, ProPay enables sellers to obtain their own credit card merchant accounts so that payments are charged to a buyer's credit card as purchases from the actual seller, rather than from a payment service. Unlike traditional credit card merchant account service providers, ProPay does not impose startup or periodic fees or minimum volume requirements, although ProPay does hold a portion of payments received in a reserve account to cover potential chargebacks. ProPay's transaction fees are slightly higher than the fees for PayPal, Billpoint, and traditional merchant credit card merchant accounts.

CCNow is yet another online payment service. CCNow acts as the retail seller in an auction or other online transaction by purchasing the goods from the original seller and then reselling them to the buyer using the original seller as a drop shipper. CCNow collects a credit card payment from the buyer, and pays accumulated amounts to sellers (less CCNow's commission) twice per month.

BidPay differs from the payment services discussed thus far in that only the buyer need enter into a relationship with BidPay. To make an online auction purchase using BidPay, a buyer accesses BidPay's website and provides a credit card number and the relevant transaction information. BidPay charges the transaction amount plus a fee to the buyer's credit card and then mails a Western Union money order to the seller. (A similar service is offered by a competing firm, EnergyFlow.) Because BidPay notifies the seller by e-mail when it deposits the money order in the mail, the seller may choose to ship the goods at that time or may wait until receiving the money order. BidPay claims to be the largest issuer of Western Union money orders in the United States, sending hundreds of thousands of money orders to tens of thousands of sellers annually.

* * *

The status of online payment companies for regulatory purposes is currently unresolved. While P2P services engage in banking activity to the extent they accept consumer deposits and make money transfers, it remains unclear whether they qualify as banks under various regulatory definitions. Likewise, although these services transmit money, the definition of a "money transmitter" varies from state to state, and it may be unclear whether a P2P service qualifies. State laws typically require banks to maintain certain levels of cash reserves, and to monitor transactions closely. In addition, banks are subject to a variety of federal regulations.

Some states require "money transmitters" to obtain a license, and to post a surety bond.

Several states have raised questions about the legal status of P2P services, with the focus of the scrutiny on Billpoint and PayPal. In February 2002, state banking regulators in Louisiana sent PayPal a letter directing the company to cease providing money transmission services to Louisiana residents until it obtained a money transmission license. PayPal obtained the license in Louisiana as well as a number of other states. Several states have inquired whether PayPal is a bank under state law; PayPal argues that it acts as an agent on behalf of its customers rather than as a bank.

Kenneth N. Kuttner & James J. McAndrews, *Personal On–Line Payments*

ECON. POL'Y REV., Dec. 1, 2001, at 35.

* * *

Risk

Providers of on-line payment instruments are concerned about the risks of fraud, operational failure, and other liquidity and credit risks because their success depends on maintaining a system that is useful to customers and protects the provider from fraudulent withdrawal of funds from the system. Therefore, it is important to examine the risk control measures employed by these new systems to combat risk.

Fraud is perhaps the most immediate threat faced by on-line payment providers. To address this risk, all the systems register and communicate credit card information using a secure socket layer—an encrypted connection to the provider's website. The payer's information is retained by the provider, reducing the need for repeated transmission over the Internet. Another risk control is a limit on the size of payments that can be made. Some providers, for example, limit transfers to very small amounts until the user's identity and address are verified by conventional mail.

Risk is also posed by the extensive use of e-mail. The systems use this medium for various purposes: e-mail serves as a means of communication, the e-mail address acts as an addressing or locating system, and one's e-mail response to a receipt of payment is used, in part, as a means of identifying the payment recipient. A single e-mail account shared by several people naturally will diminish the effectiveness of e-mail as an identifier and a means to communicate to only one person. As a result, additional means to identify the recipient become necessary. Increasing the number of hurdles a user must overcome to transfer value may lower system risk, but at the cost of reducing system convenience.

It is worth noting that the leading personal on-line payment provider grew out of an encryption firm, which indicates that the sponsors recognize the importance of preventing counterfeit and fraudulent claims from being entered against the company. One company official stated that successful providers will have to supply world-class fraud prevention and detection systems to manage this type of risk. If these systems should mature and create a more universal, interoperable system, then the operational risks will loom larger simply because of the larger values involved. In the meantime, it is safe to say that the existing systems are already under intense scrutiny by security experts (as well as hackers) for any possible weaknesses.

Like traditional financial intermediaries, on-line payment providers also face a certain amount of credit and liquidity risk. So far, this risk has been relatively modest: the dollar amounts involved have been too small to create significant risk for the financial system. In addition, nonbank providers generally maintain the assets in money market funds or at banks, all but eliminating credit and liquidity risk. Therefore, as long as providers continue to keep their funds in short-term, high-quality assets, credit and liquidity risk will not be a major issue.

Regulatory Treatment of Payments

One important issue that could affect the acceptance of on-line payments concerns the rights of consumers when using this payment method. The use of credit and debit cards is governed by a well-established set of legal rights, in addition to any contractual terms agreed to by the card issuer and consumer. In some cases, federal regulations grant consumers a certain amount of protection against fraudulent use of their cards as well as certain rights in case of errors made by the payment provider, including certain rights to resolve errors. Furthermore, consumers' potential losses are limited under the regulations that govern those card payments.

In contrast, most personal on-line payments (in particular, those based on proprietary accounts) do not involve a credit or debit card, and therefore the consumer may not enjoy the same set of legal rights that he would in a credit or debit card payment. These rights are governed instead solely by the private contractual terms set out by the providers in the user agreement. It is not clear whether consumers are aware of this distinction, particularly as many of them fund their on-line accounts with a credit card in the first place.

Regulatory Treatment of Payment Providers

Some personal on-line payment providers are banks and some are not, and this distinction gives rise to differences in regulatory treatment. Bank providers, for example, are required to hold a certain share (3 or 10 percent, depending on the level of deposits) as non-interest-bearing reserves, while nonbank providers currently have no such requirement. In addition, unlike nonbank providers, banks are required to hold a minimum level of capital. Banks are also subject to reporting requirements and periodic examination by supervisory authorities such as the Comptroller of the Currency, the Federal Reserve, the Federal Deposit Insurance Corporation, and state banking agencies. Finally, banks can avail themselves of deposit insurance for account balances up to $100,000, while nonbank providers cannot offer this protection.

Because nonbank providers of personal on-line payments typically have chosen to invest in low-risk assets, the providers resemble "narrow banks"—institutions that hold only riskfree, liquid assets, and by doing so avoid the threat of bank runs. Because of this feature, narrow banking is sometimes proposed as a way to render deposit insurance unnecessary. (Nonbank payment providers are not required to disclose this information, though.) Consequently, there is probably little demand for traditional deposit insurance. Fraud, however, is a major concern. In light of this concern, some on-line payment providers have offered private insurance against fraudulent use of their customers' accounts, to enhance the attractiveness of their service. (This differs from deposit insurance, however, which insures against bank insolvency.)

These issues raise the question of whether nonbank personal on-line payment providers are in effect banks. The answer depends on the definition of "bank." If a bank is an institution that "takes deposits and makes loans," the answer would be no, as these providers typically invest in money market assets, rather than loans.[13] This is not the only definition of a bank, however. An alternative definition, codified in the Glass–Steagall Act, focuses on the role of banks as deposit takers. The Act precludes any institution other than a state-licensed money transmitter or a state or national bank from engaging in "the business of receiving deposits subject to check or to repayment upon presentation of a passbook, certificate of deposit, or other evidence of debt, or upon request of the depositor."[14] From an economic perspective, as receivers of funds subject to withdrawal or transfer upon the instruction of customers, nonbank on-line payment providers might be deemed to fit this definition. Alternatively, certain nonbank providers of arguably similar services—for instance, money transmitters such as Western Union and traveler's check firms such as American Express—are legally recognized and are licensed in several states to provide these services.

The resemblance of personal on-line payment providers to narrow banks also raises the issue of the complementarity between lending and deposit taking emphasized in various theories of banking. Some recent theories * * * suggest that the provision of transaction deposits naturally lends itself to wider banking activity, such as lending. In those theories, the provision of transaction deposits creates a form of liquidity that can be utilized to make loans more cheaply than those offered by other firms. If those theories are correct, and apply to the personal on-line payment

13. The definition paraphrases the definition of a bank contained in the Bank Holding Company Act of 1956, which considers a bank an institution that "(i) accepts demand deposits or deposits that the depositor may withdraw by check or similar means for payment to third parties or others; and (ii) is engaged in the business of making commercial loans" (Bank Holding Company Act of 1956, Section 2(C)(1) codified at 12 U.S.C. 1841(c)).

14. Glass–Steagall Act, Section 21A(2) codified at 12 USCS § 378(a)(2).

providers, then the providers might be transformed, over time, into more bank-like firms to take advantage of this economy. In contrast, the transmitters of small-value wire transfers and traveler's checks, although similar to personal on-line payment providers, have not transformed themselves into lenders, as these theories might imply.

* * *

C. ESCROW SERVICES

The online payment services discussed above help to speed up the fulfillment of purchase transactions, by giving the seller immediate access to the buyer's payment. They also provide a measure of security to sellers, by making it unnecessary for them to run the risk of bounced checks or chargebacks. These services, however, offer no protection to buyers, who remain subject to the risk that the seller will accept payment and then fail to ship the goods.

Online escrow services offer buyers protection against the risk of nondelivery.

> Escrow services generally operate like PayPal and Billpoint, except that an escrow service holds the buyer's payment until after the goods have been shipped and the buyer has had an opportunity to inspect them. Escrow services generally charge a higher fee than payment-only services and their tracking and insurance requirements can also add significant costs to a transaction. However, because escrow services provide substantially more protection for the buyer, their fees are more likely to be paid by the buyer, while payment-only services (and credit card association rules) generally prohibit sellers from imposing a surcharge to offset fees.

David E. Sorkin, *Payment Methods for Consumer-to-Consumer Online Transactions,* 35 AKRON L.REV. 1, 14–15 (2001). For an example of an online escrow service, see www.Escrow.com.

NOTES & QUESTIONS

Who should regulate? Before the advent of the Internet, most consumers obtained their banking services from a brick-and-mortar bank located near where they lived. Many banks now offer online banking services, allowing consumers to obtain banking services from a bank located in a distant state. With Internet-only banks, the consumer may not even know where the bank is located, and the same is likely to be true of P2P payment services like PayPal and Billpoint. Should out-of-state banks and national payment services be regulated (1) by the state where the consumer using their services is located, (2) by the state where the enterprise is headquartered, or (3) by the federal government?

D. MICROPAYMENTS

When you visit your favorite news website each morning, would you be willing to pay a fraction of a cent to read the story in the sports section about the big game last night? Or would you perhaps pay a few cents to read all the articles in the sports section? Would you be willing to pay a penny to read your favorite columnist on the humor site you frequent? Pricing schemes of this sort are a possible application of online micropayments.

A micropayment may be defined as a financial payment in an amount that is small relative to the transaction costs that would be incurred in making the payment using traditional payment mechanisms. For example, it is impractical to use a credit card for purchases of less than five dollars or so, due to the transaction fees extracted by the merchant's bank, the cardholder's bank, the acquirer, the card association, and other companies involved in processing the transaction.

In the late 1990's micropayments were heralded as a breakthrough payment technology for Internet commerce, one that would make possible a broad array of new business models. Micropayments seemed to be the ideal way to sell low-value digital products for small amounts of money, amounting to a large revenue stream in the aggregate. But micropayments never caught on.[8]

Micropayment systems generally function by setting up a payment intermediary that maintains an account in the name of a user, and allows the user to load it with funds from his checking account or credit card. The user then spends against the funded amount, with the intermediary transferring funds to the merchant. Purchase transactions do not directly involve any bank or credit card system, but rather involve only the merchant, the user, and the payment intermediary. One example of such a system is RocketCash, www.rocketcash.com.

Why have micropayment systems failed to achieve broad acceptance? Consider the following critique:

> Micropayment systems have not failed because of poor implementation; they have failed because they are a bad idea. Furthermore, since their weakness is systemic, they will continue to fail in the future.
>
> Proponents of micropayments often argue that the real world demonstrates user acceptance: Micropayments are used in a number of household utilities such as electricity, gas, and most germanely telecom services like long distance.
>
> These arguments run aground on the historical record. There have been a number of attempts to implement micropayments, and they have not caught on in even in a modest fashion—a partial list of floundering or failed systems includes FirstVirtual, Cybercoin, Millicent, Digicash, Internet Dollar, Pay2See, MicroMint and Cybercent. If there was going to be broad user support, we would have seen some glimmer of it by now.

8. Some of the existing P2P systems, like PayPal, allow transaction amounts that approach the level of micropayments, but are not practical for transaction amounts of less than a few dollars.

Furthermore, businesses like the gas company and the phone company that use micropayments offline share one characteristic: They are all monopolies or cartels. In situations where there is real competition, providers are usually forced to drop "pay as you go" schemes in response to user preference, because if they don't, anyone who can offer flat-rate pricing becomes the market leader. * * *

Why have micropayments failed? * * * [U]sers want predictable and simple pricing. Micropayments, meanwhile, waste the users' mental effort in order to conserve cheap resources, by creating many tiny, unpredictable transactions. Micropayments thus create in the mind of the user both anxiety and confusion, characteristics that users have not heretofore been known to actively seek out.

* * *

Micropayments, like all payments, require a comparison: "Is this much of X worth that much of Y?" There is a minimum mental transaction cost created by this fact that cannot be optimized away, because the only transaction a user will be willing to approve with no thought will be one that costs them nothing, which is no transaction at all.

Thus the anxiety of buying is a permanent feature of micropayment systems, since economic decisions are made on the margin—not, "Is a drink worth a dollar?" but, "Is the next drink worth the next dollar?" Anything that requires the user to approve a transaction creates this anxiety, no matter what the mechanism for deciding or paying is.

The desired state for micropayments—"Get the user to authorize payment without creating any overhead"—can thus never be achieved, because the anxiety of decision making creates overhead. No matter how simple the interface is, there will always be transactions too small to be worth the hassle.

* * *

Beneath a certain price, goods or services become harder to value, not easier, because the X for Y comparison becomes more confusing, not less. Users have no trouble deciding whether a $1 newspaper is worthwhile—did it interest you, did it keep you from getting bored, did reading it let you sound up to date—but how could you decide whether each part of the newspaper is worth a penny?

Was each of 100 individual stories in the newspaper worth a penny, even though you didn't read all of them? Was each of the 25 stories you read worth 4 cents apiece? If you read a story halfway through, was it worth half what a full story was worth? And so on.

* * *

This still leaves the problems that micropayments were meant to solve. How to balance users' strong preference for simple pricing with the enormous number of cheap, but not free, things available on the Net?

Micropayment advocates often act as if this is a problem particular to the Internet, but the real world abounds with items of vanishingly small value: a single stick of gum, a single newspaper article, a single day's rent. There are three principal solutions to this problem offline—aggregation, subscription, and subsidy—that are used individually or in combination. It is these same solutions—and not micropayments—that are likely to prevail online as well.

Aggregation

Aggregation follows the newspaper example earlier—gather together a large number of low-value things, and bundle them into a single higher-value transaction.

Call this the "Disneyland" pricing model—entrance to the park costs money, and all the rides are free. Likewise, the newspaper has a single cost, that, once paid, gives the user free access to all the stories.

* * *

Subscription

A subscription is a way of bundling diverse materials together over a set period, in return for a set fee from the user. As the newspaper example demonstrates, aggregation and subscription can work together for the same bundle of assets.

Subscription is more than just aggregation in time. Money's value is variable—$100 today is better than $100 a month from now. Furthermore, producers value predictability no less than consumers, so producers are often willing to trade lower subscription prices in return for lump sum payments and more predictable revenue stream.

* * *

Subsidy

Subsidy is by far the most common form of pricing for the resources micropayments were meant to target. Subsidy is simply getting someone other than the audience to offset costs. Again, the newspaper example shows that subsidy can exist alongside aggregation and subscription, since the advertisers subsidize most, and in some cases all, of a newspaper's costs. Advertising subsidy is the normal form of revenue for most Web sites offering content.

* * *

Against users' distaste for micropayments, the tools of aggregation, subscription and subsidy will be the principal tools for bridging the gap between atomized resources and demand for simple, predictable pricing.

* * *

Clay Shirky, The Case Against Micropayments, www.openp2p.com/lpt/a//p2p/2000/12/19/micropayments.html.

NOTES & QUESTIONS

1. *The future of micropayments.* Do you agree with the argument above that micropayments in Internet commerce are doomed to failure? Does the popularity of PayPal suggest that certain implementations of low-value payment systems may yet find acceptance in certain market niches?

2. *Regulating micropayments.* Do you think the same chargeback scheme that governs credit card transactions should apply to micropayment transactions? Does the minute amount of money involved change the type of legal regulations that should apply?

E. STORED-VALUE CARDS

A stored-value card is a card, usually the size of a credit card, that holds data representing money. The data storage medium may be a magnetic stripe of the sort that is used on credit and ATM cards, or it may be an integrated circuit ("IC") computer chip. Some IC cards also contain a microprocessor that works like a miniature computer, which allows the card to perform more sophisticated functions; these are sometimes known as "smart cards." The cardholder adds value to the card by paying money to the card's issuer, which may be a financial intermediary like a bank, an institution such as a public transportation system or a university, or an individual merchant such as a long-distance telephone company. A stored-value card is used by inserting it into a card reader, which can both read and modify the information stored on the card. Using the card subtracts value from the card and transmits it to the payee through an electronic network. Stored-value cards may implement security features, such as password protection and encryption.

Stored-value payment systems may also be implemented without a physical card. "A virtual stored-value card is just a card number associated with a charge account, without an actual plastic card to go with it. Shoppers can use a credit card to add value to their stored-value account. They can also use their stored value as they would the underlying credit card by providing the account number to the merchant." Stacey L. Schreft, *Clicking with Dollars: How Consumers Can Pay for Purchases from E-*

tailers, ECON. REV., First Quarter 2002, at 37, 54. Person-to-person payment systems like PayPal, discussed *supra*, may be thought of as virtual stored-value cards.

Issuers of stored-value cards derive several types of benefits from them. First, the issuer receives payment from the consumer upon purchase of the card, but only pays that money to merchants as the card is used. During the interim, the issuer gets free use of the funds, known as "float." A second benefit to issuers is called "slippage." This is the amount that remains unused on some stored-value cards, either because the amount is so small that the consumer will choose not to redeem the card, the consumer forgets to use up the residual stored value, or the consumer loses the card. While float and slippage amounts are very small from the standpoint of a consumer, they provide a significant aggregate benefit to the issuer.

Electronic Fund Transfers, Proposed Amendments to Regulation E

Board of Governors of the Federal Reserve System.
61 Fed. Reg. 19,696 (May 2, 1996).

* * *

Stored–Value Systems

Over the past few years the financial services industry has shown increasing interest in providing "stored-value cards" (also referred to as prepaid or value-added cards) to consumers. These cards maintain, typically in a computer chip or magnetic stripe, a "stored value" of funds available to the consumer for access primarily at retail locations. The balance recorded on the card is debited at a merchant's POS terminal when the consumer makes a purchase.

Products that could be characterized broadly as "stored-value" cover a wide range. In their simplest form, stored-value systems are targeted at low-value uses (public transit, pay telephones, or photocopiers, for example); the amount that can be stored on the card is limited; and the card is disposed of once its value has been used up. These cards typically have a single type of use, and only one card issuer and one entity (likely to be the same as the issuer) that accepts the card as payment for goods or services.

More sophisticated systems can involve large transactions and permit consumers to store value in the hundreds of dollars on a card. The cards may have multiple uses, and there may be multiple card issuers and multiple card-accepting merchants. The cards may allow the consumer to obtain cash from ATMs instead of, or in addition to, making purchases. At least one system (now in the pilot stage) would enable the consumer to transfer stored-value balances to another person's card. Some systems would provide access to funds in foreign currencies. Cards tend to be reloadable, allowing the consumer to load value onto the card, for example, by withdrawing funds from an account at a depository institution through a teller, via an ATM, or, potentially, via a specially-equipped telephone. Some systems are designed as stand-alone products. In other cases, stored-value features may be added to debit or credit cards. Some of these more sophisticated stored-value systems are in operation as pilot programs or are under development by financial institutions or associations of institutions.

Colleges and universities are increasingly adding a stored-value feature to student identification cards, so that students can make purchases at campus locations such as cafeterias, bookstores, and vending machines. In some cases, the educational institution is both the issuer and the only card-accepting entity; in others, the card is also accepted by off-campus merchants. In addition to the stored-value features that some student card systems may have, these systems may operate with student asset accounts maintained by the university or by a depository institution on behalf of the university; these accounts are covered by Regulation E.

There are significant differences among proposed systems in the manner that they handle balances and transaction data. * * *

* * *

Types of Stored–Value Systems

In some stored-value systems, the balance of funds available is recorded on the card, but is also maintained at a central data facility at a bank or elsewhere. The systems operate off-line; there is no authorization of transactions by communication with a database at a financial institution or elsewhere. Transaction data are periodically transmitted to and maintained by a data facility. As in the case of the traditional consumer deposit account accessed by a debit card, in these stored-value card systems a consumer has the right to draw upon funds held by an institution. The maintenance of a record of value and of transactions for a given card apart from the card itself—so that transactions are traceable to the individual card—strongly parallels the functioning of a deposit account. The Board believes that the facts support a finding that such systems involve an account for purposes of the EFTA. These systems are referred to below as "off-line accountable stored-value systems."

In another type of stored-value system that also operates off-line, the record of value is maintained only on the card itself, and not in a central database. Transaction data for debits to the card's "stored value" are recorded on the card and captured at merchant terminals (where they are maintained for a limited period of time). Only the aggregate amount of transactions for a given period is transmitted by the merchant to a financial institution or other entity so that the merchant can receive credit. Given the lack of a centrally maintained, ongoing record of individual card balances or of transaction data in these systems, it is more difficult to conclude that an "account" exists for purposes of Regulation E. These systems will be referred to below as "off-line unaccountable stored-value systems."

A third type of stored-value system operates in a manner that is the functional equivalent of using a debit card to access a traditional deposit account. Notably, this type of system involves on-line access to a database for purposes of transaction authorization and data capture. That is, when the card is used at an ATM or a POS terminal, the transaction is authorized by means of on-line communication with the data facility, where the transaction data are stored (including information such as merchant identification, amount, date, and card number). The balance of funds available to the consumer is not recorded on the card itself, as in off-line stored-value systems; instead, the balance information is maintained in the data facility. Two distinctions between these systems and traditional deposit accounts accessed by debit card are (1) the value associated with a card is limited to the amount that the cardholder has chosen to make accessible through the card (as opposed to a deposit account accessed by debit card, where the entire account is accessible and funds available may fluctuate); and (2) the value associated with the card is accessible only through use of the card itself (in contrast to deposit accounts accessible by debit card, which typically may be accessed through various means, including check, withdrawal slip, ACH, or telephone bill payment).

The Board believes these systems—which are referred to as "on-line stored-value systems"—meet the definition of a consumer asset account, and thus are covered by Regulation E, based on their on-line operation and extensive data capture and retention. * * *

* * *

Computer Network Payment Products

Parallel to the development of stored-value card products, there has been an increasing interest in other products that might adopt stored-value concepts. Systems are being proposed, for example, for making payments over computer networks, such as the Internet. In these cases, a balance of funds could be accessed via a consumer's personal computer, and transferred or used in purchases via a computer network. As in the case of card-based products, there is a range of network payment products in operation or under development.

Some of these network payment products involve on-line access to a consumer account in a financial institution, and thus are fully subject to Regulation E. Other products may involve various procedures for authorizing and carrying out transactions, and may or may not be subject to the regulation. * * * In general, the Board believes that the same principles should apply to network payment products as to stored-value card products in analyzing coverage under Regulation E. For example, the Board might consider applying a *de minimis* exemption to network payment products in the same way the Board is proposing for stored-value card products.

* * *

NOTES & QUESTIONS

1. *Privacy Concerns.* Privacy tops the list of user concerns with all the emerging payment systems. Stored-value cards can be designed to make transactions anonymous, or to make them traceable to the cardholder. Do you think the government should mandate the inclusion of anonymity or traceability features? Should this be left to the market?

2. *Tax implications of stored-value transfers.* Mondex is a stored-value system that may be used both with smart cards and over the Internet. Mondex sells value to a participating financial institution, which resells it to consumers, who may use the value to make a purchase from a participating merchant. "Each Mondex smart card has its own memory and control program, allowing any two cards to exchange value. Individuals can move cash from one card to another without having to communicate with the central computer at the bank. The chips in the cards communicate with each other by means of a special terminal or device." Thomas P. Brown, Robert D. Fram & Margaret Jane Radin, *Altered States: Electronic Commerce and Owning the Means of Value Exchange,* 1999 STAN. TECH. L. REV. 2, at ¶ 79 (1999). In a private letter ruling, the Internal Revenue Service determined that neither Mondex nor the financial institutions need recognize income when they transfer value in exchange for dollars. The IRS also determined that such transfers do not give rise to IRS reporting requirements applying to certain types of payment transactions. *See* Priv. Ltr. Rul. 97–43–047 (July 30, 1997). The ruling is discussed in John D. Muller, *Selected Developments in the Law of Cyberspace Payments*, 54 BUS. LAW. 403, 434 (1998).

F. ELECTRONIC CHECKS

While the use of checks is declining in most of the leading industrialized countries, check writing in the United States and Australia continues to rise—though at a decreasing rate. *See* COMMITTEE ON PAYMENT AND SETTLEMENT SYSTEMS, RETAIL PAYMENTS IN SELECTED COUNTRIES: A COMPARATIVE STUDY § 4.3 (1999). The popularity of personal checks in some countries is due to several factors: the check writer retains possession of the money the check represents for a day or two after it is spent; a check may be written for any amount; it may be cancelled and payment stopped until it is cleared and settled on behalf of the payee; and the check writer is not responsible for its unauthorized use, as when the signature is forged.

In view of this popularity, the Financial Services Technology Consortium ("FSTC"), a group of banks, large corporations and technology companies, has attempted to develop an electronic or online counterpart to paper checks. An electronic check would not only have the advantages of a paper check and be faster and less expensive to process, but it would also be subject to fewer errors. The FSTC's attempt to develop a true electronic check—an electronic record that would be the legal equivalent of a paper check—is called the eCheck Project. The eCheck uses public key cryptography. Like a paper check, an eCheck must be signed and endorsed, but with digital signatures accompanied by public key certificates. As such, the eCheck system depends upon certification authorities and a public key infrastructure that can be used to validate these digital signatures. A digital signature is applied by inserting a plastic "electronic checkbook" card containing an embedded microprocessor into a smart-card reader attached to a computer. Beginning in 1998 the federal government worked with the FSTC to conduct trials of this technology. For more information on the eCheck Project, see eCheck, echeck.commerce.net.

G. BILLING TO ANOTHER ACCOUNT

Pay-per-call has become a popular method of paying for information products that are delivered by telephone. The consumer dials a telephone number beginning with the "900" prefix, connects to an information service, receives a disclosure of the fee for the service (which may be a flat fee or a per-minute charge), and by not hanging up agrees to pay the fee. The charge for the service is itemized on the consumer's monthly telephone bill. The consumer sends payment for the entire bill to the telephone company, which remits the appropriate amount to the information provider. Pay-per-call billing is regulated by the Federal Trade Commission. *See* Trade Regulation Rule Pursuant to the Telephone Disclosure and Dispute Resolution Act of 1992, 16 C.F.R. pt. 308.

A similar system has been developed to pay for purchases in Internet commerce:

> Some PSPs [payment service providers] are offering a novel way for consumers who lack credit cards or who seek greater security and privacy to shop online. They allow consumers to have their purchases included on their monthly bills for telephone service or Internet access. Since phone companies and Internet service providers bill customers monthly, an individual account with these service providers is essentially a charge account, but without an associated charge card. These charge accounts differ from credit-card accounts because the credit they offer cannot revolve. The account holder is expected to pay the bill in full each month, and a late fee is imposed if the bill is not paid on time. If several months pass without payment being made in full, the service is discontinued.
>
> There are many advantages of this type of payment service and few disadvantages. It is available to almost everyone with Internet access at home since both telephone service and an Internet service provider are generally required to access the Internet. It is easy for merchants and for the PSP to offer because it piggybacks on the existing systems for sending bills for phone and Internet service. Consumers are afforded additional privacy and protection against fraud when using credit cards since their account information is not transmitted to the merchant and the billing process is discreet. The expenses they incur while cybershopping appear on their phone bills, for example, as associated with a phone number or with the name of the PSP. The main disadvantage is that not many e-tailers are accepting payments in this manner.

Stacey L. Schreft, *Clicking with Dollars: How Consumers Can Pay for Purchases from E-tailers*, ECON. REV., First Quarter 2002, at 37, 50–51. For a description of one such billing system, see eCharge, www.echarge.com.

CHAPTER SEVENTEEN

TAXATION OF ONLINE ECONOMIC ACTIVITY

Sales taxes on commercial transactions and income taxes on business profits are major sources of government tax revenues. With the growth of electronic commerce, more and more transactions that formerly would have taken place offline are conducted online. This shift to online commerce may have a major impact on whether a transaction will result in tax revenues, and if so which taxing authority has the right to those revenues. Thus, with large and ever-increasing sums of money changing hands through e-commerce, it was inevitable that issues of taxation would come to the fore.

Several characteristics of Internet commerce raise new issues, or heighten the salience of existing issues, regarding taxation. First, e-commerce facilitates transactions between a consumer in one state and a seller in another state. States depend on sellers to collect sales and use taxes on most sales of goods, but the lack of a connection between the seller and the taxing state places obstacles in the way of this mode of enforcement.

Second, the infrastructure needed to support e-commerce transactions is dramatically more portable, and less location-sensitive, than the storefronts needed to support traditional retailing. Most functions involved in the everyday operation of a website may be performed from a location that is remote from the computer server that houses the files comprising the website. The website files may be quickly relocated to a different computer server located in a different state or a different country, without any significant effect on the operation of the business. This makes it more feasible to relocate that infrastructure in response to tax incentives, and thus increases the significance of tax havens.

Third, the sale of goods that are delivered via digital download, such as software, music, and data, raises characterization issues. Most states impose sales and use taxes only on transactions involving tangible goods, and on a limited range of services. If a digital good is characterized as intangible, it may not be subject to such taxation. The characterization of a transaction may also determine which country has the right to tax the transaction, and at what rate.

Fourth, sales of digital goods entail no shipping costs or delays, and so increase the likelihood of business-to-consumer sales across international borders. Such sales, which bypass any domestic transaction in the taxing state, may evade the existing tax structure.

Fifth, e-commerce reduces the barriers to entry to a national and international market, allowing small entities entrée to those broader markets. The complexities of a taxing environment consisting of 7,500 taxing jurisdictions within the United States, and numerous others internationally, may be severely burdensome for a small enterprise.

I. Domestic Taxation Issues

In the late 1990s, there was widespread concern that heavy-handed imposition of taxes by states and localities might stunt the growth of electronic commerce. Congress was unable to decide how e-commerce transactions should be taxed, and so enacted stopgap legislation, called the Internet Tax Freedom Act ("ITFA"), Pub. L. 105–277, 112 Stat. 2681–719 (1998), 47 U.S.C. § 151 note, that temporarily limited the authority of states to tax e-commerce. In its principal provisions, the ITFA (1) forbids states and localities from taxing the provision of Internet access services, grandfathering those access taxes that were imposed and actually collected prior to October 1, 1998, and (2) forbids multiple and discriminatory taxes on electronic commerce.[1] ITFA § 1101(a).

The ITFA also created the Advisory Commission on Electronic Commerce ("ACEC"), which it directed to "conduct a thorough study of Federal, State and local, and international taxation and tariff treatment of transactions using the Internet and Internet access and other comparable intrastate, interstate or international sales activities." ITFA § 1102(g)(1). The ACEC consisted of 19 members: eight representatives from state and local governments, eight representing the electronic commerce industry, and three federal government officials. The 16 non-federal commissioners were selected politically: five each by the Senate Majority Leader and the Speaker of the House, and three each by the House and Senate Minority Leaders. ITFA § 1102(b)(1)(C). As a result of the appointment procedure, the commissioners were sharply divided along ideological lines. The ACEC was to transmit to Congress a report containing those of its findings and recommendations that were agreed to by at least two-thirds of its membership. There was little upon which two-thirds of the membership could agree: only a few recommendations concerning the digital divide, privacy implications of Internet taxation, and international taxes and tariffs. The April 2000 report, however, contains useful discussion of the issues, and makes a variety of recommendations to which a majority (but not a two-thirds majority) of the commissioners subscribe.

1. A "multiple tax" is a tax imposed by two states on the same transaction. A "discriminatory tax" includes one imposed on an e-commerce transaction that is not imposed on a similar transaction conducted offline; one imposed at a different rate from the tax on corresponding offline transactions; and one that imposes a tax on a different person or entity than the corresponding offline tax does. ITFA § 1104(2) & (6).

Advisory Commission on Electronic Commerce, Report to Congress

(2000).
www.ecommercecommission.org/acec_report.pdf

I. Background

A. *The Evolution of Electronic Commerce*

* * *

Five years ago, the terms "electronic commerce" and "e-commerce" were virtually unheard of; today, they are household words. Notwithstanding the common usage of these terms today, the meaning and breadth of these terms are still very much uncertain. For example, it could be argued that e-commerce refers only to transactions conducted over the Internet. Conversely, e-commerce could include all transactions using the same telecommunications infrastructure as the Internet such as catalogue orders placed by telephone or facsimile.

For purposes of this report, "e-commerce," as defined in the Internet Tax Freedom Act, includes "any transaction conducted over the Internet or through Internet access, comprising the sale, lease, license, offer, or delivery of property, goods, services, or information, whether or not for consideration, and includes the provision of Internet access." The Act also specifically requires all recommendations to be "tax and technologically neutral and [to] apply to all forms of remote commerce." Therefore, the Commission's recommendations on taxation are intended to apply to all forms of remote commerce regardless of whether conducted over the Internet, through the telephone, via facsimile, through the common carrier or by any other means.

B. *The Impact of Electronic Commerce on the Economy*

* * *

Many private-sector research firms and academic institutions are conducting studies on the rapid rise of e-commerce and its positive ripple effects throughout the economy. Existing growth estimates vary greatly, however, due to the varying definitions and research methodologies these firms use to collect and analyze data. For example, some studies have focused on business-to-business transactions to gauge growth and economic impact while others have focused on business-to-consumer e-commerce, ranging from hardware and software to electronic retailing and backbone infrastructure and telecommunications.

On March 2, 2000, the United States Department of Commerce ("Commerce Department") Census Bureau released its first official estimate of online retail sales. According to this estimate, online retail sales equaled $5.3 billion or 0.64% of total retail sales during the fourth quarter of 1999. For purposes of this estimate, the term "retail sales" includes only sales of tangible goods (e.g., books, computer equipment, furniture and apparel) and does not include sales of services (e.g., entertainment, travel or financial services). This new e-commerce indicator will be released on a quarterly basis.[2]

* * * Early commercial ventures onto the Internet were generally limited to business models with "virtual" storefronts. These businesses operate only on the Internet and do not have physical storefronts (although they do have physical locations to facilitate back-end billing and fulfillment).

Today, traditional, physical retailers also are incorporating e-commerce tools into their business models and using the Internet to create Web sites as additional distribution channels through which to sell their goods and services. These retailers, often referred to as "click and mortar"[11] businesses, benefit from having a Web presence because many consumers still rely on the tangible experience they have gained inside a brick and mortar store when making an online purchase. There is also significant business-to-business use of the Internet to realize efficiencies in distribution, order fulfillment, billing, and other operational areas. Traditional catalogue-only sellers are also joining the ranks of virtual retailers and creating Web sites.

The trends in consumer buying behavior are more difficult to identify than emerging business models. With Internet commerce only in its fifth full year, it is still early to draw conclusions and make projections on the extent to which consumers of Internet goods and services are shifting their purchases from other retail channels, such as catalogues, or simply increasing their overall purchases.

C. *The Impact of Electronic Commerce on State/Local Government Revenues*

Some have expressed a concern that the rise in businesses conducting remote commerce, combined with a shift in consumer buying habits, will lead to a decrease in state and local sales and use tax revenues. In order to determine the immediacy of these concerns, it is necessary to examine how the rise of Internet sales has thus far altered sales tax collections. It is also important to examine all available evidence regarding the predicted future collection of these taxes.

In order to understand these trends and predictions, however, it is essential to understand how and why the use tax corollary to the sales tax operates. Currently, 45 states impose a state sales tax. All states that levy sales taxes also levy use taxes. Use taxes are most commonly due when an item is purchased from a business in another state and the business does not have sufficient presence (nexus) in the consumer's state for the sale to be subjected to sales tax. In the event that a consumer purchases an item and the sales tax is not collected, the consumer is required to remit the use

2. [For the first quarter of 2002, the Census Bureau estimated e-commerce sales at $9.8 billion, representing 1.3 percent of total retail sales.—Eds.]

11. The term "click and mortar" stems from the term "brick and mortar" and refers to those businesses that conduct business through both a physical storefront and a Web site. "Brick and mortar" businesses, also known as "Main Street retailers," are businesses that only conduct business through physical storefronts.

tax according to the location of consumption of the item. However, the rate of remittance of the use tax is low for business-to-consumer sales. One reason for these low collection rates is that taxing agencies have no practical means of identifying individual purchases or their consumers, making enforcement difficult and in many cases not cost effective. Most use tax remittances come from business-to-business sales where businesses are registered within the states and subject to audits. There is no conclusive data to indicate what the collection rates of the use tax would be on business-to-consumer sales if jurisdictions increased enforcement and public education of use tax obligations.

Most Internet commerce involves business-to-business sales. Forrester Research, Inc. estimates that business-to-business Internet commerce will grow from $43 billion in 1998, to $1.3 trillion by 2003, accounting for 9.4% of all business-to-business sales. Business-to-business Internet sales pose fewer issues regarding sales or use tax collection due to higher compliance rates resulting from audits by taxing authorities. The actual amount of use tax assessed varies from state to state depending on how extensive of an audit program a state maintains.

It is especially difficult to calculate the amount of sales and use tax not collected on business-to-consumer Internet sales or on any other remote sales. Some academic estimates suggest that uncollected taxes resulting from Internet sales will be less than 2% of all sales tax revenue in 2003.[13]

Many of these estimates do not distinguish between sales of taxable and non-taxable goods and services. Further, it should be noted that, to the extent Internet sales are displacing what would have otherwise been non-Internet remote sales to consumers, the use of the Internet to facilitate a sale does not increase the tax loss to state and local governments. To the extent Internet sales are replacing purchases that would have otherwise been made through a "brick and mortar" store that collected sales tax, revenue losses to states and local governments could occur. However, even this is complicated by the fact that some remote sellers collect sales and use taxes voluntarily, while other "click and mortar" sellers are required to collect sales taxes based on their substantial nexus in a state where their product is delivered. There is no data on how many businesses are collecting taxes on remote business-to-consumer sales.

Adding to the complexity of determining the amount of sales taxes actually collected on business-to-consumer sales, some "click and mortar" retailers are not collecting sales and use taxes on items purchased through the Internet where substantial nexus may be an issue. Certain businesses that have a large physical presence throughout the country have established their Web operations as separate entities which have a much more limited physical presence. Although their Web addresses carry the name of the parent company and they advertise their Internet sites in their stores,

13. Austan Goolsbee and Jonathan Zittrain, "Evaluating the Costs and Benefits of Taxing Internet Commerce," National Tax Journal, vol. 52 no. 3 (Sep., 1999); and Donald Bruce and William F. Fox, "E–Commerce in the Context of Declining State Sales Tax Bases," (Feb. 2000).

their Web sites are separate from their "Main Street" retail operations. Accordingly, most are only collecting and remitting sales taxes in the states where the "dot com" affiliate has substantial nexus.

* * *

II. Domestic Tax Issues & Proposals

A. *Sales and Use Taxes*

One of the most fundamental issues before the Commission concerns the application of state and local sales and use taxes to Internet and other remote retail sales. Sales taxes are "consumption-type" taxes designed to generate revenue. In general, these taxes are calculated and collected by businesses at the point of sale and remitted to the appropriate taxing authorities.

Sales taxes have been levied throughout history, and became more widely applied in the United States beginning with the Great Depression. States' authority to levy these taxes is derived from the 10th Amendment of the United States Constitution ("the Constitution"), which states, "The powers not delegated to the United States by the Constitution, nor prohibited by it to the States, are reserved to the States respectively, or to the people." Today, there are over 7,500 state and local governments levying sales taxes out of a potential 30,000 jurisdictions. The five states that do not levy a state sales tax are Delaware, New Hampshire, Montana, Oregon, and Alaska. Local sales taxes are currently authorized in 33 states.

Ordinarily imposed on the sale of tangible goods, the rates for these taxes range from 0.875% to 11%. A small number of state and local governments also impose sales tax on some services. These include, for example, personal and repair services. Besides determining their own rates, states and, in some cases, local governments define and classify items and exempt certain items within their tax codes. Many of these exemptions target necessities, such as food and prescription medicines. Throughout the year, tax rates, definitions, classifications, and exemptions included in the sales tax code may be changed.

State and local governments that levy sales taxes rely on them as a major source of revenue for their general funds. According to the United States Census Bureau, state and local governments collected approximately a total of $237 billion in sales and use taxes in 1999, comprising 24.8% of all revenues generated in that year. Through these general funds, state and local governments provide a variety of public services to their residents.

The inability of state and local governments to require remote sellers to collect use taxes can be traced back to a line of the United States Supreme Court ("the Court") cases that established the "substantial nexus" standard.[24] These cases point to the Commerce Clause of the Constitution and Congress' role to regulate interstate commerce as the

24. Quill Corp. v. North Dakota By and Through Heitkamp, 504 U.S. 298 (1992), and National Bellas Hess, Inc. v. Dept. of Revenue of State of Illinois, 386 U.S. 753 (1967).

basis for restricting states from forcing out-of-state sellers to collect use tax. With the explosion of e-commerce, there are concerns that an increasing number of consumers will purchase items through remote sales channels such as the Internet and catalogues, and sales tax revenues from face-to-face sales may diminish. At the same time, there are indications that online activity is also driving increased sales for "brick and mortar" retailers.

While the growth of e-commerce has had a positive effect on state and local government revenues, the potential impact of e-commerce on future sales tax revenues is uncertain at this time. A recent study by Forrester Research, Inc., estimates that, in 1999, state and local governments collected $140 million in sales and use taxes from business-to-consumer purchases over the Internet, but were unable to collect approximately $525 million in sales and use taxes from Internet retail purchases. * * *

While the exact impact of e-commerce on sales tax revenues may be uncertain, clearly the need for substantial sales tax simplification is necessary in this emerging digital economy. In the course of the Commission's examination of the impact of e-commerce on sales and use tax collections, there was general agreement among the Commissioners that the current sales and use tax system is complex and burdensome. Most, if not all, of the Commissioners expressed the view that fundamental uniformity and simplification of the existing system are essential. The need for nationwide consistency and certainty for sellers as well as the need to alleviate the financial and logistical tax collection burdens and liability of sellers were common themes throughout discussions.

Commissioners also identified issues raised by sales of digitized goods over the Internet. They discussed the challenge of determining the identity and location of the consumer of digitized goods and the need to protect consumer privacy rights.

B. *Business Activity Taxes*

Many states and some local governments levy corporate income and franchise taxes on companies that either operate or conduct business activities within their jurisdictions. Income taxes are either levied as taxes on the net or gross income of businesses. A franchise tax is measured by the net income of a business. While providing revenue for states, these taxes also serve to pay for the privilege of doing business in a state. With the exception of Michigan, Nevada, South Dakota, Washington, and Wyoming, all states and the District of Columbia levy general corporate income taxes. The rates for income taxes range from 1% to 9.99%.

With the growth of the Internet, companies are increasingly able to conduct transactions without the constraint of geopolitical boundaries. The increasing rate of interstate and international business-to-business and business-to-consumer transactions may raise questions over states' ability to collect income taxes from companies conducting business within their jurisdiction. According to 15 U.S.C. § 381 (commonly referred to as "P.L. 86–272"), states may not levy taxes on the net income of sellers of tangible personal property derived from interstate commerce if the only business activities within the state consist of:

> "(1) the solicitation of orders by such person, or his representative, in such State for sales of tangible personal property, which orders are sent outside the State for approval or rejection, and if approved, are filled by shipment or delivery from a point outside the State; and (2) the solicitation of orders by such person, or his representative, in such State in the name of or for the benefit of a prospective customer of such person, if orders by such customer to such person to enable such customer to fill orders resulting from such solicitation [are orders described in paragraph (1)]."

C. *Internet Access Taxes*

* * *

As provided under the [Internet Tax Freedom] Act, presently there is a moratorium on taxes on the sale of Internet access, unless such taxes were authorized by statute and enforced prior to the promulgation of the Act. The moratorium began on October 1, 1998 and will continue through October 21, 2001.[3] At the time the Act passed, 12 states and the District of Columbia asserted that they levied sales taxes on Internet access. In addition, several Colorado cities and Tucson, Arizona have attempted to impose taxes on Internet access. Since the moratorium's enactment, several states have reversed their policies on taxing Internet access. At the writing of this report, eight states are assessing sales taxes on Internet access charges.

* * *

NOTES & QUESTIONS

1. *Recommendation on nexus factors.* To address the perceived need for greater certainty regarding the extent of a state's authority to impose sales and use taxes on electronic commerce transactions, a majority of the Commissioners recommended that Congress

> [c]larify that the following factors would not, in and of themselves, establish a seller's physical presence in a state for purposes of determining whether a seller has sufficient nexus with that state to impose collection obligations: (a) a seller's use of an Internet service provider ("ISP") that has physical presence in a state; (b) the placement of a seller's digital data on a server located in that particular state; (c) a seller's use of telecommunications services provided by a telecommunications provider that has physical presence in that state; (d) a seller's ownership of intangible property that is used or is present in that state; (e) the presence of a seller's customers in a state; (f) a seller's affiliation with another taxpayer that has physical presence in that state; (g) the performance of

3. [The moratorium was extended through November 1, 2003, by the Internet Tax Nondiscrimination Act, Pub. L. No. 107–75, 115 Stat. 703 (2001).—Eds.]

repair or warranty services with respect to property sold by a seller that does not otherwise have physical presence in that state; (h) a contractual relationship between a seller and another party located within that state that permits goods or products purchased through the seller's Web site or catalogue to be returned to the other party's physical location within that state; and (i) the advertisement of a seller's business location, telephone number, and Web site address.

Note the overlap between these factors, relating to the nexus needed for taxation, and the factors that have been held not to support exercise of personal jurisdiction based on online activity, as discussed in Chapter 7, *supra*. Should the criteria for personal jurisdiction be congruent with those establishing a state's taxing authority? Are there any good reasons for divergences between the two sets of criteria?

2. *Origin-based sales tax regime.* Consider the following suggested resolution of the problem of determining when a state can require a seller to collect use taxes:

> A particularly attractive option is to collect taxes on interstate sales not, as now, on the basis of the buyer's place of residence but in the *seller's* principal place of business. Amazon.com's sales would then be taxed in the state of Washington, no matter where any particular book has been purchased and shipped.
>
> Such an origin-based sales tax regime would obviate concerns over neutrality and fairness: All sales could be taxed at the same rate by a state or locality and would be so taxed, unless a given jurisdiction decided otherwise. Business concerns over compliance costs and legal uncertainty would vanish, since no seller would have tax collection obligations except in his home state. Most important, an origin-based sales tax system would foster state competition by re-connecting taxation with representation—or, as economists might say, by aligning the economic incidence of taxation with its *political* incidence. The existing system permits states to export sales tax collection obligations to sellers beyond their borders, providing only that the sellers have a nexus. (Tellingly, virtually all states *exempt* their own industries.) Under an origin-based system, [Utah] could impose tax collection obligations for sales through the Internet or any other channel—but only on interstate sales by Utah firms. And of course there would be the healthy risk that over-taxed businesses might flee one state for a more accommodating jurisdiction. Exit rights and tax competition would over time accomplish what voting, all too often, does not—discipline in state taxing and spending.

Michael S. Greve, *Yes, Tax the 'Net; Don't subsidize e-commerce; instead, reform sales taxes*, WEEKLY STANDARD, May 15, 2000, at 11.

3. *Tax on Internet access?* Do you agree with the recommendation by a majority of the Commissioners that Congress "[m]ake permanent the current moratorium on any transaction taxes on the sale of Internet access, including taxes that were grandfathered under the Internet Tax Freedom Act."? Is there any good reason for treating Internet access any differently from other telecommunications services, with respect to taxation?

4. *Neutrality.* In a 1996 discussion paper, the United States Department of the Treasury posited neutrality as the touchstone for resolving issues of taxation in e-commerce:

> A fundamental guiding principle should be neutrality. Neutrality requires that the tax system treat economically similar income equally, regardless of whether earned through electronic means or through more conventional channels of commerce. Ideally, tax rules would not affect economic choices about the structure of markets and commercial activities. This will ensure that market forces alone determine the success or failure of new commercial methods. The best means by which neutrality can be achieved is through an approach which adopts and adapts existing principles—in lieu of imposing new or additional taxes.
>
> Recent technological developments may appear to be radical innovations primarily because they have evolved within a relatively short period of time. However, careful examination may very well reveal that few, if any, of these emerging issues will be so intractable that their resolution will not be found using existing principles, appropriately adjusted.

U.S. TREASURY DEPARTMENT, SELECTED TAX POLICY IMPLICATIONS OF GLOBAL ELECTRONIC COMMERCE ¶ 6.2 (1996), www.treas.gov/taxpolicy/internet.html. Given the issues raised in the readings above, do you think a neutrality-based approach is equal to the task?

A. SALES AND USE TAXES

All but five of the states impose sales and use taxes, which together constitute some 25 percent of all state and local tax revenues. A third of the states authorize localities to assess their own sales taxes, with the result that there are some 7,500 different taxing jurisdictions throughout the country.

Sales taxes usually apply to transactions between a seller and a consumer both located in the same state. The taxing state requires the seller to collect and remit the tax, and has the authority to enforce its laws against a non-complying seller. Use taxes raise more difficult issues. A use tax applies to a purchase by a consumer located in the taxing state, from an out-of-state seller, for use, consumption, or storage within the taxing state. State law requires the consumer in such a transaction to remit the use tax to the state. Most consumers are unaware of the obligation, however, and most of those who are aware of the obligation ignore it with impunity, since states find it impractical to enforce the use tax laws against individual consumers (except with respect to items that must be registered with the state, such as automobiles and boats).

In an effort to increase their collections of use taxes, states seek to require out-of-state sellers to collect the taxes due and remit them to the state. In *Quill Corp. v. North Dakota*, 504 U.S. 298 (1992), the Supreme Court held that a state may not, consistently with the Commerce Clause, require an out-of-state seller to collect use tax on sales to state residents, where the seller's only contact with the state consists of marketing its products to state residents and delivering them by mail or common carrier. This is so, the Court held, even if the seller has enough contacts with the state to satisfy the requirements of the Due Process Clause. The Court affirmed its prior holding that such a collection burden may be imposed only on a business that has a "substantial nexus" with the state.

> * * * Under *Complete Auto's* four-part test, we will sustain a tax against a Commerce Clause challenge so long as the "tax [1] is applied to an activity with a substantial nexus with the taxing State, [2] is fairly apportioned, [3] does not discriminate against interstate commerce, and [4] is fairly related to the services provided by the State." [*Complete Auto Transit, Inc. v. Brady,* 430 U.S. 274,] 279 [(1977)]. [*National Bellas Hess, Inc. v. Department of Revenue*, 386 U.S. 753 (1967)] concerns the first of these tests and stands for the proposition that a vendor whose only contacts with the taxing State are by mail or common carrier lacks the "substantial nexus" required by the Commerce Clause.
>
> * * *
>
> The State of North Dakota relies less on *Complete Auto* and more on the evolution of our due process jurisprudence. The State contends that the nexus requirements imposed by the Due Process and Commerce Clauses are equivalent and that if, as we concluded above, a mail-order house that lacks a physical presence in the taxing State nonetheless satisfies the due process "minimum contacts" test, then that corporation also meets the Commerce Clause "substantial nexus" test. We disagree. Despite the similarity in phrasing, the nexus requirements of the Due Process and Commerce Clauses are not identical. The two standards are animated by different constitutional concerns and policies.
>
> Due process centrally concerns the fundamental fairness of governmental activity. Thus, at the most general level, the due process nexus analysis requires that we ask whether an individual's connections with a State are substantial enough to legitimate the State's exercise of power over him. We have, therefore, often identified "notice" or "fair warning" as the analytic touchstone of due process nexus analysis. In contrast, the Commerce Clause and its nexus requirement are informed not so much by concerns about fairness for the individual defendant as by structural concerns about the effects of state regulation on the national economy. Under the Articles of Confederation, state taxes and duties hindered and suppressed interstate commerce; the Framers intended the Commerce Clause as a cure for these structural ills. * * *

The *Complete Auto* analysis reflects these concerns about the national economy. The second and third parts of that analysis, which require fair apportionment and non-discrimination, prohibit taxes that pass an unfair share of the tax burden onto interstate commerce. The first and fourth prongs, which require a substantial nexus and a relationship between the tax and state-provided services, limit the reach of state taxing authority so as to ensure that state taxation does not unduly burden interstate commerce. Thus, the "substantial nexus" requirement is not, like due process' "minimum contacts" requirement, a proxy for notice, but rather a means for limiting state burdens on interstate commerce. Accordingly, contrary to the State's suggestion, a corporation may have the "minimum contacts" with a taxing State as required by the Due Process Clause, and yet lack the "substantial nexus" with that State as required by the Commerce Clause.

* * *

* * *Undue burdens on interstate commerce may be avoided not only by a case-by-case evaluation of the actual burdens imposed by particular regulations or taxes, but also, in some situations, by the demarcation of a discrete realm of commercial activity that is free from interstate taxation. *Bellas Hess* followed the latter approach and created a safe harbor for vendors "whose only connection with customers in the [taxing] State is by common carrier or the United States mail." Under *Bellas Hess,* such vendors are free from state-imposed duties to collect sales and use taxes.[8]

Like other bright-line tests, the *Bellas Hess* rule appears artificial at its edges: Whether or not a State may compel a vendor to collect a sales or use tax may turn on the presence in the taxing State of a small sales force, plant, or office. Cf. *National Geographic Society v. California Bd. of Equalization,* 430 U.S. 551 (1977); *Scripto, Inc. v. Carson,* 362 U.S. 207 (1960). This artificiality, however, is more than offset by the benefits of a clear rule. Such a rule firmly establishes the boundaries of legitimate state authority to impose a duty to collect sales and use taxes and reduces litigation concerning those taxes. This benefit is important, for as we have so frequently noted, our law in this area is something of a "quagmire" and the "application of constitutional principles to specific state statutes leaves much room for controversy and

8. In addition to its common-carrier contacts with the State, Quill also licensed software to some of its North Dakota clients. * * * The State "concedes that the existence in North Dakota of a few floppy diskettes to which Quill holds title seems a slender thread upon which to base nexus." Brief for Respondent 46. We agree. Although title to "a few floppy diskettes" present in a State might constitute some minimal nexus, in *National Geographic Society v. California Bd. of Equalization,* 430 U.S. 551, 556 (1977), we expressly rejected a " 'slightest presence' standard of constitutional nexus." We therefore conclude that Quill's licensing of software in this case does not meet the "substantial nexus" requirement of the Commerce Clause.

confusion and little in the way of precise guides to the States in the exercise of their indispensable power of taxation." *Northwestern States Portland Cement Co. v. Minnesota,* 358 U.S. 450, 457–458 (1959).

Moreover, a bright-line rule in the area of sales and use taxes also encourages settled expectations and, in doing so, fosters investment by businesses and individuals. Indeed, it is not unlikely that the mail-order industry's dramatic growth over the last quarter century is due in part to the bright-line exemption from state taxation created in *Bellas Hess.*

* * *

This aspect of our decision is made easier by the fact that the underlying issue is not only one that Congress may be better qualified to resolve, but also one that Congress has the ultimate power to resolve. No matter how we evaluate the burdens that use taxes impose on interstate commerce, Congress remains free to disagree with our conclusions. * * * Indeed, in recent years Congress has considered legislation that would "overrule" the *Bellas Hess* rule. Its decision not to take action in this direction may, of course, have been dictated by respect for our holding in *Bellas Hess* that the Due Process Clause prohibits States from imposing such taxes, but today we have put that problem to rest. Accordingly, Congress is now free to decide whether, when, and to what extent the States may burden interstate mail-order concerns with a duty to collect use taxes.

* * *

Quill Corp. v. North Dakota, 504 U.S. at 311–18.

The Court has indicated that the "substantial nexus" requirement is satisfied only if the taxpayer has a "physical presence" in the taxing jurisdiction. *Barclays Bank PLC v. Franchise Tax Board*, 512 U.S. 298, 312 n.10 (1994). It is clear that a business with an office, storefront, sales force, or distribution point within a state is subject to the state's taxing jurisdiction; and it is equally clear that a business whose only contact with a state is the shipment of goods to residents of the state via common carrier may *not* be required to collect taxes on such sales. In between these two extremes there is a great deal of uncertainty, as it is not at all clear what constitutes a "physical presence."

NOTES & QUESTIONS

A federal solution? The Commerce Clause has been interpreted as both a grant of legislative authority to Congress, and a limitation on the legislative authority of the states. In the latter application, it is often referred to as the Dormant Commerce Clause. Unlike most constitutional decisions, a judicial decision applying the Dormant Commerce Clause is subject to override by Congress. This is because such a decision represents no more than the court's best guess regarding whether Congress would consider the challenged state law an interference with its plenary power to regulate interstate commerce. Congress retains the authority to declare that it has no objection to the state law, thereby rendering the law compatible with the Commerce Clause. Thus, Congress could legislatively override the Supreme Court's determination that a state may not require a company to collect use tax unless the company has a "substantial nexus" with the taxing state: "Congress is now free to decide whether, when, and to what extent the States may burden interstate mail-order concerns with a duty to collect use taxes." *Quill v. North Dakota*, 504 U.S. at 318. Should Congress exercise this authority in the context of electronic commerce? If so, is there any basis for not doing the same with respect to sales via catalogue, direct mail, and other long-distance marketing methods?

1. THE "SUBSTANTIAL NEXUS" REQUIREMENT

a. Integration of Online and Offline Businesses

Suppose that a seller does not itself have any physical presence in the state, but is affiliated in some way with another company that does have such a presence. Under what circumstances is the presence of that affiliated company attributable to the seller, for purposes of establishing nexus with the state?

One set of issues arises when a brick-and-mortar retailer, with a physical presence in one or more states, seeks to avoid attribution of that physical presence to its online operations. If a retailer with a physical presence in all fifty states sets up a website and begins selling goods through the site, the retailer will be required to collect use taxes on all sales to customers in states that impose such a tax. This will place the retailer at a competitive disadvantage with respect to freestanding online sellers that satisfy the nexus requirement in few or no states, which by virtue of the Supreme Court's interpretation of the Commerce Clause will be immune from such collection obligations. The retailer will also lose a potential competitive advantage with respect to brick-and-mortar sellers, which are required to collect sales tax on all transactions.

Some retailers have sought to avoid this attribution of physical presence by structuring their online operation as a legally distinct entity.

In the Matter of the Petition for Redetermination Under the Sales and Use Tax Law of Borders Online, Inc.

Bd. of Equalization of the State of California, SC OHA 97–638364; 56270. (2001).

This opinion considers the merits of a petition for redetermination for the period April 1, 1998, through September 30, 1999. At the Board hearing, petitioner protested a determination related to petitioner's sales to California purchasers.

Petitioner, an out-of-state corporation, makes online retail sales of tangible personal property (e.g., primarily books, videos, music and gift items) via the Internet. The goods petitioner sells to California purchasers are delivered by common carrier from outside California. Petitioner alleges that it is a separate and distinct legal entity from Borders, Inc. (hereafter Borders), an affiliated corporation that sells similar goods in "brick-and-mortar" stores throughout California. Petitioner further alleges that it did not maintain, occupy or use any place of business in California during the period in question. (See Rev. & Tax. Code, § 6203, subd. (c)(1).)

In a letter dated July 29, 1999, the Sales and Use Tax Department (hereafter the Department) informed petitioner that the Department had concluded that petitioner was a retailer engaged in business in California and was obligated to collect use tax from petitioner's California customers. (See Rev. & Tax. Code, § 6203, subd. (a).) The Department based its conclusion, at least in part, on the significance of a paragraph, which petitioner had posted on petitioner's web site under the heading of "RETURNS." The record of this matter reflects that this paragraph stated, in pertinent part, that:

> "You may return items purchased at borders.com to any Borders Books and Music store within 30 days of the date the item was shipped. All returns must be accompanied by a valid packing slip (your online receipt and shipping notification are not valid substitutes for a packing slip on returns to stores). Gift items may be returned or exchanged if they are accompanied by a valid gift packing slip. You may not return opened music or video items, unless they are defective."

Petitioner alleges that this paragraph first appeared on petitioner's web site some time in June of 1999. Petitioner further alleges that petitioner's internal records reflect that this paragraph was removed from petitioner's web site on or around August 11, 1999. Thus, petitioner apparently removed the paragraph in question shortly after petitioner received notice that the Department considered this paragraph to be evidence that petitioner had a use tax collection obligation under California law. Petitioner has not presented any evidence that would establish that petitioner ever expressly disavowed, either publicly or internally, the policy reflected by the paragraph in question.

Petitioner contends that, notwithstanding the restrictions stated in the posted paragraph, petitioner's customers could return merchandise at a Borders store without a valid packing slip and receive a store credit. Additionally, petitioner admits that, throughout the period in question, petitioner's California customers could obtain cash refunds by returning merchandise purchased from petitioner, together with a valid packing slip, to a Borders store. In other words, petitioner's customers' ability to obtain such cash refunds from Borders was not dependent on whether the paragraph at issue was posted on petitioner's web site. According to petitioner, Borders also provided return services to individuals who had purchased merchandise from one of Borders's or petitioner's competitors; however,

Borders did not, and would not, provide cash refunds to customers of Borders's or petitioner's competitors.

Petitioner alleges that any merchandise petitioner's customers returned to Borders was not sent back to petitioner but, instead, was added to Borders's inventory. Petitioner claims that Borders did not charge petitioner for return and exchange services. Finally, petitioner further claims that Borders absorbed any losses associated with accepting returns of defective merchandise from petitioner's customers.

OPINION

With certain exceptions that are not relevant to this matter, Revenue and Taxation Code section (hereafter Section) 6203 imposes a use tax collection obligation on ". . . every retailer engaged in business in this state and making sales of tangible personal property for storage, use, or other consumption in this state. . . ." Under subdivision (c)(2) of Section 6203, the meaning of "retailer engaged in business in this state" includes:

> "[a]ny retailer having any representative, agent, salesperson, canvasser, independent contractor, or solicitor operating in this state under the authority of the retailer or its subsidiary for the purpose of selling, delivering, installing, assembling, or the taking of orders for any tangible personal property."

When, as here, no dispute exists with respect to an out-of-state seller's status as a retailer, three additional requirements must be satisfied for the seller to be a "retailer engaged in business in this state" under Section 6203, subdivision (c)(2).

First, the out-of-state retailer must have a representative, agent, salesperson, canvasser, independent contractor or solicitor (hereafter, collectively, representative). Second, this representative must be operating in California under the authority of the out-of-state retailer or its subsidiary (i.e., the in-state representative must be authorized to act on the out-of-state retailer's behalf). Third, the out-of-state retailer's authorized representative's operations in California must include one of the following activities: selling, delivering, installing, assembling or taking orders for tangible personal property. Applying this analysis to the instant matter, these three requirements are met if: (1) Borders was petitioner's authorized representative in this state for purposes of taking returns from petitioner's California customers; and (2) the taking of such returns constitutes "selling." The first issue is a matter of fact, the second is a matter of law.

As to the first issue, the greater weight of the available evidence establishes that, for the period in question, Borders was petitioner's authorized representative in this state for the purpose of accepting returns from petitioner's California customers. As indicated above, petitioner expressly stated on its web site that Borders was petitioner's authorized representative for this purpose. Petitioner has submitted no evidence showing that Borders ever objected to being designated as petitioner's authorized representative or that petitioner ever revoked this designation. Rather, the evidence shows that petitioner removed the web site declaration of this designation in response to the Department's July 29, 1999, letter, not because Borders's status as petitioner's authorized representative had changed.

Although petitioner's express web site declaration is sufficient to establish that Borders was petitioner's authorized representative for returns, in addition to this direct evidence, circumstantial evidence sufficient to establish this fact also exists. Specifically, by petitioner's own admission, Borders provided unique and preferential return services to petitioner's customers. As discussed above, Borders purportedly would allow anyone to exchange for store credit any merchandise Borders stocked, regardless of whether that merchandise was purchased from Borders or petitioner or from one of their competitors. Such exchange transactions presumably would result in little, if any, net loss for Borders and would promote good will. However, even if petitioner were to establish, which petitioner has not, that Borders's practice of accepting returns from petitioner's customers was wholly independent of petitioner's published return policy, Borders's willingness to provide cash refunds to petitioner's customers, when Borders refused to do this for customers of Borders's or petitioner's competitors, indicates that Borders made such refunds because Borders was petitioner's authorized representative. While not exhaustive of the circumstantial evidence indicating that Borders was petitioner's authorized representative for returns in California, Borders's preferential treatment of petitioner's customers suffices to establish this fact.

As to the legal issue that remains, we conclude that, when accomplished through an authorized representative, the taking of returns constitutes "selling" under subdivision (c)(2) of Section 6203. Because neither the Sales and Use Tax Law in general, nor Section 6203 in specific, contains a definition of "selling," following the accepted canons of statutory construction, we construe this term according to its common usage. In other words, "selling" is inclusive of all activities that are an integral part of making sales.

When out-of-state retailers that make offers of sale to potential customers in California authorize in-state representatives to take returns, these retailers acknowledge that the taking of returns is an integral part of their selling efforts. Such an acknowledgement comports with common sense because the provision of convenient and trustworthy return procedures can be crucial to an out-of-state retailer's ability to make sales. This is especially evident in the realm of e-commerce.

For example, in this case, petitioner identified Borders as petitioner's authorized in-state representative for effecting the generous, convenient return policy petitioner published on its web site. It is apparent that petitioner announced this favorable return policy to induce potential customers, who might otherwise be wary of making purchases from a remote seller, to place orders. Indeed, many potential online customers would not place an order with an online retailer whose return policy was not worthy of confidence. An online retailer's ability to offer these potential customers convenient returns and exchanges at nearby reputable "brick-and-mortar" stores, as petitioner did, would assuredly help promote such confidence. Moreover, some online purchasers will not be satisfied with their purchases. An online retailer that offers convenient, local return and exchange options is much more likely to obtain repeat business from such purchasers. The important role that an online retailer's return policy plays in obtaining repeat business further underscores how integral the taking of returns is to selling in e-commerce transactions.

In *Quill Corp. v. North Dakota* (1992) 504 U.S. 298 [hereafter *Quill*], the United States Supreme Court held that, pursuant to the Commerce Clause of the United States Constitution, a state cannot impose a use tax collection obligation on out-of-state retailers unless those retailers have "substantial nexus" with that state. The *Quill* court explained that, to establish commerce-clause nexus, a state must show that the out-of-state retailer, or a representative of the out-of-state retailer, has a sufficiently substantial physical presence in the state to justify the imposition of a use tax collection obligation. *(Ibid.)* In this case, petitioner had a substantial physical presence in California through the many places of business and employees of Borders, petitioner's authorized representative in this state for the purpose of selling tangible personal property. Petitioner's substantial physical presence in this state more than suffices to establish that petitioner had commerce-clause nexus with California during the period in question. (See *ibid.*)

In sum, both the direct and circumstantial evidence are sufficient to establish that Borders, acting as petitioner's authorized representative, performed return and exchange activities in California. Such activities, when performed through an authorized representative, are an integral part of selling tangible personal property. Thus, due to Borders's actions in California on petitioner's behalf, petitioner was a "retailer engaged in business in this state" during the period in question. Accordingly, the petition should be denied as to these issues because petitioner was obligated to collect, and remit, use tax from petitioner's California customers. (Rev. & Tax. Code, §§ 6203, subds. (a) and (c)(2), 6204.)

NOTES & QUESTIONS

1. *Voluntary integration.* Barnes & Noble, Inc., another large chain of over 500 bookstores, set up a subsidiary, BarnesandNoble.com, Inc., to sell books through a website at www.bn.com. Operating under this structure, the online company collected use taxes for only four states (Tennessee, New Jersey, New York, and Virginia), thereby maintaining competitive parity with arch-rival Amazon.com, which collected taxes only on sales to Washington State and North Dakota. In an October 26, 2000 press release, Barnes & Noble, Inc. announced that it would integrate its e-commerce sales with its storefront operations, becoming a "clicks-and-mortar" operation. The integration strategy would involve (1) placing Internet Service

Counters in its stores, allowing customers to order products through the bn.com website, paying by cash, check, or credit card, and either picking up their order at a store or having it delivered; (2) instituting a combined membership loyalty program; and (3) allowing customers who make a purchase from bn.com to return unwanted items at any Barnes & Noble store.

Does this integration of operations mean that Barnes & Noble will be required to collect tax on all sales into states where it has a store location? If so, why would the company choose to lose the tax advantage it had when its online and storefront operations were separate?

Other retailers have tried to have it both ways: the online operation is structured as a separate legal entity, which contracts on a third-party basis with the brick-and-mortar company to accept returned items on its behalf.

For an argument that a brick-and-mortar seller should be required to collect taxes on sales by its online affiliate in all states where the seller has bricks and mortar, see Michael J. McIntyre, *Taxing Electronic Commerce Fairly And Efficiently*, 52 TAX L. REV. 625 (1997).

2. *Legislative action.* In 2001, the Arkansas legislature enacted legislation that requires certain online affiliates of brick-and-mortar retailers with store locations in the state to collect use taxes:

> (a)
>
> (1) Every vendor making a sale of tangible personal property directly or indirectly for the purpose of storage, use, distribution, or consumption in this state shall collect the tax from the purchaser and give a receipt therefor. This provision includes all out-of-state vendors who deliver merchandise into Arkansas in their own conveyance where such merchandise will be stored, used, distributed, or consumed within this state.
>
> * * *
>
> (3) The processing of orders electronically, by fax, telephone, the Internet, or other electronic ordering process, or the processing of orders by non-electronic means, by mail order, fax, telephone, or otherwise, does not relieve a vendor of responsibility for collection of the tax from the purchaser if both the following conditions exist:
>
> (A) The vendor holds a substantial ownership interest, directly or through a subsidiary, in a retailer maintaining sales locations in Arkansas or is owned in whole or in substantial part by such a retailer or by a parent or subsidiary thereof; and
>
> (B) The vendor sells the same or a substantially similar line of products as the Arkansas retailer under the same or a substantially similar business name, or the facilities or employees of the Arkansas retailer are used to advertise or promote sales by the vendor to Arkansas purchasers.

(4) For the purposes of this section, "substantial ownership interest" in an entity means that degree of ownership of equity interests in an entity that is not less than that degree of ownership specified by Section 267 of the Internal Revenue Code of 1986, as in effect on January 1, 2001, with respect to a person other than a director or officer.

ARK. CODE ANN. § 26–53–124. The California legislature passed similar legislation in 2000, but it was vetoed by the governor.

It is unclear whether the Arkansas "unitary nexus" legislation would survive a constitutional challenge. Other efforts to attribute one company's taxing nexus to another related company have been found inconsistent with the Supreme Court's interpretation of the Commerce Clause. *See Current, Inc. v. State Board of Equalization*, 24 Cal.App.4th 382 (Cal.Ct.App.1994); *SFA Folio Collections, Inc. v. Bannon*, 585 A.2d 666 (Conn.1991).

b. Provision of Incidental Services

Another difficulty in application of the nexus requirement arises when a remote seller's only presence in the taxing state is through its provision of limited services, such as warranty services, in the state.

The Multistate Tax Commission, on behalf of 26 states, addressed this issue in a 1995 Bulletin.[4] The Bulletin strongly endorses the view that a seller's arrangement for the provision of repair (or other) services in the taxing state, even if rendered by an independent company, supports a finding of taxing nexus.

Multistate Tax Commission, *Computer Company's Provision of In–State Repair Services Creates Nexus*

NB 95–1 (1995).

This Bulletin describes the nexus consequences under the U.S. Constitution and Public Law 86—272 to a company selling computer and/or related items through direct marketing (hereafter sometimes called "computer company") where the computer company also provides, directly or indirectly, repair services to its customers in a taxing State. While this Bulletin focuses on the provision of repair services performed in the taxing State, other activities conducted by or on behalf of a computer company in a taxing State may also independently create constitutional or federal statutory nexus.

4. The Multistate Tax Commission is an association of state governments that was created in 1967 through an interstate compact. Its principal purposes are to promote uniformity in state tax laws, and to establish appropriate apportionment of taxes applying to multistate taxpayers. Forty-five states participate in the Commission's activities. *See* Multistate Tax Commission, *About the Multistate Tax Commission*, www.mtc.gov/ABOUTMTC/Aboutmtc3.htm.

INDUSTRY PRACTICE

Computer companies selling through direct marketing routinely provide repair services to their customers either on-site or through a business location in the customer's State under the computer company's warranty. A typical fact pattern is described below. This example is for illustrative purposes and should not be interpreted to exclude other instances involving similar, but not identical, fact patterns.

An out-of-state direct marketing computer company ("Computer Co.") solicits sales through advertising in computer magazines, catalogues, and fliers mailed into the taxing State. Computer Co.'s one year warranty provides for repair services in the customer's State. The Computer Co. proclaims to its customers and/or potential customers in the taxing State through advertisements and other means that its warranty covers provision of repair services in the customer's State. The warranty is either included with the purchase of every Computer Co. computer or computer related equipment or is available at an additional fee. Computer Co. sells a computer or related equipment to a customer and end user in the taxing State. When the customer discovers a problem, the terms of the warranty provide that the customer should contact Computer Co. to arrange repair service. The customer is not authorized to call the third party repair company to arrange for the repair without first calling Computer Co. for authorization. Customer calls Computer Co. which, after determining that the problem is covered by the warranty, may first attempt to solve the problem over the telephone. The Computer Co. determines whether repair is necessary and authorizes the in-state repair. Either Computer Co. or the customer, on Computer Co.'s authorization, contacts a third party service provider who performs the service in the taxing State either at the customer's location or at a site determined by the third party service provider.

NEXUS CONSEQUENCES

The industry practice of providing in-state warranty repair services through third party repair service providers, as described above, creates constitutional nexus for imposition of use tax collection responsibility for all sales made to customers in that State and for income, franchise, or comparable tax liability (including but not limited to a gross receipts excise tax) in the taxing State where the warranty services are performed. The repair services performed in the taxing State by the third party representative do not constitute de minimis activities in the taxing State. De minimis activity that does not rise to the level of constitutional nexus is activity that represents no more than a trivial connection with the State. Activities that are regular or systematic and in furtherance of the seller's business, such as the provision of in-state repairs under the company's warranty in this case, are not trivial.

LEGAL ANALYSIS

1. CONSTITUTIONAL STANDARDS FOR USE TAX NEXUS

The limits of States' taxing authority under the Due Process and Commerce Clauses for imposition of use tax collection responsibility are set forth in Quill Corp. v. North Dakota, 504 U.S. 298 (1992), and in National Bellas Hess Inc. v. Dep't of Revenue, 386 U.S. 753 (1967). * * *

Under the Quill bright line test, repair service provided directly by a direct marketing computer company employee in the customer's State creates in-state physical presence that exceeds contact by U.S. mail or common carrier and constitutes "substantial nexus." Courts have also consistently ruled that out-of-state companies may not circumvent state jurisdiction to impose taxes by contracting with in-state persons to conduct company business that would have otherwise created nexus if the out-of-state company had used their own employees. The U.S. Supreme Court has uniformly found that the in-state presence of a representative of an out-of-state seller who conducts regular or systematic activities in furtherance of the seller's business, such as solicitation of sales or provision of services, creates nexus. Scripto, Inc. v. Carson, 362 U.S. 207 (1960); General Trading Co. v. Iowa, 322 U.S. 327 (1944); Felt & Tarrant Mfg. Co. v. Gallagher, 306 U.S. 62 (1939). See also Tyler Pipe Industries, Inc. v. Washington Dep't of Revenue, 483 U.S. 232 (1987); Standard Pressed Steel v. Dep't of Revenue, 419 U.S. 560 (1975). The Court in Quill specifically approved this line of cases and recognized that these cases all involve physical presence that creates nexus under National Bellas Hess. Quill, [504 U.S. at 306–07]. Accordingly, presence of representatives of a direct marketing computer company providing repair services in the customer's State will generate constitutional nexus.

The characterization of the relationship between the out-of-state seller and its in-state representative conducting business on the out-of-state seller's behalf does not affect the nexus determination. Scripto, Inc. v. Carson, 362 U.S. 207 (1960). See also Tyler Pipe Industries, Inc. v. Washington Dep't of Revenue, 483 U.S. 232 (1987); Standard Pressed Steel v. Dep't of Revenue, 419 U.S. 560 (1975). In Scripto, the Court held that in-state activities on Scripto's behalf by ten part-time independent contractors created nexus, even though these independent contractors worked for competing companies. The Court held that the distinction between employees and independent contractors was of no constitutional significance. As the Supreme Court in Scripto noted, the important fact is that the in-state activity is effective in creating and maintaining the in-state market. Scripto, 362 U.S. at 211–212. Similarly, in Tyler Pipe Industries, Inc. v. Washington Dep't of Revenue, 483 U.S. 232 (1987), the activities of one independent contractor residing in the taxing State were sufficient to create a taxable presence in the State on behalf of the company to impose Washington's Business and Occupations tax. In Tyler Pipe, the Court held that the critical test was

> whether the activities performed in this state on behalf of the taxpayer are significantly associated with the taxpayer's ability to establish and maintain a market in this state for the sales.

Tyler Pipe, 483 U.S. at 250. The Court found this standard was satisfied because "Tyler's sales representatives perform any local activities necessary for maintenance of Tyler Pipe's market and protection of its interests." Id. at 251. The important aspect of both decisions is that the Court, without weighing the amount of the in-state activities, noted that in-state activities carried on through an in-state representative associated with the seller's ability to establish and maintain a market in the taxing State satisfies constitutional nexus requirements. Tyler Pipe, 483 U.S. at 250; Standard Pressed Steel, 419 U.S. at 562. In-state representation can take many forms, such as representation by individuals, corporations, partnerships, or other entities. The different forms of the relationship have no constitutional significance. Hence, an out-of-state company may not circumvent the imposition of nexus in a State where a representative third party company, rather than an in-state individual representative, conducts in-state activities on its behalf. It is the performance of the in-state activities by an in-state entity on the seller's behalf that extends those nexus creating activities and in-state presence to the out-of-state seller.

The provision of warranty repair service in the customer's state is precisely the kind of presence that squarely supports the finding of substantial nexus. The provision of in-state repair services provided by a direct marketing computer company as part of the company's standard warranty or as an option that can be separately purchased and as an advertised part of the company's sales contributes significantly to the company's ability to establish and maintain its market for computer hardware sales in the State. As in Tyler Pipe, these in-state activities, which develop goodwill and increased market share, are no less important or beneficial to the out-of-state direct marketing computer company because they are performed by an independent third party repair service.

2. STANDARDS FOR INCOME AND FRANCHISE TAX NEXUS UNDER THE CONSTITUTION AND P.L. 86–272 [15 U.S.C. § 381]

There is a question of whether the substantial nexus standard for imposition of use tax collection as preserved in Quill or a lower nexus standard applies to income taxes, franchise taxes based upon income, and other comparable taxes. Regardless of the merits of these two positions, there is no question that when a company has sufficient contact with the State to support the constitutional imposition of a use tax collection and reporting obligation with respect to the State into which the company is selling, nexus exists for the application of an income, franchise, or comparable tax as well. The discussion of use tax nexus in the previous section supports the conclusion that constitutional nexus under the Commerce Clause and the Due Process Clause exists with respect to the market State's imposition of a reporting obligation under an income, franchise, or comparable tax.

* * *

APPLICATION OF THE LAW TO THE DIRECT MARKETING COMPUTER INDUSTRY PRACTICE

There is no issue of Due Process nexus because direct marketing computer companies purposefully direct advertising and catalogue solicitations to taxing State customers. Under applicable case law, in-state presence of independent contractors creates substantial nexus under the Commerce Clause for out-of-state companies that hire them to perform in-state services. Accordingly, the industry practice of direct marketing computer companies arranging for provision of in-state repair service through third parties creates nexus. The fact that the in-state warranty service is actually performed by a third party is of no constitutional consequence. * * *

The following States have indicated that their law is consistent with the constitutional and federal statutory nexus principles described in this Bulletin and that they will enforce these nexus standards with respect to computer companies selling computers and/or related items through direct marketing for purposes of determining, as indicated by parenthetical notation, an obligation to collect, report and remit use taxes on the sale and purchase of a computer and/or related items and/or an obligation to report and pay income taxes, franchise taxes based on income, or comparable taxes [listing 25 states and the District of Columbia] * * *.

The MTC Bulletin has no independent legal force: it amounts to a public statement by the subscribing states that they will deem a company engaged in the described activities to have nexus with the state satisfying constitutional and federal statutory requirements, and will seek to enforce their tax laws accordingly. In the following case, that position was tested in court.

State v. Quantex Microsystems, Inc.

809 So.2d 246 (La.Ct.App.2001).

■ GONZALES, J.

In this appeal, the State of Louisiana and the Secretary of the Department of Revenue and Taxation (Department) challenge a judgment dismissing their claim for unpaid taxes against Quantex Microsystems, Inc. (Quantex), a vendor of computer products.

FACTUAL AND PROCEDURAL BACKGROUND

Quantex, a New York corporation, with its principal place of business in New Jersey, sells computer products via the mail, the telephone, and the internet. It solicits business through national publications and on the internet but does not specifically direct any advertisements to Louisiana. Quantex has no offices, property, bank accounts, or direct employees in Louisiana. In the years 1995 through 1997, Quantex made computer sales of approximately $7,480,000.00 for delivery in Louisiana. As part of the limited warranty provided with the purchase of its computer products, Quantex represents to its customers that it may, at its sole discretion, provide on-site service to its customers for the replacement of defective hardware parts for one year from the date of purchase. According to

Quantex, however, this service is provided by the manufacturer of the computer products and not by Quantex.

On December 30, 1997, the Department filed suit against Quantex, seeking payment of unpaid use, income, and franchise taxes for tax years 1994, 1995, 1996, and 1997, plus penalties and interest. The Department alleged Quantex had "established a physical presence in the State of Louisiana" by providing for "repairs, service and/or support for products purchased for use in Louisiana through the use of agents, employees and/or independent contractors operating in Louisiana...." Quantex answered the suit, denying that it had a physical presence in Louisiana.

On September 9, 1999, Quantex filed a motion for summary judgment, seeking dismissal of the Department's claims for sales and use taxes. A hearing on the motion was held on October 25, 1999, and on October 26, 1999, the trial court signed a judgment, granting Quantex's motion and dismissing the Department's demands against Quantex. The Department appeals from the judgment, contending the trial court erred in finding that "an out-of-state corporation's use of independent contractors to provide on-site computer repair services in Louisiana cannot constitute [a] substantial nexus" to support state taxation.

* * *

SUMMARY JUDGMENT

The Department argues the trial court erred in granting Quantex's motion for summary judgment, based on its conclusion that "pursuant to the U.S. Supreme Court decision in *Quill Corporation* ..., Quantex Microsystems, Inc. lacks the substantial nexus with Louisiana required for the State to be able [to] impose taxes."

* * *

APPLICABLE LOUISIANA TAXATION LAW

Because the applicable substantive law determines the materiality of facts in a summary judgment setting, we now turn to a discussion of the Louisiana taxation law applicable to this case. *J. Ray McDermott, Inc. v. Morrison,* 96–2337 (La.App. 1 Cir. 11/7/97), 705 So.2d 195, 203, *writs denied,* 97–3055, 97–3062 (La.2/13/98), 709 So.2d 753, 754.

Generally, Louisiana imposes a sales tax on the retail sale in this state of each item of tangible personal property. La. R.S. 47:302. In addition to a sales tax, Louisiana imposes a use tax on items purchased in other states, but brought into Louisiana for use, consumption, distribution, and storage for use and consumption. La. R.S. 47:302. A use tax ordinarily serves to complement the sales tax of a state by eliminating the incentive to make major purchases in states with lower sales taxes. *McDermott,* 705 So.2d at 203. Every dealer located outside the state making sales of tangible personal property for distribution, storage, use, or other consumption in Louisiana shall, at the time of the sales, collect the applicable tax from the purchaser. La. R.S. 47:304(B). Any dealer who neglects, fails, or refuses to collect the tax shall be liable for and pay the tax himself. La. R.S. 47:304(C).

The Louisiana sales/use tax law is not intended to levy a tax on interstate commerce; however, our law is intended to levy a tax on the sale at retail, the use, the consumption, the distribution, and the storage to be used or consumed in this state, of tangible personal property after it has come to rest in this state and has become a part of the mass of property in this state. This includes the collection of taxes on sales of tangible personal property that are promoted through the use of catalogs and other means of sales promotion and for which federal legislation or federal jurisprudence enables the enforcement of the use tax law upon the conduct of such business. La. R.S. 47:305(E)(1).

* * *

At issue in this appeal is whether Quantex's activity in Louisiana has a "substantial nexus" with Louisiana to warrant the imposition of taxation. * * * [T]he crucial factor governing nexus is whether the activities performed in the taxing state on behalf of the taxpayer are significantly associated with the taxpayer's ability to establish and maintain a market in the taxing state. *Tyler Pipe Industries, Inc. v. Washington,* 483 U.S. 232, 250 (1987).

In granting summary judgment in favor of Quantex in this case, the trial court determined the existence of independent contractors performing warranty work in the taxing state was insufficient to establish the necessary physical presence to support state taxation. In our *de novo* review, we determine the trial court erred in finding no genuine issues of material fact in dispute.

Quantex's service guide clearly represents to buyers of its computer products that it may provide service for defective hardware parts for one year from the date of purchase. This warranty represented to the purchasers of $7,480,000.00 worth of Quantex computer products sold for delivery in Louisiana during the relevant period that representatives of Quantex may have been physically present in Louisiana performing this service.

In discovery responses provided to the Department in December of 1998, Quantex first claimed that, since January 1, 1994, it had used an independent contractor, Vanstar Corporation, to perform warranty work. In a supplemental discovery response provided to the Department in October of 1999, Quantex denied responsibility for or involvement in the providing of service, instead claiming that Fountain Technologies, Inc., the alleged manufacturer of the computer products sold by Quantex, was responsible for handling service. According to Quantex,

> On site service is handled by the manufacturer of the computer system sold by Quantex, Fountain Technologies, Inc., whose headquarters is in New Jersey. Fountain Technologies, Inc. has no office in Louisiana. While the on site service is Fountain's respon-

sibility, Fountain does not directly perform any of the on site service on systems sold by Quantex to Louisiana residents.

Fountain includes an amount in the purchase price of each computer system sold to Quantex, which amount serves to reimburse Fountain for arranging on site service. Quantex does not pay for such on site services calls except for the amount paid to Fountain Technologies, Inc. as described above.

The company Fountain Technologies, Inc. used to provide such service was Van Star. In December, 1998, Fountain Technologies, Inc. entered into an agreement with Warranty Corporation of America which is the company they use for on site service today. Warranty Corporation of America is located at 3110 Crossing Park Road, Norcross, Georgia.

The above responses indicate there are disputed factual issues regarding whether Quantex itself provided on-site service during the relevant periods or whether on-site service was provided by Fountain Technologies, Inc. Further, factual issues remain regarding the extent of the on-site service actually performed during the relevant period and whether that activity was significantly associated with Quantex's ability to establish and maintain a market in Louisiana. Further, a review of federal and state jurisprudence indicates the parameters of the "physical presence" requirement have not been sufficiently developed to determine whether on-site service performed by independent contractors on behalf of Quantex or Fountain Technologies, Inc., or the extent of such service, would be adequate to support taxation in this case. Additional discovery on these issues will be necessary on remand.

* * *

[T]he judgment of the trial court is REVERSED, and this matter is REMANDED for further proceedings consistent with this opinion. * * *

■ FOGG, J. dissenting.

I respectfully dissent. The majority reverses this grant of summary judgment upon a determination that "disputed factual issues" exist concerning (1) "whether Quantex itself provided on-site service during the relevant periods, or whether on-site service provided by Fountain Technologies, Inc.;" (2) "the extent of the on-site service actually performed during the relevant period;" and (3) whether the on-site service "was significantly associated with Quantex's ability to establish and maintain a market in Louisiana." For the following reasons, I believe that none of these constitute "genuine issues of material fact" and that, once the undisputed material facts are analyzed under the pertinent jurisprudence, Quantex is entitled to judgment as a matter of law.

* * *

* * * The applicable substantive law is fully discussed in the case of *Quill Corp. v. North Dakota,* 504 U.S. 298 (1992), the most recent United States Supreme Court case that addresses the right of a state to collect

sales and use taxes from an out-of-state vendor. *Quill* held that substantial nexus means that the out-of-state vendor must maintain a *physical presence* in the taxing state. Maintaining property or employees in the taxing state is required to constitute a physical presence. This physical presence is a bright-line rule for the imposition of sales and use taxes. *Quill Corp.,* 504 U.S. at 311. Therefore, in order for Louisiana to impose sales and use taxes on Quantex, Quantex must have a substantial nexus in this state in the form of a physical location or employees in the state.

Initially, the majority finds that Quantex's answers and supplemental answers to interrogatories are inconsistent, and therefore, raise a genuine issue of material fact. I disagree with this conclusion for two reasons. First, reviewing the interrogatories in question, I find no inconsistency. Rather, reading these answers together I believe the supplemental answer simply clarifies the original answer. Read together they state that Quantex does not contract with any person to provide service or warranty work in the State of Louisiana. Neither answer indicates that Quantex itself may have "provided on-site service during the relevant periods" as concluded by the majority; rather, Quantex consistently states that it did not provide such service. Second, even if the answers are determined to be conflicting, they could only conflict in stating which company, Vanstar or Warranty, handled service. Critical to Louisiana's right to tax is the presence of a company's property or personnel within the state. *Quill,* 504 U.S. at 311. Under either scenario, neither property nor employees of Quantex were located in Louisiana. Therefore, under either factual scenario, Quantex had no physical presence in Louisiana; a determination of whether Vanstar or Warranty handled the on-site service is not material.

The majority also finds that summary judgment is not proper because a genuine issue of material fact exists because the record does not disclose the extent of the on-site service actually performed during the relevant period. The extent of on-site service that occurs in the State of Louisiana is irrelevant to a determination of taxability in this case because there is no evidence at all before the trial court that any of the service was performed by employees of Quantex. Without such evidence, *Quill* mandates a finding of no taxability. The frequency of service provided by another company is not material to this case.

Finally, the majority finds that an issue of material fact exists as to whether the on-site service was significantly associated with Quantex's ability to establish and maintain a market in Louisiana. Under *Quill,* we should not reach this issue as Quantex has no physical presence in Louisiana. In the case of *Tyler Pipe Industries, Inc. v. Washington,* 483 U.S. 232 (1987), cited by the majority, Tyler Pipe had a physical presence in the State of Washington as it had sales representatives in that state. Any facts that would determine whether on-site service by third parties was significantly associated with Quantex's ability to establish and maintain a market in Louisiana are irrelevant to an analysis of taxability under the Commerce Clause, and therefore, are not material facts.

Considering the analysis used to determine taxability of out-of-state vendors under the Commerce Clause as set forth in *Quill*, the above factual questions do not constitute genuine issues of material fact that would preclude summary judgment. I believe Quantex made a prima facie showing that the motion should be granted. * * *

NOTES & QUESTIONS

1. *California's switch.* Although California was one of the 25 states that subscribed to the principles enunciated in Multistate Tax Commission Bulletin 95–1, *supra*, it later disassociated itself from that view and adopted a regulation taking the opposite position:

> § 1684. Collection of Use Tax by Retailers
>
> (a) *Retailers Engaged in Business in State.* Retailers engaged in business in this state * * * and making sales of tangible personal property, the storage, use, or other consumption of which is subject to the tax must register with the Board and, at the time of making the sales, or, if the storage, use or other consumption of the tangible personal property is not then taxable, at the time it becomes taxable, collect the tax from the purchaser and give the purchaser a receipt therefor.
>
> * * *
>
> A retailer is not "engaged in business in this state" based solely on its use of a representative or independent contractor in this state for purposes of performing warranty or repair services with respect to tangible personal property sold by the retailer, provided that the ultimate ownership of the representative or independent contractor so used and the retailer is not substantially similar. For purposes of this paragraph, "ultimate owner" means a stock holder, bond holder, partner, or other person holding an ownership interest.

CAL. CODE REGS. tit. 18, § 1684(a).

One commentator explains that California's switch is attributable to pressure from business representatives. "In California, the [Board of Equalization] and policymakers have taken several different actions to protect Internet activities against taxation * * *. Ernest J. Dronenburg Jr., the BOE chair, has assured the business community that the BOE intends to take the lead in keeping the Internet free of taxation. He said that 'it was the BOE's feeling that taxation of Internet activities and online services will have a chilling effect on the development of one of the most compelling and promising emerging industries. The worst thing that can happen is for Internet development to be stifled by new state and federal taxes.' " Kim Marshall & Marc Lewis, *What We Know Today About "Substantial Nexus,"* 13 STATE TAX NOTES 967, 972 (1997).

Some 40 states have taken the position that third-party warranty work *can* result in nexus.

2. *Nexus resulting from software transactions.* Software is normally licensed, not sold. This means that a software vendor retains a property interest in software that it supplies. Does this retained interest constitute the software vendor's presence in a state where multiple copies of the software have been furnished? In *Quill Corp. v. North Dakota*, 504 U.S. 298, 315 n. 8 (1992), the Court suggested that a vendor's distribution of licensed software in the taxing state might constitute substantial nexus, if the quantity distributed was more than minimal: "Although title to 'a few floppy diskettes' present in a State might constitute some minimal nexus, in *National Geographic Society v. California Bd. of Equalization*, 430 U.S. 551, 556 (1977), we expressly rejected a ' " 'slightest presence' " ' standard of constitutional nexus." A Texas administrative agency, taking up this suggestion, held that a software vendor's shipment to Texas of 40–60 computer programs each year, under licensing agreements, created substantial nexus supporting the imposition of sales and use tax. Texas Comptroller of Public Accounts, Hearing No. 36,237 (Jul. 21, 1998). But a Tennessee court held that nexus requires a literal physical presence, so that the presence in the state of multiple copies of America Online's licensed software did not constitute such a presence. *America Online, Inc. v. Johnson*, No. 97–3786–III (Tenn. Chancery Ct. Mar. 13, 2001).

3. *Nexus resulting from server location.* Does the hosting of a website on a server located in a taxing state constitute nexus with the state? There is little caselaw on the issue, but California has addressed it legislatively:

> § 1684. Collection of Use Tax by Retailers
>
> (a) * * * The use of a computer server on the Internet to create or maintain a World Wide Web page or site by an out-of-state retailer will not be considered a factor in determining whether the retailer has a substantial nexus with California. No Internet Service Provider, On-line Service Provider, internetwork communication service provider, or other Internet access service provider, or World Wide Web hosting services shall be deemed the agent or representative of any out-of-state retailer as a result of the service provider maintaining or taking orders via a web page or site on a computer server that is physically located in this state.

CAL. CODE REGS. tit. 18, § 1684(a).

This is consistent with a proposal offered by a majority of the members of the Advisory Commission on Electronic Commerce in its April 2000 report to Congress. The proposal sets forth a list of factors that would not alone establish a seller's nexus with a state, including: "a seller's use of an Internet Service Provider ('ISP') that has physical presence in a state" and "the placement of a seller's digital data on a server located in that particular state." ACEC Report at 19, discussed *supra*. It is also consistent with the position taken by the Organisation for Economic Co-operation and Development in interpreting the permanent establishment provision of its Model Tax Treaty. *See* Part II, *infra*.

2. THE BURDEN OF COLLECTING SALES AND USE TAXES

A company that sells its products to purchasers located in more than a few states, and that has sufficient nexus with those states so that state and local governments may impose use taxes consistently with Commerce Clause limitations, faces a daunting task in calculating the amount of tax due on a transaction. A number of factors go into the calculation:

(1) The location of the purchaser determines which jurisdiction's tax rules apply. Taxing jurisdictions are not limited to the 46 states that assess sales or use taxes: according to one study, there are also 4,696 cities, 1,602 counties, and 1,113 other taxing jurisdictions that overlay their own taxes on top of the state's taxes. Thus, one transaction may generate tax liabilities to the state, county, and city where the purchaser is located, each at its own rate.

(2) The applicable tax rate depends on the type of item that is sold. Some categories of goods are taxed at higher rates than others, and certain categories, such as food and clothing, are often exempt. Most types of services are typically exempt.

(3) The taxability of the transaction may depend on the status of the buyer. A jurisdiction may exempt non-profit purchasers, government agencies, or those who purchase for resale.

(4) Some jurisdictions occasionally announce a "tax holiday," which suspends the imposition of taxes for a brief period of time.

The complexity of the state sales and use tax system is not, of course, new to electronic commerce. Mail order companies that aim at a national market have long been required to comply with this multifarious set of rules. In holding that the Commerce Clause prevents Illinois from imposing tax-collection duties on a mail-order business that lacks a "substantial nexus" to the state, the Supreme Court made reference to these collection burdens:

> For if Illinois can impose such burdens, so can every other State, and so, indeed, can every municipality, every school district, and every other political subdivision throughout the Nation with power to impose sales and use taxes. The many variations in rates of tax, in allowable exemptions, and in administrative and record-keeping requirements could entangle National's interstate business in a virtual welter of complicated obligations to local jurisdictions with no legitimate claim to impose "a fair share of the cost of the local government."

National Bellas Hess, Inc. v. Department of Revenue, 386 U.S. 753, 759–60 (1967).

Help is available from third-party companies that produce tax-compliance products. In recent years, those products have become computer-based, so that a seller is enabled to comply with the taxing rules more or less automatically. This type of software has been adapted for use by e-commerce sellers, allowing automatic calculation of the tax applicable on transactions with purchasers located anywhere in the country, or anywhere in the world.

NOTES & QUESTIONS

Overcoming compliance burdens with technology. Given the availability of software that masks the complexity of the sales and use tax system and automatically computes the tax due on any transaction, should the courts revisit the issue whether the cost of compliance amounts to an undue burden on interstate commerce, in violation of the Commerce Clause?

3. CHARACTERIZATION OF DIGITAL GOODS

Most sales and use taxes apply to tangible personal property, with certain exceptions, and to a limited range of services. Is software within the category of "tangible personal property"? Does it matter whether the software is delivered embedded in a physical medium, like a CD–ROM, or is delivered by digital download? What about other types of digital goods, such as music, photographs, data from information providers, and e-books?

South Central Bell Telephone Co. v. Barthelemy

643 So.2d 1240 (La.1994).

■ HALL, JUSTICE.

We granted writs in this case to decide whether certain computer software constitutes "tangible personal property" taxable under the sales and use tax imposed by the City of New Orleans pursuant to Section 56 of the City Code. The district court classified the two types of computer software at issue—switching system and data processing software—as intangible, nontaxable property, and thus granted partial summary judgment in favor of the taxpayer, South Central Bell Telephone Co. (Bell). The court of appeal affirmed. We classify computer software as tangible, taxable property, and thus reverse and remand.

I.

During the pertinent taxing periods, January 1, 1986 through April 30, 1990, Bell operated a telephone system in Orleans Parish. As part of its system, Bell set up in the parish sixteen telephone central offices. Each telephone central office is a system, in and of itself, as well as part of the larger telephone system. Simply put, each central office is a place where the caller's telephone line is connected to the line of the person being called, if that person is served by the same central office, or, if not, to a line connected to another telephone central office. Depending upon the location of the person being called, a given call may pass through multiple central offices.

Each central office consists of, among other things, switching equipment. Switching equipment includes computer processors that are directed and operated by computer software programs. Each central office is unique; consequently, each central office requires specifically tailored software designed to meet that office's operations.

During the pertinent taxing periods, Bell licensed specific switching system software programs for use in specific central offices pursuant to license agreements confected out of state with three vendors, AT & T Technologies, Inc., Northern Telecomm and Erickson. Under these license agreements, Bell acquired the limited right to use such switching system software programs; the license agreements limited Bell's right to use designated switching system software to designated switches in designated telephone central offices. More particularly, the license agreements prohibited Bell's transfer of such software to any switch other than the designated one; prohibited Bell's sublicense, assignment, sale or transfer of the programs; prohibited Bell's use of the programs after the license expired; and required that Bell maintain strict confidentiality with regard to the programs. The license agreements also reserved to the vendors ownership of, and proprietary rights in, the switching system software programs.

The vendors delivered the switching system software programs to Bell via magnetic tapes. Once received, the software programs were loaded onto Bell's switching system processors, and the magnetic tapes were either used or discarded. The vendors either billed Bell for City taxes on the magnetic tapes, or Bell automatically accrued such taxes on the magnetic tapes. Bell was neither billed by the vendors, nor accrued such taxes on the switching system software itself, however. The switching system software is thus one of the two types of software at issue in this case.

The second type of software at issue in this case is data processing software. This software guides the functions of the computers located in Bell's data processing center in Orleans Parish. Bell's data processing center handles basic accounting functions, including processing customer billings and payments, storing and managing customer data and maintaining a voucher and disbursement system. Bell acquired the right to use the data processing software through its affiliate, BellSouth Services, Inc. (BellSouth). BellSouth entered into a master license agreement regarding the software out of state. BellSouth also tested, evaluated and adapted the software out of state. BellSouth then transmitted the software electronically via telephone lines to Bell's modem in Orleans Parish. As with the switching system software, the license agreements limited Bell's rights to use the software and reserved to the vendors ownership of, and proprietary rights in, the data processing software.

* * *

The taxes at issue in this case are use taxes levied by the City on Bell's use of the two types of software programs under § 56–21 of the City Code * * *.

In October 1990, following an audit, the City notified Bell of a proposed tax deficiency assessment for, among other things, Bell's use of the two types of computer software * * *. Bell paid the full amount of the proposed tax deficiency under protest. Thereafter, in November 1990, Bell commenced the instant action, seeking to recover the taxes paid under protest and contending that the items at issue were not taxable under the pertinent provisions of the City Code.

Each party filed cross-motions for summary judgment. After a hearing on the motions, the trial court denied the City's motion and granted Bell's motion in part, finding "that the sale/use tax of the City of New Orleans is not applicable to the licensing of the data process[ing] software or to the switching software." In written reasons for judgment, the district court stated "that under the essence of transaction test" neither type of software at issue was taxable. * * *

Affirming, the court of appeal reasoned that computer software does not fall within the definition of "tangible personal property"; rather, it falls within the definition of incorporeal property as it constitutes "intellectual property." In support of the latter conclusion, the court cited jurisprudence from other jurisdictions holding that computer software is intangible because the essence of the transaction is the acquisition of intangible information or knowledge. *South Cent. Bell Tel. Co. v. Barthelemy,* 93–1072, p. 5 (La.App. 4th Cir. 1/27/94), 631 So.2d 1340, 1343. * * *

On the City's writ application, we granted certiorari to consider the correctness of that decision. 94–0499 (La. 4/29/94), 637 So.2d 451.

II.

The city use tax is imposed by § 56–21 of the Code of the City of New Orleans:

> There is hereby levied, for general municipal purposes, a tax upon the sale at retail, the use, the consumption, the distribution and the storage for use or consumption in the city of each item or article of *tangible personal property,* upon the lease or rental of such property and upon the sale of services within the city....

"Tangible personal property" is defined in § 56–18 of the City Code as follows:

> [P]ersonal property which may be seen, weighed, measured, felt or touched, or is in any other manner perceptible to the senses. The term "tangible personal property" shall not include stocks, bonds, notes or other obligations or securities.

Construing this provision, we held in *City of New Orleans v. Baumer Foods, Inc.,* 532 So.2d 1381 (La.1988), that "the term 'tangible personal property' in the City Code's use tax is synonymous with corporeal movable property as used in the Louisiana Civil Code." 532 So.2d at 1383. * * * The application of property law concepts in this tax context is an exception to the general rule that tax laws are *sui generis,* B. Oreck, Louisiana Sales & Use Taxation § 2.2 (1992) (hereinafter Oreck). The reasoning behind applying property concepts in such a tax context is that the use of the common law term "tangible personal property" by the legislature, or by the various political subdivisions, was not intended to import the common law into Louisiana for purposes of sales and use tax law, nor to require the development of an entirely new body of property law for sales and use tax purposes only, but rather, the term was intended to be interpreted consistently with our civilian[5] property concepts embodied in the Civil Code. * * *

The pertinent Civil Code provisions are Louisiana Civil Code articles 461, 471 and 473. Article 461 distinguishes between corporeals and incorporeals, providing:

> Corporeals are things that have a body, whether animate or inanimate, and can be felt or touched.
>
> Incorporeals are things that have no body, but are comprehended by the understanding, such as the rights of inheritance, servitudes, obligations, and right of intellectual property.

Article 471 further defines corporeal movables as "things, whether animate or inanimate, that normally move or can be moved from one place to another." Article 473 further defines incorporeal movables as "rights, obligations, and actions that apply to a movable thing.... Movables of this kind are such as bonds, annuities, and interests or shares in entities possessing juridical personality."

* * *

* * * Hence, the civilian concept of corporeal movable encompasses all things that make up the physical world; conversely, incorporeals, i.e., intangibles, encompass the non-physical world of legal rights.

The term "tangible personal property" set forth in the City Code, and its synonymous Civil Code concept "corporeal movable," must be given their properly intended meaning. Physical recordings of computer software are not incorporeal rights to be comprehended by the understanding. Rather, they are part of the physical world. For the reasons set out below, we hold the computer software at issue in this case constitutes corporeal property under our civilian concept of that term, and thus, is tangible personal property, taxable under § 56–21 of the City Code.

III.

* * *

The taxation of computer software has * * * been considered by numerous courts across the country. These courts have split on the issue and have employed various analyses in reaching their decisions. The first case generally recognized as addressing the tangibility of computer software for tax purposes was *District of Columbia v. Universal Computer Assoc., Inc.*, 465 F.2d 615 (D.C.Cir.1972), which held computer software to be intangible, and therefore not taxable. The cases following soon thereafter, likewise held computer software to be intangible for sales, use and

5. [The term "civilian" refers to the civil-law basis of Louisiana state law, which is derived from France; as opposed to the common-law basis of the law of the other 49 states, which is derived from England.—Eds.]

property tax purposes. See e.g. *State v. Central Computer Serv., Inc.,* 349 So.2d 1160 (Ala.1977); *County of Sacramento v. Assessment Appeals Bd. No. 2,* 32 Cal.App.3d 654, 108 Cal.Rptr. 434 (1973); *First Nat'l Bank of Springfield v. Dep't of Revenue,* 85 Ill.2d 84, 51 Ill.Dec. 667, 421 N.E.2d 175 (1981); *Greyhound Computer Corp. v. State Dep't of Assessments & Taxation,* 271 Md. 674, 320 A.2d 52 (1974); *Commerce Union Bank v. Tidwell,* 538 S.W.2d 405 (Tenn.1976); *First Nat'l. Bank of Fort Worth v. Bullock,* 584 S.W.2d 548 (Tex.Civ.App.1979).

However, as computer software became more prevalent in society, and as courts' knowledge and understanding of computer software grew, later cases saw a shift in courts' attitudes towards the taxability of computer software, and courts began holding computer software to be tangible for sales, use and property tax purposes. This trend began with two cases decided just one day apart—*Comptroller of the Treasury v. Equitable Trust Co.,* 296 Md. 459, 464 A.2d 248 (1983) and *Chittenden Trust Co. v. King,* 143 Vt. 271, 465 A.2d 1100 (1983). The trend continued throughout the 1980's, see e.g. *Citizens & S. Sys., Inc. v. South Carolina Tax Comm'n,* 280 S.C. 138, 311 S.E.2d 717 (1984); *Hasbro Indus., Inc. v. Norberg,* 487 A.2d 124 (R.I.1985); *Creasy Sys. Consultants, Inc. v. Olsen,* 716 S.W.2d 35 (Tenn.1986); *Measurex Sys., Inc. v. State Tax Assessor,* 490 A.2d 1192 (Me.1985); *Bridge Data Co. v. Director of Revenue,* 794 S.W.2d 204 (Mo. 1990) (*en banc*); *Pennsylvania & West Virginia Supply Corp. v. Rose,* 179 W.Va. 317, 368 S.E.2d 101 (1988), though the trend was not uniform, see e.g. *CompuServe, Inc. v. Lindley,* 41 Ohio App.3d 260, 535 N.E.2d 360 (1987); *General Business Sys., Inc. v. State Board of Equalization,* 162 Cal.App.3d 50, 208 Cal.Rptr. 374 (1984); *Maccabees Mut. Life Ins. Co. v. State Dep't of Treasury,* 122 Mich.App. 660, 332 N.W.2d 561 (1983); *Northeast Datacom, Inc. v. City of Wallingford,* 212 Conn. 639, 563 A.2d 688 (1989).

The issue has also been the subject of numerous articles in various legal periodicals. Most commentators agree that computer software is tangible for sales, use and property tax purposes, and thus taxable, at least to some degree. * * *

In addition, computer software has generally been held to constitute "goods" under the Uniform Commercial Code. See, e.g., *Schroders, Inc. v. Hogan Sys., Inc.,* 137 Misc.2d 738, 522 N.Y.S.2d 404 (Sup.1987); *Chatlos Sys., Inc. v. National Cash Register Corp.,* 635 F.2d 1081 (3d Cir.1980); *RRX Indus., Inc. v. Lab–Con, Inc.,* 772 F.2d 543 (9th Cir.1985); *Communications Groups, Inc. v. Warner Communications, Inc.,* 138 Misc.2d 80, 527 N.Y.S.2d 341 (N.Y.City Civ.Ct.1988). * * *

Although interesting and helpful as background, the extensive jurisprudence and writings from other jurisdictions are not determinative or controlling of the issues presented in this case. We return to a discussion of the characteristics of computer software and classification thereof as tangible or intangible under Louisiana law.

IV.

A.

To correctly categorize software, it is necessary to first understand its basic characteristics. In its broadest scope, software encompasses all parts of the computer system other than the hardware, i.e., the machine; and the primary non-hardware component of a computer system is the program. * * * In its narrowest scope, software is synonymous with program, which, in turn, is defined as "a complete set of instructions that tells a computer how to do something." * * *

When stored on magnetic tape, disc, or computer chip, this software, or set of instructions, is physically manifested in machine readable form by arranging electrons, by use of an electric current, to create either a magnetized or unmagnetized space. * * * The computer reads the pattern of magnetized and unmagnetized spaces with a read/write head as "on" and "off", or to put it another way, "0" and "1". This machine readable language or code is the physical manifestation of the information in binary form. * * *

* * *

B.

South Central Bell argues that the software is merely "knowledge" or "intelligence," and as such is not corporeal and thus not taxable. We disagree with South Central Bell's characterization. The software at issue is not merely knowledge, but rather is knowledge recorded in a physical form which has physical existence, takes up space on the tape, disc, or hard drive, makes physical things happen, and can be perceived by the senses. * * * As the dissenting judge at the court of appeal pointed out, "In defining tangible, 'seen' is not limited to the unaided eye, 'weighed' is not limited to the butcher or bathroom scale, and 'measured' is not limited to a yardstick." 93–1072, at p. 8–9, 631 So.2d at 1348 (dissenting opinion). That we use a read/write head to read the magnetic or unmagnetic spaces is no different than any other machine that humans use to perceive those corporeal things which our naked senses cannot perceive. * * *

The software itself, i.e. the physical copy, is not merely a right or an idea to be comprehended by the understanding. The purchaser of computer software neither desires nor receives mere knowledge, but rather receives a certain arrangement of matter that will make his or her computer perform a desired function. This arrangement of matter, physically recorded on some tangible medium, constitutes a corporeal body.

We agree with Bell and the court of appeal that the form of the *delivery* of the software—magnetic tape or electronic transfer via a modem—is of no relevance. However, we disagree with Bell and the court of appeal that the essence or real object of the transaction was intangible property. * * * As the court of appeal explained, and as Bell readily admits, the programs cannot be utilized by Bell until they have been recorded into the memory of the electronic telephone switch. 93–1072, at p. 6, 631 So.2d at 1343. The essence of the transaction was not merely to obtain the intangible "knowledge" or "information", but rather, was to obtain recorded knowledge stored in some sort of physical form that Bell's computers could use. Recorded as such, the software is not merely an incorporeal idea to be comprehended, and would be of no use if it were. Rather, the software is given physical existence to make certain desired physical things happen.

One cannot escape the fact that software, recorded in physical form, becomes inextricably intertwined with, or part and parcel of the corporeal object upon which it is recorded, be that a disk, tape, hard drive, or other device. * * * That the information can be transferred and then physically recorded on another medium is of no moment, and does not make computer software any different than any other type of recorded information that can be transferred to another medium such as film, video tape, audio tape, or books.

* * * The court of appeal distinguished the purchase of * * * books, films, video and audio tapes, etc. ..., which hold stories, ideas, information and knowledge in physical form, by reasoning that the true essence of such transactions is the purchase of the tangible medium, not the intangible property (the artist's expressions) contained in that medium, and that without the specific tangible medium, the artist's expressions are useless, whereas computer software is separable from the tangible object upon which it is recorded. This distinction simply does not exist. As the dissenting judge at the court of appeal pointed out:

> [I]t is now common knowledge that books, music, and even movies or other audio/visual combinations can be copied from one medium to another. They are also all available on computer in such forms as floppy disc, tape, and CD–ROM. Such movies, books, music, etc. ... can all be delivered by and/or copied from one medium to another, including electrical impulses with the use of a modem. Assuming there is sufficient memory space available in the computer hard disc drive such movies, books, music, etc. ... can all be recorded into the permanent memory of the computer such as was done with the software in this case.

93–1072, at p. 4–5, 631 So.2d at 1346–47 (dissenting opinion). * * *

* * *

* * * When the magnetic tapes, upon which the switching software was physically recorded, came to rest in the City of New Orleans, or alternatively, when the software was physically recorded into the memory of the electronic telephone switch, the use tax attached. Likewise, once the data processing software was transmitted via telephone line and then physically recorded into the memory of Bell's computer, the software came to rest in corporeal or tangible form in the City of New Orleans and the use tax attached.[7]

7. We need not address the issue of whether use of software, through telephonic transmission, which is never reduced to physical recordation and at rest in the City of

C.

The court of appeal found that computer software constitutes "intellectual property" and thus classified such software as an incorporeal under Louisiana Civil Code article 461. * * *

* * *

We find this line of reasoning flawed and inconsistent with our civilian property concepts outlined above. As the dissenting court of appeal judge in this case perceptively pointed out, this reasoning confuses the corporeal computer software *copy* itself with the incorporeal *right* to the software. Explaining this often confused distinction, the dissenting judge noted that the incorporeal right to software is the copyright, which in this case, as is typical in such license agreements, was reserved to the vendors. 93–1072, at p. 2, 631 So.2d at 1345 (dissenting opinion). What Bell acquired, and what the City was attempting to tax, was not the copyright to the software, but the copy of the software itself. It was not the copyright that operated the telephone central office switching equipment, but rather the physical copy of the software.

* * *

We reject Bell's argument that what was purchased was the license or right to use the computer software, and that such license is intangible. * * * [T]he license to use the software, without transferring the software, would be of no use to Bell, and the license to use the software is inseparable from the physical manifestation of the software in recorded form.

We likewise decline to adopt the canned versus custom distinction invoked by a few state legislatures, commentators and courts. "Canned" software is software which has been pre-written to be used by more than one customer, or mass marketed; "custom" software is specially designed for exclusive use by one particular customer. * * * Under the canned versus custom distinction, canned programs are classified as taxable on the theory that the buyer acquires an end product; whereas, custom programs are classified as non-taxable services on the theory that the buyer acquires professional services. * * *

While the Louisiana Department of Taxation's current sales tax regulation regarding software adopts the "custom" versus "canned" distinction, * * * it has been observed that this distinction departs entirely from the general Louisiana property law concepts applicable for making the tangible versus intangible distinction. * * * To put it simply, whether the software is custom or canned, the nature of the software is the same.

Another problem with the custom/canned distinction, as illustrated by the facts in this case, is that often the software at issue is mixed, i.e., canned software is modified to the buyer's specifications, and fits neatly

New Orleans, is subject to the City's use tax, as that issue is not raised by the facts of this case.

into neither category. As the court of appeal commented, "the uncontroverted facts in this case tend to establish that the programs at issue were a combination of canned and custom programs. The programs were pre-made but apparently significant adaptations were required before [Bell] could use them." 631 So.2d at 1344.

* * *

In sum, once the "information" or "knowledge" is transformed into physical existence and recorded in physical form, it is corporeal property. The physical recordation of this software is not an incorporeal right to be comprehended. Therefore we hold that the switching system software and the data processing software involved here is tangible personal property and thus is taxable by the City of New Orleans.

* * *

■ WATSON, JUSTICE, concurring in part and dissenting in part.

The software at issue was transmitted by two methods: (1) encoded on magnetic tape; or (2) electronically transferred via telephone wires and modems. The ordinary definition or generally prevailing meaning (C.C. art. 11) of "tangible personal property" would not cover either type of software.

However, state jurisprudence gives the phrase an altered meaning which may be extended to cover the taped software. Applying the expansive reasoning of the jurisprudence, the lynch pin of holding the software to be tangible personal property seems to be that it is on a floppy disc, a tape or a compact disc and the value of the software is included in the price of the disc, tape or CD. The simplest example of this type of taxation is the purchase of a software program (such as WordPerfect, Windows or Excel) at a local computer store. Who can argue that only the value of the floppy discs and the manual may be taxed and not the program?

On the other hand, subscribers to "bulletin boards" can use modems and telephone connections to download software programs without being taxed. The analysis of software being taxed because it is bought on a tape or disc cannot be stretched logically to include data transmitted by modems and telephone wires.

I respectfully concur on taxing the South Central Bell software purchased on tapes, but dissent as to software received electronically.

NOTES & QUESTIONS

1. *A standard definition.* The definition of "tangible personal property" that was interpreted in this case is very similar to the definition of this term in the sales- and use-tax provisions of most other states and localities.

2. *Canned vs. custom software.* Most states recognize a distinction between "canned" and "custom" software: they treat the former as tangible personal property, subject to sales and use tax, but the latter as a service that is not subject to such taxes.

3. *Is digital downloading different?* Does the dissenting judge explain the grounds for his conclusion that software delivered via digital download has a different status for sales- and use-tax purposes than does software delivered via a tangible medium? Can you articulate any grounds for making such a distinction? Is there an argument that a downloaded item, like an electronic newspaper, is a "service," even though the corresponding physical item, in this case a paper newspaper, is clearly a "good"?

4. *Other digital products.* All digital products, including software, data, music and movies in digital format, and electronic books, consist of a string of ones and zeros embedded on a physical medium like a hard drive or CD, or streamed across the network. Is there any justification for differentiating among the various digital products in determining the applicability of sales and use taxes?

II. INTERNATIONAL TAXATION ISSUES

A. WEBSITE OPERATIONS AS PERMANENT ESTABLISHMENTS UNDER TAX TREATIES

The most important function of tax treaties is to prevent double taxation—the taxation of an item of income by each of two countries. Double taxation can occur when an enterprise that is a resident of one country earns income from its operations in another country, and both the country where the income arises (the "source country") and the country where the business resides (the "residence country") claim the right to tax that income. All tax treaties to which the United States is a party seek to prevent double taxation through a rule that allows a country to tax business income only to the extent that the income is attributable to "a permanent establishment" located within the taxing country. Under this approach, the authority to tax an item of business income is allocated between countries: it is taxable in the source country, to the extent it is attributable to a permanent establishment in that country, and is taxable in the residence country to the extent it is not so attributable. At least that is the theory. In reality, there are many thorny issues that arise in determining what activities of an enterprise constitute a permanent establishment, and what income is attributable to a particular permanent establishment.

What is a permanent establishment, and what novel issues arise in applying the permanent establishment approach in the context of electronic commerce? To address these issues we will consider how the issue is treated under the Organisation for Economic Co-operation and Development[6] Model Tax Convention on Income and on Capital ("OECD Model Treaty"). Nearly all U.S. tax treaties are based upon this model.

The OECD Model Treaty defines "permanent establishment" as "a fixed place of business through which the business of an enterprise is wholly or partly carried on." OECD Model Treaty Art. 5(1). Certain types

6. The OECD is an international organization composed of thirty member countries, the majority of which are among the world's most industrialized and trade-oriented countries. The OECD addresses economic and social issues including trade, education,

of activities are per se permanent establishments, including offices, factories, and mines. Art. 5(2). Other types of activities are specified as *not* constituting a permanent establishment; for present purposes, the most important of these is the maintenance of a fixed place of business solely for the purpose of carrying on "activity of a preparatory or auxiliary character." Art. 5(4)(e). An enterprise's use of an independent agent to carry on business activities does not create a permanent establishment. Art. 5(6). A permanent establishment does result, however, from use of a "dependent agent," one who "is acting on behalf of an enterprise and has, and habitually exercises, * * * an authority to conclude contracts in the name of the enterprise." Art. 5(5).

Unanswered questions arose when applying the Treaty's definition of permanent establishment to electronic commerce. Does hosting a website on a server constitute a permanent establishment where the server is located? Is a website-hosting ISP an agent of the company whose website it hosts, so as to give rise to a permanent establishment where the ISP is located? Can computer equipment that operates automatically, without human intervention, ever constitute a permanent establishment?

The resolution of these issues may have a substantial impact on how e-commerce business operations are structured. There is a great deal of variation among countries with respect to the rates at which they tax business profits. All else being equal, a business will prefer to be subject to the taxing jurisdiction of a no- or low-tax country, rather than that of a high-tax country. Under treaties to which the United States is a party, which country can tax business profits depends on where the business has a permanent establishment. If treaty rules allow a business to determine the location of the permanent establishments to which its profits are attributable by hosting its website on a particular server or by distributing its computer operations in a particular way, the business will have every incentive to do so.

To address these and related issues, in December 2000 the OECD issued a modification of its official Commentary on Article 5 of the Model Treaty. The Commentary represents the majority view of OECD member countries concerning interpretation of the Treaty, and is highly influential in guiding interpretation. Because it is much easier to update the Commentary than to update the Treaty itself, responses to technological developments are sometimes found only in the Commentary.

OECD, CLARIFICATION ON THE APPLICATION OF THE PERMANENT ESTABLISHMENT DEFINITION IN E-COMMERCE: CHANGES TO THE COMMENTARY ON THE MODEL TAX CONVENTION ON ARTICLE 5

(2000).

1. This document contains the changes to the Commentary on the OECD Model Tax Convention adopted by the Committee on Fiscal Affairs

technology, taxation, development, health, and education, through conducting studies, collecting statistics, producing reports, and issuing recommendations. *See* www.oecd.org.

on 22 December 2000 concerning the issue of the application of the current definition of permanent establishment in the context of e-commerce. It follows two previous drafts which were released for comments by Working Party No. 1 in October 1999 and March 2000.

* * *

6. As this document shows, the Committee has been able to reach a consensus on the various issues concerning the application of the current definition of permanent establishment in the context of e-commerce (subject to the two dissenting views described at the end of this paragraph and of paragraph 14 below). This consensus includes the important views that a web site cannot, in itself, constitute a permanent establishment, that a web site hosting arrangement typically does not result in a permanent establishment for the enterprise that carries on business through that web site and that an ISP will not, except in very unusual circumstances, constitute a dependent agent of another enterprise so as to constitute a permanent establishment of that enterprise. However, Spain and Portugal do not consider that physical presence is a requirement for a permanent establishment to exist in the context of e-commerce, and therefore, they also consider that, in some circumstances, an enterprise carrying on business in a State through a web site could be treated as having a permanent establishment in that State. * * *

7. As a number of commentators and delegates have noted, it is unlikely that much tax revenues depend on the issue of whether or not computer equipment at a given location constitutes a permanent establishment. In many cases, the ability to relocate computer equipment should reduce the risks that taxpayers in e-commerce operations [will] be found to have permanent establishments where they did not intend to. Also, in circumstances where a taxpayer would want to have income attributed to a country where its computer equipment is located, that result can be achieved through the use of a subsidiary even if no permanent establishment is considered to exist. It is crucial, however, that taxpayers and tax authorities know where the borderlines are and that taxpayers not be put in a position to have a permanent establishment in a country without knowing that they have a business presence in that country (a result that is avoided by the conclusion that a web site cannot, in itself, constitute a permanent establishment).

8. Since a large part of the draft released in March 2000 discussed a minority view that some human intervention was required for a permanent establishment to exist and since many commentators have argued that this was the case, the Committee wishes to explain the position reached on that issue and reflected in the changes that have been adopted.

9. Having further examination of the issue, the conclusion has been reached that human intervention is not a requirement for the existence of a permanent establishment.

* * *

12. * * * [U]sually, enterprises that have fixed places of business carry on their business through personnel. This, however, does not, and was not intended to, rule out that a business may be at least partly carried on without personnel.

13. * * * [T]he Committee believes that a requirement of human intervention could mean that, outside the e-commerce environment, important and essential business functions could be performed through fixed automated equipment located permanently at a given location without a permanent establishment being found to exist, a result that would be contrary to the object and purpose of Article 5.

14. The changes to the Commentary on Article 5 which appear below make it clear that, in many cases, the issue of whether computer equipment at a given location constitutes a permanent establishment will depend on whether the functions performed through that equipment exceed the preparatory or auxiliary threshold, something that can only be decided on a case-by-case analysis. Some countries did not like that outcome and the uncertainty that may result from it. They suggested that, in the case of e-tailers, it would have been better to simply conclude that a server cannot, by itself, constitute a permanent establishment. In order to reach a consensus, however, most of these countries have accepted the view expressed above, noting that they will take into account the need to provide a clear and certain rule in their own appreciation of what are preparatory or auxiliary activities for an e-tailer. The United Kingdom, however, has taken the view that in no circumstances do servers, of themselves or together with web sites, constitute permanent establishments of e-tailers and intends to make an observation to that effect when the changes to the Commentary on Article 5 are included in the Model Tax Convention.

15. In order to illustrate that it is possible for functions performed through computer equipment to go beyond what is preparatory or auxiliary, an example has been included in the last sentence of paragraph 42.9. It was noted during the discussion that this example is merely illustrative and should not be considered to determine the point at which the preparatory or auxiliary threshold is exceeded since many countries consider that this could be the case even if only some of the functions described in that example are performed through the equipment.

CHANGES TO THE COMMENTARY ON ARTICLE 5

Add the following heading and paragraphs 42.1 to 42.10 immediately after paragraph 42 of the Commentary on Article 5

Electronic commerce

* * *

42.2 Whilst a location where automated equipment is operated by an enterprise may constitute a permanent establishment in the country where it is situated (see below), a distinction needs to be made between computer equipment, which may be set up at a location so as to constitute a permanent establishment under certain circumstances, and the data and software which is used by, or stored on, that equipment. For instance, an Internet web site, which is a combination of software and electronic data, does not in itself constitute tangible property. It therefore does not have a location that can constitute a "place of business" as there is no "facility such as premises or, in certain instances, machinery or equipment" * * * as far as the software and data constituting that web site is concerned. On the other hand, the server on which the web site is stored and through which it is accessible is a piece of equipment having a physical location and such location may thus constitute a "fixed place of business" of the enterprise that operates that server.

42.3 The distinction between a web site and the server on which the web site is stored and used is important since the enterprise that operates the server may be different from the enterprise that carries on business through the web site. For example, it is common for the web site through which an enterprise carries on its business to be hosted on the server of an Internet Service Provider (ISP). Although the fees paid to the ISP under such arrangements may be based on the amount of disk space used to store the software and data required by the web site, these contracts typically do not result in the server and its location being at the disposal of the enterprise * * *, even if the enterprise has been able to determine that its web site should be hosted on a particular server at a particular location. In such a case, the enterprise does not even have a physical presence at that location since the web site is not tangible. In these cases, the enterprise cannot be considered to have acquired a place of business by virtue of that hosting arrangement. However, if the enterprise carrying on business through a web site has the server at its own disposal, for example it owns (or leases) and operates the server on which the web site is stored and used, the place where that server is located could constitute a permanent establishment of the enterprise if the other requirements of the Article are met.

42.4 Computer equipment at a given location may only constitute a permanent establishment if it meets the requirement of being fixed. In the case of a server, what is relevant is not the possibility of the server being moved, but whether it is in fact moved. In order to constitute a fixed place of business, a server will need to be located at a certain place for a sufficient period of time so as to become fixed * * *.

42.5. Another issue is whether the business of an enterprise may be said to be wholly or partly carried on at a location where the enterprise has equipment such as a server at its disposal. The question of whether the business of an enterprise is wholly or partly carried on through such equipment needs to be examined on a case-by-case basis, having regard to whether it can be said that, because of such equipment, the enterprise has facilities at its disposal where business functions of the enterprise are performed.

42.6 Where an enterprise operates computer equipment at a particular location, a permanent establishment may exist even though no personnel of that enterprise is required at that location for the operation of the equipment. The presence of personnel is not necessary to consider that an enterprise wholly or partly carries on its business at a location when no personnel are in fact required to carry on business activities at that location. This conclusion applies to electronic commerce to the same extent that it applies with respect to other activities in which equipment operates automatically, e.g. automatic pumping equipment used in the exploitation of natural resources.

42.7 Another issue relates to the fact that no permanent establishment may be considered to exist where the electronic commerce operations carried on through computer equipment at a given location in a country are restricted to the preparatory or auxiliary activities covered by [Article 5(4)(e)]. The question of whether particular activities performed at such a location fall within [Article 5(4)(e)] needs to be examined on a case-by-case basis having regard to the various functions performed by the enterprise through that equipment. Examples of activities which would generally be regarded as preparatory or auxiliary include:

—providing a communications link—much like a telephone line—between suppliers and customers;

—advertising of goods or services;

—relaying information through a mirror server for security and efficiency purposes;

—gathering market data for the enterprise;

—supplying information.

42.8 Where, however, such functions form in themselves an essential and significant part of the business activity of the enterprise as a whole, or where other core functions of the enterprise are carried on through the computer equipment, these would go beyond the activities covered by [Article 5(4)(e)] and if the equipment constituted a fixed place of business of the enterprise (as discussed in paragraphs 42.2 to 42.6 above), there would be a permanent establishment.

42.9 What constitutes core functions for a particular enterprise clearly depends on the nature of the business carried on by that enterprise. For instance, some ISPs are in the business of operating their own servers for the purpose of hosting web sites or other applications for other enterprises. For these ISPs, the operation of their servers in order to provide services to customers is an essential part of their commercial activity and cannot be considered preparatory or auxiliary. A different example is that of an enterprise (sometimes referred to as an "e-tailer") that carries on the business of selling products through the Internet. In that case, the enterprise is not in the business of operating servers and the mere fact that it may do so at a given location is not enough to conclude that activities performed at that location are more than preparatory and auxiliary. What needs to be done in such a case is to examine the nature of the activities performed at that location in light of the business carried on by the enterprise. If these activities are merely preparatory or auxiliary to the business of selling products on the Internet (for example, the location is used to operate a server that hosts a web site which, as is often the case, is used exclusively for advertising, displaying a catalogue of products or providing information to potential customers), [Article 5(4)(e)] will apply and the location will not constitute a permanent establishment. If, however, the typical functions related to a sale are performed at that location (for example, the conclusion of the contract with the customer, the processing of the payment and the delivery of the products are performed automatically through the equipment located there), these activities cannot be considered to be merely preparatory or auxiliary.

42.10 A last issue is whether [Article 5(5)] may apply to deem an ISP to constitute a permanent establishment. As already noted, it is common for ISPs to provide the service of hosting the web sites of other enterprises on their own servers. The issue may then arise as to whether [Article 5(5)] may apply to deem such ISPs to constitute permanent establishments of the enterprises that carry on electronic commerce through web sites operated through the servers owned and operated by these ISPs. While this could be the case in very unusual circumstances, [Article 5(5)] will generally not be applicable because the ISPs will not constitute an agent of the enterprises to which the web sites belong, because they will not have authority to conclude contracts in the name of these enterprises and will not regularly conclude such contracts or because they will constitute independent agents acting in the ordinary course of their business, as evidenced by the fact that they host the web sites of many different enterprises. It is also clear that since the web site through which an enterprise carries on its business is not itself a "person" as defined in Article 3, paragraph 5 cannot apply to deem a permanent establishment to exist by virtue of the web site being an agent of the enterprise for purposes of that paragraph.

NOTES & QUESTIONS

1. *Relevance of permanent establishment criterion.* Consider the Committee's statement: "In many cases, the ability to relocate computer equipment should reduce the risks that taxpayers in e-commerce operations [will] be found to have permanent establishments where they did not intend to. Also, in circumstances where a taxpayer would want to have income attributed to a country where its computer equipment is located, that result can be achieved through the use of a subsidiary even if no permanent establishment is considered to exist." Does this mean that website hosting companies can circumvent the interpretation of permanent establishment at will? Does this call into question the continuing relevance of the permanent establishment criterion?

2. *Website as permanent establishment where viewed.* Does a website constitute a permanent establishment in every country where it may be viewed on a user's screen? Does the OECD Commentary address that issue? Consider the following view:

> According to the new OECD Commentary, a web site is "a combination of software and electronic data" and "does not in itself constitute tangible property". This description of a web site is inaccurate. The issue to be decided is whether a remote seller's web site appearing on the computer screen of a potential customer constitutes a permanent establishment of the remote seller when it operates as a virtual office. The images appearing on that screen are tangible. Like all visible matter, they are made up of small particles of matter that are themselves invisible to the eye. Although the form of those images is controlled by software, the images themselves are not software. They are real and tangible, not an apparition. Nor are they intangible, as that term has been understood in legal parlance for centuries.
>
> In the author's view, the proper test is a functional test. A virtual office should be considered a permanent establishment of its owner if it is used to perform the functions of a traditional office. Of course, the various exceptions applicable to a "bricks and mortar" office should apply to a virtual office as well. Thus, a virtual office used merely for preliminary or auxiliary activities, within the meaning of Art. 5(4) of the OECD Model * * *, would not be treated as a permanent establishment. In general, a virtual office would constitute a permanent establishment only if it is used to make actual sales of goods or services on a more than casual basis.

Michael J. McIntyre, *U.S. Taxation of Foreign Corporations in the Digital Age*, 55 (9/10) BULL. FOR INT'L FISCAL DOCUMENTATION 498 (2001).

4. *Residence-country vs. source-country taxation*. The permanent establishment criterion is relevant under a taxing regime in which taxing authorities agree that income should be taxed by the country in which it is earned (the source country), rather than the country where the enterprise earning the income resides (the residence country). The OECD's Model Tax Treaty calls for a regime of source-country taxation, and therefore relies on the permanent establishment criterion to determine which country is deemed to be the source of income. But the rise of e-commerce may give impetus to a shift to a residence-country regime. According to a U.S. Treasury Department discussion paper:

> The United States, as do most countries, asserts jurisdiction to tax based on principles of both source and residence. If double taxation is to be avoided, however, one principle must yield to the other. Therefore, through tax treaties, countries tend to restrict their source-based taxing rights with respect to foreign taxpayers in order to exercise more fully their residence-based taxing rights. This occurs in a number of ways. The permanent establishment concept represents a preference for residence-based taxation by setting an appropriate threshold for source-based taxation of active business income. By setting a threshold, in most cases it is not

necessary to identify the source of active business income and the income is only subject to tax in the country of residence. * * *

The growth of new communications technologies and electronic commerce will likely require that principles of residence-based taxation assume even greater importance. In the world of cyberspace, it is often difficult, if not impossible, to apply traditional source concepts to link an item of income with a specific geographical location. Therefore, source based taxation could lose its rationale and be rendered obsolete by electronic commerce. By contrast, almost all taxpayers are resident somewhere. An individual is almost always a citizen or resident of a given country and, at least under U.S. law, all corporations must be established under the laws of a given jurisdiction. However, a review of current residency definitions and taxation rules may be appropriate.

U.S. TREASURY DEPARTMENT, SELECTED TAX POLICY IMPLICATIONS OF GLOBAL ELECTRONIC COMMERCE ¶ 7.1.5 (1996), www.treas.gov/taxpolicy/internet.html. Do you agree that "[i]n the world of cyberspace" it is more difficult than elsewhere to attribute income to a particular geographic location?

NOTE: PERMANENT ESTABLISHMENTS AND TAX HAVENS

The question whether a server hosting an e-commerce website constitutes a permanent establishment may have a significant effect on whether an e-commerce business elects to locate its website on a server in a tax-haven country. A tax haven is a country that seeks to entice enterprises to locate their operations, in whole or in part, within its borders, by offering extremely favorable tax treatment of the enterprises' income and property. Tax-haven countries typically do not have tax treaties with other, non-haven countries.

Why do not all enterprises relocate their operations to tax-haven countries? Favorable tax treatment is only one of the many elements that an enterprise must consider in determining where to locate its operations. Proximity to raw materials and to markets, availability and wages of employees with the required skills, issues of physical security, the location's physical, financial, and legal infrastructure, the owners' or managers' preferences regarding country of residence, and other considerations frequently greatly outweigh an enterprise's desire to minimize its tax liability. Most enterprises, therefore, choose to locate in a country that does not offer the most favorable tax treatment.

The availability of electronic commerce as a method of operating a business may substantially affect this calculus. Consider a business that interacts with its customers solely via a website, and that sells digital goods. Nearly all of the business's operations may be conducted through a computer server that hosts the company's website, and holds the digital goods that are its products. Such a server operates primarily autonomously, and to the extent that human intervention is required, that intervention may be conducted from a remote location via the network. Many of the considerations that convince businesses to locate in high-tax jurisdictions therefore become irrelevant. There are no physical inputs, so proximity to raw materials is irrelevant. The website is accessible wherever there is Internet access, and the cost of shipping digital goods does not depend significantly on the geographic distance between the server and the customer, so proximity to markets is irrelevant. Most employees, managers, and owners need not be located anywhere near the computer server: an independent contractor with technicians who maintain the computer server is all that is required. Tax treatment therefore becomes a relatively more significant consideration, and it may make economic sense to host the company's website on a server located in a country whose only advantage consists of favorable tax treatment.

If location of an e-commerce business's website on a server located in a tax haven is sufficient to create a permanent establishment in that country, then, based on the above considerations, it may become both feasible and economically rational for such businesses to relocate their websites to such locations. If this in fact should occur, it would mean a shift of the business-income tax base from high- to low-tax jurisdictions.

Based on the OECD's interpretation of the permanent establishment rules as applied to websites, what would an e-commerce company have to do to establish a permanent establishment in a low-tax jurisdiction? How much benefit would accrue to the enterprise from such a move?

B. CHARACTERIZATION ISSUES

Income may be characterized as business income, royalties, dividends, interest, income from sale of goods, income from provision of services, and in various other ways. The characterization of income plays an important role in determining its tax consequences.

In most cases, characterization of income resulting from e-commerce transactions presents no difficulty. For example, a sale of tangible personal property gives rise to business income from the sale of goods, regardless of whether the item was ordered from a website, by telephone, or by mail.

On the other hand, transactions in digital goods raise a characterization issue because the transaction may be viewed either as a *license* of the copyrighted work (such as software or music), or as a *sale* of goods, with the purchaser obtaining the right to use the work but not to make or distribute additional copies of it.

The characterization of the income resulting from a transaction involving a digital good has several consequences relating to international taxation.[7]

7. The characterization of income is also relevant for domestic taxation in a variety of contexts. For example, the applicability of use tax may depend on whether an item is characterized as a good or a service. *See* Part I(A)(3), *supra*.

First, the characterization may determine whether the income is treated as U.S.- or foreign-source income. Consider a U.S. vendor's sale of software to a purchaser in a foreign country. If a transaction involving software is treated as *sale of a good*, then under U.S. sourcing rules the income from the sale will be allocated between the United States and the country where the purchaser is located. 26 U.S.C. § 863(b). To the extent the income is treated as foreign-source, it will contribute to a tax credit for the taxpayer against tax paid on the income to the foreign country. If, on the other hand, the transaction is treated as a *transfer of copyright*, the source of the income will be the country of the seller's residence, in this example the United States. 26 U.S.C. § 865(a), (d)(1)(A). Finally, if payment for the use of the software is structured as a *royalty*, the source of the income is the place of use, which in this example is likely to be the foreign country. 26 U.S.C. § 862(a).

Second, the characterization may determine which country has the right to tax the income. Under the OECD Model Treaty, both business income and royalty income are taxable in the country where the purchaser or licensee is located (the source country) only to the extent the income is attributable to a permanent establishment of the seller or licensor in the source country. Many treaties to which the United States is a party diverge from this principle, however, and allow royalty (but not business) income to be taxed in the source country even absent a permanent establishment there.

Third, the characterization of income may determine the rate at which it is taxed, and whether any deductions are allowed. Royalty income is generally subject to a gross receipts tax, which applies a tax rate to the entire amount of the income. Business income is taxed on a net basis, applying a tax rate to income after deducting the cost of goods sold and any other allowable deductions.

The OECD Model Treaty defines "royalties" as "payments of any kind received as consideration for the use of, or the right to use any copyright of literary, artistic or scientific work." Art. 12(2). The question therefore arises whether, under a treaty based on the OECD model, the payment a purchaser makes to acquire a piece of software or some other digital good should be treated as a payment for the right to use the copyright in it, and therefore as royalty income to the seller.

An OECD Technical Advisory Group recommends an approach under which a typical transaction in a copyrighted digital good would be characterized as business rather than royalty income:

> 17.2 Under the relevant legislation of some countries, transactions which permit the customer to electronically download digital products may give rise to use of copyright by the customer, *e.g.* because a right to make one or more copies of the digital content is granted under the contract. Where the essential consideration is for something other than for the use of, or right to use, rights in the copyright (such as to acquire other types of contractual rights, data or services), and the use of copyright is limited to

> such rights as are required to enable downloading, storage and operation on the customer's computer, network or other storage, performance or display device, such use of copyright should be disregarded in the analysis of the character of the payment for purposes of applying the definition of "royalties".
>
> 17.3 This is the case for transactions that permit the customer (which may be an enterprise) to electronically download digital products (such as software, images, sounds or text) for that customer's own use or enjoyment. In these transactions, the payment is made to acquire data transmitted in the form of a digital signal for the acquiror's own use or enjoyment. This constitutes the essential consideration for the payment, which therefore does not constitute royalties but falls within Article 7 or Article 13, as the case may be. To the extent that the act of copying the digital signal onto the customer's hard disk or other non-temporary media constitutes the use of a copyright by the customer under the relevant law and contractual arrangements, this is merely an incidental part of the process of capturing and storing the digital signal. This incidental part is not important for classification purposes because it does not correspond to the essential consideration for the payment (*i.e.*, to acquire data transmitted in the form of a digital signal), which is the determining factor for the purposes of the definition of royalties. There also would be no basis to classify such transactions as "royalties" if, under the relevant law and contractual arrangements, the creation of a copy is regarded as a use of copyright by the provider rather than by the customer.
>
> 17.4 By contrast, transactions where the essential consideration for the payment is the granting of the right to use a copyright in a digital product that is electronically downloaded for that purpose will give rise to royalties. This would be the case, for example, of a book publisher who would pay to acquire the right to reproduce a copyrighted picture that it would electronically download for the purposes of including it on the cover of a book that it is producing. In this transaction, the essential consideration for the payment is the acquisition of rights to use the copyright in the digital product, *i.e.* the right to reproduce and distribute the picture, and not merely for the acquisition of the digital content.

OECD Technical Advisory Group on Treaty Characterisation of Electronic Commerce Payments, Tax Treaty Characterization Issues Arising from E–Commerce, at ¶ 16 (Feb. 1, 2001).

The United States Treasury Department adopted a similar approach in its regulations. A transaction in a computer program is treated as a sale of a good, rather than a license giving rise to royalties, as long as the purchaser does not acquire (1) the right to make copies of the computer program for purposes of distribution to the public; (2) the right to prepare derivative computer programs based upon the copyrighted computer program; (3) the right to make a public performance of the computer program;

or (4) the right to display the computer program publicly. 26 C.F.R. § 1.861–18. These constitute the exclusive rights reserved to the copyright holder under the Copyright Act, 17 U.S.C. § 106, other than the right to make such copies of the software as are necessary to utilize it. The regulation makes no distinction between software that is delivered embedded in some storage medium, such as a CD–ROM or floppy diskette, and software that is delivered by digital download across the network. 26 C.F.R. § 1.861–18(g)(2) ("The rules of this section shall be applied irrespective of the physical or electronic or other medium used to effectuate a transfer of a computer program.").

This regulation is intended only for the purpose of interpreting provisions of U.S. tax treaties: it is inapplicable to domestic tax issues, and to digital goods other than computer programs. The Treasury Department has stated that it "may consider whether to apply the principles of these regulations to all transactions in digitized information as part of a separate guidance project." T.D. 8785 (Oct. 7, 1998). Can you think of any reason why different rules should apply to other types of digital goods?

Note that many of the rules discussed above depend upon the location of the purchaser. Ordinarily the seller knows the location of the purchaser, since the seller ships a good to a particular address. But what if a good is delivered via digital download across the network? For example, a website may offer software or music for sale via its website, accepting a credit-card number, or perhaps even anonymous digital cash, as payment. In that case, the seller need never learn the location of the purchaser. This scenario presents an unanswered question. Sellers that wish to have the benefit of foreign-source income, generating a deduction against the double taxation they pay on a transaction, may find it to their advantage to require the purchaser to disclose his location—at least to the extent of identifying the location as "United States" or "outside the United States." Geolocation technology may present a viable alternative, though it remains to be seen how much credence U.S. taxing authorities will accord to locational information generated by such technology.

NOTE: VALUE ADDED TAX ON SALES OF DIGITAL GOODS

In May 2002 the European Union issued a Directive imposing tax-collection obligations on sellers of digital goods located outside the European Union. *See* Council Directive 2002/38/EC of 7 May 2002 amending and amending temporarily Directive 77/388/EEC as regards the value added tax arrangements applicable to radio and television broadcasting services and certain electronically supplied services, 2002 O.J. (L 128) 41. European Union countries impose a consumption tax, called Value Added Tax ("VAT"), on a variety of commercial activities including retail sales. The tax rate varies from country to country, with the "standard" rate ranging from a low of 15% (in Luxembourg) to a high of 25% (in Denmark and

Sweden).[8] Sellers located in an EU country are required to collect this tax on sales of digital goods regardless of whether the purchaser is located within or outside the EU. Sellers located outside the EU, however, have not been required to collect the tax. This placed European sellers at a competitive disadvantage with respect to non-European sellers.

The new Directive, which EU member states must implement through national laws by July 1, 2003, provides that sellers located outside the EU who supply "electronic services" to consumers within the EU must register with one of the EU member states. "Electronic services" include

> 1. Website supply, web-hosting, distance maintenance of programmes and equipment.
>
> 2. Supply of software and updating thereof.
>
> 3. Supply of images, text and information, and making databases available.
>
> 4. Supply of music, films and games, including games of chance and gambling games, and of political, cultural, artistic, sporting, scientific and entertainment broadcasts and events.
>
> 5. Supply of distance teaching.

Directive at Annex L. The seller must collect the VAT on all sales of such services to consumers within the EU, and must remit it to the member state with which it has registered. That member state apportions the remittances among all the member states, based on the locations of the purchasers. The new rule affects only sales to individual consumers. Sales to businesses for resale are not affected, because these businesses are required to collect VAT on their sales to the ultimate consumer.

Under the Directive, the VAT rate to be collected by a seller outside the EU will depend on the location of the *purchaser*. This rule has engendered a good deal of criticism from non-EU sellers. In sales of goods that are delivered via digital download, rather than by shipping to a physical address, the seller may not know the location of the purchaser. Current technology does not allow the location of an online purchaser to be determined sufficiently quickly, cheaply, and accurately to be feasible for this purpose. The seller may ask the purchaser to self-report her location, but the purchaser will have an incentive to report a location in a low-VAT-rate jurisdiction, or even to report that she is located outside the EU and therefore not required to pay VAT to the seller. If the purchaser reports that she is located in a country with a 15% VAT rate, but she is actually located in a country with a 25% rate, the seller will at least in theory be liable for the difference. Sellers within the EU do not face this difficulty, since they are generally permitted to collect VAT at the rate in effect where the *seller* is located.

8. The "standard" rate is the highest rate charged by a given EU country. Each country taxes various categories of transactions at rates lower than the standard rate, in some cases at a zero rate.

Before the advent of electronic commerce, the fact that EU-based sellers were required to collect VAT but non-EU-based sellers were not did not place EU-based sellers at a significant competitive disadvantage. For goods that must be delivered by shipment to a physical address, the volume of sales from a seller outside the EU directly to a consumer within the EU was limited by high shipping and other transaction costs, making it more feasible to sell the goods to EU-based resellers instead. But when the product is delivered by digital download, these barriers are largely eliminated. With sellers outside the EU starting on roughly the same footing as those within the EU, the 15–25% VAT disadvantage became a serious issue.

If you were a U.S.-based seller of digital goods seeking to access the global market, how might the EU's new rules affect your business plan? How likely is it that EU enforcement authorities will be able to detect under-collections of VAT by sellers located outside the EU, and to enforce the VAT assessments? The state and local taxing jurisdictions in the United States do not currently require sellers located outside the United States to collect sales taxes on sales to their residents. If you were a state or federal policymaker in the United States, how might you respond to the EU's action?

*

BIBLIOGRAPHY

Chapter 1

Yochai Benkler, *Net Regulation: Taking Stock and Looking Forward*, 71 U. COLO. L. REV. 1203 (2000).

James Boyle, *Governance of The Internet: A Nondelegation Doctrine For The Digital Age?*, 50 DUKE L.J. 5 (2000).

James Boyle, *Foucault in Cyberspace: Surveillance, Sovereignty, and Hard-wired Censors*, 66 U. CIN. L. REV. 177 (1997).

Robert L. Dunne, *Deterring Unauthorized Access to Computers: Controlling Behavior in Cyberspace Through a Contract Law Paradigm*, 35 JURIMETRICS J. 1 (1994).

Frank H. Easterbrook, *Cyberspace and the Law of the Horse*, 1996 U. CHI. LEGAL F. 20 (1996).

Brendon Fowler et al., *Can You Yahoo!? The Internet's Digital Fences*, 2001 DUKE L. & TECH. REV. 12.

Llewellyn Joseph Gibbons, *No Regulation, Government Regulation, or Self-Regulation: Social Enforcement or Social Contracting for Governance in Cyberspace*, 6 CORNELL J.L. & PUB. POL'Y 475 (1997).

Jack L. Goldsmith, *Against Cyberanarchy*, 65 U. CHI. L. REV. 1199 (1998).

Jack L. Goldsmith & Alan O. Sykes, *The Internet and the Dormant Commerce Clause*, 110 YALE L. J. 785 (2001).

I. Trotter Hardy, *The Proper Legal Regime for "Cyberspace,"* 55 U. PITT. L. REV. 993 (1994).

David R. Johnson & David Post, *Law and Borders—The Rise of Law in Cyberspace*, 48 STAN. L. REV. 1367 (1996).

Mark A. Lemley, *The Law and Economics of Internet Norms*, 73 CHI.-KENT L. REV. 1257 (1998).

Mark A. Lemley & Lawrence Lessig, *The End of End-to-End: Preserving the Architecture of the Internet in the Broadband Era*, 48 U.C.L.A. L. REV. 925 (2001).

Mark A. Lemley & David McGowan, *Legal Implications of Network Effects*, 86 CAL. L. REV. 479 (1998).

Lawrence Lessig, Code and Other Laws of Cyberspace (1999).

Lawrence Lessig, *The Law of the Horse: What Cyberlaw Might Teach*, 113 HARV. L. REV. 501 (1999).

Joseph P. Liu, *Legitimacy and Authority in Internet Coordination: A Domain Name Case*, 74 IND. L.J. 587 (1999).

Neil Weinstock Netanel, *Cyberspace Self-Governance: A Skeptical View from Liberal Democratic Theory*, 88 CALIF. L. REV. 395 (2000).

David G. Post, *Anarchy, State, and the Internet: An Essay on Law–Making in Cyberspace*, 1995 J. ONLINE L. art. 3.

Margaret Jane Radin & R. Polk Wagner, *The Myth Of Private Ordering: Rediscovering Legal Realism in Cyberspace*, 73 CHI.-KENT L. REV. 1295 (1998).

Joel R. Reidenberg, *Lex Informatica: The Formulation of Information Policy Rules Through Technology*, 76 TEX. L. REV. 553 (1998).

John Rothchild, *Protecting the Digital Consumer: The Limits of Cyberspace Utopianism*, 74 IND. L.J. 893 (1999).

Saskia Sassen, *The Internet and the Sovereign State: The Role and Impact of Cyberspace on National and Global Governance*, 5 IND. J. GLOBAL LEGAL STUD. 545 (1998).

CARL SHAPIRO & HAL R. VARIAN, INFORMATION RULES: A STRATEGIC GUIDE TO THE NETWORK ECONOMY (1999).

Jonathan Weinberg, *ICANN and the Problem of Legitimacy*, 50 DUKE L.J. 187 (2000).

Timothy Wu, *Application–Centered Internet Analysis*, 85 VA. L. REV. 1163 (1999).

Chapter 2

ROSEMARY J. COOMBE, THE CULTURAL LIFE OF INTELLECTUAL PROPERTIES: AUTHORSHIP, APPROPRIATION AND THE LAW (1998).

Mark A. Lemley, *The Modern Lanham Act and the Death of Common Sense*, 108 YALE L.J. 1687 (1999).

Jessica Litman, *Breakfast with Batman: The Public Interest in the Advertising Age*, 108 YALE L.J. 1717 (1999).

Ira S. Nathenson, *Internet Infoglut and Invisible Ink: Spamdexing Search Engines with Meta Tags*, 12 HARV. J.L. & TECH. 43 (1998).

Maureen A. O'Rourke, *Defining the Limits of Free-riding in Cyberspace: Trademark Liability for Metatagging*, 33 GONZ. L. REV. 277 (1997/1998).

Chapter 3

John M. Carson et al., *Claim Jumping on the Newest Frontier: Trademarks, Cybersquatting, and the Judicial Interpretation of Bad Faith*, 8 UCLA ENT. L. REV. 27 (2000).

Anupam Chander, *Dominion in Cyberspace*, 81 TEX. L. REV. __ (forthcoming 2003).

David J. Franklyn, *Owning Words in Cyberspace: The Accidental Trademark Regime*, 2001 WISC. L. REV. 1251 (2001).

A. Michael Froomkin, *Wrong Turn in Cyberspace: Using ICANN to Route Around the APA and the Constitution*, 50 DUKE L.J. 17 (2000).

Laurence R. Helfer & Graeme B. Dinwoodie, *Designing Non–National Systems: The Case of the Uniform Domain Name Dispute Resolution Policy*, 43 WM. & MARY L. REV. 141 (2001).

Jay P. Kesan & Rajiv C. Shah, *Fool Us Once Shame on You—Fool Us Twice Shame on Us: What We Can Learn from the Privatizations of the Internet Backbone Network and the Domain Name System*, 79 WASH. U. L.Q. 89 (2001).

Stacey H. King, *The "Law That It Deems Applicable": ICANN, Dispute Resolution, and the Problem of Cybersquatting*, 22 HASTINGS COMM. & ENT. L.J. 453 (2000).

Jessica Litman, *The DNS Wars: Trademarks & the Internet Domain Name System*, 4 J. SMALL & EMERGING BUS. L. 149 (2000).

David J. Loundy, *A Primer on Trademark Law and Internet Addresses*, 15 J. MARSHALL J. COMPUTER & INFO. L. 465 (1997).

Catherine T. Struve & R. Polk Wagner, *Realspace Sovereigns in Cyberspace: Problems with the ACPA*, 17 BERKELEY TECH. L. J. __ (forthcoming 2002).

Chapter 4

Symposium, *Intellectual Property and Contract Law in the Information Age: The Impact of Article 2B of the Uniform Commercial Code on the Future of Transactions in Information and Electronic Commerce*, 13 BERKELEY TECH. L.J. 809 (1998).

Lorin Brennan, *Why Article 2 Cannot Apply to Software Transactions*, 38 DUQ. L. REV. 459 (2000).

Rochelle C. Dreyfuss, *UCITA in the International Marketplace: Are We About to Export Bad Innovation Policy?*, 26 BROOK. J. INT'L L. 49 (2000).

Paul Fasciano, *Internet Electronic Mail: A Last Bastion for the Mailbox Rule*, 25 HOFSTRA L. REV. 971 (1997).

William W. Fisher III, *Property and Contract on the Internet*, 73 CHI.-KENT L. REV. 1203 (1998).

Dennis Karjala, *Federal Preemption of Shrinkwrap and On–Line Licenses*, 22 U. DAYTON L. REV. 511 (1997).

Ian R. Kerr, *Spirits in a Material World: Intelligent Agents as Intermediaries in Electronic Commerce*, 22 DALHOUSIE L.J. 189 (1999).

Mark A. Lemley, *Intellectual Property and Shrinkwrap Licenses*, 68 S. CAL. L. REV. 1239 (1995).

Mark A. Lemley, *Beyond Preemption: The Law and Policy of Intellectual Property Licensing*, 87 CAL. L. REV. 111 (1999).

Jean–Francois Lerouge, *The Use of Electronic Agents Questioned Under Contractual Law: Suggested Solutions on a European and American Level*, 18 J. MARSHALL J. COMPUTER & INFO. L. 403 (1999).

Michael J. Madison, *Legal–Ware: Contract and Copyright in the Digital Age*, 67 FORDHAM L. REV. 1025 (1998).

Stephen T. Middlebrook & John Muller, *Thoughts on Bots: The Emerging Law of Electronic Agents*, 56 Bus. Law. 341 (2000).

Bonnie A. Nardi et al., *Collaborative Programmable Intelligent Agents*, Comm. of the ACM, vol. 41, No. 3 (Mar. 1, 1998).

David A. Nimmer et al. *The Metamorphosis of Contract into Expand*, 87 Cal. L. Rev. 17 (1999).

Raymond T. Nimmer, *UCITA: A Commercial Contract Code*, 17 No. 5 Computer Law. 3 (2000).

Maureen O'Rourke, *Copyright Preemption After the ProCD Case: A Market–Based Approach*, 12 Berkeley Tech. L. J. (1997).

Margaret Jane Radin, *Humans, Computers, and Binding Commitment*, 75 Ind. L.J. 1125 (2000).

Pamela Samuelson, *Intellectual Property and Contract Law for the Information Age: Foreword to a Symposium*, 87 Cal. L. Rev. 1 (1999).

Suzanne Smed, *Intelligent Software Agents and Agency Law*, 14 Santa Clara Computer & High Tech. L.J. 503 (1998).

Lawrence B. Solum, *Legal Personhood for Artificial Intelligences*, 70 N.C. L. Rev. 1231 (1992).

M. Mitchell Waldrop, *Software Agents Prepare to Sift the Riches of Cyberspace*, Science, vol. 265, No. 5174 (Aug. 12, 1994).

Chapter 5

Adrienne J. Breslin, *Electronic Commerce: Will It Ever Truly Realize Its Global Potential?*, 20 Penn St. Int'l L. Rev. 275 (2001).

Susanna Frederick Fischer, *Saving Rosencrantz and Guildenstern in a Virtual World? A Comparative Look at Recent Global Electronic Signature Legislation*, 7 B.U. J. Sci. & Tech. L. 229 (2001).

A. Michael Froomkin, *The Essential Role of Trusted Third Parties in Electronic Commerce*, 75 Or. L. Rev. 49 (1996).

A. Michael Froomkin, *The Metaphor is the Key: Cryptography, the Clipper Chip and the Constitution*, 143 U. Pa. L. Rev. 709 (1995).

Jonathan E. Stern, *The Electronic Signatures in Global and National Commerce Act*, 16 Berkeley Tech. L.J. 391 (2001).

Jane K. Winn, *The Emperor's New Clothes: The Shocking Truth About Digital Signatures and Internet Commerce*, 37 Idaho L. Rev. 353 (2001).

Robert A. Wittie & Jane K. Winn, *Electronic Records and Signatures Under the Federal E–SIGN Legislation and the UETA*, 56 Bus. Law. 293 (2000).

Chapter 6

Jean Braucher, *Rent–Seeking and Risk–Fixing in the New Statutory Law of Electronic Commerce: Difficulties in Moving Consumer Protection Online*, 2001 Wisc. L. Rev. 527.

Joseph J. Cella III & John Reed Stark, *SEC Enforcement and the Internet: Meeting the Challenge of the Next Millennium,* 52 BUS. LAW. 815 (1997).

Gail Hillebrand & Margot Saunders, *E–Sign and UETA: What Should States Do Now?,* 5 NO. 10 CYBERSPACE LAW. 2, 5 NO. 11 CYBERSPACE LAW. 8 (Parts I & II) (2001).

Mark S. Nadel, *The Consumer Product Selection Process in an Internet Age: Obstacles to Maximum Effectiveness and Policy Options*, 14 HARV. J.L. & TECH. 187 (2000).

Esther C. Roditti, *Is Self–Help a Lawful Contractual Remedy?*, 21 RUTGERS COMPUTER & TECH. L.J. 431 (1995).

John Rothchild, *Making the Market Work: Enhancing Consumer Sovereignty Through the Telemarketing Sales Rule and the Distance Selling Directive*, 21 J. CONSUMER POL'Y 279 (1998).

James M. Snyder, *Online Auction Fraud: Are the Auction Houses Doing All They Should or Could to Stop Online Fraud?*, 52 FED. COMM. L. J. 453 (2000).

Jeff Sovern, *Protecting Privacy with Deceptive Trade Practices Legislation*, FORDHAM L. Rev. 1305 (2001).

Chapter 7

Ian C. Ballon, *Rethinking Cyberspace Jurisdiction in Intellectual Property Disputes*, 21 U. PA. J. INT'L ECON. L. 481 (2000).

Terrence Berg, www.wildwest.gov*: The Impact of the Internet on State Power to Enforce the Law*, 2000 B.Y.U.L. Rev. 1305.

Michael A. Geist, *Is There a There There? Toward Greater Certainty for Internet Jurisdiction*, 16 BERKELEY TECH. L.J. 1345 (2001).

Jane C. Ginsburg, *Extraterritoriality and Multiterritoriality in Copyright Infringement*, 37 VA. J. INT'L L. 587 (1997).

Martin Redish, *Of New Wine and Old Bottles: Personal Jurisdiction, the Internet, and the Nature of Constitutional Evolution*, 38 JURIMETRICS J. 575 (1998).

Katherine C. Sheehan, *Predicting the Future: Personal Jurisdiction for the Twenty–First Century*, 66 U. CIN. L. REV. 385 (1998).

Allan R. Stein, *The Unexceptional Problem of Jurisdiction in Cyberspace*, 32 INT'L LAW. 1167 (1998).

Howard B. Stravitz, *Personal Jurisdiction in Cyberspace: Something More is Required on the Electronic Stream of Commerce*, 49 S.C. L. REV. 925 (1998).

Michael Traynor, *Conflict of Laws, Comparative Law, and The American Law Institute*, 49 AM. J. COMP. L. 391 (2001).

Chapter 8

PHILLIP E. AGRE & MARC ROTENBERG, TECHNOLOGY & PRIVACY: THE NEW LANDSCAPE (1998).

ANITA L. ALLEN, UNEASY ACCESS: PRIVACY FOR WOMEN IN A FREE SOCIETY (1988).

Ann Bartow, *Our Data, Ourselves: Privacy, Propertization, and Gender*, 34 U.S.F. L. REV. 633 (2000).

Julie E. Cohen, *Examined Lives: Informational Privacy and the Subject as Object*, 52 STAN. L. REV. 1372 (2000).

Lorrie Faith Cranor, *The Role of Privacy Advocates and Data Protection Authorities in the Design and Deployment of the Platform for Privacy Preferences*, in PROCEEDINGS OF THE TWELFTH CONFERENCE ON COMPUTERS, FREEDOM AND PRIVACY (2002).

AMITAI ETZIONI, THE LIMITS OF PRIVACY (1999).

A. Michael Froomkin, *The Death of Privacy?*, 52 STAN. L. REV. 1471 (2000).

SIMSON GARFINKEL & DEBORAH RUSSELL, DATABASE NATION: THE DEATH OF PRIVACY IN THE 21ST CENTURY (2001).

Jerry Kang, *Information Privacy in Cyberspace Transactions*, 50 STAN. L. REV. 1193 (1998).

Lawrence Lessig, *The Architecture of Privacy*, 1 VAND. J. ENT. L. & PRAC. 56 (1999).

Jessica Litman, *Information Privacy/Information Property*, 52 STAN. L. REV. 1283 (2000).

Patricia Mell, *Seeking Shade in a Land of Perpetual Sunlight: Privacy as Property in the Electronic Wilderness*, 11 BERKELEY TECH. L. J. 1 (1996).

Richard S. Murphy, *Property Rights in Personal Information: An Economic Defense of Privacy*, 84 GEO. L.J. 2381 (1996).

Margaret Jane Radin, *Incomplete Commodification in the Computerized World*, in THE COMMODIFICATION OF INFORMATION (Neil Weinstock Netanel & Niva Elkin–Koren eds., 2002).

Joel R. Reidenberg, *E–Commerce and Trans–Atlantic Privacy*, 38 HOUS. L. REV. 717 (2001).

Joel R. Reidenberg, *Resolving Conflicting International Data Privacy Rules in Cyberspace*, 52 STAN. L. REV. 1315 (2000).

Joel R. Reidenberg & Françoise Gamet–Pol, *The Fundamental Role of Privacy and Confidence in the Network*, 30 WAKE FOREST L. REV. 105 (1995).

Marc Rotenberg, *Fair Information Practices and the Architecture of Privacy (What Larry Doesn't Get)*, 2001 STAN. TECH. L. REV. 1.

Pamela Samuelson, *Privacy as Intellectual Property*, 52 STAN. L. REV. 1125 (2000).

Paul Schwartz, *Privacy and Democracy in Cyberspace*, 52 VAND. L. REV. 1609 (1999).

Daniel J. Solove, *Privacy and Power: Computer Databases and Metaphors for Informational Privacy*, 53 STAN. L. REV. 1393 (2001).

PETER P. SWIRE & ROBERT E. LITAN, NONE OF YOUR BUSINESS: WORLD DATA FLOWS, ELECTRONIC COMMERCE, AND THE EUROPEAN PRIVACY DIRECTIVE (1998).

Eugene Volokh, *Freedom of Speech and Information Privacy: The Troubling Implications of a Right to Stop People from Speaking About You*, 52 STAN. L. REV. 1049 (2000).

ALAN F. WESTIN, PRIVACY AND FREEDOM (1967).

Chapter 9

THE DIGITAL DILEMMA: INTELLECTUAL PROPERTY IN THE INFORMATION AGE (National Research Council ed., 2000).

Stacey M. Byrnes, *Copyright Licenses, New Technology and Default Rules: Converging Media, Diverging Courts?*, 20 LOY. L.A. ENT. L. REV. 243 (2000).

Kenneth D. Crews, *The Law of Fair Use and the Illusion of Fair–Use Guidelines*, 62 OHIO ST. L.J. 599 (2001).

Stacey L. Dogan, *Infringement Once Removed: The Perils of Hyperlinking to Infringing Content*, 87 IOWA L. REV. 829 (2002).

Jane C. Ginsburg, *Can Copyright Become User–Friendly? Review of Jessica Litman, Digital Copyright*, 25 COLUM.-VLA J.L. & ARTS __ (forthcoming 2002).

Jane C. Ginsburg, *Copyright and Control Over New Technologies of Dissemination*, 101 COLUM. L. REV. 1613 (2001).

Jane C. Ginsburg, *Copyright Use and Excuse on the Internet*, 24 COLUM.-VLA J.L. & ARTS 1 (2000).

PAUL GOLDSTEIN, COPYRIGHT'S HIGHWAY: FROM GUTENBERG TO THE CELESTIAL JUKEBOX (1996).

Wendy J. Gordon, *Excuse and Justification in the Law of Fair Use: Distinguishing Empirical from Normative Market Failure*, in THE COMMODIFICATION OF INFORMATION (Neil Weinstock Netanel & Niva Elkin–Koren eds., 2002).

Wendy J. Gordon, *Fair Use as Market Failure: A Structural and Economic Analysis of the Betamax Case and its Predecessors*, 82 COLUM. L. REV. 1600 (1982).

Paul J. Heald & Suzanna Sherry, *Implied Limits on the Legislative Power: The Intellectual Property Clause as an Absolute Constraint on Congress*, 2000 U. ILL. L. REV. 1119.

Raymond S. R. Ku, *The Creative Destruction of Copyright: Napster and the New Economics of Digital Technology*, 69 U. CHI. L. REV. 263 (2002).

Marshall Leaffer, *The Uncertain Future of Fair Use in a Global Information Marketplace*, 62 OHIO ST. L.J. 849 (2001).

Mark A. Lemley, *Dealing with Overlapping Copyrights on the Internet*, 22 U. DAYTON L. REV. 547 (1997).

Mark A. Lemley & Eugene Volokh, *Freedom of Speech and Injunctions in Intellectual Property Cases*, 48 DUKE L.J. 147 (1998).

JESSICA LITMAN, DIGITAL COPYRIGHT (2001).

Jessica Litman, *The Exclusive Right to Read*, 13 CARDOZO ARTS & ENT. L.J. 29 (1994).

Joseph P. Liu, *Owning Digital Copies: Copyright Law and the Incidents of Copy Ownership*, 42 WM. & MARY L. REV. 1245 (2001).

Lydia Pallas Loren, *The Changing Nature of Derivative Works in the Face of New Technologies*, 4 J. SMALL & EMERGING BUS. L. 57 (2000).

Lydia Pallas Loren, *Digitization, Commodification, Criminalization: The Evolution of Criminal Copyright Infringement and the Importance of the Willfulness Requirement*, 77 WASH. U. L.Q. 835 (1999).

Douglas J. Masson, *Fixation on Fixation: Why Imposing Old Copyright Law on New Technology Will Not Work*, 71 IND. L.J. 1049 (1996).

Robert P. Merges & Glenn Harlan Reynolds, *The Proper Scope of the Copyright and Patent Power*, 37 HARV. J. ON LEGIS. 45 (2000).

Neil Weinstock Netanel, *Locating Copyright Within the First Amendment Skein*, 54 STAN. L. REV. 1 (2001).

David Nimmer, *Ignoring the Public, Part I: On the Absurd Complexity of the Digital Audio Transmission Right*, 7 UCLA ENT. L. REV. 189 (2000).

Ruth Okediji, *Givers, Takers, And Other Kinds Of Users: A Fair Use Doctrine For Cyberspace*, 53 FLA. L. REV. 107 (2001).

Ruth Okediji, *Toward an International Fair Use Doctrine*, 39 COLUM. J. TRANSNAT'L L. 75 (2000).

R. Anthony Reese, *Copyright and Internet Music Transmissions: Existing Law, Major Controversies, Possible Solutions*, 55 U. MIAMI L. REV. 237 (2001).

R. Anthony Reese, *The Public Display Right: The Copyright Act's Neglected Solution to the Controversy over RAM "Copies,"* 2001 U. ILL. L. REV. 83.

Lee Tien, *Publishing Software as a Speech Act*, 15 BERKELEY TECH. L. J. 629 (2000).

Alfred C. Yen, *A Preliminary Economic Analysis of Napster: Internet Technology, Copyright Liability, and the Possibility of Coasean Bargaining*, 26 U. DAYTON L. REV. 247 (2001).

Alfred C. Yen, *Internet Service Provider Liability for Subscriber Copyright Infringement, Enterprise Liability, and the First Amendment*, 88 GEO. L.J. 1833 (2000).

Chapter 10

Jonathan Band & Makoto Kono, *The Database Protection Debate in the 106th Congress*, 62 OHIO ST. L.J. 879 (2001).

Yochai Benkler, *Constitutional Bounds of Database Protection: The Role of Judicial Review in the Creation and Definition of Private Rights in Information*, 15 BERKELEY TECH. L.J. 535 (2000).

Jane C. Ginsburg, *Copyright, Common Law, and Sui Generis Protection of Databases in the United States and Abroad*, 66 U. CIN. L. REV. 151 (1997).

Paul Goldstein, *Copyright and Its Substitutes*, 1997 WIS. L. REV. 865.

Paul J. Heald, *The Extraction/Duplication Dichotomy: Constitutional Line–Drawing in the Database Debate*, 62 OHIO ST. L.J. 933 (2001).

Dennis S. Karjala, *Copyright and Misappropriation*, 17 U. DAYTON L. REV. 865 (1992).

Mark A. Lemley, *Beyond Preemption: The Law and Policy of Intellectual Property Licensing*, 87 CAL. L. REV. 111 (1999).

Maureen A. O'Rourke, *Shaping Competition on the Internet: Who Owns Product and Pricing Information?*, 53 VAND. L. REV. 1965 (2000).

Malla Pollack, *Delimiting Database Protection at the Juncture of the Commerce Clause, the Intellectual Property Clause, and the First Amendment*, 17 CARDOZO ARTS & ENT. L.J. 47 (1999).

J.H. Reichman & Pamela Samuelson, *Intellectual Property Rights in Data?*, 50 VAND. L. REV. 51 (1997).

Pamela Samuelson, *Digital Information, Digital Networks, and the Public Domain*, __ LAW & CONTEMP. PROBS.. __ (forthcoming 2002).

Pamela Samuelson & Suzanne Scotchmer, *The Law and Economics of Reverse Engineering*, 111 YALE L.J. 1575 (2002).

Jane K. Winn & James R. Wrathall, *Who Owns the Customer? The Emerging Law of Commercial Transactions in Electronic Customer Data*, 56 BUS. LAW. 213 (2000).

Chapter 11

Tom W. Bell, *Fair Use vs. Fared Use?: The Impact of Automated Rights Management on Copyright's Fair Use Doctrine*, 76 N.C. L. REV. 557 (1998).

Dan L. Burk & Julie E. Cohen, *Fair Use Infrastructure for Rights Management Systems*, 15 HARV. J.L. & TECH. 41 (2001).

Julie E. Cohen, *Lochner in Cyberspace: The New Economic Orthodoxy of "Rights Management,"* 97 MICH. L. REV. 462 (1998).

Mark Gimbel, *Some Thoughts on the Implications of Trusted Systems for Intellectual Property Law*, 50 STAN. L. REV. (1998).

Kamiel J. Koelman & Natali Helberger, *Protection of Technological Measures*, in COPYRIGHT AND ELECTRONIC COMMERCE: LEGAL ASPECTS OF ELECTRONIC COPYRIGHT MANAGEMENT (P. Bernt Hugenholtz ed., 2000).

Lawrence Lessig, *Reading the Constitution in Cyberspace*, 45 EMORY L.J. 869 (1996).

Lawrence Lessig, *The Limits in Open Code: Regulatory Standards and the Future of the Net*, 14 BERKELEY TECH. L.J. 759 (1999).

Glynn S. Lunney, Jr., *The Death of Copyright: Digital Technology, Private Copying, and the Digital Millennium Copyright Act*, 87 VA. L. REV. 813 (2001).

David Nimmer, *A Riff on Fair Use in the Digital Millennium Copyright Act*, 148 U. PA. L. REV. 673 (2000).

Pamela Samuelson, *Intellectual Property and the Digital Economy: Why the Anti–Circumvention Regulations Need to be Revised*, 14 BERKELEY TECH. L. J. 519 (1999).

Mark Stefik, *Shifting the Possible: How Trusted Systems and Digital Property Rights Challenge Us to Rethink Digital Publishing*, 12 BERKELEY TECH. L. J. 137 (1997).

Mark Stefik & Alex Silverman, *The Bit and the Pendulum: Balancing the Interests of Stakeholders in Digital Publishing*, 16 No. 1 COMPUTER LAW. 1 (1999).

Eugene Volokh, *Cheap Speech and What It Will Do*, 104 YALE L.J. 1805 (1995).

Chapter 12

John R. Allison & Mark A. Lemley, *Taking Stock: The Law and Economics of Intellectual Property Rights: Who's Patenting What? An Empirical Exploration of Patent Prosecution*, 53 VAND. L. REV. 2099 (2000).

James R. Barney, *The Prior User Defense: A Reprieve for Trade Secret Owners or a Disaster for the Patent Law?*, 82 J. PAT. & TRADEMARK OFF. SOC'Y 261 (2000).

Rochelle Cooper Dreyfuss, *Are Business Method Patents Bad for Business?*, 16 SANTA CLARA COMPUTER & HIGH TECH. L.J. 263 (2000).

Jared Earl Grusd, *Internet Business Methods: What Role Does and Should Patent Law Play?*, 4 VA. J.L. & TECH. 9 (1999).

Mark A. Lemley, *Rational Ignorance at the Patent Office*, 95 NW. U. L. REV. 1495 (2001).

Mark A. Lemley, *Reconceiving Patents in the Age of Venture Capital*, 4 J. SMALL & EMERGING BUS. L. 137 (2000).

LAWRENCE LESSIG, THE FUTURE OF IDEAS: THE FATE OF THE COMMONS IN A CONNECTED WORLD (2001).

Douglas Lichtman et al., *Taking Stock: The Law and Economics of Intellectual Property Rights: Strategic Disclosure in the Patent System*, 53 VAND. L. REV. 2175 (2000).

Robert Merges, *As Many as Six Impossible Patents Before Breakfast: Property Rights for Business Concepts and Patent System Reform*, 14 BERKELEY TECH. L.J. 577 (1999).

R. Carl Moy, *Subjecting Rembrandt to the Rule of Law: Rule–Based Solutions for Determining the Patentability of Business Methods*, 28 WM. MITCHELL L. REV. 1047 (2002).

Maureen A. O'Rourke, *Toward a Doctrine of Fair Use in Patent Law*, 100 COLUM. L. REV. 1177 (2000).

Eugene R. Quinn, Jr., *Abusing Intellectual Property Rights in Cyberspace: Patent Misuse Revisited*, 28 WM. MITCHELL L. REV. 955 (2002).

Margaret Jane Radin, *Online Standardization and the Integration of Text and Machine*, 70 FORDHAM L. REV. 1125 (2002).

Leo J. Raskind, *The State Street Bank Decision: The Bad Business of Unlimited Patent Protection for Methods of Doing Business*, 10 FORDHAM INTELL. PROP. MEDIA & ENT. L.J. 61 (1999).

Pamela Samuelson et al., *A Manifesto Concerning the Legal Protection of Computer Programs*, 94 COLUM. L. REV. 2308 (1994).

Carl Shapiro, *Navigating the Patent Thicket: Cross Licenses, Patent Pools, and Standard Setting*, in INNOVATION POLICY AND THE ECONOMY, VOL. I (Adam B. Jaffe, Josh Lerner, & Scott Stern eds., 2001).

John R. Thomas, *Collusion and Collective Action in the Patent System: A Proposal for Patent Bounties*, 2001 U. ILL. L. REV. 305.

John R. Thomas, *The Patenting of the Liberal Professions*, 40 B.C. L. REV. 1139 (1999).

Chapter 13

Dan L. Burk, *The Trouble with Trespass*, 4 J. SMALL & EMERGING BUS. L. 27 (2000).

Sabra–Anne Kelin, Note, *State Regulation of Unsolicited Commercial E–Mail*, 16 BERKELEY TECH. L.J. 435 (2001).

David E. Sorkin, *Technical and Legal Approaches to Unsolicited Electronic Mail*, 35 U.S.F. L. REV. 325 (2001).

Richard Warner, *Border Disputes: Trespass to Chattels on the Internet*, 47 VILL. L. REV. 117 (2002).

Chapter 14

Edward A. Cavazos, *Computer Bulletin Board Systems and the Right of Reply: Redefining Defamation Liability for a New Technology*, 12 REV. LITIG. 231 (1992).

Lucy H. Holmes, *Making Waves in Statutory Safe Harbors: Reevaluating Internet Service Providers' Liability for Third–Party Content and Copyright Infringement*, 7 ROGER WILLIAMS U. L. REV. 215 (2001).

Raymond S. R. Ku, *Irreconcilable Differences? Congressional Treatment of Internet Service Providers as Speakers*, 3 VAND. J. ENT. L. & PRAC. 70 (2001).

Margaret Jane Radin, *Distributed Denial of Service Attacks: Who Pays?*, 6 No. 9 CYBERSPACE LAW. 2 (Dec. 2001) (Part I) and 6 No. 10 CYBERSPACE LAW. 2 (Jan. 2002) (Part II).

Chapter 15

Alejandro E. Almaguer & Roland W. Baggott III, *Shaping New Legal Frontiers: Dispute Resolution for the Internet*, 13 OHIO ST. J. ON DISP. RESOL. 711 (1998).

ETHAN KATSH & JANET RIFKIN, ONLINE DISPUTE RESOLUTION: RESOLVING CONFLICTS IN CYBERSPACE (2001).

Ethan Katsh et al., *E–Commerce, E–Disputes, and E–Dispute Resolution: In the Shadow of "Ebay Law,"* 15 OHIO ST. J. ON DISP. RESOL. 705 (2000).

E. Casey Lide, *ADR and Cyberspace: The Role of Alternative Dispute Resolution in Online Commerce, Intellectual Property and Defamation*, 12 OHIO ST. J. ON DISP. RESOL. 193 (1996).

Lucille M. Ponte, *Throwing Bad Money After Bad: Can Online Dispute Resolution (ODR) Really Deliver the Goods for the Unhappy Internet Shopper?*, 3 TUL. J. TECH. & INTELL. PROP. 55 (2001).

Richard E. Speidel, *ICANN Domain Name Dispute Resolution, the Revised Uniform Arbitration Act, and the Limitations of Modern Arbitration Law*, 6 J. SMALL & EMERGING BUS. L. 167 (2002).

Elizabeth G. Thornburg, *Going Private: Technology, Due Process, and Internet Dispute Resolution*, 34 U.C. DAVIS L. REV. 151 (2000).

Stephen J. Ware, *Domain–Name Arbitration in the Arbitration–Law Context: Consent to, and Fairness in, the UDRP*, 6 J. SMALL & EMERGING BUS. L. 129 (2002).

Chapter 16

Thomas P. Brown et al., *Altered States: Electronic Commerce and Owning the Means of Value Exchange*, 1999 STAN. TECH. L. REV. 2.

Walter Effross, *Cyber–Banking Gains Currency—And Interest*, 49 S.C. L. REV. 943 (1998).

David D. Friedman & Kerry L. Macintosh, *The Cash of the Twenty–First Century*, 17 COMPUTER & HIGH TECH. L.J. 273 (2001).

John D. Muller, *Selected Developments in the Law of Cyberspace Payments*, 54 BUS. LAW. 403 (1998).

DONAL O'MAHONY ET AL., ELECTRONIC PAYMENT SYSTEMS FOR E–COMMERCE (2d ed. 2001).

David E. Sorkin, *Payment Methods for Consumer-to-Consumer Online Transactions*, 35 AKRON L. REV. 1 (2001).

THOMAS P. VARTANIAN ET AL., 21ST CENTURY MONEY, BANKING, AND COMMERCE (1998).

Catherine Lee Wilson, *Banking on the Net: Extending Bank Regulation to Electronic Money and Beyond*, 30 CREIGHTON L. REV. 671 (1997).

Jane K. Winn, *Clash of the Titans: Regulating the Competition Between Established and Emerging Electronic Payment Systems*, 14 BERKELEY TECH. L. J. 675 (1999).

Jane K. Winn, *XML And The Legal Foundations For Electronic Commerce: Making XML Pay: Revising Existing Electronic Payments Law To Accommodate Innovation*, 53 SMU L. REV. 1477 (2000).

Chapter 17

Arthur J. Cockfield, *Transforming the Internet into a Taxable Forum: A Case Study in E–Commerce Taxation*, 85 MINN. L. REV. 1171 (2001).

Walter Hellerstein, *U.S. State Taxation of Electronic Commerce: Preliminary Thoughts on Model Uniform Legislation*, 75 TAX NOTES 819 (1997).

PUBLIC POLICY AND THE INTERNET: PRIVACY, TAXES, AND CONTRACT (Nicholas Imparato ed., 2000).

Kim Marshall & Marc Lewis, *What We Know Today About "Substantial Nexus,"* 13 STATE TAX NOTES 967 (1997).

Michael J. McIntyre, *Taxing Electronic Commerce Fairly and Efficiently*, 52 TAX L. REV. 625 (1997).

Charles E. McLure Jr., *Taxation of Electronic Commerce: Economic Objectives, Technological Constraints, and Tax Law*, 52 TAX. L. REV. 269 (1997).

*

APPENDIX A

Computer Networking and the Internet

From an engineering perspective, the Internet is a global network of networks. To understand how computers communicate over the Internet, therefore, one must first understand the nature and operation of a computer network, and then understand how computer networks can be interconnected.

Digital computers operate on data represented in the form of binary digits, called "bits."[1] Each bit holds either of two values: zero or one. Computer-to-computer communication is at bottom the transmission of a "bitstream,"[2] a string of ones and zeros, from one computer to another. Information that is encoded into bits may be transmitted through several methods, including electrical signals traveling through wires, electromagnetic waves traveling through the air, and optical signals traveling through fiber-optic cables.

Computer networking. A computer network is a group of computers interconnected in a manner that permits computer users to exchange data and to share resources such as printers and scanners. The data transmitted on a network may represent word processing documents, graphics, e-mail messages, software, databases, audio files, video files, and any other materials that can be represented digitally.

A computer network that spans a relatively small space, such as the area within a single building or office, is called a *local area network*, or "LAN." The computers comprising a network are linked together using some medium capable of transmitting data, such as coaxial cables, optical fiber, twisted-pair copper wire, or radio waves.

Computer-to-computer communication. Messages are transmitted from one networked computer to another using a method analogous to that used in transmitting mail via the postal system. A letter sent from one person to another through the mail involves three kinds of information: the address of the sender, the address of the intended recipient, and the message sent. Communication via postal mail employs a particular format that enables us

1. Many of the technical terms used in this Appendix, such as "bit," are defined in the Glossary.

2. A string of eight bits is called a "byte." Quantities of data stored on a computer or transmitted through a network are usually measured in bytes, thousands of bytes (kilobytes or kB), millions of bytes (megabytes or mB), or billions of bytes (gigabytes or gB).

to identify the different items of information involved. The message is placed in a container called an envelope. The address of the intended recipient is written on the front of the envelope in the center, and the sender's return address is written in the upper left-hand corner.

Communication from one computer to another likewise involves three kinds of information: the address of the computer sending the message, the address of the computer to which the message is being sent, and the message itself. Each computer on a local area network is assigned a unique numerical value called its *hardware address*. Like an extremely long letter, which is too big to fit into a single envelope, the message to be sent is broken into chunks of a size determined by the communications protocol that the network uses. Each chunk of message is combined with the hardware addresses of the sending computer and the receiving computer, in a structure defined by the protocol, forming a series of *frames* or *packets*. Devices on the network read the address on each packet and route it accordingly. The recipient computer opens up the packet, extracts the data representing a chunk of the message, and throws away the rest of the packet. The various message chunks are then reassembled into the message that was transmitted.

Connecting networks. Use of different network protocols by different networks poses a difficulty for computer-to-computer communication across networks. If two networks running different network protocols were simply wired together, the computers on one network would not be able to interpret the messages from computers on the other. Communication is possible only if the messages composed using the protocols of the transmitting network are translated into messages that can be properly interpreted using the protocols of the receiving network. This translation is the job of a special-purpose computer called a *gateway*, which sits between two networks. A gateway takes the packets that it receives from one network, converts them to the frame format of the other network, and then retransmits them on that network.

Computer-to-computer communication over the Internet. The Internet is simply a large number of interconnected networks. Therefore, the same problem of translation had to be solved before the Internet could function to put all computers on any of its networks in communication with each other. The solution adopted consists of having networks of computers connect to the Internet through gateways, which translate messages from the protocol used on the network into TCP/IP, the suite of communications protocols that defines the Internet. (If the network uses TCP/IP internally, no translation is required.) Like messages within a network, messages are sent from one computer to another across the Internet in the form of *packets*. The structure of a packet that is transmitted on the Internet is determined by the Internet Protocol—the "IP" of "TCP/IP." Each packet consists of (1) a *header*, which includes the addresses of the sending and destination computers, and a sequencing number indicating in which order the packet is to be reassembled with the other packets composing the message; (2) the *payload*, consisting of the data to be transmitted; and (3) a *trailer*, which contains information that is used to check whether there were any errors in transmission. Instead of hardware addresses, the sending and receiving computers are identified by *Internet Protocol addresses*, which are described below.

Once a packet is placed on the Internet, it must be routed from the sending computer to the destination computer. This is accomplished by specialized computers called *routers*. Routers are positioned wherever the networks that make up the Internet intersect. A network that transports a packet destined for a computer belonging to another network hands it off to a router that connects it with other networks. The router reads the packet's header to ascertain the packet's ultimate destination. Then, using a complex set of algorithms, the router determines the best route for the packet to take on the way to its destination, and directs it along that path. The process is repeated as the packet moves from one router to another across the Internet, in a series of hops, until it reaches its destination.

IP addresses. The addresses used to identify computers on the Internet are called *Internet Protocol addresses,* often abbreviated as *IP addresses*. IP addresses are 32 bits long. For example, the IP address of the server holding the website belonging to the White House is

11000110100010011111000001011100.

Computers are designed to handle long strings of ones and zeros, but 32–bit addresses are unwieldy for humans. To make these addresses easier for humans to work with, they are usually written as four octets. In this format, the IP address of the White House web server is written

11000110 10001001 11110000 01011100.

To make it easier still, each octet may be interpreted as a number in base two, and converted to a decimal number. An eight-digit binary number can represent decimal numbers ranging from zero (00000000) to 255 (11111111). Thus, IP addresses may be represented as four decimal numbers in the range 0–255. These four numbers are usually separated by periods, in what is called "dotted decimal" notation. Continuing with our example of the White House web server,

198.137.240.92

is the dotted decimal representation of its 32–bit IP address.

A computer's IP address must specify the network to which the computer is connected as well as the connection between the particular computer and the network. Thus, the White House web server's IP address must not only state that this is, say, connection number 5 on its network, but must also identify the network itself, namely the White House computer network. The part of the IP address that designates the network is called the *prefix* or *network ID*. The part of the IP address that designates the connection itself is called the *suffix* or *host ID*. In our example, the prefix identifying the White House computer network is

198.137.240

while the suffix identifying the connection of the web server to this network is

.92.

IP addresses are not very different from street addresses, which are composed of a house number (for example, 123) and a street name (for example, Main Street). In a street address, we can easily distinguish the house number prefix from the street name suffix because the prefix is a number while the suffix is a series of words. In an IP address, however, both the prefix and the suffix are numbers. How then do we distinguish between them? IP addresses used on the Internet belong to three classes of networks, designated A, B and C. The class of network to which an IP address belongs is determined by the decimal value of its first octet. IP addresses beginning with a number in the range from 0 to 126 belong to Class A networks. Those beginning with a number in the range from 128 to 191 belong to Class B networks. Those beginning with a number in the range from 192 to 223 belong to Class C networks.

In an IP address belonging to a Class A network, the first octet is the prefix, identifying the network, while the remaining three octets form the suffix, identifying the connection of a particular computer on that network. In a Class B address, the prefix is the first two octets and the suffix the other two. Finally, in a Class C address, the prefix is the first three octets and the suffix the remaining one.

Applying these conventions to the IP address of the White House web server, we see that

198.137.240.92

begins with a number between 192 and 223, and thus belongs to a Class C network. Therefore, its prefix consists of the first three octets,

198.137.240

and its suffix is

.92.

The prefix indicates that the network is one assigned to the White House, and the suffix refers to a particular computer on that network, namely a web server.

Whether a network receives a Class A, B or C prefix depends upon the anticipated size of the network. Since the prefix of a Class A address uses only the first octet of the IP address, the other three octets are available to designate each connection to that network. Because these three octets comprise 24 digits, Class A addresses can uniquely designate up to 2^{24} or 16,777,216 separate connections—a very large network indeed. Class B addresses can uniquely designate 2^{16} or 65,536 connections, while Class C addresses can designate only 2^8 or 256 (for technical reasons, actually 254) connections. Thus, judging from the Class C IP address of the White House web server, we can infer that there are no more than 254 network devices connected to the White House network (the White House might, however, have other computers falling under a different IP prefix).

IP address administration. IP addresses are usually assigned in blocks to networks when they connect to the Internet. To ensure that each network receives a block of IP addresses of the appropriate class, assignments of IP addresses are managed by *Regional Internet Registries* ("RIRs"). There are currently three RIRs. The *American Registry for Internet Numbers* oversees the assignment of IP addresses for North America, South America, the Caribbean, and sub-Saharan Africa; the *Asia Pacific Network Information Centre* oversees IP address assignments for Asia and the Pacific; and the *Réseaux IP Européens Network Coordination Centre* oversees IP assignments for Europe, the Middle East, and North Africa. The RIRs assign large blocks of IP addresses to Local Internet Registries and Internet service providers, which assign smaller blocks to end users.

EXERCISES

1. Obtain the IP address of your law school web server's connection to the Internet. Using a personal computer running a Microsoft Windows operating system (Windows 98 or later), connect to the Internet and start MS–DOS Prompt, which can be found under the Start menu in the Programs folder. At the command line prompt (to the right of "C:\WINDOWS>") type the word ping and then the URL of your law school web server. Hit enter and the IP address of your law school web server should be returned.

2. Based on the IP address you obtained above, what is the largest number of connections to the Internet that your law school network can accommodate? To what class of network does the IP address of your law school web server belong? Obtain the IP address of your university web server. Is the IP address of the university web server in the same class as the IP address of your law school web server? Do the IP addresses for the main university web server and the law school web server have any numbers in common? What is the significance of this fact?

3. Connect to the Internet and open up your web browser. In the text box on the address bar of the web browser, type the IP address that you obtained for your law school web server and hit enter. What happens?

APPENDIX B

THE DOMAIN NAME SYSTEM

The DNS name server hierarchy. The domain name system is the infrastructure that allows the name of a computer connected to the Internet, called a "host name," to be associated with the computer's Internet Protocol ("IP") address.[1] This process of association makes the Internet much easier to use. The software that does the work of locating a computer that is connected to the Internet and routing information from one computer to another is designed to use the numerical addresses of those computers—their IP addresses. But most humans find it difficult to remember and work with strings of numbers like 129.42.17.99, finding it much easier to deal with strings of text like www.ibm.com. Each computer connected to the Internet therefore has two equivalent designations: an IP address, designed for use by machines, and a host name, designed for use by humans. Thus, the two addresses 129.42.17.99 and www.ibm.com each designate the same machine: the computer holding the files that make up the website of IBM Corp.[2]

Domain names are strictly a convenience for us humans. If you type "129.42.17.99" into your browser, your computer will quite cheerfully display IBM's home page, without knowing or caring to know that the computer designated by that IP address is also known as www.ibm.com. Conversely, if you type a host name like www.ibm.com into your browser, hoping to view IBM's website, your computer can do nothing to help you until it determines the IP address of that web server.

In theory, all that is needed to allow translation of host names into IP numbers (and vice versa) is a list, in electronic form, that is accessible via the Internet; one line of that list would read "www.ibm.com = 129.42.17.99." But use of such a list would have several practical disadvantages. For one thing, it would be extremely long, as there are many millions of host machines connected to the Internet, which would make it time consuming to locate the needed entry. For another, the machine on which it was located, and that machine's connection to the Internet, would have

1. Many of the technical terms used in this Appendix, such as "IP address," are defined in the Glossary.

2. There need not be a one-to-one correspondence between host names and IP addresses, however. There might be a number of different host names, under the same or different top-level domains, all designating a single host computer. For example, *www.barnesandnoble.com*, *www.bn.com*, and *www.barnesandnoble.net* each refer to the same web server, which has the IP address 208.237.178.21; typing any of those URLs into a browser will retrieve the same web page, from the same machine.

to handle an enormous number of accesses, since a query would be sent each time anyone tries to access a computer via the Internet.

The domain name system ("DNS") is in essence an implementation of such a list in a manner that solves these and other practical problems. It allows your computer to determine, nearly instantaneously, that when you type "www.ibm.com" into your browser what you really mean is "129.42.17.99."

The DNS is a hierarchical, distributed system, consisting of a large number of databases maintained on many different computers. At the top of the hierarchy is a set of thirteen computer servers, called the root servers or root name servers. Each of these computers is a name server—that is, a computer connected to the Internet that holds a document listing host names and their corresponding IP addresses. These root servers are named after the letters of the alphabet, from A through M. Each of them holds the same document, called the root zone file: a list of the authoritative name servers for each of the top-level domains ("TLDs") that are sanctioned by the Internet Corporation for Assigned Names and Numbers.[3]

The root zone file looks something like this:

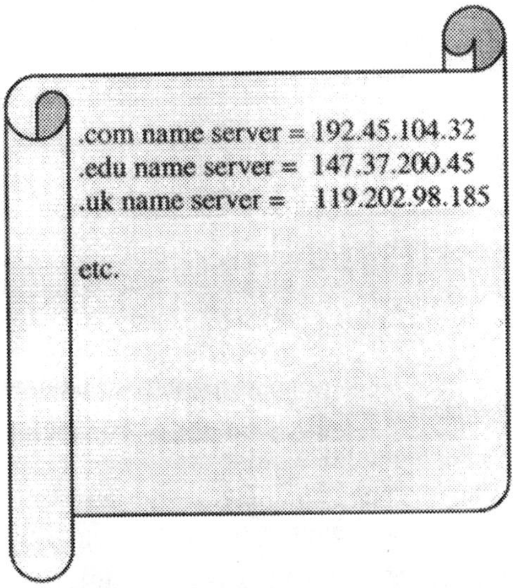

***Figure 1:* Contents of root zone file.**

It lists roughly 255 TLDs (most of which are country-code top-level domains) and the IP addresses of their corresponding authoritative name servers.

3. The "A" root server is first among equals. When the root zone file must be modified, the modifications are made to the copy of the file on the "A" root server. Servers "B" through "M" then each update their own copies of the root zone file from the "A" server's version. Ten of the root servers are located in the United States, one is in London, one in Tokyo, and one in Stockholm. The "A" root server is located in Herndon, Virginia, and is operated by Verisign, Inc., under contract with the United States government.

When you type the address of a website into your browser, the software's "resolver" component sends a query to the name server assigned to your computer,[4] requesting the IP number associated with that address. The query, in effect, looks like this:

> ''What is the IP number associated with the computer designated www.ibm.com?''

If the database on that name server holds the information you seek, it transmits that information to the resolver, and your browser uses it to access the website.[5] The response would look something like this:

> ''The computer designated www.ibm.com has the IP address 129.42.17.99.''

If the name server does not have the information needed to answer your query, it will initiate its own query, directed to one of the root servers. The query will seek the IP address of the authoritative name server for the .com TLD, and will look like this:

> ''What is the IP address of the authoritative name server for the .com top-level domain?''

The root server responds with the relevant information from the root zone file that it holds. It will look up the entry for ".com," and find the corresponding IP address. Then it will respond to your local name server:

> ''The IP address of the authoritative name server for the .com top-level domain is 192.45.104.32.''

The .com authoritative server holds its own zone file, which lists the IP addresses of the name servers associated with each of the second-level domains within the .com TLD. Each of those domains has at least two name servers associated with it. These name servers hold more detailed information about the servers associated with the domain name, as will be discussed below. When IBM Corp. registered the domain name ibm.com, it had to specify which machines it would use as its name servers. The name servers associated with a domain name can be identified through a "whois" search. As of mid–2002, the name servers assigned to IBM.com were:

INTERNET—SERVER.ZURICH.IBM.COM

NS.WATSON.IBM.COM

NS.ERS.IBM.COM

NS.ALMADEN.IBM.COM

NS.AUSTIN.IBM.COM.

4. The name server may be maintained by your ISP, if you have a dial-up connection. If you access the Internet through a local area network ("LAN"), the entity operating the LAN (which may be a university, a corporation, or some other institution) may maintain its own name server.

5. That might happen if, for example, you or somebody else had recently queried the name server for the same address: name servers keep the answers to recent queries in a cache, to speed up information retrieval.

This indicates that IBM maintains its own name servers. Smaller operations, however, may rely on name servers maintained by a registrar or a hosting service. For example, the name servers associated with ecommerce-casebook.com,

DNS2.NAMESECURE.COM

DNS1.NAMESECURE.COM,

are maintained by the registrar of the domain name, which is Name-secure.com.

Now that your local name server has learned the IP address of the authoritative name server for the .com TLD, it will address a query to that name server, asking:

''What are the IP addresses of the name servers for the domain designated ibm.com?''

The .com name server will consult its zone file, which looks something like this:

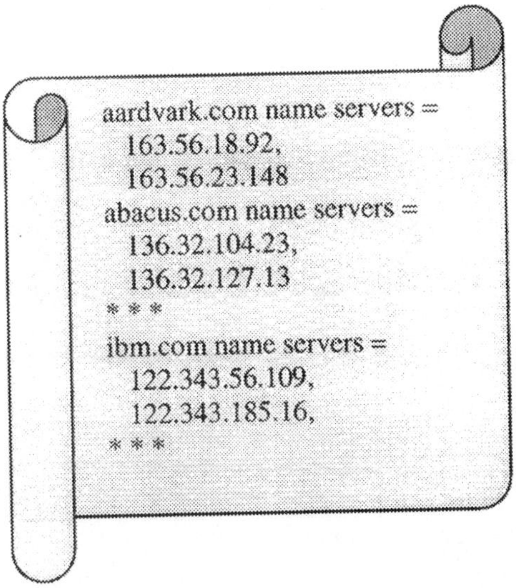

***Figure 2:* Contents of zone file for .com domains.**

Then the .com name server will report back to your local name server:

''The IP addresses of the name servers for ibm.com are 122.343.56.109, 122.343.185.16, etc.''

Each of these name servers has information about each of the host computers associated with ibm.com. One of those is the web server, which is designated www.ibm.com.[6] Since IBM is a large company with a very extensive website, there are in fact a number of other web servers associated with ibm.com, such as www–1.ibm.com, commerce.www.ibm.com, www.storage.ibm.com, etc. Each of these computers is assigned its own IP address. The name servers for ibm.com have a list of the host computers at ibm.com and their associated IP addresses. The list looks like this:

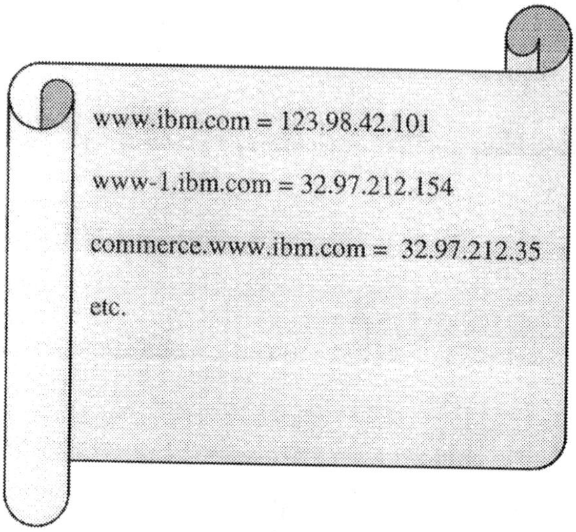

***Figure 3:* List on ibm.com's name server.**

Your name server then queries one of the name servers for ibm.com, asking:

> ''What is the IP address of the computer designated www.ibm.com?''

The ibm.com name server responds:

> ''The IP address of the computer designated www.ibm.com is 123.98.42.101.''

6. The use of "www" to designate a host machine that functions as a web server is very common, but purely conventional. Any other designation would do equally well. For example, the web server that holds the files constituting the United States Congress's website of legislative materials is designated thomas.loc.gov: the domain name is "loc.gov," and the host name is "thomas." Web servers may also be designated through a hierarchical naming scheme. Thus, www.law.upenn.edu designates a web server named "www.law" that is within the "upenn.edu" domain. A machine with this sort of designation is sometimes referred to as a "sub-host."

Your name server communicates this information to your browser's resolver component. Finally, your browser has the information it needs to contact www.ibm.com. It sends a query to IP address 123.98.42.101, to the effect:

```
''Send the home page of the website maintained at this
address.''
```

IBM's web server responds by transmitting the HTML file constituting that web page to your browser. Your browser fetches graphics files referenced in the web page, if any, then formats the page and displays it on your computer monitor as indicated by the HTML tags.[7]

The following diagram illustrates the hierarchy of name servers that allows the DNS to operate:

7. This example shows how the process of name resolution plays out without shortcuts. In practice, the name server will probably not need to query the root server to obtain the address of the authoritative name server for the .com top-level domain. Since it receives so many queries relating to .com addresses, it will likely already have that information in its cache. It may even already have in its cache the IP addresses of the name servers for ibm.com and other frequently accessed domains, so it might proceed directly to querying IBM's name server.

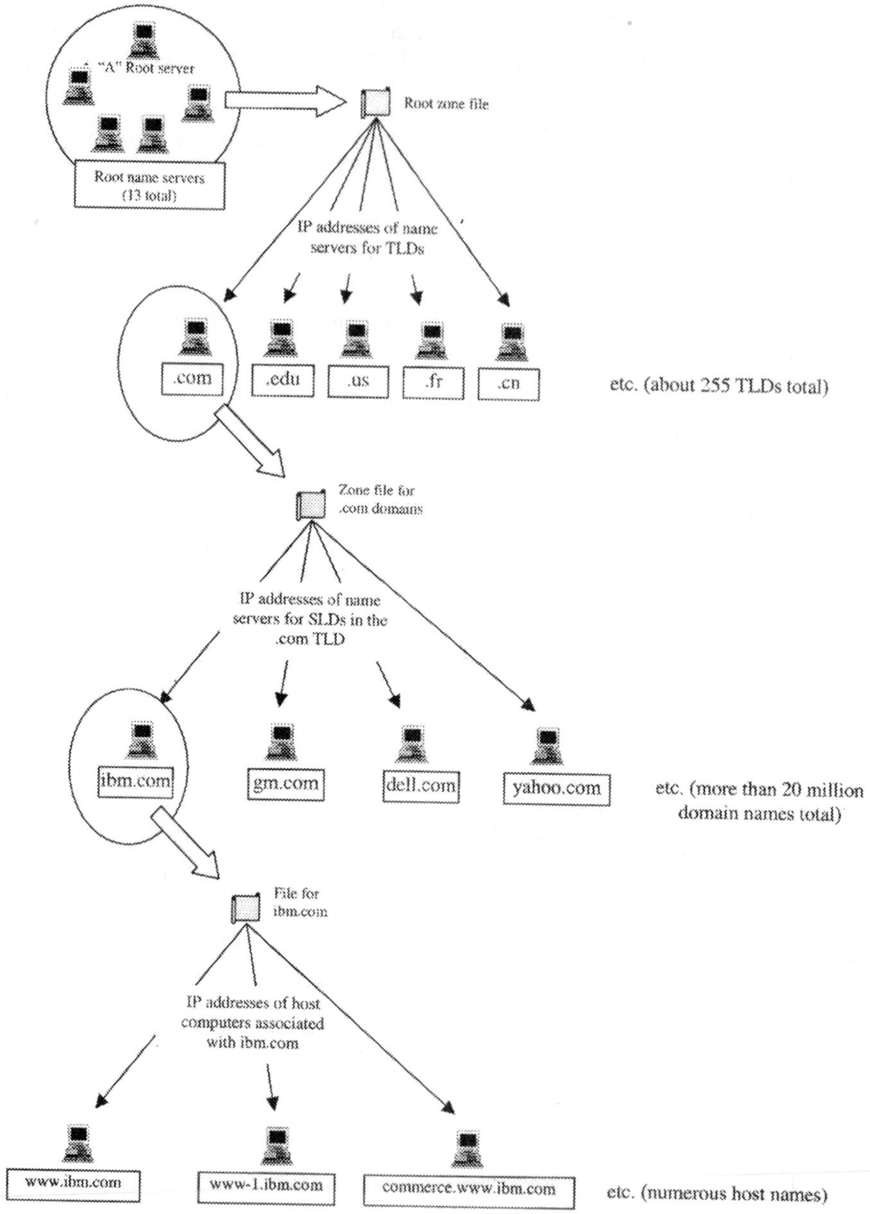

Figure 4: **Hierarchy of DNS name servers.**

The domain name hierarchy. The domain names and host names that humans use to reference resources on the Internet are created and maintained through another hierarchical infrastructure that roughly parallels the DNS hierarchy.

At the top of this hierarchy is what is referred to as the "root." The root is conceptual, and may be interpreted as the dot preceding the TLD in a domain name.

The next level of the hierarchy consists of the TLDs. As noted above, there are roughly 255 of these. Most of these, about 244 of them, are the country-code top-level domains, such as:

.ac = Ascension Island
.ca = Canada
.cn = China
.fr = France
.ls = Lesotho
.us = United States
.zw = Zimbabwe

The rest of them are the generic top-level domains ("gTLDs"), which include the original gTLDs:

.com	commercial
.net	network
.org	organization
.edu	educational
.gov	U.S. government
.mil	U.S. military
.int	international organizations,

as well as those that the Internet Corporation for Assigned Names and Numbers ("ICANN") added in 2000:

.biz	business
.aero	air-transport industry
.coop	cooperatives
.pro	professional
.museum	museums
.info	information
.name	individual names.

At the next level of the hierarchy are the second-level domains ("SLDs"). A SLD is created when a person registers that domain within a particular TLD. For example, IBM Corp. registered the SLD ibm within the .com TLD, thereby creating the domain name ibm.com. Although a name can be registered as a SLD within a particular TLD only once—nobody else can register ibm within the .com TLD—that same name can be registered independently in each other TLD. Thus, IBM Corp. also registered ibm.net, and ibm.org appears to have been registered by an individual unrelated to IBM Corp.

The next level of the hierarchy includes the host names—the designations of computers connected to the Internet—that are associated with a particular domain name. As noted above, IBM has a number of host computers functioning as web servers that are associated with ibm.com, including www.ibm.com, www–1.ibm.com, commerce.www.ibm.com, and www.storage.ibm.com. IBM has other hosts that function as mail servers. Each host is capable of holding documents that may be accessed and transmitted via the Internet. Thus, web servers hold the web pages that constitute a website, and mail servers hold e-mail messages.

The lowest level of the hierarchy consists of the electronic documents that are maintained on a particular host, and are made available via the Internet. The URL of such a document includes the host name of the computer on which it is found, a path name indicating where in that computer's filing structure the document is located, and the name of the document itself. For example, the document constituting a web page on IBM's website might have a URL like

www.ibm.com/privacy/policy.html.

This URL refers to a document named "policy.html," which is on the computer designated "www" that is associated with the ibm.com domain. The document is in a directory called "privacy."

The documents accessed via a web server may consist of:

- Web pages, which are written in text with HTML tags, and typically have a name ending with .htm or .html. Web browsers (like Netscape and Internet Explorer) are able to interpret these documents and display them on the user's computer monitor.
- Word processing documents, in the format of whatever word processing program (such as Corel WordPerfect or Microsoft Word) created them, and ending with a designation like .wpd or .doc. These documents can be displayed using the associated word processor or some compatible program.
- Documents in Adobe's Portable Document Format, ending with .pdf, which can be viewed using Adobe Acrobat.
- Graphics files, ending with .gif or .jpeg, which can be displayed using a viewer program.
- Audio files, ending with .mp3, or video files, ending with .mpeg or .mov, which can be played using compatible programs.

The following diagram illustrates the domain name hierarchy:

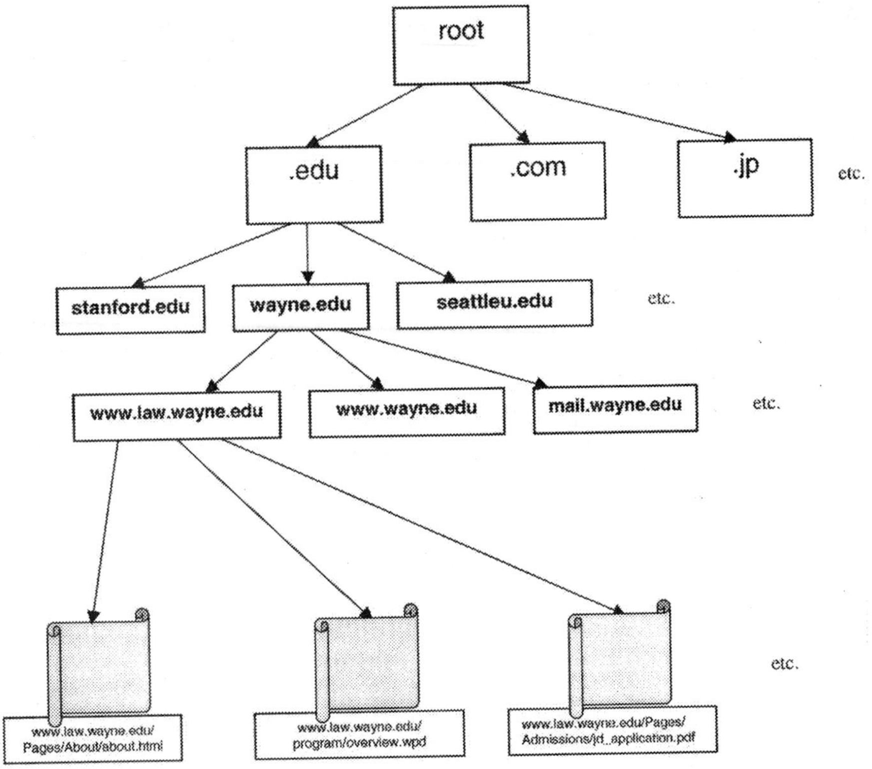

Figure 5: **Hierarchy of domain names.**

This diagram illustrates several levels of the hierarchy descending from the root, including:

- .edu and other TLDs;
- wayne.edu and other SLDs within the .edu TLD;
- several host machines on the wayne.edu domain, including the web server for Wayne State Law School, which is designated www.law.wayne.edu; and
- several documents maintained on the Wayne State Law School web server, one in HTML format, one in WordPerfect (.wpd) format, and one in Adobe PDF (.pdf) format.

Registration of domain names. To register a domain name in one of the commercial TLDs (.aero, .biz, .com, .info, .name, .net, and .org), one must apply for the name through a domain name registrar. There are several dozen of these registrars, which are accredited by ICANN, and operate under rules that ICANN establishes.[8] Registration takes place entirely

8. A current list of accredited registrars is available at ICANN's website, www.icann.org/registrars/accredited-list.html.

online, through automated systems: no human is involved at the registrar's end. The process begins with the registrant indicating the domain name that she wishes to register, such as cars.biz. The registrar checks the registry for the relevant TLD, in this case .biz, to see whether the domain name has already been registered by somebody else. If cars.biz is already registered, the registrant must select a different name. If cars.biz is available, the registrar collects certain information from the registrant, including the registrant's name, address, and telephone number, and the identity of the name servers for the domain. The registrant must pay a fee for the registration, which is set by each registrar, and typically runs about $35 a year.

Once a domain name is registered, the registrant has the right to use it in the address of resources she makes available on the Internet. For example, she could set up a website, using the URL www.cars.biz; or she could set up a mail server, on a machine with the host name mail.cars.biz, that would allow e-mail to be sent to and from addresses of the form name@cars.biz.

APPENDIX C

Michael Rappa, Business Models on the Web

digitalenterprise.org/models/models.html

(2002).

* * *

In the most basic sense, a business model is the method of doing business by which a company can sustain itself—that is, generate revenue. The business model spells-out how a company makes money by specifying where it is positioned in the value chain.

Some models are quite simple. A company produces a good or service and sells it to customers. If all goes well, the revenues from sales exceed the cost of operation and the company realizes a profit. Other models can be more intricately woven. Broadcasting is a good example. Radio, and later television, programming has been broadcast over the airwaves free to anyone with a receiver for much of the past century. The broadcaster is part of a complex network of distributors, content creators, advertisers (and their agencies), and listeners or viewers. Who makes money and how much is not always clear at the outset. The bottom line depends on many competing factors.

Internet commerce will give rise to new kinds of business models. That much is certain. But the web is also likely to reinvent tried-and-true models. Auctions are a perfect example. One of the oldest forms of brokering, auctions have been widely used throughout the world to set prices for such items as agricultural commodities, financial instruments, and unique items like fine art and antiquities. The Web has popularized the auction model and broadened its applicability to a wide array of goods and services.

Business models have been defined and categorized in many different ways. This is one attempt to present a comprehensive and cogent taxonomy of business models observable on the web. The proposed taxonomy is not meant to be exhaustive or definitive. Internet business models continue to evolve. New and interesting variations can be expected in the future.

* * *

The models are implemented in a variety of ways, as described below with examples. Moreover, a firm may combine several different models as part of its overall Internet business strategy. For example, it is not uncommon for content driven businesses to blend advertising with a subscription model.

* * *

Type of Model:	Description:
Brokerage Model	Brokers are market-makers: they bring buyers and sellers together and facilitate transactions. Brokers play a frequent role in business-to-business (B2B), business-to-consumer (B2C), or consumer-to-consumer (C2C) markets. Usually a broker charges a fee or commission for each transaction it enables. The formula for fees can vary. Brokerage models include:
	Marketplace Exchange—full range of services covering the transaction process, from market assessment to negotiation and fulfillment, for a particular industry. The exchange can operate independently of the industry, or it can be backed by an industry consortium. The broker typically charges the seller a transaction fee based on the value of the sale. There also may be membership fees. [Orbitz, ChemConnect]
	Business Trading Community—or vertical web community, is a comprehensive source of information and interaction for a particular vertical market. A community may contain product information, daily industry news and articles, job listings and classifieds. [VerticalNet]
	Buy/Sell Fulfillment—customer specifies buy or sell orders for a product or service, including price, delivery, etc. The broker charges the buyer and/or seller a transaction fee. [CarsDirect, Respond.com]
	Demand Collection System—the patented "name-your-price" model pioneered by Priceline. Prospective buyer makes a final (binding) bid for a specified good or service, and the broker arranges fulfillment. [Priceline.com]
	Auction Broker—conducts auctions for sellers (individuals or merchants). Broker charges the seller a listing fee and commission scaled with the value of the transaction. Auctions vary in terms of the offering and bidding rules. Reverse auctions are a common variant. [eBay]
	Transaction Broker—provides a third-party payment mechanism for buyers and sellers to settle a transaction. [PayPal, Escrow.com]
	Bounty Broker—offers a reward for finding a person, thing, idea, or other desired, but hard to

Type of Model:	Description:
Brokerage Model	find item. The broker may list items for a flat fee and a percent of the reward for items that are found. [BountyQuest]
	Distributor—is a catalog operation that connects a large number of product manufacturers with volume and retail buyers. Broker facilitates business transactions between franchised distributors and their trading partners. [Questlink, ConvergeTrade]
	Search Agent—is an agent (i.e., a software agent or "robot") used to search-out the price and availability for a good or service specified by the buyer, or to locate hard to find information. [MySimon, DealTime]
	Virtual Mall—hosts online merchants. The Mall typically charges setup, monthly listing, and/or per transaction fees. More sophisticated malls provide automated transaction services and relationship marketing opportunities. [ChoiceMall]
Advertising Model	The web advertising model is an extension of the traditional media broadcast model. The broadcaster, in this case, a web site, provides content (usually, but not necessarily, for free) and services (like e-mail, chat, forums) mixed with advertising messages in the form of banner ads. The banner ads may be the major or sole source of revenue for the broadcaster. The broadcaster may be a content creator or a distributor of content created elsewhere. The advertising model only works when the volume of viewer traffic is large or highly specialized.
	Portal—is a point of entry to the web, usually a search engine that includes diversified content or services. The high volume makes advertising profitable and permits further diversification of site services [Yahoo!]
	Personalized Portal—allows customization of the interface and content. This increases loyalty as a result of the user's own time invested in personalizing the site. [MyYahoo!]
	Niche Portal—cultivates a well-defined user demographic. For example, a site that attracts home buyers, young women, or new parents, can be highly sought after as a venue for certain advertisers who are willing to pay a premium to reach that particular audience. [iVillage.com]
	Classifieds—list items for sale or wanted for purchase. Listing fees are common, but there also may be a membership fee. [Monster.com, Match.com]

Type of Model:	Description:
Advertising Model	**Registered Users**—content-based sites that are free to access but require users to register (other information may or may not be collected). Registration allows inter-session tracking of users' site usage patterns and thereby generates data of greater potential value in targeted advertising campaigns. [NYTimes Digital]
	Query-based Paid Placement—sell favorable link positioning (i.e., sponsored links) or advertising keyed to particular search terms in a user query, such as Overture's trademark "pay-for-performance" model. [Google, Overture]
	Contextual Advertising—freeware developers who bundle ads with their product. For example, a browser extension that automates authentication and form fill-ins, also delivers advertising links or pop-ups as the user surfs the web. Contextual advertisers can sell targeted advertising based on an individual user's surfing behavior. [Gator, eZula]
Infomediary Model	Data about consumers and their consumption habits are valuable, especially when that information is carefully analyzed and used to target marketing campaigns. Independently collected data about producers and their products are useful to consumers when considering a purchase. Some firms function as infomediaries (information intermediaries) assisting buyers and/or sellers understand a given market.
	Advertising Networks—service that feeds banner ads to a network of sites, thereby enabling advertisers to deploy large marketing campaigns. By using cookies, the Ad Network operator collects data on web users that can be used to analyze marketing effectiveness. [DoubleClick]
	Audience Measurement Services—online audience market research agencies [Nielsen//Netratings]
	Incentive Marketing—the customer loyalty program model. Provides incentives to customers such as redeemable points or coupons for making purchases from associated retailers. Data collected about users is sold for the purpose of targeted advertising. [Coolsavings, MyPoints, Greenpoints]
	Metamediary—facilitates transactions between buyer and sellers by providing comprehensive information and ancillary services, but does not get involved in the actual exchange of goods or services between the parties. [Edmunds]

Type of Model:	Description:
Merchant Model	Wholesalers and retailers of goods and services. Sales may be made based on list prices or through auction. In some cases, the goods and services may be unique to the web and not have a traditional "brick-and-mortar" storefront.
	Virtual Merchant—or "e-tailer", a merchant that operates over the web. [Amazon.com]
	Catalog Merchant—mail-order business with a web-based catalog. Combines mail, telephone and web ordering. [Lands' End]
	Click and Mortar—traditional brick-and-mortar retail establishment with web storefront. [Barnes & Noble]
	Bit Vendor—a merchant that deals strictly in digital products and services and, in its purest form, conducts both sales and distribution over the web. [Eyewire]
Manufacturer Model	A model predicated on the power of the web to allow a manufacturer (i.e., a company that creates a product or service) to reach buyers directly and thereby compress the distribution channel. The manufacturer model can be based on efficiency, improved customer service, or a better understanding of customer preferences. [Apple Computer]
	Brand Integrated Content—Traditionally, manufacturers rely on advertising to build customer awareness. Commercials via broadcasters like radio, television and mass market publishers (newspapers and magazines), or through product placement in TV and motion pictures, has been a mainstay of modern business. The Web enables a manufacturer to integrate their brand more intimately with the content. The innovator in this respect is the luxury automobile maker, BMW. The company's bmwfilms is a creative blend of advertising with entertainment that paves the way for a new approach that might be called "advertainment"—taking the idea of product placement advertising to the extreme.
Affiliate Model	In contrast to the generalized portal, which seeks to drive a high volume of traffic to one site, the affiliate model, provides purchase opportunities wherever people may be surfing. It does this by offering financial incentives (in the form of a percentage of revenue) to affiliated partner sites. The affiliates provide purchase-point click-through to the merchant. It is a pay-for-performance model—if an affiliate does not generate sales, it represents no cost to the merchant. The affiliate model is inherently well-suited to the

Type of Model:	Description:
Affiliate Model	web, which explains its popularity. Variations include, banner exchange, pay-per-click, and revenue sharing programs. [Barnes & Noble, Amazon.com]
Community Model	The viability of the community model is based on user loyalty. Users have a high investment in both time and emotion in the site. In some cases, users are regular contributors of content and/or money. Having users who visit continually offers advertising, infomediary or specialized portal opportunities. The community model may also run on a subscription fee for premium services.
	Voluntary Contributor Model—similar to the traditional public broadcasting model—the listener or viewer contributor method used in not-for-profit radio and television broadcasting. The model is predicated on the creation of a community of users who support the site through voluntary donations. Not-for-profit organizations may also seek funding from charitable foundations and corporate sponsors that support the organization's mission. The web holds great potential as a contributor based model because the user base is more readily apparent. [The Classical Station (WCPE.org)]
	Knowledge Networks—or expert sites, that provide a source of information based on professional expertise or the experience of other users. Sites are typically run like a forum where persons seeking information can pose questions and receive answers from (presumably) someone knowledgeable about the subject. The experts may be employed staff, a regular cadre of volunteers, or in some cases, simply anyone on the web who wishes to respond. [AllExperts]
Subscription Model	Users are charged a periodic—daily, monthly or annual—fee to subscribe to a service. It is not uncommon for sites to combine free content with "premium" (i.e., subscriber-or member-only) content. Subscription fees are incurred irrespective of actual usage rates. Subscription and advertising models are frequently combined.
	Content Services—beyond newspapers and magazines, the Web has encouraged the use of the subscriber model for music and video, as well. [Listen.com, Netflix]
	Person-to-Person Networking Services—are conduits for the distribution of user-submitted information, such as individuals searching for former school mates. [Classmates]

Type of Model:	Description:
Subscription Model	**Trust Services**—an independent third party that engenders trust between unfamiliar parties entering into a transaction. The need of trust increases with the value and complexity of the product or service that is sold. Trust services typically come in the form of membership associations that abide by an explicit code of conduct, and in which members pay a subscription fee. [Truste]
	Internet Services Providers—offer Internet connectivity and related services on a monthly subscription. [AOL]
Utility Model	The utility model is based on metering usage, or a "pay as you go" approach. Unlike subscriber services, metered services are based on actual usage rates. Traditionally, metering has been used for essential services (e.g., electricity water, long-distance telephone services). Internet service providers (ISPs) in some parts of the world operate as utilities, charging customers for connection minutes, as opposed to the subscriber model common in the U.S.

* * *

IMPORTANT NOTE:

First published on the Web in 1999, this is a "work-in-progress" that is updated frequently to reflect the evolving subject matter.

The purpose of this work is purely educational.

Examples of business models are provided for illustration only. No judgment is made about the profitability or business viability of a particular model.

* * *

 Michael Rappa is the Alan T. Dickson Distinguished University Professor of Technology Management at North Carolina State University in Raleigh, North Carolina. The latest version of this work is located at "Managing the Digital Enterprise," an open courseware site accessible on the Web at http://digital-enterprise.org.

*

GLOSSARY

ACH (from **Automated Clearing House**) **Network**: An electronic fund transfer system that provides for the interbank clearing of payments among participating depository financial institutions. Both consumers and businesses may initiate electronic credit and debit transfers using this network. The "originator" of an ACH transfer issues instructions that cause funds to be moved electronically from one account to another. For example, an employer may be the originator of an ACH transaction that transfers an employee's salary from the employer's account to the employee's account. A consumer may authorize a vendor to initiate a transaction transferring money from the consumer's account to the vendor's account, in payment for a purchase made in Internet commerce.

Application (also known as **application software**): Software that performs some function other than running the computer system itself. Application software includes database programs, word processors, e-mail readers, web browsers, spreadsheets, and other types of programs. Application software needs "systems software"—the operating system and system utilities—to run on a computer.

Architecture: The design of a computer system or a network. If a system design has an "open architecture," the system can easily be connected to hardware and software regardless of its manufacturer. Such a system typically uses off-the-shelf components, and conforms to publicly available technical standards. A system with a "closed architecture" is based on proprietary specifications, making it more difficult to connect it to other hardware or software.

ARPAnet (from **Advanced Research Projects Agency Network**): A packet-switched, computer communications network that began operating in 1969, connecting university and research sites, funded by the U.S. Department of Defense Advanced Research Projects Agency (the central research organization of the U.S. Department of Defense). By 1983 ARPAnet was composed of over 300 computers, and it adopted TCP/IP as its communications protocol. Starting in the mid–1980s, the networks participating in ARPAnet gradually switched over to become part of NSFnet, which became the Internet. ARPAnet shut down in 1989.

ASCII (from **American Standard Code for Information Exchange**): A coding system used by digital computers for representing characters and certain control functions as a string of seven bits. The seven bits yield 128 possible combinations, allowing ASCII to represent the letters of the Latin alphabet set, the numerals from 0–9, and common punctuation marks. ASCII is used to create text documents—that is, documents consisting of only the basic characters and formatting, without any graphics, special formatting, different fonts, etc.

Backbone: The part of a communications network consisting of the transmission paths running at the highest speeds, and carrying a major portion of the network's data traffic. Backbone paths usually span long geographical distances. Regional networks are attached to the backbone.

Bandwidth: The rate at which data may be transmitted across a network. The bandwidth of digital devices is usually expressed as "bits per second." A dial-up connection to the Internet typically has a maximum bandwidth of 56,000 bits per second, which is often abbreviated as "56 kb/sec" or "56K." A digital subscriber line ("DSL") connection to the Internet may have a downstream bandwidth (that is, the rate at which data may be downloaded from the Internet) of several million bits per second (mb/sec), but home DSL connections more typically run at 300–750 kb/sec. A cable modem might run at 1 mb/sec. The highest-speed backbone lines currently in use, called OC–192 lines, have a maximum bandwidth of about 10,000 mb/sec.

BBS: *See* **Bulletin board system**.

Bit (from "**b**inary dig**it**"): The smallest unit of information that is processed by a digital computer. A bit can take either of two states, which are typically interpreted as one and zero. A string of bits may be interpreted as a number in binary (base two) notation. To convert a number in base two to a number in decimal (base ten) notation, we take the digit (either one or zero) at each place of the number, and multiply it by two raised to a power determined by the place of that digit in the number. Thus, a single "1" bit is interpreted as 2^0, or 1 in decimal notation. The series of bits "10" is interpreted as

$$(1 \times 2^1) + (0 \times 2^0),$$

or 2 in decimal notation. Likewise,

$$100 = (1 \times 2^2) + (0 \times 2^1) + (0 \times 2^0) = 4$$

$$101 = (1 \times 2^2) + (0 \times 2^1) + (1 \times 2^0) = 5$$

$$111 = (1 \times 2^2) + (1 \times 2^1) + (1 \times 2^0) = 7$$

$$1000 = (1 \times 2^3) + (0 \times 2^2) + (0 \times 2^1) + (0 \times 2^0) = 8$$

etc.

A string of eight bits is called a "byte." Each byte may be interpreted as a decimal number in the range 0 to 255. A byte of information can represent a character in the ASCII coding system, which is used to construct text documents.

Bot: From "robot," referring to a computer program that autonomously searches for and retrieves information from materials residing on computers connected to the Internet. The term is used for many different types of software agents and macros. Bots are used, for example, to index information on the Web so that search engines can search it, and to perform comparison shopping functions by searching out information on multiple websites.

Brick-and-mortar retailer: A retailer that operates, in the traditional manner, from a physical storefront which consumers may enter to view and purchase goods. Used to distinguish such retailers from those that make sales at a distance, such as via the Internet, catalogs, or telemarketing.

Bulletin board system (abbreviated as **BBS**): A computer-based forum on which users may post messages and electronic files. Before the Internet was widely available, BBS access was typically obtained by dialing a telephone number specific to each BBS. Proprietary online services also hosted, and continue to host, BBSs dedicated to a wide variety of subject matters. Many websites include a BBS, and web portals may include hundreds of BBSs each dedicated to a particular subject matter.

Byte: *See* **bit.**

CA: *See* **Certification authority.**

Cache: *See* **Web cache.**

ccTLD: *See* **Country code top-level domain.**

Certification Authority (abbreviated as **CA**): An entity that issues a digital certificate attesting to some fact about the holder of the certificate. In the context of digitally signing electronic messages using public key cryptography, the role of the CA is to certify that a public key really belongs to the person who proffers it. The certificate will contain, at a minimum, the name of a person and his public key. The CA digitally signs the certificate using its own private key. A user of the certificate, upon decrypting it using the CA's public key, can be confident that the person named in the certificate is the true owner of the public key set forth in the certificate. Thus, if a person receives an electronic message that is digitally signed and that can be decrypted using the public key contained in the certificate, she can be reasonably sure that the message was actually sent by the person named in the certificate.

Chat: A text-based discussion among two or more people that is conducted via a network. Chats are hosted by websites on the Internet, by proprietary online service providers like America Online, and through the Internet Relay Chat ("IRC") system. IRC servers located around the world host hundreds of IRC channels on different topics. A user's input to an IRC channel is immediately disseminated to everyone connected to that channel.

Clickstream: The data trail that an Internet user leaves behind as he performs such operations as entering data into search engines and visiting web pages. Clickstream data may be collected by an ISP, a website operator, or an interloper. For example, a website operator may be able to collect information identifying every page that the user accessed on the site, and any search terms that the user entered while searching for information on the site. Clickstream data may be collected anonymously, or, through the use of cookies, web bugs, GUIDs, and other techniques, may be associated with the user or his computer.

CMS (from **copyright management system**): *See* **Digital rights management system.**

Conditions of Use: *See* **Terms of Service.**

Cookie: A unique identifier, contained in a text file that a computer hosting a website causes to be written to the hard drive of a computer that accesses it. Each time that computer requests pages from the website thereafter, the identifier is sent back to the website, and serves to identify the computer. The identifier stored in a cookie may be used to associate all of the clickstream data collected from that computer into a single dossier. The website can use the information in the dossier to target customized information or advertisements to the user, based on inferences about the user's preferences as revealed by the clickstream data.

Copyleft: A license, accompanying a work entitled to copyright protection, that allows anyone to use, copy, distribute, and modify the work as long as the modified version is made freely available under the same license. Copyleft has been most widely used in connection with software. The most prominent version of copyleft is the General Public License that accompanies software developed in the GNU Project. *See* www.gnu.org. The open-source operating system Linux is likewise distributed under the GNU General Public License. GNU is sponsored by the Free Software Foundation, a Boston-based non-profit entity founded in 1985 by Richard Stallman.

Copyright management system (abbreviated as **CMS**): *See* **Digital rights management system.**

Country code top-level domain (abbreviated as **ccTLD**): A two-letter suffix, making up the right-most element of a domain name, designating the country controlling the assignment of second-level domains ending with that suffix. For example, the URL http://www.parl.gc.ca points to a website (belonging to the Parliament of Canada) within the ".ca" ccTLD. The government of Canada controls assignment of second-level domains, such as ".gc," within the .ca ccTLD. The two-letter abbreviations are derived from a list of country codes maintained by the International Organization for Standardization. *See* www.iso.org.

Cybersquatting: A derogatory term used to describe the practice of registering an Internet domain name for purposes that are deemed inappropriate. The term applies most particularly to registration of a domain name incorporating a word that corresponds to a trademark belonging to somebody else. The Anticybersquatting Consumer Protection Act, a U.S. federal law enacted in 1999, gives trademark owners a cause of action against cybersquatters. Sometimes also referred to as "cyberpiracy."

Database: A collection of information organized in some useful manner, and stored in electronic form on a computer. Information stored in a database may be sorted, searched, or selected according to particular criteria using a software application called a database program.

Digital certificate: A digital document, encrypted using public key cryptography, that attests to the ownership of a particular public key, by associating that key with a particular person.

Digital rights management system (abbreviated as **DRMS**): A technological device, usually implemented through computer code, that controls access to or use of an accompanying information product. Also referred to as "copyright management system" or "trusted system." A DRMS may create an audit trail for payment of royalties, or may provide a set of rules technologically enforcing limitations on use of the information, such as by preventing redistribution or copying.

Digital signature: A procedure that uses public key cryptography and related technologies to establish that an electronic document was sent by the person it purports to be from, and has not been tampered with during transmission across the network.

Directive: *See* **European Union Directive.**

DNS: *See* **Domain name system.**

DNS hijacking: An unauthorized change to a name server's database that has the effect of directing a user's computer to the wrong website when the user types in a URL.

Domain name: A string of characters forming the core of the addressing scheme that allows resources to be made available on the Internet. A domain name consists of a second-level domain together with the top-level domain in which it is registered. For example, nytimes.com is a domain name consisting of the second-level domain "nytimes," which is registered within the top-level domain ".com." The owner of nytimes.com, which happens to be The New York Times Company, may make information available on the Internet by placing it on a computer server that is accessed via the domain name. Thus, the New York Times maintains a website at www.nytimes.com, which designates the computer server holding the files that constitute its website. A domain name also forms the portion of an e-mail address to the right of the "@" symbol. Thus, employees of the New York Times are assigned e-mail addresses of the form [employee-name]@nytimes.com.

As of mid–2002, there were about 30.5 million registered domain names (21 million of them in the .com top-level domain). After several years of rapid growth in domain name registrations, the number of registered domain names is currently declining, as domain name expirations exceed new registrations. Domain names may be registered with any of several dozen registrars. For more information on domain names, see **Appendix B**.

Domain name registrar: *See* **Registrar.**

Domain name server: A computer holding a database that associates resources on the Internet with IP addresses. Domain name servers, also called name servers, are an integral part of the DNS, allowing a resource on the Internet (such as a website) to be located via the host name of the computer on which it resides. Name servers respond to queries from web browsers and from other name servers. When a user types the address of a website into her browser, her computer sends a query to a name server, asking for the IP address of that website. The name server may respond with the requested IP address, if that address is in the server's cache. If not, the name server may respond with the address of another name server, or it may send a query to that other name server. Ultimately a name server that has the needed information is reached, and it returns the IP address to the user's computer, whose browser uses that address to access the website. For more information on name servers, see **Appendix B**.

Domain Name Supporting Organization (abbreviated as **DNSO**): One of the three sub-organizations within ICANN that develop policy relating to management of the Internet. *See* www.dnso.icann.org.

Domain name system (abbreviated as **DNS**): The infrastructure that associates host names and URLs with IP addresses, and allows a computer running a web browser to locate and access resources on the Internet. The DNS includes domain name registrars, which assign domain names to registrants and maintain registries listing the domain names that have been assigned; name servers, which hold databases associating Internet resources with IP addresses; and root servers, which contain the authoritative lists of name servers for each top-level domain. When you type a URL into your web browser, your computer accesses the DNS to ascertain the IP address corresponding to that URL, which enables your computer to send a request to the server holding the desired web page, resulting in delivery of the HTML file constituting that page to your computer for display on your monitor. Primary responsibility for managing the DNS resides with the Internet Corporation for Assigned Names and Numbers. For more information on the DNS, see **Appendix B.**

DRMS: *See* **Digital rights management system.**

European Union Directive: A set of legal rules on a particular subject, established through a lawmaking process at the European Union community level, and promulgated by the European Commission, that EU member states are required by treaty to implement through enactment of national laws. *See generally* europa.eu.int.

File Transfer Protocol (abbreviated as **FTP**): A protocol used to transfer files over the Internet. FTP is used to upload and download files to and from an FTP server.

Fully qualified domain name (abbreviated as **FQDN**): The complete name of a specific computer on the Internet, consisting of the host name followed by a domain name. For example, www.cisco.com is the fully qualified domain name corresponding to a web server that Cisco Systems, Inc. maintains at the domain name cisco.com. A server that holds a website typically is assigned the host name "www," but any other name would do. For example, the website containing legislative materials of the United States Congress is on a computer with the FQDN thomas.loc.gov. A FQDN contains the information required to obtain the computer's IP address by querying a name server.

General Public License: *See* **Copyleft.**

Generic top-level domain (abbreviated as **gTLD**): A multiple-letter suffix, making up the rightmost element of a domain name, signifying the highest level domain to which the address belongs. Some gTLDs accept domain name registrations only from a restricted class of registrants, while others are unrestricted. Until November 2000, the generic top-level domains, and their intended uses, were:

.com	commercial
.net	network
.org	organization
.edu	educational
.gov	U.S. government
.mil	U.S. military
.int	international organizations.

In November 2000, the Internet Corporation for Assigned Names and Numbers added seven new top-level domains:

.biz	business
.aero	air-transport industry
.coop	cooperatives
.pro	professional
.museum	museums
.info	information
.name	individual names.

See also **Country-code top-level domain**.

GIF (from **Graphics Interchange Format**): A file format for images that is widely used on the Web.

gTLD: *See* **Generic top-level domain.**

GUID (from **globally unique identifier**): A unique identifier that is assigned to a computer or some other resource on the Internet. A GUID may be implemented in software, such as through a cookie that is written to a computer's hard drive. It may also be implemented in hardware, such as by manufacturing it into a computer's central processing unit. A GUID associated with a computer may be read by another computer, across the network. The GUID may be written into a document, serving to identify the computer that produced the document.

Hit: Each access, by a computer running a web browser, of a page (or a page component, such as a graphic image) on a website. The number of hits a website receives in a particular period of time is a measure of its popularity. The hit count is especially important to e-commerce websites, since the number of visitors a website receives is a major determinant of the amount that an advertiser pays to advertise on the site.

Home page: The web page that is presented when a user enters the basic form of a website's URL into her browser. Typically, the home page of a site is reached by entering a URL consisting of the domain name preceded by "www."

Hosting service or **hosting provider:** *See* **Internet service provider.**

Host: A computer that has access to other computers via the Internet. In particular, a host refers to a computer that is assigned an IP address (and a corresponding fully qualified domain name) and that holds the files constituting a website. Most host computers that hold websites are by convention named "www," as in www.gm.com, but need not be, e.g. europa.eu.int.

HTML (from **Hypertext Markup Language**): The computer language used to create pages on the World Wide Web. Each web page contains codes embedded in the text, called "HTML tags," that establish how the document will be displayed on the recipient's computer monitor. HTML tags are composed of alphanumeric characters that can be typed with any text editor or word processor. The HTML tags define the format, layout, size of graphics, fonts, and other features of the displayed page. The codes also define and create the hypertext links that point to other web pages. Many word processors can automatically export their documents in HTML format. The HTML code constituting a web page may be viewed in popular browsers by clicking a command labeled something like "View Page Source."

HTTP (from **Hypertext Transport Protocol**): The protocol that is used in transmitting information residing on the World Wide Web across the Internet.

Hyperlink: A string of text or a graphic in an electronic document that, when clicked with a mouse, results in the accessing of some other electronic document via HTTP. Most commonly, a hyperlink is contained within a web page, and when clicked causes a different web page to be displayed on the computer monitor. Hyperlinks may also be incorporated into word-processing documents, e-mail messages, spreadsheets, and other types of documents. Instead of a web page, a hyperlink may point to some other type of electronic document, such as a word-processing document, a graphic, or an audio or video file. Rather than retrieving a separate document, clicking on a hyperlink might result in jumping to another place in the document one is viewing. A textual hyperlink is, by convention, often identified by displaying it in blue, underlined text. Also called a "link."

ICANN: *See* **Internet Corporation for Assigned Names and Numbers.**

Identity theft: One person's use of another person's identifying information to obtain goods and services fraudulently. An identity thief who learns the victim's name, date of birth, and Social Security number might open a credit card account in the victim's name, go on a spending spree, and then leave the bills unpaid. Since the card is in the victim's name, the card issuer will believe that the charges were incurred by the victim, and will seek to hold the victim accountable. Although in theory the victim should not suffer due to the actions of the identity thief, in practice it can take months or years, and enormous efforts, before the victim clears her name and regains her credit standing. The Federal Trade Commission maintains a website about identity theft at www.consumer.gov/idtheft.

Internet: The global network of computer networks that communicate using the TCP/IP protocol. The Internet consists of physical connections among computers in more than 100 countries and a set of protocols that allows those computers to communicate with one another. The Internet is the successor to the NSFnet, which itself built on a networking concept pioneered by the ARPAnet. In 1995, the National Science Foundation transferred responsibility for the communications backbones of the Internet to several large commercial Internet service providers. Regional service providers link to these backbones, and smaller ISPs link to the regional providers. The Internet is the infrastructure over which several popular network services are run, including the World Wide Web and electronic mail. For more information on computer networking and the Internet, see **Appendix A.**

Internet Assigned Numbers Authority (abbreviated as **IANA**): An entity chartered by the Internet Society that formerly managed Internet addresses, domain names, and protocol parameters. In these functions it has been replaced by the Internet Corporation for Assigned Names and Numbers, which performs what is referred to as "the IANA function." *See* www.iana.org.

Internet Corporation for Assigned Names and Numbers (abbreviated as **ICANN**): A non-profit California corporation, formed in 1998, that performs a variety of Internet management functions under contract with the United States government. ICANN establishes the official set of top-level domains, and allocates blocks of IP network addresses. It manages the domain name system and root server system. ICANN also accredits and maintains a list of registrars that process domain name registrations. ICANN is run by a Board consisting of a President/CEO, nine At–Large Directors and nine Directors selected by ICANN's three supporting organizations. The supporting organizations are the Address Supporting Organization, for IP addresses; the Domain Name Supporting Organization, for the domain name system; and the Protocol Supporting Organization, for Internet protocols. Five of the current At–Large Directors were selected by a vote of Internet users worldwide. ICANN is funded primarily by fees from the registries and registrars at the core of the domain name system. *See* www.icann.org.

Internet service provider (abbreviated as **ISP**): An entity that provides its customers with access to the Internet. The term is sometimes also used in reference to an entity that provides space on its servers to maintain a customer's website and make it accessible to the Internet (also known as a "hosting service," "hosting provider," or "online service provider"), and to online services like America Online that offer both access to the Internet and additional proprietary services like databases, forums, and access to online merchants.

Internet Society (abbreviated as **ISOC**): An international membership organization founded in 1992, located in Reston, Virginia, dedicated to promoting the development of the Internet. With more than 150 organizational members and 6,000 individual members in 100 countries, ISOC supports Internet bodies such as the Internet Engineering Task Force, www.ietf.org, and the Internet Architecture Board, www.iab.org. ISOC works with governments, organizations and the general public to promote

Internet research, information, education, and standards. It also helps developing nations design their Internet infrastructure. *See* www.isoc.org.

InterNIC (from **Internet Network Information Center**): The domain name registration project that was formed in 1993 by agreements between Network Solutions, Inc., the National Science Foundation, General Atomics, and AT & T. InterNIC formerly made the rules pertaining to domain names, administered the registration process, and maintained the official database of registered domain names. At present, "InterNIC" is a registered service mark of the United States Department of Commerce, and refers to a set of functions performed by the Internet Corporation for Assigned Names and Numbers. *See* www.internic.org.

IP (Internet Protocol) address: The unique address of a computer or other device attached to the Internet. An IP address is usually represented as four decimal numbers in the range 0–255, separated by periods. For example, the IP address associated with the computer hosting the website of Dell Computer Corp., which is named www.dell.com, is 143.166.83.63. For more information on IP addresses, see **Appendix A.**

Link: ***See* Hyperlink.**

Listserv: ***See* Mailing list.**

Lock-in: A situation in which a product or technology with a head start or large market share may hold an insurmountable advantage over its rivals, even though the rivals may produce a better product. Users of the product or technology experience a strong incentive to stick with it, despite the existence of superior alternatives, due to the costs of acquiring or learning how to use an alternative, or the disadvantages resulting from the fact that few others use the alternative. Examples of lock-in are the QWERTY typewriter keyboard, the disincentive to change ISPs once you have an assigned e-mail address, and the triumph of the VHS format for VCRs over the Betamax format.

Mail Abuse Prevention System (abbreviated as **MAPS**): A non-profit entity that maintains, and makes available to subscribers, a list of the IP addresses of websites and hosting services that it believes promote the sending of unsolicited commercial e-mail. Internet service providers and other Internet users can use the list, called the Realtime Blackhole List, to filter or reject incoming e-mail. *See* mail-abuse.org.

Mailing list: A list of e-mail addresses that receive e-mail messages automatically distributed by mailing-list software. To send a message to the members of a mailing list, a subscriber of the list sends a single message to a designated address, and the software automatically broadcasts it to all members of the list. Each mailing list is dedicated to a particular subject matter, and is managed by a list owner, who may also (but need not) act as a moderator. Open lists allow anyone to subscribe. Subscription to a closed list requires approval of the list owner. For example, "cyberia-l" is a mailing list dedicated to legal issues relating to the Internet. It is an open list, to which anyone can subscribe by sending an e-mail message reading "subscribe cyberia-l" to the address listserv@listserv.aol.com. To have an e-mail message automatically distributed to all members of the cyberia-l list, a subscriber addresses the message to cyberia-l@listserv.aol.com. The most popular brands of mailing-list software are Listserv and Majordomo; a mailing list is therefore sometimes referred to generically as a "listserv" or "listserve."

Metatag: An HTML tag, used in the code that constitutes a web page, that describes the contents of the page. The text of a metatag is not displayed on the website visitor's computer monitor, but can be read by another computer across the network. For example, a search engine may read a web page's metatags in determining whether that page is relevant to a search query that it is processing. Metatags have been used in ways that some consider improper, such as when a website places a competitor's trademarks in its metatags, so that a user searching for the competitor's website will be referred to the metatagged site instead. Other websites have placed popular search terms (such as "sex") in their metatags, so that a user searching for one type of site will be referred to another type of site entirely. As a result of these practices, some search engines ignore metatags when evaluating a website.

MP3: A file format that is widely used for storing recorded music in digital form. Music from a CD may be converted to MP3 format, allowing it to be transmitted across the Internet, downloaded from a website, stored on a computer's hard drive, and played on a computer or a portable MP3 player. The term refers to Audio Layer 3 of the MPEG–1 audiovisual standard created by the Motion Picture Experts Group in the early 1980s. MP3 files are compressed to about one-twelfth of their original size, reducing the bandwidth needed for file transfer. This compression results in a loss of sound fidelity that is insignificant for most users.

Name server: *See* **Domain name server.**

Netiquette (from **network etiquette**): Appropriate behavior when using the Internet or another online service. Netiquette, like etiquette, is a set of informal customs, not a legal regime.

Network effects: The increase in value of a product that results when more people use it. Not all products are subject to network effects, but products that engender network effects are common in the online environment. E-mail, the Internet, telephones, and the Windows computer operating system are all examples of products characterized by network effects. Thus, an e-mail system is of no value if only one person has access to it; when a second person is added, it starts to have value; and the value of an e-mail system is increased for all existing participants each time an additional person joins the system. Network effects can cause a product to dominate a market, through lock-in, even if it is not superior to its competition. *See* **lock-in**.

Newsgroup: An online message board or discussion group devoted to a particular topic. One person posts a comment or question, another person replies, others respond to the replies, and the resulting discussion is organized in a chain of postings called a "message thread." The term usually refers to newsgroups that are part of the USENET. USENET newsgroups are organized by topic and subtopic. Thus, the newsgroup alt.art might be devoted to discussions about art generally, while the newsgroups alt.art.renaissance and alt.art.modernist would host discussions on more specific art-related topics. (The "alt" refers to "alternatives" to USENET's original categories of topics.) *See* **USENET.**

NSFnet (from **National Science Foundation Network**): A high-speed computer network funded by the National Science Foundation, created in the mid–1980s, initially linking five supercomputer research sites, and later including university networks. NSFnet adopted TCP/IP as its communication protocol. As other networks were connected, this collection of connected computers became the Internet. *See* **ARPAnet.**

OECD: *See* **Organisation for Economic Co-operation and Development.**

Online service provider: *See* **Internet service provider.**

Opt in vs. opt out: Two different approaches to obtaining the consent of a person to some proposed course of action affecting him. In the online context, these approaches come into play when an online entity, such as a website operator, a vendor, or an ISP, offers some option to an online user. Under an opt-in approach, if the user takes no action in response, she is deemed to consent to the proposed course of action. Under opt out, silence is interpreted as the absence of consent. For example, an online vendor might tell its customers that it will share their personal information with unaffiliated third parties only with the customer's consent. Under an opt-in approach, a customer is deemed to assent to such information disclosure *only if* she takes some action, such as checking a box on a website form, indicating that she assents. Under opt out, the customer is deemed to assent *unless* she takes some action indicating that she does *not* assent.

Organisation for Economic Co-operation and Development (abbreviated as **OECD**): An international organization composed of thirty member countries, the majority of which are among the world's most industrialized and trade-oriented countries. The OECD addresses economic and social issues including trade, education, technology, taxation, development, health, and education, through conducting studies, collecting statistics, producing reports, and issuing recommendations. *See* www.oecd.org.

Packet switching: A technology for transmitting messages across a network from one computer to another. The message is divided into chunks of a predetermined size, and each chunk is assembled into a packet that includes the addresses of the sending and destination computers. Each packet is then routed independently across the network. Once they reach their destination the message chunks are reassembled in their original order, reconstituting the message as sent. The delivery of messages sent across the Internet is controlled by the Transmission Control Protocol, and the internal structure and reassembly of packets is controlled by the

Internet Protocol; these two protocols in tandem, referred to as TCP/IP, allow communication to occur across the Internet. Packet switching is distinguished from circuit switching, the system used for transmitting telephone calls across the telecommunications network, which dedicates a particular path to the signals comprising a telephone conversation for the duration of the call. For more information on packets, see **Appendix A**.

PICS (from **Platform for Internet Content Selection**): A set of specifications for attaching machine-readable labels to the content of websites. A browser that is PICS-enabled can read and interpret the labels, and then take some action specified by the user based on the labels' content, such as displaying a warning or denying access. The labels may be created through self-rating by a website operator, or by some third party. PICS was developed for the primary purpose of enabling parents to control their children's access to materials on the Web. It has been promoted as a technology that encourages self-regulation and thereby avoids the need for government regulation. PICS was developed by the World Wide Web Consortium. *See* www.w3.org/PICS/.

PKI: *See* **Public key infrastructure.**

Portal (or **web portal**): A website that offers a wide variety of services, such as news, stock quotes, weather, search functions, shopping, e-mail, discussion forums, etc.

Protocol: A set of design rules for some computer-implemented process. In the Internet context, the term usually refers to the rules for encoding and transmitting data across the network. For example, TCP/IP, the set of protocols governing transmission of information on the Internet, defines how packets of data are structured, addressed, delivered, and reassembled.

Public key cryptography: A method of encrypting and decrypting information in digital format. Each person who wishes to use public key cryptography to send messages has his own pair of keys, and each pair of keys is unique. Of each pair of keys, one is designated the *public key* and the other the *private key*. The owner of a key pair makes his public key generally available to the world, while keeping the private key strictly to himself. The two keys making up a key pair are related to each other mathematically so that (1) a message encrypted with the public key can *only* be decrypted using the corresponding private key, (2) a message that can be decrypted with a particular public key can *only* have been encrypted with the corresponding private key, and (3) it is impossible to derive the private key from the public key in any reasonable amount of time. Public key cryptography, together with digital certificate technology, is well adapted for sending encrypted and authenticated information via the Internet.

Public key infrastructure (abbreviated as **PKI**): The system by which digital certificates are created, maintained, accessed, revoked, and otherwise managed. The PKI includes entities that are in the business of issuing digital certificates, along with legal rules and industry practices that foster the integrity and utility of digital signatures.

Realtime Blackhole List: *See* **Mail Abuse Prevention System.**

Registrant: A person who registers a domain name. The registrant of a domain name gains the right to use that domain name in the address of resources made available on the Internet, such as a website or e-mail accounts.

Registrar: An entity that grants a registrant the right to use a second-level domain name within a particular top-level domain. Also referred to as a "domain name registrar." Upon receiving a request to register a domain name, the registrar first checks to see whether it has already been registered. If the domain name is available, the registrar collects registration information from the registrant, collects a fee, and causes an entry to be made on the relevant registry indicating that the domain has been registered. Registrars for the commercial gTLDs are accredited by the Internet Corporation for Assigned Names and Numbers. A list of accredited registrars is available at www.icann.org/registrars/accredited-list.html.

Registration of a domain name: The process of establishing the right to use a domain name. A person registers a domain name by contacting a domain name registrar (via its website), ascertaining the availability of that name, providing the required registration information to the registrar, and paying the required fee. The registrant of a domain name gains the right to use that domain name in the address of resources made available on the Internet, such as in the URL of a website (www.domain-name.com) or in e-mail addresses (person@domain-name.com). For more information about registering domain names, see **Appendix B**.

Registration of a mark: Placement of a trademark or service mark on a register maintained by a government authority, as a means of claiming rights to use the mark and providing notice to others of the claim of such rights. In the United States, the user of a mark can acquire certain rights in the mark solely through its use, but registration confers additional rights. Trademarks may be registered with state agencies, with the United States Patent and Trademark Office if the mark is used in interstate commerce, or with both. State registration benefits are realized only in the state of registration. Federal registration of a mark allows the owner to use the mark throughout the United States for the goods or services described in the registration, and to exclude others from uses of the mark that may cause confusion. Federal registration conveys benefits for ten years if the trademark is appropriately used in accordance with the registration application during that time, and is renewable for additional ten-year periods, indefinitely. A registration application typically asks for a description of the mark, an explanation of how the registrant is using it or plans to use it in the future, and a statement that the registrant believes no one else has a right to use it. You can register a mark even if you have not yet used it, as long as you intend to use it. To show that you claim rights to a particular trademark in goods, you may use the "TM" symbol if the trademark is unregistered or registered only with a state agency, and the "R" symbol inside a circle if it is federally registered.

Registry: A database, pertaining to a particular top-level domain, containing registration information about second-level domains that have been registered within that top-level domain. Under rules established by the Internet Corporation for Assigned Names and Numbers, the operator of the registry for each commercial top-level domain is required to provide public access to information maintained in the registry via a "whois" lookup.

Request for Comments (abbreviated as **RFC**): One of a series of more than 2,500 documents on computer networking topics created by volunteer members of the Internet Engineering Task Force. The RFC publication process plays a central role in the establishment of Internet-related standards. A proposed RFC is first published as an Internet Draft, and if it gains the approval of the IETF is issued as an RFC. An RFC may be adopted as a standard by technology creators and users. *See* www.ietf.org/rfc.

Reverse domain name hijacking: A derogatory term referring to the practice in which a trademark owner inappropriately asserts trademark rights to prevent another person from using a domain name she has registered, and to gain control of that domain name. In the context of the Uniform Domain Name Dispute Resolution Policy, the term is defined as "using the [UDRP] in bad faith to attempt to deprive a registered domain-name holder of a domain name." *See* Rules for Uniform Domain Name Dispute Resolution Policy, Rule 1, www.icann.org/dndr/udrp/uniform-rules.htm.

Root name servers: The system of thirteen computers that form the foundation of the domain name system. Each root server holds an authoritative copy of a file listing each of the top-level domains, and the IP address of the primary name server for each TLD. The primary name server for each TLD contains, in turn, a list of the name servers associated with each domain name registered within that TLD. The name server associated with a particular domain name lists the IP address of each host computer associated with that domain. When you type into your browser a URL, such as www.ecommercecasebook.com, your ISP's name server queries one of the root name servers, and requests the IP address of the primary name server for the relevant TLD, in this case .com. Your name server then queries the primary name server for the .com TLD, and requests the IP address of the name server associated with ecommercecasebook.com. Next, your name server queries the name server associated with ecommercecasebook.com, and requests the IP address of the host designated as www.ecommercecasebook.com. Finally, your browser sends a page request to that IP address, and receives the data constituting the web page at that address. For more information on root name servers, see **Appendix B**.

Second-level domain (abbreviated as **SLD**): The portion of a domain name that comes immediately to the left of the rightmost dot. So, in the domain name ecommercecasebook.com, the second level domain is ecommercecasebook. The second-level domain in combination with the top-level domain constitutes a domain name. A person wishing to use a domain name registers a second-level domain within a particular top-level domain.

Server: A computer that manages some resource on a network. For example, a web server is a computer that holds the files constituting a website, and makes them available via the Internet. A file server is a computer that stores files belonging to users on a network. A print server is a computer that manages the network's printers. A network server manages the network's traffic. A server can also be a software program that manages resources.

Spam: Derogatory term for e-mail messages that are sent in bulk, to recipients who have not requested them, for commercial purposes. Also known as "unsolicited commercial e-mail," or "UCE."

Spammer: One who sends spam.

Spider: A software program that accesses various resources available on the Internet and indexes the content for use by search engines. *See* **bot.**

Sysop (from **system operator**): A person or entity that runs an online bulletin board or some other online communications forum.

TCP/IP (from **Transmission Control Protocol/Internet Protocol**): A communications protocol that is used to transmit data across the Internet. The delivery of messages is controlled by the Transmission Control Protocol, and the internal structure and reassembly of packets is controlled by the Internet Protocol.

Terms of Service (abbreviated as **TOS**): The terms under which a service or content provider makes its offerings available. Also known as "Conditions of Use" or "Terms of Use." The terms are often presented in fine print as "boilerplate" on an interior page of a website, with a hyperlink labeled "Terms of Service" (or simply "Terms") on the home page.

TLD: *See* **Top-level domain.**

Top-level domain (abbreviated as **TLD**): The highest level domain category in the hierarchy established by the Internet domain naming system. The TLD is the portion of a URL that comes to the right of the rightmost dot. Thus, in the URL www.ecommercecasebook.com, the TLD is .com. There are two types of TLDs: the generic top-level domains (such as .com, .org, and .edu) and the country-code top-level domains (such as .ca, .uk, and .ch). *See* **Generic top-level domain**, **Country-code top-level domain**.

TOS: *See* **Terms of Service.**

UCE (from **unsolicited commercial e-mail**): *See* **spam**.

UDRP (from **Uniform Domain Name Dispute Resolution Policy**): A procedure, promulgated by the Internet Corporation for Assigned Names and Numbers, for resolving disputes over the rights to domain names that involve claims of bad-faith use of another's trademarks. The UDRP applies to disputes concerning domain names in all the commercial top-level domains, and to domain names in certain country-code top-level domains. It defines the disputes that it covers, and provides guidelines for the conduct of administrative proceedings to resolve disputes. *See* www.icann.org/udrp/.

URL (from **Uniform Resource Locator**): The address that defines the location of a specific document on the Web. The URL http://lawtech.stanford.edu/who/index.html may be dissected as follows. The prefix "http" (hypertext transport protocol) specifies the communications protocol that is used to access a web page. ".edu" is the top-level domain, and "stanford" is the second-level domain; "stanford.edu" is the domain name. "lawtech" is the name of the host computer, or web server, on which the files reside. "who" is a subdirectory of files on that web server. "index.html" is the name of the HTML document that constitutes the referenced web page.

USENET (from **user network**): A system of discussion forums that can be accessed via the Internet. The USENET consists of more than 50,000 newsgroups, each dedicated to a particular subject. It is a distributed system that is maintained on many different servers around the world. *See* **Newsgroup**.

Web: *See* **World Wide Web.**

Web browser: A software application that runs on a personal computer and is used to access web pages and other materials on the World Wide Web. Web browsers interpret the HTML codes contained in a web page, and use those codes to format the content of the web page and display it on the user's computer monitor.

Web bug: An instruction in the HTML code constituting a web page that causes your computer to transmit information across the network to some other computer, under the pretext of obtaining a graphic image *from* that other computer. Web bugs exploit HTML functions originally designed to display graphic images. The HTML code of a web page with a graphic image contains an instruction that tells your web browser to grab the image from another computer, and to place it on the web page you are viewing. The HTML protocol allows your browser to append a string of text to your computer's request for the image, and to send the text to the server holding the image. A web bug gathers information that the operator of the site harboring the bug wishes to obtain from *your* computer, and places it in this string of text. The information thus transmitted may include the visiting computer's IP address, the URL of the page on which the bug is placed, the time the page containing the bug was displayed, and the identification code contained in any cookie that was placed by that server. The image that the web bug causes your browser to fetch generally consists of a single pixel that is the same color as the pixel of the web page over which it is placed, and that therefore has no visible effect on your own computer's display.

A web bug is much more powerful than a cookie. A cookie transmits information only to the server that holds the website that you are viewing. A web bug can transmit information to any server, without any action by you, and without any notice to you. Network advertisers place web bugs on thousands of websites, including the most popular sites on the Web, and are thus in a position to assemble detailed profiles of your online activities. Web bugs are sometimes euphemistically referred to as "clear GIFs," "1 x 1 GIFs," or "web beacons."

Web caching: A technology for maintaining frequently accessed web pages on a local computer server, conserving bandwidth and enabling the pages to be retrieved more quickly. If a requested web page is in a local cache, the page is supplied from the cache, rather than from the computer on the Internet from which it originated. The caching software checks for updates to stored pages and downloads them. Pages are purged from the cache after a certain amount of time has passed without a new request.

Web page: A document that is written in text with formatting information provided by HTML codes, and that resides on a web server and may be accessed via the Internet using the HTTP protocol.

Web portal: *See* **Portal.**

Whois search: A search of domain name registration information that is maintained in domain name registries. Domain name registrars collect information from each domain name registrant, including contact information for the registrant and the name server for the domain name. This information is maintained in domain name registries, indexed under each domain name. In performing a whois search, you enter a domain name and receive the registration information pertaining to that domain name.

World Wide Web: A collection of electronic documents that is maintained on computer servers throughout the world, and that may be accessed via the Internet using the HTTP protocol, together with other materials that are linked to those documents. The documents that make up the Web are in the form of web pages, consisting of text with formatting information provided by HTML codes, that are arranged into websites, and connected to one another through hyperlinks. A web page may also link to electronic documents written in non-HTML formats (such as Portable Document Format or Microsoft Word), and to graphics, audio, and video files. A web page is accessed by entering its URL into a web browser running on a computer that is connected to the Internet, or by clicking on a hyperlink pointing to that page from another document.

The Web is not the same as the Internet: the Internet is a network of computers that communicate using the TCP/IP protocol, while the Web consists of information that travels over the Internet. And the Web is not the only information traveling via the Internet: for example, e-mail and the USENET are not part of the Web.

World Wide Web Consortium (abbreviated as **W3C**): An association of nearly 500 member organizations that seeks to promote the smooth operation and evolution of the Web by developing protocols that facilitate transmission of information via the Web. The W3C was founded in 1994 by Tim Berners–Lee, who is generally credited as the inventor of the Web, and who now serves as the W3C's director. Most of the W3C's staff members are located at three universities and research institutions in the United States, France, and Japan. W3C's members include technology companies, content providers, corporate users of the Web, research laboratories, standards bodies, and governments. *See* www.w3c.org.

Zone file: A database residing on a name server that contains lists of the computer servers that are connected to the Internet and their corresponding IP addresses.

INDEX

References are to Pages.

†

GAY L.A.

ALSO BY LILLIAN FADERMAN:

Speaking for Ourselves: American Ethnic Writing
(with Barbara Bradshaw)

From the Barrio: A Chicano Anthology (with Omar Salinas)

Lesbians in Germany (with Brigitte Eriksson)

Surpassing the Love of Men: Romantic Friendship and Love Between Women from the Renaissance to the Present

Scotch Verdict

Odd Girls and Twilight Lovers: A History of Lesbian Life in 20th Century America

Chloe Plus Olivia: An Anthology of Lesbian Literature from the 17th Century to the Present

I Begin My Life All Over: The Hmong and the American Immigrant Experience (with Ghia Xiong)

To Believe in Women: What Lesbians Have Done for America

Naked in the Promised Land

ALSO BY STUART TIMMONS:

The Trouble with Harry Hay: Founder of the Modern Gay Movement

GAY L.A.

A History of Sexual Outlaws, Power Politics, and Lipstick Lesbians

LILLIAN FADERMAN
STUART TIMMONS

BASIC BOOKS
A Member of the Perseus Books Group
New York

Published by Basic Books,
A Member of the Perseus Books Group

Designed by Brent Wilcox

Library of Congress Cataloging-in-Publication Data
Faderman, Lillian.
Gay L.A. : a history of sexual outlaws, power politics, and lipstick lesbians / by Lillian Faderman and Stuart Timmons.
p. cm.
Includes index.
ISBN-13: 978-0-465-02288-5 (alk. paper)
ISBN-10: 0-465-02288-X (alk. paper)
1. Homosexuality—California—Los Angeles—History. 2. Gays—California—Los Angeles—History. 3. Gay liberation movement—California—Los Angeles—History. I. Timmons, Stuart, 1957- II. Title.
HQ76.3.L7F33 2006
306.76'609794—dc22

2006023470

06 07 08 09/ 10 9 8 7 6 5 4 3 2

For Phyllis—who makes everything possible

LF

For Jim Kepner, witness, activist, archivist, and friend

ST

And in memory of those Angelenos we have recently lost:

Betty Berzon

Vern Bullough

Frankie Hucklenbroich

Gavin Lambert

Brian Miller

William Moritz

Johnny Nojima

Jean O'Leary

Savina Teubal

Brenda Weathers

CONTENTS

ACKNOWLEDGMENTS

Our deep appreciation goes to all the Los Angeles gay men and lesbians who made the history we have written about in these pages. Hundreds of them opened their hearts and memories for this project. We are grateful to them for giving us hours of their time and so generously sharing their lives with us and our readers.

For their unfailing personal support, thanks to our families and friends, including Shirley Magidson, Trebor Healey, Bill Fishman, David Byrd, Joe Bessera, John Callahan, Cindy Friedman, Josy Cattogio, Phyllis Irwin, Beatrice Valenzuela, Steve Yarbrough, Cathy Conheim, and Donna Brooks. For Lillian's tireless work as editor, Stuart offers his lasting gratitude.

We thank those who kindly read all or parts of our manuscript and gave us their invaluable feedback, including Jehan Agrama, Malcolm Boyd, John Callahan, Jeanne Cordova, Terry DeCrescenzo, Bill Fishman, Linda Garber, Rich Jennings, Sharon A. Lilly, David Link, Ariana Manov, Mark Thompson, and Carolyn Weathers. We are grateful to those who hosted us during research trips, including Katherine Gabel and Connie Eddy, Robin Tyler and Diane Olson, Joey Cain, David Link, and Gay Timmons.

No history can be written without the help of archivists. Special thanks to Jay Johnson of the Los Angeles City Archives; Romaine Ahlstrom and the staff of the Huntington Library; Misha Schutt, David Moore, Joseph Hawkins, and Ashlie Mildfelt of the ONE National Gay and Lesbian Archives; Jo Duffy, Ann Giani, Marcia Schwemer, and Jeri Deitrick of the June Mazer Lesbian Archives; James Henley and Patricia

Johnson of the Sacramento Archives and Museum Collection Center; Lauren Buisson of the UCLA Arts Library Special Collections; Carolyn Coles and the many helpful professionals at the Los Angeles Public Library; John Cahoon of the Seaver Center; and the staff of the Southern California Library for Social Studies and Research, the Rosenbach Museum and Library, the Los Angeles Law Library, the Academy of Motion Picture Arts and Sciences, and the California State Archives.

For their invaluable help in providing materials or access to subjects, we thank Michael Marchand, Terry DeCrescenzo, Carolyn Weathers, Paul D. Cain, Donna Brooks, Jane Cantillon, Craig Collins, Rick Mechtley, Chuck Stallard, Tony Friedkin, Jim Weatherford, Ariana Manov, Ann Bradley, and Tony Barnard. Our gratitude goes to our agent Sandra Dijkstra. Lillian would like to thank the Historical Society of Southern California for a research grant that made her early work on this project possible. We are grateful for the research assistance provided by Phyllis Irwin, Kathy Hall, Jeanne Stanley, and Erin Cross.

The Doctor and Jonnie.
Author's collection.

An interracial "drag gay ball" at the Club Alabam on Central Avenue, L.A.'s "Harlem," 1945.
Shades of L.A. Archives/courtesy Los Angeles Public Library.

Introduction

Los Angeles [was] a city of heretics, . . . a city of refugees from [the rest of] America. [Their] banishment was partly dreamed and partly real.

—Frank E. Fenton, *A Place in the Sun*, 1942[1]

YEARS BEFORE autobiographical novelist John Rechy presented gay Los Angeles as a "City of Night," he witnessed a small homosexual riot. It happened in the spring of 1959, at Cooper's Doughnuts, a downtown coffee shop on a seedy stretch of Main Street between two of L.A.'s older gay bars, the Waldorf and Harold's. Since their glamour days as early as the 1930s, both bars had grown shabby, but they offered refuge to the outcasts of that depressed enclave, who also made Cooper's Doughnuts their hangout. Cooper's was an all-night haunt, a place to get cheap coffee and doughnuts, a good place to camp or cruise or converse. Most patrons were queens, butch hustlers, their friends, and their customers. Many were Latino or black. The queens wore the half-drag of Capri pants and men's shirts, which, they hoped, would enable them to escape arrest for "masquerading" as women (though they knotted their shirts at the midriff in the feminine style of the day). Because the patrons were obvious or suspected homosexuals, Cooper's became a frequent target for the Los Angeles Police Department, which prided itself on being one of the most determined enemies of homosexuality in the nation.

That night in May, a patrol car circled the block a few times, parked, and two police officers entered Cooper's, demanding to see identification from those seated at the long rectangular counter. As usual, the police stated no reasons for their harassment. Pointing to Rechy and two others, they said, "You, you, and you—come with us," and ordered the men into their squad car. But just as would happen a decade later and a continent away at the Stonewall Inn, that night in Los Angeles the crowd rebelled. The arbitrary arm of the law had come down "one time too many," Rechy says:

> First people started throwing the doughnuts they were eating at the cops. Then paper cups started flying. . . . Then coffee-stirring sticks and other things started flying at them.

Under siege, the officers fled to their squad car without their prisoners, summoning backup. More squad cars arrived, sirens blaring. Rioters were arrested and jailed. Main Street was cordoned off and remained closed until the next day. Rechy and the other detainees were able to slip away, he says, smiling more than forty-five years later at the confusion that gave him freedom.[2] This was perhaps the first homosexual uprising in the world. But the historic moment went unreported and unrecorded.

That nearly-forgotten incident is emblematic of why we felt this book needed to exist, but there were myriad other reasons as well. We found traces of a thriving lesbian and gay life in Los Angeles in overlooked archival sources dating back to the nineteenth century. We found that there was much to say about the secret but lively community established in the 1920s and '30s by those who came to Hollywood to work in the movie industry. We were fascinated and disturbed by the stories gay men told us of how the L.A. vice squad sent officers who were handsome young males ("Hollywood rejects," they were called) into gay bars in the 1950s to serve as decoys to entrap homosexuals, and by the stories gay women told us of how they were hassled by the police simply because they walked down a Los Angeles street dressed in pants and a tailored jacket. We were moved by the stories of now-elderly women and men who told us how years ago they had lived and found love and compan-

ionship in the city. We discovered that, historically, more lesbian and gay institutions started in Los Angeles than anywhere else on the planet, and that L.A.'s multifaceted, multiracial, and multicultural lesbian and gay activism continues to have tremendous impact worldwide. These stories of Los Angeles lesbian and gay life and political achievements have never been sufficiently documented. As historians and lovers of that city, we wondered how such a history could have been discounted or left uncommemorated, and we grew determined to fill in what we considered a huge gap in the record of lesbian and gay America.

Together and separately, we sat in numerous archives, poring over old newspaper clippings, city council minutes, police ledgers, court transcripts, organizational papers, letters, pictures, and mementos. We interviewed approximately 300 people, aged from sixteen to eighty-something, mostly lesbians and gay men, of all races and ethnicities. We visited them in their mansions in the Hollywood Hills, tiny apartments in Compton, assisted-living facilities for the elderly, and group homes for troubled lesbian, gay, bisexual, and transgender teens.

The process of uncovering this history offered poignant moments. Lillian will always remember, for example, her interview with a stately seventy-three-year-old woman, a retired physician, who said that fifty years earlier she came to Los Angeles from Chile to study medicine, fell in love, and realized she could never again go home because she could not live in Santiago as she lived in L.A. She produced a picture of herself, a young woman in a dress and pumps, on the arm of a "handsome young man," Jonnie—who was in fact her now-deceased woman lover of forty years. Stuart will not forget the interview in which he asked a longtime Hollywood resident whether he happened to have any photographs relating to gay life, and the octogenarian obligingly pulled out an album of sepia snapshots pasted to tattered black pages that were dated "1937": The pictures were of film industry workers at a backyard party, lounging with movie stars whose faces are still familiar.

Though we have been fortunate in being able to uncover extraordinary material about lesbian and gay Los Angeles of earlier eras, our work has sometimes been frustrating because we know that much has been lost. For example, we found a tantalizing photograph at the Central

branch of the Los Angeles Public Library, documenting a 1945 ball at the Club Alabam, which was in the heart of the black district, on 42nd Street and Central Avenue. Dexter Gordon and Charles Mingus played in the Club Alabam's house band, and Mae West, William Randolph Hearst, and Orson Wells listened to jazz there together with Duke Ellington, Jackie Robinson, and Joe Louis.[3] The 1945 photograph, however, shows two dozen young men, African American and white, wearing cocktail gowns, stoles, and Joan Crawford–style lipstick. The caption under the photo reads: "Crowds of people line up in front of the stage at the Club Alabam. Event was a 'drag' gay ball for the best dressed."[4] None of the individuals is identified, and their personal stories are lost to history.

In our quest for more information about such early drag balls, we discovered through a 1949 Halloween Bal Masque program that one particular drag ball had been staged annually for eighteen years, since 1931. We also discovered that various drag events were produced with regularity at half-a-dozen venues in South Central Los Angeles,[5] where the lively nightlife, dating back to at least the 1930s, had rivaled that of Harlem. But precise facts are sometimes murky. For example, several of our sources pointed us to Brothers, a South Central L.A. nightclub of the 1940s, which clearly had a speakeasy mystique and outlaw charm. It was located "off an alley or back of a place," and "you had to know somebody who knew somebody to take you there. That's the way it was."[6] Other details about Brothers, however, are contradictory. Some of our sources identified the eponymous "brothers" who owned the club as being two black lesbians.[7] Others, such as Clora Bryant, a woman trumpeter who was a habitué there, said that the name was "Brother's," not a plural but a possessive, and that "Brother," the owner, was a man, garbed in flowing robes.[8] Despite that contradiction, all sources do agree that Brothers was, as Bryant characterized it, "a hangout for guys who go for guys and whatever. [At Brothers] you could get whatever." Like at the Club Alabam, jazz musicians would drop in to Brothers after-hours, and movie stars would come to partake of the scene.[9] Such provocative traces of L.A.'s Harlemesque nightlife remain vivid, but the fine points—for instance, was Brothers run by two lesbians or by a man in flowing robes?—seem irrecoverable.

Such frustrations fueled our search. We wanted to locate the photographs, examine the written records, and talk with the people who knew about the hidden gay world of Los Angeles in bygone eras. We wanted to prevent fading memories from being snuffed out forever and more photos from becoming permanently obscure. We also wanted to capture more recent history, to find out how Angelenos were able to establish the biggest, wealthiest, longest-lived gay and lesbian international church, community center, and national magazine; how they became major players in city and state politics and in the movie industry that influences the world; how they entertain themselves in a city devoted to entertainment; how the steady stream of lesbian and gay immigrants that flock to L.A. for refuge have been able to make a life for themselves.

We opted to deal with both men and women in this book, even though, as we discovered, they often moved in separate circles and trod different paths around Los Angeles. Occasionally, they even waged internecine battles against one another. But, as we discovered too, they also saw each other as natural allies who shared common enemies. Through much of their history in L.A., both women and men had to hide who they were because of prejudice against homosexuality, and both suffered in their daily lives from the hostilities of a homophobic society. Although men were more likely to be prosecuted under the Los Angeles and California laws that targeted homosexuals, women too were threatened by many of those laws and even sent to jail under them. Realizing that they shared not only enemies but also ways of being that the rest of the world disdained, they banded together—"fronting" for each other, trusting one another with the secrets of their lives, sharing insider humor about, for instance, their challenges to "appropriate gender behavior." When external enemies attacked, they made common cause, and together they celebrated remarkable political victories. In the vastness that is Los Angeles, lesbians and gay men have formed multiple separate communities as well as a viable unified community.

We chose to call our book *Gay L.A.* because, as our older informants told us, "gay" in the 1930s, '40s, '50s, and '60s was the term that included homosexual men, lesbians, transgenders, and even bisexuals. Some of

our younger informants call themselves "queer." Others prefer more specific designations that signify subtleties of sexual expression, or gender identification, or even racial variations on those phenomena, such as "boi," "MTF," or "stud." We have tried always to identify our narrators by the designation they prefer, but we have chosen "gay" as our umbrella term, just as it was the umbrella term historically for both men and women who loved their own sex, as well as those whose gender presentation or gender identification was unconventional.

We divided the research and composition tasks between us, but so that these pages would read smoothly, in one narrative voice, Lillian edited the writing. As coauthors, we are admittedly an odd couple. Lillian's experiences with gay L.A. began in 1956, in the seamy working-class gay girls bars on 8th and Vermont, where the butch and femme patrons could not escape the knowledge that they were outlaws; Stuart arrived in Los Angeles twenty years later to attend UCLA, and became active in a gay liberation movement and a gay world that celebrated its pride at huge sunlit parades. Stuart, a journalist and biographer, has been politically and culturally engaged in L.A. gay life for the last thirty years. Lillian has been an academic and a writer of lesbian histories for those same thirty years. We came to our partnership not only with our gender, generational, and past and present class differences but also with different worldviews, allegiances, and talents developed over the past decades. But our goal has been to uncover the histories of gay L.A.'s women and men of all ages, socioeconomic positions, ethnicities, and political affiliations; and we believe our own diversity has helped us to re-create those histories in all their fascinating complexity.

I: THE SILENT ERA

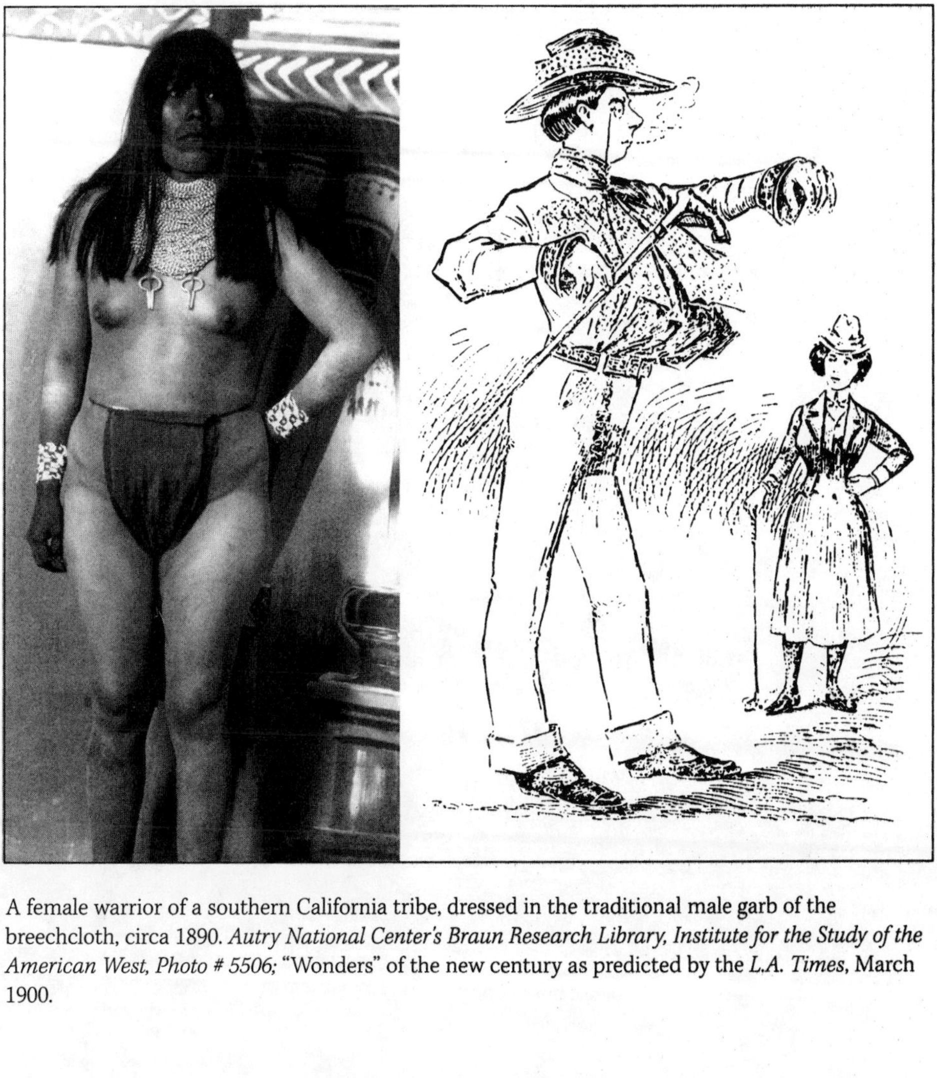

A female warrior of a southern California tribe, dressed in the traditional male garb of the breechcloth, circa 1890. *Autry National Center's Braun Research Library, Institute for the Study of the American West, Photo # 5506;* "Wonders" of the new century as predicted by the *L.A. Times*, March 1900.

CHAPTER 1

City of Angels and Devils

BEFORE THE CITY OF ANGELS

From the very beginning of the world it was meant that there should be homosexuals. . . .

—Naahwera, a Mohave traditional singer[1]

Under Spanish and Mexican influence, the Gabrielino Indian village of Yang-na was gradually transformed into the city of Los Angeles, and most of the Indians who had lived there were forcibly relocated or killed. Though in the early 1850s about half the population of Los Angeles was still Indian (4,000 whites and 3,700 Indians),[2] the new settlers knew little about the history of Native Americans and even less about their institutionalized gender and sexual practices. The white settlers' ignorance was perhaps fortunate for the Indians, who had already suffered greatly under the colonial Spaniards' imperative to impose on the Indians their Christian views of "sin." Captain Pedro Fages, who came in 1775 to the area that is now Santa Barbara, discovered to his horror that the men among the Chumash Indians were "addicted to the unspeakable vice of sinning against nature," and he dubbed their same-sex relations "excess so criminal that it seems even forbidden to speak its name."[3] The Spanish missionaries, who arrived in California soon after Fages, were also aghast at what they saw as "the sins of Sodom." "Horrible customs," Father Geronimo Boscana called the unconventional gender behavior and the homosexuality that often accompanied it when he observed the Indians

around the Southern California mission of San Juan Capistrano.[4] Father Pedro Font's comment about these "nefarious practices" among the Indians of Northern California was chilling: "There will be much to do when the Holy Faith and Christian religion [take over]."[5] Although adultery and polygamy were deemed terrible sins by the padres, such sins paled compared to the sexual inversion they saw often among the local natives.[6]

The Spaniards had observed primarily male behavior. Typical of European men of the era, female same-sex relations, and even gender inversion, was the stuff of fantasy for them.[7] They were enamored of Garci Rodriguez de Montalvo's fifteenth-century protolesbian tale about a mythical island called "California," where Queen Califia lived with her beloved subjects, all of them masculine women. "And there were no males among them at all," Montalvo wrote. He described the women as having "energetic bodies and courageous, ardent hearts." Like the Amazons of Greek myth, they waged bloody war on other lands, killing most of the males but carrying away a few so that they might copulate with them for the sake of procreation. Female babies were kept among them; male babies were slaughtered.[8] In 1535, Hernan Cortes, sharing his era's enchantment with the story of these fierce, manless women, wrote the name "California" on a map of a strip of land on the west coast of North America. It has remained its name ever since—though the protolesbian source was long forgotten.

The missionaries did indeed find "much to do" in ridding the land of the gender and sexual behavior that shocked them, since Indians up and down California had always recognized that some males, as well as some females, were different from conventional men and women. The Indians had given those who were different an honorable place in their communities.[9] The Yurok called biological males who preferred to live and dress as women *wergern* and esteemed them as more spiritual than most people. The *wergern* were often made shamans. The Yuki called them *iwop-naiip* and permitted them to marry men. Among the Juaneño of the Southern California coast they were called *kwit,* and men considered

them very desirable wives because they were robust workers in the household. Among the Yokuts, farther north and east, the cross-gendered males had honored spiritual roles, being charged with preparing corpses for burial or cremation.[10] Anthropologists generally used the French word *berdache* for Native American males as well as females who assumed gender and sex roles usually associated with the opposite sex; but more recent writers, pointing out that *berdache* means "kept boy" or "male prostitute," have rejected that term in favor of others such as "two-spirit people"[11]—an apt retort to the missionaries who dubbed sexual and gender behaviors they could not understand as bestial and godless.

The Native Americans, having had no notion in the eighteenth century that the Spanish padres would consider their culturally condoned practices to be bestial and godless, spoke freely to missionaries such as Father Boscana, who then wrote of his chagrin in discovering among the Southern California Gabrielino and Luiseno Indians that the male *berdache* were allowed to marry men, even tribal chiefs, and that the entire tribe approved of such marriages, even arranging "a grand feast" in celebration. Boscana was particularly horrified that certain boys were selected from an early age and instructed "in all the duties of the women—in their mode of dress—of walking, and dancing; so that in almost every particular, they resembled females." In his retrospective account, written in the 1820s, he noted with relief that this "detested race" (that is, the *berdache*) no longer existed in Southern California, thanks to the eradicating work of the padres.[12]

The missionaries did indeed make every effort to extirpate such behaviors out of the Native Americans, separating male same-sex couples by sending one member of the couple off to a distant mission and devising various cruel punishments for the recalcitrant. For example, Francisco Palou wrote that when the friars encountered a Santa Clara male Indian who wore women's clothes, they ordered the Spanish soldiers to strip him naked and force him to sweep the plaza in the nude for three days, to his intense shame. After his punishment, he was commanded to give up women's clothes forever. Palou observed that, rather than comply, the Indian fled his home and went elsewhere so that he might continue to live as a *berdache*.[13]

The Native Americans had surely learned by the nineteenth century that they must keep their gender and sexual preferences secret from the padres, so that it soon appeared to missionaries such as Boscana that the "detested race" had indeed been eliminated. But records published more than a hundred years after Boscana show that *berdache* customs and behaviors, among males as well as females, continued in Southern California tribes, including the Gabrielino, Luiseno,[14] and Chumash.[15] The Southern California Quechan Indians, who called *berdache* males *elxa',* continued to believe they had more power than the ordinary man and were a peaceful influence on the tribe.[16] Among the Quechan, divergent sexual behavior was not limited to the *elxa'.* Casual homosexuality among men and women was common and was not socially condemned.[17] Among the Mohave, *berdache* males, who were called *alyha,* continued to wear skirts and were initiated into their role through a testing ceremony in which the community would sing to the initiate; the true *alyha* would then publicly accept the role by dancing to the song "with much intensity."[18] Once initiated, *alyha* were believed to have been mystically transformed into their adopted sex. The Mohave thus created a social role that accommodated people that we could call "transgenders."

Biological females who desired to live as men also had institutionalized roles that continued in some tribes into the twentieth century.[19] The Southern California Kamia had traditionally honored such females by attributing the birth of agriculture to one of them, Warharmi, who was said to have been a "bearer of seeds of the cultivated plants" as well as an "introducer of Kamia culture."[20] Like the Kamia, the Mohave believed that these biological females, whom they called *hwame,* had existed ever since the world began and that they had always worn male garments and taken on male roles. The Mohave thought that whether a female would be a *hwame* or a male would be an *alyha* was determined in utero, through the pregnant mother's dreams. In puberty, the true *hwame* and *alyha* manifested their proclivities by preferring pursuits that were generally associated with the opposite sex. The *hwame* and *alyha* behaved much as did the "sexual inverts" described by European sexologists such as Richard von Krafft-Ebing and Havelock Ellis: For ex-

ample, as an early-twentieth-century Mohave Indian told the anthropologist George Devereux, young *hwames* "like to chum with boys and adopt boys' ways." As he described them, "They throw away their dolls and metates, and refuse to shred bark or perform other feminine tasks. They turn away from the skirt and long for the breech-clout."[21]

Devereux's informant, speaking of his own era, the early twentieth century, when modern European concepts about gender and sexuality had taken a strong hold among Indians, said that Mohave families attempted to dissuade young people from becoming *hwame* or *alyha.* Nevertheless, he declared, when the families failed in their efforts, "they will realize that it cannot be helped." They then invited the community to a ceremony and bestowed upon the young person the status of "*hwame*" or "*alyha.*" Another informant described such an initiation ceremony in which a girl became a *hwame:* "Proud of being stared at," he said, "she traipses and dances back and forth in a stooped posture over a flat stretch of damp land. That is how she acts if she is to be a true *hwame.*"[22] The *hwame* then assumed a name that reflected masculine status and thereafter s/he was always referred to as "he."[23]

According to some twentieth-century sources, the *hwame* adult could assume almost all aspects of the masculine role among the Mohave, but she was not permitted to be a tribal leader—though in earlier eras and among other tribes such females could hold even that most honored position. For example, in pre-conquest days, Coronne, who appears to have been "*hwame,*" was the chief of the Indians who inhabited the Southern California area that became San Juan Capistrano: According to Boscana's 1820s account, she was "of huge proportions, . . . very coarse . . . having no wish to marry [nor] feelings of love for any man." The area she ruled over was called Putuidem, which refers to an enlarged umbilicus that projects out—suggesting perhaps Coronne's pseudophallus.[24]

As in many of the Southern California tribes, the Mohave *hwame* could marry women and were considered "excellent providers." Because the Mohave believed that the paternity of a child would change if the pregnant woman had sexual relations with a new person, it was thought that a *hwame* could even become a father by having sex with her pregnant mate. The *hwame* and her partner sometimes formed a

family not unlike the contemporary lesbian family, the *hwame* being acknowledged as a parent of the baby her partner bore. According to Devereux's informants, she would "take care of [the child] with pride, and love it very sincerely."[25]

Such community tolerance of same-sex marriage, cross-gendered behaviors, homosexual family life, and sexual fluidity had scarce parallel among the invading Euro Americans who, in the mid-nineteenth century, soon outnumbered the Indian population in Southern California.

"IN DRESS NOT BELONGING TO HIS OR HER OWN SEX"

The City of Los Angeles should change its name to that of Sodom or Gomorroh [sic].[26]

—"Los Angeles Disgraced," *California Argus,* 1896

Los Angeles in the 1840s was a Mexican town of ranchos and cattle, hundreds of miles from the center of the Gold Rush, but it grew rapidly as a result of the Rush. Money poured into L.A. not only from the sale of cows that were driven north to feed the gold miners but also from the gamblers and other lawless high-rollers who were driven south by the northern vigilante committees.[27] In 1850, California was admitted to the Union. Three years later, when Harris Newmark, a businessman, arrived in Los Angeles, he observed a town of "free-and-easy customs," in which people could "do practically as they pleased." There were no city ordinances against gambling, nor against drunkenness, drugs, prostitution, or high-noon showdowns in the middle of the street—all were common in neighborhoods such as Calle de los Negroes, also called "Nigger Alley" (the present-day Los Angeles Street), a district as wild as the wildest in the West.[28] By the mid-nineteenth century, Los Angeles' wild ways had earned it a nickname: "City of the Devils."[29]

Men far outnumbered women in Los Angeles, as they did everywhere in California according to the 1850 census, which recorded 12.2 males for every one female in the state.[30] Single Euro American females were slower to come to California since many of the get-rich-quick dreams and schemes that drew men west were closed to women—un-

less they came as "men," which some did, exchanging petticoats and tight bodices for men's garb. They escaped the restrictions of Victorian womanhood by passing as members of the putative stronger sex, and they claimed the right to men's adventures.[31] Other women did not try to pass, but they "butched it up," relying on their masculine demeanor to keep them safe in a man's world. Harris Newmark recalled fifty years later a "muscular-looking woman" he had met in Los Angeles in the 1860s. According to Newmark, she called herself "Captain Jinx," a revealing sobriquet she borrowed from a popular song about a cocky gentleman who proclaims:

I taught the ladies how to dance, how to dance, how to dance.
I taught the ladies how to dance,
For I'm a captain in the Army.

Newmark's Victorian reticence did not permit him to speculate openly about Captain Jinx's sex life, but he seemed to be hinting at her inversion when he observed that she "half-strode, half jerked her way along the street. . . . She was very strong for women's rights, she said; and she certainly looked it."[32]

Frontier societies' willingness to tolerate such cross-gendered individuals was not ubiquitous. In Denver, for example, an 1875 ordinance concerning "Offenses Against Good Morals and Decency" made a man's or woman's appearance in public places "in dress not belonging to his or her own sex" a misdemeanor punishable by a fine of up to one hundred dollars.[33] Los Angeles in 1875 was still comparatively loose and lawless, and there were no such ordinances. But as L.A. grew from a Wild West town to a more staid city, the public became more ambivalent in its view of unconventional gender behavior. Near the end of the century, Los Angeles, too, adopted a law to force men to look like men and women to look like women. The law came as a result of an unrestrained yearly Saturnalia, All Fool's Night, that rivaled Mardi Gras in its sexual rowdiness and campy gender-play by both sexes.

All Fool's Night was the culminating event of La Fiesta, a weeklong ballyhoo of gaudy pageants and frolics dreamed up by the Los Angeles

Merchants Association in 1894 during a period of worrisome economic depression. Despite its trappings of "Old Spanish Days," La Fiesta followed the European tradition of Carnival, including a temporary suspension of city government, the election of a Fiesta Queen, and even the mock-jailing of the police. By 1895, La Fiesta and All Fool's Night were drawing a "merry, roistering crowd" of 100,000 to L.A.'s commercial area, to the great delight of businessmen.[34]

But the festivities also drew the ire of conservative Protestant groups that had been rapidly gaining power in Los Angeles. The religious Right of the era was shocked not only by the drunken revelries of All Fool's Night and what one newspaper account described as "a general male and female 'turn-loose'"[35] but also, and most especially, by the sight of men and women in drag. The religious Right could not decide which was the more reprehensible—men dressed as women or women dressed as men. In an article titled "Methodist Preachers Inveigh Against a Feature of the Fiesta," it was "the actions of young ladies dressed in men's clothes" that were particularly disturbing.[36] But what disturbed the author of "Hell Turned Loose on Los Angeles" the most was "the behavior of those [men] clad as women, [which] was disgusting in the extreme, and almost too vile to detail."[37] The newspapers granted that some of those cross-dressers may merely have been "out for a frolic, with no further idea than 'a little fun' if such it may be called," but other cross-dressers "used the license of the occasion to [display] all their vicious and evil propensities."[38]

The threat of the City of Angels transmogrifying into a Sodom or Gomorrah through the sins of the All Fool's Night cross-dressers posed a dilemma to the city councilmen: They were torn between the continued need to shore up a sagging economy by attracting tourists to L.A. and the pressures exerted by a mobilized religious Right. The forces of the Right seemed to win out. "The general sentiment of the people of this city is now against permitting the use of public streets as the scene of riotous revelry and debauchery," the Los Angeles City Council declared.[39] The council ordered the city attorney to investigate the California State Penal Code to see whether gender disguise was against the law. The city attorney could find nothing about disguise in the penal code except for

an 1874 law, clearly aimed at bandits and highway men, that declared it unlawful to wear "any mask, false whiskers, or any personal disguise" for the purpose of evading recognition while committing a crime. Since that particular law (Sec. 185) could not be easily applied to cross-dressers, the city council asked the city attorney to draft a Los Angeles ordinance that would specifically make it illegal "for a man to masquerade as a women, or a woman as a man."[40] But the council, in their ambivalence, stalled for three years before they considered the ordinance. Finally, in 1898, they inveighed against the "indecencies" All Fool's Night encouraged, banned the festivity along with its drag revelries, and passed Ordinance 5022.[41] This city law forbidding "masquerading" proved to be the bane of drag queens for the better part of the next century and of butch-dressing lesbians throughout the mid-century.

Constraints on gender fluidity did not apply to nineteenth- and early-twentieth-century stage performances, however, and Los Angeles was highly entertained by the gender-benders of the vaudeville and variety stage. Male impersonators particularly were popular figures in L.A. theaters. Despite their young-rake dash and highly sexualized swagger, male impersonators on stage were even considered "family entertainment" (as were female impersonators),[42] since the connection between theatrical impersonation and sexual deviancy in real life had not yet been widely made by American audiences. Ella Wesner, for instance, who had had a long amorous relationship with Josie Mansfield, the former mistress of Erie Railroad millionaire Jim Fisk, was one of the most popular male impersonators of her day. Wesner was described in 1870s newspapers as having "a face quite masculine and jet black curling hair, which she wears cut short."[43] She appeared on stage in formal men's attire, singing songs with lyrics such as:

Lovely woman was made to be loved,
To be fondled and courted and kissed;

And the fellows who've never made love to a girl,
Well, they don't know what fun they have missed.[44]

But at no time during her theatrical career was there ever a public discussion of her lesbianism, Americans still being reluctant to recognize the possibility of sexual deviancy in an attractive woman—even one dressed in drag and singing songs about loving girls. When Wesner conducted extensive theatrical tours in California, her earnings of $200 per week were touted as "the largest salary ever paid to any single star in America."[45] Male impersonators continued to star at top L.A. theaters as late as the 1920s. Kitty Doner, for instance, trumped Fannie Brice as the headliner at the Orpheum and other leading variety theaters. The newspapers described her as "the top-notcher of all male impersonators" and proclaimed that her "delineations of the so-called stronger sex [were] classic."[46]

On stage, men, too, could get away with gender impersonation for a period that extended into the twentieth century. L.A.'s first recorded theatrical female impersonation occurred in 1848 at the American Theater on Temple Street, where, at an opening night performance, General Andreas Pico took a fancy to the lovely woman who appeared as "Lady Elizabeth." The Lady was a man.[47] Throughout the nineteenth century, in L.A., as in many American cities, female impersonators were a staple on the stage, including the ethnic stage. In 1894, for example, when "Gauze," a male singer with the black Georgia Minstrels, appeared at the Los Angeles Theater, s/he was glowingly described in a review as having "a well cultivated voice and much grace as a female impersonator."[48] The Chinese community in Los Angeles also loved theatrical gender-benders. "Chinese female impersonators come high," an 1891 writer observed, "but the Chinese managers [of the Los Angeles Chinatown theaters] must have them." One theater troupe alone boasted of having five female impersonators in its company.[49]

Even into the 1920s, female impersonators strutted on stage, and in film, too. Frederic Covert was famous in Los Angeles theaters and the movies for his drag "vanity" and "peacock" dances. He slyly flaunted his homosexuality through his professional name, Ko Vert.[50] In 1923, Julian

Eltinge, the top female impersonator in America and also a homosexual, was playing to sell-out audiences at L.A.'s Orpheum Theater.[51] As the theater historian Laurence Senelick has argued, before the 1930s, gay men and lesbians were often able to use the stage to "experiment with gender shuffling in a context that won them approbation and indulgence." Drag on stage was seen as art and entertainment.[52]

The Los Angeles antimasquerading ordinance was revised in 1922 to declare that if one dressed in the clothes of the opposite sex on the streets, he or she would be sent to jail for six months and fined $500.[53] However, before the mid-twentieth century, the ordinance (which became Municipal Code 52.51 in 1936) was most often enforced against men. One woman onstage impersonator, Jean Southern, devised a stunt that tested the law (and, more to the point for her, garnered valuable publicity on the eve of her appearance at the Orpheum Theater): Southern, a 1924 newspaper reported, "stuck a cigarette in her mouth, pulled her cap down over her forehead, and walked jauntily out into the street swinging a cane." She then accosted a policeman and engaged him in conversation, waiting to see whether he would recognize that "he" was really "she." The policeman is shown in a *Los Angeles Times* photograph, not very interested in discovering that the "boy" who stands beside him is in fact a girl. Jean Southern was not hauled off to the station. Perhaps gender-bending females enjoyed relative impunity, despite the words of Ordinance 5022, because they were still essentially beneath the radar screen of the law—which was doled out and enforced by men. "There is little in this age of sheiks and shebas a man can do that a girl can't—even to the extent of making the world believe she is a man," the *Times* declared with amusement.[54]

Gender-bending males, on the other hand, could find the courts and community severe, though there were occasional instances of public indulgence, such as the town's response to Billie Dodson, known as "the man milliner of El Monte." According to a 1907 report in the *Los Angeles Times,* Dodson "walks like a girl . . . talks like a girl . . . cooks

and sews like a girl." He was a "sissy," the writer bluntly observed, and yet he had "the respect of every man in that little town whose people are direct descendants of the rough old Forty-Niners." Dodson was admired, the article explained, because of his life of self-sacrifice. He had grown effeminate taking care of his invalid mother, and, when she died, taking over the role of mother and housewife for his younger siblings and his bereft father. The writer was also insistent that Billie was not a "degenerate," pointing out that although he entertained college boys at night and his ways were "sissified," he "nevertheless lacked the offensive and unwholesome suggestion that usually lingers about an effeminate man."[55]

However, a more typical response to unusual male gender behavior was a 1911 newspaper column in which effeminate men were branded "Los Angeles Undesirables." "Willie Boys," the columnist called them, and wrote contemptuously of the most overt variety, "Silk Stocking Percy":

> He wears his hair à la sow-lick, bedaubs his white lips with rouge and pencils his eyebrows and tucks his pale baby-blue silk kerchief, soused with French perfume, into his coat sleeve. . . . He wiggles like a wild fish when he walks down the street and carries a cane and a pair of gloves to keep him warm.

"Put him down!" the columnist concluded in a sneer.[56]

Flamboyant sissies may have been targeted for public disapproval, but men who actually tried to pass as women were subject to serious legal trouble. Frank Butcher had been working in women's clothes as a cook, but was hauled off to jail when his employer recognized that "she" was a male. In 1913, his transvestism was considered criminal by the authorities, who also questioned his sanity. Butcher was ordered to appear before the Lunacy Commission of the Los Angeles Superior Court. He came corseted, gloved, wearing a large picture hat, and he proclaimed his "overwhelming desire to wear skirts and woman's finery." The court was not sympathetic. The deputy sheriff was instructed to outfit him in male clothing and to lock up his "lady duds."[57]

UNBECOMING "THE WEAKER SEX"

California is altogether anomalous, and it is not more extraordinary for a woman to plough, dig and hoe with her own hands if she have the will and strength to do so, than for men to do all their household labor. . . never seeing the face of a woman.[58]

—Eliza W. Farnham, 1856

Both middle-class and working-class nineteenth-century women who can be viewed as "protolesbian" were attracted to a city like Los Angeles for similar reasons: the possibility of escaping the pressure of relatives and the peering of neighbors, the hope of forming a community with like-minded women who had also run from the constrictions back home, the dream that work opportunities such as were lacking for women in more traditional communities might abound in a rapidly growing new city. Mary Blake, writing in the nineteenth century of leaving New England and going West with another woman, said that even on the train trip she was already feeling a "release from conventionalities" and "a rubbing off of that dust of conservativism."[59]

Even as early as 1849, "women's righters" such as Eliza Farnham were advising women without men to "go West." A widow whose most intimate relationships were with other women, Farnham came West with her children and "Miss Sampson," whom she described as being "at this time a member of my family," and with whom she labored on the farm they shared, "rejoicing every evening over the progress of the day."[60] Farnham told independent women that in California, unlike the rest of the country that was hidebound by tradition, they might do anything. She bragged of being her own carpenter, of dressing "à la monsieur" rather than in the constricting skirts of the day, and of sharing with other women "the purely sensuous enjoyments" of a pioneering and independent life.[61]

Caroline Churchill, who proudly proclaimed herself a "strong-minded woman" (a term used by enemies of women's rights to describe both suffragists and "manly women," that is, inverts), observed a generation later, in 1876, that in California opportunities for "strong-minded women"

abounded, more than anywhere else in the country, because although they were not ubiquitously liked they were nevertheless permitted to go about their business. She wrote of their successes in "money making and other business endeavors," and she claimed to have met several prosperous women physicians in California.[62]

The number of women physicians in the Los Angeles area expanded further with the founding of the University of Southern California, which was opened to both sexes in 1878, when most universities elsewhere in the country still shunned women. The USC College of Medicine was soon flooded with applications from "strong-minded women" who wanted to become doctors, such as the very "manly" Ida B. Parker, who came to Los Angeles from Kansas, graduated from USC medical school, and established a private practice in Southern California.[63] By now, women who wished to escape the constraints visited on them by conservative tradition knew they might find unprecedented possibilities in the young West.

Their opportunities were increased by L.A.'s real estate boom of the 1880s. Many of those who became rich in the boom were single women who had migrated to Los Angeles from other parts of the country. Emma Adams observed in an 1888 book that Los Angeles was unique because it was a "brisk city" of fresh opportunities for pioneers, and it was possible there for "as large a proportion of women as men to increase their fortunes" through the real estate investment business. In Los Angeles, she said, women could attend real estate auctions, boldly bid on property, negotiate sales aggressively—all endeavors that were virtually closed to women, no matter how independent, in most other places in America.[64] Adams observed that of the five single women who happened to be visiting the house where she was at that time residing, every one owned her own home, bought through her own endeavors.[65] So many unmarried women were making a fortune in L.A. real estate during those years that, beginning in 1888, a group of women established what was probably the country's first "Woman's Investment Company."

It was not unusual for such westering women to live their lives with other women, as did Eliza Farnham, though which of them had anything like what our era would call a "lesbian identity" is difficult to know for certain. By the turn of the century, the literate knew that sexologists had

articulated the terrible connection between "congenital taint" and the "real inverts"—those twilight crawlers with whom "the respectable" would not wish to identify.[66] In her memoir about a lesbian life in turn-of-the century New York, Mary Casal observed a severe class split among middle-class and working-class women who were homosexual. Once in a while, Casal admitted, she and her woman lover would "go slumming [to] invert resorts" in the Bowery, but always they felt "out of place" among the kinds of people they met there. "Our lives were on a much higher plane than those real inverts," Casal proclaimed, distinguishing herself and her lover from the sorts of lesbians that hung out in "invert resorts."[67] Casal's desire to draw such class distinctions was undoubtedly as pronounced among educated, middle-class lesbians in Los Angeles as it was among those in New York. Genteel women might live together in deeply intimate relationships, but they would not be seen in the rendezvous of the sexual outlaws.

As an early-twentieth-century homosexual police informant, L. L. Rollins acknowledged there was at least one "queer" dance hall in Los Angeles similar to the New York Bowery haunts that Casal describes, where working-class lesbians gathered together with their male counterparts.[68] But though working-class women who were lesbian in early-twentieth-century Los Angeles sometimes shared space with gay men, they appear seldom to have suffered, as the men did, from police entrapment or persecution for their sexual activities. There were multiple reasons for this: Lesbians of any class were less likely to use the sorts of semipublic cruising grounds that gay men favored—such as a dark park (where women had reason to fear male sexual assault) or a tavern (where patronage required discretionary income, which single working-class women did not have in abundance). Because of the facts of physiology that make "quickie" upright sex less appealing to women than to men, female-female sex acts were rarely carried on in any of the other places that were likely targets for police surveillance, such as public restrooms. Also, so few women officers were employed by the police department that schemes to entrap lesbians would have been impracticable; and the notion of sexual pleasure in which a penis was lacking was anyway not taken seriously by many men who made and enforced the laws.

In the middle decades of the twentieth century, lesbians, especially those of the working class, were often charged with "masquerading" by the police, that is, wearing pants and short hair when real women were supposed to wear dresses and tresses. But in earlier decades, city ordinances and municipal codes notwithstanding, law enforcement was surprisingly unpredictable, and even sympathetic, with regard to masquerading women. For example, in 1915, Professor Eugene de Forest, a "well-known teacher of dramatics," had been engaged, according to an L.A. newspaper account, to "a well-known Los Angeles woman," their marriage pending the finalization of Professor de Forest's divorce from the wife "he" had married in 1911. It was discovered that the professor, who would today be called "transgendered," was really a female, and she was arrested for masquerading. But her plea that, though physically a woman, she was "in nature a man" appears to have moved the court. She was never sentenced. Two years later, when the professor fell ill and was admitted to Los Angeles County Hospital, she was even able to convince hospital authorities, who had wanted to put her in the women's ward, that she must be placed in the men's ward.[69]

There were other such remarkable instances of the Los Angeles courts' leniency toward women who tried to pass as men in the early twentieth century. "Lionel Francis Michael Higgins," who had married a woman, was discovered to be a female herself after she misappropriated $12,000 from her L.A. employer. She diverted a jail sentence by claiming "sexual maladjustment." Instead of being imprisoned, she was sent to General Hospital: "The best that can be done is to permit her to continue to be as masculine as possible," the examining doctor told the court.[70]

The Los Angeles courts continued to be surprisingly liberal with regard to masquerading women throughout the 1920s. In 1927, a young woman by the name of Katherine (Kit) Wing posed as a man and married a sixteen-year-old, Eileen Garnett. Two years later, Wing was living as the husband of another young woman, nineteen-year-old Stella Harper. When Wing's bigamy was discovered, she was arrested. But the district attorney ordered her released, declaring that although she had committed technical perjury by misrepresenting the Garnett girl's age at the time of the marriage, "Miss Wing was not otherwise guilty in going through the cere-

mony or masquerading as a man" since the statutes applied "only where someone [had] been damaged." Wing convinced the district attorney that she had donned masculine attire only because she thought it would enable her to get more work as a barber. "Except for the one matrimony slip, I cannot see that she has done anything particularly out of the way," the DA concluded. He pointed out that "Hollywood girls" sometimes even wore "gob's [i.e., sailor's] clothes at the beach," and that it seemed to him there was "no standard attire for men or women these days."[71]

What can account for that astonishing liberality? Was it because Los Angeles by the 1920s had been feeling the challenge of becoming an important metropolis, of living up to the examples of other sophisticated major metropolises where female gender play was rampant, such as Berlin or Paris?[72] Was it because the advent of the "twentieth century" (after centuries of "teens") had seemed to herald a necessary break from tradition, including old-fashioned gender tradition? Los Angeles in 1900 seemed to brace itself for a break that would be huge: A cartoon of that year showed a couple of the new century, the man flinging his decidedly limp wrists from embroidered mutton-chop sleeves, peering through a monocle under a beribboned hat; the woman wearing a starched collar, suit jacket, and porkpie hat, and leaning on a golf club.[73]

Or had the liberality toward female gender behavior come about because Los Angeles was still reeling from the confusion over the 1911 election, which gave California women the vote eight years before it was bestowed on women in most of America? As in the rest of the country, the nineteenth-century "women's righters" of California had often been treated with disdain, their demands on behalf of women being associated with sexual deviancy. Arguing against inserting a Married Women's Property Rights clause into the first California Constitution, one delegate to the Constitutional Convention voiced the sentiments of many: "The God of nature made women frail, lovely, dependent," he declared. "The doctrine of women's rights is the doctrine of [the tribe of] mental hermaphrodites."[74] Decades later, Los Angeles antisuffragists echoed his hostility, characterizing women who wanted the vote as unfeminine and sexual freaks. L.A. newspapers constantly hammered on the connection between a woman's desire for full citizenship and her gender abnormality.

"She wears her brother's shirt and likewise his suspenders . . . and now she's learning how to vote and lift her voice in caucus. . . . She is that trial to the soul, the modern mannish woman," one article proclaimed.[75] "Woman suffrage should be defeated because it tends to unsex society," another insisted. "Politics is a realm unsuited to the normal woman."[76]

But L.A. women could not be daunted by these tactics, and they continued to pressure male voters to enfranchise them. Suffragists were more successful in Los Angeles than anywhere else in the state. California women won the vote no thanks to Northern California, where the antisuffrage vote was so heavy in San Francisco and Alameda Counties on October 10, 1911, that the *Los Angeles Times* actually predicted on October 11 that the California woman's suffrage amendment had lost.[77] In fact, the suffrage amendment won, but only by 3,587 votes, 2,000 of that margin coming from Los Angeles, where the vote to enfranchise women was 15,000 to 13,000. California became the sixth state in America (following Wyoming, Colorado, Idaho, Utah, and Washington) in which women could vote.[78]

What interpretation could be given to those facts, especially in view of the concerted efforts to depict suffrage women as "manly" and freakish? Neither the majority of men voters in L.A. nor the women who pushed them to vote for suffrage were, apparently, afraid of "unsexing," whatever that meant. The district attorney who could not see that "Kit" Wing had "done anything particularly out of the way" in marrying two women, and who insisted even that old standards of appropriate gender dress no longer applied, seems to have been echoing Angeleno ambivalence of that era about what rules were still pertinent to female behavior. For at least a few years in Los Angeles, the old certainties about how a woman must look and act had been destabilized, or had even disappeared.

Word seemed to have gotten out that women who were disdained elsewhere because of their gender or sexual behavior needed to cross the continent all the way to the Pacific, where they would find not only sunshine but also anonymity and even a modicum of safety.[79] Kit Wing had come to Los Angeles from Springville, Utah, possibly hoping—along with so many women who wanted to escape the scrutinizing eyes of relatives or neighbors—not only that she could lose herself in a distant and

growing city but also that she might discover a like-minded community. According to Box-Car Bertha, a hobo celebrity of the early decades of the twentieth century, it was common for lesbian hoboes to ride the rails (often in couples, one dressed in drag so that they might pass as a straight pair) and head for California. There were more female hoboes in California than anywhere else in the country, Box-Car Bertha observed in her memoirs that looked back on the 1920s and '30s.[80]

The Los Angeles newspapers were fascinated by the discovery of odd female immigrants into the city, especially if they passed as men: for example, "Man-Woman Is Seen as Romeo" a 1924 headline declared in telling of a "Paul J. Beach," who was found upon "his" death to be a woman. A picture of Beach in men's clothes and the woman s/he had married in the Midwest, before the couple came to Los Angeles, accompanied the article, as did a love letter from another woman declaring that she dreamt of having Beach's "nice, big, broad shoulder to lean on."[81] "Faint Reveals 'He's' a Woman," another headline announced about Peggy Dolan from Brooklyn, who, posing as a man, had made her way to Los Angeles. Her sex was discovered when "he" was taken to Los Angeles General Hospital after passing out in downtown L.A., the *Los Angeles Times* wrote sympathetically alongside a picture of a smiling boyish Peggy.[82]

SOCIAL VAGRANTS

> *Disgusting in the extreme was the function described by this young social vagrant . . . which took place a few evenings ago in the richly furnished and perfumed apartments of a wealthy man in the heart of Los Angeles.*
>
> —The Fisher Report, 1914[83]

Despite the Los Angeles City Council's attempts to regulate "riotous revelry and debauchery" of the queer variety, an underground gay male subculture took root. Already in the 1880s and early 1890s, there were many places where like-minded men might find one another in the developing city: L.A. moralists complained about the visibility of "sissy-boys on

Broadway," a major Los Angeles boulevard.[84] Night-time trysting places, known only to gay men and police, included Central Park (which in 1918 became Pershing Square) and Westlake Park. There were also traces of a gay subculture in some of the city's numerous saloons. In 1896, a soldier by the name of Holcomb complained to Los Angeles police that he had been robbed of $135 at the Thalia Beer Hall. His assailants were a black man, Charles Berry, and "some of the 'fairies' employed at the Thalia in the capacity of 'beer-slingers' and song and dance artists." The "fairies," the victim claimed, "assisted Berry in getting away with the money."[85] (L.A.'s nineteenth-century underworld appears to have been similar to that of New York, where, according to Earl Lind, a female impersonator who frequented the Bowery, criminal types generally felt comfortable with "fairies" because they knew that society considered homosexuals to be "far worse defilers of the law than themselves." Lind says the "crooks" and the "fairies" were often bed partners.)[86]

Masked balls provided cover for forbidden behavior. One such affair in the summer of 1887 was condemned as attracting "drunken prostitutes of both sexes" who conducted "vile orgies" at Merced Hall.[87] At Turnverein Hall, similar "disgraceful debauches" drew flocks of "prostitutes and their associates, thugs, hoodlums, thieves, and disreputables of all types and classes."[88] Just months after the infamous masked ball at the Merced, British immigrant Frederick Purssord converted the Merced into a lodging house, apparently for homosexual men.[89] Purssord, a colorful character who practiced electrical therapy on nude patients while nude himself, also owned a series of Turkish baths. Police had for years considered him to be "operating as a degenerate." One neighbor complained to a *Los Angeles Times* reporter, "He is the most indecent man I have ever known."[90] In 1913, he was arrested on a charge of "lewd and dissolute conduct" and was reported to have committed suicide in the city jail.[91]

Though the word "homosexual" was never mentioned in California laws, the "infamous crime against nature," which referred primarily to homosexual sodomy, first appeared in the California State Penal Code in 1872. Sodomy, regardless of who the participants were, was punishable by a term in a state prison.[92] As a Los Angeles judge instructed one nine-

teenth-century jury on a sodomy case, "Every person who assaults another with intent to commit the infamous crime against nature is guilty of a felony, and it is wholly immaterial whether the person so assaulted consents or not."[93] (Clearly, the "assault" was not against the consenting partner but rather against society.) As Los Angeles court records reveal, the Los Angeles police did not scruple to invade privacy if they had reason to suspect that two men were "violating nature." In 1888, police hauled two protesting men at 1:00 A.M. from the bed they shared at a lodging house on North Main Street and took them to the downtown jail. The following morning, Charles Murphy and John Fisher found themselves described in newspapers as "vile criminals."[94]

Fisher, the younger of the two men, escaped charges by testifying against Murphy. The pretrial hearing transcripts reveal a shady L.A. underworld of cheap lodging houses equipped with peepholes for spying, clerks who doubled as prostitutes, and policemen who came running if summoned to witness the commission of the crime against nature. John Fisher claimed to have been introduced to Charles Murphy by a mutual friend. After Murphy bought Fisher dinner, they ended up in a lodging house, where the woman clerk rented them a room for twenty-five cents. In hesitant testimony, Fisher confessed that once they had disrobed and were in bed, Murphy turned him "on my stomach." It was at that point that the clerk (who must have been spying at a peephole) entered their room, lifted her Mother Hubbard dress, and asked, "Do you fellows want some fucking?" She said she charged $2.50 for her services. When Murphy declined, the woman left and fetched the son of the lodging house owner, who testified that he looked through the peephole and witnessed Murphy "on top, just the same as he would be on a woman." He summoned a policeman, who told the court he saw that Murphy's "privates [were] erected" when he arrested the two men.[95]

The clerk who had offered her sexual services for $2.50 was not charged by the court, nor was the lodging house cited for spying on customers. But Murphy was sentenced to a couple of years in Folsom Prison.[96] He can be said to have gotten off lightly compared to the frontier-town treatment of other men who were suspected of sodomy. In 1896, Charles Wheeler was accused of having sex with an adolescent boy.

The boy's father, James Wilde, along with his uncle, tracked Wheeler down, held a knife at his throat to prevent an outcry, and castrated him.[97] The brothers then gave Wheeler a dime and referred him to the county hospital, where he was refused treatment. When the Wilde brothers were charged with mayhem, they expressed astonishment that they had been held accountable for their actions. The judge who tried them agreed. "The facts of the case," he said, alluding not to the brothers' castration of Wheeler but rather to Wheeler's alleged (though never proven) commission of sodomy, "are so revolting that one may well blush for human depravity." He dismissed the charges against the brothers for their rush to judgment and bloody deed and then declared: "The rules I follow can strike terror to no decent man."[98] Such was Wild West judgment of homosexual sodomy when Los Angeles was a frontier town.

Sodomy was a felony in California, but oral sex did not appear in the California State Penal Code as a punishable offense until 1915 (though those who were caught engaging in oral sex might be arrested under misdemeanor "vagrancy" statutes or as "lewd and dissolute persons," as was Frederick Purssord).[99] Perhaps because its misdemeanor status diminished the legal consequences, gay men in Los Angeles (as well as gay women, according to a 1914 report)[100] apparently began favoring "the twentieth-century way" once personal hygiene was improved in the city.[101] The oral sex trend may be accounted for by other factors too, such as the invention of the zipper (first introduced in 1893 and produced widely in 1912), which made "quickie" sex possible in parks at midnight—a boon to those homosexual men who lived in urban boarding houses or other dwellings that afforded little privacy.[102]

In 1915, however, California adopted a law that made oral sex as illegal as sodomy.[103] The law was passed as a direct result of the 1914 arrests for fellatio of thirty-one men in Long Beach, a Southern California town near Los Angeles. The arrests of these men unleashed a tsunami of homophobia in the newspapers that described the relationships among them as "a holocaust of vice" and the men themselves as "social va-

grants." The incident offers a more detailed glimpse of early twentieth-century gay life in Southern California.

The men were all alleged to be members of two local private clubs. After their arrests, the *Los Angeles Times,* as well as other California newspapers such as the distant *Sacramento Bee,* printed a "List of the Guilty Ones" who, the papers claimed, "were organized for immoral purposes." The men's occupations were listed beside their names so that the public would make no mistake about who they were; and in cases in which the arrestees' occupations were unknown, one newspaper described them as "professional perverted sexualists." The sensationalistic newspaper accounts were fatal for John Lamb, a forty-year-old bachelor who was a banker and an officer in his church. When officers attempted to arrest him, it was reported, he ran for several blocks, "fought them all over Pacific Park," and was led to the station with "his clothes torn and hair disheveled."[104] Released on bail, he swallowed cyanide on a rocky beach near San Pedro. The note he left confirmed that he committed suicide because the *Los Angeles Times* had published his name in its list of "Guilty Ones": "I am crazed by reading the paper this morning," Lamb wrote to his sister. He was not alone in his anguish. So many terrified men sought to buy poison at local drugstores that Long Beach officials temporarily banned the sale of toxic substances.[105]

Southern California was in a frenzy at the notion that widespread homosexual activity was being carried on in the area—at least according to the *Los Angeles Times,* which was bent on fanning the flames by printing hysterical letters such as one from a South Pasadena mother who wrote that she would prefer "having my boy a murderer or a drunkard" rather than one of those "awful vampires."[106] The *Times* assumed the righteous outrage of its readers when it reported that the men had all been members of the "606 Club" and "96 Club" (cf. "69"), which held weekly "drags" where members donned kimonos, powdered their faces, and indulged in orgies to the strains of ragtime piano. The arresting police described these men as "flutters" and "fruiters."[107]

Residents of Long Beach were embarrassed that their town was the site of such scandal, especially since Long Beach was promoting its plan to host what was billed as "the largest religious revival meeting" in

Southern California history.[108] Fistfights broke out over allegations that Long Beach was a home to moral laxness. The newspapers of rival towns such as Venice, another Southern California beach community, mocked Long Beach (à la Mark Twain) as a "Holy City."[109]

It was the overly zealous Long Beach Police Department that triggered the revelations that brought scandal to their own town. During the summer of 1914, the department hired W. H. Warren and B. C. Brown as "vice specialists" to help conduct purity campaigns aimed specifically at men who engaged in homosexual activity. Brown and Warren were central not only in the "606" and "96" cases in November of that year: In a prior sweep, they had been hired by the Los Angeles Police Department and had arrested dozens of men in L.A. Their work appears to be the first instance on record of Southern California police entrapment of homosexuals. Brown, the younger of the two, had delicate features; Warren was said to have rugged good looks.[110] The two men may have been hired partly because the police thought their physical attributes (one femininely pretty, the other masculinely handsome) would entice homosexual men of all tastes to respond sexually, for which these "vice specialists" would then arrest them.

Despite the police badges that were issued to Warren and Brown in Los Angeles and Long Beach, they had had no police training and were closer to bounty hunters than legitimate officers of the law. They seem to have regarded their work as not so much a moral crusade as a lucrative business: They were paid by the head for each man they arrested.[111] Brown boasted of "collaring" up to fifteen "social vagrants" per day, for a bounty of $10 apiece, which would net him $150 for one day's work—a small fortune in 1914.[112] Both Brown and Warren had ambitions about franchising their talents and techniques, and they attempted to sell their services to the police departments of San Francisco, Venice, Santa Monica, and even Portland, with the promise to cleanse those towns of homosexuals just as they were cleansing Los Angeles and Long Beach.

Their tactics were a model for the ways in which Southern California police entrapped gay men for much of the twentieth century. Brown and Warren would hang out in a public restroom or the changing room of a bathhouse and wait "until they saw a man whom they thought to be

given to this sort of thing." They would take turns in attracting their mark's attention by putting a finger through a hole in the partition board that divided the stalls. If the man responded by looking through the hole, he would see a mouth close to the aperture. If the man then stuck his penis through the hole, Brown or Warren would stamp indelible ink on it, and then arrest him. The inked penis would serve at the station house as irrefutable evidence of the man's guilt. It is, of course, probable that many of the men arrested in the public toilet—among them cement workers, house painters, bartenders, merchants, and day laborers[113]—were not "homosexual" but "jockers" or "wolves" (men who did not regard themselves as homosexual but occasionally had sexual relations with younger or more effeminate men), or they may simply have been tempted by the ostensible offer of quick sexual relief. Nevertheless, the mayor and police chief of Long Beach signed a proclamation that the work of Warren and Brown had "rid the city of a dangerous class which threatened the morals of the youth of the community."[114]

Warren and Brown also played major roles in the trial of Herbert Lowe, a thirty-nine-year-old florist, who was one of the men arrested as a member of the "606" and "96" clubs. Most of those arrested had avoided the further publicity of a trial by quietly paying considerable fines or, if unable to pay, accepting a half-year jail term. Lowe decided to fight the charges against him, which occasioned in the newspapers the raciest gossip since the trial of Oscar Wilde, to whom he was compared. Officers testifying against Lowe said that he had rented to vice specialist Brown an apartment that the *Los Angeles Times* sneeringly called "Lowe's Love Shack." Brown claimed that Lowe visited him at night, invited him to the next meeting of the 96 Club, and flirtatiously helped him button up a bathing suit he had borrowed from Lowe.

After he was certain of Lowe's proclivities, Brown said, he arranged for Warren and two other officers to spy while he offered himself as bait. One of the officers stationed himself in the attic, crouching, with his eye to a hole in the wallpaper; another spied through a window. Expecting the arrival of Lowe, Brown climbed into bed. Allegedly, Lowe let himself into the apartment, pulled back the blankets on the bed, knelt, and kissed Brown several times all over his body. It was then, the

Los Angeles Times reported of the courtroom testimony, that Lowe was interrupted by a sharp noise. "Warren or his friend had accidentally betrayed his presence and slipped on the gravel. Lowe looked up toward the window, startled, and arose. Just then Warren and the other officers rushed in and arrested him." The four officers all testified in court that Lowe had confessed to them that he was a "social vagrant" and had offered them a $1,500 bribe in return for his freedom. Lowe denied every allegation.[115]

The public was evidently fascinated by whatever salacious bits of the case they might read, and the *Los Angeles Times* tried to exploit that fascination into a lynch mob mentality by running editorials opining that "degenerates" such as Lowe ought to be "pilloried in the sunlight . . . [to be] abhorred by all mankind." They dubbed the members of the 606 and 96 clubs "devils" and demanded "prominent publication of the name of every wretch convicted of a horrible enormity besides which ordinary prostitution is chastity itself."[116] But despite the public's fascination with the sensational story, the paper's call to pillory fell flat. Los Angeles had undergone something of a change from a generation earlier when Charles Wheeler—the accused but never convicted "sodomite"—suffered a Wild West castration.

Roland Swaffield, Lowe's attorney, was able to put law and order on the defensive, charging that Warren was nothing more than a blackmailer, that his modus operandi was usually to "catch some fellows at the bath house and get all the money they had on them . . . and tell the fellow that he was free and not to come around again."[117] He argued that Herbert Lowe was a well-known and trusted member of the community and that Warren and Brown were outsiders, carpetbaggers. He convinced the jury that a man they saw in their town every day, who looked perfectly harmless, could not be a "degenerate . . . capable of horrible enormity." On top of that, Lowe had not been accused of sodomy—and it was only sodomy that was a felony under the law.

But it was attorney Swaffield's very emotional closing statement that sealed his case before the jury. He heaped on the "vice specialists" whatever guilt the public may have felt over the suicide of Lamb: It was Warren and Brown, Swaffield asserted, who were "dripping with the blood of

John Lamb." In the end, he achieved both sympathy and "reasonable doubt." It took the jury less than half an hour to acquit Herbert Lowe.

"Jury Acquits in Six-O-Six" blared the headline in the fickle *Los Angeles Times,* ostensibly reflecting the public's relief that the popular florist was found innocent; "Stool-Pigeons and Police Given No Credence," the subheadline declared. But the *Times* could not relinquish yet again presenting the specter of the queer peril: Next to the article about Lowe's vindication was printed a full-length portrait of a man in an off-the-shoulder gown and feathered headdress, captioned "Harry A. Wharton, a prominent member of the [606] club, [who] boasted one of the finest wardrobes among the 'queer' people." Nor could the police relinquish their pursuit. They had lost the case against Lowe, but now they were looking for Harry Wharton because they wished to arrest him as a "degenerate."[118] The California legislature, too, was intent on making sure that members of clubs such as the "606" would not get off lightly in the future: Within a year, the California State Penal Code included a new statute, 288a, which turned oral sex into a felony.

Lowe's trial had been something of a circus. Hundreds of curious spectators fought for courtroom seats, where they would hear such details as were unprintable even in sensationalistic 1914 newspapers. Those details have been preserved only through the notes and letters of Eugene Fisher, an investigator hired by the *Sacramento Bee*'s owner, C. K. McClatchy, to bring him juicy tidbits that he might publish about the wild immorality of Southern Californians. Fisher noted in his letters to his employer (in language that McClatchy could not use in his newspaper) that testimony in court showed that Lowe had "practiced the infamy [of which he was accused] for more than nine years, being the one who will 'go down' on another or will himself willingly and gladly submit to the outrage." He observed further, for McClatchy's delectation alone, that "in the majority of these cases . . . their offense is nothing more nor less than 'cocksucking.'"[119]

Eugene Fisher was also hired by McClatchy that same year to dig for homosexual dirt in Los Angeles. His reports reveal a thriving, socially

diverse gay life. "Here in Los Angeles, City of the Angels, boasted center of learning and culture on the Pacific Coast, [homosexual] depravity is growing and spreading like a hideous ulcer, seeking with insidious arts and wiles ever to claim new victims among the boys and girls," Fisher wrote in the inimitable style of the era.[120] The *Sacramento Bee,* reveling in the story of another city's moral turpitude, sensationalized Fisher's reports even further, blaring headlines such as "Vast Scandal in Los Angeles Is Reported as Suppressed"[121] and claiming that five hundred men had recently been secretly arrested for social vagrancy in Los Angeles (though the extant evidence suggests the number was closer to fifty).[122]

Through his notes and letters to McClatchy, Fisher also left a record of the varied gay social scene in 1914 Los Angeles. In the course of his investigations, the police introduced him to L. L. Rollins, who was living in the downtown area of Bunker Hill, already a neighborhood known to police for its queer denizens. Rollins, Fisher wrote, was a "social vagrant"; he offered Fisher firsthand knowledge about the "society of queers," men who cruised at night near the Los Angeles City Hall. Fisher claimed that Rollins also informed him of various other semipublic activities that were already available to L.A. gay men in 1914, such as a party at a Main Street dance hall to which he had gone with two other men, where they had been allowed to stay only because they could satisfy the proprietor that they were indeed "queer."[123]

If Fisher and his informant can be believed, class distinctions among homosexual men in L.A. were already pronounced. "Queer practices" were often conducted in modest apartments that were "scattered throughout the city"; but Rollins also knew about a higher class of "queers," ritzy homosexuals who held soirees in suites at the elegant Alexandria Hotel (where, only a few years later, the gay actor Ramon Novarro was rumored to have had a romance with Rudolph Valentino, who worked there). At the Yale Hotel on Hill Street, Rollins recollected, he had been entertained by a wealthy friend he called "Dad."[124] Young men known as "chickens," Rollins said, were often invited to Los Angeles parties for the pleasure of the socially prominent "queers" in attendance. He described an event, hosted by two millionaires who lived together in Venice Beach, that ended in an orgy of "unnatural practices." Fisher re-

ported with particular relish the details of another homosexual soiree about which Rollins told him—a formal dinner that included next to everyone's plate "a candy representation of a man's privates, which was sucked and enjoyed by each guest to the evident amusement of all."[125]

As the population of Los Angeles grew in the first decades of the twentieth century, homosexual communities and their meeting places also grew. Word of the increasing variety of "queer" venues spread not only to men who desired other men but also to the police who tried to quash them in the service of what they believed was the public will. Homosexual men were victimized by L.A.'s "militant moralists [and] connoisseurs of sin," to use the words of William Huntington Wright. Wright pointed out in a 1913 article in *The Smart Set* that public parks in Los Angeles were now being patrolled, "snooping [was becoming] the popular pastime," and privacy was "impossible." He suggested that L.A. was losing its battle to become cosmopolitan, and he attributed the loss to the recent major influx of migrants from unsophisticated small towns. Los Angeles, Wright said, was being taken over by those who had "brought their Midwestern Puritanism with them."[126] This struggle that Wright characterized between provinciality and sophistication persisted in Los Angeles for some time. It accounts for a virulent tension between the law enforcement officials who would hire men like "vice specialists" Warren and Brown, and a cosmopolitan gay community that burgeoned despite them.

Marlene Dietrich preferred men's suits and shoes in real life, too. *Courtesy of the Academy of Motion Picture Arts and Sciences.*

CHAPTER 2

Going Hollywood

THE INVASION OF A "GREAT SECRET SOCIETY"

A walk along Hollywood Boulevard or any other locale in this mad town will bring any casual observer face to face with the alarming percentage of nances and Sapphic ladies as abound in these parts. Such parties and entertainments as they have are held in their own apartments or bungalows, until for a truth, it seems that they form a great secret society within, yet apart from those they refer to as "disgustingly normal." They come from all parts of the country, and whether the discovery of themselves came in this environment, or whether they knew before they arrived what they wanted, cannot be ascertained.

—"Hollywood Lowdown," 1932[1]

Actors, writers, and designers came to Hollywood largely from vaudeville and the legitimate stages of Europe and Broadway. As artists, they were accustomed to bohemian living, unconfined by the narrow sexual strictures that kept most individuals married and monogamous. The screenwriter Frances Marion recalled that from the beginning, their unconventional reputations preceded them into provincial Los Angeles: When she arrived in 1914 there was already a movement afoot by a committee called the "Conscientious Citizens," made up of "mostly churchgoers," who gathered 10,000 signatures "to force the invaders [those who had come to work in the new movie studios] out of Los Angeles." It was hard

for Frances Marion to find an apartment, she wrote in her diary, because tacked over numerous rental signs was the edict "No Jews, actors, or dogs allowed."[2] But the Conscientious Citizens could not succeed in keeping the objects of their disdain out of the area that became Hollywood.

Indeed, by the 1920s people who preferred life on the social edge found Hollywood more attractive than almost anywhere else in America. "The law of the colony is that everyone is entitled to do as he or she sees fit in all personal matters," a Hollywood fan magazine explained in 1921. "If you don't like it you may stay away, but you must not knock."[3] Workers in the movie industry and those who were drawn to the "great secret society" (not mutually exclusive groups) helped to swell Hollywood's population from 36,000 residents at the beginning of the 1920s to 165,000 by the end of the decade.[4] The conscientious citizens' battle with the bohemians did not let up, but the bohemians fought back and even used their new Hollywood prestige to try for a time to raise the sophistication quotient in the rest of America. In 1922, when the Hollywood Women's Club cried for a curfew in the streets, a *Photoplay* magazine columnist shared his outrage with his readers: "Everybody has to be in bed and be good," he wrote in a sarcastic article about the club's curfew campaign. "All wild parties are off. Hollywood [must] become a strictly moral, residential district." He hoped to encourage movie fans everywhere to feel urbane disdain for the Hollywood Women's Club's offer to "aid the police by reporting all unseemly activities and all elements of the kind they want to suppress."[5]

It must have been difficult indeed for the conventional citizenry of what had so recently been a small California town to digest not only the risqué movies being produced in early Hollywood but also the vast changes going on in their neighborhoods. As bohemians who valued nonconformity and adventurous experimentation, many of the men and women of the early film industry would have been anything but perfect 0s ("exclusively heterosexual") on the Kinsey Scale. They were fluid both in sexuality and in gender presentation, and their daring was encouraged: For example, when Julian Eltinge appeared in drag in the 1917 silent film *The Countess Charming,* one of Hollywood's first magazines, *Photo-Play Journal,* described him glowingly as "the celebrated female

impersonator, who plays the Countess Raffeisky, a dainty woman of rare beauty";[6] in 1921, *Four Horsemen of the Apocalypse* (Rudolph Valentino's breakthrough film) presented glimpses of lesbians caressing in a café and military officers posing in women's clothes; in that same year, Alla Nazimova not only flaunted her sexual predelictions around town but also announced to the press, "I am to play a boy in my next picture."[7] Throughout the 1920s, the lesbian cavortings of silent film stars such as Evelyn Brent, Nita Naldi, Pola Negri, and Lilyan Tashman were Hollywood's open secret.[8]

The scandalized church groups and women's clubs of Hollywood found themselves fighting a losing battle. Despite the efforts of the Hollywood police who sided with them and the establishment of the Hays Office that tried to force censorship on what came out of (and went on in) the industry,[9] the movie colony continued to be so provocative that even the *New York Times* had to admit that Hollywood was "gayer, newer, brighter, and younger than anything in the history of man."[10] It was with good reason that the gay director George Cukor dubbed the late 1920s and early '30s Hollywood's "Belle Epoque."[11]

In most places in America, the Depression triggered a reactionary mood in which homosexuality was seen as tantamount to evil, degeneracy, perversion, and ugliness. A popular 1931 novel, *Loveliest of Friends*, summed up the widely shared excesses of revulsion for what was sexually unfamiliar: Lesbians were "crooked, twisted freaks of nature who stagnate[d] in dark and muddy waters, and [were] . . . cloaked with the weeds of viciousness and selfish lust."[12] But many movie industry people of those same years, though cognizant of the need to be subtle, continued to think of the sexually unconventional as interesting, provocative, and exciting. In 1932, when Salka Viertel was beginning to write the script for Greta Garbo's film *Queen Christina*, the producer Irving Thalberg asked her whether she'd seen the German lesbian movie *Mädchen in Uniform* (1931). He suggested that Viertel "keep in mind" that Queen Christina's affection for her lady-in-waiting might "indicate something like that" and told her that "if handled with taste it would give us interesting scenes."[13] Marlene Dietrich's early director, Josef von Sternberg, traded on the actress's androgyny in *Morocco* (1930) and *Blonde Venus*

(1931), admitting in his biography that he'd "wished to touch lightly on a Lesbian accent."[14] In 1933, the trade paper *Variety* reported that (in spite of the Hays Office's attempts to censor "sex perversion or any inference to it" in the movies) producers were "going heavy on the panz stuff." *Variety* cited gay touches in several forthcoming films, including *Cavalcade* (based on a play by the homosexual author Noel Coward), *Our Betters* (based on a play by Somerset Maugham, also a homosexual), and *The Warrior's Husband* (a comedy about Amazons).[15]

Those Hollywood insiders not fascinated by homosexuality in this era were at the very least blasé. In that respect, Hollywood was unlike other American cities, where men could be thrown in jail for not being sufficiently butch, as the dancer Danny Aikman recalled about his return to Wichita, Kansas, to visit his ailing mother: "I was just walking down the street . . . wearing this flowered shirt I got in California. They'd never seen anything like it in Wichita. And the police arrested me and charged me with dressing like a woman. Because I wore a shirt with flowers on it!"[16] But within the industry, gender-bending and homosexuality were often treated as in-jokes: "Were you at the Club New Yorker [in Hollywood] the other night when Jean Malin [a female impersonator] announced that he was 'all fagged out'? Whoops!" the "Rambling Reporter" for a Hollywood trade paper quipped in September 1932.[17] The following month he observed Marlene Dietrich walking through the lobby of the Roosevelt (a Hollywood hotel); she was dressed "in men's gray flannel trousers, man's suit coat (with shoulder pads out far enough to make her hips look small), a man's shirt, man's cufflinks, . . . her best mannish walk," and, the reporter added, "she lunched in Bullock's in the same outfit and walk the day before."[18] The "Rambling Reporter" knew that his movie-industry readers would "get" his implications and be pleased with their own sophistication.

Hollywood's relative urbanity in the 1920s and '30s might be explained in part by the influence of the Europeans who came to work in the film industry and/or to escape the emerging fascism of Europe. They brought with them the values of the very tolerant Weimar Republic (where popular nightlife often featured "an enticing line of homosexuals dressed as women [and] a choice of feminine and collar-and-tie lesbians"),[19] or an otherwise Continental attitude toward unconventional sexuality. These

immigrants included artists such as Salka and Berthold Viertel, Bertolt Brecht, Joseph von Sternberg, Fritz Lang, Thomas Mann, Billy Wilder, Aldous Huxley, and Christopher Isherwood. Some of them came to Hollywood with a spouse, but their conjugal bonds were seldom conventional. Huxley's wife, Maria, for example, was introduced to female homosexuality in Italy and had an open marriage with Aldous, even helping him to arrange his sexual encounters with other women in Hollywood, which left her free to explore lesbian affairs. As one of her intimates commented, "Maria—like a whole generation of European women of sophistication—never saw the connection between sex and marriage."[20] Salka and Berthold Viertel, as well as countless other Hollywood couples, had similar open arrangements, promoting a notion of sexual freedom in Hollywood that had few counterparts elsewhere in America.[21]

ALL THE VERY GAY PLACES

> *When I was in Hollywood [in the 1930s] it was considered a wild and, in a manner of speaking, a morally "lost" place. The whole world thought of it as a place of mad nightlife, riotous living, sexual orgies, . . . uncontrolled extravagances, unbridled love affairs and—in a word—SIN.*
>
> —Mercedes de Acosta[22]

Despite Mercedes de Acosta's conviction that "the whole world" knew of Hollywood's "extravagances," by the Depression-ridden 1930s the extremes of the movie colony's sexual libertarianism were generally hidden from the outside world. They had by then learned to play "the movie game," which meant creating public images that were generally far more conventional than real—though within the parameters of Hollywood, people were much freer to indulge in the "mad," "extravagant," and "unbridled." Hollywood sexual freedom often played itself out in nightclubs and bars that resembled the colorful nightspots of Europe and the clubs of Manhattan.[23] When Prohibition ended, a decade of underground speakeasy culture had created more than a passing acquaintance between high society tipplers and the social strata regarded as taboo and

even criminal. In some major cities, a queer milieu carried over into the new state-licensed bars for a brief but shining moment known in New York as the "pansy craze." In fact, the craze grew so overt in New York that one Broadway nightspot even called itself the Pansy Club.[24] In Los Angeles, the fad was sufficiently established so that the drag entertainer Ray Bourbon could open his own nightclub, the Hollywood Rendezvous. Wags of the period described him as "the Master of the Murky Mouthful, exponent of darting dirtiness . . . [who sings songs] that would make Will Hays [after whom the Hollywood censorship commission was named] screech, 'I *hate* you!'"[25]

Gays, straights, and the sexually flexible—such as Marlene Dietrich, William Haines, James Cagney, Fifi Dorsay, and Mae West—gathered together regularly in post-Prohibition nightclubs that featured gay entertainment.[26] At B.B.B.'s Cellar, the floorshow was called "Boys Will Be Girls," and Fred Monroe did impersonations of the female stars in his audience.[27] At the Bali nightclub on Sunset Strip, the composer and singer Bruz Fletcher, whom the newspapers described as a favorite of nightclub-hopping film stars, entertained the cognoscenti with gay double-entendres in songs such as "Bring Me a Lei from Hawaii," "Keep an Eye on His Business," and "The Simple Things":

I want a cozy little nest, somewhere in the West,
Where the best of all the worst will always be.
I want an extensive, expensive excursion
To the realms of "in," "per," and "di"-version.
It's the simple things in life for me.[28]

The trade papers enthused over the nightclubs' gay shows and the glamorous Hollywood audiences they attracted: For example, they called B.B.B.'s Cellar "the best after-theater spot for the money in town" and "a great drop-in spot for picture names."[29]

The L.A. police were not as tolerant: Their 1932 raid on the Cellar was described by *Variety* as part of "a drive on the Nance and Lesbian amusement places in town."[30] However, since a variety of venues abounded for so-called "Nances and Lesbians," the "drive" met with little success. Men

who wished to make gay contact with other men might go, for example, to various hotel bars and the most elegant of the nightclubs—the Mocambo, the Trocadero, Ciro's—which were primarily heterosexual but permitted gay customers to cruise there as long as they behaved with discretion: no touching, no flamboyant clothes, no effeminate gestures.

And, of course, at Hollywood parties, behind the high walls and hedges of private homes, there was freedom either to be openly gay or to dabble in gayness. Several Hollywood historians have suggested that for those who were sexually flexible such parties could further careers. Alla Nazimova's biographer, Gavin Lambert, notes that on Sunday afternoons in her home, which she called "the Garden of Alla," Nazimova hosted poolside parties that were "occasionally mixed, [but] more often 'young girls' only." Lambert implies that Nazimova's lesbian parties served as an entrée for hopeful actresses into the Hollywood scene, whether or not they had previously considered themselves lesbian.[31]

The composer Cole Porter, the actor William Haines, and the directors Edmund Goulding and George Cukor also hosted parties that had similar purposes of providing not only gay social outlets but career opportunities, too, for young men who were (or were willing to play at being) gay and were capable of tight-lipped discretion. Mark Bortles, who worked in the industry during these years, recalls that "getting in with George Cukor or other gay industry figures at private Hollywood parties could help young gay men make a lot of connections." But, he noted, "if you talked the doors got closed."[32] Cukor's parties metamorphosed as the evening wore on. In the early hours, his guests would include heterosexuals as well as close bisexual women friends such as Katherine Hepburn, Greta Garbo, and Tallulah Bankhead, but later at night his hillside home became a gay-male oasis. Over forty years, much of gay Hollywood passed through his parties. Gays flocked there, in the words of the producer Joseph Mankiwiecz, "because George was their access to the crème of Hollywood."[33]

Donald Bogle, a historian of black Hollywood, suggests a parallel social phenomenon in the parties of Ben Carter, an African American casting agent, who was "at the center of early gay black Hollywood." African Americans appeared in Hollywood films during these years

almost exclusively as chauffeurs, maids, and extras; but Bogle observes that Carter's frequent gatherings included many young black men, who could promote their limited but relatively well-paying Hollywood careers by opening themselves "for a little [gay] mischief."[34]

Those who worked behind the camera in Hollywood could also make connections at private gay gatherings. Paramount designer Howard Greer, who was responsible for the costumes in highly successful films such as *Bringing Up Baby,* threw gay parties to which "every male dressmaker in Hollywood" came, often hoping to land a job on Greer's staff. His gatherings included a mix of gay Hollywood types of the era—ingénues, muscle men, drag queens, celebrities—as his description of one such party in a 1937 letter reveals: "I flew hither and yon, asking the young, the handsome and the virile," Greer wrote. "On the following Thursday my little villa was thronged with belles. (I'd very carefully asked no women.)"[35] He hired local female impersonators from "a queer night club that ha[d] just started." He rigged up a studio spotlight to illuminate the curve of his stairway, where "really amazing" drag queens portrayed Bea Lillie and Ethel Merman. But the highlight of the evening, Greer says, was "when the torch singer sang one of Mr. Cole Porters' songs, . . . I thought Mr. Porter was going to deficate [*sic*]."[36]

Such private gay parties were a safe haven. When Prohibition was repealed in 1933, law enforcement officers, afraid of losing all vestiges of control over Hollywood nightlife, flexed their muscles by cracking down more often on Hollywood clubs that welcomed the sexually diverse. They were especially hostile to places that offered floorshows in which "men masquerade[d] as women, and women pose as men." When Hollywood Vice Squad officers raided Jimmy's Backyard, they carted off the female impersonators, who were each sentenced to six months in jail.[37] A 1933 *Variety* reported in its inimitable style:

> Vigilance of the local gendarmes closed all the pansy joints in Hollywood. Flounce factories had quite a run for the past two years, then the coppers discovered an ordinance which prohibited the appearance of anyone in a café in drag unless employed in the café. That killed the lavender spots.[38]

Variety was wrong. The Hollywood clubs in which those of all sexual persuasions met and mingled continued to flourish.[39] To the end of the 1930s, titillating guidebooks such as Jack Lord and Lloyd Huff's *How to Sin in Hollywood* gave nuggets of advice to readers: "When your urge's mauve" (that is, when you want to visit a "lavender spot"), "go to Tess's Café Internationale [a lesbian nightclub] on Sunset Boulevard at 11:00 P.M." where you can "watch the little girl customers who . . . look like boys."[40] The most popular of the late 1930s clubs was the Baroness Catherine d'Erlanger's Café Gala, which was also called, in the language of Yiddish humor, the "Ca-fegaleh."[41] Beverly Alber, a singer at the Gala, remembers it as "a marvelous gay supper club where straights came to see the entertainment."[42]

But in a milieu in which those who are supposedly gay mix with those who are supposedly straight, lines may easily blur. When unconventional artists were brought together socially during the early decades of the Hollywood industry, many of them dared to be "unstraight."[43] In Hollywood, they could carry on their lives with at least a modicum of openness as long as they played the movie game and hid the fact of their sexual flexibility from their fans. But even if constrained to disguise the root of their sensibilities, these Hollywood artists with their "unstraight" styles profoundly influenced both the heterosexual and the homosexual worlds of their day and ours.

"THE WOMEN EVEN WOMEN CAN ADORE"

> *She has sex but no particular gender. Her ways are mannish. The characters she played loved power and wore slacks, and they never had headaches or hysterics. They were also quite undomesticated. [Her] masculinity appealed to women, and her sexuality to men.*
>
> —Kenneth Tynan, *The Sound of Two Hands Clapping*[44]

In recent years, a whole industry has been created of books devoted to establishing the lesbianism or lesbian experiences of one Hollywood star or another. Many of those books are poorly documented or patently sensationalistic. Some, however, are ostensibly reliable, based on solid evidence

such as correspondence or other primary documents, or interviews with narrators who knew the subject well. Cases have been made for claiming as lesbian, or "Gillette blades" (the Hollywood slang for "bisexuals"), or at least "unstraight" numerous Hollywood character actresses, including Spring Byington, Judith Anderson, Hope Emerson, Constance Collier, Agnes Moorehead, Marie Dressler, Patsy Kelly, Hattie McDaniel, Ethel Waters, and Marjorie Main; as well as more glamorous stars, such as Pola Negri, Nita Naldi, Janet Gaynor, Alla Nazimova, Ona Munson, Peggy Fears, Lilyan Tashman, Elissa Landi, Billie Burke, Dolores Del Rio, Louise Brooks, Tallulah Bankhead, Claudette Colbert, Joan Crawford, Katherine Hepburn, Marlene Dietrich, and Greta Garbo.[45]

Why were so many of the female stars of early Hollywood unconventional in their sexuality? In addition to the historical bohemianism of the acting profession, another answer may be that girls who chose the rigorous course of training for a career in the early decades of the twentieth century were already "abnormal" in the sense that they rejected the time-honored prescription that had been laid out for women's lives: to marry young and to procreate. To be ambitious, to wish to succeed outside the domestic sphere—those were considered masculine traits in the previous century, when the early women stars were adolescents. They were not unlike the pioneering women doctors or lawyers, who were also often impervious to socialization into traditional femininity and its concomitant sexuality.[46]

Nineteenth-century sexologists such as Havelock Ellis considered the rejection of women's role a telling sign of "female sexual inversion" that was tantamount to lesbianism. Ellis' case studies in *Sexual Inversion in Women,* which often included the "symptomatic" childhood traits and predilections of typical female "sexual inverts," read strikingly like the early traits and predilections of many women stars of the 1930s. Ellis quotes the recollections of a "Miss V.," for instance: "As a child I loved to stay in the fields, refused to wear a sunbonnet, used to pretend I was a boy, climbed trees, and played ball. . . . When my hair was clipped, I was delighted and made everyone call me 'John.' I used to like to wear a man's broad-brimmed hat and make corn-cob pipes."[47] Katherine Hepburn recollected of her youth (much like Ellis' Miss V.), "From the age of nine

to age thirteen, I shaved my head. I called myself 'Jimmy'. . . [and] loved to wear knickers and [my] brother's shirts."[48] She boasted that "there was not a single tree in town [I] could not climb."[49]

Greta Garbo described herself in her youth as a "strapping boy."[50] Marlene Dietrich admitted: "I used to dress up in boy's clothes when I was a little girl. I have always liked the freedom of men's garments";[51] and when young, she called herself "Paul."[52] "Billie" was the name Joan Crawford preferred as a young person, and she saw herself as "very much a tomboy and a scrapper."[53] Crawford even admitted in a *Modern Screen* interview in 1930 that in her youth she "wasn't like other girls"; she rejected all things feminine, preferring "to shinny trees and climb fences."[54] Examples abound of early women film stars' admissions of their masculine identification in youth.

These women were too complex to be dubbed simply "sexual inverts." (We suspect that many of Havelock Ellis' subjects were also much more complex than his reductive term for them suggests.) Yet they were certainly unstraight. Their androgyny—expressed in their clothes, voice, body language, and the hint of sexual flexibility that was implicit in their gender-bending—was a good part of their allure. Hollywood understood the potential of that appeal when it planned the advertising for Dietrich's first films: The publicity for *Morocco* (1930) featured a picture of the star in black top hat and tails, captioned by the slogan, "Marlene Dietrich—The Woman All Women Want to See." The image of Dietrich in male drag was so successful that she was again dressed in top hat and tails for *Blonde Venus* (1932). When Dietrich went to a private Hollywood party around that time wearing white flannel trousers, a very masculine blue blazer, and a yachting cap, she made such a sensation that the studio took a photo of her in that outfit and planned to issue thousands of copies with the caption, "The Woman Even Women Can Adore."[55]

But part of playing the movie game was to present the glamour actresses' androgyny and all that it might stand for as an indefinable quality rather than patent lesbianism—which would have shocked rather than enchanted the general public. Hollywood's formula was to compel the viewer by a species of sex appeal whose nature was never quite articulated, and thereby to attract both male and female fans. One of Alla Nazimova's

women lovers described her as being "like a naughty little boy" when they were alone,[56] but Nazimova was most successful when she understood that her public image needed to be nuanced and ambiguous. "I am a mystery for the Americans, and that is my biggest advertisement," she realized,[57] and like other silent screen stars of flexible sexuality, such as Pola Negri and Nita Naldi,[58] she perfected the vamp image, masking lesbian characteristics in a kind of hypersexuality: The vamp "lolled about on tiger skins and shot glances, seductive or sinister, from beneath hooded lids,"[59] pulling men to her not because she desired them but rather to teach them how weak they were. Nazimova's aggressive sexuality was patently masculine, though its lesbian connections were hidden.

Though fans had little notion of what lay beneath the androgynous screen images that seduced them, behind the high, protective walls of Hollywood, at private gatherings, unstraight actresses felt they did not need to play the movie game. The director Billy Wilder recalled, in a 1988 interview, how fifty years earlier Marlene Dietrich had spoken openly in front of his party guests about her lesbian experiences, declaring: "Women are better."[60] Bankhead and Dietrich even felt safe enough with their Hollywood crowd to conceive a bawdy jest as a comment on local gossip that the two of them were having an affair: They smeared gold dust between them in telling places and appeared thus at a Hollywood gathering, "providing indisputable evidence that the gossips were right," and then "laugh[ing] like schoolgirls over the prank."[61] In 1932, when Paramount briefly considered replacing Dietrich with Bankhead in the tuxedo role in *Blonde Venus,* Bankhead is reported to have quipped loudly at the offer, "Oh, goodie, I always wanted to get into Marlene's pants."[62]

Other women stars, too, felt that they did not need to play the movie game in front of Hollywood intimates; they could reveal themselves. Scott Berg, a personal friend of Katharine Hepburn's, reports that soon after he met her, Hepburn introduced her companion of many years, Phyllis Wilbourn, as her "Alice B. Toklas" (the woman who was Gertrude Stein's lover and literary assistant). When Wilbourn remarked, "I wish you wouldn't say that. It makes me sound like an old lesbian, and I'm not," Hepburn, assuming that Berg, a Hollywood gay man, would appreciate the in-joke, retorted, "You're not what, dearie, old or a lesbian?" But

in public, Wilbourn was presented as being merely in Hepburn's employ.[63] Such a guise before the public was common. Nazimova, for instance, played the movie game by calling Glesca Marshall, her lover for the last sixteen years of her life, her "secretary." "She had to," Nazimova's friend Robert Lewis observed. "Employment depended on keeping your nose clean." Hollywood, which Lewis ambivalently called "the dirtiest place in America," was "the most eager to keep everything clean [in front of the public]."[64]

Though Hepburn never ceased to be what her close friend George Cukor called "mannish,"[65] she eventually learned to play the game by being circumspect about her personal life. She dared to express the depth of her feeling for Wilbourn openly only at Wilbourn's funeral, when, as an observer wrote, "Kate suddenly dropped to her knees and sobbed."[66] Perhaps Hepburn had learned to be careful in public when she discovered, shortly after coming to Hollywood in 1932 with the actress Laura Harding (with whom, Hepburn admitted, she was "fascinated"),[67] that their relationship was gossiped about so loudly in Hollywood that "even New York was buzzing with it."[68] Hepburn writes in *Me,* her autobiography, that when she first met Spencer Tracy even he (whom she presents in her book as the love of her life) "imagined that [she] was a lesbian."[69]

One of Hepburn's intimates, Irene Selznick (the daughter of Louis B. Mayer and the wife of David O. Selznick), described Hepburn as "a double-gaiter." When the biographer Scott Berg told Irene Selznick that he was reluctant to make assumptions about Hepburn's relationships with women since Hepburn had always claimed that "nobody really knows what goes on between two people when they're alone," Selznick replied, "That's my point." She then chastised Berg for his naïveté, saying of Hepburn's friends such as Dorothy Arzner, Nancy Hamilton, and Laura Harding, "You're too young to have known all those other women, those single women. I knew them. I knew who they were."[70]

Before she became a movie actress, Hepburn had been married to Ludlow Ogden Smith, a Philadelphia socialite, but the marriage was not a happy one,[71] and a recent Hepburn biographer offers some evidence to suggest that Smith was homosexual.[72] Hepburn left him to go off to Hollywood with Laura Harding. A couple of years later, Hepburn and Laura

Harding flew to Mexico, where Hepburn divorced Smith. The two women continued to live together in Hollywood for years, though Hepburn came to understand that she needed to be very guarded about her unstraight life when she talked to her fans. She did not hide Harding from public view, but she called her in fan magazines, such as *Motion Picture* in 1937, her "inseparable secretary-companion."[73] In later years, Hepburn seemed even more anxious to obfuscate her relationship with Laura Harding, lying about the length of time she and Harding were together, claiming in her autobiography that "after about two years, Laura went back to New York." But as the 1937 *Motion Picture* article indicates, Laura Harding, who came to Hollywood with Hepburn in 1932, was still there with her five years later.

The fan magazines much preferred, of course, that stars play the movie game by giving them an exciting story about a heterosexual romance rather than one about an "inseparable secretary-companion." The magazine writers seemed to breathe a collective sigh of relief when the androgynous Hepburn, whom movie critics were describing as having "a strident, raucous, rasping voice" and "a broad-shouldered, boyish figure,"[74] became a party to "the most celebrated Hollywood love story of the century."[75] They glommed on to the story of Hepburn's love affair with Spencer Tracy with delight; that Tracy was a married man who said he couldn't divorce his wife because he was Catholic made little difference. Several Hollywood historians, such as Richard Gully in *Vanity Fair* and Anne Edwards in *Publishers Weekly,* have suggested that Tracy was, in fact, bisexual, and that he and Hepburn, who were undeniably close friends, were also "beards" for one another.[76]

Fandom did not want to be bothered with complex truths, nor with being forced to analyze the nature of the tremendous appeal to both women and men of the Dietrichs and Hepburns and other sexually flexible, gender-bending stars. Most fans would not have wanted to learn that the styles they admired in those stars were actually rooted in a particular subculture, the name of which they could not have brought themselves even to whisper. But those who lived their lesbian experiences in 1930s Hollywood, and communicated in their films the styles that were iconographically lesbian, were a powerful influence across

America. Josef von Sternberg, the director of Dietrich's early films, recalls in his biography that he had not realized it would "stimulate a fashion" when Dietrich, a transvestite off the screen, too, appeared in men's attire in *Morocco;* but he was astonished that that was precisely the effect the film had, that it caused multitudes of straight American women for the first time in history to "ignore skirts in favor of . . . male attire."[77] It was the influence on American women of Dietrich (as well as other androgynous actresses such as Garbo and Hepburn) that the songwriters Richard Rogers and Lorenz Hart had in mind when they wrote "I'm One of the Boys":

I've always had a passion
To wear the latest fashion.
That's why I have to look like this today.
I'm one of the boys, just one of the boys.
I go to the tailor that Marlene employs.
No dresses from France are so modern as these,
And under my pants are BVD's.[78]

The new look and comportment popularized by the androgynous, unstraight women stars of the 1930s truly alarmed reactionary forces in America, who soon reacted. By the mid-1930s, the film industry, already financially hit by the Depression, had reason to panic about the pressure that churchly groups were exerting on the studios to make movies that were "100 percent pure or else,"[79] as the *Hollywood Reporter* lamented after a Catholic boycott spread across the country. The efforts to shut down the sinful film industry continued throughout the decade. Censorship advocates were opposed to anything in movies that smacked of human sexuality, but they were particularly vehement against homosexuality. "Don't go near the films. You must do without them if you want to save your soul," Cardinal William O'Connell, the archbishop of Boston, hysterically admonished "all good women, Catholic and non-Catholic" in 1938. What bothered him more than anything else about the movies of the 1930s, he revealed in a speech to a Congress of Catholic Women, were their lesbian and feminist messages: "Just as there is something

queer in being an effeminate man, it is equally queer to find a mannish woman. There is something abnormal in a woman attempting to dress in men's clothes," he proclaimed, concluding that the "modern pagan ideas [in the movies] shattered the ideal . . . that women's first and principal place is in the home."[80]

But whether or not such pronouncements frightened off heterosexual women, the unstraight across America must surely have taken heart from those alluring androgynous images of stars who, they could sense (despite fan magazine lies), were somehow like them. Young women who loved women could learn how to look and act "lesbian" even without access to an urban lesbian subculture. As the author of a 1933 book supporting movie censorship observed disapprovingly, the movies were giving young females lesbian ideas: He quotes a sixteen-year-old girl who happily proclaims, "I have one girlfriend that I love a good deal. . . . It is on her that I make use of the different ways of kissing that I see in the movies," and a seventeen-year-old who reports that she practices with her girlfriend the love scenes they see in movies: "We sometimes think we could beat Greta Garbo."[81]

The early women stars who played out their sexual flexibility and androgyny in the private setting of the Hollywood community—and then subtly communicated who they were through Hollywood films—have always fired the imagination of the unstraight everywhere. The 1930s images showing Garbo kissing her lady-in-waiting in *Queen Christina*, Marlene Dietrich flirting with women in *Morocco* and *Blonde Venus*, and Katherine Hepburn in her boy clothes in *Sylvia Scarlett* form what has been called "the foundation of lesbian film culture."[82] These films became icons of lesbian history not only because of the unstraight characters they presented but also because lesbian viewers intuited the complex sexuality of the women who played those characters. And the lesbian viewers did not have to rely solely on intuition: Despite the stars' attempts to play the movie game and keep confined to their Hollywood circles whatever was not straight in their lives, the secrets were whispered among lesbians in Chattanooga and Boise as well as in New York and Boston. Hollywood gay gossip has somehow always jumped the town's boundaries.

THE FRATERNITY

> *Jim soon had a well-defined and well-interpreted picture of Hollywood and the abnormal underworld which here existed closer to the surface than anywhere else in America. It was said that of all the handsome leading men all but a few were abnormal and even these few were under constant surveillance by the others, waiting for a single indication to include them in the fraternity.*
>
> —Gore Vidal, *The City and the Pillar*[83]

When it became widely known in Hollywood that Cary Grant and Randolph Scott (who had been lovers for years) were leaving their wives on weekends to spend private time together at their beach house, RKO executives, fearing that the gossip would leak beyond the industry borders, gave Grant an ultimatum: He must choose between continuing the relationship with Scott and having his contract renewed.[84] In contrast, when Janet Gaynor and Mary Martin, who were also lovers, took a vacation together (leaving their homosexual husbands at home), fan magazines considered it "charming for them to enjoy some time for 'girl talk'"—as their desire to be alone was naively dubbed. Gender ambiguity and "romantic friendships"[85] such as female stars could enjoy without suspicion were verboten for male stars, who were pressured to conform to the "red-blooded" image of virility that Hollywood manufactured and marketed.

But the film colony was a bohemian and artistic world that offered unprecedented opportunities for gay expression.[86] As William Mann has pointed out in *Behind the Scenes,* men with gay sensibilities were well represented among the shapers of early Hollywood—as set and costume designers as well as actors, directors, and screenwriters.[87] Nevertheless, the coercion to be discreet, to play the movie game, was severe. The male gay "underworld," as Gore Vidal characterized it, may have "existed [in Hollywood] closer to the surface than anywhere else in America"; but before the 1950s (when women, too, started to come under suspicion and scrutiny), it was far more important for gay and unstraight men than it was for lesbians and unstraight women to keep the secrets of their extraordinary world hidden from those outside the industry enclave. Even

inside Hollywood, gay men were often much more nervous than their female counterparts. Noel Coward, who had come to Hollywood from London to write screenplays, warned his friend, the aspiring photographer Cecil Beaton, "Your sleeves are too tight, your voice is too high and precise. You mustn't do it. It closes so many doors . . . I take ruthless stock of myself in the mirror before going out. A polo jumper or unfortunate tie exposes one to danger."[88]

Malcolm Boyd, who worked as a publicist and producer, recalls being forced to similar discretions: "If you wanted to stay, the rules were quite clear. I didn't let my guard down." When gay men did relax their guard, they paid for it with anxiety, Boyd suggests; he recalls a romantic dinner in a restaurant following an afternoon in bed with a lover: "I wasn't thinking, and we were actually holding hands. Then one of the top journalists in town walked up, with his wife. I felt panicked. I woke up fast. It killed the romance—the entire night was ruined. I had let my guard down."[89]

Leonard Spigelgass, a screenwriter, observed that within the industry enclave there was an "awful ambivalence" about male homosexuality. It "was held in major contempt." And yet it was also "the most exclusive club." Those who were strictly straight in Hollywood were kept out of it—to their ostensible envy, because they were thus barred from the cultured world of Cole Porter, Larry Hart, George Cukor, Somerset Maugham, and Noel Coward: "On the one hand, if you said, 'They're homosexual,' 'Oh, my, isn't that terrible' was the reaction," Spigelgass recalled. "On the other hand, if you said, 'My God, the other night I was at dinner with Cole Porter,' the immediate reaction was, 'What did he have on? What did he say? Were you at the party? Were you at one of those Sunday Brunches?'"[90]

If any suspicion of homosexual behavior leaked out beyond Hollywood, the popular media could be merciless in its language of shock and disgust. When the director William Desmond Taylor arrived in Hollywood in 1915, he kept his private life discreet to the point that he was considered "mysterious"; but his houseman was arrested in Westlake Park for procuring boys whose services only the director could afford.[91] When an unknown assailant murdered Taylor in 1922, panicked Paramount representatives, fearing that an investigation would reveal Taylor's

homosexuality, hurried to the murder scene. Desperate to avoid a scandal, they tried to remove all gay traces before the police arrived. According to some accounts, they even planted "evidence" suggesting that Taylor had numerous girlfriends.[92] But they could not avert the suspicions of the popular media. Newspapers around the country reported that Taylor belonged to an "unnatural love cult . . . comprised entirely of men";[93] that his houseman and his former secretary were "both said to be 'queer persons'"[94] and that Taylor's companions were "people of doubtful character—men who sew and crochet and embroider, women of queer reputation."[95] There was also much speculation about whether Taylor was "abnormal himself." The newspapers angrily complained of a Hollywood cover-up when the *Los Angeles Times* suppressed the rumors about Taylor's homosexuality: "It is quite true the movie world would prefer the thing handled in silence, even ignored," one reporter declared. "The movie interests would spend millions of dollars not to catch the murderers; but to prevent the real truth from coming out, to avert the exposure of Hollywood, to squelch before it is born the scandal of the century."[96]

The reporter was right about the studios' willingness to pay those with the power "to prevent the real truth from coming out": The Motion Picture Production Association made generous "contributions" to city officials; moonlighting police officers were hired to guard movie productions at good salaries. They helped the studios continue to hush up scandals for at least the next half-century: As an L.A. police historian, Joe Domanick, points out, studios "needed to protect [their] stars and other key players from career-destroying scandals. . . . Carousing wild men like Errol Flynn and homosexual stars were constantly being picked up by the LAPD, but never booked."[97]

Behind-the-scenes connections could not, of course, protect every star. Suspicions of homosexuality caused a mini-riot in El Porto, a small beach community south of Los Angeles, where the movie star William Haines and his lover Jimmy Shields had summered for years and hosted parties for their gay film friends. The Hollywood trade-paper columns had factually noted such parties: "George Cukor, Billy Haines, and a lot of others are week-ending at Laguna these week-ends";[98] but the small beach community was not as blasé as Hollywood appeared to be. In the

summer of 1936, Haines, Shields, and several friends (Cukor possibly among them) were attacked by a mob that alleged Shields had molested a minor. The crowd hurled tomatoes at the men, beat them, and booted them out of town. The scandal effectively ended Haines' career. To protect his own reputation, Cukor ceased to see Haines for years; Shields left the country for a time.[99] Hollywood gay elders remember to this day the horror of "Billy Haines being tarred and feathered out at the beach."[100]

But despite the dangers outside of Hollywood, "the fraternity" was ubiquitous within Hollywood. In 1932, the columnist for the "Hollywood Lowdown" snickered, "Discretion forbids particular mention of names in this case, but at least two prominent young men of the films owe their rapid rise to such arrangement with older men in the picture game who are not averse to helping young boys along."[101] Harry Hay, a gay man who was an actor in the 1930s, recalled that "the sexual path to the screen was more than fifty per cent," though he added that, in his experience, gay social connections could be as valuable as sexual ones: "I knew a couple of producers from underground gay scenes and got parts occasionally from them—never from my agent."[102] The career of Ralph Graves, a handsome silent-screen actor, was also helped along by gay connections—though Graves himself was unstraight rather than gay. He admitted to the film historian Anthony Slide that he'd "been in bed with a couple of fairies," including Noel Coward and Somerset Maugham during their Hollywood stints; and that he'd spent "two years of my life, every day, every night" in an "unholy relationship" with the comedy director Mack Sennett.[103] A young Tyrone Power, according to his biographer, "was approached by several wealthy homosexuals" when he first hit Hollywood, and he became a "kept boy,"[104] as Gary Cooper was said to have been in the 1920s.[105] Though male homosexuality was met with opprobrium by the outside world, within a secret Hollywood enclave, men who were open to it had a decided advantage.

Paradoxically, as despised as male homosexuality was in much of America, gay style, as it was presented through Hollywood personalities, had an in-

fluence on American men, just as lesbian style did on American women. Perhaps the most notable purveyor of gay style in the early decades of the twentieth century was Rudolph Valentino. "The Great Lover," as he was known, was so attractive to women fans that a top-selling brand of condoms was hopefully named "Sheik," after his eponymous role in *The Sheik* (1921). But women were not the only ones who found him attractive, as one of his contemporaries coyly suggested in describing "the spell Valentino cast over the entire female population—and some others."[106]

Valentino's style—his clothes, his grooming—were iconographically queer, and they created an absolute panic among homophobes, as a *Chicago Tribune* column revealed in 1925 when Valentino visited Chicago wearing what the writer sardonically described as "a symphony in green." But Valentino's green suit was only one of his items of apparel that caused the *Chicago Tribune* columnist to write hysterically, "Our gorge rises; our back hair prickles; we want to chew tobacco and spit; we want to . . . assert our masculinity." There was also the beaver collar on Valentino's coat and his slave bracelet. "What in the name of all things masculine is a slave bracelet?" the writer wailed. The worst of Valentino's offenses against butch America, according to the column, was that he was a style-setter, and his style was decidedly gay:

> It gives us a horrible sinking feeling at the pit of the stomach to know that within the next few days tailors and clothing stores will be swamped with requests for green suits, that overcoat buyers will demand beaver collars, that jewelers will be besought for slave bracelets—whatever they are—"just like Valentino's" (spoken with a lisp). Sadly we acknowledge to ourselves that this will happen.[107]

The following year, when Valentino's style-setting did not abate, he was again attacked in the *Chicago Tribune,* where the writer opined, in a column titled "Pink Powder Puffs," that someone ought to "quietly drown" Valentino because he encouraged men not only to pomade their hair but also to powder their faces. Valentino's deleterious influence, the columnist insisted, was even responsible for the installation of powder vending machines in men's washrooms, where men could now "hold a

kerchief beneath the spout, pull the lever, then take the pretty pink stuff and pat it on their cheeks in front of the mirror!" If one had to choose between male and female homosexual styles, the writer concluded with angry resignation, "better a rule by masculine women than by effeminate men."[108] Valentino's justified fury at the *Chicago Tribune* column created only another occasion for media mockery. Even the *Los Angeles Times* sneered at the actor's effeminacy with comments about his "pounding, indignant heart beneath a fresh gardenia," and headlines such as "Rudy's So Sore, It's Just Awful" and "Why, He Wants to Fight Duel with Vile Detractor."[109]

Valentino's threat to the nation's masculinity was exacerbated by various rumors about his affairs with his fellow actor Ramon Novarro and later with the French actor André Daven.[110] His wives, Jean Acker and Natacha Rambova, had both been romantically involved with Alla Nazimova (who was said to have orchestrated their marriages to Valentino);[111] and both his wives' sexuality and gender behavior (Jean Acker drove a motorcycle) helped to fuel further speculation that he himself was gay. It was also widely known in Hollywood that Acker did not spend her honeymoon night with Valentino, and that she left him the day after her marriage to resume a lesbian relationship with Grace Darmond.[112] The only other well-publicized "heterosexual relationship" Valentino had in Hollywood was with Pola Negri, who, after a dramatically staged mourning for him when he died, went on to live the rest of her life in a lesbian relationship.[113] Though the jury is still out among Valentino biographers about whether the actor was truly gay,[114] the popular press had little doubt that he was, and that his flamboyant style, rooted in homosexuality, was posing a clear threat to the traditional definition of the American male.

LAVENDER COUPLING

. . . our neuter relationship
(Publicized as "super" in Movieland):
So—between films, while he romped with men . . .

I drew plans and built a new suite
Apart from my would-be mate. . . .
("On your left, you see the great movie star's
Gorgeous Garden of Alla without an 'h'.")

—From Alla Nazimova's 1926 poem, "Not That It Matters," on her "lavender marriage" with the actor Charles Bryant[115]

Already by 1921, in the wake of the Fatty Arbuckle scandal about his alleged rape and murder of a young woman, studios were beginning to include a "morality clause" in their contracts; in effect, these clauses said that "an actor who commits any act tending to offend or outrage public morals and decency will be given five days' notice of the cancellation of his contract."[116] Though the morality clause was instituted in response to heterosexual wrongdoing, homosexuals had reason to fear it. Once the movies became a wildly lucrative business, studio bosses, who had a great deal to lose monetarily if a star's personal life "offended or outraged" the fans, became absolutely dictatorial about the public image of their stars, on screen as well as off. The studio bosses believed that in return for fat contracts, their stars were under obligation to appear—if not actually to be—"moral." If homosexuality was immoral in the mind of the general public, gay and lesbian actors needed to convince the public that they were straight, even to the extent of concocting pap for the media about their personal lives.[117]

Fan magazines adored articles about who was dating or marrying or pining for whom, and actors were usually happy to cooperate, whether or not their romances were real. The straight storybook love affairs gay actors invented not only kept them from coming under fire but also garnered great publicity, which was life's blood to Hollywood stars. Lesley Ferris dates bogus Hollywood couplings back to the 1920s, suggesting that the studios were as desperate then as they were in later decades "to cover up and divert attention from same-sex relationships."[118] Hollywood insiders adopted an extensive secret vocabulary to describe publicity pairings that involved nonheterosexuals, such as "twilight tandems," "beards," "front dating," and "lavender marriages."

Some of these actors married repeatedly. Cary Grant, his long-term affair with Randolph Scott notwithstanding, was married five times, generally in great unhappiness.[119] Tyrone Power's two marriage attempts were likened by his biographer to the attempts of a light-skinned black person to "pass." While married, Power patronized Smitty Hanson, a discreet gay hustler who was trusted by a number of Hollywood actors.[120] The more successful a gay or unstraight actor became, the more intense grew studio (and self-imposed) pressures on him or her to hide true proclivities. But Hollywood front marriages were not limited to the actors. Even a power player such as Mike Connolly, whose "Rambling Reporter" column could make or break reputations, might feel the pressure. Connolly, a gay man, often made homophobic quips in his columns, such as referring to gay men on Fairfax Avenue, a predominantly Jewish neighborhood, as "gefilte swish." Connolly had lived in a long-term relationship with another man, but, inspired by the successful ruse of Rock Hudson's front marriage to Phyllis Gates, the lesbian secretary of his agent, Connolly, too, arranged to marry a woman friend. He called off the "engagement" when he realized it would bring more attention to his homosexuality rather than less: A rival columnist had queried, "Which columnist with a raised pinky is going to shock all of Hollywood and get married?"[121]

Male actors, even those who played character roles, could never afford to risk fandom's knowledge of their homosexuality, though character actresses felt freer. The comedian Patsy Kelly, for instance, whose walk was characterized by one fan magazine writer as being "as near a sailor's roll as the swagger of an old salt,"[122] dared to declare in the fan magazine *Motion Picture* that she had been living for several years with another actress, Wilma Cox. Obviously, she was not free to use the "L" word in the 1930s, but she could say that the home she'd made with Wilma was decorated in blue and white because those were Wilma's favorite colors; that instead of dating, "often Wilma and I have a few folks in for the evening," and that she had no thoughts of marrying because "I'm having too much fun as I am. . . . I like my life. I'm happy."[123] No male actor would dare make such declarations in the 1930s.

The screen director, Dorothy Arzner, who appeared on sets almost always in virtual drag, openly attributed her ability as a director to her

"masculine characteristics," as she told *Motion Picture Studio Insider* in 1937.[124] Though she, too, certainly never admitted in print to being a lesbian—no one among her contemporaries did, except for the author of *The Well of Loneliness*—neither did she feel compelled to hide the fact that she had lived for almost half a century, until death did them part, with a woman, Marion Morgan, who was the director of a highly successful dance troupe and choreographer of Arzner's first four films.[125] Though Arnzer was not totally unscathed by her openness (Lucille Ball's biographer claims that Ball was "embarrassed by widespread gossip about Miss Arzner's lesbianism" and was unhappy about working with her),[126] nevertheless, by virtue of her "masculinity," Arzner was taken seriously in what was considered a man's profession. She was the only woman to have a significant career behind the megaphone from the 1920s to the 1940s.

Though androgyny was sometimes part of their appeal, glamour actresses usually strove to make the public think of them as heterosexual—notwithstanding Tallulah Bankhead's revisionist wisecrack in the 1950s that she became "a Lez" when she was younger "because I needed the publicity. I had to get a job, [and] in the '20s and '30s, a Lesbian was tops in desirability, especially with a girlfriend as a side dish."[127] Alla Nazimova realized that—in contradiction to the complex sexuality she communicated through her screen image—she had to pretend for the fans that in "real life" she was uncomplicated and traditional. For years she claimed to be married to actor Charles Bryant, though the marriage was never legalized and Bryant apparently preferred his own sex, as Nazimova's 1926 poem suggests (see above). She felt compelled to take publicity photos that showed her sitting on Bryant's knee, leaning against his shoulder, and smiling up at him in adoration.[128] When Nazimova forgot herself, acting out too publicly her lesbian relationship with Glesca Marshall, the "Rambling Reporter" reminded her, through a snide reference to "a certain foreign actress" and her "wife," that indiscretion robbed her of the charm of mystery.[129]

Gay and lesbian actors who were buddies sometimes paired up, genuinely liking one another enough to spend years of their lives cohabiting, though continuing to have homosexual relationships that were well hidden from the fans. The silent-screen star Lilyan Tashman, whose lesbian

life has been documented by several Hollywood historians,[130] was married to gay actor Edmund Lowe. Together they were the darlings of the fan magazines and gossip columnists, cooperating often for articles such as *Photoplay*'s "How to Hold a Husband/Wife in Hollywood":

> He: "I like elegance. There's always a delicate odor of sachet about my shirts and handkerchiefs. Lilyan puts it there."
>
> She: "A woman can easily learn how to make herself attractive, how to make her home attractive."[131]

Sleek and sophisticated Tashman, who was described by the movie magazine writer Gladys Hall as "the most gleaming, glittering, moderne, hard-surfaced, and distingué woman in all of Hollywood," even told Hall in a 1931 interview about her joyous anticipation of "maternity, nursing bottles, formulas, layettes, obstetricians, and teething problems."[132] She never gave birth to a child. As the Hollywood historian William Mann explains about such public pretense, stars like Tashman and Lowe were merely following "the protocol of the times."[133] They accepted the fact that their Hollywood careers demanded they play the movie game by appearing to be heterosexual, regardless of where they fell on the Kinsey Scale.

But even stars who resisted the game were made a party to it: Not even Greta Garbo, who was notoriously disgusted by the media's attempts to pry into her personal business, could escape. In the privacy of Hollywood, Garbo made little attempt to mask her life. Aldous Huxley recalled the first time he went to Garbo's home, where he met her lesbian lover, Mercedes de Acosta, and then Garbo herself, "dressed like a boy."[134] In the early 1930s, Garbo permitted her affair with Mercedes, as well as her perpetual transvestism, to be common Hollywood knowledge. The *Hollywood Reporter* regularly ran items such as "Greta Garbo buys men's suits for herself—from Watson, the Tailor,"[135] and discussed her "self-made man" look. The "Rambling Reporter" called Garbo "ambidextrous," referred to Mercedes as her "new love," and noted her visits to "lavender" speakeasies.[136] When Mercedes de Acosta was replaced in Garbo's affections by Salka Viertel, the *Hollywood Reporter* even carried an item hinting at their triangle.[137]

But such gossip seldom escaped the confines of Hollywood, and Garbo's letters to Mercedes show that she worked to keep hints of their relationship from leaking out to fandom. Garbo's nervousness about being "outed" outside of Hollywood was so intense that she often admonished Mercedes with words such as "You must not put my name on any letter. . . . And please be sure to glue envelopes well together as your letters usually come opened."[138]

The fan magazines were complicitous in keeping Garbo's secret because they knew that moviegoers wanted desperately to believe that Hollywood's hottest star was uncomplicatedly and romantically heterosexual, and they were overjoyed when they were able to report an ostensible affair between Garbo and John Gilbert. (Gilbert claimed privately that when he proposed marriage to Garbo, her response was, "Ah, you don't want to marry one of the fellows.")[139] Garbo did have heterosexual relationships—most biographers agree in placing the director Reuben Mamoulian, the conductor Leopold Stokowski, and the actor Brian Aherne among her lovers; but in their zealousness, fan magazines as well as gossip columnists for the nontrade papers also matched her with her gay male buddies. Hedda Hopper, writing in the *Los Angeles Times,* for instance, exuded about Garbo's road trip with the health guru, Gayelord Hauser (who was, in fact, in a long-term domestic relationship with another man, Frey Brown): "Those marriage rumors are again being revived. I do know that [Greta and Gayelord] took a picnic lunch and spent the whole day sitting together on a piece of land, trying to make up their minds whether a home should be built on it."[140]

As years went by and Garbo married no one, the fan magazines, scrambling for an explanation to give their readers, put out the word that it was because she never got over a youthful love for the Swedish director Mauritz Stiller (who was dead and had been gay).[141] "Why is it that the most alluring woman on the screen today has never married? What strange reason exists which keeps the most excitingly beautiful Garbo from committing matrimony?" one fan magazine asked, then informed readers that "the answer to the riddle of why Garbo never married . . . [despite her romance with John Gilbert] that thrilled the whole world" was to be found "in that far away grave in Sweden."[142] It is not improbable that Greta

Garbo's famous wish to "be alone" was born of her disgust with such constant attempts to place her in heterosexual dyads, her distaste for the movie game, and her fear that the public would discover that her real predilections were much more complex than *Photoplay* could process.

A LOSING GAME

> *"I think a woman wants to be dominated by a man. Men are much cleverer than women. A dominating woman cannot be happy."*
>
> —Marlene Dietrich, *Los Angeles Herald Examiner*, July 15, 1951

During the postwar years, while Joseph McCarthy baited reds and gays and women trotted back to nurseries and kitchens, the movies and the tastes of fans changed dramatically. As Gary Carey observed in his biography of Louis B. Mayer: "More and more pictures were dedicated to upholding the dignity of motherhood, family life, and other sacred values of middle-class America."[143] The girlish foppery of Armand as played by both Rudolph Valentino and Robert Taylor in Hollywood productions of *Camille* (1921 and 1936) would have caused bloody riots in the movie houses of the 1950s. The studios would have thought it suicidal in the 1950s to make films such as *Morocco* or *Queen Christina* in which the leading ladies were dressed as men. In 1937, Hepburn's "hoydenish" appearance[144] was considered charming by the fans, but twenty years later, in 1957, the fan magazines were complaining that "she allowed herself to be photographed without make-up . . . and, even worse, dressed hideously in mannish garb—sloppy slacks, sweaters, and men's trousers and suits."[145] Androgynous women stars such as Hepburn, Dietrich, and Garbo were out, and superfemmes such as Marilyn Monroe and Jayne Mansfield were in. Gay actors such as Rock Hudson were typed as heterosexual wolves (despite the open secret in Hollywood that he was a homosexual wolf). Gay fans may have continued to discern who was unstraight in Hollywood, but heterosexual moviegoers were more snug than ever in their oblivion, unless, that is, scandal magazines called homosexuality to their attention. The stars and studios did all they could to keep the fans in the dark.

Though actors and actresses had to play the movie game in earlier eras too, in the 1950s it became very serious business: To convince the public of their normality they stooped to such absurd utterances as Dietrich's hypocritical statement, quoted above, about a woman's place. Studios exacerbated the actors' anxieties to appear "normal" by routinely admonishing them that they must be accompanied by a person of the opposite sex at all public appearances, and they must never be seen at gay bars.[146] They must, above all, keep themselves out of the scandal magazines—*Confidential, Whisper, Blast, Uncensored, Rave, Top Secret,* and a host of others—which had suddenly emerged and enjoyed vast circulation in the 1950s. (*Confidential*'s readership, for example, was about 5 million in 1957,[147] outstripping both the *Saturday Evening Post* and *Look.)* Unlike the fan magazines, which had avoided stories that readers would find shocking (and thereby protected the stars), the scandal magazines traded in shock. Before the proliferation of scandal magazines, what happened in Hollywood behind high walls and hedges would stay there. But the scandal magazines' staff pounced on the film colony, scaling barriers that could never be fortified enough against them, and produced salacious, career-sabotaging headlines about infidelity, divorce, legal trouble, alcohol and drug problems—and especially about homosexuality, which, in the 1950s, was thought to be more scandalous than all the other topics put together. The actor George Nader, who was part of the mid-1950s gay circle around Rock Hudson, recalls: "We lived in fear of an exposé, or even a veiled suggestion that someone was homosexual. Such a remark would have caused an earthquake at the Studio. Every month, when *Confidential* came out, our stomachs began to turn. Which of us would be in it?"[148]

Hollywood powerbrokers sometimes found ways to protect their "star assets," even gay ones, from the perils of scandal magazines. The agent Henry Willson, himself a homosexual, was one of the most powerful players in 1950s Hollywood, known as the man who "discovered, named, represented, promoted, pimped and protected"[149] a stable of male stars. Willson invented the "postwar hunk," including Tab Hunter, Rock Hudson, Troy Donahue, and dozens more. Not only did Willson hire Los Angeles Police Department (LAPD) off-duty "goons [and] leg-breakers" to silence

the ex-lovers of his clients who threatened to sell their stories to the tabloids but he also engaged in deals with those tabloids. For example, he negotiated with *Confidential* in 1955 to protect his prize client, Rock Hudson, from a ruinous gay exposé by feeding them Tab Hunter instead (who had by then left Willson for another agent): Willson informed *Confidential* about a police report on a gay party in Glendale where Hunter had been arrested with twenty-six other men for same-sex dancing.[150] *Confidential* was happy with the exchange: They luridly characterized the incident as a "gay pajama party." (In his memoirs, published when he was seventy-three, Hunter admitted his homosexuality but denied there was anything other than harmless drinking and dancing at that particular party.) But studio heads, too, could and did maneuver to save a star: Hunter found himself "magically" rescued by Harry Weiss, the attorney who, he says, "was on call to agents, producers, and studio bosses."[151]

Gay stars who were not under a powerful protective wing had good reason to be terrified of Robert Harrison, the publisher of *Confidential*, because he was absolutely obsessive in his preoccupation with revealing their homosexuality. According to Steve Govoni, the son of *Confidential*'s managing editor, Harrison would spend many thousands of dollars if necessary to check facts and line up witnesses who would corroborate the stories of Hollywood's homosexual peccadilloes. Govoni claims that the magazine never simply made up a story out of whole cloth. *Confidential*, as well as most of the other scandal magazines, hired spies in moving companies (to tell them who was moving in or out of a dwelling), among sales clerks (who informed them of tidbits such as Dan Dailey's purchase of a dress for his own use), and in houses of prostitution. They had paid informants among waiters and hatcheck girls and hotel maids and bail bondsmen; and they employed an army of private detectives, wiretap experts, and hidden-microphone specialists.[152]

Against such forces, stars were helpless. In the sexually conservative and suspicious 1950s, women were under as much scrutiny as men. Lizabeth Scott was very much a Dietrich type; she had cool, blonde good looks and what Hedda Hopper described in various columns as a "caramel contralto" voice[153] and "a million dollar figure."[154] She was selected in 1946 as one of *Modern Screen* magazine's "Stars of the Month,"

and she made eighteen pictures in nine years, four of them in 1947. But she was not wily in playing the movie game, and she failed to produce a requisite "beard." In a 1946 article, she claimed to have no time for romance, and by 1949 Dorothy Manners was profiling her before the public as a "confirmed career girl."[155] In a 1951 interview that Hedda Hopper titled "Star By-passes Romance for Career," Scott knew enough not to be entirely dismissive when Hopper snooped for a man in the actress's life: In answer to the question, "What about romance?" Scott replied (much as Patsy Kelley did in the 1930s), "Right now, I'm having a ball, Hedda. I wouldn't give it up for anything"; yet she was quick to add, "Tomorrow is another day. I may meet that certain guy and flip completely."[156] But her attempts to pose as heterosexual were too perfunctory.

Robert Harrison was thus alerted to search for dirt, which he found and blared to millions of readers in a September 1955 *Confidential* article: "Lizabeth Scott in the Call Girls' Call Book." The article presented Scott not only as a lesbian who wore pants and was called "Scotty" but also as a habitué of an exclusive Los Angeles house of prostitution, where she enjoyed the services of "a trio of cuddle-for-cash cuties." Instead of ignoring the article, as Dietrich had done two months earlier when *Confidential* ran a story that exposed her lesbianism ("The Untold Story of Marlene Dietrich"), Lizabeth Scott sued the magazine. Papers around the country carried news of the suit and, of course, the reasons for it. *Confidential*'s allegations thus reached not only the magazine's audience but tens of millions of newspaper readers. Scott's career was effectively ended. She made only three more pictures, two in 1957 and one in 1972. It became clear through her fate that stars could no longer assume that their gay secrets would be protected by Hollywood's high walls and hedges.

Fronting in the 1950s: the lesbian and gay "Cufflink Crowd," sitting boy-girl-boy-girl, at a straight nightclub. *Courtesy Tom Gibbon.*

Lovers Tom Gibbon and Bob Clark, members of the "Cufflink Crowd," who were careful never to attend all-male parties. *Courtesy Tom Gibbon.*

CHAPTER 3

L.A. Noir

THE UNDESIRABLES

The door opened silently and I was looking at a tall blond man in a white flannel suit with a violet satin scarf around his neck. There was a cornflower in the lapel of his white coat and his pale blue eyes looked faded out by comparison. The violet scarf was loose enough to show that he wore no tie and that he had a thick soft brown neck, like the neck of a strong woman. . . . He had the general appearance of a lad who would wear a white flannel suit with a violet scarf around his neck and a cornflower in his lapel.

—Raymond Chandler, *Farewell, My Lovely,* 1940[1]

As the 1940s began, Los Angeles literally darkened. Following the 1941 attack on Pearl Harbor, cities on the West Coast instituted blackouts, fearing they would be the next target. City dwellers were instructed to blacken windows and to cover with dark paint their skylights and the top halves of automobile headlights.[2] Wartime cast shadows everywhere. This period that was so dominated by darkness and dark suspicions introduced a long era in which the unfamiliar was despised and persecuted, even by public officials whose job it was to protect. The literary and film style of "noir," marked by shadowy lighting and a theme of urban corruption, reflected a new L.A. reality.

Within weeks after the Pearl Harbor bombing, 23,000 Japanese Americans from Los Angeles alone were sent to relocation camps.[3] But most other minorities too, including homosexuals, were deemed outsiders, dangerous to the "real" citizens of Los Angeles, and they were thus targets for police harassment, false arrest, and beatings. The LAPD even turned a blind eye to assaults by others on these outsiders, allowing, for instance, enlisted servicemen to beat scores of Mexican American youths with impunity during the 1943 "Zoot Suit Riots."[4] Survivors of the era who witnessed both racism and homophobia by the police are hard put to say which was worse. Stella Rush, a white gay woman who was close friends with a black man, recalls their being followed by the police after leaving a gay bar: They were stopped, questioned, and bullied—under suspicion not only that they were "a lezzie and a fairy" but also (simply because they were a black man and a white woman together) that he was a dope pusher and she was his victim, or that he was a pimp and she was a whore.[5]

The LAPD's increasing nervousness about "undesirable" populations was exacerbated by L.A.'s sudden and massive expansion. The war demanded ships and planes. Huge ship-building facilities and aerospace plants such as Lockheed, Douglas, Northrup-Grumman, and Hughes were soon established in the Los Angeles area. Hundreds of thousands of migrants came into L.A. to fill the newly created jobs. More than 230,000 workers, most of them men initially, were employed in the aerospace industry alone.

As the men were drafted into the military, women came to take their places, making more money than ever, wearing pants, learning independence, and generally becoming very different people than they'd been before. With increased job opportunities for women, the number who had the wherewithal to live as lesbians multiplied.[6] Gay male activity in Los Angeles also expanded during the war, as gay men who lived in L.A. at the time attest: Because L.A. has a port and vast numbers of soldiers landed there, far from watchful eyes "back home" and yearning for rest and recreation, they enjoyed unprecedented opportunities for gay experiences. Kenneth Marlowe observes that during wartime Pershing Square "was even gayer than its regular scene. And servicemen who

couldn't find an available female date could always find physical satisfaction waiting for them. Many took advantage of it."[7]

The military tried to prevent the inevitable, officers warning their soldiers about big-city homosexual snares before they hit the shore: "We were solemnly told that all the queers in California wore red neckties and hung out at the corner of Hollywood and Vine," a former marine remembers.[8] The military even attempted to keep its men away from L.A. gay spots by posting bold-lettered signs on the doors of the Hollywood Boulevard bars, Slim Gordon's and Bradley's; the downtown bars, the Gay Inn, the Gayway Café, and Smittys; and every other venue they suspected drew a gay crowd (eventually including, for servicewomen, the gay girls' bar, the If Club): "OUT OF BOUNDS TO MILITARY PERSONNEL," the signs proclaimed. But there were many places that military officials missed, and before the war was over, more than a dozen gay bars were doing business on or near Hollywood Boulevard alone. The bars were a huge success with soldiers looking for gay life. For example, at the men's bar of the downtown Biltmore Hotel, which had been a cruising spot even before the war, uniformed soldiers would be "packed three-deep," according to a gay patron.[9]

The war eventually helped to foster the building of permanent homosexual communities in Los Angeles. By one estimate, a quarter million "war migrants," both straight and gay, settled in Los Angeles during the first eight years of the 1940s. When military men and women completed their tours of duty, more came back to Los Angeles than to any other city.[10] Most returned for its sunshine and space and economic opportunities. But servicemen and -women who were gay found L.A. especially attractive because its size promised both anonymity and the possibility of being able to find a community. L.A.'s gay underground expanded greatly with the influx of these new populations, as did places where gay people could meet one another.

For symbolic and functional reasons, the beach was especially attractive to gay people. It represented the very edge of the continent, far away from "back home." It was an ideal cruising ground, where one could legitimately wear minimal clothing and look at others who were similarly unattired. During and after the war, veritable oases of gay life could be

found in the open at many Los Angeles beaches, where the atmosphere was celebratory, carnival-like, even lawless.

Lesbians remember congregating and sunning at a stretch of Venice Beach near a popular gay girls bar.[11] In Santa Monica, "Bitch Beach," as it was campily called, was, according to Jim Kepner, "a square mile of lesbians and gay men, being free like nowhere else I'd seen." Gay bars fronted the boardwalk; and lesbians and gay men of the era remember especially the Tropical Village—dubbed "the TV" by its regulars—an indoor-outdoor beach bar with a Polynesian décor that, as Kepner wrote, always attracted a huge crowd, "hunky beach boys in swim trunks, gentlemen in suits and ties—lesbians in equal number, hunky butches, some in male drag, femmes off *Vogue* covers."[12] One patron recalls that the singer Johnny Ray not only drank there, but occasionally stood up and performed for the crowd.[13]

At Muscle Beach in Venice, an open-air seaside gymnasium, Bob Mizer, a shy man who lived with his mother in Los Angeles, found eager models for his Hollywood-studio-style homoerotic photography.[14] Mizer established the Athletic Model Guild (AMG) in 1945. His pictures capitalized on the image of the "California boy," always tanned, frequently blond, and sporting little more than a mischievous grin. Many of his models were gay Hollywood hopefuls, though some—like Steve Reeves, who played Hollywood's Hercules—were straight. In exchange for their modeling services, Mizer supplied them with the photos they needed for their professional pursuits. By advertising his glossy beefcake prints in a magazine that he established, *Physique Pictorial,* Mizer helped to create a huge underground gay market and to sell the promise of a gay male paradise in Los Angeles. *Physique Pictorial* also provided the first national outlet for other gay photographers, including Bruce of Los Angeles, and artists such as Tom of Finland and "Art Bob."[15] Mizer also influenced later gay artists, such as David Hockney, who said that AMG photographs motivated him to settle in Los Angeles and inspired his own famous paintings of blond boys basking in the sun.[16]

Despite Mizer's successes, however, he found himself in trouble with the law. He was arrested on obscenity charges in 1947 and sentenced to six months in prison. The authorities were shocked by his photos of men

in Roman wrestler stances with oiled bodies and generously padded posing straps, antique-looking columns in the background, a modern Southern California swimming pool in the foreground.

To Chief of Police William Parker, the galloping growth of the city and the changes it brought in the years after the war were extremely troubling. Joe Domanick, the LAPD historian, observes that Parker nervously gave his police force terse orders: "Confront and command. Control the streets at all times. Always be aggressive. Stop crimes before they happen. Seek them out. Shake them down. Make that arrest."[17] For Los Angeles' gay men and lesbians, along with people of diverse racial and ethnic groups, life became much harder with the advent of Chief Parker ("Wild Bill Parker" gays and lesbians called him)[18] since they were the ones most often being sought out, shaken down, and arrested. Under Chief Parker's ascendancy, arrests for "sex perversion" crimes, involving primarily male homosexuals, jumped dramatically.[19]

For homosexuals, LAPD's persecution had also been exacerbated in the years after the war by the chilling medicalization of their "state" through the influence of the police department's leading criminal psychiatrist, Paul de River. De River believed that homosexuals, men and women, were a grave danger to society: They were seducers of children, he opined, and in their "wild sexual orgies" they even committed murder. In his book *The Sexual Criminal,* which became a text for police officers nationwide, it was claimed that he had examined "carefully and scientifically more sex perverts than any other person in the United States at the present time."[20] He recommended preventative treatment for those he called "sexual criminals" by imposing on them Spartan living, hard work, and—most important of all—electric shock therapy, "a minimum of two shocks a week."[21]

In an article titled "Increase in Sex Crimes Laid to War Influence," the *Los Angeles Times* reported that L.A. police claimed to have accumulated records on "10,000 . . . known sex offenders."[22] Politicians who seemed to believe that persecution of homosexuals gave them political

capital encouraged LAPD hounding: Police sweeps of gay bars and arrests of both gay men and lesbians on the streets were invariably worse immediately before elections, as if to demonstrate to the public that the incumbents were "cleaning up" sin and crime. Politicians' war on homosexuals was manifested in other ways as well. An Assembly Subcommittee on Public Morals for Southern California recommended that eight Hollywood and Sunset Strip establishments be closed because they were "gathering places for perverts." The subcommittee also recommended that the legislature "prohibit the sale of liquor in taverns to unescorted women," which meant that bars that catered primarily to gay women would be put out of business entirely.[23] The Los Angeles City Council, mindful of the subcommittee's recommendations, then enacted stringent laws "to drive degenerates out of public places, especially bars."[24]

The politicians, like their henchmen the police, insisted that merely by virtue of their homosexuality all gay people were outlaws. However, the more liberal California Supreme Court ruled against several legislative and police actions regarding gay life and gay venues. For example, when a bar's license was suspended in 1951 because the owner permitted "persons of known homosexual tendencies to congregate," the California Supreme Court "set aside" the suspension, decreeing that homosexuals had the right to patronize an establishment as long as they committed no overt acts of sexual misconduct on the premises.[25] In 1956, the California Legislature tried to challenge the supreme court's decree by passing a law that prohibited the licensing of gay bars on the grounds that they were "resorts for sexual perverts"; but in 1959, the court, citing its earlier finding, declared the 1956 law unconstitutional.[26]

In Los Angeles, too, the court was far more liberal than local politicians and the LAPD. For example, the 1898 city ordinance, passed to prohibit All Fool's Night masquerading, was used by the LAPD in mid-century to prosecute gay men as well as gay women who dressed in drag or in any way that was not considered gender-appropriate: The clothes Marlene Dietrich, Greta Garbo, and Katherine Hepburn wore regularly in the 1930s could have landed a woman a jail sentence during L.A.'s noir years. Arrests under the old ordinance were challenged twice by gay women in 1950: Both actually won their cases, the courts declaring that

a woman cannot be found guilty under the ordinance simply because she is wearing "slacks together with a coat similar to that commonly worn by men, plus the fact that her hair is worn short instead of long," unless there is "further evidence of an intent to conceal her identity."[27] But despite the court's declaration, which was published in the Los Angeles Municipal Code book and must surely have been known by the LAPD and the politicians who encouraged them, cross-dressing lesbians continued to be treated as criminals throughout the 1950s: They were harassed, arrested, and thrown into the city jail's "Big Daddy Tank" (just as gay men were thrown in the "Fruit Tank" of the same institution).[28]

THE MEN'S STORY

Young and good-looking policemen . . . go into a gay bar, act as they think a gay fellow should act, and wait for someone to talk to them. They offer someone a ride or accept a ride and that does it. Some of them play fair, inasmuch as they wait for the gay one to make a pass at them, but many others wait only long enough to get in the car before declaring the arrest. The officer's word, of course, will be taken as true, and they always count on the victim not wanting publicity. They know he will pay the fine and be quiet.

—Helen Branson, owner of a 1950s Hollywood gay bar for men[29]

Los Angeles, the newcomers said, was paradise. Jim Weatherford, who came to L.A. from West Virginia, likened it to the tropical island of Aruba, where he had guarded oil refineries during the war. William Bryan, who came from Cleveland, was sold on the balmy weather, which, he says, allowed him to wear his most successful cruising outfit, a Milkes-brand athletic undershirt, year-round. Malcolm Boyd, who entered the city via the broad boulevards and manicured gardens of Beverly Hills before finding a cramped Hollywood room for $5 a week, called it Babylon.[30] But while Los Angeles was a virtual paradise for post–World War II gay newcomers from other parts of the country, it held distinct danger.

Marvin Edwards remembers one night in 1950 when he learned firsthand about the danger. He'd arrived the year before from Detroit with

Dorr Legg, his older lover, who would soon become a legendary homophile organizer. When they parted after about a year together in Los Angeles, Edwards began to frequent a bar they'd previously visited as a couple: the Crown Jewel, located in downtown L.A., on 8th Street near Olive, not far from the central public library. Outside, over the door, a glowing neon crown beckoned. Patrons recall the bar as dark, elegantly appointed, and popular. Those who were respectably employed in downtown offices regularly packed the place after work. In contrast to rougher gay bars in the area, the Crown Jewel had a coat-and-tie dress code that customers were expected to follow.

That night in 1950 when Edwards returned to the Crown Jewel, he struck up a long conversation with an attractive man, and eventually they left the bar together. They weren't aware of it, but officers of the Los Angeles Police Department tailed the two men to Edwards' rented cottage. Edwards was lucky to be spared the worst of the traumas that many gay men endured at mid-century—arrest, booking, pleading, sentencing, and even jail time. But the officers informed his landlady that he'd brought a man to spend the night under her roof. She told Edwards that she could not tolerate that sort of thing. He would, of course, have to leave. Homeless, young Edwards left L.A. permanently.[31]

Harassment such as Edwards suffered was common. As Mike Rothmiller reports in his book *L.A. Secret Police,* officers were given specific orders to "go after" homosexuals.[32] Vice Squad officers often staked out homosexual bars, both gay and lesbian, and wreaked havoc on the lives of the patrons. Sometimes they raided the bars, carting selected patrons to the police station. Sometimes Vice Squad officers noted the license plate numbers of cars parked near a bar and informed the hapless patrons' employers. Job loss was common in such cases, and for those whose contracts included "morals clauses," such as teachers, or those who worked in L.A.'s booming aerospace industry, which required a security clearance, entire careers could be lost.

Harassment was only one of the techniques that the Vice Squad used to carry out its homophobic policies. Entrapment, such as that described by men's gay bar owner Helen Branson, was the squad's most pernicious method. Law enforcement departments across the country

practiced entrapment, using undercover officers to respond to and even solicit sexual come-ons, which would permit them to make an arrest. But LAPD officers were said by victims to excel in this cruel practice because "Hollywood rejects," attractive would-be actors who failed to find work in the movies, were employed by the vice squad to carry out entrapment scams.[33] Their looks and histrionic training enabled them to play the role of decoy especially effectively, as those who were fooled by them still remember.[34]

Some undercover Vice Squad officers became known among gay men, who would caution one another about familiar faces. Tom Gibbon says he narrowly escaped an all-too-typical nightmare one afternoon in the early 1950s: "I was at a bar called Johnny Frenchman's in Malibu. I'd had a few belts and went to use the can." On his way, he spotted two good-looking men sitting at a table who, he thought, had been previously pointed out to him as being from the LAPD Hollywood Division Vice Squad. He recalls that while he was using the small restroom's toilet, "suddenly I hear this voice say, 'Hi, how ya doing?'" His instinctive feeling was that it was one of the Vice Squad officers:

> I immediately thought, "Oh shit! There it goes—the job, the whole thing." When I leave the toilet, I'm careful not to look directly, because that can mean immediate trouble, but out of the corner of my eye I can see that the guy was standing at the urinal, jacking. As I head for the door, he turns, dick hard, and stands in my way. So if I try to leave the bathroom, I'd actually have to touch it, which would be a sure arrest. I didn't know what I was going to do. Somehow, I pushed his shoulder and threw him off balance just long enough to get out of there.[35]

When Gibbon made his way back to the bar, the bartender belatedly tipped him off that the man who had been in the restroom with him was indeed a Vice Squad officer.

Stanley Markowitz was not so astute and thus not so lucky. Markowitz recalls a 1957 incident at the Hollywood Greyhound station: "There was a very good-looking guy standing at the urinal, pulling on himself. He started asking was I a student." When Markowitz admitted

that he took classes at Los Angeles City College, the man mentioned the names of specific teachers and spoke of the classes he had recently taken at the college. "I thought for sure he was a student. When he asked what I liked to do with guys, I told him. And bam—out came the cuffs. I bolted, ran smack into a wall. Broke my wrist, but still got arrested."[36] He later found out that the man was a legendary undercover officer, especially prized by the Vice Squad for his ability to gain the trust of gay men and to lead them into admitting their homosexuality—for which he would arrest them.

Charges might be trumped up with no provocation against men whom Vice Squad officers found in places the LAPD knew as "resorts of homosexuals." Rudy Ruano, a Guatemalan who aspired to become a ballet dancer, moved to Los Angeles where he quickly discovered the gay bars. One night he was in a crowded bar: "This gorgeous man came over and started talking to me. Absolutely gorgeous," Ruano remembers. Naïve to potential danger, he appreciated both the attention and the chance to practice his English. "He bought me a beer, then a second one. After an hour and a half, we were talking so much, then he said, 'Excuse me, I'll be right back.'" The man left and, moments later, returned with several uniformed police officers. "He said, 'This one and this one, and you'—pointing at me."

On the word of his accuser, an undercover Vice Squad officer, Ruano was jailed in the Glass House, the newly constructed downtown police station. Unable to afford an attorney, he endured two terrifying days waiting for a public defender. She urged him to plea-bargain. She told him the officer said that Ruano had proposed performing oral copulation on him. "I couldn't believe it. I told her, 'I can hardly speak English that well.' She said, 'It's your word against his.' So I agreed. They changed the status of my charge from lewd conduct to disturbing the peace." Ruano managed to stay employed and productive, but he feels that the arrest imposed four decades of anxiety on his life. "It's been difficult for me to arrange citizenship because of that. I want to become a citizen, but because of that little thing, it caused a lot of damage."[37]

"Entrapment was absolutely common," Duncan Donovan says, recalling many friends who suffered that fate throughout the 1950s and '60s.

Donovan remembers that frequently the phone rang late at night in the house he shared with his partner, Thomas Patrick, the deputy district attorney for Los Angeles County. "Always some young man who'd gotten picked up in a park, in a bar, in a restroom. We'd get up, get dressed, and drive across the county to help him out." Though Patrick was, of course, closeted, as his job required, his name was known as someone who could be of assistance to gay men in trouble. According to Donovan, Patrick would counsel men about whether they needed legal aid and how to deal with their arraignments. In doing so, he knew that he was taking an enormous career risk. But he had won some of the city's most explosive cases, such as the 1951 "Bloody Christmas" scandal, in which eight LAPD officers were indicted for severely beating Latino detainees; and he banked on his clout in the DA's office to help him survive those risks.[38]

But most gay men who were arrested in L.A. were not lucky enough to have Patrick's assistance. Jack had been an award-winning teacher in the Pasadena School District in the 1950s. But because he was arrested on a "Vag Lewd" charge, he lost not only his job but also the right ever to teach again, anywhere. Not yet forty, he moved hundreds of miles away to run a family motel, the only work he could find. His profession, his friends—his entire life—were virtually wiped out.[39] John Rechy remembers a friend, new to gay life, who was also ruined. Ed, who had never before had a gay sexual relationship, went to his first gay bar where he met a man who began flirting with him. When Ed suggested they "get together," the man, a Vice Squad officer, arrested him for solicitation. Rechy's friend was taken to jail. The judge before whom he appeared declared him mentally unstable. Ed was forcibly institutionalized and not permitted to communicate with anyone for six months. In the mental institution, he was threatened with shock therapy. "He was forever emotionally branded," Rechy says, "and he became a recluse for the rest of his life."[40]

Gay people who were brought to court could be in very serious trouble. Until 1975, oral and anal sex were felonies in California. Oral sex could be punishable by up to fifteen years in prison; anal sex could earn an offender a life sentence. But the most common charge against gay men was "lewd and lascivious conduct"—"Vag Lewd" under antivagrancy statutes. The notorious section 674 of the California Penal Code was termed by the

gay press in the 1960s as "the catch-all that catches all."[41] Two subdivisions of 647 particularly targeted gay men: 647(a) prohibited soliciting or engaging in lewd or dissolute conduct, and 647(d) prohibited loitering in or around a public toilet for the purpose of soliciting or engaging in lewd or dissolute conduct. (The other subdivisions addressed prostitution and begging.) Though 647 offenses were misdemeanors, those convicted under the statute were required to register as sex offenders for the rest of their lives. Gay men of that era say that a 674 arrest was often tantamount to "being ruined." Some tell stories about their depression and alcoholism following such an arrest. Some remember the suicides of others who had been arrested.

Defendants who plea-bargained in 647 arrests were usually given two years' probation and were forbidden to associate with known homosexuals or frequent places where known homosexuals congregate. So intimidated were gay men at mid-century that many believed that even private gay gatherings were illegal: Some Angelenos of that era tell stories of jumping out of the windows of private homes if the LAPD arrived at a gay party, as police sometimes did with the excuse that neighbors had complained of loud music or drunkenness.

Sometimes, arrests were the result not of entrapment but rather police discovery of real homosexual trysts in semipublic places. To gay men, these midnight-hour encounters could seem safer than bringing a sexual partner home, where one risked the discomforts and dangers of being turned in by snoopy neighbors. L.A.'s gay hunting grounds became legendary for the ease with which men found each other for connection and release. The homosexual poet Hart Crane, visiting California in the 1920s, declared of Pershing Square: "The number of faggots cruising around here is legion." (Crane even encountered a movie personality who regularly made homosexual contact in Pershing Square.)[42] The square had a "national reputation" among gay men,[43] and visitors staying at the adjacent Biltmore Hotel knew through the gay grapevine that they would find what they were looking for in the Persh-

ing Square underbrush. For years, in daylight hours, too, as one 1960s writer observed, the Square continued to be a premier homosexual spot, and it even attracted tourists who would "come down and walk through it just to see all the loud, swishing, painted queens who were parading noisily up and down the walk and carrying on with vile disregard for the 'other people.'"[44]

L.A.'s year-round good weather and growing gay population made possible the establishment of numerous outdoor trysting places, such as Echo Park Lake, Westlake Park, and North Hollywood Park. At Griffith Park, which encompasses five square miles, wild orgies involving scores of men were common. The orgies could even take place in daylight because Griffith Park had vast areas where the overgrown scrub provided a venue that was like a veritable outdoor gay bathhouse for "sex-hunters," as John Rechy calls them. Rechy, who explored gay cultures all over America in his autobiographical novel *City of Night,* observes now that he knew of no other city in the 1960s "that had a daytime scene as thriving as Los Angeles did in Griffith Park."[45] The LAPD often made arrests in such semipublic trysting places, but they could not dent the exuberant gay male eroticism there for long because as the numbers of gay men in L.A. continued to increase, the Vice Squad could not keep up.

Aside from the men's semipublic sexual encounters, there is no question that acts that were considered to be merely a social nuisance when engaged in by heterosexuals were treated as criminal when engaged in by homosexuals. Straight couples caught petting in a park or a "lovers' lane," for example, were likely to be shooed away, but gay couples were inevitably arrested. Even the most innocuous behavior was criminalized. At mid-century, bars that catered to lesbians and gay men could be shut down by the LAPD if same-sex couples were dancing there, or even simply sitting with an arm around a shoulder. To evade such harassment, at mixed gay-and-lesbian bars such as the Canyon Club in Topanga Canyon it was understood by the patrons that if the Vice Squad should make an appearance on the property, the management would flash lights on the

dance floor to signal to the same-sex couples that they must switch to a partner of the opposite sex.[46] At Gino's, a gay club in Hollywood, an advance warning system would change the music selection to the "Star Spangled Banner," which effectively ended dancing.

Gay men learned that not only would they be persecuted by the police (who called them "fruits"),[47] but that even in direst need they could not count on them for protection. Steve Hodel, a retired LAPD homicide detective, recalls one of the worst examples, which happened in the 1960s: A gay man who had been stabbed called the police as he was dying. The responding LAPD officer ridiculed the man's vocal mannerisms and mocked his dying breaths. The policeman was not disciplined, Hodel says, even though his unprofessionalism and cruelty were captured and preserved on tape.[48] Gay men could not escape the knowledge that the LAPD regarded them not only as laughable but also as ultimate criminals. Even those who were blackmailed often felt they had nowhere to turn. Without recourse to justice, it was not uncommon that they would be bled broke.[49]

The Crown Jewel, the downtown bar in which Vice Squad officers spotted Marvin Edwards and then tailed him and his new friend, was owned by Harry Weiss, the proprietor of two other gay bars and a lawyer since 1941. In the 1950s and '60s, Weiss regularly defended gay men who were arrested for homosexual activity. Though he was himself homosexual, many gay men perceived him as being unsympathetic to the plight of his clients. According to Tom Gibbon and James Miller, who knew the mid-century L.A. gay scene well, Weiss had friends in high places, from the police department on up, and there were widespread rumors about the intricate complicity between Weiss and the law.[50] Gibbon and Miller believe to this day that, in true "noir" fashion, Weiss often tipped off officers about whom to arrest; then arresting officers handed their prey a business card bearing attorney Weiss' name and number; and—to complete the circle—Weiss kicked back part of his substantial legal fees to the arresting officers.

Though Weiss was closeted, his flamboyance—including a penchant for white linen suits, fine fedoras, and other affectations—made his ho-

mosexuality evident to those in the know, even judges. Bill Regan recalls an incident in which a judge in open court referred to Weiss as "the faggot lawyer," meaning not only that he defended "faggots" but also that he was himself one.[51] But gay men in trouble put aside their worries and flocked to him. They grudgingly agree that he was effective. Weiss was "the top gay attorney," says Aristide Laurent. "He had a bad reputation, but he also had a reputation for being well connected, which meant your best chance for beating the charges."[52] He was "the go-to guy [for] all the boys who were arrested," recalls Guy Richards. "He'd help them get out of jail; then he'd go to the judge and say, 'due to lack of evidence currently available,' or some such thing, until he got the case postponed and postponed—and finally got the judge that he wanted: another queen." If the judge that Weiss managed to have assigned to the case was indeed a gay male crony, Weiss would campily tell his client, according to Richards, "*She'll* save you."[53]

Despite the various criticisms of Weiss among gay men, his business flourished, for it was not easy to find an attorney in Los Angeles who would help a gay man in trouble. Perhaps most attorneys were reluctant to take gay clients because they feared that the stigma of defending an accused sex offender could damage their professional reputations. In any event, of the thousands of local attorneys practicing then, only two were popularly known for defending homosexuals.

The other was Gladys Towels Root, who had for years been called the "Defender of the Damned." Root began practicing law in 1929 and was rumored to have defended more sex offenders than any other attorney in the United States. She, too, was a flamboyant character, as tall as Weiss was short, with a theatrical appearance that may have been calculated to disarm. In the style she regularly wore to court—opera gloves, hat towering as high as three feet above her head, rings set with stones only a little smaller than hens' eggs—she looked like the drag queens she often defended on masquerading charges. (Duncan Donovan once rode with her in an elevator that could barely accommodate her hoop skirt.) Her office was equally extravagant: paneled with mirrors and carpeted in pink; her pink draperies were embroidered with her initials in sequins, all setting off her wide desk, which was fashioned

entirely of mirrors. But Duncan Donovan's partner, Thomas Patrick, the deputy district attorney for L.A. County, observed her often in the courtroom and declared her "brilliant."[54]

Both Root and Weiss earned considerable fortunes for stooping to represent a friendless, pariah community. Though some gay men who remember the 1950s characterize both attorneys as "wonderful advocates [in the court room], . . . who shamed the justices into seeing their point of view,"[55] others still resent that Root and Weiss grew rich off the entrenched homophobia of the legal system to which all gay men were vulnerable. The average fee they charged their homosexual clients, from $2,000 to $3,000, was, for many in the early 1950s, a huge burden—the equivalent of a year's salary. Some who were defended by them also questioned their insistence that a client plea-bargain (regardless of the facts of the case), which meant that even a defendant who might be totally guiltless ended up with a record as a sex offender. Most of their clients went along with this tactic to avoid the scandalous publicity of a trial and the strong possibility of a felony conviction (a plea generally meant getting away with a misdemeanor charge). And in most cases, of course, they despaired of fair treatment in the system anyway. As many older gay men still insist, the police, who were always believed over an accused "degenerate," were very willing to practice perjury on the stand. Duncan Donovan, who was present for numerous courtroom proceedings involving charges against homosexuals, says, "Vice Squad officers had memorized what they should say. . . . They would hit the points of what should have occurred in order to get a conviction. 'Improper touching.' 'Offer to provide sexual services.' 'Solicitation of sexual services.'"[56]

Many homosexual men shrugged off these terrible legal hassles as part of the cost of being gay, and most were lucky enough to stay one step ahead of the heat. But some began to question whether they really deserved to suffer the threat of police harassment and the expensive legal price tag that accompanied it just because they were homosexual. Their realization of their essential innocence—the innocence of a human being who pursues innate needs that hurt no one else—became the start of homophile organizing.

THE WOMEN'S STORY

> *When I went to gay bars I always drank something nonalcoholic, because I thought, "If they raid the place I don't want to be so stupid drunk that I don't know what I'm doing." So I would order a 7-Up or something.*
>
> —Lisa Ben, on going to L.A. gay girls' bars in the 1940s and '50s[57]

In Los Angeles before World War II there were only a few places that catered primarily to lesbians, and they were very different from the many bars that emerged in the years after the war. The prewar bars were usually in the tradition of the upscale nightclub, and they promoted an exotic glamour, much like the lesbian bars of Weimar Berlin. They included Jane Jones' and Tess's (called in its various iterations Tess's Continental and Tess's Café Internationale). The eponymous Jane Jones was a big woman with a basso profundo voice who'd been a singer in movie musicals.[58] Tess's was owned by Tess—a woman who dressed in basic black, pearls, and a great deal of makeup—and her partner Sylvia—who looked like Radclyffe Hall and always carried around a long cigarette holder. Both Tess's and Jane Jones' featured male impersonators such as Tommy Williams and Jimmy Renard, tall, broad-shouldered women singers who wore tuxes and bow ties and had tenor voices. Gay women who frequented those nightclubs remember still Jimmy Renard's rendition of "Tonight We Love" and the evening that Tommy Williams brought Marlene Dietrich to Tess's and sang to her.[59] Unlike nightclubs such as Jimmy's Backyard and The Barn that had a large gay male clientele and featured female impersonators, Jane Jones' and Tess's suffered neither raids nor closings by the police because the phenomenon of the lesbian was not yet taken very seriously in 1930s Los Angeles.

Even into the mid-1940s, upscale lesbian nightclubs were still relatively safe. At the Flamingo in Hollywood, Beverly Shaw entertained wearing drag on her top half—a man's jacket and bow tie; and sexy-lady clothes on her bottom half—a short skirt and high heels. At the Gypsy Room on the Sunset Strip in those years, women could be openly demonstrative with one another, as Dottie remembers: "There were a lot

of women in tuxedos and a lot in beautiful gowns. Dancing was the thing. We could hug our partner and dance as close as we wanted. We never worried about the place being raided."[60] Perhaps the Gypsy Room patrons were not harassed by the law (as waltzing male couples undoubtedly would have been) because it was still socially acceptable for two women to dance together in the 1940s, and there were so few of these elegant women-only nightclubs that they may have been beneath the notice of the LAPD.

But lesbian nightspots multiplied in the years after the war, their clientele boosted by the many gay women who had come to Los Angeles to work in the defense industries and then stayed on. Working-class beer-and-pool-table bars for gay girls were soon scattered around many of the poorer areas of Los Angeles. They were different from the Sunset Strip and Hollywood nightclubs in that their patrons were regulars: women who "hung out" there and sometimes imposed on newcomers stringent rules that governed butch/femme dress and behavior.[61] Their working-class style and lingo felt alienating to middle-class lesbians. Terry DeCrescenzo, who had been a social worker, remembers that when she walked into the If Club, "a stereotypical dyke bar," as she describes it, the butches there called to each other, "Here comes a dish of ice cream." She was terrified. "I was in there for eight minutes," she says.[62] Middle-class lesbians generally stayed away from such bars, just as middle-class heterosexuals stayed away from those bars' straight equivalents. As Min, who was a business woman, and her partner Marion, who was the director of nursing in a Los Angeles hospital, now recall of their one foray into a gay girls beer bar:

> Some friends sent us to this place in Torrance—probably as a joke. We took one look around and then almost knocked each other over trying to get out. It was a different socioeconomic group. First of all, we didn't want beer, and we didn't want to play pool. We wanted a cocktail and to listen to nice music. And secondly everyone there was either a stomping butch, dressed like a man, or a frou-frou femme. We sure didn't fit.[63]

But for many working-class lesbians ("the industrial set," as Rikki Streicher, a lesbian bar owner, called them),[64] those bars were a haven to

which they retreated often—so that by the 1950s, there was a considerable choice of nightspots where L.A. gay girls might go: the Lakeshore near Westlake Park and the If Club on 8th and Vermont, both of which had started in the decade before but continued to flourish; the Cork Room, the Star Room, and the Paradise Club, where butch-and-femme couples less fashionable than those at the Gypsy Room could dance; the Pink Glove in the Valley that imposed a $5 cover charge on straight customers to keep them away; the Redhead in East L.A., which welcomed only Mexican American lesbians; the Open Door (just across the street from the If Club) where lesbian blue-collar and pink-collar workers rubbed shoulders with prostitutes—and M & M, a bar with a similar mix that catered primarily to Latinas, where Nancy Valverde remembers being dressed "very butch" when a john said to her, "If you weren't so pretty I'd pop you one," and a femme waitress coming to her defense by throwing a beer bottle and an ashtray at the man.[65]

Lesbians did not suffer from sexual entrapment by LAPD Vice Squad decoys, but the relative indulgence they had once enjoyed in Los Angeles had quite disappeared by mid-century. The upheavals of the war, when females took on freedoms and responsibilities formerly relegated to males, made many in the postwar years long for a return to an imaginary past, when all women were homemakers and, "by nature," nurturers of men.[66] The mere concept of the lesbian mocked that longing. Thus gay women living in the mid-century were aware of the danger that awaited should their lesbianism become known. Those who dressed in masculine clothes or frequented bars were often harassed by overzealous and hostile police officers, but even those who were not bar habitués or cross-dressers or visibly homosexual in any way worried about the increased opprobrium in which lesbians were held. No matter how moral or socially productive they were as citizens, they knew that they were also outlaws and were cognizant that even their private acts of love could send them to prison under California law.[67] They felt they needed to be constantly looking over their shoulders, keeping their lives

secret from all but a trusted few, devising ingenious ways to disguise their lesbianism.

For middle-class lesbians, especially those who were employed in the few professional positions open to women at mid-century (for example, teacher, nurse, social worker), social life was most often carried on in private homes because they knew that in the main public venue for lesbians, the gay girls bar, they would be vulnerable to police harassment. As Maggie, a former physical education teacher, recalls, after narrowly escaping a Vice Squad raid at a gay bar on Santa Monica beach in 1952 ("I was at the window, and I jumped out onto the sand and ran"), she never again went to a public place where gay people gathered: "I'd worked too hard to get where I was, and I didn't want to jeopardize it."[68]

But working-class and young lesbians who lived with their families or in dwellings too small to host social gatherings did not have the luxury of rejecting the bars if they wanted to find partners, or enjoy community, or merely be in the presence of their peer group. "The bars were the only place to meet women. There was no other place," Liz, who was born in 1926, recalls about the 1950s and '60s.[69] K.C. remembers a Gardena beer bar where white and Latina lesbians mixed in camaraderie during the early 1960s: "It was like going to a friend's home or a community center." The bar was the hub and starting point of all her social activities, she says, even her softball playing, which was sponsored by the bar.[70] Sharon A. Lilly says of Anna's, a Silver Lake bar where she spent her weekend nights in 1962, "It was always packed—all of us young people, nobody over twenty-three or twenty-four, dancing together. I loved it."[71]

But what was to lesbians a community center was to the police as bad as a bawdy house, and they worked hard to find ways to shut the bars down. Though lesbians may not have been entrapped sexually, the LAPD Vice Squad did not scruple to entrap them and the proprietors of their bars in other ways. For example, gay girls bars would be closed down on the charge that they had "served liquor to an intoxicated person"—though, as a transcript of a 1959 court hearing on a lesbian bar raid indicates, the liquor had been *bought for* that intoxicated person, a lesbian, by an undercover Vice Squad officer.[72] Undercover officers might return

to a bar repeatedly before finding a reason to call for a raid of the premises, as they did at the Party Pad, a gay girls bar on Vermont Avenue. The Party Pad was declared "injurious to public morals" when the undercover officer testified that he "observed a female dressed in a man's attire place her arm around the body of a female dressed in female attire, pull this person to her, and kiss her on the neck and face."[73]

Proprietors of gay bars tried various ways to avoid trouble with the police: Some encouraged a mixed crowd—lesbians, gay men, and sympathetic straights—so that the nature of the bar would be less obvious.[74] At the Star Room, a lesbian bar on the edge of Watts, where women were permitted to dance together, the owner circulated on the floor and shone a flashlight between couples, admonishing them that if a beam did not appear on the opposite wall they were dancing too close and would get her into trouble with the Vice Squad.[75] But despite various precautions, the Vice Squad might still pounce, and patrons might still be dragged off in paddy wagons and booked on trumped-up charges.[76]

From all accounts, bar raids were utterly terrifying. The methods and manners of raiding officers seemed close to those brutal Gestapo tactics against which America had recently been fighting. Though she never learned the reason for the raid, Stella Rush remembers that in 1948 she witnessed a police invasion of the Tropical Village:

> The cops burst in. There were at least six of them. They shoved us off in corners, demanding names, IDs. Losing your job was on everyone's mind . . . and finding money for a lawyer.
>
> I said to the cops, "What's the charge?"
>
> One cop answered, "We haven't charged anyone yet." Another one shouted at me, "None of your business. We're asking the questions." They interrogated you with the utmost contempt, grilling you like you'd committed some terrible crime.[77]

Police brutality, mysterious and false charges, humiliation of innocent bar patrons—all continued throughout the 1950s and into the '60s, as Eileen Cusimano recalls. Early one evening after work, she and her partner had stopped to have a beer at a gay girls bar:

> The place was raided. The police came in. Everyone froze. They walked around the room, indiscriminately arresting people. They arrested my girlfriend. I think they chose her to arrest because she was tall and good looking and stood out in the crowd. "Because you're drunk in public," they told her.
>
> I said, "That's a lie. We only had one beer."
>
> This policeman yelled at me, "You shut up or we're taking you in, too."
>
> They shoved six of the women into a paddy wagon, and then they took them to Lincoln Heights jail. They booked them all for public drunkenness. None of them was drunk. It was strictly terrorism. I couldn't get my girlfriend out until the next morning. They all had to go to court. The charges were dismissed for all of them, but what a horrible time they went through.[78]

Arrests in lesbian bars seldom led to extended sentences, but the primary goal of police harassment seems to have been to intimidate the women and frighten them away from such meeting places. It was the job of officers of the law to keep them in check, keep their numbers down, and control the proliferation of their bars—which, ironically, were burgeoning in mid-century. In the 1960s, as L.A.'s population continued to grow and the city and county to spread out, such bars began cropping up even in small communities and neighborhoods to serve local gay girls who preferred not to travel the freeways—Joan's Place in Long Beach; the Bull Dog, the Big Horn, and the Hialia in the Valley; the Big Candle in Inglewood; the Westwinds in Venice; the Daily Double in Pasadena; Arnie's on Washington and Dee's Merry-Go-Round on Manchester and Vermont, which attracted mostly black gay girls; the Plush Pony on Alhambra, which attracted mostly Chicana gay girls.

As the number of gay girls bars continued to increase, so did police harassment in them increase. Eileen Leaffer, a sociologist who studied L.A. lesbian bar society in 1967, observed that LAPD Vice Squad officers hung around gay girls bars so often that bar regulars could distinguish them from tourists or "fish queens" (men whose preferred sex act was cunnilingus, and who hoped to meet lesbians in the bars who would be amenable). The regulars in the bars were careful to warn new patrons as

soon as they befriended them about the plainclothes officers in their midst ("He's not kosher. You know . . . Vice").[79]

LAPD harassment of lesbians outside the bars increased as well. By the 1950s, a woman's presumed homosexuality alone seems to have been sufficient justification to flash the badge. Masculine-looking lesbians, or those congregating around a lesbian bar, or a butch-and-femme couple simply walking down the street together were slapped with charges that were often as false as those devised in bar raids. Meko, an African American woman, says that she and her friends were "hauled in" by the LAPD regularly on weekends—sometimes just for standing in front of the If Club or the Open Door: "They'd lie and say that we were prostituting, and they'd take us off to jail. We'd have to stay there until we got bailed out." Sometimes, Meko remembers, they were arrested just for walking in pairs, going from one bar to another on 8th and Vermont, especially if one of them was a "hard dresser" (the term among black lesbians for a woman who wore masculine clothes): "They'd say that we were 'fondling' each other. We'd have to pay a fine for 'fondling,' which was a misdemeanor."[80]

Driving was no safer: Many patrons of gay girls bars now recall that they did not dare even to park their cars in the vicinity of a bar: "The police might see it and wait for you to come out. Then they'd follow you and arrest you for anything."[81] Mid-century LAPD officers all seemed to share the conviction that a woman's mere *status* as a lesbian was tantamount to her criminality.

The most common reason for police harassment of lesbians on the streets of Los Angeles in the mid-century was "masquerading"—wearing clothing that was deemed appropriate only for men. It is difficult to imagine in our day how disturbed some people have been in the past, even in a major metropolis such as Los Angeles, at the mere sight of a woman in pants (Garbo, Dietrich, and Hepburn notwithstanding), and how intense the efforts were to keep ladies garbed in skirts. During the war years, as many women donned trousers to work in defense factories, a panic gripped traditionalists. Fletcher Bowron, the mayor of Los

Angeles, declared to his city council in 1942 that he loathed "to see masculine women much more than feminine traits in men." It was bad enough that women were losing their womanliness in defense factories; City Hall, at least, must be free of gender desecration, he said. Bowron admonished the council members not to let the war "undermine these things we like to consider feminine and ladylike." "Good taste and good sense" must prevail, the mayor decreed, exhorting the council to pass a regulation that would prevent female employees at City Hall from wearing pants.[82]

The 1950s witnessed even more concern over the undermining of things considered feminine and ladylike; and cross-dressing women were a visible emblem of how some females refused to assume their traditional roles, stubbornly continuing to claim male prerogative. The forces of reaction came down upon them. Despite the two 1950 court decisions that found that women who dressed in men's clothes were not breaking the law, throughout the 1950s cross-dressing women were more persecuted in Los Angeles than they ever had been before. Up to World War II, female transvestites had apparently continued to be treated with relative tolerance in L.A.: In 1940, a woman barber who was en route to buy supplies for her shop was arrested by the Vice Squad and charged with being dressed to impersonate a man. But the businessmen in her neighborhood came to her defense by testifying that she was not "impersonating" because they all knew she was a woman as well as a person of fine character; and—as one sympathetic newspaper reporter (erroneously) stated—there was anyway "nothing in the statute books which prohibits a woman from donning men's clothing." The felony booking charge against her for impersonation was dropped.[83]

Women who cross-dressed in the postwar years were not as lucky. Like the woman arrested for "male impersonation" in 1940, Nancy Valverde was also a barber, but her run-ins with the law fifteen years later were brutal. During the time Nancy was a student in barber school, she was arrested "almost every weekend" because she wore short hair and men's clothes: "Drapes I'd get off the rack and a tailor would alter them. A sweater with tweed in front and wool in back that cost me

twenty-seven dollars. The cops would get me for masquerading and then add on stuff, like they'd say I was drunk too, even though I was cold sober." Usually the police would take her to Lincoln Heights Jail, where she would spend a night or two before her case was heard in court the following Monday. "The cops would bring my clothes in as Exhibit A. Sometimes they'd sit behind me, goading me, laughing, saying things like, 'Better not fuck around with my wife.'"[84] Valverde says the police worried her so much that "whenever I'd see a black-and-white I'd run and hide until they were gone." In 1959, tired of repeated jail stays when she didn't run fast enough, she went to the Los Angeles County Law Library on Hill Street, checked the penal code, and found that the courts had already decided in 1950 that women were not breaking the law simply because they wore men's clothes. She provided her lawyer with that information and he used it in her defense. Finally, she says, she stopped being thrown in jail.

But though her arrests ceased, malicious police harassment did not. Once she became a barber, her neighborhood policeman found an extralegal way to trouble her, and even to threaten her livelihood: "He'd walk his beat where I worked. He just didn't like the way I dressed. He'd knock on the barbershop window with his nightstick, really loud, and my customers would jump to the ceiling. It's a good thing I had steady hands or I would've nicked their ears off lots of times."[85]

Valverde admits to having been defiant in her younger years when she was repeatedly accosted by the police: "They used to tell me, 'I want to see you in a dress.' I said to them, 'Sit down and wait 'cause you're gonna get tired.'"[86] But it was not her defiance alone that caused the police to persecute her. Even if a butch woman complied with the rules of dress and did nothing to challenge law officers, she ran the risk of police harassment anyway, sometimes for surprising reasons. Frankie Hucklenbroich, who stood at five foot eleven, tells of dressing up in a skirt, high heels, a woman's blouse, and a tailored jacket when she was job hunting one day in 1957. At the end of the afternoon she'd gone to meet her girlfriend at Coffee Dan's, a restaurant in Hollywood whose clientele included gay people and oblivious heterosexuals:

> And suddenly these cops are descending on me and telling me to get up and step outside. They wanted to arrest me. I kept asking, "What have I done?" I hadn't a clue. Everyone was looking. Finally one of the cops said that I was a man dressed up in women's clothes! "No! I'm a woman!" I kept telling them. They ended up calling a police matron who took me into the ladies room and made me prove that I wasn't a guy.[87]

Frankie's story may be uncommon, but the stories of mid-century lesbians who were arrested for cross-dressing—in all big American cities—are not. An urban myth soon emerged in lesbian communities that had little basis in legal reality: The police could not arrest a woman for masquerading if she was wearing three articles of women's clothing. Flo Fleischman believed the myth, just as most gay women did: "In those days," she says "if you were dressed in drag you went to jail; so though I'd wear mostly men's clothes, I'd also be sure to be wearing a bra and girl's underpants and some other thing—nail polish or earrings or a man-tailored shirt that buttoned like a blouse or maybe pants that zipped up on the side."[88] Gay women held on to the "three articles" myth as though it were a talisman. But it did little to help them avoid capricious arrests.[89]

Because the police were so hostile to them, lesbians often internalized the notion of their criminal status and saw themselves as outlaws, separate from much of the human community, regardless of who they really were and what they really felt about their fellow beings. The costs of that outlaw self-definition could be dear, to themselves certainly, but also to the larger society. One Los Angeles woman illustrates those costs by telling the sad story of an incident that occurred in 1965:

> I'm driving on the freeway. . . . It's about empty . . . sunset . . . and this VW bug is in the fast lane. I'm in the right lane. I don't know if the guy had a heart attack or what happened. He came careening across at a right angle and smacked into the concrete. I had all this paranoia that if I [stopped and called Emergency] the cops are going to pick up a dyke and stuff like that . . . so I was afraid to stop. I always regretted it. I don't know what happened [to the man]. I panicked and got the hell out of there because I was dressed like a dyke.[90]

The memory and her sense that—because of police hostility against people like her—she had failed her own rules of responsible and decent behavior have haunted her ever since.

Some middle-class gay women in the 1950s and 1960s did risk occasional forays into the L.A. gay girls bars, and even played with being outlaws, donning a "noir" persona for a night out, though the experience was never without at least a twinge of discomfort. Violet, who was a graduate student, recounts how in the first years of their romance, she and her lover, Ruth, a nursing administrator, sometimes enjoyed the feeling of going incognito to a forbidden place such as the Cork Room or the Star Room, where they could dance together: "There was an element of thrill to it. Not only were we doing something 'decent citizens' wouldn't like, but there was also the danger . . . a double thrill."[91] They were aware of the huge price they'd pay should their nighttime selves be discovered; and though they liked being in a roomful of lesbians, they did not dare befriend anyone there because it was impossible to know whom they might trust. A night out at the bar was like a parenthesis in the line of their lives that they strove to make as conventional as possible. Violet retained her ex-husband's last name, calling herself "Mrs."; and she and Ruth dressed conservatively in the daylight, hiding their other personae beneath a mask of tasteful makeup.

Even the potential thrill of being an outlaw for the evening could not outweigh the fear of the Vice Squad and the discomfort with bar habitués that middle-class gay women generally felt. A couple of upscale nightclubs did open in the late 1950s; both were in the more-hidden San Fernando Valley rather than on the Sunset Strip, where such places had been prominent earlier: "Beverly Shaw, Sir," who had been at the Flamingo in the 1940s, resurfaced at the Club Laurel, singing "songs tailored to your taste" in sultry and stylish imitation of Marlene Dietrich; Joanie Presents was presided over by Joan Hannan, an exotic blonde who'd made a name for herself among lesbians as the drummer in the movie *Some Like It Hot.* Such places felt a bit safer to some middle-class gay women, not only

because those clubs were, like the Sunset Strip nightclubs of the 1930s and '40s, more elegant than the bars but also because of their location: "They were out of the City of Los Angeles. They were in the County and that was less risky. I'd be fired by my agency in a snap if I'd been caught in a bar raid in the City," Betsy, who was a television ad executive, explains.[92]

Most middle-class Los Angeles gay women at mid-century avoided public lesbian venues wherever they were located, and they felt they had to find other ways to construct a social life. But it was a challenge for a gay woman who did not go to bars to find a community or even a few close friends: How could you carry on trusted friendships when you feared you couldn't risk revealing your secret? How could you even meet others like you when you and they felt compelled to hide? Harriet Perl recalls that when she taught at Hamilton High School, she and her partner played poker every weekend at the home of another couple of women teachers. "We were pretty sure they were gay because we used to put our coats in their bedroom, and we saw they had only one bed." But though the two couples met for poker during a period of six or seven years, "never, never, never did we dare admit anything to one another, not them and not us."[93] Because they could not chance telling the truth about their most important relationship, the friendship stayed superficial.

The need to hide also placed lesbians in painfully ludicrous situations. Donna, who had been a physical therapist, remembers that though most of the women in her department at the Downey hospital where both she and her partner worked were gay, they all went to great lengths to pretend they were "spinster ladies":

> We bought our first house, but we decided we'd better let people think Adele was living elsewhere. She actually kept a room on the hospital campus, though she never stayed there. The supervisor of the physical therapy department was in the same kind of situation. She lived with a woman on the nursing staff. Even though most of us knew about them, they'd arrive at work with the nurse crouched down on the floor of their car so that nobody would see them driving in together. Then the nurse had to wait until she thought no one was looking before she could sneak out of the car.[94]

Such demeaning fear of exposure was universal among professional women who were gay in those years, so forming friendships through work, as heterosexuals often did, was not an option for many of them. As Harriet Perl characterized it, in the 1950s, "being gay, even in L.A., was like being on the outskirts of civilization. It wasn't any easier to be gay in L.A. in those days than it would have been in Amarillo, Texas, or South Bend, Indiana."[95]

But in a metropolitan area as large and diverse as Los Angeles, there were certainly gay women who were able somehow to find compatible circles of lesbian friends. Mary, who was a social worker, found a tightly knit network of women who would come together regularly for house parties in her home in the hills of Silver Lake. The group called itself the "Hilltop dancing girls" because romantic dancing (such as they would not have risked in the public space of lesbian bars in the mid-century) was a prominent part of their private social get-togethers. Mary recalled in "Old Trees with White Blossoms," a 1998 ethnography about elderly lesbians, that through the decades and into old age, she and her friends continued as "a crucial support system" for each other when they became ill or lost their lovers.[96] Myra Riddell, however—another mid-century social worker who also found a group of gay professional women with whom to socialize—remembers that though it was a relief in one sense ("Here you could shake off the mask you wore at work") there was still discomfort: She characterizes her gay women friends as having been "up-tight, scared to death, always careful never to admit to anyone outside your little circle who you were." No matter what else you were in your life, it was virtually impossible at mid-century to escape the feeling that if the world knew you were a lesbian, you would be regarded first and foremost as a criminal.[97]

HIDING IN PLAIN SIGHT

Our closest friends in the '50s were two gay men, a couple like us. We did the straight world with them—parties, dancing at the Coconut Grove. My partner and I would have loved to go places we could dance together, but the gay bars were too dangerous. We had

a dear friend, a gay man, who'd lost his teaching credential because of an incident at a bar. You had to be realistic.

—Dr. Mandy B., a medical doctor in the 1950s[98]

The old Hollywood tradition of lavender coupling was still popular in mid-century L.A., particularly among those lesbians and gay men who needed to present a front to the world.[99] Gay men and lesbians would take one another to work-related holiday parties, dinners with the boss, homes of relatives who had asked uncomfortably often, "When are you going to find a nice girl [or nice boy] and get married?" They would go together to fancy restaurants and theaters and straight nightclubs, or on vacations to exotic places, where women without male escorts couldn't get in and male couples would not be welcomed. Millie remembers that she and her partner would "dress sexy," in high heels and fur stoles, and go to dinner at Freres Taix or the Biltmore Hotel and then concerts at the Philharmonic with two handsome gay men who worked, as they did, for a real estate firm. "When we got out of the car, Bob would say, 'Okay, boy-girl, boy-girl.' He'd take my arm, and Michael took Sylvia's arm. Then, when we got back into the car, he'd say, 'Okay, boy-boy, girl-girl,' and Sylvia and I would cuddle together in the back seat all the way home."[100] In addition to being convenient, front dating permitted gay people to be in control over what was potentially hurtful. They could deceive the hostile straight world that was so sure it could "spot a queer anywhere."

Another charm of these friendships was the secret fun gay men and women shared about their challenge to gender orthodoxies. Mayor Fletcher Bowron and his ilk may have loathed "masculine women" and "feminine traits in men," but role reversals often became a source of humor for male and female homosexuals. Beverly Hickok, who worked as a riveter in L.A. during the war, says that she and her girlfriend went to gay beaches and to casual restaurants with Leon and Joey, a gay male couple. Their reason for being together was not that they felt they needed to pass as straight but that they simply liked each other and enjoyed the in-jokes that revolved around gender reversal. Joey, a hairdresser, was "effeminate," and he gave Beverly her first short haircut, a boy-style bob. He would tell her he couldn't understand why she liked to

work as a riveter; she would tell him she couldn't understand his interest in hairstyling. "We really loved camping together," Beverly remembers.[101]

Norman Stanley recalls with great affection that in the late 1940s and the '50s he "ran around with this little dyke named Peggy." She was, he adds, "cute as hell and she used her masculine charms effectively on everybody." He relishes the memory of the amusing times they had in making people believe that they were heterosexuals. When they were with their partners, Patricia and George, Norman says, "We were, for all the world, two straight couples." But one New Year's Eve they didn't want to play that role, and the four of them went to a gay nightclub on La Cienega. They were refused admission. "The doorman said, 'No straights allowed!' George got us in by saying, 'If you don't let us in, Mary, I'll slap you with my purse!' For weeks we talked about how we'd become straight!"[102]

The fun in these friendships might come also from a contradictory game—being able to act out conventional gender behavior without the annoying concomitant of raising romantic (heterosexual) expectations. Jo Duffy says she and her partner loved going to restaurants and bars with gay male friends: "They were so solicitous of us. They treated us always like we were proverbial queens."[103] A gay man might have felt that he was misleading a straight woman if he opened the car door or lit a cigarette for her, or played at being chivalrous in any other way; but with a lesbian he could engage in such traditional masculine behaviors with pleasure and impunity. Millie recollects that because she and her partner were "socialized to be so girlie," it was in fact very useful to have Michael and Bob in their lives since they would "come help with the 'man chores' around the house—fixing wiring or lifting heavy things."[104] The women felt they could allow themselves to be feminine with gay men, and the men could be knightly or butch with lesbians, because such role playing in each other's presence led to no awkward expectations: There was a mutual understanding between them that conventional gender behavior (assumed or discarded at will) was divorced from conventional sexual desire.

Twilight tandems between lesbians and gay men were generally based on socioeconomic similarities, shared cultural interests and social concerns, and the chemistry necessary for any good friendship. Gay people of color often banded together in friendship groups because

they perceived a double discrimination against them in public gay venues; they were subject not only to police harassment but also sometimes to discrimination by other gay people. Saundra Tignor, an African American woman, remembers that shortly after coming to L.A. from Washington, D.C., she and her partner visited the Canyon Club, which, she says, "definitely had a racial policy." The two women were seated right away, but after a few minutes the manager came to them and told them to leave. When Saundra asked, "Is it because I'm black?" he admitted that was indeed the reason. "I was shocked . . . out here in this land of palm trees and honey. It was very hurtful."[105]

The solution that some middle-class African American gay people found was to create private clubs for both men and women that would meet in people's homes. Mynun and Gayle talk about occasionally going to bars where there were some African American lesbians, such as the Sugar Shack; but other bars, they say, seemed less welcoming: "I never wanted to go someplace and be rejected," Mynun remembers. "So because we weren't going to pay to be mistreated, we quickly fell in with a crowd of gay people, men and women, and we entertained together on a big scale." Their group was about 80 percent African American, and the rest American Indian, Latino, and white. Their parties were more than amusements, they say. Men, women, and their children from previous heterosexual relationships, too, created an extended family together:

> Anything you wanted to eat or drink. . . .
>
> Great dancing. . . .
>
> All the women dressed up in cocktail dresses and pearls or good slack suits; the men in tuxes or other fine clothes. I never saw a pair of jeans at one of those parties.
>
> But the added good thing was that we didn't have to farm our kids out—we could have the children at the parties too, and everyone was respectful of them. Some of the men were nellie, but they weren't going to do drag at our parties.
>
> I loved the men. They were such fun to be with. They tell Miss Thing she looks good when she looks good.
>
> We loved each other; we really cared about each other.[106]

To many gay people, who were (realistically) worried in the homophobic mid-century that they could lose their jobs and even be thrown into jail if their homosexuality became known, it also seemed that heterogenderal friendships helped keep them safe. Tom Gibbon and his partner Bob Clark both worked for corporations. When Gibbon was suddenly picked up by the LAPD and questioned most of one night about whether he was "queer," he and Clark feared that the police had had them under surveillance. So they decided in 1950 that, for the sake of their jobs and general well-being, they must never again attend gatherings at which only men were present. They created what they called the "Cufflink Crowd," a "tight social circle" of lesbian and gay male couples who were of their class and shared their interests. Most of his crowd preferred to stay away from gay nightspots because they were "in the closet," Gibbon says. "You had to be if you cared about your job." Usually they entertained in their homes, but even at their private parties they were careful to look "appropriate"—the men always wearing coats and ties and the women wearing dresses; and the group's forays into public places of entertainment were always arranged to appear "boy-girl, boy-girl," as is illustrated by the picture of the Cufflink Crowd's visit to a Las Vegas hotel to see Pearl Bailey perform at a dinner show. As convenient as their heterogenderal arrangements were, however, fronting ultimately became less important than genuine friendship. Gibbon says that most of his "Cufflink Crowd," who are now in their eighties, "remained friends for life" and still see one another.[107]

The mid-twentieth century was the bleakest period in L.A. history for homosexuals: Police persecution and the popular prejudices of a reactionary era made gay men and lesbians aware almost always of being threatened and excluded by the straight world. If you were a gay person, it was difficult to escape the feeling that you were forced to live in hiding, to keep the dearest and most important part of your life a deep, dark secret. But through fronting and friendships, some gays and lesbians found creative ways to expand their social parameters, bring some light into the noir, and foil the bad guys.

The Mattachine founders in a rare group shot: (clockwise) Dale Jennings, Harry Hay, Rudi Gernreich, unidentified, Bob Hull, and Chuck Rowland. *Photo: John Gruber.*

CHAPTER 4

Organizing Underground

LITTLE BEGINNINGS

Considering Mattachine, Bilitis, ONE, all seem to be cropping up on the West Coast rather than here [in New York]. . . . What is it in the air out there? Pioneers still? Or a tougher circumstance which inspires battle?

—L[orraine] H[ansberry] N[emerov], 1957[1]

In 1942, a circle of lesbian friends pooled their money and purchased a row of rental houses in Los Angeles. They created an early lesbian enclave in the heart of the city, constructing communal areas, such as a swimming pool, where they would meet each other regularly; and the homes in which they did not live, they leased only to other lesbians. They were not consciously political. They "just thought it would be pleasant to live next door to friends" and to form a community that would serve as an extended family. They provided not only fellowship for one another but also social services. For example, when a sixty-year-old resident of the community suffered a ruptured aneurysm, and doctors, observing severe impairment, wanted to institutionalize her permanently, her lesbian neighbors organized constant rotating shifts to dress and undress her, feed her, and keep her stimulated by conversation. Against the doctors' dire predictions ("She will survive as a vegetable"), she recovered normal speech and became fully functioning after three years.[2]

Such an instance of community was possible in Los Angeles long before the start of a gay movement because the homosexual population had reached a critical mass. Los Angeles by the 1940s was already largely a city of immigrants, people who came from somewhere else in search of what they could not find back home. Of course, Los Angeles would have been particularly attractive both to those who sought fleeting homosexual sex and to those who saw themselves as *being* homosexual. The city promised the sophistication and panache associated with Hollywood, the freedom that comes from relative anonymity, and the urban-area odds of meeting others who shared one's interests.

Edythe Eyde (who later became known as "Lisa Ben") came to Los Angeles as a young woman in 1945 for the same reason many were attracted to the city—to escape a stifling family back home.[3] In Northern California she'd had intense crushes on women, but she had never heard words such as "gay" or "lesbian," nor did she have any notion that there were millions like her. In Los Angeles, she soon met gay girl neighbors who took her dancing at the If Club and to softball games where most of the players and fans were lesbian. In the bar, Eyde recalls, she could not allay her fears that the police would burst in and "take me off in a paddy wagon and put me in the pokey."[4] Hoping it would help her meet gay girls in a less dangerous setting, she decided to publish a small periodical. She chose the name *Vice Versa: America's Gayest Magazine* because, she says, gay life was considered a "vice" and "the opposite of the lives . . . approved of by society."[5] Though in Berlin in the 1920s there had been three magazines directed at lesbians—*Die Freundin, Frauenliebe,* and *Garçonne*—in America, there had never before been anything like it.[6]

Production and distribution of *Vice Versa* were elementary affairs. Eyde was employed as a secretary for a minor executive at RKO, and he'd told her that even when he had no work to give her she must look busy. She was thus able to produce a hand-typed issue of *Vice Versa* every month, from June 1947 to February 1948, with a run of twelve copies per issue (an original and five carbons typed twice). Her underground readership was much larger than twelve, however, because readers passed the magazine on to other lesbians after they'd read it. The first issues of *Vice Versa* were mailed to friends or distributed at the If Club, until Eyde

was told by a more seasoned patron of the bar, "Hey, you shouldn't bring those things in here because if [the Vice Squad] catch you with them they'll put you in jail." Eyde recalls that until then she'd been utterly naïve about the danger of distributing a lesbian magazine:

> I said, "Why? There's no four letter words or dirty stories in it."
> She said, "It doesn't matter. If it's gay they'll put you in jail."
> So that tipped me off. I didn't do that anymore. I used to blithely mail them out [too]. . . . But these girls made me wise. So then I would just hand them out personally to people whom I would meet somewhere else.[7]

Eyde wrote each issue almost singlehandedly, the only repeat contributor being a straight male friend who was sympathetic to lesbians.[8] She never used her own name, nor any other name, in *Vice Versa,* nor did she even identify the magazine's provenance[9] (though her reviews of L.A. theater productions made its origin obvious). Despite her care about secrecy, however, Eyde was astonishingly militant for her day, even something of a cheerleader for the gay girl and lesbian life. She echoed Radclyffe Hall's 1928 British novel, *The Well of Loneliness,* in writing that "the third sex must be recognized as equally 'honorable' as those who are heterosexual," but her early gay pride was a sharp contrast to Hall's moroseness. Eyde dared to take on, as she described it, the "self-styled judges, who smugly carve the standards for society,"[10] to proclaim vehemently, "the Third Sex is here to stay," and to anticipate the lesbian feminism that would come three decades later when she declared: "A woman may live independently from a man if she chooses and carve out her own career. Never before have circumstances and conditions been so suitable for those of lesbian tendencies."[11]

In creating *Vice Versa,* Eyde was addressing an imaginary community, one much broader than what she saw at softball games or at the bar—a widespread gay women's intellectual and political community such as had not yet come into existence in America. Her idea to hand produce a little magazine may have been triggered when she attended meetings of the Los Angeles Science Fiction Society, whose members

(including several gay men) sometimes wrote for what she has described as "homemade [science fiction and fantasy] magazines."[12] Perhaps she was also inspired to create a magazine for lesbians when she saw on the RKO lot actresses such as Liz Scott "flouncing around . . . with a girlfriend, arm and arm, real cozy."[13] In Los Angeles, such interesting images abounded like nowhere else in the country and could fire the imagination of a romantic young woman, as Eyde was. Though homophobia and the paranoia that homophobia sometimes provoked were very present in the L.A. of the 1940s, so were unique stimuli that could permit a gay girl to envision a homophile magazine.

When Howard Hughes bought RKO in 1948, Eyde lost her job. Though she found work at other movie studios, it was usually in a secretarial pool: "I could read what they were typing and they could read what I was typing," she recalls.[14] By then she knew she'd been engaged in risky business. *Vice Versa* came to an end. But the shortlived Los Angeles magazine stands as an icon that marks the beginning of homophile publishing in America.

BEYOND THE "LEGION OF THE DAMNED"

> *Yes, your title [for the science fiction magazine* Toward Tomorrow*] has my eyes turned "toward tomorrow" also. What lies ahead? Can we incorporate ourselves? Can we first organize into a defensive body to fight for our rights?*
>
> —from a gay correspondent, "Walt" [Wally Jordan], to Jim Kepner, March 19, 1943[15]

Long before the 1969 Stonewall Rebellion, gay men were fantasizing about the possibility of banding together to fight for their rights. During the war years, when those in the military had the opportunity to make contacts with others like them from far-flung cities and towns, it helped embolden some enough to dream of themselves as an underground legion. In the summer of 1943, an air force sergeant who signed his letter only "George" wrote to Jim Kepner in Los Angeles about the "Legion of the Damned," a group to which he believed Kepner belonged: "I am very

much interested in joining this organization if it will better my unfortunate status and give me the rights and privileges that I feel all bisexuals are entitled to." George acknowledged that an organization of homosexuals might come under police scrutiny, but he was willing to take the risk: "If I knew that [the Legion of the Damned] was backed by the right kind and number of other nerve-torn individuals such as myself, it would be a great relief to me. . . . Please write me as soon as possible."[16]

George had heard about the Legion of the Damned from Wally Jordan, another serviceman, who lived in a small town in Wisconsin. Jordan, Kepner's science fiction pen pal, had tried to enlist him not only in the fantastical Legion but also in the "Sons of Hamidy," which he'd described as yet another underground homosexual organization. It had been founded in 1888, Jordan wrote, by "a few socially and politically prominent men [who] decided that a Universal Union of all Hamidy's men . . . would benefit mankind greatly."[17] Named for a Greek hero, Harmodius,[18] the group, Jordan claimed, was reactivated in 1934 and had "operatives" in major cities. A fund had even been established to pay those who "brought another H in for enlistment." Some bad recruits "almost blew the lid off," Jordan said, complicating the plot of his story as any good science fiction/fantasy writer might, but now a plan had been set to make the Sons of Hamidy a national group: "Any member of our klan" would be eligible to join; "heteros," "criminals," and "degenerates" would be kept out.[19]

Kepner sought information on the Sons of Hamidy for decades but was finally forced to conclude that it, as well as the Legion of the Damned, was a figment of his correspondents' imaginations. However, the idea of a homosexual organization was indeed in the air. In the late 1920s, in his native Minnesota, an adolescent named Chuck Rowland (later a key figure in Los Angeles homophile groups) read an article about homosexuals in *Sexology* magazine and decided that it was "perfectly obvious that what we have to do is organize."[20] In fact, there had already been attempts to organize: In Chicago, a German immigrant, Henry Gerber, had joined with a handful of other men in 1925 to create a group he called the Society for Human Rights, a name inspired by Magnus Hirschfeld's Scientific-Humanitarian Committee, which had started in Berlin in the 1890s.[21] Gerber hoped to gather a large base of

homosexuals and to educate them, as well as lawmen and politicians, through lectures and a newsletter. He felt his way carefully, devising a purposely vague charter, which was actually registered with the state in Illinois. But despite his care, Gerber's efforts were cut short when members of the group were arrested and subjected to lurid headlines naming them homosexuals and thus criminals. Though the charges were ultimately dropped, Gerber conceded defeat: "We were up against a solid wall of ignorance, hypocrisy, meanness, and corruption. The wall had won."[22]

But after World War II, male homosexuals began to make serious efforts to attack the wall again. In 1945, gay ex-GIs in New York formed an underground social organization, the Veterans Benevolent Association.[23] By 1948, the center of action had moved west along with the burgeoning migration, as the writer Joseph Hansen reports. In that year, he was approached by a man on a Hollywood street who invited him to join "an association of homosexuals that would hold meetings in each other's houses to talk over the ins and outs and highs and lows, the gaiety and grief attached to living such a life and to perhaps come up with ideas to make things better." Hansen, like many homosexual men at the time, quietly dismissed the idea as "pathetic."[24]

In that same year, Harry Hay, who had been an aspiring actor and screenwriter, wrote his first homosexual rallying cry. It was a manifesto in which he drew an alarming comparison between the murder of homosexuals in Nazi Germany and the recent firings of gay men in a homosexual purge at the State Department, which had already come under the influence of McCarthyism.[25] Hay had been well seasoned in movement strategies through the Communist Party, which he had joined in the 1930s, in rebellion against his affluent family. In the hopes of pleasing the party he had even married a woman who was a fellow member; however, after ten years of marriage he came to realize that his homosexual desires would never dim, and he was ready to devote himself to what was still practically unimaginable—a political movement of homosexuals.[26]

In his manifesto, Hay announced that he wanted other men to join him in an organization he would call Bachelors Anonymous. Like the

imaginary Sons of Hamidy, who, according to Wally Jordan's fanciful account, wore silver signet rings bearing the initials SOH,[27] members of Hay's equally imaginary "International Fraternal Order of Bachelors" would wear lapel pins so that homosexuals could discreetly recognize one another in public. The name he chose for the group was calculated, of course, to mask its nature. During the postwar era, secret fraternal organizations, a nineteenth-century craze, had enjoyed a surge in popularity, and Hay believed that such a structure provided both privacy and a sense of brotherhood that would not only defuse fear but would also appeal to homosexuals and encourage organizing. By 1950, Hay's new lover, Rudi Gernreich (who would become the well-known fashion designer), embraced Hay's manifesto, and within a year a nucleus of founding members had come together in L.A. to bring the group into being.[28] Hay then decided to call the new organization "Mattachine," which referred to medieval folk jesters who always wore masks when they performed in public. The masked Mattachine, Hay believed, would be an appropriate mascot for the organization because a mask hid identity.[29]

Unlike Gerber's earlier Society for Human Rights and other brief attempts to organize homosexuals in America, Mattachine managed to grow over many years and marked the beginning of the national homophile movement.[30] Hay's Hollywood-honed charisma and training as a stage actor were useful to the group's establishment. Early members of Mattachine's inner circle were swept up not only by his vision but also by his ability to communicate that vision dynamically.

The group exercised extreme caution. They used the word "homophile" to deflect the criminal- and mental-illness connotations of "homosexual." ("Phila" means "love.") They were super-careful in bringing others into the organization. In such venues as the basement of the First Unitarian Church of Los Angeles, the group conducted semipublic discussions on the problem of homosexuality. Many of the homosexual men who attended were so nervous about even being caught listening that they brought along a female "date" as a beard. The Mattachine leaders observed their audience: Only guests who evinced particular enthusiasm for the subject were quietly invited to join the secret society. Mattachine also adopted a cell structure, which was designed to protect

members from exposure and ruin.[31] No master lists were kept. The leaders and the rank-and-file were separate, and the latter did not know who the former were. Secrecy was key to Mattachine's existence, as was crucial at a time when homosexuals had much to fear.

Though Mattachine operated under the realistic conviction that extreme discretion was necessary to avoid the fate of Gerber's group, secrecy also had its own charm. An interracial group of homosexuals that was formed in Los Angeles about the time that Hay began Mattachine—the Cloistered Order of Conclaved Knights of Sophisticracy (more commonly known as the Knights of the Clock)[32]—modeled their elaborate rituals on groups such as the Masons. They conducted a solemn, candlelit installation ceremony, ending in the words: "May each of us then search his heart and find there gifts deep and fine to bring to the service of his brother Knights."[33] The Knights, primarily a social club (though Harry Hay recalled they were also known for sex parties),[34] aimed to offer social services, too, such as helping interracial gay couples find housing.[35] But the Knights remained a small group. No one among them had the charismatic leadership ability and visionary eloquence of Mattachine's Harry Hay.

Initially, Mattachine had a hard time growing. The fear and loathing of the homosexual at mid-century had left a terrible mark. John Gruber remembers that those who came to the early meetings often harbored such self-hatred that they "had to start at a pretty low level of group therapy" such as "'We're not ill. We're not insane.'" Even that basic premise was too much for some, who ran from the meetings in sick terror. But others bravely stayed. Gruber still recalls that people were standing up and saying, "'This is my second time here. I swore the first time I'd never come back, but you got me thinking.'" He adds, "So we were doing something right."[36]

The organization did not grow rapidly, however, until word spread of an incredible, unprecedented legal victory: In the spring of 1952, Dale Jennings, one of Mattachine's core members, was arrested on a morals charge, and he admitted that he was a homosexual. But, he said, he'd been entrapped by a member of the Los Angeles Vice Squad, who was lying in his accusation that Jennings was guilty of lewd conduct. Jen-

nings' plea was in marked contrast to that of Herbert Lowe, the man who had been caught forty years earlier in the Long Beach sweep and was exonerated only because he emphatically *denied* that he was a homosexual. Mattachine seized the opportunity to fight the entrapment battle openly. Hay found Jennings an attorney, and the group held fundraisers to pay his legal expenses. Jennings' acquittal caused a sensation on the gay male grapevine. A dozen Mattachine chapters immediately proliferated in Southern California and then quickly spread to Northern California and beyond.

But the organization's frenetic growth heralded the demise of its leadership: The new rank-and-file soon rebelled against the secret-cell structure, which had been central to Hay's conception of security. Jim Kepner, who was brought to his first Mattachine rank-and-file meeting in 1953 by one of the organization's few women members, Betty Perdue, recalled complaints that Harry Hay was a mysterious, shadowy figure who sat in some unknown realm and pulled the strings. "Everyone quotes Harry Hay but no one ever sees him," the new members said with resentment.[37] Worse, rumors of the founders' communism ran rampant just as McCarthyism was reaching a boiling point in the national consciousness. The rumors were inflamed through an attack on Mattachine by the L.A. columnist Paul Coates, who wrote of the organization as a "strange new pressure group" with Communist ties.[38] At two tumultuous conventions in the summer of 1953, tensions reached a crisis over the issues of secrecy and communism. Harry Hay and other early Mattachine founders, including Rudi Gernreich, Dale Jennings, John Gruber, and Chuck Rowland, resigned when they were dubbed Communists who "would disgrace us all."[39]

It was not only Communists that Mattachine feared would "disgrace us all." From its very beginnings, the organization eschewed men who affected a "swishy" style because the Mattachine founders, as radical as they were, felt compelled to present a conservative public face. Jamie Green remembers the emphasis placed on "presentability." "To be invited to Mattachine," he says, "you had to be wearing a Brooks Brothers three-piece suit. Those who were unusual dressers or had unusual hairstyles were not invited. If you made the mistake of bringing someone who was too flamboyant, you

could be asked to leave."[40] John Gruber says that though the organization was "so mindful of freedom for the dispossessed, at the same time we knew there had to be limits for the movement to survive."[41]

The prohibition against those who were "loud in voice or dress" was unwritten. It clearly extended to "queens"—a broad term that included gay men who were effeminate as well as "drag queens"—those who dressed and identified as women, and who would probably be regarded as "transgendered" today. Miss Destiny, a mid-century L.A. gay man who achieved fame as the fabulous queen in John Rechy's *City of Night*, observed that queens were "outcast among outcasts."[42] But queens, including drag queens, believed themselves to be part of the gay world, and before more sophisticated ideas about gender were conceptualized they all simply called themselves "gay."

It is ironic that the city's emerging gay rights movement shunned its queens; they had, after all, been the most targeted for social opprobrium and legal harassment at least since 1895, when the Los Angeles City Council put an end to All Fool's Night because the revelries encouraged drag queens. In 1914, the newspapers, outraged against the men of the 606 and 96 Clubs, expressed particular disgust that they "wore kimonos and powdered their faces." In the 1930s and '40s, a main reason that the LAPD gave for raiding clubs where homosexuals congregated was that those places attracted "female impersonators and their following."

But despite consistent harassment and scant help from their fellow gays, queen culture flourished in Los Angeles. Jim Kepner remembered that when he arrived in 1943 he found an ongoing society of queens; he had a sexual encounter with one of them, having been "snatched into Vaseline Alley off Angels' Flight downtown by Carioca, a mad Latin queen who said she was chosen successor to venerable Wilhemina, Queen of Bunker Hill."[43] A generation later, Tony Albanese, who came to L.A. hoping to live as a woman, frequented downtown gay bars on Main Street such as Harold's, the Waldorf, and the 1-2-3, where he encountered some males in garish drag, others indistinguishable from real women, all resembling, as he ambivalently characterized them, "creatures of another world" with their "cacophony of psychedelic patter,

falsetto laughter, screeching and cackling."[44] Albanese fell in with a group of transgender immigrants from Hawaii and Samoa who lived in a downtown apartment replete with "female clothing strewn all around and noxious perfumes."[45] One of the Hawaiians introduced Albanese (who by then had adopted the drag name of Denise D'Anne) to a wealthy older man who kept company with beautiful "girls." His home in the Hollywood Hills was called the "Girl Factory," and he had already helped four males become "girls" by sending them to a sex-change clinic in Casablanca, Morocco.[46]

Miss Destiny, who championed the mid-century queen world, seemed to be commenting directly on Mattachine's disinclination toward those who were "too flamboyant" when she wrote that a political movement among the sexually different would not succeed "until we stop hat[ing] the types that we are not comfortable with." "After all," she added, "how can any homosexual afford to be intolerant? All adjustments that hurt no one else ought to be accepted and understood—at least by homosexuals."[47] But it would be another generation before the community embraced the idea of unity through the concept of "GLBT."

Los Angeles Mattachine never recovered from the loss of its founders. Though the organization continued elsewhere, in L.A. it lost members because it lost direction. In 1956, throwing out the founders' common sense along with their Communist taint, Mattachine's president stated: "We do not advocate a homosexual culture or community, and we believe that none exists." The group's research director reported that his aim was "to help professional researchers find the cause of homosexuality and end the problem."[48]

However, L.A. Mattachine's early flame was not extinguished. It had already started burning in a torch of a different kind. In October 1952, a Mattachine group in West Hollywood had begun talking about creating the first homosexual magazine in America that would have national distribution. The following month, they met at the Studio Bookshop in Hollywood and chose the name "ONE, Incorporated" for their new group.

They referred to themselves often as "the Corporation"—a "capitalist" mask that was calculated to put to rest the putative connections between Communists and the homophiles. Their official name, ONE, suggested by an African American member, Bailey Whittaker (a.k.a. Guy Rousseau), came from Thomas Carlyle's line, "A mystic bond of brotherhood makes all men one." Several members of the group had been members of Knights of the Clock, the pointedly interracial homophile organization. One of the signers of ONE's incorporation papers was the partner of Don Slater, Antonio Reyes, who came to L.A. when he was sixteen, and under the tutelage of Rita Hayworth's uncle, Eduardo Cansino, became a celebrated flamenco dancer. (Reyes and Slater met while cruising in the underbrush of Pershing Square and became lovers for the next fifty years.) Merton Bird, an African American accountant, and John Nojima, a Japanese American survivor of the Manzanar Relocation Camp, were also founding members of ONE, Inc., though race was not among the primary issues ONE addressed.

ONE Magazine began publication in January 1953 with a bland first cover that could have adorned any literary quarterly, but it quickly became more and more daring. By the fourth issue, the editors made the magazine's real purpose evident on the cover, with a mock red-scare headline: "Are You Now Or Have You Ever Been a Homosexual?" By November, the phrase "The Homosexual Magazine" appeared on the cover, signaling to gay people that at last here was a periodical that dared to speak directly to them.

Against heavy odds in the midst of the reactionary McCarthy era, *ONE* made a considerable impact nationally, appearing on newsstands in several U.S. cities and selling about 5,000 copies a month, many of which passed through multiple hands.[49] By articulating issues in cover stories, such as "Homosexual Marriage," "Homosexual Servicemen," and "Religion and the Homosexual," *ONE* set a community agenda that would last for the next fifty years and more. It changed its subtitle to "The Homosexual Viewpoint," hoping to speak for homosexuals everywhere. It also provided a public address for often-desperate homosexual correspondents all over the country. An overwhelming refrain in the letters *ONE* received from male readers was about police entrapment

"wherein a plain clothesman will approach a person and pose as a fellow-sufferer," as one correspondent sadly phrased it.[50] Many correspondents who had endured such entrapment experiences turned to *ONE* for legal advice as well as solace.

The "Corporation" rented two rooms on the second floor at 232 South Hill Street, a deteriorating area of downtown Los Angeles. The office, with its beat-up creaky wooden floors and its ceiling-high orange-crate bookshelves, was as shabby as the neighborhood.[51] The men and the few women who staffed the magazine labored with great devotion and scant pay. Jim Kepner, typically, was working full-time at a milk-carton factory and volunteering an equal number of hours writing for *ONE* under at least five pen names. As the magazine's presence became more known, the staff was harassed by visits from police and even FBI officers. Others visited too, believing that ONE's expertise with homosexuals could be put to good use, such as the two Chicago priests who made their way up the creaky stairs bearing a letter of introduction from the Cook County sheriff. The priests assumed that ONE was like Alcoholics Anonymous—that is, that ONE aimed to help unfortunates recover from their homosexual addiction. "They asked if we could send two staff members to Chicago at county expense to run [recovery] groups for gay prisoners and [to train] counselors in their parishes." (The ever-fiery Don Slater, judging them unenlightened, ordered them from the premises.)[52]

The threat of the law was the most troubling to *ONE*'s editors. The Comstock Act of 1873 forbade the mailing of materials that were "obscene, lewd, lascivious or filthy," and the mere mention of homosexuality, which was illegal throughout the country when *ONE* began publication, could be considered all those things. Subscribers, too, worried: Simply by receiving a magazine which dealt openly with homosexuality they were engaging in a dangerous enterprise. Almost two-thirds of the subscribers chose to pay an extra $1.00 a year (a subscription was only $2.00) to have *ONE* mailed to them first class, in a sealed envelope, with no return address.[53]

The editors and subscribers were right to worry. As Stella Rush, who had just joined the staff, remembers, in August 1953, seven months after *ONE*'s beginning, "a couple of men suddenly showed up to search our

office. They confiscated our pure, sanitary little magazine," she says, astonished still. "Maybe they were looking for guys going down on guys in the toilet. But nobody had time for that. It was a very busy and business-like place."[54] The intruders had been sent by the Los Angeles postmaster, Otto Oleson, whose order to confiscate the magazine came from federal post office authorities in Washington, D.C.[55] The August issue had sported a cover that announced the lead article was titled "Homosexual Marriage?"

ONE's staff sought the legal aid of Eric Julber, a twenty-nine-year-old heterosexual attorney just two years out of Loyola Law School. He had recently made the newspapers when he presented evidence that the LAPD had brutalized his client, a black man accused of drug possession. Julber got him acquitted.[56] Julber recalls now his visit from a *ONE* delegation, which was made up of Dorr Legg, Dale Jennings, Don Slater, and Jim Kepner. They asked him to help them get back from the post office the seized copies of the magazine. "I told them, 'I never had anything to do with gay people, know nothing about that way of life. . . . But I do know about one thing—civil liberties and the right to be free from censorship.'" Julber says he agreed to work with *ONE* gratis, recognizing that this was potentially a "landmark case" that could make his reputation as a civil rights attorney. But he did not have the opportunity to show his skills in court: The solicitor general in Washington determined in three weeks that the August issue was not obscene, and the confiscated copies were returned.[57]

The *ONE* seizure case certainly did not enhance Julber's reputation; instead, he had to suffer the jaundiced view of his fellow attorneys, who, when they heard that he had agreed to help *ONE,* remarked, "You're kidding! What are you doing? People are going to think you're one of them."[58] Nevertheless, Julber continued working pro bono with *ONE,* reviewing each issue before publication, making sure—in a paradox that represented the era—that the homophile magazine did not advocate homosexuality. In the October 1954 issue, he wrote an article explaining what the law considered obscene, opining in that article that the subject of homosexuality among women could be treated "with greater freedom."[59]

Ironically, it was that issue of *ONE* that the post office seized once again, naming as the most obscene piece a (dismayingly innocent) story

about lesbians, "Sappho Remembered." Two other pieces in the October 1954 issue were also named obscene: an advertisement for a Swiss homosexual magazine, *Der Kreis,* which alluded to the magazine's "beautiful photos," and a playfully satiric poem, "Lord Samuel and Lord Montagu," which hinted at homosexuality in British history. Again Julber agreed to take the case gratis. Afraid that his own expertise about obscenity cases was insufficient, he tried to "get some heavy-weight backup from the ACLU." He told a director of the Southern California branch, "I think there's a violation of the First Amendment. How about becoming co-counsel?" To Julber's astonishment, the director's answer was, "I don't think we'd be interested in a case like that."[60]

Julber carried on alone. He appeared before Federal District Judge Thurmond Clarke, whom he remembers as "a beefy former USC football player," who declared in 1956 that the October 1954 issue of *ONE* was unmailable because it contained "filthy and obscene material." The judge flatly concluded, "The suggestion advanced that homosexuals should be recognized as a segment of our people and be accorded special privileges as a class is rejected."[61] *ONE* and Julber then took the case to the Ninth Circuit Court of Appeals, only to get similar results: In February 1957, the three-judge panel of the court of appeals deemed the magazine issue under question "morally depraved and debasing." Jim Kepner characterized the verdict as "a crushing decision so broad we could hardly continue the magazine if it stood." Having no alternative but to press ahead, they asked Julber to try to take the case to the United States Supreme Court.[62]

It is utterly amazing that at a time when a federal district court refused to recognize homosexuals as "a segment of our people," the Supreme Court, which had never before heard a lawsuit involving homosexuality, would listen to *ONE*'s case. It is even more amazing that the Supreme Court agreed that the post office, by imposing "stricter standards" on the magazine than would be imposed on a nonhomosexual magazine, was "discriminating" and denying *ONE*'s staff "equal protection." On January 13, 1958, the Supreme Court reversed the lower courts. Mere homosexual content in a magazine was no longer obscene, and a homosexual magazine could be sent through the U.S. mails.[63]

How could *ONE*'s editors not gloat over the huge victory? "We took on the whole federal government for a period of four years—and they spent big money, with top lawyers brought from Washington, to squish us," Dorr Legg remarked. "And they didn't! We won."[64] But as Don Slater wrote in the next issue of *ONE,* it was not the magazine alone that achieved a victory: "*ONE Magazine* has made not only history but law as well and has changed the future for all U.S. homosexuals. Never before have homosexuals claimed their rights as citizens."[65] The Los Angeles magazine's unprecedented win in the Supreme Court was a turning point for homosexual America that would be crucial to the gay movement that was to come: No homosexual publication could ever again be declared obscene merely because it was about homosexuality.

ONE, Incorporated, expanded its reach with each passing year. In the summer of 1956, ONE began a second publication, *ONE Confidential,* directed at "members of the corporation" rather than the general subscriber. That same summer saw the development of a new branch of the corporation that caused great excitement (and which eventually caused catastrophic division). Dorr Legg, the business manager and main mover and shaker behind ONE, Incorporated, had been a visionary since his participation in the Knights of the Clock, when he hoped to establish social services for interracial homosexual couples. Now he continued to dream of homophile activism that would have long-range impact. As manager of the corporation, he lamented the "tremendous gaps existing in higher education . . . concerning the homophile's place in history and his true status." Legg hoped to close the gaps.[66] He found strong support for his project among the erudite but self-taught Jim Kepner, the college-educated Julian "Woody" Underwood, and Merritt Thompson,[67] a retired dean of education at the University of Southern California whose academic credentials provided prestige and legitimacy to the venture. Gerald Heard, a much-published British philosopher and a friend of Christopher Isherwood's, joined the core group to hammer out the curriculum. The ONE Institute of Homophile

Studies,[68] the first gay studies program in the country, began offering courses in the fall of 1955.

The founders credited themselves with outstripping even Hirschfeld's Berlin Institute for Sexual Science in attempting "a specialized study of the whole field of homosexuality,"[69] including history, biology, psychology, anthropology, sociology, law, religion, philosophy, world literature, and "problematics"—which taught students how to apply their new knowledge to create strategies and goals for the homophile movement.[70] Saturday afternoon classes in these topics were offered to the public at ONE, Inc.'s office. (Kepner noted that classes, though earnest, were not large, and that "constant off-key singing, or caterwauling screeches" from an elderly singing teacher down the hall "often interrupted our classes, producing a levity out of sync with the content or tone of our lectures.")[71] ONE's educational division gave rise to yet another publication, *ONE Institute Quarterly of Homophile Studies*, and to a series of annual conferences, known as ONE's Mid-Winter Institute, which was held at various downtown L.A. hotels—another first for a homosexual group—though when the hotel staff approached, the participants were sure to lower their voices so that the nature of their discussions would not be overheard.

ONE was also becoming *the* place where homosexuals knew they could turn when in trouble or perplexity—virtually the first "gay center" in America. Charles Rowland, a member of ONE, soon took the idea of a gay center even further. In the Southern California tradition of "thinking big" and establishing new churches, he began the Church of One Brotherhood, which for a brief period hosted ecumenical Sunday morning services at the Hill Street office. Through the church he also tried to raise money for a freestanding building that would be called the "Walt Whitman Guidance Center," where homosexuals would be provided with all the elements of a social service agency, such as counseling, employment assistance, legal referrals, and medical service. Rowland estimated that hundreds of homosexuals arrived in Los Angeles monthly, including many gay teenagers whose dreams of stardom drew them to Hollywood. They became part of a legion of homosexuals "without jobs, without funds, without friends, without adequate job training or education." The Walt Whitman Guidance Center was to be their lifeline.[72]

It would be another generation before something resembling the prescient Rowland's Center could be built; nevertheless, the ever-increasing demands for help forced ONE to create a "Division of Social Services" in its two-room office, led by the indefatigable Dorr Legg. Despite slender resources, the "division" offered a gamut of services, including job placement for gay people. Surviving case forms also show that families of homosexuals, too, turned to ONE when in need: For instance, a mother used ONE's social service when her twenty-year-old son, an air force officer, faced a court-martial. The fact of his homosexuality had been leaked by a gay acquaintance who had been caught and grilled by military authorities. The mother believed her son was "unwilling to face [the] actualities of the case and [the] need for vigorous, drastic action," and solicited ONE's help.[73]

The little office was soon deluged. There were letters, such as those from small-town gay men asking whether ONE could assist them in moving to Los Angeles. There were long-distance calls from all over America from homosexuals or their families seeking advice.[74] There were "the Talkers" who "come up to the office and Talk and Talk and Talk," as the staff lamented. "It slows work down. . . . [But] they must find an outlet somehow, apparently, so we listen and listen."[75] The nation's only openly homosexual office had become a Camelot. Volunteers labored selflessly, as Dale Jennings, honored in 1953 for his work with ONE, recognized in his praise for fellow workers, "sitting there in unsuspected glory. Each of us here tonight is a hero, each has a place in history."[76]

But as revolutionary and remarkable as these "heroes" were, their organization did not escape numerous crippling problems, which foreshadowed those that were to plague the gay movement throughout the generations that followed. The sheer volume of work and simmering tensions over what "the homosexual viewpoint" should be brought intense pressures to the idealistic staff. Jim Kepner, who devoted his life to homophile causes, described his labors at ONE as "a diet of bitterness."[77] A struggle over power and over the very purpose of the organization itself created an ultimate schism for ONE, Inc. Personal tensions heightened. Some members of ONE's board were leery of Charles Rowland's enduring

Red-tinged militancy; or they were harshly critical of his far-reaching plan for the Walt Whitman Guidance Center, deeming it pie in the sky.[78] Dorr Legg, always the dominant force at ONE, Inc.,[79] lost interest in the magazine and advocated that the corporation expand its educational function, which riled Don Slater, who had been *ONE Magazine*'s creative mainstay. Slater also accused Legg of unethical tactics when he trumped Slater's bid in 1965 to win a majority on the board. Slater then mobilized his supporters, rented a truck, and removed ONE's furniture, business files, and library, claiming that *his* group was "ONE." The corporation sued Slater et al. Slater then formed a new group, the Homosexual Information Center, and published a gay magazine he called *Tangents,* lifting the name from Jim Kepner's column in *ONE.* Though Slater and his allies eventually signed an agreement promising to return all ONE business records to Legg, he kept many of them until his death in 1997.[80]

For several years the funding issue was just as thorny as the personality issues at ONE because huge donors, such as emerged a generation later, were scarce at mid-century. But though the personality problems went unresolved, the funding problem was eased when ONE received a windfall through an eccentric multimillionaire named Reed Erickson. The small-boned bodybuilder who wore a red pompadour and flaunted a pet leopard was born Rita Erickson and had been the first woman to graduate from Louisiana State University in mechanical engineering. Erickson, through sex-change procedures in 1965, was a pioneering female-to-male transsexual. After working with Harry Benjamin, the sex reassignment guru, Erickson, who had inherited a family fortune that he parlayed into $40 million, decided to use the wealth to fund a nonprofit educational foundation that would serve those whose "human potential was limited by adverse physical, mental, or social conditions." For twenty years, beginning in 1964, he poured millions of dollars into the gay/lesbian/transgender movements. Many of those dollars went to the ONE Institute for the Study of Human Resources. Eventually, Erickson purchased for ONE the Milbank Estate in L.A.'s Country Club Park. Now ONE could offer the academic programs such as Dorr Legg and his supporters had only dreamed about—in a twenty-seven-room mansion surrounded by lush acreage and worthy of its proximity to Hollywood. (In

more recent years, the mansion has been the setting of films such as *Rumor Has It* and *Running with Scissors*.)[81]

In addition to establishing a homophile movement, L.A. members of Mattachine and ONE played another vital role in gay American history as subjects in the first study to look at homosexual men outside a clinical context. In the 1940s, when Evelyn Hooker was teaching psychology classes at UCLA and performing experiments on neurotic rats, Sammy From, a gay man who was one of her brightest graduate students, befriended her. He introduced Hooker to a circle of several other gay men and two lesbians who shared a Silver Lake house; he took her to gay bars and drag clubs; he took her to parties where she met such gay luminaries as Paul Goodman and Christopher Isherwood.[82] He had made it his mission to introduce Dr. Hooker to a broad swath of gay society before he proposed that she study "people like us," that is, functional gay men who had no need for psychotherapy. When Hooker mentioned From's proposal to a heterosexual colleague, he encouraged her to take advantage of a veritable open field: She could gather empirical data about homosexual men, which had never before been done. Hooker began collecting male homosexuals' life histories and Rorschach test results in Los Angeles, but changes in her own life took her away from the city and her nascent study. She returned in 1951, still feeling, as she characterized it, "absolutely haunted" by the study she had not finished.[83]

It was then that Hooker applied for a grant from the National Institute of Mental Health. She proposed to compile data on men who were a 6 on the Kinsey scale, that is, exclusively homosexual. (As a control, she would administer the same tests to an equal number of Kinsey 0s, exclusive heterosexuals, mostly fireman and police officers.) Hooker received the NIMH grant only after federal investigators came to visit; she suspected that, because they feared a homosexual would not be impartial, only by eyeballing and interviewing her could they confirm her claim to heterosexuality. She apparently passed their test, though Hooker, nearly six feet tall and sometimes described as mannish, had oc-

casionally been mistaken for a drag queen, as happened when a police officer tried to prevent her from using the women's restroom at a Halloween drag ball in Santa Monica because he assumed she was really a man.[84] She took the dangers of her work in stride but used sensible precautions: Anticipating being swept up in a raid in the course of her gay bar visits, she carried a signed letter from the chancellor of UCLA describing the nature of her research.[85] By 1956, Hooker was ready to publish her first study, "A Preliminary Analysis of Group Behavior of Homosexuals,"[86] for which she had relied primarily on members of Los Angeles Mattachine and ONE as "an [established] pool of people she could dive into."[87]

Her research with gay men continued. Hooker had used her contacts in homophile organizations to locate other L.A. gay men whom she could use in her studies. Skip Foster, who later worked for her as a graduate researcher, first met her when the two sat together at a ONE banquet in a downtown hotel. He recalls how this "cultivated and interesting" mind zeroed in on him. She wanted to know about Foster's social network: Not only was he very familiar with L.A.'s gay bars, he also had a long-standing group of nearly two dozen gay friends who played volleyball together at Will Rogers State Beach on weekends. Hooker supplied him with a new Webcore tape recorder, which he used first to interview his beach companions; then (as Foster's lover at the time often complained) he hung out in the gay bars until closing time for a full year, earning his living by pursuing interviews through last call. "She wanted to know everything," he says—about people, bars, and all the gay institutions that were hidden away from the straight world.[88] Her work culminated in *The Hooker Report* in 1969.

The research that Hooker did in Los Angeles had national consequences. By concluding that homosexuality was not a mental illness, her studies provoked a series of attacks in the 1950s, but they played a pivotal role a generation later in the American Psychiatric Association's decision to remove homosexuality from its list of mental diseases. Judd Marmour, a psychiatrist and a leading advocate of the APA's 1973 reform, recalled that it was Hooker's L.A. studies that were "the reference point we always went back to."[89]

OVERCOMING "GOOD MANNERS"

If you mind your own business and use "good manners" you will not get into any trouble at all.

—"Attorney Stresses Nothing to Fear," *The Ladder,* 1957[90]

The women's story in Los Angeles was not the same as the men's when it came to mid-century organizing because, though lesbians and gay men often shared friendship and social life, their biggest battles with the outside world were different. Middle-class lesbians, like homosexuals of any class, suffered the threat of being rejected by family and friends, but they had little occasion to worry about the police. They were not entrapped by "Hollywood rejects" hired by the LAPD. They did not run the risk of being busted for public cruising or T-room sex. They were seldom stopped by policemen on the streets. Their greatest enemy was generalized "homophobia," which was a much more amorphous adversary than the LAPD and one that seemed impossible to tackle in such repressive times. Middle-class lesbians had good reason to worry about being fired from those very few professions that were open to females at mid-century if their sexuality became known. But, as the attorney for the *The Ladder* (the magazine of the first American lesbian organization) stressed in 1957, if they "mind[ed their] own business and use[d] 'good manners,'" they had "nothing to fear." To mind one's own business was, of course, the diametrical opposite of participating in a homophile movement.

Working-class lesbians in Los Angeles had considerable reason to be concerned that the police might arrest them in a bar raid or for masquerading, but as female and poor they also had to worry about everyday survival. They were in no position to see themselves as a united political force,[91] and middle-class lesbians were certainly not inclined to take up the battle for their working-class sisters. (Unlike middle-class gay men who, through their sexual tastes, were sometimes brought close to working-class men, homosexual women of different social classes seldom mixed.) What could bring lesbians together in a political organization?

Formal organizing among lesbians at mid-century was also hampered by other factors. Women as a whole were still political neophytes who

had been voting in America for only three decades when the homophile movement emerged. Collectively, lesbians, no less than heterosexual women, had little experience in joining organizations the aim of which was to fight political battles. Their reluctance to take a public stance as homophiles was exacerbated by the fact that those who came of age in the postwar years were of the cohort dubbed the "Silent Generation." Activism was foreign even to most men of that cohort, but for women, who had been doubly repressed by virtue of their gender, it was generally inconceivable. That even a few lesbians managed to fight the good fight in the 1950s homophile movement is astonishing.

Neither Mattachine nor ONE was able to politicize more than a few lesbians. To most women, the organizations seemed irrelevant, to say the least. First of all, they were male-founded, male-dominated, and male-focused, and even their rhetoric of "brotherhood" seemed to exclude women. Even worse, women viewed the organizations' defense of gay men's penchant for semipublic sexual encounters in the same way that many members of Mattachine had viewed the Communist issue: It was a Trojan horse that threatened to discharge trouble on all homosexuals, but lesbians could avoid it simply by dissociating themselves. Many lesbians had little sympathy anyway with gay male sexuality, which seemed to them so different from female sexuality. The attorney Herb Selwyn recalls that when he warned a Mattachine group in the 1950s about Vice Squad stakeouts in the parks, one of the few lesbian members present observed with disdain: "The boys are so horny. They just can't wait."[92]

The homophile organizers in L.A. did try from the movement's inception to include lesbians. Like the leaders of early European cogendered homosexual organizations—who argued in the nineteenth century that the presence of homosexuality among women as well as men proved that it ought to be regarded as a "natural state" rather than criminal behavior[93]—Mattachine leaders understood the political value of a cogendered organization. Rudi Gernreich, who knew of the earlier European

homophile groups from his youth in Vienna, brought "Flo," a lesbian fashion model with whom he'd worked, to the first organizing meeting. (Harry Hay remembered that Flo was "very pessimistic" about the possibility that homosexuals could organize, and she did not return).[94] Gernreich later brought another of his lesbian models, Catherine Cassidy, but she, too, did not last long in the organization. Ruth Bernhard, a bisexual who later became one of the most noted photographers of the female nude in America, was recruited as well, and she became the lone woman among seven men who formed part of the inner circle of leadership. (Bernhard left the group in 1953 and went to San Francisco, where she worked with Ansel Adams and Imogene Cunningham.)[95] From time to time, other lesbians joined Mattachine and occasionally even played substantial roles in the organization.[96] But without a burning reason to organize formally, such as gay men who suffered police entrapment had, few Los Angeles lesbians were convinced of the group's significance to their lives, and the number of women members remained miniscule.

Daughters of Bilitis, the first lesbian organization in America, was founded in San Francisco in 1955 and had a bit more success attracting women in Los Angeles than did Mattachine or ONE, though middle-class lesbians seldom joined Daughters, either. Del Martin, a founder of Daughters, pointedly complained that lesbians who had "some measure of professional status" not only refused to support homophile groups but even "damned [them] for bringing Lesbianism into the open, fearing that as the public became more aware, people might take a second look at them."[97] The accusation certainly held an element of truth: The more homosexuality was discussed in public, the more difficult it would become for two mature, unmarried women to pass as "housemates."

However, it was not merely fear of exposure, nor all the other factors mentioned above, that kept middle-class lesbians away from Daughters of Bilitis. The declared aim of the organization—to "integrate the [lesbian] into society" by "educating" her and helping her "make her adjustment"—was patronizing to middle-class lesbians, as were the preachy articles in *ONE,* such as "Café Saturday Night," which appeared in 1954. "Why the fly front pants?" the lesbian writer taunted butch lesbians:

> [Why] the men's shorts (you brag that you wear them) and the men's jackets that always look too big in the shoulders? Your answer—a hundred times over from 100 different people—would be, "I'm more comfortable this way. I never could stand women's clothes. I've always dressed this way!" (You must have looked adorable at age 7 in your bow tie and long chain!).

The author concluded with a proclamation for her lesbian readers: "We are accepted or not, THRU OUR CONDUCT! Our homosexual SOCIETY can be accepted and approved—it's up to YOU![sic]"[98] But the middle-class lesbian at mid-century had already learned very well how to comport herself in the outside world; she did not require an organization to "adjust" her. If she was able to maintain her middle-class status, it was because such survival techniques had become second nature to her. She would brook no condescending edicts from the homophiles.

But perhaps lesbians who were middle-class professionals rarely joined homophile organizations in the 1950s mostly because they lacked what political scientist Doug McAdam has identified as being crucial before minorities can organize formally—an understanding that they might have some sort of "latent political leverage."[99] "Political leverage" of any kind was unimaginable to those whose very livelihood depended on their success in hiding. In lieu of homophile organizations, however, what the Los Angeles middle-class lesbian had (if she was lucky) was a social group on which she could depend for the long haul, such as the circle of lesbians who became neighbors in 1942 and pulled together to help one of their number recover from her aneurysm; or the "Hilltop dancing girls" who met to dance in the Los Feliz area from the 1940s until death did them part;[100] or the extensive Malibu Canyon friendship circle of lesbian real estate brokers, architects, veterinarians, social workers, entertainment executives, and professors, who met in one another's homes for lavish catered parties. ("We were the A List," a member of the group now recalls.)[101] Such companionable communities offered security in the knowledge that one was not alone. It took a couple of decades more and a revolution in consciousness before middle-class lesbians were finally able to band together politically in feminist organizations.[102]

Even Daughters of Bilitis had not been formed with the intent of being a political organization. Rather, the founding members, made up largely of pink-collar and white-collar workers, wanted to establish a social alternative to the dangerous bar scene. Once the group named itself, enlarged the membership, and began discussing the social discrimination from which lesbians suffered, its purpose broadened beyond the social.[103] A year after Daughters' founding in San Francisco, Del Martin sought to expand the organization and turned to L.A. first as the most likely city outside the Bay Area where such a group might take hold. She found several lesbians who agreed to establish a chapter,[104] though it was only when a founding member and past president of San Francisco Daughters, Helen Sandoz (a.k.a. Helen Sanders or Sandy), moved to Los Angeles in 1958 that a chapter was finally formed. The woman who became her partner, Stella Rush (a.k.a. Sten Russell), remembers that Sandoz arrived in L.A. with a list of likely-prospect names and that the two of them drove all over Los Angeles County trying to convince other lesbians to join the fledgling organization.

Finally, about fifteen women came to the early meetings, which were usually held in Sandoz and Rush's living room. Rush recalls those meetings as being like pioneering consciousness-raising groups combined with group therapy: "We'd talk about our problems and fears—like how we risked losing our jobs if we didn't lie about who we were. We'd assure each other that it was society that made us lie, and not that we were bad people because we weren't allowed to be honest."[105] For the first time in Los Angeles, a group of white-collar and pink-collar lesbians were regularly gathering together to discuss systematically the problems that were visited on them by a homophobic society.

Ann Bannon (the author of the Beebo Brinker series), who lived in Los Angeles from 1956 to 1962, attended those early Daughters' gatherings, and her memories give insight into why women would have found the meetings salubrious, but also why they did not join in great number. She remembers that Daughters' meetings were a great relief after the dark, stifling gay places she had known in New York:

> In Greenwich Village I'd met people mainly in smoky bars. In L.A. everything seemed so expansive and beautiful. It seemed to spill over into the

> gay community [and Daughters]. We sat in a real home—a bottle of wine, a plate of cookies, all those attractive women, talking about real things, like how do we counteract society's refusal to know we drink orange juice and eat cereal in the morning, just like them.

But for her, the meetings were, paradoxically, more dangerous than the bars because in the bars she could be anonymous; at Daughters, where everyone soon learned a great deal about everyone else, she had no cover; and she feared the news that she was a lesbian could leak to her husband, who might claim their two small children. Bannon says she admired the group's desire to address publicly the difficult issues with which lesbians had to contend: "They discussed social change. Some of the women had been in the military, and they were angry at the hypocrisy of military policies about lesbians. I remember them even talking about would we be able to get a group together, to demonstrate. But," she says, "because of my circumstances, it was too scary for me, I couldn't join them."[106]

In fact, Daughters did not take their grievances to the streets in those years. To the extent that the consciousness-raising of their discussions made the Daughters understand the ways in which homophobia impinged on their lives, the L.A. organization may certainly be said to have been political; but the women of L.A. Daughters had no consensus about an immediate and dramatic struggle they needed to undertake, such as Mattachine men did in fighting the LAPD's nefarious entrapment policies. L.A. Daughters, like all the other branches of the organization that sprang up in the late 1950s and through the early '60s, was plagued by a fogginess of purpose. Barbara Gittings, who became a founding member of the New York branch, remembers, "Our motives were pretty hazy. We didn't have any clear sense of what we were going to do. It just seemed enough that Lesbians were getting together. . . . The discussions were awfully vague and groping. We kept seeking for ways of making the meetings interesting, without having clearly said to ourselves, 'What exactly are we meeting for?'"[107]

That unspoken question was apposite. To take on the whole world for its injustice was too overwhelming. Thus Daughters lacked an immediate

political raison d'être, such as Mattachine had when it challenged Dale Jennings' prosecution. The women's group could effect no dramatic victory. For those reasons, unlike Mattachine, it would have no spectacular growth spurts.

Helen Sandoz tried valiantly to make L.A. Daughters grow by expanding its political meaning—associating her group with the larger homophile movement, insisting that the fate of the lesbian was inextricably linked to that of the gay man because they were both "homosexuals." To that end, she circulated to Daughters' members extensive legal and medical literature on homosexual men. (Little attention had been paid to lesbians in such literature at that time.) And she tried to get members to attend ONE-organized lectures, which were usually about problems specific to gay men. So strongly did Sandy believe that lesbians must make community with gay men that in the late-1960s, while *The Ladder* and other Daughters chapters were becoming feminist,[108] she refused to join forces with the women's movement, claiming that she appreciated its goals but "did not approve much of the rhetoric," and that she wanted anyway "to concentrate on getting rights for both gay men and lesbians in the homophile movement." Her good intentions alienated many members. Stella Rush recalls: "We had a number of girls whose experiences with men had been so bad that they wouldn't even come if we had a male speaker or met jointly with the guys [from Mattachine or ONE]."[109]

Sandy also tried to expand the base of the membership by bringing more working-class lesbians into the organization. But, as in most of the homophile movement, Daughters was dedicated to the proposition that all lesbians ought to look "respectable," which meant that in public meetings, especially those with heterosexual speakers, Daughters members were obliged to "dress appropriately," that is, in skirts or dresses. Stella Rush remembers "one poor butch" who owned nothing but pants when she joined Daughters, and who had no notion of how one dressed to look "appropriate": "She got the president of Daughters to go shopping with her for a woman's suit that she could wear to attend some big meeting with an outside speaker."[110] But working-class lesbians generally had

no desire to be as accommodating to the Daughters' rules as this woman was, and they did not regard the organization as a safe space.

ONE Magazine also had mixed success in attracting L.A. lesbians. *ONE*'s guiding hand, Dorr Legg, was determined, as the Mattachine founders had been, to make *ONE* cogendered. He supported a February 1954 all-lesbian issue as well as a regular feature, "The Feminine Viewpoint: By and About Women." As a representative of *ONE Magazine* and ONE, Inc., he reached out to Daughters' members not only in California but in New York and Chicago as well; he also promoted *The Ladder* when it began publication, and he helped with its Los Angeles distribution, hoping to demonstrate ONE's willingness to make common cause with lesbians.[111] The other editors of the magazine were equally anxious to appeal to women. They brought a lesbian couple, Ann Carll Reid (née Irma Wolf and nicknamed "Corky") and Eve Elloree (née Joan Corbin), onto the editorial board with four men. Elloree, whose clever and charming drawings lent sophistication to the magazine, was made art editor. Reid was also elected the "chairman" of ONE, Inc.; the other eight board members were all men.

Ann Carll Reid shared the goal of Legg and the others at *ONE* to involve more women in the magazine. As an editor and frequent author of the "Feminine Viewpoint" columns, she made impassioned pleas for women contributors in the pages of *ONE*, trying to shake lesbians out of their complacency: "Why are we, the women, reluctant to express our viewpoint?" she challenged. "Fear? Shame? Indolence? Snobbery? Which?"[112] But so reluctant were lesbians to be contributors to *ONE* that the magazine was reduced to publishing stories about lesbians written by men under women's pseudonyms to improve the ostensible gender balance of *ONE*. Even "Sappho Remembered," the lesbian short story that became a cause célèbre when the Los Angeles post office's seizure of the magazine led to a Supreme Court trial, was written not by "Jane Dahr," as the magazine announced, but by James Barr, the author of a much-publicized 1950 gay novel, *Quatrefoil*.[113]

To rephrase Ann Carll Reid's question, why did she and Eve Elloree "*not* feel fear or shame or indolence or snobbery" about "expressing their viewpoint" in a homophile magazine? Their courage in working at *ONE* is beyond question, but it is interesting to speculate about the reasons they (and the few other lesbians who contributed regularly to *ONE*) could jump in where others feared to tread. Surely their familiarity with *Vice Versa*, Edythe Eyde's little Los Angeles magazine, had helped "prepare the way," as a ONE, Inc. publication declared in 1956: Both women had been avid readers of *Vice Versa* in the 1940s, and so the concept of a magazine by and about homosexuals was not as startling to them as it would have been to most lesbians in the early '50s.[114]

But the subtleties of class and the imperatives under which middle-class professional women lived at mid-century—even in expansive Los Angeles—explain a good deal as well. Reid, described by Eyde as "a dear, elfin, little girl, real cute,"[115] was a white-collar worker at a downtown advertising agency who often held lunch meetings with her ONE board at a nearby coffee shop.[116] Elloree, who had been a student for a couple of years at San Jose State College before coming to Los Angeles to make a home with Reid, worked only as art editor for *ONE*, an unpaid position.[117] Both women, Elloree later recollected, felt free to hang out at the If Club and keep company with "a Hollywood crowd."[118] Stella Rush, writing under the name Sten Russell, was *ONE*'s other most frequent contributor. Like Reid and Elloree, she had some college education, but she did not work in a professional job—she was a draftsman. There is no doubt that producing a homophile magazine in the reactionary mid-century demanded great courage of anyone. Yet all three women were fortunate to feel freer to do such work than did those who, as Del Martin wrote, "had some measure of professional status" and were terrified of losing it in the midst of the McCarthy era.

But regardless of what enabled the women at *ONE* to do their work, its value was uncontestable, as the many letters to the magazine confirm. Only about 10 percent of *ONE*'s correspondents were female,[119] but over the sixteen years of the magazine's existence they wrote numerous letters, asking for advice, bemoaning their loneliness, pleading for an introduction to other women like them. Their letters were often poignant,

such as the one from a Philadelphia woman: "I have been miserable these last few months because I have no one to discuss my problems with. But now that I have found your magazine I feel much better about my whole situation."[120] Sometimes the letters were utterly desperate, such as the one from a woman who asked for the name of "understanding lawyers in the Chicago area" because she could not "relate my true reason behind my difficulty" to her present lawyer. *"Very Urgent—Danger is involved,"* she wrote at the bottom of the page.[121] A married women in Granby, Quebec, confessed her lesbianism to the person she addressed as *ONE*'s "Feminine Editor" and lamented that "in this Province it is very difficult [for two women] to get together and live together, as our laws are very strict." She begged the "Feminine Editor" to "pass along my name and address to someone or a Club" who might exchange correspondence with her.[122] A New Britain, Connecticut, lesbian, after imploring the editor to "find me someone to correspond with as I am helpless in my own vicinity for reasons that you can readily understand," closed with a P.S.: "Please excuse my [hand]writing as I am very nervous."[123] It was no light thing for a lesbian to write to a homophile magazine in the 1950s.

Ann Carll Reid responded gently to all such letters, though she had to tell those writers who requested introductions to other women that the "postal authorities" would charge *ONE* with "inciting to illegal acts" if it served as a pen pal club.[124] But she, as well as the other editors, generally offered the magazine's crew as social service workers at a time when a social service organization for lesbians was inconceivable. "If you feel that any of the members of the staff of *ONE* can be helpful to you, please feel free to write to us,"[125] the editors told the women correspondents, and even coaxed them: "Please my dear friend, come out of that shell . . . and we will gladly help you in every way we possibly may."[126] The L.A. magazine's mere existence in itself was already, according to lesbian correspondents, a huge help for those who dared to read it. They looked to ONE in the 1950s to envision for them a freer world and to promise it would come to pass.

By the next decade, the outlines of such a world were appearing. The women's movement, which worked to better women's lot and also to overthrow their political reticence, was bringing about significant change; and lesbians—who as independent women suffered most under sexism—were in the forefront (as they had been in the first wave of the women's movement, during the nineteenth and early twentieth centuries).[127] They led feminist groups and they established lesbian groups. Feminism even miraculously revived L.A. Daughters by the end of the '60s. As *The Ladder* reported, the Los Angeles branch, after being dormant for a while, had "come to life like a fabled sleeping giant, with a large and very active group." Its president was a Latina, Delia Villarreal.[128] Villarreal's tenure was short-lived; but in 1971, another young Latina, Jeanne Cordova, became president, and her energy allowed the group to hold on even as other organizations for feminist lesbians were proliferating. L.A. Daughters opened the first lesbian social services center in the country, ambitiously offering "educational, recreational, and sociopolitical services, activities, and actions on behalf of our community" every night of the week in a little building it had procured on Vermont Avenue. "Our community," as Jeanne Cordova now defined it in the L.A. Daughters' newsletter she edited, had spread its concerns beyond lesbians: As its feminist goals now mandated, it was "dedicated to the personal and social liberation of all women."[129]

Gay men in Los Angeles were also changing with the times, and public perception of them was beginning to change, too. By the mid-1960s, the efforts of the homophiles to educate the straight world about homosexuality finally seemed to be producing traces of national impact. *ONE,* which had labored for more than a decade to bring homosexuality into the public forum, had reason to feel it had succeeded in 1964, when *Life* magazine ran a two-part feature on homosexual men, "Homosexuality in America: A Secret World Grows Open and Bolder," citing Los Angeles as the birthplace of the homophile movement. The *Life* article created tremendous visibility for the love that had dared not speak a name ever since the European invasion. Though the writer of the article was not precisely sympathetic to male homosexuals, he did attempt to be some-

what evenhanded, unlike the national media, which had seldom been fair when discussing homosexuality in the past.

What was more significant, the *Life* article announced to the public that the old perception of homosexuals as cowering in the twilight was in need of drastic revision, that a serious transformation was beginning. The writer of the *Life* article observed that the Los Angeles Police Department had arrested 3,069 men for homosexual offenses the previous year, but even the LAPD could not help but notice that a minirevolt was already occurring on the streets: "The pervert is no longer as secretive as he was," Inspector James Fisk despaired, inadvertently prophesying a sea change that was soon to come. "He's aggressive, and his aggressiveness is getting worse."[130]

II: THE BOLD ONES

Defiant gay activists from The Patch inside the LAPD Harbor Division Station, October 1968. This was one of two sustained Los Angeles public protests against gay bar raids prior to 1969. Troy Perry at far left. *Courtesy Lee Glaze.*

CHAPTER 5

Rumblings of a Gay Revolution

While it is possible that [the new morality] might lead to corruption and collapse, we have every reason to believe that what will ultimately emerge will be stronger, freer, and more decent than anything we knew in the past.

—Myron Roberts, "Our Changing Morality," *Los Angeles Magazine*, 1963[1]

THE "AGGRESSIVENESS" of Los Angeles homosexuals that Inspector James Fisk observed in 1964 was trivial compared to what it would become in the wake of a vast social upheaval that mounted throughout the decade. The 1965 Watts riots, the first race riots in which whites rather than blacks ran for cover, captured worldwide headlines and helped set off a new radicalism among black people all over the country. "Black Power" became a dramatic rallying cry as militants rejected the nonviolent rhetoric of Dr. Martin Luther King, Jr., and the gradualism of liberal schemes such as President Lyndon Johnson's War on Poverty. Ignited by images of a city burning and the rhetoric of righteous anger, the politically dispossessed of all stripes—including opponents of the war in Southeast Asia, Chicanos, students, hippies, the New Left, and radical feminists—adopted the stance of militancy for their own causes. In Los Angeles, Chicanos rejected the assimilationist

"Mexican Americans" and proclaimed themselves members of "La Raza." They formed organizations such as the Brown Berets and captured attention by dramatic demonstrations not only against the Establishment's war in Vietnam but also against discrimination, oppression, and malign neglect.[2]

Fueled by the nearby examples of Watts and the Chicano movement, as well as the attention of the Hollywood media that loved the color and drama of the new "youth culture," the disaffected young in L.A. also grabbed headlines.[3] In the fall and winter of 1966, thousands of them, dubbed by the *Los Angeles Times* the "Disturbing-the-Peace Corps,"[4] gathered nightly on the Sunset Strip for nearly a month; they protested the curfew laws that ordered them off the streets by 10:00 P.M. as well as the arbitrary arrests of long-haired boys and unconventional dressers. When the number of young protestors swelled to 2,000, the police called in bulldozers and tanks to clear them away.[5]

Among the protestors were many young gay people who relished the freedom to blur gender lines in the unisex drag that the counterculture now encouraged. "We used to dress up in the most outrageous outfits on weekends, and the [hippie] styles gave cover to us gay kids," Lee Mentley recalls. The young gays with whom he ran would start the evening by listening to records at Wallach's Music City on Sunset and Vine, and then make their way down the Boulevard among the hippie kids (who were often sexually flexible), stopping at the Whisky A-Go-Go, Gazzari's, the Fifth Estate Coffee House, and Pandora's Box, and ending up in the nearby gay bars such as the Farm.[6] "It's the freaks who walk up and down the streets that cause the problems," a city official complained of the boys who dressed as girls used to, with their long hair and jewelry; and the girls who dressed as boys used to, with their Levi's jeans and T-shirts.[7]

Despite the 1966 bulldozer-and-tank police assault, the young continued to flock to L.A. from small towns and cities to try their fortunes or to escape the narrowness of "back home"; and they continued to haunt the perennially flamboyant Sunset Strip, where they would meet their own kind and could savor the arty cutting edge, such as the new music scene that drew huge crowds of the countercultural young. Gay kids who

had no place to go but the streets—the runaways and throwaways—were legion among the newcomers. (They would become a chief reason for the establishment in 1972 of the Los Angeles Gay Community Services Center.)

The hip and high and gay who marched up and down the Strip and found crash pads here and there in West Hollywood or Silver Lake or Venice Beach rejected the sociopolitical rigidity of the noir years and fervently embraced new politics and a new consciousness. Influenced by sensitivity marathons, Eastern mysticism, and mind-expanding drugs, which fueled utopian visions, they became part of the countercultural "flower children" of the "love generation," and they believed themselves destined to bring "enlightenment" and radical reform to the troubled world they were inheriting.[8] They had a champion in the *Los Angeles Free Press,* which had been established in 1964 as a community alternative to the major media that avoided stories of interest to progressives. The news about the city's campaign to drive nonconformists, including homosexuals, from Pershing Square, for example, was virtually ignored by the *Los Angeles Times,* but it merited front-page headlines in the *Free Press.*[9] The militancy of the *Free Press* about progressive issues alternated with laid-back permissiveness. The *Free Press* would even publish overt "Personal" ads, not yet welcomed in the mainstream media, including ads from "Groovy Guys" (which had become a new slang term for "gay men") and "Gay Girls." The *Los Angeles Free Press* was the voice of young hippies who rejected the conventionality of their parents' culture and identified with the "different." "What if all the minorities, both born and voluntary, got together to cooperatively rent houses, shops, ballrooms, coffeeshops, ALL over town?" a writer for the *Free Press* asked in 1967, dreaming of a community of the "different."[10]

The great population of social and sexual nonconformists in 1960s Los Angeles was often visible at the Human Be-Ins, held regularly in Griffith Park and Elysian Park, where the inhibitions of convention were enthusiastically challenged. "Man, everybody TOUCH!" a counterculture poet demanded at a Griffith Park Be-In. "We are too many and only this rapport can make us one." He called out to "L.A. hippies, angels, freaks, heads, old hairs, long hairs, Mods, Minis, mendicants," telling

them, "We have a communion to build!"[11] This "communion," in which "TOUCH" was literal as much as figurative and old notions of appropriate and sanctified behavior were vehemently rejected, helped not only to foster the Sexual Revolution but also to loosen old taboos against same-sex touch.

In fact, the loosening of taboos that ushered in the Sexual Revolution had begun in Los Angeles even by the end of the 1950s, when laws regarding "obscenity" were challenged: A book dealer was arrested for selling the lesbian pulp novel *Sweeter Than Life*, and he fought the city ordinance that made it a crime to stock "obscene" books. The United States Supreme Court found in his favor in 1959. Justice William Brennan, speaking for the Court, declared that such a city ordinance "inhibits constitutionally protected expression [and] cannot stand."[12] But it was the Hollywood film industry that was especially instrumental in spreading a developing new ethos all over America. As early as 1961, film censorship, which had been codified by the Hays Commission in the 1930s, was compromised when the Motion Picture Association of America declared: "In keeping with the culture, the mores, and the values of our time, homosexuality and other sexual aberrations may now be treated with care, discretion, and restraint."[13] The Motion Picture Association of America ceased to pronounce any film "prohibited"; instead, it "advised caution" or recommended certain films for "mature audiences only." Through Hollywood, censorship was on its way to meeting its demise across America.

HOLLYWOOD A-GO-GO

> *I see gay guys dancing their souls out, their faces sweating. . . . I see queens stepping out of their closets and finding the world outside isn't as bad as they thought. . . . THEY ARE OUT! I see them taking the banner from the "free people" (I mean the hippies or flower children. . .) and wearing the most beautiful feathers they can find.*
>
> —Sam Winston, *Los Angeles Advocate*, July 1968[14]

In 1961, an estimated 140,000 homosexual men and women lived in the greater Los Angeles area.[15] The sheer numbers of homosexuals who were congregated in L.A., combined with the example of the widespread militancy of groups that had once been tractable, would soon make its gay revolution inevitable. Already Los Angeles was one of the easiest cities in the world in which one might be "different"—which included being gay. Milton, who was employed at Universal Studios, recalls a sign he saw on the lot that had been posted in the mid-1960s, which at that time probably had no equal on the planet: "Universal Does Not Discriminate Against Gays."[16]

Though Hollywood had always been a haven for homosexuals, in the 1960s it became more overtly gay than ever. According to a 1968 book titled *Hollywood, Gay Capitol of the World,* it was now nothing short of a lavender paradise: "If he wanted," the writer proclaimed, "the gay individual in Hollywood could spend just about his entire life, perform nearly every function, entertain and provide for himself, in a purely gay milieu."[17] In 1969, according to one source, the male homosexual population in Hollywood alone was 25,000.[18] Lesbians, too, had formed residential enclaves by the 1960s (generally in less affluent areas such as suburban North Hollywood) where they might spend much of their lives in company with one another. In the early 1960s, North Hollywood had a dozen lesbian softball teams sponsored by various bars, as well as numerous bowling leagues, restaurants, and private key clubs.[19] Lesbians were also brought together during these years as fans at sports events such as the Roller Derby—televised weekly in Los Angeles—which featured dashing women skaters who were almost all gay.[20]

The growth in the male homosexual population in Los Angeles did not go unnoticed by the straight media, though lesbians generally continued to remain beneath the media radar. In the early 1960s, L.A. newspapers still damned gay men as pariahs. The worst media treatment of gay men came in 1963 from a small paper, the *Hollywood Citizen-News,* which launched a muckraking assault on "sexual deviates"—coining the term "S.D."—in a four-part series based on little that was actually news. The "exposé" was triggered apparently by the newspaper's discovery of

the Los Angeles homophile movement: "These S.D.'s are organized," the writer complained. "They have their own newspapers, picture magazines, and code."[21] "SEX DEVIATES MENACE L.A.," the first headline of the series blared. The article declared that homosexuals posed the "greatest threat to health and morals in the Southland," and it distorted statistics on the venereal disease problem among gay men. The article also accused gays of being responsible for 60 percent of crime in L.A. and (bafflingly, without a shred of evidence) declared them all to be "potential killers."[22] The *Hollywood-Citizen News* called on the state legislature to make it easier to close gay bars since they were the main "S.D." meeting places.

In the midst of the newspaper's assault, an unlikely ally leapt to the defense of the beleaguered "S.D." Paul Coates, the columnist who bashed the Mattachine Society in the 1950s, recognized by the '60s that news of homosexuals in Hollywood was no news. Coates scoffed at the *Hollywood Citizen-News*'s "discovery" that Hollywood's "star-studded streets are being gingerly trod by coveys of quaint young men." "It should come as no surprise," he added with surprising understanding, "that the cinema hamlet is a traditional mecca for homosexuals. . . . They came here for a kind of social acceptance. And they found it."[23]

The *UCLA Law Review* also leapt to the defense of homosexuals in the mid-1960s. An exhaustive study, "The Consenting Adult Homosexual and the Law: An Empirical Study of Enforcement and Administration in Los Angeles County," demonstrated gross police and legal injustices against homosexuals and recommended the elimination of unfair laws.[24] The study team, led by Jon Gallo, interviewed dozens of judges and prosecuting attorneys, and were told by most of them off the record that "the legal system was behind the social mores of the day" and "[homosexual lewd conduct cases] were a waste of judicial time, prosecutorial time, and police time." "If they had their 'druthers,'" Gallo observed, "they'd rather not be dealing with such cases."[25] Obviously, for many Angelenos, citizens and officials both, times had already changed dramatically since the 1950s. The Sexual Revolution, the mass of young people who were rebelling against the conventionality of the reactionary decade in which they grew up, the alternative media and meeting spaces that supported

them, and the old L.A. flamboyance all made the rhetoric of moral crusades such as that of the *Hollywood Citizen-News* seem to many to be anachronistic.

But the police, as untroubled by anachronism as was the newspaper, continued to hound homosexuals, both men and women, throughout the 1960s. Bill Stephens recalls the "Barbra-Streisand sweep" one evening in 1967, when LAPD officers raided gay bars and made mass arrests on lewd conduct charges. Stephens, who was among those arrested, says that there had been a Barbra Streisand television special that evening, and after watching it, he had gone to meet friends for a drink at the Ram's Head, a Silver Lake beer bar. He ended up at the police station: "They took sixty of us out of five gay bars," Stephens remembers. (He added that it was that harrowing experience that radicalized him. He decided to go to law school and spend his professional life defending gay people.)[26]

Connie Eddy recalls another night at her favorite Pasadena bar, the Daily Double: She'd gotten up from her table to go to the restroom just as three sheriff's deputies came in, and she had to pass by one of them as he stood near the pool table. By the time she returned and resumed her seat there was a strange hush in the room because "everyone was too afraid to talk." The deputies were going from table to table, questioning the nervous patrons. The deputy she'd passed earlier came to her table and asked her name. She told him.

> He said, "Stand up, please."
> I said, "Why?"
> He said, "I want you to come outside with me."
> "Why?" I asked again.
> "Do what I tell you," he said. "I want you to get in the car. I'm taking you to the police station, for bumping into me—for harassing me when you walked by me at the pool table."

She insists she had not even touched the officer when she walked by. But he handcuffed her, though she begged him not to and assured him she was not resisting arrest. She was taken to Temple City Jail in a squad

car and booked. Then she was put in a jail cell with women who had been arrested on drug charges. She was kept all night. "I was frightened to death. They let me out the next morning, and I called my mother to come pick me up. I had to go to court. They gave me a public defender who said to plead 'no contest.'" The commissioner admonished her: "You swore at the officer. You won't do that again, will you?" She dared not answer anything but no. Her case was dismissed.

Connie says she went back to the bar to talk to the owner, wanting to figure out why the deputy had picked on her. The owner speculated that Connie had been singled out only because she'd caught the officer's eye since she was femininely dressed. "It was like 'Who are we going to pick up tonight?' And I was the straightest-looking person there. They wanted to scare the hell out of me."[27] For the LAPD, nothing had changed since the noir years.

But despite such harassment, bars for lesbians and gay men proliferated dramatically all over Los Angeles and its outlying areas as more homosexuals came to the city and felt freer to show themselves in semipublic places. It was a game of cat-and-mouse, and the mice were growing bolder. In 1966, there were 119 bars that catered to gay men and lesbians in and around Los Angeles.[28] In 1969, the number of bars in those areas had risen to 162.[29]

Gay men's bars have always been more numerous than those exclusively for lesbians, but the number of lesbian bars and those in which lesbians were welcomed grew larger than ever in the 1960s. Through the hippie movement, which rendered whatever was bourgeois a target of disdain, many young lesbians who had come from the middle class had declassed themselves. They were unworried about finding jobs that were "respectable" and "worthy" of their class, and they took risks that their 1950s counterparts had feared to take. Sharon A. Lilly (who became a high school principal years later) remembers that while she was still in high school, in the early 1960s, she and a gay male friend, their phony IDs in their Levis' pockets, would hang out at Anna's, a bar on east Sunset Boulevard, where Latinos, blacks, and whites mixed. "It was filled with boys and girls our age—sixteen to twenty-four. Flamboyant kids. We'd dance and dance and dance. Boys and boys. Girls and girls. Girls and

boys."[30] Unlike McCarthy-era middle-class lesbians who felt especially vulnerable because they worked at jobs funded by the government (for example, teacher, social worker) the declassed hippie was not terrified about confronting "the pigs" in bar raids. Francesca Miller, a middle-class African American woman who dropped out of college in the 1960s because she was "into having fun and doing drugs," remembers that in 1969, when the police raided the Farm, a West Hollywood gay bar frequented by young gay men and lesbians, the saucy patrons "blew kisses at them."[31]

Though some lesbian and gay teenagers managed to procure borrowed or forged IDs that would represent them as being over twenty-one and thus old enough to enter bars, for those who could not pass as adults, a new spate of coffee shops served as a sort of community center where they might socialize with other young gay people. During the 1950s on Hollywood Boulevard, gay teens hung out at coffee shops, such as the Marlin Inn, that catered exclusively to homosexuals, and those such as Coffee Dan's where an oblivious straight crowd sipped their coffee and nibbled their BLTs alongside drag queens and butches.[32] In the 1960s, more and more coffee shops opened where young gay boys and occasionally gay girls congregated. Some attracted a mixed crowd, as an Angeleno who had been a teenage habitué recalled of a Melrose Avenue coffeehouse, the 8727 Club, which catered to "gay, straight, hip, and the 'gee, I dunno' group."[33] The mix was a good cover. The proprietors of coffeehouses that had an all-gay clientele sometimes felt constrained to be as careful as bar owners: Bill Stephens, whose hangouts as a gay teen were the St. Genisius on Hollywood Boulevard and Alberto's in Westwood, remembers that the management at both, disturbed by frequent police visits, forbade the kids to booth-hop. But they carried on anyway by "sending a cup of coffee or a soda through a waitress to someone you liked," Stephens recalls. "Then you might meet and talk on the street. You could also send notes through the waitresses."[34]

Gay coffee shop hangouts were by no means limited to teens. Older gay males sometimes frequented such places to find teenage boys who

were looking for adult companions. The over–twenty-one crowd of lesbians and gay men had their own coffee shops, such as the Gold Cup on Hollywood Boulevard and Arthur J's on Santa Monica Boulevard. Francesca Miller remembers Arthur J's as a phenomenally popular all-night hangout where gay people flocked after the bars closed. Arthur J's was thought by gay men to be a great place to score. Aristide Laurent, who was a regular in the 1960s, recalls that the sexual carryings-on had been so rampant in the men's rooms at Arthur J's that the waitresses were ordered to toss a cup of ammonia on the floor hourly so the fumes would preclude anyone from spending more time than was required to use the toilet.[35]

The Sexual Revolution was clearly not lost on homosexuals. Inspired by the topless craze that was sweeping high fashion and low nightclubs, gay clubs, such as Goliath's on Melrose Avenue, featured nude male go-go dancers. Some gay men felt nudged to liberation by the phenomenon: "I remember going into one of those clubs, which was absolutely packed, and seeing a naked boy dancing up on the bar. It felt like a new wind of freedom was blowing through the place," one man recalls.[36] Sexual freedom became a major issue in L.A. gay male culture in the 1960s, and there were bars for every variety of sexual tastes. The Red Plume aped *Playboy* by appropriating its icon for outrageously gay usage: Customers were waited on by male "bunnies" wearing little more than a bow tie and a smile.[37] Madness Inc. served the leather trade. At Cannibal, the patrons could witness live sex acts.[38] Drag came back to the Sunset Strip and Hollywood. Ciro's nightclub on the Strip, which had long been shuttered, reopened as a gay venue featuring the young female impersonator, Jim Bailey. "Drags have gone mod," the author of *Hollywood, Gay Capitol of the World,* said in 1968 of miniskirted and vinyl-booted queens in the Hollywood bars.[39]

Sexually charged gay motorcycle clubs also multiplied in Los Angeles during the 1960s. The Satyrs had been the only gay motorcycle club in America when it was established in L.A. in 1954, but now the Blue Max, Oedipus, and the Kingmasters clubs all competed with the Satyrs in bringing men out of the bars and to the campgrounds of the San

Bernardino and Santa Monica Mountains, where they explored literal new heights of sexual and personal freedom.

OLD GAYS IN NEW TIMES

> *Homosexuals reading the "non-discrimination" clause in Government contracts, which sets the official key for employment policies throughout the nation, might wonder with some reason whether the term "sexual orientation" should not be added to those specifying "race, creed," etc., and thus become a part of those conditions which should have no relevance to employment opportunities for every American.*
>
> —Robert Gregory, *ONE Magazine*, 1961[40]

Though some Los Angeles homophile groups remained quite timid throughout the roaring '60s, others became bolder, defining themselves unequivocally as members of a minority and asking for the rights that were opening up to racial and ethnic minorities, as did *ONE*'s managing editor, Robert Gregory, in his claim that homosexuals should be added to the government's list of protected groups. But for the most part, there was a split between "old gays" who brought into the 1960s their 1950s fears, and "new gays" who observed the social upheavals that were taking place in Los Angeles and the world and wanted to force change even among the homophiles.

Jeanne Cordova, briefly the president of Los Angeles Daughters of Bilitis, recalls that the "old gays" in Daughters, who were generally middle-aged, were uncomfortable with the feminist thrust that she and the few other women in their twenties tried to impose on the organization. The older lesbians were still afraid that if they appeared too subversive they would be more vulnerable to their enemies, and they were annoyed when Cordova invited a group from "Women Against the War" to address Daughters. Cordova recalls that the old gays were especially "furious" with the in-your-face title that her "new gay" editorial committee had selected for the Los Angeles Daughters' newsletter, *Lesbian Tide* (cf. *The Ladder*).[41] By mutual agreement, the *Lesbian Tide* soon became

independent. Daughters of Bilitis had been the only organized precursor to the lesbian-feminist movement, but it was unable to hold on to young members in the 1970s because it could not overcome sufficiently its birth in a very different era. With the rise of lesbian feminism, L.A.'s Daughters dissolved for good.

Other homophile organizations fared better because they reflected more of the ethos of the 1960s. ONE's dream of a big donor, which had miraculously come true in the person of Reed Erickson, the female-to-male transsexual multimillionaire, was realized in a milieu very different from that of the 1950s, when ONE had been born. Erickson's Educational Foundation announced in its brochure—in very 1960s flower-power rhetoric—that "the foundation of the Foundation is Love," and that one of its chief goals was "to bring to awareness of Love Reflecting Through in the lives of those (the children, the animals, and some of the 'lepers' of our society) who have become accustomed to rejection and cruelty."[42] With Erickson's money, the ONE Institute for the Study of Human Resources could fulfill its mission, couched in New Age language, to "assist gay people and members of other sexual minorities to attain their fullest potential in our society." ONE became the first institution to offer graduate degrees in gay studies, and it was eventually accredited by the state.[43]

Some Los Angeles groups that were founded in the 1960s began by sounding like their 1950s predecessors, but their rhetoric and purpose became increasingly aggressive. The Society of Anubis, its purported eight hundred members equally divided between lesbians and gays, tamely declared when it began in 1967 that "the membership . . . strives to present to the public a true picture of the homosexual as a worthwhile member of society."[44] Gradually, however, Anubis became bolder. When the organization received a state charter two years later, the lesbian president, Helen Niehaus, boasted, "What makes it even sweeter is the specific purpose for which we are chartered." The group had made it clear on the application that a primary intention was "to support legislation for the enactment of just and enlightened sex laws."[45] Though

Anubis (named after an Egyptian god who was a "balancer of the scales" and a "healer") was hardly a radical organization, it caught something of the temper of the times in its willingness to fight. After two female undercover agents infiltrated the organization in 1969 and, at a birthday party for an Anubis member, returned with Vice Squad and Alcoholic Beverage Control officers to stage a raid, Helen Niehaus blocked their cameras with her body. She was threatened with arrest but stood her ground. No arrests were made, though Anubis was cited for selling alcohol and permitting dancing without a license.[46] The experience made Anubis even more political, and members were regularly reminded that their "voting potential" as lesbians and gays "could be pivotal."[47]

A few Los Angeles homophile groups were even bolder. In 1966, thousands of bemused Angelenos witnessed the first gay parade on record, which was part of the "First National Homophile Protest" to end the ban on gays in the military.[48] On May 12, a long line of cars bearing on their hoods signs four feet tall that declared "Ten Percent of all GI's are Homosexual" and "Write LBJ Today!"[49] wound a twenty-mile route from downtown Los Angeles to Hollywood. The protest, one of five demonstrations in cities across the nation, was planned by the National Conference of Homophile Organizations, though Los Angeles was the only city to stage a parade. The energy behind the march came from the old homophiles: Don Slater, who had been an editor of *ONE Magazine* and, after a bitter dispute with Dorr Legg about movement priorities, founded *Tangents* (a magazine that was a cross between homophile and new gay),[50] provided his office as headquarters for the caravan. Harry Hay, the deposed founder of Mattachine, acted as president of the Los Angeles committee. A core of homophile stalwarts provided most of the manpower in raising the money and driving the parade cars. As *Tangents* reported, "Almost nightly from Topanga Canyon on the North to Long Beach on the South, teams of workers placed fliers under windshield wipers of cars parked in the vicinity of bars known to cater to the gay crowd."[51]

The parade got a nibble of attention from the media. The CBS affiliate in Los Angeles ran a brief film clip of the caravan, and Slater, Hay, and his partner, John Burnside, were interviewed on local television and radio.

Though the impact of this first gay parade was minimal—and more than forty years later gay people were still fighting the same battle over homosexuals in the military—Harry Hay observed that the homophile movement had "never had so much news coverage before."[52] The coverage was inconsistent at best. For example the *Los Angeles Times* declined to send a reporter to cover the parade "unless someone was hurt."[53] Homophiles, however, coming from an era in which the media would keep mum about them if there was nothing bad to say, were thankful for crumbs of attention that were not unmitigated vilification. The homophiles did not understand what the gay revolutionaries of the next generation would figure out brilliantly: how to manipulate the media.

A NEW ROAR: THE GAY REVOLUTION BEGINS

John Q. Public has to wake up to the fact that he has to accept us. We exist. Straights have to learn to live with it. . . . If they close up our clubs we'll all have to take to the streets.

—Lee Glaze, quoted in the *Los Angeles Advocate*, August 1968[54]

Gay leaders emerged in Los Angeles during the 1960s who understood that different times called for different approaches. A few of the radical founders of the L.A. homophile movement joined them; indeed, they jumped eagerly into the new radicalism that the social climate now permitted. Jim Kepner wrote for daring journals such as the early *Advocate*, and he joined younger gay militants in actions such as a 1967 protest about police harassment at an L.A. gay bar, the Black Cat;[55] Don Slater hosted the first meeting of the Los Angeles Gay Liberation Front at his *Tangents* office on Cahuenga Boulevard. But the new gays were inventive in ways that would have been inconceivable to the older generation.

For example, gay activist Vernon Mitchell (a retired aircraft engineer) opened in West Hollywood the nation's first free clinic that would serve "homosexuals, hippies, and others reluctant to go to the Health Department [to] get reliable VD exams and treatment."[56] Gay men had often feared that if they sought treatment for venereal infections they and their sex partners would be reported to the Health Department and,

since most forms of homosexual sex were illegal in California, be accused of committing a felony. Mitchell's clinic (which would have been inconceivable almost anywhere else at the time) was a product of L.A.'s vibrant alternative culture in which the dispossessed, despairing of the Establishment, were finding their own solutions to problems.

The most notable organization that formed in Los Angeles in the mid-1960s, PRIDE, was far more radical in rhetoric and action than any of the earlier homophile organizations had dared to be.[57] PRIDE (probably the first application of the word to gay politics) was an acronym for Personal Rights in Defense and Education. Members of the organization called their opening meetings "Pride Night" and referred to the Hub, the gay bar that hosted them, as "Pride Hall." PRIDE was founded in 1966 by Steve Ginsberg, who was determined to disassociate the group from what he perceived of as the stodginess of the homophile movement. "The main hang-up is the difference between the activist militant groups, which take to the streets, like our organization, and the prissy little old ladies of some of the older groups," Ginsberg proclaimed (with the brashness of youth) to the *Los Angeles Free Press*.[58] In the context of the 1960s' sexual revolution, PRIDE's leaders adamantly refused to obfuscate their sexuality. Ginsberg, who was a twenty-seven-year-old landscape gardener, wore leather to meetings, emphasizing the determination of a new breed of gay male activists to claim freedom by flaunting rather than buttoning down.

Instead of dismissing young bar-goers as "riffraff" and shrinking from them, as Ginsberg believed the homophiles had, PRIDE hoped to embrace gay youth of all classes as part of a vital gay community. The September 1966 PRIDE newsletter proudly announced, "Ours is a young group. . . . We have great contact with the kids in the bars, who have always been neglected by the other groups."[59] But though PRIDE defended the bars, and even hoped to attract to their organization "the kids [from] the bars," they also believed that gays needed a variety of social outlets, including "a healthy atmosphere to meet in."[60] PRIDE aimed big, announcing its immediate goal—which was revolutionary

in its day—to open a gay community center.[61] Pot-of-gold donors such as Reed Erickson were still scarce, however, and the group never succeeded in raising the necessary money for a gay center, though it did organize "healthy" community activities such as a hiking club and a bowling league, and even provided "marriage" counseling for gay people—anticipating by years activities that eventually became common in many urban gay areas.

But PRIDE's most revolutionary contribution was to organize angry protests against those who tried to rob gay people of pride—most notably, the Los Angeles Police Department, which had not ceased its attacks on gays. PRIDE was behind one of the earliest demonstrations against the police harassment of homosexuals. The response to a Vice Squad raid in the first moments of 1967 at two gay bars in the Silver Lake section of Sunset Boulevard anticipated the Stonewall Rebellion by two and a half years: Twelve plainclothes Vice officers had positioned themselves in a large crowd at the Black Cat to observe the goings-on. At 11:30, when a costume contest ended at New Faces, a bar down the street, dozens of men in drag crowded into the Black Cat. As the Rhythm Queens, a trio of black women, sang a rock version of "Auld Lang Syne," balloons fell from the ceiling and gay men exchanged the traditional midnight kiss. That was when uniformed police, who had been alerted by the undercover officers, rushed in and began to swing billy clubs, tear down leftover Christmas ornaments, break furnishings, and beat several men brutally.[62] Sixteen customers and employees were arrested and forced to lie face down on the sidewalk until squad cars came to take them away. Plainclothes officers chased two men across Sanborn Avenue to the New Faces bar. There, the officers knocked the woman owner down and beat her two bartenders unconscious.[63] One of the bartenders, Robert Haas, suffered a ruptured spleen from the beating. He remained in critical condition for days, and when he recovered, was charged with felony assault on an officer.[64] Six men were charged with lewd conduct: They were seen kissing other men on the lips for up to ten seconds.[65] A jury found them all guilty.

But after a couple of years of witnessing other minority groups demand their rights, and even take to the streets for them, many Los An-

geles homosexuals were now unwilling to absorb such outrage without response. PRIDE spoke for them, organizing multiple protests outside the Black Cat.[66] Hundreds of onlookers supported the parading picketers, and activists passed out 3,000 leaflets to motorists explaining why they were there.[67] Though this may have been the first gay protest in America to attract significant numbers, the demonstrations never caught the attention of the media, and the Black Cat did not take the role in gay history attributed to the Stonewall Rebellion two and a half years later. Topography played a role in the significance of both events: Los Angeles is an area spread out over 450 square miles, where (unlike New York's Greenwich Village, the site of Stonewall) people seldom take casual walks. The Black Cat protests attracted multitudes of people who drove across town to participate, but chance passers-by (such as many of the Stonewall protestors had been) were scarce.

Nevertheless, the Black Cat protests continued for several days. Fund-raising efforts for the convicted six eventually drew support from San Francisco as well as from New York.[68] Herb Selwyn, a heterosexual lawyer and longtime supporter of gay causes, acting on behalf of two of the six men, Benny Baker and Charles Talley, appealed their convictions based on the equal protection clause of the Fourteenth Amendment: Two heterosexuals, he argued, who might be briefly kissing in a bar on New Year's Eve, as the gay men had been, would not have been subjected to police harassment, beating, and arrest. His brief reached as far as the United States Supreme Court, though the Court finally declined to hear the case.[69]

But a new activism had begun in gay L.A. Gay-Ins, inspired by Be-Ins, started in Los Angeles in March 1968. At the second Gay-In, held in Griffith Park in July, the speakers became political, exhorting huge crowds that LAPD entrapment practices must be tolerated no longer.[70] The response to a police bar raid several months later showed that L.A. gays were ceasing to accept harassment as part of the built-in cost of being gay. The Patch, owned by the comedian Lee Glaze, whose tag was "The Blond Darling," attracted many gay men and some lesbians (including the women who skated in the Roller Derby). Glaze had been warned by the police commission that if he wanted his bar, in the L.A.

suburb of Wilmington, to stay in business he had to prohibit not only drag but also groping, male-male dancing, and more than one person at a time in the restrooms.

Because business dropped dramatically after Glaze tried to comply, he boldly reinstated dancing, telling the *Los Angeles Advocate* that "homosexuals have got to start taking stands on these issues," and that he was "confident that bans against male-male dancing will be declared unconstitutional if a case ever gets before the Supreme Court."[71] As Glaze now recalls, "The cops were harassing me up one side and down the other." He responded in his inimitable way: Whenever Vice Squad officers came in to inspect the bar, Glaze, who knew them all by sight, would put "God Save the Queen" on the juke box to warn customers.[72]

One weekend night in August 1968, when the bar was packed with five hundred or so patrons and the dancing was wild, Vice Squad officers burst in with half a dozen uniformed policemen behind them. They stomped around to intimidate the patrons, demanded to see IDs, and made arrests. Glaze jumped on stage and shouted, "It's not against the law to be homosexual, and it's not a crime to be in gay bar!" The raid swiftly became a political rally. Glaze urged the patrons to band together and fight for gay rights. "We're Americans, too!" a man shouted.[73] Glaze announced to the cheering crowd that The Patch would pay for a bail bondsman for those who had been arrested. They marched to a flower shop belonging to one of the patrons, and Glaze bought all the gladioli, mums, carnations, roses, and daisies (but not pansies). At 3:00 A.M., demonstrators carried huge bouquets into the Harbor Division Station and staged a flower-power protest as they awaited the release of the arrested men.[74] With irrepressible camp, Glaze announced that he was taking out an injunction against the Bolshoi Ballet because sometimes its director permitted acts of male-male dancing. The officer behind the desk called for reinforcements.[75]

Despite the rising militancy in Los Angeles, gay people remained largely obscured to the public eye—except, of course, when homosexual men

were being attacked in the mainstream press. Alternative newspapers such as the *Los Angeles Free Press* were cropping up in urban areas throughout the 1960s, but there was no national media that spoke directly to young urban gay people who were observing minority militancy everywhere and were perplexed by, and impatient with, the gentlemanly rhetoric of the homophile publications such as *ONE* and *Tangents,* which were considered stuffy and outdated. To communicate with the world—and, more important, with each other—a new gay movement needed a media infrastructure.

That infrastructure began with a periodical that continues to this day and enjoys the largest circulation of any gay publication in America. It was born in an unlikely place: the print shop that produced scripts for the daily soap operas at ABC Studios. Richard Mitch, the driving force behind the periodical, had joined PRIDE in 1966 after being arrested at the Red Raven bar under the preposterous charge that he had performed oral sex on the dance floor. Mitch was a writer for a chemical industry journal, and he volunteered his skills to help put together PRIDE's mimeographed newsletter. Over the summer of 1967, Mitch and his lover, Bill Rau, conceived of the idea of upgrading the newsletter to a real newspaper. Their production could proceed openly because all the men in the print shop, where Rau worked with Sam Allen and Aristide Laurent, were gay. They undertook to make the newspaper look more professional than the newsletter by typing it in columns on an expensive IBM electric typewriter and setting the headlines in press type.[76] Five hundred copies of the paper's premiere issue were printed in the ABC Studios basement.[77] They chose to call the new paper *The Advocate* because the name sounded "forward-going and legal."[78] That 1967 issue contained a front-page headline that was the first use on record of the slogan "Gay Power."[79] When dissension in the PRIDE organization imperiled *The Advocate,* Richard Mitch negotiated to buy the publication for $1.00.[80] *The Advocate* eventually spread far beyond Los Angeles, becoming the first national gay news publication.

Like many gay people at mid-century who were concerned about their "day jobs," Mitch hid his identity in the gay world under a pseudonym—Dick Michaels.[81] Michaels hoped to create a paper that would

provide in-depth factual coverage of news related to gay men. (Though the paper attempted to include some lesbian coverage, it was perfunctory and generally limited to cultural items such as reviews in 1968 of the play *The Killing of Sister George* and the film *Therese and Isabelle*.) Michaels' personal obsession, triggered by his false arrest, was to investigate LAPD abuses whenever possible, and articles with such titles as "Anatomy of a Raid" and "The Fine Art of Entrapment" became staples in the paper, which included lighter fare, too, such as an April 1968 article about L.A.'s first "Gay-In" in Griffith Park, described as "a throng of about 200 wild fairies having a festive affair."[82]

Michaels was also an astute businessman who realized he might create a wider appeal for his product if he included columns about everyday-life interests such as might be found in the *Los Angeles Times:* a fitness column, "Body Buddy"; amusing features such as "Cooking with Auntie Lou"; advice columns such as "Smoke from Jeannie's Lamp," written by a heterosexual woman, Jeanne Barney; and "Astro-Logic" (an astrology column by Aristide Laurent, who confesses today that he "knew nothing about astrology").[83] Michaels also appealed to his gay readership through a large all-male personal ad section, "Trader Dick" (a play on the sexual slang terms "dick" and "trade," and the Pacific Coast chain of restaurants, Trader Vic). The Trader Dick section of the paper became increasingly provocative and—of course—popular and profitable.

Despite the sexual daring of his newspaper and his willingness to be confrontational in his attacks on the police, Michaels often betrayed a surprisingly conservative nature, both personally and in what he wanted to be the tenor of his paper. Not only was he adamant about keeping his real name a secret throughout his years at *The Advocate,* but also he refused to permit his picture to appear in a gay context and he stayed away from gay events for fear he would be photographed.[84] Though a paper such as *The Advocate* probably could not have existed were it not for the radical milieu into which it was born, Michaels preferred to feature gay men who were clean-cut and moderate in their demeanor. For instance, Troy Perry, the founder of the Metropolitan Community Church (and dapper in or out of his clerical collar), enjoyed frequent coverage in Michaels' newspaper; but Morris Kight, a prominent spokesman

for the L.A. Gay Liberation Front and an old hippie in style, had a difficult time getting the notice he merited.

For about two years, the paper's official name was the *Los Angeles Advocate,* and its beat was local. However, because "local" was Los Angeles and included Hollywood, *The Advocate* sometimes reported on stories that were also covered in the national press. It was *The Advocate*'s mission to rescue such stories from homophobic distortions. For example, the 1968 murder of the silent film star Ramon Novarro by two brothers working as hustlers made lurid headlines all over the country, but the only gay-sensitive (and factual) account of the trial was in *The Advocate,* where Jim Kepner wrote that the prosecution "seemed less concerned with [the murderers] than with convicting the semi-retired screen star of homosexuality."[85] *The Advocate* also doggedly challenged the authorities as other papers feared or neglected to do on homosexual issues. In 1969, for example, when a slight-of-stature male nurse named Howard Efland died after injuries sustained at the hands of LAPD Vice officers, a coroner's inquest described the death as "excusable homicide" due to Efland's resisting arrest; the *Los Angeles Advocate* was the only paper that recorded outrage at the law enforcement officials' patent lie.[86]

Shortly before the paper dropped the geographic modifier from its name, Mitch hired Rob Cole, a seventeen-year veteran at the *Dallas Morning News* and its former city editor, to infuse professional journalism standards into the newspaper. *The Advocate* was soon widely recognized as "the news arm of the gay movement."[87] Gay readers everywhere saw it as the source to which they might go for crucial stories that were blacked out of the mainstream press.

Dick Michaels, who had paid one dollar for ownership of *The Advocate* a few years earlier, sold the paper in 1974 to investment banker David Goodstein for $350,000.[88] Its initial print run of 500 copies had by then swelled to an audited circulation of 44,000 per issue,[89] and *The Advocate* was changing with the rapidly growing readership. Goodstein soon fired the original staff. Jeanne Barney, who continued to write for the paper, recalls that Goodstein announced to the staff that he wanted the paper to appeal to "the upwardly mobile homosexual who has a home in the hills, drives a luxury car and orders alcohol by brand." (Her

reaction: "That's all very nice—but what about the rest of us?"[90]) Aristide Laurent, who had been with *The Advocate* since its beginnings as the PRIDE newsletter, recalls that he felt as though "[his] country ha[d] been taken over."[91] Goodstein moved *The Advocate* headquarters to the affluent area of San Mateo in Northern California. It came back to Los Angeles ten years later in a much altered form.

Homosexuals understood at mid-century that their greatest adversaries were the churches, which dubbed them sinful; the mental health profession, which dubbed them sick; and the law, which took its clues from the other authorities and thus justified their cruelty. Though activists waited until 1970 to try to change the mental health profession, they embarked on a well-organized campaign to educate the churches in 1964. A group of homophiles in San Francisco started the Council on Religion and the Homosexual, an interfaith coalition under the sponsorship of the powerful Glide Memorial Church, formed in the expectation that if the churches could be made tolerant of homosexuals, law enforcement would follow suit. The following summer, an independent group calling itself the Council on Religion and the Homophile was established in Los Angeles. The Council on Religion and the Homophile argued that the public's "misunderstanding of and mistreatment of homophiles" was "unchristian," and that "open communication between churchmen and homophiles" was necessary to end intolerance.[92]

A few Los Angeles churches had long been sympathetic to homosexuals. Even during the 1950s, Stella Rush recalls, the Unitarian church to which she belonged was so concerned with police harassment of both progressives and gays that it instructed all the parishioners about what they should do if they were ever accosted by the police: "We should never say where we worked. 'Give only name, rank, and serial number.'"[93] But such liberalism was rare among the churches. In a city with more church denominations than any place else on earth, lesbians and gay men who were religious had few safe harbors at mid-century, though in the midst of the 1960s Sexual Revolution, some ministers were gradually

coming to understand that they were obliged "to reexamine their traditional attitudes toward all sexual matters, including male and female homosexuality," as one clergyman wrote.[94] But most homosexuals who wanted a church affiliation still had to be closeted.

JJ Vega, who as a teenager in the 1960s had been a member of Assembly of God, a Pentecostal church in La Puente, remembers that six or seven of her friends at church were also teenage lesbians. Though some of them, like JJ and "George" (née Nancy), felt painfully awkward when forced to be feminine, they were told they must always wear dresses, could not use masculine names, and must do the "altar call" in order to have their demons chased out of them. JJ quit the church, but church members continued to pursue her. When she began living with another woman after she graduated from high school, they paid her harassing visits, telling her she was "living in sin" and must leave her partner.[95] Her experience was all too typical for gays and lesbians who were hungry for spirituality and had nowhere to turn but the established churches.

The raid at The Patch in 1968 was at least indirectly responsible for the establishment of a new church in L.A. that would eventually provide safe harbor to many lesbians and gays worldwide. Troy Perry, a Pentecostal minister who was expelled by his Tennessee congregation because he was discovered to be gay, had moved to Southern California and had found work as a manager in the yardage department at Sears. The night of The Patch raid, he had come to the bar with a date, Tony Valdez, who was one of those arrested. After Valdez's release, Perry tried to comfort him with talk of God, but Valdez would not be comforted: "We're just a bunch of dirty queers," he said. "God doesn't care [about us]." Perry believes the incident was an epiphany for him, stirring him to the realization that he must found "a church for all of us who are outcast."[96]

Chuck Rowland had tried to found the Church of One Brotherhood years earlier, in 1956, but that era was not ready, and Rowland's efforts were short-lived. Twelve years later, the times were right. Such a church would have been inconceivable in Baptist and Pentecostal Tennessee, or almost anywhere else, but Southern California had been home to countless cults and tiny denominations as well as gigantic single churches built around one charismatic figure, such as Aimee Semple McPherson

and the Angelus Temple that she founded in the 1920s. Thus the idea of a gay church was credible—though not to everyone: Perry recalls that he presented his plan to a friend, who scoffingly asked, "How are you going to organize a bunch of queens, and get them to follow any religion . . . or do anything together?" Perry was himself uncertain, but he took out an ad in *The Advocate.*

Twelve men and women responded, and in October 1968, in the living room of his rented Huntington Park house, Perry conducted the first service of the Metropolitan Community Church, named for its birth in metropolitan Los Angeles.[97] Milan Charles, who had been a member of Rowland's failed Church of One Brotherhood, at last found a spiritual home: He became one of the early members of the Metropolitan Community Church.[98]

Perry had hit on the way to fill a gaping need of the many lesbians and gay men who had been thrown out of their churches or, like JJ Vega, were made to flee, but still longed for a spiritual life. From the initial dozen worshippers, the congregation grew so rapidly that Perry had to scramble almost every week to find a larger venue. "You better attend church every Sunday if you want to know where the Church is going to be," the congregants would quip.[99] When Perry obtained the 385-seat Encore Theater on Melrose Avenue for Metropolitan Community Church services, that, too, filled. The services were seriously Christian, but not without gay levity. For instance, Lucia Chappelle recalls that the music director, Willie Smith, "all dressed in white, would just fly out on the stage holding a microphone and shout, 'All right you queens! On your feet for Jesus!'"[100] Perry performed some of the first public gay wedding ceremonies in the country, beginning with the wedding of two Latino men in 1969.[101] In addition to tending to the spiritual needs of its parishioners, the Metropolitan Community Church offered a spate of social services, including a Crisis Intervention Counseling hotline and an "Alcoholics Together" group.[102]

Perry wanted to bring gay and lesbian community diversity into his congregation, and he was especially receptive to women and people of color. He welcomed as ushers butch women in formal dress suits;[103] he eventually helped to establish De Colores, an all-lesbian group within the

church; and he encouraged the ordination of lesbians as ministers in MCC. Flo Fleischman, who was a counselor in the church's Crisis Intervention Counseling Program, recalls that when her group was planning a conference, a gay male psychologist asked, "How many of you women will do the cooking?" She went to Troy Perry to complain and was delighted with his response: "The next Sunday in his sermon, he chewed the guys out. . . . 'I want you men to know that the women are not here to cook and clean for us!'"[104]

Perry's faithful parishioners soon made it possible for the church to purchase a large building in the West Adams district, and attendance at Sunday services swelled to more than 1,000.[105] The phenomenon did not escape national attention, and Perry was soon being interviewed for *Time* and *Newsweek*, and even appeared on Regis Philbin's celebrity television show, together with Vincent Price and Sal Mineo.[106]

Troy Perry was far from radical in his style or politics. (Lucia Chappelle remembers that the church was so conservative that she found only one other church member who openly opposed the Vietnam War.)[107] But his conception that homosexuals deserved a church where they would not be damned as sinners was radical in the 1960s, as were the gay activist causes in which he encouraged his parishioners to participate. When the Los Angeles Gay Liberation Front was formed in 1969, Perry became a member and an unlikely bedfellow of the radical, hippie activist, Morris Kight.

The culminating event of the decade came with L.A.'s May 1969 election in which City Councilman Paul Lamport lost his bid for a second term because gay people united to defeat him. Lamport's biggest accomplishment had been his campaign for the "Walk of Fame" tourist attraction—blocks and blocks of movie stars' names etched on the sidewalks of Hollywood Boulevard.[108] He also proudly counted among his achievements the passage of an antiloitering ordinance, aimed primarily at chasing male homosexuals, whom he referred to as "molesters and troublemakers," from the streets of Hollywood.[109] Some gays were convinced

that Lamport, who was endorsed by the LAPD chief, Tom Reddin, was "the man behind" the Silver Lake bar raids of New Year's Eve, 1967.[110] His 13th Council District encompassed not only Hollywood but also Silver Lake and Echo Park, a cumulative area that contained perhaps the greatest concentration of gay population and gay businesses in the nation.

Lamport's election defeat is one of the earliest instances of the power of the gay vote. *The Advocate,* which Lamport denounced for producing "a steady stream of filth and perversion,"[111] along with the gay-friendly *Los Angeles Free Press,* had united with "assorted militants"[112] in order to promote Lamport's challenger Bob Stevenson and, as *The Advocate* vowed, "to really swing an election."[113] "It's inconceivable to me that these characters presume to attempt control of an election in our district," Lamport told the media, complaining that homosexuals were so rampant in the area that he was "afraid to let [his] twelve-year old son walk through Hollywood to attend a Boy Scout meeting."[114]

The coalition to defeat him succeeded. Bob Stevenson won the election, and when he died suddenly in office, his wife, Peggy, who was voted in to replace him, made the rising gay community integral to her political machine. From the May 1969 election on, candidates realized that they could not win the 13th Council District without gay support. Even Paul Lamport came to that realization: In the next election, 1973, hoping to recapture his seat, he campaigned in gay bars of the 13th District, such as the Butch Gardens in Silver Lake. He admitted to the media that in the 1969 election the gay community had defeated him: "I didn't know anything about [the gay community]," he said in a mea culpa, "I'd never taken it seriously. Now, I do."[115]

The young radical gays in L.A. who stridently rejected what they saw as the overly cautious approach of the homophile generation that went before them were perhaps no different from many of the young, past and present: Lacking historical memory about how bad things once were and how much had already been overcome, they crassly characterized their warrior predecessors as being no more vigorous than "prissy old

ladies." But, in fact, the homophiles who emerged in the 1950s and the new gays who emerged in the '60s each helped move the political center with regard to homosexuality as far to the left as it might go in their respective day. The new gays could shake their sabers somewhat louder and push left somewhat further because Los Angeles had metamorphosed by the 1960s to sanction the rumblings of a revolution.

Most of those who would found L.A.'s radical gay groups as well as its radical lesbian groups at the end of the 1960s and in the early '70s began as political and social left-wingers (as did their 1950s predecessors). They cut their teeth on the 1960s Vietnam and civil rights struggles and the counterculture, where they learned to theorize doubts about the infallibility of society's wisdom pertaining to issues of war, race, and morality. Before they began their work as gay liberationists, the new gays learned to conceptualize minority oppression not as a problem for the oppressed individual to suffer alone but as a social ill that a mass movement might eradicate. As one veteran of civil rights and union organizing, who became a gay activist, recalled: "All of us, to a person, had been involved in other struggles." Finally, they asked, "What about *our* liberation?"[116]

This picture of Lee Heflin, Stanley Williams, and John Platania of the Gay Liberation Front appeared in *Life* magazine in 1971. *Photo: Grey Villet/* Time *and* Life *Pictures/Getty Images*

CHAPTER 6

Into the Streets

A little theory may have gotten whipped up in Boston, but in Los Angeles we put it into effect. Lesbians and gays did a lot of marching and demonstrating in the streets of L.A. because here you can do it all year round, like you can't in the East with their long cold winters.

—Jeanne Cordova, 1970s organizer[1]

SUPERFICIAL OBSERVERS of Los Angeles have delighted in characterizing the city as a kind of Land of the Lotus-Eaters in which the residents spend their days puffing pot while soaking up the sun's rays or lolling on white couches decorated with egregious zebra-hide cushions—as a New York lesbian claimed of her 1970 visit to L.A.: "These surfer girls weren't political, at least not in the New York feminist sense I was used to," she wrote with East Coast chauvinism about L.A. lesbians, quipping that the 1970 gay pride parade down Hollywood Boulevard did not start until 7:00 P.M. because "no one wanted to forfeit another good beach day; it was a challenge to be political and to stay tan, too."[2] (In fact, the parade was scheduled to start at 7:00 P.M. only because the hostile LAPD, hoping for its failure, would not permit the marchers to begin earlier.)[3]

Radical gay men and lesbians who lived in Los Angeles during this time bristle at such feeble satire at their expense. They say L.A. was a hub of passionate politics long before Stonewall. Not only had PRIDE

brought modern radical gay activism to Los Angeles by the mid-'60s, but lesbians in L.A. who came of age in the uninhibited and politically lively 1960s were very different from their postwar "Silent Generation" lesbian predecessors. Though a bit slower to fight for their own rights as lesbians, they were on the front lines of L.A.'s civil rights, antiwar, and feminist movements. Even in Venice Beach, the area of Los Angeles where the New York visitor claimed that in 1970 the sole interest of the lesbians she met was in getting a full-body tan, lesbians were in fact helping lead radical grassroots actions such as "Free Venice," a campaign for rent control and against the gentrification that was forcing poor people out of area.[4] Early in the 1970s, Venice Beach was where lesbians were soon in the forefront in establishing the Westside Women's Center, with, as Ariana Manov characterizes it, a "'fuck-you-and-the-establishment-you-rode-in-with' attitude." Lesbians at the Center published the first West Coast feminist newspaper, *Sister,* and they fashioned groundbreaking programs, such as the Fat Underground, the training of women to work in the building trades, and the Radical Therapy Collective—all in the service of women in general and lesbians in particular.[5]

The Westside Women's Center had as its model even earlier L.A. grassroots groups that offered social services to lesbians. The Los Angeles Women's Center on Crenshaw opened in 1969 (its building decorated by a red-and-white sign of the woman symbol, with a clenched fist in the circle signifying radical feminism); the Daughters of Bilitis started a center in December 1970; and the Gay Women's Services Center was founded in February 1971 by Del Whan, a lesbian who had been in the Peace Corps and had spent the 1960s in the civil rights and antiwar movements. The Gay Women's Services Center became the first organization in America that was incorporated as a social service agency exclusively for lesbians.[6]

The Gay Women's Services Center, which hoped to meet the needs of those in direst straits, expanded its services in 1971 and '72 under the leadership of a lesbian couple, Sharon Raphael and Mina Meyer. The Center's staff bailed gay women out of jails, rescued them from mental institutions, and provided shelter until they could get on their feet again; but the Center also served women who were not facing calamity: Activities were of-

fered every evening of the week—rap groups, dances, a music night in which women brought their own instruments and played together—all of which provided welcomed alternatives to gay women who would otherwise have spent their nights in the bars. The Center was staffed entirely by volunteers. To keep the facility afloat and pay the rent ($95 a month), they held a spaghetti dinner once a week and passed the hat.

Because they thought it essential for gay women to be able to find the Center, the leadership battled the telephone company over its refusal to print the word "gay" in the phone directory. The Center prevailed with the help of a phone company administrator who happened to be a lesbian: "Gay Women's Services Center" became the first telephone book listing of the G-word in L.A. (The word "homosexual" first appeared in the Los Angeles phone directory in 1968, when the Homosexual Information Center was listed.) The Gay Women's Services Center also announced its existence to potential clientele by sporting signs on its doors and windows that announced here was a "Services Center" for "Gay Women"[7]—a heroic public proclamation for 1971.

THE L.A. GAY MOVEMENT AND THE LEFT

> *In the Gay Liberation Front we were all radical, antiwar, antigovernment, anticapitalist soldiers. We said that gay liberation was just one of the many battles against the existing power structure. . . . We were in solidarity under the greater umbrella of "revolution" against the system, on all fronts, worldwide.*[8]
>
> —Sharon A. Lilly, a member of the Gay Liberation Front in 1970

McCarthyism had been dead for almost a decade, and the opprobrium in which homosexuality was held had so lessened during the liberal 1960s that the Left could afford to be more receptive to gay radicals than it had been to their homophile counterparts in the 1950s, when it was expunging homosexuals from its organizations. But because the Left had been unsympathetic to homosexuals it was initially hard for some gay leftists to claim the gay struggle as one for "*our* liberation." Morris Kight, who ultimately became a principal leader of the radical gay movement in Los

Angeles, first dipped his toe gingerly into gay politics: He carried a sign at various left-wing demonstrations that proclaimed himself to be a "Heterosexual in Support of Gay Rights."[9]

However, after the huge media focus on the New York Stonewall Rebellion in June 1969, the gay cause became a cause célèbre among the Left, and Leftist gays everywhere suddenly felt free. Autonomous chapters of the Gay Liberation Front sprang up across the country.[10] Morris Kight helped found the Los Angeles chapter a few months after the riots at the Stonewall Inn. The L.A. Gay Liberation Front, which defined itself as "the militant arm of the gay movement,"[11] borrowed the language of the Left for its slogans: "Gay Power to Gay People. Right On with the Revolution. All Power to All People." The very name "Gay Liberation Front" proclaimed the organization's roots in the Left, as did the rhetoric of their newsletter, *Front Lines:* The gay people's struggle for freedom, Morris Kight declared in a 1970 *Front Lines* editorial, had "in its wake the freedom of all those crippled by a racist, sexist, imperialistic system, [and gays would] soon break the chains."[12]

The Los Angeles Gay Liberation Front's intense commitment to a gay revolution was rooted in more than mere rhetoric. In 1970, the Los Angeles Gay Liberation Front (GLF) had opened a little thrift shop on Griffith Park Boulevard; its profits were to be funneled into GLF causes. "Gaywill Funky Shoppe," its sign proclaimed. It was run by Ralph Schaffer, a volunteer who lived in the store's back room. It was there that he was found murdered, his hands tied behind his back. His comrades believed that he had been martyred because of the sign that announced the shop as gay. Their determination to make the world a more hospitable place for gay people became profoundly personal, and their anguish over his murder radicalized them further.[13]

But GLFers considered themselves soldiers of the broader revolution, too. The group pointedly elected as its first chair Greg Byrd, an African American. Morris Kight had worked in the Bureau of Indian Affairs and was in the forefront of the protests against Dow Chemical Company's production of napalm; John Platania had registered as a conscientious objector and had worked with the United Farm Workers Union. Don Kilhefner had served in the Peace Corps in Ethiopia and was active in the Peace and Freedom Party. Some of the earliest meetings of GLF were held

at Revolution House, a mahogany-paneled, oriental-carpeted mansion dedicated to revolutionary people as a "safe house" by a wealthy anonymous donor. At Revolution House, all the revolutionary causes—social, economic, racial, and sexual—were represented. The Gay Liberation Front melded well: Its members were invited by other Revolution House groups to join their antiwar demonstrations and even to be openly gay at the Revolutionary People's Constitutional Convention. John Morgan Wilson recalls the frenetic enthusiasm among GLFers. Their excitement as young revolutionaries was palpable. "There was such a flux and a flow and an energy," he says. "Everyone was growing in leaps and bounds."[14]

Lesbian feminism, too, emerged from left-wing organizations in Los Angeles and employed the language of the Left. "We'd talk revolution—about how things had to change totally, and revolution was the only way," Sharon A. Lilly, a member of GLF and later a founding member of the Lesbian Feminists, remembers. "Revolution became like a religion for all of us."[15] Simone Wallace says that all the women at the Los Angeles Women's Center to which she belonged were—even *had to be* (if they were to fit in)—"very Maoist."[16] Sue Talbot and Liebe Gray, who were also habitués of the Women's Center, says they were really "Trotskyites."[17] All agree that they were very much to the Left, and that just as lesbian feminism grew out of the Left, women in the Left often grew into lesbian feminism. The Socialist Feminist Network, for instance, had been formed to address the ills visited on women in a capitalist society; "sleeping with the enemy" soon came to be regarded as a cause of those ills, and lesbianism (a political choice any woman could make) as a solution.

Though the gay and lesbian movements shared their Leftist genesis with the homophile movement that preceded them, their approaches to battling a homophobic society were very different because their times were very different. The homophiles were amazingly courageous for their day; but the insouciant, colorful antics such as "kiss-ins" and "gay-ins," which became almost routine in the next generation, would have caused immediate arrests and shut down organizations in the 1950s, when bravery was required

simply to attend a private Mattachine or Daughters meeting. By the 1970s, lesbians and gay men could, and did, stage the wildest of public larks, often using the Leftist revolutionary technique of guerrilla theater to inform the "het" population that "we're coming out, and you better get used to it."

In Los Angeles, they did it with special élan. When Marsha Salisbury and her lover Debby Quinn were told by the manager at an International House of Pancakes that they'd have to leave if they continued holding hands at their table, they left—and brought back with them a dozen other women who staged the first lesbian kiss-in.[18] Lesbian kiss-ins soon flourished in L.A., as did gay-men's kiss-ins. To express their displeasure at the omission of women and lesbian artists at the Los Angeles County Museum of Art, Joan Robbins and other lesbian activists called the local television stations to announce the "First National Lesbian Kiss-In," to be held right in front of the museum. The women made the evening news—as they had hoped they would.[19]

GUERILLA TACTICS

The time will come when we will march, arm in arm, ten abreast down Hollywood Boulevard, proclaiming our pride in our homosexuality.

—Charles Rowland, in the 1950s,
predicting the future of L.A. homosexuals[20]

Gay men and lesbians in the L.A. Gay Liberation Front believed that flamboyant militant actions were indispensable tools for bringing about social change. By the first months of 1970, GLFers, in an incredible burst of energy, were making themselves felt everywhere. They slapped day-glo stickers of crossbones superimposed on the head of a pig (i.e., "police") on telephone poles and in restrooms to warn cruising gay men about police surveillance. They staged noisy demonstrations at the *Los Angeles Times* because it refused to publish positive news about gay people. (The paper soon changed its ways, even running a sympathetic five-part article titled "The Woman Homosexual" in June 1970.)[21] They ceaselessly picketed Barney's Beanery, a famous West Hollywood eatery, on whose wall hung the illiterate sign, "Fagots Stay Out." It had been a fixture at

Barney's for two decades, but now it came down (though it later went up again before it was removed for good in 1984).[22] They targeted offensive presentations of gay people on television, protesting the appearance of Gay Gaylord, a recurring character on the *Carol Burnett Show* in the sketch, "As the Stomach Turns." The show's producers eliminated the character and expressed unprecedented contrition for the entertainment industry's hypocritical public homophobia, writing to GLF, "We hope you will accept our apology for having offended you."[23]

The Gay Liberation Front also battled against the L.A. gay bars' antiquated rules against touching, which dated back at least to the 1950s when the Alcoholic Beverage Control would revoke a bar's license if same-sex couples on the premises were caught merely placing an arm around a shoulder. Terrified still of having their liquor licenses pulled, many bar owners continued to enforce the taboo throughout the 1960s. But gay militants now proclaimed such rules to be discriminatory: "Our bars shouldn't be any harder on us than the heterosexual bars are on their customers, and I have been to straight bars where they have almost had sex on tabletops," observed the Reverend Troy Perry.[24] The Gay Liberation Front took on the fight, aiming at a West Hollywood bar, the Farm. The Farm's proprietor, Eddie Nash, a Lebanese immigrant born Adel Nasrallah, owned a half dozen other West Hollywood bars that attracted a gay clientele.[25] Nash tried to enforce the "no touching" rule rigorously, even though on any weekend night the Farm would be packed with more than five hundred people, hip to groin. One gay Liberation Front activist made an appointment to confront the Farm's manager. "I explained to him that with his 'no touching' policy, he was trampling on the civil rights of the very people that made his business possible. . . . He said to me, 'You don't know who you are dealing with,' and with that he put his thumb down on the desk and twisted it as though he was crushing an ant." The activist, frightened but furious, says he conjured up his nerve and raised the threat: "You don't know who you are dealing with. We will bomb your bars."[26]

On September 8, 1970, armed with nothing more lethal than fliers and posters, a crowd of determined GLF men and women descended on the Farm and launched a pacifist attack. When they proceeded to hold hands they were "86'd," that is, kicked out of the Farm. "This is blatant

oppression by a bar we gays frequent and support with our money," GLF proclaimed in the fliers that the "Radical Caucus Committee" distributed as they marched in front of the Farm every weekend for a month.[27] "Why Can't We Hold Hands in Our Own Bars?" the fliers asked. "We Can—There Is No Law Against It!" they answered.[28] After nearly a month of noisy demonstrations, the owner of the Farm capitulated and met with Morris Kight to negotiate. Activists nailed a triumphant sign outside the bar: "GAY PEOPLE'S VICTORY! THE FARM IS LIBERATED!"

On subsequent fliers, GLF informed Los Angeles gays that because the Farm was a "liberated bar," GLF was now urging gay patronage. Eddie Nash had learned to understand the power of gay organizing so well that he became a major contributor to the Gay Community Services Center when it was established the next year by former GLF leaders.[29]

A major goal of the Gay Liberation Front was to pull homosexuals out from the shadows—where they'd been relegated by a hostile society and their own fears—and into the sunshine. The GLF organized three "Gay-Ins" in 1970, each attracting thousands of frolickers who dared to be openly gay under "GAY POWER" and "GAY IS GOOD" balloons and banners.[30] Some Dionysian revelers went even further, painting their bodies with slogans such as "Fuck Forever."[31] The LAPD assigned large contingents of policemen and Vice Squad officers to patrol and intimidate Gay-In participants. But the times had already changed so much in Los Angeles that GLF was able to get a lawyer to file a temporary restraining order claiming violation of civil rights.[32]

When GLF staged the first Los Angeles gay pride parade in June 1970, the police again tried to interfere: GLF was denied a parade permit by the hostile chief of police, Ed Davis, who told newspaper reporters that he would approve a march of "thieves and burglars" more happily than one of homosexuals; but the Gay Liberation Front managed to convince the American Civil Liberties Union (ACLU)—which had refused to help the homophiles in the 1950s—to come to their aid in 1970.[33] On June 28 of that year saw the fulfillment of Chuck Rowland's 1950s prophecy about

the proud day to come when homosexuals would march, "arm in arm, ten abreast, down Hollywood Boulevard"—though Chief Davis was able to get one last lick in by preventing the parade from starting before 7:00 P.M..

One of the most effective Gay Liberation Front actions of 1970 was staged in October at an international Conference on Behavioral Modification, at the Biltmore Hotel in downtown L.A. As Carolyn Weathers recalls, she, together with other GLF members, "interspersed our hippie-clad selves among the suited psychiatrists." In the midst of Phillip Feldman's presentation on an aversion therapy cure for homosexuality that used electric shocks, one GLFer rose up and cried, "Are we going to stand for this shit?" The others shouted, "Hell, no!" and stormed the stage, grabbed the mike, and screamed at the audience, "We're sick all right—sick of having ourselves defined by sexist straight psychiatrists." Don Kilhefner, who counseled gay youth for the Gay Liberation Front, told the stunned doctors, "You have imprisoned us in your mental institutions and brainwashed us into hating ourselves. I'm working with a teenage boy right now who wants to kill himself because of you people—and you're going to, by God, sit there and listen to us for a change." Several of the doctors rose up to support them, and a dialogue ensued. The 1970 incident in L.A., one of the first in which gays challenged the mental health establishment's classification of them as "sick," helped lead to the removal in 1973 of "homosexuality" from the American Psychiatric Association 's diagnostic manual of mental disorders.[34]

Despite the explosion of unprecedented activism that some GLFers described as "a demonstration a day," the mainstream media largely ignored the Gay Liberation Front. Because this lack of visibility severely limited GLF's social impact, the group looked for an action that the mainstream media could not possibly ignore. In summer 1970, when Don Jackson, a Gay Liberation Front member, proposed a scheme in which gay people would take over a small county, GLF found a way to break through the media impasse: The organization announced that 479 homosexuals were prepared to relocate to Alpine County, a Northern California mountain community of 1,000, whose motto was "A Great Place to Raise Children." A

new law had just shortened voting requirements from a year's residency to only ninety days, which meant that within three months, gay people might become a political majority in Alpine. GLF's scheme created "utter terror" and "a shock wave through the whole State and beyond,"[35] which made the Gay Liberation Front gloat in its newsletter, *Front Lines:*

> The lid really blew off the establishment's teapot when the GLF-LA told the world about the plans for taking over the tiny county of Alpine, California. Everyone in the State power structure from Ronnie Reagan to the Board of Supervisors of Alpine to "Dr." Carl MacIntire, organizer of the recent "Victory in Vietnam" fiasco in Washington, D.C., have been running around like lunatics trying to find some legal (or even not so legal) way to prevent the takeover of the otherwise insignificant area by gays.[36]

Did GLF really intend to move gay people to Alpine en masse? Members of GLF were not always positive themselves which of their actions were serious and which were pulling the collective leg or yanking the chain of their enemy. As John Platania characterized it: "There was always an aspect of fairyland non-reality in what we did, but there was always a potential of some reality. Our vision sounded like madness. People would sometimes look at me like, 'That boy has had one tab too many.' Some people took it seriously. They saw the possibility." Without a clear consensus about whether Alpine was in earnest or a hoax, GLF devised precise procedures for their "invasion," and even obtained bids from two consulting firms to draft detailed building plans for the gay occupation—for which they could never have paid.[37]

But their scheme tested the limits of democracy and threw down a gauntlet before any who had been critical of GLF's tactics: "The entire plan is to be carried out in a totally legal manner," they proclaimed. "If the establishment really means what it says about working within the system, this is the time to prove it."[38] GLF leadership encouraged gays to prepare for a tough winter in Alpine, and Don Kilhefner and others called a news conference and deadpanned deadly seriousness about the

gay takeover, pointing out what homosexuals had been denied in America because of discrimination:

> It would mean gay territory. It would mean a gay government, a gay civil service, a county welfare department which made public assistance payments to refugees from persecution and prejudice. It would mean the establishment of the world's first museum of gay arts, sciences, and history, paid for with public funds.

Kilhefner added, to ratchet up the jolt to heterosexual America, "Almost any state in the union has an Alpine."[39]

The Establishment fell for it: Carl MacIntire, a fundamentalist minister, even announced on his radio program, which was aired on numerous stations around America, that he would lead a group of "good Christians" into Alpine to prevent this "disgrace to our country." "Christian" jabs encouraged the future settlers (or hoaxers) further. "This time, the lions will win, Dr. McIntire," GLFers jeered. [40]

MacIntire was not alone in giving the Gay Liberation Front plenty of exposure. The *Los Angeles Times* ran half a dozen stories about the Alpine takeover; major magazines and national networks followed suit. But after an actual visit to Alpine (accompanied by an FBI undercover spy whose identity all the GLFers knew),[41] GLF hinted that the group had been perpetrating a hoax and called the action off.[42] For as long as it lasted, though, the "zap" gloriously fulfilled the Gay Liberation Front's desire to attract the attention of the national media.

Agitation such as the GLF perpetrated sometimes did affect the democratic process and promote social change—if only because it made less radical demands seem reasonable by contrast. But perhaps, too, agitation forced society to reexamine antiquated notions, as happened with Penal Code 288a, the 1915 California law that had made oral sex a felony punishable by a sentence of up to fifteen years in a state prison.

In fact, the law had seldom been enforced against consenting adults in their own homes; but it was nevertheless a Sword of Damocles over the heads of all homosexuals, since even if it had not been used against them, it *could* be.[43] Albert Gordon, a Los Angeles attorney, agreed to work with Morris Kight in 1974 to devise a plan to challenge the hypocritical law. They enlisted in the battle against the oral sex statute a gay male couple, a lesbian couple, and a heterosexual couple. Gordon, who had left his job as a janitor and started law school at the age of fifty after one of his two gay sons was entrapped, had by now become the leading pro bono lawyer to L.A.'s gay community. He asked each member of the couples to sign a confession that stated: "On or about May 8, 1974, in the County of Los Angeles, State of California, we did participate in the act of oral copulation with each other."

In what Gordon admitted was "a little circus," he informed the Los Angeles Police Department that the "felons" would be available for arrest on June 13—at the L.A. Press Club. Needless to say, the cameras were poised, and no policemen showed up. Anticipating a no-show by the LAPD, Gordon had arranged for Morris Kight to make a "citizen's arrest." Kight drove the "Felons 6," as they called themselves, to the Rampart Division Police Station—with the press in attendance. But the police would not bite; the station commander refused to make the arrests: "We didn't see the crime in action" was his excuse.[44]

The next stop for the Felons 6 and their media entourage was the office of the assistant district attorney, who issued a statement such as the Long Beach men whose lives had been ruined in 1914 would have dearly loved to hear: "It is the policy of our office not to file criminal charges where consenting adults, in private, engage in sexual acts which might be considered violations of the penal law."[45] If that was the district attorney's policy, Gordon and other lawyers who fought for gay rights could argue that California Penal Code 288a—which read, simply, "Any person participating in an act of copulating the mouth of one person with the sexual organ of another is punishable by imprisonment in the State prison for a term not exceeding fifteen years"—was misleading and must be changed.

And it was changed: In 1975, Assemblyman Willie Brown, who had long been sympathetic to gays, authored a Consenting Adults Bill, and all California laws against consensual homosexual acts were revoked.[46]

"OH, YOU LESBIAN FEMINISTS!"

We lesbians had to march in the gay pride parade together with the guys who were dragging a twenty-foot papier-mâché penis down Hollywood Boulevard!

—Brenda Weathers on the 1971 gay pride parade in Los Angeles[47]

Though men and women managed to work together on some crucial issues in groups such as the Gay Liberation Front during the 1970s, the merger was not always a happy one. Encouraged by both a very articulate feminist movement and the gay movement, lesbians, after generations of virtual silence, now dared to speak up in large numbers. But, as many complained, gay men seemed deaf to their voices. Lesbians in the Los Angeles gay movement said they often felt as though they were being asked, in spirit if not in fact, to make the coffee and take the minutes.[48] Their feeling of inconsequentiality was exacerbated because Gay Liberation Front men often lived together in all-male collectives, where meetings might be held informally. Lesbian GLF members were resentful because it seemed to them that sometimes important decisions were made at these meetings. On top of that, the women complained, they had devoted themselves to many Gay Liberation Front actions that had little direct relevance to them, such as the month-long protests at the mostly-men's bar, the Farm—and yet they could see no reciprocal efforts from gay men. About lesbian concerns, the gay movement seemed largely mute.

But the most unbridgeable gap between them was sexuality. The women were troubled that, despite radical rhetoric, the new gay movement was spending too much of its energies on battles that were no different from those of the old homophile movement (such as fighting the LAPD's hostility to gay men's semipublic sex encounters). Some of the women were deeply annoyed, too, that they felt forced to witness gay male sexual displays. "The big thing that drove us nuts," they recall of GLF's joint gay and lesbian dances, "was the men's promiscuity. To the men it was liberation finally to be able to grope each other in public. But the women were put off by this nonemotional sex flaunting."[49] The men resented the women for mischaracterizing their newfound freedom and trying to squelch it.

Many lesbians were now deciding they had less in common with gay men than with straight women, that heterosexual feminist gripes about the male of the species were little different from their own. But perhaps the coup de grâce to lesbian participation in GLF came with the men's decision that the GLF would form a coalition with the Black Panthers. Though the Gay Liberation Front women had understood from the start that GLF intended to be in solidarity with all revolutionary groups, they came to resent not only that lesbian concerns were too often placed on the back burner but also that the issue of the Panthers (quintessentially macho with their values of muscle and power) now seemed to have more significance for male GLFers than any issue raised by their GLF lesbian sisters. "The men invented this idea and were entirely behind it," Michele Ross, a GLF member, wrote angrily in the *Los Angeles Free Press* in October 1970. "The women were not. We feel we must find our own identity and our own causes as gay women."[50]

For a while, the lesbians in the Gay Liberation Front continued to try to attract more women to the group, hoping that if they were better represented at meetings they might be able to modify the male-dominated agenda. Brenda Weathers wrote in the GLF newsletter:

> Attendance by the sisters [at Gay Liberation Front meetings] has been at best very sparse. The most frequently voiced reason for this seeming lack of enthusiasm seems to be that the meetings and committees are male dominated and oriented. Often I have heard sisters say, "there's no place for me there." Well . . . GET OUT OF THE BACK SEAT, SISTERS, AS WELL AS OUT OF THE CLOSETS![51]

But despite her pleas, lesbians persisted in staying away from GLF meetings. (So meager was lesbian attendance that some former GLF men today erroneously recall the organization to have been all male.)[52]

Like lesbians in the 1950s, the women could not see the relevance for them of a male-directed gay organization, but they also had other reasons for staying away. Many lesbians had become feminists by now, and they had a choice of political homes in L.A. In October 1970, most of the GLF women split from that organization and moved to the Los Angeles

Women's Center, which welcomed lesbians. The former Gay Liberation Front members started the "Gay Women's Liberation" group.[53]

The women who became refugees from GLF chose the Women's Center and not the National Organization for Women because they found the Center's radical Leftist politics more compelling—though L.A. NOW, founded in 1967 by women who had been active in the peace movement, was, in fact, the most radical chapter of the organization in the country.[54] Unlike New York NOW, which had purged its lesbian president, Ivy Bottini, in 1970,[55] Los Angeles NOW that same year elected as its president Toni Carabillo, a magnetic woman who also happened to be a lesbian. Other lesbians, such as Carabillo's partner, Judy Meuli, held key leadership positions in NOW. Though they were not officially "out," in L.A. NOW their lesbianism was an open secret, known to all the lesbians and to any straight women in the organization who cared to know.[56]

But that it should have been any kind of secret was abhorrent to radical lesbians. They would never join so tame a group. However, they were determined to make NOW deal openly with the lesbian issue. Nancy Robinson recalls that Gay Women's Liberation, to which she belonged, invaded a NOW meeting and performed guerilla theater tactics in an effort to push NOW to change: "We stormed in, all marching behind our lesbian banner, passing out our literature, shouting that they had to read it."[57] Though the radical lesbians had disrupted a speech by Assemblyman Mervyn Dymally, they were invited to stay and tell the NOW audience about the reason for their rage.[58] It was that meeting that led directly to L.A. NOW's drafting a powerful resolution in support of lesbians. The resolution declared in part:

> Whereas, the lesbian is doubly oppressed, both as a woman and as a homosexual . . .
>
> Whereas, the prejudice against the lesbian is manifested in the courts as well . . .

> Whereas, because she is so oppressed and so exploited, the lesbian has been referred to as "the rage of all women condensed to the point of explosion" . . .
>
> Therefore Be It Resolved . . . that NOW acknowledges the oppression of lesbians as a legitimate concern of feminism.

Ivy Bottini, who moved to L.A. after she had been ousted as president of New York NOW, conjectures that such a resolution could only have been written in Los Angeles. Life in L.A. was freer, she says: "The women in the New York chapter who were lesbians had high-powered jobs and were terrified of losing them. The women of L.A. NOW weren't so afraid to deal with the lesbian issue because they had more creative jobs, where they knew there was a lot of freedom and acceptance."[59] Not all members of L.A. NOW worked in creative jobs, of course. But what is certain is that L.A., at the far western part of the continent, felt freer to challenge NOW's East Coast founder, Betty Friedan, who had declared lesbians to be the "lavender menace of the women's movement." At the 1971 national conference, which happened to be held in Los Angeles, NOW invited an attractive heterosexual actress, Eve Norman ("Eve Normal" she was jokingly called by the L.A. lesbians of NOW),[60] to read the lesbian-rights resolution at a plenary session. The national delegates to the conference, far from the watchful eye of Friedan, resoundingly rejected her intolerance, and the resolution was adopted as national policy.[61]

Yet despite L.A. NOW's pro-lesbian stance, radicals continued to regard the organization as much too button-down. Though most of them, like the NOW members, had been raised in the 1950s as children of the staid middle class, in their romance with militancy during the 1970s they declassed themselves with a vengeance. They loathed what they described as the "polyester pant-suit crowd" of NOW. True radicals sported jeans and flannel and, unlike middle-class lesbians of the earlier generation or the more restrained lesbians of NOW, they declared their lesbianism loudly and proudly, whether they saw themselves as "gay women" or as "lesbian feminists."

Both "gay women" and "lesbian feminists" believed by 1971 that "the women had to do it for themselves." Until huge crises arose later in the

decade that demanded that gay men and lesbians work together against a common enemy, lesbians' collaboration with gay men became minimal. But not only did they split from the men; "gay women" and "lesbian feminists" also split from one another. In this era of identity politics, identities came to be defined more and more finely (or narrowly): Del Whan, who had spent the 1960s fighting as a radical for minority rights, believed that homosexuality was a civil rights issue rather than a feminist issue, and that she'd been most deprived of rights not because she was a woman but because she was gay. She had joined the Gay Liberation Front in late 1969 and then the Los Angeles Women's Center, but her realization that she preferred to work in a "gay women's movement" where she could promote gay women's causes led to her renting the Echo Park storefront that became the Gay Women's Services Center.[62] Brenda and Carolyn Weathers and Sharon A. Lilly, who had started out, as did Del Whan, in the L.A. Gay Liberation Front, soon became radical feminists at the Los Angeles Women's Center. They despaired about working in the male-dominated gay movement, but they also did not want to work with women's organizations such as NOW that had large heterosexual memberships. They changed their name to the "Lesbian Feminists" in February 1971 when, according to Marsha Salisbury, "a straight woman from NOW saw us stage [a kiss-in] and said, 'Oh, you lesbian feminists!' We liked that name, so we had a vote that decided that's what we'd call ourselves."[63] The name became a term used by radical lesbians everywhere.

Lesbian Feminists hoped to devote their energies to developing new cultural institutions that were both lesbian and feminist. Throughout the 1970s, an unprecedented variety of lesbian-feminist institutions and experiments spoke to the social, political, and even health needs of lesbians.[64] Many of those institutions and experiments that began in Los Angeles capitalized on what was distinctive there, such as the weather or a willingness to explore what more traditionalist cultures considered far out and even "crackpot."[65] The Feminist Women's Health Center, staffed largely by lesbians, helped women take control of their bodies. They were taught by the staff how to do their own speculum exams, what homeopathic remedies to use for vaginal infections, and how to get rid of an annoying period in one fell swoop through menstrual extraction. A radical

feminist educational group, the Califia Community ("Califia" in honor of the namesake of California, the legendary queen of golden-armored women warriors), was established in 1975 by two lesbians, Betty Brooks and Marilyn Murphy. Califia drew women to Malibu Canyon and other forest camps for bare-breasted retreats. There, imbued with utopian ideals, they labored seriously at finding solutions to problems such as class prejudice and race prejudice.[66] As "Southern California" as phenomena such as the Feminist Women's Health Center and Califia were, they caught on and spread elsewhere: The women's self-help health effort that the Los Angeles group began inspired a national movement and the eventual founding of the Federation of Feminist Women's Health Centers,[67] and Califia was one of the earlier prototypes for the outdoor lesbian mass gatherings that soon became popular all over the country.

Lesbians in 1970s Los Angeles developed a culture that had commonalities with that of urban-American lesbians elsewhere; but it was distinct, too, because it was shaped in part by the artistic and creative talents that Los Angeles has always attracted in abundance.[68] In 1973, the Woman's Building opened in L.A. in an elegant old edifice of the former Chiounard Art Institute. It became the birthplace of a new lesbian-feminist art movement in America. Though not all those who patronized its galleries, studios, classrooms, coffeehouse, bookstore, theater, and travel agency were lesbian, all were feminists and lesbian-friendly. (Cheri Gaulke and Sue Maberry, who met at the Woman's Building in the 1970s and are partners still, say that "the *energy* of the Woman's Building was absolutely lesbian.")[69] Founded by the lesbian artist Arlene Raven, along with Judy Chicago and Sheila de Bretteville, the Los Angeles Woman's Building was intended primarily as a venue for women artists and writers from all over the world who would work there to create a new women's culture.

Gaulke, a lesbian performance artist who came to L.A. in 1975, says she was drawn to the Woman's Building because of the liberty it offered to develop new kinds of art. The New York art world, Gaulke says, was more rigid than L.A.'s because it was fixated on a male-dominated gallery system and

obsessed with male-defined "success." Los Angeles artists could be looser because they had been disenfranchised anyway from the "marketplace of art" that the New York gallery system imposed. "In many ways that was a good thing," Gaulke says, "because it meant that they had the freedom to be more daring. The lesbian-feminist artists in Los Angeles could really enjoy that freedom." The effect on her and other lesbians was transformational. "The Woman's Building became a research and development lab. And what they developed was not just art; it was a whole movement."[70]

Those who were there exude still about how "thrilled the women were to find themselves finally in a lesbian environment that had nothing to do with the bars," how fabulous and important it seemed to be engaged in forming a "women's culture" that would be unique to the history of the world.[71] Women's culture (by which was usually meant "lesbian culture") was truly one in which "the women had to do it for themselves" at the Woman's Building, from defining art and the role of the artist to deciding what should and should not go into Woman's Building space and how to raise the money to keep it all afloat. Among the courses offered was a "Program of Sapphic Education," the goal of which, Terry Wolverton recalls, was "to inspire art-making" and "to help us figure out our ethics and purpose as a lesbian people."[72] Instructors and students pioneered in art forms that were revolutionary in the 1970s—performance art, autobiographical art, collaborative projects—which, in good part because of their efforts, are now considered legitimate artistic expressions.

One of the most ambitious attempts to contribute to lesbian culture by the artists of the Woman's Building was the 1977 Lesbian Art Project, affectionately called LAP. Wolverton explains that those who worked on LAP wanted not only to study lesbian culture but also to reshape it, to rescue it from the "oppression mentality" that it had fallen into during the dark decades. "Why do lesbians gather in dark and dismal bars?" they asked. "Why do they dress so drably?" LAP artists tempered their politics with Hollywood dash, resurrecting the sophistication of a bygone era by staging events such as the 1978 Valentine's Day "Dyke of Your Dreams Dance," where the participants dressed like Ginger Rogers and Fred Astaire, or like the tuxedo-and-gown lesbian set who used to frequent the Sunset Strip night clubs in the 1930s and '40s.

The women of the Lesbian Art Project foreshadowed by almost a decade the Lipstick Lesbian veneration of style, which first took hold in L.A. in the later 1980s. Wolverton says LAP craved to promote "glamour, elegance, joie de vivre." In a gesture of playful nose-thumbing at more somber lesbian feminists, the women named themselves the Natalie Barney Collective, after a wealthy and very fashionable lesbian of the early twentieth century. They hoped to "revolutionize" anew the lesbian's conception of herself by getting her out of her very proletarian, very 1970s, plaid-shirt-and-jeans uniform and into the costumes that Hollywood thought of as glamorous:

> We tried to change the atmosphere of the lesbian social event. We put our artistry to work. We designed beautiful invitations that would highlight the specialness of the occasion. We flew gorgeous banners. We enclosed the dance floor with hanging panels that pictured women outlined in glitter. We encouraged an atmosphere of playfulness—women dressed in antique evening gowns, tails, top hats. 'Delightism' is what we tried to foster. 'This is what we should give to ourselves,' we were saying.[73]

The lesbians of the Woman's Building were not alone in their desire to promote glamour among L.A. lesbian feminists while, paradoxically, not doing violence to radical lesbian-feminist values. The Women's Saloon and Parlor, a popular restaurant that opened in 1975 on Fountain Avenue in East Hollywood, was run by Colleen McKay, whom former patrons describe as "tall, willowy, elegant . . . like Romaine Brooks," the early-twentieth-century artist who was Natalie Barney's lover.[74] The very name "Women's Saloon and Parlor" was an attempt to capture all-in-one the upscale connotations of "salon," the genteel connotations of "parlor," and the working-class hangout connotations of "saloon." Lesbian-feminist patrons came to hear lesbian-feminist poets read their poems and musicians such as the New Miss Alice Stone Ladies Society Orchestra play their retro-ragtime. Those who were there remember the setting as "classy" and "arty," with a décor designed by women artists.[75] "Beautiful, 'Hollywoody' women" composed the clientele, Simone Wallace recalls.[76]

But Colleen McKay made it clear that "Hollywood" was not all that the Women's Saloon and Parlor was about; she said that she opened the

establishment "as a way to invade society and reinforce what feminists believe."[77] Any patron with a thin wallet was welcome to work off her drinks by washing dishes.[78] When workers picketed against the Gay Community Services Center (see chap. 7), the Saloon's staff refused to serve anyone who crossed the picket line.[79]

Women's music also flourished in Los Angeles. Olivia Records had started in 1973 as a lesbian collective in Washington, D.C., but before the release of Olivia's first album, Meg Christian's *I Know You Know,* the collective decided to move to Los Angeles. Ginny Berson, a founder of Olivia Records, recalls that before Olivia settled in Los Angeles she and Meg Christian had made an exploratory trip to the West, and they were awed by L.A.'s difference from D.C. In Washington, heterosexual feminists were actually "hostile to lesbians," according to Berson. In L.A., lesbians were integral to "everything that was feminist."[80] But the company chose to settle in Los Angeles "first of all, because L.A. was the center of the record industry." Berson also explains, "While we might have found a center in Nashville or New York, we didn't think a lesbian record company would do very well in Nashville; and in New York, the entertainment industry was one of many big things; in L.A. it was *the* big thing."[81] Olivia, women-owned-and-operated (from the technicians to the talent), soon opened the music industry to lesbians in ways it had never been opened before.

The number of lesbians in Los Angeles multiplied exponentially during the 1970s, when radical women who had ostensibly been heterosexual opened up to the notion of lesbianism as a political choice that any radical feminist might make. Simone Wallace, who was married when she started attending the Women's Center, remembers the Center's "Gay-Straight Dialogues," where she heard and saw, for the first time she was aware of, women who called themselves lesbian. "I felt, 'this is a world I know nothing about.' It was scary, disturbing. But it was also tremendously exciting and interesting." She eventually concluded, as did many at the Women's Center, that "my [heterosexual] lifestyle was not in keeping with my politics." She came out as lesbian.[82] "At one point, all the women were straight,"

Donna Cassyd recalls of the Los Angeles Women's Center, "and then suddenly we were all lesbian. It was like . . . 'Who did it happen to today?'. . . Lesbians were popping up like California poppies," she says.[83]

In the 1970s, women came out as lesbian into a world that would have been inconceivable to the generations that preceded them. The title of the 1955 nonfiction lesbian pulp *We Walk Alone* ("Of the love that dwells in twilight . . . in Lesbos Lonely Groves," the cover announced) encapsulated how many lesbians felt at mid-century, but such wails of loneliness were inconceivable to the "new lesbians." They knew themselves to be part of a vast community. Their knowledge was supported by a flourishing lesbian press in Los Angeles[84] as well as all over America. They had retreats and national conferences with thousands of participants, which made them feel, at least for the duration of the event, that the world was lesbian.

Los Angeles pioneered in such vast gatherings, beginning with the 1971 Gay Women's West Coast Conference, which attracted to its Metropolitan Community Church venue "gay women" (including a large Daughters of Bilitis contingent) as well as "lesbian feminists" and (to the surprise of the organizers) delegates from not just all over the West Coast, but also the East Coast, the South, and the Midwest. Jeanne Cordova, organizer of the conference, remembers that the "old gays" and the "lesbian feminists "were shocked to see each other."[85] The daughters of the Silent Generation were encountering the daughters of the Sexual Revolution. What might the generations make of one another? The lesbian feminists took off their shirts and danced about wildly and freely, in weaving circles, as at a bacchanal,[86] while the old gays looked on, bemused.

The splash of the first conference made Cordova dream of an event even more ambitious. A 1973 West Coast Lesbian Conference was national and international, attracting to its UCLA venue almost 2,000 women from twenty-six states and several countries—"the largest single gathering of lesbians known in history" to that date.[87] As was perhaps inevitable in bringing together so many diverse people, conflicts were epidemic in these conferences. One of the first political conflicts over transgenders took place at the West Coast Lesbian Conference when some lesbian attendees wanted to stop a male-to-female transsexual singer and guitarist, Beth Elliot, from performing. The Los Angeles organizers of the conference "didn't

care about transsexuals one way or another," according to Jeanne Cordova. "L.A. activists weren't purists, and we certainly weren't threatened by transsexuals' participation. There were so few of them."[88] But many of the conferees from elsewhere insisted that male-to-female transsexuals like Elliot had not only enjoyed patriarchal power over women but also continued to exude "male energy." According to Cordova, a contingent who called themselves the "Gutter Dykes of San Francisco," led by "two orange-headed dykes with crew cuts," gathered near the stage and started a protest: "They were screaming, 'That's not a woman! He's a fake! He's a transsexual!' It was like an earthquake—at first a little earthquake. Then an 8.5," Cordova remembers now.[89] Robin Morgan, a keynote speaker, exacerbated the fury with an impassioned harangue, excoriating Beth Elliot as "an opportunist, an infiltrator, and a destroyer—with the mentality of a rapist."[90]

Nor was the Elliot incident the only war of the weekend. The subtitle of the conference had been billed as "Lesbian Oppression—What Are Our Solutions?" and many of the participants aired their own feelings of oppression with immense anger, often at the lesbians sitting right beside them. For example, when the women from a lesbian mothers workshop complained that the child-care arrangements at the conference were insufficient, another lesbian yelled at them, "You should have thought about that before you fucked him."[91]

Yet the conference brought together lesbians from all over the country, and many made political coalitions. A Lesbian Mothers Union, for example, was started at that same contentious lesbian mothers workshop. The conference was also very meaningful to women on an individual level. Those who were not embroiled in the various battles remember it still as a turning point in their lives. Mary Margaret Smith says that though she'd been a lesbian for years, she had never seen more than two lesbians together before, "and at the UCLA Conference there were two thousand, women of all ages, all colors." She remembers, "Someone had handed me some kind of flier. I hid my face in it and cried because I was so overwhelmed."[92] Donna Cassyd, who had thought of herself as a heterosexual feminist on the first day of the conference, recalls now that the conference helped her find a new identity: "Being there was so wonderful, incredible, joyful. We took our shirts off and listened to women's music. I thought, 'This is so amazing.' Everything about

myself that had felt isolated was affirmed now. It made sense then to add 'lesbian' to 'feminist,' to become a lesbian-feminist."[93]

INSTITUTIONALIZING

We were demanding a place at the table. Once we had it, there was no reason to stand outside demanding it.

—John Platania, a Gay Center founder[94]

Members of the Gay Liberation Front, imbued with the romance of the Left, had been cynical about the possibility of effecting social change without a revolution. But to their astonishment, it was happening. By the early 1970s, it began to seem that "the system" was actually opening up a bit—that the law was not always hostile, that those in power might listen, that demands might be granted. Leftist GLF was faced with a dilemma: It could either deny the success of its labors or take credit for victory. GLF chose the latter. In announcing that the Gay Liberation Front was disbanding in September 1971, Morris Kight proclaimed, "Many of the goals that the Gay Liberation Front of Los Angeles started out to achieve have been achieved."[95] Though some GLFers were astonished at Kight's autocratic pronouncement, it did indeed appear to be time to move on to a new phase.

In this new phase, the leaders were no longer focused on the outside world—hoping to shock heterosexuals out of their complacency by guerilla tactics; rather, they directed their attention inward, to the lesbian and gay community—trying to figure out what it needed to do to improve its collective and individual quality of life. To that end, members of the Gay Liberation Front, led by Morris Kight, John Platania, and Don Kilhefner, used GLF's "Survival Committee" to set up social services very much like those that Chuck Rowland had dreamed of in the 1950s. They established the Van Ness Recovery House, a rehabilitation facility that would serve gay alcoholics. They set up Liberation House, which provided "crisis housing" to indigent gays, mostly young runaways and throwaways.[96] Then, John Platania, who had worked for the L.A. Community Development Agency, drew up a detailed development plan for a nonprofit corporation. His plan was the start of the Los Angeles Gay Community Services Center.[97]

The Gay Community Services Center began with Leftist rhetoric that was like that of GLF. The Center's purpose was "to meet the real needs of an oppressed minority." The word "Community" in the Center's name, according to early organizers, signified "having that kind of relationship to others in a group of people in which a person receives according to his/her needs and gives according to his/her ability." All volunteers were to understand these principles. For instance, the medical clinic was to be staffed completely by gay doctors, nurses, and technicians "who welcome the opportunity to serve their brothers and sisters."[98]

But such lofty ideals were sometimes compromised by the realities of "institutionalization." The L.A. Gay Community Services Center became the first gay entity to be granted nonprofit status by the Internal Revenue Service, thanks to Alan Gross, a heterosexual Los Angeles attorney who served pro bono as the Center's legal counsel. Gross made numerous visits to the IRS in Washington and was able to convince the feds by 1972 that the Center qualified as a "nonprofit."[99] When that status came up for review, the founders, formerly the most fiery radicals of the GLF, realized they must play the system's game: In defending the nonprofit status, Don Kilhefner, the Center's first executive director, informed the IRS: "The Center *does not advocate any* sexual orientation or lifestyle. It is common in our Gay Awareness groups to have several participants increase their ability to enjoy heterosexual relationships."[100] The ploy, purposely misleading, worked. The leadership was so successful at such maneuvering that in 1975 the Los Angeles Gay Community Services Center became the first institution with the word "gay" in its name to receive federal funding; the Center was also granted licensure by the state of California—all in an era of official antigay policy.[101]

Despite the founders' necessary practicality, however, the Gay Community Services Center's early clientele recall that in its first years it remained "hippie radical."[102] The Center's first building, a dilapidated Victorian on Wilshire Boulevard and Union Street where rap groups, planning meetings, and a variety of services were conducted, was certainly hippie shabby, with its creaky, steep stairs and rooms furnished only with old sofas and pillows.[103] Fund-raising, recalls Steve Lachs, was Morris Kight calling him or other affluent gays to say, "We seem to be

unable to see our way to meeting the phone bill this month," and asking Lachs, or any of the other "suits," whether he could offer a check for the needed amount.[104] It was rumored that in particularly desperate times, young male board members would even hit the Boulevard to turn tricks and thus be able to cover the Gay Community Services Center's rent.[105]

Gay people were willing to give their money (and perhaps even their bodies) to assure the Center's survival because they perceived it as, what one observer called, a wonderful, exciting "beehive" of "boisterousness and serendipity,"[106] with an incredible panoply of effective social programs for a community that had always been malignly neglected. No obstacle seemed to slow it down. During the Gay Community Services Center's first year, its staff reported that 1,700 to 2,500 gays and lesbians passed through its doors each week, numbers that grew even higher as word spread of this institution that had no equal anywhere.[107]

Shabby as it may have appeared, the mere existence of the Center was considered a major victory for the community. John Morgan Wilson remembers "a complete sense of celebration in that house."[108] The frenzy of activity that had characterized GLF now characterized the Gay Community Services Center. Someone was always on duty to welcome visitors. A crisis hotline received calls twenty-four hours a day. The venereal disease clinic for gay men is illustrative of the Center's luck and pluck in creating something remarkable with practically no money in these years. Benjamin Teller, a physician and the founder of the VD clinic, had read about the L.A. Gay Community Services Center in a 1971 underground paper in Atlanta, Georgia, during his stint as a public health physician. When he came to Los Angeles, he not only volunteered to run the Center's free clinic without pay but also managed to persuade pharmaceutical companies to donate drugs; and, as the founders dreamed, he recruited doctors, nurses, lab techs, and administrators who were willing to work pro bono to "give back" to their community. (Some did it despite their worries for their careers: One of the doctors would sign only his first name on charts—though eventually he mustered the courage to become an open activist.)[109]

In creating a venereal disease clinic in which gay men felt comfortable, the Center addressed the long-standing crisis of the spread of venereal disease among gay men, which County of Los Angeles officials had

never been able to solve.[110] Dr. Teller's master strategy was to create an ethic: Gay men must take personal responsibility for being tested periodically so that the chain of transmission could be broken. To achieve this ethic, a gay-positive culture had to be created. Teller dreamed up a poster of two bare-chested, good-looking, long-haired men embracing under the banner "Don't Give Him Anything But Love." He proposed to the Los Angeles County Health Department that if they would agree to do all the Center's lab work free of charge, the Center would provide a safe space for testing; this meant that sexually transmitted diseases might be identified and treated earlier and the long-run cost to the county would be reduced. Ed Edelman, who was the county supervisor for the Hollywood and West Hollywood areas, recalls that because the Center was thus saving the county money, he felt justified in becoming a strong ally and helping it obtain government funding.[111]

The most important services for the gay community, which had long suffered vilification and discrimination, were in the area of mental health. Individual counseling by mental health professionals was available to anyone in the gay community, but nonprofessionals were also trained by Betty Berzon and Don Clark, both professional therapists, in how to facilitate "consciousness-raising groups specifically for lesbian and gay people." The most basic of guidelines had to be formulated, since they were not self-evident in 1971: for example, "Use the weight of your authority to approve homosexual thoughts, behavior and feelings, in general, when reported by your client. This is important to counteract past experience with disapproval of authority figures."[112]

John Morgan Wilson describes himself as having been "a guy in a lot of confusion and pain" who was "drinking and doing a lot of drugs." The Center's therapy groups, which he attended when he was in his early thirties, provided him with a "safety net," he says. "That old Union Street Center saved my life."[113] Older clients shared that sense of salvation. "Most of my gay friends were not interested in 'being gay,'" says Ken Bartmess, who had been a dancer twenty years earlier, in the 1950s. The groups at the Center helped him build "a positive gay identity"—a concept that was completely new.[114] Veterans of less fortunate times were being healed.

The Alcoholism Center for Women, which rose from the ashes of a bitter strike against the Gay Community Services Center in 1975. *Photo: Denise Crippen/Courtesy Carolyn Weathers.*

CHAPTER 7

Big Battles

WHEN THE man who would become the first openly gay judge in the world announced to a friend that he would march down Hollywood Boulevard in the 1971 gay pride parade, the friend cautioned: "Steve, you can't. You have a career."[1] But Steve Lachs was not the only person with a "career" to come out as a homosexual in the early 1970s. Suddenly, in the wake of gay visibility that the radicals had succeeded in effecting, and the Sexual Revolution that acknowledged that sex was not always connubial, a whole new group of men and women were daring to admit publicly that they, too, were gay. They were not hippies or radicals who had dropped out of society, but professional and business people who were invested in the system. Because they wanted to forge a new image for the group to which they had secretly belonged, one of a "respectable" and "responsible" gay community, they had to begin by coming out, one person at a time.

Then, as they learned, to be effective—to make their impact felt as gay citizens and consumers; to create a community such as had never been, one served by a multiplicity of gay institutions and businesses—they also had to build a broad-based public presence. Thus they had to find ways to work together with diverse gays, such as radicals who had little interest in their "respectability." Coalition building was far from easy. Homosexuals would find that, other than attraction to the same sex and the threat of persecution, as a group of individuals their similarities could be illusions and their differences could be enormous. In

ethnicity, socioeconomics, aesthetics, politics, temperament, philosophy—they were as unlike one another as members of any random grouping might be. How could these differences be put aside in favor of a common good?

No collection of diverse individuals can find it uncomplicated to work together for an extended period toward a huge objective. But among some gays and lesbians the difficulty may have been further exacerbated because society had for so long oppressed them for their sexual desire or sexual identity. Now, suddenly, in the course of a general social liberalization, it appeared that they might have their day in the sun—that is, if other gays or lesbians did not elbow them out and claim the best rays for themselves. Internecine battles flared between personalities as well as classes, races, genders—between every conceivable grouping in the Tower of Babel that was the L.A. gay community. The community's upsetting tendency to "eat its own" was so prevalent that it was dubbed "oppression sickness."[2] It was only when enemies appeared at the gates—as happened when Senator John Briggs attacked California homosexuals through a deadly ballot initiative—that the entire gay and lesbian community seemed able to put aside its differences and work together toward victory.

INTERNECINE WARFARE

> *"Unfortunately there were bits of personal friction involved in this misunderstanding . . . and a resentment at feeling that I, and others, were often being manipulated like puppets."*
>
> —One of several resignation letters by Jim Kepner to ONE Inc.[3]

Even the earliest movement for homosexual rights in Los Angeles had suffered from internecine battles, such as the 1953 revolt against Harry Hay and his fellow radicals by the Mattachine Society.[4] In the early 1970s, "respectable" lesbians and gay men who entered the movement were upset by the ragged revolutionaries because they presented an image more disheveled and an agenda more radical than the "respectable" wished to promote. When the GLF sought donations from

those they called the "capitalist pigs" in the Hollywood Hills, some moneyed gays muttered to one another that access to their resources "was not going to [those in] tie-dye shirts."[5] From their earliest days of founding the Gay Community Services Center, GLFers dreaded the time when "the gray suits would finally come [in] and take over," even though they acknowledged that it must eventually happen if the Center was going to thrive and expand.[6]

Arguments over politics and approach also erupted constantly in the Los Angeles movement: What was the right public image? What should the gay agenda include? What were the right strategies for winning? Who had the authority to speak for a diverse community? How ought activists to treat one another to salve the wounds of being outcasts? How could lesbians and gay men work together effectively?

Though all wanted to believe that "an army of lovers shall not fail," sometimes the lover aspect caused the worst arguments of all and interfered with the army's goals. John Platania says that he and the other founders of the early Gay Community Services Center "were all sleeping with each other." Employees of the Center recall that sex was not uncommon in the men's rooms and did not raise many eyebrows.[7] For gay people in those days before the AIDS epidemic, every transgressive affair was a personal affirmation and a political act. (As one 1970 poster proclaimed, "Gay Liberation. Dig it. Do it.") Among lesbians, too, the heady excitement of working together toward revolutionary change could be mistaken for attraction or love, though the women generally had fewer sexual encounters than their male counterparts. The emotional vulnerability and erotic rivalries triggered by intimacy between movement workers easily hampered the important labors at hand.

All manner of conflicts were inevitable at all levels—from the most committed leaders to the rank-and-file folks who provided bodies for demonstrations—because each was, after all, an activist who had taken a profound personal risk in publicly supporting a gay cause. Each wanted to put his or her proverbial two cents worth in, and each felt that his or her contribution must be respected—no matter how paltry, contentious, or offbeat. One woman at a gay pride parade organizational meeting in the mid-1970s claimed to abhor the mealy-mouthed euphemisms "gay"

and "lesbian." Instead, she vehemently insisted, the parade should adopt the terms "men who suck cock" and "women who eat pussy." "And she was absolutely serious," recalls Rob Wray, who covered the meetings for *News West*.[8] In contrast, a correspondent to the newsletter of the Southern California Women for Understanding, an organization of homosexual business and professional women, was uncomfortable with the in-your-face connotations of the word "lesbian"; she argued that women had a right to reclaim the term "gay," which had once been the preferred term of homosexual females as well as males. "Why should the men get it, and scot-free at that?" she asked angrily.[9]

Human foibles and egos abounded. The question of who would emerge as a leader in the relatively open field of gay power could take on almost comic overtones. Mike Manning recalls an early 1970s gay press conference in which he witnessed a discreet shoving match between Troy Perry and Morris Kight, each hoping to capture the eye of a rolling television camera.[10] Morris Kight's dedication and prodigious activism earned him the nickname of L.A.'s "gay godfather" for more than three decades; but despite wide regard for Kight, his faults could not escape notice. The writer John Rechy, who knew Kight over the years, observed that "his sense of self-importance approached megalomania." When Rechy appeared on a television panel to which Kight had not been invited, the activist, furious about the slight, called the author the next day and proclaimed, "The gay community is very angry at you," as though Kight and community were one.[11] Kight was by no means unique. A growing cadre of alpha types had emerged, each righteously certain of his or her queer convictions and promethean destiny.

Throughout the 1970s and into the '80s, lesbians who were political had their own points of internecine contention. Grievances such as those that simmered constantly around the radical lesbian-feminist community came to a boiling point at the West Coast Women's Music and Comedy Festival in 1981. As the feminist newspaper, *Off Our Backs,* described it: "Over 400 women of color, Jewish women, and whites gathered in the dark, . . . shouting at each other, without mikes or organization, trying to gain the floor and be heard." The Latina lesbians com-

plained that "there was racism (conscious or not) among women attending the festival and the festival planners," evidenced by the fact that the Latin American Solidarity Day speeches "had to compete with the nearby proximity of . . . a crafts' fair and lake." Though women who could not afford to pay for a ticket were allowed to do a work exchange, leftist contingents complained, using anti-Semitic taunts against the producer, Robin Tyler, that the $65 admission for the four-day festival was excessive and that she was making too much money.[12] Flo Kennedy, a black activist lawyer who was an emcee at the festival and came to Tyler's defense, was called by other people of color an "elitist nigger." When Tyler repeatedly made the plea, "Please don't trash the festival," she was drowned out by the angry mob's continued protests that the festival was racist and classist.[13] Battles such as these devastated countless lesbian efforts and many of those who dared to emerge as leaders in the radical lesbian community.

The worst internecine battle, however, came at the Gay Community Services Center after it had enjoyed for several years the status of jewel in the crown of the Los Angeles gay and lesbian community. The battle evolved from a series of skirmishes that had been pitting leftists against "suits"; people of color against whites; and especially radical lesbian feminists against gay men, whom they accused of male chauvinism. For example, in 1972, Mina Meyer, a member of the board, became an administrator at the Gay Community Services Center and worked to establish the first lesbian clinic in the world—though it came into being only after a characteristic struggle. Meyer, part of the new generation of lesbians who vehemently refused to be submerged in gay male concerns, says that when she took the job at the Center there were few programs explicitly for lesbians, and she resented having to fight to create them:

> For instance, I asked the men who hired me about a women's clinic.
>
> They said, "Women don't get VD."
>
> I said, "If you're going to have a clinic for men, I want one for women."
>
> They said, "Okay. Find a woman doctor."
>
> Everything I wanted to do for lesbians was like pulling teeth. When the guys wanted to open the men's clinic, it was the whole Gay

> Community Services Center that worked on it. But I had to put the women's clinic together on my own.

Nevertheless, she found a physician, Jane Patterson, who was willing to volunteer her time at a clinic for women and even to be trained by the Feminist Women's Health Center in self-help procedures so that she could teach her lesbian patients. Meyer also got lesbian nurses and technicians to volunteer their time, and eventually three more women physicians joined the staff. Despite her disgruntlement with the men at the Gay Community Services Center, Meyer believes that the women's clinic there was a huge boon to the lesbian community. "Women came in who were in their forties, fifties, sixties," she says. "They'd never had a pap smear because they didn't want a male doctor messing around with them. Now, finally, they could be safe with a lesbian doctor."[14]

The Gay Community Services Center was also home to women who did not need to avail themselves of services such as the clinic. It was what PRIDE in its pioneering vision had dreamt of years earlier—a safe and healthy place. Sylvia Rhue, an African American woman, recalls, "I didn't drink, smoke, dance, or like loud music"; the Center suited who she was much better than the lesbian bars where, she says, she once saw "this woman on her knees from a drug-induced stupor." She adds, laughing, "I always thought I'd rather have a woman on her knees in prayer. A Boinkable Bible Babe." The lesbian rap group she joined at the Center was "like this wonderful brave new world," she says. "There we were, all together, talking seriously, trying to understand one another." For her, the Center extended beyond its services: It was there she found her social group as well as romance.[15]

Nevertheless, trouble was brewing in paradise. Those who felt unjustly treated in one manner or another sometimes tried to suppress their complaints for fear of broadcasting the stereotype of gay people as divisive or bitchy, but that merely exacerbated tensions.[16] Many internal memos were addressed in a rhetoric of total harmony to "Brothers and Sisters"; reports were often concluded with "lovingly submitted." But discord was a daily reality. Some of the greatest tensions were over money: The Center began as a labor of love that had been staffed by vol-

unteers, but when grants made it possible to pay workers, the social ecology changed. Jaime Green recalls the anguish he and others felt when that happened. "The activists were pushed out by the professionals when the salaries began," he says. "I remember when people started having job descriptions. Job descriptions?! That's when the activists started drifting away."[17]

Tensions came to a head in 1975. The conflict that almost became the coup de grâce for the Gay Community Services Center began when Lillene Fifield, a lesbian on the University of Southern California staff, volunteered her grant-writing skills and presented a proposal to a federal agency, the National Institute for Alcohol and Alcohol Abuse (NIAAA), which succeeded in netting the Gay Community Services Center's Alcoholism Program for Women a three-year grant worth $1 million. It was a windfall absolutely unprecedented for any gay group in the world. Now, with a fortune suddenly coming in, it seemed to the Center's fiscal director that it would be right to funnel some of that money out of the women's program and spend it on pressing institutional problems: The men's VD clinic was always short of funds, he pointed out, and also money was needed for the Center's new home because the ancient ramshackle Victorian in which it had been housed was condemned and would be demolished.

The director of the Alcoholism Program for Women, Brenda Weathers, who had assisted Fifield in writing the grant proposal, discovered the fiscal director's intent. She stormed into Don Kilhefner's office, protesting that the federal grant was earmarked for the women's program. To Weathers' outrage, Kilhefner tried to placate her, saying, "We're all brothers and sisters here, so when we get this kind of money we have to spread it around so everybody benefits."[18] When the Center management persisted in diverting the funds despite her vehement objections, Weathers notified Washington. Federal investigators were sent to examine the Center's books. Kilhefner preempted further actions by agreeing that Weathers and her program should be permitted to take the money from the Center's jurisdiction and establish a separate facility to serve women (primarily lesbians) with alcoholism problems.[19] The federal agency then transferred the grant to Weathers' new

nonprofit, called the Alcoholism Center for Women, which continues to this day.[20]

The fight over the grant money emboldened those in charge of various programs to articulate their own growing discontent over issues of money and power. People of color complained that few nonwhites were given authority. The lesbians believed that the overwhelmingly-male board had formed a power bloc that was, psychologically if not in fact, made up of "reactionary gray suits," men who had no compunction about stealing funds from a women's program to shore up programs for men. Several program directors published an in-house newsletter, *It's About Time,* decrying the "deplorable conditions" at the Center.

When *It's About Time* fell into the hands of Supervisor Ed Edelman's gay aide, David Glascock, he warned that the Gay Community Services Center's internal squabbling must cease or it would lose its public charter as well as the federal revenue-sharing funds that Edelman's office had helped the Center obtain. The "insurgents" were then asked by the management to sign a "statement of fidelity," which they refused to do because it seemed too much like signing a loyalty oath. Eleven of them were fired—six lesbians and five gay men.[21] This was barely the beginning of the Center's problems.

Those fired did not go away. They called themselves the Gay Feminist 11, and a defense coalition was formed to support them. The coalition demanded that the Gay Feminist 11 be reinstated immediately, that the Center's "bureaucracy" meet with them in an open community forum, and that no "scabs" be hired to replace the fired workers. When the management was not responsive, a strike was called in front of the Gay Community Services Center's new facility on Highland Avenue.

The socialist Lavender and Red Union, which met at the Center, pushed itself to the forefront of the strike and promoted it as a workers' issue,[22] complaining that "the workers" were underpaid and overworked and could no longer tolerate the Center's "patriarchal management systems" or its "racism, sexism, and classism."[23] Michael Weinstein, who was a leader in the Lavender and Red Union, says that his group "came together with the strikers [in] fighting for the heart and soul of the com-

munity, and trying to have the community embrace an agenda of activism, equality, radicalism."[24]

They believed that the Gay Community Services Center was straying from those principles that were central to its founding and its very mission, and they made utopian demands, such as equal pay for all workers, from the highest supervisor to the lowest janitor.

Jeanne Cordova, who was one of those fired, says that she and some others of the Gay Feminist 11 fought the strike proposal for which the Lavender and Red Union agitated. The Gay Community Services Center "wasn't a supermarket," she argued. "It's the place my baby gay brother might go to ask for a bed when my Catholic parents throw him out. It's a place for kids who are beaten by their fathers for being faggots." But despite the reluctance of some of the Gay Feminist 11, the strike went forward: Picketers demanded the unionization of the Center, forbade "scabs" to cross their line, and sang union songs such as "Solidarity Forever." Because some of the strikers were people of color, the Center's administrators were dubbed racists and "capitalist pigs." (The charges were particularly galling to the Center's founders. Don Kilhefner had been known as a Maoist. Morris Kight was assumed to be a Communist. Gay Liberation Front wags had called them "Peking and Moscow."[25] Just a few years earlier, they had hurled the "capitalist pig" epithet at others.)

Cordova writes that she kept protesting: "This is not a labor issue. Our fight is about lesbian feminism versus male-dominated hierarchy." But the fight generally continued to be presented to the public as a "workers' protest." She complains that the strike was set up by the socialist faction, which was less concerned for lesbian and gay welfare than interested in "bringing down capitalism."[26] (Lillene Fifield agrees that the strike had been set up—but by the Right rather than the Left: arranged by the FBI, who wanted to destroy the first and largest gay center in America. She speculates that a handsome young habitué at the Center, who claimed to be gay though he socialized with no one, was a plant, a provocateur, who agitated with "lefter than thou" rhetoric and maneuvered the strike.)[27]

Regardless of the strike's purpose or the fired staff members' grievances or whether the strike was manipulated, it created a civil war within the community that almost succeeded not in "bringing down capitalism," of course, but in bringing down the Gay Community Services Center. Three of the four physicians who staffed the women's clinic refused to cross the picket line, effectively closing the clinic.[28] Contributions to the Center dried up. Mary Margaret Smith, who had been a donor, heard that a group called the Gay Feminist 11 was striking because they'd been mistreated. "I didn't want to be caught up in controversy," she says, "And I certainly didn't want to give them my money if they weren't treating women right."[29] Others who had been contributors had absolutely no idea what the strike was about but knew only that there was discord at the Center and refused to donate until it was settled. The strikers' angry chants such as "Shut it down or we'll burn it down!" drove supporters farther away.

The lesbians on the staff who did not strike attempted to explain their position in a sixteen-page broadside, "Women Speak Out About the Gay Community Services Center," in which they declared that though they were dedicated "to providing services for the lesbian/women's community—not the gay community," at this time the Center was "the only viable means of transmitting those services in Los Angeles."[30] But their explanation met with little sympathy among radical feminists and leftists, who composed much of the activist community at the time. All those who crossed the picket line to work at the Center were ostracized as strikebreakers.

The conflict rent the lesbian community in two. *Lesbian News* (which was to become the major L.A. lesbian publication) was started by Jinx Beers during the strike in an effort to present a moderate voice after some of her friends were ejected from the Westside Women's Center because they were "scabs." A riot almost broke out the evening a group of women who continued to work at the Center went to the Women's Saloon for dinner. "'Gunfight' at the L.A. Saloon," the headline of the first issue of *Lesbian News* read. They were refused service, and the Saloon's proprietor, Colleen McKay, shut down for the night rather than tolerate their presence.[31]

Lillene Fifield, who had obtained the million-dollar grant for the Alcoholism Program for Women, was, ironically, punished the most by strike sympathizers. Fifield says now that the men at the Center had indeed been capable of being "very oppressive" to women; but she believed the Center was precious because it was where gay men and women who'd been abused by society "would begin to heal," and she thought it inappropriate for the staff to "air our dirty laundry for all the world to see." She thus chose to continue in her post as the director of women's programming, despite the strike. She says she was "made a villain" at every workshop and community event. "I was thrown out of everywhere. Even at the Woman's Building. I was told I was not welcome." Strikers overturned her car and slashed the tires.[32]

The boycott of the Gay Community Services Center continued for three years. Josy Catoggio says that when the Center received money from the Comprehensive Employment Training Act (CETA) in 1978 and hired her to be the office manager for women's programming, she was called a scab by other lesbians even though there was no longer a picket line in front of the Highland Avenue building.[33] Finally, however, in the fall of 1978, the dispute was settled out of court. The Center revised its personnel policies and procedures "in an effort to insure that the rights of present and future workers will be secure," and the strikers were awarded "token reparations" ($90 apiece). The Center capitulated further by making a public apology to them in the L.A. gay papers.[34] That year, the Center's board, sensitive to the accusation that women were not given important positions, appointed Carol Nottley as the head financial officer and Susan Kuhner as the Center's assistant director.[35]

The male-heavy board truly did try to placate lesbians over the next few years, hoping to stave off serious trouble before it took root. After a group of young women led by Christi Kissell climbed the Center's roof in the middle of the night and painted the word "Lesbian" on the Gay Community Services Center sign, the board, understanding the temper of the times, voted to make the change permanent. In 1982, in a move to cut costs, the board briefly entertained the idea of eliminating the Women's Resource Office because supposedly all the Center's departments served women. But when the board's meeting was invaded by five

angry lesbians who demanded that the Center offer more, not fewer, programs geared specifically toward women, their demands were quickly met: The board established Lesbian Central—an office run by a paid administrator devoted exclusively to lesbian concerns, as well as a meeting space and a library.[36]

But class, gender, and race problems reoccurred with regularity. Money was often behind these difficulties. The Center had grown rapidly because of the generous Democratic administration of President Jimmy Carter. It was federal money from the Department of Housing and Urban Development that permitted the Center's board to pay off the last $250,000 of its mortgage on its Highland Avenue home, and it was Comprehensive Employment and Training Act money that permitted the rapid expansion of Center programs. But with the advent of the Reagan era, such government support was cut off. Another way had to be found to fund a Center that was dedicated to social services for gay people. That way—the only way, board members insisted—was to convince private donors that the Gay and Lesbian Community Services Center was a serious, "respectable" institution.[37] They sought to hire as the Center's executive director someone who would convey that impression and would also have the ability to charm major donors (who were almost invariably men since women tended to be less affluent, not yet having made real progress anywhere in America in their fight for equal pay).

Steve Schulte, who had received a political science degree from Yale before coming to L.A. and had worked for the Los Angeles City Council, was hired as executive director in 1979. His talents were not only executive. He had moonlighted as a nude model for Colt Studios, and his beefcake pictures were wildly popular. On his first day at the Center, one employee remembers, "every man in the building ran out of his office" to get a look at the Colt legend.[38] Even board members called him "eye candy."[39] Schulte was given a dual mandate: to "clean up" the Center[40] and to raise big bucks. Under Schulte, the pull away from the Center's radical roots became downright deracination.

It was clear that the Gay Community Services Center needed "a certain sense of structure, order, and credibility" and "could not remain this

ragtag, spontaneous agency," Schulte recalls. "We were moving to become a mainstream social service institution." The gay center was making its final transformation from a culture of community activists to one of corporate management.

Schulte was determined, first of all, to create a more professional work environment by ending the "casualness about dress and rules" (which for many of the Center's staff and clientele had surely been part of its gay charm). "I'll never forget," he says, "a guy named Mike at the info desk . . . a very attractive black guy who had a great body and who worked shirtless at the front desk" (where he was the first sight of all visitors to the Center). "I had to tell him he could no longer work shirtless."[41]

During Schulte's years as director, administration burgeoned at the Center, which created further conflicts with the volunteers and low-paid staff. Cosmo Bua, who ran the information desk after "Mike," voices the complaint of many of the workers of that period by saying that the administrative offices, housed on the upper floor of the new building, swelled to the point that "if the Center was a boat, it would tip over. There was too much on top." Bua says that because so much money was spent on administration, basic services, which had been crucial to the initial concept of a "gay community services center," were eliminated, such as the hotline to counsel gay people facing crises. "People would call, suicidal, and there'd be nothing. It was appalling."[42] For the first time in the Center's history, a "minimum donation policy" was instituted, so that clients would realize, as an internal memo said, "the value of the services they are receiving."[43]

Schulte believes that, these criticisms notwithstanding, he never lost sight of the real goal, to "end up serving more people."[44] Some who worked at the Center in those years believe that that is precisely what happened. JJ Vega, who was a Center caseworker from 1982 to 1985, talks, for instance, of "the hoards of gay kids who came in from Hollywood Boulevard" who were given food, clothing, and shelter at the Center, treated by the physicians and psychologists, and "taken to museums, camping, things they never before knew."[45] But to that end, raising

money was crucial. Steve Schulte considered it part of his job "to go to Trumps [a fashionable West Hollywood restaurant owned by Sheldon Andelson] and wine and dine someone and get their money" for Center programs. His sexual charisma was a not-inconsequential aid to the robust donor program that the board instituted in order to free the Center from the vicissitudes of government funding.

The board of directors courted those who were affluent enough to join a group such as Friends of the Center or the Silver Circle and commit themselves to donations of at least $1,000 a year. Terry DeCrescenzo, one of the few women who served as chair of the board during those years, recalls that at a 1981 dinner held to attract donors six hundred people quickly signed up to join the Silver Circle.[46] The *Center News,* the Gay and Lesbian Community Services Center newsletter, often read like the society page of a metropolitan newspaper, as an announcement for one of the Center's annual fund-raisers illustrates:

> Vintage Hollywood extravagance will be on tap for this Summer's 8th Annual Lawn Party, to be hosted at Wolf's Lair—a dream castle perched high in the hills above Lake Hollywood. Celebrating the theme "Camelot in White," the lawn party site at the home of Bob Crane and Tom McClay features spacious gardens, sunny terraces and luxurious decorator touches. The affair will be catered by Trumps, which promises a sumptuous hors d'oeuvres and cocktail buffet.[47]

Potential donors were also wooed by candlelight dinners at the homes of the board members or were taken on tours of the Center, which was redecorated so that they would be impressed that nothing at the Center was "ragtag."

Yet another bloody battle brewed when the position of executive director became vacant once again because Schulte left to run for the city council. This battle combined all the major points of dissension: class, race, and gender—and even included the issues of "looksism" and

ageism to boot. The board continued to believe that because money-raising must be the executive director's major task, it should hire for that position someone who could excel at bringing in the dollars. Women, it was long thought, would have less success in appealing to affluent male donors than someone with the impressive charms of a Steve Schulte.

Del Martinez, a lesbian who was a licensed social worker and the recipient of a prestigious award from the National Social Work Association for her successes as a community organizer, made it to the shortlist of candidates to succeed Schulte. But the board ultimately rejected her for the position because, as one member complained, "She's not polished enough to reach out to our major donors."[48] When Terry DeCrescenzo, who was board president in 1983, continued to urge Martinez's appointment, DeCrescenzo's failure to consider appearance and style was met with great consternation. One of the most powerful members told her, "I recommend you stand down. You don't have our confidence." Another member said bluntly, "We have to face it! Fat and Mexican don't play in raising money!"[49]

Martinez's supporters did not have to be present at the board's executive sessions to know that she was rejected because she was middle-aged, Latina, and a woman with working-class style. Many of the lesbians who worked at the Center or used its services had hoped that if Martinez became executive director, she would pay more attention to lesbian interests than the gay male directors had been willing to do. They felt that despite the concessions of Lesbian Central and the Center's name change to include "Lesbian," women were still getting short shrift. So they were furious when Martinez was passed over by the board in favor of John Brown, a man in his thirties, whose credentials were far inferior to hers: Martinez says, angry to this day, "It was a mockery."[50] Many of the women staff members, including the director of Lesbian Central, Lauren Jardine, agreed. They resigned in outraged protest.[51]

Jardine then approached Martinez about forming an all-lesbian center, one that would speak to lesbian needs, first and foremost, as the Gay and Lesbian Community Services Center never had. Since private donations were absolutely crucial to the success of her ambitious plans, Martinez and Jardine threw themselves into fund-raising efforts. They

named the center they were designing "Connexxus" because it was to serve as a nexus that would "connect us" all, that is, all members of the lesbian community. An upscale lesbian organization, Southern California Women for Understanding (SCWU), agreed to help with a generous stipend and a sponsorship, which would permit Connexxus to raise money under SCWU's own nonprofit status. The vision that Martinez and Jardine shared for Connexxus was unique. They wished it to be all things to all lesbians, to reach out to "the baby dykes"[52] as well as to those who would go to a Connexxus-sponsored event at the Sheraton Universal Hotel to hear a white lesbian attorney and an African American lesbian entrepreneur discuss the topic "It Doesn't Take a Lot of Money to Make Money."[53]

Though there had been earlier lesbian centers in Los Angeles, Connexxus was the first to attempt to become a funded institution and to involve so broad a spectrum of the population. It was the first to operate with the unalloyed blessings of a bona fide city, West Hollywood, which provided space and even some funding. Because Connexxus was located in West Hollywood, far from many areas where lesbians who needed social services lived, Martinez worked to establish neighborhood satellites. (Connexxus's Centro de Mujeres was opened in East Los Angeles and continues to function there still.) In grand Hollywood manner, Martinez also planned—as she told potential donors—that Connexxus would eventually develop a business/services/entertainment complex for lesbian-owned businesses, professional offices, arts organizations—even a health club.[54] For a time, Connexxus seemed to be succeeding. It was reportedly serving 15,000 women yearly and finding ways to meet its annual budget of $240,000.[55]

But it was forced to shut down in 1990. The problem of money, which had been of such concern to the Gay and Lesbian Community Services Center, plagued Connexxus as well; but, unlike the Center, Connexxus could not find solutions. Though its programs directed at the diversity of the lesbian community had become increasingly elaborate, the funds to make those programs viable dried up. Most lesbians, like most women, enjoyed less discretionary income than men, who could spend more on charitable giving and were more used to being donors. Try as

they might, Connexxus could not find ways to persuade women to open their wallets wider. After the first great flush of excitement over a center exclusively for lesbians, donations dropped. The horror of the AIDS epidemic, which soon occasioned the government's pouring of money into the Gay and Lesbian Community Services Center, also diverted private donations, as well as governmental support, from an all-lesbian institution because lesbians were the population least likely to be threatened by AIDS.

Sadly, what Martinez and Jardine had hoped would be the greatest strength of Connexxus, that it would "connect us," became one of the reasons for its failure: The diverse socioeconomic and ethnic groups that made up the huge lesbian community of Los Angeles ultimately found (once again) that they could not happily share space—neither on the board nor at the Center. Working-class lesbians and many lesbians of color refused to stifle their conviction that Connexxus was too white and too middle class, that it catered too much to the affluent (who could afford to donate to the institution); and middle-class lesbians believed that Connexxus was not only too radical but also "downwardly mobile,"[56] and they were not inspired to donate.

Before disbanding, Connexxus distributed the money that was left in its coffers to the June Mazer Lesbian Collection, a repository and archive that it had helped fund, and to the Centro de Mujeres, which was determined to keep going despite the death of its parent agency. Torie Osborn, who had become executive director of the Gay and Lesbian Community Services Center in 1988—the Center's first woman executive director since its establishment seventeen years earlier—vowed to provide at the Center all the services for lesbians that had been available through Connexxus.[57]

It had been the tragic AIDS epidemic, which was destroying a generation of male leaders, that finally made "lesbian ascendancy" possible at the Center and in gay organizations everywhere. Torie Osborn, who had run Holly Near's Redwood Records and had come to Hollywood to "get into mainstream show business," was a perky, attractive young woman with enough charm and charisma to be acceptable to the Center's Board and acceptable to the grassroots women as well. (One of them, so delighted

over Osborn's appointment, spray painted "It's a Girl!" in front of the director's parking space.) Though Osborn was not precisely a Steve Schulte, she did not disappoint: For the first time, lesbians became donors in significant numbers. They were especially encouraged by an annual "Women's Night," a Hollywood gala, often replete with celebrities, the brainchild of Osborn and Jean O'Leary, a national lesbian leader who had settled in Los Angeles. (Women's Night presently raises about a half-million dollars for the Center in the course of one evening.) Osborn also ingratiated herself with male donors, and many of those who died of AIDS remembered the Center in their wills. Resources and budget doubled in her four years at the helm.[58] The taboo against a woman executive director at the Center finally vanished, bringing at long last détente about the gender issue. To date, all the subsequent executive directors at the Center have been women.

THE ENEMY AT THE GATES

> *Lesbian separatists worked with men; street people with stockbrokers. . . . People who would hardly speak to each other learned to put aside their own goals—and their anger—to work together. . . . Although the whole campaign is one we shouldn't even have had to fight, it's given us a sense of common purpose that we lacked.*
>
> —Gayle Wilson on the "No" on 6 Campaign[59]

Despite constant internal battles, for nearly a decade there seemed to be no stopping gay progress in Los Angeles. Since the 1969 city council election victory in which gay activists were instrumental in replacing homophobe Paul Lamport with gay-friendly Bill Stevenson, gays had gained steady political momentum. Remembering Lamport's defeat, some candidates began to campaign in gay bars. Bob Geoghegan, a member of Councilman Ed Edelman's staff, recalls that politicians were still sometimes attacked by their political opponents if they addressed themselves to the "untouchable community";[60] but these attacks did not stick, and gay Angelenos handsomely rewarded the attention of gay-friendly politicians. By the early 1970s, there was a political pool to

The very "manly" Dr. Ida B. Baker, who established a private practice in Southern California. *Author's collection.*

Harry Wharton, who "boasted one of the finest wardrobes among the 'queer people,'" 1914. *Courtesy Sacramento Archives and Museum Collection Center.*

Left, attorneys with Herbert Lowe, one of dozens of men accused in a "social vagrant" scandal in Southern California; right, B. C. Brown and W. H. Warren, bounty hunters of homosexuals. These pictures appeared in the *Los Angeles Times* in 1914.

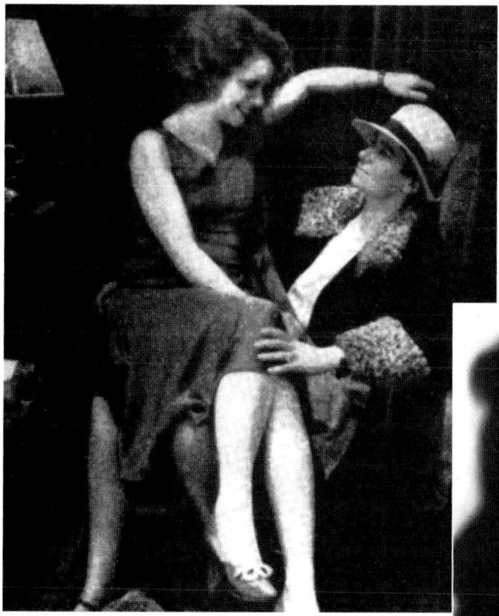

Dorothy Arzner and her star, Clara Bow, 1929. *UCLA Arts Library, Dorothy Arzner Collection.*

On screen and in private, several "unstraight" Hollywood women, such as Katharine Hepburn, dressed as men and lived as they wanted. *Author's collection.*

In the 1920s, Rudolph Valentino cast a spell "over the entire female population—and some others." *Author's collection.*

. . . the little girl customers . . .

The guidebook, *How to Sin in Hollywood*, told tourists where to go to see lesbian "boy-girls." Drawing by Lloyd Hoff, 1940

At quiet backyard parties, a gay movie queen and a gay director mingled with gay worker bees: George Cukor (in glasses), Tallulah Bankhead, and two unknowns (1937). *Photo: Rex Evans/courtesy Jim Weatherford.*

Rock Hudson, pressured by fan magazines to marry, wed lesbian Phyllis Gates. *Courtesy of the Academy of Motion Picture Arts and Sciences.*

Attorney Gladys Towels Root, "Defender of the Dammed," 1950s. Herald Examiner *Collection/Los Angeles Public Library.*

Jimmy Renard, male impersonator in L.A. nightclubs during the 1930s and '40s. *Author's collection.*

Marvin Edwards, all too briefly enjoying Los Angeles, 1949. *Author's collection.*

Nancy Valverde was regularly stopped by the LAPD for "masquerading." *Author's collection.*

"Lisa Ben," editor-in-chief of *Vice Versa. Courtesy of the ONE National Gay and Lesbian Archives.*

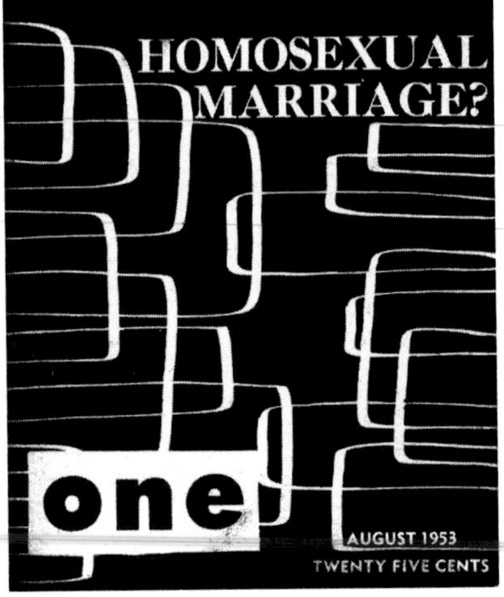

From "gay pride" to " gay marriage," *ONE Magazine* predicted the gay agenda by half a century. *Author's collection.*

Butch-femme '50s style: a member of the Satyrs motorcycle club; Miss Destiny, on the cover of *ONE* magazine. *Photo left: John Gruber/ photo right: Author's collection.*

Meko and Juanita, at the Open Door, early 1960s. *Author's collection.*

Members of one of L.A.'s numerous Lesbian softball teams. *Author's collection.*

Transgender millionaire Reed Erickson (center) on a date, early 1960s. *Courtesy of the ONE National Gay and Lesbian Archives.*

Stella Rush, one of the few lesbians to write for *ONE Magazine*, published under the name Sten Russell. *Author's collection.*

Morris Kight (far left) and Don Kilhefner (bearded) were known among GLF wags as "Moscow and Peking." *Courtesy of the ONE National Gay and Lesbian Archives.*

A new twist on Hollywood glamour: artists William Moritz and Robert Opel prepare to go out on the town. *Photo: Philip Stuart/Author's collection.*

Old gays in new times: Joan Hannan of "Joanie Presents" and Lee Glaze of "The Patch," 1969. *Courtesy Lee Glaze.*

L.A. Golden Boys circa 1970. *Courtesy Bruce Reifel.*

"Oh, you lesbian feminists!": Sharon A. Lilly and Brenda Weathers. *Courtesy Sharon A. Lilly.*

The Lesbian Tide Collective (right) helped promote a movement of kiss-ins and dances. *Photo courtesy Jeanne Cordova.*

Early 1971. *Courtesy Carolyn Weathers.*

Standing together at the Gay Community Services Center on Wilshire Boulevard: Chris Brownlie and Mary Adair on right. *Photo: Tony Barnard/UCLA Special Collections.*

New power players: from left, Judge Rand Schrader, Sheldon Andelson, Theresa DeCrescenzo, Betty Berzon, Steve Schulte, Judge Steve Lachs, and Duke Comegys. *Courtesy Theresa DeCrescenzo.*

Openly gay councilman Steve Schulte.
Courtesy of the ONE National Gay and Lesbian Archives.

Lawyers and lovers, MECLA leaders Roberta Bennett and Diane Abbitt
Courtesy of the ONE National Gay and Lesbian Archives.

National gay leader and adopted Angeleno, Jean O'Leary. *Press photo.*

Richard Deacon of *The Dick Van Dyke Show* (center) with Ah Men Founder Don Cook; unidentified man at left. *Courtesy of the ONE National Gay and Lesbian Archives.*

Beth Chayim Chadashim president Davi Cheng with scribe Neil Yerman, repairing a rescued Torah. *Courtesy Davi Cheng.*

Comedy team Patty Harrison and Robin Tyler. Their contracts were dropped by the ABC network when word got out that they were lesbians. *Courtesy Robin Tyler.*

West Hollywood's first mayor, Valerie Terrigno. *Courtesy of the ONE National Gay and Lesbian Archives.*

Rudy Ruano, before leaving Guatemala in the early 1960s.
Courtesy Rudy Ruano.

A 1991 cover of *Lesbian News*, which began in L.A. as a two-page mimeographed newsletter in 1975.
Courtesy Ella Matthes.

Ivy Bottini, a leader in the women's movement, gay rights struggles, and gay eldercare.
Courtesy Ivy Bottini.

Designers and costumers came out from behind the scenes for the AIDS fight. *Photo: Craig Collins.*

Charlene Nguon sued her southern California school district for outing her as a lesbian. *Courtesy ACLU of Southern California.*

Butchlalis de Panochtitlan: Nadine Romero, Mari Garcia, Raquel Gutierrez and Claudia Rodriguez. *Photo: Evelyn Reyes.*

Robin Eans and Sandy Sachs, the owners of Girlbar in West Hollywood, where the term "lipstick lesbian" was coined. *Photo: Dean Keefer, Courtesy Sandy Sachs.*

After years of working in the shadows, gays themselves finally became the focus of a Hollywood classic in *Brokeback Mountain. Photo: Kimberly French/courtesy Focus Features.*

splash in, and groups such as the Gay Community Alliance were formed: As Mike Manning, one of the founders of the Alliance, recalls, its approach was multileveled. The organization reached out to all gays—not only those who might donate campaign money but also "the kids in the bars"—to register, vote, and think of themselves as a political force. They developed a voter slate and a dedicated team of campaign volunteers. They raised funds for printing and mailing leaflets that would help convince gay people that their vote was crucial if gay power was to be taken to "the next level."[61]

Such efforts paid off throughout the 1970s. In 1973, Burt Pines won his campaign for city attorney with the help of a large gay constituency, which he had wooed in part by campaigning in gay bars.[62] Pines recalls, "Once I learned how [gay people] were being treated, it really troubled me. It seemed so unfair."[63] He fulfilled his campaign promises, making a seismic shift in the official response to homosexuality with two rulings: the first, that the city attorney's office would no longer prosecute people for holding hands, dancing, or making sexual propositions "just because [the act] occurs in a gay bar";[64] and the second, that the Los Angeles Police Department not only would cease to harass homosexuals but also would be *required* to hire qualified homosexuals as police officers.[65]

Ed Edelman, a two-term city councilman, followed Pines' campaign trail through gay bars in 1974 ("I never weighed the risk," he recalls)[66] and won a seat in the supervisorial district that encompassed Hollywood, West Hollywood, and Silver Lake. It was then that Edelman kept his campaign promise to hire David Glascock to serve as a liaison with the gay community, making one of the earliest openly gay political appointments in the nation. Glascock had been a driving force behind the Gay Community Alliance; he had also been convicted for a homosexual act, and he had tended a bar on Cahuenga Boulevard, where drag queens congregated. But if the media thought they could use that information to shame the new supervisor, they were wrong. The days were dead in L.A. when a politician could be made hysterical if it was discovered that a homosexual was on his staff: "We hired [Glascock] because we knew he was a homosexual," Edelman bluntly told reporters. "If we're going to

solve our problems in the gay community, we want someone who understands those problems."[67]

On the Los Angeles City Council, too, there were members who were very friendly to the gay community. Peggy Stevenson held on to the seat in her largely gay district, which she had inherited from her husband. Joel Wachs, elected in 1971, was a "perennial bachelor" who remained closeted during all his twenty-eight years on the council, but he invariably served as a powerful ally to gay interests. Some elected officials in L.A. were gay-friendly in part because they had come to understand their own lesbian and gay relatives. One of Mayor Tom Bradley's daughters is a lesbian.[68] Ed Edelman, who became known as the "archangel of the center" for his help in securing government funding, acknowledges that he has a sister who is a lesbian.[69] David Russell, the son of Councilwoman Pat Russell, became the lover of the *Advocate*'s publisher, David Goodstein.[70] Though officials of that day never joined Parents and Friends of Lesbians and Gays, family sympathy made a difference in their political understanding.

Considering the positions taken by the city attorney and the gay allies on the Board of Supervisors and the Los Angeles City Council, Police Chief Ed Davis had good reason to know that the LAPD's antigay witch hunts would no longer fly. Even the *Los Angeles Times* seemed to be against him: Chief Davis sent the newspaper a bitter letter complaining about its "strong editorial support of homosexuality" and canceling his subscription.[71]

But despite changing times, "Crazy Ed," as the chief of police was called in the gay community, refused to relinquish his hostility. In 1975, the same year Governor Jerry Brown signed the "consenting adults" bill to legalize gay sex, Davis orchestrated what may have been the most expensive (and silly) gay raid in history. John Embry, the publisher of *Drummer* magazine, had invited members of what he called the "leather fraternity" to the Mark IV bathhouse on Melrose Avenue for a private party to benefit the Gay Community Services Center. The entertainment included a mock slave auction. Val Martin, the rugged star of the SM movie *Born to Raise Hell*, offered to serve as auctioneer. (Martin, a

Colombian immigrant, worked both as an actor and an SM hustler with a pioneering specialty in fisting. His business card read, "Give me a call and I'll give you a hand.")[72] Martin had just "sold" the first gay volunteer to Terry LeGrand, who in turn gave him to Jeanne Barney, the heterosexual woman who was at that time an editor for *Drummer* magazine, to do her yard work. Then a massive police assault began.

Records indicate that 105 police officers participated in the raid (though the LAPD would not admit to more than 65).[73] Helicopters, dozens of squad cars, and a bus surrounded the bathhouse—the bus had been specially chartered as a mammoth paddy wagon. "There was total chaos and pandemonium," recalls Aristide Laurent. "I tried to leave and saw cops coming over the walls. . . . There were lights, a helicopter, and just so many cops." Jeanne Barney, who helped coordinate the event says, "No one could believe the helicopters. Then the loudspeakers. Then sheer terror." She shudders as she remembers that the police packed forty men into the bus; they took Barney in a separate car.[74]

The busload of arrestees, all shackled with plastic handcuffs, waited for hours in a crowded holding cell before they were processed at the police station. Laurent remembers one man who had a tragicomic cause to panic: "He had a dildo in his pants 'for effect,' and he was afraid of what would happen if the cops—or other inmates—found it. So he had to get behind a couple of us—all of us are in handcuffs—and we had to, without looking, get his pants open . . . unzip them . . . pull the dildo out, and kick it under the candy machine in the holding cell."[75] Sheer terror of another order set in when the charges were filed: The LAPD booked all forty men on an 1871 statute for trafficking in human slaves, a felony.

Furious with the LAPD's overkill, the community mobilized. "For the first time . . . I saw people really come together," says Jeanne Barney. "Everyone was so incensed at this: We got the West Hollywood sweater queens, the leather queens, the drag queens, the Morris Kight people . . . an amazing show of solidarity."[76] Morris Kight organized a town meeting at Troupers Hall in Hollywood, where Troy Perry raised money for the arrestees' defense by defiantly auctioning off more volunteers. (The

heterosexual attorney, Al Gordon, who took the case pro bono, stepped up to the auction block and was immediately purchased by his wife.) A liberal councilman, Zev Yaroslavsky, showed up and denounced the arrests to television cameras. Davis represented his extreme tactics as compensatory, because for years the LAPD had been "cowed," he said, into "being too lenient [by] the most powerful lobby in the city, the homosexual community."[77] Nevertheless, Peggy Stevenson, who chaired the council committee that had jurisdiction over the Police Commission's budget, succeeded in getting deducted from the LAPD's vice budget for the next year a sum equal to what the raid had cost.[78]

That was the year, 1976, that the mayor of Los Angeles, Tom Bradley, issued a proclamation signed by the city council, officially establishing a Gay Pride Week in Los Angeles.[79] The following year, 1977, when Mayor Bradley's office conducted a poll posing the statement, "Homosexuals who are qualified should be permitted to hold any Los Angeles City job for which they are qualified," only 21 percent disagreed, and more than 60 percent agreed.[80] Chief Davis's attack on the gays had backfired thunderously.

Continued gay political gains in Los Angeles were largely due to the Municipal Elections Committee of Los Angeles (MECLA), which became the most powerful gay political force ever seen in the city—or the nation. The group, which initially named itself Orion, developed from gay consciousness-raising sessions. Orion consisted originally of seven young, attractive, upper-middle-class men (of the type that Armistead Maupin has called "A-Gays").[81] Their sessions led them to the conviction that they must lend their clout to gay political concerns because it was important to change the public image of homosexuals from socially marginal individuals to a power with which politicians must reckon.[82]

Like the Gay Community Alliance, they were interested in creating gay-friendly politicians, but they operated on a much different scale. In a city that is so devoted to glamour and power, it would have been sur-

prising if such a group had not emerged in the midst of the gay movement. Judge Steve Lachs, who was then an attorney and one of the founders of the Orion group, recalls that they made vehement distinctions between themselves and the "hippies," from whom they felt they needed to wrest the position of representing the gay community.[83] Peter Scott, who was also a successful attorney and had Marlboro-Man good looks, was a model of the A-Gays that the group hoped to attract in order to do its political work; thus he became the group's first president. What the group needed to do, they decided, was not to raise public consciousness through street demonstrations where scruffy Gay Liberation Front–types would take over, but rather to become a political action committee (the first openly gay PAC in the nation). Their PAC would raise large sums of money for gay-friendly political candidates through elegant and prestigious social gatherings.

The first challenge they undertook was with the advice of David Mixner, a hot-shot political consultant who was not yet out of the closet but was known for his tactical insights. Mixner was well connected both in Hollywood and in American politics' top circles (including the Clintons): He suggested that the Orion group try to influence the next municipal elections for the Los Angeles City Council. An overt homophobe, John Gibson, who had served on the city council since the 1950s and was its president, was running for another term and seemed destined to continue as president. No gay organization in the world had ever attempted to raise big money to influence a political campaign, and initially the group was at a loss for how to begin. (Someone actually suggested they hold a bake sale.) Steve Lachs, who had also been active in fund-raising for the Jewish community, proposed some tried-and-true techniques, as he remembers now: He suggested first of all that the group contact wealthy potential donors individually and explain, on a one-to-one basis, what they hoped to do: "Spend an hour with one wealthy person who's gay," Lachs said, "and you'll get far more than you'll make from a bake sale." He suggested, too, that they stage carefully planned events to which affluent gays would want to come and where they would be persuaded to make large contributions to the cause.

For its first event, the group rented the banquet room of the Carriage Trade, the popular gay bar and restaurant. Lachs recalls how they orchestrated that evening. First, he gave "the very emotional speech"; then another member, Rob Eichberg, made the pitch. Lachs had prearranged for a corporate attorney to raise his hand on cue and make the initial donation. "This sounds wonderful," the gay attorney said. "I pledge $1,000," a generous sum in 1976. Eichberg and Lachs played the room until $20,000 was pledged. Because it was necessary to deposit the funds into a bank account, the Orion group decided to give itself a new name, one that would reflect its political concerns but not reveal its sexual orientation lest timid donors fear to write "gay" or "homosexual" on a check.[84] They became the Municipal Elections Committee of Los Angeles (MECLA).

The organization was at that time all male, and the authors of *Out for Good,* a history of the national gay rights movement, have suggested that at this event (and in MECLA, generally) there had been "little ideology, other than the ideology of power and influence."[85] Be that as it may, for the very first time, a group of A-Gays had gotten together not simply to demonstrate power (or indulge their pleasure, which had already happened often in Los Angeles, for example, at the 1930s parties of George Cukor and Cole Porter). MECLA's end product was big bucks, raised specifically for the gay rights battle, which included the rights of those homosexuals who had no power. Monetary munificence on the scale that MECLA achieved that night at the Carriage Trade had been unprecedented in the community. Thus began serious gay fund-raising.

To help them spend the money it raised for best effect, MECLA was guided by David Mixner, whose savvy strategies brought L.A. politicians to believe that gay power and the gay vote were tremendous, that failure to get the gay vote could be fatal to a political career, and that MECLA, a chief power broker, could deliver it. Politicians were soon coveting invitations to "MECLA Breakfasts" at venues such as the Bel Age Hotel in West Hollywood, where candidates who had first been vetted by MECLA's board addressed potential donors over eggs Florentine. As an aide to a high-ranking elected official observed to a newspaper reporter at a MECLA event: "Powerful? You bet they're powerful. I have never

seen anything like the gays [for raising money] from a minority group. . . . We pay attention, I can tell you that."[86]

In 1977, MECLA expanded its board from nine men to five women and ten men. The board's president, Peter Scott, claimed that feminist consciousness was behind the realization that women ought to be brought into MECLA: "Either you believe that women are equal or you don't. If you do, you have to recognize that they don't have equal opportunity, so it's your duty to bootstrap them up," he declared[87]—though he did not mean that MECLA's boardroom doors would be open to just any woman. Both men and women invited to serve on MECLA's board in the 1970s had to pledge to make contributions of at least $1,200 a year to MECLA.[88] Such a policy, which shut out gays and lesbians who were not affluent, soon set off smoldering resentments among some sectors of the community; they complained that "the people in the hills and the elitists" had commandeered gay politics, acting as though the movement were a commodity to be purchased. "MECLA Doesn't Speak For Us!" picketers proclaimed at one of the group's pow-wows. Such malcontents barely registered, however. MECLA aimed high and continued to recruit the wealthy.

Roberta Bennett and Diane Abbitt, a lesbian couple who became L.A. lawyers, were soon major players in MECLA. They had been leaders in both national and local NOW, heading its Lesbian Rights Task Force and organizing its lesbian "Alternative Lifestyles Conference." But they decided that "it was real crazy not to work with the gay male community"—against the advice of lesbian activists such as Jeanne Cordova, who told them, remembering her experiences at the Center, "What's wrong with you? Don't you know that anything lesbians do when they work with the boys gets co-opted by them and the women never get credit for anything?"[89] Bennett and Abbitt recall that the first time they attended a MECLA reception, they felt that finally they had found their movement home: "It was far more sophisticated than anything we had done with NOW. It was exciting, challenging, and it felt good.

These people were opening a new avenue of activism—the traditional political arena."[90]

MECLA men convinced the two women of the importance of raising money to give to political candidates who were supportive of gay rights. The lesbian community had never really been seriously tapped as *political* donors, but Bennett and Abbitt warmed to the challenge. The men had them listen to a tape of the first fund-raising event at the Carriage Trade "to see how it was done."[91] Then Bennett and Abbitt organized their own luncheon at the Carriage Trade Restaurant. They invited forty or fifty affluent lesbians who wore high heels and dresses (and whose class equivalents in the preceding generation would not have dreamed of setting foot in a semipublic lesbian gathering). Bennett and Abbitt told them, "We want you to hear about how the Municipal Elections Committee is working within the system in order to defeat discrimination in the gay community." They raised "big money," Bennett says. "The boys were very impressed."[92] She and Abbitt were each eventually elected co-chairs of MECLA.

Never before had upper-middle-class lesbians participated as a group in *any* homosexual cause. Eventually about one-third of the MECLA membership was female. As Esther, a Los Angeles physician, believes, the appeal of MECLA was twofold for women like her: She approved heartily of the organization's determination to "give the gay community a political voice in Sacramento and L.A., and Washington, too," but MECLA's "prosperous, grand fetes" also held a great attraction for her: "It was fun to get dressed up and see who else was dressed up."[93] Through MECLA's "fashionable" events, affluent lesbians became major donors in the movement for gay rights.

The greatest battle for MECLA and for the entire Los Angeles lesbian and gay community came in the wake of a disaster in liberal Dade County, Florida. An orange juice pitchwoman, Anita Bryant, had succeeded in getting the electorate to repeal an ordinance, very like one in Los Angeles, that forbade discrimination in jobs and housing on the

basis of sexual orientation. The right-wing victory in Dade was soon followed by reversals of gay gains in three more cities. It did not take much prescience for the *Los Angeles Times* to understand—as it announced in an article titled "Gay Rights: Is a Backlash Forming?"—that next "the war [would] be waged in California."[94]

Gay Americans were shocked by Anita Bryant's victory. "No one thought she'd win," recalls David Mixner of an election day that, to homosexuals nationwide, became known, with gallows' wit, as "Horrible Tuesday."[95] But shock was not paralysis. All over America, in cities that had never had more than a dimly lit gay bar or two, gay organizations were formed to fight the right-wing attacks.[96] In Los Angeles, Troy Perry and Morris Kight organized the Coalition for Human Rights, and, days after the Florida vote, they were able to get 9,000 protesters to gather in the streets.[97]

The horror of Horrible Tuesday brought some immediate respite to the usual internecine lesbian and gay community battles. Kight, who had been a chief villain in the Gay Feminist 11 strike at the Gay Community Services Center, cleverly understood (as had gay male leaders since Magnus Hirschfeld in the nineteenth century) that the predominant negative stereotype that simplistically characterized homosexuals as wildly promiscuous men could be tempered and complicated by showing that women were also homosexuals. Kight declared that "co-sexual parity" must be a priority of the Coalition for Human Rights.[98] Class divisions were also tackled because the leaders realized that numbers counted. David Mixner, the most respected strategist among affluent gays, declared that gay people would win an upcoming war in California only if they fought in a single, united campaign, rather than one campaign of wealthy conservatives ("the Suits") and another of grassroots radicals ("the Streets"). To that end, Mixner approached Ivy Bottini, at that time the head of women's programming at the Gay Community Services Center. He told Bottini, who had not only impeccable lesbian credentials but also a working-class background, "We need the grassroots working on this campaign too. And if you come in, they'll come in."[99]

As the *Los Angeles Times* and gay activists predicted, war did come to California. It was brought by a Southern California state senator, John

Briggs, a right-wing Republican candidate for governor who believed he would bolster his odds by making gay people a scapegoat. Briggs hoped to replicate Bryant's success in Florida through a "California Save Our Children" ballot initiative. His supporters gathered half a million signatures, almost two hundred thousand more than what was required for the initiative to qualify for the 1978 California ballot. The chilling text of the initiative, which became Proposition 6, declared that "one of the most fundamental interests of the State is the establishment and preservation of the family unit"—and for that reason, public school administrators, counselors, teachers, and teachers' aides must be fired if it was discovered that they engaged in "the advocating, soliciting, imposing, encouraging, or promoting of private or public homosexual activity." That is, not only homosexuals would be fired but also all public school employees who indicated they were in any way supportive of the rights of gay people.[100]

Ivy Bottini had for years considered herself a lesbian separatist; but she realized that the right wing was now aiming for a far bigger victory than what they had achieved in one county in Florida: They were waging their antigay war statewide in the largest state in the nation. Their win would herald the end of homosexual progress. On the brink of such a war, Bottini recalls, separatism was a luxury that lesbians could not afford—though she admits that her first organizational meeting with gay men had been an emotional struggle for her: "I felt, 'I'm in enemy territory.' The men had been so separate from the lesbian community that I'd made my home." Yet she believed, as many in the lesbian and gay community came to believe, that she had no choice but to put aside differences.[101]

Once the Briggs initiative qualified for the ballot, lesbians and gays knew that the assault would not be limited to schoolteachers and school administrators (whose numbers are legion in the gay community): The Right, if they were not stopped, would ultimately attack all homosexuals. The 1950s would be repeated. Lesbians and gay men who had California licenses to practice a profession—physicians, lawyers, social workers, psychologists—felt that they had particular reason to worry: They would probably be next once Proposition 6 passed; the State of

California could well try to revoke their licenses, too. Thus even organizations that had been primarily social, such as Southern California Women for Understanding, realized that it was vital they join forces in the fight—that this was a witch-hunt that must be answered aggressively because closet doors would anyway be flung open by the enemy. Mere discretion, which middle-class lesbians such as those who belonged to SCWU had always tried to practice, could no longer be depended upon for protection. Southern California Women for Understanding now vowed to adopt "an aggressive stance with the media, asking for coverage and the opportunity to appear, in order to counter the vicious stereotyping" of homosexuals.[102]

One serious split remained in the lesbian and gay community as they waged war against Briggs. A faction believed that homosexuals could not win against the initiative without a heterosexual "twist." They hired an experienced strategist, Don Bradley, a straight man, who devised a campaign that deftly avoided explicitly gay issues, coining slogans such as "No on 6: Who Will Be Next?"[103] The No on 6 campaign was not alone in its strategy to be coy about *who* was leading the protest against Proposition 6 and *why.* The Coalition for Human Rights had been so named because it was hoped that people of color would agree that right-wing assaults were not gay-specific and thus would make common cause with homosexuals. MECLA, too, was circumspect: In keeping with the strategy to impress upon the electorate that Proposition 6 had implications beyond gay people, Peter Scott, representing the organization, characterized the Briggs initiative to the *Los Angeles Times* as "really a Jim Crow–type law."[104] But grassroots lesbians and gays hated the strategy. They feared that the real issue, right-wing homophobia, was being "washed down in the big morass of human rights."[105] They formed the Union for Lesbians and Gay Men, proclaiming that Bryant and others had made a categorical assault on homosexuals, and that to present it as an attack against all minorities was mendacity.

Ultimately, however, the fierce hostility of the external enemy made factionalism impractical. Radical groups such as the militant lesbian and gay Action Coalition to Defeat the Briggs Initiative realized that an effective strategy was vital, and they developed a slogan much like the

one that Don Bradley had coined for No on 6: "Discrimination: Who's Next?"[106] Groups such as New Alliance for Gay Equality (better known by its acronym, New AGE), formed by MECLA members to fight Proposition 6, soon realized that MECLA's skillful fund-raising would be insufficient without grassroots workers who would register voters, make campaign signs, and help turn out the vote. Los Angeles lesbians and gays had work to do that required all of them.

To cover No on 6 campaign expenses, Troy Perry went on a much-publicized fast until he raised $100,000. No on 6 wanted to purchase media spots on television and radio, and for that, vast sums were needed. Even those who felt they had been burnt in the past by gay factionalism did their part. John Morgan Wilson, for example, threw a fund-raising party whose guests included Christopher Isherwood, Don Bachardy, Vito Russo, and the film star Bud Cort. "I gave [the No on 6 campaign] a pot full of money," he says, "but I didn't want to get near the leaders," whom he associated with past discord.[107] Money also came from those who had never given to a lesbian or gay cause before. Gayle Wilson, a wealthy Los Angeles realtor (Mixner calls her "the pioneer of Lipstick Lesbians")[108] put together the first fund-raiser for the campaign, a women's luncheon at the chic Beverly Hilton Hotel in Beverly Hills, to which she invited as guest speaker Midge Costanza, who had just left her position as President Carter's assistant. The 250 lesbians who were present donated $45,000 at the luncheon. The money was used to open an "Anti-Briggs Campaign" office.[109]

The diversity of lesbians and gays, which had been a huge source of conflict in the past, now worked to their benefit because they were able to produce results in diverse communities. When the Beverly Hills Chamber of Commerce made the mistake of endorsing Proposition 6, Gayle Wilson, along with her movie-star friend, Cher, launched a walk-out and boycott of Beverly Hills businesses. (The Chamber of Commerce not only rescinded its endorsement of Proposition 6 within twenty-four hours but also came out publicly against it.)[110] The gay Los Angeles Stonewall Democratic Club mapped out an intensive, and successful, strategy to secure resolutions against Proposition 6 from the Demo-

cratic State Central Committee, the California Democratic Council, and the Democratic Committees from cities all over the state.[111] Lesbian and gay radicals such as Robin Podolsky, who had been a shop steward and a trade union organizer, joined the Action Coalition to Defeat the Briggs Initiative and focused on voter registration, fund-raising, and pamphleteering in working-class and people-of-color communities. Podolsky says that "one of [her] best memories" is the time she walked with other members of the coalition in the precincts of the African American community of Watts and talked about "discrimination and how anyone who suffered discrimination historically must understand that this was terrible trouble." The Action Coalition, Podolsky says, "raised incredible amounts of money" by throwing parties in bars, and then used it to take out ads in the *Los Angeles Times.* She is still pleased that her radical group "rivaled the rich organizations" in fund-raising, but the monies all went to a united cause.[112]

One source, however, could not be easily tapped: lesbians and gays in the entertainment industry. As David Mixner recalls, Rock Hudson wrote a check for $49, because campaign finance law required that any contribution of fifty dollars or more be reported. Celebrities and anyone else who felt the need to remain closeted feared to be thus exposed, and they contributed no more than the safe amount. Those celebrities who were straight-identified could afford to be less timid (the rumors about the homosexuality of some of them notwithstanding): Burt Lancaster, John Travolta, Donna Summer, Neil and Joyce Bogart (who were founders of Casablanca Records, the disco label that had signed The Village People as well as the gay icon Donna Summer)—all contributed large sums to the campaign.[113]

Republican celebrities helped through their endorsements, too. In the summer before the election, a closeted member of Ronald Reagan's entourage contacted New AGE, asking whether a statement against Proposition 6 from the former Hollywood actor/California governor would be helpful. Mixner and Peter Scott were invited to meet with Reagan in his West L.A. office, where he confirmed that he would support their fight, and he soon issued a public statement that Proposition 6 had

"a potential for real mischief." Ivy Bottini says that Reagan's statement was "the kiss of death for Briggs."[114] Bob Hope, a fellow Republican who also wielded great power in the movie town and beyond, soon followed Reagan in opposing Briggs.[115] Before such well-known conservatives had expressed their opposition in public, potential-voter polls still showed 61 percent in favor of the Briggs initiative and 31 percent against. After a spate of announcements by the influential saying they opposed Proposition 6, polls moved to a virtual tie.[116] In the November election, Proposition 6 was defeated by 58 percent to 42 percent, with a margin of more than a million votes. "We even won [ultra-conservative] Orange County," Mixner, who had helped raise close to a million dollars for the campaign, delights in recalling.[117]

Ironically, Briggs' attack actually strengthened the gay community and healed many wounds. The combat against an external enemy made the community comprehend, as nothing ever had before, the adage "If we do not hang together, we shall surely hang separately." After the resounding defeat of the initiative, Ivy Bottini voiced the sentiments of many lesbians in declaring, "I loved working with those men! Let me tell you, I will NEVER AGAIN be a separatist!"[118] The war they fought together created a parity between Los Angeles lesbians and gay men. Finally, power (at least for political purposes) was genuinely shared, and lesbians were no longer merely token in mixed organizations. It could no longer seem to them that the men invariably co-opted everything for their own ends and ignored the women. Though there would be battles between them again in the future (such as the one spurred by the center's rejection of Del Martinez), during the Briggs campaign gay men and lesbians became closer than they'd been since their mid-century lavender tandems.

For the duration of the campaign, the community suppressed almost all the other bitterly cherished factions, too, even those of race, class, and political philosophy. As Jinx Beers declared in the *Lesbian News* right after the election: "What we now know is that all it takes is a strong central issue and we *can* pull together—even if most of the time we don't want to." Beers also thanked the enemies—Briggs and Bryant—"for giving us the opportunity and incentive to educate the general pub-

lic." The widespread revelation of the shocking malice of homophobes and the innocence of gay people would, she predicted, go a long way toward helping lesbians and gays win future wars against their foes.[119]

The Briggs initiative had other salubrious effects as well. It pulled countless Los Angeles gay people out of the closet and got them used to supporting gay causes personally and financially. Its political results were measurable: MECLA credited the Briggs threat with 25,000 newly registered voters sympathetic to gay rights. The triumph was so total that in the words of the *Los Angeles Times*, the senator's "flamboyant campaign had provoked a pro-gay backlash."[120]

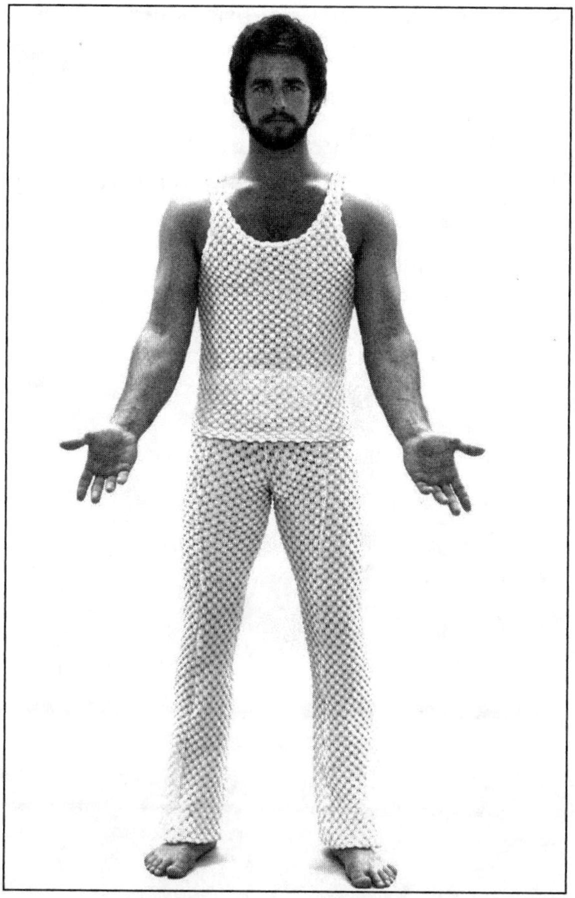

By marketing distinctive fashions, Ah Men brought a bit of gay Hollywood to the provinces. *Courtesy of the ONE National Gay and Lesbian Archives.*

CHAPTER 8

Glitz and Glam

GOLDEN BOYS

Admen are finding gold in marketing to upscale gays. . . . After all, if a silver-and-malachite saltcellar can be sold for $1,000 in the first hour of Los Angeles' recent Gay and Lesbian Lifestyle Expo, can Maseratis and Kieselstein-Cord belts be far behind?

—"But Will It Play in West Hollywood?"
Los Angeles Magazine, 1981[1]

West Hollywood by the mid-1970s had come to epitomize a new gay lifestyle, one that promoted a brotherhood of pleasure as a statement of gay liberation. Steve Schulte and his lover, who were part of still another great gay exodus from less-welcoming areas, moved to West Hollywood from Iowa. Schulte became—in very Hollywood fashion—both a male pinup model and an elected official: "I never would have imagined how many guys our age, like brothers and pals, were right there—open, attractive, and fun. Like ours, their lives had changed," he reminisces of those 1970s halcyon days. "There was euphoria and hopefulness in West Hollywood. . . . It was quite astonishing to find that, and to become part of it very quickly."[2]

West Hollywood—with its witty moniker "Boystown" (a reference to the 1948 Spencer Tracy film about a colony of orphaned newsboys)[3] and its double-entendre zip code, "90069"—had long been a gay male enclave. In the 1920s, the area, which bordered on Beverly Hills and was

part of Los Angeles County, had attracted speakeasies and bootleggers because it was not under the jurisdiction of the harsh Los Angeles (City) Police Department. It had drawn gay men for the same reason and continued to draw them through the years. It was a gay dreamland.

In the 1970s, the residents of West Hollywood became emboldened, expressing their gay freedom not just after dark, but brazenly in the sun: holding hands, flirting, and cruising all over the district. Boystown became even more of what it had been in earlier years; only now, gay-owned and gay-targeted businesses boomed there and glitzy consumption flourished. West Hollywood appeared to be not just a gay ghetto, but an entire gay town—though one with little class or racial diversity and, outside of a few nightclubs and bars such as Peanuts and the Palms, unreflective of the lesbian community.

On Santa Monica Boulevard, West Hollywood's main thoroughfare, one business advertised its services in pink neon cursive that resembled a beauty salon sign—but rather than "Perms and Hair-Tinting" the sign, which was on one of West Hollywood's first gyms, offered simply "Muscles." A few blocks up, the Big Weenie hot dog stand sign advertised its wares on a billboard with the slogan "Big Weenies Are Better!" All American Boy, a Boulevard boutique that sold casual clothes, was advertised most effectively by its young male customers who favored the form-fitting knit shirts that emblazoned the store's "All American Boy" logo—which read as a delicious irony on the pumped pectorals of America's outcasts.[4] The home décor industry virtually settled in West Hollywood, its panoply of costly shops displaying terra cotta, marble, wrought iron, fabrics, antiques, and all the other trappings of domestic elegance. In the mid-1970s, a surreal cobalt-colored glass high-rise that housed more than a hundred décor showrooms opened there.

It is ironic that, in L.A. as elsewhere, gay radicals, who prided themselves on their antimaterialism, were actually responsible for the inception of a new gay consumerism when they made the gay community widely visible. For a time, gay consumerism meant more than conspicuous consumption: It was also something of a political act. Any business owned by gay people might present itself as a "gay business," and to support it was to support the gay cause. But as the visible gay community

expanded, the businesses that qualified for community support proliferated: Even straight-owned companies began to vie for gay favor in a market economy where numbers are everything.

Gay men became the hot new demographic for corporate America once it was announced by business researchers not only that there were vast numbers of gays but also that the household income of gay males far exceeded the average in America; and that, as Los Angeles–based Walker-Struman Research announced, "eighty-three percent of gay men order drinks by brand name, more than seventy-five percent prefer bottled water, and about seventy percent are under forty years of age."[5] A *New Yorker* cartoon summed up the effect such discoveries had on big business: It depicted a pack of anxious-looking executives sitting in a posh boardroom, the distinguished CEO peering at an intimidated underling. The caption read, "I know the advertising department is gay, Haskell, but are they gay enough?"[6]

Salivating thus over gay dollars even straight companies began buying ads in gay publications. And gay people responded, still at least partly for political reasons: "Gay money," it was thought, demonstrated and fostered "gay power" (though for some, silver-and-malachite saltcellars were not without charm). As *Los Angeles Magazine* suggested in its article "But Will It Play in West Hollywood?" because gay L.A.—youthful, affluent, and fashion-conscious—epitomized the demographics that impressed advertisers, it was thought to be an entrepreneurial nirvana.

Many of the flourishing Los Angeles businesses based themselves on a gay cultural myth that had been well promoted through the mid-century Athletic Model Guild, the *Advocate*'s Groovy Guy contests, and, most of all, the movies: the fable that L.A. was a town chock-full of golden-haired, surfer-bodied, actor-handsome youths. Gay-targeted business often played on the fantasy that *you, too,* can look like those Golden Boys if you wear . . . eat . . . do . . . whatever the business was selling. Ah Men, for example, a West Hollywood men's clothing boutique, used the Golden Boy as their main advertising come-on—featuring gorgeous Hollywood models—to sell a fashion fantasy. Ah Men captured the local gay market and, through its mail orders, brought a bit of gay

Hollywood to the provinces. It also made inroads among straight consumers, particularly men who worked in the entertainment industry.

Ah Men had already been popular with the West Hollywood crowd by the late 1950s. Don Cook, the founder, was selling see-through mesh pants, jumpsuits, low-rise slacks, and underwear styles that Macy's would never carry—"incredibly faggy" clothes, as even many gay men admitted. Nevertheless, Ah Men's styles eventually had great play: the *Los Angeles Times* published articles on Cook, his store, and his mail-order business; and Hollywood celebrities such as Richard Deacon, the acerbic gay actor who appeared on the *Dick Van Dyke Show,* posed for publicity photos with him.[7] Occasionally trading the Golden Boy image in for other kinds of prestige, Cook was even able, in the late 1970s, to persuade stars such as Sammy Davis, Jr. to let themselves be photographed in satin and leather for Ah Men catalogs.[8] Gay men as well as straight in small towns around the nation were able to "go Hollywood" by purchasing paisley bikinis and camouflage caftans modeled in the Ah Men catalogs by some of Hollywood's handsomest and sexiest. Cook's success paved the way for similar boutiques in West Hollywood, such as International Male, which earned millions in the 1970s by selling the gay look.[9]

GOLDEN BOYS DANCE, DANCE, DANCE

> *Hundreds of bodies writhe in the disco tempos of the latest hits. You can feel every bass note clear through every fiber of your body, and the pulsating rhythms make you want to dance, dance dance!*
>
> —*Data Boy,* on West Hollywood's Studio One[10]

Some Los Angeles businesses did not use sex to sell gay products—instead, sex itself was the product. Gay baths, bars, and that distinctly 1970s enterprise, discotheques, boomed and became money machines in Los Angeles. The biggest such business was West Hollywood's Studio One, conceived in 1972 when Scott Forbes, a Beverly Hills optometrist, asked Lee Glaze how he was able to draw an instant gay crowd when he revived Ciro's nightclub on the Sunset Strip. The ever-

generous Glaze offered the use of his vast gay mailing list.[11] Two years later, Forbes opened Studio One (a name evocative of its Hollywood location) in a cavernous factory building that he outfitted with strobes and speakers in a hall of mirrors that became a temple of amplified sound and masculine vanity.

One thousand or more gay men gathered nightly at Studio One to "dance, dance, dance." Forbes' disco temple featured a deejay that a 1974 *Billboard* magazine named number one in Los Angeles. Studio One was also widely regarded as the number one dance spot, straight or gay. Music industry promoters vied to have their records played there;[12] it was featured on national television; and it was dubbed by many newspapers and magazines as one of the most exciting discos in the country. The cachet of Studio One was enhanced by its Back Lot Theater (another name chosen to evoke movie-studio proximity), which featured entertainers ranging from Joan Rivers to Wayland Flowers and his outrageous, foul-mouthed puppet, Madame.

Scott Forbes' disco became a legend; and its owner, the former optometrist who was now called the "disco king" by the press, became an overnight millionaire. His phenomenal prominence in promoting gay pleasure even rendered him a political power in the gay community. Forbes served on the boards of gay L.A.'s most important or prestigious organizations and agencies, such as the Gay Community Services Center and the Municipal Elections Committee of Los Angeles (MECLA).

To the media, Forbes often spoke of his business in tones of political pride: "Studio One was designed, planned, and conceived for gay people, gay male people," he announced to the *Los Angeles Times*. "Any straight people here are guests of the gay community."[13] Forbes insisted that his discothèque filled a vital community need: It celebrated sexual freedom for gay men. As he told the *Times* reporter, although many came to dance, just as many came primarily "for sexual purposes."[14] His admission elicited shocked letters to the editor: "What is this society coming to?" one reader lamented. "Don't people want any more out of another human being than their body for sexual pleasures?"[15] Apparently they did not: 1,600 invited guests packed the house for the disco's sixth anniversary. The crowd rarely thinned over the years.

The beauties of gay Hollywood could have the time of their lives at Studio One. But what to them was all the rage outraged others. Gay activists complained bitterly of Studio One–types who would rather dance than fight for gay rights, disparaging them as "disco bunnies—blond, built, and brainless."[16] Activists were also outraged at clubs that practiced hateful exclusionary policies, and Studio One was a prime target of their anger. Forbes' statement to the *Los Angeles Times* that his disco was simply "for . . . gay male people" was duplicitous by its omission of who counted in his definition of "gay male people." Studio One turned away almost everyone not meeting its Hollywood Golden Boy standard. Nonwhites were especially excluded: "to keep the club from getting too dark," as Mark Haile, a journalist for *BLK,* an African American gay magazine, says bitterly.[17] All but the most remarkably attractive blacks, Latinos, and Asian "gay male people" were generally asked for three pieces of picture identification—an effective ploy for weeding out the "undesirables." (Mark Haile observed a rite of passage for young gays of color: They would go to Studio One armed with three pieces of ID "so they could say they got in the door." But they didn't stay long: "It was too light.")[18] Dave Johnson, the activist son of actor Russell Johnson (of *Gilligan's Island* fame), reported in the *Los Angeles Free Press* that he had staked the place out and seen thirty-five instances in less than an hour in which people of color, and white females as well, were refused admission.[19]

Studio One was not alone among West Hollywood bars to practice exclusionary policies, which were an ironic by-product of the expansion of the gay community and the success of the gay movement. Tak Yamamoto recalls that in the 1960s, West Hollywood clubs "didn't have a policy of white-male dominance" because club owners needed all the customers they could get.[20] With the gay population explosion they could afford to turn away the "less desirable" since there were so many of the "more desirable" who were dying to get through their doors, bringing fame and fortune to the owner with their glamorous presence. Francesca Miller says that at one 1970s disco, where "the guys were really into flaunting muscles and male beauty," a guard at the door asked women for five pieces of identification. The presence of females, straight or gay,

must have cramped the men's uninhibited sexual expression, she suggests. Miller also theorizes that lesbians were no longer needed as beards for gay men who "didn't want to be reminded of the past, like the 1950s, when gay men thought they had to have women around to protect them from the police."[21]

When the *Los Angeles Times* confronted Forbes in 1976 on allegations of racism and sexism at Studio One, he dug himself in deeper by claiming that he needed to keep out "the bad element."[22] Irate picketers, organized by the Gay Community Mobilization Committee, demonstrated in front of Studio One until they were granted a meeting with Forbes, who promised reform. When nothing changed at Studio One, the issue grew into a political crusade that revealed where the real power in the gay movement lay during those years. Because of Forbes' checkbook activism—his generous advertising in the gay press and his donations to gay causes—most community institutions did not support the boycott, and the media were reluctant even to write about the complaints against Studio One. The offensive door policy, as well as the protests, continued for years.

Other establishments that had excluded the non–Golden Boys reformed more quickly in response to the protest: Eddie Nash, who had earlier bowed to the Gay Liberation Front's pressure to allow same-sex dancing at the Farm, also owned Dude City in Hollywood, which banned women, and the Paradise Ballroom downtown, which banned blacks.[23] Troy Perry mobilized effective protests against Nash, and the bans were lifted right away. But Scott Forbes felt that he and Studio One could afford to be impervious to such pressure as long as the beauties kept flocking.

In earlier decades, gay men could find sex at bathhouses that were not explicitly gay, such as Brooks Baths on Beverly Boulevard, where the Orthodox Jewish clientele were oblivious to the patrons who were definitely not there for religious-ritual bathing. In the 1970s, however, "tubs" proliferated in Los Angeles. Some were consciously designed as gay sex

clubs and usually required that a client become a member (and sign a waiver agreeing that no offense would be taken at the sight of homosexual activity). For many in that pre-AIDS era, gay L.A.'s new lifestyle meant that after the bars closed at 2:00 A.M. it was time to move on to the all-night and all-day baths. Some recall now that they lost entire weekends in such establishments.

The tubs often "specialized." The Corral Club in the Valley was reputed to have had a sling in every room for the leather crowd; Glen's Baths attracted young Latinos and their admirers.[24] Other baths were like Studio One, with a door policy that would ensure a "hot crowd" of the gorgeous and young. The 8709, a bathhouse nestled quietly just at the border of West Hollywood, was the most notable of the gorgeous-and-young tubs. One habitué recalls a night at the 8709 when almost every one of the five hundred or so "stunning" men there appeared to be under thirty.[25]

Gay activists may have objected to such discrimination, but pickets were not as feasible in front of a bathhouse as they might be in front of a disco, and exclusionary policies continued unabated in L.A. tubs. At Basic Plumbing on Fairfax, a "dry bath"[26] where men prowled dark corridors under red lights, customers were asked to lift their shirts before being allowed entry. Those with less-than-toned torsos were kept out. As Rick St. Dennis recalls, "pull-up-your-shirt places" became widespread in 1970s L.A.: "If you weren't built a certain way or you were too heavy, you'd get rejected."[27]

The 8709 became the most legendary of the Los Angeles bathhouses. Though located on an inconspicuous street corner, on the inside of the 8709 there was an elaborate maze, much black paint, and rooms large and small. According to legend, closeted actors entered through a secret door that led to an unlit, anonymous orgy room. The 8709 also attracted an endless stream of blond surfer types who migrated, erotically charged, from the disco down the street. One customer of the 8709 reminisces still about being "fortunate enough to go there" and recalls how he was "always amazed by the beautiful men."[28] Another remembers "walking through the large orgy room that was packed so tight with bodies you couldn't move." He says: "That was

very much real fine!"[29] Because the ground floor backed onto a deli, 8709 customers could order food through a small window, precluding any need to leave.

By marketing a deliriously sybaritic sexuality, the 8709 became extraordinarily lucrative. Sheldon Andelson, the 8709's co-owner, made his appearances in the gay community dressed "casually in cashmere and hand-sewn shoes," accompanied often by a pair of elegant whippets who waited for him in his Jaguar.[30] Andelson was a successful lawyer; but he also had mainstream political ambitions, supported in part by revenues from the 8709. Paradoxically, it was his political ambitions that ultimately struck the death knell of his profitable bathhouse. In 1982, Governor Jerry Brown nominated Andelson to a seat on the University of California Board of Regents. Such a nomination had been unprecedented for an open homosexual, and Andelson felt elated and fulfilled. The bathhouse, however, became an albatross, threatening to break the neck of his nomination.

Andelson's co-ownership of a gay bathhouse was doubly problematic because the AIDS epidemic was under way by then, and the baths were considered by many to be among the most dangerous vectors for AIDS. He faced a huge dilemma. When, just before his nomination, the Municipal Elections Committee of Los Angeles (of which he had been a leading member since 1979) called for the closing of all bathhouses because they were hazardous to public health, Andelson was resentful. David Mixner writes that MECLA's position "threatened [his] economic base" and also "struck him as a personal betrayal."[31] However, a television reporter discovered his co-ownership of the 8709 just as his prestigious appointment was being debated in the California State Senate. Governor Brown had already made a huge leap forward by nominating a homosexual for the Board of Regents, but if it were known that the homosexual in question had a hand in L.A.'s premier gay orgy spot—in the midst of the AIDS epidemic, no less—the governor might be embarrassed to retraction. Andelson let himself be convinced by David Mixner and Peter Scott that he must not let that happen: He must procure for the community a phenomenal symbol of gay power and prestige by sacrificing the bathhouse. Andelson divested himself.

"SUCCESSFUL, ACHIEVING WOMEN"

Among lesbian feminists, there was a thing called downward mobility. Well, I've never heard of any revolution fighting for less. *Women already have less; we need to be fighting for* more.

—Robin Tyler in the *Lesbian News*[32]

As many gay men pursued unrestrained sexual freedom in the 1970s, many gay women pursued professional success. Both groups sought what earlier eras had denied them most stringently and what the late 1970s finally made possible. Jeanne Cordova, who had been president of the Los Angeles chapter of Daughters of Bilitis, followed a trajectory in her development that was emblematic of the history of a sizable segment of the lesbian community. Attractive, young, and fiery, she quit the homophile Daughters because the organization seemed to her not at all attractive, young, and fiery. She then became a chief player among radical gays and was the editor of the *Lesbian Tide,* a magazine of the lesbian-feminist movement. Cordova says now that 1975 was "the last year of radicalism." In the second half of the decade, the gay movement "went civil rights, reformist, fund-raising."

This was a defensive move, she believes, necessitated by the war the community had to wage against homophobes such as Anita Bryant who were trying to destroy gay life. "We saw that the radical movement, where we'd wanted to create an egalitarian society and tried to use guerrilla tactics to that end, didn't do the job." The Dade County vote, Cordova claims, made gay people realize that they had to find more practical ways to survive. They understood that the point was no longer to get thousands of people into the streets, but rather to raise hundreds of thousands of dollars, which would enable them "to present television commercials to millions" and thereby to sway votes.[33]

The memory of the landslide defeat of Briggs, as well as flourishing gay economics, had made "survival" a moot point in the late 1970s. Cordova converted her magazine, the *Lesbian Tide,* which had been quite radical, to a "more middle-of-the-road publication."[34] The magazine was renamed *The Tide,* and Cordova became very concerned about its pol-

ish: "If we had continued to publish the same kind of shoddy pictures and stories like you'd find in some of the East Coast magazines, who would read it out here in L.A.?" she asks now. "We knew the audience we had to reach."

Cordova also learned about advertising and promotion, which cracked open new opportunities for her. The Los Angeles gay pride parade committee asked her to publish its parade booklet, which announced parade events and featured business ads that paid publication costs. She discovered then that the gay community included myriad real estate brokers, doctors, lawyers—all manner of business and professional people who had goods and services to offer and wanted to reach other gays and lesbians. In 1982, she began the *Community Yellow Pages,* a Los Angeles gay and lesbian directory. It was big business: "An incredible success. People loved it. I went from making $7,000 one year to $70,000 the next, and in a few years accumulated over $1 million."

Some of those who continued to be part of the radical community were bitterly critical of Cordova's transformation to a capitalist, and they lamented those leaders who, as they saw it, had abandoned responsibility to lead and teach in favor of "going mainstream for financial motives." Cordova, however, sees her metamorphosis as being consistent with a larger pattern: "It's an inevitable part of social change that grassroots radicalism should give way to middle-class assimilation. Though I have mixed feelings about it, I know that movements lose their sharp radical edge. No one can stop it." Movements dissipate like waves, she says, "and then another wave comes in."[35]

Southern California Women for Understanding came in with the next wave. It had been birthed through the Whitman-Radclyffe Foundation, a nonprofit, public-interest organization, formed first in Northern California in the early 1970s for the purpose of "enhanc[ing] the quality of life for gay people." Despite the nod to lesbians in the group's name ("Radclyffe," as in Radclyffe Hall; Walt Whitman was, of course, the group's other namesake), the foundation was made up largely of gay men,

though Betty Berzon, the Los Angeles–based therapist and gay leader, served on its national board of directors and helped to establish a Southern California branch in 1974. Few women belonged to the Southern California branch, for the usual reasons: It was "too male-dominated and too male-oriented and [lesbians] were turned off to any deeper involvement."[36] But in 1976, Berzon called together two dozen lesbians who were in business and the professions and formed a "support group," the Southern California Women for the Whitman-Radclyffe Foundation. When the Whitman-Radclyffe Foundation announced, however, that its primary interest had become helping gay alcoholics, Southern California Women opted out. The members formed an independent organization, Southern California Women for Understanding.[37]

Betty Berzon had hoped to establish what had never yet existed—a political group made up exclusively of upper-middle-class lesbians. But when Myra Riddell, another Los Angeles psychotherapist, was elected Southern California Women's first president, the group's focus became at least as social as it was political. (However, even in its transformation it was revolutionary since a formally established social group made up exclusively of upper-middle-class lesbians had also never yet existed.) It did not take long for the most careful and closeted women to be drawn to SCWU events by the rumors that they were attracting A-list lesbians. Frieda, who had been a professor and an associate dean at a Los Angeles university, remembers:

> I was never an organizational person, but I was curious to see what they were concerned about . . . well . . . mostly to see what the people who went there were like. They had a dance in a beautiful old private house in Mt. Washington. They had a . . . ballroom . . . with a gallery above it. I went up to the gallery and looked down. And I saw a whole floor full of good-looking, elegantly dressed women. That was really nice. That really impressed me.[38]

Her partner, Marion, a retired psychiatrist, says that she had always been a "fag hag" because she loved the impeccable sophistication and re-

fined tastes of the gay men she knew, but Southern California Women for Understanding attracted lesbians who were "just as polished."[39]

Though it was a vigorously social group, its steering committee members decided, in the midst of the Briggs battle, that SCWU could accomplish what they believed to be an important political goal: "to change the [public] image of lesbians by presenting our membership as successful, achieving women."[40] Fearing that such women might still be reluctant to participate in a gay women's group, the leadership penned a secret policy statement: Expressing concerns about appearance that were not much different from those that had been harbored by middle-class lesbians at mid-century, they wrote that the women they hoped to attract were no less repelled than were heterosexuals by lesbians who fit the "negative stereotype"—the old-style butches-and-femmes and the poorly dressed and ill-mannered lesbian-feminists. Southern California Women for Understanding planned to draw in more "successful, achieving women" by methods not unlike those that Delta Delta Delta might use to seduce prospective sorority members: They would demonstrate that the women who already belonged to SCWU were attractive and socially desirable, and they would provide "a non-threatening setting"[41]—poolside champagne brunches, golf tournaments, dance cruises, casino nights on board the *Queen Mary*[42]—all aimed at capturing the "successful, achieving" lesbian through snob appeal.

Cognizant that such elitism might lay them open to claims of racism, which would have been genuinely disturbing to many of these women,[43] SCWU made a special effort to place high-achieving lesbians of color in prominent positions, such as Joyce Gonzalez, a radio station manager, who was made a member of the first steering committee; and Estilita Grimaldo, the owner of an all-women's travel agency, who became the editor of the newsletter by its third issue.

The leaders worked hard to create "nonthreatening" social events, though many of the early attendees, who had never before set foot out of the closet, did not take their initial steps easily. SCWU's first party was held at the secluded hilltop home of Dr. Jane Patterson: The chances that neighbors or anyone else would see who was walking into the house

were nil; everyone was invited by someone known to her; and yet, Myra Riddell recalls, "a lot of the women later told us that they drove around the hills for thirty or forty minutes before they could gather the courage to come in." But Southern California Women for Understanding's tactic of attracting women through social events before raising their "lesbian political consciousness" eventually worked well. Women who had found it difficult to attend a secluded lesbian party were before long taking giant steps, meeting at the Beverly Hilton Hotel with politicians and religious leaders to tell them what gay people needed and wanted.

SCWU became increasingly political. It formulated as a chief goal "to seek power and influence . . . in order to serve the community at large."[44] The organization not only worked on political campaigns, beginning with No on 6, but it was also interested in helping gays who needed help. For example, SCWU established scholarships for lesbian students and helped to fund Connexxus, the social service agency for lesbians. As early as the summer of 1983, SCWU began raising money and volunteers for the AIDS war.[45] SCWU membership burgeoned to more than 1,000, and chapters spread to Long Beach, Laguna, Orange, Garden Grove, Covina, North Hollywood, Altadena, Ventura, San Bernardino, Fullerton—all over Southern California. Southern California Women for Understanding was soon calling itself "the largest lesbian support group in the country."[46]

The leaders of SCWU who wanted to focus on the political aspects of the organization were ecstatic when they discovered a star for the cause in Jean O'Leary, an articulate, polished, handsome young woman with political know-how and surprising connections. O'Leary not only had been an executive director of the National Gay and Lesbian Task Force but had also spearheaded a campaign for the introduction of a Federal Gay Rights Bill into the House of Representatives. She was an openly gay delegate at the 1976 Democratic Convention, and she was also an intimate of Midge Costanza's, the special assistant to President Carter. It was O'Leary who convinced Costanza to arrange for lesbian and gay leaders to be invited in March 1977 to a meeting in the White House—the first such meeting in history. And in November 1977, O'Leary grabbed attention again when she was credited with leading the effort

for the passage of a resolution supporting lesbian rights at the International Women's Year Conference in Houston.

Southern California Women for Understanding had discovered her even before those last victories. So delighted were they with their find—a famous lesbian who was determined to "work within the system and challenge it to broaden its scope"[47]—that in February 1977 they rented a huge hall that seated thousands at the Convention Center so that she might address the lesbians of Los Angeles. The delight was mutual. O'Leary decided to move to Los Angeles after appearing at SCWU events because she felt "a quiet power" there: "Things weren't radical, weren't out in the streets," she recalls. "People in L.A. moved things with money and influence. I knew this had to be the next level. L.A. was the place to be."[48]

GIRLS' NIGHT OUT

We were the "glam" lesbians. We set a lot of fashion trends. We weren't political at all.

—Heather Leavitt, of the women at Peanuts in West Hollywood[49]

Not all L.A. lesbians were bent on power and influence, nor were they interested in radical lesbian feminism. Some just wanted to dance. Though their numbers were fewer than that of the "Golden Boys," Los Angeles was home to "Golden Girls," too. The gay historian John D'Emilio has suggested that throughout the 1970s gay men and lesbians were living lives that were diametrical opposites of one another: the men in "glitzy, high-tech, [urban] discos, . . . spending money, focused on themselves, and searching for sex"; the women "in self-sufficient, rural communities, . . . financially marginal, focused on group process, and nurturing loving relationships."[50] But D'Emilio had overlooked L.A.'s glam lesbians.

Lesbian bars proliferated and became big business during the late 1970s and into the 1980s. By 1983, there were more than forty lesbian bars in Los Angeles and its environs that aimed to be much more upscale than the old If Club or Open Door—as their names, such as "Executive

Suite" and "Cinema Lady," often announced.[51] The clientele for such bars had swelled for a variety of reasons: First of all, the Sexual Revolution had made women's undisguised pursuit of sex partners, even in public places, more permissible than it had been in earlier eras. Feminism, which helped to de-stigmatize love between women, encouraged more women to feel comfortable exploring lesbianism. Although lesbians generally continued to lag behind gay men in terms of income,[52] the feminist movement's battles for equal pay for equal work had succeeded in shrinking the gap, which meant that lesbians had more discretionary money to spend on entertainment. Finally, in an era of sexual revolution and rescinded antigay laws, more lesbians of middle-class background, whose earlier counterparts had socialized primarily in private homes, now dared to let their lesbianism show in semipublic settings.[53]

Lesbians who frequented the glamorous nightclubs had little in common with the radical lesbian feminists who sported T-shirts and jeans or SCWU types in business suits. The Palms, on Santa Monica Boulevard, attracted women who looked like the descendents of the ingénues that had frequented Tess's or Jane Jones' on the Sunset Strip two generations earlier. Marci says that the clients at the Palms "modeled themselves after Hollywood starlets." (Rather than emulating Dietrich or Garbo, as the women at Tess's used to, their ideal was Farrah Fawcett, the glamorous television star of the 1970s.) "The women who went to the Palms practically all had long blonde hair, though there were a few gorgeous black and Chicana lesbians there, too," Marci recalls. "Everyone was dressed like a movie star—lots of exotic jewelry, tight black dresses, high heels. And they always drank something sophisticated like cognac or martinis."[54]

Many of these women had found a niche in Hollywood production; they worked in behind-the-scenes jobs such as publicity, film editing, and script writing, professions that had become increasingly welcome to females. But lesbians who found employment in the movie industry in the late 1970s still feared that Hollywood had not yet recovered from the repressive mid-century, in which a Lizabeth Scott could be ruined if ru-

mored to be gay. Marci speculates that the Palms lesbians dressed as they did because they were "still closeted at work and didn't want to look 'out' anywhere they went." The few women who dared to look "butchy" at the Palms, Marci says, were usually self-employed. She remembers a Palms habitué who owned her own insurance company: "She made over two million dollars a year. She could afford to look any way she pleased. But her style was tailored, polished, complete. More like Radclyffe Hall than a beer-hall butch."[55]

By the early 1980s, the style favored at the Palms had spread to other Los Angeles bars, such as Flamingo's in the Silver Lake district, where, Suzanne Gage remembers, "there was a lot of dressing to kill, a big lipstick lesbian crowd." The style eventually appeared in lesbian bars of the suburbs, too, such as Vermie's in Pasadena, where Melissa Etheridge, still an unknown, presented a new model for the "lesbian look," stunning the packed audiences with her long blonde mane and her raw sexual energy.[56]

Heather Leavitt, who frequented Peanuts as well as the Palms, recalls that the women at Peanuts were "light-years away" from some of their lesbian contemporaries: "All the crunchy Birkenstock lesbians were to the north" (in the Valley of North Hollywood, Studio City, Sherman Oaks, and Van Nuys). In West Hollywood, it was all about "the look." "The look" at Peanuts meant, she says, "beautiful": silk shirts ("polyester was a sin"), jeans by Calvin Klein or Jordache ("long before Jordache was popular in the straight community"), Gucci shoes, puka-shell necklaces, lots of gold. If the women at the Palms looked like starlets, some of those at Peanuts actually were—or they were the daughters of Hollywood stars. According to Heather, at the Palms the women spent their money freely; at Peanuts, they spent their parents' money freely. "These were very privileged girls; Peanuts was on the border of Beverly Hills, and the parking lot was full of Mercedes and Porches."

The Peanuts lesbians were not only as image-conscious as their male counterparts at Studio One; they were also as wildly uninhibited. The Sexual Revolution in which they'd grown up had demolished the manacles of restraint, as Heather recalls when she describes the night of a "wet T-shirt contest":

> All the participants were under twenty-one. I wasn't even eighteen yet. We were all hot, young, tempestuous, and tempting. One gal—Frenchy, a blonde cutie—and I . . . we took our T-shirts off, and the audience's jaws dropped. I screamed, "Is this what you want?" They whistled and cheered. . . . We were so into pot and coke, and others kept pulling us into the bathroom for a snort. . . . It wasn't about relationships at Peanuts. It was about sex—everywhere, in the cars parked in the lot, in the bathrooms. We were young and dumb and full of come. But it was such a free and open time.

Even before West Hollywood was incorporated in the mid-1980s, Heather claims, gay people already felt that they owned that city. It never occurred to the lesbians at Peanuts to worry about a raid; the days when gay people feared they could get arrested for dancing together in public, or when police might hassle patrons merely for being in a lesbian bar, were ancient history. Though there were young lesbians and gay men who continued to be politically and historically aware, Heather says that those she ran with "believed that the big battles had all been won." She adds, "In their memory, they had never even existed."[57]

However, though the external struggles seemed to have been won, internal struggles, both old and new, continued to rage within the L.A. lesbian community. The lesbian sex wars, for instance, were essentially about the right to promulgate styles of lesbian sexuality condoned by neither Southern California Women for Understanding nor most lesbian feminists. Lesbian SM became a point of controversy in Los Angeles after a secret group, the Sado-Masochists Organization of Lesbians of Los Angeles (SMOLLA), expanded and morphed into Leather and Lace, and (after some resistance on the part of the newspaper) ran announcements of its meetings in the *Lesbian News.* Leather and Lace, established in 1982, featured SM theatricality—rituals, uniforms, dramatic trappings such as racks (as well as "warm, friendly rap groups, where the women could feel safe").[58] According to Leather and Lace's founder,

Sheree Rose, the group fell apart after three years, split over an issue that had been percolating in the L.A. lesbian community since the early 1970s.[59] Wendy, a beautiful, tall bottom, wanted to be allowed to join in the activities, to which some members objected because Wendy was a post-op male-to-female transsexual.

Other lesbian SM groups emerged in Los Angeles to take the place of Leather and Lace, such as Wild Women, Dominant Society (which men could join as submissives), Femmes and Butches ("an SM club for women who liked the old-fashioned way"), and LA RAWW (Los Angeles Radical and Wild Women). LA RAWW attracted to its parties "a hundred women going wild with SM sex, food, and a social place to talk," Rose says.[60] Eventually semipublic venues emerged as well, such as Cunt Club, Club Utero, and Ozone—all lesbian sex clubs.

But none of these sex clubs—private or semipublic—achieved great longevity, even in edgy, theatrical Hollywood. Vivian Escalante, who started Cunt Club, explains that there was great initial enthusiasm for such ventures (which sometimes included playful spoofs on bygone glamour, such as "gorgeous cigarette girls" carrying portable display trays from which they peddled lubricants and condoms instead of cigarettes). But unlike gay men, who have been able to support a multiplicity of such venues, lesbians, Escalante says, "are very shy."[61] Wet T-shirt contests and parking lot sex could be wildly successful at Peanuts, where one might indulge or not, but RAWW and the Cunt Club were too unambiguous to draw a large and steady lesbian clientele. Most of the lesbian sex clubs folded within a year or so, though others sometimes cropped up to replace them.

Nevertheless, the new open focus on lesbian sex and glamour did not go unnoticed or unlamented by committed old-school lesbian-feminists, such as Irene Weiss, a founder of Califia Community. Weiss, believing that the biggest battles with external enemies were still not won, sent out an impassioned plea to the "new lesbians" (whom she accused of preferring kinky sex to lesbian politics) to "rethink and reexamine" their priorities: "I call on you to pour your heart, soul, blood and guts, into *organizing*."[62] Weiss' plea fell on young ears that were deaf. The L.A. radical lesbians of the early 1970s had not succeeded in birthing a large new

generation in their own image. Much of the younger generation of lesbians lived in a different world—one in which the "sex, drugs, rock and roll," and, for some, edgy sexual experimentation seemed more compelling than antiquated politics.[63]

The "glam" lesbian trend, which started in Los Angeles, spread to big cities all over America by the end of the 1980s. Writing in *Out/Look Magazine* in 1989, Arlene Stein speculated that lipstick lesbians and other glam-lesbian types flourished not because there no longer were problems of homophobia or sexism that lesbians had to fight, but rather the phenomenon marked a triumph of "commercialization and popularization of feminist culture and the avant-garde art world," in which many lesbians participated.[64] But there were other reasons that new looks and lifestyles grew. The super-seriousness of radical lesbian feminism sounded too shrill and even gratuitous in the ears of the young. What were the radicals still fighting about so vehemently? The battles over freedom for women had been won, they insisted. The wage gap was closing, there were even affirmative action policies that helped women get into professional schools, and there were already women doctors and lawyers galore. In L.A., thanks to a tolerant cultural climate, lesbians could finally step out of the shadows and indulge openly in their pleasures. If problems of homophobia or sexism still existed, they believed, one had to look hard to find them.

"DISCO SUCKS"

Take off your watch, take off your rings.
You don't want to lose those things
When you fist-FUNK!
Won't you fist-funk with me?

—Lyrics by Craig Lee for Lotus Lame and the Lame Flames[65]

Though West Hollywood's relentless disco beat epitomized gay nightlife in the 1970s and early '80s, the very different subculture of punk rock, for which Los Angeles was a major center, also attracted young gay people. On the surface, disco (exuberantly bright and glitzy) and punk (darkly

nihilistic) appeared to be diametrical opposites. Punkers mocked the West Hollywood lifestyle and coined the slogan "Disco Sucks."[66] But despite differences, the two subcultures surprisingly shared some attributes—particularly a gay sensibility (though in different guises) and a significant gay infrastructure.

Clubs such as Studio One usually excluded heterosexuals, but punk clubs played to a gay-straight mix and provided an avant garde haven for artists, actors, and musicians of all persuasions. Gay talent was not often identified as gay, but it infused L.A.'s dynamic punk scene with style and wit. Gay punks could be camouflaged in the sexual ambiguity and amorality of punk culture. Punks disdained the "straight" world, broadening the very word "straight" to signify "bourgeois conformity." They snubbed whatever smacked of the bourgeoisie and sometimes called themselves the "hip-eoisie." This blanket rejection of "normalcy" afforded refuge for homosexuality, though decidedly not of the West Hollywood variety.

Punks affected an alienated persona, but gay punks found West Hollywood alienating beyond endurance. Creative spirits burning to be different, descendants of bohemians, they were put off by what they saw as the glitzy pretensions and straightjacket conformity of West Hollywood. The punk clubs, located mostly in less-upscale areas, east of La Brea, were open to all races, classes, genders, and kinks; and for many gay men, the habitués of punk clubs were far more sexually thrilling than the predictable disco crowd. Those who felt like misfits in any world—straight or gay—could get happily lost in the camaraderie of the punk world, its live bands, and its edgy performance art.

But most punks who had gay sexual experiences did not identify as homosexual any more than they identified as heterosexual or even bisexual. Jack Marquette, who promoted punk nightclubs, recalls that many in that scene "thrived on sexual ambiguity,"[67] but they maintained a determined refusal to categorize their lifestyles. Their "orientation" (the very concept of which they would disdain) was best classified as "decline to state." John Callahan, who was openly gay, says that few in his crowd declared their homosexuality because "public sexual orientation was passé."[68]

Although sexual ambiguity may have been almost universal among them, however, the punk world was not always entirely accepting of males who were unambiguously homosexual. The punk persona, taking its roots in rock and roll to the extreme, gloried in crude and rude posturing. For men, punk sexual ambiguity alternated with punk machismo that could express itself in homophobia as hostile as a hardhat's. Craig Lee, a musician in several punk bands and the composer of "Fist Funk," was harassed for his homosexuality: The tires on his car were slashed; he was often taunted as a "fag," both by his audience and in print; and long before he fell ill, it was maliciously rumored that he had AIDS.[69] Such hassling caused many to hide the fact of their homosexual identity behind the more permissible "decline to state." Because of punk's macho affectations, the homosexual exploits of many male punkers had to be fueled by drugs and alcohol, and were seldom talked about. Some, like Darby Crash of the Germs, were revealed to be gay only posthumously.

Perhaps many of the punk musicians were encouraged to be discreet because they had big dreams of landing a lucrative contract from the nearby music industry. Nevertheless, there were some famous male punk rockers who appear to have been primarily or exclusively homosexual, including Gerardo Velasquez of Nervous Gender, Kid Congo of the Cramps, and Tomata du Plenty of the Screamers. A handful of punk icons flaunted gayness outrageously, such as the African American drag diva Vaginal Crème Davis, who created a band called Cholita: The Female Menudo (for which she performed as a Latina—swapping ethnic identity as well as gender).

Out or not, gays could easily conceal themselves in the fashions of punk. Though punks would have considered the gay male "clone look" (muscle-revealing pastel Izod shirts and 501 jeans) or the lipstick lesbian look (Gucci shoes and gold chains) as oppressively conformist as the businessman's three-piece suit, they created their own "look" that

was as studied as the styles at Studio One or Peanuts, and one that young gays could love. Gay-boy punks were permitted to affect androgyny by dyeing their hair jet black and wearing eyeliner and face powder.[70] Gay girl punks could merge easily with other girl punks who were not lesbian-identified. Phranc, a Los Angeles–based musician who performed in Castration Squad and other punk bands such as Nervous Gender, recalls that the female-punk look could be very gender-bending: Even feminine punk rockers would wear "skinny ties and other boy things."[71]

Though homosexual practices were usually covert among male punks, among punk girls they were open and even signified a declaration of female sexual freedom, which punks resoundingly approved. Sheree Rose remembers her own early sojourns into the punk rock club scene: "There was an amorphous sexual energy," she says. "Who you slept with didn't have anything to do with gender. The men knew that the women were sleeping together. It was no problem."[72] According to Fran, who was also a punk rocker, everyone acknowledged that pansexuality was the female-punk "norm": "You'd go to a club, come back to the crash pad shit-faced, and end up sleeping with another girl as likely as with a guy, and you didn't have to hide it." In between visits to punk rock venues such as Florentine Gardens and Brave Dog, Fran would visit bars such as Peanuts, and, as she observes now, the distinctions were more apparent than real: "The girls [at Peanuts] were different from those at the punk clubs mostly because they had a gay identity. We punks did the same things in bed that they did. It was just that we never called ourselves 'gay.'"[73] Phranc, who was the public darling of sexually flexible punk rockers like Fran, agrees that although pansexuality was the punk female norm, a "lesbian identity" was rare in punk culture: "Everyone among the punk rocker girls was experimenting with sex, but I can think of only one other person besides me who actually called herself a dyke. The rest just did it."[74]

Punk females "were not at all political," Phranc says. "They were into 'anything goes.' It was all personal pleasure and fashion." Despite their sexual fluidity and gender ambiguity, the girl punks were nothing at all

like the radical feminists of the decade before who had experimented with lesbian relationships as "the next important step" and wore "boy things" as a politically correct uniform. Like the lipstick lesbians, girl punks provided another model of style for young females who enjoyed sex with other females—one that was far more loose and light and trendy than anything lesbian feminists could be comfortable with.[75]

Lesbian feminists also disapproved of punk rock because of its trappings and symbols of violence (including swastikas, worn sometimes "just to piss people off").[76] But punk rock could be political in ways that even lesbian feminists would condone. Groups such as Age of Consent presented gay and feminist social critiques in rap songs such as "Missionary Position" and "Schizo Gay: Gay All Night and Straight All Day." Female punk rockers, disdaining conventional femininity, demanded what most women were still too timid to claim. Fran was a devotee of women's punk rock bands, including the Slits, Castration Squad, and Red Fear, which flaunted aggressive female pansexuality. She remembers that those performers "had so much strength, power, and presence," which was "really attractive and appealing to a girl like me who was looking for a way to be."[77]

Gay wit and imagination had a strong influence on the L.A. punk scene. Many of its prime venues, such as the Brave Dog, the long-lived Anti-Club on east Melrose, and a series of bohemian "events" called "Theoretical parties," were conceived and successfully run by gay men such as Jack Marquette and Jim Van Tyne. Alternating with the extreme of machismo, hints of gayness were sometimes provocative political statements because of their power to *épater le bourgeois.* Local punk rock bands called themselves by names such as Circle Jerks, the Weirdos, and the Dickies. L.A.'s first punk club, the Masque, featured Arthur J and the Gold Cups, a band name that referred (for those in the know) to two prime L.A. hangouts for gay hustlers. Gayness influenced punk culture and, in turn, exploited its outrageous challenges to convention. For instance, Craig Lee's lyrics for "Fist-Funk" lampooned gay sexual extremes

and also introduced the shocking concept of fist fucking to heterosexual audiences. Under Lee's creative direction, the Lame Flames performed songs such as "Fist Funk" dressed in black SM caps and red jockstraps over black lace stockings and teddies, creating a defiantly queer effect.[78]

The gay and lesbian young who were rejected by the bouncers guarding the doors of West Hollywood's party temples—and many more who never even wanted to knock on those doors—found a temple of their own among the rejects and rejectors that defined the punk demimonde. Though it was a new frontier, it was also an old one: It was the latest incarnation of L.A.'s long-standing bohemian world, where lesbians, gays, and those who "decline to state" had always danced on the edge.

III: SMASH HITS, DEVASTATING BOMBS, STUNNING COMEBACKS

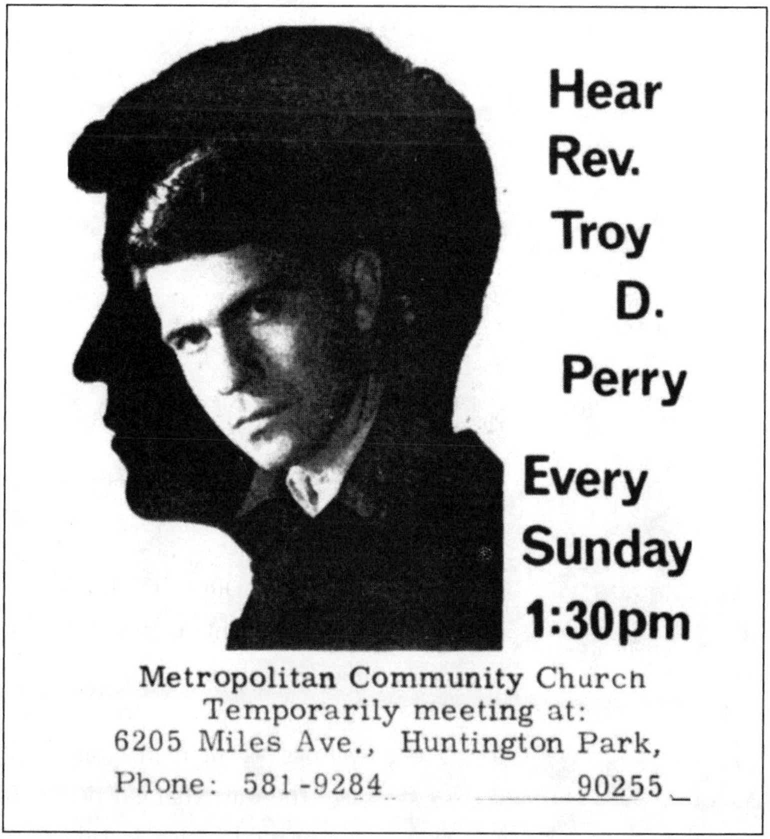
Hear
Rev.
Troy
D.
Perry
Every
Sunday
1:30pm
Metropolitan Community Church
Temporarily meeting at:
6205 Miles Ave., Huntington Park,
Phone: 581-9284 90255

The face that launched a worldwide church: Troy Perry, 1968. *Courtesy Aristide Laurent.*

CHAPTER 9

Building Worlds of Our Own

TEMPLES OF OUR OWN

> *Gay people came to our church out of the shadows, out of the closets, out of the half-world.*
>
> —The Reverend Troy Perry, founder of Metropolitan Community Church[1]

The early movement slogan—"Gay Liberation. Dig It. Do It."—that exhorted gay people to claim their sexuality, the nightclubs such as Studio One and Peanuts that invited them to uninhibited release of sexual energy, the panoply of erotic possibilities that were opening to gays in a city so large and diverse—all reflect a crucial part of the history of liberated gay L.A. But another crucial part concerns the ways that gay people built daytime lives in Los Angeles, how they formed vital institutions that compensated for those from which they had been barred, what they ultimately did with the media savvy and money that has always been part of gay L.A., how they tended to the most vulnerable members of their community—the sick and old and young, and how they dealt with devastating setbacks.

One of the most remarkable of the daytime stories is about the birth of religious institutions in Los Angeles that went on to impact gay life all over America and beyond. Troy Perry and his Metropolitan Community Church are the central figures in that story. From its humble beginnings in 1968, when twelve men and women met in the living room of Perry's

rented house in a Los Angeles suburb, the Metropolitan Community Church has grown to be the largest gay institution in the world. It has 275 congregations in twenty-three countries and houses of worship in all but four of the United States. It owns property worth about $100 million. In California, there are twenty-five MCC churches; in Texas there are fifteen. It is probably the world's largest employer of gays and lesbians.[2] Troy Perry's Metropolitan Community Church was, for a while, alone in providing the gay community with spiritual sustenance, but his success eventually led to the huge proliferation of MCCs as well as other gay and lesbian religious institutions. Steeped in the Bible and practiced in the rolling oratory of the fundamentalist South, Troy Perry became the major gay religious leader. Often described as "kinda hot," his strong features, penetrating hazel eyes, and towering six feet were a huge draw, as personal qualities often are with a charismatic preacher. It was inevitable that some gay male parishioners would fall in love with him, but Perry believed that a gay minister must be even more scrupulous than nongay religious leaders in delineating boundaries. When MCC eventually ordained more ministers, Perry used earthy humor to deliver a steadfast rule that would place the gay church above the scandals plaguing other denominations: "Don't fuck the flock."[3]

The flock continued to expand. By 1972, contributions were sufficient for MCC to purchase a former opera house in the depressed but architecturally-grand West Adams district. Perry, ever conscious of the rejection gay people had suffered in traditional religious institutions, was determined to create for them a bona fide and beautiful church. He had the walls papered with expensive silk and thick new carpets laid. It was not about style, Perry says: "It was about self-esteem. I wanted people to know that theirs was a 'real church.'" As one parishioner from the Hollywood Hills enthused, "It was one of the most elegant places to go. The choir all in robes; all these gay people in bright sunlight!"[4]

In his position as religious leader of an oppressed minority, Perry was determined to involve his congregants in committed social activism. Parishioner Lucia Chappelle recalls that in the 1970s, "someone would call a protest—against ABC television for supporting Anita Bryant, the *Los Angeles Times* for refusing to use the word 'gay' instead of 'homosex-

ual,' the Hollywood police for discriminatory policies—and then our telephone trees would be buzzing, and 80 percent of the people who showed up at the demonstration would be from the Metropolitan Community Church."[5] Perry says that his work to ensure that gays and lesbians would fight for their rights and "never take a backseat" was modeled on the goals of the black church in America in its historical struggles for civil rights.[6] (Gay wits, drawing on the parallel with another cleric who was a civil rights activist, called Perry "our Martin Luther Queen.")

Metropolitan Community Church also shared with black churches the terrible experience of noxious enemies. Frank Zerilli, who worked at MCC in its early years, recalls that hate mail came so frequently that it was "stacked a foot thick." In a mood of dark humor, MCC workers filed such mail under "Letters from Christians."[7] In January 1973, the "Christians" struck in person: The assistant pastor, Lee Carlton, returning at night from a funeral, found the church in flames. Zerilli, who arrived a few hours later, described the scene as "heart-wrenching," especially since MCC was "the first property ever owned by the gay community in America." Parishioners were convinced that the fire was an act of arson, and though official investigators claimed to find no evidence that the 1973 fire had been purposely set,[8] parishioners believed their theory was confirmed when other Metropolitan Community Churches were later torched.[9]

Nonetheless, the destruction of the edifice made the institution stronger. The following Sunday, so many people were intent on showing their support for the church and broadcasting the message that gays would not be intimidated that no building could be found to accommodate the crowd of more than 1,000 people. The Sunday service was held *en plein aire*. Councilman Bob Stevenson arranged to close 22nd Street to accommodate the horde of worshippers, who were accompanied by a horde of media. When the Metrochords, a gay singing group, expressed concern at this public exposure and asked for screens to sing behind, Perry was furious, as was MCC's music director Willie Smith, who told the complaining singers, "Sissy, the closet done burned down!"[10] That day, Perry says, "broke the back of people's worries about coming out of the closet." It also marked the beginning of an accelerated growth for the

church, which was soon able to build far beyond the borders of Los Angeles, nationally and internationally, from South Africa to the Philippines to all over Europe and Latin America. The new Mother Church that was erected in the middle of Boystown is now valued at $9 million.[11]

From the beginning, Perry also earned the gratitude and respect of gays and lesbians who weren't Christian. "We can't bar other people the way we've been barred," he explained to his congregation in the early 1970s;[12] he opened the doors not only to all who wanted to come worship but also to those who wanted simply to use the church as a meeting place—even to the Wicca priestess Z. Budapest and the lesbian witches of the Susan B. Anthony Coven #1, which met in the church's social hall. At Perry's earliest Sunday services, Jewish gays were also part of the congregation, the men sitting wrapped in their prayer shawls as Perry preached in his Pentecostal style. Jewish lesbians attended MCC in its early years, too, and some even adapted Perry's example into viable models for their own women-centered institutions. Savina Teubal, a native of Argentina, came to Los Angeles to be a screenwriter, but instead became a feminist biblical scholar and the founder of Sarah's Tent, a Jewish women's religious group. Teubal said that she was inspired to establish Sarah's Tent, named for the Old Testament matriarch, after she attended MCC. "I was fervently interested in new movements that went against convention. The thought that Metropolitan Community Church could gather together so many people in a rebellious religious movement was inspiring to me. It reminded me of the Peronistas screaming against the Oligarchs, and the Communist rallies that I went to in Buenos Aires." It was the example of Perry's challenges to religious orthodoxy, she acknowledged, that helped her to rethink the meaning of women in the Bible and to invent feminist rituals and celebrations for Jewish women.[13]

Perry warmly welcomed gay Jews into Metropolitan Community Church, but he suggested in 1972 that perhaps they might want to form their own *minyan* (a prayer group of ten or more Jews). With Perry's encouragement, the Jewish congregants enlisted two Los Angeles rabbis,

Norman Eichberg and Erwin Herman, to help start a Metropolitan Community Temple within MCC.[14] Gay and lesbian religious Jews began going to Troy Perry's church because "Troy showed that religion is just as important to lesbian and gay people as it is to straight people," Mina Meyer, one of the first lesbians to be part of Metropolitan Community Temple, explains. "But we Jews didn't feel comfortable in straight synagogues. They didn't recognize our families as families." She recalls seeing at the earliest services "old Jewish gay men, in their fifties, sixties, and seventies. They hadn't been to a Jewish service since their bar mitzvah. They sat there crying. How much this meant to them!"[15] Harriet Perl, who was in her fifties when she joined the Temple, says, "When I first heard about it, I couldn't figure out why anyone would want to have a gay temple. I'd spent my whole adult life having nothing to do with Judaism. But this temple's traditions reminded me of being Jewish as a child. . . with my grandmother. . . . I felt like I could finally come back to that."[16]

On January 26, 1973, still housed at the Metropolitan Community Church, the Jews adopted for their group the Hebrew name Beth Chayim Chadashim, meaning House of New Life. It was that evening that MCC was mysteriously burned, though the Jewish arc, along with the Christian altar, was undamaged. The arc contained a newly acquired Torah[17]—one that had miraculously survived the Nazi invasion of Czechoslovakia and now miraculously survived the church fire. Homeless, with the Torah in tow, Beth Chayim Chadashim (BCC) was offered temporary space for services in the school building of the Leo Baeck Temple in West Los Angeles.[18] Among the traditionally observant, the existence of a gay temple became a point of hot debate. Even the Union of American Hebrew Congregations (later known as the Union for Reform Judaism) protested angrily when Rabbi John Sherwood proposed that Beth Chayim Chadashim be recognized.[19] The battle was quelled within months, however, and in 1974, the Union's national board gave its final approval for BCC's inclusion into the group of 1 million members.[20] This approval marked the first time that a gay congregation had been accepted by the governing body of an established religion.[21]

Beth Chayim Chadashim had been largely male to that point, though lesbians were welcome. Mina Meyer was BCC's first treasurer; Sharon

Raphael was the first social action chair. Mina Meyer was even invited to give the first sermon at the first BCC Yom Kippur service.[22] But for the most part, the Beth Chayim Chadashim patriarchy-quotient was no different from that of the straight world. Its members had backgrounds in various denominations—Orthodox, Conservative, and Reform—but its rituals were heavily Orthodox, which soon caused some lesbian feminists, such as Mina, to leave. The very traditional language of the prayers, "full of 'He's' and 'Him's'," as Harriet Perl says, "pricked our feminist sensibilities." Perl gathered the few remaining lesbian members, and together they challenged the men about the sexist liturgy. To make their point, Harriet read the Declaration of Independence, substituting "women" for "men." "That made the guys pretty uncomfortable," she recalls, "but they really listened, and there was never a need for a gender fight." Perl, a retired English teacher, was asked to sit with the men and figure out with them, each holding a prayer book, how they could "degenderize" its language. In 1974, BCC became the very first religious body with a de-androcentrized liturgy.[23]

Despite the nonsexist language of its liturgy, BCC had trouble attracting women in its early years. The BCC board of directors, appointing an Affirmative Action Committee that would be responsible for implementing a new policy, pledged that women would meticulously be given equal time and space in all functions of the temple: "For example, if men present sermons twice a month, then women shall present sermons twice a month." In 1975, the congregation also put out a call in lesbian periodicals and elsewhere for Jewish lesbians to "take their place in the temple . . . [and] help in creating a deeper involvement of women."[24] The congregation's sincerity about gender parity could hardly be questioned when Beth Chayim Chadashim, which had been served until 1983 only by rabbinical students, was finally in a position to hire an ordained rabbi: Janet Marder was their choice. Though Marder was a heterosexual woman, with the exception of two years, from 1992 to 1994, when Marc Blumenthal, a gay man, was the rabbi, all subsequent rabbis have been lesbians.

Metropolitan Community Church had similar gender issues to work through, and the unity of the institution was seriously threatened when lesbian congregants perceived the men to be insensitive to their needs.

The Christian liturgy included as many "He's" and "Him's" as the Jewish one. Taking Beth Chayim Chadashim as its model, a committee of MCC feminist men and women tried to get the church to adopt inclusive language, but the battles raged for years. Lucia Chappelle recalls that when a resolution for an inclusive language hymnal was proposed at the 1981 General Conference, one MCC clergyman cried out, "Father! Father! . . . Why do they want to take my Father away from me?"[25] When the resolution failed, committed feminists began De Colores, a women's outreach church within MCC, creating their own liturgy with prayers such as "We praise you, El Shaddai, breasted one, for giving us the courage to reach out to womyn."[26] However, the AIDS epidemic of the 1980s and '90s, which effectively destroyed a generation of male leaders, called on lesbians to make peace and assume leadership within the church. They became elders in MCC in unprecedented numbers. In 2005, when Troy Perry retired, the Reverend Elder Nancy Wilson, who had been a member of De Colores twenty years earlier, was named worldwide head of the Metropolitan Community Churches.

Some gay churches that had their roots in Los Angeles have grown branches elsewhere, as did their prototype, MCC. Carl Bean, a gay African American who had been an entertainer at Harlem's prestigious Apollo Theater and on Broadway, was drawn to Los Angeles in 1972 by its entertainment industry; but when he first walked into Metropolitan Community Church, he recalls, he was "so overcome by a sense of joy and community" that he cried. Bean sought ordination and in 1982 founded the Unity Fellowship of Christ Church, a church primarily for African American lesbians and gays. The church has grown to twelve congregations scattered around the United States, some of them, such as the New York congregation, with as many as 2,000 members on the rolls.[27]

Like MCC, BCC also inspired the founding of gay religious institutions elsewhere. There were no other gay Jewish institutions in the world when Beth Chayim Chadashim began in 1972, but several were soon created after the model of BCC: for example, in New York, Beth Simchat

Torah, established in 1973; in Philadelphia, Congregation Beth Ahavah, established in 1975; in Chicago, Congregation Or Chadesh, established in 1976; and in San Francisco, Congregation Sha'ar Zahav, established in 1977. The gay congregation of L.A. also grew. Members of Beth Chayim Chadashim were able to purchase a synagogue building in 1977. When Rabbi Denise Eger left her position at Beth Chayim Chadashim after a messy personal problem with the temple's board, she started another gay temple, the upscale Kol Ami in West Hollywood. That congregation too purchased its own building.

Both gay synagogues in L.A. now offer religious services that depart little from the Reform tradition and are in most ways like other Reform synagogues that attract young, middle-class Jewish families. Rabbi Eger remembers that when she became the rabbi at Beth Chayim Chadashim in the 1980s, in the midst of the AIDS epidemic, "my life was spent going from one hospital to another, one funeral to another."[28] Now, with the epidemic much more under control, Beth Chayim Chadashim is in the midst of the gay baby boom. Congregants have been so fertile or so active in adopting that the synagogue has started a religious school for five- and six-year-olds. "I officiated not only at the baby-naming ceremonies for most of the children," the current rabbi, Lisa Edwards, says, "but also at the weddings of most of their parents."[29] The Congregation Kol Ami membership, too, now includes about one hundred children under the age of sixteen, and the synagogue is becoming increasingly family-oriented. In fact, the gay and lesbian parents in Kol Ami have even deliberated about whether to opt out of the gay pride parade—where, they fear, proximity to contingents such as the leathermen may be troubling to young kids.[30]

The institutionalization of gay churches and synagogues has not satisfied many gay people who wish for something other than what they see as mere permutations of Judeo-Christianity, and who blame Western religion as the root and rod of homophobia. Some Los Angeles lesbians, led by witch Z. Budapest, turned to Wicca. Some gay men, led by the Mattachine Society's old founder, Harry Hay, and the Gay Liberation Front activist Don Kilhefner, fostered another branch of paganism. Hay and Kilhefner were convinced that the gay movement needed a

radical spiritual culture to restore its meaning. Hay claimed that through years of research he had learned that gay people shared a unique consciousness, for which they had been honored rather than derided in non-Western societies.[31] Kilhefner and Hay, along with Mitch Walker, a psychologist, issued a call in 1979 for a "spiritual gathering of radical faeries," where gay men would enjoy "gay space" and goddess-worship (both influenced by tenets of lesbian separatism and spiritual feminism). That first gathering saw the beginning of numerous retreats that attracted thousands of gay men from all over the world and inspired the establishment of faerie households and rural communes.[32] Not only gay churches and synagogues, but also various sects have proliferated easily in Los Angeles because nonconventional spirituality has traditionally been freer there than anywhere in the country. Any and all spiritual bents can be satisfied.

MEDIA OF OUR OWN

When I realized that nobody would ever again produce me because they found out I was a lesbian, that's when I understood that I had to become a producer myself.

—Robin Tyler, comic and gay-and-lesbian event producer[33]

The rich and glamorous Hollywood entertainment industry has been essential to a large segment of the gay L.A. community, giving it employment and style. But the industry was slow to acknowledge to the outside world that "gay" existed, let alone that it was ubiquitous in Hollywood. In 1962, Hollywood's first post–Production Code forays into homosexuality on the screen, *The Children's Hour* and *Advise and Consent*, both concluded with the suicides of the "homosexually-inclined" characters. Throughout the decade, there was no such creature as a reasonably well-adjusted homosexual in the movies, and nary a gay character was permitted to escape death: For example, in *The Fox* (1967), the neurotic, hysterical lesbian is accidentally-on-purpose felled by a giant phallus in the form of a tree; in *The Sergeant* (1968), the gay male character (again) kills himself because it is so awful to be homosexual.

In the 1970s, when gay people were becoming increasingly visible throughout America, Hollywood was practically silent on the subject of homosexuality, though there were a few exceptions, such as *The Boys in the Band* (1970), which offered a host of gay stereotypes, each of them miserable. A movie made for television in 1971, *That Certain Summer,* finally dared to transcend stereotypes: The *New York Times* called it the first film "to take a mature and non-remonstrative approach to the subject of homosexuality." Ironically, it was around that sympathetic film that gays made an early organized attempt to put pressure on the industry. A media task force, formed by the new Gay Community Services Center when the movie was being filmed, demanded a meeting with the producers and script writers because they assumed *That Certain Summer* would contain the usual negative images of homosexuals. They were welcomed by the producer, Robert Wise, recalls Deni Ponty, a task force member: "He told us, 'I'm surprised you're here. I work with a lot of you boys.' I said, 'It's the 'you boys' we're here about." Ultimately, their conference was cordial. The task force was discouraged from further actions, however, when one of the writers privately scolded them, saying that he had been fighting effectively "behind the scenes" for gay progress, which such a meeting would endanger.[34] The task force did no more, and Hollywood was slow to improve.[35]

In the 1980s, several films finally attempted to feature sympathetic gay characters—for example, *Making Love* and *Personal Best* (both in 1982), and *Liana* (1983). But despite such projects, and despite the gayness of the town, Hollywood actors or their studios still remained as hypervigilant as their counterparts of the 1930s, '40s, and '50s had been in making sure that their heterosexual image remained beyond question in the world outside. The fiasco over the attempt to turn Patricia Nell Warren's best-selling gay novel, *The Front Runner,* into a Hollywood movie illustrated the point dramatically. Paul Newman had bought the rights to Warren's novel in the early 1980s and intended to play the role of the coach who falls in love with his champion runner. But Newman's studio would not permit it unless the script was rewritten to show him falling in love with a female teacher. Newman walked away from the project. In 1986, the producer Jerry Wheeler bought the rights and tried to find a

star who would play the coach. According to Kim Garfield, Wheeler's publicist on the project, he solicited "every good-looking male star in Hollywood for the coach role." Tommy Lee Jones told him, "I ain't gonna play no fuckin' faggot." Burt Reynolds said, "I'd love to play the part, but if I do, everyone will think I'm gay (as they already do), and because I've lost weight they'll also think I have AIDS." Wheeler approached another star who said he was interested in the role, but he'd have to check with his agent. The next day, Wheeler found a newspaper-wrapped parcel at the door of his office. Inside the newspaper was a dead fish and a note: "Don't call any of my clients again or this will be your head."[36]

Time wrote bemusedly about Wheeler's casting frustrations in 1988: "Didn't anybody want to appear in his film? . . . What was the catch? Did he want someone to play a rapist, a child molester, or a drooling maniac? No. Those would have been easy parts to fill. Wheeler wanted a rugged star to play a college track coach who happens to be gay." Huge gay gains all over America notwithstanding, *Time* concluded, "Hollywood still feels that homosexual roles spell trouble."[37] Wheeler gave up the struggle to make the film in 1989; he died of AIDS in 1990.

If it was considered damaging for an actor simply to play the role of a homosexual, how much more damaging it was to be perceived as one, particularly if that perception threatened to spread beyond the relatively safe enclave of industry people. Sheila Kuehl, who played Zelda Gilroy on the television series, *The Many Loves of Dobie Gillis,* says that even in the uptight late 1950s, when she joined the industry, "everyone was thought to be bisexual" in Hollywood. "It was bohemian, an element of freedom," she notes. But many a promising Hollywood career came to an abrupt end if an industry executive believed that viewers, who lived in the world far from Hollywood, might suspect an actor of any kind of sexuality other than hetero. Sheila Kuehl's Zelda had been the most popular female character on the program, the only one to appear for four consecutive years. She was tapped to do a new series, a spin-off in which Zelda would be the main character. "But suddenly the pilot sank like a stone," Kuehl says. Her director told her that the president of CBS had watched her performance and opined that she came off as "too butch." That is, her homosexuality was discernible. The Zelda Gilroy project was killed.[38]

Michael Kearns, too, had a promising career as an actor. His big break came when he was cast in a wholesome, family-oriented television series, *The Waltons.* Kearns played John Boy's older brother in the close-knit rural family. He had leading-man good looks, talent, and youth (he was twenty-two when he landed the plum role in the series). His agent, who knew Kearns was gay, worried that if word got out beyond the industry, his promising career would be damaged. Kearns recalls that the agent admonished him "not to go to gay bars and not to go out without a woman!" Kearns played the Hollywood game, taking care to be absolutely closeted in public. But a friend who had ghost-written a gay book, *The Happy Hustler* (piggy-backing on the best-seller *The Happy Hooker*), asked him to pose for the cover picture, and he accepted the job. When Michael Kearns was revealed to be "the Happy Hustler," his Hollywood career came to a standstill and never fully recovered.[39]

Robin Tyler also had a Hollywood career that flashed and then expired. She had come to Hollywood with Patti Harrison, her lover and stage partner in what was the first feminist comedy act ever. They appeared on a midnight talk show, which Fred Silverman, the head of ABC, happened to see; the next day, their agent at the William Morris Agency called them to announce, "ABC is going to give you your own show, like *Laverne and Shirley!*" When Harrison and Tyler expressed reluctance about signing the contract that ABC offered them because of its morals clause, Silverman told them, "Look, I know you're lesbians. It's okay. Just don't act up publicly." They taped four episodes. ABC seemed pleased until one night they appeared at 10:00 P.M. on the Crofft Comedy Hour, and immediately after, Tyler appeared again—on the 11:00 P.M. news. There was a clip of her, speaking at a gay rally. The newscaster referred to her as "Robin Tyler, avowed lesbian." "Fred Silverman wouldn't see us anymore," Tyler remembers. Their contracts were dropped.[40]

But unlike Hollywood actors of an earlier era who were forced to sink into oblivion when rumors of their homosexuality got out, Kuehl, Kearns, and Tyler found the limelight again—because now there was an audience of fans made up of the large, openly gay community. Kuehl, who became a lawyer, ran for the State Assembly with the gay community solidly be-

hind her, and she won—the first openly gay person even to have gotten through a California primary. When Kuehl ran for the California State Senate, again with the gay community's strong support, she won that race, too. Kearns found a successful career in Los Angeles gay theater. Robin Tyler became a producer of major lesbian and gay events, such as the 1979 and 1987 Marches on Washington and the Millennium March in 2000. She also became a leader in campaigns such as California's gay marriage struggle and the successful battle to derail a Paramount Television talk show that was to be hosted by arch homophobe Laura Schlesinger.

Los Angeles naturally draws a big population (a good part of it gay) that is gifted in media-making and distributing. Because producers of mainstream media continued to censor homosexuality even as the gay community grew stronger in the 1970s, L.A. gays developed their own media. Sometimes their efforts remained regional or countercultural, such as a gay-produced radio program, *IMRU,* which started in Los Angeles in 1971 and has continued uninterruptedly to the present. *IMRU* (the name refers to the ubiquitous gay graffiti, "IM1, R U12?") airs on KPFK, a progressive, listener-sponsored FM station, and brings gay and lesbian news and culture to the Southern California community. Outfest, L.A.'s gay and lesbian film festival, established in 1982 by the Lesbian and Gay Media Coalition, became the largest film festival (gay or otherwise) in Southern California, the film capital. Outfest has premiered such successful art house films as the transgender classic *Priscilla, Queen of the Desert,* and has grown to annual ticket sales of half a million dollars. Outfest also offers weekly screenings year-round and offshoots such as the Fusion Festival, billed as "the only multicultural gender inclusive film festival of its kind."

Other efforts have had a broader impact. The success of gay and lesbian bookstores such as those in Los Angeles not only encouraged the proliferation of lesbian and gay publishing houses nationally, but also showed the mainstream publishers and bookstores that there was a lucrative gay

market. Simone Wallace, co-owner of Sisterhood Bookstore, says that during the store's first twenty years, from 1972 to 1992, the volume of sales increased dramatically every year. She recalls lines that ran down the street and around the block when popular lesbian authors, such as Lily Tomlin and Jane Wagner, who published *The Search for Signs of Intelligent Life,* came for signings.[41] A gay bookstore, A Different Light, was opened in the Silver Lake area in 1979, and its manager, Richard Labonte, brought in for signings major authors—Christopher Isherwood, Allan Ginsburg, William Burroughs, and Larry Kramer. A Different Light was packed with gay people from all over Los Angeles and quickly expanded to a chain of stores in West Hollywood, New York, and San Francisco. L.A.'s A Different Light succeeded in attracting the lesbian market, too, with an ambitious Lesbian Writers Series, beginning in 1984.[42]

Ironically, the remarkable success of stores such as Sisterhood and A Different Light mandated their eventual failure. As Ann Bradley, creator of the Lesbian Writers Series, points out, there were no "Gay and Lesbian" sections in mass-market chain bookstores at the time stores like Sisterhood and A Different Light began. The profitability of gay and lesbian books not only made New York publishers understand that there was money in the publication of such books, but also made Barnes and Noble and Borders understand that they had neglected a significant market. Soon the pioneers could not compete against the big chains. The owners of A Different Light were forced to close one of its L.A. stores, and then its New York branch and, finally, they sold the two other stores. Sisterhood shut its door in 1999. Nevertheless, such bookstores were responsible for what had been a great national boom in gay and lesbian publishing during the '80s and '90s.

Some L.A. gay productions, despite their humble origins, have "gone mainstream" themselves. Gay periodicals, born long ago into the L.A. counterculture as modest little magazines or mimeographed newsletters (for example, *Vice Versa* in the 1940s, *ONE* in the '50s, *The Advocate* in the '60s, *Lesbian News* in the '70s), grew in the 1980s to address a large national

community and to reflect huge sociopolitical shifts among lesbians and gays. The most successful of the magazines capitalize on their proximity to Hollywood, promoting lesbian and gay glamour along with the news.

The Advocate, which started publishing in Los Angeles in 1967 as the newsletter of PRIDE, is today a glossy *"People"* magazine for America's "mainstream" gay population. In 1984, ten years after it had been taken off to the Bay Area by publisher David Goodstein, it returned to Southern California and settled in Hollywood. Under Goodstein, the ads and images of *The Advocate* had hyped gay male sexuality to the dwarfing of all else, and with the advent of AIDS, the magazine had gone into decline.[43] According to Mark Thompson, who was an *Advocate* editor, it was suffering from serious "moral confusion": How could a paper that ran ads for poppers and bathhouses (as *The Advocate* had under Goodstein) make its living off of a community that was now dying from a disease exacerbated by such marketed sexuality?[44]

In Hollywood, *The Advocate* was reinvented, and it became the top-circulating gay magazine in the country. The catalyst for its success was Richard Rouilard, who revamped the entire publication, including its design and content. Even the masthead was overhauled under Rouilard's direction: In an attempt to broaden the subscriber base (and compensate for the loss of readers who were succumbing to AIDS), *The Advocate,* for the first time, announced itself as "The National Gay *and Lesbian* Magazine."

Rouilard had been editor of the society pages of the *Los Angeles Herald Examiner.* With a penchant for flash that he had polished in his previous job, he aimed for *The Advocate* to become glossy and glamorous, a magazine that would be read by upwardly mobile gays everywhere. He often ran glitzy cover stories about the "beautiful people," especially the gay community's icons in Hollywood, such as Madonna, and handsome male stars (who in their interviews were usually very quick to make their sexual orientation clear: "I'm not gay . . . though I'm gay-friendly"). Rouilard managed to bring not only the magazine and Los Angeles gay culture to national attention, but himself as well. "I'm not just a homosexual," Rouilard quipped. "I'm a publici-sexual."[45] (*Time* magazine featured him in a November 1991 article as a "California trendsetter.")

But he also made *The Advocate* a widely respected publication. He hired new talent (including several lesbians) who produced professionally written and beautifully photographed stories on serious subjects such as gay bashing around the country. The mainstream press had generally been neglecting such incidents. But with the aid of a Manhattan publicist, Rouilard was able to bring *The Advocate* to the attention of editors such as those at the *Washington Post, USA Today,* and the Associated Press, who soon began following up on stories they had read about in Rouilard's magazine.[46]

The Advocate led the way for a whole spate of slick, national gay magazines, though none has ever achieved *The Advocate*'s prominence or longevity. In 2005, Planet Out, which owns Gay.com and other gay-specific internet interests, purchased all the assets of Los Angeles–based LPI Media (Liberation Publications Incorporated), of which *The Advocate* was a part, for a total of $31.1 million.[47]

The *Lesbian News,* like *The Advocate,* started out as a tiny, poorly produced newsletter. Its libertarian founder, Jinx Beers, says that she merely wanted to present an alternative voice to the hegemony of lesbian radicalism in 1975 Los Angeles.[48] Under Beers, the publication metamorphosed from the first issue of two 8.5 x 11-inch mimeographed sheets of typing paper to a multisectioned newspaper of up to one hundred pages, which included political columns, advice columns, horoscopes, lesbian news from around the world, and numerous ads addressed not only to Southern California lesbians but also to those all over America. In 1989, she sold the publication to Deborah Bergman, who had been a reporter for the *Los Angeles Times.*

Unlike Beers, Bergman had never been known as an activist of any stripe in the lesbian community. She undertook the paper as a business proposition. Under her ownership, the *Lesbian News* became the first publication in the country that promoted the image of lesbian glamour, featuring Hollywoodized lesbians—feminine, long-haired, voluptuous—in alluring ads for upscale cruises and trendy bars (usually described as "the hottest spot in town"). Bergman reversed, almost single-handedly,

the print image of the lesbian as declassed and grim, which had been the most visible lesbian image of the 1970s. The *Lesbian News* was in good part responsible for popularizing the "lipstick lesbian," who had been born in L.A. and has more recently been made famous worldwide through the television series, *The L Word.*

Bergman, having changed the style of the paper, sold the *Lesbian News* for a hefty sum in 1994 to the L.A. entrepreneur Ella Matthes. Like Bergman, Matthes was not known for lesbian political activism: "I don't think I really know what 'politically correct' means," she still says;[49] but she tries to present the community's diversity in *Lesbian News,* hiring columnists who are African American, Latina, Asian, white, queer, lesbian, transgendered, baby dyke—the whole panoply.

Matthes' philosophy, however, is light-years away from the values of those lesbians of the 1970s who raised consciousness about the importance of such inclusion. She says she wants *Lesbian News* always to be "a Cadillac instead of a Ford," and almost every one of its glossy covers features a photo of a Hollywood-gorgeous woman. The more glamorous the cover, Matthes observes, the more popular the issue. "If there isn't a catchy cover, the magazines just sit there." The most popular issue to date had a cover picture of Gwen Stefani, in eye-popping décolletage, with the headline, "The Reigning Queen of Rock & Roll Talks to Us About Fame, Fashion, and her Lesbian Fans."[50]

As print pioneer of the glam image, *Lesbian News* has an estimated monthly readership of about 120,000 (counting the hand-to-hand circulation of issues, Matthes says) and is distributed in big cities everywhere—through mailed subscriptions, chains such as Barnes & Noble and Borders, and lesbian venues such as bars and centers. Matthes acknowledges the tremendous influence of Hollywood in *Lesbian News* since it was taken over from Jinx Beers in 1989. "It wouldn't still be around if we weren't in Hollywood. People love that. Hollywood sells." She says she hopes eventually to make *Lesbian News* an "all-glossy" magazine and wants to include even more articles on "the trends, how to dress, how to do your hair, how to buy great things for little dollars."[51]

The successes of *The Advocate* and *Lesbian News* encouraged numerous emulators in L.A. and elsewhere: By the end of the 1990s, there were

ten lesbian and/or gay periodicals in Los Angeles alone; and advertisers, who now believed they had found a virtual gold mine in the gay consumer, were beating down the doors of the gay media. As the *Los Angeles Times* observed, though the rest of the publishing industry was barely holding its own, in gay periodicals advertising pages had swelled 35 percent in 1997 and another 20 percent in 1998. The gay L.A. newspaper *Frontiers* exceeded even those impressive figures, expanding over a period of four years from 100 pages to 180 pages, as its ads increased by 80 percent and its distribution spread to forty cities. Though the future of such publications is becoming somewhat unclear since more of the mainstream media are finding gay news to be "newsworthy,"[52] for that brief period, the gay print media, led by L.A., had become, as the *Los Angeles Times* wrote, "the biggest growth sector in publishing."[53]

A CITY OF OUR OWN

> *Together, this council and all of us can create the environment we need to feel safe and to prosper. We've made history together.*
>
> —Valerie Terrigno, newly elected lesbian mayor of the newly incorporated City of West Hollywood, November 1984[54]

West Hollywood, a strip of 1.9 square miles that bridges Hollywood and Beverly Hills, was an unincorporated territory of Los Angeles County prior to 1984. For gay people, particularly men, it was certainly a party town, but it was also home: An estimated 40 percent of West Hollywood's 36,000 residents were gay. Another 30 percent of the population were seniors, primarily Jewish. The gays and the seniors had one clear common cause: Eighty-eight percent of West Hollywood residents were renters, and they hoped that if West Hollywood were incorporated, it would be possible to pass rent-control legislation, as the city of Santa Monica had done, and stem the runaway rent escalation occasioned by the rise in property values.[55] Gays and seniors in a friendly coalition agitated together for cityhood, wearing red, white, and blue "Vote for Cityhood" badges and packing the county's hearings on West Hollywood incorporation.[56]

Although rent control was the ostensible issue that ignited the drive for cityhood, gay residents wanted cityhood for a more emotional reason, too: West Hollywood had become a sort of "Israel" for some gays—a promised land, the best and only hope for "a city of our own." Of the thirty-five candidates vying for seats on the city council of the proposed city, seventeen were gay. As the *Los Angeles Times* observed: "Nowhere in the country have so many openly gay candidates run in one political race."[57] The coalition between the area's seniors and gays brought astounding victory: Not only was West Hollywood granted cityhood by a wide margin of voters in the November 1984 election, but also three gay people won their bids to sit on the five-member city council—Valerie Terrigno (who had been the director of Crossroads, a Hollywood Boulevard nonprofit job counseling agency that also provided emergency food and shelter for its largely gay clientele), Steve Schulte (who had been the executive director of the Gay Community Services Center), and John Heilman (an attorney). A gay judge, Rand Schraeder, who had been a Gay Liberation Front member, was selected to administer the oath of office to them all.

Thirty-one-year-old Valerie Terrigno, whom the media had described as "a blonde-haired, brown-eyed Golden Girl,"[58] had won the highest number of votes in the election, and she was chosen "by acclamation" of her fellow council members to be West Hollywood's first mayor.[59] Thus in quick order, West Hollywood had become the nation's first gay-majority government, and Terrigno had become the nation's first "out" lesbian mayor.[60] She also became the darling of the media everywhere, and for a time her celebrity vied with that of Hollywood's stars. A French television crew filmed her for three weeks. Reporters from *People* magazine followed her incessantly.[61] Requests for interviews numbered thirty a day. A delegation came to ask her to run for governor. She was invited to speak in South Africa, Japan, all over Europe. In Italy, she was called "the Virgin Madonna."[62]

Terrigno and the council were true to their campaign promises. The council's first significant action was to approve a rent rollback and a ban on evictions. The second significant action, at the start of 1985, was Mayor Terrigno's introduction of domestic partnership legislation,

which meant that the partners of gay employees of the City of West Hollywood would receive medical insurance and other benefits. The passage of this legislation marked "the first legal recognition [by an American city] ever of same-sex relationships."[63]

Terrigno and the West Hollywood City Council went on a weekend retreat for an "encounter session." West Hollywood, they determined, was to be an unadulterated dream product of its Southern California heritage: a laid-back city of "a purer democracy, in which good intentions would not be smothered by the weight of bureaucracy."[64] The council passed other sweeping gay rights ordinances forbidding discrimination against homosexuals. The gay community cheered on Mayor Terrigno as she invaded Barney's Beanery with screwdriver in hand and, for the very last time, removed the offensive "FAGOTS STAY OUT" sign from its wall.

Among gay people worldwide, West Hollywood was soon seen as a "gay Camelot," as letters to Mayor Terrigno suggested: for example, from a French woman, "Felicitation on your victory. You are an escample [*sic*] for a French people homosescule [*sic*]"; from a Turkish man, "Homosexuality is completely forbidden [in Turkey]. Please, please, help me, take me near you—dear my friend, my sister."[65] Befitting gay aesthetic sensibility, the new city also underwent brightening and beautification as the mayor ordered that flowers be planted on the sad-looking median strip of traffic-heavy Santa Monica Boulevard.[66]

But the "victory" that Terrigno had declared for herself and the city soon turned to ashes. Shortly after her election, Terrigno recalls, she had been awakened at 3:00 A.M. when her dog started barking. Looking out the window, she saw men in brown polyester three-piece suits going through her trash. "The FBI," she says now.[67] Terrigno was under suspicion for embezzling federal funds—not in her role as mayor, but rather as director of Crossroads, the position she'd held before her election. Records reveal that Crossroads had been under investigation months before, when the Federal Emergency Management Agency, that had provided Crossroads with some its funding, began auditing its financial records because $24,000 of a $30,000 grant allocated to Crossroads in the winter of 1983–84 could not be accounted for. (Terrigno insists even now that when she took the job at Crossroads in 1983 she had inherited

a financial mess that she had tried desperately and in vain to straighten out.) Morris Kight, eminence grise in the gay community by now and founder and first director of Crossroads, placed her under further suspicion by publicly accusing her of having mismanaged and possibly misappropriated funds given Crossroads by the Community Development Department.[68]

The investigation that ensued tore the gay community apart. Though a "Grassroots Justice for Valerie Terrigno Committee" denounced the charges against her as "a farce and a setup,"[69] little money was raised for her defense. Sheldon Andelson paid the entertainment mega-lawyer Howard Weitzman to be her attorney. Some, like Gene La Pietra, a West Hollywood power broker and the owner of a gay Latino disco palace, insist that Terrigno was crucified by the law and in the press because she was a lesbian mayor of a gay city: "They came after her like they were going after Mafioso," La Pietra says.[70] But many in West Hollywood were furious, believing that, because of her, "the reputation of the whole gay community will be smeared" and that "even if she is proven innocent, it will still be damaging [to the gay city] if she is shown to have been an incompetent administrator."[71]

In October 1985, less than a year after her remarkable victories, Valerie Terrigno was indicted on charges that she embezzled almost $11,000 in federal funds,[72] hardly a significant enough sum, her supporters pointed out, to warrant the prolonged government investigation of her, which the supporters called simply "a witch hunt." In May 1986, Terrigno was convicted of twelve counts against her. She was sentenced to sixty days in a halfway house and ordered to perform 1,000 hours of community service.[73] La Pietra says of Terrigno's ordeal, "It destroyed her." Although it did not destroy West Hollywood, the city found itself reeling from the tragic destabilization.

And at the same time, as the number of AIDS cases rose alarmingly, it had an even worse tragedy with which to deal.

A lesbian wedding party on the church steps. *Photo courtesy Jay Vega.*

CHAPTER 10

"Our Own"

Sometimes you need to be with your own and embrace who you are.

— Rita Gonzales, member of Lesbianas Unidas[1]

SEVERAL GAY people of color played key roles in ONE, the pioneering homophile organization of the 1950s and '60s.[2] In the early 1970s, groups such as the Gay Liberation Front were, according to Bruce Reifel, a GLF member, "the biggest ethnic mish-mash you ever did see."[3] Among the builders of L.A.'s gay institutions that were later perceived as "mainstream," people of color again played key roles: John Platania, who planned the Gay Center, grew up on the Akwasasne-Mohawk reservation; Greg Byrd, an African American, was the Gay Liberation Front's first president; Jeanne Cordova, a Latina, was a prime mover and shaker in lesbian and gay efforts throughout the 1970s and into the '80s. But more often in Los Angeles, gays of color and gay Euro Americans inhabited separate spaces.

Not only have gays of color had to struggle with battles that are particular to their parent communities but also they have felt that participation in white-dominated institutions and events was too much like "an excursion into whiteness." Los Angeles geography has exacerbated that problem. Gay institutions have tended to be located in areas where few people of color live. L.A.'s distinct ethnic neighborhoods, spread out

over 450 square miles, and its clogged freeways and inefficient public transit system have created de facto segregation. When even "getting there" can be a major problem, how can gays of color believe they are welcome at gay film festivals, Women on a Roll dances, the Stonewall Democrats, the "Maybe Baby" groups?

Indeed, some gays of color have proclaimed, they should not even want to join activities that diminish the totality of who they are. The African American writer Alycee Lane admonished readers of *BLK,* the L.A.-based gay magazine, that it was pathetic for people of color to participate in a gay pride parade down the streets of white districts. A healthy integration of sexuality and ethnicity could be achieved only if people of color dared to "celebrate being lesbian and gay in our own neighborhoods":

> What is African-American gay and lesbian pride that is *only* articulated in the "safety" of white communities? It is not pride at all; *it is a bottomless self-hate,* for in those alien places we often subsume our blackness for the gay thing, and in our own neighborhoods, we subsume our gayness for the black thing. We divide ourselves into expendable parts. We *are* those expendable parts.[4]

In recent years, many gay people of color in Los Angeles have taken on the challenge to subsume neither ethnicity nor sexuality, while Euro American gays have been challenged to try harder to bring diversity into the larger community institutions.

COMING TO GAY L.A.

> *I knew other Guatemalan immigrants who became millionaires. But we didn't come for the money. We gay ones came for the freedom.*
>
> —Francisco Ico del Rio, immigrant from Guatemala City in 1962[5]

Gay men and women who were not born in the United States were long drawn to Los Angeles, often because they suffered harassment in their homelands and had heard of the city's legendary openness. Francisco Ico

del Rio remembers the tone of romance and excitement in a letter that he received from a gay friend who had escaped the confines of Guatemala. The friend wrote about how from the moment he flew over L.A. it had seemed to him like a magical dream:

> He said it was like a field of black velvet covered with shimmering colored sequins. He talked about the endless wide freeways, about Hollywood Boulevard [where] everywhere were handsome hustlers showing their things through their pants. There was more freedom and more acceptance in Los Angeles. He urged us all to come.[6]

Del Rio and eight other Guatemalan men soon joined the lone gay explorer, who had succeeded in landing a job and an apartment in L.A. In Guatemala, del Rio complains, he'd been able to meet his boyfriend only in dark movie theaters because they could not risk being seen together. "If you said or did anything that looked too gay," he recalls, "your gay friends would warn you against the danger by whispering, 'You're throwing feathers!'" In Guatemala, another of the immigrants, Rudy Ruano, says, he had been beaten and threatened with death by his own brother because he was gay.[7]

In 1962, del Rio and the other men from Guatemala City shared a one-bedroom apartment on Franklin Avenue, splitting the $200 monthly rent. After paying his bills, del Rio purchased a new shirt every weekend so that he would "look sharp" in bars where Latinos mixed with Anglos—the Vieux Carré, the Gaslight, the Hideaway, and the Redwood Room. He was warned about the wiles of the Vice Squad, but he and his friends still marveled at the remarkable freedom their new home afforded. Rudy Ruano says he was astounded that by simply walking out the door of his Hollywood apartment he could "pick up four or five guys in a day."[8]

Gays in Mexico were drawn to L.A. for similar reasons. Andreas, who came in 1975, says that in Chihuahua "you are either a drag queen or a total closet case." There, too, family violence against homosexuals was not uncommon. "Brothers and fathers would think it was necessary to their honor to beat you up and drive you away or even kill you."

He went first to El Paso, where he met up with a circle of other Mexican immigrants and was befriended by Chino, "this fabulous queen [and] our real leader." Chino's brother, an actor, had secured a job at ABC Studios, and he helped Chino find work there as a wardrobe assistant on shows such as *Welcome Back Kotter,* where he dressed a young John Travolta. "One by one, we all decided that El Paso was too small and we moved to L.A.," says Andreas, recalling that he drove to Los Angeles with a lesbian couple, Lupe and Whiskey. Chino helped his friends get jobs, showed them gay clubs such as the Beer Can and Circus Disco, and most importantly, encouraged a sense of community among them. Andreas describes how for gay immigrants, who suffer from poverty, loneliness, and social limitations, such networks of compatriots were vital in holding at bay the alienation of a big city. "You *so* needed to be part of something."[9]

Other gay people of color came to Los Angeles not because they feared being beaten up or harassed back home, but because they could not let themselves be a part of anything gay under the eyes of their traditional families. Marcia Kawahara says that as long as she remained on Kawaii, in the presence of her "very heterosexual" Okinawan family and community, she had to deny her own sexuality because "I was afraid of sullying the family name." When she was a counselor for the Hawaiian police department, Kawahara had worked with juvenile female runaways. "The girls were considered 'status offenders,'" she says, "and I secretly felt that that's what I was too—a status offender." At the age of forty-eight, she realized that only if she ran away ("became a fugitive," as she characterizes it) could she let herself be gay. In L.A., she ultimately found what she could not even begin to look for back home—an entire community of Asian lesbians, many of them college students, who "took me in and treated me like a gray eminence."[10]

Some "immigrants" to gay L.A. had fewer miles to travel but felt nevertheless that they were crossing a border when they left their homes. Though covert same-sex sexual relations have been common in the bar-

rios and ghettos of America,[11] to claim a homosexual identity has been problematic for people of color, and some have felt that to do it they must relocate to another part of the city, whether permanently or just for the evening. Jolino Beserra, who was born in East L.A. and raised in the San Gabriel Valley, recalls that "anyone that I knew who was gay was just beat up."[12] Jef Huereque says that though he had worked hard in the Chicano movement in East L.A., he found "little to no tolerance about homosexuality there," particularly for gay males.[13] If they wished to let their gayness show, it was safer to go elsewhere.

In the 1940s, '50s, and '60s, when semipublic meeting places for gay people were relatively scarce, it was not uncommon for blacks, Latinos, and whites to share bars,[14] such as the If Club, the Open Door, the Star Room, and the Sugar Shack for lesbians; the Piccadilly, the Waldorf, the Golden Carp, and the Vieux Carré for gay men. A lone bar opened for Chicana gay women in East L.A. in the 1960s and continues to this day, its name changing through the years from Redhead to Reds to Redz. But more often, Chicanas who lived outside of East L.A. mixed in bars with white women, as K.C. recalls of the lesbian bar she frequented in Gardena in the 1960s: "Sunday mornings we would all congregate there, a bunch of Mexicans and white girls. We'd usually gather up beers and sodas, go to a local park and play softball for a couple of hours, then end up back at the bar together."[15] Jeanne Cordova remembers a similar hangout, Tulley's in Pico Rivera, where she was a regular in the '60s. The working-class white and Latina patrons would meet over drinks there, play softball every weekend, and "sleep with each other."[16]

Even into the 1970s, the troubling attitudes toward homosexuality in their parent communities made some gay Latinos and Latinas continue to look to other parts of the city to claim a gay identity. JJ Vega, a Chicana who was a working-class woman in those years, says that it was access to places outside her barrio, such as North Hollywood, that changed her life. In predominantly white lesbian bars such as the Big Horn, she recalls, not only did she feel free as she never could in her own neighborhood but also she was able to meet women who would tell her about lesbian books and movement ideas, women who opened a new world to her.[17]

Joey Terrill remembers several gay venues in Hollywood that were ethnically mixed, such as the After Dark and the Paradise Ballroom; such places permitted his "escape from the East Side, from a constricted, Catholic upbringing; from the entrenched homophobia of the gangs and the cholos." Terrill, who was raised by a single mother in East L.A., believes that any racism he may have encountered in Hollywood was balanced by a feeling, like JJ Vega's, that there he had "possibility" and could be "a fish in a new ocean." Also like Vega, Terrill believes that the social mobility that comes from cross-class relationships between gays, which could be enjoyed outside the barrio, saved many Mexican American gays from "economic dead-ends, jail, or getting killed in a drive-by."[18]

There was no gay male equivalent to Reds in an L.A. barrio until 1999, when Chico, a men's gay bar, opened in Montebello. The clientele has not always been comfortable with its proximity to home, though. One Chico patron, interviewed by the *Los Angeles Times* in 2001, declined to give his name because he did not dare let the men in his family know that he is gay. He observed that still, even in the twenty-first century, "to have something like this [a men's gay bar in the barrio] is so taboo."[19] It was because the taboo was so powerful that closeted Chicano males, even those who "passed" in barrio gangs, felt constrained to seek refuge in the 1970s in gay bars that were at least a few miles away from home, such as Ken's River Club in East Hollywood.

The trek across the city did not always end in a welcome for people of color, and positive experiences such as Vega's and Terrill's were by no means universal. One white Hollywood man recalls that in the 1960s "we were all closet bigots. It was considered real déclassé to go to bed with a Mexican."[20] Others say that cross-racial relationships occurred often but were rarely acknowledged. Gene La Pietra observes that it was "okay to go into cubicles at the baths and sleep with every black and Mexican, but not to be seen with them publicly," and that this hypocrisy "was tolerated at the highest levels of gay society."[21] Not all white gays would "tolerate" such hypocrisy and discrimination, of course. When it became known that the Canyon Club excluded African Americans, many white patrons boycotted it in protest.[22] But often race relations among whites

and people of color in the gay community were not much different from those in the heterosexual community.

Racial discrimination in predominantly white venues encouraged the growth of clubs aimed specifically at gay people of color (though located usually outside the barrios and ghettos), such as Mugi's and Faces, whose clientele was mostly Asian gay men;[23] and the Silver Platter, which served recent gay Latino immigrants. The River Club hosted both Asian and Latino men. Catch One was opened by Jewel Williams in 1973 and was soon the city's premier disco palace for black gays. Now the longest-running gay black dance club in Los Angeles and the largest in the world, its cachet grew in the 1980s, when it was known to be a hang-out for Madonna and other celebrities of her ilk. But at Catch One, whites were in the minority. There, the tables were turned. The African American journalist Mark Haile recalls that there was "some sense of tolerance" for the whites as long as the West Hollywood Madonna-groupies respected that it was "an African American space." (But, Haile adds, "there was almost a palpable sigh of relief" among black gays when the Catch One fad ended for whites.)

Some of these bars even served as community centers for gay people of color. Fund-raisers might be staged there for causes that were important to them. Fliers and periodicals might be distributed on the premises that would alert them to the existence of the gay ethnic community beyond the bar. A couple of these places became major community forces. At Catch One, Jewel Williams held Sunday afternoon tea dances to benefit the Carl Bean AIDS Hospice in South Central Los Angeles. She offered meeting space to organizations such as United Lesbians of African Heritage, Prime Plus (a group of older black lesbians), and "Sistah Session" raps. She invited Jesse Jackson to speak at Catch One in 1988, making him the first major presidential candidate to address a black gay audience anywhere.[24] Gene La Pietra's Circus Disco in Hollywood has had an equivalent significance for the Latino gay community. La Pietra's bar hosted numerous community fund-raisers, including an appearance by Cesar Chavez to encourage solidarity between gays and progressives. As Jewel Williams observes, many gays of color

came to these dance palaces for pleasure on the night they turned twenty-one, but they were also ushered into a world of political activity and social support for their ethnicity as well as their sexuality.[25]

As these clubs became safe havens, gay people of color developed new cultures. Circus Disco was started by Gene La Pietra because his non-white friends had been barred from Studio One. Andreas recalls how the news that the Circus was to be a gay Latino disco was at first met with incredulity among his social set: "We couldn't quite imagine that." But when the doors opened, patrons found "good sound, great light systems, and the best music we'd ever heard." No one could have guessed how many gay Latinos were waiting for a dance palace of their own:[26] Circus Disco, which held more than 1,000, was packed every weekend. (It has now expanded to a venue that holds 3,000 and is still packed every weekend.) The habitués created styles of dancing that became vital to the gay Latino scene. An in-crowd formed. "If you didn't know the steps, you were dead," Andreas remembers.

Joey Terrill believes that not only the dancing but also the fashions had a profound purpose. "We were all making art and communicating with each other," he says. "I never thought of it per se as 'Latino.' It just so happened we all *were*. . . . We were all from the East Side and we were going into Hollywood." Before leaving his mother's home, Terrill would don platform shoes and baggy pants, stowing a woman's vintage beaded sweater in a plastic bag, and hop on the bus. Once he had crossed into Hollywood, he felt safe enough to complete his outfit by putting on the glittering sweater.[27]

Andreas believes that the sense of style at Circus Disco was distinctly Latino. "It was a melding of the 1940s and the 1970s, somehow always with a Latin flavor. Imagine a Fred Astaire tux with jelly sandals."[28] Andreas and his friends would transform an item, such as an apron that might be purchased for a dollar at a thrift shop, by making it into a tie, a vest, and a handkerchief. Outfits were often so fabulous that they set a trend and became a fine source of chauvinistic pride: "All

dressed up, us Latin queens would go to Circus to perform. The look of West Hollywood was tame and lame. They tried to copycat us, but really couldn't."[29]

Gay Latinos also found other venues far from the barrios where they could be openly gay, such as Griffith Park, the great oasis dividing Hollywood from the San Fernando Valley. There, on Sunday afternoons, on a hill overlooking the city, a van with good speakers would become a mobile disco booth, and upwards of eight hundred gay Latino young people, male and female, would create a surreal social scene. "You'd see these beautifully dressed and coiffed people—the girls in stilettos, dancing in the dirt. You'd cruise; you'd get picked up—all the while looking at the fabulous city of Los Angeles."[30]

NEW HUNGERS

> *Our premise is simple. It is demoralizing ALWAYS to be in the minority, and we find that it is a refreshing change of pace for most [people] of color to be surrounded by [those] of similar interests and background.*
>
> —Founders of Debreta's, an L.A. African American lesbian group[31]

Clubs such as Catch One and Circus Disco tried to transcend their function as mere pleasure palaces, but most clubs, whether for gays of color, whites, or an ethnic mix, specialized in drinking and cruising. Horacio Roque Ramirez observes that the clubs "seem like heaven when you first go into them," but they have serious limits when it comes to sustaining community.[32] Terry Gock, a psychotherapist and the founder of Asian Pacific Lesbians and Gays, describes some gay clubs not only as "skuzzy" but also as places that foster competition and its concomitant, rejection: They can exacerbate a terrible feeling of isolation, despite their ostensibly social atmosphere.[33]

But alternatives to them appeared slim in other decades. Some people of color had tried to organize formally in the 1970s. Gay and lesbian Chicanos, concerned that there was "nothing, really, for Mexican Americans in the gay community,"[34] formed a group called Unidos in 1970. In 1974,

Estilita Grimaldo Smith, a Panamanian businesswoman (who ran Womantours out of the Woman's Building), started Latin American Lesbians of Los Angeles for women who had roots in Argentina, Chile, Columbia, El Salvador, Mexico, Nicaragua, Panama, and Peru.[35] But neither organization lasted long.

Informal social groups for people of color had more staying power. For example, Debreta's was started in 1977 by an African American lesbian couple, Bobreta Franklin and Deborah Johnson. When they'd first considered forming such a group, Franklin and Johnson acknowledged that they had white lesbian friends and had never encountered bigotry among them, yet something vital was lacking in those relationships. "We needed an atmosphere where we could see people like ourselves and know that we weren't the only ones, where we could talk about the oppression we had, both in the lesbian community and the African American community, and know that we'd really be understood on both fronts."[36] Debreta's sponsored cruises, theater parties, dances, picnics—but members could not ignore that by virtue of their being an organization of black lesbians their import went beyond the mere social. To "raise consciousness" in the outside world, for example, they rented the ballrooms of Hiltons or Marriotts as openly African American gay women; to raise their own consciousness, they conducted raps about the meaning and consequence of their dual identities. Though Debreta's may have started as a social group in 1977, it became part of what Johnson and Franklin called in 1981 "a growing group self-awareness among Third World gays" who were now "actively mobilizing and building coalitions."[37]

But even groups that had no such express awareness were important because they brought together gay people of color who felt they could not be comfortably ethnic in the white-dominated gay community. Gay politics of the 1970s and early '80s were often alienating to them. For example, lesbian-feminist separatism made little sense to black lesbians, who felt that they were more oppressed because of their race than their sexuality or gender, and that they needed to maintain alliances with their black brothers. Even the terms "lesbian" and "gay" felt odd to some people of color. Ayofemi Folayan, an African American women, explains:

"There were lots of black women who loved women in the 1970s, but 'gay' and 'lesbian' was a white thing."[38]

The declassed, radical, dress-down style of white lesbian feminists was also offensive to many people of color. Gayle, an office worker in the 1970s, remembers sartorial splendors at the elegant parties she attended with other black lesbians and gay men in Los Angeles:

> The air was always filled with perfume and cigarette smoke. The guys were in suits or silk shirts and slacks. Sometimes the ladies wore long gowns in pastel colors, or bell-bottoms with fancy tops. I used to wear these gorgeous Palazzo pants. And the hard-dresser butches—they liked tailored suits or jackets with contrasting slacks, pointy-collar shirts and French cuffs. One butch always wore plaid jackets that had pink that was boxed with blues or greens.

Even outside of private parties—for example, at the "Sunday cocktail hour" at Catch One, style prevailed, according to Gayle.[39] The fancy dress that would have scandalized most leftist lesbians and gays was seen by blacks who aspired to better their socioeconomic position as an important marker of respectability rather than something to eschew as "politically incorrect."

A major turning point for gays in African American communities occurred in the early 1980s, when gay-friendly institutions (that were not bars) began to be established in their own neighborhoods. "When Carl Bean started the Unity Fellowship of Christ Church, it tapped into a very below-the-surface crowd of people who didn't consider themselves activists, or involved, at all," says Mark Haile. He observes that the members of Unity Fellowship (which continues to this day) include those engaging in gay sex who are not gay-identified, people who do call themselves lesbian or gay, and often their straight families. Elegant fund-raisers are held by Gentlemen Concerned, Ladies Concerned, Sisters of Love—all groups within the church, to help support

Bean's Minority AIDS Project as well as Rue's House, which Jewel Williams founded for HIV-infected women and children of color. The garden parties and barbeques of these groups ("which do not face towards West Hollywood," Mark Haile says) include both working-class and middle-class black gay people.

"OUR PEOPLE, OUR PROBLEM, OUR SOLUTION"

> *Sure we supported our black brothers and were involved in fighting AIDS, and we even worked with some mostly-white groups. But we wanted to have something we could call our own, where black lesbians could connect just with each other—a black woman-space, where we could find each other as black women.*
>
> — Lisa Powell, a founder of United Lesbians of African Heritage[40]

Agencies such as the Gay and Lesbian Community Services Center and Connexxus hoped from the beginning, as GLF had before them, to provide a "healthy place" for the entire mix of the gay community. They continued to try to offer something for everyone: At the Center in 1988, for instance, the Black Lesbian Therapy Group met on Wednesdays, Gay and Lesbian Latinos Unidos (GLLU) met on Thursdays, Womyn of Color Rap met on Fridays, and so forth.[41] Leaders at the Center and other community institutions, wanting to integrate, also brought a few people of color into prominent positions. The logic was that others would then follow because they would understand they were welcome. But such attempts at inclusion could be awkward, as Lucia Chappelle, an African American lesbian, wryly points out: "The story of my life in the queer community has been, 'Oh, my God! A black lesbian! Grab her!'"[42] Those few lesbians and gays of color who were willing to work in predominantly white groups could be spread thin by being made token representatives on every gay L.A. institutional or organizational board in sight. Terry Gock says that in the 1980s he left the board of the Gay and Lesbian Center after a year because, although he admired the organization's work, he was weary of being the lone Asian board member. He also

stopped attending the Stonewall Democratic Club because of the "extra work" required of the only Asian person at most meetings.

Resentments emerged when gay people of color felt they were being exhausted because the community wanted to rid themselves of perceived racism but did not know how. (Robin Podolsky, who was a founder of White Women Against Racism, says that her group began in the 1980s, when lesbians of color at Califia finally became exasperated and told the white lesbians: "All right, you guys have to do it for yourself. Do it like Alcoholics Anonymous. Unlearn your racist reflexes.")[43] Some who straddled the white and the people of color communities, such as Yolanda Retter, a longtime activist whose background is German and Peruvian, tried to serve as gadflies on the L.A. gay white-body-politic, urging it to look to its own racism and also telling gay people of color that they must find their own voice.

Suspicion continued even when predominantly white groups tried hard to bring in people of color, because mistrust had been built through the years. When Jim McDaniels, an African American raised in a white enclave in Orange County, became the facilitator of ACT UP's new People of Color Coalition, one member of the group remarked, "It's so great to have you here because you know how to navigate the white power structure of ACT UP." McDaniels was stunned to realize that some members of the People of Color Coalition saw ACT UP—which had prided itself on being an open populist alternative to an unresponsive power structure—as merely another part of the white power structure. "They just felt uncomfortable and unwelcome . . . completely disenfranchised from the one place you'd think they'd feel enfranchised. To them it was that 'white boys and girls club.' It might as well have been academia or a country club or the Republican Party."[44]

A number of groups for lesbians and/or gay men of color emerged in the 1980s, but most remained fairly small because potential members were often reluctant to join an organization in which they would be expected

to espouse a gay political message in public and risk "outing" themselves to their parent community. Lisa Powell, director of United Lesbians of African Heritage (ULOAH), says that shortly after her group was formed, they tried to get a contingent of members to march in the Martin Luther King Day parade, which was held in an African American neighborhood, on Crenshaw Boulevard. "But," Powell recalls, "we could hardly get any of the women to agree to 'walk down Crenshaw,'" a phrase that has now become shorthand among black lesbians in L.A. for the test of being "out": "Would you walk down Crenshaw?"[45] Cleo Manago, the African American gay activist who organized the first gay contingent to march in the Martin Luther King Day parade, says he also had trouble mustering more than a skeleton crew to hold up the banner.[46]

Still, an inexorable momentum had begun in the 1980s, and such groups continued to form. Even organizations that started ostensibly as social groups came to realize that they were necessarily political because their members belonged to a dual minority, with inevitable issues that needed to be addressed. Rita Gonzales recalls that when she was invited to her first Lesbianas Unidas retreat she announced, "It's good to be with other Latinas, but I'm not very political." The response of Lydia Otero, president of Lesbianas Unidas, "scared the heck out of me," she says, but also made her understand a cogent concept: Otero shouted, "You're a lesbian? You're Latina? You're political!"[47]

The very act of forming a gay people of color group became in itself valuable because it helped members not only to define their identity but also to think of themselves as a community and cause others to think of them in the same way: The motto of the Black AIDS Institute, "Our people, our problem, our solution," expresses the empowering concept. Simply by its existence, the activist Mario Perez Ceballos insists, "Gay and Lesbian Latinos Unidos began to change the tone of how gay politics was conceived of . . . in L.A."[48]

Gay people of color groups in Los Angeles eventually proliferated, and the demographics of the city, with its abundant cornucopia of races, ethnicities, and sexualities, have made it possible to search out ever-closer matches to one's identity. There are not only enough lesbian and gay Latino artists to form an organization such as VIVA but also enough gay

Central American writers who rebel against the "dominant Chicano establishment in L.A." to form Equipo Y Vos, a separate group devoted only to people like them.[49] (Chicanos might laugh at their being considered an "establishment" by anyone; but Equipo's founder, Horacio Roque Ramirez, explains of his separate group that "it's calming to have that national identity, those national roots, to have history.")

One common pattern of division and multiplication in Los Angeles has been this: A few African American or Asian American or Latino gay men who felt alienated in gay organizations that were predominantly white formed a group. A few lesbians happily joined the group since it was concerned with issues of their race as well as of homosexuality. Their presence attracted more women, and eventually there was a critical mass of lesbians in the group. The communication among the lesbians led to their realization that their needs were not being met in an organization that addressed their race, and perhaps some aspects of their homosexuality, but not their gender. As their numbers grew, they demanded more voice, and gay men of color were not always open to granting their demands. The lesbians defected from the founding organization, and there were enough of them in populous and diverse L.A. to form a new group that shared not only the identities of race and sexuality, but even gender.[50]

The National Gay and Lesbian Black Leadership Forum, which was founded in Los Angeles by Phill Wilson in 1986, became one instance of such division and multiplication. As its name suggests, the organization was intended for both men and women, and it hoped to cultivate the concept of leadership within the black community. Up to a thousand African American gays were attracted each year to its national conference held in downtown L.A. hotels. But although the Black Leadership Forum had intended gender equality, it could not escape the same gender discontents that often troubled the larger lesbian and gay community. Saundra Tignor joined because it "fought on both the racial and sexual fronts." But its cogendered aspect, she says, "failed to meet women's needs."[51]

Tignor, along with other Black Leadership Forum members Lisa Powell and Yolanda Whittington, broke off in 1989. Powell recalls, "We wanted to prioritize for ourselves as women."[52] They founded their own

organization, United Lesbians of African Heritage (ULOAH). Once they could claim an organization all their own, it became psychologically more appealing to participate as a group with other organizations that were cross-gender and cross-color, such as ACT UP and Queer Nation, in what Powell recalls as "those high and heady days of phone trees and taking it to the streets."[53] But the ULOAH activity that raised the most interest in its membership defines the group pointedly by its triple identity of race, sexual orientation, and gender. The annual Sistahfest, which attracts to Los Angeles women from everywhere in America as well as Africa, Europe, and the Caribbean, is an all-black-lesbian love fest, as Betty Smith glowingly describes it:

> Hundreds and hundreds of black women—being together, dancing together. We all sit by the campfire and people stand up and say things they'd never say anywhere. We wouldn't like it if it was racially or sexually mixed. It's so personal, like if you went to a psychiatrist and someone wanted to sit in. . . . None of us is a stranger at Sistahfest. It's family. It's one of the best things that ever happened to Black women. It's *our own*, created by *us*.[54]

The Sistahfest phenomenon fulfills those longings that make many gay people, nonwhite and white alike, search the huge city for the precise fit: It affirms identity; it provides a trusted group; it offers a place. While there, one is not a stranger.

Groups formed and split off in similar ways among the other gay L.A. people of color communities, too. For example, the women of Gay and Lesbian Latinos Unidos broke off to form Lesbianas Unidas; the women of Asian Pacific Lesbians and Gays broke off to form Los Angeles Asian/Pacific Islander Sisters (LAAPIS). Other divisions and proliferations also became possible in L.A. because the gay population continued to grow and to increase in diversity. Mark Haile has observed that ethnic gay groups in Los Angeles can be described as a series of "begats."[55] He uses the gay Asian community as an example, with Asian Pacfic Lesbians and Gays begatting not only the Gay Asian Pacific Support Network and LAAPIS but also the Gay Asian Rap Group. Those groups

begat Barangay—the gay Filipino group, as well as the L.A. chapter of Trikone, the South Asian group. The begats continue: A former member of LAAPIS explains that the latest proliferations are a result of burgeoning immigration into Los Angeles of non-English-speaking Asians: "They want to be with lesbians who speak their own language."[56] But even that division threatens to divide further. The Vietnamese lesbian group, O-Moi, for example, has struggled with splits between those who speak Vietnamese *well* and those who are losing the language because they have become too Americanized.[57] The strength of Los Angeles as a huge cornucopia also presents a huge challenge to unity since identity can be defined more and more narrowly.

The abundance of L.A.'s diversity has fostered not only the splintering of groups but also the founding of very specialized groups. Roland Palencia witnessed the loss of a generation of gay Latino artists to AIDS and the attendant loss of cultural expression and record.[58] In response, Palencia, who had been a founder of Gay and Lesbian Latinos Unidos, now formed VIVA, a group of gay Latino artists. The group's task was daunting because, as the playwright Luis Alfaro observed, "the Chicano community was still holding on to the belief that Queer Latinos did not exist," and gay Latinos were reluctant to expose themselves to their parent community.[59] The times were right for change, however. VIVA won funding from the U.S. Conference of Mayors and produced a blitz of readings, art openings, and other cultural events in L.A., including the creation of Teatro VIVA, which used performance art and cross-dressing to explore themes that were urgent or troubling for the gay Latino community, such as the importance of safe sex or how to disclose HIV status to families. Though AIDS drove most of its programs, VIVA's leaders believed that lesbians' voices were crucial. (They made the point that "gay" is not limited to male-male sex.) Lesbians were elected to the board and hired on the staff. They launched an annual women's event, Chicks and Salsa, which drew huge audiences of Latina lesbians. Some lesbian writers and artists of VIVA, such as Terri de la Peña, Cheri Moraga, and Laura Aguilar, went on to win national reputations.

VIVA lasted for almost a decade, enough time, the artist Miguel Angel Reyes says, to give gay Latino/Latina artists what they had never had: a

feeling not only that there was a critical mass to comprise an audience interested in what the gay Latino artist had to say or show but also that these artists "belonged somewhere." Knowing that there are both peers and an audience gets the artist started, Reyes suggests. And then "after awhile, you realize, you're fine now."[60]

Though Los Angeles is made up largely of areas that are segregated by ethnicity, class, or sexuality, Angelenos are occasionally brought together in surprising concord, as they have been in the Silver Lake area. A troubling gay/straight divide developed more than a generation ago between Silver Lake's working-class Latino families, who make up 40 percent of the population in the area, and gays (both white and people of color). Straddling Sunset Boulevard between Hollywood and downtown, Silver Lake had long served as a small, quiet gay enclave; but in the late 1970s, its cheap rents, Craftsman architecture, and bohemian ambiance drew larger numbers of gays into the district.[61] Gay realtors encouraged the trend, appealing especially to affluent homosexuals with the marketing slogan "West Hollywood Is Moving East."[62] Silver Lake's gay population was soon more than 20 percent.

The working-class community did not appear to welcome them. Gay people were deeply troubled by the blunt expressions of mistrust, such as that of a Salvadorean mother who admitted to a *Los Angeles Times* reporter, "I tell my children to be careful because they have to play in the street. I tell them to watch out for two things—cars and gays."[63] A series of muggings and several murders, as well as the firebombing of the Frog Pond, a Silver Lake gay restaurant, created serious tensions. Some gays were certain that local street youth were attacking gay people out of homophobic contempt. Others, however, pointed out that the attacks might be less hate crimes than the acts of poor residents who worried about the effects of gentrification. "Gays were moving in and fixing up the houses, and there was a perception that they would price Latinos out," said Michael McKinley, a Beverly Hills hairdresser who still lives in Silver Lake.[64]

An integrated lesbian and gay group, the Sunset Junction Neighborhood Alliance, decided to tackle the problem head-on.[65] Rejecting the idea of a demonstration, which could be regarded as hostile, they chose a quintessentially L.A. solution: They threw an outdoor party that evolved into a street fair (entertainment was provided by "guest" stars such as the Supremes). The Neighborhood Alliance also reached out to Latino community organizations, such as El Centro del Pueblo, a social service nonprofit, to broker a truce with the street gangs. Michael McKinley, a leader of the Neighborhood Alliance, was inspired to employ local gang members to work as security guards for the fair. Gang members were initially reluctant to be associated with what was perceived as a gay and lesbian event. But, McKinley says, they were won over because it gave them visibility and an unwonted respect from agencies such as the LAPD.[66] The first year, the LAPD, concerned with protecting the gays, warned the Neighborhood Alliance of a "bloodbath," but the fair proceeded without incident. Now, more than twenty-five years later, the annual Silver Lake Street Fair has grown from an initial crowd of 5,000 to more than 100,000, including gay cholos and yuppies, families and the elderly.[67] The fair's harmony, gay residents of Silver Lake report, laps over into everyday life—"like the Mexican restaurants . . . with the gay flag as part of their décor," the lesbian couple Lori Ball and Lisa Ginsburg say, "and the gay Salsa dancing at Rudolfo's Sunset Junction."[68]

Faces of AIDS activism: above Barry Diller, Steve Tisch, Barbra Streisand, and David Geffen. Below, Mark Kostopoulos. *Top photo: © 1992 Michael Jacobs/MJP/Courtesy APLA; lower photo: Chuck Stallard.*

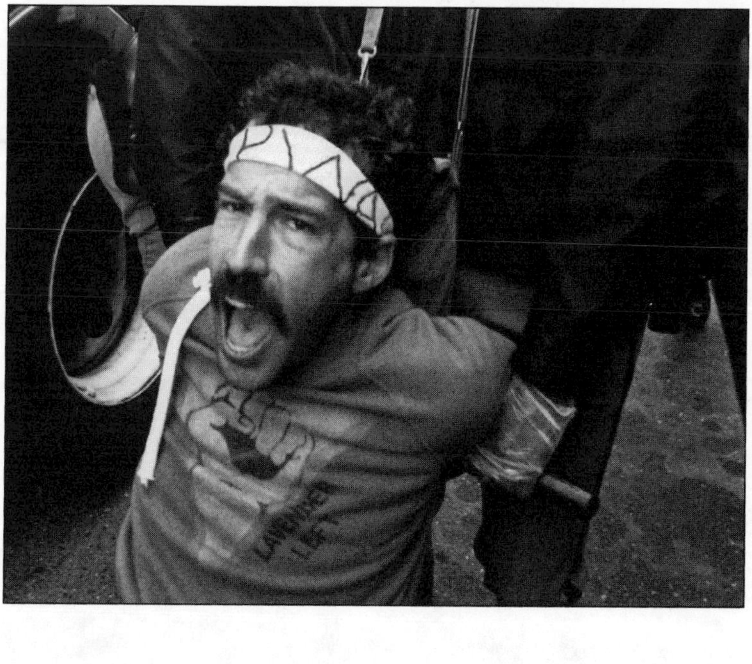

CHAPTER 11

Devastation

A SUDDEN SIEGE

AIDS changed everything, literally overnight.

—Gene La Pietra[1]

IT HIT LIKE the bomb that kills people but lets buildings stand–except this bomb killed selectively, and the victims were mostly gay. The modern plague that would wipe out millions started killing just a few at a time: in private rooms at L.A.'s Cedars-Sinai Hospital; in crowded corners of County General; in hillside homes and in Skid Row alleys. Michael Gottlieb, a Los Angeles epidemiologist, was the man who "discovered" AIDS. He identified five male homosexuals with an unusual form of pneumonia at UCLA Medical Center during the summer of 1981 and made them the subject of the first article describing the mysterious new ailment.[2] Within weeks, the illness was noticed in New York and San Francisco, and gay ghettos began their long state of siege.

As the gay actor and activist Michael Kearns observes, "AIDS changed what it meant to be gay. We had to face the fact there was no going back, that what we called gay life was lost forever."[3] AIDS, Acquired Immune Deficiency Syndrome (named by the Los Angeles researcher Bruce Voeller),[4] wiped out a golden age of sexual freedom. It decimated a

generation of gay men coming into their prime years of mature leadership as activists and political insiders. It killed choreographers, curators, artists, and designers, plundering the arts and entertainment industries of much of their best talent. It leveled closets and crippled communities. Its destructive ripple effect altered nearly every aspect of gay life.

For the straight world as well, AIDS wreaked havoc, evoking a dangerous level of public fear. The general population so dreaded contracting AIDS by the impossible transmission route of donating blood that the Red Cross had to declare a "blood emergency" in Los Angeles and Orange counties.[5] In the television industry, as *TV Guide* reported, "the comparative openness and liberalism of the '70s has disappeared. In their place is a climate of fear." Female stars began insisting that their leading men be straight.[6]

AIDS also wrought economic devastation on newly built businesses in the gay world. Before the epidemic, gay chic was beginning to draw straight clientele to gay discos, where straights and gays might mingle freely, much as their counterparts had in the Sunset Strip and Hollywood nightclubs of the 1930s. Gene La Pietra, owner of Circus Disco, recalls a news story that claimed that AIDS could be transmitted by casual contact. "The very next day," he says, "the whole club scene changed. It suddenly wasn't fashionable for straight people to have a gay friend."[7] Mixed nights ended in his club, as in most others. Heterosexuals continued to frequent those clubs only if the proprietors offered "straight dance nights." Within twenty-four months of Gottlieb's article, gay bars in the Hollywood/West Hollywood area reported a 20 percent drop in business, and the six bathhouses in the area suffered a revenue plunge of 50 percent.[8]

Public health concerns were sometimes confused with homophobic attacks, and vice versa. Some gay establishments angrily denied the danger of AIDS and tried to keep operating as usual. When *Frontiers* published its first cover story about the disease,[9] copies of the newspaper were thrown out of gay bars, whose owners thought it bad for business. A debate, not fully resolved to this day, began to call for the closing of the bathhouses—or, at the very least, for a regulation that would require the proprietors to hire monitors who would police the goings-on with flash-

lights to prevent unsafe sexual behavior. In an environment of scant information, the community was unmoored. No AIDS antibody test was available until 1985, and gay men lived in painful suspense, waiting in terror for the first symptom. One gay Hollywoodite who became sick early in the epidemic voiced the bewilderment and terrible sense of injustice that was common: "I don't think I overdid anything," he said. "I was just part of the flow."[10]

Gay life had indeed changed. The looming question now was whether AIDS had the power to revive closets, snuff out hard-won gains, and propel the gay community back to the 1950s.

For all its devastation, AIDS had the opposite effect. It triggered a resurgence of activism, as well as ingenuity and generosity the likes of which Los Angeles had never before seen. One of the first responses was archetypically "Southern California" in its New Age quality: Louise Hay, a former fashion model and motivational speaker, founded the "Hayride," a weekly support group. Hay offered spiritual encouragement, urged men to clutch teddy bears, and sold tapes with her message of positive thinking. Other responses addressed the effects of the epidemic more realistically. Gay bartenders, who witnessed countless gay men lose their health, jobs, and savings, set out coffee cans to collect change for a relief fund and threw benefit beer busts. A group of friends launched an organization called Aid for AIDS that focused on immediate cash relief for people with HIV living below the poverty line, where illness was propelling many. In 1982, the Gay Community Services Center called an emergency meeting to discuss the AIDS services they would need to provide.

The incidence of AIDS among lesbians has been low. Those few who have contracted the disease have usually gotten it through means other than same-sex sexual relations. (As *Time* quipped at the height of the epidemic, if you want to avoid AIDS, become a lesbian.) Nevertheless, L.A. lesbians were active in the earliest efforts to help when they saw that gay men were being felled by the disease. Ivy Bottini recalls that

when her friend Ken Schnorr developed symptoms in 1982, doctors were still unsure of what his ailment was, and when she called the Centers for Disease Control for advice she was given only vague answers. Along with members of the politically sophisticated Municipal Elections Committee of Los Angeles (MECLA), she became a founding supporter of AIDS Project Los Angeles (APLA),[11] which, in the decade that followed, served more than 11,000 Angelenos.

From the beginning, AIDS Project Los Angeles was cochaired by a man and a woman, starting with Diane Abbitt and Joel Weisman. Lesbians were heavily involved in all aspects of the organization. Women's presence helped emphasize to the public that AIDS was a tragedy not just for gay men but for humanity—that although the disease targeted the gay male community, their friends outside were anguished for them and would fight by their side. Abbitt and her partner at the time, Roberta Bennett, also worked together with their old cohorts, David Mixner, Peter Scott, and Duke Comegys (a Los Angeles–based heir to Texas oil money), all of whom had already demonstrated in groups such as MECLA their ability to get the ear of elected officials.[12] Now their focus was on convincing those in power that AIDS drugs must be made available immediately. AZT was given early approval, Abbitt says, because she and her group were able to convince Henry Waxman—the congressman from Los Angeles who was head of the U.S. Congress' Health Committee—that the drug should be put on an expedited track.[13]

Lesbians also opened their purses to AIDS causes. Roberta Bennett, who served on the board of APLA for six years and was active in its money-raising drives, says she never had difficulty getting lesbians to donate and even to open a food bank that would serve people with AIDS.[14] Some lesbians, such as Sue Talbot and Liebe Gray, who were volunteers in APLA, say that they had been lesbian separatists before the epidemic called on them to help their brothers.[15] Just as the separate factions of L.A.'s gay community had banded together during the campaign against the Briggs initiative to fight an external enemy, so did they band now to fight a much more relentless internal enemy.

Their unified focus came with a price. Many gay women like Talbot and Gray turned their energies from lesbian concerns to the battle against AIDS—which accounts, in part, for the failure during the height of the epidemic of L.A. institutions that served lesbians, such as Connexxus and the Woman's Building. Other organizations within the community also found that their energies could no longer be focused on the old concerns, which seemed somewhat frivolous and self-indulgent in comparison to the cataclysmic disaster of AIDS. For instance, Gay and Lesbian Latinos Unidos (GLLU) had formed out of distrust for white-dominated groups; but at the height of the epidemic, members set aside their suspicions and worked closely with those groups. They translated into Spanish AIDS informational material that the Gay and Lesbian Community Services Center published, and they marched side by side with predominantly white organizations at AIDS demonstrations and protests: "'My group/your group' didn't seem right at that point," Rita Gonzales says.[16] AIDS became GLLU's main concern as its energies were put into founding Bienestar ("well-being" in Spanish), a Latino HIV-care nonprofit agency, which now has scores of employees and twelve locations in L.A. But Bienestar's establishment seriously shifted the focus of GLLU from an organization that dealt with all aspects of Latino gay and lesbian concerns to one that addressed the overwhelming problem of AIDS. Roland Palencia observes, "Ironically, we have the biggest [gay] Latino institution, and yet it's primarily around a disease; it's not around an entire community."[17]

Hollywood became a great asset in the fight against AIDS because movie stars were hugely effective in generating donations and spreading public awareness. One of the first actors to take an active role was Zelda Rubenstein, the diminutive star of the film *Poltergeist,* who donned a ruffled apron and admonished a series of bare-chested "sons" to "Play Safely" in ads that appeared on buses; Rubenstein also made videos that were shown between pop music numbers at gay bars.

Other Hollywood stars, such as Burt Lancaster, Angela Lansbury, and Joan Rivers, were quick to lend their clout. Elizabeth Taylor became the face of AIDS activism, as she continues to be. But the star whose impact was most powerful in these early efforts was Rock Hudson, whose AIDS diagnosis in 1985 shook the world. The closeted actor (who "came out" only in a posthumous memoir) lent his name to an AIDS Project Los Angeles event that year. As he languished in the hospital, a dinner featuring tributes to him from Elizabeth Taylor, Betty Ford, Burt Reynolds, and even a polite letter from Ronald and Nancy Reagan raised $1.1 million.[18] When ruggedly handsome and big-screen-familiar Rock Hudson made his famous Hollywood face the face of AIDS, Americans began to view the crisis differently.

AIDS Project Los Angeles, continuing to use its proximity to the entertainment industry to brilliant advantage, began an annual Commitment to Life event. The first, a dinner at which Elizabeth Taylor was the star attraction, raised $1.3 million.[19] Subsequent fund-raisers featured luminaries such as Barbra Streisand, Bruce Springsteen, and Whitney Houston. They filled L.A.'s Shrine Auditorium and the Universal Amphitheater. At 1998's Commitment to Life event, the recently outed industry executive Barry Diller wryly announced: "My money-grubbing, money-raising friends and cochairs have just delivered $3.2 million."[20]

But APLA did not rely on Hollywood alone to bring in money for AIDS causes. The Los Angeles AIDS Walk it sponsored was expected in its first year to raise a few hundred thousand dollars. It attracted a broad swath of the public and brought in more than $1 million. Since its inception, it has raised a total of more than $50 million. The event became a model for AIDS Walks all over the country. AIDS Project Los Angeles and other AIDS groups also organized candlelight marches for the growing numbers of grieving, angry survivors. With tearstained faces and dripping candles, thousands flooded the streets annually, from Pasadena to West Hollywood, honoring the dead and calling for a cure.[21]

But even as marches, agencies, and public awareness increased, so did death. By 1987, more than 71,000 cases of AIDS had been diagnosed nationally, and AIDS-related deaths had exceeded 41,000. *San Diego Update,* which covered the Los Angeles beat, carried an obituary

section illustrated with photos, mostly of AIDS casualties in their thirties and forties. As one reader recalls, "It got to the point where you opened the paper with a knot in your stomach because you didn't know who was dead."[22]

Death was as visible on the streets as in the papers. John Morgan Wilson remembers how, walking down Santa Monica Boulevard in the 1980s, "you would see homeless men dying of AIDS on the sidewalk. They couldn't pay their rent and got evicted." But AIDS did not distinguish between the rich and the poor. Within a few years, many of the most prominent, powerful, wealthy, and talented of the gay L.A. community were also dead or dying: the pillars of MECLA and the board of directors of the Gay and Lesbian Community Center—Sheldon Andelson, Rob Eichberg, Peter Scott, Judge Rand Schrader, Duke Comegys; Scott Forbes, the Disco King; Paul Monette, a National Book Award winner; the up-and-coming writers Gil Cuadros and Steven Corbin; the artist Mundo Meza. A whole generation of leaders of gay L.A., as well as their presumed inheritors, were disappearing.

The pain and pang of it all were especially apparent at a Hollywood performance of *The Normal Heart,* Larry Kramer's play about AIDS. John Morgan Wilson says that when he turned around in his seat in the theater and looked back, he saw, in the glimmer of the stage lights, dozens of I.V. poles holding bags of intravenous medicine that dripped into the veins of patients who were sitting in the audience. "They came to see this play pulling their I.V. units on wheels," he recalls. "It was about them."[23]

AN ARMY TO FIGHT AGAINST AIDS

We were loud and rude. . . . We didn't fit the MECLA mold at all.

—Bruce Mirken, AIDS activist and journalist[24]

Even in the war against AIDS, internal struggles arose. The government response to AIDS seemed hopelessly inadequate in the face of the mounting toll of suffering, and some gay people insisted that what was required now was not simply fund-raising and grieving but grassroots

militancy. They feared that the nonprofit power structure—dominated by MECLA types who hoped to work within the system—was not angry enough and not effective enough in the battle. In 1986, an external threat in the form of a hostile ballot proposition crystallized for them the conviction that "loud and rude" was a more appropriate response to the enemy than the "MECLA mold's" well-modulated tones.[25]

Right-wing politicians had hoped that AIDS, which they imagined as a "gay plague," would be a wedge to help them turn back gay rights once and for all. In California, the furthest extremist among them, Lyndon La Rouche, introduced a 1986 ballot measure that made John Briggs' initiative look downright gay-friendly. La Rouche's Proposition 64 called for mandatory HIV testing, barred exposed Californians from working with children or food, and, most terrifying, raised the specter of quarantine relocation camps for those found to be HIV-infected. (An Orange County congressman who endorsed the initiative vowed to expand on La Rouche's idea by making it a federal crime for infected persons to kiss.)[26] Despite the efforts of Hollywood celebrities such as Elizabeth Taylor, early polls indicated that La Rouche could win by a wide margin. Torie Osborn (the young lesbian who was to become executive director of the Gay and Lesbian Community Services Center two years later) was hired to run a Southern California "No on 64" office and, with David Mixner, to plan a media campaign against the proposition. Affluent L.A. gays donated $3 million to the campaign.[27]

But, as the journalist Bruce Mirken recalls, other gay people whose approach was very different from that of the No on 64 campaign office now decided that it was "time to wake up and get involved." They formed a coalition that distributed 60,000 fliers in gay bars and neighborhoods across L.A. calling for a protest at La Rouche's headquarters. More than 4,000 people joined their march, invading the streets of L.A.'s quiet Atwater Village. (La Rouche, who promoted the slogan "Spread panic, not AIDS," denounced the march itself as a "public health threat.")[28] The combined efforts of the No on 64 campaign and those who took to the streets of Atwater helped to defeat the proposition by a huge margin: 71 percent to 29 percent. The street-fight against La Rouche provided the momentum and model for a new style in the AIDS war.

Following the victory over La Rouche, the Stop AIDS Quarantine Committee, a group that had been formed by Michael Weinstein and Chris Brownlie as part of the March-on-Atwater coalition, turned to other compelling AIDS problems. Weinstein and Brownlie, old comrades from the Lavender and Red Union, called a public hearing that addressed the County's failure to provide decent AIDS health care. More than a third of L.A.'s HIV-infected population relied on the Los Angeles County–USC Hospital, where the grim clinic was known only as "5P21" for its room number. Patients were forced to wait up to six weeks for an appointment at County. In the interim, they went untreated; some died.[29]

At the Stop AIDS Quarantine Committee hearing, hundreds of people got up to speak, and the meeting, which started in the morning, lasted well into evening. In the midst of their testimonies, Chris Brownlie was suddenly flattened by an attack of pneumonia and was rushed to the hospital. For three days, he lay on a gurney in a hallway because no room was available. Only a plea from Michael Weinstein to Supervisor Edelman finally got Brownlie into a hospital room. Weinstein had grown from a youthful radical to an admirer of Sheldon Andelson's expert politicking. Now, however, he realized that gay political circumstances had changed yet again. He saw clearly that "AIDS was so horrifying, and the treatment of AIDS patients was so horrifying, that rubbing elbows wasn't going to cut it."[30]

What would cut it—he and many others came to believe—was a response that was tailored to the times and the dire crisis of the epidemic. AIDS activism required a high-impact form of organized protest, backed by complex political strategy: It had to be forceful, intelligent, and most of all it had to convey the urgency of the situation. Such massive, enraged, and organized civil disobedience was on display in 1987 at the March on Washington, a national protest with a sizable Los Angeles contingent. The march included a same-sex wedding of hundreds of couples on the steps of the U.S. Supreme Court, followed by a group arrest of dozens protesting federal homophobia. But it was the blunt signs and rude day-glo stickers of an organization recently formed in New York, the AIDS Coalition to Unleash Power, that provided a new

blueprint for the grief-stricken and the angry. "The Government Has Blood on Its Hands!" the stickers read. "You Say Don't Fuck. We Say Fuck You!" And next to a picture of President Reagan, "He Kills Me." John Fall recalls seeing the New Yorkers' signs and thinking instantly, "Oh, how obvious. That's what we're going to do!"[31] He was not alone in that epiphany. Another Angeleno who was present at the march, Mark Kostopoulos, of the gay socialist group Lavender Left, began organizing ACT UP/LA the minute he returned to Los Angeles.

Like the Gay Liberation Front nearly twenty years earlier, ACT UP spread to dozens of cities. Los Angeles formed the second-largest group of this decentralized and autonomous movement. In contrast to AIDS Project Los Angeles, ACT UP/LA had no interest in quiet political diplomacy. Instead, with playful media mastery it promoted open expressions of fury about AIDS and how little was being done to end it.

Kostopoulos and the Lavender Left notified local gay groups that they would be holding a "Town Hall Meeting to Beat AIDS."[32] Hundreds of people braved a torrential downpour to attend.[33] The group's tone was emphatically angry, and its thrust was emphatically activist. Michael Weinstein demanded "an army to fight against AIDS." From the outset, the group based its strategy on a firmly progressive analysis of the epidemic: For example, the organization proclaimed that AIDS disproportionately affects poor men and women of color, and they called for a free, nationalized health care system.[34] Kostopoulos charged that the government was "prolonging and creating the AIDS crisis."[35] ACT UP/LA would attack not only the medical and drug industry profiteering, which it derisively called "AIDS, Inc.," but also every level of government for its "inadequate and harmful" response.[36] Though the members were nearly all gay, ACT UP/LA was *not* to be a gay activist group. John Fall remembers that the distinction was clear: "Our focus was on AIDS–and we were gay."

ACT UP/LA stopped traffic on the streets and ambushed bureaucrats in spectacular actions. The group seemed to operate by raw passion. As one veteran described the experience of working in ACT UP/LA, it was "an adrenaline rush that lasted for nearly four years."[37] But passion was balanced by strategic discipline and a fine ability to coolly negotiate

complex budgets with government bureaucracies. ACT UP was a movement of *organized* outrage, deliberately nonviolent. Guile and cheekiness were among its methods. For example, gay men and lesbians in ACT UP/LA dressed up as heterosexual couples and infiltrated a Catholic prayer breakfast. At the right moment—when Archbishop Roger Mahoney, who had been denouncing safe sex, stepped up to the microphone—the ACT UPers shouted "Hypocrite!" and "Murderer!" and kept shouting until they were dragged out of the dining room by aging Knights of Columbus.

The cheek had great charm for the participants. But Craig Collins recalls that "anger was at all times seething below the surface."[38] "We all knew people who were simply dying," says John Fall. "The sense was, because we're gay, they're gonna let us all die." Those in ACT UP could not fail to be mindful that every minute counted. The doctrinaire aspects of Lavender Left dissolved quickly. When meetings stretched into four-hour debates and those attending were "held hostage by these ideological discussions about socialism, we just wouldn't tolerate it," John Fall remembers. Frustrated with the cautious bureaucratese of AIDS agencies, they chose a course of direct action. "The organization would not be what it said, but what it did," says Peter Cashman, who termed the group "a new beast" in activism.

The impatience of ACT UP/LA members, many of whom were HIV positive, drove them to master the most effective methods to get their message out. "We got professional very quickly," says Fall, who wrote the group's press releases. Entertainment industry professionals aided their efforts. For instance, for eight months after his diagnosis, Steven Kolzak, the casting agent responsible for the hit television show *Cheers,* had kept silent about his medical condition, but after the death of a producer friend who never mentioned that he had AIDS, Kolzak became part of ACT UP and went public, even to speaking out in middle-America's *TV Guide.*[39] ACT UPers also learned that the drama of civil disobedience was very effective in helping the organization attract desired media attention, and that arrests practically guaranteed a spot on television news. They also learned that cameras provided protection from police abuse.

Initially, some had feared being arrested at ACT UP protests because of the stigma of a police record and the trauma they associated with incarceration. But when they learned that a bail fund and volunteer attorneys would help ACT UP members get quick release, more and more members began to volunteer to be carted off to the station. When John Fall was merely cited rather than arrested, "everyone's reaction was, 'Oh, you just got a citation?'"[40] Many ACT UPers let themselves be arrested because they felt they had nothing to lose. "We all thought we were dead men anyway. That makes it very easy for you to risk your life in front of a policeman," recalls Gunther Freehill.[41]

ACT UP members developed a distinct sartorial aesthetic: leather jackets, Doc Marten boots, black jeans, and among the most daring, the new fad of piercings. Their tough-guy style sometimes had an amusing effect: During one jailhouse stay, ACT UPers were asked by other inmates, "When did you join the Silent Death gang?" It took a few moments for them to understand that, because they were all wearing "Silence = Death" T-shirts of pink and black, they'd been perceived as a new Los Angeles gang, complete with colors.

Many in ACT UP were suffering from various stages of the disease; some had never been tested or were asymptomatic. Nevertheless, they all shared a wordless sense of destiny. Those who were uninfected often claimed, when they were arrested in actions, to be HIV positive in solidarity with the infected. If they felt dispossessed by their government, they felt all the more connected to one another. When comrades were released from jail, ACT UPers threw parties. When comrades died, ACT UPers stopped traffic with political funerals, holding signs that read "Murdered by Government Indifference." They exhorted one another to bravery and wrote of their battles in heroic terms, as did the male-to-female transgender "AIDS diva" Connie Norman, who was dying of AIDS.

She urged her fellow warriors:

> Someday this plague will be over and we will survive as a people to tell the tales. Don't forget to tell how much we honored life. Don't forget to tell how hard many of us have fought for it. Life is and has always been

precious to us and our community's response to this plague proves it. . . . Remember our heroes and heroines.[42]

GETTING HEARD

It was a branded presence. You knew something very different was going on here; a very different notion of what political activism can be.

—Craig Collins on ACT UP's Coffee Pot Brigade in the Gay Pride Parade[43]

Christopher Street West, the organization sponsoring L.A.'s gay pride parade, did not know what hit it. After contingents of lesbian and gay business and professional groups, politicians waving from convertibles, sound trucks pulsating with dance music, and oiled boys grinding in swimsuits, a new contingent marched. Its message was neither bland nor sexy, and it was causing a huge stir at the 1989 parade. "The reactions," recalls one marcher, "ranged from drunken disco queens being completely flabbergasted to people jumping in to join us."[44] Contrary to Christopher Street West rules, ACT UP had simply attached itself to an accommodating group. It had not registered or submitted its controversial message for approval. Among the palms framing Santa Monica Boulevard, two men bore a smartly painted black banner shaped like a giant funeral ribbon; its shocking pink inscription read, "Wake Up and Smell the Coffee!" Directly behind that, an eight-foot white Chippendale coffee pot danced like a surreal Disney character, its own banner announcing, "Homophobia Is Brewing!" Behind these heralds, from out of mammoth coffee cups, loomed huge portraits. One, of L.A. Sheriff Sherman Block, carried the slogan "Arrested Equals Tested," which reflected the proposed legislation he was backing. Over the portrait of a known homophobe, Pete Schabarum, the L.A. County supervisor, was stenciled the word "GUILTY!" Holding chrome percolators and wearing their "Silence = Death" T-shirts, the ACT UP contingent marched. Each expertly crafted prop was the labor of movie- and television-studio professionals: graphic designers, lighting designers, costumers, artists. ACT UP roared like a flood down the main drag of Boystown.

The media strategy and artistry that was the daily bread of many local activists became one of the most powerful weapons in ACT UP/L.A.'s arsenal. The subversive artists who created the "Coffee Pot Brigade" knew well how to make statements that would grab the attention of the media. They even sang—as when responding to Archbishop Roger Mahony's proclamation in 1989 that young people should avoid "being trapped into the 'safe-sex' myth," which, he said, "is both a lie and a fraud."[45] On the same December day that ACT UP/New York made headlines by disrupting a mass in St. Patrick's Cathedral, ACT UP/LA unleashed an action titled "Slice Mahony's Baloney." Dressed in red-and-white cassocks, their cheeks rouged, tinseled halos wobbling over their heads, they visited five cathedrals in Los Angeles. They gleefully mocked Catholic demands for lifelong celibacy among homosexuals by dubbing themselves "the Altered Boys." They waited for parishioners to enter or leave the cathedrals, then burst into parodies of hymns and carols, such as one sung to the tune of "We Three Kings":

We Gay Queens of Hollywood are
Bearing condoms, O yes we are.
Vine and Fountain, Magic Mountain,
Schlepping from bar to bar.

The action proceeded peacefully, except for a parishioner at Good Shepherd Cathedral in Beverly Hills who punched a protestor. News coverage was substantial. It was also, as Craig Collins, who coordinated the media, recalls, "the first positive treatment of anything ACT UP." He explained to one reporter, who was puzzled about the group's stridency, "These people are going to die." Collins says that he still remembers "the look on her face as she got that." And, he adds, "it showed up in her story."[46]

Not everything that AIDS activists promoted, however, was tinsel and carols, though to protect ACT UP, individuals who inflicted property damage to make a symbolic point claimed to be representing "independent affinity groups." Days before the "Mahony's Baloney" action, four L.A. Roman Catholic churches were splattered with red paint and plas-

tered with posters labeling the archbishop a murderer. "Greater Religious Responsibility" took credit for the action. Religious officials and authorities immediately denounced the vandalism, which ACT UP denied having a hand in—while also voicing sympathy with the vandals via its spokesperson Helene Schpak, who told the *Los Angeles Times,* "We believe any [action] is appropriate to protest a policy of death."[47]

Another "affinity group" briefly halted the 1990 Rose Parade when activists brandished a banner that read "Emergency—Stop the Parade—70,000 Dead from AIDS," which was flashed on television worldwide. Though such actions were never officially connected to ACT UP, they potently embodied one of the group's infamous day-glo sticker philosophies: "We're ACT UP. Fuck you."

ACT UP/LA achieved a significant victory in getting the County to take seriously the need to put energy and dollars into improving public health care for AIDS patients. This did not happen overnight. With the growing number of newly diagnosed AIDS cases, many of them nonwhite and uninsured, a gruesome health care apartheid developed. In a *Los Angeles Times* editorial, activists had denounced the shockingly inadequate facilities at County Hospital for people with AIDS:

> People with temperatures of 103 or higher sit for hours on hard wooden benches waiting for help. Some receive chemotherapy in crowded hallways, vomiting in bags. Others in the same hallways, stripped to the waist, have IVs hooked to their arms.[48]

Duly shamed, the L.A. County Board of Supervisors voted to improve AIDS care at County Hospital, but progress was glacial.[49] To goad them into action, activists held a weeklong vigil, setting up a tent city where protestors slept overnight and demonstrated during the day. They constructed an ongoing mock AIDS ward outside the hospital gates: Some activists dressed as doctors; others, many genuinely ill, lay on cots, and they acted out the horror of the disease. Demanding a fifty-bed AIDS

ward and treatment that would be equal to what was available for the affluent, activists braved cold and rain. Connie Norman, the earthy, opinionated male-to-female transsexual, finagled the donation of a trailer in which she heated gallons of soup to keep protestors warm and fed. At one of the daily rallies, Chris Brownlie, the man who three years earlier had languished on a gurney in a hallway inside the nearby building, stepped up to the podium. Bruce Mirken recalls Brownlie as a powerful speaker who built to an electrifying crescendo: "'It's not about the T cells, the fevers, the day-to-day struggles,' Chris said. Then he burst into this scream. 'It's about caring! And the policy of the County is not to care!'"[50]

Near the end of the vigil, Supervisor Ed Edelman appeared before the crowd and offered cautious encouragement. It had been Edelman who steered millions of public dollars toward gay health care for nearly two decades, but his past helpfulness could not stand him in good stead among this outraged crowd. To these impatient activists, his speech was "pathetically wishy-washy." They booed him offstage. Edelman appeared shocked;[51] he had not understood that with this generation of activists, old alliances carried little weight. (Despite the crowd's hostility, Edelman continued his support. He arranged for County funding that would help Weinstein's new AIDS Hospice Foundation; its first facility was named the Chris Brownlie Hospice.)

Because of ACT UP's rowdy persona and insistence on action over talk, it found itself largely shunned by L.A.'s gay political elite. "MECLA, which set the agenda in the L.A. gay community, was opposed to ACT UP,"[52] recalls Peter Cashman. So was *Frontiers*, the largest local gay publication, which refused to cover the activities of ACT UP. But by 1989, the epidemic had become so bad that diverse groups within the gay community finally realized that, as Rita Gonzales says, "my group/your group didn't seem right." Rank-and-file activists and leaders of the gay establishment finally converged in a demonstration at the Federal Building. The huge mob was fiercely determined to send a message to the feds, who had been dragging their feet on issues such as safe-sex education and compassionate early approval of drugs. They created a cacophony of drumming and banging, ear-splitting whistles, and the incessant

shouting of "Shut it down!" "No business as usual!" Eighty activists volunteered to be arrested: Among them were the Reverend Troy Perry, a veteran of many arrests; Torie Osborn, now director of the Gay and Lesbian Community Services Center; Gil Gerard, director of the Minority AIDS Project; and the *Frontiers* publisher, Bob Craig.

Federal officers wore latex gloves, plastic shields over their faces, and panicked expressions. Terrified, they roughly dragged the eighty activists into custody. Perry said that in twenty years of activism, he'd never experienced such brutal treatment. But the protestors could not be daunted. One told a reporter, "I'm about to get arrested, and I'm a little afraid. But I'm willing to get arrested because I'm more afraid of doing nothing."[53] While the officers, wearing their protective latex gloves, manhandled them, the arrestees kept chanting, "Your gloves don't match your shoes!"[54]

NOT JUST WHITE GAY MEN

> *It's the radicals who change history, like the suffragette who was killed by the racehorse. I want to live my life that way. The exhilaration of it. That's the kind of life I had in ACT UP.*
>
> —Cyndy Crogan, lesbian member of ACT UP[55]

West Hollywood became one of the most AIDS-proactive cities in the nation because its local government and its large gay population were willing to support services. But West Hollywood remained Boystown, which helped fueled perceptions that AIDS was a gay white male disease. The medical truth was far different, but it was slow to be widely recognized. It was not until 1991, when Magic Johnson declared he would retire from the Los Angeles Lakers basketball team because he was infected with HIV, that the myth of AIDS as a gay white disease substantially eroded. Johnson's revelation reverberated—as the *Los Angeles Times* observed—everywhere: "in playgrounds, health clinics, the offices of activists, and [to] government figures in Washington, D.C." The telephones at AIDS clinics all over Southern California were flooded with calls from people suddenly wanting an HIV test.[56]

The need for AIDS care facilities was great in L.A.'s vast communities of color, located primarily east of La Brea and south of Olympic, in areas where the populations were poor and less likely to have private health insurance. By 1992, almost 40 percent of all the AIDS cases that were reported countywide were Latinos or African Americans. And that official statistic did not reflect the large number of infected people who would not reveal their illness because of cultural stigma or the fear of deportation if they were undocumented immigrants.[57] Over time, as infection rates soared among people of color, AIDS service institutions were opened in their communities. But there was no established model of care specific to them; as the founder of the AIDS clinic in Watts concluded: "What's good for West Hollywood doesn't necessarily work for South-Central" (an African American district). Gay activists of color organized to serve their specific communities. The Minority AIDS Project, the first and largest community-based black gay AIDS organization, was founded by the Reverend Carl Bean of Unity Fellowship of Christ Church. Bienestar, the HIV service agency for Latinos, soon spread to locations in such diverse areas as El Monte, Van Nuys, Wilmington, Hollywood, San Bernardino, and Boyle Heights. In response to the high incidence of the disease among L.A.'s nonwhite plurality, ACT UP began publishing its newsletter in Spanish and established the People of Color Caucus.

About 10 percent of ACT UP/LA activists were lesbians.[58] Almost none were infected, but they came to the organization for the same reasons that lesbians had joined AIDS Project Los Angeles and other AIDs groups—because of a sense of "the unfairness of genocide,"[59] because "you begin to appreciate people when you might lose them,"[60] because of a desire to be helpful amidst the devastation. Many had been caregivers for gay male friends with AIDS or had worked professionally with AIDS patients. (As Torie Osborn observes, the number of lesbians in health care has always been astronomical: "When straight nurses didn't want to work in AIDS wards, lesbian nurses did it," she says. "They *wanted* to do it.")[61]

Robin Podolsky, a performance artist and writer, had been active in the mainstream feminist movement, but with the advent of the epidemic, her perspective changed: "I took the straight world's response to AIDS personally, their terrible indifference and smugness," she explains. "I knew if it were lesbians who had AIDS, straight women [in the feminist movement] would feel indifferent, too. My allegiance shifted." She was among the ACT UP/LA members who participated in the huge vigil and campout at County Hospital to protest that one of the biggest hospitals in the world couldn't give adequate AIDS care to the poor; with other ACT UP members she took over the Federal Building and was one of the eighty dragged off to jail; and she devoted her writing and art to AIDS causes.[62] Much rarer in ACT UP was a lesbian member such as Mary Lucey, who says she came to ACT UP because she had been diagnosed as HIV positive and her doctor told her that she had only thirteen months to live. Lucey recalls that when the facilitator asked at the first meeting she attended who had the disease, she was the only woman in the room to raise her hand.[63]

Other lesbians became active in ACT UP not only because they wished to help gay men with AIDS but also because they had been won over by ACT UP's willingness to make coalitions with other progressive causes and protest groups, such as abortion clinic defense.[64] The lesbians admired ACT UP's style and believed they could learn important methods from the passionate ACT UPers. Cyndy Crogan, who was an activist with Fired Up For Choice, a predominantly lesbian organization that fought against right-wingers who were blockading access to abortion clinics, says she first learned of ACT UP when she worked by the side of ACT UP members. "That's my tribe over there," she thought as she watched ACT UP's "radical approach at clinic hits."

Among the ACT UP men, Crogan observed a haughty "sense of entitlement," a "male characteristic" about which lesbian feminists had been bitterly critical. But Crogan says that the ACT UP men's feeling of entitlement soon empowered her, too: "I was swept up with it. I became part of their power. I learned how to claim power myself." She liked it, also, she says, that ACT UPers merged playfulness with serious structure. "I learned from ACT UP the incredible planning that needs to go

into anything that comes off well. It's so organized, like a corporation." Crogan says that her years in ACT UP taught her that a group cannot be effective without a sense of urgency, and she has applied it to her lesbian political work, such as organizing a Los Angeles Dyke March: "From ACT UP men I learned to oppose having 'crowd control' in the Dyke March. It's too engraved in women to be nice. Until women get angry, they won't be free. That's what the men taught me."[65]

Women assumed leadership roles in ACT UP through their own initiative, but also through the inexorable loss of men. Mark Kostopoulos, the founding member who became so identified with ACT UP, chose Helene Schpak to be his successor, and it was she who ultimately facilitated more than half the meetings. The women had learned from the examples of ACT UPers, and they were as brash as the boys—for instance, burning Bibles in a portable barbecue near a clinic to distract and taunt Operation Rescue volunteers.[66] ACT UP women also had their own muscle and could be fearless hand-to-hand combatants. At one abortion clinic action, Helene Schpak recalls, Mary Lucey and her partner Nancy McNiel had just entered an elevator with two men from Operation Rescue who began to push the women belligerently just as the doors were closing. Schpak, witnessing that bit of the scene, raced upstairs to help Lucey and McNiel. When the doors opened, she says, "the guys were on the floor. Those two women had beat the crap out of them!"[67]

Despite the horrors of the plague, gay progress did not cease. L.A. saw a mass exit from the closet of those who were infected ("mainly because they had nothing to lose," the writer David Ehrenstein noted).[68] Widespread homophobia was much less possible once it became clear to heterosexuals that beloved friends and relatives were gay and needed help in their fight against AIDS. Los Angeles did eventually rise to the terrible challenge of the epidemic, thanks in good part to the work of groups such as AIDS Project Los Angeles and ACT UP/LA. Dave Johnson, who had been active in the Studio One boycott and was openly HIV positive, was appointed the city's first AIDS coordinator. Michael Weinstein's

group, which had begun as the Stop AIDS Quarantine Committee and became the AIDS Healthcare Foundation, received monetary support from the City of Los Angeles and Los Angeles County, as well as from the federal government; this support helped the foundation evolve into a huge provider of AIDS care services, with clinics not only in the West but also in Africa and Mexico.

Some ACT UP/LA activists became "suits," getting jobs with non-profits or government AIDS organizations. They carried over a sense of urgency into the realm of bureaucracy. Occasional old associates worried that as "suits" they would sell out to "AIDS, Inc"; but those like Gunther Freehill, who became an administrator with the Los Angeles County Office of AIDS Programs and Policy, say their past activism in fiercely radical groups such as ACT UP gave them a militant resolve that will forever inform everything they do on behalf of people with AIDS.[69]

Former T.V. star Sheila Kuehl became the first openly gay state legislator in California. Kuehl pioneered a law to protect gay students. *Courtesy Sheila Kuehl.*

CHAPTER 12

Stunning Comebacks

If there is a place that seems like home and heart, it's San Francisco. New York is mind. And Los Angeles is power and politics.

—National gay movement historian, John D'Emilio, 1993[1]

GAY ANGELENOS had become expert in waging massive protests over AIDS issues, and their honed skills were put to spectacular use in subsequent political battles. In September 1991, Pete Wilson, the Republican governor of California, vetoed Assembly Bill 101, which would have outlawed job discrimination against homosexuals. "We were betrayed," Laurie McBride, a gay rights lobbyist in Sacramento, complained. "Before he was elected, Pete Wilson looked me right in the eye and said he would help craft a bill that he would sign. He's reneged."[2] The governor claimed that AB101 would be burdensome to small businesses because it would impose excessive regulation. Gay L.A., after years of weathering the brutal AIDS war, was in no mood to be put off by such an absurd excuse. The dramatic fury of the gay community became, according to Wilson's aide, Dan Schnur, "one of the single biggest frustrations of the first two years [of Wilson's governorship]."[3]

The flashpoint for the fury was Rob Roberts of Queer Nation, who had been fasting until AB101 would be made law. He had set up a camp he called "Queer Village" in a West Hollywood park, and other activists

joined him nightly. When news of Wilson's veto broke, the crowd that had already been building at Queer Village took to the streets. Within hours, word had spread all over Los Angeles, and, despite the city's handicap of its vast sprawl, massive demonstrations began. Hoards of protestors eventually descended not only on West Hollywood, Beverly Hills, and Silver Lake, but also on the San Fernando Valley, Anaheim, and at the Los Angeles International Airport, where they took over a runway. For seventeen days, night after night, gay men and women congregated to stage protests throughout the Los Angeles Basin. Protests also broke out in cities up and down the state, but the L.A. response was described as "the most massive and sustained civil unrest in California since the 1960s."[4]

As many as 50,000 gay people came out of their various exclusionary niches of class, gender, race, political affiliation[5]—and again banded together against an external enemy. "We hit the streets, leaderless. It was one of those times when the situation catalyzes everyone. People showed up that we'd never seen before," the veteran lesbian activist Robin Podolsky recalls.[6] Members of the Log Cabin Republicans shouted their protests alongside the pierced radicals of Queer Nation and the United Lesbians of African Heritage and the Stonewall Democratic Club. "I remember us chanting on Santa Monica Boulevard, 'Out of the gyms and into the streets,'" recalls Michael du Plessis of Queer Nation. To the astonished delight of the protestors, gay people did pour out the gyms, and even out of the bars.[7]

In Boystown, gays burned Governor Wilson in effigy. In the Silver Lake district, people emerged from their houses and cheered the demonstrators on. On the fourth night of the demonstrations, they brought their protests downtown to the Ronald Reagan State Building, where a protestor shattered a heavy glass door and the LAPD SWAT Team was called out. When in the midst of the nightly demonstrations the foolhardy governor appeared in Los Angeles for a Republican fundraiser at the County Art Museum, thousands of demonstrators surrounded the building, chanting "Pete Wilson, you fucking weasel! Come out and face the people!" They sat on the street, intoning "Aaaahhh," an eerie mantra and war cry right in the middle of traffic-heavy Wilshire Boulevard. They followed the governor to the Plaza Hotel in Century

City, where the police in full riot gear were called in and, clubs in hand, moved down on them.

Many were beaten and arrested. (The police actions at the Century Plaza Hotel led to the largest gay-and-lesbian class action suit ever against the police department.)[8] But the L.A. gay community had already experienced beatings and arrests in AIDS protests, and they were less flappable than virgin demonstrators might have been. They had both passion and sangfroid, as Cyndy Crogan, who participated in AIDS demonstrations as well as the AB 101 protests, suggests: "I thought then, 'If my life ends right here, in this action, what better way to die. That's when life means the most.'"[9]

They had also learned methods from militant AIDS campaigns, and the seeming disorder of the protestors had its own logic. For instance, Jehan Agrama, who was president of the media watch organization, Gay & Lesbian Alliance Against Defamation (GLAAD), explains that groups worked in tandem: "Queer Nation would be invasive and rude. GLAAD would just stand quietly handing out fliers. The effect was great."[10] Though the protests were ostensibly leaderless, they were far from disorganized. The switchboard of the Gay and Lesbian Community Services Center spread the word daily about the changing locations of the nightly demonstrations.[11] The Center also provided a truck and an amp system from which speakers would rally the community. ACT UP sent trained legal observers out to note instances of police brutality.[12] The protestors knew well how to use the media. As the police were descending aggressively on them at the Century Plaza Hotel, Jehan Agrama grabbed a microphone and sang, "We are a gay and gentle people, singing, singing for our lives." Television cameras zoomed in, the police were confused and fell back, and the demonstrators took the opportunity to regroup.[13]

The AB 101 demonstrations became a symbol of some pride to L.A. gay activists, who, as Torie Osborn observes, had been irritated because Los Angeles had not been given the respect it merited as a political force among gays nationally. But with the 1991 L.A. protests, she says, "the baton moved." Gays in Los Angeles such as Osborn credit their seventeen days of protest with persuading Governor Wilson to look again at

the problem of job discrimination.[14] The following year, Wilson reconsidered his veto, signing into law a similar version of a gay rights bill. "The gay community is an extremely potent force politically and is taken extremely seriously," Dan Schnur, the governor's aide, conceded.[15]

MAKING THE MEDIA BEHAVE

We're here to tell you how to do it better. This is how we prefer to be called: not "avowed homosexual," but "gay" or "lesbian"; not "AIDS victim" but "person with AIDS."

—Jehan Agrama, co-chair of GLAAD,
in 1990s meetings with the news media[16]

From the beginning, the entertainment industry, fueled by gay talent and surrounded by a gay culture, kept its truths secret and promulgated lies in films when it mentioned homosexuality at all. It was rarely challenged. In 1980, the Alliance of Gay and Lesbian Artists (AGLA) was founded as a support group for actors struggling to be part of the gay movement while employed in the industry. They became early media watchdogs, issuing criticism for negative portrayals of gays and publicly offering awards for positive ones—to Cher who played a lesbian in *Silkwood,* to *Hill Street Blues* for addressing the plight of a gay policeman, to Phil Donahue for his sympathetic discussions about homosexuality. Julie Harris and Alan Bates presented awards at AGLA's annual gala, which filled the Huntington-Hartford Theater.[17] The group's watchdog role, however, conflicted with the members' careers as workers in the industry. Chris Uszler, who had been the executive director of the organization, recalls that AGLA fell apart because many members were reluctant to be confrontational with Hollywood executives from whom they might be seeking employment.[18] But in the next years a variety of gay L.A. groups began to tackle Hollywood. Their agitation finally succeeded in raising consciousness and conscience in the industry.

The worst fears of members of the Alliance of Gay and Lesbian Artists—that producers and directors would not hire them if they openly agitated for homosexual concerns—were somewhat eased when

producers and directors themselves became founding members of Hollywood Supports, an organization dedicated to reversing discrimination against gays in the entertainment industry. Established in 1992 by the former Fox chairman, Barry Diller, and the MCA president, Sidney Sheinberg, Hollywood Supports attracted prominent Hollywood power brokers such as David Geffen.[19] With such clout on their side, a network of gay and lesbian industry employees could finally persuade Hollywood to declare support aloud. All the major guilds, agencies, and studios (including the conservative Fox as well as Disney, which suffered a three-year Southern Baptist boycott for its new policies) were soon offering domestic partner benefits for gay and lesbian employees.

Other groups also formed in the late 1980s and early '90s to call Hollywood to conscience. The usual gay L.A. split between fiery radicals who wanted to take it to the streets and the A-Gays who wanted to play power politics emerged again in the Hollywood battle. But, as Jehan Agrama observes, both sides understood the global impact of what the industry wrought, and both sides had the same goal—to make Hollywood change. Their difference in approach became a kind of strength: Together they played good cop/bad cop.

Jehan Agrama, a lesbian producer, and Richard Jennings, a gay attorney for Paramount Studios, both quit their jobs and devoted their energies to the Los Angeles Gay & Lesbian Alliance Against Defamation, founded in 1989.[20] Agrama and Jennings demanded meetings with Hollywood executives and media representatives, presented their impressive credentials as members of the entertainment industry, and said that GLAAD was willing to "educate." Had the times not been right, they might not have gotten past the door to begin with. But years of gay movement progress had made the times right.

Agrama says the news media began calling GLAAD to discuss coverage of stories about gay people. Jay Leno told Barbara Walters on a television special that he would not do humor that was offensive to gays and lesbians, and he consulted with GLAAD about whether certain jokes were "appropriate."[21] GLAAD also took out ads in the *Hollywood Reporter* and *Variety* in the form of "open letters" that called Hollywood to task. When *Basic Instinct,* a movie about a lesbian serial killer, was being filmed in 1991,

GLAAD protested that "while none of us supports censorship, we are tired of having the diversity of our lives censored by the media." The organization demanded that Hollywood portray real-life lesbian and gay images rather than noxious sensationalism.[22] Their protest did not stop the filming, but it garnered GLAAD international support and, as its star Sharon Stone told Barbara Walters, as much publicity as the film itself got.[23]

The Los Angeles Queer Nation's approach was very different from that of GLAAD. Queer Nation prided itself on being, as one member, Judy Sisneros, described it, a "small, broke, rowdy group of queer activists."[24] They had learned through the examples of AIDS activism how to use the media to call attention to their cause and get their message out. They, too, felt provoked in the early 1990s when "the stuff coming out of Hollywood was really indefensible," Queer National Michael du Plessis recalls.[25] In 1992, they invaded the 6:00 A.M. Oscar nominations press conference and handed out fliers with their blunt messages. The press leapt at the chance to talk to radical queer activists, hoping for sensationalistic stories about which movie stars were hiding in the closet.[26] "Gay Groups Plan an Oscar 'Outing,'" *New York Newsday* proclaimed, explaining in terms calculated to titillate, "Shouting 'FIRE' in a crowded theater may not be protected free speech, but some radical gay activists believe shouting 'dyke' and 'queer' at actors reputed to be gay during next Monday's Oscar telecast is."[27] Queer Nation threatened that as part of its "Stop Hollywood Homophobia" action they would storm the stage at the Dorothy Chandler Pavilion, where the Academy Awards were being held. Even major newspapers delightedly ran front-page stories with headlines such as "Angry Gay and Lesbian Activists Plan to Upstage Oscar Tonight."[28]

As the stars strolled down the red carpet the evening of the awards, Queer Nation members sat down on the street outside the Dorothy Chandler Pavilion and chanted: "We're not here to educate. / We're here to ruin your date."[29] Mounted police immediately surrounded them. Queer Nation hoped to gain worldwide attention for the cause by disrupting Hollywood's most glittering event, and they succeeded. Several were arrested, and the incident was covered by the media all over the planet.

That same year, the joint efforts of GLAAD and Queer Nation nipped in the bud plans for a Rush Limbaugh television talk show on CBS. Lim-

baugh's nationally syndicated radio programs were a thorn to gay people, who perceived him not only as a bigot but also a fomenter of violence against them. When Limbaugh was invited to L.A. to stand in for the television host Pat Sajak as a trial run for his own CBS talk show, GLAAD and Queer Nation, along with ACT UP, were ready for him. Dozens of members of the organizations managed to get seats in his audience. Queer Nation and ACT UP were planning to shout Limbaugh down. Before that could happen, Sylvia Rhue, a GLAAD board member who had planned just "to sit there and scowl and offer quiet passive resistance," found herself on national television when she uttered an objection to one of Limbaugh's antiwomen diatribes. "He came up and stuck a microphone in my face," she says. A shouting match ensued between them, the audience, packed by the three gay organizations, cheering Rhue on. "He couldn't handle me; he couldn't handle the crowd who was on my side. Limbaugh totally lost it." And he lost his television program because the gay groups had made him betray his inability to deal with a live and hostile audience.[30]

Like GLAAD, Queer Nation takes credit for helping to change Hollywood. "A lot happened as a result of our Oscar action and other protests," Judy Sisneros says. "Look at what the movies have produced over the last decade."[31] But the two groups were vital complements to one another. When the comic Andrew Dice Clay's gay-bashing concert film *Dice Rules* (distributed by Carolco Pictures, the same company that produced *Basic Instinct*) was being marketed, Queer Nation gathered on the Sunset Strip at 3:00 A.M. and defaced the Andrew Dice Clay billboard by throwing Christmas tree ornaments filled with enamel paint on it, scrawling the word "HOMOPHOBIA" over it, and disconnecting the electric lights that illuminated it.[32] GLAAD, in contrast, met with theater executives and explained their objections to the film.

But because the militants acted out in rowdy ways, Jehan Agrama says, it was easier for GLAAD, with its button-down style, to approach executives: "Would you rather do business with those guys or with us?" GLAAD representatives could imply. The desired end was achieved through double-barreled pressure. In this instance, GLAAD convinced the Loews Theaters chain, most of the United Artists chain, Cinemark,

and the American Multi-Cinema chain to refuse to screen the Andrew Dice Clay film. They succeeded in part because the radicals once again moved the center to the left: Queer Nation's unruly Sunset Strip action made GLAAD's polite demands that the theater chains boycott the film appear reasonable by contrast.

The metamorphosis in Hollywood that resulted from gay pressure was reflected throughout the 1990s in the GLAAD awards dinners. In 1991, Universal studio heads despaired when GLAAD announced that *Fried Green Tomatoes,* a movie that hinted at a lesbian love story, would be given the GLAAD Award for Best Film at the annual awards dinner. "They freaked out about it. This was one award they didn't want," Agrama says, since they thought that the film would lose revenue at the box office if it were widely acknowledged to be lesbian. But as the decade progressed, not only did the nominees show up for GLAAD's annual awards dinners but the studios began to buy out entire tables. The dinner has become a mini–Academy Awards, attracting celebrities such as Elizabeth Taylor, Carrie Fisher, Whoopie Goldberg, Sharon Stone, and Roseanne, and it raises more than $1 million for the organization.[33] It is produced by some of the best talent in the industry and held at places such as the Century Plaza Hotel (of AB 101–protest fame) and the Kodak Theater (which also hosts the maxi–Academy Awards). For an extra $1,000 donation to GLAAD, a dinner guest can share the cocktail hour with celebs.[34]

GIRLS RULE

> Republican leader in the California Legislature Jim Brulte: *"Sheila, one question. If you're a lesbian, how come all my guys like you so much?"*
>
> Assemblywoman from Los Angeles Sheila Kuehl: *"Discrimination demonizes the truly fabulous."*
>
> —First California State Assembly session of 1995.[35]

By the 1990s, many L.A. lesbians, whose predecessors had been silent in the 1950s and separatist in the 1970s, had taken a place at the larger gay community table. In part because the AIDS epidemic decimated so

much of the gay male leadership, lesbians even sat often at the table's head. They ran many of the major L.A. gay institutions, from the Gay and Lesbian Community Services Center,[36] where they served as executive directors as well as chairs of the board, to both of the gay synagogues, where they served as rabbis. Lesbian ascendancy is not peculiar to Los Angeles, of course, but since that city's population is so immense, there are probably more lesbians in prominent positions there than anywhere in the world.[37]

Their leadership has not been limited to the gay community. The women's movement too opened the door to high places, and the decrease in homophobia has meant that "out" lesbians might step in. They've represented Southern California in the legislature, and they've been appointed or elected judges and mayors and directors of city offices. Some of those who found themselves in prominent positions in the 1990s had been lesbian-feminist separatists twenty years earlier. A new era permitted them to carry what had once been radical feminist values into the Southern California "establishment"—where they no longer seemed so radical.

Renee Cowhig came to Los Angeles from Boston in 1973 to escape her rigid Irish Catholic working-class family. "I grew up in Boston," she says, "where the cops chip your teeth in the gay bars and toughs chase you around." In L.A., she joined the Women's Center and worked on the radical feminist newspaper *Sister.* With another lesbian feminist, Ariana Manov, she devised a program for women, including herself, to learn building-trade skills, and they received federal CETA funds to run the program. Their ambition was born out of the lesbian-feminist polemic arguing that gender should not be tied to career opportunities and that nontraditional jobs should be open to women. Cowhig made her reputation as a building and safety manager following the Northridge earthquake. Santa Monica hired her in 1994 to be the head of the Division of Maintenance and Management for the entire city, where she supervises 120 workers, mostly male, and is out as a lesbian. At Maintenance headquarters, she also runs an annual summer program, Rosie's Girls (the reference is to Rosie the Riveter), that is funded by the City of Los Angeles and incarnates her 1970s utopian dreams: to teach hundreds of adolescent females carpentry, welding, and electrician skills.[38]

Judy Abdo, an out lesbian who was elected to the Santa Monica City Council and then became mayor for two terms in the 1990s, believes that her successes were possible in Santa Monica because that town has long been "home to beatniks, hippies, Jane Fonda and Tom Hayden"; it was also "neighbor to the Church in Ocean Park, where at Sunday night dances in the '70s gays and straights would share the dance floor." Abdo's explanation for the liberality of the area is that "people who live life on the edge go for the edges of places. Santa Monica is the edge of the city, county, country. You go west and there's no place else to go." During her first term as mayor, Santa Monica even paid for her to attend the National Lesbian Conference in Atlanta. "It's that kind of city," she says.[39]

But neighboring L.A. has also become "that kind of city." The 1980s rise to judgeships of out gay men, such as Rand Schrader and Steve Lachs, was followed by the 1990s rise to judgeships of out lesbians. Stephanie Sautner, a former New York City police detective, came to Los Angeles to study law, joined the L.A. Gay and Lesbian Bar Association, and stayed, first becoming deputy city attorney and then, after Governor Wilson's veto of AB 101, deciding in outrage to run for judge as an openly lesbian candidate. She won her municipal court judicial bid in 1992 and later became a judge in the superior court. Rita Baird, who had also been a member of the Gay and Lesbian Bar Association, says that Judge Rand Schrader served as a mentor and model for her. Like him, she determined to be out in her legal career. Baird says that in Southern California it has been a "nonissue" in her advancement. Governor Gray Davis appointed her to the superior court, and her fellow judges elected her a court commissioner. The only way in which being an out gay woman has had significance, Baird says, is that "it is probably important for young lawyers' growth and development to know that the judge before them is a lesbian, and that she will do a good job and they will get a fair hearing."[40]

Since the 1990s, L.A. has also been represented in the California State Legislature by out lesbians. In 1994, Sheila Kuehl, a.k.a. Zelda Gilroy, one of the "loves of Dobie Gillis," became the first openly gay state assemblyperson. She had come out publicly in 1991 on *Good Morning, America; Entertainment Today;* and *Geraldo;* but when she announced her intention to run, three years later, *People* magazine headlined the

"scoop": "Zelda Jumps Out of the Closet and into a State Government Race." The sensationalism could not hurt her race in Southern California, even among her constituents who were not especially pro-gay, as she wryly tells:

> During the time of that campaign I was sitting in a Santa Monica restaurant and this big, burly guy comes barreling up to my table and bangs on it. He says, "Sheila, I hate all politicians, because they lie. I hate them all, except for you—because you've already told us the worst thing about yourself, so why would you lie about anything else?"[41]

Kuehl ran her first assembly race against six men, but her credentials as a law professor and the head attorney at the California Women's Law Center made the voters in her district, the west end of Los Angeles and the San Fernando Valley, pay attention. (That she had once been Zelda also helped in starstruck Southern California.) When one of her opponents suggested that she was not fit for office because she was a lesbian, his smear campaign backfired on him. "People find it distasteful if you're not talking about the issues," she says. She herself brought up her homosexuality whenever she thought it relevant to make a point: for example, "It's like the experience of my gay-and-lesbian community . . . talents being wasted, people being treated like outsiders." Polls showed that she won because the issues on which she ran—education, the environment, and public safety—mattered most to her constituency. In other districts, it is possible that she would not have done so well in 1994, despite her focus on the issues; but in her district, with its affluent and well-educated population, she received 20 percent more of the vote than her closest contender.

Kuehl says that although her sexual orientation was of no interest to her constituents, she feared that it might make a difference to her colleagues. On her first day in the legislature, a newly elected Christian conservative announced on the assembly floor, "I don't want to make a mistake. What do I call you, Ms. or Mr.?" But his hostile voice was in the minority. At lunch that day, she was approached by John Vasconcellas, Antonio Villaraigosa, Kevin Murray (an African American), and a half dozen other assemblymen, who told her, "We don't want you to eat

lunch by yourself, so we're gonna be the 'gay-and-lesbian caucus.'" She was voted the first-ever freshman chair of the California Assembly's judiciary committee, and, before her successful bid for the state senate in 2000, she became Speaker Pro Tem in the assembly.

Beginning with her second year in office, Kuehl had been introducing a bill to protect gay, lesbian, and transgendered students from harassment in California schools. It passed in 1999 as Assembly Bill 537, after the African American assemblyman, Herb Wesson, made "the most eloquent speech," Kuehl says. Publicly proclaiming to her and Carole Migden, a lesbian from Northern California who by then had joined Kuehl in the assembly, "Ms. Kuehl, Ms. Migden, this is not just your fight," Wesson demonstrated that Kuehl did indeed have a "caucus."

The following year she ran for the state senate on issues such as gun control and education. She won handily in an area that includes Hollywood, West Hollywood, Beverly Hills, Universal City, Malibu, Pacific Palisades, Brentwood, and Sherman Oaks—the richest district in the state, which is also socially liberal and well-populated by industry people.[42]

As Kuehl was contemplating her senate run, she encouraged another out lesbian politician from Los Angeles to run for the assembly. Jackie Goldberg had been president of the school board and in 1992 was elected to the Los Angeles City Council, representing Echo Park, an ethnically diverse, working-class district near downtown Los Angeles—an area with a population very different from the ones that put Sheila Kuehl in office. Goldberg had not been out when she ran for the city council because, she says, she and her partner, Sharon Stricker, were raising an adopted son and they feared he would be harassed by his classmates if it were known that he had lesbian mothers. But by the 1990s, L.A. gays would not tolerate what they saw as the hypocrisy of the closet. Goldberg admits that even close friends were angry when she did not come out during her city council campaign. The Stonewall Democratic Club, resenting her silence, outed her in the *Los Angeles Times.* (When she expressed concern to her son, then a high school senior and a basketball player, his response was, "Oh, Mom, no big deal. Jocks don't read the paper.")[43] Once outed, Goldberg actively targeted the gay voter. "I'd start out at midnight, go to all the gay bars. I'd stand on a bar stool and make

my speech." Goldberg says now that her outing actually helped her race because many gay people who might not have voted, did; and since they made up at least 15 percent of her district, she won easily.

As a councilwoman she was sensitive to that strong constituency. As early as 1985, inspired by the neighboring city of West Hollywood, a task force had been appointed by the L.A. city government to study the issue of domestic partnership legislation. They recommended that the City of Los Angeles offer a full package of benefits for the domestic partners of all its employees. This was the first time in history that a *major* city had even considered the issue, though the recommendation was not adopted until 1993, when Goldberg drafted legislation to put those recommendations into effect. Thirteen of the fifteen council members voted in favor of it. As a result of its adoption, even businesses vying for city contracts are now informed: "If you do business with the City of Los Angeles, you must provide domestic partner benefits to all your employees."[44]

By the time Jackie Goldberg ran for the California State Assembly, in 1999, being openly lesbian in L.A. was clearly no hindrance. She received almost 75 percent of the vote and was even endorsed by *L'Opinion,* the major citywide Spanish paper, because, she explains, on the city council she'd fought to make Los Angeles the first major city with a living-wage ordinance, and the working-class Latinos in her district were grateful. That she was a lesbian, Goldberg says, was entirely irrelevant to them.[45]

In 2000, gay Angelenos, who had had good reasons in recent years to believe that their fellow citizens were behind them, received a shocking blow: Sixty-one percent of the California electorate, under right-wing-fomented hysteria, voted to approve Proposition 22, the Knight initiative that stated: "Only marriage between a man and a woman is valid or recognized in California." The proposition not only blocked gay marriage for Californians, but also preempted the possibility that a gay marriage that was valid in another state would be recognized in California. In 2003, Goldberg authored Assembly Bill 205 to cushion the worst effects of Proposition 22, which denied any legal recognition to gay commitments. The bill, which was approved by the California legislature, gave gay and lesbian domestic partners a panoply of rights, including community property protections, housing protections, and surviving-partner benefits.

Many California gays refuse still to relinquish their aspirations for the full spectrum of federal rights and the recognition that only marriage can provide, but with the exception that domestic partners cannot file a joint tax return, the bill completely mirrors California's marriage laws. It was signed by Governor Gray Davis and went into effect in 2005.[46]

The 2004 California elections brought six openly gay people to the state legislature: four out lesbians—Goldberg in the assemby; Kuehl, Migden, and Chris Kehoe in the senate; and two out gay men—Mark Leno and John Laird in the assembly, making the California State Legislature the only one in the union to have now a true gay-and-lesbian caucus.[47]

TAKING CARE OF OUR OWN

> *The Society for Senior Gay and Lesbian Citizens [will] help relieve the suffering of less fortunate Gay and Lesbian Senior Citizens who are forced to stare down the double-barreled gun of POVERTY and LONELY ISOLATION. . . . [Our] primary emphasis will be on COMMUNITY LIVING. . . . It is very cruel to expect a person to retreat back into the closet once they reach retirement age.*
>
> —Fund-raising appeal for a proposed L.A. "residence for needy older Gay and Lesbian Citizens," 1980[48]

Since homophobia has abated over the last couple of generations, fewer gays have felt compelled to marry someone of the opposite sex and leave the gay world—which means that they live in the gay community longer; and because people are also living longer, there are more elderly among L.A. gays than ever before. The community is expanding at the other end, too. More young people are becoming part of the gay world because in the current social milieu the young, including gays, have been discovering their sexuality earlier. Thus the gay population is not only larger than ever but also younger and older.

Attempts to address the special needs of the elderly in the gay community were frustrated in the past because money went to what appeared to be more pressing needs—for example, providing mental health services to a community that had been wounded; getting gay-

friendly politicians elected; addressing the AIDS crisis. In 1980, Robert Arthur, a popular movie actor of the 1930s and '40s, established a non-profit public-benefit corporation, the Society for Senior Gay and Lesbian Citizens (SSGLC), its purpose being, as its logo announced, "Taking Care of Our Own." The main goal was to provide the first residential facility of its kind in the world, giving "food, shelter, and a place of acceptance and understanding to those Gay and Lesbian Citizens who find themselves alone and without adequate financial support in their senior years."[49]

SSCLC could not raise sufficient money for such a utopian facility, but in 1982, as an intermediate step, it was able to procure a "Project Rainbow" office at the Angelus Plaza, a 1,093-unit apartment complex for the elderly on Bunker Hill, which had once been a gay area. It was now estimated that from 4 to 10 percent of the residents were homosexual. Project Rainbow hoped to offer to them social gatherings, legal aid, field trips, and "mobile volunteer visiting." In an article headlined "Antidote to Loneliness," the *Los Angeles Times* announced that the city council's president, Joel Wachs, and an L.A. resident, Christine Jorgensen (who, in 1952, became the world's most famous transsexual), were on hand, along with hundreds of gay activists, to celebrate the official opening of the Project Rainbow Center at Angelus Plaza. A proclamation from Mayor Tom Bradley declaring a Gay/Lesbian Senior Citizens Week in Los Angeles hung in the Project Rainbow office.[50]

But not all the elderly residents of Angelus Plaza were thrilled to have openly gay people in their midst. A retired naval officer who had just moved in to Angelus Plaza when the Project Rainbow office opened protested that he had spent "thirty years keeping such people out of the navy [and] the first notice that caught [my] eye was an announcement of a lesbian women's meeting." A ninety-three-year-old resident complained of the gay and lesbian seniors who now openly shared the complex with him: "They're not natural. They belong with dogs and monkeys. . . . They ought to build a little island and send them all there."[51] What the lesbian and gay seniors needed was a residential facility of their own. But the AIDS crisis was already hitting the gay community. Charitable giving as well as government monies would soon be

diverted to AIDS.[52] Young men were dying as in a holocaust, and a project for the elderly had to be put on the back burner.

Ivy Bottini, the veteran activist and leader in L.A.'s gay community, says that for twenty years she kept trying to raise the issue of housing for indigent lesbian and gay senior citizens, but it was "never the right time." Finally, she and John Fournier, who was head of Senior Services at the Gay and Lesbian Community Services Center, brought together representatives from various gay groups that dealt with the elderly. As they testified, it was not only indigent gays who needed special housing: "Even if we do have some money when we're old, we go into retirement homes and there we have to go back into the closet," they said. "If we have a partner, we have to take two rooms. That's horrible, too!" The group decided it would establish a nonprofit corporation, Gay and Lesbian Elder Housing, that would work to provide residential space for a socioeconomic spectrum of gay and lesbian elderly, including those who needed affordable housing.[53]

Unlike a generation earlier, when such a project was unfeasible, now L.A. gay money and political clout finally came together to serve what had been the most neglected gay population.[54] Eric Garcetti, a city council member, helped the group procure a piece of land in Hollywood, on Ivar Street and Selma Avenue. The Los Angeles City Council voted unanimously to transfer $6 million to the project. Plans got under way to build Encore Hall (appropriately named for its entertainment-industry site), which would be a complex of 104 one- and two-bedroom apartments for lesbian and gay seniors. An L.A. lesbian heiress donated $1.5 million to the project because she "wanted to make sure that more lesbians would be involved." Another woman donor instituted the "1,000 Women Campaign," pledging to give $100,000 if 1,000 other women would each give $100.[55] Gay and Lesbian Elder Housing finally raised $20 million to complete the project. In July 2005, officials and advocates for lesbian and gay seniors held a groundbreaking ceremony at Encore Hall's construction site for "the nation's first affordable housing facility aimed at older GLBT adults."[56] Thirty percent of the apartments have been set aside for people with AIDS or gay seniors "who are in immediate danger of being homeless." In the "Gayle Wilson Pool" (named for the deceased lesbian

activist and real estate millionaire), senior aerobics will be taught. A large community center on the site will offer classes, plays, and musical entertainment.[57]

Since the 1920s, Hollywood has been a seductive magnet for attractive young people who have arrived from all over the country, suitcase in hand, at the Greyhound bus station, or by train at Union Station, hoping, often naïvely, to find a career in the movie industry. Gays, especially young gay men with artistic bent and dreams, were disproportionately represented among them. For many of those who did not make it, the choices could be grim: They could go home again; they could find menial jobs to keep themselves fed; they could hustle in the sex industry. Because existing social agencies had little interest in their particular problems, one of the reasons for the establishment of the Gay Community Services Center in 1972 was to help just such a population by providing shelter and food, so they would not feel forced to prostitute themselves. The center was soon being contacted regularly by the Los Angeles Probation Department to help deal with "displaced" gay youth, especially in the Hollywood area. In 1982, Los Angeles City Council members who had long political ties to the gay community, including Zev Yaroslavsky, Peggy Stevenson, and Joel Wachs, helped the Gay Community Services Center in securing a block grant to purchase property in Hollywood for a facility for homeless lesbian and gay teenagers. Martel House, as it was called, was professionally staffed and provided counseling, education, and social services in a supportive "home" environment.

Los Angeles is still the number one destination for homeless youth in the country, and it is estimated that 30 percent of them are gay, lesbian, bisexual, or transgendered (GLBT).[58] The Gay and Lesbian Center (the present name of the Gay and Lesbian Community Services Center) has expanded its services for them over the years. Its Jeffrey Griffith Youth Center is a drop-in facility on Santa Monica Boulevard. The site was chosen because gay boys often work that district, known as Hustlers' Row, for food and a place to stay.[59] The youth center now serves about 7,000

GLBT young people each year with counseling, free meals, showers, and clothing. The Gay and Lesbian Center also has a residential program, Kruks/Tilsner, which houses young people whose ages range from eighteen to twenty-four (about 60 percent are male, 30 percent female, 8 percent transgendered, and 2 percent undeclared) for up to eighteen months.[60] Most of the youths are "rescued off the streets" where they, too, have been engaging in survival prostitution. The Center has vans that travel the area so that program personnel can spot likely candidates and offer to take them to the shelter.[61]

Such resources proliferate in Los Angeles. The existence of one inspires others. Several other programs to serve youth were born at the Gay and Lesbian Center or have been influenced—sometimes in unlikely ways—by the center. A Los Angeles high school teacher, Virginia Uribe, wandered into the center's Lesbian Central office around 1982. She was close to fifty years old, had long been a lesbian, but had been too scared to seek out gay events; this was her first excursion into a large group of homosexuals. "I found a great cross-section of people, just like in the rest of the world (except the men I saw around the Center were a lot better looking than guys in the rest of the world). They welcomed me in. I finally felt like I was a part of something," she says. The experience made her especially sensitive to a student at her school, an effeminate young man. "The other kids spat at him," she remembers. "They threw eggs at him. He was never given a chance to be 'a part of something.'" When he fought back, he was expelled from school.

Remembering her happy experiences of inclusion and her student's wretched exclusion, Uribe put up a sign in her class announcing that she would conduct a "Gay Support Group" during lunch hours.

The group came to be called "Project 10" (with reference to the statistic that about 10 percent of the population is gay). Within a month, twenty-five students were attending Project 10 meetings. Books on gay subjects were ordered for the high school library, and a bulletin board announced gay news such as the celebration of National Coming Out Day. Uribe's goal was to keep gay youth in school and to keep them from despair. It was, she says, the first such program in the country to address the needs of gay kids in mainstream schools.[62] Once teachers elsewhere

began hearing about Project 10, they would call the very supportive principal at Fairfax High School, Warren Steinberg, to say, "We need a Project 10 at our school. How do we do it?" Project 10 became the inspiration for "Gay-Straight Alliance" groups, which now exist in almost all the secondary schools in Los Angeles and in many schools all over America. Uribe suggests that Project 10 even triggered the impulse behind the "Dignity for All Students" bill, sponsored by Sheila Kuehl, which added protection from harassment on account of "sexual orientation and gender" to the California State Education Code.[63]

But Uribe's Project did encounter opposition. Lou Sheldon of the Traditional Values Coalition wrote to state legislators saying, "Did you know they are teaching a sodomy class at Fairfax High School? They are teaching the kids how to get AIDS." He attacked Uribe directly as a lesbian, calling her "a fox guarding the henhouse." U.S. Senator Jesse Helms ordered an investigation into whether Project 10 was receiving federal funds. (It was not.) In 1988, Sheldon convinced a right-wing assemblywoman on the Education Committee to introduce a resolution to suspend all state money coming into Los Angeles schools until Project 10 was stopped.

The City of Los Angeles and the L.A. media came to Uribe's defense. All the members of the Los Angeles Board of Education not only signed a "big scroll" honoring Uribe,[64] but also expressed the board's strong commitment to diversity and reiterated that commitment in a 1990 document that established guidelines for dealing with diversity throughout the school district. An entire page of supportive letters appeared in the *Los Angeles Times,* along with a powerful editorial defending her and the program. City council members castigated Sheldon and his followers directly for opposing a program that had been established for the purpose of "keeping kids from killing themselves."

Another major program for youth that was inspired by L.A.'s Gay and Lesbian Center is Terry DeCrescenzo's Gay and Lesbian Adolescent Social Services (GLASS). DeCrescenzo was president of the Center's board of directors when Martel House was being established. Through her own experience working at the Los Angeles County Probation Department she had seen that gay and lesbian adolescents, sometimes only twelve

years old, desperately needed even more than Martel House (aimed at teens and young adults) could offer. In existing agencies, gay kids were abused, treated as though they were mentally ill, and held up to ridicule. She decided she would focus her career on helping such children. Again, L.A. money made it possible. In 1984, she obtained a large unsecured personal loan from the gay activist-millionaire Sheldon Andelson, who had just started his own bank, and with that money DeCrescenzo opened GLASS's first group home to address the needs of L.A.'s huge population of GLBT throwaway children. Eventually, seven group homes were opened, and GLASS became a model for gay adolescent residential programs "from Indiana to Israel."[65]

For a time, however, GLASS' survival was in question. DeCrescenzo says that in the early 1990s, her program was constantly being harassed by the Department of Social Services (DSS). GLASS was attacked with allegations such as had always been the nightmare of gay adults who work with youth:

> DSS didn't even want to know from gay kids. When I started talking about transgendered kids, they were really unhappy. They went on a fishing expedition. They got one of our kids and said, "We heard you're having sex with one of the staff." He said, "No!" They said, "We know you're lying." The investigation went on for two years. They even had people go to the Gay Pride Festival and find our kids and say, "We hear you're having sex with the staff." They terrorized the staff and the kids.

Finally, seven men on the staff were accused of sexual malfeasance. The children were removed from the group homes—those on probation as juvenile delinquents were led away in shackles. DeCrescenzo was served with a "lifetime exclusion order," forbidding her from working ever again in social services in California, or even from being in the presence of a minor. Sensationalistic media accused her of "pimping the boys off to major donors," DeCresenzo says. She fought the charges in court, and ultimately not one of them could be upheld. GLASS was, nevertheless, put on a five-year probationary period. "For a long time, the staff members were afraid to be alone with a kid, even for a minute," she says.

Those difficult years came to an end, and GLASS now continues to flourish, serving 1,500 adolescents a year on a $10 million budget. The adolescents, most from poor Latino and African American families, are referred to GLASS from the Los Angeles Department of Mental Health, the Department of Children and Family Services, and the Probation Department. Many of them had been street kids who supported themselves by drug dealing and prostitution. Many had grown up "in the system," moving from one foster home to another because their parents were incarcerated, abusive, drug addicts, or otherwise dysfunctional. Michael Marchand, the director of GLASS's day treatment program, says the children wind up at GLASS, generally, because their gender behavior had been an uncomfortable issue in their other placements. He gives the example of one very effeminate boy who was constantly being beaten up by the other children in his previous group home and was told by the staff, "If you didn't act like such a sissy, they wouldn't pick on you." The only way he knew to prevent a beating was to smear his feces all over himself.[66]

Although the children in GLASS are not always kind to one another, no one ever gets harassed because they are not "appropriately" masculine or feminine. Sexuality appears to be of less concern to GLASS adolescents than gender expression. Many of the girls are "studs" or wear boys' clothes exclusively. A few of the boys wear makeup and feminine clothes. Some say they will have a sex-change operation when they are older. "Lucy" has been in GLASS for three years. He was raped by a seventeen-year-old boy when he was six or seven, taken from his drug-addicted mother by Child Protective Services, and placed in Five Acres and then Vista del Mar group homes for children. There, he says, the kids would call him faggot and "give me shit everyday because I always loved to do girl's things." He sees himself as a lesbian—that is, he prefers girls and feels that he, too, is a girl. At GLASS, he met another transgendered male-to-female adolescent who "showed me how to walk and talk like a girl should"; now his GLASS counselor "tells me how to carry myself like a lady. She says, 'Don't put your makeup on in class. Don't curse. Don't burp.' She gives me tips about lipstick and eye shadow and blush, and we talk about ladies clothing, like what you should buy." Lucy remembers

that "Before, I used to be a demon. I'd bite people. I'd go AWOL from my placement." Now, he says, "everyone tells me I'm a beautiful spirit."[67]

"Jessica," who has been at GLASS for two years, "likes boys" and feels "like a woman," but he has never had a "serious relationship." When his mother could not take care of him, he went to live with his aunt, and at thirteen he was raped by her husband's cousin. Jessica was sent to group homes and foster care where he was beaten up so often that he began to cut himself on his arms—"to get some of the pain out," he says. Jessica was in a mental hospital for six months before winding up at GLASS. He goes to Oasis, a continuation school for gay and lesbian youth during the day, and lives in a GLASS group home. His GLASS counselor, he says, "buys me teddy bears every time I get an A at school."[68]

Many of the children at GLASS suffer insurmountable depression because of past trauma. Some are suicidal; several, like Jessica, are "cutters." But others are clearly making it. "Mary," who had run away from her mother's house "because of all the men raping girls, and all the drugs and gang-banging going on," met up with a pimp who put her on the streets. She was sent to GLASS after she was arrested and told a probation worker she was bisexual. She has a girlfriend now—"a stud," Mary says, "who looks like a guy"—who is also in the GLASS residency program. Mary has been at GLASS for eighteen months. She is on the honor roll in high school and is taking a class at West Los Angeles Junior College. She also has a job working with elementary school children in an after-school enrichment program. "I put my past in a box and threw it away," she says. "I'm never going to look for that box again." But, she observes, not all the kids she knows in GLASS have such happy stories. "A lot of them, maybe 60 percent of them, just have to step out on the street and they can get in trouble again. They [go] AWOL, do drugs. They don't take things seriously here anymore than they did anywhere else."[69]

Still, her success story is not unique. "Junior," who is seventeen years old, has been at GLASS for a year. She calls herself a "stud" and says she knew she was gay from the time she was twelve, when she lived with her mother and five brothers in a barrio in Wilmington. Her mother was a cocaine addict, and Junior started selling drugs before she was in her teens. Junior's life has been violent. She was raped by one of her mother's hus-

bands, her mother's boyfriends, her uncles. She was a cutter and attempted suicide repeatedly. She was living in foster homes, juvenile hall, and a mental hospital more than she was living with her mother, who was incarcerated when Junior was fourteen. Junior seldom went to school. Now, she says, she has 144 high school units, her grades are high, and she is president of the Activities Board at GLASS, which she sees as a great honor—"I never would have thought it could happen." Her therapist and her girlfriend at GLASS have made all the difference, she claims. Now she knows what she wants to do. "The big thing," she says, "is I don't want to be like my mom." She hopes to go to college when she graduates from SEA Girls Academy, the charter school to which GLASS sends her. "I want to become a psychotherapist. I knew a lot of therapists, at the mental hospital and places, who don't know how to do it because they haven't been through what their clients have. I've been there. I'll know how to do it."[70]

GLASS not only runs group homes but also subsidizes foster parents (75 percent of whom are lesbian or gay), offers services such as job-skill training, and supports a doctor's office on wheels that provides health care to street kids. Some of GLASS's money comes from public agencies, but the gay and lesbian community in Los Angeles has also supported GLASS well. There are donors' brunches, for instance, where a GLASS resident, seventeen-year-old "Leticia," reads her poems; they have titles such as "Look—Do You See Me or Just a Placement Child?" and "Where I've Been and Where I'm Going," the latter being an autobiographical piece about being molested and having to grow up too fast.[71]

Terry DeCrescenzo says that it helps that GLASS is based in Los Angeles, a city of celebrities and wealth. "We had a fund-raiser for Gay and Lesbian Adolescent Social Services to which we invited ten donors, at $5,000 a plate, to have dinner with Ellen DeGeneres and her mother. We sold half the tickets the first day. Nobody batted an eye at the cost."[72] Gay L.A.'s legendary obsession with power and glamour can be turned to good use, as she observes, in the service of the most vulnerable members of the community.

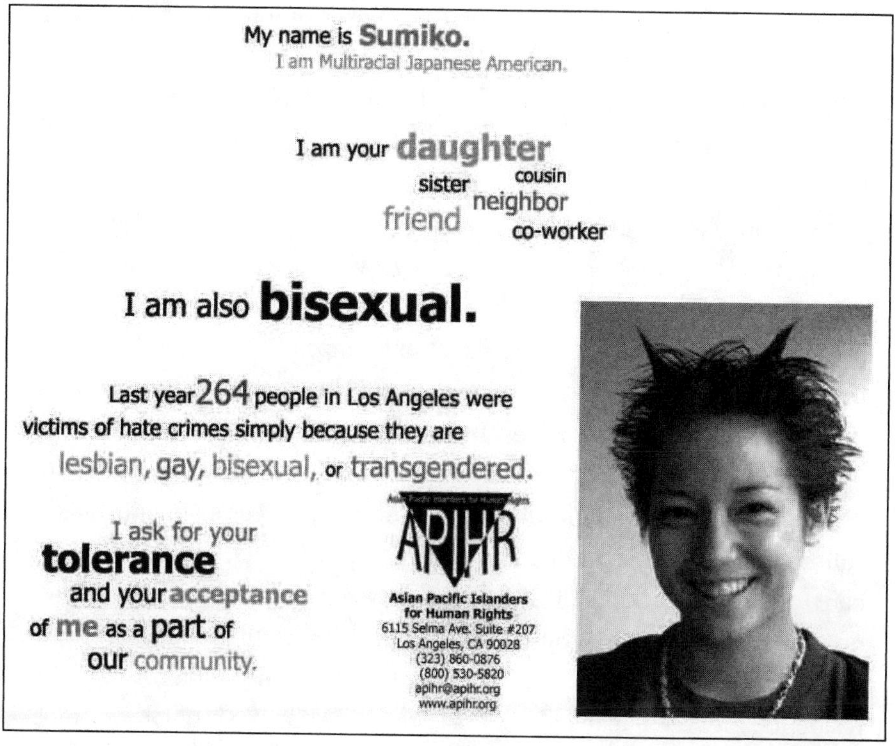

My name is Sumiko.
I am Multiracial Japanese American.
I am your daughter
sister
cousin
neighbor
friend
co-worker
I am also bisexual.
Last year 264 people in Los Angeles were victims of hate crimes simply because they are lesbian, gay, bisexual, or transgendered.
I ask for your tolerance and your acceptance of me as a part of our community.
APIHR
Asian Pacific Islanders for Human Rights
6115 Selma Ave. Suite #207
Los Angeles, CA 90028
(323) 860-0876
(800) 530-5820
apihr@apihr.org
www.apihr.org

One of the community ads placed by Asian Pacific Islanders for Human Rights. *Courtesy APIHR.*

EPILOGUE

The Twenty-first Century

As with most social trends, especially the ones involving tomorrow, what is true of the world is doubly true of America, and what is doubly true of America is quadruply true of Los Angeles.

—Pico Iyer, "Where Worlds Collide"[1]

THE CHANGES in gay life over the past half-century have been astonishing. They have surpassed by far the fantasies that Wally Jordan spun in his 1943 letters to Jim Kepner about the Sons of Hamidy, the marvelous (nonexistent) organization of socially and politically prominent homosexuals. In 2002, a blue ribbon committee was appointed to select a new chief of police for Los Angeles, and a seat on it was reserved for the openly lesbian executive director of the Gay and Lesbian Center, Lorri Jean. In 2004, during the L.A. mayoral race, Antonio Villaraigosa, campaigning energetically in the gay community, chided the incumbent for making only ten gay appointments out of 364 slots. "That's offensive!" Villaraigosa said.[2] He won the election.

That gay people would not only cease to be persecuted by police and politicians but would also be wooed by them under official policy; that they would not only have public faces but those faces would be of all races and ethnicities; that transgender people (who had been even more despised than the homosexuals with whom they were associated)

should come out in the daylight and organize; that unbiased portrayals of gays should someday be beamed from L.A. into the world's living rooms and be shown on the big screen everywhere—these were beyond Jordan's wildest dreams.

CORNUCOPIA

I was already an ethnic minority there. That was hard enough. I didn't want to stick out as a sexual minority, too. In Los Angeles I don't feel like I stick out that much.

—Kim Swindle-Bautista, a Korean who was adopted and raised in Indiana[3]

Los Angeles, always a magnet for the adventurer, the disaffected, the haven-seeker, continues to be a Promised Land for gay people from everywhere. It is a global village to which gay immigrants continue to be drawn because life back home can be immeasurably more difficult. Ewa, a Polish chess champion, was first sent to the United States for an international tournament. She says she immediately longed to stay, though it was "very stressful" for her to learn to speak English. She fought to remain in Los Angeles because she "hated how closed" Poland was for gay people. "*Lesbijka* has a very negative connotation there," she says. "I had to always keep secret who I was." In L.A. she easily found an open lesbian culture: "For a person who had to hide all the time, coming into a roomful of women who could sit in a circle and talk openly about their women lovers . . . well, it was so amazing."[4]

In recent years, there has been an enormous flowering in and around L.A. of gay organizations for immigrants, as well as for people of color, who are increasingly willing to be out. For example, there is now a Russian and Eastern European Gay and Lesbian Group that meets on the border of West Hollywood. There is GALAS, the Gay and Lesbian Armenian Society of Los Angeles. There is ELAD for "Ebony Lesbians of Afrikaan Descent." Not only is there O-Moi for Vietnamese lesbians,[5] but also an organization of gay and lesbian Asian Pacific Islanders has de-

signed services and programs for twenty-seven Asian ethnicities in Los Angeles. The proliferation of gay Latino organizations has been especially impressive (though not unexpected because Los Angeles now includes more same-sex Latino households than any other place in America);[6] there is Latinas Understanding the Need for Action (LUNA) for Latina lesbians and bisexuals, Sabores for "Gay, Lesbian, Transgender and Bisexual Youth," Latinas and Friends for Latina lesbians and those who love them, a reconstructed Gay and Lesbian Latinos Unidos, Que Onda Queers, "Groupo de Apoyo Para Lesbianas Latinas," Gay Latinos/Latinas Bible Study, Tu for Spanish-speaking transgenders, and Vida for Spanish-speaking HIV+ transgenders.[7]

Though many groups meet a quick demise after the initial burst of enthusiasm, others invariably crop up to take their place. The tenor of these organizations keeps evolving. For example, Luis Lopez, a policy analyst, who says he was "amazed at the lack of civic engagement from the largest concentration of gay Latinos in the country,"[8] founded "Honor PAC," a political action committee for LGBT Latinos. ("Honor" translates as "pride" in Spanish). Lopez, thirty-two, had never heard of MECLA (Municipal Elections Committee of Los Angeles), which flourished almost thirty years earlier, but he understands the political potential of gay Latinos who are now coming into the middle class in large numbers. His goals are similar to those MECLA had, except that he hopes to work specifically with Latinos to raise money and support candidates that "serve the unique needs and interests of Latina/o/LGBT communities."[9]

L.A.'s abundance makes possible a profusion of alternatives for a profusion of gay populations. For gay Latinos who are not politically active, for example, bars and clubs continue to proliferate: Red's, Circus Disco, the Plaza, and Chico now have competition from such venues as Club Bravo, Coco Bongo, Fuego, Club Infierno, El Maguey, El Calor, Olé Olé, OZZ, Club Tomboys, Club Tempo, Club Temptations, and Club Papi.[10] Those who see themselves outside the common working-class affinity of gays of color can also find limitless new affinities in Los Angeles. Julia Salazar says that though her parents speak Spanish, she never learned the language, and professionally and socially she has blended in with an

upper-middle-class gay community whose ethnicity is not a major factor in their lives.[11] Monserrat Fontes, a lesbian writer whose family is from Mexico, points out that Mexicans have been "the working backbone of this state," and she is involved in registering Latina women to vote; but, she says, "I don't even know where the Chicana lesbian groups are. I'm doing more than I can handle now. Call me and I'll send money, but that's about it."[12] Both Salazar and Fontes have been in long-term relationships with women who are not Latina. Davi Cheng, whose family came to Los Angeles via China and Hong Kong, says she "never felt comfortable in an Asian lesbian group." She converted to Judaism in 1997 and organized a klezmer band at the gay and lesbian synagogue, Beth Chayim Chadishm, where she also became president of the congregation.[13]

As more gays of color have been willing to take a proverbial "walk down Crenshaw"—Lisa Powell's phrase for being out anywhere, even in one's parent community—they have altered the previously monochromatic public face of gay L.A. Charlene Nguon, for example, a suburban Los Angeles high school student from an Asian family, has become the poster girl for a minor's right to privacy regarding sexual orientation. Nguon, who refused to stop "hugging, kissing, and holding hands with her girlfriend," brought a lawsuit against the school district when her principal informed her parents of her homosexual behavior. Her suit, supported by the American Civil Liberties Union of Southern California as well as her family, argues that "a student has a right not to have her sexual orientation disclosed to her parents, even if she is out of the closet at school." Nguon also seeks to create a district-wide policy that would not treat gay students differently from their straight counterparts when they express affection.[14] Such visibility speaks eloquently to parent communities of color that have often in the past dismissed homosexuality as a "white disease," to the pain of their gay children.

Gay people of color in Los Angeles have also been waging campaigns that tackle directly the homophobia of their parent communities, such as

the Asian Pacific Islanders for Human Rights ads in numerous Asian language newspapers that are published in Los Angeles: Each ad features the image of an attractive Asian lesbian, gay, or transgendered young person, stating, for example, "I am your daughter/cousin/sister/friend/neighbor/co-worker. I am also a lesbian. . . . I ask for your tolerance and acceptance of me as part of our community."[15]

There is some evidence that such efforts by gays of color have been working—that the parent communities are beginning to acknowledge the gay sexuality of some of its members and to understand gays as another legitimate minority group. In January 2006, the Asian Pacific American Legal Center of Southern California, along with 250 other civil rights and church groups, including the NAACP, the Mexican-American Legal Defense and Education Fund, and the National Black Justice Coalition, filed a joint amicus brief asking the California Court of Appeals to apply a 1948 California Supreme Court decision, Perez v. Sharp—which struck down laws banning interracial marriage—to gay marriage. Karen Wang, vice president of the Asian Pacific American Legal Center, declared, "People of color in California are sadly familiar with marriage discrimination, as many of our communities were targets of racially restrictive marriage rules in the past [and must] stand together in support of marriage equality [for gays]."[16] The connection she draws between racism and homophobia represents a moving victory for gay people of color. Their parent communities have begun to come to their defense. Although support is certainly not universal in communities of color,[17] that it should be so publicly and well articulated would have been unimaginable in earlier eras.

It is also a moving victory for gay people in general. L.A.'s Mattachine Society first voiced in the 1950s the revolutionary concept that gays were a "cultural minority." Discrimination against homosexuals, they said, is no different from discrimination against other minorities. Both prejudices are rooted in the dominant society's unjust and irrational impulse to demonize the "other." Wang's assertion that "the civil rights of all communities are inseparably linked" is what gay people have tried to argue all along.

TRANS LOS ANGELES

Many mixed race people are saying that race, as a means of categorizing people, no longer works. Transgender people are showing us that gender, as a similar construct, has no meaning either.

—"Era of the Gender Crosser," *Los Angeles Times*, 2001[18]

Transgender people have always been drawn to L.A. where they could find community or pass far more easily than they could in smaller towns; and historically, performing a gender other than the one into which they were born may have felt more comfortable in a city of performers than it would have been elsewhere. It is not surprising that George Jorgensen, an ex-G.I. who grabbed headlines in 1952 when Danish doctors helped him become "Christine Jorgensen," decided to settle in Los Angeles. She aspired to the profession of "Hollywood photographer or actress," she announced, and was soon "deluged [with] fabulous contract offers." She lived as a celebrity in L.A.[19] It was also in L.A., in 1970, that "Virginia Prince," the male publisher of the magazine *Transvestia* (1960–1976), coined the word "transgender," which became an umbrella term to describe both those who were transsexuals such as Jorgensen, and those who were transvestites, as Prince was.[20]

But Christine Jorgensen and the performativity of Hollywood culture notwithstanding, for much of L.A.'s history, transgenders had a difficult time with the police, and, as the mid-twentieth-century drag queen Miss Destiny observed, they were "outcast among outcasts."[21] For years, transgender activists agitated for more sensitivity among law enforcement officers, and Los Angeles has witnessed important changes in official attitudes.[22] The captain of West Hollywood's Sheriff's Station, Richard Odenthal, worked with transgender support groups at the end of the twentieth century to create a "briefing program" for his deputies when he realized that some officers were "having trouble dealing with the growing transgender population in the city." West Hollywood became officially supportive of transgenders. Odenthal observed that although some deputies were sympathetic to begin with, others "needed a bit more time, and some still did not like the idea." But, he added, their prej-

udices would not be tolerated: "They know that they are expected to behave professionally." A seven-member task force was appointed by city officials "to study the needs" of the transgender population.[23]

As in other big American cities, the transgender community in L.A. is organizing seriously, sponsoring "Transgender Days of Remembrance" to memorialize those who were killed in the past by hate crimes; Transgender Leadership Summits to help groups all over California strategize methods for local organizing; and annual Transunity Conferences, which are "pride" events for "transsexual, transgender, gender-queer, and cross-dressing individuals and those who love and care for them," and have been drawing more than 1,000 people each year.[24] As the *Los Angeles Times* suggested in a two-part article on transgenders in 2001, the community has "found a voice" because it has been "buoyed by the successes of gay liberation and freed by medical advances."[25]

The first attempt to bring transgenders together in Los Angeles was in 1980, but the secretive group remained small and wound down after a few years.[26] Bamby Salcedo, an MTF from Mexico, migrated to L.A. in 1986, at the age of eighteen, when a friend wrote her that in Hollywood "there was a lot of 'family,'" that is, other male-to-female transsexuals. "I did what many of us do," says Salcedo, who was unable to speak English. "I came to Santa Monica Boulevard and started doing sex work." Salcedo, who had been sexually abused as a child and started sniffing glue by age nine, found that drugs were easily available on the streets of Hollywood. After years of taking heroin, meth, and crack, she concedes, she was "pretty much a garbage can."[27] She complains that there was little by way of community services in L.A. to pull transwomen like her back from the edge.[28]

But in more recent years, Salcedo says, AIDS programs have been helping L.A. transwomen. She believes her life took a turn when she was invited to a party of trans "girls" sponsored by the Latino AIDS service, Bienestar. "The other girls I knew before were either from the street or in prison. I'd never seen such a party of girls . . . like a fun, clean party." Salcedo signed up as a client with Bienestar and completed an addiction treatment program. She was offered employment as a Bienestar case manager and works in an office on Sunset Boulevard, decorated with

posters by Frida Kahlo, whose bright palette is reflected in the makeup of the "girls" who are employed there. Salcedo's job is to refer transwomen to clinics and other services. But she hopes also to expand transgender organizing, observing that the few MTFs she knows who have been politically active have worked mostly for AIDS groups. "For transgenders there's so many other issues that our community [largely working-class, people of color MTFs] needs to address. Drug abuse. Incarceration. Homelessness. Prostitution." Because there is no organization for transwomen, Salcedo has joined the board of the FTM Alliance.

Much of the transgender leadership in Los Angeles has come from transmen—female-to-male transgenders—though they have needed to overcome barriers in order to organize. As might be expected, female-to-male transgenders (FTM) have been less flamboyant in their life styles than many male-to-female transgenders. Masen Davis, a founder of the FTM Alliance, points out that one of their biggest obstacles to organizing has been that many FTMs hope only to get on with their lives in their chosen gender, and in vast Los Angeles, where one can don a new identity as easily as a costume, that hope is not unrealistic. But the increasing visibility of transgenders (including their big-screen visibility in the successful 2005 Hollywood film *Transamerica*) has stimulated the growth of the FTM Alliance. Transman Daniel Gould, a staff person for the Alliance, says the group is reaching a broader population also because biological females are now identifying as FTM at a young age and have more family support than their counterparts did in the past. A Significant Others group, which the Alliance had intended originally for partners of transpeople, is now serving many parents of minors who are transgender. Most of the children range in age from eleven to fourteen, but the youngest, Gould says, is five.[29]

The issues of gender and identity have become increasingly complex and increasingly conceptualized in big cities such as Los Angeles. It has long been recognized that not all transvestites are gay: "Virginia Prince," for example, insisted that transvestites were generally heterosexual, married, and fathers—as he himself was.[30] It is now also recognized that

not all transsexuals, pre- or post-op, become "straight." Many prefer bisexuality or homosexuality. A *Los Angeles Times* article on L.A. transsexuals, "Fitting into Their Own Skin," featured one couple, Boe Randal, an FTM who was born Karen Ann, and his spouse, Mona Rios, an MTF who was born William John.[31] The possible permutations of sexual identity among transsexuals are copious.

The possible permutations of gender identity are also copious. Transsexualism is merely one choice among many. Raquel Gutierrez, a founder of Butchlalis de Panochtitlan, a Los Angeles performance group of "butch stars of pussylandia . . . for gender muthaphukkin," explains the vast array of options for those who do not accept the usual roles. She points out the subtle gradations between numerous gender concepts, such as "butch," "stud," boi," and "baby daddy." For instance, "butch," in the historical sense, she says, is reliant on its binary opposite, "femme." Gutierrez rejects the term "butch" for herself because it is too limited and she does not need a femme to be who she is. She calls herself a "boi," and at twenty-nine says she looks like a fifteen-year-old boy. She believes the "boi" concept "relates to a sophisticated understanding of gender presentation," permitting her, Peter Pan–like, to "play with gender maturity or the lack of it." Gutierrez is not interested in becoming a transman "because the surgery is too big, and anyway I'm content as I am. I don't feel that much of a man." She finds gradations not only in gender and sexual identities but in all aspects of identity. She says she "exhausted [her] identity as a 'lesbian of color'" when that community was critical of her dating a white woman. But, as she affirms, there is a panoply of identities from which to chose in expansive gay L.A.[32]

HOLLYWOOD IN THE TWENTY-FIRST CENTURY

Everything I had hoped would be true when I was eighteen years old mostly is in Hollywood.

—David Taylor, the executive director of Out at Warner Brothers[33]

For most of Hollywood's history, the strong gay and lesbian presence there, which has always helped fashion American culture, was kept

more or less secret from the outside world. Gay Hollywood today, if not precisely rushing from the closet, is coming out gradually. The ubiquitous presence of gays in various parts of the industry has ceased to be a Hollywood secret. Working openly now—as producers, directors, programming heads, screenwriters—gays bring increasingly complex gay themes and characters into movies and television, and they have even established new television networks that speak directly to a national gay audience. Though most gay actors still share the fear of their earlier counterparts that their onscreen credibility in heterosexual roles would be compromised if they declared themselves, straight actors are no longer as panicked (as Tommy Lee Jones was when offered the lead in *The Frontrunner* in the 1980s) about playing gay. Some gay actors are coming out—women while they are working and men after they stop working: for example, Ellen DeGeneres, Rosie O'Donnell, Lily Tomlin, Tab Hunter, Richard Chamberlaine, and George Takei.

The distance Hollywood movies have been able to travel with regard to the subject of homosexuality is particularly impressive if one compares, for example, the 1946 film about Cole Porter's life, *Night and Day,* which totally suppressed his homosexuality, with the twenty-first-century version: In *De-Lovely* (2004), the Cole Porter character is shown kissing his virtually naked male lover, hosting one of his famous Hollywood parties where the guests are a bevy of obviously gay male beauties, and staring seductively into the eyes of a singer and future trick as he coaches the young man on the vocal intricacies of "Night and Day." Though the movie industry still has a way to go before gay and lesbian audiences can feel they are being depicted in all their diversity and complexity, films of the early twenty-first century have shown Asian American lesbians living happily ever after *(Saving Face);* African American lesbians and white lesbians happily giving male chauvinist pigs their comeuppance *(She Hate Me* and *Broken Flowers);* male homosexuals who are supermacho and those who are effete *(Alexander* and *Capote);* lesbian cheerleaders who double as secret agents *(D.E.B.S.);* and gay men who are the only sane beings in a dysfunctional world *(The Family Stone).*

The phenomenon of *Brokeback Mountain,* the gay cowboy love story, heralds even more remarkable change. It opened to the highest per-screen

attendance average of any movie of its year (2005). Its success at the box office—earning about $150 million worldwide in its first two months—indicated that its appeal went far beyond the "gay niche."[34] Multiplex theaters in such unlikely places as Tulsa, Oklahoma, had to add extra screens to satisfy audience demands for showings.[35] It swept the major critics' awards (voted best picture by the New York Film Critics Circle, the Los Angeles Film Critics Association, the San Francisco Film Critics, the Boston Society of Film Critics, the Dallas-Fort Worth Film Critics Association, the Utah Film Critics, the Iowa Film Critics, the St. Louis Film Critics Association, etc.).[36] It swept the Golden Globes awards. [37] It had more Oscar nominations than any film that year and received three Academy Awards, including one for the best adapted screenplay and one for the best director.[38]

By 2005, gay men and lesbians had also become a staple on network television. If, as culture critic Larry Gross has suggested, television is the greatest source of "common information and images that create and maintain a world view and a value system,"[39] the old view and system that had long worked against gay people appears to be under deadly attack. Hollywood now brings a profusion of images of likable and human gay characters to the general populace.[40] Stories about lesbian parenting, unconventional gender identity, and coping with HIV infection are common fare on mainstream legal and medical shows. The multiseason runs of broadcast and cable programs in which gay characters or personalities are prominent—such as *Will and Grace*, the *Ellen* talk show, *Six Feet Under*, *ER*, *Queer Eye for the Straight Guy*, and *The L Word*—have given birth to yet a new surge of broadcast programs that includes major gay episodes or features gays regularly.[41] Some gay media pundits have worried that this rapid proliferation merely indicates a transitory "gay craze," and that the fickle medium will retreat to its old malign neglect. Time will, of course, tell, but as of the first half-dozen years of the new century gay characters have been presented in ways that are increasingly daring. In the first scene of the ABC weekly comedy series, *Crumbs*, for example, the very sympathetic main character wakes up in bed next to another man. The program's out writer-producer, Marco Pennette, says that when he shared this idea for an opening scene with executives at ABC they "didn't blink": "We can show this on TV in 2005. The world will keep spinning."[42]

Perhaps the growing inclusion of gay people on broadcast television was nudged by the sudden appearance of three gay television networks, which threatened to siphon off what was perceived as an affluent gay audience. The first, Here! TV, began in 2003 and soon had competition from Logo, a network backed by MTV and Viacom. Logo, established in 2005, became the first-ever basic cable channel to devote itself exclusively to programs with LGBT content. (Q Television Network began in 2004, with satellite and digital cable subscribers in urban areas across the country, but met its demise within two years. The broadband channel OutzoneTV.com soon sprang up to take its place.

Whether gay networks will be able to sustain a place in a competitive market also remains to be seen, but their birth is a quintessential example of the current risk taking and stretching in the industry. Meredith Kadlec, vice president of original programming at Here! TV, observes of the innovative concept of gay networks: "In Hollywood, the old adage is, 'Everything has been done before.' But not in this realm!" What can be done that is new in soap opera?—Here! TV's *Dante's Cove,* a soap opera about Kevin and his gay pals battling supernatural forces in their town. What can be done in a comedy-drama serial that is original?—Logo's *Noah's Arc,* about a screenwriter in Los Angeles who is an African American gay man. Action films?— Here! TV's produced-for-television movie about a lesbian hero who "kicks ass and gets the girl."[43]

Onscreen gay ubiquity has been greatly aided by the growing number of "out" gay people in high places in the industry. Since the 1992 founding of Hollywood Supports by the former Fox chair, Barry Diller, and the MCA president, Sidney Sheinberg, the Hollywood closet, whose door had been soldered shut in mid-century, opens wider and wider, at least for those who work behind the camera. The president of entertainment at Showtime is out, for example, as is the president of entertainment at the WB television network.[44] They acknowledge their responsibility to the larger world. As the WB president of entertainment observed shortly

after his appointment: "It would be really remiss of me if I didn't try to find shows on this network that accurately reflect gay life."[45] At the major studios, David Taylor, who is an executive assistant to a vice president at Warner Home Videos, observes, "There's no tolerance for prejudice. It's explicit. Diversity is encouraged." Since 2002, Warner Brothers has been sponsoring Out at Warner Brothers, an industry affinity group of gays and lesbians, which now has hundreds of members and is a major presence at gay events such as the Outfest Film Festival.[46]

Lesbians have not yet had the same degree of prominence and success as have gay men in behind-the-camera Hollywood (reflecting perhaps the male-female success ratio in much of the outside world). But young lesbians in the industry are reassured in their ambitions by the out lesbians who have made it, and the current milieu encourages them to be out, too. Ashley Kaplan, the twenty-four-year-old manager of development for Evolution, a reality television production firm, says that her role model is Caroline Strauss, the out president for original programming at HBO, who has been responsible for shows such as *Six Feet Under,* which regularly presents gay characters.[47] Meredith Kadlec says that since joining the industry in 1994 (two years after the founding of Hollywood Supports) she has never been closeted: "If there are people at some industry meeting who don't know, I find a way to drop it into the conversation." She believes that homosexuality is even a "plus" in Hollywood: "There's a 'hip' factor in being a lesbian."[48] (Joe Libonati, a thirty-year-old publicist for NBC, says that for men, too, "in this city and industry, being gay helps tremendously.")[49]

Young lesbians in the industry have also organized in order to encourage one another. POWER UP (Professional Organization of Women in Entertainment Reaching Up) was founded in 2000 "to promote the integration and visibility of gay women in all areas of the industry." The 1,500-member group finances short films made by its members, and Stacy Codikow, POWER UP's founder, proudly points to its various successes—such as the production of a short movie of *D.E.B.S.* (by the African American filmmaker Angela Robinson), which was then bought by Screen Gems and made into a successful full-length feature film.[50]

Among the most encouraging developments for lesbians in the industry has been the comedy-drama series, *The L Word,* which the television executive and producer Ilene Chaiken pitched to Showtime after witnessing the triumphs of *Will & Grace* and *Queer as Folk.*[51] Chaiken's project was an instant success in its first year, and Showtime "renewed it faster than any series in its history."[52] *The L Word,* about a group of lipstick lesbians in West Hollywood, affects lesbian life in the real world, too. GirlBar, a West Hollywood venue, packs in hundreds of *L Word* look-alikes, who also gather at places such as the Falcon, an upscale West Hollywood restaurant, for huge *L Word* viewing parties.[53] But the series' impact goes further: Just as groups of lesbians in the 1950s used to gather on Sundays in living rooms around the country to hear the weekly radio programs of Tallulah Bankhead (whom they knew was a lesbian by her enchanting whiskey voice and their own gaydar), so have they been gathering, in greater numbers now, around television sets or DVDs everywhere to watch *The L Word.* Hollywood lipstick-lesbian style thus spreads across America.

The gay styles that Hollywood promotes spread across America for men, too, as they have since the 1920s when Rudolph Valentino influenced the look of the American male.[54] Cowboy wear had been long out of fashion, but—as the *New York Times* observed in 2006—though *Brokeback Mountain* failed to win as best picture at the Academy Awards, the movie's representation of "two plain cowboys who fell in love in plain old Western wear" conquered in another way: It "hit the fashion bull's-eye." The fashion writer David Colman suggested on the front page of the *New York Times* "Styles" section that the film brought cowboy clothes "striding back into style," evidenced by nationwide interest in the fashion right after the film was released: Ralph Lauren opened two New York stores devoted to "a vintage Western feel"; a "venerable Denver retailer" reported sales of Western shirts up 25 percent; and just before the Academy Awards, "on eBay, Western hats, belt buckles, and shirts were up 25 percent in the last month alone."[55]

What transpires in L.A. sooner or later affects the rest of the world—at the least because of the city's position as the center of entertainment that speaks to the masses. Frank Rich's rhetorical question in a *New York*

Times review of *Brokeback Mountain*—"What if they held a culture war and no one fired a shot?"—defines a vital aspect L.A.'s power: A Hollywood film's tremendously moving depiction of homosexual love, which is being seen everywhere, may bloodlessly win a culture war.[56]

Social trends that point to the future have always been "quadruply" more pronounced in Los Angeles, as Pico Iyer has suggested. Its location at the edge of the continent, far from "back home," has sharpened its cutting edge and sanctioned experimentation such as would have been impossible elsewhere. From its beginnings as a frontier town, it has permitted, or has seemed to permit, what was unconventional, creative, daring. Michael Weinstein, who created the international AIDS Healthcare Foundation, explains that it was easier to do that from Los Angeles than it would have been elsewhere because the city is still something of the "Wild West," without a long-established power structure in place "that you have to be part of or pay homage to, such as exists in New York or San Francisco."[57] Terry Wolverton says that she left Grand Rapids, Michigan, so that she could develop her lesbian art and writing: "The Midwest operates on a philosophy of limitations. In L.A., no matter how unusual an idea is, there are enough people who'll tell you, 'Yeah, let's give it a try.' In L.A., you can invent new institutions in which you can be yourself."[58]

That ethos helps to explain why it was Los Angeles that gave birth to the country's first gay organizations, churches, synagogues, magazines, community centers. L.A.'s growth to gargantuan magnitude and its vast diversity also help to explain why gay men and women flocked there: In Los Angeles, they knew, they could find both anonymity and community, which have been vital to gays' survival and development. During the last half-century, gay life has been transformed in cities all over America. But in Los Angeles these transformations have occurred on a huge scale; and the gay consciousness and lifestyles that have developed there have had tremendous influence on how gay life is lived everywhere.

NOTES

INTRODUCTION

1. Frank Fenton, *A Place in the Sun* (New York: Random House, 1942).

2. ST interview with John Rechy, 71, August 29, 2005.

3. Michael Datcher, "Blue Spirits Rising: The Re-emergence of the L.A. Jazz Scene," *American Visions* 8, no. 2 (April–May 1993): 42.

4. Item S–001–368 120, Shades of Los Angeles Collection, Los Angeles Public Library.

5. In Jim Heimann, *Sins of the City: The Real Los Angeles Noir* (San Francisco: Chronicle Books, 1999), 154.

6. Steven L. Isoardi, "Central Avenue Sounds, oral history transcript, 1990," Clora Bryant interviewed by Steven L. Isoardi, Los Angeles: Oral History Program, University of California, Los Angeles, 1994, 105–107.

7. ST interview with Mark Haile, December 13, 2005; and Mark Haile, *The BLK Guide to Southern California for Black People in the Life* (Los Angeles: BLK Publishing Company, 1997), 11.

8. Bryant interview.

9. Ibid. See also Clora Bryant et al., eds., *Central Avenue Sounds: Jazz in Los Angeles.* (Berkeley, CA: University of California Press, 1998), 352.

CHAPTER 1

1. In George Devereux, "Institutionalized Homosexuality of the Mohave Indians," *Human Biology* 9 (1937): 501.

2. Cary McWilliams, *Southern California Country: An Island on the Land* (New York: Duell, Sloan, and Pierce, 1943), 44.

3. Herbert Ingram Priestly, ed. and trans., *A Historical, Political, and Natural Description of California by Pedro Fages* (1937; rpt. Ramona, Calif.: Ballena Press, 1972), 48, 33.

4. Geronimo Boscana, "Chinigchinich: A Historical Account of the Origins, Customs, and Traditions of the Indians at the Missionary Establishment of San Juan Capistrano, Alta California: Called Acagchemem Nation," trans. Alfred Robinson, in Alfred Robinson, *Life in California During a Residence of Several Years in That Territory . . . to Which Is Annexed a Historical Account of the Origins and Customs of the Indians of Alta California* (New York: Wiley and Putnam, 1846), 283–284.

5. Herbert E. Bolton, ed. and trans., *Font's Complete Diary: A Chronicle of the Founding of San Francisco* (Berkeley: University of California Press, 1931), 105.

6. Albert L. Hurtado, *Intimate Frontiers: Sex, Gender, and Culture in Old California* (Albuquerque: University of New Mexico Press, 1999), 5. See also Albert L. Hurtado, "Sexuality in

California's Franciscan Missions: Cultural Perceptions and Sad Realities," *California History* 71, no. 3 (Fall 1992): 370–385, 451–453.

7. See Lillian Faderman, *Surpassing the Love of Men: Romantic Friendship and Love Between Women from the Renaissance to the Present* (New York: William Morrow, 1981).

8. Garci Rodriguez de Montalvo, *The Labors of the Very Brave Knight Esplandian,* trans. William Thomas Little (Binghamton, N.Y.: Medieval and Renaissance Texts and Studies, 1992), 456–458.

9. Will Roscoe identifies honored roles and spiritual sanction for "third and fourth genders" among Native Americans throughout North America: See *Changing Ones: Third and Fourth Genders in Native North America* (New York: St. Martin's Press, 1998). See also Walter Williams, *The Spirit and the Flesh: Sexual Diversity in American Indian Culture* (Boston: Beacon Press, 1986).

10. A. L. Kroeber, *Handbook of the Indians of California* (1925; rpt. Berkeley: California Book Company), 46, 180, 647, 748–749.

11. See Sue-Ellen Jacobs, Wesley Thomas, and Sabine Lang, eds., *Two-Spirit People: Native American Gender Identity, Sexuality, and Spirituality* (Urbana: University of Illinois Press, 1997).

12. Boscana, "Chinigchinich," 283–284.

13. Francisco Palou, *Palou's Life of Fray Junipero Serra,* ed. and trans. Maynard J. Geiger (Washington, D.C.: Academy of American Franciscan History, 1955), 198–199.

14. John P. Harrington, "Cultural Element Distributions 19: Central California Coast," *University of California Anthropological Records* 7, no. 1 (1942): 32, 45. The contemporary Gabrielino playwright Cindi Alvitri says that to this day homosexuality is kept highly secret among the Tongva (Gabrielino): ST interview with Alvitri, April 7, 2005.

15. Of the Chumash, whose territory extended to Malibu Beach, A. L. Kroeber reported in 1925 that males were observed "in the dress, clothing, and character of women." Kroeber, *Handbook,* 497.

16. Ibid., 517.

17. Jack D. Forbes, *Warriors of the Colorado: The Yumas of the Quechan Nation and Their Neighbors* (Norman: University of Oklahoma Press, 1960), 57.

18. Devereux, "Institutionalized Homosexuality," 508.

19. Ramona Ford lists several West Coast (California and Oregon) tribes in which there were "female cross-gender roles": see "Native American Women: Changing Status, Changing Interpretations," in *Writing the Range: Race, Class and Culture in the Women's West,* ed. Elizabeth Jameson and Susan Armitage (Norman: University of Oklahoma Press, 1997), 52. See also Sue-Ellen Jacobs, "Berdache: A Brief Review of the Literature," *Colorado Anthropologist* 1 (1968); Evelyn Blackwood, "Sexuality and Gender in Certain Native American Tribes: The Case of Cross-Gender Females," *Signs: Journal of Women in Culture and Society* 10, no. 1 (1984): 27–42; Harriet Whitehead, "The Bow and the Burden Strap: A New Look at Institutionalized Homosexuality in Native North America," in *Sexual Meanings: The Cultural Construction of Gender and Sexuality,* ed. Sherry Ortner and Harriet Whitehead (Cambridge: Cambridge University Press, 1981), 80–115.

20. E. W. Gifford, "The Kamia of the Imperial Valley," *Bureau of American Ethnology Bulletin* 97 (Washington, D.C.: U.S. Government Printing Office, 1931), 6, 12.

21. Devereux, "Institutionalized Homosexuality," 503.

22. Ibid., 504.

23. Ibid., 511.

24. Boscana, "Chinigchinich," 330–332.

25. Devereux, "Institutionalized Homosexuality," 514.

26. "Los Angeles Disgraced," *California Argus,* May 9, 1896, in La Fiesta Scrapbook, Braun Research Library, Southwest Museum, Los Angeles (MS 207S1).

27. *Tarnished Angels: Paradisiacal Turpitude in Los Angeles,* ed. W. W. Robinson from an 1897 Los Angeles "Souvenir Sporting Guide" (Los Angeles: Ward Ritchie Press, 1964), 13.

28. Harris Newmark, *Sixty Years in Southern California, 1853–1913* (1916; rpt. Boston: Houghton Mifflin, 1930), 29–31, 266–267.

29. "Along El Camino Real," *Los Angeles Times,* January 31, 1939, 14.

30. Christine Fischer, "Women in California in the Early 1850s," in *Women in the Life of Southern California,* ed. Doyce B. Nunis, Jr. (Los Angeles: Historical Society of Southern California, 1996), 48.

31. For women who passed as men in other parts of the West, see, for example, "Little Jo Monoghan," in James Horan, *Desperate Women* (New York: G. P. Putnam's Sons, 1952); Mrs. E. J. Guerin, *Mountain Charley; or the Adventures of Mrs. E. J. Guerin, Who Was Thirteen Years in Male Attire* (rpt. Norman: University of Oklahoma Press, 1968); Mabel Rowe Curtis, *The Coachman Was a Lady: The Story of the Life of Charley Parkhurst* (Watsonville, Calif.: Pajaro Valley Historical Association, 1959). Albert Richardson, writing in 1867, said that it was so common for women to dress as men and go West that "help wanted" ads in mining country had to state: "No young women in disguise need apply," Albert D. Richardson, *Beyond the Mississippi: From the Great River to the Great Ocean, 1857–1867* (Hartford, Conn.: American Publishing Company, 1867), 200. Richardson also described the women in drag whom he had met in the West as all belonging to "the wretched class against which society shuts its iron doors."

32. Newmark, *Sixty Years,* 278.

33. Evelyn A. Schlatter, "Drag's a Life: Women, Gender, and Cross-Dressing in the Nineteenth Century West," in *Writing the Range: Race, Class and Culture in the Women's West,* ed. Elizabeth Jameson and Susan Armitage (Norman: University of Oklahoma Press, 1997), 338.

34. "Scenes on the Streets," April 18, 1895, unsourced clipping, item 1178, Max Meyburg, La Fiesta de Los Angeles Scrapbook, 1894–1931, Seaver Center, Los Angeles.

35. "Down with the Queen," *Los Angeles Record,* April 11, 1896, in La Fiesta Scrapbook, Braun Research Library, Southwest Museum, Los Angeles (MS 207 S1).

36. "Methodist Preachers Inveigh Against a Feature of the Fiesta," *Los Angeles Express,* March 16, 1896, in La Fiesta Scrapbook, Southwest Museum; and "Hell Turned Loose on Los Angeles," *Los Angeles Independent,* May 9, 1896, in Scrapbook, Braun Research Library, Southwest Museum.

37. "Hell Turned Loose on Los Angeles," Scrapbook, Braun Research Library, Southwest Museum (MS 207S1).

38. Ibid.

39. Los Angeles City Council Minutes, April 4, 1898: City of Los Angeles Records, vol. 25, February 21, 1898, to June 24, 1898, 248–249, in Los Angeles City Archives.

40. Los Angeles City Council Meeting reported in *Los Angeles Times,* March 26, 1895, 8.

41. City Council minutes, April 4, 1898: City of Los Angeles Records, vol. 25, Feb. 21, 1898, to June 24, 1898, 248–249, Los Angeles City Archives.

42. Impersonation acts were popular in nineteenth-century theater all over America. See Laurence Senelick, "The Evolution of the Male Impersonator on the Popular Stage," *Essays in Theater* 1, no. 1 (1982): 31–44; Laurence Senelick, "Boys and Girls Together: Sub-cultural Origins of Glamour Drag and Male Impersonation on the Nineteenth-Century Stage," 80–95; and Elizabeth Drorbaugh, "Sliding Scales: Notes on Storme DeLarverie and the Jewel Box Production Review," 120–143, in *Crossing the Stage: Controversies on Cross Dressing,* ed. Lesley Ferris (New York: Routledge, 1993); Gillian M. Rodger, "Male Impersonation on the North American Variety and Vaudeville Stage" (PhD diss., University of Pittsburgh, 1998), 66–69. For a discussion of the popularity of vaudeville in early-twentieth-century Los Angeles see Stan Steiner, "Vaudeville in Los Angeles, 1910–1926: Theaters, Management, and the Orpheum," *Pacific Historical Review* 61, no. 1 (February 1992): 103–113.

43. Rodger, "Male Impersonation," 66. (Rodger is quoting an August 6, 1870, newspaper, the *Clipper.*)

44. Ibid., 96.

45. Ibid., 72.

46. *Los Angeles Times,* September 1, 1924, A7.

47. Marshall L. Wright, *Before There Was a Hollywood: An Early History of Entertainment in Los Angeles, 1830–1930* (Los Angeles: self-published, 1998); in the Los Angeles Public Library Reference Collection.

48. "The Stage," *Los Angeles Times,* March 18, 1894, 19; also "Amusements," *Los Angeles Times,* February 2, 1893, 4.

49. "The Stage," *Los Angeles Times,* July 6, 1891, 4.

50. "Ko Vert, Female Impersonator, Wants Divorce," *Los Angeles Times,* September 30, 1922, II, 8. Ko Vert's one-day marriage was described as "a surprise to the film world."

51. Eltinge postured as a homophobe, but historians have documented his homosexuality: See, for example, Daniel Loftman Hurewitz, "Made in Edendale: Bohemian Los Angeles and the Politics of Identity, 1918–1953" (PhD diss., University of California, Los Angeles, 2001); Sharon Ullman, *Sex Seen: The Emergence of Modern Sexuality in America* (Berkeley: University of California Press, 1997); and Stan Steiner, "The Orpheum Theater of Los Angeles: An Overview," *Southern California Quarterly* 72, no. 4 (Winter 1990): 339–372.

52. Senelick, "Boys and Girls Together," 93.

53. The new ordinance regulated both masquerading and the issuance of permits to masqueraders. It was passed June 14, 1922, and given the number 43939, sections 1 and 2: See City of Los Angeles Records, vol. 128: 805, and vol. 129: 132–133. In 1936 this ordinance became 52.51 and 52.52 of the Los Angeles Municipal Code.

54. "Boy Role Easy for Her," *Los Angeles Times,* February 20, 1924, A10, and "Looking Through the Lens at Bits of Life," ibid.

55. "Billie's Way Is Feminine: Man-Milliner of El Monte 'a Perfect Lady,'" *Los Angeles Times,* January 13, 1907, II, 3.

56. "Flirtatious Willies Kept Upon the Run," *Los Angeles Times,* September 10, 1911, II, 9.

57. "Feminine Togs Not for Him; 'Lady Cook' Must Return to His Own Attire," *Los Angeles Times,* February 27, 1912, II, 14.

58. Eliza W. Farnham, *California, In-Doors and Out; or, How We Farm, Mine, and Live Generally in the Golden State* (New York: Dix, Edwards, and Company, 1856), 28.

59. Mary E. Blake, *On the Wing: Rambling Notes of a Trip to the Pacific* (Boston: Lee and Shepard, 1883), 2.

60. Farnham, *California, In-Doors and Out,* 27, 106.

61. Ibid., 188–189, 177–178.

62. Caroline M. Churchill, *Over the Purple Hills, or Sketches of Travel in California* (Denver: C. M. Churchill, 1876), 255–256.

63. The names of numerous women physicians who practiced medicine in turn-of-the-century Los Angeles are included in George H. Kress, *History of the Medical Profession in Southern California* (Los Angeles: Times-Mirror, 1910).

64. Emma H. Adams, *To and Fro, Up and Down: Southern California, Oregon, and Washington Territory* (Chicago: Cranston and Stowe, 1888), 67, 229.

65. Ibid., 229–230.

66. See Faderman, *Surpassing the Love of Men,* 239–253, for a discussion of how the nineteenth-century sexologists "morbidified" love between women.

67. Mary Casal, *The Stone Wall: An Autobiography* (Chicago: Eyncourt Press, 1930), 183.

68. In Eugene Fisher report on Los Angeles "degenerates," Sacramento City Archives, folder CD1 002 060.

69. "Man by Nature Really Woman," *Los Angeles Times,* September 30, 1917, V, 12.

70. "Science Aids Masquerader," *Los Angeles Times,* November 19, 1938, A3.

71. "Girl 'Husband' Gets Liberty," *Los Angeles Times,* January 15, 1929, A14.

72. See chap. 2.

73. "What We May Expect When the New Shirtwaist for Men Is 'In Flower,'" *Los Angeles Times,* August 15, 1900, I, 1.

74. Delegate to the California Constitutional Convention, Charles Botts, quoted in Donald Hargis, "Women's Rights in California, 1849," *Historical Society of Southern California Newsletter,* December 1955, 320–334.

75. "Uncle Walt," *Los Angeles Times,* May 11, 1911, I, 14.

76. Quoted in Jane Apostol, "Why Women Should Not Have the Vote: Anti-Suffrage Views in the Southland in 1911," in *Women in the Life of Southern California,* ed. Doyce B. Nunis, Jr. (Los Angeles: Historical Society of Southern California, 1996), 267–281.

77. Ibid.

78. Ibid.

79. In his dissertation on Bohemian Los Angeles and the politics of sexual identity, Daniel Hurewitz speculates that gay men and lesbians were attracted early to Los Angeles because it was a haven in which nontraditional behavior would be tolerated: Hurewitz, "Made in Edendale." Already at the beginning of the twentieth century, Los Angeles prided itself on being something of an art colony: "Los Angeles, always aspiring to be at the head of every procession, can exhibit a group of such as artists as is unknown to any other community of the same size and years," a 1901 newspaper article declared, observing the "artistic temperament" of those artists who lived in L.A.'s "Little Bohemia": "Los Angeles Becoming a Recognized Art Center," *Los Angeles Times,* June 23, 1901, C1.

80. *Sisters of the Road: The Autobiography of Box-Car Bertha,* as told to Dr. Ben L. Reitman (1937; rpt. New York: Harper and Row, 1975), 39, 60, 283, 290.

81. "'Mr.' Beach Held Romeo," *Los Angeles Times,* December 18, 1924, A1. See also the "Peter Stratford" case, "Grave Hides Strange Tale," (obit. of "Peter Stratford") *Los Angeles Times,* May 4, 1929, A2.

82. "Faint Reveals 'He's' a Woman," *Los Angeles Times,* September 28, 1932, 11.

83. The *Sacramento Bee* had hired Eugene Fisher to investigate a 1914 Long Beach scandal, discussed below. A folder of his field notes and correspondence is preserved at the Sacramento City Archives (folder CD1 002 060). Fisher's most detailed account of the episode consists of nineteen pages, hereafter referred to as the "Fisher Report." For another discussion of the Long Beach scandal see Ullman, *Sex Seen.*

84. "Some Phases of the Woman Question," *Los Angeles Times,* September 29, 1895, 15. By 1911, "effeminate undesirables" were said to be found on "any corner of the principal streets of Los Angeles"; "Flirtatious Willies."

85. "Says He Was Robbed," *Los Angeles Times,* February 2, 1896, 34.

86. Earl Lind [Ralph Werther], *The Female Impersonators* (1922; rpt. New York, Arno Press, 1975), 123.

87. "An Infamy; Vile Orgies at a Dance in a Public Hall," *Los Angeles Times,* June 3, 1887, 5.

88. Ibid. See also "End of the Carnival," *San Francisco Examiner,* April 14 [undated (1894?), in Seaver Center Scrapbook, 1894–1931, Seaver Center, Los Angeles], which refers to the Turnverein's young male athletes appearing in a Los Angeles parade "wearing little more than a feather."

89. See "By Laudanum," *Los Angeles Times,* November 24, 1887, 2. See also "Is Jailed in Turkish Bath," *Los Angeles Times,* January 22, 1913, II, 1.

90. Purssord's record as a "degenerate" is discussed in the Fisher Report. His career as an electrical therapist is discussed in "Adam's Garb Is Doctor's," *Los Angeles Times,* November 2, 1906, I, 13. "He is the most indecent man . . . ," ibid. Fisher describes Purssord as French; the U.S Census for 1900 lists him as British.

91. Purssord's suicide is discussed in the Fisher Report.

92. For a detailed account of this topic, see George Painter's Web-published "The Sensibilities of Our Forefathers: The History of Sodomy Laws in the United States–California," http://www.sodomylaws.org/sensibilities/california.htm.

93. *People v. Ed Wilson,* CR 2218, December 11, 1896, Judge J. W. McKinley, Los Angeles Hall of Records.

94. "Vile Criminals," *Los Angeles Times,* March 26, 1888, 8.

95. *People v. Charles Murphy,* CR 243, April 4, 1888, Los Angeles Hall of Records.

96. Los Angeles County Jail Register, April 1888–January 1897, Seaver Center, Los Angeles.

97. "Terrible Revenge; Two Brothers Take the Law Into Their Own Hands," *Los Angeles Times,* March 17, 1896, 3.

98. Ibid.

99. Sweeping vagrancy ordinances were common in the nineteenth century and after (see chap. 3) to run "undesirables," including homosexuals, out of town at the discretion of the police.

100. Fisher Report.

101. See, for example, "Wanted: Free Baths," *Los Angeles Times,* July 31, 1898, B4, in which the editors urged the city council to subsidize public baths.

102. Anecdotal information suggests that fellatio continued to be the preferred sexual activity of Los Angeles gay men through the mid-twentieth century: for example, ST interview with Harry Hay, May 17, 1987; ST interview with Oreste Pucciani, October 3, 1982. Also, a gay *male* publication, *Gay Girls* [sic] *Guide to the M.S. and the Modern World, 3rd Edition* (Fall 1957), notes on p. 19: "With the great increase in universal bathing facilities and personal hygiene in the 20th Century, oral techniques occupy a more prominent place than at any time in previous history." Pamphlet collection, ONE National Gay and Lesbian Archives, University of Southern California, Los Angeles.

103. The new law was enacted June 1, 1915. See *Statutes and Amendments to the Codes of California,* 1915, chap. 586, p. 1022. See also Painter, "The Sensibilities of Our Forefathers: The History of Sodomy Laws in the United States–California."

104. Letter from Eugene Fisher to C. K. McClatchy (owner of the *Sacramento Bee*), December 5, 1914. Sacramento City Archives (folder CD1 002 060).

105. "Takes His Life Through Shame: Note Asserts Innocence, but Unprovable," *Los Angeles Times,* November 15, 1914, I, 8.

106. "Are They Insane? A Woman's Query," *Los Angeles Times,* November 18, 1914, II, 5.

107. Fisher Report.

108. "Revival at Long Beach," *Los Angeles Times,* December 14, 1914, II, 1.

109. "Long Beach Morality Argument Ends in Fight" and "Long Beach, California—The Home of 'Social Vagrants.' Oh You 'Holy' City!" *Venice Daily Vanguard,* November 16, 1914, 1, 2. A *Los Angeles Times* article concluded, "What a Holy City Long Beach is!" in "Long Beach Uncovers Social Vagrant Clan," November 14, 1914, II, 8. See Mark Twain's *The Man That Corrupted Hadleyburg and Other Stories* (New York: Harper Brothers, 1900).

110. Eugene Fisher to C. K. McClatchy, November 20, 1914, Sacramento City Archives.

111. "Recital of Shameless Men," *Los Angeles Times,* November 19, 1914, p. 1.

112. Undated handwritten notes of Fisher, Sacramento City Archives.

113. Eugene Fisher to C. K. McClatchy, November 20, 1914.

114. "Long Beach Uncovers Social Vagrant Clan," *Los Angeles Times,* November 14, 1914, II, 8.

115. "Attorney Aims Blow at Detective Witness," *Los Angeles Times,* December 11, 1914.

116. "Publicity Is Needed and Then More Publicity," *Los Angeles Times,* November 26, 1914, II, 8.

117. "Long Beach Recital of Shameless Men," *Los Angeles Times,* Novemebr 14, 1914, II, 1.

118. "Jury Acquits in Six-O-Six," *Los Angeles Times,* December 12, 1914, II, 9.

119. Eugene Fisher to C. K. McClatchy, November 23, 1914, and Eugene Fisher to C. K. McClatchy (undated). Sacramento City Archives.

120. Fisher Report.

121. "Vast Scandal in Los Angeles Is Reported as Suppressed," *Sacramento Bee,* November 18, 1914, 1.

122. The *Bee*'s substantial file on this scandal contains no evidence for five hundred arrests. The Fisher Report does state that Warren and Brown made "fifty or more arrests . . . in the decency campaign which was carried on in Los Angeles."

123. Fisher Report.

124. Eugene Fisher to C. K. McClatchy, December 5, 1914, ibid.

125. Ibid.

126. Wright quoted in Cary McWilliams, *Southern California Country,* 158.

CHAPTER 2

1. "Hollywood Lowdown," *Broadway Brevities,* April 11, 1932, 10. "Hollywood Lowdown" was a regular column in *Broadway Brevities,* a New York City tabloid of the 1920s and '30s; its frequent gay references, though often scathing, contained verifiable details.

2. Frances Marion, *Off with Their Heads: A Serio-Comic Tale of Hollywood* (New York: Macmillan, 1972), 2–4.

3. Mary Winship, "Oh, Hollywood," *Photoplay,* May 1921, 112.

4. Merry Ovick, *Los Angeles: The End of the Rainbow* (Los Angeles: Balcony, 1994), 168.

5. Cal Yorke, "Plays and Players," *Photoplay,* January 1922, 95.

6. "Julian Eltinge," *Photo-Play Journal,* October 1917, 27.

7. Gavin Lambert, *Nazimova* (New York: Knopf, 1997), 201, 248.

8. Anthony Slide, "The Silent Closet," *Film Quarterly* (Summer 1979): 27.

9. To forestall government censorship, the Hays Office was established within the Motion Picture Producers and Distributors of America as a mechanism for self-censorship. Toward the top of the list of what Hollywood pledged not to show in films was references to homosexuality.

10. Mildred Adams, "The City of Angels Enters Heaven," *New York Times,* August 3, 1930, 5.

11. William Mann, *Behind the Screen: How Gays and Lesbians Shaped Hollywood* (New York: Viking, 2001), 84. See also Toto le Grand, "The Golden Age of Queens," part 4, *Bay Area Reporter* 4, no. 21 (October 1974).

12. Sheila Donisthorpe, *Loveliest of Friends* (New York: Charles Kendall, 1931).

13. Salka Viertel, *The Kindness of Strangers* (New York: Holt, Rinehart, and Winston, 1969), 175.

14. Josef von Sternberg, *Fun in a Chinese Laundry* (New York: MacMillan, 1965), 247.

15. "Tsk, Tsk, Such Goings On," *Variety,* February 28, 1933, 2.

16. In Barry Paris, *Louise Brooks: A Biography* (New York: Alfred A. Knopf, 1989), 400.

17. "Rambling Reporter," *Hollywood Reporter,* September 29, 1932, 2.

18. Ibid., October 20, 1932, 2.

19. Louise Brooks, *Lulu in Hollywood* (New York: Alfred A. Knopf, 1982), 96–97. See also Mel Gordon, *Voluptuous Panic: The Erotic World of Weimar Berlin* (Los Angeles: Feral House, 2006).

20. David King Dunaway, *Huxley in Hollywood* (New York: Harper and Row, 1989), 72.

21. As George Chauncey points out in *Gay New York: Gender, Urban Culture, and the Making of the Gay Male World, 1890–1940* (New York: Basic Books, 1994), New York, too, had its areas of gay sophistication in the early decades of the twentieth century, including Greenwich Village and Harlem. See also Lillian Faderman, *Odd Girls and Twilight Lovers: A History of Lesbian Life in Twentieth-Century America* (New York: Columbia University Press, 1991), especially chap. 3, "Lesbian Chic: Experimentation and Repression in the '20s."

22. Mercedes de Acosta, "Here Lies the Heart," manuscript version 02:04, chap. 32, 336, in Rosenbach Museum and Library, Philadelphia. We thank Dr. Kathleen Hall for providing us with this material.

23. By the 1920s, dance halls, cabarets, and speakeasies had sprung up all over Hollywood: Jim Heimann, *Out with the Stars: Hollywood Nightlife in the Golden Era* (New York: Abbeville

Press, 1985), 23–24. According to Axel Madsen, there were already several all-lesbian bars in Los Angeles by the 1920s. He cites The Big House on Hollywood Boulevard and the Lakeshore Bar near Westlake Park: *The Sewing Circle: Hollywood's Greatest Secret: Female Stars Who Loved Other Women* (New York: Birch Lane Press, 1995), 96–97. However, Madsen sometimes errs on dating: For example, he presents the Open Door, a bar that was established in the 1950s, in his discussion of lesbian bars of the 1920s and '30s.

24. For a discussion of New York's "pansy craze," see Chauncey, *Gay New York,* 314–321.

25. Jack Lord and Lloyd Huff, *How to Sin in Hollywood* (Hollywood: Jack Lord, 1940), 39.

26. Richard Barrios, *Screened Out: Playing Gay in Hollywood from Edison to Stonewall* (New York: Routledge, 2003), 103.

27. *Los Angeles Times,* December 21, 1932, A5.

28. Fletcher is the subject of Tyler Alpern's extensive biographical Web site, http://www.tyler-alpern.com/bruz.html. Fletcher rated more than one hundred mentions in the *Los Angeles Times* between 1935 and 1939.

29. "B.B.B.'s Cellar," *Variety,* October 4, 1932, 53.

30. "Coast Raid on Panze Joints," *Variety,* October 4, 1932, 52.

31. Gavin Lambert, *Nazimova* (New York: Alfred A. Knopf, 1997), 210.

32. ST interview with Mark Bortles, September 6, 2004. Cukor and Cole Porter vied for pre-eminence as partygivers and were jealous of one another's success, as their guests understood. "I had lunch at Cole's and dinner at George's," one partygoer recalled, "but you never told one about the other," Patrick McGilligan, *George Cukor: A Double Life* (New York: St. Martin's Press, 1991).

33. McGilligan, *George Cukor,* 120–126.

34. Donald Bogle, *Bright Boulevards, Bold Dreams: The Story of Black Hollywood* (New York: Ballantine Books, 2005). Bogle also discusses other African American gay and bisexual actors of the period such as Hattie McDaniel.

35. April 2, 1937, Howard Greer to James Broughton, p. 4, box 2, folder 101, James Broughton Papers, Collection 1, Special Collections, Kent State Library, Ohio. "Belle" is mid-century gay slang for an attractive young gay man. We thank Tyler Alpert for providing us with this material.

36. Ibid.

37. Heimann, *Out with the Stars,* 72–73.

38. "Hollywood Goes Beer Quaffing," *Variety,* November 21, 1933, 59.

39. See also Daniel Loftman Hurewitz's discussion of Hollywood nightclubs in the 1930s in "Made in Edendale: Bohemian Los Angeles and the Politics of Sexual Identity" (PhD diss., University of California, Los Angeles, 2001), 112–117.

40. Jack Lord and Lloyd Huff, *How to Sin in Hollywood* (Hollywood: Jack Lord, 1940), 39.

41. ST interview with Duncan Donovan, April 1, 2004. "Fegaleh," meaning a little bird, is Yiddish slang for "fairy."

42. LF interview with Beverly Alber, 78, February 15, 2004. See also Lester Strong and David Hanna, "Hollywood Watering Holes '30s Style," *Harvard Gay and Lesbian Review,* July 31, 1996.

43. W. K. Martin uses this term in *Marlene Dietrich* (New York: Chelsea House, 1995).

44. Kenneth Tynan regarding Marlene Dietrich in *The Sound of Two Hands Clapping* (New York: Holt, Rinehart, and Winston, 1975), 58.

45. Of the books included in these notes, we have found the most useful with regard to establishing actresses' sexuality are Anthony Slide's *The Silent Players;* William Mann's *Behind the Screen;* Gavin Lambert's *Nazimova;* Barry Paris' *Louise Brooks;* Steven Bach's *Marlene Dietrich;* Maria Riva's *Marlene Dietrich;* Lawrence Quirk and William Schoell's *Joan Crawford;* Brendan Gill's *Tallulah;* Karen Swenson's *Greta Garbo;* Barry Paris' *Garbo: A Biography;* Hugo Vickers' *Loving Garbo;* Robert Schanke's *That Furious Lesbian;* and Judith Mayne's *Directed by Dorothy Arzner.* See also Graham Russell Gao Hodges, *Anna May Wong: From Laundryman's Daughter to Hollywood Legend* (New York: Palgrave, 2004), and the Mercedes de Acosta Collection at the

Rosenbach Museum and Library, especially letters from Greta Garbo, Marlene Dietrich, Ona Munson, Polly Kirk, and Eva LeGalliene.

46. For a discussion of pioneering professional women who were "unstraight," see Lillian Faderman, *To Believe in Women* (New York: Houghton Mifflin, 1999).

47. Havelock Ellis, *Studies in the Psychology of Sex: Sexual Inversion in Women* (1897; rpt. New York: Random House, 1942), 230.

48. Christopher Anderson, *Young Kate* (New York: Henry Holt, 1988), 140.

49. A. Scott Berg, *Kate Remembered* (New York: G. P. Putnam and Sons, 2003), 45.

50. Raymond Daum, *Walking with Garbo* (New York: HarperCollins, 1991), 22.

51. Jack Grant, *Screen Book,* excerpted in *Hollywood and the Great Fan Magazines,* ed. Martin Levin (New York: Arbor House, 1970), 47+.

52. Steven Bach, *Marlene Dietrich: Life and Legend* (New York: William Morrow, 1992), 19.

53. Lawrence J. Quirk and William Schoell, *Joan Crawford: The Essential Biography* (Lexington: University Press of Kentucky, 2002), 2.

54. Adele Whitley Fletcher, "They Weren't Born Beautiful," *Modern Screen,* September 1930, 40–41.

55. Maria Riva, *Marlene Dietrich, by Her Daughter* (New York: Alfred A. Knopf, 1993), 87.

56. Mercedes de Acosta in Lambert, *Nazimova,* 178.

57. Robert A. Schanke, "Alla Nazimova: The Witch of Makeup," in Robert A. Schanke and Kim Marra, eds., *Passing Performances: Queer Readings of Leading Players in American Theater History* (Ann Arbor: University of Michigan Press, 1998), 133.

58. The sexuality of Nita Naldi and Pola Negri is discussed in Anthony Slide, "The Silent Closet," *Film Quarterly* (Summer 1999): 24–32.

59. Vamp image described in "Garbo Is Still Queen," *Motion Picture,* August 1936, 37+.

60. Bach, *Marlene Dietrich,* 74, 245–246.

61. Brendan Gill, *Tallulah* (New York: Holt, Rinehart, Winston, 1972), 51–52.

62. Martin, *Marlene Dietrich,* 91. Maria Riva claims that Bankhead never actually succeeded in that desire: Riva, who was briefly an actress and toured in a play with Bankhead, recalls that Bankhead, "completely naked, liked chasing me down hotel corridors. Poor Tallulah, she hadn't managed to get 'into Dietrich's pants' at Paramount, [and] now figured she'd get into the daughter's," Riva, *Marlene Dietrich, by Her Daughter,* 554.

63. Berg, *Kate Remembered,* 4–5. Other biographers, too, who knew the two women personally offer evidence that suggests that Phyllis was more than an employee to Katherine: See, for example, James Prideaux, *Knowing Hepburn and Other Curious Experiences* (Winchester, Mass.: Faber and Faber, 1996), 62.

64. Quoted in Lambert, *Nazimova,* 315. Wilbourn had played a similar role for the actress Constance Collier until Collier's death. There is some indication that Greta Garbo was once interested in Wilbourn. Garbo's friend and correspondent, Cecil Beaton, teased Garbo in a 1948 letter: "There's not much point in trying to find out if you've been seeing Constance Collier's companion." In Hugo Vickers, *Loving Garbo: The Story of Greta Garbo, Cecil Beaton, and Mercedes de Acosta* (New York: Random House, 1994), 145.

65. Patrick McGilligan, *George Cukor: A Double Life* (New York: St. Martin's Press, 1991), 82, 85.

66. Berg, *Kate Remembered,* 350.

67. Ibid., 83.

68. Katharine Hepburn, *Me: Stories of My Life* (New York: Alfred A. Knopf, 1991), 131–132.

69. Ibid., 400.

70. Selznick is quoted in Berg, *Kate Remembered,* 266–267.

71. Ibid., 81.

72. James Robert Parish, *Katherine Hepburn: The Untold Story* (New York: Advocate Books, 2005), 66, 121. Parish characterizes their relationship as "a marriage of convenience" (96).

73. Don Camp, "Hepburn Goes in for Hobbies in a Great Big Way," *Motion Picture,* February 1937, 40+.

74. Quoted in Homer Dickens, *The Films of Katharine Hepburn* (1971; rev. ed. New York: Carol Publishing, 1990), 43.

75. Joel Ryan, *Katharine Hepburn: A Stylish Life* (New York: Byron Preiss Visual Publications, 1999), 83.

76. Gully and Edwards quoted in Parish, *Katherine Hepburn,* 208.

77. Sternberg, *Fun in a Chinese Laundry,* 246.

78. "I'm One of the Boys," in *The Hollywood Party* (1933), quoted in Brett L. Adams, "Latitude in Mass-Produced Culture's Capitol: The New Woman and Other Players in Hollywood, 1920–1941," *Frontiers: A Journal of Women's Studies* 25, no. 2 (June 2004): 65–96.

79. *Hollywood Reporter,* June 18, 1934, 1–2.

80. "Cardinal Raps Public Filth," *Los Angeles Times,* April 28, 1938, 9.

81. Herbert Blumer, *Movies and Conduct* (New York: Macmillan, 1933), 45, 71. See Jack Lait and Lee Mortimer, who attributed the "epidemic of homosexuality" among young women almost twenty years later to "knowledge that many of the movie set prefer it that way," in *U.S.A. Confidential* (New York: Crown, 1952), 42–43.

82. Caroline Sheldon, "Lesbians in Film: Some Thoughts," in *Gays in Film,* ed. Richard Dyer (New York: Zoetrope, 1984), 5–26. For the influence of the 1930s' lesbian images on lesbians today, see also Andrea Weiss, *Vampires and Violets: Lesbians in Film* (New York: Penguin, 1992), especially "A Queer Feeling When I Look at You," chap. 2, and Patricia White, *UnInvited: Classical Hollywood Cinema and Lesbian Representability* (Bloomington: Indiana University Press, 1999).

83. Gore Vidal, *The City and the Pillar* (New York: Dutton, 1948), 109.

84. Donald Spoto, *Blue Angel: The Life of Marlene Dietrich* (1992; rpt. New York: Cooper Square Press, 2000), 124.

85. Historically, passionate relationships between women were often seen by the uninitiated as merely "romantic friendships" rather than lesbian love, perhaps because in a more puritanical era people preferred not to entertain the notion of autonomous female sexuality such as lesbianism required: See Lillian Faderman, *Surpassing the Love of Men: Romantic Friendship and Love Between Women from the Renaissance to the Present* (New York: William Morrow, 1981).

86. We have found the most useful with regard to establishing male actors' sexuality: Mann, *Behind the Screen* and *Wisecracker: The Life and Times of William Haines* (New York: Viking, 1998); Slide, "The Silent Closet"; McGillian, *George Cukor;* Anthony Slide, *Silent Players: A Biographical and Autobiographical Study of 100 Silent Film Actors and Actresses,* (Lexington: University Press of Kentucky, 2002); Joseph Morella and George Mazzei, *Genius and Lust: The Creative and Sexual Lives of Cole Porter and Noel Coward* (New York: Carroll and Graf, 1995); Hector Arce, *The Secret Life of Tyrone Power: The Drama of a Bisexual in the Spotlight* (New York: William Morrow, 1979); Larry Swindell, *The Last Hero: A Biography of Gary Cooper* (New York: Doubleday, 1980); Allan R. Ellenberger, *Ramon Novarro* (Jefferson, N.C: McFarland, 1999); and Arthur Laurents, *Original Story By: A Memoir of Broadway and Hollywood* (New York: Alfred A. Knopf, 2000).

87. Mann's focus, as his subtitle suggests, is "How Gays and Lesbians Shaped Hollywood: 1910–1969."

88. Morella and Mazzei, *Genius and Lust,* 103.

89. ST interview with Malcolm Boyd, 80, September 3, 2004.

90. Leonard Spigelgass quoted in David Grafton, *Red, Hot, and Rich: An Oral History of Cole Porter* (New York: Stein and Day, 1987).

91. Sidney D. Kirkpatrick, *A Cast of Killers* (New York: E. P. Dutton, 1986), 229.

92. Ibid.

93. Edward Doherty, *Denver Post,* March 3, 1922.

94. *New York Herald,* February 6, 1922.

95. *New York News,* February 6, 1922.

96. Ibid.

97. Joe Domanick, *To Protect And Serve: The LAPD's Century of War in the City of Dreams* (New York: Pocket Books, 1994), 121. See also Charles Higham and Roy Moseley, *Cary Grant: The Lonely Heart* (New York: Harcourt Brace Jovanovich, 1989), 147, for an example of the police covering up the gay arrest of a star.

98. "Rambling Reporter," *Hollywood Reporter,* July 3, 1934, 2.

99. William J. Mann, *Wisecracker: The Life and Times of William Haines* (New York: Viking, 1998), 260.

100. ST interview with Duncan Donovan, 84, April 1, 2004.

101. "Hollywood Lowdown," *Broadway Brevities,* April 11, 1932, 10.

102. ST interview with Harry Hay, 76, January 3, 1988.

103. Slide, *Silent Players,* 159.

104. Arce, *The Secret Life of Tyrone Power,* 69.

105. Swindell, *The Last Hero,* 104–105.

106. Dagmar Godowska, *First Person Plural: The Lives of Dagmar Godowska* (New York: Viking Press, 1958), 71.

107. "Thank God for Five-Yard McCarty," *Chicago Tribune,* November 10, 1925.

108. "Pink Powder Puffs," *Chicago Tribune,* July 18, 1926.

109. "Rudy's So Sore, It's Just Awful," *Los Angeles Times,* July 21, 1926, 2.

110. Ellenberger, *Ramon Novarro,* 15, and David Brett, *Valentino: A Dream of Desire* (London: Robson Books, 1998).

111. Lambert, *Nazimova,* 223.

112. Ibid., 223–224. See also Emily W. Leider, *Dark Lover: The Life and Death of Rudolph Valentino* (New York: Farrar, Strauss and Giroux, 2003), 99–101.

113. On Negri see William Mann, *Wisecracker,* 109; John Baxter, *The Hollywood Exiles* (New York: Taplinger, 1976), 46–47; and Pola Negri, *Memoirs of a Star* (Garden City, N.Y.: Doubleday, 1970).

114. See Leider, *Dark Lover,* passim.

115. In Lambert, *Nazimova,* 397–400.

116. Quoted in Cal Yorke, "Plays and Players," *Photoplay,* December 1921, 80.

117. Aspirants to stardom also went along with the game, not only to bolster their images but sometimes, too, for the sake of glamour and a good meal: Tab Hunter recounts that before he became a star, he was willing to do publicity dating with actresses: "Having ourselves described as 'an item' or 'deeply involved' was a small price to pay for access to lavish parties overflowing with delicacies otherwise unavailable to actors living on saltines, sardines, and soda pop." Tab Hunter with Eddie Muller, *Tab Hunter Confidential: The Making of a Movie Star* (Chapel Hill, N.C.: Algonquin Books of Chapel Hill, 2005), 73–74.

118. Lesley Ferris, "Kit and Guth," in Schanke and Marra, *Passing Performances,* 197–220. The practice of lavender marriage in Hollywood extended even to those who were not in front of the camera, according to the actor Rex Evans and his partner Jim Weatherford. As they recall, decorator Jimmy Pendleton, who was "as gay as could be," married "a Texas rich woman who was the ugliest thing." Weatherford says that Pendleton's wife "gave him one night out a week to be with his gay friends." ST interview with Jim Weatherford, June 29, 2004.

119. Charles Higham and Roy Moseley, *Cary Grant: The Lonely Heart* (New York: Harcourt Brace Jovanovich, 1989).

120. Arce, *Tyrone Power,* 113.

121. Val Holley, *Mike Connolly and the Manly Art of Hollywood Gossip* (Jefferson, N.C.: McFarland, 2003), 103.

122. Ramona Bergere, "She Does as She Pleases," *Modern Screen,* March 1937, 18.

123. Gladys Hall, "'Tis the Likes of Kelly," *Motion Picture*, January 1937, 32+.

124. "A Woman's Touch," *Motion Picture Studio Insider*, July 1937, 20.

125. Judith Mayne's *Directed by Dorothy Arzner* (Bloomington: Indiana University Press, 1994) discusses Arzner's career as well as her lesbian relationships. See also Weiss, *Vampires and Violets*.

126. Charles Higham, *Lucy: The Real Life of Lucille Ball* (New York: St. Martin's Press, 1984), 52.

127. Quoted in Barry Paris, *Louise Brooks* (New York: Alfred A. Knopf, 1989), 419.

128. Lambert, *Nazimova*, 162.

129. *Hollywood Reporter*, July 31, 1935.

130. For example, McGilligan, *George Cukor;* Barry Paris, *Garbo: A Biography* (London: Pan Books, 1996); Mann, *Behind the Screen*; Lambert, *Nazimova*.

131. "How To Hold a Husband/Wife in Hollywood," *Photoplay*, June 1929, 106.

132. Gladys Hall, "Lil's Baby!" August 25, 1931, typescript in the Gladys Hall file, Academy of Motion Picture Arts and Sciences.

133. Mann, *Behind the Screen*, 115.

134. Huxley quoted in Basil Rathbone, *In and Out of Character* (Garden City, N.Y.: Doubleday, 1956), 143.

135. "Rambling Reporter," *Hollywood Reporter*, November 21, 1931, 2.

136. "Ambidextrous" and "new love" quoted in Karen Swenson, *Greta Garbo: A Life Apart* (New York: Scribner, 1997), 259–260. "Lavender" speakeasy in "Rambling Reporter," *Hollywood Reporter*, January 7, 1932, 2.

137. "The Lowdown," *Hollywood Reporter*, January 27, 1932, 2. Mercedes de Acosta writes of her romances with Garbo, Dietrich, and other famous actresses in *Here Lies the Heart* (1960; rpt. New York: Arno Press, 1975). In the various drafts of this autobiography, now at the Rosenbach Museum in Philadelphia, she was even more explicit about these love relationships than she was in the published version. Among Mercedes de Acosta's papers at the Rosenbach are also letters sent to her by Dietrich and Garbo regarding their relationship. See also Robert A. Schanke, *"That Furious Lesbian": The Story of Mercedes de Acosta* (Carbondale: Southern Illinois University Press, 2003), and Hugo Vickers, *Loving Garbo: The Story of Greta Garbo, Cecil Beaton, and Mercedes de Acosta* (New York: Random House, 1994).

138. Greta Garbo to Mercedes de Acosta, April 29, 1950, box 23, file 30, Rosenbach Museum and Library.

139. Quoted in Weiss, *Vampires and Violets*, 32.

140. "Hedda Hopper's Hollywood," *Los Angeles Times*, January 15, 1941, 12.

141. Stiller's homosexuality is discussed in Swenson, *Greta Garbo: A Life Apart*, 56.

142. Marcella Burke, "Why Garbo Has Never Married," in *Hollywood and the Great Fan Magazines*, ed. Martin Levin (New York: Arbor House, 1970), 74+.

143. Gary Carey, *All the Stars in Heaven: Louis B. Mayer's M-G-M* (New York: E. P. Dutton, 1981), 215.

144. Don Camp, "Hepburn Goes in for Hobbies in a Great Big Way," *Motion Picture*, February 1937, 40+.

145. Romano Tozzi, *Films in Review*, December 1957, 484.

146. ST interviews with Jim Weatherford, June 29, 2004, and Michael Kearns, September 21, 2004.

147. Robert S. Sennett, *Hollywood Hoopla: Creating Stars and Selling Movies in the Golden Age of Hollywood* (New York: Billboard Books, 1998), 61.

148. Rock Hudson and Sara Davidson, *Rock Hudson: His Story* (New York: William Morrow, 1986), 74.

149. Robert Hofler, *The Man Who Invented Rock Hudson: The Pretty Boys and Dirty Deals of Henry Willson* (New York: Carroll & Graf, 2006). It was Willson who arranged a front marriage

between Hudson and Phyllis Gates: Trudy Ring, "Behind the Screen," *Advocate*, February 28, 2006, 47, and Robert Hofler, "Outing Mrs. Rock Hudson," ibid., 46–47.

150. Hofler, *The Man Who Invented Rock Hudson*.

151. Hunter with Muller, *Tab Hunter Confidential*, 51–52.

152. Steve Govoni, "Now It Can Be Told," *American Film*, February 1990, 28–33+.

153. Quoted in Max Pierce, "In Search of Lizabeth Scott, the Sphinx from Scranton," *Films of the Golden Age*, Summer 2002, 21.

154. Hedda Hopper, "Star By-passes Romance for Career," *Los Angeles Times*, October 14, 1951, E1.

155. Pierce, "In Search of Lizabeth Scott," 24.

156. Hopper, "Star By-passes Romance."

CHAPTER 3

1. Raymond Chandler, *The Big Sleep* and *Farewell, My Lovely* (New York: The Modern Library, 1995), 279–280.

2. Kevin Starr, *Embattled Dreams* (New York: Oxford University Press, 2002), 36. Total blackouts followed the immediate attack on December 7, 1941, and partial blackouts continued.

3. "Facts of Japanese Inquiry Released," *Los Angeles Times*, March 20, 1942, 9.

4. Starr, *Embattled Dreams*, on LAPD treatment of Latinos: "For years, in fact, the LAPD and the sheriff's department had been making war on young men of Mexican descent. . . . The sheer presence of young Mexicans on street corners in the barrio . . . was seen by patrolling police or sheriff's deputies as de facto proof of a crime in process or about to happen. . . . Beatings were frequent, as were frame-ups" (98).

5. LF interview with Stella Rush, 79, November 10, 2004.

6. Edith Eyde [a.k.a. Lisa Ben] made such observations firsthand in her Los Angeles–based lesbian magazine, *Vice Versa*: "Here to Stay," September 1947, 4–5.

7. Kenneth Marlowe, *The Male Homosexual* (Los Angeles: Sherbourne Press, 1965), 46. Also, ST interview with Norman Stanley, 78, September 17, 2004.

8. Alan Berube, *Coming Out Under Fire: The History of Gay Men and Women in World War Two* (New York: Free Press, 1990), 114.

9. Ibid., 123.

10. Carey McWilliams, *California, the Great Exception* (New York: Current Books, 1949), 13–14.

11. LF interview with Beverly Hickok, 85, September 17, 2004.

12. Jim Kepner, "The Loves of a Longtime Activist: An Autobiography and Gay Movement History, Sort Of, in 181 Vignettes" (unpublished ms., 1993). LF interview with Laura Sherman, 77, July 26, 2004. Beverly Hickok, *Against the Grain: Coming Out in the 1940s* (Philadelphia: Xlibris, 2003), 50–51.

13. Stanley interview.

14. *The Complete Reprint of Physique Pictorial, 1951–1964*, vol. 1 (Cologne, Germany: Taschen, 1997), 6–17.

15. Tom of Finland Foundation, *Tom of Finland: Retrospective* (North Hollywood: London Press, 1988), 5.

16. Michael Duncan, "Bob Mizer at Western Projects," *Art in America* 93, no. 3 (March 2005): 146. See also Stuart Timmons, "Wanted: Athletic Models," *The Advocate*, July 30, 1992, 56–60.

17. Joe Domanick, *To Protect and to Serve: The LAPD's Century of War in the City of Dreams* (New York: Pocket Books), 12. The philosophy established by Parker was continued by his protégé, Daryl Gates, LAPD Chief from 1979 to 1992.

18. Correspondence from Norman Stanley to Sallie Fiske, March 15, 1961, private collection.

19. According to LAPD statistics, in 1947, the police made 1,656 arrests for "sex perversion." Three years later, when Parker became chief, arrests increased 86.5 percent: Los Angeles Police Department, *Annual Report,* 1947 and 1950. Even admired public figures who were gay, such as the tennis star Bill Tilden and the civil rights organizer Bayard Rustin, suffered career-wrecking lewd conduct arrests by the zealous LAPD.

20. Eugene D. Williams, introduction to *The Sexual Criminal: A Psychoanalytic Study,* by Paul de River, 2nd ed. (1949; rpt. Springfield, Ill.: Charles C. Thomas, 1956).

21. De River, *The Sexual Criminal: A Psychoanalytic Study,* 276–277.

22. "Increase in Sex Crimes Laid to War Influence," *Los Angeles Times,* November 11, 1948, A6.

23. "Closing of Eight Bars Urged by Assembly Group," *Los Angeles Times,* February 6, 1948, 1. These sanctions also targeted prostitution.

24. "Degenerate Ban Voted," *Los Angeles Times,* March 12, 1949, A1.

25. *Stoumen v. Reilly* (California 1951), in *Lesbians, Gay Men and the Law,* ed. William B. Rubenstein (New York: The New Press, 1993), 205–206. See also Nan Boyd, *Wide Open Town: A History of Queer San Francisco to 1965* (Berkeley: University of California Press, 2003).

26. Rubenstein, *Lesbians, Gay Men and the Law,* 206.

27. *People v. Guynn,* 1950, CR A 2551; *People v. Granato,* 1950, CR A, 2552: *Los Angeles Municipal Code,* 1956, vol. 2, 28 (52.51).

28. The 1958 LAPD Annual Report reveals that the police felt embattled by judicial decrees which, the department said, had "hamstrung" officers and "hoodwinked an apathetic public." Nevertheless, the report said, the LAPD would not be daunted in "its resolve to keep the city free from corruption": VICE section, 14.

29. Helen Branson, *Gay Bar* (San Francisco: Pan Graphic Press, 1957),42.

30. ST interviews with Jim Weatherford, 84, June 29, 2004; William Joseph Bryan, 78, March 16, 2004; and Malcolm Boyd, 81, June 27, 2004.

31. ST interview with Marvin Edwards, 73, June 7, 2004.

32. Mike Rothmiller, *L.A. Secret Police: Inside the LAPD Elite Spy Network* (New York: Pocketbooks, 1992), 73.

33. The term "Hollywood reject" became so widespread it rated inclusion in a national gay lexicon: Bruce Rodgers, *Gay Talk: A Sometimes Outrageous Dictionary of Gay Slang* (New York: Paragon Books, 1972).

34. ST interview with Stanley Markowitz, 75, June 7, 2004.

35. ST interview with Tom Gibbon, 78, June 12, 2004.

36. Markowitz interview.

37. ST interview with Rudy Ruano, 60, September 16, 2004.

38. Donovan interview.

39. ST interview with Jack (pseud.), 79, June 4, 2004.

40. ST interview with John Rechy, August 29, 2005.

41. Ed Jackson, "647: The Catch-All That Catches All," *Los Angeles Advocate,* June 1968, 9.

42. Quoted in William Mann, *Behind the Screen: How Gays and Lesbians Shaped Hollywood, 1910–1969* (New York: Viking: 2001), 87.

43. Kenneth Marlow, *The Male Homosexual* (Los Angeles: Sherbourne Press, 1965), 46.

44. Ibid.

45. Rechy interview, 71, August 29, 2005.

46. A number of our narrators recounted stories of a flashing red-light signal at the Canyon Club. However, one woman who went often to the Canyon Club says, "The guy who owned it was a cop, and the police never showed up"; she speculates, "Maybe he flashed the lights to add atmosphere. Maybe it was just a game." LF interview with Myra Riddell, 77, November 9, 2004.

47. Rothmiller, *L.A. Secret Police,* 73.

48. ST interview with Steve Hodel, 65, September 14, 2005.

49. Kevin Brownlow recalls that from its first days, Hollywood proved "a paradise" for blackmailers: *The Parade's Gone By* (New York: Alfred A, Knopf, 1968), 39. Organized crime used to target homosexuals for a blackmail scheme they referred to as "fruitshakes."

50. Gibbon interview; ST interview with James Miller, July 5, 2004.

51. ST interview with Bill Regan, 73, July 1, 2004.

52. ST interview with Aristide Laurent, 63, August 25, 2004.

53. ST interviews with Guy Richards, 73, June 21 and July 1, 2004.

54. Donovan interview. See also Cy Rice, *Defender of the Damned: Gladys Towels Root* (New York: The Citadel Press, 1964).

55. Weatherford interview.

56. Donovan interview. The attorney Bill Stephens, who defended men against entrapment charges, corroborated Donovan's obvservation. ST interview with Bill Stephens, 64, August 27, 2004.

57. Lisa Ben, taped interview with Paul Cain. We are indebted to Mr. Cain for sharing his transcription with us.

58. Jane Jones' bar is described in Lester Strong and David Hanna, "Hollywood Watering Holes, 30's Style," *Harvard Gay and Lesbian Review*, July 31, 1996.

59. Tess's various venues and names are described in Jack Lord and Lloyd Hoff, *How to Sin in Hollywood* (Hollywood: self-published, 1940), 38–39; in a taped interview with Rikki Streicher, July 1981, June Mazer Lesbian Archives, West Hollywood, California; in Beverly Hickok, *Against the Current: Coming Out in the 1940s* (Philadelphia: Xlibris, 2003); in Hickok interview; and in Hanna, "Hollywood Watering Holes."

60. LF interview with Dottie, 77, February 14, 2004.

61. Eileen Leaffer makes a similar distinction between lesbian nightclubs and bars in "Gay Life: An Ethnography of Lesbian Society" (unpublished paper, Occidental College, Department of Sociology, 1967), 1, June Mazer Lesbian Archives.

62. LF interview with Terry DeCrescenzo, April 4, 2004.

63. LF interview with Min, 80, and Marion, 76, February 12, 2004.

64. Streicher taped interview, June Mazer Lesbian Archives.

65. LF interview with Nancy Valverde, 73, October 5, 2004.

66. See, for example, Betty Friedan's *The Feminine Mystique* (New York: Penguin, 1963), for a discussion of how American women were encouraged after World War II to limit their pursuits exclusively to domestic life.

67. Though there is little evidence that lesbians were prosecuted under the 1915 California law against oral sex, because the law was part of the Penal Code, they knew they could be. See "The History of Sodomy Laws in the United States: California," http://www.sodomylaws.org/sensibilities/california.htm: The author identifies only four published cases that dealt with "consensual relations between women" in the United States.

68. LF interview with Maggie (pseud.), 76, February 13, 2004.

69. Liz quoted in Janise Gravlin, "Old Trees with White Blossoms: An Ethnography of Aging Lesbians" (master's thesis, University of California, Los Angeles, 1998), 57–58.

70. LF interview with K.C. (pseud.), 61, April 22, 2004. Softball attracted many young gay women in Los Angeles, and not all teams were generated in the bars. Elena Martinez (pseud.), who played with corporate-sponsored Buena Park and Huntington Park teams in the 1950s and '60s, says that those teams were largely lesbian, but she and her friends seldom hung out at the lesbian bars because they wanted to play well and they feared that drinking would interfere with their ability (LF interview, April 19, 2004). Softball games provided some social outlet where working-class and young gay women could meet other women. However, because softball was widely associated with lesbianism by mid-century and was played in public, many feared to participate, believing (ironically) that the bars, which were hidden from public view, were a safer venue.

71. LF interview with Sharon A, Lilly, 58, April 8, 2004. Elizabeth Lapovsky Kennedy and Madeline D. Davis have also observed, in their study of mid-century working-class lesbians in Buffalo, New York, that lesbian bars served as centers of community: *Boots of Leather, Slippers of Gold: The History of a Lesbian Community* (New York: Routledge, 1993). See also Joan Nestle, *A Restricted Country* (Ithaca, N.Y.: Firebrand Books, 1987), regarding community in lesbian bars in New York City.

72. Hearing before the Alcoholic Beverage Control Appeals Board of the State of California, December 16, 1959, "In the Matter of the Accusation Against William Ford and Ernestina D. Jones," proprietors of The Party Pad in Los Angeles, folder #404, file 50897, "Proceedings," 56.

73. "Proposed Decision," 8, 2, ibid.

74. Strong and Hanna, "Hollywood Watering Holes, 30's Style," 30. Allan Berube's narrators also observed that bars during World War II attempted to cater to mixed crowds in order to camouflage the character of the establishments and thus avoid police harassment: *Coming Out Under Fire*, 113–114.

75. LF interviews with Violet, 71, February 14, 2004, and Saundra Tignor, 67, August 20, 2004.

76. Raids on lesbian bars were also frequent in other big cities during those years: See, for example, Maxine Wolfe, "Invisible Women in Invisible Places: The Production of Social Space in Lesbian Bars," in *Queers in Space: Communities, Public Spaces, Sites of Resistance*, ed. Gordon Brent Ingram, Anne-Marie Bouthillette, and Yolanda Retter (Seattle: Bay Press, 1997), 301–324; Nestle, *A Restricted Country*; "The Gay Bar—Whose Problem Is It?" *The Ladder*, December 1959, 4–13+; and *Improper Bostonians*, comp. The History Project (Boston: Beacon Press, 1998).

77. LF interview with Stella Rush, 79, November 10, 2004.

78. LF interview with Eileen Cusimano, 67, October 6, 2004.

79. Leaffer, "Gay Life."

80. LF interview with Meko, 64, July 23, 2004.

81. LF interview with Sally (pseud.), 69, February 18, 2004.

82. "Mayor Fletcher Bowron Against Slacks for Women at City Hall," *Los Angeles Times*, April 22, 1942, 1.

83. "Woman Barber Wins Leniency," *Los Angeles Times*, May 1, 1940, A2.

84. LF interview with Nancy Valverde, November 5, 2004.

85. Valverde interviews.

86. Ibid.

87. LF interview with Frankie Hucklenbroich, 65, March 20, 2004. See also Frankie Hucklenbroich, *A Crystal Diary* (Ithaca, N.Y.: Firebrand, 1997), and Lillian Faderman, *Naked in the Promised Land* (New York: Houghton Mifflin, 2003).

88. LF interview with Flo Fleischman, 74, April 7, 2004.

89. Cross-dressing lesbians everywhere sought means—whether creative, silly, or demeaning—to evade masquerading laws by wearing three articles of women's clothing. A New Orleans woman, for example, remembers that in addition to wearing panties and bra, she sewed lace on all her socks so that the police would believe they were indeed an article of women's clothing: in Maxine Wolfe, "Invisible Women in Invisible Places."

90. Lou, in Gravlin, "Old Trees with White Blossoms," 40.

91. Violet interview.

92. LF interview with Betsy, 78, July 25, 2004.

93. LF interview with Harriet Perl, 83, February 14, 2004.

94. LF interview with Donna, 70, January 11, 2004.

95. Perl interview.

96. In Gravlin, "Old Trees with White Blossoms," 79.

97. LF interview with Myra Riddell, 77, November 9, 2004.

98. LF interview with Dr. Mandy (pseud.), 74, February 15, 2004.

99. Lesbians and gay men fronted for one another elsewhere as well in mid-century: See, for example, David K. Johnson, *The Lavender Scare: The Cold War Persecution of Gays and Lesbians in the Federal Government* (Chicago: University of Chicago Press, 2004), 150–154.

100. LF interview with Millie, 79, October 7, 2004.

101. Hickok interview.

102. Stanley interview.

103. LF interview with Jo Duffy, 78, July 27, 2004.

104. Millie interview.

105. LF interview with Saundra Tignor, 67, August 20, 2004.

106. LF interview with Mynun, 63, and Gayle, 64, April 5, 2004.

107. ST interview with Tom Gibbon, 82, and Bob Clark, 80, June 21, 2004.

CHAPTER 4

1. *The Ladder,* May 1957, 28. Under the name Lorraine Hansberry, the author went on to write the groundbreaking play *Raisin in the Sun* in 1959.

2. Mina Robinson (a.k.a. Mina Meyer), "The Older Lesbian" (master's thesis, California State University, Dominguez Hills, 1979).

3. Numerous interviews with "Lisa Ben" have been published in recent years. See, especially, Leland Moss, "An Interview with Lisa Ben," *Gaysweek,* January 23, 1978, 14–16; Eric Marcus, *Making History: The Struggle for Gay and Lesbian Equal Rights, 1945–1990* (New York: HarperCollins, 1992); Zsa Zsa Gershick, *Gay Old Girls* (Los Angeles: Alyson, 1998); Rodger Streitmatter, *Unspeakable: The Rise of the Gay and Lesbian Press in America* (Winchester, Mass.: Faber and Faber, 1995); Vern Bullough, ed., *Before Stonewall: Activists for Gay and Lesbian Rights in a Historical Context* (interview with Lisa Ben by Florence Fleischman) (New York: Harrington Press, 2002); Paul D. Cain, *Leading the Parade: Conversations with America's Most Influential Lesbians and Gay Men* (Lanham, Md.: Scarecrow Press, 2002). We are grateful to Paul Cain for permitting us to see his unedited interview transcript. Eyde has given various reasons for changing her name to Lisa Ben ("lesbian"). In some interviews, she says she became Lisa Ben when the editors of the *Ladder* refused to let her publish a piece under the name "Ima Spinster." In others, she says she took the name Lisa Ben when invited to record a song for a Capitol Records album.

4. Marcus, *Making History,* 6.

5. Ibid., 8.

6. Beginning in the late nineteenth century in Europe, there were also several journals and magazines directed at "sexual inverts" (primarily men), including, in Germany, *Der Eigene* and *Jahrbuch für sexuelle Zwischenstufen* (the journal of Magnus Hirschfeld's Scientific-Humanitarian Committee); in Switzerland, *Der Kreis;* in France, *Le Cercle;* in Denmark, *Vennen.*

7. Gershick, *Gay Old Girls,* 49–50.

8. Cain transcript.

9. Gershick, *Gay Old Girls,* 49.

10. Film review of *Children of Loneliness, Vice Versa* 1, no. 1 (June 1947): 9–13.

11. "Here to Stay," *Vice Versa* 1, no. 4 (September 1947): 4–5.

12. Cain transcript. Jim Kepner, who was also a member of that group, cautiously discussed gay rights as a utopian "fantasy" with science fiction/fantasy fans that he suspected were gay.

13. Gershick, *Gay Old Girls,* 62.

14. Cain transcript.

15. Kepner Papers, ONE National Gay and Lesbian Archives, University of Southern California, Los Angeles.

16. George to James Kepner, July 1945, Kepner Papers. The phrase "bisexual" is clearly a euphemism for "homosexual."

17. Wally Jordan to James Kepner, May 14, 1943, Kepner Papers.

18. Harmodius, with his lover, fellow Athenian Aristogeitan, killed the tyrant Peisistratus in 514 B.C. Statues and a song immortalized the lovers; in 1827, Edgar Allen Poe translated the hymn, lauding "Harmodious the gallant and good" and Aristogeitan as "deliverers of Athens from shame."

19. Jordan to Kepner, May 14, 1943, Kepner Papers.

20. Marcus, *Making History*, 29.

21. Henry Gerber, "The Society for Human Rights," *ONE Magazine*, September 1962, 5–10.

22. Ibid.

23. On the Veteran's Benevolent Association, see Jonathan Katz, *Gay American History: Lesbians and Gay Men in the U.S.A.* (New York: Harper and Row, 1976), 635, and John D'Emilio, *Sexual Politics, Sexual Communities: The Making of a Homosexual Minority in the U.S., 1940–1970* (Chicago: University of Chicago Press, 1983), 32.

24. Joseph Hansen, *A Few Doors West of Hope: The Life and Times of Dauntless Don Slater* (Los Angeles: Homosexual Information Center, 1998).

25. See Stuart Timmons, *The Trouble with Harry Hay: Founder of the Modern Gay Movement* (Boston: Alyson, 1990), 136–137, and David K. Johnson, *The Lavender Scare: The Cold War Persecution of Gays and Lesbians in the Federal Government* (Chicago: University of Chicago Press, 2004), 170–171.

26. Harry Hay's life is discussed in Timmons, *The Trouble with Harry Hay*; Harry Hay and Will Roscoe, *Radically Gay: Gay Liberation in the Words of Its Founder* (Boston: Beacon Press, 1996); and Vern Bullough's entry in *Before Stonewall: Activists for Gay and Lesbian Rights in Historical Context*, ed. Vern Bullough (New York: Harrington Park Press, 2002).

27. Jordan to Kepner, March 19, 1943, Kepner Papers: "A silver ring . . . will be all you'll need to recognize them."

28. The founding date of the Mattachine Society has been variously set: See Timmons, *The Trouble with Harry Hay*, 132–138, 140, 143–145.

29. Cf. "the closet," a mid-twentieth-century term that refers to being secretive about one's homosexuality.

30. There are parallels between Gerber's fledgling movement and that of the L.A. homophiles. Each conceptualized an educational component, aimed both at building the awareness of gay men and at external law reform. "I realized at once that homosexuals themselves needed nearly as much attention as the laws pertaining to their acts." Gerber, "The Society for Human Rights," 5–10.

31. Though Mattachine's cell structure paralleled that of the Communist Party, it was, in fact, more closely based on such secret organizations as the Masons: See Timmons, *The Trouble with Harry Hay*, 156.

32. The organization was also called Knights of the Clocks: Jim Kepner, undated memo, Knights of the Clock folder, ONE National Gay and Lesbian Archives; also, Wayne R. Dynes, "W. Dorr Legg," in *Before Stonewall: Activists for Gay and Lesbian Rights in a Historical Context*, ed. Vern Bullough (New York: Harrington Park Press, 2002), 98.

33. "Installation Procedure," Knights of the Clock folder, subject file, ONE National Gay and Lesbian Archives.

34. ST interview with Harry Hay, 76, October 10, 1988.

35. Marvin Cutler [Dorr Legg], ed., *Homosexuals Today* (Los Angeles: ONE Press, 1956), 93.

36. ST interview with John Gruber, 77, June 23, 2005.

37. ST interview with Jim Kepner, August 22, 1986.

38. "Well, Medium and Rare," Paul Coates, *Los Angeles Daily Mirror*, March 12, 1953. See also Kenneth Frank, "Homosexuals, Inc.," 1950s file, undated clipping, ONE National Gay and Lesbian Archives. Frank, who proclaims, "Don't sell the twisted twerps short!" fancifully describes Mattachine as having 9,000 members and branches in "principal cities across the country"; he also comments on Hay's Communist ties and calls the organization "decidedly pinko."

39. Marcus, *Making History,* 59.

40. ST interview with Jamie Green, 71, March 11, 2006.

41. ST interview with John Gruber, 77, June 23, 2005. In interviews with Stuart Timmons, neither Hay nor the other Mattachine founders ever mentioned—and likely regretted—this political compromise. See Timmons, *The Trouble with Harry Hay.*

42. "The Fabulous Miss Destiny," *ONE Magazine,* September 1964, 6–12.

43. Jim Kepner, "The Loves of a Long-Time Activist: An Autobiography and Gay Movement History, Sort of" (unpublished manuscript, Los Angeles, 1993), 93, collection of ST. Kepner reports that "[when] Mexican doctors began performing sex-change operations, Carioca died on a Calexico butcher's table."

44. Denise D'Anne (Tony Albanese) as told to Cathy Cade, "Going the Distance: The Life of Denise D'Anne" (unpublished manuscript, 2003), 34.

45. Ibid.

46. Ibid, 45.

47. "The Fabulous Miss Destiny."

48. Ken Burns, quoted in Jim Kepner, "My First Sixty-five Years in Gay Liberation: Myself and Our Movement" (unpublished ms., c. 1980), 12, 1956 section, ONE National Gay and Lesbian Archives. The title of Kepner's ongoing manuscript shifted as he aged (see also chap. 6, note 9).

49. Five thousand is the figure cited by Streitmatter in *Unspeakable,* 28. Martin Block cites 3,400 copies in 1955, *ONE's* "peak year": in Marcus, *Making History,* 41. See also Craig Loftin, "Passionate Anxieties: McCarthyism and American Sexual Identity, 1945–1965" (PhD diss., University of Southern California, 2005).

50. J. B. Berkvam to ONE, Inc., received July 5, 1957: ONE, Inc., Social Service file, 1957, ONE National Gay and Lesbian Archives.

51. ST interview with Skip Foster, June 27, 2005.

52. Kepner, "My First Sixty-five Years," 24.

53. Joyce Murdock and Deb Price, *Courting Justice: Gay Men and Lesbians v. the Supreme Court* (New York: Basic Books, 2001), 27.

54. LF interview with Stella Rush (Sten Russell), 79, November 10, 2004.

55. ST interview with Eric Julber, 80, June 24, 2005.

56. Julber recalls a *Los Angeles Daily News* headline "Police Brutality Victim Acquitted."

57. By ONE's Legal Counsel (Eric Julber), "The Law of Mailable Material," *ONE Magazine,* October 1954, 5.

58. Julber interview.

59. (Julber), "The Law of Mailable Material," 6.

60. Julber interview.

61. Clarke quoted in "The Post Office Case," *ONE Confidential,* March 1956, 17.

62. Kepner, "My First Sixty-five Years," 19.

63. Murdoch and Price discuss the Supreme Court decision at length in *Courting Justice,* 27ff.

64. Interview with Dorr Legg in Cain, *Leading the Parade,* 5.

65. Don Slater, *ONE Magazine,* February 1958, 17.

66. "A Milestone in Education," *ONE Confidential,* December 1956, 3.

67. Merritt Thompson was closeted and used the pseudonym Tom Merritt.

68. Kepner, "My First Sixty-five Years," 24. See also Dorr Legg, *Homophile Studies in Theory and Practice* (Los Angeles: ONE Institute Press, 1994).

69. Legg, *Homophile Studies.*

70. "Milestone," 3.

71. Kepner, "My First Sixty-five Years," 34.

72. Cutler, *Homosexuals Today,* 81.

73. ONE case form (unnumbered), Social Service file, 1957, ONE National Gay and Lesbian Archives.

74. "You and the Law," *ONE Confidential,* August 1956, 12.

75. "Crackpots in Our Hair," *ONE Confidential,* December 1956, 2.

76. Dale Jennings, "Address to the Mattachine Society Banquet," November 14, 1953, Homosexual Information Center Archives.

77. Kepner, "My First Sixty-five Years," 4.

78. "Kwack, Kwack," *ONE Confidential,* 1956.

79. ST interview with Bob Mitchell, 90, June 19, 2005: Mitchell referred to himself as a "cardboard president" of ONE, Inc.'s board.

80. See Timmons, *The Trouble with Harry Hay,* 215–218, and Cain, *Leading the Parade,* 7–8.

81. Holly Devor, "How One Transsexual Man Supported ONE," 383–392, and Dynes, "W. Dorr Legg," 94–102, in *Before Stonewall.*

82. Laud Humphreys, "An Interview with Evelyn Hooker," *Alternative Lifestyles* 1, no. 2 (May 1978): 194. Isherwood later became her tenant.

83. Ibid., 195.

84. ST interview with John Gruber, 77, July 2, 2004.

85. Bruce Shenitz, "The Grand Dame of Gay Liberation," *Los Angeles Times Magazine,* June 10, 1990, 25.

86. Evelyn Hooker, "A Preliminary Analysis of Group Behavior of Homosexuals," *Journal of Psychology* 42 (1956): 217–225.

87. Gruber interview, July 2, 2004.

88. ST Interview with Skip Foster, June 27, 2005.

89. In Shenitz, "The Grand Dame," 20.

90. *The Ladder,* 1957, 15–16.

91. Some scholars have argued that working-class lesbians created their own protopolitical movements through the communities they formed in lesbian bars: See, for example, Joan Nestle, *A Restricted Country* (Ithaca, N.Y.: Firebrand, 1987), and Elizabeth Kennedy and Madeline Davis, *Boots of Leather, Slippers of Gold* (New York: Routledge, 1993), on lesbians in New York City and Buffalo.

92. ST interview with Herb Selwyn, 80, January 16, 2005. Similarly, Flo Fleischman complains of ONE Institute, which she visited in the late 1950s: "There was nothing to interest women, no women's values. Nothing but talk about restroom sex and entrapment": LF interview with Flo Fleischman, 74, April 7, 2004.

93. For example, Magnus Hirschfeld's Scientific Humanitarian Committee, established in Germany in 1897 to fight Paragraph 175 (which penalized male homosexuality), actively recruited women. Hirschfeld's 1896 book, *Sappho und Sokrates,* also emphasized that homosexuality was a "natural" phenomenon, common to both sexes.

94. Timmons, *The Trouble with Harry Hay,* 149.

95. On Bernhard's participation in early Mattachine, see ibid., 154. On Bernhard's career, see Tee Corinne, "Ruth Bernhard," in *The Queer Encyclopedia of the Visual Arts,* ed. Claude J. Summers (San Francisco: Cleis Press, 2004), 52–53.

96. Marilyn (Boopsie) Reiger played a crucial role in changing Mattachine from a secret society to a more transparent organization: See Martin Meeker, "Behind the Mask of Respectability: Reconsidering the Mattachine Society and Male Homophile Practice, 1950s and 1960s," *Journal of the History of Sexuality* 10, no. 1 (2001): 78–16; D'Emilio, *Sexual Politics,* 76–79; and Timmons, *The Trouble with Harry Hay,* 176–177.

97. Del Martin and Phyllis Lyon, *Lesbian/Woman* (1972; rpt. New York: Bantam, 1983), 210–211.

98. Inez Wagner, "Café Saturday Night," *ONE Magazine,* February 1954, 24.

99. Doug McAdam, *Political Process and the Development of Black Insurgency, 1930–1970* (Chicago: University of Chicago Press, 1982), 36–38.

100. See p. 99.

101. LF interview with Myra Ridell, 77, November 9, 2004.

102. For a discussion of NOW, Southern California Women for Understanding, and Connexxus, see chaps. 7 and 8.

103. Though the founders of Daughters of Bilities were not aware in 1955 of Mattachine's existence, by the following year, the two organizations had discovered one another. Del Martin acknowledged commonality between the all-lesbian Daughters and the primarily male Mattachine Society, and in the first issue of *The Ladder,* the Daughters' newsletter, she made sure to credit Mattachine as being the pioneer in "a nationwide movement to bring understanding to and about the homosexual minority." But at the same time, she observed crucial differences between the primary political interests of lesbians and gay men that explained why an all-lesbian organization was necessary. Lesbian concerns centered not on "difficulty with law enforcement," Martin wrote, but on issues of status—on the bigotry, intolerance, and discrimination they suffered merely by *being* lesbian: Del Martin, "President's Message," *Ladder* 1, no. 1 (October 1956): 6. John D'Emilio also discusses the influence of Mattachine on Daughters of Bilitis in its formative stages: *Sexual Politics,* see esp. 103–104. However, despite Martin's recognition of the pioneering role that the men's homophile organization played, serious conflicts developed between Daughters and the men's groups, culminating in 1961 when the ONE Institute composed a "Homosexual Bill of Rights" and Daughters opposed it, arguing that to announce such a bill would "set the homophile movement back into oblivion . . . and would leave us wide open as a target of ridicule from those who already dislike us": Del Martin, "How Far Out Can We Go," *The Ladder,* January 1961, 4–5.

104. In 1956 and '57, Del Martin appealed to Ann Carll Reid (Corky), then a writer for *ONE Magazine,* and Alison Hunter (Vicki), who was briefly the women's editor at *ONE Magazine,* to help her establish a Los Angeles chapter of Daughter of Bilitis. (Alison Hunter was a "floating name" used by several people who wrote for *ONE.*) Reid responded (April 2, 1956) that she would help in any way she could, DOB file, ONE National Gay and Lesbian Archives. An organizing meeting was held in Los Angeles in January 1957 ("Daughters Hold Brunch in L.A.—Plans for Chapter Underway," *The Ladder,* February 1957, 10), but the chapter was not established until 1958.

105. Rush interview.

106. LF interview with Ann Bannon, April 3, 2004.

107. Jonathan Katz interview with Barbara Gittings, in *Gay American History* (New York: Harper and Row, 1976), 425–426.

108. Kristen Esterberg suggests that Daughters of Bilitis went through three distinct phases of development, moving from an "integrationist" organization which took the position that lesbians were just like heterosexual women except for what they did in bed, to an organization allied with the militant segment of the homophile movement, to a feminist organization: "From Accommodation to Liberation: A Social Movement Analysis of Lesbians in the Homophile Movement," *Gender and Society* 8, no. 3 (1994): 424–443. However, the various Daughters chapters, which were organized eventually in other Southern and Northern California towns as well as in New York, Chicago, and Rhode Island, retained some autonomy in their direction. Regardless of the position the chapters took, the organization struggled always for membership.

109. Rush interview; also, Stella Rush's essay on Helen Sandoz in *Before Stonewall* (see note 32).

110. Rush interview.

111. Dorr Legg correspondence, in Daughters of Bilitis file, ONE Institute Papers, ONE National Gay and Lesbian Archives, and *ONE Magazine,* October–November, 1956, 37. Despite Legg's "nonsexist" efforts, lesbian leaders were often suspicious of him: See Martin, "How Far Can We Go?" Flo Fleischman recalls Legg as "a sexist": Fleischman interview.

112. "The Feminine Viewpoint," *ONE Magazine,* February 1956, 26–27.

113. Jane Dahr (James Barr Fugate), "Sappho Remembered," *ONE Magazine*, October 1954, 12–15. Stella Rush resigned from *ONE* in anger because, she complained, *ONE* men felt "justified in writing the most drastic opinions under a feminine pseudonym if a feminine [writer] happens to be lacking at the moment": Letter to ONE board, July 26, 1961, Tangentgroup, online, http://www.tangentgroup.org/history/RusgResig.html. Jim Kepner, in his essay "The Women of ONE" (ONE National Gay and Lesbian Archives), mentions several other women who played fairly minor roles on the magazine and in ONE, Inc.

114. Cutler, *Homosexuals Today*, 91. Edythe Eyde remembers Reid and Elloree as being among the readers of *Vice Versa* that she knew personally: Cain transcript.

115. Cain transcript.

116. Kepner, "My First Sixty-five Years," 8.

117. Ibid., 45.

118. Tee Corinne's telephone interview with Joan Corbin, December 10, 2000, in "Queer Caucus for Art," http://www.artcataloging.net/. (This article is no longer posted online.)

119. E-mail communication to ST from Craig Loftin, May 3, 2006.

120. Letter from Miss O. E. Fisher, October 12, 1957, ONE, Inc., Social Services file, 1957, ONE National Gay and Lesbian Archives.

121. Letter from Elizabeth Mellikant, January 23, 1956, ONE, Inc. Social Services file, 1956, ONE National Gay and Lesbian Archives.

122. Letter addressed to "Miss D'Ann Carroll [Ann Carll Reid], Feminine Editor," from Margot Robert, July 11, 1956, *ONE Magazine* letters, ONE National Gay and Lesbian Archives.

123. Letter addressed to "Dear Editor," from Clare Robertson, August 13, 1955, ONE National Gay and Lesbian Archives.

124. Ann Carll Reid to Miss Toni Lyon, July 5, 1954, ONE National Gay and Lesbian Archives. (ONE also received countless such requests from men for gay contacts, especially in rural areas.)

125. Letter from Ann Carll Reid to Clare Robertson, October 3, 1955, ONE National Gay and Lesbian Archives.

126. Letter from William Lambert (Dorr Legg) to Miss R. A. Tolmie, Augusta, Georgia, August 17, 1955, ONE, Inc., Social Services file, 1955, ONE National Gay and Lesbian Archives.

127. See Lillian Faderman, *To Believe in Women: What Lesbians Have Done for America* (New York: Houghton Mifflin, 1999).

128. Gene Damon (Barbara Grier), "The Year of the Chapter," *The Ladder*, December 1969–January 1970.

129. L.A. DOB Center announcement in *Lesbian Tide*, December 1971, 16–17, and inside cover.

130. Paul Welch, "Homosexuality in America: A Secret World Grows Open and Bolder," *Life*, July 27, 1964.

CHAPTER 5

1. Myron Roberts, "Our Changing Morality," *Los Angeles Magazine*, December 1963, 1960s file, ONE National Gay and Lesbian Archives.

2. The Brown Berets were among the chief organizers of the Chicano Moratorium in 1970, a protest that attracted 25,000 and was the largest North American Latino demonstration until the 2006 protests over immigration policies.

3. Social historian Andrew Kopkind writes that it took a few years after the Watts riots before "white radicals began to speak of 'revolution' or 'Revolution'": Arthur Kopkind, "Looking Backward: The Sixties and the Movement," *Ramparts*, February 1963. Perhaps Kopkind was thinking of the "Siege of Chicago" and Tom Hayden's threat during the 1968 Democratic Convention that "the period of organized, peaceful, and orderly demonstrations is coming to an end." "WE WILL BECOME WARRIORS," Hayden roared after pointing out that for blacks, peace-

ful tactics such as the 1963 March on Washington for Jobs and Freedom had less effect than the militant tactics of the Watts riots: Hayden's speech reported in *Los Angeles Free Press*, September 13, 1968. In Los Angeles, however, young people became "warriors" by 1966.

4. Art Seidenbaum, "Spectator, 1967," *Los Angeles Times*, January 10, 1967, DI.

5. ST interviews with David Crittendon, 59, October 12, 2004, and Lee Mentley, 56, August 19, 2005.

6. Mentley interview.

7. Art Berman, "Shutdown of Teenage Clubs Demanded by Businessmen," *Los Angeles Times*, November 15, 1966, 1.

8. Los Angeles in the mid- and late 1960s had an ongoing hippie "summer of love," both before and after the 1967 Haight-Ashberry "Summer of Love."

9. Ridgely Cummings, "Pershing Square Is Defoliated: City Says 'Get Out' to Eccentrics, Pensioners, Non-Conformists," *Los Angeles Free Press*, September 3, 1964, 1.

10. William T. Margolis, "A Plot to Overthrow the Overground," *Los Angeles Free Press*, March 10, 1967, 10–11.

11. Ibid.

12. Reported in "Obscenity Ordinance Ruling," *The Ladder*, January 1960, 20.

13. Quoted in Larry Gross and James D. Woods, *The Columbia Reader on Lesbians and Gay Men in Media, Society, and Politics* (New York: Columbia University Press, 1999), 292.

14. Sam Winston (Sam Allen), "The Bead Reader," *Los Angeles Advocate*, July 1968, 8.

15. "Cancer-Like Vice Spreads in Los Angeles," *Los Angeles Times*, January 29, 1961, G1, an article about prostitution, pornography, and narcotics, which mentions homosexuals in relation to a leap in the incidence of venereal disease.

16. ST interview with Milton, 62, June 15, 2004.

17. L. Jay Barrow, *Hollywood, Gay Capitol of the World: The Homosexual and How He Lives* (Van Nuys, Calif.: Triumph News Company, 1968), 14.

18. "Are You a Man?" (flier), Paul Lamport file, ONE National Gay and Lesbian Archives.

19. Robin Rauzi, "Lesbians Have Been Drawn to Area's Suburban Lifestyle Since Long Before 'Ellen,'" *Los Angeles Times*, April 27, 1997, B4 (Valley section); and LF interview with Jo Duffy, 78, July 27, 2004.

20. LF interview with Del Martinez, 71, August 12, 2005.

21. Carol Collins, "Sex Deviates Menace L.A.; Southland's VD Rises 1,000 Pct!" *Hollywood Citizen-News*, February 4, 1963, 1.

22. Carol Collins, "Parker Hits SD Coddling: Jail Terms Urged by City Officers," *Hollywood Citizen-News*, February 6, 1963, 1.

23. Paul Coates, "The Sick, Sick, Sick Young Men," undated clipping, c. February 1963, 1963 clippings file, ONE National Gay and Lesbian Archives. Coates' title parodies the 1959 "Ballad of the Sad Young Men."

24. Jon J. Gallo et al., "The Consenting Adult Homosexual and the Law: An Empirical Study of Enforcement and Administration in Los Angeles County," *UCLA Law Review* 13, no. 3 (March 1966): 643–832.

25. ST interview with Jon Gallo, 63, August 18, 2005.

26. Stephens interview.

27. LF interview with Connie Eddy, 62, July 23, 2004.

28. About a dozen of those bars were exclusively lesbian; another dozen were frequented by both lesbians and gay men: *The Address Book*, comp. Bob Damron, mid-1966, ONE National Gay and Lesbian Archives.

29. *Bob Damron's Address Book*, 1969, ONE National Gay and Lesbian Archives.

30. LF interview with Sharon A. Lilly, 58, April 8, 2004.

31. LF interview with Francesca Miller, 57, July 24, 2004.

32. Personal recollections of LF. See also John Rechy, "The City of Lost Angels," in *Beneath the Skin: The Collected Essays of John Rechy* (New York: Caroll and Graf, 2004), 30.

33. Don Noyes-More, *California Boomer: Keeper of the Story* (Plymouth, Vt.: Five Corners Publications, 2000), 61.

34. Stephens interview. Stephens noted that gay teens also enjoyed a circuit of house parties in the same era, where hundreds paid a dollar admission to an "old man" of twenty-five.

35. ST interview with Aristide Laurent, 63, June 30, 2004.

36. ST interview with L.N., June 18, 1997.

37. Barrow, *Hollywood, Gay Capitol,* 89.

38. Ibid., 67.

39. Ibid., 109. Owner Lee Glaze renamed Ciro's The Patch II.

40. Robert Gregory, editorial, *ONE Magazine,* August 1961, 4–5.

41. LF interview with Jeanne Cordova, 56, August 21, 2004. The magazine's confrontational tone was not immediately apparent: The first issue of the *Lesbian Tide* betrayed its roots in a 1950s organization, declaring that Los Angeles Daughters of Bilitis was "nonpolitical," that it staged "PEACEFUL" events, and that feminists were objectionable in their "I hate men" rhetoric: *Lesbian Tide,* July–August 1971, 1–3.

42. Erickson Educational Foundation brochure, Reed Erickson Collection, box 2, ONE National Gay and Lesbian Archives.

43. Institute for the Study of Human Resources brochure, Reed Erickson Collection, box 18, ONE National Gay and Lesbian Archives. See also Holly Devor, "How One Transsexual Man Supported ONE," 383–392, and Wayne Dynes, "W. Dorr Legg," 94–102, in *Before Stonewall: Activists for Gay and Lesbian Rights in a Historical Context,* ed. Vern Bullough (New York: Harrington Press, 2002). ONE offered a master's degree and doctorate in "Homophile Studies." Soon after ONE received the coup of accreditation, Erickson, who was addicted to drugs, claimed that his putative "wife," Evangelina, was suing him for 50 percent of his fortune, his sister and former wife were blackmailing him for money, and he could no longer afford to support the Institute. Beginning in 1984 to his death, Erickson tried unsuccessfully to evict ONE from the Milbank estate. (See correspondence between Reed Erickson and Dorr Legg, especially 1/3/83 and 1/14/83, box 18.) The Institute ceased offering degrees in 1986, but after Erickson's death, ONE was granted half interest in the estate by the courts. In 1997, ONE sold its share of the property; its library was moved to the ONE National Gay and Lesbian Archives at USC.

44. Brochure, "Society of Anubis, Inc.," Anubis file, ONE National Gay and Lesbian Archives.

45. *Anubis Bulletin,* March 1969, Anubis file, ONE National Gay and Lesbian Archives.

46. The Anubis raid is discussed in the *Los Angeles Free Press,* January 2, 1970, 2; and in *The Ladder,* April–May 1970, 31.

47. For example, letter to Anubis membership from Voter Registration chairman, January 21, 1970, Anubis file, ONE National Gay and Lesbian Archives.

48. Don Slater, "Protest on Wheels," *Tangents,* May 1966.

49. Stuart Timmons, *The Trouble with Harry Hay: Founder of the Modern Gay Movement* (Boston: Alyson, 1990), 220–222.

50. After his departure from ONE in 1965, Slater set up the Homosexual Information Center on Cahuenga Boulevard. Because he called his new magazine *Tangents,* the Center was alternately known as "the Tangents Group."

51. Slater, "Protest on Wheels."

52. Ibid.

53. Ibid.

54. "Patch Fights Three-Way Battle," *Los Angeles Advocate,* August 1968, 3+.

55. Kepner, who became an activist in the 1940s, remained so until his death in 1997. He joined Mattachine, ONE, the Council on Religion and the Homophile, and virtually every Los

Angeles–based gay organization throughout the 1960s and '70s, often serving on their boards and producing their newsletters.

56. Vernon Mitchell (obituary), *Los Angeles Times*, December 26, 1991; "Can Homosexuals Trust the Health Dept.? Two Views of the VD Danger: Mike Kinghorn says 'No!' 'We Must!' says Jim Kepner," *PRIDE Newsletter*, September 9, 1966, 2.

57. Other cities also showed signs of incipient gay radicalism in the 1960s. For example, Marc Stein points out that in Philadelphia, in 1965, three teenagers held "the first gay sit-in" in protest over the refusal of Dewey's Restaurant to serve homosexuals and people wearing "nonconformist clothing." See "The First Gay Sit-In," http://www.hnn.us/aritcles/116522.html. The New York City Mattachine Society staged a "Sip-In" in 1966 to protest a bar's refusal to serve avowed homosexuals: See John D'Emilio, *Sexual Politics, Sexual Community: The Making of a Homosexual Minority in the United States, 1940–1970* (Chicago: University of Chicago Press, 1983), 207–208. Susan Stryker's documentary, *Screaming Queens* (2005), concerns another early protest, in San Francisco in 1966, of transgender people. Columbia University chartered the first gay student organization in 1967.

58. Steve Ginsberg, "Pride Organizes Homophiles: New Group Wants Militant Civil Rights Drive," *Los Angeles Free Press*, 1966 (clipping), PRIDE file, ONE National Gay and Lesbian Archives.

59. *PRIDE Newsletter*, September 9, 1966, 4.

60. Ginsberg, "PRIDE Organizes Homophiles."

61. Ibid.

62. Jim Highland, "Raid!" *Tangents*, January 1967, 5. The Black Cat in Los Angeles was not related to the San Francisco Black Cat.

63. "Bushwhacker Declared Historic Site," undated memo (circa 1980), signed by Jim Kepner, Black Cat file, ONE National Gay and Lesbian Archives.

64. "Guilty As Charged," unsigned, undated manuscript, Black Cat file, ONE National Gay and Lesbian Archives.

65. Untitled clipping, *Open City*, October 11, 1967, Black Cat file, ONE National Gay and Lesbian Archives.

66. The gay protesters were joined by a Leftist nongay group, the Right of Assembly and Movement Committee. See also John Bryan, "Police Outrages Help Create Los Angeles Homosexual Rights Drive," *Los Angeles Free Press*, March 10, 1967, 5.

67. "Bushwhacker Declared Historic Site," ONE National Gay and Lesbian Archives.

68. Two San Francisco groups, the Council on Religion and the Homosexual and the Tavern Guild, supported the L.A. demonstration: "Monster of a Protest Set for Saturday," *Los Angeles Free Press*, February 10, 1967, 1. Jim Kepner appealed to the Manhattan chapter of the Daughters of Bilitis for support: Jim Kepner to DOB, New York City, March 2, 1967.

69. Joyce Murdoch and Deb Price, *Courting Justice: Gay Men and Lesbians v. the Supreme Court* (New York: Basic Books, 2001), 143–146.

70. "Gay-In in Griffith Park" (photo essay), *Los Angeles Advocate*, July 1968, 18. See also Moira Rachel Kenny, *Mapping Gay L.A.: The Intersection of Place and Politics* (Philadelphia: Temple University Press, 2001), 170–171.

71. "Patch Fights Three-Way Battle," *Los Angeles Advocate*, August 1968, 3+.

72. ST interview with Lee Glaze, 66, September 19, 2004.

73. Dick Michaels, "Patch Raids Police Station," *Los Angeles Advocate*, September 1968, 6–7.

74. Ibid.

75. Glaze interview.

76. ST interview with Aristide Laurent, 63, August 25, 2004.

77. Dudley Clendenin and Adam Nagourney, *Out For Good: The Struggle to Build a Gay Rights Movement In America* (New York: Simon and Schuster, 1999), chap. 18, "Citizen Goodstein."

78. Laurent interview.

79. "U.S. Capitol Turns on to Gay Power," *Los Angeles Advocate*, September 1967, 1.

80. Minutes, PRIDE, March 27, 1968, PRIDE file, ONE National Gay and Lesbian Archives. See also Mark Thompson, ed., *The Long Road to Freedom: The Advocate History of the Gay and Lesbian Movement* (New York: St. Martin's Press, 1992), xix.

81. Bill Rau, Dick Michaels' partner, became Bill Rand. Sam Allen wrote for the *Los Angeles Advocate* under the name Sam Winston.

82. P. Nutz [Aristide Laurent], "First L.A. Gay-In: Ultra High Camp," *Los Angeles Advocate*, April 1968, 3–4.

83. Laurent interview.

84. ST interview with Rob Cole, 75, July 25, 2005.

85. Jim Kepner, "The Posthumous Trial of Ramon Novarro, *Los Angeles Advocate*, October 1969, 5+; "Brothers Convicted of Novarro Murder Face Life," *Los Angeles Advocate*, November 1969, 1; "Paul Ferguson's Story: 'Tom Did It!'" *Los Angeles Advocate*, December 1969, 5+; "Tom Ferguson Blames Paul, then Confesses," *Los Angeles Advocate*, January 1970, 5+.

86. Notes from ST interview with Jim Kepner, May 25, 1990.

87. Cole interview.

88. For more on Goodstein's regime at the *Los Angeles Advocate*, see Clendenin and Nagourney, *Out for Good*, "Citizen Goodstein," 245–260.

89. Cole interview.

90. Written communication, Jeanne Barney to ST, July 11, 2005.

91. Laurent interview.

92. "What Is The C.R.H.?" *Concern: Newsletter of the Southern California Council on Religion and the Homophile*, February 1967, 1.

93. LF interview with Stella Rush, 79, November 10, 2004. As progressive as the Unitarian Church was, however, when Harry Hay approached its famous Rev. Steve Fritchman in 1952 with the request that he lend his support to the Mattachine Society, he was rebuffed: as discussed in Timmons, *The Trouble with Harry Hay*, 147.

94. Rev. Ted McIlvenna, quoted in *Concern* 5 (February 1967): 2.

95. LF interview with JJ (Jay) Vega, 50, September 18, 2004.

96. Troy Perry, *Don't Be Afraid Any More: The Story of Reverend Troy Perry and the Metropolitan Community Churches* (New York: St. Martin's Press, 1990), 34; and *Out for Good*, 179–180.

97. Perry, *Don't Be Afraid*, 36.

98. ST interview with Troy Perry, 65, August 30, 2005.

99. *God, Gays, and the Gospel: This Is Our Story*, documentary video (Los Angeles: Universal Fellowship of Metropolitan Community Churches, 1984).

100. ST interview with Lucia Chappelle, 53, August 3, 2005.

101. Perry interview.

102. John Dart, "A Church for Homosexuals," *Los Angeles Times*, December 8, 1969, C1.

103. ST interview with Joey Terrill, 49, July 31, 2004.

104. LF interview with Flo Fleischman, 74, April 7, 2004.

105. ST interview with Frank Zerelli, 60, July 8, 2004.

106. Display advertisement, *Los Angeles Times*, January 17, 1970, A3.

107. Chappell interview.

108. "Ex-Councilman Paul H. Lamport Dies," *Los Angeles Daily News*, April 3, 1984.

109. "Lamport Raps Stand of Two Newspapers," *Hollywood Citizen-News*, May 16, 1969.

110. Jim Kepner reported this suspicion to subscribers of his newsletter, *Pursuit Letter* no. 1, April 28, 1969, Paul Lamport file, ONE National Gay and Lesbian Archives.

111. Ibid.

112. "Lamport Raps Stand of Two Newspapers."

113. Ibid.

114. Quoted in "Cross Currents," *The Ladder*, October–November 1969, 32–33.

115. "Tiger Changing Stripes: Lamport Tours the Bars," *Los Angeles Advocate*, March 28, 1973.
116. ST interview with John (Jon) Platania, 65, July 28, 2005.

CHAPTER 6

1. LF interview with Jeanne Cordova, 56, August 21, 2004.
2. Karla Jay, *Tales of the Lavender Menace: A Memoir of Liberation* (New York: Basic Books, 1999), 168–171,
3. ST interview with Troy Perry, 65, August 30, 2005.
4. LF interview with Ariana Manov, 57, May 2, 2004.
5. Manov interview.
6. Sharon Raphael, "Coming Out: The Emergence of the Movement Lesbian" (PhD diss., Case Western Reserve University, 1974), 53.
7. The Gay Women's Service Center is described in Raphael, "Coming Out," 53–55; LF interview with Mina Meyer, 64, and Sharon Raphael, 62, April 5, 2004; and LF interview with Del Whan, 65, July 14, 2005.
8. E-mail correspondence to LF from Sharon A. Lilly, July 13, 2005.
9. Jim Kepner, "My First Sixty-six Years," in "Gay Liberation: Myself and Our Movement" (1989), 1969 section: "Praising Morris and Righting the Record" (unpublished ms.), ONE National Gay and Lesbian Archives, University of Southern California, Los Angeles. The title of Kepner's ongoing manuscript shifted as he aged (see also chap. 4, note 48).
10. Eighty chapters of the GLF formed after Stonewall. See http://www.angelfire.com/on2/glf2000/Page2.html.
11. Flier, "Gay Liberation Front," GLF-LA file, ONE National Gay and Lesbian Archives.
12. Morris Kight, "Where We've Been; Where We Are Going," *Front Lines* 1, no. 1 (December 1970): 2, 7–8.
13. ST interview with Gary Hundertmark, 57, September 14, 2004.
14. Wilson interview.
15. LF interview with Sharon A. Lilly, 58, April 8, 2004.
16. LF interview with Simone Wallace, 58, July 25, 2004.
17. LF interview with Sue Talbot, 57, and Liebe Gray, 58, October 4, 2004.
18. Marsha Salisbury et al., at the Lesbian Feminist Reunion, held at the ONE National Gay and Lesbian Archives, July 25, 2004.
19. LF interview with Donna Cassyd, 64, July 28, 2004.
20. Eric Marcus, *Making History: The Struggle for Gay and Lesbian Equal Rights, 1945–1990* (New York: HarperCollins, 1992), 32.
21. Lynn Lilliston, "The Woman Homosexual," *Los Angeles Times*, June 21–25, 1970.
22. It was resurrected three times before its permanent removal by Valerie Terrigno, first mayor of West Hollywood.
23. Letter dated January 8, 1971, from Bob Wright, associate producer, *Carol Burnett Show*, to John Bexter, GLF file, ONE National Gay and Lesbian Archives.
24. Letter from Troy Perry to Don Kilhefner (GLF), October 3, 1970, GLF file, ONE National Gay and Lesbian Archives.
25. See also "Eddie Nash Convicted on Seven Drug Counts," *Los Angeles Times*, October 6, 1982, B1, and "Murder Probe Figure Faces New Charges," *Los Angeles Times*, December 2, 1981, B11.
26. Written communication to ST from Jack Willis (pseud.).
27. "Down on the Farm," undated GLF flier, Gay Liberation Front L.A. Demonstrations file, ONE National Gay and Lesbian Archives.
28. "Why Can't We Hold Hands in Our Own Bars?" GLF flier, c. September, 1970, Gay Liberation Front L.A. Demonstrations file, ONE National Gay and Lesbian Archives.

29. ST interview with Jaime Green, 72, June 24, 2004.

30. Gay-In organizers claimed their purpose to be "to get our gay brothers and sisters out of their closets and to show society again that we intend to claim full participatory rights." *Front Lines* 1, no. 1 (December 1970): 6.

31. Mark Thompson, ed., *Long Road to Freedom: The Advocate History of the Lesbian and Gay Movement* (New York: St. Martin's Press, 1994), 36.

32. Complaint for Violation of Civil Rights, *Gay Liberation Front v. Edward M. Davis et al.*, August 7, 1970, U.S. District Court, Central District of California.

33. "Homosexuals Receive ACLU Aid in Parade Permit Fight," *Los Angeles Times*, June 13, 1970, B4. A detailed history of the Los Angeles gay pride parade, which is called "Christopher Street West" (a name chosen to obfuscate the parade's purpose to hostile Angelenos while communicating clearly to gays, who would have heard of the Stonewall Rebellion on Christopher Street) may be found at http://www.lapride.org/pages/cswhistory.html.

34. E-mail correspondence from Carolyn Weathers to LF, April 23, 2004; and other informants at the Lesbian Feminists reunion, July 25, 2004, at ONE National Gay and Lesbian Archives. San Francisco gays and feminists protested a similar meeting in May 1970.

35. Weathers and Lilly interviews.

36. "Alpine Co., Here We Come!" *Front Lines* 1, no. 1 (December 1970): 1+.

37. Proposals for "Master Planning the Alpine County Project" were submitted by Ladd & Kelsey and Architects and Economic Research Associates ($15,000 and $35,000 respectively), both dated December 2, 1970, GLF-LA file, ONE National Gay and Lesbian Archives.

38. "Alpine Co. Here We Come!"

39. "Homosexuals Weigh Move to Alpine County," *Los Angeles Times*, October 19, 1970.

40. "Alpine Co., Here We Come!"

41. Morris Kight interview, "Gay Liberation Front: 20th Anniversary," CD produced by Bob Dallmeyer, June 1989.

42. Weathers and Lilly interviews.

43. In one case, *People v. Manicap*, 1953, a heterosexual couple and another woman were charged and convicted of consensual oral sex on the testimony of LAPD officers, who had spied in their windows. That the three were African American may have encouraged this rare prosecution: CA Crim. 4992.

44. ST interview with Tom Coleman, 57, August 16, 2005; and e-mail correspondence to LF from Jeanne Cordova, January 19, 2006. Cordova and Troy Perry were among the Felons 6.

45. Gudron Fonfa, "Most Wanton Women," *The Lesbian Tide: A Feminist Lesbian Publication Written by and for the Rising Tide of Women Today*, July 1974, 8+.

46. California Statutes, 1975, chs. 71 and 877, pp. 131 and 1957.

47. Brenda Weathers interview.

48. Sharon Zecha, March 25, 1971 speech, rpt. in *Everywoman* 2, no. 10 (July 9, 1971).

49. LF interview with Jeanne Cordova, 56, October 3, 2004.

50. Michele Ross, "Gay Women's Lib Center," *Los Angeles Free Press*, October 23, 1970.

51. Brenda Weathers, *Front Lines* 1, no. 1 (December 1970): 6.

52. E-mail correspondence to ST from Stanley Williams, August 7, 2005.

53. "New Gay Women's Liberation Office at the Women's Center," *Women's Liberation Newsletter*, October 1970.

54. Michelle Moravec, "In Their Own Time: Voices from the Los Angeles Women's Movement, 1967–1976" (bachelor's thesis, University of California, Los Angeles, 1991), and Adele Wallace, "The Los Angeles Women's Movement: A Research Guide," Library and Information Science Special Project, San Jose State University, 1999.

55. LF interview with Ivy Bottini, 78, August 19, 2004. Bottini, who became a resident of Los Angeles, recalls that at the 1971 national NOW conference in L.A., "Word had just gotten out about what happened to me. I was a hero. It was so different from what I'd left in New York."

56. Personal recollection of LF.

57. Nancy Robinson at the Lesbian Feminist Reunion, held at the ONE National Gay and Lesbian Archives, July 25, 2004.

58. Lesbian Feminist Reunion.

59. Bottini interview.

60. Personal recollection of LF.

61. "Victory at Los Angeles," a headline in *The Ladder* blared, December 1971–January 1972, 14–16.

62. Whan interview.

63. Lesbian Feminist Reunion.

64. Formal groups such as most lesbians feared to join in earlier eras now boomed in L.A. In 1971, the three major lesbian groups, Daughters of Bilitis, the Gay Women's Services Center, and the Lesbian Feminists, were so active that women had to make hard choices about which of a plethora of interesting events to attend on any given night. The groups decided it was essential to form an "Intergroup Council" of lesbians/gay women so that they might coordinate calendars, discuss common problems, air differences, and plan joint events, such as the Gay Women's West Coast Conference, which they cosponsored in June of that year. By the next year the council had become so large, representing so many lesbian groups from Los Angeles and nearby cities such as Orange County and San Diego, that it was renamed the Southern California Coalition of Lesbian Organizations. The times were a far cry from a generation earlier, when lesbians were hiding out in bars or secret little enclaves and L.A. Daughters of Bilitis was starved for members.

65. Terry Wolverton reveals a meaning of the term "crackpot" that, she suggests, is apt for much of the L.A. lesbian experimentation of the 1970s: "During the process of alchemical transformation, as one substance is transmuted into another, the pot cracks. The old container is insufficient to house the new substance. Thus a 'crackpot' may be someone undergoing just such a transformation of the self." *Insurgent Muse: Life and Art at the Women's Building* (San Francisco: City Lights Books, 2002), 60.

66. The founders of Califia had been to Sagaris, a radical feminist institute in Vermont, and thought that California women "could do it better." ST interview with Josy Cattogio, 54, August 2005. About 20 percent of the Califia participants were heterosexual. See Marilyn Murphy, "Califia Community," in *Learning Our Way: Essays in Feminist Education*, ed. Charlotte Bunch and Sandra Pollack (New York: Crossing Pressing, 1983), 138–153; and Betty Brooks, "All the Teachers Are the Taught and All the Taught Are the Teachers," in Califia Community file, ONE National Gay and Lesbian Archives.

67. The Feminist Women's Health Center also specialized in safe abortions once they became legal in 1973. LF interview with Suzanne Gage, 52, September 10, 2004. Gage, who worked at the Feminist Women's Health Center, also founded in 1980 the Lesbian Well-Women's Clinic.

68. Lesbian life in 1970s Los Angeles is also discussed in Yolanda Retter, "Lesbian Spaces in L.A., 1970–90," in *Queers in Space: Communities, Public Places, Sites of Resistance*, ed. Gordon Ingram, Anne-Marie Bouthillette, and Yolanda Retter (Seattle: Bay Press, 1997).

69. LF interview with Sue Maberry, 55, and Cheri Gaulke, 56, July 27, 2004.

70. Gaulke interview.

71. LF interview with Ann Giagni, 55, July 27, 2004.

72. LF interview with Terry Wolverton, 50, August 19, 2004. See also Wolverton, *Insurgent Muse*.

73. Wolverton interview.

74. Maberry and Gaulke interview.

75. Gray interview.

76. Wallace interview.

77. McKay quoted in Jeanne Cordova, "When We Were Outlaws: A Memoir of the '70s" (unpublished ms., 2004 version).

78. Gray interview.

79. Cordova, "When We Were Outlaws."

80. Berson interview. If Olivia Records profited by its L.A. connection, the L.A. lesbian-feminist community also profited: Olivia's artists lent their talents to fund-raisers for the Woman's Building as well as to L.A. lesbian-feminist theater, such as Liebe Gray's 1976 play, *To See the Elephant,* about six nineteenth-century women who travel across America in hot pursuit of Calamity Jane (played by the Olivia Records star Cris Williamson), who is their passion: LF interview with Liebe Gray, 58, October 4, 2004.

81. LF interview (telephone) with Ginny Berson, August 3, 2005.

82. Wallace interview.

83. LF interview with Donna Cassyd, 64, July 28, 2004.

84. Several periodicals were published in 1970s Los Angeles that were either lesbian or lesbian-friendly, including *The Lesbian Tide,* started by Jeanne Cordova as the newsletter of the Los Angeles chapter of Daughters of Bilitis. For nine years *The Lesbian Tide* enjoyed the largest circulation of any lesbian magazine of the era. The *Lesbian News,* which began in 1975, is still in production. Lesbian-friendly periodicals included *Sister,* published by a collective at the Westside Women's Center and produced largely by lesbians, as well as *Everywoman* and *Chrysalis.*

85. "Joan," "The Gay Women's West Coast Conference," *Everywoman* 2, no. 10 (July 9, 1971), and Cordova interview, August 21, 2004.

86. E-mail correspondence from Carolyn Weathers to LF, January 15, 2006.

87. Raphael, "Coming Out," 77, and Cordova interview, August 21, 2004. Sheila Kuehl, then associate dean of students, virtually sneaked the conference onto campus one weekend in the spring, arranging to have rooms and auditoriums opened, but never indicating to UCLA authorities the nature of the group that would be using them: LF interview with Sheila Kuehl, July 24, 2004. In 1960, the Daughters of Bilitis held what was billed as the first "National Lesbian Conference" in San Francisco with approximately two hundred participants.

88. E-mail correspondence to LF from Jeanne Cordova, January 19, 2006.

89. Cordova interview, August 21, 2004.

90. Quoted in Joanne Meyerowitz, *How Sex Changed: A History of Transsexualism in the United States* (Cambridge, Mass.: Harvard University Press, 2002), 260.

91. Recollection of Kate Kauffman, quoted in "Changing the World, Building New Lives," http://www.CathyCade.com. Despite the various conflicts, the UCLA conference also inspired the Lesbian Rights Task Force of Los Angeles NOW to undertake an annual lesbian conference at USC, beginning in 1975. The NOW lesbian conference was coyly called "Women and Alternate Lifestyles."

92. LF interview with Mary Margaret Smith, 55, April 7, 2004.

93. Cassyd interview.

94. ST interview with John (Jon) Platania, 65, July 28, 2005.

95. Kight quoted in Thompson, *Long Road to Freedom,* 55.

96. ST interview with Joey Terrill, 49, July 31, 2005.

97. John [*sic*] Platania, "The Gay Community Services Center: A proposal directed toward the planning, programming, funding, and implementation of a multiple human services center open to homosexual women and men of the Greater Los Angeles Area," July 1971, collection of ST, courtesy Jon Platania.

98. Richard Nash, "Power to Gay People: A Los Angeles Experiment in Community Action," *After You're Out: Personal Experiences of Gay Men and Lesbian Women,* ed. Karla Jay and Allen Young (New York: Pyramid Books, 1975), 248–255.

99. E-mail correspondence to LF from Terry DeCrescenzo, January 17, 2006.

100. Don Kilhefner to James Griffith (IRS), May 14, 1973, ONE National Gay and Lesbian Archives.

101. John Kyper, "Gay Community Centers," Los Angeles, box 104-106, ONE National Gay and Lesbian Archives.

102. Terrill interview.

103. Dudley Clendinen and Adam Nagourney, *Out for Good: The Struggle to Build a Gay Rights Movement in America* (New York: Simon and Schuster, 1999), 84.

104. Lachs interview.

105. Remarks by Don Kilhefner and Morris Kight, "Speaking the Vision," Plummer Park, November 7, 1986.

106. ST interview with Steve Schulte, 59, September 8, 2005.

107. Lynn Lilliston, "Help Center for the Gay Community," *Los Angeles Times*, July 6, 1973, B1.

108. Wilson interview.

109. ST interview with Ben Teller, 64, September 2, 2005.

110. Ibid.

111. ST interview with Ed Edelman, 74, September 5, 2005.

112. "Gay Clients," developed by Don Clark and Betty Berzon, box 104-106, ONE National Gay and Lesbian Archives.

113. Wilson interview.

114. ST Interview with Ken Bartmess, 80, June 27, 2005.

CHAPTER 7

1. ST interview with Steve Lachs, 60, July 21, 2004.

2. Robin Stevens, "Eating Our Own," *The Advocate*, August 13, 1992, 32.

3. February 27, 1955, Homosexual Information Center Library, California State University, Northridge.

4. See chap. 4.

5. ST interview with Rick St. Dennis, 56, August 27, 2005.

6. ST interview with John (Jon) Platania, August 17, 2005.

7. ST interviews with Deni Ponty, 57, July 15, 2005; Josy Cattogio, 54, September 1, 2005; and Cosmo Bua, 53, September 6, 2005.

8. ST interview with Rob Wray, 49, September 7, 2005.

9. *Southern California Women Newsletter*, November–December 1978, 4. (The name of the newsletter was altered throughout the years as the group changed affiliation; see references below to Southern California Women for the Whitman-Radclyffe Foundation, Southern California Women for Understanding, etc.)

10. ST interview with Mike Manning, 57, August 28, 2005.

11. John Rechy, eulogy, "Tribute to Morris Kight," January 29, 2000, ST's personal collection.

12. E-mail correspondence from Robin Tyler to LF, September 15, 2005.

13. Loraine Hutchins, "Festival," *Off Our Backs* 11, no. 10 (November 1981): 1+.

14. LF interview with Mina Meyer, 64, April 5, 2004. The strike had essentially destroyed the women's clinic. When Josy Catoggio joined the Center in 1978, Sheldon Andelson, head of the board, discussed with her the idea of establishing another women's health clinic, but Catoggio felt that by then the Feminist Health Center had sufficiently filled the gap and the Gay Community Services Center's efforts would be redundant: ST interview with Josy Catoggio, 54, August 1, 2005.

15. LF interview with Sylvia Rhue, 56, October 7, 2004.

16. ST interview with Michael Weinstein, 53, September 20, 2005.

17. ST interview with Jaime Green, 72, June 24, 2004.

18. Carolyn Weathers, "An Early History of the Alcoholism Center for Women" (unpublished document), LF's personal collection.

19. Letter from Don Kilhefner to Dr. Gilbert Shaw, chief administrator of the federal granting agency (NIAAA), proposing that "APW be enabled to establish its autonomy and operate independently of GCSC," May 8, 1975. We are grateful to Terry DeCrescenzo for drawing this correspondence to our attention.

20. LF interview with Brenda Weathers, 67, April 5, 2004.

21. "Gay Center May Drop One Million Dollar Program," *NewsWest*, May 30, 1975.

22. LF interview with Robin Podolsky, 48, April 6, 2004.

23. "Chronology of Recent Events at the Gay Community Services Center," April 29, 1975, in GCSC file, June Mazer Lesbian Archives, West Hollywood, California.

24. Weinstein interview.

25. ST interview with Bruce Reifle, 63, September 29, 2005.

26. Jeanne Cordova, "The Strike," in "When We Were Outlaws: A Memoir" (unpublished ms., 2004 version).

27. LF interview with Lillene Fifield, 62, July 28, 2004.

28. "Doctors Say 'No' to GSCS Clinic," *Lesbian News*, October 1975, 2.

29. LF interview with Mary Margaret Smith, 55, April 7, 2004.

30. "Women Speak Out About GCSC," ONE National Gay and Lesbian Archives, University of Southern California, Los Angeles.

31. "'Gunfight' at the L.A. Saloon," *Lesbian News*, September 1975, 1; and LF interview with Jinx Beers, 72, August 27, 2005.

32. Fifield interview.

33. LF interview with Josy Catoggio, 53, July 26, 2004.

34. "GCSC Dispute Settled," *Lesbian News*, September 1978, 1, and e-mail correspondence to LF from Jeanne Cordova, January 19, 2006.

35. LF interview with Carol Nottley, 65, October 10, 2005.

36. LF telephone interview with Beth Nottley, 48, October 21, 2005.

37. Carol Nottley interview.

38. Bua interview.

39. ST interview with Ben Teller, 64, September 2, 2005.

40. Carol Nottley interview. The Los Angeles Gay Community Services Center took a leap toward professionalization in 1977, when Carol Nottley was recruited from a Beverly Hills certified public accounting firm to become the Center's chief financial officer. During her tenure, Nottley says, she often had to struggle with the staff who were left over from the more radical early years. "They didn't like structure. They just wanted a place that was theirs."

41. Schulte interview.

42. Bua interview. See also the *Los Angeles Times* article reporting critics' complaints that Schulte, "in his zest to legitimize and sanitize the center, turned his back on people who depended on it for basic services like food and legal aide": Alan Citron, "Homosexual Quits Job to Run for Office," *Los Angeles Times*, December 22, 1983, WS1.

43. Memo dated 2/15/78, Gay Community Services Center, box 103-118, ONE National Gay and Lesbian Archives.

44. Schulte interview. Gay Community Services Center services to the needy did expand with the influx of money and they continue to this day, but the name has been changed to the "Gay and Lesbian Center" to reflect a broader purpose. In the 1990s, the Center began a fund-raising campaign (with a lead donation of $1 million) to establish the Village, a separate lesbian/gay venue, which offered programs that were not "crisis oriented." The Lily Tomlin/Jane Wagner Cultural Arts Program at the Village includes theatrical productions and art exhibits, as well as book discussion groups, courses such as "Taking the Mystery Out of Remodeling Your Home," and a comprehensive program for lesbian and gay seniors: LF interviews with Lorri Jean (CEO of

the Gay and Lesbian Center), 47, April 30, 2004, and Julia Salazar (Director of Community Outreach and Education), 47, August 19, 2004.

45. LF interview with JJ (Jay) Vega, September 18, 2004.

46. LF interview with Terry DeCrescenzo, April 4, 2004.

47. "Annual Summer Lawn Party Set for August 27," *The Center News*, Summer 1989, 1.

48. Information from LF interview with Rita Baird, 58, July 25, 2004: Los Angeles Gay Community Services Center board member from 1983 to 1986.

49. DeCrescenzo interview.

50. LF interview with Del Martinez, 71, August 12, 2005.

51. Ibid.

52. Ibid.

53. *Connexxus Newsletter*, January 10, 1985.

54. Martinez interview. See also fund-raising flier, "The Vision Connects Us: So Far It's Working," 1988, Connexxus Papers, June Mazer Lesbian Archives, West Hollywood, California.

55. Garland Richard Kyle, "Connexxus May Well Be the Most Cost-Effective Human Service Organization in All of Los Angeles County," *Frontiers* 6, no. 23 (March 9–March 23, 1988): 70–71.

56. Moira Rachel Kenney, *Mapping Gay L.A.: The Intersection of Place and Politics* (Philadelphia: Temple University Press, 2001), 136.

57. Martinez interview. The Gay and Lesbian Community Services Center's Lesbian Central had been disbanded by then. Julia Salazar (who worked at the Center from 1982 to 1995) says, "There were several really integral women on the board, such as Gwen Baba, a philanthropist, and they felt lesbians shouldn't want to be shuffled into that little space. We met as a group and said, 'What if we made the entire center a place for women, not just this room?'" In 1988, Salazar was asked to create more women's programming, including courses such as "Dating Skills for Women," "Effective Public Speaking," "Astrology for Women," "Buying Your First House," and creative writing classes: Salazar interview.

58. LF interview with Torie Osborn, April 30, 2004. Also, Torie Osborn, *Coming Home to America: A Roadmap to Gay and Lesbian Empowerment* (New York: St. Martin's Press, 1996).

59. Wilson quoted in "Gayle Wilson—Elitist," *Southern California Women Newsletter*, November–December 1978, 1.

60. ST interview with Bob Geoghegan, 61, September 5, 2005.

61. Manning interview, and "Gay Community Alliance," subject file, ONE National Gay and Lesbian Archives.

62. Gay political activists, including Dave Glascock, volunteered for Pines' campaign, sensitizing Pines to the injustice of certain city policies and practices. The gay philanthropist Lloyd Wrigler was Pines' most generous contributor. District Attorney Vince Bugliosi campaigned in gay bars a year before Pines did so.

63. ST interview with Burt Pines, 66, September 22, 2005.

64. Frank del Olmo, "Pines to Curb 'Gay Bar' Prosecutions," *Los Angeles Times*, April 23, 1974, A1.

65. "'No Legal Bars to Homosexuals as Officers'—Pines," *Los Angeles Times*, May 10, 1975, A1. See also, "Thank You, Burt," *NewsWest*, May 30, 1975, in which the new L.A. gay paper acknowledged gay Angelenos' debt to Burt Pines. Pines remained gay-friendly and in 1981 was appointed by Governor Jerry Brown to head a California State commission studying discrimination against homosexuals, the elderly, and the handicapped.

66. ST interview with Ed Edelman, 74, September 5, 2005.

67. "Edelman Says He Knew of Gay Aide's Past Conviction," *Los Angeles Times*, January, 14, 1975, B3.

68. ST interview with Troy Perry, 65, September 16, 2005, and ST interview with Mark Haile, 49, December 13, 2005.

69. Edelman interview.

70. ST interview with Mark Thompson, 53, October 29, 2005.

71. "Chief Davis Cancels His Subscription," letter to the editor, *Los Angeles Times*, August 20, 1975, A12.

72. ST interview with Jeanne Barney, July 19, 2005.

73. "Southland," *Los Angeles Times*, June 29, 1976, B2.

74. Barney interview.

75. ST interview with Aristide Laurent, 63, August 25, 2004.

76. Barney interview.

77. "LAPD Has Been Cowed by Gays, Davis Charges," *Los Angeles Times*, May 21, 1976, E1.

78. Perry interview. Peggy Stevenson understood that she was reelected to her council seat in good part because of the gay vote, and she was the Los Angeles City Council's most important ally of the gay community in those years.

79. "The Los Angeles Gay and Lesbian History Map," "Los Angeles Lesbians" file, ONE National Gay and Lesbian Archives.

80. "Results of Poll Conducted by Mayor Bradley's Pollsters, 1977," Gay Press file, ONE National Gay and Lesbian Archives.

81. The term was coined in 1976 in Maupin's *Tales of the City*.

82. Orion's purpose and membership described in LF interview with Diane Abbitt, 62, October 17, 2005.

83. Lachs interview.

84. Ibid.

85. Dudley Clendenin and Adam Nagourney, *Out for Good: The Struggle to Build a Gay Rights Movement in America* (New York: Simon and Schuster, 1999), 357.

86. Doyle McManus, "Gay Rights Group Displays Power," *Los Angeles Times*, March 18, 1979, C5.

87. As told to LF in Abbitt interview. It is perhaps significant that MECLA decided to add women to its board the month after the June 1977 success of Anita Bryant's vicious Dade County, Florida, campaign to repeal gay rights. Bryant's campaign argued that the gay movement was really about increasing opportunities for gay men to have sex with impunity. As even the homophiles recognized thirty years earlier, the presence of lesbians in the organization would show that its purpose was more serious.

88. Abbitt interview.

89. LF interview with Roberta Bennett, 63, December 18, 2004, and Robbi Simon, "herstories/theirstories" (an interview with Roberta Bennett and Diane Abbitt), *Southern California Women for Understanding Newsletter*, December 1982–January 1983, 10–11.

90. Simon, "herstories/theirstories," and Bennett and Abbitt interviews.

91. Bennett and Abbitt interviews.

92. Bennett interview.

93. LF interview with Esther (pseud.), 74, December 19, 2004.

94. "Gay Rights: Is a Backlash Forming?" *Los Angeles Times*, July 29, 1978, F1. See also the discussion of Anita Bryant's and John Briggs' campaigns against gay rights in Clendenin and Nagourney, *Out for Good*.

95. ST interview with David Mixner, 59, September 4, 2005.

96. Jim Kepner, "Becoming a People: A 4,000-Year Chronology of Gay and Lesbian History" (Los Angeles: self-published, 1995), 110, ST collection.

97. "New Group Already at Work: March Its First Success," *NewsWest*, June 23, 1977, 7.

98. Ibid.

99. LF interview with Ivy Bottini, 78, August 19, 2004.

100. Initiative text from *Southern California Women Newsletter*, 1978.

101. Bottini interview.

102. Myra Riddell, "Notes from the Chair," *Southern California Women/Whitman-Radclyffe Foundation News,* 1977.

103. Clendenin and Nagourney, *Out for Good,* 382–383. Despite the straight shield and obfuscating ploys, gay talent really ran the campaign. For example, Sally Fiske, a television anchor, came out as a lesbian on the local "Evening News" because she was outraged by Briggs. When she was fired from her job, she became the public relations director of No on 6.

104. Doug Shuit, "Bitter Fight Expected on Gay Teacher Issue," *Los Angeles Times,* June 2, 1978, B3.

105. LF interview with Suzanne Gage, 52, September 10, 2004.

106. LF interview with Robin Podolsky, 48, April 6, 2004.

107. ST interview with John Morgan Wilson, 60, July 18, 2005.

108. Mixner interview.

109. Bottini interview. See also: "Gayle Wilson—Elitist," *Southern California Women Newsletter,* November–December 1978, 1.

110. Mixner interview.

111. Stonewall Democratic Club Announcement of Its Agenda for Summer and Fall of 1978, Stonewall Democratic Club files, ONE National Gay and Lesbian Archives.

112. Podolsky interview.

113. Mixner interview.

114. Bottini interview.

115. Mixner interview.

116. Jinx Beers, editorial, *Lesbian News,* November 1978, 1.

117. Mixner interview.

118. Quoted in "One Hell of a Campaign—And We Won!" *Southern California Women Newsletter,* November–December 1978, 1.

119. Jinx Beers, editorial, *Lesbian News,* December 1978, 10–11.

120. "Gay Rights Group Displays Power," *Los Angeles Times,* March 18, 1979.

CHAPTER 8

1. Lucinda Pennington, "But Will It Play in West Hollywood?" *Los Angeles Magazine,* May 1981, 117–118.

2. ST interview with Steve Schulte, 59, September 8, 2005.

3. The real Boystown had been started by Father Flanagan in 1917 to care for orphaned newsboys.

4. Jim Morris, a retired African American bodybuilder who had won the title of Mr. America in 1973, owned the gym and pioneered personal training. "Big Weenies" T-shirts were popular among gay and even straight Angelenos. Following every fad of his day, the owner, Charles Roberts, even organized the Big Weenie jogging team.

5. Quoted in Pennington, "But Will It Play in West Hollywood?" Assertions about gay affluence have been highly controversial in the community. See John W. Stiles, "The Myth of Gay Affluence: Why Does the World Think We're So Well Off? And How Is It Hurting Us That They Do?" *OutSmart,* June 2004; and M. V. Lee Badgett, "Income Inflation: The Myth of Affluence Among Gay, Lesbian and Bisexual Americans," *Income Inflation* (joint publication of the Policy Institute of the National Gay and Lesbian Task Force and the Institute for Gay and Lesbian Strategic Studies, Washington, D.C., 2000), http://www.thetaskforce.org/downloads/income.pdf.

6. "But Will It Play in West Hollywood?" ("Gay" in this *New Yorker* cartoon referred, of course, to men and did not include lesbians, who were perceived by big business as barely better off financially than their straight female counterparts.)

7. Photos in the Ah Men file, ONE National Gay and Lesbian Archives, University of Southern California, Los Angeles.

8. "Listen," *Los Angeles Times,* December 7, 1979, K6.

9. Doug Edwards, "Business: Gene Burkard, the Man Behind International's Mail Male," *The Advocate,* June 28, 1979. Burkard began his business in San Diego before opening a West Hollywood shop.

10. "Studio One a Big Hit!" clipping, *Data Boy Southern California* (July 1977), Studio One file, ONE National Gay and Lesbian Archives.

11. ST interview with Lee Glaze, 66, September 19, 2004.

12. Dennis Hunt, "Disco DJ: Producer of the Beat," *Los Angeles Times,* Jan 12, 1979, F14.

13. Jack Slater, "Discotheques Dance to Another Tune," *Los Angeles Times,* August 11, 1976, G1.

14. Ibid.

15. Jan Lang, "A Higher Goal," letters to the editor, *Los Angeles Times,* August 29, 1976, E18.

16. Personal recollections of ST.

17. ST interview with Mark Haile, 49, December 13, 2005. Ironically, Manny Slali, an Arab Mexican, was the *Billboard*-anointed deejay who made the club's reputation in its early years: "Disco DJ: Producer of the Beat," *Los Angeles Times,* January 12, 1979, F14.

18. Haile interview.

19. Dave Johnson, "Studio One Hit with Charges of Racism, Sexist Discrimination," *Los Angeles Free Press,* June 13, 1975. See also Eric Wat, "Three Pieces of ID," in *The Making of a Gay Asian Community: An Oral History of Pre-AIDS Los Angeles* (Lanham, Md.: Rowman and Littlefield, 2002), 55–58.

20. Wat, "Three Pieces of ID," 56. Asians, blacks, and Latinos, who compose large segments of L.A.'s gay population, were eventually welcomed by enterprising gay businessmen who built vast dance clubs catering to them.

21. LF interview with Francesca Miller, 57, July 24, 2004.

22. "Discotheques Dance," *Los Angeles Times,* August 11, 1976.

23. ST interview with Troy Perry, 65, August 30, 2005. Perry recalls that Hal Gitman, the manager of Dude City, told him that "gay men don't want women in the bar." Perry replied, "Nonsense. I've never met a gay man yet who'll let a woman get in the way of his cruising."

24. For more on the history of L.A.'s baths, see Eddie Coronado's extensive Web site, http://www.gaytubs.com/losangels.htm.

25. E-mail correspondence, "Jack" (age unknown) to Eddie Coronado, October 10, 1999.

26. Clubs exclusively for sex, with no pretense of bath facilities, were known as "dry baths." The phenomenon grew in the 1970s.

27. ST interview with Rick St. Dennis, 56, August 27, 2005. A gay businessman, Marty Benson, opened several bathhouses catering to older and heavier men; he became extremely rich in the process.

28. "Jack" to Eddie Coronado, October 10, 1999; and "Richard" (age unknown), September 27, 1999.

29. E-mail correspondence, "Raul" (age unknown) to Eddie Coronado, September 20, 1999.

30. "Today," biography and excerpts of award acceptance speeches, p. 1 (c. 1993), Andelson file, ONE National Gay and Lesbian Archives.

31. David Mixner, *Stranger Among Friends* (New York: Bantam Books, 1996), 163.

32. Lauren Hanson, "The Life and Times of Robin Tyler," *Lesbian News,* July 1991, 50.

33. LF interview with Jeanne Cordova, 56, October 3, 2004.

34. Scott Anderson, "The Gay Press," *The Advocate,* December 13, 1979, 22. Cordova points out that even the great radical media icon, the *Los Angeles Free Press,* had become "much less political and more sexual" before its demise in 1977: Cordova interview, October 3, 2004.

35. Cordova interview, October 3, 2004.

36. *Southern California Women for Understanding Newsletter,* Summer 1976.

37. SCWU Steering Committee minutes, June 8, 1978, SCWU Papers, June Mazer Lesbian Archives, West Hollywood, California.

38. LF interview with Frieda (pseud.), 74, August 20, 2004.

39. LF interview with Marion (pseud.), 78, August 20, 2004.

40. SCWU Steering Committee minutes, January 5, 1978.

41. "Surprise Information," policy statement, SCWU Activities Committee file, June Mazer Lesbian Archives.

42. SCWU Activities Committee file, June Mazer Lesbian Archives.

43. Such complaints were leveled against SCWU even by its own members. In the February 1977 newsletter, for example, Dr. Shevvy Healy complained that because SCWU charged an admission of $7.50 for Jean O'Leary's speech at the Convention Center, black and Chicana women had been unable to attend (p. 5). See also Irene Robertson's impassioned defense in the following newsletter, March 1977, in which she says that SCWU works to combat the stereotype that there are no affluent black and Chicana lesbians (p. 2).

44. Board of Directors Minutes: SCWU Goals, August 23, 1984, SCWU Papers, June Mazer Lesbian Archives.

45. Executive Committee minutes, July 21, 1983, SCWU Papers; Agenda, Board of Directors, August 25, 1983, SCWU Papers, June Mazer Lesbian Archives.

46. *Lesbian News,* August 1982, 3.

47. Flier announcing O'Leary's speech in SCWU Activities Committee file, SCWU Papers, June Mazer Lesbian Archives.

48. LF interview with Jean O'Leary, February 16, 2004.

49. LF interview with Heather Leavitt, 40, July 20, 2004.

50. John D'Emilio, *Making Trouble* (New York: Routledge, 1992), 258.

51. See Southern California Women for Understanding's list of lesbian bars in which they intended to distribute their newsletter: "SCWU Board Decides to Bar None," *SCWU Newsletter,* February–March 1983.

52. In 1981, annual gay-male-household incomes averaged $30,000 and lesbian incomes averaged less than $20,000: Lucinda Pennington, "But Will It Play in West Hollywood?" *Los Angeles Magazine,* May 1981, 118.

53. Seventy-five percent of the members of the upscale Southern California Women for Understanding admitted in the organization's survey that they "liked" lesbian bars: "SCWU Board Decides to Bar None."

54. LF interview with Marci (pseud.), 55, July 25, 2004.

55. Marci interview. Styles changed from year to year in lesbian bars of the 1970s. Suzanne Gage says that when she arrived at the Palms in the early 1970s, the women had "an androgynous, studied look—leotards or spaghetti straps, tight jeans, belts with studs. Country Western was big." But even then, "going to the Palms was like making an appearance," Gage notes. "Everyone is checking you out. This is Hollywood, after all." LF interview with Suzanne Gage, 52, September 10, 2004.

56. Gage interview.

57. Leavitt interview.

58. LF interview with Sheree Rose, August 30, 2004.

59. See chap. 7 for the transsexual conflict at the West Coast Lesbian Conference in 1973.

60. Rose interview.

61. LF interview with Vivian Escalante, 51, December 3, 2005.

62. Irene Weiss, letter to the editor, *Lesbian News,* August 1982, 28.

63. Some SM lesbians, including Sheree Rose, have been active in both radical feminist politics and SM and say that they are not mutually exclusive.

64. Arlene Stein, "All Dressed Up and No Place to Go: Style Wars and the New Lesbianism," *Out/Look,* Winter 1989, 36.

65. Performed by Lotus Lame and the Lame Flames, a girl-punk band masterminded by Lee.

66. "Disco Sucks" was a movement that spanned British and U.S. cities starting in 1979; some felt it was clearly antigay, despite the gay leadership in punk rock: See Peter Braunstein, "The Last Days of Gay Disco," *Village Voice*, June 24–30, 1998.

67. ST interview with Jack Marquette, 54, September 18, 2005.

68. ST interview with John Callahan, 61, September 23, 2005.

69. Brendan Mullen, Stuart Timmons and Geza X, "Craig Lee, 1956–1991," *LA Weekly*, October 18, 1991.

70. Personal observation of ST, c. 1983.

71. LF interview with Phranc, 47, August 18, 2004.

72. Rose interview.

73. LF interview with Fran (pseud.), 40, August 1, 2004. Bisexuality among the female punk rockers in Hollywood during the early 1980s is also described in Aimee Cooper, *Coloring Outside the Lines: A Punk Rock Memoir* (Elgin, TX.: Rowdy's Press, 2003).

74. Phranc interview.

75. Fran interview.

76. Phranc interview. In an effort to address this issue, the Dead Kennedys performed a song called "Nazi Punks Fuck Off!"

77. Fran interview.

78. Another of Lee's songs, "Bad Sex," thrilled straight hedonists with gay wisdom: "I feel like my life is under a hex / All I wanted was love, all I got was bad sex."

CHAPTER 9

1. ST interview with Troy Perry, 65, September 16, 2005.

2. Statistics: e-mail correspondence to LF from the Rev. Nancy Wilson, November 16, 2005; MCC press advisory, October 29, 2005; John Dart, "Gay-Oriented Church Joins Ecumenical Group," *Los Angeles Times*, February 21, 1997, B1; *Our Facts: 2004 Annual Report, MCC Metropolitan Community Churches*, May 16, 2005.

3. Perry interview, September 16, 2005.

4. Ibid.

5. LF interview with Lucia Chappelle, 52, August 27, 2005.

6. Perry interview, September 16, 2005.

7. ST interview with Frank Zerilli, 60, July 8, 2004.

8. "Probers Say Church Blaze Was Not Arson," *Los Angeles Times*, February 24, 1973, A27.

9. Dudley Clendenin and Adam Nagourney discuss arson at other Metropolitan Community Churches in *Out for Good: The Struggle to Build a Gay Rights Movement in America* (New York: Simon and Schuster, 1999), chap. 12.

10. ST interview with Lucia Chappelle, 52, September 1, 2005.

11. Wilson communication.

12. LF interview with Chappelle. Chappelle was a congregation member beginning in 1971.

13. LF interview with Savina Teubal, 77, February 17, 2004. See also Teubal's books, *Sarah, The Priestess: The First Matriarch of Genesis* (Athens, OH: Swallow Press, 1984), and *Hagar the Egyptian: The Lost Tradition of the Matriarchs* (New York: HarperCollins, 1990).

14. ST interview Troy Perry, August 30, 2005. Rabbi Eichberg was the father of MECLA's Rob Eichberg.

15. LF interview with Mina Meyer, 64, April 5, 2004.

16. LF interview with Harriet Perl, 83, February 14, 2004.

17. Perry interview, August 30, 2005.

18. "New Life for Jewish Temple," typescript, Beth Chayim Chadashim file, ONE National Gay and Lesbian Archives, University of Southern California, Los Angeles.

19. http://www.mljewish.org, vol. 9, no. 14. This article is no longer available online, but see John Sherwood, "Reform Judaism and Homosexuality," http://www.mljewish.org/cgi-bin/retrieve.cgi?VOLUME=10&NUMBER=63&FORMAT=html.

20. "Hebrew Group Okays Beth Chayim Temple," *Los Angeles Times*, July 20, 1974, 26.

21. See Jeannette Vance, "The Impact of HIV/AIDS on Queer Spiritual Communities: Metropolitan Community Church and Beth Chayim Chadashim" (master's thesis, Claremont Graduate School, 2000); see also Gary David Comstock, *Unrepentant, Self-Affirming, Practicing: Lesbian/Gay/Bisexual People Within Organized Religion* (New York: Continuum, 1996).

22. Meyer interview, and LF interview with Sharon Raphael, 62, April 5, 2004.

23. Perl interview.

24. "Women Take Their Place in the Temple," *Lesbian News*, September 1975, 2.

25. LF interview with Chappelle.

26. Paula Schoenwether, "Celebration of Our Birth," in "Worship Resources from the Women of De Colores M.C.C. and Friends" (Los Angeles: self-published by De Colores, undated), 1.

27. Lynn Simross, "The 'Rev.' Responds to Calling," *Los Angeles Times*, August 15, 1985; and Darryl Fears, "Gay Blacks Feeling Strained Church Ties," *Washington Post*, November 2, 2004, A3.

28. LF interview with Rabbi Denise Eger, 45, October 18, 2005.

29. LF interview with Rabbi Lisa Edwards, 53, October 16, 2005.

30. Eger interview.

31. Hay had been researching the Native American *berdache* tradition since the 1950s. Walter Williams' *The Spirit and the Flesh: Sexual Diversity in American Indian Culture* (Boston: Beacon Press, 1986) and Will Roscoe's *The Zuni Man-Woman* (Albuquerque: University of New Mexico Press, 1991) both acknowledge his studies in this area.

32. See also Stuart Timmons, *The Trouble with Harry Hay: Founder of the Modern Gay Movement* (Boston: Alyson, 1990); Mark Thompson, *Gay Spirit: Myth and Meaning* (New York: St. Martin's Press, 1987); and Arthur Evans, *Witchcraft and the Gay Counterculture: A Radical View of Western Civilization and Some of the People It Has Tried to Destroy* (Boston: Fag Rag Books, 1978).

33. LF interview with Robin Tyler, 62, August 22, 2004.

34. ST interview with Deni Ponty, 57, July 15, 2005.

35. During the 1979 filming in Greenwich Village of *Cruising*, a movie portraying homosexuality and SM as ending in murder, gays staged a protest, which, the film historian Vito Russo claimed, "was the beginning of a heightened sensitivity around Hollywood." Interview with Vito Russo in Eric Marcus, *Making History: The Struggle for Gay and Lesbian Equal Rights, 1945–1990* (New York: HarperCollins, 1992), 393. *That Certain Summer* may have been dismissed by Russo because it was a film made for television.

36. LF interview with Kim Garfield, 71, October 13, 2005.

37. "A Reluctance to Play Gay," *Time*, July 4, 1988, 61.

38. LF interview with Sheila Kuehl, 63, July 24, 2004.

39. ST interview with Michael Kearns, 54, June 18, 2004.

40. Tyler interview, August 22, 2004, and LF interview with Robin Tyler, August 28, 2005; LF interview with Patti Harrison, 70, August 28, 2005; Lauren Hanson, "The Life and Times of Robin Tyler," *Lesbian News*, July 1991, 32+.

41. LF interview with Simone Wallace, 58, July 25, 2004.

42. LF interview with Ann Bradley, 50, April 6, 2004.

43. Mark Thompson, ed., *The Long Road to Freedom: The Advocate History of the Gay and Lesbian Movement* (New York: St. Martin's Press, 1994), xxvi.

44. ST interview with Mark Thompson, 53, October 29, 2005.

45. Elizabeth Venant, "Richard Rouilard Is Proud, Outrageous and . . . in Your Face," *Los Angeles Times*, January 2, 1992, E1. Rouilard's transformation of *The Advocate* caused a huge jump in subscriptions, though his lavish spending cut his tenure short. However, his innovations left a lasting mark on the nation's leading gay publication.

46. Ibid.

47. *The Advocate,* January 17, 2006, 26.

48. LF interview with Jinx Beers, 72, August 28, 2005.

49. LF interview with Ella Matthes, August 27, 2005.

50. Ibid. The Gwen Stefani cover was dated May 2005. Similarly, editors of *The Advocate* and *Frontiers* have complained that their publications did not sell unless the cover featured an alluring male. The magazines have also been criticized by various segments of the community for the lack of diversity on their covers.

51. Matthes interview.

52. In 2005, for example, the Los Angeles gay pride parade received coverage in 120 broadcast media (Lorri Jean, "Pride and Paris," *Lesbian News,* August 2005, 10), and gay marriage as well as the groundbreaking Western film, *Brokeback Mountain,* became a topic of focus in all major newspapers.

53. *Los Angeles Times,* November 12, 1999, C1.

54. Quoted in Kevin Roderick, "New City Debuts in Rousing Old-Time Meeting," *Los Angeles Times,* November 30, 1984, C3.

55. Stephen Braun, "West Hollywood Decision Delayed," *Los Angeles Times,* July 29, 1984, WS1.

56. Stephen Braun, "West Hollywood: Vote May Make It First Gay-Run City," *Los Angeles Times,* October 14, 1984, C1.

57. Ibid.

58. "The Friends of Valerie Terrigno," *Los Angeles Reader,* November 22, 1985, 1.

59. Roderick, "New City Debuts."

60. Stephen Braun, "The Trouble With Terrigno," *Los Angeles Times Magazine,* June 1, 1986, 17; Dorit Phyllis Gary, "Mayor Terrigno," *L.A. Weekly,* July 5–11, 1985.

61. Braun, "The Trouble with Terrigno," 19.

62. ST and LF interview with Valerie Terrigno, 51, October 16, 2005.

63. West Hollywood lobbyist Helene Myshar. The city council of Berkeley, California, also proposed domestic partnership legislation that year, but West Hollywood preceded Berkeley in enacting such legislation.

64. Chris Woodyard and Deborah Anderluh, "West Hollywood's First Mayor Indicted," *Los Angeles Herald Examiner,* October 24, 1985, A1, and Braun, "The Trouble with Terrigno," 17.

65. Braun, "The Trouble with Terrigno," 19.

66. Terrrigno interview.

67. Ibid.

68. Gary, "Mayor Terrigno," 24.

69. "Terrigno Supporters Demonstrate," *The News,* April 4, 1986, 20.

70. ST interview with Gene La Pietra, 57, October 21, 2005.

71. Gary, "Mayor Terrigno," 24.

72. George Ramos and Stephen Braun, "Probers Accuse Terrigno of Embezzling U.S. Funds," *Los Angeles Times,* October 24, 1985, 1.

73. "Terrigno Sentenced to 60 Days in Halfway House," *The News,* May 16, 1986.

CHAPTER 10

1. LF interview with Rita Gonzales, 53, October 2, 2004.

2. See chap. 4.

3. ST interview with Bruce Reifel, 63, September 29, 2005.

4. Alycee J. Lane, "Pride at Home: Celebrating Being Lesbian and Gay in Our Own Neighborhoods," *BLK,* July 1990, 13. *BLK* was started in Los Angeles by Alan Bell in 1988 as a free publication for distribution in L.A.'s black gay bars. It soon became a national publication. Bell's

company also published *Black Lace*, a quarterly erotic magazine for black lesbians, and *Blackfire*, an erotic bimonthly for gay men.

5. ST interview with Francisco Ico del Rio, April 6, 2004.

6. Ibid.

7. ST interview with Rudy Ruano, 60, September 16, 2004.

8. Ibid.

9. ST interview with "Andreas" (pseud.), 53, December 20, 2004.

10. LF interview with Marcia Kawahara, 65, September 6, 2004.

11. The phrase "the down low" is used by African Americans to describe such covert relations.

12. ST interview with Jolino Beserra, 48, November 6, 2005.

13. ST interview with Jef Huereque, 52, December 11, 2005.

14. Few Asians went to gay bars in those years. As Eric Wat points out, the gay Asian American population grew, along with the larger Asian American population, when the Japanese and Chinese were joined by immigrants from the Philippines, Korea, and Southeast Asia: *The Making of a Gay Asian Community: An Oral History of Pre-AIDS Los Angeles* (Lanham, MD: Rowman and Littlefield, 2002).

15. LF interview with K.C. (pseud.), 61, April 22, 2004.

16. E-mail correspondence to LF from Jeanne Cordova, January 23, 2006.

17. LF interview with JJ (Jay) Vega, 50, September 18, 2004.

18. ST interview with Joey Terrill, 49, July 31, 2005.

19. Hilary E. MacGregor, "In Montebello, Producer Puts Down Roots at New Breed of Gay Bar," *Los Angeles Times*, May 23, 2001, E-1.

20. ST interview with Rick St. Dennis, 56, August 27, 2005.

21. ST interview with Gene La Pietra, 57, October 21, 2005.

22. ST interviews with Tom Gibbon, 82, June 21, 2004, and Bill Stephens, 64, August 27, 2004.

23. See Wat, *The Making of a Gay Asian Community*.

24. Erin Aubry Kaplan, "Crown Jewel: The Catch One Turns 30 This Year," *LA Weekly*, September 12–18, 2003; LF interviews with Mary Margaret Smith, 55, April 7, 2004, and Karen Ocamb, 54, August 20, 2004; *GBF*, April 2004, 30; "Major Events in Black Gay History," *BLK*, June 1989, 12.

25. Interview with Jewel Williams in "Lesbian Pride: One Day at a Time," *LA Weekly*, June 23, 1989; and ST interview with Mark Haile, 49, December 13, 2005.

26. Other gay Latino clubs that permitted dancing included La Plaza, in Hollywood (only after their lip sync drag shows in Spanish), Tabasco's, and El Barcito, both in Silver Lake. The dance floors at these clubs, however, could accommodate from a few dozen to perhaps one hundred people—never the numbers that flocked to the warehouse-like Circus.

27. Terrill interview.

28. Andreas interview.

29. Ibid.

30. Ibid.

31. Deborah Johnson and Bobreta Franklin, "Debreta's Then and Now," *Southern California Women for Understanding Newsletter*, May 1981, 13–14; also LF interview with Bobretta Franklin, 59, August 21, 2004.

32. ST interview with Horacio Roque Ramierez, 36, December 14, 2005. Some historians have suggested that working-class bars were indeed the site of community building. See, for example, Elizabeth Lapovsky Kennedy and Madeline D. Davis, *Boots of Leather, Slippers of Gold: A History of a Lesbian Community* (New York: Routledge, 1993), and Helen Branson, *Gay Bar* (San Francisco: Pan Graphic Press, 1957).

33. ST interview with Terry Gock, 52, December 2, 2005.

34. "Mexican-American Gays to Have Own Organization," *The Advocate*, August 19–September 1, 1970, 3. Steve Jordan, an L.A. Latino, called the initial meetings at MCC.

35. Interview with Estilita Grimaldo Smith in *Sister,* April 1974; and "Latin American Lesbians," *The Tide,* July 1974, 15.

36. Franklin interview.

37. Johnson and Franklin, "Debreta's Then and Now," 13–14.

38. LF interview with Ayofemi (Stowe) Folayan, 54, July 27, 2004. Folayan's observation about the "whiteness" of terms such as "gay" or "homosexual" was confirmed in the 1980s for health workers as they tried to stem the spread of AIDS in black and Latino communities. They learned to use instead terms such as "men who have sex with men."

39. LF interview with Gayle, 57, April 5, 2004.

40. LF interview with Lisa Powell, 46, August 20, 2004.

41. See, for example, "GLCSC Happenings," *The Center News,* July–August 1988, 8.

42. LF interview with Lucia Chappelle, 52, August 27, 2005.

43. LF interview with Robin Podolsky, 48, April 6, 2004.

44. ST interview with Jim McDaniels, 43, November 14, 2005.

45. Powell interview.

46. Haile interview.

47. Gonzales interview.

48. ST interview with Mario Perez Ceballos, 29, December 12, 2005.

49. ST interview with Horacio Roque Ramierez, 36, December 14, 2005.

50. Aside from gender conflicts—which were by no means limited to communities of color—gay ethnic groups could find themselves attacked from within as being too bourgeois, too influenced by the "white agenda," or too radical: See Karen Ocamb, "Phill Wilson: L.A.'s New AIDS Coordinator Talks," *BLK,* October 1990, 7.

51. LF interview with Saundra Tignor, 67, August 20, 2004.

52. Powell interview.

53. Ibid.

54. LF interview with Betty Smith, 66, December 14, 2004.

55. Haile interview.

56. LF interview with Kim Swindle-Bautista, 36, December 15, 2004. LAAPIS functions primarily as an e-mail list now. Kim Swindle-Bautista (a Korean woman who was adopted as a child and raised in the United States) explains that the organization essentially dissolved in 1998, after hosting a successful national conference at UCLA (sponsored by the Pacific Bell Telephone Company) of the Asian and Pacific-Islander Lesbian and Bisexual Women's Network. "We just burned out," she says.

57. Gina Masequesmay, "Negotiating Multiple Identities in a Queer Vietnamese Support Group," *Journal of Homosexuality* 45, no. 2 (Fall 2003): 193–215.

58. Latino artists who died of AIDS at this time include Ludar Feldenstein, Mundo Meza, Teddy Sandoval, Corey Roberts Auli, Gil Cuardros, and Jack Vargas.

59. Luis Alfaro, "Out of the Shadows: A Testimonio Against Loneliness," *Anthology of Angels,* ed. Luiz Sampaio (Los Angeles: VIVA, 1999), 3.

60. ST interview with Miguel Angel Reyes, 41, December 5, 2005.

61. Gay filmmakers as early as Mack Sennett were headquartered in Silver Lake, earning the area the nickname "the Swish Alps" (an appellation also applied to the Hollywood Hills): George Ramos, "Silver Lake: Residents of All Stripes Are Drawn to an Evolving Community," *Los Angeles Times,* November 18, 1984, C1.

62. Sam Kaplan, "Gay Street Fair: Out of the Closet and Into the Community," *Los Angeles Times,* August 26, 1980, F1.

63. Ramos, "Evolving Community."

64. Conor Dougherty, "Influx of Newcomers Changing Sunset Junction Neighborhood: Spotlight on Silver Lake," *Los Angeles Business Journal,* December 9, 2002.

65. ST interview with Michael McKinley, 47, December 30, 2005.

66. Ibid.

67. Ibid.

68. LF interview with Lori Ball, 40, and Lisa Ginsburg, 42, July 23, 2004.

CHAPTER 11

1. ST interview with Gene La Pietra, 57, October 21, 2005.

2. Michael Gottlieb et al., "Pneumocystis Pneumonia—Los Angeles," *Morbidity and Mortality Weekly Report* 30 (1981): 250–252.

3. E-mail correspondence from Michael Kearns to ST, October 31, 2005.

4. Mary McNamara, "Life Is Forever Altered as an Epidemic Turns 20," *Los Angeles Times*, June 2, 2001, B1. Voeller argued that the original name, Gay Related Immune Disorder, was inflammatory and unscientific.

5. "Blood Emergency Declared," *Los Angeles Times*, September 12, 1983, A2.

6. Mary Murphy, "The AIDS Scare: What It's Done to Hollywood," *TV Guide*, October 22, 1988, 4–9.

7. ST interview with Gene La Pietra, 57, October 21, 2005.

8. Alan Citron, "AIDS Haunts Gay Sex Life," *Los Angeles Times*, July 17, 1983, WS1.

9. Larry Kramer, "1,183 and Counting," *Frontiers* 1, no. 24 (March 30–April 13, 1983): 1+.

10. Ibid.

11. LF interview with Ivy Bottini, 78, August 19, 2004.

12. Several of the early members of MECLA had by now quit that organization and founded the Book Study Group, a secret society whose main purpose was to raise money among wealthy gays primarily to support political candidates who would help in the fight against AIDS: LF interview with Jean O'Leary, February 18, 2004, and Diane Abbitt, 62, October 17, 2005.

13. Abbitt interview.

14. LF interview with Roberta Bennett, 63, December 18, 2004.

15. LF interview with Sue Talbot, 57, and Liebe Gray, 58, October 4, 2004.

16. LF interview with Rita Gonzales, 53, October 2, 2004.

17. ST interview with Roland Palencia, 48, November 8, 2005.

18. Marylouise Oates, "Show Biz Shows Its Stuff at AIDS Benefit," *Los Angeles Times*, September 21, 1985, 5, 1. Because President Reagan had not acknowledged the AIDS epidemic until this date, some at the event booed his message.

19. Dudley Clendinen and Adam Nagourney, *Out for Good: The Struggle to Build a Gay Rights Movement in America* (New York: Simon and Schuster, 1999), 515.

20. Bill Higgins, "Gala AIDS Fundraiser Is Sedate but Still Starry," *Los Angeles Times*, February 16, 1998.

21. "3,000 Marchers Seek More AIDS Research," *Los Angeles Times*, May 27, 1983, A18.

22. ST interview with Bruce Mirken, 49, September 23, 2005.

23. ST interview with John Morgan Wilson, 60, July 18, 2005.

24. Mirken interview.

25. Clendinen and Nagourney suggest (*Out for Good*, 541) that "class frictions in California's gay community were put aside" in the campaign against Proposition 64; but as Mirken observes, frictions were rife.

26. "Dannemeyer Backs AIDS Quarantine," *Los Angeles Times*, July 3, 1986, 1+.

27. LF interview with Torie Osborn, April 30, 2004.

28. "Prop. 64 Feud Between Gays, LaRouche Backers Grows," *Los Angeles Times*, September 17, 1986, 1+.

29. Larry Day, "County Clinics in Crisis," *ACT UP/LA* (newsletter), February–March 1990, 4.

30. ST interview with Michael Weinstein, 53, September 20, 2005.

31. ST interview with John Fall, 42, October 30, 2005.

32. "Bring the Spirit of Washington Home!" flier, ACT UP/LA Collection, ONE National Gay and Lesbian Archives, University of Southern California, Los Angeles.

33. Richard Labonte, "200 Form ACT UP Group for Los Angeles," *San Diego Update,* undated clipping, ACT UP/LA Collection, ONE National Gay and Lesbian Archives.

34. David Lee Perkins, "ACT UP/LA," outreach letter, p. 3, ACT UP/LA Collection, ONE National Gay and Lesbian Archives.

35. Labonte, "200 form ACT UP Group."

36. "Bring the Spirit" flier.

37. Mirken interview. ACT UP's prime years in L.A. lasted from 1988 to 1991, though activity continued well into the 1990s.

38. ST interview with Craig Collins, 53, October 25, 2005.

39. Murphy, "The AIDS Scare."

40. Fall interview.

41. ST interview with Gunther Freehill, 52, October 27, 2005.

42. Connie Norman, "Tribal Rights," *San Diego Update,* October 6, 1993.

43. Collins interview.

44. Ibid. ACT UP was able to secure a legitimate place in the parade in subsequent years. The 1990 theme spun the right-wing panic about flag burning into an AIDS statement. Dressed in red, white, and blue jerseys made by volunteer Hollywood costumers, AIDS activists bore signs that demanded "STOP DESECRATION OF FAGS."

45. Russell Chandler, "Bishops Oppose Condoms . . . ," *Los Angeles Times,* November 10, 1989, A1. Rebelling against conservative proposals of "abstinence only" for HIV protection, these activists insisted that HIV positive men could have sex and still be responsible. They advocated condom distribution and safe-sex awareness when it was still a new concept.

46. Collins interview.

47. Hector Tobar, "Silent Activists' March Disrupts Mahony Mass," *Los Angeles Times,* December 26, 1989, B3. The group was parodying Mahony's statement in an official church paper titled *Called to Compassion and Responsibility* that safe sex was "a lie and a fraud."

48. Peter Cashman, John Fall, and Enric Morello, "Fumbling on AIDS Causes Waste, Suffering," *Los Angeles Times,* February 13, 1989, 2+.

49. In August 1988 the L.A. supervisors ordered a twenty-bed ward to open within one month. It took more than one year. David Lacaillade, Draft History of L.A. County AIDS Issues (undated), collection of Cyndy Crogan.

50. Mirken interview.

51. Ibid.

52. ST interview with Peter Cashman, 56, October 18, 2005. Other members of ACT UP confirm that MECLA distanced itself, although the MECLA co-chair, Diane Himes, expressed support for the "righteous anger" of emerging political groups to Timothy Stirton in his article, "The New Gay Activism," *Frontiers* 7, no. 7 (July 27–August 10, 1988): 22.

53. "80 Arrested as AIDS Protest Is Broken Up," *Los Angeles Times,* November 7, 1989, 1.

54. Sandy Dwyer, "Activists Confront Feds," *The News,* October 13, 1989, 1.

55. LF interview with Cyndy Crogan, 49, April 7, 2004.

56. Scott Harris, "Announcement Hailed as a Way to Teach Public Taboos," *Los Angeles Times,* November 8, 1991, A32.

57. Lucille Renwick, "A Different Front in the AIDS War," *Los Angeles Times,* October 4, 1992, 21.

58. Benita Roth, "Feminist Boundaries in the Feminist-friendly Organization: The Women's Caucus of ACT UP/LA," *Gender and Society* 12, no. 2 (April 1998): 129–145. Other estimates

have been higher. An ACT UP member, Judy Sisneros, says lesbians composed 15 percent: LF interview with Judy Sisneros, 49, April 6, 2004.

59. Osborn interview.

60. LF interview with Robin Podolsky, 48, April 6, 2004.

61. Osborn interview.

62. Podolsky interview.

63. ST interview with Mary Lucey, 49, October 17, 2005.

64. With an army of Christian fundamentalists culled from a vast base of Orange County churches, Operation Rescue had been blocking the doors of women's health clinics, intimidating women into giving up their plans to abort. Feminist Majority Foundation, an organization concerned with a woman's right to choose abortion, wanted male "muscle" to protect L.A. family planning clinics from the antichoice group. Katherine Spillar of the Feminist Majority's Clinic Defense Alliance campaign recalls, "At that time, ACT UP/LA was huge. They could mobilize tremendous numbers of people": ST interview with Katherine Spillar, 50, November 14, 2005.

65. Crogan interview.

66. Sisneros interview.

67. ST interview with Helene Schpak, 53, October 14, 2005.

68. Mary McNamara, "Life Is Forever Altered as an Epidemic Turns 20," *Los Angeles Times*, June 3, 2001.

69. Written communication to ST from Gunther Freehill, October 24, 2005.

CHAPTER 12

1. Quoted in Bettina Boxall, "L.A.'s New Gay Muscle," *Los Angeles Times Magazine*, March 28, 1993, 32.

2. Sandy Harrison, "Hail of Protests Greets Veto," *Los Angeles Daily News*, October 1, 1991, N1.

3. See Boxall, "L.A.'s New Gay Muscle," 28.

4. Torie Osborn, *Coming Home to America: A Roadmap to Gay and Lesbian Empowerment* (New York: St. Martin's Press, 1996), 140.

5. LF interview with Torie Osborn, April 30, 2004. See also Bruce Mirken and Stuart Timmons, "This Is War: A Broken Promise, a Week in the Streets, a City Transformed," *Los Angeles Reader*, October 11, 1991, 6.

6. LF interview with Robin Podolsky, 48, April 6, 2004.

7. ST interview with Michael du Plessis, 44, January 12, 2006.

8. LF interview with Cyndy Crogan, 49, April 4, 2004.

9. Ibid.

10. LF interview with Jehan Agrama, August 19, 2004.

11. Osborn, *Coming Home to America*, 144–145.

12. Crogan interview.

13. E-mail correspondence to LF from Jehan Agrama, January 14, 2006.

14. In Boxall, "L.A.'s New Gay Muscle."

15. Ibid.

16. Agrama interview.

17. "Portrayals of Homosexuals Honored," *Los Angeles Times*, September 19, 1984, E7.

18. ST interview with Chris Uszler, 54, January 19, 2006. Though AGLA dissolved after a few years, Uszler says that the group had considerable success in "making gays more visible in the movies and raising the gay profile."

19. Geffen did not come out until 1992, but prior to that time he contributed millions of dollars to gay and AIDS charities such as AIDS Project Los Angeles and GLAAD, and he was the producer of the lesbian film *Personal Best*, in 1982: See "David Geffen," *Pink*, Fall 2004, 28.

20. GLAAD had started in New York in 1985 for the purpose of countering the misinformation that was being spread about gays and AIDS. It was modeled after the Jewish Anti-Defamation League.

21. Agrama interview.

22. "Media Watch: GLAAD/LA," *Lesbian News*, June 1991, 34.

23. Ibid.

24. E-mail correspondence to ST from Judy Sisneros, January 19, 2006.

25. Du Plessis interview. In 1991, in addition to *Basic Instinct, JFK* included a baroque gay orgy scene among suspects in the president's assassination, and *Silence of the Lambs* portrayed a serial killer who donned "drag" by flaying his female victims and draping himself in their skins.

26. Queer National Kathleen Chapman remembers, "It was being heavily rumored that QN was going to release a list of queer Hollywood celebrities on the day of the Oscars, and the media got absolutely obsessed with that, in some ways more than they were about a possible disruption of the awards ceremony. QN was allegedly going to be handing out maps of the queer stars' homes, and the press really wanted to get its hands on that. As a way of throwing the whole outing issue back in the faces of the media, on the day of the Oscars, some in QN had a press conference . . . at which we released a list of celebrities who we *refused* to claim as queer." E-mail correspondence to ST January 19, 2006.

27. Jane Galbraith, "Part of Campaign Protesting Negative Stereotypes in Films: Gay Groups Plan an Oscar 'Outing." *New York Newsday*, March 26, 1992, 58.

28. Cathy Dunphy, "Angry Gay and Lesbian Activists Plan to Upstage Oscar Tonight," *Toronto Star*, March 30, 1992, A1.

29. "Ten Arrested at Ceremony Protest," *Los Angeles Daily News*, March 31, 1992, N1.

30. LF interview with Sylvia Rhue, 56, October 7, 2004. Los Angeles GLAAD and friends were also responsible for derailing a planned Paramount television talk show of another homophobic radio star, Dr. Laura Schlesinger. "Stop Dr. Laura" campaign member Robin Tyler called for a protest march on Paramount Studios. Their demonstration got worldwide coverage, and GLAAD was bequeathed $1 million by a donor who was impressed with the action: LF interview with Robin Tyler, 62, August 22, 2004.

31. LF interview with Judy Sisneros, 49, April 6, 2004.

32. LF interview with Sandy (pseud.), 49, April 7, 2004.

33. Agrama interview.

34. LF interview with Terry DeCrescenzo, April 4, 2004.

35. LF interview with Sheila Kuehl, 63, July 24, 2004.

36. The name was changed to the Los Angeles Gay and Lesbian Center in 1996. A longtime board member, LuAnn Boylan, observes, "We dropped Community Services' because we thought the Center was a lot broader than what those words came to mean. We still offer services to those in need, and that will always be our first priority, but we also celebrate the *wellness* of the community." LF interview with LuAnn Boylan, 57, April 7, 2004.

37. According to http://www.gaydemographics.org, Los Angeles has approximately three times the number of same-sex households as New York City. The statistic is based on the federal U.S. 2000 census: "2000 Census Information on Same-Sex Couples."

38. LF interview with Renee Cowhig, 56, July 26, 2004.

39. LF interview with Judy Abdo, 60, July 23, 2004.

40. LF interview with Rita Baird, 58, July 25, 2004.

41. Kuehl interview.

42. Ibid.

43. LF interview with Jackie Goldberg, 60, and Sharon Stricker, 61, August 20, 2004.

44. Ibid.

45. Ibid. Goldberg's ties with labor and progressives go back to her involvement with the free speech movement at U.C. Berkeley.

46. T. A. Gilmartin, "Jackie Goldberg Doesn't Care What You Call It: AB 205 Is (Almost) Marriage," *Lesbian News*, December 2004, 26–27.

47. Two more out L.A. gays were elected to the superior court in 2004: Zeke Zeidler and Donna Groman. Elsewhere in the United States, openly gay people were elected to state legislatures for the first time in 2004 in North Carolina, Idaho, and Missouri. Vermont elected its first openly gay state senator. Oregon elected Rives Kistler to its supreme court—the first openly gay person to be elected to statewide office there. Portland elected its first openly gay city council member. At the federal level, three openly gay people won reelection to Congress: Barney Frank (Massachusetts), Tammy Baldwin (Wisconsin), and Jim Kolbe (Arizona), http://www.victoryfund.org.

48. Robert Arthur, president of the Society for Senior Gay and Lesbian Citizens, fund-raising brochure. We are grateful to Carol Nottley, a member of the SSGLC board of directors, for bringing this brochure to our attention.

49. SAGE, a center for the elderly, had opened in New York City earlier, but it focused "more narrowly on home visits and self-protection," according to Vito Bruno, director of services for Project Rainbow: Lois Timnick, "Antidote to Loneliness: L.A. Opens Seniors' Gay, Lesbian Center," *Los Angeles Times*, July 18, 1982, 1+.

50. Ibid.

51. Ibid.

52. On the scarcity of money in the 1980s for all community needs outside of AIDS, see "Lesbians vs. Gays: War Over Money in the Age of AIDS," *Lesbian News*, October 1989, 1+.

53. LF interview with Ivy Bottini, 78, August 19, 2004. Bobreta Franklin, a board member on the project, points out that there are gay and lesbian elder communities elsewhere, such as The Palms in Manosota, Florida, which is connected to Leisure World, but none of these communities feature low-cost housing for the needy: LF interview with Bobreta Franklin, 59, August 21, 2004. See also Bobreta Franklin, "Sunset of Our Lives: Retirement Communities for Lesbians" (about African American lesbian senior citizens. Franklin's interview subjects were all members of United Lesbians of African Heritage's seniors' group). (Master's thesis, Pacific Oaks College, Pasadena, California, 2004).

54. In the 1990s, there were other plans to establish residential facilities for L.A. gay and lesbian elders, such as those drawn up by Pat Parks, a leader in the Coalition of Older Lesbians (COOL), but none came to fruition at that time: COOL member Laura Sherman (pseud.), 77, July 26, 2004. There have also been a variety of organizations in gay L.A. that focus specifically on the elderly. Prime Plus, for example, is a group for African American lesbian seniors under the auspices of United Lesbians of African Heritage (ULOAH). ULOAH's executive director, Lisa Powell, says that Prime Plus offers help and security for older black lesbians, who would otherwise have to return to the closet in order to get such assistance from the broader and less tolerant African American community: LF interview with Lisa Powell, 46, August 20, 2004.

55. Bottini interview.

56. "Low-Income GLBT [Gay, Lesbian, Bisexual, Transgendered] Seniors Get Housing," *Update*, July 20, 2005, 4.

57. Ibid.

58. LF interview with Lorri Jean, 47, April 30, 2004.

59. Jean and Boylan interviews.

60. E-mail correspondence to LF from LuAnn Boylan, April 13, 2004.

61. Boylan interview.

62. The Harvey Milk School in New York, which is an alternative school exclusively for LGBT youth, had started shortly before Project 10; but, Uribe says, she wanted "no dumping ground for gay kids." Her aim was to reduce discrimination in mainstream institutions rather than to segregate young people in gay institutions: LF interview with Virginia Uribe, 70, July 26, 2004. Since

the late 1980s, there have been alternative schools, such as Oasis, a continuation school for LGBT youth in Los Angeles.

63. Ibid.

64. Jackie Goldberg, who was on the Los Angeles School Board during these years, says that "once the board members met Virginia, who looks like a grandmother, they were very comfortable with her and the project. For kids who were gay to have a place to go didn't seem to them like a bad idea at all." Goldberg interview.

65. DeCrescenzo interview.

66. LF interview with Michael Marchand, December 3, 2005. We are grateful to Michael Marchand and Terry DeCrescenzo for arranging interviews for us with GLASS adolescents.

67. LF interview with "Lucy," (pseud.) 16, December 3, 2005.

68. LF interviews with "Jessica," (pseud.) 16, December 3, 2005.

69. LF interview with "Mary," (pseud.) 17, December 3, 2005.

70. LF interview with "Junior," (pseud.) 17, December 3, 2005.

71. LF interview with "Leticia," (pseud.) 17, December 3, 2005.

72. DeCrescenzo interview.

EPILOGUE

1. Pico Iyer, "Where Worlds Collide," *Harper's Magazine,* August 1995.

2. Karen Ocamb, "Villaraigosa Names Lesbian to Police Commission," *IN Magazine* (Los Angeles), February 14, 2006.

3. LF interview with Kim Swindle-Bautista, 36, December 15, 2004.

4. LF interview with Ewa (pseud.), 47, August 16, 2004. See also Diana Fisher, "Immigrant Closets: Tactical Micro-Practices-in-the-Hyphen," *Journal of Homosexuality* 45, no. 2 (Fall 2003): 185, about L.A.'s gay immigrant Russian community.

5. For a discussion of the complex diversity in the Southern California Vietnamese lesbian community, see Gina Masequesmay, "Negotiating Multiple Identities in a Queer Vietnamese Support Group," *Journal of Homosexuality* 45, no. 2 (Fall 2003): 193–215.

6. Jason Cianciotto, *Hispanic and Latino Same-Sex Couple Households in the United States: A Report from the 2000 Census* (Washington, D.C.: National Gay & Lesbian Task Force Policy Institute and the Latino/a Coalition for Justice, 2005), 45.

7. List gleaned from "Community Access" pages of *Lesbian News,* May 2004.

8. ST interview with Luis Lopez, 32, December 29, 2005.

9. Honor PAC fact sheet, 2005 (ST collection).

10. Most of these bars and clubs advertise regularly in *Divas* and *Revista Adelante,* bilingual magazines for Southern Californian lesbian, gay, and transgender people.

11. LF interview with Julia Salazar, 47, August 19, 2004.

12. LF interview with Monserrat Fontes, 64, July 24, 2004.

13. LF interview with Davi Cheng, 48, December 5, 2005.

14. Tamar Lewin, "Openly Gay Student's Lawsuit Over Privacy Will Proceed," *New York Times,* December 2, 2005.

15. With the support of several funding agencies, these ads, featuring photographs of gay, bisexual, lesbian, and transgender Asians of various backgrounds, have appeared over several years in nearly a dozen languages, including Tagolog, Vietnamese, and Hindi.

16. Lambda Legal Defense Fund news release, January 10, 2006.

17. See Lynette Clemetson, "Both Sides Court Black Churches in the Battle Over Gay Marriage," *New York Times,* March 1, 2004, A1, for a discussion of the rift in the black community over this issue.

18. Professor Robert Dawidoff, quoted in Mary McNamara, "Era of the Gender Crosser," *Los Angeles Times,* February 27, 2001, A1.

19. "Man Turned Woman Deluged by Show Offers: Fabulous Contracts Held Out for Appearances," *Los Angeles Times*, December 7, 1952, 43.

20. See V. Prince, "Charles to Virginia: Sex Research as a Personal Experience," in *The Frontiers of Sex Research*, ed. Vern Bullough (Buffalo, N.Y.: Prometheus Books, 1979), 167–175, and Vern Bullough, "Virginia Prince," in *Before Stonewall: Activists for Gay and Lesbian Rights in Historical Context*, ed. Vern L. Bullough (Binghamton, N.Y.: Harrington Park Press, 2002), 372. Magnus Hirschfeld coined the term "transsexual" in 1925.

21. See chap. 4.

22. In 1979, the City of Los Angeles also enacted Municipal Code 49.72a: "It shall be an unlawful employment practice for an employer to fail or refuse to hire, or to discharge any individual . . . on the basis (in whole or in part) of such individual's sexual orientation. . . . As used in this ordinance, the term 'sexual orientation' shall mean an individual having . . . or projecting a self-image not associated with one's biological maleness or one's biological femaleness." Despite City of Los Angeles policy, however, there continue to be allegations of police abuse against transsexuals. For example, an Amnesty International newsletter quotes a Native American transgender woman in Los Angeles: "The police are not here to serve; they are here to get served. . . . Every night I'm taken into an alley and given the choice between having sex or going to jail"; http://www.amnestyusa.org/outfront/stonewalled/abuse.

23. Odenthal is quoted in McNamara, "Era of the Cross Gender."

24. Susan Forrest, "TransUnity: Gender Explosion," http://la.indymedia.org/news/2005/06/128166.php.

25. McNamara, "Era of the Cross Gender."

26. Jeff, an FTM transsexual, was the convener, and his early work inspired the founding of FTM International in San Francisco, though little was done to establish a public group in Los Angeles for the next twenty years: ST interview with Jeff, 49, November 9, 2005.

27. ST interview with Bamby Salcedo, 37, January 11, 2005.

28. Salcedo quotes L.A. County estimates that in Los Angeles, 75 percent of transwomen are working-class Latinas.

29. ST interview with Masen Davis, 34, and Daniel Gould, 37, November 1, 2005.

30. Virginia Prince, "Homosexuality, Transvestism, and Transsexualism," *American Journal of Psychotherapy* 11 (1957): 80–85.

31. Mary Mcnamara, "Fitting into Their Own Skins," *Los Angeles Times*, February 28, 2001, E1. This is part 2 of a series that began in the February 27 issue.

32. LF interview with Raquel Gutierrez, 29, December 7, 2005.

33. LF and ST interview with David Taylor, 35, October 17, 2005.

34. "Broke-ing the Bank," *The Advocate*, February 28, 2006, 40.

35. Adam B. Vary, "The Brokeback Mountain Effect," *The Advocate*, February 28, 2006, 37.

36. *Daily Variety*, March 10, 2006.

37. Gay films triumphed at the 2005 Golden Globes. *Brokeback Mountain* won four awards, including one for "best dramatic film." The other top awards were given to *Transamerica*, about a transsexual, and *Capote*, about the gay writer.

38. The failure of the Academy of Motion Picture Arts and Sciences to name *Brokeback Mountain* "best picture" created in gay circles all over America a huge chorus of accusations of homophobia, but some gay critics point out that more complex reasons may explain why the award went to a film about racism, *Crash*, rather than to *Brokeback Mountain:* See, for example, Charles Karel Bouley, "Homophobia? Hogwash!" http://www.advocate.com, March 9, 2006.

39. Larry Gross, "Out of the Mainstream: Sexual Minorities and the Mass Media," in *Gay People, Sex, and the Media*, ed. Michella A. Wolf and Alfred P. Kielwasser (New York: Harrington Park Press, 1991), 22. See also Larry Gross, *Up from Invisibility: Lesbians, Gay Men, and the Media in America* (New York: Columbia University Press, 2001).

40. Cultural critics such as Suzanna Danuta Walters have warned against assuming that increased homosexual visibility in the media will lead to an increase in tolerance. Walters points out that the decade in which *Ellen* and *Will & Grace* came to television was also the decade in which the Defense of Marriage Act was passed and the electorate all over America voted in favor of antigay referenda. Nevertheless, she concedes, the 1990s also brought revolutionary gay images into the American living room, such as the much-noted lesbian-kiss scene with Mariel Hemingway on *Roseanne*: in Suzanna Danuta Walters, *All the Rage: The Story of Gay Visibility in America* (Chicago: University of Chicago Press, 2001).

41. In 2005, ABC offered *Crumbs, Emily's Reasons Why Not,* and *Hot Properties*; NBC offered *Inconceivable, My Name Is Earl,* and *The Book of Daniel*; CBS offered *Out of Practice.*

42. Greg Hernandez, "All in the Family," *The Advocate,* September 27, 2005, 60.

43. LF interview with Meredith Kadlec, 37, October 18, 2005.

44. Mike Goodridge, "The WB's New VIP," *The Advocate,* September 28, 2004, 53.

45. Ibid.

46. Taylor interview.

47. LF interview with Ashley Kaplan, 24, October 17, 2005.

48. Kadlec interview.

49. ST interview with Joe Libonati, 30, October 17, 2005.

50. LF interview with Stacy Codikow, 42, August 18, 2004.

51. Michele Kort, "Welcome Back to the L Word," *The Advocate,* February 1, 2005, 43.

52. Ibid.

53. Shana Naomi Krochmal, "'L Word' Tour of West Hollywood," *Planet Out Entertainment,* April 4, 2005, http://www.planetout.com.

54. See chap. 2.

55. David Colman, "Fashion Goes West," *New York Times,* March 9, 2006, E1.

56. Frank Rich, "Brokeback Mountain: A Landmark in the Troubled History of America's Relationship to Homosexuality," *New York Times,* December 18, 2005.

57. ST interview with Michael Weinstein, 53, September 20, 2005.

58. LF interview with Terry Wolverton, 50, August 19, 2004.

INDEX

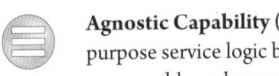

Agnostic Capability (324) How can multi-purpose service logic be made effectively consumable and composable?

Agnostic Context (312) How can multi-purpose service logic be positioned as an effective enterprise resource?

Agnostic Sub-Controller (607) How can agnostic, cross-entity composition logic be separated, reused, and governed independently?

Asynchronous Queuing (582) How can a service and its consumers accommodate isolated failures and avoid unnecessarily locking resources?

Atomic Service Transaction (623) How can a transaction with rollback capability be propagated across messaging-based services?

Brokered Authentication (661) How can a service efficiently verify consumer credentials if the consumer and service do not trust each other or if the consumer requires access to multiple services?

Canonical Expression (275) How can service contracts be consistently understood and interpreted?

Canonical Protocol (150) How can services be designed to avoid protcol bridging?

Canonical Resources (237) How can unnecessary infrastructure resource disparity be avoided?

Canonical Schema (158) How can services be designed to avoid data model transformation?

Canonical Schema Bus (709)

Canonical Versioning (286) How can service contracts within the same service inventory be versioned with minimal impact?

Capability Composition (521) How can a service capability solve a problem that requires logic outside of the service boundary?

Capability Recomposition (526) How can the same capability be used to help solve multiple problems?

Compatible Change (465) How can a service contract be modified without impacting consumers?

Compensating Service Transaction (631) How can composition runtime exceptions be consistently accommodated without requiring services to lock resources?

Composition Autonomy (616) How can compositions be implemented to minimize loss of autonomy?

Concurrent Contracts (421) How can a service facilitate multi-consumer coupling requirements and abstraction concerns at the same time?

Contract Centralization (409) How can direct consumer-to-implementation coupling be avoided?

Contract Denormalization (414) How can a service contract facilitate consumer programs with differing data exchange requirements?

Cross-Domain Utility Layer (267) How can redundant utility logic be avoided across domain service inventories?

Data Confidentiality (641) How can data within a message be protected so that it is not disclosed to unintended recipients while in transit?

Data Format Transformation (681) How can services interact with programs that communicate with different data formats?

Data Model Transformation (671) How can services interoperate when using different data models for the same type of data?

Data Origin Authentication (649) How can a service verify that a message originates from a known sender and that the message has not been tampered with in transit?

Decomposed Capability (504) How can a service be designed to minimize the chances of capability logic deconstruction?

Decoupled Contract (401) How can a service express its capabilities independently of its implementation?

(pattern list continued on inside back cover)

Praise for this Book

"With the continued explosion of services and the increased rate of adoption of SOA through the market, there is a critical need for comprehensive, actionable guidance that provides the fastest possible time to results. Microsoft is honored to contribute to the *SOA Design Patterns* book, and to continue working with the community to realize the value of Real World SOA."

- Steven Martin, Senior Director, Developer Platform Product Management, Microsoft

"*SOA Design Patterns* provides the proper guidance with the right level of abstraction to be adapted to each organization's needs, and Oracle is pleased to have contributed to the patterns contained in this book."

- Dr. Mohamad Afshar, Director of Product Management, Oracle Fusion Middleware, Oracle

"Red Hat is pleased to be involved in the *SOA Design Patterns* book and contribute important SOA design patterns to the community that we and our customers have used within our own SOA platforms. I am sure this will be a great resource for future SOA practitioners."

- Pierre Fricke Director, Product Line Management, JBoss SOA Platform, Red Hat

"A wealth of proven, reusable SOA design patterns, clearly explained and illustrated with examples. An invaluable resource for all those involved in the design of service-oriented solutions."

- Phil Thomas, Consulting IT Specialist, IBM Software Group

"This obligatory almanac of SOA design patterns will become the foundation on which many organizations will build their successful SOA solutions. It will allow organizations to build their own focused SOA design patterns catalog in an expedited fashion knowing that it contains the wealth and expertise of proven SOA best practices."

- Stephen Bennett, Director, Technology Business Unit, Oracle Corporation

"The technical differences between service orientation and object orientation are subtle enough to confuse even the most advanced developers. Thomas Erl's book provides a great service by clearly articulating SOA design patterns and differentiating them from similar OO design patterns."

- Anne Thomas Manes, VP & Research Director, Burton Group

"*SOA Design Patterns* does an excellent job of laying out and discussing the areas of SOA design that a competent SOA practitioner should understand and employ."

- Robert Laird, SOA Architect, IBM

"As always, Thomas delivers again. In a well-structured and easy-to-understand way, this book provides a wonderful collection of patterns each addressing a typical set of SOA design problems with well articulated solutions. The plain language and hundreds of diagrams included in the book help make the complicated subjects of SOA design comprehensible even to those who are new to the SOA design world. It's a must-have reference book for all SOA practitioners, especially for enterprise architects, solution architects, developers, managers, and business process experts."

- Canyang Kevin Liu, Solution Architecture Manager, SAP

"The concept of service oriented architecture has long promised visions of agile organizations being able to swap out interfaces and applications as business needs change. SOA also promises incredible developer and IT productivity, with the idea that key services would be candidates for cross-enterprise sharing or reuse. But many organizations' efforts to move to SOA have been mired—by organizational issues, by conflicting vendor messages, and by architectures that may amount to little more than Just a Bunch of Web Services. There's been a lot of confusion in the SOA marketplace about exactly what SOA is, what it's supposed to accomplish, and how an enterprise goes about in making it work.

SOA Design Patterns is a definitive work that offers clarity on the purpose and functioning of service oriented architecture. SOA Design Patterns not only helps the IT practitioner lay the groundwork for a well-functioning SOA effort across the enterprise, but also connects the dots between SOA and the business requirements in a very concrete way. Plus, this book is completely technology agnostic–*SOA Design Patterns* rightly focuses on infrastructure and architecture, and it doesn't matter whether you're using components of one kind or another, or Java, or .NET, or Web services, or REST-style interfaces.

While no two SOA implementations are alike, Thomas Erl and his team of contributors have effectively identified the similarities in composition services need to have at a sub-atomic level in order to interact with each other as we hope they will. The book identifies 85 SOA design patterns which have been developed and thoroughly vetted to ensure that a service-oriented architecture does achieve the flexibility and loose coupling promised. The book is also compelling in that it is a living document, if you will, inviting participation in an open process to identify and formulate new patterns to this growing body of knowledge."

- Joe McKendrick, Independent Analyst, Author of ZDNet's SOA Blog

"If you want to truly educate yourself on SOA, read this book."

- Sona Srinivasan, Global Client Services & Operations, CISCO

"An impressive decomposition of the process and architectural elements that support service-oriented analysis, design, and delivery. Right-sized and terminologically consistent.

Overall, the book represents a patient separation of concerns in respect of the process and architectural parts that underpin any serious SOA undertaking. Two things stand out. First, the pattern relationship diagrams provide rich views into the systemic relationships that structure a service-oriented architecture: these patterns are not discrete, isolated templates to be applied

mechanically to the problem space; rather, they form a network of forces and constraints that guide the practitioner to consider the task at hand in the context of its inter-dependencies. Second, the pattern sequence diagrams and accompanying notes provide a useful framework for planning and executing the many activities that comprise an SOA engagement."

- Ian Robinson, Principal Technology Consultant, ThoughtWorks

"Successful implementation of SOA principles requires a shift in focus from software system means, or the way capabilities are developed, to the desired end results, or real-world effects required to satisfy organizational business processes. In *SOA Design Patterns,* Thomas Erl provides service architects with a broad palette of reusable service patterns that describe service capabilities that can cut across many SOA applications. Service architects taking advantage of these patterns will save a great deal of time describing and assembling services to deliver the real world effects they need to meet their organization's specific business objectives."

- Chuck Georgo, Public Safety and National Security Architect

"In IT, we have increasingly come to see the value of having catalogs of good solution patterns in programming and systems design. With this book, Thomas Erl brings a comprehensive set of patterns to bear on the world of SOA. These patterns enable easily communicated, reusable, and effective solutions, allowing us to more rapidly design and build out the large, complicated and interoperable enterprise SOAs into which our IT environments are evolving."

- Al Gough, Business Systems Solutions CTO, CACI International Inc.

"This book provides a comprehensive and pragmatic review of design issues in service-centric design, development, and evolution. The Web site related to this book [SOAPatterns.org] is a wonderful platform and gives the opportunity for the software community to maintain this catalogue...."

- Veronica Gacitua Decar, Dublin City University

"Erl's *SOA Design Patterns* is for the IT decision maker determined to make smart architecture design choices, smart investments, and long term enterprise impact. For those IT professionals committed to service-orientation as a value-added design and implementation option, Patterns offers a credible, repeatable approach to engineering an adaptable business enterprise. This is a must read for all IT architect professionals."

- Larry Gloss, VP and General Manager, Information Manufacturing, LLC

"These SOA patterns define, encompass, and comprise a complete repertoire of best practices for developing a world-class IT SOA portfolio for the enterprise and its organizational units through to service and schema analysis and design. After many years as an architect on many SOA projects, I strongly recommend this book be on the shelf of every analyst and technical member of any SOA effort, right next to the SOA standards and guidelines it outlines and elucidates the need for. Our SOA governance standards draw heavily from this work and others from this series."

- Robert John Hathaway III, Enterprise Software Architect, SOA Object Systems

"A wise man once told me that wisdom isn't all about knowledge and intelligence, it is just as much about asking questions. Asking questions is the true mark of wisdom and during the writing of the *SOA Design Patterns* book Thomas Erl has shown his real qualities. The community effort behind this book is huge meaning that Thomas has had access to the knowledge and experience of a large group of accomplished practitioners. The result speaks for itself. This book is packed with proven solutions to recurring problems, and the documented pros and cons of each solution have been verified by persons with true experience. This book could give SOA initiatives of any scale a real boost."

- Herbjörn Wilhelmsen, Architect and Senior Consultant, Objectware

"This book is an absolute milestone in SOA literature. For the first time we are provided with a practical guide on how the principle centric description of service orientation from a vendor-agnostic viewpoint is actually made to work in a language based on patterns. This book makes you talk SOA! There are very few who understand SOA like Thomas Erl does, he actually put's it all together!"

- Brian Lokhorst, Solution Architect, Dutch Tax Office

"Service oriented architecture is all about best practices we have learned since IT's existence. This book takes all those best practices and bundles them into a nice pattern catalogue. [It provides] a really excellent approach as patterns are not just documented but are provided with application scenarios through case studies [which] fills the gap between theory and practice."

- Shakti Sharma, Senior Enterprise Architect, Sysco Corp

"An excellent and important book on solving problems in SOA [with a] solid structure. Has the potential of being among the major influential books."

- Peter Chang, Lawrence Technical University

"*SOA Design Patterns* presents a vast amount of knowledge about how to successfully implement SOA within an organization. The information is clear, concise, and most importantly, legitimate."

- Peter B. Woodhull, President and Principal Architect, Modus21

"*SOA Design Patterns* offers real insights into everyday problems that one will encounter when investing in services oriented architecture. [It] provides a number of problem descriptions and offers strategies for dealing with these problems. SOA design patterns highlights more than just the technical problems and solutions. Common organizational issues that can hinder progress towards achieving SOA migration are explained along with potential approaches for dealing with these real world challenges. Once again Thomas Erl provides in-depth coverage of SOA terminology and helps the reader better understand and appreciate the complexities of migrating to an SOA environment."

- David Michalowicz, Air and Space Operations Center Modernization Team Lead, MITRE Corporation

"This is a long overdue, serious, comprehensive, and well-presented catalog of SOA design patterns. This will be required reading and reference for all our SOA engineers and architects. The best of the series so far!

[The book] works in two ways: as a primer in SOA design and architecture it can easily be read front-to-back to get an overview of most of the key design issues you will encounter, and as a reference catalog of design techniques that can be referred to again and again ..."

- Wendell Ocasio, Architecture Consultant, DoD Military Health Systems, Agilex Technologies

"Thomas has once again provided the SOA practitioner with a phenomenal collection of knowledge. This is a reference that I will come back to time and time again as I move forward in SOA design efforts.

What I liked most about this book is its vendor agnostic approach to SOA design patterns. This approach really presents the reader with an understanding of why or why not to implement a pattern, group patterns, or use compound patterns rather than giving them a marketing spiel on why one implementation of a pattern is better than another (for example, why one ESB is better than another). I think as SOA adoption continues to advance, the ability for architects to understand when and why to apply specific patterns will be a driving factor in the overall success and evolution of SOA. Additionally, I believe that this book provides the consumer with the understanding required to chose which vendor's SOA products are right for their specific needs."

- Bryan Brew, SOA Consultant, Booz Allen Hamilton

"A must have for every SOA practitioner."

- Richard Van Schelven, Principal Engineer, Ericsson

"This book is a long-expected successor to the books on object-oriented design patterns and integration patterns. It is a great reference book that clearly and thoroughly describes design patterns for SOA. A great read for architects who are facing the challenge of transforming their enterprise into a service-oriented enterprise."

- Linda Terlouw, Solution Architect, Ordina

"The maturation of Service-Orientation has given the industry time to absorb the best practices of service development. Thomas Erl has amassed this collective wisdom in *SOA Design Patterns*, an absolutely indispensible addition to any Service Oriented bookshelf."

- Kevin P. Davis, Ph.D

"The problem with most texts on SOA is one of specificity. Architects responsible for SOA implementation in most organizations have little time for abstract theories on the subject, but are hungry for concrete details that they can relate to the real problems they face in their environment. *SOA Design Patterns* is critical reading for anyone with service design responsibilities. Not only does the text provide the normal pattern templates, but each pattern is applied in

detail against a background case study to provide exceptionally meaningful context to the information. The graphic visualizations of the problems and pattern solutions are excellent supplementary companions to the explanatory text. This book will greatly stretch the knowledge of the reader as much for raising and addressing issues that may have never occurred to the reader as it does in treating those problems that are in more common occurrence. The real beauty of this book is in its plain English prose. Unlike so many technical reference books, one does not find themselves re-reading sections multiple times trying to discern the intent of the author. This is also not a reference that will sit gathering dust on a shelf after one or two perusings. Practitioners will find themselves returning over and over to utilize the knowledge in their projects. This is as close as you'll come to having a service design expert sitting over your shoulder."

- James Kinneavy, Principal Software Architect, University of California

"As the industry converges on SOA patterns, Erl provides an outstanding reference guide to composition and integration—and yet another distinctive contribution to the SOA practice."

- Steve Birkel, Chief IT Technical Architect, Intel Corp.

"With *SOA Design Patterns,* Thomas Erl adds an indispensable SOA reference volume to the technologist's library. Replete with to-the-point examples, it will be a helpful aid to any IT organization."

- Ed Dodds, Strategist, Systems Architect, Conmergence

"Again, Thomas Erl has written an indispensable guide to SOA. Building on his prior successes, his patterns go into even more detail. Therefore, this book is not only helpful to the SOA beginner, but also provides new insight and ideas to professionals."

- Philipp Offermann, Research Scientist, Technische Universität Berlin, Germany

"*SOA Design Patterns* is an extraordinary contribution to SOA best practices! Once again, Thomas has created an indispensable resource for any person or organization interested in or actively engaged in the practice of Service Oriented Architecture. Using case studies based on three very different business models, Thomas guides the reader through the process of selecting appropriate implementation patterns to ensure a flexible, well-performing, and secure SOA ecosystem."

- Victor Brown, Managing Partner and Principal Consultant,
Cypress Management Group Corporation

SOA Design Patterns

The Prentice Hall Service-Oriented Computing Series from Thomas Erl aims to provide the IT industry with a consistent level of unbiased, practical, and comprehensive guidance and instruction in the areas of service-oriented architecture, service-orientation, and the expanding landscape that is shaping the real-world service-oriented computing platform.

For more information, visit www.soabooks.com.

SOA Design Patterns

Thomas Erl

(with additional contributors)

PRENTICE HALL

UPPER SADDLE RIVER, NJ • BOSTON • INDIANAPOLIS • SAN FRANCISCO

NEW YORK • TORONTO • MONTREAL • LONDON • MUNICH • PARIS • MADRID

CAPETOWN • SYDNEY • TOKYO • SINGAPORE • MEXICO CITY

Library of Congress Cataloging-in-Publication Data:

Erl, Thomas.

SOA design patterns / Thomas Erl. — 1st ed.

p. cm.

ISBN 0-13-613516-1 (hardback : alk. paper) 1. Web services.
2. Computer architecture. 3. Software patterns. 4. System design. I. Title.

TK5105.88813.E735 2008

006.7—dc22

2008040488

ISBN-13: 978-0-13-613516-6
ISBN-10: 0-13-613516-1
Text printed in the United States on recycled paper at R.R. Donnelley in Crawfordsville, Indiana.
Second printing June 2009

The following patterns: Exception Shielding, Threat Screening, Trusted Subsystem, Service Perimeter Guard, Data Confidentiality, Data Origin Authentication, Direct Authentication, Brokered Authentication are courtesy of the Microsoft Patterns & Practices team. For more information please visit http://msdn.microsoft.com/practices. These patterns were originally developed by Jason Hogg, Frederick Chong, Dwayne Taylor, Lonnie Wall, Paul Slater, Tom Hollander, Wojtek Kozaczynski, Don Smith, Larry Brader, Sajjas Nasir Imran, Pablo Cibraro, Nelly Delgado and Ward Cunningham

Editor-in-Chief
Mark L. Taub

Managing Editor
Kristy Hart

Copy Editor
Language Logistics

Indexer
Cheryl Lenser

Proofreader
Williams Woods Publishing

Composition
Jake McFarland
Bumpy Design

Graphics
Zuzana Cappova
Tami Young
Spencer Fruhling

Photos
Thomas Erl

Cover Design
Thomas Erl

To the SOA pioneers that blazed the trail we now so freely base our roadmaps on, and to the SOA community that helped me refine the wisdom of the pioneers into this catalog of patterns.

- Thomas Erl

Contents

PART IV: SERVICE COMPOSITION DESIGN PATTERNS

Foreword

The entire history of software engineering can be characterized as one of rising levels of abstraction. We see this in our languages, our tools, our platforms, and our methods. Indeed, abstraction is the primary way that we as humans attend to complexity—and software-intensive systems are among the most complex artifacts ever created.

I would also observe that one of the most important advances in software engineering over the past two decades has been the practice of patterns. Patterns are yet another example of this rise in abstraction: A pattern specifies a common solution to a common problem in the form of a society of components that collaborate with one another. Influenced by the writings of Christopher Alexander, Kent Beck and Ward Cunningham began to codify various design patterns from their experience with Smalltalk. Growing slowly but steadily, these concepts began to gain traction among other developers. The publication of the seminal book *Design Patterns* by Erich Gamma, John Vlissides, Ralph Johnson, and Richard Helm marked the introduction of these ideas to the mainstream. The subsequent activities of the Hillside Group provided a forum for this growing community, yielding a very vibrant literature and practice. Now the practice of patterns is very much mainstream: Every well-structured software-intensive system tends to be full of patterns (whether their architects name them intentionally or not).

The emerging dominant architectural style for many enterprise systems is that of a service-oriented architecture, a style that at its core is essentially a message passing architecture. However, therein are many patterns that work (and anti-patterns that should be avoided).

Thomas' work is therefore the right book at the right time. He really groks the nature of SOA systems: There are many hard design decisions to be made, ranging from data-orientation to the problems of legacy integration and even security. Thomas offers wise counsel on each of these issues and many more, all in the language of design patterns. There are many things I like about this work. It's comprehensive. It's written in a very accessible

pattern language. It offers patterns that play well with one another. Finally, Thomas covers not just the technical details, but also sets these patterns in the context of economic and other considerations.

SOA Design Patterns is an important contribution to the literature and practice of building and delivering quality software-intensive systems.

—*Grady Booch, IBM Fellow*
September, 2008

Acknowledgments

This book was in development for over three years, a good portion of which was dedicated to external reviews. Patterns were subjected to three review cycles that spanned a period of over twelve months and involved over 200 IT professionals. Pre-release galleys of my first and second manuscript drafts were printed and shipped to SOA experts and patterns experts around the world. Additionally, I had the full manuscript published at SOAPatterns.org for an open industry review. Even though these review phases added much time and effort to the development of this book, they ultimately elevated the quality of this work by a significant margin.

Special thanks to Prentice Hall for their patience and support throughout the book development process. Specifically, I'd like to thank Kristy Hart and Jake McFarland for their tremendous production efforts and tireless commitment to achieving printed perfection, Mark Taub who stood by this book project through a whirlwind of changes, reviews, more changes, extensions, and delays, Stephane Nakib and Heather Fox for their on-going guidance, and Eric Miller for his assistance with publishing the online review version of the first manuscript draft. I am fortunate to be working with the best publishing team in the industry.

Special thanks also to Herbjörn Wilhelmsen, Martin Fowler, Ralph Johnson, Bobby Woolf, Grady Booch, Gregor Hohpe, Baptist Eggen, Dragos Manolescu, Frank Buschmann, Wendell Ocasio, and Kevin Davis for their guidance and uninhibited feedback throughout the review cycles.

My thanks and gratitude to the following reviewers that participated in one or more of the manuscript reviews (in alphabetical order by last name):

Mohamad Afshar, Oracle

Sanjay Agara, Wipro

Stephen Bennett, Oracle

Steve Birkel, Intel

Brandon Bohling, Intel

Grady Booch, IBM

Bryan Brew, Booz Allen Hamilton

Victor Brown, CMGC

Frank Buschmann, Siemens

Enrique G. Castro-Leon, Intel

Peter Chang, Lawrence Technical University

Jason "AJ" Comfort, Booz Allen Hamilton

John Crupi, JackBe

Veronica Gacitua Decar, Dublin City University

Ed Dodds, Conmergence

Kevin P. Davis, PhD

Dominic Duggan, Stevens Institute of Technology

Baptist Eggen, Dutch Department of Defense

Steve Elston, Microsoft

Dale Ferrario, Sun Microsystems

Martin Fowler, ThoughtWorks

Pierre Fricke, Red Hat

Chuck Georgo, Public Safety and National Security

Larry Gloss, Information Manufacturing

Al Gough, CACI International Inc.

Daniel Gross, University of Toronto

Robert John Hathaway III, SOA Object Systems

William M. Hegarty, ThoughtWorks

Gregor Hohpe, Google

Ralph Johnson, UIUC

James Kinneavy, University of California

Robert Laird, IBM

Doug Lea, Oswego State University of New York

Canyang Kevin Liu, SAP

Terry Lottes, Northrop Grumman Mission Systems

Chris Madrid, Microsoft

Anne Thomas Manes, Burton Group

Dragos Manolescu, Microsoft

Steven Martin, Microsoft

Joe McKendrick

J.D. Meier, Microsoft

David Michalowicz, MITRE Corporation

Per Vonge Nielsen, Microsoft

Wendell Ocasio, DoD Military Health Systems, Agilex Technologies

Philipp Offermann, University of Berlin

Dmitri Ossipov, Microsoft

Prasen Palvakar, Oracle

Parviz Peiravi, Intel

Nishit Rao, Oracle

Ian Robinson, ThoughtWorks

Richard Van Schelven, Ericsson

Shakti Sharma, Sysco Corp

Don Smith, Microsoft

Michael Sor, Booz Allen Hamilton

John Sparks, Western Southern Life

Sona Srinivasan, CISCO

Linda Terlouw, Ordina

Phil Thomas, IBM

Steve Vinoski, IEEE

Herbjörn Wilhelmsen, Objectware

Peter B. Woodhull, Modus21

Bobby Woolf, IBM

Farzin Yashar, IBM

Markus Zirn, Oracle

Olaf Zimmermann, IBM

There were many more individuals who directly or indirectly supported this effort. Amidst the flurry of correspondence over the past three years, I was unable to keep track of all participants. If you were part of the SOA design patterns project and you don't see your name on this list, then do contact me via www.thomaserl.com.

Contributors

In alphabetical order by last name:

Larry Brader

David Chappell, Oracle

Frederick Chong

Pablo Cibraro, Lagash Systems SA

Ward Cunningham

Nelly Delgado, Microsoft

Florent Georges

Charles Stacy Harris, Microsoft

Kelvin Henney, Curbralan

Jason Hogg, Microsoft

Tom Hollander

Anish Karmarkar, Oracle

Sajjas Nasir Imran, Infosys

Berthold Maier, Oracle

Hajo Normann, EDS

Wojtek Kozaczynski

Mark Little, Red Hat

Brian Lokhorst, Dutch Tax Office

Brian Loesgen, Neudesic

Matt Long, Microsoft

David Orchard, Oracle

Thomas Rischbeck, IPT

Chris Riley, SOA Systems

Satadru Roy, Sun Microsystems

Arnaud Simon, Red Hat

Paul Slater, Wadeware

Don Smith

Sharon Smith, Microsoft

Dwayne Taylor

Tina Tech

Bernd Trops, SOPERA GmbH

Clemens Utschig-Utschig, Oracle

Lonnie Wall, RDA Corporation

Torsten Winterberg, Oracle

Dennis Wisnosky, U.S. Department of Defense

Chapter 1

Introduction

While recently delivering a week-long workshop at a client location, I was required to spend a fair amount of time waiting in the reception area every day. The client was a very large company in the finance industry, and in order to enter their offices, I had to first request a visitor's pass from the security guard and then wait until someone from the office came down to the lobby to escort me back up.

Upon entering the building for the first time, I noticed that the front door was stuck. It took me two or three tries to force it open. The security guard later told me that a delivery person had accidentally struck the door with some sort of cart, warping the frame and damaging the handle. They weren't expecting replacement parts to be installed for another two weeks and were not allowed to keep the door open.

While waiting for my escort that day, I noticed numerous people (mostly office staff) trying to access the building via the jammed door, each going through the same experience I did. People tried different approaches, some more effective than others. At one point there was an actual line-up impatiently waiting for the person at the front to figure it out. Just about everyone who eventually entered complained about the door to the guard.

On the next day of the workshop I was again waiting in the lobby watching the same story unfold. I saw familiar faces struggling with the door again; getting it ajar seemed more a matter of luck than technique, so it was difficult to remember how one opened it the day before. On this day, the security guard ran toward the door to help people open it whenever he could. However, over time, he found himself rushing back and forth a lot, dealing with the door and tending to people at the reception desk who needed to register and request passes.

The third day came around, and I was surprised to encounter the guard standing outside by the entrance. I could see through the glass walls that someone else was taking care of reception duties. As I approached the door, the guard greeted me, and I assumed he was going to open it to let me in. Instead, he asked me not to enter and proceeded to give me a short lesson on how to open the door with two swift moves. The lesson consisted of a brief explanation and a short demonstration. I thanked him and moved to go inside, but he stopped me, shut the door, and then said "Ok, now you do it." And so I did.

While waiting in the lobby that morning, I watched him give that same lesson to just about everyone who needed to enter. Sometimes the guard had a whole class as a group of office employees who arrived at the same time were taught together.

As I walked toward the building on the fourth day, I noticed the guard was no longer at the door. Recalling "the moves" I'd learned the day before, I proceeded to open it with relative ease. As I entered the lobby, I could see that the same guard was alone again to manage the reception area. Then, while waiting for my escort as usual, I witnessed droves of people entering the building with little to no problems.

It was even more impressive the following day during my last morning. People were coming and going without breaking a stride. It was as if the door had actually been fixed. At the end of that last day of training, I said good-bye to the guard and complimented him on how he dealt with the door issue. "You're a true problem solver," I said. "Yes, I know," he responded with a grin, "I'm the smart one."

On the taxi ride back to the airport, I thought some more about the damaged door and the solution the guard came up with. I did some rough math, taking into account how long it took the average person to get past the jammed door during the first two days and how many people I saw streaming into the building every morning. I estimated that over the last two days (after each employee was given a lesson by the guard) about 35,000 seconds were saved, translating into around 9.7 hours.

I never did find out when that door was eventually fixed, but assuming it took another week as expected, that time savings could easily be doubled or tripled. That's potentially 20–30 extra working hours the company received, thanks to one person's ingenuity.

This experience reminded me of why I felt strongly about putting together this catalog of design patterns. That guard spent the second day trying a variety of ways to deal with a problem until he found a proven method that was effective, easy to learn, and repeatable by anyone. On the third day he transferred that knowledge to all who needed it, and on the remaining days they put that knowledge to good use. In the end, the cumulative benefit was significant because all of the employees who saved time were able to spend that time solving new problems for the benefit of the company.

While problem solving is a fundamental skill we all possess, not everyone should have to solve the same problems. This is the basic rationale behind design patterns. There are jammed doors along the path to completing just about any IT project, perhaps even more so with SOA initiatives simply because their scope tends to be larger and more ambitious. I hope you'll find this book an effective resource for "learning the moves" to counter problems you might have to face in pursuit of realizing your own service-oriented solutions.

1.1 Objectives of this Book

A design pattern is simply a proven design solution for a common design problem that is formally documented in a consistent manner. This book was written with one primary goal in mind: to provide a master pattern catalog and pattern language for SOA and service-orientation. This sole objective has driven this collection of design patterns through numerous rounds of reviews, revisions, and community participation.

1.2 Who this Book is For

This book is intended for IT practitioners who:

- want to learn proven design solutions and practices for building SOA implementations
- want to prepare themselves for common challenges associated with the definition and design of services and service-oriented solutions
- want to learn about SOA and service-orientation by studying detailed aspects of fundamental design
- want to learn about the different types of service-oriented architectures and understand exactly how they are distinct from other architectural models
- want to gain a deep insight into the complexion of modern-day service-oriented solution design

This book can essentially be considered a reference text for use by anyone involved with the construction of service-oriented solutions.

1.3 What this Book Does Not Cover

The following sections highlight specific subject areas not addressed in this book.

Topics Covered by Other Books

This title is dedicated to documenting design patterns only. Because most of the patterns in this catalog were specifically created in support of service-orientation, there are many cross-references to design principles whenever they are related or relevant to a particular pattern. These design principles are covered separately in *SOA Principles of Service Design,* a companion guide for this book.

Furthermore, this book does not contain a tutorial about Web services or service-oriented computing. There are several publications that have already covered these areas in detail. Suggestions are provided in the upcoming *Recommended Reading* section.

Web Service and REST Service Design Patterns

The Web services technology platform has historically influenced the evolution of service-oriented computing, affecting the complexion and feature-set of typical service-oriented architecture implementations. As a result, numerous design patterns in this book make reference to the use of Web services, and the majority of examples provided show services being implemented as Web services.

Furthermore, a series of REST-inspired design patterns were also developed for this pattern catalog but were not considered ready for inclusion in this first edition of the printed *SOA Design Patterns* book. These patterns have been published in the *Candidate* section of the SOAPatterns.org Web site where they will be subjected to on-going reviews, along with other candidate patterns.

It is important to note that the purpose of this book is to provide a catalog of design patterns that help solve problems specific to the realization of SOA and service-orientation. As has been established in previous series titles, Web services and REST services provide implementation *options* for building services as part of service-oriented solutions.

SOA Standardization Efforts

There are several efforts underway by different standards and research organizations to produce abstract definitions, architectural models, and vocabularies for SOA. These projects are in various stages of maturity, and several overlap in scope.

The mandate of this book series is to provide the IT community with current, real-world insight into the most important aspects of service-oriented computing, SOA, and service-orientation. A great deal of research goes into each and every title to follow through on this commitment. This research includes the detailed review of existing and upcoming technologies and platforms, relevant technology products and technology standards, architectural standards and specifications, as well as interviews conducted with key members of leading organizations in the SOA community.

As of the writing of this book there has been no indication that any of the deliverables produced by the aforementioned independent efforts will be adopted as industry-wide SOA standards. In order to maintain an accurate, real-world perspective, these models and vocabularies can therefore not be covered or referenced in this book.

However, given the unpredictable nature of the IT industry, there is always a possibility that one or more of these deliverables will attain industry standard status at some point in time. Should this occur, this book will be supplemented with online content that describes the relationship of the standards to the content of this book and further maps concepts, terms, and models to whatever conventions are established by the standards. This information would be published on SOABooks.com, as described in the *Updates, Errata, and Resources* page. If you'd like to be automatically notified of these types of updates, see the *Notification Service* section for more information.

NOTE

This comment refers to SOA-related specifications only. There are numerous standards initiatives that have produced and continue to produce highly relevant technology specifications, such as those used for XML and Web services. These are referenced, explained, and otherwise documented wherever appropriate in all series titles.

1.4 Recommended Reading

As already mentioned, this book establishes a master pattern catalog for SOA design patterns. Many of these patterns have roots in the following previously published pattern catalogs that are recommended reading, especially if you are new to the world of design patterns:

- *Design Patterns: Elements of Reusable Object-Oriented Software* (E. Gamma, R. Helm, R. Johnson, J. Vlissides, Addison-Wesley 1994)
- *Patterns of Enterprise Application Architecture* (M. Fowler, Addison-Wesley 2003)
- *Enterprise Integration Patterns* (G. Hohpe, B. Woolf, Addison-Wesley 2003)
- *Pattern-Oriented Software Architecture, Volumes 1–5* (F. Buschmann, K. Henney, M. Kircher, R. Meunier, H. Rohnert, D. Schmidt, P. Sommerlad, M. Stal, Wiley 1996–2007)

How the patterns in these and other publications have influenced the SOA design patterns in this book is further discussed in the *Historical Influences* section in Chapter 5.

While this book includes basic patterns that describe foundational parts of SOA and service-orientation in detail, it does not provide a great deal of introductory coverage of SOA or service-oriented computing as a whole. If you are new to SOA and service-orientation, you can consider reading the following titles that are part of this book series:

- *SOA Principles of Service Design*
- *Service-Oriented Architecture: Concepts, Technology, and Design*

Furthermore, in preparation for those patterns that are focused on design solutions that entail the use of Web service technologies, you can use this book as a companion reference guide:

- *Web Service Contract Design and Versioning for SOA*

Note also that the following additional series titles are in development, each of which further explores and builds upon the SOA design patterns documented in this book:

- *SOA with Java*
- *SOA with .NET*
- *ESB Architecture for SOA*
- *SOA Governance*
- *SOA with REST*

You can check on the availability of these titles at SOABooks.com and you can further read up on fundamental topics pertaining to SOA and service-orientation at WhatisSOA.com and SOAPrinciples.com. Finally, you can take advantage of an online master glossary for this book series at SOAGlossary.com.

1.5 How this Book is Organized

This book begins with Chapters 1 and 2 providing introductory content and case study background information respectively. The remainder of the book is grouped into the following parts:

- Part I: Fundamentals
- Part II: Service Inventory Design Patterns
- Part III: Service Design Patterns
- Part IV: Service Composition Design Patterns
- Part V: Supplemental
- Part VI: Appendices

Part I: Fundamentals

Chapters 3, 4, and 5 in this first part set the stage for all of the design patterns that follow in the subsequent parts by covering key terminology and design issues and by providing an exploration of architecture design principles and the service-oriented architecture types that are later referenced by the individual design pattern descriptions. Also provided is an explanation of how pattern profiles in this book are structured, along with additional sections that cover relevant design topics, such as Web services, service design principle references, and pattern types.

Part II: Service Inventory Design Patterns

"Service inventory" is a term used to represent a collection on independently standardized and governed services. Design patterns associated with the design of the service inventory technology architecture are provided in the following chapters:

- *Chapter 6: Foundational Inventory Patterns* – The baseline design characteristics of a service inventory architecture are addressed by a series of closely related design patterns that are presented in a proposed application sequence.
- *Chapter 7: Logical Inventory Layer Patterns* – How services within a service inventory can be grouped into logical layers is covered by a set of design patterns that represent the most common types of service layers.
- *Chapter 8: Inventory Centralization Patterns* – A set of patterns dedicated to centralizing key parts of a service inventory architecture is provided to build upon the preceding fundamental architectural patterns.
- *Chapter 9: Inventory Implementation Patterns* – This more specialized collection of patterns addresses a variety of implementation design issues and options for service inventory architectures.
- *Chapter 10: Inventory Governance Patterns* – Design patterns relating to the post-implementation governance of a service inventory architecture are provided.

Part III: Service Design Patterns

This part is comprised of a set of chapters specific to the design of services and service architecture:

- *Chapter 11: Foundational Service Patterns* – A set of basic design patterns that help establish fundamental service design characteristics via a suggested application

sequence. Collectively, these patterns form the most basic application of service-orientation within a service boundary.

- *Chapter 12: Service Implementation Patterns* – A collection of specialized design patterns that provide design solutions for a range of service architecture-specific issues.
- *Chapter 13: Service Security Patterns* – These patterns primarily shape the internal logic of services to equip them with security controls that counter common threats.
- *Chapter 14: Service Contract Design Patterns* – A set of design patterns focused on service contract design concerns both from a contract content and architectural perspective.
- *Chapter 15: Legacy Encapsulation Patterns* – How services can encapsulate and interact with legacy systems and resources is addressed by this set of patterns.
- *Chapter 16: Service Governance Patterns* – For services already deployed and in use, these patterns address common governance issues related to typical post-implementation changes.

Part IV: Service Composition Design Patterns

Service composition design and runtime interaction are addressed by the patterns in the following chapters:

- *Chapter 17: Capability Composition Patterns* – A pair of core patterns that establish the basis of service capability composition as it pertains to composition design and architecture.
- *Chapter 18: Service Messaging Patterns* – This large collection of patterns is focused on inter-service message exchange and processing and provides design solutions for a wide range of messaging concerns.
- *Chapter 19: Composition Implementation Patterns* – Service composition architecture design and runtime composition integrity are addressed by these patterns.
- *Chapter 20: Service Interaction Security Patterns* – A set of patterns focused exclusively on security issues pertaining to runtime service interaction and data exchange.
- *Chapter 21: Transformation Patterns* – Design patterns specific to the runtime transformation of messages via intermediary processing layers.

Part V: Supplemental

- *Chapter 22: Common Compound Design Patterns* – Many of the previously documented design patterns can be combined into compound patterns that solve larger, yet still common design problems. This chapter provides examples of some of the more relevant combinations, including Enterprise Service Bus (704) and Orchestration (701).
- *Chapter 23: Strategic Architecture Considerations* – This chapter essentially provides a strategic context for all of the content covered in previous chapters by revisiting the key goals of service-oriented computing and highlighting how the attainment of each individual goal can impact the different SOA types first established in Chapter 4.
- *Chapter 24: Principles and Patterns at the U.S. Department of Defense* – A brief exploration of how service-orientation design principles and key design patterns are used at the DoD in relation to the Business Operating Environment (BOE).

Part VI: Appendices

- *Appendix A: Case Study Conclusion* – The storylines for the three case studies first introduced in Chapter 2 and then further explored in subsequent chapters are concluded.
- *Appendix B: Candidate Patterns* – The pattern review process is highlighted along with an explanation of how patterns still under review are classified as candidates.
- *Appendix C: Principles of Service-Orientation* – Summarized descriptions of the eight service-orientation design principles are provided for reference purposes.
- *Appendix D: Patterns and Principles Cross-Reference* – This appendix organizes design patterns for quick reference purposes as they pertain to service-orientation design principles.
- *Appendix E: Patterns and Architectural Types Cross-Reference* – Design patterns are cross-referenced with the four service-oriented architecture types established in Chapter 4.

Note that an alphabetical listing of all design patterns together with their page numbers is provided on the inside cover of this book.

1.6 Symbols, Figures, Style Conventions

The books in this series conform to a series of conventions, as explained here.

Symbol Legend

This book contains more than 400 diagrams that are labeled as *figures*. The primary symbols used throughout the figures are individually listed in the symbol legend located on the inside of the front cover.

How Color is Used

Most symbols have distinct colors associated with them so that they are easily recognized within the different figures. One exception to this convention is when portions of a figure need to be highlighted for a particular reason. In this case, symbols may be colored in red. The conflict symbol (which looks like a lightning bolt) is always red because it is used to highlight points of conflict.

Data Flow and Directionality Conventions

Some of the figures in this book deviate from traditional conventions associated with depicting data flow. This is further explained in the *Service Consumer* section in Chapter 3.

Pattern Documentation Conventions

Each pattern in this book is documented in a consistent format according to a set of predefined notation conventions that are explained in the *Pattern Notation* section in Chapter 5. Note that certain general style conventions are changed subsequent to Chapter 5, as explained on the flipside of the Part II divider page (page 110).

1.7 Additional Information

The following sections describe available supplementary information and resources for the books in the *Prentice Hall Service-Oriented Computing Series from Thomas Erl.*

Updates, Errata, and Resources (www.soabooks.com)

Information about other series titles and various supporting resources can be found at SOABooks.com. You are encouraged to visit this site regularly to check for content changes and corrections.

Visio Stencil (www.soabooks.com)

Prentice Hall has produced a Visio stencil containing the color symbols used by the books in this series. This stencil can be downloaded at SOABooks.com.

Community Patterns Site (www.soapatterns.org)

All of the pattern profile summary tables documented in this book are also published online at SOAPatterns.org, as part of an open site for the SOA community dedicated to SOA design patterns. This site allows you to provide feedback regarding any of the design patterns and you can further submit your own pattern candidates. More information about candidate patterns is provided in Appendix B.

Master Glossary (www.soaglossary.com)

This Web site provides a master online glossary for all series titles. The content on this site continues to grow and expand with new glossary definitions as new series titles are developed and released.

Supplementary Posters (www.soaposters.com)

SOAPosters.com provides a set of color posters available for free download as supplements for the books in this series.

The SOA Magazine (www.soamag.com)

The SOA Magazine is a regular publication provided by SOA Systems Inc. and Prentice Hall and is officially associated with the *Prentice Hall Service-Oriented Computing Series from Thomas Erl.* The SOA Magazine is dedicated to publishing specialized SOA articles, case studies, and papers by industry experts and professionals. The common criterion for contributions is that each explores a distinct aspect of service-oriented computing.

Referenced Specifications (www.soaspecs.com)

Various series titles reference or provide tutorials and examples of industry specifications and standards. The SOASpecs.com Web site provides a central portal to the original specification documents created and maintained by the primary standards organizations.

Notification Service

If you'd like to be automatically notified of new book releases in this series, new supplementary content for this title, or key changes to the previously listed Web sites, use the notification form at SOABooks.com.

Contact the Author

To contact me directly, visit my bio site at www.thomaserl.com.

Chapter 2

Case Study Background

This book covers a range of design patterns that can be incorporated into a variety of environments. Numerous case study examples are provided to supplement design pattern descriptions with some real-world context. All of these examples relate to the background established in this chapter. To make navigation easier, light gray shading has been applied to all case study content subsequent to this chapter.

The upcoming sections provide background information for three case studies based on the following profiles:

- Cutit Saws, a medium-sized private company with a central IT environment, positioning itself as an acquisition target for larger corporations.
- Alleywood Lumber, a large private corporation with a central IT environment and online clients.
- Forestry Regulatory Commission, a large public organization with distributed and partially outsourced IT environments and a very large client base.

As illustrated in Figure 2.1, these organizations have relationships with each other. Cutit Saws is a supplier of chainsaws and chains for Alleywood Lumber, and both of these companies are (to different extents) governed by policies maintained by the Forestry Regulatory Commission.

The next three sections describe each organization's individual set of goals and challenges, establishing the starting point for three separate but intertwined storylines that carry on throughout Parts II, III, and IV of the book and then conclude in Appendix A.

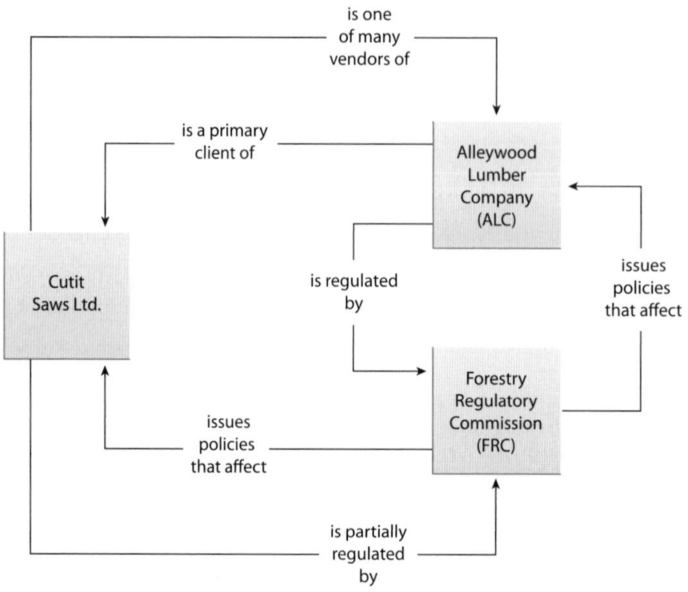

Figure 2.1

The three organizations from our case studies have direct and indirect relationships. Cutit and Alleywood have a typical vendor/client arrangement, but the FRC can issue policies that affect both companies.

2.1 Case #1 Background: Cutit Saws Ltd.

Cutit Saws is a niche manufacturer and reseller of high-end hydraulic diamond chainsaws. It has established itself in the tool vendor marketplace by developing a series of unique chainsaw designs that provide effective penetration against especially dense matter.

NOTE

Those of you who read *SOA Principles of Service Design* may already be familiar with Cutit Saws because the Cutit environment formed the basis for a set of detailed examples focused on service design in that book. The background information provided in this section carries forward the Cutit storyline and therefore represents the state of their IT enterprise after the events described in *SOA Principles of Service Design* have transpired.

Note, however, that knowledge of prior examples is not required to understand or work with the case study content in this book.

History

Cutit began as a small company founded by a group of inexperienced business partners based on a set of unique and patented chainsaw blade designs. The effectiveness of these chains eventually led to an unexpected measure of growth, turning Cutit Saws into a successful venture but also placing it into a position it was not prepared for.

Cutit recently released a new diamond blade chain design that became an immediate success. The manufacturing process for this chain is more complex than for previous models, requiring the use of simulations and additional quality assurance steps. As a result, the Cutit team cannot keep up with the demand, and backorders are increasing daily.

With competitors looming and threatening to release similar (reverse-engineered) chain designs, Cutit is under severe time pressure to increase the efficiency and responsiveness of its overall supply-chain process.

Technical Infrastructure and Automation Environment

Much of Cutit's legacy environment is represented by or in some way integrates with a central, custom-developed accounting and inventory management system maintained by a dozen IT staff. This environment was originally designed by one of the company principals but has since become somewhat of an albatross as it has been unable to accommodate the increasing extensibility and scalability demands.

The Cutit team acknowledged the limitations of their modest IT enterprise, and with a realization of how these limitations could severely inhibit the growth potential of the company, they decided to make some changes.

They turned their attention toward SOA and proceeded with the first stage of a larger transition project. The result was the delivery of four services that effectively automated their Lab Project business process, allowing for the efficient simulation of formula applications.

Business Goals and Obstacles

Cutit's primary motivation with their on-going SOA transition project is to establish an IT enterprise that can be more easily extended and modified in response to business change. In recent months, the source of business change has been internal, due to the unanticipated development and success of their newest blade design. Although a fortunate turn of events, this has resulted in chaos for the IT staff.

Another factor that influenced the decision to standardize their environment on SOA is the fact that Cutit owners are planning to position their company as an acquisition target in the coming years. By maximizing revenue generation between now and then, they hope to demand lucrative purchasing terms. They also feel that a standardized and optimized service-enabled IT environment will make the company a more attractive acquisition.

To realize these goals, Cutit continues to focus on their fundamental supply-chain processes. With the Lab Project portion of their manufacturing process completed, they now turn their attention to automating and service-enabling the inventory transfer and back-order fulfillment process that is carried out immediately after chain manufacturing is completed.

2.2 Case #2 Background: Alleywood Lumber Company

Alleywood is a large-sized corporation but still considered a medium-sized contender in the global lumber industry. The company is comprised of three mills distributed in the U.S. and Canada and a head office based out of Chicago. It processes a variety of lumber and supplies for both domestic and international clients.

History

The Alleywood organization has been privately owned by the Alleywood family for three generations. However, recent legislation and foreign trade regulations have made it difficult for it to compete with some of the larger, more internationally established lumber corporations.

The Alleywood family reluctantly agreed to make the company available for sale. Several interested parties emerged, and subsequent to much negotiation and communication, Alleywood was purchased by the McPherson Corporation. Terms were agreed to last year, and the transition is just now beginning to take place.

McPherson is a conglomerate that owns several companies, including the Tri-Fold Paper Mills. One of the reasons McPherson chose Alleywood was to develop its own supply chain from raw wood to refined paper goods.

Although Alleywood retained most of its 900 employees, its upper management was almost completely replaced. A primary goal of the new CIO is to revamp Alleywood's IT environment so that it can be more easily connected to the already services-enabled Tri-Fold enterprise.

Technical Infrastructure and Automation Environment

Alleywood has historically relied on a central ERP system. Outdated by today's standards, it was implemented about eight years ago as part of a very large migration project, replacing many mainframe systems. Since then, the ERP vendor has been assimilated by a larger vendor, and in its current form, the product has become unsupported and obsolete. Due to declining profits over the past two years, no effort was made to upgrade the system.

Business Goals and Obstacles

The focal point of this transition is the collection of central repositories that contain accounting, inventory, financial history, and related corporate data. This information needs to be ported into the new environment in such a manner that the consolidated IT enterprise is still efficient and responsive to business change. For example, Alleywood needs to be constantly able to adapt to regulatory policy changes issued by the FRC. It has been able to do so on its own with relative success but now must continue to adapt to these changes without impacting connectivity with the Tri-Fold environment.

It was decided from the onset that this environment would be developed from the ground up in support of an enterprise-wide SOA. Services will be custom-built and optimized wherever possible. The Tri-Fold environment is already very service-centric, in that services encapsulating ERP modules have been somewhat standardized in alignment with the recently delivered custom services designed to represent other segments of the Tri-Fold enterprise.

Therefore, in addition to building new services for Alleywood, a strategic objective of this transition will be to reuse key services already developed as part of the Tri-Fold service inventory.

Other critical decision points that need to be addressed are:

- Whether the old data models from Alleywood's legacy databases will be preserved or whether the initiative should encompass a remodeling project as part of the overall data export requirements.
- Whether services reused from Tri-Fold should be centrally maintained by Tri-Fold architects or whether they can be evolved independently by Alleywood architects.
- Whether all services will be custom built for Alleywood or whether a new ERP platform will form the basis of the revised enterprise.

2.3 Case #3 Background: Forestry Regulatory Commission (FRC)

There are many independent regulatory commissions that act as objective extensions of the government to administer policies for specific industries. The FRC is dedicated to overseeing commercial activity related to the forestry industry. As part of that role it is responsible for managing and enforcing policies that pertain to private companies involved with the forestry and lumber trade.

History

As an organizational entity, the FRC has been in existence for over 50 years. It has undergone many changes during that time, as its funding has fluctuated and its directives are repeatedly augmented. In its current state, it exists as a relatively autonomous agency with three main administration offices, 112 satellite locations, and a staff of over 20,000.

Each of the main offices represents one of three primary FRC business divisions:

- Policy Management
- Field Support
- Assessments and Appeals

Although they have always worked together to further the overall goals of the FRC, these divisions have been physically isolated and have developed individual corporate cultures. In many ways, these offices exist as independent organizations.

As the forestry industry expands, so must the FRC. It has grown steadily over the past ten years and expects this trend to continue.

Technical Infrastructure and Automation Environment

The FRC has a massive inventory of products, custom-built systems, middleware, and repositories. No one knows for sure how many applications actually exist, but estimates range from 300 to 450. Of these, a large percentage was built by external solution providers. At last count, the FRC has nearly 900 registered IT vendors.

Those automation solution projects that were outsourced began with formal proposal submission processes governed by dedicated review committees. In the past, the primary criteria applied to the assessment of vendor proposals was the claimed expertise, promised delivery timeline, and, of course, the estimated cost.

Other solutions have been developed in-house. With a total IT staff of over 1,000, the FRC has numerous resources at its disposal. Each of the three administration offices has an IT division with its own departmental structure and organizational hierarchy. There are regular meetings between IT managers from all divisions, but outside of that, there is infrequent communication or coordination. Resources are rarely shared between offices, and when they are, strict charge-back policies are in place to ensure that any loan is eventually compensated.

Business Goals and Obstacles

A year ago an annual financial report was delivered to the president of the FRC and its board of directors revealing that operational IT costs have been higher than ever before. This led to a follow-up strategic meeting for which historical reports were prepared, providing an analysis of IT expenses over the past 10 years.

It became evident that, unlike other departments, the cost increases for IT were severely disproportionate with the FRC's rate of growth. For example, five years ago the FRC expanded by 5%. Its IT costs, however, increased by 9%. This last year, the FRC grew by 3%, but the IT budget jumped by 13%. Every year, the three IT divisions are consuming a larger portion of the overall FRC budget. If this alarming trend would be allowed to continue, the FRC would be forced to downsize other departments just to support IT.

Subsequent to a series of tense meetings with the IT directors from each office, an in-depth audit of past IT expenditures was commissioned. The results indicated that every time the FRC expanded or underwent internal policy changes, the underlying IT environments were required to compensate by either building new systems or modifying existing ones. Almost all primary systems are currently integrated with others to some extent. These integration channels were costly to implement and have become especially expensive to change and maintain.

Over time, so many point-to-point integration channels have been created that a change to one can have a significant ripple effect across several others. Therefore, even a minor alteration can result in a costly development, integration, and regression testing effort. This has quietly escalated to a point where IT costs have become unmanageable.

Subsequent to these revelations, the president of the FRC decides that a reorganization is in order, beginning with upper IT management. All IT directors are replaced, and the position of CTO is established. IT divisions will no longer have the independence they've enjoyed so far; now each of the new directors must report to the CTO, and it is up to this individual to figure out how to turn this all around. Following a further independent analysis project, it is decided that a major move toward SOA provides the best option to solving FRC's IT problems.

Part I

Fundamentals

Chapter 3

Basic Terms and Concepts

It's been well established that service-oriented computing represents an ambitious platform with the potential to transform the complexion of an enterprise. Design patterns in support of this platform therefore tackle a spectrum of design problems, ranging from the encapsulation of granular functionality to the strategic partitioning of the enterprise into service-enabled domains.

A constant among all the patterns documented in this book is that each, in some shape or form, impacts or relates to technology architecture. A service, a solution comprised of services, a collection of related services—each has a pre-determined architectural design, each claims its own distinct part of the overarching enterprise architecture, and all are collectively designed to work in concert to realize common strategic goals.

Purpose of this Introductory Chapter

This chapter establishes the fundamental links between service-oriented computing, service-orientation, and technology architecture. You will find this content useful if you are new to SOA or if you need to look up definitions to some of the terms used throughout this book. Also, the upcoming architecture-related definitions provide background information for the service-oriented architecture types explained in Chapter 4. Those types are then subsequently referenced in pattern descriptions.

> **NOTE**
>
> This chapter borrows some content from SOAGlossary.com.

3.1 Architecture Fundamentals

To prepare for the upcoming discussion of service-orientation and technology architecture in Chapter 4, let's begin by establishing some fundamental terminology. The next sections establish the following basic architecture-related IT terms:

- *Technology Architecture* – The fundamental physical design of something.
- *Technology Infrastructure* – The underlying, supporting technology environment, including software and hardware.
- *Software Program* – A standalone system that may be a custom-developed application or a purchased product.

We are by no means attempting to formally define these terms for the IT industry. These definitions are simply part of the common vocabulary used by the books in this series to ensure consistency and clarity across all titles. Figure 3.1 further illustrates their meaning.

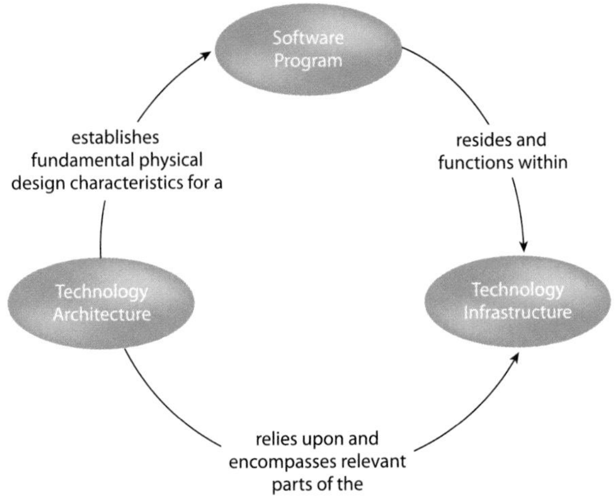

Figure 3.1
An overview of how the enterprise elements represented by these terms relate to each other.

A Classic Analogy for Architecture and Infrastructure

It's well-known how the IT community borrowed the term "architecture" from its traditional association with the design and construction of buildings and structures. Its origin also helps us establish an analogy that is useful for distinguishing a technology architecture from a technology infrastructure.

A building has a physical design expressed in an architecture blueprint or specification. However, the building exists within a surrounding environment. This environment may or may not provide a lot of support for the building to fulfill its purpose. For example, an office or residential building located within a city is supported by the streets, power plants, utility pole cables, sewer systems, and other resources provided by the city environment. This supporting environment is analogous to technology infrastructure.

In order for a building to take advantage of these infrastructure extensions, its physical design needs to integrate them as part of its official architecture. Therefore, an architecture specification for a building will encompass the parts of its surrounding infrastructure that are relevant to the building. As a result, there is no firm boundary between what constitutes the building architecture and the environmental infrastructure. This same overlap exists in the IT world, as explained in the following definitions.

Technology Architecture

A technology architecture expresses fundamental and foundational aspects of physical design for some piece of technology. Whereas computer hardware products will have their own individual technology architectures, within a typical IT enterprise, we are most concerned with the architecture of software programs.

For a program we purchase, we may want to understand its internal design to ensure that it is compatible with the environment already established within our enterprise. For programs we build, it becomes our responsibility to define the physical design ourselves.

When designing a new software program, we need to take into consideration the environment in which it will need to be deployed and in which it will need to carry out its purpose. In most established enterprises, implementation environments already exist in the form of servers, operating systems, and runtime and middleware platforms. As explained in the next section, all of these parts are considered technology infrastructure. And, as with buildings and cities, the software program's architecture is comprised of new parts interwoven with the relevant parts of the infrastructure that already exist as part of the surrounding environment.

The scope of technology architecture can vary depending on what it is we are designing. Some well-known types include:

- *Component Architecture* – In a distributed computing environment, this represents the physical structure of an individual software program that exists as a component.
- *Application Architecture* – A technology architecture with a physical boundary limited to the deployment environment of a particular application or system. In a distributed computing environment, an application architecture can encompass multiple component architectures.
- *Integration Architecture* – The technology architecture of two or more connected applications or systems including whatever technologies, resources, or extensions were added to enable their integration. Many integration architectures include middleware platforms and associated adapter or bridging extensions.
- *Enterprise Technology Architecture* – Unlike component, application, and integration architectures, which are often documented in design specifications *prior* to the creation of programs, enterprise technology architectures frequently result as a documentation of what already exists within an enterprise environment. An enterprise technology architecture specification can encompass (or may just reference) all previously listed forms of architecture and may also act as a formal documentation of the enterprise infrastructure as well.

As shown in Figure 3.2, each of these architecture types represents a different scope, whereby one tends to encompass the other.

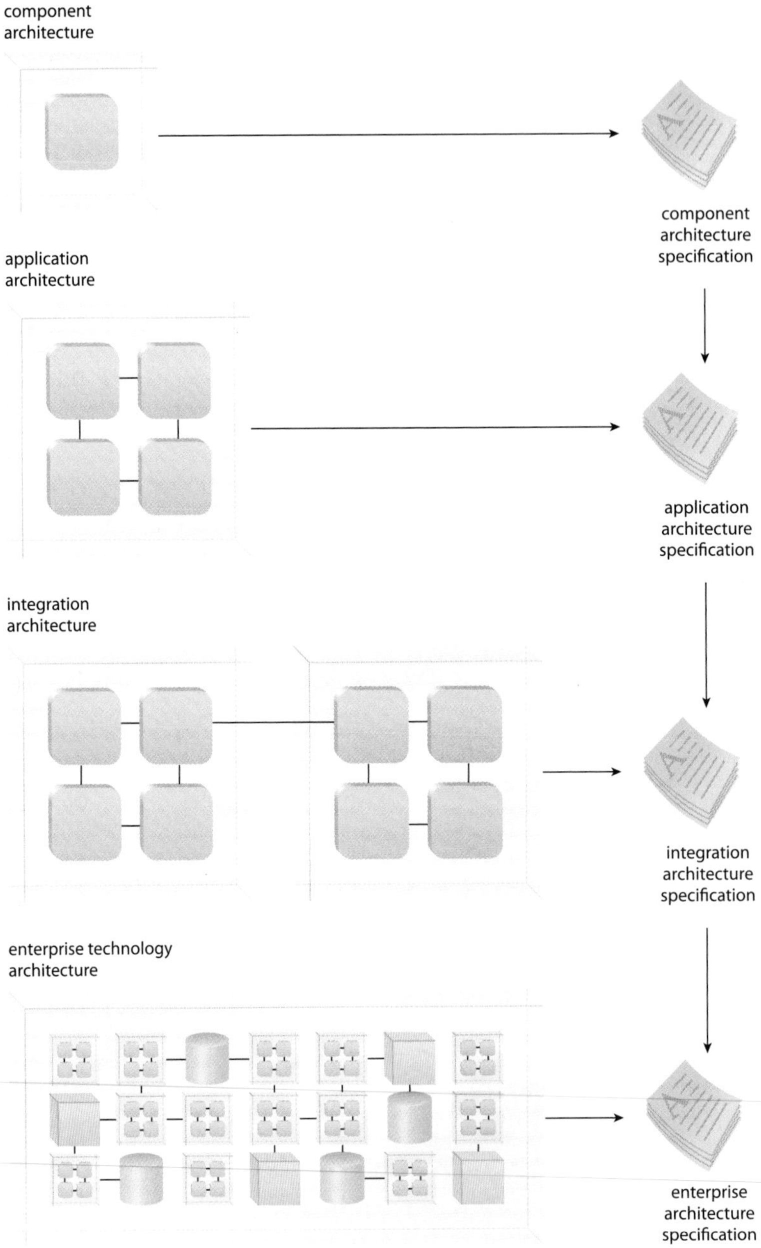

Figure 3.2

Common traditional levels of documented technology architecture.

In a service-oriented environment the scope of technology architecture can also vary. The distinct forms of service-oriented architectures and how they roughly correspond to the previously listed traditional architecture types is explained separately in the section *The Four Types of Service-Oriented Technology Architecture* in Chapter 4.

NOTE

As just mentioned, you can define an architecture for a piece of hardware or a software program, which is why you will sometimes see the term "architecture" further qualified as hardware architecture or software architecture. Because our focus in SOA projects is primarily on software design, why then do we continue using the broader "technology architecture" term? As revealed by many patterns in this book, architecture in the world of service-oriented computing relies on a combination of software and hardware resources, both of which find their way into typical architecture specifications.

Technology Infrastructure

Within a typical IT enterprise, technology infrastructure represents the environment in which software programs are deployed. As with the term "architecture," infrastructure can also be qualified with "software" or "hardware" to identify certain parts of this environment.

Common forms of hardware infrastructure include:

- servers and workstations
- routers, firewalls, and networking equipment
- back-up power supplies, cables, and other computer equipment

Types of software typically considered part of an enterprise's technology infrastructure include:

- operating systems and system APIs
- runtime environments and system-level service agents
- databases and directories
- transaction management programs and message queues
- middleware and adapters
- user account management and security technologies

What generally distinguishes a technology that is part of infrastructure from one that is exclusive to a particular component or application architecture is that it is made available to multiple applications or systems and therefore exists as a resource of the enterprise (and is therefore also separately owned and governed). An example of a common software program that can be either classified as part of infrastructure or specific to an application architecture is a database (Figure 3.3).

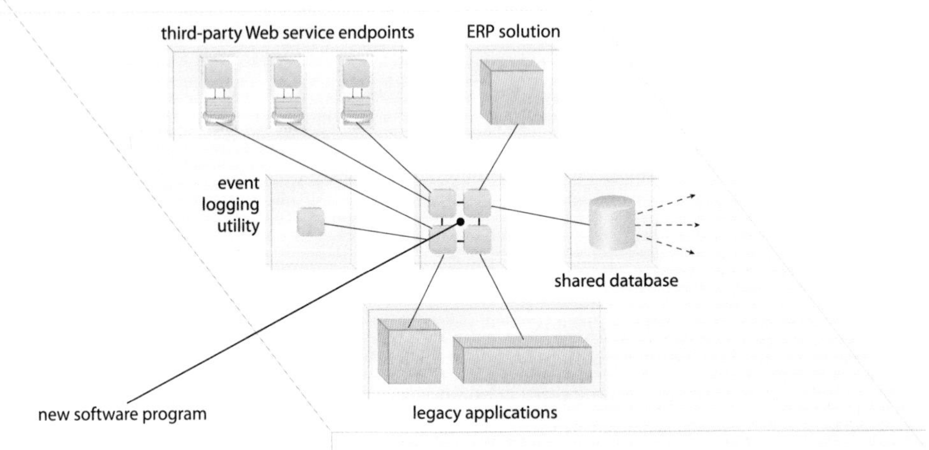

Figure 3.3
A software program implemented within an enterprise finds itself dependent on various resources in the surrounding infrastructure.

As previously mentioned, relevant pieces of technology infrastructure find their way into almost all forms of architecture documentation because they become part of the architecture itself. An enterprise technology architecture specification often documents some or all of an enterprise's infrastructure in a reference format that is made available to authors of other architecture design documents.

The infrastructure of an enterprise will frequently determine the processing potential of technology architectures that reside within it and are built upon it. This potential threshold is then further leveraged or constrained by the design of the architecture itself. Consequently, a software program is required to exist and execute within the boundaries and thresholds established by both its underlying infrastructure and architecture (as explained in Figure 3.4).

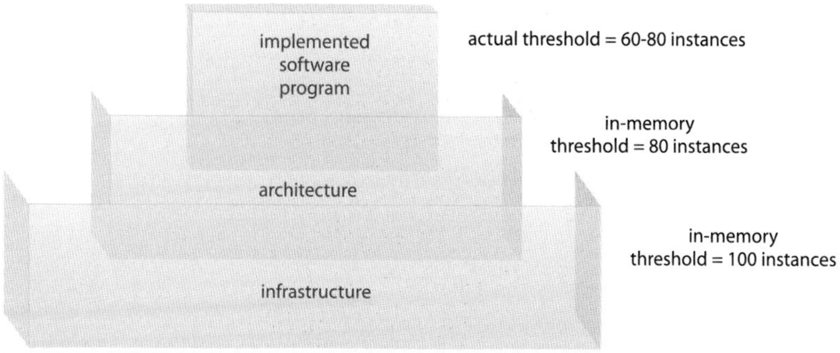

Figure 3.4

Technology infrastructures and architectures collectively establish boundaries that determine the processing thresholds of software programs. In this example, the maximum instances of a program that can be concurrently invoked is less than what the infrastructure can support because of limitations introduced by the architecture and the software program's own implementation.

Software Program

A software program is simply an existing system, application, or solution. It may represent a purchased product or a custom-designed program. In relation to technology architecture, a software program can be considered an implementation of the design documented in an architecture specification, as well as the logic that resides and executes within the supporting environment also specified by the technology architecture.

Part of a software program's design can be documented within an application architecture specification. Usually this part is backend-centric with an emphasis on the program's overall structure (including components it may be comprised of), technologies, and resource requirements. A typical application architecture specification is therefore frequently supplemented with additional types of design documents, such as functional specifications that illustrate the flow and style of the program user interfaces and detailed design documents that establish programming routines and algorithms.

Depending on the conventions, methodologies, or preferences of the IT department, this additional design information may or may not be considered part of the program's official technology architecture (Figure 3.5).

> **NOTE**
>
> The upcoming *Relationship to Design Framework* section briefly provides some reference content for readers of *SOA Principles of Service Design*. If this does not interest you, feel free to skip ahead to the *Service-Oriented Computing Fundamentals* section.

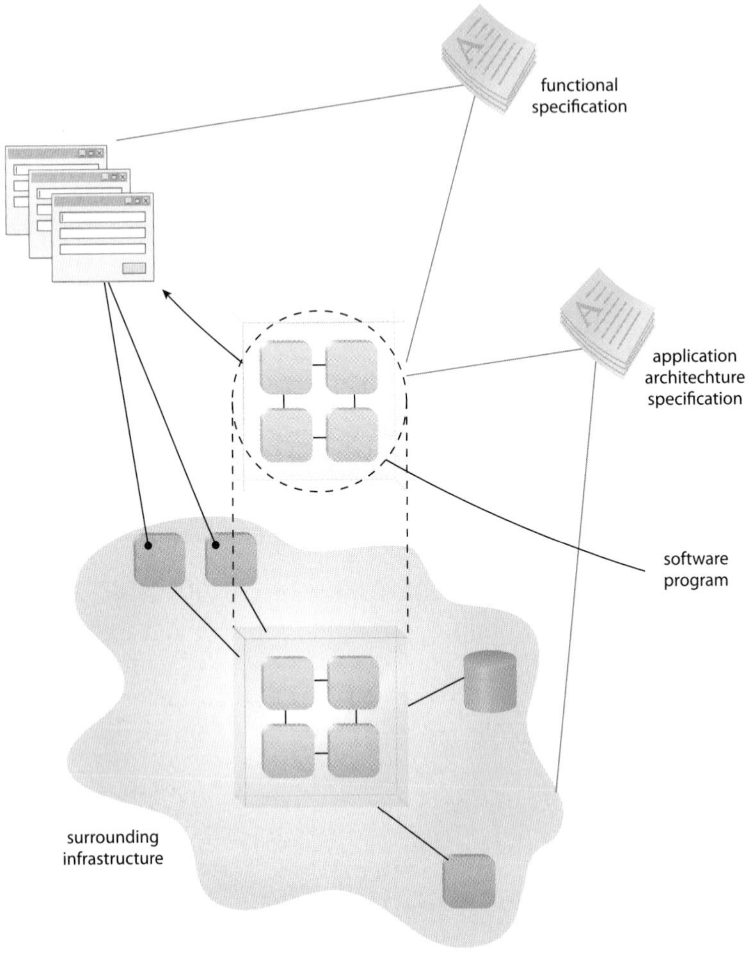

Figure 3.5

The physical design of a software program is partially defined by its application architecture along with relevant parts of the surrounding infrastructure. Other documents, such as a functional specification, establish additional design characteristics, such as the program's user-interfaces.

Relationship to Design Framework

Chapter 3 of *SOA Principles of Service Design* documents a base design framework that includes the following terms:

- *Design Characteristic* – A property of a software program or technology architecture that results from how it was designed. A design characteristic can be any concrete quality, such as the fact that the program is componentized, provides fine or coarse-grained functions, and so on.

- *Design Principle* – An accepted industry practice with a specific design goal. The service-orientation design paradigm is comprised of a set of design principles that are applied together to achieve the goals of service-oriented computing (as explained in the upcoming *Service-Orientation and Technology Architecture* section).
- *Design Pattern* – A proven solution to a common design problem documented in a consistent format. (See the *Fundamental Terminology* section in Chapter 5 for a full definition of this term.)
- *Design Standard* – Design conventions customized individually by organizations in order to reliably deliver solutions in support of the organization's specific business goals. Design standards can support and optimize the application of design principles and design patterns for particular environments and can help ensure the consistent realization of design characteristics. Conversely, design principles and patterns can form the basis of design standards that are then further customized. (Note that design standards should not be confused with *industry* standards, such as XML and WSDL.)

Figure 3.6 illustrates how closely this design framework can tie into the architecture-related vocabulary we just covered. In the end, principles, patterns, and architecture all revolve around and influence design.

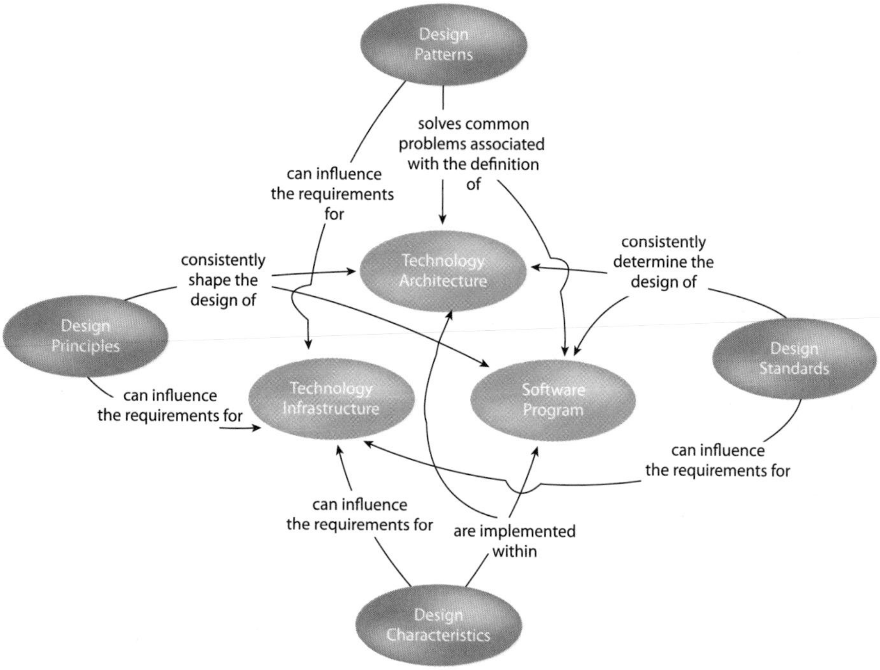

Figure 3.6

How the elements of a design framework can be associated with architecture-related elements.

SUMMARY OF KEY POINTS

- Technology architecture represents the physical structure and aspects of physical design for a piece of technology. Traditional variations of technology architecture include component, application, integration, and enterprise technology architecture. (These will be compared to service-oriented architecture types in Chapter 4.)
- Technology infrastructure represents the structure and complexion of a technical environment most commonly confined to the boundary of an organization's enterprise. Technology architectures encompass portions of relevant infrastructure.
- Technology architectures encompass portions of relevant infrastructure.
- A software program is a system or application that is partially defined by and also resides within a technology architecture.

3.2 Service-Oriented Computing Fundamentals

The upcoming sections provide descriptions of common terms used throughout this book.

Service-Oriented Computing

Service-oriented computing is an umbrella term that represents a new generation distributed computing platform. As such, it encompasses many things, including its own design paradigm and design principles, design patterns, a distinct architectural model, and related concepts, technologies, and frameworks.

Service-oriented computing builds upon past distributed computing platforms and adds new design layers, governance considerations, and a vast set of preferred implementation technologies, several of which are based on the Web services framework.

In this book we make reference to the strategic goals of service-oriented computing as they relate to the application of service-orientation and the design of service-oriented architecture. These goals are briefly described in the section *The Method of Service-Orientation* in Chapter 4.

Service-Orientation

Service-orientation is a design paradigm intended for the creation of solution logic units that are individually shaped so that they can be collectively and repeatedly utilized in support of the realization of the specific strategic goals and benefits associated with SOA and service-oriented computing.

Solution logic designed in accordance with service-orientation can be qualified with "service-oriented," and units of service-oriented solution logic are referred to as "services." As a design paradigm for distributed computing, service-orientation can be compared to object-orientation (or object-oriented design). Service-orientation, in fact, has many roots in object-orientation and has also been influenced by other industry developments, as shown in Figure 3.7.

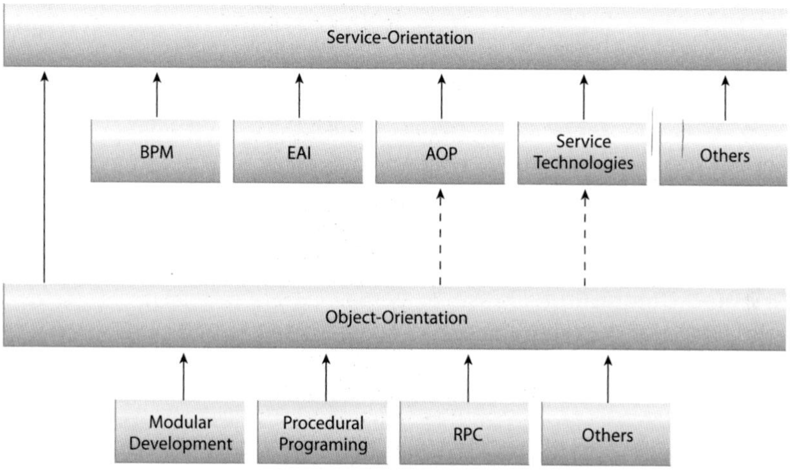

Figure 3.7

Service-orientation is very much an evolutionary design paradigm that owes much of its existence to established design practices and technology platforms.

The service-orientation design paradigm is primarily comprised of eight design principles, which are listed in the section *The Method of Service-Orientation* in Chapter 4. These principles are further summarized in Appendix C and referenced by all subsequent design pattern descriptions so as to highlight potential relationships between the application of a pattern and the application of related design principles.

Service-Oriented Architecture (SOA)

Service-oriented architecture represents an architectural model that aims to enhance the agility and cost-effectiveness of an enterprise while reducing the burden of IT on the overall organization. It accomplishes this by positioning services as the primary means through which solution logic is represented. SOA supports service-orientation in the realization of the strategic goals associated with service-oriented computing. Historically, the term "service-oriented architecture" (or "SOA") has been used so broadly by the media and within vendor marketing literature that it has almost become synonymous with service-oriented computing itself.

As a form of technology architecture, an SOA implementation can consist of a combination of technologies, products, APIs, supporting infrastructure extensions, and various other parts. The actual complexion of a deployed service-oriented architecture is unique within each enterprise; however it is typified by the introduction of new technologies and platforms that specifically support the creation, execution, and evolution of service-oriented solutions. As a result, building a technology architecture around the service-oriented architectural model establishes an environment suitable for solution logic that has been designed in compliance with service-orientation design principles.

Chapter 4 establishes distinct types of service-oriented architecture and documents four key characteristics that each variation should possess in order to fully support service-orientation. These architecture types are then further referenced by design pattern descriptions in order to highlight the potential scope or applicability of a given pattern.

Service

A *service* is a unit of solution logic (Figure 3.8) to which service-orientation has been applied to a meaningful extent. It is the application of service-orientation design principles that distinguishes a unit of logic as a service compared to units of logic that may exist solely as objects or components.

Subsequent to conceptual service modeling, service-oriented design and development stages implement a service as a physically independent software program with specific design characteristics that support the attainment of the strategic goals associated with service-oriented computing.

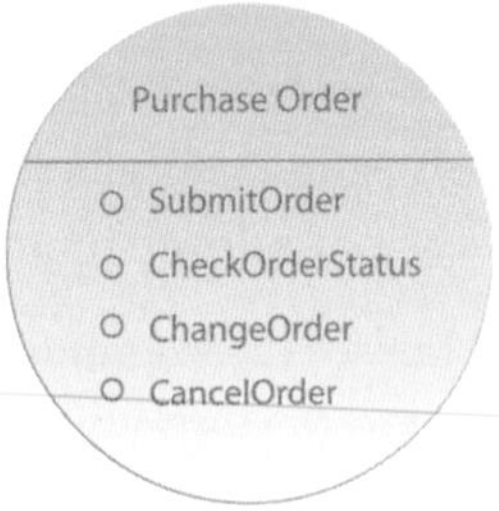

Figure 3.8
The chorded circle symbol is used to represent a service, primarily from a contract perspective.

A service corresponds, in scope, to the service architecture type described in Chapter 4. The design patterns in Part III of this book are further dedicated to or related to the design of services.

Service Capability

Each service is assigned its own distinct functional context and is comprised of a set of functions or *capabilities* related to this context. Therefore, a service can be considered a container of capabilities associated with a common purpose (based on a common functional context). The individual bullet items within the service symbol from Figure 3.8 are capabilities.

The term *service capability* has no implication as to how a service is implemented. Therefore, this term can be especially useful during service modeling stages when the physical design of a service has not yet been determined (at which point it is further qualified as a *service capability candidate*). As explained later in the *Service Implementation Mediums* section, once it is known whether a service exists as a Web service, a REST service, or a component, terms such as "service method" or "service operation" can be used instead.

Service Consumer

When a program invokes and interacts with a service it is labeled as a *service consumer*. It is very important to understand that this term refers to the temporary runtime role assumed by a program when it is engaging a service in a data exchange.

For example, you can create a desktop application that is capable of exchanging messages with a service. When it is interacting with the service, the desktop application is considered a service consumer.

You can also design a service to invoke and interact with other services (which, in fact, forms the basis of a service composition, as explained in the next section). In this case, the service itself will temporarily act as the service consumer (Figure 3.9).

Many of the examples in the upcoming chapters show consumers as services. Furthermore, due to the unpredictable nature of data flow through service compositions, the directionality between consumers and services is intentionally not standardized in diagrams provided in this book (which is a deviation from the left-to-right convention used with traditional client-server illustrations).

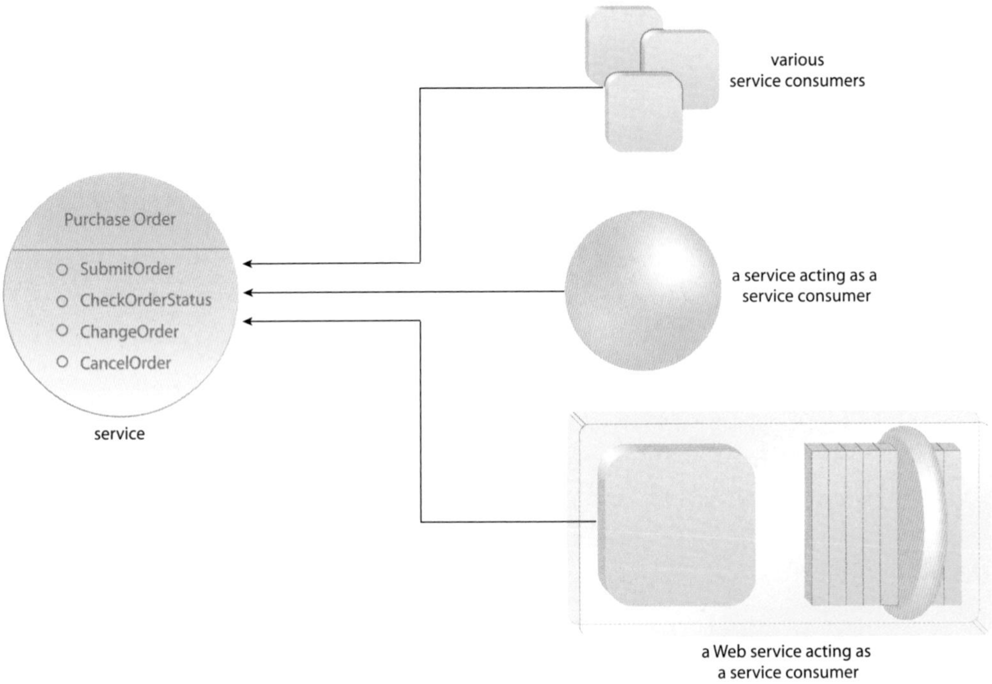

Figure 3.9

The Purchase Order service being accessed by a variety of programs acting as service consumers.

A common alternative term for service consumer is *service requester*. Also, a term often used to represent the runtime role a service assumes when it is being invoked by a service consumer is *service provider*. These terms originated with the W3C and are therefore often used when services are built as Web services, as shown in Figure 3.10.

Many of the patterns in this book deal with design issues that are related to the interaction between service and consumer. Be sure to constantly keep in mind that any service can also be a service consumer.

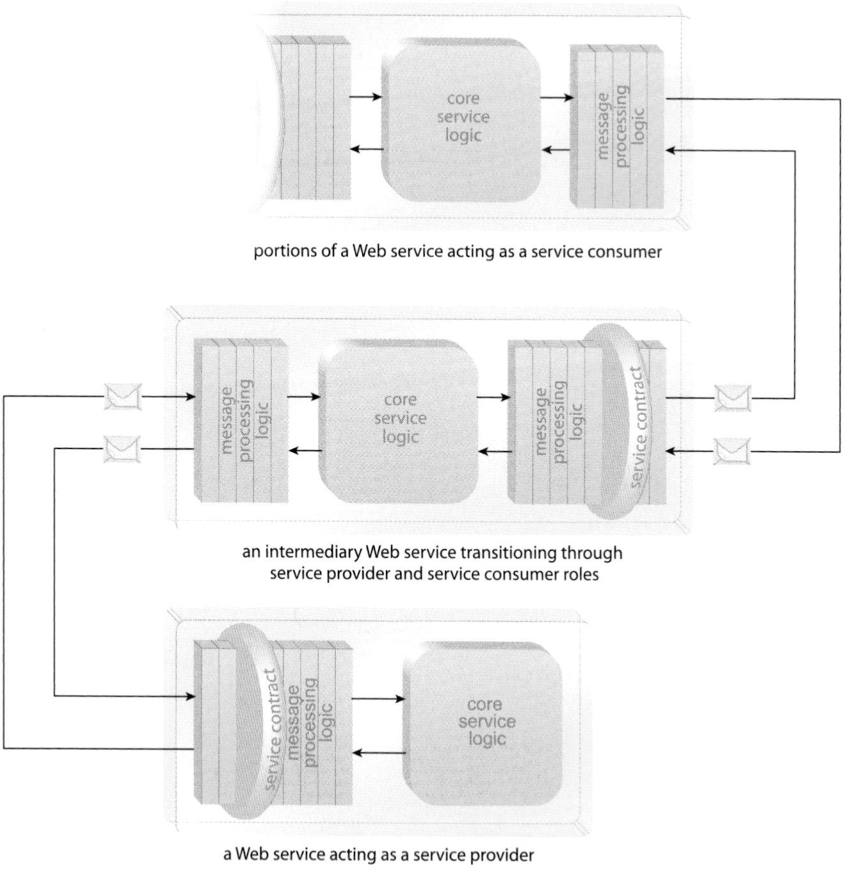

Figure 3.10

Three variations of a Web service showing the different physical parts of its architecture that come into play, depending on the role it assumes at runtime. Note how a service that transitions through service provider and consumer roles is further classified as an intermediary.

Service Composition

A *service composition* is an aggregate of services collectively composed to automate a particular task or business process (Figure 3.11). To qualify as a composition, at least two participating services plus a composition initiator need to be present. Otherwise, the service interaction only represents a point-to-point exchange.

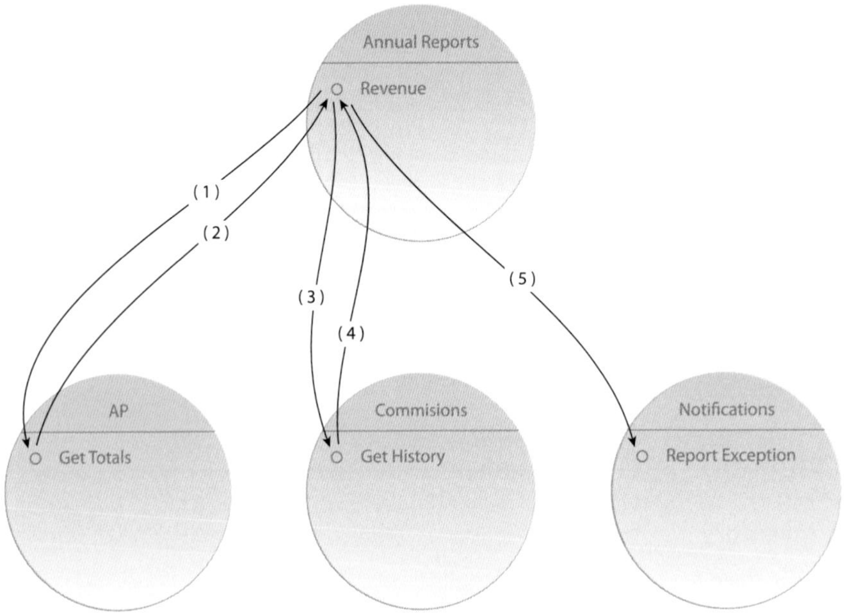

Figure 3.11

A service composition comprised of four services. The arrows indicate a sequence of modeled message exchanges. Note arrow #5 representing a one-way, asynchronous data delivery.

Much of the service-orientation design paradigm revolves around preparing services for effective participation in numerous complex compositions—so much so that the Service Composability design principle is dedicated solely to ensuring that services are designed in support of repeatable composition. A service composition in itself also represents one of the four SOA types explained in Chapter 4.

The design of a composition entails various architectural considerations in order to ensure that runtime service activities can be carried out as expected. Part IV of this book provides a set of chapters with patterns focused on composition design and related runtime processing.

NOTE

There are several additional terms associated with service composition design, including:

- composition controller
- composition controller capability
- composition initiator
- composition member
- composition member capability
- composition sub-controller
- service activity

Definitions for these terms are available at SOAGlossary.com.

Service Inventory

A *service inventory* is an independently standardized and governed collection of complementary services within a boundary that represents an enterprise or a meaningful segment of an enterprise (Figure 3.12). When an organization has multiple service inventories, this term is further qualified as *domain service inventory,* as explained in the pattern description for Domain Inventory (123).

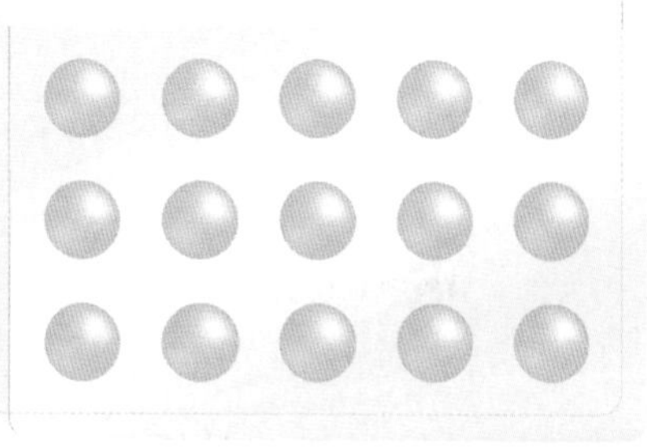

Figure 3.12

The standard symbol used to represent a service inventory in this book is the open blue container.

Service inventories are typically created through top-down delivery processes that result in the definition of *service inventory blueprints.* The subsequent application of service-orientation design principles and custom design standards throughout a service inventory is of paramount importance so as to establish a high degree of native inter-service interoperability. This supports the repeated creation of effective service compositions in response to new and changing business requirements.

The service inventory architecture is one of four SOA types explained in the following chapter. Part II of this book further provides a collection of fundamental and specialized patterns dedicated to service inventory design.

Where Did the Term "Service Inventory" Come From?

"When building services as part of an SOA project, there is an emphasis on developing them as standalone programs that are expected to be flexible and robust so that they can be readily reused and composed. Service-oriented design has therefore been heavily influenced by commercial product design techniques, to the extent that a service delivered as a black box is somewhat comparable to a software product. Inspired by commercial terminology, a collection of services for a given segment of an enterprise is referred to as a *service inventory*. And, similarly, the technology architecture that supports this collection of services is referred to as the *service inventory architecture*.

What's the difference between a service inventory and a service catalog? The same manner in which an inventory of products is documented with a product catalog, an inventory of services is documented with a service catalog. It's therefore still appropriate to refer to a collection of services as a service catalog; however, when applying design patterns and defining the actual concrete architecture, terms like "service inventory" (or even "service pools") tend to work better."

– "Introducing SOA Design Patterns," SOA World Magazine, June 2008

Service-Oriented Analysis

Service-oriented analysis represents one of the early stages in an SOA initiative and the first phase in the service delivery cycle. It is a process that often begins with preparatory information gathering steps that are completed in support of a service modeling sub-process that results in the creation of conceptual service candidates, service capability candidates, and service composition candidates.

The service-oriented analysis process is commonly carried out iteratively, once for each business process. When applied as part of a top-down approach, the scope of a planned service inventory will generally determine the extent of the service-oriented analysis effort. All iterations of a service-oriented analysis then pertain to that scope, with the goal of producing a service inventory blueprint. (Visit SOAMethodology.com for an explanation of the iterative service-oriented analysis process.)

A key success factor of service-oriented analysis is the hands-on collaboration of both business analysts and technology architects. The former group is especially involved in the definition of service candidates with a business-centric functional context because they understand the business processes used as input for the analysis and because service-orientation aims to align business and IT more closely.

The service definition process that is commonly carried out as part of a service-oriented analysis will usually contain steps that correspond to the foundational service patterns provided in Chapter 11.

Service Candidate

When conceptualizing services during the service modeling part of the service-oriented analysis phase, services are defined on a preliminary basis and still subject to change and refinement before they are handed over to the service-oriented design project stage responsible for producing the physical service architecture. The term *service candidate* is used to help distinguish a conceptualized service from an actual implemented service.

3.3 Service Implementation Mediums

It is important to view and position SOA as an architectural model that is neutral to any one technology platform. By doing so, an enterprise is given the freedom to continually pursue the strategic goals associated with SOA and service-orientation by leveraging on-going technology advancements.

Currently, a service can be built and implemented as a:

- component
- Web service
- REST service

Essentially, any implementation technology that can be used to create a distributed system may be suitable for service-orientation.

Many of the design patterns in this book are not specific to any one of these three implementation mediums, but some are. For example, several examples in this book are based on the use of Web services because this service implementation medium has been historically the most popular.

The remaining sections in this chapter briefly introduce each of these implementation options. However, because this book is dedicated to design patterns, complete descriptions of these technologies are intentionally deferred to other series titles.

Services as Components

A *component* is a software program designed to be part of a distributed system. It provides a technical interface comparable to a traditional application programming interface (API) through which it exposes public capabilities as *methods,* thereby allowing it to be explicitly invoked by other programs (Figure 3.13).

Figure 3.13

The symbols used to represent a component. The symbol on the left is a generic component that may or may not have been designed as a service, whereas the symbol on the right is explictly labeled to indicate that it has been designed as a service.

Components typically rely on platform-specific development and runtime technologies. For example, components can be built using Java or .NET tools and are then deployed in a runtime environment capable of supporting the corresponding component communications technology requirements, as implemented by the chosen development platform.

> **NOTE**
>
> Building service-oriented components is one of the topics covered in the upcoming books *SOA with Java* and *SOA with .NET.*

Services as Web Services

A *Web service* is a body of solution logic that provides a physically decoupled technical contract consisting of a WSDL definition and one or more XML Schema definitions and also possible WS-Policy expressions. The Web service contract exposes public capabilities as *operations,* establishing a technical interface but without any ties to a proprietary communications framework (Figure 3.14).

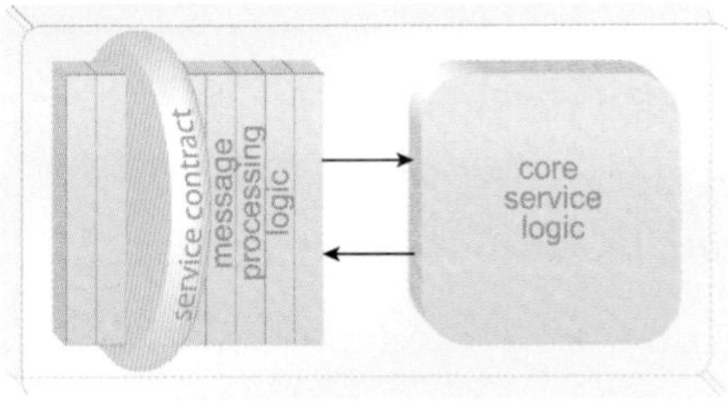

Figure 3.14

The typical Web service architecture containing a service contract, a component, and message processing logic comprised of event-driven agents, as per the pattern Service Agent (543).

Service-orientation can be applied to the design of Web services. The fact that Web services provide an architectural model whereby the service contract is physically decoupled and vendor-neutral is conducive to several of the design goals associated with service-orientation.

NOTE

Coverage of Web services in relation to SOA is provided by the books *Web Service Contract Design and Versioning for SOA* and *Service-Oriented Architecture: Concepts, Technology, and Design.*

REST Services

Representational State Transfer (REST) provides a means of constructing distributed systems based on the notion of *resources. REST services* (or *RESTful Services*) are lightweight programs that are designed with an emphasis on simplicity, scalability, and usability. REST services can be further shaped by the application of service-orientation principles.

As previously explained in the *Web Service and REST Service Design Patterns* section in Chapter 1, several REST-inspired candidate design patterns have been developed for this pattern catalog and are published at SOAPatterns.org.

NOTE

How REST services can be built in support of SOA and service-orientation is explored in the upcoming series titles *SOA with REST*, *SOA with Java*, and *SOA with .NET*.

SUMMARY OF KEY POINTS

- Service-orientation is a design paradigm that can be applied to any suitable distributed computing technology platform.
- There are currently three common implementation mediums suitable for building services: components, Web services, and REST services.

Chapter 4

The Architecture of Service-Orientation

4.1 The Method of Service-Orientation

4.2 The Four Characteristics of SOA

4.3 The Four Common Types of SOA

4.4 The End Result of Service-Orientation

Service-oriented computing is fundamentally about attaining a specific target state. It asks that we take extra design considerations into account with everything we build so that all the moving parts of a service-oriented solution support the realization of this state and foster its growth and evolution. This target state is attractive because it has associated with it a specific set of goals and benefits.

To fully understand service-oriented technology architecture requires knowledge of:

- how these goals and benefits are achieved (the method)
- what entails the attainment of these goals and benefits (the end-result)

This understanding allows us to assess what requirements and demands are placed upon technology architecture.

Purpose of this Introductory Chapter

The focus of this chapter is on establishing the relationship between service-orientation and service-oriented architecture by highlighting common architectural characteristics required to support the goals of service-orientation. This chapter furthermore documents types of service-oriented architecture that are referenced later in design pattern descriptions.

4.1 The Method of Service-Orientation

To realize the strategic benefits of service-oriented computing requires that each piece of solution logic be designed consistently and in a manner that fully supports the expected target environment. This is the role of service-orientation. It is the fundamental method by which service-oriented solutions are created.

Principles of Service-Orientation

There are eight distinct design principles that are part of the service-orientation design paradigm. Each addresses a key aspect of service design by ensuring that specific design characteristics are consistently realized within every service. When collectively applied to a

meaningful extent, service-orientation design principles shape solution logic into something we can legitimately refer to as "service-oriented."

Below are the eight service-orientation design principles together with their official definitions:

- *Standardized Service Contract* – Services within the same service inventory are in compliance with the same contract design standards.
- *Service Loose Coupling* – Service contracts impose low consumer coupling requirements and are themselves decoupled from their surrounding environment.
- *Service Abstraction* – Service contracts only contain essential information and information about services is limited to what is published in service contracts.
- *Service Reusability* – Services contain and express agnostic logic and can be positioned as reusable enterprise resources.
- *Service Autonomy* – Services exercise a high level of control over their underlying runtime execution environment.
- *Service Statelessness* – Services minimize resource consumption by deferring the management of state information when necessary.
- *Service Discoverability* – Services are supplemented with communicative meta data by which they can be effectively discovered and interpreted.
- *Service Composability* – Services are effective composition participants, regardless of the size and complexity of the composition.

Figure 4.1 provides some perspective as to how these principles affect the design of a service. The application of the principles on the right side tend to result in concrete design characteristics being added to a service, whereas the principles on the left usually act as regulatory influences, ensuring a balanced application of service-orientation as a whole.

As just mentioned, a solution is considered service-oriented once service-orientation has been applied to a meaningful extent. A mere understanding of the design paradigm, however, is insufficient. To apply service-orientation consistently and successfully requires a technology architecture customized to accommodate its design preferences, initially when services are first delivered and especially when collections of services are accumulated and assembled into complex compositions.

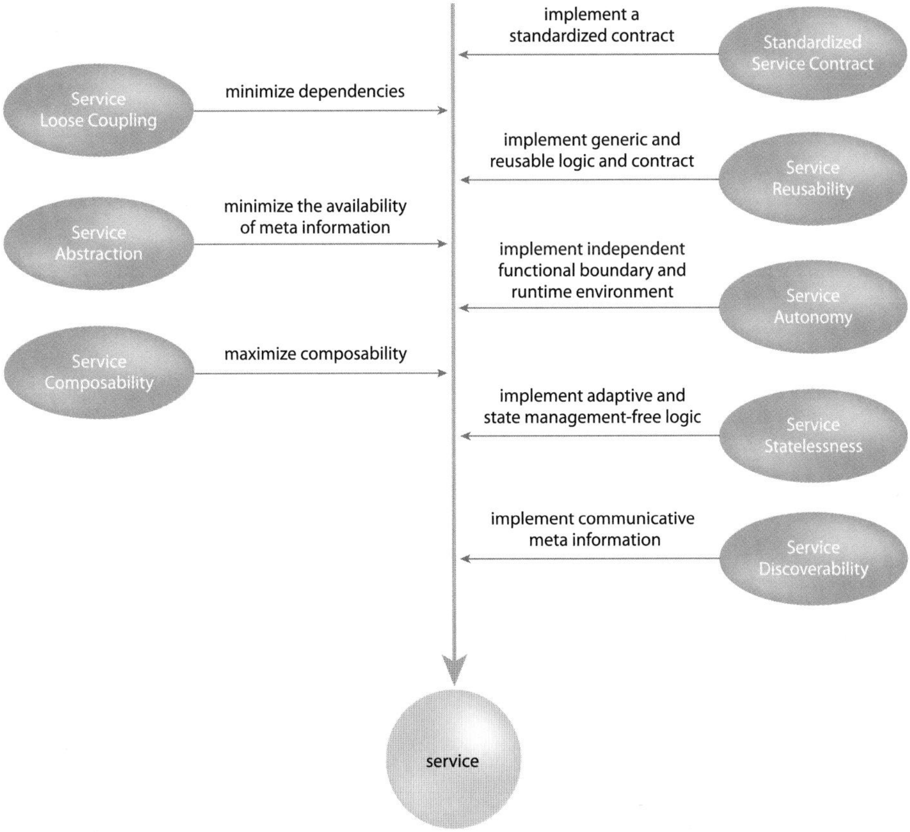

Figure 4.1

How service-orientation design principles relate to each other and how they collectively shape service design.

NOTE

Design principles are referenced throughout this book but represent a separate subject-matter that is covered in *SOA Principles of Service Design*. Introductory coverage of service-orientation is also available at SOAPrinciples.com.

Strategic Goals of Service-Oriented Computing

Service-orientation emerged as a design approach in support of achieving the following goals and benefits associated with SOA and service-oriented computing:

- *Increased Intrinsic Interoperability* – Services within a given boundary are designed to be naturally compatible so that they can be effectively assembled and reconfigured in response to changing business requirements.
- *Increased Federation* – Services establish a uniform contract layer that hides underlying disparity, allowing them to be individually governed and evolved.
- *Increased Vendor Diversification Options* – A service-oriented environment is based on a vendor-neutral architectural model, allowing the organization to evolve the architecture in tandem with the business without being limited to proprietary vendor platform characteristics.
- *Increased Business and Technology Domain Alignment* – Some services are designed with a business-centric functional context, allowing them to mirror and evolve with the business of the organization.
- *Increased ROI* – Most services are delivered and viewed as IT assets that are expected to provide repeated value that surpasses the cost of delivery and ownership.
- *Increased Organizational Agility* – New and changing business requirements can be fulfilled more rapidly by establishing an environment in which solutions can be assembled or augmented with reduced effort by leveraging the reusability and native interoperability of existing services.
- *Reduced IT Burden* – The enterprise as a whole is streamlined as a result of the previously described goals and benefits, allowing IT itself to better support the organization by providing more value with less cost and less overall burden.

NOTE

Formal descriptions for these strategic goals are available at WhatIsSOA.com and in Chapter 3 of *SOA Principles of Service Design*.

When studying the design patterns in this book that support service-orientation, it is important to keep these goals (and the target state they represent) in mind. Understanding the ultimate state attainable provides us with a constant strategic context for each pattern. In other words, it helps provide insight into why certain parts of a service-oriented environment need to be designed in certain ways, which may not always be evident when reading through the pattern descriptions individually.

SUMMARY OF KEY POINTS

- A key ingredient to attaining the strategic goals and benefits associated with service-oriented computing is the successful application of the service-orientation design paradigm.
- Service-oriented architecture needs to be designed in support of service-orientation in order to support the realization of these strategic goals and benefits.
- Understanding the strategic goals helps clarify the design solutions proposed by SOA design patterns.

4.2 The Four Characteristics of SOA

Having just explained the service-orientation design paradigm and its associated goals, we now need to turn our attention to the physical design of a service-oriented solution or environment.

In support of achieving the goals of service-orientation, there are four base characteristics we look to establish in any form of SOA:

- *Business-Driven* – The technology architecture is aligned with the current business architecture. This context is then constantly maintained so that the technology architecture evolves in tandem with the business over time.
- *Vendor-Neutral* – The architectural model is not based solely on a proprietary vendor platform, allowing different vendor technologies to be combined or replaced over time in order to maximize business requirements fulfillment on an on-going basis.

- *Enterprise-Centric* – The scope of the architecture represents a meaningful segment of the enterprise, allowing for the reuse and composition of services and enabling service-oriented solutions to span traditional application silos.
- *Composition-Centric* – The architecture inherently supports the mechanics of repeated service aggregation, allowing it to accommodate constant change via the agile assembly of service compositions.

These characteristics help distinguish SOA from other architectural models and also define the fundamental requirements a technology architecture must fulfill to be fully supportive of service-orientation. As we explore each individually, keep in mind that in real-world implementations the extent to which these characteristics can be attained tends to vary.

Business-Driven

Traditional technology architectures were commonly designed in support of solutions delivered to fulfill tactical (short-term) business requirements. Because the overarching, strategic (long-term) business goals of the organization aren't taken into consideration when the architecture is defined, this approach can result in a technical environment that, over time, becomes out of alignment with the organization's business direction and requirements (Figure 4.2).

This gradual separation of business and technology results in a technology architecture with diminishing potential to fulfill business requirements and one that is increasingly difficult to adapt to changing business needs.

When a technology architecture is business-driven, the overarching business vision, goals, and requirements are positioned as the basis for and the primary influence of the architectural model. This maximizes the potential alignment of technology and business and allows for a technology architecture that can evolve in tandem with the organization as a whole (Figure 4.3). The result is a continual increase in the value and lifespan of the architecture.

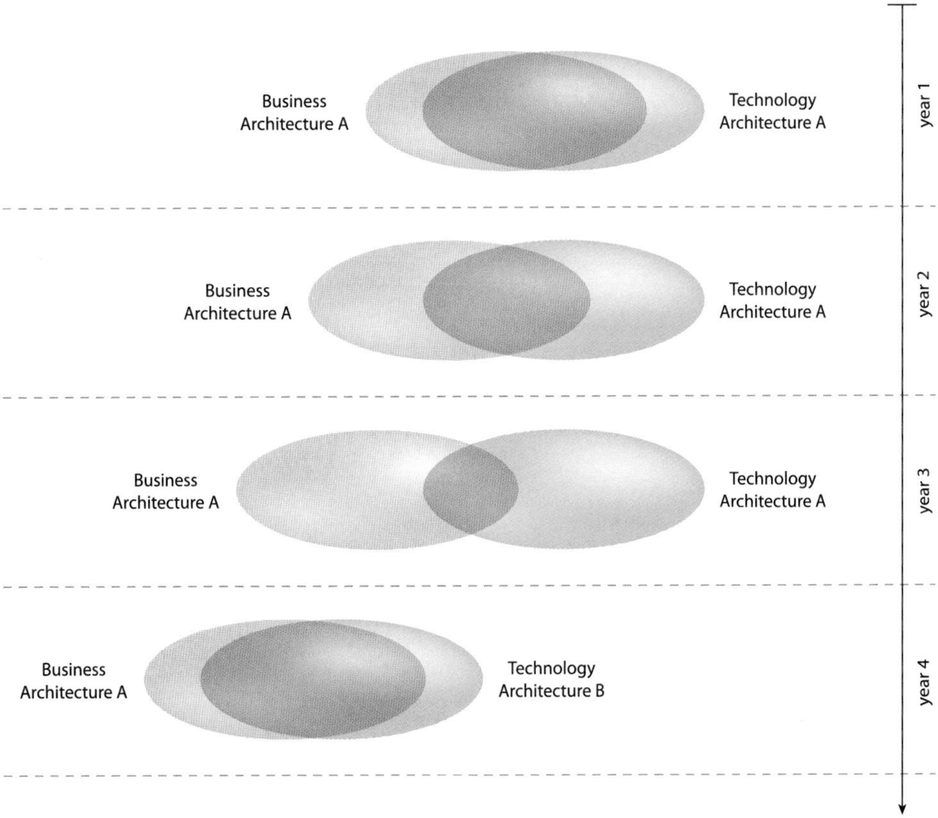

Figure 4.2

A traditional technology architecture (A) is often delivered in alignment with the current state of a business but can be incapable of changing in alignment with how the business evolves. As business and technology architectures become increasingly out of synch, business requirement fulfillment decreases, often to the point that a whole new technology architecture (B) is needed, which effectively resets this cycle.

Vendor-Neutral

Designing a service-oriented technology architecture around one particular vendor platform can lead to an implementation that inadvertently inherits proprietary characteristics. This can end up inhibiting the future evolution of an inventory architecture in response to technology innovations that become available from other vendors.

An inhibitive technology architecture is unable to evolve and expand in response to changing automation requirements, which can result in the architecture having a limited lifespan after which it needs to be replaced to remain effective (Figure 4.4).

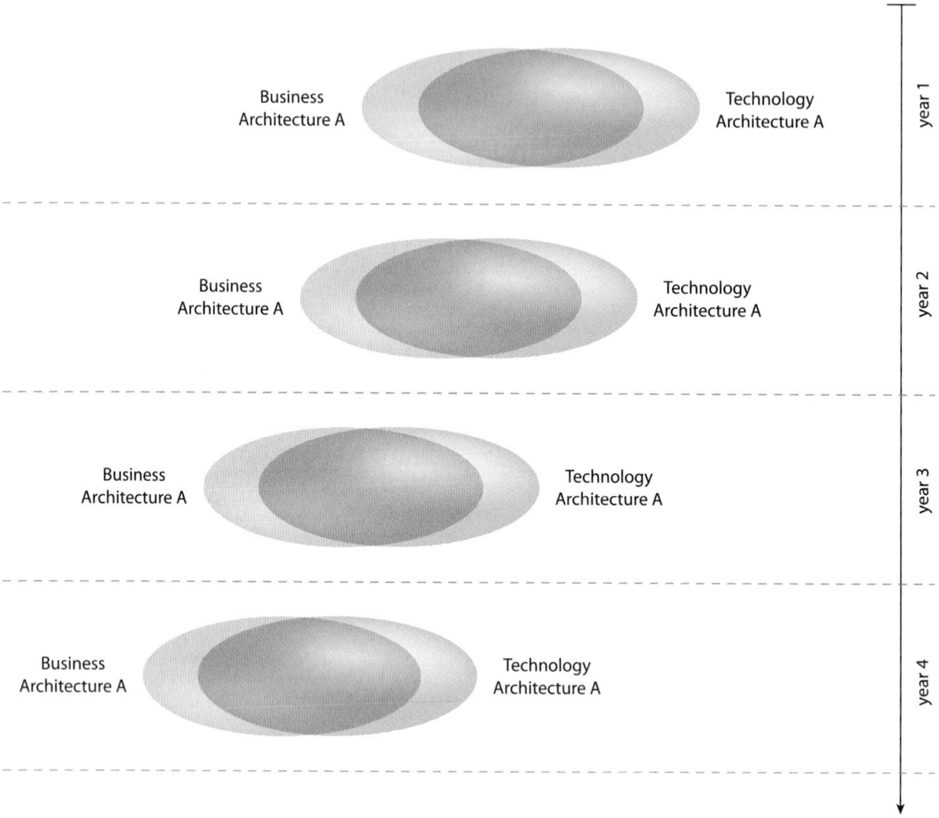

Figure 4.3
By defining a strategic, business-centric scope to the technology architecture, it can be kept in constant synch with how the business evolves over time.

It is in the best interest of an organization to base the design of a service-oriented architecture on a model that is in alignment with the primary SOA vendor platforms, yet neutral to all of them. A vendor-neutral architectural model can be derived from a vendor-neutral design paradigm used to build the solution logic the architecture will be responsible for supporting. The service-orientation paradigm provides such an approach, in that it is derived from and applicable to real world technology platforms while remaining independent of them.

NOTE

Just because an architecture is classified as vendor-neutral doesn't mean it is also *aligned* with current vendor technology. Some models produced by independent efforts are out of synch with the manner in which mainstream SOA technology exists today and is expected to evolve in the future and can therefore be just as inhibitive as vendor-specific models.

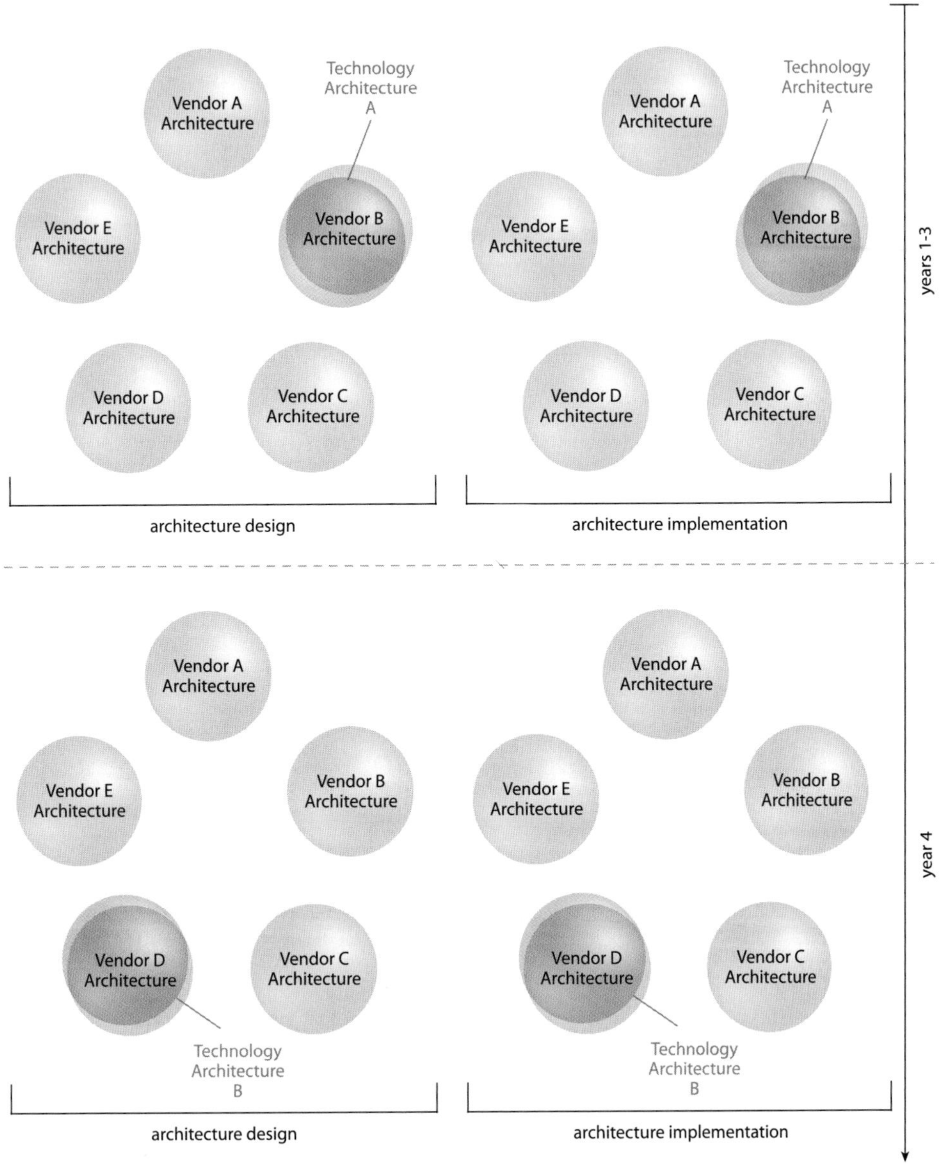

Figure 4.4

Vendor-centric technology architectures are often bound to corresponding vendor platform roadmaps. This can reduce opportunities to leverage technology innovations provided by other vendor platforms and can result in the need to eventually replace the architecture entirely with a new vendor implementation (which starts the cycle over again).

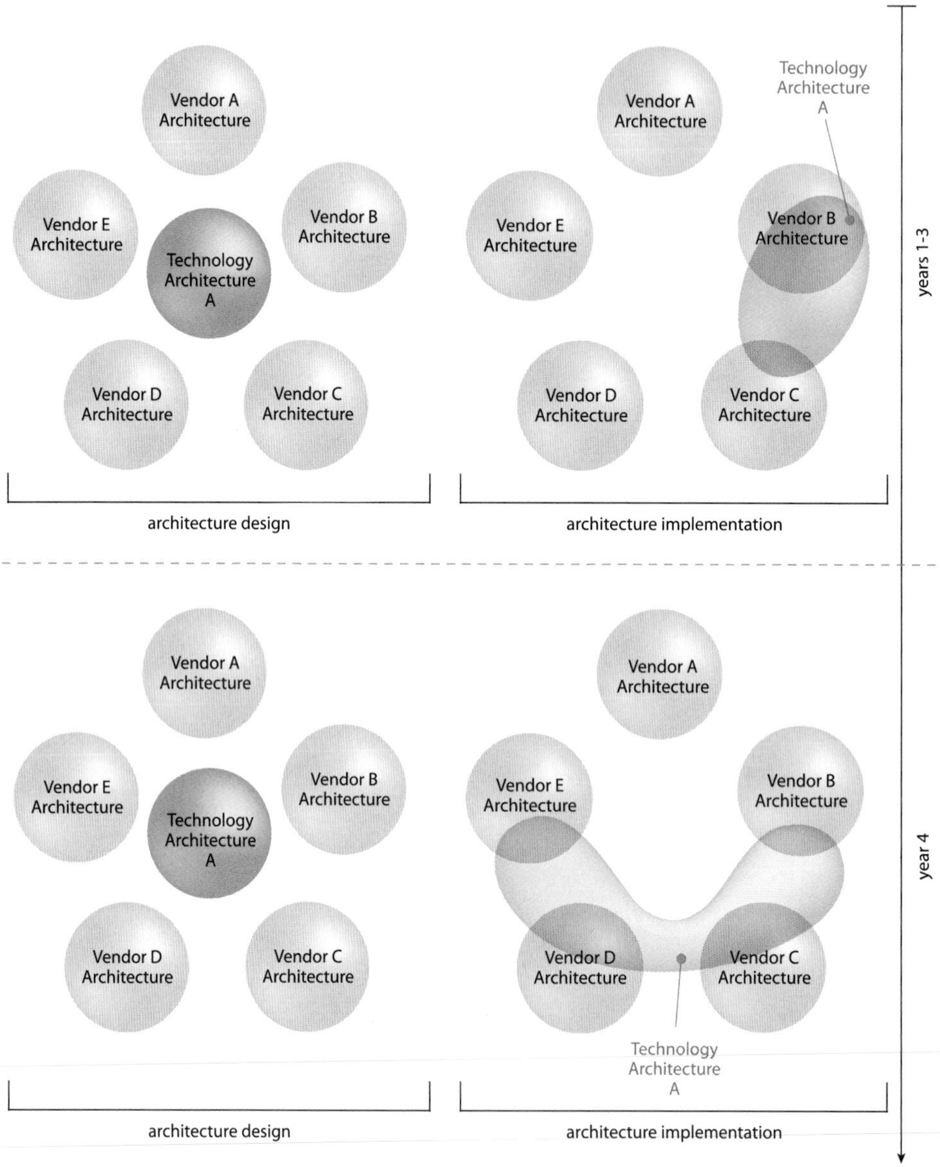

Figure 4.5

If the architectural model is designed to be and remain neutral to vendor platforms, it maintains the freedom to diversify its implementation by leveraging multiple vendor technology innovations. This increases the longevity of the architecture as it is allowed to augment and evolve in response to changing requirements.

Enterprise-Centric

Just because solutions are based on a distributed architecture doesn't mean that there still isn't the constant danger of creating new silos. In fact, it has been common to build distributed solutions comprised of single-purpose components. Software programs labeled as services that are designed in this manner naturally result in silos (Figure 4.6) that continue to bloat the enterprise and lead to traditional integration requirements.

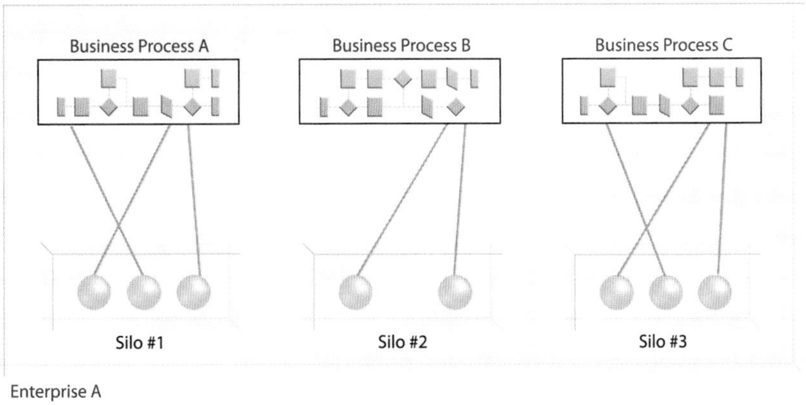

Figure 4.6
Single-purpose services delivered to automate specific business processes end up establishing silos within the enterprise.

When applying service-orientation, services are positioned as *enterprise resources,* which implies that service logic is designed with the following primary characteristics:

- The logic is available beyond a specific implementation boundary.
- The logic is designed according to established design principles and enterprise standards.

Essentially, the body of logic is classified as a resource of the enterprise. This does not necessarily make it an enterprise-*wide* resource or one that must be used throughout an entire technical environment. In other words, an enterprise resource does not belong solely to any one application or solution environment.

As further established in the pattern description for Service Encapsulation (305), an enterprise resource essentially embodies the fundamental characteristics of service logic.

> **NOTE**
>
> See the *Enterprise vs. Enterprise-wide* section in Chapter 5 for a comparison of how these two terms are used in this book.

In order to leverage services as enterprise resources, the underlying technology architecture must establish a model that is natively based on the assumption that software programs delivered as services will be shared by other parts of the enterprise or will be part of larger solutions that include shared services. This baseline requirement places an emphasis on standardizing parts of the architecture (as per the canonical patterns introduced in Chapter 5) so that service reuse and interoperability can be continually fostered (Figure 4.7).

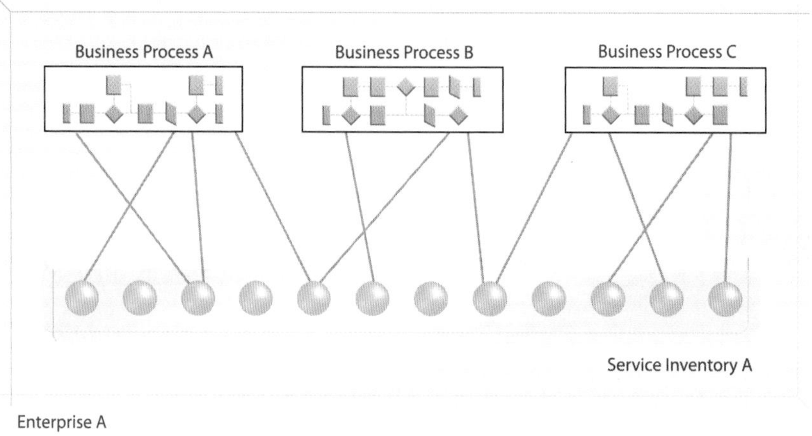

Figure 4.7
When services are positioned as enterprise resources they no longer create or reside in silos. Instead they are made available to a broader scope of utilization by being part of a service inventory.

Composition-Centric

More so than in previous distributed computing paradigms, service-orientation places an emphasis on designing software programs as not just reusable resources, but as flexible resources that can be plugged into different aggregate structures as part of a variety of service-oriented solutions.

To accomplish this, services must be composable. As advocated by the Service Composability principle, this means that services must be capable of being pulled into a variety of composition designs, regardless of whether they are initially required to participate in a composition when they are first delivered (Figure 4.8).

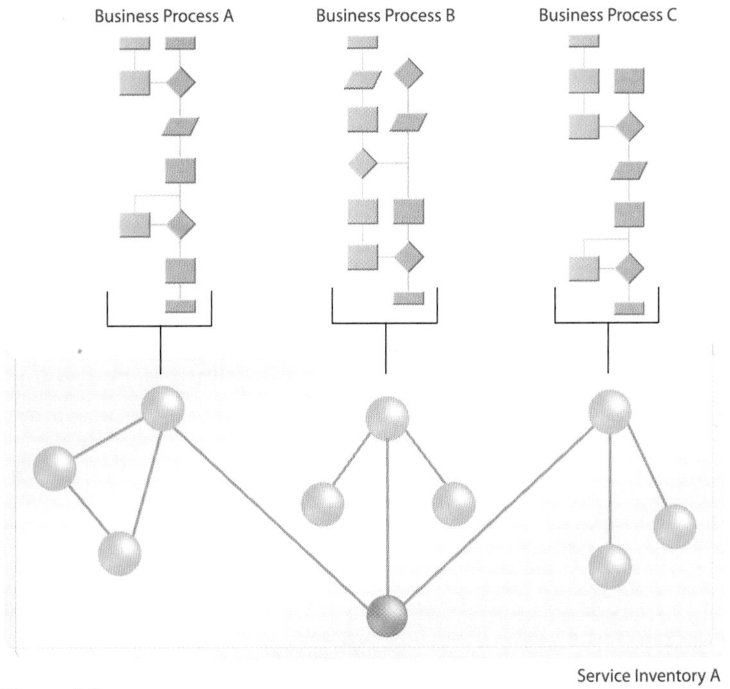

Figure 4.8

Services within the same service inventory are composed into different configurations. The highlighted service is reused by multiple compositions to automate different business processes.

To support native composability, the underlying technology architecture must be prepared to enable a range of simple and complex composition designs. Architectural extensions (and related infrastructure extensions) pertaining to scalability, reliability, and runtime data exchange processing and integrity are essential to support this key characteristic.

> **NOTE**
>
> In the next section we introduce four specific types of service-oriented architecture. The aforementioned architectural characteristics are fundamental to all of these SOA types; however, it is worth singling out the service inventory as the primary starting point for their implementation. We revisit these four characteristics at the beginning of Chapter 6 to highlight how they relate to fundamental inventory patterns.

SUMMARY OF KEY POINTS

- The four fundamental characteristics that any form of SOA needs to have in support of service-orientation are Business-Driven, Vendor-Neutral, Enterprise-Centric, and Composition-Centric.
- Whereas the Business-Driven and Vendor-Neutral characteristics help shape the overall context and model of a service-oriented architecture, the Enterprise-Centric and Composition-Centric characteristics place demands on the actual technology and infrastructure extensions that the architecture is based upon.
- The fundamental inventory patterns in Chapter 6 are closely related to these four characteristics.

4.3 The Four Common Types of SOA

As we've already established, every software program ends up being comprised of and residing in some form of architectural combination of resources, technologies, and platforms (infrastructure-related or otherwise). If we take the time to customize these architectural elements, we can establish a refined and standardized environment for the implementation of (also customized) software programs.

The intentional design of technology architecture is very important to service-oriented computing. It is essential to establishing an environment within which services can be repeatedly recomposed to maximize business requirements fulfillment. As evidenced by the range of architectural design patterns in this book, the strategic benefit to customizing the scope, context, and boundary of an architecture is significant.

To better understand the basic mechanics of SOA, we now need to study the common types of technology architectures that exist:

- *Service Architecture* – The architecture of a single service.
- *Service Composition Architecture* – The architecture of a set of services assembled into a service composition.
- *Service Inventory Architecture* – The architecture that supports a collection of related services that are independently standardized and governed.
- *Service-Oriented Enterprise Architecture* – The architecture of the enterprise itself, to whatever extent it is service-oriented.

Although they are roughly comparable to the four traditional architecture types described in the *Architecture Fundamentals* section in Chapter 3, each is distinct due to the unique requirements and dynamics of service-orientation (Figure 4.9). The next four sections explore these SOA types individually.

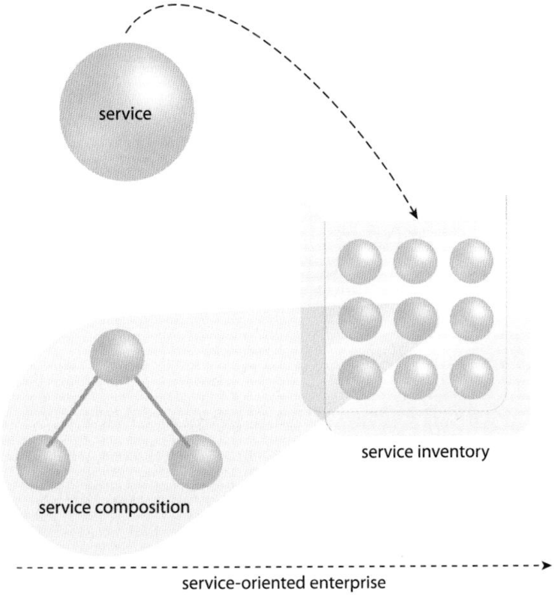

Figure 4.9
Services (top left) are delivered into a service inventory (right) from which service compositions (bottom left) are drawn. These basic elements establish the fundamental service-orientation dynamic but also represent the three common SOA types that can reside within a service-oriented enterprise (bottom).

Service Architecture

A technology architecture limited to the physical design of a software program designed as a service is referred to as the *service architecture*. This form of technology architecture is comparable in scope to a component architecture, except that it will typically rely on a greater amount of infrastructure extensions to support its need for increased reliability, performance, scalability, behavioral predictability, and especially its need for increased autonomy. The scope of a service architecture will also tend to be larger because a service can, among other things, encompass multiple components.

Whereas it was not always that common to document a separate architecture for a component in traditional distributed applications, the importance of producing services that need to exist as independent and highly self-sufficient and self-contained software programs requires that each be individually designed. Figure 4.10 shows a highly simplified view of a sample service architecture.

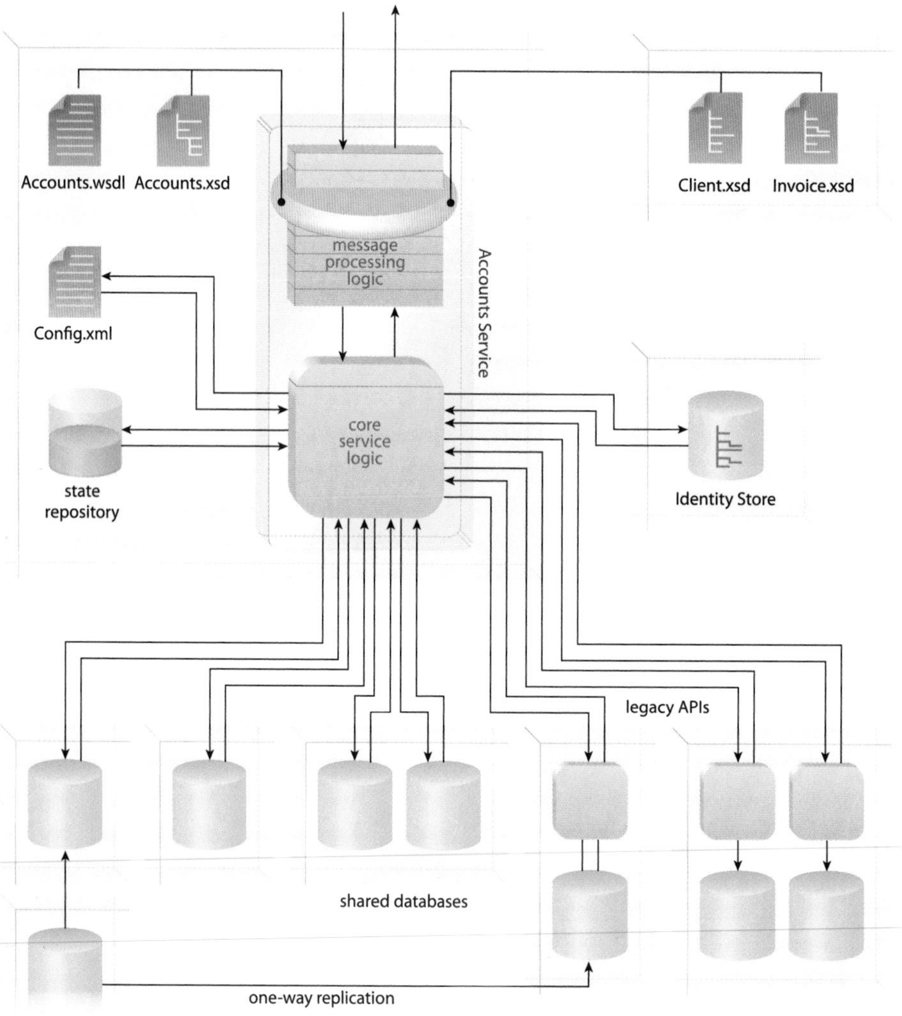

Figure 4.10

An example of a high-level service architecture view for the Accounts Web service, depicting the parts of the surrounding infrastructure utilized to fulfill the functional requirements of all capabilities (or operations). Additional views can be created to show only those architectural elements related to the processing of specific capabilities. Further detail, such as data flow and security requirements, would normally also be included.

Information Hiding

Service architecture specifications are typically owned by service custodians and, in support of the Service Abstraction design principle, their contents are often protected and hidden from other project team members (Figure 4.11).

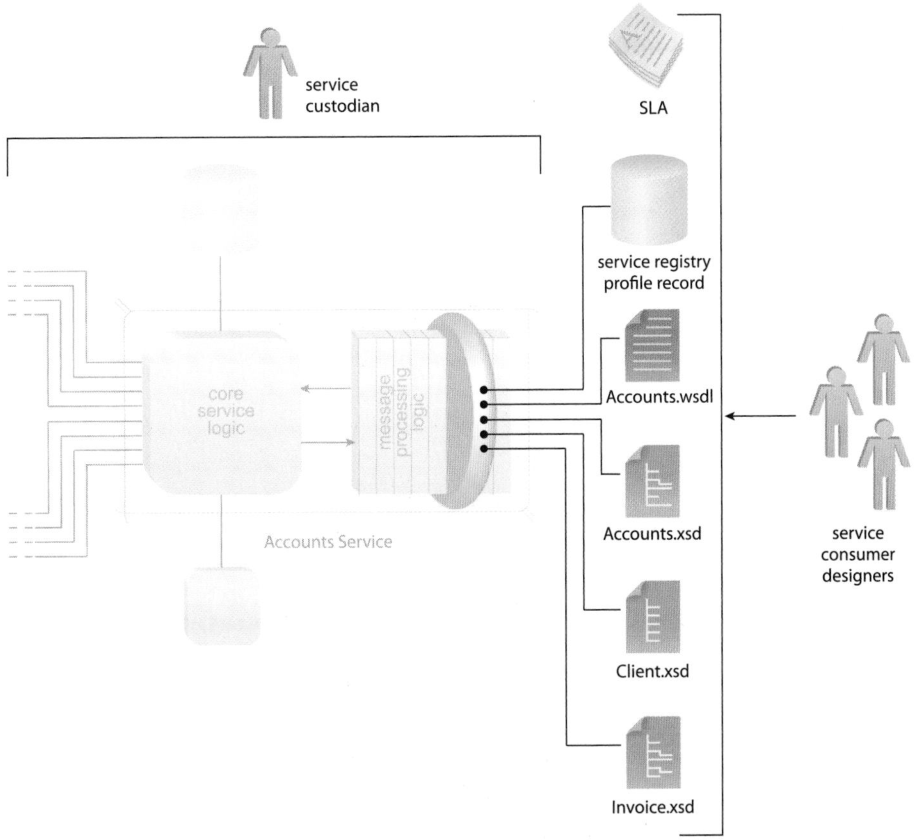

Figure 4.11
The custodian of the Accounts service intentionally limits access to architecture documentation. As a result, service consumer designers are only privy to published service contract documents.

Design Standards

The application of design standards and other service-orientation design principles (Figure 4.12) further affects the depth and detail to which a service's technology architecture may need to be defined. For example, implementation consideration raised by the Service Autonomy and Service Statelessness principles can require a service architecture to extend deeply into its surrounding infrastructure by defining exactly what physical environment it is deployed within, what resources it needs to access, what other parts of the enterprise may

be accessing those same resources, and what extensions from the infrastructure it can use to defer or store data it is responsible for processing.

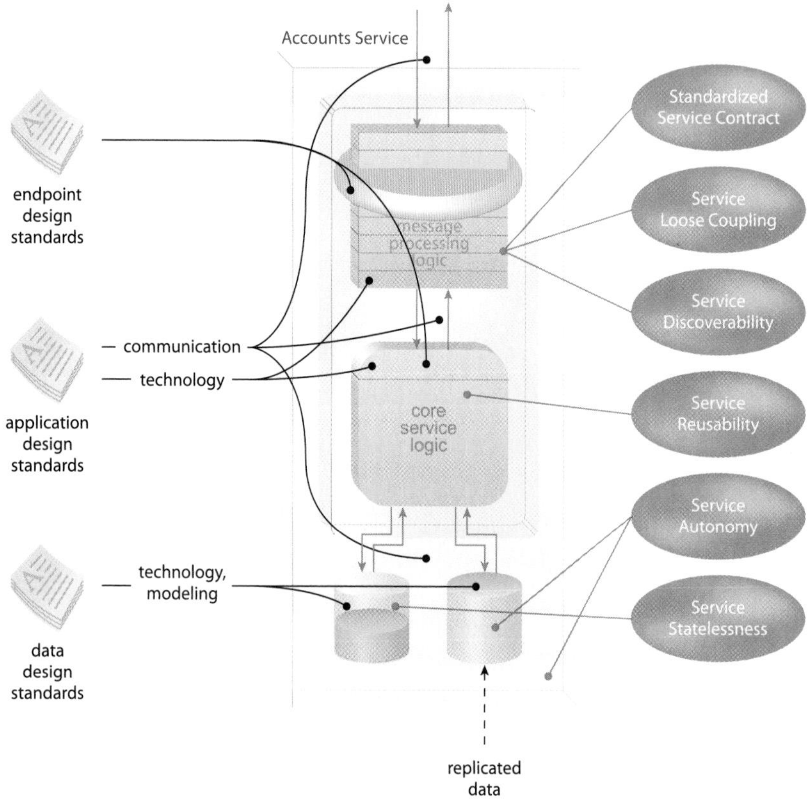

Figure 4.12

Custom design standards and service-orientation design principles are applied to establish a specific set of design characteristics within the Accounts service architecture.

Service Contracts

A central part of a service architecture is typically its technical contract (Figure 4.13). Following standard service-oriented design processes, the service contract is usually the first part of a service to be physically delivered. The capabilities expressed by the contract further dictate the scope and nature of its underlying logic and the processing requirements that will need to be supported by its implementation.

This is why some consideration is given to implementation during a service's modeling phase (which occurs prior to its physical design).

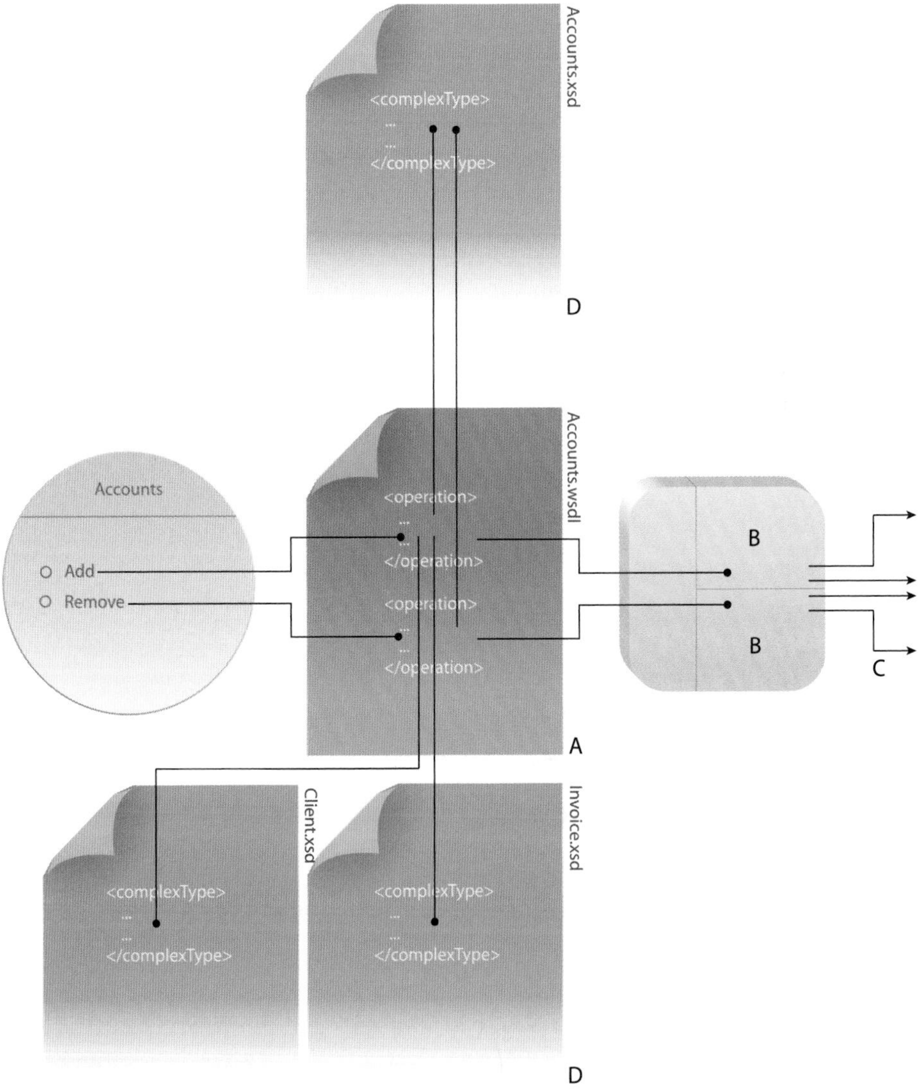

Figure 4.13

The service contract is a fundamental part of the Accounts service architecture. Its definition gives the service a public identity and helps express its functional scope. Specifically, the WSDL document (A) expresses operations that correspond to segments of functionality (B) within the underlying Accounts service logic. The logic, in turn, accesses other resources in the enterprise to carry out those functions (C). To accomplish this, the WSDL document provides data exchange definitions via input and output message types established in separate XML Schema documents (D).

NOTE

Many organizations use standard *service profile documents* to collect and maintain information about a service throughout its lifespan. Chapter 15 of *SOA Principles of Service Design* explains the service profile document and provides a sample template.

Service Agents

Another infrastructure-related aspect of service design is any dependencies the service may have on service agents—event-driven intermediary programs capable of transparently intercepting and processing messages sent to or from a service (Figure 4.14). Service agents can be custom-developed or may be provided by the underlying runtime environment, and they form the basis of a pattern appropriately titled Service Agent (543).

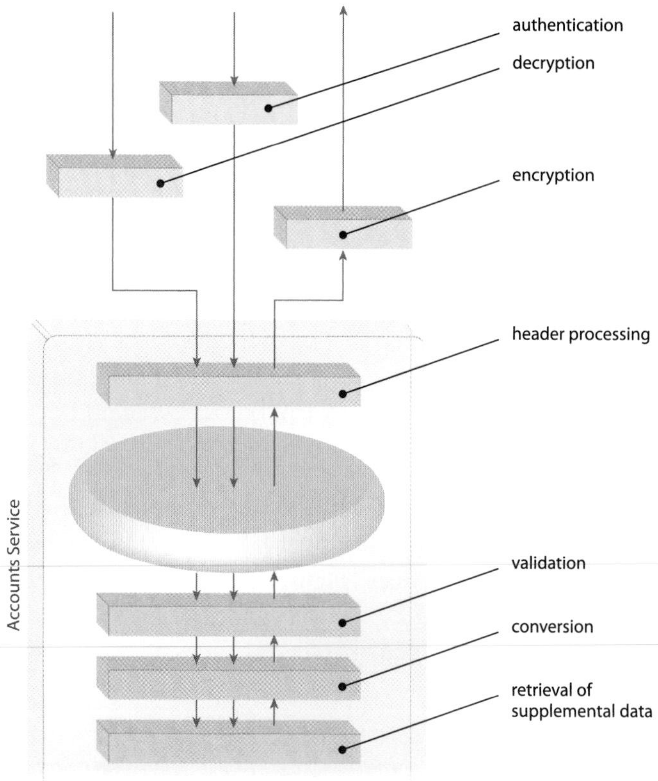

Figure 4.14

A variety of service agents are part of the Accounts service architecture. Some perform general processing of all data while others are specific to input or output data flow.

Within a service architecture the specific agent programs may be identified along with run-time information as to how message contents are processed or even altered by agent involvement. Service agents may themselves have their own architecture specifications that can be referenced by the service architecture.

Service Capabilities

A key consideration with any service architecture is the fact that the functionality offered by a service resides within one or more individual capabilities (Figure 4.15). This often requires the architecture definition itself to be taken to the capability level.

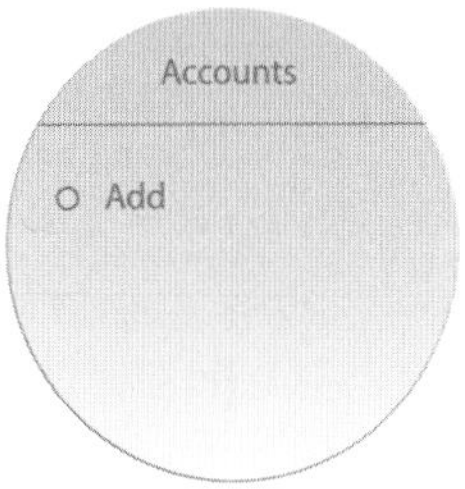

Figure 4.15
The Accounts service with an Add capability.

Each service capability encapsulates its own piece of logic, although the underlying logic may itself be modularized allowing different capabilities to share the same routines. Some of this logic may be custom-developed for the service, whereas other capabilities may represent or need to access one or more back-end resources (including other services). Therefore, individual capabilities end up with their own, individual designs that may need to be so detailed that they are documented as separate "capability architectures," all of which relate back to the parent service architecture.

Service Composition Architecture

The fundamental purpose of delivering a series of independent services is so that they can be combined into service compositions—fully functional solutions capable of automating larger, more complex business tasks (Figure 4.16).

Each service composition has a corresponding *service composition architecture*. In much the same way an application architecture for a distributed system includes the individual architecture definitions of its components, this form of architecture encompasses the service architectures of all participating services (Figure 4.17).

NOTE

Standard composition terminology defines two basic roles that services can assume within a composition. The service responsible for composing others takes on the role of *composition controller*, whereas composed services are referred to as *composition members*.

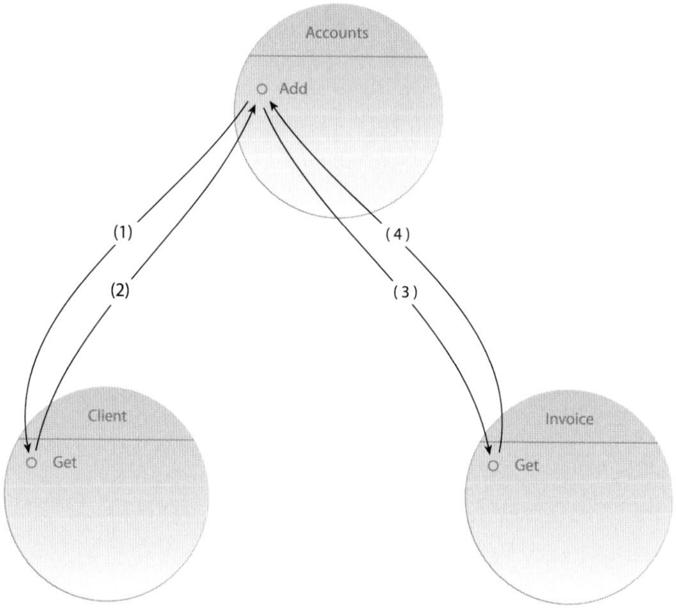

Figure 4.16
The Accounts service composition from a modeling perspective. The numbered arrows indicate the sequence of data flow and service interaction required for the Add capability to compose capabilities within the Client and Invoice services.

A composition architecture (especially one that composes services that encapsulate disparate legacy systems) may be compared to a traditional integration architecture. This comparison is usually only valid in scope, as the design considerations emphasized by service-orientation ensure that the design of a service composition is much different than that of integrated applications.

For example, one difference in how composition architectures are documented is in the extent of detail they include about reusable services involved in the composition. Because these types of service architecture specifications are often guarded (as per the requirements raised by the Service Abstraction principle), a composition architecture may only be able to make reference to the technical interface and service-level agreement (SLA) published as part of the service's public contract (Figure 4.18).

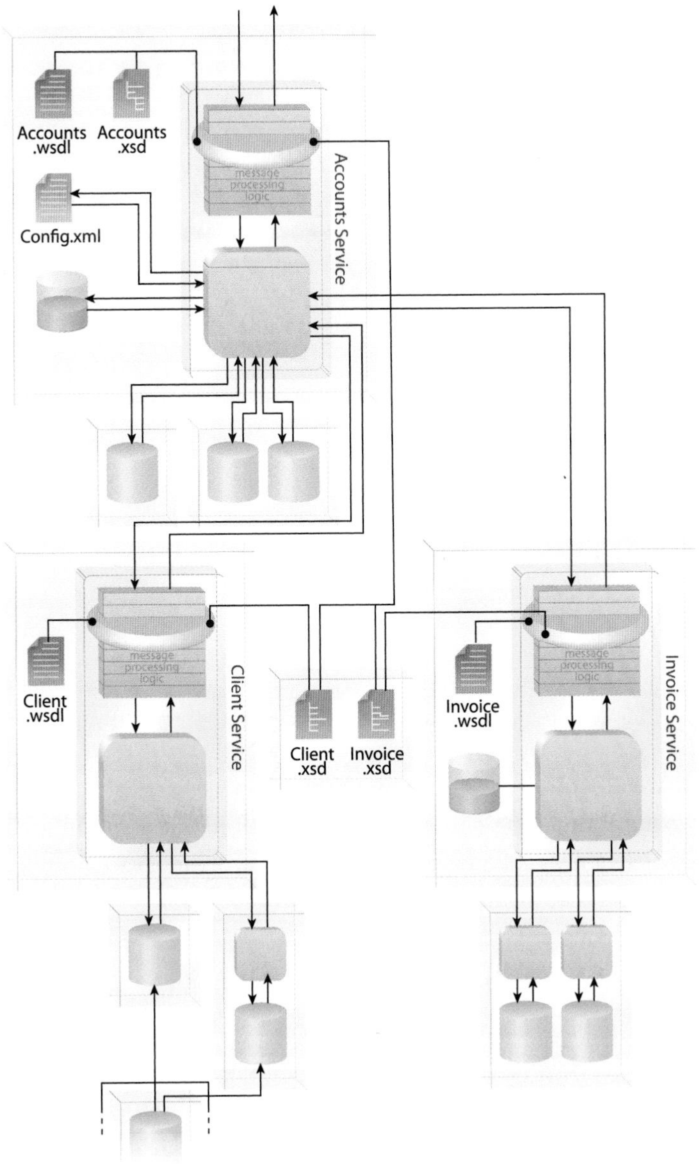

Figure 4.17

The same Accounts service composition from Figure 4.16 viewed from a physical architecture perspective illustrating how each composition member's underlying resources provide the functionality required to automate the process logic represented by the Accounts Add capability.

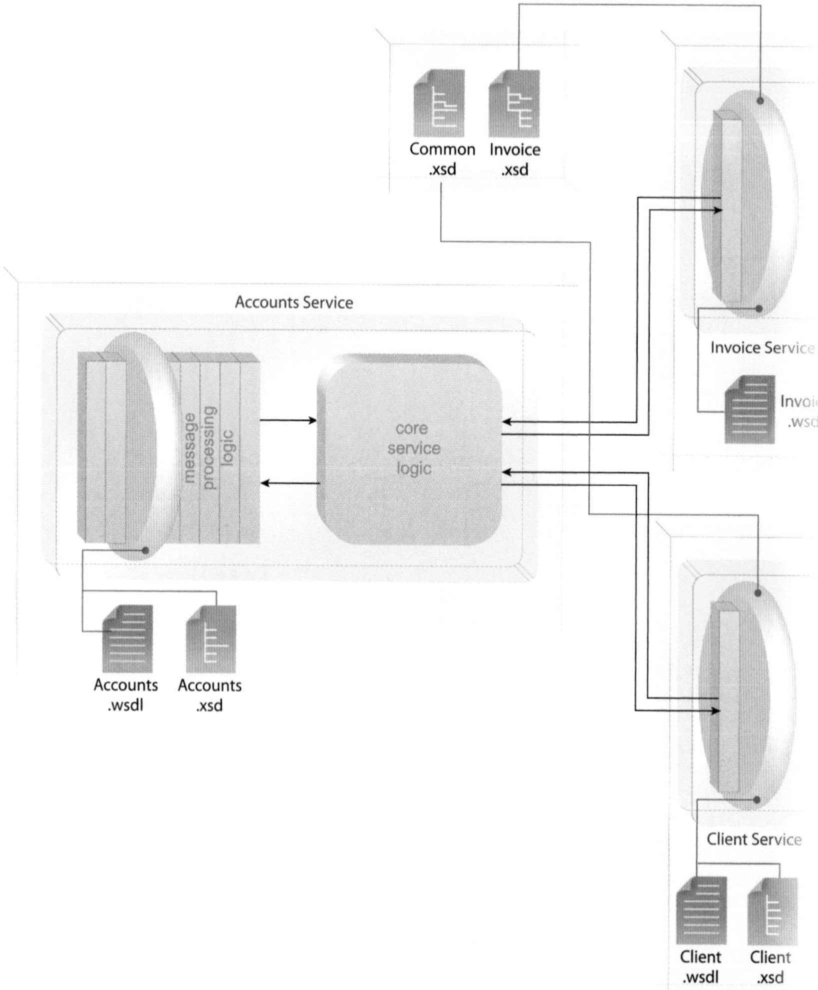

Figure 4.18

The physical service architecture view from Figure 4.17 is not available to the designer of the Accounts service. Instead, only the information published in the contracts for the Invoice and Client services can be accessed and referenced in the Account service composition architecture.

> **NOTE**
>
> Even though compositions are comprised of services, it is actually the service capabilities that are individually invoked and executed in order to carry out the composition logic. This is why design patterns, such as Capability Composition (521) and Capability Recomposition (526) make specific reference to the composed capability (as opposed to the composed service).

Nested Compositions

Another rather unique aspect of service composition architecture is that a composition may find itself a nested part of a larger parent composition, and therefore one composition architecture may encompass or reference another (Figure 4.19).

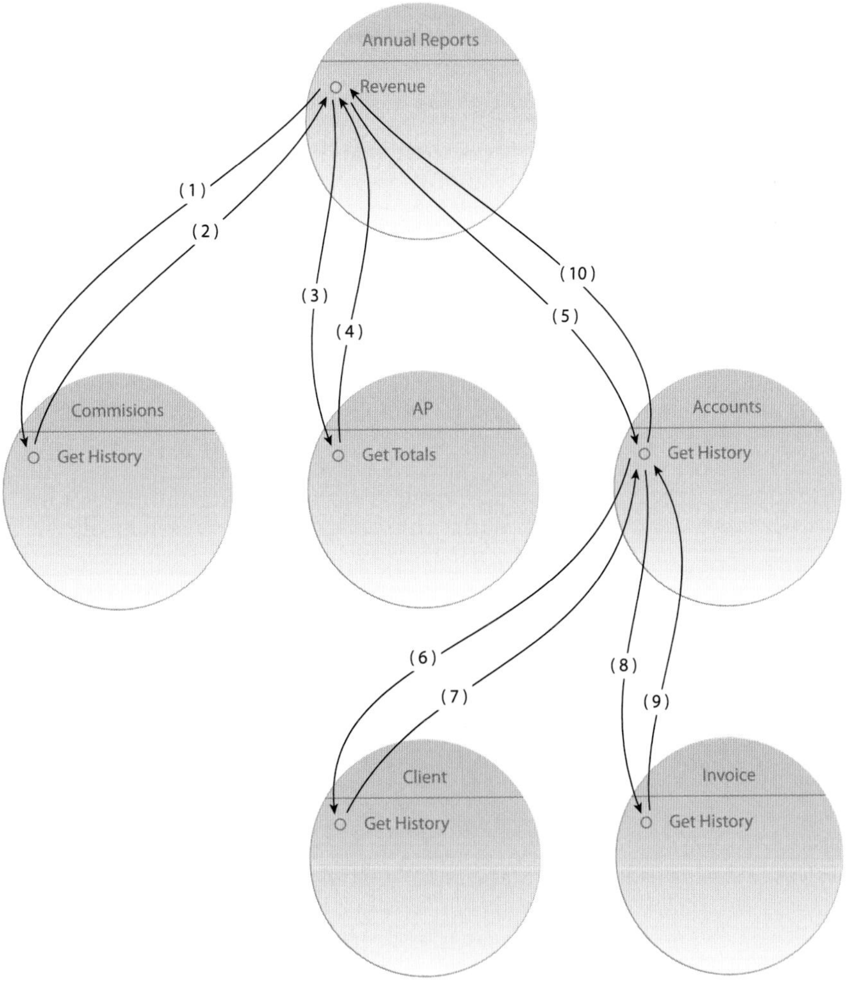

Figure 4.19

The Accounts service finds itself nested within the larger Annual Reports composition that composes the Accounts Get History capability which, in turn, composes capabilities within the Client and Invoice services.

Task Services and Alternative Compositions

Service composition architectures are much more than just an accumulation of individual service architectures (or contracts). A newly created composition is usually accompanied by a task-specific service that is positioned as the composition controller. The details of this service are less private, and its design is an integral part of the architecture because it usually provides most of the composition logic required.

Furthermore, the business process the service is required to automate may involve the need for composition logic capable of dealing with multiple runtime scenarios (exception-related or otherwise), each of which may result in a different composition configuration (Figure 4.20). These scenarios and their related service activities and message paths are a common part of composition designs. They need to be understood and mapped out in advance so that the composition logic encapsulated by the task service is fully prepared to deal with the range of runtime situations it faces.

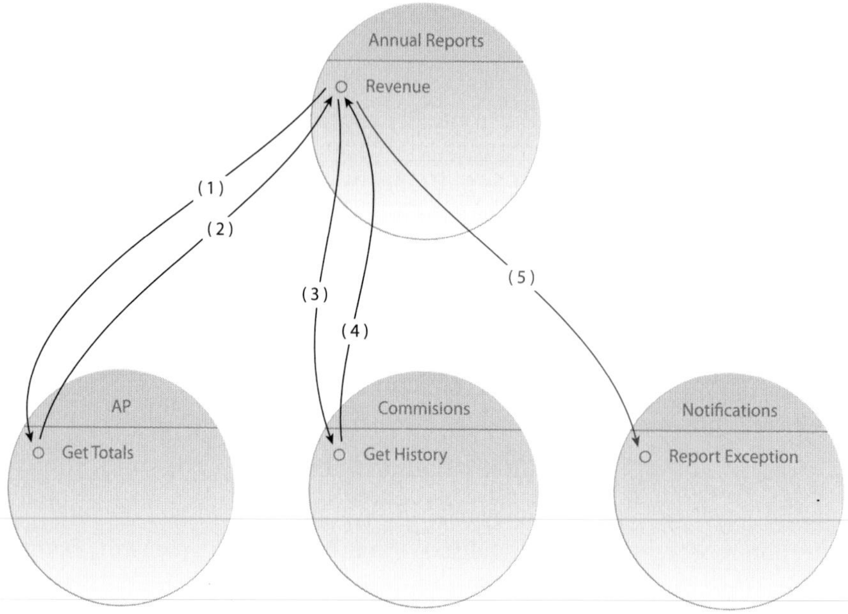

Figure 4.20

A given business process may need to be automated by a range of service compositions in order to accommodate different runtime scenarios. In this case, alternative composition logic within the Annual Report's Revenue capability kicks in to deal with an exception condition. As a result, the Notification service is invoked prior to the Accounts service even being included in the composition. (This scenario represents an alternative composition design to the one shown in Figure 4.19.)

Compositions and Infrastructure

A composition architecture will be heavily dependent on the activity management features of the underlying runtime environment responsible for hosting the services participating in the composition. Security, transaction management, reliable messaging, and other infrastructure extensions, such as support for sophisticated message routing, may all find their way into a typical composition architecture specification. Numerous patterns in this book address these types of extensions.

> **NOTE**
>
> It's often difficult to determine where a service architecture ends and where a composition architecture begins. One service can compose others, which can make a given composition architecture seem like an extension of a service architecture. Often these lines are drawn when the Service Abstraction principle is applied, thereby defining clean boundaries around service architectures that are hidden from the overall composition design.

Service Inventory Architecture

Services delivered independently or as part of compositions by different IT projects risk introducing redundancy and non-standardization. This can lead to a non-federated enterprise in which clusters of services mimic an environment comprised of traditional siloed applications.

The result is that though often classified as a service-oriented architecture, many of the traditional challenges associated with design disparity, transformation, and integration continue to emerge and undermine strategic service-oriented computing goals.

As first explained in Chapter 3, a service inventory is a collection of independently standardized and governed services delivered within a pre-defined architectural boundary. This collection represents a meaningful scope that exceeds the processing boundary of a single business process and ideally spans numerous business processes. The scope and boundary of a service inventory architecture can vary, as explained in the Enterprise Inventory (116) and Domain Inventory (123) pattern descriptions.

Ideally, the service inventory is first conceptually modeled, leading to the creation of a service inventory blueprint. It is often this blueprint that ends up defining the required scope of the architecture type referred to as a service inventory architecture (Figure 4.21).

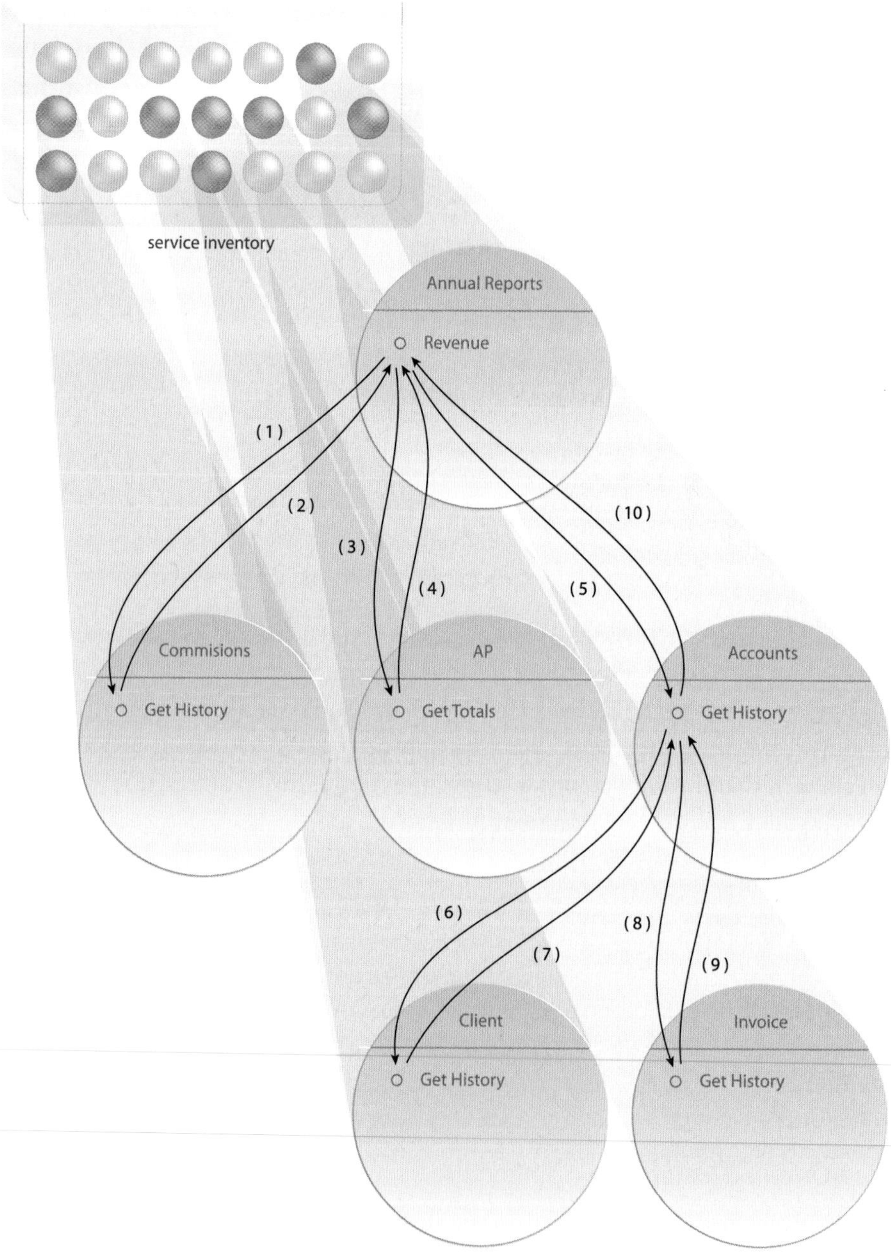

Figure 4.21

Ultimately, the services within an inventory can be composed and recomposed, as represented by different composition architectures. To that end, many of the design patterns in this book need to be consistently applied within the boundary of the service inventory.

From an enterprise design perspective, the service inventory can represent a concrete boundary for a standardized architecture implementation. This means that because the services within an inventory are standardized, so are the technologies and extensions provided by the underlying architecture.

As evidenced by the inventory boundary design patterns in Chapter 6, the scope of a service inventory can be enterprise-wide, or it can represent a domain within the enterprise. For that reason, this type of architecture is not called a "domain architecture." It relates to the scope of the inventory boundary, which may encompass multiple domains.

NOTE

When the term "SOA" or "SOA implementation" is used, it is most commonly associated with the scope of a service inventory. In fact, with the exception of some design patterns that address cross-inventory exchanges, most of the patterns in this book are expected to be applied within the boundary of a service inventory.

It is difficult to compare a service inventory architecture with traditional types of architecture because the concept of an inventory has not been common. The closest candidate would be an integration architecture that represents some significant segment of an enterprise. However, this comparison would be only relevant in scope, as service-orientation design characteristics and related standardization efforts strive to turn a service inventory into a highly homogenous environment .

NOTE

For more information about how service-orientation differs from and attempts to address the primary challenges associated with silo-based, standalone application environments, see SOAPrinciples.com. To learn more about defining service inventory blueprints, visit SOAMethodology.com.

Service-Oriented Enterprise Architecture

This form of technology architecture essentially represents all service, service composition, and service inventory architectures that reside within a specific IT enterprise.

A service-oriented enterprise architecture is comparable to a traditional enterprise technical architecture only when most or all of an enterprise's technical environments are service-oriented. Otherwise it may simply be a documentation of the parts of the enterprise that have adopted SOA, in which case it exists as a subset of the parent enterprise technology architecture.

In multi-inventory environments or in environments where standardization efforts were not fully successful, a service-oriented enterprise architecture specification will further document any transformation points and design disparity that may also exist.

Additionally, the service-oriented enterprise architecture can further establish enterprise-wide design standards and conventions to which all service, composition, and inventory architecture implementations need to comply, and which may also need to be referenced in the corresponding architecture specifications. (Canonical Resources (237) represents a pattern that may introduce such standards.)

NOTE

This chapter is focused on technology architecture only. It is worth pointing out that a "complete" service-oriented enterprise architecture would encompass both the technology and business architecture of an enterprise (much like traditional enterprise architecture).

Architecture Types and Scope

Figure 4.22 illustrates how each of the previously described service-oriented architecture types establishes its own scope. Service architectures fall within composition architectures and both are natural parts of a service inventory architecture. The service-oriented enterprise architecture represents a parent architecture that encompasses all others.

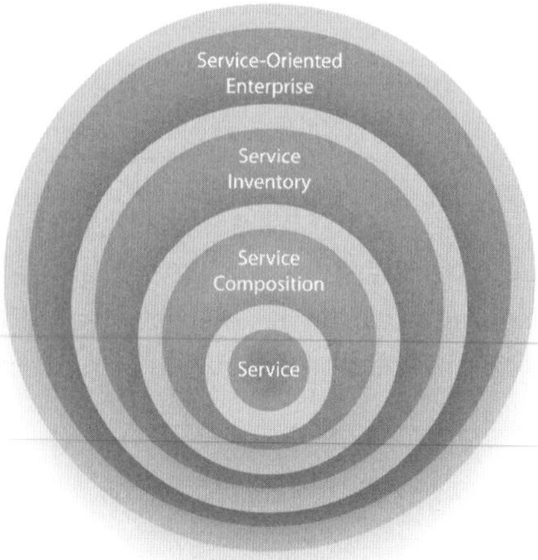

Figure 4.22

A layered model of how service-oriented architecture types encompass each other. This view highlights the common levels of SOA that exist within a typical enterprise.

Architecture Types and Inheritance

The environment and conventions established by the enterprise are carried over into individual service inventory architecture implementations that may reside within a

single enterprise environment. These inventories further introduce new and more specific architectural elements (such as runtime platforms and middleware) that then form the foundation of service and composition architectures implemented within the inventory boundary.

As a result, a natural form of architectural inheritance is formed. This relationship between architecture types is good to keep in mind as it can identify potential (positive and negative) dependencies that may exist.

Other Forms of Service-Oriented Architecture

All of the architecture types explored so far relate mostly to a private IT enterprise environment. While these represent the most common variations, they are by no means the only ones. The following two sections discuss some examples of additional architecture types with different scopes and characteristics.

Inter-Business Service Architecture

This is an architecture that spans enterprises and therefore is prone to encompass diverse environments and incompatible design conventions. A focal point is often the use of transformation technologies, security, and access to subsets of inventory logic.

Note that an inter-business service architecture is different from a traditional B2B environment. Data exchange is designed around communication across partner service inventories via predefined service endpoints and can include specialized compositions that also span inventories.

Service-Oriented Community Architecture

With the advent of community-centric data exchange standards, such as the Web Services Choreography Description Language (WS-CDL) and a growing marketplace of third-party services, the option is there to define a service-oriented architecture dedicated to collaboration among community members.

NOTE

Patterns, such as Service Perimeter Guard (394), Inventory Endpoint (260), and many of the security patterns in Chapters 13 and 20, are often used to support this SOA type.

Additional variations of service-oriented architecture can exist. For example, hybrid architectures comprised of a combination of traditional and service-oriented elements may be created as a result of pilot or partially completed transition projects, or they may exist as an intermediate architecture while a larger-scale migration is still underway.

SUMMARY OF KEY POINTS

- A service architecture represents the technology architecture that pertains to a service and any of the enterprise resources its capabilities may need to access or rely upon.
- A service composition architecture corresponds to a service composition and therefore encompasses the individual architectures of its member services as well as any additional architectural elements that may be required to carry out the composition logic.
- A service inventory architecture typically represents a significant scope that encompasses all service and composition architectures related to the boundary of a pre-defined service inventory.
- A service-oriented enterprise architecture represents all service inventories within an enterprise and further defines cross-inventory communication options and enterprise design standards.

4.4 The End Result of Service-Orientation

Automated business communities and the IT industry have an endless bi-directional relationship where each influences the other. Business demands and trends create automation requirements that the IT community strives to fulfill. New method and technology innovations produced by the IT community help inspire organizations to improve their existing business and even try out new lines of business. (The advent of the Internet is a good example of the latter.)

The IT industry has been through the cycle depicted in Figure 4.23 many times. Each iteration has brought about change and generally an increase in the sophistication and complexity of technology platforms.

Sometimes a series of iterations through this progress cycle leads to a foundational shift in the overall approach to automation and computing itself. The emergence of major platforms and frameworks, such as object-orientation and enterprise application integration,

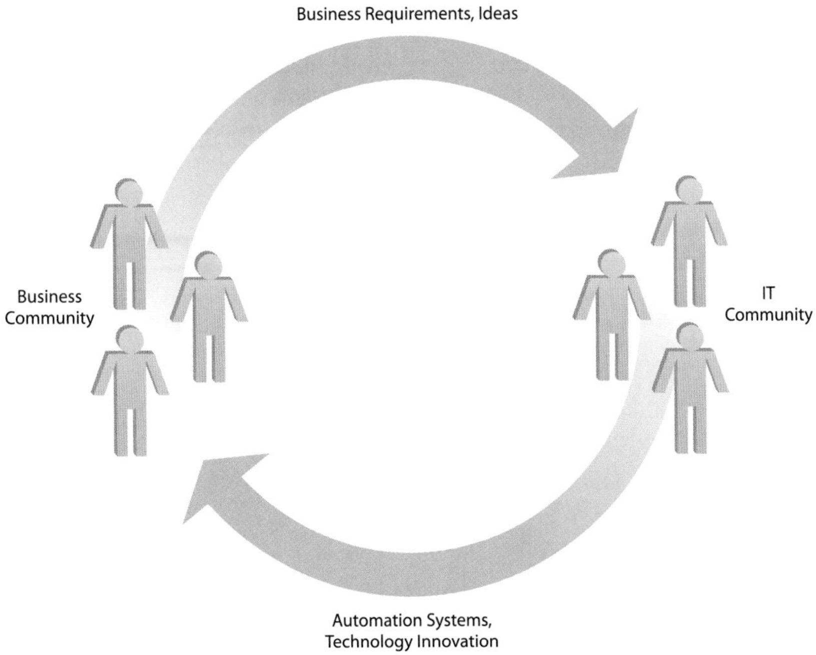

Figure 4.23

The endless progress cycle establishes the dynamics between the business and IT communities.

are examples of this. Significant changes like these represent an accumulation of technologies and methods and can therefore be considered landmarks in the evolution of IT itself. Each also results in the formation of distinct technology architecture requirements.

Service-oriented computing is no exception. The platform it establishes provides the potential to achieve significant strategic benefits that are a reflection of what business communities are currently demanding, as represented by the following previously described goals:

- Increased Intrinsic Interoperability
- Increased Federation
- Increased Vendor Diversification Options
- Increased Business and Technology Domain Alignment
- Increased ROI
- Increased Organizational Agility
- Reduced IT Burden

It is the target state resulting from the attainment of these strategic goals that an adoption of service-orientation attempts to achieve. In other words, these goals represent the desired end-result of applying the method of service-orientation.

How then does this relate to service-oriented technology architecture? Figure 4.24 hints at how the pursuit of these specific goals results in a series of impacts onto all architecture types brought upon by the application of service-orientation.

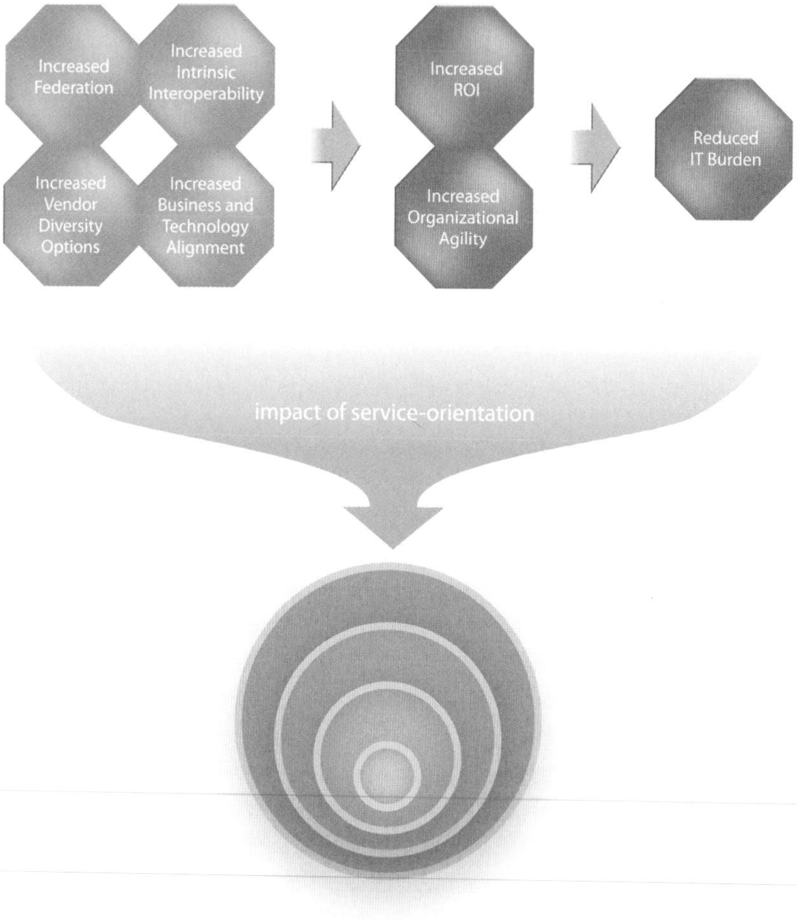

Figure 4.24

The common strategic goals and benefits of service-oriented computing are realized through the application of service-orientation. This, in turn, impacts the demands and requirements placed upon the four types of service-oriented technology architectures. (Note that the three goals on the right [green] represent the ultimate target benefits achieved when attaining the four goals on the left [gray].)

NOTE

For those of you interested in how each of the strategic goals relates to specific design patterns, see Chapter 23.

Almost all of the design patterns in this book are specifically intended to support the application of service-orientation by solving common problems that may arise as a result of the impact placed upon the different architecture types. This is an important perspective to keep in mind when working with SOA design patterns, as it is always helpful to understand that all patterns in this catalog share this common objective.

Ultimately, the successful implementation of service-oriented architectures will support and maintain the benefits associated with the strategic goals of service-oriented computing. As concluded by Figure 4.25, the progress cycle that continually transpires between business and IT communities results in constant change. Standardized, optimized, and overall robust service-oriented architectures fully support and even enable the accommodation of this change as a natural characteristic of a service-oriented enterprise.

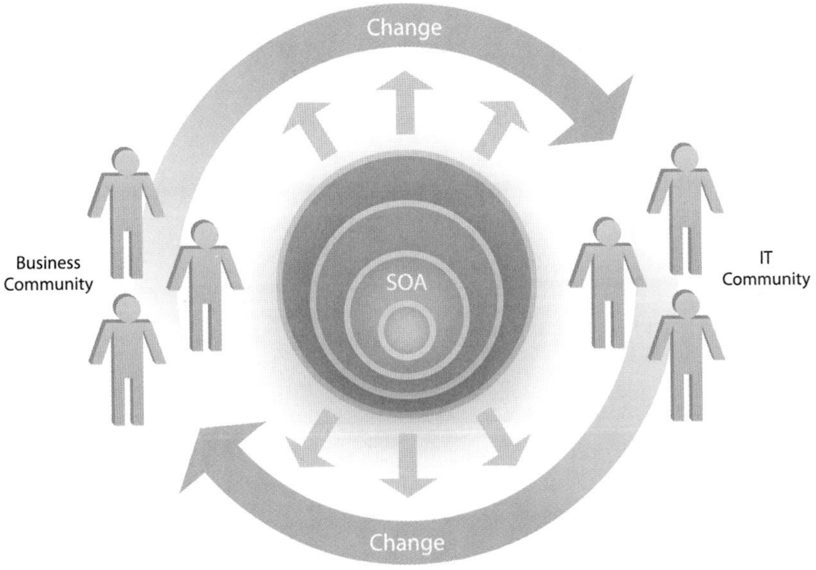

Figure 4.25

Ultimately, service-orientation and service-oriented technology architectures support the two-way dynamic between business and IT communities, allowing each to introduce or accommodate change throughout an endless cycle.

SUMMARY OF KEY POINTS

- Service-orientation places various demands on all types of service-oriented architectures.
- Specific requirements can be defined when studying each of the goals of service-oriented computing.

Chapter 5

Understanding SOA Design Patterns

The first step to forming an effective working relationship with SOA design patterns is attaining a sound comfort level with pattern-related terminology and notation. This provides us with the knowledge required to navigate through the upcoming chapters with insight as to how the patterns can be applied individually and in various combinations.

Purpose of this Introductory Chapter

This important chapter covers these fundamental topics and further describes how design pattern descriptions are organized into standardized profiles. The remaining sections single out specific pattern types and discuss some common design considerations.

5.1 Fundamental Terminology

What's a Design Pattern?

The simplest way to describe a pattern is that it provides a proven solution to a common problem individually documented in a consistent format and usually as part of a larger collection.

The notion of a pattern is already a fundamental part of everyday life. Without acknowledging it each time, we naturally use proven solutions to solve common problems each day. Patterns in the IT world that revolve around the design of automated systems are referred to as *design patterns*.

Design patterns are helpful because they:

- represent field-tested solutions to common design problems
- organize design intelligence into a standardized and easily "referencable" format
- are generally repeatable by most IT professionals involved with design
- can be used to ensure consistency in how systems are designed and built
- can become the basis for design standards
- are usually flexible and optional (and openly document the impacts of their application and even suggest alternative approaches)

- can be used as educational aids by documenting specific aspects of system design (regardless of whether they are applied)
- can sometimes be applied prior and subsequent to the implementation of a system
- can be supported via the application of other design patterns that are part of the same collection

Furthermore, because the solutions provided by design patterns are proven, their consistent application tends to naturally improve the quality of system designs.

Let's provide a simple (non SOA-related) example of a design pattern that addresses a user interface design problem:

Problem: *How can users be limited to entering one value of a set of predefined values into a form field?*

Solution: *Use a drop-down list populated with the predefined values as the input field.*

What this example also highlights is the fact that the solution provided by a given pattern may not necessarily represent the only suitable solution for that problem. In fact, there can be multiple patterns that provide alternative solutions for the same problem. Each solution will have its own requirements and consequences, and it is up to the practitioner to choose.

In the previous example, a different solution to the stated problem would be to use a list-box instead of a drop-down list. This alternative would form the basis of a separate design pattern description. The user-interface designer can study and compare both patterns to learn about the benefits and trade-offs of each. A drop-down list, for instance, takes up less space than a list box but requires that a user always perform a separate action to access the list. Because a list box can display more field lines at the same time, the user may have an easier time locating the desired value.

NOTE

Even though design patterns provide proven design solutions, their mere use cannot guarantee that design problems are always solved as required. Many factors weigh in to the ultimate success of using a design pattern, including constraints imposed by the implementation environment, competency of the practitioners, diverging business requirements, and so on. All of these represent aspects that affect the extent to which a pattern can be successfully applied.

What's a Compound Pattern?

A compound pattern is a coarse-grained pattern comprised of a set of finer-grained patterns. Compound patterns are explained in detail at the beginning of Chapter 22.

What's a Design Pattern Language?

A *pattern language* is a set of related patterns that act as building blocks in that they can be carried out in *pattern sequences* (or *pattern application sequences*), where each subsequent pattern builds upon the former. As explained shortly in the *Historical Influences* section, the notion of a pattern language originated in building architecture as did the term "pattern sequence" used in association with the order in which patterns can be carried out.

Some pattern languages are open-ended, allowing patterns to be combined into a variety of creative sequences, while others are more structured whereby groups of patterns are presented in a suggested application sequence. In this case, the pattern sequence is generally based on the granularity of the patterns, in that coarser grained patterns are applied prior to finer-grained ones that then build upon or extend the foundation established by the coarse-grained patterns. In these types of pattern languages, the manner in which patterns can be organized into pattern sequences may be limited to how they are applied within their groups.

Structured pattern languages are helpful because they:

- can organize groups of field-tested design patterns into proposed, field-tested application sequences
- ensure consistency in how particular design goals are achieved (because by carrying out sets of inter-dependent patterns in a proven order, the quality of the results can be more easily guaranteed)
- are effective learning tools that can provide insight into how and why a particular method or technique should be applied as well as the effects of its application
- provide an extra level of depth in relation to pattern application (because they document the individual patterns plus the cumulative effects of their application)
- are flexible in that the ultimate pattern application sequence is up to the practitioner (and also because the application of any pattern within the overall language can be optional)

This book in its entirety provides an open-ended, master pattern language for SOA. The extent to which different patterns are related can vary, but overall they share a common

objective and endless pattern sequences can be explored. The relationship diagrams explained in the upcoming *Pattern Relationship Figures* section will often hint at common application sequences for a given pattern.

Chapters 6 and 11 single out sets of closely related patterns and structure them into groups organized into recommended application sequences that essentially establish primitive design processes. As a result, these collections of patterns could be classified as "mini" structured pattern languages that are still part of the overall master pattern language.

What's a Design Pattern Catalog?

A design pattern catalog is simply a documented collection of related design patterns. Therefore, this book is also referred to as a catalog for design patterns associated with SOA and service-orientation.

SUMMARY OF KEY POINTS

- A design pattern is a formal documentation of a proven solution to a common problem.
- A design pattern language is a group of related design patterns that can be applied in a variety of creative application sequences.
- A design pattern catalog is a collection of related design patterns documented together.
- This book contains a design pattern catalog that documents a master pattern language for SOA.

5.2 Historical Influences

Because service-orientation has deep roots in past distributed computing design platforms, many of the SOA design patterns have origins and influences that can be traced back to established design concepts, approaches, and previously published design pattern catalogs.

As illustrated in Figure 5.1, object-orientation, EAI, enterprise application architecture, and software architecture in general represent areas for which well-recognized design pattern catalogs exist, each of which has influenced design patterns in this book. Starting with the original pattern language created by Christopher Alexander, let's briefly discuss these influences separately.

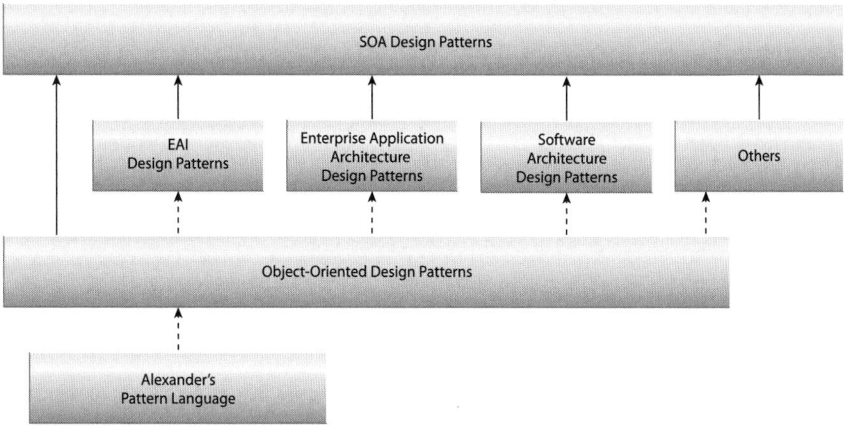

Figure 5.1
The primary influences of SOA design patterns.

Alexander's Pattern Language

It's been well documented how the notion of the design pattern owes its existence to the work of Christopher Alexander. Just about every design pattern publication pays tribute to Alexander's pattern language as a fundamental influence and source of inspiration.

Alexander pioneered the concept of patterns in relation to building architecture and related areas, such as city and community structure. He documented a collection of patterns and organized them into a pre-defined series he called a "sequence." The result was an architectural pattern language that inspired the IT community to create their own patterns for the design of automated systems.

Alexander's work is more than just a historical footnote for design patterns; it provides insight into how patterns in general should and should not be structured and organized.

For example, some lessons learned from Alexander's work include:

- *Pattern language sequences need to add value.* Often related patterns are better documented independently from each other even if there is some potential for them to be organized into a sequence. The primary purpose of any application sequence established by a pattern language is *not* to provide a logical organization for a set of related patterns but to demonstrate a proven process that provides value on its own.
- *Patterns do not need to be normalized.* There is often a perception that each design pattern should own an individual domain. In reality, the problem and solution space represented by individual patterns sometimes naturally overlaps. For example, you can easily have two patterns that propose different solutions to the same problem.

Beyond just the idea of organizing solutions into a pattern format, Alexander helped advocate the importance of clarity in how pattern catalogs need to be documented. He preached that patterns need to be individually clear as to their purpose and applicability and that pattern languages need to further communicate the rationale behind any sequences they may propose.

> **NOTE**
>
> As provided by research from Dr. Peter H. Chang from Lawrence Technological University, earlier origins also exist. For example, George Polya published the book *How to Solve It* (Princeton University Press) back in 1945, which included a "problem solving plan" that can be viewed at www.math.utah.edu/~pa/math/polya.html (based on the second edition released in 1957). Furthermore, Marvin Minsky published the paper *Steps Toward Artificial Intelligence* for MIT in 1960 that included coverage of pattern recognition and made further reference to Polya's work.

Object-Oriented Patterns

A variety of design patterns in support of object-orientation surfaced over the past 15 years, the most recognized of which is the pattern catalog published in *Design Patterns: Elements of Reusable Object-Oriented Software* (Gamma, Helm, Johnson, Vlissides; Addison-Wesley, 1995). This set of 23 patterns produced by the "Gang of Four" expanded and helped further establish object-orientation as a design approach for distributed solutions. Some of these patterns have persisted within service-orientation, albeit within an augmented context and new names.

For example, the following patterns in this book are related:

- Capability Composition (521) is associated with Composite
- Service Façade (333) is derived from Façade
- Legacy Wrapper (441) is derived from Adapter
- Non-Agnostic Context (319) is associated with Mediator
- Decoupled Contract (401) is associated with Bridge

Concepts established by several additional object-orientation patterns have factored into other SOA patterns. The incorporation of these patterns within service-orientation is a testament to their importance and evidence of how object-orientation as a whole has influenced the evolution of SOA.

Another relevant object-oriented-related influence is the paper "Using Pattern Languages for Object-Oriented Programs" published by Kent Beck and Ward Cunningham for the 1987 OOPSLA conference. This paper is notable not only for its brevity, but for its vision and its explicit emphasis on the use of sequences in organizing patterns.

> **NOTE**
>
> The comparative analysis in Chapter 14 of *SOA Principles of Service Design* provides a study of how object-oriented design concepts and principles relate to service-orientation.

Software Architecture Patterns

As design patterns became a mainstream part of IT, a set of important books emerged establishing formal conventions for pattern documentation and providing a series of common design patterns for software architecture in general. These pattern catalogs were developed in five separate volumes over a period of a dozen years as part of the *Pattern-Oriented Software Architecture* series (F. Buschmann, K. Henney, M. Kircher, R. Meunier, H. Rohnert, D. Schmidt, P. Sommerlad, M. Stal, Wiley 1996–2007).

Because of the general nature of the patterns, the contributions made by this series are too voluminous to document individually. Here are some examples of how SOA design patterns relate:

- Service Layers (143) is associated with Layers
- Service Broker (707) compound pattern is associated with Broker
- Concurrent Contracts (421) is associated with Extension Interface
- Metadata Centralization (280) is associated with Lookup
- Event-Driven Messaging (599) is derived from Publisher-Subscriber
- Process Abstraction (182) is associated with Whole-Part
- Atomic Service Transaction (623) is associated with Coordinator and Task Coordinator
- Partial State Deferral (356) is associated with Partial Acquisition

It is also worth noting that Volume 4 of the series (entitled *A Pattern Language for Distributed Computing*) focuses on connecting existing patterns relevant to building distributed systems into a larger pattern language. This book documents the roots of various previously published patterns, including those that are part of other pattern catalogs listed in this section.

Enterprise Application Architecture Patterns

As distributed computing became an established platform for solution design, an emphasis on enterprise architecture emerged bringing with it its own set of design patterns, many of which built upon object-oriented concepts and patterns. A respected pattern catalog in this field was published in *Patterns of Enterprise Application Architecture* (Fowler, Addison-Wesley, 2003).

You might notice that many of the influences originating from enterprise architecture patterns are located in the two pattern languages provided in Chapters 6 and 11. Service-orientation is, at heart, a design paradigm for distributed computing, and although distinct, it still relies and builds upon the fundamental patterns and concepts associated with enterprise application architecture in general.

For example, the following patterns in this book are related:

- Service Encapsulation (305) is associated with Gateway and Service Layer
- Decoupled Contract (401) is associated with Separated Interface
- Service Façade (333) is derived from Remote Façade
- Stateful Services (248) is derived from Server Session State
- Partial State Deferral (356) is derived from Lazy Load
- State Repository (242) is derived from Database Session State

Studying these types of influences can lead to further revelations as to how SOA has evolved into a unique architectural model.

EAI Patterns

Several pattern catalogs centered around the use of messaging to fulfill integration requirements emerged during the EAI era. These patterns establish sound approaches for robust messaging-based communication and address various integration-related challenges.

A recognized publication in this field is *Enterprise Integration Patterns* (Hohpe, Woolf, Addison-Wesley, 2004).

Because EAI is one of the primary influences of service-orientation, this book contains service interaction patterns based on the use of messaging primarily in support of service composition scenarios.

Some examples of SOA patterns related to design patterns documented in *Enterprise Integration Patterns*:

- Service Messaging (533) is derived from Message, Messaging, and Document Message
- Data Model Transformation (671) is derived from Message Translator
- Canonical Schema (158) is associated with Canonical Data Model
- Service Agent (543) is associated with Event-Driven Consumer
- Process Centralization (193) is associated with Process Manager
- Intermediate Routing (549) is derived from Content-Based Router

Several references to additional EAI patterns are interspersed in the upcoming chapters (Chapter 18, in particular).

SOA Patterns

The intention behind this collection of SOA patterns is not to replace or compete with the catalogs provided by previous publications, but instead to build upon and complement them with a catalog focused solely on attaining the strategic goals associated with service-orientated computing.

This catalog is comprised of new patterns, existing patterns that have been augmented, and patterns that are intentionally similar to patterns in other catalogs. The latter group is included so that these patterns can be explained within the context of SOA and to also formally highlight them as a supporting part of the service-orientation design paradigm.

Learning about the design solutions and techniques provided by SOA design patterns can provide insight into the mechanics required to enable service-orientation and also help clarify exactly how SOA represents a distinct architectural model. When exploring these distinctions, it is important to take into account:

- which of the past design techniques are preserved and emphasized
- which of the past design techniques are de-emphasized
- new design techniques
- new approaches to carrying out existing techniques

Note that there are several more useful design patterns in the previously mentioned books which are not mentioned in this pattern catalog. Some provide detailed solutions that are not necessarily specific to SOA, but still very helpful.

SUMMARY OF KEY POINTS

- The pattern language invented by Christopher Alexander inspired the use of design patterns in the IT world.
- The object-orientation platform has an established set of design patterns that are at the root of several of the patterns in this catalog. Additional influences can be traced back to patterns created for enterprise application architecture, EAI, and general software architecture pattern catalogs.

5.3 Pattern Notation

Throughout this book design patterns need to be referenced and explained in text and illustrations. A simple notation is used to consistently represent different types of patterns.

Pattern Symbols

As shown in Figure 5.2, specific symbols are used to represent:

- a design pattern
- a compound design pattern
- a group of related design patterns

Additionally, colors are incorporated to indicate if a displayed design pattern is just being referenced and not actually discussed, versus one that is the current topic of discussion.

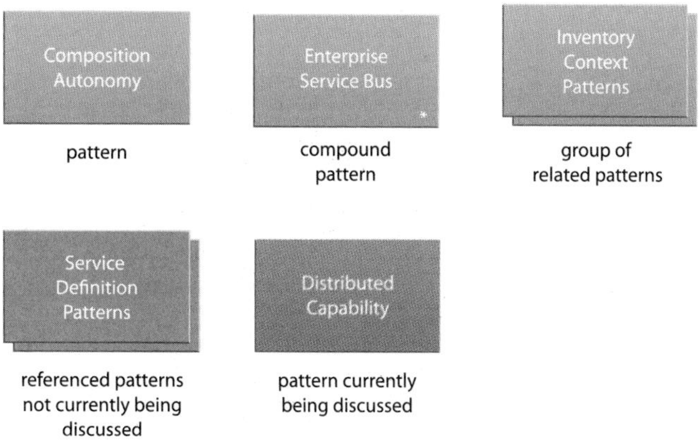

Figure 5.2

The standard symbols used to represent different types of design patterns and how design patterns relate to the current subject being covered.

Pattern Figures

The symbols displayed in Figure 5.2 are used in the following three primary types of diagrams:

- pattern application sequence figures
- pattern relationship figures
- compound pattern hierarchy figures

Let's take a closer look at each:

Pattern Application Sequence Figures

When documenting design pattern languages, it is helpful to display the suggested sequence in which patterns should be applied. Figures 5.3 and 5.4 show pattern application sequences for groups of related patterns and for individual patterns belonging to a particular group, respectively.

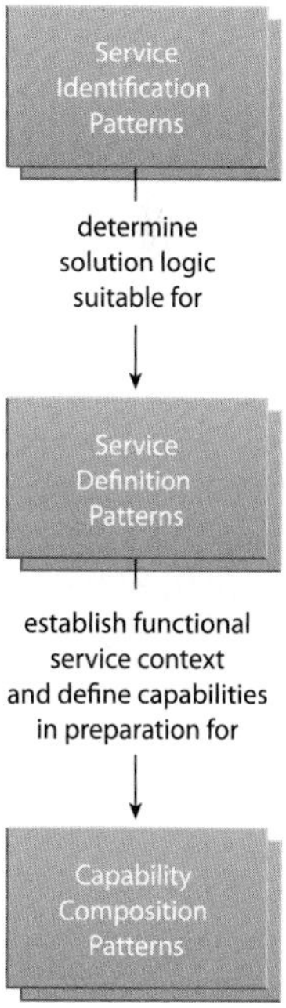

Figure 5.3

The pattern groups from Chapters 11 and 17 displayed in a recommended application sequence.

Pattern Relationship Figures

As explained in the upcoming *Pattern Profiles* section, this book explores numerous inter-pattern relationships and provides one pattern relationship diagram (Figure 5.5) for each documented design pattern.

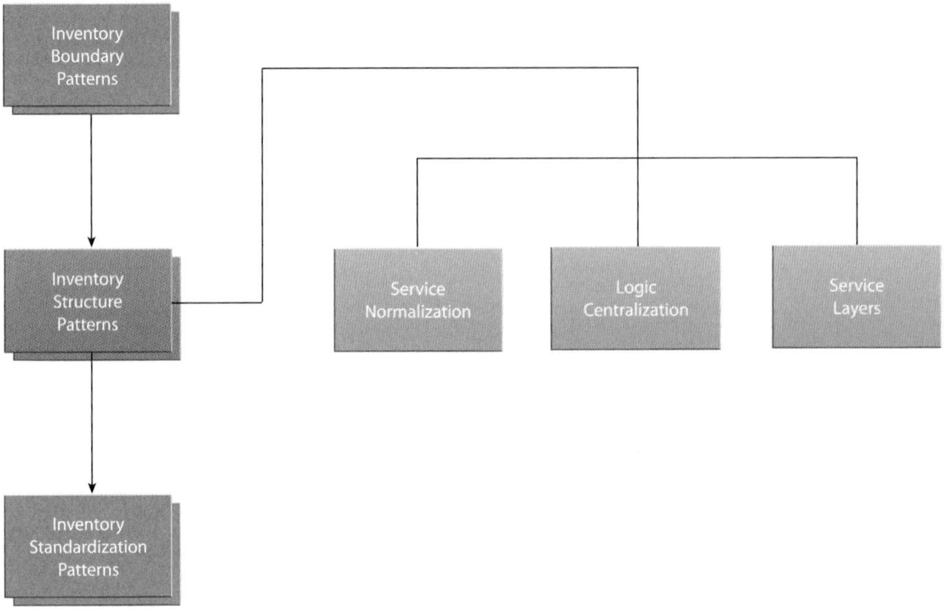

Figure 5.4

The inventory structure patterns group from Chapter 6 is highlighted in this diagram. In this case, there is no recommendation as to the order in which the three patterns on the right should be applied.

A style convention applied to all pattern relationship diagrams is the use of color, as follows:

- Each pattern relationship diagram explores the relationships of one pattern. Therefore, that design pattern is highlighted in red, as per the previously established symbol notation.
- Pattern relationships are documented in a unidirectional manner. For relationships where the pattern currently being discussed affects or relates to other patterns, a red line is used along with an arrow pointing to the other pattern. When the relationship line documents how other patterns relate to the current pattern, the lines are green, and the arrows are reversed.

Note that directionality of relationships is preserved in different diagrams. For example, the green relationship line emitting from Service Normalization (131) and pointing to Logic Centralization (136) in the preceding figure would be reversed (and colored red) in the pattern relationship figure for Service Normalization (131).

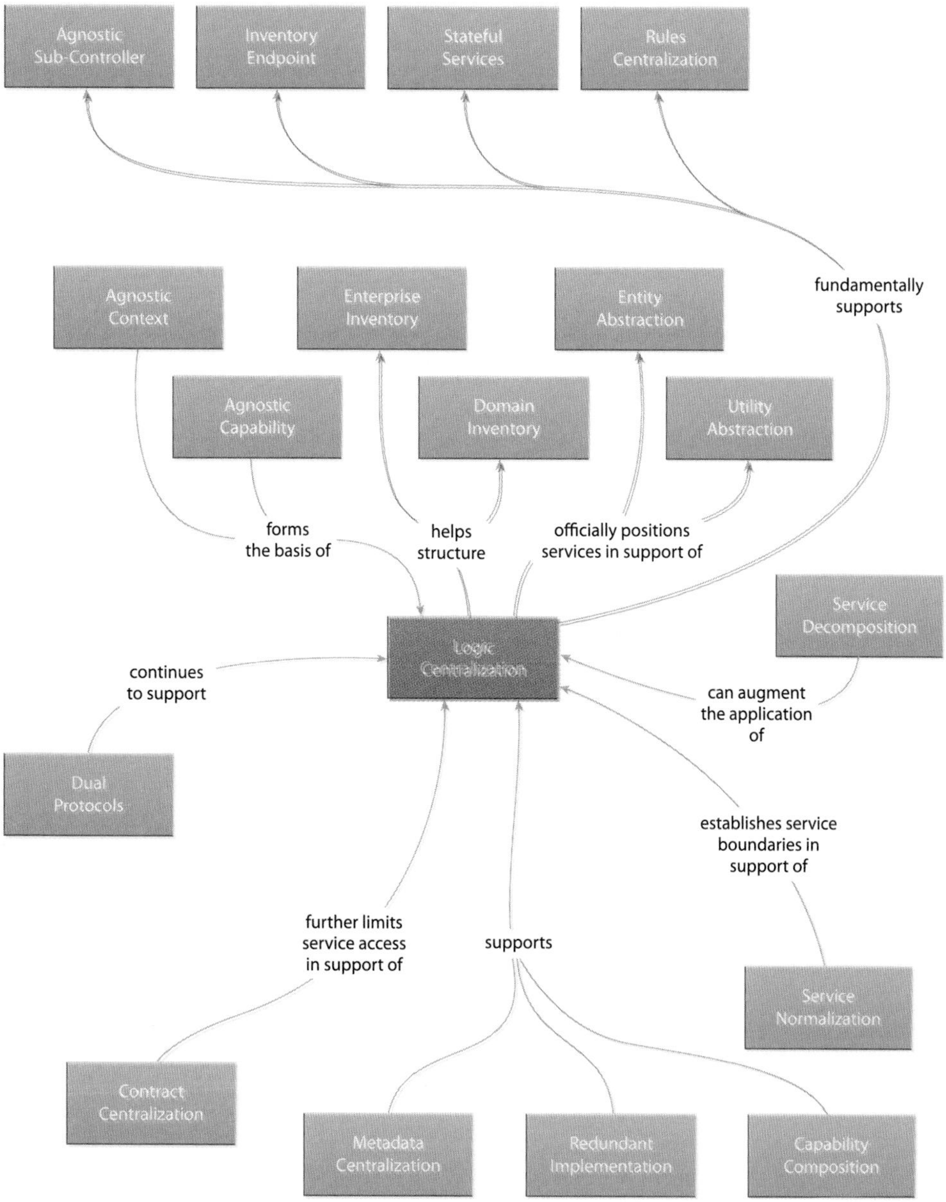

Figure 5.5

An example of a pattern relationship diagram.

Compound Pattern Hierarchy Figures

Compound patterns are comprised of combinations of design patterns. When illustrating a compound pattern, a hierarchical representation is usually required, where the compound pattern name is displayed at the top, and the patterns that comprise the compound are shown underneath.

These types of diagrams (Figures 5.6 and 5.7) can be considered simplified relationship figures in that they only identify which patterns belong to which compound, without getting into the details of how these patterns relate. Compound patterns are documented separately in Chapter 22, but compound hierarchy figures are displayed throughout the upcoming chapters.

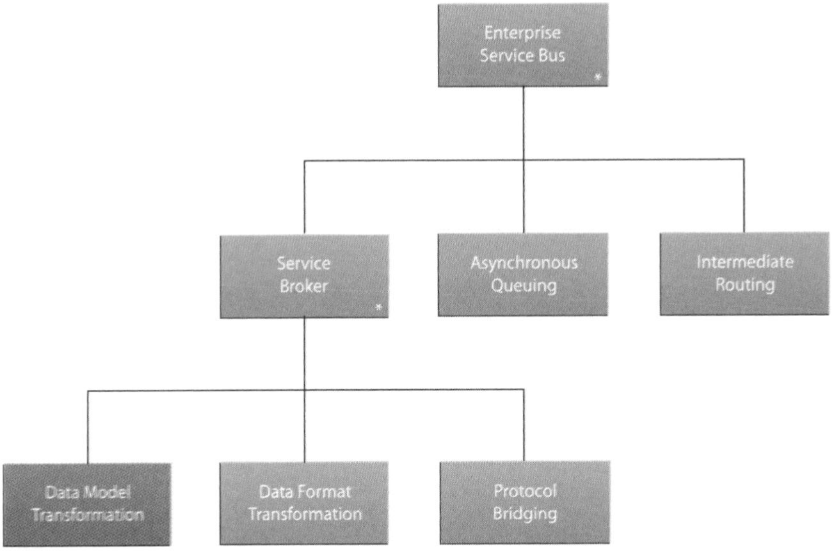

Figure 5.6

Enterprise Service Bus (704) is a compound pattern comprised of several core patterns, one of which is a compound pattern in its own right and therefore represents a nested pattern hierarchy. In this case, Data Model Transformation (671) is highlighted, indicating that it is the current pattern being discussed.

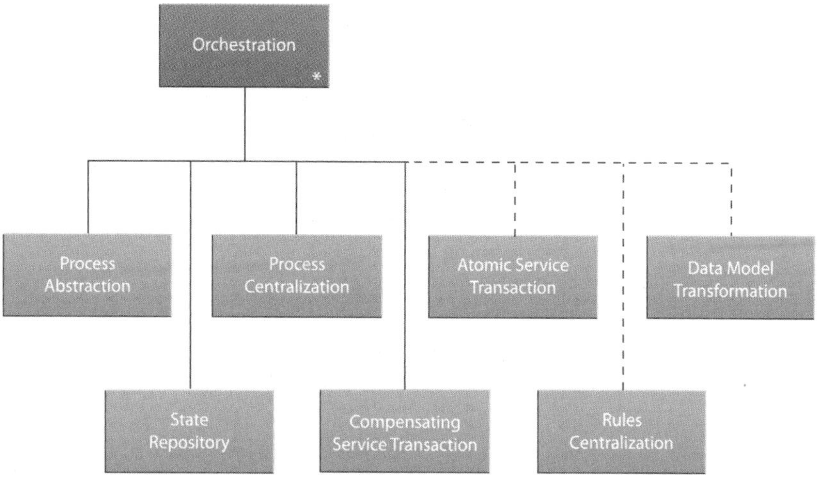

Figure 5.7

There are additional patterns associated with Orchestration (701) that can be considered optional extensions. In this case, the hierarchy lines are dashed.

> **NOTE**
>
> Another notation used for some forms of compound patterns involves showing patterns combined with a plus ("+") symbol. These diagrams are limited to Chapter 22 and are formally described there.

Capitalization

All design pattern names (including names of compound patterns) are capitalized throughout this book. The names for groups of related patterns are capitalized when displayed in Figures but not when referenced in body text.

Page Number References

As you may have already noticed in earlier parts of this chapter, each pattern name is followed by a page number in parentheses. This number, which points to the first page of the corresponding pattern profile, is provided for quick reference purposes. Its use has become a common convention among pattern catalogs. The only time the number is not displayed is when a pattern name is referenced within that pattern's profile section.

5.4 Pattern Profiles

Each of the patterns in this catalog is described using the same profile format and structure based on the following parts:

- Requirement
- Icon
- Summary
- Problem
- Solution
- Application
- Impacts
- Relationships
- Case Study Example

The following sections describe each part individually.

Requirement

This is a concise, single-sentence statement that presents the fundamental requirement addressed by the pattern in the form of a question. Every pattern description begins with this statement.

For example:

How can a service be designed to minimize the chances of capability logic deconstruction?

Note that the inside cover of this book lists all of the patterns together with their respective requirement statements.

Icon

Each pattern description is accompanied by an icon image that acts as a visual identifier.

An example of a pattern icon:

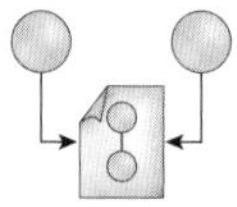

The icons are displayed together with the requirement statements in each pattern profile as well as on the inside book cover.

Summary

Following the requirement statement, a summary table is displayed, comprised of statements that collectively provide a concise synopsis of the pattern for quick reference purposes.

The following parts of the profile are summarized in this table:

- Problem
- Solution
- Application
- Impacts

Additionally, the profile table provides references to related service-orientation design principles and service-oriented architectural types via the following sections:

- Principles
- Architecture

The parts of the pattern description not represented in the summary table are the *Relationships* and *Case Study Example* sections.

> **NOTE**
>
> All pattern summary tables in this book are also published online at SOAPatterns.org.

Problem

The issue causing a problem and the effects of the problem are described in this section, typically accompanied by a figure that further illustrates the "problem state." It is this problem for which the pattern provides a solution. Problem descriptions may also include common circumstances that can lead to the problem (also known as "forces").

Solution

This represents the design solution proposed by the pattern to solve the problem and fulfill the requirement. Often the solution is a short statement followed by a diagram that concisely communicates the final solution state. "How-to" details are not provided in this section but are instead located in the *Application* section.

Application

This part is dedicated to describing how the pattern can be applied. In can include guidelines, implementation details, and sometimes even a suggested process.

Impacts

Most patterns come with trade-offs. This section highlights common consequences, costs, and requirements associated with the application of a pattern.

Note that these consequences are common but not necessarily predictable. For example, issues related to typical performance requirements are often raised; however, these issues may not impact an environment with an already highly scalable infrastructure.

Relationships

The use of design patterns can tie into all aspects of design and architecture. It is important to understand the requirements and dependencies a pattern may have and the effects of its application upon other patterns.

These diagrams are not exhaustive in that not all possible relationships a given design pattern can have are shown. Through the use of pattern relationship figures, this section merely highlights common relationships with an emphasis on how patterns support or depend on each other.

> **NOTE**
>
> Because there are two patterns in each relationship, almost every relationship is shown twice in this book: once in the *Relationships* section of each of the two patterns. To avoid content redundancy, most relationships are only described once. Therefore, if you find a relationship shown in a diagram that is not described in the accompanying text, refer to the description for the other pattern involved in that relationship. Note, however, that some relationships are considered self-explanatory and are therefore not described at all.
>
> Details regarding the format of pattern relationship figures are provided in the *Pattern Notation* section earlier in this chapter.

Case Study Example

Most pattern profiles conclude with a case study example that demonstrates the sample application of a pattern in relation to the storylines established in Chapter 2.

SUMMARY OF KEY POINTS

- Each design pattern is documented with the same profile structure.
- Design pattern profiles begin with a requirements statement and an icon and then provide a summary table followed by sections with detailed descriptions.

5.5 Patterns with Common Characteristics

Each pattern in this book is distinct and unique and is considered an equal member of the overall pattern catalog. However, it is worth highlighting certain groups of similar patterns to better understand how they were named and why they share common characteristics.

NOTE

The following sections do not attempt to group patterns into formal categories. The upcoming chapters in Parts II, III, and IV already are subdivided by chapters representing specific pattern types. These sections here only point out that within and across these types, collections of patterns share common qualities and were labeled to reflect this.

Canonical Patterns

Canonical design patterns propose that the best solution for a particular problem is to introduce a design standard. The successful application of this type of pattern results in a canonical convention that guarantees consistent design across different parts of an inventory or solution.

The canonical design patterns in this book are:

- Canonical Protocol (150)
- Canonical Schema (158)
- Canonical Expression (275)
- Canonical Resources (237)
- Canonical Versioning (286)

Centralization Patterns

Centralization simply means limiting the options of something to one. Applying this concept within key parts of a service-oriented architecture establishes consistency and fosters standardization and reuse and, ultimately, native interconnectivity.

The following centralization patterns are covered in the upcoming chapters:

- Logic Centralization (136)
- Metadata Centralization (280)
- Process Centralization (193)
- Rules Centralization (216)
- Schema Centralization (200)
- Contract Centralization (409)
- Policy Centralization (207)

A common characteristic across centralization patterns is a trade-off between increased architectural harmony and increased governance and performance requirements. As explained shortly in the *Measures of Pattern Application* section, patterns can be applied to different extents. A key factor when assessing the application measure for centralization patterns is at what point the benefit outweighs the architectural impact.

NOTE

Centralization patterns are also very much related to the use of design standards. To constantly require that certain parts of a service-oriented architecture are centralized requires that supporting conventions be regularly followed.

SUMMARY OF KEY POINTS

- Canonical and centralization patterns need to be consistently applied to realize their benefits.
- Canonical and centralization patterns require the use of supporting design standards.

5.6 Key Design Considerations

"Enterprise" vs. "Enterprise-wide"

Having discussed the notion of services as enterprise resources back in Chapter 4, it is important that there is a clear distinction between something that exists as a resource as part of an enterprise and something that is actually an enterprise-*wide* resource.

- An enterprise resource is not a resource that is necessarily made available across the entire enterprise. Instead, it is a resource positioned for use within the enterprise, outside of and beyond any one particular application boundary. In other words, it is a "cross-silo" resource.
- An enterprise-wide resource, on the other hand, is truly intended for use across all service inventories within an enterprise.

This difference in terminology is especially relevant to design patterns associated with specific enterprise boundaries, such as Domain Inventory (123). Note also that a service positioned as an enterprise resource is expected to be an inventory-wide resource, meaning that it is interoperable from anywhere within the inventory boundary.

Design Patterns and Design Principles

Most of the upcoming design patterns reference design principles where appropriate to highlight a dependency or relationship or perhaps to describe the effect a design pattern may have on service-orientation.

Specifically, the relationship between service-orientation design principles and patterns can be defined as follows:

- Design principles are applied collectively to solution logic in order to shape it in such a manner that it fosters key design characteristics that support the strategic goals associated with service-oriented computing.

- Design patterns provide solutions to common problems encountered when applying design principles—*and*—when establishing an environment suitable for implementing logic designed in accordance with service-orientation principles.

In many ways, design principles and patterns are alike. Both provide design guidance in support of achieving overarching strategic goals. In fact, it would not be unreasonable to think of the eight service-orientation principles as super patterns that are further supported by the patterns in this book.

Service-orientation design principles have another role in that they collectively define service-orientation as a design paradigm. Ultimately, it is best to view design patterns as providing support for the realization of design principles and their associated goals. (Design principles were introduced in the *Principles of Service-Orientation* section in Chapter 4.)

NOTE

We just stated that design principles could be thought of as super patterns. Why then weren't they documented as such? When the manuscript for this book was undergoing a review by Ralph Johnson and his pattern review group at UIUC, the question came up as to how to determine whether something is a legitimate pattern.

Ralph responded by stating, "When people ask me, 'Is this a pattern?' I usually say, 'That is not the right question.' The right question is whether pattern form is the best way to communicate this material." This is a good way to think of the purpose of this book.

Each pattern provides a specific solution to a distinct problem. The guidance provided by a design principle is much broader and can, in fact, end up solving a variety of problems. Therefore, design principles are better off documented in their form.

Design Patterns and Design Granularity

Design granularity, as it pertains to service-orientation, is itself something worth being familiar with prior to reading the upcoming chapters. Provided here are brief descriptions of common granularity-related terms:

- *Service Granularity* – The overall quantity of functionality encapsulated by a service determines the service granularity. A service's granularity is set by its functional context, which is usually established during the service modeling phase.
- *Capability Granularity* – The quantity of functionality encapsulated by a specific service capability determines the level of corresponding capability granularity.

- *Data Granularity* – The quantity of data exchanged by a specific service capability determines the level of its data granularity.
- *Constraint Granularity* – The extent of validation logic detail defined for a given service capability within the service contract determines the capability's level of constraint granularity. Generally, the more specific the constraints and the larger the amount of constraints, the more fine-grained the capability's constraint granularity is.

The effect of design patterns on service-related design granularity can vary. For example, when applying multiple patterns (or compound patterns) to the same service, the end-levels of design granularity may be distinctly defined by that combination of patterns (and they may fluctuate between the application of one pattern to another).

Measures of Design Pattern Application

It is important to acknowledge that most patterns do not propose a black or white design option. Design patterns can often be applied at different levels. Although the effectiveness of a given pattern will generally be equivalent to the extent to which it is realized, there may be practical considerations that simply limit the degree to which a pattern can be applied in the real world (as is often the case when designing service logic that is required to encapsulate legacy functionality).

This consideration affects both design patterns and design principles. For example, individual service-orientation design principles can rarely be applied to their maximum potential. The point is to pursue the design goals of a design pattern or principle to whatever extent feasible and to strive for an end-result that realizes the pattern or principle to a meaningful extent.

SUMMARY OF KEY POINTS

- Some specific terminology is used within design pattern profiles. The distinction between "enterprise" and "enterprise-wide" is especially important.
- Design pattern profiles contain references to related design principles, revealing links between the patterns and the realization of service-orientation itself.
- As with design principles, most design patterns can be applied to various measures. Sometimes it isn't possible to fully apply a design pattern due to environmental constraints.

Part II

Service Inventory Design Patterns

The patterns in this chapter are fundamental to defining a service-oriented architectural model with an emphasis on service inventory architecture. The design problems solved by these patterns help structure the architecture for the sole purpose of establishing a flexible and agile environment suitable for solution logic designed in accordance with service-orientation.

This chapter is structured so that the patterns are organized into a proposed application sequence. It is important to acknowledge that you are not required to follow this recommended sequence and that these patterns exist individually as part of the master pattern language provided by the book as a whole. You can therefore consider this chapter a "mini" structured pattern language that is part of a greater open-ended pattern language. As such, these patterns can be combined with patterns from other chapters into a variety of creative sequences.

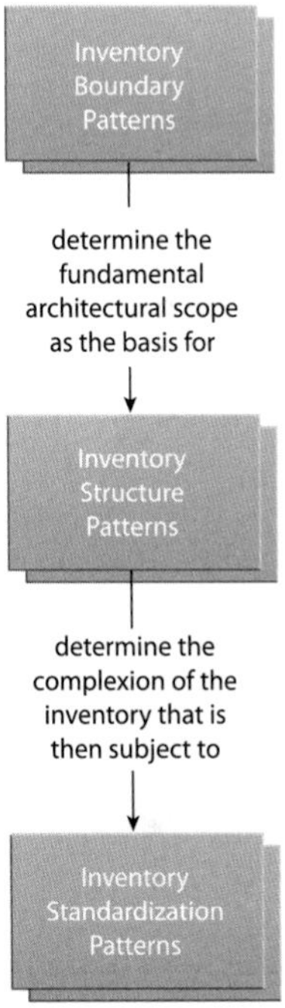

Figure 6.1
The patterns in this chapter are organized into groups that are ordered into a proposed application sequence in support of defining a layered inventory architecture.

As shown in Figure 6.1, the upcoming patterns are organized into the following groups:

1. *Inventory Boundary Patterns* – The scope of an architecture is defined by identifying the boundary of its corresponding service inventory and related characteristics.
2. *Inventory Structure Patterns* – The high-level structure and the overall complexion of the inventory itself is determined, which further influences the requirements that the eventual architecture implementation will need to fulfill.
3. *Inventory Standardization Patterns* – Key inventory-wide design standards are established to ensure a baseline level of service interoperability.

The design patterns within a given group are explained at the beginning of each of the upcoming sections.

NOTE

Throughout this chapter you'll notice references to "agnostic" services and logic. If this term is new to you, skip ahead to the *Agnostic Logic and Non-Agnostic Logic* section at the beginning of Chapter 7 for an explanation. Also if you are not familiar with the term "service inventory," be sure to read the definition provided in Chapter 3.

How Inventory Design Patterns Relate to SOA Design Characteristics

It is interesting to note that the four fundamental design characteristics of a service-oriented architecture (established back in Chapter 4) are closely related to the application of the design patterns in this chapter, as shown in Table 6.1. The nature of these relationships will become clear when reading the pattern descriptions.

	Business Driven	Vendor Neutral	Enterprise Centric	Composition Centric
Enterprise Inventory	x	x	x	x
Domain Inventory	x	x	x	x
Logic Centralization	x		x	x
Service Normalization				x
Service Layers	x		x	x
Canonical Schema			x	x
Canonical Protocol			x	x

Table 6.1

How fundamental inventory design patterns (left) relate to the required base characteristics (top) of service-oriented architecture.

How Foundational Inventory and Service Patterns Relate

As mentioned earlier, this chapter provides a structured collection of patterns provided in a recommended application sequence. Chapter 11 provides a similarly organized set of patterns arranged in a suggested application sequence focused solely on service design. The fact that this chapter precedes Chapter 11 is not meant to indicate that the process established by this pattern application sequence should be completed prior to service design. Inventory design patterns are simply covered first in this book because they tend to be broader and coarser-grained in nature than those specific to service design.

In most modern SOA methodologies, iterative modeling and design processes are used to allow the design of an inventory architecture to be accomplished concurrently with service modeling and identification so that the definition of one can lead to the refinement of the other. It is completely up to you as to how these pattern groups are used in incorporated into project delivery cycles.

How Case Studies are Used in this Chapter

It's been a few chapters since we introduced the case study backgrounds, so it's worth a reminder that each of the upcoming design patterns is supplemented with a brief case study example. For this particular chapter, all examples relate back to the Alleywood Lumber Company environment established in the *Case #2 Background: Alleywood Lumber Company* section in Chapter 2.

As described in that chapter, Alleywood is facing an overhaul of their existing environment. An enterprise SOA initiative will require them to produce a collection of services that continue to represent their existing business lines, while also providing native interconnectivity with existing Tri-Fold services. By progressing through the upcoming sequence of patterns, Alleywood's service-oriented technology architecture and a preliminary service inventory are defined.

6.1 Inventory Boundary Patterns

As explained in Chapters 3 and 4, a service inventory represents an independently standardized and governed collection of related services, and each such inventory is supported by its own, individual service-oriented technology architecture implementation. Therefore, a fundamental step in the creation of any service inventory is the definition of its scope in relation to the enterprise within which it resides.

The design patterns Enterprise Inventory (116) and Domain Inventory (123) shown in Figure 6.2 establish the boundary of the service inventory. Only one of these two patterns can be applied within a given IT enterprise.

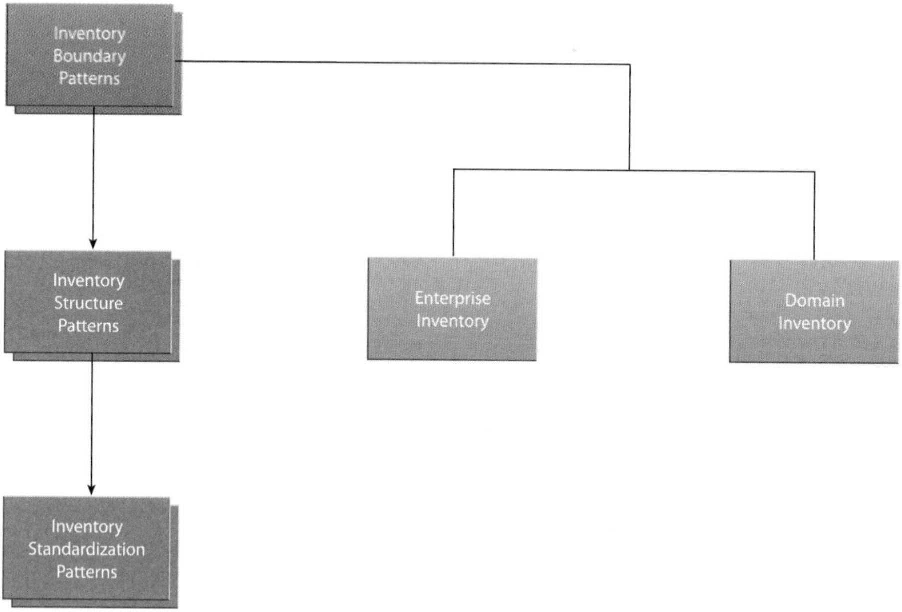

Figure 6.2

These inventory boundary patterns establish well-defined perimeters that determine the physical scope of an inventory.

Enterprise Inventory

How can services be delivered to maximize recomposition?

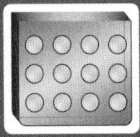

Problem	Delivering services independently via different project teams across an enterprise establishes a constant risk of producing inconsistent service and architecture implementations, compromising recomposition opportunities.
Solution	Services for multiple solutions can be designed for delivery within a standardized, enterprise-wide inventory architecture wherein they can be freely and repeatedly recomposed.
Application	The enterprise service inventory is ideally modeled in advance, and enterprise-wide standards are applied to services delivered by different project teams.
Impacts	Significant upfront analysis is required to define an enterprise inventory blueprint and numerous organizational impacts result from the subsequent governance requirements.
Principles	Standardized Service Contract, Service Abstraction, Service Composability
Architecture	Enterprise, Inventory

Table 6.2
Profile summary for the Enterprise Inventory pattern.

Problem

Throughout an enterprise, services can be delivered as part of various on-going development projects. Because each project has its own priorities and goals, services and supporting implementation architectures can easily be designed in isolation, optimized to fulfill tactical requirements.

The result is a collection of potentially disparate service clusters and technology architectures. The differences in these implementation environments can lead to serious problems when attempting to compose services into new configurations that span the initial architectural boundaries (Figure 6.3).

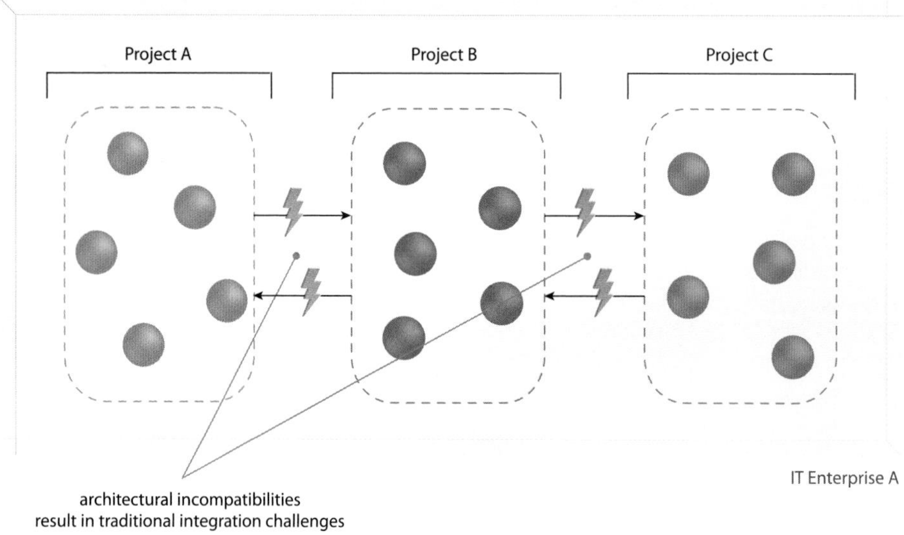

Figure 6.3

All services are built with the same vendor platform, but they are delivered via separate projects without taking into account a common architectural boundary. The end-result is an environment reminiscent of a silo-based enterprise that relies on constant integration effort to enable interoperability.

Solution

A service-oriented enterprise architecture is established to form the basis for a single enterprise service inventory. Services delivered as part of any project are designed specifically for implementation within the enterprise inventory's supporting architecture, guaranteeing wide-spread standardization and intrinsic interoperability.

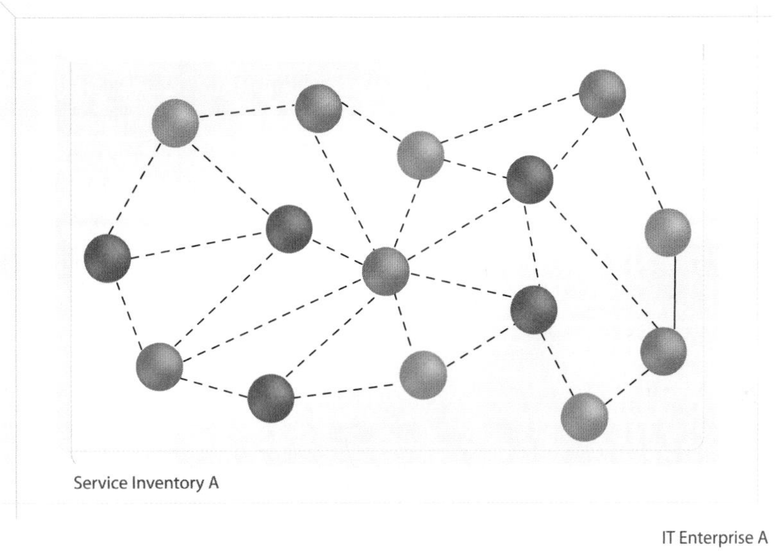

Figure 6.4

An enterprise service inventory establishes an enterprise-wide architectural boundary that promotes native interoperability and recomposition among all services.

Application

If the planned enterprise service inventory is significant in scope, then the organization needs to ensure it is capable of carrying out the corresponding SOA adoption effort.

Various factors come into play, each of which may introduce the need to reduce the scope or explore an alternative approach:

- the maturity of available technology for the planned services (especially for services being positioned as highly reusable enterprise resources)
- the maturity of governance technology platforms required to manage and evolve the service inventory as it is being built and after it is in place
- the order of magnitude associated with the amount of change and disruption brought on by the adoption
- the amount of legacy environments that are expected to constrain service encapsulation

- the financial resources required to carry out the adoption
- cultural and political obstacles that may arise as a result of the proposed changes and the required standardization effort

Therefore, this pattern is recommended for the following types of environments:

- small-to-medium-sized organizations with sufficient resources
- medium-to-large-sized organizations with highly controlled IT environments, a history of enterprise-wide standardization, or with the cultural flexibility to successfully adopt the required level of standardization
- medium-to-large-sized organizations that have the resources to build an enterprise service inventory while concurrently operating and maintaining their existing legacy systems
- new organizations that have no legacy systems and no IT history (and can therefore build an IT enterprise with a clean slate)

An enterprise service inventory does not need to encompass an *entire* enterprise. The purpose of this pattern is to establish a single service inventory with a scope sufficiently meaningful to warrant its creation.

Furthermore, the application of this pattern does not result in the creation of physical services. It establishes the concept of a service inventory on an enterprise-wide scale, for which services are conceptually defined through a planning and analysis effort that ties into the definition of a service inventory blueprint. To accomplish all of this typically requires a top-down analysis project that is completed by iteratively carrying out the service-oriented analysis and service modeling processes.

The following steps provide a suggested process:

1. Carry out planning and analysis stages to determine a preliminary scope for the service inventory that appears to be manageable based on the previously listed factors.
2. Collect all of the necessary enterprise business specifications that document business models and requirements that fall within the scope of the planned inventory (as well as those that are enterprise-wide). These specifications can include business entity models, logical data models, ontologies, taxonomies, business process definitions, and numerous other information and business architecture documents.

3. Using the enterprise-wide business models collected in Step 2, apply Entity Abstraction (175) and Process Abstraction (182) to establish a base set of business service layers.

4. Carry out the service-oriented analysis process iteratively by decomposing business process definitions that fall within the scope of the planned inventory. This results in the definition of service candidates that are continually refined. (See SOAMethodology.com for an example of a top-down process that iterates through the service-oriented analysis stage.)

NOTE

Several of the previously listed steps also apply to the upcoming pattern Domain Inventory (123). The primary distinctions are scope and quantity. The ultimate goal of Enterprise Inventory is to establish a *single* service inventory that spans as much of the IT enterprise as possible, whereas Domain Inventory (123) allows for multiple (usually smaller) inventories to exist within an enterprise.

Impacts

To achieve unity across an enterprise-wide service inventory, a large (and sometimes monumental) amount of top-down analysis may be required so that service candidates can be modeled and aligned with each other prior to their actual delivery. This can lead to an expensive and time-consuming up-front analysis project.

Alternative methodologies can be employed to phase in the delivery of services with less initial analysis. One example is the "meet-in-the-middle" approach that allows for analysis to occur on an on-going basis while services are built and implemented. There is then a commitment to "re-align" the services at a later point after the analysis produces a mature enterprise-wide inventory blueprint. Although a proven strategy that overcomes the time-burden of top-down approaches, this method can introduce additional complexities and increased expense.

Common issues that challenge the creation of an enterprise service inventory are documented in the *Problem* section of the pattern description for Domain Inventory (123) because this pattern provides an alternative approach that directly addresses concerns associated with Enterprise Inventory.

Relationships

Enterprise Inventory establishes an architectural boundary with a physical structure that is further subject to the application of a series of additional inventory-related patterns. Inventory Endpoint (260) in particular can complement this pattern by providing standardized access to consumers outside the enterprise. Domain Inventory (123) provides the primary alternative to this pattern.

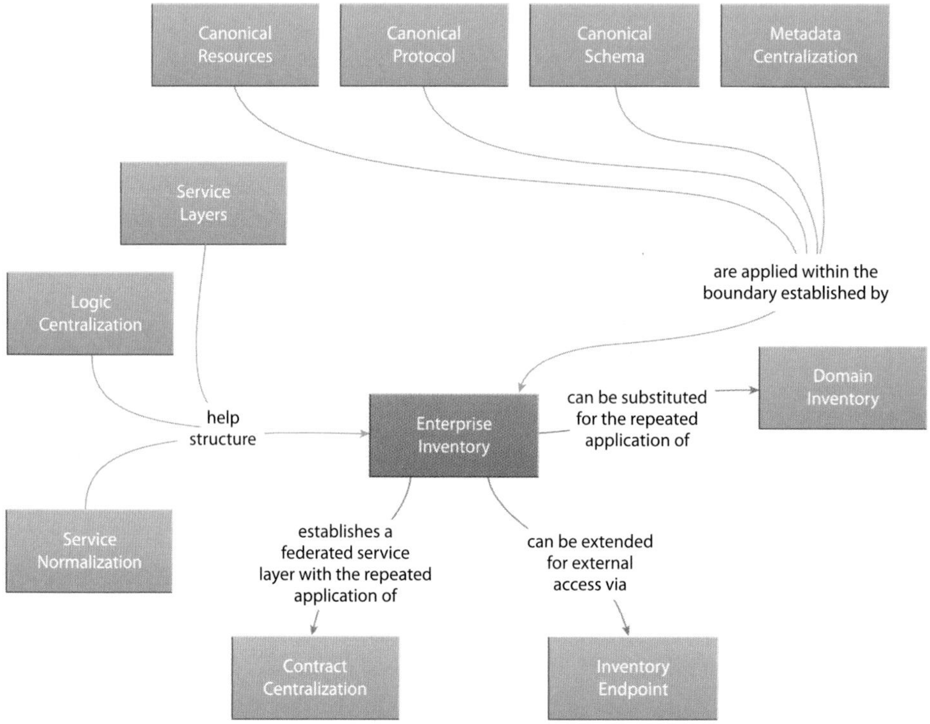

Figure 6.5
Enterprise Inventory determines scope, but it relies on other patterns to establish the inventory structure.

CASE STUDY EXAMPLE

Armed with enterprise architecture standards that dictate technical constraints and further establish a centralized, Web services-centric communications framework, Alleywood and Tri-Fold teams have been able to incorporate strategic business requirements and goals to define a target inventory architecture.

To further set its physical boundary, additional analysis is required to determine what logic the planned service inventory will actually be required to encompass. Business analysts and subject matter experts are employed to participate in a series of service-oriented analysis and service modeling processes where existing and extended business processes are studied and used as a source from which to derive a variety of services.

These processes are carried out iteratively to produce a service inventory blueprint for the collection of services Alleywood is planning to deliver. By performing these processes and applying the service definition patterns described in Chapter 11, a set of initial service candidates is defined (Figure 6.6).

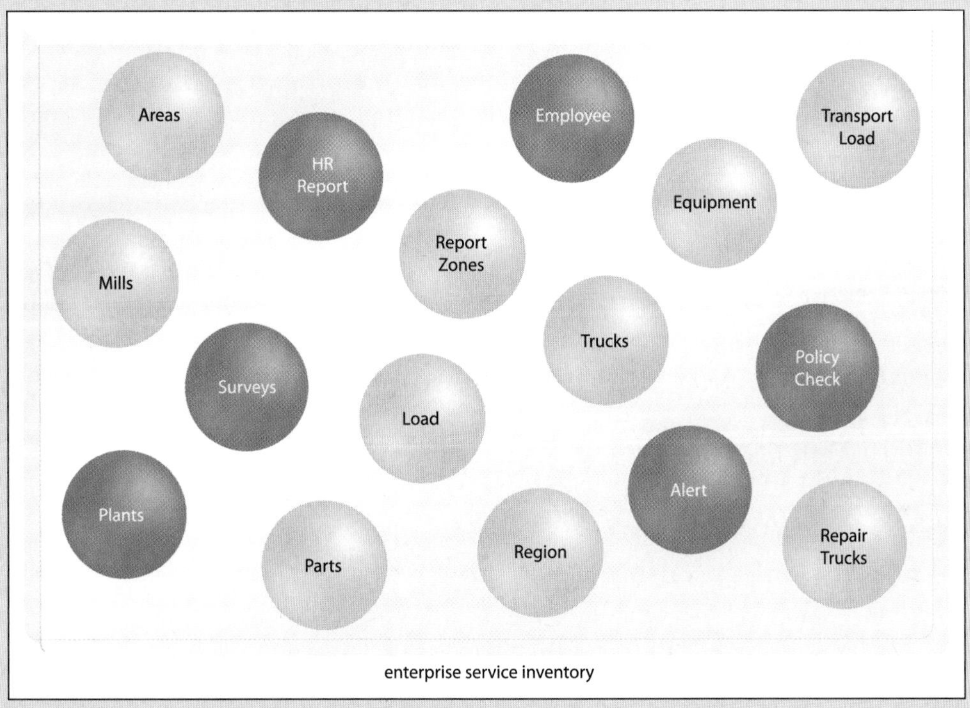

Figure 6.6

The initial set of services that comprise an enterprise service inventory that spans Alleywood and Tri-Fold environments. Gray services belong to Alleywood while purple-colored services originated with Tri-Fold.

Domain Inventory

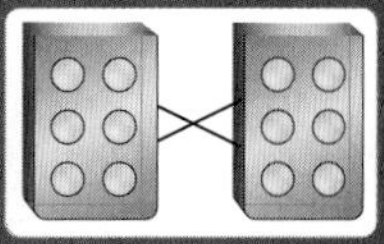

How can services be delivered to maximize recomposition when enterprise-wide standardization is not possible?

Problem	Establishing an single enterprise service inventory may be unmanageable for some enterprises, and attempts to do so may jeopardize the success of an SOA adoption as a whole.
Solution	Services can be grouped into manageable, domain-specific service inventories, each of which can be independently standardized, governed, and owned.
Application	Inventory domain boundaries need to be carefully established.
Impacts	Standardization disparity between domain service inventories imposes transformation requirements and reduces the overall benefit potential of the SOA adoption.
Principles	Standardized Service Contract, Service Abstraction, Service Composability
Architecture	Enterprise, Inventory

Table 6.3
Profile summary for the Domain Inventory pattern.

Problem

In larger environments it can be impractical or even unrealistic to define and maintain a single service inventory for an entire enterprise. Standardization and governance issues can raise numerous concerns, most of which tend to be organizational in nature (Figure 6.7).

> **NOTE**
>
> Several of the issues raised in Figure 6.7 relate to the governance of SOA projects and implementations. Organizational and technology-related governance topics (and patterns) will be covered separately in the upcoming title *SOA Governance* as part of this book series.

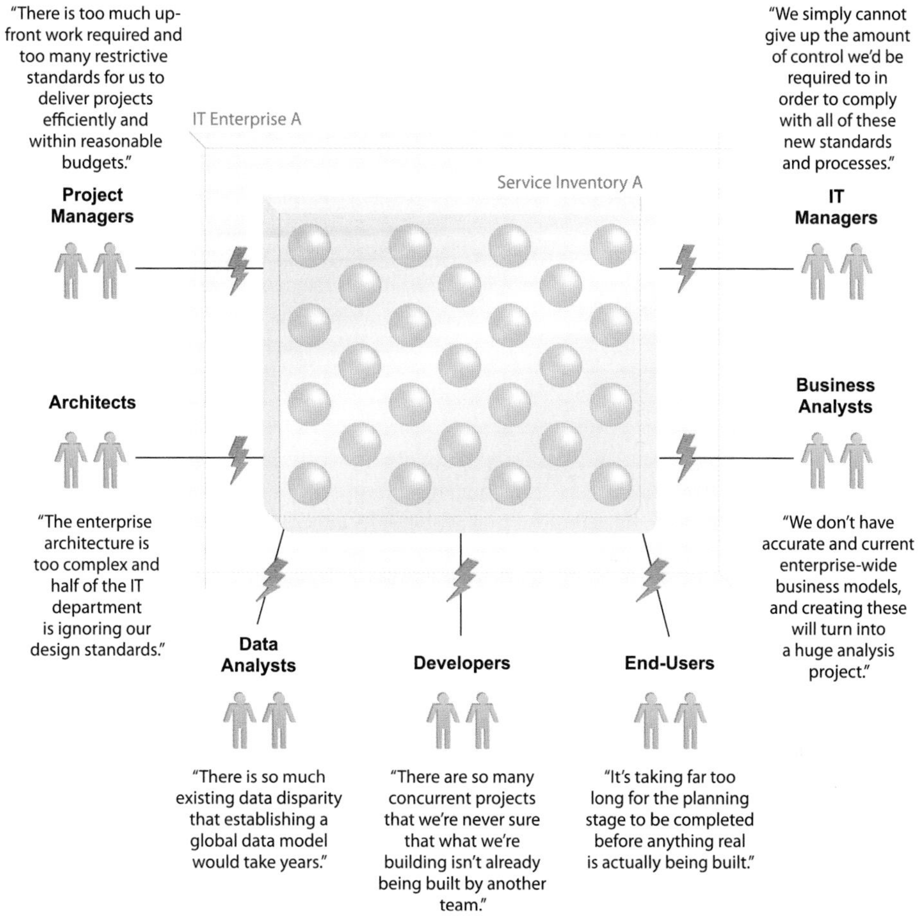

Figure 6.7

Common organizational issues that hinder efforts to establish a single enterprise service inventory.

Solution

Multiple service inventories are created for one enterprise. The scope of each represents a well-defined enterprise domain. Within domains, service inventories are standardized and governed independently (Figure 6.8).

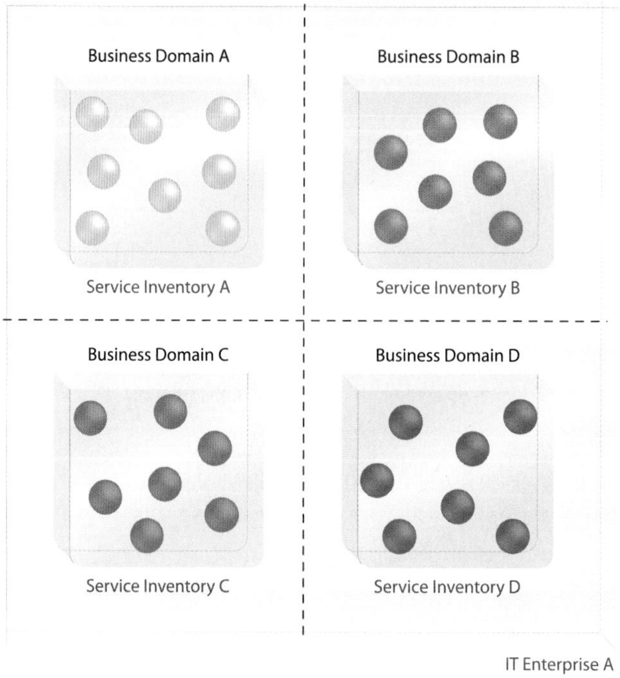

Figure 6.8

An enterprise partitioned into domain service inventories, each representing a pre-defined domain.

Application

Whether or not to apply this pattern is tied to the question of whether an enterprise service inventory is feasible within a given environment. Many factors (most of which are specific to the organization) weigh in on this decision point. However, some general guidelines are available.

For example, domain service inventories are an appropriate alternative when any of the following supporting factors exist:

- The implementation environment is a large enterprise without strong executive sponsorship and wide-spread support for the SOA initiative.
- The enterprise does not have an established, global data models and creating them is considered unrealistic.
- The organization is incapable of changing the complexion of its IT departments in support of a more centralized governance model.

The application of this pattern can bypass these obstacles and accelerate the transition toward service-orientation in that an enterprise-level migration can be delivered in phases that each result in the creation of a manageable collection of services. For many organizations, this pattern provides the only realistic option for adopting SOA.

The key to creating effective domain inventories is to clearly define the domains in advance, thereby establishing a sub-divided view of an enterprise prior to building any one inventory.

Organizations will often have options as to how the domains are defined. Here are some common examples:

- Organizational business areas represented by specific IT departments or groups. These business areas would then establish the basis for business domains.
- Organizational business domains not represented by separate IT departments or groups. These domains can still form the basis of service inventory boundaries but require cooperation across IT departments.
- Remote offices, each with its own IT department and development center. This can result in geographical-based domains.

Ideally, domain inventories correspond to enterprise business domains, such as those based on an organization's lines of business. This allows each inventory to be tuned to and evolve with its corresponding set of business models in full support of establishing the business-driven architecture characteristic.

Impacts

Multi-domain service inventory implementations make some impositions, in that they allow for individual inventories to be standardized differently. This generally results in the need to introduce targeted transformation for cross-domain interoperability as part of the overall enterprise architecture.

The ultimate benefits associated with achieving a unified and federated enterprise service-oriented architecture are scaled back to whatever extent domain inventories are created.

Transformation requirements that emerge to enable cross-domain data exchange impact the development and design effort of corresponding service compositions and also add performance overhead to their runtime execution. Furthermore, the independence by which each inventory can be built and evolved will often lead to the creation of redundant services across domains.

Relationships

The same design patterns that structure an enterprise inventory will end up structuring an inventory defined via Domain Inventory (only the scope will be smaller). However, unlike Enterprise Inventory (116), the application of this pattern will generally result in the need for transformation patterns, such as Protocol Bridging (687) and Data Model Transformation (671). Inventory Endpoint (260) will also play a more prominent role to facilitate cross-inventory communication.

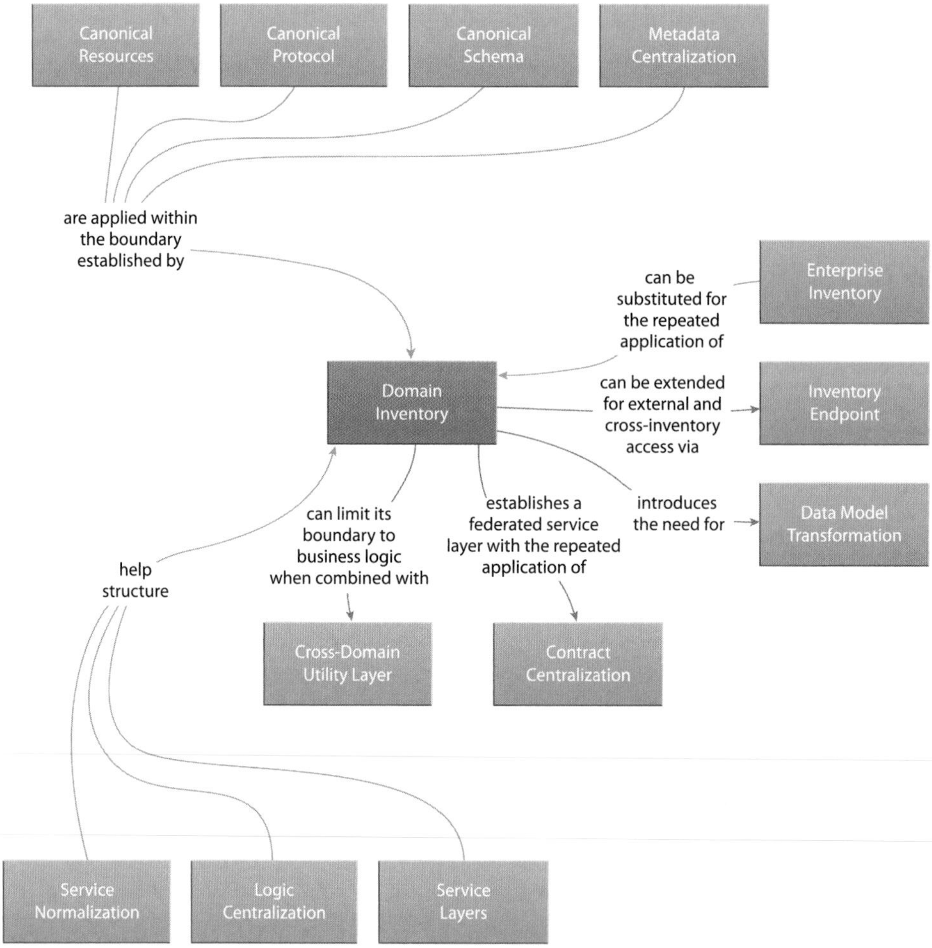

Figure 6.9

Domain Inventory shares many of the same relationships as Enterprise Inventory (116) but introduces new requirements that can be fulfilled by additional patterns more specific to a domain-based environment.

CASE STUDY EXAMPLE

The original goal of McPherson enterprise architects was to establish a global collection of services that would span Alleywood and Tri-Fold platforms. Although it was understood that this would require an unprecedented standardization and federation effort, the strategic benefits seemed to justify it.

However, subsequent to the creation of a more detailed transition plan and associated metrics and cost estimates, many further discussions with management and key IT personnel within Alleywood, Tri-Fold, and other McPherson departments resulted in the identification of several concerns:

- The cost of the standardization effort is much higher than expected, primarily due to the outstanding data architectures that need to be defined.
- Incompatibilities have been identified between some of the preliminary data remodeling that has been performed by Alleywood and the schemas that have already been implemented as part of Tri-Fold's ERP environment. To bring these into alignment would require changing existing Tri-Fold service implementations.
- Alleywood management has complained about several design standards that have been imposed upon them in order to deliver services in compliance with Tri-Fold requirements. Due to the difference in implementation technology, Alleywood feels these standards introduce awkward and inefficient design characteristics into their planned service designs.
- Alleywood and Tri-Fold use different business modeling methodologies. This has resulted in different forms of business model specifications. Furthermore, meetings between analysts from each organization have been strained due to differences in philosophy and conventions associated with business analysis processes.

These and other reasons have prompted a change in the original strategic plan. Instead of creating a single pool of federated services, separate domain inventories will be established (Figure 6.10). This will allow Alleywood and Tri-Fold teams to design and govern their services independently from each other.

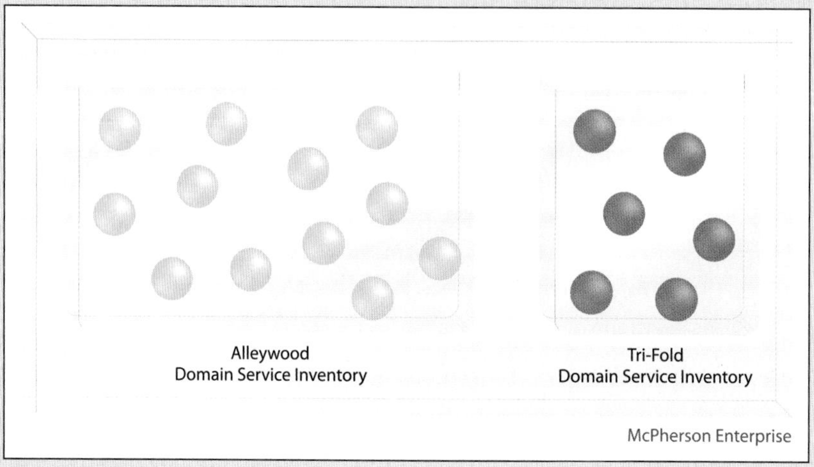

Figure 6.10

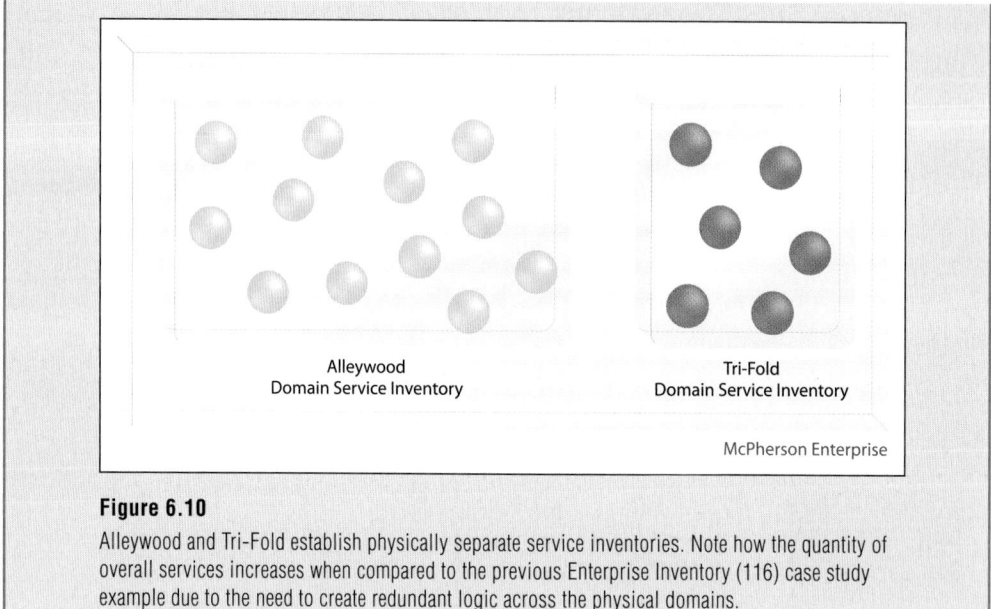

Alleywood and Tri-Fold establish physically separate service inventories. Note how the quantity of overall services increases when compared to the previous Enterprise Inventory (116) case study example due to the need to create redundant logic across the physical domains.

6.2 Inventory Structure Patterns

Once the inventory boundary is determined, the complexion and organization of the inventory itself needs to be determined on a fundamental level. The next set of patterns helps define the underlying inventory structure by establishing basic service boundaries and classifications.

As shown in Figure 6.11, Service Normalization (131) and Logic Centralization (136) influence the inventory structure by requiring that future services be in alignment with each other and that future agnostic services in particular be positioned as the sole endpoint for the logic they represent.

There is no proposed sequence within this pattern group. These patterns simply establish modeling and design parameters on an inventory-wide basis.

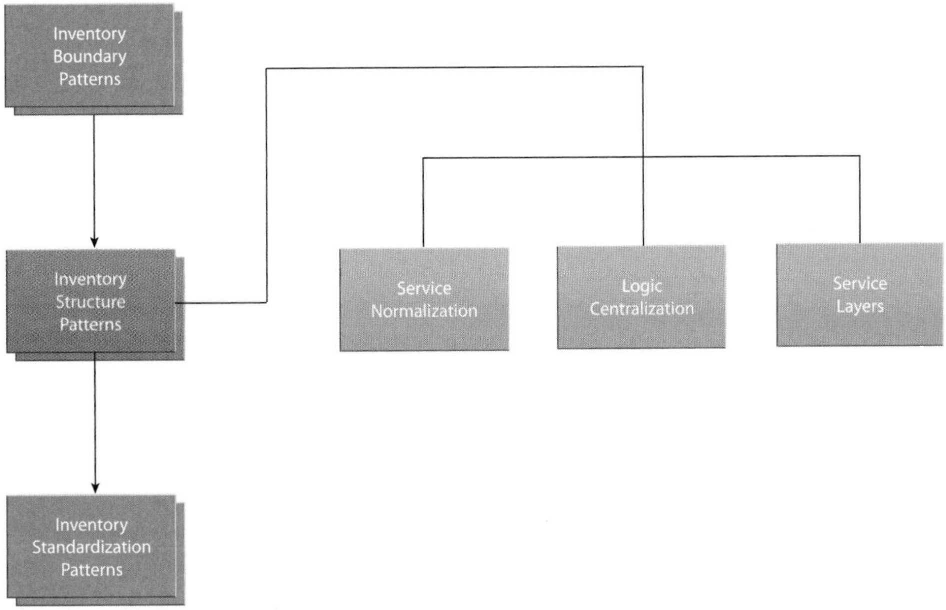

Figure 6.11

The inventory structure patterns align and position services within an inventory and further organize the inventory into logical abstraction layers.

Service Normalization

How can a service inventory avoid redundant service logic?

Problem	When delivering services as part of a service inventory, there is a constant risk that services will be created with overlapping functional boundaries, making it difficult to enable wide-spread reuse.
Solution	The service inventory needs to be designed with an emphasis on service boundary alignment.
Application	Functional service boundaries are modeled as part of a formal analysis process and persist throughout inventory design and governance.
Impacts	Ensuring that service boundaries are and remain well-aligned introduces extra up-front analysis and on-going governance effort.
Principles	Service Autonomy
Architecture	Inventory, Service

Table 6.4

Profile summary for the Service Normalization pattern.

Problem

The boundary of a service is defined by its functional context and the collective boundaries of its capabilities. Even within a pre-defined inventory boundary, when services are delivered by multiple project teams there is a risk that some will provide functionality that will overlap with others.

This leads to a denormalization of the inventory (Figure 6.12), which can cause several problems, such as:

- an inability to establish service capabilities as the official endpoints for bodies of agnostic logic
- a more convoluted architecture wherein services with overlapping functionality can become out of synch, providing the same functions in different ways

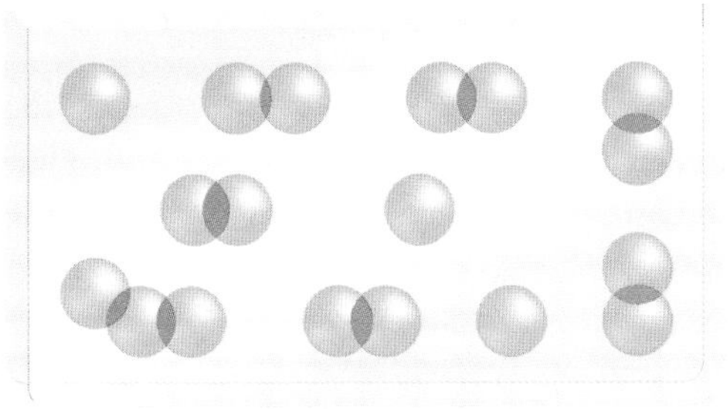

Figure 6.12
A service inventory containing services with overlapping functional boundaries that introduce denormalization.

Solution

Services are collectively modeled before their individual physical contracts are created. This provides the opportunity for each service boundary to be planned out so as to ensure that it does not overlap with other services. The result is a service inventory with a higher degree of functional normalization (Figure 6.13).

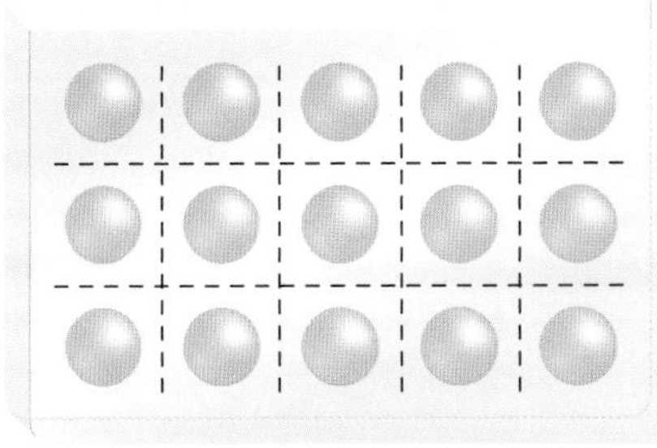

Figure 6.13
When services are delivered with complementary and well-aligned boundaries, normalization across the inventory is attained. Note also how the quantity of required services is reduced.

Application

The goals of this pattern are best realized by pursuing service-level autonomy (as associated with the Service Autonomy design principle) during the service modeling stage.

Common steps include:

1. Identifying and decomposing a business process definition that pertains to the inventory boundary.
2. Allocating the individual parts of the process into appropriate new or existing conceptual service candidates.

3. Validating that no two service boundaries overlap.

These steps are part of a greater service modeling process that takes other modeling considerations into account. To fully apply Service Normalization requires that this process be carried out iteratively, once for every business process that is associated with the scope of the service inventory. Through these iterations, the functional contexts and boundaries of service candidates are repeatedly refined and validated.

The end-result is a service inventory blueprint that provides a normalized view of all services within the inventory. This approach is typically part of a top-down delivery effort.

NOTE

The service modeling process explained in *Service-Oriented Architecture: Concepts, Technology, and Design* contains steps that address normalization issues. However, because larger modeling efforts may result in this process being carried out concurrently by different teams, a subsequent inventory blueprint-wide review is always recommended. Other approaches for achieving the goals of Service Normalization may also exist as part of different methodologies.

Impacts

The guarantee of inventory-wide normalization requires that all services be conceptually modeled prior to delivery, as part of an inventory service blueprint specification. Depending on the scope of the planned inventory, this can result in a separate analysis project that needs to be completed before any service can actually be built.

Continual governance effort is further required to ensure that services maintain normalization throughout the inventory as they are revised and evolved over time.

Relationships

Service Normalization lays the foundation for Contract Centralization (409) by ensuring that no two services share the same functionality. This allows contracts to be positioned as the sole entry point into service logic and further enables those services to be independently evolved, as per Service Refactoring (484). Schema Centralization (200) and Policy Centralization (207) further support this pattern by avoiding contract-related redundancy.

To successfully preserve a normalized inventory requires the consistent enforcement of Logic Centralization (136), making these two patterns very closely related.

Contract Denormalization (414) is referred to in Figure 6.14 only to indicate that, despite its name, it does not interfere with the goals of this pattern. As explained in Chapter 16, Proxy Capability (497) must violate this pattern out of necessity when services require post implementation decomposition.

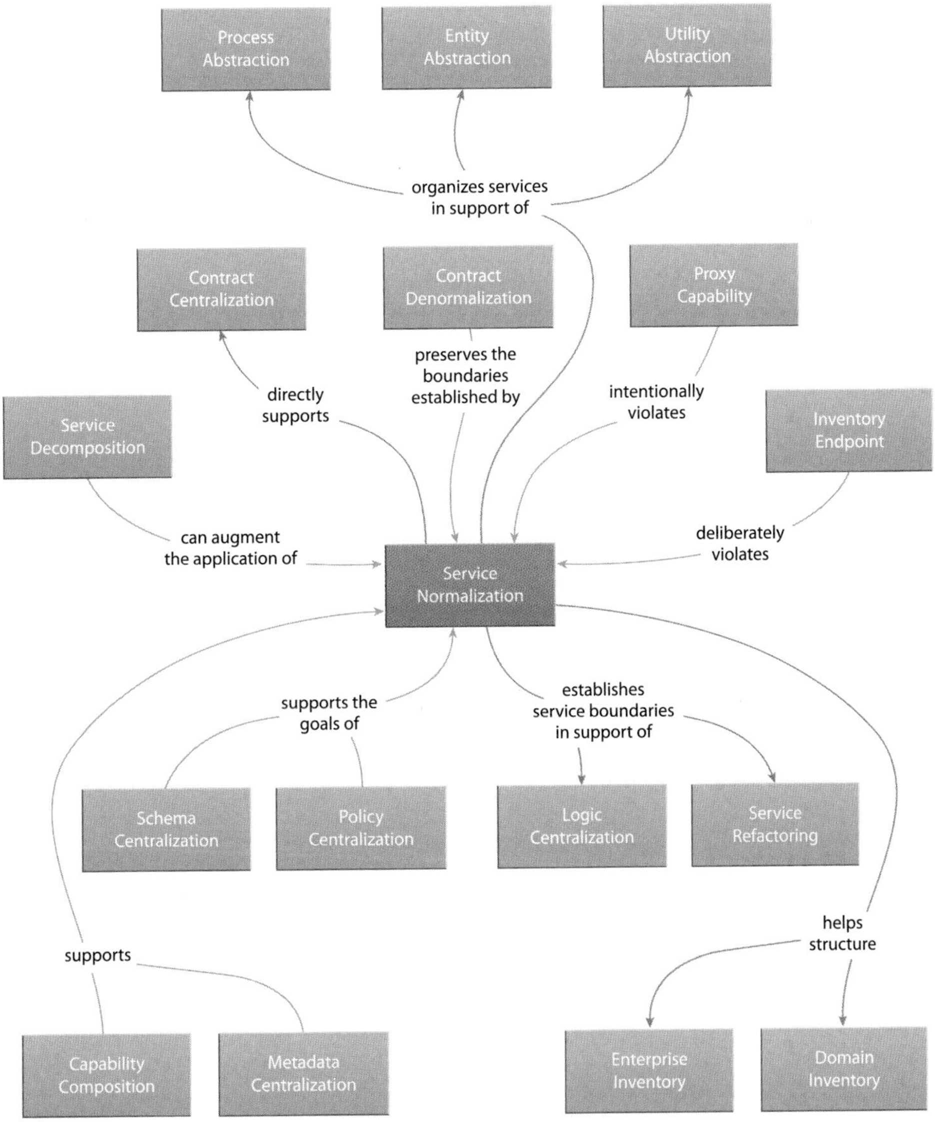

Figure 6.14

Service Normalization fundamentally organizes a service inventory but relies on the successful application of other patterns to retain this state.

CASE STUDY EXAMPLE

Because the initial version of the Alleywood inventory service blueprint was defined via a collaborative effort comprised of different groups of architects and business analysts delivering different service candidates, there is a risk that some of the proposed service contexts functionally overlap with others.

A blueprint-wide review is conducted to look for any potential denormalization of the established service boundaries. A few are detected and subsequently corrected by adjusting the parent contexts of the affected services. One such example is shown in Figure 6.15.

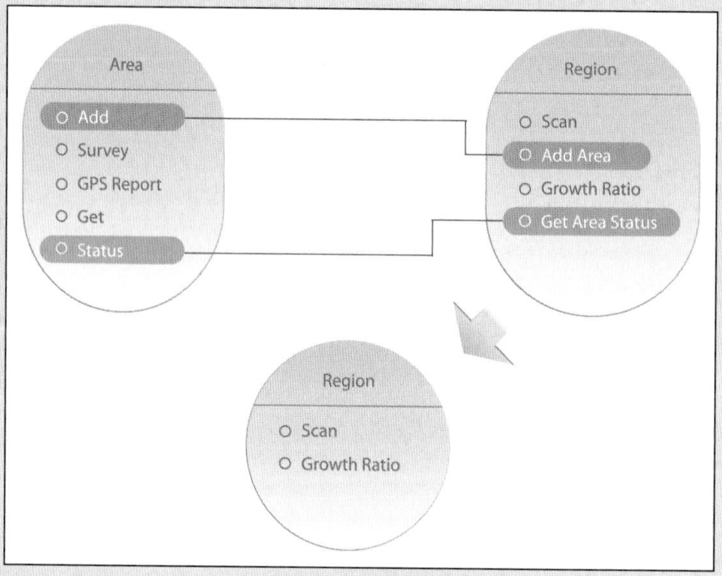

Figure 6.15

Those who modeled the Region service assumed it would encompass area-related processing. However, an Area service was also being delivered by a separate modeling team. As a result, the Region service capabilities associated with area record processing are removed to avoid functional overlap and increase overall inventory normalization.

Logic Centralization

How can the misuse of redundant service logic be avoided?

Problem	If agnostic services are not consistently reused, redundant functionality can be delivered in other services, resulting in problems associated with inventory denormalization and service ownership and governance.
Solution	Access to reusable functionality is limited to official agnostic services.
Application	Agnostic services need to be properly designed and governed, and their use must be enforced via enterprise standards.
Impacts	Organizational issues reminiscent of past reuse projects can raise obstacles to applying this pattern.
Principles	Service Reusability, Service Composability
Architecture	Inventory, Composition, Service

Table 6.5

Profile summary for the Logic Centralization pattern.

Problem

As we established in earlier chapters, reuse represents a key characteristic that typically needs to be realized on a broad scale for some of the more strategic goals associated with service-orientation to be attained. However, even if well-designed agnostic services are consistently delivered into a service inventory, it does not guarantee that project teams building new solutions will use them.

For various reasons, it may be easier, simpler, or just more practical to avoid involving reusable services in order to concentrate on the fulfillment of short-term, tactical delivery goals. This approach may be convenient, but it eventually results in a denormalized service inventory where functional redundancy is common (Figure 6.16).

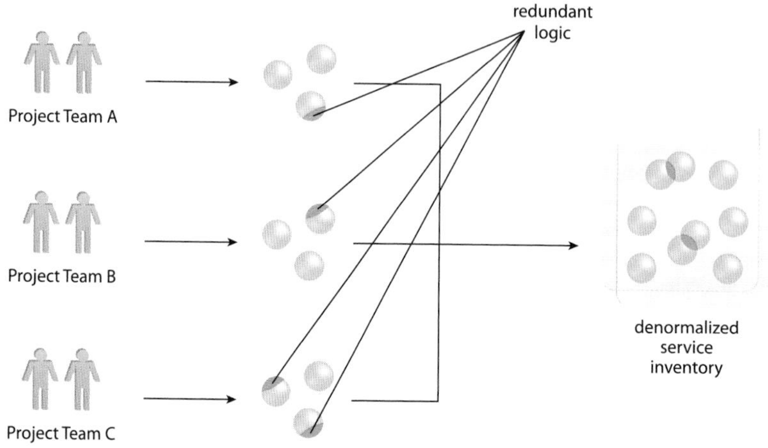

Figure 6.16

Different project teams delivering services with redundant logic leads to functional overlap among services in the inventory.

Solution

To pursue the strategic goals associated with service reuse, the characteristic of reuse itself must form the basis of supporting internal design standards. The foremost of these standards needs to dictate that services classified as agnostic must become a primary (or even sole) means by which the logic they represent is accessed. This forms the basis for Logic Centralization, as depicted in Figure 6.17. The level to which the centralization of logic succeeds as an enterprise-wide standard determines the extent to which the repeated ROI of services can be realized.

Application

When services are built by different project teams, there is always the risk that one team will develop a service with new logic that exists as part of an already-implemented agnostic service.

Common reasons for this are:

- The project team is not aware of the agnostic service's existence or capabilities because the service is not sufficiently discoverable or descriptive.
- The project team refuses to use the existing agnostic service because it is considered burdensome to do so.

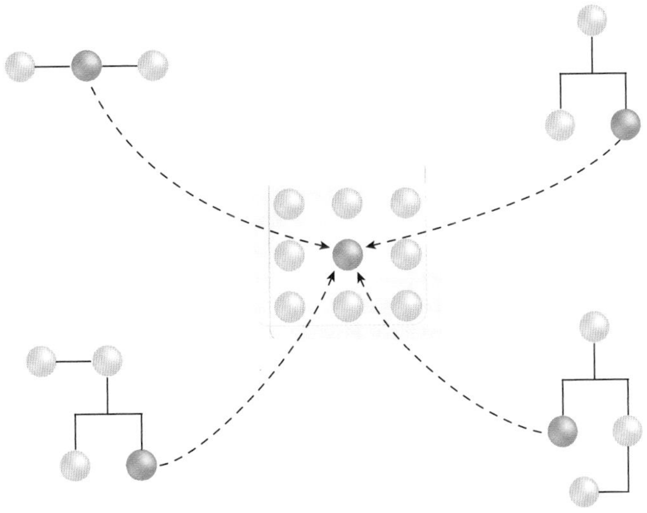

Figure 6.17
Service consumers are required to reuse functionality provided by a single designated agnostic service.

While the former scenario can be avoided through the application of Metadata Centralization (280), the latter is where an inventory-wide design standard is required. In fact, the manner in which this pattern is applied is through the creation and enforcement of a standard that requires that services act as the sole entry point for the functional boundaries they represent within a given inventory.

This type of standard essentially dictates that agnostic services must always be used as intended, even if they do not yet possess all required functions. For example, if a new capability needed by a project team clearly falls within the boundary of an existing service, the corresponding functionality needs to be added to that service instead of ending up elsewhere (Figure 6.18).

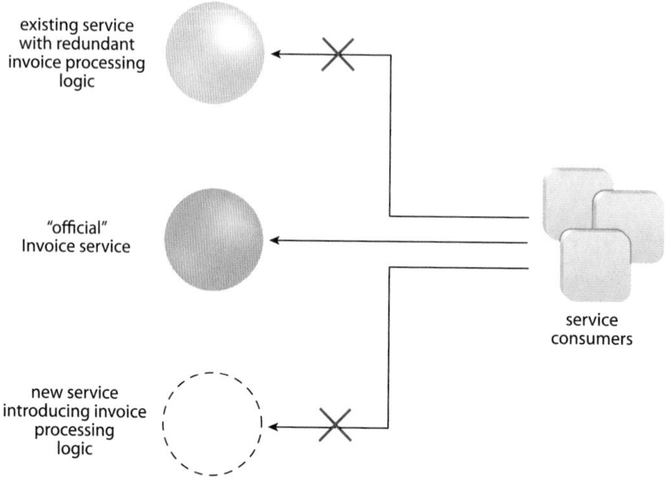

Figure 6.18

In this case, only one service is considered the "official" entry point for invoice-related processing.

Impacts

As straightforward as Logic Centralization may sound, it can be difficult to achieve, especially with broadly scoped service inventories. For larger organizations working toward an enterprise service inventory attaining a state where all development project teams agree to not build redundant logic and instead use existing services may seem like an unattainable ideal.

Introducing Logic Centralization into an organization that does not have a history of fostering reuse or using design standards in general will almost always raise cultural issues with people and IT departments affected by service delivery projects.

For example:

- Existing project plans and processes are impacted by requiring the involvement of reusable services as part of their development projects.
- There may be resistance to giving up control of solution designs if teams are forced to include existing agnostic services or produce new services that need to be reusable.

These concerns need to be addressed prior to the delivery of agnostic services to avoid compromising the strategic value of a service inventory. If only partial support for the delivery and usage of reusable services is received within an IT division, the risk of ending up with a denormalized and potentially convoluted inventory architecture is significant.

Relationships

Logic Centralization is a core design pattern very much focused on centralizing *agnostic* logic, which is why it is commonly associated with Entity Abstraction (175) and Utility Abstraction (168) and also why its application is influenced by Agnostic Context (312) and Agnostic Capability (324).

Whereas Service Normalization (131) primarily solves a service modeling problem, Logic Centralization addresses service usage concerns. In a way, Logic Centralization helps attain the goals of Service Normalization (131).

Contract Centralization (409) also has a very close relationship with Logic Centralization because together they position official services that can only be accessed via official entry points (contracts), which is fundamental to establishing a healthy federated endpoint layer.

There are also numerous peripheral relationships with additional specialized patterns, such as Metadata Centralization (280), which supports the discovery of services to which Logic Centralization has been applied, and Redundant Implementation (345), which supports the scalability demands that tend to fall upon centralized services. Additional examples are shown at the top and bottom of Figure 6.19.

Perhaps its most important relationship is with Capability Composition (521), a pattern that introduces the fundamental rule that logic outside of a service's boundary must be composed.

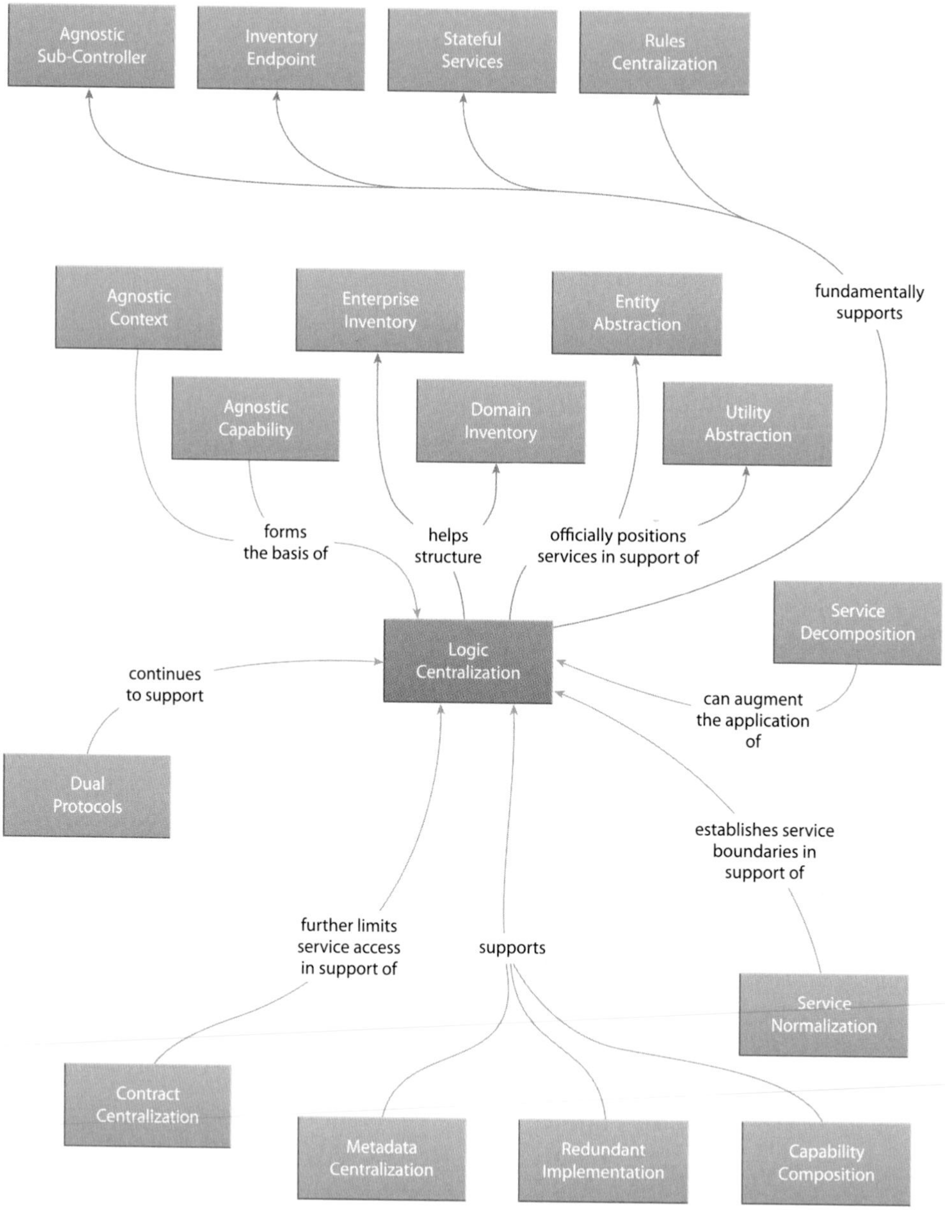

Figure 6.19

Logic Centralization supports the goals of many design patterns but is itself also supported by others.

CASE STUDY EXAMPLE

The preceding Service Normalization (131) example introduced the Area and Region services that had been modeled concurrently and therefore resulted in the definition of overlapping functional boundaries. Alleywood architects speculate that if this overlap had not been corrected during the analysis phase, two services providing redundant functionality would have been delivered within the same service inventory.

Whenever Alleywood service consumer designers would have required the affected Area capabilities, they would have chosen to use either one of the two services, or they would have perhaps only discovered one of the two and simply used that one only. Either scenario risks the misuse of the Region service for area-related functions because no requirement exists to use one over the other.

To prevent this from ever happening, especially with subsequent service delivery projects that may not have the benefit of up-front modeling phases, a special enterprise standard is established. It essentially dictates that for any body of agnostic logic, only one official service is positioned as the endpoint. This standard applies even though the possibility of multiple endpoints will continue to exist.

In Alleywood's case, the enforcement of this standard is tied to the use of a service registry from where any project team can locate the official service for a particular type of capability. Therefore, Alleywood applies this pattern together with Metadata Centralization (280).

Service Layers

How can the services in an inventory be organized based on functional commonality?

Problem	Arbitrarily defining services delivered and governed by different project teams can lead to design inconsistency and inadvertent functional redundancy across a service inventory.
Solution	The inventory is structured into two or more logical service layers, each of which is responsible for abstracting logic based on a common functional type.
Application	Service models are chosen and then form the basis for service layers that establish modeling and design standards.
Impacts	The common costs and impacts associated with design standards and up-front analysis need to be accepted.
Principles	Service Reusability, Service Composability
Architecture	Inventory, Service

Table 6.6

Profile summary for the Service Layers pattern.

> **NOTE**
>
> This pattern should not be confused with Service Layer (Fowler, Stafford). Whereas the goal of Service Layers is to establish logical domains represented by collections of related services, the application of Service Layer results in an externally facing interface layer for a specific application.

Problem

Within a typical service inventory there will tend to be services that have similar functional contexts. However, these services may be designed and implemented differently, depending on the nature of the delivery project. This leads to a missed opportunity to establish consistency in how service boundaries are defined and in the nature of the logic they encapsulate. The result is an inventory of services that cannot easily (or cleanly) be partitioned into groups for the purpose of sub-domain based abstraction and governance (Figure 6.20).

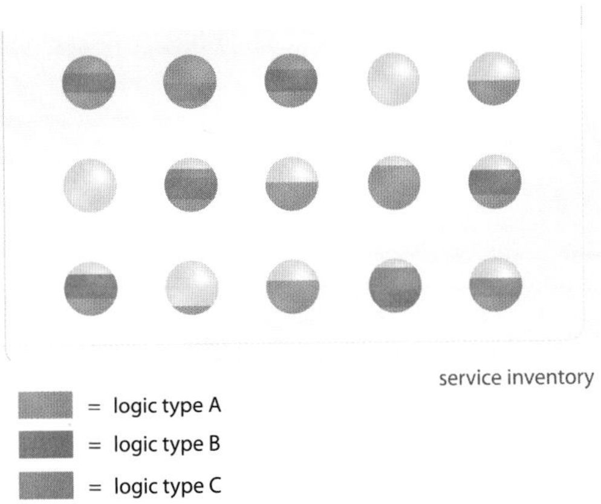

Figure 6.20

Arbitrarily delivered services exist as hybrids where many encapsulate different forms of logic. This can inhibit their reusability and long-term governance.

Solution

A service inventory architecture can formally establish classification profiles to represent common types of services within a given inventory. These profiles are referred to as *service models,* each of which represents a unique set of design characteristics associated with a well defined service category. Service models form the basis for this pattern in that a collection of services that conform to one model establish a logical architectural layer of related functionality (Figure 6.21).

Applying Service Layers ensures that services matching common types are designed with the same fundamental characteristics, as derived from common service models. These services can form logical domains within the inventory, which can be evolved and governed as groups (Figure 6.22).

> **NOTE**
>
> Because service layers are closely related to service models, this pattern could have easily been called Service Models instead. The term "Service Layers" was chosen because it represents the end-result of repeatedly applying service models to service inventories.

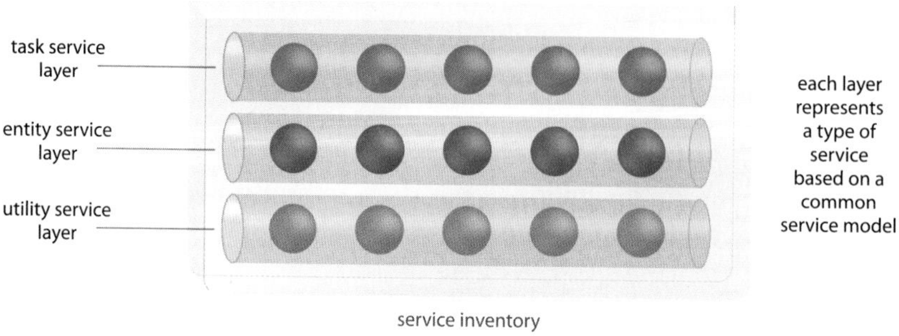

Figure 6.21

Related services are designed according to service models, thereby establishing logical service layers. In this case, the service inventory is structured with three service layers that correspond to the three abstraction patterns described in Chapter 7. (Note the pipe symbol is used to represent a service layer in this book.)

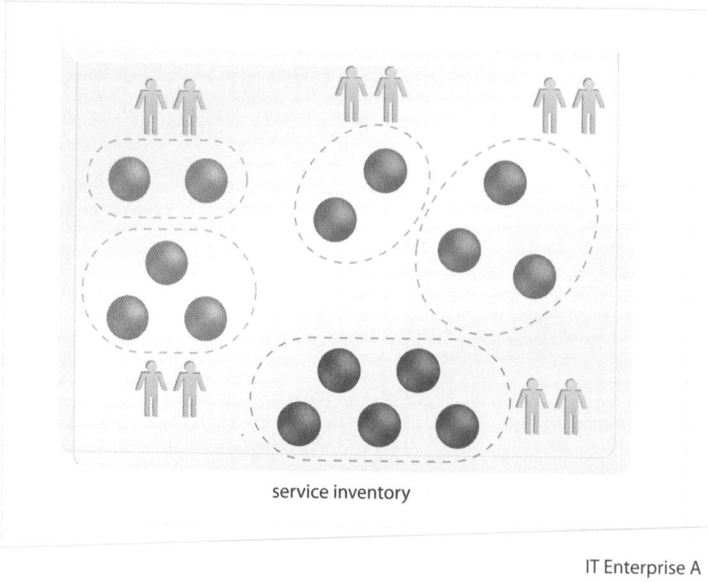

Figure 6.22

Layers (and sub-layers) can form groups of services. Long-term governance ownership of these groups can be assigned to dedicated custodians most suited to the nature of the underlying service models.

Application

Layers of services are generally defined prior to the implementation of a service inventory. During the modeling of a service inventory blueprint, the functional nature of planned service candidates helps determine what layers are most suitable. Therefore, any given service inventory can have different layers. The only rule is that there be a minimum of two.

The most fundamental layers are:

- a layer that represents single-purpose (non-agnostic) logic
- a layer that represents multi-purpose (agnostic) logic

By abstracting non-agnostic logic into one part of an inventory, agnostic logic can be defined and evolved in support of fostering reusability.

While there is always the option of customizing service layers, the safest starting point is to base them on common industry service models. These fundamental models have been proven to solve known design problems and are further explored in Chapter 7 as part of the descriptions for Process Abstraction (182), Entity Abstraction (175), and Utility Abstraction (168). As illustrated in Figure 6.23, service compositions tend to naturally span service layers established by common service models.

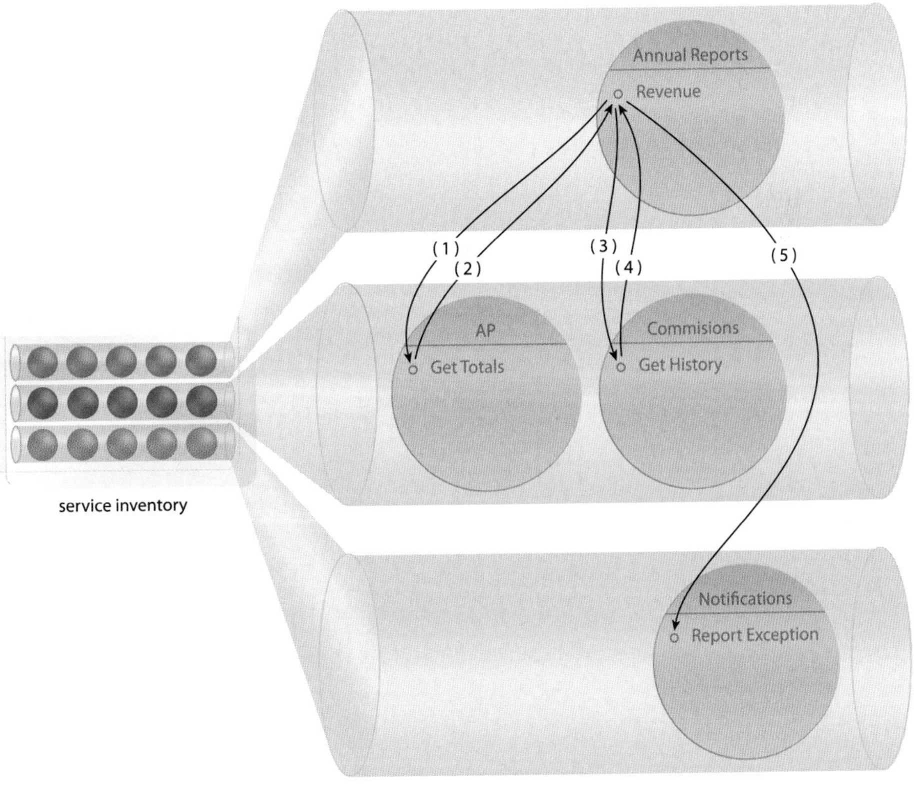

Figure 6.23
Shown here is a service inventory organized into process, entity, and utility layers (left) and a service composition drawn from this inventory comprised of services that span these layers (right).

Impacts

Determining what service models should or shouldn't be used within a service inventory requires a familiarity with the types of logic that reside within the inventory's boundary. Therefore, service layers often evolve out of repeated iterations of the service-oriented analysis phase and sometimes even require revisions to previously modeled service candidates. As a result, their use can increase the time and effort required to define a service inventory blueprint.

An exception to this is when service models have already been established as enterprise design standards, in which case they can be used as the basis for planned service layers right from the start.

Furthermore, once layers have been chosen, they become inventory-wide design standards in that every subsequently defined service needs to fit into one of the established service layers. After services have been built according to the underlying service models, it can be very difficult to change the structure of the established layers without disrupting the service inventory.

Relationships

Service Layers introduces logical separation into inventory boundaries and therefore naturally builds upon Enterprise Inventory (116) and Domain Inventory (123). Both Service Normalization (131) and Logic Centralization (136) help establish firm boundaries for individual services that allow for them to be organized into layers in support of this pattern.

As shown in Figure 6.24 and explored throughout Chapter 7, this pattern forms the basis of Utility Abstraction (168), Entity Abstraction (175), and Process Abstraction (182).

NOTE

Service Layers is at the root of the abstraction patterns that are core to the compound pattern Three-Layer Inventory (715).

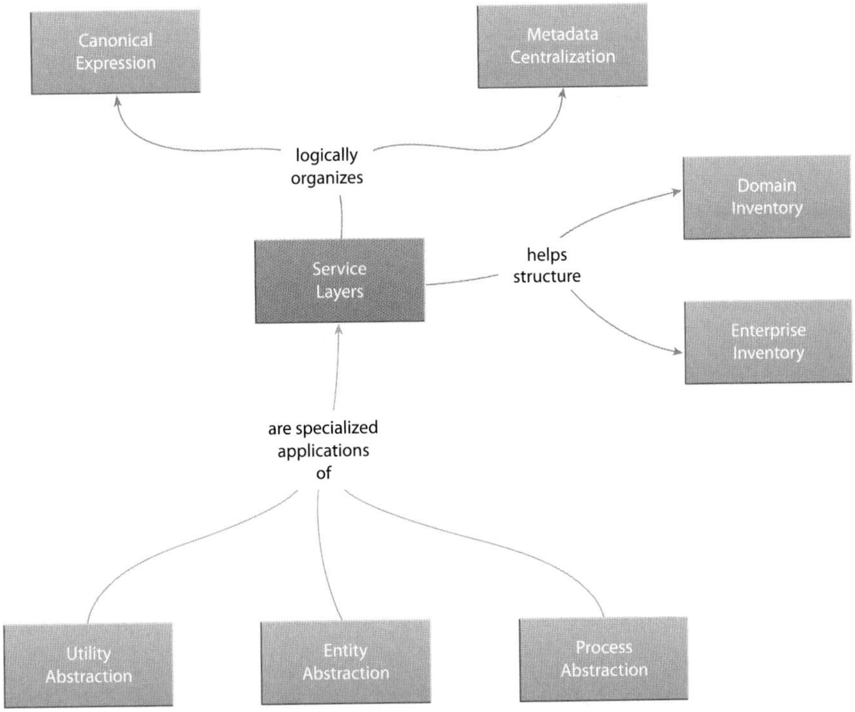

Figure 6.24

Service Layers relates to preceding and upcoming patterns by adding a logical structure to the service inventory.

CASE STUDY EXAMPLE

As they proceed through service-oriented analysis stages, architects and analysts for Cutit, Alleywood, and the FRC individually decide that the task, utility, and entity service models will be used to standardize layers of services within their respective planned service inventories.

See the case study examples in Chapter 7 for details as to how specific layers are created by these organizations as a result of adopting the pattern.

6.3 Inventory Standardization Patterns

Design patterns and design standards were defined as two separate but related parts of a typical design framework back in Chapter 4. A design pattern provides a proven solution to a common design problem, and a design standard is a mandatory convention applied across multiple systems. Whereas a design pattern is industry-recognized, a design standard is internal and specific to an IT enterprise.

Even though they are distinct, design standards are a lot like design patterns. In fact, design standards can be seen as "pre-solving" specific design issues in order to ensure consistent system designs. It is therefore not uncommon for a design pattern to become the basis of design standard, which is essentially what this group of patterns is all about.

These next patterns (Figure 6.25) do not just propose possible solutions to common problems, but they propose that to solve this set of specific problems, the solutions themselves must become actual design standards.

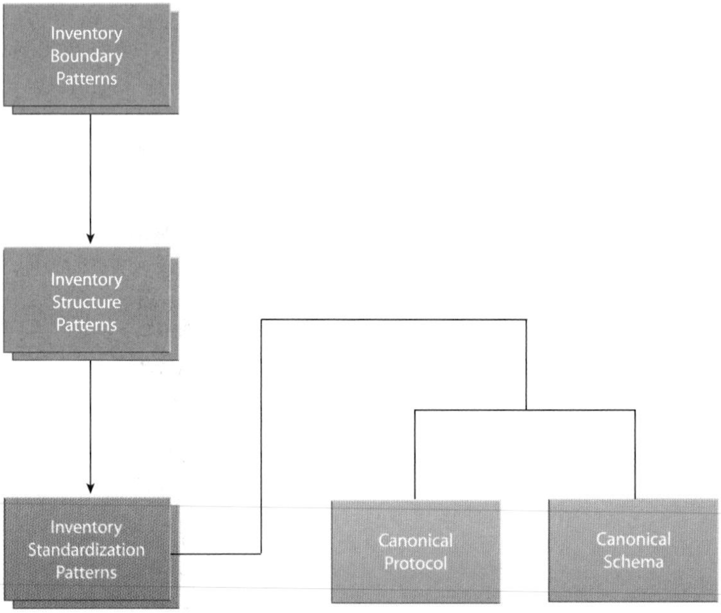

Figure 6.25

The two standardization patterns enforce fundamental design conventions in support of fostering intra-inventory interoperability.

Though there is no particular order in which these patterns need to be applied, it is sometimes necessary for Canonical Protocol to be established prior to the Canonical Schema because the communications technology represents the fundamental medium by which data (and associated data models) are delivered and processed.

Canonical Protocol

How can services be designed to avoid protocol bridging?

Problem	Services that support different communication technologies compromise interoperability, limit the quantity of potential consumers, and introduce the need for undesirable protocol bridging measures.
Solution	The architecture establishes a single communications technology as the sole or primary medium by which services can interact.
Application	The communication protocols (including protocol versions) used within a service inventory boundary are standardized for all services.
Impacts	An inventory architecture in which communication protocols are standardized is subject to any limitations imposed by the communications technology.
Principles	Standardized Service Contract
Architecture	Inventory, Service

Table 6.7
Profile summary for the Canonical Protocol pattern.

What Do We Mean by "Protocol"?

Within the context of this pattern, "protocol" represents technologies required to establish baseline communication. From a Web services perspective this would include the standardization of a transport protocol, such as HTTP, as well as a messaging protocol, such as SOAP. Other more specific message formats that may also be commonly referred to as protocols, would likely not fall within the scope of this pattern, especially if they introduce specific structures via pre-defined schemas. In this case, they may be more relevant to Canonical Schema (158).

Problem

Each service exists as a standalone software program. When these programs need to exchange information, they have to form a connection using a communications technology. When programs are designed to use different communications technologies, they are incompatible and cannot exchange information without involving a separate program that can translate one communications technology to another, as per Protocol Bridging (687).

Building services with different implementation technologies is not uncommon, but allowing services based on different communication technologies to exist within the same architecture can result in limitations. For example, groups of services based on the same communication framework are likely to be delivered as part of the same project. The day any of these services needs to be pulled into a new composition consisting of services delivered by a different project (and using different communication protocols), incompatibility issues could make their connectivity and reuse challenging and perhaps impossible (Figure 6.26).

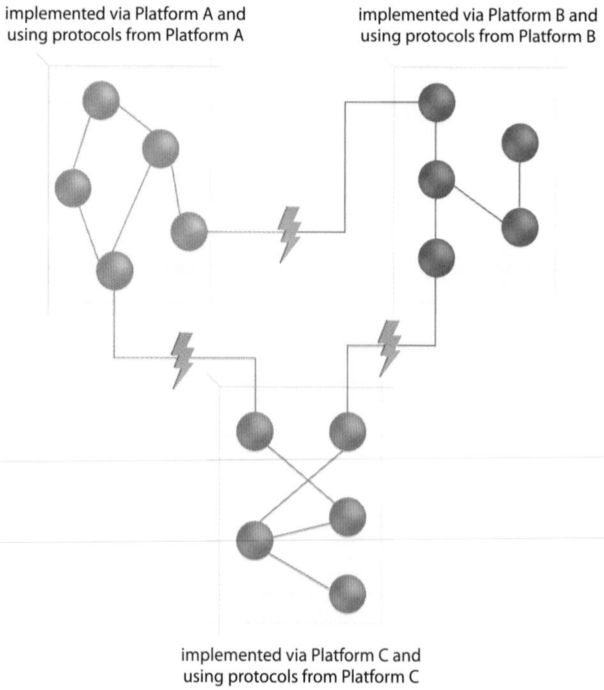

Figure 6.26

Different groups of services (likely delivered via different projects) establish communication boundaries through the use of incompatible communication protocols.

Solution

The technology architecture is designed to limit enablement of cross-service interaction to a single or primary communications protocol or protocol version. All other technologies associated with supporting the protocol's underlying communications framework are also standardized. This guarantees baseline technological compatibility across services (Figure 6.27).

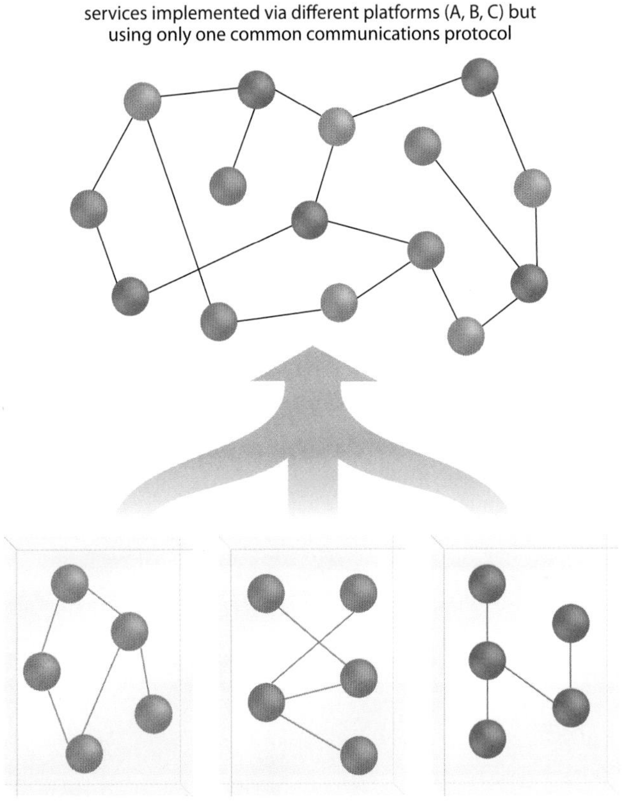

Figure 6.27

Though still delivered by different projects via different vendor platforms, these services conform to one centralized communications technology, making them technologically compatible.

NOTE

This design pattern advocates the standardization of protocols used for inter-service communication only. Traditional protocols, such as those used to communicate with proprietary components or databases, are not affected by this pattern as long as they remain part of the logic encapsulated by services.

Application

To ensure that all services an inventory architecture is intended to support can effectively interact and be repeatedly recomposed requires that a centralized communications technology be carefully chosen.

A common framework that fulfills this role is the Web services platform because it leverages industry-standard transport and messaging protocols (e.g., HTTP and SOAP) that are widely supported yet still vendor-neutral. However, even when using Web services, this design standardization pattern must still be applied to overcome possible disparity resulting from the mismatch of protocol-related *versions* (as illustrated in Figure 6.28). The WS-I Basic Profile is therefore likely a key part of applying this pattern as a means of ensuring technological compatibility among the various versions of Web service technology standards.

Alternative communication options can also be explored within controlled environments. For example, a proprietary vendor protocol can be chosen, as long as all services within its inventory are standardized to conform to its use.

NOTE

When applying this design pattern to Web services, any Web services-related industry standards and technologies associated with inter-service communication are affected. This can include WSDL, XML Schema, SOAP, WS-Policy, and various WS-* standards. This pattern does not dictate how these technologies are applied, only that their use—and, in particular, their version—are standardized.

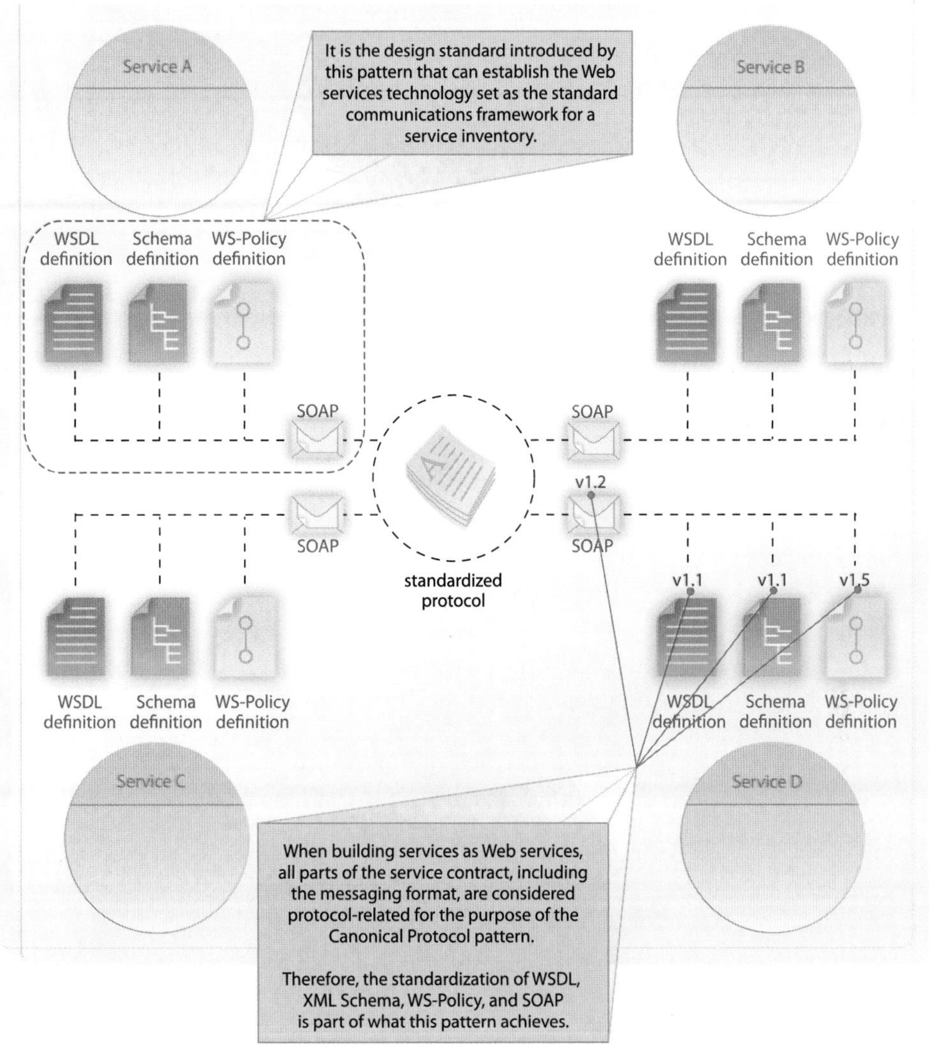
Service A
It is the design standard introduced by this pattern that can establish the Web services technology set as the standard communications framework for a service inventory.
Service B
WSDL definition
Schema definition
WS-Policy definition
WSDL definition
Schema definition
WS-Policy definition
SOAP
SOAP
v1.2
SOAP
SOAP
standardized protocol
v1.1
v1.1
v1.5
WSDL definition
Schema definition
WS-Policy definition
WSDL definition
Schema definition
WS-Policy definition
Service C
Service D
When building services as Web services, all parts of the service contract, including the messaging format, are considered protocol-related for the purpose of the Canonical Protocol pattern.
Therefore, the standardization of WSDL, XML Schema, WS-Policy, and SOAP is part of what this pattern achieves.

Figure 6.28

All parts of the Web service contract are affected by this design pattern.

Impacts

Some key considerations when standardizing on one communication protocol are:

- *Maturity and Reliability* – Whichever protocol is chosen, service interaction throughout the resulting technology architecture will be constrained by whatever limitations this framework imposes. Therefore, the maturity and overall adequacy of the communications technology must be carefully assessed.
- *Longevity* – If there are any concerns that vendors may discontinue or abandon the technology, the associated risks would need to be taken into account.
- *Cost* – Building services to support a primary communication protocol can bring with it a series of hidden expenses. Some may be related to accommodating deficiencies in the protocol (as per the maturity, reliability, and longevity considerations just raised), while other costs can be incurred if the protocol is part of a proprietary platform that requires licensing fees.

When the preferred protocol imposes constraints in any of these areas, Dual Protocols (227) can be viewed as a viable alternative to (or even a first step toward) this pattern.

NOTE

This design pattern could be considered a specialized implementation of Canonical Resources (237) in that it is very much about standardizing technology across an inventory. However, it is singled out here because a communication protocol is more than just an architectural extension. It represents the fundamental means by which all parts of a distributed solution work together.

Relationships

Canonical Protocol's architectural focus naturally results in relationships with other architecture-centric design patterns, such as Canonical Resources (237), Enterprise Inventory (116), and Domain Inventory (123).

By standardizing the medium by which services exchange business and activity data, a foundation for service interoperability is established. Therefore, this pattern is closely related to Service Messaging (533), Messaging Metadata (538), and also Schema Centralization (200).

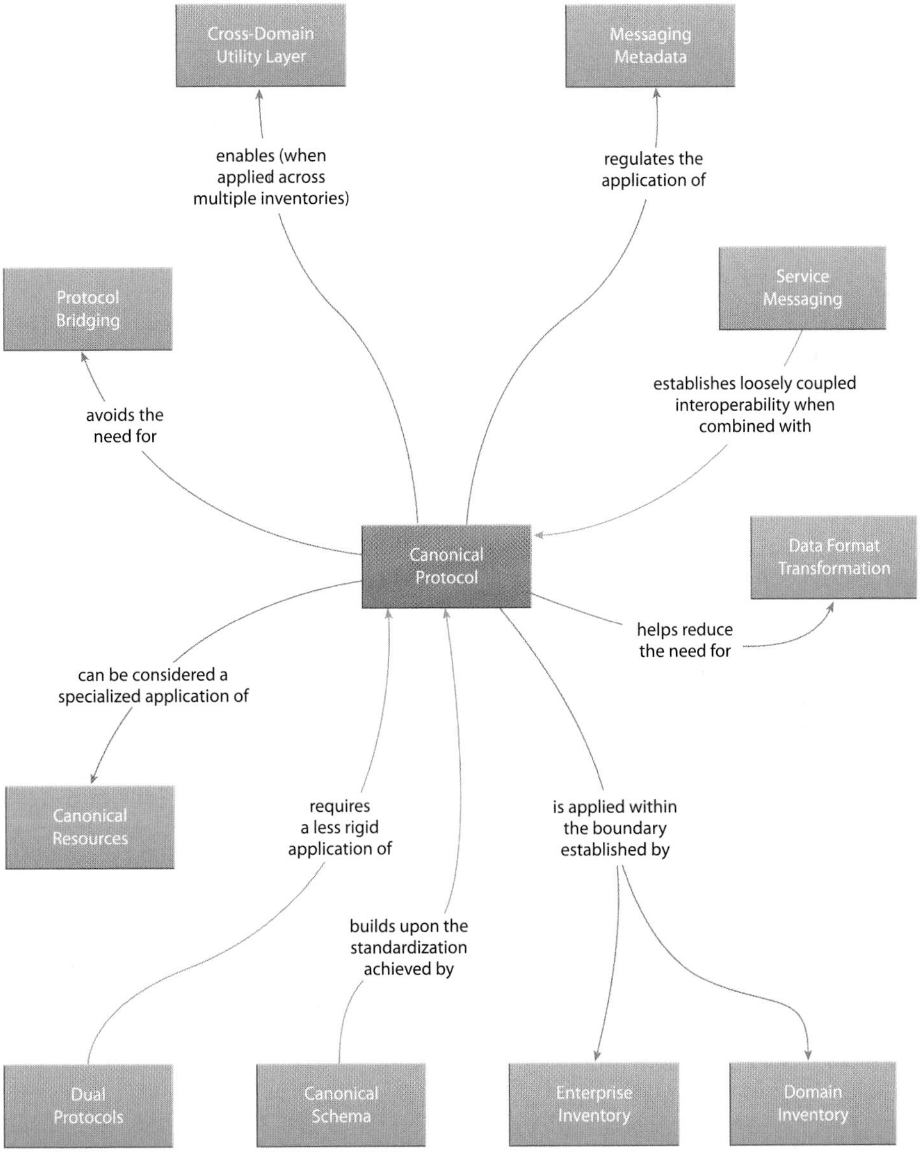

Figure 6.29

Canonical Protocol proposes an inventory-wide design standard that solves foundational interoperability issues and therefore relates to inventory and messaging patterns.

CASE STUDY EXAMPLE

Alleywood's IT environment has historically been Java-based. The services planned as part of the current project were naturally going to be developed and implemented using Java technologies. The importance of Canonical Protocol was acknowledged as architects determined that it would make the most sense for all services to be accessible via a central JMS messaging framework.

However, subsequent discussions with Tri-Fold architects and enterprise architects from McPherson resulted in a requirement to move toward a Web services-based communications framework instead.

This was a strategic decision based primarily on the fact that Tri-Fold's services are comprised of endpoints into a larger ERP, plus a set of custom .NET components. Neither environment supports JMS, but both support Web services, as does Alleywood's Java-based platform (Figure 6.30).

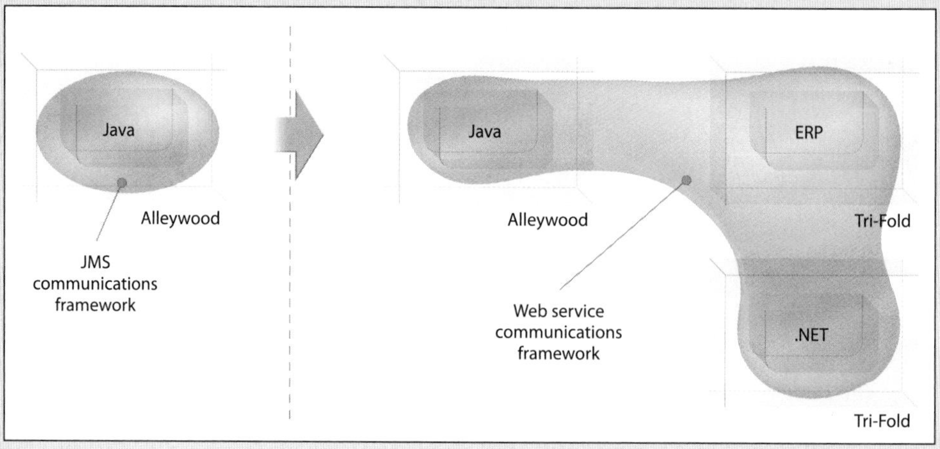

Figure 6.30

Although the application of this pattern was already considered when attempting to standardize on JMS, subsequent requirements broadened the scope of the centralized communications framework to encompass three platforms. This led to the decision to standardize on the use of Web services.

Canonical Schema

How can services be designed to avoid data model transformation?

Problem	Services with disparate models for similar data impose transformation requirements that increase development effort, design complexity, and runtime performance overhead.
Solution	Data models for common information sets are standardized across service contracts within an inventory boundary.
Application	Design standards are applied to schemas used by service contracts as part of a formal design process.
Impacts	Maintaining the standardization of contract schemas can introduce significant governance effort and cultural challenges.
Principles	Standardized Service Contract
Architecture	Inventory, Service

Table 6.8
Profile summary for the Canonical Schema pattern.

> **NOTE**
>
> Canonical Schema should not be confused with Canonical Data Model (Hohpe, Woolf). With Canonical Schema, services and consumers utilize and conform to an already-developed data model, avoiding the need for transformation. The classic Canonical Data Model pattern assumes that data model transformations are necessary and recommends that they be designed in such a manner that they adhere to a standard data model instead of resulting in pair-wise permutations.

Problem

For a service to send or receive data, it needs to know in advance exactly how that data will be organized and structured. For example, a business document such as an invoice can have its own data model structure that determines how invoice information is organized, what the different parts of an invoice document are called, and what data types and validation constraints should be associated with these parts.

When different services are delivered by different project teams, each team may decide to structure an invoice data model in a different way. When those services need to exchange invoice data at a later point in time, they will not be compatible and will require Data Model Transformation (671) to convert one invoice document structure into another.

This generally introduces the need to design and develop a custom transformation layer consisting of mapping logic and rules that resolve differences between disparate schemas. This logic can be implemented as part of the service hosting environment and carries out its transformation *every time* data needs to be exchanged via the affected service capabilities (and is therefore considered undesirable).

Solution

The need for Data Model Transformation (671) can be avoided by ensuring that service contracts are designed with compatible schemas from the beginning. This is achieved by applying data design standards to the data models within service contracts (see Figure 6.31).

Application

Canonical Schema is commonly applied to services implemented as Web services because this allows for data models to be defined using the industry standard XML Schema expression language. In this case, XML Schema definitions representing the same type of documents or information sets need to be kept in alignment so that complex and simple data types remain in synch across different service contracts.

Once standardized schemas are in place, this pattern is realized via a formal process through which service contracts are designed, which ensures consistent application of the Standardized Service Contract design principle.

Impacts

In larger enterprises, the scope of data model standardization may need to be limited to individual domains so as to make the standardization effort and the subsequent governance responsibilities more manageable. In fact, it is the considerations raised by this pattern that often motivates organizations to apply Domain Inventory (123) over Enterprise Inventory (116).

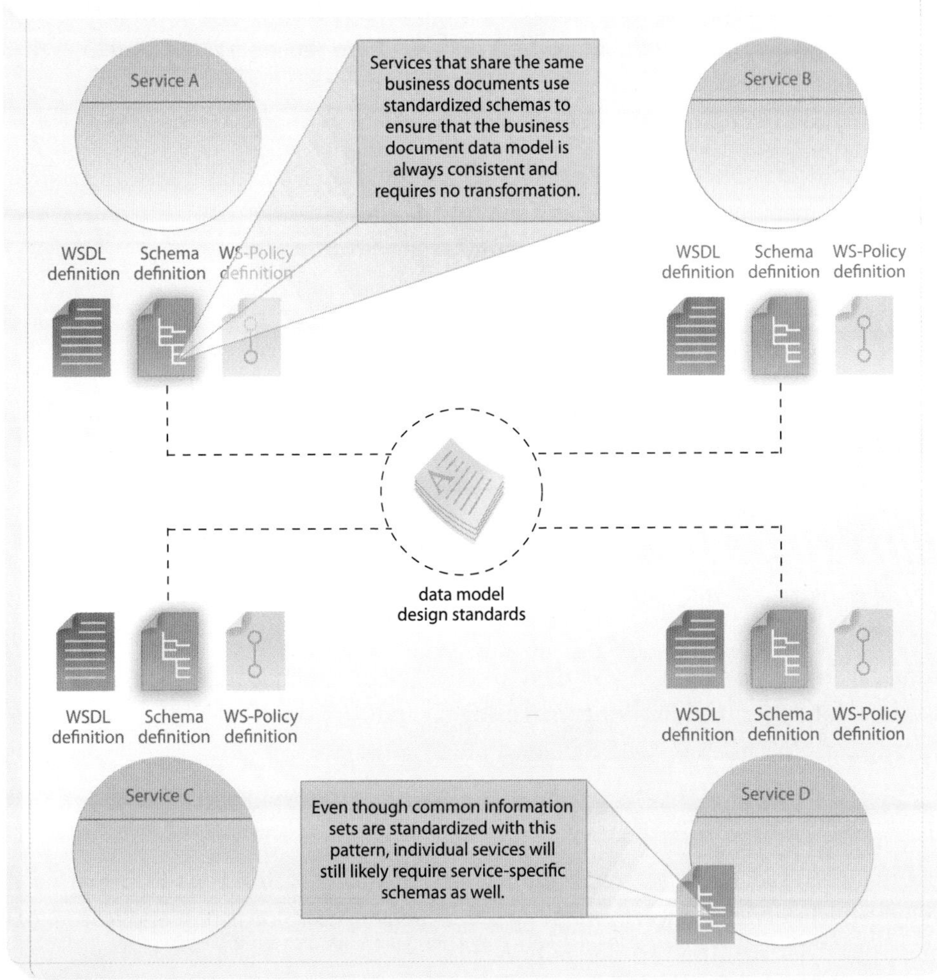

Figure 6.31

Multiple services implemented as Web services have standardized XML schema definitions as a result of applying this pattern.

Relationships

Data models are typically standardized within the boundaries of inventories defined by Enterprise Inventory (116) or Domain Inventory (123), resulting in a healthy inventory architecture with a reduced need for Data Model Transformation (671).

Also, by establishing a key design standard in support of service interoperability, Canonical Schema forms several close relationships with other patterns, such as Schema Centralization (200) and Canonical Protocol (150).

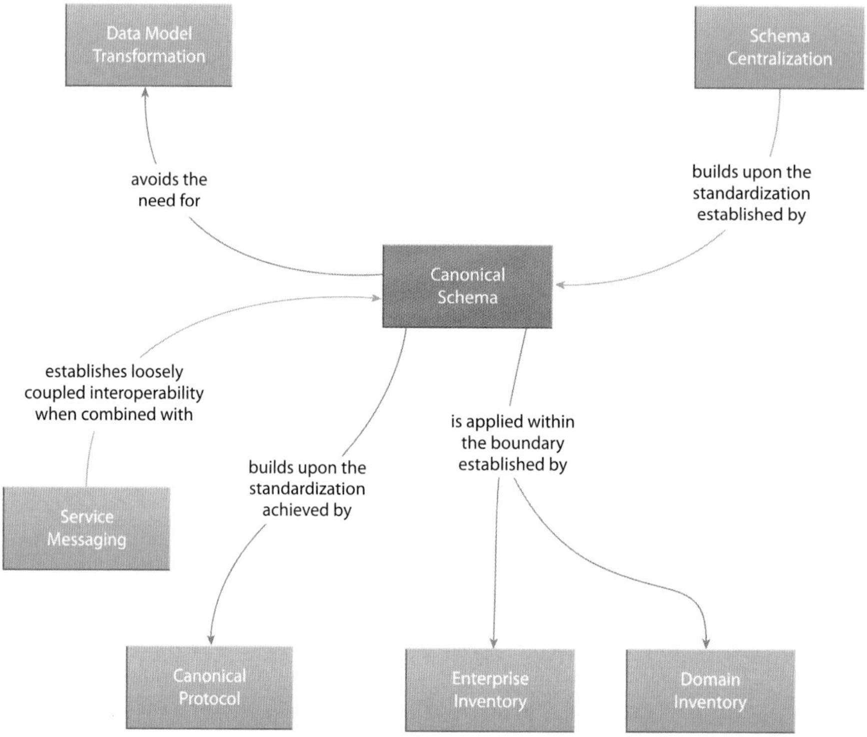

Figure 6.32

Canonical Schema achieves an important type of standardization that is fundamental to inventory architectures.

CASE STUDY EXAMPLE

The three disparate environments that were somewhat unified by the application of Canonical Protocol (150) and the introduction of a Web services framework are expected to share a fair amount of data.

Architects realize that the mere use of Web services will not standardize data exchange beyond the communication protocol itself. As it currently stands, the same types of data used by the individual environments is represented by different data models, as defined by the underlying database structures that were independently created. For an order

Service Layers (143) establishes a general means of organizing the services within an inventory into logical groups. Each layer is based on a type of service and therefore represents a set of services that conform to this type. These types correspond to industry classifications referred to as *service models*.

Following are the three most common service models:

- *Utility Service Model* – A type of service that provides generic processing logic that is not classified as business logic (as explained in the upcoming *Business Logic and Agnostic Logic* section). Utility logic is often referred to as “cross-cutting” logic because it is ideally agnostic and reusable and therefore multi-purpose in nature.
- *Entity Service Model* – A business-centric service type that is derived from one or more business entities. Entity services are also agnostic and therefore expected to be highly reusable.
- *Task Service Model* – Also a business service model, but one that is intentionally non-agnostic because its functional scope is limited to single-purpose business process logic.

These three service models correspond to the three inventory layer patterns described in this chapter as follows:

- Utility Abstraction (168) establishes a service layer comprised of utility services.
- Entity Abstraction (175) results in a service layer that represents entity services.
- Process Abstraction (182) creates a non-agnostic service layer that consists of task services.

Combining Layers

As explained by Three-Layer Inventory (715), it is a recommended practice to use all three of these design patterns together. For most organizations, they collectively represent an effective grouping of common service logic.

However, this is not absolutely required. The rule established by Service Layers (143) is that at least two layers must exist. Given that it is generally desirable to have one layer abstract non-agnostic logic, this means that Process Abstraction (182) can be applied together with either Utility Abstraction (168) or Entity Abstraction (175), as shown in Figure 7.1.

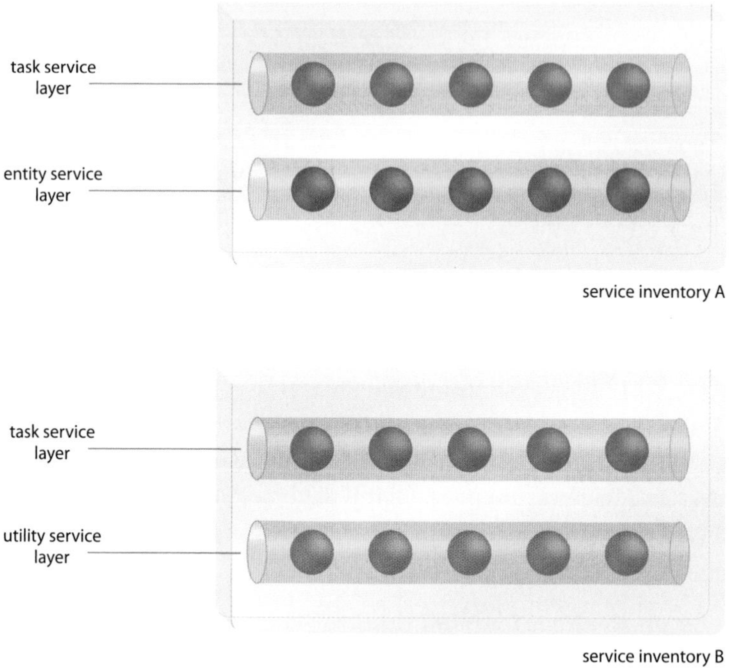

Figure 7.1

Two different service inventories, each with only two service layers. Inventory A establishes an entity service layer that is most likely comprised of services that also encapsulate common utility logic. Inventory B limits its agnostic services to the utility layer, which probably results in entity-specific logic being redundantly dispersed throughout the task service layer.

Service layer combinations that are less common include the following:

- *Utility + Entity* – If these layers are intended to represent agnostic and reusable services, then this layer combination will rely on composition via consumer programs that are not service-oriented. This can still foster reuse but the overall composability potential of services will be limited.
- *Task Only* – A service inventory structured with a single task service layer makes little sense because it would essentially be comprised of a series of independent, silo-based applications. Although it is common to find a set of single-purpose programs that represent some or all of an IT enterprise, from a service-orientation perspective, there is not much gain to this design. Agnostic service layers are required to establish services as reusable enterprise resources.

NOTE

Organizations can choose to derive custom variations of these fundamental abstraction patterns and can even create new service models and abstraction layers altogether. Sometimes this approach is warranted when a service inventory spans domains and a unique, business domain-specific service model is required.

Business Logic and Utility Logic

When discussing service models and service layers (and service design in general), a distinction is always made between business logic and non-business logic. Logic is classified as being business-centric when it is derived from business analysis models and specifications. Examples of such documents include workflow or business process definitions, BPM specifications, ontologies, taxonomies, logical data models, business entity references diagrams, and a variety of other documents related to business architecture, data architecture, and information architecture in general.

Anything having to do with *representing* the manner in which an organization carries out its business can generally be classified as a form of business logic. When it comes to service encapsulation, we are primarily interested in business logic that can be automated.

Automating business logic requires more processing than is generally documented by the aforementioned business analysis documents. There are various underlying mechanics and resources that come into play at a technology level. Those parts of the processing logic that are not related to or derived from business logic are classified as utility logic, as explained in the upcoming description of Utility Abstraction (168).

Agnostic Logic and Non-Agnostic Logic

The term "agnostic" originated from Greek where it means "without knowledge." Therefore, logic that is sufficiently generic so that it is not specific to (has no knowledge of) a particular parent task is classified as *agnostic* logic. Because knowledge specific to single purpose tasks is intentionally omitted, agnostic logic is considered multi-purpose. On the flipside, logic that *is* specific to (contains knowledge of) a single-purpose task is labeled as *non-agnostic* logic.

Another way of thinking about agnostic and non-agnostic logic is to focus on the extent to which the logic can be repurposed. Because agnostic logic is expected to be multi-purpose, it is subject to the Service Reusability principle with the intention of turning it into highly

reusable logic. Once reusable, this logic is truly multi-purpose in that it, as a software program (or service), can be used to automate multiple business processes.

Non-agnostic logic does not have these types of expectations, which is why non-agnostic services are deliberately designed as single-purpose software programs.

NOTE

The word "agnostic" also has specific meaning within some religious communities. If you are uncomfortable using this term, you can substitute it with terms like "neutral" or "unbiased." Although the underlying meaning is not quite as clear with these terms, they may still be effective in making the distinction between these logic types.

Service Layers and Logic Types

Each of the design patterns in this chapter defines a service layer that is based on a distinct combination of the four logic types we just covered, as shown in Table 7.1.

	Business Logic	Utility Logic	Agnostic Logic	Non-Agnostic Logic
Utility Service Layer		x	x	
Entity Service Layer	x		x	
Task Service Layer	x			x

Table 7.1

An overview of how common service layers relate to the fundamental logic types. Any service that ends up containing logic that spans two or more layers cannot be cleanly grouped into a layer structure such as this, and is therefore often labeled as a *hybrid service.*

Note the absence of a service layer that represents both utility and non-agnostic logic. Such a service layer can be created, but it is not common and therefore not documented as a separate pattern. Generally, the need to assemble services together into compositions is driven by business-centric tasks or processes. This establishes the task service layer as the primary part of a service inventory that abstracts non-agnostic logic.

Utility Abstraction

How can common non-business centric logic be separated, reused, and independently governed?

Problem	When non-business centric processing logic is packaged together with business-specific logic, it results in the redundant implementation of common utility functions across different services.
Solution	A service layer dedicated to utility processing is established, providing reusable utility services for use by other services in the inventory.
Application	The utility service model is incorporated into analysis and design processes in support of utility logic abstraction, and further steps are taken to define balanced service contexts.
Impacts	When utility logic is distributed across multiple services it can increase the size, complexity, and performance demands of compositions.
Principles	Service Loose Coupling, Service Abstraction, Service Reusability, Service Composability
Architecture	Inventory, Composition, Service

Table 7.2

Profile summary for the Utility Abstraction pattern.

Problem

Among the logic required to automate just about any business task, there will be some that can be considered generic, "cross-cutting" processing functionality that has no relationship to formal business models. IT environments typically have a variety of technologies, products, databases, and other resources that offer features or functions useful for many purposes. This type of non-business centric logic can be considered utility logic.

The functionality associated with the automation of a business process will often include utility processing functions that find themselves bundled together into the same service with business process logic, business rules, and other forms of business logic (Figure 7.2).

This packaging results in hybrid services that make the individual strategic design and governance of utility logic practically impossible. For example, if generic processing

functionality capable of addressing multiple cross-cutting concerns is embedded together with business process-specific logic, it becomes challenging to make the generic processing logic separately available for reuse.

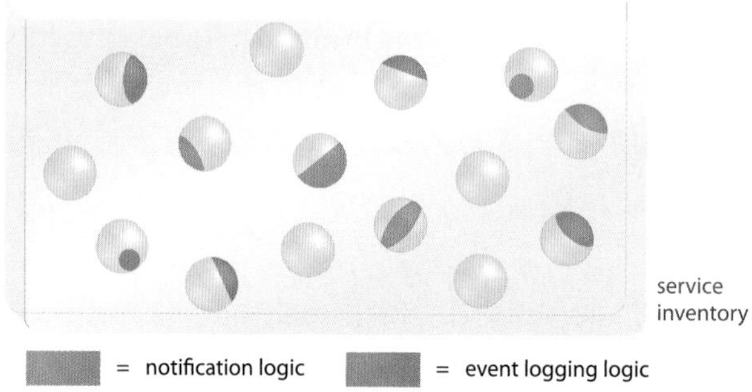

Figure 7.2

Utility logic is embedded within services that also contain business-centric functionality. As a result, much of the utility logic is redundantly implemented and not reusable.

Solution

Agnostic non-business-centric utility functions are defined and grouped into separate utility services. Because these utility services provide common functions that are not specific to any one task, they can be reused to automate multiple tasks. The result is a utility service layer (Figure 7.3) that is typically defined, owned, and governed by technology experts (usually without involvement of business experts).

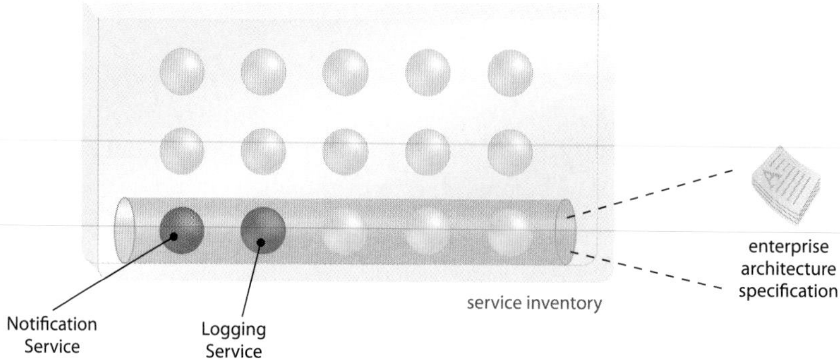

Figure 7.3

Cross-cutting utility logic is identified with the help of enterprise technology architecture specifications and then abstracted into a layer of dedicated services based on the utility service model.

Application

Utility processing is common to all enterprises, but the process of abstracting cross-cutting functionality into reusable units of logic can be difficult. One challenge constantly associated with utility service designs is the definition of appropriate service contexts. Unlike business service contexts that can be derived from existing business models, the functional context of utility services is often left to the judgment of architects and developers. It can therefore be challenging to set a service context that is suitable for long-term reuse and service contract longevity.

Here are some guidelines:

- Avoid overly coarse-grained services that bundle lots of capabilities together. These can be difficult to reuse and establish awkward functional contexts that can lead to bloated services over time.
- Define a very clear functional context for each service but give it the flexibility to evolve with the inventory. Unlike business services that tend to have strict boundaries, utility service boundaries can be augmented somewhat as long as the parent context is preserved.
- Use Canonical Expression (275) to ensure the creation of easy-to-understand service contracts. Because utility services tend to be produced by technology experts, there is often the danger that their public-facing contract details will be too technology-centric and cryptic.

During the service modeling process, the logical utility layer is already preconceived and conceptualized. Subsequently, when service contracts are ready to be defined, a special process geared toward utility service design needs to be applied so that the unique issues associated with this type of service can be addressed.

Establishing a formal utility service layer that spans a service inventory requires constant attention to how logic is partitioned and grouped within functional service contexts. Despite best efforts, you should be prepared to eventually split up coarse-grained utility services, as per Service Decomposition (489). You can prepare for this by applying Decomposed Capability (504) in advance.

Impacts

Adding this service layer to an inventory that already separates its services into multiple business-centric layers will predictably increase the size and design complexity of service compositions. Due to the additional inter-service communication required, runtime performance will also be affected.

Furthermore, the definition of utility service layers can make some impositions on how traditional development projects may have been carried out. However, the fact that object-oriented analysis and design (as well as aspect-oriented programming) have raised an awareness of the benefits of abstracting cross-cutting utility logic, these requirements will not be too foreign to most organizations.

Relationships

Because its application also results in agnostic service layers—and therefore is fundamentally influenced by Agnostic Context (312)—Utility Abstraction shares many of the same pattern relationships as Entity Abstraction. The primary difference is the absence of business-centric influences.

Notable relationships specific to Utility Abstraction are Service Agent (543), which emulates its non business-centric functional context and Cross-Domain Utility Layer (267), which essentially results in a broad application of Utility Abstraction. Rules Centralization (216), Service Perimeter Guard (394), and Stateful Services (248) also can be considered specialized implementations of this pattern.

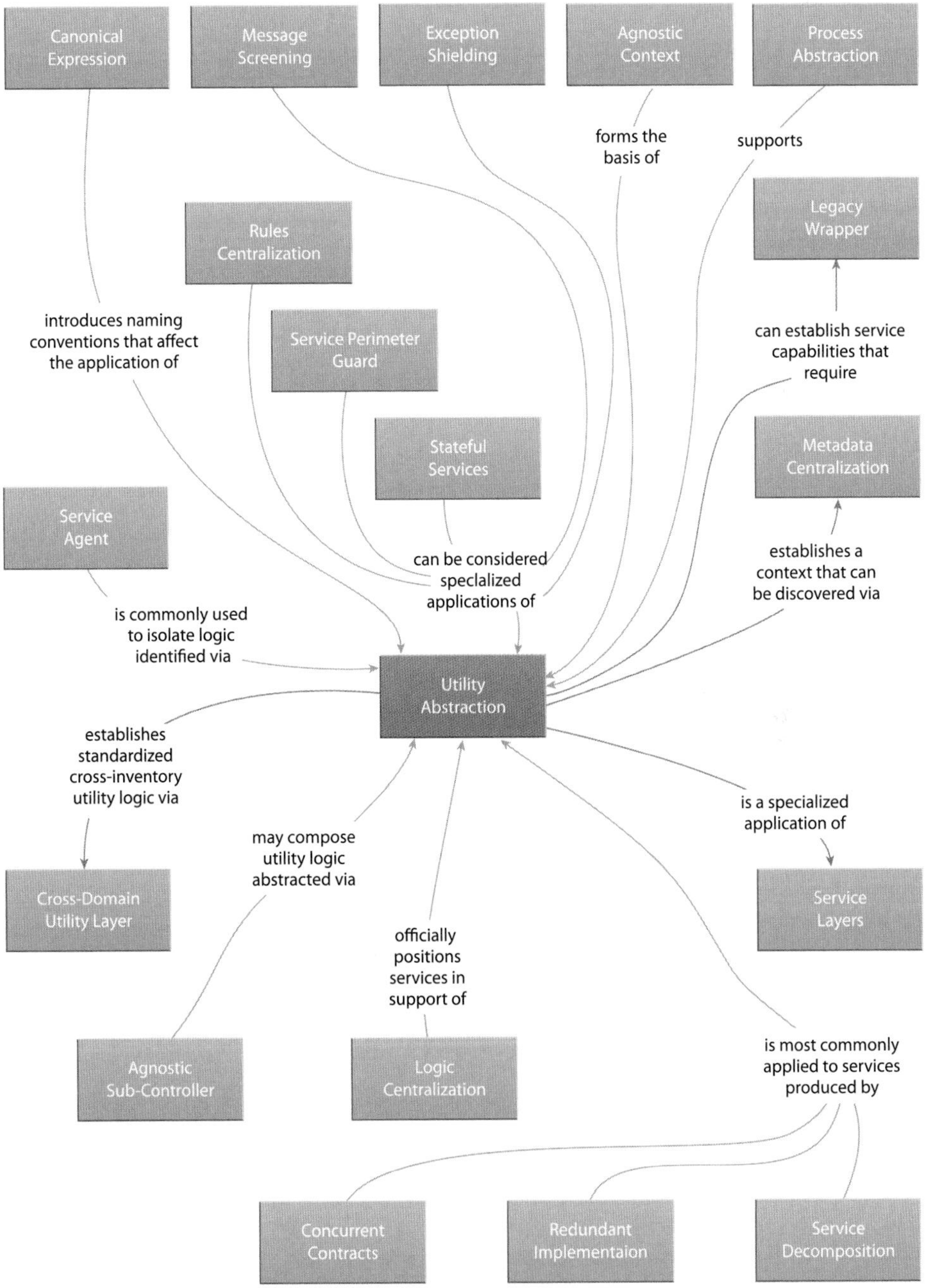

Figure 7.4

Utility Abstraction tends to relate to design patterns that are not business-centric but still concerned with the design of agnostic logic.

CASE STUDY EXAMPLE

Cutit's immediate priority is to streamline their internal supply chain process. The order process in particular needs to be supported by the planned services so that orders and back-orders can be fulfilled as soon as possible.

A service-oriented analysis effort is carried out with the assumption that all three common service layers (utility, entity, task) will be used as the basis for the inventory's logical structure. This stage includes detailed service modeling and business process decomposition, resulting in the identification of several key relationships between different Cutit artifacts.

Here are some examples:

- Everything originates with the manufacturing of chain blades in the Cutit lab, which requires the use of specific *materials* that are applied as per predefined *formulas*.
- The assembly of *chains* results in products being added to the overall *inventory*.
- *Saws* and *kits* are items Cutit purchases from different manufacturers to complement their chain models.
- *Notifications* need to be issued when stock levels fall below certain thresholds or if other urgent conditions occur.
- Finally, a periodic *patent sweep* is conducted to search for recently issued patents with similarities to Cutit's planned chain designs.

These artifact relationships are incorporated into service modeling steps that produce the preliminary service inventory blueprint shown in simplified form in Figure 7.5. The analysis reveals a series of service candidates, most of which are business-centric in nature. The Patent Sweep and Notifications service candidates, however, have functional contexts that do not correspond to any modeled business specifications. They are therefore classified as utility services and together establish the beginning of Cutit's inventory utility service layer.

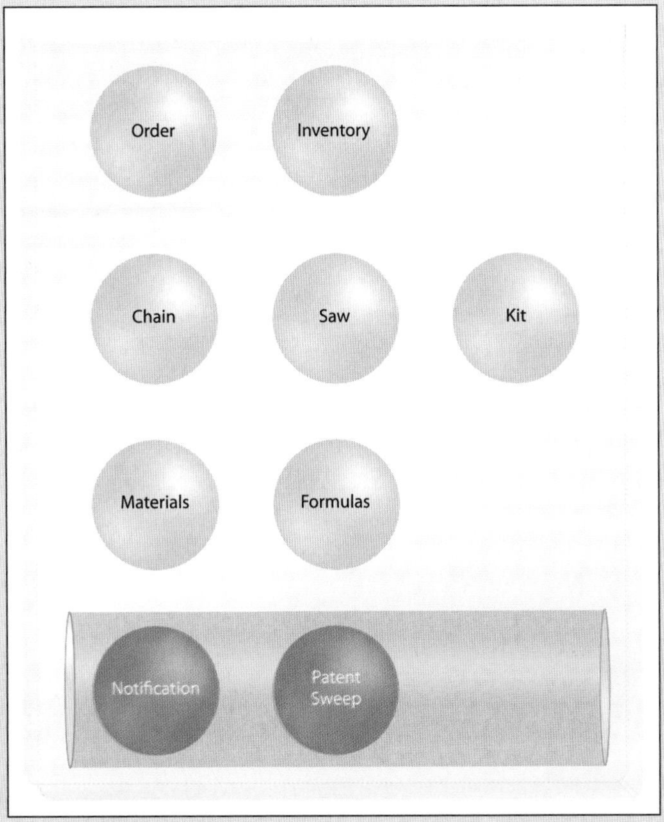

Figure 7.5

The initial set of services planned to support the following types of processes: keeping track of orders and back-orders, chain manufacturing, tracking required manufacturing materials, and the inventory management of manufactured and purchased products. To support these tasks, two utility services are defined. Note that task services are intentionally excluded from this diagram so that they can be introduced in the case study example for Process Abstraction (182).

Entity Abstraction

How can agnostic business logic be separated, reused, and governed independently?

Problem	Bundling both process-agnostic and process-specific business logic into the same service eventually results in the creation of redundant agnostic business logic across multiple services.
Solution	An agnostic business service layer can be established, dedicated to services that base their functional context on existing business entities.
Application	Entity service contexts are derived from business entity models and then establish a logical layer that is modeled during the analysis phase.
Impacts	The core, business-centric nature of the services introduced by this pattern require extra modeling and design attention and their governance requirements can impose dramatic organizational changes.
Principles	Service Loose Coupling, Service Abstraction, Service Reusability, Service Composability
Architecture	Inventory, Composition, Service

Table 7.3
Profile summary for the Entity Abstraction pattern.

Problem

When attempting to abstract business logic there is a natural tendency to group together logic associated with a specific task or business process. Any potentially reusable business logic is embedded together with single-purpose, process-specific logic. Therefore, the reusability potential for this logic is lost (Figure 7.6).

Additionally, the business analysts who have entity-level expertise are often different from those who have process-level expertise. When entity and process logic are grouped together in support of automating a particular task, it is usually owned by the analysts responsible for the business process definition. This can result in missed opportunities to incorporate design considerations specific to business entity rules, characteristics, and relationships.

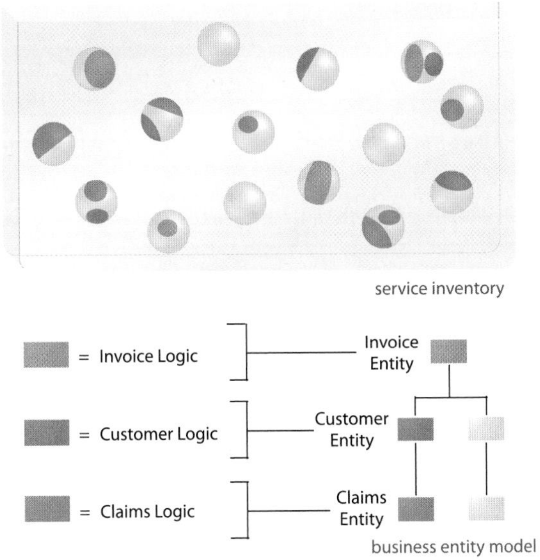

Figure 7.6

Solution logic associated with the processing of specific business entities is added to (most likely task-centric) services as required and therefore is dispersed (and redundantly implemented) throughout the service inventory.

Solution

To carry out its business, each organization deals with different "business things," like people, documents, products, and partner organizations. These things (or artifacts) are referred to as *business entities*. As organizations change the way they do business, new tasks may be required, or existing tasks may need to be altered. But throughout all of this change, new or revised tasks usually continue to involve the same business entities.

When looking for ways to design multi-purpose services that have a lot of reuse potential, it is therefore considered a safe bet to build services based on business entities. These entity services are naturally multi-purpose because each can be reused to help automate different tasks. This pattern partitions business logic that is evidently multi-purpose into a separate set of services with agnostic functional contexts based on business entities (Figure 7.7).

Application

To apply this pattern, the service modeling process needs to be carried out to identify and group logic appropriate for entity service encapsulation. Subsequently, the service-oriented design process for entity services must be completed to create standardized

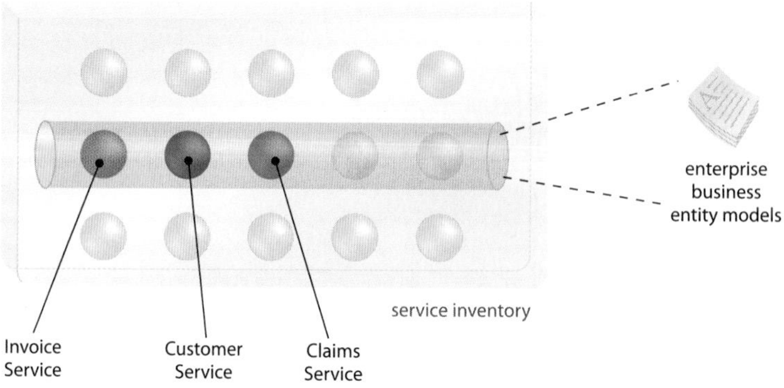

Figure 7.7
A layer of entity services, each of which encapsulates processing associated with a specific business entity (or a group of related entities).

service contracts based on business entity contexts. Often a logical data model or an enterprise entity model provides the source for these contexts.

The resulting service layer is comprised of a (usually large) collection of agnostic business services that can be reused across numerous different business processes. Each entity service can be owned and governed by a group that includes business analysts with the appropriate subject matter expertise to preserve its integrity and to ensure the service continually evolves in alignment with the business.

Note that the granularity of entity services can sometimes vary. Although deriving a single service context from a single business entity results in a cleanly modeled service layer, this approach is not always possible. Practical considerations sometimes require that a service context be based on multiple entities—or a single entity may form the basis for multiple service contexts (Figure 7.8).

NOTE

This pattern may not be suitable for organizations with business entities that are volatile and subject to frequent change. In this case other, more stable sources for agnostic business contexts need to be sought. Alternatively, a new business entity specification can be developed wherein more abstract business entities are defined that are less prone to change. For example, in a company that has constantly changing products, it can be more effective to base entity service contexts on an abstract product entity instead of individual product types that may have limited longevity.

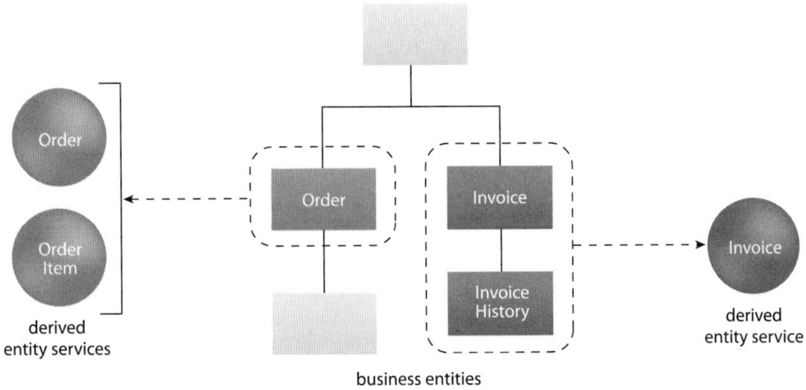

Figure 7.8
The parts of a business entity model encapsulated by entity services can vary.

Impacts

Although there is tremendous business benefit to establishing an entity service layer, it can impose change on several levels, not limited to just analysis and design processes. Because this pattern positions a significant portion of business logic as reusable enterprise resources (services), a great deal of attention needs to be focused on its subsequent governance and evolution.

The application of this pattern can shift organizational structures, change the complexion of project teams, and introduce new skill set requirements. Therefore, Entity Abstraction should be incorporated as early in the planning stages as possible, so as to give all of those involved with service modeling and service design enough time to understand and accept the nature of this service layer.

One of the key success factors to maintaining an effective entity service layer is establishing a suitable ownership structure for the entity services. Because this can necessitate joint ownership between business subject matter experts and technology experts, it may require the formation of new groups and policies.

Relationships

Entity Abstraction can be viewed as a business-centric application of Agnostic Context (312). It is therefore closely related to patterns that support the definition of agnostic business services, such as Logic Centralization (136).

As discussed in Chapter 16, coarse-grained entity services tend to require the application of Service Decomposition (489) at some stage. They also raise further business logic-related design considerations that carry over to contract design, which is where patterns such as Validation Abstraction (429) and Legacy Wrapper (441) may be required.

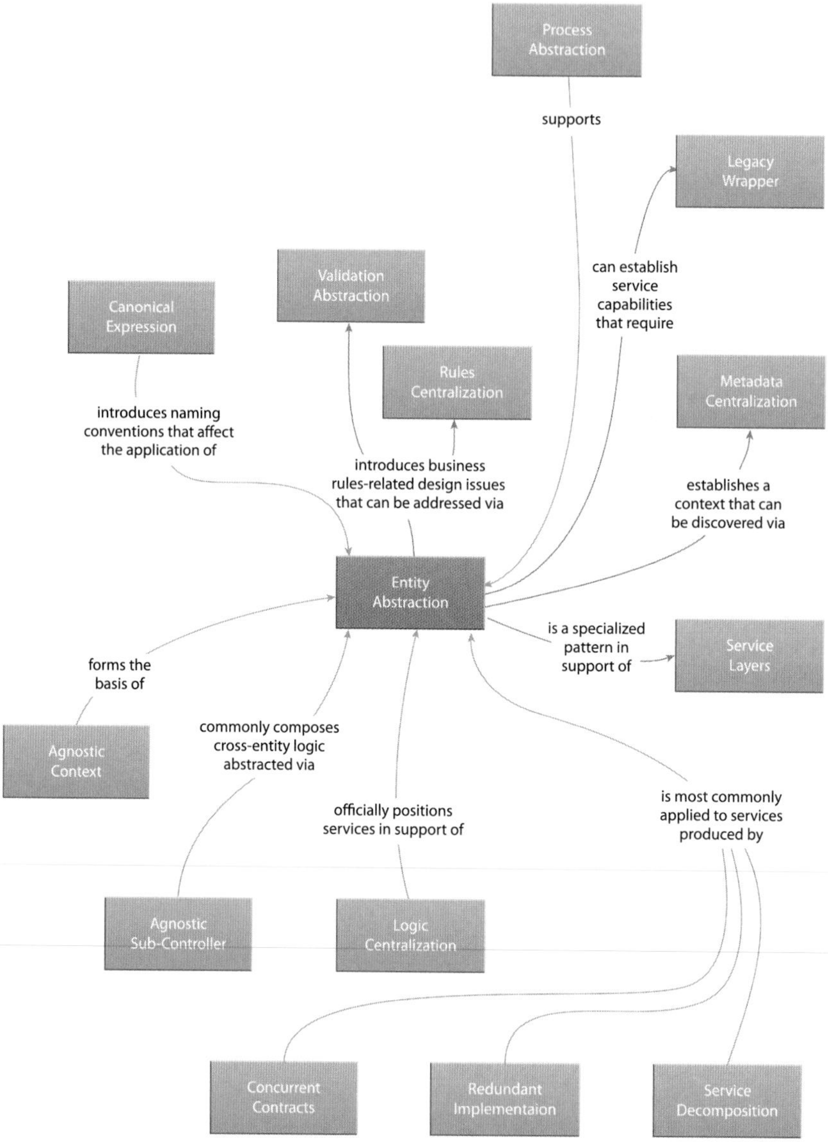

Figure 7.9

Entity Abstraction combines agnostic and business-centric functional contexts, which is why it relates to a range of different design patterns.

CASE STUDY EXAMPLE

Using an elaborate entity relationship diagram (that has long covered an entire wall in one of their IT meeting rooms), Alleywood architects collaborate with business analysts to carry out their own service-oriented analysis with a focus on identifying core business entities.

After iterating through and decomposing numerous business processes, a series of artifacts are documented, along with their inter-relationships:

- *Employees* use *equipment* to process natural wood in the field. The equipment needs to be maintained with an inventory of *parts.*
- Accumulated wood is placed on *trucks,* which haul *loads* to the *mills* where the wood is processed and refined.
- Mills are located in different *regions,* some of which are governed by different regulations.
- *Alerts* are issued for warning and emergency situations, such as when an employee is injured or a truck breaks down.
- *Policy checks* are periodically performed to look for amended or newly issued regulations that may affect existing wood processing plans.
- Finally, *resource surveys* are conducted to search through a central repository of workers available for field jobs.

Of these artifacts, it is determined that Alerts and Resource Survey are to be classified as utility service candidates because they do not correspond to recognized business entities.

There is some debate as to whether Policy Check should be considered an entity service even though their business entity diagram does not contain a policy entity. In the end, they decide to also classify this as a utility service candidate because they could not foresee the need for a functional context dedicated to policies (especially considering that the only policies they are concerned with are those issued by the FRC).

As shown in Figure 7.10, eight entity service candidates are defined, establishing a fair-sized entity service layer. With the exception of Employee, each of these entity-centric functional contexts corresponds to one business entity within their entity relationship diagram. The same business analysts responsible for maintaining that diagram agree to remain involved with the ownership and evolution of these entity services.

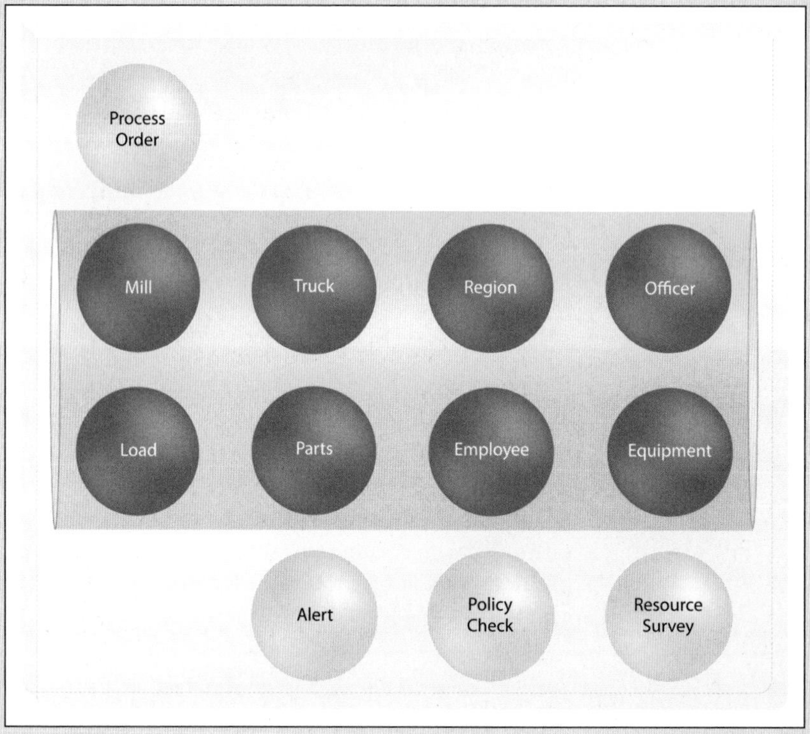

Figure 7.10

The services within the entity layer represent the bulk of the service logic defined so far and will therefore be required to shoulder a great deal of the processing associated with Alleywood's primary automation tasks.

The Employee service candidate was actually derived from three separate, employee-related business entities for which the creation of separate services was not deemed justifiable.

Note that because Alleywood does not have a single business entity to represent an order, a task service is established to encapsulate all of the composition logic required to process order documents.

Process Abstraction

How can non-agnostic process logic be separated and governed independently?

Problem	Grouping task-centric logic together with task-agnostic logic hinders the governance of the task-specific logic and the reuse of the agnostic logic.
Solution	A dedicated parent business process service layer is established to support governance independence and the positioning of task services as potential enterprise resources.
Application	Business process logic is typically filtered out after utility and entity services have been defined, allowing for the definition of task services that comprise this layer.
Impacts	In addition to the modeling and design considerations associated with creating task services, abstracting parent business process logic establishes an inherent dependency on carrying out that logic via the composition of other services.
Principles	Service Loose Coupling, Service Abstraction, Service Composability
Architecture	Inventory, Composition, Service

Table 7.4
Profile summary for the Process Abstraction pattern.

Problem

Services can be designed to resemble traditional silo-based applications wherein agnostic and non-agnostic logic is grouped together in each service. This can happen when services are delivered individually by separate project teams or service-orientation is disregarded as part of the delivery method.

This approach has several repercussions:

- It reduces opportunities for applying the Service Reusability design principle on a broad scale.
- It imposes governance complexity when expertise associated with business entities and business processes lie with different individuals.

- It makes it difficult to apply Non-Agnostic Context (319), thereby reducing the chances of successfully abstracting single-purpose cross-entity logic into legitimate services.

As illustrated in Figure 7.11, this grouping can further result in the fragmented implementation of task logic.

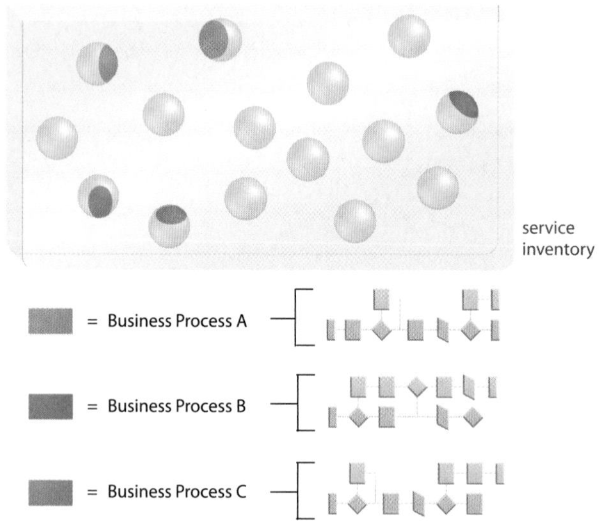

Figure 7.11

Parent business process-specific logic is grouped with other logic that is likely agnostic, resulting in some dispersal. The primary negative effect is that by combining task-specific and task-agnostic logic, the opportunity to establish agnostic services in support of Agnostic Context (319) and other related patterns, such as Logic Centralization (136), is hindered.

Solution

Business logic that spans multiple entity service boundaries is abstracted into a distinct functional context associated with the task service model. This establishes a parent service layer responsible for containing workflow and service composition logic required to carry out the parent business process (Figure 7.12).

The abstraction established by this process service layer can increase organizational agility because it is the parent business logic that is commonly subject to business change. As a result, being able to access and maintain this logic in a separate set of services can decrease

the effort required to respond to change while shielding agnostic services in other layers from the impact of the change. This is because when a mature inventory of services is available, business changes will often only translate into a need to recompose agnostic services without modifying them.

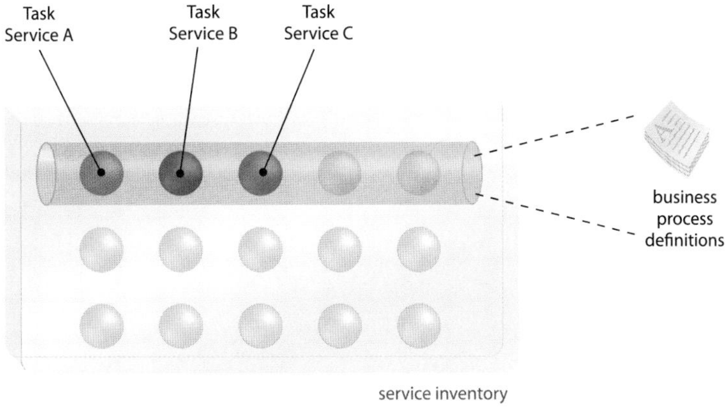

Figure 7.12

Solution logic limited to the fulfillment of parent business processes is abstracted into separate task services. This establishes a parent task service layer that abstracts non-agnostic business process logic responsible for composing agnostic services.

Application

It may appear as though this pattern is applied out of necessity in support of Utility Abstraction (168) and Entity Abstraction (175). Because these two patterns force the isolation of business process-agnostic logic, any logic that is specific to parent business processes must be located in its own layer.

However, logic residing in a parent business process layer does not need to be encapsulated by services. The formation of a task service layer is the result of repeatedly applying Service Encapsulation (305) and Non-Agnostic Context (319) to this logic so as to shape it into well-defined services.

Services based on a task-centric context are very similar in concept to traditional silo-based applications, in that they are associated with the execution of a specific business process. Therefore, these types of services are more easily incorporated into established project delivery lifecycles and subsequent ownership arrangements.

The intentional abstraction of process logic into a separate service layer needs to be established alongside the definition of other service layers to ensure that subsequent modeling and design processes properly carry out the allocation of this logic. As with the inventory structure patterns from Chapter 5, this pattern is realized via analysis and design processes, such as those explained in Chapter 3.

Note also that while it is common to associate a task service with a single business process, this limitation is not required. As with any service, a task service can be comprised of multiple capabilities, each of which represents a separate process or task. The only rule is that these processes be related to a common overarching functional context.

Often the desire to limit a task service to a single process is related to scalability and autonomy concerns. Given that a task service will generally contain a great deal of composition logic, it is usually beneficial to limit its functional scope to a single composition so that it does not impose performance burden upon one composition when being invoked to compose another.

These types of runtime performance issues is one of the reasons this pattern is combined with Process Centralization (193) as part of the application of Orchestration (701).

Impacts

The deliberate separation of business process logic into dedicated services generally positions task services as parent controllers of service compositions. Because essential agnostic logic will have been abstracted into other services, task services will almost always depend on multiple agnostic services to carry out their business process logic. An organization needs to be prepared to implement and support service compositions in order for this pattern to be effectively applied.

Furthermore, this pattern places logic into services that could otherwise be located into other types of service consumer programs. This in itself introduces additional design and development effort.

Relationships

Because Process Abstraction provides a service classification dedicated to encapsulating non-agnostic logic, its application filters out single-purpose logic in support of defining agnostic services, as per Entity Abstraction (175) and Utility Abstraction (168).

The key foundation of this pattern is Non-Agnostic Context (319), which establishes the intentionally single-purpose scope that results in the creation of task services.

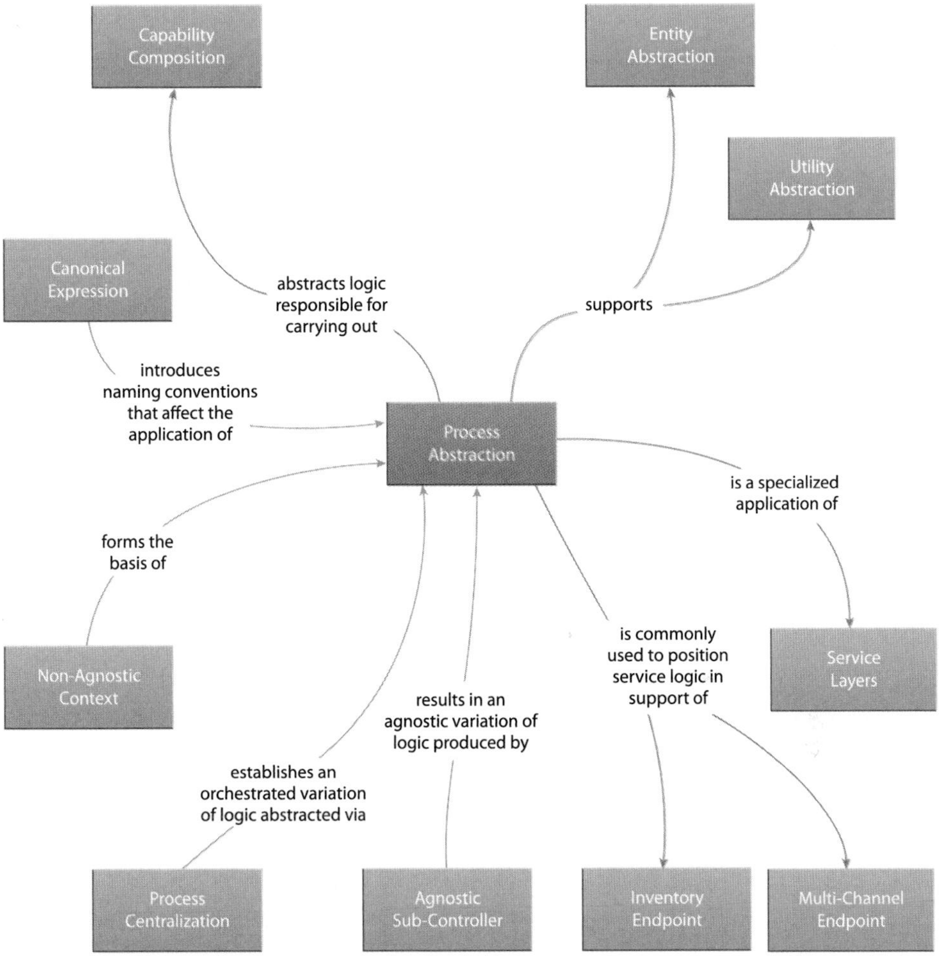

Figure 7.13

Process Abstraction is vital to establishing a parent business task service layer wherein single purpose logic can be placed so that agnostic services can be comprised of pure, multi-purpose logic.

Note also that Process Abstraction is a core part of Orchestration (701). The concept of abstracting parent process logic into a logical layer forms the basis for modern orchestration platforms that are commonly based on Web service composition technologies, such as WS-BPEL. In fact, when part of this compound pattern, the application of Process Abstraction results in a variation of the task service model called the *orchestrated task service*.

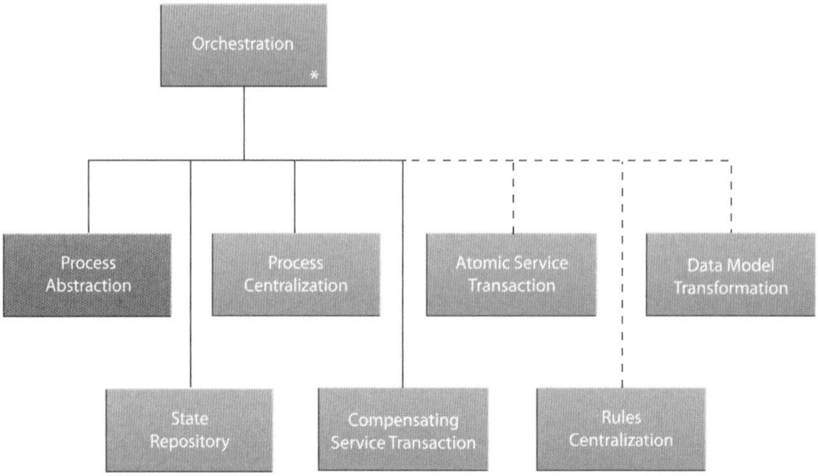

Figure 7.14
Process Abstraction is one of four core patterns that comprise Orchestration (701).

CASE STUDY EXAMPLE

There are literally hundreds of services planned as part of the FRC's long-term effort to build an enterprise service inventory. Phase one of the roll-out schedule is comprised of the delivery of a core set of services that represent fundamental functions within the organization. The goal is to establish services as an accepted functional medium within the respective divisions before moving toward large-scale, cross-divisional process automation.

Following are some of the results of a large-scale service inventory analysis effort:

- *Policies* are official documents based on a series of *regulations* governed by the FRC's Policy Management division.
- The Field Support division sends out FRC *officers* to inspect various forestry *organization sites* and issue *evaluations*.
- Based on these evaluations and other factors, the Assessment and Appeals division issues *assessment* reports.
- Negative assessments can require that organizations pay *fines*. However, these assessments can also be *appealed*.

- Various types of intra- and inter-divisional *reports* are anticipated, many of which will require runtime *conversion* of disparate data models and formats.

As with the Cutit and Alleywood examples, most of the service candidates are again based on the entity service model and the Reports and Divisional Conversion service candidates at the bottom of Figure 7.15 represent the utility service layer.

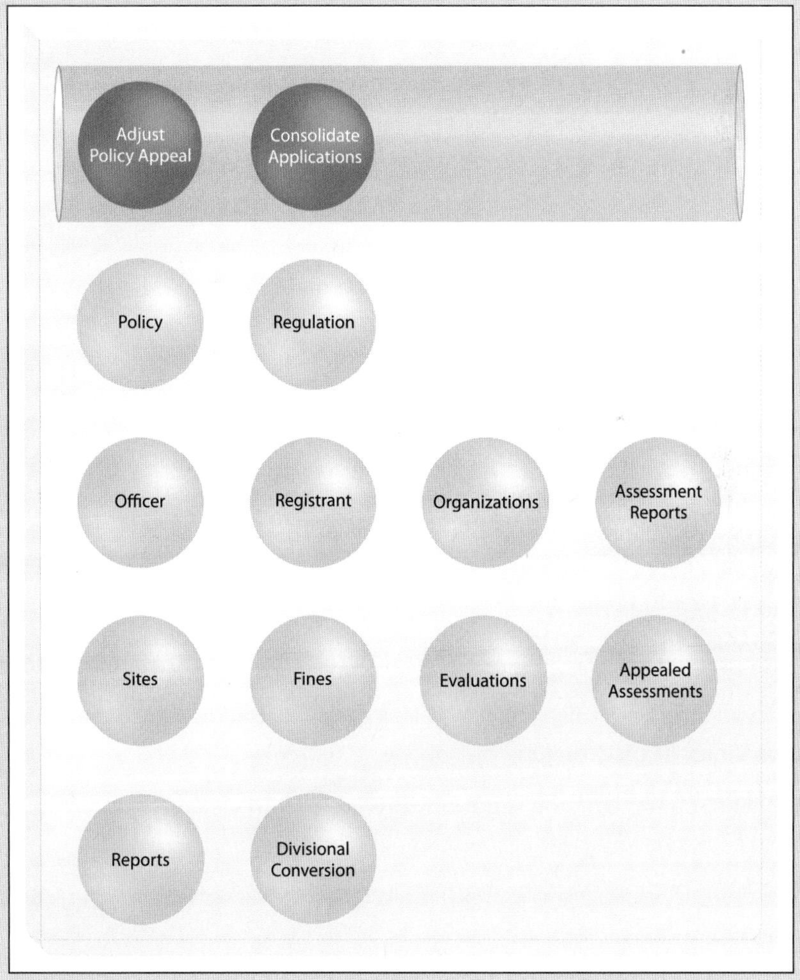

Figure 7.15

Three groups of services, each core to the business operation of an FRC division.

To understand why Adjust Policy Appeal is classified as a task service, we need to go beyond the artifact relationships to learn more about the analysis work carried out by FRC architects and analysts.

Adjust Policy Appeal is a specific business process that was decomposed and studied during the service-oriented analysis process. It essentially represents a business task whereby statistics from successful and failed appeals are collected and assessed to indicate possible changes made to various metrics (fees, date ranges, etc.) used in FRC policies. This business process requires the involvement of various previously defined services, including Policy, Appealed Assessments, and Reports.

It therefore contains logic comprised of:

- functions that can be completed by entity and utility services
- functions specific to the Adjust Policy Appeal business process, such as decision logic, composition logic, and unique calculations

Whereas the former type of functionality is carried out by agnostic entity and utility services, the latter type is specific to the Adjust Policy Appeal business process and therefore considered non-agnostic. This makes it suitable for encapsulation within a task service as part of the task service layer.

NOTE

The additionally displayed Consolidate Applications task service represents a separate business process not explained here. However, the justification for its logic being part of a task service is the same as with Adjust Policy Appeal.

Chapter 8

Inventory Centralization Patterns

Process Centralization

Schema Centralization

Policy Centralization

Rules Centralization

The design patterns in the preceding chapter focused on organizing a service inventory into logical domains, which means their application doesn't affect the physical location of individual services. For example, all of the services within an entity abstraction layer are not expected to reside on the same computer or server.

These next patterns, however, do address physical aspects of service inventory architecture, as follows:

- Process Centralization (193) advocates that logic associated with different business processes should be kept in the same location.
- Schema Centralization (200) positions standardized schemas as physically independent parts of the inventory architecture so that they can be shared across services and also used independently from services.
- Policy Centralization (207) helps establish global and domain-level policies that are physically isolated and can therefore also be shared by and applied to multiple services.
- Rules Centralization (216) is focused on separating processing logic and data storage specific to the management of business rules data.

Because these are centralization patterns, each introduces some extent of inventory-wide standardization. This is an important and recurring application requirement (and impact) for all patterns in this chapter.

Furthermore, unlike the patterns in the preceding chapters which have so far been quite fundamental to inventory design, the physical inventory centralization patterns can be considered more specialized. Although they are recommended, these patterns are not absolutely required to establish a basic service inventory.

Process Centralization

How can abstracted business process logic be centrally governed?

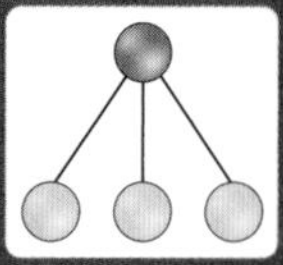

Problem	When business process logic is distributed across independent service implementations, it can be problematic to extend and evolve.
Solution	Logic representing numerous business processes can be deployed and governed from a central location.
Application	Middleware platforms generally provide the necessary orchestration technologies to apply this pattern.
Impacts	Significant infrastructure and architectural changes are imposed when the required middleware is introduced.
Principles	Service Autonomy, Service Statelessness, Service Composability
Architecture	Inventory, Composition

Table 8.1

Profile summary for the Process Centralization pattern.

Problem

Within environments containing larger service inventories, the single-purpose requirement to concurrently support the automation of multiple business processes is common. Business process logic that spans business entities (process logic that cannot be represented by any one entity service) can be placed into individual task services (as shown in Figure 8.1).

While these services exist as peer members of a service inventory, the fact that they are independently implemented results in an enterprise's business process logic being physically distributed across multiple locations. When changes come along, the ability to efficiently extend, streamline, or even combine business process logic is inhibited because the underlying logic of each affected task service needs to be revisited, opened up, and changed, as required.

Furthermore, due to the nature of varying workflow logic, some business processes cannot be carried out in real-time. Instead, they may impose long-running service activities that can span minutes, hours, and even days. Independent task service implementations need to be equipped with state deferral extensions to facilitate these requirements. While this is

technically feasible, it can become somewhat tedious to repeat these implementation extensions across numerous individual service environments, especially when the task services are highly distributed across different physical servers (and perhaps even across different vendor runtime platforms).

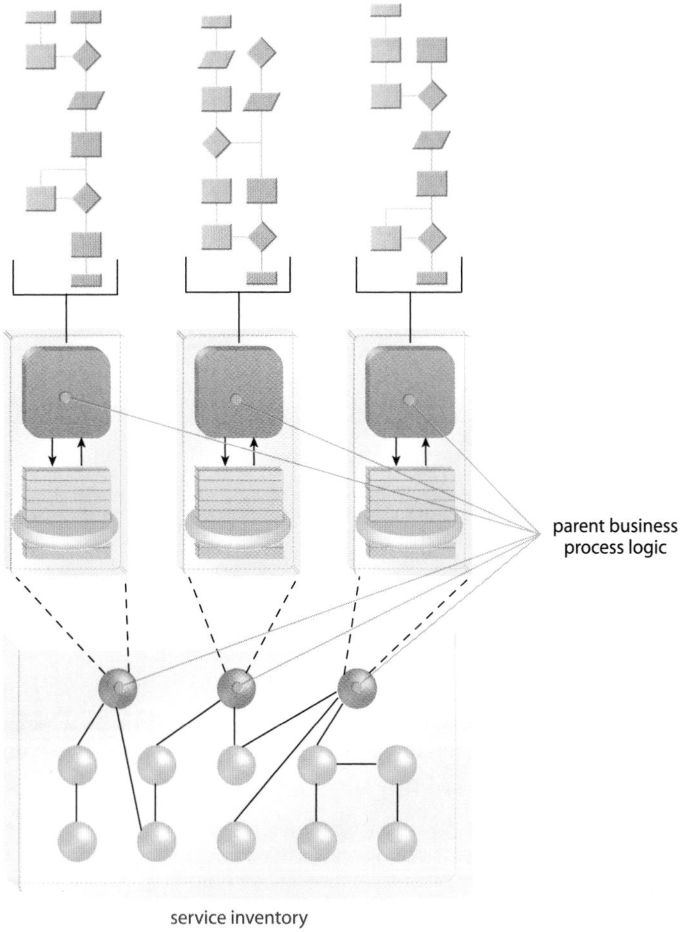

Figure 8.1

Task services are commonly implemented as individual Web services. Because each program contains embedded business process logic, it results in a physically decentralized architecture.

Solution

Parent business process logic (representing some or all of the business processes within a given domain) is centralized into one location. An orchestration platform hosts and executes this logic while allowing for its on-going, centralized maintenance (Figure 8.2).

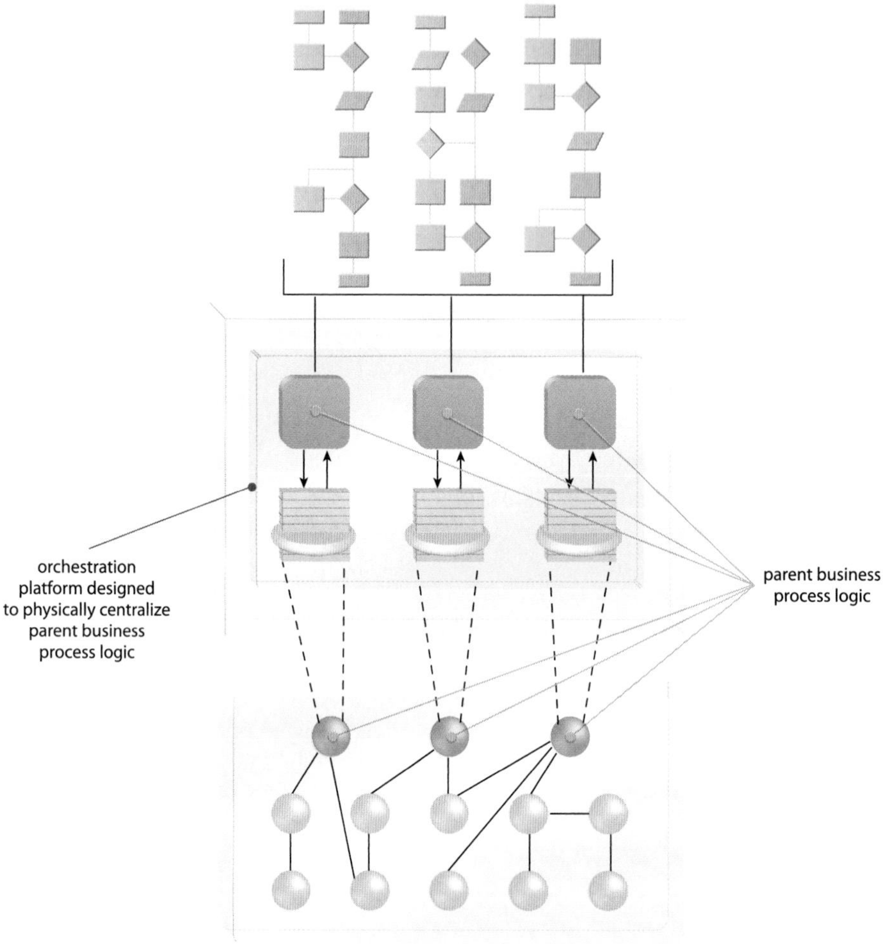

Figure 8.2

Task services can continue to be implemented as separate Web services, but as part of an orchestration platform their collective business process logic is centrally located and governed (resulting in "orchestrated" task services).

Application

Modern variations of orchestration platforms that emerged during the EAI era provide a fundamental medium for centralizing process logic. When combined with support for open business process definition languages (such as WS-BPEL), these platforms become suitable for establishing a primary parent composition layer within SOA.

To realize this design pattern, a modern orchestration platform is required. Such an environment is typically comprised of the following:

- a graphical front-end tool allowing users to express and maintain business process logic
- a back-end middleware runtime environment capable of hosting orchestrated task services and the corresponding collection of business process definitions created with the front-end tool
- features that comply with industry standards related to business process logic expression and execution, such as WS-BPEL

In a nutshell, the composition logic for a specific business process is defined using the front-end tool and then encapsulated by a specific orchestrated task service. The backend platform hosts the service in the same environment as others, allowing these services to carry out their composition logic with a range of supporting features, including state management and various service agents.

NOTE

Orchestration (701) is not absolutely required to apply this pattern. Placing logic for multiple business processes into a single task service can also be considered an application of Process Centralization. However, for reasons explained in the description for Process Abstraction (182), this practice is not always recommended.

Impacts

Introducing orchestration technology into an enterprise can be expensive and disruptive. The infrastructure requirements to host and run the necessary middleware can increase the size and overall operational costs of the IT environment as a whole. It is therefore best to decide whether an orchestration layer can be established early in the technology architecture planning process.

The overall impact of this design pattern depends on the extent to which service-related middleware already exists as part of the enterprise. If no middle tier exists, its introduction will affect the surrounding infrastructure and the complexion of the overall technology architecture including existing service inventories.

Furthermore, the front- and back-end products required to support orchestration are rarely implemented in isolation. When creating an orchestration environment, the middleware platform is typically expanded to encompass a range of centralized service governance functions.

NOTE

This pattern can also be applied after a service inventory has already been established. As long as Process Abstraction (182) was used to define a layer of task services, the proper separation of agnostic and non-agnostic logic will exist to allow for the non-agnostic (process-specific) logic to be cleanly migrated to a central location.

Relationships

This pattern raises a number of architectural considerations that consequently establish relationships with a variety of patterns. Because Process Centralization represents a core part of Orchestration (701), Canonical Resources (237) comes into play, especially when more than one orchestration product is a possibility.

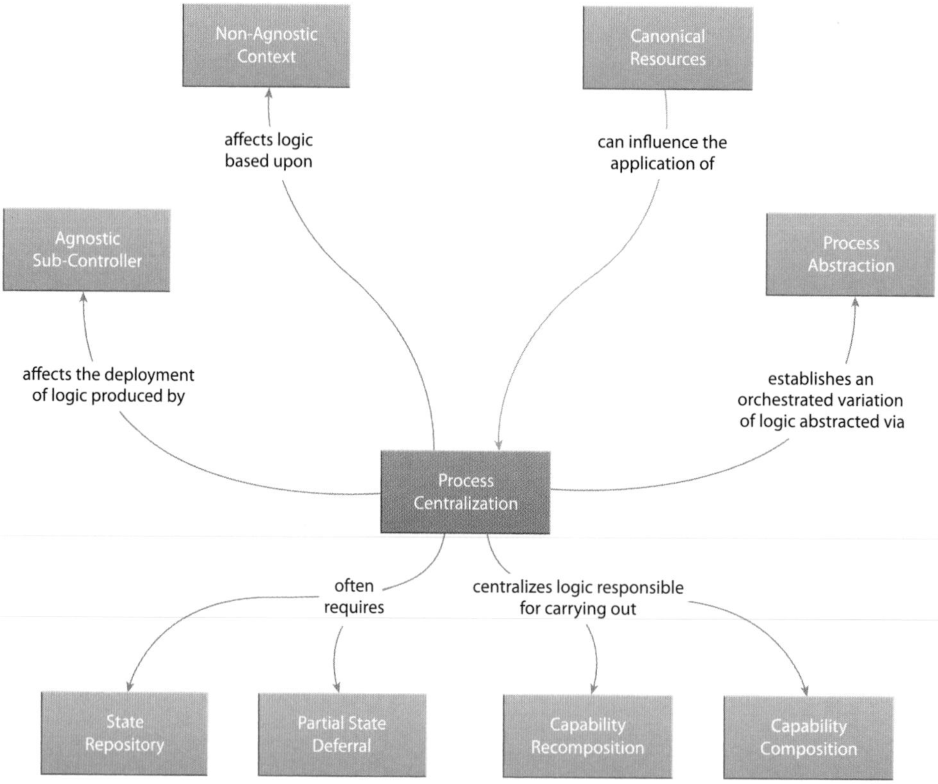

Figure 8.3

Process Centralization establishes a physical process hub within an architecture, and therefore can affect the application of several other patterns.

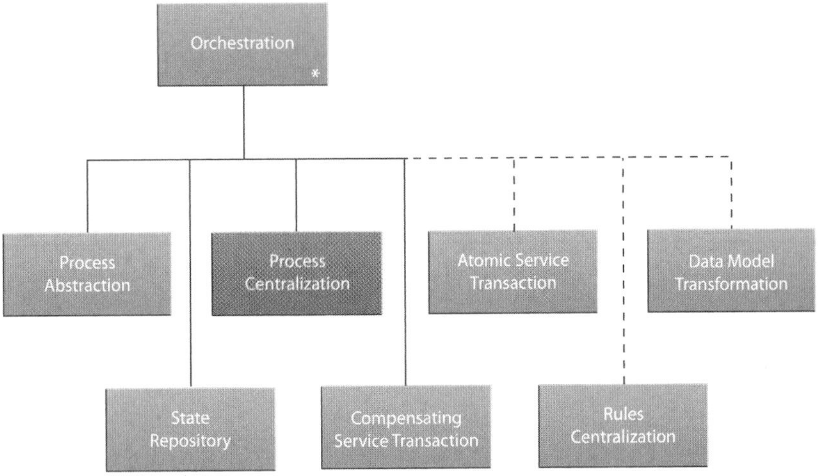

Figure 8.4

Process Centralization is most commonly associated with its role as part of the core patterns that represent Orchestration (701).

Process-centralized environments naturally require state management extensions, as per State Repository (242) and Partial State Deferral (356), due to the tendency of orchestrated task services to be more stateful and to allow for the temporary storage of state data in support of long-running process activities.

Finally, because this pattern is only focused on the physical location of process logic, it equally supports both Capability Composition (521) and Capability Recomposition (526).

CASE STUDY EXAMPLE

During a larger service modeling exercise, the McPherson Enterprise team realizes that as part the initial planned roll-out there will be the need to support six different complex service compositions within just the Tri-Fold environment alone. After completing subsequent project phases, it is estimated that the quantity of service compositions could easily triple (including compositions that will need to access services in the Alleywood inventory).

From the beginning, it was assumed that some sort of orchestration platform would be needed to establish a true enterprise middleware implementation in support of their SOA project. These latest findings appear to support this conclusion, but the team is

still uncertain as to whether to make the use of the orchestration environment mandatory for all task services (effectively turning each task service into an orchestrated task service), or whether to make this decision on an individual basis.

The former option would establish the equivalent of an enterprise design standard, requiring that all task logic be expressed in WS-BPEL and that it be carried out in the centralized orchestration environments.

Some team members feel that such a standard would be overkill and would not allow for the delivery of more optimized task services that would exist as standalone Web services. Others feel it could compromise attaining desired levels of Service Autonomy that have been identified for some composition requirements.

After some discussion, the decision to establish a design standard based on Process Centralization was postponed. The team agrees to give their new orchestration product a nine month period to prove that it is suitable for the range of processing requirements their compositions will need to fulfill.

Schema Centralization

How can service contracts be designed to avoid redundant data representation?

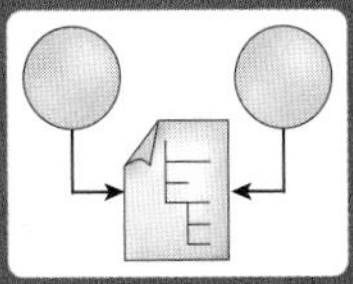

Problem	Different service contracts often need to express capabilities that process similar business documents or data sets, resulting in redundant schema content that is difficult to govern.
Solution	Select schemas that exist as physically separate parts of the service contract are shared across multiple contracts.
Application	Up-front analysis effort is required to establish a schema layer independent of and in support of the service layer.
Impacts	Governance of shared schemas becomes increasingly important as multiple services can form dependencies on the same schema definitions.
Principles	Standardized Service Contract, Service Loose Coupling
Architecture	Inventory, Service

Table 8.2
Profile summary for the Schema Centralization pattern.

Problem

When building services for larger enterprise environments, the context established by each service boundary will usually not be exclusive to one body of data. For example a Claims service will represent a collection of claims-related functions and will therefore be primarily responsible for processing claims data. However, even though it will be positioned as a primary endpoint for that body of functionality, it will likely not be the only service to work with claims data.

As a result, the need for duplicate schema data models emerges, leading to the definition of service contracts with redundant content (Figure 8.5). Even if the data models across these contracts are standardized, the redundant and decentralized implementation of contract schemas introduces constant governance challenges primarily associated with keeping schema data models in synch.

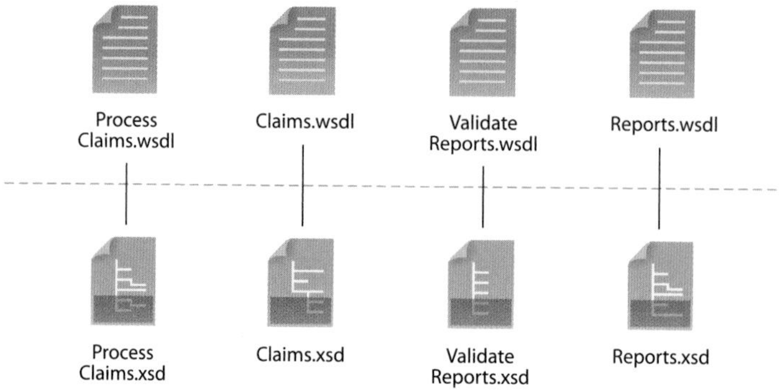

Figure 8.5

A set of WSDL definitions for which a corresponding set of XML schemas has been custom tailored. This has the appearance of a very clean contract architecture, but it actually can introduce significant schema content redundancy as indicated by the red-shaded areas.

Solution

Schemas can be designed and implemented independently from the service capabilities that utilize them to represent the structure and typing of message content. As a result, a schema architecture can be established and standardized somewhat separately from the parent service layer. For example, if one schema representing claims data is defined, any service with a capability that needs to process claims data would use the same schema (Figure 8.6).

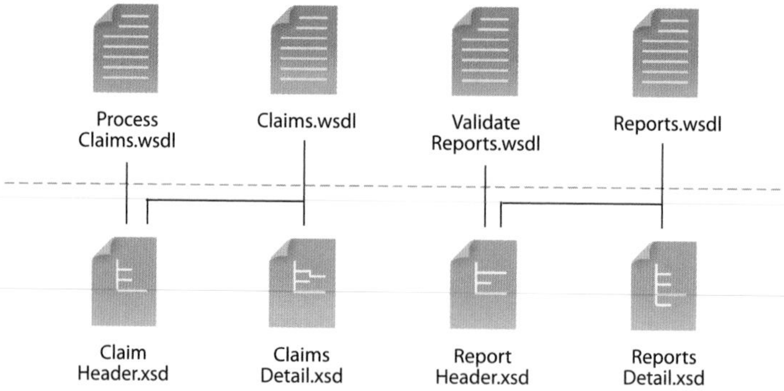

Figure 8.6

WSDL definitions that share common XML schemas end up sharing the same message data models. Note how the reduction of redundant content also results in smaller-sized schemas.

Application

What is primarily advocated by this pattern is the creation of an independent schema (or data representation) architecture. This architecture may already exist within an organization, especially if serious XML Schema standardization efforts have already been carried out. However, if schemas need to be defined as part of the SOA initiative, then it is recommended that they be created prior to the completion of individual service contracts.

Ideally, the incorporation of the separate schema layer is taken into account subsequent to the completion of the service inventory blueprint, in preparation for the delivery of the physical service inventory.

The following sequence is suggested:

1. Complete a service inventory blueprint to establish a conceptual representation of planned services within an inventory.
2. Determine the required centralized schema definitions to represent the common business entities and information sets likely to be processed by services in this inventory.
3. Create the schema definitions by applying design standards to ensure consistency and normalization.
4. Create the WSDL definitions using the standard schemas wherever appropriate and supplementing the contract with any required service-specific schemas.

NOTE

Even though this design pattern advocates the avoidance of redundant schema content, in most environments it is common to supplement centralized schemas with service-specific schemas. It can be impractical and even impossible to centralize all schemas within an inventory.

Impacts

Because of the dependencies formed on the shared schema definitions, their initial design is crucial. After multiple service contracts form links to a schema, the evolution of the schema definition becomes a key part of the overall service inventory governance. Any change to a centralized schema can affect numerous service contracts.

For larger organizations, this level of data standardization can pose daunting challenges, many of which revolve around the maintenance of the shared schemas and the enforcement of associated design standards.

Relationships

The schema layer established by Schema Centralization can be built upon and further incorporated as part of a Contract Centralization (409) effort and, due to its emphasis on reducing data model redundancy, also carries forward the goals of Service Normalization (131) into the data tier.

An interesting relationship can exist between this pattern and Validation Abstraction (429) in that the creation of official, centralized schemas can bring with it more detail than all services may actually require. This can end up countering some of the optimization and information hiding goals of Validation Abstraction (429).

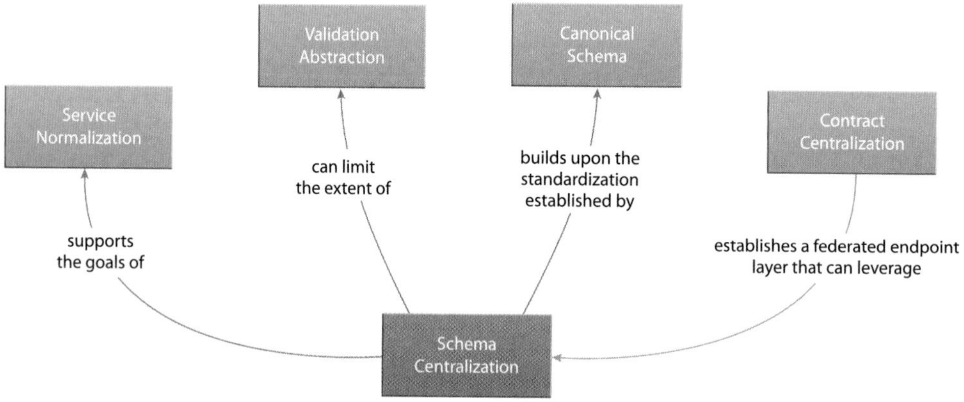

Figure 8.7
Schema Centralization has few relationships because its scope is limited to an independent, underlying data model tier.

CASE STUDY EXAMPLE

The processing logic behind the four Cutit services is reviewed by architects in an effort to identify where common data sets are used.

The following areas are found:

- The Run Chain Inventory Transfer, Inventory, and Chain services are required to process data associated with a chain manufacturing record.
- The Run Chain Inventory Transfer, Inventory, and Order services are required to process data associated with a chain inventory record.
- The Run Chain Inventory Transfer and Order services are required to process order records.

As a result, the project team employs data analysts to create standardized data models (as XML schemas) for chain manufacturing, chain inventory, and order record documents, as shown in Figure 8.8.

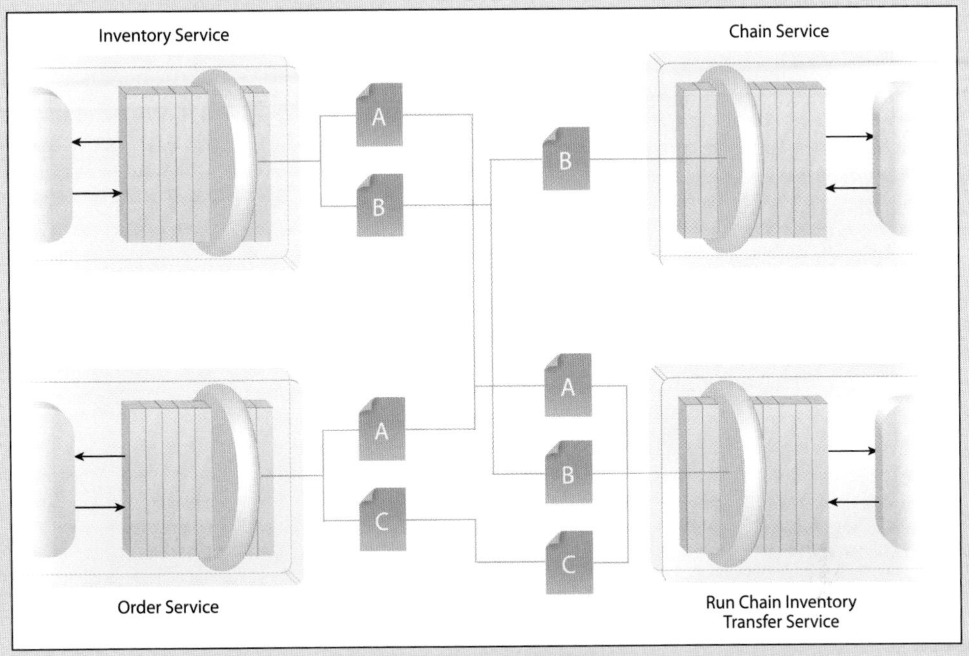

Figure 8.8

The XML schemas (A, B, C) defined for the individual Cutit Web services are synchronized wherever common data sets are identified. (A represents the inventory record, B represents the chain manufacturing record, and C represents the order record.)

The Cutit team now decides to streamline the overall data representation architecture by avoiding redundant schema content. The result is a service contract structure similar to what is displayed in Figure 8.8, only central physical schemas are shared across services (Figure 8.9).

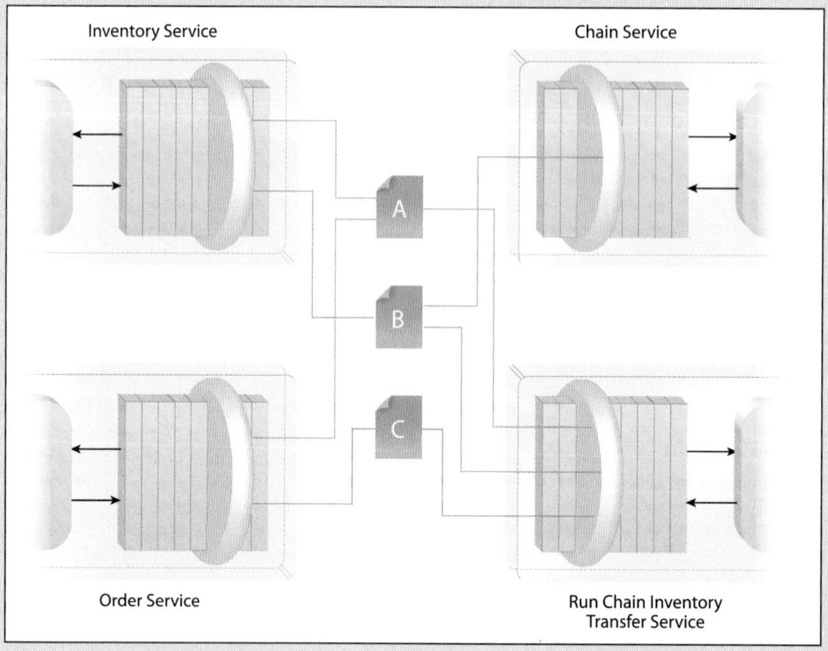

Figure 8.9

Schemas A, B, and C are centrally positioned and linked to via the service contracts that are required to process the corresponding data sets. (Additional service-specific schemas still exist but are not shown in this figure.)

Assuming Schema A in the preceding diagram is inventory.xsd, and Schema C is order.xsd, the WSDL definition for the Order service might begin as follows:

```
<definitions targetNamespace=
  "http://cutitsaws.com/contract/order"
  xmlns:tns="http://cutitsaws.com/contract/order"
  ...>
  <types>
    <xsd:schema xmlns:xsd="http://www.w3.org/2001/XMLSchema">
      <xsd:import namespace=
        "http://cutitsaws.com/schema/inventory"
        schemaLocation=
        "http://cutitsaws.com/schema/inventory.xsd"/>
      <xsd:import namespace=
        "http://cutitsaws.com/schema/order"
        schemaLocation=
        "http://cutitsaws.com/schema/order.xsd"/>
    </xsd:schema>
```

```
    ...
  </types>
...
</definitions>
```

Example 8.1

The Order service contract imports the centralized inventory and order schemas, which are also shared by other service contracts.

NOTE

The application of this pattern is further explored in Chapter 6 of *SOA Principles of Service Design* as part of the case study example and in Chapter 14 of *Web Service Contract Design and Versioning for SOA*.

Note also that the *Web Service Contract Design and Versioning for SOA* book establishes a convention with regards to the spelling of the term "XML Schema." The word "schema" is capitalized when referring to the XML Schema language or specification and it is lower case when discussing schema documents in general.

For example, the following statement makes reference to the XML Schema language:

"One feature provided by XML Schema is the ability to..."

And this sentence explains the use of XML schema documents:

"When defining an XML schema it is important to..."

This spelling convention is also used in this book.

Policy Centralization

How can policies be normalized and consistently enforced across multiple services?

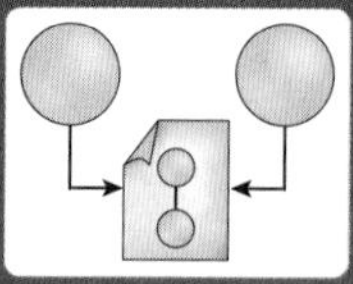

Problem	Policies that apply to multiple services can introduce redundancy and inconsistency within service logic and contracts.
Solution	Global or domain-specific policies can be isolated and applied to multiple services.
Application	Up-front analysis effort specific to defining and establishing reusable policies is recommended, and an appropriate policy enforcement framework is required.
Impacts	Policy frameworks can introduce performance overhead and may impose dependencies on proprietary technologies. There is also the risk of conflict between centralized and service-specific policies.
Principles	Standardized Service Contracts, Service Loose Coupling, Service Abstraction
Architecture	Inventory, Service

Table 8.3
Profile summary for the Policy Centralization pattern.

Problems

Services may be required to process a variety of individual policies (also called *policy expressions*). Areas commonly addressed by policies include security and transaction requirements, as well as a variety of quality-of-service (QoS) properties.

Regulatory policies may affect a range of services, whereas other policies may be service-specific. A service built as a Web service can establish policy requirements as part of its contract via the use of WS-Policy expressions, or it may apply policies within its underlying service logic.

When common policies are repeated across multiple service contracts, they introduce redundancy into the service inventory (Figure 8.10). This leads to bloated policy content and increases the governance burden required to ensure that common policies are kept in synch over time.

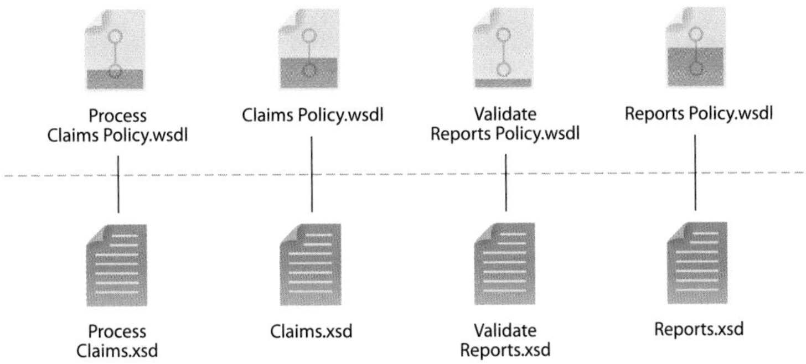

Figure 8.10

Each of the four displayed WSDL documents is extended with individual WS-Policy definitions. The red shading indicates the extent of redundancy across policies.

Solution

Policies that apply to multiple services can be abstracted into separate policy definition documents or service agents that are part of an inventory-wide policy enforcement framework. Abstracted policies can be positioned to apply to multiple services, thereby reducing redundancy and providing centralized policy governance (Figure 8.11).

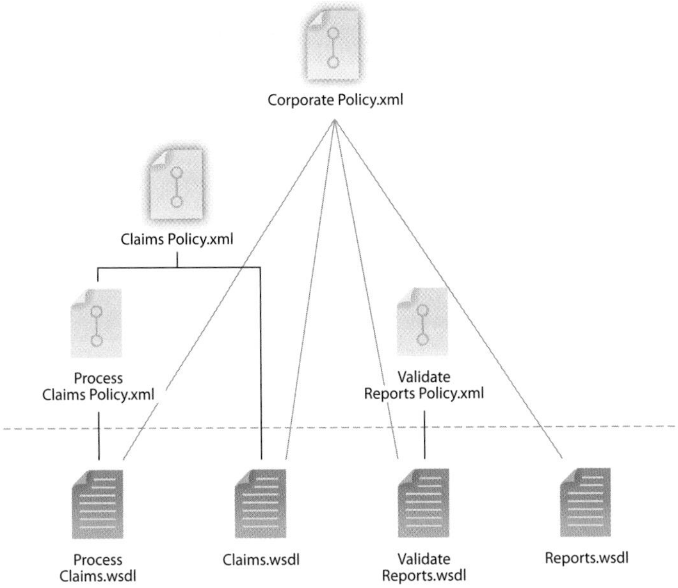

Figure 8.11

A global policy definition (Corporate Policy.xml) is established and applies to all WSDL documents, and a further domain policy (Claims Policy.xml) is created and linked to two WSDL definitions. This new policy structure eliminates redundancy of policy content and ensures consistent policy enforcement.

Application

A policy framework needs to be added to the inventory architecture so that policies can be separately defined and associated with services and then validated, enforced, and even audited at runtime.

The WS-Policy framework includes a separate WS-PolicyAttachments specification that explains binding mechanisms for policies. Policy definitions can be embedded within or linked to WSDL documents. To apply this pattern one or more policies typically need to be grouped together into a policy definition that is made available so that Web service contracts to which the policies apply can add the appropriate references.

Middle-tier platforms (such as those provided by ESB products) can provide policy features supported by runtime agents that carry out policy compliance checking. In these environments, global and domain-level policies can also be established via service agents that act as *policy enforcement points* (Figure 8.12).

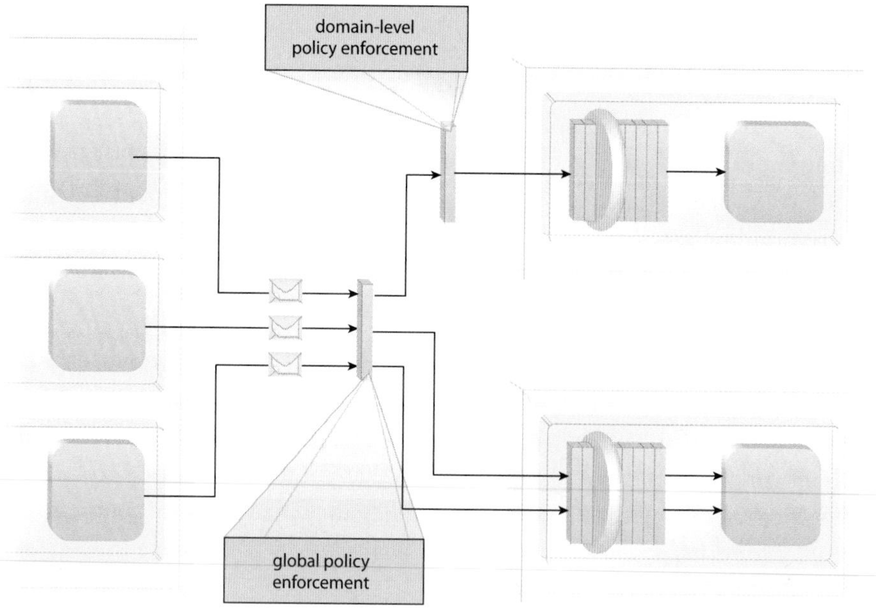

Figure 8.12

Service agents, as part of an inventory-wide policy framework, intercept incoming messages to check for policy compliance. One agent (bottom) enforces a global policy that applies to all services, while the second agent (top) enforces a domain-level policy after global policy compliance was confirmed.

NOTE

Policy requirements are often collected early on during the service delivery lifecycle. For example, service modeling processes allow analysts to determine potential policies while the service is still in the conceptual stage. Policy logic is typically documented within the service profile where policies can be defined on a service or capability level.

Impacts

Policy definition is an additional step in the service delivery lifecycle that needs to be taken into consideration early on. Part of the analysis involved with defining policies is determining what types of policies should *not* be made part of the technical service contract.

Some policies may be subject to unexpected change and therefore more likely to demand new contract versions. Other policies may be more suited for a service-level agreement (SLA) that exists as a document used by humans (usually the owners of potential consumer programs). Therefore, the Service Abstraction principle is a key factor in ensuring that the constraint granularity of contract capabilities remains reasonable.

Once global or domain-level policies are established, they need to be maintained with a great amount of care. One change or addition to a shared policy will affect all services that rely upon it. This, in turn, affects all service consumers that have formed dependencies on the corresponding service contracts. A governance structure is therefore required, comprised of assigned roles (such as policy custodians) and processes that ensure that common policies are properly evolved.

Furthermore, increased up-front analysis is required prior to the delivery of WS-Policy definitions so that policies are designed with the right balance of constraints and flexibility to accommodate the range of contracts that may be required to use them. A common problem when working with centralized policies is that conflicts can arise between policies at different levels. For example, a new global policy may inadvertently contradict a service-level policy for a particular service. Formal analysis and governance processes can help avoid these situations.

Additionally, the service agents and proxies that establish the policy enforcement points within the inventory architecture can add performance overhead and independent failure modes, which the surrounding infrastructure needs to be able to accommodate. Each centralized policy effectively adds a layer of runtime processing and service dependency.

Finally, when implementing a policy framework based on the use of service agents (as part of an ESB product, for example), it is relatively common for the WS-Policy standard to not be fully supported. Instead, the framework may require that policies be defined via front-end tools that output a proprietary policy format. Once deployed, this can lead to undesirable vendor lock-in scenarios that counter the objectives of the vendor-neutral architecture characteristic (explained in Chapter 4). The use of proprietary policy formats further can prevent inter-organization data exchange unless both organizations happen to be using the same products.

Relationships

Because Policy Centralization essentially establishes an independent policy layer that extends service contracts, it directly relates to and benefits from Contract Centralization (409).

This pattern continues the concepts established by Service Normalization (131) in that it avoids redundancy across policies via centralization, and because Policy Centralization can affect the content of a service contract, there is a further relationship with Validation Abstraction (429).

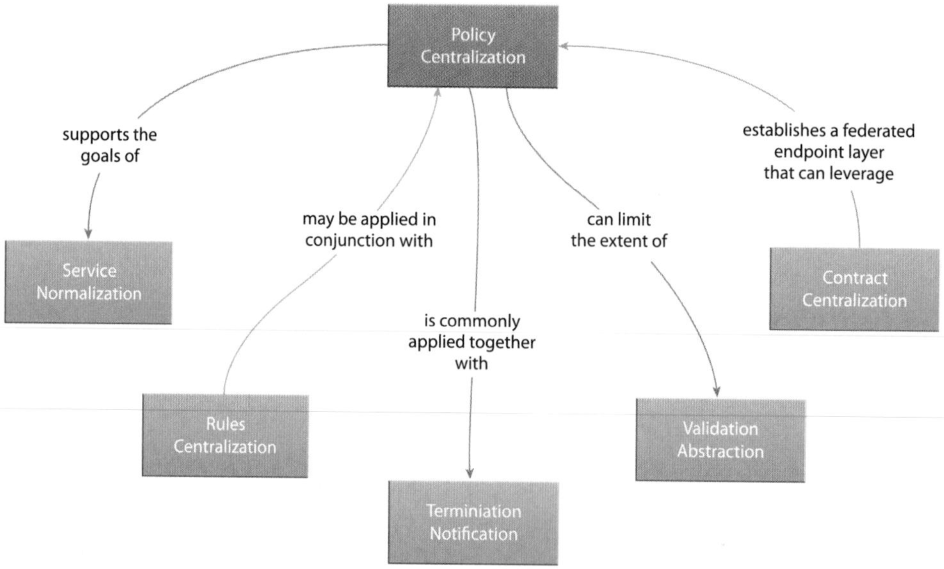

Figure 8.13

Policy Centralization positions policies within a service inventory architecture and therefore affects other patterns that either relate to the service contract layer or to the nature of policy logic.

NOTE

The nature of policy logic can vary, but the fact that policies are often based on security regulations can also tie the application of this pattern to several of the security patterns provided in Chapters 13 and 20.

ESB products have been credited with popularizing policy enforcement and the concept of centralized policies, which is why this pattern is one of the common extensions to Enterprise Service Bus (704).

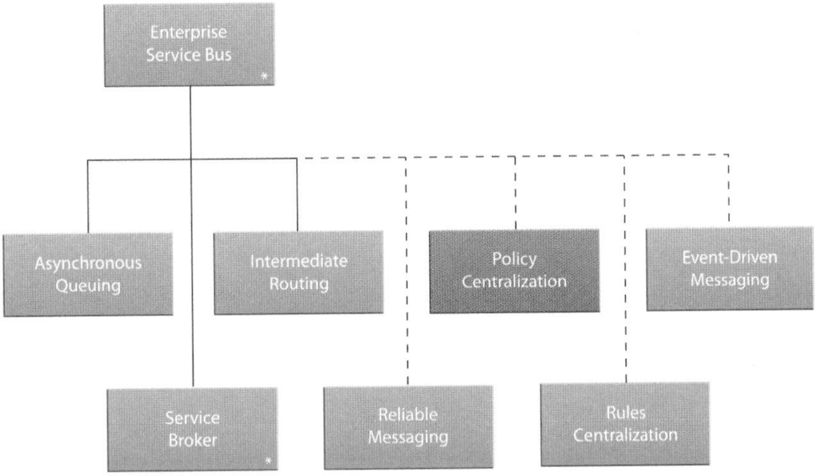

Figure 8.14

When supported, the addition of Policy Centralization brings an important layer of quality assurance to the base messaging, routing, and brokerage patterns that comprise Enterprise Service Bus (704).

NOTE

Another policy-related pattern that was developed for this book but not included in this edition is Canonical Policy Vocabulary. This pattern establishes standardized policy vocabularies required when customizing policies for use within a service inventory. You can learn more about this pattern at SOAPatterns.org.

CASE STUDY EXAMPLE

When finalizing the service contracts described in the Schema Centralization (200) case study example, Cutit architects incorporate a policy that requires that all messages transmitted to any Web service comply to the SOAP 1.2 standard.

The initial approach was to add this policy to each individual Web service contract, as shown in Figure 8.15.

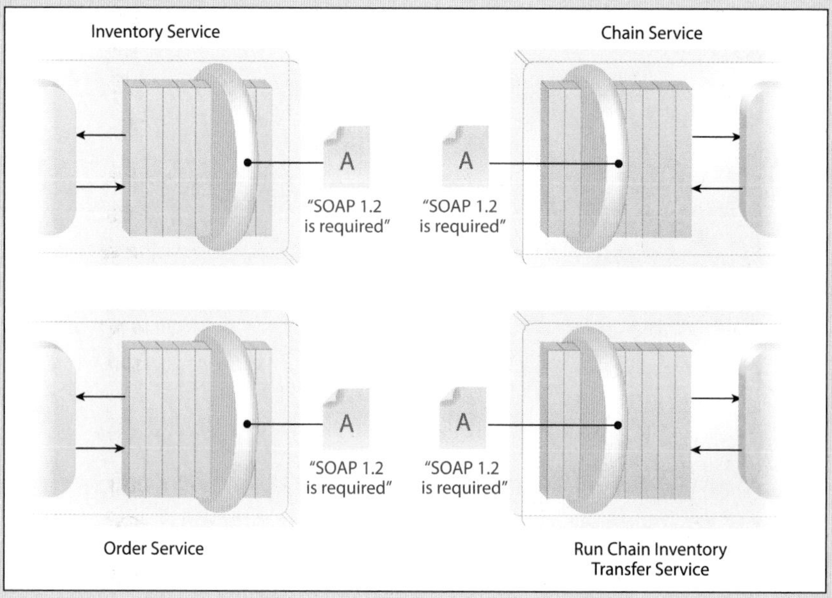

Figure 8.15

The same policy (A) is added redundantly across all Web service contracts.

After the architecture design specification was reviewed, concerns were raised about the redundancy introduced by adding identical policies across multiple contracts. Should the policies ever need to be augmented or removed, it would require a significant governance effort, especially if this approach was taken with all of the services in the Cutit inventory.

Subsequent to some research, a Cutit architect discovers that the middleware product they were considering would allow them to leverage the ability to centralize a policy so that it could be shared across multiple Web service contracts. A prototype is assembled with the architecture illustrated in Figure 8.16, demonstrating a single policy being dynamically applied to multiple Web service contracts.

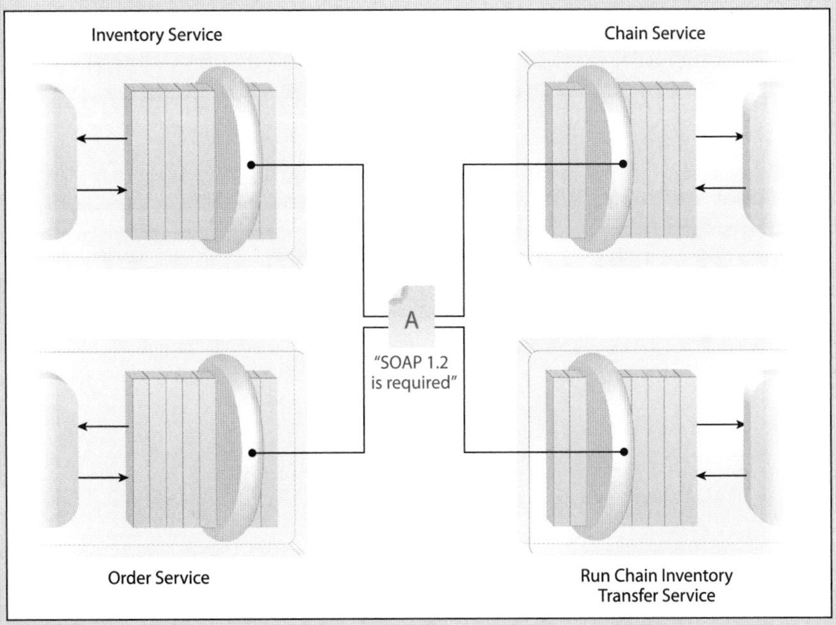

Figure 8.16
A single global policy (A) is established, thereby replacing the redundant policy definitions entirely.

Assuming Policy A in the preceding diagram resides in globalPolicies.xml, the `portType` element in the WSDL definition for the Order service might contain a `wsp:PolicyURIs` attribute, as follows:

```
<definitions targetNamespace=
  "http://cutitsaws.com/contract/order"
  xmlns:tns="http://cutitsaws.com/contract/order"
  ...>
  ...
  <portType name="ptOrder"
    wsp:PolicyURIs="pol:globalPolicies.xml">
    <operation name="SubmitOrder">
      <input message="tns:msgSubmitOrderRequest"/>
      <output message="tns:msgsubmitOrderResponse"/>
    </operation>
    ...
  </portType>
...
</definitions>
```

Example 8.2
The Order service contract with an external reference to a global policy definition that is shared by other services.

NOTE

Besides the use of the `wsp:PolicyURIs` attribute, there are several other ways to externally reference and attach policies to WSDL definitions, as explored in Chapter 16 of *Web Service Contract Design and Versioning for SOA.*

Rules Centralization

How can business rules be abstracted and centrally governed?

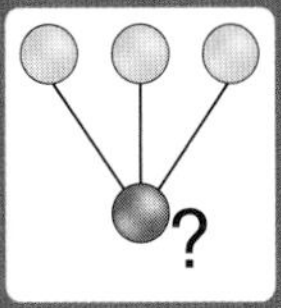

Problem	The same business rules may apply across different business services, leading to redundancy and governance challenges.
Solution	The storage and management of business rules are positioned within a dedicated architectural extension from where they can be centrally accessed and maintained.
Application	The use of a business rules management system or engine is employed and accessed via system agents or a dedicated service.
Impacts	Services are subjected to increased performance overhead, risk, and architectural dependency.
Principles	Service Reusability
Architecture	Inventory

Table 8.4
Profile summary for the Rules Centralization pattern.

Problem

The workflow logic within any given business process is driven by and structured around rules specific to how the logic must be carried out, as per the policies, regulations, and preferences of the organization. Individual business service capabilities frequently must carry out their encapsulated logic in accordance with these rules.

It is not uncommon for the same rule to be applied to different scenarios involving different business entities. This results in a need to incorporate one rule within multiple bodies of service logic. As an organization changes over time, so do certain business rules. This can lead to modifications within individual entity business services as well as business process logic encapsulated by task services or otherwise (including the occasional utility service). Having to revisit multiple services each time a business rule changes can be counter-productive.

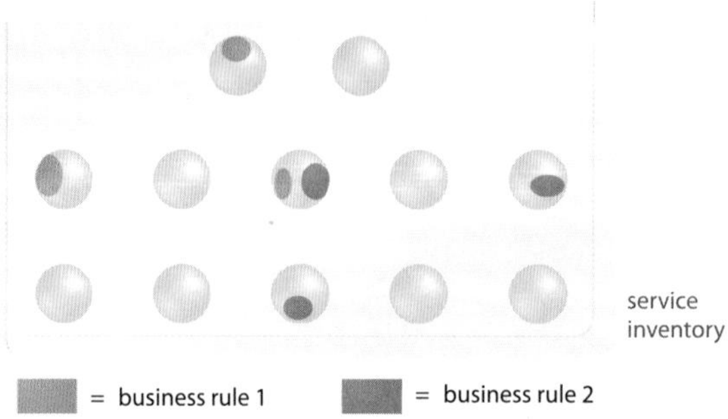

Figure 8.17

Just two business rules can find their way into several different business services and, in this case, even a utility service. A global change to either rule will therefore impact multiple services.

Solution

Business rules can be physically abstracted into a dedicated part of the architecture under the management of specialized rules engines and platforms. This centralizes access to business rule logic and avoids redundancy. It further centralizes the governance of business rules so that they can be modified and evolved from a single location.

Application

Different business rules management systems exist, each introducing a relatively proprietary runtime and administration platform. A central service can be established to provide an official access point for the creation, modification, retrieval, and application of business rules.

Modern runtime platforms also offer native rules repositories and processing logic that is made accessible via a set of system service agents and APIs. This allows any service to interface with business rules-related logic without having to compose a separate service.

NOTE

Centralized rule services are most often classified as members of the utility service layer because they provide generic processing functionality that leverages technology resources and because their functional context is not derived from any organization-specific business models. Even though rule data is business-centric, to the rules service it is just data that it is required to manage and dispense.

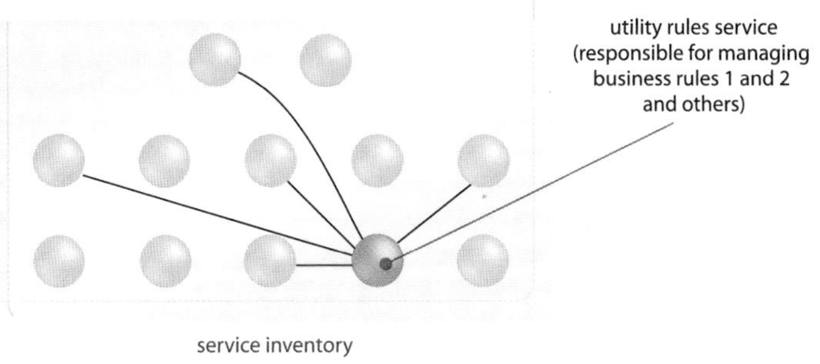

Figure 8.18

All business rules are encapsulated by a single rules service accessed at runtime by other services that need to retrieve or apply business rule logic. (Service agents are also commonly used to provide native access to abstracted rules, as explained shortly.)

Impacts

Because this pattern is applied across an entire service inventory, it can impact an architecture in several ways:

- While it achieves the centralization of business rules data within an inventory, Rules Centralization also ends up *decentralizing* business logic associated with business services. For example, business rules related to the processing of invoices would normally be encapsulated by an Invoice entity service. However, this pattern would move those business rules into a separate location.
- The performance requirements of affected services are increased due to the need for business rules to be retrieved or applied at runtime. Caching mechanisms can alleviate this impact to an extent (usually when rules are temporarily stored as state information for a particular service composition).
- If existing runtime platform features cannot be leveraged to establish centralized rules management, this pattern generally results in the introduction of a separate business rules management product. This extension can increase the size, complexity, and overall operational cost of a technology architecture and must furthermore be sufficiently reliable to consistently accommodate service usage patterns. A rules management system prone to runtime failure can paralyze an entire service inventory.

- Accessing centralized business rules via native system agents and APIs will impose tight architectural dependencies upon services. If many business services use these runtime features, the overall service inventory could become "locked in" to a particular vendor platform.
- Because the actual business rule logic is physically separated, the scope of logic encapsulated by several business service capabilities is incomplete (as per their parent contexts), and their overall autonomy is decreased.

Another issue worth noting is the actual management of centralized business rules. Often a technical administrator is in charge of the rules system, but multiple business domain experts may be needed to maintain the business rules themselves. This can lead to ownership challenges in that the custodian of a business service must also be involved with the maintenance of a subset of the business rules within the central rules repository in addition to the governance of the business service itself.

Relationships

Business rules can be found just about anywhere within a typical service-oriented solution, which is why the abstraction and centralization of rules data can affect the content of a service contract, as per Validation Abstraction (429).

Because this pattern may result in the creation of specialized rules utility services, it is naturally related to Agnostic Context (312) and Utility Abstraction (168), as well as Cross-Domain Utility Layer (267). As a reusable utility service, a rules service may need to encapsulate proprietary rules engines or products, which can lead to the need for Legacy Wrapper (441) and which also ties into the regulatory influence of Canonical Resources (237). Finally, policies will often need to incorporate or introduce rules, which is why this pattern may be applied together with Policy Centralization (207).

Centralized business rules are commonly leveraged to increase the sophistication with which ESB products carry out messaging, routing, and brokerage-related functions. In ESB environments, the variation of this pattern resulting in native agents and APIs is more common than the creation of dedicated rules services. Similarly, this pattern can be leveraged by Orchestration (701) so that business rule logic can be incorporated into workflow and composition logic.

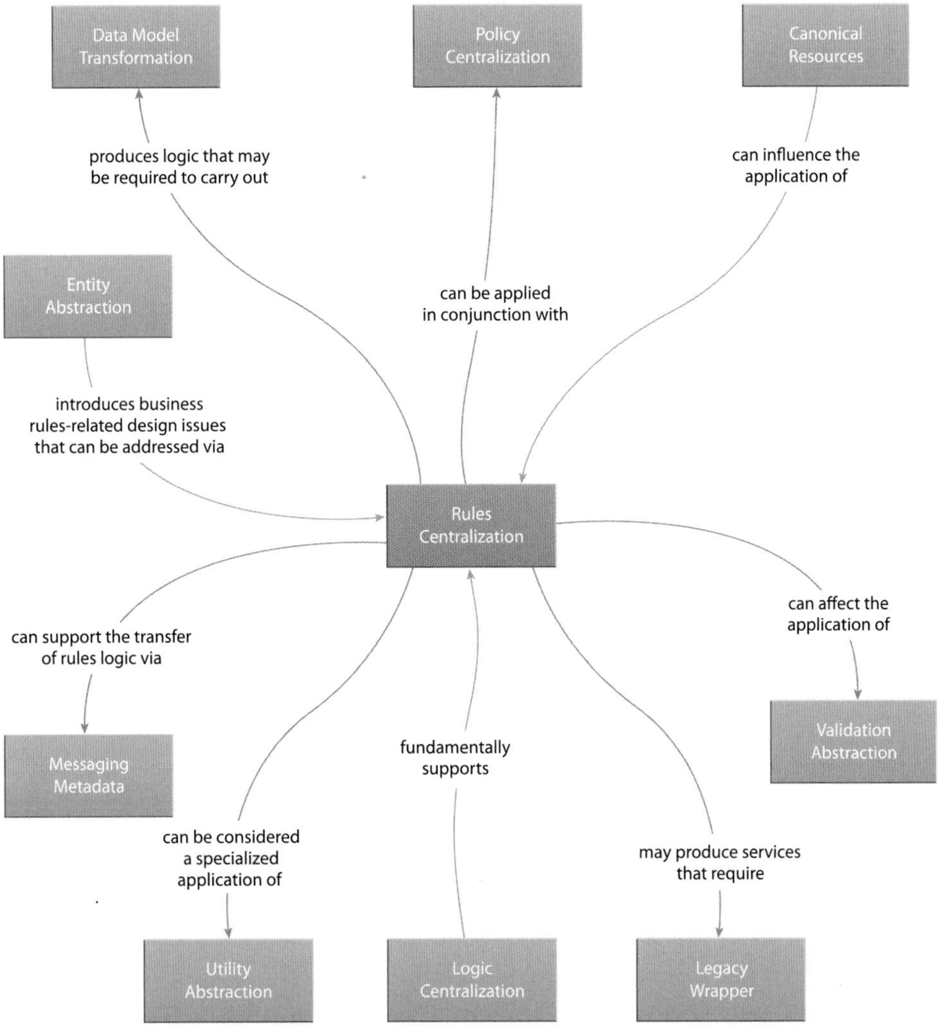

Figure 8.19

The Rules Centralization pattern establishes utility logic that can affect the application of a variety of other patterns.

> **NOTE**
>
> In the upcoming case study example the repeated references to policies relate to regulatory policies, as opposed to technical policies that were the focal point of the preceding case study example for Policy Centralization (207).

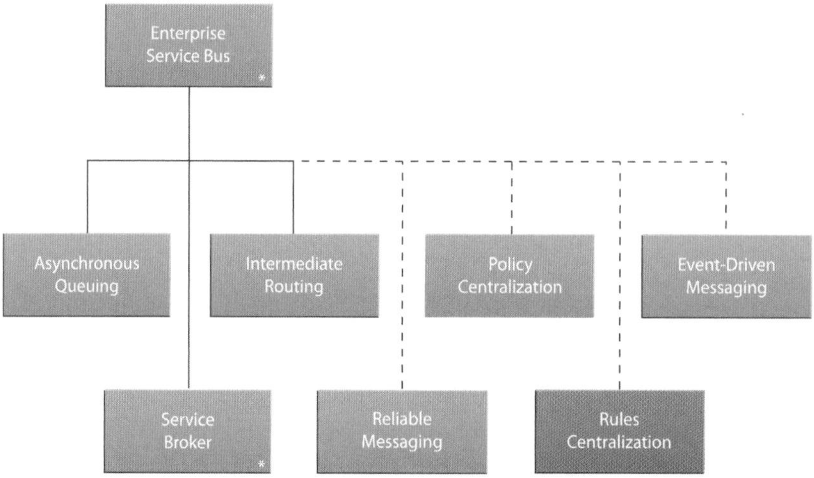

Figure 8.20

One of the optional parts of Enterprise Service Bus (704) is that of native Rules Centralization, allowing much of the core ESB functions to be driven by business rule logic.

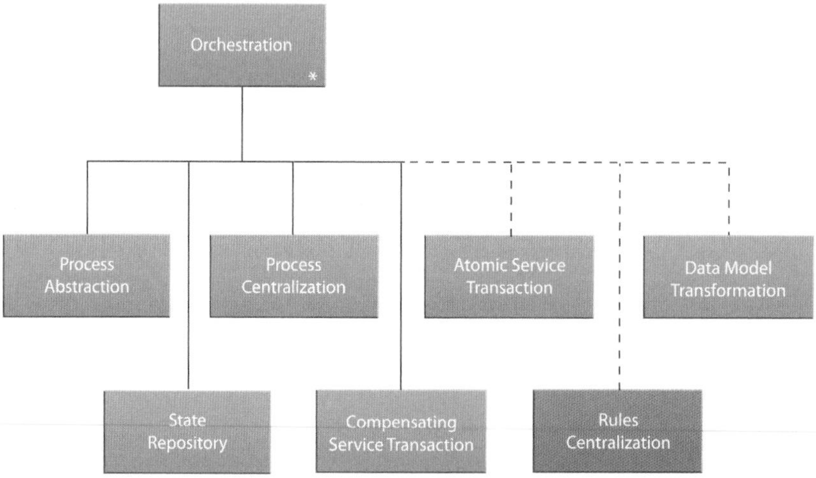

Figure 8.21

Business rules processing can also be part of an orchestration environment, which is why this pattern is considered an optional extension of Orchestration (701).

CASE STUDY EXAMPLE

The FRC manages a large amount of policies that regulate the commercial forestry industry. Different policies apply to different types of forestry companies, but ultimately, many of the policy rules and requirements are inter-related. If one policy needs to be changed, then that change can affect a series of other policies that are in some way connected or dependent.

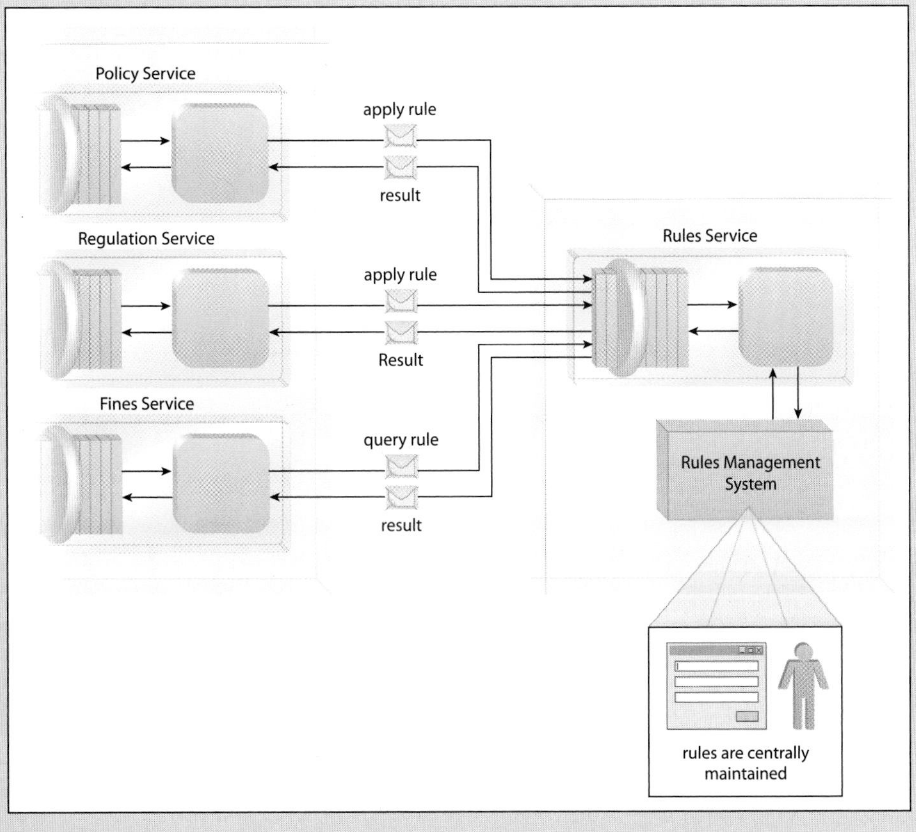

Figure 8.22

The Rules service encapsulating a proprietary rules management system provides central access to rules-related processing logic for other services. The rules management product also centralizes all business rules data for maintenance by a dedicated administrator.

Within the FRC service inventory there are many services (mostly entity-centric) that require access to policy business rules. During the early service modeling stages, it was determined that these rules should not be managed by these services individually. Doing so would result in an unacceptable amount of logic redundancy.

Because so many of the policies tied back into a core set of business rules, it was deemed necessary to establish a service responsible for the management, issuance, and application of policy-related business rules. This Rules service was classified as a utility service and became a central part of their inventory.

Chapter 9

Inventory Implementation Patterns

Dual Protocols

Canonical Resources

State Repository

Stateful Services

Service Grid

Inventory Endpoint

Cross-Domain Utility Layer

To address further common design issues relating to service inventory architecture, this chapter provides a set of specialized patterns that help solve implementation-level problems.

Each of these five patterns targets a specific area of inventory architecture:

- Dual Protocols (227) provides a flexible solution that addresses the challenges of establishing a canonical communications protocol.
- Standardization of underlying technologies is advocated by Canonical Resources (237).
- State Repository (242) and Stateful Services (248) provide alternative solutions for runtime state data deferral.
- Service Grid (254) proposes a sophisticated solution for state deferral and fault tolerance.

The following additional two patterns are focused on solving extra-inventory architectural concerns for environments in which multiple domain inventories exist or for when communication external to the inventory boundary needs to be accommodated:

- Inventory Endpoint (260) establishes somewhat of a specialized proxy service that interacts with external consumers on behalf of services within the inventory boundary.
- Cross-Domain Utility Layer (267) proposes a design solution that changes the face of domain inventories by stretching a common layer of utility services across inventory boundaries.

Whereas the objective of Inventory Endpoint (260) is to preserve the integrity of services within a boundary at the cost of increasing logic redundancy, the goals behind Cross-Domain Utility Layer (267) are to open up portions of these boundaries for the purpose of reducing enterprise-wide redundancy and increasing reuse.

NOTE

Some of the patterns in this chapter reference the term "service activity." Be sure to revisit the definition in Chapter 3 if the term is not familiar to you.

Dual Protocols

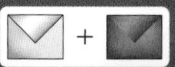

How can a service inventory overcome the limitations of its canonical protocol while still remaining standardized?

Problem	Canonical Protocol (150) requires that all services conform to the use of the same communications technology; however, a single protocol may not be able to accommodate all service requirements, thereby introducing limitations.
Solution	The service inventory architecture is designed to support services based on primary and secondary protocols.
Application	Primary and secondary service levels are created and collectively represent the service endpoint layer. All services are subject to standard service-orientation design considerations and specific guidelines are followed to minimize the impact of not following Canonical Protocol (150).
Impacts	This pattern can lead to a convoluted inventory architecture, increased governance effort and expense, and (when poorly applied) an unhealthy dependence on Protocol Bridging (687). Because the endpoint layer is semi-federated, the quantity of potential consumers and reuse opportunities is decreased.
Principles	Standardized Service Contract, Service Loose Coupling, Service Abstraction, Service Autonomy, Service Composability
Architecture	Inventory, Service

Table 9.1

Profile summary for the Dual Protocols pattern.

NOTE

For a definition of what the term "protocol" refers to in this pattern, see the *What Do We Mean by "Protocol?"* section in the pattern description for Canonical Protocol (150).

Problem

As advocated by Canonical Protocol (150), it is preferred for all services within an inventory to interact using the same communications technology. However, when inventory-wide protocol standardization is not possible or when the chosen communications technology is inadequate for certain types of data exchanges, it can compromise service interoperability, thereby undermining the overall goals of Canonical Protocol (150).

Solution

Two levels of services are delivered within the same inventory:

- a primary level based on the preferred protocol
- a secondary level based on an alternative protocol

This allows the secondary protocol to be used whenever the primary protocol is deemed deficient or inappropriate. This solution furthermore allows services based on the secondary protocol to be promoted to the primary protocol when appropriate.

Application

A popular example of a transport plus messaging protocol combination that is chosen for standardization but that is part of a technology platform that may not be suitable for all types of services is SOAP over HTTP. Even though services built as Web services can establish a standardized communications framework based on these technologies, this choice can raise some issues.

For example:

- SOAP introduces message-processing overhead that may be unreasonable for service capabilities that need to exchange granular amounts of data or that need to be invoked multiple times by the same consumer during the same business process.
- The additional messaging-related processing may be considered inappropriate for services that physically co-exist on the same server and do not require remote communication.
- The service may require a special feature that cannot be accommodated by the Web services technology platform due to an absence of vendor support or a gap or deficiency in a supported Web service standard.

As stated earlier, issues such as these can make it difficult to justify Canonical Protocol (150) on an inventory-wide basis.

Dual Protocols therefore provides a compromise that is essentially based on the standardization of two canonical protocols. For example, when applying this pattern to a Web services-based service inventory, services built as Web services are typically classified as the primary service level because the use of Web services supports several other design benefits and patterns that leverage its industry standards.

However, for circumstances where Web services do not represent a suitable implementation option for services, a secondary protocol is chosen (Figure 9.1). Most commonly, this alternative protocol is based on a particular component platform (such as Java or .NET). In this case, components are designed as self-contained services subject to the full set of service-orientation design principles (including the standardization of the component interface via the Standardized Service Contract principle).

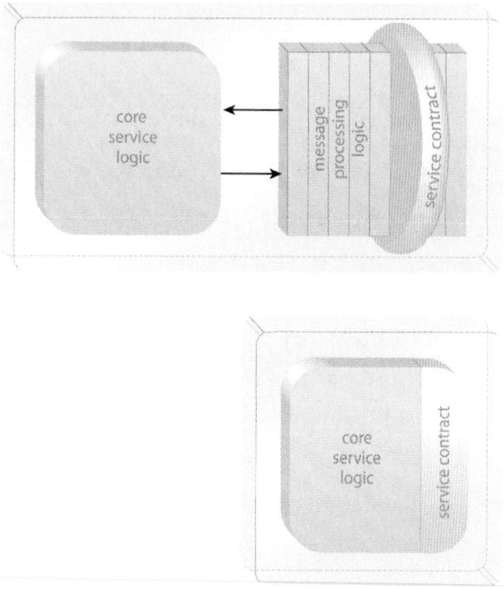

Figure 9.1

A service implemented as a Web service (top) and a service implemented as a component (bottom). Both have standardized service contracts and are subject to all service-orientation design principles.

Figure 9.2 illustrates how primary services existing as Web services can co-exist with secondary services existing as components. Both primary and secondary service levels represent official endpoints as part of a semi-federated service endpoint layer.

There are significant risks when applying this pattern as explained in the upcoming *Impacts* section. To minimize this impact, the following guidelines are recommended:

- Contract Centralization (409) must always be respected, which means that services based on the primary protocol must be accessed via the primary protocol when invoked by secondary services. In the case of Web services, this require that component-based services not directly access the underlying components or resources of Web services-based services.
- Consider some or all services in the secondary level as transition candidates. If this pattern was chosen due to a lack of maturity in the primary protocol, then secondary services can be earmarked for an upgrade to the primary level once the technology has sufficiently evolved.
- During a transitional period, use Concurrent Contracts (421) to enable a service to be accessible via either protocol. This way, it can begin to interoperate using the primary protocol while continuing to support consumers that rely upon the secondary protocol.
- Apply Redundant Implementation (345) wherever feasible in support of secondary services. This is especially relevant when component-based secondary services are primarily composed by the core service logic of Web services-based services to avoid remote communication. Redundant Implementation (345) will support the autonomy of both primary and secondary service levels.

Note that some secondary services may never transition and therefore always remain based on the secondary protocol. This may be due to the nature of their functionality or the convenience of keeping them for intra-service composition purposes only.

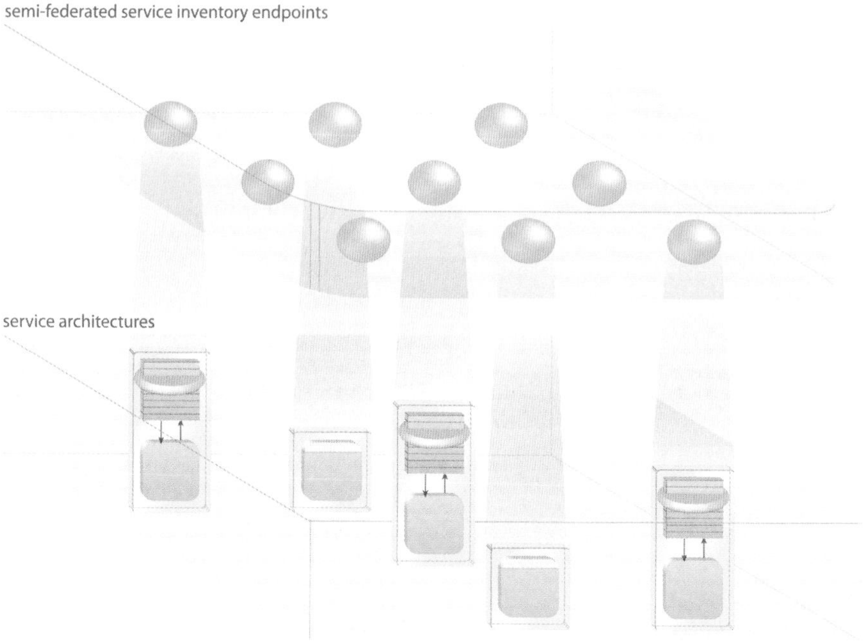

Figure 9.2

From an endpoint perspective the service contracts are all standardized, but their implementations are based on different communication protocols.

As shown in Figure 9.3, the first guideline in the previous list establishes some ground rules as to how primary and secondary services should and should not interact.

The key requirement to successfully applying this pattern is for services to continue adhering to Standardized Service Contract, Service Loose Coupling, and Service Abstraction design principles to avoid many of the negative, indirect coupling types that can lead to governance problems.

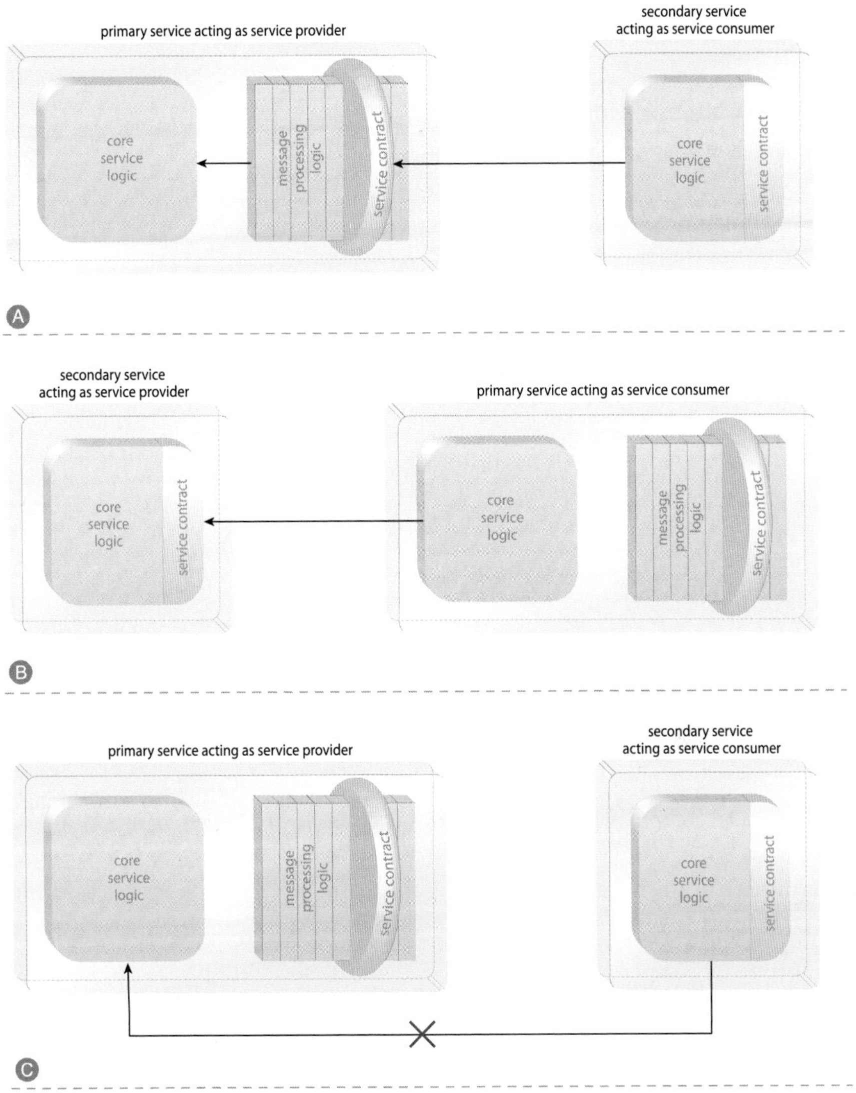

Figure 9.3

Regardless of protocol, all services must invoke each other via their official service contracts (A, B). Bypassing the contract may seem convenient when the underlying service logic of the primary service supports the same protocol as the secondary service (C), but it is an anti-pattern that will eventually inhibit the application of this pattern and further weaken the overall service inventory foundation.

> **NOTE**
>
> An alternative approach to applying this pattern is to limit the secondary protocol to utility services only. When working with Web services as the primary protocol and a native component technology as the secondary protocol, this approach can reduce the size of Web service compositions by limiting them to business services. These business Web services can then compose component-based utility services, as required.
>
> Although this pattern description is focused on components and Web services as implementation mediums, REST services and the use of HTTP as an application protocol provide another viable option. To learn more, visit SOAPatterns.org and read up on the REST-inspired patterns currently in development.

Impacts

This design pattern must be used in moderation. It imposes some significant architectural constraints and sacrifices that need to be carefully assessed before committing to an architecture based on primary and secondary protocols.

For example:

- The use of Concurrent Contracts (421) to provide secondary services with two interfaces while they are being transitioned from secondary to primary status can lead to overly complex governance requirements. If this pattern is applied to a large service inventory with a large percentage of secondary services, the transition effort may be unwieldy.
- The repeated application of Redundant Implementation (345) in support of secondary services can rapidly increase infrastructure budgets and the overall configuration management effort required to keep all deployments of a given service in synch.
- Depending on which technologies are chosen for primary and secondary protocol levels, this pattern may limit the application of other key design patterns, such as Canonical Schema (158) and Schema Centralization (200).
- The examples in this chapter were focused on Web services comprised of components that shared the same protocol technology as the component-based services. If this pattern is applied to primary and secondary service levels that are based on disparate protocols, it will introduce the need for the constant application of Protocol Bridging (687).

- This pattern introduces the on-going risk of imposing too much technology coupling upon consumers, thereby making plans to migrate to a fully federated service inventory difficult to fully attain.

There are concrete benefits to carrying out this design pattern in the right way, but it introduces a whole new dimension to a service-oriented architecture adoption, and the associated risks need to be planned for in advance.

Relationships

The extra requirements that come with applying Dual Protocols often need to be addressed with the application of additional supporting patterns, such as Redundant Implementation (345), Concurrent Contracts (421), and Protocol Bridging (687).

Although this pattern fundamentally preserves the goals of Logic Centralization (136) and Contract Centralization (409), it ends up augmenting the default approach of carrying out Canonical Protocol (150) by essentially allowing two canonical protocols.

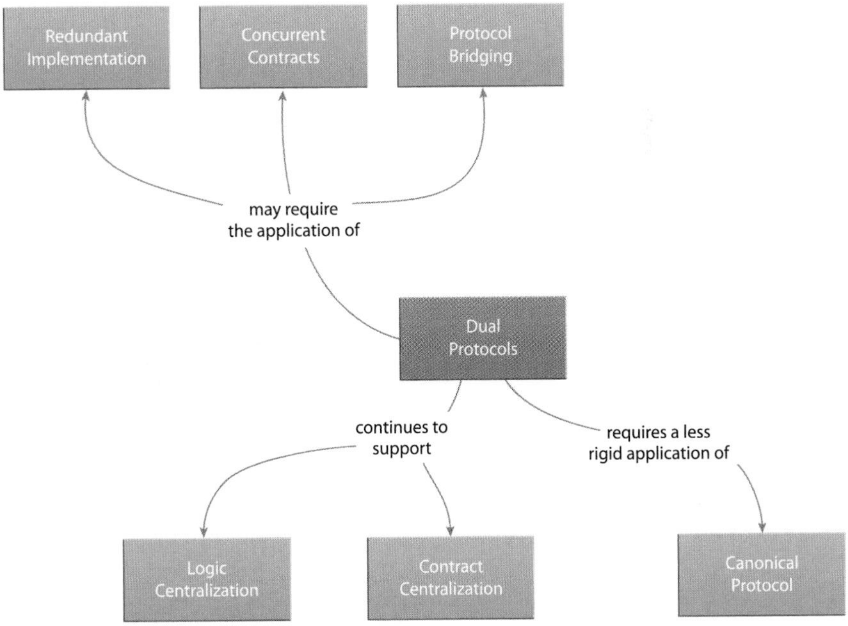

Figure 9.4

Dual Protocols can increase the flexibility and complexity of an inventory architecture and therefore requires the support of other key patterns.

CASE STUDY EXAMPLE

The Field Support office at the FRC has relied on a custom-built, distributed Web application for over five years. This system is relatively out of date by today's standards and is primarily comprised of a series of COM components and Web service scripts deployed across the traditional three physical tiers: Web server, application server, and a dedicated database server. The DCOM protocol that was popular during the 1990s is still used to communicate between the Web and application servers.

Although the IT group that has been maintaining this system is being mandated to support a broad adoption of Web services, they will not receive funding for another two years to complete this transition. Yet, in the meantime, they are still required to make parts of their system (including database access) available via SOAP messaging from other FRC applications.

To accomplish this, they first consider simply deploying a set of Web services that act as endpoints into their environment. This would satisfy immediate requirements without too much up-front effort or investment.

However, upon further discussion with architects from FRC's EA department, they begin to realize that the Web services they would be delivering would not conform to standardized schemas and would therefore not properly represent the business services within the Field Support division. They would essentially just be integration endpoints.

In the long-term, many consumer programs could form dependencies on these services, thereby entrenching their contracts. When this department is ready to move over to a full-scale services architecture, the "real" services that would then be modeled would be incompatible with these endpoints.

As a result, they would either have to disrupt the existing connections by replacing the original Web services with properly modeled ones, or they would need to classify those Web services as a legacy part of their environment that would then need to be further wrapped within newly standardized services, as per Legacy Wrapper (441). Neither option is desirable.

To avoid this situation, they decide to proceed with a preliminary service inventory architecture that supports two standard communication protocols: DCOM and SOAP. A service inventory blueprint is created for their environment, and a specific subset of the modeled service candidates is chosen for initial delivery. Some, providing new internally needed functionality, will still be delivered as COM components, while others

(especially those with which external applications need to communicate) will be built as Web services.

A strategic plan is put in place, allowing services comprised of COM components to gradually transition to Web services via component technology upgrades and the incorporation of Web service contracts.

Canonical Resources

How can unnecessary infrastructure resource disparity be avoided?

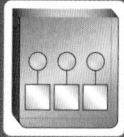

Problem	Service implementations can unnecessarily introduce disparate infrastructure resources, thereby bloating the enterprise and resulting in increased governance burden.
Solution	The supporting infrastructure and architecture can be equipped with common resources and extensions that can be repeatedly utilized by different services.
Application	Enterprise design standards are defined to formalize the required use of standardized architectural resources.
Impacts	If this pattern leads to too much dependency on shared infrastructure resources, it can decrease the autonomy and mobility of services.
Principles	Service Autonomy
Architecture	Enterprise, Inventory

Table 9.2

Profile summary for the Canonical Resources pattern.

What Do We Mean by "Resource"?

Within the context of this pattern, a resource refers to an extension of the infrastructure that provides general processing functions.

Examples include:

- databases, directories, and data warehouse products
- state deferral mechanisms (such as a standard state database, standard tables within a database used for temporary storage, or grid technology)
- security processing extensions (such as a central directory or a standardized set of security technologies and/or processing agents)
- activity management extensions (such as context and transaction management frameworks)
- reliability extensions (such as a sequence-based messaging framework)

> Note that a resource may or may not be shared. Note also that this pattern does not advocate sharing resources.

Problem

Services delivered without architectural design standards or developed outside of an organization (as part of an outsourced project, for example) run the risk of introducing disparate yet still redundant infrastructure resources. This can bloat an inventory architecture and unnecessarily introduce complexity, leading to increased administration and operational costs and other governance burdens associated with maintaining a bloated enterprise environment (Figure 9.5).

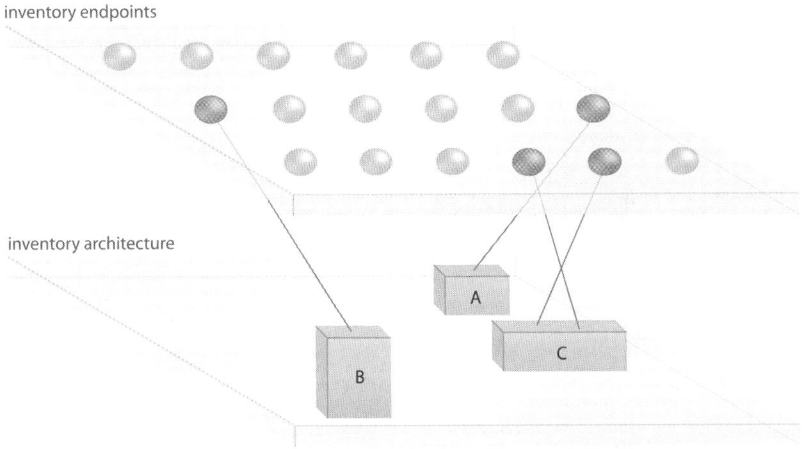

Figure 9.5

Services use different infrastructure resources for the same purpose, resulting in inconsistent architectural dependencies. In this diagram, A, B, and C could represent disparate databases or other out-of-the-box products from different vendors.

Solution

Utility Abstraction (168) is often used to wrap common infrastructure resources and then make them available via a standardized contract to the rest of the service inventory. When this is not possible, common resources are identified and standardized in order to maintain consistency across service designs and throughout the inventory in general (Figure 9.6).

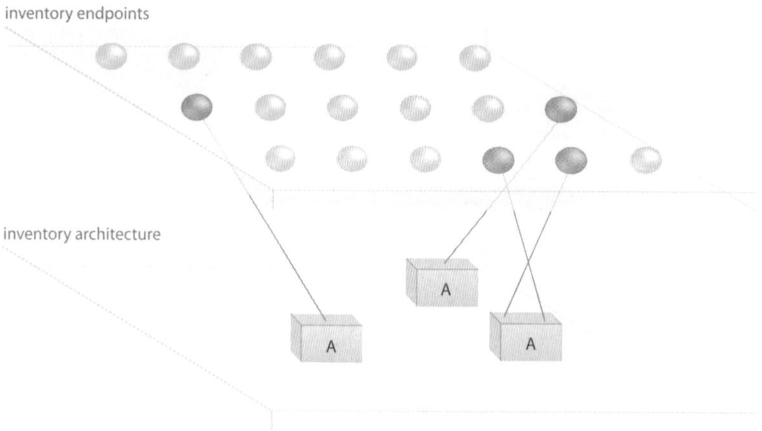

Figure 9.6

Services use the same standardized infrastructure resource for the same purpose. Note, however, that they do not share the same implementation of the resource.

Application

This pattern is specifically focused on infrastructure products, platforms, and extensions (collectively referred to as "resources") that provide common features useful to multiple services. These infrastructure-centric resources are essentially identified and standardized.

It is important to not allow the application of this pattern to inhibit the Vendor-Neutral design characteristic (introduced in Chapter 4) of a service inventory architecture. Therefore, the nature of the design standards that result from this pattern is preferably such that the chosen resource becomes the default option for a given requirement or purpose. This leaves the flexibility for alternatives to be considered if requirements exist that cannot be adequately fulfilled by the standardized resource.

Impacts

The repeated application of this pattern can lead to a natural tendency to want to share and reuse standardized products for cost or development efficiency purposes. This may often be warranted, but it can also inadvertantly reduce the autonomy of services beyond what it should be.

Relationships

This pattern relates to others primarily as a regulatory influence. Design patterns that implement new architectural resources or extensions are encouraged to avoid introducing disparate infrastructure-related products and technologies that fulfill the same overall purpose. This affects all of the patterns listed at the top of Figure 9.7.

The end result of applying Canonical Resources is similar to enforcing an enterprise design standard, which is why Canonical Protocol (150) can be viewed as a variation of this pattern focused only on communication technologies.

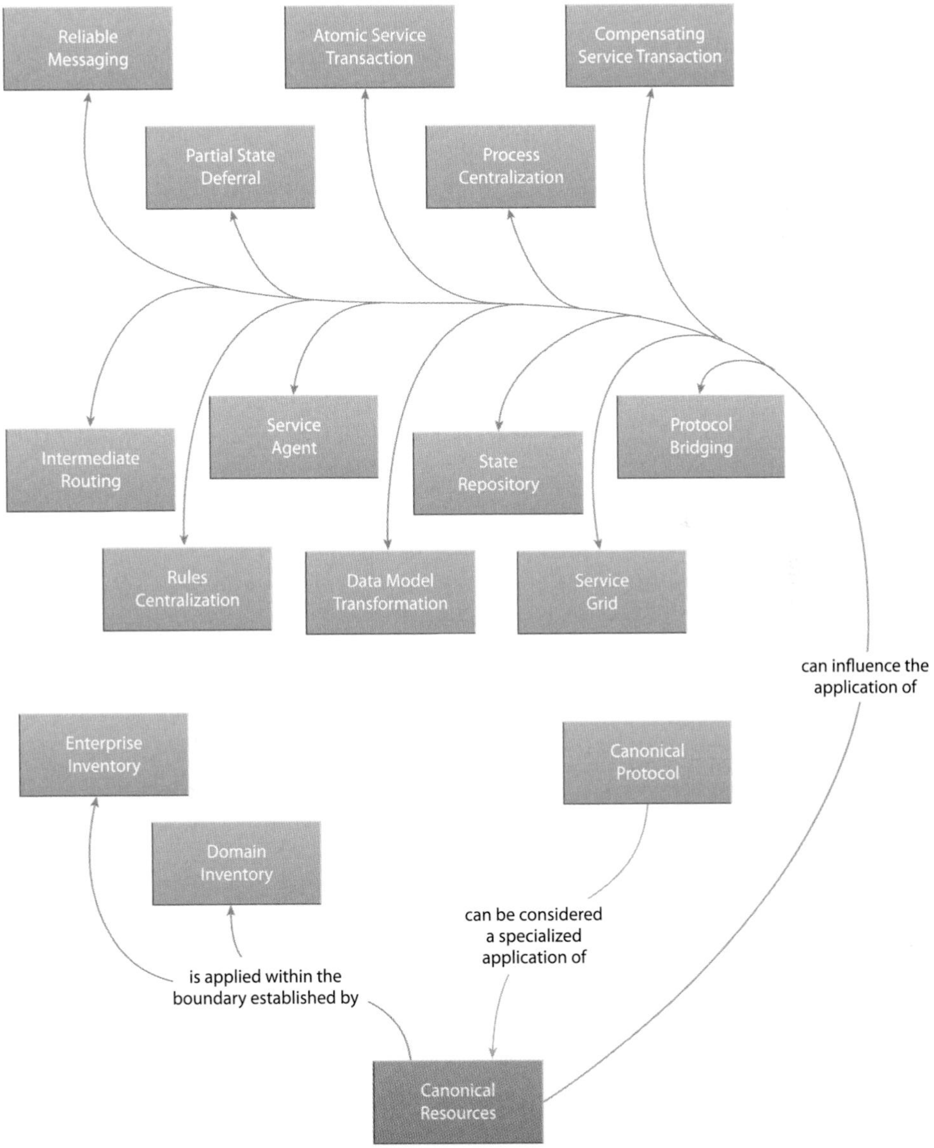

Figure 9.7
Canonical Resources helps standardize the underlying inventory architecture and therefore influences the application of many other architectural patterns.

CASE STUDY EXAMPLE

As the FRC service inventory continues to grow, more sophisticated service compositions can be assembled to automate larger, more complex business processes. Some of these tasks require an increased level of integrity to ensure that if any one composition member fails, all of the activity carried out to that point can be reversed.

This need for cross-service transactions originally inspired a solution comprised of custom SOAP headers combined with a proprietary third-party product that introduced a series of service agents to process the headers and manage the overall transaction.

During a subsequent runtime platform upgrade, support for the WS-Coordination and WS-AtomicTransaction standards was provided, enabling ACID-style transactions to span multiple Web services, as per Atomic Service Transaction (623). New compositions leveraged this to establish an industry-standard transaction management system whereby participating services could issue standardized messages in order to vote on the outcome of the overall transaction.

However, when services using the proprietary transaction management product had to be combined with recently delivered services into new compositions, there was an evident incompatibility that required significant reworking to overcome. Essentially, the old services had to be upgraded in order to support both styles of transaction management.

It became clear that transaction management, as an architectural extension, had to become standardized across the inventory. The WS-Coordination and WS-AtomicTransaction standards were chosen for this purpose.

State Repository

How can service state data be persisted for extended periods without consuming service runtime resources?

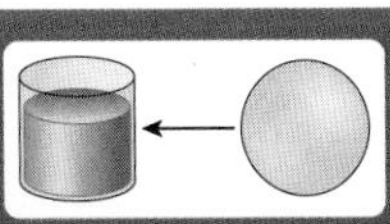

Problem	Large amounts of state data cached to support the activity within a running service composition can consume too much memory, especially for long-running activities, thereby decreasing scalability.
Solution	State data can be temporarily written to and then later retrieved from a dedicated state repository.
Application	A shared or dedicated repository is made available as part of the inventory or service architecture.
Impacts	The addition of required write and read functionality increases the service design complexity and can negatively affect performance.
Principles	Service Statelessness
Architecture	Inventory, Service

Table 9.3
Profile summary for the State Repository pattern.

Problem

It is often necessary to retrieve and cache bodies of data to which service capabilities require repeated access during the course of a service activity. However, some complex compositions introduce extended periods of processing during which this data is not required. While idle, this cached data continues to be stored in memory and consumes runtime resources (Figure 9.8).

This excess consumption can severely compound during periods of high concurrent usage, depleting the overall available runtime service. As this occurs repeatedly with different services throughout an inventory, overall scalability thresholds can decrease.

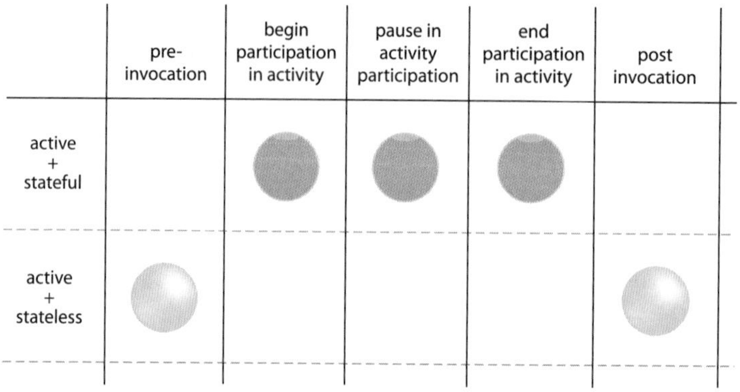

Figure 9.8

During the lifespan of a service instance it may be required to remain stateful and keep state data cached in memory even as its participation in the activity is paused. (The orange color is used to represent the state data.)

Solution

A state repository is established as an architectural extension made available to any service for temporary state data deferral purposes (Figure 9.9). This alleviates services from having to unnecessarily keep state data in memory for extended periods.

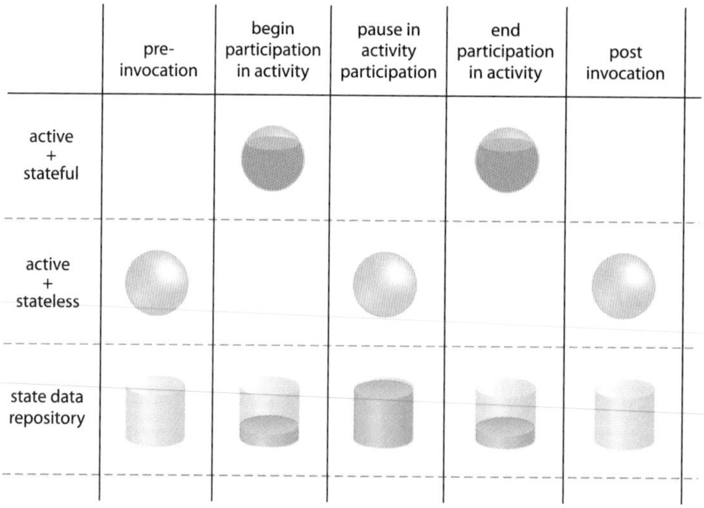

Figure 9.9

By deferring state data to a state repository, the service is able to transition to a stateless condition during pauses in the activity, thereby temporarily freeing system resources.

> **NOTE**
>
> See the *Measuring Service Statelessness* section in Chapter 11 of *SOA Principles of Service Design* for a detailed description of state data and additional scenarios involving state data repositories.

Application

Typically, a dedicated database is provided for state deferral purposes. The database is located on the same physical server as the services that will be utilizing it, so as to minimize runtime performance overhead associated with the writing and retrieval of the data. Another approach is to create dedicated tables within an existing database. Though less effective, this still provides a state deferral option suitable for temporary data storage.

Alternatives to State Repository include Stateful Services (248) and State Messaging (557), which can be considered especially when the state data does not need to be persisted over long periods of time. Howver, it is also fairly common for State Repository to be used in conjunction with these patterns to provide more flexible (albeit more complex) state management mechanisms that may be especially suitable for providing customized state deferral options for different types of state data.

Impacts

Incorporating the state deferral logic required to carry out this pattern can increase service design complexity, leading to more development effort and expense.

Although State Repository can improve scalability, having to write data to and retrieve data from a physical hard drive generally imposes more runtime performance overhead than having to carry out the same functions against data stored in memory. For service activities with strict real-time performance requirements, this state deferral option needs to be carefully assessed.

Relationships

Establishing a state management system via State Repository naturally relates to other state deferral-related patterns, such as Stateful Services (248), Partial State Deferral (356), State Messaging (557), and Service Grid (254). All of these patterns may end up using the central state database introduced by this pattern. Canonical Resources (237) can further help ensure that no one inventory will have more than one type of state management database unless absolutely required.

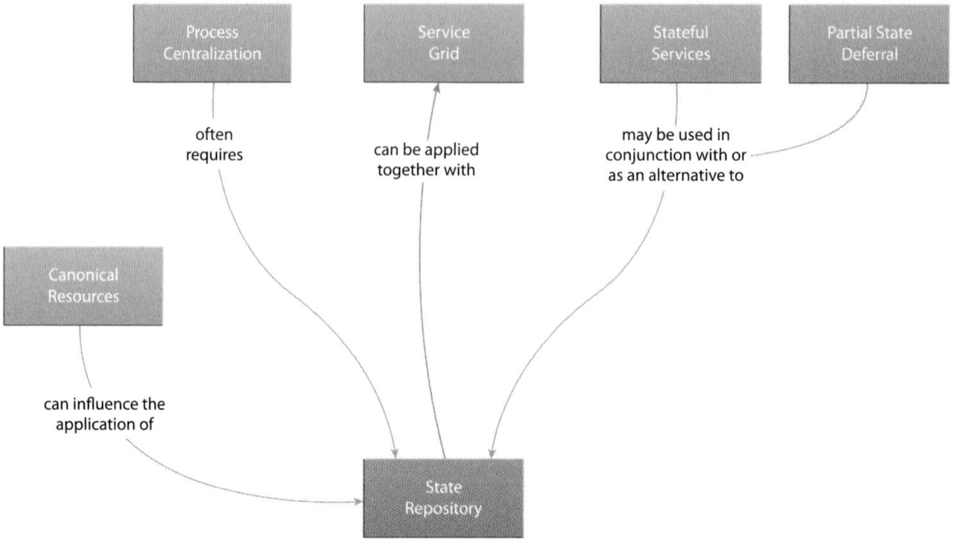

Figure 9.10
State Repository is fundamental to just about any state management design considerations and related patterns.

Process Centralization (193) will almost always require the application of this pattern to provide a means of persisting state data associated with the many business processes that orchestration environments are required to execute and manage (especially in support of long-running processes). This is why State Repository is one of the core patterns that comprise Orchestration (701).

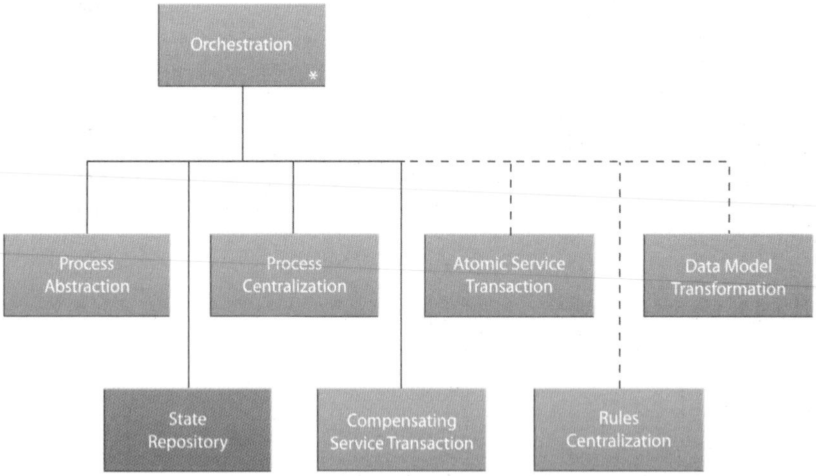

Figure 9.11
State Repository is a fundamental part of the compound pattern Orchestration (701).

CASE STUDY EXAMPLE

The Alleywood Policy Check service (Figure 9.12) is responsible for issuing periodic queries against public FRC Web services that provide access to the most current policy information. These queries help confirm that current policies used by Alleywood are still valid or have changed.

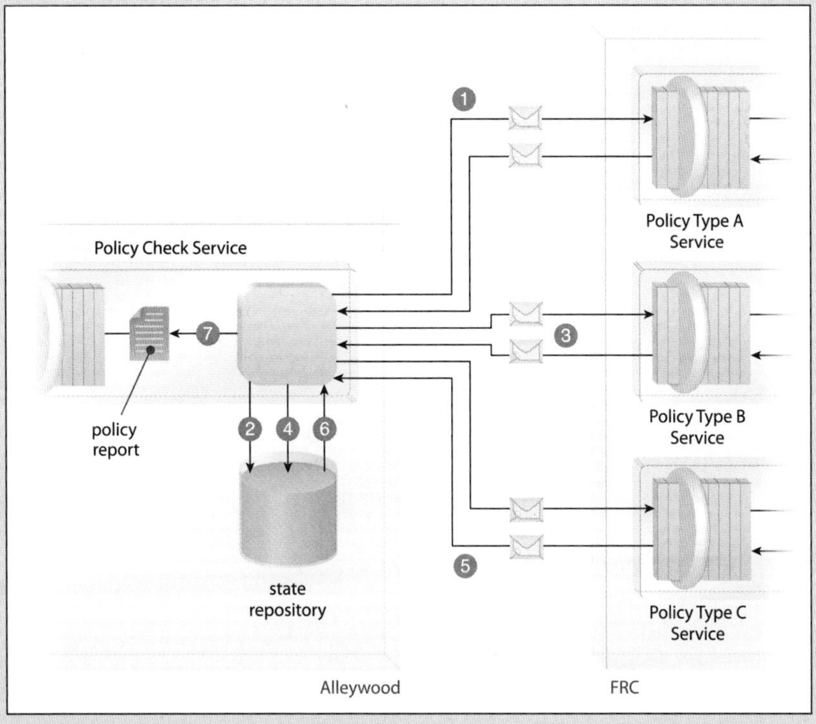

Figure 9.12

The Policy Check service issues a query against the first FRC service (1) and then writes the results to the state repository (2) before requesting data from the next FRC service (3). That information is then also written to the state repository (4), and after the Policy Check service retrieves the last batch of data from the third FRC service (5), it retrieves the data from the state repository (6) and assembles the requested policy report (7).

The FRC exposes three separate Web services that provide report-style data for different policy types. Alleywood, being a larger-sized company, is required to remain in compliance with all three types of policies. This service therefore needs to query each FRC service before it can produce a consolidated report.

Query times can vary, depending on concurrent usage of the FRC services and the databases they access. Sometimes it can take minutes to receive a response, and other times the response times out or fails altogether. The initial version of the Policy Check service had many problems due to these irregular access conditions. It became one of the most unreliable parts of the Alleywood service inventory and consumed unusually high amounts of memory.

As a result, the Policy Check service is refactored to write each batch of data it receives to a state repository. Even if access to an FRC service fails, the data collected so far is preserved in this database, while the Policy Check service retries its access. It then continues to wait until it has received all the information it needs, at which point it retrieves all of the data back from the state repository and merges it into the requested report.

Stateful Services

How can service state data be persisted and managed without consuming service runtime resources?

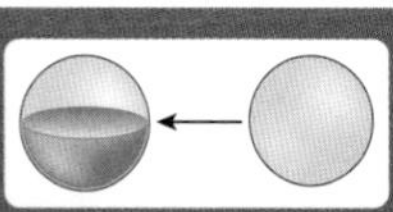

Problem	State data associated with a particular service activity can impose a great deal of runtime state management responsibility upon service compositions, thereby reducing their scalability.
Solution	State data is managed and stored by intentionally stateful utility services.
Application	Stateful utility services provide in-memory state data storage and/or can maintain service activity context data.
Impacts	If not properly implemented, stateful utility services can become a performance bottleneck.
Principles	Service Statelessness
Architecture	Inventory, Service

Table 9.4
Profile summary for the Stateful Services pattern.

Problem

The coordination of large service activities requires the constant management of state data. Placing the burden of retaining and processing this data upon business services increases their individual memory consumption as well as the duration for which they are required to remain stateful (Figure 9.13).

Solution

Intentionally stateful utility services are created to provide regular state deferral and storage functions and/or to provide runtime coordination functions to manage the flow and participation of service activities. This alleviates the need for any one business service from having to retain or manage state data for extended periods (Figure 9.14).

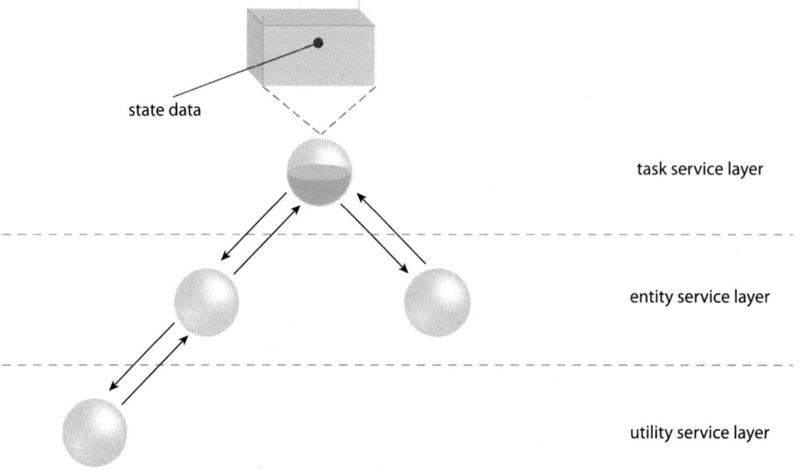

Figure 9.13

The task controller service of a modest composition is required to retain and manage all of the service activity's state data until the activity is completed.

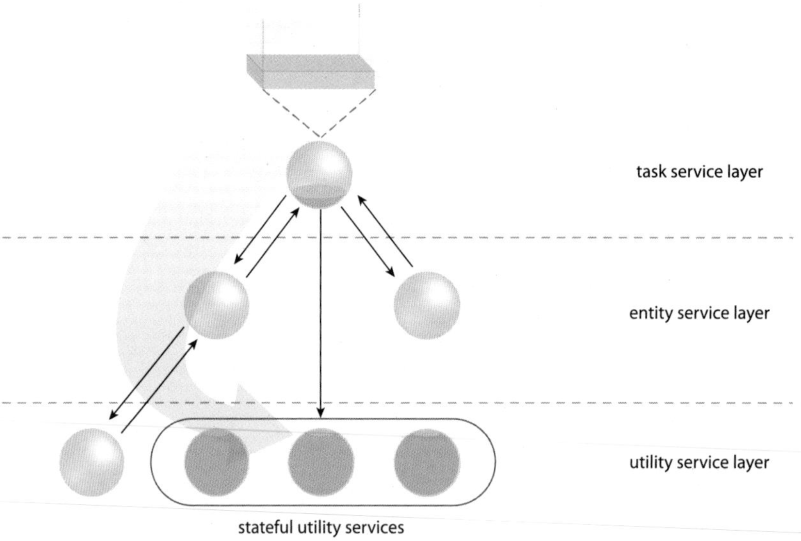

Figure 9.14

With the use of stateful utility services, state management responsibilities are deferred.

Application

This pattern is commonly applied in two ways:

- The stateful utility services provide state management deferral functions that are explicitly used by other services as required.
- The stateful utility services are part of a service activity management framework (such as WS-Coordination) within which they act as runtime activity coordinators.

Either way, what distinguishes services dedicated to state management is that they are deliberately stateful parts of the enterprise. Therefore, these specialized services intentionally violate the Service Statelessness principle so as to support its application in other services.

NOTE

When stateful utility services act as coordinators during the execution of a service activity, the type of state data they process is commonly referred to as *context data* in that it represents information pertaining to the context of the current service activity.

Impacts

In high concurrency situations, stateful utility services can be required to manage numerous service activities and activity instances at the same time. If they are not supported by the proper infrastructure, the overall performance and scalability of the service inventory as a whole can be compromised, thereby undermining their purpose.

Also the use of stateful utility services adds more "moving parts" to a given service composition, thereby increasing its complexity.

Relationships

This pattern establishes a specialized variation of the utility service and is therefore related to Utility Abstraction (168). Some implementations may still require a state management database behind the scenes, leading to the need to also apply State Repository (242) and the option to utilize State Messaging (557) to temporarily off-load state data is also possible. Additionally, both State Repository (242) and State Messaging (557) represent viable alternatives to Stateful Services altogether.

When stateful utility services exist as Web services, Service Messaging (553) is required for basic communication, and Messaging Metadata (538) provides a means of supplementing state data deliveries with additional activity details. As further explored in the next pattern description, Stateful Services also relates closely to Service Grid (254).

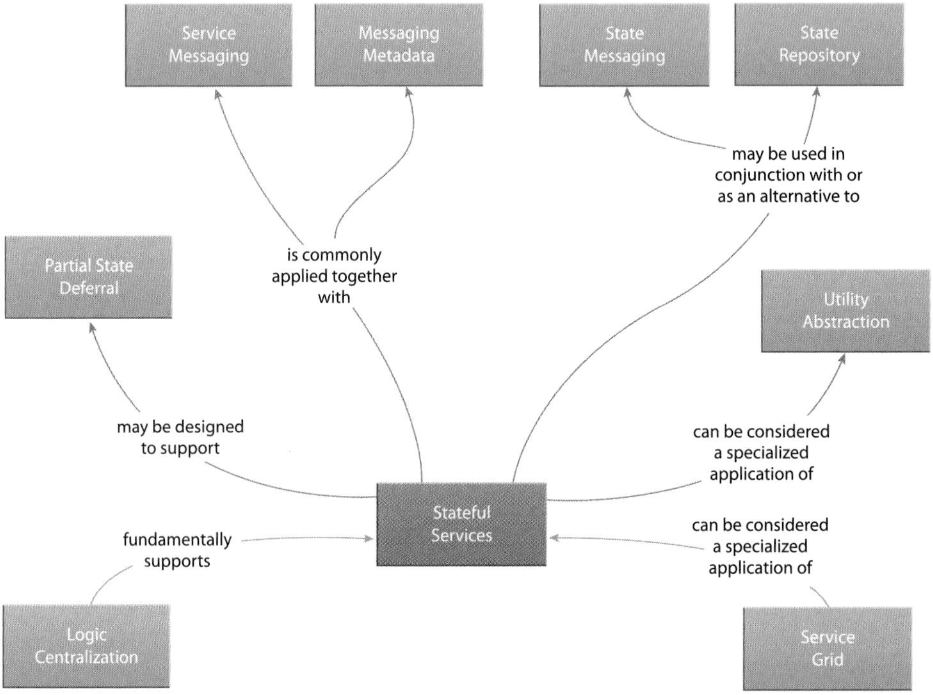

Figure 9.15

Stateful Services results in the creation of utility services that centralize state and activity management, primarily via messaging.

CASE STUDY EXAMPLE

The transaction framework described in the case study example for Canonical Resources (237) established WS-Coordination as a standardized context management system intended to facilitate all ACID-style transactions within the FRC service inventory.

Under the covers this framework is comprised of a set of stateful utility services that are pre-defined as part of the WS-Coordination specification. These services require that regular services participating in a transaction first register for the transaction and then communicate to them the status of their involvement. Once a service has completed its participation, it de-registers itself from the transaction.

The rules by which the stateful WS-Coordination services manage transactions are defined separately in the WS-AtomicTransaction specification. For example, a voting mechanism is introduced whereby participating services are polled as to whether their contribution to a given transaction was successful or not. Services can respond with "Commit" or "Abort" messages that indicate their status. If just one "Abort" message is received (or if one vote is missing from the registered services), then the transaction is in fact aborted, and a "Rollback" message is sent to all participants.

Together, WS-Coordination and WS-AtomicTransaction provide an industry-standard transaction management framework for the FRC that manages service activity data (referred to as context information) on behalf of other custom services. This alleviates custom FRC services from having to provide some of the logic required to coordinate service activity-specific details.

However, after working with this framework, it is soon discovered that there is an additional opportunity to delegate state management-related processing. Specifically, FRC architects notice redundant logic creeping into a number of entity services required to work with a set of code lists common to the forestry industry. Often these code lists need to be placed into memory and then repeatedly accessed as transactions are carried out.

FRC architects would like to see this type of state data managed separately by stateful utility services. Because the WS-Coordination system services are pre-defined, architects are not comfortable augmenting them to incorporate this new functionality. Instead, they opt to create a custom Code service that will be used to complement the WS-Coordination framework by allowing all services participating in transactions to read and write code lists (Figure 9.16).

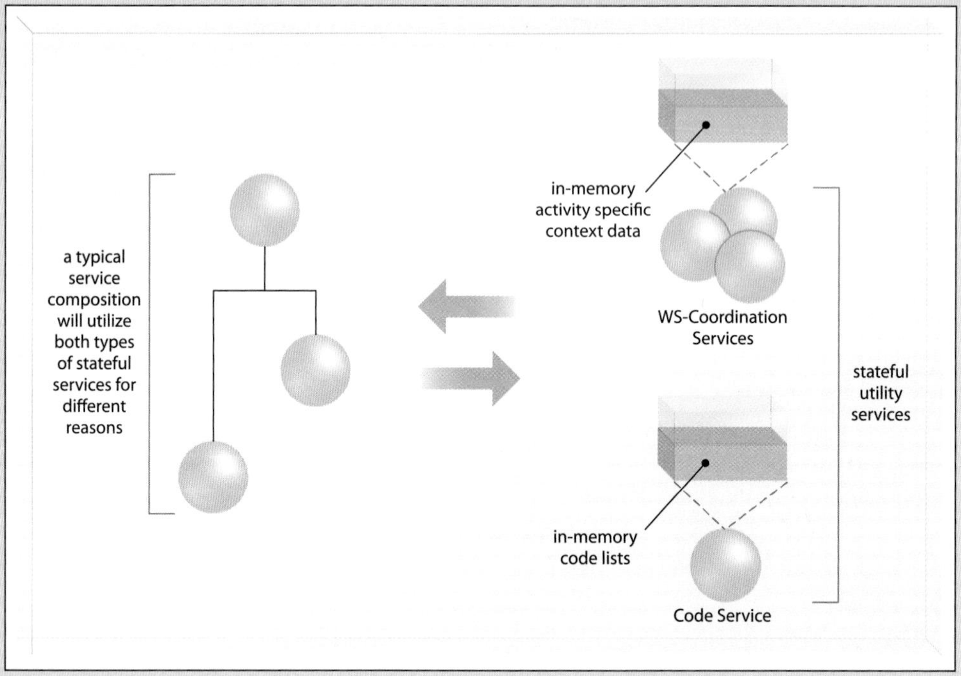

Figure 9.16

The FRC employs stateful system services provided the WS-Coordination framework, as well as a custom-developed, stateful Code service.

NOTE

The preceding case study example used the WS-Coordination framework as an example of a framework that supports the application of this pattern. The actual mechanics behind cross-service transactions are further explained in the pattern description for Atomic Service Transaction (623).

Service Grid

By David Chappell

How can deferred service state data be scaled and kept fault-tolerant?

Problem	State data deferred via State Repository or Stateful Services can be subject to performance bottlenecks and failure, especially when exposed to high-usage volumes.
Solution	State data is deferred to a collection of stateful system services that form a grid that provides high scalability and fault tolerance through memory replication and redundancy and supporting infrastructure.
Application	Grid technology is introduced into the enterprise or inventory architecture.
Impacts	This pattern can require a significant infrastructure upgrade and can correspondingly increase governance burden.
Principles	Service Statelessness
Architecture	Enterprise, Inventory, Service

Table 9.5
Profile summary for the Service Grid pattern

Problem

Conventional state deferral mechanisms have thresholds that can impede the usage potential of services.

For example:

- When services defer state data to a central database, as per State Repository (242), it can result in performance bottlenecks relative to the extent that the repository is shared and the available resources of the underlying infrastructure. Furthermore, a state database can become a single point of failure for all services that rely on it (Figure 9.17).
- When services defer state data to utility services, as per Stateful Services (248), failover concerns are even greater than with State Repository (242) because the state data is kept in memory and may not be recoverable after a failure condition. Additionally, stateful utility services may become performance bottlenecks due to an absence of built-in load balancing functionality.

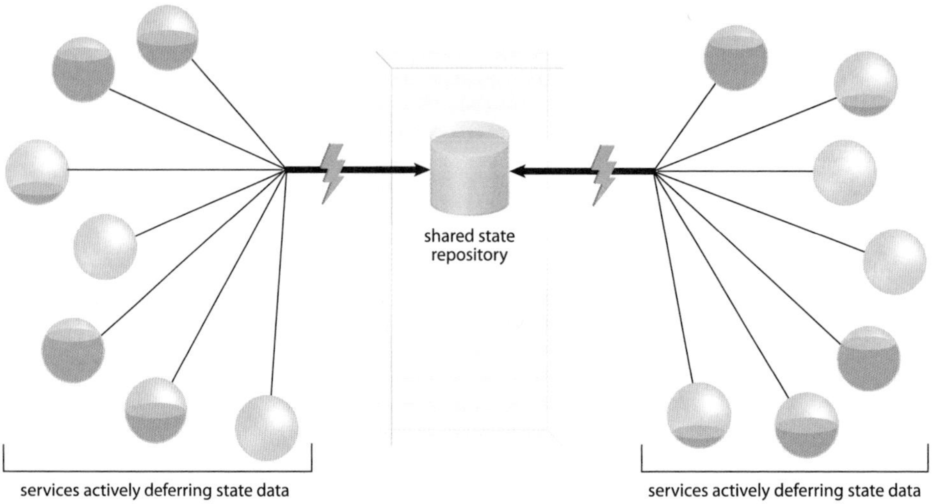

Figure 9.17
A central state repository can raise performance and reliability concerns when it is subject to high concurrent usage.

In some platforms, State Repository (242) and Stateful Services (248) can be supported by infrastructure extensions that provide failover. However, these extensions are often based on "failure and restart" approaches that involve a transaction manager-like rollback and recovery. While this provides some level of fault tolerance, it will typically result in loss of data, runtime disruption and exceptions, and may further require manual intervention by humans.

Solution

Deferred service state data is persisted and stored by a dedicated collection of grid services—stateful services which are part of a services-based grid platform and act as an extension of the infrastructure.

Within this platform, multiple, redundant instances of the grid services are constantly available and remain consistently synchronized. This allows each grid service to provide its own individual memory cache that is replicated across multiple redundant instances that reside on and are load balanced across different server machines (Figure 9.18). Additional grid service instances can be further spawned, as required.

The resulting environment can establish high scalability and fault tolerance of deferred state data throughout an entire service inventory and even across multiple inventories.

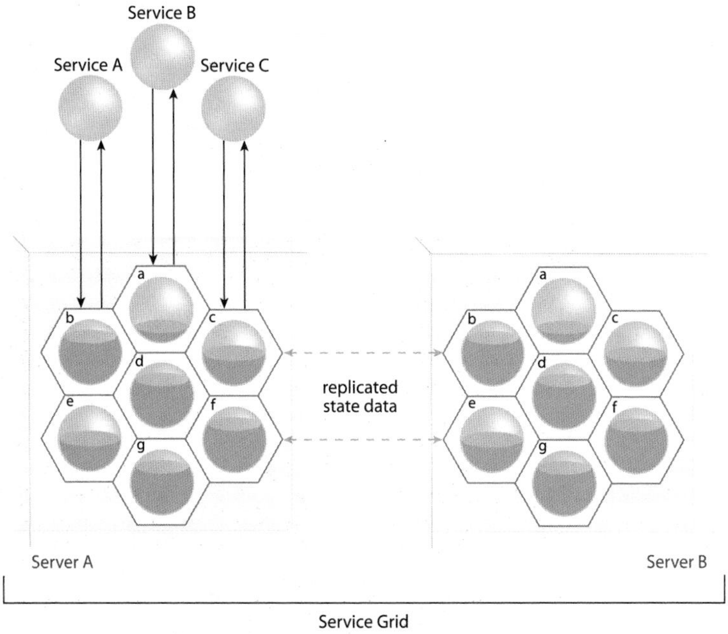

Figure 9.18

A service grid establishes replicated instances of stateful grid services across different server machines, resulting in increased scalability and reliability of state data. (A grid service is represented by the standard service symbol enclosed in a honeycomb cell.)

Application

How Service Grid is actually implemented can vary, depending on the specific platform or vendor product that is chosen. A common process is for a custom service to pass state data to a grid service, which then responds with a unique identifier (called a *state key*) that represents the body of state data. The service receives and holds onto the state key while it remains active, and can then use this key to access and retrieve some or all of the previously deferred state data.

> **NOTE**
>
> The notion of a state key also forms the basis of a separate pattern that allows the same body of state data to be shared across multiple services and service compositions. This and other specialized patterns associated with Service Grid are being published at SOAPatterns.org and will further be documented in a separate book by David Chappell.

Behind the scenes, the inner mechanics of the service grid ensure that whatever state data is received is constantly duplicated via distributed, redundant grid service instances. If the custom service makes a change to the state data or retrieves portions of it, these events are replicated to the corresponding redundant grid service instances so that they remain synchronized.

Should a grid instance fail, any one of its counterparts assumes its place and continues to make the state data available to the original custom service. Intelligent load-balancing functionality may be present to direct deferral or retrieval requests from the custom service to the grid service instance residing on the physical server that is being used the least at that point in time. Furthermore, advanced grid computing extensions can be added to offload the execution of service logic into the service grid in order to reduce network data serialization latency between custom and grid services.

Throughout all of this, regular custom services that interact with grid services are shielded from the inner workings of the service grid platform and may simply view grid services as generic stateful utility services. A service grid implementation can include or be further extended with State Repository (242) for long-term state storage requirements.

This pattern is especially effective in large-scale service inventories or across multiple inventories because of its horizontal scalability potential. It is not uncommon for service grid implementations to be comprised of dozens or hundreds of servers. The constant availability of the state deferral mechanism provided by the grid services reduces the resource impact on regular custom services, thereby increasing their scalability as well. When broadly utilized, this load sharing dynamic can establish a service grid as a prevalent and intrinsic part of the overall service-oriented enterprise.

NOTE

The actual type of interface or technical contract exposed by grid services can vary, depending on the grid platform.

Impacts

The need to add multiple physical servers, coupled with product license costs and additional required infrastructure extensions can make the adoption of Service Grid costly. It may be further desirable for a service grid to be isolated on its own high-speed network in order to accommodate the constant cross-server synchronization that needs to occur.

As a result of the required expansion of infrastructure, grid-based environments will naturally increase the governance burden of one or more service inventory architectures, resulting in on-going operational effort and costs.

Relationships

The application of Service Grid essentially results in the application of Stateful Services (248), but State Repository (242) can also become part of a grid platform, depending on its configuration. Partial State Deferral (356) is generally supported by grid services, that may further require the use of Messaging Metadata (538) to exchange state keys.

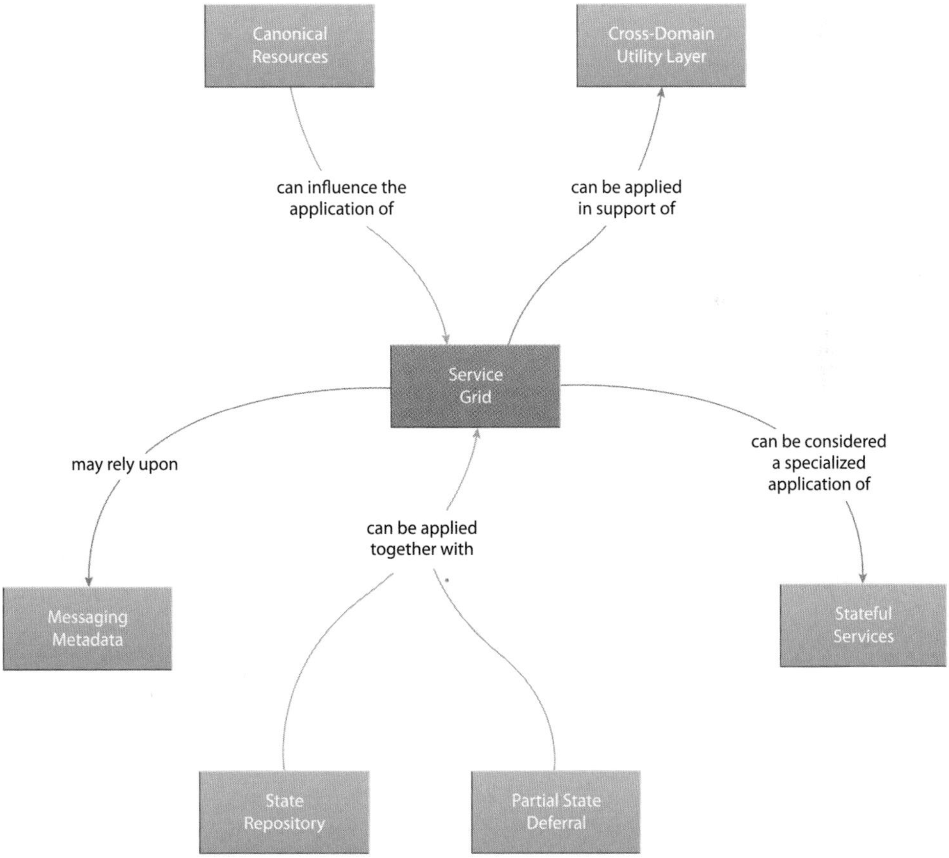

Figure 9.19

Service Grid naturally relates to other state management patterns and others associated with its inner mechanics.

When positioned as an enterprise-level resource, Service Grid can establish infrastructure that can be leveraged by multiple service inventories. Because of the utility-centric nature of grid services, this can effectively enable or extend the application of Cross-Domain Utility Layer (267).

CASE STUDY EXAMPLE

In the case study example for Stateful Services (248), the FRC proceeded with an architecture whereby they built a Code service to act as a state management resource. Soon after this went into production, many additional requirements for various specialized state deferral scenarios emerge.

Additionally, FRC architects witness how the individually deployed Code service becomes increasingly popular. After warnings from systems administrators that the service is nearing its concurrent usage threshold, a spike in usage causes it to exhaust available memory, triggering runtime exceptions and ultimately resulting in a system failure that cascades across the various service compositions that were using the service.

This experience convinces architects to immediately begin investigating options to increase scalability and reliability of this and other state management services they were planning to deliver. In the short-term, they apply Redundant Implementation (345) to provide some relief, but their attention soon turns toward Service Grid.

Based on current usage statistics, they find it difficult to warrant the investment of a full-blown grid computing platform. However, a subsequent study of upcoming projects and a review of their service inventory blueprint convinces them that this will eventually be needed and that a service grid platform should be established soon so that it can evolve with the rest of the service inventory architecture. This will allow the planned services and compositions to incorporate the grid services and the use of state keys right away as part of their initial design. The savings in avoided refactoring costs alone reassures the architects of their decision to proceed with Service Grid.

Inventory Endpoint

How can a service inventory be shielded from external access while still offering service capabilities to external consumers?

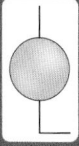

Problem	A group of services delivered for a specific inventory may provide capabilities that are useful to services outside of that inventory. However, for security and governance reasons, it may not be desirable to expose all services or all service capabilities to external consumers.
Solution	Abstract the relevant capabilities into an endpoint service that acts as a the official inventory entry point dedicated to a specific set of external consumers.
Application	The endpoint service can expose a contract with the same capabilities as its underlying services, but augmented with policies or other characteristics to accommodate external consumer interaction requirements.
Impacts	Endpoint services can increase the governance freedom of underlying services but can also increase governance effort by introducing redundant service logic and contracts into an inventory.
Principles	Standardized Service Contract, Service Loose Coupling, Service Abstraction
Architecture	Inventory

Table 9.6

Profile summary for the Inventory Endpoint pattern.

Problem

As described in Chapter 4, a service inventory represents a collection of independently standardized and governed services. When opportunities arise for services to share their capabilities with service consumers that reside outside of the inventory (whether they are consumers within the same organization but part of a different inventory or consumers external to the organization itself), interoperability, privacy, and security-related concerns often arise, making the option of simply exposing internal inventory services to external consumers less than desirable (Figure 9.20).

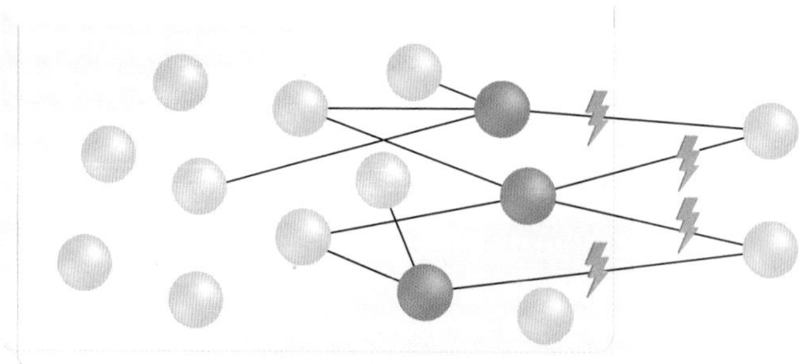

Figure 9.20
External service consumers accessing native inventory services can impose runtime demands and introduce new risks.

Solution

A special type of intermediary service is positioned as the official service inventory entry point for consumers external to the inventory that need to access native services within the inventory (Figure 9.21). This endpoint service can be configured to accommodate consumer interaction preferences and can further contain broker and mediation logic to help facilitate communication with internal inventory services.

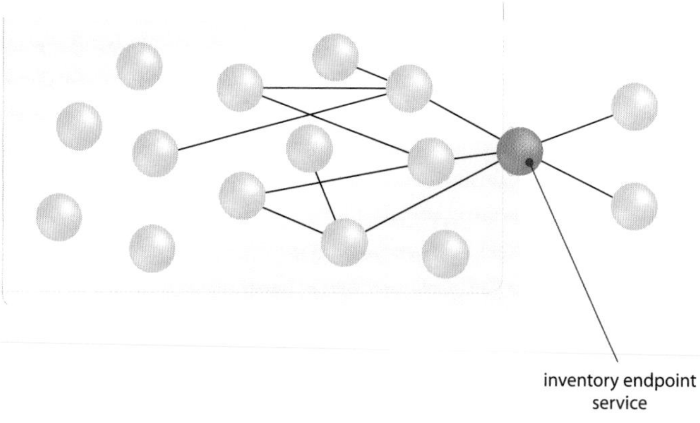

Figure 9.21
A new service introduced to facilitate external consumer requirements can ensure that other native inventory services are not affected.

Application

By abstracting capabilities from a collection of services into a single contract, services positioned as endpoints for an inventory offer several benefits, including:

- Increased governance freedom for the underlying services, as they can be changed and extended without affecting the endpoint service contract. Even if underlying service functionality needs to be altered, logic could be introduced into the endpoint service to accommodate for the changes so that external consumers remain unaffected and unaware.
- The endpoint service contract can be fully customized to accommodate the external consumer programs. This allows for the addition of data and security constraints, policy assertions and alternatives, and even the support of additional transport protocols unique to the consumer interaction requirements. By abstracting these implementation requirements into a single service, underlying inventory services are not required to change.
- A separate endpoint service can be created for each group of external consumers. This allows the aforementioned customization to be specific to a range of consumer types. For example, one endpoint service can be created for consumers from a different domain inventory, and a separate endpoint service can be positioned for consumer programs residing outside of the organization itself.
- Beyond providing alternative contract representation for inventory services, an endpoint service can also provide Protocol Bridging (687) for consumers that use disparate protocols or data exchange technologies.

Endpoint services are typically single-purpose with non-agnostic functional contexts and are therefore generally classified as task services. Some organizations, however, prefer to consider the endpoint service as its own service model, especially since endpoint services may be required to encapsulate inventory-specific task services.

Although they are often delivered and owned by the custodian of the inventory for which they act as endpoints, they are not always considered members of that inventory because they are required to conform to different design standards and are not made available for native compositions. Endpoint services are often literally maintained at the periphery of inventory boundaries. Therefore, the first step to working with endpoint services is to establish an effective ownership structure that will allow these services to evolve with both their underlying inventories and their consumers.

For endpoint services created to interact with consumers from external organizations, special implementation requirements are almost always needed. These can include the need for deployment within a DMZ on an isolated server and various infrastructure extensions associated with security and sometimes scalability.

The core service logic for an endpoint service is generally comparable to logic shaped by Service Façade (333) in that it is mostly comprised of routines that relay data requests and responses to and from the external consumers and the underlying inventory services. However, when endpoint services are required to provide new policies or enforce new constraints, additional logic is needed. Furthermore, endpoint services are commonly relied upon to act as brokers by carrying out Data Model Transformation (671), Data Format Transformation (681), and even Protocol Bridging (687).

Impacts

While Inventory Endpoint increases the freedom with which inventory services can be evolved and governed over time, they do result in the introduction of new services and service contracts that will need to be maintained as an addition to the service inventory itself. This governance responsibility and the associated ownership issues that need to be addressed can introduce a significant amount of cost and effort because of the on-going maintenance required to keep them in synch with internal service and external consumer requirements. This pattern may even lead to the need for a new IT group altogether (especially if multiple endpoint services are produced).

Relationships

The use of Inventory Endpoint raises both contract design and architectural issues, which therefore relates this pattern to service design patterns, such as Service Façade (333) and Concurrent Contracts (421), as well as implementation-related patterns like Composition Autonomy (616) and Redundant Implementation (345).

In fact, this pattern can sometimes appear as a specialized variation of Concurrent Contracts (421) in that it introduces the need to establish a new services that functionally overlap with existing ones (and therefore also violates Service Normalization (131) to an extent).

As shown by the relationships to the three patterns that comprise Service Broker (707) on the right side of Figure 9.22, one of the most common responsibilities of the inventory endpoint service is to overcome the communication disparity between inventory services and external consumers. This is simply because consumers outside of the inventory are generally subject to different design standards and conventions.

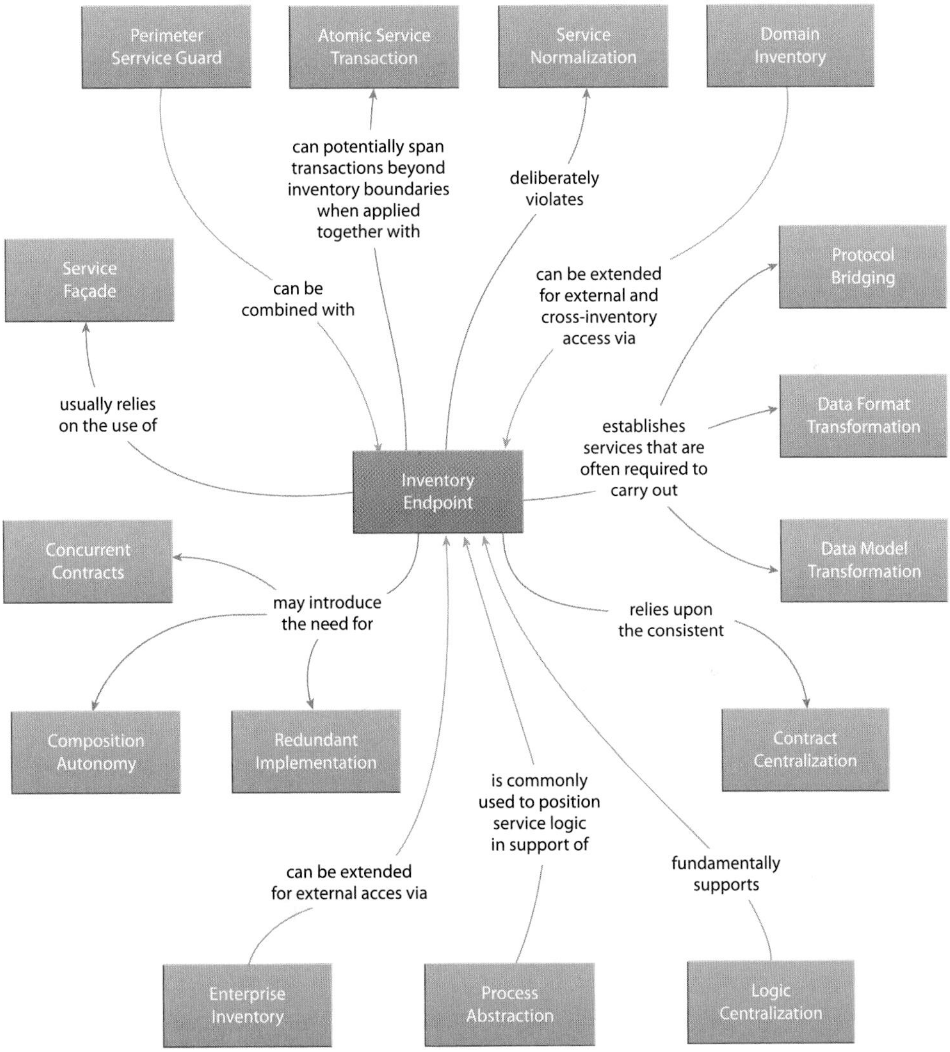

Figure 9.22

Inventory Endpoint provides a specialized design solution that touches on a range of design issues.

> **NOTE**
>
> The application of Enterprise Service Bus (704) will also often naturally apply Inventory Endpoint by establishing external endpoints that encapsulate broker and mediation logic. The distinction with this pattern is that the endpoint is specific to a service inventory.

CASE STUDY EXAMPLE

A new Tri-Fold service composition is assembled to automate the recently modeled Plant Supply business process. This is a complex composition involving eight services and a great deal of activity management. To further complicate the design, the Plant Supply task service is required to access the following three services that reside within the Alleywood service inventory:

- a Trucks service responsible for processing information related to the delivery of materials to the plants
- a Load service that provides functionality pertaining to "in transport" materials being delivered
- a Mills service that represents the origin of delivered loads

The initial composition design has the Plant Supply task service invoking each of the three Alleywood services individually, thereby being subject to remote access performance challenges and data model transformation requirements, in addition to further disparity in how security and activity meta data is represented (Figure 9.23).

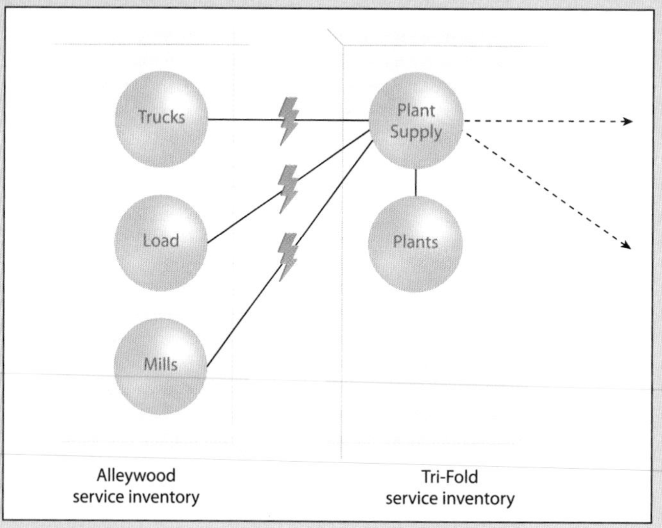

Figure 9.23

Repeated cross-domain access by the Tri-Fold Plant Supply task service compounds the impact of the disparity between the independent service inventories.

Once performance calculations are added up and after the design complexity of this proposed composition is mapped out, the approach is rejected. Instead, by applying Inventory Endpoint, a new service is introduced into the Alleywood inventory called the Plant Supply Endpoint service.

This service establishes a contract custom designed for the Tri-Fold Plant Supply service so that no external transformation is required (Figure 9.24). Internally, this service performs all necessary conversion and also encapsulates the required composition logic to interact with the Alleywood Trucks, Load, and Mills services.

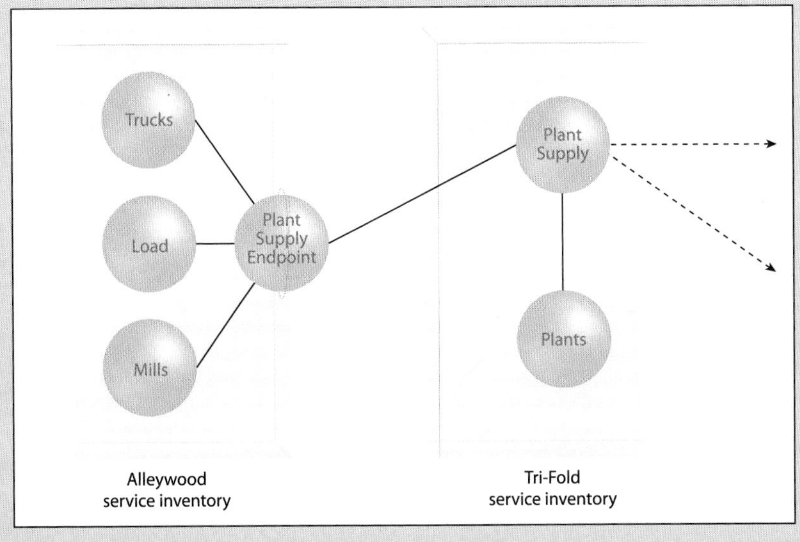

Figure 9.24

The new Plant Supply endpoint service eliminates unnecessary remote communication and carries out all required composition and transformation logic.

Cross-Domain Utility Layer

How can redundant utility logic be avoided across domain service inventories?

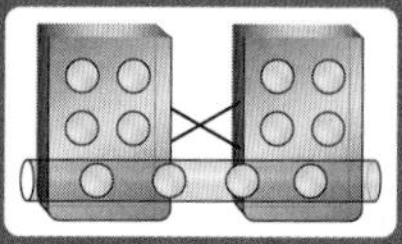

Problem	While domain service inventories may be required for independent business governance, they can impose unnecessary redundancy within utility service layers.
Solution	A common utility service layer can be established, spanning two or more domain service inventories.
Application	A common set of utility services needs to be defined and standardized in coordination with service inventory owners.
Impacts	Increased effort is required to coordinate and govern a cross-inventory utility service layer.
Principles	Service Reusability, Service Composability
Architecture	Enterprise, Inventory

Table 9.7
Profile summary for the Cross-Domain Utility Layer pattern.

Problem

The primary reason for enterprises to proceed with multiple domain service inventories is to allow for the governance of individual inventories by separate groups that represent the respective domains. More often than not, these inventories are associated with organizational business domains, and the governance issues pertain to the design and evolution of business service layers. The rationale is to tolerate the use of different standards and increased redundancy across business service layers within domains for the benefit of acheiving manageable SOA adoption and governance.

However, the utility layers within these domains have no ties to business models, and often the corresponding utility services encapsulate enterprise resources that are common to all domains. As a result, some utility logic created for one domain will tend to be functionally similar (or even identical) to others. The resulting redundancy and design disparity within multiple utility service layers (across different inventories) is therefore wasteful and unnecessary (Figure 9.25).

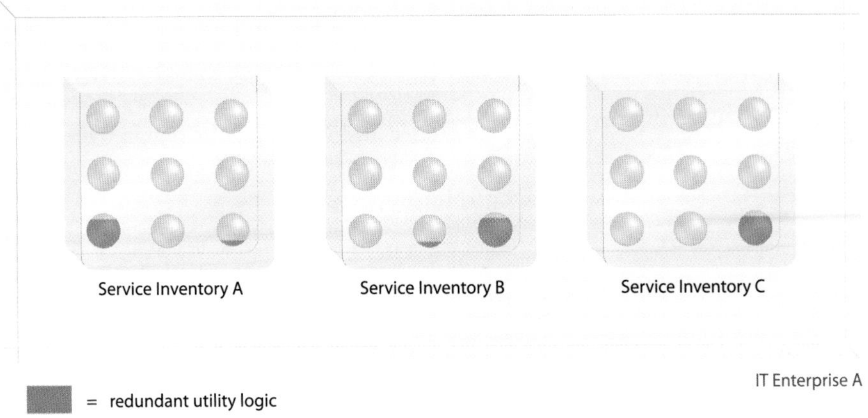

Figure 9.25

By having to duplicate functionality across domain service inventories, more utility logic and services are created than are actually required.

Solution

A common utility service layer is positioned for use by multiple domain service inventories, establishing a centralized collection of normalized (non-redundant) utility services accessible to and reusable by services across domains (Figure 9.26).

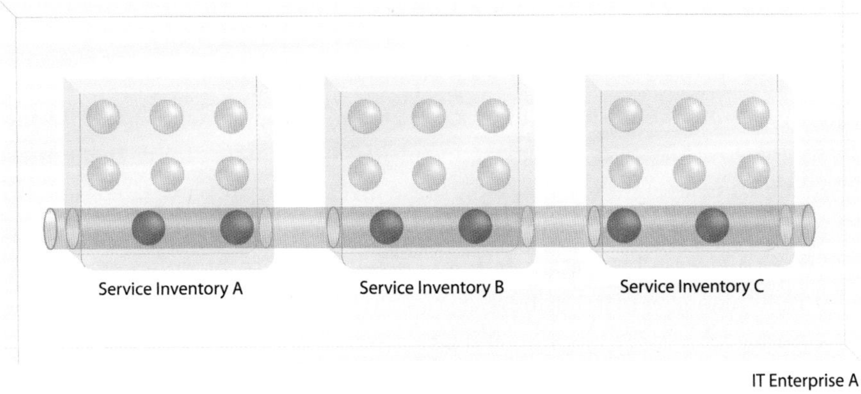

Figure 9.26

A cross-domain utility service layer establishes a set of common services that address broad, cross-cutting concerns. Notice how a smaller quantity of utility services is required (compared to Figure 9.25) due to reduced redundancy.

Application

It is recommended that in addition to design standards that require domains to use utility services, standard processes also exist across domains to allow for the identification and reuse of cross-domain utility services. This service layer is very much a part of the enterprise architecture and should therefore be established prior to domain service inventory definition.

Note that a cross-domain utility service layer does not need to replace a domain inventory's utility layer in its entirety. Domain-specific utility services can be defined as required and then further complemented by cross-domain utility services (Figure 9.27).

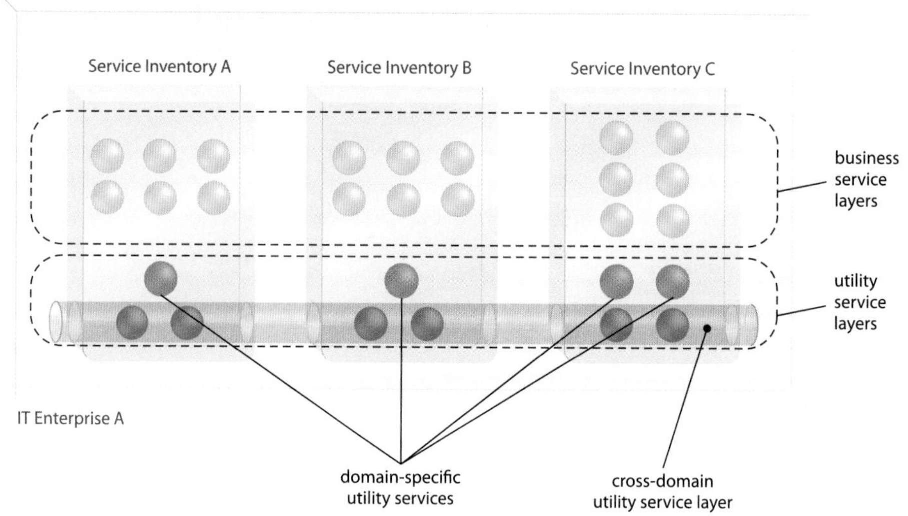

Figure 9.27

An enterprise architecture comprised of three inventories that share a cross-domain utility service layer but also allow for domain-specific utility services to be created.

Impacts

One of the reasons to create domain service inventories is to allow for each domain to evolve independently, which is a more manageable approach for some organizations. Requiring that all inventories use the same common set of utility services reduces this independence somewhat.

It furthermore complicates the overall governance processes that need to be in place; instead of domain-specific groups that own and maintain domain services, there may now

need to be an enterprise governance group that owns the cross-domain utility service layer and ensures that these services are properly utilized within each domain.

Note also that if service inventory domains are based on geographical boundaries, or if domains consist of vastly disparate technical environments, the governance logistics for applying this pattern can prove difficult.

Relationships

Cross-Domain Utility Layer changes the complexion of a service-oriented enterprise by impacting multiple domain inventory architectures and therefore has naturally close relationships with Domain Inventory (123), Utility Abstraction (168), and Agnostic Context (312), while also providing an opportunity to establish broad baseline interoperability in support of Canonical Protocol (150).

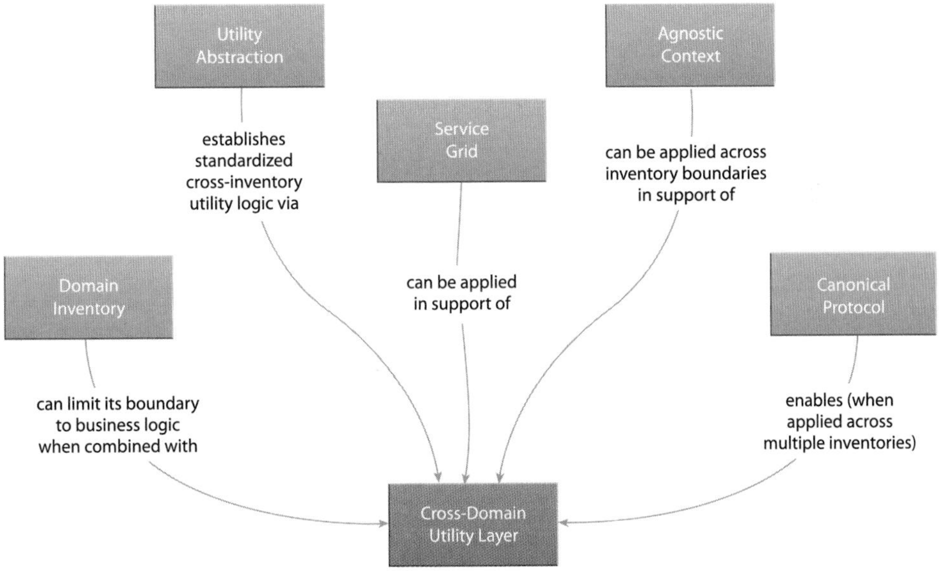

Figure 9.28

Cross-Domain Utility Layer increases the reach of shared utility services in support of increased recomposition of utility capabilities.

CASE STUDY EXAMPLE

When both Alleywood and Tri-Fold service inventory blueprints are completed, they are reviewed by the McPherson Enterprise Group. Although each is comprised of well-defined, normalized collections of services, it is evident that there is significant

functional redundancy, especially within the utility service layers. In fact, the utility logic defined is almost identical, primarily due to these services being positioned for access to shared resources.

The reasons behind splitting the original enterprise service inventory into separate physical domains were primarily rooted within resource and governance issues associated with business concerns. However, there is no real objection to applying this pattern to establish an enterprise-wide utility service layer. Although the initial layer is comprised of all utility services either inventory needs (Figure 9.29), Alleywood and Tri-Fold will be able to create inventory-specific utility services as well.

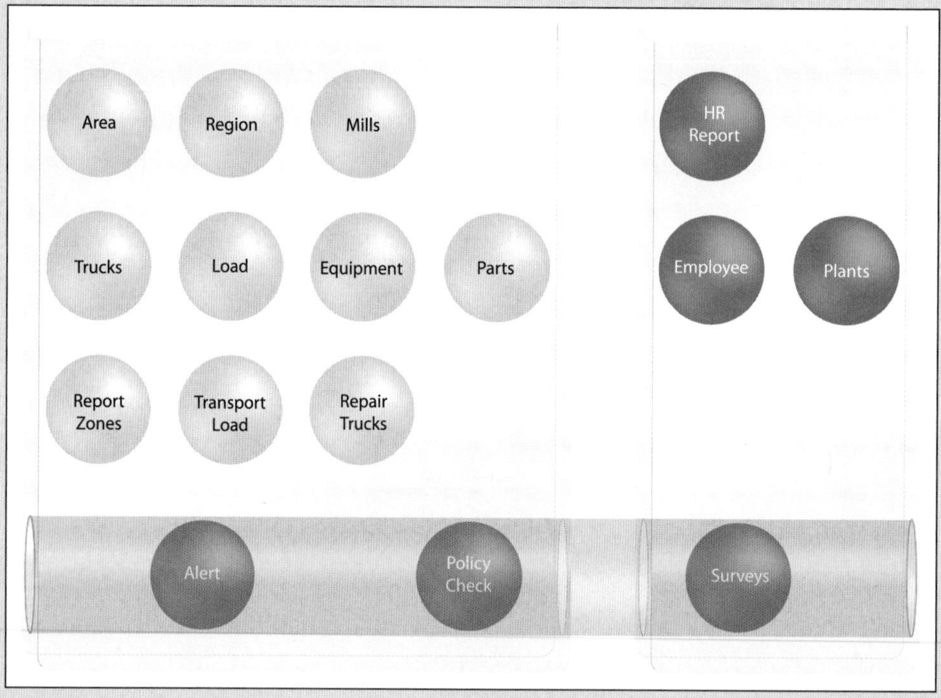

Figure 9.29

A cross-domain utility service layer that effectively replaces both previously defined inventory-specific utility service layers.

Chapter 10

Inventory Governance Patterns

Canonical Expression

Metadata Centralization

Canonical Versioning

When first designing a service inventory, there are steps that can be taken to ensure that the eventual effort and impact of having to govern the inventory is reduced. This chapter provides a set of patterns that supply some fundamental design-time solutions specifically with the inventory's post-implementation evolution in mind.

Canonical Expression (275) refines the service contract in support of increased discoverability, which goes hand-in-hand with Metadata Centralization (280), a pattern that essentially establishes a service registry for the discovery of service contracts. These patterns are further complemented by Canonical Versioning (286), which requires the use of a consistent, inventory-wide versioning strategy.

All of these patterns are considered fundamental to inventory governance in that they support and are influenced by the Service Discoverability principle, which actually shapes service meta information in such a manner that it can be effectively discovered and interpreted.

NOTE

The governance patterns in this chapter focus on fundamental technical and design-related governance issues only. The upcoming title *SOA Governance* as part of this book series will provide a collection of additional technical and organizational best practices and patterns.

Canonical Expression

How can service contracts be consistently understood and interpreted?

Problem	Service contracts may express similar capabilities in different ways, leading to inconsistency and risking misinterpretation.
Solution	Service contracts are standardized using naming conventions.
Application	Naming conventions are applied to service contracts as part of formal analysis and design processes.
Impacts	The use of global naming conventions introduces enterprise-wide standards that need to be consistently used and enforced.
Principles	Standardized Service Contract, Service Discoverability
Architecture	Enterprise, Inventory, Service

Table 10.1
Profile summary for the Canonical Expression pattern.

Problem

Service contracts delivered or extended by different projects and at different times are naturally shaped by the architects and developers that work with them. The manner in which the service context and the service's individual capabilities are defined and expressed through the contract syntax can therefore vary. Some may use descriptive and verbose conventions, while others may use terse and technical formats. Furthermore, the actual terms used to express common or similar capabilities may also vary.

Because services are positioned as enterprise resources, it is fully expected that other project teams will need to discover and interpret the contract in order to understand how the service can be used. Inconsistencies in how technical service contracts are expressed undermine these efforts by introducing a constant risk of misinterpretation (on a technical level). The proliferation of these inconsistencies furthermore places a convoluted face on a service inventory, increasing the effort to effectively navigate various contracts to study possible composition design options.

Solution

Standardized naming conventions can be applied to the delivery of all service contracts so as to ensure the consistent expression of service contexts and capabilities (Figure 10.1).

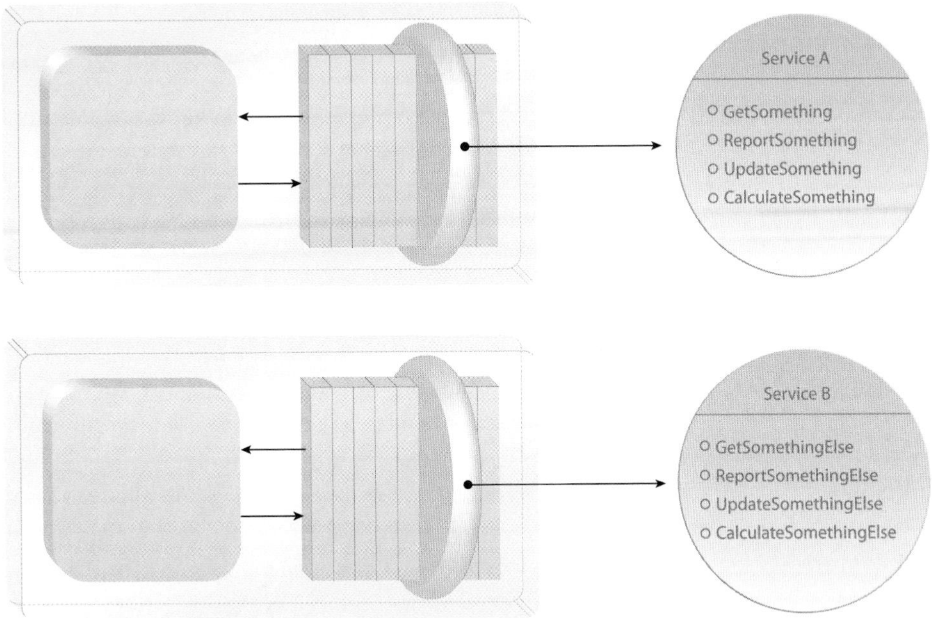

Figure 10.1
The expression of service contracts is aligned across services.

Application

A set of naming and functional expression conventions needs to be established as formal design standards. The realization of consistent contract design is then attained via the disciplined use of these conventions within common analysis and design processes.

An example of a standard associated with contract expression is the CRUD (create, read, update, delete) convention traditionally used to outfit components with a predictable set of methods. Entity services in particular often require these types of data processing functions, and using standardized verbs to express them supports the application of this pattern.

With Web services in particular, this pattern will tend to impact the design of WSDL definitions, as illustrated in Figure 10.2.

> **NOTE**
>
> This pattern can be applied regardless of whether the service contract is decoupled.

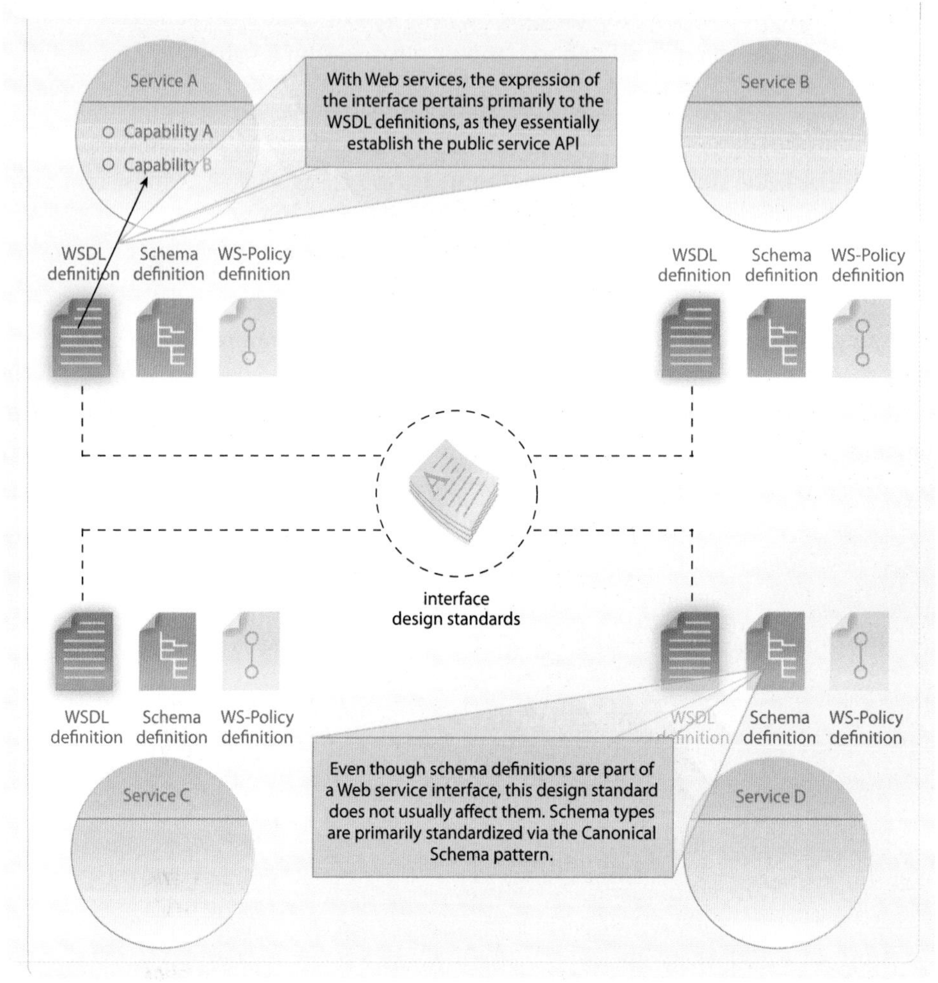

Figure 10.2

The WSDL definitions of the four services are affected by Canonical Expression.

Impacts

The relevance of Canonical Expression may at first appear trivial. However, when building a collection of services, especially within larger enterprise environments, a consistent functional expression significantly reduces tangible risk factors.

The primary requirement to successfully applying this pattern is the incorporation and enforcement of the required design standards. If a formal design process has already been

established in support of Decoupled Contract (401) and Canonical Schema (158), then the effort to include a step dedicated to Canonical Expression is usually minor.

Note also that unlike Canonical Schema (158), which often must be limited to domain service inventories due to its governance impact, this pattern can more easily be positioned as an enterprise-wide standard. This benefits the enterprise as a whole as consistent expression is established across all domains.

Relationships

The naming conventions introduced by Canonical Expression influence how several other patterns are applied (as listed at the top of Figure 10.3). This pattern fundamentally supports the goals of Contract Centralization (409) and Metadata Centralization (280) by enhancing the intuitiveness of service identification and reuse.

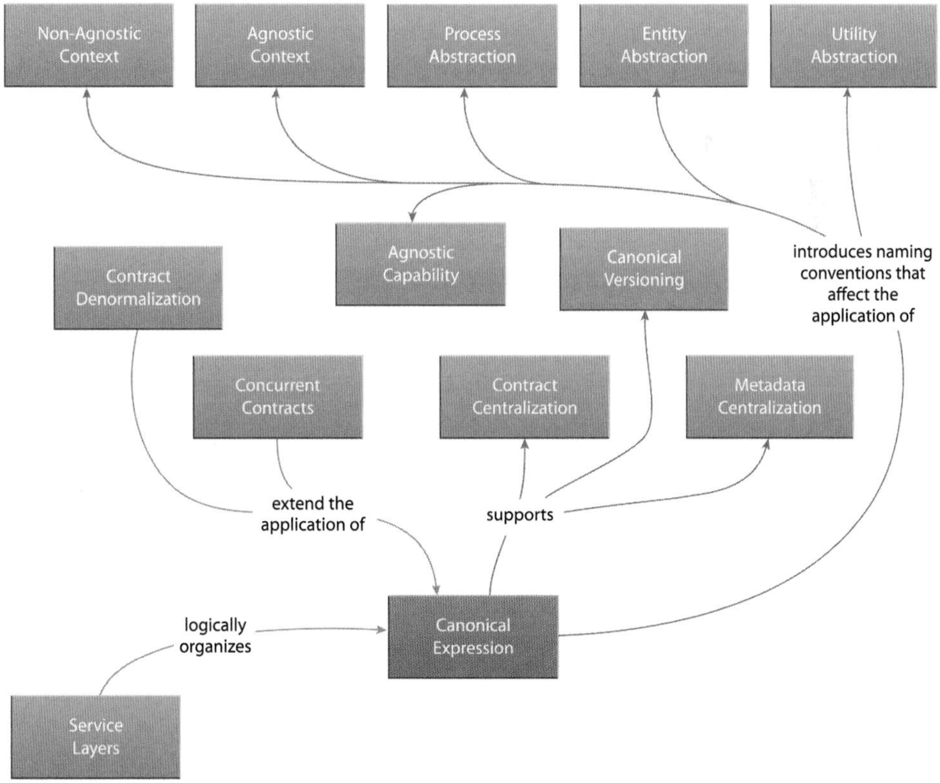

Figure 10.3

Canonical Expression keeps the external expression of service contracts consistent, thereby affecting contract and context-related patterns.

CASE STUDY EXAMPLE

An early pilot version of the Inventory Processing service has been used for testing purposes. It consists of a Web service that was auto-generated using a development tool that derived the Web service contract from component class interfaces that exist as part of the custom legacy inventory management system.

Although this Web service has been valuable for various assessment purposes, once architects take a closer look at the actual Web service contract code, they detect some content that raises concerns:

- The Web service operations inherited the cryptic legacy component method names.
- Several of the Web service operations have input and output message schemas that are derived from input and output legacy method parameters that are too granular for message-based service interaction.
- There is no real concept of an inventory record because it was not supported within the legacy component API.

These and other issues prompt Cutit to move ahead with a formal design process that requires the definition of service contracts prior to the development of underlying logic. This design process is completed subsequent to a formal analysis and modeling process during which architects collaborate with business analysts to define conceptual service candidates. These candidates then form the basis of the physical service designs.

Architects and developers can now avoid irregularities and problematic characteristics within service contracts because they have gained control of the definition of these contracts.

Metadata Centralization

How can service metadata be centrally published and governed?

Problem	Project teams, especially in larger enterprises, run the constant risk of building functionality that already exists or is already in development, resulting in wasted effort, service logic redundancy, and service inventory denormalization.
Solution	Service metadata can be centrally published in a service registry so as to provide a formal means of service registration and discovery.
Application	A private service registry needs to be positioned as a central part of an inventory architecture supported by formal processes for registration and discovery.
Impacts	The service registry product needs to be adequately mature and reliable, and its required use and maintenance needs to be incorporated into all service delivery and governance processes and methodologies.
Principles	Service Discoverability
Architecture	Enterprise, Inventory

Table 10.2

Profile summary for the Metadata Centralization pattern.

Problem

When growing a service inventory and fostering fundamental qualities such as those realized by Service Normalization (131) and Logic Centralization (136), there is a constant risk of project teams inadvertently (or sometimes even intentionally) delivering new services or service capabilities that already exist or are already in development (Figure 10.4).

This leads to undesirable results, most notably:

- the introduction of redundant service logic, which runs contrary to Logic Centralization (136)
- the introduction of overlapping service contexts, which runs contrary to Service Normalization (131)

- an overall less effective service inventory and technology architecture, bloated and convoluted by the added redundancy and denormalization and in need of additional governance effort

All of these characteristics can undermine an SOA initiative by reducing its strategic benefit potential.

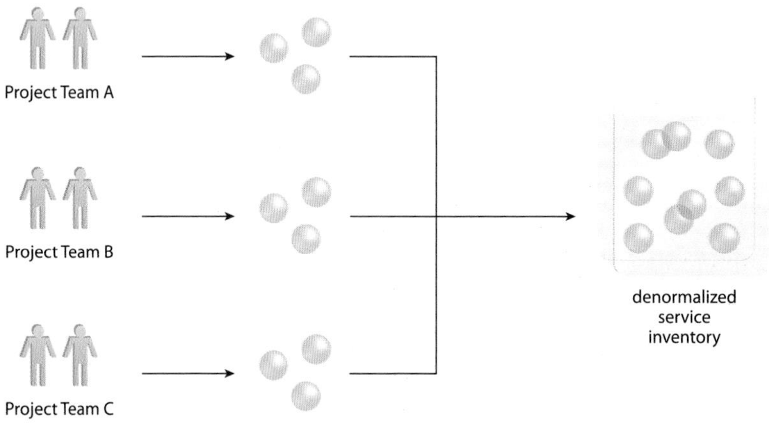

Figure 10.4

Without an awareness of the full range of existing and upcoming services, there is a constant risk that project teams will deliver service logic that already exists or is already in development.

Solution

A service registry is established as a central part of the surrounding infrastructure and is used by service owners and designers to:

- register existing services and capabilities
- register services and capabilities in development

As emphasized in discovery-related governance patterns, the registration process requires that discovery information be recorded in a highly descriptive and communicative manner so that it can be used by project teams to:

- locate and interpret existing services and learn about their functional contexts and boundaries
- locate and interpret service capabilities and learn about their invocation and interaction requirements

By providing a current and well-maintained registry of service contexts and capabilities, effective service discovery can be achieved (Figure 10.5).

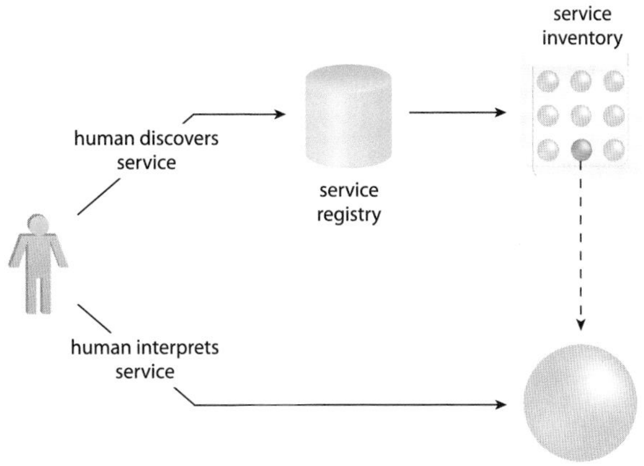

Figure 10.5

The fundamental discovery process during which a human locates a potential service via a service registry representing the service inventory and then interprets the service to determine its suitability.

> **NOTE**
>
> Metadata Centralization is clearly a design pattern associated with the Service Discoverability design principle and the discovery of services in general. Why then is it not simply called Service Discovery?
>
> Service discovery itself is a process that is carried out once an enterprise has successfully applied Metadata Centralization to its architecture and the Service Discoverability design principle to its services. The process of service discovery is therefore related to a set of SOA governance patterns documented separately in the upcoming title *SOA Governance* that will be released as part of this book series.

Application

The application of this pattern requires the following common steps:

1. Regularly apply the Service Discoverability principle to all service contracts being modeled and designed.
2. Use service profiles and supporting processes to standardize the documentation of service and capability metadata. For example, a common part of service profiles is a standard vocabulary used for keywords that are attached to the service registry records.

3. Implement a reliable service registry product and position it as a standard part of the supporting infrastructure.

Finally, formal processes for the registration and discovery of services and capabilities need to be established.

> **NOTE**
>
> This pattern can be applied to a single service inventory or multiple domain inventories, depending on the ability of the service registry product to associate domains with service profile records. For a service profile template and descriptions of service discovery and interpretation processes, see Chapters 16 and 12, respectively, in *SOA Principles of Service Design*.

Impacts

Service registration and discovery processes are key success factors for the effective governance of a service inventory. If the processes are not respected or followed consistently by project teams or if the registry is not kept current, then the value potential of Metadata Centralization will severely diminish.

From a design perspective, however, this pattern will introduce the need for metadata standardization, as per the Service Discoverability principle. It will further require that metadata documentation and registration become part of the standard service delivery lifecycles.

There may further be a need to create a new organizational role in support of realizing Metadata Centralization. A person or a group would act as service registry custodian and assume responsibility for collecting the required metadata and maintaining the registry.

Relationships

Metadata Centralization essentially establishes a service registry, which is key to ensuring the long-term successful application of Logic Centralization (136) and Contract Centralization (409). If the correct services and their contracts can be effectively located (discovered), then the risk of inadvertently introducing redundant logic into an environment is reduced, further supporting Service Normalization (131).

Agnostic services represent the primary type of service for which metadata needs to be centralized for discovery purposes, which is why this pattern is especially relevant to services defined as a result of Entity Abstraction (175) and Utility Abstraction (168).

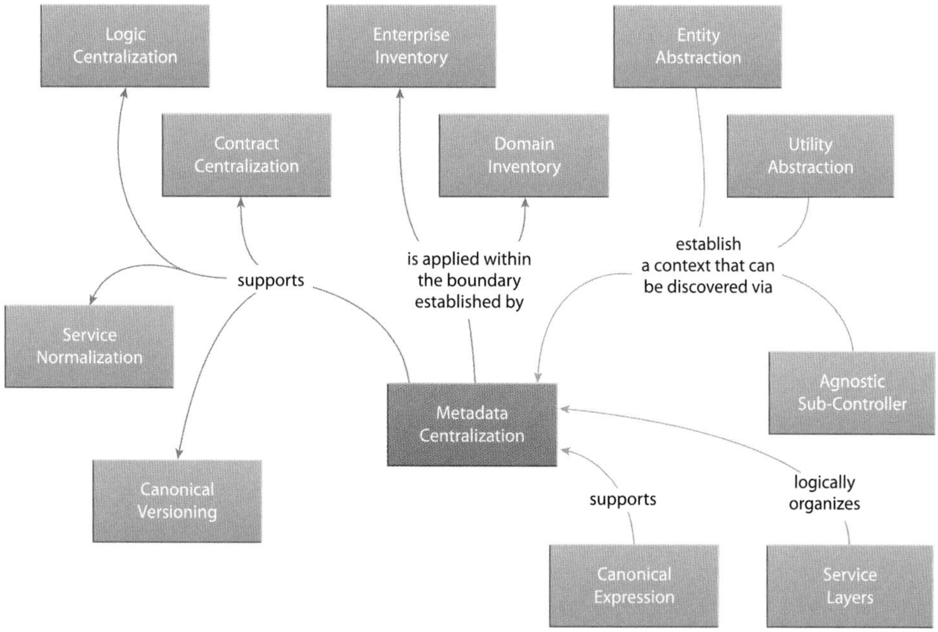

Figure 10.6

Metadata Centralization facilitates discovery and therefore relates to other patterns that rely on design-time awareness in order to be consistently applied.

CASE STUDY EXAMPLE

As explained in the Logic Centralization (136) example from Chapter 6, the original functional overlap between the Alleywood Areas and Region services could have gone undetected, resulting in the quality and integrity of the service inventory being negatively affected. For this reason, it was determined early on that a service registry would be required to support Service Normalization (131) and ensure the consistent application of Logic Centralization (136).

However, due to the decision to establish separate domain service inventories, architects struggle with the option of implementing a separate service registry for each inventory. Although it would continue to allow each group to govern their respective service collection independently, it would establish two different repositories.

It is anticipated that Alleywood and Tri-Fold services will need to interoperate. Those creating cross-inventory compositions will therefore need to issue separate queries in order to discover the required service capabilities.

The awkwardness of this governance architecture eventually prompts McPherson to establish a central enterprise service registry instead (Figure 10.7). This registry is governed by the McPherson Enterprise Group and allows Alleywood and Tri-Fold project teams to search each others' inventories.

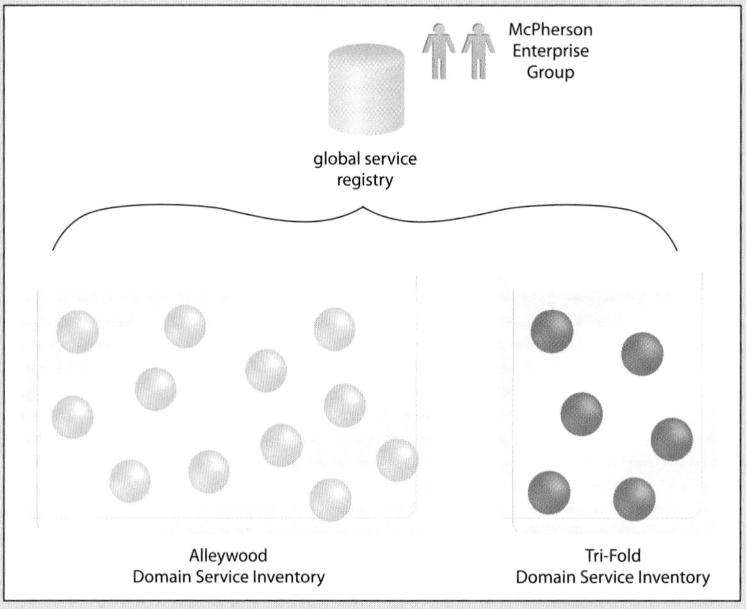

Figure 10.7
A global registry that spans services across Alleywood and Tri-Fold inventories.

Canonical Versioning

How can service contracts within the same service inventory be versioned with minimal impact?

Problem	Service contracts within the same service inventory that are versioned differently will cause numerous interoperability and governance problems.
Solution	Service contract versioning rules and the expression of version information are standardized within a service inventory boundary.
Application	Governance and design standards are required to ensure consistent versioning of service contracts within the inventory boundary.
Impacts	The creation and enforcement of the required versioning standards introduce new governance demands.
Principles	Standardized Service Contract
Architecture	Service, Inventory

Table 10.3

Profile summary for the Canonical Versioning pattern.

Problem

When service contracts within the same service inventory are subjected to different versioning approaches and conventions, post-implementation contract-level disparity emerges, compromising interoperability and effective service governance (Figure 10.8). This can negatively impact design-time consumer development, runtime service access, service reusability, and the overall evolution of the service inventory as a whole.

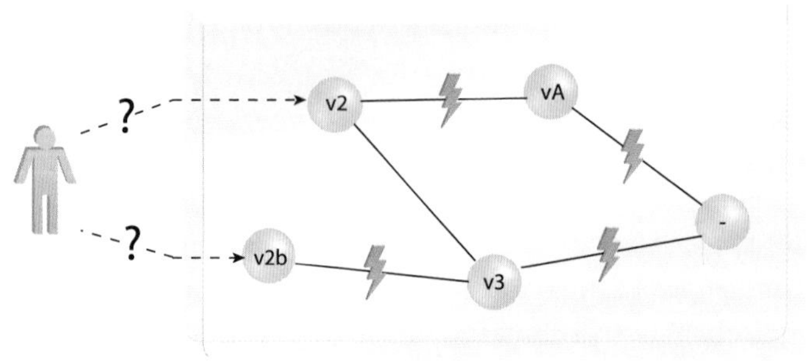

Figure 10.8
Services that have been versioned differently become challenging to compose and interoperate and also difficult to interpret.

Solution

Service contracts within the same inventory are versioned according to the same conventions and as part of the same overall versioning strategy (Figure 10.9). This ensures a consistent governance path for each service, thereby preserving contract standardization and intra-inventory compatibility and interoperability.

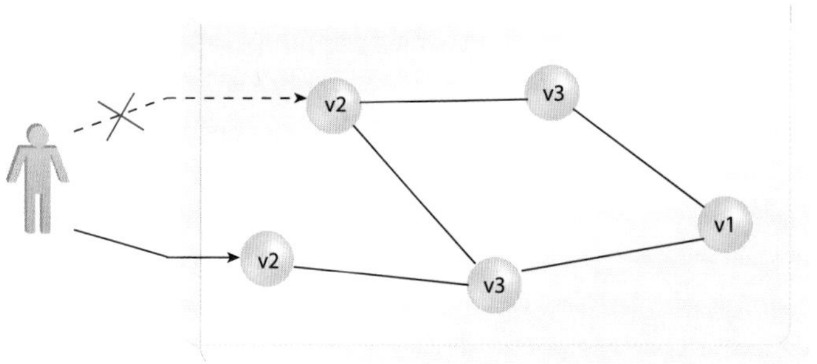

Figure 10.9
When services are versioned according to the same overarching strategy, they can retain their original standardization and interoperability and are more easily understood by consumer designers.

Application

This pattern generally requires that a single versioning strategy be chosen, comprised of a series of rules and conventions that essentially become governance standards.

Canonical Versioning approaches can vary depending on the complexion of the enterprise, existing versioning or configuration management methodologies that may already be in

place, and the nature of the overall governance strategy that may have also been established.

There are three common strategies that provide a baseline set of rules:

- *Strict* – Any compatible or incompatible change results in a new version of the service contract. This approach does not support backwards or forwards compatibility and is most commonly used when service contracts are shared between partner organizations and when changes to a contract can have legal implications.
- *Flexible* – Any incompatible change results in a new version of the service contract, and the contract is designed to support backwards compatibility but not forwards compatibility.
- *Loose* – Any incompatible change results in a new version of the service contract and the contract is designed to support backwards compatibility and forwards compatibility.

NOTE

The terms "backwards compatibility" and "forwards compatibility" are explained in the description for Compatible Change (465) in Chapter 16. For examples of each of these versioning strategies, see Chapters 20–23 in *Web Service Contract Design and Versioning for SOA*.

Impacts

There is the constant risk that project teams will continue to use their own versioning approaches, or rely too heavily on patterns like Concurrent Contracts (421), which allows them to simply add new contracts to an existing service.

The successful application of any versioning strategy will require strong support for the adherence to its rules and conventions to the extent that the chosen versioning approach becomes an inventory-wide standard on par with any other design standard. This introduces the need for a new organizational role that is tasked with enforcing the processes and syntactical characteristics that are defined as part of the strategy.

Relationships

Canonical Versioning essentially formalizes the application of Compatible Change (465), Version Identification (472), and Termination Notification (478), in that the overarching

strategy established by this pattern will determine how and to what extent each of these more specific versioning patterns is applied.

The application of Metadata Centralization (280) results in a service registry that enables effective discovery of different contract versions and Canonical Expression (275) implements characteristics in service contracts that improve their legibility. Both of these patterns therefore aid the goals of Canonical Versioning.

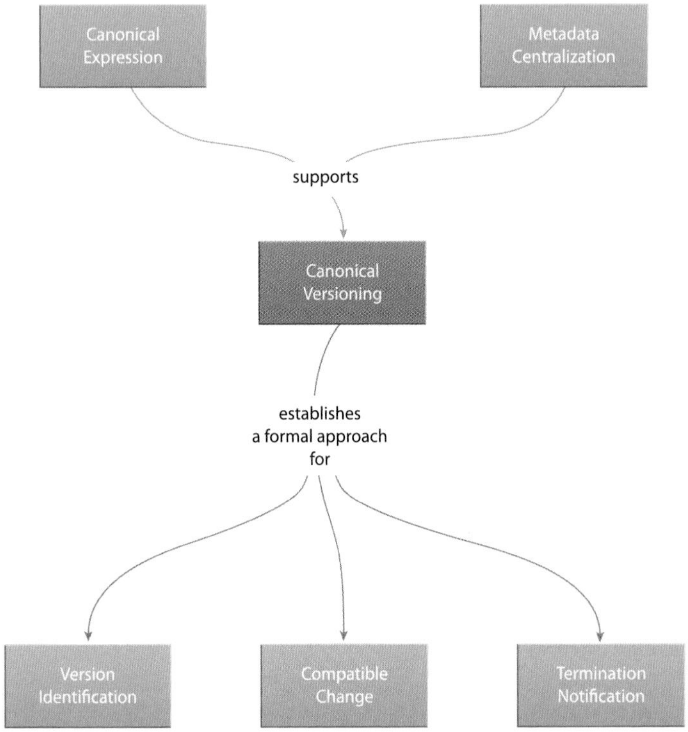

Figure 10.10
Canonical Versioning is primarily related to other versioning patterns.

> **NOTE**
>
> Before continuing with this case study example, be sure to read up on the Policy Check service that was defined in the State Repository (242) case study example and then later positioned to support multiple inventories as part of the example for Cross-Domain Utility Layer (267).

CASE STUDY EXAMPLE

The FRC announced that due to new government legislation, it has revised some of its policies. This changes the policy data that was being made available electronically via its public Web services.

The Alleywood Policy Check service was originally positioned to shield the rest of the Alleywood service inventory from these types of changes by providing the sole access point for FRC policy data. Although its service logic can be augmented to accommodate changes to the FRC services, architects soon realize that they cannot prevent having to issue a new version of the Policy Check contract because the FRC has added new content and structure into their policy schemas.

Being the first time they've had to contend with a major versioning issue, the Alleywood team decides that some formal approach needs to be in place before they proceed. After some research into common versioning practices and further deliberation, they produce a versioning strategy comprised of a set of specific conventions and rules:

Version Identification (472) will be applied as follows:

- Version information will be expressed in major numbers displayed left of the decimal point and minor version numbers displayed to the right of the decimal point (e.g., "1.0").
- Minor and major contract version numbers will be expressed using the WSDL `documentation` element by displaying the word "Version" before the version number (e.g., `<documentation>Version 1.0</documentation>`)
- Major version numbers will be appended to the WSDL definition's target namespace and prefixed with a "v" as shown here: `http://alleywoodlumber/contract/po/v1`

Compatible Change (465) will be applied as follows:

- A compatible change in the WSDL definition increments the minor version number and does not change the WSDL definition target namespace.
- A compatible change in the XML Schema definition increments the minor version number and does not change the XML Schema or WSDL definition target namespaces.
- An incompatible change in the WSDL definition increments the major version number and forces a new WSDL target namespace value.

- An incompatible change in the XML Schema definition increments the major version number and forces a new target namespace value for both the XML Schema and WSDL definitions.

The previously described scenario results in a set of incompatible changes that requires that the major version number of the Policy Check service contract be incremented from 1.0 to 2.0.

This example demonstrates the beginning of the Policy Check XML Schema and WSDL definitions after this change has occurred:

```
<xsd:schema xmlns:xsd=
  "http://www.w3.org/2001/XMLSchema"
  targetNamespace="http://alleywoodlumber/schema/pc/v2"
  xmlns="http://alleywoodlumber/schema/pc/v2"
  version="2.0">
  <xsd:annotation>
    <xsd:documentation>
      Version 2.0
    </xsd:documentation>
  </xsd:annotation>
  ...
</xsd:schema>

<definitions name="Policy Check" targetNamespace=
  "http://alleywoodlumber/contract/pc/v2"
  xmlns="http://schemas.xmlsoap.org/wsdl/"
  xmlns:tns="http://alleywoodlumber/contract/pc/v2"
  xmlns:pc="http://alleywoodlumber/schema/pc/v2"
  xmlns:xsd="http://www.w3.org/2001/XMLSchema">
  <documentation>
    Version 2.0
  </documentation>
  ...
</definitions>
```

Example 10.1

Fragments from the Policy Check Web service contract documents that show the effects of applying a versioning strategy.

The Alleywood architects acknowledge that defining the versioning approach is only the first step. In order for Canonical Versioning to be fully realized, these new rules and standards must be applied to any future service contracts that need to be versioned. This leads to the creation of a new process that is placed under the jurisdiction of the governance group.

Part III

Service Design Patterns

Chapter 11

Foundational Service Patterns

Functional Decomposition

Service Encapsulation

Agnostic Context

Non-Agnostic Context

Agnostic Capability

The design patterns in this chapter represent the most essential steps required to partition and organize solution logic into services and capabilities in support of subsequent composition. In many ways, these patterns can be considered fundamental service-orientation theory.

As shown in Figure 11.1, the patterns are organized into a proposed application sequence. As much as the individual patterns provide proven solutions, the suggested application sequence itself is also proven, which is why this chapter is structured accordingly.

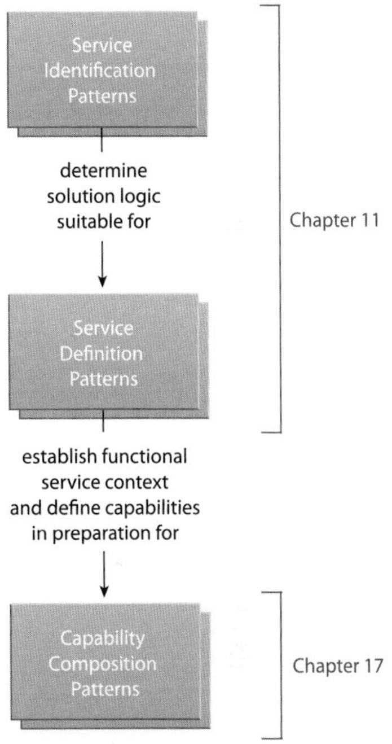

Figure 11.1
The patterns in this chapter follow a sequence that is carried over in Chapter 17.

The patterns are divided into two groups that lead up to the application of the composition patterns in Chapter 17, as follows:

1. *Service Identification Patterns* – The overall solution logic required to solve a given problem is first defined, and the parts of this logic suitable for service encapsulation are subsequently filtered out.
2. *Service Definition Patterns* – Base functional service contexts are defined and used to organize available service logic. Within agnostic contexts, service logic is further partitioned into individual capabilities.
3. *Capability Composition Patterns* – The previous patterns establish the boundaries of capability utilization, which naturally leads to the composition patterns described in Chapter 17.

When you string the service identification and service definition patterns together in their suggested application sequence, you will end up with a sequence of steps that can be considered a primitive service modeling process. The purpose of this process is only to raise the more fundamental considerations when shaping services into candidates for subsequent design. In real-life applications, the steps represented by these patterns would be part of a larger, customized process and methodology.

NOTE

If you haven't already, be sure to also read the *How Foundational Inventory and Service Design Patterns Relate* section at the beginning of Chapter 6.

CASE STUDY BACKGROUND

Due to the emphasis on the fundamental process established by the pattern sequence, all case study examples in this chapter revolve around a simple business task presenting a modest set of requirements that are fulfilled through the application of these patterns.

The following process description provides the necessary background information for subsequent examples.

The Chain Inventory Transfer Business Process

Whenever Cutit Saws manufactures a new chain, it undergoes a short process that takes the newly assembled chain from the manufacturing to the inventory control departments, as follows:

1. The assembled chain is released by the manufacturing team and delivered to a Quality Inspector.
2. The chain undergoes a manual inspection for defects, which includes endurance and alignment tests.
3. If the chain passes these tests, it is forwarded to the Inventory Controller (a person). If any one of the tests fail, the chain is sent back to the manufacturing team, along with a test report that is not electronically recorded.
4. The Inventory Controller generates an inventory record for the chain to officially add it to the inventory.
5. As part of creating an inventory record, the chain is assigned a predefined model number. If back orders for this model exist, the chain is also associated with the next back order in line.
6. As part of a back order, the chain is then forwarded to the shipping department along with a corresponding order document.
7. If the chain model is not on back order, the chain is simply added to the existing inventory stock.

As illustrated in Figure 11.2, this process consists of a combination of automated and manual steps.

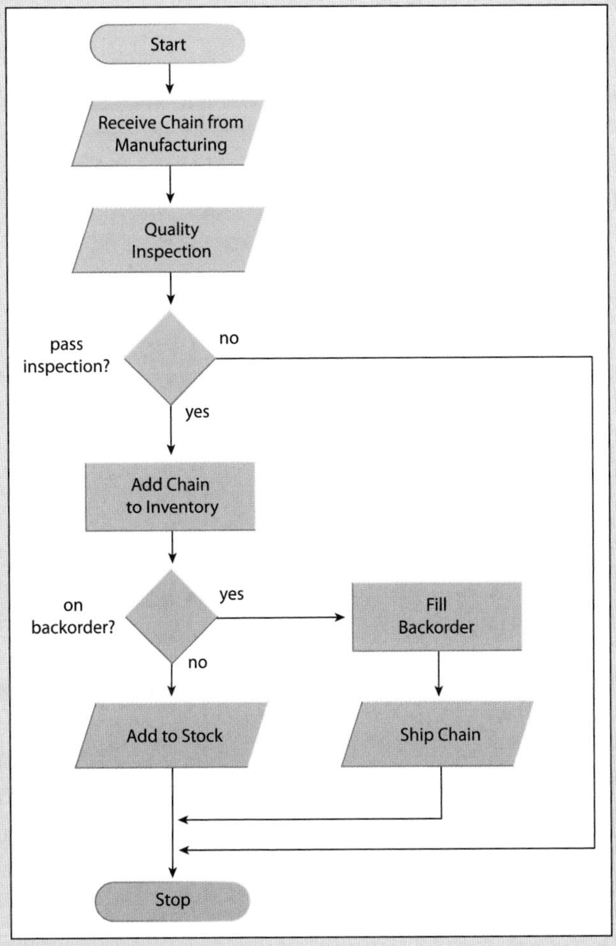

Figure 11.2
The Chain Inventory Transfer business process transitions a newly manufactured chain to the inventory warehouse from where it is either shipped or stored.

NOTE

This case study example continues into Chapter 17.

11.1 Service Identification Patterns

These initial design patterns (Figure 11.3) essentially carry out a separation of concerns in support of service-orientation during which solution logic is decomposed and the portions suitable for service encapsulation are identified. The result is a foundation of unorganized logic ready to be shaped into legitimate services via the application of the subsequent service definition patterns and the principles of service-orientation.

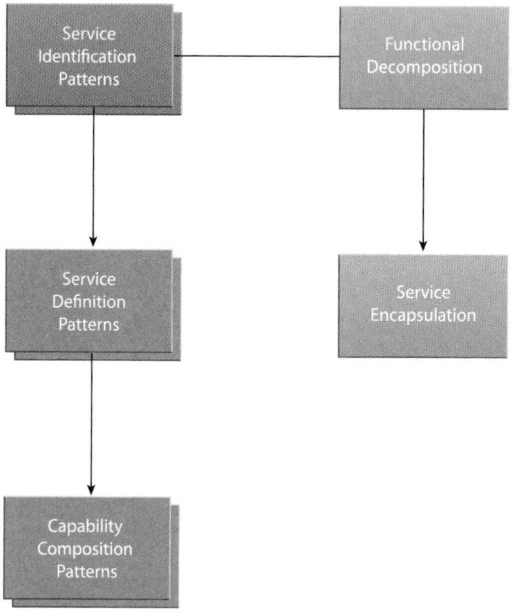

Figure 11.3

The two patterns in this section raise specific considerations that apply to the process of carrying out a separation of concerns.

NOTE

You might notice that these upcoming patterns are the only two design patterns in this book that are not directly related to any service-orientation design principles (as per the *Principles* field in the upcoming profile summary tables).

These patterns are so foundational that there is not yet an opportunity to involve or connect them with the specific design considerations raised by common service-orientation principles. However, one could argue that because they are so fundamental to establishing services that they are, in fact, related to all parts of service-orientation.

Functional Decomposition

How can a large business problem be solved without having to build a standalone body of solution logic?

Problem	To solve a large, complex business problem a corresponding amount of solution logic needs to be created, resulting in a self-contained application with traditional governance and reusability constraints.
Solution	The large business problem can be broken down into a set of smaller, related problems, allowing the required solution logic to also be decomposed into a corresponding set of smaller, related solution logic units.
Application	Depending on the nature of the large problem, a service-oriented analysis process can be created to cleanly deconstruct it into smaller problems.
Impacts	The ownership of multiple smaller programs can result in increased design complexity and governance challenges.
Principles	n/a
Architecture	Service

Table 11.1
Profile summary for the Functional Decomposition pattern.

Problem

Most business tasks or business processes requiring automation constitute large problems. An accepted approach to solving a large automation problem has been to build an application. Prior to the advent of distributed computing, custom-developed applications were primarily designed as monolithic executables—single, self-contained bodies of solution logic (Figure 11.4).

Repeatedly solving large problems by building monolithic solution logic results in an enterprise comprised of single-purpose applications residing in siloed implementation boundaries.

For many organizations such environments have posed significant challenges associated with extensibility and cross-application connectivity. Furthermore, a siloed technology landscape can become bloated and expensive to maintain and change—so much so that

many of these applications have remained in modernized technical environments as entrenched legacy systems that continue to inhibit the overall evolution of the enterprise.

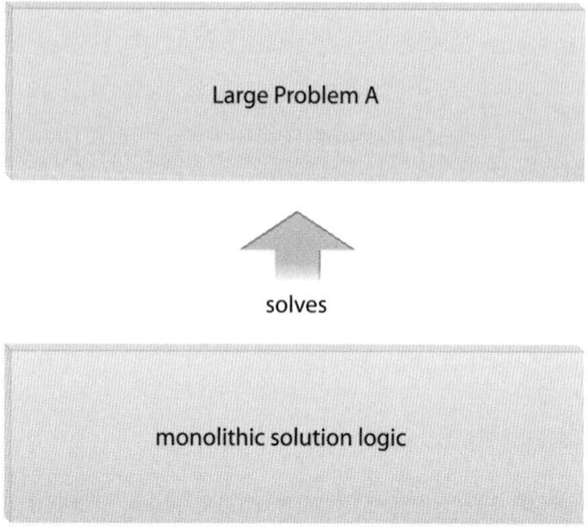

Figure 11.4
One approach to solving a large problem is to build a correspondingly large body of solution logic.

Solution

Functional Decomposition is essentially an application of the separation of concerns theory. This established software engineering principle promotes the decomposition of a larger problem into smaller problems (called *concerns*) for which corresponding units of solution logic can be built.

The rationale is that a larger problem can be more easily and effectively solved when separated into smaller parts. Each unit of solution logic that is built exists as a separate body of logic responsible for solving one or more of the identified, smaller concerns (Figure 11.5). This design approach is well-established and forms the basis for previous and current distributed computing platforms.

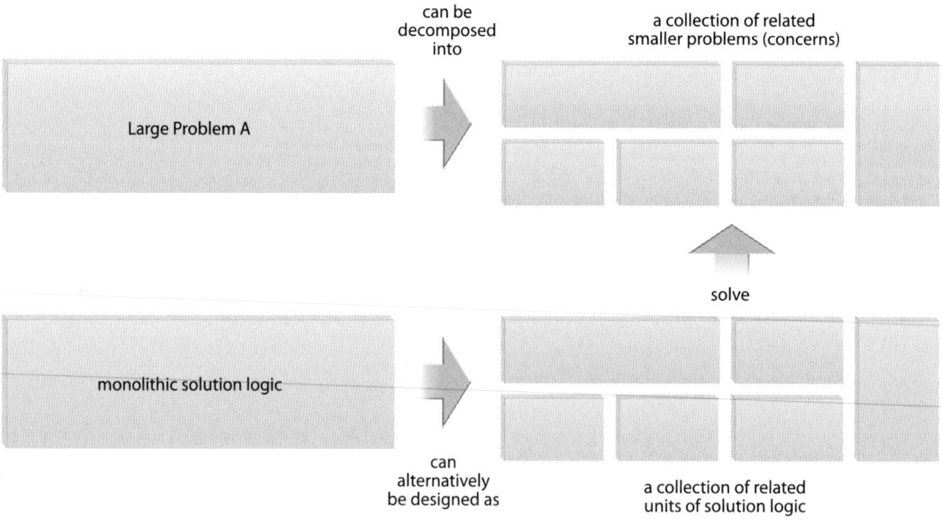

Figure 11.5
Distributed computing is based on an approach where a large problem is decomposed and its corresponding solution logic is distributed across individual solution logic units. On its own, this pattern results in the decomposition of the larger problem into smaller problems, as shown in the top part of this figure. The actual definition of solution logic units occurs through the application of subsequent patterns in this chapter.

NOTE

One of the key considerations when applying this pattern as part of the overall application sequence is that many of the individually defined units of solution logic will eventually be expected to be able to help solve additional large problems in order to achieve the target state explained in the pattern description for Capability Recomposition (526) and illustrated in Figure 17.5.

Application

As previously stated, Function Decomposition is essentially realized by carrying out the separation of concerns in support of service-orientation. A primary means by which service-orientation is distinguished from other distributed design approaches is the manner in which separation is achieved and how units of solution logic are defined.

This pattern is therefore not applied independently. It represents the starting point for a process that begins with functional separation and then continues through to shape separated logic into services, as per the subsequent patterns in this chapter.

In practice, this form of decomposition is generally achieved via a service modeling process that begins with a preliminary identification of individual concerns. The large problem corresponds to a business process that needs to be automated. The functional decomposition of this business process results in the definition of granular process steps, each of which can be considered an individual concern.

Impacts

Distributed units of solution logic require individual attention with regards to interconnectivity, security, reliability, and maintenance in order to ensure that each chain in the link of runtime activity processing is and remains adequately reliable and self-sufficient. An environment consisting of a large amount of smaller software programs therefore imposes more design complexity and governance challenges than one comprised of a single monolithic application.

Furthermore, the effectiveness of this pattern is limited by the quality of the problem definition. For a business process (representing the larger problem) to be properly decomposed, it needs to be documented in an accurate and detailed manner so that individual process steps are sufficiently granular. If the quality of the business process definition is poor, then the resulting concerns will form a weak foundation for subsequent service definition.

Relationships

On a fundamental level, you could say that Functional Decomposition forms the basis for all of the patterns in this book. But when identifying direct relationships, the only pattern that really qualifies is Service Encapsulation (305). Functional Decomposition essentially prepares the concerns that are subsequently addressed by solution logic that begins to take shape with the application of Service Encapsulation (305).

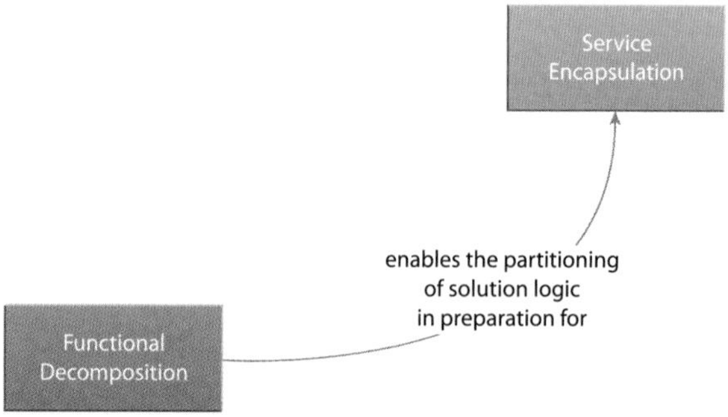
Service Encapsulation
enables the partitioning
of solution logic
in preparation for
Functional Decomposition

Figure 11.6

This displayed relationship simply establishes how the reasoning behind decomposing functionality is to make the decomposed parts available for potential encapsulation by services.

CASE STUDY EXAMPLE

The requirement for the Chain Inventory Transfer process to be established and automated wherever appropriate represents a large business problem. Using the process description documented previously in Figure 11.2 as a starting point, the Cutit team decomposes this problem into a set of concerns roughly equivalent to the primary process steps, as follows:

Concern 1 – How can the chain's quality be guaranteed?

Concern 2 – How can the chain be recorded as part of the inventory?

Concern 3 – How can the chain be cross-referenced with any corresponding back orders?

Concern 4 – How can the chain be associated with the correct back order?

Concern 5 – How can the chain be delivered to fulfill the back order?

(Note that in larger business process definitions it is more common to bundle groups of related, more granular steps to represent individual concerns.)

For each of these concerns, corresponding solutions are defined:

Solution for Concern 1 – The chain is manually inspected.

Solution for Concern 2 – The chain is electronically recorded as part of the inventory control system.

Solution for Concern 3 – Upon recording the chain, the system performs a cross-check for corresponding back orders, using the model number as the search criteria.

Solution for Concern 4 – The next back order in the queue is pulled up from the order management system and filled using the chain's inventory record.

Solution for Concern 5 – The chain is manually shipped.

In many cases, the identification of concerns can occur prior to the definition of the actual business process workflow. In this case, the concerns are represented by a set of related business requirements that are solved via the execution of steps within a larger business process definition.

Service Encapsulation

How can solution logic be made available as a resource of the enterprise?

Problem	Solution logic designed for a single application environment is typically limited in its potential to interoperate with or be leveraged by other parts of an enterprise.
Solution	Solution logic can be encapsulated by a service so that it is positioned as an enterprise resource capable of functioning beyond the boundary for which it is initially delivered.
Application	Solution logic suitable for service encapsulation needs to be identified.
Impacts	Service-encapsulated solution logic is subject to additional design and governance considerations.
Principles	n/a
Architecture	Service

Table 11.2
Profile summary for the Service Encapsulation pattern.

Problem

A collection of related software programs that represent a larger, decomposed body of solution logic can continue to exist within a siloed application boundary. In fact, many past distributed systems were built this way. The decision to partition the solution logic into smaller units was often motivated by the following considerations:

- increasing scalability by separating the parts of the system more subject to high volume and concurrency
- improving security by isolating specific parts of the system with special access and privacy requirements
- increasing reliability by distributing critical parts of a system across multiple physical servers
- achieving nominal reuse within the system boundary (or within a limited part of the enterprise)

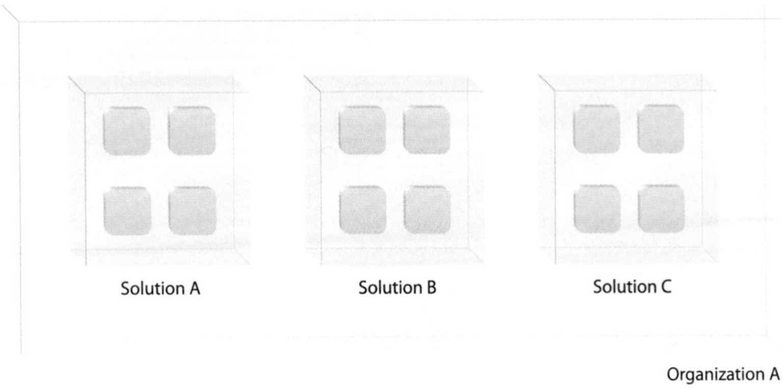

Figure 11.7
An enterprise consisting of distributed, yet still siloed solutions.

When an enterprise is comprised of siloed (or quasi-siloed) distributed solutions (Figure 11.7), it can encounter many design and governance challenges, such as:

- significant amounts of waste and redundancy
- inefficient application delivery
- bloated, oversized technical environments
- complex infrastructure and convoluted enterprise architecture
- complex and expensive integration
- ever-increasing IT operational costs

Details regarding these issues are documented in the *Life Before Service-Orientation* section of *SOA Principles of Service Design* and also at SOAPrinciples.com.

Solution

Solution logic suitable for classification as an enterprise resource can be encapsulated by and exposed as a service. This essentially means that the logic itself may form the basis for a new service, or the logic may be encapsulated by an existing service (most likely as a new capability). This results in an environment where services are shared (Figure 11.8).

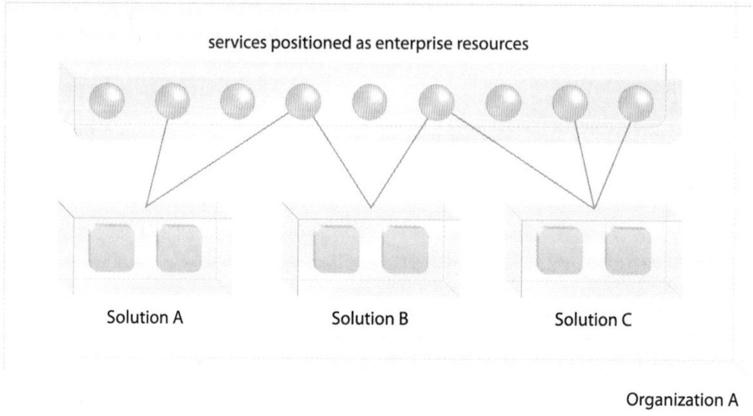

Figure 11.8
An enterprise wherein individual solutions use logic encapsulated as services and vice versa.

Application

The first required step is to identify and filter out solution logic that is actually suitable as an enterprise resource. Not all solution logic falls into this category. There will be bodies of logic that are tailored for individual distributed applications and for which other design approaches may be more appropriate.

Here are some guidelines:

- *Does the logic contain functionality that is useful to parts of the enterprise outside of the immediate application boundary?*

  If it does, the logic has increased value potential that may warrant its classification as an enterprise resource. This type of logic generally forms the basis of an agnostic service, as per Agnostic Context (312).

- *Does logic designed to leverage enterprise resources also have the potential to become an enterprise resource?*

  This form of logic emerges after evident agnostic logic is initially separated. It may be required for service-orientation to be applied to this type of logic so that it remains uniform with agnostic services and so that some or all of its functionality can also be positioned as an enterprise resource. This option is further explored in Non-Agnostic Context (319).

- *Does the implementation of the logic impose hard constraints that make it impractical or impossible to position the logic as an effective enterprise resource?*

  Regardless of whether the nature of the logic makes it suitable as an enterprise resource, there may be real-world limitations that prevent it from being effectively encapsulated by a service.

Using criteria such as this, the solution logic suitable for service encapsulation can be identified, allowing unsuitable logic to be filtered out (Figure 11.9).

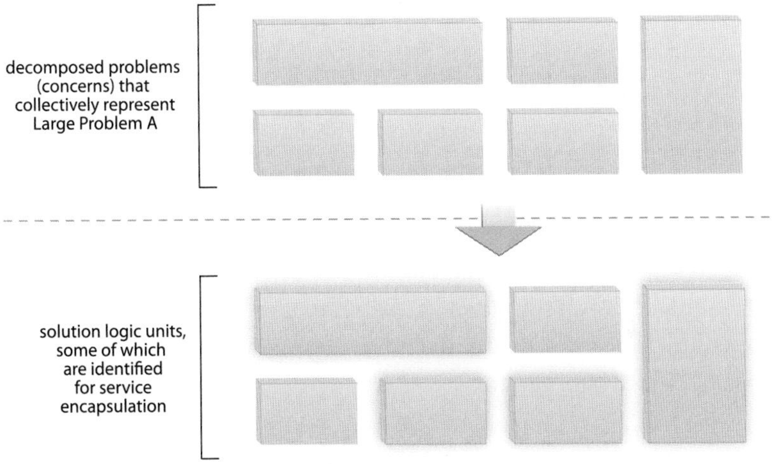

Figure 11.9

A subset of the decomposed monolithic solution logic is identified as being suitable for service encapsulation (as represented by the highlighted blocks).

For encapsulated solution logic to become an effective member of a service inventory, it needs to be further shaped by other patterns and principles so that it is designed to support the strategic goals associated with service-oriented computing.

A solid knowledge of the service-orientation design paradigm is therefore necessary in order to best determine when logic is and is not suitable for service encapsulation. As a rule of thumb, if service-orientation design principles cannot be applied to a meaningful extent, the logic will not likely warrant service encapsulation.

As previously stated, how this logic is determined is based on the methodology used and the maturity of the existing service inventory. Logic identified as being suitable for service encapsulation may be assigned to an existing service, or it may form the basis of a new service.

Impacts

Because the application of this pattern results in the identification and filtering of logic (in preparation for the upcoming group of service definition patterns), there is no immediate impact.

However, it should be noted that its application is limited to the filtering process only. Logic that is not considered suitable for service encapsulation is given no further consideration by this or any other patterns in this chapter. Therefore, this pattern sequence must be part of a larger analysis process that encompasses the modeling of solution logic that will not be encapsulated within services.

Relationships

Logic deemed suitable for service encapsulation is subsequently grouped into single or multi-purpose services, as per Non-Agnostic Context (319) and Agnostic Context (312).

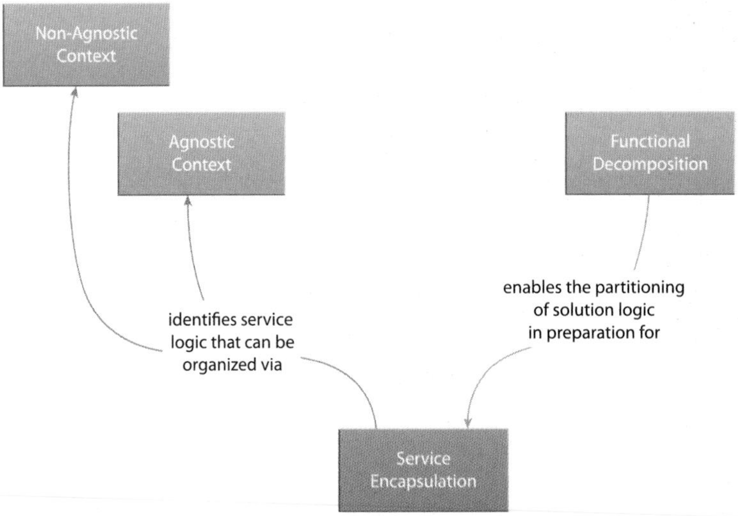

Figure 11.10
Service Encapsulation determines what logic will eventually comprise services.

CASE STUDY EXAMPLE

Upon reviewing the individual solutions defined as a result of applying Functional Decomposition (300), the Cutit team determines which parts are suitable for service encapsulation, as follows:

- Solutions for Concerns 1 and 5 are not suitable because they represent steps that are manually performed.
- Solutions for Concerns 2, 3, and 4 are suitable because they represent logic that can be automated and has no known limitations for it to be potentially useful on an enterprise basis.

Solutions for Concerns 1 and 5 remain part of the overall solution design—only they won't be delivered as services. The remaining solutions (for Concerns 2, 3, and 4) are further subject to the upcoming service definition patterns.

11.2 Service Definition Patterns

The identification of logic suitable for service encapsulation and the grouping and distribution of that logic within distinct functional contexts establishes fundamental service boundaries. These boundaries become increasingly important as an inventory of services is assembled and inventory-related patterns, such as Service Normalization (131), are applied to avoid functional overlap.

To define the most suitable boundary for a service requires that the most suitable functional context be established. This determines what functionality belongs within and outside of a service boundary. This next set of patterns (Figure 11.11) help make this determination by providing criteria for whether service logic is to be considered agnostic or non-agnostic and further guidance for how agnostic service logic in particular can be organized into separate capabilities.

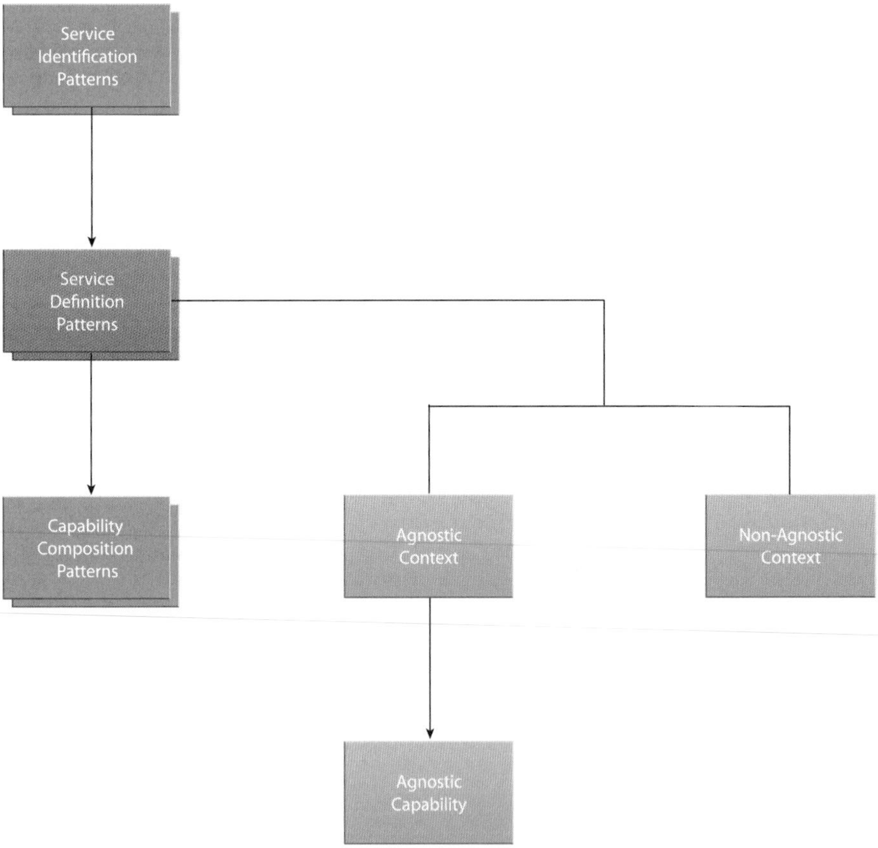

Figure 11.11
Service definition patterns organize service logic into specific contexts, thereby establishing service boundaries.

Agnostic Context

How can multi-purpose service logic be positioned as an effective enterprise resource?

Problem	Multi-purpose logic grouped together with single purpose logic results in programs with little or no reuse potential that introduce waste and redundancy into an enterprise.
Solution	Isolate logic that is not specific to one purpose into separate services with distinct agnostic contexts.
Application	Agnostic service contexts are defined by carrying out service-oriented analysis and service modeling processes.
Impacts	This pattern positions reusable solution logic at an enterprise level, potentially bringing with it increased design complexity and enterprise governance issues.
Principles	Service Reusability
Architecture	Service

Table 11.3

Profile summary for the Agnostic Context pattern.

> **NOTE**
>
> For a description of the term "agnostic" and related background information, see the *Agnostic Logic and Non-Agnostic Logic* section at the beginning of Chapter 7.

Problem

The solution logic required to solve a single concern will frequently include logic that is also suitable for solving other concerns. Grouping single and multi-purpose functionality together into one unit of logic will limit or even eliminate the potential for reuse (Figure 11.12).

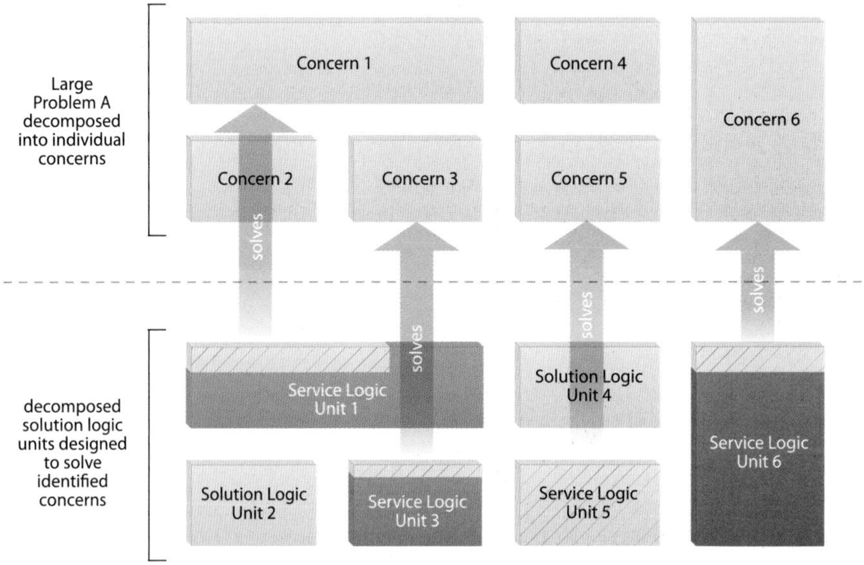

Figure 11.12

Decomposed units of solution logic will naturally be designed to solve concerns specific to a single, larger problem. Units 1, 3, and 6 represent logic that contains multi-purpose functionality trapped within a single-purpose (single concern) context. Single-purpose (non-agnostic) logic is represented by the striped pattern in this diagram.

Solution

Solution logic that is agnostic to the larger problem is separated from logic that is specific to the larger problem. One or more services with distinct agnostic functional contexts are then identified within which the agnostic logic is located (Figure 11.13).

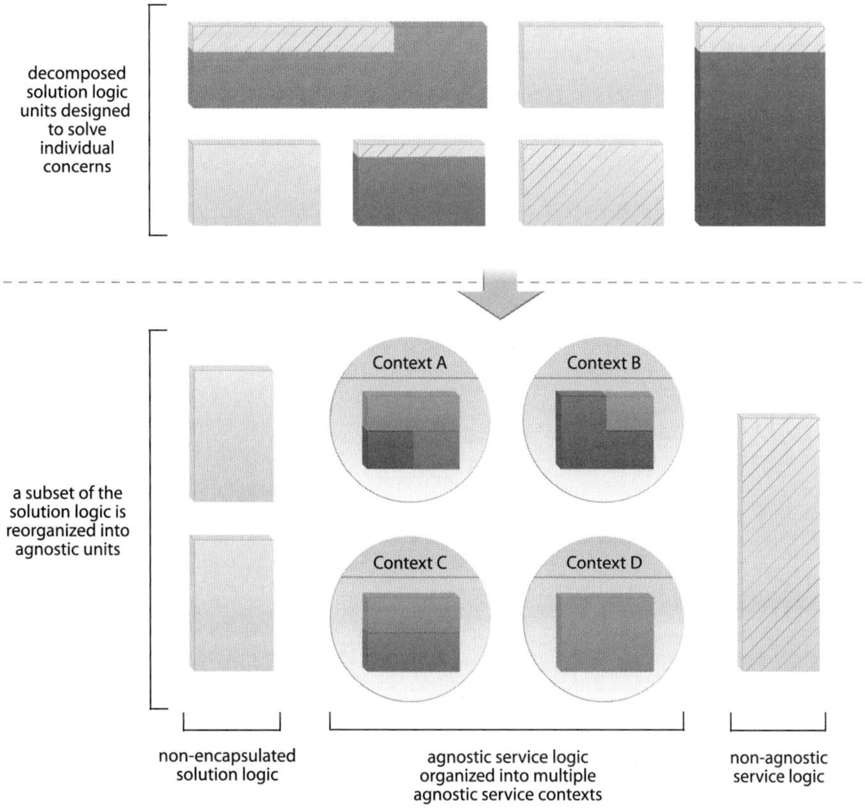

Figure 11.13

The application of this pattern results in a subset of the solution logic being further decomposed and then distributed into services with specific agnostic contexts.

Application

Solution logic is further decomposed and reorganized as a result of carrying out formal analysis and modeling processes. Agnostic logic is defined and continually refined into a set of candidate service contexts. These contexts can be based on pre-defined agnostic service model classifications, such as those that form the basis of Entity Abstraction (175) and Utility Abstraction (168).

Impacts

The application of this design pattern essentially results in the creation of services with reuse potential, which ties directly into several strategic service-oriented computing benefits, including an increased and repeatable return on investment.

Achieving these benefits tends to increase the overall quantity of services required to solve a given problem, which leads to additional design considerations and performance overhead associated with service compositions.

The governance effort of agnostic services is significantly more than if the corresponding solution logic was dedicated to a single application. Additionally, the governance of the overall architecture is also impacted as the quantity of agnostic services within an inventory grows.

Relationships

From a service design perspective, Agnostic Context is one of the most distinctive patterns associated with service-orientation. It therefore has several relationships with other patterns that apply specialized variations of Agnostic Context, such as Entity Abstraction (175) and Utility Abstraction (168). The closest relationship is between Agnostic Context and Agnostic Capability (324), as the latter is applied to services that have already been deemed agnostic.

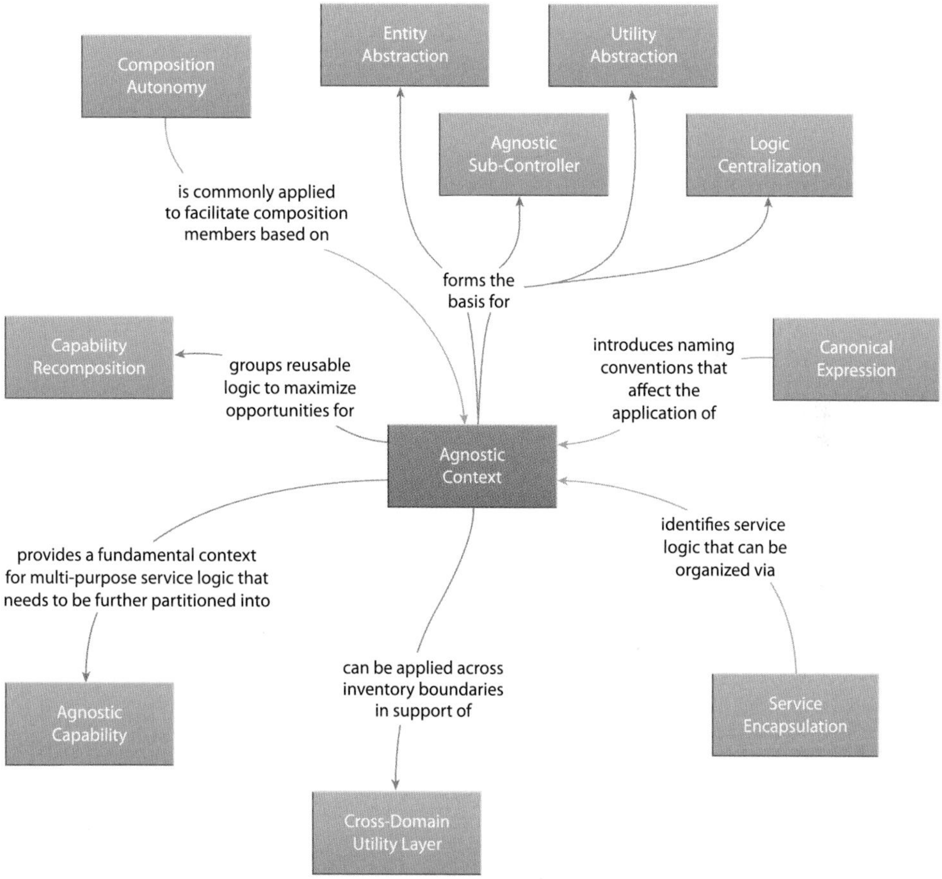

Figure 11.14

Agnostic Context is core to service design and is responsible for forming the basis of several fundamental architectural design patterns.

CASE STUDY EXAMPLE

Cutit analysts and architects review the logic identified as being potentially suitable for service encapsulation and break down this logic into individual actions, as follows:

Solution for Concern 2

- create a new inventory record
- retrieve chain specification information by serial number
- enter chain information, including the assignment of pre-defined model number
- save new inventory record

Solution for Concern 3

- issue a query for back orders keyed on model number
- retrieve a list of outstanding back order records sorted by order date
- if no back orders exist, terminate process

Solution for Concern 4

- retrieve the back order record with the oldest date (the next back order in line)
- change status of order from "back order" to "completed"
- save revised order record

Upon assessing the suitability for these actions to be classified as reusable (and forming the basis of entity or utility-centric agnostic functional contexts), the Cutit team reorganizes the logic into different groupings (Figure 11.15) and comes up with the following preliminary agnostic service contexts:

Inventory Processing

- create a new inventory record
- enter chain information, including the assignment of pre-defined model number
- save new inventory record

Chain Information

- retrieve chain specification information by serial number

Order Processing

- issue a query for back orders keyed on model number
- retrieve a list of outstanding back order records (if any) sorted by order date
- retrieve the back order record with the oldest date (the next back order in line)
- change status of order from "back order" to "completed"
- save revised order record

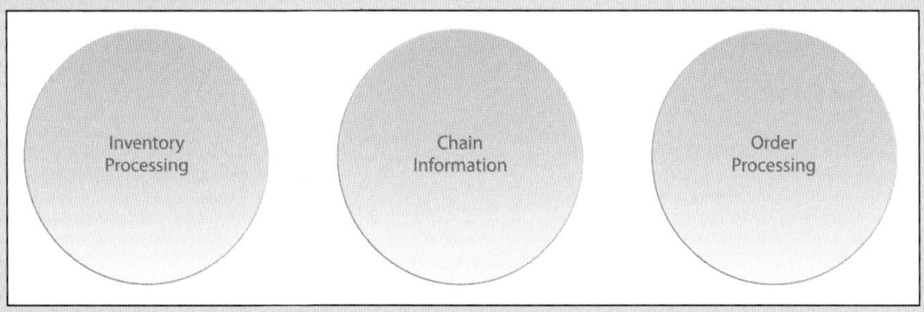

Figure 11.15

The agnostic service contexts established as a result of applying this pattern; all three services are based on Entity Abstraction (175).

Non-Agnostic Context

How can single-purpose service logic be positioned as an effective enterprise resource?

Problem	Non-agnostic logic that is not service-oriented can inhibit the effectiveness of service compositions that utilize agnostic services.
Solution	Non-agnostic solution logic suitable for service encapsulation can be located within services that reside as official members of a service inventory.
Application	A single-purpose functional service context is defined.
Impacts	Although they are not expected to provide reuse potential, non-agnostic services are still subject to the rigor of service-orientation.
Principles	Standardized Service Contract, Service Composability
Architecture	Service

Table 11.4
Profile summary for the Non-Agnostic Context pattern.

Problem

When applying service-orientation, there is a great deal of emphasis on abstracting and positioning solution logic that is agnostic to business tasks and parent business processes. This forms the very basis of the Service Reusability principle and associated patterns.

The result is that non-agnostic logic gets filtered out and often relegated to encapsulation within software programs that are not part of the service inventory but instead exist peripherally as dedicated service consumers (also referred to as "composition initiators"). This is represented by the top part of Figure 11.16.

In this case, service-orientation is not applied to non-agnostic solution logic, which limits its potential to ever become an effective enterprise resource, which can compromise the quality of the service compositions the logic may be responsible for controlling.

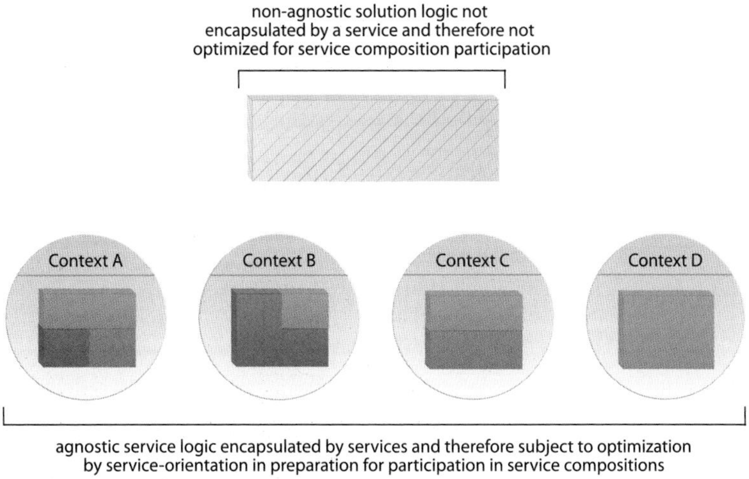
non-agnostic solution logic not
encapsulated by a service and therefore not
optimized for service composition participation
Context A
Context B
Context C
Context D
agnostic service logic encapsulated by services and therefore subject to optimization
by service-orientation in preparation for participation in service compositions

Figure 11.16

The non-agnostic solution logic is not encapsulated into a service and therefore may reduce the effectiveness of service compositions that may include the agnostic services at the bottom of this figure.

Solution

Suitable non-agnostic solution logic is encapsulated by a service with a correspondingly non-agnostic functional context (Figure 11.17). This positions the logic as part of a service inventory. A secondary benefit is that, as a service, this logic is further available for any potential unforeseen involvement in service compositions.

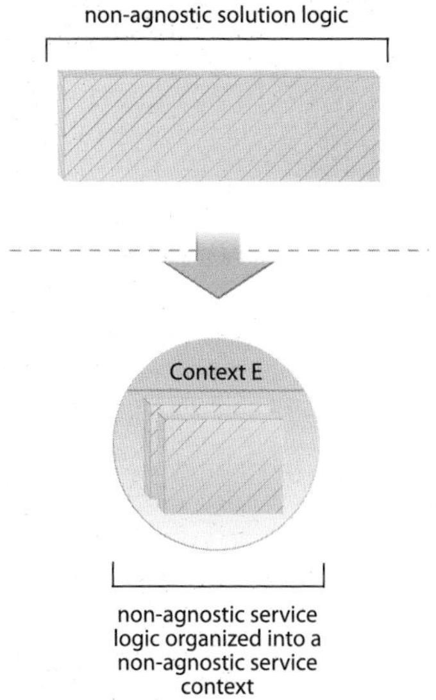
non-agnostic solution logic
Context E
non-agnostic service
logic organized into a
non-agnostic service
context

Figure 11.17

The non-agnostic service logic is encapsulated within a service based on a correspondingly non-agnostic service context (E).

Application

Non-agnostic service logic is shaped via the same governing design principles as agnostic services with the exception of Service Reusability and with a lesser initial emphasis on service contract design.

NOTE

If reusable functionality is discovered within the boundary of a non-agnostic service, it can be made available via Agnostic Sub-Controller (607).

This pattern is most commonly applied in combination with Process Abstraction (182) to establish a standard task service layer. However, it is not limited to encapsulating parent business process logic. Other custom, single-purpose service models can be created and based on a non-agnostic functional context.

There are no rules as to whether this pattern should be applied before or after Agnostic Context (312). The mainstream service modeling process described at SOAMethodology.com suggests identifying agnostic service candidates prior to non-agnostic candidates so that multi-purpose logic can be filtered out first, but it is really up to your preferences and whatever methodology you end up using.

Either way, the end result of completing both Agnostic Context (312) and Non-Agnostic Context is that all of the solution logic considered suitable for service encapsulation ends up organized into a set of well-defined service contexts (Figure 11.18).

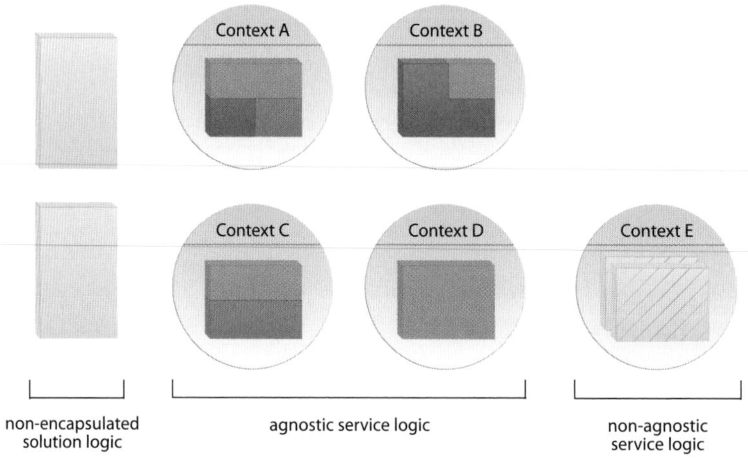

Figure 11.18

Context E joins A through D as future members of a service inventory. The non-encapsulated logic (left) remains separated.

> **NOTE**
>
> As explained in the description for Process Abstraction (182), non-agnostic logic is not required to reside in a service. The assumption when applying this pattern is that the logic allocated for a non-agnostic service was identified as being suitable for encapsulation as per the prior application of Service Encapsulation (305). When applying Non-Agnostic Context as part of a service modeling process, logic designated for a non-agnostic service can still be relocated to a non-service-oriented program. Herbjörn Wilhelmsen published a study at SOAMag.com that compares the pros and cons of abstracting single-purpose logic into services and non-service-oriented applications.

Impacts

Because service-orientation still needs to be applied to the underlying solution logic of a non-agnostic service, its initial delivery will be more expensive and more time-consuming than if it were to simply exist in a program external to the service inventory. The ultimate return on this investment can therefore be significantly lower than with agnostic services.

> **NOTE**
>
> It is the application of this pattern to a body of non-agnostic logic that determines whether this logic is considered a composition initiator or a composition controller. The former is a non-service-oriented program generally responsible for triggering composition logic, whereas the latter is a service responsible for encapsulating composition logic.

Relationships

When studying Non-Agnostic Context, it is important to remember that it is applied subsequent to Service Encapsulation (305). Even though the context is specific to one purpose, it is still considered a service.

The types of services that most commonly require this pattern are those based on task-centric service models. This explains the relationships between Process Abstraction (182) and Process Centralization (193), which are associated with the task service and orchestrated task service models respectively.

A key relationship also defined in Figure 11.19 is that between Non-Agnostic Context and Capability Composition (521). The single-purpose nature of the logic encapsulated by services based on non-agnostic contexts is generally associated with composition logic required to automate a business task. Therefore, this pattern fully supports and even enables Capability Composition (521) and Capability Recomposition (526).

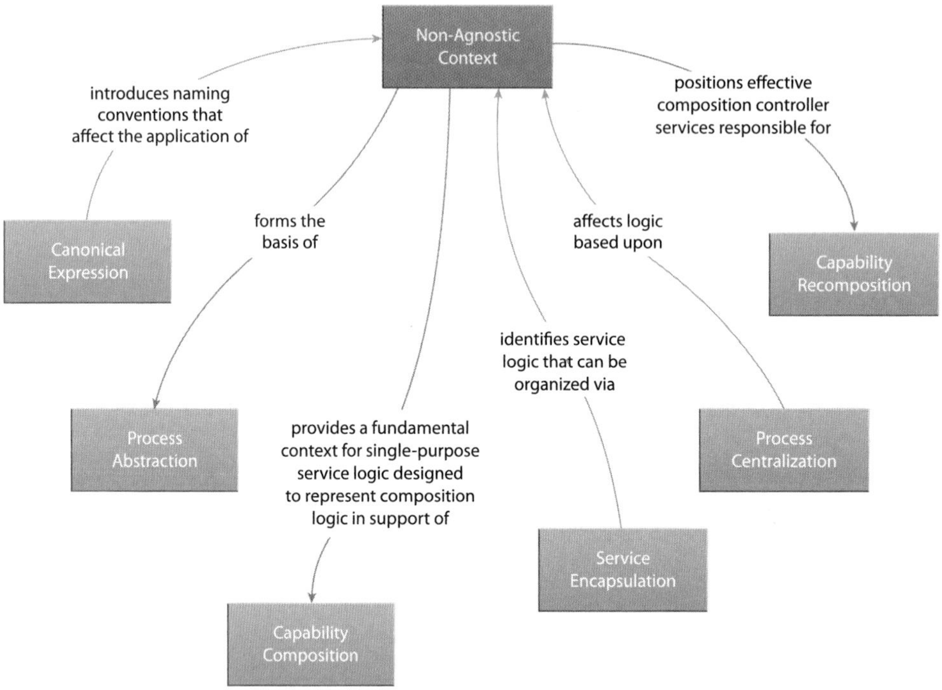

Figure 11.19

Non-Agnostic Context establishes a service context that is intentionally single-purpose and very much related to patterns that address parent process design issues.

CASE STUDY EXAMPLE

The definition of a non-agnostic service context for the Chain Inventory Transfer process is quite straightforward primarily because the process is so simple. A parent service context is created to represent the process itself and to assume the responsibility of executing the workflow logic described previously in Figure 11.2.

As shown in Figure 11.20, because this service context is defined by the scope of the business process, it is accordingly named.

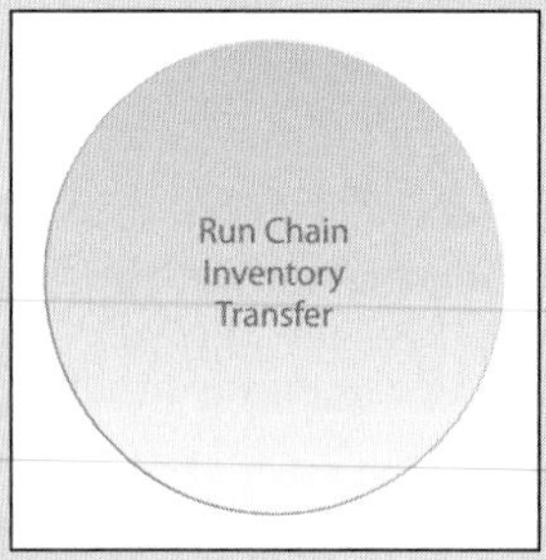

Figure 11.20

An intentionally non-agnostic service context representing the parent business process is defined. In the Chapter 17 case study examples, this service will be responsible for composing the agnostic services defined earlier in the example for Agnostic Context (312).

Agnostic Capability

How can multi-purpose service logic be made effectively consumable and composable?

Problem	Service capabilities derived from specific concerns may not be useful to multiple service consumers, thereby reducing the reusability potential of the agnostic service.
Solution	Agnostic service logic is partitioned into a set of well-defined capabilities that address common concerns not specific to any one problem. Through subsequent analysis, the agnostic context of capabilities is further refined.
Application	Service capabilities are defined and iteratively refined through proven analysis and modeling processes.
Impacts	The definition of each service capability requires extra up-front analysis and design effort.
Principles	Standardized Service Contract, Service Reusability, Service Composability
Architecture	Service

Table 11.5
Profile summary for the Agnostic Capability pattern.

Problem

When defining service capabilities that were derived from concerns related to a specific problem, there is the natural tendency for those capabilities to be specific to those concerns, regardless of that fact that they reside within an agnostic service context.

This can result in a set of capabilities that may appear to be agnostic but actually provide functionality that is very specific to the concerns associated with the original large problem (or business process) for which they were originally defined (Figure 11.21).

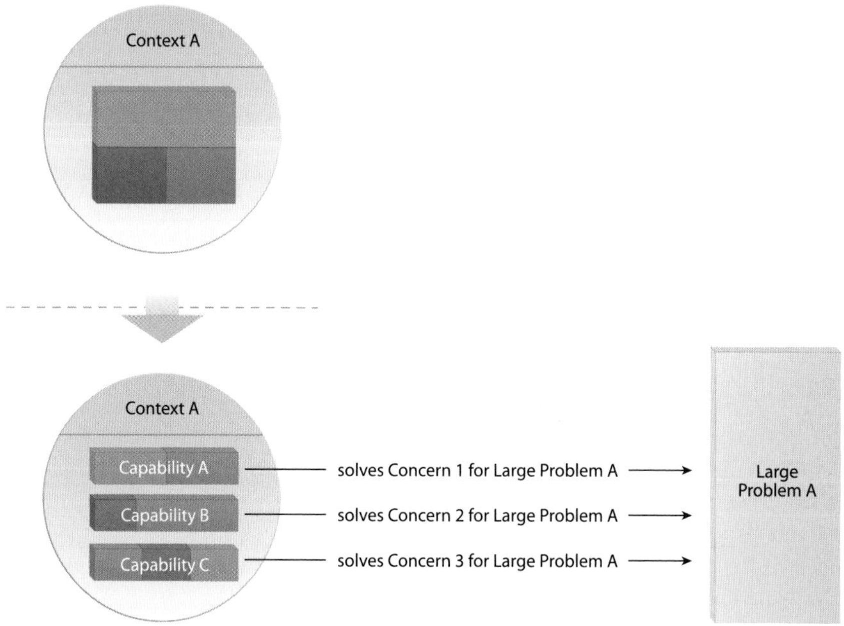

Figure 11.21

The three capabilities provided by Service Context A are defined to solve the specific requirements of the corresponding concerns of Large Problem A. This can reduce and perhaps even eliminate reuse opportunities.

Solution

Agnostic service capabilities are defined and each is subjected to additional analysis beyond its initial definition, allowing it to be refined until it reaches a point where it is sufficiently balanced so that it remains aligned to the parent service's agnostic context while also accommodating the functional requirements of a range of common service consumers. This enables each service capability to address a concern that is truly common (multi-purpose), thereby allowing it to help solve multiple larger problems (Figure 11.22).

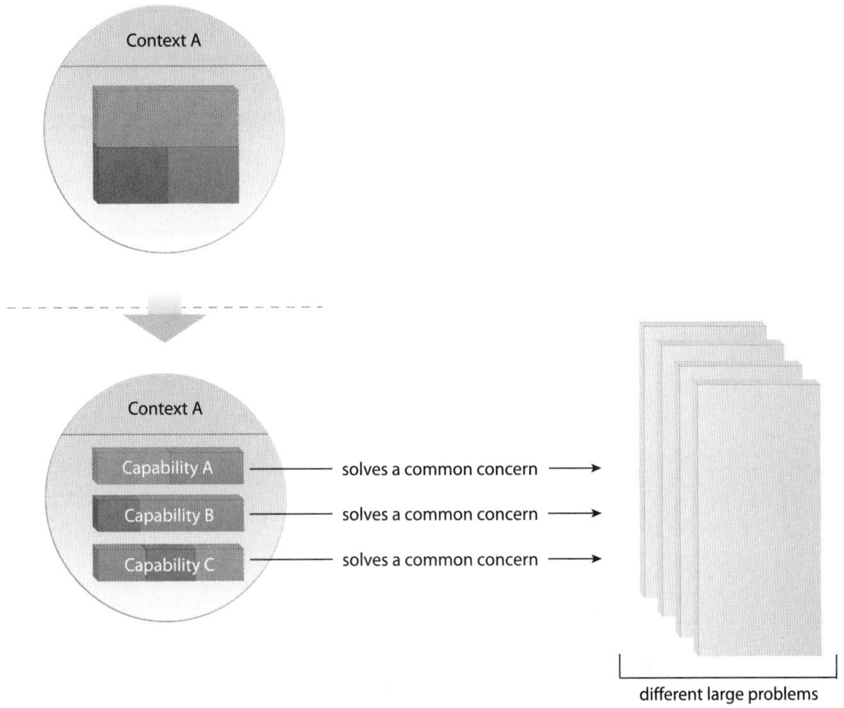

Figure 11.22

Through the application of this pattern, the service logic grouped within a specific service context is made available as a set of well-defined and complementary capabilities.

Application

By carrying out service-oriented analysis and service modeling processes, candidate service capabilities are identified, defined, and grouped into candidate service contexts. Through repeated iterations of these processes, the definition and organization of the capabilities are further refined.

This pattern essentially positions each capability as an independent function able to solve a concern that is common to multiple business processes or tasks. Well-defined agnostic capabilities lie at the heart of fundamental service-orientation principles, such as Service Reusability and Service Composability.

Impacts

The quality of a service capability definition improves with each iteration through a service-oriented analysis process, whereby its functionality and expression (via the service contract) are repeatedly validated or refined. However, all of these iterations add to the up-front analysis time and effort required to produce the service.

Additionally, inadvertent "over modeling" can lead to capabilities that are too vague and too generic or that perhaps offer more functionality than will actually be required. These consequences can be avoided by sticking to analysis processes that are focused on specific business domains.

Relationships

Agnostic Capability can be considered a continuation of Agnostic Context (312), making these two patterns naturally related. But when studying how services are assembled into compositions, the ultimate role of the defined agnostic capabilities becomes evidently integral to the application of both Capability Composition (521) and Capability Recomposition (526).

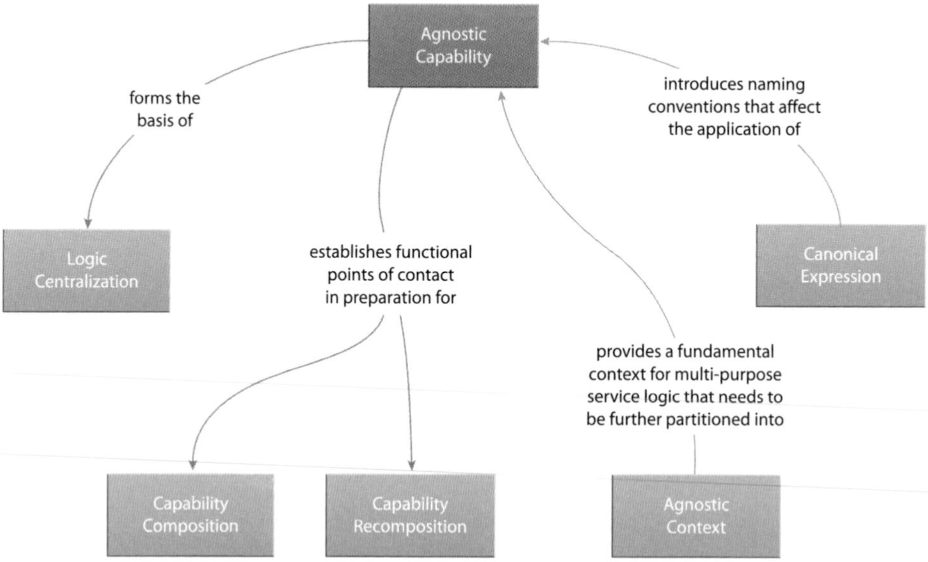

Figure 11.23

Agnostic Capability provides the externally facing functions that form the basis of service contracts.

CASE STUDY EXAMPLE

The Cutit team proceeds to establish service capabilities for its three entity services (Figure 11.24), as follows:

- The actions associated with the Inventory Processing context are studied and consolidated into a single capability called "Create Record."
- The one action allocated to the Chain Information context is shaped into a generic capability called "Retrieve Chain Record."
- The actions grouped within the Order Processing context are refined into three separate capabilities called "Retrieve Order Record," "Retrieve Back Order List," and "Edit Order."

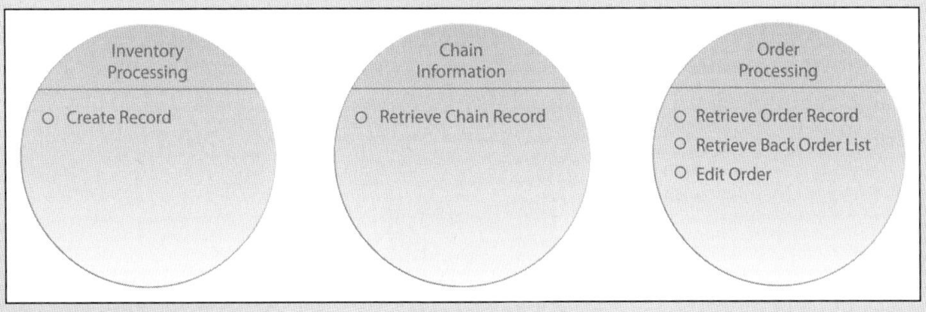

Figure 11.24
The three service definitions, each with capabilities that address the processing requirements of the Chain Inventory Transfer business process.

Although there is an opportunity to proceed into the actual design and development stages with these service definitions, the team insists that they perform some additional service modeling. Several new business processes are analyzed, allowing the functionality (and associated algorithms) behind each capability to be better optimized. Another side-benefit of these additional iterations is the streamlining of the service definitions themselves, as shown in Figure 11.25.

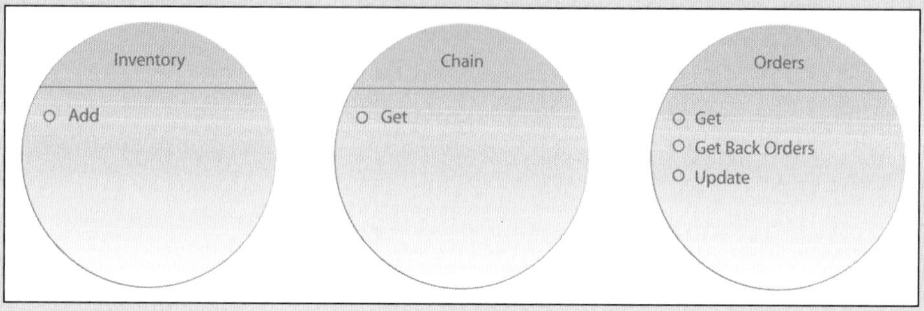

Figure 11.25
After some further service modeling, the definitions are refined with agnostic capabilities.

Chapter 12

Service Implementation Patterns

Service Façade

Redundant Implementation

Service Data Replication

Partial State Deferral

Partial Validation

UI Mediator

Each of the following design patterns impacts or augments the service architecture in a specific manner, thereby affecting its physical implementation. Most are considered specialized, meaning that they are to be used for specific requirements and may not be needed at all (and are rarely all used together).

Arguably the most important pattern in this chapter is Service Façade (333) because it introduces a key component into the service architecture that can help a service evolve in response to on-going change.

Redundant Implementation (345), Service Data Replication (350), and Partial State Deferral (356), on the other hand, help establish a more robust service implementation by addressing common performance and scalability demands. Unlike Service Façade (333), which actually alters the complexion of the service architecture, these three patterns can be more easily applied subsequent to a service's initial deployment.

Partial Validation (362) is a consumer-focused pattern that helps optimize runtime message processing and UI Mediator (366) is a pattern specialized to bridging potential usability gaps between services and the presentation layer.

Service Façade

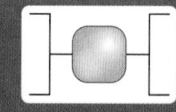

How can a service accommodate changes to its contract or implementation while allowing the core service logic to evolve independently?

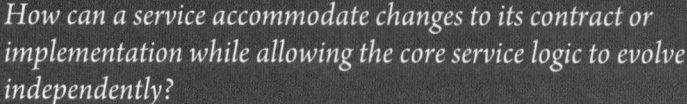

Problem	The coupling of the core service logic to contracts and implementation resources can inhibit its evolution and negatively impact service consumers.
Solution	A service façade component is used to abstract a part of the service architecture with negative coupling potential.
Application	A separate façade component is incorporated into the service design.
Impacts	The addition of the façade component introduces design effort and performance overhead.
Principles	Standardized Service Contract, Service Loose Coupling
Architecture	Service

Table 12.1
Profile summary for the Service Façade pattern.

Problem

A given service will contain a core body of logic responsible for carrying out its (usually business-centric) capabilities. When a service is subject to change either due to changes in the contract or in its underlying implementation, this core service logic can find itself extended and augmented to accommodate that change. As a result, the initial bundling of core service logic with contract-specific or implementation-specific processing logic can eventually result in design-time and runtime challenges.

For example:

- A single body of service logic is required to support multiple contracts, thereby introducing new decision logic and requiring the core business routines to process different types of input and output messages.

- The usage patterns of shared resources accessed by the service are changed, resulting in changes to the established service behavior that end up negatively affecting existing service consumers.
- The service implementation is upgraded or refactored, resulting in changes to the core business logic in order to accommodate the new and/or improved implementation.
- The service is subjected to decomposition, as per Service Decomposition (489).

Figure 12.1 illustrates the first of these scenarios.

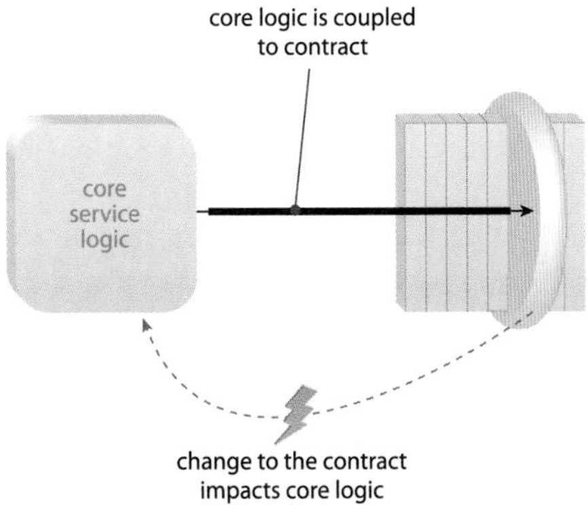

Figure 12.1

If the core service logic is coupled directly to the contract, any changes to how the service interacts with consumers will require changes to the core service logic. (This represents only one of several of the problem scenarios addressed by this pattern.)

Solution

Façade logic is inserted into the service architecture to establish one or more layers of abstraction that can accommodate future changes to the service contract, the service logic, and the underlying service implementation (Figure 12.2).

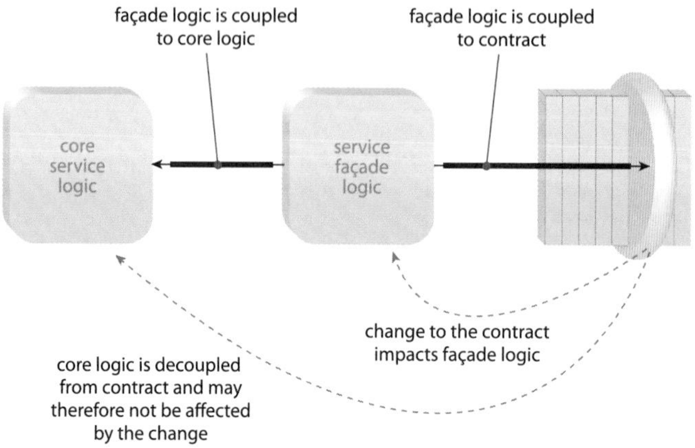

Figure 12.2

Façade logic is placed in between the contract and the core service logic. This allows the core service logic to remain decoupled from the contract.

> **NOTE**
>
> Service Façade is a versatile pattern that can be applied in many different ways within a given service architecture. The upcoming *Application* section explores several possible application scenarios to demonstrate how service façade logic can be potentially utilized. This section is therefore noticeably longer than the average *Application* section for other patterns.

Application

Service façade logic is considered part of the overall service logic but distinct from the core service logic, as follows:

- The core service logic is expected to provide the range of functions responsible for carrying out the capabilities expressed by the service contract.
- The service façade logic is primarily responsible for providing supplemental, intermediate processing logic in support of the core service logic.

Service façade logic is generally isolated into a separate component that is part of the service architecture. Common types of logic that tend to reside within a service façade component include:

- *Relaying Logic* – The façade logic simply relays input and output messages between the contract and the core service logic or between the core service logic and other parts of the service architecture. For examples of this, see the descriptions for Proxy Capability (497) and Distributed Capability (510).
- *Broker Logic* – The façade logic carries out transformation logic as per the patterns associated with Service Broker (707). This may be especially required when a single unit of core service logic is used together with multiple service contracts, as per Concurrent Contracts (421).
- *Behavior Correction* – The façade logic is used compensate for changes in the behavior of the core service logic in order to maintain the service behavior to which established consumers have become accustomed.
- *Contract-Specific Requirements* – When service facades are coupled to contracts in order to accommodate different types of service consumers, they can find themselves having to support whatever interaction requirements the contracts express. This can include special security, reliability, and activity management processing requirements. While all of this processing can also be located within the core service logic, it may be desirable to isolate it into façade components when the processing requirements are exclusive to specific contracts.

Service façade components can be positioned within a service architecture in different ways, depending on the nature and extent of abstraction required. For example, a façade component can be located between the core service logic and the contract. Figure 12.3 elaborates on the problem scenario first introduced in Figure 12.1 by showing how a design based on core service logic coupled to the contract can lead to restrictive architectures after multiple contracts enter the picture.

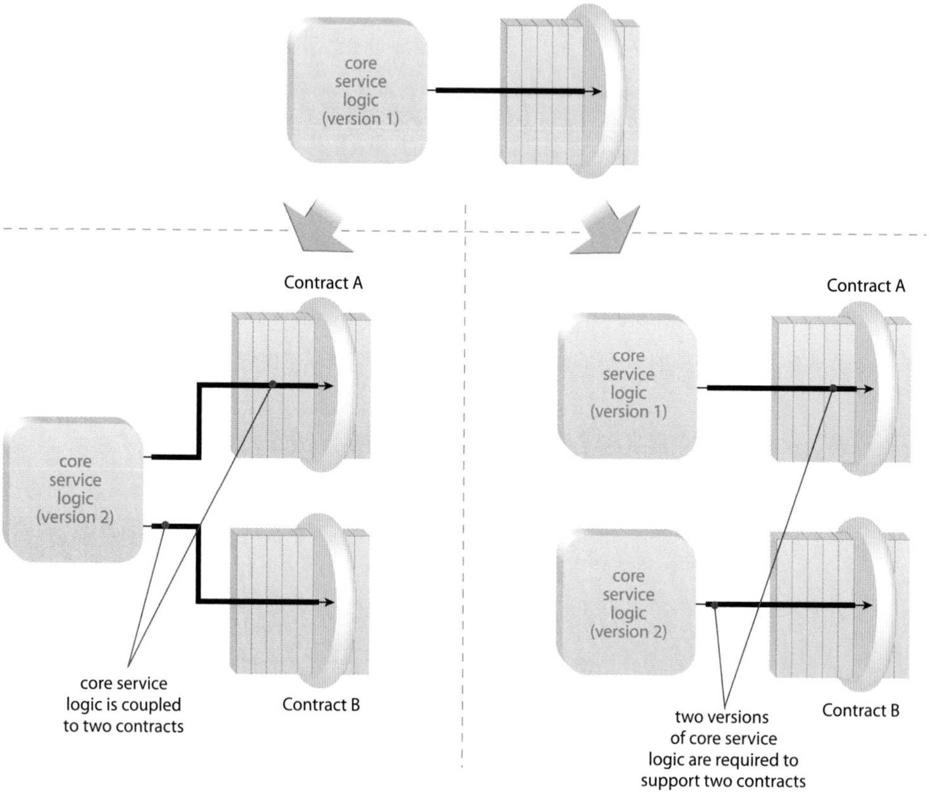

Figure 12.3

When designing services we are encouraged to tailor underlying service logic in support of independently customized and standardized service contracts. This results in a high level of logic-to-contract coupling, while allowing the contract itself to be decoupled from its implementation. Although this is considered desirable from a contract coupling perspective, it can lead to undesirable design options for supporting multiple service contracts with just a base unit of core service logic. The first architecture (left) requires a new version of the core service logic that is now coupled to two contracts, while the second (right) requires the creation of a new service altogether, leading to redundant core service logic.

Figure 12.4 illustrates how the abstraction achieved through the use of service façade components allows for the addition of multiple service contracts without major impact to the core service logic. Service façade components are intentionally tightly coupled to their respective contracts, allowing the core service logic to remain loosely coupled or even decoupled. What this figure also highlights is the opportunity to position consumer-specific service logic as an independent (and perhaps even reusable) part of the service architecture.

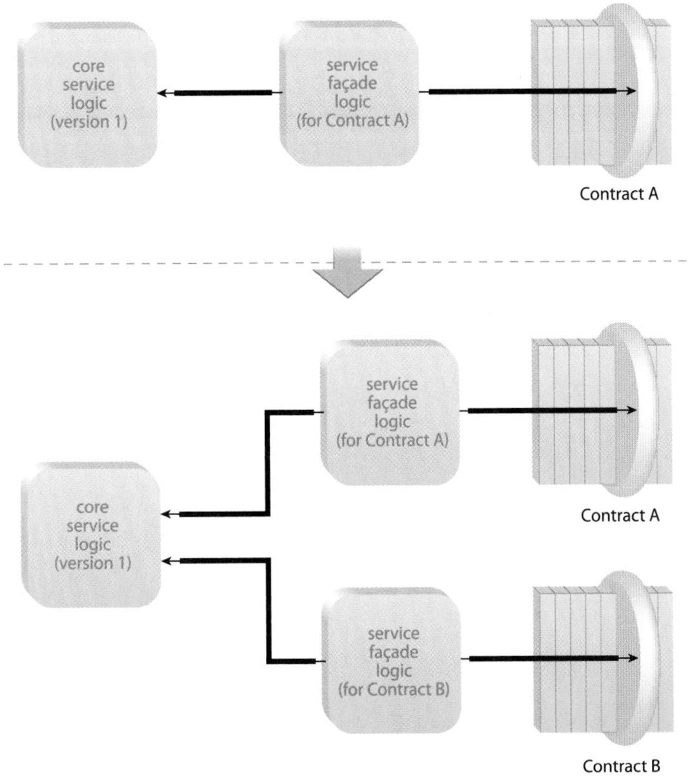

Figure 12.4

New service contracts can be accommodated by repeating this pattern to introduce new façade components, thereby potentially shielding the core service logic.

When service façade logic is used to correct the behavior of changed core service logic, it is also typically positioned between the contract and core service logic. This allows it to exist independently from logic that is coupled to (and thereby potentially influenced by) specific parts of the underlying implementation.

Figure 12.5 shows how core service logic coupled to both the implementation and the contract may be forced to pass on changes in behavior to established service consumers. Figure 12.6 then demonstrates how a layer of service façade processing can be designed to regulate service-to-consumer interaction in order to preserve the expected service behavior.

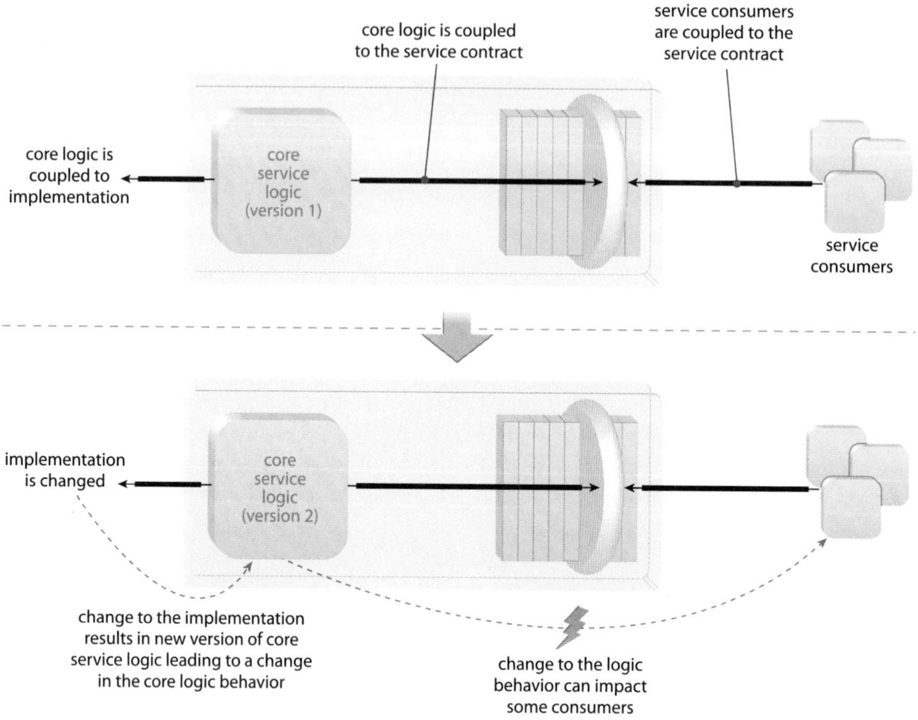

Figure 12.5

Parts of the implementation encapsulated and bound to by version 1 (top) of the core service logic are subject to change, resulting in the release of a second version (bottom) that brings with it a noticeable change in behavior. Service consumers coupled to the service contract are affected by this change because the new core service logic is also directly coupled to the contract.

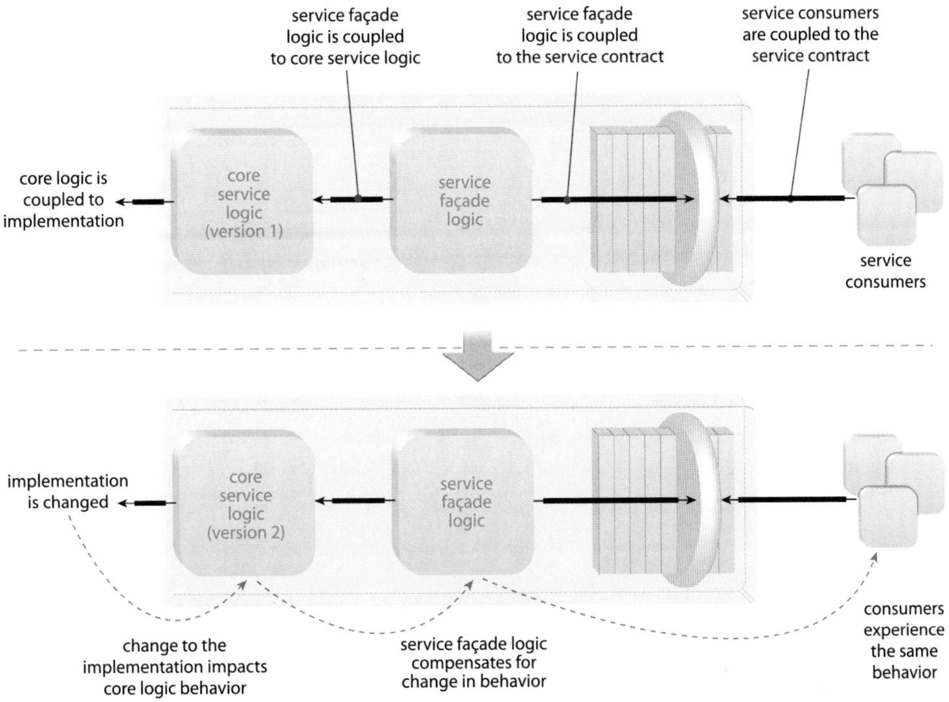

Figure 12.6

The core service logic is updated due to the change in implementation, but the behavioral changes are caught by the service façade component which contains additional routines to preserve the original behavior while still interacting with version 2 of the core service logic.

Finally, it is worth pointing out that service façade logic is not limited to acting as an intermediary between the core service logic and the service contract. Figure 12.7 shows an architecture in which components are positioned as facades for underlying implementation resources. In this case, this pattern helps shield core service logic from changes to the underlying implementation by abstracting backend parts.

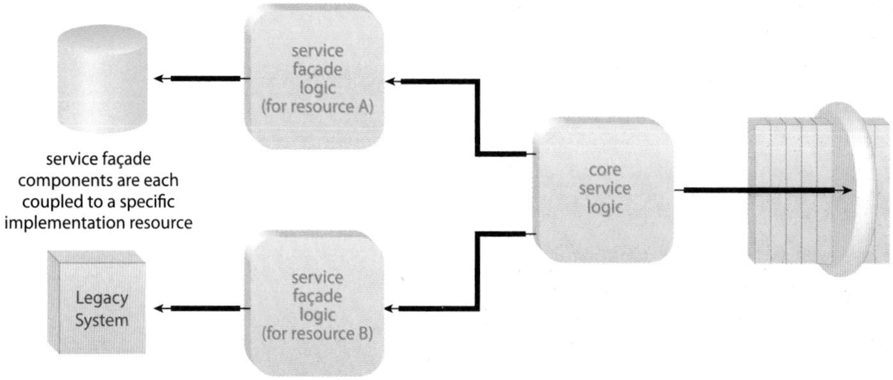

Figure 12.7

One service façade component abstracts a shared database (resource A) whereas another abstracts a legacy system (resource B). This abstraction helps protect the core service logic from changes to either of these parts of the underlying service implementation.

Impacts

Creating façade components results in an increased amount of physical logic decomposition. This naturally introduces additional design and development effort, as well as extra cross-component communication requirements. Although some performance overhead is expected, it is generally minor as long as façade and core service components are located on the same physical server.

Some governance overhead can also be expected, due to the increased amount of components per service.

Relationships

The structural solution provided by Service Façade helps support the application of several other patterns, including Service Refactoring (484), Service Decomposition(489), Proxy Capability (497), Agnostic Sub-Controller (607), Inventory Endpoint(260), Distributed Capability (510), Concurrent Contracts (421), and Contract Denormalization (414). This pattern is ideally combined with Decoupled Contract (401) in order to provide the maximum amount of design and refactoring flexibility throughout a service's lifespan.

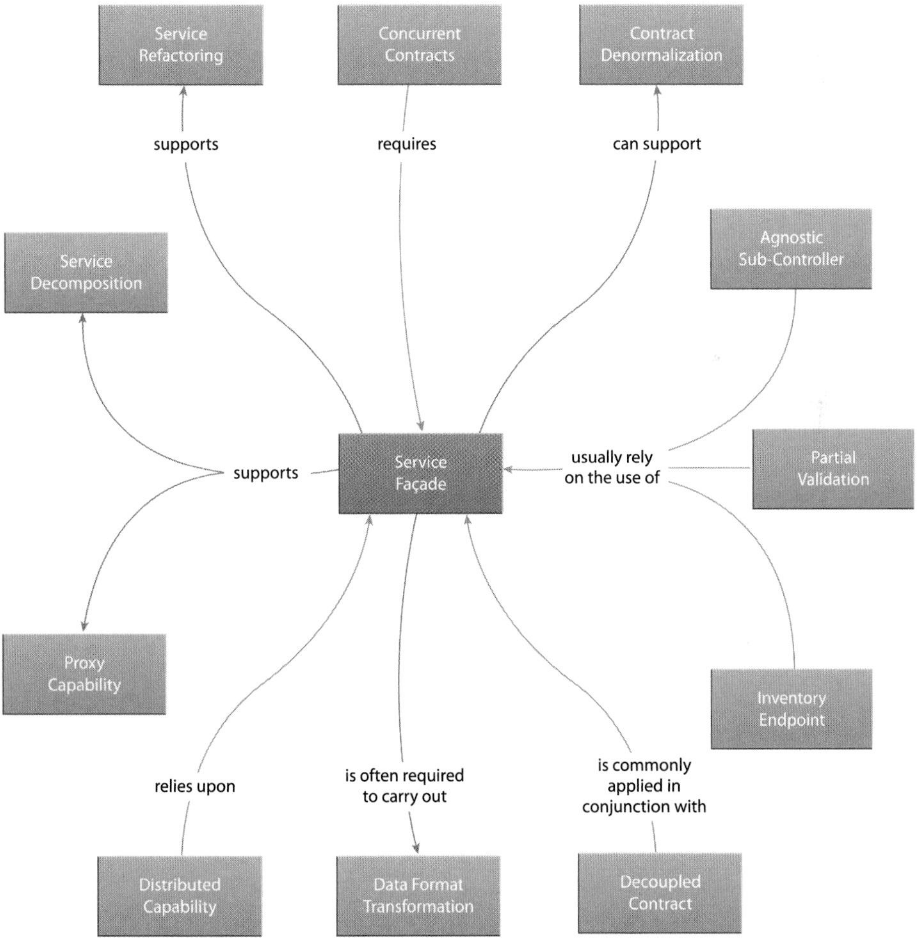

Figure 12.8
Service Façade establishes a key part of the service logic that ends up supporting several other service design patterns.

CASE STUDY EXAMPLE

The FRC is developing an entity service called Appealed Assessments, which is dedicated to producing a range of reports related to already assessed claims that have been successfully or unsuccessfully appealed. Depending on the nature and scope of the requested report, this service may need to access up to six different repositories in order to gather all of the required data.

A component-based architecture already exists in which a separate wrapper utility component has been created to represent and provide standardized access to all six repositories. This Data Controller component provides all the logic required to fulfill the capabilities of the planned Assessment Reports service in addition to several other generic data access and reporting functions.

Instead of creating new logic to accomplish the same data access tasks, FRC wants to use the Data Controller component as the core service logic for the Appealed Assessments service. However, they are told by the group that owns this component that it can't be altered in support of this service. Furthermore, the component is expected to undergo some changes in the near future that may result in it having to support one additional database plus accommodate the planned consolidation of two existing legacy repositories. As a result, the component needs to remain an independently governed part of the architecture.

The FRC architects decide to design a service façade component that will be used to bind to the official WSDL contract for the Appealed Assessments service. The façade component is appropriately named Data Relayer, and its primary responsibility is to receive service consumer requests via the standardized WSDL contract, relay those requests to the corresponding internal wrapper components, and then relay the responses back to the service consumer.

The Data Relayer component contains a modest amount of logic, most of which is focused on validating data reports received from the Data Controller component and (if necessary) converting them to the format and data model required by the Appealed Assessments service's WSDL `message` construct and associated XML schema complex types.

The resulting service architecture (Figure 12.9) allows the original Data Controller component to evolve independently while establishing the Data Relayer component as an intermediate façade dedicated to the Appealed Assessments service.

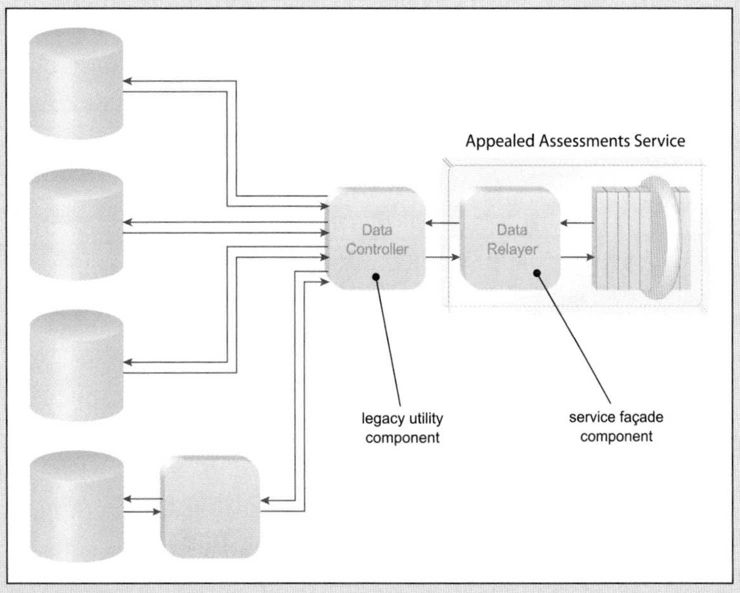

Figure 12.9

The Data Relayer service façade component is designed into the architecture of the Appealed Assessments service. Note the bottom database is accessed via a separate API component. This environment (called "MainAST103") is explained in the Legacy Wrapper (441) case study example.

This architecture further accommodates the expected changes to the Data Controller component. Should any of these changes affect the format or data of the reports generated by the Data Controller functions, the Data Relayer component can be augmented to compensate for these changes so that the Appealed Assessments service contract remains unchanged and so that consumers of this service remain unaffected.

The case study example for Legacy Wrapper (441) continues this scenario by introducing the need to add a legacy wrapper component into the Appealed Assessments service architecture.

NOTE

You may have noticed that in Figure 12.9 Data Controller is further labeled as a "legacy" component. This is because even though it is conceptually similar to a utility service, it is an older component that has not been subjected to service orientation. It therefore is not considered a member of the service inventory but is instead (from an SOA perspective) a part of the legacy environment.

Redundant Implementation

How can the reliability and availability of a service be increased?

Problem	A service that is being actively reused introduces a potential single point of failure that may jeopardize the reliability of all compositions in which it participates if an unexpected error condition occurs.
Solution	Reusable services can be deployed via redundant implementations or with failover support.
Application	The same service implementation is redundantly deployed or supported by infrastructure with redundancy features.
Impacts	Extra governance effort is required to keep all redundant implementations in synch.
Principles	Service Autonomy
Architecture	Service

Table 12.2
Profile summary for the Redundant Implementation pattern.

Problem

Agnostic services are prone to repeated reuse by different service compositions. As a result, each agnostic service can introduce a single point of failure for each composition. Considering the emphasis on repeated reuse within service-orientation, it is easily foreseeable for every complex composition to be comprised of multiple agnostic services that introduce multiple potential points of failure (Figure 12.10).

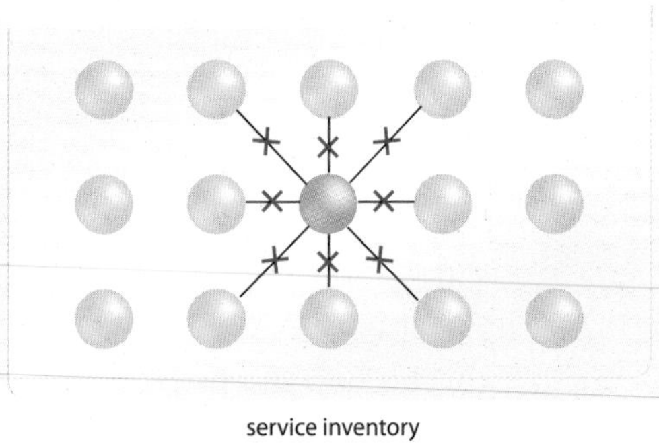

Figure 12.10
When a highly reused service becomes unexpectedly unavailable, it will jeopardize all of its service consumers.

Solution

Multiple implementations of services with high reuse potential or providing critical functionality can be deployed to guarantee high availability and increased reliability, even when unexpected exceptions or outages occur (Figure 12.11).

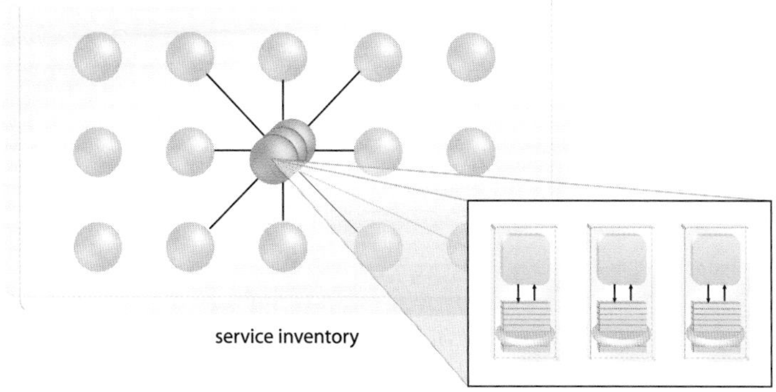

Figure 12.11

Having redundant implementations of agnostic services provides fail-over protection should any one implementation go down.

Application

When services are actually redundantly deployed, there are several ways in which this pattern can be applied:

- Different redundant service implementations can be established for different sets of service consumers.
- One service implementation is designated as the official contact point for consumers, but it is further supported by one or more backup implementations that are used in case of failure or unavailability.

Figure 12.12 illustrates the first variation where the same service is deployed twice; once for access by internal service consumers and again for use by external consumers. This scenario also highlights how this pattern can be applied to various extents. For example, The core service logic may be exactly duplicated in both implementations, but the contracts may, in fact, be different to accommodate the different consumer types, as per Concurrent Contracts (421).

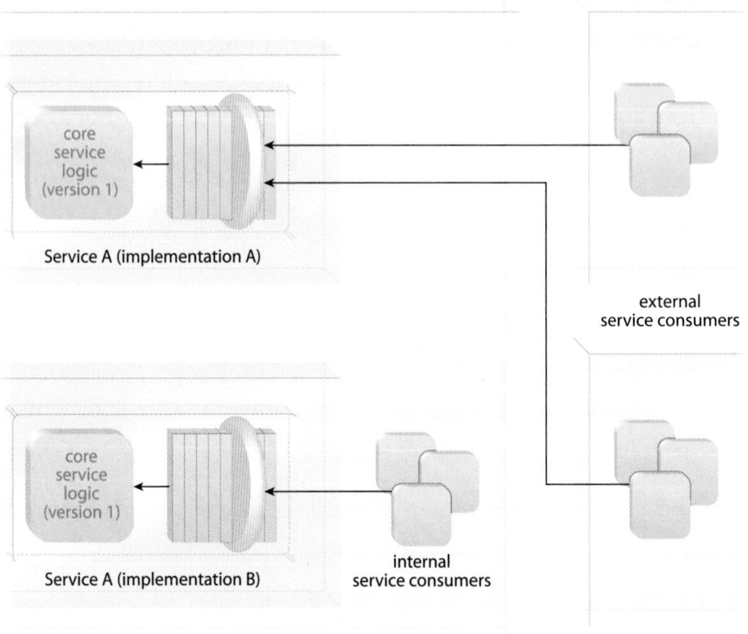

Figure 12.12

Service A has multiple service contracts as well as a redundant implementation, allowing this service to facilitate a wide range of consumer programs.

Impacts

While the application of Redundant Implementation will improve the autonomy, reliability, and scalability of services and the service inventory as a whole, it clearly brings with it some tangible impacts, the foremost of which are increased infrastructure requirements and associated, operational-related governance demands.

For example, additional hardware and administration effort may be needed for each redundantly implemented service and additional governance is required to further keep all duplicated service architectures in synch to whatever extent necessary.

Relationships

Agnostic services naturally have the most concurrent usage demands and therefore have the greatest need for this pattern, which is why it is important for services defined via Entity Abstraction (175) and Utility Abstraction (168). However, even non-agnostic services, such as those realized via Inventory Endpoint (260) may require Redundant Implementation due to reliability demands.

Composition Autonomy (616) will often repeatedly apply Redundant Implementation to ensure that services participating in the composition can achieve increased levels of autonomy and isolation.

Furthermore, establishing a redundant deployment of a service that requires access to shared data sources will usually demand the involvement of Service Data Replication (350).

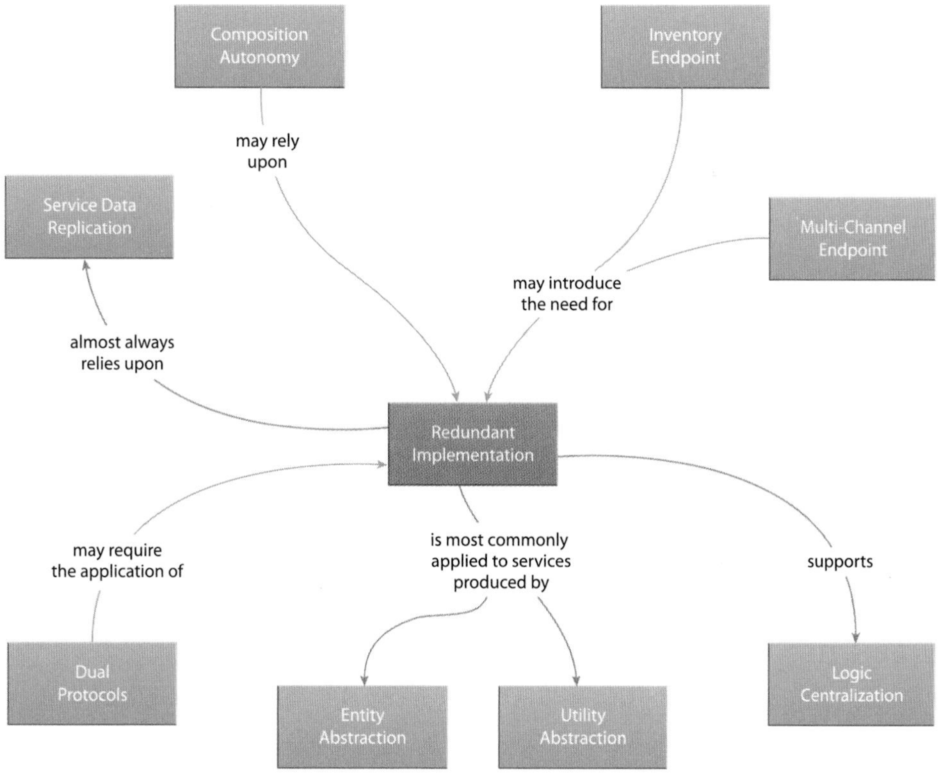

Figure 12.13

Redundant Implementation's support for the Service Autonomy design principle affects several other more specialized (autonomy-related) patterns.

CASE STUDY EXAMPLE

As illustrated in the case study example for Cross-Domain Utility Layer (267), the Alleywood and Tri-Fold service inventories have been architected to share a set of common utility services.

Subsequent to implementing this new cross-domain architecture, some of these utility services naturally became very popular. The Alert service in particular was hit with a consistently high amount of concurrent usage throughout any given work day. Being the service responsible for issuing important notifications when specific pre-defined exception conditions occurred (including policy and security violations), the Alert service was classified as a mission critical part of the overall enterprise architecture.

As a result, a firm requirement was issued, disallowing the Alert service from ever reaching its usage threshold and further requiring chances of service failure be minimized.

To accommodate these requirements, three redundant implementations of the Alert service were created, resulting in four total service implementations. Two were deployed within each environment (Alleywood and Tri-Fold), the second in each environment considered the backup to the first. Intelligent routing agents performed load balancing and failover across each pair of Alert services, as required.

Service Data Replication

How can service autonomy be preserved when services require access to shared data sources?

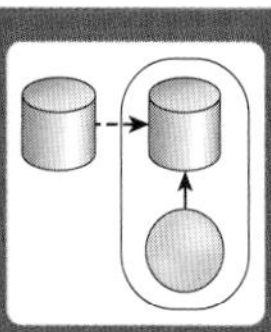

Problem	Service logic can be deployed in isolation to increase service autonomy, but services continue to lose autonomy when requiring access to shared data sources.
Solution	Services can have their own dedicated databases with replication to shared data sources.
Application	An additional database needs to be provided for the service and one or more replication channels need to be enabled between it and the shared data sources.
Impacts	This pattern results in additional infrastructure cost and demands, and an excess of replication channels can be difficult to manage.
Principles	Service Autonomy
Architecture	Inventory, Service

Table 12.3
Profile summary for the Service Data Replication pattern.

Problem

Various steps can be taken to increase the overall autonomy and behavioral predictability of services. The components that underlie custom-developed services, for example, can be isolated from other programs into their own process space or even onto dedicated servers. These are relatively straightforward measures because the components, the service contract, and even the extra hardware that may be required are all new to the environment.

However, what usually stands in the way of achieving high levels of autonomy is the fact that even the most isolated service will likely still need to interact with some central database in order to access or even update business data. These repositories are usually shared not just with other services, but with various parts of the enterprise, including the legacy applications they may have been originally built for (Figure 12.14).

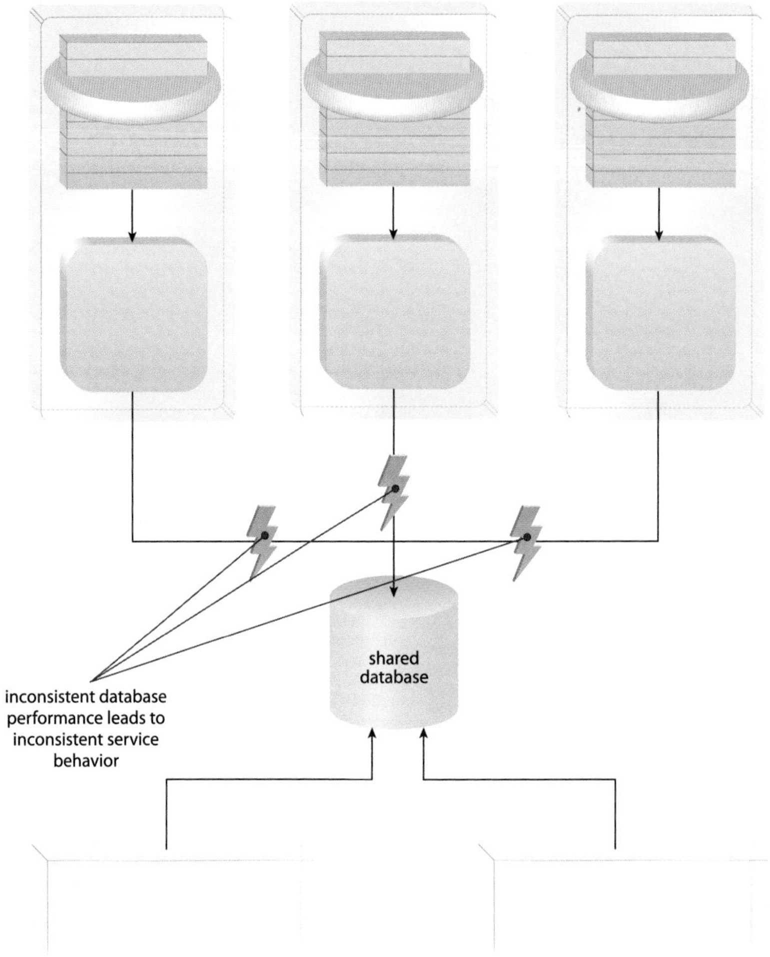
shared
database
inconsistent database
performance leads to
inconsistent service
behavior

Figure 12.14

Multiple services accessing the same shared database will likely encounter locking and performance constraints that will inhibit their individual autonomy.

Although an organization could choose to rebuild their existing data architecture in support of a new service inventory, the cost, effort, and potential disruption of doing so may be prohibitive.

Solution

Service implementations can be equipped with dedicated databases, but instead of creating dedicated data stores, the databases provide replicated data from a central data source. This way, services can access centralized data with increased autonomy while not requiring exclusive ownership over the data (Figure 12.15).

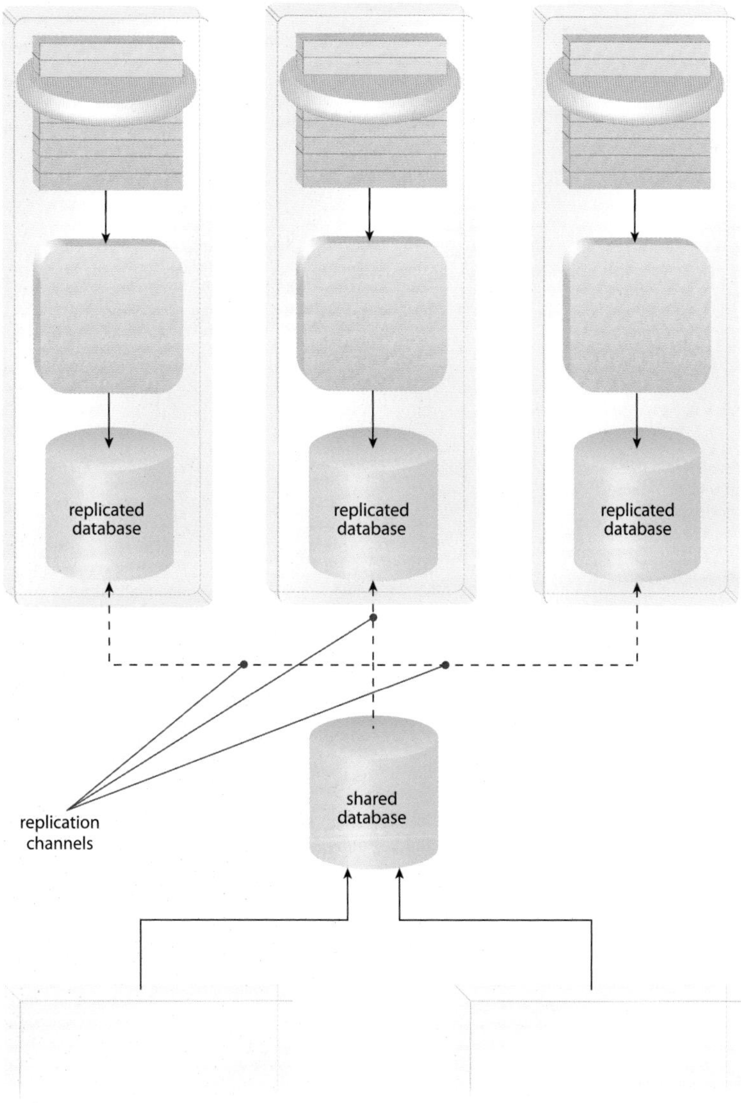

Figure 12.15

By providing each service its own replicated database, autonomy is increased and the strain on the shared central database is also reduced.

Application

This design pattern is especially relevant to agnostic services that are heavily reused and need to facilitate multiple compositions. When this pattern is applied to a large amount of services within a given inventory, it can dramatically reshape the underlying infrastructure of an enterprise's data environment.

Sophisticated data replication architectures may need to be created, and additional design techniques may need to be applied to the databases themselves in order to avoid bottlenecks that can result from an excess of concurrent access and locking. Some replication strategies can even introduce the need for additional satellite databases that provide fully replicated data sets on behalf of a central database but become the contact point for service databases requiring only a subset of the replicated information.

Some services (especially those providing reporting-related capabilities) may only require read access to data, which can be fulfilled by a one-way data replication channel. Most services, though, end up requiring both read and update abilities, which leads to the need for two-way replication.

Furthermore, modern replication technology allows for the runtime transformation of database schemas. As long as the performance and reliability is acceptable, this feature can potentially enable the replicated database to be tuned for individual service architectures.

Impacts

As stated earlier, repeated application of this design pattern can result in costly extensions to the infrastructure in order to support the required data replication in addition to costs associated with all of the additional licenses required for the dedicated service databases. Furthermore, in order to support numerous two-way data replication channels, an enterprise may need to implement a sophisticated and complex data replication architecture, which may require the need to introduce additional, intermediate databases.

Relationships

Service Data Replication is a key pattern applied in support of realizing the Service Autonomy design principle. It ties directly into the application of Redundant Implementation (345) and Composition Autonomy (616) because both aim to reduce service access to shared resources and increase service isolation levels. To access or manage replicated data may further involve some form of legacy interface, as per Legacy Wrapper (441).

Data replication can also play a role in service versioning and decomposition. As shown in Figure 12.11, a replicated data source may be required to support isolated capability logic as defined via Distributed Capability (510), or it may be needed to support already decomposed capability logic resulting from Proxy Capability (497).

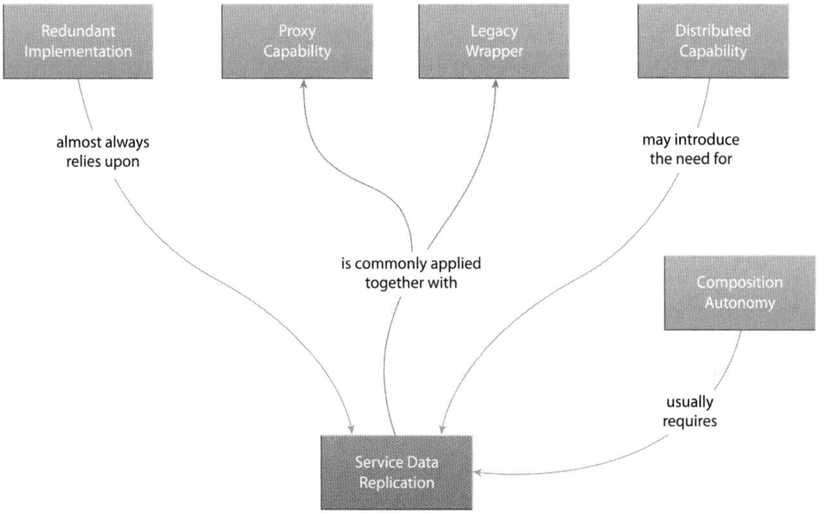

Figure 12.16

Service Data Replication helps reduce the requirements for shared data access and therefore supports a series of autonomy-related patterns.

CASE STUDY EXAMPLE

The FRC Assessment Reports service is responsible for generating and dispensing historical reports for specific registered companies. These reports are used to evaluate and determine annual fines and registration fees (which increase based on the number of violations).

To carry out its reporting functions, this service is required to query the following four databases:

- Registrant Contact (primarily provides company profile information)
- Registrant Activity (includes all incidents, violations, appeals, payments, and other types of historical data)
- Assessment Fees (contains past and current fee schedules and related information)
- Assessment Activity (consists entirely of historical assessments data)

Based on existing design standards that enforce Logic Centralization (136), the first three repositories need to be accessed via the Registrant and Assessment services.

Except for the Assessment Fees database, all of the repositories are used by other legacy applications within the FRC enterprise and now also by other services. Therefore, report generation times can fluctuate, depending on how much shared access is occurring when the Reports service is issuing its queries.

Recently, a new business requirement came about whereby field agents for the FRC would be able to perform assessments on-site while visiting and meeting with registered companies. To perform this task remotely introduced the need for field staff to use portable tablet devices capable of issuing the queries.

To accommodate remote access (especially in regions with limited connectivity) and the increased usage imposed by the new field agent user group, it was decided to improve the response times of assessment report generation by establishing dedicated databases for the Registrant and Assessment Reports services (Figure 12.12).

These databases would be entirely comprised of data replicated from the Registrant Contact, Registrant Activity, and Assessment Activity repositories. Only the subset of data actually required for the reports was replicated and refreshed on a regular basis. The result was a significant increase in autonomy for both Registrant and Assessment Reports services, allowing report generation to be delivered more consistently.

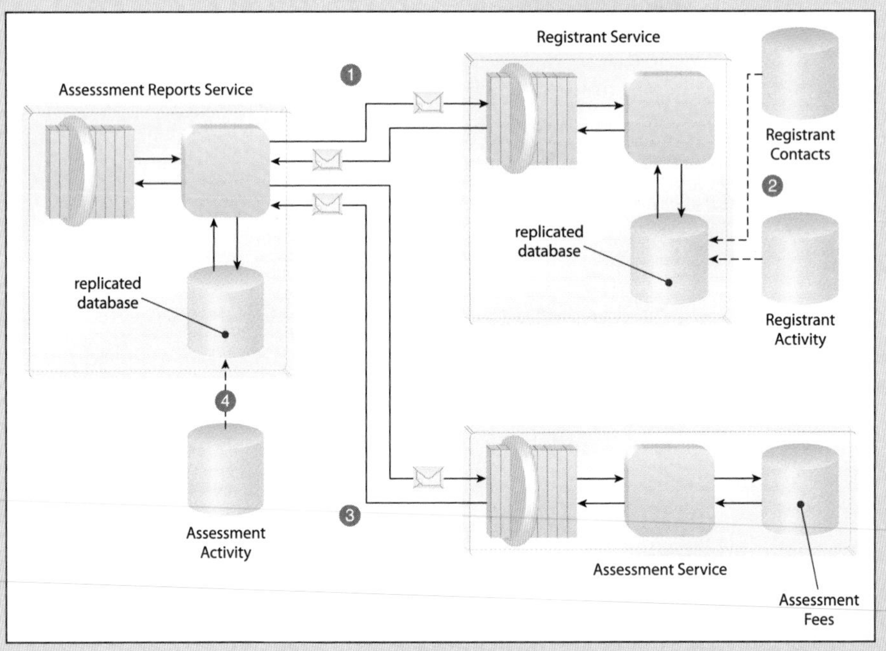

Figure 12.17

The Assessment Reports service first invokes the Registrant service to request Registrant profile and activity data (1). The Registrant Service retrieves this data via a dedicated database comprised of data replicated from the Registrant Contact and Registrant Activity repositories (2). Next, the Assessment Reports service requests assessment fee data via the Assessment service (3). This service already has a dedicated database that does not require replication. Finally, the Assessment Reports service retrieves data from its own replicated Assessment Activity database (4).

Partial State Deferral

How can services be designed to optimize resource consumption while still remaining stateful?

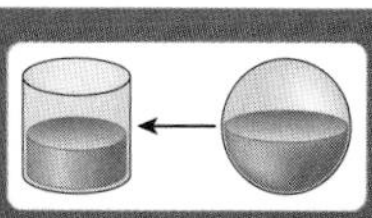

Problem	Service capabilities may be required to store and manage large amounts of state data, resulting in increased memory consumption and reduced scalability.
Solution	Even when services are required to remain stateful, a subset of their state data can be temporarily deferred.
Application	Various state management deferral options exist, depending on the surrounding architecture.
Impacts	Partial state management deferral can add to design complexity and bind a service to the architecture.
Principles	Service Statelessness
Architecture	Inventory, Service

Table 12.4
Profile summary for the Partial State Deferral pattern.

Problem

When services are composed as part of larger runtime activities, there is often a firm need for the service to remain active and stateful while other parts of the activity are being completed.

If the service is required to hold larger amounts of state data, the state management requirements can result in a significant performance drain on the underlying implementation environment. This can be wasteful when only a subset of the data is actually required for the service to accommodate the activity.

In high concurrency scenarios environments, the actual availability of the service can be compromised where accumulated, wasted resources compound to exceed system thresholds (Figure 12.18).

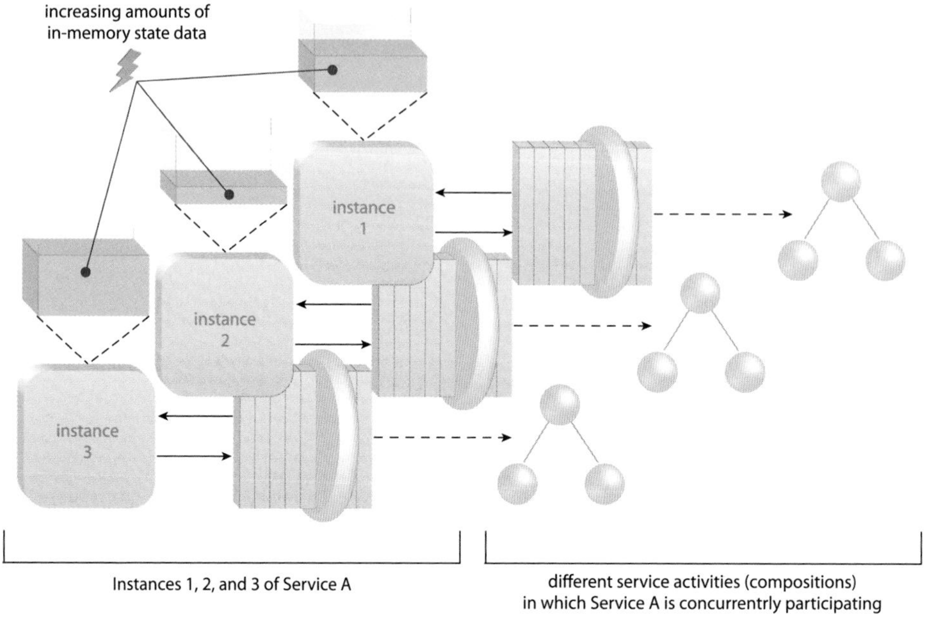

Figure 12.18

In concurrent usage scenarios, stateful services will require that multiple service instances be invoked, each with its own measure of state-related memory consumption requirements.

Solution

The service logic can be designed to defer a *subset* of its state information and management responsibilities to another part of the enterprise. This allows the service to remain stateful while consuming less system resources (Figure 12.19). The deferred state data can be retrieved when required.

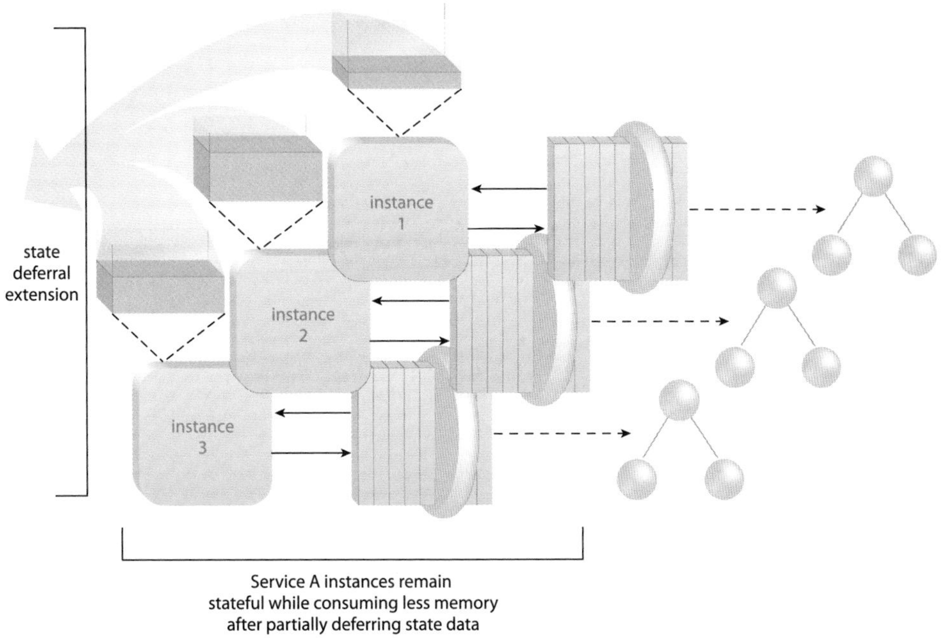
state
deferral
extension
instance
1
instance
2
instance
3
Service A instances remain
stateful while consuming less memory
after partially deferring state data

Figure 12.19

Applying this pattern results in the same amount of concurrent service instances but less overall state-related memory consumption.

Application

This design pattern is almost always applied for the deferral of large amounts of business state data, such as record sets or code lists. The general idea is for these bodies of data to be temporarily off-loaded. To accomplish this, an effective state delegation option is required. This may preclude the use of State Repository (242) unless virtual databases can be utilized to make the writing and retrieval of data efficient and responsive.

Partial State Deferral can be effectively used in conjunction with Stateful Services (248) or State Messaging (557) so that state data transmissions can occur without writing to disk. Any state deferral extension can be used in support of this pattern, as long as the performance hit of transferring state data does not introduce unreasonable lag time to the overall activity so that the extension does not undermine the performance gain sought by the pattern itself.

Services designed with this pattern can be further optimized to minimize lag time by retrieving deferred state data in advance.

> **NOTE**
>
> For descriptions of different types of state data and levels of service statelessness, see SOAGlossary.com.

Impacts

Most state management deferral options require that the service move and then later retrieve the state data from outside of its boundary. This can challenge the preference to keep the service as a self-contained part of an inventory and can also bind its implementation to the technology architecture. The resulting architectural dependency may result in governance challenges should standard state management extensions ever need to be changed.

Furthermore, the routines required to program service logic that carries out runtime state data deferral and retrieval add design and development complexity and effort. Finally, if the aforementioned optimization is not possible, the retrieval of large amounts of business data as part of a sequential processing routine will introduce some extent of lag time.

> **NOTE**
>
> The target state sought by this design pattern corresponds to the *Partially Deferred Memory* statelessness level described in Chapter 11 of *SOA Principles of Service Design*.

Relationships

This specialized pattern has relationships with the other state management-related patterns, namely State Repository (242), Service Grid (254), State Messaging (557), and Stateful Services (248), and also provides a common feature used in orchestration environments, as per Process Centralization (193). The application of Canonical Resources (237) can further affect how this pattern is applied.

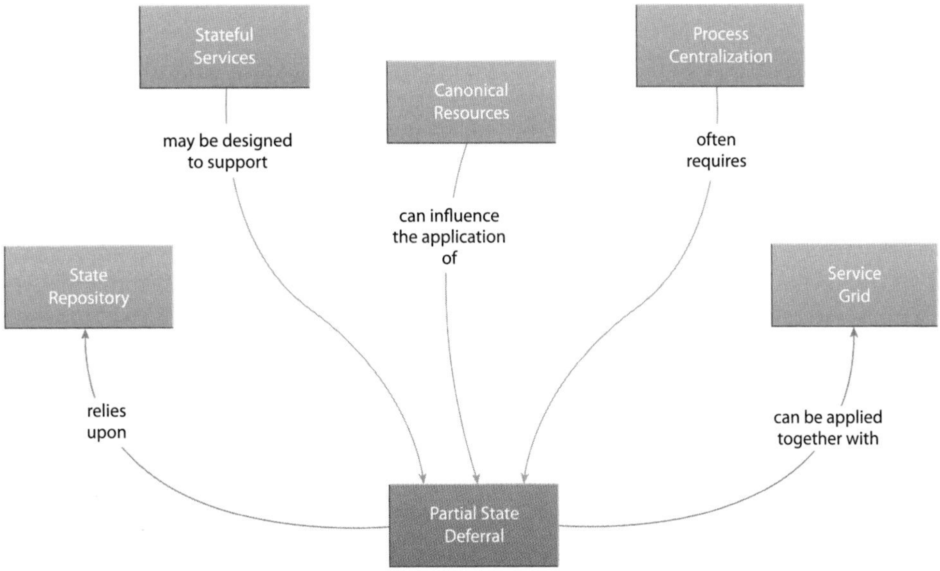

Figure 12.20
Partial State Deferral has basic relationships with other patterns that support or benefit from state management delegation.

CASE STUDY EXAMPLE

The FRC Area Policy Report service (also described in the Composition Autonomy (616) case study example section) is required to access the Area service and then the Policy Checks service, the latter of which is located on a remote server. Because policy data does not change on a frequent basis and because on any given day most queries issued by the Area Policy Report service are generally related to the same areas, an opportunity is discovered to optimize the composition architecture by applying Partial State Deferral.

Essentially, whenever one or more instances of the Area Policy Report task service are active, the retrieved policy data is stored in a local state repository. Because during the course of a normal working day the majority of reports relate to the same group of areas, the stored policy data is useful to most instances of this service.

As shown in Figure 12.21, instances of the Area Policy Report task service remain stateful but are not required to explicitly retrieve or store the policy data.

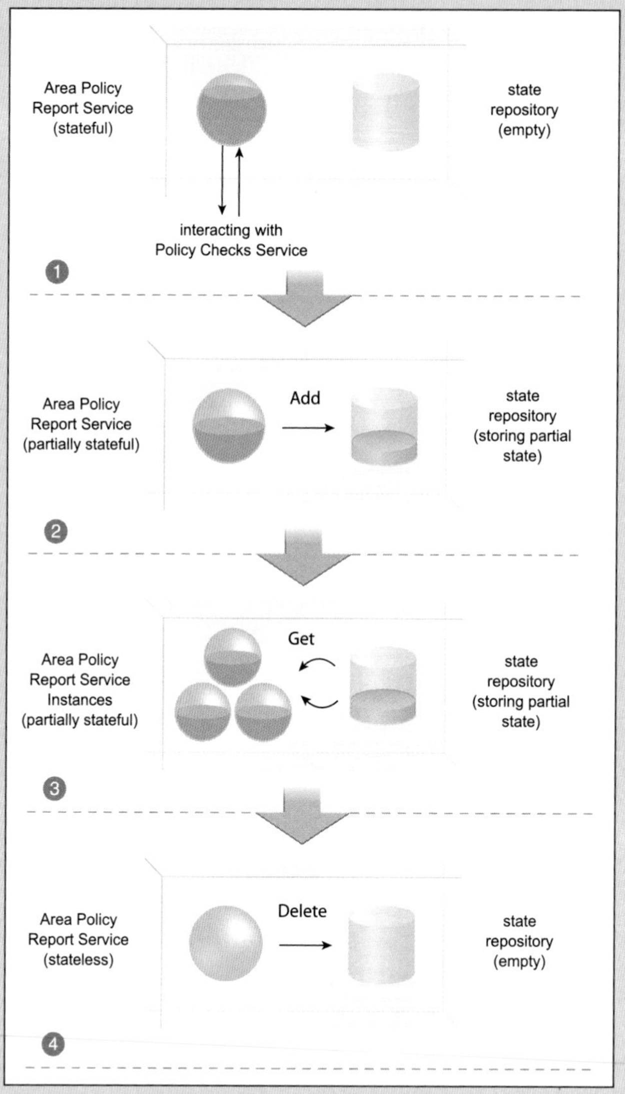

Figure 12.21

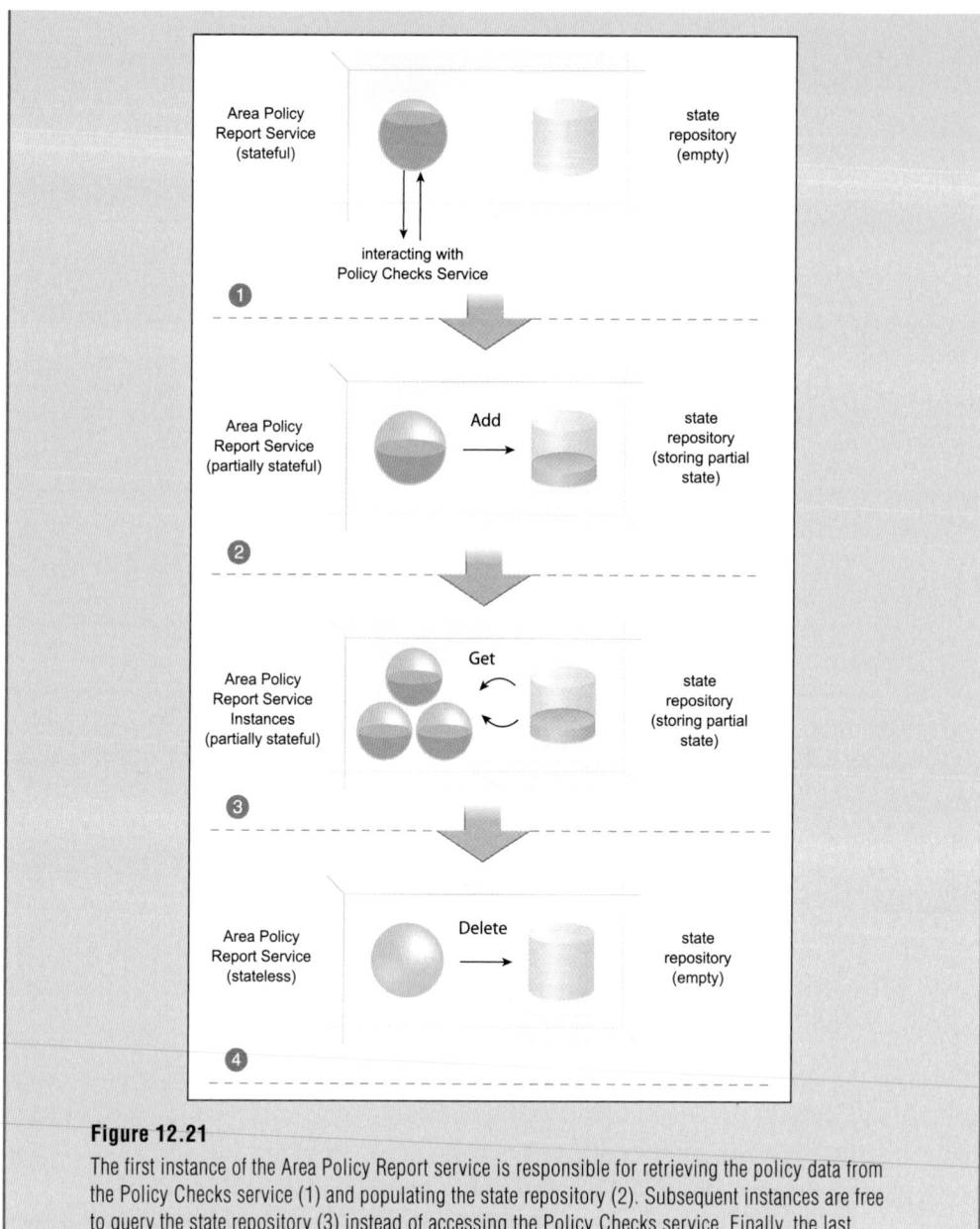

The first instance of the Area Policy Report service is responsible for retrieving the policy data from the Policy Checks service (1) and populating the state repository (2). Subsequent instances are free to query the state repository (3) instead of accessing the Policy Checks service. Finally, the last instance is responsible for clearing the state repository (4).

Partial Validation

By David Orchard, Chris Riley

How can unnecessary data validation be avoided?

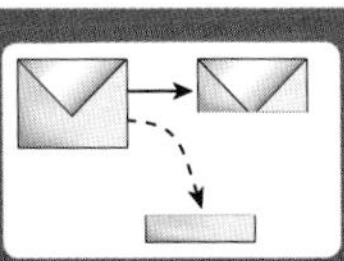

Problem	The generic capabilities provided by agnostic services sometimes result in service contracts that impose unnecessary data and validation upon consumer programs.
Solution	A consumer program can be designed to only validate the relevant subset of the data and ignore the remainder.
Application	The application of this pattern is specific to the technology used for the consumer implementation. For example, with Web services, XPath can be used to filter out unnecessary data prior to validation.
Impacts	Extra design-time effort is required and the additional runtime data filtering-related logic can reduce the processing gains of avoiding unnecessary validation.
Principles	Standardized Service Contract, Service Loose Coupling
Architecture	Composition

Table 12.5
Profile summary for the Partial Validation pattern.

Problem

Agnostic services are designed with high reuse potential in mind, and therefore there is a constant emphasis on providing generic capabilities that can accommodate a wide range of possible consumers.

Although this approach leads to increased reuse opportunities, it can also impose unreasonable validation requirements upon some consumers. A typical example is when a capability is designed to be intentionally coarse-grained in order to provide a broad data set in its response messages. The set of data may only be useful to a subset of the service consumers the remaining of which will be forced to validate the message data upon receiving it but then discard data that is not relevant to their needs (Figure 12.22).

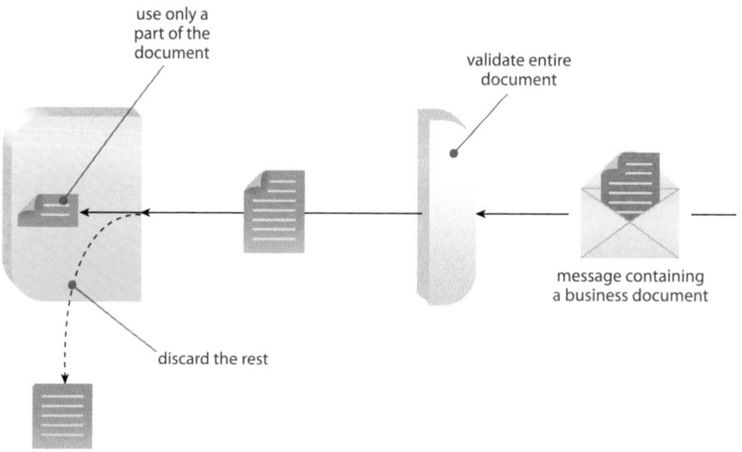

Figure 12.22

When a service consumer requires only a subset of the data provided to it by the agnostic service, it is expected to validate the entire data set (message payload) before discarding the unnecessary message data.

Solution

The service consumer is intentionally designed to not fully comply to the service contract. Instead, its validation logic is tuned to only look for and validate message data relevant to its needs, thereby ignoring the rest (Figure 12.23). This reduces consumer processing requirements and decreases the extent to which some consumers need to couple themselves to the service contract.

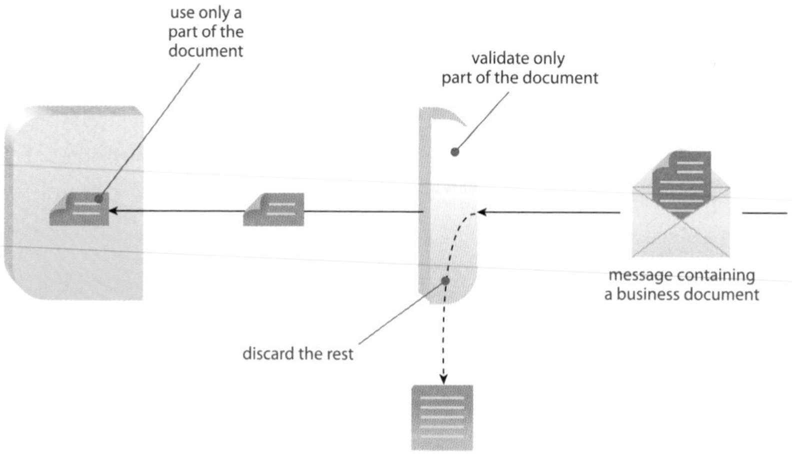

Figure 12.23

Because the irrelevant data is ignored prior to validation, it is discarded earlier and avoids imposing unnecessary validation-related processing upon the consumer.

Application

Partial Validation is applied within the consumer program implementation. Custom routines are added to allow for the regular receipt and parsing of incoming service messages, while then avoiding actual validation of irrelevant data.

A typical algorthim used by these routines would be as follows:

1. Receive response message from service.
2. Identify the parts of the message that are relevant to the consumer's processing requirements.
3. Validate the parts identified in Step 2 and discard the balance of the message contents.
4. If valid, retain the parts identified in Step 2. Otherwise, reject the message.

Partial Validation routines can be located within the core consumer business logic or they can be abstracted into an event-driven intermediary, as per Service Agent (543). When services assume the consumer role by composing other services, this type of logic may also be suitable for abstraction via Service Façade (333).

Impacts

The custom programming required by this pattern can add to the design complexity of the overall consumer program logic. Furthermore, the extra processing required by the consumer to look for and extract only relevant data can impose its own processing overhead.

Relationships

Depending on how Partial Validation is applied, it may make sense to combine it with Service Agent (543) or Service Façade (333). Although not directly related to the application of Validation Abstraction (429), these two patterns do share common goals.

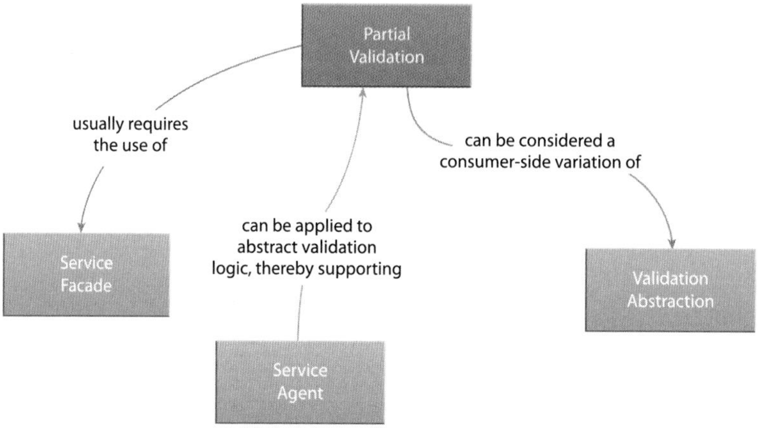

Figure 12.24

Partial Validation introduces internal, consumer-side processing logic and therefore has limited relationships with other patterns.

CASE STUDY EXAMPLE

The FRC Assessment Reports service (described earlier in the Service Data Replication (350) case study example) is required to access the Registrant service in order to request registrant profile data for one of its reports (see Figure 12.12). These reports are often parameter-driven, meaning that they can vary in scope and content depending on the reporting parameters provided to the Assessment Reports service by a given consumer.

Because of this variance in report content and because the Assessment Reports service is always required to invoke the same Get operation that returns entire profile documents, it often ends up with more registrant data than it actually needs. Its original design simply accepted and validated incoming messages and then made the entire message contents available to the report generation routines. However, as the amount of concurrent usage increases, so does the complexity of some reports, leading to increased resource requirements for this service.

Due to the enterprise-wide initiative to reduce infrastructure costs, architects do not receive funding to apply Redundant Implementation (345) in order to establish a second implementation of this service for load balancing purposes. This forces them to revisit the service design in order to investigate optimization opportunities.

They soon discover that the internal service logic can be refactored by applying Partial Validation. This enables the service to continue performing its report generation logic while decreasing its processing and memory consumption due to a dramatic reduction in runtime message validation.

UI Mediator

By Clemens Utschig-Utschig, Berthold Maier, Bernd Trops, Hajo Normann, Torsten Winterberg

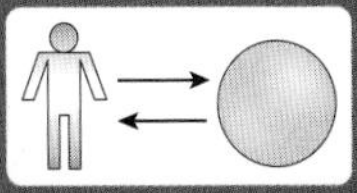

How can a service-oriented solution provide a consistent, interactive user experience?

Problem	Because the behavior of individual services can vary depending on their design, runtime usage, and the workload required to carry out a given capability, the consistency with which a service-oriented solution can respond to requests originating from a user-interface can fluctuate, leading to a poor user experience.
Solution	Establish mediator logic solely responsible for ensuring timely interaction and feedback with user-interfaces and presentation logic.
Application	A utility mediator service or service agent is positioned as the initial recipient of messages originating from the user-interface. This mediation logic responds in a timely and consistent manner regardless of the behavior of the underling solution.
Impacts	The mediator logic establishes an additional layer of processing that can add to the required runtime processing.
Principles	Service Loose Coupling
Architecture	Composition

Table 12.6
Profile summary for the UI Mediator pattern.

Problem

Service-oriented solutions are commonly designed as service compositions that may be comprised of services with varying runtime behaviors and processing demands. When the process being automated by the solution is driven by human interaction via user-interfaces, the quality of the user experience can vary due to these behavioral and environmental irregularities.

Whereas a human user expects immediate responses to requests issued via the user-interface, the underlying services may be not be designed or able to provide these responses in a synchronous and timely manner (Figure 12.25). Poor or inconsistent user experience can lead to a decrease in the usage and overall success of the solution.

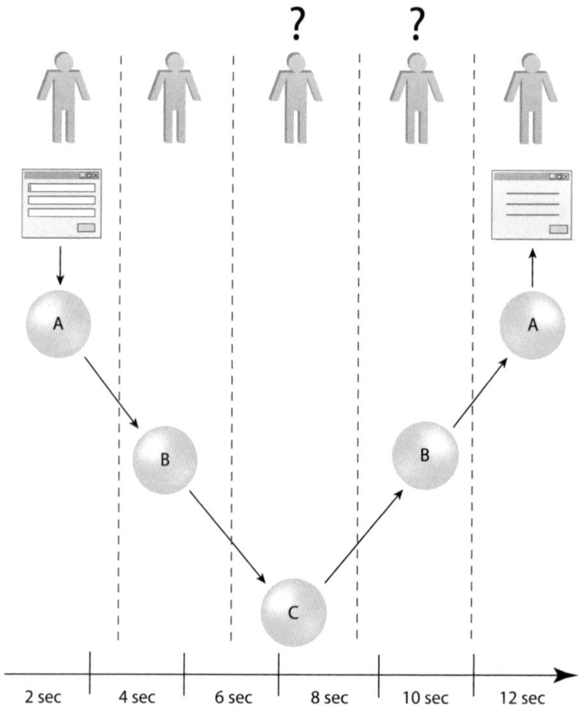

Figure 12.25

While services A, B, and C require several seconds to automate a task initiated via a user-interface, the human user receives no indication as to the progress of the task and is left waiting until a result is finally displayed.

Solution

A mediator service is positioned between a service or service composition and the front-end solution user-interfaces. It is responsible for providing the user with continuous feedback and for gracefully facilitating various runtime conditions so that the underlying processing of the services does not affect the quality of the user experience (Figure 12.26).

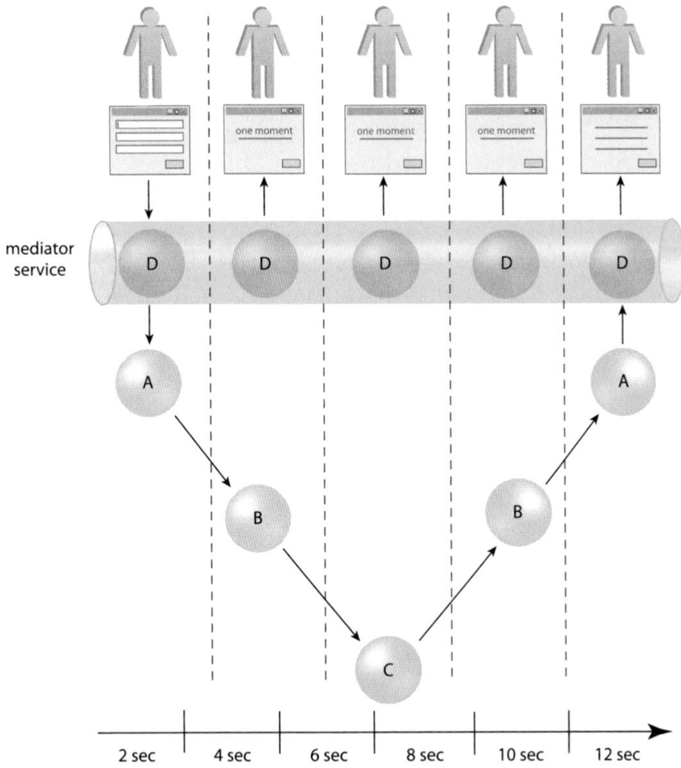

Figure 12.26

The mediator service (D) regularly updates the user interface while services A, B, and C work behind-the-scenes to complete the task.

Application

There are two common methods of applying this pattern:

- Build a mediator service with its own service contract.
- Build a mediator service agent.

The first approach requires that a mediator utility service be created and that the user-interface be designed to bind solely with this service for the duration of a specific task. The mediator service exposes a generic contract with weakly typed capabilities that simply relay request and response messages between the user-interface and underlying service(s). This type of mediator service will contain logic that determines how and when to interact with the user-interface independently.

The second approach requires that this pattern be applied together with Service Agent (543). When locating mediator logic within event-driven agents, request and response messages between the user-interface and services are transparently intercepted, triggering events that kick-off the mediation logic. Agents must be designed to remain stateful during the completion of the task so that they can interact with the user-interface as required.

Common user-interface mediation routines include:

- displaying forms or pages with a progress or status indicator while services are processing a given request
- displaying forms that request additional data from the user
- routing a user task to the next step independently from underlying service processing
- simulating synchronous human-to-solution exchanges while underlying service activities are carried out asynchronously
- gracefully responding to exception or time-out conditions

The mediator essentially preserves a constant correlation between a user session and the process being automated by services. For this purpose, the mediator service or agent may even maintain a correlation ID that is assigned to all incoming and outgoing messages. However, in order for mediation logic to remain agnostic, it will generally not contain any business process-specific rules or logic. Its capabilities are limited to generic interaction routines.

Impacts

When delivering the mediator logic as a service or a service agent, additional runtime processing is added to the automation of the overall business task due to the insertion of the mediator service layer within the overall composition (and also due to the frequent interaction carried out independently by the mediator logic).

Furthermore, when the mediator exists as a service with its own published contract, user-interfaces are required to bind directly to and interact with the mediator service during the span of an entire business task. This naturally decouples the user-interfaces from the underlying service composition, which can be advantageous if the business logic is subject to change. However, if the mediation logic is agnostic and positioned as part of a reusable utility service, the parent composition logic may actually be responsible for controlling its involvement, leading to a tighter coupling.

Relationships

Because it represents a form of utility logic, UI Mediator is based on Utility Abstraction (168). Service Agent (543) simply provides an optional implementation medium for this pattern.

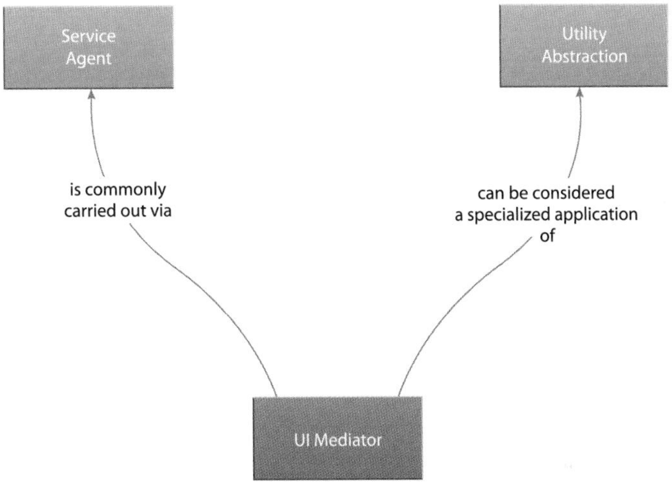

Figure 12.27
As a specialized utility service, UI Mediator has few relationships.

CASE STUDY EXAMPLE

Prior to the purchase of Alleywood Lumber, McPherson had been carrying out an ongoing BPM initiative to help automate existing manual processes and to optimize outdated automated processes. With the assimilation of Alleywood operations, McPherson analysts subject a series of former Alleywood business processes to their established business modeling practices.

The first process relates to the online commercial and retail sale of lumber. Alleywood has a simple Web site in place that allows clients to perform the following tasks sequentially:

1. Initiate a search on the availability of different types of lumber.
2. Assemble an order from the available items.
3. Indicate the shipping details.

The Web site contains scripts that run on the Web server and integrate with an outdated legacy database in which lumber items are stored. Because this database is shared throughout the Alleywood enterprise, its performance and response time can vary dramatically. This primarily affects the time it takes to complete Step 1.

Analysts investigate the history of this commerce site by studying usage logs. After consolidating some of the statistics using a special tool, they discover that the search action can take up to 60 seconds to complete. They further find out that 30% of users who initiate a search abandon the Web site when the query time exceeds 20 seconds, whereas when the query time is less than 5 seconds, 90% of searches result in actual orders.

These metrics are compiled into a report that provides a series of recommendations as to how the online lumber ordering site can be improved, with an emphasis on user experience. This report is passed on to the architecture team, which responds by making a number of changes:

- Service Data Replication (350) is applied to establish a dedicated database for the site.
- A Retail Lumber service is created to provide standardized data access to the database.
- UI Mediator is applied using Service Agent (543) to ensure that long query times or unexpected erratic behavior do not affect the user experience.

The mediator logic contains the following built-in rules:

- If there is no response from the Retail Lumber service within 5 seconds, display a progress indicator page in the user's browser.
- If there is no response from the Retail Lumber service after 15 seconds, display a Web page with a message explaining that the system is currently not available but that the requested information will be e-mailed to the user shortly (the e-mail address is captured as part of the login credentials required to access the site).
- If the Retail Lumber service responds with no data, display the original form along with a message indicating that different search parameters must be provided.

The mediator agent helps establish an improved user experience that appears to be synchronous and interactive, regardless of the behavior of the Retail Lumber service and its underlying database.

Chapter 13

Service Security Patterns

Exception Shielding

Message Screening

Trusted Subsystem

Service Perimeter Guard

Because service-oriented solutions are typically composed of aggregated services, each moving part within a composition architecture can become a potential target for a security breach. The individual service architectures themselves therefore often need to be equipped with extra controls that enable them to withstand common forms of attacks from malicious consumers.

The following chapter provides four patterns that extend service design in support of increased protection from security threats. Exception Shielding (376) ensures that any error or exception information generated by a service is safe before it is released to consumers. Message Screening (381) is more concerned with inbound data as it provides additional logic that checks messages received from consumers for potentially harmful content. Trusted Subsystem (387) establishes a mechanism whereby consumers cannot directly access service resources with their credentials, and Service Perimeter Guard (394) introduces a new type of utility service that carries out common security functions for external consumers on behalf of internal services.

CASE STUDY BACKGROUND

After Alleywood's reengineered online Lumber Ordering system (described in the case study example for UI Mediator (366) from Chapter 12) is released, McPherson decides to promote it beyond local clients, as part of an international marketing campaign. As a result, the online ordering site attracts many new visitors from foreign regions. Some visit the site just to check out Alleywood's retail inventory, while others find the costs of retail lumber attractive enough to place orders that need to be shipped to remote locations.

However, an unexpected side-effect of the site's increased exposure is an increase in attempted attacks. After just a few days online, the ordering site begins to crash on a daily basis. Days later, the frequency of system failure increases to several times a day. Alleywood architects scramble to find out why this is happening, and they work closely together with McPherson security specialists to investigate the event and usage logs.

What is subsequently revealed is a series of vulnerabilities in the service architecture of the Retail Lumber service. The security team insists that the site and compromised

resources be taken off-line until this issue is resolved. They are concerned that hackers will gain enough environmental information to attack other parts of the enterprise.

As a result of a thorough threat analysis, Alleywood architects propose a site redesign, in which these vulnerabilities in the Retail Lumber service architecture are addressed using well-known service security patterns (as explained in the upcoming examples in this chapter).

Exception Shielding

By Jason Hogg, Don Smith, Fred Chong, Tom Hollander, Wojtek Kozaczynski, Larry Brader, Nelly Delgado, Dwayne Taylor, Lonnie Wall, Paul Slater, Sajjad Nasir Imran, Pablo Cibraro, Ward Cunningham

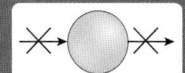

How can a service prevent the disclosure of information about its internal implementation when an exception occurs?

Problem	Unfiltered exception data output by a service may contain internal implementation details that can compromise the security of the service and its surrounding environment.
Solution	Potentially unsafe exception data is "sanitized" by replacing it with exception data that is safe by design before it is made available to consumers.
Application	This pattern can be applied at design time by reviewing and altering source code or at runtime by adding dynamic sanitization routines.
Impacts	Sanitized exception information can make the tracking of errors more difficult due to the lack of detail provided to consumers.
Principles	Service Abstraction
Architecture	Service

Table 13.1
Profile summary for the Exception Shielding pattern.

Problem

When an exception condition occurs inside a service implementation, the service may issue a response message to convey the exception to the consumer. As shown in Figure 13.1, the response message may inadvertently contain unsafe information that can be exploited to attack the service and its surrounding environment.

For example, a detailed fault message can disclose information about the resources accessed by the service logic that threw the exception. An attacker could then deliberately cause the service to throw an unhandled exception in an attempt to obtain and exploit sensitive information, such as connection strings, server names, SQL queries, XPath commands, stack traces, and data schemas.

Furthermore, if an exception is expected, a pre-defined error message with information about the cause of the fault could be returned to the consumer. Such a message may have been designed by an architect or developer without knowledge of its security implications and may therefore also contain sensitive information that poses a security risk.

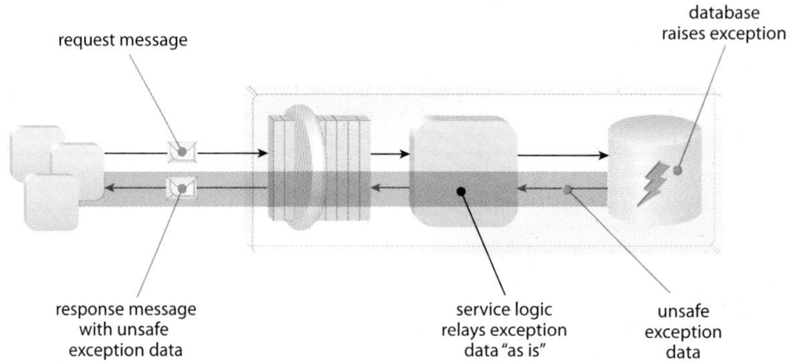

Figure 13.1

Subsequent to an exception, the service logic passes on potentially unsafe information to service consumers.

Solution

Unsafe exception-related data is "sanitized," a process by which this information is identified and replaced with exception information that is safe by design. Sanitized exception messages do not contain sensitive data nor a detailed stack trace, either of which might reveal potentially harmful details about the service's inner workings. After a service is subjected to a sanitization process, it is limited to returning only those exception details that are deemed safe (Figure 13.2).

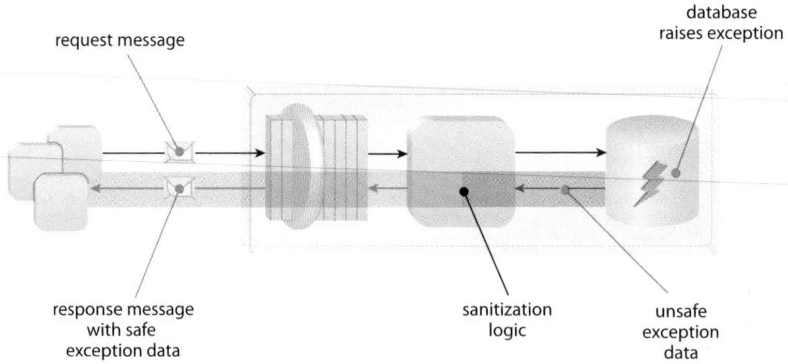

Figure 13.2

Potentially unsafe information is sanitized by routines added to the service logic, thereby releasing only safe exception information to service consumers.

The exception sanitization process can be further formalized, allowing output messages containing exception details to be standardized across services. This enables maintenance staff to troubleshoot and centrally manage exceptions on an inventory-wide basis.

Application

Sanitization routines can be applied at design-time during the initial service delivery or as part of a service refactoring effort. This results in pre-defined exception details that are considered "safe by design." However, this pattern is also focused on the incorporation of runtime exception shielding logic.

The basic exception shielding process with runtime sanitization logic occurs as follows:

1. The consumer submits a request message to the service.
2. The service attempts to process the request and throws an exception. The exception may contain safe or unsafe information.
3. Exception shielding routines residing in the service logic check the exception information. If it is safe by design, it is already considered sanitized and is returned to the consumer unmodified. If the exception is identified as unsafe, it is replaced with safe exception information.
4. The service returns the safe exception message to the consumer.

Exception shielding routines are commonly built into individual services because it is generally preferable to keep shielding logic as close to the service as possible. For this purpose, the shielding routines may be part of the core service logic or separated into an intra-service agent or handler.

This pattern can also be applied in combination with Utility Abstraction (168) in order to centralize common shielding logic into a utility service that can be reused by other services. However, this approach would usually be used as a "safety net" to complement existing exception shielding logic within the service.

Note that an unhandled exception can be wrapped by another exception. The exception shielding logic needs to be sophisticated enough to ensure that all outer exceptions are checked for wrapped exceptions before allowing them to be returned to the consumer.

Unsanitized exception data can also be safely captured in an event log, allowing maintenance staff to identify and troubleshoot exceptions. This type of information can assist with intrusion detection and incident response, and monitoring tools can further capture and respond to safe exception information by automatically notifying administrators when

these exceptions occur. The event log itself must, of course, be secured to prevent unauthorized access.

This same information can also be used by developers to diagnose design-time errors. In some cases, tools might require that a given fault message contains an ID that help desk staff can use to more effectively troubleshoot and trace problems. The exception shielding logic can be designed to generate such an identifier for each exception.

Impacts

Because the exception information provided to consumers is sanitized, it lacks details that can be valuable when trying to track or trace error information. Often, consumers are given a GUID that must subsequently be searched for in error logs in order to retrieve exception details necessary to resolve certain exceptions. Being able to dynamically turn exception shielding functions on and off can help alleviate these situations.

Also while exception shielding logic can increase the amount of runtime filtering and processing the service must perform, because this processing is only instantiated when exceptions actually occur, the impact is trivial and should not affect regular service operation.

Furthermore, developers building exception shielding logic require an understanding of the range of potential security threats this logic is intended to protect the service from. Otherwise, incomplete or ineffective exception logic can lead to a false sense of security.

Relationships

Exception Shielding represents a form of utility logic that can be further supported by Service Agent (543), Utility Abstraction (168), and Service Perimeter Guard (394) when isolating it especially for the purpose of reuse across services.

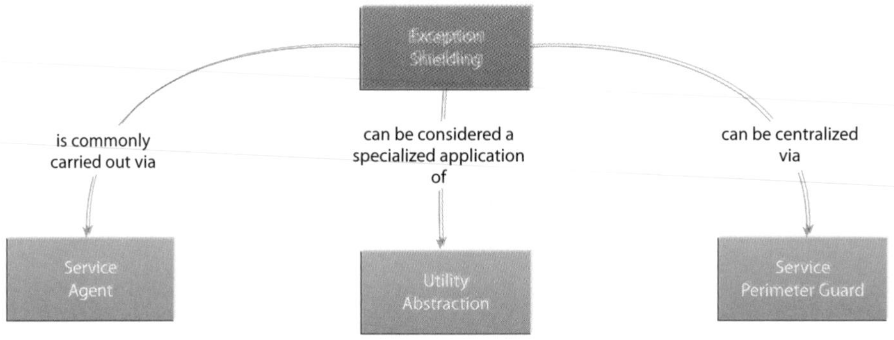

Figure 13.3
Exception Shielding shares the same types of relationships as other utility-centric patterns.

CASE STUDY EXAMPLE

External hackers have been regularly triggering exceptions in the Retail Lumber service that accesses Alleywood's retail database. The database had been responding by providing detailed information about the nature of the exception and a number of environmental details about the surrounding implementation. The Retail Lumber service was unwittingly relaying these details to malicious consumers via SOAP fault messages.

As part of the redesign project, Alleywood architects incorporate runtime exception shielding routines to prevent unintentional information within unhandled exceptions from being exposed externally. Because Alleywood's operations team requires exception information in order to troubleshoot legitimate issues, these routines first write exception information to a secure central log where it can be analyzed. Each of these log entries includes a unique identifier that is included with the sanitized general error message that replaces each exception. When partner organizations contact the help desk, this number can be used to trace back to the specific exception that caused the issue.

Alleywood was fortunate because the application server upon which their Web services were running allowed for pre and post-message processing logic to be inserted declaratively into the SOAP message processing pipeline. As a result, Alleywood was able to standardize the exception shielding logic and then reconfigure each of their services to utilize this new behavior.

Message Screening

By Jason Hogg, Don Smith, Fred Chong, Tom Hollander, Wojtek Kozaczynski, Larry Brader, Nelly Delgado, Dwayne Taylor, Lonnie Wall, Paul Slater, Sajjad Nasir Imran, Pablo Cibraro, Ward Cunningham

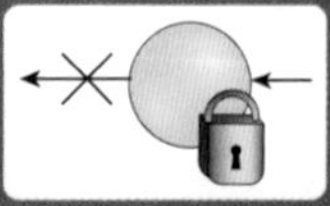

How can a service be protected from malformed or malicious input?

Problem	An attacker can transmit messages with malicious or malformed content to a service, resulting in undesirable behavior.
Solution	The service is equipped or supplemented with special screening routines that assume that all input data is harmful until proven otherwise.
Application	When a service receives a message, it makes a number of checks to screen message content for harmful data.
Impacts	Extra runtime processing is required with each message exchange, and the screening logic requires additional, specialized routines to process binary message content, such as attachments. It may also not be possible to check for all possible forms of harmful content.
Principles	Standardized Service Contract
Architecture	Service

Table 13.2
Profile summary for the Message Screening pattern.

Problem

If a service-bound message contains invalid data, it can cause the service or other downstream systems that process the received data to behave in an undesirable manner (Figure 13.4). This data may be accidentally inserted by a consumer or intentionally added by an attacker.

> **NOTE**
>
> Sending harmful content to a program in this way is known as an *injection attack*.

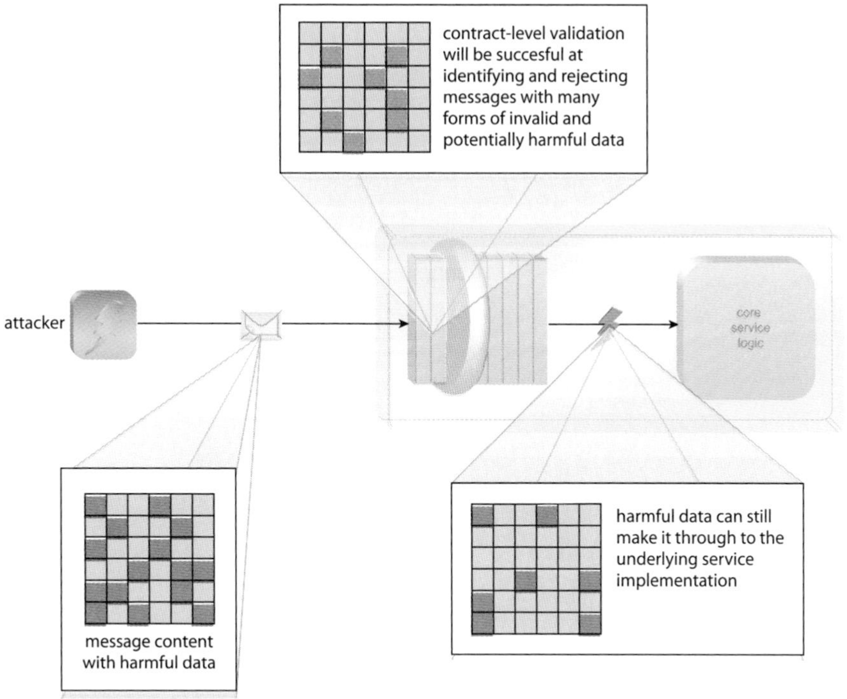

Figure 13.4

Parts of the message content transmitted by an attacker can make their way through to the service implementation. (The red squares represent potentially harmful data.)

Solution

When designing the service logic, it is assumed that all input data is harmful until proven otherwise. Specialized threat screening routines are therefore added to the internal service logic. The routines in this logic enforce well-defined policies that specify which parts of a message are required for the service to process the request. Because these filtering routines reside within the service, it remains protected without reliance on consumer-side validation logic (Figure 13.5).

Application

Applying this pattern requires that the necessary message screening routines be added to the service in such a manner that they are invoked when input data is received by any service capability. These routines will generally be designed to perform a set of standard screening tasks, such as:

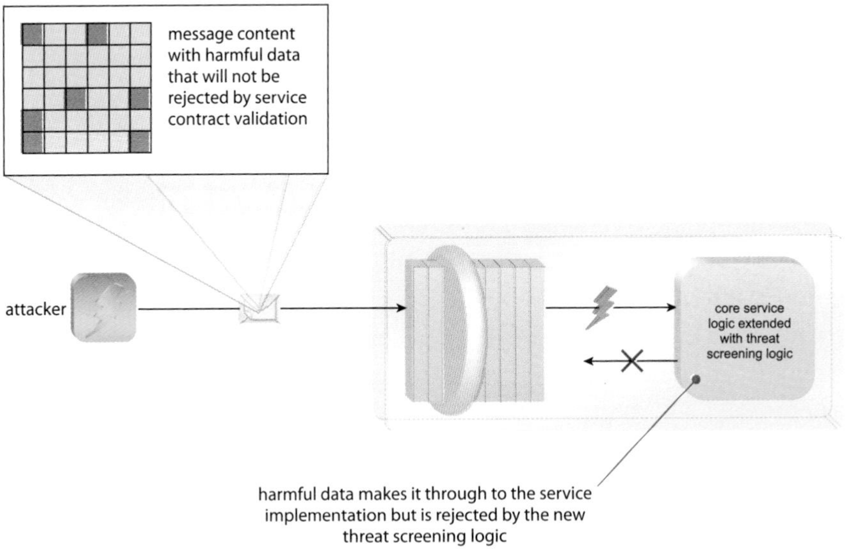
message content
with harmful data
that will not be
rejected by service
contract validation
attacker
core service
logic extended
with threat
screening logic
harmful data makes it through to the service
implementation but is rejected by the new
threat screening logic

Figure 13.5

Because the service logic is equipped with extra message screening routines, malicious or malformed data can still be detected and rejected before it has a chance to do harm.

- Comparing the size of the request message against the maximum allowable size that is specified for request messages for a given capability.
- Parsing the entire request message for malicious content. (For Web services, malicious content could be placed in either the SOAP message header or body, so both would need to be checked.)

When designing threat screening logic, a number of considerations need to be taken into account, as follows:

- If a message is encrypted with message layer security, it may not be possible to inspect data for malicious content unless the message is decrypted beforehand or the screening logic has access to the decryption key.
- Custom threat screening logic is required to check binary message content, such as attachments. Such logic must be capable of recognizing each type of binary attachment that it encounters to ensure that it is free of malicious content. This form of binary data validation will often require the involvement of anti-virus filters or similar mechanisms.

- Message screening logic must be very efficient when it conducts its validation checks. Otherwise, it can turn into a system bottleneck and might itself become the target of a denial of service attack. A balance needs to be attained whereby the maximum message size is large enough to allow legitimate messages to be accepted, but small enough to prevent attacks.
- There is the option to combine this pattern with Utility Abstraction (168) or Service Agent (543) so as to isolate message screening logic into a separate utility service or an external intermediary service agent. However, this can establish a potential single point of failure that may become the target of aggressive attacks. It is often preferable to keep exception shielding logic close to the service and to consider this approach as a "safety net."
- XML schemas can be further enhanced in support of this pattern by reducing the use of coarse-grained data types (such as `xsd:string`), which can be more prone to accepting a wider range of potentially harmful data. Similarly, XML message payloads that contain a CDATA field can be used to inject illegal characters that are ignored by the XML parser. If CDATA fields are necessary, they need to be inspected for malicious content.

So far we have been focusing on the receipt of input data via request messages issued by service consumers. It is also worth noting that harmful data could be obtained by the service implementation while it is responding to a legitimate consumer request message.

If the service logic, for example, receives data via another (less secure) service or by accessing non-secured data sources, it may inadvertently become a potential carrier of malicious input. In this case, it is the consumer receiving the response message from the service that is at risk. This scenario can be mitigated by applying this pattern to data received by the service implementation from non-trusted sources.

Impacts

Building and maintaining message screening logic requires specialized skills to ensure that as many threats as possible can be checked for. Depending on the extent to which screening logic is designed and how well the routines are actually built, this pattern may be only partially effective and could easily lead to a false sense of security. It is therefore important to design message screening routines in conjunction with a formal threat model.

Furthermore, the extra runtime processing required to thoroughly check incoming data for a range of security threats can be demanding and may introduce latency. This impact can

be somewhat reduced by deferring this logic to a highly autonomous and scalable utility service.

Depending on the nature of the surrounding infrastructure, it may simply not be possible to perform all desired checks. For example, service capabilities that accept binary attachments may not be able to validate every type of potential attachment format.

Relationships

Because it represents another form of utility-centric processing logic, Message Screening shares the same relationships as Exception Shielding (376).

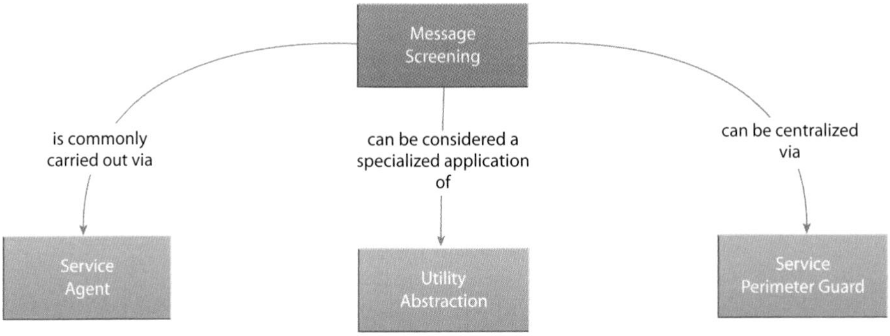

Figure 13.6

The potential pattern relationships of Message Screening are all associated with its separation and isolation because this form of logic can often be reused.

CASE STUDY EXAMPLE

In addition to the exceptions raised during the attacks explained in the previous case study example, Alleywood's Retail Lumber service had also been receiving a range of messages that contained both malformed and malicious content. Some of this data had been accidentally sent by a malfunctioning consumer; however, most was clearly part of a coordinated injection attack on the service. This part of the attack was attributed to the majority of problems that eventually occurred because so much harmful data was readily accepted as valid input.

A McPherson security specialist works with the development team in order to establish a set of screening routines that would be carried out with each incoming message received by the Retail Lumber service. Architects get involved, and soon a discussion

ensues about whether it would make more sense to abstract this logic into its own utility service that could be reused by the Retail Lumber service and others.

Alleywood architects feel this approach would make sense from an inventory standardization and normalization perspective and consider a number of different options including developing a new utility service that would implement the screening logic. Subsequent to some further modeling effort it is revealed that this design would require that consumers first call this service prior to the Retail Lumber service. The McPherson security consultant quickly points out that services cannot trust consumers in this manner.

As a result, the development team is asked to proceed with incorporating the screening logic directly into the Retail Lumber service design. Rather than having each service implement this functionality into its business logic, the architects create a single message validation routine and then declaratively specify that this logic use the same message processing interception mechanism within which exception shielding logic is applied—only this time the message screening logic is run before the message is processed.

Trusted Subsystem

By Jason Hogg, Don Smith, Fred Chong, Tom Hollander, Wojtek Kozaczynski, Larry Brader, Nelly Delgado, Dwayne Taylor, Lonnie Wall, Paul Slater, Sajjad Nasir Imran, Pablo Cibraro, Ward Cunningham

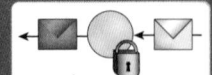

How can a consumer be prevented from circumventing a service and directly accessing its resources?

Problem	A consumer that accesses backend resources of a service directly can compromise the integrity of the resources and can further lead to undesirable forms of implementation coupling.
Solution	The service is designed to use its own credentials for authentication and authorization with backend resources on behalf of consumers.
Application	Depending on the nature of the underlying resources, various design options and security technologies can be applied.
Impacts	If this type of service is compromised by attackers or unauthorized consumers, it can be exploited to gain access to a wide range of downstream resources.
Principles	Service Loose Coupling
Architecture	Service

Table 13.3
Profile summary for the Trusted Subsystem pattern.

Problem

When underlying service resources, such as databases, can be accessed directly by consumer programs, the security of the resource can be compromised by malicious attackers and/or consumer programs can form unhealthy dependencies on parts of the service architecture that can lead to negative forms of consumer-to-service coupling (Figure 13.7).

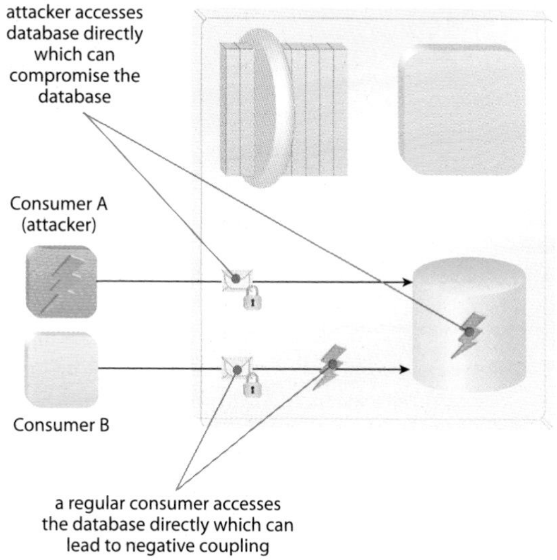
attacker accesses database directly which can compromise the database
Consumer A (attacker)
Consumer B
a regular consumer accesses the database directly which can lead to negative coupling

Figure 13.7

Allowing either malicious and non-malicious consumers to access the service's database directly leads to significant problems.

Solution

The service acts as a trusted subsystem of its underlying resources. Consumers can only access the resources via the service and the service uses its own credentials instead of the consumer's credentials to carry out access to the resources.

> **NOTE**
>
> This pattern also addresses the problem of when delegation is simply not supported by a service architecture (which in itself is a common situation).

Application

The service is positioned as the sole means by which the underlying resources can be accessed by service consumer programs. This will frequently require the joint application of Contract Centralization (409).

Consumers are further limited to authentication and authorization via the service and their credentials are not delegated to the underlying resource. Instead, the service uses its own credentials.

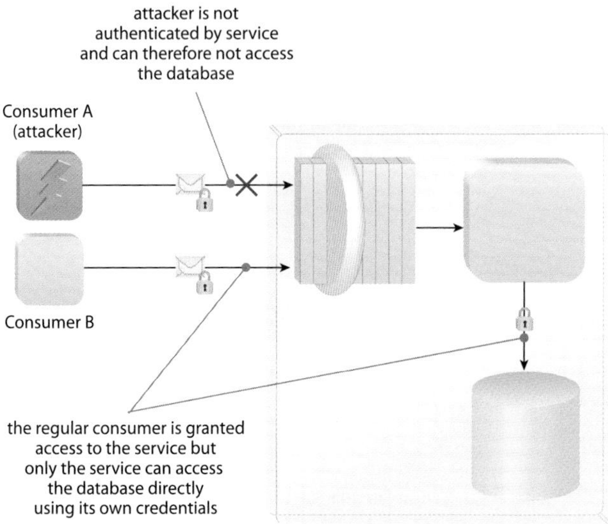
attacker is not authenticated by service and can therefore not access the database
Consumer A (attacker)
Consumer B
the regular consumer is granted access to the service but only the service can access the database directly using its own credentials

Figure 13.8

Neither a malicious or non-malicious consumer can access the database directly. Only the service itself can access the database with its own credentials.

When accessing a remote resource, the service must be designed to carry out the following steps upon the arrival of a request message with credentials:

1. Authenticate and authorize the message via Direct Authentication (656) or Brokered Authentication (661).
2. Send a request to the remote resource accompanied by the service's own credentials (or the service account under which the trusted subsystem process is being executed).
3. Upon receiving and processing a response from the resource, issue its own response back to the consumer.

To carry this out successfully, the remote resources must be able to verify that the mid-stream caller (the service) is trusted and not just any system process. Requiring this type of verification enhances security by making it more difficult for attackers to simulate a trusted subsystem and perform "man-in-the-middle" attacks.

As referenced earlier, each subsystem establishes a trust boundary. When multiple services are composed together to solve more complex problems, each can simultaneously act as a trusted subsystem and the resource that is accessed by a trusted subsystem. Figure 13.9 illustrates how this scenario establishes two overlapping trust boundaries.

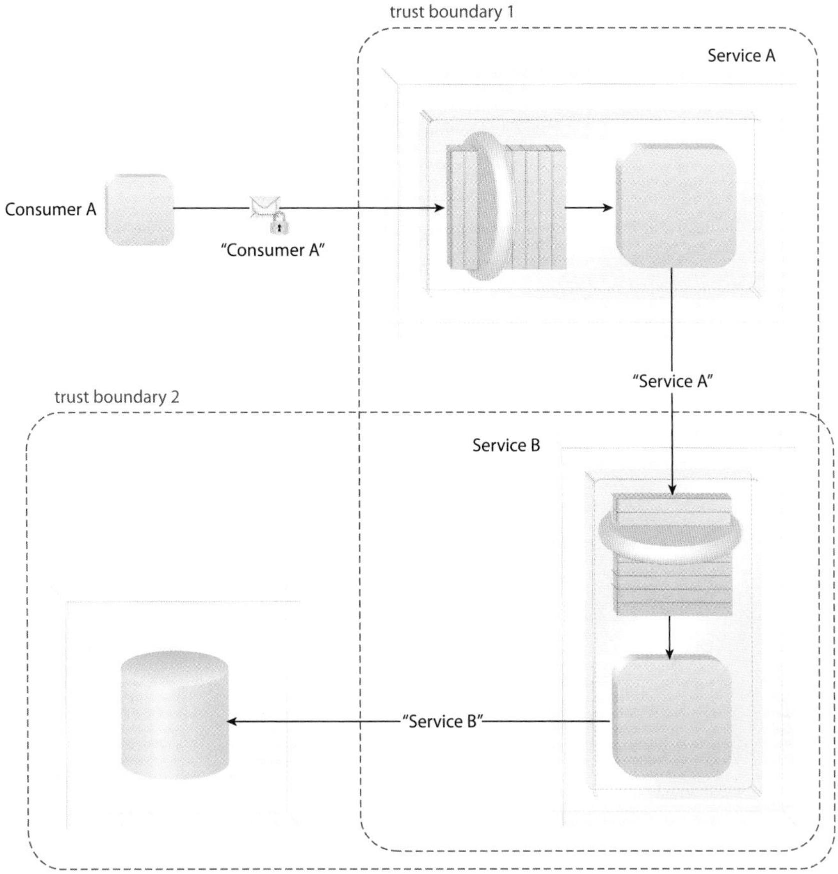

Figure 13.9
Service B acts as a trusted subsystem and also as the resource of a different trusted subsystem (Service A).

Several approaches and technologies can be used to implement this pattern:

- *Service accounts are used within the trusted subsystem* – A common method of implementing verification with the Kerberos protocol is to use a service account that is effective only within a particular trusted subsystem.
- *Local accounts are used on each host* – When it is not possible to authenticate using Kerberos service accounts, you can create a local account on each host within the trusted subsystem. These types of accounts are often referred to as "mirrored accounts," as each will have the same login and password. Mirrored accounts generally require complex passwords that need to be frequently changed.

- *An X.509 PKI is used for authentication within the trusted subsystem* – The X.509 PKI can issue a certificate for each application within a trusted subsystem. To access resources the service must use an X.509 certificate as the basis for authentication. In addition, the certificate must be on the list of certificates that are authorized to access the resource.
- *IPSec is used between computers in the trusted subsystem so that communication is secure* – IPSec secures messages between two hosts at the network layer to provide data confidentiality, data integrity, and replay detection. It can be configured to initiate secure communication with the Kerberos protocol, X.509 certificates, or a pre-shared key. IPSec performs considerably better than message-layer security, but it does not allow for granular control of resources. This is because, with IPSec, a trusted subsystem can only be established between computers that participate in the trusted subsystem and not on a specific program accessing a specific resource.

NOTE

In some situations, resources might need to perform actions based on the identity of the consumer. For example, a database may require the consumer identity to enable data entitlement logic or to create an audit trail. In this case, the consumer's identity will still need to be "flowed" to the backend resource. Flowing the identity of a consumer while avoiding delegation can be performed by including a unique consumer identifier within either the message body or a custom SOAP header.

Impacts

If a service implementing Trusted Subsystem is compromised, it can be used to exploit any downstream resources it has access to. For this reason, services acting as trusted subsystems often become prime targets for attackers to probe for vulnerabilities within the enterprise.

Relationships

Because this pattern pertains to the authentication of consumers, it is naturally associated with Direct Authentication (656) and Brokered Authentication (661) in that when an alternative to delegation is required it is applied in combination with one of these two patterns.

Trusted Subsystem essentially acts as an extension to Contract Centralization (409) by reinforcing centralized service contract access with secure, centralized access to backend service resources.

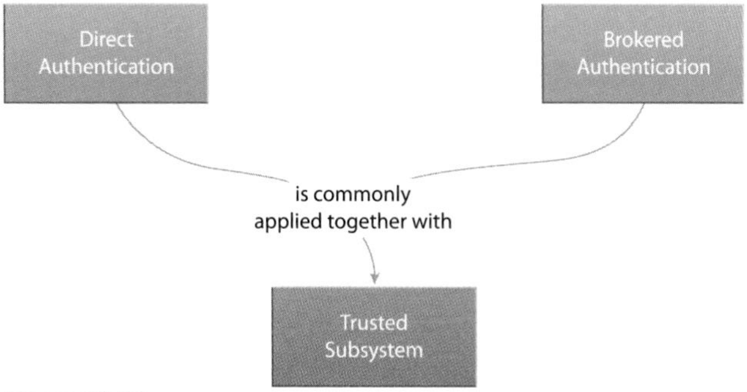

Figure 13.10

Even though Trusted Subsystem can be applied with other authentication-centric patterns, its role is to limit the propagation of the consumer credentials that are authenticated.

CASE STUDY EXAMPLE

The initial version of the Retail Lumber service exposed only basic catalog functionality, providing read-only information similar to what was already on the HTML-based Web site. As a result, Alleywood's architects did not feel that their services required authentication. But due to increased demand by business partners for access to more functionality, such as order processing and tracking, they must now consider additional security mechanisms including authentication.

The security team recommends that the service architecture be further enhanced, and in their report, they raise a series of issues:

- How will the external consumers be authenticated?
- Specifically which backend resources will consumers need direct access to?
- How should consumer identity information be propagated to backend systems?
- What auditing requirements exist?
- Where are dependent resources located within the corporate network, and what requirements exist for authenticating such resources?
- What (if any) advantages can be utilized by resource sharing techniques such as connection pooling?

The architecture team reviews each of these questions to better define the access and security requirements for the planned authenticated consumer message requests.

Subsequent to reviewing the results of their analysis together with the security team, it is determined to proceed with an authentication design whereby consumer credentials are not used for direct access to any service resources.

Instead, a service account is established. Calls from the Retail Lumber service to back-end databases will not access resources directly under the identity of the caller but will instead be transitioned to the service account. This approach also has the advantage of enabling connection pooling for use between the service and its databases.

However, Alleywood's architects also had to consider how to support data entitlement rules, meaning that the calls from the Retail Lumber services had to incorporate a unique identifier for the originating user, allowing the backend databases to only return information relevant to that consumer. Alleywood decides to pass this information in a custom SOAP header. McPherson's security specialists also point out that it is critical to ensure this custom SOAP header is also signed to guarantee that the identifier is not modified in transit. They therefore further proceed with Data Origin Authentication (649).

Service Perimeter Guard

By Jason Hogg, Don Smith, Fred Chong, Tom Hollander, Wojtek Kozaczynski, Larry Brader, Nelly Delgado, Dwayne Taylor, Lonnie Wall, Paul Slater, Sajjad Nasir Imran, Pablo Cibraro, Ward Cunningham

How can services that run in a private network be made available to external consumers without exposing internal resources?

Problem	External consumers that require access to one or more services in a private network can attack the service or use it to gain access to internal resources.
Solution	An intermediate service is established at the perimeter of the private network as a secure contact point for any external consumers that need to interact with internal services.
Application	The service is deployed in a perimeter network and is designed to work with existing firewall technologies so as to establish a secure bridging mechanism between external and internal networks.
Impacts	A perimeter service adds complexity and performance overhead as it establishes an intermediary processing layer for all external-to-internal communication.
Principles	Service Loose Coupling, Service Abstraction
Architecture	Service

Table 13.4
Profile summary for the Service Perimeter Guard pattern.

Problem

External consumers require access to one or more services deployed in a private network. Direct access to the private network would expose services to external attackers that can gain internal information and use it to compromise the services and the network (Figure 13.11).

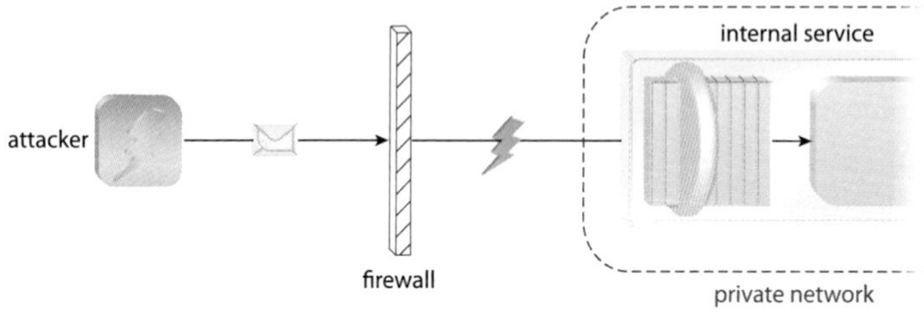

Figure 13.11

A consumer that gains access to an internal service can exploit it directly through attacks.

Solution

An intermediary service is positioned at the perimeter of the private network and is established as the sole contact point for external consumers on behalf of one or more internal services (Figure 13.12).

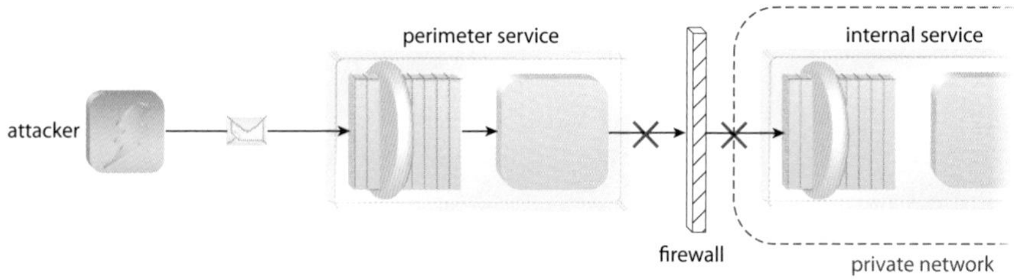

Figure 13.12

The perimeter service processes the attacker's message and upon determining its malicious intent, rejects it. This spares the underlying internal service from exposure and unnecessary security-related processing.

Application

This type of service is typically deployed in a perimeter network (also known as the DMZ or demilitarized zone), which has access to resources in the private network through a firewall. It operates at the application layer and is intended to work in conjunction with existing firewall technologies (and not to replace them).

An external consumer will send a request message addressed to the perimeter service's external contract, which the perimeter service then forwards to the appropriate internal service. Similarly, when the internal service responds, the perimeter service relays the response to the external consumer. Throughout this exchange, the location and contract of the internal service remains hidden from the external consumer.

One of the primary advantages of Service Perimeter Guard is that it can establish centralized security processing on behalf of other services. This enables an architecture to be built around a perimeter service capable of implementing other security patterns, such as Brokered Authentication (661), Message Screening (381), and Exception Shielding (376).

> **NOTE**
>
> This pattern is similar in concept to Inventory Endpoint (260) but differs in two primary ways. First, Service Perimeter Guard is primarily about security-related processing, and its design solution is focused on providing a secure endpoint on behalf of other services. Secondly, Inventory Endpoint (260) is intended to specifically establish an entry point for an entire inventory of services. Service Perimeter Guard, on the other hand, has no such limitation. It can be used to represent one or several internal services. Note also that Inventory Endpoint (260) and Service Perimeter Guard can be applied to the same service.

Impacts

The use of perimeter services can add complexity and processing overhead and can further introduce performance bottlenecks when required to route and apply security processing to large numbers of messages.

As the single point of entry for a private network, this type of service can also become a primary target for attackers. This requires perimeter services to be thoroughly hardened. Also, the use of this pattern does not reduce the need to secure internal services, especially in relation to the communication that needs to occur between internal and perimeter services.

Relationships

The abstraction established by Service Perimeter Guard provides a point of isolation that can centralize Direct Authentication (656), Brokered Authentication (661), and Message Screening (381) on behalf of multiple other services. This pattern can further be combined with Inventory Endpoint (260) to establish centralized security processing for an entire inventory of services.

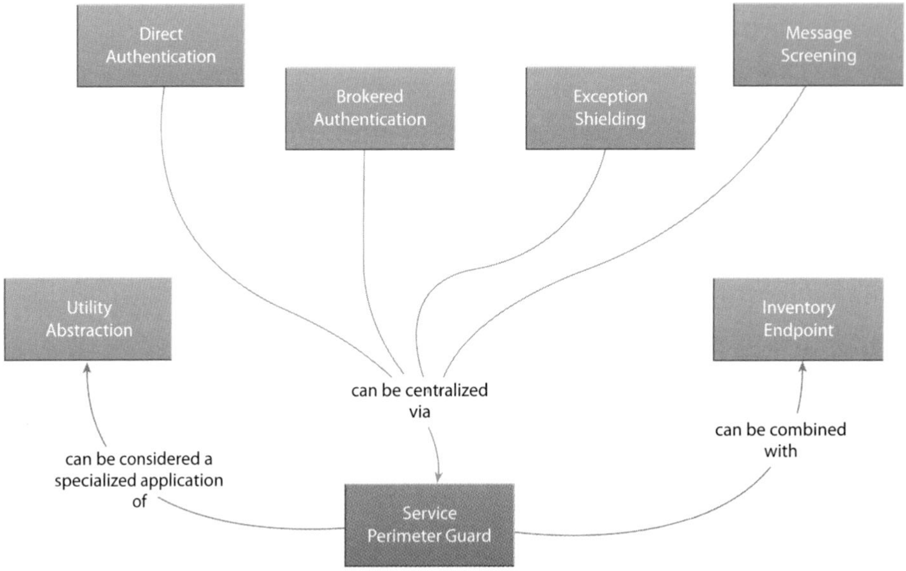

Figure 13.13

The security-centric wrapper service established by this pattern can centralize a variety of security-related processing logic.

CASE STUDY EXAMPLE

The redesign of the Retail Lumber service architecture is nearly completed when news of a new development project surfaces. Apparently, business requirements have emerged for Alleywood to also provide a Wholesale Lumber service to be made available for access to a new set of partner organizations in the lumber distribution sector.

Unlike the Retail Lumber service, which essentially provides an online access point for a broad public client-base, the Wholesale Lumber service will establish a programmatic interface for a limited number of partner organizations.

In order to avoid the problems encountered with the original Retail Lumber service, Alleywood decides to apply the same security patterns to the Wholesale Lumber service. However, after taking a look at the requirements specification for this service, it becomes apparent that some additional security measures need to be added.

Specifically, the service will also need to be accessed by other internal services that need to perform some of the same queries and orders for bulk lumber shipments to be issued

to various departments within Tri-Fold. Even though Tri-Fold has its own service inventory, it is technically not an external consumer, and this service could end up being part of several Tri-Fold service compositions.

The security team is uncomfortable with the idea of exposing a service to both external and internal consumers and recommends establishing a wrapper service that acts as the endpoint for external interaction only.

A perimeter service is subsequently designed to perform all authentication of external consumers. Architects further realize that the introduction of this service further provides an opportunity to further support the application of Exception Shielding (376), Trusted Subsystem (387), and Message Screening (381), by adding some extra "safety net" security processing logic.

This alleviates the Wholesale Lumber service from having to carry out most of this security-related logic and also prompts yet another redesign of the Retail Lumber service. The original idea architects had to move some of the more common security logic into a utility service is now justified. To accomplish this without impacting existing consumers, architects further apply this pattern together with Proxy Capability (497).

After the application of the four patterns described in this chapter, the Alleywood architects finally receive the green light to go live with the updated Lumber Order system.

Chapter 14

Service Contract Design Patterns

Decoupled Contract

Contract Centralization

Contract Denormalization

Concurrent Contracts

Validation Abstraction

Service-orientation places a great deal of emphasis on the design of service contracts. The Standardized Service Contract design principle in fact requires that all contracts within a given service inventory conform to the same conventions so as to establish a truly federated endpoint layer. From an inventory architecture perspective, this requirement is addressed by Canonical Schema (158) and Canonical Expression (275), as explained in previous chapters.

For example, both Decoupled Contract (401) and Contract Centralization (409) are considered essential to service design (especially when building services as Web services), because when combined, these patterns position the contract as an independent yet still central part of the service architecture.

The remaining patterns in this chapter provide various techniques for accommodating multiple consumer types. They can be applied independently or together. For example, Concurrent Contracts (421) can be used to establish multiple endpoints for a service, each of which can be further optimized via Contract Denormalization (414) and Validation Abstraction (429).

Furthermore, it is worth noting that Contract Denormalization (414) and Concurrent Contracts (421) can be part of the initial service design, or they can be applied after a service has been in use for some time. In the latter case, these two patterns could be considered governance-related as much as the design patterns in Chapter 16.

Decoupled Contract

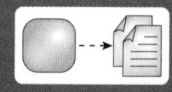

How can a service express its capabilities independently of its implementation?

Problem	For a service to be positioned as an effective enterprise resource, it must be equipped with a technical contract that exists independently from its implementation yet still in alignment with other services.
Solution	The service contract is physically decoupled from its implementation.
Application	A service's technical interface is physically separated and subject to relevant service-orientation design principles.
Impacts	Service functionality is limited to the feature-set of the decoupled contract medium.
Principles	Standardized Service Contract, Service Loose Coupling
Architecture	Service

Table 14.1
Profile summary for the Decoupled Contract pattern.

Problem

Services can be built using component-centric distributed development technologies, such as .NET and Java. Although these development environments provide adequate platforms for building components as services, they usually require that the technical contract be physically bound to the underlying service logic when the service is built solely as a component. This essentially requires that the service contract be expressed via the same native technologies used to build the components (Figure 14.1).

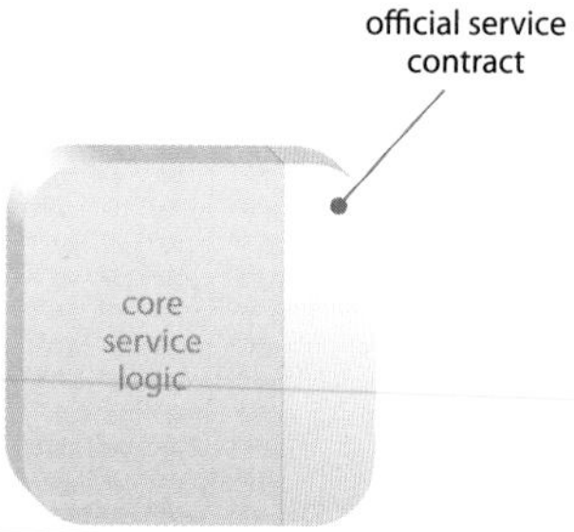

Figure 14.1
A component designed as a service, exposing an official service contract.

As a result, the utilization and evolution of services is inhibited because they can only be used by consumer programs compatible with their technology. Even though bridging and transformation products are available, this limitation generally results in increased integration effort and a

reduced number of potential service consumers (which translates into reduced reuse potential).

Furthermore, requiring that consumers be bound to a native implementation technology results in a negative form of coupling (known as technology coupling) that establishes direct dependencies on the continued existence of that technology. Should the service owner ever want to upgrade or replace the underlying logic with logic built using a different development platform, it would be very difficult to accomplish without effectively breaking all existing consumer dependencies (Figure 14.2).

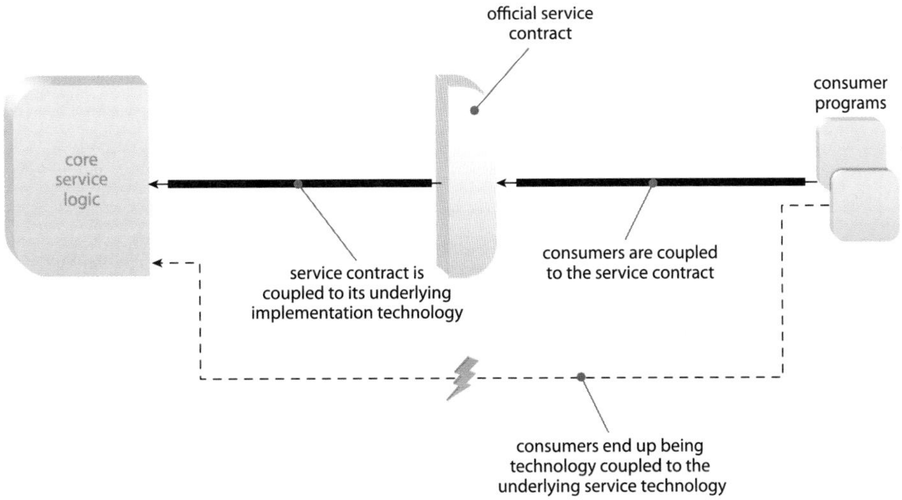

Figure 14.2

Because service consumers are required to couple themselves to a service contract that is itself coupled to the native component technology, the consumers become technology coupled.

Solution

The service contract is created as a physically separate part of the overall service implementation. This decouples the contract from the underlying service implementation, allowing it to be independently designed and governed (Figure 14.3).

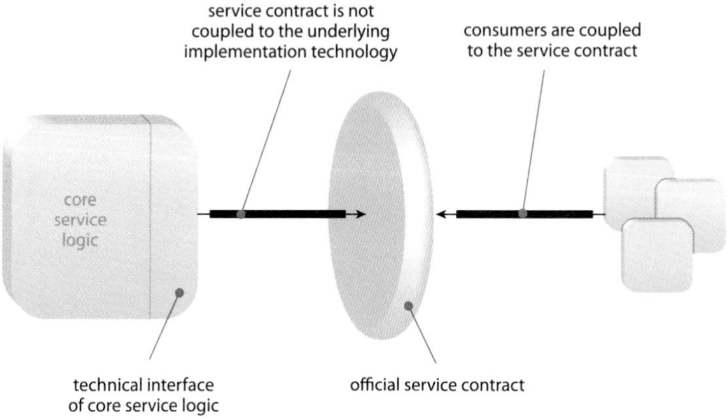

Figure 14.3

By decoupling the service contract, the service implementation can be evolved without directly impacting service consumers. This can increase the amount of refactoring opportunities and the range of potential consumer programs (and corresponding reuse).

Application

Web services represent the most popular means of applying this design pattern, as they force the service contract to be expressed in separate description documents using industry standard meta languages.

Service inventories based on the use of contracts that support industry standards are considered to have the greatest freedom for long-term governance and vendor diversification. Therefore, Web service contracts are effective as long as the underlying runtime platforms are deemed sufficiently mature to support the range of processing logic required by all service capabilities and any potential composition configurations in which they may need to take part (Figure 14.4).

A common risk associated with expressing service contracts using Web service technologies is the established approach of auto-generating Web service contract description documents (WSDL, XML Schema, and WS-Policy definitions) via modern development tools. This technique can result in implementation coupling, a negative coupling type whereby contracts express implementation details, such as physical data models or proprietary component method parameters.

Consumer programs that then bind to these types of service contracts form design-time dependencies on their physical implementation details. When the underlying service implementation is required to change, all existing service consumers can be immediately affected. This inflexibility can paralyze the evolution of a service and introduce the requirement for multiple, premature service versions (Figure 14.5).

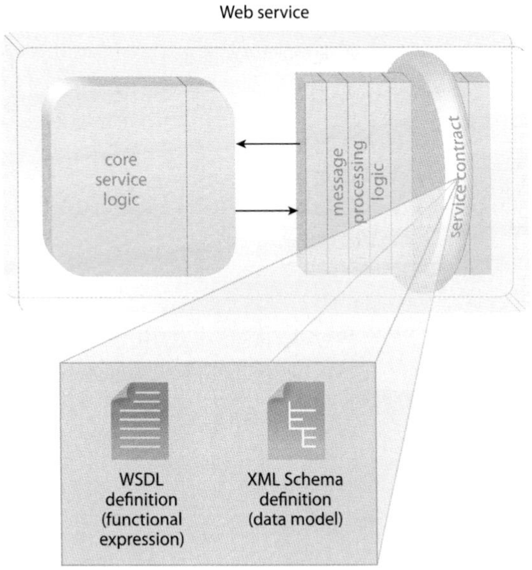

Figure 14.4

When the decoupling of a contract from its implementation is realized by delivering the service as a Web service, it introduces the need to formally define the functional expression and data representation parts of the service contract via WSDL and XML Schema (and optional WS-Policy) definitions.

Figure 14.5

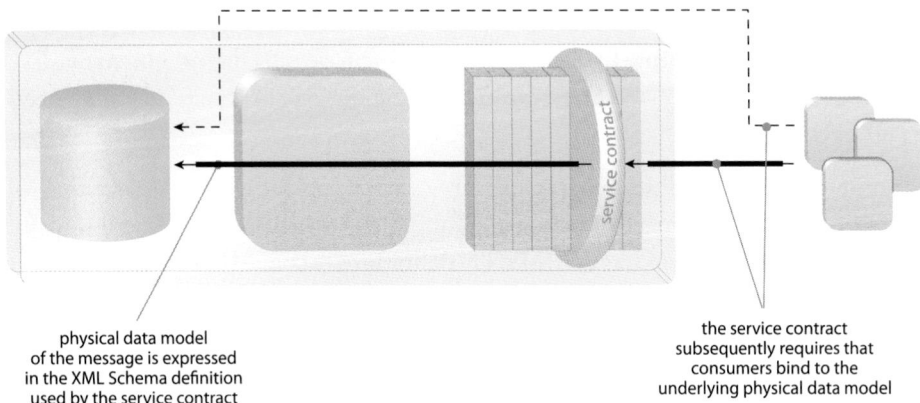

An example of how implementation coupling of the service contract can propagate implementation coupling to service consumers.

The Service Loose Coupling design principle addresses this issue by advocating the independent creation of a service contract so that the contract's content can also remain decoupled from any existing or future logic and resources it may be required to encapsulate. This further allows the contract to be shaped according to existing design standards (as per the Standardized Service Contract principle) and establishes it as an endpoint into service logic freed from ties to underlying implementation details (Figure 14.6).

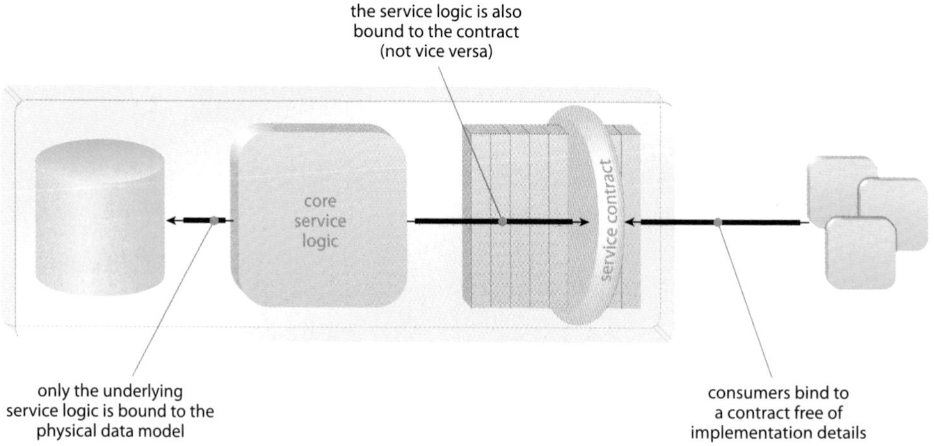

Figure 14.6

Revisiting the previous example, if the service contract can be kept free of implementation details, consumers can avoid binding to them.

Impacts

When decoupled contracts are employed, the service and its consumers will be tied to any limitations associated with the maturity of the vendor platform's support for relevant contract and related communications technologies. Deficiencies within the contract technology platform can inhibit the utilization of the service. Standardizing on a technology decoupled contract design can then impose any deficiencies on the service inventory as a whole.

Relationships

Decoupled Contract is fundamental to many design techniques that revolve around the use of Web services or directly benefit from the existence of a physically separate service contract.

Patterns associated with the post-implementation augmentation of service contracts, such as Service Decomposition (489), Proxy Capability (497), Distributed Capability (510),

and Contract Denormalization (414), all can be more effectively applied to a service with a decoupled contract.

Contract Centralization (409) and Service Refactoring (484) benefit tremendously from this pattern due to the independence it achieves between contract and implementation. Service Façade (333) is often applied to add another level of abstraction between core service logic and the decoupled contract, and these two patterns furthermore enable the realization of Concurrent Contracts (421).

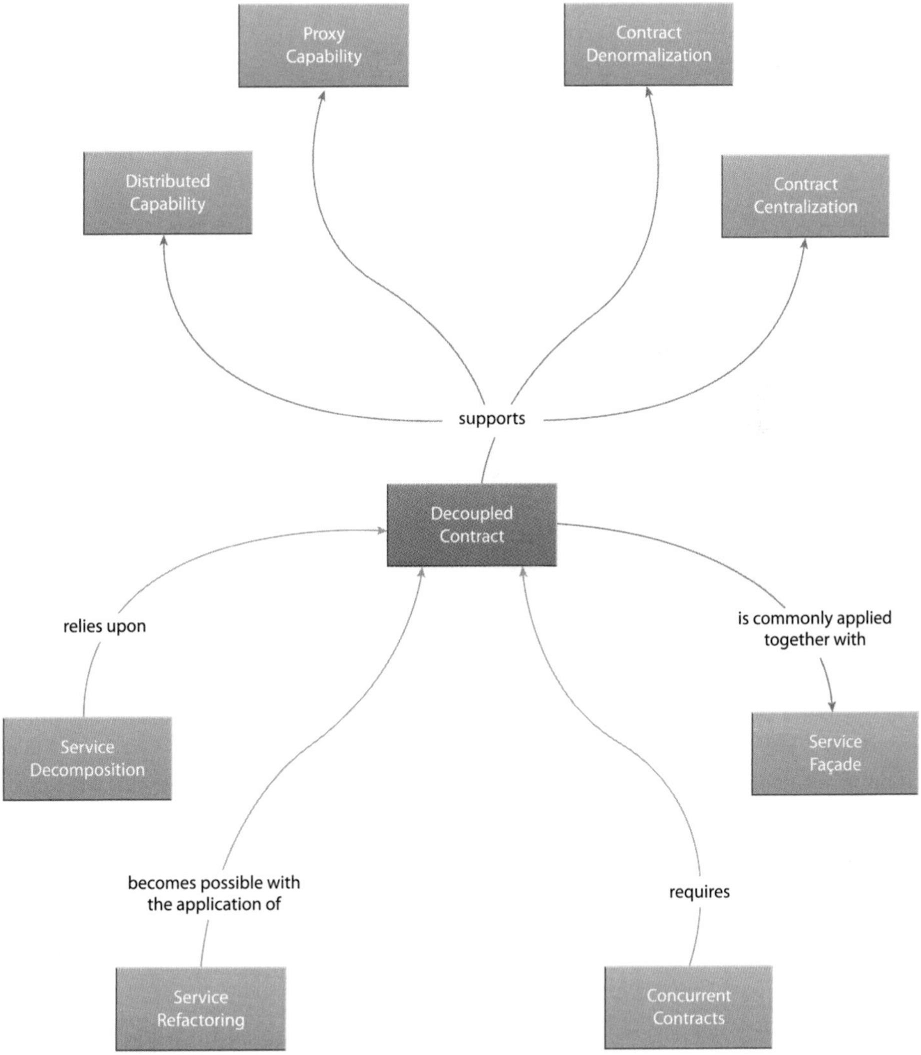

Figure 14.7

Decoupled Contract establishes an important separation of logic, technology, and technical interface that can be leveraged by many other design patterns.

CASE STUDY EXAMPLE

The case study example for Service Façade (333) in Chapter 12 introduced a utility component called "Data Controller" that is responsible for providing centralized access to a set of databases. Although the nature of this component is similar in concept to a utility service, the fact that it was delivered prior to the SOA initiative and does not conform to the design standards applied to newly developed services has prompted FRC architects to categorize it as a part of their legacy environment.

As explained in the Service Façade (333) example, this component was used by the Appealed Assessments service to provide the data it required to generate specific reports. As new projects emerge, new services are designed. One project in particular is tasked with delivering the Fines and Evaluations services. Upon a review of their processing requirements, it is determined that both of these services will require access to the databases represented by the Data Controller component.

The project team is reluctant to have each service couple itself to a legacy program that was recently changed (see the Legacy Wrapper (441) case study example in Chapter 12) and may still be subject to further change. Each of these modifications would impact each of the services, increasing the potential governance burden.

After some discussions with the owners of the Data Controller component, it is decided that this component will be redesigned as a utility *service* for inclusion in the FRC service inventory. One of the first challenges to address is the fact that the Data Controller exists as a standalone Java EJB. By way of Canonical Protocol (150), the FRC service inventory was standardized on the Web services technology framework, allowing all service endpoints to be comprised of decoupled service contracts (WSDL and XML Schema definitions).

For the Data Controller to comply to this requirement, it too needs to be equipped with a decoupled service contract that exists independently from its underlying service logic. Subsequent to a redesign, the Data Controller is deployed as a Web service. Its decoupled contract makes it possible for it to expose a standardized service contract independently from its implementation (Figure 14.8). This will allow the underlying logic and technology to undergo changes and refactoring efforts without affecting the contract and all of the service consumers that bind to it.

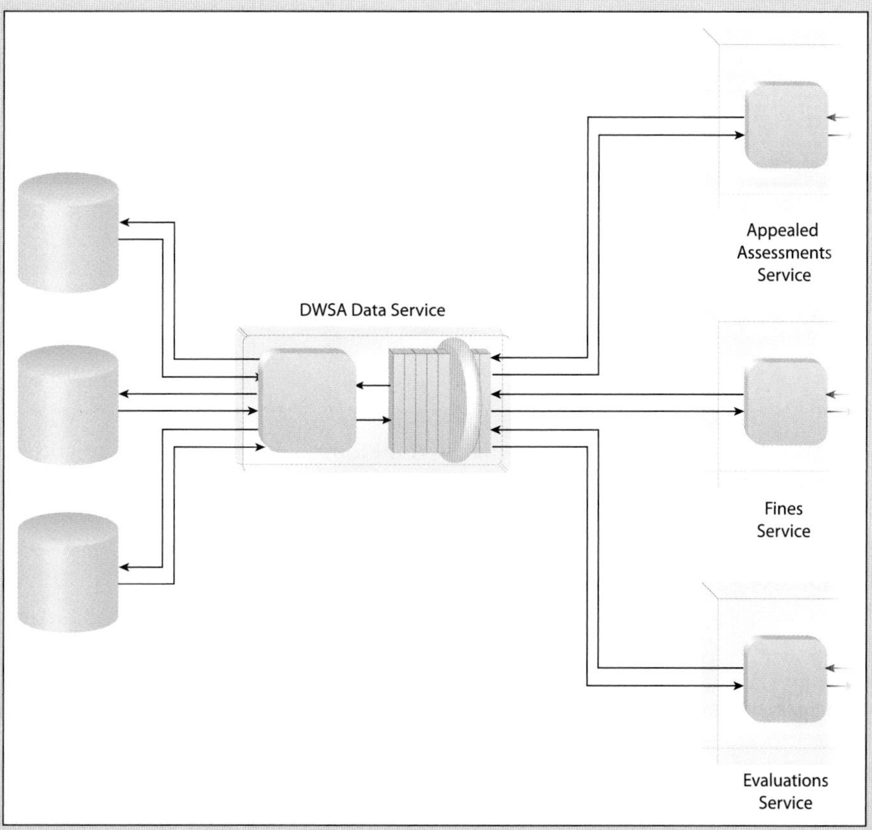

Figure 14.8

Appealed Assessments, Fines, and Evaluations services now all access the new DWSA Data service (formerly the Data Controller component) via its decoupled contract.

NOTE

As shown in Figure 14.8, the redesign also results in a new name for the service. Because of Canonical Expression (275), the service is given the name "DWSA Data," which the architects feel better expresses its functional context. DWSA is short for "Data Warehouse Subdivision A," the part of the overall data warehouse that provides a collection of statistical data relevant to appeals, fines, and assessments.

Contract Centralization

How can direct consumer-to-implementation coupling be avoided?

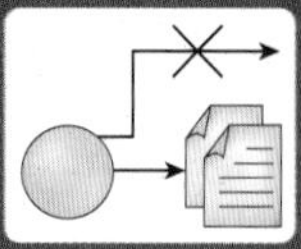

Problem	Consumer programs can be designed to access underlying service resources using different entry points, resulting in different forms of implementation dependencies that inhibit the service from evolving in response to change.
Solution	Access to service logic is limited to the service contract, forcing consumers to avoid implementation coupling.
Application	This pattern is realized through formal enterprise design standards and the targeted application of the Service Abstraction design principle.
Impacts	Forcing consumer programs to access service capabilities and resources via a central contract can impose performance overhead and requires on-going standardization effort.
Principles	Standardized Service Contract, Service Loose Coupling, Service Abstraction
Architecture	Composition, Service

Table 14.2
Profile summary for the Contract Centralization pattern.

Problem

Even when services within an enterprise are deployed with published, standardized service contracts, those designing consumer programs can be tempted to look for alternative entry points into service logic. For example, it may be easier or more efficient to bypass the service contract and simply access its underlying logic directly using native protocols (Figure 14.9).

Subsequently, the service contract loses its significance, and the service ends up with numerous tight dependencies (usually in the form of integration channels) to various parts of its implementation. This inhibits the evolution and governance of the service and undermines many of the objectives of service-orientation.

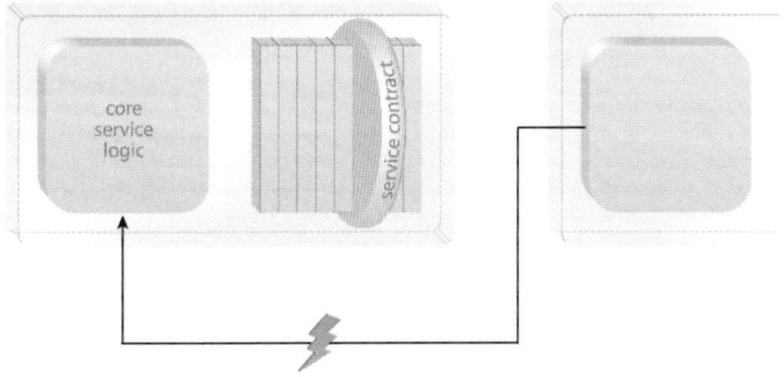

Figure 14.9

A service consumer program simply bypasses the service contract to access underlying logic directly.

Solution

Contract Centralization establishes a design standard that positions the service contract as the sole entry point into service logic. This allows for a consistent form of loose coupling with all service consumer programs (Figure 14.10).

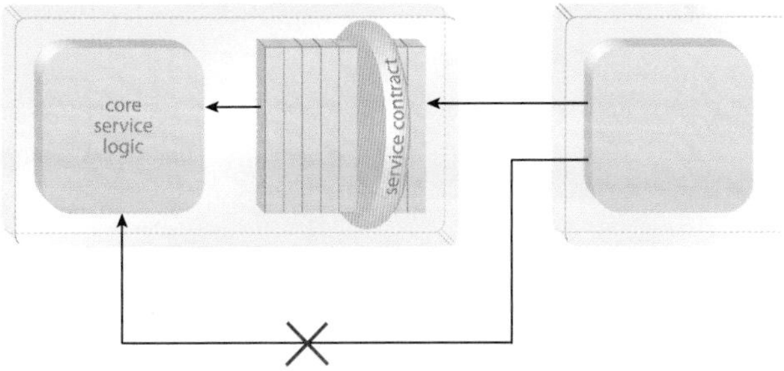

Figure 14.10

Through Contract Centralization we place the service contract front and center within a service architecture. This is why much of service-orientation is focused on contract design.

Application

The application of this pattern establishes a distinction between the official published service contract and other parts of the service that can also be accessed via separate technical endpoints. For example, a consumer could interface with an underlying service component via that component's API. This API still represents a technical contract, but not the "official" service entry point. This would therefore be considered a non-centralized form of service coupling.

If Contract Centralization is enforced to a meaningful extent, the service contract becomes a focal point for a great deal of interaction. From a long-term evolutionary perspective, therefore, Web services and REST services provide an effective means of establishing a centralized contract while remaining decoupled from the service's underlying environment, as per Decoupled Contract (401).

On the other hand, contract technology that requires the use of proprietary communication protocols will limit service access to those consumer programs compatible with the proprietary requirements of the contract. In this case, the repeated application of this pattern can result in a proliferation of technology coupling throughout an inventory.

Impacts

Integration architecture has a well-rooted history that predates the emergence of middleware and the EAI movement. Few of the past integration architectures were based on a concept like centralization, and more often than not, connections were made to whatever application entry points were the most convenient and efficient to fulfill immediate requirements.

Requiring architects, developers, project managers, and other team members to now forsake all of the options they've had in the past in favor of a design standard that is being established for the long-term good of the enterprise can be difficult. Resistance to centralization is common, and tactical requirements, such as time-to-market priorities and budget restrictions, can motivate some project teams to simply disregard this pattern altogether.

Furthermore, requiring that all service consumers access a body of logic through a single entry point can result in a classic convergence of performance issues, especially when having to reroute multiple existing integration channels to interface with a service contract. Contract Centralization needs to be expected and planned for, especially with agnostic services because they are subject to the greatest concurrency demands.

Relationships

By looking at the variety of relationships in Figure 14.11, it is evident how important Contract Centralization is to service-orientation. It is a part of establishing an effective endpoint layer within inventories and the repeated utilization of agnostic services, such as those based on Entity Abstraction (175) and Utility Abstraction (168), relies on the base requirement that they only be accessed via their contracts which, in turn, fully supports the long-term, independent governance of services subject to Service Refactoring (484).

Contract Centralization is responsible for positioning service contracts as a fundamental service access tier that can be further extended via complementary policy and schema layers, as per Policy Centralization (207) and Schema Centralization (200).

It is important to acknowledge that the centralization of service contracts is supported (and often enabled) by Decoupled Contract (401) and Service Normalization (131). Decoupled contracts can be much more easily centralized and separately positioned from underlying service implementations and the normalization of services further ensures that centralized contracts do not end up representing redundant logic.

One of the closest relationships is between Contract Centralization and Logic Centralization (136), as explored further in the description for the compound pattern Official Endpoint (711).

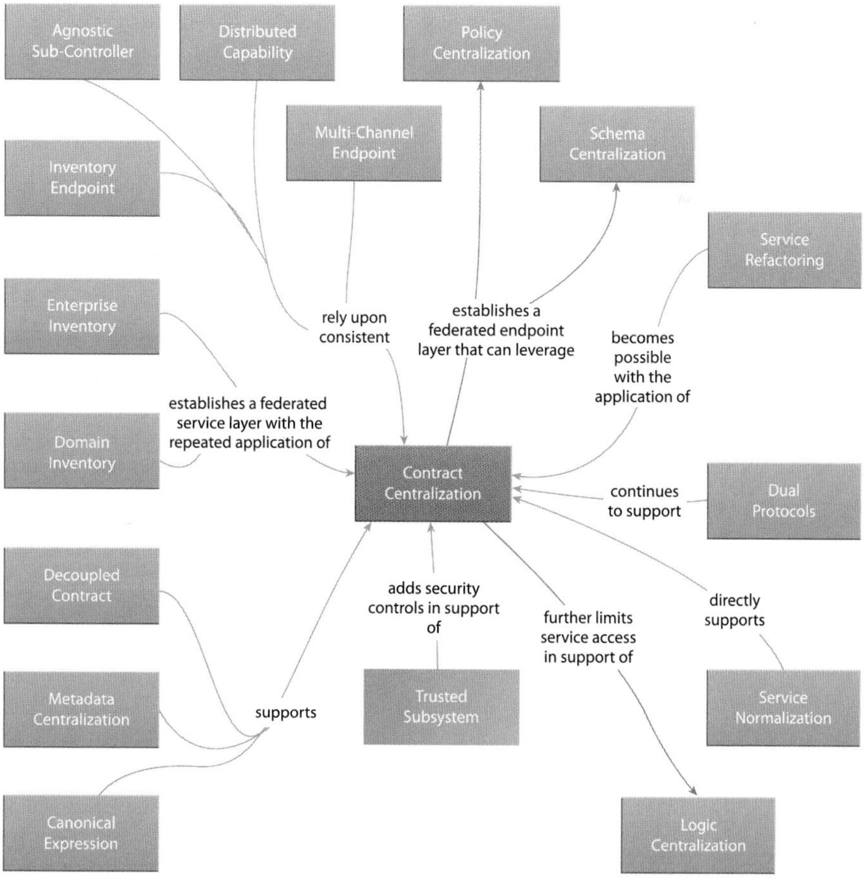

Figure 14.11

Contract Centralization is a lot like an enterprise design standard in that it regulates how services are accessed and therefore has relationships with both service logic and contract-related patterns.

CASE STUDY EXAMPLE

Enterprise architects within the FRC make a strategic decision to position the delivery of all new service contracts as the sole allowable entry points into the corresponding service logic. This requires a great deal of communication and some education for existing IT staff that have become accustomed to achieving interoperability via specialized integration channels.

This move results in a formal, enterprise-wide design standard that affects all new services being delivered. Any legacy system logic a service capability may encapsulate can no longer be directly accessed by external applications. Although they expect resistance to this standard for some time, every effort is made to uphold it.

A remaining challenge, however, still looms. The legacy environments encapsulated by some of the planned services already have established integration channels with other applications. The team does not want to make the introduction of Contract Centralization too disruptive for the rest of the enterprise. At the same time, it wants to take any possible steps toward maximizing its independence to govern these services.

A decision is therefore made to assess each of the existing integration channels and to identify encapsulated systems with the most channels and the most integration-related activity. Those at the top of the list are scheduled for a transition toward supporting the contract-centralized architecture. The initial plan is to move them over within six to eight months, depending on available resources and other priorities.

Contract Denormalization

How can a service contract facilitate consumer programs with differing data exchange requirements?

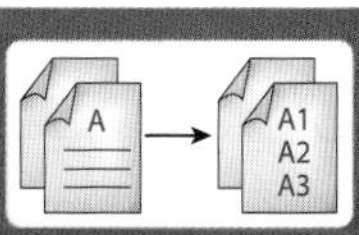

Problem	Services with strictly normalized contracts can impose unnecessary functional and performace demands on some consumer programs.
Solution	Service contracts can include a measured extent of denormalization, allowing multiple capabilities to redundantly express core functions in different ways for different types of consumer programs.
Application	The service contract is carefully extended with additional capabilities that provide functional variations of a primary capability.
Impacts	Overuse of this pattern on the same contract can dramatically increase its size, making it difficult to interpret and unwieldy to govern.
Principles	Standardized Service Contract, Service Loose Coupling
Architecture	Service

Table 14.3
Profile summary for the Contract Denormalization pattern.

Problem

Because services can be utilized within a variety of compositions, it is difficult to express each capability in such a way that it is suited for each possible consumer program.

For example, a capability may not return a sufficient amount of data in response to a consumer request, or more commonly, it provides too much data, thereby imposing transmission and processing overhead upon the consumer program (Figure 14.12).

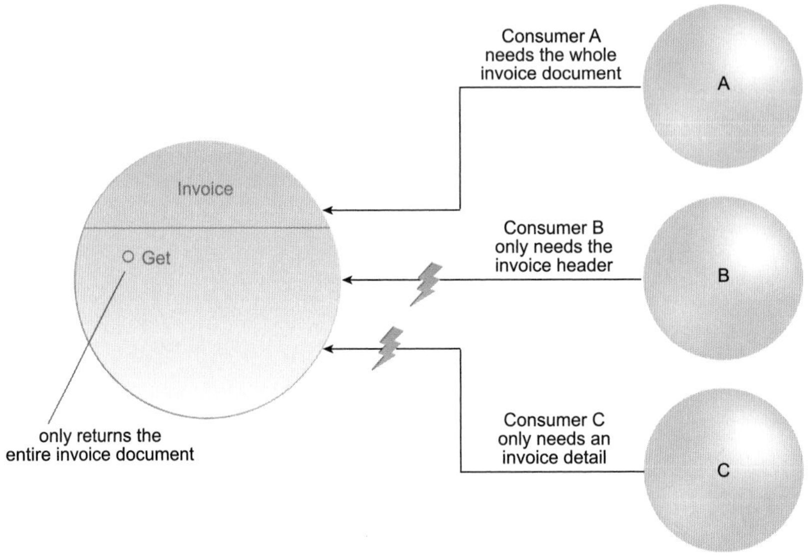

Figure 14.12

The Invoice service provides a Get capability that is not able to facilitate the varying granularity levels different service consumer programs prefer.

Solution

Unlike pursuing normalization across a service inventory, as per Service Normalization (131), where denormalization can impact the autonomy and governance of individual services, the level of acceptable normalization across a service contract is more flexible.

This flexibility allows for increased contract design options, including strategic incorporation of the denormalization of expressed functionality. In other words, the processing of one service capability does not need to be limited to one capability. Capabilities with redundant functionality offered at different levels of granularity can be provided to support multiple consumer and composition requirements (Figure 14.13).

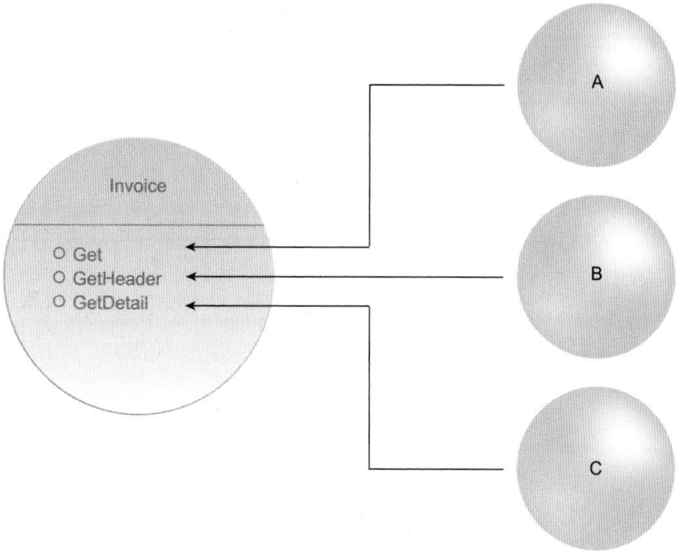

Figure 14.13

Equipped with additional (albeit redundant) capabilities, the Invoice service is able to better accommodate the individual requirements of the three consumers.

Application

Depending on the nature of the capability logic, there are some common ways that this pattern is applied:

- The same capability can be offered at different levels of granularity. As already illustrated in Figure 14.13, an entity service can contain different Get-related capabilities that can get an entire document, get just the document header, or get one or more document detail items (or a specific document property). The latter two variations introduce functionality that overlaps with the first and are therefore considered redundant.
- A new capability is added to an existing task service. Even though the task service encapsulates a body of business process logic, one or more capabilities can be added to expose segments of the process logic (normally in the form of modest subprocesses). This can establish alternate entry points into business process logic, but from an endpoint perspective, the capabilities appear to encapsulate redundant logic.

Even though this pattern intentionally introduces functional redundancy into the contract, there is typically no need to add significant functional processing to the underlying service logic. If all related capability definitions can be processed by the same set of components, the corresponding routines can be parameterized and shared.

Impacts

Overuse of this pattern can lead to overly large and convoluted service contracts. If multiple variations of each primary capability are added, the contract can become unmanageable and difficult to evolve. The effectiveness of agnostic services especially can suffer from poor functional expression.

Furthermore, adding capability variations that expose redundant functionality may require the creation of multiple, also redundant schema definitions. A Web service implementation, for example, could easily be comprised of numerous schema files, making its governance increasingly challenging.

Relationships

Contract Denormalization introduces additional capabilities into a contract, most of which will repeat the expression of functionality. This is why Service Façade (333) is commonly applied in support of this pattern; it allows for a single façade component to interact with other components and routines on the service back-end in order to facilitate redundant contract capabilities without the need for redundant service logic.

The flexibility to apply this pattern is further increased via Decoupled Contract (401) primarily because it provides the freedom to fully customize a service contract independently for its underlying implementation.

Service Normalization (131) does not directly relate to the application of Contract Denormalization, but it is interesting to note that despite its name, this pattern does not interfere with the pursuit of normalizing service boundaries. The boundaries remain the same; only the contract content changes.

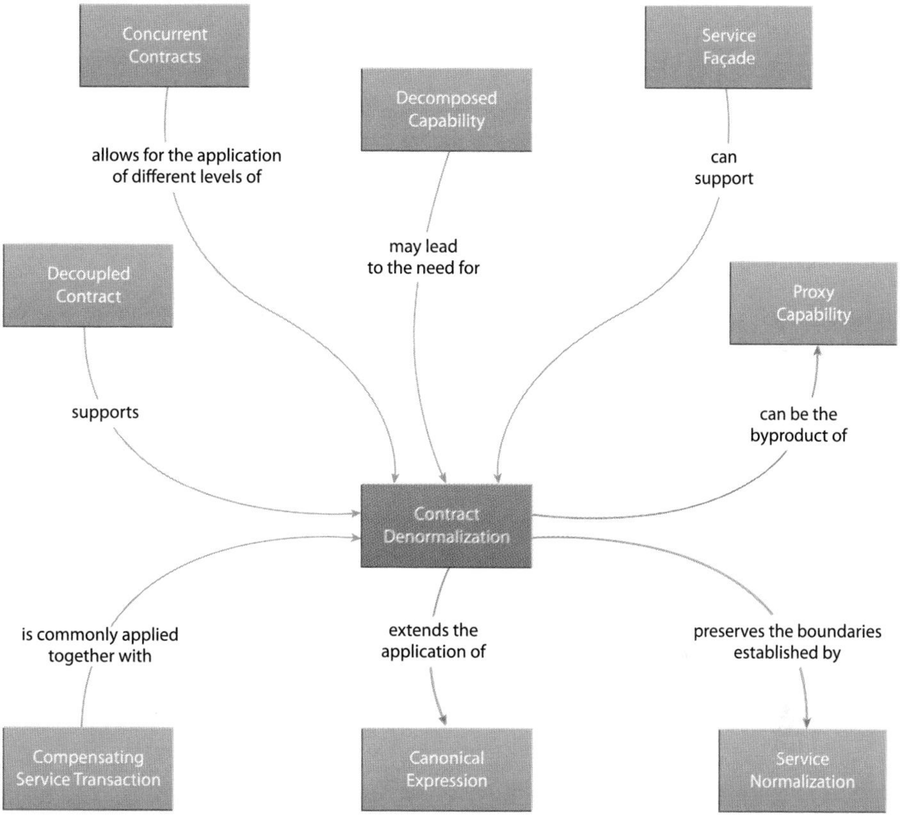

Figure 14.14

Contract Denormalization allows for the extension of contracts with redundant capabilities and therefore relates mostly to patterns that can support this requirement.

CASE STUDY EXAMPLE

The Officer entity Web service has been used by the FRC to provide centralized access to all processing and data associated with regulations officers. This service was initially delivered with a single Update operation that accepted a single complex type comprised of an entire officer record, including historical data, as shown here:

```
<definitions name="Officer"
  targetNamespace="http://frc/officer/wsdl/"
  xmlns="http://schemas.xmlsoap.org/wsdl/"
  xmlns:off="http://frc/officer/schema/"
  xmlns:soap="http://schemas.xmlsoap.org/wsdl/soap/"
  xmlns:tns="http://frc/officer/wsdl/"
```

```
  xmlns:xsd="http://www.w3.org/2001/XMLSchema">
  <types>
    <xsd:schema targetNamespace="http://frc/officer/">
      <xsd:import namespace="http://frc/officer/schema/"
        schemaLocation="Officer.xsd"/>
    </xsd:schema>
  </types>
  <message name="UpdateOfficer">
    <part name="RequestA" element="off:OfficerDoc"/>
  </message>
  <message name="UpdateOfficerConfirm">
    <part name="ResponseA" element="off:ReturnCodeA"/>
  </message>
  <portType name="OffInt">
    <operation name="Update">
      <input message="tns:UpdateOfficer"/>
      <output message="tns:UpdateOfficerConfirm"/>
    </operation>
  </portType>
  ...
</definitions>
```

Example 14.1

A subset of the original Officer WSDL definition comprised of a single Update operation.

Limiting the service to this one operation was originally considered reasonable because the backend database used to house officer data was modeled in such a manner that it could only accept changes to historical log entries when those changes were accompanied by a number of parent values associated with the officer profile record itself.

However, the database in question was just replaced with a new product designed with a more flexible data model. In response to recent bandwidth concerns, a number of service contracts are revisited to explore the design of leaner, more optimized data exchanges.

When architects review the Officer Web service contract, they see an opportunity to provide a more streamlined input message format for when only updates to historical logs are required. Due to the change in data model, these logs can now be updated with only the parent officer ID value.

The development team then proceeds to denormalize the contract by adding a new operation named UpdateLog. As shown in Example 14.2, the UpdateLog operation is now part of the Web service interface, alongside the original Update operation.

```
<definitions name="Officer" ...>
  ...
  <message name="UpdateOfficerLog">
    <part name="RequestB" element="off:OfficerLog"/>
  </message>
  <message name="UpdateOfficerLogConfirm">
    <part name="ResponseB" element="off:ReturnCodeB"/>
  </message>
  <portType name="OffInt">
    <operation name="Update">
      <input message="tns:UpdateOfficer"/>
      <output message="tns:UpdateOfficerConfirm"/>
    </operation>
    <operation name="UpdateLog">
      <input message="tns:UpdateOfficerLog"/>
      <output message="tns:UpdateOfficerLogConfirm"/>
    </operation>
  </portType>
  ...
</definitions>
```

Example 14.2

The revised, denormalized Officer WSDL definition with Update and UpdateLog operations.

Concurrent Contracts

How can a service facilitate multi-consumer coupling requirements and abstraction concerns at the same time?

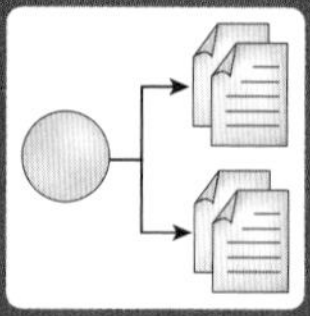

Problem	A service's contract may not be suitable for or applicable to all potential service consumers.
Solution	Multiple contracts can be created for a single service, each targeted at a specific type of consumer.
Application	This pattern is ideally applied together with Service Façade (333) to support new contracts as required.
Impacts	Each new contract can effectively add a new service endpoint to an inventory, thereby increasing corresponding governance effort.
Principles	Standardized Service Contract, Service Loose Coupling, Service Reusability
Architecture	Service

Table 14.4
Profile summary for the Concurrent Contracts pattern.

Problem

By default, a service has a contract that expresses the full range of its abilities. However, it can be challenging to design this contract in such a manner that it accommodates different types of service consumers.

For example, the service contract may need to incorporate special processing extensions (such as policy assertions) not supported by all consumer programs. Or the service may need to be made available to semi- or non-trusted consumers that could potentially abuse some of its capabilities.

Having one contract support a range of consumer types is challenging both from design and governance perspectives and can ultimately lead to security concerns and constraints that limit the service's overall effectiveness (Figure 14.15).

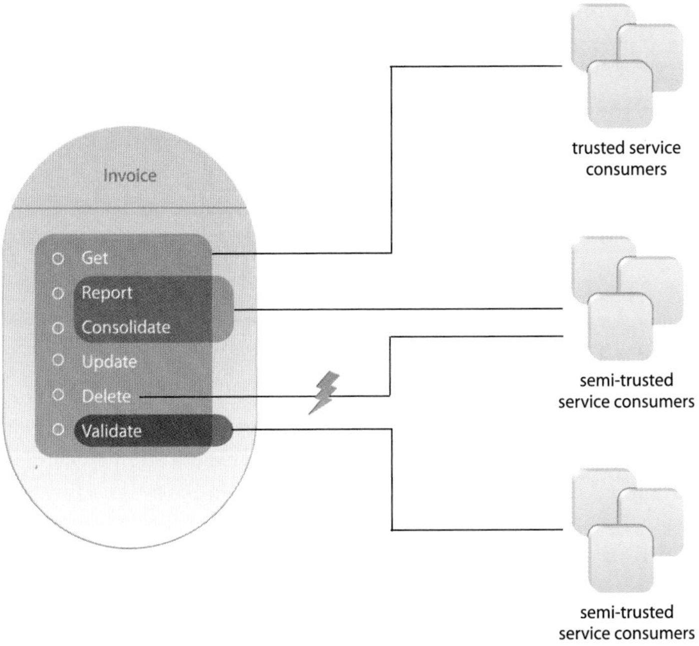

Figure 14.15

It can be undesirable to expose a service contract to all potential consumers, especially when some are less trusted than others. For example, exposing the full Invoice service contract to consumers that should only have access to a subset of its capabilities introduces the risk that consumers will attempt to access other capabilities anyway.

Solution

To accommodate different types of consumers, separate service contracts can be created for the same underlying service implementation. Even though this introduces redundancy in functional representation, it allows each contract to be extended and governed individually. It also provides the option of exposing a subset of the service capabilities to specific consumers (Figure 14.16).

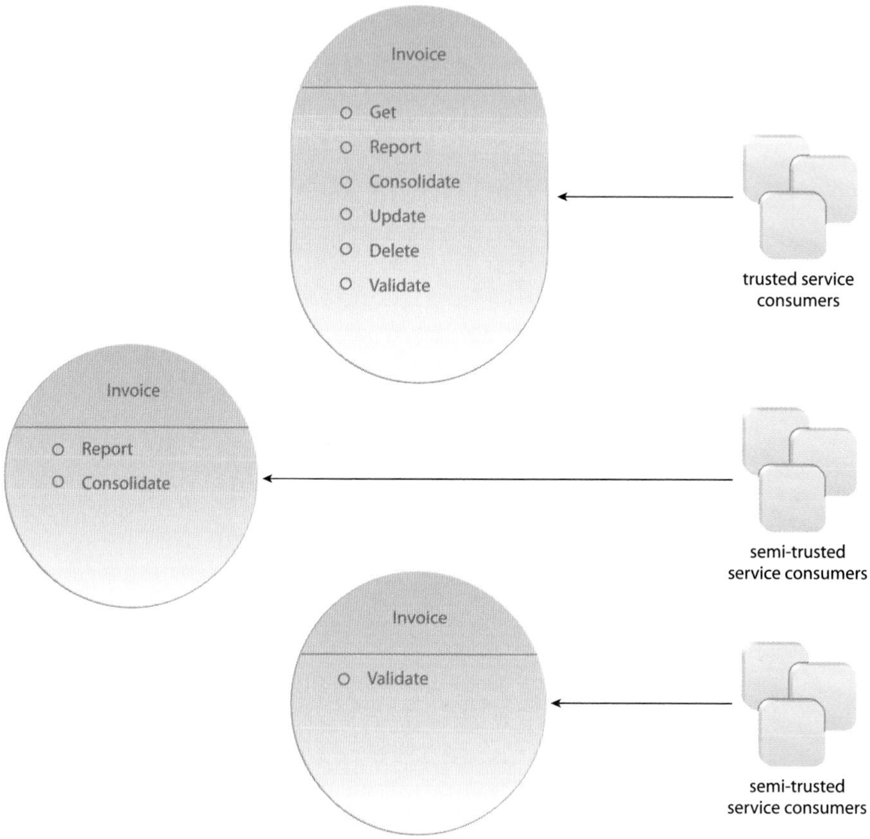

Figure 14.16

Separate contracts are created for the three service consumer categories. In some environments this may require the further qualification of the service name; for example, the three contracts may be named Invoice Admin, Invoice Reporting, Invoice Vendor.

Application

This pattern needs to be applied with care and moderation. Introducing multiple contracts leads to increased governance complexity and effort, as explained shortly in the *Impacts* section.

Often additional contracts are not considered necessary until well after the deployment of the service and its original contract. Therefore, it is recommended that new contracts not be created too reactively. Instead, each new consumer base (a group of related types of service consumer programs) should be well-defined so that it is confirmed that a new contract is warranted and that the nature of its expressed capabilities is clearly thought out.

The application of this pattern in general is more easily carried out if the service was originally designed according to Service Façade (333). A separate façade can actually be created for each new contract, as shown in Figure 14.17.

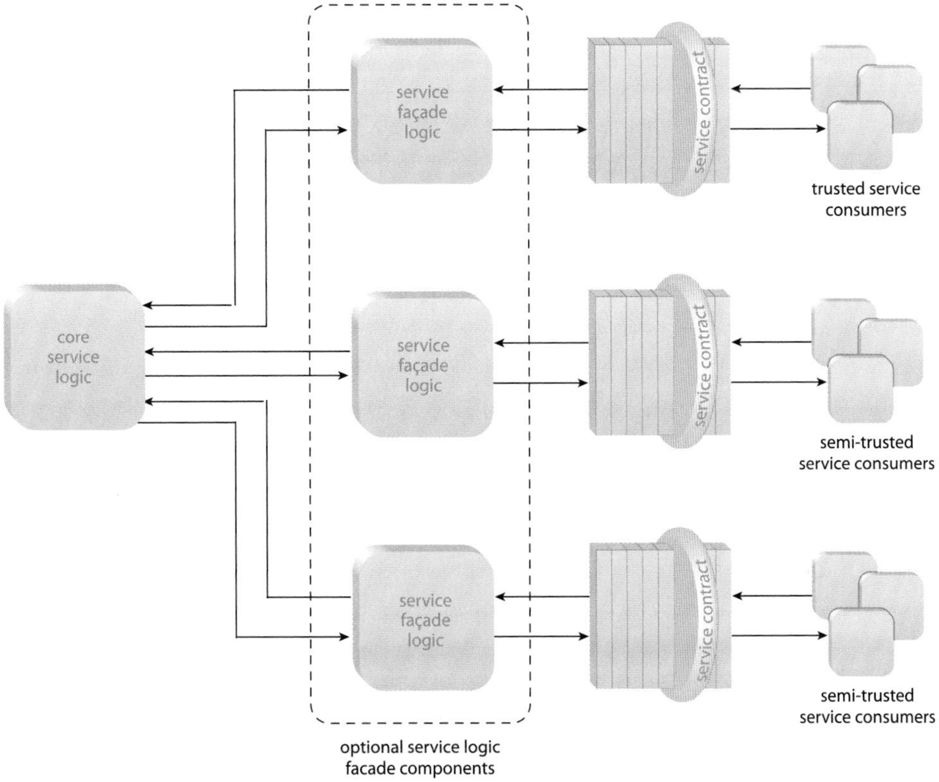

Figure 14.17

Multiple service contracts can be implemented with the support of Service Façade (333), which allows for contract-specific abstraction from the core underlying logic. This is especially relevant when contracts need to vary in terms of data representation support and security requirements.

There will be a natural tendency to want to modify the validation of contracts for different consumers. This also needs to be carefully assessed. Ideally, the contracts remain in alignment in how they express their respective capability sets. However, certain policies and security constraints may be applicable only to certain types of consumers (especially when having to facilitate both internal and external consumer bases).

Therefore, as a rule of thumb, it is best to limit the variation in validation logic to access control only. Validation logic based on underlying service business logic should remain the same across all contracts for the single service implementation. If different business rules or business constraints apply to different types of consumers, that decision logic may be best embedded within the underlying service logic, as per Validation Abstraction (429).

Impacts

From the perspective of the consumer, adding new contracts to the same service is the equivalent of adding new services. This pattern can therefore lead to the bloating of a service inventory and can further confuse consumer designers trying to discover or choose the appropriate variation of a contract. Additionally, new contracts will tend to introduce governance requirements so as to ensure that each establishes a legitimate endpoint.

Relationships

For Concurrent Contracts to be applied, the service contract itself should ideally be fully decoupled from the underlying service logic as per Decoupled Contract (401), and Service Façade (333) should ideally be applied to provide façade logic that supports multiple contracts without the need for redundant service logic.

Both Contract Denormalization (414) and Validation Abstraction (429) are employed to help optimize service contracts in support of the Service Abstraction design principle and also to facilitate different types of service consumers. Concurrent Contracts allows for varying levels of these two patterns to be applied to individual contracts, all for the same service. However, it could turn out that there is less of a need for Contract Denormalization (414) given that denormalized capabilities could simply exist in a different contract (Figure 14.18).

```
<definitions name="EformApplication" ...>
  ...
  <portType name="AppInt">
    <operation name="Add">
      <input message="tns:AddApp"/>
      <output message="tns:AddAppConfirm"/>
    </operation>
    <operation name="Update">
      <input message="tns:UpdateApp"/>
      <output message="tns:UpdateAppConfirm"/>
    </operation>
    <operation name="Get">
      <input message="tns:GetApp"/>
      <output message="tns:GetAppResults"/>
    </operation>
  </portType>
  ...
</definitions>
<wsp:Policy xmlns:wsp="...">
  ...
  <wsp:ExactlyOne>
    <wsp:SpecVersion wsp:Usage="wsp:Required"
      wsp:Preference="10"
      wsp:URI="http://schemas.xmlsoap.org/ws/2004/03/rm"/>
    <wsp:SpecVersion wsp:Usage="wsp:Required"
      wsp:Preference="1"
      wsp:URI="http://schemas.xmlsoap.org/ws/2003/02/rm"/>
  </wsp:ExactlyOne>
</wsp:Policy>
```

Example 14.4

A second service contract is created specifically for service consumers transmitting application documents electronically. In this version, the Delete operation is removed, and a policy is introduced requiring consumers to support one of two WS-ReliableMessaging specifications.

Validation Abstraction

How can service contracts be designed to more easily adapt to validation logic changes?

Problem	Service contracts that contain detailed validation constraints become more easily invalidated when the rules behind those constraints change.
Solution	Granular validation logic and rules can be abstracted away from the service contract, thereby decreasing constraint granularity and increasing the contract's potential longevity.
Application	Abstracted validation logic and rules need to be moved to the underlying service logic, a different service, a service agent, or elsewhere.
Impacts	This pattern can somewhat decentralize validation logic and can also complicate schema standardization.
Principles	Standardized Service Contract, Service Loose Coupling, Service Abstraction
Architecture	Service

Table 14.5

Profile summary for the Validation Abstraction pattern.

Problem

When building services as Web services, a great deal of validation logic can be expressed using the XML Schema and WS-Policy languages. These standards provide a comprehensive range of features that allow for the definition of very precise and sophisticated validation rules and constraints. By deferring the majority of validation constraints to the service contract, the underlying service logic is alleviated from having to concern itself with the validity and legitimacy of incoming message contents.

However, as part of the technical service contract, this validation logic expresses fixed terms of engagement to which all potential consumer programs need to comply. The day the underlying business rules or requirements (upon which some of the validation constraints may be based) change, it may not be possible to make the corresponding changes to the established contract without releasing a new version. New contract versions introduce governance burden, especially with agnostic services that have many consumers (Figure 14.19).

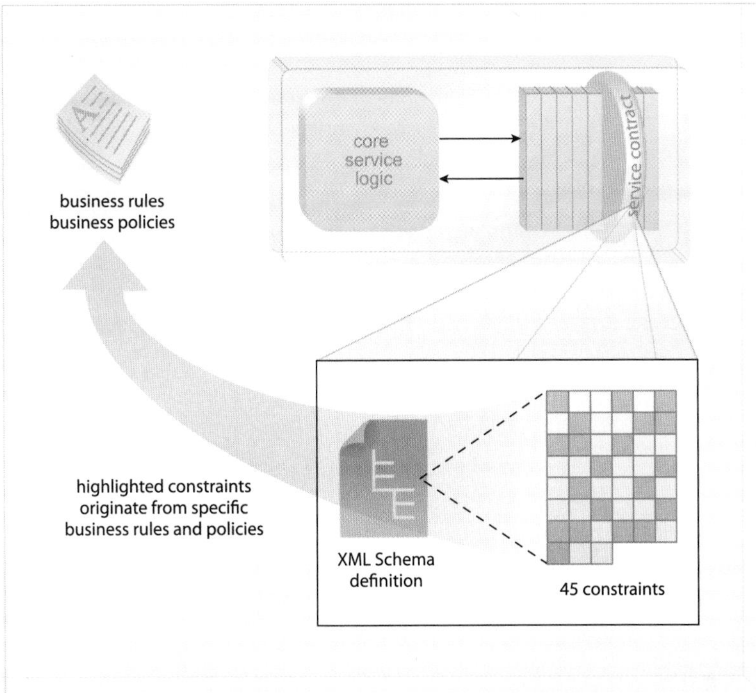

(the estimated chance that this service contract will be invalid within one year is 32%)

Figure 14.19

Many validation constraints that find their way into contract schemas are tied directly back to business rules and policies that may be subject to change. (In this figure, the dark green squares represent constraints based on business rules and policies.)

Solution

Depending on the nature of the message data being exchanged, there may be opportunities to decrease the constraint granularity of contract capabilities. This leads to a reduction in the quantity and restrictiveness of validation logic embedded in the service contract by deferring select validation constraints elsewhere.

The less validation logic in the contract, the lower the risk of the contract being impacted by overarching business changes. Therefore, the potential longevity of a service contract is extended (Figure 14.20).

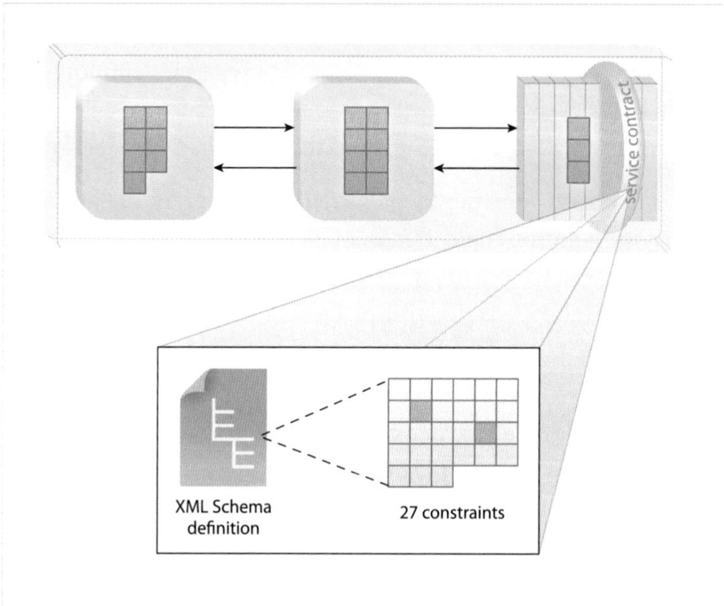

Figure 14.20
By reducing the overall quantity of constraints and especially filtering out those more prone to change, the longevity of a service contract can be extended.

Application

This is an example of a pattern that supports service design but imposes change upon the underlying schema and policy definitions. In other words, it asks that schemas and policies be somewhat more conservatively designed in support of service longevity.

Examples of the types of validation logic that Validation Abstraction tends to target include:

- detailed and granular validation constraints that express very specific conditions
- constraints based upon precise value characteristics (such as null values or the minimum or maximum allowable length of a document value)
- constraints based on embedded enumeration values or code lists
- policy expressions that define specific properties or behaviors derived from business rules

Another area in which this pattern can be effectively applied is the actual typing of message data. Instead of tuning data types to current document definition requirements, an approach can be adopted whereby more lenient data types are employed. This especially affects the simple types used within XML schemas to represent specific document values. Furthermore, attachments can even be utilized to bypass contract-level typing altogether.

As with the other deferred constraints, the actual validation of the affected values occurs within the underlying solution logic. For validation and policy-based constraints that still need to be communicated to consumer program designers, descriptions of the constraints can be added to supplemental service contract documentation, such as the SLA.

Impacts

One of the benefits of decoupled service contracts is that they provide a central location for the placement of validation logic. All of the constraints messages need to comply to can be enforced at the outer rim of the service boundary so that only valid messages make their way through to the underlying service logic.

Applying this pattern removes validation logic from the contract layer, decentralizing it and thereby requiring it to be maintained in different locations. Although this increases maintenance effort, this increase is generally not equivalent to the governance impact of having to introduce a new version of a service contract or a new capability.

Relationships

When applying Validation Abstraction, it is important to take Policy Centralization (207) and Schema Centralization (200) into account because when contracts use centralized policies or schemas, their validation logic may not be able to be abstracted as much as this pattern advocates.

One of the major types of logic this pattern looks to remove or hide from the service contract is business rules. Therefore, Rules Centralization (216) is related, as is Entity Abstraction (175) due to the fact that it produces services that encapsulate business entity logic (which generally includes associated business rules) and also posses contracts with multiple capabilities that may be affected by this pattern.

Where exactly abstracted validation logic goes is not dictated by this pattern, which is why Service Agent (543) and Rules Centralization (216) provide possible options. When applying Concurrent Contracts (421), this pattern can be used to customize each contract to facilitate different consumer requirements.

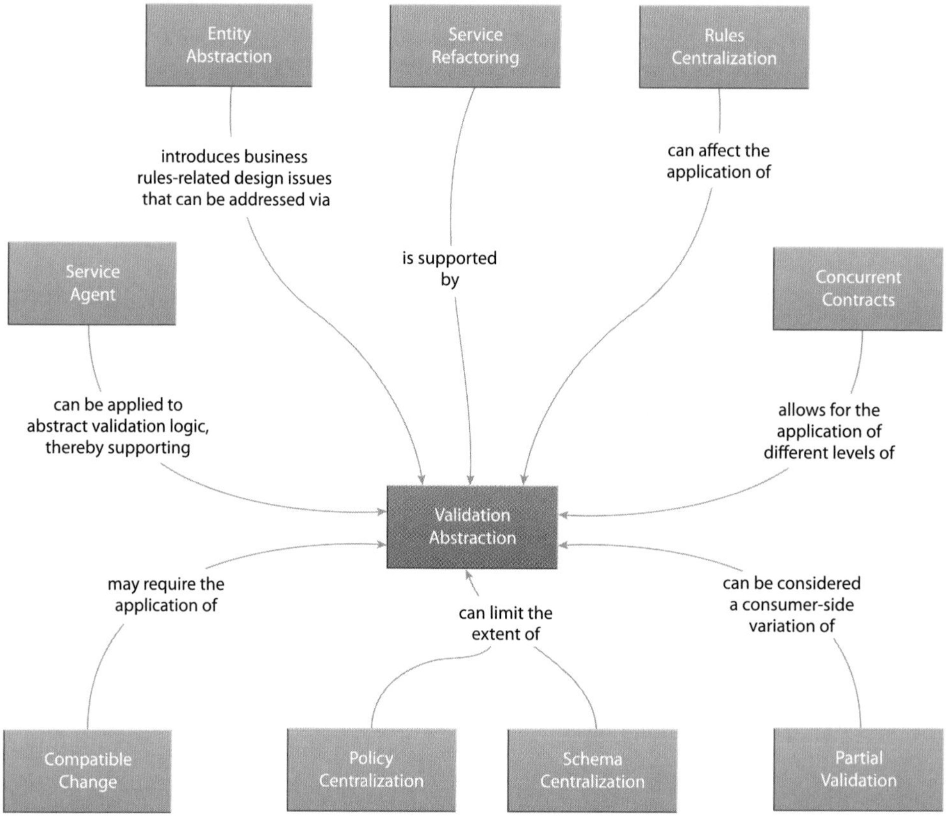

Figure 14.21

Validation Abstraction's goal of streamlining service contract content can directly tie into the application of some patterns, while also meeting resistance from others.

CASE STUDY EXAMPLE

The case study example for Concurrent Contracts (421) introduced portions of the WSDL definition for the EformApplication service contract, including the following construct for the Add operation:

```
<operation name="Add">
  <input message="tns:AddApp"/>
  <output message="tns:AddAppConfirm"/>
</operation>
```

The existing validation logic for externally received application logic is comprised of the following rules:

- Applications must be accompanied by an ID value auto-generated by the client user-interface used by the person to fill out and then submit the application electronically on behalf of the company. This ID must consist of two sets of three digits separated by a hyphen.
- The name of the company submitting the application. The name value is limited to 100 characters.
- The federal tax number of the company. This value is limited to 12 digits.
- The company's FRC classification, as selected via a pre-populated drop-down list by the person filling out the online application.
- Additional remarks provided by the person completing the application via an open, multi-line text field.

The original XML Schema types associated with the AddApp message mirror these validation rules, as follows:

```
<xsd:schema xmlns:xsd="http://www.w3.org/2001/XMLSchema"
  targetNamespace="http://frc/applications"
  xmlns="http://frc/genproc">
  <xsd:element name="submission" type="AppType"/>
  <xsd:complexType>
    <xsd:sequence>
      <xsd:element name="submission" type="AppType"
        maxOccurs="unbounded"/>
    </xsd:sequence>
  </xsd:complexType>
  <xsd:complexType name="AppType">
    <xsd:sequence>
      <xsd:element name="AppID" type="AppIDType"/>
      <xsd:element name="Name" type="NameType"/>
      <xsd:element name="TaxNum" type="TaxNumType"/>
      <xsd:element name="Class" type="ClassType"/>
      <xsd:element name="Comments" type="xsd:string"/>
    </xsd:sequence>
  </xsd:complexType>
  <xsd:simpleType name="AppIDType">
    <xsd:restriction base="xsd:string">
      <xsd:pattern value="\d{3}\-\d{3}\"/>
```

```
    </xsd:restriction>
  </xsd:simpleType>
  <xsd:simpleType name="NameType">
    <xsd:restriction base="xsd:string">
      <xsd:length value="100"/>
    </xsd:restriction>
  </xsd:simpleType>
  <xsd:simpleType name="TaxNumType">
    <xsd:restriction base="xsd:integer">
      <xsd:totalDigits value="12"/>
    </xsd:restriction>
  </xsd:simpleType>
  <xsd:simpleType name="ClassType">
    <xsd:restriction base="xsd:string">
      <xsd:enumeration value="CDA"/>
      <xsd:enumeration value="TRU"/>
      <xsd:enumeration value="CMI"/>
      <xsd:enumeration value="TER"/>
      <xsd:enumeration value="LBR"/>
      <xsd:enumeration value="LBA"/>
      <xsd:enumeration value="MAG"/>
      <xsd:enumeration value="IST"/>
      <xsd:enumeration value="GER"/>
    </xsd:restriction>
  </xsd:simpleType>
</xsd:schema>
```

Example 14.5

The original schema definition for the EformApplication service contract.

It was initially considered reasonable for the AddApp operation to have a relatively fine-grained level of constraint coupling because the application documents received by this service were submitted only by Web client logic also developed by the FRC. If the business validation rules changed, then both the Web forms and the schema types for the EformApplication service contract were also changed correspondingly.

However, a recent requirement emerged to allow non-Web client-based programs to also submit and retrieve application data. Security policies do not allow for another external endpoint to be published for application processing, which means that the EformApplication contract now needs to accommodate data exchanges with both Web clients and B2B-style partner service consumers.

To date, the EformApplication service has been in production for five months during which one classification code had to be removed and two new codes had to be added.

Once external partner consumer programs bind to the published EformApplication contract, it becomes cumbersome and risky to change validation constraints, such as embedded code lists. The team responsible for this service decides to loosen the validation rules in the contract by replacing the enumerated class code list with an allowable input string of three characters, as shown here:

```
<xsd:schema xmlns:xsd="http://www.w3.org/2001/XMLSchema"
  targetNamespace="http://frc/applications"
  xmlns="http://frc/genproc">
  <xsd:element name="submission" type="AppType"/>
  <xsd:complexType>
    <xsd:sequence>
      <xsd:element name="submission" type="AppType"
        maxOccurs="unbounded"/>
    </xsd:sequence>
  </xsd:complexType>
  <xsd:complexType name="AppType">
    <xsd:sequence>
      <xsd:element name="AppID" type="AppIDType"/>
      <xsd:element name="Name" type="NameType"/>
      <xsd:element name="TaxNum" type="TaxNumType"/>
      <xsd:element name="Class" type="ClassType"/>
      <xsd:element name="Comments" type="xsd:string"/>
    </xsd:sequence>
  </xsd:complexType>
  <xsd:simpleType name="AppIDType">
    <xsd:restriction base="xsd:string">
      <xsd:pattern value="\d{3}\-\d{3}\"/>
    </xsd:restriction>
  </xsd:simpleType>
  <xsd:simpleType name="NameType">
    <xsd:restriction base="xsd:string">
      <xsd:length value="100"/>
    </xsd:restriction>
  </xsd:simpleType>
  <xsd:simpleType name="TaxNumType">
    <xsd:restriction base="xsd:integer">
      <xsd:totalDigits value="12"/>
    </xsd:restriction>
  </xsd:simpleType>
  <xsd:simpleType name="ClassType">
```

```
    <xsd:restriction base="xsd:string">
      <xsd:length value="3"/>
    </xsd:restriction>
  </xsd:simpleType>
</xsd:schema>
```

Example 14.6

The revised XML Schema definition with coarser-grained constraint granularity due to the abstraction of classification code validation.

Chapter 15

Legacy Encapsulation Patterns

Legacy Wrapper

Multi-Channel Endpoint

File Gateway

Introducing a collection of standardized service endpoints into an established IT enterprise will almost always result in a need to manage the marriage of service-orientation with legacy encapsulation. This chapter provides a set of patterns dedicated to addressing common challenges with service encapsulation of legacy systems and environments.

Legacy Wrapper (441) establishes the fundamental concept of wrapping proprietary legacy APIs with a standardized service contract, while Multi-Channel Endpoint (451) builds on this concept to introduce a service that decouples legacy systems from delivery channel-specific programs. File Gateway (457) further provides bridging logic for services that need to encapsulate and interact with legacy systems that produce flat files.

Legacy Wrapper

By Thomas Erl, Satadru Roy

How can wrapper services with non-standard contracts be prevented from spreading indirect consumer-to-implementation coupling?

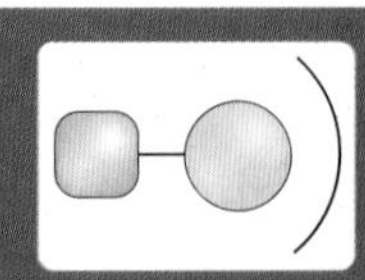

Problem	Wrapper services required to encapsulate legacy logic are often forced to introduce a non-standard service contract with high technology coupling requirements, resulting in a proliferation of implementation coupling throughout all service consumer programs.
Solution	The non-standard wrapper service can be replaced by or further wrapped with a standardized service contract that extracts, encapsulates, and possibly eliminates legacy technical details from the contract.
Application	A custom service contract and required service logic need to be developed to represent the proprietary legacy interface.
Impacts	The introduction of an additional service adds a layer of processing and associated performance overhead.
Principles	Standardized Service Contract, Service Loose Coupling, Service Abstraction
Architecture	Service

Table 15.1

Profile summary for the Legacy Wrapper pattern.

Problem

Legacy systems must often be encapsulated by services established by proprietary component APIs or Web service adapter products. The resulting technical interface is frequently fixed and non-customizable. Because the contract is pre-determined by the product vendor or constrained by legacy component APIs, it is not compliant with contract design standards applied to a given service inventory.

Furthermore, the nature of API and Web service adapter contracts is often such that they contain embedded, implementation-specific (and sometimes technology-specific) details. This imposes the corresponding forms of implementation and technology coupling upon all service consumers (Figure 15.1).

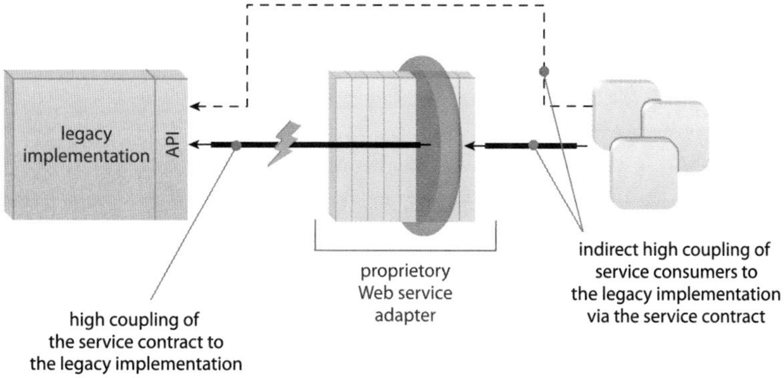

Figure 15.1

High contract-to-logic coupling resulting in high implementation coupling by service consumers.

Solution

Although a legacy system API or a Web service adapter will expose an official, generic entry point into legacy system logic, it is often unadvisable to classify such an endpoint as an official member of a service inventory. Instead, it can be safer to view legacy APIs and Web service adapters as extensions of the legacy environment providing just another proprietary interface that is available for service encapsulation.

This perspective allows for the creation of a standardized legacy wrapper service that expresses legacy function in a standardized manner. The result is a design that enables the full abstraction of proprietary legacy characteristics (Figure 15.2), which provides the freedom of evolving or replacing the legacy system with minimal impact on existing service consumers.

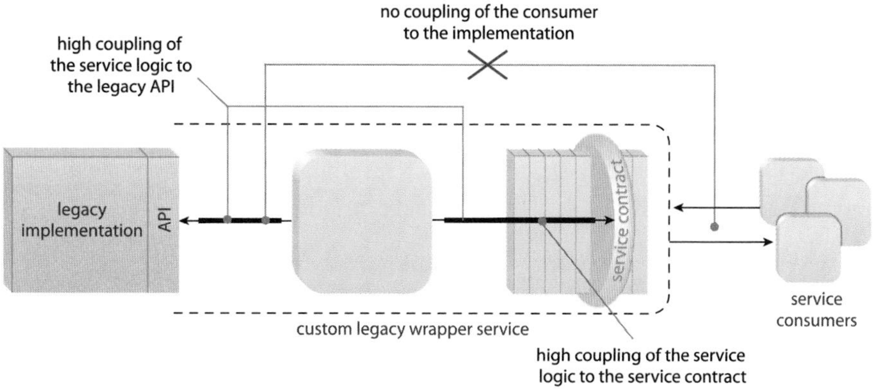

Figure 15.2

Tight coupling of the service logic to both the legacy API and the service contract alleviates service consumers from implementation coupling.

Application

The application of this pattern is typically associated with the introduction of a new service contract. However, when wrapping only the parts of a legacy resource that fall within a pre-defined service boundary, this pattern may result in just the addition of a new capability to an existing service contract.

Either way, the wrapper service (or capability) will typically contain logic that performs transformation between its standardized contract and the native legacy interface. Often, this form of transformation is accomplished by eliminating and encapsulating technical information, as follows:

- *Eliminating Technical Information* – Often legacy input and output data contain highly proprietary characteristics, such as message correlation IDs, error codes, audit information, etc. Many of these details can be removed from the wrapper contract through additional internal transformation. For example, error codes could be translated to SOAP faults, and message correlation IDs can be generated within the wrapper service implementation. In the latter case, the consumers can communicate with the wrapper service over a blocking communication protocol such as HTTP and hence would not need to know about correlation IDs.
- *Encapsulating Technical Information* – When service consumers still need to pass on legacy-specific data (such as audit-related information) the message exchanged by the legacy wrapper contract can be designed to partition standardized business data from proprietary legacy data into body and header sections, respectively. In this case, both the legacy wrapper service and its consumer will need to carry out additional processing to assemble and extract data from the header and body sections of incoming and outgoing messages.

The former approach usually results in a utility service whereas the latter option will tend to add the wrapper logic as an extension of a business service. It can be beneficial to establish a sole utility wrapper service for a legacy system so that all required transformation logic is centralized within that service's underlying logic. If capabilities from multiple services each access the native APIs or Web service adapter interfaces, the necessary transformation logic will need to be distributed (decentralized). If a point in time arrives where the legacy system is replaced with newer technology, it will impact multiple services.

> **NOTE**
>
> Some ERP environments allow for the customization of local APIs but still insist on auto-generating Web service contracts. When building services as Web services, these types of environments may still warrant encapsulation via a separate, standardized Web service. However, be sure to first explore any API customization features. Sometimes it is possible to customize a native ERP object or API to such an extent that actual contract design standards can be applied. If the API is standardized, then the auto-generated Web service contract also may be standardized because it will likely mirror the API.

Impacts

Adding a new wrapper layer introduces performance overhead associated with the additional service invocation and data transformation requirements.

Also, expecting a legacy wrapper contract alone to fully shield consumers from being affected from when underlying legacy systems are changed or replaced can be unrealistic. When new systems or resources are introduced into a service architecture, the overall behavior of the service may be impacted, even when the contract remains the same. In this case, it may be required to further supplement the service logic with additional functions that compensate for any potential negative effects these behavioral changes may have on consumers. Service Façade (333) is often used for this purpose.

Relationships

Legacy Wrapper makes legacy resources accessible on an inter-service basis. It can therefore be part of any service capability that requires legacy functionality. Entity and utility services are the most common candidates because they tend to encapsulate logic that represents either fixed business-centric boundaries or technology resources. Therefore, this pattern is often applied in conjunction with Entity Abstraction (175) and Utility Abstraction (168).

Patterns that often introduce proprietary products or out-of-the-box services, such as Rules Centralization (216), also may end up having to rely on Legacy Wrapper to make their services part of a federated service inventory. Service Data Replication (350) can be combined with this pattern to provide access to replicated proprietary repositories, and File Gateway (457) may be applied to supplement the wrapper contract with specialized internal legacy encapsulation logic.

Because of the broker-related responsibilities that a legacy wrapper service will generally need to assume, it is further expected that it will require the application of Data Format Transformation (681) or Data Model Transformation (671), and possibly Protocol Bridging (687).

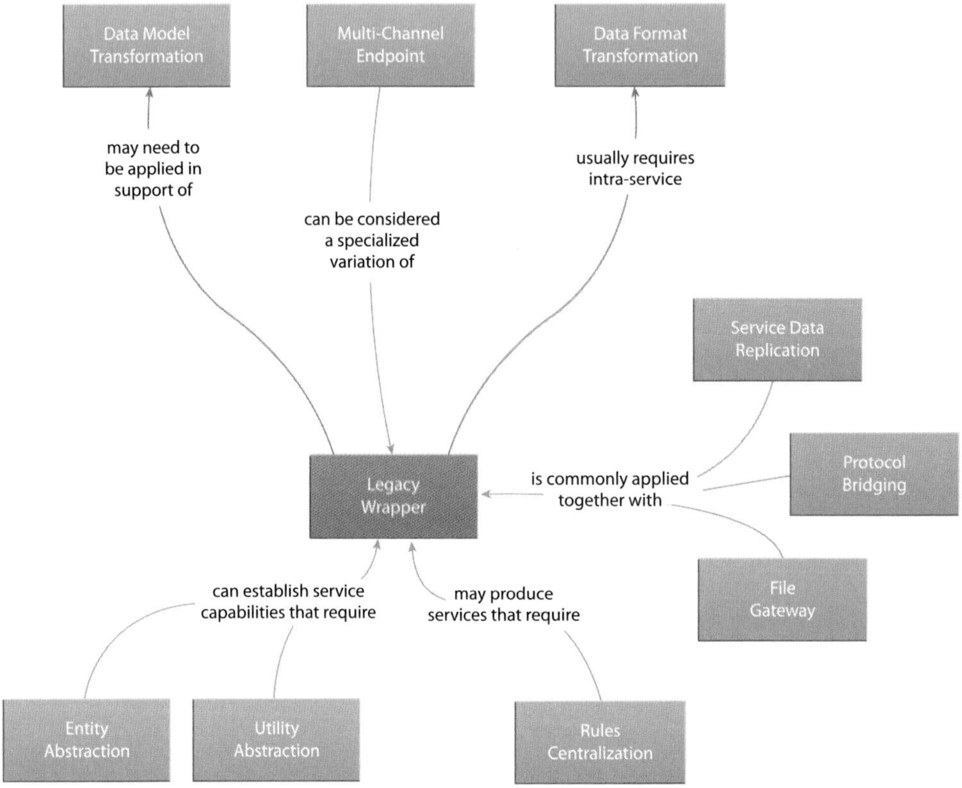

Figure 15.3

Legacy Wrapper provides a convenient means of bringing legacy logic into a service inventory without compromising the integrity of the service contracts. It therefore is of interest to any pattern that may require access to legacy resources.

Legacy Wrapper is a therefore frequently applied together with Enterprise Service Bus (704) in order to leverage the broker capabilities natively provided by ESB platforms.

CASE STUDY EXAMPLE

Subsequent to the implementation of the Appealed Assessments service (described in the Service Façade (333) case study example), the Data Controller component is modified to no longer provide access to one of the four data repositories. Instead, architects plan to add the lost data access functionality to the Appealed Assessments service's Data Relayer component. This would make that component less of a service façade, while continuing to preserve the functionality promised by the Appealed Assessments service contract.

However, an idea for another option emerges. The repository in question is part of a legacy environment (called MainAST103) that runs on mainframe technologies and limits data access to a generic CICS API but also provides the option of auto-generating a wrapper Web service interface to mirror this API. At first this seems interesting, but when the auto-generated WSDL (with embedded XML Schema content) is studied, the FRC architects want no part of it.

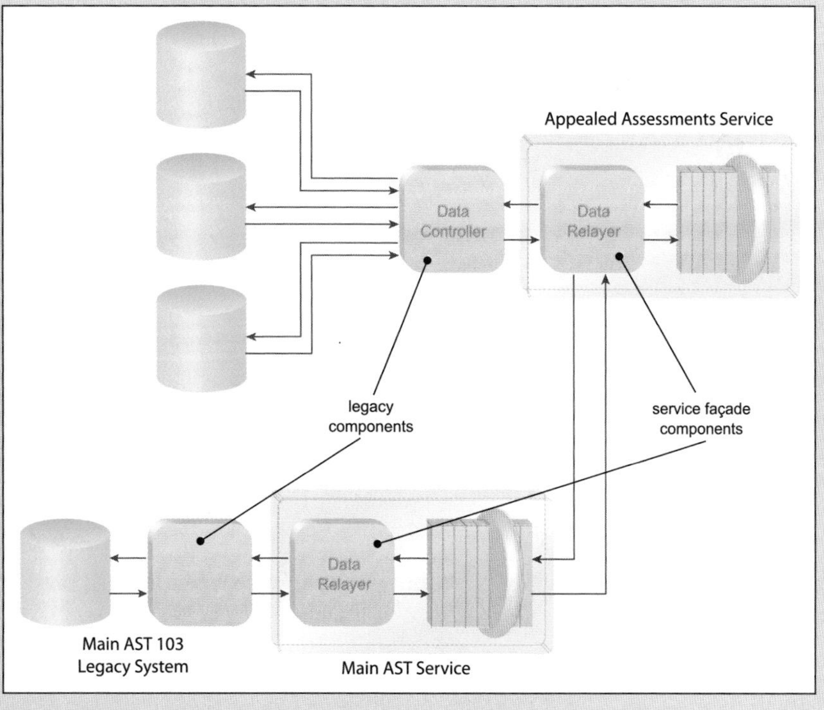

Figure 15.4
The revised Appealed Assessments service architecture.

Instead, they opt to create a new MainAST utility service (Figure 15.4) to "wrap" this legacy mainframe system and associated API. The functional context of this utility service is limited to this one CICS API accessed via MQ messaging, and its core service logic is dedicated to converting requests, responses, and data to and from the standardized Web service contract models and the native, proprietary legacy API formats.

Provided here are some fragments of the input and output messages exchanged by the CICS API:

```
000100        01 ASSESSMENT-APPEAL-REQUEST.
000200        05 ASSESSMENT-APPEAL-CONTROL-DATA.
000300        10 SECURITY-TOKEN       PIC X(10).
000500        10 MESSAGE-ID           PIC X(20).
000600        10 MESSAGE-CORR-ID      PIC X(20).
000700        05 ASSESSMENT-APPEAL -DATA.
000800        10 AGENCY-ID            PIC X(20).
000900        10 ASSESSMENT-NUMBER    PIC X(10).
001000        10 APPEAL-REASON-CODE   PIC X(10).
001100        10 APPEAL-DATE          PIC X(08).
```

Example 15.1

A fragment of the COBOL COPYBOOK description for the input message of the legacy CICS API. Note that because communication with the MainAST 103 legacy program is carried out through MQ-based messaging, technical information such as security tokens, message IDs and correlation IDs are expected and used for authorization and message correlation purposes.

```
000100        01 ASSESSMENT-APPEAL-RESPONSE.
000200        05 ASSESSMENT-APPEAL-RESPONSE-CONTROL-DATA.
000300        10 MESSAGE-ID                        PIC X(20).
000400        10 MESSAGE-CORR-ID                   PIC X(20).
000700        05 ASSESSMENT-APPEAL-RESPONSE-DATA.
000800        10 RETURN-CODE                       PIC 9(2).
000900        10 ERROR-TYPE                        PIC X(2).
000900        10 ERROR-CODE-DESC                   PIC X(20).
001000        10 APPEAL-RESULT-CODE                PIC X(10).
```

Example 15.2

A fragment of the COBOL COPYBOOK for the response message. This response message also contains technical information, such as message and correlation IDs. As is typical with mainframe-based APIs, the result of the transaction invocation (and possible errors) are communicated through the return code, error code, error descriptions, etc.

CASE STUDY EXAMPLE

Whenever a lumber company decides to appeal an FRC policy violation assessment, it needs to initiate a separate appeals process for which it also is required to pay a new fee.

The FRC further offers an EDI system that can be accessed by authorized companies (or their attorneys) to submit these payments. The FRC also operates a call center that takes calls from company accounting departments through which payments can also be made. In this case, the call center representative collects the payment information over the phone and enters it into an internal system.

Each method of payment translates into a different delivery channel for payment data. Historically, these channels were independently supported by different systems. The call center system is a custom-developed application that integrates with the central accounting system, whereas the EDI interface is essentially a dated B2B system that has been in place for 10 years and acts as a wrapper for a legacy database.

Payment data is collected in different formats and stored in different repositories. Once a month, batch exports are carried out to extract payment data from the B2B database into the accounting system.

With talk of allowing FRC field agents to collect payments remotely and submit them via mobile devices, architects want to take steps to avoid introducing yet another application and data silo. They decide to introduce an intermediary processing layer based on the multi-channel service. This layer splits the backend call center application and the EDI environment away from the front-end call center application and external EDI consumers.

File Gateway

By Satadru Roy

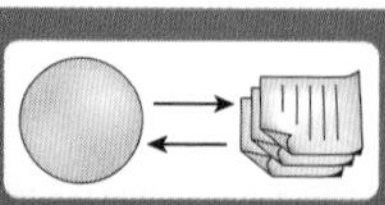

How can service logic interact with legacy systems that can only share information by exchanging files?

Problem	Data records contained in flat files produced by a legacy system need to be processed individually by service logic, but legacy systems are not capable of directly invoking services. Conversely, service logic may need to produce information for the legacy system, but building file creation and transfer functionality into the service can result in an inflexible design.
Solution	Intermediary two-way file processing logic is positioned between the legacy system and the service.
Application	For inbound data the file gateway processing logic can detect file drops and leverage available broker features to perform Data Model Transformation (671) and Data Format Transformation (681). On the outbound side, this logic intercepts information produced by services and packages them (with possible transformation) into new or existing files for consumption by the legacy system.
Impacts	The type of logic provided by this pattern is unsuitable when immediate replies are required by either service or legacy system. Deployment and governance of two-way file processing logic can further add to operational complexity and may require specialized administration skills.
Principles	Service Loose Coupling
Architecture	Service

Table 15.3

Profile summary for the File Gateway pattern.

Problem

Quite often, service-enabled applications need to process information that is produced only periodically by legacy systems as flat files that can contain a large number of data records separated by delimiters. Any application that needs to access the data in these files will usually be required to iterate through each record to perform necessary calculations.

However, such applications also have to take on the additional responsibility of polling directories to check when the files are actually created and released by the legacy system. Once detected, these files then may need to be parsed, moved (or removed), renamed, transformed, and archived before processing can be considered successful. This has traditionally resulted in overly complex and inflexible data access architectures that revolve around file drop polling and file format-related processing.

The limitations of this architecture further compound when this form of processing needs to be encapsulated by a service. Legacy systems are designed with the assumption that other legacy consumers are accessing the flat files they produce and therefore have no concept of a service, let alone a means of invoking services (as depicted in Figure 15.8).

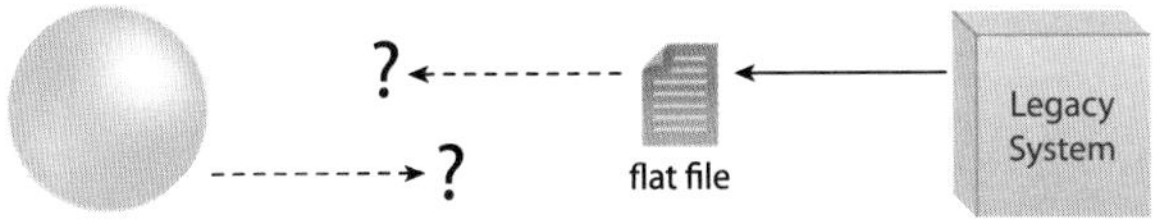

Figure 15.8
The flat files produced by legacy system are intended for customized legacy consumers, not for services.

Solution

Service-friendly gateway logic is introduced, capable of handling file detection and processing and subsequent communication with services. This allows services to consume flat files as legacy consumer systems would. It further introduces the opportunity to optimize this logic to improve upon any existing limitations in the legacy environment (Figure 15.9).

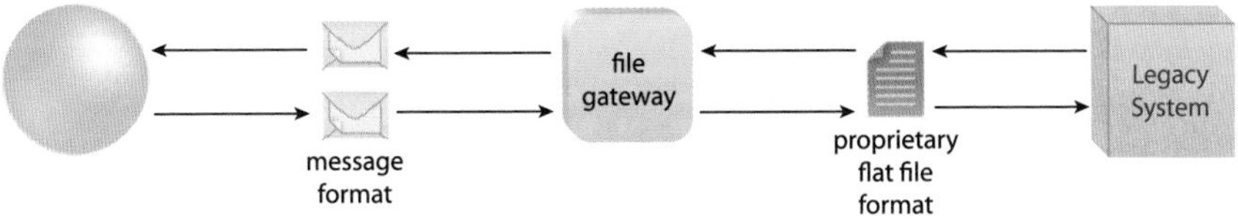

Figure 15.9
File gateway logic acts as a mediator between a service and a flat-file-based legacy system.

Application

The gateway logic introduced by this pattern is most commonly wrapped in a separate utility component positioned independently from business services and is therefore capable of acting as an intermediary between legacy systems and services requiring access to the

legacy data. However, the option also exists to limit this logic to individual service architectures.

This file processing logic will typically be comprised of routines that carry out the following tasks:

- File drop polling with configurable polling cycles.
- File and delimiter parsing and data retrieval with configurable parameters that determine how many records should be read and processed at one time.
- File data transformation, as per Data Format Transformation (681) and possible Data Model Transformation (671).
- Service invocation and file data transfer to services.
- File cleanup, renaming, and/or archiving.

Note that making the polling frequency and number of records processed at a time configurable allows the file processing logic to control the volume of messages sent to a service over a period of time. If a given service takes longer than usual to process a batch of records, these two settings can be tweaked to allow the service to catch up and, similarly, the rate can be increased if the service is processing incoming messages quicker than they are generated.

When services need to share data with legacy systems only capable of receiving flat files, this logic can act as the recipient and broker of messages responsible for transforming them into the legacy format. For example, for the first batch of incoming data the file gateway component can write records out to a flat file with special character-based delimiters separating each data record from another. Subsequent incoming data could then be appended to this file until a pre-specified file size limit is reached, after which it creates a new file and repeats this process.

Impacts

Most of the impacts of this pattern are related to the impacts of file transfer in general. Because the process of transferring files is inherently asynchronous, it naturally introduces (often significant) latency to just about any data exchange scenario.

It can further be challenging to position file gateway components as reusable utility services due to the frequent need to configure the parameters of file transfer and processing for each service-to-legacy system file transfer.

Careful planning for mangement, administration, and monitoring is also required to maintain expectations related to message processing volumes and performance.

Relationships

As explained previously, File Gateway commonly introduces utility services that depend on Data Format Transformation (681) and possible Data Model Transformation (671) to perform the conversion logic necessary for flat file data to be packaged and sent to services.

When viewing file transfer itself as a communications protocol, this pattern can be viewed as a variation of Protocol Bridging (687) as it essentially overcomes disparity in legacy and service communication platforms.

The application of Legacy Wrapper (441) may require File Gateway when a legacy system producing flat files needs to be wrapped by a standardized service contract and Service Agent (543), Service Callback (566), and Event-Driven Messaging (599) can be further applied to establish more sophisticated processing extensions around the file gateway logic.

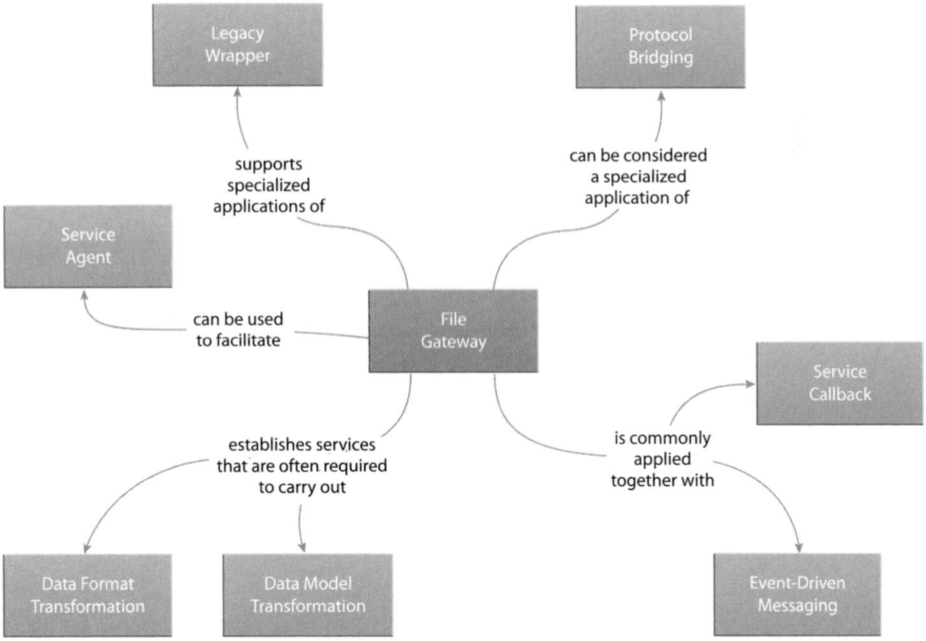

Figure 15.10

File Gateway establishes relationships with all of the transformation patterns associated with Service Broker (707).

File Gateway is also commonly applied together with Enterprise Service Bus (704) whereby the file gateway component is deployed within the bus platform and is designed to leverage its inherent broker and routing features.

NOTE

This pattern leverages and builds upon a number of established EAI patterns, such as File Transfer (Hohpe, Woolf).

CASE STUDY EXAMPLE

The FRC EDI system explained in the preceding example for Multi-Channel Endpoint (451) is currently subjected to a monthly batch extract of payment data that is manually imported into the accounting system. The batch extract produces a large set of flat files, with each file containing payment information for one transaction.

The FRC has also been developing a new Accounts Web service responsible for providing access to information pertaining to corporate accounts held by companies registered with the FRC. This service needs to be extended with a GetPaymentHistory operation that will retrieve payment records for a given account.

The payment details collected by the call center are immediately entered into the accounting database and are therefore readily accessible by the Accounts service. However, because the balance of the payment details that are stored in the EDI legacy repository are only imported monthly, the service will rarely gain access to current data.

Upon further investigation, architects discover an API provided by the legacy environment that allows extracts to be performed at any time. With this interface available to them, they decide to design an architecture with the following parts:

- a file gateway component capable of interacting with the API
- a WS-Addressing framework capable of supporting endpoint references

With this architecture, each time the GetPaymentHistory operation is called, the following processing steps occur:

1. The Accounts service invokes the file gateway component and passes it its data request along with its destination address, as per Service Callback (566).

2. The file gateway component initiates a file extract.
3. When the extraction is complete and requested data is available, the component contacts the Accounts service via the provided destination address.
4. The Accounts service is invoked and receives the data.

The internal file gateway logic is further optimized to poll the target directory for file drops in advance on a periodic basis so that the time required to initiate a batch extract for the most current data is reduced because a base of recent payment data has already been extracted.

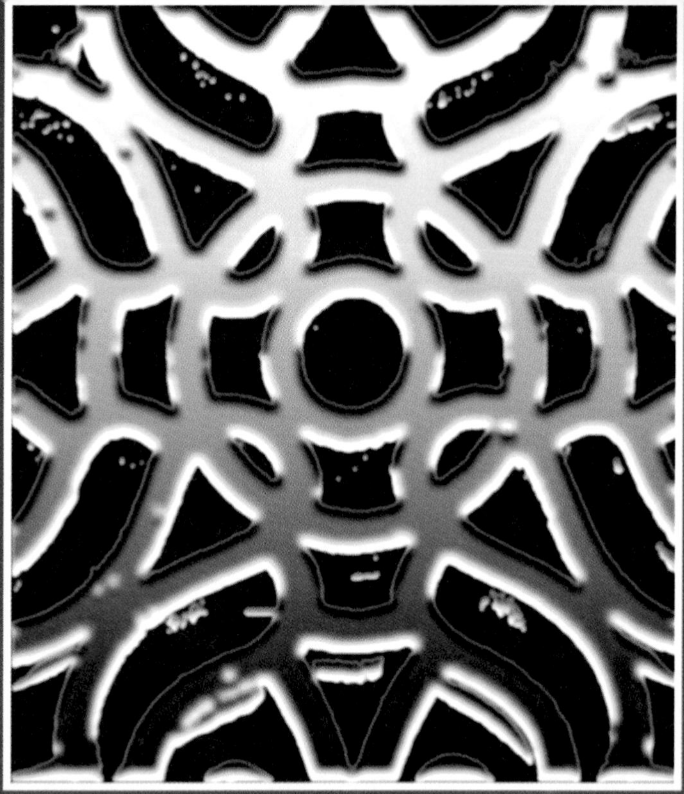

Chapter 16

Service Governance Patterns

- Compatible Change
- Version Identification
- Termination Notification
- Service Refactoring
- Service Decomposition
- Proxy Capability
- Decomposed Capability
- Distributed Capability

NOTE

The governance patterns in this chapter focus only on design-related governance issues that pertain to service architecture. The upcoming book *SOA Governance* as part of this book series will provide a collection of broader technical and organizational best practices and patterns.

Despite best efforts during analysis and modeling phases to deliver services with a broad range of capabilities, they will still be subjected to new situations and requirements that can challenge the scope of their original design. For this reason, several patterns have emerged to help evolve a service without compromising its responsibilities as an active member of a service inventory.

Compatible Change (465) and Version Identification (472) are focused on the versioning of service contracts. Similarly, Termination Notification (478) addresses the retirement of services or service contracts.

The most fundamental pattern in this chapter is Service Refactoring (484), which leverages a loosely (and ideally decoupled) contract to allow the underlying logic and implementation to be upgraded and improved.

The trio of Service Decomposition (489), Decomposed Capability (504), and Proxy Capability (497) establish techniques that allow coarser-grained services to be physically partitioned into multiple fine-grained services that can help further improve composition performance. Distributed Capability (510) also provides a specialized, refactoring-related design solution to help increase service scalability via internally distributed processing deferral.

Compatible Change

By David Orchard, Chris Riley

How can a service contract be modified without impacting consumers?

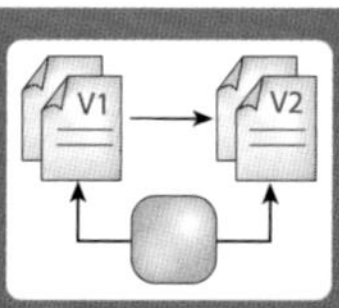

Problem	Changing an already-published service contract can impact and invalidate existing consumer programs.
Solution	Some changes to the service contract can be backwards-compatible, thereby avoiding negative consumer impacts.
Application	Service contract changes can be accommodated via extension or by the loosening of existing constraints or by applying Concurrent Contracts (421).
Impacts	Compatible changes still introduce versioning governance effort, and the technique of loosening constraints can lead to vague contract designs.
Principles	Standardized Service Contract, Service Loose Coupling
Architecture	Service

Table 16.1
Profile summary for the Compatible Change pattern.

Problem

After a service is initially deployed as part of an active service inventory, it will make its capabilities available as an enterprise resource. Consumers will be designed to invoke and interact with the service via its contract in order to leverage its capabilities for their own use. As a result, dependencies will naturally be formed between the service contract and those consumer programs. If the contract needs to be changed thereafter, that change can risk impacting existing consumers that were designed in accordance with the original, unchanged contract (Figure 16.1).

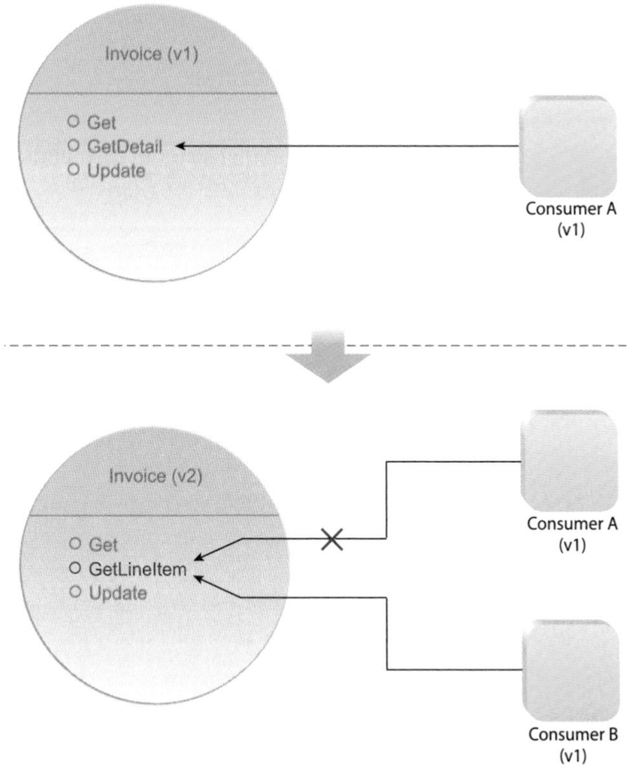

Figure 16.1

The name of a service capability is modified after version 1 of a service contract is already in use. As a result, version 2 of the contract is incompatible with Consumer A.

Solution

Wherever possible, changes to established service contracts can be made to preserve the contract's backwards compatibility with existing consumers. This allows the service contract to evolve as required, while avoiding negative impact on dependent compositions and consumer programs (Figure 16.2).

Application

There are a variety of techniques by which this pattern can be applied, depending on the nature of the required change to the contract. The fundamental purpose of this pattern is to avoid having to impose *incompatible* changes upon a service contract that do not

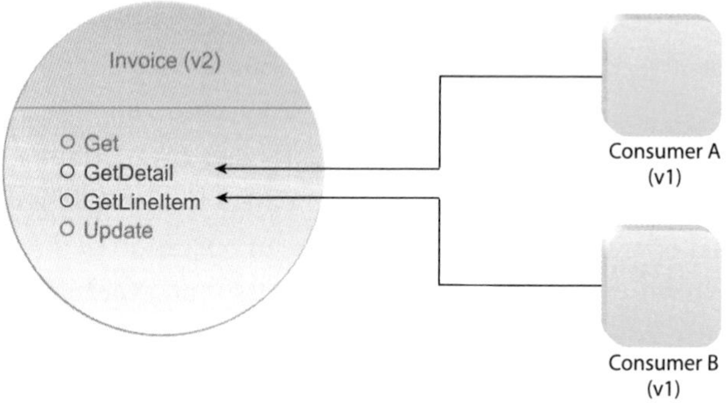

Figure 16.2

The existing capability is not renamed. Instead, a new capability with a new name is added alongside the original capability, thereby preserving compatibility with both Consumers A and B.

preserve backwards compatibility and therefore risk breaking and invalidating existing service-consumer relationships.

Here is a collection of common changes for Web service contracts, along with descriptions of how (or to what extent) these changes can be applied in a backwards-compatible manner:

- *Adding a New Operation to a WSDL Definition* – The operation can simply be appended to the existing definition, thereby acting as an extension of the contract without impacting any established contract content.
- *Renaming an Existing Operation* – As explained in the previous diagrams, an operation can be renamed by adding a new operation with the new name alongside of the existing operation with the old name. This approach can be further supplemented with Termination Notification (478), if there is a requirement to eventually retire the original operation while allowing consumers dependent on that operation a grace period to be updated in support of the renamed operation.
- *Removing an Existing Operation* – If an operation needs to be permanently deleted from the WSDL definition, there are no options for accomplishing this change in a compatible manner. Termination Notification (478) is highly recommended in this case in order to give consumer designers sufficient opportunity to transition their programs so that they are no longer using the to-be-terminated operation. Also, the technique of turning removed operations into functional stubs that respond with descriptive error data can also be employed to minimize impact on consumers that could not be transitioned.

- *Changing the MEP of an Existing Operation* – To alter an operation's message exchange pattern requires that its input and output message definitions (and possibly its fault definition) be modified, which is normally an incompatible change. To still proceed with this change while preserving backwards compatibility requires that a new operation with the modified MEP be appended to the WSDL definition together with the original operation. As when renaming an operation in this manner, Termination Notification (478) can be used to assist an eventual transition.
- *Adding a Fault Message to an Existing Operation* – The addition of a fault message (when considered separately from a change to the MEP) may often appear as a compatible change because the option of issuing a fault message does not affect the core functionality of an operation. However, because this addition augments the service behavior, it should be considered a change that can only be compatible when adding the fault message as part of a new operation altogether.
- *Adding a New Port Type* – Because WSDL definitions allow for the existence of multiple port type definitions, the service contract can be extended by adding a new port type alongside an existing one. Although this represents a form of compatible change, it may be more desirable to simply issue a new version of the entire Web service contract.
- *Adding a New Message Schema Element or Attribute* – New elements or attributes can be added to an existing message schema as a compatible change as long as they are optional. This way, their presence will not affect established service consumers that were designed prior to their existence.
- *Removing an Existing Message Schema Element or Attribute* – Regardless of whether they are optional or required, if already established message schema elements or attributes need to be removed from the service contract, it will result in an incompatible change. Therefore, this pattern cannot be applied in this case.
- *Modifying the Constraint of an Existing Message Schema* – The validation logic behind any given part of a message schema can be modified as part of Compatible Change, as long as the constraint granularity becomes coarser. In other words, if the restrictions are loosened, then message exchanges with existing consumers should remain unaffected.
- *Adding a New Policy* – One or more WS-Policy statements can be added via Compatible Change by simply adding policy alternatives to the existing policy attachment point.

- *Adding Policy Assertions* – A policy assertion can be added as per Compatible Change (465) to an existing policy as long as it is optional or added as part of a separate policy as a policy alternative.
- *Adding Ignorable Policy Assertions* – Because ignorable policy assertions are often used to express behavioral characteristics of a service, this type of change is generally not considered compatible.

> **NOTE**
>
> This list of changes corresponds to a series of sections within Chapters 21, 22, and 23 in the book *Web Service Contract Design and Versioning for SOA*, which explores compatible and incompatible change scenarios with code examples.

Impacts

Each time an already published service contract is changed, versioning and governance effort is required to ensure that the change is represented as a new version of the contract and properly expressed and communicated to existing and new consumers. As explained in the upcoming *Relationships* section, this leads to a reliance upon Canonical Versioning (286) and Version Identification (472).

When applying Compatible Change in such a manner that it introduces redundancy or duplication into a contract (as explained in several of the scenarios from the *Application* section), this pattern can eventually result in bloated contracts that are more difficult to maintain. Furthermore, these techniques often lead to the need for Termination Notification (478), which can add to both the contract content and governance effort for service and consumer owners.

Finally, when the result of applying this pattern is a loosening of established contract constraints (as described in the *Modifying the Constraint of an Existing Message Schema* scenario from the *Application* section earlier), it can produce vague and overly coarse-grained contract content.

Relationships

To apply this pattern consistently across multiple services requires the presence of a formal versioning system, which is ideally standardized as per Canonical Versioning (286). Furthermore, this pattern is dependent upon Version Identification (472) to ensure that changes are properly expressed and may also require Termination Notification (478) to transition contract content and consumers from old to new versions.

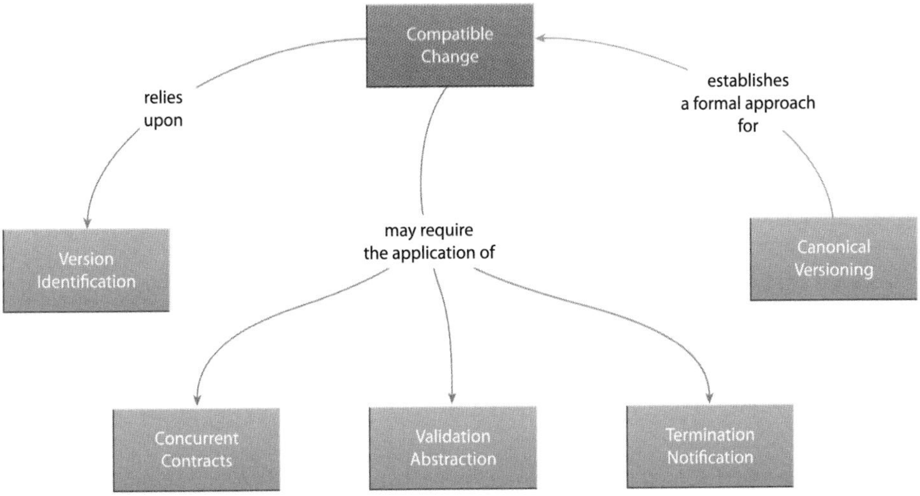

Figure 16.3
Compatible Change relates to several other service governance patterns but also may depend on some contract design patterns.

CASE STUDY EXAMPLE

As described in the case study example for Contract Denormalization (414), the Officer service contract was recently extended by FRC architects to include a new UpdateLog operation.

Before the architects can release this contract into the production environment, it must go through a testing process and be approved by the quality assurance team. The first concern raised by this team is the fact that a change has been made to the technical interface of the service and that regression testing must be carried out to ensure that existing consumers are not negatively impacted.

The architects plead with the QA manager that these additional testing cycles are not necessary. They explain that the contract content was only appended by the addition of the UpdateLog operation, and none of the previously existing contract code was affected, as shown in the highlighted parts of this example:

```
<definitions name="Officer"
  targetNamespace="http://frc/officer/wsdl/"
  xmlns="http://schemas.xmlsoap.org/wsdl/"
  xmlns:off="http://frc/officer/schema/"
  xmlns:soap="http://schemas.xmlsoap.org/wsdl/soap/"
```

```
  xmlns:tns="http://frc/officer/wsdl/"
  xmlns:xsd="http://www.w3.org/2001/XMLSchema">
  <types>
    <xsd:schema targetNamespace="http://frc/officer/">
      <xsd:import namespace="http://frc/officer/schema/"
        schemaLocation="Officer.xsd"/>
    </xsd:schema>
  </types>
  <message name="UpdateOfficer">
    <part name="RequestA" element="off:OfficerDoc"/>
  </message>
  <message name="UpdateOfficerConfirm">
    <part name="ResponseA" element="off:ReturnCodeA"/>
  </message>
  <message name="UpdateOfficerLog">
    <part name="RequestB" element="off:OfficerLog"/>
  </message>
  <message name="UpdateOfficerLogConfirm">
    <part name="ResponseB" element="off:ReturnCodeB"/>
  </message>
  <portType name="OffInt">
    <operation name="Update">
      <input message="tns:UpdateOfficer"/>
      <output message="tns:UpdateOfficerConfirm"/>
    </operation>
    <operation name="UpdateLog">
      <input message="tns:UpdateOfficerLog"/>
      <output message="tns:UpdateOfficerLogConfirm"/>
    </operation>
  </portType>
  ...
</definitions>
```

Example 16.1

The WSDL definition from Example 14.1 is revisited to show how the change made during the application of Contract Denormalization (414) was backwards-compatible.

Because existing content was not changed and only new content was added, they claim that the contract is fully backwards-compatible. The QA manager agrees that this indicates a reduced risk but insists that the revised service be subjected to some testing to ensure that the addition of the new operation logic did not affect its overall behavior.

Version Identification

By David Orchard, Chris Riley

How can consumers be made aware of service contract version information?

Problem	When an already-published service contract is changed, unaware consumers will miss the opportunity to leverage the change or may be negatively impacted by the change.
Solution	Versioning information pertaining to compatible and incompatible changes can be expressed as part of the service contract, both for communication and enforcement purposes.
Application	With Web service contracts, version numbers can be incorporated into namespace values and as annotations.
Impacts	This pattern may require that version information be expressed with a proprietary vocabulary that needs to be understood by consumer designers in advance.
Principles	Standardized Service Contract
Architecture	Service

Table 16.2
Profile summary for the Version Identification pattern.

Problem

Whether a contract is subject to compatible or incompatible changes, any modification to its published content will typically warrant a new contract version. Without a means of associating contract versions with changes, the compatibility between a service and its current and new consumers is constantly at risk, and the service also becomes less discoverable to consumer designers (Figure 16.4).

Furthermore, the service itself also becomes more burdensome to govern and evolve.

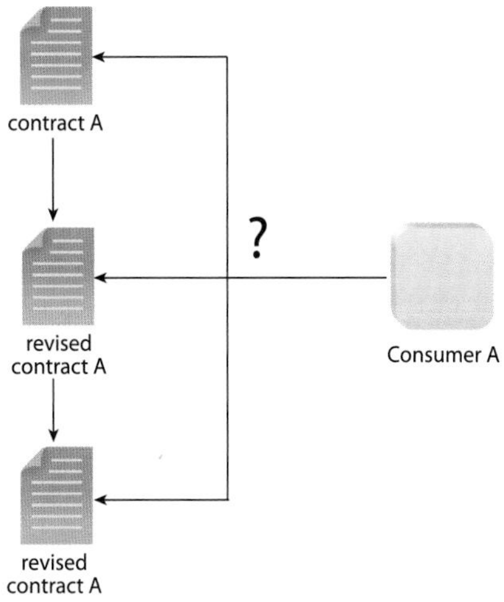

Figure 16.4
As a service contract is required to change, a service consumer is left in the dark as to whether it is still compatible.

Solution

The service contract can be designed to express version identifiers that allow the consumer to confidently determine whether it is compatible with the service. The use of version identifiers further supports Concurrent Contracts (421) for versioning purposes, thereby allowing a consumer to choose the correct contract based on its expressed version, as shown in Figure 16.5.

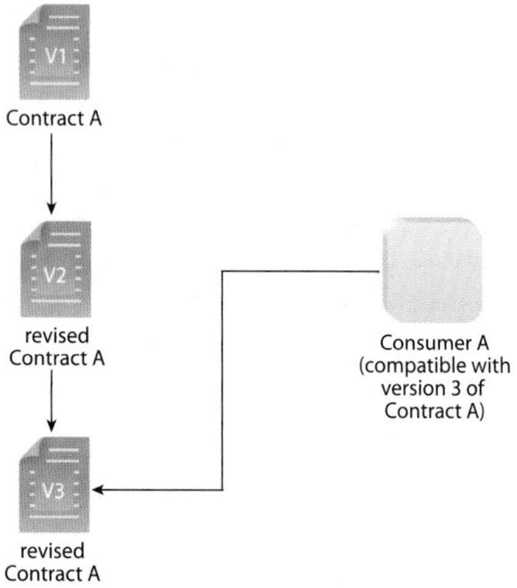

Figure 16.5

Because the service contracts express versioning information, Consumer A can proceed to invoke version 3 of the service contract because it was designed to be compatible with that specific version.

Application

Versions are typically identified using numeric values that are incorporated into the service contract either as human-readable annotations or as actual extensions of the technical contract content. The most common version number format is a decimal where the first digit represents the major version number, and digits following the decimal point represent minor version numbers.

What the version numbers actually mean depends on the conventions established by an overarching versioning strategy. Two common approaches are described here:

- *Amount of Work* – Major and minor version numbers are used to indicate the amount of effort that went into each change. An increment of a major version number represents a significant amount of work, whereas increases in the minor version numbers represent minor upgrades.
- *Compatibility Guarantee* – Major and minor version numbers are used to express compatibility. The most common system is based on the rule that an increase in a major version number will result in a contract that is not backwards-compatible, whereas increases in minor version numbers are backwards-compatible. As a result, minor version increments are not expected to affect existing consumers.

Note that these two identification systems can be combined so that version number increases continue to indicate compatible or incompatible changes, while also representing the amount of work that went into the changes.

With Web service contracts specifically, a common means of ensuring that existing consumers cannot accidentally bind to contracts that have been subject to non-backwards-compatible changes is to incorporate the version numbers into new namespace values that are issued with each new major version increase.

NOTE

Whereas version numbers are often incorporated into the target namespaces for WSDL definitions, date values are commonly appended to target namespaces for XML Schema definitions. See Chapters 20, 21, and 22 in the *Web Service Contract Design and Versioning for SOA* book for code examples and more details.

Impacts

Version identification systems and conventions are typically specific to a given service inventory and usually part of a standardized versioning strategy, as per Canonical Versioning (286). As a result, they are not standardized on an industry level and therefore, when expressed as part of the technical contract, impose the constant requirement that service consumers be designed to understand the meaning of version identifiers and programmatically consume them, as required.

When services are exposed to new or external consumers, these same requirements apply, but the necessary enforcement of standards may be more difficult to achieve.

Relationships

This pattern is commonly applied together with (or as a result of) the application of Canonical Versioning (286) and is further an essential part of carrying out Compatible Change (465).

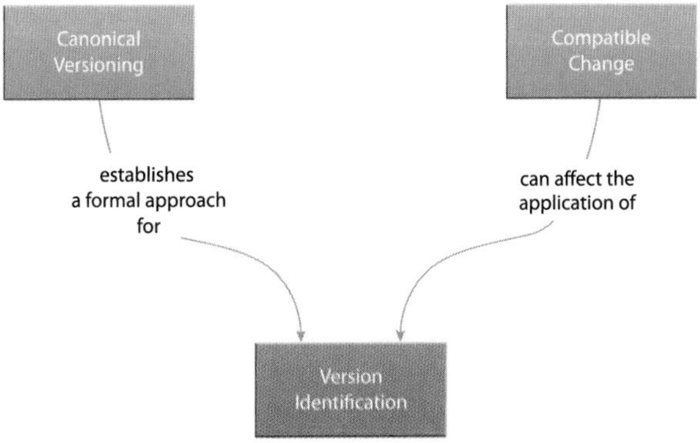

Figure 16.6

Version Identification relates primarily to other contract versioning patterns.

NOTE

Version Identification is comparable to Format Indicator (Hohpe, Woolf) when applied to express a version number as part of a message. Format Indicator differs in that it is message-centric and also enables the expression of other meta information, such as foreign keys and document formats.

CASE STUDY EXAMPLE

As explained in the example for Compatible Change (465) example, the quality assurance team performs some further testing on the Officer service with its extended service contract. Subsequent to carrying out these tests they clear the new service for release into production, subject to one condition: The service contract must express a version number to indicate that it has been changed.

This version number follows existing versioning conventions whereby a backwards-compatible change increments the minor version number (the digit following the decimal point). The FRC architects agree that this is a good idea and are quick to add a human-readable comment to the Officer WSDL definition by using the `documentation` element as follows:

```
<definitions name="Officer"
  targetNamespace="http://frc/officer/wsdl/"
  xmlns="http://schemas.xmlsoap.org/wsdl/"
  xmlns:off="http://frc/officer/schema/"
  xmlns:soap="http://schemas.xmlsoap.org/wsdl/soap/"
  xmlns:tns="http://frc/officer/wsdl/"
  xmlns:xsd="http://www.w3.org/2001/XMLSchema">
  <documentation>Version 1.1</documentation>
  ...
</definitions>
```

Example 16.2
The WSDL definition from Example 16.1 is annotated with a version number.

Several months after version 1.1 of the Officer service was deployed, two new projects get started, each pertaining to the HR system that is currently in place. One of the FRC enterprise architects is involved with both project teams to ensure compliance with design standards. After reviewing each design specification, she notices some commonality. The first solution requires event logging functionality, and the other solution has a requirement for error logging. She soon realizes that there is a need for the FRC to create a separate utility Logging service.

After proposing her recommendation, the Logging service is built in support of both solutions. Weeks later during a review of the service inventory blueprint, an analyst points out that the UpdateLog operation that was added to the Officer service contract should, in fact, be located within the new Logging service.

The FRC architecture team agrees to make this change, though it isn't considered an immediate priority. Several weeks thereafter, the Officer service is revisited, and the logic behind the UpdateLog operation is removed. As a result, the UpdateLog operation itself is deleted from the contract.

Following the versioning conventions set out by the quality assurance team, this type of change is classified as "incompatible," meaning that it imposes a non-backwards-compatible change that will impact consumer programs that have already formed dependencies on the Officer service's UpdateLog operation. Consequently, they are required to increment the major version number (the digit before the decimal) and further append the Officer WSDL definition's target namespace with the new version number, as follows:

```
<definitions name="Officer"
  targetNamespace="http://frc/officer/wsdl/v2"
  xmlns="http://schemas.xmlsoap.org/wsdl/"
  xmlns:off="http://frc/officer/schema/"
  xmlns:soap="http://schemas.xmlsoap.org/wsdl/soap/"
  xmlns:tns="http://frc/officer/wsdl/v2"
  xmlns:xsd="http://www.w3.org/2001/XMLSchema">
  <documentation>Version 2.0</documentation>
  <types>
    <xsd:schema targetNamespace="http://frc/officer/">
      <xsd:import namespace="http://frc/officer/schema/"
        schemaLocation="Officer.xsd"/>
    </xsd:schema>
  </types>
  <message name="UpdateOfficer">
    <part name="RequestA" element="off:OfficerDoc"/>
  </message>
  <message name="UpdateOfficerConfirm">
    <part name="ResponseA" element="off:ReturnCodeA"/>
  </message>
  <portType name="OffInt">
    <operation name="Update">
      <input message="tns:UpdateOfficer"/>
      <output message="tns:UpdateOfficerConfirm"/>
    </operation>
```

```
  </portType>
  ...
</definitions>
```

Example 16.3

The UpdateLog operation is removed from the revised Officer WSDL definition, resulting in an incompatible change that requires a new target namespace value.

Termination Notification

By David Orchard, Chris Riley

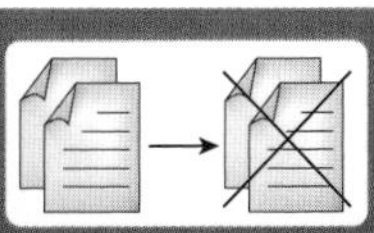

How can the scheduled expiry of a service contract be communicated to consumer programs?

Problem	Consumer programs may be unaware of when a service or a service contract version is scheduled for retirement, thereby risking runtime failure.
Solution	Service contracts can be designed to express termination information for programmatic and human consumption.
Application	Service contracts can be extended with ignorable policy assertions or supplemented with human-readable annotations.
Impacts	The syntax and conventions used to express termination information must be understood by service consumers in order for this information to be effectively used.
Principles	Standardized Service Contract
Architecture	Composition, Service

Table 16.3

Profile summary for the Termination Notification pattern.

Problem

As services evolve over time, various conditions and circumstances can lead to the need to retire a service contract, a portion of a service contract, or the entire service itself.

Examples include:

- the service contract is subjected to a non-backwards-compatible change
- a compatible change is applied to a service contract but strict versioning policies require the issuance of an entirely new version of the service contract
- a service's original functional scope is no longer applicable in relation to how the business has changed
- a service is decomposed into more granular services or combined together with another service

In larger IT enterprises and especially when making services accessible to external partner organizations, it can be challenging to communicate to consumer owners the pending termination of a service or any part of its contract in a timely manner.

Failure to recognize a scheduled retirement will inevitably lead to runtime failure scenarios, where unaware consumer programs that attempt to invoke the service are rejected (Figure 16.7).

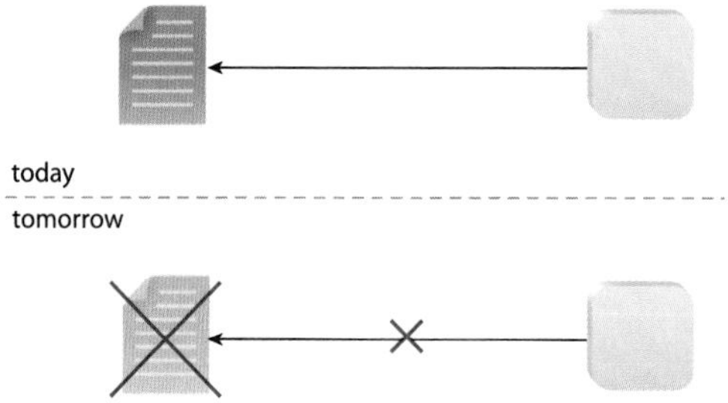

Figure 16.7

The consumer program (right) invokes a service via its contract as usual today, but when the contract is terminated on the next day, the attempted invocation fails.

Solution

Service contracts are equipped with termination details, thereby allowing consumers to become aware of the contract retirement in advance (Figure 16.8).

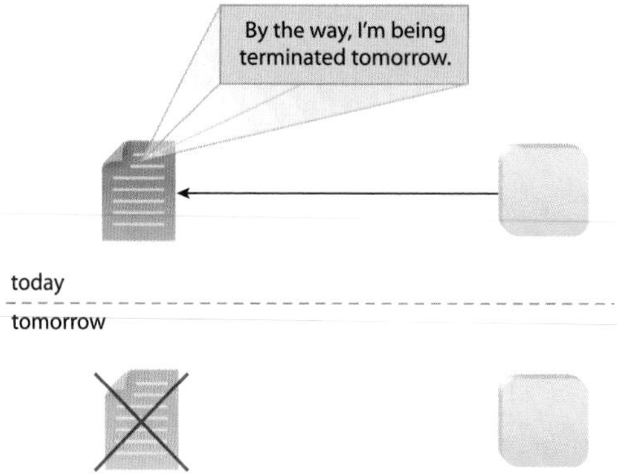

Figure 16.8

The service contract includes a standardized statement that communicates when it is scheduled for termination. As a result, the consumer does not attempt to invoke it after the contract has been terminated.

Application

This pattern is most commonly applied by supplementing technical contract content with human-readable annotations that simply provide the termination date. However, with Web service contracts, there is also the option of leveraging the WS-Policy language to express termination notifications via ignorable policy assertions. This enables consumer programs to be designed to programmatically check for termination information.

It is also worth noting that in addition to expressing service contract termination, there are other purposes for which Termination Notification can be applied, such as:

- *Indicating the retirement of a specific capability or operation* – This is especially relevant when choosing one of the transition techniques described in Compatible Change (465) where an original operation is preserved and a similar, but changed, operation is added.
- *Indicating the retirement of an entire service* – This same approach can be used to communicate that an entire service program itself is scheduled for retirement.
- *Indicating the retirement of a message schema* – Although policy assertions may not be suitable for this purpose, regular annotations can be added to schemas to explain when the schema version will be terminated and/or replaced.

Note also that governance standards can be put in place as part of an overarching Canonical Versioning (286) strategy to express termination notification information via standardized annotations or non-ignorable policy assertions. In the latter case, this can require that all Web service contracts contain termination assertions, regardless of whether they are due for termination. For those contracts that are not being terminated, a pre-defined value indicating this is placed in the assertion instead of a date (or the assertion is left empty).

Impacts

All of the techniques explained in this pattern description require the use of non-standardized extension content for service contracts. This is because there is no industry standard for expressing termination information. Termination Notification relies on the existence and successful enforcement of governance standards and therefore has a direct dependency on Canonical Versioning (286).

Relationships

As just mentioned, how this pattern is applied is often governed by Canonical Versioning (286). Both Compatible Change (465) and Proxy Capability (497) can lead to the need for Termination Notification.

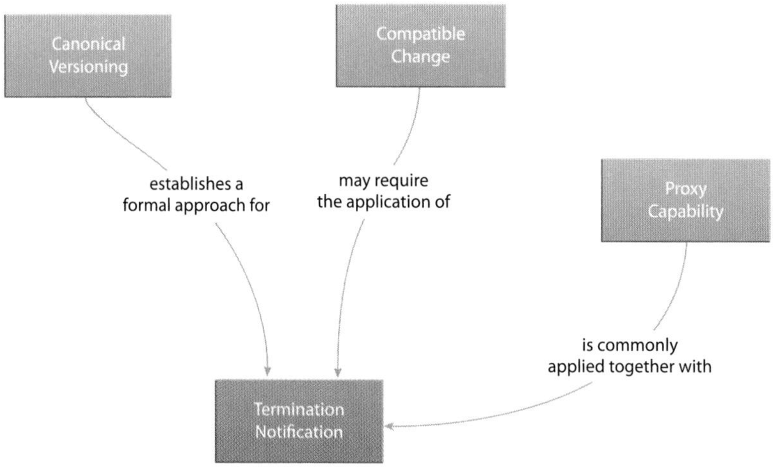

Figure 16.9

Termination Notification relates primarily to other versioning patterns but also can support Proxy Capability (497).

> **NOTE**
>
> Termination Notification is similar in concept to Message Expiration (Hohpe, Woolf), a pattern that advocates adding a timestamp to a message to indicate when the message itself is no longer considered valid.

CASE STUDY EXAMPLE

In the example for Version Identification (472) example the FRC team removed the UpdateLog operation from the Officer WSDL definition, resulting in a non-backwards-compatible change. After a meeting with some of the custodians of the consumer programs affected by this incompatible change, FRC architects begin to realize that the change will result in significant effort on the part of consumer owners and that it could take several months before all of the consumer programs are updated to work with the new utility Logging service. Furthermore, several of the individuals responsible for owning consumers were not available and will need to be informed of the pending change at a later point.

As a result of these circumstances, the FRC team decides to postpone the change, allowing the Officer service to maintain its UpdateLog operation for the next six months while the Logging service is also available. They work with the quality assurance team on a plan to accommodate this transition, as follows:

1. Establish a new design standard that disallows any new consumer programs from accessing the Officer service's UpdateLog operation.
2. Notify all team leads via e-mail of the date on which the UpdateLog operation will be removed.
3. Incorporate this termination date into the Officer WSDL definition by means of a non-ignorable policy assertion.

Step 3 is implemented as follows:

```
<definitions name="Officer" ... >
  ...
  <binding name="bdPO" type="tns:OffInt">
    <operation name="Update">
      <soapbind:operation
        soapAction="http://frc/update/request"
        soapActionRequired="true" required="true"/>
      <input>
        <soapbind:body use="literal"/>
      </input>
      <output>
        <soapbind:body use="literal"/>
      </output>
    </operation>
    <operation name="UpdateLog">
      <wsp:Policy>
        <pol:termination wsp:Ignorable="true">
          Mar-01-2009
        </pol:termination>
      </wsp:Policy>
      <soapbind:operation
        soapAction="http://frc/updateLog/request"
        soapActionRequired="true" required="true"/>
      <input>
        <soapbind:body use="literal"/>
      </input>
      <output>
        <soapbind:body use="literal"/>
```

```
      </output>
    </operation>
      ...
  </binding>
  ...
</definitions>
```

Example 16.4

The `operation` element within the Officer WSDL definition's `binding` construct is modified to include a custom ignorable WS-Policy assertion that expresses the scheduled termination date of the UpdateLog operation.

NOTE

For more examples of Termination Notification see Chapter 23 of *Web Service Contract Design and Versioning for SOA*.

Service Refactoring

How can a service be evolved without impacting existing consumers?

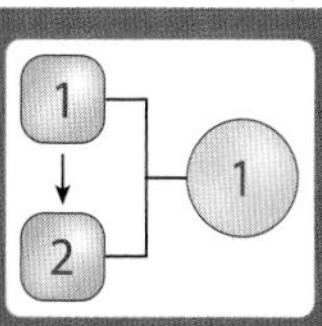

Problem	The logic or implementation technology of a service may become outdated or inadequate over time, but the service has become too entrenched to be replaced.
Solution	The service contract is preserved to maintain existing consumer dependencies, but the underlying service logic and/or implementation are refactored.
Application	Service logic and implementation technology are gradually improved or upgraded but must undergo additional testing.
Impacts	This pattern introduces governance effort as well as risk associated with potentially negative side-effects introduced by new logic or technology.
Principles	Standardized Service Contract, Service Loose Coupling, Service Abstraction
Architecture	Service

Table 16.4
Profile summary for the Service Refactoring pattern.

Problem

Subsequent to its initial delivery, unforeseen performance and business requirements may demand more from a service than it is capable of providing (Figure 16.10). Replacing the service entirely may be undesirable, especially when several consumer programs have already formed dependencies upon its established service contract.

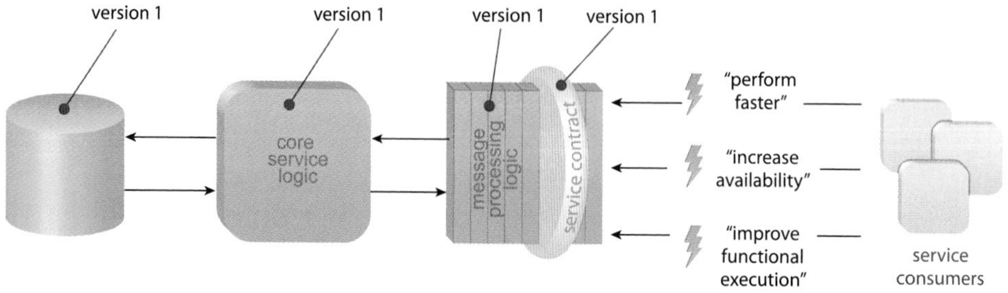

Figure 16.10

Consumers of an existing service demand new requirements for which the service was not originally designed. The red symbols indicate the different parts of this service architecture that could be independently versioned.

Solution

Software refactoring is an accepted software engineering practice whereby existing software programs can be gradually improved without affecting the manner in which they behave. When applied to service design, this approach provides more opportunity for services to evolve within an organization without disrupting their existing consumers. As shown in Figure 16.11, with the application of this pattern the underlying logic and implementation of a service can be regularly optimized, improved, or even upgraded while preserving the service contract.

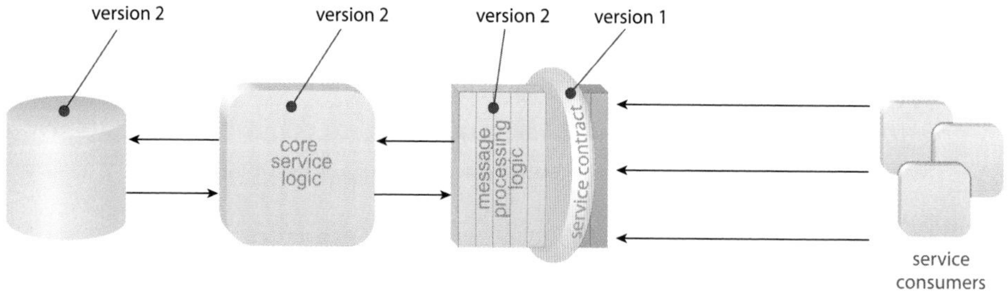

Figure 16.11

All parts of a service architecture abstracted by its contract can potentially be refactored without compromising existing consumer relationships. The service contract and the remaining, externally facing message processing agents (red) are not affected by the refactoring effort.

Application

Software refactoring practices allow programs to be improved through a series of small upgrades that continue to preserve their interfaces and overall behavior. By limiting the scope of these upgrades, the risk associated with negatively impacting consumers is minimized. The emphasis of software refactoring techniques is on the cumulative result of these individual refactoring steps.

This pattern can be more successfully applied when the service has already been subjected to the application of Decoupled Contract (401) and the Service Loose Coupling design principle. The separation of service logic from a fully decoupled contract provides increased freedom as to how refactoring can be carried out, while minimizing potential disruption to existing service consumers.

> **NOTE**
>
> Several books covering refactoring techniques and specialized patterns are available. Two well-known titles are *Refactoring: Improving the Design of Existing Code* (Fowler, Beck, Brant, Opdyke, Roberts) and *Refactoring to Patterns* (Kerievsky), both by Addison-Wesley. The site www.refactoring.com provides additional resources as well as a catalog of proven "refactorings."

Impacts

The refactoring of existing service logic or technology introduces the need for the service to undergo redesign, redevelopment, and retesting cycles so as to ensure that the existing guarantees expressed in the service contract (which includes its SOA) can continue to be fulfilled as expected (or better).

Because already established and proven logic and technology is modified or replaced as a result of applying this pattern, there is still always a risk that the behavior and reliability of a refactored capability or service may still somehow negatively affect existing consumers. The degree to which this risk is alleviated is proportional to the maturity, suitability, and scope of the newly added logic and technology and the extent to which quality assurance and testing are applied to the refactored service.

Relationships

The extent to which Service Refactoring can be applied depends on how the service itself was first designed. This is why there is a direct relationship between this pattern and Service Normalization (131), Contract Centralization (409), and Decoupled Contract (401). The abstraction and independence gained by the successful application of those patterns allows services to be individually governed and evolved with minimal impact to consumer programs.

Furthermore, depending on the nature of the refactoring requirements, Service Decomposition (489), Concurrent Contracts (421), or Service Façade (333) may need to be applied to accommodate how the service is being improved.

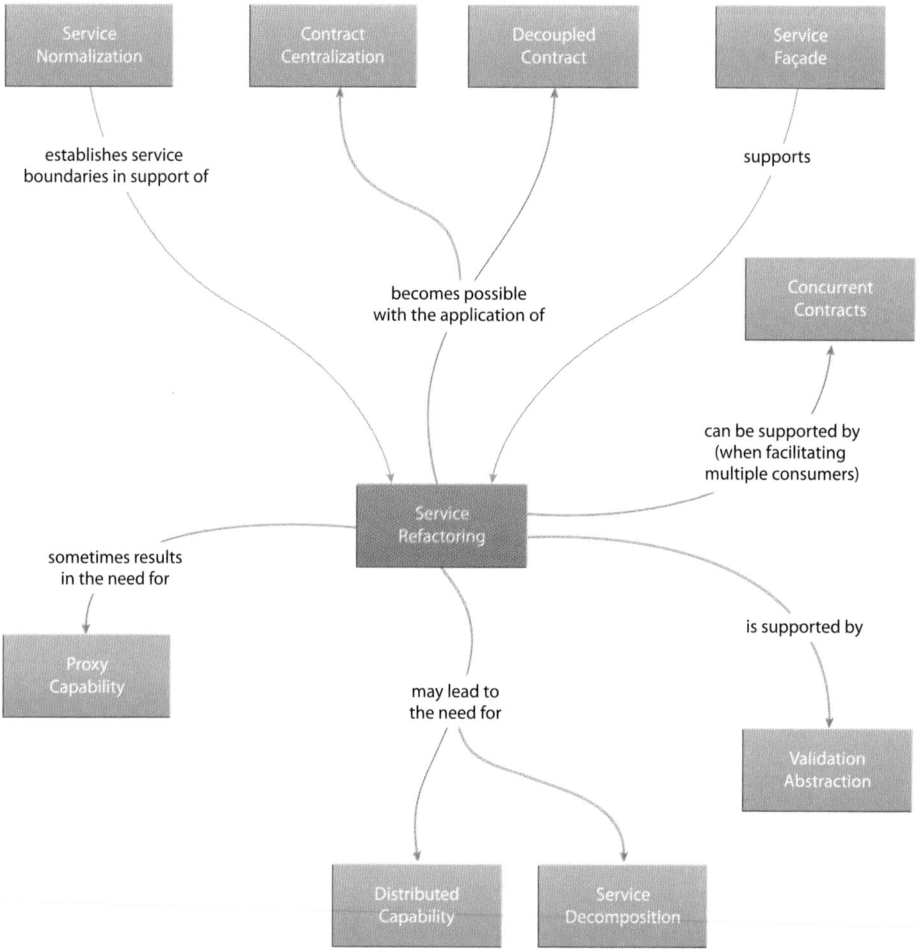

Figure 16.12

Service Refactoring relies on several key contract-related patterns to ensure that refactoring-related changes do not disrupt existing service consumers.

CASE STUDY EXAMPLE

The Alleywood Employee service was implemented some time ago. It originally established a standardized service contract that acted as an endpoint into the HR module of a large ERP system. Since the McPherson buyout, various products have been upgraded or replaced to contemporize the overall IT enterprise. As part of this initiative, this ERP system was re-evaluated.

The ERP vendor had been bought out by a competing software manufacturer, and the ERP platform was simply made part of a larger product line that offered an alternative ERP. The McPherson group believed that the original Alleywood ERP environment would soon be retired by its new owner in order to give their ERP product a greater market share.

As a result, it was decided to completely replace this product. This, of course, affected many services, including the Employee service. However, because its contract was decoupled and had been fully standardized, it was in no way dependent on any part of the underlying ERP environment.

A new HR product and a custom-developed employee reporting application were introduced, allowing developers to refactor some of the core service logic so that the concurrent usage thresholds of the more popular service capabilities could be increased while the service contract and the service's overall expected behavior are preserved.

This limited the impact of the HR product to the service only. Besides a brief period of unavailability, all Employee service consumers were shielded from this impact and continued to use the Employee service as normal.

Service Decomposition

How can the granularity of a service be increased subsequent to its implementation?

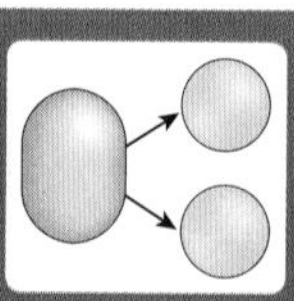

Problem	Overly coarse-grained services can inhibit optimal composition design.
Solution	An already implemented coarse-grained service can be decomposed into two or more fine-grained services.
Application	The underlying service logic is restructured, and new service contracts are established. This pattern will likely require Proxy Capability (497) to preserve the integrity of the original coarse-grained service contract.
Impacts	An increase in fine-grained services naturally leads to larger, more complex service composition designs.
Principles	Service Loose Coupling, Service Composability
Architecture	Service

Table 16.5
Profile summary for the Service Decomposition pattern.

Problem

When modeling services during the initial analysis phases it is common to take practical considerations into account. For example, what may ideally be represented by a set of fine-grained business service candidates is later combined into a smaller number of coarse-grained services primarily due to performance and other infrastructure-related concerns motivated by the need to keep service composition sizes under control.

After a service inventory architecture matures and more powerful and sophisticated technology and runtime products are incorporated, larger, more complex service compositions become a reality. When designing such compositions, it is generally preferable to keep the footprints of individual services as small as possible because only select service capabilities are required to automate a given parent business task. However, when forced to work with overly coarse-grained services, composition performance can be negatively affected, and the overall composition designs can be less than optimal (Figure 16.13).

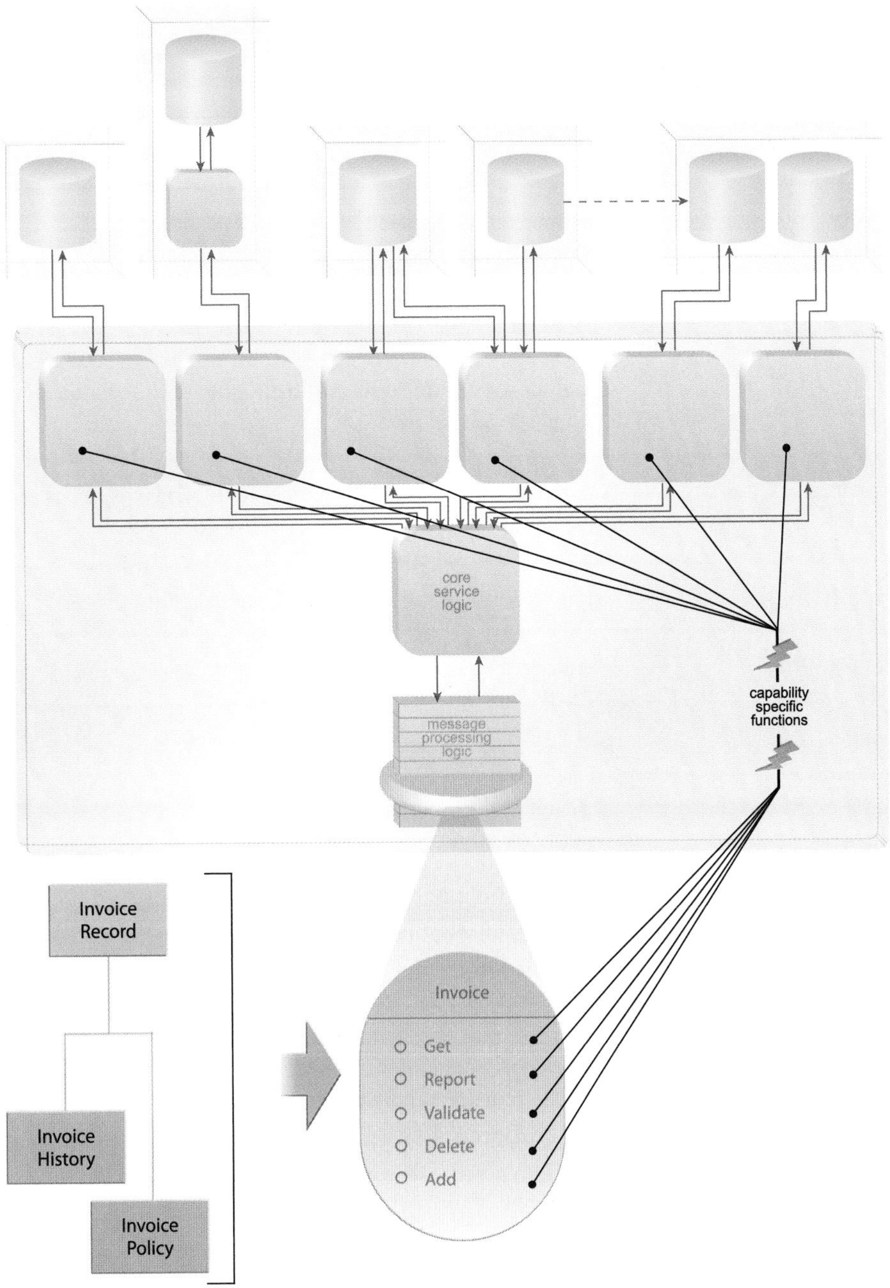

Figure 16.13

An Invoice service with a functional context originally derived from three separate business entities ends up existing as a large software program with a correspondingly large footprint, regardless of which capability a composition may need to compose.

NOTE

Another circumstance under which this problem condition can occur is when services are being produced via a meet-in-the-middle delivery process, where a top-down analysis is only partially completed prior to service development. In this delivery approach, the top-down process continues concurrently with service delivery projects. There is a commitment to revising implemented service designs after the top-down analysis progresses to a point where necessary changes to the original service inventory are identified. For more details regarding SOA project delivery strategies, see Chapter 10 in *Service-Oriented Architecture: Concepts, Technology, and Design.*

Solution

The coarse-grained service is decomposed into a set of fine-grained services that collectively represent the functional context of the original service but establish distinct functional contexts of their own (Figure 16.14).

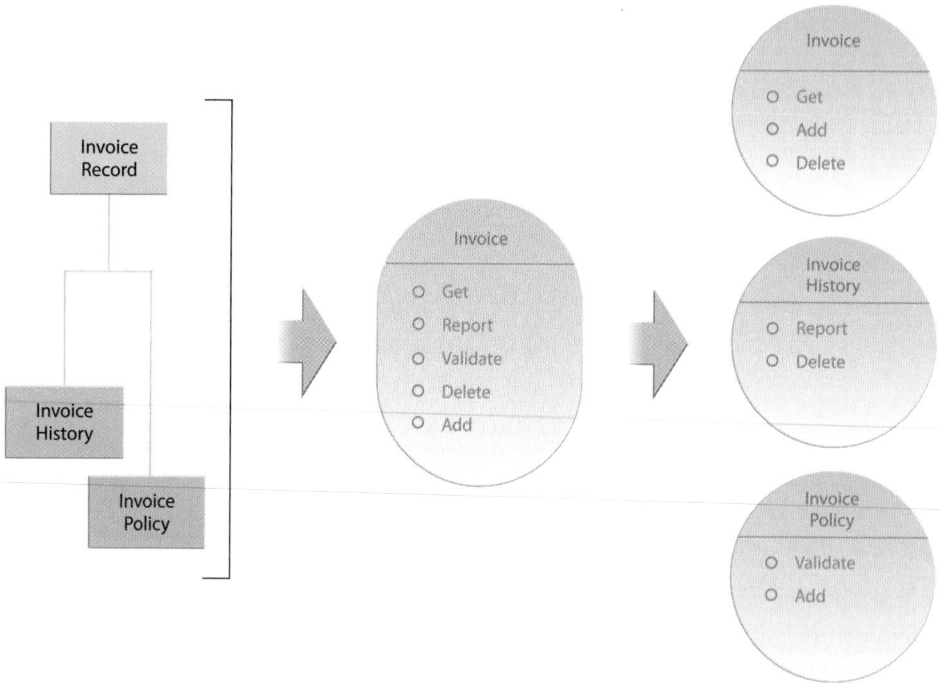

Figure 16.14

The original, coarse-grained Invoice service is decomposed into three separate services, one of which remains associated with general invoice processing but only encapsulates a subset of the original capabilities.

Application

Carrying out this pattern essentially requires that the existing, coarse-grained service be broken apart and its logic reorganized into new, finer-grained functional boundaries.

Therefore, the first step is usually to revisit the service inventory blueprint and decide how the service can be re-modeled into multiple service candidates. As part of this process, new capability candidates will also need to be defined, especially if Decomposed Capability (504) was not taken into account during the service's original design. After the modeling is completed, the new services are subject to the standard lifecycle phases, beginning with contract design (based on the modeled service candidates) and all the way through to final testing and quality assurance phases (Figure 16.15).

Unless it is decided to also retrofit previous consumer programs that formed dependencies on the original service, Proxy Capability (497) will likely need to be applied to preserve the original service contract for backwards compatibility.

NOTE

The concepts behind this pattern can also be applied in reverse, where two or more fine-grained services are combined into one coarse-grained service. The use of Proxy Capability (497) would still apply for preserving the original service contracts. This is the basis of a pattern called Service Consolidation which, at the time of this writing, was classified as a candidate pattern that is available for review at SOAPatterns.org.

Impacts

The extent to which Service Decomposition can impact a service inventory depends on how established a service is and how many consumer programs have formed relationships on it. The more consumers involved, the more complicated and disruptive this pattern can be.

Because this pattern is commonly applied after an inventory architecture has matured, its application needs to be carefully planned together with the repeated application of Proxy Capability (497).

The preventative use of Decomposed Capability (504) can ease the impact of Service Decomposition and will also result in a cleaner separation of functional service contexts.

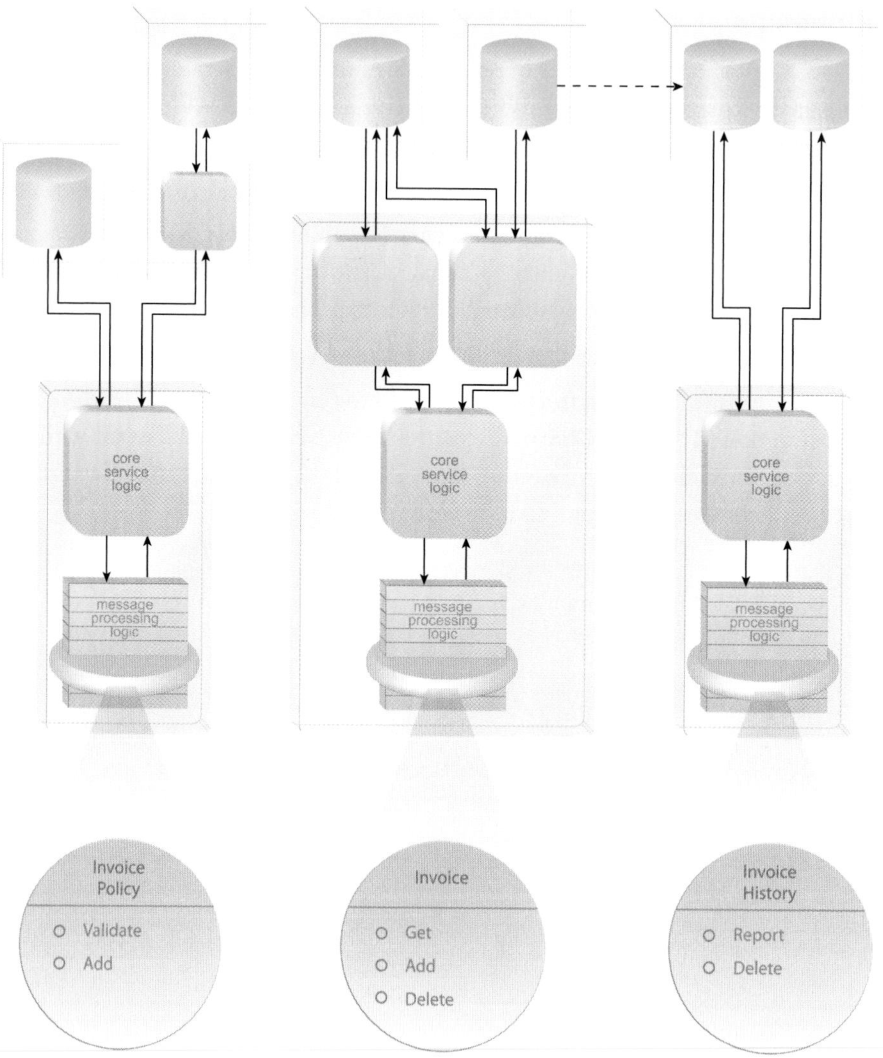

Figure 16.15

The new, fine-grained services each provide fewer capabilities and therefore also impose smaller program sizes.

Relationships

Service Decomposition has a series of relationships with other service-level patterns, most notably Service Refactoring (484). When a service is upgraded as a result of a refactoring effort, the application of Service Decomposition may very well be the means by which this is carried out.

As explained in the pattern description for Proxy Capability (497), Service Decomposition relies on that pattern to implement the actual partitioning via the redevelopment effort required to turn one or more regular capabilities into proxies. As a result, this pattern shares several of the same patterns as Proxy Capability (497).

Service Decomposition is most frequently applied to agnostic services, therefore tying it to Entity Abstraction (175) and Utility Abstraction (168). However, the result of this pattern can introduce a measure of service redundancy due to the need for Proxy Capability (497) to violate Service Normalization (131) to some extent.

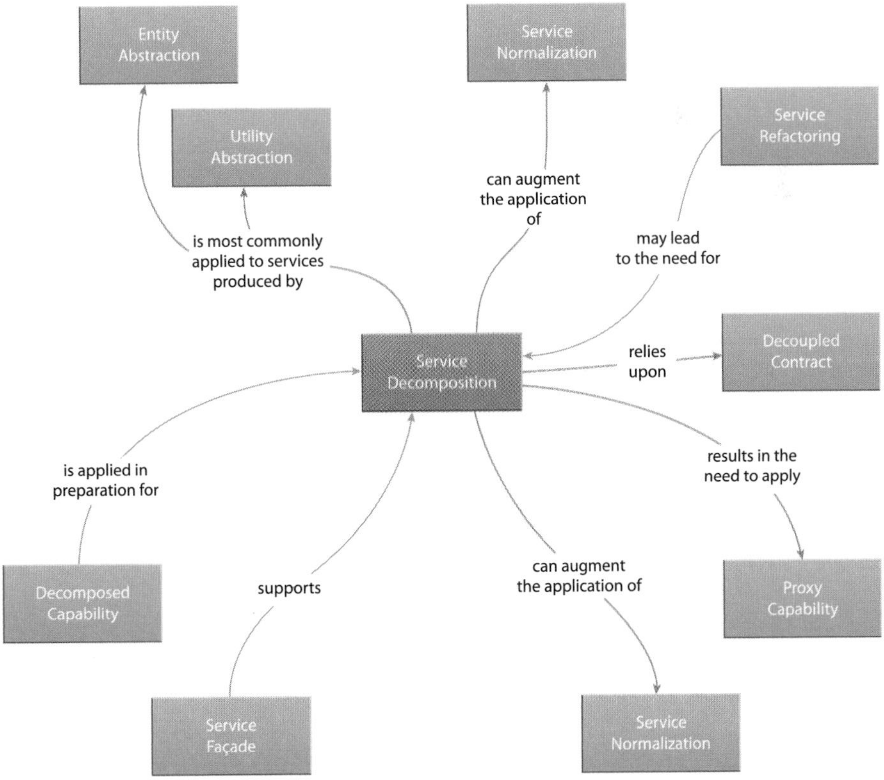

Figure 16.16

Service Decomposition is a refactoring-related approach to splitting up service logic that ties into numerous patterns that shape service logic and contracts.

CASE STUDY EXAMPLE

The case study example for Service Refactoring (484) explained how the Employee service was reengineered for a number of reasons. One of the results of this effort is that the service is now more scalable and can handle increased usage loads. The primary reason scalability was addressed is in preparation for new, upcoming service compositions that will require access to employee data and functionality. Those compositions were in the planning stages at that time and are now in production.

Some preliminary statistics show that despite the increase in usage thresholds, the Employee service is still excessively strained, and there have already been complaints about latency and memory overhead associated with the service's invocation and participation as part of the overall composition.

At first the team responsible for the Employee service considers Redundant Implementation (345) to help alleviate this situation. While this would address some of the latency issues, it would not solve the memory overhead issue.

The team then explores the option of splitting the functionality in the Employee service into two separate services. From a back-end perspective, there is an opportunity to do this in a relatively clean-cut manner. Currently, the service encapsulates functionality from an HR ERP system and a custom-developed reporting application. However, as a member of the entity service layer, the architects and business analysts involved would like to preserve the business entity-based functional context in each of the two services it would be split into. Therefore, they don't want to make the decision based on the current service implementation architecture alone.

They turn to the information architecture group responsible for maintaining the master entity relationship diagram to look for suitable employee-related entities that might form the basis of separate services. They locate an Employee Records entity that has a relationship with the parent Employee entity. Employee Records represents historical employee information, such as overtime, sick days, complaints, promotions, injuries, etc.

The team reviews the current entity service functionality and additional capabilities that may need to be added (such as those modeled as part of the service inventory blueprint but not yet implemented). They also look into the back-end systems being encapsulated. The custom-developed reporting application does not provide all of the required features to support a service dedicated to Employee Records processing. The team would need for this service to continue accessing the HR ERP system, plus

eventually upcoming Employee Records capabilities will need to further access the central data warehouse.

On the bright side, their original usage statistics indicate that some of the latency issues resulted from the Employee service being tied up executing long-running reporting queries. If this type of functionality were to exist in a separate service, the primary Employee capabilities would be more scalable and reliable, and the Employee service would be "lighter" and a more effective composition participant.

After taking all these factors into consideration, the team feels that it makes sense to break off historical reporting functionality into a separate service appropriately called "Employee Records." The first challenge they face is that the existing Employee service contract is already being used by many consumer programs. If they move capabilities from this service to another, they will introduce significant disruption. For this situation, they apply Proxy Capability (497), as explained in the next case study example.

NOTE

The preceding scenario describes one possible option as to how a service can be decomposed. Another design option is to split the one entity service into an entity and utility service in order to accommodate more practical concerns. Either way, how a service is decomposed is ultimately best determined by a thorough analysis to ensure that your business requirements are fully met.

Proxy Capability

How can a service subject to decomposition continue to support consumers affected by the decomposition?

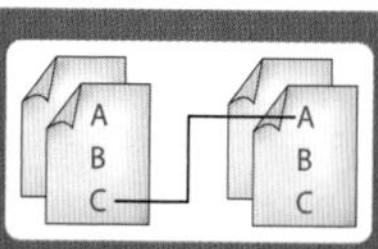

Problem	If an established service needs to be decomposed into multiple services, its contract and its existing consumers can be impacted.
Solution	The original service contract is preserved, even if underlying capability logic is separated, by turning the established capability definition into a proxy.
Application	Façade logic needs to be introduced to relay requests and responses between the proxy and newly located capabilities.
Impacts	The practical solution provided by this pattern results in a measure of service denormalization.
Principles	Service Loose Coupling
Architecture	Service

Table 16.6
Profile summary for the Proxy Capability pattern.

Problem

As per Service Decomposition (489), it is sometimes deemed necessary to further decompose a service's functional boundary into two or more functional boundaries, essentially establishing new services within the overall inventory. This can clearly impact existing service consumers who have already formed dependencies on the established service contract (Figure 16.17).

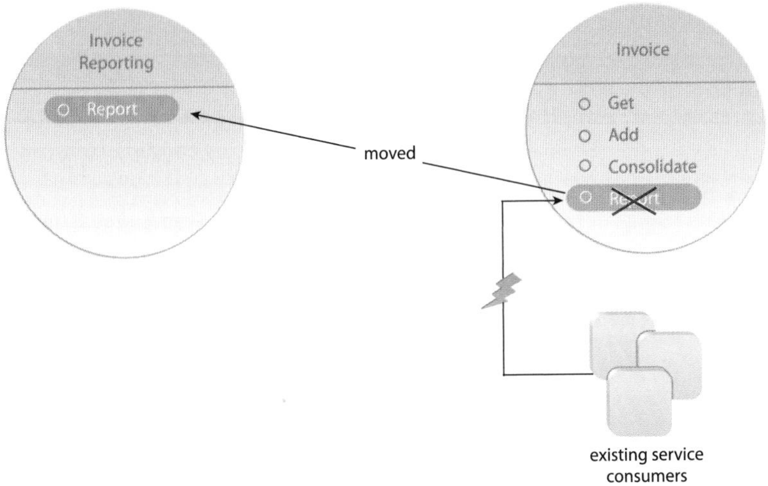

Figure 16.17
Moving a service capability that is part of an established service contract will predictably impact existing service consumers.

Solution

Capabilities affected by the decomposition are preserved, while those same capabilities are still allowed to become part of new services. Although the service's original functional context is changed and its official functional boundary is reduced, it continues to provide capabilities that no longer belong within its context or boundary. These are proxy capabilities that are preserved (often for a limited period of time) to reduce the impact of the decomposition on the service inventory (Figure 16.18).

This does not prevent the capabilities in the new services from being independently accessed. In fact, access to the capability logic via its new service contract is encouraged so as to minimize the eventual effort for proxy capabilities to be phased out.

Application

Proxy Capability relies on the application of Service Façade (333) in that a façade is established to preserve affected service capabilities. The only difference is that instead of calling capability logic that is still part of the same service, the façade calls capabilities that are now part of new services (Figure 16.19).

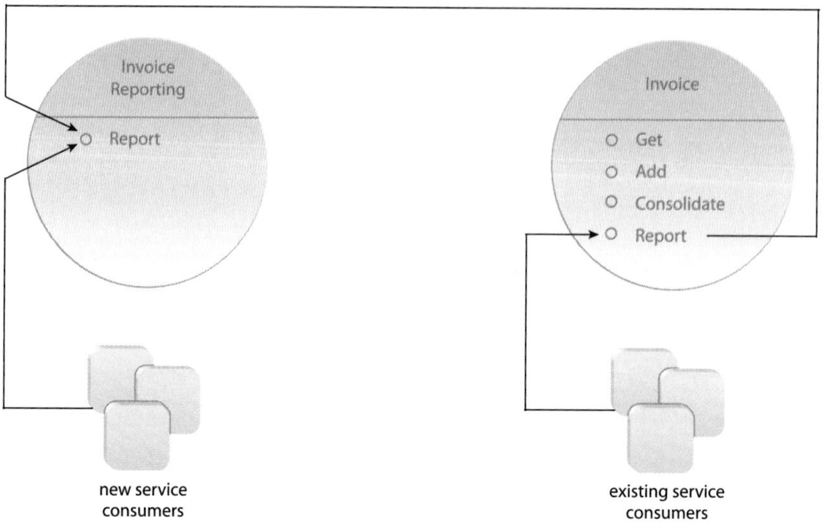

Figure 16.18

By preserving the existing capability and allowing it to act as a proxy for the relocated capability logic, existing consumers will be less impacted.

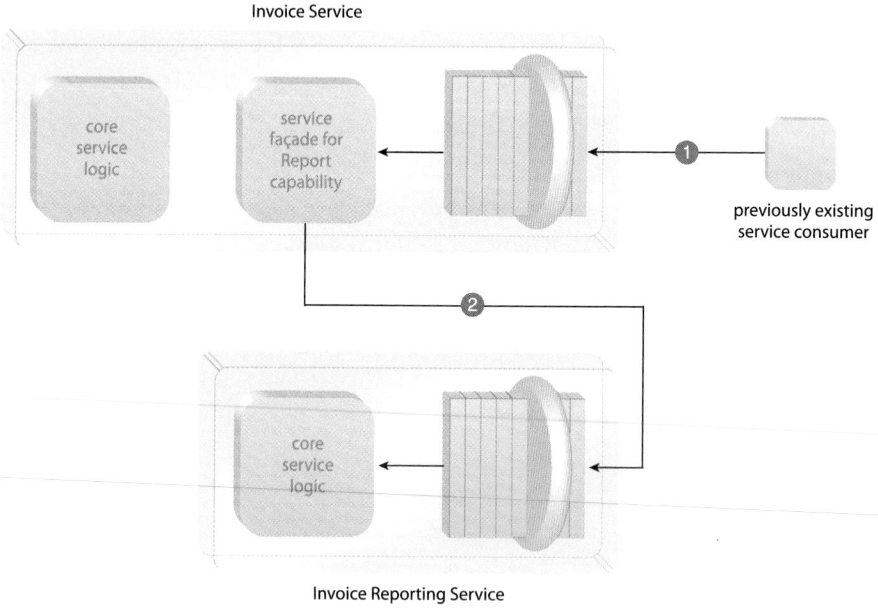

Figure 16.19

When an existing consumer requests an Invoice service operation that has been moved due to the decomposition of the service (1), a newly added façade component relays the request to the capability's new location (2), in this case the Invoice Reporting service.

> **NOTE**
>
> Termination Notification (478) is also commonly applied together with Proxy Capability in order to communicate the scheduled expiry of proxy capabilities.

Impacts

Although the application of this pattern extends the longevity of service contracts while allowing for the creative decomposition of service logic, it does introduce a measure of service denormalization that runs contrary to the goals of Service Normalization (131).

Proxy capabilities need to be clearly tagged with metadata communicating the fact that they no longer represent the official endpoint for their respective logic to avoid having consumers inadvertently bind to them.

Furthermore, this pattern alone does not guarantee that a proxy capability will continue to provide the same behavior and reliability of the original capability it replaced.

Relationships

Whereas Distributed Capability (510) prepares a service for the eventual application of Service Decomposition (489), Proxy Capability actually implements the decomposition while preserving the original service contract.

This is supported by Decoupled Contract (401), which allows the contracts of both the original and the decomposed services to be individually customized in support of the proxy capability. Service Façade (333) also plays an integral role in that it can be used to relay requests (act as the proxy) to and from the newly decomposed service.

And as previously mentioned, this pattern does end up going against the goals of Service Normalization (131). From an endpoint perspective especially, this pattern introduces the appearance of redundant functionality, a trade-off that is accepted in support of service evolution.

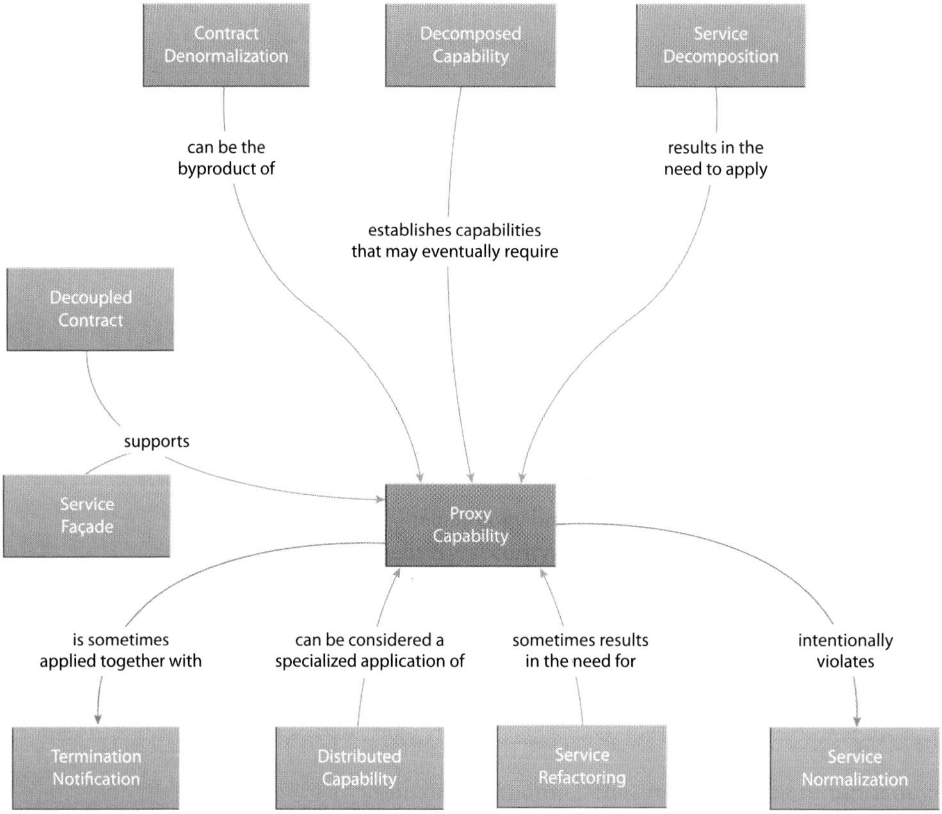

Figure 16.20

Proxy Capability alters the structure of a service in support of the creation of a new service and therefore touches several patterns related to service logic structure and the service decomposition process.

CASE STUDY EXAMPLE

In the case study example for Service Decomposition (489) we explained how the Alleywood team came to the decision to split their existing Employee service into separate Employee and Employee Record services.

To see this through, they need to find a way to achieve the following:

1. Establish a new Employee Record service.
2. Move the corresponding functionality from the Employee service to the new Employee Record service.

3. Complete Steps 1 and 2 without changing the original Employee service contract so as to not impact existing service consumers.

To complete Step 1 they model the new Employee Record service, as shown in Figure 16.21.

To accomplish Steps 2 and 3 they employ Proxy Capability for each of the capabilities in the Employee service that needs to be moved to the Employee Record service. Figure 16.22 illustrates how two of the original Employee service capabilities map to four of the Employee Record service capabilities.

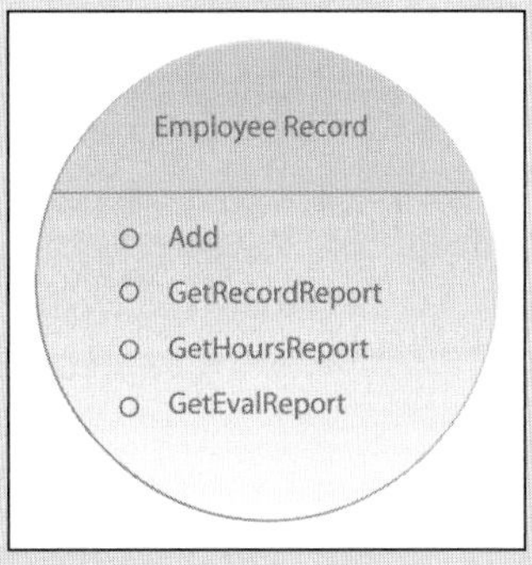

Figure 16.21
After some analysis, the new Employee Record service candidate is modeled with four capability candidates.

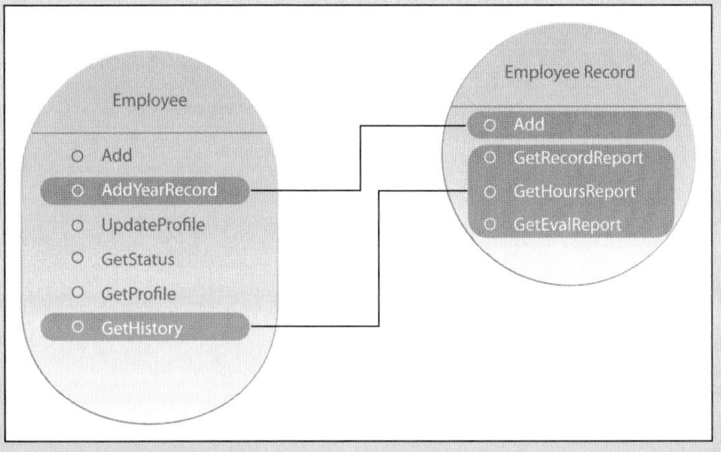

Figure 16.22
The Employee service's AddRecord and GetHistory capabilities are positioned as proxies for the Employee Record's Add, GetRecordReport, GetHoursReport, and GetEvalReport capabilities.

The Employee Record service is eventually designed and delivered as a fully functional, standalone service. However, the Employee service contract remains unchanged, plus additional logic is added in the form of a façade component. This functionality responds to requests for the original AddRecord and GetHistory capabilities and then relays those requests over to the Employee Record. The eventual responses are then received and passed back to the Employee service consumer.

However, one issue remains. In order for the GetHistory operation to work, it must make three calls to the Employee Record service (one to each of the three GetReport operations).

The team considers whether to add a corresponding GetHistory operation to the Employee Record service just for the proxy work that the Employee service must perform. But, they are concerned that the additional operation will be confusing to other consumers. They decide instead to try to accelerate the retirement of the Employee GetHistory operation.

Decomposed Capability

How can a service be designed to minimize the chances of capability logic deconstruction?

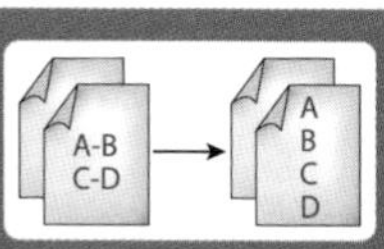

Problem	The decomposition of a service subsequent to its implementation can require the deconstruction of logic within capabilities, which can be disruptive and make the preservation of a service contract problematic.
Solution	Services prone to future decomposition can be equipped with a series of granular capabilities that more easily facilitate decomposition.
Application	Additional service modeling is carried out to define granular, more easily distributed capabilities.
Impacts	Until the service is eventually decomposed, it may be represented by a bloated contract that stays with it as long as proxy capabilities are supported.
Principles	Standardized Service Contract, Service Abstraction
Architecture	Service

Table 16.7
Profile summary for the Decomposed Capability pattern.

Problem

Some types of services are more prone to being split after they have been developed and deployed. For example, entity services derive their functional context from corresponding business entities that are documented as part of common information architecture specifications. Often, an entity service context will initially be based around a larger, more significant business entity or even a group of related entities.

This can be adequate for immediate purposes but can eventually result in a number of challenges (Figure 16.23), including the following:

- As the service is extended, many additional capabilities are added because they are all associated with its functional context, leading to a bulky functional boundary that is difficult to govern.
- The service, due to increased popularity as a result of added capabilities or high reuse of individual capabilities, becomes a processing bottleneck.

Despite a foreknowledge of these challenges, it may still not be possible to create a larger group of more granular services because of infrastructure constraints that restrict the size of potential service compositions. Sometimes an organization needs to wait until its infrastructure is upgraded or its vendor runtime platform matures to the point that it can support complex compositions with numerous participating services. In the meantime, however, the organization cannot afford to postpone the delivery of its services.

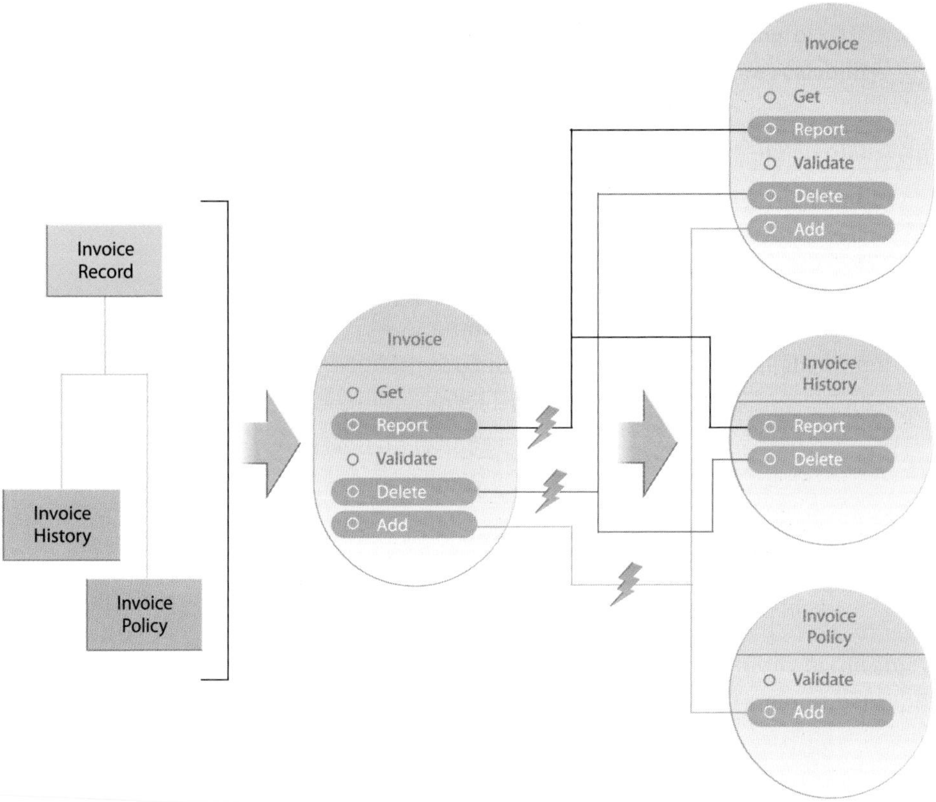

Figure 16.23

An Invoice entity service (middle) derived from a group of Invoice-related business entities (left) exposes coarse-grained capabilities that are difficult to decompose when service decomposition requirements present themselves. Each of the affected Invoice service capabilities needs to be split up in order to accommodate the new services (right).

Solution

Services can be initially designed with future decomposition requirements in mind, which generally translates into the creation of more granular capabilities. With an entity service, for example, granular capabilities can be aligned better with individual business entities. This way, if the service needs to be decomposed in the future into a collection of services that represent individual business entities, the transition is facilitated by reducing the need to deconstruct capabilities (Figure 16.24).

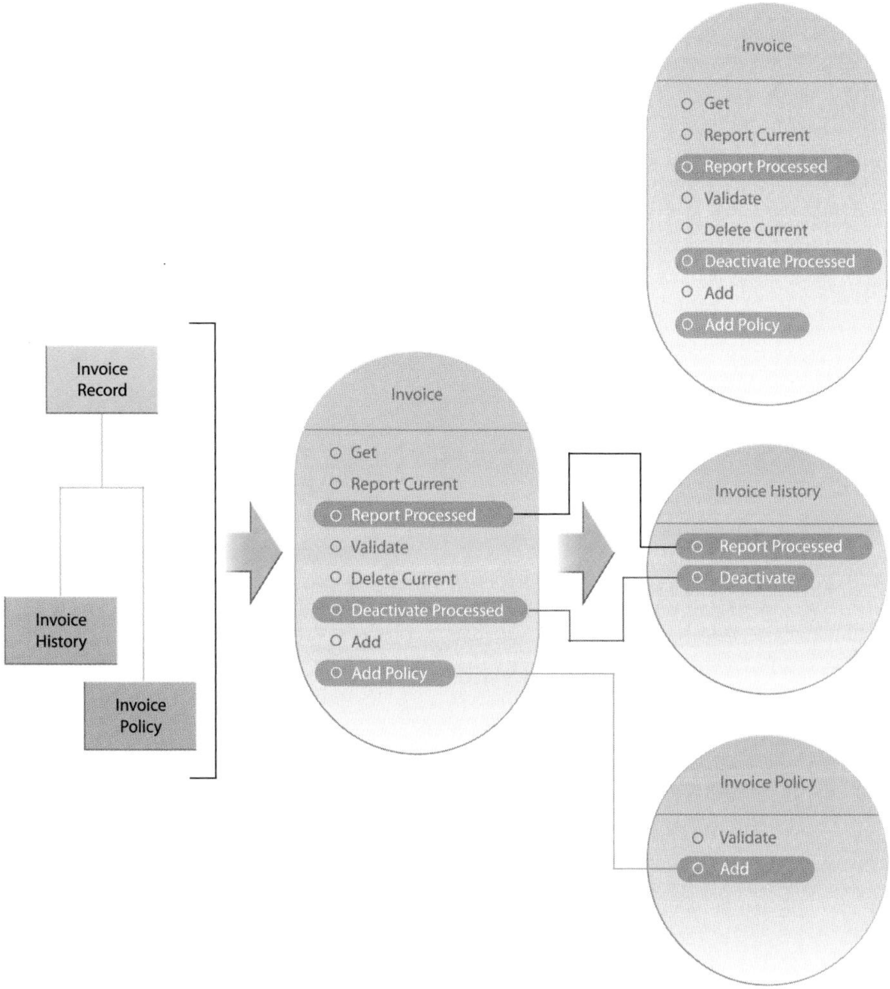

Figure 16.24

The Invoice service (middle) derived from the same business entities (left) introduced in Figure 16.23 now exposes a series of more granular capabilities, several of which correspond directly to specific business entities. This increases the ease at which subsequent service decomposition can be accomplished. The decomposed services (right) are no longer in conflict because the capabilities affected by the decomposition are clearly mapped to the new services. Those same capabilities also remain in the Invoice service contract (top right) as per Proxy Capability (497).

Application

This pattern introduces more up-front service modeling effort in order to determine the appropriate service capability definitions. Specifically, the following considerations need to be taken into account:

- how the current functional scope can potentially be divided into two or more functional contexts
- how capabilities can be defined for these new functional contexts

This modeling effort follows a process whereby a collection of service candidates are defined in association with the scope of the service in question. These service candidates represent future services that can result from a decomposition of the current service and therefore provide a basis for capability candidates to be defined in support of the decomposition.

> **NOTE**
>
> This pattern differs from Contract Denormalization (414) in that the latter introduces redundant, granular capabilities for the purpose of supporting consumer requirements. Decomposed Capability allows for targeted granular capabilities (which may or may not be redundant) in order to facilitate the long-term evolutionary requirements of the service and the service inventory as a whole.

Impacts

The initial service contract that results from applying this pattern can be large and difficult to use. The increased capability granularity can impose performance overhead on service consumers that may be required to invoke the service multiple times to carry out a series of granular functions that could have been grouped together in a coarse-grained capability. This may lead to the need to apply Contract Denormalization (414), which will result in even more capabilities.

Even after the service has been decomposed, the existing consumers of the initial service may still need to be accommodated via proxy capabilities as per Proxy Capability (497), requiring the original service contract to remain for an indefinite period of time.

Also, it is sometimes difficult to predict how a service will be decomposed when initially defining it. There is the constant risk that the service will be populated with fine-grained capabilities that will never end up in other services and may have unnecessarily imposed performance burden upon consumers in the meantime.

Relationships

The key relationship illustrated in Figure 16.25 is between Decomposed Capability and Service Decomposition (489) because this pattern is applied in advance with the foreknowledge that a service will likely need to be decomposed in the future. It can therefore also be viewed as a governance pattern in that its purpose is to minimize the impact of a service's evolution. For this same reason, it relates to Proxy Capability (497) that will usually end up being applied to one or more of the capabilities decomposed by this pattern.

As already mentioned, the more fine-grained capabilities introduced by this pattern may require that Contract Denormalization (414) also be applied.

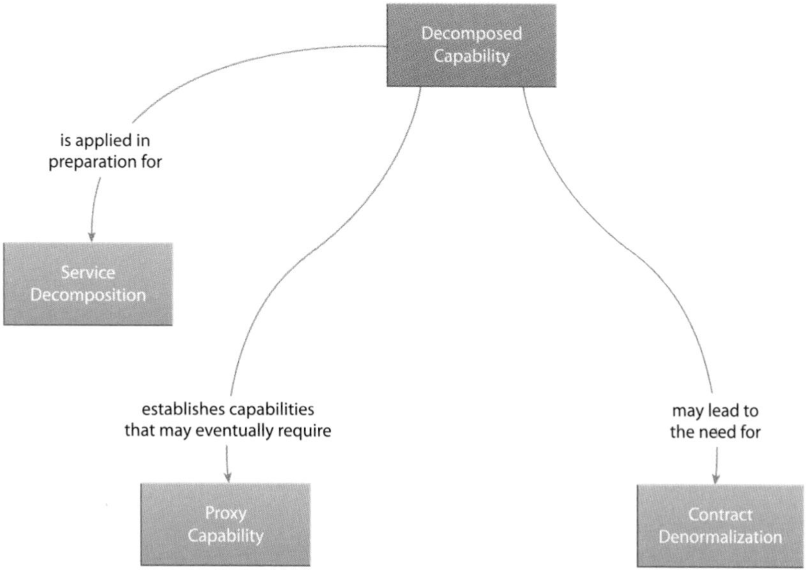

Figure 16.25

Decomposed Capability prepares a service contract for eventual decomposition, making it closely related to patterns associated with Service Decomposition (489).

CASE STUDY EXAMPLE

The case study example for Proxy Capability (497) demonstrated how the decomposition of a service can lead to subsequent design issues, even when establishing capabilities that act as proxies for existing consumers. If the capabilities for the newly derived service don't cleanly match the functional context and granularity of the capabilities of the original service, then awkward and inefficient proxy mapping may result. Depending on how

long the retirement of old capabilities can take, the decomposition of a service can actually increase some of the functional burden it was intended to improve.

Let's focus again on the Employee and Employee Record services explained in the preceding example. If we step back in time when the Employee service was first modeled, we can give the architects and analysts responsible for defining the original service candidate the opportunity to apply Decomposed Capability before proceeding with the physical design and implementation of this service.

In the case of Alleywood, the service would have been based on the two already discussed business entities (Employee and Employee Record) plus a third existing employee-related business entity called Employee Classification. These entities would have determined the capability definition from the beginning in that the original Employee entity service would essentially be viewed as three entity services bundled into one.

Capabilities for this service would have been defined with future decomposition in mind, and the result would have looked a lot like Figure 16.26.

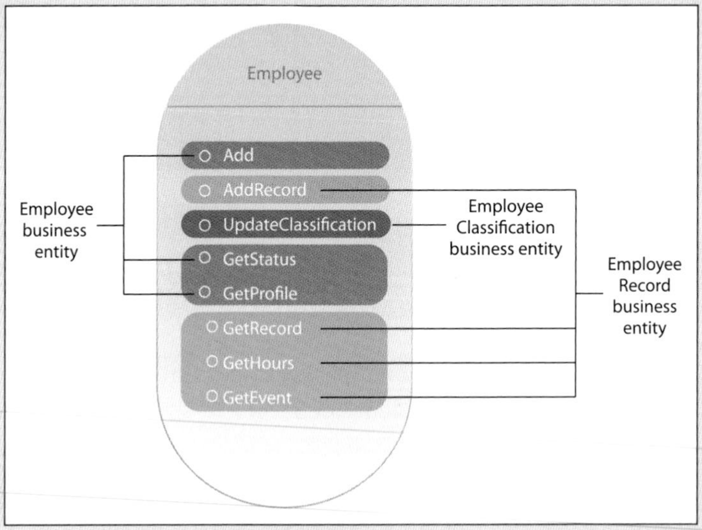

Figure 16.26
The original Employee service modeled to accommodate future decomposition by containing capabilities directly associated with known employee-related business entities. Note that not all of the capability names need to be the same as they will be when the service is decomposed into derived services.

Distributed Capability

How can a service preserve its functional context while also fulfilling special capability processing requirements?

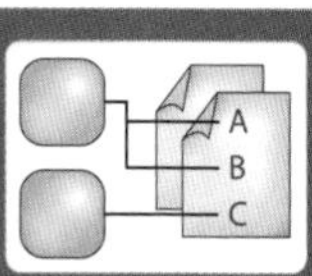

Problem	A capability that belongs within a service may have unique processing requirements that cannot be accommodated by the default service implementation, but separating capability logic from the service will compromise the integrity of the service context.
Solution	The underlying service logic is distributed, thereby allowing the implementation logic for a capability with unique processing requirements to be physically separated, while continuing to be represented by the same service contract.
Application	The logic is moved and intermediary processing is added to act as a liaison between the moved logic and the main service logic.
Impacts	The distribution of a capability's logic leads to performance overhead associated with remote communication and the need for new intermediate processing.
Principles	Standardized Service Contract, Service Autonomy
Architecture	Service

Table 16.8
Profile summary for the Distributed Capability pattern.

Problem

Each capability within a service's functional context represents a body of processing logic. When a service exists in a physically implemented form, its surrounding environment may not be able to fully support all of the processing requirements of all associated capabilities.

For example, there may be a capability with unique performance, security, availability, or reliability requirements that can only be fulfilled through specific architectural extensions and special infrastructure. Other times, it is the increased processing demands on a single capability that can tax the overall service implementation to such an extent that it compromises the performance and reliability of other service capabilities (Figure 16.27).

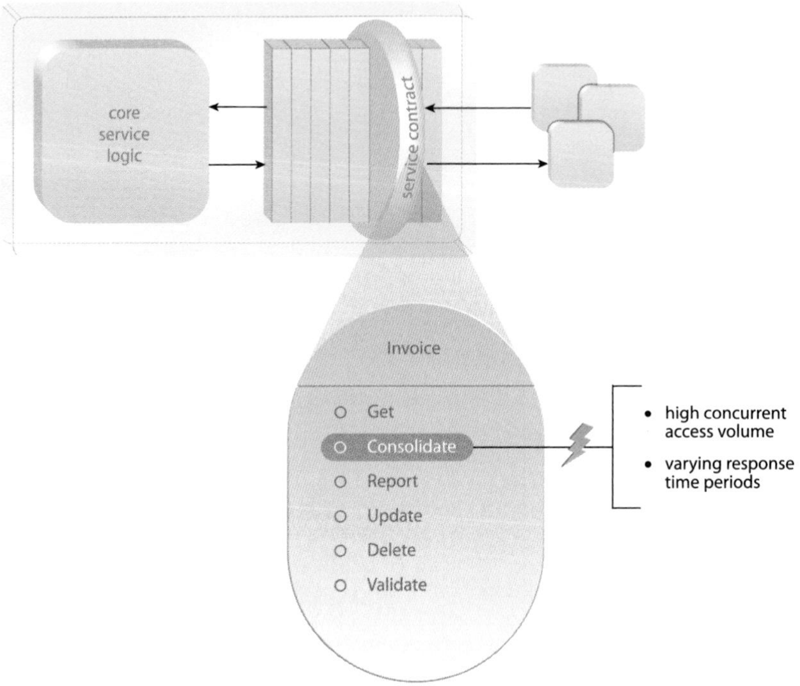

Figure 16.27

The Consolidate operation of the Invoice Web service is subject to high concurrent usage and long response periods when it is required to perform complex consolidation calculations. These factors regularly lock up server resources and therefore compromise the performance and reliability of other service operations.

The logic supporting such a capability can be split off into its own service implementation. However, this would result in the need to break the original functional context for which the service was modeled.

Solution

Capability logic with special processing requirements is distributed to a physically remote environment. Intermediate processing logic is added to interact with local and distributed service logic on behalf of the single service contract (Figure 16.28).

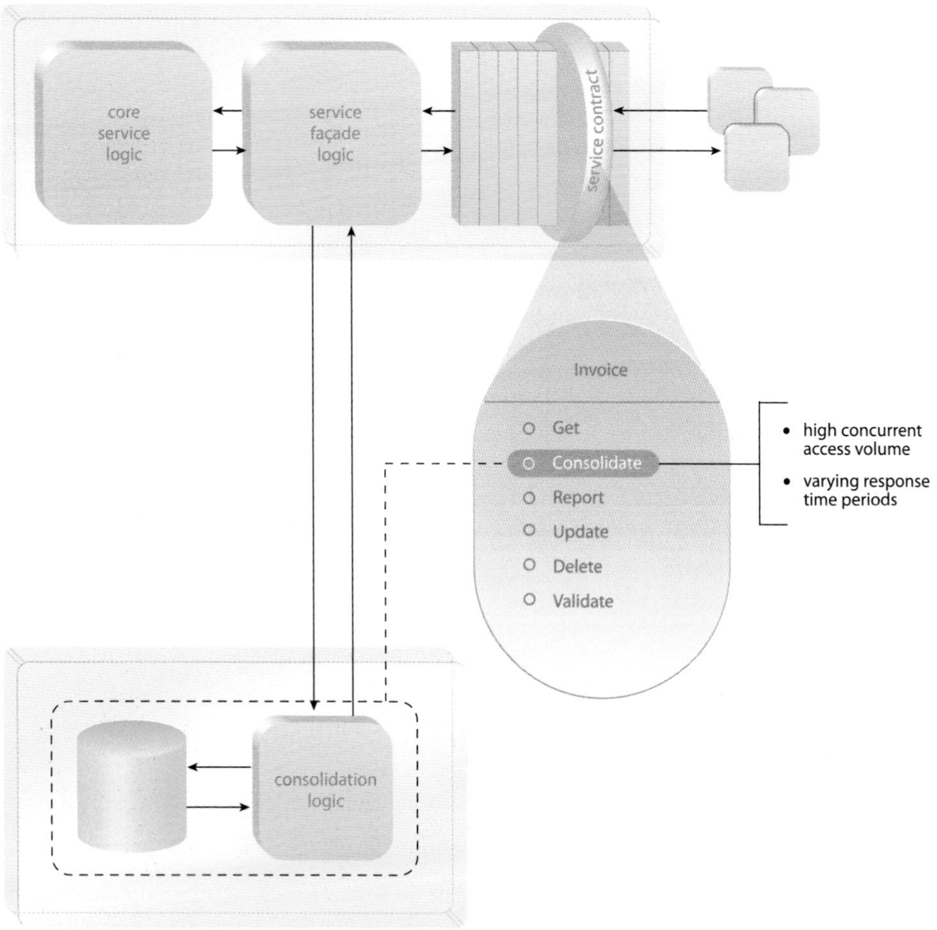

Figure 16.28

The logic for the Consolidate operation is relocated to a separate physical environment. A service façade component interacts with the consolidation logic on behalf of the Invoice service contract.

Application

This pattern is commonly realized through the application of Service Façade (333) in order to establish the intermediate logic that essentially acts as the controller of a "component composition." The component(s) representing the distributed capability logic interact with the façade logic via remote access.

Performance requirements can be somewhat streamlined by embedding additional processing logic within the façade so that it does more than just relay request and response message values. For example, the façade logic can contain routines that further parse and

extract data from an incoming request message so that only the information absolutely required by the distributed capability logic is transmitted.

An alternative to using Service Façade (333) is Service Agent (543). Event-driven agents can be developed to intercept request messages for a specific service capability. These agents can carry out the validation that exists within the corresponding contract (or perhaps this validation is deferred to the capability logic itself) and then simply route the request message directly to the capability. The same agents can process the outgoing response messages from the capability as well.

Impacts

This pattern preserves the purity of a service's functional context at the cost of imposing performance overhead. The positioning of the contract as the sole access point for two or more distributed implementations of service logic introduces an increased likelihood of remote access whenever the service is invoked.

If the capability logic was separated to guarantee a certain response time during high volume usage, then this may be somewhat undermined by the remote access requirements. On the other hand, overall service autonomy tends to be positively impacted as the autonomy level of the separated capability logic can be improved as a result of its separation.

Relationships

When structuring a service to support distributed capability processing, the service implementation itself exists like a mini-composition, whereby a façade component takes on the role of both component controller and single access point for the distributed service logic. This is why this pattern has such a strong reliance on Service Façade (333) and why it is supported by Decoupled Contract (401) in particular.

Contract Centralization (409) is also an essential part of the service design because it ensures that the contract will remain the sole access point, regardless of the extent the underlying logic may need to be distributed.

When a distributed capability needs to share access to service-related data, Service Data Replication (350) can be employed to help facilitate this access without the need to introduce intra-service data sharing issues. Additionally, this pattern is often the result of applying Service Refactoring (484) and can therefore be considered a continuation of a refactoring effort, especially when applied after the service's initial deployment.

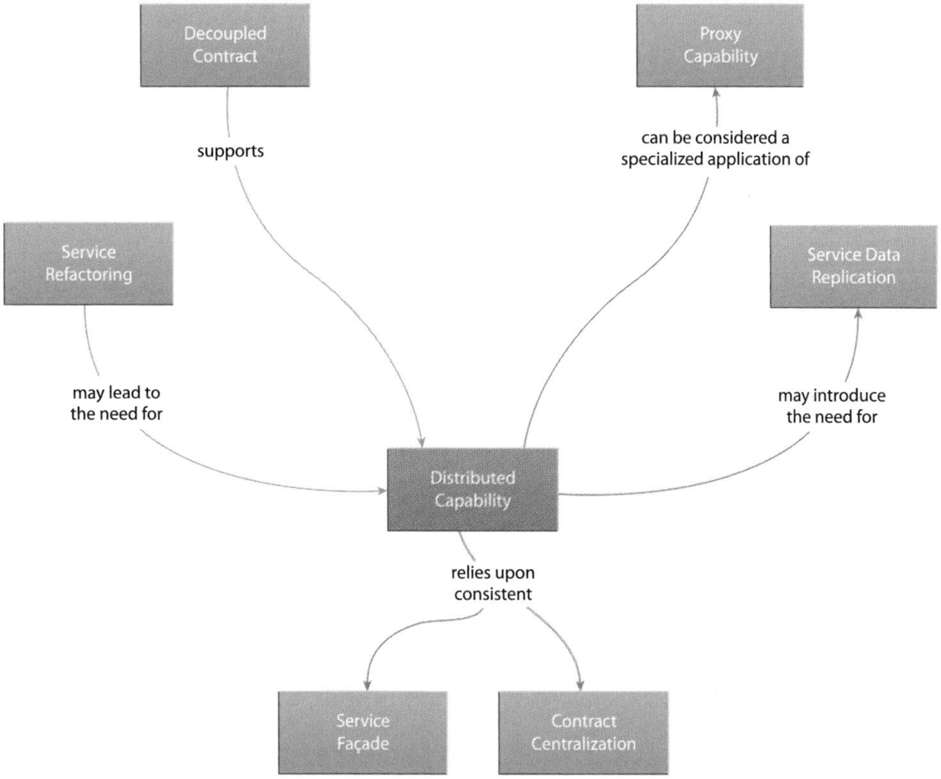

Figure 16.29

Distributed Capability supports the internal decomposition of service logic and therefore has relationships with both service logic and contract-related patterns.

CASE STUDY EXAMPLE

The newly deployed Employee Record service that was defined as a result of applying Service Decomposition (489) and Proxy Capability (497) (see the corresponding case study examples) has become increasingly popular. It is currently being reused within eight service compositions and a new development project is going to be requesting its participation in yet another composition.

For this next composition, the project team is asking that new functionality be added to allow the service to produce highly detailed reports that include various record details and statistics relating to employee hours and ratings from past evaluations. To accommodate this requirement, a new capability is added, called GetMasterReport.

This capability is designed into the Web service contract as an operation that is able to receive parameterized input messages and output large documents comprised of various statistical information and record details.

Preliminary tests show that some of the "from" and "to" value ranges accepted by the operation can take minutes to process because the underlying logic is required to access several databases and then perform a series of calculations before it can produce the required consolidated report.

There are concerns that this one capability will tie up the service too often so that its overall scalability will decrease, thereby affecting its reliability. As a result, the team decides to separate the logic for the GetMasterReport operation to a dedicated server. The Employee Record service is equipped with a façade component that relays requests and responses to and from the separated MSTReportGenerator component.

NOTE

No diagram is provided for this example because the service architecture would be portrayed almost identically to the Invoice service example from Figure 16.28.

Part IV

Service Composition Design Patterns

Chapter 17

Capability Composition Patterns

Capability Composition

Capability Recomposition

The patterns in this chapter provide the means by which to assemble and compose together the service logic that was successfully decomposed, partitioned, and streamlined via the previously explained service identification and definition patterns (Figure 17.1).

These composition patterns essentially establish capabilities as the fundamental means by which service logic is aggregated to solve one or more larger problems. Studying these patterns reveals how composition logic becomes a natural part of service design.

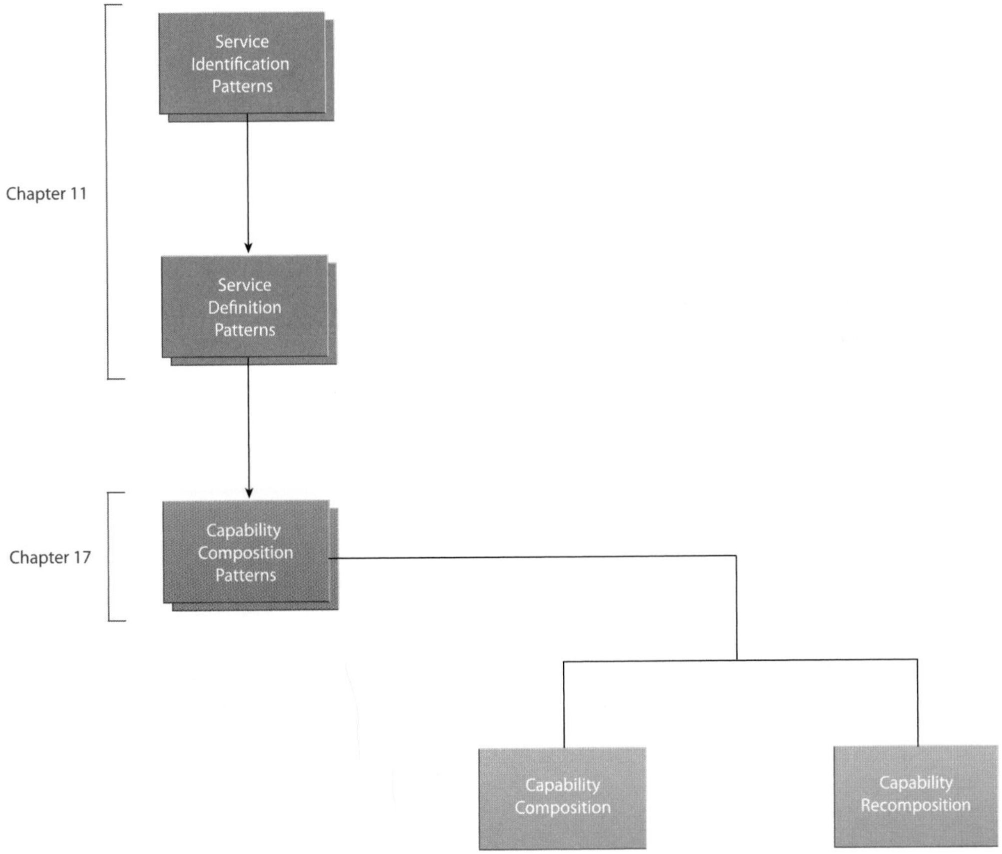

Figure 17.1

Capability composition patterns build upon service identification and definition patterns to establish the concept of service composition.

Capability Composition

How can a service capability solve a problem that requires logic outside of the service boundary?

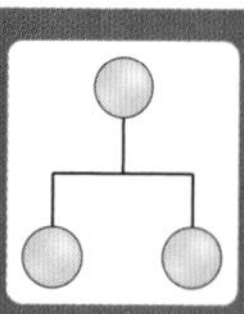

Problem	A capability may not be able to fulfill its processing requirements without adding logic that resides outside of its service's functional context, thereby compromising the integrity of the service context and risking service denormalization.
Solution	When requiring access to logic that falls outside of a service's boundary, capability logic within the service is designed to compose one or more capabilities in other services.
Application	The functionality encapsulated by a capability includes logic that can invoke other capabilities from other services.
Impacts	Carrying out composition logic requires external invocation, which adds performance overhead and decreases service autonomy.
Principles	All
Architecture	Inventory, Composition, Service

Table 17.1
Profile summary for the Capability Composition pattern.

Problem

Although the nature of a capability may be in alignment with a service's overall functional context, the logic required to carry out the capability may need to go beyond the designated service context boundary.

The service boundary could be increased, but this would change its original context and further introduces the danger of functional overlap and service denormalization because the expanded boundary could infringe on the functional boundaries of other services.

Solution

A service capability does not execute logic that resides outside of the service's functional boundary. Instead, it invokes the appropriate capability in a different service based on the appropriate functional boundary (Figure 17.2).

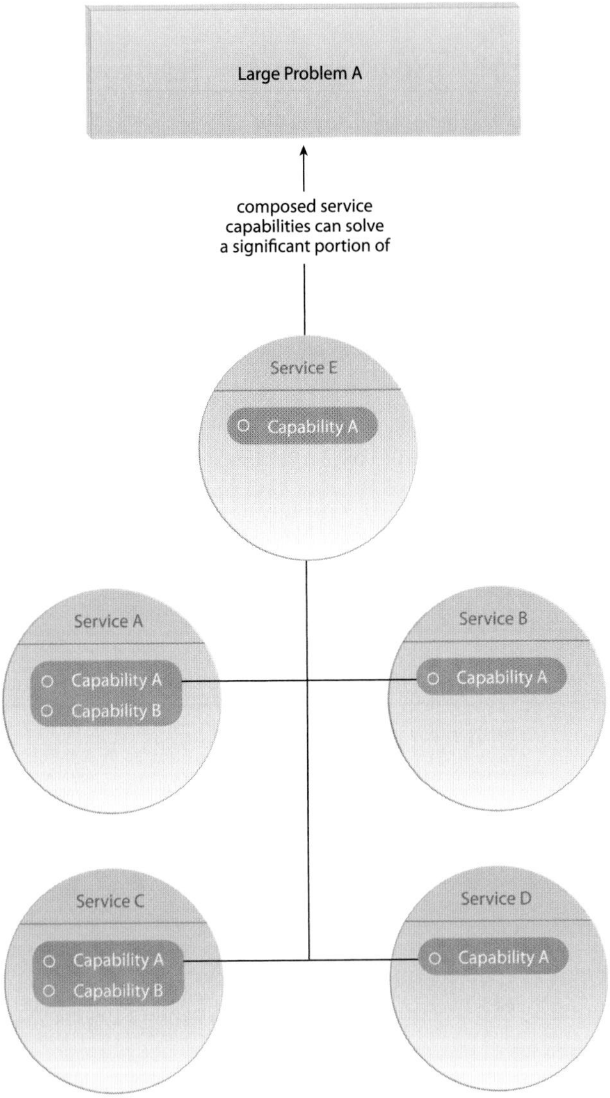

Figure 17.2

The individual capabilities of services can be aggregated to collectively help solve the large problem from which they were originally derived.

Application

This pattern is applied throughout a service delivery lifecycle. For example:

- During the service modeling phase, composition candidates are assembled to define conceptual aggregates comprised of individually composed capability candidates.
- The service design process requires that the functional processing requirements of a service capability be analyzed so as to identify the potential involvement of capabilities.
- When in development, distributed invocation logic may need to be embedded within the capability routines, especially when required to access capabilities residing in other physical services.

Note that if an external body of logic is defined for which no service capability yet exists, then that logic needs to be created as part of a new capability (not as part of the existing capability). The new capability may or may not form the basis of a new service.

Impacts

When capabilities are distributed across numerous services, some of which may reside in remote locations, cross-service capability invocation can impose measurable runtime performance overhead.

Also the overall autonomy of a service is reduced due to the fact that its capability is dependent on another service. This eventuality represents an important design dynamic within service compositions that the application of the Service Autonomy design principle helps prepare a service for.

Furthermore, requiring that a new capability be created when the required external logic does not exist can lead to unexpected scope increases in service delivery projects.

Relationships

Because service-oriented computing is a distributed computing platform, it is fully expected that a solution is comprised of parts that are aggregated together. However, Capability Composition does more than just enable service aggregation. It ensures that Service Normalization (131) and Logic Centralization (136) are fully supported by requiring external service invocation through service boundary enforcement.

It is further important that this pattern be viewed as a step toward what services and their supporting architectures must ultimately realize: Capability Recomposition (526).

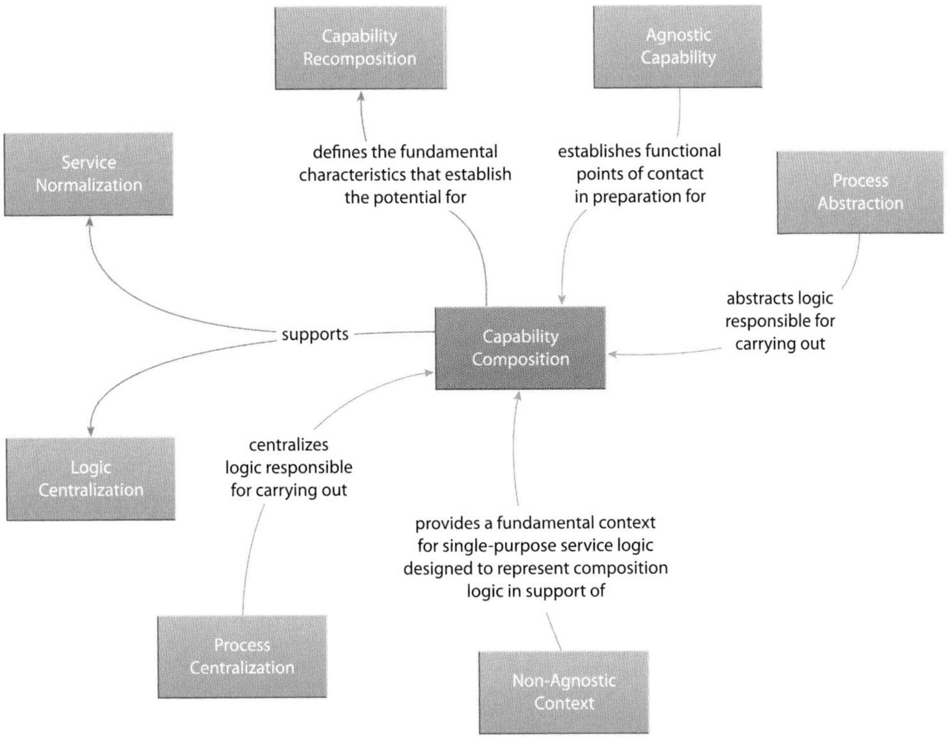

Figure 17.3

Capability Composition represents the ability for services to be composed but not necessarily repeatedly.

NOTE

The following case study example is a continuation of the examples in Chapter 11.

CASE STUDY EXAMPLE

The segment of the Cutit Chain Inventory Transfer process that requires the creation of an inventory record and the cross-referencing of associated back orders could represent a body of logic that is always required with each newly created inventory record. Therefore, this query could be automatically carried out as part of the Inventory service's Add capability.

However, this pattern dictates that the Add capability only create an inventory record and nothing more. Issuing data queries against order information is outside of the capability's functional boundary and also beyond the parent service scope of inventory-related processing.

The ability for a back order query to be issued is already present within the Order service's GetBackOrders capability. Therefore, if the Inventory service's Add capability requires this functionality, it simply needs to invoke that capability via the Order service. Although this imposes performance requirements associated with multiple service invocation, it guarantees that no one service will functionally overlap with others.

The application of this pattern on a broader scale results in the assembly of all four services into a coordinated composition capable of automating the Chain Inventory Transfer business process, as shown in Figure 17.4.

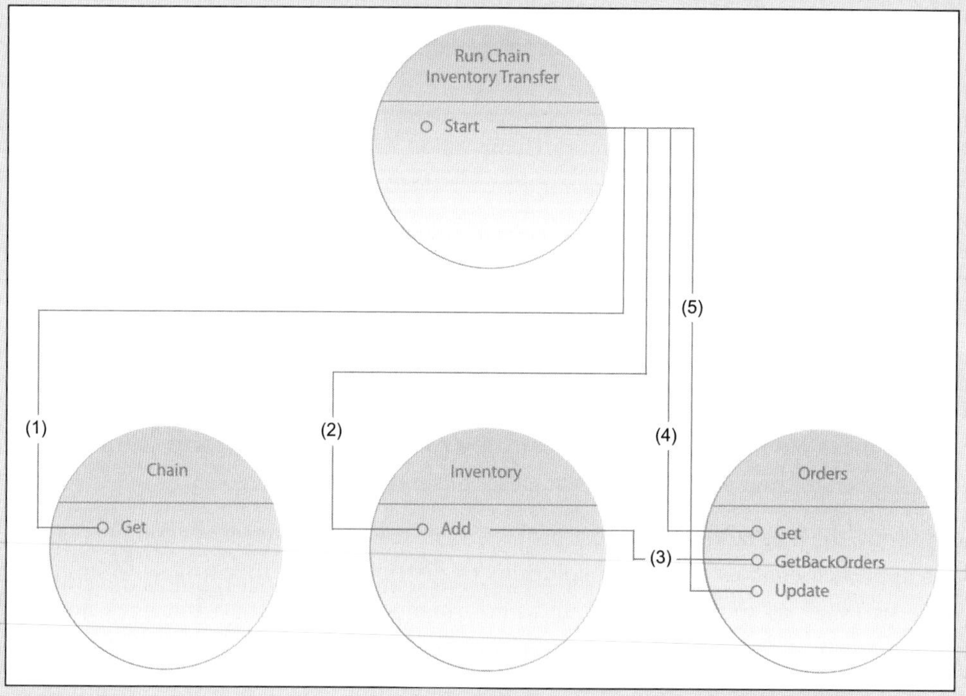

Figure 17.4

The final composition of the services defined via the application of this pattern to all capabilities in support of the coordinated automation of the Chain Inventory Transfer process. Note composition step 3 representing the newly introduced feature of the Inventory service's Add capability to perform automatic back order checks.

Capability Recomposition

How can the same capability be used to help solve multiple problems?

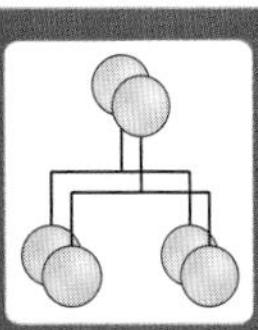

Problem	Using agnostic service logic to only solve a single problem is wasteful and does not leverage the logic's reuse potential.
Solution	Agnostic service capabilities can be designed to be repeatedly invoked in support of multiple compositions that solve multiple problems.
Application	Effective recomposition requires the coordinated, successful, and repeated application of several additional patterns.
Impacts	Repeated service composition demands existing and persistent standardization and governance.
Principles	All
Architecture	Inventory, Composition, Service

Table 17.2
Profile summary for the Capability Recomposition pattern.

Problem

A distributed solution can be comprised of services designed for a specific composition. This is often the case when collections of services are delivered by independent projects. Because these services are tuned to automate a particular business process, little consideration is given to their potential to solve other business problems.

As a result, the outstanding business problems get solved with new collections of services. This approach enables individual solutions to distribute logic in response to immediate concerns (such as special security and performance requirements) but does not foster reuse to any meaningful extent.

Typical effects associated with missing reuse opportunities arise, reminiscent of silo-based environments—for example, the proliferation of redundant logic, wasteful delivery projects, and an increasingly bloated enterprise.

Solution

A key fundamental pattern and one that is essential to the realization of most strategic service-oriented computing goals is that of Capability Recomposition. The successful application of this pattern allows agnostic logic to be repeatedly reused as part of different service aggregates assembled to solve different problems (Figure 17.5).

Application

Though fundamental, this is a pattern very much dependent on others in that it builds upon and leverages many of the patterns in this book. In fact, the extent to which Capability Recomposition can be realized is dependent on the extent to which other SOA patterns have been and will continue to be successfully applied.

So what's the difference between this design pattern and the repeated application of Capability Composition (521)? For the logic encapsulated by a capability to be repeatedly composable, it must be designed in such a manner that it can facilitate numerous scenarios and concurrent invocation. These are not requirements for realizing Capability Composition (521).

It is worth noting that the Service Composability design principle is dedicated to supporting the goals of this pattern. The design considerations raised by this principle help ensure that other service-orientation principles are sufficiently applied so that each service capability is prepared for recomposition.

Impacts

Just as this pattern results in strategic benefits from the combined application of other patterns, it also inherits their collective challenges and complexities. Service composition itself represents a design technique that may impose a learning curve upon those responsible for solution design. It is comprised of a unique process that requires a combination of creativity and awareness of how services can be effectively combined within the constraints of the underlying architecture and infrastructure.

Furthermore, the importance of governing agnostic services is greatly amplified, as these represent the parts of a service inventory most prone to repeated composition. Performance, security, version control, and interaction requirements of each agnostic service can impact the design of any given service composition. Service ownership also plays a key role in ensuring that agnostic services are properly evolved throughout participation in multiple compositions.

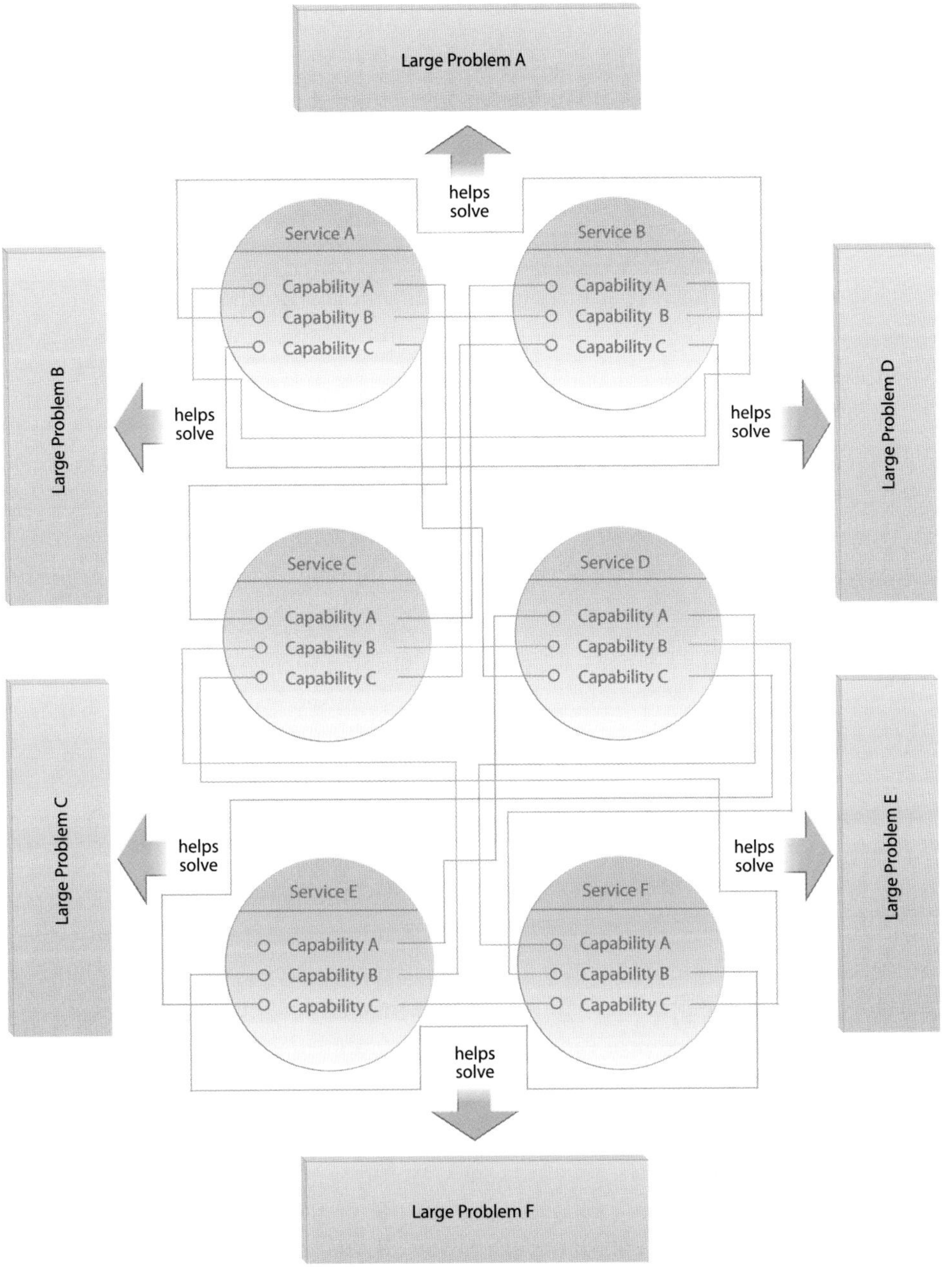

Figure 17.5

The individual capabilities of the original services can be repeatedly aggregated together with additional capabilities into different composition configurations. This enables capabilities to collectively solve the large problem for which they were originally delivered in addition to several other problems.

Relationships

Many patterns in this book support Capability Recomposition. This multitude of supportive relationships is key to understanding the dynamics behind service-orientation. Ultimately, the repeated composition of service capabilities is what leads to the attainment of several of the key strategic benefits and goals associated with service-oriented computing.

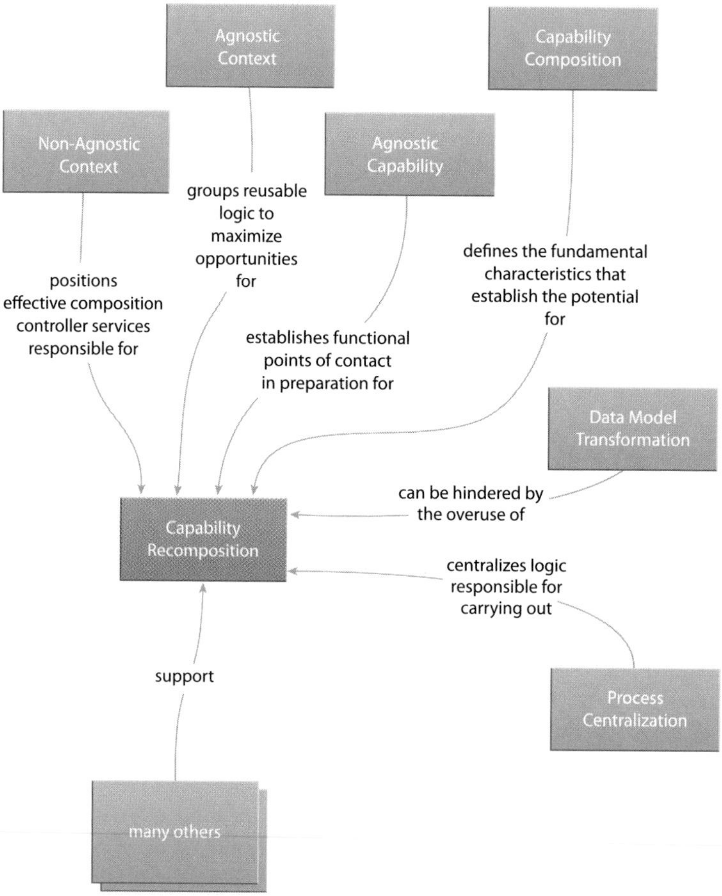

Figure 17.6

Numerous patterns relate to and support Capability Recomposition.

CASE STUDY EXAMPLE

All of the services created for the automation of the Chain Inventory Transfer process offer logic that is reusable and expressed via standardized service contracts. This makes the logic well-suited for recomposition for the purpose of automating other business processes and solving other problems.

Chapter 18

Service Messaging Patterns

- Service Messaging
- Messaging Metadata
- Service Agent
- Intermediate Routing
- State Messaging
- Service Callback
- Service Instance Routing
- Asynchronous Queuing
- Reliable Messaging
- Event-Driven Messaging

Numerous factors can come into play when designing the possible runtime activity that can occur between services within a composition. These patterns provide various techniques for processing and coordinating data exchanges between services.

Service Messaging (533) establishes the base pattern that others in this chapter further specialize and build upon. Messaging Metadata (538), for example, extends Service Messaging (533) by providing the opportunity to supplement messages with additional meta details. Transparent intermediary processing is provided by Service Agent (543) as well as the more specialized Intermediate Routing (549).

The Service Instance Routing (574), Service Callback (566), and State Messaging (557) patterns explore creative ways to leverage a messaging framework in order to communicate between service instances, form asynchronous messaging interactions, and defer state data to the message layer, respectively.

Finally, Asynchronous Queuing (582) and Reliable Messaging (592) provide inventory-level extensions that can improve the quality and integrity of message-based communication, and Event-Driven Messaging (599) establishes the well-known publish-and-subscribe messaging model in support of service interaction.

Service Messaging

How can services interoperate without forming persistent, tightly coupled connections?

Problem	Services that depend on traditional remote communication protocols impose the need for persistent connections and tightly coupled data exchanges, increasing consumer dependencies and limiting service reuse potential.
Solution	Services can be designed to interact via a messaging-based technology, which removes the need for persistent connections and reduces coupling requirements.
Application	A messaging framework needs to be established, and services need to be designed to use it.
Impacts	Messaging technology brings with it QoS concerns such as reliable delivery, security, performance, and transactions.
Principles	Standardized Service Contract, Service Loose Coupling
Architecture	Inventory, Composition, Service

Table 18.1
Profile summary for the Service Messaging pattern.

Problem

Common implementations of distributed solutions rely on remote invocation frameworks, such as those based on RPC technology. These communication systems establish persistent connections based on binary protocols to enable the exchange of data between units of logic.

Although efficient and reliable, they are primarily utilized within the boundaries of application environments and for select integration purposes. Positioning an RPC-based component as an enterprise resource with multiple potential consumers can lower its concurrency threshold because of the overhead associated with creating, sustaining, and terminating the required persistent RPC binary connections.

Solution

Messaging provides an alternative communications framework that does not rely on persistent connections. Instead, messages are transmitted as independent units of communication routed via the underlying infrastructure (Figure 18.1).

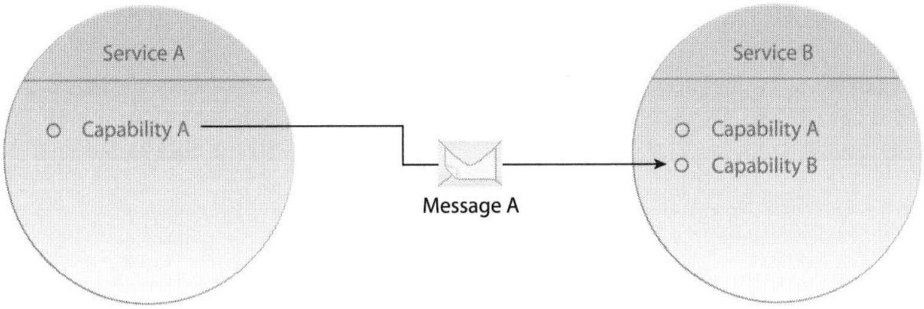

Figure 18.1
Services interact via the transmission of messages—self-contained units of communication.

Application

A messaging framework supported by the enterprise's technical environment needs to be implemented to an extent that it is capable of supporting service interaction requirements. Many established design patterns for messaging frameworks exist, most of which emerged from experience with enterprise integration platforms.

Impacts

Some messaging frameworks cannot provide an adequate level of QoS to support the high demands that can be placed on services positioned as reusable enterprise resources.

To fully enable the application of Capability Recomposition (526) and many of the supporting patterns, the message framework must provide a means of:

- guaranteeing the delivery of each message or guaranteeing a notification of failed deliveries
- securing message contents beyond the transport
- managing state and context data across a service activity
- transmitting messages efficiently as part of real-time interactions
- coordinating cross-service transactions

Without these types of extensions in place, the availability, reliability, and reusability of services will impose limitations that can undermine the strategic goals associated with SOA in general. As explained in the upcoming *Relationships* section, several, more specialized patterns address these individual issues.

Relationships

As one of the most fundamental design patterns in this catalog, Service Messaging ties directly into interoperability design considerations. The success of this pattern is therefore often dependent on the extent to which Canonical Protocol (150) and Canonical Schema (158) are applied within a given inventory.

Service Agent (543) forms a functional relationship with Service Messaging in that event-driven agent programs transparently intercept and process message contents. Messaging Metadata (538) is also closely related because it essentially extends the typical message to incorporate meta details.

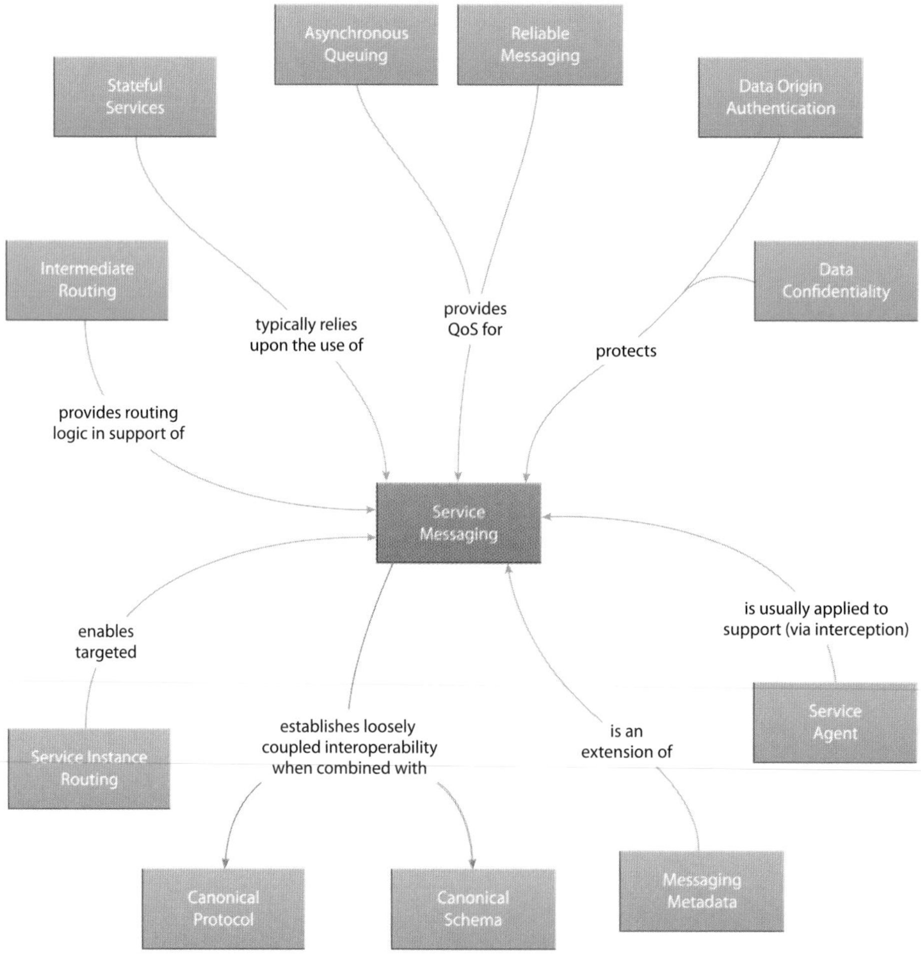

Figure 18.2

Service Messaging establishes the basis for many, more specialized communication and messaging-related patterns.

NOTE

As mentioned in Chapter 5, this pattern is related to several patterns documented in Hohpe and Woolf's book *Enterprise Integration Patterns*, including Message, Messaging, and Document Message and can further be linked to Message Channel and Message Endpoint. Numerous additional specialized messaging patterns documented in this book were established during the EAI era and can still help solve design problems in support of service-oriented solutions, especially in relation to enabling asynchronous message exchanges.

CASE STUDY EXAMPLE

Prior to the SOA initiative, most of the FRC's distributed solutions were based solely on RPC technology. This communications framework was very efficient and reliable but also posed several recurring challenges:

- Components established persistent connections that consumed excessive memory. At peak volume periods, server resource thresholds were regularly surpassed, introducing noticeable latency to all users.
- Most component interaction was based on the exchange of granular parameter data or entire records sets grouped into a proprietary binary format. The resulting communication requirements led to numerous roundtrips between clients and servers, further taxing resources and tightly binding components together.
- It was very difficult to change existing distributed designs due to the numerous cross-component dependencies that were formed. Communication patterns were rigid and primarily synchronous, leaving little opportunity to streamline interaction scenarios.

As part of this service delivery project and the overarching SOA initiative, the majority of the new services are being developed and implemented using Web service technology. Therefore, the use of messaging for inter-service communication is a natural requirement.

In order to leverage the many WS-* extensions that have been identified as key parts of the enterprise service-oriented architecture the FRC is planning, SOAP is chosen as the standard message format.

Relationships

This fundamental pattern can be seen as an extension of Service Messaging (533). Service compositions that rely on industry standard transaction management, security, routing and reliable messaging will utilize specialized implementations of this pattern, as represented by the variety of message-related patterns shown in Figure 18.5.

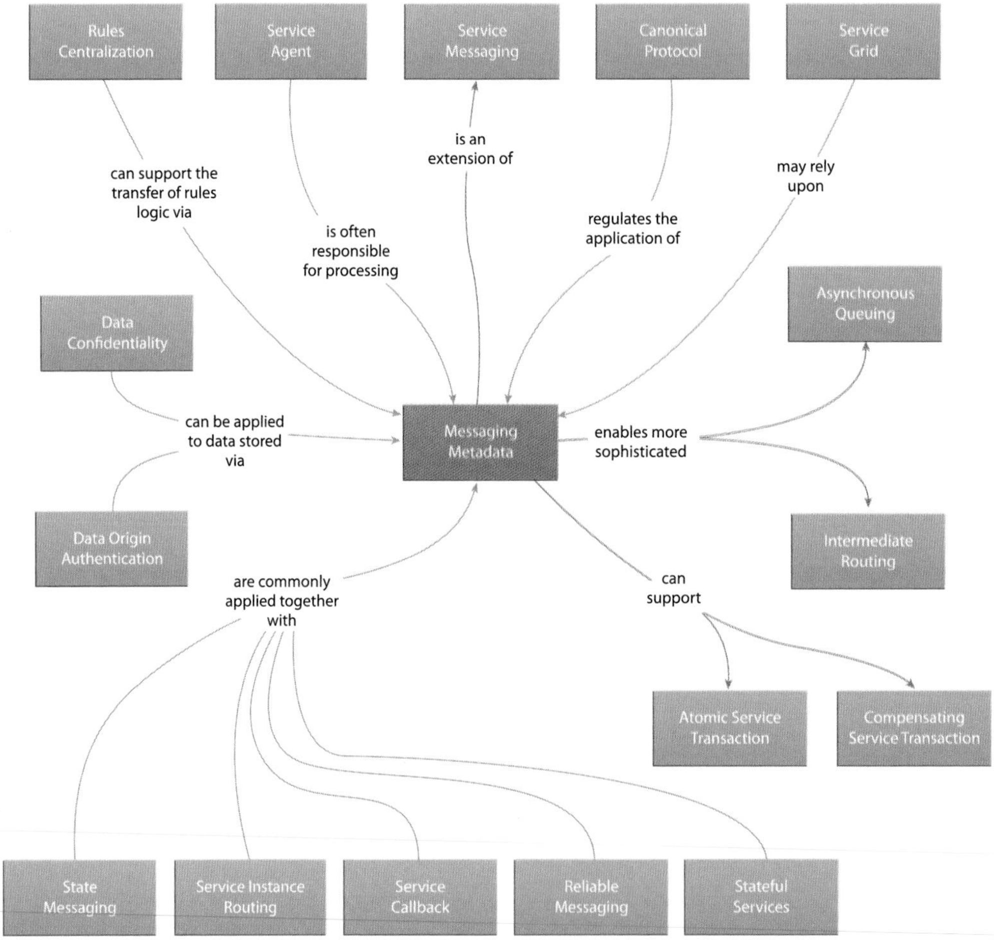

Figure 18.5
Messaging Metadata is commonly associated with patterns that provide extensions to composition architectures.

CASE STUDY EXAMPLE

When messages are routed through various intermediate services within the Cutit Saws environment, they are equipped with a metadata construct that establishes a correlation identifier. Cutit architects use the WS-Addressing `MessageID` element to express correlation values via industry standard header blocks within their SOAP messages, as follows:

```
<Envelope xmlns="http://schemas.xmlsoap.org/soap/envelope/"
  xmlns:wsa="http://schemas.xmlsoap.org/ws
  /2004/08/addressing">
  <Header>
    <wsa:MessageID>
      uuid:938993-226
    </wsa:MessageID>
  </Header>
  <Body>
    ...
  </Body>
</Envelope>
```

Example 18.1

The `MessageID` construct defines a SOAP header block as per the conventions established in the WS-Addressing specification.

NOTE

For more examples of how this pattern is applied with Web services and WS-* standards, see Chapters 6, 7, and 17 in *Service-Oriented Architecture: Concepts, Technology, and Design* and Chapters 4, 11, 15, 18, and 19 in *Web Service Contract Design and Versioning for SOA*.

Service Agent

How can event-driven logic be separated and governed independently?

Problem	Service compositions can become large and inefficient, especially when required to invoke granular capabilities across multiple services.
Solution	Event-driven logic can be deferred to event-driven programs that don't require explicit invocation, thereby reducing the size and performance strain of service compositions.
Application	Service agents can be designed to automatically respond to predefined conditions without invocation via a published contract.
Impacts	The complexity of composition logic increases when it is distributed across services, and event-driven agents and reliance on service agents can further tie an inventory architecture to proprietary vendor technology.
Principles	Service Loose Coupling, Service Reusability
Architecture	Inventory, Composition

Table 18.3
Profile summary for the Service Agent pattern.

Problem

Service composition logic consists of a series of service invocations; each invocation enlisting a service to carry out a segment of the overall parent business process logic. Larger business processes can be enormously complex, especially when having to incorporate numerous "what if" conditions via compensation and exception handling sub-processes. As a result, service compositions can grow correspondingly large (Figure 18.6).

Furthermore, each service invocation comes with a performance hit resulting from having to explicitly invoke and communicate with the service itself. The performance of larger compositions can suffer from the collective overhead of having to invoke multiple services to automate a single task.

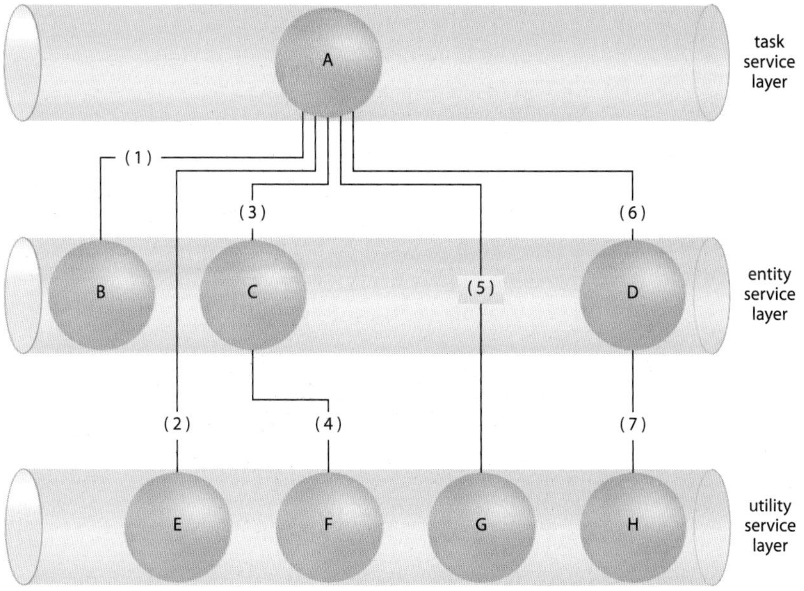

Figure 18.6
A service sequentially composing several others to carry out a particular task.

Solution

Service logic that is triggered by a predictable event can be isolated into a separate program especially designed for automatic invocation upon the occurrence of the event (Figure 18.7). This reduces the amount of composition logic that needs to reside within services and further decreases the quantity of services (or service invocations) required for a given composition.

Application

The event-driven logic is implemented as a service agent—a program with no published contract that is capable of intercepting and processing messages at runtime. Service agents are typically lightweight programs with modest footprints and generally contain common utility-centric processing logic.

For example, vendor runtime platforms commonly provide "system-level" agents that carry out utility functions such as authentication, logging, and load balancing. Service agents can also be custom-developed to provide business-centric and/or single-purpose logic as well.

As first introduced in Figure 4.14 in the *Service Architecture* section of Chapter 4, the message processing logic that is a natural part of any Web service implementation actually consists of a series of system (and perhaps custom) service agents that collectively carry out necessary runtime actions.

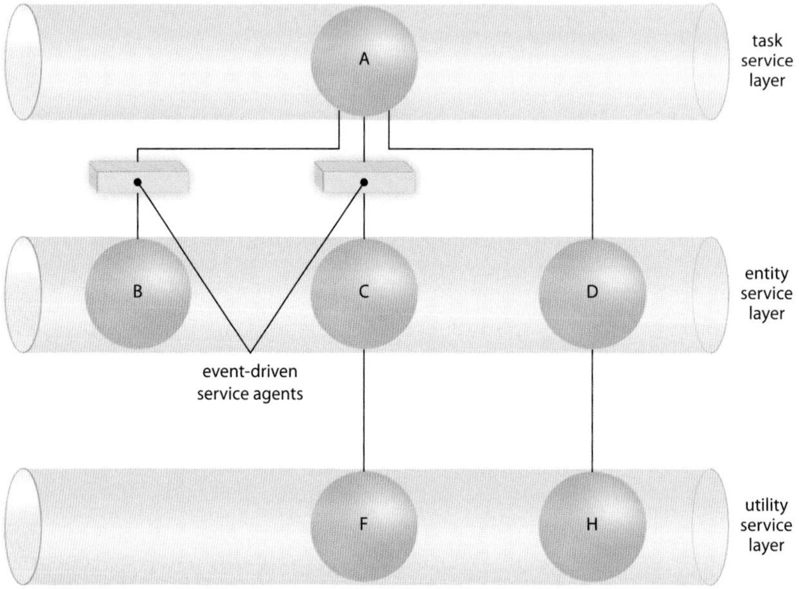

Figure 18.7

Two service agents replace the need for the explicit invocation of utility services E and G. By deferring common logic to service agents, the overall quantity of explicitly invoked services decreases.

NOTE

Service agents are most commonly deployed to facilitate inter-service communication, but they can also be utilized within service architectures. In fact, intra-service use of agents can avoid some of the vendor dependency issues that arise with inter-service agent usage, as explained next in the *Impacts* section.

Impacts

Event-driven agents provide yet another layer of abstraction to which multiple service compositions can form dependencies. Although the perceived size of the composition may be reduced, the actual complexity of the composition itself does not decrease. Composition logic is simply more decentralized as it now also encompasses service agents that automatically perform portions of the overall task.

Overuse of this design pattern can result in an inventory architecture that is difficult to build services for. With too many service agents transparently performing a range of functions, it can become too challenging to design composition architectures that take all possible agent-related processing scenarios into account. Furthermore, some service agent programs may end up conflicting with other service agents or other service logic.

Governance can also become an issue in that service agents will need to be owned and maintained by a separate group that needs to understand the inventory-wide impacts of any changes made to agent logic. For example, system service agents can be subject to behavioral changes as a result of runtime platform upgrades. An agent versioning system will be further required to address these challenges.

Relationships

The event-driven programs created as a result of applying this pattern become a common and intrinsic part of service-oriented inventory architectures. The type of logic they encapsulate is comparable to utility logic, and therefore similar design considerations are most commonly applied. Either way, Service Agent's most fundamental relationships are with Service Messaging (533) and Messaging Metadata (538).

As previously mentioned, the overuse of this pattern can lead to an undesirably high level of dependency on a vendor platform. This can be due to the need to build custom service agents with proprietary programming languages or because services rely too heavily on the proprietary agents provided by vendor runtime environments. Canonical Resources (237) can alleviate this, but it does not directly regulate the *quantity* of produced agents.

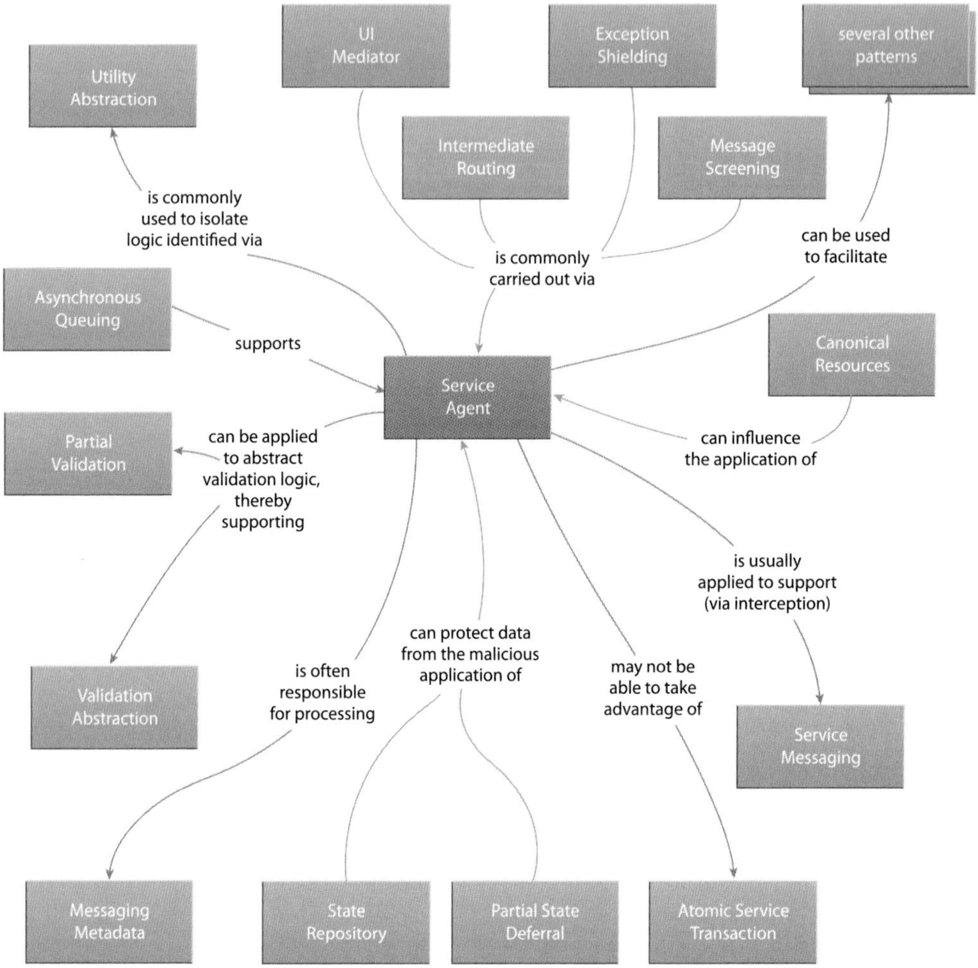

Figure 18.8

This diagram reveals the extent to which Service Agent can be utilized when applying SOA design patterns. Note the "several other patterns" block at the top right indicating that further relationships exist.

NOTE
Service Agent is closely related to Event-Driven Consumer (Hohpe, Woolf).

CASE STUDY EXAMPLE

Within an average day at one of the Alleywood mills, trucks haul loads of raw trees to a primary bay where the amount of usable wood is assessed and then unloaded for further processing. This process is tracked in that the arrival and departure of every truck is logged, along with each received load.

As workers record this information via mobile hand-held devices with keypads, the data is processed by the Truck and Load services, which are commonly composed by a separate task service responsible for specific types of load deliveries.

As part of a typical service composition, the Truck service is required to invoke and send data to the Load service depending on the size and nature of a given load. Alleywood architects have positioned two custom service agents that facilitate this exchange by providing supplementary logging and validation functions (Figure 18.9).

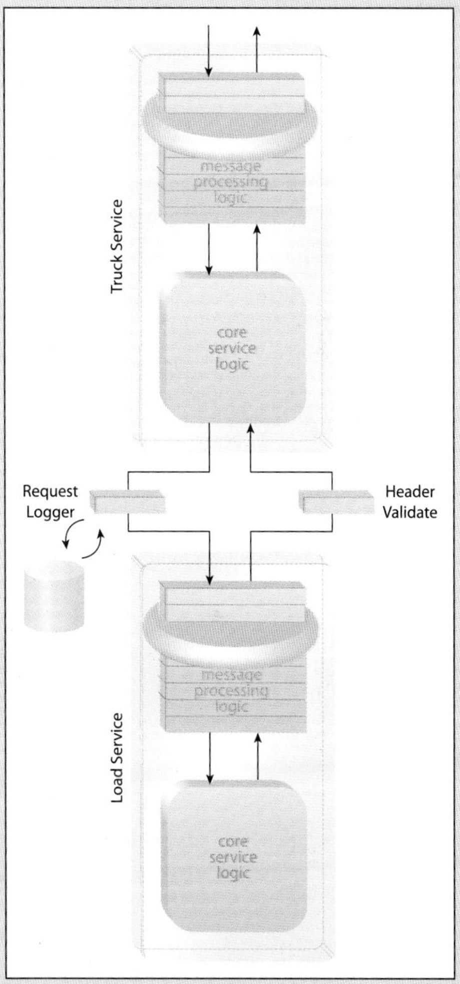

Figure 18.9
Two service agents are employed in a request-response data exchange.

The Request Logger agent captures any data related to loads that are below a minimum quantity or contain a high percentage of "non-processable" raw materials. These are written to a separate database and form the basis of analytical statistics used by Alleywood process engineers. The Header Validation agent simply validates a set of custom headers used for load and truck tracking purposes.

Both service agents perform functions that are common to other services. The Request Logger agent, for example, has several rules built into it, enabling it to silently log a series of what are considered "abnormal conditions." Similarly, the Header Validation agent is designed to validate all custom Alleywood headers.

Intermediate Routing

By Mark Little, Thomas Rischbeck, Arnaud Simon

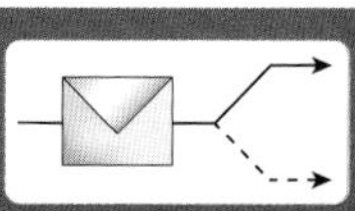

How can dynamic runtime factors affect the path of a message?

Problem	The larger and more complex a service composition is, the more difficult it is to anticipate and design for all possible runtime scenarios in advance, especially with asynchronous, messaging-based communication.
Solution	Message paths can be dynamically determined through the use of intermediary routing logic.
Application	Various types of intermediary routing logic can be incorporated to create message paths based on message content or runtime factors.
Impacts	Dynamically determining a message path adds layers of processing logic and correspondingly can increase performance overhead. Also the use of multiple routing logic can result in overly complex service activities.
Principles	Service Loose Coupling, Service Reusability, Service Composability
Architecture	Composition

Table 18.4

Profile summary for the Intermediate Routing pattern.

Problem

A service composition can be viewed as a chain of point-to-point data exchanges between composition participants. Collectively, these exchanges end up automating a parent business process.

The message routing logic (the decision logic that determines how messages are passed from one service to another) can be embedded within the logic of each service in a composition. This allows for the successful execution of *predetermined* message paths. However, there may be unforeseen factors that are not accounted for in the embedded routing logic, which can lead to unanticipated system failure.

For example:

- The destination service a message is being transmitted to is temporarily (or even permanently) unavailable.

- The embedded routing logic contains a "catch all" condition to handle exceptions, but the resulting message destination is still incorrect.
- The originally planned message path cannot be carried out, resulting in a rejection of the message from the service's previous consumer.

Figure 18.10 illustrates these scenarios.

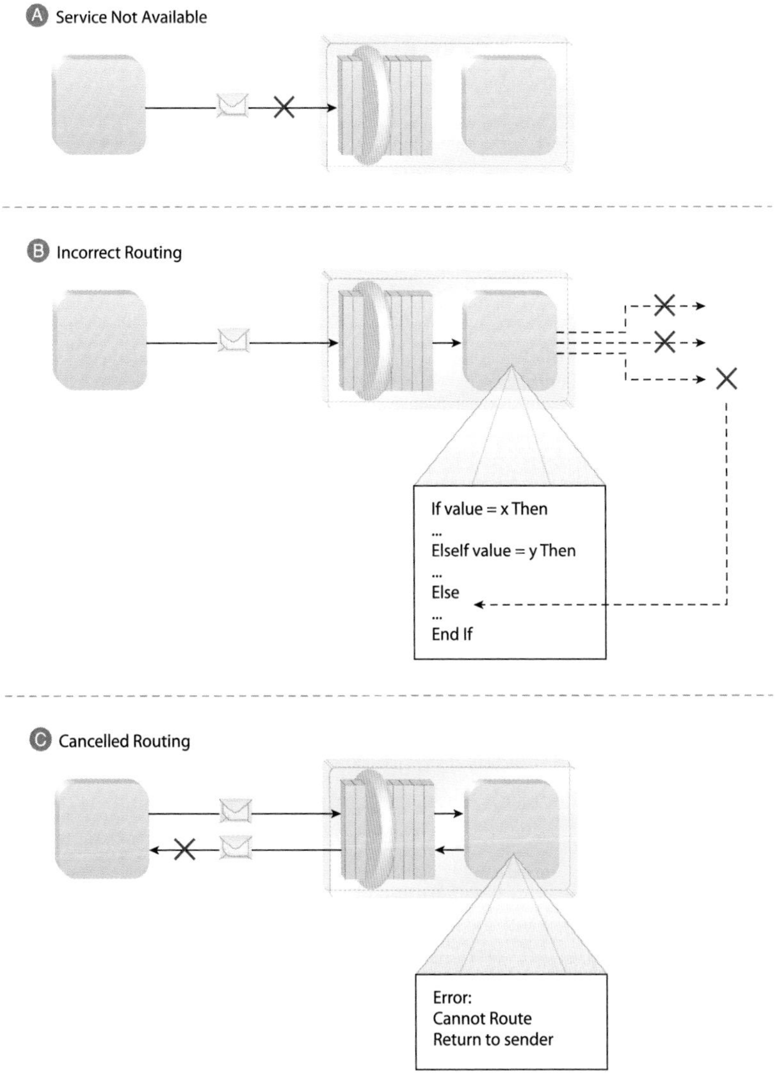

Figure 18.10

A message transmission fails because the service is not available (A). Internal service routing logic is insufficient and ends up sending the message to the wrong destination (B). Internal service logic is incapable of routing the message and simply rejects it (C), effectively terminating the service activity.

Alternatively, there may simply be functional requirements that are dynamic in nature and for which services cannot be designed in advance.

Solution

Generic, multi-purpose routing logic can be abstracted so that it exists as a separate part of the architecture in support of multiple services and service compositions. Most commonly this is achieved through the use of event-driven service agents that transparently intercept messages and dynamically determine their paths (Figure 18.11).

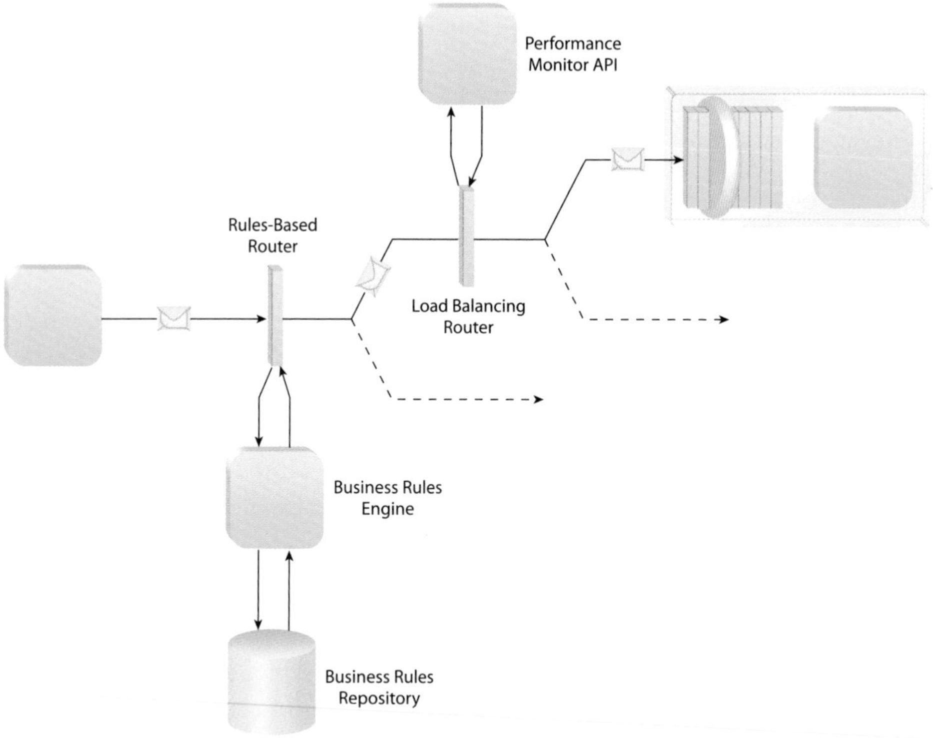

Figure 18.11

A message passes through two router agents before it arrives at its destination. The Rules-Based Router identifies the target service based on a business rule that the agent dynamically retrieves and interprets, as a consequence of Rules Centralization (216). The Load Balancing Router then checks current usage statistics for that service before it decides which instance or redundant implementation of the service to send the message to.

Application

This pattern is usually applied as a specialized implementation of Service Agent (543). Routing-centric agents required to perform dynamic routing are often provided by messaging middleware and are a fundamental component of ESB products. These types of out-of-the-box agents can be configured to carry out a range of routing functions. However, the creation of custom routing agents is also possible and not uncommon, especially in environments that need to support complex service compositions with special requirements.

Common forms of routing functionality include:

- *Content-Based Routing* – Essentially, this type of routing determines a message's path based on its contents. Content-based routing can be used to model complex business processes and provide an efficient way to recompose services on the fly. Such routing decisions may need to involve access to a business rules engine to accurately assess message destinations.
- *Load Balancing* – This form of routing agent has become an important part of environments where concurrent usage demands are commonplace. A load balancing router is capable of directing a message to one or more identical service instances in order to help the service activity be carried out as efficiently as possible.
- *1:1 Routing* – In this case, the routing agent is directly wired to a single physical service at any point in time. When messages arrive, the agent is capable of routing them to different service instances or redundant service implementations. This accommodates standard fail-over requirements and allows services to be maintained or upgraded without risking "disruption of service" to consumers.

Regardless of the nature of the routing logic, it is desirable to be able to update and modify routing parameters dynamically—ideally even by business analysts so that they can adapt and control the business logic in real-time. This is particularly important when business logic is subject to frequent change. If changes are *extremely* frequent, it can be further beneficial to model the routing logic through the extraction of complex *business rules* that describe declarative logic on top of the message content and use the outcome to make the routing decision.

A more frugal alternative is to employ content-based routing using XPath or XQuery expressions. However, these languages require technically more involved personnel for their control and maintenance.

NOTE

While event-driven agents represent the most common implementation of this pattern, routing logic can also be incorporated into actual intermediary services that process and forward messages based on the same factors as those previously listed.

Impacts

The usage of routing agents allows the automation of complex decisions and the quick adaptation to changing business requirements. However, the complexity and flexibility of incorporating intermediate routing logic into composition architectures is not without disadvantages:

- Dynamic modification of routing rules at runtime can introduce the risk of having previously untested logic set into production. If possible, routing rule-set changes should first be put through a conventional staging process.
- Dynamic routing paths can be elaborate and therefore difficult to manage and update, leading to a risk of unexpected failure conditions. A centralized routing rule management system can help alleviate the risk of introducing potential points of failure.
- Physically separated routing logic will naturally add performance overhead when compared to direct service-to-service communication, where the routing logic is embedded within the consumer program.

Additionally, security can be a concern when applying this pattern. You may want to control who will and will not process a message containing sensitive data. An inventory architecture with many built-in intermediate routing agents can provide native functionality that conflicts with some security requirements.

Relationships

Routing functionality is a fundamental part of messaging frameworks and can therefore be associated with most messaging-related design patterns. The separation of metadata provided by Messaging Metadata (538) allows for the more advanced forms of routing described earlier in the *Application* section. Also when implementing routing logic with Service Agent (543), Canonical Resources (237) can influence the platform and technologies used to build and host the agent programs.

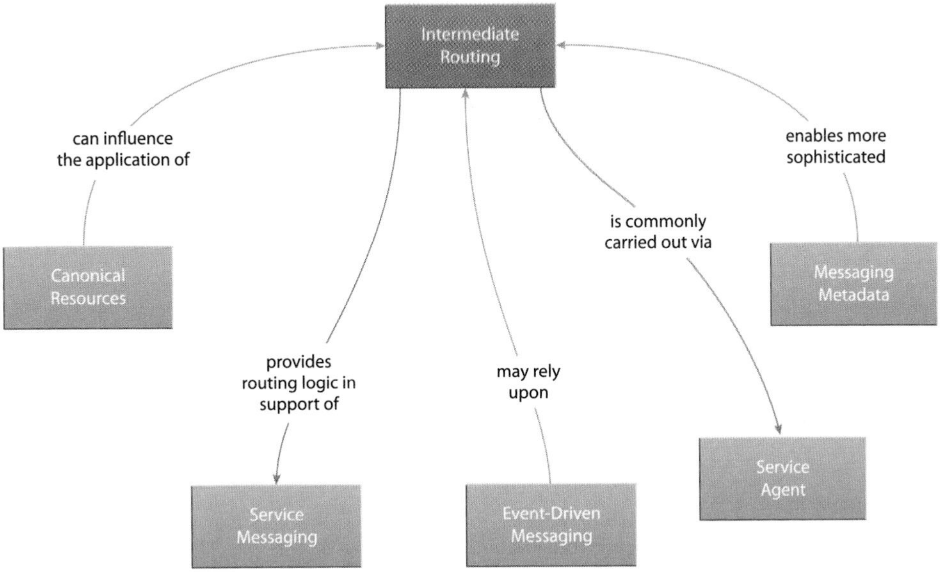

Figure 18.12

Intermediate Routing provides specialized, agent-related processing in support of message transmissions and therefore has relationships with several messaging patterns.

Because of their messaging-centric feature-sets, ESB platforms are fully expected to carry out routing functionality in support of sophisticated service activity process. Intermediate Routing is therefore one of the three core patterns that represent Enterprise Service Bus (704).

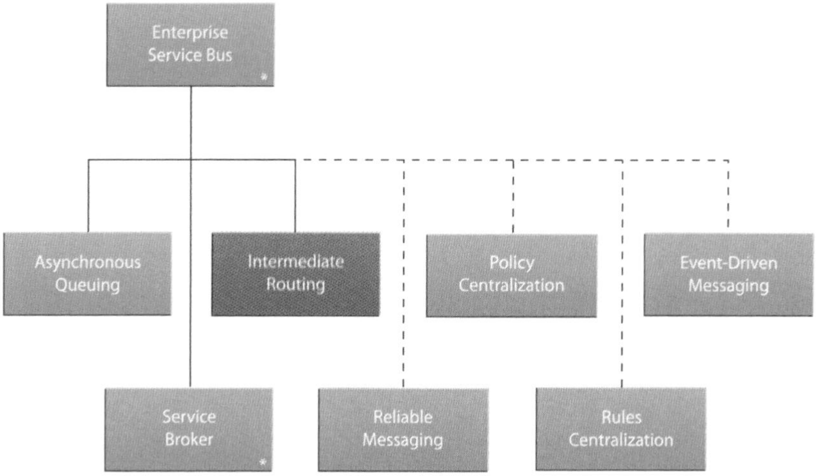

Figure 18.13

Intermediate Routing is one of the patterns that comprise Enterprise Service Bus (704).

NOTE

Depending on how it is applied, the runtime routing logic established by Intermediate Routing is comparable to Content-Based Router (Hohpe, Woolf), Dynamic Router (Hohpe, Woolf), and Message Router (Hohpe, Woolf). Several more message routing patterns are described in the *Enterprise Integration Patterns* catalog. Intermediate Routing highlights the most common routing options used for service composition architectures.

CASE STUDY EXAMPLE

The Flight Plan Validation service described later in the example for Data Format Transformation (681) forwards flight plan documents after they have successfully been transformed and validated.

As part of the FRC Aerial Firefighting Coordination business process, content-based routers are employed to route these documents through the appropriate service, based on the following factors:

- the SOAP body of the received flight plan messages
- SOAP headers that may indicate limited availability or delayed arrival of aircrafts
- the severity level of the current wildfire
- the location to which the aircrafts will need to travel (usually the location of the fire)

The routing intelligence is complex and even subject to further changes due to international regulatory compliance requirements. As shown in Figure 18.14, all of these factors determine the ultimate decision as to which service to forward the message to.

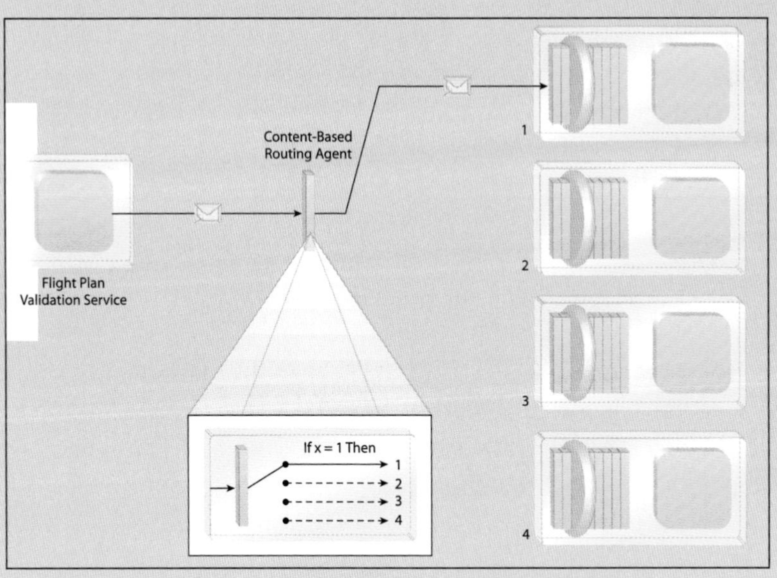

Figure 18.14

The content-based routing agent receives the message from the Flight Plan Validation service and then dynamically determines where to route it to. Note that in this case, the service may be sending the message to a logical address that is processed by the agent, which then forwards it to the appropriate physical address.

State Messaging

By Anish Karmarkar

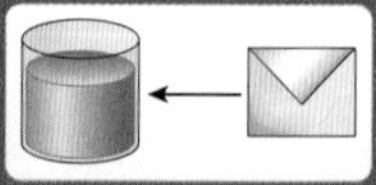

How can a service remain stateless while participating in stateful interactions?

Problem	When services are required to maintain state information in memory between message exchanges with consumers, their scalability can be comprised, and they can become a performance burden on the surrounding infrastructure.
Solution	Instead of retaining the state data in memory, its storage is temporarily delegated to messages.
Application	Depending on how this pattern is applied, both services and consumers may need to be designed to process message-based state data.
Impacts	This pattern may not be suitable for all forms of state data, and should messages be lost, any state information they carried may be lost as well.
Principles	Standardized Service Contract, Service Statelessness, Service Composability
Architecture	Composition, Service

Table 18.5
Profile summary for the State Messaging pattern.

Problem

Services are sometimes required to be involved in runtime activities that span multiple message exchanges. In these cases, a service may need to retain state information until the overarching task is completed. This is especially common with services that act as composition controllers.

By default, services are often designed to keep this state data in memory so that it is easily accessible and essentially remains alive for as long as the service instance is active (Figure 18.15). However, this design approach can lead to serious scalability problems and further runs contrary to the Service Statelessness design principle.

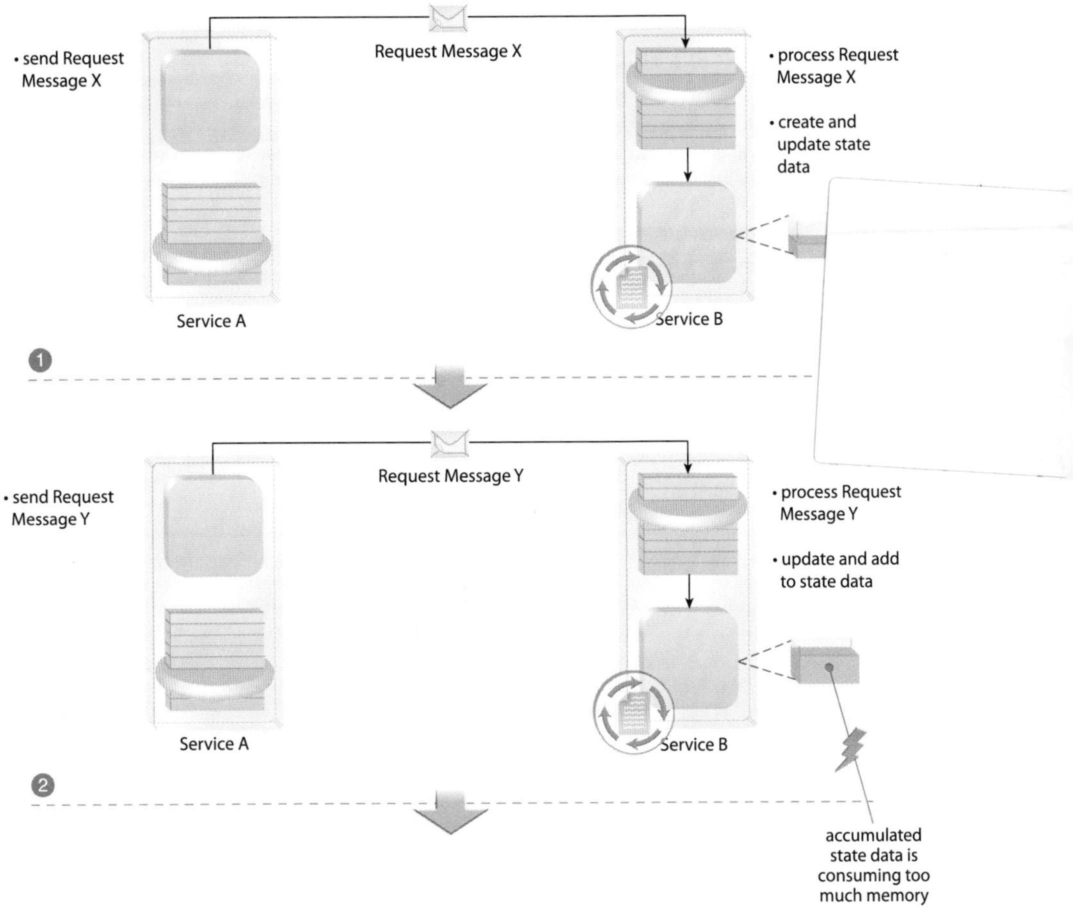

Figure 18.15

This figure shows just a part of a larger conversational exchange betwen two services. Service A, acting as a service consumer, issues a Request Message X to Service B (1). Service B creates the necessary data structures to maintain the state associated with processing Request Message X and updates the data structures after processing is completed. Service A then issues another request to Service B (2), which Service B then processes, resulting in an update of the state data that also increases the quantity of state data Service B must retain (which, ultimately, results in scalability problems).

Solution

Instead of the service maintaining state data in memory, it moves the data to the message. During a conversational interaction, the service retrieves the latest state data from the next input message (Figure 18.16).

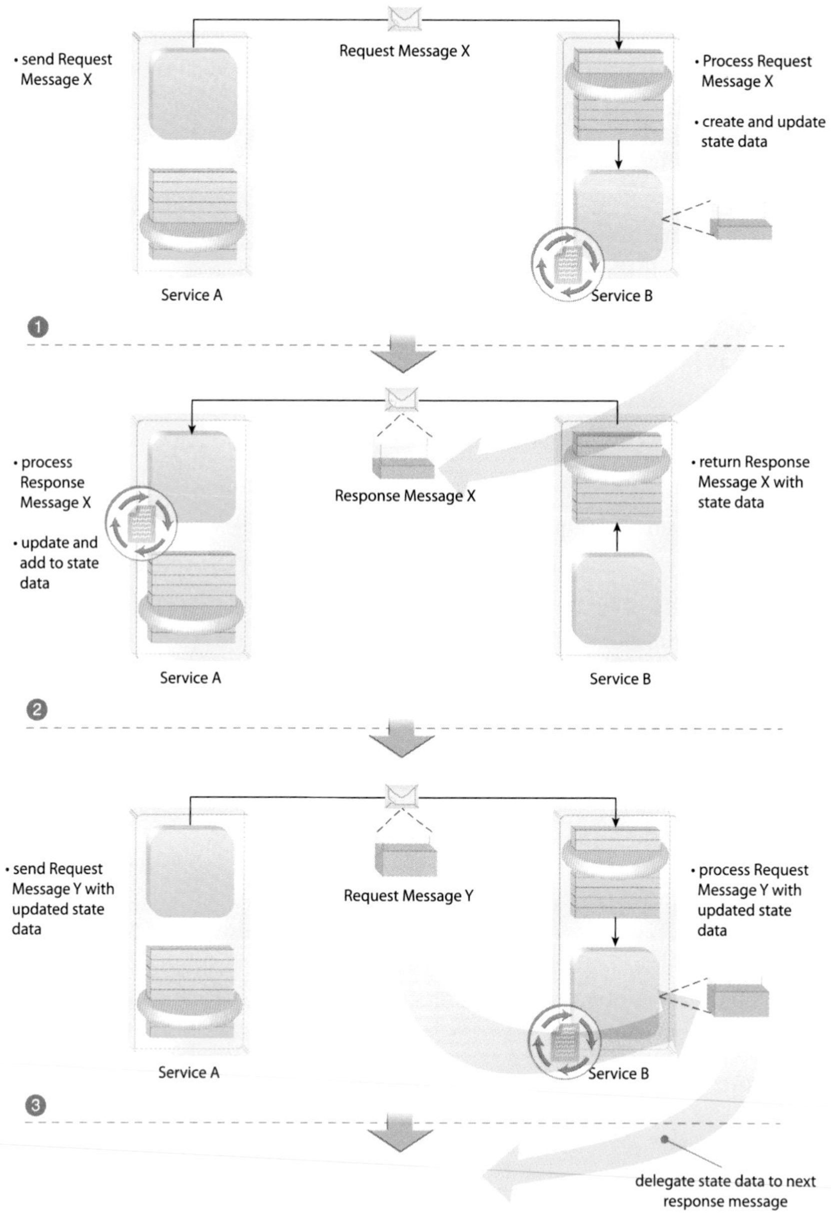

Figure 18.16

Service A, acting as a service consumer, issues Request Message X to Service B (1). Service B creates the necessary data structures to maintain the necessary state and updates the data structures after processing this message. Service B then adds the state data to Response Message X, which it then returns back to Service A (2). Service A processes the response and then generates Request Message Y containing updated state data, which is then received and processed by Service B (3).

Application

There are two common approaches to applying this pattern, both of which affect how the service consumer relates to the state data:

- The consumer retains a copy of the latest state data in memory and only the service benefits from delegating the state data to the message. This approach is suitable for when this pattern is implemented using WS-Addressing, due to the one-way conversational nature of Endpoint References (EPRs).
- Both the consumer and the service use messages to temporarily off-load state data. This two-way interaction with state data may be appropriate when both consumer and service are actual services within a larger composition. This technique can be achieved using custom message headers.

With either approach, this pattern requires that the messaging infrastructure be capable of distinguishing between message body content (or payload data) and supplementary metadata commonly stored in message headers. Whereas with WS-Addressing these message headers can be processed by many modern messaging products and platforms, the custom header approach requires extra custom development effort.

It is important to note that both techniques introduce the need for proprietary service logic. While WS-Addressing standardizes the EPR wrapper elements used to house state data, it does not standardize the expression of the state data itself. When using custom headers, the need for proprietary processing logic required to extract and process state data from messages will span to both consumer and service.

NOTE

For examples of pre-defined SOAP headers that are suitable for sophisticated, two-way conversational message exchanges, view the WS-Context specification accessible via SOASpecs.com.

Impacts

When following the two-way model with custom headers, messages that are lost due to runtime failure or exception conditions will further lose the state data, thereby placing the overarching task in jeopardy.

It is also important to consider the security implications of state data placed on the messaging layer. For services that handle sensitive or private data, the corresponding state information should either be suitably encrypted and/or digitally signed, and it is not uncommon for the consumer to not gain access to protected state data.

Furthermore, because this pattern requires that state data be stored within messages that are passed back and forth with every request and response, it is important to consider the size of this information and the implications on bandwidth and runtime latency. As with other patterns that require new infrastructure extensions, establishing inventory-wide support for State Messaging will introduce cost and effort associated with the necessary infrastructure upgrades.

Relationships

State Messaging is based on Service Messaging (533) and further utilizes Messaging Metadata (538) to represent state information within header blocks. This pattern can also be used in conjunction with Service Instance Routing (574) in such a way that only part of the state is maintained by the consumer, while the other part is managed by the service. This can lead to reduced message sizes and memory requirements.

Asynchronous Queuing (582) and Reliable Messaging (592) can be further utilized to provide increased robustness within the underlying infrastructure so that the state data remains protected against runtime failures and errors, even while in transit.

Also, as mentioned earlier, the use of state data with security requirements may demand that this pattern be combined with Data Confidentiality (641) and/or Data Origin Authentication (649).

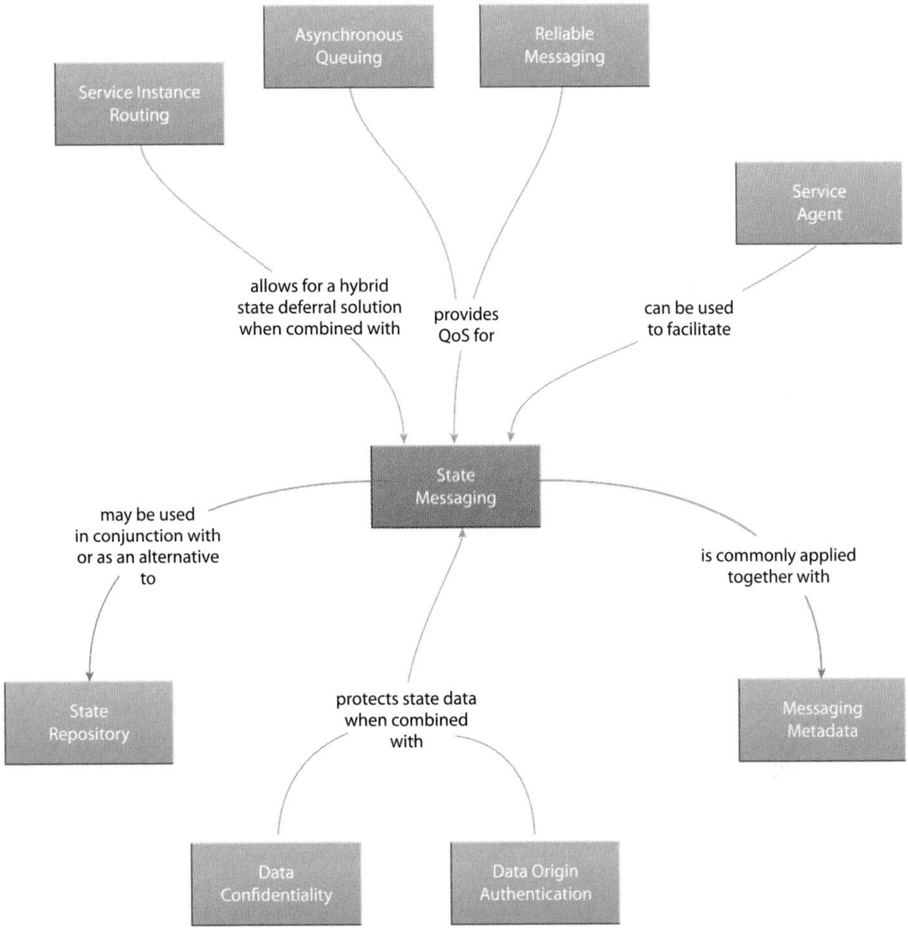

Figure 18.17

State Messaging is associated with other message patterns but also those that provide often required quality-of-service and security extensions.

CASE STUDY EXAMPLE

In order to reduce operational costs at the FRC, management has decided to look for opportunities to downsize infrastructure. Several meetings with IT staff have generated some ideas, one of which is to simply shift some of the processing responsibilities out of the FRC enterprise and onto partner organizations. One application of this approach relates to the FRC's approval process for industrial machinery that forestry companies are required to undergo before they can purchase and put new lumber processing machines to use.

Up until now, the FRC has automated these approvals so that all parts of the approval process are carried out by the Approval service. This includes cases where all or some of the process steps are completed by partners.

Each occurrence of the process generates an application document that stores specifications and other required details about the machinery. These documents can become relatively large, and the FRC receives many of these applications daily. As a result, they are required to store large amounts of information, a good portion of which is state data that corresponds to documents that are part of incomplete approval processes.

In an effort to delegate processing and infrastructure requirements to partners, it is decided to re-engineer the Approval service so that it supports State Messaging. Specifically, by moving the state associated with a given approval process to the message layer, the responsibility for storing and maintaining approval documents can be delegated to the partner consumer applications until such a time that the process is completed (at which point the documents become part of the FRC archive).

At first, FRC architects build a prototype based on the use of custom headers with the intention of providing Alleywood and other partners the opportunity to delegate state data to messages as well.

After exploring scenarios involving this prototype further, the architects realize that they cannot proceed with this design due to a firm requirement that the FRC maintain control of state data during external interaction with partners. Allowing partners to access and even modify the status of an application, for example, would be strictly prohibited. As a result, the architects decide to standardize on the use of reference parameters provided by WS-Addressing Endpoint References (EPRs).

The following example shows a request message sent to the FRC that initiates the approval process:

```
<Envelope xmlns="http://www.w3.org/2003/05/soap-envelope"
  xmlns:wsa="http://www.w3.org/2005/08/addressing"
  xmlns:frc="http://frc/ns/approval">
  <Header>
    <wsa:To>
      http://frc/submitApp
    </wsa:To>
    ...
  </Header>
  <Body>
    <frc:ApprovalStep1>
```

```
      ...
    </frc:ApprovalStep1>
  </Body>
</Envelope>
```

Example 18.2

A SOAP message containing an application for approval. This message is the first in a series of messages that must be exchanged to complete the approval process.

The next example displays the corresponding response message generated by the FRC. It contains the `frc:ServiceEPR` construct (representing the EPR for the service), which includes a reference parameter element called `frc:AppApprovalState` that contains the status of the application (among other state details):

```
<Envelope xmlns="http://www.w3.org/2003/05/soap-envelope"
  xmlns:frc="http://frc/ns/approval"
  xmlns:wsa="http://www.w3.org/2005/08/addressing">
  <Header>
    ...
  </Header>
  <Body>
    <!-- Response from FRC -->
    <frc:ApprovalStep1Response>
      <frc:ServiceEPR>
        <wsa:Address>
          http://frc/submitApp
        </wsa:Address>
        <wsa:ReferenceParameters>
          <frc:AppApprovalState>
            ...
          <frc:AppApprovalState>
          ...
        </wsa:ReferenceParameters>
      </frc:ServiceEPR>
      ...
    </frc:ApprovalStep1Response>
  </Body>
</Envelope>
```

Example 18.3

The FRC's response message that provides the state data located in the `wsa:ReferenceParameters` construct that is further wrapped within the `frc:ServiceEPR` construct, which represents a new EPR for the Approval service. Note that this message does not indicate the final approval but only approval from one of several FRC departments.

After receiving the message from Example 18.3, the partner organization issues the message shown in Example 18.4 to the destination within the FRC provided by the preceding message's EPR. In this case the state data is located in the `frc:AppApprovalState` construct in the SOAP header (as required by WS-Addressing):

```
<Envelope xmlns="http://www.w3.org/2003/05/soap-envelope"
  xmlns:wsa="http://www.w3.org/2005/08/addressing"
  xmlns:frc="http://frc/ns/approval">
  <Header>
    <wsa:To>
      http://frc/submitApp
    </wsa:To>
    <frc:AppApprovalState wsa:IsReferenceParameter="true">
      ...
    </frc:AppApprovalState>
  </Header>
  <Body>
    <!-- Message sent for approval step 2 -->
    <frc:ApprovalStep2>
      ...
    </frc:AppovalStep2>
  </Body>
</Envelope>
```

Example 18.4

The second message sent to the FRC for Step 2 of the approval process provides state data within the reference parameter `frc:AppApprovalState` as a SOAP header block. This header is used by the FRC service to recreate the current state of the application.

Service Callback

By Anish Karmarkar

How can a service communicate asynchronously with its consumers?

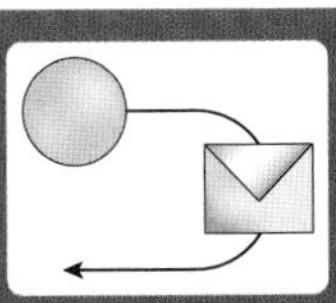

Problem	When a service needs to respond to a consumer request through the issuance of multiple messages or when service message processing requires a large amount of time, it is often not possible to communicate synchronously.
Solution	A service can require that consumers communicate with it asynchronously and provide a callback address to which the service can send response messages.
Application	A callback address generation and message correlation mechanism needs to be incorporated into the messaging framework and the overall inventory architecture.
Impacts	Asynchronous communication can introduce reliability concerns and can further require that surrounding infrastructure be upgraded to fully support the necessary callback correlation.
Principles	Standardized Service Contract, Service Loose Coupling, Service Composability
Architecture	Inventory, Service, Composition

Table 18.6
Profile summary for the Service Callback pattern.

Problem

When service logic requires that a consumer request be responded to with multiple messages, a standard request-response messaging exchange is not appropriate. Similarly, when a given consumer request requires that the service perform prolonged processing before being able to respond, synchronous communication is not possible without jeopardizing scalability and reliability of the service and its surrounding architecture (Figure 18.8).

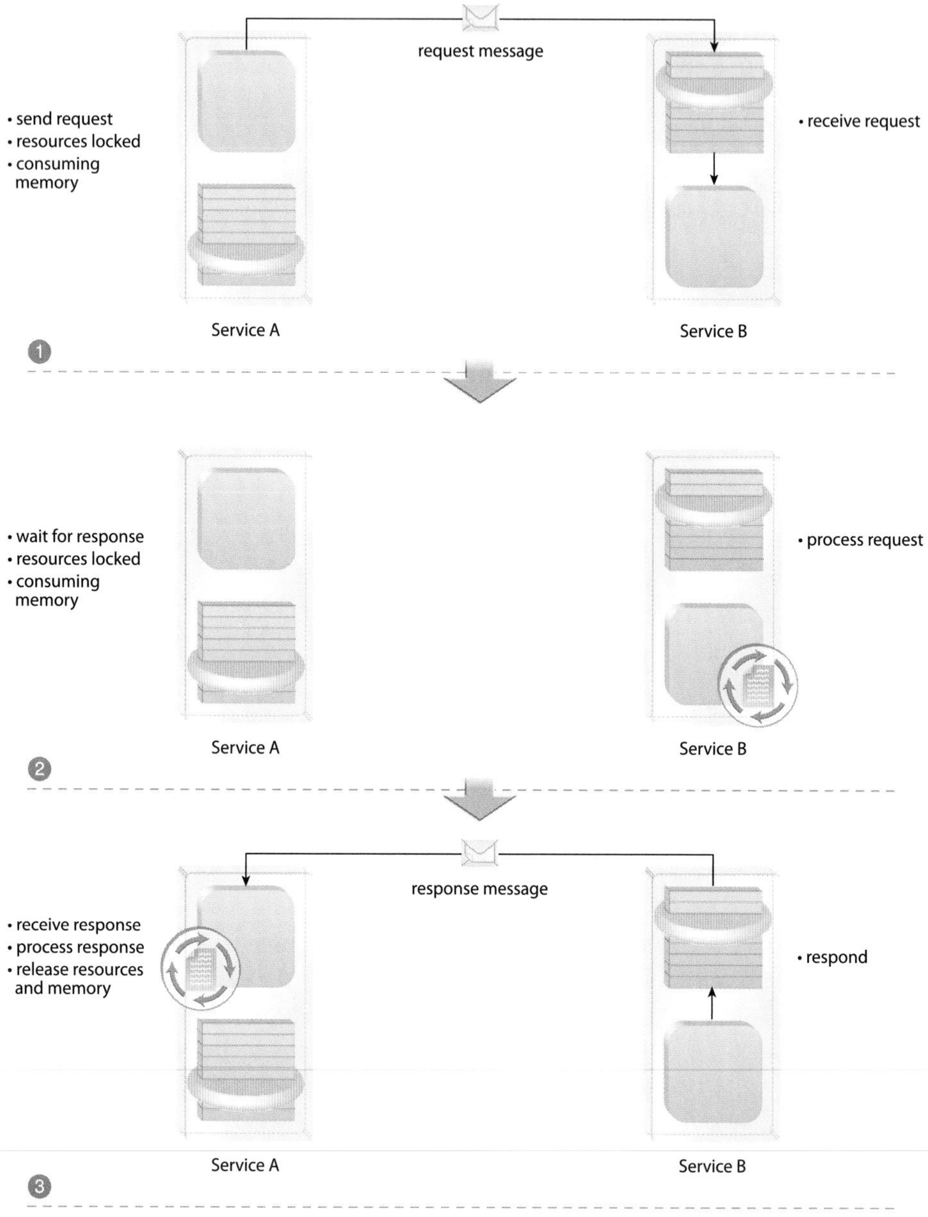

Figure 18.18

Service A, acting as the service consumer, issues a request message to Service B (1), and because it is part of a synchronous data exchange, Service A is required to wait (2) until Service B processes the request message and then transmits a response (3). During this waiting period, both service and consumer must be available and continue to use up memory.

Solution

Services are designed in such a manner that consumers provide them with a callback address at which they can be contacted by the service at some point after the service receives the initial consumer request message (Figure 18.19). Consumers are furthermore asked to supply correlation details that allow the service to send an identifier within future messages so that consumers can associate them with the original task.

> **NOTE**
>
> A callback address does not need to represent the address of the consumer that provided it. The callback address can point to a different location altogether.

Application

Services designed to support this pattern must be able to preserve callback addresses and associated correlation data, especially when using this technique for longer running service-side processes that may include extended periods of inactivity (such as when waiting for human interaction to occur). While this may be built into the actual service architecture, the management of this information is often assumed by the surrounding inventory infrastructure, especially when implementing this pattern with established standards, such as WS-Addressing.

On the consumer side, this pattern can be supported through the use of event-driven agent programs that are positioned to listen for service response messages. This again may be provided by the infrastructure extensions themselves.

Furthermore, because a consumer will not be expecting an immediate response to its original request, it will commonly move on to other tasks while the service continues with its processing. The consumer architecture may therefore need to be able to support the scenario where service requests are received and temporarily stored until the consumer is ready to process them. This is why this pattern is often implemented with the support of messaging queues.

Also, because the callback address does the job of redirecting service responses, the service needs to ensure that the callback address is a trusted destination for its messages.

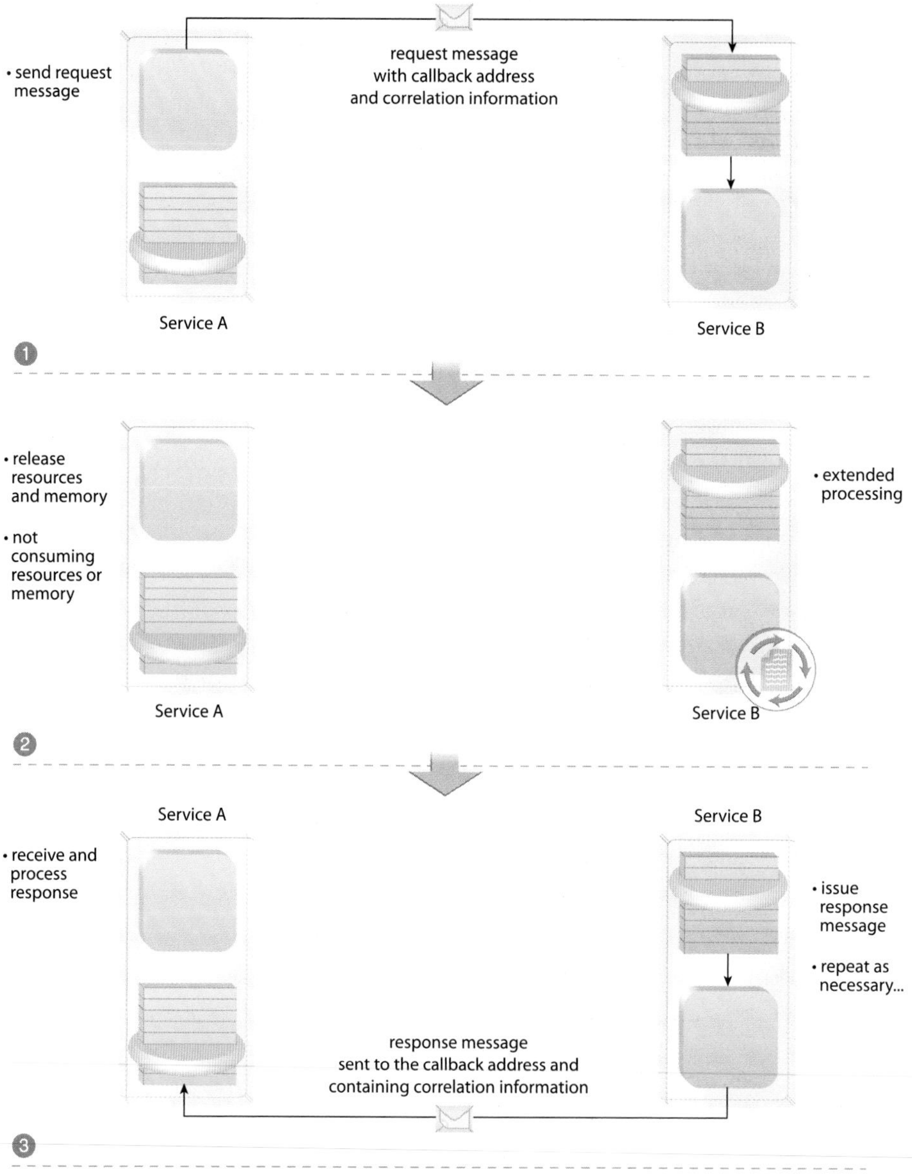

Figure 18.19

Service A sends a message containing the callback address and correlation information to Service B (1). While Service B is processing the message, Service A is unblocked (2). Service B, at some later point in time, sends a response containing the correlation information to the callback address to Service A (3). While Service B retains this callback address, it can continue to issue subsequent response messages to Service A.

Impacts

The asynchronous nature of the messaging introduced by this pattern can reduce reliability due to the absence of the immediate feedback received with standard synchronous exchanges. Reliable Messaging (592) can be applied to alleviate this risk.

Establishing an architecture whereby all services within a given inventory support WS-Addressing can introduce significant costs associated with necessary infrastructure upgrades. However, not all services will likely require this pattern, which may allow for its application to be limited to select composition architectures.

Relationships

Service Callback is based on the use of Service Messaging (533) and will normally require the application of Messaging Metadata (538) to represent the callback and correlation details separately from the message body content. In fact, Messaging Metadata (538) can be considered a critical requirement with respect to transferring the callback address and correlation information.

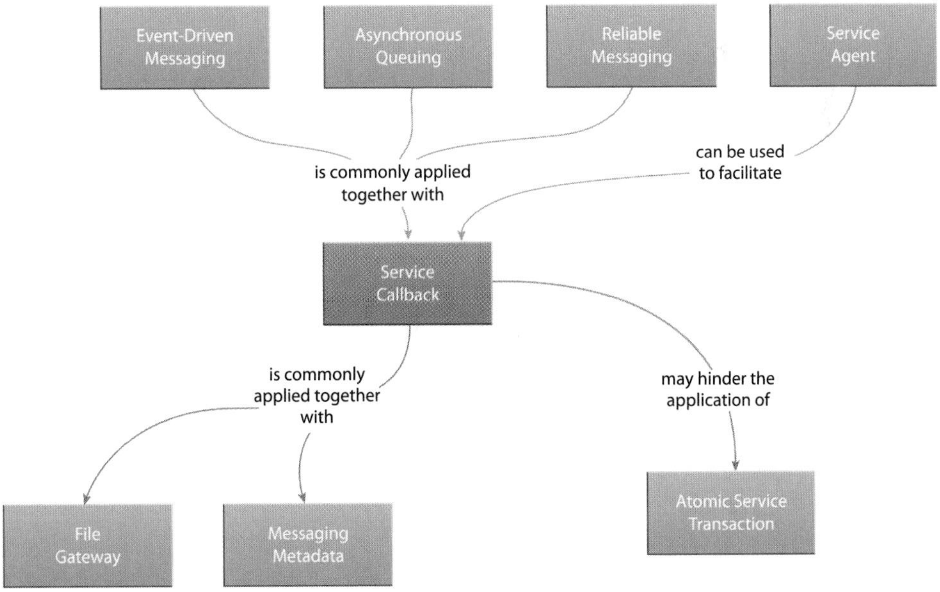

Figure 18.20

The decoupled nature of Service Callback naturally leads to relationships with other messaging patterns.

Furthermore, the need to coordinate asynchronous requests and possible multiple responses will typically involve Service Agent (543), especially when this pattern is applied as a result of infrastructure extensions.

While Service Callback may be considered an alternative to Asynchronous Queuing (582), it is common to use message queues together with issuing messages that contain callback addresses. This pattern can be supported through the use of Event-Driven Messaging (599) and Reliable Messaging (592).

NOTE

Service Callback incorporates concepts established in prior messaging patterns, including Return Address (Hohpe, Woolf) and Correlation Identifier (Hohpe, Woolf).

CASE STUDY EXAMPLE

Cutit Saw's recently released diamond blade chain design has become a runaway success, so much so that Cutit cannot keep up with the demand surge. This has not only resulted in large time gaps in order fulfillment, but also in higher costs as Cutit's IT department has had to track backorders manually. As a result, Cutit's response time has slowed dramatically. This, in turn, has raised concerns with Alleywood, one of its primary clients.

Cutit currently responds to purchase orders synchronously, and when backorders are required, the original purchase order is simply rejected. The manual process that was put in place before the success of the new blade design required Cutit to monitor their inventory and inform Alleywood about availability, as well as ask them to resubmit purchase orders after the items are back in stock. This not only scales poorly, but McPherson's new CIO does not like the cost that this process imposes on Alleywood.

Subsequent to a formal complaint lodged by the CIO in which McPherson threatens to equip all Alleywood workers with chainsaw blades from a competitor, Cutit's management scrambles to make changes. Senior architects are sent to the Alleywood office to meet with IT delegates in an attempt to work out a better system. The end-result is an agreement that Cutit will improve its response time by building a dedicated Backorder service capable of automating the backorder process asynchronously.

In support of this, Alleywood agrees that its consumer programs will provide callback addresses with each purchase order message sent to the Cutit Backorder service.

Specifically, they are required to provide the WS-Addressing `wsa:From` header block with each of their SOAP request messages. This header block specifies the callback address where asynchronous responses will need to be sent by the Backorder service.

If all the items in the purchase order are in stock, this service responds (to the callback address) asynchronously with an order fulfillment statement containing expected delivery date and shipping information. As backordered items become available, the service sends updates to this same callback address with new delivery date and shipping information until the purchase order is finally fulfilled.

In addition to the use of the `wsa:From` header block, the `wsa:MessageID` header is incorporated to represent correlation identifiers. Also the `wsa:RelatesTo` header is added with a special `RelationshipType` value of "http://cutitsaws.com/po/response" and the message ID of the request message. This information is used by Alleywood to correlate responses from Cutit to the original purchase order request.

The following code sample shows a purchase order request message from Alleywood to Cutit:

```
<Envelope xmlns="http://www.w3.org/2003/05/soap-envelope"
  xmlns:wsa="http://www.w3.org/2005/08/addressing">
  <Header>
    <wsa:From>
      <wsa:Address>
        http://mcpherson/alleywood/cutitPO
      </wsa:Address>
    </wsa:From>
    <wsa:MessageID>
      http://mcpherson/6B29FC40-CA47-1067-B31D-00DD010662DA
    </wsa:MessageID>
    <wsa:Action>
      ...
    </wsa:Action>
  </Header>
  <Body>
    <! - PO details ->
    ...
  </Body>
</Envelope>
```

Example 18.5

A purchase order request message that uses the `wsa:From` construct to specify the callback address where Cutit can send one or more responses asynchronously.

This next example shows the subsequent response message issued by Cutit back to Alleywood's callback address:

```
<Envelope xmlns="http://www.w3.org/2003/05/soap-envelope"
  xmlns:wsa="http://www.w3.org/2005/08/addressing">
  <Header>
    <wsa:To>
      http://mcpherson/alleywood/cutitPO
    </wsa:To>
    <wsa:RelatesTo RelationshipType=
      "http://cutitsaws.com/po/response">
      http://mcpherson/6B29FC40-CA47-1067-B31D-00DD010662DA
    </wsa:RelatesTo>
    <wsa:Action>
      ...
    </wsa:Action>
  </Header>
  <Body>
    <!-- PO response from Cutit -->
    ...
  </Body>
</Envelope>
```

Example 18.6

This response message is sent to the location specified in the `wsa:From` header from the corresponding request message. It uses the `wsa:MessageID` element from that request message as its correlation identifier. Note also how the value of the `wsa:RelatesTo` construct matches that of the `wsa:MessageID` construct from Example 18.5.

Service Instance Routing

By Anish Karmarkar

How can consumers contact and interact with service instances without the need for proprietary processing logic?

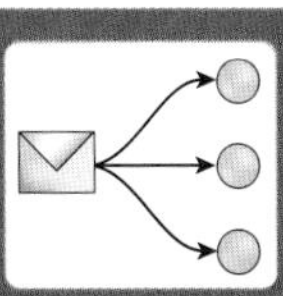

Problem	When required to repeatedly access a specific stateful service instance, consumers must rely on custom logic that more tightly couples them to the service.
Solution	The service provides an instance identifier along with its destination information in a standardized format that shields the consumer from having to resort to custom logic.
Application	The service is still required to provide custom logic to generate and manage instance identifiers, and both service and consumer require a common messaging infrastructure.
Impacts	This pattern can introduce the need for significant infrastructure upgrades and when misused can further lead to overly stateful messaging activities that can violate the Service Statelessness principle.
Principles	Service Loose Coupling, Service Statelessness, Service Composability
Architecture	Inventory, Composition, Service

Table 18.7

Profile summary for the Service Instance Routing pattern.

Problem

There are cases where a consumer sends multiple messages to a service and the messages need to be processed within the same runtime context. Such services are intentionally designed to remain stateful so that they can carry out conversational or session-centric message exchanges.

However, service contracts generally do not provide a standardized means of representing or targeting instances of services. Therefore, consumer and service designers need to resort to passing proprietary instance identifiers as part of the regular message data, which results in the need for proprietary instance processing logic (Figure 18.21).

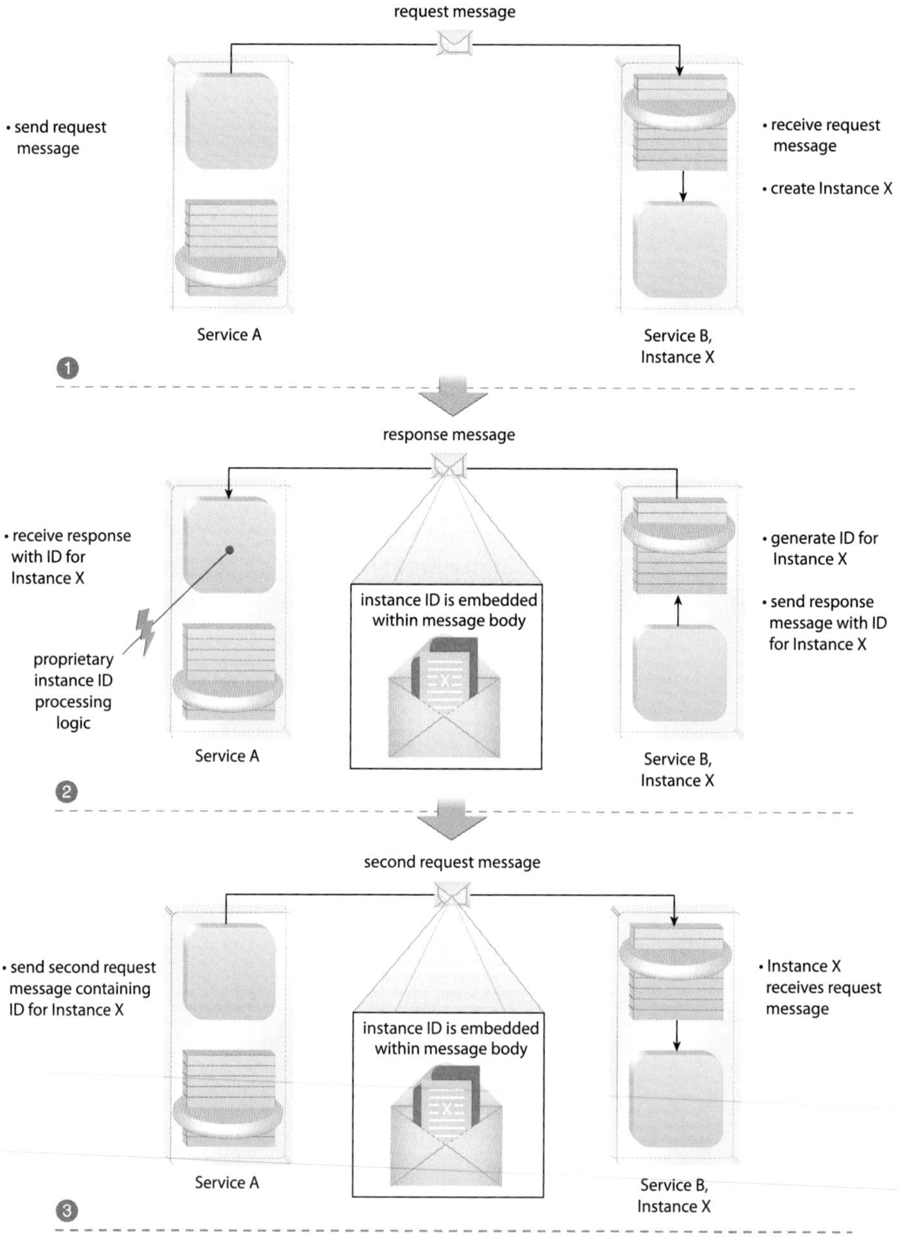

Figure 18.21

Service A, acting as a service consumer, issues a request message to Service B. An instance of Service B is created (1) using proprietary internal service logic that labels the instance as "Instance X." Service B returns an identifier for Instance X as part of the response message body back to Service A (2). Proprietary processing logic within Service A locates and extracts the embedded instance identifier and then embeds it into a second message that it sends to Instance X of Service B (3).

Note that in the scenario depicted in Figure 18.21, the lifecycle of the instances and the routing of the messages are managed by Service B. Throughout this exchange, Service A remains aware of any instance identifiers generated by Service B. Given that every such conversation can be different, there is no uniformity, and instance details are always required to be processed by custom logic that ends up increasing the coupling between the service and any of its consumers.

Solution

The underlying infrastructure is extended to support the processing of message metadata that enables a service instance identifier to be placed into a reference to the overall destination of the service (Figure 18.22). This reference (also referred to as an *endpoint reference*) is managed by the messaging infrastructure so that messages issued by the consumer are automatically routed to the destination represented by the reference.

As a result, the processing of instance IDs does not negatively affect consumer-to-service coupling because consumers are not required to contain proprietary service instance processing logic. Because the instance identifiers are part of a reference that is managed by the infrastructure, they are opaque to consumers. This means that consumers do not need to be aware of whether they are sending messages to a service or one of its instances because this is the responsibility of the routing logic within the messaging infrastructure.

Application

The echoing of the service instance identifier in conversational messages needs to be incorporated on the consumer-side messaging framework and architecture. An infrastructure that supports service instance routing is therefore required. When building services as Web services, this pattern is typically applied using infrastructure extensions compliant with the WS-Addressing specification.

NOTE

This pattern also forms the basis for providing additional *service-side* support for conversations or sessions. In such cases, the lifecycle management of instances is delegated to the infrastructure and codified by container contracts available via application server containers.

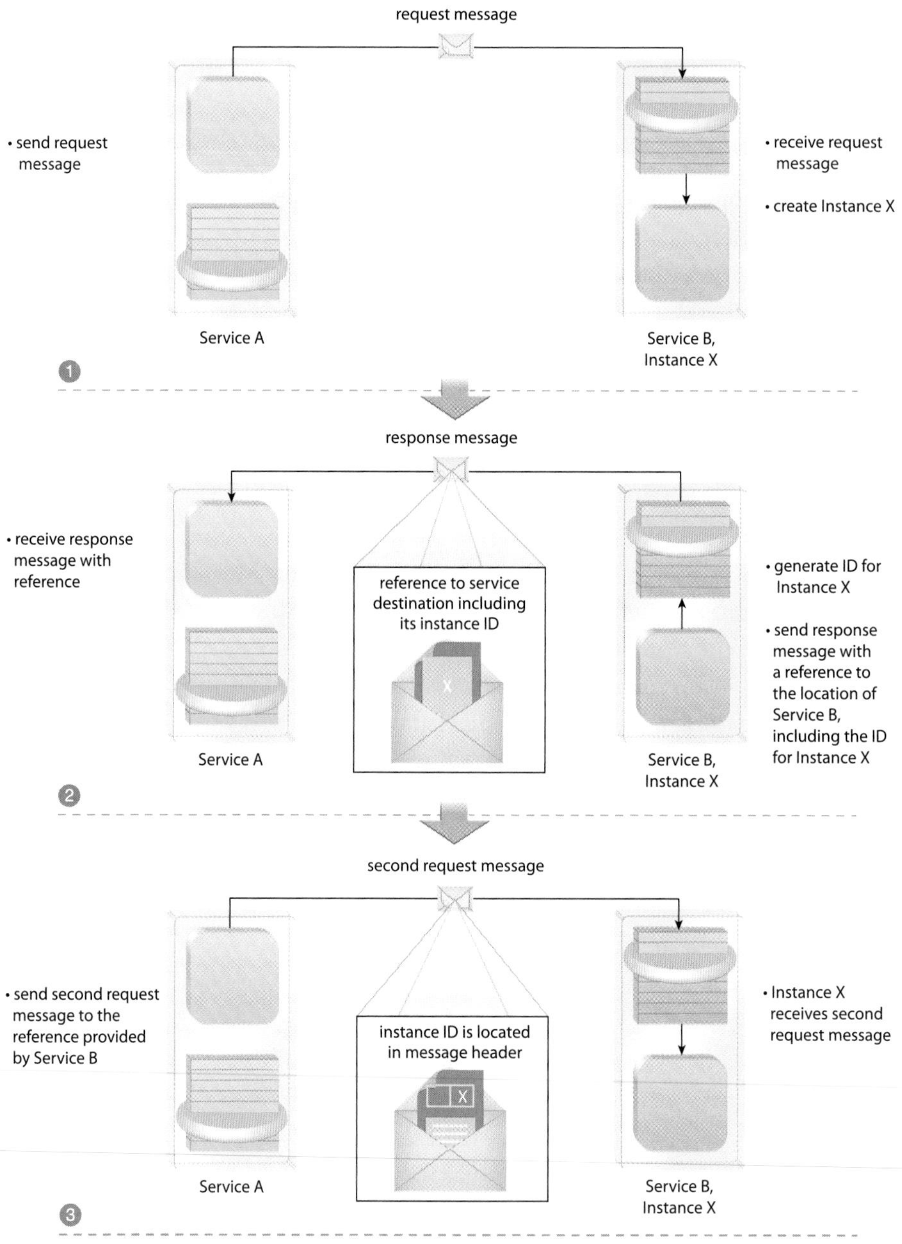

Figure 18.22

Service A, acting as a service consumer, issues a request message to Service B. Instance X of Service B is created (1), and a new message containing a reference to the destination of Service B (which includes the Instance X identifier) is returned back to Service A (2). Service A issues a second message that is routed to Instance X of Service B (3) without the need for proprietary logic. The instance identifier is located in the header of this message and is therefore kept separate from the message body.

Impacts

Applying this pattern across an entire service inventory requires that the necessary infrastructure extensions be established as part of the inventory architecture. This can lead to increased costs and governance effort.

Service Instance Routing can be used to create highly stateful services designed to carry out prolonged conversational message exchanges. While stateful interaction is often required, it is easy to apply this pattern to such an extent that it runs contrary to the Service Statelessness principle, thereby undermining the importance of long-term service scalability.

Furthermore, because service instance identifiers are valid only during the lifecycle of the instance, there is the danger that stale identifiers may be inadvertently used for invocation. Controls are required to ensure that identifiers are destroyed after the end of each service instance.

Relationships

Service Instance Routing is naturally related to Messaging Metadata (538) because it applies to messages that generally require the use of message headers. The actual mechanics behind the implementation of the infrastructure extensions necessary for this pattern often rely on the use of event-driven intermediaries to carry out the message header process, which is why this pattern is frequently associated with Service Agent (543).

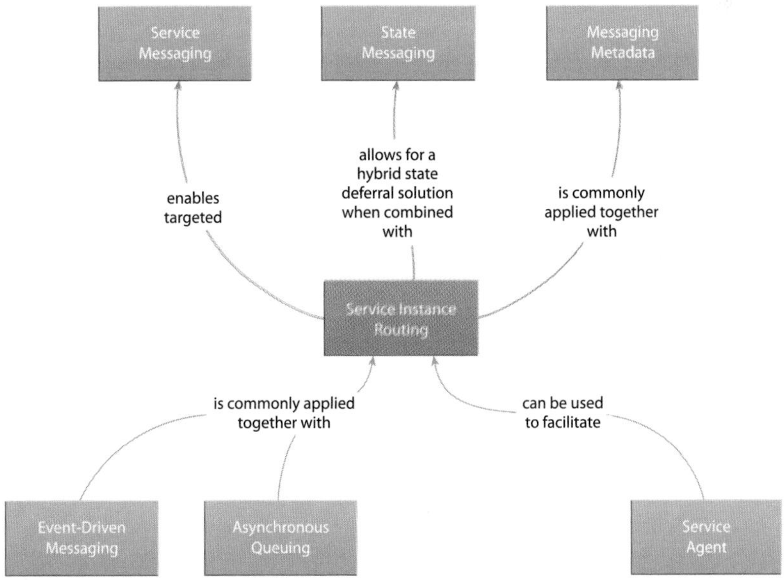

Figure 18.23

The modification of service reference structure and echoing of instance identifiers as opaque tokens affects several other messaging patterns.

CASE STUDY EXAMPLE

Based on a recent marketing research report, management at Cutit Saws has decided to make their products available to the public. To accomplish this, Cutit architects are asked to establish an online presence with a standard Web site that contains a shopping cart that customers can use to pick and choose products for purchase and delivery.

The new External Order Web service is created as the backend engine for the new Web site. This service is contacted each time the online shopping cart is used. Once invoked, its instance remains in memory, and the service is considered stateful.

One instance of the External Order service instance corresponds to one online shopping cart. The Web site scripts need to obtain some sort of identifier to the External Order service instance so that they can continue interacting with it while the human end-user manages the shopping cart.

After reviewing these very specific requirements, architects choose to invest in an infrastructure upgrade that introduces support for WS-Addressing Endpoint References (EPRs). EPRs essentially provide them with a standardized means of expressing the address of a Web service along with a set of parameters (called reference parameters) that can be used to specify the service instance.

The following excerpt highlights a fragment of the Cutit implementation of WS-Addressing EPRs by showing the contents of the Create Shopping Cart request message:

```
<Envelope xmlns="http://www.w3.org/2003/05/soap-envelope">
  <Header>
    ...
  </Header>
  <Body>
    <cu:CreateShoppingCart
      xmlns:cu="http://cutitsaws.com/shopping">
      ...
    </cu:CreateShoppingCart>
  </Body>
</Envelope>
```

Example 18.7

A request message for creating a new shopping cart.

The next example displays the corresponding response message issued from the External Order service, which returns the WS-Addressing EPR `cu:ShoppingCartEPR`, as follows:

```
<Envelope xmlns="http://www.w3.org/2003/05/soap-envelope"
  xmlns:wsa="http://www.w3.org/2005/08/addressing">
  <Header>
    ...
  </Header>
  <Body>
    <!-- Response from Cutit -->
    <cu:CreateShoppingCartResponse
      xmlns:cu="http://cutitsaws.com/shopping">
      <cu:ShoppingCartEPR>
        <wsa:Address>
          http://cutitsaws.com/shoppingcart
        </wsa:Address>
        <wsa:ReferenceParameters>
          <cu:InstanceID>
            6B29FC40-CA47-1067-B31D-00DD010662DA
          </cu:InstanceID>
        </wsa:ReferenceParameters>
      </cu:ShoppingCartEPR>
    </cu:CreateShoppingCartResponse>
    ...
  </Body>
</Envelope>
```

Example 18.8

Note how this message contains a reference parameter called `cu:InstanceID` in addition to the standard network endpoint details. This reference parameter contains the identifier of the service instance that the consumer is expected to use for subsequent requests.

This final example shows the contents of the message sent back to the External Order service instance:

```
<Envelope xmlns="http://www.w3.org/2003/05/soap-envelope"
  xmlns:wsa="http://www.w3.org/2005/08/addressing"
  xmlns:cu="http://cutitsaws.com/shopping">
  <Header>
    <wsa:To>
      http://cutitsaws.com/shoppingcart
    </wsa:To>
    <cu:InstanceID wsa:IsReferenceParameter="true">
      6B29FC40-CA47-1067-B31D-00DD010662DA
    </cu:InstanceID>
```

```
    ...
  </Header>
  <Body>
    <! - Message sent to a particular shopping cart -->
    <cu:AddItem>
      ...
    </cu:AddItem>
  </Body>
</Envelope>
```

Example 18.9

This `cu:AddItem` message is targeted to a specific instance of the Cutit External Order service.

Asynchronous Queuing

By Mark Little, Thomas Rischbeck, Arnaud Simon

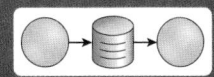

How can a service and its consumers accommodate isolated failures and avoid unnecessarily locking resources?

Problem	When a service capability requires that consumers interact with it synchronously, it can inhibit performance and compromise reliability.
Solution	A service can exchange messages with its consumers via an intermediary buffer, allowing service and consumers to process messages independently by remaining temporally decoupled.
Application	Queuing technology needs to be incorporated into the surrounding architecture, and back-up stores may also be required.
Impacts	There may be no acknowledgement of successful message delivery, and atomic transactions may not be possible.
Principles	Standardized Service Contracts, Service Loose Coupling, Service Statelessness
Architecture	Inventory, Composition

Table 18.8
Profile summary for the Asynchronous Queuing pattern.

Problem

Synchronous communication requires an immediate response to each request and therefore forces two-way data exchange for every service interaction. When services need to carry out synchronous communication, both service and service consumer must be available and ready to complete the data exchange. This can introduce reliability issues when either the service cannot guarantee its availability to receive the request message or the service consumer cannot guarantee its availability to receive the response to its request.

Because of its sequential nature, synchronous message exchanges can further impose processing overhead, as the service consumer needs to wait until it receives a response from its original request before proceeding to its next action. As shown in Figure 18.24, prolonged responses can introduce latency by temporally locking both consumer and service.

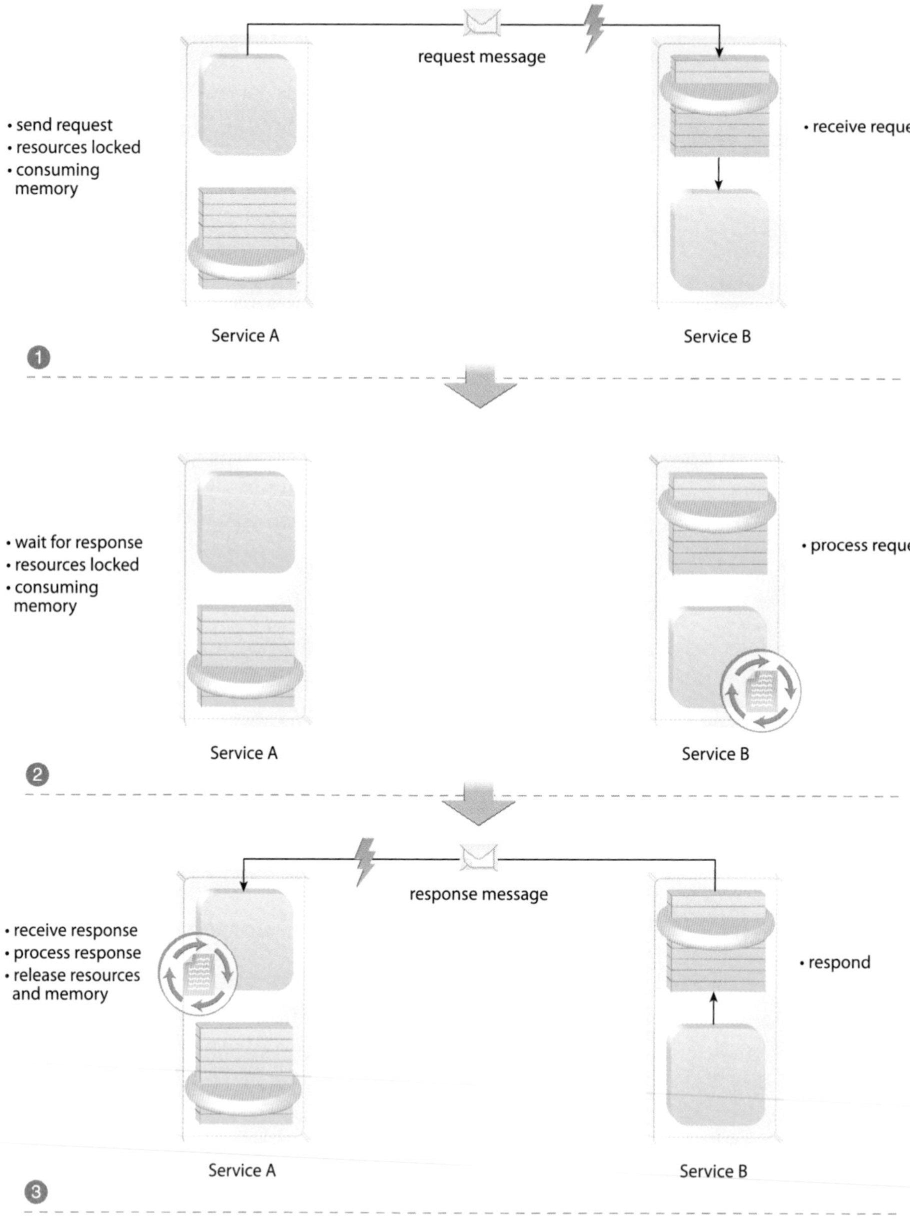

Figure 18.24

Service A, acting as the service consumer, issues a request message to Service B (1), and because it is part of a synchronous data exchange, Service A is required to wait (2) until Service B processes the request message and then transmits a response (3). During this waiting period, both service and consumer must be available and continue to use up memory. Because Asynchronous Queuing and Service Callback (566) both enable asynchronous messaging as an alternative to synchronous communication, this figure is identical to Figure 18.18, except for the red lightning bolt symbols which hint at the reliability problem also addressed by this pattern.

Another problem forced synchronous communication can cause is an overload of services required to facilitate a great deal of concurrent access. Because services are expected to process requests as soon as they are received, usage thresholds can be more easily reached, thereby exposing the service to multi-consumer latency or overall failure.

Solution

A queue is introduced as an intermediary buffer that receives request messages and then forwards them on behalf of the service consumers (Figure 18.25). If the target service is unavailable, the queue acts as temporary storage and retains the message. It then periodically attempts retransmission.

Similarly, if there is a response, it can be issued through the same queue that will forward it back to the service consumer when the consumer is available. While either service or consumer is processing message contents, the other can deactivate itself (or move on to other processing) in order to minimize memory consumption (Figure 18.26).

Application

In modern ESB platforms, the use of a queue can be completely transparent, meaning that neither consumer nor service may know that a queue was involved in a data exchange. The queuing framework can be supported by intelligent service agents that detect when a queue is required and intercept message transmissions accordingly.

The queue can be configured to process messages in different ways and is typically set up to poll an unavailable target recipient periodically until it becomes available or until the message transmission is considered to have failed. Queues can further be used to leverage asynchronous message exchange by incorporating topics and message broadcasts to multiple consumers, as per Event-Driven Messaging (599).

Many vendor queues are equipped with a back-up store so that messages in transit are not lost should a system failure occur. Especially when supporting more complex compositions, Asynchronous Queuing is commonly applied in conjunction with Reliable Messaging (592).

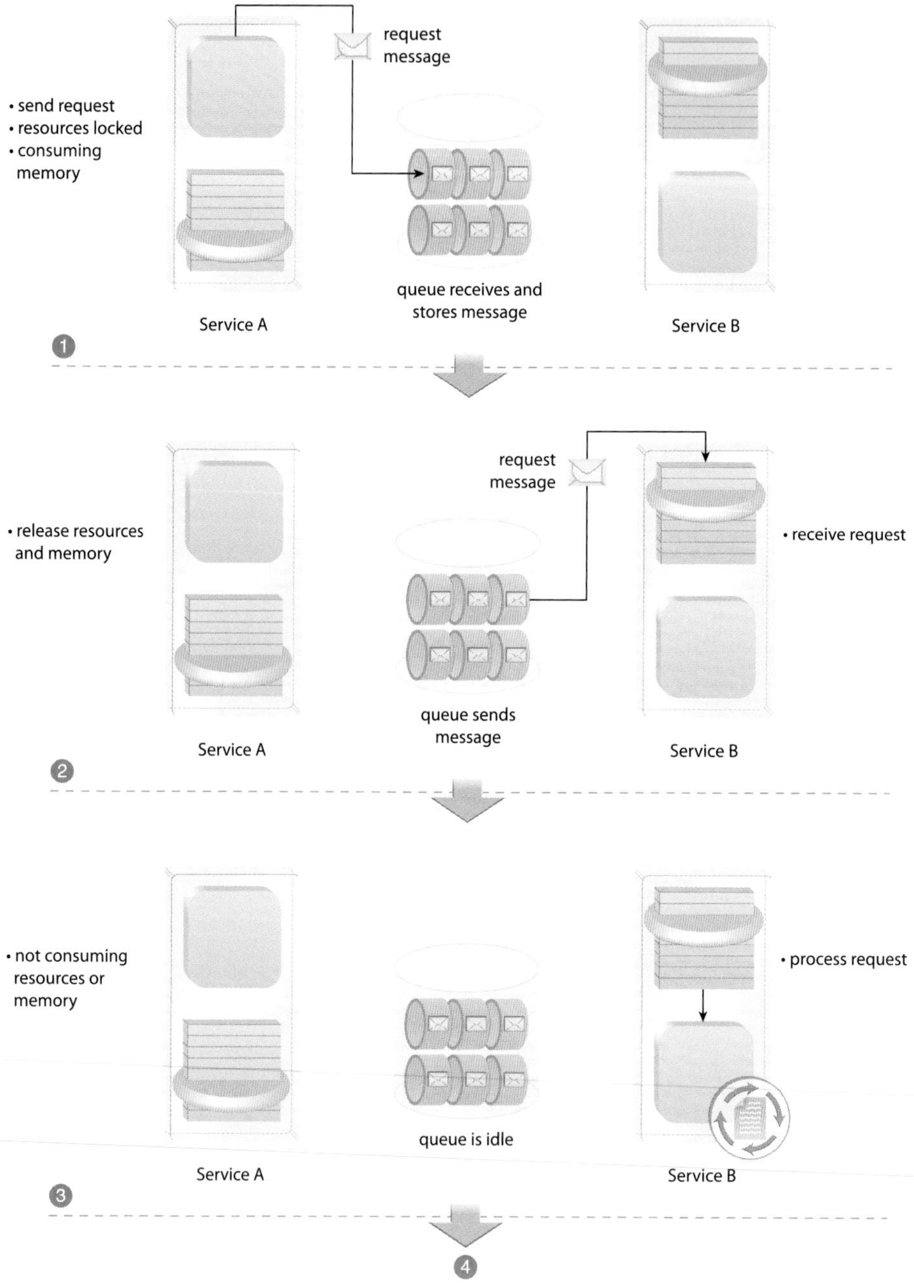

Figure 18.25

Service A sends a message to Service B, which is intercepted and stored by an intermediary queue (1). The queue the forwards the message to Service B (2), and while Service B is processing the message, Service A remains released from memory (3).

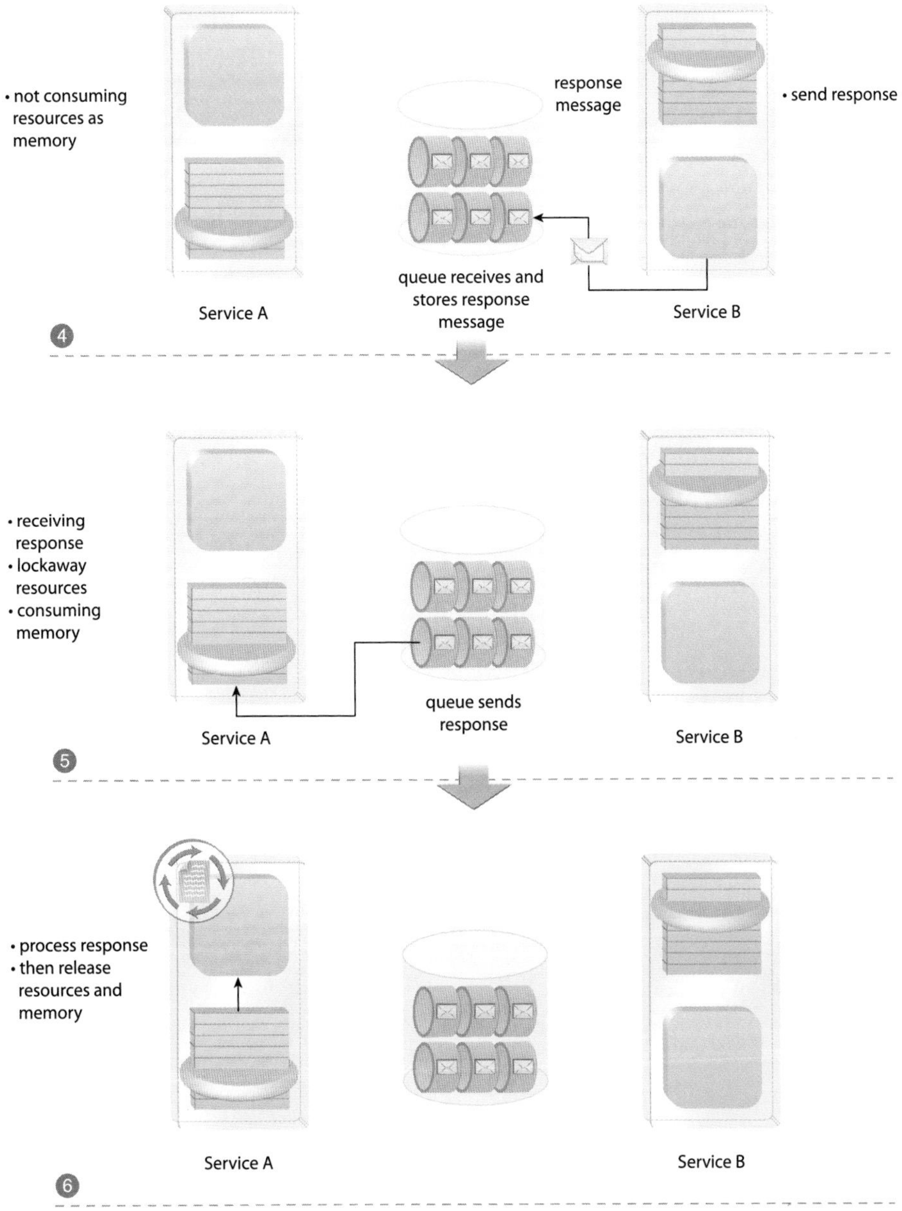

Figure 18.26

After completing its processing, Service B issues a response message back to Service A, which is also received and stored by the intermediary queue (4). Service A receives the response (5) and completes processing of the response, all the while Service B is deactivated (6).

NOTE

In some platforms, services to which the queue is expected to forward messages need to be pre-registered with the queue in advance. There are other common characteristics about the use of messaging queues that are not explained in this pattern, such as a "pull" based architecture wherein services are required to poll the queue to retrieve messages instead of the "push" model described so far. This pattern does not intend to describe the usage of messaging queues in general; it is focused solely on asynchronous messaging in response to the problem defined in the preceding *Problem* section.

Impacts

The use of intermediary queues allows for creative asynchronous message exchange patterns that can optimize service interaction by eliminating the need for a required response to each request. However, asynchronous message exchanges can also lead to more complex service activities that are difficult to design. It may be challenging to anticipate all of the possible runtime scenarios at design-time, and therefore extra exception handling logic may be necessary.

An asynchronous data exchange that involves a queue can also be more difficult to control and monitor. It may not be possible to protect asynchronous activities with Atomic Service Transaction (623) because of the time-response constraints usually associated with transactions and their requirements to hold resources in suspension until either commit or rollback instructions are issued.

Furthermore, an advantage to synchronous messaging is that because a response is always required, it acts as an immediate acknowledgement that the initial request message was successfully delivered and processed. With asynchronous message exchange patterns, no response is expected, and the message issuer therefore is not necessarily notified of successful or failed deliveries. However, most queuing systems allow the monitoring and administration of in-flight message transmissions. Messages in the queue can be further examined and managed during transit, which in larger systems can greatly simplify administrative control and the isolation of communication faults.

Relationships

Asynchronous Queuing is a design pattern dedicated to accommodating message exchanges and therefore is naturally related to Service Messaging (533). Event-driven agents form a fundamental part of the queuing framework, which explains the relevance of Service Agent (543). Furthermore, Messaging Metadata (538) can play a role in how messages are processed, stored, or routed via these agents.

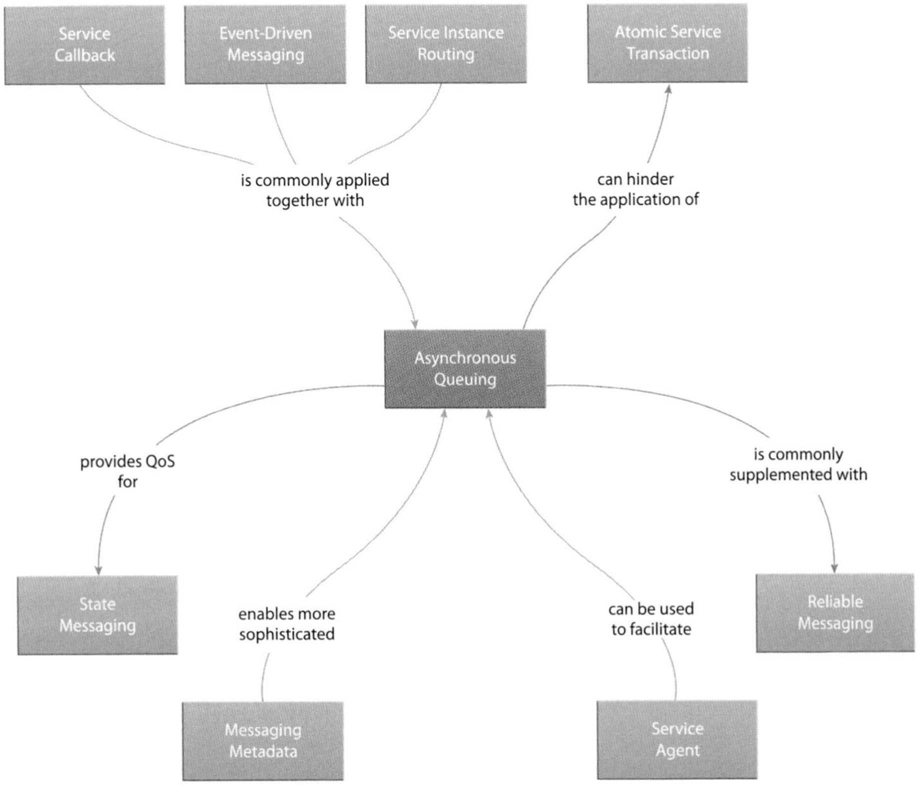

Figure 18.27

The message-centric focus of Asynchronous Queuing naturally leads to relationships with other messaging patterns.

ESB platforms are fundamentally about decreasing the coupling between different parts of a service-oriented solution, which is why this pattern is a core part of Enterprise Service Bus (704), as shown in Figure 18.28.

An optional design pattern associated with the ESB is Reliable Messaging (592), which is a pattern commonly applied in conjunction with Asynchronous Queuing. Together, these two patterns provide key QoS extensions that make the use of ESB products attractive, especially in support of complex service compositions.

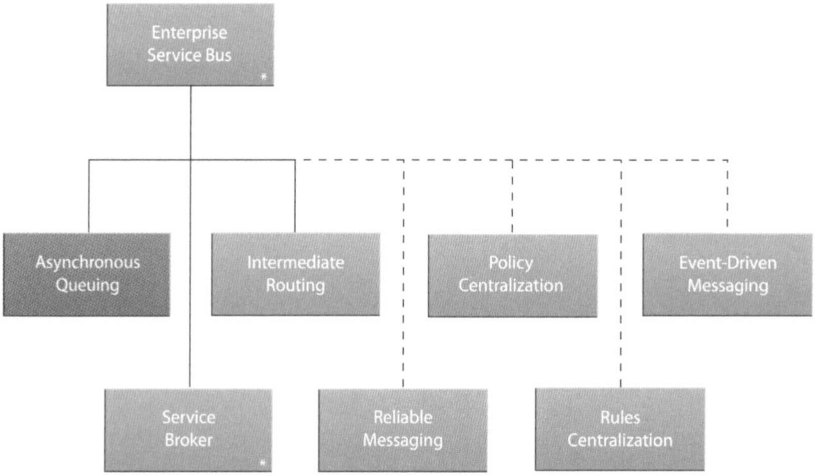

Figure 18.28

Asynchronous Queuing is a design pattern that can be applied independently but also represents one of the core patterns that comprise Enterprise Service Bus (704).

CASE STUDY EXAMPLE

The FRC continues to employ an integrated legacy environment for the transfer of batch extracts from an ERP system to a proprietary purchase order administration (POAdmin) product. The ERP environment provides an API capable of outputting exported data from its native CSV format to a predefined XML structure. An ERP wrapper Web service was further made available by the vendor in order to enable access to extracted data via SOAP.

Generating the extracts was time consuming, especially if purchase order data for a range of dates was requested. The batch files could also be very large, which required longer transfer times. As a result, there have been a variety of performance issues due to

the fact that the POAdmin program had to remain locked and suspended while waiting for the response from the ERP API, which required a synchronous exchange (Figure 18.29). This also caused the occasional system crash as the POAdmin request would timeout, resulting in the POAdmin program to freeze.

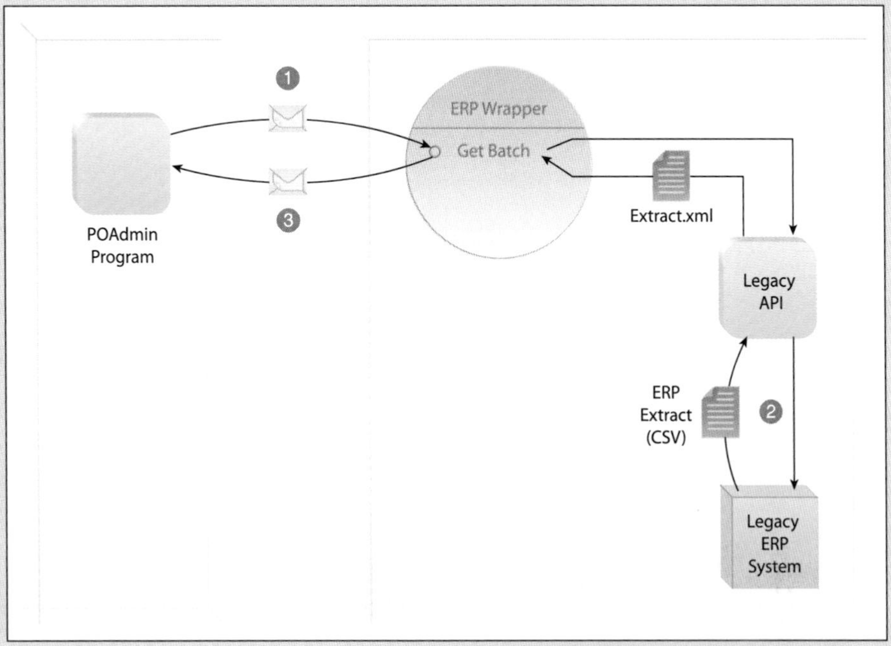

Figure 18.29

The legacy POAdmin program initiates a synchronous exchange by issuing a request message to the ERP Wrapper service (1). While the underlying ERP environment retrieves the requested batch extract (2), the POAdmin program continues to wait in suspension until it finally receives a response comprised of the extract in XML format (3).

Network outages have also occurred, leading to interruptions half-way through a transfer. In this situation, the whole transfer would need to be repeated. This required frequent administrative intervention, and management perceived the solution as brittle and inefficient.

As illustrated in Figure 18.30, the FRC project team decides to re-architect this environment to improve the reliability of this exchange but also to provide more appropriate access to the ERP environment for additional services that may need to work with its data.

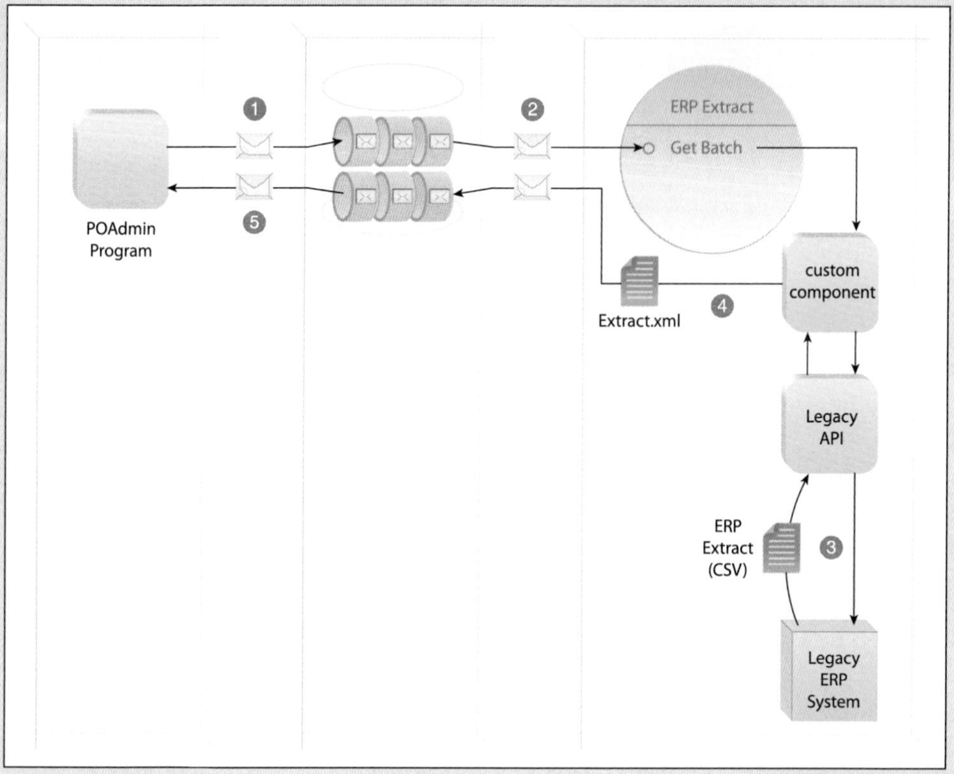

Figure 18.30

The POAdmin program sends a request that is received by the queue (1). The queue then forwards the message to the new ERP Extract service (2), which then passes it along to a custom component. This component interacts with the ERP API to retrieve the requested extract data (3) and then forwards this directly to the queue (4). The queue then interacts with the POAdmin API to provide the program the data it originally requested.

This new architecture introduces a queue to store and then forward all requests on behalf of the POAdmin program. The queue is configured to issue an immediate response to POAdmin in order to simulate the synchronous exchange. A new, standardized Web service is then brought in to replace the previous ERP Wrapper service. This new ERP Extract service provides a one-way operation that simply receives the request message from the queue. It then interacts with an (also newly provided) custom component that interfaces with the ERP API.

Once the extract is received, this component directly forwards the result to the queue, which in turn accesses the POAdmin API to transmit the purchase order data extract.

Reliable Messaging

By Mark Little, Thomas Rischbeck, Arnaud Simon

How can services communicate reliably when implemented in an unreliable environment?

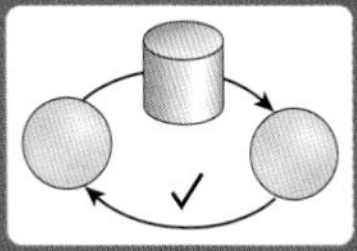

Problem	Service communication cannot be guaranteed when using unreliable messaging protocols or when dependent on an otherwise unreliable environment.
Solution	An intermediate reliability mechanism is introduced into the inventory architecture, ensuring that message delivery is guaranteed.
Application	Middleware, service agents, and data stores are deployed to track message deliveries, manage the issuance of acknowledgements, and persist messages during failure conditions.
Impacts	Using a reliability framework adds processing overhead that can affect service activity performance. It also increases composition design complexity and may not be compatible with Atomic Service Transaction (623).
Principles	Service Composability
Architecture	Inventory, Composition

Table 18.9

Profile summary for the Reliable Messaging pattern.

Problem

When services are designed to communicate via messages, there is a natural loss of quality-of-service due to the stateless nature of underlying messaging protocols, such as HTTP. Unlike with binary communication protocols where a persistent connection is maintained until the data transmission between a sender and receiver is completed, with message exchanges the runtime platform may not be able to provide feedback to the sender as to whether or not a message was successfully delivered (Figure 18.31).

Furthermore, because the probability of failure is exacerbated as the service count (and the number of corresponding network links) grows with service compositions increasing in size and complexity, the inability of an infrastructure to introduce guaranteed message delivery can introduce measurable risk factors into service composition architectures (especially those that rely heavily on agnostic services).

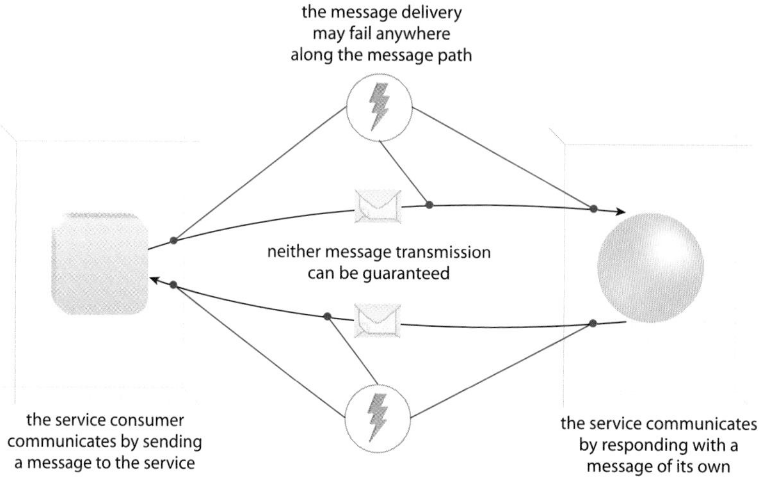
the message delivery
may fail anywhere
along the message path
neither message transmission
can be guaranteed
the service consumer
communicates by sending
a message to the service
the service communicates
by responding with a
message of its own

Figure 18.31

During the course of a regular message exchange, there are no guarantees. Various runtime conditions may cause the message delivery to fail.

Solution

The inventory architecture is equipped with a reliability framework that tracks and temporarily persists message transmissions and issues positive and negative acknowledgements to communicate successful and failed transmissions to message senders.

Application

A complete reliability framework is typically comprised of infrastructure and intermediary processing logic capable of:

- guaranteeing message delivery during failure conditions via the use of a persistence store
- tracking messages at runtime
- issuing acknowledgements for individual or sequences of messages

The repository used for guaranteed delivery may provide the option to store messages in memory or on disk so as to act as a back-up mechanism for when message transmissions fail. This central storage also eases the management and administration of service-oriented solutions because it allows administrators to track the status of messages and trace the causes behind unresolved delivery problems.

Reliability agents further manage the confirmation of successful and failed message deliveries via positive (ACK) and negative (NACK) acknowledgement notifications. Messages may be transmitted and acknowledged individually, or they may be bundled into message sequences that are acknowledged in groups (and may also have sequence-related delivery rules).

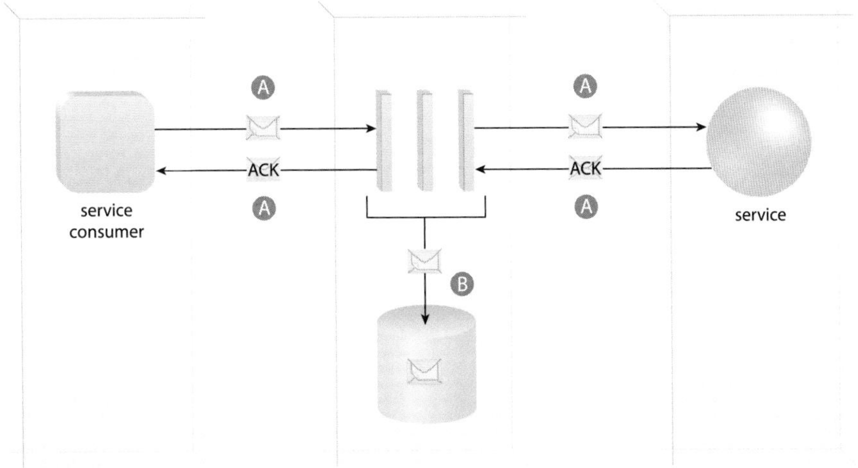

Figure 18.32

When building services as Web services, this pattern is commonly applied by implementing a combination of the WS-ReliableMessaging standard (A) and guaranteed delivery extensions, such as a persistent repository (B). This figure highlights the typical moving parts of the resulting reliability framework.

Impacts

Reliable Messaging introduces a layer of processing that includes runtime message capture, persistence, tracking, and acknowledgement notification issuance. All of these features add moving parts to an inventory architecture that demand additional performance and guarantee requirements and increase the complexity of service-oriented solutions proportional to the size of their service compositions.

Furthermore, due to the temporary storage of messages, the incorporation of positive and negative acknowledgement notifications, and the use of various delivery rules (including those based on group message delivery via sequences), it may not be possible to wrap services using reliability features into atomic transactions, as per Atomic Service Transaction (623).

Relationships

Applying this pattern directly affects messaging-related patterns in that it changes how messages are transmitted and delivered. The quality of Service Messaging (533) is improved, and Messaging Metadata (538) is commonly utilized to manage and track messages via reliability agents that can be considered specialized implementations of Service Agent (543). Considerations arise from the application of Canonical Resources (237) can help ensure that an inventory architecture standardizes on a single reliability framework.

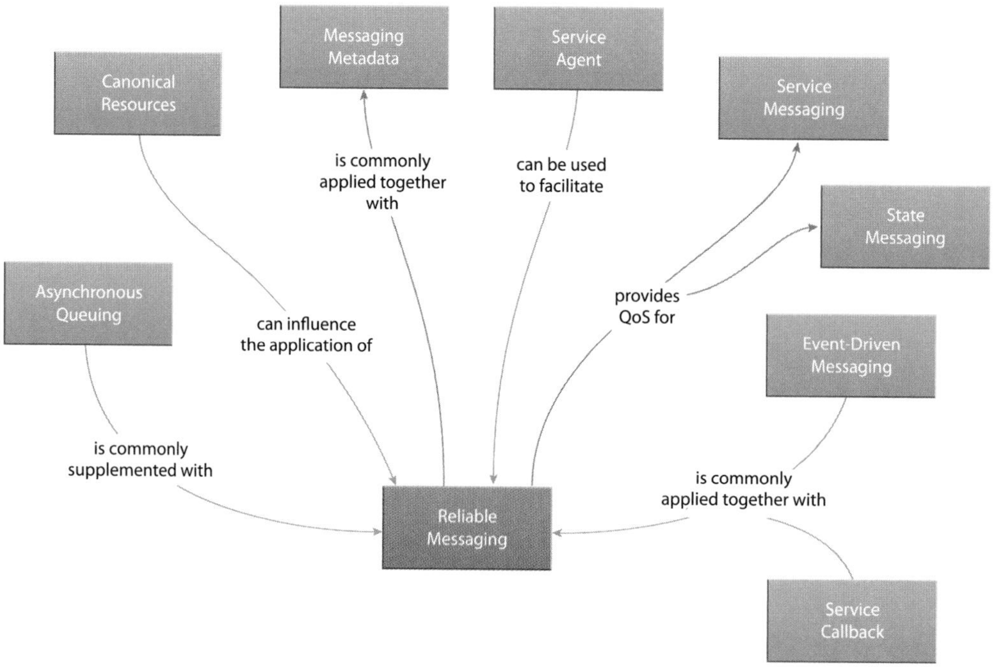

Figure 18.33
The messaging-centric focus of this pattern makes it naturally affect other messaging-related patterns.

Because of the importance of guaranteeing message delivery and improving the overall quality of base messaging frameworks, the runtime functionality established by applying Reliable Messaging is typically associated with ESB platforms (Figure 18.34).

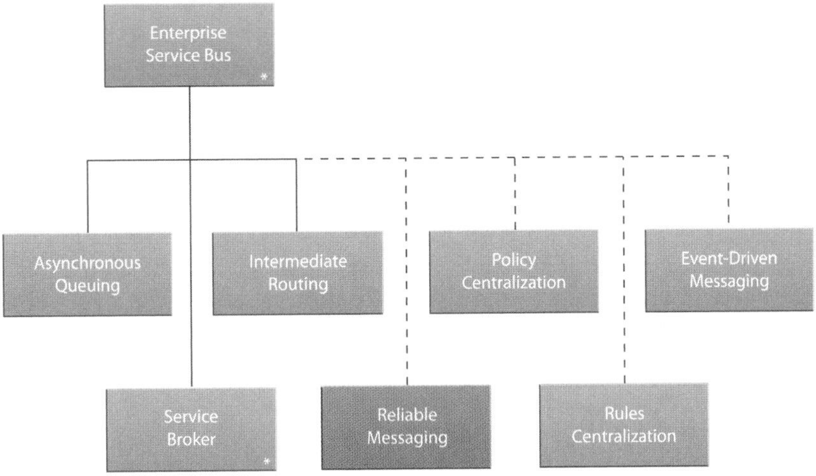

Figure 18.34

Reliable Messaging can be applied by itself, but is also a pattern commonly realized via Enterprise Service Bus (704).

NOTE

Reliable Messaging encompasses much of what Guaranteed Delivery (Hohpe, Woolf) advocates in relation to persisting messages and then further supplements this with additional reliability extensions.

CASE STUDY EXAMPLE

The FRC receives a great number of documents from external companies. Every day, in fact, thousands of messages are received via existing Web service endpoints, containing applications, requests, appeals, and even payment details.

Each month statistics are collected by IT administrators that show the quantity of messages received along with metrics associated with the number of failed deliveries, rejected deliveries, messages tagged as security threats, and general delivery errors. One statistic that has always been closely watched is "lost messages." This represents messages that were received by the Web service but then went missing once forwarded to additional internal services.

The FRC has only been using Web services as their primary access point for external communication for the past six months. During that time, the lost message count has been consistently high. It was originally thought that the Web services platform itself required further tuning, but now, a half year later, it is considered a persistent problem that is simply unacceptable.

A new project is started specifically to address this and other quality of service issues with the externally facing Web services. Subsequent to an internal analysis and an assessment of the marketplace, the FRC architecture team decides to bring in an ESB product that provides built-in reliable messaging. Web services are redeployed within this new environment, and additional development and configuration effort is performed to incorporate the automatic acknowledgement system provided by the reliable messaging extensions.

This new architecture helps attain increased quality of service by reducing lost messages. The approach is to first group messages by type and then send each group to a corresponding internal service responsible for processing a type of message.

Each group of messages transmitted to an internal service is received with a positive or negative acknowledgement that communicates the success or failure of the deliveries (Figure 18.35). Upon receiving a negative acknowledgement, the Web service logs the failure and all of the message details. This establishes a permanent record of all failed delivery attempts.

As shown in the following example, the use of reliable messaging headers allows the FRC to assign an identifier to the message along with a message number that indicates the position of the current message within the overall sequence group.

```
<Envelope xmlns="http://schemas.xmlsoap.org/soap/envelope/"
    xmlns:wsu="http://schemas.xmlsoap.org/ws/2002/07/utility"
    xmlns:wsrm="http://schemas.xmlsoap.org/ws/2004/03/rm">
  <Header>
    <wsrm:Sequence>
      <wsu:Identifier>
        uuid:038857-524
      </wsu:Identifier>
      <wsrm:MessageNumber>
        9
      </wsrm:MessageNumber>
    </wsrm:Sequence>
```

```
  </Header>
  <Body>
    ...
  </Body>
</Envelope>
```

Example 18.10

Through the use of reliable messaging metadata headers, this message is assigned a number that indicates where the message is located within the overall message sequence.

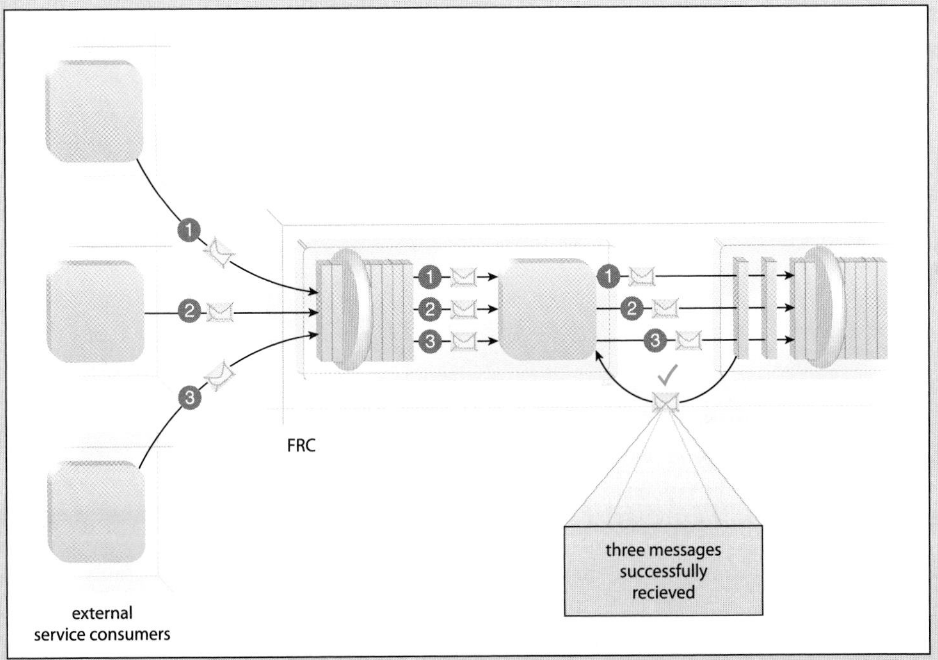

Figure 18.35

The externally facing FRC Web service receives a range of messages (1, 2, 3) from companies that have automated their data exchange with the FRC. With the reliable messaging extensions in place, messages are first grouped into sequences and then sent to the appropriate internal service for further processing.

Although the team is pleased with the manner in which they have instilled their inventory architecture with support for WS-ReliableMessaging, they acknowledge that this represents only a partial application of this pattern due to the absence of an intermediate persistence repository.

Event-Driven Messaging

By Mark Little, Thomas Rischbeck, Arnaud Simon

How can service consumers be automatically notified of runtime service events?

Problem	Events that occur within the functional boundary encapsulated by a service may be of relevance to service consumers, but without resorting to inefficient polling-based interaction, the consumer has no way of learning about these events.
Solution	The consumer establishes itself as a subscriber of the service. The service, in turn, automatically issues notifications of relevant events to this and any of its subscribers.
Application	A messaging framework is implemented capable of supporting the publish-and-subscribe MEP and associated complex event processing and tracking.
Impacts	Event-driven message exchanges cannot easily be incorporated as part of Atomic Service Transaction (623), and publisher/subscriber availability issues can arise.
Principles	Standardized Service Contract, Service Loose Coupling, Service Autonomy
Architecture	Inventory, Composition

Table 18.10

Profile summary for the Event-Driven Messaging pattern.

Problem

In typical messaging environments, service consumers can choose between one-way and request-response message exchange patterns (MEPs), but both need to originate from the consumer. Events may occur within the service provider's functional boundary that are of interest to the consumer. Following traditional MEPs, the consumer would need to continually poll the service in order to find out whether such an event had occurred (and to then retrieve the corresponding event details).

This model is inefficient because it leads to numerous unnecessary service invocations and data exchanges (Figure 18.36). It can further introduce delays as to when the consumer receives the event information because it may be only able to check for the event at predetermined polling intervals.

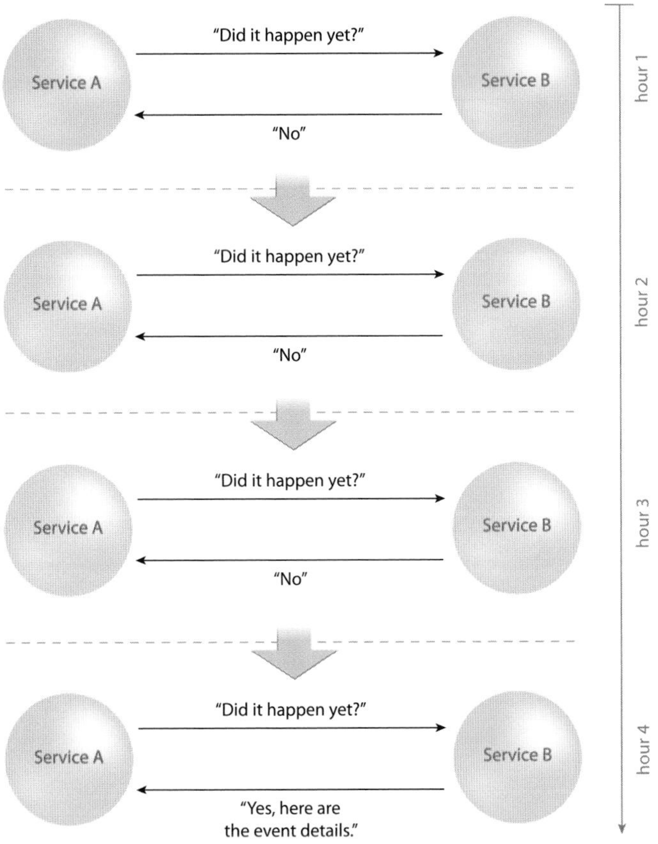

Figure 18.36

Service A (acting as a service consumer) polls Service B on an hourly basis for information about an event that Service A is interested in. Each polling cycle involves a synchronous, request-response message exchange. After the fourth hour, Service A learns that the event has occurred and receives the event information.

Solution

An event management program is introduced, allowing the service consumer to set itself up as a *subscriber* to events associated with a service that assumes the role of *publisher*. There may be different types of events that the service makes available, and consumers can choose which they would like to be subscribed to.

When such an event occurs, the service (acting as publisher) automatically sends the event details to the event management program, which then broadcasts an event notification to all of the consumers registered as subscribers of the event (Figure 18.37).

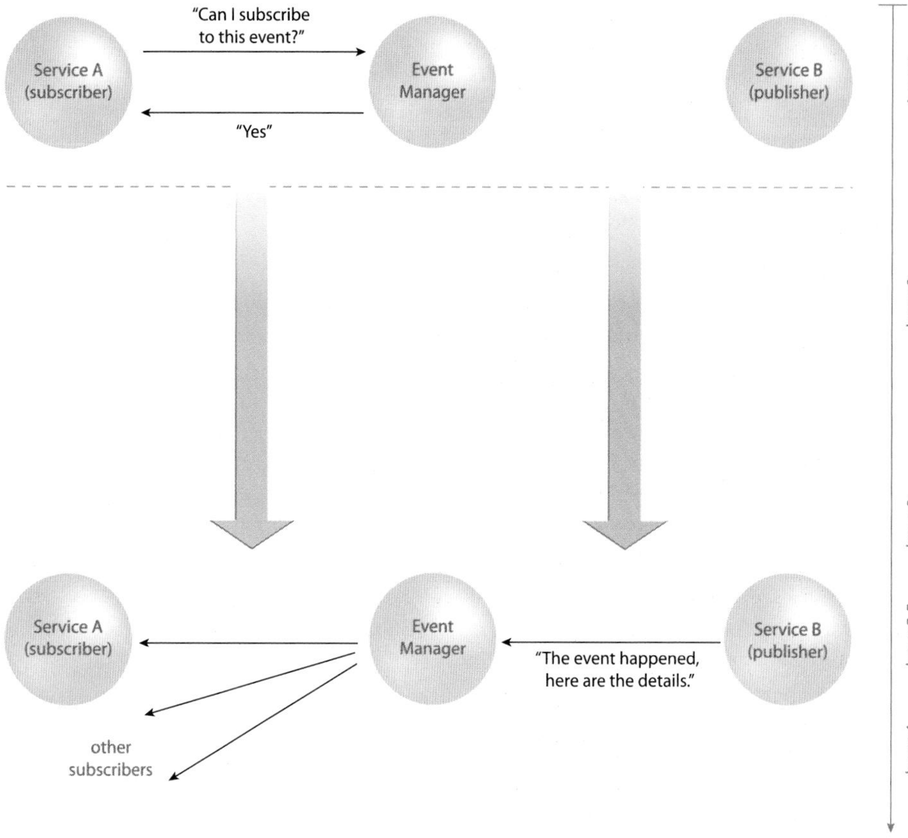

Figure 18.37

Service A requests that it be set up as a subscriber to the event it is interested in by interacting with an event manager. Once the event occurs, Service B forwards the details to the event manager which, in turn, notifies Service A (and all other subscribers) via a one-way, asynchronous data transfer. Note that in this case, Service A also receives the event information earlier because the event details can be transmitted as soon as they're available.

NOTE

The solution proposed by this pattern is closely related to the event-driven architecture (EDA) model. The upcoming *ESB Architecture for SOA* title that will be released as part of this book series will explore how event-driven messaging is supported via Enterprise Service Bus (704) and will further provide more detailed, ESB-specific design patterns.

Application

An event-driven messaging framework is implemented as an extension to the service inventory. Runtime platforms, messaging middleware, and ESB products commonly provide the necessary infrastructure for message processing and tracing capabilities, along with service agents that supply complex event processing, filtering, and correlation.

Impacts

Event-Driven Messaging is based on asynchronous message exchanges that can occur sporadically, depending on whenever the service-side events actually occur. It therefore may not be possible to wrap these exchanges within controlled runtime transactions.

Furthermore, because notification broadcasts cannot be predicted, the consumer must always be available to receive the notification message transmissions. Also, messages are typically issued via the one-way MEP, which does not require an acknowledgement response from the consumer.

Both of these drawbacks can raise serious reliability issues that can be addressed through the application of Asynchronous Queuing (582) and Reliable Messaging (592).

Relationships

The unique messaging model established by Event-Driven Messaging extends the base model provided by Service Messaging (533) and is itself often extended via other specialized messaging patterns, such as Asynchronous Queuing (582) and Reliable Messaging (592).

The publish-and-subscribe model that underlies Event-Driven Messaging provides advanced, asynchronous messaging functionality that can build upon the routing and messaging logic provided natively by ESB platforms (Figure 18.39).

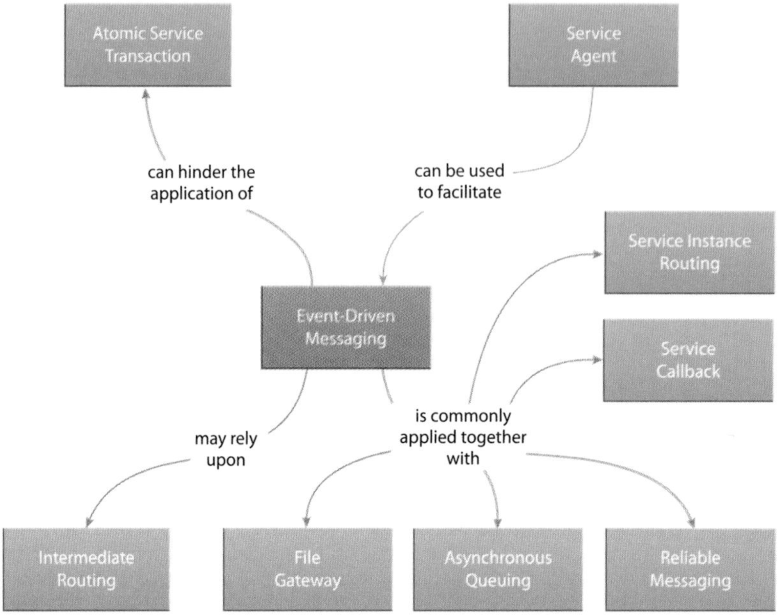

Figure 18.38

Event-Driven Messaging provides distinct functionality that relies upon a combination of other messaging and agent-related patterns.

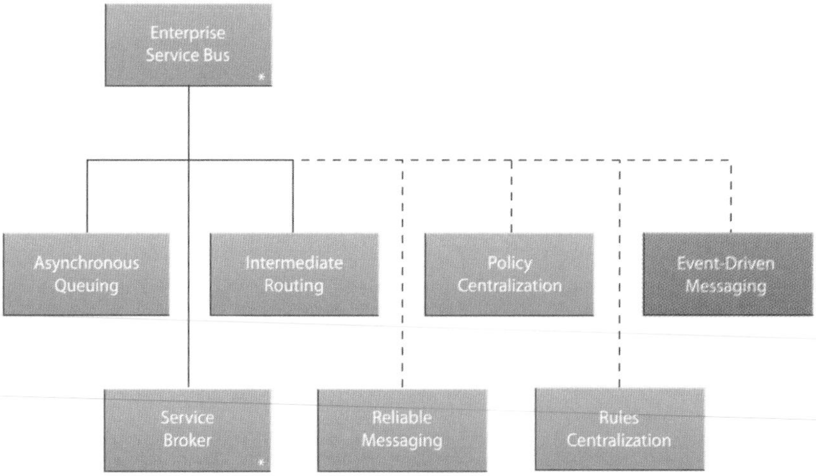

Figure 18.39

Event-Driven Messaging is considered an optional extension to Enterprise Service Bus (704).

NOTE

Event-Driven Messaging is broad pattern that relates to a number of established messaging patterns, including Publish-Subscribe Channel (Hohpe, Woolf) and Event Message (Hohpe, Woolf).

CASE STUDY EXAMPLE

The FRC manages a fleet of field agents that visit lumber mills and other sites owned by companies in the lumber and forestry industries. Often these visits are to follow up on complaints or concerns by company representatives. For example, the field officer may need to help educate mill operators as to how a new FRC policy affects their existing operations. However, at times field officers are also sent out to perform surprise inspections to ensure that certain procedure-related policies are, in fact, being followed.

To better support these officers, the FRC has issued mobile devices that display the agenda for a given day and any related logistical or contract information. These devices were custom-developed, and FRC architects had to make a decision as to whether they should be designed to periodically poll the central FRC scheduling system for updates or whether a push mechanism should be used instead. After interviews with relevant FRC staff (both field officers and those maintaining the internal system that contains the data required by the officers), they opted for the push approach.

Even though the periodic polling routine would have been less expensive and time-consuming to build, their interviews revealed that there are times where internal staff need to get urgent messages out to field officers. For example, in case of a natural disaster or other type of emergency. In this situation it is unacceptable to have to wait until the mobile device issues its next polling command; the notification needs to go out immediately.

To implement such a system, FRC architects turn to Event-Driven Messaging, which that allows them to set up each mobile device as a subscriber to events governed by a central service acting as a publisher. Whenever relevant events occur, a message broadcast is transmitted to all field officers. The system is further able to distinguish between different types of subscribers and messages. Individual officers are subscribed to their schedule, and therefore an officer only receives an update when an agenda change affects that officer. However, other types of messages (such as those that notify about an emergency) are automatically sent out to all subscribers.

Chapter 19

Composition Implementation Patterns

Agnostic Sub-Controller

Composition Autonomy

Atomic Service Transaction

Compensating Service Transaction

Depending on the processing requirements of a service composition, certain design options can be considered as a means of improving the composition architecture. The patterns in this chapter provide a mixed set of design solutions that address implementation-level issues pertaining primarily to runtime service activity management and composition structure.

When working with task services, Agnostic Sub-Controller (607) provides a method by which sub-process logic can be reused as a nested composition structure. Composition Autonomy (616) is focused on increasing the collective performance and behavioral predictability of a service composition and is closely related to the Service Autonomy design principle. Both Atomic Service Transaction (623) and Compensating Service Transaction (631) enhance the integrity of runtime service activities by wrapping them in coordinated boundaries.

Agnostic Sub-Controller

How can agnostic, cross-entity composition logic be separated, reused, and governed independently?

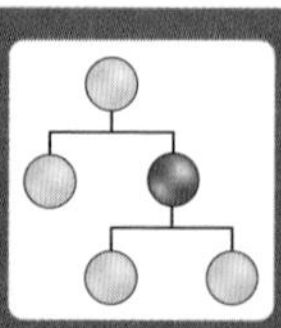

Problem	Service compositions are generally configured specific to a parent task, inhibiting reuse potential that may exist within a subset of the composition logic.
Solution	Reusable, cross-entity composition logic is abstracted or made accessible via an agnostic sub-controller capability, allowing that subset of the parent composition logic to be recomposed independently.
Application	A new agnostic service is created or a task service is appended with an agnostic sub-controller capability.
Impacts	The addition of a cross-entity, agnostic service can increase the size and complexity of compositions and the abstraction of agnostic cross-entity logic can violate modeling and design standards established by Service Layers (143).
Principles	Service Reusability, Service Composability
Architecture	Composition, Service

Table 19.1
Profile summary for the Agnostic Sub-Controller pattern.

> **NOTE**
>
> The term "sub-controller" is not new to this pattern. It is used to represent any service or service capability that composes services and is itself also composed. See SOAGlossary.com for a full definition.

Problem

When following Non-Agnostic Context (319), non-agnostic logic, at the time it is originally defined, is considered single purpose and non-reusable. By applying Process Abstraction (182), this type of logic is isolated within a task service that is typically positioned as the parent controller of a composition. When also having services based upon Entity Abstraction (175), the task service will generally be comprised of composition logic that needs to span multiple business entity boundaries in order to compose the respective entity services.

Subsequent to its definition and usage, it may be discovered that the task service contains segments of cross-entity logic that are, in fact, agnostic. This type of logic is most comparable to sub-processes that represent composition sequences so common that they are considered reusable. However, because this logic resides embedded within a larger body of non-agnostic logic, its reuse potential cannot be realized (Figure 19.1).

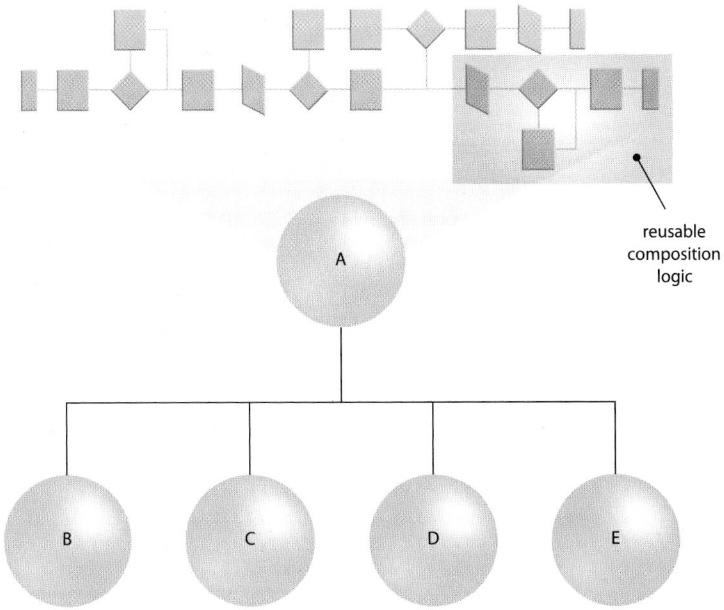

Figure 19.1
A subset of the parent process logic is deemed reusable but it is trapped among the other non-agnostic process logic encapsulated by the task service.

Solution

The newly discovered, cross-entity agnostic logic is separated into an agnostic service or an agnostic capability is added to the original task service. Either way, the result is a body of composition logic that itself can now be independently recomposed, thereby establishing an agnostic sub-controller (Figure 19.2).

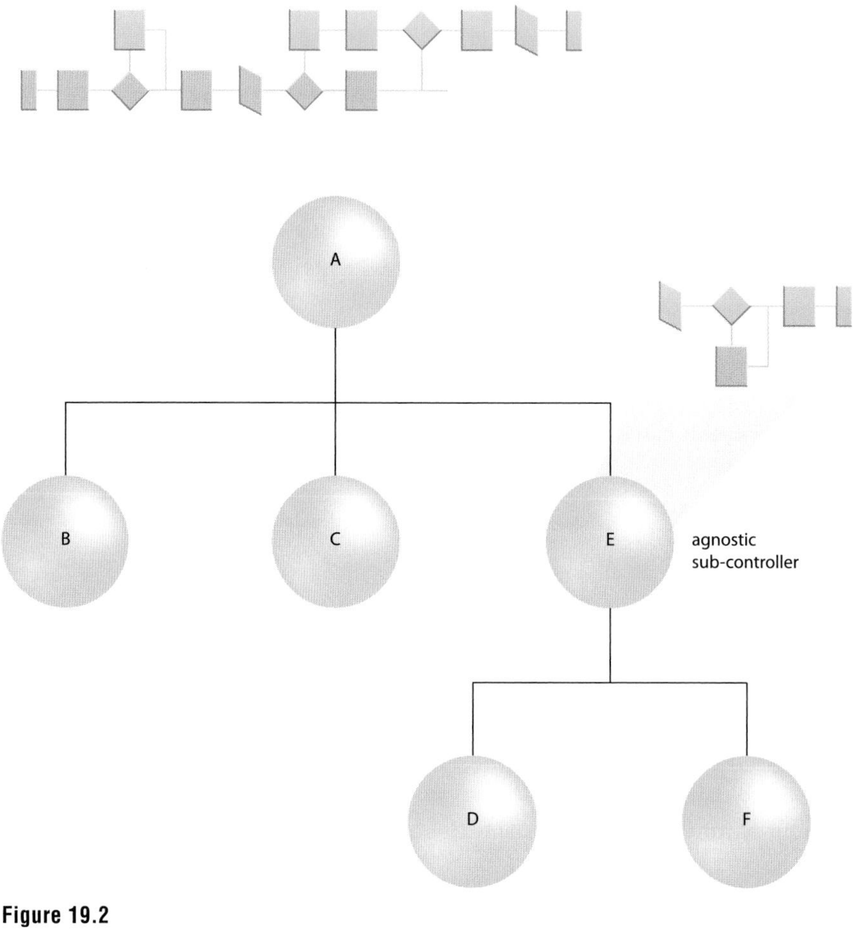

Figure 19.2

A traditional, single-purpose composition is often configured in a two-tier hierarchy, with all of the composition logic residing in the parent task service. Alternatively, the composition can be structured into additional tiers so that the composition is comprised of a parent controller service and one or more nested compositions represented by sub-controller services. These nested compositions may be necessary to carry out the parent task, but individually they can also provide logic that can be used independently to automate a smaller task, or they may have logic that can be used to automate other larger tasks. Either way, they can be structured to represent and abstract agnostic logic for reuse purposes.

Application

There are two common methods for abstracting agnostic, cross-entity logic, each with its own set of trade-offs:

- *New Agnostic Service* – The logic forms the basis of a new agnostic service. The challenge may lie in positioning this service within any of the layers previously established by Service Layers (143). Because it will usually represent cross-entity logic, it may be possible to assign it a coarse-grained business entity-based scope, thereby qualifying it as a standalone entity service.
- *New Agnostic Capability* – The logic remains within the task service but it is made accessible via a new capability exposed by the task service contract. Although a practical approach, this can disturb the clean separation previously achieved by Process Abstraction (182).

With either technique, supporting infrastructure will need to be upgraded to prepare for the reuse of the newly found agnostic logic.

Impacts

The main challenge with the application of this pattern is its effect on the overall logical structure of the service inventory. Depending on the scope and nature of the agnostic sub-controller logic, its isolation into a separate service or capability can easily violate one or more of the patterns associated with Service Layers (143). The resulting confusion and misalignment of functional service contexts may not be warranted.

It is recommended that the actual reuse potential of the identified logic be first established and confirmed before proceeding with this pattern.

Relationships

Agnostic Sub-Controller is applied to service logic that is likely to have previously been non-agnostic, which is why this pattern has relationships with Process Abstraction (182), Process Centralization (193), and Agnostic Context (312).

Service Façade (333) is often employed to help structure the internal logic of an agnostic sub-controller service, and Contract Centralization (409) is important and relevant to the successful long-term usage of this type of service (as with any service).

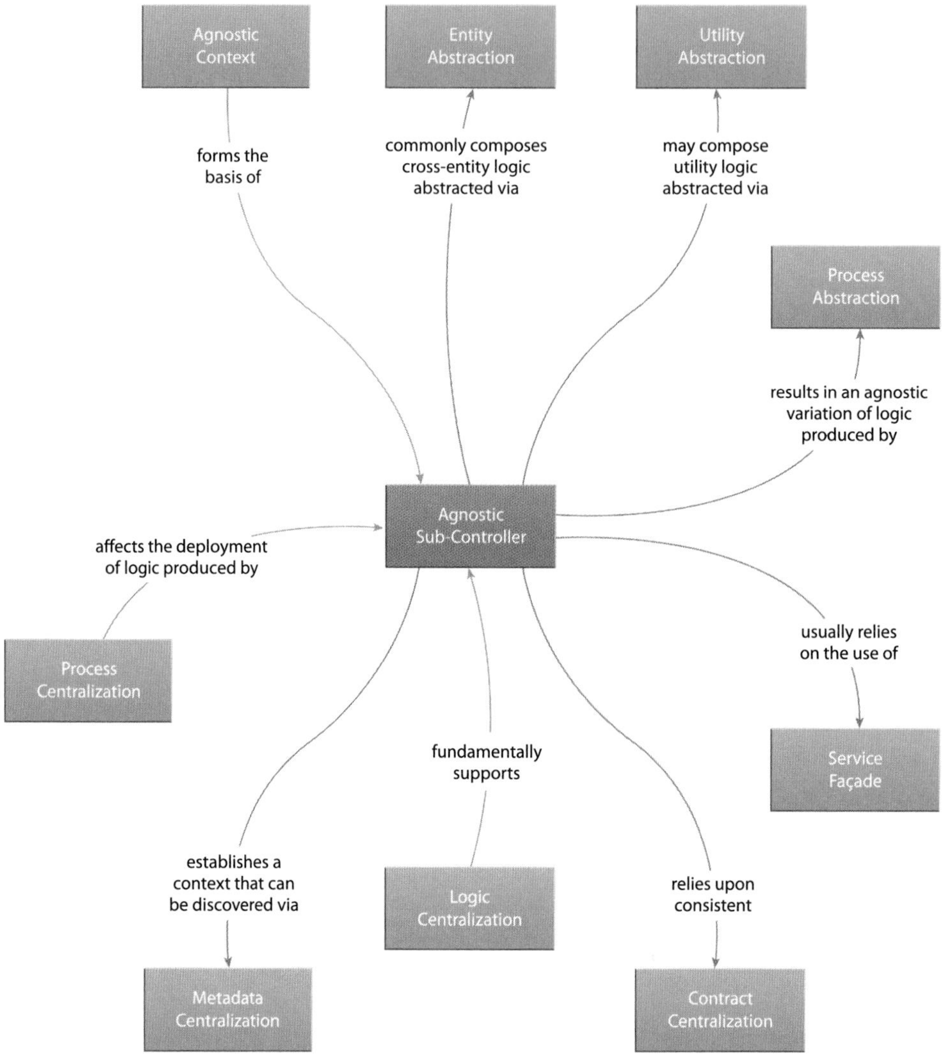

Figure 19.3

Agnostic Sub-Controller is in the unique position of having relationships with patterns focused on non-agnostic and agnostic logic.

CASE STUDY EXAMPLE

The original design of the Alleywood Report Zones task service encapsulates all the composition logic required to assemble a consolidated report by retrieving data from the Region, Area, and Policy Checks entity services, as shown in Figure 19.4.

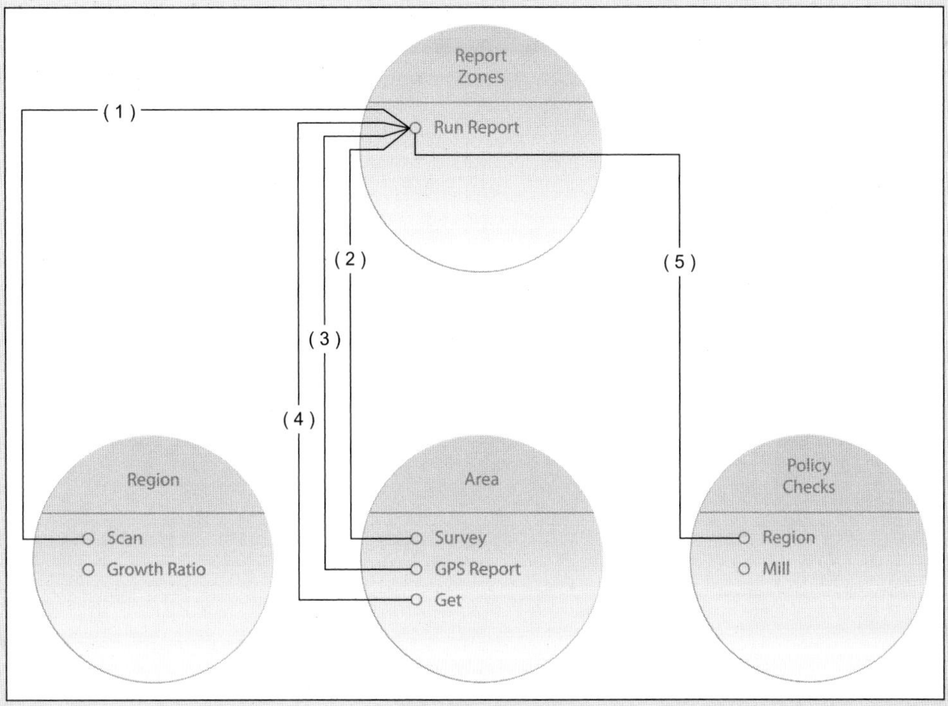

Figure 19.4
The initial service composition hierarchy established by the Report Zones task service responsible for carrying out the Report Zones business task.

This composition automates the Report Zones business process, which collects a range of information about the regions and areas that fall within a particular zone and then cross-references this data with any relevant FRC issued policies.

The process is comprised of the following steps:

1. Perform a scan of one or more regions to identify all affected areas.
2. For each area, carry out a zoning survey and retrieve the most current GPS report data. Based on the results of these queries, request the corresponding area records.

3. Consolidate the area record data by establishing a special, temporary view record comprised of textual and image information.
4. Perform policy checks for all area records to ensure that any FRC policies that may affect an area are identified.

As illustrated in Figure 19.4, the Report Zones service invokes the Scan capability of the Region service to collect region data and then invokes three separate capabilities from the Area service to further gather Area information that pertains to the previously identified regions. It then carries out its own embedded logic to establish a custom view of the area data before passing information over to the Policy Checks utility service.

During a meeting with a Tri-Fold project team, Alleywood analysts hear about a Geo-Analysis solution they are currently designing that requires similar reporting functionality. Only, the Tri-Fold task service already receives region data as input values passed to the task service's capability. The Tri-Fold team is therefore planning to build composition logic that queries the Area and Policy Checks services only, as shown in Figure 19.5.

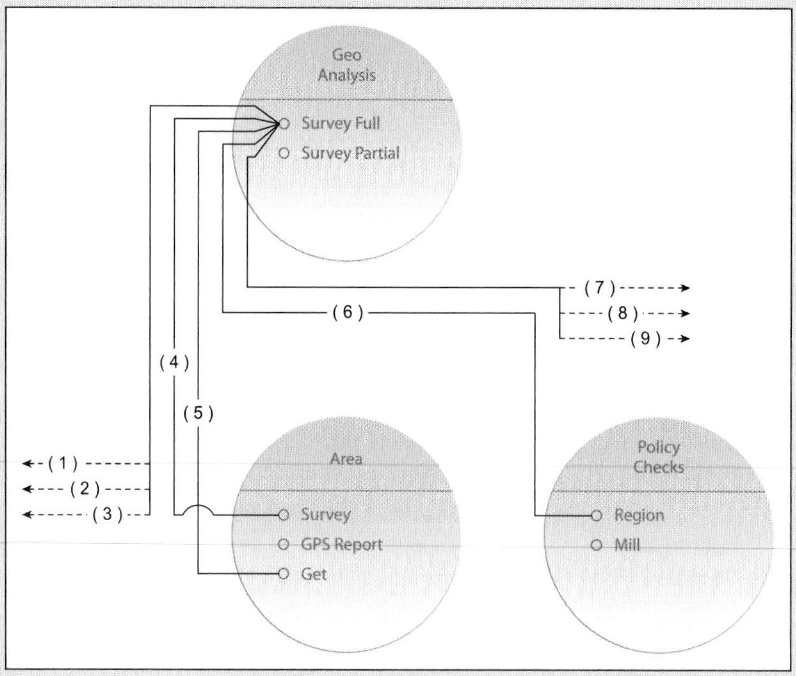

Figure 19.5

The Area and Policy Checks services are invoked as part of a larger composition involving six other services (not shown).

Another difference between the Report Zones and Geo-Analysis tasks is that the latter does require image data and therefore does not invoke the Area service's GPS Report capability.

However, after some discussion among the project teams, it is proposed that there is sufficient common functionality to warrant the creation of an agnostic sub-controller, especially given that additional reuse opportunities for this logic are also anticipated. This new agnostic Area Policy Report service is created. It abstracts the collection and consolidation of area data and the retrieval of corresponding policies, as shown in Figure 19.6.

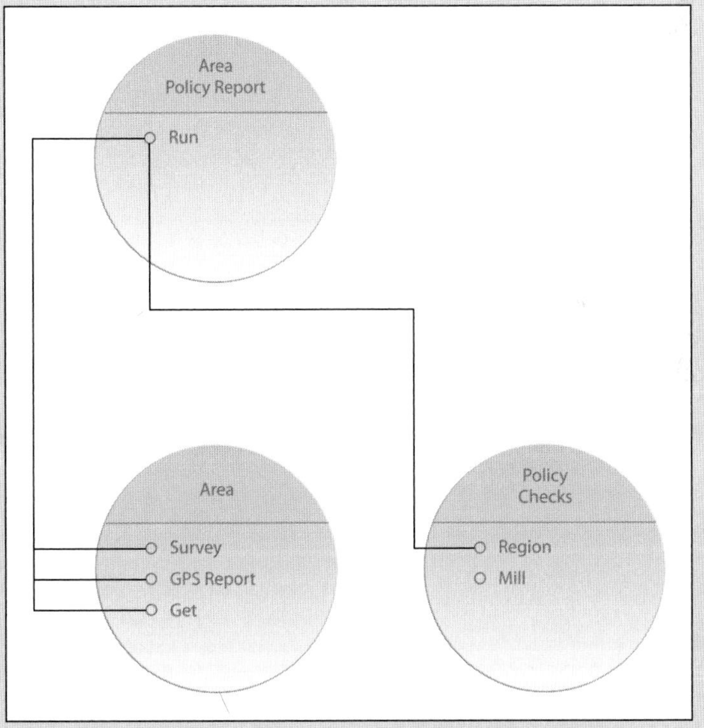

Figure 19.6

The new Area Policy Report service isolating the recently discovered agnostic, cross-entity logic. The relationship lines between capabilities are not numbers because the capabilities the service invokes and the sequence in which they are invoked is determined by the input value received via its Run capability.

At first there is some resistance to the idea of introducing a new service into the inventory only to provide this one small body of agnostic composition logic. A debate ensues as to whether it would make more sense to simply add a Policy Report capability to the Area service or to perhaps create a new Policy entity service with an Area Report capability. By reviewing the service inventory blueprint, the teams discover that a Policy entity service has in fact been modeled and is planned for delivery later in the year.

However, subsequent discussions lead to the conclusion that a separate agnostic service is the best design option for this case. It allows the reporting functionality to be abstracted and extended across two different entity services, as required. Besides being able to locate this logic in a separate physical service implementation, concerns regarding how this cross-entity logic could be incorporated within existing entity services (without violating established entity service boundaries) is avoided by simply classifying it as a utility service.

As it enters the design phase, the Area Policy Report service is subjected to the same design rigor as any other agnostic service. The result is a flexible set of composition logic encapsulated by the Run capability, allowing the service to receive a range of input values. This, for example, enables this agnostic sub-controller to support both the Report Zones and Geo-Analysis tasks by providing optional GPS image data to the former (Figure 19.7).

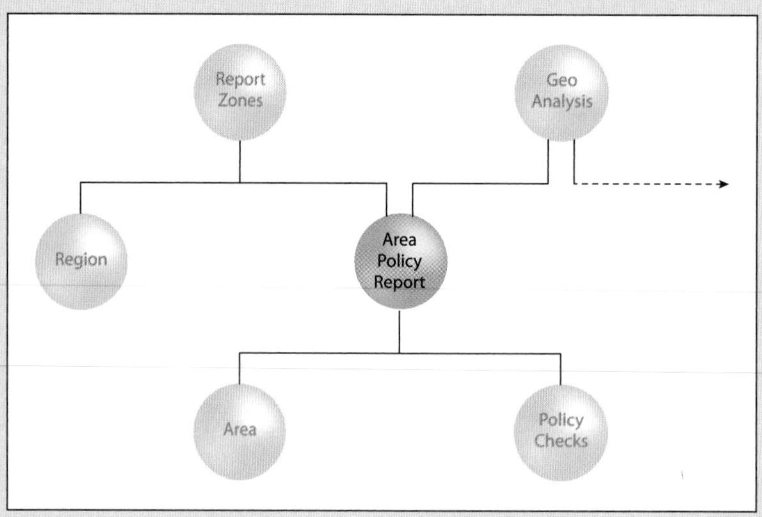

Figure 19.7

The agnostic Area Policy Report service being shared by the Report Zones and Geo-Analysis compositions.

Composition Autonomy

How can compositions be implemented to minimize loss of autonomy?

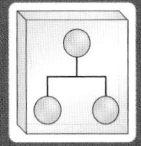

Problem	Composition controller services naturally lose autonomy when delegating processing tasks to composed services, some of which may be shared across multiple compositions.
Solution	All composition participants can be isolated to maximize the autonomy of the composition as a whole.
Application	The agnostic member services of a composition are redundantly implemented in an isolated environment together with the task service.
Impacts	Increasing autonomy on a composition level results in increased infrastructure costs and government responsibilities.
Principles	Service Autonomy, Service Reusability, Service Composability
Architecture	Composition

Table 19.2
Profile summary for the Composition Autonomy pattern.

Problem

Services are ideally individually autonomous so that they can provide a high degree of behavioral predictability when repeatedly reused and shared across multiple compositions. However, a natural result of typical distributed service composition is a *loss* of autonomy by any service composing another simply due to the fact that the service is required to invoke solution logic that resides outside of its controlled execution environment.

When individual services provide high levels of individual autonomy, the collective autonomy of the composition is correspondingly elevated, and this is generally adequate for most service compositions. But when one or more composition participants have a poor level of autonomy or when the requirements of the composition as a whole demand a higher degree of robustness and reliability, then a distributed composition may be insufficient (Figure 19.8).

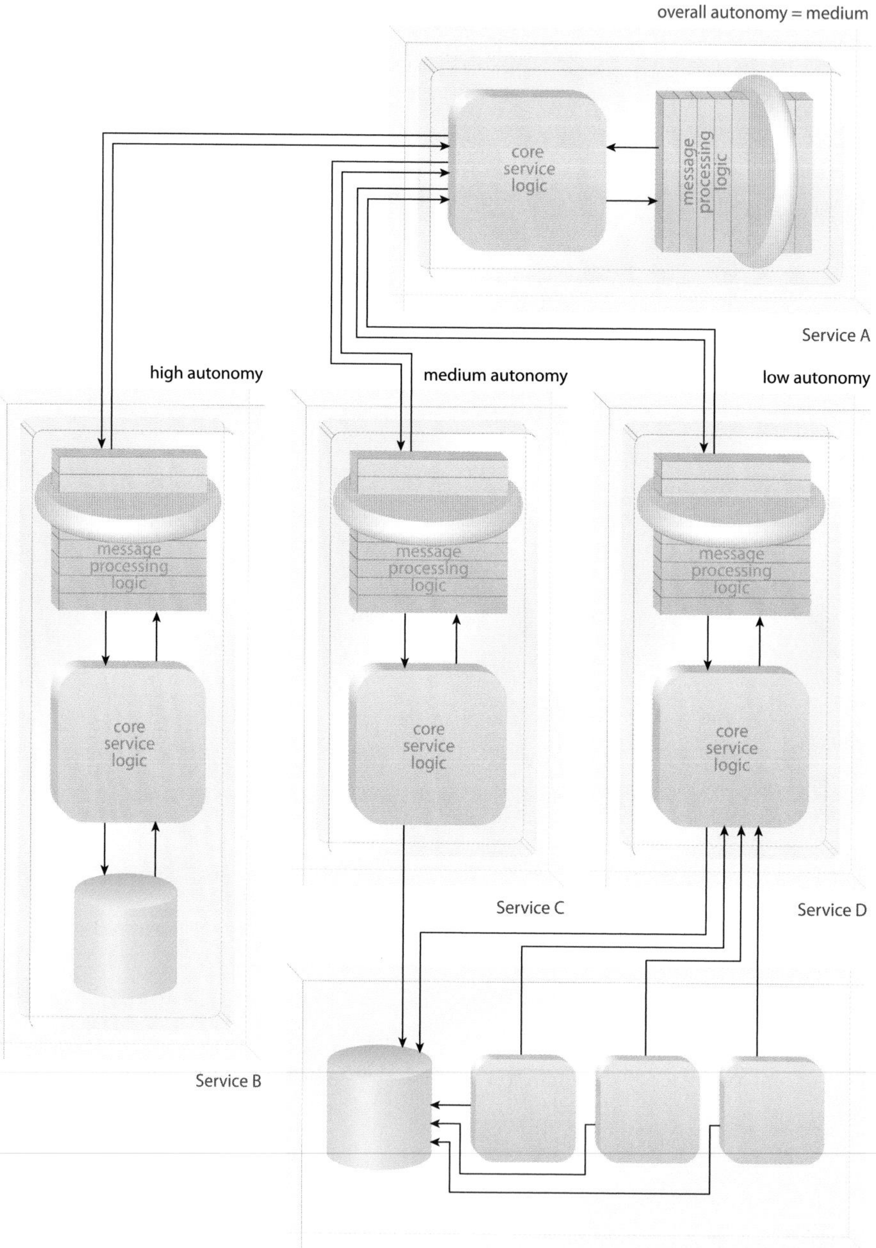

Figure 19.8

In a highly distributed environment, a service composition's overall autonomy will be collectively determined by the autonomy of its individual composition members. When services are designed in accordance with the Service Autonomy design principle, this collective autonomy will generally be sufficient. However, there are times when a higher degree of composition autonomy is required. As shown in this figure, Service D offers the lowest level of autonomy because its logic is accessed by external programs.

Solution

The services participating in the composition are deployed within an isolated environment so as to give the composition as a whole a high level of autonomy (Figure 19.9).

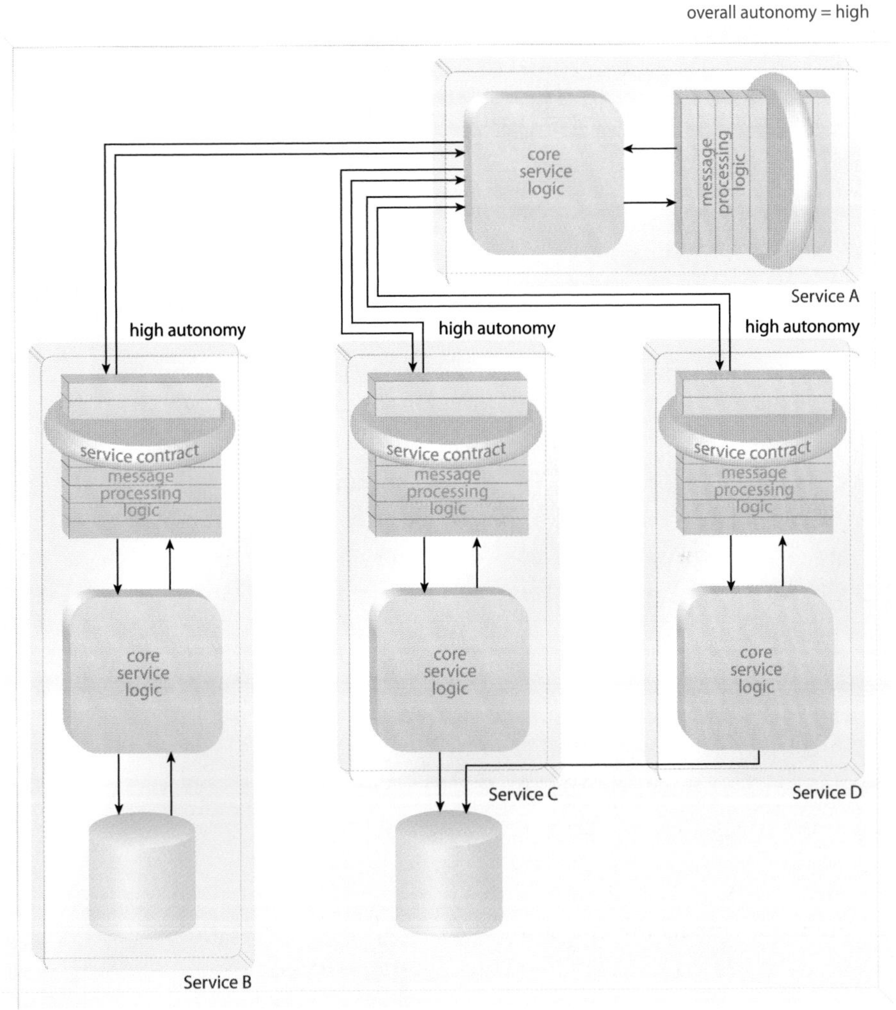

Figure 19.9

By grouping the services of a composition into a separate deployment environment, the collective autonomy is maximized because the implementation is dedicated to the composition, and none of the services are otherwise shared. Services C and D in particular benefit from this new implementation as they are no longer subject to shared access.

Application

To increase the autonomy of a composition the following steps can be taken:

- Two or more composed services are deployed on the same physical server to avoid remote communication.
- The composed services are isolated to avoid shared access.
- The agnostic composed services are redundantly implemented, as per Redundant Implementation (345).
- Services requiring data access are supplied with dedicated or replicated data stores, as per Service Data Replication (350).

It's important to keep in mind that a service composition is a design-time representation of the aggregated service capabilities required to automate a specific business task. This has the following implications when applying this pattern:

- Even though entire services are redundantly deployed, only a subset of the capabilities will likely be utilized by the composition.
- Depending on the complexity of the business task, a variety of runtime scenarios can result in different capability compositions, some of which may need to involve services outside of the dedicated composition environment.

NOTE

There are variations in the extent to which this design pattern can be applied, several of which correspond to autonomy levels described in Chapter 10 of *SOA Principles of Service Design*.

Impacts

Because the requirements for increasing the overall autonomy of a service composition usually involve upgrading or extending the existing enterprise infrastructure, there are obvious costs and impacts that need to be taken into consideration.

Redundant implementations of agnostic services further add governance effort and expense so that these independent implementations are kept in synch with their shared counterparts.

Relationships

Because of its narrow emphasis on supporting the goals of the Service Autonomy design principle, this pattern has just a handful of relationships. Fundamentally, Composition Autonomy is concerned with maximizing the reliability and availability of services based on Agnostic Context (312).

Service Data Replication (350) and Redundant Implementation (345) help establish an appropriate level of isolation for service compositions. Often, security needs will dictate the decision to isolate externally facing services and any services they may compose, which may lead to the need to apply Composition Autonomy in support of Inventory Endpoint (260).

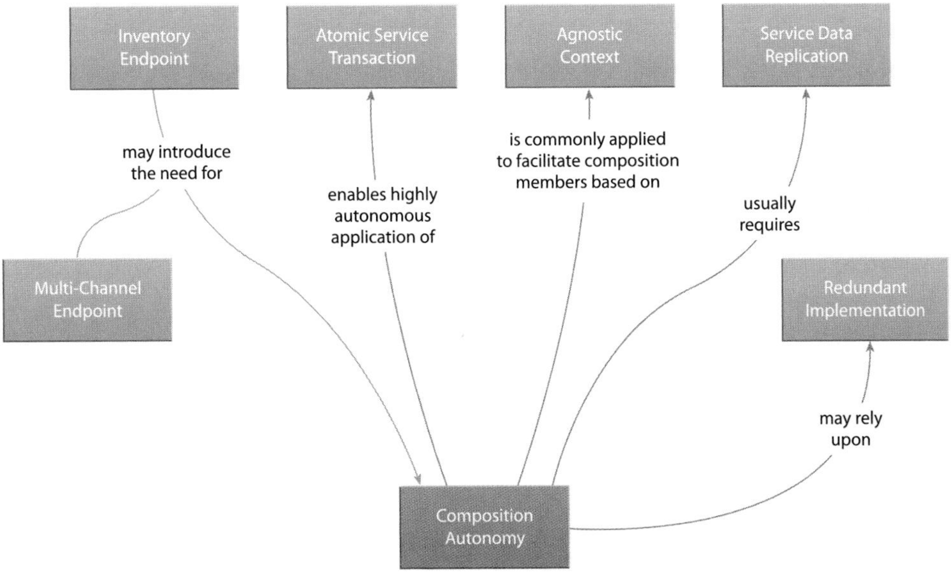

Figure 19.10

Composition Autonomy is implementation-centric and will generally require the application of more specialized patterns to realize required levels of composition isolation.

CASE STUDY EXAMPLE

Since it was first implemented, the Area Policy Report composition (described earlier in the Agnostic Sub-Controller (607) example) has become increasingly popular. Six separate parent compositions now utilize its relatively simple functions to receive consolidated area and policy reports. Each of these parent compositions may, at any time, invoke multiple instances of this service.

Initially there were no problems as the requested reports were relatively small and the usage demands were manageable. However, the request for larger, more complex reports has increased, as has the extent of concurrent usage. On any given day, a peak usage of over 60 instances of the Area Policy Report service is reached.

These demands have predictably resulted in a noticeable increase in latency, which has led to a need to better optimize this service. Upon investigating the physical composition architecture, it is discovered that the Area Policy Report task service is located on a different server than the Area and Policy Checks services it is responsible for composing (Figure 19.11).

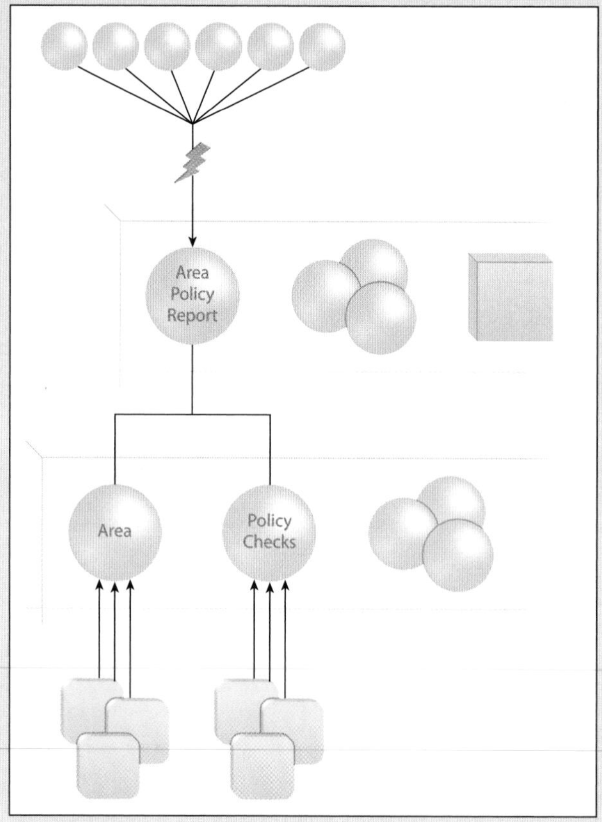

Figure 19.11

All services reside in shared processing environments, thereby reducing the overall autonomy of the composition.

The Area Policy Report service is co-located with eight other task services and a small legacy application, all on one physical server. Being more established agnostic resources, the Area and Policy Checks services have been deployed on a powerful, multi-processor server. Yet, as agnostic resources, these services are individually reused by many other compositions.

Upon further review of usage statistics, analysts identify the Area entity service as the primary bottleneck. Sometimes the Area Policy Report service is required to call the Area service more than once for a single report, plus the quantity of data that needs to be retrieved by the Area service can sometimes be significant (especially when large amounts of GPS image data are requested).

Because there are several solution delivery projects underway that have identified the need to compose the Area Policy Report service, the demand for this composition will only increase. As result, the decision is made to apply Composition Autonomy, but only to a limited extent.

A dedicated server is set up, allowing a redundant implementation of the Area service to be deployed together with the sole implementation of the Area Policy Report service. The Policy Checks utility service is not part of this new isolated environment at this point, as it continues to perform within acceptable parameters. However, the option is always there for a redundant implementation of this service to also be added to this environment (Figure 19.12).

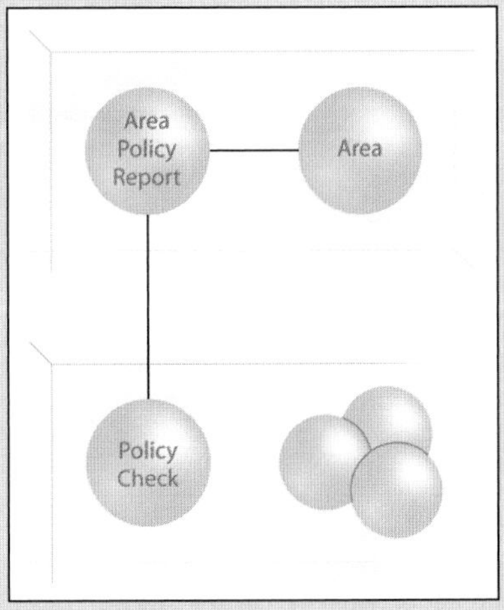

Figure 19.12

The new environment dramatically increases composition autonomy by isolating the two services responsible for performing the bulk of the composition logic.

Atomic Service Transaction

How can a transaction with rollback capability be propagated across messaging-based services?

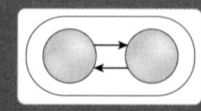

Problem	When runtime activities that span multiple services fail, the parent business task is incomplete and actions performed and changes made up to that point may compromise the integrity of the underlying solution and architecture.
Solution	Runtime service activities can be wrapped in a transaction with rollback feature that resets all actions and changes if the parent business task cannot be successfully completed.
Application	A transaction management system is made part of the inventory architecture and then used by those service compositions that require rollback features.
Impacts	Transacted service activities can consume more memory because of the requirement for each service to preserve its original state until it is notified to rollback or commit its changes.
Principles	Service Statelessness
Architecture	Inventory, Composition

Table 19.3
Profile summary for the Atomic Service Transaction pattern.

Problem

During the course of a runtime service activity, a variety of issues can arise, relating either to the delivery of data between participating services or to problems occurring within service boundaries.

If a serious failure condition is encountered and insufficient exception handling logic is available within all affected services, then the overarching business process will not be allowed to complete successfully, nor will it be allowed to complete a pre-defined failure condition.

Instead, services may simply be left hanging in suspension indefinitely or until they time out. Outstanding changes that some services may have made to databases or other resources can end up causing problems or even corrupting parts of the enterprise because other required changes were never completed (Figure 19.13).

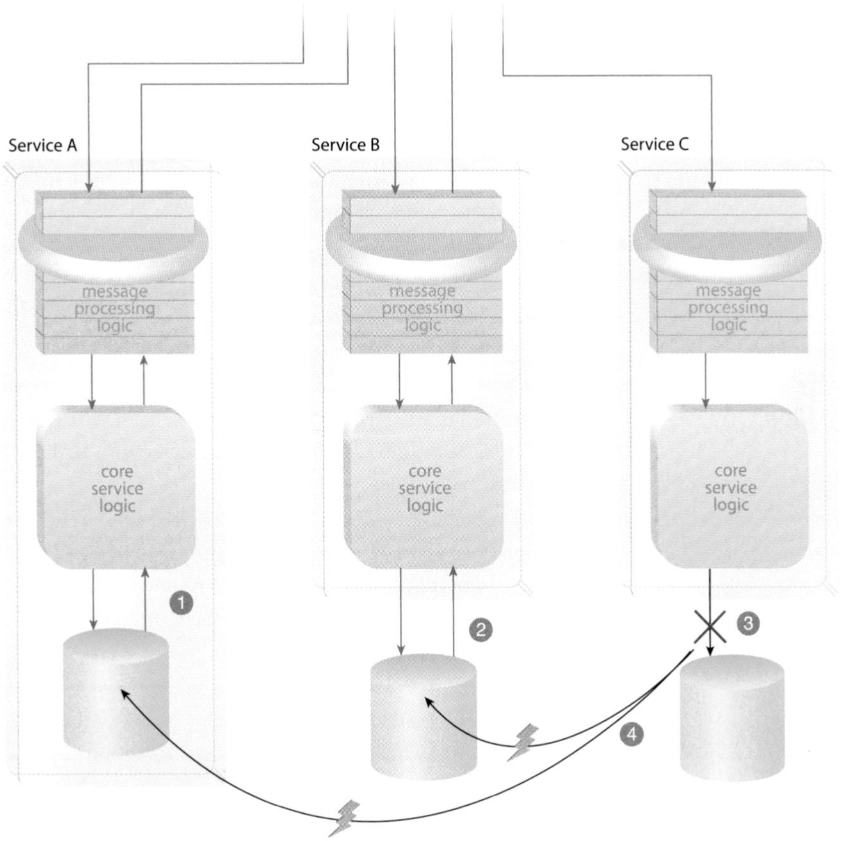

Figure 19.13

This figure shows three services being sequentially invoked in support of automating a parent business task. The first two services successfully complete their required database updates (1, 2), but the third service fails at its attempt to update its database (3). According to the rules of the business process, either all three updates must succeed or none at all. However, because the first two updates have already been completed, the failed update of the third database compromises the quality of the data in the first two (4).

Solution

A transaction system can require that services within a particular composition register themselves as part of a transaction prior to completing their changes. Then, as the service activity is underway, participating services communicate with the transaction system as to their status (Figure 19.14).

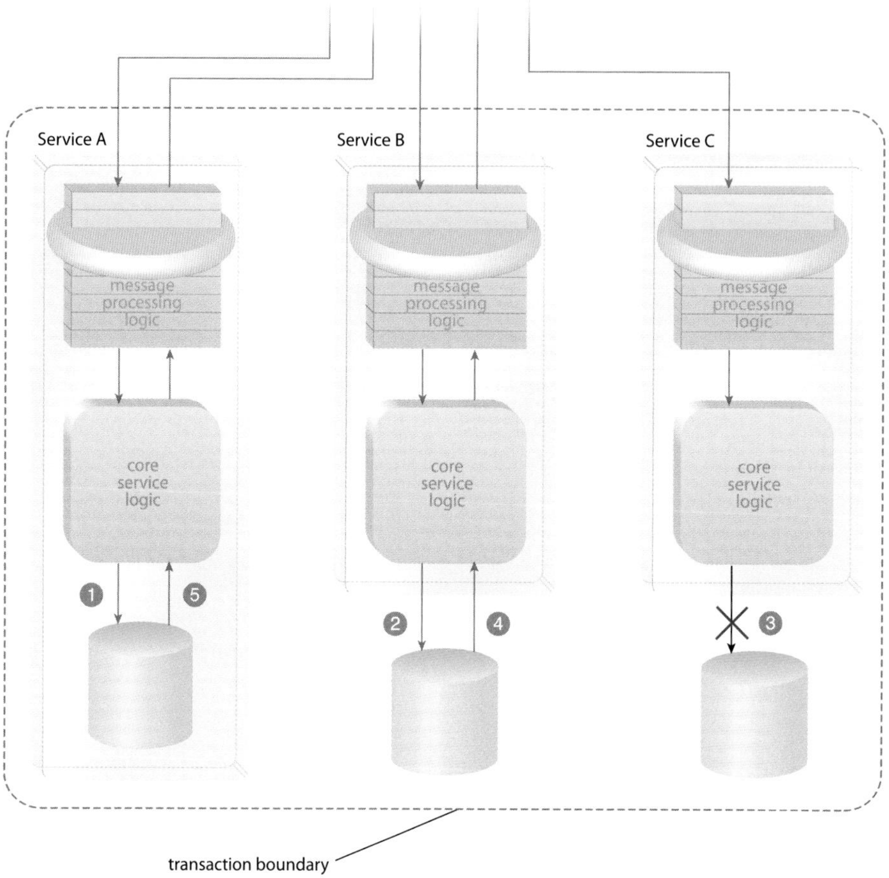

Figure 19.14

As per the previous figure, Services A and B complete their respective tasks successfully. However each time they do, they initiate a local transaction, temporarily saving the current state of the database prior to making their changes (1, 2). After Service C fails its database update attempt (3), Services A and B restore their databases back to their original states (4, 5). The business task is effectively reset or rolled back across services within the pre-defined transaction boundary.

At some point, the system queries all services to ask whether their functions were carried out successfully. If any one service responds negatively (or if any one service does not respond at all), a rollback command is issued, requesting that all services now restore any changes made up until that point. However, if all services respond favorably, then a commit command is issued asking all services to commit their changes.

Application

Depending on the transaction management system being used, the application of this design pattern can vary. Fundamentally, though, some mechanism needs to be in place so that all services within a given composition can be tracked at runtime and then contacted to receive status updates and for notification of commit or rollback commands.

For services delivered as components, runtime transaction management systems are capable of natively establishing transaction boundaries across services, especially when they rely on traditional binary protocols that create persistent connections.

When services are built as Web services, the WS-Coordination and WS-AtomicTransaction standards provide an industry standard mechanism to support transaction propagation across Web service implementations. Figure 19.15 illustrates how, when using WS-Coordination, a coordinator service is positioned to define the transaction boundary and manage transaction activity.

> **NOTE**
>
> For more information about WS-Coordination and related standards, visit SOASpecs.com and WS-Standards.com and see Chapter 6 in *Service-Oriented Architecture: Concepts, Technology, and Design.*

Impacts

For services to effectively participate in an atomic transaction, they need to capture a snapshot of a resource prior to making changes to it. This previous condition is often loaded into memory as state data and will continue to consume memory until the service receives the commit or rollback command. In larger transactions involving multiple services, this amount of memory consumption can add up and reduce overall service scalability (an issue especially important to shared agnostic services).

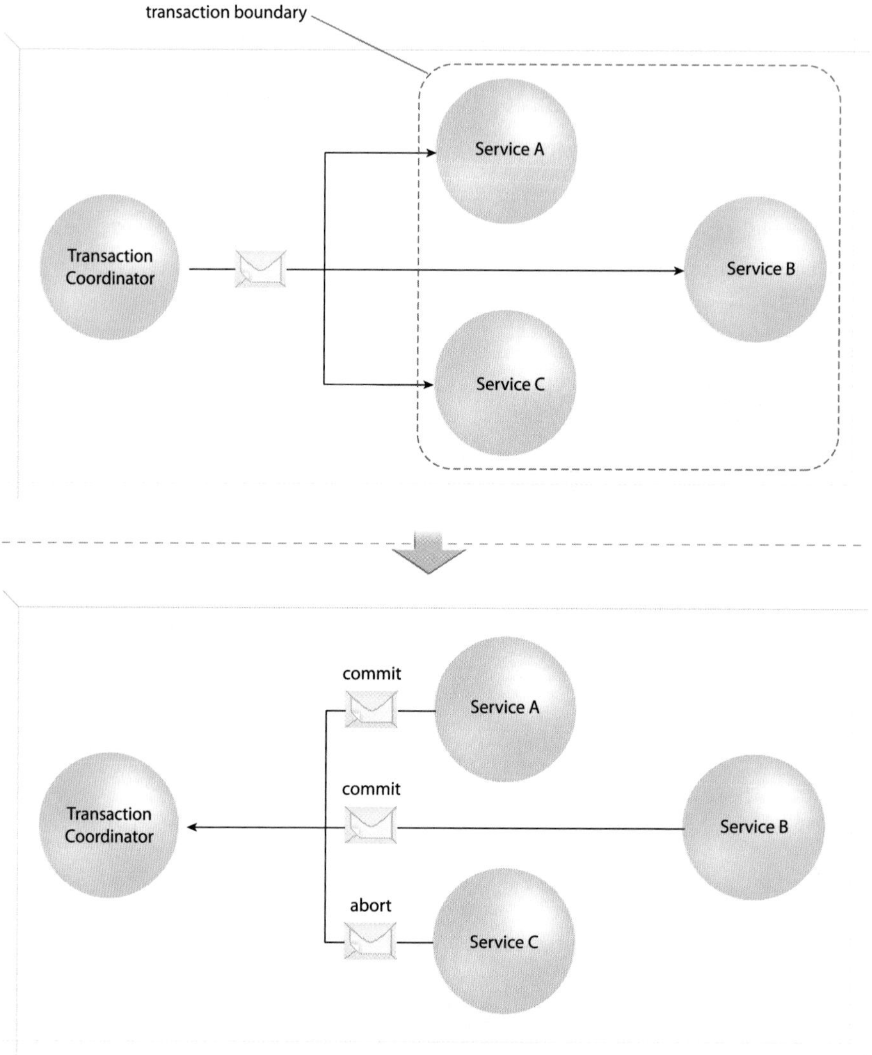

Figure 19.15

The transaction coordinator establishes the transaction boundary as per participating services that register for this transacted activity. These services are then queried as to whether the transaction should be committed or rolled back. Because Service C's database update attempt failed, it votes to abort the transaction, which is what subsequently happens.

Relationships

This pattern can touch on many runtime activity-related parts of an inventory architecture, which is why it has so many relationships with patterns concerned with messaging, agent, and composition processing.

Atomic transactions are often initiated and coordinated via the parent business process layer as per Process Abstraction (182) and are extra effective when all participants can be physically isolated as per Composition Autonomy (616).

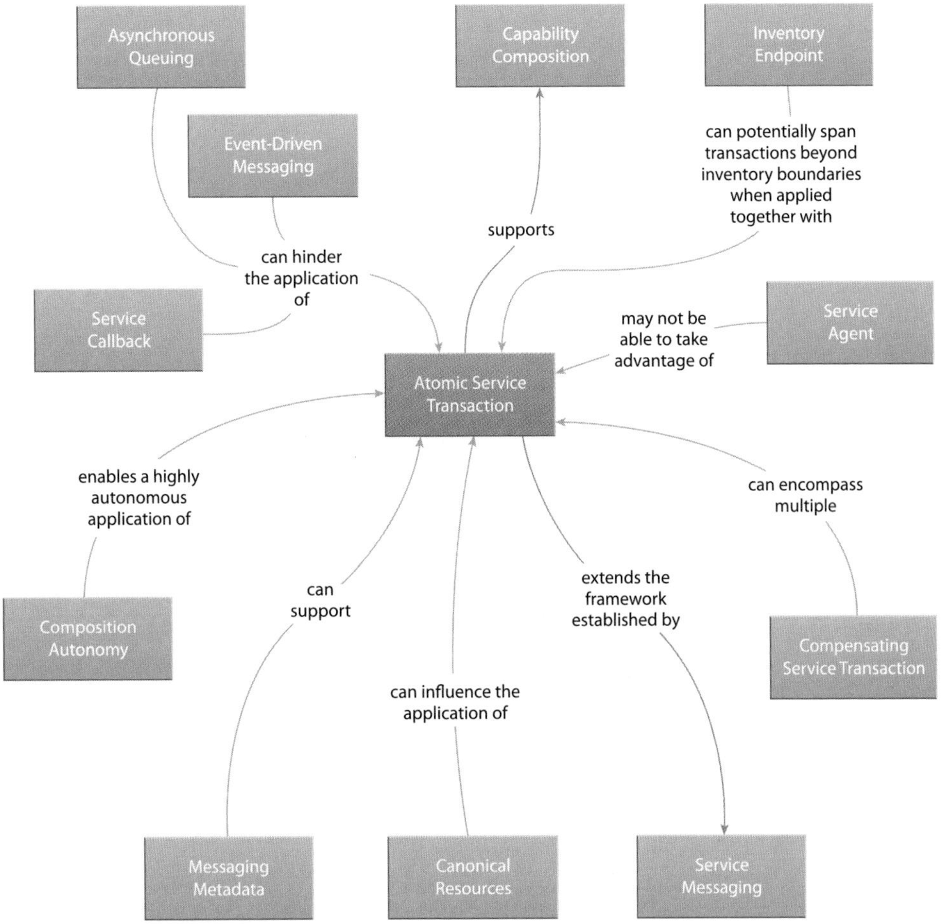

Figure 19.16

Atomic Service Transaction establishes a framework for coordinating transactions that involve numerous services and therefore relates to a variety of other patterns that provide runtime processing features.

However, asynchronous-based messaging patterns, such as Event-Driven Messaging (599) and Asynchronous Queuing (582), are often incompatible with this pattern due to its need to lock resources and its common reliance on synchronous data exchanges.

When centralizing process logic as part of an orchestration environment, the scope and complexity of service compositions can increase, primarily due to the rich feature set usually provided by orchestration products. Orchestrated logic therefore benefits from the runtime control provided by Atomic Service Transaction, which is why this pattern represents a common extension to Orchestration (701).

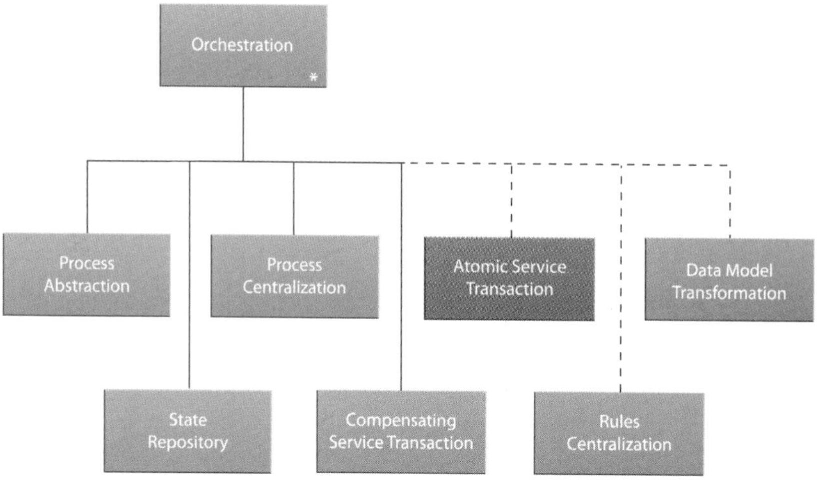

Figure 19.17
Atomic Service Transaction represents an optional part of Orchestration (701).

CASE STUDY EXAMPLE

Several service compositions created in support of the Alleywood and Tri-Fold accounting systems require that either all parts of the composition succeed or fail. Through the use of transaction metadata, messages can be equipped with header blocks that express transaction details, as shown in Example 19.1. This functionality effectively allows a transaction to span numerous Web services.

```
<Envelope xmlns="http://schemas.xmlsoap.org/soap/envelope/"
  xmlns:wscoor="http://schemas.xmlsoap.org/ws/2002/08/wscoor"
  xmlns:wsu="http://schemas.xmlsoap.org/ws/2002/07/utility">
  <Header>
    <wscoor:CoordinationContext>
      <wsu:Expires>
```

```
        2009-03-03T00:00:00.0000000-09:00
      </wsu:Expires>
      <wsu:Identifier>
        uuid:isidf843249-454580-dfs
      </wsu:Identifier>
      <wscoor:CoordinationType>
        http://schemas.xmlsoap.org/ws/2003/09/wsat
      </wscoor:CoordinationType>
    </wscoor:CoordinationContext>
  </Header>
  <Body>
    ...
  </Body>
</Envelope>
```

Example 19.1

This header block establishes that the `Expires` and `Identifier` element values are associated with an atomic transaction (as defined in the `CoordinationType` element).

These are just some of the examples of technologies that currently support industry standard messaging metadata. Furthermore, these metadata types can be combined into the same header section, allowing each message to be outfitted with a rich set of meta information types.

Compensating Service Transaction

By Clemens Utschig-Utschig, Berthold Maier, Bernd Trops, Hajo Normann, Torsten Winterberg, Brian Loesgen, Mark Little

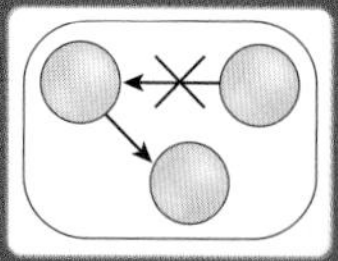

How can composition runtime exceptions be consistently accommodated without requiring services to lock resources?

Problem	Whereas uncontrolled runtime exceptions can jeopardize a service composition, wrapping the composition in an atomic transaction can tie up too many resources, thereby negatively affecting performance and scalability.
Solution	Compensating routines are introduced, allowing runtime exceptions to be resolved with the opportunity for reduced resource locking and memory consumption.
Application	Compensation logic is pre-defined and implemented as part of the parent composition controller logic or via individual "undo" service capabilities.
Impacts	Unlike atomic transactions that are governed by specific rules, the use of compensation logic is open-ended and can vary in its actual effectiveness.
Principles	Service Loose Coupling
Architecture	Inventory, Composition

Table 19.4
Profile summary for the Compensating Service Transaction pattern.

Problem

When services being composed at runtime encounter failure conditions, runtime exceptions are raised either by individual services or by the platform hosting the service composition instance.

Services may or may not have adequate internal logic to gracefully handle some exceptions, thereby preserving the integrity of the remaining composition. However, with serious or unanticipated exceptions, services often have no choice but to propagate the exception to other services in the composition. Similarly, when the runtime platform itself generates an exception, it may be required to halt the execution of the composition or terminate the

composition instance altogether. One approach to solving this problem while preserving the integrity of the composition is the usage of transactions.

When applying Atomic Service Transaction (623), these situations are resolved by enabling all services to rollback to their original state before the composition instance is destroyed. In order to obtain this type of functionality, back-end resources (such as database tables and records, as well as other systems) will typically need to be locked for the duration of the transaction (Figure 19.18).

Depending on the length and scope of the transaction, this can severely degrade performance and can also reduce the scalability of the overall service inventory.

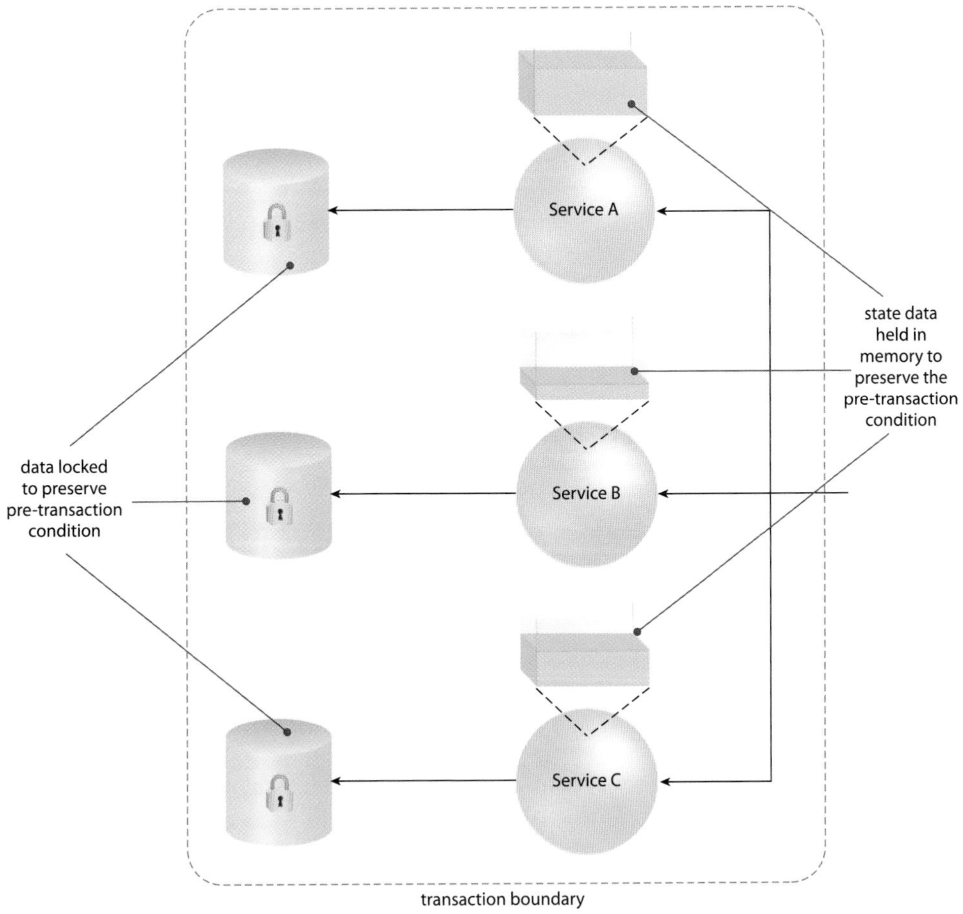

Figure 19.18

Services involved in an atomic transaction are required to lock up resources for the duration of the transaction.

Solution

Instead of being wrapped in an atomic transaction, the service composition is supplemented with compensating logic. This logic differs from atomic transactions in that it does not require services to maintain the original state or lock resources for the duration of the transaction.

As long as there is no firm requirement for compensations to restore a runtime activity back to its original state, exception conditions can be handled gracefully without jeopardizing the integrity of the composition (Figure 19.19).

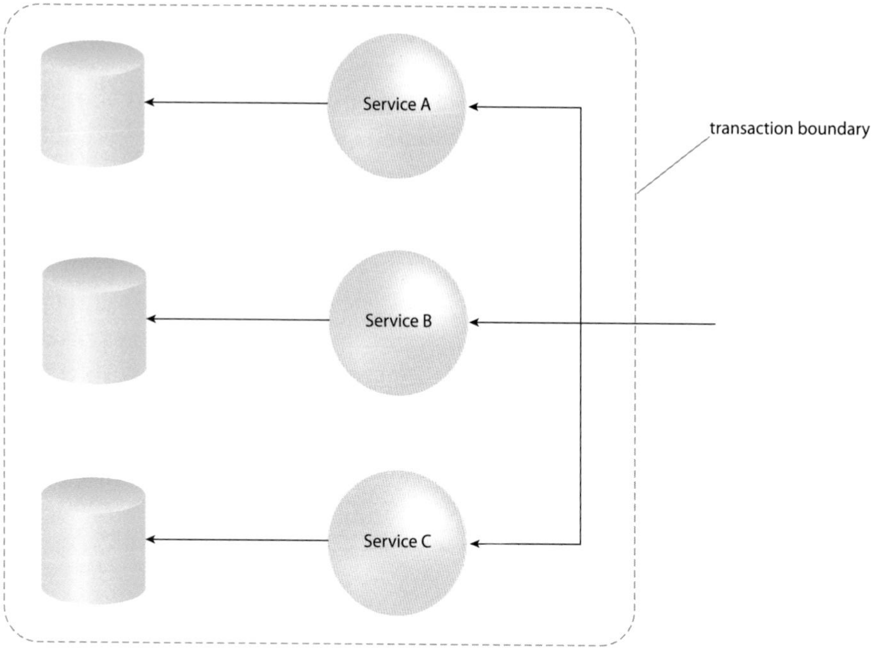

Figure 19.19

Compensating transactions do not require that resources be locked or that the original state be preserved.

Application

Compensating logic is typically defined at these levels:

- composition member
- composition controller

A service is considered a composition member when it is being composed by parent composition logic. At this level, compensating routines can extend a service via the addition of *undo* capabilities. For every capability that alters the state of the underlying service implementation (including any repositories or other resources accessed by the service logic), a corresponding undo capability is added. This allows the parent composition logic to respond to an exception condition by calling the undo capability of each service that was invoked up until that point.

The composition controller may be a task service that is composing other services or it may represent parent composition logic that is part of a platform based on Orchestration (701). When applied within middleware environments, the role of a composition controller is comparable to that of a transaction manager.

Either way, this logic can be extended with compensating routines that also respond to exception conditions with pre-determined exception handling logic. The only difference is that, in this case, the logic resides with the task logic, as per Process Abstraction (182).

At the controller level, the compensating logic may optionally invoke the individual undo capabilities of composition member services. It can also be designed to carry out additional functions, such as sending out a notification message or starting up a new instance of the composition after the previous instance was terminated. In most cases, compensation logic will invalidate the last "commited" state, as opposed to canceling back to the original pre-state.

The undo logic can vary from carrying out a simple notification to restoring some or all of the resources modified by the service. Another approach is to have the undo capability simply tag affected resources (such as an updated database record) with a marker that indicates its invalidation.

When redundant service capabilities are appended to a contract via Contract Denormalization (414), correspondingly redundant undo capabilities (that provide undo functionality at different levels of granularity) can also be added.

NOTE

When designing services as Web services and applying Orchestration (701), the WS-BPEL language provides a common means of defining compensating processes as part of the overall parent composition logic. For more information about WS-BPEL, visit SOASpecs.com and see Chapters 6 and 16 in *Service-Oriented Architecture: Concepts, Technology, and Design*.

Impacts

Because the nature and extent of compensating logic is left up to the designer, it can vary in quality and effectiveness. Creating a series of undo capabilities that perform little or no logic that actually undoes anything can lead to a false assumption that an exception was effectively handled, when in fact it wasn't. This is especially the case when composition designers are not allowed access to the underlying logic of composition member services and must therefore simply assume that undo capabilities provided by service contracts are handling failure conditions properly.

Additionally, for services that do perform a range of data or resource access functions, having to append the service contract with an undo capability for each existing capability that alters the service implementation state can bloat the service contract.

Relationships

Compensating Service Transaction shares several of the same relationships as Atomic Service Transaction (623) and also has its own relationship with that pattern as any one compensating transaction can encompass one or more individual atomic transactions.

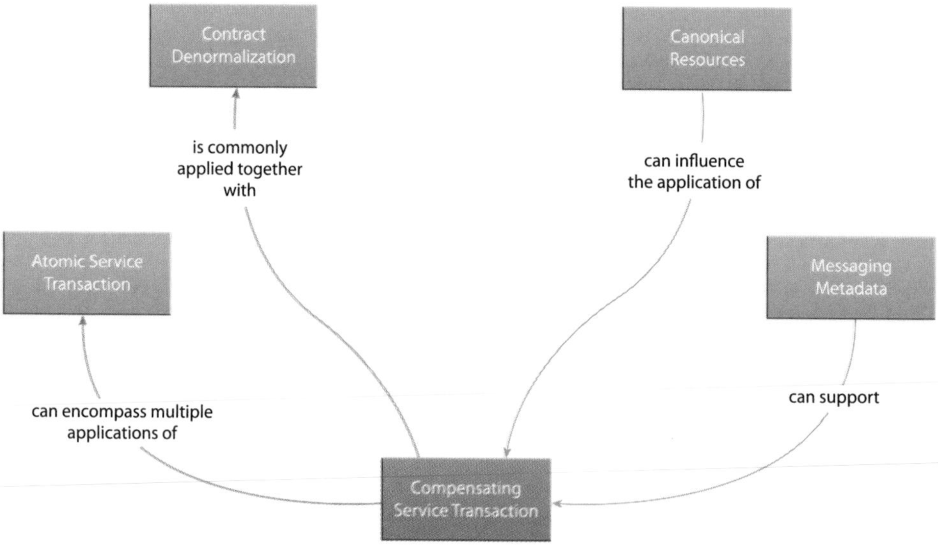

Figure 19.20

Compensating Service Transaction relates to several messaging and composition design patterns.

The ability to define and carry out compensation logic positions Compensating Service Transaction as a core part of Orchestration (701).

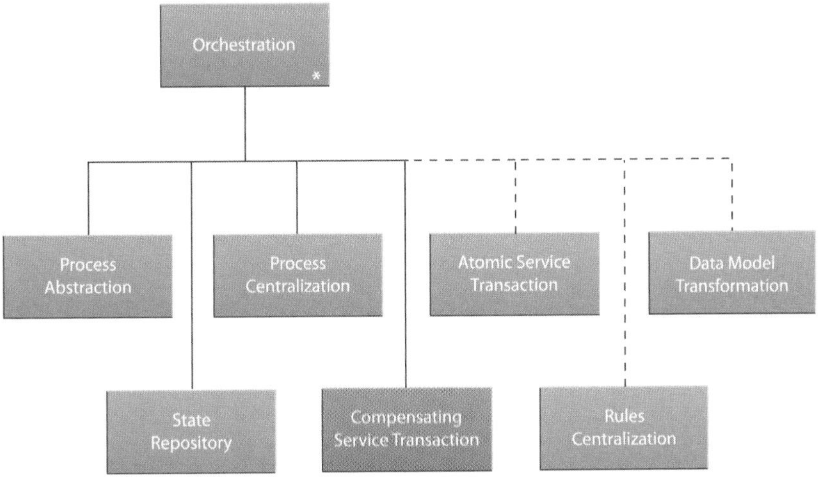

Figure 19.21
Compensating Service Transaction represents a key part of Orchestration (701).

CASE STUDY EXAMPLE

The Inventory Web service developed by Cutit establishes a central access point to their inventory management system, which governs three separate warehouses. This service contains a Transfer operation that allows a consumer to move stock from one warehouse to another. The stock in each warehouse is referred to as an individual inventory.

As shown in Example 19.2, the Transfer operation executes a WS-BPEL routine that carries out a tightly coupled transaction whereby the stock from one inventory (`removeInventory`) must be successfully moved to another (`stockToInventory`). Should the Transfer operation fail, the original state of the stock must be restored in both inventories.

```
<scope name="InventoryMgmt">
  <invoke name="RemoveInventory"
    partnerLink="InventorySystem"
    portType="ns1:InventoryService"
    operation="removeInventory"
    inputVariable="RemoveInventory_Input"
    outputVariable="RemoveInventory_Output"/>
```

```
  <invoke name="Invoke_StockToInventory"
    partnerLink="InventorySystem"
    portType="ns1:InventoryService"
    operation="stockToInventory"
    inputVariable="newStockInventory_Input"
    outputVariable="newStockInventory_Output"/>
</scope>
```

Example 19.2

This WS-BPEL routine carries out a transaction that must be committed if successful or rolled back in the event of a failure condition.

Transfers can require a great deal of runtime processing, especially when a single transfer consists of a bundle of numerous individual stock items. Due to the nature of the inventory management system API, the Transfer operation is required to repeatedly access the system to perform queries in relation to the source warehouse. It must then carry out another set of queries for the destination warehouse to ensure that there is room for the stock to be transferred. Finally, updates need to be performed, which again requires repeated access.

Throughout all of this interaction, the Inventory service further needs to lock inventory records until the transfer is completed. This has resulted in an unreasonable strain on the Inventory service and the underlying inventory management system, and has further affected other parts of the Cutit enterprise.

As a result, Cutit architects decide to change the functionality of the Transfer operation so that it carries out a compensating transaction. To implement this, the WS-BPEL code is redeveloped to incorporate a compensation handler designed to call an undo operation, as shown here:

```
<scope name="InventoryMgmt">
  <faultHandlers>
    <catch faultName="ns2:NoSpaceAvailableFault">
      <compensate name="Compensate_Withdraw"/>
    </catch>
  </faultHandlers>
  <sequence name="Sequence_1">
    <scope name="WithdrawInventory">
      <compensationHandler>
        <invoke name="undoWithdrawInventory"
          partnerLink="InventorySystem"
          portType="ns1:InventoryService"
          operation="undoWithdraInventory"
```

```
        inputVariable="undoWithdrawInventory_Input"
        outputVariable="undoWithdrawInventory_Output"/>
    </compensationHandler>
    <invoke name="RemoveInventory"
      partnerLink="InventorySystem"
      portType="ns1:InventoryService"
      operation="withdrawInventory"
      inputVariable="WithdrawInventory_Input"
      outputVariable="WithdrawInventory_Output"/>
  </scope>
  <invoke name="Invoke_StockToInventory"
    partnerLink="InventorySystem"
    portType="ns1:InventoryService"
    operation="stockInventory"
    inputVariable="newStockInventory_Input"
    outputVariable="newStockInventory_Output"/>
 </sequence>
</scope>
```

Example 19.3

A compensation routine that invokes an undo operation (highlighted) in the event that the StockToInventory call fails. The `catch` construct catches the fault condition and then invokes the undoWithdrawInventory operation.

Chapter 20

Service Interaction Security Patterns

Data Confidentiality

Data Origin Authentication

Direct Authentication

Brokered Authentication

When designing mission-critical enterprise solutions, which are often comprised of complex service compositions, services can be subjected to a variety of different usage scenarios, each of which can introduce unique security risks and requirements. Designing effective compositions therefore requires that services be prepared for a range of runtime interaction security challenges.

The upcoming Data Confidentiality (641) and Data Origin Authentication (649) patterns focus on applying security at the message level to protect sensitive message data from unintended exposure and tampering. Direct Authentication (656) and Brokered Authentication (661) establish security controls that enable services to verify that only intended consumers will gain access to sensitive message data.

NOTE

The simplified code fragments in the upcoming case study example sections highlight different security technologies that are not explained in this book. Specifically, code associated with the following standards is provided:

- WS-Security
- XML Encryption
- XML Signature
- SAML

To learn more about any of these specifications, visit www.soaspecs.com. For more formal and detailed examples of messages that incorporate encryption and digital signatures in particular, view Appendix D of the *WS-I Sample Application Security Architecture* document (which can also be accessed at SOASpecs.com).

Data Confidentiality

By Jason Hogg, Don Smith, Fred Chong, Tom Hollander, Wojtek Kozaczynski, Larry Brader, Nelly Delgado, Dwayne Taylor, Lonnie Wall, Paul Slater, Sajjad Nasir Imran, Pablo Cibraro, Ward Cunningham

How can data within a message be protected so that it is not disclosed to unintended recipients while in transit?

Problem	Within service compositions, data is often required to pass through one or more intermediaries. Point-to-point security protocols, such as those frequently used at the transport-layer, may allow messages containing sensitive information to be intercepted and viewed by such intermediaries.
Solution	The message contents are encrypted independently from the transport, ensuring that only intended recipients can access the protected data.
Application	A symmetric or asymmetric encryption and decryption algorithm, such as those specified in the XML-Encryption standard, is applied at the message level.
Impacts	This pattern may add runtime performance overhead associated with the required encryption and decryption of message data. The management of keys can further add to governance burden.
Principles	Service Composability
Architecture	Inventory, Composition, Service

Table 20.1
Profile summary for the Data Confidentiality pattern.

Problem

Message data can flow over insecure networks—either within an organization's inernal network or across public networks. A conventional approach is to protect message data at the transport layer by encrypting the connection between a service and its consumer through technologies such as SSL and TLS. These technologies provide point-to-point data protection that hides message data from eavesdroppers between two points in a network.

Transport layer security is effective for many point-to-point data exchanges because the services and consumers involved are pre-defined, and the risk of unwanted exposure to

sensitive data via nontrusted intermediaries tends to be low. However, when messages are exchanged as part of a composition or via message paths with various intermediaries, they can be exposed to the following threats for which point-to-point transport layer security does not provide protection:

- Agents and other services may be able to gain access to message data because while they are in possession of the message data, it is not encrypted.
- Sensitive data might be further vulnerable while temporarily persisted in a message queue, database, or file, and eavesdropper programs located along a network might be capable of gaining access to this data whenever it leaves a secure area (such as a protected memory space) or crosses a communication line that is not encrypted (such as a public network).

Figure 20.1 illustrates where data can be exposed along a message path.

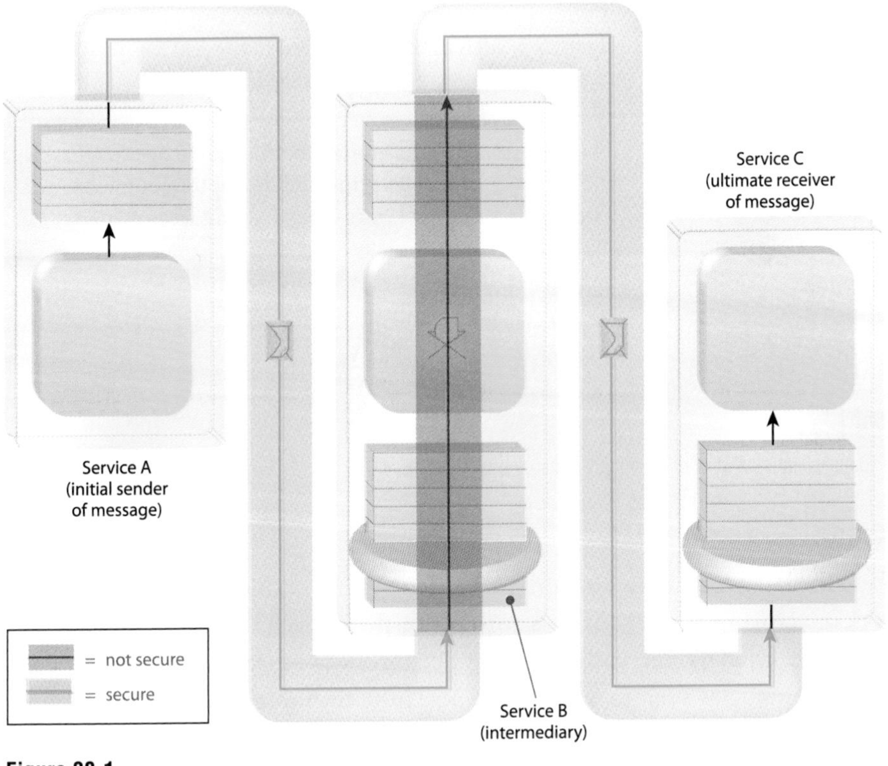

Figure 20.1

Point-to-point or transport layer security measures can only protect a message while in between service transmissions (green zone). It does not protect the message while in the service's possession (red zone).

Solution

To fully protect a message's contents, message layer encryption technologies are applied so that the security of the data is embedded and remains with the message and is only available to authorized recipients (Figure 20.2).

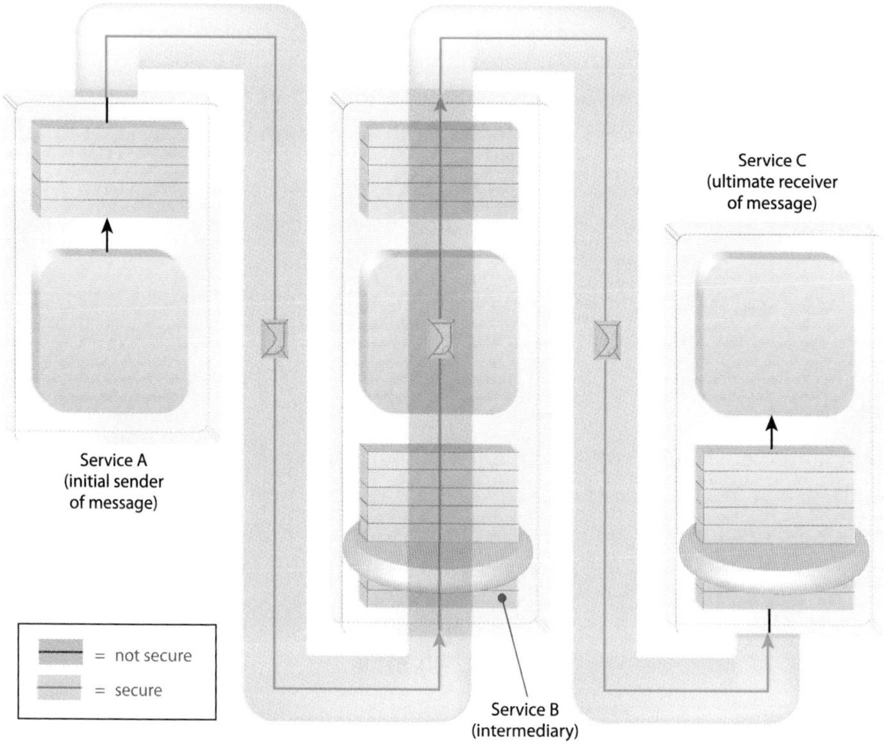

Figure 20.2

Data Confidentiality protects the message while in transit between services and while in the possession of unauthorized intermediaries.

Application

This design pattern is most commonly applied to Web services via the XML-Encryption technology referenced from within the WS-Security standard. XML-Encryption converts unencrypted message data, known as *plaintext*, into encrypted data called *ciphertext*. Plaintext data is encrypted with an algorithm and a cryptographic key. The resulting ciphertext is then converted back to plaintext by the intended message recipient who possesses a key that can decrypt the data.

There are two common types of cryptography that provide data confidentiality: *symmetric* and *asymmetric*. While both follow a similar process, each has its own unique characteristics.

With symmetric cryptography, the sender and recipient share a common key that is used to perform both encryption and decryption. Symmetric cryptography relies on a common secret key and a symmetric encryption algorithm, which transforms data between plaintext and ciphertext. With asymmetric cryptography (also known as public key cryptography), the sender encrypts data with one key, and the recipient uses a different key to decrypt the ciphertext. The encryption key and its matching decryption key are often referred to as a public/private key pair.

In cases where more than one message exchange occurs between a service and consumer, a "high-entropy" shared secret can be negotiated so that the first exchange includes a shared secret that is encrypted and based on the newly generated shared secret; additional message exchanges are performed symmetrically.

Impacts

Cryptographic operations are computationally intensive, which may have an impact on system resource usage. Also the task of managing and safeguarding encryption keys can introduce significant governance overhead depending on the quantity of keys used, the type of encryption chosen, and the overall key management infrastructure.

Furthermore, the security provided by Data Confidentiality is not absolute. Factors that need to be taken into account include the following:

- Encryption does not prevent data tampering. For example, attackers can still replace encrypted data bits in transit, which can cause the message recipient to decrypt the data to something other than the original plaintext. This vulnerability is addressed by Data Origin Authentication (649).

- If too much data is encrypted with the same symmetric key, an attacker can intercept several messages and attempt to cryptographically attack the encrypted messages with the goal of obtaining the symmetric key. To minimize this risk, session-based encryption keys with a relatively short life span are typically used.
- Much of the strength of symmetric encryption algorithms comes from the randomness of their encryption keys. If keys originate from a source that is not sufficiently random, attackers may narrow down the number of possible values for the encryption key.
- Asymmetric encryption requires more processing resources than symmetric encryption. For this reason, asymmetric encryption is usually optimized by adding a one-time, high-entropy symmetric key to encrypt a message and then asymmetrically encrypt the shared key. This reduces the size of the data that is asymmetrically encrypted, which also improves performance.
- Use of encryption algorithms that have not been subjected to rigorous review by trained cryptologists may contain undiscovered flaws that can be exploited by attackers. Therefore, well-known encryption algorithms that have withstood years of rigorous attacks and scrutiny should be used.
- Different countries may recognize different standards for data protection.

Relationships

Because the purpose of Data Confidentiality is to secure message contents, it relates directly to Service Messaging (533) and also Messaging Metadata (538), as encryption can be applied to message headers in addition to the message body content. For example, security credentials, as used by Direct Authentication (656) and Brokered Authentication (661), are often stored in message headers and can therefore be protected via encryption.

This pattern is often combined with Data Origin Authentication (649) to realize complete message layer security so that intermediary processing layers, such as those established by Service Agent (543), cannot be used to gain unauthorized access to message data.

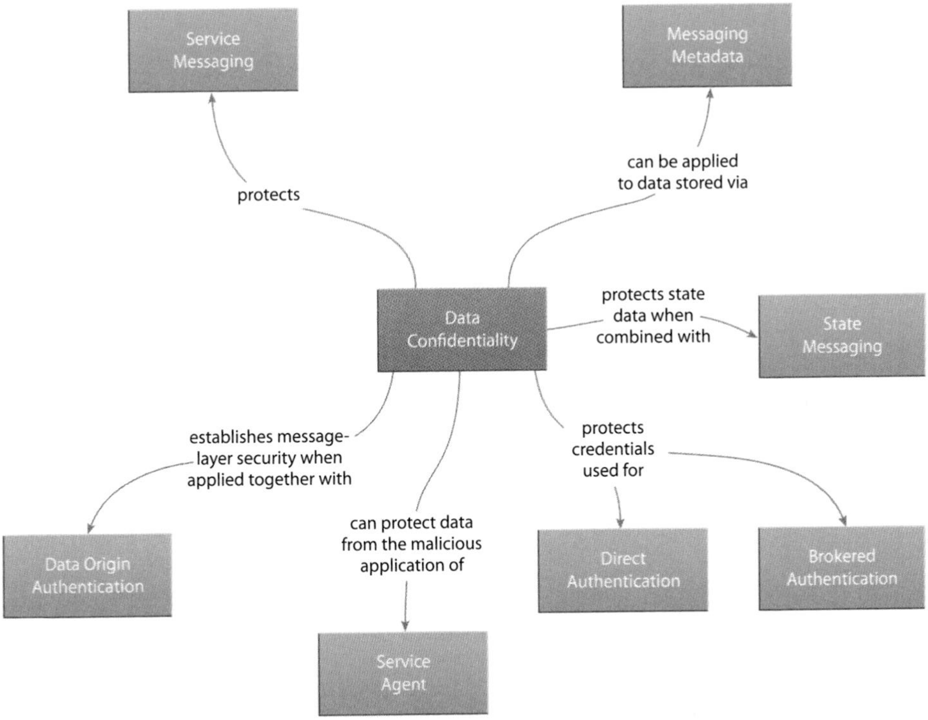

Figure 20.3
Data Confidentiality combines messaging and security considerations.

CASE STUDY EXAMPLE

Every company involved with the forestry industry must be registered with the FRC. They are required to pay annual dues to remain in good standing and may also be forced to pay penalties as a result of policy violations.

The processing of payments can be regularly made online via a set of exposed Web services that can issue invoices, collect the payment transfer, and then confirm payments via electronic receipts. To interface with these externally facing services, organizations have the choice of submitting SOAP messages with plaintext or WS-Security-based content. The transmission channel between the organization and the FRC is encrypted via standard SSL.

Cutit Saws does not initially see the value in taking the time to outfit their payment messages with special message layer security. They only issue payments once a year and

have never been fined for any policy violations. They therefore simply send a plaintext message, as follows:

```
<Envelope xmlns="http://schemas.xmlsoap.org/soap/envelope/" ...>
  <Body>
    <frc:Payment>
      <frc:InvoiceNumber>
        738345
      </frc:InvoiceNumber>
      <frc:Amount>
        $137.14
      </frc:Amount>
      <frc:Date>
        02.06.08
      </frc:Date>
    </frc:Payment>
  </Body>
</Envelope>
```

Example 20.1

A sample SOAP message with no encryption.

Alleywood, on the other hand, has become accustomed to being fined for policy violations on a regular basis. They are therefore required to issue payments to the FRC on a monthly basis.

The service consumer built by Alleywood to interact with the FRC Payment service is fully enabled to leverage their existing Web services security infrastructure. Example 20.2 shows a sample message sent from Alleywood to which Data Confidentially has been applied:

```
<Envelope xmlns="http://schemas.xmlsoap.org/soap/envelope/" ...>
  <Body>
    <xenc:EncryptedData xmlns="..." Type="...">
      <xenc:EncryptionMethod Algorithm=
        "http://www.w3.org/2001/04/xmlenc#aes128-cbc"/>
        <xenc:CipherData>
          <xenc:CipherValue>
            08FJF0239J
          </xenc:CipherValue>
        </xenc:CipherData>
      </xenc:EncryptionMethod>
```

```
    </xenc:EncryptedData>
  </Body>
</Envelope>
```

Example 20.2

A SOAP message with message layer encryption.

As shown in Figure 20.4, the FRC Payment service exposes separate operations for plain and encrypted messages. In either case, the service ensures that the payment values within the message body are encrypted before the message is further routed throughout the extensive FRC enterprise.

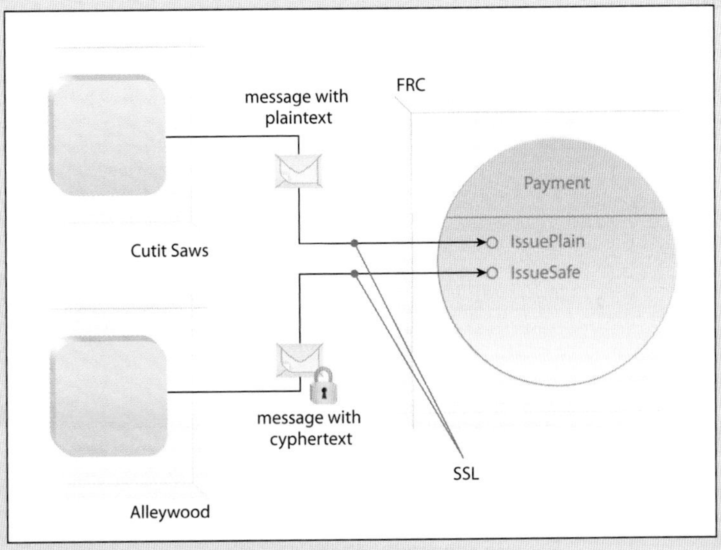

Figure 20.4

The transport channels between the FRC Payment service and external service consumer programs are encrypted via SSL, regardless of whether the messages themselves provide further message layer encryption.

Data Origin Authentication

By Jason Hogg, Don Smith, Fred Chong, Tom Hollander, Wojtek Kozaczynski, Larry Brader, Nelly Delgado, Dwayne Taylor, Lonnie Wall, Paul Slater, Sajjad Nasir Imran, Pablo Cibraro, Ward Cunningham

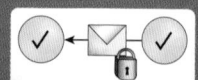

How can a service verify that a message originates from a known sender and that the message has not been tampered with in transit?

Problem	The intermediary processing layers generally required by service compositions can expose sensitive data when security is limited to point-to-point protocols, such as those used with transport-layer security.
Solution	A message can be digitally signed so that the recipient services can verify that it originated from the expected consumer and that it has not been tampered with during transit.
Application	A digital signature algorithm is applied to the message to provide "proof of origin," allowing sensitive message contents to be protected from tampering. This technology must be supported by both consumer and service.
Impacts	Use of cryptographic techniques can add to performance requirements and the choice of digital signing algorithm can affect the level of security actually achieved.
Principles	Service Composability
Architecture	Composition

Table 20.2
Profile summary for the Data Origin Authentication pattern.

Problem

A message sent by a consumer to a service may need to be processed by one or more intermediaries (routers, firewalls, message queues, and so on). The data contained in the message will ultimately influence the behavior of the service after it is received.

There is a risk that an attacker could manipulate messages in transit in order to maliciously alter service behavior (Figure 20.5). Message manipulation can take the form of data modification within the message or even the substitution of credentials that change the message's apparent origin, thereby allowing an attacker to impersonate a legitimate consumer.

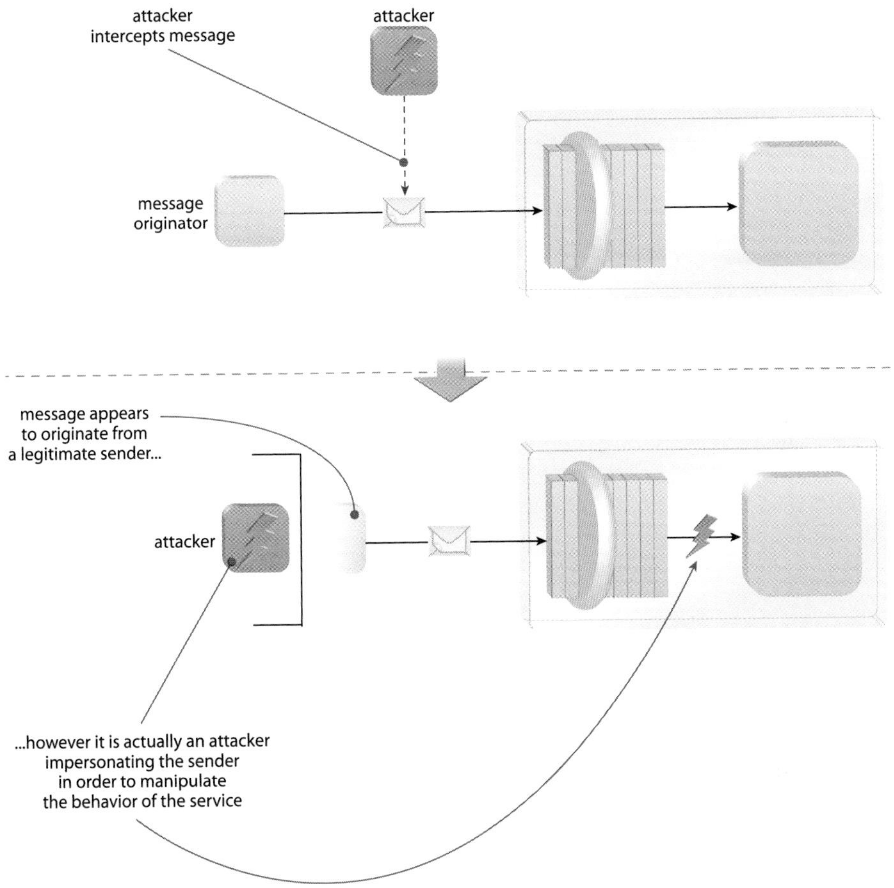

Figure 20.5

An attacker can design or modify an intermediary such that it intercepts a message in order to forward harmful data to a service that views it as a legitimate consumer.

Solution

Digital signature technology is used to enable message recipients to verify that messages have not been tampered with in transit and that they originate from a trusted sender (Figure 20.6).

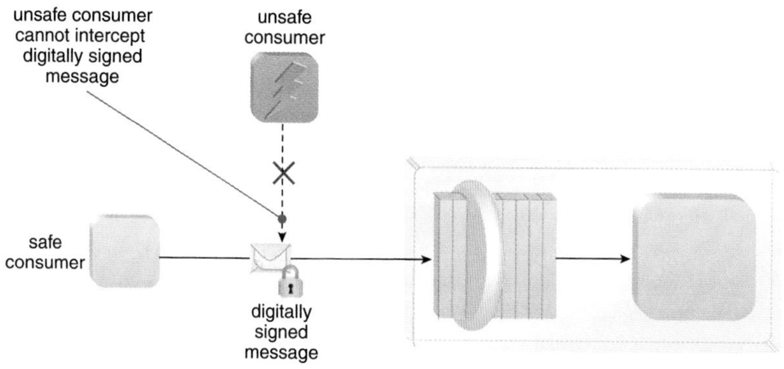

Figure 20.6

In this scenario, the attacker could be attempting to take a valid message and substitute someone else's credentials thereby impersonating the other party, or perhaps the attacker is trying to modify an existing message to the behavior of the service. Either way, when a message is digitally signed, the service can verify the message origin and reject the message if its origin is deemed invalid.

Application

Data Origin Authentication within Web services is typically applied via an XML signature technology from within WS-Security, which enables the recipient of a message to verify that:

- the message has not been altered while in transit (referred to as the message's *data integrity*)
- the message originated from the expected sender (known as the message's *authenticity*)

As with Data Confidentiality (641), this pattern can also be applied with *symmetric* and *asymmetric* variations. Only instead of cryptography, the application of this pattern results in symmetric or asymmetric signatures.

A symmetric signature, commonly known as a Message Authentication Code (MAC), is created by using a shared secret to sign and verify the message. MACs are generated by taking as input a checksum based on the message content and a shared secret. Each MAC can be verified only by a message recipient that has both the shared secret and the original message content that was used to create the MAC.

The most common type of MAC used in Web services is the Hashed Message Authentication Code (HMAC), an algorithm that uses a shared secret and a hashing algorithm to create the signature that is then embedded into the message. The recipient verifies this signature by using the shared secret and the message content to recreate the HMAC and by comparing it to the actual HMAC that was sent in the message.

Asymmetric signatures, on the other hand, are processed with two different keys: One (the private key) is used for creating the signature and another (the public key) for verifying it. These keys are related and are commonly referred to as a *public/private key pair*. The public key is generally distributed with the message, whereas the private key is kept secret by the owner (and is never sent in a message). A signature that is created and verified with an asymmetric public/private key pair is referred to as a *digital signature*.

For both signing and encryption purposes, asymmetric keys are often managed through a Public Key Infrastructure (PKI). Information that describes the consumer is bound to its public key through endorsement from a trusted party to form a certificate that allows a message recipient to verify the private key in a received message signature to the public key in the sender's certificate.

NOTE

The XML-Signature technology can be used to provide symmetric or asymmetric algorithms to SOAP message content. Additional digital signature technologies are available that explicitly use an asymmetric algorithm. These technologies may or may not be part of a SOAP message security architecture.

XML-Signature is part of the WS-Security framework. For more information, visit SOASpecs.com.

It is also worth noting that asymmetric digital signatures can be used to support requirements for non-repudiation. This is because access to the private key is usually restricted to the owner of the key, which makes it easier to verify proof-of-ownership, a value that a client presents to demonstrate knowledge of either a shared secret or a private key to support client authentication. In cases where the consumer denies having performed the action, digital signatures can provide evidence to the contrary. Although digital signatures can help prove non-repudiation, their use may not be sufficient to provide actual legal proof.

Symmetric signatures, on the other hand, cannot support non-repudiation because shared secrets are known by multiple parties. This makes it more difficult to prove that a specific party used the shared secret to sign the message.

Impacts

This pattern shares similar impacts as Data Confidentiality (641) because it too utilizes keys and is subject to the same performance and governance related consequences and also the same types of security risks.

Relationships

Because of its close relationship with achieving message layer security, Data Origin Authentication has almost the identical set of relationships as Data Confidentiality (641).

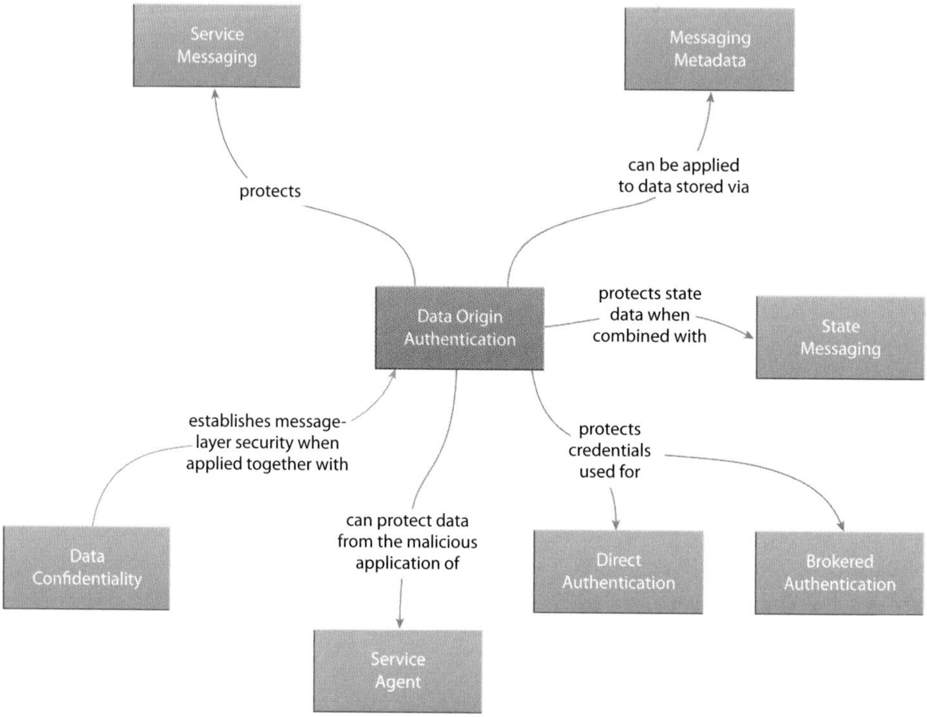

Figure 20.7

As with Data Confidentiality (641), this pattern is focused on applying security to the message and therefore shares the same pattern relationships.

CASE STUDY EXAMPLE

A couple of weeks after the FRC Payment service (introduced in the Data Confidentiality (641) example) went live, an FRC administrator performing a routine review of system logs notices something unusual. For the past three days, the Payment service has periodically redirected messages received from external organizations to an internal dead letter queue even though no exceptions seem to have triggered this. Upon further investigation, the administrator locates the redirected messages and notices that they do not contain valid payment submissions. Instead, they are populated with cryptic content that can't be deciphered by humans.

The administrator immediately calls in the head of FRC's security department. Subsequent to an emergency review, the security manager orders the Payment service shut down. Following some further analysis by the security team, it appears as though the Payment service has been subjected to periodic attacks by Cutit Saws. The Cutit IT manager is quickly contacted, and after some further joint analysis, it is discovered that although the messages indicate that they originated from Cutit Saws, they were, in fact, sent by an malicious consumer program that was impersonating the Cutit consumer. Because Cutit has been sending their messages in plaintext, they had been easily intercepted and modified.

This revelation leads to a new policy that is brought into effect within the next week requiring that all external organizations digitally sign their messages when accessing the Payment service. The Cutit team that was originally hesitant to invest in building security into their message transmissions is now happy to comply, still feeling a bit shook up by this security breach.

Cutit applies Data Origin Authentication, enabling the FRC Payment service to verify the origin of their messages. Should an attacker now try to modify message contents, the manipulations will be detected and the messages rejected.

The following example provides some insight into the new SOAP header that is added to Cutit messages:

```
<Envelope xmlns="http://schemas.xmlsoap.org/soap/envelope/" ...>
  <Header>
    <wsse:Security>
       <ds:Signature Id="23rml23r0"
        xmlns="http://www.w3.org/2000/09/xmldsig#">
        <ds:SignedInfo>
          <ds:CanonicalizationMethod Algorithm=
            "http://www.w3.org/TR/2001/
              REC-xml-c14n-20010315"/>
            <ds:SignatureMethod Algorithm=
              "http://www.w3.org/2000/09/
              xmldsig#dsa-sha1"/>
            <ds:Reference
              URI="http://www.w3.org/TR/2000/
              REC-xhtml1-20000126/">
            <ds:DigestMethod Algorithm=
              "http://www.w3.org/2000/09/xmldsig#sha1"/>
            <ds:DigestValue>
              83KFHFR923JLS9
```

```
          </ds:DigestValue>
        </ds:Reference>
      </ds:SignedInfo>
      <ds:SignatureValue>
        KVMV034045IGKF-R
      </ds:SignatureValue>
      <ds:KeyInfo>
        ...
      </ds:KeyInfo>
    </ds:Signature>
  </wsse:Security>
 </Header>
 ...
</Envelope>
```

Example 20.3

The FRC now requires that all external organizations issue digitally signed messages when issuing payment data. This example provides a snippet of a SOAP header containing a digital signature.

Direct Authentication

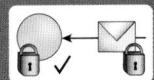

By Jason Hogg, Don Smith, Fred Chong, Tom Hollander, Wojtek Kozaczynski, Larry Brader, Nelly Delgado, Dwayne Taylor, Lonnie Wall, Paul Slater, Sajjad Nasir Imran, Pablo Cibraro, Ward Cunningham

How can a service verify the credentials provided by a consumer?

Problem	Some of the capabilities offered by a service may be intended for specific groups of consumers or may involve the transmission of sensitive data. Attackers that access this data could use it to compromise the service or the IT enterprise itself.
Solution	Service capabilities require that consumers provide credentials that can be authenticated against an identity store.
Application	The service implementation is provided access to an identity store, allowing it to authenticate the consumer directly.
Impacts	Consumers must provide credentials compatible with the service's authentication logic. This pattern may lead to multiple identity stores, resulting in extra governance burden.
Principles	Service Composability
Architecture	Composition, Service

Table 20.3
Profile summary for the Direct Authentication pattern.

Problem

Services are commonly required to handle sensitive or private data that cannot be made available to all potential consumer programs. Furthermore, certain service capabilities may carry out internal processing that should only be triggered by certain types of consumers. Making these capabilities openly available to any consumer will jeopardize the security of the service and any resources it may access or have access to (Figure 20.8).

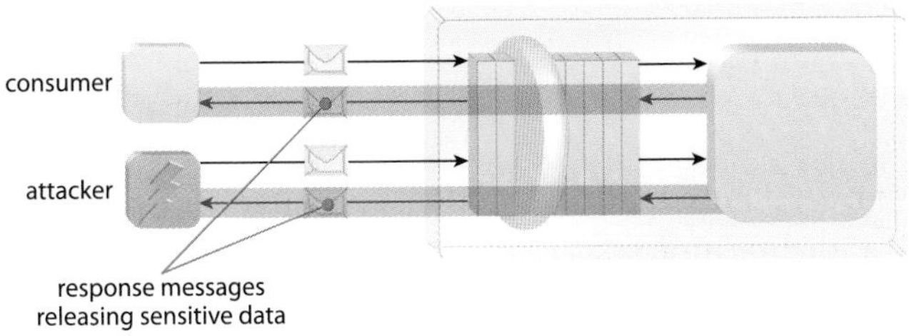

Figure 20.8
When a service is openly accessible, intended consumers and attackers can gain access to potentially sensitive data and logic.

Solution

The service requires the consumer to present credentials for authentication so that additional controls, such as authorization and auditing, can be implemented. The credentials that the consumer presents to the service must include a unique identifier and a shared secret in order for the service to perform authentication. An example of a unique identifier is a username and a shared secret can be a password or a password alternative.

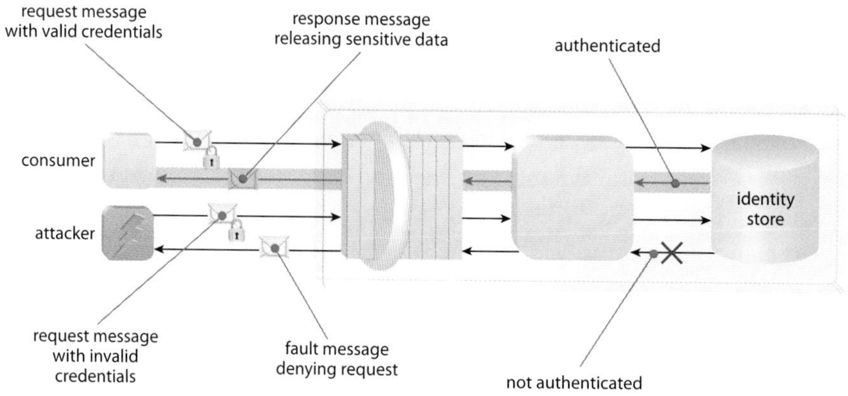

Figure 20.9

By having the service authenticate consumer requests against an identity store, only safe consumers can access sensitive data and logic.

Application

With Direct Authentication, the service is designed to take "direct" responsibility for authentication. As depicted in Figure 20.9, the application of this pattern usually results in a process whereby the service consumer accesses the service and provides credentials that are then authenticated by the service via an identity store that holds the credentials of valid consumers for a particular identity domain. The service verifies that the credentials represent a unique consumer and that it has established "proof-of-possession" of a shared secret. If authentication is successful, the requested data is sent to the consumer, and if not, a fault message is sent to the consumer.

Note that proof-of-possession can be established by the consumer when it provides the actual shared secret to the service or by supplying a password equivalent. One common

password equivalent is a password created using a keyed-hash message authentication (HMAC) function, which uses a checksum calculated from the message and the shared secret in order to generate a password alternative. In order for the service to verify the integrity and authenticity of the message, it retrieves the user's password from the identity store, calculates the checksum of the message, and then uses the HMAC function to recreate the password alternative. If it matches that provided by the consumer, then both the integrity and authenticity of the message has been verified. For the service to authenticate credentials, it must have direct access to the identity store, including appropriate permissions for accessing identity information.

The data stores required by this pattern can be centralized or decentralized. The former model establishes a remote store that is shared by multiple services. This can lead to runtime latency and behavioral fluctuations, depending on usage volume. A decentralized model enables some or all services to own their own individual identity stores. Although this increases autonomy, it can add to the governance burden of keeping multiple identity stores constantly synchronized.

Impacts

Consumers and services must trust each other to manage keys securely. If either mismanage the keys, the service can be repeatedly and unknowingly attacked.

A benefit to Direct Authentication is that if the shared secret is compromised, then only the relationship between one service composition and one consumer is jeopardized. Other compositions using alternative identity stores may not be affected as long as each consumer retains unique credentials. However, because Direct Authentication on its own does not provide single sign-on functionality, consumers will often need to be repeatedly authenticated across services within a service composition. Although this can be avoided by caching the consumer password, it is still not recommended.

Additionally, a malicious consumer can attempt to impersonate a safe consumer by intercepting the transmission of the shared secret. It therefore is advisable that the transport of messages containing credentials be secured.

Also at risk is the identity store itself. Comprehensive security measures must be applied to ensure that its collection of passwords is not breached. This is especially a concern when regular database products are customized to act as repositories for security credentials.

Relationships

As explained in the *Relationships* sections for Data Confidentially (641) and Data Origin Authentication (649), messages that are exchanged with security credentials can be protected by message layer security controls. These credentials are used to support Direct Authentication.

This pattern relies on the cross-service standardization achieved by Canonical Resources (237) so that composed services that authenticate each other use a common security architecture. In this type of environment, Direct Authentication is usually chosen over Brokered Authentication (661).

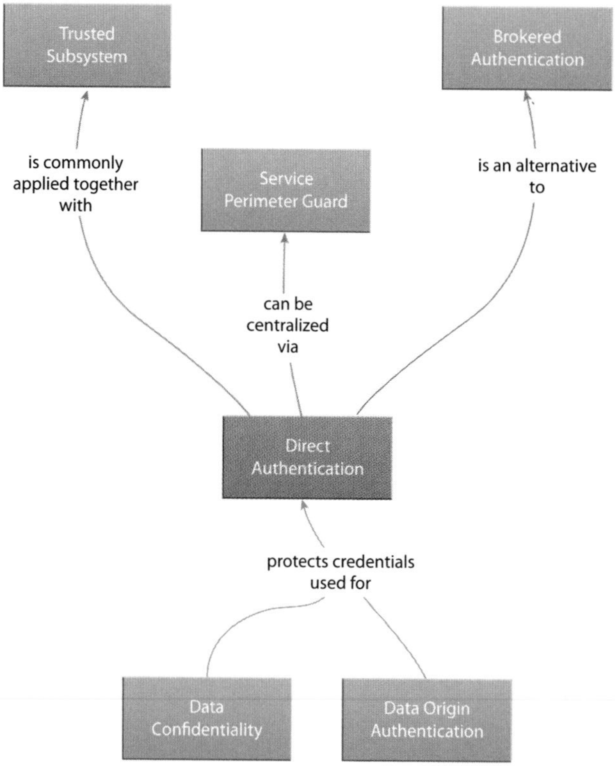

Figure 20.10

Direct Authentication is commonly applied together with other security patterns.

CASE STUDY EXAMPLE

For the previously introduced FRC Payment service to forward messages to their next, destinations, the service needs to supplement them with security credentials for internal authentication. The WS-Security framework has been standardized within the FRC environment and is used for this purpose.

The following simplified example shows a message extract containing metadata in the `Header` construct that expresses authentication credentials:

```
<Envelope xmlns="http://schemas.xmlsoap.org/soap/envelope/" ...>
  <Header>
    <wsse:Security>
      <wsse:UsernameToken>
        <wsse:Username>
          sam009ev
        </wsse:Username>
        <wsse:Password Type="wsse:PasswordDigest">
          idkxm203984lsdf
        </wsse:Password>
      </wsse:UsernameToken>
    </wsse:Security>
  </Header>
  <Body>
    ...
  </Body>
</Envelope>
```

Example 20.4

The FRC uses WS-Security metadata in headers for the internal transmission of security credentials via SOAP messages.

Brokered Authentication

By Jason Hogg, Don Smith, Fred Chong, Tom Hollander, Wojtek Kozaczynski, Larry Brader, Nelly Delgado, Dwayne Taylor, Lonnie Wall, Paul Slater, Sajjad Nasir Imran, Pablo Cibraro, Ward Cunningham

How can a service efficiently verify consumer credentials if the consumer and service do not trust each other or if the consumer requires access to multiple services?

Problem	Requiring the use of Direct Authentication (656) can be impractical or even impossible when consumers and services do not trust each other or when consumers are required to access multiple services as part of the same runtime activity.
Solution	An authentication broker with a centralized identity store assumes the responsibility for authenticating the consumer and issuing a token that the consumer can use to access the service.
Application	An authentication broker product introduced into the inventory architecture carries out the intermediary authentication and issuance of temporary credentials using technologies such as X.509 certificates or Kerberos, SAML, or SecPAL tokens.
Impacts	This pattern can establish a potential single point of failure and a central breach point that, if compromised, could jeopardize an entire service inventory.
Principles	Service Composability
Architecture	Inventory, Composition, Service

Table 20.4

Profile summary for the Brokered Authentication pattern.

Problem

Services can have a wide variety of consumers, many of which will be unknown when the service is first designed (Figure 20.11). Establishing trust directly between a consumer and service, as per Direct Authentication (656), often requires out-of-band communication that can hinder consumers and services from interacting dynamically.

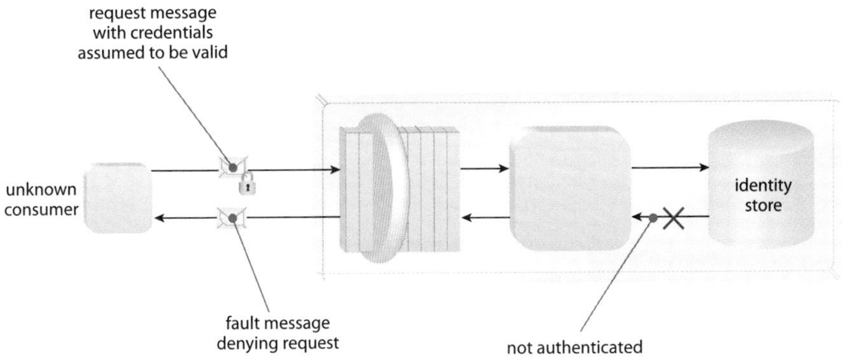

Figure 20.11
A consumer attempts to access a service with credentials that turn out to be incorrect.

Furthermore, even when Direct Authentication (656) is successfully applied, if a given consumer requires access to numerous services as part of the same runtime service activity, it may be asked to provide separate credentials for each service (Figure 20.12). In this case, the consumer may need to cache credentials for use with additional runtime activities, which may result in the consumer having to persist a password temporarily, which introduces additional security threats.

Solution

An authentication broker is added as an architectural extension capable of validating consumer credentials without the need for consumers to have direct relationships with the services they need to access. Both consumers and services trust the authentication broker, allowing it to become a centralized authentication and credential issuing mechanism within the overall inventory architecture (see Figure 20.13).

This centralized security platform can simplify the development of individual services and can further reduce the governance burden associated with identity management.

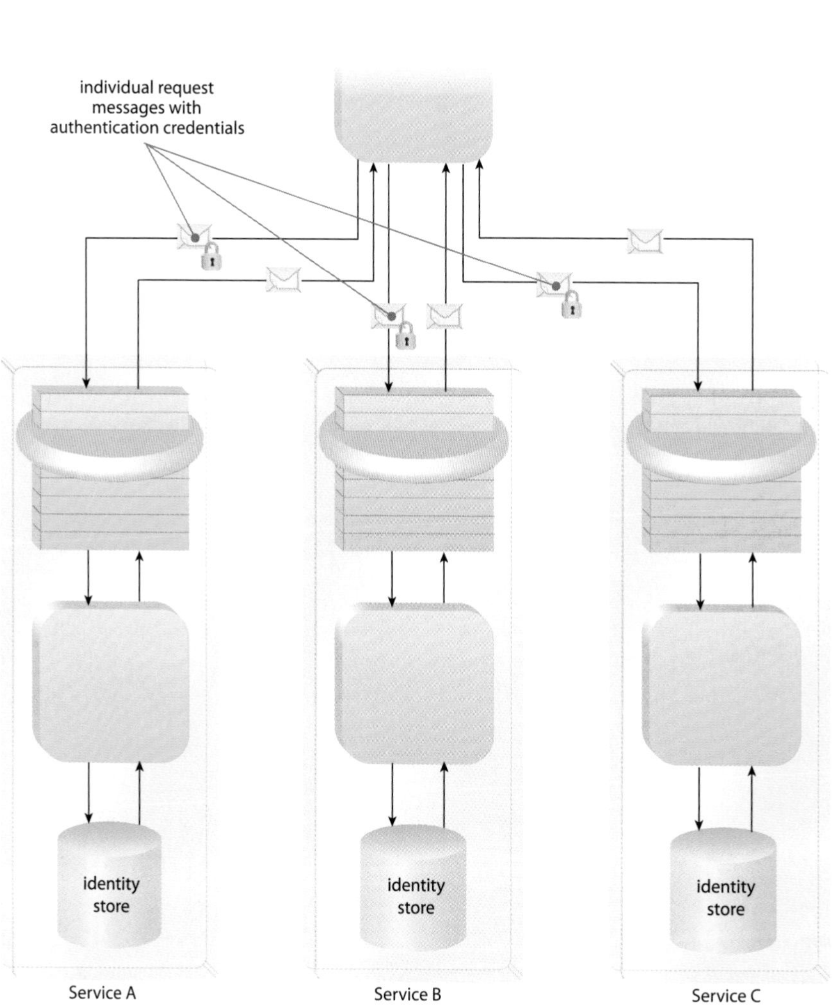

Figure 20.12

Using Direct Authentication (656), a consumer is forced to send credentials to and get authenticated by each service it composes.

Application

This pattern is generally applied by the deployment of an authentication broker product or platform. The internal architectures of these products can vary in how they carry out the broker functions. However, for the most part, they follow the process illustrated in Figure 20.13 (note the use of the small lock symbol that represents a token).

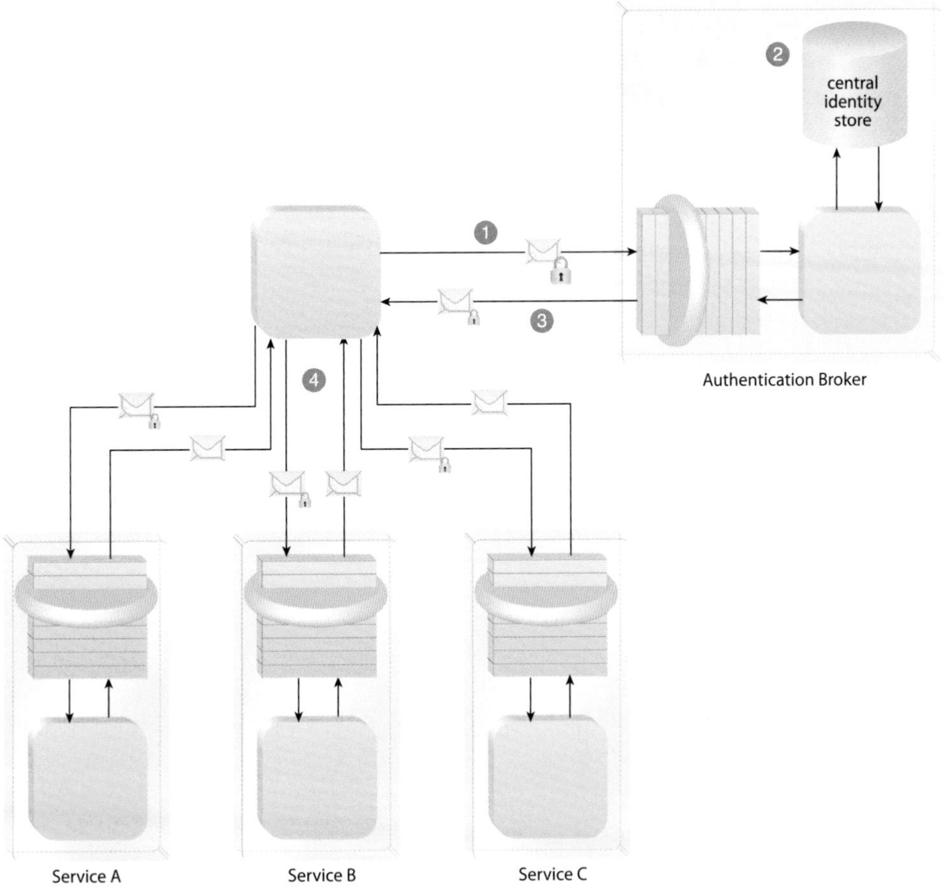

Figure 20.13

The consumer submits a request with credentials to the authentication broker (1), which the broker authenticates against a central identity store (2). The broker then responds with a token (3) that the consumer can use to access Services A, B, and C (4), none of which require their own identity store.

Figure 20.13 demonstrates how authentication brokers can be capable of issuing tokens to consumers that are used for future interactions. For example, if the consumer requests access to a specific service, the broker can issue a token to an authorized consumer that is specifically scoped for that service, potentially allowing the consumer to repeatedly interact with the service using the same token issued by the broker.

There are a variety of security technologies associated with authentication brokers:

- the X.509 PKI infrastructure that uses a Certificate Authority for signing and issuing X.509 certificates

- the Kerberos protocol, which uses an Authentication service and a Ticket Granting service for issuing Kerberos tickets
- the WS-Trust specification, which describes a protocol used by Security Token Services (STS) for issuing tokens such as SAML and SecPAL

Claims held in security tokens can contain sensitive data and must therefore be protected in transit via Data Confidentiality (641) or the use of a transport-layer security, such as SSL. Security tokens must be signed by the issuing authentication broker. If they are not, their integrity cannot be verified, which could result in attackers trying to issue false tokens. Furthermore, without the security token being signed, there would be no way for a service to verify that the token was issued by a trusted authentication broker.

Note also that trust relationships can be established between different authentication brokers. In other words, one broker can issue security tokens that are used across organizational boundaries and autonomous security domains, each of which can have their own broker.

Impacts

The centralized trust model that Brokered Authentication uses could create a single point of failure. Some types of authentication brokers, such as the Kerberos Key Distribution Center (KDC), must be constantly online and available to issue security tokens to consumers. Should such an authentication broker become unavailable at any point, it could cripple service communication. This can be mitigated somewhat via Redundant Implementation (345) or by implementing backup authentication brokers.

Additional tradeoffs associated with the validity periods of issued tokens also need to be considered. For example, the Kerberos protocol typically issues tokens for eight hours, whereas X.509 certificates will often be issued for much longer validity periods (often around a year), in which case sophisticated revocation systems, such as those provided by Certificate Revocation Lists (CRLs) and the Online Certificate Status Protocol (OCSP), are required.

Furthermore, should an authentication broker ever be compromised, attackers may gain access to confidential identify information or even the ability to falsely issue security tokens, enabling them to gain access to and perform malicious activities against many services.

Relationships

Brokered Authentication is an alternative to Direct Authentication (656) but shares most of the same pattern relationships. The broker functionality provided by this pattern is often conveniently centralized via Service Perimeter Guard (394).

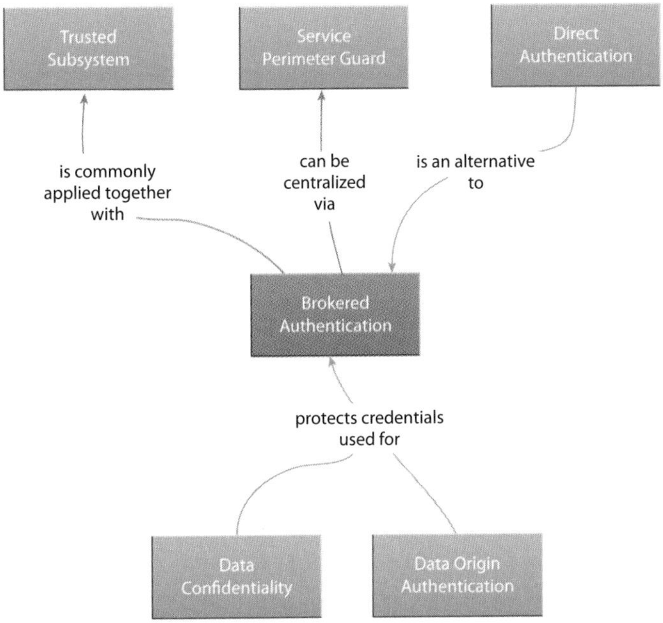

Figure 20.14

Brokered Authentication shares the same relationships as Direct Authentication (656) but is also commonly applied together with Service Perimeter Guard (394).

CASE STUDY EXAMPLE

The FRC Payment service explained in the preceding examples is required to forward collected payment information to the following four services:

- Audit service
- Logging service
- Accounts Receivable service
- Notification service

The first three require that the Payment service (acting as the consumer) be authenticated. The initial Direct Authentication (656) design FRC architects used required that each of these three services separately authenticate the Payment service. After a while, it became evident that a few issues made this architecture unacceptable:

- Due to governance reasons, each service ended up with its own identity store.

- It became increasingly difficult to keep the identity stores in synch.
- Runtime latency was introduced as a result of having to repeatedly re-authenticate a consumer multiple times.

After explaining these issues in a business case for their manager, the FRC architects gained funding for the purchase of an authentication broker.

This product uses a Security Token Service (STS) in its perimeter network that serves the purpose of authenticating users from remote consumer locations, and then uses a SAML token signed by the STS. The issuance of these tokens is managed automatically through trust policies that specify the services supported by the broker. The broker is further configured to require that the Payment service authenticate to the STS using X.509 certificates issued by a separate Certificate Authority (CA). The trust policies on the STS specify which CAs are allowed to issue certificates and attributes from certificates that should be mapped from the certificate to the SAML token that is issued.

The following example shows a snippet of the SAML code used in a token:

```
<Envelope xmlns="http://schemas.xmlsoap.org/soap/envelope/" ...>
  <Header>
    <wsse:Security>
      <saml:Assertion ...>
      <saml:Conditions ...>
      <saml:AuthorizationDecisionStatement>
        <saml:Actions>
          ...
          <saml:Action>
            Access Audit
          </saml:Action>
        </saml:Actions>
        ...
      </saml:AuthorizationDecisionStatement>
    </wsse:Security>
  </Header>
  <Body>
    ...
  </Body>
</Envelope>
```

Example 20.5

A SOAP message containing a SAML token.

Chapter 21

Transformation Patterns

When introducing service-oriented architectures into legacy environments or when delivering services via bottom-up approaches, it is not uncommon to encounter interoperability challenges that can only be overcome by programs with brokerage features.

These three common patterns have been part of integration architectures for many years and continue to be valuable and even essential in modern-day SOA implementations. Each addresses an aspect of data exchange:

- *Communications Protocol* – Software programs can be built to communicate with different technologies or different versions of the same technology. Either way, when disparity between wire-level protocols exist, some form of intermediary program is required to "bridge" these differences.
- *Data Format* – Even if the underlying communications protocol is compatible, two programs that need to exchange data may offer this data via different character sets, file formats, or data formats (such as XML and CSV). For this, an additional type of intermediary processing logic is required to convert one format to the other.
- *Data Model* – Even when the communications protocol and data formats are compatible, for software programs to exchange any form of structured data (such as business documents), the definition of the model that the data structure is based on (the data model) can be different at transmitting and receiving ends. This leads to a requirement for the runtime transformation of information from one data model into another.

Protocol Bridging (687), Data Format Transformation (681), and Data Model Transformation (671) respectively address these three interoperability obstacles. Although their methods are well-established and proven, the required use of these patterns can indicate an inability to achieve the standardization required to realize service-orientation to its full extent within a given environment.

Each pattern introduces a layer of intermediary processing that has similar impacts on performance, design complexity, and development effort. The overuse of these patterns is therefore considered an anti-pattern.

Data Model Transformation

How can services interoperate when using different data models for the same type of data?

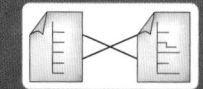

Problem	Services may use incompatible schemas to represent the same data, hindering service interaction and composition.
Solution	A data transformation technology can be incorporated to convert data between disparate schema structures.
Application	Mapping logic needs to be developed and deployed so that data compliant to one data model can be dynamically converted to comply to a different data model.
Impacts	Data model transformation introduces development effort, design complexity, and runtime performance overhead, and overuse of this pattern can seriously inhibit service recomposition potential.
Principles	Standardized Service Contract, Service Reusability, Service Composability
Architecture	Inventory, Composition

Table 21.1
Profile summary for the Data Model Transformation pattern.

Problem

For any service-enabled part of an enterprise where Canonical Schema (158) has not been successfully applied, services delivered as part of different projects run a high risk of representing similar data using different schemas (Figure 21.1).

This will typically not affect immediate service implementations, as the schemas may very well have been standardized across the initial solution or composition. However, when these same services need to be recomposed, schema incompatibilities can impose significant interoperability challenges.

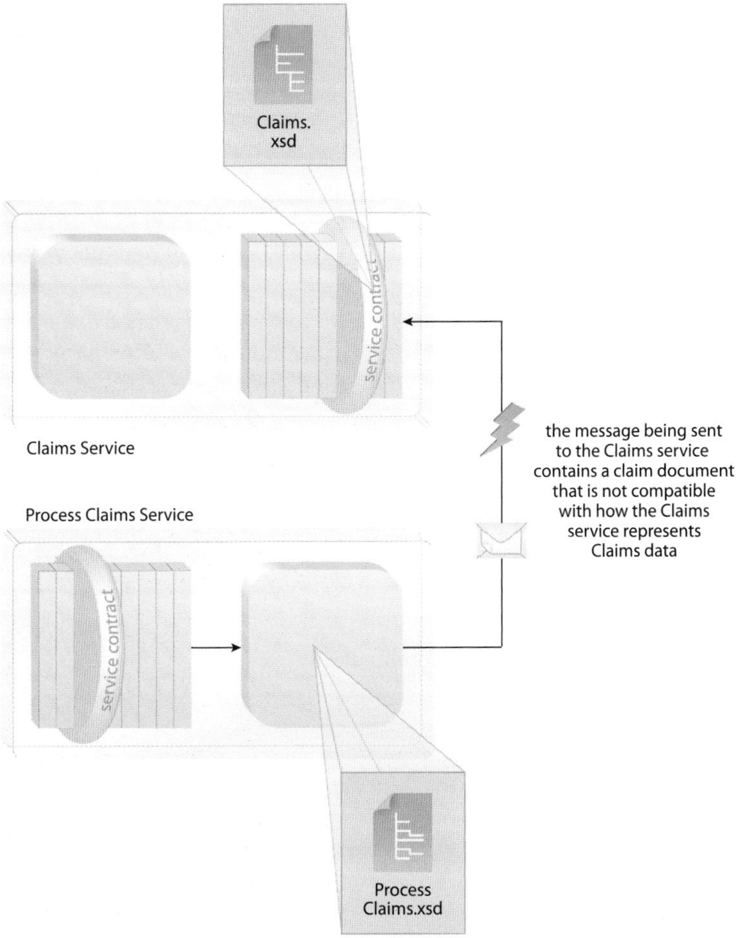

Figure 21.1

The Process Claims service represents a claim record using a different schema than the one required by the Claims service contract. This incompatibility prevents the cross-service exchange of a claims document.

Solution

Data model transformation logic can be introduced to carry out the runtime conversion of data, so that data complying to one data model can be restructured to comply to a different data model (Figure 21.2). This extends a non-standardized messaging framework, enabling it to dynamically overcome disparity between the schemas used by a service contract and messages transmitted to that contract.

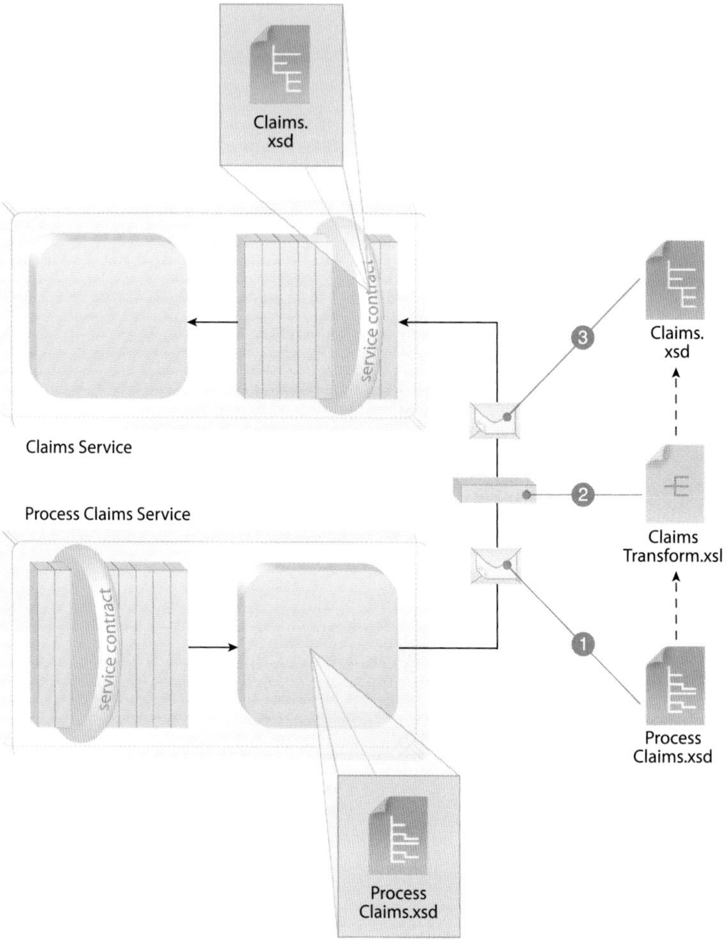

Figure 21.2

An XSLT style sheet containing data model mapping logic (2) is added as a form of intermediary processing that is executed at runtime. With each transmission, the data model of the claims document is converted from the schema used by the Process Claims service (1) to the data model compliant with the schema used by the Claims service (3). This runtime transformation logic can reside with either service architecture or as part of a separate middleware platform.

Application

Formalized data transformation is an established concept that dates back to the EAI era where data model incompatibilities were often resolved via broker services that existed as part of middleware platforms.

When services are implemented as Web services, XSLT is generally used to define the mapping logic that is subsequently executed to perform the transformation at runtime. In fact, the use of XSLT style sheets represents the most common application of this pattern.

Although Data Model Transformation is a fundamental and essential part of most service-oriented architectures, it represents a pattern that is used only out of necessity. Many of the service contract patterns described in this book, in fact, result in a reduction or even an elimination of data transformation requirements. However, the realities of legacy encapsulation, the application of Domain Inventory (123), and common governance challenges usually introduce schema disparity that still must be dealt with.

This pattern solves an important problem, but it is equally important to be constantly aware of the fact that it is only applied when other patterns cannot be realized to their full potential. Due to the constant emphasis on "transformation avoidance" throughout service-orientation, it is recommended to consider this pattern as a last resort to solving interoperability problems.

NOTE

Data Model Transformation further addresses the transformation required between different versions of the same data model. For XML schemas, XSLT can also be used for this purpose.

Impacts

The use of this pattern has several consequences:

- The development of the mapping logic adds time and effort to the creation of service compositions.
- The incorporation of data model transformation logic introduces design complexity into a service composition and the service inventory as a whole.
- Data model transformation logic introduces a runtime layer wherein the execution of mapping logic adds performance overhead every time services with disparate schemas need to exchange data.

Relationships

Canonical Schema (158) has a well-known "tug-of-war" relationship with Data Model Transformation, in that this pattern generally needs to be applied to whatever extent Canonical Schema (158) is not realized.

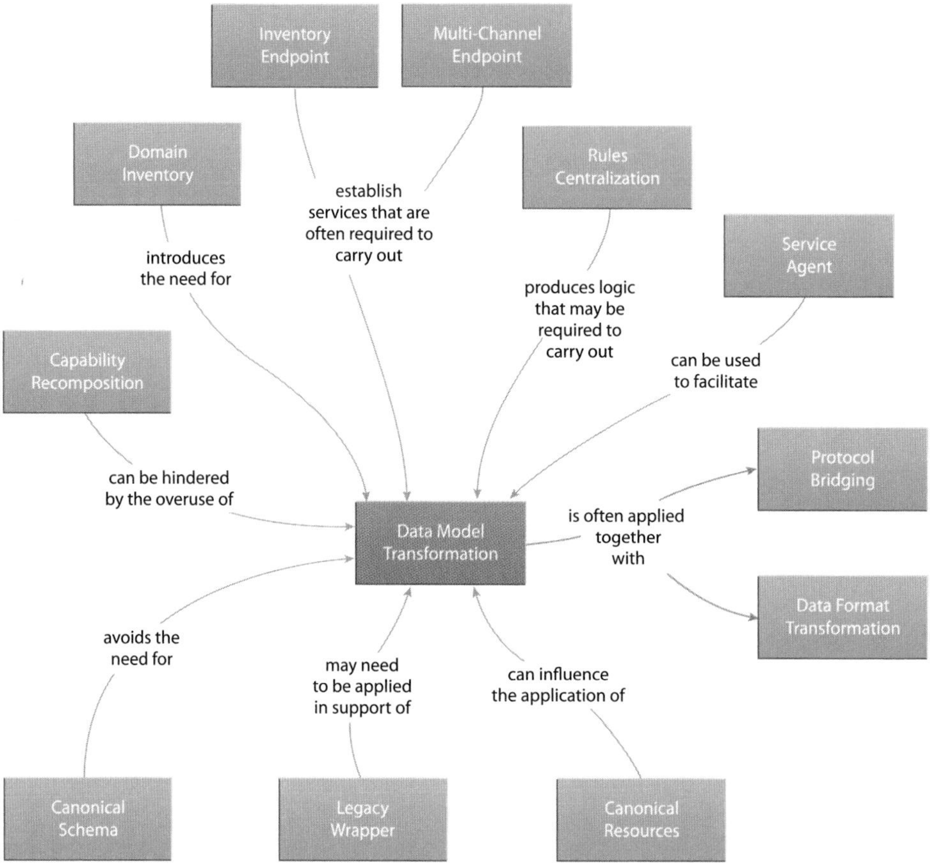

Figure 21.3

Perhaps the most common broker pattern used in composition architectures, Data Model Transformation has many ties to a diverse collection of patterns that are affected by its application.

When in use, it can help overcome disparity between services that may be introduced by patterns like Domain Inventory (123) and Inventory Endpoint (260). It also addresses conversion requirements that may result from Legacy Wrapper (441) and Rules Centralization (216).

Although it provides important functionality, its overuse is an anti-pattern that can undermine the goals of Capability Recomposition (526).

As shown in Figures 21.4 and 21.5, Data Model Transformation is a core part of Service Broker (707) and Enterprise Service Bus (704) and also the only broker-related pattern associated as an optional extension of Orchestration (701).

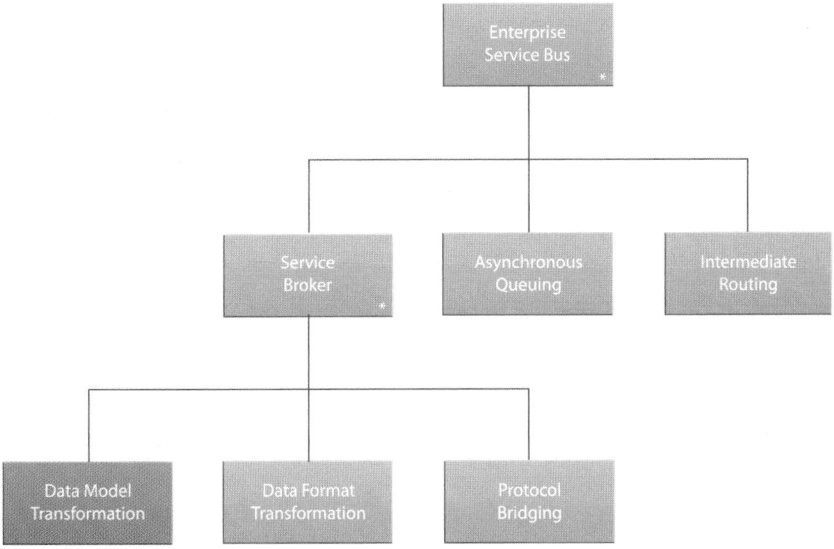

Figure 21.4

Data Model Transformation is one of three transformation-related design patterns that comprise Service Broker (707) and Enterprise Service Bus (704).

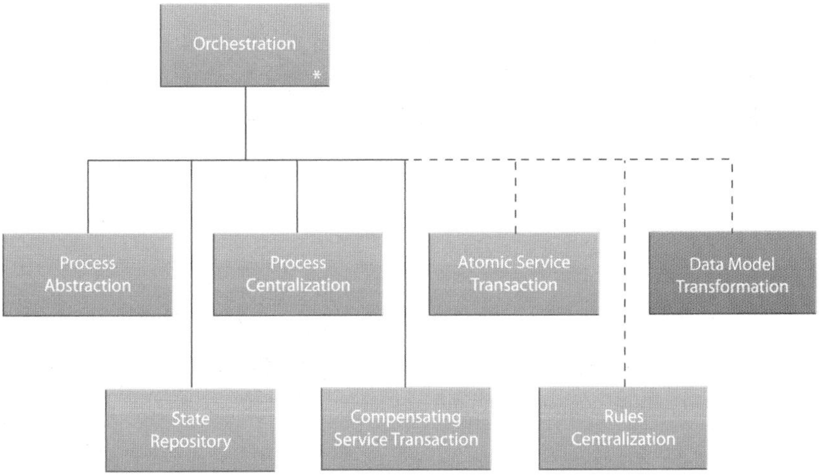

Figure 21.5

Data Model Transformation is also one of the optional patterns associated with Orchestration (701).

CASE STUDY EXAMPLE

A year before they were acquired, one of Alleywood's largest clients established an online business exchange system that required Alleywood to receive purchase orders and produce invoices based on the Universal Business Language (UBL) schema. Since that time, Alleywood has continued to use UBL for a variety of accounting documents. Tri-Fold, on the other hand, has always used its own proprietary XML Schema definition for these same types of documents.

Now that Alleywood and Tri-Fold have developed their respective domain service inventories, internal interoperability requirements begin to emerge leading to the need for Alleywood and Tri-Fold services to exchange accounting data. The first document that needs to be addressed is the purchase order.

A fragment of Tri-Fold's XML Schema definition for a purchase order is shown here:

```
<xsd:schema xmlns:xsd="http://www.w3.org/2001/XMLSchema"
  xmlns:tri="..." targetNamespace="..."
  elementFormDefault="qualified">
  <xsd:element name="order-form" type="tri:order-form.type"/>
  <xsd:element name="customer" type="tri:customer.type"/>
  <xsd:element name="delivery" type="tri:delivery.type"/>
  <xsd:element name="goods" type="tri:goods.type"/>
  <xsd:complexType name="order-form.type">
    <xsd:sequence>
      <xsd:element ref="tri:customer"/>
      <xsd:element ref="tri:delivery"/>
      <xsd:element ref="tri:goods"/>
    </xsd:sequence>
    <xsd:attribute name="id" type="xsd:string"
      use="required"/>
    <xsd:attribute name="timestamp" type="xsd:dateTime"
      use="required"/>
  </xsd:complexType>
  ...
</xsd:schema>
```

Example 21.1

Code from the Tri-Fold purchase order XML Schema definition.

A sample purchase order document instance of this schema would look something like this:

```
<order-form xmlns="..." id="20080212-AA"
  timestamp="2008-02-12T13:20:54-06:00">
  <customer ref="alleywood">
    <name>Alleywood Lumber Company</name>
    <street>128 Wood Avenue</street>
    <city zip="60601" state="IL">Chicago</city>
    <contact phone="+1 555 55 55" name="John Smith"/>
  </customer>
  <delivery date="2008-02-24+P1D">
    <street>42 Forest Street</street>
    <city zip="60601" state="IL">Chicago</city>
  </delivery>
  <goods quantity="5" ref="sp-457">
    <amount total="5412.45" unit="1082.49"/>
    <note>Special Paper</note>
  </goods>
</order-form>
```

Example 21.2

The beginning of a Tri-Fold purchase order document that corresponds to the schema from Example 21.1.

In contrast, Alleywood's UBL-based purchase order document is twice the size. Here is an excerpt from a document instance comparable to Tri-Fold's:

```
<Order xmlns="..." xmlns:cbc="..." xmlns:cac="...">
  <cbc:ID>20080212-AA</cbc:ID>
  <cbc:IssueDate>2008-02-12</cbc:IssueDate>
  <cbc:IssueTime>13:20:54-06:00</cbc:IssueTime>
  <cac:BuyerCustomerParty>
    <cac:Party>
      <cac:PartyIdentification>
        <cbc:ID>...</cbc:ID>
      </cac:PartyIdentification>
    </cac:Party>
    <cac:BuyerContact>
      <cbc:Name>John Doe</cbc:Name>
      <cbc:Telephone>+1 555 55 55</cbc:Telephone>
    </cac:BuyerContact>
  </cac:BuyerCustomerParty>
  <cac:SellerSupplierParty>
    <cac:Party>
      <cac:PartyIdentification>
        <cbc:ID>...</cbc:ID>
      </cac:PartyIdentification>
    </cac:Party>
```

```
  </cac:SellerSupplierParty>
  ...
</Order>
```

Example 21.3

A code snippet from a much more verbose Alleywood purchase order document.

> **NOTE**
>
> To view the corresponding schema used by Alleywood, see http://docs.oasis-open.org/ubl/os-UBL-2.0/xsd/maindoc/UBL-Order-2.0.xsd at the OASIS Web site.

To overcome the significant disparity in data representation between the Alleywood and Tri-Fold XML schemas, an XSLT stylesheet is developed, providing mapping logic that allows a runtime XSLT processor to transform the Alleywood UBL purchase order into an XML document that complies with the Tri-Fold purchase order schema.

The portion of the XSLT stylesheet that pertains to the transformation of customer data is shown here:

```
<xsl:stylesheet
  xmlns:xsl="http://www.w3.org/1999/XSL/Transform"
  xmlns:xsd="http://www.w3.org/2001/XMLSchema"
  xmlns:ubl="...." xmlns:cbc="..."
  xmlns:cac="..." xmlns:tri="..."
  exclude-result-prefixes="xsd ubl cbc cac"
  version="2.0">
  <xsl:output indent="yes"/>

  <!-- Create the Tri-Fold reference from the Alleywood ID URI. -->
  <xsl:function name="tri:ref" as="xsd:string">
    <xsl:param name="elem" as="element()"/>
    <xsl:sequence select=
      "substring-after($elem/cbc:ID, '#')"/>
  </xsl:function>
  ...

  <!-- This represents the main entry point for
    the entire order. -->
  <xsl:template match="ubl:Order">
    <tri:order-form id="{ cbc:ID }" timestamp="{
      dateTime(cbc:IssueDate, cbc:IssueTime) }">
```

```
      <xsl:apply-templates select="
        cac:BuyerCustomerParty, cac:Delivery,
        cac:OrderLine/cac:LineItem"/>
    </tri:order-form>
  </xsl:template>

  <!-- Process the customer contact information. -->
  <xsl:template match="cac:BuyerCustomerParty">
    <xsl:variable name="ref"   select="
      tri:ref(cac:Party/cac:PartyIdentification)"/>
    <xsl:variable name="party" select="tri:party($ref)"/>
    <tri:customer ref="{ $ref }">
      <tri:name>
        <xsl:value-of select="$party/name"/>
      </tri:name>
      <tri:street>
        <xsl:value-of select="$party/street"/>
      </tri:street>
      <tri:city zip="{ $party/zip }"
        state="{ $party/state }">
          <xsl:value-of select="$party/city"/>
      </tri:city>
      <xsl:apply-templates select="cac:BuyerContact"/>
    </tri:customer>
  </xsl:template>

   <!-- Transform the customer contact information. -->
   <xsl:template match="cac:BuyerContact">
     <tri:contact name="{ cbc:Name }"
       phone="{ cbc:Telephone }"/>
   </xsl:template>
   ...
</xsl:stylesheet>
```

Example 21.4

A look at the XSLT stylesheet used to enable the receipt of an Alleywood purchase order by a Tri-Fold service. Only the markup code responsible for transforming customer contact data is shown.

Data Format Transformation

By Mark Little, Thomas Rischbeck, Arnaud Simon

How can services interact with programs that communicate with different data formats?

Problem	A service may be incompatible with resources it needs to access due to data format disparity. Furthermore, a service consumer that communicates using a data format different from a target service will be incompatible and therefore unable to invoke the service.
Solution	Intermediary data format transformation logic needs to be introduced in order to dynamically translate one data format into another.
Application	This necessary transformation logic is incorporated by adding internal service logic, service agents, or a dedicated transformation service.
Impacts	The use of data format transformation logic inevitably adds development effort, design complexity, and performance overhead.
Principles	Standardized Service Contract, Service Loose Coupling
Architecture	Inventory, Composition, Service

Table 21.2
Profile summary for the Data Format Transformation pattern.

Problem

Services can be fundamentally incompatible with resources or programs that only support disparate data formats. For example, a service may have been standardized to send and receive XML-formatted data but is required to also retrieve data from a legacy environment that only supports the CSV format (Figure 21.6).

Solution

A layer of data format transformation logic is introduced. This logic is specifically designed to convert one or more data formats into one or more different data formats (Figure 21.7).

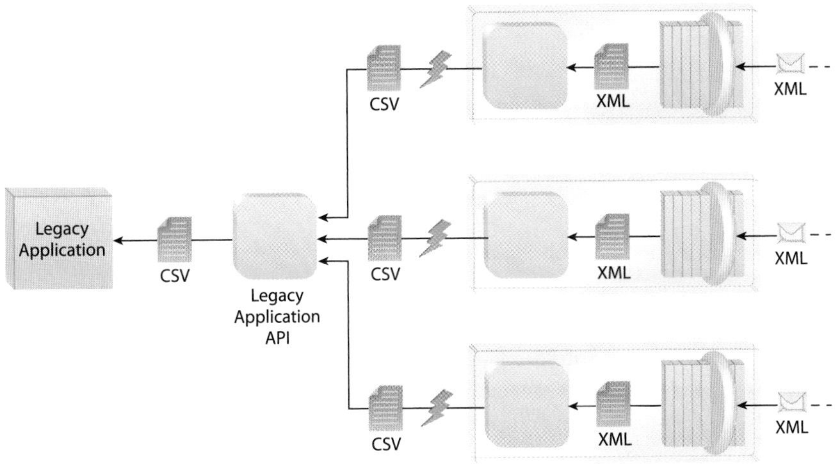

Figure 21.6

Three different services accustomed to processing XML formatted data need to access a legacy application API that only accepts CSV formatted data.

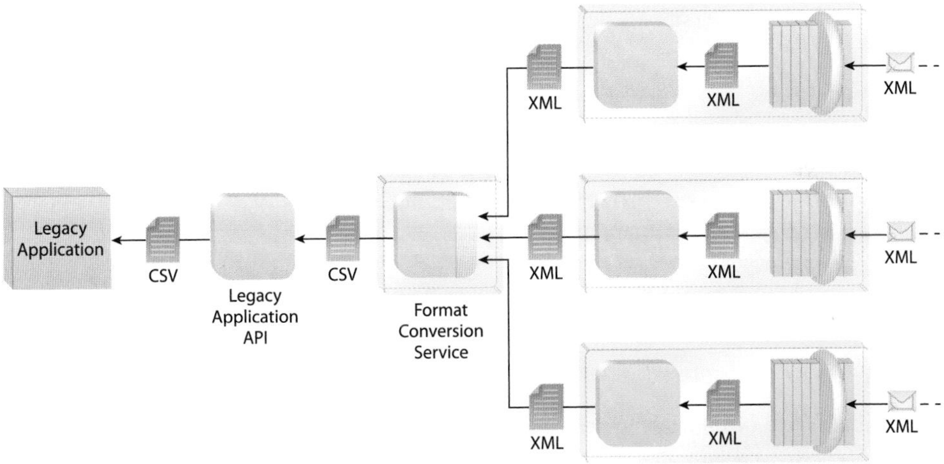

Figure 21.7

A Format Conversion utility service is added to the architecture. This service abstracts the legacy application API and provides XML-to-CSV and CSV-to-XML functions. Note that in the depicted architecture, the Format Conversion service exists as a component being reused by multiple components that are part of Web services, as per Dual Protocols (227).

Application

Data format transformation logic can exist within a service's internal logic, within a service agent, or (as shown earlier in Figure 21.7) as a separate service altogether. Middleware with brokerage features will often provide out-of-the-box services and agents that perform a variety of data format conversions.

Furthermore, because the conversion of one data format to another will naturally transform the source data model, the application of this design pattern can be seen as also applying Data Model Transformation (671). However, as previously explained, Data Model Transformation (671) is most commonly used separately for the conversion of one formal data model to another when both source and destination formats are the same.

Impacts

As with any of the three design patterns associated with the parent compound pattern Service Broker (707), the introduction of a transformation layer for data format conversion will have the following impacts:

- An increase in solution development effort when the required transformation logic needs to be custom-programmed. However, custom development effort may not be necessary when using a middleware platform already equipped with the required conversion functionality.
- An increase in design complexity, as this pattern will introduce a new layer in an already distributed environment.
- An increase in performance requirements because the format conversion will need to be executed every time interaction between disparate format sources is required. This is especially a concern with the transformation of data formats because of the tendency to carry out bulk or batch format conversions.

These impacts are often considered natural requirements that come with introducing a service layer into an enterprise with legacy applications and resources.

Relationships

Data Format Transformation is typically utilized to help integrate custom service logic with legacy systems, which makes it commonly required when applying Legacy Wrapper (441). The actual transformation logic may be the responsibility of a façade component that is tasked with converting proprietary to standardized formats, as per Service Façade (333).

When protocols are standardized using Canonical Protocol (150), data formats are usually standardized as well. This is because most communication protocols are associated with common data formats. For example the CSV format is often used with FTP and SCP protocols, and XML is primarily associated with HTTP. Therefore, when Data Format Transformation is required, it is often in conjunction with Protocol Bridging (687).

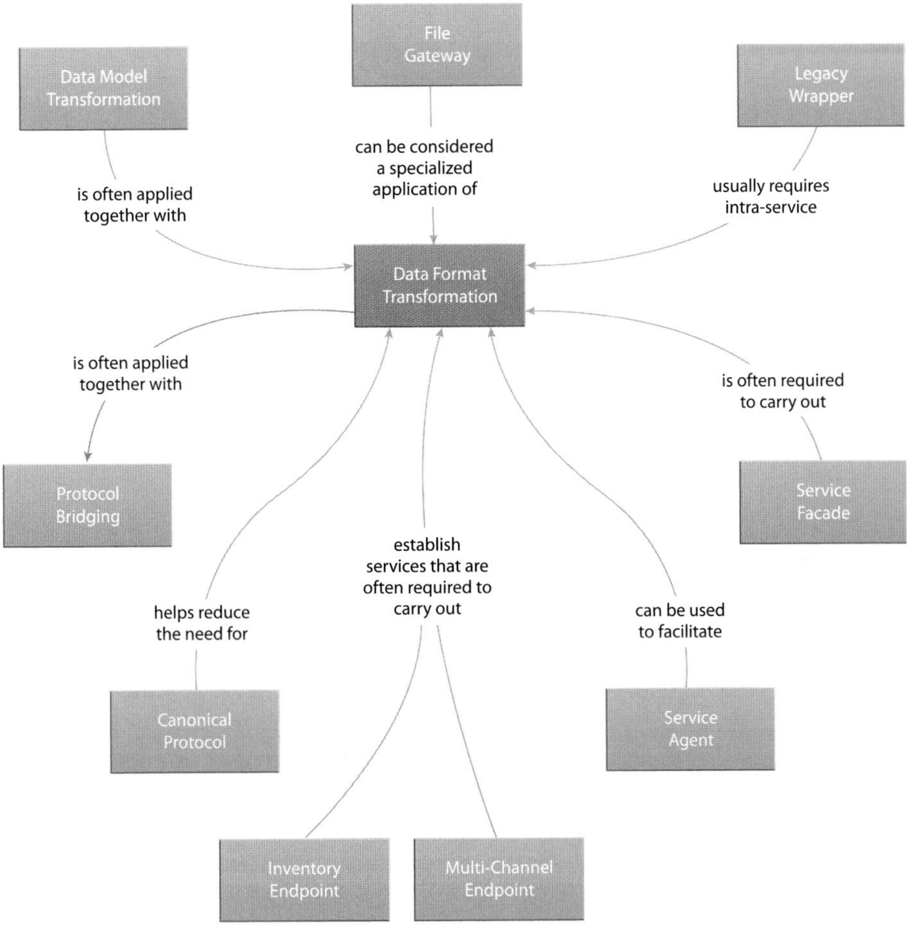

Figure 21.8

Data Format Transformation is commonly employed to deal with traditional integration issues resulting from legacy encapsulation, which is why this pattern relates to Legacy Wrapper (441) and broker-related patterns.

Also worth noting is that this pattern represents one of the three core patterns of Service Broker (707). Because Service Broker (707) is a also a core part of Enterprise Service Bus (704), ESB platforms are fully expected to support the conversion of different data formats.

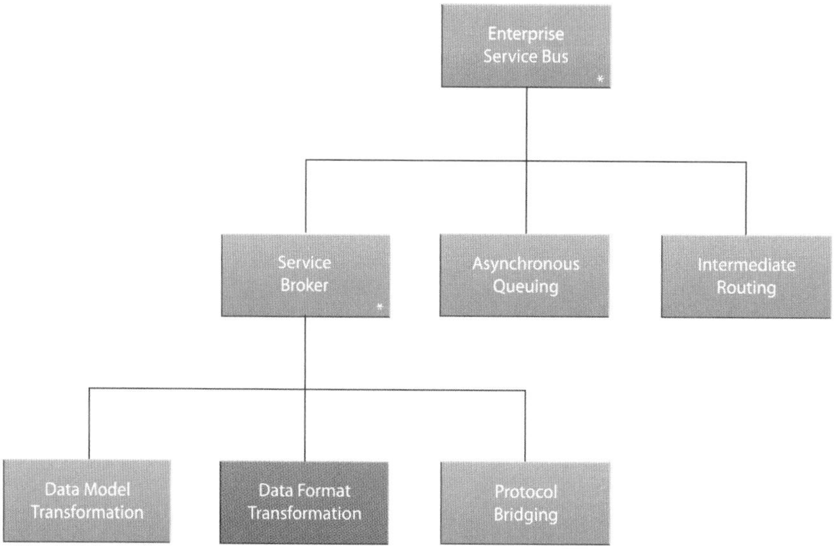

Figure 21.9

Data Format Transformation is one of three transformation-related design patterns that comprise Service Broker (707) and Enterprise Service Bus (704).

CASE STUDY EXAMPLE

Besides commercial forestry activity, another area the FRC is involved in is forestry-related disaster prevention. A large part of this program regulates critical response plans for forest wildfires.

One business process in particular governs the issuance of flight plans from fixed-wing and helicopter aircrafts capable of acting as "water bombers" for aerial firefighting. To coordinate such an effort, especially when having to call in aircrafts from different regions, a complex flight planning process is encapsulated and carried out via a central Flight Plan Validation service.

Because this service is responsible for processing flight plans sent from different sources, it has been designed to handle different data input formats. For example, the default flight plan format is XML, but the service is capable of receiving proprietary formats, such as AFTN (Aeronautical Fixed Telecommunication Network), AMHS (Aeronautical Message Handling System), as well as SMTP.

As shown in Figure 21.10, the Flight Plan Validation service converts AFTN, AMHS and SMTP message attachments to the expected XML message format, which is then forwarded to additional services.

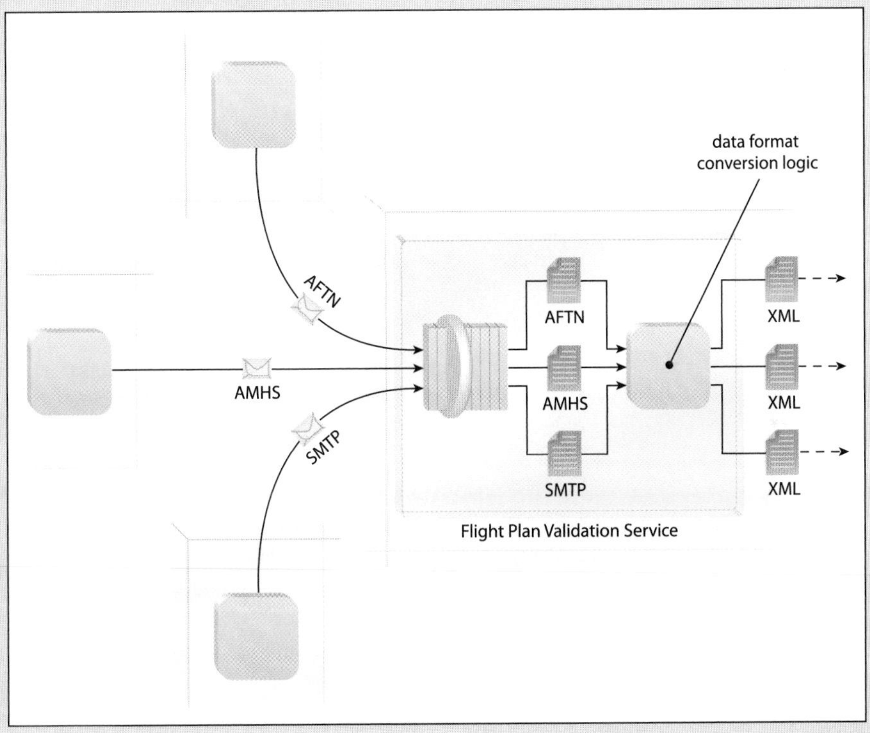

Figure 21.10

Different organizations providing critical assistance in aid of a forestry fire supply aircrafts that become part of an aerial firefighting effort. Flight plans are submitted to the FRC, which is responsible for the coordination effort. The FRC Flight Plan Validation service is designed to support the receipt of multiple flight plan format types and to then convert these formats into XML.

Protocol Bridging

By Mark Little, Thomas Rischbeck, Arnaud Simon

How can a service exchange data with consumers that use different communication protocols?

Problem	Services using different communication protocols or different versions of the same protocol cannot exchange data.
Solution	Bridging logic is introduced to enable communication between different communication protocols by dynamically converting one protocol to another at runtime.
Application	Instead of connecting directly to each other, consumer programs and services connect to a broker, which provides bridging logic that carries out the protocol conversion.
Impacts	Significant performance overhead can be imposed by bridging technologies, and their use can limit or eliminate the ability to incorporate reliability and transaction features.
Principles	Standardized Service Contract, Service Composability
Architecture	Inventory, Composition

Table 21.3
Profile summary for the Protocol Bridging pattern.

> **NOTE**
>
> If you haven't already, be sure to read the section *What Do We Mean by "Protocol?"* in the description for Canonical Protocol (150) before proceeding.

Problem

Services delivered by different project teams or at different times can be built using different communication technologies (Figure 21.11). For example, services can use completely disparate frameworks (such as JMS and DCOM) or different versions of the same communications technologies (such as HTTP plus SOAP versions 1.1 and 1.2).

This is a common scenario when design standards are not prevalent in an enterprise and services are primarily designed in support of tactical requirements. As a result, service interoperability outside of immediate composition boundaries is severely diminished, leading to missed opportunities to reuse and recompose services for new purposes. Over time, this

leads to "islands" of disparate service compositions that are reminiscent of traditional, silo-based application environments.

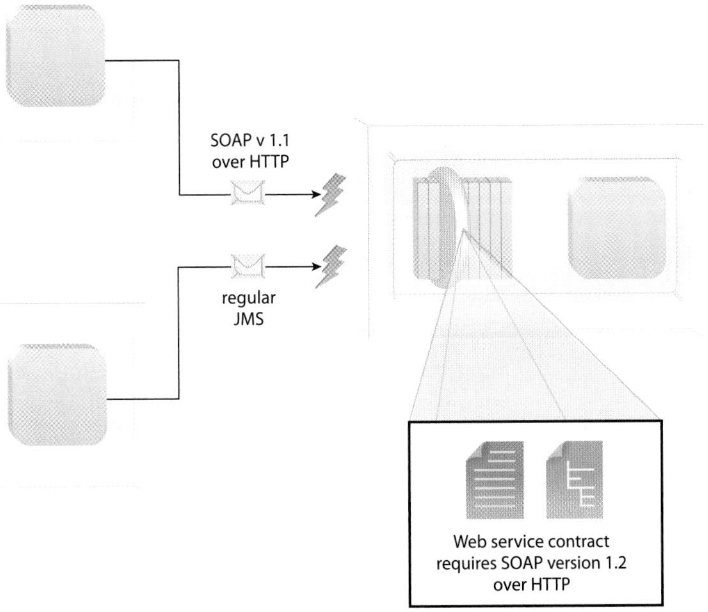

Figure 21.11

The consumer programs (left) cannot access the service because the communications protocols used by the consumers are not supported by the service. The service only accepts messages that comply to SOAP version 1.2 transmitted via HTTP.

Solution

Protocol bridging technology is used to overcome the disparity between different communications frameworks by enabling the runtime conversion of protocols (Figure 21.12).

Application

This pattern is commonly employed when legacy systems need to act as service consumers or when legacy logic needs to be encapsulated by services. As mentioned earlier, it is also used to overcome communication gaps when disparate sets of services are delivered.

A protocol bridging layer is composed of a set of adapters that act as on-/off-ramps for a given transport protocol. These adapters may be off-the-shelf products provided by the broker or a third-party vendor, or they may be generated to mirror specific service contracts using a proprietary protocol dialect.

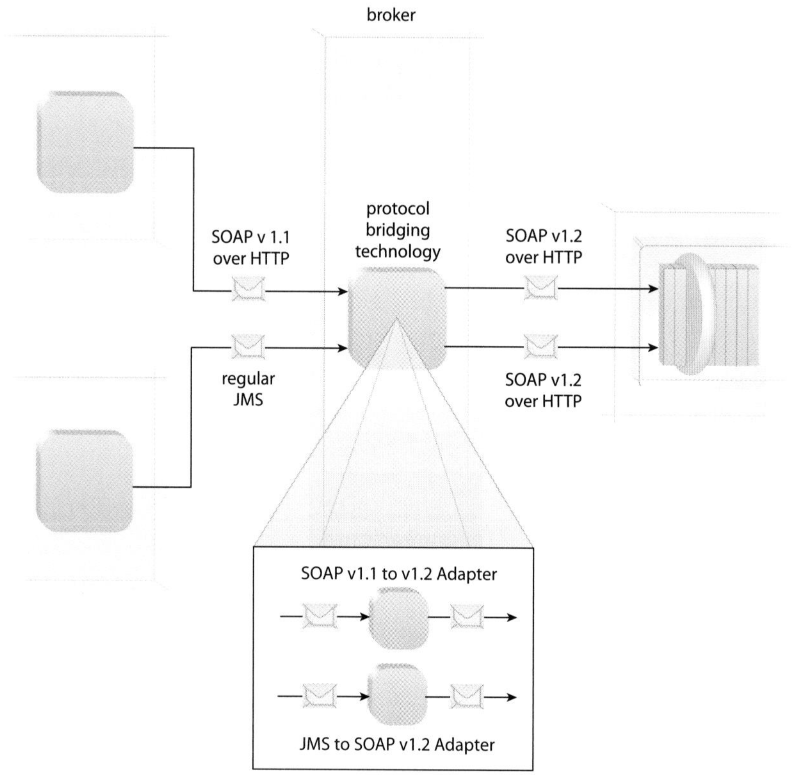

Figure 21.12

The consumer programs interact with a middle-tier broker that provides protocol bridging features. Separate protocol adapters are used to translate the two incompatible protocols to the required SOAP version 1.2 over HTTP. The broker then transmits the messages to the service on behalf of the consumers.

When a protocol bridge receives a message, it transforms it and performs whatever other work is required to make the message comply with the target protocol (or protocol version).

Protocol bridging can be used to expose or access services via multiple protocols, depending on whether adapters are implemented on the consumer or provider end. A multi-protocol conversion program can offer support for numerous protocols (HTTP, JMS, UDP, TCP, etc.) that can be natively exposed as independent protocol transformation services.

Impacts

While necessary to overcome baseline communications disparity, Protocol Bridging is a pattern only used out of necessity. From an architectural perspective, it is considered an undesirable option because of the design complexity and runtime performance overhead it imposes. Even though it can support interoperability between services, it does so at a less than optimal level. Service compositions relying on this pattern often end up having decreased levels of availability and reliability.

Protocol Bridging originated with early EAI platforms and is therefore still considered an integration-related design approach. The manner in which it involves protocol adapters and translation logic can be overly complex because of the binary encoding used by many transport protocols. In some cases, protocol conversions may even result in inaccurate semantic meanings being applied to message contents.

Though an expected part of brokerage functionality, some platforms may support limited sets of protocols with an emphasis on conversion to and from SOAP and HTTP only.

Relationships

Protocol Bridging is a pattern that has long been used to solve traditional integration problems and therefore finds itself closely related to Legacy Wrapper (441) and Dual Protocols (227). The nature of its bridging technology can also be influenced by Canonical Resources (237) when choices are available.

The extent to which this pattern is applied to intra-service bridging requirements only is based on how successful the application of Canonical Protocol (150) has been in achieving a sole inter-service communications technology.

As a part of Service Broker (707), Protocol Bridging is commonly associated with the compound pattern Enterprise Service Bus (704), as shown in Figure 21.14.

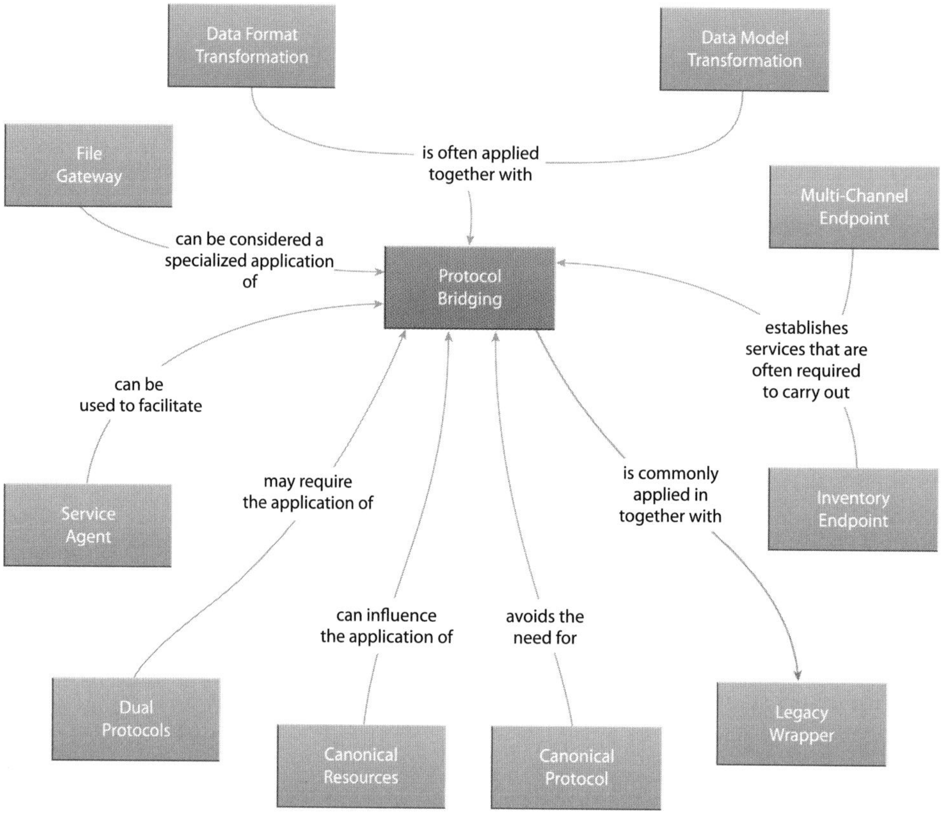

Figure 21.13

Protocol Bridging provides low-level conversion of different communication technologies and therefore relates to patterns such as Inventory Endpoint (260) and Legacy Wrapper (441) that require this type of functionality, as well as standards-based patterns that seek to avoid it.

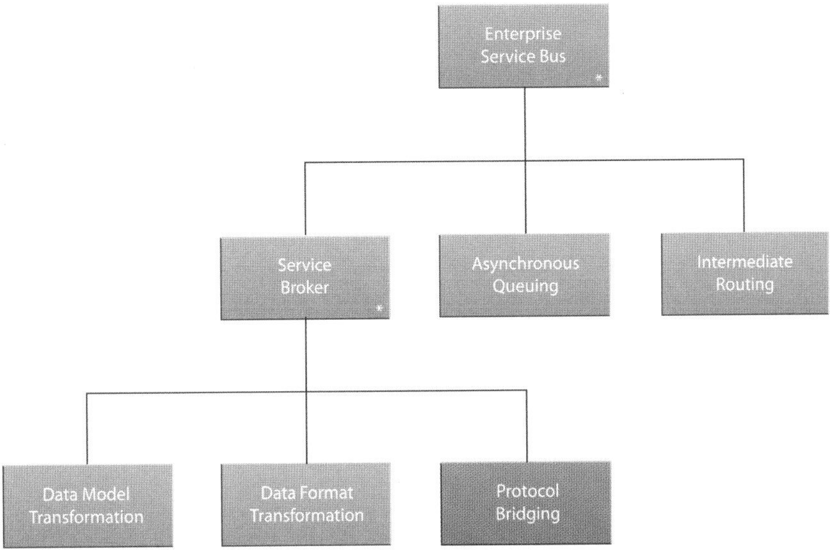

Figure 21.14

Protocol Bridging provides fundamental integration functionality that positions it as a core pattern of both Service Broker (707) and Enterprise Service Bus (704).

CASE STUDY EXAMPLE

The Cutit Run Inventory Transfer Process service composition originally depicted in the case study example for Schema Centralization (200) had been recently re-designed to incorporate standardized schemas so as to avoid the need for Data Model Transformation (671).

This composition consists of the following services:

- Chain service
- Inventory service
- Order service
- Run Inventory Transfer Process service

Subsequent to receiving new requirements, the Cutit architecture team is asked to incorporate access to a legacy repository providing historical inventory data. This database can only be accessed via a vendor-provided adapter that is limited to the use of SOAP 1.1 messaging.

Cutit architects are able to apply Protocol Bridging by leveraging the broker features from their existing middleware platform to establish a means of allowing the Inventory service to query the database via its published adapter interface. However, before proceeding with this design, they decide to go a step further and apply Legacy Wrapper (441) so that the inventory archive database's proprietary API is wrapped with a standardized contract. This establishes the Inventory Archive service which provides a contract fully capable of supporting SOAP 1.2 messages by encapsulating and centralizing the necessary protocol transformation logic.

Part V

Supplemental

Chapter 22

Common Compound Design Patterns

Orchestration

Enterprise Service Bus

Service Broker

Canonical Schema Bus

Official Endpoint

Federated Endpoint Layer

Three-Layer Inventory

Singled out in this chapter are some of the more common and important combinations of the patterns documented in previous chapters. Each such combination is classified as a *compound design pattern*.

"Compound" vs. "Composite"

A "composite" is generally something that is comprised of interconnected parts. For example, you could legitimately refer to a service composition as a composite of services because the individual parts need to be designed into an aggregate in order to act as a whole. A "compound," on the other hand, can simply be considered the result of combining a specific set of things together. A chemical compound consists of a combination of ingredients that result in something new when mixed together.

The patterns in this chapter are referred to as "compound patterns" because they document the effects of applying multiple patterns together. One of the most interesting parts of this exploration is that certain combinations of patterns result in design solutions that are already quite common, such as with Enterprise Service Bus (704) and Service Broker (707).

> **NOTE**
>
> Also worth mentioning is that a design pattern named "Composite" has been in existence for some time as a fundamental part of object-oriented design.

Compound Patterns and Pattern Relationships

Every pattern profile in the previous chapters included a *Relationships* section that provided some insight into inter-pattern dependencies and how the application of one pattern can affect another.

Compound patterns are also about relationships, but in a different way. The patterns that comprise a compound pattern have a relationship with the compound pattern itself. Whether these patterns have dependencies with or impact each other is immaterial. When studying them as members of a compound pattern, we are only interested in the results of their combined application.

Joint Application vs. Coexistent Application

When we discuss the notion of combining patterns into compounds, it is important to clarify how patterns can be combined.

A compound pattern can represent a set of patterns that are applied together to a particular program or implementation in order to establish a specific set of design characteristics. This would be referred to as *joint application.*

The compound patterns with patterns that are jointly applied are:

- Official Endpoint (711)
- Federated Endpoint Layer (713)
- Three-Layer Inventory (715)

Alternatively, the patterns that comprise a compound pattern can represent a set of related features provided by a particular program or environment. In this case, a *coexistent application* of patterns establishes a "solution environment" that may be realized by a combination of tools and technologies.

Compound patterns comprised of patterns that coexist to establish such an environment are:

- Orchestration (701)
- Enterprise Service Bus (704)
- Service Broker (707)
- Canonical Schema Bus (709)

The notation used to express compound patterns comprised of patterns that are jointly applied versus those applied in a coexistent manner differs, as shown in Figure 22.1.

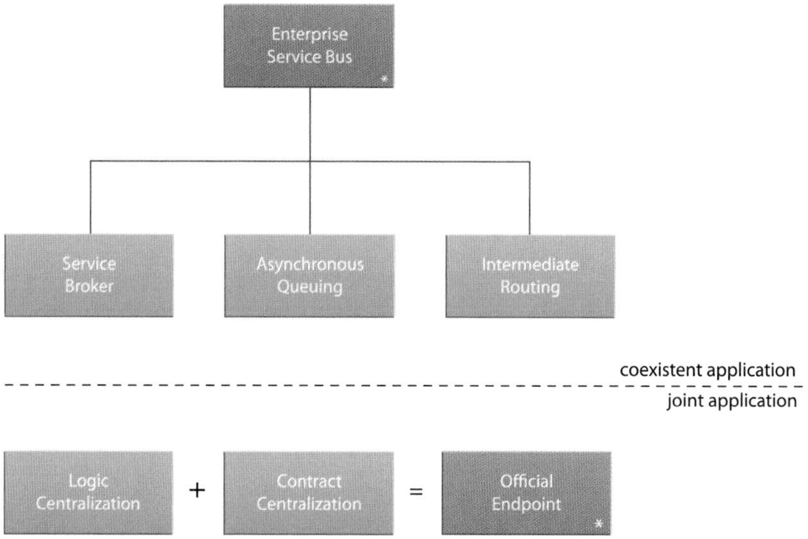

Figure 22.1

Compound patterns comprised of patterns that are applied to coexist are expressed in a hierarchy, whereas those that are made up of patterns that are applied jointly are represented via a formula-style notation.

Compound Patterns and Pattern Granularity

Even though this chapter classifies a set of patterns as "compound patterns," it is important to note that just about any pattern can turn out to be a compound pattern. Every one of the other patterns described in this book can be decomposed into a set of more granular patterns. Their joint or coexistent combination then results in the original pattern, thereby also making it a compound pattern.

For example, Chapter 18 establishes Asynchronous Queuing (582) and Intermediate Routing (549) as providing fundamental, messaging-related solutions. In the upcoming *ESB Architecture for SOA* book, a set of more granular queuing and routing design patterns are described that can be considered as collectively representing Asynchronous Queuing (582) and Intermediate Routing (549) as compound patterns.

The reason this perspective is important is because whether or not a pattern is labeled as being a compound pattern is always relative. It is just a matter of the granularity at which the pattern is documented in relation to other patterns in the same catalog.

As a result, the compound patterns in this chapter are only classified as such because of the granularity at which the rest of the patterns are defined in this book. In a different publication or context, these patterns may be classified differently.

Orchestration

By Thomas Erl, Brian Loesgen

An orchestration platform is dedicated to the effective maintenance and execution of parent business process logic. Modern-day orchestration environments are especially expected to support sophisticated and complex service composition logic that can result in long-running runtime activities.

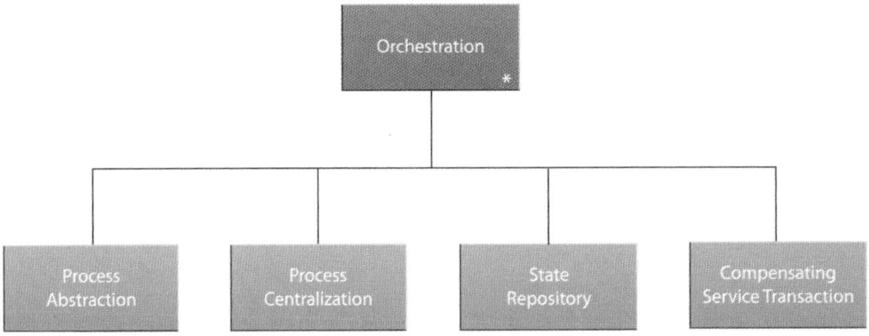

Figure 22.2

The base patterns that comprise Orchestration.

The Orchestration compound pattern is comprised of the following design patterns:

- Process Abstraction (182) is responsible for separating non-agnostic logic from agnostic logic, which forms the basis of the parent composition logic that resides within the orchestration platform and is executed by the orchestration engine.
- Process Centralization (193) limits the physical distribution of abstracted process logic into one (or a group) of locations. This allows for the centralized maintenance of parent composition logic via specialized tools provided by the orchestration platform.
- State Repository (242) enables orchestration environments to support long-running service activities by providing a native state management repository that can be leveraged as a state deferral mechanism.
- Compensating Service Transaction (631) further supports long-running processes by allowing parent composition logic to be supplemented with compensation sub-processes that address exception conditions.

Figure 22.3 illustrates how the combination of the first three of these patterns establishes an orchestration environment from an implementation perspective, and Figure 22.4 highlights how this base platform is commonly extended with features that correspond to design solutions provided by other patterns covered in this book.

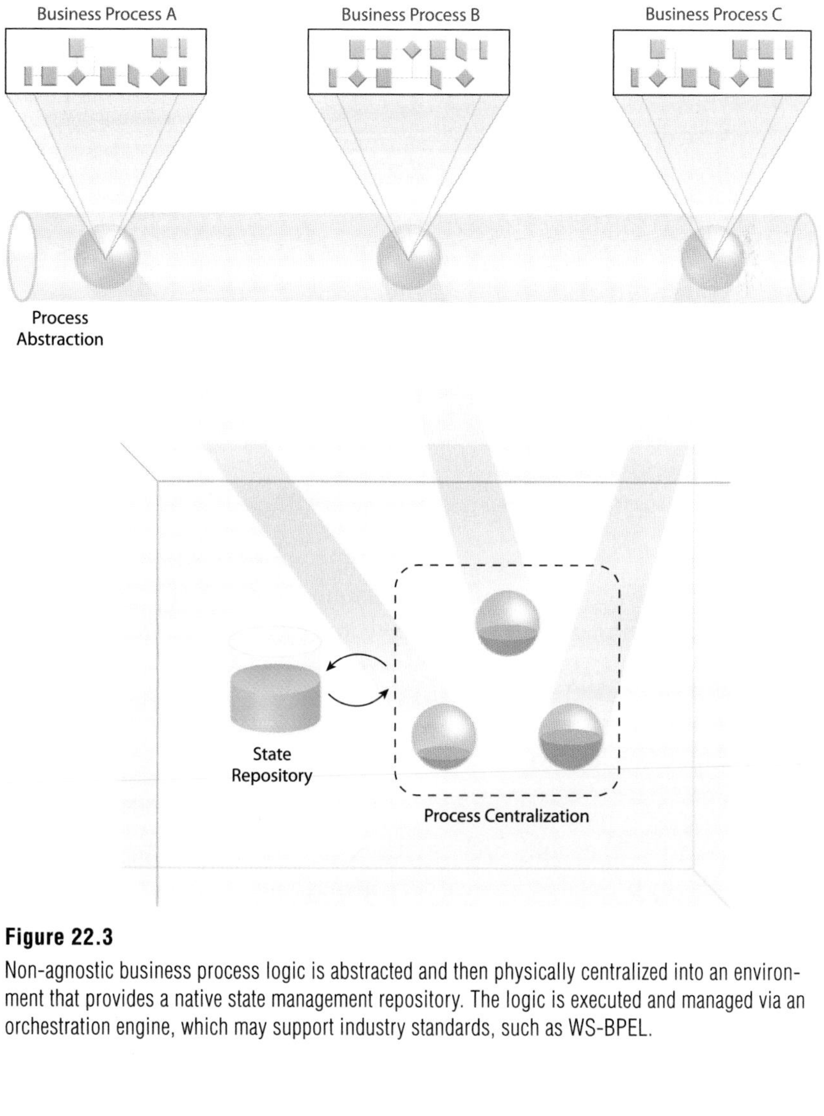

Figure 22.3

Non-agnostic business process logic is abstracted and then physically centralized into an environment that provides a native state management repository. The logic is executed and managed via an orchestration engine, which may support industry standards, such as WS-BPEL.

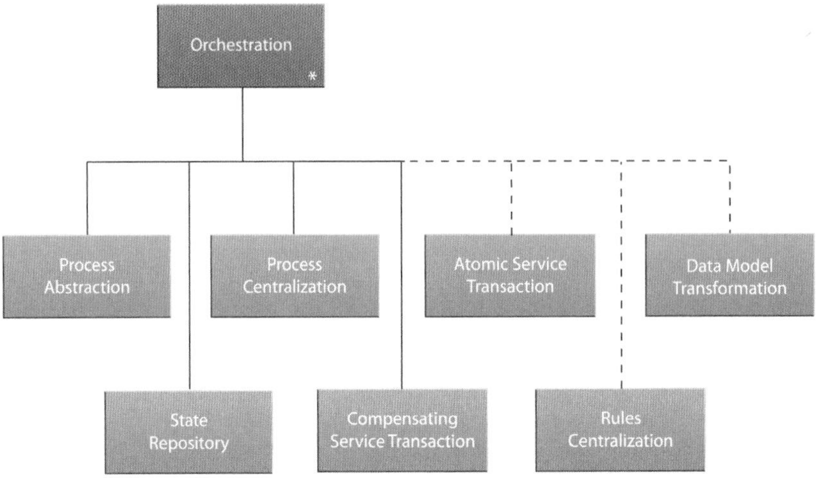

Figure 22.4

The extended Orchestration compound pattern shows how solutions provided by other design patterns expand upon the core model.

Enterprise Service Bus

By Thomas Erl, Mark Little, Thomas Rischbeck, Arnaud Simon

An enterprise service bus represents an environment designed to foster sophisticated interconnectivity between services. It establishes an intermediate layer of processing that can help overcome common problems associated with reliability, scalability, and communications disparity.

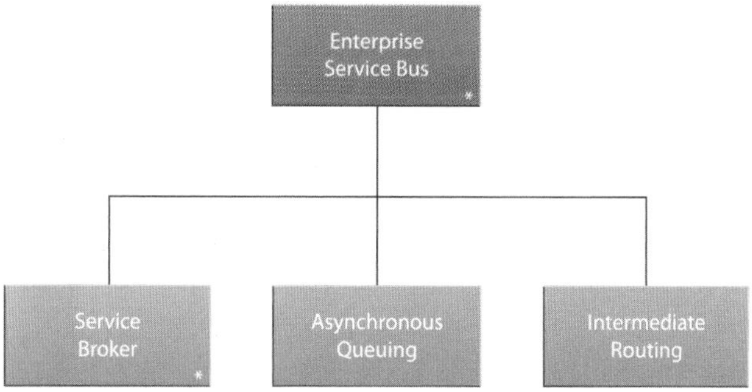

Figure 22.5
The base patterns that comprise Enterprise Service Bus.

Enterprise Service Bus is considered a compound pattern comprised of the following core patterns that coexist to provide a base set of interoperability-enablement features:

- Service Broker (707), which itself is a compound pattern that consists of a set of integration-centric patterns used to translate between incompatible data models, data formats, and communication protocols.
- Asynchronous Queuing (582), which establishes an intermediate queuing mechanism that enables asynchronous message exchanges and increases the reliability of message transmissions when service availability is uncertain.
- Intermediate Routing (549), which provides intelligent agent-based routing options to facilitate various runtime conditions.

How this set of patterns can be combined to establish a middleware-based messaging mechanism is illustrated in Figure 22.6. The expanded pattern hierarchy shown in Figure 22.7 reveals additional patterns that are common, optional extensions of Enterprise Service Bus.

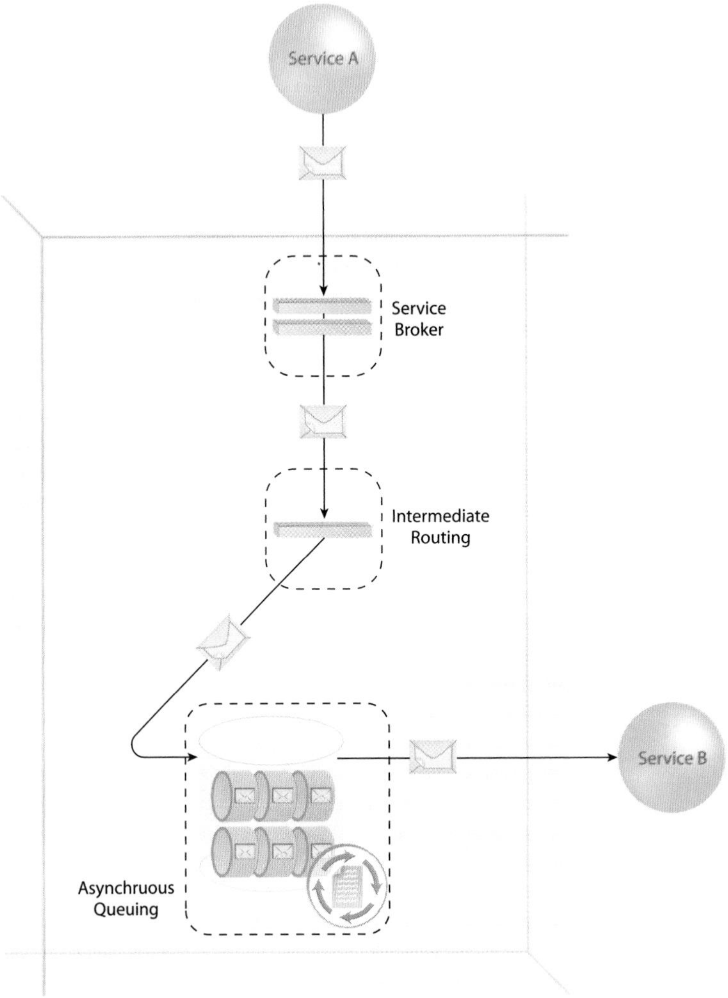

Figure 22.6

A message undergoing various processing steps carried out by an ESB in order to successfully transform and deliver the message contents to their destination. Note that this scenario depicts all three solutions working in tandem to process a single message. Other message transmissions may not require all of this functionality. It is simply the coexistence of specific patterns that constitutes an ESB.

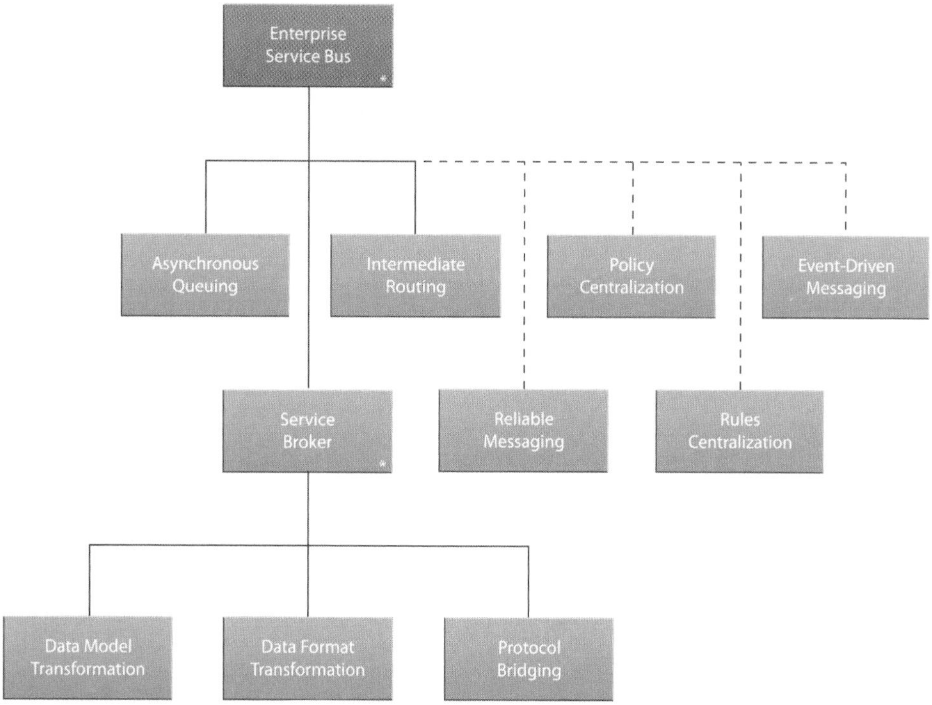

Figure 22.7

The expanded Enterprise Service Bus pattern hierarchy showing the core patterns (top left) and patterns that commonly extend the base ESB (top right), plus the patterns that comprise Service Broker (707) (bottom).

Service Broker

By Mark Little, Thomas Rischbeck, Arnaud Simon

Broker functionality has been a common part of middleware platforms, providing multi-faceted runtime conversion features that enable integration between disparate systems.

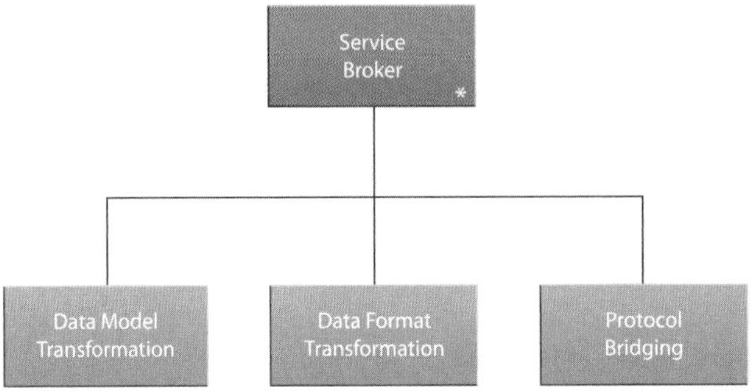

Figure 22.8

The patterns that comprise Service Broker.

The Service Broker compound pattern is comprised of Data Model Transformation (671), Data Format Transformation (681), and Protocol Bridging (687). Although all of these patterns are used only out of necessity, establishing an environment capable of handling the three most common transformation requirements can add a great deal of flexibility to a service-oriented architecture implementation, and also has the added bonus of being able to perform more than one transformation function at the same time.

Broker-related features are a fundamental part of ESB platforms, which is why this pattern exists as part of Enterprise Service Bus (704), as depicted in Figure 22.9.

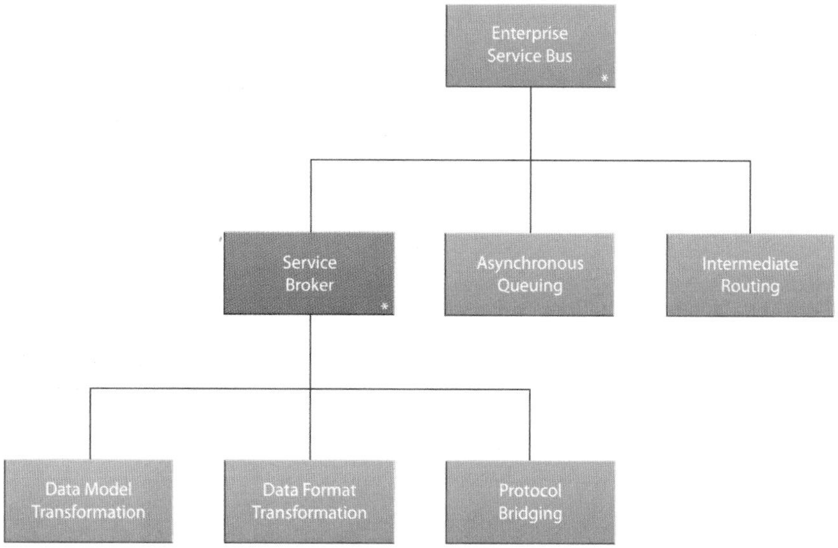

Figure 22.9
The Service Broker pattern hierarchy itself is nested within the hierarchy of Enterprise Service Bus (704).

Canonical Schema Bus

By Clemens Utschig-Utschig, Berthold Maier, Bernd Trops, Hajo Normann, Torsten Winterberg, Thomas Erl

While Enterprise Service Bus (704) provides a range of messaging-centric functions that help establish connectivity between different services and between services and resources they are required to encapsulate, it does not inherently enforce or advocate standardization. In fact, it can be argued that the native broker functions provided by some ESB platforms can discourage standardization by making it "too convenient" to integrate disparate services.

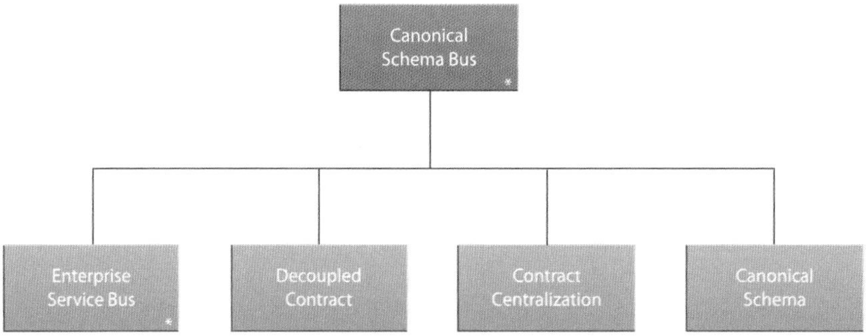

Figure 22.10
The patterns that comprise Canonical Schema Bus.

Building upon the platform established by Enterprise Service Bus (704), this pattern adds Decoupled Contract (401) and Contract Centralization (409) together with Canonical Schema (158) to position entry points into the logic, data, and functions offered via the service bus environment as independently standardized service contracts (Figure 22.11).

Canonical Schema Bus restricts entry to points to centralized and canonical service contracts and further limits the use of Service Broker (707) related patterns to intra-service transformation requirements. This places the onus of having to conform to standardized contracts upon any service or program that needs to consume them. The ultimate goal of this pattern is to promote and enforce contract-level standardization throughout a service inventory.

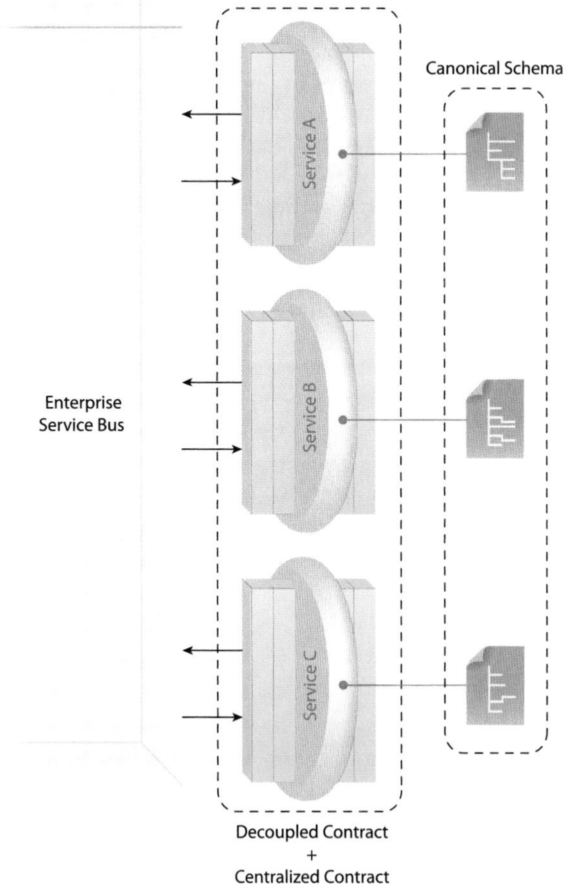

Figure 22.11

This pattern requires that access to ESB encapsulated functions and resources be limited to standardized service contracts.

Official Endpoint

As important as it is to clearly differentiate Logic Centralization (136) from Contract Centralization (409), it is equally important to understand how these two fundamental patterns can and should be used together:

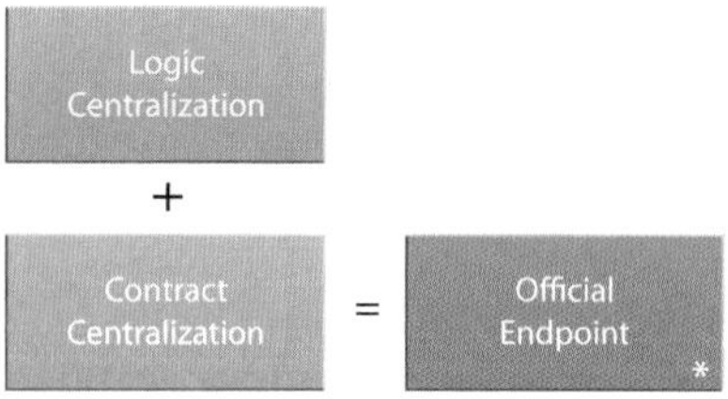

Figure 22.12
The patterns that comprise Official Endpoint.

- While Logic Centralization (136) asks designers to build consumer programs that only invoke designated services when specific types of information processing are required, it does not address how this logic is to be accessed.
- While Contract Centralization (409) asks designers to build consumer programs that access a service only via its published contract, it does not indicate which services should be accessed for specific purposes.

Applying these two patterns to the same service realizes the Official Endpoint compound pattern (Figure 22.13). The repeated application of Official Endpoint supports the goal of establishing a federated layer of service endpoints, which is why this compound pattern is also a part of Federated Endpoint Layer (713).

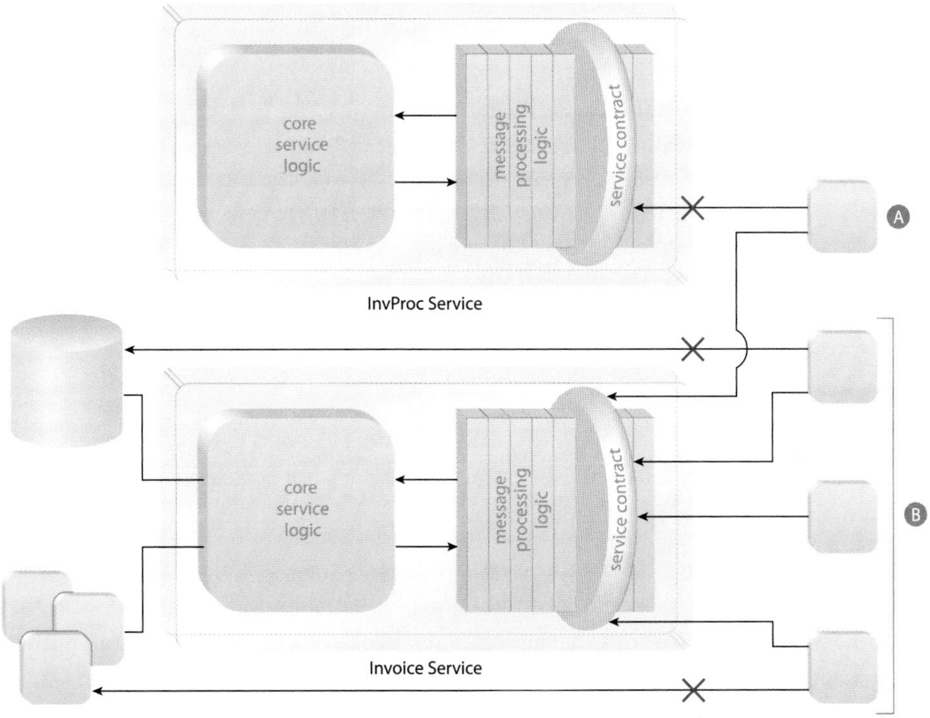

Figure 22.13

As per Logic Centralization (136), a consumer program (A) requiring invoice functionality can only access the Invoice service, which is the designated service for this logic. As per Contract Centralization (409), consumer programs (B) can only access the Invoice service via its centralized contract. The combination of these patterns establishes the Invoice service as an "official" endpoint.

Federated Endpoint Layer

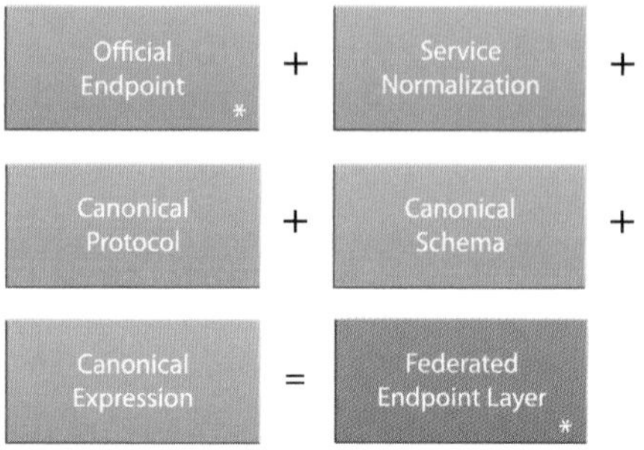

Figure 22.14
The patterns that comprise Federated Endpoint Layer.

Federation, within the context of this compound pattern (and also as it relates to the Increased Federation strategic goal explained in Chapter 4), represents a state where different services combine to form a united front (Figure 22.15), while allowing their respective, underlying environments to continue to be governed independently (Figure 22.16).

Federation is an important concept in service-oriented computing. It represents the desired state of the external, consumer-facing perspective of a service inventory, as expressed by the collective contracts of all the inventory's services. The more federated and unified this collection of contracts (endpoints) is, the more easily and effectively the services can be repeatedly consumed and leveraged.

The various patterns that make up this compound pattern are applied as follows:

- Each service positions the service contract as its sole entry point for a distinct functional boundary, as per Contract Centralization (409) and Logic Centralization (136) that comprise Official Endpoint (711).
- Service Normalization (131) is applied to the inventory (most likely via the prior definition of a service inventory blueprint) to ensure that no functional boundaries overlap.
- The service contracts (endpoints) themselves are standardized so that they support the same primary protocol, share the same data models for business documents, and express themselves consistently, as per Canonical Protocol (150), Canonical Schema (158), and Canonical Expression (275), respectively.

Figure 22.15

The abstracted view of a federated service inventory, as represented by a series of standardized service contracts.

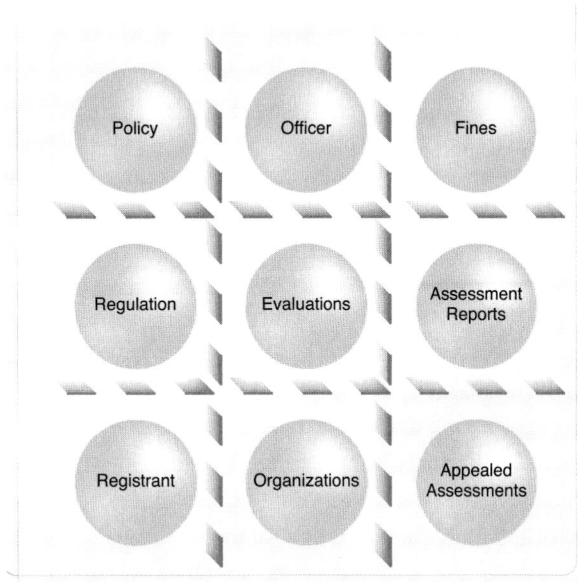

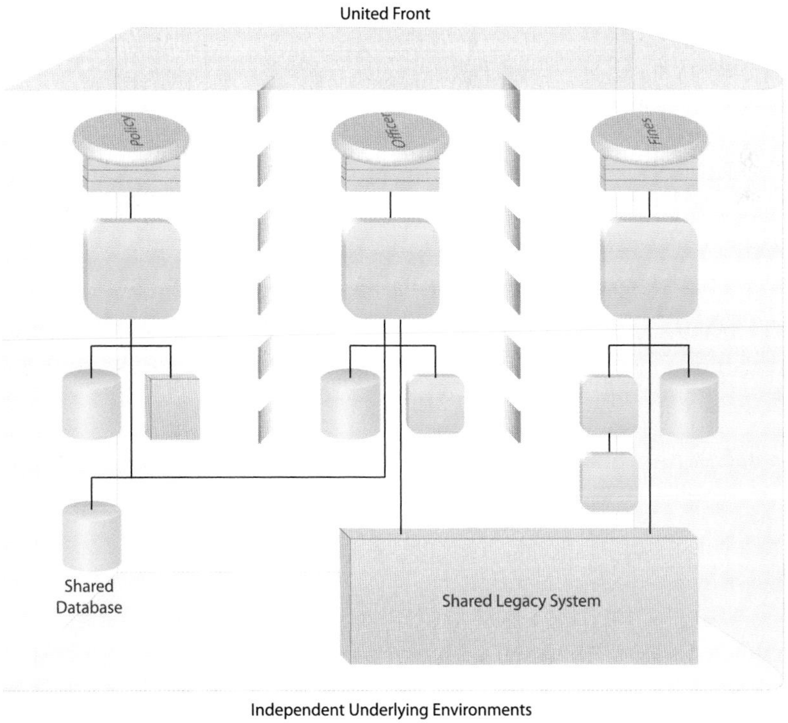

Figure 22.16

If you were to tip Figure 22.13 over on its side, you might see how, though providing a united front, the federated endpoints each abstract different service implementations.

Three-Layer Inventory

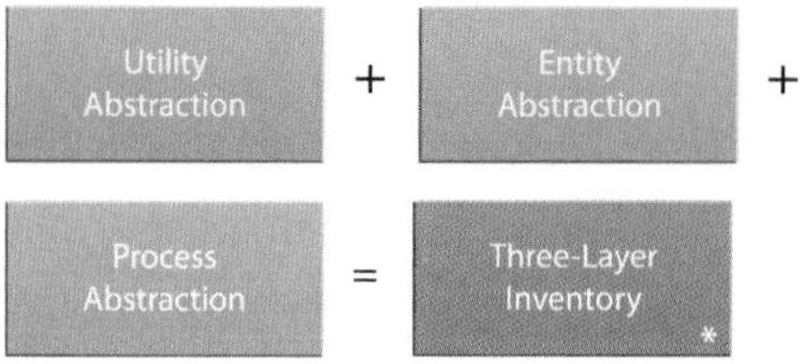

Figure 22.17
Each service layer represents a type of service based on one of three common service models.

This compound pattern is simply comprised of the combined application of the following three fundamental inventory design patterns associated with Service Layers (143).

- Utility Abstraction (168)
- Entity Abstraction (175)
- Process Abstraction (182)

The Three-Layer Inventory exists because the combined application of these three patterns is recommended for the following reasons:

- Each of the three abstraction patterns is proven to represent a common classification of service logic. The combined logic required to automate business processes for most organizations can be represented by these three service layers.
- The service layers are fully complementary in that each layer is distinct and does not overlap with another. As explained in the introductory section of Chapter 7, the three layers establish an effective separation of non-agnostic and agnostic plus business-centric and non-business-centric logic.
- The service models upon which these service layers are based are generic. This not only makes them common, but also customizable. For example, a typical variation of the utility service model is a state management service, as per in Stateful Services (248).

Even if an organization has unique or unconventional business requirements, it is advisable to begin a service inventory blueprint definition effort with this pattern. Once the service modeling process is underway, it will become evident as to whether defined services fit well into the three service models that establish these layers.

Figure 22.18 shows the common view of a service inventory partitioned via these three layers.

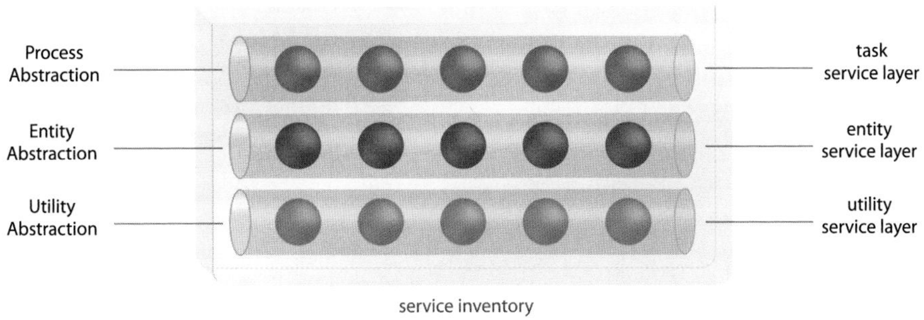

Figure 22.18

Each service layer represents a type of service based on one of three common service models.

Chapter 23

Strategic Architecture Considerations

Increased Federation

Increased Intrinsic Interoperability

Increased Vendor Diversification Options

Increased Business and Technology Alignment

Increased ROI

Increased Organizational Agility

Reduced IT Burden

All of the design patterns in this book provide design solutions in support of service-orientation. As first explained in Chapter 4, the end-result of successfully realizing service-orientation is a target state defined by a specific set of strategic goals. This chapter revisits these goals and highlights some of the key patterns that relate to their attainment.

> **NOTE**
>
> The patterns mentioned in each of the upcoming sections are not the only patterns that are recommended or required to achieve a given strategic goal. These sections simply provide examples in order to demonstrate how SOA design patterns can be mapped to the strategic goals of service-oriented computing. The unique requirements, environments, and constraints faced by individual IT enterprises will almost always warrant the use of additional patterns and practices. Furthermore, it's important to understand that these goals are inter-related. The attainment of one supports the attainment of others.

Increased Federation

As previously explained, federation can be classified as the unification of disparate environments while continuing to allow them to be independently governed. Within the context of service-orientation, this results in an emphasis on establishing endpoints as standardized, official "points of contact" for services (Figure 23.1).

Service-orientation is focused on service contract content and the positioning of the service contract as an architectural element. This eventually results in a federated environment that needs to be attainable and maintainable by the underlying architecture. As a result, every type of service-oriented technology architecture tends to be contract-centric.

Examples of related patterns:

- Both Enterprise Inventory (116) and Domain Inventory (123) result in concrete architectural boundaries within which contract-related design standards are applied. Therefore, these two patterns establish the scope in which federation is typically pursued.

- Logic Centralization (136), Contract Centralization (409), and, as a result, Official Endpoint (711) directly support this goal by producing clear design standards that ensure that each service that is part of a federated inventory has a well-defined functional scope and can only be accessed via its standardized contract. This is further aided by Service Normalization (131), which ensures that service boundaries do not overlap.
- It is important to single out Decoupled Contract (401) as a contributor as well, as it is the physical separation of contract from implementation which helps preserve federation over time (in relation to the considerations raised by the Service Abstraction design principle).
- Service Layers (143) and its three variations tie into federation by assisting with the organization and classification of services within a federated service inventory.
- The inherent standardization that is required by contracts for a collection of services to establish a united endpoint layer is supported by patterns such as Canonical Schema (158), Canonical Protocol (150), and Canonical Expression (275). Even Canonical Versioning (286) plays a factor, especially when attempting to maintain a federated state as services continue to evolve over time.
- Of course, Federated Endpoint Layer (713) is directly based on the target state advocated by this goal, but another compound pattern that can be applied more so from an infrastructure perspective in pursuit of maintaining federation is Canonical Schema Bus (709).

In many enterprises, the extent of attainable federation can be maximized by applying these patterns to services built as Web services, primarily due to the native realization of Decoupled Contract (401) that Web service implementations naturally provide.

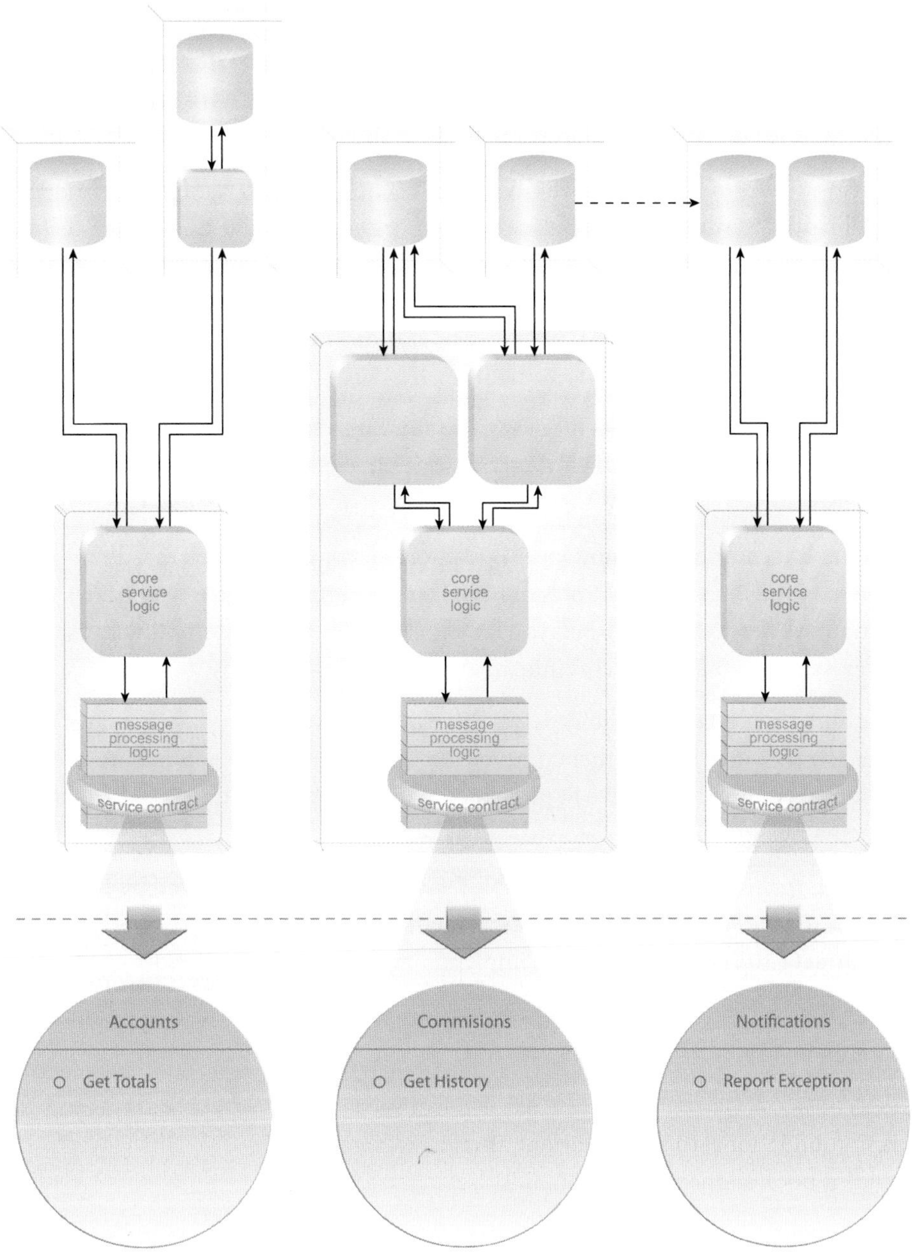

Figure 23.1

Regardless of the diversity and disparity of the underlying service implementations, from an endpoint perspective (bottom), a federated service layer establishes a consistent set of access points.

Increased Intrinsic Interoperability

The goal of increasing native interoperability represents a core state where units of service-oriented solution logic (services) are inherently compatible and therefore able to exchange data without the need to be separately integrated (Figure 23.2).

This intrinsic level of inter-connectivity relies on the federated contract-related requirements already described and can place further demands on the underlying technology architecture.

Examples of related patterns:

- On the most fundamental level, Capability Recomposition (526) establishes the baseline expectation that different services can incorporate into different compositions, thereby requiring the target state envisioned by this goal.
- From a practical perspective, contract design standards-centric patterns, such as Canonical Schema (158), Canonical Protocol (150), and Schema Centralization (200) each directly enable and enhance interoperability. Canonical Schema Bus (709) further assists this goal by enforcing contract design standards in ESB-centric environments.
- The preceding patterns and others that relate to the exchange of information between services benefit from the successful application of patterns that help position the technical service contract as an independent, yet standardized part of the service architecture. Decoupled Contract (401) and Contract Centralization (409) relate to this, as do more specialized patterns like Contract Denormalization (414) which can enhance interoperability by catering to different types of service consumers.
- Of course, Enterprise Inventory (116) and Domain Inventory (123) establish the extent to which services are expected to be natively interoperable, but Cross-Domain Utility Layer (267) is also worth mentioning as a means of improving baseline interoperability across domain boundaries.

These are just examples of patterns that help foster baseline interoperability. Because this goal is so foundational to service-orientation, in some way or another, the majority of patterns in this book support interoperability between services.

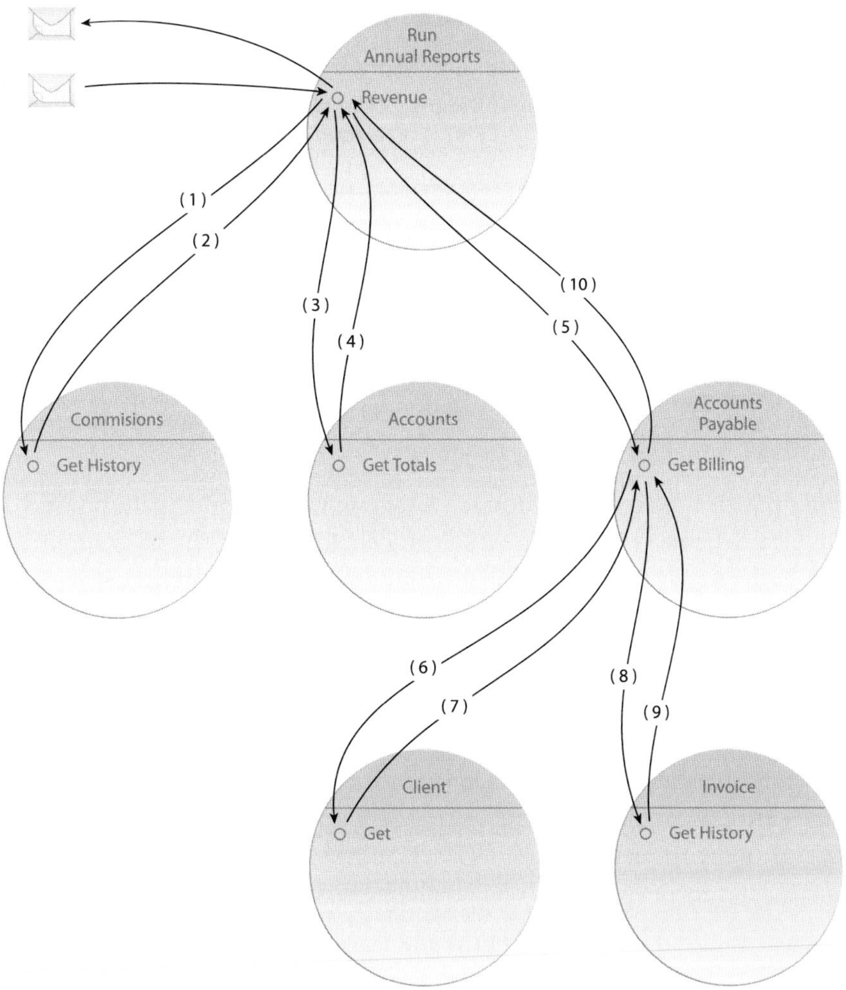

Figure 23.2

Message data travels throughout services to enable the automation of a composition. The smoother this communication, the more efficient the composition logic executes. Intrinsic interoperability strives to establish an environment in which data can be passed without constraint among numerous variations of aggregated services.

Increased Vendor Diversification Options

It is not a goal of service-orientation to increase the vendor diversity within enterprises. Instead, the objective is to provide a constant *option* for diversification so that when existing products and technologies are no longer adequate, they can be extended or even replaced with whatever else the marketplace has to offer without disrupting the established, federated service layer (Figure 23.3).

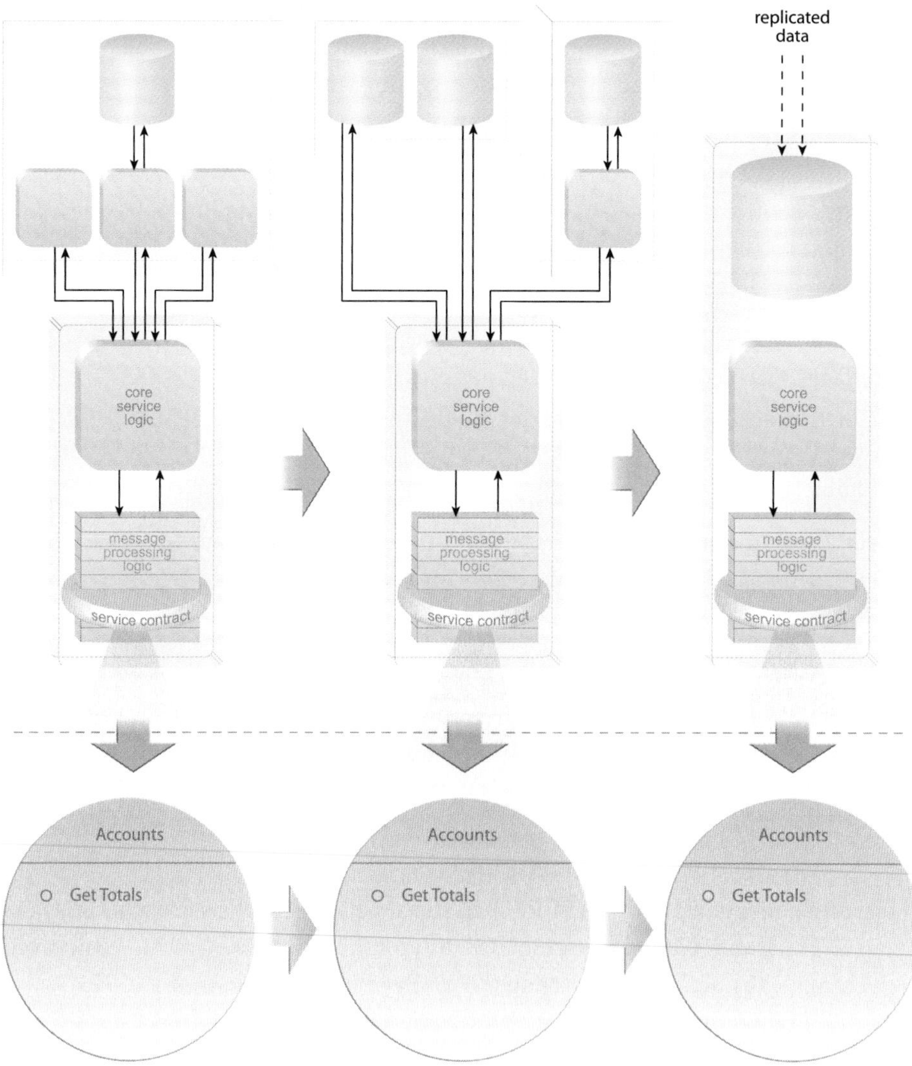

Figure 23.3

The vendor technology that underlies a service's implementation architecture may change and evolve over time, but its service contract remains the same.

The key is to allow this option to exist without having to replace a technology architecture when vendor diversification is required. This essentially imposes the requirement that architecture models remain as vendor-neutral as possible.

Examples of related patterns:

- A key design-time factor in support of this goal is how a service architecture is structured internally. For example, Service Façade (333) can help establish a healthy decoupling of various, vendor-specific resources from the core service logic so as to allow those resources to be more easily changed and replaced, as per Service Refactoring (484). On the other hand, Service Agent (543) can lead to less desirable dependencies on vendor platforms when over-applied.
- Sometimes the best solution is to wrap proprietary technology resources into non-business-centric services so as to maintain an extent of decoupling of business logic and vendor technology. For this purpose, Utility Abstraction (168) and Legacy Wrapper (441) can be applied.
- How a service relates to its underlying resources is generally determined by how it interfaces with them. Legacy-related patterns, such as File Gateway (457), can be useful in addition to the intra-service application of the transformation patterns Data Model Transformation (671), Data Format Transformation (681), and Protocol Bridging (687).
- Several patterns are simply applied via the purchase and deployment of vendor products. Examples of this include State Repository (242), Metadata Centralization (280), Service Data Replication (350), and Partial State Deferral (356).
- Patterns associated with middleware platforms, such as those established by Enterprise Service Bus (704), Orchestration (701), and Service Grid (254), can inhibit the attainment of this goal due to the fact that such platforms can encompass large portions of the infrastructure that underlie a service inventory architecture, which can lead to the architecture as a whole becoming overly dependent on supporting vendor technology.
- The preceding point ties into more specialized patterns, such as Process Centralization (193), Policy Centralization (207), Intermediate Routing (549), Asynchronous Queuing (582), Reliable Messaging (592), Event-Driven Messaging (599), Atomic Service Transaction (623), Compensating Service Transaction (631), as well as security-related patterns including Data Confidentiality (641), Data Origin Authentication (649), Direct Authentication (656), and Brokered Authentication (661).

However, it is worth noting that all of these patterns can be applied with the support of industry standards which can naturally increase the freedom to diversify vendor technologies.

- One pattern that can be considered in opposition with this goal is Canonical Resources (237). It advocates keeping underlying service implementation technologies the same in order to reduce diversity. However, the objectives of this pattern are expected to yield to the need to diversify vendor technology when having to maintain business alignment or when attempting to maximize business requirements fulfillment.

Several additional patterns can also be applied via (and are even inspired by) industry technology standards.

Increased Business and Technology Alignment

The motivation behind building a technology environment that is synchronized with the current state of a business but also designed to continuously adapt to how the business changes over time is to avoid having to reach a decision point where we have to choose between living with an outdated automation environment and replacing it altogether.

Service-orientation fosters design characteristics that enable service-oriented solutions to be extended, reconfigured, or replaced using already available resources (services) without disrupting the already established layer of federated service endpoints (Figure 23.4).

Examples of related patterns:

- In their earliest stages, services can be aligned with business intelligence as a result of service modeling processes in which foundational patterns, such as Functional Decomposition (300), Service Encapsulation (305), Agnostic Context (312), Non-Agnostic Context (319), and Agnostic Capability (324) first surface to help define the functional contexts and boundaries of services.
- The definition of services in relation to business logic is further supported by the application Service Layers (143), in particular Process Abstraction (182) and Entity Abstraction (175).

- Canonical Schema (158) and Schema Centralization (200) can also be considered supporting patterns in that they allow for the definition of independent data models for business documents that are then used and shared by business-centric services.
- From a broader and more strategic perspective, however, Capability Recomposition (526) represents the key to maintaining alignment with the business in that it is through the ability to repeatedly compose services into new aggregates that changing or new business requirements can be continually fulfilled in an effective manner.

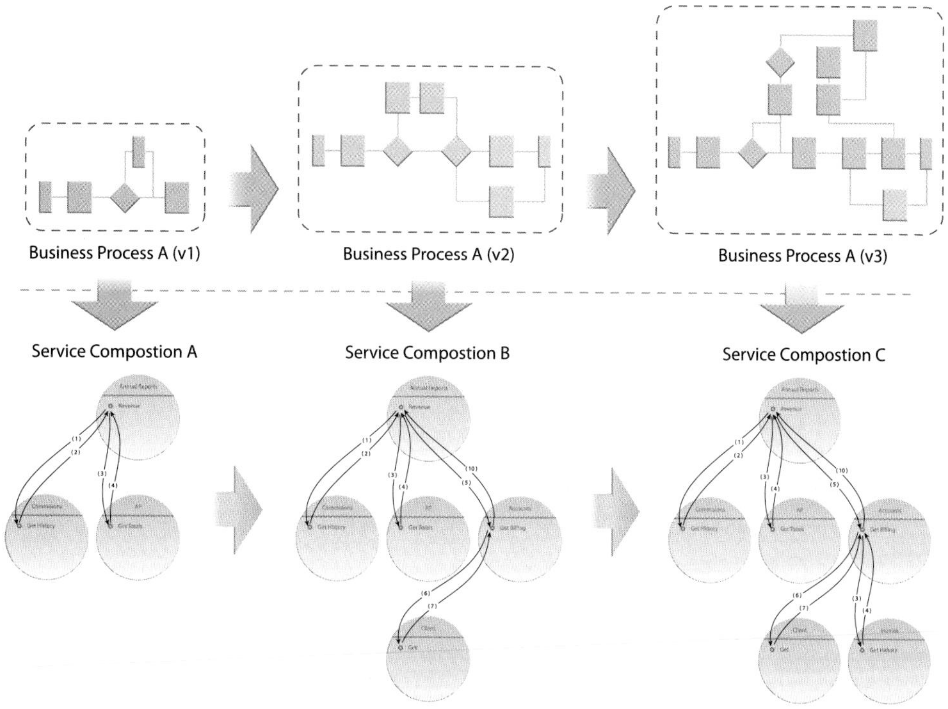

Figure 23.4

A business process (top) will evolve and change over time, and services can be continually composed and recomposed (bottom) to accommodate this change.

Increased ROI

The majority of services for a given inventory are expected to be agnostic, which means they are delivered as IT assets capable of providing repeated value to the organization over time. This leads to cost savings and a measurable return on the initial investment that was required to deliver them (Figure 23.5).

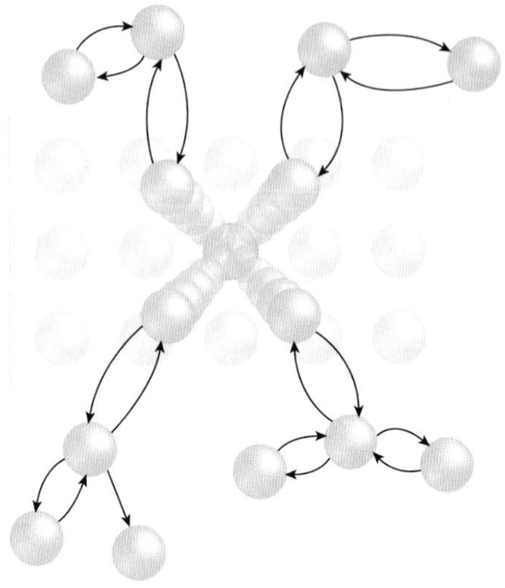

Figure 23.5
An agnostic service becomes a valuable IT asset that can be repeatedly leveraged by being reused as part of multiple compositions. In this figure, each composition invokes multiple instances of the same service.

However, the extent to which each service can realize its ROI potential is directly related to its supporting service, composition, and inventory architectures.

Examples of related patterns:

- On a basic level, this goal is fundamentally supported when agnostic services and their capabilities are first defined via Agnostic Context (312) and Agnostic Capability (324).
- Agnostic services are then further formalized via the application of Entity Abstraction (175) and Utility Abstraction (168), but it's important to also acknowledge Process Abstraction (182) as means by which non-agnostic logic can be separated in support of agnostic service definition.
- Both Logic Centralization (136) and Service Normalization (131) position a body of agnostic service logic as a reusable resource while reducing the chances of overlapping logic from being introduced into the service inventory.
- Numerous patterns help establish a service architecture and supporting infrastructure that enables a given service to be reliably reused and scaled in response to increasing usage demands. Examples include Redundant Implementation (345), Service Data Replication (350), State Repository (242), Stateful Services (248), and Service Grid (254).
- Additionally, patterns like Metadata Centralization (280) and Canonical Expression (275) that help establish governance infrastructure further support the design-time identification and interpretation of services for reuse purposes.

- Finally, it is through Capability Recomposition (526) that reuse and the attainment of increased returns on initial investments are achieved.

Several other more specialized patterns can also play a key part in maximizing reuse by solving design problems specific to creating agnostic services or in relation to their runtime usage.

Increased Organizational Agility

Organizational agility refers to a state at which an enterprise is sufficiently service-oriented so that it can adapt to business change more responsively. This enables the organization as a whole to respond to new requirements or challenges with less time and effort (Figure 23.6). The result is a measurable advantage that increases its efficiency and even its overall competitiveness. To achieve this level of organizational agility, all types service-oriented technology architectures must themselves be inherently flexible and agile.

Because this strategic goal is reliant upon the attainment of several of the previously listed goals, it also benefits from the previously listed patterns that apply to those goals.

For example:

- During their inception, services modeled and designed as per Agnostic Context (312) and Agnostic Capability (324) and further shaped by variations of Service Layers (143) fundamentally establish the ability to continually apply Capability Recomposition (526) in response to new and changing business requirements
- Service Refactoring (484) and the various governance-related patterns further enable services to be more efficiently evolved and adapted.
- Runtime platform patterns, such as Orchestration (701), Enterprise Service Bus (704), and Service Grid (254), can establish effective levels of centralized operation and maintenance in addition to providing sophisticated infrastructure that allows services to be scaled and increases the overall robustness of an inventory architecture.
- The standardization realized by the successful application of canonical patterns, such as Canonical Schema (158), Canonical Protocol (150), and Canonical Versioning (286), is fully leveraged when needing to maximize organizational responsiveness with reduced solution delivery effort.

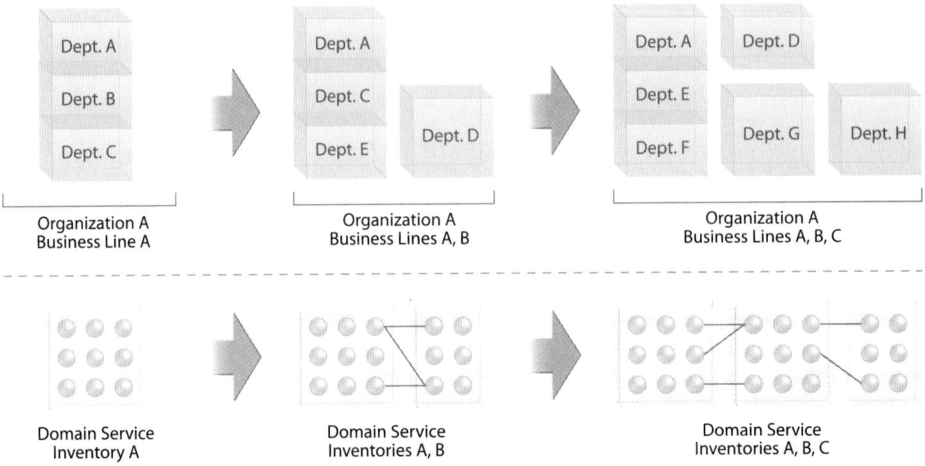

Figure 23.6

An organization will naturally evolve its business vision over time. Inventories of services can grow and can be reconfigured to support these changes, allowing the IT enterprise to move in tandem with the business.

Reduced IT Burden

This ultimate strategic benefit is the result of the combined attainment of increased ROI and increased organizational agility. A service-oriented IT enterprise can essentially offer its parent organization more responsiveness with less effort and cost.

This benefit is strategic in that for it to be continuously realized, the supporting technology environment needs to be properly governed and evolved to keep up with both business change and technology innovation. Providing the maximum business value to the organization in a manner that reduces the impact of IT is the ultimate target state of service-oriented computing. This state is achieved by realizing flexible and effective service, composition, and inventory architectures in full support of strategic business goals—and—maintaining this flexibility and effectiveness by fully leveraging every iteration of the business-technology cycle, thereby allowing both business and IT communities to evolve in support of each other (Figure 23.7).

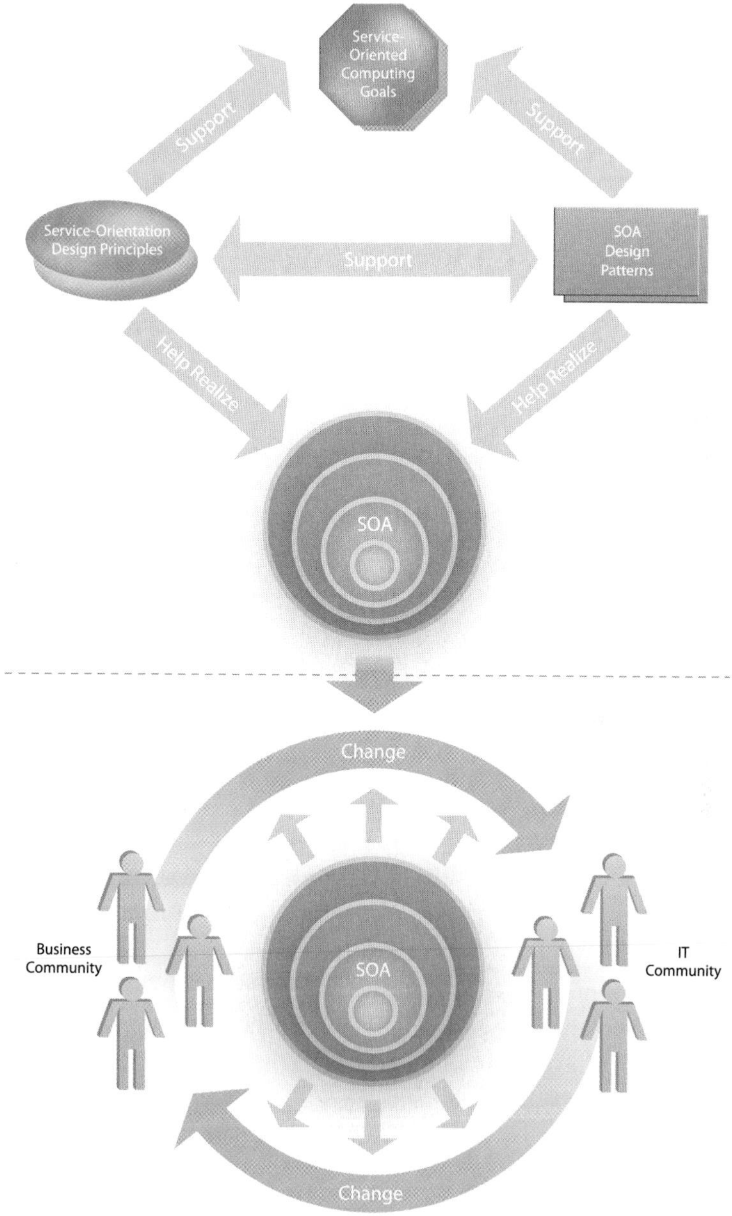

Figure 23.7

The strategic goals of service-oriented computing represent a target state that service-orientation provides a method of achieving. The successful application of service-orientation helps shape and define requirements for different types of service-oriented architectures that end up establishing an IT automation model designed to fully support the endless two-way cycle of change through which business and IT communities continually transition. Amidst all of this, SOA design patterns introduce a critical success factor by providing proven design solutions and practices that support (and are supported by) service-orientation.

Chapter 24

Principles and Patterns at the U.S. Department of Defense

By Dennis Wisnosky, Chief Architect, Business Mission Area, U.S. Department of Defense

The Business Operating Environment (BOE)

Principles, Patterns, and the BOE

The Future of SOA and the DoD

SOADoD.org

"The Department of Defense (DoD) is perhaps the largest and most complex organization in the world. It manages more than twice the budget of the world's largest corporation, employs more people than the population of a third of the world's countries, provides medical care for as many patients as the largest health management organization, and carries five hundred times the number of inventory items as the world's largest commercial retail operation."

—DoD Enterprise Transition Plan, September 2005

In 2005, the U.S. Congress passed the National Defense Authorization Act for FY2005 to modernize and streamline automated business systems within the DoD with the purpose of improving organizational agility and increasing the value of IT in general, while also reducing the historically escalating operational IT costs.

This legislation resulted in the creation of the Business Enterprise Architecture (BEA), which serves as the master blueprint for guiding and constraining the DoD's investments in business systems. These investments total to approximately 53% of the DoD's IT budget, roughly equivalent to the sum of the remainder of the budget for the entire U.S. Federal Government.

In 2006, the Business Mission Area (BMA) decided to plan and manage these investments via an architectural approach based upon SOA as a means of achieving modularity, interoperability, and the DoD's overall goals of "net-centricity" and disciplined information sharing.

NOTE

Net-centricity is the realization of a networked environment that includes infrastructure, systems, processes, and people. Its purpose is to enable net-centric operations—a completely different approach to warfighting, intelligence, and business functions.

Through SOA, the DoD's business IT solutions are being united via an infrastructure and standards-based pattern termed the *Business Operating Environment (BOE)*. The other DoD mission areas (Warfighting, DoD Intelligence, and the Defense Information Environment) are following this same approach. As a result, many of the projects and interrelated sub-projects that drive these mission areas are fundamentally based on the development of services through SOA and service-orientation.

The Business Operating Environment (BOE)

Due to the scale, complexity, and diversity faced by project teams when progressing with SOA adoption and roll-out efforts, the DoD developed a strategy with guiding principles that correlate with service-orientation design principles and with approaches that apply many established SOA design patterns. This strategy is represented by the BOE, and because it encompasses many SOA design patterns, it can therefore itself be considered compound pattern (Figure 24.1).

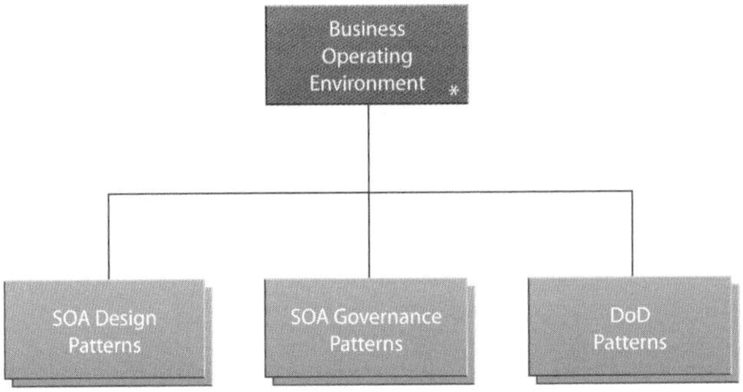

Figure 24.1
The BOE can be represented as a broad compound pattern encompassing SOA design and governance patterns, as well as a number of patterns specific to the DoD.

The emphasis of the BOE is to enable the incremental, phased adoption of SOA within DoD enterprise environments by framing individual service-oriented architecture implementations in support of the overarching business vision and supporting enterprise architectures. Within the BMA, it is intended as a key realization of the DoD's vision for a Global Information Grid and to also integrate and leverage the DoD common SOA infrastructure by establishing a set of core enterprise services and standards to be used across all DoD Components (departments, divisions, organizations that comprise the DoD) and Mission Areas.

This framing approach essentially relies on the identification of the key parts and requirements of an effective service-oriented technology architecture implementation and then guides the development, acquisition, and incorporation of services across multiple business units within the overall enterprise. As such, it sets a model for various parts of the enterprise to follow as they transition to and standardize on service-orientation. The BOE defines and helps propagate a common shared vision of how IT enterprises create and deploy services, resulting in a target state whereby shifts in business and IT strategy can be accommodated at the speed of service composition.

Within the DoD, the BOE essentially establishes a modernized, services-based IT ecosystem.

Principles, Patterns, and the BOE

The BOE is based upon a set of guiding principles formulated to keep the delivery of business capabilities aligned with the net-centric guidance of the DoD while providing support for business transformation. BOE guiding principles individually correspond and relate to a number of SOA design patterns, as well as the service-orientation principles (Figure 24.2) documented in Thomas Erl's *SOA Principles of Service Design*.

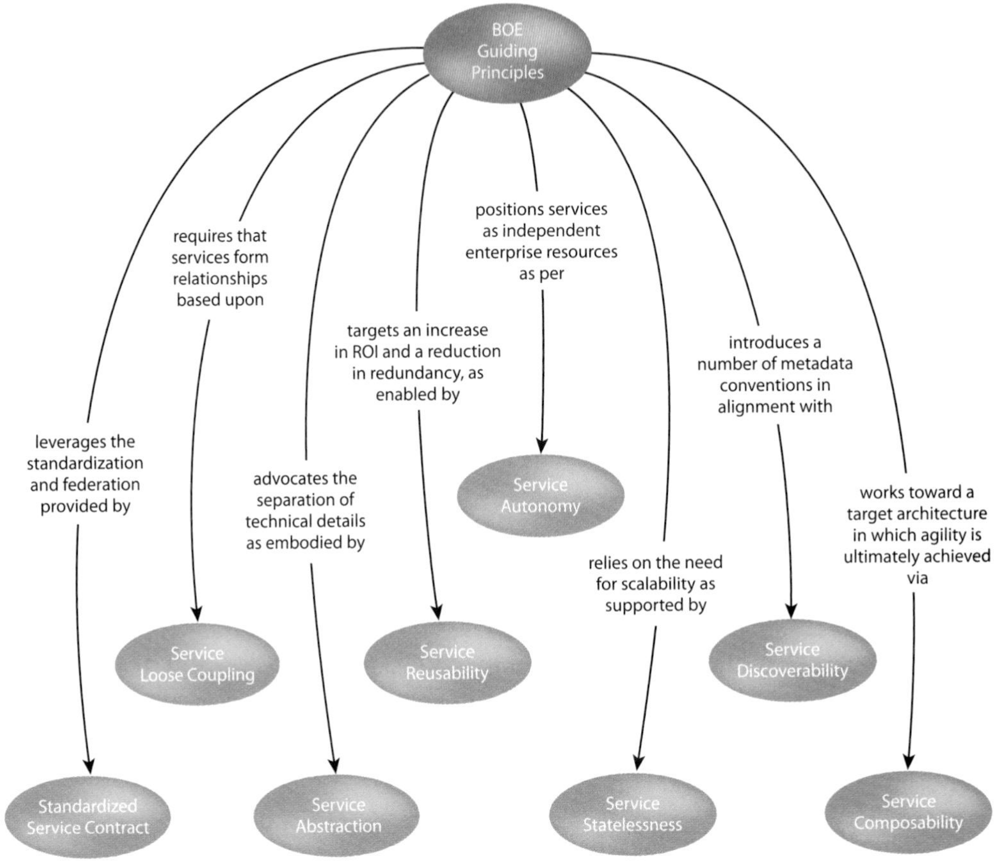

Figure 24.2
BOE guiding principles have a strong relationship with service-orientation principles and share many common goals.

The following sections highlight how BOE guiding principles relate to SOA design patterns and service-orientation design principles.

NOTE

To avoid confusion between BOE and service-orientation principles, BOE principles are referred to as "guiding principles" in the upcoming sections.

Incorporation of Information Assurance (IA)

Information assurance relates specifically to information security. This guiding principle states that the development and application of the BOE will incorporate IA requirements as a core part of the DoD infrastructure and in conformance with pre-defined security standards and directives. Security patterns, such as Direct Authentication (656), Brokered Authentication (661), Data Confidentiality (641), and Data Origin Authentication (649), can play a key role in supporting the goals of this guiding principle.

Adherence to Standards

Vendor neutrality and openness is advocated throughout a technology architecture and realized through the adherence to open standards for consistent system and data interoperability. This is supported by the Standardized Service Contract principle but can also be associated with service-orientation as a whole when it represents the standard paradigm for solution design.

Data Visibility, Accessibility, and Understandability to Support Decision Makers

In support of attaining the goals of DoD Business Transformation and carrying out various related activities (including those described in the DoD Net-Centric Data Strategy and the DoD Net-Centric Services Strategy), business data and services need to be easily located, understood, and reused by authorized users.

To follow this guiding principle, pre-defined protocols and other forms of standardization are applied to information sharing in general. While this is directly supported by the Standardized Service Contract, Service Discoverability, and Service Reusability principles, it also requires the successful application of patterns such as Canonical Schema (158), Contract Centralization (409), and Canonical Protocol (150) to ensure consistent interoperability.

When working with data from legacy repositories, common Service Broker (707) patterns, such as Data Model Transformation (681) and Protocol Bridging (687), may be further required. Also worth noting is that due to their utility-centric nature, data services are generally reliant upon the application of Utility Abstraction (168).

Loosely Coupled Services

The BOE is very much focused on the creation of independent business services in support of the overall DoD SOA initiative (and building upon core infrastructure capabilities provided by the Defense Information Systems Agency). Its ultimate goal is to establish a

"suite" of loosely coupled services and service-oriented solutions to automate cross-enterprise business processes.

While this is clearly aligned with the Service Loose Coupling design principle, it is also supported by the Service Autonomy principle due to the emphasis on establishing independent services that can be readily composed. Service Statelessness may also play a part in realizing the goals of this guiding principle when scalability issues arise.

Because the goal of establishing collections of loosely coupled services is foundational to service-oriented computing in general, this guiding principle can be supported by the application of most SOA design patterns.

Authoritative Sources of Trusted Data

Metadata repositories should be provided for business data asset and service producers so that such data sources can be registered and become visible to potential consumers. When associated with the discovery of data services this can relate to the Service Discoverability principle as well as Metadata Centralization (280).

Positioning data assets and services as authoritative sources of data relies upon the application of Official Endpoint (711), the compound pattern comprised of Logic Centralization (136) and Contract Centralization (409).

When following this guiding principle on a data architecture level, Schema Centralization (200) can become necessary to ensure that individual document schemas provide standardized representations of data sources as well as providing data service consumers with the means to understand the data provided.

Metadata-Driven Framework for Separation from Technical Details

Users and consumers are separated from technical and implementation details by requiring access to only the metadata describing the character and invocation interfaces of the services, as opposed to the underlying technology platforms and approaches used for implementation. This builds upon the search, discovery, and registry extensions established by the preceding guiding principle to create an environment wherein service implementations can be independently governed and evolved without impacting those that use and bind to them.

The Service Abstraction principle embodies the fundamental concepts of information hiding in support of these goals so that services are positioned as black boxes that can be subject to a variety of governance patterns, such as Service Refactoring (484) and Service Decomposition (489).

Support Use of Open Source Software

Open source software solutions will be viewed and used on an equal basis with regular commercial offerings, thereby enabling the DoD to leverage the cost savings and source code availability of open source software.

With the increasing amounts of services-centric open source projects, following this guiding principle opens the door to applying the Service Reusability and Service Composability principles in new ways by building pure open source or hybrid (open source plus commercial) service-oriented solutions.

Emphasize Use of Service-Enabled Commercial Off-the-Shelf (COTS) Software

For COTS product acquisitions to be considered, they must provide built-in support for standardized service interface contracts or for readily producing the same from COTS services that can be customized and pulled into existing service inventories, as per the policies and standards outlined as part of the BOE. A related aspect of this requirement is that COTS functions or capabilities that duplicate common functionality provided by the DoD and BMA enterprise services should be factored out in favor of invoking or using the DoD services.

This relates to several service-orientation principles, including Service Reusability, Service Composability, and Standardized Service Contract. To overcome limitations within (existing or new) COTS products, it may also be necessary to apply legacy-centric patterns, such as Legacy Wrapper (441) or any of the Service Broker (707) patterns.

Participation in the DoD Enterprise

Services produced by projects that follow the BOE approach are in compliance with the overarching DoD enterprise and can interoperate with existing services, such as the DoD enterprise services, regardless of tier.

Principles focused on repurposing services (such as Service Reusability, Service Discoverability, and Service Composability) are critical to achieving this goal, as are core design patterns associated with inter- and intra-inventory interoperability.

Support Mobility — Users & Devices

BOE technology and services should support a wide range of mobile and intermittently-connected devices. This requires that the Service Reusability principle be applied with different types of consumers in mind. Multi-Channel Endpoint (451) can directly address the requirements of this guiding principle, especially when legacy encapsulation is part of the overall service architecture.

The Future of SOA and the DoD

As SOA adoption continues to grow throughout DoD Components (the Office of the Secretary of Defense, the DoD Services, the Combatant Commands, DoD Agencies and Field Activities, etc.), so does the awareness of service-orientation and the necessity for standards, patterns, and principles to be applied appropriately and consistently. In support of these objectives, the BOE remains the driving and guiding force behind the numerous SOA projects that are currently underway in the BMA.

SOADoD.org

There are numerous public documents available about the SOA initiatives at the U.S. Department of Defense. SOADoD.org is a new portal site dedicated to providing specifications, project descriptions, and other resources pertaining to the on-going SOA adoption effort at the DoD.

—Dennis Wisnosky, Chief Architect, Business Mission Area,
U.S. Department of Defense

Part VI

Appendices

Appendix A

Case Study Conclusion

The case study examples provided throughout the chapters in this book have demonstrated the application of patterns in a diverse variety of scenarios, while also providing insight into the technologies commonly used for a given pattern. The following sections briefly summarize the effects of key patterns applied to the three organizations that were studied. Each section also discusses how these patterns helped attain the business goals of the organization, as originally established in Chapter 2.

Cutit Saws Ltd.

The justification for Cutit to invest in an SOA initiative was based on a very clear goal of wanting to take advantage of the recent increase in their product demand and to parlay this into prolonged revenue growth so as to position their company as a prime acquisition target.

The application of the foundational service patterns Functional Decomposition (300), Service Encapsulation (305), Agnostic Context (312), Non-Agnostic Context (319), and Agnostic Capability (324) helped Cutit define a set of services to automate their previously archaic supply-chain process. The resulting Inventory, Chain, Order, and Run Chain Inventory Transfer services were combined into a service-oriented solution that addressed the key goal of improving the automation of their inventory transfer process, while establishing individual services that were ready-made to adapt to future business change.

These and other services were further refined via Canonical Expression (275), and optimized through the application of patterns such as Messaging Metadata (538), Service Callback (566), Service Instance Routing (574), and Compensating Service Transaction (631). The overall Cutit service inventory was also well structured and standardized with the help of Schema Centralization (200) and Policy Centralization (207).

Alleywood Lumber Company

The Alleywood IT enterprise found itself in a more complicated situation, having been acquired by McPherson and forced to find ways to cooperate and interoperate with the IT department of the also-acquired Tri-Fold company. Alleywood's strategic goals were primarily focused on ensuring that the merging and integration of its IT assets within the overall McPherson enterprise was successful.

Throughout the examples, Alleywood faced numerous situations that were solved by the application of design patterns. Perhaps the most significant was the decision by McPherson architects to proceed with Domain Inventory (123), which allowed the Alleywood enterprise to build and govern its own service inventory independently from the one established by Tri-Fold.

While this empowered Alleywood architects to build services and proceed with their SOA adoption on their own terms, overarching standards were still applied by McPherson architects via Canonical Protocol (150) and Canonical Schema (158) across both Alleywood and Tri-Fold inventory domains.

This innovative strategy of defining domain service inventories while still achieving an extent of cross-domain standardization enabled McPherson to attain a high level of baseline interoperability across all services. This, coupled with the cross-domain reuse achieved by Cross-Domain Utility Layer (267) and the master service registry established by Metadata Centralization (280), laid a solid foundation for the attainment of the long-term strategic goal of creating a global IT environment that is diverse, yet still harmonized and streamlined.

While designing and delivering various services, the Alleywood team faced many design problems that were addressed with the help of design patterns. The most memorable scenario perhaps was the security breach that they had to contend with when their Retail Lumber service was attacked and eventually decommissioned. The resulting cooperative effort between Alleywood and McPherson architects and security specialists resulted in a project during which Exception Shielding (376), Trusted Subsystem (387), and Message Screening (381) were applied to produce a vastly improved service design that was protected well beyond the attacks it had previously been subjected to.

Another significant stage in the evolution of Alleywood's service inventory was the application of service governance patterns, such as Service Decomposition (489), Proxy Capability (497), and Distributed Capability (510), which helped augment the Employee service to such an extent that a new Employee Records service was spawned with little disruption to the remaining inventory services.

Forestry Regulatory Commission (FRC)

The FRC's SOA effort was championed by their newly hired CTO who, along with a new set of directors, assumed control over a vast, legacy-ridden IT enterprise. The adoption of SOA was viewed as the wholesale solution to overcoming the skyrocketing operational costs that had been consuming more and more of the FRC's budget over the past years.

Subsequent to defining the planned service inventory, various FRC project teams went about modeling, designing, and building services. Because so much legacy logic needed encapsulation, the Legacy Wrapper (441) example typified a common service implementation, whereby outdated or proprietary APIs and interfaces needed to be wrapped by standardized service contracts. Other legacy encapsulation patterns, such as Multi-Channel Endpoint (451), helped further bring legacy assets into the service inventory so that they could be made available to a wider variety of consumers without imposing negative coupling requirements.

A key part of the overall SOA initiative was also establishing governance controls so that the planned inventory of services could be more effectively and efficiently maintained and evolved. This is where patterns such as Version Identification (472), Compatible Change (465), and Termination Notification (478) played important roles.

During its initial adoption stages, the FRC invested heavily in infrastructure upgrades which resulted in highly sophisticated messaging frameworks supported by the application of patterns such as Asynchronous Queuing (582), Intermediate Routing (549), Event-Driven Messaging (599), and Reliable Messaging (592). This allowed for the development of mission-critical solutions (e.g., the Flight Plan Validation service) that could leverage the quality-of-service features provided by the messaging framework, as well as the loosely coupled nature of message-based communication itself.

Combined with the architectural enhancements brought about by patterns such as Stateful Services (248) and Service Data Replication (350), the FRC has built an inventory of services that are scalable, reliable, and repeatedly composable into a variety of sophisticated solutions.

Appendix B

Candidate Patterns

The patterns documented in this book were in development for nearly 40 months prior to publication in printed format. During this period, the pattern catalog underwent exhaustive reviews by SOA experts and practitioners, key members of the patterns community, as well as members of the vendor and academic communities. Additionally, an open public review of the first draft of the manuscript of this book was held for several months at SOAPatterns.org during which 234 individual reviews were collected. The *History* and *Acknowledgements* pages at this Web site provide further details regarding past review stages and cycles.

The feedback collected as a result of this review process helped validate many patterns, but also helped identify those patterns that were either invalid or not yet ready to be considered fully proven or field-tested. At the time of this writing, a subset of the original patterns were deemed "not ready" for inclusion in the official SOA design pattern catalog and were therefore classified as *candidate patterns*.

Draft versions of these patterns are published in the *Candidate Patterns* part of the SOAPatterns.org Web site, where they are made available for public review until such a point that they are considered fully validated. After that, they are moved to the master SOA design patterns catalog.

Some notable patterns that were classified as candidates are those inspired by REST. A set of patterns co-authored by IBM's Raj Balasubramanian (also co-author of the upcoming series title *SOA with REST*) was originally developed for this book but then excluded, as per recommendations from industry experts in the REST community. There was concern over the maturity of the REST-related technologies and concepts upon which the patterns were based. These patterns are expected to remain candidates for at least a year before they are individually re-assessed.

Other candidate patterns include several grid-related patterns contributed by David Chappell from Oracle and the Service Virtualization pattern from Satadru Roy of Sun Microsystems.

You are encouraged to visit SOAPatterns.org to view these and other candidate patterns and to also provide your comments and opinions using the online feedback forms. Note that SOAPatterns.org is different from SOAPatterns.com. The former is a community site dedicated to SOA patterns in general, whereas the latter acts as the official Web site for this book.

Appendix C

Principles of Service-Orientation

The first draft of the *SOA Design Patterns* manuscript was originally written for a book that was to be called "SOA: Principles and Patterns." After the manuscript became too bulky for one book, it was decided to split it up into two titles: one about design patterns and one about design principles.

The latter was published in a book called *SOA Principles of Service Design,* which preceded *SOA Design Patterns.* Eight specific design principles were documented in this book, each explored in a dedicated chapter. Collectively, these principles comprise the service-orientation design paradigm, as explained earlier in Chapters 3 and 4.

As much as patterns inter-relate, principles too can relate to patterns as well as to each other. You may have noticed that the profile tables for the patterns in this book reference these principles wherever common relationships might exist. A cross-reference of these relationships is provided in Appendix D.

As an additional reference resource, the original profile tables for the principles themselves are provided in this appendix, as follows:

- Standardized Service Contract (Table C.1)
- Service Loose Coupling (Table C.2)
- Service Abstraction (Table C.3)
- Service Reusability (Table C.4)
- Service Autonomy (Table C.5)
- Service Statelessness (Table C.6)
- Service Discoverability (Table C.7)
- Service Composability (Table C.8)

You are also encouraged to visit SOAPrinciples.com for more background information about service-orientation.

NOTE

The profile tables in this appendix contain excerpts from *SOA Principles of Service Design* and therefore also include some terms and references specific to that book.

Standardized Service Contract	
Short Definition	*"Services share standardized contracts."*
Long Definition	*"Services within the same service inventory are in compliance with the same contract design standards."*
Goals	• To enable services with a meaningful level of natural interoperability within the boundary of a service inventory. This reduces the need for data transformation because consistent data models are used for information exchange. • To allow the purpose and capabilities of services to be more easily and intuitively understood. The consistency with which service functionality is expressed through service contracts increases interpretability and the overall predictability of service endpoints throughout a service inventory. Note that these goals are further supported by other service-orientation principles as well.
Design Characteristics	• A service contract (comprised of a technical interface or one or more service description documents) is provided with the service. • The service contract is standardized through the application of design standards.
Implementation Requirements	The fact that contracts need to be standardized can introduce significant implementation requirements to organizations that do not have a history of using standards. For example: • Design standards and conventions need to ideally be in place prior to the delivery of any service in order to ensure adequately scoped standardization. (For those organizations that have already produced ad-hoc Web services, retro-fitting strategies may need to be employed.) • Formal processes need to be introduced to ensure that services are modeled and designed consistently, incorporating accepted design principles, conventions, and standards.

	• Because achieving standardized Web service contracts generally requires a "contract first" approach to service-oriented design, the full application of this principle will often demand the use of development tools capable of importing a customized service contract without imposing changes. • Appropriate skill-sets are required to carry out the modeling and design processes with the chosen tools. When working with Web services, the need for a high level of proficiency with XML schema and WSDL languages is practically unavoidable. WS-Policy expertise may also be required. These and other requirements can add up to a noticeable transition effort that goes well beyond technology adoption.
Web Service Region of Influence	Because this principle is focused solely on the content of the service contract, its influence is limited to the contract and related processing logic within a typical Web service. 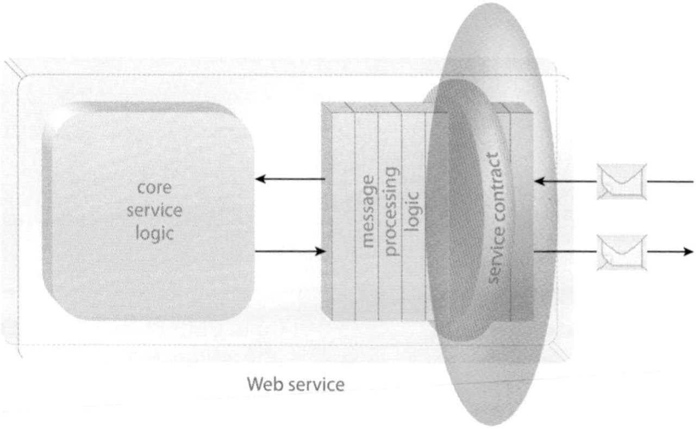

Table C.1

A profile for the Standardized Service Contract principle.

Service Loose Coupling	
Short Definition	*"Services are loosely coupled."*
Long Definition	*"Service contracts impose low consumer coupling requirements and are themselves decoupled from their surrounding environment."*
Goals	By consistently fostering reduced coupling within and between services we are working toward a state where service contracts increase independence from their implementations and services are increasingly independent from each other. This promotes an environment in which services and their consumers can be adaptively evolved over time with minimal impact on each other.
Design Characteristics	• The existence of a service contract that is ideally decoupled from technology and implementation details. • A functional service context that is not dependent on outside logic. • Minimal consumer coupling requirements.
Implementation Requirements	• Loosely coupled services are typically required to perform more runtime processing than if they were more tightly coupled. As a result, data exchange in general can consume more runtime resources, especially during concurrent access and high usage scenarios. • To achieve the right balance of coupling, while also supporting the other service-orientation principles that affect contract design, requires increased service contract design proficiency.

Web Service Region of Influence	As we explore different coupling types in the next section, it will become evident that applying this principle touches numerous parts of the typical Web service architecture. However, the primary focal point, both for internal and consumer-related design considerations, remains the service contract. 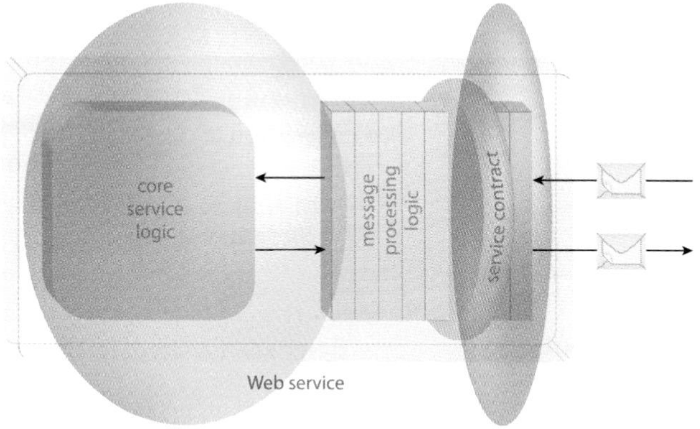

Table C.2

A profile for the Service Loose Coupling principle.

Service Abstraction	
Short Definition	*"Non-essential service information is abstracted."*
Long Definition	*"Service contracts only contain essential information and information about services is limited to what is published in service contracts."*
Goals	Many of the other principles emphasize the need to publish *more* information in the service contract. The primary role of this principle is to keep the quantity and detail of contract content concise and balanced and prevent unnecessary access to additional service details.
Design Characteristics	• Services consistently abstract specific information about technology, logic, and function away from the outside world (the world outside of the service boundary). • Services have contracts that concisely define interaction requirements and constraints and other required service meta details. • Outside of what is documented in the service contract, information about a service is controlled or altogether hidden within a particular environment.
Implementation Requirements	The primary prerequisite to achieving the appropriate level of abstraction for each service is the level of service contract design skill applied.
Web Service Region of Influence	The *Region of Influence* part of this profile has been moved to the *Types of Meta Abstraction* section (in the book *SOA Principles of Service Design*) where a separate Web service figure is provided for each form of abstraction.

Table C.3

A profile for the Service Abstraction principle.

<table>
<tr><th colspan="2">Service Reusability</th></tr>
<tr><td>Short Definition</td><td>"Services are reusable."</td></tr>
<tr><td>Long Definition</td><td>"Services contain and express agnostic logic and can be positioned as reusable enterprise resources."</td></tr>
<tr><td>Goals</td><td>The goals behind Service Reusability are tied directly to some of the most strategic objectives of service-oriented computing:<ul><li>To allow for service logic to be repeatedly leveraged over time so as to achieve an increasingly high return on the initial investment of delivering the service.</li><li>To increase business agility on an organizational level by enabling the rapid fulfillment of future business automation requirements through wide-scale service composition.</li><li>To enable the realization of agnostic service models.</li><li>To enable the creation of service inventories with a high percentage of agnostic services.</li></ul></td></tr>
<tr><td>Design Characteristics</td><td><ul><li>The service is defined by an agnostic functional context—The logic encapsulated by the service is associated with a context that is sufficiently agnostic to any one usage scenario so as to be considered reusable.</li><li>The service logic is highly generic—The logic encapsulated by the service is sufficiently generic, allowing it to facilitate numerous usage scenarios by different types of service consumers.</li><li>The service has a generic and extensible contract—The service contract is flexible enough to process a range of input and output messages.</li><li>The service logic can be accessed concurrently—Services are designed to facilitate simultaneous access by multiple consumer programs.</li></ul></td></tr>
<tr><td>Implementation Requirements</td><td>From an implementation perspective, Service Reusability can be the most demanding of the principles we've covered so far. Below are common requirements for creating reusable services and supporting their long-term existence:</td></tr>
</table>

	• A scalable runtime hosting environment capable of high-to-extreme concurrent service usage. Once a service inventory is relatively mature, reusable services will find themselves in an increasingly large number of compositions. • A solid version control system to properly evolve contracts representing reusable services. • Service analysts and designers with a high degree of subject matter expertise who can ensure that the service boundary and contract accurately represent the service's reusable functional context. • A high level of service development and commercial software development expertise so as to structure the underlying logic into generic and potentially decomposable components and routines. These and other requirements place an emphasis on the appropriate staffing of the service delivery team, as well as the importance of a powerful and scalable hosting environment and supporting infrastructure.
Web Service Region of Influence	This principle can affect all parts of a Web service. Contract design, the use of system messaging agents, and the underlying core logic can all be shaped by a service's reusability requirements. When we view the service as an IT asset that requires an investment but provides the potential for repeated returns, we can appreciate why more care needs to be taken when designing each part of the service architecture. 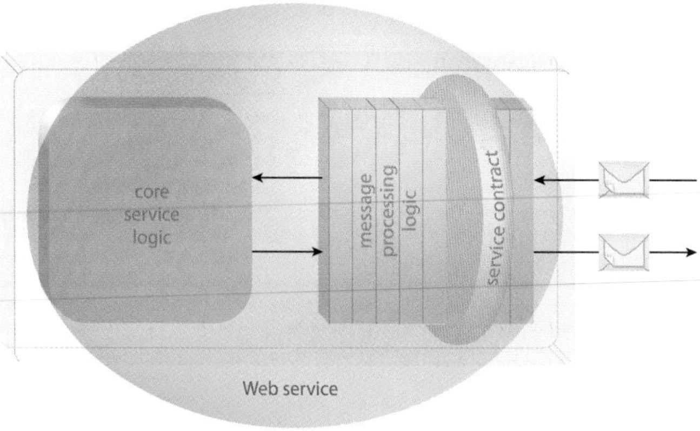

Table C.4

A profile for the Service Reusability principle.

Service Autonomy	
Short Definition	*"Services are autonomous."*
Long Definition	*"Services exercise a high level of control over their underlying runtime execution environment."*
Goals	• To increase a service's runtime reliability, performance, and predictability, especially when being reused and composed. • To increase the amount of control a service has over its runtime environment. By pursuing autonomous design and runtime environments, we are essentially aiming to increase post-implementation control over the service and the service's control over its own execution environment.
Design Characteristics	• Services have a contract that expresses a well-defined functional boundary that should not overlap with other services. • Services are deployed in an environment over which they exercise a great deal (and preferably an exclusive level) of control. • Service instances are hosted by an environment that accommodates high concurrency for scalability purposes.
Implementation Requirements	• A high level of control over how service logic is designed and developed. Depending on the level of autonomy being sought, this may also involve control over the supporting data models. • A distributable deployment environment, so as to allow the service to be moved, isolated, or composed as required. • An infrastructure capable of supporting desired autonomy levels.

Web Service Region of Influence	Service Autonomy is almost exclusively focused on the service implementation, with an emphasis on the core service logic and any resources it may need at runtime. However, the service contract is also affected due to normalization considerations (as explained later). 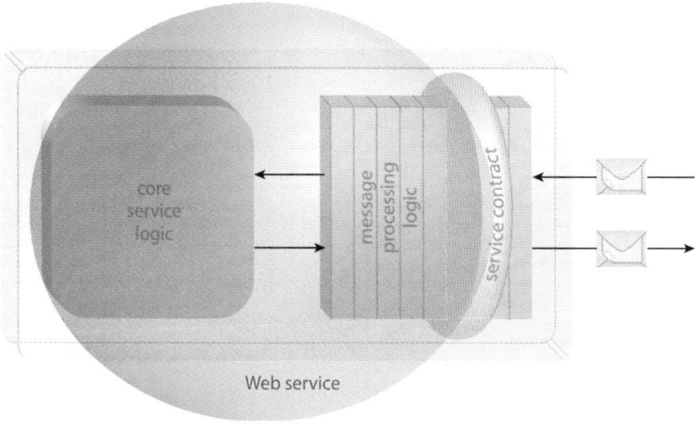

Table C.5
A profile for the Service Autonomy principle.

Service Statelessness	
Short Definition	*"Services minimize statefulness."*
Long Definition	*"Services minimize resource consumption by deferring the management of state information when necessary."*
Goals	• To increase service scalability. • To support the design of agnostic service logic and improve the potential for service reuse.
Design Characteristics	What makes this somewhat of a unique principle is the fact that it is promoting a condition of the service that is temporary in nature. Depending on the service model and state deferral approach used, different types of design characteristics can be implemented. Some examples include: • Highly business process-agnostic logic so that the service is not designed to retain state information for any specific parent business process. • Less constrained service contracts so as to allow for the receipt and transmission of a wider range of state data at runtime. • Increased amounts of interpretative programming routines capable of parsing a range of state information delivered by messages and responding to a range of corresponding action requests.
Implementation Requirements	Although state deferral can reduce the overall consumption of memory and system resources, services designed with statelessness considerations can also introduce some performance demands associated with the runtime retrieval and interpretation of deferred state data. Here is a short checklist of common requirements that can be used to assess the support of stateless service designs by vendor technologies and target deployment locations: • The runtime environment should allow for a service to transition from an idle state to an active processing state in a highly efficient manner.

	• Enterprise-level or high-performance XML parsers and hardware accelerators (and SOAP processors) should be provided to allow services implemented as Web services to more efficiently parse larger message payloads with less performance constraints. • The use of attachments may need to be supported by Web services to allow for messages to include bodies of payload data that do not undergo interface-level validation or translation to local formats. The nature of the implementation support required by the average stateless service in an environment will depend on the state deferral approach used within the service-oriented architecture.
Web Service Region of Influence	Building a service to maximize the stateless condition affects the service contract design but can also directly influence how service logic is designed, right down to the individual programming routines and even the core algorithms that lie beneath each service capability. 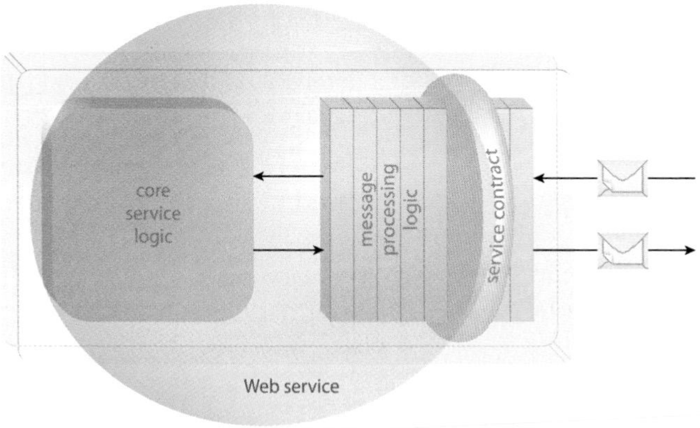

Table C.6
A profile for the Service Statelessness principle.

Service Discoverability	
Short Definition	*"Services are discoverable."*
Long Definition	*"Services are supplemented with communicative meta data by which they can be effectively discovered and interpreted."*
Goals	• Services are positioned as highly discoverable resources within the enterprise. • The purpose and capabilities of each service are clearly expressed so that they can be interpreted by humans and software programs. Achieving these goals requires foresight and a solid understanding of the nature of the service itself. Depending on the type of service model being designed, realizing this principle may require both business and technical expertise.
Design Characteristics	• Service contracts are equipped with appropriate meta data that will be correctly referenced when discovery queries are issued. • Service contracts are further outfitted with additional meta information that clearly communicates their purpose and capabilities to humans. • If a service registry exists, registry records are populated with the same attention to meta information as just described. • If a service registry does not exist, service profile documents are authored to supplement the service contract and to form the basis for future registry records. (See Chapter 15 in *SOA Principles of Service Design* for more details about service profiles.)

Implementation Requirements	• The existence of design standards that govern the meta information used to make service contracts discoverable and interpretable, as well as guidelines for how and when service contracts should be further supplemented with annotations. • The existence of design standards that establish a consistent means of recording service meta information outside of the contract. This information is either collected in a supplemental document in preparation for a service registry, or it is placed in the registry itself. You may have noticed the absence of a service registry on the list of implementation requirements. As previously established, the goal of this principle is to implement design characteristics within the service, not within the architecture.
Web Service Region of Influence	Even though we ultimately want a discovery mechanism in place, it is also ideal for service contracts to be independently discoverable and interpretable. From a Web service perspective, this principle is focused solely on the service contract documents. 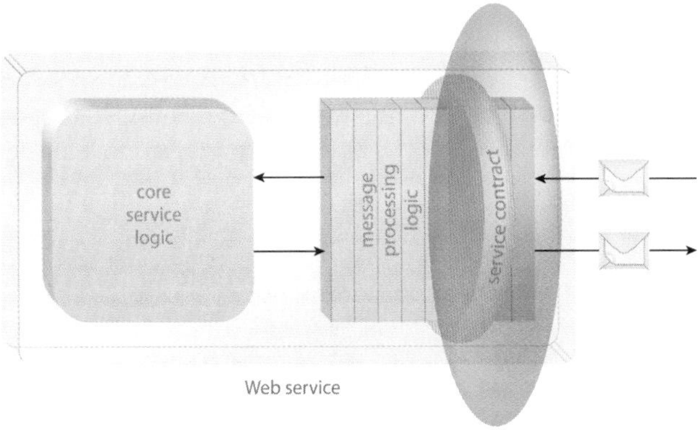

Table C.7
A profile for the Service Discoverability principle.

Service Composability	
Short Definition	*"Services are composable."*
Long Definition	*"Services are effective composition participants, regardless of the size and complexity of the composition."*
Goals	When discussing the goals of Service Composability, pretty much all of the goals of Service Reusability apply. This is because service composition often turns out to be a form of service reuse. In fact, you may recall that one of the objectives we listed for the Service Reusability principle was to enable wide-scale service composition. However, above and beyond simply attaining reuse, service composition provides the medium through which we can achieve what is often classified as the ultimate goal of service-oriented computing. By establishing an enterprise comprised of solution logic represented by an inventory of highly reusable services, we provide the means for a large extent of future business automation requirements to be fulfilled through... you guessed it: service composition.
Design Characteristics for Composition Member Capabilities	Ideally, every service capability (especially those providing reusable logic) is considered a potential composition member. This essentially means that the design characteristics already established by the Service Reusability principle are equally relevant to building effective composition members. Additionally, there are two further characteristics emphasized by this principle: • The service needs to possess a highly efficient execution environment. More so than being able to manage concurrency, the efficiency with which composition members perform their individual processing should be highly tuned. • The service contract needs to be flexible so that it can facilitate different types of data exchange requirements for similar functions. This typically relates to the ability of the contract to exchange the same type of data at different levels of granularity.

	The manner in which these qualities go beyond mere reuse has to do primarily with the service being capable of optimizing its runtime processing responsibilities in support of multiple, simultaneous compositions.
Design Characteristics for Composition Controller Capabilities	Composition members will often also need to act as controllers or sub-controllers within different composition configurations. However, services designed as designated controllers are generally alleviated from many of the high-performance demands placed on composition members. These types of services therefore have their own set of design characteristics: • The logic encapsulated by a designated controller will almost always be limited to a single business task. Typically, the task service model is used, resulting in the common characteristics of that model being applied to this type of service. • While designated controllers may be reusable, service reuse is not usually a primary design consideration. Therefore, the design characteristics fostered by Service Reusability are considered and applied where appropriate, but with less of the usual rigor applied to agnostic services. • Statelessness is not always as strictly emphasized on designated controllers as with composition members. Depending on the state deferral options available by the surrounding architecture, designated controllers may sometimes need to be designed to remain fully stateful while the underlying composition members carry out their respective parts of the overall task. Of course, any capability acting as a controller can become a member of a larger composition, which brings the previously listed composition member design characteristics into account as well.

Table C.8

A profile for the Service Composability principle.

Appendix D

Patterns and Principles Cross-Reference

For quick reference purposes, this appendix provides a master cross-reference of service-orientation design principles and SOA design patterns based on the principles listed in the *Principles* cell of the profile tables that begin each pattern description. Note that these design principles are briefly explained in Appendix C and more information about the service-orientation design paradigm is available at SOAPrinciples.com.

Design Principle	Referenced by Patterns
Standardized Service Contract	Agnostic Capability (324)
	Asynchronous Queuing (582)
	Canonical Expression (275)
	Canonical Protocol (150)
	Canonical Schema (158)
	Canonical Versioning (286)
	Capability Composition (521)
	Capability Recomposition (526)
	Compatible Change (465)
	Concurrent Contracts (421)
	Contract Centralization (409)
	Contract Denormalization (414)
	Data Format Transformation (681)
	Data Model Transformation (671)
	Decomposed Capability (504)
	Decoupled Contract (401)
	Distributed Capability (510)
	Domain Inventory (123)

Design Principle	Referenced by Patterns
Standardized Service Contract	Dual Protocols (227) Enterprise Inventory (116) Event-Driven Messaging (599) Inventory Endpoint (260) Legacy Wrapper (441) Message Screening (381) Non-Agnostic Context (319) Partial Validation (362) Policy Centralization (207) Protocol Bridging (687) Schema Centralization (200) Service Callback (566) Service Façade (333) Service Messaging (533) Service Refactoring (484) State Messaging (557) Termination Notification (478) Validation Abstraction (429) Version Identification (472)
Service Loose Coupling	Asynchronous Queuing (582) Capability Composition (521) Capability Recomposition (526) Compatible Change (465) Compensating Service Transaction (631) Concurrent Contracts (421)

(continues)

(continued)

Design Principle	Referenced by Patterns
Service Loose Coupling	Contract Centralization (409) Contract Denormalization (414) Data Format Transformation (681) Decoupled Contract (401) Dual Protocols (227) Entity Abstraction (175) Event-Driven Messaging (599) File Gateway (457) Intermediate Routing (549) Inventory Endpoint (260) Legacy Wrapper (441) Messaging Metadata (538) Multi-Channel Endpoint (451) Partial Validation (362) Policy Centralization (207) Process Abstraction (182) Proxy Capability (497) Schema Centralization (200) Service Agent (543) Service Callback (566) Service Decomposition (489) Service Façade (333) Service Instance Routing (574) Service Messaging (533) Service Perimeter Guard (394) Service Refactoring (484)

Design Principle	Referenced by Patterns
Service Loose Coupling	Trusted Subsystem (387) UI Mediator (366) Utility Abstraction (168) Validation Abstraction (429)
Service Abstraction	Capability Composition (521) Capability Recomposition (526) Decomposed Capability (504) Domain Inventory (123) Dual Protocols (227) Enterprise Inventory (116) Entity Abstraction (175) Exception Shielding (376) Inventory Endpoint (260) Legacy Wrapper (441) Policy Centralization (207) Process Abstraction (182) Service Perimeter Guard (394) Service Refactoring (484) Utility Abstraction (168) Validation Abstraction (429)
Service Reusability	Agnostic Capability (324) Agnostic Context (312) Agnostic Sub-Controller (607) Capability Composition (521) Capability Recomposition 526)

(continues)

(continued)

Design Principle	Referenced by Patterns
Service Reusability	Composition Autonomy (616) Concurrent Contracts (421) Cross-Domain Utility Layer (267) Data Model Transformation (671) Entity Abstraction (175) Intermediate Routing (549) Logic Centralization (136) Multi-Channel Endpoint (451) Rules Centralization (216) Service Agent (543) Service Layers (143) Utility Abstraction (168)
Service Autonomy	Canonical Resources (237) Capability Composition (521) Capability Recomposition (526) Composition Autonomy (616) Distributed Capability (510) Dual Protocols (227) Event-Driven Messaging (599) Process Centralization (193) Redundant Implementation (345) Service Data Replication (350) Service Normalization (131)

Design Principle	Referenced by Patterns
Service Statelessness	Asynchronous Queuing (582)
	Atomic Service Transaction (623)
	Capability Composition (521)
	Capability Recomposition (526)
	Messaging Metadata (538)
	Partial State Deferral (356)
	Process Centralization (193)
	Service Grid (254)
	Service Instance Routing (574)
	State Messaging (557)
	State Repository (242)
	Stateful Services (248)
Service Discoverability	Canonical Expression (275)
	Capability Composition (521)
	Capability Recomposition (526)
	Metadata Centralization (280)
Service Composability	Agnostic Capability (324)
	Agnostic Sub-Controller (607)
	Brokered Authentication (661)
	Capability Composition (521)
	Capability Recomposition (526)
	Composition Autonomy (616)
	Cross-Domain Utility Layer (267)
	Data Confidentiality (641)
	Data Model Transformation (671)

(continues)

(continued)

Design Principle	Referenced by Patterns
Service Composability	Data Origin Authentication (649)
	Direct Authentication (656)
	Domain Inventory (123)
	Dual Protocols (227)
	Enterprise Inventory (116)
	Entity Abstraction (175)
	Intermediate Routing (549)
	Logic Centralization (136)
	Non-Agnostic Context (319)
	Process Abstraction (182)
	Process Centralization (193)
	Protocol Bridging (687)
	Reliable Messaging (592)
	Service Callback (566)
	Service Decomposition (489)
	Service Instance Routing (574)
	Service Layers (143)
	State Messaging (557)
	Utility Abstraction (168)

Appendix E

Patterns and Architecture Types Cross-Reference

Provided in this appendix is a cross-reference table with the four SOA architecture types established in Chapter 4 referenced against SOA design patterns, based on the architecture types listed in the *Architecture* cell of each pattern profile table.

Architecture Type	Referenced by Patterns
Service	Agnostic Capability (324) Agnostic Context (312) Agnostic Sub-Controller (607) Brokered Authentication (661) Canonical Expression (275) Canonical Protocol (150) Canonical Schema (158) Canonical Versioning (286) Capability Composition (521) Capability Recomposition (526) Compatible Change (465) Concurrent Contracts (421) Contract Denormalization (414) Data Confidentiality (641) Data Format Transformation (681) Decomposed Capability (504) Decoupled Contract (401) Direct Authentication (656) Distributed Capability (510)

Architecture Type	Referenced by Patterns
Service	Dual Protocols (227) Entity Abstraction (175) Event-Driven Messaging (599) Exception Shielding (376) File Gateway (457) Functional Decomposition (300) Legacy Wrapper (441) Logic Centralization (136) Message Screening (381) Multi-Channel Endpoint (451) Non-Agnostic Context (319) Partial State Deferral (356) Policy Centralization (193) Process Abstraction (182) Proxy Capability (497) Redundant Implementation (345) Schema Centralization (200) Service Callback (566) Service Data Replication (350) Service Decomposition (489) Service Encapsulation (305) Service Façade (333) Service Grid (254) Service Instance Routing (574) Service Layers (143) Service Messaging (533)

continues

(continued)

Architecture Type	Referenced by Patterns
Service	Service Normalization (131) Service Perimeter Guard (394) Service Refactoring (484) State Messaging (557) State Repository (242) Stateful Services (248) Termination Notification (478) Trusted Subsystem (387) Utility Abstraction (168) Validation Abstraction (429) Version Identification (472)
Composition	Agnostic Sub-Controller (607) Asynchronous Queuing (582) Atomic Service Transaction (623) Brokered Authentication (661) Capability Composition (521) Capability Recomposition (526) Compensating Service Transaction (631) Composition Autonomy (616) Contract Centralization (409) Data Confidentiality (641) Data Format Transformation (681) Data Model Transformation (671) Data Origin Authentication (649) Direct Authentication (656)

Architecture Type	Referenced by Patterns
Composition	Entity Abstraction (175) Intermediate Routing (549) Logic Centralization (136) Messaging Metadata (538) Partial Validation (362) Process Abstraction (182) Process Centralization (193) Reliable Messaging (592) Service Agent (543) Service Callback (566) Service Instance Routing (574) Service Messaging (533) State Messaging (557) Termination Notification (478) UI Mediator (366) Utility Abstraction (168)
Inventory	Asynchronous Queuing (582) Atomic Service Transaction (623) Brokered Authentication (661) Canonical Expression (275) Canonical Protocol (150) Canonical Resources (237) Canonical Schema (158) Canonical Versioning (286) Capability Composition (521)

continues

(continued)

Architecture Type	Referenced by Patterns
Inventory	Capability Recomposition (526) Compensating Service Transaction (631) Cross-Domain Utility Layer (267) Data Confidentiality (641) Data Format Transformation (681) Data Model Transformation (671) Domain Inventory (123) Enterprise Inventory (116) Logic Centralization (136) Service Normalization (131) Dual Protocols (227) Entity Abstraction (175) Event-Driven Messaging (599) Inventory Endpoint (260) Metadata Centralization (280) Partial State Deferral (356) Policy Centralization (207) Process Abstraction (182) Process Centralization (193) Reliable Messaging (592) Rules Centralization (216) Schema Centralization (200) Service Agent (543) Service Callback (566) Service Data Replication (350)

Architecture Type	Referenced by Patterns
Inventory	Service Grid (254) Service Instance Routing (574) Service Layers (143) Service Messaging (533) State Repository (242) Stateful Services (248) Utility Abstraction (168)
Enterprise	Canonical Expression (275) Canonical Resources (237) Cross-Domain Utility Layer (267) Domain Inventory (123) Enterprise Inventory (116) Metadata Centralization (280) Service Grid (254)

Table E.1

About the Author

Thomas Erl is the world's top-selling SOA author, Series Editor of the *Prentice Hall Service-Oriented Computing Series from Thomas Erl,* and Editor of *The SOA Magazine* (www.soamag.com). With over 100,000 copies in print world-wide, his books have become international bestsellers and have been formally endorsed by senior members of major software organizations, such as IBM, Microsoft, Oracle, BEA, Sun, Intel, SAP, CISCO, and HP.

His most recent titles *SOA Design Patterns* and *Web Service Contract Design and Versioning for SOA* were co-authored with a series of industry experts and follow his first three books *Service-Oriented Architecture: A Field Guide to Integrating XML and Web Services, Service-Oriented Architecture: Concepts, Technology, and Design,* and *SOA Principles of Service Design.*

Thomas is currently working with over 20 authors on the upcoming titles: *SOA Governance, SOA with .NET, SOA with Java, ESB Architecture for SOA,* and *SOA with REST.* He is also overseeing the SOAPatterns.org initiative, a community site dedicated to SOA patterns.

Thomas is the founder of SOA Systems Inc. (www.soasystems.com), a company specializing in vendor-neutral SOA consulting and training services. Thomas is also the founder of the internationally recognized SOA Certified Professional program (www.soacp.com and www.soaschool.com). Thomas is a speaker and instructor for private and public events and is regularly invited to Gartner summits. He has delivered many workshops and keynote speeches, and is on the program committee for the International SOA Symposium. Articles and interviews by Thomas have been published in numerous publications, including *The Wall Street Journal* and *CIO Magazine.*

For more information, visit: www.thomaserl.com.

About the Contributors

Provided in this section are biographies for some of the contributors. For a cross-reference of contributors and patterns, see the *Index of Patterns* page located before the main index at the end of this book.

David Chappell

David Chappell is Vice President and Chief Technologist for SOA at Oracle, where he is driving the vision for Oracle's SOA Grid initiative. David has more thanr 20 years of experience in the software industry. He is well known worldwide for his writings and public lectures on the subjects of service-oriented architecture (SOA), the enterprise service bus (ESB), message oriented middleware (MOM), enterprise integration, and is a co-author of many advanced Web Services standards. As author of *Enterprise Service Bus* (O'Reilly, 2004), David has had tremendous impact on redefining the shape and definition of SOA infrastructure. David is also currently working on a separate title dedicated to grid-enabled service-oriented architecture, a topic he has already written extensively about.

Kevlin Henney

Kevlin Henney is an independent consultant and trainer based in the UK. His areas of interest and practice are software architecture and patterns, programming languages and techniques, and agile development processes and practices. He is and has been a columnist for a number of software development magazines and sites, including Better Software, The Register, Java Report, and C++ Report. Kevlin is co-author of Volumes 4 and 5 in the *Pattern-Oriented Software Architecture series* (A Pattern Language for Distributed Computing and On Patterns and Pattern Languages).

Florent Georges

Florent is a freelance IT consultant in Brussels who has been involved in the XML world for more than 11 years and is a recognized expert within the XSLT and XQuery communities. Soon after discovering Web services, he had the opportunity to work with them for several years with major European institutions and companies in the financial and IT consultancy sectors in Brussels and London, such as ING and Atos Origin. In 2008 Florent won the SOACP contest by tying for the highest score among all participants in a series of certification workshops associated with the 2008 International SOA Symposium. As a result, Florent received his SOA Architect certification with a special "Top Gun" designation. Florent maintains a blog at www.fgeorges.org.

Jason Hogg

Jason Hogg is an Architect inside the Microsoft Services Managed Solutions Group. Jason has been with Microsoft for six years where he has also worked inside Microsoft's Patterns & Practices and Microsoft Research divisions. While at Microsoft Jason has specialized in topics relating to the design of distributed applications, with an emphasis on SOA, security, and interoperability. Prior to joining Microsoft Jason, worked for 12 years as a consultant in the United States, Great Britain, and Australia at organizations including The United Nations, WorldNow, J Sainsbury's, British Airways, and BankWest . Jason holds an MSc (CompSci) from the University of Washington.

Anish Karmarkar

Anish Karmarkar, Ph.D., is a Consulting Member of Technical Staff at Oracle and is part of the standards and strategy team responsible for SOA, Web services, and Java specifications. He has 17 years of research, development, and standards experience in various aspects of distributed systems and protocols. Anish is a co-editor of various Web services standards, including SOAP 1.2, WS-ReliableMessaging, WS-ReliableMessaging Policy, WS-MakeConnection, WS-I Basic Profile, WS-I Reliable Secure Profile, WS-I Attachments Profile, RRSHB, amongst others. He is also a co-editor of the SCA set of specifications. As an active participant and a founding member in various Web services and SOA-related Working Groups, Technical Committees, Expert Groups in W3C, OASIS, JCP, and OSOA collaboration, he has played a significant role in the development of Web services and SCA standards and specifications. Anish has been on the Board of Directors of the OSGi Alliance since 2006, co-chair of the OASIS SCA BPEL Technical Committee, and Oracle's alternate representative on the JCP "Big Java" Executive Committee. He has also served as the vice-Chair of WS-I Basic Profile Working Group. He received his Ph.D. in Computer Science from Texas A&M University in 1997.

Mark Little

Dr. Mark Little is Engineering Director at Red Hat where he is the Technical Development Manager for the JBoss SOA Platform. Prior to this he was the lead on the JBossESB and JBossTS projects, where he is still the Development Manager. Mark has over 20 years of experience in using and developing distributed systems, that includes being Chief Architect at Arjuna Technologies and a Distinguished Engineer at Hewlett Packard, where he lead the transactions team to produce the world's first Web Services transactions product. Mark spends a lot of time working in various standards bodies, including OASIS and W3C, and has co-authored several of the WS-* standards. He has presented regularly at conferences, workshops and events such as JavaOne, HP World, JBoss World, the SOA Symposium, and the World Wide Web Conference where he has also been a co-chair on the Web Services track. Mark is also a co-author of a number of books including *Java Transaction Processing* and the upcoming title *ESB Architecture for SOA*.

Brian Lokhorst MSc, BSc, SOACP

Brian Lokhorst is a Solution Architect for the new Declarations Management System (DMS) of the Dutch Tax and Customs Administration (DTCA). Previously, Brian worked as an integration-technology architect in the program responsible for getting the DTCA transformed into a service oriented organization. He advised on the gradual migration towards a service-oriented way of thinking, with a special focus on Web services and the use of ESB-technology for its technical implementation. As technical team lead and senior infrastructure developer Brian was responsible for a B2B-integration implemented with Web services and ESB-technology between two government agencies. Prior to that he was responsible for developing the ICT service portfolio architecture and the architecture of software factories for the DTCA. Brian is a Certified SOA Architect and an IBM Certified RUP 7.1 Solution Designer. Brian holds an MSc in Business Economics & ICT from the University of Groningen and a BSc in International Business Economics from the School of Business and Economics at Windesheim University.

Brian Loesgen

Based in San Diego, Brian Loesgen is a Principal Consultant with Neudesic, a firm that specializes in .NET development and Microsoft server integration. Brian is a five-time Microsoft MVP for BizTalk Server and has extensive experience building sophisticated enterprise and mobile solutions. In addition, Brian has been involved with advanced Enterprise Service Bus solutions, and was a key architect and developer of the "Microsoft ESB Guidance" released by Microsoft in Oct 2006. He is a co-author of six books, including

BizTalk Server 2004 Unleashed, and is currently working on *SOA with .NET.* He has written technical white papers for Intel, Microsoft, and others and has spoken at numerous major technical conferences worldwide. Brian is a co-founder and past-President of the International .NET Association (ineta.org). He is the President of the San Diego .NET user group, leads the San Diego Software Industry Council SOA SIG, and is a member of the Editorial Board for the .NET Developer's Journal. Brian is also a member of the Microsoft Connected Systems Division Virtual Technical Specialist Team, and is part of Microsoft's Connected Systems Advisory Board. Brian's blog is at blog.BrianLoesgen.com.

Berthold Maier

Berthold Maier works for Oracle Consulting Germany as Chief Architect and has more than 15 years experience as a developer, coach, and architect building complex, mission-critical applications and integration architectures. Within the last seven years at Oracle he has held several positions in the German consulting organization with a focus on Java/JEE, Integration, SOA, BPM, DB, ECM, security, and, most recently, enterprise architecture management.

Since December 2006 Berthold has been the acting Chief Architect for the entire Oracle consulting division in Germany. In this position he is responsible for reference architectures pertaining to integration and JEE, and for the Oracle Consulting Development Frameworks. He is also the originator and architect of the Accelerate Consulting Framework based on MDA, SOA and ADF. Berthold is a well-known speaker and author, and is also a co-founder of the Masons-of-SOA, an inter-company network founded by architects of Oracle Germany, Opitz, SOPEra (Eclipse Project Swordfish founders), and EDS.

Hajo Normann

Hajo Normann is an SOA/BPM evangelist and architect at EDS. His interest for business focused, enterprise-wide, cross-siloed bundles of functionality (services) first emerged in 2001 while acting as the architect and technical team lead for a shared service platform at a large German bank. In 2003, Hajo modeled business processes at the Federal Office and is now working on a governmental project focused on BPMN models and executable WS-BPEL processes. Much of Hajo's research has been concentrated on the missing links between SOA and BPM and he is regularly engaged in discussions and thought exchange with BPM and ESB thought leaders at Oracle Headquarters. Hajo co-leads the German DOAG SIG SOA, co-founded the Masons-of-SOA, acts as an Oracle ACE Director, and is a frequent speaker at public events.

Chris Riley, SOACP

Chris Riley is a Senior Consultant and Instructor with SOA Systems Inc. and has been part of many engagements across North America. In his capacity as a consultant, Chris is working with Fortune 500 organizations (such as Pearson, Kodak, SAIC, and State of Indiana) in the financial services, consumer products, education, and government sectors in their pursuit of enterprise SOA. He specializes in helping organizations move from traditional distributed computing processes to SOA using open standards. Prior to SOA Systems, Chris ran the Professional Service department for Cape Clear Software as Director of Architecture helping North American customers implement Enterprise Service Bus technology. In this role, Chris also coordinated and supported webinars and speaking engagements promoting ESB and SOA with Gartner and Forrester, as well as public forums, such as the Integration Consortium, Toronto Java User Group and SOA Seminar Series. Previous to Cape Clear, Chris worked at Extricity, Inc. as a Senior Solution Consultant and PTC as a manager of Technical Services.

Thomas Rischbeck

Thomas is an IT architect and business developer with the Swiss-based [ipt] consultancy group. He has many years of experience in the delivery of complex e-business architectures in the government and logistics domains. Thomas advises clients on their enterprise architecture and works on various technical and organizational topics with a focus on SOA infrastructure and SOA governance. Thomas has a strong foundation in asynchronous integration middleware and distributed and parallel architectures. Prior to joining [ipt], Thomas worked as a senior engineer with the Hewlett Packard middleware division (ex Bluestone). At HP he was the lead developer for the JMS message broker and its integration into the HP application server. After the HP-Compaq merger in 2001, Thomas took on the role of solutions architect with Arjuna Ltd. Thomas holds a B.Sc. in Computing Science and a Ph.D. in Parallel Computing, both from the University of Newcastle upon Tyne. He is a frequent speaker and also active as an author for the upcoming book *ESB Architecture for SOA*.

Satadru Roy

Satadru Roy is a Senior SOA Architect with Sun Microsystems, Canada where he consults with clients to provide architecture and design guidance for their SOA initiatives. Satadru has extensive consulting experience in various domain verticals and he has also worked for well-known infrastructure software vendors, such as BEA Systems, Inc. He has extensive experience in middleware, application integration and BPM, and is a strong proponent of

open source-based integration technologies. Satadru is one of the co-authors of the upcoming *SOA with Java* title.

Arnaud Simon

Arnaud Simon is a Red Hat senior middleware consultant and co-author of the upcoming book *ESB Architecture for SOA*. Prior to Red Hat Arnaud was an IT Architect working for IPT, a European systems integrator based in Switzerland. Before that he was leading the Message Service Team for Arjuna Technologies Limited, a spin-off from Hewlett-Packard where he was a senior research and development engineer. Arnaud obtained his Ph.D in Computing Science from INRIA and completed research posts at both INRIA and Newcastle University.

Bernd Trops

Bernd Trops is the Director of Professional Services at SOPERA GmbH. Since the mid-90s he worked for several companies (including GemStone, Brokat, WebGain, and Oracle) as a Systems Engineer and coach on countless OO and J2EE projects.

During his Oracle days Bernd held the position of SOA Architect with focus on large-scale initiatives. One notable project included the Deutsche Posts Service Back Bone, which eventually became the foundation for the Eclipse SOA Runtime Framework's core Project Swordfish. Today he is responsible for consulting and training at SOPERA, which supports an OpenSource SOA platform contributed to the Eclipse Foundation. Bernd is also a co-founder of the Masons-of-SOA.

Clemens Utschig-Utschig

An eight year Oracle veteran, Clemens works for the SOA Product Management team at Oracle Headquarters in the USA where he is responsible for product strategy and developer adoption. During the early days of Java Clemens founded the local Java Community and years later he was nominated as Austria's representative into the EMEA Java/XML community. Clemens spent years consulting in Switzerland and Dubai and performed workshops all around Europe. In 2004 he was the first consultant from EMEA to be invited for an internship with Oracle where he spent a month developing the XML Datacontrol for the JSR-227 reference-implementation that is since part of the official samples. Since his transfer into the SOA/integration engineering group, Clemens is responsible for cross product integration and currently acts as advisor for SOA to Fusion Applications development. He is an advisory member of the Applications Architecture Board and a member of

the OASIS SCA assembly Technical Committee. In 2006 Clemens was designated as the youngest Oracle ACE for contributions to the developer community on OTN, and graduated the same year as the youngest Certified Project Manager from Stanford University. He is a frequent speaker at conferences and has published articles in known industry journals. Clemens is an advisory member of Oracle's Arch2Arch community, serves in the advisory board for SOA at the Germany-based JAX/SOACon conference, and is co-founder of the Masons-of-SOA.

Torsten Winterberg

Torsten Winterberg works for the Oracle Advantage Partner OPITZ Consulting as the director of the Application Development division. He is a long-time developer, coach, and architect with specializations in the areas of Java EE, BPM, BPEL, ESB, BAM and SOA in general. He is a known speaker in the German Java community and has written numerous articles on SOA-related topics. He is currently focused on the design and architecture aspects of projects based on the Oracle SOA Suite. Torsten is part of the Masons of SOA and is co-authoring an article series on "Hot SOA topics not tackled yet by others" for the German Javamagazin. He is also a member of the advisory board for two big German conferences (Jax, W-Jax), was BPM track chair for Jax 2008, and helps lead the DOAG Special Interest Group SOA. Torsten was recognized by Oracle for his evangelist role by being the designated Oracle ACE Director since 2007.

Dennis Wisnosky

Dennis Wisnosky is Chief Technical Officer of the US Department of Defense (DoD) Business Mission Area within the office of the Deputy Under Secretary of Defense for Business Transformation (OUSD (BT)). He is recognized as a creator of the Integrated Definition language, the standard for modeling and analysis in management and business improvement efforts. Wisnosky holds a bachelor's degree in physics and mathematics from California University of Pennsylvania, a master's in management science from the University of Dayton, and a master's in electrical engineering from the University of Pittsburgh.

Index of Patterns

Index

A

E

F

G–H

I

J–K

L

M

Q–R

S

T

U

V

W

X–Z

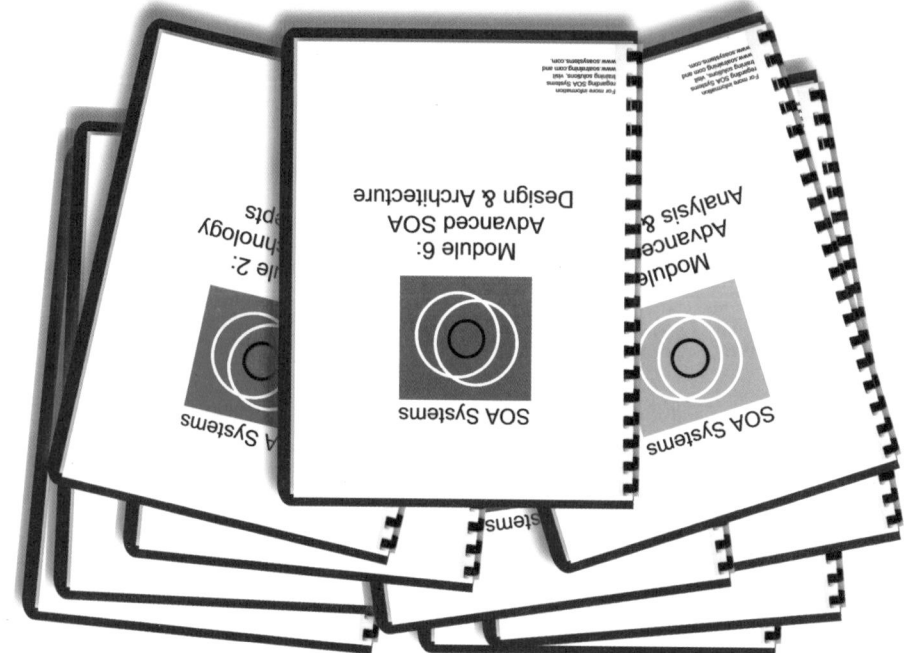

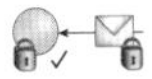

Direct Authentication (656) How can a service verify the credentials provided by a consumer?

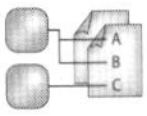

Distributed Capability (510) How can a service preserve its functional context while also fulfilling special capability processing requirements?

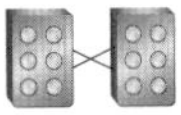

Domain Inventory (123) How can services be delivered to maximize recomposition when enterprise-wide standardization is not possible?

Dual Protocols (227) How can a service inventory overcome the limitations of its canonical protocol while still remaining standardized?

Enterprise Inventory (116) How can services be delivered to maximize recomposition?

Enterprise Service Bus (704)

Entity Abstraction (175) How can agnostic business logic be separated, reused, and governed independently?

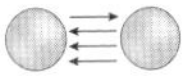

Event-Driven Messaging (599) How can service consumers be automatically notified of runtime service events?

Exception Shielding (376) How can a service prevent the disclosure of information about its internal implementation when an exception occurs?

Federated Endpoint Layer (713)

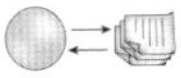

File Gateway (457) How can service logic interact with legacy systems that can only share information by exchanging files?

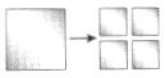

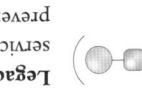

Functional Decomposition (300) How can a large business problem be solved without having to build a standalone body of solution logic?

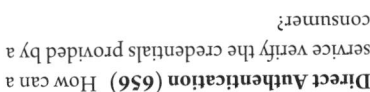

Intermediate Routing (549) How can dynamic runtime factors affect the path of a message?

Inventory Endpoint (260) How can a service inventory be shielded from external access while still offering service capabilities to external consumers?

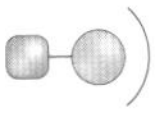

Legacy Wrapper (441) How can wrapper services with non-standard contracts be prevented from spreading indirect consumer-to-implementation coupling?

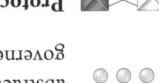

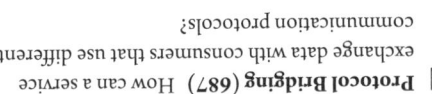

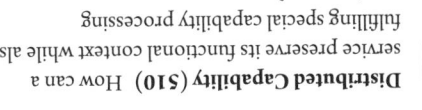

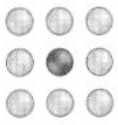

Logic Centralization (136) How can the misuse of redundant service logic be avoided?

Message Screening (381) How can a service be protected from malformed or malicious input?

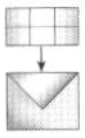

Messaging Metadata (538) How can services be designed to process activity-specific data at runtime?

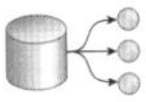

Metadata Centralization (280) How can service metadata be centrally published and governed?

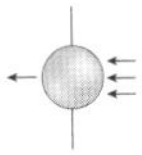

Multi-Channel Endpoint (451) How can legacy logic fragmented and duplicated for different delivery channels be centrally consolidated?

Non-Agnostic Context (319) How can single-purpose service logic be positioned as an effective enterprise resource?

Official Endpoint (711)

Orchestration (701)

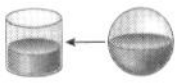

Partial State Deferral (356) How can services be designed to optimize resource consumption while still remaining stateful?

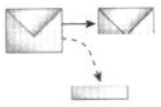

Partial Validation (362) How can unnecessary data validation be avoided?

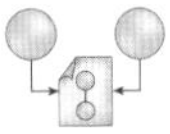

Policy Centralization (207) How can policies be normalized and consistently enforced across multiple services?

Process Abstraction (182) How can non-agnostic process logic be separated and governed independently?

Process Centralization (193) How can abstracted business process logic be centrally governed?

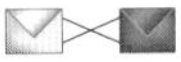

Protocol Bridging (687) How can a service exchange data with consumers that use different communication protocols?

1–58778–081–X

9 781587 780813 90000